France

Lille, Flanders
& the Somme
p178

Around Paris
p159

Normandy
p212

Brittany
p252

Paris
p56

Champagne
p296

Alsace &
Lorraine
p318

The Loire
Valley
p366

Burgundy
p409

Atlantic
Coast
p610

Massif
Central
p537

French Alps &
the Jura
Mountains
p478

Dordogne,
Limousin
& the Lot
p561

Lyon &
the Rhône
Valley
p452

French Basque
Country
p644

Toulouse Area
p692

Languedoc-
Roussillon
p713

Provence
p761

The Pyrenees
p670

The French Riviera
& Monaco
p827

Corsica
p877

THIS EDITION WRITTEN AND RESEARCHED BY

Nicola Williams,

Alexis Averbuck, Oliver Berry, Stuart Butler, Jean-Bernard Carillet,
Kerry Christiani, Gregor Clark, Emilie Filou, Catherine Le Nevez,
Daniel Robinson

Contents

MONACO P864

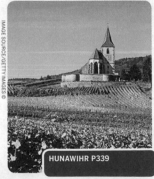

HUNAWIHR P339

VISIONS OF OUR LAND/GETTY IMAGES ©

IMAGE SOURCE/GETTY IMAGES ©

Contents

BRUNO DE HOGUES/GETTY IMAGES ©

PONT DU GARD P721

Contents

UNDERSTAND

SURVIVAL GUIDE

SPECIAL FEATURES

Welcome to France

France seduces travellers with its unfalteringly familiar culture, woven around cafe terraces, village-square markets and lace-curtained bistros with their plat du jour chalked on the board.

Cultural Savoir Faire

France is about world-class architecture and art, outstanding museums, Roman temples and Renaissance châteaux. It seduces with iconic landmarks known the world over, and rising stars yet to be discovered. The country's cultural repertoire is staggering in volume and diversity. And this is where the beauty of *la belle France* lies: when super stars such as Mademoiselle Eiffel, royal Versailles and the celebrity French Riviera have been ticked off, there's still plenty more to thrill. (France is, after all, the world's top tourist destination with more than 80 million visitors a year.)

Gastronomy

Food is of enormous importance to the French and each region has its own specialities alongside French classics. The daily culinary agenda takes no prisoners: breakfasting on warm croissants from the *boulangerie*, stopping in at Parisian bistros, and shopping at the market are all second nature to the French – and it would rude to refuse. But French gastronomy goes far deeper than just eating well. Its experiential nature means there is always something tasty to observe, learn and try, wherever you are – be it flipping crepes in Brittany or chinking Champagne flutes in ancient Reims cellars, the culinary opportunities are endless.

Art de Vivre

The rhythm of daily life – dictated by the seasons in the depths of *la France profonde* (rural France) – exudes an intimacy that gets under your skin. Don't resist. Rather, live the French lifestyle. Embrace the luxury of simple everyday rituals being transformed into unforgettable moments, be it a coffee and croissant in the Parisian cafe where Sartre and Simone de Beauvoir met to philosophise, a stroll through the lily-clad gardens Monet painted, or a walk on a beach in Brittany scented with the subtle infusion of language, music and mythology brought by 5th-century Celtic invaders.

Outdoor Action

And then there is the *terroir* (land) and the varied journey it weaves from northern France's cliffs and sand dunes to the piercing blue sea of the French Riviera and Corsica's verdant oak forests. Outdoor action is what France's lyrical landscape demands – and there's something for everybody. Whether you end up walking barefoot across wave-rippled sand to Mont St-Michel, riding a cable car to glacial panoramas above Chamonix, or cartwheeling down Europe's highest sand dune, France does not disappoint. Its great outdoors is thrilling, with endless opportunities and the next adventure begging to be had. *Allez!*

Why I Love France

By Nicola Williams

France has been home for two decades yet I can't shake off that uncanny feeling I'm on holiday – French *art de vivre* (art of living) is just too good and I'm mad about it. From my Haute-Savoie house on Lake Geneva's southern shore, the dark green hills of the Jura and *un café* in the wisteria-draped village bar are my wake-up call. Weekends of endless possibilities punctuate the gentle rhythm of village life: ravishing art museums in Lyon and Paris, hiking and skiing in the Alps, paddle boarding on the glittering lake, road trips to Beaujolais and Burgundy and other regions so different they could be another country. France's sheer variety never ceases to amaze me.

For more about our authors, see page 1016

Above: Vallée de l'Ariège (p689)

France

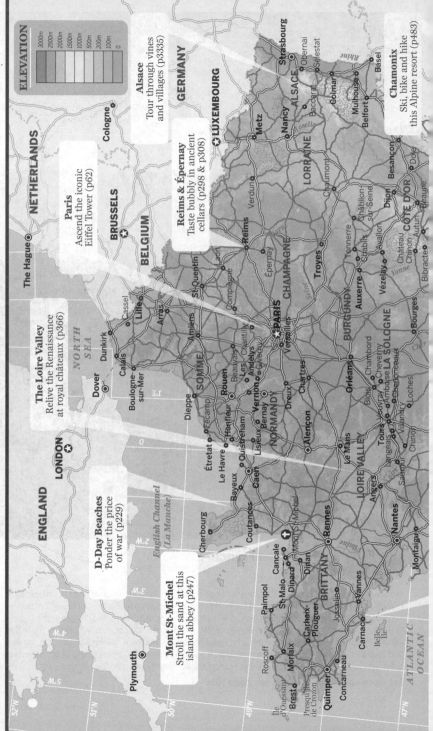

ENGLAND

D-Day Beaches
Ponder the price of war (p229)

Mont St-Michel
Stroll the sand at this island abbey (p247)

The Loire Valley
Relive the Renaissance at royal châteaux (p366)

Paris
Ascend the iconic Eiffel Tower (p62)

Alsace
Tour through vines and villages (p3335)

Reims & Épernay
Taste bubbly in ancient cellars (p298 & p308)

Chamonix
Ski, bike and hike this Alpine resort (p483)

NETHERLANDS

The Hague

London

Plymouth

Cologne

BRUSSELS
BELGIUM

LUXEMBOURG
Luxembourg

GERMANY

Strasbourg
Obernai
Sélestat

L Basel

Metz
Nancy
ALSACE
Colmar
Baccarat
Mulhouse
Belfort

LORRAINE

Chaumont

Verdun

Besançon
CÔTE D'OR
Dole

Reims
Épernay

CHAMPAGNE
Troyes

BURGUNDY

Auxerre
Tonnerre
Chablis
Vézelay
Avallon
Dijon
Beaune
Autun
Château-
Chinon
Bibracte

Châtillon-
sur-Seine

Yonne

Laon
St-Quentin
Compiègne

Lille
Arras
Amiens
SOMME

Cassel
Dunkirk
Calais
Boulogne-
sur-Mer
Dieppe

NORTH
SEA

Dover

Les Chantilly
Beauvais
Andelys
Giverny

PARIS
Versailles

Chartres
Dreux

Orléans
Blois
Chambord
Cheverny
LA SOLOGNE
Chenonceau
Bourges
Loches

Fécamp
Rouen
Vernon
Bernay
Étretat
Le Havre
Honfleur
Lisieux
Ouistreham
NORMANDY
Caen
Bayeux
Alençon

Le Mans

LOIRE VALLEY
Tours
Vouvray
Amboise
Azay-le-
Rideau
Langeais
Villandry
Saumur
Angers
Chinon

English Channel
(La Manche)

Cherbourg

Coutances

St-Malo
Cancale
Dinard
Dinan
Mont St-Michel

Paimpol
Roscoff
Morlaix
Brest
Presqu'île
de Crozon
Quimper
Concarneau

Carhaix-
Plouguer
Josselin

Rennes

BRITTANY

Vannes
Carnac

Belle
Île

Nantes

Montaigu

ATLANTIC
OCEAN

Île
d'Ouessant

ELEVATION
3000m
2500m
2000m
1500m
1000m
500m
200m
100m
0

0   100 km
0   50 miles

N

52°N
51°N
50°N
49°N
47°N

5°W
4°W
3°W
2°W
1°W
0
1°E

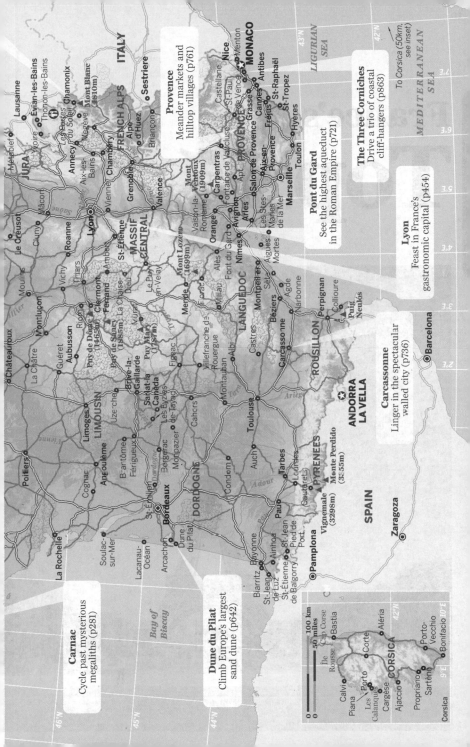

Carnac
Cycle past mysterious megaliths (p281)

Dune du Pilat
Climb Europe's largest sand dune (p642)

Provence
Meander markets and hilltop villages (p761)

The Three Corniches
Drive a trio of coastal cliff-hangers (p863)

Pont du Gard
See the highest aqueduct in the Roman Empire (p721)

Lyon
Feast in France's gastronomic capital (p454)

Carcassonne
Linger in the spectacular walled city (p736)

ITALY

FRENCH ALPS

Mont Blanc (4810m)

JURA

MASSIF CENTRAL

LIMOUSIN

DORDOGNE

LANGUEDOC

ROUSSILLON

PROVENCE

MONACO

Nice

LIGURIAN SEA

MEDITERRANEAN SEA

To Corsica (50km, see inset)

PYRENEES
Mont Perdido (3355m)

Vignemale (3298m)

SPAIN

ANDORRA LA VELLA

Barcelona

Zaragoza

Pamplona

CORSICA

Bay of Biscay

La Rochelle

Bordeaux

Toulouse

Lyon

Marseille

France's
Top 15

Eiffel Tower

1 Seven million people visit the Eiffel Tower (p62) annually, and with the recent revamp of its 1st-floor 'museum' space there's even more reason to go. From an evening ascent amid twinkling lights to lunch in one of the restaurants, every visit is unique. Pedal beneath it, skip the lift and trek up it, munch a crêpe next to it, snap a selfie in front of it or visit it at night. Best are the special occasions when all 324m of the iconic tower glows a different colour.

Mont St-Michel

2 The dramatic play of tides on this abbey-island in Normandy is magical and mysterious. Said by Celtic mythology to be a sea tomb to which souls of the dead were sent, Mont St-Michel (p247) is rich in legend and history, which are keenly felt as you make your way barefoot across rippled sand to the stunning architectural ensemble. Walk around it alone or, better still, hook up with a guide in nearby Genêts for a dramatic day hike across the bay.

PAWEL LIBERA/GETTY IMAGES ©

JETHIC/ISTOCK PHOTO ©

Champagne

3 Better known-brand Champagne houses in the main towns of Reims and Épernay are famed the world over. However, our tip is that much of Champagne's finest liquid gold is created by passionate, small-scale *vignerons* (winegrowers) in drop-dead gorgeous villages, therefore rendering the region's scenic driving routes the loveliest way of tasting fine bubbly amid rolling vineyards. Our favourite: exploring the region's best Champagne museum, the Musée de la Vigne et du Vin (p308) in Le Mesnil-sur-Oger, following by tasting and lunch in the village at Le Mesnil. Épernay p308

Loire Valley Châteaux

4 If it's aristocratic pomp and architectural splendour you're after this is the place to linger. Flowing more than 1000km into the Atlantic, the Loire is one of France's last *fleuves sauvages* (wild rivers) and its banks provide a 1000-year snapshot of French high society. The valley is riddled with beautiful châteaux sporting turrets and ballrooms, lavish cupolas and chapels. If you're a hopeless romantic seeking the perfect fairytale castle, head for moat-ringed Azay-le-Rideau (p394), Villandry (p393) and its gardens, and less-visited Château de Beauregard (p381). Château d'Azay-le-Rideau p394

3

KODACHROME25/GETTY IMAGES ©

Chamonix Action

5 The birthplace of
mountaineering and
winter playground to the
rich, famous and not-so-
famous, this iconic ski
resort in the French Alps
has something for every-
one. Snowsport fiends fly
down slopes on skis or
boards in order to savour
the breathtaking views of
Mont-Blanc and surround-
ing mountains. But there's
absolutely no obligation to
do so: non-skiers can hop
aboard the Aiguille du Midi
(p483) cable-car – and
onwards to Italy aboard
the Télécabine Panoramic
Mont Blanc – for the ride of
a lifetime above 3800m.

Pont du Gard

6 This Unesco World Heritage Site (p721) near Nîmes in southern France is gargantuan: 35 arches straddle the Roman aqueduct's 275m-long upper tier, containing a watercourse that was designed to carry 20,000 cu metres of water per day. View it from a canoe on the River Gard or stroll across the top. Oh, and don't forget your swimming gear for a spot of post-Pont daredevil diving and jumping from the rocks nearby – a plunge that will entice the most reluctant of young historians. Flop afterwards onto a floating deck a little way downstream.

Alsatian Wine Route

7 It is one of France's most popular drives (p335) – and for good reason. Motoring in this far northeast corner of France takes you through a kaleidoscope of lush green vines, perched castles and gentle mist-covered mountains. The only pit stops en route are half-timbered villages and roadside wine cellars, where fruity Alsace vintages can be swirled, tasted and bought. To be truly wooed, drive the Route des Vins d'Alsace in autumn, when vines are heavy with grapes waiting to be harvested and colours are at their vibrant best.

6

7

DENNIS MACDONALD/GETTY IMAGES ©

JUSTIN FOULKES/LONELY PLANET ©

Carcassonne at Dusk

8 That first glimpse of La Cité's sturdy stone witch's-hat turrets above Carcassonne (p736) in the Languedoc is enough to make your hair stand on end. To properly savour this fairytale walled city, linger at dusk after the crowds have left, when the old town belongs to its 100 or so inhabitants and the few visitors staying at the handful of lovely hotels within its ramparts. Don't forget to look back when you leave to view the old city, beautifully illuminated, glowing in the warm night.

D-Day Beaches

9 A trip to these peaceful, broad stretches of fine sand and breeze-blown bluffs is one of France's most emotional journeys. On 6 June 1944 beaches here became a cacophony of gunfire and explosions, the bodies of Allied soldiers lying in the sand as their comrades-in-arms charged inland. Just up the hill from Omaha Beach, the long rows of symmetrical gravestones at the Normandy American Cemetery & Memorial (p231) bear solemn, silent testimony to the horrible price paid for France's liberation from Nazi tyranny.
Omaha Beach p231

Carnac Megaliths

10 Pedalling past open fields dotted with the world's greatest concentration of mysterious megaliths (p281) gives a poignant reminder of Brittany's ancient human inhabitants. No one knows for sure what inspired these gigantic menhirs, dolmens, cromlechs, tumuli and cairns to be built. A sun god? Some phallic fertility cult? Post-ride, try to unravel the mystery from the soft-sand comfort of La Grande Plage (p281), Carnac's longest and most popular beach with a 2km-long stretch of pearly white sand.

JEAN-PIERRE LESCOURRET/GETTY IMAGES ©

Lyonnais Bouchons

11 The red-and-white checked tablecloths, closely packed tables and decades-old bistro decor could be anywhere in France. It's the local cuisine that makes *bouchons* (p467) in Lyon unique, plus the quaint culinary customs, such as totting up the bill on the paper tablecloth, or serving wine in a glass bottle wrapped with an elastic band to stop drips, or the 'shut weekends' opening hours. Various piggy parts drive Lyonnais cuisine, but have faith – this French city is said to be the gastronomic capital of France. Dine and decide.

Hilltop Villages

12 Impossibly perched on a rocky peak above the Mediterranean, gloriously lost in back country, fortified or château-topped... southern France's portfolio of *villages perchés* is vast and impressive, and calls for go-slow touring – on foot, by bicycle or car. Most villages are medieval, built from golden stone and riddled with cobbled lanes, flower-filled alleys and hidden squares silent but for the glug of a fountain. Combine a village visit with lunch alfresco – La Table de Ventabren (p785) near Aix-en-Provence is one such dreamy address that you'll never want to leave. Èze p864

Provençal Markets

13 No region is more of a market-must than this one. Be it fresh fish by the port in seafaring Marseille, early summer's strings of pink garlic, melons from Cavaillon all summer long or wintertime's earthy 'black diamond' truffles, Provence thrives on a bounty of fresh produce – grown locally and piled high each morning at the market. Every town and village has one, but those in Carpentras (p812) and Aix-en-Provence (p780) are the best known. Stock up on dried herbs, green and black olives marinated a dozen different ways, courgette flowers and oils. Carpentras p812

Dune du Pilat

14 The Dune du Pilat (p642) is a 'mountain' that just has to be climbed. Not only is the coastal panorama from the top of Europe's largest sand dune a stunner – it takes in the Banc d'Arguin bird reserve and Cap Ferret across the bay – but the nearby beaches have some of the Atlantic coast's best surf. Cycle here from Arcachon and top off the trip with a dozen locally farmed oysters and a couple of tasty *crepinettes* (local sausages).

The Three Corniches, Nice

15 It's impossible to drive this dramatic trio of coastal roads, each one higher and with more hairpin bends than the next, without conjuring up cinematic images of Grace Kelly, Hitchcock, the glitz of Riviera high life, and the glamour of the Monaco royal family – all while absorbing views of the sweeping blue sea fringing Europe's most mythical coastline. To make a perfect day out of it, shop for a picnic at the cours Saleya morning market before leaving Nice. Nice p830

Need to Know

For more information, see Survival Guide (p957)

Currency
Euro (€)

Language
French

Money
ATMs at every airport, most train stations and on every second street corner in towns and cities. Visa, MasterCard and Amex widely accepted

Visas
Generally not required for stays of up to 90 days (or at all for EU nationals); some nationalities need a Schengen visa

Mobile Phones
European and Australian phones work, but only American cells with 900 and 1800 MHz networks are compatible; check with your provider before leaving home. Use a French SIM card to call with a cheaper French number

Time
Central European Time (GMT/UTC plus one hour)

When to Go

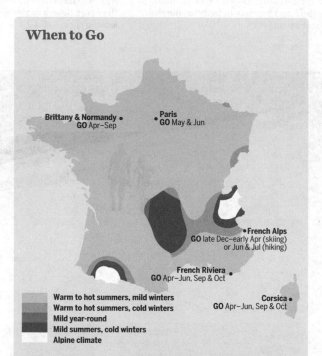

Brittany & Normandy •
GO Apr–Sep

• Paris
GO May & Jun

•French Alps
GO late Dec–early Apr (skiing)
or Jun & Jul (hiking)

French Riviera •
GO Apr–Jun, Sep & Oct

Corsica •
GO Apr–Jun, Sep & Oct

- Warm to hot summers, mild winters
- Warm to hot summers, cold winters
- Mild year-round
- Mild summers, cold winters
- Alpine climate

High Season
(Jul & Aug)

➡ Christmas, New Year and Easter equally busy

➡ Queues at sights and on the road, especially August

➡ Late December to March is high season in Alpine ski resorts

➡ Book tables and accommodation in the best restaurants well in advance

Shoulder (Apr–Jun & Sep)

➡ Accommodation rates drop in southern France and other hotspots

➡ Spring: warm weather, flowers, local produce

➡ The *vendange* (grape harvest) is reason to visit in autumn

Low Season
(Oct–Mar)

➡ Prices up to 50% less than high season

➡ Sights, attractions and restaurants open fewer days and shorter hours

➡ Hotels and restaurants in quieter rural regions (such as the Dordogne) are closed

Useful Websites

France Guide (www.france guide.com) Official French government tourist office website

France.fr (www.france.fr) Official country website

France 24 (www.france24. com/en/france) French news in English

Paris by Mouth (www.parisby mouth.com) Dining and drinking; one-stop site for where and how to eat in the capital with plenty of the latest openings

David Lebovitz (www. davidlebovitz.com) American pastry chef in Paris and author of several French cook books; insightful postings and great France-related articles shared on his Facebook page

French Word-a-Day (http:// french-word-a-day.typepad. com) Fun language learning

Lonely Planet (www.lonely planet.com/france) Destination information, bookings and traveller forum

Important Numbers

France country code	☑33
International access code	☑00
Europe-wide emergency	☑112
Ambulance (SAMU)	☑15
Police	☑17
Fire	☑18

Exchange Rates

Australia	A$1	€0.70
Canada	C$1	€0.69
Japan	¥100	€0.72
NZ	NZ$1	€0.64
UK	UK£1	€1.26
US	US$1	€0.76

For current exchange rates see www.xe.com

Daily Costs

Budget: less than €120

➡ Dorm bed: €15–25

➡ Double room in a budget hotel: €90

➡ Free admission to many attractions first Sunday of month

➡ Lunch *menus*: €12–18

Midrange: €120–200

➡ Double room in a midrange hotel: €90–190

➡ Lunch *menus* (set meals) in gourmet restaurants: €20–40

Top end: more than €200

➡ Double room in a top-end hotel: €190–350

➡ Lower weekend rates in business hotels

➡ Top restaurant dinner: *menu* €65, à la carte €100–150

Opening Hours

Opening hours vary throughout the year. We list high-season opening hours in this guide, but remember that longer summer hours often decrease in shoulder and low seasons.

Banks 9am–noon & 2–5pm Monday to Friday or Tuesday to Saturday

Restaurants Noon–2.30pm and 7–11pm six days a week

Cafes 7am–11pm

Bars 7pm–1am

Clubs 10pm–3am, 4am or 5am Thursday to Saturday

Shops 10am–noon & 2–7pm Monday to Saturday

Arriving in France

Aéroport de Charles de Gaulle (Paris; CDG; www.aeroports deparis.fr) Trains, buses and RER run to the city centre every 15 to 30 minutes between 5am and 11pm, after which night buses kick in (12.30am to 5.30am). Fares are €9.50/17/7.60 by RER/ bus/night bus or around €50 for the 30-minute taxi journey.

Aéroport d'Orly (ORY; ☑01 70 36 39 50; www.aeroports deparis.fr) Linked to central Paris by Orlyval rail then RER (€10.90) or bus (€7.50–12.50) every 15 minutes between 5am and 11pm. The 25-minute journey by taxi costs €40–55.

Getting Around

Transport in France is comfortable, quick, usually reliable and reasonably priced.

Train Run by state-owned SNCF France's rail network is first-class, with extensive coverage and frequent departures. Check timetables on www.sncf.com.

Car Leave cities and large towns (where a car is hard to park and a hindrance) for *la France profonde* (rural France) and a car comes into its own, allowing discovery of villages, hamlets and rural landscapes impossible to visit with public transport. Cars can be hired at airports and train stations. Drive on the right, but be aware of France's potentially hazardous 'priority to the right' rule.

Bus Cheaper and slower than trains. Useful for remote villages that aren't serviced by trains.

Bicycle Certain regions (Loire Valley, Lubéron in Provence and Burgundy) beg to be explored by two wheels and have dedicated cycle paths, some along canal towpaths or between orchards and vineyards.

For much more on **getting around**, see p975

First Time France

For more information, see Survival Guide (p957)

Checklist

➜ Check passport validity and visa requirements

➜ Arrange travel insurance

➜ Check airline baggage restrictions

➜ Book accommodation; reserve big-name restaurants

➜ Buy tickets online for the Louvre, Eiffel Tower et al

➜ Download France-related travel apps and music

What to Pack

➜ Travel plug (electrical adapter) for France's two-pin plugs

➜ Sunscreen, sunhat and sunglasses (southern France)

➜ Rainproof jacket & umbrella (northern France)

➜ Pocketknife with corkscrew: most French wines have corks (make sure to pack this in your checked-in luggage)

➜ Walking shoes – for mountains, hilltop villages, cobbled streets and pedestrian old towns

➜ Light scarf or sarong – to cover bare shoulders in churches

➜ An adventurous appetite (a French culinary necessity)

Top Tips for Your Trip

➜ Almost every village and town has a weekly morning market brimming with fruit, veg and other regional produce – and there's no finer opportunity for mingling with locals! Take your own shopping bag or basket.

➜ To get the best out of a French road trip, avoid *autoroutes* (highways) and main roads. Opt instead for back roads and country lanes that twist past farms, châteaux, vineyards and fruit orchards – scenic routes are highlighted in green on road maps (print and digital) published by French cartographer Michelin (www.viamichelin.com).

➜ For authentic local dining experiences avoid restaurants that tout a '*menu touristique*' or display a sample meal of plastic food on the pavement outside. While it might be tempting to favour restaurants with a menu in English, the very best (and best-loved by locals) rarely offer a translation.

What to Wear

➜ It might be the cradle of haute couture, but Paris sports a mixed bag of styles. To avoid standing out from the urban crowd, smart-casual is the way to go. The further south you are, the more relaxed fashion becomes. Even so, no bikini tops or bare male chests s'*il vous plaît*, unless you're on the beach.

➜ Countrywide, dress up rather than down in nicer midrange restaurants, clubs and bars – no jeans and trainers, unless you're at the local village bar (though black or 'smarter' jeans will probably be OK).

Sleeping

Advance reservations during high season are highly recommended. See p958 for more information.

➜ **Chambres d'hôte** (B&Bs) Small and friendly, B&Bs ooze bags of French charm and *art de vivre*.

➜ **Hotels** From luxuriant châteaux to simple village *auberges* (inns), hotels cater to every taste and budget. Breakfast is rarely included in rates.

➜ **Camping** Ecologically chic and often creative, camping is an affordable way of experiencing *la belle France* alfresco.

Cent Savers

➡ **Eat cheap** Lunchtime *formules* (two courses) and *menus* (three courses) in restaurants are a snip of the price of evening dining.

➡ **Discount admission** City museum passes provide cheaper admission to sights.

➡ **Savvy sleeping** It's cheaper for families staying in hotels to ask for a double room with extra bed rather than a triple. Families of four or more will find self-catering accommodation cheaper.

➡ **Picnic perfection** With its bucolic scenery and outstanding produce, France is picnic paradise. Buy a baguette from the *boulangerie* (bakery) and fill it with Camembert, pâté or *charcuterie* (cold meats). Finish sweet with *macarons* (Paris), buttery *Kouign amann* (Breton butter cake), cherries (southern France) or – for blue-blooded gourmets – Champagne and Reims' *biscuit roses*.

Bargaining

With the exception of the odd haggle at the market, little bargaining goes on in France.

Tipping

➡ **Restaurants** A 15% service charge is included in the bill, but many still leave a few euros. '*Service non compris*' means service is not included.

➡ **Bars & Cafes** For drinks at the bar, don't tip. For drinks brought to your table, tip like a restaurant.

➡ **Hotels** Bellhops expect €1 to €2 per bag; no need to tip the concierge, cleaners or front-desk staff.

Etiquette

➡ **Conversation** Use the formal '*vous*' when speaking to anyone unknown or older than you; informal '*tu*' is reserved for close friends, family and children.

➡ **Churches** Dress modestly (cover shoulders).

➡ **Drinks** Asking for *une carafe d'eau* (free jug of tap water) in restaurants is acceptable. Never end a meal with a cappuccino or cup of tea. Play French and order *un café* (espresso).

➡ **French Kissing** Exchange *bisous* (cheek-skimming kisses) – right cheek first – with casual acquaintances and friends.

Eating

In cities there are a multitude of places to eat. To dine fine and eat local, book ahead, particularly for weekends. In rural France, the same goes for *bonnes tables* (literally 'good tables') and Sunday lunch, a fiesty, afternoon-long affair. See p34 and p934 for more information.

➡ **Restaurants & bistros** Range from unchanged for a century to contemporary minimalist; urban dining is international, rural dining staunchly French.

➡ **Brasseries** Open from dawn until late, these casual eateries are great for dining in between standard meal times.

➡ **Cafés** Ideal for breakfast and light lunch; many morph into bars.

Language

Step into *la France profonde* (rural France) and you'll need those French phrases you mastered before setting off.

① What are the opening hours?
Quelles sont les heures d'ouverture?
kel son lay zer doo·vair·tewr

French business hours are governed by a maze of regulations, so it's a good idea to check before you make plans.

② I'd like the set menu, please.
Je voudrais le menu, s'il vous plait.
zher voo·dray ler mer·new seel voo play

The best-value dining in France is the two- or three-course meal at a fixed price. Most restaurants have one on the chalkboard.

③ Which wine would you recommend?
Quel vin vous conseillez?
kel vun voo kon·say·yay

Who better to ask for advice on wine than the French?

④ Can I address you with 'tu'?
Est-ce que je peux vous tutoyer?
es ker zher per voo tew·twa·yay

Before you start addressing someone with the informal 'you' form, it's polite to ask permission first.

⑤ Do you have plans for tonight/tomorrow?
Vous avez prévu quelque chose ce soir/demain?
voo za·vay pray·vew kel·ker shoz ser swar/der·mun

To arrange to meet up without sounding pushy, ask friends if they're available rather than inviting them directly.

What's New

Eiffel Tower Face-lift

On the 1st floor of Paris' emblematic tower, two glitzy new glass pavilions house interactive history exhibits; outside them, peer d-o-w-n through vertigo-inducing glass flooring to the ground 57m below. (p62)

Capital Art Excitement

No two Paris museum openings have been more eagerly awaited than the Musée Picasso (p89) and Frank Gehry's extraordinary Fondation Louis Vuitton (p70); both finally opened to the public in October 2014.

Baie de Somme

This sparkling estuary with ravishing sands is an increasingly chic weekend getaway for Parisians – and it's going to get hotter as WWI commemorative events unfurl (until 2018; p198).

Grande Mosquée de Strasbourg

Twenty years in the making, this architecturally striking mosque – the largest ever built on French soil – marks a new dawn for Muslims in France. (p325)

Le Camino, Le Puy-en-Velay

Few journeys across France are as spiritual as the Chemin de St-Jacques pilgrimage route across the Massif Central, through the Lot Valley and French Basque country, to Santiago de Compostela in Spain. This new museum tells the story. (p557)

The Confluence, Lyon

The renaissance of Lyon's industrial wasteland, where the Rhône and Saône rivers meet, continues: its crowning glory, the Musée des Confluences, opened in December 2014 glittering in steel-and-glass crystal. (p461)

Le Train de l'Ardèche, Rhône Valley

After a six-year closure, the exquisite little tourist train is back in business, carving its sublimely sinuous route along the precipitous gorges of the Doux River. (p477)

La Tyrolienne, Val Thorens

The French Alps is not all about winter snow sports. Enter the world's highest zip line. We dare you! (p508)

Fort de Brégançon, Bormes-les-Mimosas

Seven French presidents summered here between 1968 and 2013. Now it's the public's turn to enjoy this former state residence, a fortress atop a small island in the French Riviera. (p859)

Musée Renoir, Cagnes-sur-Mer

Renoir's Riviera home and studio, secreted away in citrus and olive groves, has been reopened and is more engaging than ever – admire *Les Grandes Baigneuses* (The Women Bathers; 1892) and unknown sculptures by the Impressionists. (p844)

MuCEM, Marseille

No single building better reflects the miraculous makeover of this mythical Mediterranean port than MuCEM, snug in a 17th-century fortress and breathtaking latticed shoe-box linked by a sky-high footbridge. (p764)

For more recommendations and reviews, see lonelyplanet.com/france

If You Like...

Gorgeous Villages

There is no humbler pleasure than exploring villages of gold stone, pink granite or whitewash. Cobbled lanes ensnare ornate fountains, flowery squares and houses strung with wisteria, vines or drying peppers.

Pérouges Day trip it from Lyon for cider and sugar-crusted *galettes* between yellow-gold medieval stone. (p474)

St-Émilion A medieval village perched dramatically above Bordeaux vines. (p638)

St-Jean Pied de Port Ancient pilgrim outpost en route to Santiago de Compostela in Spain. (p667)

Yvoire On Lake Geneva's southern shore, this flowery, château-clad Savoy village is a privileged address. (p497)

The Luberon A part of Provence lavishly strewn with hilltop villages; red-rock Roussillon is pure brilliance. (p817)

Èze Fuses a stunning hilltop village with sweeping Riviera panoramas. (p866)

The Dordogne Beautiful *bastides* (fortified hilltop towns) at every turn. (p563)

Wine Tasting

Be it tasting in cellars, watching grape harvests or sleeping *au château*, French wine culture demands immediate road-testing.

Bordeaux The Medoc, (p635) St-Émilion (p638) and Cognac (p626) set connoisseurs' hearts aflutter.

Burgundy Sample renowned vintages in Beaune, the Côte d'Or and Chablis. (p416)

Châteauneuf-du-Pape Vines planted by 14th-century popes yield southern France's most illustrious red. (p809)

Gigondas Taste raved-about reds in this gold-stone village in Provence, or try its equally luxuriant Jurassien counterpart, Pupillin. (p814)

Bandol and Cassis Wine tasting in these two villages (p865; p780) is as much about the setting as the wonderful wine.

Route des Vins d'Alsace Pair wine tasting with castle-topped villages in this storybook region, rich in rieslings, pinots and sylvaners. (p332)

Castles

The Loire Valley is the prime stop for French châteaux, dripping in period gold leaf. But venture elsewhere and you'll be surprised by what hides behind lumbering stone walls.

Versailles France's largest and grandest château, a stone's throw from Paris. (p162)

Chambord Renaissance countrygetaway castle where French kings and queens had a ball. (p379)

Azay-le-Rideau Classic French château with moat, turrets and sweeping staircase. (p394)

Villandry The formal French gardens framing this Renaissance Loire Valley château are glorious. (p393)

Cathar fortresses, Languedoc Now ruined, these dramatic, heat-sizzled hilltop castles evoke 13th-century persecution. (p756)

Château des Comtes Foix, Vallée de l'Ariège A château with amazing views of the Pyrenees. (p690)

Coastal Paths

From white cliff to red rock, pebble cove to gold sand strip, France's coastline is dramatically different. Explore on a windswept *sentier du littoral* (coastal trail), scented with sea salt and herbal scrub.

St-Tropez This *sentier du littoral* leads from fishing coves to celebrity-laced sands. (p857)

Bandol Stride the coast between inland vines and waterfront rock formations. (p865)

Chemin de Nietzsche Spectacular, steep rocky footpath near Nice where the German philosopher once hung out. (p866)

Corsica Hike from Bonifacio to a lighthouse, or past Genoese watchtowers along Cap Corse's Customs Officers' Trail. (p877)

Côte d'Opale Savour opal blues from windwept clifftops near Cap Blanc-Nez and Cap Griz Nez. (p192)

Coastal capers Fall in love with Brittany's Belle Île (p286) or Île d'Ouessant (p271), or chic Île de Ré (p625) in the Atlantic.

Île de Porquerolles Mediterranean island beauty strung with sea-facing cycling and hiking trails. (p863)

Markets

Art-nouveau hangar or tree-shaded village square... French markets spill across an enticing mix of spaces. Every town and village has one – they operate in the mornings and at least once a week. Bring your own bag.

Lyonnais markets Les Halles and Croix Rousse are Lyon's two buxom market divas, endowed with stalls heaving with fruit, veg, meat and runny St Marcellin cheese. (p471)

Place des Lices No town square is as celebrity-studded as St-Tropez. (p858)

Marché des Capucins Enjoy oysters and white wine at Bordeaux' Saturday-morning market. (p633)

Marché Couvert Once a bishop's palace, now a temple to local produce in Metz. (p361)

Uzès Languedoc's most splendid farmers market. (p721)

Carpentras No French region is as known for its markets as Provence, and this Friday-morning *marché* steals the Provençal show. (p814)

Islands & Beaches

The country's 3200km-long coastline morphs from white chalk cliffs (Normandy) to treacherous promontories (Brittany) to broad expanses of fine sand (Atlantic Coast)

Top: Galerie des Glaces, Château de Versailles (p162)
Bottom: Bonifacio (p897), Corsica

and pebbly or sandy beaches (Mediterranean Coast).

Îles d'Hyères France's only marine national park and a pedestrian paradise fringed with near-tropical beaches. (p863)

Plage de Pampelonne Stars love this hip beach in St-Tropez, darling, and for good reason – it's glam and golden. (p856)

Île de Ré Follow the flock from Paris to this chic, beach-laced island off the west coast. (p625)

Belle Île Its name means 'Beautiful Island'and that is just what this island is off the Breton coast. (p286)

Corsica Plage de Palombaggia and Plage de Santa Giulia near Porto-Vecchio are to die for. (p902)

Les Landes Surfers' secret backed by dunes on the Atlantic Coast. (p651)

Côte d'Opale Rousing, wind-buffeted beaches across from the white cliffs of Dover. (p192)

Gorges de l'Ardèche River beaches are all the rage and those around Pont d'Arc are great fun; arrive by kayak. (p477)

Incredible Train Journeys

There is nothing quite like watching mountains, valleys, gorges and rivers jog past kalaidescope-style from the window of an old-fashioned steam train or mountain railway.

Mer de Glace Ride a mountain train from Chamonix to Montenvers, then a cable car to this glacial sea of ice. (p485)

Tramway du Mont Blanc Travel in the shade of Europe's biggest mountain aboard France's highest train from Megève. (p493)

Le Train Jaune Mind-blowing Pyreneen scenery aboard a mountain train in Roussillon. (p41)

Pine Cone Train Narrow-gauge railway from Nice. (p840)

Chemin de Fer Touristique du Haut-Quercy Savour the sun-baked vineyards, oak forests and rivers of the Lot in southwest France aboard a vintage steam train. (p605)

La Vapeur du Trieux Journey riverside on this steam train from Breton harbour to an artists' village. (p265)

Le Petit Train de la Rhune Chug past miniature Pottok ponies to the summit of the most famous Basque mountain. (p666)

The Trembler Tremble as you cross sand-covered tracks too close to the water on this seaside train – a Corsican icon – between Île Rousse and Calvi. (p888)

Rural Escapes

Solitude is sweet and if you know where to go, there's ample opportunity to stray off the beaten track and play Zen sans the crowds.

Marais Poitevin Paddle in perfect peace through this tranquil, bird-filled wetland dubbed 'Green Venice'. (p619)

Vallée d'Aspe The 21st century has yet to reach this quiet Pyrenean valley, sprinkled with tiny hamlets and rural farms. (p681)

Essoyes Watch the vine-streaked landscapes of Champagne fade into watercolour distance in this riverside village, Renoir's summer home. (p317)

Le Crotoy The mood is laidback and the panorama superb in this picturesque fishing town on the northern bank of the Baie de Somme. (p198)

Forêt de Paimpont Recharge your batteries in this immense Breton forest, far from the coastal crowds. (p290)

Ota and Evisa Rolling hills, chestnut groves and picturesque

villages in the Corsican hills above Porto. (p891)

Parc Naturel Régional du Vercors Experience life on a farm at À la Crécia, a rural retreat in the French Alps. (p523)

Domaine de Palissade Trek on horseback through this remote, coastal nature park in the Camargue, kissed pink by salt pans and flamingoes. (p792)

Mountain Vistas

On sunny days views from atop France's highest mountains are, quite literally, breathtaking. Cable cars and mountain railways often take out the legwork.

Aiguille du Midi, Chamonix If you can handle the height (3842m), unforgettable summit views of the French, Swiss and Italian Alps await. (p483)

Pic du Lac Blanc, Alpe d'Huez Scale the 3330m year-round by cable car – magical views ripple across the French Alps into Italy and Switzerland. (p526)

Massif de l'Estérel, French Riviera Stupendous views of red rock, green forest and big blue – only on foot! (p855)

Ballon d'Alsace See where Alsace, Franche-Comté and Lorraine converge from this rounded, 1247m-high mountain. (p348)

Puy de Dôme, Auvergne Gulp at extinct volcanoes, pea-green and grassy, from this icy summit reached by foot or cog railway. (p547)

Cirque de Gavarnie Near Lourdes, a mind-blowing mountain amphitheatre ringed by icy Pyrenean peaks. (p687)

Pic du Midi Eye-popping panorama of the entire Pyrenees; catch a cable car from La Mongie. (p687)

Month by Month

TOP EVENTS

Festival d'Avignon,
July

Fête du Citron,
February

Fête des Lumières,
December

Cannes Film Festival,
May

Monaco Grand Prix,
May

January

With New Year festivities done and dusted, it's time to head to the Alps. Crowds on the slopes thin out once school's back, but January remains a busy month. On the Mediterranean, mild winters are wonderfully serene in a part of France that's mad busy the rest of the year.

🏃 Vive le Ski!

Grab your skis, hit the slopes. Most resorts in the Alps, Pyrenees and Jura open mid to late December, but January is the start of the French ski season in earnest. Whether a purpose-built station or lost Alpine village, there's a resort to match every mood and moment.

🏃 Hunting Black Diamonds

No culinary product is more aromatic or decadent than black truffles. Hunt them in the Dordogne and Provence: the season runs late December to March, but January is the prime month. (p568)

February

Crisp cold weather in the mountains – lots of china-blue skies now – means ski season moves into top gear. Alpine resorts get mobbed by families during the February school holidays and accommodation is at its priciest.

🎊 Nice Carnival

(www.nicecarnaval.com) Nice makes the most of its mild climate with this crazy Lenten carnival. As well as parade and costume shenanigans, merrymakers pelt each other with blooms during the legendary flower battles. Dunkirk in northern France celebrates Mardi Gras with equal gusto. (p836)

🎊 Citrus Celebrations

Menton on the French Riviera was once Europe's biggest lemon producer, hence its exotic Fête du Citron (Lemon Festival). These days it has to ship in a zillion lemons from Spain to sculpt into gargantuan carnival characters. (p874)

March

The ski season stays busy thanks to ongoing school holidays (until mid-March) and warmer temperatures. Down south, spring ushers in the bullfighting season and *Pâques* (Easter).

🎊 Féria Pascale

(www.feriaarles.com) No fest sets passions in France's hot south blazing more than Féria de Pâques, held at Easter in Arles to open the bullfighting season. There are four days of street dancing, music, concerts alfresco and bull-fighting. (p788)

April

Dedicated ski fiends can carve glaciers in the highest French ski resorts until mid-April or even later at highest altitudes. Then it's off with the ski boots and on with the hiking gear as peach and almond trees flower pink against a backdrop of snow-capped peaks.

◉ Counting Sheep

During the ancient Fête de la Transhumance in late April or May, shepherds walk their flocks of sheep up to lush green summer pastures; St-Rémy de Provence's fest is among the best known. Or head to villages in the Pyrenees and Massif Central to witness this transit. (p683)

May

There is no lovelier month to travel in France, as the first melons ripen in Provence and outdoor markets burst with new-found colour. Spring is always in.

⚔ May Day

No one works on 1 May, a national holiday that incites summer buzz, with *muguets* (lilies of the valley) sold at roadside stalls and given to friends for good luck. In Arles, Camargue cowboys show off their bull-herding and equestrian skills at the Fête des Gardians. (p788)

⚔ Pèlerinage des Gitans

(www.gitans.fr) Roma flock to the Camargue on 24 and 25 May and again in October for a flamboyant fiesta of street music, dancing and dipping their toes in the sea. (p794)

☆ Starring at Cannes

(www.festival-cannes.com) In mid-May, film stars and celebrities walk the red carpet at Cannes,

Europe's biggest cinema extravaganza. (p847)

◉ Monaco Grand Prix

(www.grand-prix-monaco. com) How fitting that Formula One's most glamorous rip around the streets of one of the world's most glam countries at the Monaco Grand Prix. (p867)

June

As midsummer approaches, the festival pace quickens alongside a rising temperature gauge, which tempts the first bathers into the sea. Looking north, nesting white storks shower good luck on farmsteads in Alsace.

☆ Fête de la Musique

(www.fetedelamusique. culture.fr) Orchestras, crooners, buskers and bands fill streets with free music during France's vibrant nationwide celebration of music on 21 June.

☆ Paris Jazz Festival

(http://parisjazzfestival. paris.fr) No festival better evokes the brilliance of Paris' interwar jazz age than this annual fest in the Parc de Floral. (p111)

July

If lavender's your French love, now is the time to catch it flowering in Provence. But you won't be the only one. School's out for the summer, showering

the country with endless tourists, traffic and too many *complet* (full) signs strung in hotel windows.

◉ Tour de France

(www.letour.fr) The world's most prestigious cycling race ends on av des Champs-Élysées in Paris on the third or fourth Sunday of July, but you can catch it for two weeks before all over France – the route changes each year but the French Alps are a hot spot. (p111)

⚔ Bastille Day

Join the French in celebrating the storming of the Bastille on 14 July 1789 – countrywide there are firework displays, balls, processions, parades and lots of hoo-ha all round.

☆ Festival d'Avignon

(www.festival-avignon.com) Rouse your inner thespian with Avignon's legendary performing arts festival. Street acts in its fringe fest are as inspired as those on official stages. (p802)

☆ Jazz à Juan

(www.jazzajuan.fr) Jive to jazz cats in Juan-les-Pins at this mythical Riviera music fest, which has been around for 50-odd years. Jazz à Juan requires tickets, but the fringe 'Off' part of the music festival does not. (p843)

⚔ Festival de Cornouaille

(www.festival-cornouaille. com) Traditional Celtic music takes over the Breton town of Quimper during this inspiring summer festival in late July. (p275)

August

It's that mad summer month when the French join everyone else on holiday. Paris, Lyon and other big cities empty; traffic jams at motorway toll booths test the patience of a saint; and temperatures soar. Avoid. Or don your party hat and join the mad crowd!

🎆 Celts Unite!

(www.festival-interceltique. com) Celtic culture is the focus of the Festival Interceltique de Lorient, when hundreds of thousands of Celts from Brittany and abroad flock to Lorient to celebrate just that. (p254)

🎆 Bubbles!

There's no better excuse for a flute or three of bubbly than during the first weekend in August when Champagne toasts its vines and vintages with the Route du Champagne en Fête. Free tastings, cellar visits, music and dancing. (p304)

September

As sun-plump grapes hang heavy on darkened vines and that August madness drops off as abruptly as it began, a welcome tranquillity falls across autumnal France. This is the start of France's *vendange* (grape harvest).

☉ The Rutting Season

Nothing beats getting up at dawn to watch mating stags, boar and red deer at play. Observatory towers are hidden in woods around Château de Chambord but the Loire is choc-a-bloc with Renaissance hunting pads, so it doesn't matter which one you visit. (p379)

🏛 Braderie de Lille

The mountains of empty mussel shells engulfing the streets after three days of mussel-munching have to be seen to be believed. Then there's the real reason for visiting Lille the first weekend in September – its huge flea market is Europe's largest. (p187)

October

The days become shorter, the last grapes are harvested and the first sweet chestnuts fall from trees. With the changing of the clocks on the last Sunday of the month, there's no denying it's winter.

☆ Nuit Blanche

In one last ditch attempt to stretch out what's left of summer, Paris museums, monuments, cultural spaces, bars, clubs and so on rock around the clock during Paris' so-called 'White Night', aka one fabulous long all-nighter! (p112)

November

It's nippy now. Toussaint (All Saints' Day) on 1 November ushers in the switch to shorter winter opening hours for many sights. Many restaurants close two nights a week now, making dining out on Monday a challenge in some towns.

🍷 Beaujolais Nouveau

At the stroke of midnight on the third Thursday in November the first bottles of cherry-red Beaujolais *Nouveau* wine are cracked open – and what a party it can be in Beaujolais, Lyon and other places nearby! (p474)

December

Days are short and it's cold everywhere bar the south of France. But there are Christmas school holidays and festive celebrations to bolster sun-deprived souls, not to mention some season-opening winter skiing in the highest-altitude Alpine resorts from mid-December.

🏛 Alsatian Christmas Markets

Visitors meander between fairy-light-covered craft stalls, mug of *vin chaud* (warm mulled wine) in gloved hand, at Alsace's traditional pre-Christmas markets.

🎆 Fête des Lumières

(www.lumieres.lyon.fr) France's biggest and best light show, on and around 8 December, transforms the streets and squares of Lyon into an open stage. (p462)

Itineraries

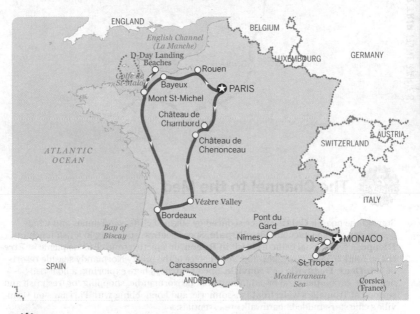

10 DAYS Essential France

No place screams 'France!' more than **Paris**. Spend two days in the capital, allowing time for cafe lounging, long bistro lunches and romantic strolls along the Seine and Canal St-Martin. Day three, enjoy Renaissance royalty at **Château de Chambord** and **Château de Chenonceau** in the Loire Valley. Or spend two days in Normandy instead, marvelling at **Rouen's** Notre Dame cathedral, the **Bayeux** tapestry, sea-splashed **Mont St-Michel** and – should modern history be your passion – the **D-Day landing beaches**.

Day five, zoom south to view some of the world's most precious cave art in the **Vézère Valley**, Dordogne. Key sites are around the towns of Les Eyzies-de-Tayac-Sireuil and Montignac. Or consider Sarlat-la-Canéda, showcase to some of France's best medieval architecture, as a base. Day seven experience 12 hours in **Bordeaux** – overnight in a B&B in the old wine-merchant quarter and enrol in a wine-tasting course at the Maison du Vin de Bordeaux. Next day it's a three-hour drive to the walled city of **Carcassonne**, Roman **Nîmes** and the **Pont du Gard.** Finish on the French Riviera with a casino flutter in Grace Kelly's **Monaco**, a portside aperitif in Brigitte Bardot's **St-Tropez** and a stroll around Matisse's **Nice**.

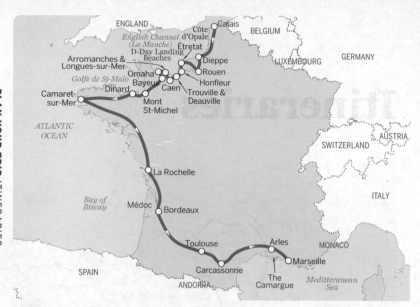

The Channel to the Med

Step off the boat in **Calais** and be seduced by 40km of cliffs, sand dunes and windy beaches on the spectacular **Côte d'Opale**. Speed southwest, taking in a fish lunch in **Dieppe**, a sensational cathedral visit in **Rouen**, or a picturesque cliffside picnic in **Étretat** en route to your overnight stop: your choice of the pretty Normandy seaside resorts of **Honfleur**, **Deauville** or **Trouville**. Spend two days here exploring: a boat trip beneath the gargantuan and breathtaking Pont de Normandie, shopping for fresh fish and seafood at Trouville's waterfront Poissonnerie, and hobnobbing with Parisians on Deauville's chic star-studded boardwalk are essentials.

Devote day three to Normandy's **D-Day landing beaches**. Start with the Mémorial – Un Musée pour la Paix in **Caen**, the best single museum devoted to the Battle of Normandy and a must-see, then follow a westward arc along the beach-laced coast, taking in the caisson-strewn sands at **Arromanches**, gun installations at **Longues-sur-Mer**, and the now-serene 7km-long stretch of 'bloody **Omaha**'. Come dusk, rejuvenate spent emotions over fresh scallops and *calvados* (apple-flavoured brandy). Or, if art is more your cup of tea, skip the beaches and go for the stunning representation of 11th-century warfare embroidered across 70m of tapestry in **Bayeux**.

Day four and the iconic, postcard-perfect **Mont St-Michel** and its beautiful sandy bay beckons – hiking barefoot across the sands here is an exhilarating experience. End the week in Brittany with a flop in an old-fashioned beach tent in **Dinard** and a bracing stroll on spectacular headlands around **Camaret-sur-Mer**.

Week two begins with a long drive south to chic **La Rochelle** for a lavish seafood feast. Spend a night here, continuing the gourmet theme as you wend your way south through Médoc wine country to **Bordeaux**. Next morning, stop in 'ville rose' **Toulouse** and/or **Carcassonne** before hitting the Med. The **Camargue** – a wetland of flamingos, horses and incredible bird life – is a unique patch of coast to explore and Van Gogh thought so too. Follow in his footsteps around **Arles**, breaking for a gastronomic lunch at L'Atelier or La Chassagnette before continuing on to gritty **Marseille**.

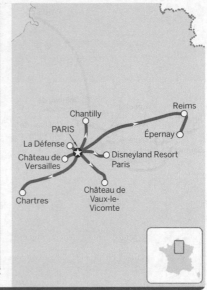

 Brittany to Bordeaux

For an exhilarating dose of Breton culture, Atlantic sea air and outstanding wine full of southern sun, there is no better trip than this. It starts fresh off the boat in **St-Malo**, a walled city with sturdy Vauban ramparts that beg exploration at sunset. Linger at least a day in this gritty port. Walk across at low tide to Île du Grand Bé and lap up great views atop a 14th-century tower in pretty St-Servan. Motor along the **Côte d'Émeraude** the next day, stopping in **Dinard** en route to **Roscoff** 200km west. Devote day four to discovering Brittany's famous cider in **Argol** on the **Presqu'île de Crozon**, megaliths around **Carnac**, and a turreted medieval castle in **Josselin**. Push south next along the Atlantic coast, stopping in **Nantes** if you like big cities (and riding mechanical elephants), or continuing to the peaceful waterways of Green Venice, aka the **Marais Poitevin**. **Bordeaux** is your final destination for day six, from where a bevy of Bordeaux wine-tasting trips tempt. End the journey on a high atop Europe's highest sand dune, **Dune du Pilat**, near oyster-famed Arcachon.

 A Week Around Paris

What makes capital city **Paris** even more wonderful is the extraordinary green and un-urban journey of Renaissance châteaux and sparkling wine that unfurls within an hour of the city. Day one has to be France's grandest castle, **Château de Versailles**, and its vast gardens. The second day, feast on France's best-preserved medieval basilica and the dazzling blue stained glass in **Chartres**, an easy train ride away. Small-town **Chantilly** is a good spot to combine a laid-back lunch with a Renaissance château, formal French gardens and – if you snagged tickets in advance – an enchanting equestrian performance. On the fourth day, catch the train to elegant **Reims** in the heart of the Champagne region. Scale its cathedral for dazzling views before tucking into the serious business of Champagne tasting. Dedicated bubbly aficionados can hop the next day to **Épernay**, France's other great Champagne city. On day six enjoy a lazy start then catch an afternoon fountain show at **Château de Vaux-le-Vicomte**, followed by a candlelit tour of the château. End the week with a look at futuristic **La Défense** or, for those with kids, **Disneyland Resort Paris**.

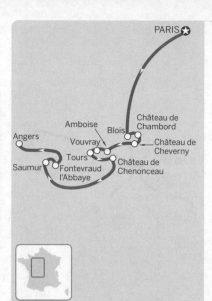

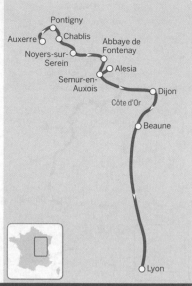

5 DAYS — Along the Loire Valley

For five days of aristocratic pomp and architectural splendour within spitting distance of transport hub **Paris**, there is no finer destination than the regal, château-studded Loire Valley. First up is the Unesco-hallmarked city of **Blois**. On day two, make the most of the limited time you have by hooking up with an organised château tour from here: queen of all castles **Château de Chambord** and the charmingly classical **Château de Cheverny**, with its hound-packed kennels, make a great combo. On the third day, continue southwest along France's longest river, the Loire, to **Amboise**, final home of Leonardo da Vinci; and solidly bourgeois **Tours**, from where **Château de Chenonceau**, beautifully strung across the River Cher 34km east, is an easy hop the next morning. If wine is a love, try to build some *dégustation* (tasting) of some local **Vouvray** wines in vineyards east of Tours into your itinerary. End your trip with France's elite riding school in **Saumur** and the movingly simple abbey church **Fontevraud l'Abbaye** – or push on northwest to **Angers** with its black chateau and Apocalypse tapestry. Château de Verrières is a befitting overnight address in this château-rich neck of the woods.

6 DAYS — Burgundy & Beyond

Red-wine lovers can enjoy the fruits of Burgundy with this itinerary, which begins in the Roman river-port of **Auxerre**, 170km southeast of Paris. Explore its ancient abbey, Gothic cathedral and cycle along towpaths in the afternoon. On day two consider an easy bike ride to Burgundy's last surviving example of Cistercian architecture in pretty **Pontigny**, 25km north. Stay overnight or push on to nearby **Chablis**, where bags more bike rides and gentle hikes between Burgundy vineyards await – allow plenty of time here to taste the seven *grands crus* of this well-known wine-making town. Day four, meander south to the picture-postcard village of **Noyers-sur-Serein**, then head east to the breathtaking, Unesco-listed **Abbaye de Fontenay**, before winding up for the night in **Semur-en-Auxois**, 25km south. **Alésia**, where Julius Caesar defeated Gaulish chief Vercingétorix in 52 BC, is not far from here and makes for a fascinating day out. On the last day discover **Dijon** and its beautiful medieval and Renaissance buildings. From here, should you have more time, take a road trip through the wine-making area of **Côte d'Or** to **Beaune**, or south to **Lyon** in the Rhône Valley.

🕙 10 DAYS — The South of France

For sun, sea and celebrity action, hit the hot south. Start in **Nice**, star of a coastline that unfurls in a pageant of belle-époque palaces and iconic sands. Drive along the Riviera's trio of legendary **corniches** – coastal views are mind-blowing – and day three take the train to glitzy **Monaco**. Then move to fishing port **St-Tropez** where millionaire yachts jostle for space with street artists. Rise early the next morning for the place des Lices market and frolic away the afternoon on the sand at Plage de Pampelonne. Day six is a toss-up between a dramatic drive along the **Corniche des Maures** to **Bormes-les-Mimosas** and the staggering **Route des Crêtes** mountain pass, or a boat trip to the *très belle* **Îles d'Hyères**. Head inland next to **Aix-en-Provence**, a canvas of graceful 19th-century architecture, stylish cafes and hidden squares. From Aix, it's a hop and a skip to **Ventabren** where lunch or dinner alfresco at La Table de Ventabren is what eating in Provence is all about. Devote your last two days to the wild **Gorges du Verdon**, Europe's largest canyon, two hour's drive northeast, or the gentler **Luberon** with its bounty of photogenic hilltop villages.

🕔 5 DAYS — Spring in the Alps

A trip to the French Alps often translates as one week of skiing in one place. Yet take the time to explore the region after the snow has melted – spring or early summer is best – and you'll be pleasantly surprised. Warm up with old-town ambling, lakeside strolling and warm-weather swimming in fairy-tale **Annecy**, a lakeside town just 45km from Geneva, Switzerland. On day two move on to **Chamonix** at the foot of Mont Blanc, Western Europe's highest peak: ride a cable car up to the **Aiguille du Midi** or, if the sky is not crystal-clear, ride a train up to the **Mer de Glace** glacier. Yet more unforgettable views of Mont Blanc seduce along hiking trails in **St-Gervais** and **Megève**, chic, picturesque Alpine villages with medieval old towns. Let the adrenalin rip, or push on via **Chambéry** to the **Parc National de la Vanoise**, where spectacular hiking in **Les Trois Vallées** easily pleases outdoor junkies. A fitting finale to your Alpine foray is the dizzying drive through the **Parc National des Écrins** to **Briançon**, the loveliest of all the medieval villages in the French Alps, famous for its Vauban fortifications.

Plan Your Trip

Eat & Drink Like a Local

Indulging in France's extraordinary wealth of gastronomic pleasures is reason alone to travel here – cruising around inspires hunger, gastronomic adventure and experimental know-how. For more on food and wine, see The French Table (p934) chapter.

The Year in Food

Feasting happens year-round, and what's cooking changes with the seasons.

Spring (Mar–May)

Markets burst with asparagus, artichokes and fresh goat's cheese, Easter cooks up traditional lamb for lunch, and the first strawberries redden.

Summer (Jun–Aug)

Melons, cherries, peaches, apricots, fresh figs, garlic and tomatoes brighten market stalls. Breton shallots are hand-harvested, and on the Atlantic and Mediterranean coasts, food lovers gorge on seafood and shellfish.

Autumn (Sep–Nov)

The Camargue's nutty red rice is harvested. Normandy apples fall from trees to make France's finest cider, and the chestnut harvest begins in the Ardèche, Cévennes and Corsica. In damp woods, mushrooming and the game season begins.

Winter (Dec–Feb)

Nets are strung beneath silvery groves in Provence and Corsica to catch olives. Pungent markets in the Dordogne and Provence sell black truffles, and in the Alps, skiers dip into cheese fondue. Christmas means Champagne and oysters, foie gras, chestnut-stuffed turkey and yule logs.

Food Experiences

Meals of a Lifetime

➡ **Le Grand Véfour** (p127) The ultimate haute cuisine experience in an 18th-century Parisian landmark.

➡ **Petit Pierre Reboul** (p785) Aix-en-Provence's culinary star and king of creative French.

➡ **Restaurant Hostellerie de Plaisance** (p640) Twin-star gastronomy by chef Philippe Etchebest in St-Émilion.

➡ **La Ribaudière** (p640) Michelin-starred cuisine packed with homegrown vegies near Cognac.

➡ **Le Bistrot** (p490) Gastronome paradise in Chamonix courtesy of Michelin-starred chef Mickey.

➡ **Le Vieux Logis** (p573) Local Dordogne products – including seasonal truffles – crafted into creative cuisine in Périgord Noir.

➡ **Le Coquillage** (p263) Triple-starred Michelin temple set to French perfection in a château in Brittany.

Cheap Treats

➡ **Croque monsieur** Toasted ham and cheese sandwich; cheesy 'madames' are egg-topped.

➡ **Chestnuts** Served piping hot in paper bags on street corners in winter.

➡ **Socca** Chickpea-flour pancake typical to Nice in the French Riviera (p837).

➡ **Pan Bagnat** Crusty Niçois tuna sandwich dripping in fruity green olive oil.

➡ **Flammekueche** (*tarte flambée* in French) Alsatian thin-crust pizza dough topped with sour cream, onions and bacon.

➡ **Ice cream** By the best *glaciers* (ice-cream makers) in France: **Berthillon** (p133) in Paris, **Fenocchio** (p837) in Nice, and **Glaces Geronimi** (p890) or **Raugi** (p882) in Corsica. Myrtle, chestnut, lavender, artichoke or camembert ice anyone?

➡ **Crêpes** Large, round, thin pancakes cooked at street-corner stands while you wait.

Dare to Try

➡ **Andouillette** Big fat sausage made from minced pig intestine; try it in Lyon, France's gastronomic heart and known for its piggy cuisine.

➡ **Oursins** (sea urchins) Caught and eaten west of Marseille in February.

➡ **Epoisses de Bourgogne** Create a stink with France's undisputed smelliest cheese from Burgundy.

➡ **Escargots** (snails) Eat them in Burgundy, shells stuffed with garlic and parsley butter, and oven-baked.

➡ **Cuisses de grenouilles** (frogs' legs) Catching wild frogs and frog farming has been outlawed in France since 1980, but frogs' legs are imported from Southeast Asia, ensuring this French culinary tradition is alive and kicking.

➡ **Foie** (liver) Die-hard aficionados in the Dordogne eat fresh fattened duck or goose liver, raw and chilled, with a glass of sweet Monbazillac wine.

➡ **Pieds de cochon** (pig trotters) Just that, or go for the oven-baked trotters of a *mouton* (sheep) or *veau* (calf).

Local Specialities

Gourmet appetites know no bounds in France, paradise for food lovers with its varied cuisine, markets and local gusto for dining well. Go to Burgundy for hearty wine-based cooking, Brittany and the Atlantic coast for seafood, and Basque Country for a slice of Spanish spice.

Normandy

Cream, apples and cider are the essentials of Norman cuisine (p217), which sees mussels simmered in cream and a splash of cider to make *moules à la crème normande* and tripe thrown in the slow pot with cider and vegetables to make *tripes à la mode de Caen*. Creamy Camembert is the local cow's milk cheese, and on the coast *coquilles St-Jacques* (scallops) and *huîtres* (oysters) rule the seafood roost. Apples are the essence of the region's main tipples: tangy cider and the potent *calvados* (apple brandy), exquisite straight or splashed on apple sorbet.

Burgundy

Vine-wealthy Burgundy honours a culinary trinity of beef, red wine and Dijon mustard. Savour bœuf bourguignon (beef marinated and cooked in young red wine with mushrooms, onions, carrots and bacon), followed by the pick of Burgundy AOC cheeses. Or eat a snail, traditionally served by the dozen and oven-baked in their shells with butter, garlic and parsley – mop the juices up with bread.

Wine-tasting in the Côte d'Or vineyards, source of world-famous Côte de Nuits and Côte de Beaune wines, is obligatory when in Burgundy; laid-back Irancy, less known around the globe but much-loved by locals, is an insider favourite.

The Dordogne

This southwest region is fabulously famous for its indulgent black truffles (p568) and poultry, especially ducks and geese, whose fattened livers are turned into *pâté de foie gras* (duck- or goose-liver pâté), which, somewhat predictably, comes straight or flavoured with Cognac and truffles. *Confit de canard* and *confit d'oie* are duck or goose joints cooked very slowly in their own fat. Snails are another tasty treat – savour one stuffed with foie gras. Walnuts from the region's abundant walnut groves go into *eau de noix* (caramel-coloured walnut liqueur).

Lyon

All too often Lyon is dubbed France's gastronomic capital. And while it doesn't compete with France's capital when it comes to variety of international cuisine, it certainly holds its own when it comes to titillating taste buds with the unusual and inventive. Take the age-old repertoire of feisty, often pork-driven dishes served in the city's legendary *bouchons* (small bistros): breaded fried tripe, big fat *andouillettes* (pig-intestine sausage), silk-weaver's brains (a herbed cheese spread, not brains at all) – there is no way you can ever say Lyonnais cuisine is run of the mill. A lighter, less meaty speciality is *quenelle de brochet,* a poached dumpling made of freshwater fish (usually pike) and served with sauce Nantua (a cream and freshwater-crayfish sauce).

Equally fine is the Lyonnais wine list where very fine Côtes de Rhône reds vie for attention with local Brouilly and highly esteemed Mâcon reds from nearby Burgundy. In *bouchons,* local Beaujolais is mixed with a dash of blackcurrant liqueur to make a blood-red *communard* aperitif.

Alsace

No Alsatian dish is more classic than *choucroute alsacienne* – sauerkraut flavoured with juniper berries and served hot with sausages, bacon, pork and/or ham knuckle. It's meaty, Teutonic and served in *winstubs* (traditional Alsatian taverns). *Wädele braisé au pinot noir* (ham knuckles braised in wine) also come with sauerkraut. Crack open a bottle of light citrusy sylvaner, crisp dry Alsatian riesling or full-bodied pinot noir to accompany either, and round off the filling feast with a *tarte alsacienne,* a scrumptious custard tart made with local fruit like mirabelles (sweet yellow plums) or *quetsches* (a variety of purple plum). Beer might be big in Alsace but it's a big no-no when it comes to sauerkraut. Sweet tooths will adore Alsatian gingerbread and Kougelhopf (sugared, ring-shaped raisin cake).

Provence & the Riviera

Cuisine in this sun-baked land is laden with tomatoes, melons, cherries, peaches, olives, Mediterranean fish and Alpine cheese. Farmers gather at the weekly market to sell their fruit and vegetables, woven garlic plaits, dried herbs displayed in stubby coarse sacks, and olives stuffed with a multitude of edible sins. *À la Provençal* still means anything with a generous dose of garlic-seasoned tomatoes, while a simple *filet mignon* sprinkled with olive oil and rosemary fresh from the garden makes the same magnificent Sunday lunch it did generations ago.

Yet there are exciting culinary contrasts in this region, which see fishermen return with the catch of the day in seafaring Marseille; grazing bulls and paddy fields in the Camargue; lambs in the Alpilles; black truffles in the Vaucluse; cheese made from cow's milk in Alpine pastures; and an Italianate accent to cooking in seaside Nice.

Bouillabaisse, Marseille's mighty meal of fish stew, is Provence's most famous contribution to French cuisine. The chowder must contain at least three kinds of fresh saltwater fish, cooked for about 10 minutes in a broth containing onions, tomatoes, saffron and various herbs, and eaten as a main course with toasted bread and *rouille* (a spicy red mayonnaise of olive oil, garlic and chilli peppers).

When in Provence, do as the Provençaux do: drink pastis. An aniseed-flavoured, 45% alcoholic drink, it was invented in Marseille by industrialist Paul Ricard in 1932. Amber-coloured in the bottle, it turns milky white when mixed with water. An essential lunch or dinner companion is a chilled glass of the region's irresistibly pink, AOC Côtes de Provence rosé wine.

Brittany

Brittany is a paradise for seafood lovers (think lobster, scallops, sea bass, turbot, mussels and oysters from Cancale) as well as kids, thanks to the humble crêpe and *galette,* an ancient culinary tradition that has long-ruled Breton cuisine. Pair a sweet wheat-flour pancake or savoury buckwheat *galette* with *une bolée* (a stubby terracotta goblet) of apple-rich Breton cider, and taste buds enter gourmet heaven. Royal Guillevic and ciders produced by the Domaine de Kervéguen are excellent-quality artisanal ciders to try. If cider is not your cup of tea, order a local beer like Coreff or non-alcoholic *lait ribot* (fermented milk). *Chouchen* (hydromel), a fermented honey liqueur, is a typical Breton aperitif.

Cheese is not big, but *la beurre de Bretagne* (Breton butter) is. Traditionally sea-salted and creamy, a knob of it naturally goes into crêpes, *galettes* and the most outrageously buttery cake you're likely to ever taste in your life – *kouign amann* (Breton butter cake). Bretons, unlike the rest of the French, even butter their bread. Butter handmade by Jean-Yves Bourdier – buy it at his shop in **St-Malo** (www.lebeurre bordier.com; 9 rue Orme) – ends up on tables of top restaurants around the world.

Seaweed is another Breton culinary curiosity, and 80% of French shallots are grown here.

Languedoc-Roussillon

No dish better evokes Languedoc than *cassoulet,* an earthy cockle-warming stew of white beans and meat that fires passionate debate. Everyone knows best which type of bean and meat hunk should be thrown in the *cassole,* the traditional earthenware dish it is cooked and brought to the table in. Otherwise this region's trademark cuisine *campagnarde* (country cooking) sees fishermen tend lagoon oyster beds on the coast, olives pressed in gentle hills inland, blue-veined 'king of cheeses' ripening in caves in Roquefort, fattened geese and gaggles of ducks around Toulouse, sheep in salty marsh meadows around Montpellier, and mushrooms in its forests. A Spanish accent gives cuisine in neighbouring Roussillon a fiery twist of exuberance.

Basque Country

Among the essential ingredients of Basque cooking are the deep-red Espelette chillies that add bite to many dishes, including the dusting on the signature *jambon de Bayonne,* the locally prepared Bayonne ham. Eating out in this part of France near Spain is a delight thanks to its many casual *pintxo* (tapas) bars serving garlic prawns, spicy chorizo sausages and other local dishes tapas-style. Wash the whole lot down with a glass of local cider *(sidrea* in basque), lighter, sweeter and more sparkling than ciders in northern France, best poured in a glass at arm's length.

Basques love cakes, especially *gâteau basque* (layer cake filled with cream or cherry jam). Then there's Bayonne chocolate...

How to Eat & Drink Like a Local

It pays to know what and how much to eat, and when – adopting the local culinary pace is key to savouring every last exquisite moment of the French day.

When to Eat

➜ **Petit déjeuner (breakfast)** The French kick-start the day with a *tartine* (slice of baguette smeared with unsalted butter and jam) and *un café* (espresso), long milky *café au lait* or – especially kids – hot chocolate. In hotels you get a real cup but in French homes, coffee and hot chocolate are drunk from a cereal bowl – perfect bread-dunking terrain. Croissants (eaten straight, never with butter or jam) are a weekend treat along with brioches (sweet breads), *pains au chocolat* (chocolate-filled croissants) and other *viennoiserie* (sweet baked goods).

➜ **Déjeuner (lunch)** A meal few French would go without. The traditional main meal of the day, lunch translates as a starter and main course with wine, followed by an espresso. Sunday lunch is a long, languid affair taking several hours. Indeed, a fully fledged, traditional French meal – lunch or *dîner* – can comprise six courses, each accompanied by a different wine. Standard restaurant lunch hours are noon to 2.30pm.

➜ **Aperitif** The *apéro* (predinner drink) is sacred. Paris cafes and bars get packed out from around 5pm onwards as workers relax over a chit-chat-fuelled *kir* (white wine sweetened with blackcurrant syrup) or beer.

➜ **Goûter** An afternoon snack, devoured with particular relish by French children. A slab of milk chocolate inside a wedge of baguette is a traditional favourite.

➜ **Dîner (dinner)** Traditionally lighter than lunch, but a meal that is increasingly treated as the main meal of the day. Standard restaurant times are 7pm to 10.30pm.

Where to Eat

➜ **Auberge** Country inn serving traditional fare, often attached to a small hotel.

➜ **Ferme auberge** Working farm that cooks up meals from local farm products; usually only dinner and frequently only by reservation.

➜ **Bistro** (also spelled *bistrot*) Anything from a pub or bar with snacks and light meals to a small, fully fledged restaurant.

➜ **Neobistro** Particularly trendy in Paris where this contemporary take on the traditional bistro embraces everything from checked-tablecloth tradition to contemporary minimalism.

➡ **Brasserie** Much like a cafe except it serves full meals, drinks and coffee from morning until 11pm or later. Typical fare includes *choucroute* (sauerkraut) and *moules frites* (mussels and fries).

➡ **Restaurant** Born in Paris in the 18th century, restaurants today serve lunch and dinner five or six days a week.

➡ **Buffet** (or *buvette*) Kiosk, usually at train stations and airports, selling drinks, filled baguettes and snacks.

➡ **Cafe** Basic light snacks as well as drinks.

➡ **Crêperie** (also *galetterie*) Casual address specialising in sweet crêpes and savoury *galettes* (buckwheat crêpes).

➡ **Salon de thé** Trendy tearoom often serving light lunches (quiche, salads, cakes, tarts, pies and pastries) as well as green, black and herbal teas.

➡ **Table d'hôte** (literally 'host's table') Some of the most charming B&Bs serve *table d'hôte* too, a delicious homemade meal of set courses with little or no choice.

➡ **Winstub** Cosy wine tavern in Alsace serving traditional Alsatian cooking and local wines.

➡ **Estaminet** Flemish-style eatery of Flanders and *le nord,* cooking up regional fare.

Menu Decoder

➡ **Carte** Menu, as in the written list of what's cooking, listed in the order you'd eat it: starter, main course, cheese then dessert.

➡ **Menu** Not at all what it means in English, *le menu* in French is a two- or three-course meal at a fixed price. It's by far the best-value dining and most bistros and restaurants chalk one on the board. Lunch *menus* – usually incredibly good value – occasionally include a glass of wine and/or coffee; dinner *menus* in gastronomic restaurants sometimes pair a perfectly matched glass of wine with each course.

➡ **À la carte** Order whatever you fancy from the menu (as opposed to choosing a fixed *menu*).

➡ **Formule** Not to be confused with a *menu, une formule* is a cheaper lunchtime option comprising a main plus starter or dessert.

➡ **Plat du jour** Dish of the day, invariably good value.

➡ **Menu enfant** Two- or three-course kids' meal at a fixed price (generally for children up to the age of 12); usually includes a soft drink.

➡ **Menu dégustation** Fixed-price tasting *menu* served in many top-end restaurants, consisting of five to seven modestly sized courses.

➡ **Amuse-bouche** A complimentary savoury morsel intended to excite and ignite taste buds, served in top-end and gastronomic restaurants at the very beginning of a meal.

➡ **Entrée** Starter, appetiser.

➡ **Plat** Main course.

➡ **Fromage** Cheese, accompanied with fresh bread (never crackers and no butter); always served after the main course and *before* dessert.

➡ **Dessert** Just that, served *after* cheese.

Plan Your Trip

Travel with Children

Be it kid-friendly extraordinaire capital or rural hinterland, France spoils families with its rich mix of cultural sights, activities and entertainment – some paid for, some free. To get the most out of travelling *en famille*, plan ahead.

France for Kids

Savvy parents can find kid-appeal in almost every sight in France, must-sees included. Skip the formal guided tour of Mont St Michel, for example, and hook up with a walking guide to lead you and the children barefoot across the sand to the abbey; trade the daytime queues at the Eiffel Tower for a tour after dark with teens; don't dismiss wine tasting in Provence or Burgundy outright rent bicycles and turn it into a family bike ride instead. Opportunities are endless.

Museums & Monuments

Many Paris museums organise creative *ateliers* (workshops) for children, parent-accompanied or solo. Workshops are themed, require booking, last 1½ to two hours, and cost €5 to €15 per child. French children have no school Wednesday afternoon, so most workshops happen Wednesday afternoon, weekends and daily during school holidays. Most cater for kids aged seven to 14 years, although in Paris art tours at the Louvre start at four years and at the Musée d'Orsay, five years.

Countrywide, when buying tickets at museums and monuments, ask about children's activity sheets – most have something to hook kids. Another winner is to arm your gadget-mad child (from 6yrs) with an audioguide. Older children can check out

Which Region?

Paris
Interactive museums, choice dining for every taste and budget, and beautiful green parks seemingly at every turn make the French capital a top choice for families.

Normandy
Beaches, boats and some great stuff for history-mad kids and teens give this northern region plenty of family lure.

Brittany
More beaches, boats, pirate-perfect islands and bags of good old-fashioned outdoor fun. Enough said.

French Alps & the Jura Mountains
Winter in this mountainous region in western France translates as one giant outdoor (snowy) playground – for all ages.

French Riviera & Monaco
A vibrant arts scene, a vivacious cafe culture and a beach-laced shore riddled with seafaring activities keeps kids of all ages on their toes.

Corsica
Sailing, kayaking, walking, biking, or simply dipping your toes or snorkel mask in clear turquoise waters: life on this island is fairytale *belle* (beautiful).

what apps each museum or monument might have for smartphones and tablets.

Outdoor Activities

Once the kids are out of nappies, skiing in the French Alps is the obvious family choice. Ski school École du Ski Français (p961) initiates kids in the art of snow plough (group or private lessons, half- or full day) from four years old, and many resorts open fun-driven *jardins de neige* (snow gardens) to children from three years old. Families with kids aged under 10 will find smaller resorts like Les Gets, Avoriaz (car-free), La Clusaz, Chamrousse and Le Grand Bornand easier to navigate and better value than larger ski stations. Then, of course, there is all the fun of the fair off-piste: ice skating, sledging, snowshoeing, mushing, indoor swimming pools...

The French Alps and Pyrenees are prime walking areas. Tourist offices have information on easy, well-signposted family walks – or get in touch with a local guide. In Chamonix the cable-car ride and two-hour hike to Lac Blanc followed by a dip in the Alpine lake is a DIY family favourite; as are the mountain-discovery half-days for ages three to seven, and outdoor-adventure days for ages eight to 12 run by Cham' Aventure (p486). As with skiing, smaller places such as the Parc Naturel Régional du Massif des Bauges cater much better to young families than the big names everyone knows.

White-water sports and canoeing are doable for children aged seven and older; the French Alps, Provence and Massif Central are key areas. Mountain biking is an outdoor thrill that teens can share – try Morzine. Or dip into some gentle sea-kayaking around *calanques* (deep rocky inlets), below cliffs and into caves in the Mediterranean, a family activity suitable for kids aged four

upwards. Marseille in Provence and Bonifacio on Corsica are hot spots to rent the gear and get afloat.

Entertainment

Tourist offices can tell you what's on – and the repertoire is impressive: puppet shows alfresco, children's theatres, children's films at cinemas Wednesday afternoon and weekends, street buskers, illuminated monuments after dark, an abundance of music festivals and so on. A sure winner are the *son et lumière* (sound-and-light) shows projected on some Renaissance châteaux in the Loire Valley; the papal palace in Avignon; and cathedral façades in Rouen, Chartres and Amiens. Outstanding after-dark illuminations that never fail to enchant include Paris' Eiffel Tower and Marseille's MuCEM.

Dining Out

French children, accustomed to three-course lunches at school, expect a starter *(entrée)*, main course *(plat)* and dessert as their main meal of the day. They know the difference between Brie and Camembert, and eat lettuce, grated carrot and other salads no problem. Main meals tend to be meat 'n' veg or pasta, followed by dessert and/or a slice of cheese. Classic French mains loved by children include *gratin dauphinois* (sliced potatoes oven-baked in cream), *escalope de veau* (breaded pan-fried veal) and *bœuf bourguignon* (beef stew). Fondue and *raclette* (melted cheese served with potatoes and cold meats) become favourites from about five years, and *moules frites* (mussels and fries) a couple of years later.

Children's *menus* (fixed meal at a set price) are common, although anyone in France for more than a few days will soon tire of the ubiquitous spaghetti bolognaise or *saucisse* (sausage), or *steak haché* (beef burger) and *frites* (fries) followed by ice cream that most feature. Don't be shy in asking for a half-portion of an adult main – restaurants generally oblige. Ditto in budget and midrange places to ask for a plate of *pâtes au beurre* (pasta with butter) for fussy or very young eaters.

It is perfectly acceptable to dine *en famille* after dark, providing the kids don't run wild. Few restaurants open their doors, however, before 7.30pm or 8pm, making brasseries and cafes – many serve food continuously from 7am or 8am until midnight – more appealing for families with younger children. Some restaurants have high chairs and supply paper and pens for children to draw with while waiting for their meal.

Baby requirements are easily met. The choice of infant formula, soy and cow's milk, nappies (diapers) and jarred baby food in supermarkets and pharmacies is similar to any developed country, although opening hours are more limited (few shops open Sunday). Organic *(bio)* baby food is harder to find.

Drinks

Buy a fizzy drink for every child sitting at the table and the bill soars. Opt instead for a free *carafe d'eau* (jug of tap water) with meals and *un sirop* (flavoured fruit syrup) in between – jazzed up with *des glaçons* (some ice cubes) and *une paille* (a straw). Every self-respecting cafe and bar in France has dozens of syrup flavours to choose from: pomegranate fuelled grenadine and pea-green *menthe* (mint) are French-kid favourites, but there are peach, raspberry, cherry, lemon and a rainbow of others, too. Syrup is served diluted with water and, best up, costs a good €2 less than a Coke. Expect to pay around €1.50 a glass.

Children's Highlights

Gastronomic Experiences

➡ Afternoon tea to remember at Ladurée (p124), Paris

➡ Breton crêpes (p252)

➡ Berthillon (p133) ice cream, Paris; Geronimi (p890) and Raugi (p882) ice cream, Corsica

➡ Waffles with sweet vanilla cream, served since the 18th century, at Meert (p184) tearoom, Lille

➡ Oysters on an oyster farm, Gujan Mestras (p643), near Bordeaux

➡ Grape-juice tasting (parents taste alcoholic equivalent), La Balance Mets et Vins (p533), Arbois

➡ Frogs' legs and a lakeside bike ride, La Bicyclette Bleue (p475), La Dombes

➡ Snail discovery and tasting at Languedoc snail farm-museum, La Caracole (p724), near Alès

➡ Joining in the chestnut harvest at La Ferme de la Borie (p743), an organic farm in Haut-Languedoc

➡ Hand-milling mustard seeds with stone at mustard factory Moutarderie Fallot (p423) in Beaune

➡ Get acquainted with fabulous fungi at the Musée du Champignon (p402), a mushroom farm in a cave near Samur

Energy Burners

➡ Skiing, snowboarding, sledging and dog-mushing (from four years), French Alps and Pyrenees (p478)

➡ Scaling Aiguille du Midi by gondola and crossing glaciers into Italy (from four years), Chamonix (p483)

➡ Around an island by bike (over five years) or parent-pulled bike trailer (over one year), Île de Ré (p625) and Île de Porquerolles (p863)

➡ White-water sports (over seven years), Gorges du Verdon (p822), Gorges du Tarn (p746) and Gorges de l'Ardèche (p477)

➡ Canoeing (over seven years) beneath the Pont du Gard near Nîmes (p721) or along the Dordogne River around La Roque Gageac (p574)

➡ Donkey treks (over 10 years) including Robert Louis Stevenson in the wild Cévennes (p742)

➡ Horse-riding with cowboys in the Camargue (p792)

➡ Zipping between trees on wires at Acrobastille (p518) (from five years), Grenoble

Best Free Stuff

➡ Scaring yourself silly by standing on glass floors up up high and looking down down down – at Paris' Eiffel Tower (p62), Aiguille du Midi (p483) above Chamonix, Marseille's Villa Méditeranée (p765)

➡ Crazy about castles? No fortress is finer to explore than Marseille's feisty Fort St-Jean (p765)

➡ Watching fairy-tales come to life before your eyes in half-timbered, castle-topped villages along the Route des Vins d'Alsace (p332)

➡ Montpellier Parc Zoologique (p725) – city zoo

➡ Watching spectacular Pyrenean scenery unfold aboard mythical mountain train, Le Train Jaune (p757) in the Languedoc

➡ Dune du Pilat (p642): the largest 'sandcastle' any child is ever likely to see

➡ World-class freebie festivals that kids love: Avignon's fringe Festival Off (p802), Lyon's Fête des Lumières (p462) and the Carnaval de Nice (p836)

Wildlife Watch

➡ Vultures in Parc National des Pyrénées (p687)

➡ Seals in northern France's Baie de Somme (p198)

➡ Wolves in Parc National du Mercantour (www.mercantour.eu), **Parc Animalier des Monts de Guéret** (☑05 55 81 23 23; www.loups-chabrieres.com; adult/child €9.50/7; ☉10am-8pm May-Aug, 1.30-6pm Sep-Apr) and Parc du Gévaudan (p750)

➡ Dancing horses in Saumur (p398), Versailles (p161) and Chantilly (p171)

➡ Bulls and flamingos in the Camargue (p791)

Rainy Days

➡ Romp through sewage tunnels with rats, Musée des Égouts (p62) de Paris

➡ Aquariums in Paris (p65), Monaco (p865), Boulogne-sur-Mer, (p195) St-Malo (p256), Brest (p269), La Rochelle (p621), Lyon (p462) and Biarritz (p652)

➡ Ogle at skulls, Les Catacombes (p108), Paris

➡ Play cavemen in caves riddled with prehistoric art in the Vézère Valley, with the world's largest collection of stalactites at Aven Armand (p748), Languedoc

➡ Delve into the depths of the ocean at Cité de l'Océan (p652), Biarritz

➡ Inspect insects, lots of insects, at Micropolis (p750) near Millau; and Insectopia (p604), Lot Valley

➡ Sweeter than sweet museums: Musée du Bonbon Haribo (p722), Uzès; Planète Musée du Chocolat (p653), Biarritz

Tech Experiences

➡ Science workshops at Paris' Cité des Sciences (p81) (from three years) and Palais de la Découverte (p68) (from 10 years)

➡ Learn how planes are built (from six years), Jean Luc Lagardère Airbus factory (p698), Toulouse

➡ Enter wannabe-mechanic heaven, Cité de l'Automobile and Cité du Train (p349), Mulhouse

➡ Meddle in science at Strasbourg's interactive Le Vaisseau (p326) science and technology museum

➡ Spin in a fish on a hi-tech vintage carousel or ride a house-sized mechanical elephant at Les Machines de l'Île de Nantes (p612), Nantes

---

WHAT TO PACK

Babies & Toddlers

➡ A front or back sling: France's cobbled streets, metro stairs and hilltop villages were not built with pushchairs (strollers) in mind. Several must-see museums, notably Château de Versailles, don't let pushchairs in.

➡ A portable changing mat, handwash gel etc (baby-changing facilities are a rarity)

➡ A canvas screw-on seat for toddlers (few restaurants have high chairs)

➡ Car seat: rental companies rent them but at proportionately extortionate rates. In France children under 10 years or less than 1.40m in height must, by law, be strapped in an appropriate car seat.

Six to 12 Years

➡ Binoculars for young explorers to zoom in on wildlife, sculpted cathedral façades, etc

➡ A pocket video camera to inject fun into 'boring' adult activities

➡ Activity books, sketchpad and pens, travel journal and kid-sized day pack

➡ Water bottle, always handy (and great fun to fill up at water fountains found all over France, marked 'eau potable')

➡ Fold-away microscooter and/or rollerblades

➡ Kite (for beaches in Brittany, Normandy and on the Atlantic coast with strong winds)

Teens

➡ France-related apps

➡ French phrasebook

➡ Mask, snorkel and flippers to dive in from a multitude of magnificent beaches on the Atlantic coast and Med; only two or three marked trails countrywide rent the gear.

→ The 100-year old Funiculaire du Capucin (p548) in Le Mont-Dore, Massif Central, is one mighty cool way to climb a mountain.

Hands-On History & Culture

→ Time-travel to 1920s Paris: chase vintage sailboats with a stick in Jardin du Luxembourg (p105), just like Parisian kids did a century ago

→ Relive the battle between Julius Caesar and Vercingétorix at Alésia in 52 BC, with reconstructed Roman fortification lines et al, at Burgundy's first-class MuséoParc Alésia (p430)

→ Become acquainted with the fine art of perfumerie in Grasse (p852; perfume studios, museum, workshops) and nearby Mouans-Sartoux (p851; flower gardens)

→ Play medieval builders at Chantier Médiéval de Guédelon (p434), Burgundy

→ Go Roman (over five years) at Ludo, Pont du Gard, near Nîmes (p721)

Theme Parks

→ Cité de l'Espace (p695; outer space), Toulouse

→ Disneyland (p161), Paris

→ Vulcania (p547; volcanoes), Massif Central

→ Futuroscope (p618) (film), Poitiers

Boat Trips

→ Canal boating, Burgundy (p419) and Languedoc (p732)

→ Sailing around caves and pearly-white cliffs, Bonifacio (p897), Corsica

→ Sea-kayaking in Les Calanques (p780), Marseille

→ River boating aboard a flat-bottomed *gabarre*, Périgord and Lot Valleys (p576)

→ White-water rafting in the Gorges du Verdon (p822), Provence

Planning

When to Go

Consider the season and what you want to do/see: teen travel is a year-round affair (there's always something to entertain, regardless of the weather), but parents with younger kids will find the dry, pleasantly warm days of spring and early summer best suited to kidding around the park –

every town has at least one *terrain de jeux* (playground).

France's festival repertoire is another planning consideration.

Accommodation

In Paris and larger towns and cities, serviced apartments equipped with washing machine and kitchen are suited to families with younger children. Countrywide, hotels with family or four-person rooms can be hard to find and need booking in advance. Functional, if soulless, chain hotels like Formule 1, found on the outskirts of most large towns, always have a generous quota of family rooms and make convenient overnight stops for motorists driving from continental Europe or the UK (Troyes is a popular stopover for Brits en route to the Alps). Parents with just one child and/or a baby in tow will have no problem finding hotel accommodation – most midrange hotels have baby cots and are happy to put a child's bed in a double room for a minimal extra cost.

In rural France, family-friendly B&Bs and *fermes auberges* (farmstays) are convenient. For older children, tree houses decked out with bunk beds and Mongolian yurts create a real family adventure; see the Accommodation section of the Directory A–Z for more.

Camping is huge with French families: check into a self-catering mobile home, wooden chalet or tent; sit back on the verandah with glass of wine in hand and watch as your kids – wonderfully oblivious to any barriers language might pose – run around with new-found French friends.

Plan Your Trip
Outdoor Activities

France takes outdoor activities and elevates them to a fine art. In the birthplace of the Tour de France, the cycling is world-class; in Mont Blanc's backyard the skiing is second to none. And everywhere the hiking is, ah, just *magnifique* – from Corsica's coastal wilds to the volcanic cones of Massif Central.

Best Outdoor Experiences

Best Off-Piste Descent
Whoop as you make a 2800m vertical descent on La Vallée Blanche in Chamonix – it's the ride of a lifetime.

Best Long-Distance Hike
Scale the wildest heights of the Pyrenees on the GR10, taking you from the Mediterranean to the Atlantic.

Best Cycling
Cruise past turreted châteaux and trace the curves of France's longest river in the Loire Valley.

Best Surf
Grab your board and hit the fizzing surf on the Atlantic Coast. Hossegor is big-wave heaven.

Best Kayaking & Canyoning
Make a splash in the astonishingly turquoise water of the Gorges du Verdon, Europe's largest canyon.

Skiing & Snowboarding

When to Go

The ski season goes with the snow, running from early or mid-December to around mid-April. The higher you go, the more snow-sure the resort and the longer the season. Crowds and room rates skyrocket during school holidays (Christmas, February half-term, Easter), so avoid these times if you can. There is summer glacier skiing in two resorts: Les Deux Alpes (p524) and Val d'Isère (Espace Killy; p513) from roughly mid-June to August.

Skiing & Snowboarding Destinations

Just whisper the words 'French Alps' to a skier and watch their eyes light up. These mountains are the crème de la crème of European skiing, with the height edge and giddy Mont Blanc views. Return time and again (and many do) and you'll still never ski them all! Two of the world's largest areas are here – Les Portes du Soleil (p494), with 650km of runs, and Les Trois Vallées (p507) with 600km of runs – as well as Europe's highest resort, Val Thorens (p507), at 2300m. Crowned by Mont Blanc, Chamonix (p483) skiing is the stuff of legend, especially the do-before-you-die La Vallée Blanche (p486) off-piste descent. Speed is of the essence in the glacier-licked freerider favourites of Les Deux Alpes and Val d'Isère, as well as Alpe d'Huez (p526), where the brave can tackle Europe's longest black run, the 16km La Sarenne.

Beginners and intermediates will find tamer skiing and boarding in the Pyrenees (p670) and Le Mont-Dore (p548) in Massif Central. Cross-country (*ski de fond*) is big in the thickly forested Jura (p529), the host of the famous **Transjurassiene** (www.transjurassienne.com) race, and at the Espace Nordique Sancy (p549) in the Massif Central, with 250km of trails to glide and skate on.

Ski Passes, Tuition & Equipment Hire

Prices for ski passes (*forfaits*) covering one or more ski areas vary according to the popularity of the resort, but can be anything from €30 to €52 per day to €120 to €260 per week (six days). Most passes are now hands-free, with a built-in chip that barriers detect, and can be prebooked online – a wise idea if you want to beat the slopeside queues. Children usually pay half-price and under fives ski for free (bring proof of age).

All-inclusive rental will set you back around €32/175 per day/six days for skiing/snowboarding equipment, and €15/65 for cross-country. Most resorts have one or more ski schools with certified instructors. Group lessons cost roughly €40/160 for one/six half-days. Kids can start learning from the age of four.

Information

➡ **Where to Ski and Snowboard** (Chris Gill and Dave Watts; www.wheretoskiandsnowboard. com) Up-to-the minute guide to the slopes.

➡ **If You Ski** (www.ifyouski.com) Resort guides, ski deals and the lowdown on ski hire and schools.

➡ **Météo France** (www.meteofrance.com) Weather and daily avalanche forecast during the ski season.

➡ **École du Ski Français** (ESF; www.esf.net) The largest ski school in the world, with first-class tuition. Search by region.

SKI RUN CLASSIFICATIONS

➡ **Green** Easy-peasy runs for absolute beginners.

➡ **Blue** Gentle, well-groomed runs for novices.

➡ **Red** Intermediate – groomed but steeper and narrower than blue runs.

➡ **Black** Difficult runs for experts, often with moguls and steep, near-vertical drops.

➡ **France Montagnes** (www.france-montagnes. com) Official website of French ski resorts, with guides, maps, snow reports and more.

Hiking & Walking
When to Go

There is some form of walking available year-round in France. Spring and autumn are great seasons to hike in Corsica and on the French Riviera, which swelter in summer. The season is short and sweet in the Alps, running from mid-June to September.

Hiking & Walking Destinations

Hikers have a high time of it in the Alps, with mile after never-ending mile of well-marked trails. Lifts and cable cars take the sweat out of hiking here in summer. Chamonix is the trailhead for the epic 10-day, three-country Tour du Mont Blanc (p487), but gentler paths, such as the Grand Balcon Sud (p487), also command Mont Blanc close-ups. Some of the finest treks head into the more remote, glacier-capped wilds of the Parc National des Écrins (p524), with 700km of trails – many following old shepherd routes – and the equally gorgeous Parc National de la Vanoise (p517).

But the Alps are tip-of-the-iceberg stuff. Just as lovely are walks threading through the softly-rounded heights of the Vosges (p347) and through the forest-cloaked hills of Jura (p529), spreading down to Lake Geneva. The extinct volcanoes in the Massif Central (p537), interwoven with 13 *Grandes Randonnées* (long-distance footpaths), and the mist-shrouded peaks and swooping forested valleys of the Parc National des Pyrénées (p679) offer fine walking and blissful solitude. In the Cévennes, you can follow in Robert Louis Stevenson's footsteps on the GR70 Chemin de Stevenson (p742) from Le Puy to Alès – with or without a donkey.

The coast, you say? Corsica is a hiker's paradise – the GR20, the 15-day trek that crosses the island north to south (p908), is one of France's most famous, but there are dozens of shorter, easier walks. Or combine walking with swimming on the *sentiers*

littoraux in the Alpes-Maritimes. More bracing hikes await on the GR21 skirting the chalky cliffs of Côte d'Albâtre in Normandy (p220), the Côte d'Opale's GR120, taking in the colour-changing seascapes of the English Channel (p192), and Brittany's forested Presqu'île de Crozon peninsula (p273), with 145km of signed trails.

Information

➔ **Club Alpin Français** (French Alpine Club; www.ffcam.fr) Has guides for alpine sports and manages 127 *refuges* (mountain huts).

NATIONAL PARKS AT A GLANCE

PARK	FEATURES	ACTIVITIES	WHEN TO GO
Parc National de la Vanoise (p517)	postglacial mountain landscape of Alpine peaks, beech-fir forests & 80 sq km of glaciers, forming France's first national park (530 sq km); chamois, ibex, marmots, golden eagles, bearded vultures	alpine & cross-country skiing, walking, mountaineering, mountain biking	spring, summer & winter
Parc National de Port-Cros (www.portcrosparcnational.fr)	island marine park off the Côte d'Azur forming France's smallest national park & Europe's first marine park (700 hectares & 1288 hectares of water); puffins, shearwaters, migratory birds	snorkelling, birdwatching, swimming, gentle strolling	summer & autumn (for birdwatching)
Parc National des Calanques (p780)	rocky promontories rising out of turquoise water; idyllic coves & beaches, some accessible only by kayak	hiking, sea kayaking, swimming, snorkelling	spring & summer
Parc National des Cévennes (p741)	wild peat bogs, granite peaks, ravines & ridges bordering the Massif Central & Languedoc (910 sq km); red deer, beavers, vultures, wolves, bison	walking, donkey trekking, mountain biking, horse riding, cross-country skiing, caving, canoeing, botany (2250 plant species)	spring & winter
Parc National des Écrins (p524)	glaciers, glacial lakes & mountaintops soaring up to 4102m in the French Alps (1770 sq km); marmots, lynx, ibex, chamois, bearded vultures	walking, climbing, hang-gliding & paragliding, kayaking	spring & summer
Parc National des Pyrénées (p679)	100km of mountains along the Spanish border (457 sq km); marmots, izards (Pyrenean chamois), brown bears, golden eagles, vultures, buzzards	alpine & cross-country skiing, walking, mountaineering, rock-climbing, white-water sports, canoeing, kayaking, mountain biking	spring, summer & winter
Parc National du Mercantour (www.mercantour.eu)	Provence at its most majestic with 3000m-plus peaks & dead-end valleys along the Italian border; marmots, mouflons, chamois, ibex, wolves, golden & short-toed eagles, bearded vultures; Bronze Age petroglyphs	alpine skiing, white-water sports, mountain biking, walking, donkey trekking	spring, summer & winter

➡ **IGN** (www.ign.fr) Topographic maps covering every corner of France, plus walking guides. The hiker's best friend.

➡ **GR-Infos** (www.gr-infos.com) Multilingual site with route descriptions and maps for France's long-distance trails.

➡ **Parcs Nationaux de France** (French National Parks; www.parcsnationaux.fr) Official site for info on France's seven national parks.

➡ **Cicerone** (www.cicerone.co.uk) Walking guides to Haute Savoie, Dordogne, Languedoc, Massif Central and Corsica, among others.

Cycling & Mountain Biking

When to Go

Slip onto a bicycle saddle to maximise breezes when the heat turns up. Summer is prime time for road cycling on the coast and mountain biking – *vélo tout terrain* (VTT) – in the French Alps and Pyrenees, with the season running from mid-June to September. Elsewhere, there's some form of cycling available year-round, be it in vine-ribboned valleys or along France's great waterways.

Cycling & Mountain Biking Destinations

France is fabulous freewheeling country, with routes leading along its lushly wooded valleys and mighty rivers begging to be explored in slow motion. The options are boundless, but among the best are the soothingly lovely, château-studded Loire Valley – Loire à Vélo (p367) maintains 800km of signposted routes from Cuffy to the Atlantic; the peaceful towpaths shadowing the 240km, Unesco-listed Canal du Midi (p711); and Provence's 236km Autour du Luberon (p820), taking you from one gold-stone village to the next. You can pair wine tasting with a pedal through the vines in Burgundy (p409), the Beaujolais region (p474), the southern Rhône Valley (p475) or the Route des Vins d'Alsace (p332). Bicycle trails also crisscross the sun-baked Île de Ré (p625), dangling off the Atlantic coast.

Naturally, if you're up for a challenge, the gruelling inclines and exhilarating descents of the Alps and Pyrenees will ap-

peal. Resorts such as Alpe d'Huez (p526), Morzine (p494) and Les Deux Alpes (p524) are downhill heaven, as is the Parc National des Pyrénées (p679), where ski stations open up to mountain bikers in summer with *sentiers balisés* (marked trails) and obstacle-riddled bike parks for honing technique. Most cable cars let you take your bike for free or a nominal fee with a valid lift pass.

Bike hire is widely available and costs from €10 per day for a classic bike to €35 for a top-of-the-range mountain bike or ebike. Tourist office websites are a good first port of call for route maps and itineraries.

Information

➡ **Lonely Planet Cycling in France** Your definitive guide to cycling in France, with elevation charts, itineraries for all fitness levels and detailed maps.

➡ **Fédération Française de Cyclisme** (French Cycling Federation; www.ffc.fr) Going strong since 1881, this is the authority on competitive cycling and mountain biking in France.

➡ **VeloMap** (www.velomap.org) For free Garmin GPS cycling maps.

➡ **Véloroutes et Voies Vertes** (www.af3v.org) The inside scoop on 250 signposted *véloroutes* (bike paths) and *voies vertes* (greenways), plus an interactive map to pinpoint them.

Adventure & Water Sports

Kayaking & Canoeing

Kayaking and canoeing are available up and down the country, with some of the best options (including the looking-glass Lake Annecy; p497) in the French Alps, the Vézère Valley (p580), the River Gard (p721) and the Gorges de l'Ardèche (p477). Startlingly turquoise water and sheer, forest-cloaked cliffs make the Gorges du Tarn (p746) and Gorges du Verdon (p822) highly scenic spots for a paddle. Sea kayakers prefer the ragged, cove-indented Parc National des Calanques (p780) and Corsica's islet-speckled waters (p877). Expect to pay around €10 to €15 for kayak/canoe rental per day, and €25 to €50 for a half-/full-day excursion.

Surfing & Kite-surfing

The wave-thrashed, wind-lashed Atlantic coast – Arcachon (p641) and Cap Ferret (p643), for instance – and the French Basque Country make surfers swoon. You'll find some of Europe's best surf in ocean-battered Biarritz and nearby Hossegor (p651), which hosts the 10-day Quiksilver Pro France on the ASP World Surfing Tour in late September and early October. Group lessons are available everywhere for between €25 and €35. For surf spots and schools, visit www.surfingfrance.com.

Kite-surfers, meanwhile, catch breezes on the French Riviera (p827) and Corsica (around Porto-Vecchio; p902), where outfits offer courses as well as equipment rental.

Rock Climbing & Via Ferrate

For intrepid souls, the holy grail of rock climbing is France's highest of the high: 4810m Mont Blanc. Chamonix guide companies (p487) organise ascents of this monster mountain (from €920), as well as five-day rock-climbing courses in the surrounding Alps (€630 to €920). On a less daunting scale, you'll find rock climbing on sandstone ridges in the Forêt de Fontainebleau (p170) on Paris' fringes, in the jagged pinnacles of Corsica's L'Alta Rocca (p904), and in the thickly wooded Parc National des Cévennes (p741).

If you are less experienced but fancy flirting with climbing, *via ferrate* (fixed-rope routes) lace the Alps, Pyrenees, Cévennes and Corsica. Guide companies charge around €50 for half-day escapades.

Canyoning & White-Water Rafting

For a thrill, little beats throwing yourself down a foaming river in a raft or a waterfall while rappelling – cue white-water rafting and canyoning. Canyoning operators are found in mountainous, ravine-riddled areas – from the French Alps to Aiguilles de Bavella in Corsica.

White-water rafting is another sure-fire way to get the heart pumping. France's most scenic options on this front include the cliff-flanked limestone wilderness of the Gorges de l'Ardèche (p477) and the mind-blowingly spectacular Gorges du Verdon (p822), Europe's largest canyon, where you can also hydrospeed and gorge float. A half-day outing for either activity will set you back around €50.

Scuba Diving

Scuba divers bubble below the glittering surface of the Mediterranean. Among France's top dive sites are the Massif de l'Estérel (p853) on the French Riviera, with its WWII shipwrecks and pristine waters, and the Reserve Naturelle de Scandola (p891), Îles Lavezzi (p899) and Mérouville (Bonifacio; p897) in Corsica; the latter for close encounters with groupers. Starfish and wrasse are often sighted on dives in St-Jean de Luz (p658) in the French Basque Country. A single dive will set you back around €40; all equipment is provided.

Paragliding

Many a peak, perfect thermals, and glacier-frosted mountains and forests to observe while drifting down to ground level attract paragliders to Alpine resorts such as Chamonix (p483). Lake Annecy (p497) is another favourite in the Alps, while the Vallée d'Aspe (p680) is a good launch pad in the Pyrenees. In the Massif Central, there's paragliding off the top of Puy de Dôme (p547).

Tandem flights with a qualified instructor cost anything between €65 and €220. **Flight Culture** (www.flightculture.co.uk) runs learn-to-paraglide courses at the 114m-high Dune du Pilat, Europe's highest sand dune, on the Atlantic coast.

Regions at a Glance

For the French, there is Paris and the rest of the country – yet few appreciate just how varied that 'rest of the country' is. The largest country in Europe after Russia and Ukraine, hexagon-shaped France is hugged by water or mountains along every side (except its north-eastern boundary) – an instant win for lovers of natural beauty, the coast and the great outdoors. Winter skiing and summer hiking 'n' biking rule the Alps in eastern France and the Pyrenees lacing the 450km-long border with Spain in the southwest. For *très belle* beach holidays, the coastal regions of Normandy and Brittany (northern France), the Atlantic coast (with waves surfers love), Corsica, and the French Riviera (Côte d'Azur), Provence and Languedoc-Roussillon on the hot Mediterranean deliver every time. Then there is food and wine, most exceptional in Burgundy, Provence, the Dordogne, and the Rhône Valley with the city of Lyon at its helm.

Paris

Food
Art
Shopping

Bistro Dining

Tables are jammed tight, chairs spill onto busy pavements outside, dishes of the day are chalked on the blackboard, and cuisine is simple and delicious. Such is the timeless joy of bistro dining in the capital.

Museums & Galleries

All the great masters star in Paris' priceless portfolio of museums. Not all the booty is stashed inside: buildings, metro stations, parks and other public art give *Mona* a good run for her money.

Fashion & Flea Markets

Luxury fashion houses, edgy boutiques, Left Bank designer-vintage and Europe's largest flea market: Paris really is the last word in fabulous shopping.

p57

Around Paris

Châteaux
Cathedrals
Green Spaces

A Taste of Royalty

Château de Versailles – vast, opulent and *very* shimmery – has to be seen to be believed. Fontainebleau, Chantilly and Vaux-le-Vicomte are other fabled addresses in French royalty's little black book.

Sacred Architecture

The other heavyweight near Paris is Chartres' cathedral, one of Western architecture's greatest achievements, with stained glass in awesome blue.

Urban Green

Parisians take air in thick forests outside the city: Forêt de Fontainebleau, an old royal hunting ground, is a hot spot for rock climbing and family walks. Chantilly means manicured French gardens and upper-class horse racing.

p159

Lille, Flanders & the Somme

Architecture
History
Coastline

Flemish Style

Breaking for a glass of strong local beer between old-town meanders around extravagant Flemish Renaissance buildings is a highlight of northern France. Lille and Arras are the cities to target.

Gothic to WWI

Amiens evokes both serene contemplation inside one of France's most awe-inspiring Gothic cathedrals, and emotional encounters in WWI cemeteries.

Coastal Capers

Hiking along the Côte d'Opale – a wind-buffeted area of white cliffs, gold sand and ever-changing sea and sky – is dramatic and beautiful, as is a Baie de Somme bicycle ride past lounging seals.

p178

Normandy

Food
Coastline
Battlefields

Calvados & Camembert

This coastal chunk of northern France is a pastoral land of butter and soft cheeses. Its exotic fruits: Camembert, cider, fiery *calvados* (apple brandy) and super-fresh seafood.

Cliffs & Coves

Chalk-white cliff to dune-lined beach, rock spire to pebble cove, coastal path to tide-splashed island-abbey Mont St-Michel: few coastlines are as inspiring.

D-Day Beaches

Normandy has long played a pivotal role in European history, but it was during WWII's D-Day landings that Normandy leaped to global importance. Museums, memorials, cemeteries and endless stretches of soft golden sand evoke that dramatic day in 1944.

p212

Brittany

Food
Walking
Islands

Crêpes & Cider

These two Breton culinary staples are no secret but who cares? Devouring caramel-doused buckwheat pancakes in the company of homemade cider is a big reason to visit Brittany.

Wild Hikes

With its wild dramatic coastline, islands, medieval towns and thick forests laced in Celtic lore and legend, this proud and fiercely independent region promises exhilarating walks.

Breton Beauties

Brittany's much-loved islands, dotted with black sheep and crossed with craggy coastal paths and windswept cycling tracks, are big draws. Don't miss the dramatic Île d'Ouessant or the very aptly named Belle Île.

p252

Champagne

Champagne
Walking
Drives

Bubbly Tasting

Gawp at a Champagne panorama from atop Reims' cathedral then zoom in close with serious tasting at the world's most prestigious Champagne houses in Reims and Épernay.

Vineyard Trails

Nothing quite fulfills the French dream like easy day hikes through neat rows of vineyards, exquisite picture-postcard villages bedecked in flowers and a gold-stone riverside hamlet right out of a Renoir painting.

Majestic Motoring

No routes are more geared to motorists and cyclists than the Champagne Routes, fabulously picturesque and well-signposted driving itineraries taking in the region's wealthy winemaking villages, hillside vines and traditional cellars.

p296

Alsace & Lorraine

Battlefields
City Life
Villages

Emotional Journeys

Surveying the dazzling symmetry of crosses on the Verdun battlefields is painful. Memorials, museums, cemeteries, forts and an ossuary mark out the journey.

Urban Icons

With the sublime (Strasbourg's cathedral) to the space-age (Centre Pompidou in Metz), this northeast chunk of France steals urbanite hearts with its city squares, architecture, museums and Alsatian-style dining.

Chocolate-Box Villages

There is no lovelier way of getting acquainted with this part of France than travelling from hilltop castles to storknest-blessed farms to half-timbered villages framed by vines.

p318

Loire Valley

Châteaux
History
Cycling

Royal Architecture

Endowed with stunning structural and decorative gems from medieval to Renaissance and beyond, the Loire's lavish châteaux sweep most visitors off their feet.

Tempestuous Tales

This region is a dramatic storyteller: through spectacular castles, fortresses, apocalyptic tapestries and court paintings, the gore and glory, political intrigue and sex scandals of medieval and Renaissance France fabulously unfold.

Riverside Trails

The River Loire is France's longest, best-decorated river. Pedalling riverside along the flat from château to château is one of the valley's great joys.

p366

Burgundy

Wine
History
Activities

Reds & Whites

Mooch between vines and old-stone villages along Burgundy's *grand cru* vineyard route. But this region is not just about Côte d'Or reds – taste whites in Chablis and Mâcon also.

Medieval History

Nowhere is Burgundy's past as one of medieval Europe's mightiest states evoked more keenly than in the dashingly handsome capital Dijon. Complete the medieval history tour with Cluny and Cîteaux abbeys.

Great Outdoors

Hiking and biking past vineyards or cruising in a canal boat is the good life. Pedal the towpath to gloriously medieval Abbaye de Fontenay, open a bottle of Chablis and savour the best of Burgundy.

p409

Lyon & the Rhône Valley

Food
Roman Sites
Cycling

Famous Flavours

No city in France excites taste buds more than Lyon. Savour local specialities in a checkedtableclothed *bouchon* (Lyonnais bistro), washed down by Côtes de Rhône wine poured from a Lyonnais *pot*.

Roman Remains

Not content with lavishing two majestic amphitheatres on Lyon (catch a concert alfresco after dark during Les Nuits de Fourvière – magical!), the Romans gifted the Rhône Valley with a third in jazz-famed Vienne.

Two-Wheel Touring

Pedalling between vineyards in Beaujolais country or around frog-filled lakes swamped with bird life in La Dombes is a simple pleasure of valley life.

p452

French Alps & the Jura Mountains

Food
Activities
Farmstays

Culture & Cuisine

Fondue is the tip of the culinary iceberg in this Alpine region, where cow's milk flavours dozens of cheeses. Around Lake Annecy, chefs woo with wild herbs and lake perch.

Adrenaline Rush

Crowned by Mont Blanc (4810m), the French Alps show no mercy in their insanely challenging ski trails and mountain-bike descents. Did we mention Europe's longest black downhill piste and the world's highest zip line?

Back to Nature

Feel the humble rhythm of the land with an overnight stay on a farm. Bottle-feed calves, collect the eggs, eat breakfast in a fragrant garden or before a wood-burning stove, and feel right at home.

p478

Massif Central

Volcanoes
Architecture
Outdoors

Volcanoes

The last one erupted in 5000 BC but their presence is still evident: mineral waters bubble up from volcanic springs in Vichy and Volvic; volcanic stone paints Clermont-Ferrand black and there's the razzmatazz of Vulcania.

Belle Époque

A string of early 20th-century spa towns (including Vichy) add understated elegance to this region's otherwise deeply provincial bow.

Hiking & Skiing

Walking is the best way to explore this unique landscape – an uncanny, grass-green moonscape of giant molehills crossed with trails. Then there are the little-known ski slopes of Le Mont-Dore.

p535

Dordogne, Limousin & the Lot

Food
Hilltop Towns
Cruises

Mouth-Watering Markets

Black truffles, foie gras and walnuts... Gourmets, eat your heart out in this fertile part of central and southwest France, where the fruits of the land are piled high at a bevy of atmospheric weekly markets.

Mighty Bastides

Not only is Dordogne's prized collection of fortified 13th-century towns and villages a joy to explore, valley views from the top of these clifftop *bastides* are uplifting. Start with Monpazier and Domme.

Meandering Waterways

Be it aboard a canoe, raft or *gabarre* (traditional flat-bottomed boat), cruising quietly along the region's rivers is an invitation to see *la belle France* at her most serene.

p561

Atlantic Coast

Port Towns
Wine
Outdoors

Town Life

Hip dining rendezvous in an old banana-ripening warehouse in Nantes, limestone arcades and islands in La Rochelle, and brilliant art museums in wine-rich Bordeaux.

Wonderful Wines

France's largest wine-growing region, Bordeaux encompasses the Médoc with its magnificent châteaux and medieval hamlet of St-Émilion. The wine is wonderful (not to mention the Cognac).

Rural Retreats

Paddling emerald-green waterways in the Marais Poitevin, pedalling sun-baked Île de Ré and wandering between weathered, wooden oyster shacks in Arcachon Bay is what this tranquil region is all about – slowing the pace right down.

p610

French Basque Country

Food
Outdoors
Culture

Culture & Cuisine

This exuberant region beneath the mist-soaked Pyrenees evokes Spain with its fiestas, bullfights, traditional *pelota* (ball games), tapas and famous Bayonne ham.

Surf's Up

Riding waves in the glitzy beach resort of Biarritz or on surfer beaches in Les Landes is a good reason to visit this sun-slicked coastal region, snug in France's southwestern corner.

A Timeless Pilgrimage

For centuries pilgrims have made their way across France to the quaint walled town of St-Jean Pied de Port, and beyond to Santiago de Compostela in Spain. Do the same, on foot or by bicycle.

p644

The Pyrenees

Outdoors
Scenery
History

Outdoor Action

Make Parc National des Pyrénées your playground. Vigorous hikes to lofty heights, good-value downhill skiing and racy white-water sports will leave you wanting more.

Jaw-Dropping Views

France's last wilderness has rare flora and fauna, snow-kissed peaks, vulture-specked skies, waterfalls and lakes. Top views include those from Pic du Jer, Pic du Midi, Lescun, Cirque de Gavarnie, Lac de Gaube and pretty much every valley around.

Rare & Holy Cities

That same elegance that saw well-to-do 19th-century Brits and Americans winter in Pau still attracts guests today. Then there is sacred Lourdes, a provincial pilgrim city.

p670

Toulouse Area

Food
History
Cruises

Cassoulet & Armagnac

Try Emile restaurant for Toulouse's best *cassoulet* (rich bean, pork and duck stew), though this classic bean-stew dish simmers on the stove in most kitchens. Begin with an aperitif and end with an Armagnac brandy.

Towns with Tales

Red-brick Toulouse's historic mansions, quintessential fortified town Montauban, Gothic Albi, Moissac's Romanesque abbey: this compact region is packed with historical tales and historic architecture.

Canal du Midi

Pop a cork out of a bottle of Vin de Pays d'Oc and savour the go-slow, lush-green loveliness of the Canal du Midi. Stroll or pedal its towpaths, soak in a spa, or simply rent a canal boat and drift.

p692

Languedoc-Roussillon

Culture
Roman Sites
Outdoors

Neighbouring Spain

Roussillon is a hot, dusty, lively region, long part of Catalonia at the eastern end of the Pyrenees. Celebrate a traditional fiesta in Perpignan, modern art and *sardane* (Catalan folk dance) in Céret.

Aqueducts & Amphitheatres

Nîmes' amphitheatre and the gracefully arched Pont du Gard are two of the Roman Empire's best-preserved sites.

Footpaths & Waterways

Try canoeing beneath the Pont du Gard, biking towpaths to Carcassonne, boating the Canal du Midi, climbing up to Cathar fortresses, donkey trekking in the Cévennes, or hiking gorges in Haut-Languedoc.

p713

Provence

Food
Villages
Modern Art

Eating & Drinking

Sip pastis over *pétanque*, spend all evening savouring bouillabaisse (fish stew), mingle over buckets of herbs and marinated olives at the market, hunt truffles, and taste Bandol reds and Côtes de Provence rosé.

Sensual Sauntering

Travelling *à la provençal* is a sensual journey past scented lavender fields and chestnut forests, through apple-green vineyards and silvery olive groves, around markets, chapels, and medieval villages perched on rocky crags.

Avant-Garde

Provence is an art museum and has the roll-call to prove it: Matisse, Renoir, Picasso, Cézanne, Van Gogh and Signac all painted and lived here.

p761

The French Riviera & Monaco

Resorts
Glamour
Coastline

Coastal Queen

Urban grit, old-world opulence, art that moves you and a seaside promenade everyone loves – Nice, queen of the French Riviera, will always be belle of the seaside ball.

Party Time

Enjoy the Riviera high life: trail film stars in Cannes, watch Formula One, meet high society in Monaco, guzzle champers in St-Tropez, frolic in famous footsteps on sandy beaches, dine amid priceless art, dance til dawn...

Magnificent Scenery

With its glistening sea, idyllic beaches and coastal paths, this part of the Med coast begs wonderful walks. Cicadas sing on Cap Ferrat, while the sun turns the Massif de l'Estérel brilliant red.

p827

Corsica

Drives
Hiking
Boat Trips

Postcard Home

Corsican coastal towns are impossibly picturesque – alley-woven Bastia, Italianate Bonifacio, celebed Île Rousse, chichi Calvi – but it's the hair-raising coastal roads wending past medieval Genoese watchtowers and the big blue views that scream 'Send a postcard!'

Great Outdoors

Hiking high-altitude mountain trails once the preserve of bandits and *bergers* (shepherds) is a trail-junkie favourite, as are the cliffhanging Gorges de Spelunca and beautiful pink, ochre and ginger Calanques de Piana.

The Big Blue

Nowhere does the Med seem bluer. Hop on deck in Porto, Bonifacio, Calvi or Porto-Vecchio for a boat excursion, or view sapphire waters through a mask while diving and snorkelling.

p877

On the
Road

Paris

POP 2.2 MILLION

Best Places to Eat

→ Le 6 Paul Bert (p131)
→ Restaurant David Toutain (p123)
→ Le Pantruche (p128)
→ Bones (p131)
→ Hugo Desnoyer (p123)

Best Places to Sleep

→ Edgar (p114)
→ Hôtel Emile (p119)
→ L'Hôtel (p121)
→ Le Citizen Hotel (p118)
→ Hôtel du Nord – Le Pari Vélo (p118)

Why Go?

Paris has a timeless familiarity for first-time and frequent visitors, with instantly recognisable architectural icons – the wrought-iron Eiffel Tower, broad Arc de Triomphe guarding glamorous Champs-Élysées, gargoyled Notre Dame cathedral, lamplit bridges spanning the Seine and art nouveau brasseries spilling onto wicker-chair-lined terraces. Dining is a quintessential part of any Parisian experience – whether at cosy neighbourhood bistros, Michelin-starred temples to gastronomy, *boulangeries* (bakeries), *fromageries* (cheese shops) or street markets. Shopping, especially fashion shopping, is also quintessential in this stylish city, for discount and vintage fashion through to groundbreaking emerging designers and venerable haute couture houses. And Paris is one of the world's great art repositories, with priceless treasures showcased in palatial museums. But against its iconic backdrop, Paris' real magic lies in the unexpected: hidden parks, small museums and tucked-away boutiques, bistros and neighbourhood cafes where you can watch Parisian life unfold.

When to Go
Paris

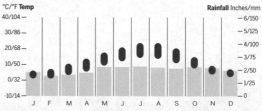

Jun & Jul Afternoon concerts every weekend during the Paris Jazz Festival.

Mid-Jul–mid-Aug Paris Plages transform the riverbanks into sandy beaches.

Oct Museums, bars and more stay open all night during Nuit Blanche.

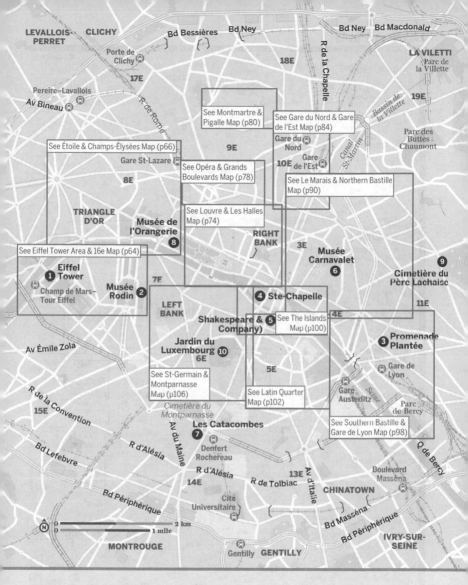

Paris Highlights

1 Ascending the **Eiffel Tower** (p62) at dusk for the best views of the City of Light

2 Indulging in a Parisian moment in the sculpture-filled gardens of **Musée Rodin** (p63)

3 Strolling the elevated **Promenade Plantée** (p95)

4 Taking in the sublime stained glass of **Sainte-Chapelle** (p95)

5 Attending a reading at **Shakespeare & Company** bookshop (p153)

6 Delving into Parisian history at **Musée Carnavalet** (p89)

7 Prowling the spine-prickling tunnels of **Les Catacombes** (p108)

8 Marvelling at Monet's *Water Lilies* at **Musée de l'Orangerie** (p77)

9 Paying respects to the famous and infamous at **Cimetière du Père Lachaise** (p85)

10 Unwinding in the city's most popular park, the **Jardin du Luxembourg** (p105)

Greater Paris

History

Paris was born in the Seine in the 3rd century BC, when the Parisii tribe of Celtic Gauls settled on what is now the Île de la Cité. Centuries of conflict between the Gauls and Romans ended in 52 BC, and in 508 Frankish king Clovis I made Paris the seat of his united Gaul kingdom. In the 9th century France was beset by Scandinavian Vikings. In the centuries that followed, these 'Norsemen' started pushing towards Paris, which had risen rapidly in importance. Construction had begun on the cathedral of Notre Dame in the 12th century, the Louvre was built as a riverside fortress around 1200, Ste-Chapelle was consecrated in 1248 and the Sorbonne opened its doors in 1253.

Many of the city's most famous buildings and monuments were erected during the Renaissance at the end of the 15th century. But in less than a century, Paris was again in turmoil, as clashes between Huguenot (Protestant) and Catholic groups increased, culminating in the St Bartholomew's Day massacre in 1572. Louis XIV (the Sun King) ascended the throne in 1643 at the age of five and ruled until 1715, virtually emptying the national coffers with his ambitious building and battling. His greatest legacy is the palace at Versailles. The excesses of Louis XVI and his queen, Marie Antoinette, in part led to an uprising of Parisians on 14 July 1789 and the storming of the Bastille prison – triggering the French Revolution.

PARIS IN...

Two Days

Kick off with a morning cruise or tour, then concentrate on the most Parisian of sights and attractions: **Notre Dame**, the **Louvre**, the **Eiffel Tower** and the **Arc de Triomphe**. In the late afternoon have a coffee or glass of wine on the av des Champs-Élysées before making your way to Montmartre for dinner. The following day take in such sights as the **Musée d'Orsay**, **Sainte-Chapelle**, **Conciergerie**, **Musée National du Moyen Âge** or **Musée Rodin**. Dine in soulful St-German before hitting the Latin Quarter's jazz clubs.

Four Days

Be sure to visit at least one Parisian street market and consider a cruise along **Canal St-Martin**, bookended by visits to **Cimetière du Père Lachaise** and **Parc de la Villette**. By night, take in a concert, opera or ballet at the **Palais Garnier** or **Opéra Bastille**, and a bar and club crawl in Le Marais and its vibrant surrounds.

One Week

With one week in the French capital, you can see a good many of the major sights covered in this chapter and take excursions from Paris proper further afield to areas around Paris such as **Versailles**.

Emperor Napoléon III 'modernised' Paris, installing wide boulevards, sculpted parks and a modern sewer system, but became embroiled in a costly and unsuccessful war with Prussia in 1870. When Parisians heard of their emperor's capture, they demanded a republic. Despite its bloody beginnings, the Third Republic ushered in the glittering, highly creative belle époque (beautiful age), celebrated for its graceful art nouveau architecture and advances in the arts and sciences.

By the 1930s, Paris was a centre for the artistic avant-garde, but the movement was cut short by the Nazi occupation of 1940. Paris was liberated in 1944 by an Allied force spearheaded by Free French units.

After the war, Paris regained its position as a creative centre and nurtured a revitalised liberalism that reached a climax in the student-led uprisings of May 1968. The Sorbonne was occupied, the Latin Quarter barricaded and some nine million people nationwide joined a general strike that paralysed the country. From the latter half of the 20th century on, France's presidents have made their mark on the cityscape by initiating *grands projets* (great projects or works), including the Mitterand-instigated book-shaped Bibliothèque Nationale de France (national library) and the city's second opera house, Opéra Bastille, and Chirac's Musée du Quai Branly.

In 2001, Bertrand Delanoë, a Socialist with support from the Green Party, became Paris' – and a European capital's – first openly gay mayor. He was re-elected in 2008. During his time in office, he pioneered innovative initiatives including the Vélib' bike-share scheme, Autolib' car-share scheme, the Paris Plages 'beaches' and the permanent pedestrianisation of the former riverside expressway now comprising Les Berges de Seine. After Delanoë stepped down in 2014, Paris elected its first-ever female mayor, Socialist Anne Hidalgo. Among her goals are turning unused office space into 60,000 new homes within six years, creating pedestrianised 'eco-districts' in each *arrondissement* and planting 20,000 trees.

⊙ Sights

Paris straddles the Seine fairly evenly. In this chapter, neighbourhoods start at the city's most famous sight, the Eiffel Tower, and move clockwise around the Right Bank to the Islands and the Left Bank.

⊙ Eiffel Tower Area & 16e

Paris' iconic spire has two glitzy new glass pavilions on its revamped 1st floor housing interactive history exhibits. The tower is surrounded by open areas on both banks of the Seine, which take in both the 7e and 16e. Both

---

FAST FACTS

➜ **Area** 105 sq km

➜ **Local industry** commerce, manufacturing, technology, tourism.

➜ **Signature drinks** France's finest are all here; don't miss a Bloody Mary from inventor, Harry's New York Bar (p140).

ℹ ARRONDISSEMENTS

Within the the *Périphérique* (ring road), Paris is divided into 20 *arrondissements* (city districts), which spiral clockwise like a snail shell from the centre. *Arrondissement* numbers (1er, 2e etc) form an integral part of all Parisian addresses (including in this book); the pull-out sheetmap has a map of the *arrondissements*. Each *arrondissement* has its own personality, but it's the *quartiers* (quarters, ie neighbourhoods), which often overlap *arrondissement* boundaries, that give Paris its village atmosphere.

are home to *very* well-heeled Parisians and some outstanding museums.

⭐ **Eiffel Tower**   LANDMARK
(Map p64; ☎08 92 70 12 39; www.tour-eiffel.fr; Champ de Mars, 5 av Anatole France, 7e; lift to top adult/child €15/10.50, lift to 2nd fl €9/4.50, stairs to 2nd fl €5/3, lift 2nd fl to top €6; ⊙lifts & stairs 9am-midnight mid-Jun-Aug, lifts 9.30am-11pm, stairs 9.30am-6.30pm Sep-mid-Jun; Ⓜ Bir Hakeim or RER Champ de Mars-Tour Eiffel) No one could imagine Paris today without it. But Gustave Eiffel only constructed this elegant, 320m-tall signature spire as a temporary exhibit for the 1889 World Fair. Luckily, the art nouveau tower's popularity assured its survival. Prebook tickets online to avoid long ticket queues.

Lifts ascend to the tower's three levels; change lifts on the 2nd level for the final ascent to the top. Energetic visitors can walk as far as the 2nd level using the south pillar's 704-step stairs.

Île aux Cygnes   ISLAND
(Isle of Swans; btwn Pont de Grenelle & Pont de Bir Hakeim, 15e; Ⓜ Javel or Bir Hakeim) Paris' little-known third island, the artificially created Île aux Cygnes, was formed in 1827 to protect the river port and measures just 850m by 11m. On the western side of the Pont de Grenelle is a soaring one-quarter scale **Statue of Liberty** replica, inaugurated in 1889. Walk east along the Allée des Cygnes – the tree-lined walkway that runs the length of the island – for knock-out Eiffel Tower views.

⭐ **Musée du Quai Branly**   MUSEUM
(Map p64; www.quaibranly.fr; 37 quai Branly, 7e; adult/child €8.50/free; ⊙11am-7pm Tue, Wed & Sun, 11am-9pm Thu-Sat; Ⓜ Alma Marceau or RER Pont de l'Alma) No other museum in Paris so

inspires travellers, armchair anthropologists and those who simply appreciate the beauty of traditional craftsmanship. A tribute to the diversity of human culture, Musée du Quai Branly presents an overview of indigenous and folk art. Its four main sections focus on Oceania, Asia, Africa and the Americas.

An impressive array of masks, carvings, weapons, jewellery and more make up the body of the rich collection, displayed in a refreshingly unique interior without rooms or high walls.

Musée des Égouts de Paris   MUSEUM
(Map p64; place de la Résistance, 7e; adult/child €4.40/3.60; ⊙11am-5pm Sat-Wed May-Sep, 11am-4pm Sat-Wed Oct-Dec & Feb-Apr; Ⓜ Alma Marceau or RER Pont de l'Alma) Raw sewage flows beneath your feet as you walk through 480m of odoriferous tunnels in this working sewer museum. Exhibitions cover the development of Paris' waste water–disposal system, including its resident rats (an estimated one sewer rat for every Parisian above ground). Enter via a rectangular maintenance hole topped with a kiosk across the street from 93 quai d'Orsay, 7e.

The sewers keep regular hours except when rain floods the tunnels. Toy rats are sold at its gift shop.

Les Berges de Seine   PROMENADE
(http://lesberges.paris.fr; btwn Musée d'Orsay & Pont de l'Alma, 7e; ⊙information point noon-7pm Sun-Thu, 10am-10pm Fri & Sat; Ⓜ Solférino, Assemblée Nationale or Invalides) A breath of fresh air, this 2.3km-long riverside promenade is Parisians' latest spot to run, cycle, skate, play board games or take part in a packed program of events. Equally it's simply a great place to hang out – in a Zzz shipping-container hut (free by reservation at the information point just west of the Musée d'Orsay), on the archipelago of floating gardens, or at the burgeoning restaurants and bars (some floating too aboard boats and barges).

Hôtel des Invalides   MONUMENT, MUSEUM
(Map p64; www.musee-armee.fr; 129 rue de Grenelle, 7e; adult/child €9.50/free; ⊙7.30am-7pm daily, to 9pm Tue Apr-Sep, hours can vary; Ⓜ Invalides) Fronted by the 500m-long Esplanade des Invalides lawns, the Hôtel des Invalides was built in the 1670s by Louis XIV to house 4000 *invalides* (disabled war veterans). On 14 July 1789, a mob broke into the building and seized 32,000 rifles before heading on to the prison at Bastille and the start of the French Revolution. Admission includes entry to all Hôtel des

Invalides sights. Hours for individual sights often vary – check the website for updates.

In the Cour d'Honneur, the nation's largest collection on the history of the French military is displayed at the Musée de l'Armée (Army Museum; Map p64; www.musee-armee.fr; 129 rue de Grenelle, 7e; included in Hôtel des Invalides admission; ⊙10am-6pm Apr-Oct, to 5pm Nov-Mar; MInvalides). South is Église St-Louis des Invalides, once used by soldiers, and Église du Dôme which, with its sparkling golden dome (1677–1735), is one of the finest religious edifices erected under Louis XIV and was the inspiration for the United States Capitol building. It received the remains of Napoléon in 1840. The extravagant Tombeau de Napoléon 1er, in the centre of the church, comprises six coffins fitting into one another like a Russian doll. Scale models of towns, fortresses and châteaux across France fill the esoteric Musée des Plans-Reliefs.

Regular classical concerts (some free, others costing up to €9) take place here year-round.

Musée Rodin GARDEN, MUSEUM

(Map p64; www.musee-rodin.fr; 79 rue de Varenne, 7e; adult/child museum incl garden €6/free, garden only €2/free; ⊙10am-5.45pm Tue & Thu-Sun, to 8.45pm Wed; MVarenne) Sculptor, painter, sketcher, engraver and collector Auguste Rodin donated his entire collection to the French state in 1908 on the proviso that they dedicate his former workshop and showroom, the beautiful 1730 Hôtel Biron, to displaying his works. They're now installed not only in the mansion itself, but in its rose-clambered garden – one of the most peaceful places in central Paris and a wonderful spot to contemplate his famous work *The Thinker*.

Purchase tickets online to avoid queuing.

Musée d'Orsay MUSEUM

(www.musee-orsay.fr; 62 rue de Lille, 7e; adult/child €11/free; ⊙9.30am-6pm Tue, Wed & Fri-Sun, to 9.45pm Thu; MAssemblée Nationale or RER Musée d'Orsay) Recently renovated to incorporate richly coloured walls and increased exhibition space, the home of France's national collection from the impressionist, postimpressionist and art nouveau movements spanning the 1840s to 1914 is the glorious former Gare d'Orsay railway station – itself an art nouveau showpiece – where a roll-call of masters and their world-famous works are on display.

Top of every visitor's must-see list is the museum's painting collections, centred on the world's largest collection of impressionist and postimpressionist art.

Just some of its highlights are Manet's *On The Beach* and *Woman With Fans;* Monet's gardens at Giverny; Cézanne's card players and still lifes; Renoir's *Ball at the Moulin de la Galette* and *Girls at the Piano;* Degas' ballerinas; Toulouse-Lautrec's cabaret dancers; Pissarro's *The Harvest;* Sisley's *View of the Canal St-Martin;* and Van Gogh's self-portraits, *Bedroom in Arles* and *Starry Night.* There are also some magnificent decorative arts, graphic arts and sculptures.

Save time by prepurchasing tickets online and head to entrance C. Admission drops to

---

ⓘ MUSEUM DISCOUNTS & FREEBIES

If you plan on visiting a lot of museums, pick up a Paris Museum Pass (http://en.paris museumpass.com; 2/4/6 days €42/56/69), or a Paris City Passport (www.parisinfo.com; 2/3/5 days €71/103/130), which also includes public transport and various extras. The passes get you into 60-odd venues in and around Paris, bypassing (or reducing) long ticket queues. Both passes are available from the Paris Convention & Visitors Bureau (p154).

Permanent collections at most city-run museums are free, including the Maison de Victor Hugo and the Musée Carnavalet. Temporary exhibitions usually command a fee.

Admission to national museums is reduced for those aged over 60 and between 18 and 25, and completely free for EU residents under 26 years and anyone under 18 years, so don't buy a Paris Museum Pass or Paris City Passport if you qualify.

National museums are also free for everyone on the first Sunday of each month. These include the Musée National d'Art Moderne in the Centre Pompidou, Musée de l'Orangerie, Musée du Quai Branly, Musée d'Orsay, Musée Guimet des Arts Asiatiques, Musée Picasso, Musée Rodin, Musée National du Moyen Âge, Cité de l'Architecture et du Patrimoine and the Musée des Arts et Métiers.

Ditto for the following, except they're only free the first Sunday of the month November to March: Arc de Triomphe, Conciergerie, Panthéon, Sainte-Chapelle and the Tours de Notre Dame. The Musée du Louvre is free on the first Sunday of the month from October to March only.

Eiffel Tower Area & 16e

400 m
0.2 miles

Ministère des Affaires Étrangères
Invalides
Invalides
R de St-Dominique
R de l'Université
R de Constantine
R de Grenelle
Pl de Grenelle
Square d'Ajaccio
Musée Rodin
R de Varenne
R de Bourgogne
Rue de Varenne
Left Bank
Bd des Invalides

Pont des Invalides
Av du Maréchal Galliéni
Esplanade des Invalides
Pl des Invalides
R Fabert
Jardin de l'Intendant
Pl Vauban
Esplanade du Souvenir Français

Seine
Q d'Orsay
Av Robert Schuman
Pl de Finlande
Bd de la Tour Maubourg
R Surcouf
R de la Comète
Pl Santiago du Chili
Square Santiago du Chili
La Tour Maubourg
R de Louis Codet
R Bixio
R de Lowendal

Av Jean Nicot
R Malar
R St-Dominique
R Amélie
R de Grenelle
R Ernest Psichari
R Duvivier
R Cler
R Valadon
Passage de l'Union
R Bosquet
Av de la Motte-Picquet
École Militaire
Av de Tourville
Av Duquesne
7e

R Cognacq-Jay
Passage Landrieu
R Cler
R du Champ de Mars
Av de la Motte-Picquet

Pont de l'Alma
Pl de la Résistance
Av Bosquet
Av de Suffren
École Supérieure de Guerre

Pont de l'Alma
Cité de l'Alma
Av Rapp
Av Franco Russe
R E Valentin
R Dupont des Loges
R Sédillot
R du Général Camou
R de Montessuy
R de l'Université
R Augereau
Av Élisée Reclus
R du'Exposition
Av de la Bourdonnais
Av Joseph Bouvard
Av Émile Deschanel
Allée Adrienne Lecouvreur
Av Anatole France

Passerelle Debilly
Av de New York
Pont de la Bourdonnais
Seine
Batobus Stop
Pont d'Iéna
Musée du Quai Branly
Q Branly
Allée Paul Deschanel
Av Gustave Eiffel
Parc du Champ de Mars
Pl Jacques Rueff
Av Charles Floquet
Pr Champfleury
Av Émile Acollas
Allée Thomy Thierry
Av Pierre Loti
Av Émile Deschanel

Av des Nations Unies
16e
Pl de Varsovie
Jardins du Trocadéro
Eiffel Tower
Champ de Mars–Tour Eiffel
Allée Léon Bourgeois
Stade Émile Anthoine
Av de New York
R du Général Lambert
R Jean Rey
Pl des Martyrs Juifs du Vélodrome d'Hiver
R de la Fédération
R Edgar Faure
Pl A Sauvy
R Desaix
R de la Fédération
Av de Suffren

Trocadéro
Pl du Trocadéro et du 11 Novembre
R Benjamin Franklin
R Fresnel
Bd Delessert
R Chardin
R Notre Dame
R Beethoven
R le Tasse
Passy
Pont de Bir Hakeim
Q de Grenelle
Bd de Grenelle
Bir Hakeim
R St-Saëns
15e
R Nélaton

5
9
4
10
13
11
15
16
8
2
18
14
17
20
19
12
7
6
1
3

Eiffel Tower Area & 16e

€8.50 after 4.30pm (after 6pm on Thursday). Combined tickets with the Musée de l'Orangerie cost €16 to visit both within four days, while combined tickets with the Musée Rodin are €15 to visit both on the same day.

Palais de Chaillot
PALACE

(Map p64; 17 place du Trocadéro et du 11 Novembre, 16e; M Trocadéro) The two curved, colonnaded wings of this palace and the terrace in between them afford an exceptional panorama of the Jardins du Trocadéro, the Seine and the Eiffel Tower. The palace's eastern wing houses the standout Cité de l'Architecture et du Patrimoine (Map p64; www.citechaillot.fr; 1 place du Trocadéro et du 11 Novembre, 16e; adult/child €8/free; ☺11am-7pm Wed & Fri-Mon, to 9pm Thu; M Trocadéro), devoted to French architecture and heritage. The western wing houses the Musée de la Marine. Also located in this wing is Musée de l'Homme, which is closed for renovations until 2015.

Aquarium de Paris Cinéaqua
AQUARIUM

(Map p64; www.cineaqua.com; av des Nations Unies, 16e; adult/child €20.50/16; ☺10am-7pm; M Trocadéro) Paris' aquarium, on the eastern side of the Jardins du Trocadéro, has a shark tank and 500-odd fish species to entertain families on rainy days. Three cinemas screen ocean-related and other films (dubbed in French, with subtitles). Budget tip: show your ticket from the nearby Musée de la Marine to get reduced aquarium admission (adult/child €16.40/10.40).

◎ Étoile & Champs-Élysées

A dozen avenues radiate out from place de l'Étoile (officially called place Charles de Gaulle). First among them is av des Champs-Élysées. This broad, tree-shaded boulevard, the name of which refers to the 'Elysian Fields' ('heaven' in Greek mythology) links place de la Concorde with the Arc de Triomphe and is lined with luxury shops. To its north, rue du Faubourg St-Honoré (8e), the western extension of rue St-Honoré, is home to renowned couture houses, jewellers, antique shops and the 18th-century Palais de l'Élysée, official residence of the French president.

★ Arc de Triomphe
LANDMARK

(Map p66; www.monuments-nationaux.fr; place Charles de Gaulle, 8e; adult/child €9.50/free; ☺10am-11pm Apr-Sep, to 10.30pm Oct-Mar; M Charles de Gaulle–Étoile) If anything rivals the Eiffel Tower as the symbol of Paris, it's this magnificent 1836 monument to Napoléon's 1805 victory at Austerlitz, which he commissioned the following year. The intricately sculpted triumphal arch stands sentinel in the centre of the Étoile ('star') roundabout. From the viewing platform on top of the arch (50m up via 284 steps and well worth the climb) you can see the dozen avenues.

Musée Jacquemart-André
ART MUSEUM

(Map p66; www.musee-jacquemart-andre.com; 158 bd Haussmann, 8e; adult/child €11/9.50; ☺10am-6pm, to 9.30pm Mon & Sat during temporary exhibits; M Miromesnil) If you belonged to the cream of Parisian society in the late 19th century, chances are you would have been invited to one of the dazzling soirées held at this mansion. The home of art collectors Nélie Jacquemart and Édouard André, this opulent residence was designed in the then-fashionable eclectic style, which combined elements from different eras – seen here in the presence of Greek and Roman antiquities,

Étoile & Champs-Élysées

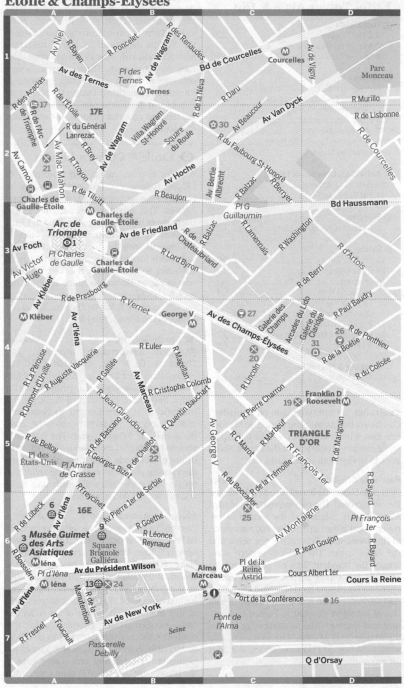

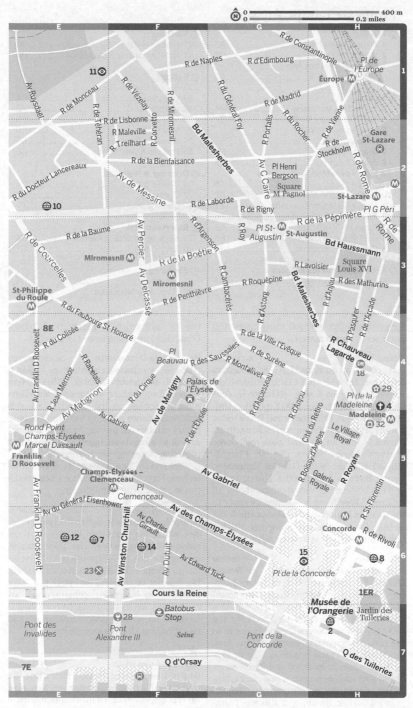

Étoile & Champs-Élysées

Egyptian artefacts, period furnishings and portraits by Dutch masters.

Grand Palais   ART MUSEUM
(Map p66; www.grandpalais.fr; 3 av du Général Eisenhower, 8e; adult/child €13/9; ⊙10am-10pm Tue-Sat, to 8pm Sun & Mon; Ⓜ Champs-Élysées–Clemenceau) Built for the 1900 Exposition Universelle (World's Fair), the Grand Palais today houses several exhibition spaces beneath its huge 8.5-tonne art nouveau glass roof. Some of Paris' biggest shows (Renoir, Chagall, Turner) are held in the Galeries Nationales, lasting three to four months. Hours, prices and exhibition dates vary significantly for all galleries. Those listed here generally apply to the Galeries Nationales, but always check the website for exact details. Reserving a ticket online for any show is strongly advised.

Petit Palais   ART MUSEUM
(Map p66; www.petitpalais.paris.fr; av Winston Churchill, 8e; permanent collections free; ⊙10am-6pm Tue-Sun; Ⓜ Champs-Élysées–Clemenceau) FREE Like the Grand Palais opposite, this architectural stunner was also built for the 1900 Exposition Universelle, and is home to the Paris municipality's Museum of Fine Arts, the Musée des Beaux-Arts de la Ville de Paris. It specialises in medieval and Renaissance objets d'art such as porcelain and clocks, tapestries, drawings and 19th-century French painting and sculpture; and also has paint-

ings by such artists as Rembrandt, Colbert, Cézanne, Monet, Gaugin and Delacroix.

Palais de la Découverte   SCIENCE MUSEUM
(Map p66; www.palais-decouverte.fr; av Franklin D Roosevelt, 8e; adult/child €9/6; ⊙9.30am-6pm Tue-Sat, 10am-7pm Sun; Ⓜ Champs-Élysées–Clemenceau) Attached to the Grand Palais, this children's science museum has excellent temporary exhibits (eg moving lifelike dinosaurs) as well as a hands-on, interactive permanent collection focusing on astronomy, biology, physics and the like. Some of the older exhibits have French-only explanations, but overall this is a dependable family outing.

Palais de Tokyo   ART MUSEUM
(Map p66; www.palaisdetokyo.com; 13 av du Président Wilson, 16e; adult/child €10/free; ⊙noon-midnight Wed-Mon; Ⓜ Iéna) The Tokyo Palace, created for the 1937 Exposition Universelle, has no permanent collection. Rather its shell-like interior of concrete and steel is a stark backdrop to interactive contemporary art exhibitions and installations. Its bookshop is fabulous for art and design magazines, and its eating/drinking options are magic.

★ Musée Guimet
des Arts Asiatiques   ART MUSEUM
(Map p66; www.museeguimet.fr; 6 place d'Iéna, 16e; adult/child €7.50/free; ⊙10am-6pm Wed-Mon; Ⓜ Iéna) France's foremost Asian art museum has a

superb collection. Observe the gradual transmission of both Buddhism and artistic styles along the Silk Road in pieces ranging from 1st-century Gandhara Buddhas from Afghanistan and Pakistan, to later Central Asian, Chinese and Japanese Buddhist sculptures and art. Part of the collection is housed in the nearby **Panthéon Bouddhique** (Map p66; 19 av d'léna, 16e; ⊘10am-5.45pm Wed-Mon, garden to 5pm) FREE with a **Japanese garden.**

Place de la Concorde   SQUARE
(Map p66; 8e; Ⓜ Concorde) Paris spreads around you, with views of the Eiffel Tower, the Seine and along the Champs-Élysées, when you stand in the city's largest square. Its 3300-year-old pink granite obelisk was a gift from Egypt in 1831. The square was first laid out in 1755 and originally named after King Louis XV, but its royal associations meant that it took centre stage during the Revolution – Louis XVI was the first to be guillotined here in 1793.

Église de la Madeleine   CHURCH
(Church of St Mary Magdalene; Map p66; www.eglise-lamadeleine.com; place de la Madeleine, 8e; ⊘9.30am-7pm; Ⓜ Madeleine) Place de la Madeleine is named after the 19th-century neoclassical church at its centre, the Église de la Madeleine. Constructed in the style of a massive Greek temple, 'La Madeleine' was consecrated in 1842 after almost a century of design changes and construction delays.

The church is a popular venue for classical-music concerts (some free); check the posters outside or the website for dates.

On the south side, the monumental staircase affords one of the city's most quintessential Parisian panoramas. From here, you can see down rue Royale to place de la Concorde and its obelisk and across the Seine to the Assemblée Nationale. The Invalides' gold dome appears in the background.

La Pinacothèque   ART MUSEUM
(Map p78; www.pinacotheque.com; 28 place de la Madeleine, 8e; adult/child from €12.30/10.80; ⊘10.30am-6pm Sat-Tue & Thu, to 9pm Wed & Fri; Ⓜ Madeleine) The top private museum in Paris, La Pinacothèque organises three to four major exhibits per year. Its nonlinear approach to art history, with exhibits that range from Mayan masks to retrospectives covering the work of artists such as Edvard Munch, has shaken up the otherwise rigid Paris art world and won over residents used to more formal presentations.

Flame of Liberty Memorial   MONUMENT
(Map p66; place de l'Alma, 8e; Ⓜ Alma Marceau) This bronze sculpture, a replica of the one topping the Statue of Liberty, was placed here in 1987 as a symbol of friendship between France and the USA. More famous is its location, above the place d'Alma tunnel where, on 31 August 1997, Diana, Princess of Wales, was

---

WORTH A TRIP

LA DÉFENSE

Architecture buffs will have a field day in Paris' business district, located in the western suburbs. Begun in the 1950s, today La Défense showcases extraordinary monumental art and is the only place in central Paris where you'll see skyscrapers.

La Défense Grande Arche metro station is the western terminus of metro line 1; regular t+ tickets are valid.

Grande Arche de la Défense (1 Parvis de la Défense; Ⓜ La Défense) La Défense's landmark edifice is the white marble Grande Arche, a cubelike arch built in the 1980s to home government and business offices. The arch marks the western end of the Axe Historique (Historic Axis), though Danish architect Johan-Otto von Sprekelsen deliberately placed the Grande Arche fractionally out of alignment. It's not possible to visit inside or access the roof.

Musée de la Défense (www.ladefense.fr; 15 place de la Défense; Ⓜ La Défense) FREE Set to reopen after renovation in early 2015, this museum evokes the area's development and architecture through drawings, architectural plans and scale models.

Info Défense (☏ 01 47 74 84 24; www.ladefense.fr; place de la Défense; ⊘9am-6pm Mon-Fri, 10am-5pm Sat & Sun; Ⓜ La Défense) Calder, Miró, Agam, César and Torricini are among the international artists behind the colourful and often surprising sculptures and murals that pepper the central 1km-long promenade. Pick up a map and excellent booklets in English outlining walks to discover its arts and surprising green spaces at the Info Défense kiosk, to the side of the moon-shaped CNIT building on the main drag.

killed in a car accident. Graffiti remembering the princess covers the entire wall next to the sculpture.

Musée de la Mode de la Ville de Paris

MUSEUM

(Map p66; www.galliera.paris.fr; 10 av Pierre 1er de Serbie, 16e; adult/child €8/free; ⊙10am-6pm Tue, Wed, Fri-Sun, 10am-9pm Thu; Ména) Paris' Fashion Museum, housed in 19th-century Palais Galliera, warehouses some 100,000 outfits and accessories – from canes and umbrellas to fans and gloves – from the 18th century to the present day. The sumptuous Italianate palace and gardens dating from the mid-19th century are worth a visit in themselves, as are the excellent temporary exhibitions the museum hosts.

⊙ Louvre & Les Halles

Louis VI created *halles* (markets) for merchants who converged on the city centre to sell their wares, and for over 800 years they were, in the words of Émile Zola, the 'belly of Paris'. Although the wholesalers moved out to the suburb of Rungis in 1971 (and were replaced by the soulless subterranean shopping mall Forum des Halles (p77), currently undergoing a major makeover), the markets' spirit lives on here. To the southwest is France's first national museum, the incomparable Louvre.

★ Musée du Louvre

MUSEUM

(Map p74; ☑01 40 20 53 17; www.louvre.fr; rue de Rivoli & quai des Tuileries, 1er; adult/child €12/free; ⊙9am-6pm Mon, Thu, Sat & Sun, to 9.45pm Wed & Fri; MPalais Royal–Musée du Louvre) Few art galleries are as prized or daunting as the Musée du Louvre, Paris' pièce de résistance no first-time visitor to the city can resist. This is, after all, one of the world's largest and most diverse museums. Showcase to 35,000 works of art – from Mesopotamian, Egyptian and Greek antiquities to masterpieces by artists such as da Vinci, Michelangelo and Rembrandt – it would take nine months to glance at every piece, rendering advance planning essential.

Today the palace rambles over four floors, up and down innumerable staircases, and through three wings: the **Sully Wing** creates

---

WORTH A TRIP

BOIS DE BOULOGNE

On Paris' western edge, the 845-hectare **Bois de Boulogne** (bd Maillot; MPorte Maillot) owes its informal layout to Baron Haussmann, who planted 400,000 trees here in the 19th century. Along with various gardens and attractions, the park has 15km of cycle paths and 28km of bridle paths through 125 hectares of forested land. Vélib' stations are found near most of the park entrances, but not within the park itself.

Be warned that the area becomes a distinctly adult playground after dark, especially along the allée de Longchamp running northeast from the Étang des Réservoirs (Reservoirs Pond), where prostitutes cruise for clients.

Le Chalet des Îles (☑01 42 88 04 69; Carrefour du Bout des Lacs; 30/60/90/120min €6/10/15.50/19, plus €50 deposit; ⊙noon-5pm Mon-Fri, 10am-6pm Sat & Sun mid-Feb–Oct; MAv Henri Martin) Rents boats for a romantic row around Lac Inférieur, the largest of the Bois' lakes and ponds.

Jardin d'Acclimatation (www.jardindacclimatation.fr; av du Mahatma Gandhi; admission €3, attraction single/carnet of 10 €2.90/15; ⊙10am-7pm Apr-Sep, to 6pm Oct-Mar; MLes Sablons) Families with young kids flock to this endearing amusement park, with swings, roundabouts and playgrounds (included in the admission fee), plus attractions such as puppet shows, boat rides, a small water park, pony rides and a little train (which cost extra).

Stade Roland Garros-Musée de la Fédération Française de Tennis (www.fft.fr; 2 av Gordon Bennett, 16e; adult/child €10.50/8.50, with stadium visit €15.50/10.50; ⊙10am-6pm Wed, Fri-Sun; MPorte d'Auteuil) Host to the French Open, the Roland Garros stadium's tennis museum traces the sport's 500-year history through paintings, sculptures and posters. Stadium tours take place at 11am and 3pm in English; reservations are required.

Fondation Louis Vuitton (www.fondationlouisvuitton.fr; av du Mahatma Gandhi, 16e; MLes Sablons) Frank Gehry's extraordinary new 'iceberg' building is topped by 3600 glass panels forming 12 giant 'sails' and competes for attention with the modern and contemporary artistic creations inside.

the four sides of the Cour Carrée (literally 'square courtyard') at the eastern end of the complex; Denon Wing stretches 800m along the Seine to the south; and northern Richelieu Wing skirts rue de Rivoli. Long before its modern incarnation, the vast Palais du Louvre originally served as a fortress constructed by Philippe-Auguste in the 12th century (medieval remnants are still visible on the lower ground floor, Sully); it was rebuilt in the mid-16th century as a royal residence in the Renaissance style. The Revolutionary Convention turned it into a national museum in 1793.

The paintings, sculptures and artefacts on display in the Louvre Museum have been amassed by subsequent French governments. Among them are works of art and artisanship from all over Europe and priceless collections of antiquities. The Louvre's raison d'être is essentially to present Western art (primarily French and Italian, but also Dutch and Spanish) from the Middle Ages to about 1848 (at which point the Musée d'Orsay takes over), as well as works from ancient civilisations that formed the starting point for Western art.

When the museum opened in the late 18th century it contained 2500 paintings and objets d'art; the 'Grand Louvre' project inaugurated by the late President Mitterrand in 1989 doubled the museum's exhibition space, and both new and renovated galleries have opened in recent years devoted to objets d'art such as the crown jewels of Louis XV (Room 66, 1st floor, Apollo Gallery, Denon). Late 2012 saw the opening of the new Islamic art galleries (lower ground floor, Denon) in the restored Cour Visconti.

The richness and sheer size of the place (the south side facing the Seine is 700m long) can be overwhelming. However, there's an array of innovative, entertaining self-guided thematic trails (1½ to three hours; download trail brochures in advance from the website) ranging from a Louvre masterpieces trail to the art of eating, plus several for kids (hunting lions, galloping horses). Even better are the Louvre's self-paced multimedia guides (€5). More-formal, English-language guided tours depart from the Hall Napoléon (Map p74), which has free English-language maps.

For many, the star attraction is Leonardo da Vinci's *La Joconde,* better known as *Mona Lisa* (Room 6, 1st floor, Denon). This entire section of the 1st floor of the Denon Wing, in fact, is hung with masterpieces – Rooms 75 and 77 have enormous French paintings from Ingres, Delacroix *(Liberty Leading the People)*

DON'T MISS

MUSÉE MARMOTTAN MONET

Housed in the duc de Valmy's former hunting lodge (well, let's call it a mansion), on the edge of the Bois de Boulogne, the intimate Musée Marmottan Monet (☏ 01 44 96 50 33; www.marmottan.com; 2 rue Louis Boilly, 16e; adult/child €10/5; ⊙10am-6pm Tue-Sun, to 8pm Thu; Ⓜ La Muette) houses the world's largest collection of Monet paintings and sketches, beginning with the seminal *Impression Soleil Levant* (1873), from which impressionism took its name. Masterpieces to look out for include *La Barque* (1887), *Cathédrale de Rouen* (1892), *Londres, le Parlement* (1901) and the various *Nymphéas* (Water Lilies) – many of which were smaller studies for the water lilies in the Musée de l'Orangerie (p77). Also on display are a handful of canvases by Renoir, Pissarro, Gauguin and Morisot.

and Géricault *(The Raft of the Medusa)*, while Rooms 1, 3, 5 and 8 contain transcendent pieces by Raphael, Titian, Botticini and Botticcelli. On the ground floor of the Denon Wing, take time for Michelangelo's *The Dying Slave* and Canova's *Psyche and Cupid* (Room 4).

But don't rush by the treasures from antiquity: both Mesopotamia (ground floor, Richelieu) and Egypt (ground and 1st floors, Sully) offer fascinating insights into ancient civilisations, as seen in the *Code of Hammurabi* (Room 3, ground floor, Richelieu) and the *Seated Scribe* (Room 22, 1st floor, Sully). Also worth a look are the mosaics and figurines from the Byzantine empire (lower ground floor, Denon), which merge into the state-of-the-art Islam collection in the Cour Visconti, and of course the armless Greek duo, the *Venus de Milo* (Room 16, ground floor, Sully) and the *Winged Victory of Samothrace* (top of Daru staircase, 1st floor, Denon, under renovation through 2015).

Also of note are the gilded-to-the-max Napoléon III Apartments (1st floor, Richelieu), Dutch masters Vermeer (Room 38, 2nd floor, Richelieu) and Rembrandt (Room 31, 2nd floor, Richelieu), and 18th- and 19th-century French painting collection (2nd floor, Sully), which features iconic works like Ingres' *The Turkish Bath* (off Room 60).

continued p76

The Louvre

A HALF-DAY TOUR

Successfully visiting the Louvre is a fine art. Its complex labyrinth of galleries and staircases spiralling three wings and four floors renders discovery a snakes-and-ladders experience. Initiate yourself with this three-hour itinerary – a playful mix of Mona Lisa obvious and up-to-the-minute unexpected.

Arriving by the stunning main entrance, pick up colour-coded floor plans at the lower-ground-floor **information desk ❶** beneath IM Pei's glass pyramid, ride the escalator up to the Sully Wing and swap passport for multimedia guide (there are limited descriptions in the galleries) at the wing entrance.

The Louvre is as much about spectacular architecture as masterly art. To appreciate this zip up and down Sully's Escalier Henri II to admire **Venus de Milo ❷**, then up parallel Escalier Henri IV to the palatial displays in **Cour Khorsabad ❸**. Cross room 1 to find the escalator up to the 1st floor and staircase-as-art **L'Esprit d'Escalier ❹**. Next traverse 25 consecutive galleries (thank you, floor plan!) to flip conventional contemplation on its head with Cy Twombly's **The Ceiling ❺**, and the hypnotic **Winged Victory of Samothrace sculpture ❻** – just two rooms away – which brazenly insists on being admired from all angles. End with the impossibly famous **The Raft of Medusa ❼**, **Mona Lisa ❽** and **Virgin & Child ❾**.

TOP TIPS

➡ **Floor Plans** Don't even consider entering the Louvre's maze of galleries without a Plan/Information Louvre brochure, free from the information desk in the Hall Napoléon

➡ **Crowd dodgers** The Denon Wing is always packed; visit on late nights Wednesday or Friday or trade Denon in for the notably quieter Richelieu Wing

➡ **2nd floor** Not for first-timers: save its more specialist works for subsequent visits

---

MISSION MONA LISA

If you just want to venerate the Louvre's most famous lady, use the Porte des Lions entrance (closed Tuesday and Friday), from where it's a five-minute walk. Go up one flight of stairs and through rooms 26, 14 and 13 to the Grande Galerie and adjoining room 6.

L'Esprit d'Escalier
Escalier Lefuel, Richelieu
Discover the 'Spirit of the Staircase' through François Morel-let's contemporary stained glass, which casts new light on old stone. DETOUR» Napoleon III's gorgeous gilt apartments.

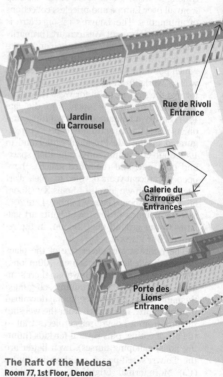

Rue de Rivoli Entrance

Jardin du Carrousel

Galerie du Carrousel Entrances

Porte des Lions Entrance

The Raft of the Medusa
Room 77, 1st Floor, Denon
Decipher the politics behind French romanticism in Théodore Géricault's *Raft of the Medusa*.

DEA/G. DAGLI ORTI/GETTY IMAGES ©

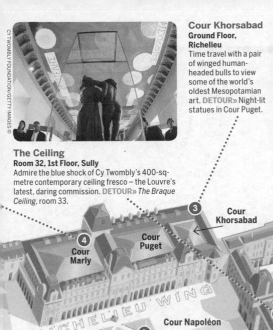

The Ceiling
Room 32, 1st Floor, Sully
Admire the blue shock of Cy Twombly's 400-sq-metre contemporary ceiling fresco – the Louvre's latest, daring commission. DETOUR» *The Braque Ceiling*, room 33.

Cour Khorsabad
Ground Floor, Richelieu
Time travel with a pair of winged human-headed bulls to view some of the world's oldest Mesopotamian art. DETOUR» Night-lit statues in Cour Puget.

Venus de Milo
Room 16, Ground Floor, Sully
No one knows who sculpted this seductively realistic goddess from Greek antiquity. Naked to the hips, she is a Hellenistic masterpiece.

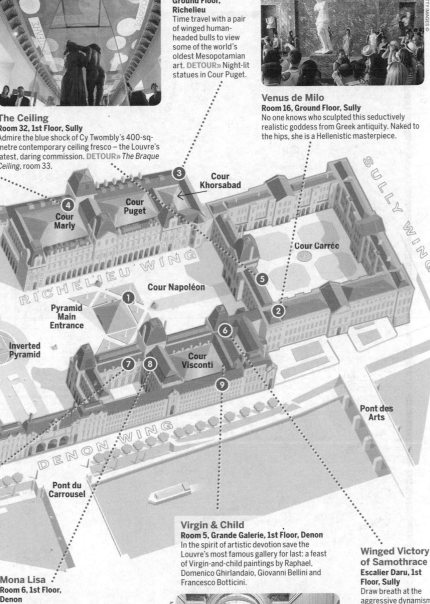

Cour Khorsabad

Cour Puget

❹ **Cour Marly**

❸

Cour Carrée

Cour Napoléon

RICHELIEU WING

SULLY WING

Pyramid Main Entrance

❶

Inverted Pyramid

❺

❷

❻

Cour Visconti

❼ ❽

❾

DENON WING

Pont des Arts

Pont du Carrousel

Virgin & Child
Room 5, Grande Galerie, 1st Floor, Denon
In the spirit of artistic devotion save the Louvre's most famous gallery for last: a feast of Virgin-and-child paintings by Raphael, Domenico Ghirlandaio, Giovanni Bellini and Francesco Botticini.

Mona Lisa
Room 6, 1st Floor, Denon
No smile is as enigmatic or bewitching as hers. Da Vinci's diminutive *La Joconde* hangs opposite the largest painting in the Louvre – sumptuous, fellow Italian Renaissance artwork *The Wedding at Cana.*

Winged Victory of Samothrace
Escalier Daru, 1st Floor, Sully
Draw breath at the aggressive dynamism of this headless, handless Hellenistic goddess. DETOUR» The razzle-dazzle of the Apollo Gallery's crown jewels.

Louvre & Les Halles

A map of the Louvre & Les Halles area. Labels visible:

Bd de la Madeleine
9e
R Cambon
R des Capucines
R Volney
R de la Paix
R Daunou
32
12
R de Port Mahon
R de la Michodière
R Gaillon
R de Monsigny
Quatre Septembre
R de Gramont
R St-Augustin
R de Louvois
R Marsollier
R Dalayrac
Passage Choiseul
R Ste-Anne
R Rameau
R Chabanais
34
Cour Vendôme
Pl Vendôme
Colonne Vendôme
11
R Danielle Casanova
R Louis Le Grand
R d'Antin
Av de l'Opéra
R Gomboust
R du Marché St-Honoré
R du Marché
R de la Sourdière
R des Petits Champs
R de Ventadour
R des Moulins
25
23
R de Castiglione
R St-Honoré
R du Marché St-Honoré
Pyramides
Paris Convention & Visitors Bureau
R Thérèse
R Villedo
39
R de
28
24
R du Mont Thabor
R d'Alger
R du 29 Juillet
30
R de Rivoli
R St-Roch
R de la Sourdière
R des Pyramides
R d'Argenteuil
R Molière
R de Richelieu
R de Montpensier
Galerie de Montpensier
45
Jardin du Palais Royal
44
8
Tuileries
Pl des Pyramides
R St-Honoré
R de l'Echelle
Av de l'Opéra
40
5
Jardin des Tuileries
10
R de Rivoli
Palais Royal Musée du Louvre
Pl du Palais Royal
43
Q des Tuileries
Av du Général Lemonnier
Terrasse des Tuileries
Terrasse des Tuileries
Jardin du Carrousel
Arc de Triomphe du Carrousel
Pl du Carrousel
R de Rohan
6
7
Cour Napoléon
Musée du Louvre
3
Q Anatole France
Pont Royal
Q des Tuileries
Seine
Pont du Carrousel
Jardin de l'Infante
7e
26
R de Verneuil
R du Bac
Q Voltaire
Faubourg St-Germain
Q Malaquais
Batobus Stop
Pont des Arts
R de l'Université
R de Beaune
R Allent
R de Lille
R des St-Pères
6e
Q Malaquais
R de Seine
Q de Conti
Pl de l'Institut

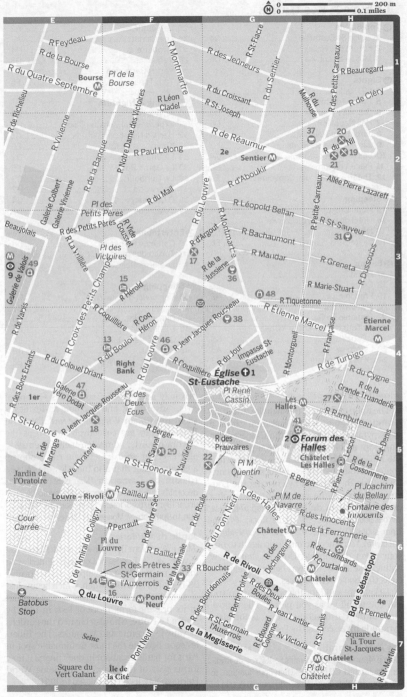

Louvre & Les Halles

continued from p71

The main entrance is through the 21m-high **Grande Pyramide** (Map p74; place du Louvre), a glass pyramid designed by the Chinese-born American architect IM Pei. If you don't have the Museum Pass (which gives you priority), you can avoid the longest queues (for security) outside the pyramid by entering the Louvre complex via the underground shopping centre **Carrousel du Louvre** (Map p74; www.carrouseldulouvre.com; 99 rue de Rivoli; ⊙8am-11pm, shops 10am-8pm; 🖥; ⓜPalais Royal–Musée du Louvre). You'll need to queue up again to buy your ticket once inside. Do note that a new online ticketing system was being implemented as this book went to press.

Tickets are valid for the whole day, so you can come and go as you please. The centrepiece of the Carrousel du Louvre is the glass Pyramide Inversée, also by Pei.

Les Arts Décoratifs   ART MUSEUM
(Map p74; www.lesartsdecoratifs.fr; 107 rue de Rivoli, 1er; aduld/child €11/free; ⊙11am-6pm Tue-Sun, to 9pm Thu; ⓜPalais Royal–Musée du Louvre) A trio of

privately administered collections – Applied Arts, Advertising and Fashion & Textiles – sit in the Rohan Wing of the vast Palais du Louvre. They are collectively known as the Decorative Arts; admission includes entry to all three. For an extra €2, you can scoop up a combo ticket that also includes the **Musée Nissim de Camondo** (Map p66; www.lesartsdecoratifs.fr; 63 rue de Monceau, 8e; adult/18-25yr/under 18yr €9/6.50/free; ⊙11am-6pm Tue, Wed & Fri-Sun, to 9pm Thu; ⓜMonceau or Villiers) in the 8e.

Jardin des Tuileries   GARDEN
(Map p74; ⊙7am-11pm Jun-Aug, shorter hours rest of year; 👶; ⓜTuileries or Concorde) Filled with fountains, ponds and sculptures, the formal, 28-hectare Tuileries Garden, which begins just west of the Jardin du Carrousel, was laid out in its present form, more or less, in 1664 by André Le Nôtre, who also created the gardens at Vaux-le-Vicomte and Versailles. The Tuileries soon became the most fashionable spot in Paris for parading about in one's finery. It now forms part of the Banks of the Seine World Heritage Site listed by Unesco in 1991.

Musée de l'Orangerie MUSEUM
(Map p66; www.musee-orangerie.fr; Jardin des Tuileries, 1e; adult/child €9/6.50; ⊘9am-6pm Wed-Mon; Ⓜ Concorde) Located in the southwestern corner of the Jardin des Tuileries, this museum, with the Jeu de Paume, is all that remains of the former Palais des Tuileries, which was razed during the Paris Commune in 1871. It exhibits important impressionist works, including a series of Monet's *Decorations des Nymphéas* (Water Lilies) in two huge oval rooms purpose-built in 1927 on the artist's instructions, as well as works by Cézanne, Matisse, Picasso, Renoir, Sisley, Soutine and Utrillo. An audioguide costs €5.

Jeu de Paume GALLERY
(Map p66; ☑01 47 03 12 50; www.jeudepaume.org; 1 place de la Concorde, 8e; adult/child €8.50/free; ⊘11am-9pm Tue, to 7pm Wed-Sun; Ⓜ Concorde) The Galerie du Jeu de Paume, which stages innovative photography exhibitions, is housed in an erstwhile *jeu de paume* (royal tennis court) in the northwestern corner of the Jardin des Tuileries and is all that remains of the Palais des Tuileries.

Place Vendôme SQUARE
(Map p74; Ⓜ Tuileries or Opéra) Octagonal place Vendôme and the arcaded and colonnaded buildings around it were constructed between 1687 and 1721. In March 1796 Napoléon married Josephine, Viscountess Beauharnais, in the building at No 3. Today the buildings surrounding the square house the posh Hôtel Ritz Paris and some of the city's most fashionable boutiques.

Jardin du Palais Royal GARDEN
(Map p74; 2 place Colette, 1er; ⊘7am-10.15pm Apr & May, to 11pm Jun-Aug, shorter hours rest of year; Ⓜ Palais Royal–Musée du Louvre) FREE The Jardin du Palais Royal is a perfect spot to sit, contemplate and picnic between boxed hedges, or shop in the trio of arcades that frame the garden so beautifully: the Galerie de Valois (east), Galerie de Montpensier (west) and Galerie Beaujolais. However, it's the southern end of the complex, polka-dotted with sculptor Daniel Buren's 260 black-and-white striped columns, that has become the garden's signature feature.

This elegant urban space is fronted by the neoclassical Palais Royal (closed to the public), constructed in 1633 by Cardinal Richelieu but mostly dating to the late 18th century. Louis XIV hung out here in the 1640s; today it is home to the Conseil d'État (State Council; Map p74).

The Galerie de Valois is the most upmarket arcade with designer boutiques such as Stella McCartney, Pierre Hardy, Didier Ludot (p148) and coat-of-arms engraver Guillaumot, at work at Nos 151 to 154 since 1785. Across the garden in the Galerie de Montpensier the Revolution broke out on a warm mid-July day just three years after the galleries opened in the Café du Foy. The third arcade, tiny Galerie Beaujolais, is crossed by Passage du Perron, a passageway above which the writer Colette (1873–1954) lived out the last dozen years of her life.

★**Forum des Halles** LANDMARK
(Map p74; www.forumdeshalles.com; 1 rue Pierre Lescot, 1er; ⊘shops 10am-8pm Mon-Sat; Ⓜ Châtelet–Les Halles) Paris' main wholesale food market stood here for nearly 800 years before being replaced by this underground shopping mall in 1971. Four floors of stores extend down to the city's busiest métro hub, while a massive renovation project – with an enormous golden-hued translucent canopy as centrepiece – is under way, with a target completion date of 2016.

★**Église St-Eustache** CHURCH
(Map p74; www.st-eustache.org; 2 impasse St-Eustache, 1er; ⊘9.30am-7pm Mon-Fri, 9am-7pm Sat & Sun; Ⓜ Les Halles) Just north of the gardens snuggling up to the bustling Forum des Halles, is one of the most beautiful churches in Paris. Majestic, architecturally magnificent and musically outstanding, St-Eustache has made spirits soar for centuries.

59 Rivoli GALLERY
(Map p74; http://59rivoli-eng.org; 59 rue de Rivoli, 1er; ⊘1-8pm daily; Ⓜ Louvre-Rivoli) FREE In such a classical part of Paris crammed with elegant historic architecture, 59 Rivoli is quite the bohemian breath of fresh air. Take time out to watch artists at work in the 30 *ateliers* (studios) strung on six floors of the long-abandoned bank building, now a legalised squat where some of Paris' most creative talent works (but doesn't live).

The ground-floor gallery hosts a new exhibition every fortnight and free gigs, concerts and shows pack the place out most weekends. Look for the sculpted façade festooned with catchy drapes, banners and unconventional recycled piping above the shop fronts.

Opéra & Grands Boulevards

0 — 200 m
0 — 0.1 miles

G

R Cadet

R Saulnier

R Richer

R Geoffroy Marie

R de la Boule Rouge

R de Trévise

16

Cité Bergère

R Bergère

11

Bd Poissonnière

R d'Uzès

R de Montyon

Passage des Deux Sœurs

15

R Cadet

R du Faubourg Montmartre

Grands Boulevards

Bd Montmartre

12

13

Galerie Montmartre

14

25

9

R Vivienne

R St-Marc

R Buffault

Passage Verdeau

6

R de la Grange Batelière

Passage Jouffroy

8

F

R de Maubeuge

R Lamartine

Pl Kossuth

R Fléchier

R Bourdaloue

Notre Dame de Lorette

Le Peletier

R Chauchat

R Rossini

R Drouot

Richelieu Drouot

R de Richelieu

2e

R Favart

R d'Amboise

R de Marivaux

E

10

R St-Georges

R le Peletier

R La Fayette

R Laffitte

R de Gramont

Bd Haussmann

R Pillet Will

R de Châteaudun

R de la Victoire

R Taitbout

R Taitbout

D

R St-Lazare

Av de Provence

Pl Adrien Oudin

R du Helder

R de Choiseul

Bd des Italiens

R de la Michodière

Cité d'Antin

C

R de Londres

Cité de Londres

R St-Lazare

Trinité

7

Square d'Estienne d'Orves

Pl d'Estienne d'Orves

R de Mogador

R de la Chaussée d'Antin

6e

Chaussée d'Antin

20

2

R de la Chaussée d'Antin

R de la Chaussée d'Antin

R Meyerbeer

R Halévy

Pl Diaghilev

R Gluck

Pl J Rouché

Palais Garnier

1

18

Opéra

Pl de l'Opéra

B

R de Budapest

Pl du Havre

St-Lazare

R du Havre

8e

R de Caumartin

Havre Caumartin

Bd Haussmann

R Joubert

R Charras

22

23

24

21

R des Mathurins

5

R Auber

Auber

R Boudreau

Pl Édouard VIII

R Scribe

Pl Ch Garnier

4

19

Bd des Capucines

17

A

R Tronchet

R Vignon

Godot de Mauroy

R de Caumartin

R de Sèze

3

1   2   3   4

◉ Opéra & Grands Boulevards

★ Palais Garnier   OPERA HOUSE
(Map p78; ☏08 25 05 44 05; www.operadeparis.fr; cnr rues Scribe & Auber, 9e; unguided tour adult/child €10/6, guided tour adult/child €14/12.50; ⊙unguided tour 10am-5pm, to 1pm on matinee performance days, guided tour by reservation; Ⓜ Opéra) The fabled 'phantom of the opera' lurked in this opulent opera house designed in 1860 by Charles Garnier (then an unknown 35-year-old architect). You can reserve a spot on an English-language guided tour or take an unguided tour of the attached museum, with posters, costumes, backdrops, original scores and other memorabilia, which includes a behind-the-scenes peek (except during matinees and rehearsals). Highlights include the Grand Staircase and horseshoe-shaped, gilded auditorium with red velvet seats, a massive chandelier and Chagall's gorgeous ceiling mural.

Musée du Parfum   MUSEUM
(Map p78; www.fragonard.com; 9 rue Scribe, 9e; ⊙9am-6pm Mon-Sat, to 5pm Sun; Ⓜ Opéra) **FREE** If the art of perfume-making entices, stop by this collection of copper distillery vats and antique flacons and test your nose on a few basic scents. Run by the parfumerie Fragonard, it's located in a beautiful old *hôtel particulier* (private mansion); free guided visits are available in multiple languages. A short distance south, a separate wing in a 20th-century theatre, the **Théâtre-Musée des Capucines** (Map p74; 39 bd des Capucines, 2e; ⊙9am-6pm Mon-Sat; Ⓜ Opéra), concentrates largely on the bottling and packaging side of perfume production.

◉ Montmartre & Pigalle

Montmartre's slinking streets lined with crooked ivy-clad buildings retain a fairy-tale charm. Crowned by the Sacré-Cœur basilica, Montmartre has lofty views, wine-producing vines and hidden village squares that have lured painters from the 19th century onwards. The best time to explore (see p82 for our walking tour) is early morning when tourists are few.

To its southwest, lively, neon-lit Pigalle is a tame red-light district that's fast becoming better known for its foodie scene.

★ Basilique du Sacré-Cœur   BASILICA
(Map p80; www.sacre-coeur-montmartre.com; place du Parvis du Sacré-Cœur; dome adult/child €6/4, cash only; ⊙6am-10.30pm, dome 9am-7pm Apr-Sep, to 5.30pm Oct-Mar; Ⓜ Anvers) Although some may poke fun at Sacré-Cœur's unsubtle design, the view from its parvis is one of those perfect Paris postcards. More than just a basilica, Sacré-Cœur is a veritable experience, from the musicians performing on the steps to the groups of friends picnicking on the hillside park. Touristy, yes. But beneath it all, Sacré-Cœur's heart still shines gold.

Place du Tertre   SQUARE
(Map p80; Ⓜ Abbesses) It would be hard to miss the place du Tertre, one of the most touristy spots in all of Paris. Although today it's filled with visitors, buskers and portrait artists, it

Montmartre & Pigalle

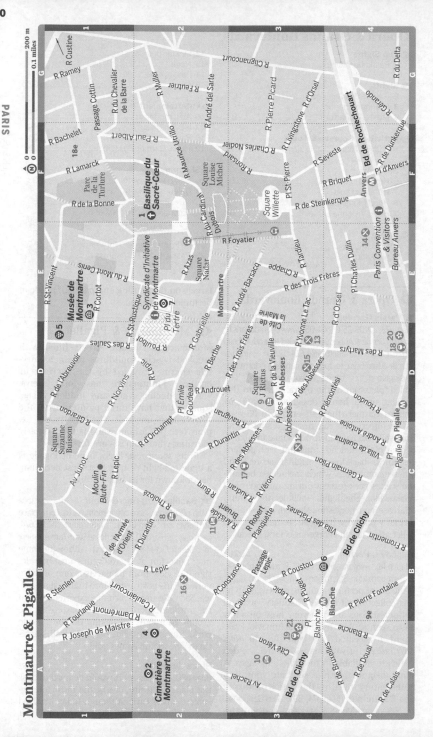

200 m
0.1 miles

2 Cimetière de Montmartre

1 Basilique du Sacré-Cœur

Parc de la Turlure

3 Musée de Montmartre

5

Square Suzanne Buisson

Moulin Blute-Fin

Square Louise Michel

Square Willette

Square Nadar

Syndicate d'Initiative de Montmartre

Square J Rictus

Montmartre

Pl du Tertre **7**

Pl Émile Goudeau

Pl des Abbesses

Paris Convention & Visitors Bureau Anvers

Anvers **M**

Pigalle **M** Pigalle

Blanche **M**

Pl Blanche

Pl St-Pierre

Pl d'Anvers

Pl Charles Dullin

14

13

15

12

16

17

11

8

10

19 21

18 20

6

4

Streets

R Custine
R Ramey
Passage Cottin
R du Chevalier de la Barre
R Bachelet
18e
R Lamarck
R de la Bonne
R St-Vincent
R du Mont Cenis
R Cortot
R St-Rustique
R Poulbot
R des Saules
R de l'Abreuvoir
R Norvins
R Lepic
R Girardon
Av Junot
R Lepic
R de l'Armée d'Orient
R Durantin
R Thiolöze
R Tourlaque
R Steinlen
R Damremont
R Caulaincourt
R Joseph de Maistre
Av Rachel
Cité Véron
Pl Blanche
Bd de Clichy
R Constance
R Cauchois
Passage Lepic
R Puget
R Lepic
R Coustou
R Véron
R Audran
R des Abbesses
R Aristide Bruant
R Robert Planquette
Villa des Platanes
R Germain Pilon
R Burq
R Durantin
R d'Orchampt
R Ravignan
R Berthe
R des Trois Frères
R André Antoine
Villa de Guelma
Pl des Abbesses
R de la Vieuville
R des Abbesses
R Houdon
R d'Orsel
R Yvonne Le Tac
R Drevet
R Piémontesi
Cité de la Mairie
R Gabrielle
R Azaïs
R Foyatier
R Cardinal Dubois
R Maurice Utrillo
R Paul Albert
R Feutrier
R Muller
R André del Sarte
R Charles Nodier
R Ronsard
R Séveste
R de Steinkerque
R Briquet
R Pierre Picard
R Livingstone
R d'Orsel
R Clignancourt
R St-Pierre
R Tardieu
R des Trois Frères
R André-Barsacq
R Chappe
R de Chappe
Montmartre
Pl du Tertre
R des Martyrs
R d'Orsel
Bd de Rochechouart
Bd de Dunkerque
R Gérando
R du Delta
9e
R Pierre Fontaine
R Blanche
R de Bruxelles
R de Douai
R de Calais
Bd de Clichy
R Fromentin

Montmartre & Pigalle

◉ Top Sights
1 Basilique du Sacré-Cœur	F2
2 Cimetière de Montmartre	A2
3 Musée de Montmartre	E1

◉ Sights
4 Cimetière de Montmartre Entrance & Conservation Office	A2
5 Clos Montmartre	D1
6 Musée de l'Érotisme	B4
7 Place du Tertre	E2

◉ Sleeping
8 Hôtel des Arts	C2
9 Hôtel Regyn's Montmartre	D3
10 Loft	A3
11 Plug-Inn Hostel	B2

◉ Eating
12 Chez Toinette	C3
13 Le Miroir	D3
14 Le Petit Trianon	E4
15 Le Relais Gascon	D3
16 Le Relais Gascon	B2

◉ Drinking & Nightlife
17 Cave des Abbesses	C3
18 La Fourmi	D4
19 La Machine du Moulin Rouge	A3

◉ Entertainment
20 La Cigale	D4
21 Moulin Rouge	A3

was originally the main square of the village of Montmartre before it was incorporated into the city proper.

★**Cimetière de Montmartre**　CEMETERY
(Map p80; ⊙8am-5.30pm Mon-Fri, from 8.30am Sat, from 9am Sun; ⓂPlace de Clichy) Established in 1798, this 11-hectare cemetery is perhaps the most celebrated necropolis in Paris after Père Lachaise. It contains the graves of writers Émile Zola (whose ashes are now in the Panthéon), Alexandre Dumas (fils) and Stendhal, composers Jacques Offenbach and Hector Berlioz, artist Edgar Degas, film director François Truffaut and dancer Vaslav Nijinsky, among others.

★**Musée de Montmartre**　MUSEUM
(Map p80; www.museedemontmartre.fr; 12 rue Cortot, 18e; adult/child €9/5; ⊙10am-6pm; ⓂLamarck–Caulaincourt) The Montmartre Museum displays paintings, lithographs and documents mostly relating to the area's rebellious and bohemian past. It's located in one of the oldest houses in Montmartre, a 17th-century manor home where over a dozen artists, including Renoir and Utrillo, once lived. Suzanne Valadon's restored studio was set to open here at the time of writing.

Musée de l'Érotisme　ART MUSEUM
(Map p80; www.musee-erotisme.com; 72 bd de Clichy, 18e; admission €10; ⊙10am-2am; ⓂBlanche) The Museum of Erotic Art attempts to raise around 2000 titillating statuary, stimulating sexual aids and fetishist items to a loftier plane, with antique and modern erotic art from four continents spread out across several floors. Some of the exhibits are, well, breathtaking, to say the least.

◉ **Gare du Nord, Gare de l'Est & Canal St-Martin**

Highlights here include Parc de la Villette, with its wonderful museums and attractions, and the ongoing urban renaissance of Canal St-Martin, one of the most vibrant neighbourhoods in Paris today.

Parc de la Villette　PARK
(www.villette.com; ⓂPorte de la Villette or Porte de Pantin) The largest park in Paris, the Parc de la Villette is a cultural centre, kids' playground and landscaped urban space at the intersection of two canals, the Ourcq and the St-Denis. Its futuristic layout includes the colossal mirrorlike sphere of the Géode cinema and the bright-red cubical pavilions known as *folies*. Among its themed gardens are the Jardin du Dragon (Dragon Garden), with a giant dragon's tongue slide for kids, the Jardin des Dunes (Dunes Garden) and Jardin des Miroirs (Mirror Garden).

Cité des Sciences　SCIENCE MUSEUM
(☏01 56 43 20 20; www.cite-sciences.fr; Parc de la Villette, 19e; adult/under 26yr €9/6; ⊙10am-6pm Tue-Sat, to 7pm Sun; ⓂPorte de la Villette) This is the city's top museum for kids, with three floors of hands-on exhibits for children aged two and up, plus two special-effects cinemas, a planetarium and a retired submarine. The only drawback is that each exhibit has a separate admission fee (though some combined tickets do exist), so you'll have to do some pretrip research in order to figure out what's most appropriate.

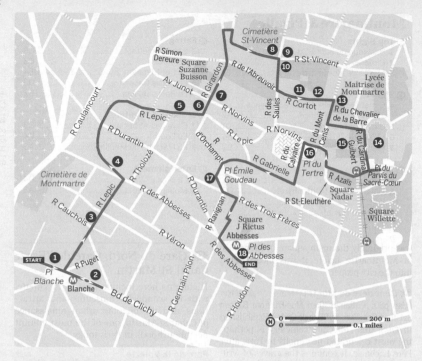

🏃 Walking Tour
Montmartre Art Attack

START Ⓜ BLANCHE
FINISH Ⓜ ABBESSES
LENGTH 2.5KM, 2.5 HOURS

Montmartre has been a place of legend ever since St Denis was executed here in about AD 250 and began his headless journey on foot to the village north of Paris that still bears his name (p79). In recent times the Montmartre of myth has been resurrected by music, books and especially films like *Le Fabuleux Destin d'Amélie Poulain* (*Amélie;* 2002), which presented the district in various shades of rose, and *Moulin Rouge* (2001), which also made it pretty but gave it a bit more edge.

For centuries Montmartre was a simple country village filled with the *moulins* (mills) that supplied Paris with its flour. When it was incorporated into the capital in 1860, its picturesque charm and low rents attracted painters and writers – especially after the Communard uprising of 1871, which began here. The late

19th and early 20th centuries were Montmartre's heyday, when Toulouse-Lautrec drew his favourite cancan dancers and Picasso, Braque and others introduced cubism to the world.

After WWI such creative activity shifted to Montparnasse, but Montmartre retained an upbeat ambience. The real attractions here, apart from the great views from the Butte de Montmartre (Montmartre Hill), are the area's little parks and steep, winding cobblestone streets, lined with houses that seem about to be engulfed by creeping vines and ivy.

Begin the walk outside the Blanche metro station on place Blanche ('White Square'). The name of this square derives from the plaster (made from the locally mined gypsum) that was carted through the area. To the northwest is the legendary ❶ **Moulin Rouge** beneath its trademark red windmill. To the right is the ❷ **Musée de l'Érotisme**, an institution that portrays itself as educational rather than titillating. Yeah, right.

Walk up rue Lepic, lined with food shops, and halfway up on the left you'll find ❸ **Café des Deux Moulins** where heroine Amélie worked in the eponymous film. Follow the curve to the west: Théo van Gogh owned the ❹ **house at No 54**, and his brother, the artist Vincent, stayed with him on the 3rd floor from 1886 to 1888.

Further along rue Lepic are Montmartre's famous twinned windmills. The ❺ **Moulin de la Blute-Fin** and, 100m east at the corner of rue Girardon, the ❻ **Moulin Radet** (now a restaurant), together formed the Moulin de la Galette, a popular open-air dance hall in the late 19th century immortalised by Pierre-Auguste Renoir in his 1876 tableau *Le Bal du Moulin de la Galette* (Dance at the Moulin de la Galette), which is displayed in the Musée d'Orsay.

Crossing through place Marcel Aymé you'll see a curious sculpture of a man emerging from a stone wall, the ❼ **Passe-Muraille statue**. It portrays Dutilleul, the hero of Marcel Aymé's short story *Le Passe-Muraille* (The Walker through Walls) who awakes one fine morning to discover he can do just what he's shown doing here. Aymé lived in the adjacent apartment building from 1902 to 1967.

Cross the street to leafy square Suzanne Buisson, turn left (north) onto rue Girardon, and pass Allée des Brouillards (Fog Alley), named after the adjacent 'Fog Castle' where several artists squatted in the late 19th century – Renoir lived at No 8 from 1890 to 1897. Descend the stairs from place Dalida into rue St-Vincent: on the other side of the wall is ❽ **Cimetière St-Vincent**, final resting place of Maurice Utrillo (1883–1955), the 'painter of walking Montmartre'.

Just over rue des Saules is the celebrated cabaret ❾ **Au Lapin Agile**. Although its name seems to suggest a 'nimble rabbit', it actually comes from *Le Lapin à Gill*, a mural of a rabbit jumping out of a cooking pot by caricaturist André Gill, which can still be seen on the western exterior wall.

Turn right (south) onto rue des Saules. Just opposite is ❿ **Clos Montmartre**, a small vineyard dating from 1933; its 2000 vines produce an average 800 bottles of wine each October, which is then auctioned off for charity. The ⓫ **Musée de Montmartre** is at 12–14 rue Cortot, the first street on the left after the vineyard. The museum is housed in Montmartre's oldest building, a manor house built in the

17th century, and was the one-time home to painters Renoir, Utrillo and Raoul Dufy. Further along at No 6 is the ⓬ **house of Eric Satie** where the celebrated composer lived from 1892 to 1898.

At the end of rue Cortot turn right (south) onto rue du Mont Cenis – the attractive ⓭ **water tower** just opposite dates from the early 20th century – then left onto rue de Chevalier de la Barre and right onto rue du Cardinal Guibert. The entrance to the ⓮ **Basilique du Sacré-Cœur** and the stunning vista over Paris from the steps are just to the south.

From the basilica follow rue Azaïs west, then turn north to ⓯ **Église St-Pierre de Montmartre**. This church was built on the site of a Roman temple to Mars (or Mercury) – some say that the name Montmartre is derived from 'Mons Martis' (Latin for Mount of Mars), others prefer the Christian 'Mont Martyr' (Mount of the Martyr).

Across from the church is ⓰ **place du Tertre**, arguably Paris' most touristy place but buzzy and fun nonetheless. Cossack soldiers allegedly first introduced the term *bistro* (Russian for 'quickly') into French at No 6 (La Mère Catherine) in 1814. On Christmas Eve 1898, Louis Renault's first car was driven up the Butte to place du Tertre, marking the start of the French auto industry.

From place du Calvaire take the steps onto rue Gabrielle, turning right (west) to reach place Émile Goudeau. At No 11b is the ⓱ **Bateau Lavoir** where Kees Van Dongen, Max Jacob, Amedeo Modigliani and Pablo Picasso once lived in an old piano factory later used as a laundry. It was dubbed the 'Laundry Boat' because of the way it swayed in a strong breeze. Picasso painted his seminal *Les Demoiselles d'Avignon* (1907) here. Initially located at No 13, the original Bateau Lavoir burned down in 1970 and was rebuilt in 1978.

Take the steps down from place Émile Goudeau and follow rue des Abbesses south into place des Abbesses, where you can't miss the ⓲ **metro station** entrance designed by Hector Guimard. In the 18th century gypsum miners excavated significant amounts of the Butte, which is why the Abbesses metro station was dug so deeply.

Gare du Nord & Gare de l'Est

N ↑ 0 ——————— 200 m
0 ——————— 0.1 miles

MONTMARTRE Bd Barbès 18E

Bd Barbès

Barbès
Rochechouart

R de la Charbonnière

Bd de la Chapelle

R de Tombouctou

Sq de
Jessaint

La Chapelle

Bd de Rochechouart

R de la Charbonnière

Pl de la
Chapelle

R Louis Blanc

Villa Garance

Hôpital
Lariboisière

R Perdonnet

R Cail

R du Delta

R Guy Patin

R Ambroise Paré

R de Maubeuge

R du Faubourg St-Denis

R Demarquay

R Pétrelle

R de Dunkerque

R du Faubourg Poissonnière

Pl de
Roubaix

Gare du
Nord

Gare du Nord
Welcome Desk

R de l'Aqueduc

R La Fayette

R Condorcet

R de Rocroy

Bd de Magenta

Pl Napoléon III

Gare du
Nord

R de Dunkerque

R d'Alsace

R Belzunce

R St-Vincent
de Paul

R Fénelon

Bd de Denain

R Bossuet

3

R d'Abbeville

R La Fayette

R des 2 Gares

R d'Alsace

1

R Pierre Sémard

9E

R d'Hauteville

Pl de
Valenciennes

R de St-Quentin

Passage Delanos

R de Bellefond

Pl
Franz
Liszt

2

R des Petits Hôtels

R d'Alsace

Poissonnière

R de Chabrol

RATP Bus
350 to Charles de
Gaulle Airport

Gare de
l'Est

R des Messageries

10E

R du 8 Mai 1945

R du Faubourg Poissonnière

Cité Paradis

R de Paradis

Sq A
Satragne

R du Faubourg
St-Martin

Gare de l'Est

R St-
Laurent

Av de Verdun

Sq
Villemin

R Philippe de Girard

5

R des Petites Écuries

R Martel

R de la Fidélité

Sq St-
Laurent

4

R Gabriel Laumain

R Jarry

Passage
du Désir

Bd de Strasbourg

R des Vinaigriers

R d'Enghien

Passage des Petites
Écuries

Cour des
Petites Écuries

R du Faubourg St-Denis

Château
d'Eau

R du Faubourg St-Martin

Bd de Magenta

R Lucien
Sampaix

7

6

R de l'Échiquier

Passage Brady

R de Nancy

9

R Hittorff

Bonne
Nouvelle

R Thorel

R de Mazagran

R Gustave Goublier

R du Château d'Eau

R Bouchardon

Jacques
Bonsergent

7

Poissonnière

8

Bd de Bonne Nouvelle

2E

R de la Lune

R de Metz

Strasbourg
St-Denis

Gare du Nord & Gare de l'Est

Cité de la Musique   MUSEUM
(www.cite-musique.fr; 221 av Jean Jaurès, 19e; ⊙noon-6pm Tue-Sat, 10am-6pm Sun; Ⓜ Porte de Pantin) The Cité de la Musique, on the southern edge of Parc de la Villette, is a striking, triangular-shaped concert hall whose mission is to introduce music from around the world to Parisians. The **Musée de la Musique** (Music Museum; adult/child €7/free; Ⓜ Porte de Pantin) inside displays some 900 rare musical instruments; you can hear many of them being played on the audioguide.

Parc des Buttes-Chaumont   PARK
(rue Manin & rue Botzaris, 19e; ⊙7am-10pm May-Sep, to 8pm Oct-Apr; Ⓜ Buttes-Chaumont or Botzaris) This quirky park is one of the city's largest green spaces; its landscaped slopes hide grottoes, waterfalls, a lake and even an island topped with a temple to Sybil. Once a gypsum quarry and rubbish dump, it was given its present form by Baron Haussmann in time for the opening of the 1867 Exposition Universelle.

◉ Ménilmontant & Belleville

A solidly working-class *quartier* (neighbourhood) until just a few years ago, Ménilmontant now heaves with restaurants, bars and clubs. Multicultural, arty Belleville is also rapidly gentrifying but remains for the most part gritty and unpretentious.

Parc de Belleville   PARK
(Ⓜ Couronnes) A few blocks east of bd de Belleville, this lovely park occupies a hill almost 200m above sea level, set amid 4.5 hectares of greenery. Little known to visitors, the park (which opened in 1992) offers some of the best views of the city.

★ Cimetière du Père Lachaise   CEMETERY
(⌨01 43 70 70 33; www.pere-lachaise.com; 16 rue du Repos & bd de Ménilmontant, 20e; ⊙8am-6pm Mon-Fri, 8.30am-6pm Sat, 9am-6pm Sun; Ⓜ Père Lachaise or Gambetta) **FREE** The world's most visited cemetery, Père Lachaise, opened in 1804. Its 70,000 ornate, even ostentatious, tombs of the rich and/or famous form a verdant, 44-hectare sculpture garden. The most visited are those of 1960s rock star Jim Morrison (division 6) and Oscar Wilde (division 89). Pick up cemetery maps at the **conservation office** (16 rue du Repos, 20e; ⊙8.30am-12.30pm & 2-5pm Mon-Fri; Ⓜ Père Lachaise), near the main bd de Ménilmontant entrance.

DON'T MISS

CANAL ST-MARTIN

The shaded towpaths of the tranquil, 4.5km-long Canal St-Martin are a wonderful place for a romantic stroll or a bike ride, while the surrounding streets teem with trendy places to drink, dine and catch live music.

Dug out in 1825, the canal was a major cargo thoroughfare by the time Marcel Carné's 1938 film *Hôtel du Nord* was set in the canalside hotel – now a cafe-bar – of the same name. Although the film (about a Romeo-and-Juliet-style suicide pact) was shot in a studio, author Eugène Dabit, whose stories formed the basis of the film, lived here when the hotel was run by his parents.

The canal's fortunes fell in the 1960s when barge transportation declined. It was slated to be concreted over and turned into a roadway until local residents rallied to save it. When the title character of *Amélie* skipped stones here in 2001, the cheap rents and quaint setting were just starting to lure artists, designers and students, who set up artists' collectives, vintage and offbeat boutiques, and a bevy of neo-retro cafes and bars.

Today Canal St-Martin is the centre of Paris' bobo (bohemian bourgeois) life, but maritime legacies endure, including old swing-bridges that still pivot 90 degrees when barges pass through the canal's double-locks. Take a canal boat **cruise** (www.canauxrama.com; adult/student & senior/4-12yr €16/12/8.50) to savour the full flavour.

Cimetière du Père Lachaise

A HALF-DAY TOUR

There is a certain romance to getting lost in Cimetière du Père Lachaise, a grave jungle spun from centuries of tales. But to search for one grave among 70,000 in this 44-hectare land of the dead is no joke – narrow the search with this itinerary.

From the main bd de Ménilmontant entrance (metro Père Lachaise or Philippe Auguste), head up av Principale, turn right onto av du Puits and collect a map from the **Bureaux de la Conservation** ❶.

Backtrack along av du Puits, turn right onto av Latérale du Sud, scale the stairs and bear right along chemin Denon to New Realist artist **Arman** ❷, film director **Claude Chabrol** ❸ and **Chopin** ❹.

Follow chemin Méhul downhill, cross av Casimir Périer and bear right onto chemin Serré. Take the second left (chemin Lebrun – unsigned), head uphill and near the top leave the footpath to weave through graves on your right to rock star **Jim Morrison** ❺. Back on chemin Lauriston, continue uphill to roundabout **Rond-Point Casimir Périer** ❻.

Admire the funerary art of contemporary photographer **André Chabot** ❼, av de la Chapelle. Continue uphill for energising city views from the **chapel** ❽ steps, then zig-zag to **Molière & La Fontaine** ❾, on chemin Molière.

Cut between graves onto av Tranversale No 1 – spot potatoes atop **Parmentier's** ❿ headstone. Continue straight onto av Greffülhe and left onto av Tranversale No 2 to rub **Monsieur Noir's** ⓫ shiny crotch.

Navigation to **Édith Piaf** ⓬ and the **Mur des Fédérés** ⓭ is straightforward. End with lipstick-kissed **Oscar Wilde** ⓮ near the Porte Gambetta entrance.

TOP TIPS

➡ **Say 'Cheese!'** Père Lachaise is photography paradise any time of day/year, but best are sunny autumn mornings after the rain.

➡ **Guided Tours** Cemetery lovers will appreciate themed guided tours (two hours) led by entertaining cemetery historian Thierry Le Roi (www.necro-romantiques.com).

BRUNO DE HOGUES / GETTY IMAGES ©

Chopin, Division 11
Add a devotional note to the handwritten letters and flowers brightening the marble tomb of Polish composer/pianist Frédéric Chopin (1810–49), who spent his short adult life in Paris. His heart is buried in Warsaw.

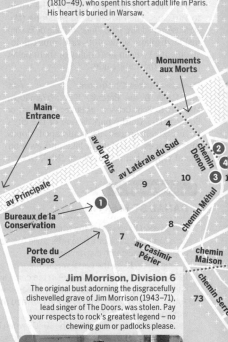

Jim Morrison, Division 6
The original bust adorning the disgracefully dishevelled grave of Jim Morrison (1943–71), lead singer of The Doors, was stolen. Pay your respects to rock's greatest legend – no chewing gum or padlocks please.

NICOLA WILLIAMS ©

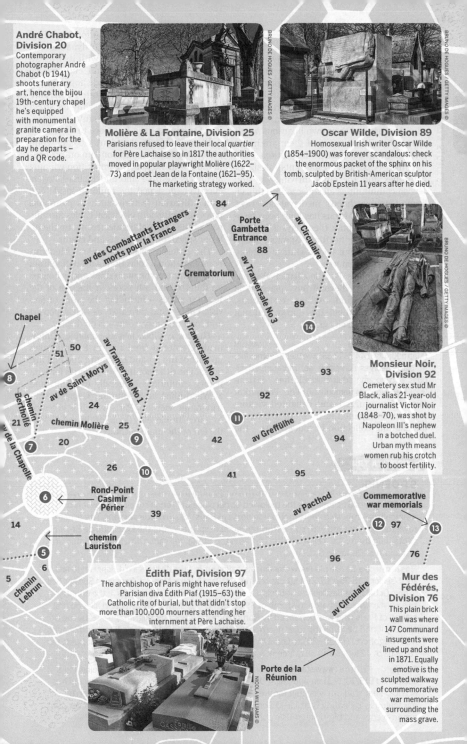

André Chabot, Division 20
Contemporary photographer André Chabot (b 1941) shoots funerary art, hence the bijou 19th-century chapel he's equipped with monumental granite camera in preparation for the day he departs – and a QR code.

BRUNO DE HOGUES / GETTY IMAGES ©

Molière & La Fontaine, Division 25
Parisians refused to leave their local *quartier* for Père Lachaise so in 1817 the authorities moved in popular playwright Molière (1622–73) and poet Jean de la Fontaine (1621–95). The marketing strategy worked.

Oscar Wilde, Division 89
Homosexual Irish writer Oscar Wilde (1854–1900) was forever scandalous: check the enormous packet of the sphinx on his tomb, sculpted by British-American sculptor Jacob Epstein 11 years after he died.

BRUNO DE HOGUES / GETTY IMAGES ©

BRUNO DE HOGUES / GETTY IMAGES ©

av des Combattants Étrangers morts pour la France

84

Porte Gambetta Entrance
88

av Circulaire

Crematorium

av Transversale No 3

89

14

Chapel

av Transversale No 2

Monsieur Noir, Division 92
Cemetery sex stud Mr Black, alias 21-year-old journalist Victor Noir (1848–70), was shot by Napoleon III's nephew in a botched duel. Urban myth means women rub his crotch to boost fertility.

50
51

8

chemin Bertholle

av de Saint Morys

av de Transversale No 1

93

21

24

92

11

7

chemin Molière

25

42

av Greffülhe

94

20

9

26

10

41

95

6

Rond-Point Casimir Périer

39

av Pacthod

Commemorative war memorials

14

chemin Lauriston

12 97

13

76

5

6

96

av Circulaire

Mur des Fédérés, Division 76
This plain brick wall was where 147 Communard insurgents were lined up and shot in 1871. Equally emotive is the sculpted walkway of commemorative war memorials surrounding the mass grave.

5

chemin Lebrun

Édith Piaf, Division 97
The archbishop of Paris might have refused Parisian diva Édith Piaf (1915–63) the Catholic rite of burial, but that didn't stop more than 100,000 mourners attending her internment at Père Lachaise.

Porte de la Réunion

NICOLA WILLIAMS ©

⊙ Le Marais & Bastille

Paris' *marais* (marsh) was converted to farmland in the 12th century. In the early 17th century, Henri IV built the place Royale (today's place des Vosges), turning the area into Paris' most fashionable residential district and attracting wealthy aristocrats who then erected their own luxurious *hôtels particulier*. Today many of them are house museums and government institutions.

Funky bars and restaurants, designer boutiques and the city's thriving gay and Jewish communities all squeeze into this vibrant neighbourhood's medieval laneways. While the lower Marais has long been fashionable, the real buzz these days is in Haut Marais (upper or northern Marais), showcasing rising design talent, vintage fashion, hip art and cool eateries.

The contiguous Bastille district also has buzzing nightlife. Beyond busy place de la Bastille, you'll find exciting restaurants, modest cafes and all the quirky, unusual shops that make a city great.

Centre Pompidou   MUSEUM
(Map p90; ☏ 01 44 78 12 33; www.centrepompidou. fr; place Georges Pompidou, 4e; museum, exhibitions & panorama adult/child €13/free; ⊙ 11am-9pm Wed-Mon; Ⓜ Rambuteau) The Pompidou Centre has amazed and delighted visitors ever since it opened in 1977, not just for its outstanding collection of modern art – the largest in Europe – but also for its radical architectural statement. The dynamic and vibrant arts centre delights with its irresistible cocktail of galleries and cutting-edge exhibitions, hands-on workshops, dance performances, cinemas and other entertainment venues. The exterior, with its street performers and fanciful fountains (place Igor Stravinsky), is a fun place to linger.

Former French President Georges Pompidou wanted an ultracontemporary artistic hub, and he got it: competition-winning architects Renzo Piano and Richard Rogers effectively designed the building inside out, with utilitarian features such as plumbing, pipes, air vents and electrical cables forming part of the external façade, freeing up the interior space for exhibitions and events.

The Musée National d'Art Moderne, France's national collection of art dating from 1905 onward, is the main draw and is housed on the 4th and 5th floors. A fraction of the 100,000 pieces – including the work of fauvists, cubists and surrealists as well as pop art and contemporary works – is on display.

The huge Bibliothèque Publique d'Information, entered from rue du Renard, takes up part of the 1st and the entire 2nd and 3rd floors. The 6th floor has two galleries for temporary exhibitions (generally excellent) and a hyperindustrial restaurant, Georges, with panoramic views of Paris, which is accessed by a free lift/elevator (look for the red door to the left of the main entrance).

WORTH A TRIP

ST-DENIS

For 1200 years St-Denis was the hallowed burial place of French royalty. Today it is a multicultural suburb a short metro ride north of Paris' 18e *arrondissement*. The ornate royal tombs, adorned with some truly remarkable statuary, and the Basilique de St-Denis containing them, are well worth the trip, as is the Stade de France, the futuristic stadium just south of Canal de St-Denis.

Basilique de St-Denis (www.monuments-nationaux.fr; 1 rue de la Légion d'Honneur; tombs adult/senior & 18-25yr €7.50/4.50, basilica free; ⊙ 10am-6.15pm Mon-Sat, from noon Sun Apr-Sep, to 5pm Oct-Mar; Ⓜ Basilique de St-Denis) Once one of the most sacred sites in the country, this basilica was built atop the tomb of St Denis, the 3rd-century martyr and alleged first bishop of Paris who was beheaded by Roman priests. A popular pilgrimage site, by the 6th century it had become the royal necropolis: all but a handful of France's kings and queens from Dagobert I (r 629–39) to Louis XVIII (r 1814–24) were buried here (today it holds the remains of 42 kings and 32 queens).

Stade de France (www.stadefrance.com; rue Francis de Pressensé, St-Denis la Plaine; tours adult/child €15/10; ⊙ 11am-4pm; Ⓜ St-Denis-Porte de Paris or La Plaine Stade de France) This 80,000-seat stadium was built for the 1998 football World Cup, which France won by miraculously defeating Brazil 3–0. Today it hosts football and rugby matches, major gymnastic events and big-ticket music concerts.

Rooftop admission is included in museum and exhibition admission – or just buy a panorama ticket to go up to the roof.

Admission to the museum is free on the first Sunday of each month.

There are cinemas and more exhibition space on the ground floor and in the basement.

West of the centre, place Georges Pompidou and the nearby pedestrian streets attract buskers, musicians, jugglers and mime artists. South of the centre on place Igor Stravinsky are fanciful mechanical fountains of skeletons, hearts, treble clefs and a big pair of ruby-red lips, created by Jean Tinguely and Niki de Saint Phalle.

Musée Picasso   ART MUSEUM

(Map p90; ☑01 42 71 25 21; www.museepicasso paris.fr; 5 rue de Thorigny, 3e; admission €11; ⊙11.30am-6pm Tue-Sun, to 9pm 3rd Sat of month; Ⓜ St-Paul or Chemin Vert) One of Paris' most beloved art collections reopened its doors in late 2014 after a massive renovation and much controversy. Housed in the stunning, mid-17th-century Hôtel Salé, the Musée Picasso woos art lovers with 5000 drawings, engravings, paintings, ceramic works and sculptures by the *grand maître* (great master) Pablo Picasso (1881–1973). The extraordinary collection was donated to the French government by the artist's heirs in lieu of paying inheritance tax.

Hôtel de Ville   CITY HALL

(Map p90; www.paris.fr; place de l'Hôtel de Ville, 4e; Ⓜ Hôtel de Ville) FREE Paris' beautiful neo-Renaissance town hall was gutted during the Paris Commune of 1871 and rebuilt in luxurious neo-Renaissance style between 1874 and 1882. The ornate façade is decorated with 108 statues of illustrious Parisians, and the outstanding temporary exhibitions (admission free) held inside in its Salle St-Jean almost always have a Parisian theme. From December to early March, an ice-skating rink sets up outside this beautiful building, creating a real picture-book experience.

Place des Vosges   SQUARE

(Map p90; place des Vosges, 4e; Ⓜ St-Paul or Bastille) Inaugurated in 1612 as place Royale and thus Paris' oldest square, place des Vosges is a strikingly elegant ensemble of 36 symmetrical houses with ground-floor arcades, steep slate roofs and large dormer windows arranged around a leafy square with four symmetrical fountains and an 1829 copy of a mounted statue of Louis XIII. The square received its present name in 1800 to honour the Vosges *département* (administrative division) for being the first in France to pay its taxes.

Maison de Victor Hugo   HOUSE MUSEUM

(Map p90; www.musee-hugo.paris.fr; 6 place des Vosges, 4e; ⊙10am-6pm Tue-Sun; Ⓜ St-Paul or Bastille) FREE Between 1832 and 1848 writer Victor Hugo lived in an apartment on the 3rd floor of Hôtel de Rohan-Guéménée, overlooking one of Paris' most elegant squares. He moved here a year after the publication of *Notre Dame de Paris* (The Hunchback of Notre Dame), completing *Ruy Blas* while living here. The house is now a small museum devoted to the life and times of this celebrated novelist and poet, with an impressive collection of his personal drawings and portraits.

★ Musée Carnavalet   MUSEUM

(Map p90; www.carnavalet.paris.fr; 23 rue de Sévigné, 3e; ⊙10am-6pm Tue-Sun; Ⓜ St-Paul, Chemin Vert or Rambuteau) FREE This engaging history museum, spanning Gallo-Roman times to the modern day, is in two *hôtels particuliers:* mid-16th-century Renaissance-style Hôtel Carnavalet and late-17th-century Hôtel Le Peletier de St-Fargeau. Some of the nation's most important documents, paintings and other objects from the French Revolution are here.

Don't miss Georges Fouquet's stunning art nouveau jewellery shop from rue Royale, and Marcel Proust's cork-lined bedroom from his bd Haussmann apartment where he wrote his 7350-page literary cycle *À la Recherche de Temps Perdu* (Remembrance of Things Past).

★ Musée des Arts et Métiers   MUSEUM

(Map p90; www.arts-et-metiers.net; 60 rue de Réaumur, 3e; adult/child €6.50/free; ⊙10am-6pm Tue, Wed & Fri-Sun, to 9.30pm Thu; Ⓜ Arts et Métiers) The Arts & Crafts Museum, dating to 1794 and Europe's oldest science and technology museum, is a must for anyone with kids – or an interest in how things tick or work. Housed inside the sublime 18th-century priory of St-Martin des Champs, some 3000 instruments, machines and working models from the 18th to 20th centuries are displayed across three floors. In the attached church of St-Martin des Champs is Foucault's original pendulum, introduced to the world at the Universal Exhibition in Paris in 1855.

Musée d'Art et d'Histoire du Judaïsme   MUSEUM

(Map p90; www.mahj.org; 71 rue du Temple, 4e; adult/child €8/free; ⊙11am-6pm Mon-Fri, 10am-6pm Sun; Ⓜ Rambuteau) To delve into the historic

Le Marais & Northern Bastille

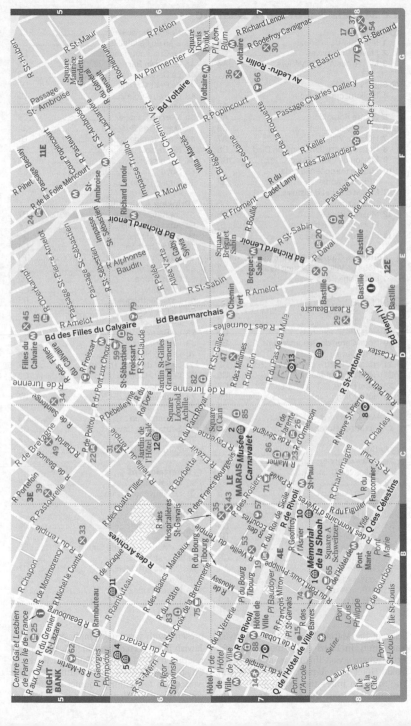

Le Marais & Northern Bastille

heart of the Marais' long-established Jewish community in Pletzl (from the Yiddish for 'little square'), visit this fascinating museum inside Hôtel de St-Aignan, dating from 1650. The museum traces the evolution of Jewish communities from the Middle Ages to the present, with particular emphasis on French Jewish history. Highlights include documents relating to the Dreyfus Affair; and works by Chagall, Modigliani and Soutine. Creative workshops for children, adults and families complement excellent temporary exhibitions.

⭐ **Mémorial de la Shoah** MUSEUM
(Map p90; www.memorialdelashoah.org; 17 rue Geoffroy l'Asnier, 4e; ⊙10am-6pm Sun-Wed & Fri, to 10pm Thu; Ⓜ St-Paul) **FREE** Established in 1956, the Memorial to the Unknown Jewish Martyr has metamorphosed into the Memorial of the Shoah – a Hebrew word meaning 'catastrophe' and synonymous with the Holocaust. Exhibitions relate to the Holocaust and German occupation of parts of France and Paris during WWII. The actual memorial to the victims of the Shoah stands at the entrance.

Maison Européenne de la Photographie PHOTOGRAPHY MUSEUM
(Map p90; www.mep-fr.org; 5-7 rue de Fourcy, 4e; adult/child €8/4.50; ⊙11am-7.45pm Wed-Sun; Ⓜ St-Paul or Pont Marie) The European House of Photography, housed in the overly renovated Hôtel Hénault de Cantorbe (dating – believe it or not – from the early 18th century), has cutting-edge temporary exhibits (usually retrospectives on single photographers), as well as an enormous permanent collection on the history of photography and its connections with France. There are frequent showings of short films and documentaries on weekend afternoons. The Japanese garden at the entrance is a delight.

Place de la Bastille SQUARE
(Map p90; Ⓜ Bastille) The Bastille was a 14th-century fortress built to protect the city gates and is the most famous monument in Paris that no longer exists. Nothing remains of the prison it became under Cardinal Richelieu, which was mobbed on 14 July 1789, igniting the French Revolution, but you can't miss the 52m-high green-bronze column topped by a gilded, winged Liberty. Revolutionaries

---

WORTH A TRIP

BOIS DE VINCENNES

Originally royal hunting grounds, the Bois de Vincennes was annexed by the army following the Revolution and then donated to the city in 1860 by Napoléon III. A fabulous place to escape the urban tumult, the woodlands also contain a handful of notable sights. Metro lines 1 (St-Mandé, Château de Vincennes) and 8 (Porte Dorée, Porte de Charenton) will get you to the eastern edges of the park. Pick up picnic supplies on rue de Midi, Vincennes' main shopping street.

Château de Vincennes (www.chateau-vincennes.fr; av de Paris, Vincennes; adult/child €8.50/free; ⊙10am-6pm mid-May–mid-Sep, to 5pm mid-Sep–mid-May; Ⓜ Château de Vincennes) Originally a meagre 12th-century hunting lodge the castle was expanded several times throughout the centuries until it reached its present size under Louis XIV. Notable features include the beautiful 52m-high keep (1370) and the royal chapel (1552), both of which are open to visits. Note that the chapel is only open between 11am and noon, and 2.30pm and 4pm.

Parc Zoologique de Paris (Zoo de Vincennes; http://parczoologiquedeparis.fr; cnr Daumesnil & rte de la Ceinture du Lac, 12e; adult/child €22/16.50; ⊙10am-6pm Mon-Fri, 9.30am-7.30pm Sat & Sun mid-Mar–mid-Oct, 10am-5pm daily mid-Oct–mid-Mar; Ⓜ Porte Dorée) Reopened in 2014 after years of renovations, Paris' largest, now state-of-the-art zoo focuses on the conservation of species and habitats, with camouflaged vantage points (no peering through fences). Its biozones include Patagonia, with sea lions to cougars; the savannah of Sahel-Sudan, with lions, white rhinos and giraffes; forested Europe, with wolves, lynx and wolverines; a Guiana rainforest with jaguars, monkeys and anacondas; and Madagascar, home to lemurs. Other highlights include Australian marsupials and manatees (sea cows).

Parc Floral de Paris (www.parcfloraldeparisjeux.com; Esplanade du Château de Vincennes or rte de la Pyramide; adult/child €5.50/2.75; ⊙9.30am-8pm Apr-Sep, shorter hours rest of year; Ⓜ Château de Vincennes) This magnificent botanical park is one of the highlights of the Bois de Vincennes. Natural landscaping and a magnificent collection of plants will keep amateur gardeners happy, while Paris' largest play area (giant climbing webs and slides, jungle gyms, sandboxes etc) will absolutely thrill families. Open-air concerts are staged throughout summer, making it a first-rate picnic destination.

Lac Daumesnil (Ⓜ Porte Dorée) Like something out of a Renoir painting, the largest lake in the Bois de Vincennes is a popular destination for walks and rowboat excursions in warmer months (from €12 per half-hour). A Buddhist temple is located nearby.

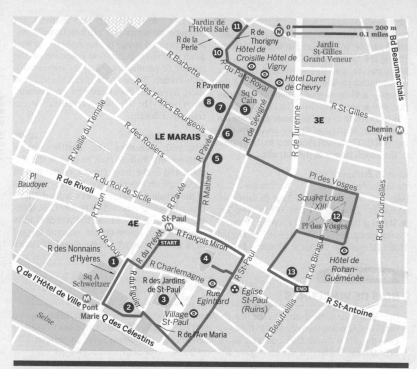

Walking Tour
Medieval Marais Meanderings

START Ⓜ ST-PAUL
FINISH Ⓜ HÔTEL DE SULLY
LENGTH 2KM, 1.5 HOURS

While Henri IV was busy having place Royale (today's place des Vosges) built, aristocrats were commissioning beautiful *hôtels particuliers* – the city's most beautiful Renaissance structures that lend the Marais a particular architectural harmony.

From rue François Miron, walk south on rue du Prévôt to rue Charlemagne. To the right at 7 rue de Jouy stands majestic **①Hôtel d'Aumont**, built around 1650 for a financier. Continue south along rue des Nonnains d'Hyères and turn left onto rue de l'Hôtel de Ville. At 1 rue du Figuier is **②Hôtel de Sens**, the oldest Marais mansion, with geometric gardens and a neo-Gothic turret. Begun around 1475, it was built as digs for the archbishops of Sens. It was restored in mock Gothic style in 1911.

Continue southeast along rue de l'Ave Maria, then northeast along rue des Jardins de St-Paul. To the left, two truncated towers are all

that remain of Philippe-Auguste's **③enceinte**, a fortified wall (1190) once guarded by 39 towers. Cross rue Charlemagne, duck into rue Eginhard and follow it to rue St-Paul and **④Église St-Paul St-Louis** (1641). At the end of rue St-Paul, turn left, then walk north up rue Malher and rue Pavée, the first cobbled road in Paris. At No 24 is the late Renaissance **⑤Hôtel Lamoignon**.

North along rue Payenne is the back of the **⑥Musée Carnavalet**; the Revolutionary-era 'Temple of Reason'; **⑦Chapelle de l'Humanité** at No 5; and the rear of **⑧Musée Cognacq-Jay**. From grassy **⑨Square George Cain** opposite 11 rue Payenne, walk northwest to more spectacular 17th-century *hôtels particuliers:* **⑩Hôtel de Libéral Bruant** at 1 rue de la Perle, and **⑪Hôtel Salé** crammed with Picassos at 5 rue de Thorigny.

Retrace your steps to rue du Parc Royal, walk south down rue de Sévigné and follow rue des Francs Bourgeois eastwards to end with sublime **⑫place des Vosges** and **⑬Hôtel de Sully**.

from the uprising of 1830 are buried beneath. Now a skirmishly busy roundabout, it's still Paris' most symbolic destination for political protests.

Promenade Plantée PARK

(Map p98; 12e; ☉8am-9.30pm May-Aug, to 5.30pm Sep-Apr; Ⓜ Bastille or Gare de Lyon) The disused 19th-century Vincennes railway viaduct was successfully reborn as the world's first elevated park, planted with a fragrant profusion of cherry trees, maples, rose trellises, bamboo corridors and lavender. Three storeys above ground, it provides a unique aerial vantage point on the surrounding architecture. Access is via staircase – usually at least one per city block – and lift (elevator; although they're invariably out of service). At street level, the Viaduc des Arts (Map p98; www.viaduc desarts.fr; 1-129 av Daumesnil, 12e; ☉hours vary; Ⓜ Bastille or Gare de Lyon) gallery-workshops run along av Daumesnil.

◉ The Islands

Paris' two inner-city islands could not be more different. The bigger Île de la Cité is full of sights, including Notre Dame, while little Île St-Louis is residential and much quieter, with a scattering of boutiques and restaurants – and legendary ice-cream maker Berthillon.

ÎLE DE LA CITÉ

The site of the first settlement in Paris, around the 3rd century BC, and later the Roman town of Lutèce (Lutetia), the Île de la Cité remained the centre of royal and ecclesiastical power even after the city spread to both banks of the Seine during the Middle Ages. The buildings on the middle part of the island were demolished and rebuilt during Baron Haussmann's great urban renewal scheme of the late 19th century.

Don't miss the charming triangular park Square du Vert Gallant at the Île de la Cité's western tip beneath the Pont Neuf.

★ Cathédrale Notre Dame de Paris CATHEDRAL

(Map p100; ☑01 53 10 07 00; www.cathedralede paris.com; 6 place du Parvis Notre Dame, 4e; cathedral free, towers adult/child €8.50/free, treasury €2/1; ☉cathedral 7.45am-6.45pm Mon-Sat, to 7.15pm Sun, towers 10am-6.30pm, to 11pm Fri & Sat Jul & Aug; Ⓜ Cité) Notre Dame, Paris' most visited unticketed site with upwards of 14 million visitors crossing its threshold a year, is a masterpiece of French Gothic architecture.

It was the focus of Catholic Paris for seven centuries, its vast interior accommodating 6000-plus worshippers. Highlights include its three spectacular rose windows, treasury and bell towers which can be climbed. From the North Tower, 400-odd steps spiral to the top of the western façade, where you'll find yourself face-to-face with frightening gargoyles and a spectacular view of Paris.

★ Sainte-Chapelle CHAPEL

(Map p100; ☑01 53 40 60 80, concerts 01 42 77 65 65; http://sainte-chapelle.monuments-nationaux.fr; 8 bd du Palais, 1er; adult/child €8.50/free, joint ticket with Conciergerie €12.50; ☉9.30am-6pm daily, to 9pm Wed mid-May–mid-Sep, 9am-5pm Nov-Feb; Ⓜ Cité) Try to save Sainte-Chapelle for a sunny day, when Paris' oldest, finest stained glass is at its dazzling best. Enshrined within the Palais de Justice (Law Courts), this gemlike Holy Chapel is Paris' most exquisite Gothic monument. Sainte-Chapelle was built in just six years (compared with nearly 200 years for Notre Dame) and consecrated in 1248.

The chapel was conceived by Louis IX to house his personal collection of holy relics, including the famous Holy Crown (now in Notre Dame).

Conciergerie MONUMENT

(Map p100; www.monuments-nationaux.fr; 2 bd du Palais, 1er; adult/child €8.50/free, joint ticket with Sainte-Chapelle €12.50; ☉9.30am-6pm; Ⓜ Cité) A royal palace in the 14th century, the Conciergerie later became a prison. During the Reign of Terror (1793–94) alleged enemies of the Revolution were incarcerated here before being brought before the Revolutionary Tribunal at the Palais de Justice next door. Top-billing exhibitions take place in the beautiful, Rayonnant Gothic Salle des Gens d'Armes, which is Europe's largest surviving medieval hall.

Pont Neuf BRIDGE

(Map p100; Ⓜ Pont Neuf) Paris' oldest bridge has linked the western end of Île de la Cité with both river banks since 1607, when the king inaugurated it by crossing the bridge on a white stallion. The occasion is commemorated by an equestrian statue of Henry IV, known to his subjects as the Vert Galant ('jolly rogue' or 'dirty old man', perspective depending).

View the bridge's seven arches, decorated with humorous and grotesque figures of barbers, dentists, pickpockets, loiterers etc, from a spot along the river or afloat upon it.

Notre Dame

TIMELINE

1160 Maurice de Sully becomes bishop of Paris. Mission: to grace growing Paris with a lofty new cathedral.

1182–90 The **choir with double ambulatory** ❶ is finished and work starts on the nave and side chapels.

1200–50 The **west façade** ❷, with rose window, three portals and two soaring towers, goes up. Everyone is stunned.

1345 Some 180 years after the foundation stone was laid, the Cathédrale de Notre Dame is complete. It is dedicated to notre dame (our lady), the Virgin Mary.

1789 Revolutionaries smash the original **Gallery of Kings** ❸, pillage the cathedral and melt all its bells except the great bell Emmanuel. The cathedral becomes a Temple of Reason then a warehouse.

1831 Victor Hugo's novel *The Hunchback of Notre Dame* inspires new interest in the half-ruined Gothic cathedral.

1845–50 Architect Viollet-le-Duc undertakes its restoration. Twenty-eight new kings are sculpted for the west façade. The heavily decorated **portals** ❹ and **spire** ❺ are reconstructed. The neo-Gothic **treasury** ❻ is built.

1860 The area in front of Notre Dame is cleared to create the parvis, an alfresco classroom where Parisians can learn a catechism illustrated on sculpted stone portals.

1935 A rooster bearing part of the relics of the Crown of Thorns, St Denis and St Geneviève is put on top of the cathedral spire to protect those who pray inside.

1991 The architectural masterpiece of Notre Dame and its Seine-side riverbanks become a Unesco World Heritage Site.

2013 Notre Dame celebrates 850 years since construction began with a bevy of new bells and restoration works.

Virgin & Child
Spot all 37 artworks representing the Virgin Mary. Pilgrims have revered the pearly-cream sculpture of her in the sanctuary since the 14th century. Light a devotional candle and write some words to the *Livre de Vie* (Book of Life).

North Rose Window
See prophets, judges, kings and priests venerate Mary in vivid blue and violet glass, one of three beautiful rose blooms (1225–70), each almost 10m in diameter.

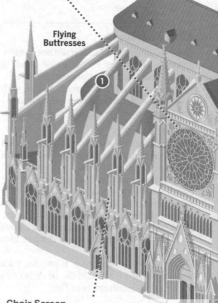

Flying Buttresses

Choir Screen
No part of the cathedral weaves biblical tales more evocatively than these ornate wooden panels, carved in the 14th century after the Black Death killed half the country's population. The faintly gaudy colours were restored in the 1960s.

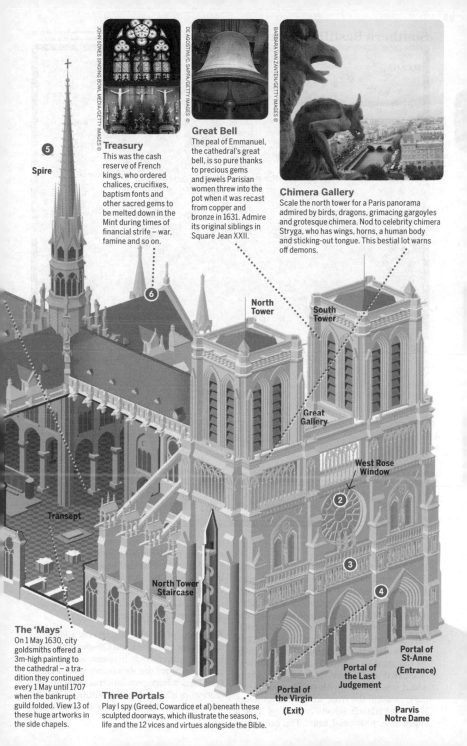

Treasury
This was the cash reserve of French kings, who ordered chalices, crucifixes, baptism fonts and other sacred gems to be melted down in the Mint during times of financial strife – war, famine and so on.

Great Bell
The peal of Emmanuel, the cathedral's great bell, is so pure thanks to precious gems and jewels Parisian women threw into the pot when it was recast from copper and bronze in 1631. Admire its original siblings in Square Jean XXII.

Chimera Gallery
Scale the north tower for a Paris panorama admired by birds, dragons, grimacing gargoyles and grotesque chimera. Nod to celebrity chimera Stryga, who has wings, horns, a human body and sticking-out tongue. This bestial lot warns off demons.

5 Spire

6

North Tower

South Tower

Great Gallery

West Rose Window

2

Transept

North Tower Staircase

3

4

The 'Mays'
On 1 May 1630, city goldsmiths offered a 3m-high painting to the cathedral – a tradition they continued every 1 May until 1707 when the bankrupt guild folded. View 13 of these huge artworks in the side chapels.

Three Portals
Play I spy (Greed, Cowardice et al) beneath these sculpted doorways, which illustrate the seasons, life and the 12 vices and virtues alongside the Bible.

Portal of the Virgin (Exit)

Portal of the Last Judgement

Portal of St-Anne (Entrance)

Parvis Notre Dame

Southern Bastille & Gare de Lyon

0 — 400 m
0 — 0.2 miles

LE MARAIS
R du Petit Musc
Colonne de Juillet ① ◎ 7 ⓜ Bastille
R de Charonne
R Jean Macé ◎ 18
R Chanzy
R Bd Henri IV
Bastille ⓜ 20
R de Charenton
Ledru–Rollin
11E
R du Faubourg St-Antoine
19
R St-Bernard
R Faidherbe
R Paul Bert 12
R Titon
14
ⓜ Sully Morland
Bastille ⓜ 8
21
R de Prague
23
R de Montreuil
4E
R Mornay
Bd Morland
R Crillon
Bd Bourdon
Bd de la Bastille
10
R de Lyon
11
R Moreau
St-Nicolas
Av Ledru–Rollin
R Charles Baudelaire
R d'Aligre
Faidherbe Chaligny ⓜ
Q Henri IV
Pont Morland
13
R Jules César
R de Bercy
24
◎ 1
R d'Austerlitz
16
15
R de Crillon
St-Antoine
R de Reuilly
Quai de la Rapée
R de Charenton
Promenade Plantée Av Daumesnil
R de Cotte
R Baccaria
R de Charenton
R Crozatier
Reuilly Diderot ⓜ
Q St-Bernard
R Traversière
R Parrot
R Abel
Bd Diderot
Promenade Plantée
Impasse Érard
6 ◎
Pont d'Austerlitz
Bd Diderot
Gare de Lyon ⓜ
R Jean Bouton Grauwin
12E
R de Charenton
Hôtel de la Porte Dorée (1.5km)
LATIN QUARTER
5 ⓜ
Gare d'Austerlitz
R Van Gogh
R de Bercy
Gare de Lyon ◎
Av Daumesnil
R du Charolais
Gare d'Austerlitz
Pont Charles de Gaulle
Av Pierre Mendès-France
R Villiot
Bd de l'Hôpital
◎ 4
Av d'Austerlitz
Seine
Q de la Rapée
Bd de Bercy
Bercy ⓜ
R de Bercy
13E
Hôpital de la Pitié–Salpêtrière
R Fulton
Q de la Gare
Pont de Bercy
22
R de Bercy
3 ⓜ
R de Pommard
Quai de la Gare
Q de Bercy
Parc de Bercy
R de Ponmard
R Jenner
R Jeanne d'Arc
R Bruant
Chevaleret
R Valéry Larbaud
P.l Jean Vilar
9
Q de Bercy
R Joseph Kessel
Cour St-Émilion
Bd Vincent Auriol
Pho 14 (900m); Tang Frères (1.1km)
R Louise Weiss
Av de France
Q François Mauriac
◎ 2
17

ÎLE ST-LOUIS

In the early 17th century, the smaller of the Seine's two islands, Île St-Louis, was actually two uninhabited islets called Île Notre Dame (Our Lady Isle) and Île aux Vaches (Cows Island). A building contractor and two financiers worked out a deal with Louis XIII to create a single island and build two stone bridges to the mainland in exchange for the right to subdivide and sell the newly created real estate. By 1664 the entire island was covered with fine houses facing the quays and the river, which remain today. Today the island's streets and quays have a village-like, provincial calm. The only sight as such, French baroque **Église St-Louis en l'Île** (Map p100; 19bis rue St-Louis en l'Île; ⊙9am-1pm & 2-7.30pm Tue-Sat, to 7pm Sun; ⓜ Pont Marie), was built between 1664 and 1726.

⊙ Latin Quarter

The centre of Parisian higher education since the Middle Ages, the Latin Quarter is so called because conversation between students and professors until the Revolution was in Latin. It still has a large population of students and academics affiliated with institutions that include the world-famous Sorbonne university.

Southern Bastille & Gare de Lyon

To the southeast is the city's beautiful botanic gardens, the Jardin des Plantes.

★ Musée National du Moyen Âge
MUSEUM

(Map p102; www.musee-moyenage.fr; 6 place Paul Painlevé, 5e; adult/child €8/free; ⊙9.15am-5.45pm Wed-Mon; ⓂCluny–La Sorbonne) The National Museum of the Middle Ages holds a series of sublime treasures, from medieval statuary, stained glass and objets d'art to its celebrated series of tapestries, *The Lady with the Unicorn* (1500). Throw in extant architecture – an ornate 15th-century mansion (the Hôtel de Cluny), and the much older *frigidarium* (cold room) of an enormous Roman-era bathhouse – and you have one of Paris' top small museums. Outside, four medieval gardens grace the northeastern corner; more bathhouse remains are to the west.

★ Panthéon
MAUSOLEUM

(Map p102; www.monum.fr; place du Panthéon, 5e; adult/child €7.50/free; ⊙10am-6.30pm Apr-Sep, to 6pm Oct-Mar; ⓂMaubert-Mutualité, Cardinal Lemoine or RER Luxembourg) Overlooking the city from its Left Bank perch, the Panthéon's stately neoclassical dome stands out as one of the most recognisable icons on the Parisian skyline. Originally a church and now a mausoleum, it has served since 1791 as the resting place of some of France's greatest thinkers, including Voltaire, Rousseau, Braille and Hugo. An architectural masterpiece, the interior is impressively vast (if slightly soulless) and certainly worth a wander. The dome is closed for renovations through 2015 (other structural work will continue through 2022).

Jardin des Plantes
GARDEN

(Map p98; www.jardindesplantes.net; place Valhubert & 36 rue Geoffroy-St-Hilaire, 5e; ⊙7.30am-7.45pm Apr-Oct, 8am-5.15pm Nov-Mar; ⓂGare d'Austerlitz, Censier Daubenton or Jussieu) FREE Founded in 1626 as a medicinal herb garden for Louis XIII, Paris' 24-hectare botanic gardens – visually defined by the double alley of plane trees that run the length of the park – are an idyllic spot to stroll around, break for a picnic (watch out for the automatic sprinklers!) and escape the city concrete for a spell. Upping its appeal are three museums from the Muséum National d'Histoire Naturelle (p99) and a small zoo (Map p102; www.mnhn.fr; 57 rue Cuvier, 5e; adult/child €11/9; ⊙9am-6.30pm Apr-Oct, shorter hours rest of year; ⓂGare d'Austerlitz, Censier Daubenton or Jussieu).

Muséum National d'Histoire Naturelle
NATURAL HISTORY MUSEUM

(Map p102; www.mnhn.fr; place Valhubert & 36 rue Geoffroy St-Hilaire, 5e; ⓂGare d'Austerlitz, Censier Daubenton or Jussieu) Despite the name, the Natural History Museum is not a single building, but a collection of sites throughout France. Its historic home is in the Jardin des Plantes, and it's here you'll find the greatest number of branches: taxidermied animals

The Islands

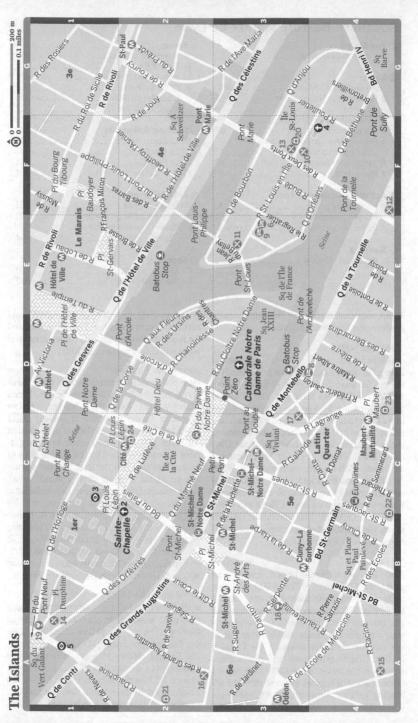

0   200 m
0   0.1 miles

The Islands

in the excellent **Grande Galerie de l'Évolution** (Map p102; adult/child €7/free; ⊙10am-6pm Wed-Mon), fossils and dinosaur skeletons in the **Galeries d'Anatomie Comparée et de Paléontologie** (Map p98; adult/child €7/free; ⊙10am-5pm Wed-Mon) and meteorites and crystals in the **Galerie de Minéralogie et de Géologie** (Map p102).

★**Institut du Monde Arabe**   ARCHITECTURE, MUSEUM
(Arab World Institute; Map p102; www.imarabe.org; 1 place Mohammed V, 5e; adult/child €8/4; ⊙10am-6pm Tue-Thu, to 9.30pm Fri, to 7pm Sat & Sun; M Jussieu) The Arab World Institute was jointly founded by France and 18 Middle Eastern and North African nations in 1980, with the aim of promoting cross-cultural dialogue. In addition to hosting concerts, film screenings and a research centre, the stunning landmark is also home to a new museum and temporary exhibition space.

Mosquée de Paris   MOSQUE
(Map p102; ☎01 45 35 97 33; www.la-mosquee.com; 2bis place du Puits de l'Ermite, 5e; adult/child €3/2; ⊙mosque 9am-noon & 2-6pm Sat-Thu; M Censier Daubenton or Place Monge) Paris' central mosque, with a striking 26m-high minaret, was completed in 1926 in an ornate art deco Moorish style. You can visit the interior to admire the intricate tile work and calligraphy. A separate entrance leads to the wonderful North African–style *hammam* (Map p102; ☎01 43 31 38 20; www.la-mosquee.com; 39 rue Geoffroy St-Hilaire, 5e; admission/spa package €18/from €43; ⊙10am-9pm Wed-Mon; M Censier Daubenton or Place Monge), *restaurant* (Map p102; ☎01 43 31 38 20; www.la-mosquee.com; 39 rue Geoffroy St-Hilaire, 5e; mains €15-26; ⊙noon-2.30pm & 7.30-10.30pm; M Censier Daubenton or Place Monge) and *salon de thé* (tearoom), and a small *souk* (actually more of a gift shop). Visitors must be modestly dressed.

Musée de la Sculpture en Plein Air   MUSEUM
(Map p102; quai St-Bernard, 5e; M Gare d'Austerlitz) **FREE** Along quai St-Bernard, this open-air sculpture museum (also known as the Jardin Tino Rossi) has more than 50 late 20th-century unfenced sculptures, and makes a great picnic spot. A salad beneath a César or a baguette beside a Brancusi is a pretty classy way to see the Seine up close.

◎ Place d'Italie & Chinatown

Spiralling out from place d'Italie, the 13e *arrondissement* has undergone a renaissance in recent years, heralded in the 1990s by the controversial Bibliothèque Nationale de France and the arrival of the high-speed metro line 14. Additions followed rapidly, among them the floating Piscine Joséphine Baker swimming pool, and Paris' most recent bridge, the Passerelle Simone de Beauvoir (2006), which provides a cycle and pedestrian link to the Right Bank. Current changes include the overhaul of the Gare d'Austerlitz area which aren't slated to stop until 2020, when the Paris Rive Gauche redevelopment project ends.

Between av d'Italie and av de Choisy is the city's largest Chinatown.

Bibliothèque Nationale de France   NATIONAL LIBRARY
(Map p98; ☎01 53 79 59 59; www.bnf.fr; 11 quai François Mauriac, 13e; temporary exhibitions adult/child from €9/free; ⊙exhibitions 10am-7pm Tue-Sat, 1-7pm Sun, closed early-late Sep; M Bibliothèque) With four glass towers shaped like half-open books, the 1995-opened National Library

Latin Quarter

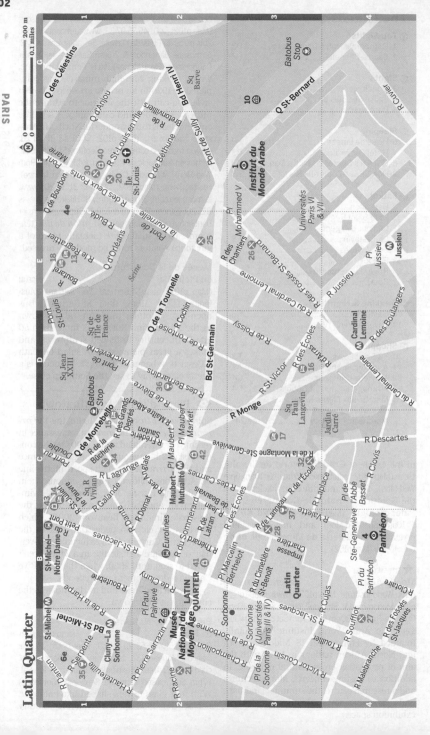

200 m
0.1 miles

G
Q des Célestins
Bd Henri IV
Sq Barye
Batobus Stop
10
Q St-Bernard

F
Q d'Anjou
R de Bretonvilliers
R St-Louis en l'Île
40
30
20
Île St-Louis
5
Q de Béthune
4e
R des Deux Ponts
Pont Marie
Pont de Sully
Institut du Monde Arabe
1
Pl Mohammed V
R des Chantiers
26

E
Q de Bourbon
R de Bude
Q d'Orléans
18
13
R le Regrattier
R Boutarel
Seine
Pont de la Tournelle
25
R du Cardinal Lemoine
R des Fossés St-Bernard
Universités Paris VI & VII
Jussieu
Pl Jussieu

D
Pont St-Louis
Sq de l'Île de France
Q de la Tournelle
R Cochin
R de Pontoise
R de Poissy
Bd St-Germain
R Jussieu
R des Boulangers
Sq Jean XXIII
Pont de l'Archevêché
Cardinal Lemoine
R du Cardinal Lemoine

C
Batobus Stop
Q de Montebello
15
R des Grands Degrés
R Frédéric Sauton
R de la Bûcherie
34
R du Maître Albert
R de Bièvre
36
R des Bernardins
Bd St-Germain
R St-Victor
R des Écoles
16
R Monge
Sq Paul Langevin
Jardin Carré
R Descartes
Pont au Double

B
St-Michel–Notre Dame
Petit Pont
R St-Julien le Pauvre
43
14
Sq R Viviani
R Galande
R Lagrange
R des Anglais
R Dante
R Domat
R St-Jacques
Maubert–Mutualité
Pl Maubert
Maubert Market
42
17
Pl Maubert
R des Carmes
R de la Montagne Ste-Geneviève
32
R de l'École
R Laplace
R Valette
R Clovis
Pl de l'Abbé Basset
Panthéon
4

A
St-Michel
6e
35
R Serpente
R Danton
R Hautefeuille
Bd St-Michel
R de la Harpe
R Boutebrie
Cluny–La Sorbonne
2
R de Cluny
Pl Paul Painlevé
Musée National du Moyen Âge
LATIN QUARTER
41
Sorbonne
Pl de la Sorbonne
R Champollion
R Pierre Sarrazin
Pl de la Sorbonne (Universités Paris III & IV)
R de la Sorbonne
Eurolines
Euronlines
R du Sommerard
R Thénard
R de Latran
R Jean de Beauvais
Pl Marcelin Berthelot
R du Cimetière St-Benoît
R des Écoles
28
R de Lanneau
37
Impasse Chartière
Latin Quarter
R St-Jacques
R Cujas
R Soufflot
Pl du Panthéon
Pl Ste-Geneviève
R Clotaire
27
R Toullier
R Victor Cousin
R Malebranche
R des Fossés St-Jacques
21
R Racine

1 2 3 4

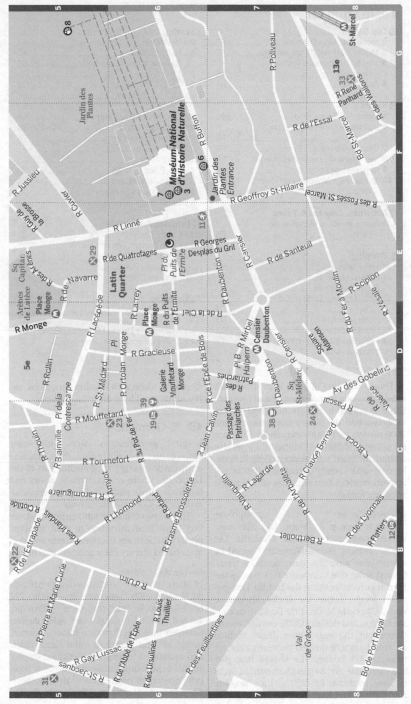

Jardin des Plantes

Muséum National d'Histoire Naturelle 3

Jardin des Plantes Entrance

R Buffon

R Geoffroy St-Hilaire

R Poliveau

St-Marcel

13e

R René Panhard

R de l'Essai

R des Wallons

Bd St-Marcel

R des Fossés St-Marcel

R Cuvier

R Jussieu

R Guy de la Brosse

R Linné

R de Quatrofages

R Georges Desplas

R du Gril

R de Santeuil

R Censier

R du Fer à Moulin

R Scipion

R de Navarre

R des Arènes

Sq Capitan

Arènes de Lutèce

Place Monge

R Monge

Latin Quarter

Pl du Puits de l'Ermite

R Daubenton

R Lacépède

R Larrey

R du Puits de l'Ermite

Place Monge

R de la Clef

R Mirbel

Censier Daubenton

R Vésale

R de Valence

Av des Gobelins

R Gracieuse

Pl Monge

R Ortolan

R St-Médard

Galerie Mouffetard Monge

R de l'Épée de Bois

R des Patriarches

Pl B R Halpern

R Daubenton

R Censier

Square Adanson

5e

R Collin

Pl de la Contrescarpe

R Bainville

R Mouffetard

R du Pot de Fer

Passage des Patriarches

Sq St-Médard

R Pascal

R Claude Bernard

R Broca

R des Lyonnais

R Flatters

R Thouin

R Tournefort

R Amyot

R Larromiguière

R Lhomond

R Jean Calvin

R Vauquelin

R Lagarde

R de l'Arbalète

R Berthollet

R Pierre et Marie Curie

R de l'Estrapade

R Clotilde

R des Irlandais

R Érasme Brossolette

R d'Ulm

R Louis Thuillier

R des Feuillantines

Val de Grâce

Bd de Port Royal

R Gay Lussac

R de l'Abbé de l'Épée

R des Ursulines

R St-Jacques

8

33

6

7

3

11

9

29

39

23

19

22

38

24

12

31

Latin Quarter

of France was one of President Mitterand's most ambitious and costliest *grands projets*. Some 12 million tomes are stored on 420km of shelves and the library can accommodate 2000 readers and 2000 researchers. Excellent temporary exhibitions (entrance E) revolve around 'the word' – from storytelling to bookbinding and French heroes. Exhibition admission includes free same-day access to the reference library.

Docks en Seine   CULTURAL CENTRE
(Cité de la Mode et du Design; Map p98; www. paris-docks-en-seine.fr; 36 quai d'Austerlitz, 13e; ⊙10am-midnight; M Gare d'Austerlitz) Framed by a lurid-lime wave-like glass façade, a transformed Seine-side warehouse now houses the French fashion institute, the Institut Français de la Mode (hence the docks' alternative name, Cité de la Mode et du Design), mounting fashion and design exhibitions and events throughout the year. Other draws include an entertainment-themed contemporary art museum **Art Ludique-Le Musée** (Map p98; http://artludique.com; 34 quai d'Austerlitz, 13e, Docks en Seine; adult/child €15/9.50; ⊙11am-7pm Mon, 11am-10pm Wed-Fri, 10am-10pm Sat & Sun; M Gare

d'Austerlitz), along with ultrahip bars, clubs and restaurants and huge riverside terraces.

◎ St-Germain

Despite gentrification since its early 20th-century bohemian days, there remains a cinematic quality to this soulful part of the Left Bank, where artists, writers, actors and musicians cross paths and *la vie germano-pratine* (St-Germain life) is *belle*.

This is one of those neighbourhoods whose very fabric is an attraction in itself, so allow plenty of time to stroll its side streets and stop at its fabled literary cafes and historic shops.

Musée des Lettres et Manuscrits   LETTERS & MANUSCRIPTS MUSEUM
(MLM; Map p106; www.museedeslettres.fr; 222 bd St-Germain, 7e; adult/child €7/5; ⊙10am-7pm Tue-Wed & Fri-Sun, to 9.30pm Thu; M Rue du Bac) Grouped into five themes – history, science, music, art and literature – the handwritten and annotated letters and works on display at this captivating museum provide a powerful emotional connection to their authors. They include Napoléon, Charles de Gaulle,

Marie Curie, Albert Einstein, Mozart, Beethoven, Piaf, Monet, Toulouse-Lautrec, Van Gogh, Victor Hugo, Hemingway and F Scott Fitzgerald; there are many, many more. It's thoroughly absorbing – allow at least a couple of hours. Temporary exhibitions also take place regularly.

Musée de la Monnaie de Paris MUSEUM
(Map p100; ☑ 01 40 46 56 66; www.monnaiedeparis. fr; 11 quai de Conti, 6e; Ⓜ Pont Neuf) Due to have reopened after extensive renovations by the time you're reading this, the Parisian Mint Museum traces the history of French coinage from antiquity onwards, with displays that help to bring to life this otherwise niche subject. It's housed in the 18th-century royal mint, the Monnaie de Paris, which is still used by the Ministry of Finance to produce commemorative medals and coins.

★ **Église St-Germain des Prés** CHURCH
(Map p106; www.eglise-sgp.org; 3 place St-Germain des Prés, 6e; ⊙ 8am-7.45pm Mon-Sat, 9am-8pm Sun; Ⓜ St-Germain des Prés) Paris' oldest standing church, the Romanesque St Germanus of the Fields, was built in the 11th century on the site of a 6th-century abbey and was the dominant place of worship in Paris until the arrival of Notre Dame. It's since been altered many times, but the **Chapelle de St-Symphorien** (to the right as you enter) was part of the original abbey and is believed to be the resting place of St Germanus (AD 496–576), the first bishop of Paris.

★ **Église St-Sulpice** CHURCH
(Map p106; http://pss75.fr/saint-sulpice-paris; place St Sulpice, 6e; ⊙ 7.30am-7.30pm; Ⓜ St Sulpice) In 1646 work started on the twin-towered Church of St Sulpicius, lined inside with 21 side chapels, and it took six architects 150 years to finish. What draws most visitors isn't its striking Italianate façade with two rows of superimposed columns, its Counter-Reformation-influenced neoclassical decor or even its frescoes by Eugène Delacroix, but its setting for a murderous scene in Dan Brown's *The Da Vinci Code*.

You can hear the monumental, 1781-built organ during 10.30am Mass on Sunday or the occasional Sunday-afternoon concert.

★ **Jardin du Luxembourg** PARK
(Map p106; numerous entrances; ⊙ hours vary; Ⓜ St-Sulpice, Rennes or Notre Dame des Champs, or RER Luxembourg) This inner-city oasis of formal terraces, chestnut groves and lush lawns has a special place in Parisians' hearts.

Napoléon dedicated the 23 gracefully laid-out hectares of the Luxembourg Gardens to the children of Paris, and many residents spent their childhood prodding 1920s wooden **sailboats** (per 30min €3; ⊙ Apr-Oct) with long sticks on the octagonal **Grand Bassin** pond, watching puppets perform Punch & Judy-type shows at the **Théâtre du Luxembourg** (Map p106; www.marionnettesduluxembourg.fr; tickets €4.80; ⊙ usually 3.30pm Wed, 11am & 3.30pm Sat & Sun, daily during school holidays; Ⓜ Notre Dame des Champs), and riding the *carrousel* (merry-go-round) or **ponies** (Map p106).

◉ Montparnasse

After WWI, writers, poets and artists of the avant-garde – Cocteau, Chagall and Picasso among them – abandoned Montmartre and crossed the Seine, shifting the centre of artistic ferment to the area around bd du Montparnasse. Montparnasse remained a creative centre until the mid-1930s. Since the construction of the Gare Montparnasse complex in the second half of the 20th century, there are few reminders of the area's bohemian past except landmark cafes, brasseries and famous graves in Montparnasse's cemetery.

Tour Montparnasse VIEWPOINT
(Map p106; www.tourmontparnasse56.com; rue de l'Arrivée, 15e; adult/child €14.50/9; ⊙ 9.30am-11.30pm daily Apr-Sep, to 10.30pm Sun-Thu, to 11pm Fri & Sat Oct-Mar; Ⓜ Montparnasse Bienvenüe) Spectacular views unfold from this 210m-high smoked-glass and steel office block, built in 1973. (Bonus: it's about the only spot in the city you can't see this startlingly ugly skyscraper, which dwarfs low-rise Paris.) Europe's fastest lift/elevator whisks visitors up in 38 seconds to the indoor observatory on the 56th floor, with multimedia displays. Finish with a hike up the stairs to the 59th-floor open-air terrace (with a sheltered walkway) and sip bubbly at the terrace's Champagne bar.

★ **Cimetière du Montparnasse** CEMETERY
(www.paris.fr; bd Edgar Quinet & rue Froidevaux, 14e; ⊙ 8am-6pm Mon-Fri, 8.30am-6pm Sat, 9am-6pm Sun; Ⓜ Edgar Quinet or Raspail) Opened in 1824, Montparnasse Cemetery, Paris' second largest after Père Lachaise, sprawls over 19 hectares shaded by 1200 trees, including maples, ash, lime trees and conifers. Among its illustrious 'residents' are poet Charles Baudelaire, writer Guy de Maupassant, playwright Samuel Beckett, sculptor Constantin Brancusi, painter Chaim Soutine, photographer Man Ray, industrialist André Citroën, Captain Alfred

106

PARIS

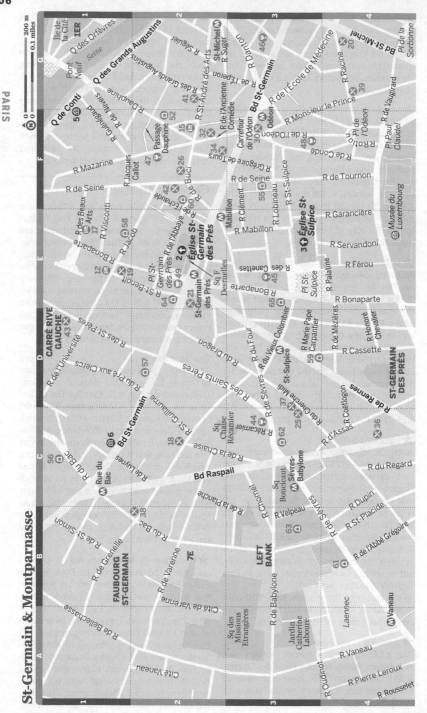

St-Germain & Montparnasse

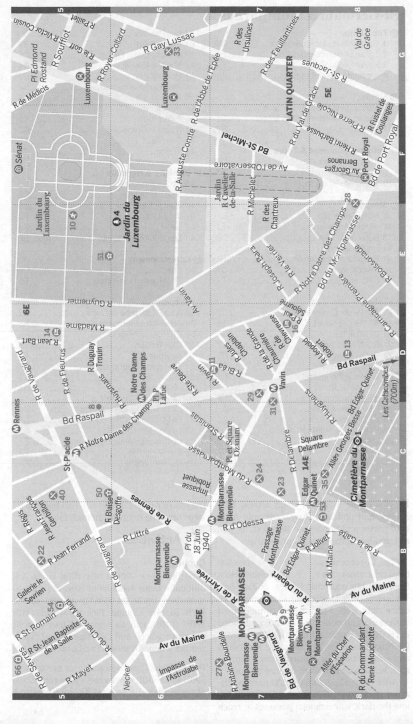

St-Germain & Montparnasse

Dreyfus of the infamous affair, actress Jean Seberg, and philosopher-writer couple Jean-Paul Sartre and Simone de Beauvoir, as well as legendary singer Serge Gainsbourg.

★ **Les Catacombes** CEMETERY
(www.catacombes.paris.fr; 1 av Colonel Henri Roi-Tanguy, 14e; adult/child €8/free; ☉10am-5pm Tue-Sun; Ⓜ Denfert Rochereau) Paris' most macabre sight is its underground tunnels lined with skulls and bones. In 1785 it was decided to rectify the hygiene problems of Paris' overflowing cemeteries by exhuming the bones and storing them in disused quarry tunnels and the Catacombes were created in 1810.

After descending 20m (via 130 narrow, dizzying spiral steps) below street level, you follow the dark, subterranean passages to reach the ossuary itself (2km in all). Exit back up 83 steps onto rue Remy Dumoncel, 14e.

🏃 Activities

Cycling

Paris has some 700km of cycling lanes. Additionally many sections of road are shut to motorised traffic on Sunday as part of the Paris Respire scheme. Pick up wheels with Vélib' (p156), join an organised tour or rent your own wheels and DIY. Most rental places require a deposit; take ID and a credit card.

Paris à Vélo, C'est Sympa BICYCLE RENTAL
(☎ 01 48 87 60 01; www.parisvelosympa.com; 22 rue Alphonse Baudin, 11e; per day €20; ☉9.30am-1pm &

2-6pm Mon-Fri, 9am-7pm Sat & Sun Apr-Oct, shorter hours winter; Ⓜ St-Sébastien Froissart)

Freescoot
BICYCLE RENTAL

(🗺 01 44 07 06 72; www.freescoot.com; 63 quai de la Tournelle, 5e; bike/tandem from €15/30; ⊙ 9am-1pm & 2-7pm Mon-Sat year-round, plus Sun mid-Apr–mid-Sep; Ⓜ Maubert-Mutualité)

Skating

Paris' most popular activity after cycling is skating, on the streets or on ice. In winter, a temporary outdoor rink is installed in front of the Hôtel de Ville. See www.paris.fr for other locations.

Nomadeshop
SKATING

(Map p98; 🗺 01 44 54 07 44; www.nomadeshop. com; 37 bd Bourdon, 4e; half/full day from €5/8; ⊙ 11am-1.30pm & 2.30-7.30pm Tue-Fri, 10am-7pm Sat, noon-6pm Sun; Ⓜ Bastille) Paris' 'Harrods for roller-heads' rents and sells equipment and accessories, including wheels, helmets, elbow and knee guards. The shop is also the departure point for Sunday's 'Randonnée en Rollers' around Paris, kicking off at 2.30pm (and lasting three hours), organised by skating club **Rollers & Coquillages** (Map p98; www. rollers-coquillages.org) FREE.

Pari Roller
ROLLERBLADING

(Map p106; www.pari-roller.com; place Raoul Dautry, 14e; ⊙ 10pm-1am Fri, arrive 9.30pm; Ⓜ Montparnasse Bienvenüe) The world's largest inline mass skate, Pari Roller regularly attracts more than 10,000 bladers. Dubbed 'Friday Night Fever', this fast-paced skate covers a different 30km-odd route each week. Most incorporate cobblestones and downhill stretches, and are geared for experienced bladers only (for your safety and everyone else's). It takes place year-round except when wet weather makes conditions treacherous.

Swimming

Paris has dozens of public swimming pools; visit www.paris.fr for a complete list. Swimmers need to don a *bonnet de bain* (bathing cap), generally sold at pools. Men are required to wear skin-tight trunks (Speedos); loose-fitting Bermuda shorts are not allowed.

Swimming in the Seine is strictly forbidden, even during Paris Plages (p111), due to boat traffic and the health hazards posed by the water quality (although it's better than it has been in a long time, with Atlantic salmon returning to the river).

Piscine Joséphine Baker
SWIMMING

(Map p98; 🗺 01 56 61 96 50; quai François Mauriac, 13e; pool adult/child €3/1.70, sauna €10/5; ⊙ 7-

8.30am & 1-9pm Mon, Wed & Fri, 1-11pm Tue & Thu, 11am-8pm Sat, 10am-8pm Sun; Ⓜ Bibliothèque or Quai de la Gare) Floating on the Seine, this striking swimming pool is style indeed (named after the sensual 1920s American singer, what else could it be?). More of a spot to be seen than to thrash laps, the two 25m-by-10m pools lure Parisians like bees to a honey pot in summer when the roof slides back.

Courses

Culinary

What better place to discover the secrets of *la cuisine française* than in Paris, the capital of gastronomy? Courses are available at different levels and durations:

Cook'n With Class
COOKING

(www.cooknwithclass.com) Nine international chefs, small classes and a Montmartre location.

École Le Cordon Bleu
COOKING

(www.cordonbleu.edu) One of the world's foremost culinary arts schools.

La Cuisine Paris
COOKING

(Map p90; http://lacuisineparis.com) A variety of courses from bread, croissants and macarons to market classes and 'foodie walks'.

Le Foodist
COOKING

(www.lefoodist.com) Cooking classes, wine pairings and hosted dinners in the Latin Quarter.

Patricia Wells
COOKING

(www.patriciawells.com) Five-day moveable feast from the former *International Herald Tribune* food critic.

PARIS FOR CHILDREN

Paris is extraordinarily kid-friendly and on a family trip you'll find no shortage of things to see, do and experience – the Going Out directory of www.parisinfo. com is a great place to start.

Top five Parisian attractions for kids:
Jardin du Luxembourg (p105)
Puppet shows, pony rides and more.
Cité des Sciences (p81)
Interactive exhibits make science fun.
Aquarium de Paris Cinéaqua (p65)
Shark tank!
Parc Zoologique de Paris (p93)
State-of-the-art zoo.
Jardin d'Acclimatation (p70)
Delightful amusement park for tots.

PARIS TOURS

PETITE CEINTURE

Long before the tramway or even the metro, the 35km Petite Ceinture (Little Belt) steam railway encircled the city of Paris. Constructed during the reign of Napoléon III between 1852 and 1869 as a way to move troops and goods around the city's fortifications, it became a thriving passenger service until the metro arrived in 1900. Most passenger services ceased in 1934 and goods services in 1993, and the line became an overgrown wilderness. Until recently, access was forbidden (although that didn't stop maverick urban explorers scrambling along its tracks and tunnels). Of the line's original 29 stations, 17 survive (in various states of disrepair). Plans for regenerating the Petite Ceinture railway corridor have progressed with the recent opening of three sections with walkways alongside the tracks. Other areas remain off limits.

In southern Paris, the Petite Ceinture du 15e (PC 15; www.paris.fr; btwn rue Olivier de Serres & rue St-Charles, 15e; ⊙9am-8.30pm May-Aug, to 7.30pm Apr & Sep, to 6pm Mar, reduced hours Oct-Feb; Ⓜ Balard or Porte de Versailles) FREE stretches for 1.3km, with biodiverse habitats including forest, grassland and prairies supporting 220 species of flora and fauna. In addition to the end points, there are three lift/elevator-enabled access points along its route: 397ter rue de Vaugirard; opposite 82 rue Desnouettes; and place Robert Guillemard. Ultimately the goal is to open the entire section of track between parcs Georges-Brassens and André-Citroën, around 3km in all.

Sections in eastern Paris, Petite Ceinture du 12e (PC 12), near the Bois de Vincennes, and western Paris, Petite Ceinture du 16e (PC 16) near the Bois de Boulogne, are also open to the public.

Wine Tasting

Musée du Vin   WINE TASTING
(☑01 45 25 63 26; www.museeduvinparis.com; rue des Eaux, 5 square Charles Dickens, 16e; museum adult/child €11.90/9.90; ⊙10am-6pm Tue-Sun; Ⓜ Passy) In addition to its displays, Paris' wine museum offers instructive tastings (€59 for two hours).

Ô Chateau   WINE TASTING
(Map p74; www.o-chateau.com; 68 rue Jean-Jacques Rousseau, 1er; ⊙4pm-midnight Mon-Sat; ☎; Ⓜ Les Halles or Étienne Marcel) Wine aficionados can thank this young, fun, cosmopolitan *bar à vins* for bringing affordable tasting to Paris. Sit at the long, trendy bar and savour your pick of 40-odd *grands vins* served by the glass (500-odd by the bottle!). Or sign up in advance for an intro to French wine (€30) or a guided cellar tasting in English over lunch (€75) or dinner (€100).

⚐ Tours

★**Parisien d'un jour –
Paris Greeters**   WALKING TOUR
(www.parisgreeters.fr; by donation) See Paris through local eyes with these two- to three-hour city tours. Volunteers – knowledgable Parisians passionate about their city in the main – lead groups (maximum six people) to their favourite spots. Minimum two weeks' notice needed.

★**THATLou**   GUIDED TOUR
(☑06 86 13 32 12; www.thatlou.com; per person excluding admission fees Louvre/d'Orsay €25/35) Absolutely inspirational, THATLou headed up by bilingual Daisy Plume organises treasure hunts in English or French for groups of two people or more in the Louvre, Musée d'Orsay (THATd'Or) and streets of the Latin Quarter (THATrue). Participants form teams and play alone or against another team, and have to photograph themselves in front of 20 to 30 works of art ('treasure'). Hunts typically last 1½ to two hours.

Fat Tire Bike Tours   CYCLING TOUR
(Map p64; ☑01 56 58 10 54; www.fattirebiketours. com) Day and night bike tours of the city, both in central Pais and further afield to Versailles and Monet's garden in Giverny.

Bateaux-Mouches   BOAT TOUR
(Map p66; ☑01 42 25 96 10; www.bateauxmouches. com; Port de la Conférence, 8e; adult/child €13.50/5.50; ⊙Apr-Dec; Ⓜ Alma Marceau) The largest river cruise company in Paris and a favourite with tour groups. Cruises (70 minutes) run regularly from 10.15am to 11pm April to September and 13 times a day between 11am and 9pm the rest of the year. Commentary is in French and English. It's located on the Right Bank, just east of the Pont de l'Alma.

Ça Se Visite
WALKING TOUR

(www.ca-se-visite.fr; adult/child on foot €12/10, scooter €15/13) Meet local artists and craftspeople on resident-led 'urban discovery tours' of the northeast (Belleville, Ménilmontant, Canal St-Martin, Canal de l'Ourcq, Oberkampf, La Villette) – on foot or *trottinette* (scooter).

Paris Walks
WALKING TOUR

(✆ 01 48 09 21 40; www.paris-walks.com; adult/child €12/8) Long established and highly rated by our readers, Paris Walks offers two-hour thematic walking tours (art, fashion, chocolate, the French Revolution etc).

Bateaux Parisiens
BOAT TOUR

(Map p64; www.bateauxparisiens.com; Port de la Bourdonnais, 7e; adult/child €14/6; Ⓜ Bir Hakeim or RER Pont de l'Alma) This vast operation runs 1½-hour river circuits with recorded commentary in 13 languages (every 30 minutes 10am to 10.30pm April to September, hourly 10am to 10pm October to March), and a host of themed lunch/dinner cruises. It has two locations: one by the Eiffel Tower, the other south of Notre Dame.

L'Open Tour
BUS TOUR

(Map p78; www.parisopentour.com; one-day pass adult/child €31/16) Hop-on, hop-off bus tours aboard open-deck buses with four different circuits and 50 stops to jump on/off at – top for a whirlwind city tour.

⚜ Festivals & Events

Innumerable festivals, cultural and sporting events and trade shows take place in Paris throughout the year. Check www.parisinfo.com to find out what's on when you're in town.

February

Salon International de l'Agriculture
FOOD

(www.salon-agriculture.com) A 10-day international agricultural fair with produce and animals turned into starter and main-course dishes from all over France, held at the Parc des Expositions at Porte de Versailles in the 15e (metro Porte de Versailles) from late February to early March.

April

Foire du Trône
FUN FAIR

(www.foiredutrone.com; Ⓜ Porte Dorée) Huge fun-fair with 350 attractions is held on the Pelouse de Reuilly of the Bois de Vincennes for eight weeks early April to late May.

Marathon International de Paris
SPORTS

(www.parismarathon.com) The Paris International Marathon, on the first or second Sunday in April, starts on the av des Champs-Élysées, 8e, and finishes on av Foch, 16e.

May & June

French Tennis Open
SPORTS

(www.rolandgarros.com) The glitzy Internationaux de France de Tennis – the Grand Slam – is a two-week affair from late May to mid-June at Stade Roland Garros on the southern edge of the Bois de Boulogne.

Portes Ouvertes des Ateliers d'Artistes de Belleville
ART FESTIVAL

(www.ateliers-artistes-belleville.org) More than 250 painters, sculptors and other artists in Belleville in the 10e open their studio doors to visitors over four days (Friday to Monday) in late May.

Gay Pride March
GAY

(www.gaypride.fr) A colourful, Saturday-afternoon parade in late June through the Marais to Bastille celebrates Gay Pride Day, with bars and clubs sponsoring floats, and participants dressing outrageously.

Paris Jazz Festival
MUSIC FESTIVAL

(www.parisjazzfestival.fr) Free jazz concerts every Saturday and Sunday afternoon in June and July in Parc Floral de Paris. Park entry applies.

July & August

Bastille Day
CULTURAL FESTIVAL

(14 July; www.paris.fr) Paris is *the* place to be on France's national day. Late on the night of the 13th, *bals des sapeurs-pompiers* (dances sponsored by Paris' firefighters, who are considered sex symbols in France) are held at fire stations around the city. At 10am on the 14th, there's a military and fire-brigade parade along av des Champs-Élysées, accompanied by a fly-past of fighter aircraft and helicopters. In the evening, a huge display of *feux d'artifice* (fireworks) is held at around 11pm on the Champ de Mars in the 7e.

Paris Plages
BEACH

(www.paris.fr) 'Paris Beaches' sees three waterfront areas transformed into sand-and-pebble beaches, complete with sun beds, beach umbrellas, atomisers, loungers and palm trees, for four weeks from mid-July to mid-August.

Tour de France
SPORTS

(www.letour.com) The last of 21 stages of this prestigious, 3500km cycling event finishes with a race up av des Champs-Élysées on the third or fourth Sunday of July, as it has done since 1975.

Rock en Seine
MUSIC FESTIVAL

(www.rockenseine.com) Headlining acts rock the Domaine National deSt-Cloud on the city's southwestern edge.

September & October

Jazz à la Villette
MUSIC FESTIVAL

(www.jazzalavillette.com) Ten-day jazz festival in early September has sessions in Parc de la Villette, at the Cité de la Musique and in surrounding bars.

Nuit Blanche
EVENT

(www.paris.fr) 'White Night' is when Paris becomes 'the city that doesn't sleep', with museums across town joining bars and clubs and staying open till the very wee hours on the first Saturday and Sunday of October.

Fête des Vendanges de Montmartre
HARVEST

(www.fetedesvendangesdemontmartre.com) This five-day festival during the second weekend in October celebrates Montmartre's grape harvest with costumes, speeches and a parade.

December

Christmas Eve Mass
CHRISTMAS

Celebrated at midnight on Christmas Eve at many Paris churches, including Notre Dame.

Le Festival du Merveilleux
FUN FAIR

(www.arts-forains.com) Normally closed to the public, the private Musée des Arts Forains, filled with yesteryear fairground attractions, opens for 11 days from late December to early January during Le Festival du Merveilleux, with enchanting rides, attractions and shows.

New Year's Eve
NEW YEAR

Bd St-Michel (5e), place de la Bastille (11e), the Eiffel Tower (7e) and especially av des Champs-Élysées (8e) are the Parisian hot spots to welcome in the new year.

🛏 Sleeping

Paris has a huge choice of accommodation, from hostels through to deluxe hotels, some of which rank among the world's finest. Yet although the city has well over 1500 establishments, you'll still need to book well ahead during the warmer months (April to October) and all public and school holidays.

Accommodation outside central Paris is marginally cheaper than within the city it-self, but it's almost always a false economy, as travelling consumes time and money. Choose somewhere within Paris' 20 *arrondissements*, where you can experience Parisian life the moment you step out the door.

➡ Hotels

Parisian hotel rooms are infamously small and expensive. Price-comparison online booking sites can save you a bundle. Cheaper hotels may not have lifts and/or air-con; some don't accept credit cards.

Good hotel-booking websites include the well-organised **Paris Hotel** (www.hotels-paris.fr), with lots of user reviews, and **Paris Hotel Service** (www.parishotelservice.com), specialising in boutique hotel gems.

➡ Hostels

Paris is awash with hostels, and standards are consistently improving. A wave of state-of-the-art hostels have recently opened their doors, with more in the works, including a 950-bed 'megahostel' by leading hostel chain **Generator** (www.generatorhostels.com), located near Canal St-Martin, 10e.

➡ Camping

On the city's edge in the Bois de Boulogne, the ecofriendly **Camping Indigo** (www.camping-indigo.com) site is open year-round.

➡ B&Bs

B&B accommodation (*chambres d'hôte* in French) is increasingly popular. The city of Paris' scheme **Paris Quality Hosts** (Hôtes Qualité Paris; www.hotesqualiteparis.fr) fosters B&Bs, in part to ease the isolation of Parisians, half of whom live alone. There's often a minimum stay of three or four nights. You can also rent private rooms through **Airbnb** (www.airbnb.com).

🛏 Eiffel Tower Area & 16e

The best bargains in this upmarket residential area are in the 15e, south and west of the Eiffel Tower.

★ Hôtel Vic Eiffel
BOUTIQUE HOTEL €

(www.hotelviceiffel.com; 92 bd Garibaldi, 15e; s/d from €99/109; 🛜; Ⓜ Sèvres-Lecourbe) Outstanding value for money, this pristine hotel with chic orange and oyster-grey rooms (two are wheelchair accessible) is a short walk from the Eiffel Tower, with the metro on the doorstep. Budget-priced Classic rooms are small but perfectly functional; midrange Superior and Privilege rooms offer increased space. Friendly staff go out of their way to help.

LOVE LOCKS

Stretching from the Latin Quarter's quai de la Tournelle to the eastern tip of the Île de la Cité, the **Pont de l'Archevêché** footbridge is one of many Parisian bridges covered in padlocks. Inscribed with initials and sometimes adorned with ribbons, the locks are attached by couples who then throw the key into the Seine as a symbol of eternal love. Although it sounds romantic, there are now so many padlocks that several bridge railings and grates have been permanently damaged by the sheer weight. One of Mme Hidalgo's first high-profile acts as Paris mayor was to remove the locks on the adorned **Pont des Arts** (west of the Île de la Cité), but just weeks after the initial cleanup the locks were back, causing a section of railing to collapse – a signal to couples that it may be time to find a new way to express their love. Flowers, perhaps?

Hôtel du Champ-de-Mars　　　　HOTEL €
(Map p64; ☑ 01 45 51 52 30; www.hotelduchampde
mars.com; 7 rue du Champ de Mars, 7e; s/d €105/130;
@ 🛜; M École Militaire) This charming 25-room cheapie (relatively speaking) in the shadow of the Eiffel Tower is on everyone's wish list – book a month or two ahead. Two ground-floor rooms overlook a flowered courtyard.

⭐**Sublim Eiffel**　　　　DESIGN HOTEL €€
(☑ 01 40 65 95 95; www.sublimeiffel.com; 94 bd Garibaldi, 15e; d from €140; ❄ 🛜; M Sèvres-Lecourbe) There's no forgetting what city you're in with the Eiffel Tower motifs in reception and rooms (along with Parisian street-map carpets and metro-tunnel-shaped bedheads) plus glittering tower views from upper-floor windows. Edgy design elements also include cobblestone staircase carpeting (there's also a lift/elevator) and, fittingly in *la ville lumière,* technicoloured in-room fibre optic lighting. The small wellness centre/hammam offers massages.

⭐**Hôtel Félicien**　　　BOUTIQUE HOTEL €€
(☑ 01 83 76 02 45; www.hotelfelicienparis.com; 21 rue Félicien David, 16e; d €120-280; ❄ @ 🛜 🏊; M Mirabeau) The price–quality ratio at this chic boutique hotel, squirrelled away in a 1930s building, is outstanding. Exquisitely designed rooms feel more five-star than four, with 'White' and 'Silver' suites on the hotel's top 'Sky floor' more than satisfying their promise of indulgent cocooning. Romantics, eat your heart out.

⭐**Hôtel Molitor**　　　　BOUTIQUE HOTEL €€€
(☑ 01 56 07 08 50; www.mltr.fr; 2 av de la porte Molitor, 16e; d from €270; ❄ @ 🛜 🏊; M Michel Ange Molitor) Famed as Paris' swishest swimming pool in the 1930s (where the bikini made its first appearance, no less) and hot spot for graffiti art in the 1990s, the Molitor is one seriously mythical address. The art deco com-

plex, built in 1929 and abandoned from 1989, has been restored to stunning effect.

🛏 Étoile & Champs-Élysées

This area is famed for its luxury hotels, famous boutiques, gastronomic restaurants and glam nightlife. Landmark hotel reopenings see the return of the **Hôtel de Crillon** (www.crillon.com), with two suites designed by Karl Lagerfeld, as well as belle époque beauty the **Ritz** (www.ritzparis.com), following head to toe renovations of its rooms, bars, restaurants, gardens and Ritz Escoffier cooking school.

BVJ Monceau　　　　　　HOSTEL €
(☑ 01 43 29 34 80; www.bvjhotel.com; 12 rue Léon Jost, 17e; dm/d per person €30/35; 🛜; M Courcelles) Set in the former studio and *hôtel particulier* of painter Henri Gervex (1852–1929), this new hostel near the Champs-Élysées has 24 spacious rooms, sleeping two to 10 people each. Bathrooms are shared. Unlike more recent additions to the Paris hostel scene, the BVJ has retained a period feel, with original moulding, a secluded courtyard and parquet floors throughout.

Hidden Hotel　　　　　BOUTIQUE HOTEL €€€
(Map p66; ☑ 01 40 55 03 57; www.hidden-hotel.com; 28 rue de l'Arc de Triomphe, 17e; d €389-454; ❄ @ 🛜; M Charles de Gaulle-Étoile) 🍃 The Hidden is one of the Champs-Élysées' best secrets. It's serene, stylish, reasonably spacious, and it even sports green credentials: the earth-coloured tones are the result of natural pigments (no paint), and all rooms feature handmade wooden furniture, stone basins, and linen curtains surrounding the beds. The queen-size Emotion rooms are among the most popular.

Hôtel Amarante Beau Manoir　　HOTEL €€€
(Map p66; ☑ 01 53 43 28 28; www.amarantebeau
manoir.com; 6 rue de l'Arcade, 8e; d €228-266; ❄ @ 🛜; M Madeleine) Among the cosier

hotels in the 8e, the 18th-century Amarante has traditional-style rooms, with exposed rafters, wooden furniture and oak panelling. It has a prime location just around the corner from place Madeleine, and free wi-fi. The breakfast room is in a beautiful cross-vaulted stone cellar.

🛏 Louvre & Les Halles

The upsides of this neighbourhood are its central location, excellent transport links and proximity to major museums and shopping. However, the immediate area around the Forum des Halles (p77) may be noisy or inconvenient during construction works until their completion in 2016.

Hôtel Tiquetonne   HOTEL €

(🖉01 42 36 94 58; www.hoteltiquetonne.fr; 6 rue Tiquetonne, 2e; d €65, with shared shower €50; 🛜; M Étienne Marcel) What heart-warmingly good value this 45-room cheapie is. This serious, well-tended address has been in the hotel biz since the 1900s and is much-loved by a loyal clientele of all ages. Rooms range across seven floors, are spick and span, and sport an inoffensive mix of vintage decor – roughly 1930s to 1980s, with brand-new bathrooms and parquet flooring in recently renovated rooms.

Hôtel Vivienne   HOTEL €

(Map p78; 🖉01 42 33 13 26; www.hotel-vivienne. com; 40 rue Vivienne, 2e; d €108-150, tr & q €160; @🛜; M Grands Boulevards) This stylish two-star hotel is amazingly good value for Paris. While the 45 rooms are not huge, they have all the mod cons; some even boast little balconies. Family rooms accommodate up to two children on a sofa bed.

Hôtel O   BOUTIQUE HOTEL €€

(Map p74; 🖉01 42 36 04 02; www.hotel-o-paris. com; 19 rue Hérold, 1er; r €229-299; ✸🛜; M Sentier or Bourse) A futuristic refuge from the busy Paris streets, Hôtel O makes use of clever design to maximise small spaces. French designer Ora-Ito echoes the natural world with elegant curves and simple, ecofriendly materials such as felt, oak and cork. Choose from one of three styles of room: Cocoon, Odyssey or the deluxe Galileo.

Le Relais du Louvre   BOUTIQUE HOTEL €€

(Map p74; 🖉01 40 41 96 42; www.relaisdulouvre.com; 19 rue des Prêtres St-Germain l'Auxerrois, 1er; s €135-180, d €175-263, tr €235-263; ✸🛜; M Pont Neuf) If you like style in a traditional sense, choose this lovely 21-room hotel just west of the Lou-

vre and across the street from Église St-Germain l'Auxerrois with its melodious chime of bells. The nine rooms facing the street and church are petite, while room 2 has access to the garden.

Hôtel de la Place du Louvre   BOUTIQUE HOTEL €€

(Map p74; 🖉01 42 33 78 68; www.paris-hotel-place-du-louvre.com; 21 rue des Prêtres St-Germain l'Auxerrois, 1er; d €135-205; ✸🛜; M Pont Neuf) Not to be confused with the Relais du Louvre next door, this fairly recent addition to the Parisian hotel scene is warmly welcomed. It has just 20 rooms split across five floors – a couple on each floor are lucky enough to ogle the majestic Louvre across the street.

★Edgar   BOUTIQUE HOTEL €€

(🖉01 40 41 05 19; www.edgarparis.com; 31 rue d'Alexandrie, 2e; d €235-295; ✸🛜; M Strasbourg St-Denis) Twelve playful rooms, each decorated by a different team of artists or designers, await the lucky few who secure a reservation at this former convent/seamstress workshop. Milagros conjures up all the magic of the Far West, while Dream echoes the rich imagination of childhood with surrealist installations. Breakfast is served in the popular downstairs restaurant, and the hidden tree-shaded square is a fabulous location.

★Hôtel Crayon   BOUTIQUE HOTEL €€€

(Map p74; 🖉01 42 36 54 19; www.hotelcrayon.com; 25 rue du Bouloi, 1er; s/d €311/347; ✸🛜; M Les Halles or Sentier) Line drawings by French artist Julie Gauthron bedeck walls and doors at this creative boutique hotel. The pencil (le crayon) is the theme, with 26 rooms sporting a different shade of each floor's chosen colour – we love the coloured-glass shower doors and the books on the bedside table guests can swap and take home. Online deals often slash rates by over 50%.

🛏 Opéra & Grands Boulevards

Shopping and entertainment options abound in this central neighbourhood.

Hôtel France Albion   HOTEL €

(🖉01 45 26 00 81; www.albion-paris-hotel.com; 11 rue Notre Dame de Lorette, 9e; s €77-103, d €97-123, f €163; ✸🛜; M St-Georges) For the quietest night's sleep, go for a room facing the courtyard of this neat-as-a-pin budget hotel. Its rooms all have en suite bathrooms and, for Paris, are decently sized (doubles from 14 sq metres), and staff are eager to please. The location, near Opéra, is fabulous.

Hôtel Monte Carlo HOTEL €
(Map p78; ☎01 47 70 36 75; www.hotelmontecarlo.
fr; 44 rue du Faubourg Montmartre, 9e; s without en
suite €59-88, with en suite €79-117, d without en suite
€69-98, with en suite €89-147, tr with en suite €125-
167; ☎; MLe Peletier) A unique budget hotel,
the Monte Carlo is a steal, with colourful, personalised rooms and a great neighbourhood
location. The owners go the extra mile and
even provide a partly organic breakfast. The
cheaper rooms don't have private bathroom
facilities, but overall it outclasses many of the
other choices in its price range.

Hôtel Chopin HISTORIC HOTEL €
(Map p78; ☎01 47 70 58 10; www.hotelchopin.fr;
46 passage Jouffroy, 9e; d €85-145; @; MGrands
Boulevards) Dating from 1846, the 36-room
Chopin is inside one of Paris' most delightful 19th-century *passages couverts* (covered
shopping arcades). The rooms don't have
much in the way of personality (and the
cheaper rooms are small and dark), but the
belle époque location is beautiful.

Hôtel Langlois HISTORIC HOTEL €€
(Map p78; ☎01 48 74 78 24; www.hotel-langlois.
com; 63 rue St-Lazare, 9e; s €150-160, d €180-190;
❇@☎; MTrinité) Built in 1870, this 27-room
hotel has kept its charm, from the tiny caged
elevator to sandstone fireplaces (sadly decommissioned) in many rooms as well as original
bathroom fixtures and tiles. Room 64 has
wonderful views of Montmartre's rooftops.

Hôtel Joyce DESIGN HOTEL €€€
(☎01 55 07 00 01; www.astotel.com; 29 rue la
Bruyère, 9e; d from €320; ❇@☎; MSt-Georges)
🍃 Located in a lovely residential area between Montmartre and Opéra, this place
has all the modern design touches (iPod
docks, individually styled rooms, a sky-lit
breakfast room fitted out with old Range
Rover seats) and makes some ecofriendly
claims – it relies on 50% renewable energy
and uses organic products. Rates start from
€230 outside high season.

🛏 Montmartre & Pigalle

Many places in this hilly, village-like (if touristy) neighbourhood have views across Paris.

Hôtel Eldorado HOTEL €
(☎01 45 22 35 21; www.eldoradohotel.fr; 18 rue
des Dames, 17e; s €43-71, d €65-94, tr €82-102; ☎;
MPlace de Clichy) This bohemian place is one
of Paris' greatest finds: a welcoming, reasonably well-run hotel with 23 colourfully decorated and (often) ethnically themed rooms, with

a private garden at the back. Unfortunately
rooms facing the garden will probably be
quite noisy as they look out onto the restaurant – earplugs may be a good idea. Cheaper-
category singles have washbasin only.

Plug-Inn Hostel HOSTEL €
(Map p80; ☎01 42 58 42 58; www.plug-inn.fr; 7 rue
Aristide Bruant, 18e; dm €25-37, d €90-105; @☎;
MAbbesses or Blanche) This 2010 hostel has
several things going for it, the first of which is
its central Montmartre location. The four- to
six-person rooms all have their own showers,
there's a kitchen, free breakfast and the staff
are even friendly (a rarity among Parisian
hostels). One drawback is that communal areas are small. No curfew at night.

Hôtel Regyn's Montmartre HOTEL €
(Map p80; ☎01 42 54 45 21; www.hotel-regyns-
paris.com; 18 place des Abbesses, 18e; s €65 155,
d & tw €115-175; @☎; MAbbesses) A good
choice if you want to stay in Montmartre
and not break the bank is this 22-room
hotel. Although the rooms are nothing to
crow about, its location is unbeatable – just
opposite the Abbesses metro station. Some
rooms have views over Paris.

★ Loft APARTMENT €€
(Map p80; ☎06 14 48 47 48; www.loft-paris.fr; 7 cité
Véron, 18e; apt €100-270; ☎; MBlanche) Book
months in advance to secure one of the stylish apartments in this gem, which offers an
intimacy that simply cannot be replicated
in a hotel. Just around the corner from the

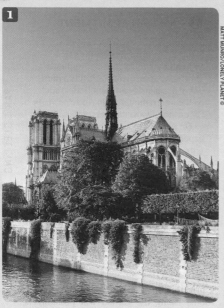

MATT MUNRO/LONELY PLANET ©

1. Cathédrale Notre Dame de Paris p95 **2.** Pont au Double p147 **3.** Paris Plages p111 **4.** Bateaux-Mouches p110

The Seine

La ligne de vie de Paris (the lifeline of Paris), the Seine, sluices through the city, spanned by 37 bridges. Its Unesco World Heritage Site–listed riverbanks offer picturesque promenades, parks and year-round activities. After dark, watch the river dance with the watery reflections of city lights. You are in Paris.

The riverbanks have been reborn with the creation of Les Berges de Seine. On the Right Bank, east of the Hôtel de Ville, 1.5km of former expressway now incorporates walkways and cycleways. Even more revolutionary is the completely car-free 2.3km stretch of the Left Bank from the Pont de l'Alma to the Musée d'Orsay (newly linked to the waterfront by a grand staircase that doubles as amphitheatre seating), with sporting equipment, games, events, restaurants and bars (some aboard boats) and floating gardens on 1800 sq metres of artificial islands (complete with knotted-rope hammocks where you can lie back and soak up the river's reclaimed serenity).

More than ever, Parisians flock to the Seine to cycle, jog, inline skate, stroll and simply hang-out; staircases along the banks lead down to the water's edge.

SEINE-SIDE HIGHLIGHTS

Picnics Idyllic spots include the Musée de la Sculpture en Plein Air (p101) and Square du Vert Gallant (p95).

Bridges Stroll the historic Pont Neuf (p95), or busker-filled Pont St-Louis or Pont au Double (p147).

Beaches Lounge along summer's Paris Plages (p111).

Islands The Île de la Cité (p95) and Île St-Louis (p98) are enchanting; the Île aux Cygnes (p62) is a little-known gem.

Cruises Board Bateaux-Mouches (p110) or hop on and off the Batobus (p157).

Moulin Rouge, this apartment block offers choices ranging from a two-person studio to a loft that can fit a large family or group. The owner, a culture journalist, is a great resource.

Hôtel des Arts HOTEL €€

(Map p80; ☑ 01 46 06 30 52; www.arts-hotel-paris.com; 5 rue Tholozé, 18e; s/d from €145/160; ☞; Ⓜ Abbesses or Blanche) The Hôtel des Arts is a friendly, attractive 50-room hotel, convenient to both place Pigalle and Montmartre. It has comfortable midrange rooms that are excellent value; consider spending an extra €20 for the superior rooms, which have nicer views. Just up the street is the old-style windmill Moulin de la Blute-Fin. Better rates are often available online.

★ Hôtel Amour BOUTIQUE HOTEL €€

(☑ 01 48 78 31 80; www.hotelamourparis.fr; 8 rue Navarin, 9e; s €145, d €170-225; ☞; Ⓜ St-Georges or Pigalle) Planning a romantic escapade to Paris? Say no more. The inimitable black-clad Amour (formerly a love hotel by the hour) features original design and artwork in each of the rooms – you won't find a more unique place to lay your head in Paris at these prices. You have to be willing to forgo television – but who needs TV when you're in love?

🛏 Gare du Nord, Gare de l'Est & Canal St-Martin

The budget-to-midrange hotels around the Gare du Nord and Gare de l'Est train stations are convenient for passengers and staying in this area is fantastic for soaking up Canal St-Martin's boho vibe.

Hôtel du Nord – Le Pari Vélo HOTEL €

(Map p90; ☑ 01 42 01 66 00; www.hoteldunord-leparivelo.com; 47 rue Albert Thomas, 10e; d €73-86, tr €96, q €125; ☞; Ⓜ République) This particularly charming place has 24 personalised rooms decorated with flea-market antiques. Beyond the bric-a-brac charm (and the ever-popular dog, Pluto), Hôtel du Nord's other winning attribute is its prized location near place République. Bikes are on loan for guests.

St Christopher's
Gare du Nord HOSTEL €

(Map p84; ☑ 01 70 08 52 22; www.st-christophers. co.uk/paris-hostels; 5 rue de Dunkerque, 10e; dm €20-44, d €90-170; @☞; Ⓜ Gare du Nord) Just steps from the Gare du Nord, this newer St Christopher's, opened in 2013, has brought more modern hostel accommodation to the city, with six floors of light-filled rooms (600 total). Dorms sleep four, six, eight and 10 people but

there is a catch – unless you reserve months in advance, they won't come cheap.

St Christopher's Canal HOSTEL €

(☑ 01 40 34 34 40; www.st-christophers.co.uk/ paris-hostels; 159 rue de Crimée, 19e; dm €20-52, d from €85; @☞; Ⓜ Riquet or Jaurès) Opened in 2008, this is certainly one of Paris' best, biggest (300 beds) and most up-to-date hostels. It features modern design, four types of dorms (12-, 10-, eight- and six-bed) and doubles with or without bathrooms. Other perks include a canal-side cafe, a bar, a female-only floor, bike rental and organised day trips.

Auberge de Jeunesse
Yves Robert HOSTEL €

(☑ 01 40 38 87 90; www.fuaj.org; 20 rue Pajol, 18e; dm/d per person €31/60; Ⓜ Marx Dormoy) 🌊 Overlooking the railway tracks behind the Gare de l'Est is this snazzy new solar-powered hostel. The spacious ground-floor area houses a cafe and communal area; rooms sleep one to six people. On the down side, it can be a hike to get anywhere else in the city, and wi-fi is only in the reception area. Breakfast included.

★ Le Citizen Hotel BOUTIQUE HOTEL €€

(Map p90; ☑ 01 83 62 55 50; www.lecitizenhotel. com; 96 quai de Jemmapes, 10e; d €199 & €269; ☞; Ⓜ Gare de l'Est or Jacques Bonsergent) Opened in 2011, the Citizen is a sign the times are a changin' on the Canal St-Martin. A team of forward-thinking creative types put their heads together for this one, and the result is 12 alluring rooms equipped with niceties such as iPads, filtered water and warm minimalist design. Artwork is from Oakland's Creative Growth Art Center for disabled artists.

🛏 Ménilmontant & Belleville

★ Mama Shelter DESIGN HOTEL €

(☑ 01 43 48 48 48; www.mamashelter.com; 109 rue de Bagnolet, 20e; s/d from €79/89; ❉@☞; 🚌 76, Ⓜ Alexandre Dumas or Gambetta) Coaxed into its zany new incarnation by uberdesigner Philippe Starck, this former car park offers what is surely the best-value accommodation in the city. Its 170 super-comfortable rooms feature iMacs, trademark Starck details like a chocolate-and-fuchsia colour scheme, concrete walls and even microwave ovens, while a rooftop terrace and cool pizzeria add to the hotel's street cred.

🛏 Le Marais & Bastille

Buzzing nightlife, hip shopping and a great range of eating options make the centrally situated Marais wildly popular. Look out for the opening of **Les Bains** (www.lesbains-paris. com), formerly thermal baths and later a steamy nightclub, which promises to be an amazing place to stay. The nearby Bastille has far fewer tourists, allowing you to see the 'real' Paris up close.

★**Cosmos Hôtel**　　　　　　　HOTEL €
(Map p90; ☑ 01 43 57 25 88; www.cosmos-hotel-paris. com; 35 rue Jean-Pierre Timbaud, 11e; s €62-75, d €68-75, tr/q €85/94; ☎; ⓜ République) Cheap, brilliant value and just footsteps from the nightlife of rue JPT, Cosmos is a shiny star with retro style on the budget-hotel scene. It has been around for 30-odd years but, unlike most other hotels in the same price bracket, Cosmos has been treated to a thoroughly modern makeover this century. Breakfast €8.

Hôtel de la Porte Dorée　　　　HOTEL €
(☑ 01 43 07 56 97; www.hoteldelaportedoree.com; 273 av Daumesnil, 12e; s €66-78, d €91-105, tr €133; ❄ @ ☎; ⓜ Porte Dorée) 🖉 A few blocks inside the bd Périphérique ring road and steps from Porte Dorée metro station, this country-manor style hotel is as family-friendly as you'll find, with crayons and paper at reception, toy boxes in the rooms and the Bois de Vincennes right nearby. Some of the 43 hardwood-floor rooms have period fireplaces.

Hôtel Beaumarchais　　　DESIGN HOTEL €
(Map p90; ☑ 01 53 36 86 86; www.hotelbeaumar-chais.com; 3 rue Oberkampf, 11e; s €75-100, d €90-145; ☎; ⓜ Filles du Calvaire) This bright 31-room design hotel, with its emphasis on sunbursts and bold primary colours, is just this side of kitsch. But it makes for a bright Paris experience. There are monthly art exhibitions and guests are invited to the *vernissage* (opening night). The boutiques and bars of the Marais are a two-minute walk away.

Hôtel Daval　　　　　　　HOTEL €
(Map p90; ☑ 01 47 00 51 23; www.hoteldaval.com; 21 rue Daval, 11e; s/d/tr/q €98/109/149/169; ❄ ☎; ⓜ Bastille) This 23-room hotel with lift/eleva-tor is a very central option if you're looking for budget accommodation just off place de la Bastille. Rooms and bathrooms are on the small side; to ensure peace and quiet, choose a back room (eg room 13).

★**Hôtel Jeanne d'Arc**　　　　HOTEL €€
(Map p90; ☑ 01 48 87 62 11; www.hoteljeannedarc. com; 3 rue de Jarente, 4e; s €72, d €98-120, q €250; ☎; ⓜ St-Paul) About the only thing wrong with this gorgeous address is everyone knows about it; book well in advance. Games

to play, a painted rocking chair for tots in the bijou lounge, knick-knacks everywhere and the most extraordinary mirror in the break-fast room create a real 'family home' air in this 35-room house.

★**Hôtel Emile**　　　　　　DESIGN HOTEL €€
(Map p90; ☑ 01 42 72 76 17; www.hotelemile.com; 2 rue Malher, 4e; s €170, d €180-230, ste €350; ❄ ☎; ⓜ St-Paul) Prepare to be dazzled – literally. Retro B&W, geometrically patterned car-pets, curtains, wallpapers and drapes dress this chic hotel, wedged between boutiques and restaurants in the Marais. Pricier 'top floor' doubles are just that, complete with a breathtaking outlook over Parisian roofs and chimney pots. Breakfast, included in the price, is on bar stools in the lobby; open the cupboard to find the 'kitchen'.

Hôtel Georgette　　　　　DESIGN HOTEL €€
(Map p90; ☑ 01 44 61 10 10; www.hotelgeorgette. com; 36 rue du Grenier St-Lazare, 3e; d €153-216; ❄ ☎; ⓜ Rambuteau) Clearly seeking inspi-ration from the Centre Pompidou around the corner, this sweet little neighbourhood hotel is a steal. The lobby is bright and ap-pealing, and rooms are a decorative ode to either pop art, op art, dada or new realism with lots of bold colours and funky touch-es like Andy Warhol–inspired Campbell's soup-can lamp shades.

**Hôtel Caron
de Beaumarchais**　　　　　BOUTIQUE HOTEL €€
(Map p90; ☑ 01 42 72 34 12; www.carondebeau marchais.com; 12 rue Vieille du Temple, 4e; d €160-198; @ ☎; ⓜ St-Paul) The attention to detail at this unique themed hotel, decorated like an 18th-century private house, is impressive. From the period card table set as if time stopped halfway through a game, to the harp and well-worked sheet music propped on the music stand, the decor evokes the life and times of the 18th-century playwright after whom the hotel is named.

Hi Matic　　　　　　　　HOTEL €€
(Map p90; ☑ 01 43 67 56 56; www.hi-matic.net; 71 rue de Charonne, 11e; d €156-176, f €196; ❄ @ ☎; ⓜ Bastille) 🖉 The upside of this 'urban hotel of the future' is its eco-cred (LED energy-saving lights, natural pigments instead of paint) and colourful, imaginative space-saving design (mattresses rolled onto tat-amis at night) that some will find fun. The drawback is that service is minimal, with computerised check-in and vending-machine-dispensed organic breakfasts, but there's an on-site manager.

Hôtel Paris Bastille　　　　HOTEL €€
(Map p98; ☎01 40 01 07 17; www.hotelparis bastille.com; 67 rue de Lyon, 12e; s/d/tr/q €200/214/265/288; ❋☎; Ⓜ Bastille) A haven of serenity near busy Bastille and Le Marais, this comfortable midrange hotel has a range of modern rooms. Although it feels slightly chain-like, it's nonetheless one of the nicest and most dependable options in the neighbourhood.

★**Hôtel Fabric**　　　　DESIGN HOTEL €€€
(Map p90; ☎01 43 57 27 00; www.hotelfabric.com; 31 rue de la Folie Méricourt, 11e; d €240-360; ❋☎; Ⓜ Oberkampf) Four-star Hôtel Fabric is a stylish ode to its industrial heritage as a 19th-century textile factory. Steely pillars prop up the red-brick lounge area with *table d'hôte* dining table and vintage touches including a Singer sewing machine. Darkly carpeted corridors open onto crisp, bright rooms with beautiful textiles and ubercool cupboards (upcycled packing crates!). Breakfast €15.

Hôtel du Petit Moulin　　　BOUTIQUE HOTEL €€€
(Map p90; ☎01 42 74 10 10; www.hoteldupetit moulin.com; 29-31 rue du Poitou, 3e; d €220-350; ☎; Ⓜ Filles du Calvaire) This scrumptious 17-room hotel, a bakery at the time of Henri IV, was designed from head to toe by Christian Lacroix. Pick from medieval and rococo Marais (rooms sporting exposed beams and dressed in toile de Jouy wallpaper), to more modern surrounds with contemporary murals and heart-shaped mirrors just this side of kitsch.

🛏 The Islands

Island accommodation, concentrated on the peaceful, romantic Île St-Louis, is geographically as central as it gets.

Hôtel Saint-Louis en l'Isle　　BOUTIQUE HOTEL €€
(Map p100; ☎01 46 34 04 80; www.saintlouisenlisle. com; 75 rue St-Louis en l'Île, 4e; d €159-249, tr €289; ❋@☎; Ⓜ Pont Marie) This elegant abode brandishes a pristine taupe façade and perfectly polished interior. Spot-on home comforts like a kettle with complimentary tea and coffee in each room or the iPod docking station next to the bed make Saint-Louis stand out. Room 52 on the 5th floor with beams and balcony is dreamy, and the stone-cellar breakfast room is a 17th-century gem. Breakfast €13.

Hôtel de Lutèce　　　　HOTEL €€
(Map p100; ☎01 43 26 23 52; www.paris-hotel-lutece. com; 65 rue St-Louis en l'Île, 4e; s €210, d €210-285; ❋☎; Ⓜ Pont Marie) A lobby salon with ancient fireplace, wood panelling, antique furnish-

ings and terracotta tiles sets the inviting tone of the lovely Lutèce, an exquisite hotel with tastefully decorated rooms and one of the city's most desirable locations. Breakfast €14.

🛏 Latin Quarter

This energetic area's popularity with students and visiting academics makes rooms hardest to find during conferences and seminars from March to June and in October.

Hôtel Esmeralda　　　　HOTEL €
(Map p100; ☎01 43 54 19 20; www.hotel-esmeralda. fr; 4 rue St-Julien le Pauvre, 5e; s €80-100, d €115-130, tr €140; ☎; Ⓜ St-Michel) Tucked away in a quiet street with million-dollar views of Notre Dame (choose room 12!), this no-frills place is about as central to the Latin Quarter as it gets. At these prices, the 19 rooms are no great shakes (the cheapest singles have washbasin only) but they're popular. Book well ahead by phone (no online bookings). Wi-fi in reception area only.

Young & Happy　　　　HOSTEL €
(Map p102; ☎01 47 07 47 07; www.youngandhappy. fr; 80 rue Mouffetard, 5e; dm €22-33, d €60-90; @☎; Ⓜ Place Monge) This friendly if frayed Latin Quarter favourite was Paris' first independent hostel. Rates include breakfast in the dark stone-vaulted cellar, and the self-catering kitchen gets a workout from guests trawling rue Mouffetard's markets and food shops. Beds are in cramped rooms with washbasins, but women are in luck with an en-suite female dorm (€28 to €38). Wi-fi in the reception area only. Book well ahead.

Hôtel Minerve　　　　HOTEL €€
(Map p102; ☎01 43 26 26 04; www.parishotel minerve.com; 13 rue des Écoles, 5e; s €125, d €146-202, tr €202; ❋@☎; Ⓜ Cardinal Lemoine) Oriental carpets, antique books, frescoes of French monuments and wall tapestries make this family-run hotel a lovely and reasonably priced place to stay. Room styles are a mix of traditional and modern (renovated 2014); some have small balconies with views of Notre Dame, while the 1st-floor rooms all have parquet floors.

Hôtel les Degrés de Notre Dame　　HOTEL €€
(Map p100; ☎01 55 42 88 88; www.lesdegreshotel. com; 10 rue des Grands Degrés, 5e; d incl breakfast €120-170; ☎; Ⓜ Maubert-Mutualité) Wonderfully old-school, with a winding timber staircase (no lift) and charming staff, this hotel a block from the Seine is good value. Breakfast, included in the rate, comes with fresh-squeezed

OJ. Rooms 47 and the spacious 501 have romantic views of Notre Dame. Rooms have not been renovated for some time, however.

Five Hotel
BOUTIQUE HOTEL €€€

(Map p102; ☑ 01 43 31 74 21; www.thefivehotel.com; 3 rue Flatters, 5e; s €255, d €285-305; ❄ �; Ⓜ Les Gobelins) Choose from one of five perfumes to fragrance your (small) room at this contemporary romantic sanctum. Its private apartment, One by the Five, has a phenomenal 'levitating' bed. Rates are often discounted by up to 50% online, making it a better deal than it first appears.

Hôtel Résidence Henri IV
HOTEL €€€

(Map p102; ☑ 01 44 41 31 81; www.residencehenri4. com; 50 rue des Bernardins, 5e; d €285, ste €365-395; ❄ sigma; Ⓜ Maubert-Mutualité) This exquisite late-19th-century cul-de-sac hotel has eight generously sized rooms (minimum 17 sq metres) and five two-room apartments (minimum 25 sq metres), with medieval-style touches. All are equipped with kitchenettes (induction cooktops, fridge, microwave and dishes), making them particularly handy for families and market goers.

🔖 Place d'Italie & Chinatown

Oops
HOSTEL €

(☑ 01 47 07 47 00; www.oops-paris.com; 50 av des Gobelins, 13e; dm €42, d €115; @ sigma; Ⓜ Gobelins) A candy-floss-pink lift/elevator scales the six colourful floors of Paris' first 'design hostel'. Good-size four- to six-bed dorms and doubles (from €27 and €70, respectively, outside high season) are all en suite and accessible all day. Some have Eiffel Tower views. Breakfast is included but there's no kitchen. No credit cards, no alcohol allowed.

⭐ Hôtel Saint Charles
HOTEL €€

(☑ 01 45 89 56 54; www.hotel-saint-charles.com; 6 rue de l'Espérance, 13e; d/tr/q €170/210/280; ❄ sigma; Ⓜ Corvisart) Live like a local at this Butte aux Cailles hotel, located on a quiet, village-like street yet close to the area's lively bars and restaurants. Some of its 57 streamlined, contemporary rooms with aubergine tones have balconies; communal outdoor areas include a timber-decked terrace and fern- and conifer-filled garden.

🔖 St-Germain

The chic, central location, superb shopping, sophisticated dining and proximity to the Jardin du Luxembourg are the top draws here

but budget accommodation is seriously short changed.

Hôtel St-André des Arts
HOTEL €

(Map p106; ☑ 01 43 26 96 16; 66 rue St-André des Arts, 6e; s/d/tr/q €81/101/129/144; sigma; Ⓜ Odéon) Located on a lively, restaurant-lined thoroughfare, this 31-room hotel is a veritable bargain in the centre of the action. The rooms are basic and there's no lift, but the public areas are very evocative of *vieux Paris* (old Paris), with beamed ceilings and ancient stone walls. Room rates include breakfast.

Hôtel Perreyve
HOTEL €€

(Map p106; ☑ 01 45 48 35 01; www.hotel-perreyve. com; 63 rue Madame, 6e; s €140, d €175-200; ❄ sigma; Ⓜ Rennes) A hop, skip and a jump from the Jardin du Luxembourg, this welcoming 1920s hotel is superb value given its coveted location. Cosy, carpeted rooms have enormous frescoes; on the ground floor, start the day in the pretty breakfast room with herringbone floors and fire-engine-red tables and chairs.

Hôtel Danemark
BOUTIQUE HOTEL €€

(Map p106; ☑ 01 43 26 93 78; www.hoteldanemark. com; 21 rue Vavin, 6e; d €185-205; ❄ @ sigma; Ⓜ Vavin) In a peaceful location near the Jardin du Luxembourg, this stone-walled hotel has 15 scrumptious, eclectically furnished rooms. All are well soundproofed and at least 20 sq metres, which is bigger than many Parisians' apartments. Also unlike many residential apartments, all have bathtubs.

⭐ L'Hôtel
BOUTIQUE HOTEL €€€

(Map p106; ☑ 01 44 41 99 00; www.l-hotel.com; 13 rue des Beaux Arts, 6e; d €275-495; ❄ @ sigma ❄; Ⓜ St-Germain des Prés) In a quiet quayside street, this award-winning hostelry is the stuff of romance, Parisian myths and urban legends. Rock- and film-star patrons fight to sleep in room 16, where Oscar Wilde died in 1900 and which is now decorated with a peacock motif, or in the art deco room 36 (which entertainer Mistinguett once stayed in), with its huge mirrored bed.

Hôtel d'Angleterre
HISTORIC HOTEL €€€

(Map p106; ☑ 01 42 60 34 72; www.hotel-dangleterre. com; 44 rue Jacob, 6e; s €175, d €250-275; @ sigma; Ⓜ St-Germain des Prés) If the walls could talk... this former garden of the British Embassy is where the Treaty of Paris ending the American Revolution was prepared in 1783. Hemingway lodged here in 1921, as did Charles Lindbergh in 1927 after completing the world's first solo nonstop flight from New York to Paris. Its 27 exquisite rooms are individually decorated. Rates include breakfast.

L'Apostrophe
DESIGN HOTEL €€€

(Map p106; 01 56 54 31 31; www.apostrophe-hotel. com; 3 rue de Chevreuse, 6e; d €299-353; ✳@☎; M Vavin) A street work-of-art with its stencilled façade, this art hotel's 16 dramatically different rooms pay homage to the written word. Spray-painted graffiti tags cover one wall of room U (for *urbain*) which has a ceiling shaped like a skateboard ramp. Room P (for Paris parody) sits in the clouds overlooking Paris' rooftops. Rates tumble to midrange territory outside high season.

🛏 Montparnasse

With fewer tourists than many other areas, Montparnasse offers good value as well as excellent links to both major airports.

La Maison
BOUTIQUE HOTEL €

(01 45 42 11 39; www.lamaisonmontparnasse.com; 53 rue de Gergovie, 14e; s €95-110, d €115-130, tr €135-160, f €165-205; ✳@☎; M Pernety) The House goes all out to recreate home, with homemade cakes and jams for breakfast in the open-plan kitchen-lounge or little courtyard garden. A candy-striped staircase leads to its 36 rooms (there's a box-sized lift too) with bold pinks, violets and soft neutral tones. Ask for an Eiffel Tower-view room.

Arty Paris
HOSTEL €

(01 40 34 40 34; www.artyparis.fr; 62 rue des Morillons, 15e; dm €22-35, s €65-100, d €75-120, tr €80-135, q €100-180; ☎; M Porte de Vanves) Freebies at this fun, all-en-suite hostel/budget hotel include lockers, croissant breakfasts and wifi. Private rooms come with plasma TVs, but since that's not why you came to Paris, you'll be more interested in the hotel's authentic local neighbourhood location by Parc Georges Brassens, moments from the T3 tram, and buses that can zip you to St-Germain, the Louvre and Montmartre.

Hôtel Carladez Cambronne
HOTEL €

(01 47 34 07 12; www.hotelcarladez.com; 3 place du Général Beuret, 15e; d €97-155, f €170-235; ☎; M Vaugirard) On a quintessentially Parisian cafe-clad square, this freshly renovated hotel has comfortable rooms. Higher-priced superior rooms come with bathtubs, more space and tend to be quieter. Communal coffee- and tea-making facilities let you make yourself at home. Very good value.

Hôtel de la Paix
DESIGN HOTEL €€

(Map p106; 01 43 20 35 82; www.hoteldelapaix. com; 225 bd Raspail, 14e; d €110-240; ✳@☎; M Montparnasse Bienvenüe) Stacked on seven floors of a 1970s building, this chic hotel's 39 light-filled modern rooms have at least one vintage feature – old pegs to hang coats on, an old-fashioned school desk, or wooden-slat house shutters recycled as a bed head. Cheaper rooms are simply smaller than dearer ones.

✴ Eating

Some people rally around local sports teams, but in Paris, they rally around *la table* – and everything on it. Pistachio macarons, shots of tomato consommé, decadent bœuf bourguignon, a gooey wedge of Camembert running onto the cheese plate: food is not fuel here – it's the reason you get up in the morning. Rather than being known for regional specialities as elsewhere in the country, the city is the crossroads for the regional flavours of France. And, as a multicultural melting pot, it's also a fantastic place to experience cuisine from around the globe.

Neobistros offer some of the most exciting dining options in Paris today. Generally small and relatively informal, they're run by young, talented chefs who aren't afraid to experiment and push the envelope of traditional French fare.

✴ Eiffel Tower Area & 16e

This museum- and monument-rich area has some fine dines too, including two inside the tower itself – brasserie **58 Tour Eiffel** (Map p64; 01 45 55 20 04; www.restaurants-tour eiffel.com; 1st level, Eiffel Tower, Champ de Mars, 7e; 2-/3-course lunch menu €21/26, dinner menu €66/75; 11.30am-4.30pm & 6.30-11pm; M Bir Hakeim or RER Champ de Mars–Tour Eiffel) and Michelin-starred **Le Jules Verne** (Map p64; 01 45 55 61 44; www.lejulesverne-paris.com; 2nd fl, Eiffel Tower, Champ de Mars, 7e; lunch menus €98, dinner menus €185-230; noon-1.30pm & 7.30-9.30pm; M Champ de Mars-Tour Eiffel or Bir Hakeim).

Choux d'Enfer
PATISSERIE €

(Map p64; 01 47 83 26 67; cnr rue Jean Rey & quai Branly, 15e; bag sweet/savoury choux €5/7, with cream filling €6-17; 10am-8pm; M Bir-Hakeim or RER Champ de Mars-Tour Eiffel) This kiosk gives street food a whole new spin. The creation of top French chefs Alain Ducasse and Christophe Michalak, it cooks up *choux* (pastry puffs). Grab a brown paper bag of nine *choux salées* (savoury cheese puffs) spiced with pepper, curry or cumin; or go sweet with almond, cocoa, coffee, lemon and vanilla *chouquettes,* with or without cream filling.

Pain & Chocolat
CAFE €

(Map p64; 16 av de la Motte-Picquet, 7e; mains €10-22, brunch menus €7-22; ⊙9am-7pm Tue-Fri, 10am-7pm Sat & Sun; MLa Tour Maubourg) You'll be glad you forewent that overpriced, under-delivering hotel breakfast when you start the day in proper Parisian style at this delightfully retro cafe. Everything is made on the premises, salads, tartines (open-faced sandwiches), egg dishes and cakes, pastries and quiches included. Don't miss the hot chocolate, made from an old family recipe.

★ Le Casse Noix
MODERN FRENCH €€

(Map p64; ☑01 45 66 09 01; www.le-cassenoix.fr; 56 rue de la Fédération, 15e; 2-/3-course lunch menus €21/26, 3-course dinner menu €33; ⊙noon-2.30pm & 7-10.30pm Mon-Fri; MBir Hakeim) Proving that a location footsteps from the Eiffel Tower doesn't mean compromising on quality, quantity or authenticity, 'the nutcracker' is a neighbourhood gem with a cosy retro interior, affordable prices and exceptional cuisine that changes by season and by the inspiration of owner/chef Pierre Olivier Lenormand, who has honed his skills in some of Paris' most fêted kitchens. Book ahead.

★ Hugo Desnoyer
BUTCHER €€

(☑01 46 47 83 00; www.hugodesnoyer.fr; 28 rue du Docteur Blanche, 16e; menu €50, mains €16-32; ⊙7am-8pm Tue-Fri, 7am-7.30pm Sat; MJasmin) Hugo Desnoyer is Paris' most famous butcher and the trip to his shop in the 16e is well worth it. Arrive by noon or reserve to snag a table and settle down to a *table d'hôte* feast of homemade terrines, quiches, foie gras and cold cuts followed by the finest meat in Paris – cooked to perfection *naturellement.* Watch out for another Desnoyer opening in 2015.

La Véraison
MODERN FRENCH €€

(☑01 45 32 39 39; www.laveraison.com; 64 rue de la Croix Nivert, 15e; 2-/3-course lunch menus €15/18, mains €19-24; ⊙12.30-2pm & 8-10pm Tue-Fri, 7.30-10pm Sat; MCommerce) The elegant simplicity of owner/chef Ulla Bosse's welcoming neighbourhood bistro (bare boards, timber tables, pistachio-coloured walls) belies the outstanding cuisine she creates in her open kitchen. The starters alone – truffled chestnut velouté, foie gras ravioli in cognac sauce, burrata cheese with orange, crispy 'Peking duck' morsels, Thai crab cakes with mango dip – are reason enough to return.

★ Restaurant David Toutain
GASTRONOMIC €€€

(Map p64; ☑01 45 51 11 10; http://davidtoutain.com; 29 rue Surcouf, 7e; menus lunch €42, dinner €68-98; ⊙noon-2.30pm & 8-10pm Mon-Fri; MInvalides) Prepare to be wowed: David Toutain pushes the envelope at his eponymous new restaurant with some of the most creative high-end cooking in Paris today. Mystery degustation courses include unlikely combinations such as smoked eel in green-apple and black-sesame mousse, or candied celery and truffled rice pudding with artichoke praline (stunning wine pairings available).

Chez Françoise
TRADITIONAL FRENCH €€€

(Map p64; ☑01 47 05 49 03; http://chezfrancoise.com; Aérogare des Invalides; 2-/3-course menus from €28/33, oysters per half-dozen €15.50-29; ⊙noon-3pm & 7pm-midnight; MInvalides) Buried beneath the enormous Air France building but opening to a retractable roofed terrace, this old-school 1949-opened restaurant – a favourite with parliamentary workers from the Assemblée Nationale – recalls the early glamour of air travel, as it is established at this former off-site terminal for transiting passengers. Specialities include *entrecôte de bœuf* and sublime oysters.

Les Ombres
MODERN FRENCH €€€

(Map p64; ☑01 47 53 68 00; www.lesombres-restaurant.com; 27 quai Branly, 7e; 2-/3-course lunch menu €32/42, dinner menu €68, mains €32-44; ⊙noon-2.15pm & 7-10.20pm; Miéna or RER Pont de l'Alma) This glass-enclosed rooftop restaurant on the 5th floor of the Musée du Quai Branly is named the 'Shadows' after the patterns cast by the Eiffel Tower's webbed ironwork. Dramatic Eiffel views are complemented by kitchen creations such as *gambas* (prawns) with black rice and fennel, or pan-seared Burgundy snails in watercress sauce. Reserve.

Les Climats
TRADITIONAL FRENCH €€€

(Map p74; http://lesclimats.fr; 41 rue de Lille, 7e; 2-/3-course lunch menus €36/42, mains €32-44, bar snacks €7-22; ⊙restaurant noon-2.30pm & 7-10.30pm Tue-Sat, bar noon-2.30pm & 6-11pm; MSolférino) Like the neighbouring Musée d'Orsay, this is a magnficent art-nouveau treasure – a 1905-built former home for female telephone, telegram and postal workers – featuring soaring vaulted ceilings and original stained glass, as well as a garden for summer lunches and a glassed-in winter garden. Exquisite dishes complement its 150-page list of wines, sparkling wines and whiskies purely from Burgundy.

PARIS EATING

DON'T MISS

PARISIAN FOOD MARKETS

Nowhere encapsulates Paris' village atmosphere more than its markets. Not simply places to shop, the city's street markets are social gatherings for the entire neighbourhood. Nearly every little quarter has its own street market at least once a week, and the city also has some wonderful covered markets and commercial streets with stalls. No markets take place on Mondays. The website www.paris.fr lists every market by *arrondissement*, including speciality markets.

Paris' top 10:

Marché aux Enfants Rouges (Map p90; 39 rue de Bretagne, 3e; ⊙8.30am-1pm & 4-7.30pm Tue-Fri, 4-8pm Sat, 8.30am-2pm Sun; Ⓜ Filles du Calvaire) Paris' oldest covered market with communal tables for lunch.

Marché Bastille (Map p90; bd Richard Lenoir, 11e; ⊙7am-2.30pm Thu & Sun; Ⓜ Bastille or Richard Lenoir) Arguably the best open-air market in Paris.

Marché d'Aligre (Map p98; http://marchedaligre.free.fr; rue d'Aligre, 12e; ⊙8am-1pm & 4-7.30pm Tue-Sat, 8am-1.30pm Sun; Ⓜ Ledru-Rollin) All the staples of French cuisine can be found in this chaotic marketplace. Offerings in its covered Marché Beauvau are more gourmet.

Marché de Belleville (Map p90; bd de Belleville, 11e & 20e; ⊙7am-2.30pm Tue & Fri; Ⓜ Belleville) Fascinating entry into the large communities of the eastern neighbourhoods; home to artists, students and immigrants from Africa, Asia and the Middle East.

Marché Edgar Quinet (Map p106; bd Edgar Quinet, 14e; ⊙7am-2.30pm Wed, 7am-3pm Sat; Ⓜ Edgar Quinet or Montparnasse Bienvenüe) Local open-air market with some great stalls sizzling up snacks.

Marché Raspail (Map p106; bd Raspail btwn rue de Rennes & rue du Cherche Midi, 6e; ⊙regular market 7am-2.30pm Tue & Fri, organic market 9am-3pm Sun; Ⓜ Rennes) Especially popular on Sundays, when it's filled with organic produce.

Rue Cler (Map p64; rue Cler, 7e; ⊙most shops 8am-7pm Tue-Sat, to noon Sun; Ⓜ École Militaire) Bustling commercial street near the Eiffel Tower with a street party atmosphere on weekends.

Rue Montorgueil, 2e A splinter of the historic Les Halles – Paris' wholesale markets, today, grocery and speciality stalls set up along the pedestrian street.

Rue Mouffetard, 5e Paris' most photogenic commercial street.

Rue Daguerre, 14e Charming local street with stall-fronted shops; liveliest on Sunday mornings.

✖ Étoile & Champs-Élysées

This area is renowned for haute cuisine – and haute prices – but if you choose to eat at one of the finer restaurants for lunch on a weekday, you'll save a bundle and still get to treat your taste buds to an extraordinary meal. Make sure to reserve. Under-the-radar restaurants are scattered in the backstreets; gourmet food and drink shops, some with attached eateries, garland place de la Madeleine (Map p66; place de la Madeleine, 8e; Ⓜ Madeleine).

★**Ladurée**   PATISSERIE €
(Map p66; www.laduree.com; 75 av des Champs-Élysées, 8e; pastries from €1.50; ⊙7.30am-11.30pm Mon-Fri, 8.30am-12.30am Sat, 8.30am-11.30pm Sun;

Ⓜ George V) One of the oldest patisseries in Paris, Ladurée has been around since 1862 and was the original creator of the lighter-than-air macaron. Its tearoom is the classiest spot to indulge on the Champs. Alternatively, pick up some pastries to go – from croissants to its trademark macarons, it's all quite heavenly.

Aubrac Corner   BURGERS €
(Map p66; www.maison-aubrac.com/aubrac-corner; 37 rue Marbeuf, 8e; sandwiches from €5, burgers €9-11; ⊙7.45am-6.30pm Mon-Fri, 11am-6pm Sat; Ⓜ Franklin D Roosevelt) At this gourmet deli of famous steakhouse Maison Aubrac, burgers come with bowls of fries or *aligot* (mashed potatoes with melted cheese); take them

downstairs into the hidden wine cellar, a refuge from the nonstop commotion outside. Afterwards, browse the deli for Laguiole (the special *aligot* cheese).

Le Hide
FRENCH €€

(Map p66; ☑ 01 45 74 15 81; www.lehide.fr; 10 rue du Général Lanrezac, 17e; 2-/3-course menus €25/34; ⏰ noon-2pm Mon-Fri & 7-10pm Mon-Sat; Ⓜ Charles de Gaulle–Étoile) A perpetual favourite, Le Hide is a tiny neighbourhood bistro serving scrumptious traditional French fare: snails, baked shoulder of lamb with pumpkin purée or monkfish in lemon butter. Unsurprisingly, this place fills up faster than you can scamper down the steps of the nearby Arc de Triomphe. Reserve well in advance.

Mini Palais
MODERN FRENCH €€

(Map p66; ☑ 01 42 56 42 42; www.minipalais.com; av Winston Churchill, 8e; lunch menu €28, mains €22-45; ⏰ 10am-2am, kitchen to midnight; Ⓜ Champs-Élysées-Clemenceau or Invalides) Set inside the fabulous Grand Palais, the Mini Palais resembles an artist's studio on a colossal scale, with unvarnished hardwood floors, industrial lights suspended from ceiling beams and a handful of plaster casts on display. Its sizzling success means that the crowd is anything but bohemian; dress to impress for a taste of the lauded modern cuisine.

Philippe & Jean-Pierre
TRADITIONAL FRENCH €€

(Map p66; ☑ 01 47 23 57 80, www.philippeetjeanpierre.fr; 7 rue de Boccador, 8e; 4-/5-course menu €40/50, mains €24-26; ⏰ noon-2.15pm & 7.15-10.45pm Mon-Sat; Ⓜ Alma Marceau) Philippe graciously oversees the elegant, parquet-floored, white tableclothed dining room, while co-owner Jean-Pierre helms the kitchen. Seasonal menus incorporate dishes like cauliflower cream soup with mushrooms and truffles, sautéed scallops with leek and Granny Smith sauce and melt-in-the-middle *moelleux au chocolat* cake. Given the service, quality and gilt-edged Triangle d'Or location, prices are a veritable bargain.

Monsieur Bleu
MODERN FRENCH €€

(Map p66; ☑ 01 47 20 90 47; www.monsieurbleu.com; Palais de Tokyo, 20 av de New York, 16e; mains €15-20; ⏰ noon-2am; Ⓜ Iéna) An 'in' address with the ubercool fashion set since opening in 2013, this darling of a restaurant has bags going for it – superb interior design by Joseph Dirand, excellent seasonal cuisine and a summer terrace with a monumental Eiffel Tower view. Find it inside Palais de Tokyo; reserve in advance.

✖ Louvre & Les Halles

Trendy restaurants are on the rise in this central area. Two of the 'hood's hottest restaurants, **Frenchie** (Map p74; dishes €10-20; ⏰ 7-11pm Mon-Fri) and **Verjus** (Map p74; 47 rue de Montpensier, 1er; small plates €8-14, sandwiches €10; ⏰ 12.30-2pm Mon-Fri; Ⓜ Bourse or Palais Royal-Musée du Louvre), both also offer walk-in, wine bar dining.

Frenchie To Go
FAST FOOD €

(Map p74; www.frenchietogo.com; 9 rue du Nil, 2e; sandwiches €8-14; ⏰ 8.30am-4.30pm Mon-Fri, 9.30am-5.30pm Sat & Sun; 🛜; Ⓜ Sentier) Despite the drawbacks – limited seating, eye-poppingly expensive doughnuts – the fast-food outpost of the burgeoning Frenchie (p126) empire is a wildly popular destination. Bilingual staff transform choice ingredients (eg cuts of meat from the Ginger Pig in Yorkshire) into American classics like pulled-pork and pastrami sandwiches, accompanied by cornets of fries, coleslaw and pickled veggies.

Claus
BREAKFAST €

(Map p74; ☑ 01 42 33 55 10; www.clausparis.com; 14 rue Jean-Jacques Rousseau, 1er; breakfasts €13-18, plat du jour €13; ⏰ 8am-5pm Mon-Fri, 9.30am-5pm Sat & Sun; Ⓜ Étienne Marcel) Dubbed the '*haute-couture* breakfast specialist' in Parisian foodie circles, this inspired *épicerie du petit-dej* (breakfast grocery shop) has everything you could possibly desire for the ultimate gourmet breakfast and brunch – organic mueslis and cereals, fresh juices, jams, honey and so on.

Breakfast or brunch on site, shop at Claus to create your own or ask for a luxury breakfast hamper to be delivered to your door. Its lunchtime salads, soups and tarts are equally tasty.

Blend
BURGERS €

(Map p74; www.blendhamburger.com; 44 rue d'Argout, 2e; burger & fries €14; ⏰ noon-11pm daily; Ⓜ Sentier) A burger cannot simply be a burger in gourmet Paris, where burger buffs dissolve into raptures of ecstacy over gourmet creations at Blend. Think homemade brioche buns and ketchup, hand-cut meat and the most inventive of toppings that transform the humble burger into something rather special. Fries cost extra.

★ Pirouette
NEOBISTRO €€

(Map p74; ☑ 01 40 26 47 81; 5 rue Mondétour, 1er; lunch menu €18, 3-/6-course dinner menu €40/60; ⏰ noon-2.30pm & 7.30-10.30pm Mon-Sat; Ⓜ Les

ⓘ PARIS FOOD BLOGS & WEBSITES
····································

Le Fooding (www.lefooding.com) French movement shaking up the ossified establishment; expect a good balance between quirky, under-the-radar reviews and truly fine dining.

Gilles Pudlowski (www.gillespudlowski. com) Indefatigable French food critic and author.

David Lebovitz (www.davidlebovitz. com) Former Bay Area pastry chef who relocated to Paris in 2004. Good insight and recommendations.

Paris by Mouth (http://parisbymouth. com) Capital dining and drinking news and reviews.

La Fourchette (www.thefork.com) User reviews and great deals of up to 50% off in restaurants in Paris.

Halles) In one of the best restaurants in the vicinity of the old 'belly of Paris', chef Tomy Gousset's kitchen crew is working wonders at this cool loft-like space, serving up tantalising creations that range from seared duck, asparagus and Buddha's hand fruit to rum baba with chantilly and lime. Some unique ingredients and a new spin for French cuisine.

La Tour de Montlhéry – Chez Denise   TRADITIONAL FRENCH €€
(Map p74; ☑ 01 42 36 21 82; 5 rue des Prouvaires, 1er; mains €23-28; ☺ noon-2.30pm & 7.30pm-5am Mon-Fri; Ⓜ Châtelet) The most traditional eatery near the former Les Halles marketplace, this boisterous old bistro with red-chequered tablecloths has been run by the same team for 30-some years. If you've just arrived and are ready to feast on all the French classics – snails in garlic sauce, veal liver, steak tartare, braised beef cheeks and housemade pâtés – reservations are in order. Open till dawn.

Le Soufflé   TRADITIONAL FRENCH €€
(Map p74; ☑ 01 42 60 27 19; www.lesouffle.fr; 36 rue du Mont Thabor, 1er; soufflés €13-19, menus €37 & €44; ☺ lunch & dinner Mon-Sat; Ⓜ Concorde or Tuileries) The faintly vintage, aqua-blue façade of this concept kitchen is reassuringly befitting of the timeless French classic it serves inside – the soufflé. The light fluffy dish served in white ramekins comes in dozens of different flavours, both savoury and sweet; *andouillette* (pig intestine sausage) is the top choice for fearless gourmets.

L'Ardoise   BISTRO €€
(Map p74; ☑ 01 42 96 28 18; www.lardoise-paris.com; 28 rue du Mont Thabor, 1er; menu €38; ☺ noon-2.30pm Mon-Sat, 7.30-10.30pm Mon-Sun; Ⓜ Concorde or Tuileries) This is a lovely little bistro with no menu as such (*ardoise* means 'blackboard', which is all there is), but who cares? The food – *fricassée* of corn-fed chicken with morels, pork cheeks in ginger, hare in black pepper, prepared dexterously by chef Pierre Jay (ex-Tour d'Argent) – is superb.

★**Frenchie**   BISTRO €€€
(Map p74; ☑ 01 40 39 96 19; www.frenchie -restaurant.com; 5-6 rue du Nil, 2e; prix fixe menu €48; ☺ 7-11pm Mon-Fri; Ⓜ Sentier) Tucked down an alley you wouldn't venture down otherwise, this bijou bistro with wooden tables and old stone walls is iconic. Frenchie is always packed and for good reason: excellent-value dishes are modern, market-driven (the menu changes daily with a choice of two dishes) and prepared with just the right dose of unpretentious creative flair by French chef Gregory Marchand.

★**Verjus**   MODERN AMERICAN €€€
(Map p74; ☑ 01 42 97 54 40; www.verjusparis.com; 52 rue de Richelieu, 1er; prix-fixe menu €60; ☺ 7-10pm Mon-Fri; Ⓜ Bourse or Palais Royal–Musée du Louvre) Opened by American duo Braden Perkins and Laura Adrian, Verjus was born out of a wildly successful clandestine supper club known as the Hidden Kitchen. The restaurant builds on that tradition, offering a chance to sample some excellent, creative cuisine (gnocchi with shiitake relish and parmesan, wild-boar confit with cherry compote) in a casual space. The tasting menu is a series of small plates, using ingredients sourced straight from producers.

Yam'Tcha   FUSION €€€
(Map p74; ☑ 01 40 26 08 07; www.yamtcha.com; 4 rue Sauval, 1er; prix-fixe menu €100; ☺ noon-2.30pm Wed-Sat, 7.30-10.30pm Tue-Sat; Ⓜ Louvre Rivoli) Chef Adeline Grattard's ingeniously fused French and Cantonese flavours (fried squid with sweet-potato noodles) has earned her no shortage of critical praise. Pair dishes on the frequently changing menu with wine or tea, or sample the special lunch menu (€60) offered Wednesday through Friday. Reserve up to two months in advance.

Passage 53   MODERN FRENCH €€€
(Map p78; ☑ 01 42 33 04 35; www.passage53.com; 53 Passage des Panoramas, 2e; lunch/dinner menu €60/130; ☺ noon-2.30pm & 7.30-10.30pm Tue-Sat; Ⓜ Grands Boulevards or Bourse) No address inside Passage des Panoramas contrasts more dra-

matically with the outside hustle and bustle than this elegant restaurant at No 53. An oasis of calm and tranquillity (with window blinds pulled firmly down when closed), this gastronomic address is an ode to the best French produce – worked to perfection in a series of tasting courses by Japanese chef Shinichi Sato. Reserve.

Le Grand Véfour　　　TRADITIONAL FRENCH €€€
(Map p74; ☑01 42 96 56 27; www.grand-vefour. com; 17 rue de Beaujolais, 1er; lunch/dinner menu €98/298; ◎noon-2.30pm & 7.30-10.30pm Mon-Fri; ⓂPyramides) This 18th-century jewel on the northern edge of the Jardin du Palais Royal has been a dining favourite of the Parisian elite since 1784; just look at who gets their names ascribed to each table – from Napoléon and Victor Hugo to Colette (who lived next door). The food is tip-top; expect a voyage of discovery in one of the most beautiful restaurants in the world.

🗡 Opéra & Grands Boulevards

L'Opéra marks the start of the Grands Boulevards, where shoppers and office workers dine. Just north of here the area becomes more residential, and the diversity of choices increases.

Stanz　　　BAGELS €
(Map p78; http://stanzbagel.com; 56 rue La Fayette, 9e; bagels €3.80-8.50; ◎10am-8.30pm Mon-Sat, 11am-5pm Sun; ⓂCadet) All-natural, handmade bagels, in classic and mini sizes, are given the Parisian gourmet treatment with toppings such as smoked ham with honey mustard, rocket and pickles or chicken and preserved lemon. Sweet varieties range from pink praline to chocolate chestnut.

Chez Plume　　　ROTISSERIE €
(Map p78; www.chezplume.fr; 6 rue des Martyrs, 9e; dishes €3.50-8.50; ◎10.15am-2.45pm Mon-Fri, 5-8pm Tue-Fri, 9.30am-8.30pm Sat, 9.30am-3pm Sun; ⓂNotre Dame de Lorette) This rotisserie specialises in free-range chicken from southwest France, prepared in a variety of fashions: simply roasted, as a crumble, or even in a quiche or sandwich. It's wonderfully casual: add a side or two (potatoes, polenta, seasonal vegies) and pull up a counter seat.

Le Zinc des Cavistes　　　WINE BAR €
(Map p78; ☑01 47 70 88 64; 5 rue du Faubourg Montmartre, 9e; lunch menu €15.50, mains €13.50-18; ◎kitchen noon-11pm; ⓂGrands Boulevards) Don't tell the masses standing dutifully in the queue at the iconic, old-fashioned restaurant Charti-

er that there's a much better restaurant right next door. Local secret Le Zinc des Cavistes is as good for a full-blown meal (duck confit with mash, chicken fricassée with crushed potatoes) as it is for sampling new vintages.

★Richer　　　NEOBISTRO €€
(Map p84; 2 rue Richer, 9e; mains €16-25; ◎kitchen noon-2.30pm & 7.30-10.30pm; ⓂPoissonière or Bonne Nouvelle) Run by the same team as across-the-street neighbour L'Office (Map p84; ☑01 47 70 67 31; 3 rue Richer, 9e; 2-/3-course lunch menus €22/27, dinner menus €28/34; ◎noon-2.30pm & 7.30-10.30pm Mon-Fri; ⓂPoissonière or Bonne Nouvelle), Richer's pared-back and exposed-brick decor is a smart setting for genius creations like trout tartare with cauliflower and tomato and citrus mousse, and quince and lime cheesecake for dessert. It doesn't take reservations, but if it's full, Richer posts a list of recommended local addresses outside. Fantastic value.

Floquifil　　　TRADITIONAL FRENCH €€
(Map p78; ☑01 84 19 42 12; www.floquifil.fr; 17 rue de Montyon, 9e; mains €14-25; ◎11am midnight Mon-Fri, from 6.30pm Sat, ⓂGrands Boulevards) If you were to envision the ultimate backstreet Parisian wine bar, it would probably look a lot like Floquifil: table-strewn terrace, dark timber furniture, aquamarine-painted walls and bottles galore. But while the by-the-glass wines are superb, you're missing out if you don't dine here (on rosemary-roasted lamb with ratatouille or at the very least a chacuterie platter).

Bistrot La Bruyère　　　BISTRO €€
(☑09 81 22 20 56; 31 rue la Bruyère, 9e; 2-/3-course lunch menus €18/21, dinner menus €28/35; ◎noon-2.30pm & 7.30-10.30pm Mon-Sat; ⓂSt-Georges) Young-gun chef Loïc Buisson is the wunderkind behind winning dishes like tomato gazpacho, pigs trotter pancakes with apple chips, tuna with fried leeks, and beef from celebrated butcher Hugo Desnoyer at this unassuming but brilliant little bistro. One to watch.

Caillebotte　　　MODERN FRENCH €€
(☑01 53 20 88 70; 8 rue Hippolyte Lebas, 9e; 2-course lunch menu €19, 3-/5-course dinner menus €35/49; ◎noon-2.30pm & 7.30-10.30pm Mon-Fri; ⓂNotre Dame de Lorette) Although named for impressionist painter Gustave Caillebotte, the clattering interior – slate tiles, blond wood and tightly packed marble-topped tables – means this isn't the place for a romantic meal. But it is the place for amazing flavour combinations like scallops with creamy fennel and coffee

❶ GLUTEN-FREE DINING

Gluten-free dining isn't easy in Paris; do your research ahead of time. Two good places to start:

Noglu (Map p78; ☑ 01 40 26 41 24; www. noglu.fr; 16 Passage des Panoramas, 2e; mains €16-20, menu €24; ⊙ noon-2.30pm Mon-Sat, 7.30-10.30pm Tue-Sat; ☑; Ⓜ Richelieu-Drouot or Grands Boulevards) Chic address building on French tradition (bœuf bourguignon) while simultaneously drawing on newer culinary trends to create some devilishly good pastries, vegetarian plates, pizzas and salads.

Helmut Newcake (Map p90; www. helmutnewcake.com; 36 rue Bichat, 10e; mains €7.80-9.80; ⊙ noon-7.30pm Tue-Sat, to 6pm Sun; Ⓜ Goncourt) Combines the French genius for pastries with a 100% gluten-free kitchen; lunch (salads, quiches, soups, pizzas) is scrumptious and market driven.

purée and sea urchin foam, by the same team as Le Pantruche.

🍴 Montmartre & Pigalle

Neobistros, wine bars and world cuisine all feature in this atmosphere-laden area. Choose carefully to avoid tourist traps.

Le Petit Trianon   CAFE €
(Map p80; ☑ 01 44 92 78 08; 80 bd de Rochechouart, 18e; mains €7.50-13.50; ⊙ 8am-2pm; Ⓜ Anvers) With its large windows and a few carefully chosen antiques, this recently revived belle époque cafe at the foot of Montmartre feels about as timeless as the Butte itself. Dating back to 1894 and attached to the century-old Le Trianon theatre, it's no stretch to imagine artists like Toulouse-Lautrec and crowds of show-goers once filling the place in the evening.

Le Relais Gascon   GASCON €
(Map p80; ☑ 01 42 58 58 22; www.lerelaisgascon.fr; 6 rue des Abbesses, 18e; mains €11.50-16.50, lunch/dinner menus €17.50/27.50; ⊙ 10am-2am; Ⓜ Abbesses) Situated just a short stroll from the place des Abbesses, the Relais Gascon has a relaxed atmosphere and authentic regional cuisine at very reasonable prices. The giant salads and *confit de canard* will satisfy big eaters, while the traditional *cassoulet* and *tartiflette* are equally delicious. Another **branch** (Map p80; ☑ 01 42 52 11 11; 13 rue Joseph de Maistre; Ⓜ Ab-

besses) is just down the street. No credit cards at the main restaurant.

★ Le Miroir   BISTRO €€
(Map p80; ☑ 01 46 06 50 73; http://restaurantmiroir. com; 94 rue des Martyrs, 18e; lunch menu €19.50, dinner menus €27-34; ⊙ noon-2.30pm & 7.30-11pm Tue-Sat; Ⓜ Abbesses) This unassuming modern bistro is smack in the middle of the Montmartre tourist trail, yet it remains a local favourite. There are lots of delightful pâtés and rillettes to start off with – guinea hen with dates, duck with mushrooms, haddock and lemon – followed by well-prepared standards like stuffed veal shoulder.

★ Le Pantruche   BISTRO €€
(☑ 01 48 78 55 60; www.lepantruche.com; 3 rue Victor Massé, 9e; lunch/dinner menus €19/35; ⊙ 12.30-2.30pm & 7.30-10.30pm Mon-Fri; Ⓜ Pigalle) Named after a nearby 19th-century theatre, classy Pantruche has been making waves in the already crowded dining hot spot of South Pigalle. No surprise, then, that it hits all the right notes: seasonal bistro fare, reasonable prices and an intimate setting. The menu runs from classics (steak with Béarnaise sauce) to more daring creations (scallops served in a parmesan broth with cauliflower mousseline).

Le Garde Temps   MODERN FRENCH €€
(☑ 01 83 76 04 66; www.restaurant-legardetemps. fr; 19bis rue Pierre Fontaine, 9e; lunch menu €17, 2-/3-course dinner menus €26/33; ⊙ noon-2pm & 7-10.30pm Mon-Fri, 7-10.30pm Sat; Ⓜ Pigalle) The chalkboard menus at this contemporary bistro are framed and hung on the walls, and thankfully the promise of gastronomic art does not disappoint. Old bistro standards have been swept away in favour of more imaginative creations (fondant of red cabbage topped with quail confit) and – here's where the Garde Temps scores big points – the dinner prices aren't much more than that hohum cafe down the street.

Cul de Poule   MODERN FRENCH €€
(☑ 01 53 16 13 07; 53 rue des Martyrs, 9e; 2-/3-course menus lunch €16/19, dinner €24/29; ⊙ noon-2.30pm & 8-11pm Mon-Sat; Ⓜ Pigalle) With plastic, orange cafeteria seats outside, you probably wouldn't wander into the Cul de Poule by accident. But the light-hearted spirit (yes, there is a mounted chicken's derrière on the wall) is deceiving; this is one of the most affordable quality kitchens in the Pigalle neighbourhood, with excellent neobistro fare that emphasises quality ingredients from the French countryside.

Chez Toinette TRADITIONAL FRENCH €€
(Map p80; ☑ 01 42 54 44 36; 20 rue Germain Pilon, 18e; mains €19-24; ☺ 7-11.30pm Mon-Sat; Ⓜ Abbesses) The atmosphere of this convivial restaurant is rivalled only by its fine cuisine (seared duck with honey, venison with foie gras). In the heart of one of the capital's most touristy neighbourhoods, Chez Toinette has kept alive the tradition of old Montmartre with its simplicity and culinary expertise. An excellent choice for a traditional French meal.

✖ Gare du Nord, Gare de l'Est & Canal St-Martin

Traditional brasseries and bistros cluster around Gare du Nord and Gare de l'Est, and great things await along Canal St-Martin's creative banks.

Du Pain et des Idées BOULANGERIE €
(Map p90; 34 rue Yves Toudic, 10e; ☺ 7am-8pm Mon-Fri; Ⓜ Jacques Bonsergent) Fabulous traditional bakery with naturally leavened bread, orange-blossom brioche and *escargots* (similar to cinnamon rolls) in four decadent flavours – pistachio and chocolate, anyone? The bakery itself dates back to 1889.

Sunken Chip FAST FOOD €
(Map p90; www.thesunkenchip.com; 39 rue des Vinaigriers, 10e; fish & chips €12-14; ☺ noon-2.30pm & 7-10.30pm Wed-Sun; 🌐; Ⓜ Jacques Bonsergent) Although it's hard to believe anyone would come to Paris in search of fish 'n' chips, it's hard to argue with the battered, fried goodness at this ideally located takeaway. Nothing frozen here: it's all line-caught fish fresh from Brittany (three varieties per day), accompanied with thick-cut chips (peeled and chopped *sur place*), malt vinegar and mushy peas.

Pink Flamingo PIZZERIA €
(Map p90; ☑ 01 42 02 31 70; www.pinkflamingo pizza.com; 67 rue Bichat, 10e; pizzas €11.50-17; ☺ 7-11.30pm Mon-Thu, noon-3pm & 7-11.30pm Fri-Sun; 🌐; Ⓜ Jacques Bonsergent) Not another pizza place? *Mais non, chérie!* Once the weather warms up, the Flamingo unveils its secret weapon – pink helium balloons that the delivery guy uses to locate you and your perfect canal-side picnic spot (GPS not needed).

★ Abri NEOBISTRO €€
(Map p84; ☑ 01 83 97 00 00; 92 rue du Faubourg Poissonnière, 9e; lunch/dinner menus €25/43; ☺ noon-2.30pm Mon, noon-2.30pm & 7.30-10pm Tue-Sat; Ⓜ Poissonnière) It's no bigger than a shoebox and the decor is borderline nonexistent,

but converts will tell you that's all part of the charm. The reason everyone's raving? Katsuaki Okiyama is a seriously talented chef with an artistic flair, and his tasting menus (three courses at lunch, six at dinner) are exceptionally good value.

On Monday and Saturday, a giant sandwich (€13, includes drink) is all that's served for lunch. Reserve well in advance.

★ Le Verre Volé BISTRO €€
(Map p90; ☑ 01 48 03 17 34; 67 rue de Lancry, 10e; mains lunch €15-17, dinner €15-26; ☺ noon-2.30pm & 7-10.30pm; Ⓜ Jacques Bonsergent) The tiny 'Stolen Glass' – a wine shop with a few tables – is just about the most perfect wine bar–restaurant in Paris, with excellent wines and expert advice. Unpretentious and hearty *plats du jour* (dishes of the day) are excellent. Reserve well in advance for meals, or stop by to pick up a bottle.

★ Chez Michel BRETON, SEAFOOD €€
(Map p84; ☑ 01 44 53 06 20; 10 rue Belzunce, 10e; menus lunch/dinner €29/35; ☺ 7pm-midnight Mon, noon-2.30pm & 7pm-midnight Tue-Fri; Ⓜ Gare du Nord) If all you know about Breton cuisine is crêpes and cider, a visit to Chez Michel is in order. The only option is to order the four-course menu, which features excellent seafood (scallop tartare, hake with Breton white beans) as well as numerous specialities like *kig ha farz* (Breton pot au feu), *keuz breizh* (Breton cheeses) and *kouign* (butter cake). An extra surcharge for certain dishes is common.

✖ Ménilmontant & Belleville

Foodies are flocking to Ménilmontant and Belleville's emerging hot spots.

Felicity Lemon NEOBISTRO €
(Map p90; ☑ 01 71 32 71 11; www.felicitylemon.com; 4 rue Lemon, 20e; small plates €4-15; ☺ noon-2.30pm Wed-Sat, 7-10.30pm Tue-Sat; Ⓜ Belleville) Excellent music, a stylish interior with vintage tables and chairs, and contemporary art for sale give this small *'cantine de quartier'* in Belleville instant sex appeal. (Yes, it is named after the private secretary of Agatha Christie's Hercule Poirot.) The tapas-inspired menu features creative dishes to share: sweet duck breast with mango, pan-fried pears and asparagus, cucumber-feta salad etc.

Le Dauphin BISTRO €€
(Map p90; ☑ 01 55 28 78 88; 131 av Parmentier, 11e; 2-/3-course lunch menus €23/27, mains €15-20; ☺ 12.30-2.30pm Tue-Fri, 7.30-11.30pm Tue-Sat;

PARIS EATING

MOVEABLE FEASTS

Street food is taking the city by storm as food trucks specialising in everything from French favourites like *tartiflette* (potato, reblochon cheese, bacon and onion gratin) to gourmet burgers and wildly flavoured ice creams roll out across Paris. Top picks:

Camion Qui Fume (www.lecamionquifume.com; burger & fries €10.50) The smoking food truck that started it all, with gourmet burgers grilled by SoCal chef (and now local food celeb) Kristin Frederick. Follow @lecamionquifume.

Cantine California (www.cantinecalifornia.com; burger & fries €11) Organic burgers, tacos and homemade desserts from San Fran transplant Jordan Feilders. Follow @CantineCali.

Mes Bocaux (Map p66; www.mesbocaux.fr; 37 rue Marceau, 8e; 2-/3-course menu €11/13.50; Ⓜ Alma-Marceau) Gourmet, organic French offerings served in jars from chef Marc Veyrat. Preorder before noon then pick up.

Ⓜ Goncourt) Advance reservations are essential at this buzzing bistro. Run by the same team as nearby Le Chateaubriand, the stark white space with marble floor, bar, ceiling and walls (and the odd mirror) is a temple to taste. Lunch is a choice of two starters and two mains (one fish, one meat), presented like a work of art on white china. Dinner is strictly à la carte.

Chatomat   MODERN FRENCH €€
(📞 01 47 97 25 77; 6 rue Victor Letalle, 20e; mains €15-20; ⏱ 7.30-10.30pm Tue-Sat & 1st Sun of month; Ⓜ Ménilmontant, Couronnes or Père Lachaise) No dinner address is worth the trek to Belleville more than this contemporary bistro with plain white walls, post-industrial flavour and bags of foodie buzz. In the kitchen of the old shop-turned-restaurant, Alice and Victor cook up just three starters, three mains and three desserts each night – and none disappoint. Book in advance.

Soya   VEGETARIAN €€
(Map p90; 📞 01 48 06 33 02; 20 rue de la Pierre Levée, 11e; lunch menus €16-20, brunch €25; ⏱ noon-3.30pm & 7-11pm Mon-Fri, 11.30am-11pm Sat, 11.30am-4pm Sun; 📷; Ⓜ Goncourt or République) A favourite for its ubercool location in an industrial *atelier* (with bare cement, metal columns and big windows), Soya is a full-on *cantine bio* (organic eatery) in what was once a staunchly working-class district. Dishes, many tofu-based, are vegetarian and the weekend brunch buffet is deliciously lazy and languid. A glass floor floods the basement area with light.

Le Chateaubriand   NEOBISTRO €€€
(Map p90; 📞 01 43 57 45 95; 129 av Parmentier, 11e; menus €60-120; ⏱ 7.30-10.30pm Tue-Sat; Ⓜ Goncourt) Le Chateaubriand is an elegantly tiled, art deco dining room with strikingly imaginative cuisine. Basque chef Iñaki Aizpitarte is well travelled and his dishes show that global exposure again and again in its odd combinations (watermelon and mackerel, milk-fed veal with langoustines and truffles). Advance reservations absolutely essential; if you don't have one, try your luck but only after 9.30pm.

✖ Le Marais & Bastille

Le Marais spills over with small restaurants of every imaginable type, and is one of Paris' premier neighbourhoods for eating out. Traditional French and neobistros vie for supremacy in Bastille.

★ Candelaria   MEXICAN €
(Map p90; www.candelariaparis.com; 52 rue Saintonge; tacos €3.20-3.75, quesadillas & tostadas €3.50, lunch menu €11.50; ⏱ noon-midnight Thu-Sat, to 11pm Sun-Wed; ❄; Ⓜ Filles du Calvaire) You need to know about this cool *taqueria* (taco shop) to find it. Made of pure, unadulterated hipness in that brazenly nonchalant manner Paris does so well, clandestine Candelaria serves delicious tacos, quesadillas and tostadas in a laid-back setting – squat at the bar in the front or lounge out back around a shared table with bar stools or at low coffee tables.

CheZaline   DELICATESSEN €
(Map p90; 85 rue de la Roquette, 11e; dishes €6.50-9; ⏱ 11am-5.30pm Mon-Fri; Ⓜ Voltaire) A former horse-meat butcher's shop (*chevaline*, hence the spin on the name) is now a fabulous deli creating seasonally changing baguettes filled with ingredients like ham and house-made pesto. Other delicacies include salads and homemade terrines. There's a handful of seats (and plenty of parks nearby). Prepare to queue.

Café Marais

MODERN FRENCH €

(Map p90; ☑01 42 71 61 46; 10 rue des Haudriettes, 3e; lunch/dinner menu €12.90/15.90; ⊙noon-3.30pm & 7-11pm Wed-Mon; Ⓜ Arts et Métiers) Exposed stone, beamed ceiling and silent B&W Charlie Chaplin movies screened on one wall create an appealing vintage feel in this small and excellent bistro – one of the best-value spots to dine in the Marais. The round of Camembert roasted with honey, homemade courgette gratin and parmesan crème brûlée are all excellent.

L'As du Fallafel

JEWISH €

(Map p90; 34 rue des Rosiers, 4e; takeaway dishes €5.50-8.50; ⊙noon-midnight Sun-Thu, to 5pm Fri; Ⓜ St-Paul) The lunchtime queue stretching halfway down the street from this place says it all. This Parisian favourite, 100% worth the inevitable wait, is *the* address for kosher, perfectly deep-fried chickpea balls and turkey or lamb shwarma sandwiches. Do as every Parisian does and takeaway.

Le Clown Bar

WINE BAR €

(Map p90; ☑01 43 55 87 35; 114 rue Amelot, 11e; mains €15-20; Ⓜ Filles du Calvaire) A historic monument next to the city's winter circus, the Cirque d'Hiver (1852), this unique address is practically a museum with its painted ceilings, mosaics on the wall, zinc bar and purist art decor style. A restaurant for decades, the mythical address was taken over in early 2014 by chef-sommelier duo Sven Chartier and Ewen Lemoigne.

Breizh Café

CAFE €

(Map p90; www.breizhcafe.com; 109 rue Vieille du Temple, 3e; crêpes & galettes €4-12; ⊙11.30am-11pm Wed-Sat, to 10pm Sun; Ⓜ St-Sébastien Froissart) Everything at the Breton Café (*breizh* is 'Breton' in Breton) is 100% authentic, be it the Cancale oysters, the 20 types of cider, or the organic-flour crêpes cooked to perfection.

Gentle Gourmet Café

CAFE, VEGAN €

(Map p98; ☑01 43 43 48 49; www.gentlegourmetcafe.com; 24 bd de la Bastille, 12e; mains €14-19; ⊙11.30am-3pm & 6-11pm Tue-Sun; 🛜🖊; Ⓜ Bastille) 🖊 If you've been overdoing the *steak-frites* in Paris, head here for a reprieve. All of its dishes are vegan and most are organic (tofu ricotta cannelloni, portobello-mushroom burger in sesame brioche buns, raw lasagne); there are also detox juices and teas. Large windows fill the cafe with natural light, but the best seats are on the terrace.

Pozzetto

ICE CREAM €

(Map p90; www.pozzetto.biz; 16 rue Vieille du Temple, 4e; cone or pot €4-5.90; ⊙11.30am-9pm Mon-Thu, to 11.30pm Fri-Sun; Ⓜ St-Paul) Urban myth says this gelato maker opened when friends from northern Italy couldn't find their favourite ice cream in Paris so they imported the ingredients to make it themselves. Twelve flavours – spatula'd, not scooped – include *gianduia* (hazelnut chocolate from Turin) and *zabaione*, made from egg yolks, sugar and sweet Marsala wine. Great Italian *caffè* too.

★ Le 6 Paul Bert

BISTRO €€

(Map p98; ☑01 43 79 14 32; 6 rue Paul Bert, 12e; 2-/3-course lunch menus €15/19, 4-course dinner menu €44; ⊙noon-2pm Tue, noon-2pm & 7.30-11pm Wed-Sat; Ⓜ Faidherbe-Chaligny) Opened by Bertrand Auboyneau of neighbouring Bistrot Paul Bert (p132) and Québecois chef Louis-Philippe Riel, Le 6 serves mindblowing multicourse menus of small(ish) plates. The exquisitely prepared and presented creations from Riel's open kitchen change daily but invariably involve unexpected flavour combinations (quail/turnip, asparagus/monkfish, artichoke/white chocolate).

★ Bones

BISTRO €€

(Map p90; ☑09 80 75 32 08; www.bonesparis.com; 43 rue Godefroy Cavaignac, 11e; bar dishes €4-16, 4-/5-course menus €47/55; ⊙kitchen 7-11pm Tue-Sat; Ⓜ Voltaire) Even if you don't score a first-service (7pm to 7.30pm) reservation for red-hot Australian chef James Henry's stripped-back new premises, you have a couple of back-up options. The second service (9.30pm to 10.30pm) is walk-in only. Or you can order Henry's signature small plates (smoked oyster, beef heart, sea-bass carpaccio, house-cured charcuterie) at the lively bar.

★ Dessance

DESSERTS €€

(Map p90; ☑01 42 77 23 62; www.dessance.fr; 74 rue des Archives, 3e; desserts à la carte €19, 4-course dessert menu €36-44; ⊙3-11pm Wed-Fri, noon-midnight Sat & Sun; 🖊; Ⓜ Arts et Métiers) Dining at Dessance is unique. Only desserts are served – with an astonishing eye for detail and creative zeal for marrying unexpected ingredients (yes, broccoli, beetroot and roquette with chocolate and caramel). Whether you opt for the four-dessert menu or à la carte, a sweet amuse-bouche kicks off the experience and a plate of mini *gourmandises* (sweet things) ends it.

★ Blue Valentine
MODERN FRENCH €€

(Map p90; ✆01 43 38 34 72; http://blue valentine-restaurant.com; 13 rue de la Pierre Levée, 11e; 2-/3-course menu €29/36, 8-course tasting menu €54; ⏱noon-2.30pm & 7.30-11pm Wed-Sun, bar 7pm-2am; Ⓜ République) This thoroughly modern bistro with retro decor in the increasingly gourmet 11e was a hit the moment it opened in late 2013. A hip crowd flocks here for well-crafted cocktails and Japanese chef Saito Terumitsu's exquisite dishes flavoured with edible flowers and a profusion of herbs. The menu is small – just three dishes to choose from per course – but memorable.

★ Le Petit Marché
BISTRO €€

(Map p90; ✆01 42 72 06 67; 9 rue de Béarn, 3e; mains €18-26; ⏱noon-4pm & 7.30pm-midnight; Ⓜ Chemin Vert) A faintly fusion cuisine is what makes this cosy bistro, footsteps from place des Vosges, stand out. Dishes such as raw tuna wrapped in sesame seeds or caramelised duck breast served with roasted bananas lend a welcome Asian kick to a menu that otherwise reassures with old French bistro favourites that have been around for centuries. Also has a summer pavement terrace.

À la Biche au Bois
TRADITIONAL FRENCH €€

(Map p98; ✆01 43 43 34 38; 45 av Ledru-Rollin, 12e; 7-10.45pm Mon, noon-2.30pm & 7-10.45pm Tue-Sat; ⏱3-course lunch menu €29.80, mains €17-22.50; Ⓜ Gare de Lyon) Game, especially *la biche,* is the speciality of the convivial 'doe in the woods', but dishes like foie gras and *coq au vin* also add to the ambience of being out in the countryside, as do the green awning and potted plants out front. The cheeses and wines are excellent, but top honours, game aside, go to the sensational *frites.*

Bistrot Paul Bert
BISTRO €€

(Map p98; ✆01 43 72 24 01; 18 rue Paul Bert, 11e; 3-course lunch/dinner menus €19/38; ⏱noon-2pm & 7.30-11pm Tue-Sat; Ⓜ Faidherbe-Chaligny) When food writers list Paris' best bistros, one of the names that consistently pop up is Paul Bert. The timeless vintage decor and perfectly executed classic dishes like *steak-frites* and hazelnut-cream Paris-Brest pastry merit booking ahead. Look out for its siblings L'Écailler du Bistrot (Map p98; ✆01 43 72 76 77; 22 rue Paul Bert, 11e; mains €17-34, seafood platter €65; ⏱noon-2.30pm & 7.30-11pm Tue-Sat; Ⓜ Faidherbe-Chaligny), for seafood, and Le 6 Paul Bert (p131), for small plates, in the same street.

Yard
MODERN FRENCH €€

(✆01 40 09 70 30; 6 rue de Mont Louis, 11e; 3-course lunch menu €18, mains €15-18; ⏱noon-2.30pm Mon, noon-2.30pm & 8-10.30pm Tue-Fri; Ⓜ Philippe Auguste) Opening to an atmospheric terrace near Père Lachaise cemetery, this bistro built on a former construction yard has been resurrected by chefs Shaun Kelly (previously of Au Passage) and Elenie Sapera (of Bones; p131) working the open kitchen and tapas bar. Daily changing menus incorporate seasonal dishes such as spring lamb with leeks. Book ahead for dinner.

Derrière
MODERN FRENCH €€

(Map p90; ✆01 44 61 91 95; www.derriere-resto.com; 69 rue des Gravilliers, 3e; lunch menus €25, mains €17-24; ⏱noon-2.30pm & 8-11pm Mon-Sat, noon-4.30pm Sun; Ⓜ Arts et Métiers) Play table tennis, sit on the side of the bed, glass of champers in hand, or lounge between book cases – such is the nature of this restaurant with courtyard seating. Chilled vibe in a trendy 'shoes-off' style aside, Derrière (literally 'behind') is deadly serious in the kitchen. Classic French bistro dishes and more inventive creations are excellent, as is Sunday brunch.

Chez Marianne
JEWISH €€

(Map p90; 2 rue des Hospitalières St-Gervais, 4e; mains €18-25; ⏱noon-midnight; Ⓜ St-Paul) Heaving at lunchtime, Chez Marianne translates to elbow-to-elbow eating beneath age-old beams on copious portions of felafel, hummus, aubergine purée and 25-odd other *zakouski* (hors d'œuvres; €14/16/18 for plate of four/five/six). Fare is Sephardic rather than Ashkenazi (the norm at most Pletzl eateries), not Beth Din kosher. A hole-in-the-wall window sells felafel in pita (€7) to munch on the move.

Bofinger
BRASSERIE €€

(Map p90; ✆01 42 72 87 82; www.bofinger.com; 5-7 rue de la Bastille, 4e; menus €36.50-59, mains €22.50-46; ⏱noon-3pm & 6.30pm-midnight; Ⓜ Bastille) Founded in 1864, Bofinger is reputedly Paris' oldest brasserie, though its polished art nouveau brass, glass and mirrors flags redecoration a few decades later. Specialities include Alsatian-inspired dishes such as *choucroute* (sauerkraut), oysters and seafood dishes. Ask for a seat downstairs and under the *coupole* (stained-glass dome).

Septime
MODERN FRENCH €€€

(Map p90; ✆01 43 67 38 29; 80 rue de Charonne, 11e; menus lunch €28-55, dinner €58; ⏱7-10pm Mon, 12.15-2pm & 7-10pm Tue-Fri; Ⓜ Charonne) Reading

PATRICIA WELLS' CULINARY SHOPPING SECRETS

Cookery teacher and author of *The Food Lover's Guide to Paris*, American Patricia Wells (www.patriciawells.com) has lived, cooked and shopped in Paris since 1980, and is considered to have truly captured the soul of French cuisine.

What is it that makes Paris so wonderful for culinary shopping? The tradition, the quality, the quantity, the atmosphere and physical beauty!

Where do you shop? All over: the Sunday organic market at Rennes (Marché Raspail, p124) – I love the dried fruits and nuts; Poilâne (p137) for bread; Quatrehomme (Map p106; www.quatrehomme.fr; 62 rue de Sèvres, 6e; ☺9am-7.45pm Tue-Sat; Ⓜ Vanneau) for cheese; and Poissonnerie du Bac (Map p106; www.poissonnerie-paris.fr; 69 rue du Bac, 7e; ☺9am-1pm & 4-7.30pm Tue-Sat, 9.30am-1pm Sun; Ⓜ Rue du Bac) for fish. I shop regularly at Le Bon Marché's La Grande Épicerie de Paris (p154); for special meals I always order things in advance and go from shop to shop – La Maison du Chocolat (Map p106; www.lamaisonduchocolat.fr; 19 rue de Sèvres, 6e; ☺10am-7.30pm Mon-Sat, to 1pm Sun; Ⓜ Sèvres-Babylone) and Pierre Hermé (p154) for chocolate and cakes, and La Dernière Goutte (Map p106; www.lader_nieregoutte.net; 6 rue du Bourbon le Château, 6e; ☺3-8pm Mon, 10.30am-1.30pm & 3-8pm Tue-Fri, 11am-7pm Sat; Ⓜ Mabillon) for wine. That is the fun of Paris and of France.

A perfect culinary souvenir from Paris? Fragonard (Map p106; ☎01 42 84 12 12, www.fragonard.com; 196 bd St-Germain, 6e; ☺10am-7pm Mon-Sat; Ⓜ Rue du Bac or St-Germain des Prés), the perfume maker, has a great shop on bd St-Germain. It has a changing litany of great things for the home. Nothing is very expensive and the offerings change every few months. The gift wrapping is worth it alone!

the menu at newly Michelin-starred Septime won't get you far, as it looks mostly like an obscure shopping list (hanger steak/chicory/roots, chicken's egg/foie gras/*lardo*). And that's if you even get a menu – if you order the excellent five-course meal (available for both lunch and dinner), you won't even know what's being served until it arrives. Reserve in advance.

The alchemists in Bertrand Grébaut's kitchen are capable of producing some truly beautiful creations, and the blue-smocked waitstaff go out of their way to ensure that the culinary surprises are all pleasant ones.

For a pre- or post-meal drink, drop by its wine bar Septime La Cave (Map p90; www.septime-charonne.fr; 3 rue Basfroi, 11e; ☺4-11pm Tue-Sat; Ⓜ Charonne). And for stunning seafood tapas, try its sister restaurant Clamato (Map p90; www.septime-charonne.fr; 80 rue de Charonne, 11e; tapas €6-19; ☺7-11pm Mon-Fri, noon-11pm Sat & Sun; Ⓜ Charonne).

✖ The Islands

Famed more for its ice cream than dining options, Île St-Louis nevertheless has some appealing options. Quality places are limited on the Île de la Cité.

★ **Café Saint Régis**   CAFE €
(Map p100; http://cafesaintregisparis.com; 6 rue du Jean de Bellay, 4e; salads & mains €14.50-28; ☺7am-2am; ☎; Ⓜ Pont Marie) Hip and historical with an effortless dose of retro vintage thrown in, Le Saint Régis – as those in the know call it – is a deliciously Parisian hang-out any time of day. From pastries for breakfast to a mid-morning pancake, brasserie lunch or early evening oyster platter, Café St-Regis gets it just right. Come midnight it morphs into a late-night hot spot.

Berthillon   ICE CREAM €
(Map p100; 31 rue St-Louis en l'Île, 4e; 2-/3-/4-ball cone or tub €2.50/5.50/7; ☺10am-8pm Wed-Sun; Ⓜ Pont Marie) Berthillon is to ice cream what Château Lafite Rothschild is to wine and Valrhona is to chocolate. Among its 70-odd flavours, the fruit-flavoured sorbets are renowned, as are its rich chocolate, coffee, *marrons glacés* (candied chestnuts) and Agenaise (Armagnac and prunes). Watch for seasonal flavours like roasted pineapple and basil, or ginger and caramel. Eat in or take away.

★ **Les Voyelles**   MODERN FRENCH €€
(Map p100; ☎01 46 33 69 75; www.les-voyelles.com; 74 quai des Orfèvres, 4e; plat du jour €12, 2-/3-course menus €17/22.50; ☺8am-midnight Tue-Sat; Ⓜ Pont

Neuf) This new kid on the block is worth the short walk from Notre Dame. The Vowels – spot the letters casually scattered between books and beautiful objects on the shelves lining the intimate 'library' dining room – is thoroughly contemporary, with a menu ranging from finger food to full-blown dinner to match. Its pavement terrace is Paris gold.

Le Tastevin TRADITIONAL FRENCH €€€
(Map p100; ☑01 43 54 17 31; www.letastevin-paris.com; 46 rue St-Louis en l'Île, 4e; mains €27-34.50, menus from €33; ⊙noon-2pm & 7-11.15pm Tue-Sun; MPont Marie) With its old-fashioned lace curtains, wood panelling and beamed ceiling, this posh old-style address in a 17th-century building smacks of charm. Its excellent cuisine is equally traditional: think *escargots* (snails), foie gras, sole, or *ris de veau* (calf sweetbreads) with morels and tagliatelli.

✖ Latin Quarter

From cheap-eat student haunts to chandelier-lit palaces loaded with history, dining options abound. Rue Mouffetard is famed for its food market and food shops.

Le Comptoir du Panthéon CAFE, BRASSERIE €
(Map p102; ☑01 43 54 75 56; 5 rue Soufflot, 5e; salads €11-13, mains €12.40-15.40; ⊙7am-1.45am; ⊛; MCardinal Lemoine or RER Luxembourg) Enormous, creative meal-size salads are the reason to pick this as a dining spot. Magnificently placed across from the domed Panthéon on the shady side of the street, its pavement ter-

race is big, busy and oh so Parisian – turn your head away from Voltaire's burial place and the Eiffel Tower pops into view.

Le Jardin des Pâtes ORGANIC, PASTA €
(Map p102; ☑01 43 31 50 71; 4 rue Lacépède, 5e; pasta €10.50-14; ⊙noon-2.30pm & 7.30-10.30pm; ⊛; MPlace Monge) 🖋 A crisp white-and-green façade handily placed next to a Vélib' station flags the Pasta Garden, a simple, smart 100% *bio* (organic) place where pasta comes in every guise imaginable – barley, buckwheat, rye, wheat, rice, chestnut and so on. Try the *pâtes de chataignes* (chestnut pasta) with duck breast, nutmeg, crème fraîche and mushrooms.

La Salle à Manger TRADITIONAL FRENCH €
(Map p102; ☑01 55 43 91 99; 138 rue Mouffetard, 5e; mains €10-14; ⊙8.30am-6.30pm; MCensier Daubenton) With a sunny pavement terrace beneath trees enviably placed at the foot of foodie street rue Mouffetard, the 'Dining Room' is prime real estate. Its 360-degree outlook – market stalls, fountain, church and garden with playground for tots – couldn't be prettier, and its salads, *tartines*, tarts and pastries ensure packed tables at breakfast, lunch and weekend brunch.

Chez Nicos CRÊPERIE €
(Map p102; 44 rue Mouffetard, 5e; crêpes €3-6; ⊙noon-2am; ⊛; MPlace Monge) The signboard outside crêpe artist Nicos' unassuming little shop chalks up dozens of fillings but ask by name for his masterpiece, 'La Crêpe du Chef',

---

INTERNATIONAL EAT STREETS

First-time visitors often mistake the international restaurants squeezed into the labyrinth of narrow streets across the Seine from Notre Dame between rue St-Jacques, bd St-Germain and bd St-Michel, 5e, for the whole of the famous 'Latin Quarter'. However, you'd be wise to simply avoid this area altogether. For the best global cuisine, try the following:

Av de Choisy, av d'Ivry and rue Baudricourt, 13e Cheap Chinese and Southeast Asian (especially Vietnamese) eateries.

Bd de Belleville, 11e & 20e North African food, especially couscous.

Rue Au Maire, 3e Small Chinese noodle shops and restaurants.

Rue Cadet, rue Richer and rue Geoffroy Marie, 9e Triangle of streets with Jewish (mostly Sephardic) and kosher food.

Rue Cail, 10e Fabulous array of Indian restaurants.

Rue de Belleville, 20e Dine on Chinese, Southeast Asian or Middle Eastern.

Rue Ste-Anne, 2e The heart of Paris' Japantown.

Rue des Rosiers, 4e Jewish restaurants (some Ashkenazic, some Sephardic, not all kosher) serving specialities from Central Europe, North Africa and Israel. Many are closed Friday evening, Saturday and Jewish holidays.

stuffed with aubergines, feta, mozzarella, lettuce, tomatoes and onions. There's a handful of tables inside; otherwise get it wrapped up in foil and head to a nearby park.

★**Café de la Nouvelle Mairie** BISTRO €€
(Map p102; 19 rue des Fossés St-Jacques, 5e; mains €14-16; ⊗8am-midnight Mon-Fri; **M**Cardinal-Lemoine) Shhhh...just around the corner from the Panthéon but hidden away on a small, fountained square, the narrow wine bar Café de la Nouvelle is a neighbourhood secret, serving blackboard-chalked natural wines by the glass and delicious seasonal bistro fare from oysters and ribs (*à la française*) to grilled lamb sausage over lentils.

★**Les Pipos** BISTRO €€
(Map p102; ☑01 43 54 11 40; www.les-pipos.com; 2 rue de l'École Polytechnique, 5e; mains €13.90-26.90; ⊗8am-2am Mon-Sat; **M**Maubert-Mutualité) A feast for the eyes and the senses, this *bar à vins* is above all worth a visit for its food. The bistro standards (bœuf bourguignon) and *charcuteries de terroir* (regional cold meats and sausages) are mouth-watering, as is the cheese board, which includes all the gourmet names (bleu d'Auvergne, St-Félicien and St-Marcellin). No credit cards.

Les Papilles BISTRO €€
(Map p102; ☑01 43 25 20 79; www.lespapillesparis.com; 30 rue Gay Lussac, 5e; 2-/3-course menus from €22/31; ⊗noon-2.30pm & 7-10pm Tue-Sat; **M**Raspail or RER Luxembourg) This hybrid bistro, wine cellar and *épicerie* (specialist grocer) with sunflower-yellow façade is one of those fabulous Parisian dining experiences. Meals are served at simply dressed tables wedged beneath bottle-lined walls, and the fare is market-driven: each weekday cooks up a different *marmite du marché* (market casserole). But what really sets it apart is its exceptional wine list.

L'AOC TRADITIONAL FRENCH €€
(Map p102; ☑01 43 54 22 52; www.restoaoc.com; 14 rue des Fossés St-Bernard, 5e; 2-/3-course lunch menus €21/29, mains €19-36; ⊗noon-2.30pm & 7.30-10.30pm Tue-Sat; **M**Cardinal Lemoine) 'Bistrot carnivore' is the strapline of this ingenious restaurant concocted around France's most respected culinary products. The concept is Appellation d'Origine Contrôlée (AOC), meaning everything has been reared or produced according to strict guidelines. The result? Only the best! Choose between meaty favourites (steak tartare) or the rotisserie menu, ranging from roast chicken to suckling pig.

Le Coupe-Chou FRENCH €€
(Map p102; ☑01 46 33 68 69; www.lecoupechou.com; 9 & 11 rue de Lanneau, 5e; 2-/3-course menus €27/33; ⊗noon-2.30pm & 7.30-10.30pm; **M**Maubert-Mutualité) This maze of candlelit rooms inside a vine-clad 17th-century townhouse is overwhelmingly romantic. Ceilings are beamed, furnishings are antique, and background classical music mingles with the intimate chatter of diners. As in the days when Marlene Dietrich dined here, advance reservations are essential.

★**Sola** FUSION €€€
(Map p100; ☑dinner 01 43 29 59 04, lunch 09 65 01 73 68; www.restaurant-sola.com; 12 rue de l'Hôtel Colbert, 5e; lunch/dinner €48/98; ⊗noon-2pm & 7-10pm Tue-Sat; **M**St-Michel) For serious gourmands, Sola is arguably the Latin Quarter's proverbial brass ring. Pedigreed chef Hiroki Yoshitake combines French technique with Japanese sensibility, resulting in gorgeous signature creations (such as miso-marinated foie gras on *feuille de brick* served on a slice of tree trunk). The artful presentations and attentive service make this a great choice for a romantic meal – go for the full experience and reserve a table in the Japanese dining room downstairs.

La Tour d'Argent GASTRONOMIC €€€
(Map p100; ☑01 43 54 23 31; www.latourdargent.com; 15 quai de la Tournelle, 5e; lunch menus €65, dinner menus €170-190; ⊗noon-2.30pm & 7.30-10.30pm Tue-Sat; **M**Cardinal Lemoine or Pont Marie) The venerable 'Silver Tower' is famous for its *caneton* (duckling), rooftop garden with glimmering Notre Dame views and a fabulous history harking back to 1582 – from Henry III's inauguration of the first fork in France to inspiration for the winsome animated film *Ratatouille*. Its wine cellar is one of Paris' best; dining is dressy and exceedingly fine.

✕ **Place d'Italie & Chinatown**

The 13e's Chinatown is a hotbed of authentic Asian food. Near place d'Italie, the villagey Butte aux Cailles is chock-a-block with interesting addresses.

Tang Frères SUPERMARKET
(48 av d'Ivry, 13e; ⊗9am-8pm Tue-Sat, to 1pm Sun; **M**Porte d'Ivry) Chinatown's beating heart centres on this enormous Asian supermarket, where you'd be forgiven for thinking you'd been transported to another continent. Spices, sauces, freezers full of frozen dumplings, and kitchen utensils are imported from Asia

along with beverages including Chinese beer. Ready-to-eat snacks are sold opposite the entrance.

Pho 14
VIETNAMESE €

(129 av de Choisy, 13e; mains €6.50-9.80; ⏱9am-11pm; Ⓜ Tolbiac) Factor in a wait at this small, simple restaurant (also known as Pho Banh Cuon 14) – it doesn't take bookings and is wildly popular with in-the-know locals for its authentic and astonishingly cheap *pho*. The steaming Vietnamese broth is richly flavoured with cinnamon and incorporates noodles and traditional beef or chicken.

Chez Nathalie
MODERN FRENCH €€

(☑ 01 45 80 20 42; www.cheznathalie.fr; 41 rue Van-drezanne, 13e; mains €21-28; ⏱noon-2.30pm Tue-Fri, 7-11pm Tue-Sat; Ⓜ Corvisart or Place d'Italie) On a quiet street with summertime terrace tables, this pocket-size restaurant is a lovely spot to dine *tête à tête*. Transparent Kartell chairs and deep-purple table tops complement the stylised menu, which fuses traditional French with world food such as rabbit tajine with dates, oranges and almonds, creamy tomato, prawn and ginger risotto, or squid pan-fried with Espelette peppers.

Restaurant Variations
BISTRO €€

(Map p102; ☑ 01 43 31 36 04; www.restaurant variations.com; 18 rue des Wallons, 13e; lunch menus €16.50-19, dinner menus €24-44; ⏱noon-2pm Mon-Fri, 7-10pm Mon-Sat; Ⓜ St-Marcel) In a pin-drop-quiet backstreet you'd never stumble on by chance, this light-filled restaurant is a diamond find. It's framed by huge glass windows and artfully decorated with large-scale photographs; square white plates showcase the colours and textures of brothers Philippe and Pierre Tondetta's Italian-accented offerings such as rack of lamb accompanied by polenta with olives and aged parmesan.

L'Auberge du 15
GASTRONOMIC €€€

(☑ 01 47 07 07 45; www.laubergedu15.com; 15 rue de la Santé, 13e; 4-course lunch menu €39, 7-/9-course menus €65/85, mains €35-45; ⏱noon-2.30pm Tue-Sat, 7.30-11pm Tue-Thu, 7-11pm Fri & Sat; Ⓜ St-Jacques or RER Port Royal) With rough-hewn stone walls, chocolate-toned decor and classic French dishes, Nicolas Castelet's charming 'inn' evokes a country retreat. Choose dining companions who share your culinary tastes – many of the mains must be ordered by a minimum of two people and the *dégustation* menus by the entire table.

✖ St-Germain

The picnicking turf of the Jardin du Luxembourg is complemented by some fabulous places to pick up picnic ingredients. Even if it's not picnic weather, the neighbourhood's streets are lined with places to dine for all budgets.

★ JSFP Traiteur
DELICATESSEN €

(Map p106; http://jsfp-traiteur.com; 8 rue de Buci, 6e; dishes €3.40-5.70; ⏱9.30am-8.30pm; 🖉; Ⓜ Mabillon) Brimming with big bowls of salad, terrines, pâté and other prepared delicacies, this deli is a brilliant bet for quality Parisian 'fast food' such as quiches in a variety of flavour combinations (courgette and chive, mozzarella and basil, salmon and spinach...) to take to a nearby park, square or stretch of riverfront.

PARIS' OLDEST RESTAURANT & CAFE

St-Germain claims both the city's oldest restaurant and its oldest cafe.

À la Petite Chaise (Map p106; ☑ 01 42 22 13 35; www.alapetitechaise.fr; 36 rue de Grenelle, 6e; lunch/dinner menus from €23/36; ⏱noon-2pm & 7-11pm; Ⓜ Sèvres-Babylone) Paris' oldest restaurant hides behind an iron gate that's been here since it opened in 1680, when wine merchant Georges Rameau served food to the public to accompany his wares. Classical decor and cuisine (onion soup, foie gras, duck, lamb and unexpected delights like truffled asparagus) make it worth a visit above and beyond its history.

Le Procope (Map p106; www.procope.com; 13 rue de l'Ancienne Comédie, 6e; 2-/3-course menus from €29/36; ⏱11.30am-midnight Sun-Wed, to 1am Thu-Sat; 🖬; Ⓜ Odéon) The city's oldest cafe welcomed its first patrons in 1686, and was frequented by Voltaire, Molière and Balzac et al. Its chandeliered interior also has an entrance onto the 1735-built glass-roofed passageway Cour du Commerce St-André. Along with house specialities like *coq au vin*, calf's head casserole in veal stock, and calf kidneys with violet mustard, it serves its own sorbets and ice creams, which it's been making here since 1686 too.

Au Pied de Fouet
BISTRO €

(Map p106; ☑ 01 43 54 87 83; www.aupieddefouet. com; 50 rue St-Benoît, 6e; mains €9-12.50; ☺ noon-2.30pm & 7-11pm Mon-Sat; Ⓜ St-Germain des Prés) Wholly classic bistro dishes such as *entrecôte* (steak), *confit de canard* (duck cooked slowly in its own fat) and *foie de volailles sauté* (pan-fried chicken livers) at this busy bistro are astonishingly good value. Round off your meal with a *tarte Tatin*, wine-soaked prunes or bowl of *fromage blanc* (a cross between yoghurt, sour cream and cream cheese).

L'Avant Comptoir
FRENCH TAPAS €

(Map p106; www.hotel-paris-relais-saint-germain. com; 3 Carrefour de l'Odéon, 6e; tapas €3-7; ☺ noon-midnight; Ⓜ Odéon) Squeeze in around the zinc bar (there are no seats and it's tiny) and order off the menu suspended from the ceiling to feast on amazing tapas dishes such as Iberian ham or salmon tartare croquettes, duck-sausage hot dogs, blood-sausage *macarons,* and prosciutto and artichoke waffles with wines by the glass in a chaotically sociable atmosphere.

Cuisine de Bar
SANDWICHES €

(Map p106; www.cuisinedebar.fr; 8 rue du Cherche Midi, 6e; dishes €9.20-13.50; ☺ 8.30am-7pm Tue-Sat, 9.30am-3.30pm Sun; ☏; Ⓜ Sèvres-Babylone) As next-door neighbour to one of Paris' most famous bakers, this isn't your average sandwich bar. Instead, it's an ultrachic spot to lunch between designer boutiques on open sandwiches cut from that celebrated **Poilâne** (Map p106; www.poilane.fr; 8 rue du Cherche Midi, 6e; ☺ 7.15am-8.15pm Mon-Sat; Ⓜ Sèvres-Babylone) bread and fabulously topped with gourmet goodies such as foie gras, smoked duck, gooey St-Marcellin cheese and Bayonne ham.

Little Breizh
CRÊPERIE €

(Map p106; ☑ 01 43 54 60 74; www.littlebreizh.fr; 11 rue Grégoire de Tours, 6e; crêpes €4.50-12; ☺ noon-2.30pm & 7-10pm; ☑ ♿; Ⓜ Odéon) As authentic as you'd find in Brittany, but with some innovative twists (such as Breton sardines, olive oil and sundried tomatoes; goat's cheese, stewed apple, hazelnuts, rosemary and honey; smoked salmon, dill cream, pink peppercorns and lemon), the crêpes at this sweet spot are infinitely more enticing than those sold on nearby street corners. Hours can fluctuate; book ahead.

Treize
CAFE €

(Thirteen – A Baker's Dozen; Map p106; ☑ 01 73 77 27 89; 16 rue des Sts-Pères, 7e; lunch menus €13-17, brunch menus €10-23, mains €13-15; ☺ 10am-6pm Tue-Sat; ☑; Ⓜ Rue du Bac or St-Germain des Prés) Pass through a passageway, cross a cobbled courtyard and at the very end you'll find the latticed doors of Treize, a charming contemporary cafe turning out savoury pies, creative salads and sweet cakes (the carrot cake has a local following), along with unique tea blends, and coffee by Parisian roaster Coutume (p144). Perfect for whiling away an afternoon.

★ Bouillon Racine
BRASSERIE €€

(Map p102; ☑ 01 44 32 15 60; www.bouillonracine. com; 3 rue Racine, 6e; weekday lunch menu €16, menus €31-42; ☺ noon-11pm; ♿; Ⓜ Cluny–La Sorbonne) Inconspicuously situated in a quiet street, this heritage-listed 1906 art-nouveau 'soup kitchen', with mirrored walls, floral motifs and ceramic tiling, was built in 1906 to feed market workers. Despite the magnificent interior, the food – inspired by age-old recipes – is by no means an afterthought.

★ Semilla
NEOBISTRO €€

(Map p106; ☑ 01 43 54 34 50; 54 rue de Seine, 6e; lunch menu €24, mains €20-50; ☺ 12.30-2.30pm & 7-10.45pm; Ⓜ Odéon or Mabillon) Stark concrete, exposed pipes and an open kitchen (where you can book front-row 'chef seats') set the factory-style scene for edgy, modern, changing dishes like pork spare ribs with sweet potato and cinnamon, mushrooms in hazelnut butter and trout with passionfruit and ginger. Desserts are outstanding. Be sure to book.

Café Trama
MODERN FRENCH €€

(Map p106; ☑ 01 45 48 33 71; 83 rue du Cherche Midi, 6e; mains €15-22; ☺ kitchen noon-2.45pm & 7.30-10pm Tue-Sat; Ⓜ Vaneau or St-Placide) Cafe classics come with a contemporary twist at this black-awning-framed local with mellow lighting, chequered tiles, vintage furniture and pavement tables. Try the pan-fried squid with rocket and orange segments, croque monsieur with truffle salt on premium Poujauran bread, or ginger and basil beef tartare with meat from famed Parisian butcher Hugo Desnoyer, along with all-natural wines.

Brasserie Lipp
BRASSERIE €€

(Map p106; ☑ 01 45 48 53 91; 151 bd St-Germain, 6e; mains €22-38; ☺ 11.45am-12.45am; Ⓜ St-Germain des Prés) Waiters in black waistcoats, bow ties and long white aprons serve brasserie favourites like *choucroute garnie* (sauerkraut with smoked or salted pork, frankfurters and potatoes) and *jarret de porc aux lentilles* (pork knuckle with lentils) at this illustrious wood-panelled establishment. (Note: salads aren't allowed as meals.) Opened by Léonard

Lipp in 1880, the brasserie achieved immortality when Hemingway sang its praises in *A Moveable Feast*.

Roger la Grenouille — TRADITIONAL FRENCH €€
(Map p100; ☑ 01 56 24 24 34; 26-28 rue des Grands Augins, 6e; lunch/dinner menus from €22/27; ☺ 7-11pm Mon, noon-2pm & 7-11pm Tue-Sat; Ⓜ St-Michel) Scattered with frog sculptures, B&W pictures of 1920s Paris and an array of old lamps, time-worn, sepia-coloured institution 'Roger the Frog' serves nine varieties of frogs' legs such as à la Provençale (with tomato) and Normande (cooked in cider and served with apple). If you're squeamish about devouring Roger, alternatives include dishes like roast sea bass with braised fennel.

Polidor — TRADITIONAL FRENCH €€
(Map p100; ☑ 01 43 26 95 34; www.polidor.com; 41 rue Monsieur le Prince, 6e; menus €22-35; ☺ noon-2.30pm & 7pm-12.30am Mon-Sat, noon-2.30pm & 7-11pm Sun; ♿; Ⓜ Odéon) A meal at this quintessentially Parisian *crèmerie-restaurant* is like a trip to Victor Hugo's Paris: the restaurant and its decor date from 1845. *Menus* of tasty, family-style French cuisine ensure a stream of diners eager to sample *bœuf bourguignon*, *blanquette de veau à l'ancienne* (veal in white sauce) and Polidor's famous *tarte Tatin*. Expect to wait. No credit cards.

LITTLE BRITTANY

Due to Gare Montparnasse's transport links to Brittany, the surrounding streets – especially rue du Montparnasse, 14e, and rue Odessa, 14e, one block west – are lined with dozens of authentic Breton crêperies. Top picks:

Crêperie Josselin (Map p106; ☑ 01 43 20 93 50; 67 rue du Montparnasse, 14e; crêpes €7-10; ☺ 11.30am-3pm & 5-11pm Tue-Fri, 11.30am-11pm Sat & Sun; ♿; Ⓜ Edgar Quinet) Filled with dark timber furniture, painted plates and screened by lace curtains; delicious *galettes* (savoury buckwheat crêpes) include Roquefort with walnuts.

Crêperie Plougastel (Map p106; ☑ 01 42 79 90 63; www.creperie-plougastel. com; 47 rue du Montparnasse, 14e; crêpes €3.10-10.90; ☺ noon-midnight; ♿; Ⓜ Edgar Quinet) Plougastel's decor might be spartan, but its *galettes* and crêpes are anything but, with generous toppings including St-Jacques scallops.

✖ Montparnasse

In the 1920s, the area around bd du Montparnasse became one of Paris' premier avenues for cafe life, and it still harbours a handful of legendary establishments.

La Cabane à Huîtres — SEAFOOD €
(Map p106; ☑ 01 45 49 47 27; 4 rue Antoine Bourdelle, 14e; dozen oysters €17, menu €21.90; ☺ noon-2.15pm & 7-10.15pm Wed-Sat; Ⓜ Montparnasse Bienvenüe) Wonderfully rustic, this wooden-styled *cabane* (cabin) with just nine tables is the pride and joy of fifth-generation oyster farmer Françis Dubourg, who splits his time between the capital and his oyster farm in Arcachon on the Atlantic coast. The fixed menu includes a dozen oysters, foie gras, *magret de canard fumé* (smoked duck breast) or smoked salmon.

Jeu de Quilles — BISTRO €€
(☑ 01 53 90 76 22; www.jdequilles.fr; 45 rue Boulard, 14e; mains €25-40; ☺ noon-2pm Wed-Sat, 8-10pm Tue-Sat; Ⓜ Mouton-Duvernet) When your next-door neighbour is the original premises of celebrated butcher Hugo Desnoyer, you have an inside track to serve exceptional meat-based dishes, and chef Benoît Reix does at this brilliant bistro. Creations such as artichoke-paste-encrusted pork or veal carpaccio pair with an extensive selection of natural wines. Reserve ahead: there are just 18 seats and locals love it.

Jadis — NEOBISTRO €€
(☑ 01 45 57 73 20; www.bistrotjadisparis.com; 208 rue de la Croix Nivert, 15e; lunch/dinner menus from €26.50/38; ☺ 12.15-2pm & 7.15-11pm Mon-Fri; Ⓜ Boucicaut) This classy, crimson-fronted neobistro on the corner of a very unassuming street remains one of Paris' most revered (ie reserve in advance). Traditional French dishes pack a modern punch thanks to risk-taking young chef Guillaume Delage. The lunch *menu* is extraordinarily good value and the chocolate soufflé – order it at the start of your meal – is divine.

La Rotonde Montparnasse — BRASSERIE €€
(Map p106; ☑ 01 43 26 48 26; www.rotondemontparnasse.com; 105 bd du Montparnasse, 6e; 3-course menu €42, mains €14.50-42; ☺ 6am-2am, menus noon-3pm & 7-11pm; Ⓜ Vavin) Opened in 1911 and recently restored to its former glory, La Rotonde may be awash with the same Les Montparnos history as its famous neighbours like Le Select et al, but the real reason to come

STARS OF THE FUTURE

Founded in 1920 by Paris' chamber of commerce and industry, **Restaurants d'Application de Ferrandi** (Map p106; www.ferrandi-paris.fr; 28 rue de l'Abbé Grégoire, 6e; Le Premier lunch/dinner menus €25/40, Le 28 lunch/dinner menus €30/45; ⊘ by reservation Le Premier 12.30pm Tue-Fri, dinner Thu, Le 28 12.30pm Wed-Fri, 7.30pm Mon & Tue, both closed school holidays; Ⓜ St-Placide) is arguably France's most prestigious culinary school, turning out a who's who of industry professionals. You can taste these future Michelin-starred chefs' creations at bargain prices at the school's two training restaurants, Le Premier (focusing on classical French cookery) and Le 28 (high-level gastronomy), overseen by Ferrandi's esteemed professors.

is for the superior food. Meat comes from Parisian butcher extraordinaire Hugo Desnoyer, salmon and chicken are organic and brasserie classics are cooked to perfection.

Au Moulin Vert TRADITIONAL FRENCH €€
(☑ 01 45 39 31 31; www.aumoulinvert.com; 34bis rue des Plantes, 14e; lunch/dinner menus from €19.50/30; ⊘ noon-2.30pm daily, 7-10.30pm Mon-Thu, 7-11pm Fri & Sat, 7-10pm Sun; 📶; Ⓜ Alésia) The Moulin Rouge ('red windmill') might be more famous but at the opposite end of town, the 19th-century 'green windmill' is a delightful, relaxed neighbourhood restaurant opening to a glass-paned winter garden and sunlit terrace. Chef Gérard Chagot's seasonal creations like duck in cherries, cod in cider and snails in garlic are served by aproned waiters at white-clothed tables.

La Closerie des Lilas BRASSERIE €€
(Map p106; ☑ 01 40 51 34 50; www.closeriedeslilas.fr; 171 bd du Montparnasse, 6e; restaurant mains €27.50-56.50, brasserie mains €25-33; ⊘ restaurant noon-2.15pm & 7-11.30pm, brasserie noon-12.30am, piano bar 11am-1.30am; Ⓜ Vavin or RER Port Royal) Brass plaques tell you exactly where Hemingway (who wrote much of *The Sun Also Rises* here) and luminaries like Picasso, Apollinaire, Man Ray, Jean-Paul Sartre and Samuel Beckett stood, sat or fell. The 'Lilac Enclosure' is split into a late-night piano bar, upmarket restaurant and more lovable (and cheaper) brasserie with a hedged-in pavement terrace.

Le Dôme BRASSERIE €€€
(Map p106; ☑ 01 43 35 25 81; 108 bd du Montparnasse, 14e; mains €43-66.50, seafood platters €66; ⊘ noon-3pm & 7-11pm; Ⓜ Vavin) A 1930s art deco extravaganza of the formal white-tablecloth and bow-tied waiter variety, monumental Le Dôme is one of the swishest places around for shellfish platters piled high with fresh oysters, king prawns, crab claws and much more, followed by traditional creamy homemade *millefeuille* for dessert, wheeled in on a trolley and cut in front of you.

Its cheaper bistro and *poissonnerie* (fishmonger) are around the corner.

Drinking & Nightlife

In a country where eating and drinking are as inseparable as cheese and wine, it's inevitable that the line between bars, cafes and bistros is blurred at best.

Drinking in Paris essentially means paying the rent for the space you take up, meaning it costs more sitting at tables than standing at the counter, more on a fancy square than a backstreet, more in the 8e than in the 18e. Come 10pm, many cafes apply a pricier night rate.

A coffee starts at around €2, a glass of wine from around €3.50, a cocktail generally costs €8 to €15 and a *demi* (half-pint) of beer between €3.50 and €7. In clubs and chic bars, prices can easily be double this.

Paris' residential make-up means clubs aren't ubiquitous. Still, electronica, laced with funk and groove, is its strong suit; salsa and Latino also maintain a huge following. Admission to clubs is free to around €20; entry is often cheaper before 1am.

Eiffel Tower Area & 16e

★ St James Paris BAR
(☑ 01 44 05 81 81; www.saint-james-paris.com; 43 rue Bugeaud, 16e; drinks €15-25, Sun brunch €65; ⊘ 7-11pm; 📶; Ⓜ Porte Dauphine) It might be a hotel bar, but a drink at St James might well be one of your most memorable in Paris. Tucked behind a stone wall, this historic mansion opens its bar each evening to nonguests – and the setting redefines extraordinary. Winter drinks are in the library, in summer they're in the impossibly romantic garden.

Étoile & Champs-Élysées

Charlie Birdy PUB
(Map p66; www.charliebirdy.com; 124 rue de la Boétie, 8e; ⊘ noon-5am; 📶; Ⓜ Franklin D Roosevelt)

GAY & LESBIAN PARIS

The city known as 'gay Paree' lives up to its name. Paris is so open that there's less of a defined 'scene' here than other cities where it's more underground, and you'll find venues right throughout the city attracting a mixed crowd.

Le Marais, especially the areas around the intersection of rue Ste-Croix de la Bretonnerie and rue des Archives, and eastwards to rue Vieille du Temple, has been Paris' main centre of gay nightlife for some three decades and is still the epicentre of gay and lesbian life in Paris. There's also a handful of bars and clubs within walking distance of bd de Sébastopol. The lesbian scene is less prominent than its gay counterpart, and centres around a few cafes and bars in Le Marais, particularly along rue des Écouffes.

The **Centre Gai et Lesbien de Paris** (CGL; Map p90; ✆01 43 57 21 47; www.centre lgbtparis.org; 63 rue Beaubourg, 3e; ⊘centre & bar 3.30-8pm Mon-Fri, 1-7pm Sat, library 6-8pm Mon-Wed, 3.30-6pm Fri, 5-7pm Sat; Ⓜ Rambuteau or Arts et Métiers), with a large library and sociable bar, is the single best source of information in Paris for gay and lesbian travellers.

Top choices are:

Open Café (Map p90; www.opencafe.fr; 17 rue des Archives, 4e; ⊘11am-2am; Ⓜ Hôtel de Ville) The wide terrace is prime for talent-watching.

Scream Club (Map p90; www.scream-paris.com; 18 rue du Faubourg du Temple, 11e; admission €15; ⊘midnight-7am Sat; Ⓜ Belleville or Goncourt) Saturday's the night at 'Paris' biggest gay party'.

3W Kafé (Map p90; 8 rue des Écouffes, 4e; ⊘8pm-3am Wed & Thu, to 5.30am Fri & Sat; Ⓜ St-Paul) The name of this sleek spot stands for 'women with women'.

Queen (Map p66; ✆01 53 89 08 90; www.queen.fr; 102 av des Champs-Élysées, 8e; ⊘11.30pm-6.30am; Ⓜ George V) Don't miss disco night!

La Champmeslé (Map p74; www.lachampmesle.com; 4 rue Chabanais, 2e; ⊘4pm-dawn Mon-Sat; Ⓜ Pyramides) Cabaret nights, fortune-telling and art exhibitions attract an older lesbian crowd.

Le Tango (Map p90; www.boiteafrissons.fr; 13 rue au Maire, 3e; admission €6-9; ⊘10.30pm-5am Fri & Sat, 6-11pm Sun; Ⓜ Arts et Métiers) Historic 1930s dancehall hosting legendary gay tea dances.

This kick-back brick-walled place just off the Champs-Élysées is easily the most inviting pub in the neighbourhood. The usual array of bar food (burgers, hot dogs, more burgers...) is available; DJs hit the decks on weekend nights.

ShowCase   CLUB
(Map p66; www.showcase.fr; Port des Champs-Élysées, 8e; ⊘11.30pm-6am Thu-Sat; Ⓜ Invalides or Champs-Élysées-Clemenceau) This gigantic electro club has solved the neighbour-versus-noise problem that haunts so many Parisian nightlife spots: it's secreted beneath the Pont Alexandre III bridge alongside the Seine. Unlike other exclusive Champs backstreet clubs, the Showcase can pack 'em in (up to 1500 clubbers) and is less stringent about its door policy, though you'll still want to dress like a star.

🍷 Louvre & Les Halles

Angelina   TEAROOM
(Map p74; 226 rue de Rivoli, 1er; ⊘8am-7pm Mon-Fri, 9am-7pm Sat & Sun; Ⓜ Tuileries) Clink china with lunching ladies, their posturing poodles and half the students from Tokyo University at Angelina, a grand dame of a tearoom dating to 1903. Decadent pastries are served here, against a fresco backdrop of belle époque Nice, but it is the superthick, decadently sickening 'African' hot chocolate (€8.20), which comes with a pot of whipped cream and a carafe of water, that prompts the constant queue for a table at Angelina.

Harry's New York Bar   COCKTAIL BAR
(Map p74; www.harrysbar.fr; 5 rue Daunou, 2e; ⊘noon-2am; Ⓜ Opéra) One of the most popular American-style bars in the prewar years, Harry's once welcomed writers like F Scott

Fitzgerald and Ernest Hemingway, who no doubt sampled the bar's unique cocktail and creation: the Bloody Mary. The Cuban mahogany interior dates from the mid-19th century and was brought over from a Manhattan bar in 1911.

Experimental Cocktail Club COCKTAIL BAR
(Map p74; www.experimentalcocktailclub.com; 37 rue St-Saveur, 2e; ☺7pm-2am daily; Ⓜ Réaumur-Sébastopol) Called ECC by trendies, this fabulous speakeasy with grey façade and old-beamed ceiling is effortlessly hip. Oozing spirit and soul, the cocktail bar – with retrochic decor by American interior designer Cuoco Black and sister bars in London and New York – is a sophisticated flashback to those *années folles* (crazy years) of Prohibition New York.

Le Garde Robe WINE BAR
(Map p74; 41 rue de l'Arbre Sec, 1er, ☺12.30-2.30pm & 7.30-11pm Mon-Fri; Ⓜ Louvre Rivoli) The Garde Robe is possibly the only bar in the world to serve alcohol alongside a 'Detox' menu. While you probably shouldn't come here for the full-on cleansing experience, you can definitely expect excellent, affordable natural wines, a casual atmosphere and a good selection of eats, ranging from the standard cheese and charcuterie plates to more adventurous veg-friendly options.

Le Rex Club CLUB
(Map p84; www.rexclub.com; 5 bd Poissonnière, 2e; ☺midnight-7am Thu-Sat; Ⓜ Bonne Nouvelle) Attached to the art-deco Grand Rex cinema, this is Paris' premier house and techno venue where some of the world's hottest DJs strut their stuff on a 70-speaker, multidiffusion sound system.

Lockwood CAFE
(Map p74; 73 rue d'Aboukir, 2e; ☺8am-2am Mon-Sat; Ⓜ Sentier) A handy address for hip coffee lovers. Savour beans from the Belleville Brûlerie (p144) during the day and well-mixed cocktails in the subterranean candle-lit *cave* at night.

Kong BAR
(Map p74; www.kong.fr; 1 rue du Pont Neuf, 1er; ☺12.15-11.30pm daily; Ⓜ Pont Neuf) Evenings at this Philippe Starck–designed riot of iridescent champagne-coloured vinyl booths, Japanese cartoon cut-outs and garden-gnome stools see Paris' glam young set guzzling Dom Pérignon, nibbling at tapas-style platters (mains

€20 to €40) and shaking their designer-clad booty on the tables.

☕ Montmartre & Pigalle

La Fourmi BAR
(Map p80; 74 rue des Martyrs, 18e; ☺8am-1am Mon-Thu, to 3am Fri & Sat, 10am-1am Sun; Ⓜ Pigalle) A Pigalle institution, La Fourmi hits the mark with its high ceilings, long zinc bar and unpretentious vibe. Get up to speed on live music and club nights or sit down for a reasonably priced meal and drinks.

La Machine du Moulin Rouge CLUB
(Map p80; 90 bd de Clichy, 18e; ☺hours vary; Ⓜ Blanche) Part of the original Moulin Rouge (well, the boiler room, anyway), this club packs 'em in on weekends with a dance floor, concert hall, champagne bar and outdoor terrace.

Cave des Abbesses WINE BAR
(Map p80; 43 rue des Abbesses, 18e; cheese & charcuterie €7-13; ☺5-9.30pm Tue-Sun; Ⓜ Abbesses) Pass through the door at the back of the Cave des Abbesses wine shop and you'll discover, no, not a storage room or a portal to another dimension, but instead a quirky little bar. It feels like one of those places only regulars know about, but don't be intimidated; sit down, order a plate of cheese and a glass of Corbières, and you'll blend right in.

☕ Gare du Nord, Gare de l'Est & Canal St-Martin

Chez Prune BAR
(Map p90; 71 quai de Valmy, 10e; ☺8am-2am Mon-Sat, 10am-2am Sun; Ⓜ République) This Soho-boho cafe put Canal St-Martin on the map

---

BEST BAR-HOPPING STREETS

Prime Parisian streets (and their surrounds) for a *soirée* (evening out):

Rue Vieille du Temple, 4e Marais cocktail of gay bars and chic cafes.

Rue Oberkampf, 11e Edgy urban hangouts.

Rue de Lappe, 11e Boisterous Bastille bars and clubs.

Rue de la Butte aux Cailles, 13e Village atmosphere and fun local haunts.

Rue Princesse, 6e Student and sports bars.

LOCAL KNOWLEDGE

RUE MONTMARTRE

In the Louvre and Les Halles neighbourhood, rue Montmartre is dotted with appealing places to sip a *café* or cocktail.

A good place to start (or end) is **Le Tambour** (Map p74; ☑ 01 42 33 06 90; 41 rue Montmartre, 2e; ⊙ 8am-6am; Ⓜ Étienne Marcel or Sentier), a mecca for Parisian night owls with its long hours (food served until 3.30am or 4am), recycled street furniture and old metro maps.

a decade ago and its good vibes and rough-around-the-edges look show no sign of fading in the near future.

L'Atmosphère   BAR

(Map p90; 49 rue Lucien Sampaix, 10e; ⊙ 9.30am-1.45am Mon-Sat, to midnight Sun; Ⓜ Jacques Bonsergent or Gare de l'Est) A nod to the 1938 flick *Hôtel du Nord* (p85), this timber-and-tile cafe along the canal has an arty, spirited ambience, well-priced drinks and good food.

Chez Jeannette   BAR

(Map p84; www.chezjeannette.com; 47 rue du Faubourg St-Denis, 10e; ⊙ 8am-2am; Ⓜ Château d'Eau) Cracked tile floors and original 1950s decor have turned Chez Jeannette into one of the 10e's most popular hot spots. Local hang-out by day, pints by night and reasonably priced meals around the clock.

🍸 Ménilmontant & Belleville

★ Le Barbouquin   CAFE

(Map p90; www.lebarbouquin.fr; 3 rue Ramponeau, 20e; ⊙ 10.30am-6pm Tue-Sat; Ⓜ Belleville) There is no lovelier spot to relax in a vintage armchair over a cup of organic tea or freshly juiced carrot and apple cocktail after a hectic morning at Belleville market. Secondhand books – to be borrowed, exchanged or bought – line one wall and the twinset of pavement-terrace tables outside sit on magnificently graffitied rue Dénoyez. Breakfast and weekend brunch.

Café Charbon   BAR

(Map p90; www.lecafecharbon.com; 109 rue Oberkampf, 11e; ⊙ 9am-2am; 🛜; Ⓜ Parmentier) With its post-industrial belle époque ambience, the Charbon was the first of the hip cafes and bars to catch on in Ménilmontant. It's always crowded and worth heading to for the dis-

tressed decor with high ceilings, chandeliers and perched DJ booth.

Café Chéri(e)   BAR

(Map p90; 44 bd de la Villette, 19e; ⊙ noon-1am; Ⓜ Belleville) An imaginative, colourful bar with its signature red lighting, infamous mojitos and *caipirinhas* and commitment to quality tunes, Chéri(e) is everyone's darling in this part of town. Gritty art-chic crowd and electro DJs Thursday to Saturday.

Zéro Zéro   BAR

(Map p90; www.radiozerozero.com; 89 rue Amelot, 11e; ⊙ 7.30pm-midnight Mon-Sat; Ⓜ St-Sébastien Froissart) Zéro Zéro screams Berlin with its banquet seating and tag-covered walls (and ceiling, and windows, and bar...). Electro and house is the sound and the house cocktail, a potent rum-and-ginger concoction, ensures a wild party spirit.

🍸 Le Marais & Bastille

★ Le Baron Rouge   WINE BAR

(Map p98; 1 rue Théophile Roussel, 12e; ⊙ 10am-2pm & 5-10pm Tue-Fri, 10am-10pm Sat, 10am-4pm Sun; Ⓜ Ledru-Rollin) Just about the ultimate Parisian wine-bar experience, this place has barrels stacked against the bottle-lined walls. As unpretentious as you'll find, it's a local meeting place where everyone is welcome and it's especially busy on Sunday after the Marché d'Aligre (p124) wraps up. All the usual suspects – cheese, charcuterie and oysters – will keep your belly full.

★ Le Mary Céleste   COCKTAIL BAR

(Map p90; www.lemaryceleste.com; 1 rue Commines, 3e; cocktails €12-13, tapas €8-12; ⊙ 6pm-2am; Ⓜ Filles du Calvaire) Predictably there's a distinct nautical feel to this fashionable, uber-cool cocktail bar in the Marais. Snag a stool at the central circular bar or play savvy and reserve one of a handful of tables (in advance online). Cocktails are creative and the perfect partner to a dozen oysters or your pick of a dozen-odd, tapas-style 'small plates' designed to be shared.

★ Le Cap Horn   BAR

(Map p90; 8 rue de Birague, 4e; ⊙ 10am-1am; Ⓜ St-Paul or Chemin Vert) On summer evenings the ambience at this laid-back, Chilean bar is electric. The crowd spills onto the pavement, parked cars doubling as table tops for well-shaken pina coladas, punch cocos and cocktails made with pisco, a fiery Chilean grape *eau-de-vie* (brandy). Find it steps from place des Vosges.

★ Broken Arm — CAFE

(Map p90; ☑ 01 44 61 53 60; 2 rue Perrée, 3e; ☺ 9am-6pm Tue-Sat, lunch noon-3.30pm; ☎; Ⓜ Temple or Arts et Métiers) Kick off with a freshly squeezed apple, kiwi and mint juice and congratulate yourself on scoring a table – inside or out – at this overpoweringly hipster address where the chic folk of Marais lunch after making an appearance in the adjoining concept store. The menu is limited but packed with goodness: excellent salads, cold platters and cakes.

Le Pure Café — CAFE

(Map p98; www.purecafe.fr; 14 rue Jean Macé, 11e; ☺ 7am-2am Mon-Fri, 8am-2am Sat, 9am-midnight Sun; Ⓜ Charonne) A classic Parisian haunt, this rustic, cherry-red corner cafe featured in the art-house film *Before Sunset,* but it's still a refreshingly unpretentious spot for a drink, cheese or chacuterie platters, fusion cuisine or Sunday brunch.

Le Loir dans La Théière — CAFE

(Map p90; 3 rue des Rosiers, 4e; ☺ 9am 7.30pm; Ⓜ St-Paul) Its cutesy name (Dormouse in the Teapot) notwithstanding, this is a wonderful old space filled with retro toys, comfy couches and scenes of *Through the Looking Glass* on the walls. It's dozen different types of tea poured in the company of excellent savoury tarts and crumble-type desserts ensure a constant queue on the street outside. Breakfast and brunch too.

La Fée Verte — BAR

(Map p90; 108 rue de la Roquette, 11e; ☺ 8am-2am Mon-Sat, 9am-2am Sun; ☎; Ⓜ Voltaire) You guessed it, the 'Green Fairy' specialises in absinthe (served traditionally with spoons and sugar cubes), but this fabulously old-fashioned neighbourhood cafe and bar also serves terrific food.

Le Barav — WINE BAR

(Map p90; ☑ 01 48 04 57 59; www.lebarav.fr; 6 rue Charles-François Dupuis, 3e; ☺ noon-3pm Mon-Fri, 6pm-12.30am Tue-Sat; Ⓜ Temple) This hipster *bar à vin,* smart in the trendy Haut Marais, oozes atmosphere – and one of the city's loveliest pavement terraces. Its extensive wine list is complemented by tasty food.

L'Ebouillanté — CAFE

(Map p90; http://ebouillante.pagesperso-orange.fr; 6 rue des Barres, 4e; ☺ noon-10pm summer, to 7pm winter; Ⓜ Hôtel de Ville) On sunny days there is no prettier cafe terrace. Enjoying a privileged position on a pedestrian, stone-flagged street just footsteps from the Seine, L'Ebouillanté buzzes with savvy Parisians sipping refreshing glasses of homemade *citronnade* (ginger lemonade), hibiscus flower cordial and herbal teas. Delicious cakes, jumbo salads, savoury crêpes and Sunday brunch (€21) complement the long drinks menu.

Aux Deux Amis — CAFE, BAR

(Map p90; ☑ 01 58 30 38 13; 45 rue Oberkampf, 11e; ☺ 8am-2am Tue-Sat; Ⓜ Oberkampf) From the well-worn, tiled floor to the day's menu scrawled in marker on the vintage mirror behind the bar (two-/three-course lunch menu €18/22), Aux Deux Amis is the quintessential Parisian neighbourhood bar. It's perfect for coffee any time and at dusk it serves tapas-style dishes. Friday brings the house speciality – *tartare de cheval* (hand-chopped horsemeat seasoned with a secret mix of herbs).

Café La Fusée — BAR

(Map p90; 168 rue St-Martin, 3e; ☺ 8am-2am daily; Ⓜ Rambuteau or Étienne Marcel) A short walk from the Pompidou, the Rocket is a lively, laid-back indie hang-out with a red-and-white striped awning strung with fairy lights outside, and paint-peeling, tobacco-coloured walls indoors. You can grab simple meals here (€8 to €13), and it's got a decent wine selection by the glass.

Boot Café — CAFE

(Map p90; 19 rue du Pont aux Choux, 3e; ☺ 8.30am-7.30pm Tue-Fri, 10am-6pm Sat; Ⓜ Filles du Calvaire) The charm of this three-table ode to good coffee is its façade, which must win the prize for 'most photographed' An old cobbler's shop, the original washed-blue façade and 'Cordonnerie' lettering have been beautifully preserved, as has the red boot sign above. Excellent coffee, roasted in Paris, to boot.

Twenty One Sound Bar — CLUB

(Map p98; 20 rue de la Forge Royale, 11e; ☺ 8pm-2am Tue-Thu, from 9pm Fri & Sat; Ⓜ Faidherbe-Chaligny) Stark steel and concrete amp up the acoustics at this hip-hop haven, with renowned (sometimes legendary) DJs mixing on the decks and regular drinks specials.

🅣 The Islands

Taverne Henri IV — WINE BAR

(Map p100; 13 place du Pont Neuf, 1er; ☺ 11.30am-11pm Mon-Sat, closed Aug; Ⓜ Pont Neuf) One of the few places to drink on Île de la Cité, this wine bar dates to 1885 and lures a fair few

LOCAL KNOWLEDGE

COFFEE REVOLUTION

Bitter Parisian coffee is becoming a thing of the past: the city is in the throes of a coffee revolution, with local roasteries priming cafes citywide for outstanding brews made by professional baristas, often using cutting-edge extraction techniques. Caffeine fiends are now spoilt for choice and while there's still plenty of substandard coffee in Paris, you don't have to go far to avoid it. Leading the charge:

Belleville Brûlerie (☑ 09 83 75 60 80; http://cafesbelleville.com; 10 rue Pradier, 19e; 300g packet €13-16; ⊙ 11.30am-6.30pm Sat; Ⓜ Belleville) Groundbreaking roastery with Saturday morning tastings 'n' cuppings.

Coutume (http://coutumecafe.com; 47 rue Babylone, 7e; ⊙ 8am-7pm Mon-Fri, from 10am Sat & Sun; 🛜; Ⓜ St-François Xavier or Vaneau) 🌿 Artisan roasters of premium beans, with a fab flagship cafe.

La Caféothèque (Map p90; www.lacafeotheque.com; 52 rue de l'Hôtel de Ville, 4e; ⊙ 9.30am-7.30pm; 🛜; Ⓜ St-Paul or Hôtel de Ville) Maze of a coffee house with tasting notes and seating made to lounge on all day.

Holybelly (Map p84; http://holybel.ly; 19 rue Lucien Sampaix, 10e; ⊙ 9am-6pm Thu-Mon, from 10am Sat & Sun; Ⓜ Jacques Bonsergent) The flagbearer for Canal St-Martin's new crop of coffee specialists; distressed decor, a serious kitchen and a pinball machine.

Tuck Shop (Map p84; 13 rue Lucien Sampaix, 10e; ⊙ 10am-5pm Tue-Fri, 11am-6pm Sat & Sun; Ⓜ Jacques Bonsergent) Superb brews at this Aussie-run vegetarian hang-out.

Telescope (Map p74; www.telescopecafe.com; 5 rue Villedo, 1er; ⊙ 8.30am-5pm Mon-Fri, 9.30am-6.30pm Sat; Ⓜ Pyramides) It may be small, but it packs a punch.

legal types from the nearby Palais de Justice (not to mention celeb writers and actors, as the autographed snaps testify). A tasty choice of *tartines*, charcuterie and cheese platters complement its extensive wine list.

🍷 Latin Quarter

Le Verre à Pied   CAFE
(Map p102; http://leverreapied.fr; 118bis rue Mouffetard, 5e; ⊙ 9am-9pm Tue-Sat, 9.30am-4pm Sun; Ⓜ Censier Daubenton) This *café-tabac* is a pearl of a place where little has changed since 1870. Its nicotine-hued mirrored wall, moulded cornices and original bar make it part of a dying breed, but the place oozes the charm, glamour and romance of an old Paris everyone loves, including stall holders from the rue Mouffetard market who yo-yo in and out.

Curio Parlor Cocktail Club   COCKTAIL BAR
(Map p102; www.curioparlor.com; 16 rue des Bernardins, 5e; ⊙ 7pm-2am Mon-Thu, to 4am Fri-Sun; Ⓜ Maubert-Mutualité) Run by the same switched-on, chilled-out team as the Experimental Cocktail Club, this hybrid bar-club looks to the interwar *années folles* of 1920s Paris, London and New York for inspiration. Its racing-green façade with a simple brass plaque on the door is the height of discretion.

Go to its Facebook page to find out which party is happening when.

Le Pub St-Hilaire   PUB
(Map p102; 2 rue Valette, 5e; ⊙ 3pm-2am Mon-Thu, 3pm-4am Fri, 4pm-4am Sat, 4pm-midnight Sun; Ⓜ Maubert-Mutualité) 'Buzzing' fails to do justice to the pulsating vibe inside this student-loved pub. Generous happy hours last several hours and the place is kept packed with a trio of pool tables, board games, music on two floors, hearty bar food and various gimmicks to rev up the party crowd (a metre of cocktails, 'be your own barman' etc).

Le Vieux Chêne   BAR
(Map p102; 69 rue Mouffetard, 5e; ⊙ 4pm-2am Sun-Thu, to 5am Fri & Sat; Ⓜ Place Monge) This rue Mouffetard institution is reckoned to be Paris' oldest bar. Indeed, a revolutionary circle met here in 1848 and it was a popular *bal musette* (dancing club) in the late 19th and early 20th centuries. These days it's a student favourite, especially during happy hour (4pm to 9pm Tuesday to Sunday, and from 4pm until closing on Monday).

Place d'Italie & Chinatown

★ Le Batofar   CLUB
(Map p98; www.batofar.org; opposite 11 quai François Mauriac, 13e; ☺ bar 12.30pm-midnight Tue, to 6am Wed-Fri, 6pm-6am Sat; Ⓜ Quai de la Gare or Bibliothèque) This much-loved, red-metal tugboat has a rooftop bar that's terrific in summer, and a respected restaurant, while the club underneath provides memorable underwater acoustics between its metal walls and portholes. Le Batofar is known for its edgy, experimental music policy and live performances, mostly electro-oriented but also incorporating hip-hop, new wave, rock, punk or jazz.

St-Germain

★ Les Deux Magots   CAFE
(Map p106; www.lesdeuxmagots.fr; 170 bd St Germain, 6e; ☺ 7.30am-1am; Ⓜ St-Germain des Prés) If ever there were a cafe that summed up St-Germain des Prés' early-20th-century literary scene, it's this former hang-out of anyone who was anyone. You will spend *beaucoup* to sip a coffee in a wicker chair on the terrace shaded by dark-green awnings and geraniums spilling from window boxes, but it's an undeniable piece of Parisian history.

★ Au Sauvignon   WINE BAR
(Map p106; 80 rue des St-Pères, 7e; ☺ 8.30am-10pm Mon-Sat, to 9pm Sun; Ⓜ Sèvres-Babylone) Grab a table in the evening sun at this wonderfully authentic *bar à vin* or head to the quintessential bistro interior, with an original zinc bar, tightly packed tables and hand-painted ceiling celebrating French viticultural tradition. A plate of *casse-croûtes au pain Poilâne* – toast with ham, pâté, terrine, smoked salmon, foie gras – is the perfect accompaniment.

Castor Club   COCKTAIL BAR
(Map p100; 14 rue Hautefeuille, 6e; ☺ 7pm-4am Wed-Sat; Ⓜ Odéon) Discreetly signed, this underground cocktail bar has an intimate upstairs bar and 18th-century cellar with hole-in-the-wall booths where you can sip superb-value cocktails (custom-made, if you like) and groove to smooth '50s, '60s and '70s tracks. Very cool.

Alain Milliat   JUICE BAR
(Map p64; ☎ 01 45 55 63 86; www.alain-milliat.com; 159 rue de Grenelle, 7e; ☺ 11am-3pm & 6pm-midnight Tue-Fri, 9am-midnight Sat, 10am-6pm Sun; Ⓜ La Tour Maubourg) Alain Milliat's fruit juices, bottled in the south of France, were once reserved for ultra-exclusive hotels and restaurants. But you can pop into his Parisian juice bar–bistro to buy one of the 33 varieties of juice and nectar, or sip them in-house. Stunning flavours include rosé-grape or green-tomato juice and white-peach nectar.

Le 10   PUB
(Map p106; http://10bar.pagesperso-orange.fr; 10 rue de l'Odéon, 6e; ☺ 6pm-2am; Ⓜ Odéon) Plastered with posters, cellar pub 'Le Dix' is a student favourite, not least for its cheap sangria. An eclectic selection emerges from the jukebox – everything from jazz and the Doors to traditional French *chansons* (à la Édith Piaf). It's the ideal spot for plotting the next revolution or conquering a lonely heart.

Brasserie O'Neil   MICROBREWERY
(Map p106; www.oneilbar.fr; 20 rue des Canettes, 6e; ☺ noon-2am; Ⓜ St-Sulpice or Mabillon) Paris' first microbrewery was opened by a French restaurateur and French brewer more than two decades ago, and still brews four fabulous beers (blond, amber, bitter brown and citrusy white) on the premises. Soak them up with thin-crusted *flammekueches* (Alsatian pizzas).

Jane Club   CLUB
(Map p106; www.wagg.fr; 62 rue Mazarine, 6e; ☺ 10.30pm-6am Fri & Sat, 3.30pm-2am Sun; ☎; Ⓜ Odéon) Formerly Le Wagg and kitted out with a kickin' new sound system, Jane Club is a temple to golden '80s, golden '90s and timeless rock and roll. You can also catch live

---

ⓘ WHAT'S ON

Paris' two top listings guides *Pariscope* (€0.50) and **L'Officiel des Spectacles** (www.offi.fr; €0.50), both in French but easy to navigate, are available from newsstands on Wednesday, and are crammed with everything that's on in the capital.

Useful websites:

LYLO (www.lylo.fr) Short for Les Yeux, Les Oreilles (meaning 'eyes and ears'), offering the lowdown on the live music, concert and clubbing scenes.

Le Figaro Scope (www.figaroscope.fr) Has a great search tool for concerts by *arrondissement* – click on the map.

Paris Nightlife (www.parisnightlife.fr) All-encompassing listings site.

ⓘ THEATRE & CONCERT TICKETS

The most convenient place to purchase concert, theatre and other cultural and sporting event tickets is from electronics and entertainment megashop **Fnac** (Map p106; ☑ 08 92 68 36 22; www.fnactickets.com), whether in person at the *billeteries* (ticket offices) or by phone or online. There are branches throughout Paris including in the Forum des Halles.

On the day of performance, theatre, opera and ballet tickets are sold for half price (plus €3 commission) at the central **Kiosque Théâtre Madeleine** (Map p66; opposite 15 place de la Madeleine, 8e; ⊙ 12.30-8pm Tue-Sat, to 4pm Sun; Ⓜ Madeleine).

---

concerts here (Pete Doherty, for example). Salsa takes place every Sunday. Hours can vary.

☆ Entertainment

Catching a performance in Paris is a treat. French and international opera, ballet and theatre companies, and cabaret dancers take to the stage in venues of mythical proportion, and a flurry of young, passionate, highly creative musicians, thespians and artists make the city's fascinating fringe art scene what it is.

Cabaret

Whirling lines of feather boa-clad, high-kicking dancers at grand-scale cabarets like the can-can creator, the Moulin Rouge, are a quintessential fixture on Paris' entertainment scene – for everyone but Parisians. Still, the dazzling sets, costumes and dancing guarantee an entertaining evening (or matinee). Tickets to these spectacles start from around €90 (from €130 with lunch, from €150 with dinner), and usually include a half-bottle of Champagne.

Moulin Rouge   CABARET
(Map p80; ☑ 01 53 09 82 82; www.moulinrouge.fr; 82 bd de Clichy, 18e; Ⓜ Blanche) Immortalised in the posters of Toulouse-Lautrec and later on screen by Baz Luhrmann, the Moulin Rouge twinkles beneath a 1925 replica of its original red windmill. Yes, it's rife with bus-tour crowds. But from the opening bars of music to the last high kick it's a whirl of fantastical costumes, sets, choreography and Champagne. Booking advised.

Live Music

Cosmopolitan Paris is a first-class stage for classical music and big-name rock, pop and independent acts, and Paris-bred world music is renowned. The city became Europe's most important jazz centre after WWII, and clubs and cellars still lure international stars. You'll also find fantastically atmospheric *chanson* venues.

Palais Omnisports de Paris-Bercy (Map p98; ☑ 01 40 02 60 60; www.bercy.fr; 8 bd de Bercy, 12e; Ⓜ Bercy), **Le Zénith** (☑ 01 55 80 09 38, 08 90 71 02 07; www.le-zenith.com; 211 av Jean Jaurès, 19e; Ⓜ Porte de Pantin) and **Stade de France** (☑ 08 92 39 01 00; www.stadefrance.com; rue Francis de Pressensé, ZAC du Cornillon Nord, St-Denis La Plaine; Ⓜ St-Denis-Porte de Paris) are Paris' big-name venues. But it's the smaller concert halls loaded with history and charm that most fans favour; **La Cigale** (Map p80; ☑ 01 49 25 89 99; www.lacigale.fr; 120 bd de Rochechouart, 18e; admission €25-60; Ⓜ Anvers or Pigalle) and **L'Olympia** (Map p78; ☑ 08 92 68 33 68; www.olympiahall.com; 28 bd des Capucines, 9e; Ⓜ Opéra) are two of many.

For a classical concert to remember, visit the 2400-seat, Jean Nouvel–designed **Philharmonie de Paris** (www.philharmoniedeparis. com; Parc de la Villette, 19e; Ⓜ Porte de Pantin) when it opens in the Parc de la Villette in 2015.

Point Éphémère   LIVE MUSIC
(www.pointephemere.org; 200 quai de Valmy, 10e; ⊙ 12.30pm-2am Mon-Sat, 12.30-11pm Sun; 🎵; Ⓜ Louis Blanc) This arts and music venue by the Canal St-Martin attracts an underground crowd from noon until past midnight, for drinks, meals, concerts, dance nights and even art exhibitions. At the time of writing there were three different food trucks setting up shop here three days a week after 7pm.

Salle Pleyel   CLASSICAL
(Map p66; ☑ 01 42 56 13 13; www.sallepleyel.fr; 252 rue du Faubourg St-Honoré, 8e; ⊙ box office noon-7pm Mon-Sat, to 8pm on day of performance, 11am to 2hr prior to performance Sun; Ⓜ Ternes) Dating from the 1920s, this highly regarded hall hosts many of Paris' finest classical-music recitals and concerts.

Le Nouveau Casino   LIVE MUSIC
(Map p90; www.nouveaucasino.net; 109 rue Oberkampf, 11e; ⊙ Tue-Sun; Ⓜ Parmentier) This club-concert annexe of Café Charbon (p142) has made a name for itself amid the bars of Oberkampf with its live music concerts (usu-

ally Tuesday, Thursday and Friday) and lively club nights on weekends. Electro, pop, deep house, rock – the program is eclectic, underground and always up to the minute. Check the website for listings.

Le Baiser Salé
LIVE MUSIC
(Map p74; www.lebaisersale.com; 58 rue des Lombards, 1er; ⊘ daily; Ⓜ Châtelet) Known for its Afro and Latin jazz, and jazz fusion concerts, the Salty Kiss combines big names and unknown artists. The place has a relaxed vibe, with sets usually starting at 7.30pm or 9.30pm.

Le Vieux Belleville
LIVE MUSIC
(www.le-vieux-belleville.com; 12 rue des Envierges, 20e; ⊘ 11am-3pm Mon-Fri, 8pm-2am Thu-Sat; Ⓜ Pyrénées) This old-fashioned bistro and *musette* at the top of Parc de Belleville is an atmospheric venue for performances of *chansons* featuring accordions and an organ grinder three times a week. It's a lively favourite with locals, so booking ahead is advised.

Bus Palladium
LIVE MUSIC
(www.lebuspalladium.com; 6 rue Pierre Fontaine, 9c; ⊘ hours vary; Ⓜ Blanche) Once the place to be back in the 1960s, the Bus is now back in business 50 years later, with funky DJs and a mixed bag of performances by indie and pop groups.

Cabaret Sauvage
WORLD MUSIC
(www.cabaretsauvage.com; 221 av Jean Jaurès, 19e; ⊘ hours vary; Ⓜ Porte de la Villette) This very cool space in the Parc de la Villette (it looks like a gigantic yurt) is host to African, reggae and raï concerts as well as DJ nights that last till dawn. Occasional hip-hop and indie acts also pass through.

Badaboum
LIVE MUSIC
(Map p90; www.badaboum-paris.com; 2bis rue des Taillandiers, 11e; ⊘ cocktail bar 7pm-2am Wed-Sat, club & concerts vary; Ⓜ Bastille or Ledru-Rollin) Formerly La Scène Bastille and freshly refitted, the onomatopoeically named Badaboum hosts a mixed bag of concerts on its up-close-and-personal stage but focuses on electro, funk and hip-hop. Great atmosphere, super cocktails and a secret room upstairs.

Au Limonaire
LIVE MUSIC
(Map p78; ☑ 01 45 23 33 33; http://limonaire.free.fr; 18 cité Bergère, 9e; ⊘ 6pm-2am Tue-Sat, from 7pm Sun & Mon; Ⓜ Grands Boulevards) This perfect little wine bar is one of the best places to listen to traditional French *chansons* and local singer-songwriters. Performances begin at 10pm Tuesday to Saturday and 7pm on Sunday. Entry is free; reservations are recommended if you plan on dining.

Cinema
The film-lover's ultimate city, Paris has some wonderful movie houses to catch new flicks, avant-garde cinema and priceless classics. Foreign films (including English-language films) screened in their original language with French subtitles are labelled 'VO' (*version originale*). Films labelled 'VF' (*version française*) are dubbed in French. Pariscope and L'Officiel des Spectacles list the full crop of Paris' cinematic pickings and screening times; online check out http://cinema. leparisien.fr.

Films set in Paris are the centrepiece of the city's film archive, the **Forum des Images** (Map p74; www.forumdesimages.fr; 1 Grande Galerie, Porte St-Eustache, Forum des Halles, 1er; ⊘ 1-10pm Tue-Fri, from 2pm Sat & Sun; Ⓜ Les Halles). Film

---

BUSKERS IN PARIS

Paris' eclectic gaggle of clowns, mime artists, living statues, acrobats, roller-bladers, buskers and other street entertainers cost substantially less than a theatre ticket (a few coins in the hat is appreciated). Some excellent musicians perform in the long, echo-filled corridors of the metro, a highly prized privilege that artists audition for. Outside, you can be sure of a good show at the following spots:

Place Georges Pompidou, 4e The huge square in front of the Centre Pompidou.

Pont St-Louis, 4e The bridge linking Paris' two islands.

Pont au Double, 4e The pedestrian bridge linking Notre Dame with the Left Bank.

Place Joachim du Bellay, 1er Musicians and fire-eaters near the Fontaine des Innocents.

Parc de la Villette, 19e (p81) African drummers on the weekend.

Place du Tertre, 18e (p79) Montmartre's original main square is Paris' busiest busker stage.

buffs also shouldn't miss the **Cinémathèque Française** (Map p98; www.cinematheque.fr; 51 rue de Bercy, 12e; exhibits adult/child €6/3; ⊗ noon-7pm Mon & Wed-Sat, to 8pm Sun; Ⓜ Bercy), with two museums, a film library and screenings.

Cinéma La Pagode   CINEMA
(Ⓓ 01 45 55 48 48; www.etoile-cinema.com; 57bis rue de Babylone, 7e; Ⓜ St-François Xavier) This 19th-century Japanese pagoda was converted into a cinema in the 1930s and remains the most atmospheric spot in Paris to catch arthouse and classic films. Don't miss a moment or two in its bamboo-enshrined garden.

Theatre

Most theatre productions, including those originally written in other languages, are performed in French. English-speaking troupes very occasionally play at smaller venues around town.

Comédie Française   THEATRE
(Map p74; www.comedie-francaise.fr; place Colette, 1er; Ⓜ Palais Royal–Musée du Louvre) Founded in 1680 under Louis XIV, this state-run theatre bases its repertoire around the works of classic French playwrights. The theatre has its roots in an earlier company directed by Molière at the Palais Royal – the French playwright and actor was seized by a convulsion on stage during the fourth performance of the *Imaginary Invalid* in 1673 and died later at his home on nearby rue de Richelieu.

Opera & Ballet

France's Opéra National de Paris and Ballet de l'Opéra National de Paris perform at Paris' two opera houses, the Palais Garnier and Opéra Bastille. The season runs between September and July.

Palais Garnier   OPERA
(Map p78; Ⓓ 08 92 89 90 90; www.operadeparis.fr; place de l'Opéra, 9e; Ⓜ Opéra) The city's original opera house is smaller than its Bastille counterpart, but has perfect acoustics. Due to its odd shape, some seats have limited or no visibility – book carefully. Ticket prices and conditions (including last-minute discounts) are available from the **box office** (Map p78; cnr rues Scribe & Auber; ⊗ 11am-6.30pm Mon-Sat).

Opéra Bastille   OPERA, BALLET
(Map p98; Ⓓ 08 92 89 90 90; www.operadeparis.fr; 2-6 place de la Bastille, 12e; Ⓜ Bastille) This 3400-seat venue is the city's main opera hall; it also occasionally stages ballet and classical concerts. Tickets go on sale online up to two weeks before they're available by telephone or

at the **box office** (Map p98; Ⓓ 01 40 01 19 70; 130 rue de Lyon, 12e; ⊗ 2.30-6.30pm Mon-Sat; Ⓜ Bastille). Standing-only tickets (*places débouts;* €5) are available 90 minutes before performances begin.

🔒 Shopping

The most exclusive designer boutiques require customers to buzz to get in – don't be shy about ringing that bell. Paris' twice-yearly *soldes* (sales) generally last around five weeks, starting in mid-January and again in mid-June.

Many larger stores hold *nocturnes* (late nights) on Thursday, remaining open until around 10pm. Sunday shopping is severely limited; the Champs-Élysées, Montmartre, Marais and Bastille areas are liveliest.

🔒 Étoile & Champs-Élysées

This ritzy area is famed for its haute couture houses (Chanel, Dior et al) concentrated in the **Triangle d'Or** (Golden Triangle) bordered by avs Georges V, Champs-Élysées and Montaigne, 8e.

Guerlain   PERFUME
(Map p66; Ⓓ spa 01 45 62 11 21; www.guerlain.com; 68 av des Champs-Élysées, 8e; ⊗ 10.30am-8pm Mon-Sat, noon-7pm Sun; Ⓜ Franklin D Roosevelt) Guerlain is Paris' most famous parfumerie, and its shop (dating from 1912) is one of the most beautiful in the city. With its shimmering mirror and marble art-deco interior, it's a reminder of the former glory of the Champs-Élysées. For total indulgence, make an appointment at its decadent spa.

🔒 Louvre & Les Halles

Legacies of the historic *halles* (markets) include cookware shops; you'll also find high-street chains here as well as beautiful *passages couverts* (covered arcades) such as **Galerie Véro Dodat** (Map p74; btwn rue Jean-Jacques-Rousseau & 2 rue du Bouloi; ⊗ vary; Ⓜ Louvre Rivoli) and **Passage des Panoramas** (Map p78; 10 rue St-Marc, 2e; ⊗ 6am-midnight daily; Ⓜ Bourse).

★ Didier Ludot   FASHION
(Map p74; www.didierludot.fr; 19-20 & 23-24 Galerie de Montpensier, 1er; ⊗ 10.30am-7pm Mon-Sat; Ⓜ Palais Royal–Musée du Louvre) In the rag trade since 1975, collector Didier Ludot sells the city's finest couture creations of yesteryear in his exclusive twinset of boutiques, hosts exhibitions, and has published a book por-

traying the evolution of the little black dress, brilliantly brought to life in his shop that sells just that, **La Petite Robe Noire** (Map p74; 125 Galerie de Valois, 1er; ⊙ 11am-7pm Mon-Sat; Ⓜ Palais Royal–Musée du Louvre).

E Dehillerin   HOMEWARES
(Map p74; www.dehillerin.com; 18-20 rue Coquillière, 1er; ⊙ 9am-12.30pm & 2-6pm Mon, 9am-6pm Tue-Sat; Ⓜ Les Halles) Founded in 1820, this extraordinary two-level store – think old-fashioned warehouse rather than shiny, chic boutique – carries an incredible selection of professional-quality *matériel de cuisine* (kitchenware). Poultry scissors, turbot poacher, professional copper cookware or Eiffel Tower–shaped cake tin – it's all here.

Colette   CONCEPT STORE
(Map p74; www.colette.fr; 213 rue St-Honoré, 1er; ⊙ 11am-7pm Mon-Sat; Ⓜ Tuileries) Uber-hip is an understatement. Ogle designer fashion on the 1st floor, and streetwear, limited-edition sneakers, art books, music, gadgets and other high-tech, inventive and/or plain unusual items on the ground floor. End with a drink in the basement 'water bar' and pick up free design magazines and flyers for some of the city's hippest happenings by the door upon leaving.

Kiliwatch   FASHION
(Map p74; http://espacekiliwatch.fr; 64 rue Tiquetonne, 2e; ⊙ 10.30am-7pm Mon, to 7.30pm Tue-Sat; Ⓜ Étienne Marcel) A Parisian institution, Kiliwatch gets jam-packed with hip guys and gals rummaging through racks of new and used streetwear. Startling vintage range of hats and boots plus art/photography books, eyewear and the latest sneakers.

🔓 Opéra & Grands Boulevards

Famous department stores are found in the Grands Boulevards; place de la Madeleine has a welter of specialist gourmet shops.

Galeries Lafayette   DEPARTMENT STORE
(Map p78; http://haussmann.galerieslafayette.com; 40 bd Haussmann, 9e; ⊙ 9.30am-8pm Mon-Sat, to 9pm Thu; Ⓜ Auber or Chaussée d'Antin) *Grande dame* department store Galeries Lafayette is spread across the main store (whose magnificent stained-glass dome is more than a century old), **men's store** (Map p78) and **homewares** (Map p78) store, and includes a gourmet emporium.

Catch modern art in the **gallery** (Map p78; www.galeriedesgaleries.com; 1st fl; ⊙ 11am-7pm Tue-Sat; **FREE**), or take in a **fashion show** (☑ bookings 01 42 82 30 25; ⊙ 3pm Fri Mar-Jul & Sep-Dec by reservation); a free, windswept rooftop panorama, or a break at one of its 19 restaurants and cafes.

Le Printemps   DEPARTMENT STORE
(Map p78; www.printemps.com; 64 bd Haussmann, 9e; ⊙ 9.35am-8pm Mon-Wed & Fri & Sat, to 10pm Thu; ☎; Ⓜ Havre Caumartin) Famous department store Le Printemps encompasses Le Printemps de la Mode (women's fashion), **Le Printemps de l'Homme** (Map p78; men's fashion), both with established and up-and-coming designer wear, and Le Printemps de la Beauté et Maison (beauty and homewares), offering a staggering display of perfume, cosmetics and accessories. There's a free panoramic rooftop terrace and luxury eateries including Ladurée.

DISCOUNT DESIGNER OUTLETS & SECONDHAND CHIC

Save up to 70% off men's, women's and kids' fashions on previous seasons' collections, surpluses, prototypes and seconds by name-brand designers at the discounted outlet stores along rue d'Alésia, 14e, west of the Alésia metro station, particularly between av de Maine and rue Raymond-Losserand. Shops here pop up regularly and close just as often, so you can never be sure what you'll find. For slashed prices on *grandes marques* (big names) under one roof, head to the 15e's **Mistigriff** (www.mistigriff.fr; 83-85 rue St-Charles, 15e; ⊙ 10.30am-7.30pm Mon-Sat; Ⓜ Charles Michels).

When Paris' well-heeled residents spring-clean their wardrobes, they take their designer and vintage cast-offs to *dépôt-vente* (secondhand) boutiques, where savvy locals snap up serious bargains. Start your search at **Chercheminippes** (Map p106; www.chercheminippes.com; 102, 109-111, 114 & 124 rue du Cherche Midi, 6e; ⊙ 11am-7pm Mon-Sat; Ⓜ Vaneau), six beautifully presented boutiques on one street selling secondhand pieces by current designers. Each specialises in a different genre (haute couture, kids, menswear etc) perfectly ordered by size and designer. There are even changing rooms.

RICHARD I'ANSON/GETTY IMAGES ©

Shopping

Paris has it all: broad boulevards lined with flagship fashion houses and international labels, famous *grands magasins* (department stores) and fabulous markets. But the real charm of Parisian shopping lies in strolling the backstreets, where tiny speciality shops and quirky boutiques sell everything from strawberry-scented Wellington boots to heaven-scented candles.

Fashion is Paris' forte. Browse haute couture creations in the **Étoile** and **Champs-Élysées** neighbourhood (p148), particularly within the Triangle d'Or (Golden Triangle). For original streetwear and vintage gear, head for **Le Marais** (p152), particularly the Haut Marais. Small boutiques fill **St-Germain's** chic streets (p153). You'll also find adorable children's wear and accessories. Parisian fashion doesn't have to break the bank: there are fantastic bargains at secondhand and vintage boutiques, along with outlet shops selling previous seasons' collections, surpluses and seconds by top-line designers.

But fashion is just the beginning. Paris is an exquisite treasure chest of gourmet food (including cheeses, macarons and foie gras), wine, tea, books, beautiful stationery, art, art supplies, antiques and collectables. Ask for *un paquet cadeau* – free (and very beautiful) gift wrapping offered by most shops.

UNIQUE SHOPPING EXPERIENCES

Passages couverts Paris' 19th-century glass-roofed covered passages were the precursors to shopping malls.

Flea markets Lose yourself in the maze of *marchés* (markets) at the enormous Marché aux Puces de St-Ouen (p152).

Street markets Scores of colourful street markets take place every week.

Grands Magasins One-stop department store shopping in resplendent art nouveau surrounds.

📍 Montmartre & Pigalle

Away from the tourist tat, look out for food shops, art, quintessential souvenirs and fashion.

Marché aux Puces de St-Ouen   MARKET

(www.marcheauxpuces-saintouen.com; rue des Rosiers, av Michelet, rue Voltaire, rue Paul Bert & rue Jean-Henri Fabre; ⊘9am-6pm Sat, 10am-6pm Sun, 11am-5pm Mon; Ⓜ Porte de Clignancourt) This vast flea market, founded in the late 19th century and said to be Europe's largest, has more than 2500 stalls grouped into a dozen *marchés* (market areas), each with its own speciality (eg Paul Bert for 17th-century furniture, Malik for clothing, Biron for Asian art). There are miles upon miles of 'freelance' stalls; come prepared to spend some time.

📍 Le Marais & Bastille

Quirky homewares, art galleries and up-and-coming designers proliferate here, especially in the hip Haut Marais. Bastille has some of the city's best markets.

★ Paris Rendez-Vous   CONCEPT STORE

(Map p90; 29 rue de Rivoli, 4e; ⊘10am-7pm Mon-Sat; Ⓜ Hôtel de Ville) Only the city of Paris could be so chic as to have its own designer line of souvenirs, sold in its own ubercool concept store inside the Hôtel de Ville. Shop here for everything from clothing and homewares to Paris-themed books, toy sailing boats and signature Jardin du Luxembourg's Fermob chairs. *Quel style!*

★ Chez Hélène   CONFECTIONERY

(Map p90; www.chezhelene-paris.com; 28 rue St-Gilles, 3e; ⊘11.30am-7.30pm Mon-Sat, 11am-1pm & 3-7pm Sun; Ⓜ Rambuteau) Pure indulgence is what this irresistible *bonbon* boutique – a child's dream come true – is about. Old-fashioned toffees and caramels, fudge, liquorice, Eiffel Tower sugar cubes, designer lollipops, artisanal marshmallows, Provençal *calissons*...the choice of quality, well-made *bonbons* (sweets) and *gourmandises* (sweet treats) is outstanding.

★ Fleux   DESIGN, HOMEWARES

(Map p90; www.fleux.com; 39 & 52 rue Ste-Croix de la Bretonnerie, 4e; ⊘10.45am-7.30pm Mon-Fri, 10.30am-8pm Sat, 1.30-7.30pm Sun; Ⓜ Hôtel de Ville) Innovative designs for the home by European designers fill this twinset of big white mazes. Products range from super chic to kitsch, clever and plain crazy. Its e-boutique stocks about 10% of what you see on the shop floor, but Fleux can post most Paris purchases home for you (at a price, *bien sûr*).

La Manufacture de Chocolat   FOOD, DRINK

(Map p90; www.lechocolat-alainducasse.com; 40 rue de la Roquette, 11e; ⊘10.30am-7pm Tue-Sat; Ⓜ Bastille) If you dine at superstar chef Alain Ducasse's restaurants, the chocolate will have been made here at Ducasse's own chocolate factory – the first in Paris to produce 'bean-to-bar' chocolate – which he set up with his former executive pastry chef Nicolas Berger. Deliberate over ganaches, pralines and truffles and no fewer than 44 flavours of chocolate bar.

You can also buy Ducasse's chocolates at his Left Bank boutique, Le Chocolat Alain Ducasse (Map p106; www.lechocolat-alainducasse.com; 26 rue St-Benoît, 6e; ⊘10.30am-7.30pm Tue-Sat; Ⓜ St Germain des Prés).

My Crazy Pop   FOOD

(Map p98; 15 rue Trousseau, 11e; ⊘11am-7pm Tue-Fri, to 8pm Sat; Ⓜ Ledru-Rollin) Wasabi, parmesan, barbecue and olive tapenade are among the amazing savoury flavours at this popcorn shop (a French first); sweet styles include gingerbread praline, salted-butter caramel and orange and cinnamon. Wander through to the viewing window at the back to watch the kernels being popped using heat and pressure only (no oil).

L'Éclaireur   CONCEPT STORE

(Map p90; www.leclaireur.com; 40 rue de Sévigné, 4e; ⊘11am-7pm Mon-Sat; Ⓜ St-Paul) Part art space, part lounge and part deconstructionist fashion statement, this shop for women is known for having the next big thing first. The nearby menswear store (Map p90; www.leclaireur.com; 12 rue Malher, 4e; Ⓜ St-Paul) on rue Malher fills an equally stunning, old warehouse-turned-art space.

Merci   CONCEPT STORE

(Map p90; www.merci-merci.com; 111 bd Beaumarchais, 3e; ⊘10am-7pm Mon-Sat; Ⓜ St-Sébastien Froissart) A Fiat Cinquecento marks the entrance to this unique concept store which donates all its profits to a children's charity in Madagascar. Shop for fashion, accessories, linens, lamps and nifty designs for the home; and complete the experience with a coffee in its hybrid used-book-shop-cafe or lunch in its stylish basement.

The Islands

Enchanting gift shops and gourmet boutiques line the Île St-Louis' little streets.

★ 38 Saint Louis
CHEESE

(Map p100; 38 rue St-Louis en l'Île, 4e; ⊘ 9am-9.30pm Tue-Sat, to 7pm Sun & Mon; Ⓜ Pont Marie) Saturday wine tastings, artisan fruit chutneys, grape juice and prepared dishes to go: there is far more to this thoroughly modern *fromagerie* than its old-fashioned façade and absolutely superb selection of first-class French *fromage* (cheese). The shop is run by a young, dynamic duo, driven by food. Buy a wooden box filled with vacuum-packed cheese to take home.

Marché aux Fleurs
Reine Elizabeth II
MARKET

(Map p100; place Louis Lépin, 4e; ⊘ 8am-7.30pm Mon-Sat, Ⓜ Cité) Blooms have been sold at this flower market since 1808, making it the oldest market of any kind in Paris. On Sunday, between 9am and 7pm, it transforms into a twittering bird market, **Marché aux Oiseaux** (Map p100; ⊘ 9am-7pm).

Latin Quarter

Late-opening bookshops and music shops fill this studenty quarter. Look out for over two dozen branches of **Au Vieux Campeur** (Map p100; www.auvieuxcampeur.fr; 48 rue des Écoles, 5e; ⊘ 11am-7.30pm Mon-Wed, Fri & Sat, to 9pm Thu; Ⓜ Maubert-Mutualité or Cluny–La Sorbonne), selling gear for every outdoor pursuit imaginable.

★ Shakespeare
& Company
BOOKS

(Map p102; www.shakespeareandcompany.com; 37 rue de la Bûcherie, 5e; ⊘ 10am-11pm Mon-Fri, from 11am Sat & Sun; Ⓜ St-Michel) This bookshop is the stuff of legends. A kind of spell descends as you enter, weaving between nooks and crannies overflowing with new and second-hand English-language books. The original shop (12 rue l'Odéon, 6e; closed by the Nazis in 1941) was run by Sylvia Beach and became the meeting point for Hemingway's 'Lost Generation'. Readings by emerging and illustrious authors take place at 7pm most Mondays; it also hosts workshops and festivals.

Fromagerie Laurent Dubois
FOOD, DRINK

(Map p100; www.fromageslaurentdubois.fr; 47ter bd St-Germain, 5e; ⊘ 8.30am-7.30pm Tue-Sat, to 1pm Sun; Ⓜ Maubert-Mutualité) One of the best *fromageries* in Paris, this cheese lover's nirvana is filled with to-die-for delicacies such

as St-Félicien with Périgord truffles. Rare, limited-production cheeses include blue Termignon and Tarentaise goat's cheese. All are appropriately cellared in warm, humid or cold environments. There's also a 15e **branch** (www.fromageslaurentdubois.fr; 2 rue de Lourmel, 15e; ⊘ 9am-1pm & 4-7.45pm Tue-Fri, 8.30am-7.45pm Sat, 9am-1pm Sun; Ⓜ Dupleix).

St-Germain

Art, antiques and chic designer boutiques wedge between cafes, museums and churches.

★ Gab & Jo
CONCEPT STORE

(Map p106; www.gabjo.fr; 28 rue Jacob, 6e; ⊘ 11am-7pm Mon-Sat; Ⓜ St-Germain des Prés) Forget mass-produced, imported souvenirs: for quality local gifts to take home, browse the shelves of Gab & Jo, the country's first-ever concept store stocking only made-in-France items. Designers include Marie-Jeanne de Grasse (scented candles), Marius Fabre (Marseille soaps), Germaine-des-Prés (lingerie), MILF (sunglasses) and Monsieur Marcel (T-shirts).

Deyrolle
ANTIQUES, HOMEWARES

(Map p106; www.deyrolle.com; 46 rue du Bac, 7e; ⊘ 10am-1pm & 2-7pm Mon, 10am-7pm Tue-Sat; Ⓜ Rue du Bac) Overrun with creatures including lions, tigers, zebras and storks, taxidermist Deyrolle opened in 1831. In addition to stuffed animals (for rent and sale), it stocks minerals, shells, corals and crustaceans, stand-mounted ostrich eggs and pedagogical storyboards. There are also rare and unusual seeds (including many old types of tomato), gardening tools and accessories.

Cire Trudon
CANDLES

(Map p106; www.ciretrudon.com; 78 rue de Seine, 6e; ⊘ 10am-7pm Tue-Sat; Ⓜ Odéon) Claude Trudon began selling candles here in 1643, and the company – which officially supplied Versailles and Napoléon with light – is now the world's oldest candle-maker (look for the plaque to the left of the shop's awning). A rainbow of candles and candlesticks fill the shelves inside.

Le Bon Marché
DEPARTMENT STORE

(Map p106; www.bonmarche.fr; 24 rue de Sèvres, 7e; ⊘ 10am-8pm Mon-Wed & Sat, to 9pm Thu & Fri; Ⓜ Sèvres Babylone) Built by Gustave Eiffel as Paris' first department store in 1852, Le Bon Marché is the epitome of style, with a superb concentration of men's and women's fashions, beautiful homewares, stationery, books and toys as well as chic dining options.

The icing on the cake is its glorious food hall, **La Grande Épicerie de Paris** (Map p106; www.lagrandeepicerie.fr; 36 rue de Sèvres, 7e; ⊙8.30am-9pm Mon-Sat; Ⓜ Sèvres Babylone).

Pierre Hermé
FOOD

(Map p106; www.pierreherme.com; 72 rue Bonaparte, 6e; ⊙10am-7pm Sun-Wed, to 7.30pm Thu & Fri, to 8pm Sat; Ⓜ Odéon or RER Luxembourg) It's the size of a chocolate box, but once you're in, your taste buds will go wild. Pierre Hermé is one of Paris' top chocolatiers and this boutique is a veritable feast of perfectly presented petits fours, cakes, chocolates, nougats, macarons and jam.

JB Guanti
ACCESSORIES

(Map p106; www.jbguanti.fr; 59 rue de Rennes, 6e; ⊙10am-7pm Mon-Sat; Ⓜ St-Sulpice or Mabillon) For the ultimate finishing touch, the men's and women's gloves at this boutique, which specialises solely in gloves, are the epitome of both style and comfort, whether unlined, silk lined, cashmere lined, lambskin lined or trimmed with rabbit fur.

A La Recherche De Jane
ACCESSORIES

(Map p100; http://alarecherchedejane.wordpress.com; 41 rue Dauphine, 6e; ⊙11.30am-7pm Wed-Sat, 1-7pm Sun; Ⓜ Odéon) This welcoming *chapelier* (milliner) has literally thousands of handcrafted hats on hand for both men and women, and can also make them to order.

🏠 Montparnasse

Discount fashion outlets and hidden local treasures make it worth exploring Montparnasse's streets.

★ Adam Montparnasse
ART SUPPLIES

(Map p106; www.adamparis.com; 11 bd Edgar Quinet, 14e; ⊙9.30am-7pm Mon-Sat; Ⓜ Edgar Quinet) If Paris' art galleries have inspired you, pick up paint brushes, charcoals, pastels, sketchpads, watercolours, oils, acrylics, canvases and more at this historic shop. Picasso, Brancusi and Giacometti were among Édouard Adam's clients. Another seminal client was Yves Klein, with whom Adam developed the ultramarine 'Klein blue' – the VLB25 'Klein Blue' varnish is sold exclusively here.

ℹ Information

DANGERS & ANNOYANCES

Paris is generally a safe city.

Metro stations best avoided late at night include: Châtelet–Les Halles and its seemingly endless corridors; Château Rouge; Gare du Nord; Strasbourg St-Denis; Réaumur Sébastopol; and Montparnasse Bienvenüe.

Bornes d'alarme (alarm boxes) are located in the centre of each platform and some station corridors.

Pickpocketing is a problem wherever there are crowds (especially of tourists). Be particularly alert around Sacré-Cœur, Pigalle, the Forum des Halles and Centre Pompidou, the Latin Quarter (especially near the Seine), the Eiffel Tower and on the metro.

In an increasingly common ruse, scammers pretend to 'find' a gold ring (after subtly dropping it on the ground) and offer it to you as a diversionary tactic to surreptitiously reach into your pockets or bags, or to demand money. Don't fall for it!

Take care crossing roads: Parisian drivers frequently ignore green pedestrian lights.

INTERNET ACCESS

Wi-fi is widely available at accommodation in Paris and is increasingly free. The city has hundreds of wi-fi points offering free two-hour sessions from 7am and 11pm at public spaces including parks, libraries and municipal buildings. Locations are mapped at www.paris.fr/wifi.

Expect to pay between €4 and €5 per hour for online access in internet cafes; **Milk** (www.milklub.com; 31 bd de Sébastopol, 1er; 1/2/3hr €3.90/6.90/8.90; ⊙24hr; Ⓜ Les Halles) has several branches in central Paris.

MEDICAL SERVICES

American Hospital of Paris (🖉01 46 41 25 25; www.american-hospital.org; 63 bd Victor Hugo, Neuilly-sur-Seine; Ⓜ Pont de Levallois) Private hospital; emergency 24-hour medical and dental care.

Hertford British Hospital (🖉01 47 59 59 59; www.ihfb.org; 3 rue Barbès, Levallois; Ⓜ Anatole France) Less expensive, private English-speaking option.

Hôpital Hôtel Dieu (🖉01 42 34 82 34; www.aphp.fr; 1 place du Parvis Notre Dame, 4e; Ⓜ Cité) One of the city's main government-run public hospitals; after 8pm use the emergency entrance on rue de la Cité.

Pharmacie Les Champs (🖉01 45 62 02 41; Galerie des Champs-Élysées, 84 av des Champs-Élysées, 8e; ⊙24hr; Ⓜ George V)

TOURIST INFORMATION

Paris Convention & Visitors Bureau (Office du Tourisme et des Congrès de Paris; Map p74; www.parisinfo.com; 27 rue des Pyramides, 1er; ⊙9am-7pm May-Oct, 10am-7pm Nov-Apr; Ⓜ Pyramides) Main branch of the Paris Convention & Visitors Bureau, about 500m northwest of the Louvre.

ℹ Getting There & Away

AIR

Aéroport de Charles de Gaulle (CDG; www.aeroportsdeparis.fr)

Aéroport d'Orly (ORY; ☑ 01 70 36 39 50; www.aeroportsdeparis.fr) Aéroport d'Orly is located 19km south of central Paris but, despite being closer than CDG, it is not as frequently used by international airlines and public transportation options aren't quite as straightforward. If you have heavy luggage or young kids in tow, consider a taxi.

Aéroport de Beauvais (BVA; ☑ 08 92 68 20 66; www.aeroportbeauvais.com) Beauvais Airport is 75km north of Paris and a few low-cost flights go through here – but before you snap up that bargain, consider if the post-arrival journey is worth it.

BUS

Gare Routiére Internationale de Paris-Galliéni (☑ 08 92 89 90 91; 28 av du Général de Gaulle; Ⓜ Galliéni) The city's international bus terminal is in the eastern suburb of Bagnolet; it's about a 15-minute metro ride to the more central République station.

TRAIN

Paris has six major train stations. For mainline train information visit the **SNCF** (www.voyages-sncf.com) website.

Gare du Nord (rue de Dunkerque, 10e; Ⓜ Gare du Nord) Trains to/from the UK, Belgium, northern Germany, Scandinavia, Moscow etc (terminus of the high-speed Thalys trains to/from Amsterdam, Brussels, Cologne and Geneva and Eurostar to London); trains to the northern suburbs of Paris and northern France, including TGV Nord trains to Lille and Calais.

Gare de l'Est (bd de Strasbourg, 10e; Ⓜ Gare de l'Est) Trains to/from Luxembourg, parts of Switzerland (Basel, Lucerne, Zurich), southern Germany (Frankfurt, Munich) and points further east; regular and TGV Est trains to areas of France east of Paris (Champagne, Alsace and Lorraine).

Gare de Lyon (bd Diderot, 12e; Ⓜ Gare de Lyon) Gare de Lyon is the terminus for trains from Provence, the Alps, the Riviera and Italy. Also serves Geneva. Located in eastern Paris.

Gare d'Austerlitz (bd de l'Hôpital, 13e; Ⓜ Gare d'Austerlitz) Trains to/from Spain and Portugal; Loire Valley and non-TGV trains to southwestern France (eg Bordeaux and Basque Country).

Gare Montparnasse (av du Maine & bd de Vaugirard, 15e; Ⓜ Montparnasse Bienvenüe) Trains to/from Brittany and places en route from Paris (eg Chartres, Angers, Nantes); TGV Atlantique Ouest and TGV Atlantique Sud-Ouest trains to Tours, Nantes, Bordeaux and other destinations in southwestern France.

Gare St-Lazare (rue St-Lazare & rue d'Amsterdam, 8e; Ⓜ St-Lazare) Normandy (eg Dieppe, Le Havre, Cherbourg).

ℹ Getting Around

TO/FROM THE AIRPORTS

Getting into town is straightforward and inexpensive thanks to a fleet of public transport options; the most expedient are listed here. Bus drivers sell tickets. Children aged four to 11 years pay half price on most of the services.

METRO ART

Many metro stations incorporate artistic themes (usually in certain sections only), including the following:

Abbesses (line 12) Hector Guimard's finest glass-canopied, twin wrought-iron lamp posts illuminating the dark-green-on-lemon-yellow Métropolitain sign.

Arts et Métiers (line 11 platform) Jules Verne-inspired copper panelling.

Bastille (line 5 platform) Revolution-era newspaper-engraving frescos.

Chaussée d'Antin-Lafayette (line 7 platform) Recalls the Marquis de Lafayette's role as general in the American Revolution.

Cluny–La Sorbonne (line 10 platform) Academia.

Concorde (line 12 platform) Some 45,000 tiles spell out the text of the *Déclaration des Droits de l'Homme et du Citoyen* (Declaration of the Rights of Man and of the Citizen), setting forth the principles of the French Revolution.

Louvre-Rivoli (line 1 platform and corridor) Statues and bas-reliefs.

Palais Royal–Musée du Louvre (line 1) Contemporary twist on Guimard's entrances incorporating 800 colourful glass balls.

AÉROPORT CHARLES DE GAULLE

Train

CDG is served by the RER B line (€9.50, approximately 50 minutes, every 10 to 15 minutes), which serves the Gare du Nord, Châtelet–Les Halles and St-Michel–Notre Dame stations in the city centre. Trains run from 5am to 11pm; there are fewer trains on weekends.

Bus

There are six main bus lines:

Les Cars Air France line 2 (€17, 1¼ hours, every 20 minutes, 6am to 11pm) Links the airport with the Arc de Triomphe. Children aged two to 11 pay half price.

Les Cars Air France line 4 (€17.50, every 30 minutes, 6am to 10pm from CDG, 6am to 9.30pm from Paris) Links the airport with Gare de Lyon (50 minutes) in eastern Paris and Gare Montparnasse (55 minutes) in southern Paris. Children aged two to 11 pay half price.

Roissybus (€10.50, 45 to 60 minutes, every 15 minutes, 5.30am to 11pm) Links the airport with the Opéra.

RATP bus 350 (€5.70, 50 minutes, every 30 minutes, 5.30am to 11pm) Links the airport with Gare de l'Est in northern Paris.

RATP bus 351 (€5.70, 60 minutes, every 30 minutes, 5.30am to 11pm) Links the airport with place de la Nation in eastern Paris.

Noctilien bus 140 & 143 (€7.60 or 4 metro tickets, hourly, 12.30am to 5.30pm) Part of the RATP night service, Noctilien has two buses that go to CDG: bus 140 from Gare de l'Est, and 143 from Gare de l'Est and Gare du Nord.

Taxi

A taxi to the city centre takes 40 minutes. During the day, pay around €50; the fare increases 15% between 5pm and 10am and on Sunday. Only take taxis at a clearly marked rank. Never follow anyone who approaches you at the airport and claims to be a driver.

AÉROPORT D'ORLY

Train

There is no direct train to/from Orly; you'll need to change transport halfway. Note that while it is possible to take a shuttle to the RER C line, this service is quite long and not recommended.

RER B (€10.90, 35 minutes, every four to 12 minutes) This line connects Orly with the St-Michel–Notre Dame, Châtelet–Les Halles and Gare du Nord stations in the city centre. In order to get from Orly to the RER station (Antony), you must first take the Orlyval automatic train. The service runs from 6am to 11pm (fewer weekends). You only need one ticket to take the two trains.

Bus & Tram

There are several bus lines and a state-of-the-art tram line that serve Orly:

Air France bus 1 (€12.50, one hour, every 20 minutes 5am to 10.20pm from Orly, 6am to 11.20pm from Invalides) This bus runs to/from the Gare Montparnasse (35 minutes) in southern Paris, Invalides in the 7e, and the Arc de Triomphe. Children aged two to 11 pay half-price.

Orlybus (€7.50, 30 minutes, every 15 minutes, 6am to 11.20pm from Orly, 5.35am to 11.05pm from Paris) This bus runs to/from the metro station Denfert Rochereau in southern Paris, making several stops en route.

Tramway T7 (€1.70, every six minutes, 40 minutes, 5.30am to 12.30am Monday to Saturday, 6.30am to 12.30am Sunday) In service since the end of 2013, this tramway links Orly with Villejuif-Louis Aragon metro station in southern Paris; buy tickets from the machine at the tram stop as no tickets are sold on board.

Taxi

A taxi to the city centre takes roughly 30 minutes. During the day, pay between €40 and €55; the fare increases 15% between 5pm and 10am and on Sunday.

AÉROPORT PARIS-BEAUVAIS

The Beauvais shuttle (€17, 1¼ hours) links the airport with metro station Porte de Maillot. See the airport website for details and tickets.

BICYCLE

The **Vélib'** (http://en.velib.paris.fr; day/ week subscription €1.70/8, bike hire up to 30min/60min/90min/2hr free/€1/2/4) bike share scheme puts 20,000-odd bikes at the disposal of Parisians and visitors to get around the city. There are some 1800 stations throughout the city, each with anywhere from 20 to 70 bike stands. The bikes are accessible around the clock.

➡ To get a bike, you first need to purchase a one-/seven-day subscription (€1.70/8), either at the docking station terminals or online.

➡ The terminals require a credit card with an embedded smartchip (though even then, not all work). Otherwise, prepurchase a subscription online.

➡ After you authorise a deposit (€150) to pay for the bike should it go missing, you'll receive an ID number and PIN code and you're ready to go.

➡ Bikes are rented in 30-minute intervals: the first half-hour is free, the second is €2, the third and each additional half-hour are €4. If you return a bike before a half-hour is up and then take a new one, you will not be charged.

➡ If the station you want to return your bike to is full, log in to the terminal to get 15 minutes for free to find another station.

➤ Bikes are geared to cyclists aged 14 and over, and are fitted with gears, an antitheft lock with key, reflective strips and front/rear lights. Bring your own helmet.

BOAT

Batobus (www.batobus.com; Port de Solférino, 7e; 1-/2-day pass €16/18; ◷10am-9.30pm Apr-Aug, to 7pm rest of year) Batobus runs glassed-in trimarans that dock every 20 to 25 minutes at eight small piers along the Seine: Eiffel Tower, Musée d'Orsay, St-Germain des Prés, Notre Dame, Jardin des Plantes, Hôtel de Ville, Musée du Louvre and Champs-Élysées. Buy tickets online, at ferry stops or tourist offices. You can also buy a 2-/3-day ticket covering L'Open Tour buses too for €45/49.

CAR & MOTORCYCLE

Driving in Paris is defined by the triple hassle of navigation, heavy traffic and parking.

Major car-rental companies have offices at airports and train stations.

Electric-car-share program **Autolib'** (www.autolib.eu) is similar to bike-share scheme Vélib': pay €9 per half-hour to rent a GPS-equipped car in 30-minute intervals, or subscribe for a week/month (€10/25) to get cheaper rates (€7/6.50 per half-hour). Cars can be collected/dropped off at 1000 stations and are designed for short hops; the car battery lasts 250km. Carry your driver's license and photo ID.

Scooter hire companies include **Left Bank Scooters** (☑ 06 82 70 13 82; www.leftbank scooters.com).

PUBLIC TRANSPORT

Paris' public transit system, mostly operated by the **RATP** (www.ratp.fr) is one of Europe's cheapest and most efficient. View and download transport maps from the RATP website.

Bus

Paris' RATP-operated bus system runs from 5.30am to 8.30pm Monday to Saturday. Certain evening-service lines continue until between midnight and 12.30am. Services are drastically reduced on Sunday and public holidays, when buses run from 7am to 8.30pm.

Normal bus rides in one or two bus zones cost one metro ticket; longer rides require more. Transfers to other buses are allowed on the same ticket as long as the change takes place 1½ hours between the first and last validation. Validate tickets in the ticket machine near the driver.

The RATP runs 47 **Noctilien** (www.noctilien.fr) night bus lines, which depart hourly from 12.30am to 5.30pm: look for navy-blue N or Noctilien signs at bus stops. You pay a certain number of standard €1.70 metro/bus tickets, depending on the length of your journey. Transfers require a separate ticket.

Metro & RER

Paris' underground network, run by RATP, consists of two separate but linked systems: the metro and the RER suburban train line. The metro has 14 numbered lines; the RER has five main lines, designated A to E and then numbered, that pass through the city centre.

➤ Each metro line has a different colour and number. Signs in stations indicate the way to the platform for your line. The *direction* signs on each platform indicate the terminus. On lines that split into several branches, the terminus served by each train is indicated on the cars, and signs on each platform give the number of minutes until the next train.

➤ Signs marked *correspondance* (transfer) show how to reach connecting trains. At stations with many intersecting lines, such as Châtelet and Montparnasse Bienvenüe, the connection can take a long time.

➤ Each metro line has its own schedule, but trains usually start at around 5.30am, with the last train beginning its run between 12.35am and 1.15am (2.15am on Friday and Saturday).

➤ The same RATP tickets are valid on the metro, RER (within the city limits, ie zone 1), buses, trams and the Montmartre funicular. A ticket – called Le Ticket t+ – costs €1.70 (half-price for children aged four to nine years) if bought individually and €13.70 for adults for a *carnet* (book) of 10. Ticket windows accept most credit cards but machines don't accept all credit cards (even some chip-enabled cards).

➤ One ticket lets you travel between any two metro stations – no return journeys – for a period of 1½ hours, with unlimited transfers. A single ticket can be used to transfer between daytime buses and trams, but not from the metro to bus or vice versa.

➤ Keep your ticket until you exit the station or risk a fine.

Tram

The metro is tailor-made for crosstown trips, but to whizz around Paris' perimeter, hop on the T3 tram. From the Pont du Garigliano, 15e, it currently skims the city's edge as far as Porte de la Chapelle, 18e. An extension to Porte d'Asnières, 17e, is due for completion in 2017, encircling some three-quarters of the city in total. Passengers use standard t+ tickets. For updates on Paris' tramways, visit www.tramway.paris.fr.

TOURIST PASSES

The Mobilis and Paris Visite passes are valid on the metro, RER, SNCF's suburban lines, buses, night buses, trams and Montmartre funicular railway. No photo is needed, but write your card number on the ticket. Passes are sold at larger metro and RER stations, SNCF offices in Paris, and the airports.

The Mobilis card allows unlimited travel for one day and costs €6.80 (two zones) to €16.10 (five zones). Buy it at any metro, RER or SNCF station in the Paris region. Depending on how many times you plan to hop on/off the metro in a day, a *carnet* might work out cheaper.

Paris Visite allows unlimited travel as well as discounted entry to certain museums and other discounts and bonuses. The 'Paris+Suburbs+Airports' pass includes transport to/from the airports and costs €22.85/34.70/48.65/59.50 for one/two/three/five days. The cheaper 'Paris Centre' pass, valid for zone 1 to 3, costs €10.85/17.65/24.10/34.70 for one/two/three/five days. Children aged four to 11 years pay half-price.

TRAVEL PASSES

If you're staying in Paris longer than a few days, the cheapest and easiest way to use public transport is to get a rechargeable **Navigo** (www.navigo.fr) pass, allowing unlimited travel on the metro, RER, buses and trams. Unless you'll be using the suburban commuter lines extensively, the basic ticket valid for zones 1 and 2 should be sufficient.

Weekly/monthly passes, beginning on a Monday/first day of the month respectively, cost €20.40/67.10. You'll also need to pay €5 for a Navigo Découverte (Navigo Discovery) card and

attach a passport photo. Passes are issued on the spot but (unlike the standard Navigo pass available to residents) not replaceable if lost or stolen. Even if you're in Paris for three or four days, it may work out cheaper than buying *carnets*.

TAXI

➤ The *prise en charge* (flagfall) is €2.50. Within the city limits, it costs €1 per kilometre for travel between 10am and 5pm Monday to Saturday (*Tarif A;* white light on taxi roof and meter).

➤ At night (5pm to 10am), on Sunday from 7am to midnight, and in the inner suburbs the rate is €1.24 per kilometre (*Tarif B;* orange light).

➤ Travel in the outer suburbs is at *Tarif C,* €1.50 per kilometre (blue light).

➤ There's a €3 surcharge for taking a fourth passenger, but drivers sometimes refuse for insurance reasons. The first piece of baggage is free; additional pieces over 5kg cost €1 extra.

➤ Flagging down a taxi in Paris can be difficult; it's best to find an official taxi stand.

➤ To order a taxi, call or reserve online with **Taxis G7** (☑3607; www.taxisg7.fr), **Taxis Bleus** (☑01 49 36 10 10; www.taxis-bleus.com) or **Alpha Taxis** (☑01 45 85 85 85; www.alphataxis.com).

➤ Increasingly big in Paris is **Uber** (www.uber.com/cities/paris) taxi, whereby you order a taxi and pay via your smartphone.

Around Paris

Best Places to Eat

➜ Le Jardin des Plumes (p168)

➜ Dardonville (p170)

➜ Le Saint-Hilaire (p177)

➜ La Capitainerie (p173)

➜ Le Tripot (p177)

Best Places to Stay

➜ La Ferme de la Canardière (p172)

➜ Best Western Le Grand Monarque (p177)

➜ La Guérinière (p169)

➜ Le Clos Fleuri (p167)

➜ Hôtel de Londres (p169)

Why Go?

Whether you're taking day trips from Paris or continuing further afield, a trove of treasures awaits in the areas around the French capital.

The Île de France région – the 12,000-sq-km 'Island of France' shaped by five rivers – and surrounding areas count some of the most extravagant châteaux in the land. At the top of everyone's list is the palace at Versailles, the opulence and extravagance of which partly spurred the French Revolution, but the châteaux in Fontainebleau and Chantilly are also breathtaking. Many beautiful and ambitious cathedrals are also here, including Senlis' Gothic wonder and the glorious cathedral crowning the medieval old city of Chartres. In Giverny, Monet's home and gardens provide a picturesque insight into the inspiration for his seminal paintings.

But Paris' surrounds don't only hark back to the past. Also here is every kid's favourite, Disneyland Resort Paris, which now has more attractions than ever.

When to Go

Chartres

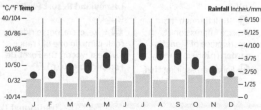

Apr–Oct Monet's former home in Giverny is open and its gardens are in bloom.

Mid-Apr–mid-Oct Chartres' landmarks light up during Chartres en Lumières.

Mid-June–mid-Sep Fountains dance to classical music in Versailles' gardens some summer evenings.

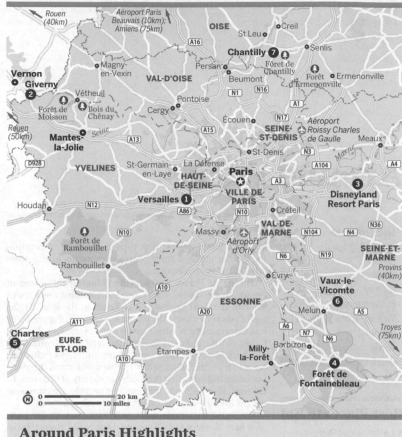

Around Paris Highlights

1 Relive the glory of the 17th- and 18th-century kingdom of France at the opulent-and-then-some **Château de Versailles** (p162)

2 Stroll through the life-size impressionist masterpiece of **Monet's garden** (p166) in Giverny

3 Follow an aspiring chef, rat Rémy, in his quest to prepare a Parisian meal aboard Walt Disney Studios Park's brand-new, larger-than-life Ratatouille ride at **Disneyland Resort Paris** (p161)

4 Hike, cycle, horse ride or rock-climb in one of France's loveliest woods, the **Forêt de Fontainebleau** (p170)

5 Gaze at the hypnotic blue stained-glass windows at the **Cathédrale Notre Dame** (p174) in Chartres

6 Visit the interior of **Château de Vaux-le-Vicomte** (p171) by candlelight

7 View the extraordinary artworks inside the lake-set **Château de Chantilly** (p171)

Disneyland Resort Paris

It took almost €4.6 billion to turn the beet fields 32km east of Paris into Europe's first Disney theme park. What started out as Euro-Disney in 1992 today comprises the traditional Disneyland Park theme park, the film-oriented Walt Disney Studios Park, and the hotel-, shop- and restaurant-filled Disney Village. And kids – and kids-at-heart – can't seem to get enough.

⊙ Sights

One-day admission fees at **Disneyland Resort Paris** (⌨ hotel bookings 01 60 30 60 30, restaurant reservations 01 60 30 40 50; www. disneylandparis.com; one day adult/child €64/58; ⊙ hours vary; Ⓜ RER Marne-la-Vallée/Chessy) include unlimited access to attractions in *either* Disneyland Park or Walt Disney Studios Park. The latter includes entry to Disneyland Park three hours before it closes. A multitude of multiday passes, special offers and packages are always available.

Disneyland Park   THEME PARK
(⊙ 10am-11pm May-Aug, to 10pm Sep, to 6pm Oct-Apr, hours can vary) Disneyland Park has five themed *pays* (lands): the 1900s-styled **Main Street USA**; **Frontierland**, home of the legendary Big Thunder Mountain ride; **Adventureland**, which evokes exotic lands in rides such as the Pirates of the Caribbean and Indiana Jones and the Temple of Peril; **Fantasyland**, crowned by Sleeping Beauty's castle; and the high-tech **Discoveryland**, with massive-queue rides such as Space Mountain: Mission 2, Star Wars and Buzz Lightyear Laser Blast.

Walt Disney Studios Park   THEME PARK
(⊙ 10am-7pm May-Sep, to 6pm Oct-Apr, hours can vary) The sound stage, production backlot and animation studios provide an up-close illustration of how films, TV programs and cartoons are produced, with behind-the-scenes tours, larger-than-life characters and spine-tingling rides including the Twilight Zone Tower of Terror. Its latest addition is the outsized Ratatouille ride, based on the winsome 2007 film about a rat who dreams of becoming a top Parisian chef and offering a multisensory rat's perspective of Paris' rooftops and restaurant kitchens aboard a trackless 'ratmobile'.

🛏 Sleeping

The resort's seven American-styled **hotels** (⌨ central booking 01 60 30 60 53) are linked by free shuttle bus to the parks. Rates vary hugely, according to the season, packages and promotional deals. Plenty of chain-style hotels are also in the vicinity of the resort.

✕ Eating

No picnic hampers/coolers are allowed but you can bring snacks, sandwiches, bottled water (refillable at water fountains) and the like. The resort also has numerous themed

❶ TOP DISNEY TIPS

➡ Crowds peak during European school holidays; visit www. schoolholidayseurope.eu to avoid them if possible.

➡ Preplan your day on Disney's website, working out which rides, shows etc you really want to see.

➡ Buy tickets in advance to avoid the ticket queue.

➡ The free Disneyland Paris App provides real-time waiting time for attractions but note that free wi-fi is only available in limited areas within the park.

➡ Once in, reserve your time slot on the busiest rides using FastPass, the park's ride reservation system (limited to one reservation at a time).

➡ Disney hotel guests are often entitled to two 'Magic hours' in Disneyland Park (usually from 8am May to October) before opening to the public; however, not all rides run during these hours.

restaurants (⌨ central reservations 01 60 30 40 50) of varying quality and value; reservations are recommended and can be made online up to two months in advance.

❶ Information

Tourist Office (⌨ 01 60 43 33 33; www. visitparisregion.com; place François Truffaut; ⊙ 9am-8pm) Near the RER and TGV train stations.

❶ Getting There & Away

Disneyland is easily reached by RER A4 (€7.50, 40 minutes to one hour, frequent), which runs from central Paris to Marne-la-Vallée/Chessy, Disneyland's RER station.

TGV trains run directly from Charles de Gaulle airport terminal 2 to Disneyland's Marne-la-Vallée/Chessy TGV station (€18, 12 minutes, up to two per hour).

By car, follow route A4 from Porte de Bercy (direction Metz-Nancy) and take exit 14.

Versailles

POP 88,470

Louis XIV transformed his father's hunting lodge into the monumental Château de Versailles in the mid-17th century, and it remains France's most famous and grand palace. Situated in the leafy, bourgeois suburb of Versailles, about 22km southwest of central Paris, the baroque château was the kingdom's political capital and the seat of the royal court from 1682 up until the fateful events of 1789 when revolutionaries massacred the palace guard. Louis XVI and Marie Antoinette were ultimately dragged back to Paris, where they were ingloriously guillotined.

◎ Sights

Château de Versailles PALACE
(☑01 30 83 78 00; www.chateauversailles.fr; passport ticket incl estate-wide access adult/child €18/free, with musical events €25/free, palace €15/free; ☺9am-6.30pm Tue-Sat, to 6pm Sun Apr-Oct, to 5.30pm Tue-Sun Nov-Mar; Ⓜ RER Versailles-Château–Rive Gauche) Amid magnificently landscaped formal gardens, this splendid and enormous palace was built in the mid-17th century during the reign of Louis XIV – the Roi Soleil (Sun King) – to project the absolute power of the French monarchy, which was then at the height of its glory. The château has undergone relatively few alterations since its construction, though almost all the interior furnishings disappeared during the Revolution and many of the rooms were rebuilt by Louis-Philippe (r 1830–48).

Some 30,000 workers and soldiers toiled on the structure, the bills for which all but emptied the kingdom's coffers.

Work began in 1661 under the guidance of architect Louis Le Vau (Jules Hardouin-Mansart took over from Le Vau in the mid-1670s); painter and interior designer Charles Le Brun; and landscape artist André Le Nôtre, whose workers flattened hills, drained marshes and relocated forests as they laid out the seemingly endless gardens, ponds and fountains.

Le Brun and his hundreds of artisans decorated every moulding, cornice, ceiling and door of the interior with the most luxurious and ostentatious of appointments: frescos, marble, gilt and woodcarvings, many with themes and symbols drawn from Greek and Roman mythology. The King's Suite of the Grands Appartements du Roi et de la Reine (King's and Queen's State Apartments), for example, includes rooms dedicated to Hercules, Venus, Diana, Mars and Mercury. The opulence reaches its peak in the Galerie des Glaces (Hall of Mirrors), a 75m-long ballroom with 17 huge mirrors on one side and, on the other, an equal number of windows looking out over the gardens and the setting sun.

The current €400 million restoration program is the most ambitious yet, and until it's completed in 2020, at least a part of the palace is likely to be clad in scaffolding when you visit.

Château de Versailles
Gardens & Park GARDEN
(except during musical events admission free; ☺gardens 9am-8.30pm Apr-Oct, 8am-6pm Nov-Mar, park 7am-8.30pm Apr-Oct, 8am-6pm Nov-Mar) The section of the vast gardens nearest the palace, laid out between 1661 and 1700 in the formal French style, is famed for its geometrically aligned terraces, flowerbeds, tree-lined paths, ponds and fountains. The 400-odd statues of marble, bronze and lead were made by the most talented sculptors of the era. The English-style Jardins du Petit Trianon are more pastoral and have meandering, sheltered paths.

Oriented to reflect the sunset, the **Grand Canal** (Chateau gardens), 1.6km long and 62m wide, is traversed by the 1km-long Petit Canal, creating a cross-shaped body of water with a perimeter of more than 5.5km.

On the southwestern side of the palace, the **Orangerie**, built under the Parterre du Midi (Southern Flowerbed), shelters tropical plants in winter.

The gardens' largest fountains include the 17th-century **Bassin de Neptune**, a dazzling mirage of 99 spouting gushers 300m north of the palace, whose straight side abuts a small pond graced by a winged dragon (Grille du Dragon). On the same days as the Grandes Eaux Musicales fountain displays, the Bassin de Neptune flows for 10 minutes.

At the eastern end of the Grand Canal, the **Bassin d'Apollon** was built in 1688. Emerging from the water in the centre is Apollo's chariot, pulled by rearing horses.

Domaine de Marie-Antoinette PALACE
(Marie-Antoinette's Estate; adult/child €10/free, with passport ticket free; ☺noon-6.30pm Tue-Sun Apr-Oct, to 5.30pm Tue-Sat Nov-Mar) Northwest of Versailles' main palace is the Domaine de Marie-Antoinette. Admission includes the pink-colonnaded **Grand Trianon**, built in 1687 for Louis XIV and his family to escape the rigid etiquette of the court, and the ochre-coloured, 1760s **Petit**

Trianon, redecorated in 1867 by consort of Napoléon III, Empress Eugénie, who added Louis XVI–style furnishings, as well as the 1784-completed **Hameau de la Reine** (Queen's Hamlet), a mock village of thatched cottages where Marie-Antoinette played milkmaid.

Versailles Stables   STABLES
Today the **Petites Écuries** (Little Stables) FREE are used by Versailles' School of Architecture. The **Grandes Écuries** (Big Stables) are the stage for the prestigious **Académie du Spectacle Équestre** (Academy of Equestrian Arts; ☑ 01 39 02 07 14; www.acadequestre. fr; 1 av Rockefeller; training session adult/child €12/6.50; ☺ 45min training session 11.15am last Sat & Sun of month). It presents spectacular **Reprises Musicales** (Musical Equestrian Shows; adult/child from €25/16; ☺ 6pm Sat, 3pm Sun), for which tickets sell out weeks in advance; book ahead online. In the stables' main courtyard is a new manège where horses and their riders train. Show tickets and training sessions include a stable visit.

**Salle du
Jeu de Paume**   ROYAL TENNIS COURT
(www.versailles-tourisme.com; 1 rue du Jeu de Paume; admission free, guided tour €9; ☺ 2-5.45pm Tue-Sun, guided tour in French 3pm Sat) In May 1789 Louis XVI convened the États-Généraux, made up of more than 1118 deputies representing the nobility, clergy and the Third Estate ('common people'), to moderate dissent. Denied entry, the Third Estate's reps met separately on this 1686-built royal tennis court, formed a National Assembly and took the Serment du Jeu de Paume (Tennis Court Oath), swearing not to dissolve it until Louis XVI accepted a new constitution.

Less than a month later, a mob in Paris stormed the prison at Bastille.

☞ Tours

Take a tour if you're pressed for time.

Paris City Vision   BUS TOUR
(☑ 01 44 55 61 00; www.pariscityvision.com; adult/child including palace entry from €116/84)

ℹ TOP VERSAILLES TIPS

Versailles is one of the country's most popular destinations, with more than five million visitors annually; advance planning will make visiting more enjoyable.

➡ Monday is out for obvious reasons (it's closed).

➡ By noon queues for tickets and entering the château spiral out of control: arrive early morning and avoid Tuesday and Sunday, its busiest days.

➡ Prepurchase tickets on the château's website or at Fnac (p146) branches and head straight to **Entrance A**.

➡ Versailles is free on the first Sunday of every month from November to March.

➡ Prams/buggies and metal-frame baby carriers aren't allowed inside the palace.

➡ To access areas that are otherwise off limits and to learn more about Versailles' history, prebook a 90-minute **guided tour** (☑ 01 30 83 77 88; www.chateauversailles. fr; tours €7 plus palace admission; ☺ English-language tours Tue-Sun, tour times vary) of the Private Apartments of Louis XV and Louis XVI and the Opera House or Royal Chapel. Tour tickets also include access to the most famous parts of the palace.

➡ The estate is so vast that the only way to see it all is to hire a four-person **electric car** (☑ 01 39 66 97 66; per hr €32) or hop aboard the **shuttle train** (www.train-versailles.com; adult/child €7.50/5.80); you can also rent a **bike** (☑ 01 39 66 97 66; per hr €6.50) or **boat** (☑ 01 39 66 97 66; per hr €15).

➡ Try to time your visit for the **Grandes Eaux Musicales** (adult/child €9/7.50; ☺ 11am-noon & 3.30-5pm Tue, Sat & Sun mid-May–late Jun, 11am-noon & 3.30-5pm Sat & Sun Apr–mid-May & Jul-Oct) or the after-dark **Grandes Eaux Nocturnes** (adult/child €24/20; ☺ from 8.30pm Sat mid-Jun–mid-Sep), truly magical 'dancing water' displays – set to music composed by baroque- and classical-era composers – throughout the grounds in summer.

➡ Audioguides are included in admission. For an offbeat insight, check out the independent app **Happy Versailles** (www.happy-visit-versailles.com; €2.69).

Versailles

A DAY IN COURT

Visiting Versailles – even just the State Apartments – may seem overwhelming at first, but think of it as a house where people ate, drank, worked, slept and conspired and you'll be on the right path.

Some two decades into his long reign, Louis XIV began turning his father's hunting lodge into a palace large enough to house his entire court (to keep closer tabs on the 6000-strong army of courtiers). Sparing no expense, the Sun King employed the greatest artists and craftspeople of the day and by 1682 he'd created the most extravagant dormitory in history.

The royal schedule was as accurate and predictable as a Swiss watch. By following this itinerary of rooms you can recreate the king's day, starting with the **King's Bedchamber ❶** and the **Queen's Bedchamber ❷**, where the royal couple was roused at about the same time. The royal procession then leads through the **Hall of Mirrors ❸** to the **Royal Chapel ❹** for morning Mass and returns to the **Council Chamber ❺** for late-morning meetings with ministers. After lunch the king might ride or hunt or visit the **King's Library ❻**. Later he could join courtesans for an 'apartment evening' starting from the **Hercules Drawing Room ❼** or play billiards in the **Diana Drawing Room ❽** before supping at 10pm.

VERSAILLES BY NUMBERS

- ➡ **Rooms** 700 (11 hectares of roof)
- ➡ **Windows** 2153
- ➡ **Staircases** 67
- ➡ **Gardens and parks** 800 hectares
- ➡ **Trees** 200,000
- ➡ **Fountains** 50 (with 620 nozzles)
- ➡ **Paintings** 6300 (measuring 11km laid end to end)
- ➡ **Statues and sculptures** 2100
- ➡ **Objets d'art and furnishings** 5000
- ➡ **Visitors** 5.3 million per year

Queen's Bedchamber
Chambre de la Reine
The queen's life was on constant public display and even the births of her children were watched by crowds of spectators in her own bedchamber. **DETOUR »** The Guardroom, with a dozen armed men at the ready.

LUNCH BREAK

Diner-style food at Sister's Café, crêpes at Le Phare St-Louis or picnic in the park.

Guardroom

South Wing

King's Library
Bibliothèque du Roi
The last resident, bibliophile Louis XVI, loved geography and his copy of *The Travels of James Cook* (in English, which he read fluently) is still on the shelf here.

SAVVY SIGHTSEEING

Avoid Versailles on Monday (closed), Tuesday (Paris' museums close, so visitors flock here) and Sunday, the busiest day. Also, book tickets online so you don't have to queue.

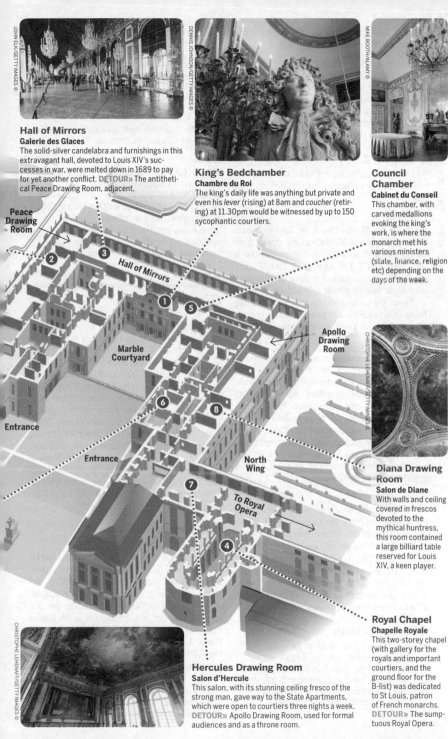

Hall of Mirrors
Galerie des Glaces
The solid-silver candelabra and furnishings in this extravagant hall, devoted to Louis XIV's successes in war, were melted down in 1689 to pay for yet another conflict. **DETOUR»** The antithetical Peace Drawing Room, adjacent.

King's Bedchamber
Chambre du Roi
The king's daily life was anything but private and even his *lever* (rising) at 8am and *coucher* (retiring) at 11.30pm would be witnessed by up to 150 sycophantic courtiers.

Council Chamber
Cabinet du Conseil
This chamber, with carved medallions evoking the king's work, is where the monarch met his various ministers (state, finance, religion etc) depending on the days of the week.

Peace Drawing Room

Hall of Mirrors

Marble Courtyard

Apollo Drawing Room

Entrance

Entrance

North Wing

To Royal Opera

Diana Drawing Room
Salon de Diane
With walls and ceiling covered in frescos devoted to the mythical huntress, this room contained a large billiard table reserved for Louis XIV, a keen player.

Royal Chapel
Chapelle Royale
This two-storey chapel (with gallery for the royals and important courtiers, and the ground floor for the B-list) was dedicated to St Louis, patron of French monarchs. **DETOUR»** The sumptuous Royal Opera.

Hercules Drawing Room
Salon d'Hercule
This salon, with its stunning ceiling fresco of the strong man, gave way to the State Apartments, which were open to courtiers three nights a week. **DETOUR»** Apollo Drawing Room, used for formal audiences and as a throne room.

Guided half-day minibus trips from Paris to Versailles.

City Discovery BUS TOUR
(☑ 09 70 44 52 90; www.city-discovery.com) Various Versailles tours from adult/child €69/41. Other options from Paris include Versailles/Giverny (€179/107), Fontainebleau (€59/36) and Disneyland Resort Paris (including entry to both parks €92/83).

✗ Eating

In the Louis XIV–created town of Versailles, rue de Satory is lined with restaurants and cafes.

Chez Lazare BISTRO €
(☑ 01 39 50 41 45; 18 rue de Satory; menus 2-course lunch €12.50, 2-/3-course dinner from €17.50/27.50; ⊙ noon-2pm & 7-10pm Mon-Thu & Sun, noon-2pm & 7-10.30pm Fri & Sat) Wicker chairs fill the pavement terrace of this popular local bistro which specialises in meat and seafood cooked on an open grill. It's not fancy but portions are generous, the atmosphere convivial and the value superb.

Angelina CAFE €€
(www.angelina-versailles.fr; snacks €14-25, mains €23-35; ⊙ 10am-6pm Tue-Sat Apr-Oct, to 5pm Tue-Sat Nov-Mar) Eateries within the estate include tearoom Angelina, famed for its decadent hot chocolate. Stop by for pastries, light dishes such as quiches, charcuterie platters and salads, or filling meals such as truffle ravioli, beef with sweet potato mash or hot smoked salmon. In addition to the branch by the Petit Trianon, there's another inside the palace.

À la Ferme REGIONAL CUISINE €€
(☑ 01 39 53 10 81; www.alaferme-versailles.com; 3 rue du Maréchal Joffre; menus lunch €15.50-22.90, dinner €21.50-26.20; ⊙ noon-2pm & 7-10pm Wed-Sun) Rustic farm objects such as cartwheels strung from old wood beams add a country air 'At the Farm'. Cuisine inspired by southwest France spans dishes such as beef with Roquefort sauce to skewers of beef, lamb, chicken and spicy sausage.

❶ Information

Tourist Office (☑ 01 39 24 88 88; www.versailles-tourisme.com; 2bis av de Paris; ⊙ 10am-6pm Mon, 9am-7pm Tue-Sun Apr-Oct, 9am-6pm Tue-Sat, 11am-5pm Sun & Mon Nov-Mar) Sells the passport to Château de Versailles and detailed visitor's guides.

❶ Getting There & Away

BUS
RATP bus 171 (€1.70 or one t+ metro/bus ticket, 35 minutes) links Paris' Pont de Sèvres metro station (15e) with place d'Armes at least every 15 minutes from around 6am to 1am.

CAR
Follow the A13 from Porte d'Auteuil and take the exit marked 'Versailles Château'.

TRAIN
RER C5 (€3.25, 45 minutes, frequent) goes from Paris' Left Bank RER stations to Versailles-Château–Rive Gauche station. The RER C8 links Paris with Versailles-Chantiers station, a 1.3km walk from the château.

SNCF operates trains from Paris' Gare Montparnasse to Versailles-Chantiers, and from Paris' Gare St-Lazare to Versailles-Rive Droite, 1.2km from the château.

Giverny

POP 516

The tiny country village of Giverny, 74km northwest of Paris, is a place of pilgrimage for devotees of impressionism, and can feel swamped by the tour-bus crowd in the summer months. Monet lived here from 1883 until his death in 1926, in a rambling house – surrounded by flower-filled gardens – that's now the immensely popular Maison et Jardins de Claude Monet. Note that it's closed from November to March, along with most accommodation and restaurants, so there's little point visiting out of season. If you are here between April and October, however, you're in for a treat.

Be aware that the village has no public toilets, ATMs or bureaux de change.

◉ Sights

Maison et Jardins de Claude Monet MUSEUM, GARDEN
(☑ 02 32 51 28 21; www.fondation-monet.com; 84 rue Claude Monet; adult/child €9.50/5, incl Musée des Impressionnismes Giverny €16.50/8; ⊙ 9.30am-6pm Apr-Oct) Monet's home for the last 43 years of his life is now a delightful house-museum. His pastel-pink house and Water Lily studio stand on the periphery of the Clos Normand, with its symmetrically laid-out gardens bursting with flowers. Monet bought the Jardin d'Eau (Water Garden) in 1895 and set about creating his trademark lily pond, as well as the famous Japanese bridge (since rebuilt).

The charmingly preserved house and beautiful bloom-filled gardens (rather than Monet's works) are the draws here.

Draped with purple wisteria, the Japanese bridge blends into the asymmetrical foreground and background, creating the intimate atmosphere for which the 'painter of light' was renowned.

Seasons have an enormous effect on Giverny. From early to late spring, daffodils, tulips, rhododendrons, wisteria and irises appear, followed by poppies and lilies. By June, nasturtiums, roses and sweet peas are in flower. Around September, there are dahlias, sunflowers and hollyhocks.

Combined tickets with Paris' Musée Marmottan Monet per adult/child cost €18.50/9, and combined adult tickets with Paris' Musée de l'Orangerie cost €18.50.

Musée des Impressionnismes Giverny   ART MUSEUM
(☑ 02 32 51 94 65; www.mdig.fr; 99 rue Claude Monet; adult/child €7/4.50, incl Maison et Jardins de Claude Monet €16.50/8; ⊙ 10am-6pm Apr-Oct) About 100m northwest of the Maison de Claude Monet is the Giverny Museum of Impressionisms. Set up in partnership with the Musée d'Orsay, among others, the pluralised name reinforces its coverage of all aspects of impressionism and related movements in its permanent collection and temporary exhibitions. Reserve ahead for two-hour **art workshops** (€12.50 including materials) offering an introduction to watercolour, drawing, sketching or pastels. Lectures, readings, concerts and documentaries also take place regularly.

🛏 Sleeping & Eating

Le Clos Fleuri   B&B €€
(☑ 02 32 21 36 51; www.giverny-leclosfleuri.fr; 5 rue de la Dîme; s/d €93/98; ⊙ Apr-Oct; ☎) Big rooms with king-size beds and exposed wood beams overlook the hedged gardens of this delightful B&B within strolling distance of the Maison et Jardins de Claude Monet.

CLAUDE MONET

....

Everyone discusses my art and pretends to understand, as if it were necessary to understand, when it is simply necessary to love.

Claude Monet

The undisputed leader of the impressionists, Claude Monet was born in Paris in 1840 and grew up in Le Havre, where he found an early affinity with the outdoors. Monet disliked school and spent much of his time sketching his professors in the margins of his exercise books. By 15 his skills as a caricaturist were known throughout Le Havre, but Eugène Boudin, his first mentor, persuaded him to turn his attention away from portraiture towards the study of colour, light and landscape.

In 1860 military service interrupted Monet's studies at the Académie Suisse in Paris and took him to Algiers, where the intense light and colours further fuelled his imagination. The young painter became fascinated with capturing a specific moment in time, the immediate impression of the scene before him, rather than the precise detail.

From 1867 Monet's distinctive style began to emerge, focusing on the effects of light and colour and using the quick, undisguised broken brushstrokes that would characterise the impressionist period. His contemporaries were Pissarro, Renoir, Sisley, Cézanne and Degas. The young painters left the studio to work outdoors, experimenting with the shades and hues of nature, and arguing and sharing ideas. Their work was far from welcomed by critics; one of them condemned it as 'impressionism', in reference to Monet's *Impression: Sunrise* (1874). Much to the critic's chagrin, the name stuck.

From the late 1870s Monet concentrated on painting in series, seeking to re-create a landscape by showing its transformation under different conditions of light and atmosphere. *Haystacks* (1890–91) and *Rouen Cathedral* (1891–95) are some of the best-known works of this period. In 1883 Monet moved to Giverny, planting his property with a variety of flowers around an artificial pond, the Jardin d'Eau, in order to paint the subtle effects of sunlight on natural forms. It was here that he painted the *Nymphéas* (Water Lilies) series. The huge dimensions of some of these works, together with the fact that the pond's surface takes up the entire canvas, meant the abandonment of composition in the traditional sense and the virtual disintegration of form. For the finest examples of Monet's works, visit Paris' Musée Marmottan Monet, Musée de l'Orangerie and Musée d'Orsay.

Each of its three rooms is named after a different flower; green-thumbed host Danielle speaks fluent English.

La Pluie de Roses
B&B €€

(☑02 32 51 10 67; www.givernylapluiederoses.fr; 14 rue Claude Monet; s/d/tr/f €120/130/175/220; ☎) You'll be won over by this adorable private home cocooned in a dreamy, peaceful garden. Inside, the three rooms are so comfy it's hard to wake up. Superb breakfast in a verandah awash with sunlight. Payment is by cash only.

La Musardière
HOTEL €€

(☑02 32 21 03 18; www.lamusardiere.fr; 123 rue Claude Monet; d €84-99, tr €123-136, f €146, 3-course menus €26-36; ⊘hotel Feb–mid-Dec, restaurant noon-10pm Apr-Oct; ☎) This two-star 10-room hotel dating back to 1880 and evocatively called the 'Idler' is set amid a lovely garden less than 100m northeast of the Maison et Jardins de Claude Monet. Savouring a crêpe in its restaurant is a pleasure.

★ Le Jardin des Plumes
MODERN FRENCH €€

(☑02 32 54 26 35; www.lejardindesplumes.fr; 1 rue du Milieu; menus 2-course lunch €29, 3-/5-/7-course dinner €39/62/82; ⊘12.15-1.45pm & 7.15-9pm Wed-Sun; ☑) Opened in 2012, this gorgeous sky-blue-trimmed property's airy white dining room sets the stage for chef Eric Guerin's exquisite, inventive cuisine, which justifies the trip from Paris alone. Its four rooms (€160 to €200) and four suites (€250 to €290) combine vintage and contemporary furnishings. It's less than 10 minutes' walk to the Maison et Jardins de Claude Monet.

ℹ Information

Tourist Office (☑02 32 64 45 01; www.cape-tourisme.fr; 80 rue Claude Monet; ⊘10am-6pm Apr-Oct) New office by the Maison et Jardins de Claude Monet.

ℹ Getting There & Away

The closest train station is at Vernon, from where buses, taxis and cycle/walking tracks run to Giverny.

BICYCLE
Café L'Arrivée de Giverny (☑02 32 21 16 01; 1 place de la Gare; per day €14; ⊘7am-11pm) Rent bikes at the Café L'Arrivée de Giverny, opposite the train station in Vernon, from where Giverny is a signposted 5km along a direct (and flat) cycle/walking track.

BUS
Shuttle buses (€8 return, 20 minutes, four daily April to October) meet most trains to and from Paris.

TAXI
Taxis (☑06 07 01 83 50, 06 81 09 00 43) usually wait outside the train station in Vernon and charge around €15 for the one-way trip to Giverny.

TRAIN
From Paris' Gare St-Lazare there are up to 15 daily trains to Vernon (€14.30, 50 minutes), 7km to the west of Giverny. Trains also run to/from Rouen in Normandy (€11.60, 40 minutes, every two hours).

Fontainebleau
POP 16,302

Fresh air fills your lungs on arriving in the smart town of Fontainebleau. It's enveloped by the 20,000-hectare Forêt de Fontainebleau, which is as big a playground today as it was in the 16th century, with superb walking and rock-climbing opportunities. The town grew up around its magnificent château, one of the most beautifully decorated and furnished in France. Although it's less crowded and pressured than Versailles, exploring it can still take the best part of a day. You'll also find a cosmopolitan drinking and dining scene, thanks to the town's lifeblood, the international graduate business school Insead.

⊙ Sights

Château de Fontainebleau
PALACE

(☑01 60 71 50 70; www.musee-chateau-fontainebleau.fr; place Général de Gaulle; adult/child €11/free; ⊘9.30am-6pm Wed-Mon Apr-Sep, to 5pm Wed-Mon Oct-Mar) The resplendent, 1900-room Château de Fontainebleau's list of former tenants and guests reads like a who's who of French royalty and aristocracy. Every square centimetre of wall and ceiling space is richly adorned with wood panelling, gilded carvings, frescos, tapestries and paintings.

Visits take in the **Grands Appartements** (State Apartments), which contain several outstanding rooms. An informative 1½-hour audioguide (included in the price) leads you around the main areas.

The first château on this site was built in the early 12th century and enlarged by Louis IX a century later. Only a single medieval tower survived the energetic Renaissance-style reconstruction undertaken by François I (r 1515–47), whose superb artisans, many of them brought from Italy, blended Italian and French styles to create what is known as the First School of Fontainebleau. The Mona Lisa once hung here amid other fine works of art in the royal collection.

During the latter half of the 16th century, the château was further enlarged by Henri II (r 1547–59), Catherine de Médicis and Henri IV (r 1589–1610), whose Flemish and French artists created the Second School of Fontainebleau. Even Louis XIV got in on the act: it was he who hired landscape artist André Le Nôtre, celebrated for his work at Versailles, to redesign the gardens.

Fontainebleau was beloved by Napoléon Bonaparte, who had a fair bit of restoration work carried out. Napoléon III was another frequent visitor. During WWII the château was turned into a German headquarters. After it was liberated by Allied forces under US General George Patton in 1944, part of the complex served as the Allied and then NATO headquarters from 1945 to 1965.

The spectacular Chapelle de la Trinité (Trinity Chapel), the ornamentation of which dates from the first half of the 17th century, is where Louis XV married Marie Leczinska in 1725 and where the future Napoléon III was christened in 1810. Galerie François 1er, a jewel of Renaissance architecture, was decorated from 1533 to 1540 by Il Rosso, a Florentine follower of Michelangelo. In the wood panelling, François I's monogram appears repeatedly along with his emblem, a dragon-like salamander. The Musée Chinois de l'Impératrice Eugénie (Chinese Museum of Empress Eugénie) consists of four drawing rooms created in 1863 for the oriental art and curios collected by Napoléon III's wife.

The Salle de Bal, a 30m-long ballroom dating from the mid-16th century that was also used for receptions and banquets, is renowned for its mythologicalfrescocoes, marquetry floor and Italian-inspired coffered ceiling. Its large windows afford views of the Cour Ovale (Oval Courtyard) and the gardens. The gilded bed in the 17th- and 18th-century Chambre de l'Impératrice (Empress' Bedroom) was never used by Marie-Antoinette, for whom it was built in 1787. The gilding in the Salle du Trône (Throne Room), which was the royal bedroom before the Napoléonic period, is decorated in golds, greens and yellows.

As successive monarchs added their own wings to the château, five irregularly shaped courtyards were created. The oldest and most interesting is the Cour Ovale (Oval Courtyard), no longer oval but U-shaped due to Henri IV's construction work. It incorporates the keep, the sole remnant of the medieval château. The largest courtyard is the Cour du Cheval Blanc (Courtyard of the White Horse), from where you enter the château. Napoléon, about to be exiled to Elba in 1814, bade farewell to his guards from the magnificent 17th-century double-horseshoe staircase here. For that reason the courtyard is also called the Cour des Adieux (Farewell Courtyard).

Château de Fontainebleau
Gardens & Park GARDEN
(🕙 9am-6.30pm May-Sep, to 5.30pm Mar, Apr & Oct, to 4.30pm Nov-Feb, palace park 24hr) FREE On the northern side of the château is the formal Jardin de Diane, which was created by Catherine de Médicis. Le Nôtre's formal, 17th-century Jardin Français (French Garden), also known as the Grand Parterre, is east of the Cour de la Fontaine (Fountain Courtyard) and the Étang des Carpes (Carp Pond). The informal Jardin Anglais (English Garden), laid out in 1812, is west of the pond. Excavated in 1609, the Grand Canal predates the canals at Versailles by more than half a century.

🛏 Sleeping

La Guérinière B&B €
(📞 06 13 50 50 37; balestier.gerard@wanadoo.fr; 10 rue de Montebello; d incl breakfast €70; @ 🤝) This charming B&B provides some of the best-value accommodation in town. Owner Monsieur Balestier speaks English and has five rooms, each named after a different flower and dressed in white linens and period furniture; some have wooden beams. Breakfast includes homemade jam and zesty marmalade.

Hôtel de Londres HOTEL €€
(📞 01 64 22 20 21; www.hoteldelondres.com; 1 place Général de Gaulle; d €95-185; ❄ @ 🤝) Classy, cosy and beautifully kept, the 16-room 'Hotel London' is furnished in warm reds and royal blues. The priciest rooms (eg room 5) have balconies with dreamy château views.

🍴 Eating

There are lovely cafe terraces on place Napoléon Bonaparte and some appealing drinking options on rue de la Corne. For

FORÊT DE FONTAINEBLEAU

Beginning just 500m south of the château and surrounding the town, the 200-sq-km **Forêt de Fontainebleau** (Fontainebleau Forest) is one of the prettiest woods in the region. The many trails are excellent for jogging, walking, cycling and horse riding; Fontainebleau's tourist office stocks maps and guides.

Rock-climbing enthusiasts have long come to the forest's sandstone ridges, rich in cliffs and overhangs, to hone their skills before setting off for the Alps. There are different grades marked by colours, starting with white ones, which are suitable for children, and going up to death-defying black boulders. The **Bleau** (http://bleau.info) website has stacks of information in English on climbing in Fontainebleau. Two gorges worth visiting are the **Gorges d'Apremont**, 7km northwest near Barbizon, and the **Gorges de Franchard**, a few kilometres south of Gorges d'Apremont. If you want to give it a go, contact **Top Loisirs** (☑ 01 60 74 08 50; www.toploisirs.fr) about equipment hire and instruction; pick-ups in Fontainebleau are possible by arrangement. The tourist office also sells comprehensive climbing guides.

fabulous *fromageries* (cheese shops), head to rue des Sablons and rue Grande.

★ **Dardonville**　　PATISSERIE, BOULANGERIE €
(24 rue des Sablons; ⊘ 7am-1.30pm & 3.15-7.30pm Tue-Sat, 7am-1.30pm Sun) Melt-in-your-mouth macarons, in flavours such as poppy seed and gingerbread, cost just €4.80 per dozen (per *dozen!*) at this exceptional pâtisserie-*boulangerie* (bakery). Queues also form out the door for its amazing breads and savoury petits fours such as tiny pastry-wrapped sausages and teensy coin-size quiches that make perfect picnic fare.

Crêperie Ty Koz　　CRÊPERIE €
(☑ 01 64 22 00 55; www.creperiety-koz.com; 18 rue de la Cloche; crêpes & galettes €3-12.80; ⊘ noon-2pm & 7-10pm Tue-Wed, noon-2pm & 7-10.30pm Thu-Sun) Tucked away in an attractive courtyard, this Breton hidey-hole cooks up authentic sweet crêpes and *simple* (single thickness) and *pourleth* (double thickness) *galettes* (savoury buckwheat crêpes). Wash them down with traditional Val de Rance cider.

Le Bistrot 9　　BISTRO €€
(☑ 01 64 22 87 84; www.lebistrot9.com; 9 rue de Montebello; mains €16-29; ⊘ noon-2pm & 7-10pm Mon-Thu, noon-2pm & 7-11pm Fri & Sat, noon-2.30pm Sun) Fronted by an awning-covered, timber-decked terrace (heated in winter), this locals' favourite has a cheerful red- and yellow-painted, bare-boards interior and delicious specialities including beef tartare, poached salmon in *beurre blanc* (white sauce), *sole meunière* (floured, fried sole served with butter sauce with lemon) and

profiteroles for dessert as well as oysters in season. Great value and lively vibe.

Le Franklin Roosevelt　　BRASSERIE €€
(☑ 01 64 22 28 73; 20 rue Grande; mains €13.50-24.50; ⊘ 10am-1am Mon-Sat) With wooden panelling, red banquette seating and atmosphere to spare, the Franklin keeps locals well fed: the *salades composées* (salads with meat or fish) are healthy and huge.

Le Ferrare　　BRASSERIE €
(☑ 01 60 72 37 04; 23 rue de France; 2-/3-course menus €12.30/13.90; ⊘ 7.30am-4pm Mon, to 10.30pm Tue-Thu, to 1am Fri & Sat; ☎) Locals pile into this quintessential bar-brasserie, which has a blackboard full of Auvergne specialities and bargain-priced *plats du jour* (daily specials; €10.80).

ⓘ Information

Tourist Office (☑ 01 60 74 99 99; www.fontainebleau-tourisme.com; 4 rue Royale; ⊘ 10am-6pm Mon-Sat, 10am-1pm & 2-5pm Sun May-Oct, 10am-6pm Mon-Sat, 10am-1pm Sun Nov-Apr; ☎) In a converted petrol station west of the château, with information on the town and forest.

ⓘ Getting There & Around

Importantly, train tickets to Fontainebleau-Avon are sold at Gare de Lyon's SNCF Transilien counter/Billet Ile-de-France machines, *not* SNCF mainline counters/machines. On returning to Paris, tickets include travel to any metro station.

Up to 40 daily SNCF Transilien (www.transilien.com) commuter trains link Paris' Gare de Lyon with Fontainebleau-Avon station (€8.75, 35 to 60 minutes).

Local bus line A links the train station with Château de Fontainebleau (€2), 2km southwest, every 10 minutes; the stop is opposite the main entrance.

A la Petite Reine (📞 01 60 74 57 57; www. alapetitereine.com; 14 rue de la Paroisse; bike hire per hr/day €8/15; ☺ 9am-7.30pm Tue-Sat, to 6pm Sun) rents bikes.

Vaux-le-Vicomte

Château de Vaux-le-Vicomte   CHÂTEAU
(📞 01 64 14 41 90; www.vaux-le-vicomte.com; adult/child €16.50/13.50, candlelight visits incl entry €19.50/17.50; ☺ 10am-6pm mid-Mar–early Nov, candlelight visits 5-11pm Sat May–early Oct) The privately owned Château de Vaux-le-Vicomte and its fabulous formal gardens, 20km north of Fontainebleau and 61km southeast of Paris, were designed and built by Le Brun, Le Vau and Le Nôtre between 1656 and 1661 as a precursor to their more ambitious work at Versailles.

The château's beautifully furnished interior is topped by a striking dome. Don't miss the stables' collection of 18th- and 19th-century carriages, or if at all possible, a candlelight visit.

During the same period as candlelight visits, there are elaborate jeux d'eau (fountain displays) in the gardens from 3pm to 6pm on the second and last Saturday of the month.

In the vaulted cellars an exhibition looks at Le Nôtre's landscaping of the gardens.

The beauty of Vaux-le-Vicomte turned out to be the undoing of its original owner, Nicolas Fouquet, Louis XIV's minister of finance. It seems that Louis, seething that he'd been upstaged at the château's official opening, had Fouquet thrown into prison, where the unfortunate ministre died in 1680.

ⓘ Getting There & Away

Vaux-le-Vicomte is not an easy place to reach by public transport. The château is 6km northeast of Melun, which is served by RER line D2 from Paris (€8.10, 30 minutes). The **Châteaubus shuttle** (☺ adult/child return €8/4) links Melun station with the château four to six times daily on Saturday and Sunday from April to mid-November; at other times you'll have to take a **taxi** (📞 01 64 52 51 50; one way €18, evening & Sun €25).

By car, follow the A6 from Paris and then the A5 (direction Melun), and take the 'St-Germain Laxis' exit. From Fontainebleau take the N6 and N36.

Chantilly

POP 10,441

The elegant old town of Chantilly, 50km north of Paris, is small and select. Its imposing, heavily restored château is surrounded by parkland, gardens and the Forêt de Chantilly, offering a wealth of walking opportunities. Chantilly's racetrack is one of the most prestigious hat-and-frock addresses in Europe, and deliciously sweetened thick crème Chantilly was created here. Just don't come on Tuesday, when the château is closed.

⊙ Sights

Château de Chantilly   CHÂTEAU
(📞 03 44 27 31 80; www.domainedechantilly. com; domain pass adult/child €20/10, show pass €30/20; ☺ 10am-6pm Wed-Mon Apr-Oct, 10.30am-5pm Wed-Mon Nov-Mar) A storybook vision surrounded by an artificial lake and magnificent gardens, the Château de Chantilly contains a superb collection of paintings within the Musée Condé.

Left in a shambles after the Revolution, the greatly restored château consists of two attached buildings, the Petit and Grand Châteaux, which are entered through the same vestibule. The estate's Grandes Écuries (Grand Stables) are just west.

A little train around the estate per adult/child costs €5/3; four-person golf carts are also available for hire (€31).

Containing the Appartements des Princes (Princes' Suites), the **Petit Château** was built around 1560 for Anne de Montmorency (1492–1567), who served six French kings as connétable (high constable), diplomat and warrior, and died doing battle with Protestants in the Counter-Reformation. The highlight here is the **Cabinet des Livres**, a repository of 700 manuscripts and more than 30,000 volumes, including a Gutenberg Bible and a facsimile of the Très Riches Heures du Duc de Berry, an illuminated manuscript dating from the 15th century that illustrates the calendar year for both the peasantry and the nobility. The **chapel**, to the left as you walk into the vestibule, has woodwork and stained-glass windows dating from the mid-16th century.

The attached Renaissance-style **Grand Château**, completely demolished during the Revolution, was rebuilt by the Duke of Aumale, son of King Louis-Philippe, from 1875 to 1885. It contains the **Musée Condé**, a series of 19th-century rooms adorned with paintings and sculptures haphazardly arranged according to the whims of the duke – he donated the château to the Institut de France on the condition the exhibits were not reorganised and would remain open to the public. The most remarkable works, hidden in the Sanctuaire (Sanctuary), include paintings by Filippino Lippi, Jean Fouquet and (it's thought) Raphael.

Château de Chantilly Gardens GARDEN

(admission included in domain pass; gardens & park only adult/child €7/3.50; ⊗ 10am-8pm Wed-Mon year-round) The Château de Chantilly's wondrous gardens encompass the formal Jardin Français (French Garden), with flowerbeds, lakes and a Grand Canal all laid out by Le Nôtre in the mid-17th century, northeast of the main building; and the 'wilder' Jardin Anglais (English Garden), begun in 1817, to the west. East of the Jardin Français is the rustic Jardin Anglo-Chinois (Anglo-Chinese Garden), created in the 1770s.

The foliage and silted-up waterways of the Jardin Anglo-Chinois surround the hameau, a mock village dating from 1774, whose mill and half-timbered buildings inspired the Hameau de la Reine at Versailles. *Crème Chantilly* was invented here.

Grandes Écuries STABLES

(Grand Stables) The Grandes Écuries, built between 1719 and 1740 to house 240 horses and more than 400 hounds, stand west of the château near Chantilly's famous hippodrome (racecourse), inaugurated in 1834. The stables house the Musée Vivant du Cheval (Living Horse Museum; ☑ 03 44 27 31 80; www.museevivantducheval.fr; adult/child including demonstration €11/5.50, stables only €4/free; ⊗ 10am-6pm Wed-Mon Apr-Oct, 10.30am-5pm Wed-Mon Nov-Mar), included in domain and

show pass admission. Displays range from riding equipment to rocking horses to artworks.

Every visitor, big and small, will be mesmerised by the one-hour equestrian show (adult/child €21/15; ⊗ 2.30pm Wed-Mon Apr-Oct), included in the show pass.

The stables' pampered equines live in luxurious wooden stalls built by Louis-Henri de Bourbon, the seventh Prince de Condé, who was convinced he would be reincarnated as a horse (hence the extraordinary grandeur!).

Forêt de Chantilly FOREST

Once a royal hunting estate, the 63-sq-km Forêt de Chantilly is criss-crossed by walking and riding trails. Long-distance trails here include the GR11, which links the Château de Chantilly with the town of Senlis; the GR1, from Luzarches (famed for its cathedral, parts of which date from the 12th century) to Ermenonville; and the GR12, which heads northeast from four lakes known as the Étangs de Commelles to the Forêt d'Halatte.

The tourist office stocks maps and guides.

🛏 Sleeping

La Ferme de la Canardière B&B €€

(☑ 03 44 62 00 96; www.fermecanardiere.com; 20 rue du Viaduc; s/d incl breakfast €135/160; ☏ ⊠) Delicately embroidered cushions, country-style furnishings and a colour scheme of soft creams and beiges cast a romantic air over this family-run property, which is everything a French B&B should be. In summer allow plenty of time for breakfast on the terrace before plunging into the pool.

Hôtel du Parc HOTEL €€

(☑ 03 44 58 20 00; www.hotel-parc-chantilly.com; 36 av du Maréchal Joffre; s €93-186, d €109-249,

---

CHÂTEAU DE WHIPPED CREAM

Like every self-respecting French château three centuries ago, the palace at Chantilly had its own *hameau* (hamlet) complete with *laitier* (dairy), where the lady of the household and her guests could play at being milkmaids. But the cows at the Chantilly dairy took their job rather more seriously than their fellow bovines at other faux *crémeries* (dairy shops), and the *crème Chantilly* served at the hamlet's teas became the talk (and envy) of aristocratic 18th-century Europe. The future Habsburg emperor Joseph II paid a clandestine visit to this *'temple de marbre'* (marble temple), as he called it, to taste it himself in 1777.

Chantilly (or more properly *crème Chantilly*) is whipped unpasteurised cream with a twist. It's beaten with icing and vanilla sugars to the consistency of a mousse and dolloped on berries. Try it in any cafe or restaurant in town.

f €135-270; @🛜) Part of the Best Western chain, this modern hotel is freshly renovated and has an unbeatable location five minutes' walk from the train station and restaurants. Cheaper rooms face busy av du Maréchal Joffre; pricier 'confort' rooms have stylish touches such as horse-themed prints. Parking costs up to €30 extra depending on the season.

✖ Eating

Le Café Noir CAFE €
(place Omer Vallon; mains €9.50-16.50, 3-course menus €19.50-26.50; ⊙kitchen noon-11.30pm Mon-Sat; 🛜📶) There's a terrace on the pavement out front of this sociable cafe but the best alfrescoco dining is in the umbrella-shaded cobbled courtyard. (If the weather's not behaving, head to the cherry-red skylit interior.) Dishes range from prawns in cognac to Milanese veal; lighter bites include salads, *tartines* and croques madame and monsieur.

Le Boudoir CAFE €
(📌03 44 55 44 49; www.leboudoir-chantilly.fr; 100 rue du Connétable; lunch menu €11.50; ⊙11am-6pm Mon, 10am-7pm Tue-Sat, 11am-7pm Sun) As a certified partner of Parisian gourmet emporium Fauchon, you can be sure of the quality at this charming tearoom. Strewn with comfy sofas, it's a perfect place to try *crème Chantilly* in all its decadence (on hot chocolate topped with lashings of the stuff) or to enjoy a light lunch (salads, savoury tarts and so on).

La Capitainerie TRADITIONAL FRENCH €€
(📌03 44 57 15 89; www.chateaudechantilly.com; 2-/3-course menus €27/31, mains €14-32, snacks €4-8.50; ⊙lunch noon-3pm, snacks noon-5.45pm Wed-Mon) Beneath the vaulted stone ceiling of the château kitchens, La Capitainerie captures history's grandeur and romance. Fare is traditional and includes *crème Chantilly* at every opportunity.

Le Vertugadin TRADITIONAL FRENCH €€
(📌03 44 57 03 19; www.vertugadin.com; 44 rue du Connétable; 3-course menus €29-30, mains €18-38; ⊙7.15-10pm Tue, noon-2pm & 7.15-10pm Wed-Sat, noon-2pm Sun) Old-style and elegant, this ode to regional cuisine – meat, game and terrines accompanied by sweet onion chutney; steak with foie gras and truffles with mashed potatoes and apple – fills a white-shuttered town house. A warming fire roars in the hearth in winter, and summer welcomes diners to the walled garden.

Le Goutillon BISTRO €€
(📌03 44 58 01 00; 61 rue du Connétable; 2-/3-course menus €15/25; ⊙noon-2pm & 7-9.30pm) With its red-and-white checked tablecloths, simple wooden tables and classic bistro fare, this cosy, very friendly French affair is as much a wine bar as a place to dine.

Self-Catering

Marché Decouvert MARKET
(place Omer Vallon; ⊙8.30am-12.30pm Wed & Sat) Chantilly's twice-weekly open-air market is good for picnic goodies.

🛈 Information

Office de Tourisme de Chantilly (📌03 44 67 37 37; www.chantilly-tourisme.com; 60 av du Maréchal Joffre; ⊙9.30am-12.30pm & 1.30-5.30pm Mon-Sat) Can help with accommodation and has details of walks through town, along Chantilly's two canals and around the racecourse, as well as walking and mountain-bike trails in the forest.

🛈 Getting There & Away

Paris' Gare du Nord links with Chantilly-Gouvieux train station (€7.50, 25 to 40 minutes) by hourly-or-better SNCF commuter trains.

Driving from Paris, the fastest route is via the Autoroute du Nord (A1/E19); use exit 7 ('Survilliers-Chantilly'). The N1 then N16 from Porte de la Chapelle/St-Denis is cheaper.

Château de Chantilly is a little more than 2km northeast of the train and bus stations. The most direct route is to walk along av de la Plaine des Aigles through a section of the Forêt de Chantilly. You'll get a better sense of the town, however, by following av du Maréchal Joffre and rue de Paris to connect with rue du Connétable, Chantilly's principal thoroughfare. A taxi from the station to the château costs about €8.

Senlis

POP 16,331

Just 10km northeast of Chantilly (53km north of Paris), Senlis is an enchanting medieval town of winding cobblestone streets, Gallo-Roman ramparts and towers. It was a royal seat from the time of Clovis in the 5th and 6th centuries to Henri IV (r 1589–1610), and contains three small but well-formed **museums** (www.musees-senlis.fr; combined ticket for all three museums adult/child €4/free, single museum €3/free) devoted to subjects as diverse as art and archaeology, hunting and the French cavalry in North Africa.

The town's greatest highlight, however, is its Gothic **Cathédrale de Notre Dame** (place du Parvis Notre Dame; ⊘8am-7pm) FREE, built between 1150 and 1191. The cathedral is unusually bright, with original stained glass. The magnificent carved-stone **Grand Portal** (1176), on the western side facing place du Parvis Notre Dame, has statues and a central relief relating to the life of the Virgin Mary. It's believed to have been the inspiration for the portal at the cathedral in Chartres.

Senlis' **tourist office** (✆03 44 53 06 40; www.senlis-tourisme.fr; place du Parvis Notre Dame; ⊘10am-12.30pm & 2-6.15pm Mon-Sat, 10.30am-1pm & 2-6.15pm Sun Mar-Oct, 10am-12.30pm & 2-5pm, 10.30am-12.30pm & 2-5pm Sun Nov-Feb) is just opposite the cathedral.

Buses (€2, 25 minutes) link Senlis with Chantilly's bus station, just next to its train station, about every half-hour on weekdays and hourly on Saturday, with around half a dozen departures on Sunday.

Chartres

POP 40,675

Step off the train in Chartres, 91km south-west of Paris, and the two very different steeples – one Gothic, the other Romanesque – of its glorious 13th-century cathedral beckon. Follow them to check out the cathedral's dazzling blue stained-glass windows and its collection of relics, including the Sainte Voile (Holy Veil) said to have been worn by the Virgin Mary when she gave birth to Jesus, which have lured pilgrims since the Middle Ages.

After visiting the town's museums, don't miss a stroll around Chartres' carefully preserved old city. Adjacent to the cathedral, staircases and steep streets lined with half-timbered medieval houses lead down-hill to the narrow western channel of the Eure River, romantically spanned by foot-bridges.

◉ Sights & Activities

Allow 1½ to two hours to walk the signpost-ed *circuit touristique* (tourist circuit) tak-ing in Chartres' key sights. Free town maps from the tourist office also mark the route.

Cathédrale Notre Dame   CATHEDRAL
(www.cathedrale-chartres.org; place de la Cathédrale; ⊘8.30am-7.30pm daily year-round,

to 10pm Tue, Fri & Sun Jun-Aug) One of West-ern civilisation's crowning architectural achievements, the 130m-long Cathédrale Notre Dame de Chartres is renowned for its brilliant-blue stained-glass windows and sacred holy veil. Built in the Gothic style during the first quarter of the 13th century to replace a Romanesque cathedral that had been devastated by fire – along with much of the town – in 1194, effective fundraising and donated labour meant construction took only 30 years, resulting in a high de-gree of architectural unity.

Today, it is France's best-preserved medi-eval cathedral, having been spared post-medieval modifications, the ravages of war and the Reign of Terror.

The cathedral's west, north and south entrances have superbly ornamented triple portals, but the west entrance, known as the **Portail Royal**, is the only one that predates the fire. Carved from 1145 to 1155, its superb statues, whose fea-tures are elongated in the Romanesque style, represent the glory of Christ in the centre, and the Nativity and the Ascen-sion to the right and left, respectively. The structure's other main Romanesque fea-ture is the 105m-high **Clocher Vieux** (Old Bell Tower), also called the Tour Sud (South Tower). Construction began in the 1140s; it remains the tallest Romanesque steeple still standing.

A visit to the 112m-high **Clocher Neuf** (New Bell Tower; adult/child €7.50/free; ⊘9.30am-12.30pm & 2-6pm Mon-Sat, 2-6pm Sun May-Aug, 9.30am-12.30pm & 2-6pm Mon-Sat, 2-6pm Sun Sep-Apr), also known as the Tour Nord (North Tower), is worth the ticket price and the climb up the long 350-step spiral stairway. Access is just behind the cathedral bookshop. A 70m-high platform on the lacy flamboyant **Gothic spire**, built from 1507 to 1513 by Jehan de Beauce after an earlier wooden spire burned down, affords superb views of the three-tiered flying buttresses and the 19th-century copper roof, turned green by verdigris.

The cathedral's 176 extraordinary **stained-glass windows**, almost all of which date back to the 13th century, form one of the most important ensembles of medieval stained glass in the world. The three most exquisite windows, dating from the mid-12th century, are in the wall above the west entrance and below the rose window. Survivors of the fire of 1194 (they were made

Chartres

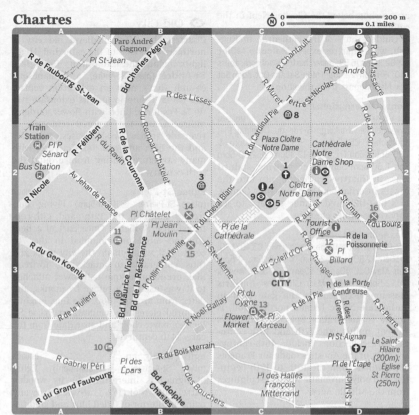

some four decades before), the windows are revered for the depth and intensity of their tones, famously known as 'Chartres blue'.

In Chartres since 876, the venerated **Sainte Voile** (Holy Veil; p176) – a yellowish bolt of silk draped over a support – is displayed at the end of the cathedral's north aisle behind the choir.

The cathedral's 110m **crypt** (adult/child €3/2.40; ⊙ up to five tours daily), a tombless Romanesque structure built in 1024 around a 9th-century predecessor, is the largest in France. Thirty-minute tours in French (with a written English translation) start at the cathedral-run **shop** (☑ 02 37 21 59 08; 18 Cloître Notre Dame) selling souvenirs, from April to October. At other times they begin

Chartres

at the shop below the Clocher Neuf in the cathedral.

Guided tours of the cathedral, in English, with Chartres expert **Malcolm Miller** (☑ 02 37 28 15 58; millerchartres@aol.com; tours €10; ☺ noon & 2.45pm Mon-Sat Apr-Oct, noon Sat Nov-Mar) depart from the shop.

Centre International du Vitrail MUSEUM
(www.centre-vitrail.org; 5 rue du Cardinal Pie; adult/child €5.50/free; ☺ 9.30am-12.30pm & 1.30-6pm Mon-Fri, 10am-12.30pm & 2.30-6pm Sat, 2.30-6pm Sun) After viewing stained glass in Chartres' cathedral, nip into the town's International Stained-Glass Centre, in a half-timbered former granary, to see superb examples close up.

Musée des Beaux-Arts MUSEUM
(29 Cloître Notre Dame; adult/child €3.40/1.70; ☺ 10am-12.30pm & 2-6pm Wed & Sat, 2-6pm Sun May-Oct, 10am-12.30pm & 2-5pm Wed & Sat, 2-5pm Sun Nov-Mar) Chartres' fine-arts museum, accessed via the gate next to Cathédrale Notre Dame's north portal, is in the former Palais Épiscopal (Bishop's Palace), built in the 17th and 18th centuries. Its collections include 16th-century enamels of the Apostles made for François I, paintings from the 16th to 19th centuries and poly-chromatic wooden sculptures from the Middle Ages.

Le Petit Chart' Train TOURIST TRAIN
(http://petittrain.olikeopen.com; adult/child €6.50/3.50; ☺ 10.30am-2pm late Mar-Oct) Departing from in front of the tourist office, Chartres' electric tourist 'train' covers the main sights in 35 minutes.

HOLY VEIL

The most venerated object in Chartres cathedral is the **Sainte Voile**, the 'Holy Veil' said to have been worn by the Virgin Mary when she gave birth to Jesus. It originally formed part of the imperial treasury of Constantinople but was offered to Charlemagne by the Empress Irene when the Holy Roman Emperor proposed marriage to her in 802. Charles the Bald presented it to the town in 876; the cathedral was built because the veil survived the 1194 fire.

◉ Old City

Chartres' beautiful medieval old city is northeast and east of the cathedral. Highlights include the 12th-century **Collégiale St-André** (place St-André), a Romanesque church that's now an exhibition centre; **rue de la Tannerie** and its extension **rue de la Foulerie**, lined with flower gardens, millraces and the restored remnants of riverside trades: wash houses, tanneries and the like; and **rue des Écuyers**, with many structures dating from around the 16th century.

Église St-Pierre CHURCH
(place St-Pierre; ☺ 10am-5pm) Flying buttresses hold up the 12th- and 13th-century Église St-Pierre. Once part of a Benedictine monastery founded in the 7th century, it was outside the city walls and thus vulnerable to attack; the fortress-like, pre-Romanesque bell tower attached to it was used as a refuge by monks, and dates from around 1000. The fine, brightly coloured clerestory windows in Église St-Pierre's nave, choir and apse date from the early 14th century.

Église St-Aignan CHURCH
(place St-Aignan; ☺ 8.30am-6pm) Église St-Aignan is interesting for its wooden barrel-vault roof (1625), arcaded nave and painted interior of faded blue and gold floral motifs (c 1870). The stained glass and the Renaissance Chapelle de St-Michel date from the 16th and 17th centuries.

✸ Festivals & Events

Chartres en Lumières LIGHTS FESTIVAL
(www.chartresenlumieres.com) From mid-April to mid-October, 27 of Chartres' landmarks are spectacularly lit every night. You can also see them from aboard **Le Petit Chart' Train late circuits** (adult/child €7.50/4.50; ☺ 10.30pm daily Jul & Aug, Fri & Sat Apr-Jun & Sep-Oct) or on **night walking tours** (adult/child €13/5; ☺ by reservation Jul & Aug) in English, bookable through Chartres' tourist office.

🛏 Sleeping

Chartres is a convenient stop en route to the Loire Valley.

Hôtel du Bœuf Couronné HOTEL €€
(☑ 02 37 18 06 06; www.leboeufcouronne.com; 15 place Châtelet; s €57-96, d €67-121; @☎) The red-curtained entrance lends a vaguely

theatrical air to this two-star Logis guesthouse in the centre of everything. Its summer-time terrace restaurant has cathedral-view dining and the XV bar mixes great cocktails.

Best Western
Le Grand Monarque
HOTEL €€€

(☑ 02 37 18 15 15; www.bw-grand-monarque.com; 22 place des Épars; d €139-206, f €206; ☺restaurant noon-2pm & 7.30-10pm Tue-Sat, noon-2pm Sun; ❋@❂) With its teal-blue shutters gracing its 1779 façade, lovely stained-glass ceiling and treasure trove of period furnishings, old B&W photos and knick-knacks, the refurbished Grand Monarque (with aircon in some rooms) is a historical gem and very central. A host of hydrotherapy treatments are available at its decadent spa; its elegant restaurant, **Georges** (three-course *menus* from €51), has a Michelin star. Staff are charming.

✖ Eating

La Passacaille
ITALIAN €

(☑ 02 37 21 52 10; www.lapassacaille.fr; 30 rue Ste-Même; 2-/3-course menus €16/19, pizzas €10.30-14.90, pasta €10.90-15.60; ☺11.45am-2pm & 6.45-10pm Thu & Sun-Tue, 11.45am-2pm & 6.45-10.30pm Fri & Sat; ❄) This welcoming spot has particularly good pizzas (try the Montagnarde with tomato, mozzarella, soft, nutty-flavoured Reblochon cheese, potatoes, red onions, cured ham and *crème fraîche*) and homemade pasta with toppings including *pistou* (pesto) also made on the premises. Tables spill onto the square out front in summer.

La Chocolaterie
PATISSERIE, TEAROOM €

(2 place du Cygne; dishes €3.80-5.50; ☺8am-7.30pm Tue-Sat, 10am-7.30pm Sun & Mon) Soak up local life overlooking the open-air flower market. This tearoom/patisserie's hot chocolate and macarons (flavoured with orange, apricot, peanut, pineapple and so on) are sublime, as are its sweet homemade crêpes and miniature madeleine cakes.

Covered Market
MARKET €

(place Billard; ☺7am-1pm Wed & Sat) Food shops surround the covered market, just off rue des Changes south of the cathedral. The market itself dates from the early 20th century.

★ Le Saint-Hilaire
REGIONAL CUISINE €€

(☑ 02 37 30 97 57; www.restaurant-saint-hilaire. fr; 11 rue du Pont St-Hilaire; 3-course menus from

€29; ☺noon-2pm & 7-9.30pm Tue-Sat) At this pistachio-painted, wood-beamed charmer, local products are ingeniously used in to-die-for dishes such as bacon-wrapped prawns with leek fondue, honey-roasted duck, and escalope of veal in hazelnut and foie gras sauce. Don't miss its lobster *menu* in season, or the aromatic cheese platters.

Le Tripot
BISTRO €€

(☑ 02 37 36 60 11; http://letripot.monsite-orange. fr; 11 place Jean Moulin; menus 3-course lunch €15.50, 3-course dinner €28-44; ☺noon-1.45pm & 7.30-9.15pm Tue & Thu-Sat, noon-1.45pm Sun) Tucked off the tourist trail and easy to miss, even if you do chance down its narrow street, this atmospheric space with low beamed ceilings is a winner for authentic and adventurous French fare such as saddle of rabbit stuffed with snails, and grilled turbot in truffled hollandaise sauce. Locals are onto it, so booking ahead's advised.

L'Escalier
BISTRO €€

(☑ 02 37 33 05 45; www.lescalier-chartres.com; 1 rue du Bourg; 2-/3-course menus €18/22; ☺noon-3pm & 7-10pm) On a steep corner near its namesake staircase in Chartres' hilly Old City, this deceptively large, very local restaurant has a wonderful terrace for summertime dining and is worth the pre- or post-meal climb for its short but superb *menu* (foie gras platters, succulent steaks and classic desserts including crème caramel). Look out for live jazz performances.

❶ Information

Tourist Office (☑ 02 37 18 26 26; www. chartres-tourisme.com; 8-10 rue de la Poissonnerie; ☺10am-6pm Mon-Sat, to 5pm Sun) Housed in the historic Maison du Saumon, with an exhibition on Chartres' history. Rents 1½-hour English-language audioguide tours (€5.50/8.50 for one/two) of the medieval city as well as binoculars (€2), fabulous for seeing details of the cathedral close up.

❶ Getting There & Away

Frequent SNCF trains link Paris' Gare Montparnasse (€15.60, 55 to 70 minutes) with Chartres, some of which stop at Versailles-Chantiers (€13.20, 45 to 60 minutes).

If you're driving from Paris, follow the A6 from Porte d'Orléans (direction Bordeaux–Nantes), then the A10 and A11 (direction Nantes) and take the 'Chartres' exit.

Lille, Flanders & the Somme

POP 5.97 MILLION

Best Places to Eat

➜ Meert (p184)

➜ La Sirène (p193)

➜ Het Kasteelhof (p188)

➜ Les Deux Frères – Chez Zénon (p190)

➜ Le Bistrot des Arts (p210)

Best Places to Stay

➜ L'Hermitage Gantois (p184)

➜ Le Cercle de Malines (p194)

➜ La Corne d'Or (p190)

➜ Hôtel Les Pilotes (p199)

➜ Au Vintage (p205)

Why Go?

True, a tan is easier to come by along the Mediterranean, but when it comes to culture, cuisine, beer, shopping and dramatic views of land and sea – not to mention good old-fashioned friendliness – the regions of the Ch'tis (residents of France's northern tip) and Picards compete with the best France has to offer. In Lille and French Flanders, the down-to-earth Flemish vibe mixes easily with French sophistication and *savoir faire*. And in Picardy and Artois, WWI memorials and cemeteries marking the front lines of 1916 render overseas visitors speechless time and again with their heart-breaking beauty. On a more cheerful note, the blessedly underrated cities of Amiens, Laon and Arras will captivate culture vultures with their glorious architectural treasures, while nature lovers will get a buzz along the sublime Côte d'Opale and fascinating Baie de Somme. Whatever your inclination, you're guaranteed leave this part of France with new experiences and wonderful memories.

When to Go
Lille

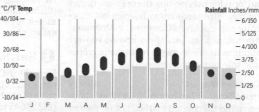

Feb & Mar Pre-Lenten carnivals bring out marching bands and costumed revellers.

Jul & Aug Splendid weather makes summer a perfect time to explore Côte d'Opale.

Sep The world's largest flea market, the Braderie, takes over Lille on the first weekend in September.

Lille, Flanders & the Somme Highlights

1 Strolling around **Lille**'s (p180) chic and photogenic centre

2 Marvelling at Amiens' breathtaking Gothic **cathedral** (p206)

3 Rambling along the spectacular, windswept **Côte d'Opale** (p192), facing the white cliffs of Dover

4 Contemplating modern art at the innovative **Louvre-Lens museum** (p191) in Lens

5 Enjoying a hefty dose of Flemish culture in the pretty hilltop town of **Cassel** (p188)

6 Getting the best views of magical **Baie de Somme** (p198) from a kayak

7 Joining the bustle of the Saturday market in Arras' gorgeous Flemish-style **Place des Héros** (p189)

8 Pondering the sacrifices at **Vimy Ridge Canadian National Historical Site** (p204)

9 Revelling in elegant architecture and fine arts in **Compiègne** (p209)

History & Geography

In the Middle Ages, the Nord *département* (the sliver of France along the Belgian border; www.tourisme-nord.fr), together with much of Belgium and part of the Netherlands, belonged to a feudal principality known as Flanders (Flandre or Flandres in French, Vlaanderen in Flemish). Today, many people in the area still speak Flemish – essentially Dutch with some variation in pronunciation and vocabulary – and are very proud of their *flamand* culture and cuisine.

The area south of the Somme estuary and Albert forms the *région* of Picardy, historically centred on the Somme *département,* which saw some of the bloodiest fighting of WWI. The popular British WWI love song 'Rose of Picardy' was penned here in 1916 by Frederick E Weatherley.

ℹ Getting There & Away

Lille, Flanders and Picardy are a hop, skip and a jump from southwest England. By train on the **Eurostar** (www.eurostar.com) (promotional fares Lille–London start at just €88 return) Lille is just 70 minutes from London's St Pancras International train station. **Eurotunnel** (www.eurotunnel. com) can get you and your car from Folkestone to Calais, via the Channel Tunnel, in a mere 35 minutes. For those with sturdy sea legs, car ferries link Dover with Calais and Dunkirk.

On the Continent, superfast Eurostar and TGV trains link Lille with Brussels (35 minutes), and TGVs make travel from Lille to Paris' Gare du Nord (one hour) and Charles de Gaulle Airport (one hour) a breeze.

LILLE

POP 233,210

Lille (Rijsel in Flemish) may be France's most underrated major city. In recent decades this once-grimy industrial metropolis, its economy based on declining industries, has shrugged off its grey image and transformed itself into a glittering and self-confident cultural and commercial hub. Highlights for the visitor include an attractive old town with a strong Flemish accent, three renowned art museums, stylish shopping, some excellent dining options and a cutting-edge, student-driven nightlife scene. The Lillois have a well-deserved reputation for friendliness – and are so proud of being friendly that they often mention it!

Thanks to the Eurostar and the TGV, Lille makes an easy, environmentally sustainable weekend destination from London, Paris or Brussels.

History

Lille owes its name – once spelled L'Isle – to the fact that it was founded, back in the 11th century, on an island in the River Deûle. In 1667 the city was captured by French forces led personally by Louis XIV, who promptly set about fortifying his prize, creating the Lille Citadelle. In the 1850s the miserable conditions in which Lille's 'labouring classes' lived – the city was long the centre of France's textile industry – were exposed by Victor Hugo.

◉ Sights & Activities

Palais des
Beaux Arts
ART MUSEUM

(Fine Arts Museum; ✆03 20 06 78 00; www.pba-lille.fr; place de la République; adult/child €6.50/free; ⊙2-5.30pm Mon, 10am-5.30pm Wed-Sun; Ⓜ République-Beaux Arts) Lille's world-renowned Fine Arts Museum displays a truly first-rate collection of 15th- to 20th-century paintings, including works by Rubens, Van Dyck and Manet. Exquisite porcelain and faience (pottery), much of it of local provenance, is on the ground floor, while in the basement you'll find classical archaeology, medieval statuary and 18th-century scale models of the fortified cities of northern France and Belgium. Information sheets in French, English and Dutch are available in each hall.

Musée d'Art Moderne,
d'Art Contemporain et
d'Art Brut – LaM
ART MUSEUM

(✆03 20 19 68 68; www.musee-lam.fr; 1 allée du Musée, Villeneuve-d'Ascq; adult/child €7/free; ⊙10am-6pm Tue-Sun) Colourful, playful and just plain weird works of modern and contemporary art by masters such as Braque, Calder, Léger, Miró, Modigliani and Picasso are the big draw at this renowned museum and sculpture park in the Lille suburb of Villeneuve-d'Ascq, 9km east of Gare Lille-Europe. Take metro line 1 to Pont de Bois, then bus line 4 (10 minutes) to Villeneuve-d'Ascq-LaM.

La Piscine Musée d'Art
et d'Industrie
ART MUSEUM

(✆03 20 69 23 60; www.roubaix-lapiscine.com; 23 rue de l'Espérance, Roubaix; adult/child €5.50/free; ⊙11am-6pm Tue-Thu, 11am-8pm Fri, 1-6pm Sat & Sun; Ⓜ Gare Jean Lebas) If Paris can turn a disused train station into a world-class museum (the Musée d'Orsay), why not transform an art deco municipal swimming pool (built 1927–32) – an architectural masterpiece inspired by civic pride and hygienic high-mindedness – into a temple of the arts? This innovative museum, 12km northeast of Gare Lille-

---

Europe in Roubaix, showcases fine arts, applied arts and sculpture in a delightfully watery environment.

Wazemmes
NEIGHBOURHOOD

(Ⓜ Gambetta) For an authentic taste of grass-roots Lille, head to the ethnically mixed, family-friendly *quartier populaire* (working-class quarter) of Wazemmes, 1.7km southwest of place du Général de Gaulle, where African immigrants and old-time proletarians live harmoniously alongside penurious students and trendy *bobos* (bourgeois bohemians).

The neighbourhood's focal point is the cavernous **Marché de Wazemmes**, Lille's favourite food market. The adjacent **outdoor market** is the place to be on Sunday morning – it's a real carnival scene! Rue des Sarrazins and rue Jules Guesde are lined with shops, restaurants and Tunisian pastry places, many owned by, and catering to, the area's North African residents.

Wazemmes is famed for its many outdoor concerts and street festivals, including **La Louche d'Or** (Golden Ladle; 1 May), a soup festival that has spread to cities across Europe.

Maison Natale de
Charles de Gaulle
HOUSE MUSEUM

(✆03 28 38 12 05; www.maison-natale-de-gaulle.org; 9 rue Princesse; adult/child incl audioguide €6/free; ⊙10am-noon & 2-5pm Wed-Sat, 1.30-5pm Sun) The upper-middle-class house in which Charles de Gaulle was born in 1890 is now a museum presenting the French leader in the context of his times, with an emphasis on his connection to French Flanders. Displays include de Gaulle's dainty baptismal robe and some evocative newsreels.

Musée de
l'Hospice Comtesse
ART MUSEUM

(✆03 28 36 84 00; 32 rue de la Monnaie; adult/child €3.50/free; ⊙10am-12.30pm & 2-6pm, closed Mon morning & Tue) Housed in a remarkably

Lille

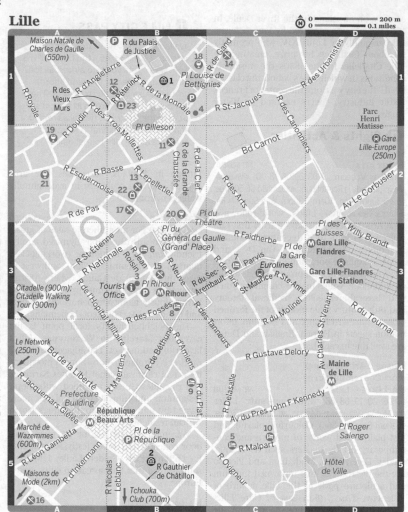

attractive 15th- and 17th-century poorhouse, this museum features ceramics, earthenware wall tiles, religious art and 17th- and 18th-century paintings and furniture. A rood screen separates the Salle des Malades (Hospital Hall) from a mid-17th century chapel (look up to see a mid-19th century painted ceiling).

Citadelle

FORTRESS

(☏03 20 21 94 39; Vauban-Esquermes; ▣12) At the northwestern end of bd de la Liberté, this massive star-shaped fortress was designed by renowned 17th-century French military architect Vauban after France captured Lille in 1667. Made of some 60 million bricks, it still functions as a French and NATO military base. Guided tours are available on Sundays in summer – contact the tourist office. This is the only way to see the inside of the Citadelle.

Outside the 2.2km-long ramparts is the city centre's largest park, where children will love the amusement park, playground and small municipal zoo.

☞ Tours

The tourist office (p187) runs various guided tours.

Lille

Citadelle Walking Tour WALKING
(adult €7.50; ⊙3pm & 4.30pm Sun Jun-Aug) This is the only way to see the inside of the Citadelle, usually a closed military zone. Sign up for the tour (in French) at least 72 hours ahead and bring a passport or national ID card. The tour lasts one hour.

Vieux Lille Walking Tour WALKING
(adult/child €11.50/9.50; ⊙10.15am Sat in English; 3pm daily in French) Departing from the tourist office, this walking tour takes in all the highlights of Lille's 17th- and 18th-century Old Town.

Flanders Battlefields Tour WWI HISTORY
(adult €44; ⊙1-5pm Sat in English) Four-hour tour of several important WWI battle sites around Ypres (just across the Belgian border). Tours depart from the tourist office.

⚜ Festivals & Events

The Braderie (p187), a flea-market extraordinaire, is held on the first weekend in September. Before the festivities you can join in the **semi-marathon** (www.semimarathon-lille.fr) that begins at 8.45am on Saturday, or a 10km run at 10.45am; both set off from place de la République.

Throughout the year, the varied art exhibitions associated with **Lille 3000** (www.lille3000.com) 'explore the richness and complexities of the world of tomorrow'.

In the lead-up to Christmas, decorations and edible goodies are sold at the **Marché de Noël** (Christmas Market; www.noel-a-lille.com; place Rihour; ⊙late Nov-30 Dec).

🛏 Sleeping

Most Lille hotels are at their fullest, and priciest, from Monday to Thursday.

Auberge de Jeunesse HOSTEL €
(☑03 20 57 08 94; www.hifrance.org; 12 rue Malpart; dm incl breakfast €23; @🛜; Ⓜ Mairie de Lille, République-Beaux-Arts) This central former maternity hospital has 163 beds in rooms for two to eight, kitchen facilities and free parking. A few doubles have ensuite showers. Lockout is from 11am to 3pm (to 4pm Friday to Sunday).

Hotel Kanaï HOTEL €€
(☑03 20 57 14 78; www.hotelkanai.com; 10 rue de Bethune; d €75-140; ❄@🛜; Ⓜ Rihour) In the heart of Lille's pedestrian zone, this enticing hotel offers reasonably priced rooms with a clean modern design; pick of the bunch are rooms 102 and 302, with large picture windows and plenty of natural light.

All come with coffee makers, attractive tiled bathrooms, crisp linen and excellent bedding. One complaint: there's no lift.

Grand Hôtel Bellevue HISTORIC HOTEL €€
(☑03 20 57 45 64; www.grandhotelbellevue.com; 5 rue Jean Roisin; d €119-199; ❄@🛜; Ⓜ Rihour) Grandly built in the early 20th century, this venerable establishment features 60 spacious rooms equipped with marble bathrooms, grey carpets, gilded picture frames and flat-screen TVs.

It's well worth springing for one of the better rooms with views of place du Général de Gaulle.

Hôtel Brueghel
HOTEL €€

(☑ 03 20 06 06 69; www.hotel-brueghel-lille.com; 5 parvis St-Maurice; s €86-102, d €94-127; ☜; Ⓜ Gare Lille-Flandres) The Brueghel is a dependable midrange hotel that occupies an appealing brick building halfway between Gare Lille-Flandres and the Grand' Place. The wood-panelled lobby has charm in spades, as does the creaky, tiny lift that trundles guests up to 65 rooms that have been recently modernised. Some south-facing rooms have sunny views of the adjacent church. A good deal.

La Villa 30
B&B €€

(☑ 03 66 73 61 30; www.lavilla30.fr; 24 rue du Plat; d incl breakfast €99-125; ☜; Ⓜ République Beaux Arts) This five-room B&B is a safe bet. The fashion-forward style reflects the owner's love for contemporary interior design, with elegant furnishings, chocolate brown, beige and grey colour schemes, and modern bathrooms. One room has a balcony. It's in a quiet street near the Palais des Beaux Arts.

★ L'Hermitage Gantois
HISTORIC HOTEL €€€

(☑ 03 20 85 30 30; www.hotelhermitagegantois. com; 224 rue de Paris; d €234-455; @☜; Ⓜ Mairie de Lille) This five-star hotel creates enchanting, harmonious spaces by complementing its rich architectural heritage – such as a Flemish-Gothic façade – with refined ultramodernism. The 67 rooms are sumptuous, with Starck accessories next to Louis XV–style chairs and bathrooms that sparkle with Carrara marble. One of the four courtyards is home to a 220-year-old wisteria. The still-consecrated chapel was built in 1637.

✕ Eating

Lille (especially Vieux Lille) has a flourishing culinary scene. Keep an eye out for *estaminets* (traditional Flemish eateries, with antique knick-knacks on the walls and plain wooden tables) serving Flemish specialities.

Dining hot spots in Vieux Lille include rue de Gand – home to a dozen small, moderately priced French and Flemish restaurants – and rue de la Monnaie and its side streets.

★ Meert
PATISSERIE €

(☑ 03 20 57 07 44; www.meert.fr; 27 rue Esquermoise; waffles from €3; ☺ 9.30am-9.30pm Tue-Sat, 9am-6pm Sun; Ⓜ Rihour) A delightful spot for morning coffee or mid-afternoon tea, this elegant tearoom dating to 1761 is beloved for its retro decor and its *gaufres* (waffles) filled with sweet Madagascar vanilla paste. The tearoom's 1830s-vintage chocolate shop next door has a similarly old-fashioned atmosphere.

Le Pain Quotidien
BOULANGERIE €

(☑ 03 20 42 88 90; www.lepainquotidien.fr; 35 place Rihour; mains €10-15; ☺ 8am-9.15pm; Ⓜ Rihour) At this popular bakery, high-ceilinged interior rooms are flanked by display cases stacked floor to ceiling with jams, organic juices and scrumptious baked goods. In warm weather there's also outdoor seating on place Rihour, making this a prime spot for morning bowls of coffee, midday sandwiches and healthy salads, and afternoon snacks.

Le Bistrot Lillois
FLEMISH €

(☑ 03 20 14 04 15; 40 rue de Gand; mains €10-15; ☺ noon-2pm & 7.30-10pm Tue-Sat) This place owes its reputation to a menu based solidly on expertly prepared regional specialities. The highlight of the menu is *os à moëlle* (marrow bone), but other dishes worth trying include *carbonade flamande* (braised beef stewed with Flemish beer, spice bread and brown sugar) and *potjevleesch* (jellied chicken, pork, veal and rabbit).

Au Vieux de la Vieille
FLEMISH €

(☑ 03 20 13 81 64; www.estaminetlille.fr; 2-4 rue des Vieux Murs; mains €12-15; ☺ noon-2pm & 7-10.30pm daily) Although locals say that it used to be better, this *estaminet* (Flemish-style eatery) remains one of the highly rated venues in central Lille for regional cuisine. The fact it has outdoor seating on picturesque cobblestoned place de l'Oignon is a plus.

Le Comptoir 44
NEOBISTRO €

(☑ 03 20 21 03 63; www.comptoir44.fr; 44 rue de Gand; mains €13-19, lunch menu €16, dinner menu €31; ☺ noon-2.30pm & 7-10.30pm) Considering its location on rue de Gand, this rustic chic bistro could have been a typical tourist trap; instead, well-prepared bistro classics and regional dishes go down a treat and are served with a smile by a dynamic team.

La Petite Cour
FLEMISH €

(☑ 03 20 51 52 81; www.lapetitecourlille.fr; 17 rue du Curé St-Étienne; mains €15-19, lunch menus €16-19, dinner menu €28; ☺ noon-2pm & 7.30-10.30pm Mon-Thu, to 11.30pm Fri & Sat) You'd never guess from outside that there's an atmospheric dining room with brick walls, wooden floors, high ceilings and a lovely inner courtyard. Foodwise, it's no less impressive, with a tempting array of Flemish staples, salads as well as meat and fish dishes.

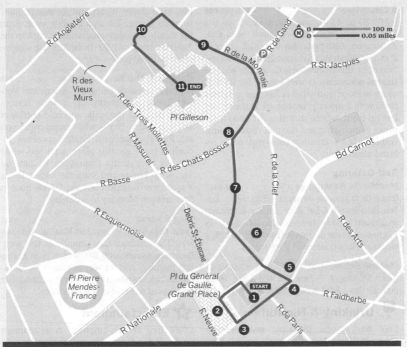

Lille Walk
Lille Discovery Stroll

START VIEILLE BOURSE
FINISH CATHÉDRALE NOTRE-DAME-DE-LA-TREILLE
DISTANCE 1KM
DURATION ONE HOUR

The best place to begin is the **❶ Vieille Bourse**, a Flemish Renaissance extravaganza ornately decorated with caryatids and cornucopia. Built in 1653, it consists of 24 separate houses set around a richly ornamented interior courtyard that hosts a used-book market. In warm weather locals often gather here to play *échecs* (chess).

West of the Vieille Bourse is **❷ place du Général de Gaulle** (or 'Grand' Place') where you can admire the 1932 art deco home of **❸ La Voix du Nord** (the leading regional newspaper), crowned by a gilded sculpture of the Three Graces. The victory column (1845) in the fountain commemorates the city's successful resistance to the Austrian siege of 1792. On warm evenings, Lillois come here by the thousands to stroll, take in the atmosphere and sip a local beer. East of the Vieille Bourse, impressive **❹ place du Théâtre** is dominat-

ed by the Louis XVI–style **❺ Opéra** and the neo-Flemish **❻ Chambre de Commerce**, topped by a 76m-high spire sporting a gilded clock. Both were built in the early 20th century. Look east along rue Faidherbe and you'll see Gare Lille-Flandres at the other end.

Vieux Lille (Old Lille), proud of its restored 17th- and 18th-century brick houses, begins just north of here. Hard to believe, but in the late 1970s this quarter was a half-abandoned slum dominated by empty, dilapidated buildings. Head north along **❼ rue de la Grande Chaussée**, lined with Lille's chic-est shops, and take a peek at **❽ À l'Huîtrière** restaurant, an art deco masterpiece. Continue north along **❾ rue de la Monnaie** (named after a mint constructed here in 1685), whose old brick residences now house boutiques and the Musée de l'Hospice Comtesse.

Turning left (west) on tiny **❿ rue Péterinck** and then left again will take you to the 19th-century, neo-Gothic **Cathédrale Notre-Dame-de-la-Treille**, which has a strikingly modern (some would say 'jarring') west façade (1999) that looks better from inside or when illuminated at night.

À l'Huîtrière   SEAFOOD €€€

(☎03 20 55 43 41; www.huitriere.fr; 3 rue des Chats Bossus; mains €35-62, lunch menu €45, dinner menu €98, oyster bar from €10; ◷noon-2pm & 7-9.30pm Mon-Sat, noon-2pm Sun) On the 'Street of the Hunchback Cats', this sophisticated restaurant is well known for its fabulous seafood and wine cellar. For a lighter meal with a lower price tag, sit at the oyster bar up front, where stunning art deco trappings – including sea-themed mosaics and stained glass – create a colourful, more relaxed atmosphere.

Self-Catering

Marché de Wazemmes   MARKET

(place de la Nouvelle Aventure; ◷8am-2pm Tue-Thu, 8am-8pm Fri & Sat, 8am-3pm Sun & holidays; ⓜGambetta) This beloved foodie space is 1.7km southwest of the tourist office, in Lille's working-class quarter of Wazemmes.

Marché Sébastopol   FOOD MARKET

(place Sébastopol; ◷7am-2pm Wed & Sat; ⓜRépublique Beaux Arts) A popular food market.

🍷 Drinking & Nightlife

Lille has several drinking and nightlife areas. In Vieux Lille the small, stylish bars and cafes along streets such as rue Royale, rue de la Barre and rue de Gand are a big hit with chic 30-somethings. On Friday and Saturday nights, in the rue Masséna student zone, a university-age crowd descends on dozens of high-decibel bars along rue Masséna (750m southwest of the tourist office) and almost-perpendicular rue Solférino (as far southeast as Marché Sébastopol).

In the warm season, sidewalk cafes make the square in front of the Opéra, the place du Théâtre, a fine spot to sip beer and soak up the Flemish atmosphere.

L'Illustration Café   BAR

(www.bar-lillustration.com; 18 rue Royale; ◷12.30pm-3am Mon-Sat, 3pm-3am Sun) Adorned with art nouveau woodwork and changing exhibits by local painters, this laid-back bar attracts artists, musicians, budding intellectuals and teachers in the mood to read, exchange weighty ideas, or just shoot the breeze. The mellow soundtrack mixes Western classical with jazz, French *chansons* and African beats.

Morel & Fils   BAR

(31-33 place du Théâtre; ◷8am-11pm Mon-Sat, 3-11pm Sun; ⓜRihour) This bar-cafe diagonally across from Lille's Opéra features eclectic

historical decor incorporating mannequins from its former life as a lingerie shop. Scan the façade for cannonballs dating back to the Austrian siege of 1792 (including one suggestively painted pink one).

Café Oz – The Australian Bar   PUB

(33 place Louise de Bettignies; ◷5pm-3am Mon-Sat) Footy and rugby on a wide screen, Australiana on the walls and cold bottles of Toohey's Extra Dry – what more could you ask for? Popular with English-speakers, including students, this place is packed when DJs do their thing from 9pm to 3am on Thursday, Friday and Saturday nights. It has a great warm-season terrace. Happy hour is 5pm to 9pm Monday to Saturday.

Vice & Versa   GAY BAR

(3 rue de la Barre; ◷3pm-3am Mon-Sat, 4pm-3am Sun) The rainbow flies proudly at this well-heeled, sophisticated bar, which is as gay as it is popular (and it's very popular). Decor includes brick walls, a camp crystal chandelier and lots of red and green laser dots.

⭐ Entertainment

Lille's free French-language entertainment guide *Sortir* (www.lille.sortir.eu, in French) is available at the tourist office, cinemas, event venues and bookshops.

Le Network   DISCO

(www.network-cafe.net; 15 rue du Faisan; ◷10.30pm-5.30am Tue & Wed, 9.30pm-5.30am Thu, 10.30pm-7am Fri & Sat, 7pm-5am Sun; ⓜRépublique Beaux Arts) At Lille's hottest discotheque, you can sip beer and boogie in the main hall, presided over by two 5m-high statues from faraway lands, or in the baroque Venetian room, decked out with velvet settees and crystal chandeliers. The door policy is pretty strict – locals dress up – but tends to be a bit more relaxed for tourists. Situated 600m northwest of the Palais des Beaux-Arts.

Tchouka Club   DISCO

(www.tchoukaclub.org; 80 rue Barthélemy Delespaul; ◷11pm-7am Fri & Sat) This till-dawn gay and lesbian disco has photo-montage wall murals, plenty of flashing lights, buff barmen in tank tops and a soundtrack that's heavy on electro, house and techno. It's so packed after 1am that you may have trouble getting in. Relaxed dress code. Situated 700m due south of the Palais des Beaux-Arts.

Shopping

Lille's snazziest clothing and housewares boutiques are in Vieux Lille, in the area bounded by rue de la Monnaie, rue Esquermoise, rue de la Grande Chausée (a window shopper's paradise!) and rue d'Angleterre. Keep an eye out for shops specialising in French Flemish edibles, including cheeses.

Maisons de Mode   FASHION
(☑03 20 99 91 20; www.maisonsdemode.com; 58/60 rue du Faubourg des Postes; ☺2-7pm Wed-Sat) Cool, cutting-edge couture by promising young designers can be found in this cluster of studio-boutiques, about 2.5km southwest of the Palais des Beaux-Arts.

L'Abbaye des Saveurs   FOOD & WINE
(☑03 28 07 70 06; www.abbayedessaveurs.com; 13 rue des Vieux Murs; ☺2-7pm Mon & Tue, 11am-7pm Wed-Sat, 11am-1.30pm Sun) A beer-lover's dream, this little shop features dozens of famous and more obscure local brews, from both the French and Belgian sides of the border.

Fromagerie Philippe Olivier   FOOD & WINE
(☑03 20 74 96 99; www.philippeolivier.fr; 3 rue du Curé St-Étienne; ☺2.30pm-7.15pm Mon, 10am-7.15pm Tue-Thu, 9am-7.15pm Fri & Sat; MRihour) This shop near place de Gaulle is an excellent source for local cheeses.

ℹ Information

International Currency Exchange (Gare Lille-Europe; ☺7.30am-8pm Mon-Sat, 10am-8pm Sun; MGare Lille-Europe) Currency exchange in Gare Lille-Europe, in Hall 3.

Tourist Office (☑03 59 57 94 00; www.lilletourism.com; place Rihour; ☺9am-6pm Mon-Sat, 10am-noon & 2-5pm Sun & holidays; MRihour) The tourist office occupies what's left of the Flamboyant Gothic–style Palais Rihour, built in the mid-1400s. It has free maps and an excellent map-brochure (€3) outlining walking tours of five city *quartiers*.

ℹ Getting There & Away

AIR

Aéroport de Lille (www.lille.aeroport.fr) Lille is connected to Biarritz, Barcelona (Spain), Bordeaux, Corsica, Geneva (Switzerland), Lyon, Marseille, Montpellier, Nantes, Nice, Strasbourg and Toulouse, among others.

BUS

Eurolines (☑08 92 89 90 91; www.eurolines.com; 23 parvis St-Maurice; underground railGare Lille-Flandres) serves cities such as Brussels

(€19, 1½ hours), Amsterdam (€37, five hours) and London (€36 to €47, 5½ hours; by day via the Channel Tunnel, at night by ferry). The bus stop is a 10-minute walk from Eurolines' ticket office; follow av Le Corbusier just past Gare Lille-Europe, then look for the stop on your left, beyond the taxi rank on bd de Leeds.

CAR

Driving into Lille is incredibly confusing, even with a good map. To get to the city centre, the best thing to do is to suspend your sense of direction and blindly follow the 'Centre Ville' signs. Parking lots are easy to find in the centre.

Avis, Europcar, Hertz and **National-Citer** have car-hire offices in Gare Lille-Europe, while domestic rental companies such as **DLM** (☑03 20 06 18 80; www.dlm.fr; 32 place de la Gare; ☺8am-noon & 2-6.30pm Mon-Fri, 9am-noon & 2-6pm Sat; underground railGare Lille-Flandres) can be found in the backstreets around Gare Lille-Flandres.

TRAIN

Lille's two main train stations, old-fashioned Gare Lille-Flandres and ultramodern Gare Lille-Europe, are 400m apart on the eastern edge of the city centre. They are one stop apart on metro line 2.

Gare Lille-Europe (MGare Lille-Europe) Topped by what looks like a 20-storey ski boot, this ultramodern station handles province-to-province TGVs, Eurostar trains to London and TGVs/Eurostars to Brussels-Nord. Example fares include:

Gare Lille-Flandres (MGare Lille-Flandres) Used by almost all intra-regional services and

> **DON'T MISS**
>
> ## BRADERIE DE LILLE
>
> On the first weekend in September Lille's entire city centre – 200km of footpaths – is transformed into the **Braderie de Lille**, billed as the world's largest flea market. The extravaganza – with stands selling antiques, local delicacies, handicrafts and more – dates from the Middle Ages, when Lillois servants were permitted to hawk their employers' old garments for some extra cash.
>
> The city's biggest annual event, the Braderie runs nonstop – yes, all night long – from 2pm on Saturday to 11pm on Sunday, when street sweepers emerge to tackle the mounds of mussel shells and old frites (French fries) left behind by the merrymakers. Lille's tourist office can supply you with a free map of the festivities.

almost all TGVs to Paris' Gare du Nord (€35 to €61, one hour, 14 to 24 daily).

Charles de Gaulle Airport €44 to €61, one hour, at least hourly.

Nice from €151, 7½ hours, one to two direct daily

London €90 to €133, 80 minutes, 10 daily (departures are from the station's far northern end).

Brussels-Nord €19 to €30, 35 minutes, at least a dozen daily.

❶ Getting Around

BUS, TRAM & METRO

Lille's two speedy metro lines (1 and 2), two tramways (R and T), two Citadine shuttles (C1, which circles the city centre clockwise, and C2, which goes counterclockwise) and many urban and suburban bus lines – several of which cross into Belgium – are run by **Transpole** (www.transpole. fr). In the city centre, metros run every two to four minutes until about 12.30am. Useful metro stops include those at the train stations, Rihour (next to the tourist office), République Beaux Arts (near the Palais des Beaux-Arts), Gambetta (near the Wazemmes food market) and Gare Jean Lebas (near La Piscine).

Tickets (€1.50) are sold on buses but must be purchased *before* boarding a metro or tram. A Pass' Journée (all-day pass) costs €4 and needs to be time-stamped just once; two/three-day passes are also available. A Pass Soirée, good for unlimited travel after 7pm, costs €2.

TAXI

Taxi Gare Lille (☏ 03 20 06 64 00)

Taxi Rihour (☏ 03 20 55 20 56)

FLANDERS & ARTOIS

Cassel

POP 2390

At the summit of French Flanders' highest hill (though at 176m it's hardly Mont Blanc), the fortified, quintessentially Flemish village of Cassel offers panoramic views of the verdant Flanders plain.

Thanks to its elevated position, Cassel served as Maréchal Ferdinand Foch's headquarters at the beginning of WWI. In 1940 it was the site of intensive rearguard resistance by British troops defending Dunkirk during the evacuation.

Cassel's citizens are enormously proud of Reuze Papa and Reuze Maman, the resident giants, who are feted on Easter Monday. A bagpipe festival is held in Cassel on a weekend in early to mid-June.

The town also boasts a few superbly atmospheric *estaminets*, home-style restaurants serving Flemish specialities.

◉ Sights

Musée Départemental de Flandre   ART MUSEUM
(☏ 03 59 73 45 60; www.museedeflandre.lenord. fr; 26 Grand' Place; adult/child €5/free; ⊙10am-12.30pm & 2-6pm Tue-Sat, 10am-6pm Sun) The main square, fringed by austere brick buildings with steep slate roofs, is where you'll find this well-organised museum, which spotlights Flanders' rich heritage and showcases Flemish art both old and new.

Moulin   WINDMILL
(3 rue St-Nicolas; adult/child €3/2.50; ⊙10am-12.30pm & 2-6pm daily Jul-Aug, 2-6pm weekends Oct-Mar) Ten generations ago, wheat flour was milled and linseed oil pressed just as it is today at this wooden windmill, perched on the highest point in town to catch the wind. The mill-keeper offers excellent 45-minute tours in which he demonstrates the internal workings of the mill and explains the historical context of windmills in French Flanders.

During the 19th century the region's skyline was dotted with 2000 such windmills.

🛏 Sleeping & Eating

Hôtel Le Foch   HOTEL €
(☏ 03 28 42 47 73; www.hotel-foch.net; 41 Grand' Place; s/d €62/71; 🐾) Just down the hill, on Cassel's main square, Hôtel Le Foch has six spacious rooms with antique-style beds, some with views of the square.

★**Het Kasteelhof**   FLEMISH €
(☏ 03 28 40 59 29; lvermeersch.free.fr/kasteelhof; 8 rue St-Nicolas; mains €10-13; ⊙noon-9pm Thu-Sun) The self-proclaimed 'highest *estaminet* in Flanders' is directly across from Cassel's hilltop windmill. It's got two cosy and crowded rooms connected by a ridiculously narrow and steep staircase which waitresses somehow manage to navigate with glasses of walnut liqueur, mugs of Flemish beer and platters full of sausages, hearty soups and casseroles.

For dessert, don't miss its Speculoos ice cream, and as you exit, peek in its store downstairs for uniquely Flemish treats that you're unlikely to find elsewhere in France.

NORTHERN BREWS

French Flanders brews some truly excellent *bière blonde* (lager) and *bière ambrée* (amber beer) with an alcohol content of up to 8.5%. While in the area, beer lovers should be sure to try some of these brands, which give the Belgian brewers a run for their money: 3 Monts, Amadeus, Ambre des Flandres, Brasserie des 2 Caps, Ch'ti, Enfants de Gayant, Grain d'Orge, Hellemus, Jenlain, L'Angélus, La Wambrechies, Moulins d'Ascq, Raoul, Septante 5, St-Landelin, Triple Secret des Moines and Vieux Lille.

Kerelshof　　　　　FLEMISH €
(☑03 28 48 06 75; 31 Grand' Place; mains €8.50-12.50; ⊘noon-2pm & 7-9.30pm Thu-Sun) This Flemish eatery has folksy decor, beamed ceilings, a pair of fireplaces trimmed in cheery shades of blue and plenty of local beers on tap. Expect regional staples prepared with *savoir faire*.

Taverne Flamande　　　　FLEMISH €
(☑03 28 42 42 59; www.taverne-flamande.fr; 34 Grand' Place; mains €10-15, menus €14-30; ⊘noon-2pm & 7-8.30pm Thu-Mon, noon-2pm Tue) This Flemish inn features a classic 1933 dining room with red banquettes, red-and-white checked tablecloths and, on cold days, a crackling fire. Specialities include *carbonade* (braised beef stewed with beer), *waterzooi* (stew) and *potjevleesch* (jellied chicken, pork, veal and rabbit).

ℹ Information

Tourist Office (☑03 28 40 52 55; www.cassel-horizons.com; 20 Grand' Place; ⊘9.30am-noon & 1.30-5.30pm Mon-Fri, 9am-noon Sat) Has various brochures.

ℹ Getting There & Away

Cassel is 57km southeast of Calais. Cassel's train station, 3km down the hill from the centre, has direct services to Dunkirk (€6.60, 25 minutes, up to 24 daily Monday to Friday, 16 on Saturday, seven on Sunday).

Arras

POP 43,690
An unexpected gem of a city, Arras (the final s is pronounced), the former capital of Artois, is worth seeing mainly for its exceptional ensemble of Flemish-style arcaded buildings and two subterranean WWI sites.

The city also makes a good base for visits to the Battle of the Somme Memorials.

◉ Sights & Activities

★ **Grand' Place &**
Place des Héros　　　　　SQUARE
Arras' two ancient market squares, the Grand' Place and the almost-adjacent, smaller Place des Héros (also known as Petite Place), are surrounded by 17th- and 18th-century Flemish-baroque houses topped by curvaceous 'Dutch' gables. Although the structures vary in decorative detail, their 345 sandstone columns form a common arcade unique in France. The squares, especially handsome at night, are about 600m northwest of the train station.

As picture-perfect as they look today, both squares were heavily damaged during WWI and most of the gorgeous façades had to be reconstructed from scratch.

Hôtel de Ville　　　　BELFRY, CELLARS
(place des Héros; belfry adult/child €2.90/1.90, Boves tour adult/child €5.20/3, combined ticket adult/child €6.80/3.70; ⊘belfry 10am-noon & 2-6pm, boves closed 3 weeks in Jan) Arras' Flemish-Gothic city hall dates from the 16th century but was completely rebuilt after WWI. Three 'giants' occupy the lobby (see p180). For a panoramic view, hop on a lift (plus 43 stairs) to the first floor of the Unesco World Heritage-listed, 75m-high **belfry**, or for a truly unique perspective on Arras head into the slimy **souterrains** (tunnels) that fan out underneath the building. Also known as *boves* (cellars), they were turned into British command posts, hospitals and barracks during WWI.

Each spring, in a brilliant juxtaposition of underground gloom and horticultural exuberance, plants and flowers turn the tunnels into the **Jardin des Boves** (Cellar Gardens), designed around a different theme each year. Tours lasting 45 minutes (in English upon request) focus on the gardens when they're there, or on the tunnels' history the rest of the year. Tours generally begin at 11am and run at least twice in the afternoon from Monday to Friday, or every 30 minutes on Saturday and Sunday.

Carrière Wellington　　　　HISTORIC SITE
(Wellington Quarry; ☑03 21 51 26 95; www.carriere-wellington.com; rue Delétoille; adult/child €6.80/3.10; ⊘10am-12.30pm & 1.30-5pm, closed late-Dec–mid-Jan) The staging ground for the spring 1917 offensive, Wellington Quarry is

WORTH A TRIP

DUNKIRK

In late May of 1940 Dunkirk (Dunkerque) became world famous and was flattened, almost simultaneously. As Nazi armies closed in, 1400 naval vessels and fishing boats braved intense German artillery and air attacks to ferry 340,000 Allied soldiers to the safety of England. This unplanned and chaotic evacuation – dubbed Operation Dynamo – failed to save any heavy equipment but was nevertheless seen as a heroic demonstration of Britain's resourcefulness and determination.

Rebuilt during one of the most uninspired periods in the entire history of Western architecture, the modern city has precious little charm but is well worth a detour for its various WWII memorials and museums. To get a feel for the 1940 evacuation of Dunkirk, drop by the not-for-profit **Mémorial du Souvenir** (www.dynamo-dunkerque.com; Courtines du Bastion 32; admission €4; ⊙ 10am-noon & 2-5pm Apr-Sep). The **Dunkirk British Memorial** (D601), honouring more than 4500 British and Commonwealth soldiers 'with no known grave', is next to a Commonwealth military cemetery about 1.5km southeast of the centre.

By train, Dunkirk is connected to Calais and Lille.

a 20m-deep network of old chalk quarries expanded during WWI by tunnellers from New Zealand. Hour-long guided tours in French and English combine imaginative audiovisuals, evocative photos and period artefacts. Signs painted in black are British and from WWI, those in red are French from WWII, when the site was used as a bomb shelter. The quarry is about 1km south of the train station.

By car, follow the 'Carrière' signs from the northeast corner of the Grand' Place (bd Faidherbe).

🛏 Sleeping

Hôtel Diamant　　　　　　　　HOTEL €
(☑ 03 21 71 23 23; www.arras-hotel-diamant.com; 5 place des Héros; s €68-78, d €80-90) This small hotel feels like a cosy doll's house and has one of the city's most desirable locations. It's an

excellent option if you can snag one of the six rooms overlooking the Petite Place and the belfry. Rooms are tiny, though, and there's no lift. The hotel also rents two fully equipped apartments in the town house next door.

Ostel Les 3 Luppars　　　　　　HOTEL €
(☑ 03 21 60 02 03; www.ostel-les-3luppars.com; 49 Grand' Place; s/d €65/80; 🐾) Occupying the Grand' Place's only non-Flemish-style building (it's Gothic and dates from the 1400s), this hotel has a private courtyard and 42 rooms, including 10 with fine views of the square and two (28 and 29) fitted out for families. The decor and breakfast are uninspired but the atmosphere is homey. Also has a sauna (€5 per person for a half-hour).

★La Corne d'Or　　　　　　　　B&B €€
(☑ 03 21 58 85 94; www.lamaisondhotes.com; 1 place Guy Mollet; d incl breakfast €125-160; 🐾) Enviably secreted west of Grand' Place on a small square, this one-of-a-kind B&B occupies a magnificent 18th-century *hôtel particulier* (private mansion), where every detail is looked after. Much more than a posh B&B, it's the equivalent of staying in an art collector's residence, with five imaginatively designed suites and a wonderful little inner courtyard. Australian host Rodney is a great resource.

Hôtel de l'Univers　　　　　　　HOTEL €€
(☑ 03 21 71 34 01; www.univers.najeti.fr; 3-5 place de la Croix Rouge; d €145-165; 🐾) Ensconced in a 16th-century former Jesuit monastery, this characterful hostelry is arrayed in a U around a quiet neoclassical courtyard. Classic draperies and bedspreads give each of the 38 rooms a touch of classic French class. That said, some rooms, including room 108, are more luminous and better laid-out than others, so ask to see a few before committing.

There's an onsite restaurant. Reserve ahead for parking in the hotel's courtyard (€10).

🍴 Eating

Many places to eat are tucked away under the arches of the Grand' Place and along adjacent rue de la Taillerie, which leads to the Place des Héros (Petite Place).

★Les Deux Frères – Chez Zénon　　　REGIONAL CUISINE €
(23 rue de la Taillerie; mains €11-14; ⊙ noon-2.30pm Tue-Sat, bar 8.30am-9pm Tue-Sat) Blink and you'll miss this pocket-sized bistro with a wonderfully congenial atmosphere, a stone's throw from the Grand' Place. Chez Zénon is always

packed and for good reason: fabulous-value regional dishes (think *potjevleesch* and pig intestine sausages with Maroilles cheese) taste fresh and home-cooked. The only hiccup is snagging a table; arrive at noon or 2pm. There's outdoor seating in summer.

Le Petit Rat Porteur   BRASSERIE €
(✓ 03 21 51 29 70; 11 rue de la Taillerie; mains €10-19, lunch menu €14; ⊘ noon-2pm & 7-9.30pm Tue-Sat, noon-2pm Sun) This buzzing brasserie is smack in the middle of the Arras tourist trail, yet it remains a local favourite. There are lots of delightful salads to start off with, followed by spot-on regional standards such as *potjevleesch* and *waterzooi*. The menu is translated into English to play to Arras' many anglophones, who are in love with this bijou brasserie – especially the vaulted cellar.

La Cave des Saveurs   FRENCH, FLEMISH €€
(✓ 03 21 59 75 24; 36 Grand' Place; mains €13-20, menus €21-37; ⊘ noon-2pm & 7-9pm Mon, Tue & Thu-Sat, noon-2pm Wed) In a vaulted brick cellar that served as a brewery before WWII, this atmospheric restaurant serves traditional French dishes as well as a few Flemish specialities such as *carbonade*.

La Faisanderie   TRADITIONAL FRENCH €€€
(✓ 03 21 48 20 76, www.restaurant-la-faisandorie. com; 45 Grand' Place; menus €27-48; ⊘ lunch Tue, Wed & Fri-Sun, dinner Tue-Sat) This respectable restaurant occupying a heritage building on the Grand' Place serves a range of French classics prepared with carefully chosen ingredients, but the real show stealer is its superb vaulted cellar.

Self-Catering

Open-Air Market   MARKET €
(place des Héros, Grand' Place & place de la Vacquerie; ⊘ 7am-1pm Wed & Sat) Around the *hôtel de ville*. The Saturday market is really huge.

ℹ Information

Tourist Office (✓ 03 21 51 26 95; www.explorearras.fr; place des Héros; ⊘ 9am-6.30pm Mon-Sat, 10am-1.30pm & 2.30-6.30pm Sun) Inside the *hôtel de ville*.

ℹ Getting There & Around

BICYCLE

Arras Vélo (✓ 06 29 71 61 91; www.arrasavelo. com; place du Théâtre; per day €10; ⊘ 9am-6pm) Rents electric bicycles, convenient for getting to the Vimy battlefields 12km north of town.

CAR

Avis (✓ 03 21 51 69 03; www.avis.fr, 6 rue Gambetta; ⊘ 9am-noon & 2-6pm Mon-Fri, 9am-noon & 4-6pm Sat) Half a block northwest of the train station.

Europcar (✓ 03 21 07 29 54; 5 rue de Douai; ⊘ 8.30am-noon & 2-5pm Mon-Fri, 9am-noon Sat) Half a block to the right as you exit the train station.

TAXI

Alliance Arras Taxis (✓ 03 21 23 69 69; ⊘ 24hr) Can take you to Somme battlefield sites (eg Vimy).

TRAIN

Arras' station is 750m southeast of the two main squares.

Amiens €12.70, 45 minutes, six to 11 daily.

WORTH A TRIP

LOUVRE-LENS

Opened with fanfare in 2012 in Lens, 18km north of Arras, the innovative **Louvre-Lens** (✓ 03 21 18 62 62; www.louvrelens.fr; 99 rue Paul Bert, Lens; ⊘ 10am-6pm Wed-Mon) showcases hundreds of treasures from Paris' venerable Musée du Louvre in a purpose-built, state-of-the-art exhibition space. Unlike its Parisian cousin, there's no permanent collection here. Instead, the museum's centrepiece, a 120m-long exhibition space called the **Galerie du Temps,** displays a limited but significant, ever-rotating collection of 200-plus pieces from the original Louvre, spanning that museum's full breadth and diversity of cultures and historical periods.

A second building, the glass-walled **Pavillon de Verre,** displays temporary themed exhibits. Rounding out the museum are educational facilities, an auditorium, a restaurant and a park.

Lens is accessible by regular TGV trains from Paris' Gare du Nord (€28.50 to €51, 65 to 70 minutes), as well as regional trains from Lille (from €6.80, 40 minutes) and Arras (from €4.50, 15 minutes).

Lens €4.50, 15 minutes, up to 29 daily Monday to Friday, 18 on Saturday, 13 on Sunday.

Lille-Flandres €11.20, 35 minutes, 14 to 19 daily.

Paris Gare du Nord (TGV) €33 to €49, 50 minutes, 11 to 14 daily.

CÔTE D'OPALE

Calais to Boulogne

There may be only 40km between Calais and Boulogne-sur-Mer, but what 40km! If you're looking for windswept beaches, sand dunes, lofty chalk cliffs, spectacular vistas and charming seaside towns, it doesn't get much better than the Côte d'Opale (Opal Coast), which stretches southward from Calais along the English Channel. One of northern France's most alluring stretches of coast, it got its name because of the ever-changing interplay of greys and blues in the sea and sky. Landscapes are not the only drawcard. The Côte d'Opale is also of strong historical significance. Here you'll find the remains of Nazi Germany's Atlantic Wall, a chain of fortifications and gun emplacements built to prevent the Allied invasion that in the end took place in Normandy. And for outdoorsy types, there are plenty of hiking paths that hug the coast.

By car, follow the D940 coastal road.

◉ Sights

Cap Blanc-Nez   LANDMARK
Southwest of Calais, the coastal dunes give way to cliffs that culminate in windswept, 134m-high Cap Blanc-Nez, which affords breathtaking views of the Bay of Wissant, the port of Calais, the Flemish countryside (pockmarked by Allied bomb craters) and the distant cliffs of Kent. The grey obelisk (erected 1922), a short walk up the hill from the parking area, honours the WWI Dover Patrol. Paths lead to a number of massive, concrete German bunkers and gun emplacements.

Cap Gris-Nez   LANDMARK
Topped by a lighthouse and a radar station serving the 600 ships that pass by each day, the 45m-high cliffs of Cap Gris-Nez are only 28km from the white cliffs of the English coast. The name – Grey Nose – is a corruption of the archaic English 'craig ness', meaning 'rocky promontory'. The area is a stopping-off point for millions of migrating birds.

Musée du Mur de l'Atlantique   WAR MUSEUM
(Atlantic Wall Museum; ☑03 21 32 97 33; www.batterietodt.com; route du Musée, Audinghen; adult/child €8.50/5; ☉10am-5.15pm daily, to 6.15pm Jul-Aug, closed mid-Nov–mid-Feb) Oodles of WWII hardware, including a massive, rail-borne German artillery piece with a range of 86km, are on display at this very well organised museum housed in a Brobdingnagian German pillbox. It is just southwest of Audinghen, 500m off D940.

Dunes de la Slack   NATURAL LANDMARK
The Sahara it ain't, but these wind-carved sand dunes that extend along the coast south of Ambleteuse conjure up images of exotic destinations. The best way to appreciate the stunning landscape is to follow the paths that criss-cross the area.

Musée 39-45   WAR MUSEUM
(☑03 21 87 33 01; www.musee3945.com; D940, Ambleteuse; adult/child €8.50/5.50; ☉10am-6pm, weekends only Mar & Nov, closed Dec-Feb) The neatly organised Musée 39-45, at the northern edge of Ambleteuse, features realistic tableaux of WWII military and civilian life, and a 25-minute film. The dashing but wildly impractical French officers' dress uniforms of 1931 hint at possible reasons why France fared so badly on the battlefield in 1940. Popular wartime songs accompany your visit.

Brasserie Artisanale des 2 Caps   BREWERY
(☑03 21 10 56 53; www.2caps.fr; ferme de Belle Dalle, Tardinghen; tours €4.50; ☉10am-7pm Tue-Sat, daily Jul & Aug) Historic farm buildings in the countryside 5km south of Wissant house one of northern France's best microbreweries. There's a great shop and tasting room, and brewmaster Christophe Noyon offers occasional 90-minute tours of the premises.

🛏 Sleeping & Eating

Hôtel Le Vivier   HOTEL €€
(☑03 21 35 93 61; www.levivier.com; place de l'Église, Wissant; d incl breakfast €60-104; 🐾) Opposite Wissant's church and a couple of blocks from the beach, this reliable pad has 39 smallish but space-efficient and bright rooms. If it's a sea view you're after, consider staying at the annexe positioned on the southern outskirts of the village. The restaurant is known for its fresh seafood. Check the website for special offers.

Hôtel-Restaurant L'Escale
HOTEL €

(☑03 21 85 25 00; www.hotel-lescale.com; rue de la Mer, Escalles; d €65-85; 🐾) Compact and cosy are the watchwords at this welcoming country retreat, and while the rooms are hardly spacious, they're well equipped and functional. The hotel has three buildings, all in the heart of Escalles. Rooms 38 and 39, which offer views of the Caps, are the pick of the bunch. The attached restaurant serves French classics with Channel Coast touches.

La Marie Galante
SEAFOOD €

(☑03 21 83 02 32; 173 rue Edouard Quenu, Audresselles; mains €14-19, menu €18-46; ⊗noon-1.30pm & 7-9pm Tue-Sun) In the scenic fishing village of Audresselles is this gem for fish and seafood lovers. The à la carte offerings might include cod, mussels, lobster or scallops, but local foodies recommend the stonking seafood platter.

★ La Sirène
SEAFOOD €€

(☑03 21 32 95 97; www.lasirene-capgrisnez.com; 376 rue de la Plage, cap Gris-Nez, Audinghen; mains €10-36, menu €29; ⊗noon-2pm & 7.30-9pm Tue-Sun Apr-Sep, lunch only Feb, Mar, Oct & Nov) You won't find a cosier place in Côte d'Opale than this much-loved hideaway, snuggled at the foot of Cap Gris-Nez. Predominantly but not exclusively a seafood restaurant, La Sirène doesn't waver in its commitment to serving only the freshest food that can be sourced at the harbour each day. For proof, try the grilled lobster. Large picture windows provide optimum sea views.

Get your act together – it's often booked out in summer.

ℹ Information

Tourist Office (☑03 21 82 48 00; www.terredes2capstourisme.fr; 1 place de la Mairie, Wissant; ⊗9.30am-noon & 2-6pm Mon-Sat, 10am-1pm & 3-6pm Sun) Has English-speaking staff and can provide useful brochures.

Calais

POP 75,240

As Churchill might have put it, 'never in the field of human tourism have so many travellers passed through a place and so few stopped to visit'. There would seem to be few compelling reasons for the 15 million people who travel by way of Calais each year to stop and explore – pity the local tourist office, whose job it is to snag a few of the Britons racing south to warmer climes – but in fact the town is worth at least a brief stopover.

The city, a mere 34km from the English town of Dover (Douvres in French), also makes a convenient launching pad for exploring the majestic Côte d'Opale.

◉ Sights

Cité Internationale de la Dentelle et de la Mode
MUSEUM

(International Centre of Lace & Fashion; ☑03 21 00 42 30; www.cite-dentelle.fr; 135 quai du Commerce; adult/child €5/2.50; ⊗10am-6pm Wed-Mon) Enter the intricate world of lace-making, the industry that once made Calais a textile powerhouse. The informative, cutting-edge exhibits trace the history of lace from the early centuries of hand-knotting (some stunning samples are on display).

The highlight is watching a century-old mechanical loom with 3500 vertical threads and 11,000 horizontal ones bang, clatter and clunk according to instructions given by perforated Jacquard cards. Signs are in French and English. Situated 500m southeast of the town hall building.

Beffroi de Calais
CLOCK TOWER

(Belfry; ☑03 21 46 20 53; place du Soldat Inconnu; adult/child €5/3; ⊗10am-noon & 2-5pm, closed Mon Oct-Apr) An imposing landmark visible from anywhere in town, Calais' 78m-high belfry was recognised as a Unesco World Heritage Site in 2005 and opened to the public in 2011. An elevator whisks you to the top, where you can admire 360-degree views of the town and surrounding landscape.

Burghers of Calais
STATUE

(place du Soldat Inconnu) In front of Calais' Flemish Renaissance-style town hall (1911–25) is Rodin's famous statue *Les Bourgeois de Calais* (The Burghers of Calais; 1895), honouring six local citizens who, in 1347, held off the besieging English forces for more than eight months. Edward III was so impressed he ultimately spared the Calaisiens and their six leaders.

Musée Mémoire 1939–1945
WAR MUSEUM

(☑03 21 34 21 57; parc St-Pierre; adult/child incl audioguide €6/5; ⊗10am-6pm, closed Dec & Jan) Housed in a concrete bunker built as a German naval headquarters, this WWII museum displays thousands of period artefacts, including weapons, uniforms and proclamations. Situated incongruously in flowery

Parc St-Pierre, next to a boules ground and a children's playground.

Blériot Plage
BEACH

The unique attraction at Calais' cabin-lined beach, which begins 1km northwest of place d'Armes, is watching huge car ferries as they sail majestically to and from Dover. The sand continues westward along the 8km long, dune-lined Blériot Plage, named after the pioneer aviator Louis Blériot, who began the first ever trans-Channel flight from here in 1909.

🛌 Sleeping

The neighbouring town of Coquelles, just west of Calais, is a convenient place to grab a night's sleep, thanks to the abundance of chain hotels just off the autoroute near the tunnel entrance.

Centre Européen de Séjour
HOSTEL €

(📞 03 21 34 70 20; www.auberge-jeunesse-calais.com; av Maréchal de Lattre de Tassigny; s/tw incl breakfast €30/48; 🔁; 🚌 3, 5, 9) Great for those on a budget, this efficiently-run venture occupies a drab building just 200m from the beach. It features a bar, a lounge area and modern (if soulless) one- to three-bed rooms with en suite bathrooms. There's an on-site restaurant (meals from €14). Note that prices drop by about 10% after two nights.

★ Le Cercle de Malines
B&B €€

(📞 03 21 96 80 65; www.lecercledemalines.com; 12 rue de Malines; d incl breakfast €68-128; 🔁) This stately 19th-century town house south of the centre is just the ticket for those seeking a stylish 'home away from home' experience in Calais. The five rooms, including a judiciously laid-out family room, are very different in design and colour scheme and are comfortably spread out on two floors; our choice is 'Rome', with a claw-footed bath.

The big living room, complete with period moulding, has a fine window onto a little flower-filled garden where you can relax after exploring the treasures of Calais. The breakfast is a real spoil and includes plenty of locally sourced and homemade goodies – it helps that the owner is a baker. Good English is spoken.

Hôtel Meurice
HOTEL €€

(📞 03 21 34 57 03; www.hotel-meurice.fr; 5-7 rue Edmond Roche; d €92-162; 🔁🔁) Sheer delight for lovers of the utterly retro, this veteran downtown hotel on a quiet street brims with character, thanks to its grand lobby staircase, antique furnishings, Hemingwayesque bar and breakfast rooms with garden views. All the rooms are different.

🍴 Eating

Restaurants ring place d'Armes and are plentiful just south of there along rue Royale.

★ Histoire Ancienne
BISTRO €€

(📞 03 21 34 11 20; www.histoire-ancienne.com; 20 rue Royale; mains €18-23, lunch menu €17, dinner menu €21-29; ⏰noon-2pm Mon-Sat, 6-9.30pm Tue-Sat) This local treasure at the heart of town rustles up French and regional dishes in a lovely 1930s Paris-style bistro setting. Does the pan fried seabass fillet taste better than the endives creamy soup? You be the judge. Service is prompt and friendly.

Le Grand Bleu
MODERN FRENCH €€

(📞 03 21 97 97 98; www.legrandbleu-calais.com; 8 rue Jean-Pierre Avron; weekday menu €19-21, dinner menu €30-51; ⏰lunch Thu-Tue, dinner Thu-Mon) Run by talented chef Matthieu Colin (ex-Ledoyen), this eatery overlooking the harbour is known for its *cuisine élaborée* (creatively transformed versions of traditional dishes) made with fresh local products. Its weekday menus offer fabulous value. One quibble: tables are tightly packed together. Book a table in the luminous veranda to enjoy the harbour views.

ℹ️ Information

Exchange rates aboard car ferries and in the terminals are atrocious. You'll find banks with cash machines downtown.

Tourist Office (📞 03 21 96 62 40; www.calais-cotedopale.com; 12 bd Georges Clemenceau; ⏰10am-6pm Mon-Sat, to 5pm Sun) Just across the bridge (north) from the train station. Has brochures on Calais and the Côte d'Opale.

ℹ️ Getting There & Away

You can cross the English Channel by ferry or rail.

BOAT

Each day, more than three dozen car ferries from Dover dock at Calais' bustling **car-ferry terminal**, situated about 1.5km northeast of place d'Armes.

P&O Ferries (📞 0825 120 156; www.poferries.com; 41 place d'Armes), **DFDS Seaways** (📞 02 32 14 68 50; www.dfdsseaways.co.uk; Ferry Terminal) and **My Ferry Link** (www.myferrylink.com) operate regular trans-Channel service. P&O accepts foot passengers; DFDS and My Ferry Link only take passengers with vehicles.

Shuttle buses (€2, roughly hourly from 11am to 6pm) link Gare Calais-Ville (the train station) with the car-ferry terminal. Departure times are posted at the stops.

BUS

Bus 505, run by **Inglard-Colvert** (☑ 03 21 96 36 12), makes three runs daily along the breathtaking Côte d'Opale coastal road (D940), stopping in Wissant (40 minutes) and other coastal communites en route to Boulogne-sur-Mer (1½ hours). The fare is €1 for any stop along this route. Find the bus stop opposite the train station.

CAR & MOTORCYCLE

To reach the Channel Tunnel's vehicle-loading area at Coquelles, about 6km southwest of Calais' town centre, follow the road signs on the A16 to 'Tunnel Sous La Manche' (Tunnel Under the Channel) and get off at exit 42.

TRAIN

Calais has two train stations, linked by trains and a *navette* (shuttle bus; €2, free with train ticket).

Gare Calais-Ville In the city centre, it has direct services to Amiens (€27.10, two hours, five or six daily), Boulogne (€8.30, 30 minutes, 22 daily Monday to Friday, nine to 12 daily on weekends) and Lille-Flandres (€18.50, 1¼ hours, about 15 daily Monday to Friday, eight to 10 daily on weekend).

Gare Calais-Fréthun A TGV station 10km southwest of town near the Channel Tunnel entrance, this is served by TGVs to Paris' Gare du Nord (from €37, 1¾ hours, eight daily Monday to Saturday, three on Sunday) as well as the Eurostar to London St Pancras (from €62, one hour, three daily).

Boulogne-sur-Mer

POP 44,070

The most interesting of France's Channel ports, Boulogne makes a pretty good first stop in France, especially if combined with a swing north through the Côte d'Opale. The Basse Ville (Lower City) is an uninspiring assemblage of postwar structures but the attractive Ville Haute (Upper City), perched high above the rest of town, is girded by a 13th-century wall. The biggest draw is Nausicaã, one of Europe's premier aquariums.

◉ Sights & Activities

Nausicaã   AQUARIUM
(☑ 03 21 30 99 99; www.nausicaa.co.uk; bd Ste-Beuve; adult/child €18.80/12.30; ⊙ 9.30am-6.30pm, closed Jan) One of Europe's premier aquariums, Nausicaã lets you get up close and personal with an amazing variety of

marine species, including jellyfish, sharks, caimans, conger eels, turtles and colourful tropical reef species. Kid-friendly activities include feeding sessions and fish petting. Also a hit with younger visitors: California sea lions and African penguins, including young 'uns hatched right here. All signs are in French and English.

Ville Haute   HISTORIC QUARTER
You can walk all the way around the Upper City – a hilltop island of centuries-old buildings and cobblestone streets – atop the rectangular, tree-shaded ramparts. The **Basilique Notre Dame** (rue de Lille; ⊙ 10am-noon & 2-5pm), its towering, Italianate dome visible from all over town, is an odd structure built from 1827 to 1866. The partly Romanesque crypt was under renovation at the time of research. The nearby **Château-Musée** (Castle Museum; ☑ 03 21 10 02 20; rue de Bernet; adult/child €5/free; ⊙ museum 10am 12.30pm & 2-5.30pm, closed Tue, courtyard 7am-7pm daily), housed in a 13th-century fortified castle, contains Egyptian antiquities, 19th-century Inuit masks, Andean ceramics and a collection of Grecian urns.

Among the impressive buildings around place Godefroy de Bouillon are the neoclassical **Hôtel Desandrouin** (17 rue du Puits d'Amour), built in the 1780s and later used by Napoléon, and the brick **Hôtel de Ville** (1735), with its square medieval belfry (ground floor accessible through the lobby).

Basse Ville   NEIGHBOURHOOD
Boulogne's Basse Ville (Lower Town) is dominated by its **fishing port** (quai Gambetta). Hungry seagulls dive and squawk overhead as they survey the fishing boats and the *poissonniers* (fishmongers) selling freshly landed *cabillaud* (Atlantic cod), *carrelet* (plaice) and sole – Boulogne's most important commercial fish – as well as *bar* (sea bass), mullet, *raie* (skate) and turbot. Take a good look so you know what you're getting next time you order *poisson* (fish).

Florelle   BOAT TOUR
(☑ 06 48 49 42 26; www.boulogne-promenade-en-mer.com; quai Gambetta; adult/child €11/8; ⊙ daily by reservation) The best way to discover Boulogne's fishing harbour and the magnificent Côte d'Opale is by joining a boat tour. This outfit offers various *promenades en mer* (boat excursions) along the coast towards Cap Blanc-Nez and Cap Gris-Nez. The shortest tour lasts one hour; the longest takes

LILLE, FLANDERS & THE SOMME BOULOGNE-SUR-MER

Boulogne-sur-Mer

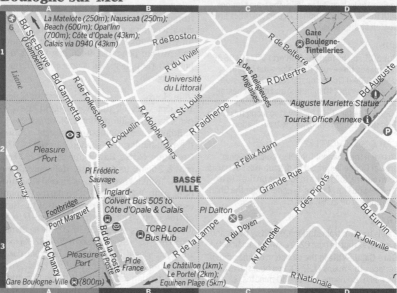

La Matelote (250m); Nausicaä (250m);
Beach (600m); Opal'Inn
(700m); Côte d'Opale (43km);
Calais via D940 (43km)

R de Boston

R du Vivier

Université
du Littoral

R de Belterre

Gare
Boulogne-
Tintelleries

R des Religieuses
Anglaises

R Dutertre

Bd Ste-Beuve
Bd Gambetta

Bd Gambetta

R de Folkestone

R Adolphe Thiers

R Coquelin

R St-Louis

R Faidherbe

Auguste Mariette Statue

Tourist Office Annexe

Bd Auguste

Lione

O Chanzy

Pleasure
Port

Pl Frédéric
Sauvage

BASSE
VILLE

R Félix Adam

Grande Rue

R des Pipots

Inglard-
Colvert Bus 505 to
Côte d'Opale & Calais

Pl Dalton

R de la Lampe

R du Doyen

Av Perrochel

Bd Eurvin

R Joinville

Footbridge
Pont Marguet

Bd de la Poste
O de la Poste

TCRB Local
Bus Hub

Pleasure
Port

Bd Chanzy

Pl de
France

Gare Boulogne-Ville (800m)

Le Châtillon (1km);
Le Portel (2km);
Equihen Plage (5km)

R Nationale

about four hours. Tours go every day in summer but are weather-dependent.

Beaches

Boulogne's **main beach** begins just north of Nausicaä, across the mouth of the Liane from a whirring wind farm on the one-time site of a steelworks. Other fine beaches include **Le Portel**, 2.5km southwest of Boulogne (bus C from place de France), and **Equihen Plage**, about 5km to the south (bus A from the train station or place de France). All the beaches are also easily accessible by bike.

🛏 Sleeping

Opal'Inn
HOTEL €

(☎03 21 32 15 15; www.hotel-opalinn.com; 168 bd Ste-Beuve; s €59, d €79-109; 🛜) One of several hotels on the seafront, this is a solid mid-range abode with contemporary decor. Lilac and chocolate hues give its 42 rooms instant appeal, and the outlook from the *chambres avec vue mer* (rooms with a sea view) is heavenly – Nausicaä and the harbour in one direction, the beach and the sea in the other.

Les Terrasses de l'Enclos
B&B €€

(☎03 91 90 05 90; www.enclosdeleveche.com; 6 rue Pressy; d incl breakfast €75-120; 🛜) To really soak up the Haute Ville's atmosphere, stay at this delightful B&B housed in a convert-

ed 19th-century mansion at the top of the old town. Easily the most elegant and best-value choice in Boulogne, it shelters five rooms that range from medium to large. They're individually decorated and furnished with grand comfort. The stone-paved courtyard is inviting, too.

Hôtel La Matelote
HOTEL €€

(☎03 21 30 33 33; www.la-matelote.com; 70 bd Ste-Beuve; d €105-202; ❄🛜❄) Boulogne's plushest hotel draws an older clientele willing to pay top euro for its Old World character, professional service and excellent amenities, including a spa bath, sauna and tiny pool. Its 35 rooms, many decorated in rich shades of red and gold, have classic wood furnishings, and some come with balconies (alas, no direct sea views). Across the road from Nausicaä.

The place lives on its reputation, but could use a little work.

🍴 Eating

Thanks to its ready supply, Boulogne is an excellent place for fresh fish (everything except the salmon is likely to have been landed locally).

⭐ Le Châtillon
SEAFOOD €

(☎03 21 31 43 96; www.le-chatillon.com; 6 rue Charles Tellier; mains €12-22, menus €19-21;

N 0 ———— 200 m
  0 ———— 0.1 miles

VILLE
HAUTE

Mariette
Av Charles de Gaulle
R St-Jean
Bd Eurvin
Pl Godefroy
de Bouillon
R de Lille
R du Château
R de l'Oratoire
R St-Martin
R d'Aumont
R Porte Gayole
R Boucher de Perthes

LILLE, FLANDERS & THE SOMME BOULOGNE-SUR-MER

lishment, with white tablecloths, paper-thin wine glasses, fine porcelain and a focus on fish, is a winner. Aside from great quality fish, what makes chef Tony Lestienne's approach so appealingly modern is the almost total absence of traditional sauces, which allows all the goodness of the fish to come through.

Self-Catering

Marché FOOD MARKET €
(place Dalton; ⊘ Wed & Sat morning) Boulogne's lively biweekly fruit and vegetable market.

ℹ Information

Tourist Office (☑ 03 21 10 88 10; www.tourisme-boulognesurmer.com; parvis de Nausicaä; ⊘10am-12.30pm & 1.45-6pm Mon-Sat, 10.30am-1pm & 2.30-5pm Sun; 🛜) Helpful staff, English brochures and free wi-fi.
Tourist Office Annexe (Square Mariette Pacha; ⊘10.30am-12.30pm & 2-5pm Mon-Sat) At the entrance of the Upper City.

ℹ Getting There & Around

BIKE

Cycleco (☑ 03 91 18 34 48; forum Jean Noël; per hr/day from €1/5; ⊘9am-7pm) Hires out regular bikes and electric bicycles, convenient for getting to the beaches at Equihen Plage and Le Portel.

BUS

Buses go to Calais via the gorgeous Côte d'Opale. They also serve Le Touquet, to the south. All buses leave from place de France.

TRAIN

The main train station, **Gare Boulogne-Ville**, is 1.2km southeast of the centre. Destinations include:

⊘5am-3pm Mon, Tue & Thu, 4am-3pm Wed & Fri, lunch 11.30am-3pm Mon-Fri) Dive into the docklands, an area of warehouses and fisheries, and you'll stumble onto one of Boulogne's worst-kept secrets: Le Châtillon. At lunchtime it's hectic with a happy mix of fisherfolk, wholesale fish merchants and tourists in the know. Unsurprisingly, seafood reigns supreme here, but there are also a few meaty mains. Tip: book a table in the much quieter upstairs room.

L'Îlot Vert MODERN FRENCH €€
(☑ 03 21 92 01 62; 36 rue de Lille; mains €18, lunch menu €17-32, dinner menu €32; ⊘noon-2pm & 7-9.30pm Mon, Tue & Thu-Sat, noon-2pm Sun) A faintly fusion-style cuisine is what makes this trendy eatery with a cutting-edge design stand out. The *carte* is short but appetising, and each item is presented like a work of art on (predictably) designer plates. Best of all, this address is on a sweet little street in the upper town, and there's a relaxing courtyard at the back.

La Matelote SEAFOOD €€€
(☑ 03 21 30 33 33; www.la-matelote.com; 80 bd Ste-Beuve; mains €30-32, lunch menus €25-35, dinner menus €40-82; ⊘noon-2pm & 7.30-9.30pm Fri-Wed, 7.30-9.30pm Thu) Facing the Nausicaä aquarium, this stylish Michelin-starred estab-

Amiens €21.10, 1½ hours, seven to 11 daily.
Calais-Ville €8.30, 20 to 40 minutes, 22 daily Monday to Friday, fewer on weekends.
Lille-Flandres or Lille-Europe €22.40, one hour, five or six direct daily.
Paris Gare du Nord €37.50, two to 2¾ hours, eight to 11 direct daily.

BAIE DE SOMME

If you're in search of inspiration and escape, the Baie de Somme is the answer, with some truly world-class nature-gazing to be enjoyed. This sparkling estuary affords delightfully watery views as the cycle of the tides alternately hides and reveals vast expanses of sand. The bay, which is notorious for strong currents and galloping tides, forms a unique habitat for all kinds of birds and marine life, including a colony of about 300 sandbank-lounging seals at Pointe du Hourdel.

Le Crotoy, on the northern bank, and St-Valery-sur-Somme, on the southern bank, both make good bases for exploring the area. Both towns are increasingly popular with Parisian weekenders and offer a good range of eateries, shops, hotels, B&Bs and operators offering various trips around the estuary. The most obvious way to explore the bay is to take a boat excursion, but you can also explore it on foot with a guide, or by kayak.

The Baie de Somme is a glorious place to experience Picard nature at its most unspoilt and spectacular – a fact that's clearly not lost on the nation's powers-that-be, who've recently made it France's 10th 'Grand Site de France' (see www.grandsite baiedesomme.fr).

Le Crotoy

POP 2300

Hugging the northern bank of the bay, Le Crotoy enjoys a wonderful setting and is a lovely place to relax in. No doubt you'll be won over by the laid-back seaside ambience and superb panoramas.

🏃 Activities

Walking across the bay on your own is an extremely bad idea; you'll need the expertise of an experienced local guide.

Promenade en Baie   WALKING TOUR
(📞 03 22 27 47 36; www.promenade-en-baie.com; 5 allée des Soupirs) This experienced opera-

tor runs excellent three-hour guided walks through the bay as well as a range of nature walks in the area. It also offers not-to-be-missed seal-watching excursions at Pointe du Hourdel, at the mouth of the Somme estuary – binoculars are provided.

🛏 Sleeping & Eating

Les Tourelles   HOTEL €€
(📞 03 22 27 16 33; www.lestourelles.com; 2-4 rue Pierre Guerlain; d €81-115; @ 🛜) 🅿 With its unmissable *tourelles* (conical turrets) and ochre façade, this bijou hotel overlooking Le Crotoy's beach stands out like a beacon on the northern bank of the bay. Thirteen rooms have fabulous bay views; try No 33, which occupies one of the two turrets. The attached restaurant (mains from €12) serves excellent regional cuisine and offers vegie and locavore options.

Kids aged four to 14 can stay in a room with 10 bunk beds (€31 per child including breakfast).

ℹ Getting There & Away

Le Crotoy is best accessed with a car. It's 74km northwest of Amiens – follow the A16 then take the D40 and D940.

St-Valery-sur-Somme

More fashionable and busier than Le Crotoy, St-Valery-sur-Somme is becoming a major tourist hotspot in northern France, and it's easy to see why. On the southern bank of the bay, this sweet little medieval town, with its attractive tree-lined promenade, delightful port and historic quarter, has charm in spades.

🏃 Activities

Chemin de Fer de la Baie de Somme   TOURIST TRAIN
(📞 03 22 26 96 96; www.cfbs.eu; quai Lejoille; adult/child €13.40/10) Railway enthusiasts and families will make a beeline for this 19th-century steam tourist train, which chuffs along the bay on a restored line between St-Valery-sur-Somme and Le Crotoy. The one-way trip lasts about one hour. It also serves Cayeux-sur-Mer, to the west.

Le Baliseur Somme II   BOAT TOUR
(📞 06 70 65 95 44; www.bateaubaiedesomme. com; quai Lejoille; adult/child from €12/8) This well-established company runs various boat excursions inside the bay aboard a

ABBAYE ET JARDINS DE VALLOIRES

Nestled in a bucolic valley, the strikingly beautiful Abbaye de Valloires (☑03 22 29 62 33; www.abbaye-valloires.com; Argoules; adult/child €13.50/9; ☺10.30am-5.30pm May-Aug, to 4.30pm Apr & Sep, guided tours hourly) dates from the 12th century and is well worth a detour for its spectacular Cistercian architecture and baroque interior.

Entirely restored in the 18th century, it's one of northern France's most complete monastic complexes, including caretaker's house, church, cloister, sacristy, chapterhouse and refectory. The interior of the church has a magnificent organ loft, sculptures, stalls and wrought-iron choir screen. Note that the abbey is only accessible on a guided tour; ask about the availability of English tours by phoning ahead.

After the tour, you're free to stroll among quiet landscaped gardens and soak in the ethereal calm surrounding the abbey. In summer various events are held here. If you want to overnight in Valloires, the abbey has an hostelry and a restaurant (open for lunch).

The abbey is a circuitous 25km northeast of Le Crotoy.

decommissioned *baliseur* (buoy tender) that was in use between 1950 and 1999. The 'Between Land and Sea' cruise includes a guided walk at low tide. Sunset cruises are also available.

Commandant Charcot IV　　　BOAT TOUR
(☑03 22 60 74 68; www.bateau-baie-somme.com; quai Lejoille; adult/child from €12/8) This company operates various boat trips inside the bay. The most interesting one goes as far as Le Hourdel, where you can spot the seal colonies (1¼ hours).

Rando-Nature en Somme　　　WALKING TOUR
(☑03 22 26 92 30; www.randonature-baiedesomme.com; quai Lejoille; adult/child from €10/5; ☺daily in summer) This well-regarded outfit organises themed guided nature walks, including the *Traversée de la baie* (crossing of the bay; three hours) and *Les Phoques et la Baie* (seal-watching at pointe Le Hourdel, at the mouth of the Somme estuary; 2½ hours).

La Maison des Guides　　　KAYAKING
(☑06 18 42 71 16; www.guides-baiedesomme.com; quai Jeanne d'Arc; from €30; ☺daily by reservation) For something unique, sign on with Matthieu Cornu who leads excellent kayak tours in the bay, including an environmentally-aware three-hour seal-watching trip.

🛌 Sleeping

Sophie et Patrick Deloison　　　B&B, APARTMENT €
(☑0624490464,0322269217;www.hebergement-baie-somme.com; 1 quai du Romerel; s/d incl breakfast €40/50, apt from €127) Right in the centre, this quaint B&B feels like a warm soft nest. The two traditional-style rooms are simple yet attractive, with flea-market antiques and knick-knacks that convey a yesteryear charm. The owners also rent out three apartments in a separate house on a quiet street–they're sizzling hot value, have loads of character and can be rented for a night.

★**Hôtel Les Pilotes**　　　BOUTIQUE HOTEL €€
(☑03 22 60 80 39; www.lespilotes.fr; 62 rue de la Ferté; d €100-210; 🖰) This boutique bonanza shelters 25 personalised rooms that sport 1960s vintage decor and beautiful pieces of retro furnishings and knick-knacks. Don't sell yourself short with a streetside room: what you want is a room at the front with fetching views of the bay through the large windows – you might even spot a seal or two. *Quel bonheur!*

Breakfast (€11) is a sumptuous affair, with excellent locally-sourced *produits fermiers* (products from the countryside). Excellent English is spoken.

Au Vélocipède　　　B&B €€
(☑03 22 60 57 42; www.auvelocipede.fr; 1 rue du Puits Salé; s/d incl breakfast €89/99; 🖰) This renovated town house facing the church is now a swish B&B run very much along the lines of a small boutique hotel. It conceals four supremely comfortable rooms designed with utmost grace and done out in taupe, beige, black and blue shades. Those up at attic level (rooms 3 and 4) are especially romantic. Cash only.

La Femme d'à Côté　　　B&B €€
(☑06 87 95 68 37; www.lafemmedacote.fr; 26 rue Questive; s €79-89, d €89-99, incl breakfast; 🖰) This delightful brick town house has lots of personality – the four boutique rooms (suites would be a better description) have exquisite feminine touches, and the walls

are adorned with black and white female photographic portraits – and its tasteful decor makes this one of the nicest choices in the Baie de Somme area.

Eating

Le Bistrot des Pilotes NEOBISTRO €
(☑ 03 22 60 38 95; 37 quai Blavet; mains €16-22; ◷ noon-2.30pm & 7.30-9.30pm daily) Market-fresh cuisine with a twist, discreet service, black-and-white tiling and a good selection of savoury seafood dishes and Picardy classics lure a discerning clientele to this bijou neobistro. The outdoor tables occupy a prime location on the waterfront, with unsurpassed bay views. Round off your meal with a rich panna cotta or a platter of local cheeses.

Au Vélocipède MODERN FRENCH €€
(☑ 03 22 60 57 42; www.auvelocipede.fr; 1 rue du Puits Salé; mains €16-19; ◷ noon-6pm Sun, Mon & Wed-Fri, noon-6pm & 7.30-9pm Sat) For contemporary market-driven cuisine, this boho-flavoured, rustic-chic restaurant is a winner. Pick from creative concoctions chalked on the board, and whatever you do, don't miss out on the exquisite homemade cakes and pastries. It fills up in the blink of an eye at lunchtime, so book a table or show up early. Past 2.30pm it morphs into a tearoom.

Le Nicol's SEAFOOD €€
(☑ 03 22 26 82 96; 15 rue de la Ferté; mains €13-21, menus €18-38; ◷ noon-2pm & 7-9pm Tue-Sun) Le Nicol's is renowned for its whopping bowls of mussels and chips at eminently affordable prices. You can have them a dozen different ways, but the smart choice is the *moules à la salicorne* (mussels cooked with samphire) – they're as you've never tasted before. It also excels with fish dishes and seafood platters. One minus: seating is tight.

Information

Tourist Office (☑ 03 22 60 93 50; www.tourisme-baiedesomme.fr; 2 place Guillaume Le Conquérant, St-Valery-sur-Somme; ◷ 9.30am-12.30pm & 2.30-6pm daily, closed Mon Oct-Mar) Has excellent English-language brochures.

Getting There & Away

St-Valery-sur-Somme is best accessed with a car. It's 72km northwest of Amiens via the A16 and the D40.

PARC ORNITHOLOGIQUE DU MARQUENTERRE

An astonishing 360 species of bird have been sighted at the 2.6-sq-km **Marquenterre Ornithological Park** (☑ 03 22 25 68 99; www.parcdumarquenterre.com; 25bis chemin des Garennes, St-Quentin-en-Tourmont; adult/child €10.50/7.90; ◷ 10am-6pm), an important migratory stopover between the UK, Iceland, Scandinavia and Siberia and the warmer climes of West Africa. Three marked walking circuits (2km to 6km) take you to marshes, dunes, meadows, freshwater ponds, a brackish lagoon and 12 observation posts, or you can tour the park by horse-drawn cart. Binoculars can be rented at the reception. It's a circuitous 10km northwest of Le Crotoy.

BATTLE OF THE SOMME, FLANDERS & ARTOIS MEMORIALS

The First Battle of the Somme, a WWI Allied offensive waged in the villages and woodlands northeast of Amiens, was designed to relieve pressure on the beleaguered French troops at Verdun. On 1 July 1916, British, Commonwealth and French troops 'went over the top' in a massive assault along a 34km front. But German positions proved virtually unbreachable, and on the first day of the battle an astounding 21,392 British troops were killed and another 35,492 were wounded. Most casualties were infantrymen mown down by German machine guns. By the time the offensive was called off in mid-November, a total of 1.2 million lives had been lost on both sides. The British had advanced 12km, the French 8km.

The Battle of the Somme has become a symbol of the meaningless slaughter of war and its killing fields have since become a site of pilgrimage. Each year, thousands of visitors from Australia, New Zealand, Canada and Great Britain follow the Circuit du Souvenir.

Between 2014 and 2018, a number of events will commemorate the Centenary of WWI throughout the region – it's well worth timing your trip around them.

Convenient bases to explore the area include Amiens, Arras and the rural towns of Péronne, Albert and Pozières.

⊙ Sights

Australian Corps
Memorial Park   WAR MEMORIAL
(www.anzac-france.com; ⊙ vehicle access 9am-6pm Apr-Oct, 9am-4pm Nov-Mar, pedestrians 24hr) Inaugurated in 2008, this memorial commemorates the engagement of more than 100,000 Australians who served in the Australian Corps in France. It stands on the hilltop site of the Battle of Le Hamel (4 July 1918), fought and won by Australian and American troops under the command of Australian Lieutenant General John Monash. The Australian Corps Memorial is 7km northeast of Villers-Bretonneux; follow the signs to 'Monument Australien/Memorial Park'.

The memorial comprises three curvaceous walls clad in green granite; the central slab is adorned with a large bronze 'Rising Sun', which is the badge worn by members of the Australian Imperial Force. The German air ace Baron Manfred von Richthofen, aka the Red Baron, was shot down a bit northwest of here – Australian ground forces claimed credit but so did a Canadian pilot.

Indian & Chinese Cemetery   CEMETERY
(Ayette) Towards the end of WWI, tens of thousands of Chinese labourers were recruited by the British government to perform non-combat jobs in Europe, including the gruesome task of recovering and burying Allied war dead. Some of these *travailleurs chinois* (Chinese labourers) as well as Indians who served with British forces are buried in this Commonwealth cemetery, which is 29km northeast of Albert, just off the D919 at the southern edge of the village of Ayette.

Many Chinese labourers died in the Spanish flu epidemic of 1918–19. Their gravestones are etched in Chinese and English with inscriptions such as 'a good reputation endures forever', 'a noble duty bravely done' and 'faithful unto death'. The nearby graves of Indians are marked in Hindi or Arabic. There's also the tomb of a single German.

Beaumont-Hamel
Newfoundland Memorial   WAR MEMORIAL
(✆03 22 76 70 86; www.veterans.gc.ca; Beaumont-Hamel) This evocative memorial preserves part of the Western Front in the state it was in at fighting's end. The zigzag trench system, which still fills with mud in winter, is clearly visible, as are countless shell craters and the remains of barbed-wire barriers. A path leads to an orientation table at the top of the 'Caribou mound', where a bronze caribou statue is surrounded by plants native to Newfoundland. Beaumont-Hamel is 9km north of Albert; follow the signs for 'Memorial Terreneuvien'.

The memorial to the 29th Division, to which the volunteer Royal Newfoundland Regiment belonged, stands at the entrance of the site. On 1 July 1916 this regiment stormed entrenched German positions and was nearly wiped out; until recently, a plaque at the entrance noted bluntly that 'strategic and tactical miscalculations led to a great slaughter'. Canadian students based at the Welcome Centre (✆03 22 76 70 86; www.veterans.gc.ca/eng/memorials; Beaumon-Hamel; ⊙9am-5pm), which resembles a Newfoundland fisher's house, give free guided tours in French or English (except from mid-December to mid-January).

La Grande Mine   LANDMARK
(La Boisselle) Just outside the hamlet of La Boisselle, this enormous crater looks like the site of a meteor impact. Some 100m across and 30m deep, the Lochnagar Crater Memorial (as it's officially known) was created on the morning of the first day of the First Battle of the Somme (1 July 1916) by about 25 tonnes of ammonal laid by British sappers in order to create a breach in the German lines.

La Grande Mine is 4km northeast of Albert along the D929.

Historial de la
Grande Guerre   WAR MUSEUM
(Museum of the Great War; ✆03 22 83 14 18; www.historial.org; Château de Péronne, Péronne; adult/child incl audioguide €7.50/4; ⊙10am-6pm, closed mid-Dec–mid-Feb) The best place to begin a visit to the Somme battlefields – especially

---

ⓘ WWI SITES RESOURCES

Area tourist offices can supply you with some excellent English-language brochures, including *The Visitor's Guide to the Battlefields* and *Australians in the Somme*, as well as the free multilingual map *The Great War Remembered*. For online information, including the program of events for the WWI Centenary, see www.somme-battlefields.com and www.somme14-18.com.

Battle of the Somme Memorials

Arras (16km); Vimy Ridge Canadian National Historical Site (28km); Indian Memorial (54km); Fromelles (58km)

D917 Lille (65km)

Ayette Indian & Chinese Cemetery

N30

D919   D30

D938   Bapaume

Beaumont

Beaumont-Hamel Newfoundland Memorial   36th (Ulster) Division Memorial   D929

Acheux

Hamel   D151   A1

D50   D73   A2

Thiepval Memorial   D107

Pozières

D919   D20   La Boisselle   D20

Longueval   D20

D11   Rancourt

Villers-Bocage   Albert   La Grande Mine   South African National Memorial (Delville Wood)   N17

N25   D23   Somme American Cemetery (24km)

D42   D329   D938

D929

D1   Somme   Péronne

Bray-sur-Somme   D1   Historial de la Grande Guerre

Corbie   Australian Corps Memorial Park   La Chapelette British & Indian Cemeteries   D6

Amiens   D1

Australian National War Memorial   A1   N17

D1029   D1029

N1   A29   Musée Franco-Australien   Villers-Bretonneux   D329   A29   St-Quentin (25km)

D23   D42   D337

---

if you're interested in WWI's historical and cultural context – is the outstanding Historial de la Grande Guerre in the town of Péronne, about 60km east of Amiens. Tucked inside Péronne's massively fortified château, this award-winning museum tells the story of the war chronologically, with equal space given to the German, French and British perspectives on what happened, how and why.

The museum contains a unique collection of visually engaging material, including period films and the bone-chilling engravings by Otto Dix, which capture the aesthetic sensibilities, enthusiasm, naive patriotism and unimaginable violence of the time. The proud uniforms of various units and armies are shown laid out on the ground, as if on freshly – though bloodlessly – dead soldiers. The lake behind the museum is a fine place for a stroll or picnic.

La Chapelette British & Indian Cemeteries   CEMETERY

(Péronne) On the D1017 at the southern edge of Péronne (towards St-Quentin), this cemetery has multifaith, multilingual headstones, with a section for the fallen of units such as the 38th King George's Own Central India Horse.

Somme American Cemetery   CEMETERY

(www.abmc.gov; Bony; ⊙9am-5pm) In late September 1918, just six weeks before the end of WWI, American units – flanked by their British, Canadian and Australian allies – launched an assault on the Germans' heavily fortified Hindenburg Line. Some of the fiercest fighting took place near the village of Bony, on the sloping site now occupied by the 1844 Latin Crosses and Stars of David of this well-maintained cemetery, which is 24km northeast of Péronne, mostly along D6, and 18km north of St-Quentin along D1044.

One regiment of the 27th Infantry Division, a National Guard unit from New York, suffered 337 dead and 658 wounded on a single day. The names of 333 men whose remains were never recovered are inscribed on the walls of the Memorial Chapel, reached through massive bronze doors. The small Visitors' Building (turn left at the flagpole) has information on the battle.

South African National Memorial & Museum   WAR MEMORIAL

(www.delvillewood.com; Longueval; ⊙10am-5.30pm Tue-Sun, closed Dec & Jan) The memorial stands in the middle of shell-pocked Delville Wood, where the 1st South African Infantry

Brigade fought against various units of the 4th German Army Corps in the third week of July 1916. Outnumbered, the South African troops were almost decimated but managed to hold on and fight back. The star-shaped museum is a replica of Cape Town's Castle of Good Hope. The memorial is in Longueval, about 13km east-northeast of Albert, mostly along the D20.

A wide avenue flanked by a double row of oak trees leads to the Great Arch, which precedes the rows of white headstones.

Thiepval Memorial   WAR MEMORIAL

(☑03 22 74 60 47; www.cwgc.org; Thiepval; ⊘ visitors centre 9.30am-5pm) The largest British war memorial in the world, this arch-shaped, 45m-high construction is visible for many kilometres in all directions. Designed by Edwin Lutyens, it was built on the site of a German stronghold that was stormed on 1 July 1916, the first day of the Battle of the Somme, which is known as the 'bloodiest day of the British army'. The site also has a large Commonwealth cemetery and an informative visitors centre. Thiepval is 7.5km northeast of Albert along the D151.

The columns of the arches are inscribed with the names of 73,367 British and South African soldiers whose remains were never recovered or identified.

Ulster Tower Memorial   WAR MEMORIAL

(☑03 22 74 87 14; Thiepval; ⊘museum 10am-5pm Tue-Sun Mar-Nov, to 6pm May-Sep) The five thousand Ulstermen who perished in the Battle of the Somme are commemorated by this mock Gothic-style tower, an exact replica of Helen's Tower at Clanboye, County Down, the place where the Ulster Division did its training. Dedicated in 1921, it has long been a Unionist pilgrimage site; a black obelisk known as the Orange Memorial to Fallen Brethren (1993) stands in an enclosure behind the tower.

It's on the D73 between Beaumont-Hamel and Thiepval; follow the signs to the 'Mémorial Irlandais'.

In a sign that historic wounds are finally healing, in 2006 the Irish Republic issued a €0.75 postage stamp showing the overwhelmingly Protestant 36th Division in action on this site, to commemorate the 90th anniversary of the Battle of the Somme.

Virtually untouched since the war, nearby Thiepval Wood can be visited on a guided tour (donation requested) at 11am and/or 3pm; call ahead for dates of scheduled group tours.

Musée Franco-Australien   WAR MUSEUM

(Franco-Australian Museum; ☑03 22 96 80 79; www.museeaustralien.com; 9 rue Victoria, Villers-Bretonneux; adult/child €5/3; ⊘9.30am-5.30pm Mon-Sat) In Villers-Bretonneux, 17km east of Amiens via the D1029, this well-organised museum displays highly personal WWI Australiana including letters and photographs that evoke life on the Western Front. It is housed in a primary school that was built with funds donated by school-children in the Australian state of Victoria.

COMMONWEALTH CEMETERIES & MEMORIALS

Almost 750,000 soldiers, airmen and sailors from Great Britain, Australia, Canada, the Indian subcontinent, Ireland, New Zealand, South Africa, the West Indies and other parts of the British Empire died during WWI on the Western Front, two-thirds of them in France. They were buried where they fell, in more than 1000 military cemeteries and 2000 civilian cemeteries that dot the landscape along a wide swath of territory – 'Flanders Fields' – running roughly from Amiens and Cambrai north via Arras and Béthune to Armentières and Ypres (Ieper) in Belgium. French and German war dead were reburied in large cemeteries after the war. American war dead of the world wars were either repatriated (61%) or reburied in large cemeteries near where they fell (39%).

The focal point of each Commonwealth cemetery, now tended by the Commonwealth War Graves Commission (www.cwgc.org), is the Cross of Sacrifice. Many of the headstones, made of Portland limestone, bear moving personal inscriptions composed by family members. Most cemeteries have a bronze Cemetery Register box that contains a visitors book, in which you can record your impressions, and a booklet with biographical details on each of the identified dead (Americans who died fighting with British forces can be spotted by their addresses). Some larger cemeteries also have a bronze plaque with historical information.

Australian National War Memorial
WAR MEMORIAL

(www.cwgc.org; Villers-Bretonneux) The names of 10,982 Australian soldiers whose remains were never found are engraved on the base of the 32m-high memorial, one of the most imposing WWI monuments in the Somme, 2km north of Villers-Bretonneux along the D23. For the full effect, climb up to the viewing platform. In front of the memorial is a large Commonwealth cemetery. The Anzac Day Dawn Service (www.anzac-france.com) is held here every 25 April at 5.30am.

The ceremony pays homage to the 313,000 Australians (out of a total population of 4.5 million) who volunteered for overseas military service; 46,000 met their deaths on the Western Front (14,000 others perished elsewhere). See www.ww1westernfront.gov.au for more information.

Vimy Ridge Canadian National Historic Site
WAR MEMORIAL

(www.veterans.gc.ca; Vimy; ⊘visitor centre 9am-5pm daily) Vimy Ridge, 11km north of Arras, was the scene of some of the bloodiest and toughest trench warfare of WWI, with almost two full years of attacks. Of the 66,655 Canadians who died in WWI, 3598 lost their lives in April 1917 taking this 14km-long stretch. Its highest point – site of a heavily fortified German position – was later chosen as the site of Canada's WWI memorial.

Overlooking the plain of Artois, the superbly designed white monument was built from 1925 to 1936. The peaceful, 1 sq km park also includes two Canadian cemeteries, a monument to France's Moroccan Division (in French and Arabic) and a Visitor Centre staffed by bilingual Canadian students who run free guided tours.

Vimy Ridge is a very evocative site, and it's easy to see why. Whereas the French, right after the war, attempted to erase all signs of battle and return the Somme region to agriculture and normalcy, the Canadians decided that the most evocative way to remember their fallen was to preserve part of the crater-pocked battlefield exactly the way it looked when the guns fell silent. As a result, the best place to get some sense of the hell known as the Western Front is the chilling, eerie moonscape of Vimy. The zigzag trench system is clearly visible, as are countless shell craters. Because countless bodies still lie buried among the trees and craters, the entire site is treated like a graveyard.

The imposing memorial features 20 allegorical figures, carved from huge blocks of white Croatian limestone, that include a cloaked, downcast female figure representing a young Canada grieving for her fallen. The two striking columns represent Canada and France. The names of 11,285 Canadians who 'died in France but have no known graves', listed alphabetically and within each letter by rank, are inscribed around the base.

A taxi from Arras costs about €25 one way (€30 on Sunday), or you can cycle along secondary roads to get here.

Fromelles (Pheasant Wood) Military Cemetery & Memorial Park
CEMETERY

(www.cwgc.org; Fromelles) In Fromelles, about 20km west of Lille, this hexagonal cemetery – the first new Commonwealth cemetery in half a century – was dedicated on 19 July 2010 following the discovery of the mass graves of 250 Australian soldiers. Just 2km northwest, the Australian Memorial Park marks the spot where, on 19 and 20 July 1916, 1917 Australians and 519 British soldiers were killed during a poorly planned offensive intended to divert German forces from the Battle of the Somme.

Another 3146 Australians and 977 British were wounded. This was 'the worst 24 hours in Australia's entire history' – in the words of Ross McMullin, writing for the Australian War Memorial (www.awm.gov.au). It seems likely that one of the soldiers on the victorious German side was a 27-year-old corporal in the 16th Bavarian Reserve Infantry Regiment named Adolf Hitler.

After the battle, the Germans buried many of the Australian and British dead in mass graves behind their lines. Most were reburied after the war, but eight pits containing the remains of 250 men were not found until 2008. To provide them with a dignified final resting place, the Fromelles (Pheasant Wood) Military Cemetery was established in 2010, the 94th anniversary of the catastrophic and pointless assault. DNA testing has established the identity of 109 Australians.

After the surviving Australians retreated to their pre-battle front lines, hundreds of their comrades-in-arms lay wounded in no-man's land. For three days the survivors made heroic efforts to rescue them, acts of bravery commemorated by the sculpture Cobbers visible in the Fromelles Memorial Park. Inaugurated in 1998, it is situated atop a row of

German blockhouses 2km northwest of the new cemetery; to get there, follow the signs to the 'Mémorial Australien'.

Nearby, in what was once no-man's land between the Australian and German front lines, is the VC Corner Australian Cemetery. There are no headstones because not a single one of the 410 souls buried here was identified.

Indian Memorial
WAR MEMORIAL

(www.cwgc.org; Neuve-Chapelle) The evocative Mémorial Indien (Neuve-Chapelle Memorial), vaguely Moghul in architecture, records the names of 4700 soldiers of the Indian Army who 'have no known grave'. The 15m-high column, flanked by two tigers, is topped by a lotus capital, the Imperial Crown and the Star of India. The units and the ranks of the fallen engraved on the walls evoke the pride, pomp and exploitation on which the British Empire was built.

This memorial is 20km west of Lille, in the village of Neuve-Chapelle.

🛏 Sleeping & Eating

Although Amiens and Arras have a good range of accommodation options, a growing number of visitors choose to stay in one of the small hotels or B&Bs in the towns closer to the battlefields, including Péronne, Albert and Pozières.

★ Au Vintage
B&B €

(☑06 83 03 45 26, 03 22 75 63 28; www.chambres-dhotes-albert.com; 19 rue de Corbie, Albert; d incl breakfast €65-85; 🕾) This B&B is an absolute spoil from start to finish. It occupies an elegant brick mansion with two rooms and a family suite that are furnished with taste and flair. Our fave is Rubis, with its super-size bathroom. Evelyne and Jacky are delightful, cultured hosts who enjoy sharing their knowledge about the battlefields with their guests – in good English.

The B&B is on a quiet street southwest of the tourist office.

Butterworth Farm
B&B €

(☑06 22 30 28 02, 03 22 74 04 47; www.butterworth-cottage.com; route de Bazentin, Pozières; d incl breakfast €65; 🕾) Beloved by Australians and Brits, this well-run venture is an excellent base. Well-tended, fresh guest rooms are in a converted barn, the façade of which is covered with wood panels. There's a garden, filled with flowers and herbs, for lounging in, and breakfasts are copious.

Hôtel Saint-Claude
HOTEL €

(☑03 22 79 49 49; www.hotelsaintclaude.com; 42 place Louis Daudré, Péronne; s €65-86, d €86-112; 🕾) Originally a *relais de poste* ('post inn'), the epicentral Saint-Claude makes a fine base. A breath of fresh air, it does away with old-fashioned furnishings – its dozen contemporary rooms are decorated in adventurous colours and come with up-to-date bathrooms. Downstairs there's a solid country restaurant.

La Basilique
HOTEL €€

(☑03 22 75 04 71; www.hoteldelabasilique.fr; 3 rue Gambetta, Albert; d €88-98; 🕾) This comfortable spot in the shadow of Albert's basilica looks and feels exactly the way an inn ensconced in the heart of a provincial French town should. That it has a well-priced restaurant serving *cuisine du terroir* (regional specialities made with quality ingredients from the countryside) and the tourist office is just across the street puts it over the top.

Le Tommy
BRASSERIE €

(☑03 22 74 82 84; 91 route d'Albert, Pozières; mains €8-12; ⏰ 11am-3pm) This no-frills, slightly eccentric eatery on the main road in Pozières is ideal for a light lunch comprising a main course and dessert, or a sandwich. It also houses a small museum with WWI memorabilia and artefacts.

👉 Tours

Tourist offices (including those in Amiens, Arras, Albert and Péronne) can help book tours of battlefield sites and memorials. Respected tour companies include **The Battlefields Experience** (☑03 22 76 29 60; www.thebattleofthesomme.co.uk), **Western Front Tours** (www.westernfronttours.com.au; ⏰ mid-Mar–mid-Nov), **Terres de Mémoire** (☑03 22 84 23 05; www.terresdememoire.com), **Chemins d'Histoire** (☑06 31 31 85 02; www.cheminsdhistoire.com) and **True Blue Digger Tours** (☑06 01 33 46 76; www.trueblue-diggertours.com).

ℹ Information

Tourist Office (☑03 22 84 42 38; www.hautesomme-tourisme.com; 16 place André Audinot, Péronne; ⏰10am-noon & 2-6pm Mon-Sat) Excellent English brochures on the battlefields can be picked up at Péronne's tourist office, 100m from the museum entrance.

Tourist Office (☑03 22 75 16 42; www.tourisme-paysducoquelicot.com; 6 rue Émile Zola, Albert; ⏰9am-12.30pm & 1.30-6.30pm Mon-Sat, 9am-1pm Sun) The tourist office in Albert offers abundant info and has English brochures on the battlefields. It can also help with accommodation bookings.

❶ Getting There & Away

You'll need your own transport to visit most of the Somme memorials (one exception is Villers-Bretonneux, which is accessible by train). The train station, well served from Amiens (€3.90, 10 minutes, 11 daily Monday to Friday, four to six daily weekends), is 600m south of the museum (take rue de Melbourne) and a walkable 3km south of the Australian National War Memorial. A round-trip taxi ride from Villers-Bretonneux to the memorial costs around €20.

PICARDY

Amiens

POP 137,030

One of France's most awe-inspiring Gothic cathedrals is reason enough to spend time in Amiens, the comfy, if reserved, former capital of Picardy, where Jules Verne spent the last two decades of his life. The mostly pedestrianised city centre, rebuilt after WWII, is complemented by lovely green spaces along the Somme river. Some 25,000 students give the town a youthful feel.

Amiens is an excellent base for visits to the Battle of the Somme Memorials.

◉ Sights & Activities

★ Cathédrale Notre Dame   CATHEDRAL
(place Notre Dame; north tower adult/child €5.50/free, audioguide €4; ⊙cathedral 8.30am-6.15pm daily, north tower afternoon only Wed-Mon) The largest Gothic cathedral in France (it's 145m long) and a Unesco World Heritage Site, this magnificent structure was begun in 1220 to house the skull of St John the Baptist. Architecture connoisseurs rave about the soaring Gothic arches (42.3m high over the transept), unity of style and immense interior, but for locals the highlight is the 17th-century statue known as the Ange Pleureur (Crying Angel), in the ambulatory directly behind the over-the-top baroque high altar.

Note that the skull of St John the Baptist is sometimes exposed – framed in gold and jewels – in the northern outer wall of the ambulatory.

The octagonal, 234m-long labyrinth on the black-and-white floor of the nave is easy to miss as the soaring vaults draw the eye upward. Plaques in the south transept arm

honour American, Australian, British, Canadian and New Zealand soldiers who perished in WWI.

To get a sense of what you're seeing, it's worth hiring a one-hour audioguide, available in six languages, at the tourist office (across the street). Weather permitting, it's possible to climb the north tower; tickets are sold in the boutique to the left as you approach the west façade.

A free 45-minute light show bathes the cathedral's façade in vivid medieval colours nightly from mid-June to mid-September and December to 1 January; the photons start flying at 7pm in winter and sometime between 9.45pm (September) and 10.45pm (June) in summer.

Maison de Jules Verne   HOUSE MUSEUM
(Home of Jules Verne; ☑03 22 45 45 75; www.amiens.fr/vie-quotidienne/culture/; 2 rue Charles Dubois; adult/child €7.50/4; ⊙10am-12.30pm & 2-6.30pm Mon & Wed-Fri, 2-6.30pm Tue, 11am-6.30pm Sat & Sun) Jules Verne (1828–1905) wrote many of his best-known works of brain-tingling – and eerily prescient – science fiction under the eaves of this turreted Amiens home. The models, prints, posters and other items inspired by Verne's fecund imagination afford a fascinating opportunity to check out the future as he envisioned it over a century ago, when going around the world in 80 days sounded utterly fantastic. Signs are in French and English.

Musée de Picardie   MUSEUM
(☑03 22 97 14 00; www.amiens.fr/musees; 48 rue de la République; adult/child €5.50/free; ⊙10am-noon & 2-6pm Tue-Sat, until 9pm Thu, 2-7pm Sun) Housed in a dashing Second Empire structure (1855–67) with a jaw-droppingly impressive central room, the Picardy Museum is surprisingly well endowed with archaeological exhibits, medieval art and Revolution-era ceramics.

Tour Perret   TOWER
(place Alphonse Fiquet) For a long time the tallest building in western Europe, the reinforced concrete Perret Tower (110m), facing the train station, was designed by Belgian architect Auguste Perret (who also planned postwar Le Havre) and completed in 1954. It is not open to visitors.

Hortillonnages   BOAT TOUR
(☑03 22 92 12 18; 54 bd Beauvillé; adult/child €5.90/4.10; ⊙2-5pm Apr-Oct) Amiens' market gardens – some 3 sq km in extent – have

Amiens

Amiens

⦿ Top Sights
1 Cathédrale Notre Dame B2

◎ Sights
2 Maison de Jules Verne B4
3 Musée de Picardie A3
4 Tour Perret C3

🛏 Sleeping
5 Grand Hôtel de l'Univers C3
6 Hôtel Le St-Louis C4
7 Hôtel Victor Hugo C2

⦿ Eating
8 Le Quai C1
9 Le T'chiot Zinc C3
10 Marché sur l'Eau C2
11 Tante Jeanne C1

◉ Drinking & Nightlife
12 Le Rétroviseur C1
13 Marott' Street B3

supplied the city with vegetables and flowers since the Middle Ages. Today, their peaceful *rieux* (waterways), home to seven working farms, more than 1000 private gardens and countless water birds, can be visited on 12-person boats whose raised prows make them look a bit like gondolas. Available later

(to 6.30pm) if weather and demand allow. A not-to-be-missed experience.

🛏 Sleeping

Amiens' hotels offer excellent value for money but often fill up with businesspeople from Monday to Thursday.

Le Quatorze
B&B €

(03 22 47 50 85, 06 16 89 19 87; www.lequatorze. fr; 14 av de Dublin; d incl breakfast €75;) At this calm haven, in a backstreet that few know of, Amiens-born-and-bred Laure offers the perfect small B&B experience, with five snug rooms mixing modern fixtures with antique charm (original tiles, family photos, wood flooring, floral wallpapers). The B&B occupies a bourgeois town house in the *quartier anglais,* a historic neighbourhood full of superb brick mansions, a 15-minute stroll east of the train station.

Avoid room 1, which feels a tad boxy due to the cubicle shower and toilets plonked in the corner.

Hôtel Victor Hugo
HOTEL €

(03 22 91 57 91; www.hotel-a-amiens.com; 2 rue de l'Oratoire; d €49-65;) Just a block from the cathedral, this bargain-priced, family-run hotel has 10 simple but comfortable rooms. Best value, if you don't mind a long stair climb, are those on the sloped-ceilinged top floor (rooms 7 and 8) with rooftop views and lots of natural light. No parking.

Hôtel Le St-Louis
HOTEL €

(03 22 91 76 03; www.amiens-hotel.fr; 24 rue des Otages; d €74-91;) The 24 rooms, some off a deck-like inner courtyard, are modern and serviceable, and double-glazing shuts out the street noise. Ask for a room on the upper floors to get more natural light.

Grand Hôtel de l'Univers
HOTEL €€

(03 22 91 52 51; www.hotel-univers-amiens.com; 2 rue de Noyon; d €95-125;) This venerable, Best Western–affiliated hostelry has an enviable parkside location in the city's heart, only one block from the train station. Rue de Noyon is pedestrianised so you won't be bothered by noise. The 40 rooms, set around a four-storey atrium, are immaculate and very comfortable; try room 26 (€110) for its double aspect and balcony. One quibble: there's no parking.

✖ Eating & Drinking

The St-Leu Quarter – picturesque, though not quite the 'northern Venice' it's touted to be – is lined with neon-lit riverside restaurants and pubs, many featuring warm-season terraces with views up to the cathedral. There are more places to eat across the river at place du Don.

Le T'chiot Zinc
BISTRO €

(03 22 91 43 79; 18 rue de Noyon; menus €14-28; noon-2.30pm & 7-10pm Mon-Sat) Inviting, bistro-style decor reminiscent of the belle époque provides a fine backdrop for the tasty French and Picard cuisine, including fish dishes and *caqhuse* (pork in a cream, wine vinegar and onion sauce).

Tante Jeanne
CRÊPERIE €

(03 22 72 30 30; 1 rue de la Dodane; mains €9-16; noon-2pm & 7-10pm Mon-Thu, 10am-2pm & 7-11pm Fri, noon-11.30pm Sat, noon-10pm Sun) Down in the Saint-Leu neighborhood, this is a good spot for an afternoon snack or a lighter meal, with crispy galettes and a variety of salads, and views from the sidewalk tables in warm weather.

Marché sur l'Eau
FOOD MARKET €

(place Parmentier; to 12.30pm Sat, to 1pm in summer) Fruit and vegetables grown in the Hortillonnages are sold at this one-time floating market, now held on dry land on Saturday mornings throughout the year. A special market is also held on the third Sunday in June, when producers don traditional outfits and bring their produce downriver in high-prowed, gondola-like boats.

Le Quai
BRASSERIE €€

(03 22 72 10 80; www.restaurant-le-quai.com; 13 quai Bélu; mains €14-23, menus €16-24; noon-2pm & 7-10pm Mon-Thu & Sun, to 11pm Fri & Sat) With its zesty decor, recession-proof prices and lovely riverside terrace, it's no wonder Le Quai is packed to the rafters at lunchtime. The cuisine is a modern twist on French and Picard traditional recipes. If homemade *burger spécial quai* (burger with beefsteak, ham and Maroilles sauce) is on the menu, order it!

Marott' Street
WINE BAR

(03 22 91 14 93; 1 rue Marotte; 2.30pm-1am Mon & Sat, noon-1am Tue-Fri) Designed by Gustave Eiffel's architectural firm in 1892, this exquisite ex-insurance office now attracts chic, well-off 30-somethings who sip sparkling wine while suspended – on clear-glass tiles – over the wine cellar.

Le Rétroviseur
BAR, BRASSERIE

(03 22 91 92 70; www.leretroviseur.fr; place du Don; 5pm-1am Mon, noon-2am Tue-Fri, 4pm-2am Sat) A highlight of Amiens' nightlife, Le Rétroviseur is as much a bar as a restaurant. The interior is super atmospheric but the terrace overlooking the small square is a great spot to just chill out in summer. It hosts live bands certain evenings. The eclectic menu features a few vegie options.

ℹ Information

Banks can be found around place René Goblet and rue des Trois Cailloux.

Tourist Office (☑ 03 22 71 60 50; www.amiens-tourisme.com; 40 place Notre Dame; ⊘ 9.30am-6pm Mon-Sat, 10am-noon & 2-5pm Sun) Can supply details on the Somme memorials (including minibus tours) and cultural events.

ℹ Getting There & Around

BICYCLE

Vélo Service (Buscyclette; ☑ 09 80 82 44 00; www.buscyclette.fr; 13 place Alphonse Fiquet; per day/weekend €3/7; ⊘ 9am-7pm Mon-Sat) A nonprofit organisation that rents bikes from the courtyard of Tour Perret, behind the main entrance.

CAR

There's free parking one or two blocks north of the Hôtel Victor Hugo, along rue Lameth, rue Cardon, rue Jean XXIII and rue de la Barette.

To hire a car to tour the memorials, try **Avis** (☑ 03 22 91 31 21; www.avis.fr; bd d'Alsace-Lorraine), at the train station.

TRAIN

Amiens is an important rail hub. Accessed through a dramatic modern entrance, the downtown train station offers direct services to all cities listed below. SNCF buses (€10, 45 minutes, about seven daily) also go to the Haute Picardie TGV station, 42km east of the city.

Arras €12.70, 45 minutes, six to 13 daily.

Boulogne €21.10, 1½ hours, seven to nine daily.

Calais-Ville €27.10, two to 2½ hours, four to five daily.

Compiègne €13.90, 1¼ hours, eight to 12 daily.

Laon €18.50, 1¼ hours, five to nine daily.

Lille-Flandres €21.70, 1½ hours, five to 13 daily.

Paris Gare du Nord €16.50 to €22.20, 1¼ to 1¾ hours, 14 to 22 daily.

Rouen €20.80, 1¼ hours, five daily.

Compiègne

POP 42,690

Heading north from Paris towards Lille (or vice versa), it's definitely worth stopping in at Compiègne. This *cité impériale* (imperial city) has a lively, prosperous air, and its *centre historique* is sheer delight.

Compiègne reached its glittering zenith under Emperor Napoléon III (r 1852–70), whose legacy is alive and well in the château – the star attraction – and its park. A forest clearing near the city was the site of the armistice that ended WWI and the French

surrender in 1940. On 23 May 1430 Joan of Arc (Jeanne d'Arc) – honoured by two statues in the city centre – was captured at Compiègne by the Burgundians, who later sold her to their English allies.

◉ Sights

★ **Palais Impérial**　　　　PALACE, MUSEUM
(☑ 03 44 38 47 00; www.musee-chateau-compiegne.fr; place du Général de Gaulle; adult/child €7/free; ⊘ 10am-6pm Wed-Mon, Grands Appartements 10am-12.30pm & 1.30-5.15pm Wed-Mon) Visitors to this 1337-room palace, originally built under Louis XV, are struck by its imposing grandeur. This was the location of Napoléon III's dazzling hunting parties, which drew aristocrats from all around Europe.

The same ticket grants access to the adjacent **Musée du Second Empire**, which illustrates the lives of Napoléon III and his family; the **Musée de l'Impératrice**, which stars Eugénie (Napoléon III's wife); and the **Musée de la Voiture**, which features vehicles that pre-date the internal combustion engine.

The sumptuous Grands Appartements, including the empress's bedroom and a ballroom lit by 15 chandeliers, can be visited with an audioguide (available in English).

Stretching east from the château, the 20-hectare, English-style Petit Parc links up with the Grand Parc and the Forêt de Compiègne, a forest that surrounds Compiègne on the east and south and is criss-crossed by rectilinear paths. The area is a favourite venue for hiking and cycling (maps available at the tourist office) as well as horse riding.

**Mémorial de l'Internement
et de la Déportation – Camp
de Royallieu**　　　　WWII MUSEUM
(Internment & Deportation Memorial; ☑ 03 44 96 37 00; www.memorial-compiegne.fr; 2bis av des Martyrs de la Liberté; adult/child incl English audioguide €3/1.50; ⊘ 10am-6pm Wed-Mon) Lying about 2.5km southwest of the city centre, the French military base of Royallieu was used as a Nazi transit camp from 1941 to 1944; several of the original buildings have housed this profoundly moving memorial museum since 2008. Of the more than 53,000 men, women and children held here (mostly Jews, prisoners of war and Resistance fighters), 48,000 were marched through town to the train station for the trip east to concentration and extermination camps, including Auschwitz.

Clairière de l'Armistice HISTORIC SITE
(Armistice Clearing; 📞03 44 85 14 18; www.musee-armistice-14-18.fr; adult/child €5/3; ⏱10am-5.30pm, closed Tue Oct-Mar) The armistice that put an end to WWI was signed in a thick forest 7km northeast of Compiègne, inside the railway carriage of the Allied supreme commander. On 22 June 1940, in the same railway car, the French were forced to sign the armistice that recognised Nazi Germany's domination of France.

Clairière de l'Armistice commemorates these events with monuments, memorabilia, newspaper clippings and stereoscopic (3D) photos. The wooden rail wagon now on display is of the same type as the original one.

Taken for exhibition to Berlin, the original carriage was destroyed in April 1945 on the Führer's personal orders lest it be used for a third surrender – his own. Some of the furnishings that can be seen in the replica, hidden away during WWII, were the ones actually used in 1918.

From Compiègne, take the road to Soissons and follow the signs.

🛏 Sleeping

Ibis Budget HOTEL €
(📞08 92 68 31 04; www.ibisbudgethotel.com; 1 rue Pierre Sauvage; d €49; 📶) Yes, yes, we know it's a chain hotel, but this abode gets by on its super handy location, a waddle away from restaurants, monuments and the train station. It offers identical-looking chain hotel rooms with off-the-shelf furnishings and petite bathrooms but it's clean, practical and well soundproofed. There's no private parking, though.

Hôtel du Nord HOTEL €€
(📞03 44 83 42 30; www.hoteldunordcompiegne.com; 1 place de la Gare; s €80-85, d €90-95; 📶) Near the train station, this 20-room establishment is perfectly poised for all Compiègne's attractions. Rooms are compact, in chocolate, beige and taupe tones and with crisp linens, and most bathrooms have been modernised. Bag a room with a view on to the Oise river. Downstairs, the restaurant serves French classics with a creative twist in a panoramic dining room overlooking the river.
Check website for weekend deals.

🍴 Eating

⭐ **Le Bistrot des Arts** NEOBISTRO €€
(📞03 44 20 10 10; www.lebistrotdesarts.com; 35 cours Guynemer; mains €13-20, menus €14-29; ⏱noon-2pm & 7-9pm Mon-Fri, 7-9.30pm Sat) This much-lauded bistro filled with character and atmosphere is known for its consistently delicious and wonderfully priced cuisine, which has a modern edge but is firmly based in the classic French tradition. The menu changes regularly, but mains might include beef stewed with beer, served with homemade fries. Midway between the tourist office and the train station, facing the river.

Le Bistrot du Terroir TRADITIONAL FRENCH €€
(📞03 44 40 06 36; www.bistrot-du-terroir.fr; 13 Rue Eugène Floquet; mains €12-21, lunch menus €14-29, dinner menu €29; ⏱noon-2pm & 7-10pm Mon-Thu, to 11pm Fri & Sat) At first glance, you know Le Bistrot du Terroir is a find. Tucked in a side street near the tourist office, this cosy little place with a wooden interior serves delicious French cuisine, made with seasonal products, mixing traditional recipes with *nouvelle* ideas. Sample the sinful roasted lamb and finish yourself off with the divine *crème brûlée* with fig marmalade.

ℹ Information

Tourist Office (📞03 44 40 01 00; www.compiegne-tourisme.fr; place de l'Hôtel de Ville; ⏱9.15am-12.15pm & 1.45-6.15pm Mon-Sat) This centrally located office abuts the flamboyant Gothic 16th-century *hôtel de ville*.

ℹ Getting There & Away

Compiègne, 65km northeast of Paris, can be easily visited on a day trip from the capital.

Local buses, which depart from the train station, are free Monday to Saturday. Buses 1 and 2 serve the tourist office and château.

TRAIN
Compiègne is linked by train to Paris' Gare du Nord (€15, 40 to 70 minutes, 16 to 29 daily) and Amiens (€13.90, one to 1¼ hours, eight to 12 daily).

Laon
POP 27,090

Aficionados of medieval architecture, rejoice. The claw-shaped, hilltop Ville Haute (Upper City) is enclosed within a 7km-long wall that is pierced by three fortified gates. It boasts a magnificent Gothic cathedral and no less than 84 listed historic monuments, the densest concentration in France. The narrow streets, alleyways and courtyards are particularly rewarding territory for keen-eyed wandering. And what view! About 100 vertical metres below sits the Ville Basse (Lower

City), completely rebuilt after being flattened in WWII. Amazingly, despite its beauty, Laon is still way off the radar of most visitors.

Laon served as the capital of the Carolingian empire until it was brought to an end in 987 by Hugh Capet, who for some reason preferred ruling from Paris.

◎ Sights

Cathédrale Notre Dame   CATHEDRAL
(☉9am-8pm) A model for a number of its more famous Gothic sisters – Chartres, Reims and Dijon among them – this medieval jewel was built (1150–1230) in the transitional Gothic style on Romanesque foundations. The 110m-long interior, remarkably well lit, has three levels of columns and arches and a gilded wrought-iron choir screen; some of the stained glass dates from the 12th century. The structure is best appreciated with an audioguide (€5), available next door at the tourist office.

⌂ Sleeping & Eating

Hôtel Les Chevaliers   HOTEL €
(☑03 23 27 17 50; 3 rue Sérurier; s/d €63/69; ☏) Parts of this recently renovated hostelry, right around the corner from the Haute Ville's *hôtel de ville*, date from the Middle Ages. Ask for rooms 11 and 12, which have exposed beams and brick walls and enjoy superb views.

La Maison des 3 Rois   B&B €€
(☑03 23 20 74 24; www.lamaisondes3rois.com; 17 rue St-Martin; d incl breakfast €90-100; ☏) Nestled in an exquisitely renovated 14th-century *maison de maître* (nobleman's house) in the Haute Ville, this is Laon's hidden gem. Each room has its own personality – some with floorboards or tiles, others with low beamed ceilings. La Petite Suite is ideal for families. A steal.

Estaminet Saint-Jean   REGIONAL CUISINE €
(☑03 23 23 04 89; 23 rue St-Jean; mains €13-15; ☉noon-2pm & 7-9.30pm Tue & Thu-Sat, noon-2pm

Wed & Sun) Specialising in traditional Flemish and Picard cuisine accompanied by your choice of 30 beers, this classic neighbourhood inn with a flavour of bygone days is especially good value at lunchtime. Try the *poulet au Maroilles* (chicken with Maroilles cheese).

❶ Information

Tourist Office (☑03 23 20 28 62; www.tourisme-paysdelaon.com; Hôtel Dieu, place du Parvis; ☉10am-12.30pm & 1-5.30pm Mon-Sat, 2-5.30pm Sun; ☏) Can supply you with a free town map and excellent English brochures on Laon and the surrounds. Also offers audioguides for excellent one- to three-hour walking tours of the Ville Haute and the cathedral, guided tours (in French, with guides who may speak English), wi-fi and free internet access. Situated next to the cathedral in a 12th-century hospital decorated with 14th-century frescos.

❶ Getting There & Around

Laon is 67km northwest of Reims (in Champagne).

CAR
The Ville Haute's one-way streets circle round and round – if they don't drive you crazy they'll at least make you dizzy. Parking is available at the eastern end of the Ville Haute, around the Citadelle.

TRAIN
The train station, in the Ville Basse, is linked to Amiens (€18.50, 1½ hours, four to 12 daily), Paris' Gare du Nord (€23.50, 1½ hours, 19 daily Monday to Friday, eight on Saturday and Sunday) and Reims (€10.20, 40 minutes, three to nine daily).

The Ville Haute is a steep 20-minute walk from the train station – the stairs begin at the upper end of av Carnot – but it's more fun to take the automated, elevated **Poma funicular railway** (return €1.20; ☉every 5min 7am-8pm Mon-Sat), which links the train station with the upper city in 3½ minutes flat.

Normandy

POP 3.3 MILLION

Best Places to Eat

➡ Le Bouchon du Vaugueux (p237)

➡ La Rose des Vents (p217)

➡ Marché aux Poissons (p241)

➡ La Reine Mathilde (p228)

➡ Made in Normandy (p218)

Best Places to Stay

➡ Hôtel de la Chaîne d'Or (p225)

➡ La Maison de Famille (p237)

➡ L'Espérance (p240)

➡ Hôtel de Bourgtheroulde (p217)

➡ Detective Hôtel (p222)

Why Go?

From the Norman invasion of England in 1066 to the D-Day landings of 1944, Normandy has long played an outsized role in European history. This rich and often brutal past is brought vividly to life by the spectacular island monastery of Mont St-Michel; the Bayeux Tapestry, world-famous for its cartoon scenes of 11th-century life; and the cemeteries and memorials along the D-Day beaches, places of solemn pilgrimage. Lower-profile charms include a variety of dramatic coastal landscapes, lots of pebbly beaches, some of France's finest museums, quiet pastoral villages and architectural gems ranging from Rouen's medieval old city – home of Monet's favourite cathedral – to the maritime charms of Honfleur to the striking postwar modernism of Le Havre. Camembert, apples, cider, cream-rich cuisine and the very freshest fish and seafood provide further reasons to visit this accessible and beautiful region of France.

When to Go

Rouen

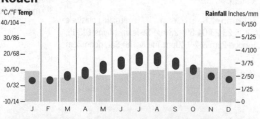

Jun D-Day commemorations are held on the landing beaches.

Jul Fêtes Médiévales in Bayeux celebrate the city's glorious history with medieval re-enactments.

Sep Deauville's American Film Festival is the accessible cousin of Cannes.

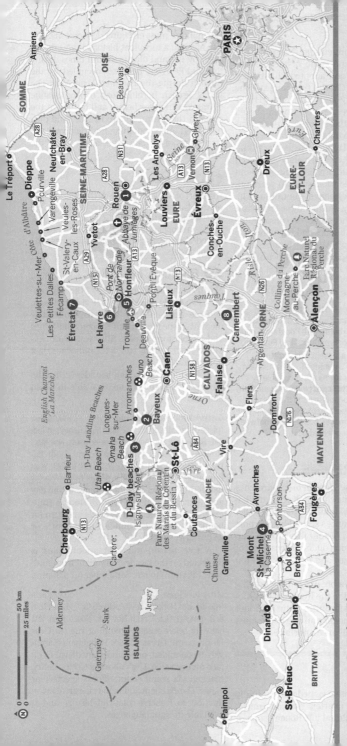

Normandy Highlights

1 Strolling among half-timbered houses and Gothic churches in **Rouen's old town** (p214)

2 Travelling back to 1066 with the world's oldest comic strip, the **Bayeux Tapestry** (p225)

3 Pondering the price of freedom at the **D-Day beaches** (p229) and nearby war cemeteries

4 Watching the tide rush in from the ramparts of **Mont St-Michel** (p247) and its extraordinary monastery

5 Savouring super-fresh seafood at ha'bourside restaurants such as **Au P'tit Mareyeur** (p244) in charming Honfleur

6 Experiencing postwar modernism at its most elegant in **Le Havre** (p223)

7 Marvelling at the famous twin cliffs and free-standing limestone arches of **Étretat** (p222)

8 Enjoying rich **Norman cuisine** (p217), from creamy Camembert and fresh oysters to tangy cider and appley Calvados

History

Vikings invaded present-day Normandy in the 9th century, and some of them established settlements and adopted Christianity. In 911 French king Charles the Simple, of the Carolingian dynasty, and Viking chief Hrölfr agreed that the area around Rouen should be handed over to these Norsemen – or Normans, as they came to be known.

Throughout the Hundred Years War (1337–1453), the Duchy of Normandy seesawed between French and English rule. England dominated the region for some 30 years until France gained permanent control in 1450. In the 16th century, Normandy, a Protestant stronghold, was the scene of considerable fighting between Catholics and Huguenots.

The liberation of Western Europe from Nazi occupation began on the beaches of Normandy on D-Day, 6 June 1944.

❶ Getting There & Around

Car ferries link Dieppe with the English port of Newhaven; Le Havre and Ouistreham (Caen) with Portsmouth; and Cherbourg with Poole and Portsmouth and the Irish ports of Dublin and Rosslare.

Normandy is easily accessible by train from Paris – Rouen is just 70 minutes from Paris' Gare St-Lazare. Most major towns are accessible by rail, and with the **Visi'ter card** (www.ter-sncf.com) travel for one to four people around the Basse Normandie region is remarkably cheap on weekends and holidays. However, bus services between smaller towns are infrequent at best.

SEINE-MARITIME

The Seine-Maritime *département* stretches along the chalk-white cliffs of the Côte d'Albâtre (Alabaster Coast) from Le Tréport via Dieppe to Le Havre, France's second-busiest port (after Marseille). Its history firmly bound up with the sea, the region offers visitors a mix of small seaside villages and dramatic cliff-top walks.

When you fancy a break from the bracing sea air, head inland to the lively, ancient metropolis of Rouen, a favourite haunt of Monet and Simone de Beauvoir and one of the most intriguing cities in France's northeast.

Rouen

POP 110,700

With its soaring Gothic cathedral, beautifully restored medieval quarter, excellent museums and vibrant cultural life, Rouen is one of Normandy's most engaging destinations. The city has had a turbulent history. It was devastated by fire and plague several times during the Middle Ages, and was occupied by the English during the Hundred Years War. The young French heroine Joan of Arc (Jeanne d'Arc) was tried for heresy and burned at the stake in the central square in 1431. And during WWII, Allied bombing raids laid waste to large parts of the city, especially south of the cathedral.

❶ Orientation

The heart of the old city is rue du Gros Horloge, which is two blocks north of the city centre's main east–west thoroughfare, rue Général Leclerc. The main shopping precinct is due north of the cathedral, on pedestrianised rue des Carmes and nearby streets.

◉ Sights & Activities

North of the cathedral, parts of the city centre – especially between rue de la République and rue Jeanne d'Arc – still have a distinctly medieval aspect, with half-timbered buildings and cobblestone streets. Alleyways worth exploring include tiny **rue des Chanoines**, just 90cm wide.

At the tourist office, audioguides (€5) of the city and the cathedral are available in seven languages.

Cathédrale Notre Dame　　　　CATHEDRAL
(place de la Cathédrale; ◷ 2-6pm Mon, 9am-7pm Tue-Sat, 8am-6pm Sun Apr-Oct, shorter hours Nov-Mar) Rouen's stunning Gothic cathedral, built between the late 12th and 16th centuries, was famously the subject of a series of canvasses painted by Monet at various times of the day and year. The 75m-tall **Tour de Beurre** (Butter Tower) was financed by locals in return for being allowed to eat butter during Lent – or so the story goes.

A free **sound-and-light spectacular** is projected on the façade every night from mid-June (at 11pm) to late September (at 9.30pm).

Gros Horloge　　　　CLOCK TOWER
(rue du Gros Horloge; adult/child €6/3; ◷ 10am-1pm & 2-7pm Apr-Oct, 2-6pm Nov-Mar, closed Mon, last entry 1hr before closing) Spanning rue du Gros Horloge, the Great Clock's Renaissance archway has a gilded, one-handed medieval clock face on each side. High above, a Gothic belfry, reached via spiral stairs, affords spectacular views. The excellent audioguide is a great introduction to Rouen's colourful history and is available in eight languages.

Rouen

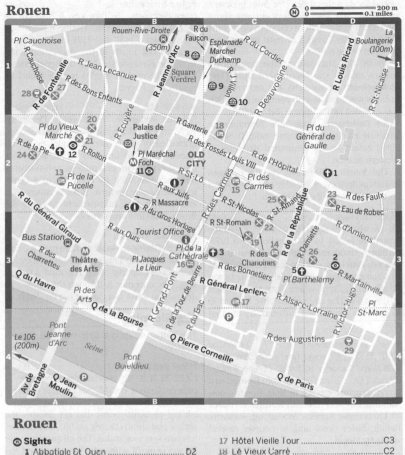

Palais de Justice   ARCHITECTURE

(place Maréchal Foch & rue aux Juifs) The ornately Gothic Law Courts, little more than a shell
at the end of WWII, have been restored to
their early-16th-century glory. The spire- and
gargoyle-adorned courtyard is accessible on

NORMANDY ROUEN

weekdays via a metal detector from pedestrianised rue aux Juifs. Visitors curious about the French justice system can sit in on a court session – under French law, most proceedings are open to the public.

Under the staircase at the courtyard's eastern end is the **Monument Juif** (Jewish Monument; rue aux Juifs), the only relic of Rouen's medieval Jewish community, which was expelled by Philippe le Bel in 1306.

An impressive, stone-built Romanesque structure constructed around 1100, it is the oldest extant Jewish communal structure in Western Europe.

The tourist office runs two-hour **tours** (€6.50) at 3pm every Tuesday and at 10.30am on the last Friday of every month.

Place du Vieux Marché SQUARE
This is where 19-year-old Joan of Arc was executed for heresy in 1431. Dedicated in 1979, thrillingly modernist **Église Jeanne d'Arc** (place du Vieux Maré; ⊙10am-noon & 2-6pm, closed Fri & Sun mornings), with its fish-scale exterior, stands on the spot where Joan was burned at the stake. The church's soaring interior is lit by some marvellous 16th-century stained glass.

Musée des Beaux-Arts ART MUSEUM
(☑02 35 71 28 40; www.rouen-musees.com; esplanade Marcel Duchamp; adult/child €5/free, 3 museums adult €8; ⊙10am-6pm Wed-Mon) Housed in a grand structure erected in 1870, Rouen's outstanding fine-arts museum features canvases by Caravaggio, Rubens, Modigliani, Pissarro, Renoir, Sisley (lots) and, of course, several works by Monet.

Musée de la Céramique MUSEUM
(☑02 35 07 31 74; www.rouen-musees.com; 1 rue du Faucon; adult/child €3/free, 3 museums adult €8; ⊙2-6pm Wed-Mon) The Ceramics Museum, housed in a 17th-century building with a fine courtyard, is known for its 16th- to 19th-century faience (tin-glazed earthenware) and porcelain.

Musée Le Secq
des Tournelles MUSEUM
(☑0235884292; www.museelesecqdestournelles.fr; 2 rue Jacques Villon; adult/child €3/free, 3 museums adult €8; ⊙2-6pm Wed-Mon) Home to one of the world's premier collections of wrought iron, this riveting museum showcases the extraordinary skills of pre-industrial-age iron- and locksmiths. Housed in a desanctified 16th-century church.

Église St-Maclou CHURCH
(place Barthelemy; ⊙10am-noon & 2-5.30pm Sat & Sun) This Flamboyant Gothic church was built between 1437 and 1521 (and renovated in 2013) but much of the decoration dates from the Renaissance. Half-timbered houses inclined at curious angles can be found on nearby side-streets.

Aître St-Maclou HISTORIC QUARTER
(186 rue Martainville; ⊙9am-6pm) Decorated with lurid woodcarvings of skulls, crossbones, gravediggers' tools and hourglasses (a reminder that your time, my friend, is running out), this macabre ensemble of half-timbered buildings was used for centuries as a cemetery for plague victims. Built between 1526 and 1533, it now houses Rouen's École des Beaux-Arts (fine arts school).

Abbatiale St-Ouen CHURCH
(place du Général de Gaulle; ⊙10am-noon & 2-6pm Tue-Thu, Sat & Sun) This 14th-century abbey is a marvellous example of the Rayonnant Gothic style. The entrance is through the lovely garden on the south side, facing rue des Faulx.

🛏 Sleeping

The tourist office can help you find a room (€3 fee).

Hôtel des Carmes HOTEL €
(☑02 35 71 92 31; www.hoteldescarmes.com; 33 place des Carmes; d €57-82, ste €83-108; 🐾) This sweet little hotel, built in 1850, offers 12 smallish but pleasant rooms that get cheaper the higher you climb (there's no lift). The annexe has two spacious suites. The oil paintings are by the owner's wife, who also designed the decor.

La Boulangerie B&B €
(☑06 12 94 53 15; www.laboulangerie.fr; 59 rue St-Nicaise; d €77-92, q €154 incl breakfast; 🐾) Tucked into a quiet side street 1.2km northeast of the cathedral, this adorable B&B, above an historic bakery, has three pleasingly decorated rooms and, for stays of a week or more, apartments. Your charming hosts, Franck and Aminata, are a gold mine of local information.

Hôtel Vieille Tour HOTEL €
(☑02 35 70 03 27; www.hotelcentrerouen.fr; 42 place de la Haute Vieille Tour; d €55-85; 🐾) Central, friendly and good value, this hotel has 20 bright, quiet rooms with big windows and simple, practical furnishings. Situated in a postwar building facing 'Parking Cathédrale'.

Le Vieux Carré
HOTEL €

(☑02 35 71 67 70; www.hotel-vieux-carre.com; 34 rue Ganterie; r €60-68; ☎) Set around a little medieval courtyard, this quiet, half-timbered hotel has a delightfully old-fashioned *salon de thé* (tearoom) and 13 small, practical rooms, all of which were renovated in 2012 and '13.

Auberge de Jeunesse Robec
HOSTEL €

(☑02 35 08 18 50; www.fuaj.org; 3 rue de la Tour; dm/s/d incl breakfast €22.80/34/58; ☺reception 8-11.45am & 5.30-10pm; ☎) The two- to eight-bed rooms at this modern, 88-bed hostel are comfortable and functional. Situated 2km east of the cathedral off route de Darnétal; from the city centre, take bus T2 or T3 to the 'Auberge de Jeunesse' stop.

Hôtel Le Cardinal
HOTEL €€

(☑02 35 70 24 42; www.cardinal-hotel.fr; 1 place de la Cathédrale; s €78-98, d €88-118; ☎) Facing the cathedral's famous west façade, this 15-room hotel is one of best midrange deals in central Rouen. All but two of the bright rooms have romantic cathedral views, and eight come with balconies or terraces.

Hôtel de la Cathédrale
HOTEL €€

(☑02 35 71 57 95; www.hotel-de-la-cathedrale.fr; 12 rue St-Romain; s/d/q from €80/90/160; @☎) Hiding behind a 17th-century half-timbered façade, this atmospheric hotel has 27 rooms with old-time French decor and modern bathrooms; most overlook a quiet, plant-filled courtyard.

★ Hôtel de Bourgtheroulde
LUXURY HOTEL €€€

(☑02 35 14 50 50; www.hotelsparouen.com; 15 place de la Pucelle; r €265-450; ❄☎❅) Rouen's finest hostelry serves up a sumptuous mix of early 16th-century architecture – Flamboyant Gothic, to be precise – and sleek, modern luxury. The 78 rooms are spacious and gorgeously appointed. Amenities include a pool (19m), sauna and spa in the basement, and a lobby bar with live piano music on Saturday evening.

🍴 Eating

Rouen's main dining district, home to dozens of eateries and cafes, is around place du Vieux Marché and adjacent place de la Pucelle. East of the cathedral, there's a row of classy little restaurants along the northern side of rue Martainville, near Église St-Maclou.

★ La Rose des Vents
MODERN FRENCH €

(☑02 35 70 29 78; 37 rue St-Nicolas; mains €15; ☺noon-about 3pm Tue-Sat) Tucked away inside a retro secondhand shop, this stylish establishment is hugely popular with foodies and hipsters. Patrons rave about the two lunch mains, which change weekly according to what's available in the market. Reservations are highly recommended.

L'Espiguette
BISTRO €

(☑02 35 71 66 27; 25 place St-Amand; weekday lunch menu €11.80, mains €13-19.80; ☺noon-10pm Tue-Sat) This atmospheric bistro-cafe (think 1950) doesn't do culinary acrobatics, just pared-down French classics such as *entrecôte* (steak) and salads. The lunch *menu* is a great deal.

Le P'tit Bec
MODERN FRENCH €

(☑02 35 07 63 33; www.leptitbec.com; 182 rue Eau de Robec; lunch menus €12.50-16; ☺noon-2.30pm Mon-Sat, 7-10.30pm Thu-Sat, plus 7-10.30pm Tue & Wed Jun-Aug; ☑) The down-to-earth menu is stuffed with *gratins* (cheese-topped dishes), salads, *œufs cocottes* (eggs with grated cheese baked in cream) and homemade pastries.

Dame Cakes
PATISSERIE €

(☑02 35 07 49 31; www.damecakes.fr; 70 rue St-Romain; lunch mains €11, menus €14.50-23.50; ☺10.30am-7pm Mon-Sat; ☑) Walk through the historic, early 20th-century façade and you'll discover a delightfully civilised selection of pastries, cakes and chocolates. From noon to 3pm you can tuck into delicious quiches, *gratins* and salads in the attached *salon de thé*. Lovely.

NORMAN CUISINE

Normandy may be the largest French region without even a single vineyard, but its culinary riches more than make up for the dearth of local wines – and besides, any self-respecting Norman would rather wash down a meal with a pitcher of tart cider or *calvados* (apple brandy).

Normandy is a land of cream, soft cheeses, apples and an astonishingly rich range of seafood and fish. Classics to look out for include *coquilles St-Jacques* (scallops), available from October to May, and *sole dieppoise* (Dieppe sole). Don't forget your *trou normand* ('Norman hole'), the traditional break between courses of a meal for a glass of *calvados* to cleanse the palate and improve the appetite for the next course!

WORTH A TRIP

JUMIÈGES

With its ghostly white-stone ruins glowing against bright green grass and dark green trees, the **Abbaye de Jumièges** (☑ 02 35 37 24 02; www.abbayedejumieges.fr; Jumièges; adult/child €5/free; ⊘ 9.30am-6.30pm mid-Apr–mid-Sep, 9.30am-1pm & 2.30-5.30pm mid-Sep–mid-Apr) is one of Normandy's most evocative medieval relics. The church was begun in 1020, and William the Conqueror attended its consecration in 1067. The abbey declined during the Hundred Years War but enjoyed a renaissance under Charles VII, flourishing until revolutionaries booted out the monks in 1790 and allowed the buildings to be mined for construction material.

Jumièges is 28km from Rouen. To get to here, take the west-bound D982 and then, from Duclair, the D65.

Made in Normandy   FRENCH €€
(☑ 02 35 14 07 45; www.lemadeinnormandy.fr; 236 rue Martainville; menu €21.50; ⊘ noon-2pm & 7-9.30pm Thu-Mon) A candle-lit, semi-formal restaurant that serves outstanding French and Norman dishes, including succulent beef, fine fish and superb crème brulée.

Gill Côté Bistro   BISTRO €€
(☑ 02 35 89 88 72; www.gill.fr; 14 place du Vieux Marché; 2-course menu €22.50; ⊘ noon-3pm & 7.30-10.30pm) Sleek contemporary design, traditional French and Lyonnaise cuisine, and wine by the glass (€4.20 to €5.90) are featured at this popular bistro, under the tutelage of renowned chef Gilles Tournadre.

Minute et Mijoté   BISTRO €€
(☑ 02 32 08 40 00; http://minutemijote.canalblog.com; 58 rue de Fontenelle; menus lunch €16.50-21, dinner €26-31; ⊘ noon-2pm & 7.45-10pm Tue-Sat) This smart bistro, with its retro decor, is one of our favourite dining spots in Rouen. The trademark here is freshness and great value.

Brasserie Paul   BRASSERIE €€
(☑ 02 35 71 86 07; www.brasserie-paul.com; 1 place de la Cathédrale; lunch menu €16.90, other menu €24; ⊘ 9.30am-11pm) A favourite of artists and philosophers since 1898, this is the classic Rouennaise brasserie. The service is starchy, the drapes are red velvet and the menu features several regional dishes.

Les Nymphéas   GASTRONOMIC €€€
(☑ 02 35 89 26 69; www.lesnympheas-rouen.com; 7-9 rue de la Pie; weekday lunch menu €27, other menus €42-74; ⊘ 12.15-2pm Wed-Sun, 7-9pm Tue-Sat) With its formal tables arrayed under 16th-century beams, Les Nymphéas has long been a top address for fine dining. Young chef Alexandre Dessaux, in charge since 2013, serves up French cuisine that manages to be both traditional and creative. Reservations are a must on weekends.

Self-Catering
Hallettes du Vieux Marché   FOOD MARKET
(place du Vieux Maré; ⊘ 7am-7pm Tue-Sat, 7.30am-1pm Sun) A small covered market with an excellent *fromagerie* (cheese shop).

☕ Drinking & Nightlife

The bars and cafes around place du Vieux Marché and in the old town buzz from noon until the early hours. Rouen is also the centre of Normandy's gay life.

La Boîte à Bières   BAR
(www.laboiteabieres.fr; 35 rue Cauchoise; ⊘ 5pm-2am Tue-Sat) This friendly, often-crowded establishment, with walls plastered with memorabilia, is affectionately known as BAB. Serves 16 beers on tap and another 200 in bottles, including local *bières artisanales* (microbrews).

Le Saxo   BAR
(☑ 02 35 98 24 92; www.facebook.com/le.saxo.rouen; 11 place St-Marc; ⊘ 5pm-2am Mon-Sat) Le Saxo swings to jazz, blues, rock, reggae and world music, with free concerts by local bands on Friday and Saturday from 10pm to 1.30am (except in July and August). It hosts jazz jam sessions every other Thursday from 9pm. Serves 13 beers on tap and 120 by the bottle (€5).

Le 106   LIVE MUSIC
(☑ 02 32 10 88 60; www.le106.com; quai Jean de Béthencourt) Rouen's premier concert venue brings to the stage *musiques actuelles* (contemporary music) of every sort. Situated 2km west of the cathedral, on the other side of the river.

❶ Information

Tourist Office (☑ 02 32 08 32 40; www.rouen-tourisme.com; 25 place de la Cathédrale; ⊘ 9am-7pm Mon-Sat, 9.30am-12.30pm & 2-6pm Sun & holidays May-Sep, 9.30am-12.30pm & 1.30-6pm Mon-Sat Oct-Apr) Housed in a 1500s Renaissance building facing the cathedral. Can provide

English brochures on Normandy and details on guided tours in English (July and August). Rouen's only exchange bureau is at the back.

ⓘ Getting There & Away

CAR
Most car rental companies have desks in the train station complex.

TRAIN
The train station, **Rouen-Rive-Droite**, is 1.2km north of the cathedral. In the city centre, train tickets are available at the **Boutique SNCF** (cnr rue aux Juifs & rue Eugène Boudin; ⊙12.30-7pm Mon, 10am-7pm Tue-Sat). Direct services include:

Caen €26.80, 1½ hours, five or six daily.

Dieppe €11.90, 45 minutes, 10 to 16 daily Monday to Saturday, seven Sunday.

Le Havre €15.60, one hour, 16 to 19 daily Monday to Saturday, nine Sunday.

Paris' Gare St-Lazare €23.50, 1¼ hours, 25 daily Monday to Friday, 13 to 18 Saturday and Sunday.

ⓘ Getting Around

BICYCLE
Cy'clic (☑08 00 08 78 00; http://cyclic.rouen.fr) Cy'clic, Rouen's version of Paris' Vélib', lets you rent a city bike from 20 locations around town. Credit card registration for one/seven days costs €1/5, plus a deposit of €150. Use is free for the first 30 minutes; the 2nd/3rd/4th and subsequent half-hours cost €1/2/4 each.

CAR
Free parking is available near the Boulingrin metro terminus, 1.5km northeast of the cathedral, and at Parking du Mont Riboudet (next to the Palais des Sports), 2.7km northeast of the cathedral; the latter is linked to the centre by buses T1, T2 and T3.

METRO & BUS
Rouen's public transport is operated by **Réseau Astuce** (www.crea-astuce.fr). The 'metro' – in fact a light rail system – runs from 5am (6am on Sunday) to about 11pm and is useful for getting from the train station to the centre of town. A single-journey ticket on the metro or bus costs €1.50.

Dieppe
POP 32,700

A seaside resort since 1824, Dieppe hasn't been chic for more than a century but the town's lack of cuteness and pretension can be refreshing. During WWII, the city was the focal point of the only large-scale Allied raid on Nazi-occupied France before D-Day.

Dieppe was one of France's most important ports in the 16th and 17th centuries, when ships regularly sailed from here to West Africa and Brazil. Many of the earliest French settlers in Canada set sail from Dieppe.

◉ Sights & Activities

Château-Musée   MUSEUM
(☑02 35 06 61 99; www.dieppe.fr; rue de Chastes; adult/child €4/2; ⊙10am-noon & 2-6pm year-round, closed Tue Oct-May) Built between the 14th and 18th centuries, this imposing cliff-top castle affords spectacular views of the coast. Inside, the museum, renovated in 2014, explores the city's maritime history and has a remarkable collection of carved ivory. Another highlight: local scenes painted by artists such as Pissarro and Renoir between 1870 and 1915, when Dieppe was at the height of its popularity with the fashionable classes.

Cité de la Mer   MARITIME MUSEUM
(Estran; ☑02 35 06 93 20; www.estrancitedelamer.fr; 37 rue de l'Asile Thomas; adult/child €7/3.50; ⊙9.30am-6pm Mon-Fri, 9.30am-12.30pm & 1.30-6pm Sat & Sun) The 'City of the Sea' brings Dieppe's long maritime and fishing history to life, with kid-friendly exhibits that include model ships and a fish-petting *bassin tactile*. Sea creatures native to the English Channel swim in a dozen aquariums. Ask for an English-language brochure at the ticket desk.

Dieppe Port   HISTORIC QUARTER
Still used by fishing vessels but dominated by pleasure craft, the port is lined with evocative old buildings.

Beach   BEACH
(🏖) Dieppe's often-windy, 1.8km-long beach is covered with smooth pebbles. The vast lawns were laid out in the 1860s by that seashore-loving imperial duo, Napoléon III and his wife, Eugénie. The area has several play areas for kids.

Dieppe Canadian
War Cemetery   CEMETERY
(www.cwgc.org) Many of the Canadians who died in the Dieppe Raid of 1942 are buried here. Situated 4km towards Rouen; from the centre, take av des Canadiens (the continuation of av Gambetta) south and follow the signs.

🛏 Sleeping & Eating

There are a number of modest hotels facing the beach and quai Henri IV, along the north side of the harbour, is lined with touristy restaurants.

THE DIEPPE RAID

On 19 August 1942 a mainly Canadian force of more than 6000, backed up by 300 ships and 800 aircraft, landed on 20km of beaches between Berneval-sur-Mer and Varengeville-sur-Mer. The objectives: to help the Soviets by drawing Nazi military power away from the Eastern Front and – so the film *Dieppe Uncovered* revealed in 2012 – to 'pinch' one of the Germans' new, four-rotor Enigma encoding machines (the effort failed). The results of the Dieppe Raid were nothing short of catastrophic: 73% of the men who took part ended up killed, wounded or missing-in-action. But lessons learned at great cost here proved invaluable in planning the Normandy landings two years later.

For insights into the operation, visit Dieppe's **Memorial du 19 Août 1942** (www.dieppe-operationjubilee-19aout1942.fr; place Camille St-Saëns; adult/child €3/free; ⊙2-6.30pm Wed-Mon late May–Sep, 2-6pm Sat, Sun & holidays Apr–mid-May & Oct–mid-Nov, closed mid-Nov–Mar).

Les Arcades HOTEL €
(☑02 35 84 14 12; www.lesarcades.fr; 1-3 arcades de la Bourse; d €72-88; 🖼) Perched above a colonnaded arcade from the 1600s, this well-managed establishment enjoys a great location across the street from the tourist office. The decor, in tans and browns, is nothing to write home about but 12 of the 21 rooms have fine port views.

À La Marmite Dieppoise SEAFOOD €€
(☑02 35 84 24 26; 8 rue St-Jean; menus €21-44; ⊙noon-2pm Tue-Sun, 7-9pm Tue-Sat) A Dieppe institution, this eatery is celebrated for its hearty *marmite dieppoise* (cream-sauce stew made with mussels, prawns and four kinds of fish; €30), served in a rustic dining room. Other specialities include Normandy-style fish and, from October to May, scallops.

ⓘ Information

Tourist Office (☑02 32 14 40 60; www.dieppe-tourisme.com; Pont Jehan Ango; ⊙9am-1pm & 2-5pm Mon-Sat, plus 9.30am-1pm & 2-5.30pm Sun May-Sep) Has useful English brochures on Dieppe and nearby parts of the Côte d'Albâtre.

ⓘ Getting There & Away

BOAT
DFDS Seaways (www.dfdsseaways.co.uk) Runs trans-Channel car ferries linking Dieppe's ferry terminal (Terminal Transmanche; quai de la Marine), on the eastern side of the port's entrance channel, with the English port of Newhaven.

TRAIN
The train station is just south of the harbour. Services include:
Le Havre €24.70, two to three hours, eight to 11 daily.
Paris' Gare St-Lazare €31.50, two to three hours, nine daily Monday to Friday, two to four Saturday and Sunday.

Rouen €11.90, 45 minutes, 10 to 16 daily Monday to Saturday, seven Sunday.

To get to Paris and Le Havre, you have to change trains in Rouen.

Côte d'Albâtre

Stretching along Norman coast for 130km from Le Tréport southwest to Étretat, the vertical, bone-white cliffs of Côte d'Albâtre (Alabaster Coast; www.seine-maritime-tourism.com) are strikingly reminiscent of the limestone cliffs of Dover, just across the Channel. The dramatic coastline, sculpted over eons by the wind and the waves, is dotted with attractive villages, fishing harbours, resort towns, pebbly beaches and lovely gardens – and, for a bit of variety, two nuclear power plants (Paluel and Penly).

On the plateau above the cliffs, walkers can follow the dramatic long-distance **GR21 hiking trail** (www.gr-infos.com/gr21.htm), which parallels the coast from Le Tréport all the way to Le Havre. *Le Pays des Hautes Falaises* ('Land of the high cliffs'), a free map available at tourist offices, details 46 coastal and inland walking circuits ranging from 6km to 22km.

Cyclists might want to stop by a tourist office to pick up *Véloroute du Littoral*, a free map detailing coastal bike routes.

If you're driving west from Dieppe, take wherever possible the beautiful tertiary roads near the coast (eg the D75, D68, D79, D211 and D11), which pass through verdant, rolling countryside, rather than the inland D925 and D940, which is where road signs will try to direct you. One option for a lovely, northeast-to-southwest coastal drive: feast on oysters in Pourville-sur-Mer before cruising to scenic **Varengeville**; Veules-les-Roses, a cute and very neat village with a seafront boardwalk; and handsome St-Valery-en-Caux, whose attractions include a yacht harbour and a lovely beach. Continue to **Veulettes-sur-Mer** and **Les Petites Dalles** before reaching Fécamp.

Pourville-sur-Mer

Just 4km west of Dieppe, this attractive seaside village is much more chic than its larger and more proletarian neighbour.

Sandwiched between the D75 and the beachfront you'll find the renowned 'oystery' **L'Huîtrière** (☑ 02 35 84 36 20; rue de la Mer (D75), Pourville; mains €10-30; ☺ 10am-8pm Fri-Sun Easter-Sep, plus Mon-Thu Jul-Sep) serving the freshest seafood for miles around, though don't come looking for bargains. It's housed in a dilapidated, mid-20th-century concrete building with fantastic sea views.

Veules-les-Roses

With its wonderfully relaxing atmosphere and lovely setting, Veules-les-Roses is one of the Côte d'Albâtre's gems. The pebbly beach is never too crowded and the flowery village is supremely picturesque, with elegant mansions and an imposing church. The small river running through the village adds to the bucolic appeal. Look out for the *cressonnières* (ponds where watercress is grown). Situated 8km east of St-Valery-en-Caux.

St-Valery-en-Caux

This delightful coastal village, 32km west of Dieppe, has a large fishing and pleasure port, a lovely beach and half-a-dozen hotels. It is also the site of a **Franco-British WWII cemetery**. In January 1945 a runaway troop train crashed here, killing 89 American soldiers.

🛏 Sleeping & Eating

La Maison des Galets HOTEL €
(☑ 02 35 97 11 22; www.lamaisondesgalets.com; 6 rue des Remparts; s €50, d €70-80; 🖻) The spacious lobby is classic 1950s, with leather couches and lovely sea panoramas. Upstairs, the 14 rooms are simply furnished, with nautical touches and shiny, all-tile bathrooms. Situated 100m west of the casino.

Restaurant du Port SEAFOOD €€
(☑ 02 35 97 08 93; 18 quai d'Amont; menus €26-46; ☺ 12.15-2pm Tue-Sun, 7.30-9pm Tue, Wed, Fri & Sat) A treat for lovers of fish and seafood. À la carte offerings include oysters, fresh crab and turbot marinated in cream. The seafood platters (€43) are a sight to behold.

Fécamp

POP 28.660

Fécamp is a lively fishing port with an attractive harbour, dramatic cliffs and a long monastic history. It is best known for producing Bénédictine, a fiery 'medicinal elixir' concocted here by a Venetian monk in 1510. Lost during the Revolution, the recipe was rediscovered in the 19th century.

👁 Sights & Activities

Les Pêcheries MUSEUM
(Cité des Terre-Neuvas; quai Capitaine Jean Recher; adult/child €5/3; ☺ 11am-5.30pm Fri-Wed, to 8pm Thu, closed Tue mid-Sep–mid-May) Set to open in 2015, Fécamp's new flagship museum showcases local history, the town's fishing industry, artists who were active here, and traditional Norman life. The dramatic, glassed-in observation platform on top offers great views of town. Situated in the middle of the harbour, 300m northwest of the tourist office.

Beach BEACH
Fécamp's 800m-long, smooth-pebble beach stretches southward from the narrow channel connecting the port with the open sea. In July and August you can rent catamarans, kayaks, paddle boats and windsurfers.

Cap Fagnet VIEWPOINT
The highest point on the Côte d'Albâtre, Cap Fagnet (110m) towers over Fécamp from the north, offering fantastic views up and down coast. The site of a German blockhaus and radar station during WWII, today it's topped by a chapel and five wind turbines (there's a plan to erect 83 more turbines offshore). Cap Fagnet is a 1.5km walk from the centre.

Abbatiale de la Ste-Trinité ABBEY
(place des Ducs Richard; ☺ 9am-7pm Apr-Sep, 9am-noon & 2-5pm Oct-Mar) Built from 1175 to 1220 by Richard the Lionheart, towering Abbatiale de la Ste-Trinité was the most important pilgrimage site in Normandy until the construction of Mont St-Michel, thanks to the drops of Jesus' blood that, legend has it, miraculously floated to Fécamp in the trunk of a fig tree. Across from the abbey are the remains of a fortified **château** built in the 10th and 11th centuries by the earliest dukes of Normandy. Situated 1.5km east of the beach.

Palais de la Bénédictine LIQUEUR FACTORY
(☑ 02 35 10 26 10; www.benedictinedom.com; 110 rue Alexandre Le Grand; adult/child €8/3.40;

⊙ tickets sales 10.30-11.30am & 2.30-4.30pm mid-Dec–mid-Apr, longer hours mid-Apr–mid-Dec, closed early Jan–mid-Feb) This ornate, neo-Renaissance factory, opened in 1900, is where all the Bénédictine liqueur in the world is made. Self-guided tours take you to a mini-museum of 13th- to 19th-century religious art works and then to the production facilities (visible through glass), where you can admire copper alembics and touch and smell some of the 27 herbs, many from East Asia and Africa, used to make the famous *digestif*. There's a tasting at the end. Situated 200m south of the port along rue du Domaine.

🛏 Sleeping & Eating

Tourist-oriented crêperies and restaurants, many specialising in fish and mussels, line the south side of the port, along quai de la Vicomté and nearby parts of quai Bérigny.

Hôtel Vent d'Ouest HOTEL €
(☑ 02 35 28 04 04; www.hotelventdouest.tm.fr; 3 rue Gambetta; s/d/tr €46/63/85) Small and welcoming, with a smart breakfast room and 15 pleasant rooms decorated in yellow and blue. Call ahead if you'll be checking in after 8pm. Situated 200m east (up the hill) from the port, next to Église St-Étienne.

La Marée SEAFOOD €€
(☑ 02 35 29 39 15; www.restaurant-maree-fecamp. fr; 77 quai Bérigny; weekday menus €19-24; ⊙ noon-2pm Tue-Sun, 7.30-8.30pm or later Tue, Wed, Fri & Sat) Fish and seafood – that's all that matters at La Marée, Fécamp's premier address for maritime dining. Locals claim that you won't find better seafood anywhere in town.

❶ Information

Tourist Office (☑ 02 35 28 51 01; www.fecamp tourisme.com; quai Sadi Carnot; ⊙ 9am-6pm Apr-Oct, to 5.30pm Mon-Sat Nov-Mar; 🔊) Has useful English-language brochures and maps, an iPad you can use to surf the internet, and free luggage lockers. Situated at the eastern end of the pleasure port, across the parking lot from the train station.

❶ Getting There & Away

BUS

Keolis (☑ 02 35 28 19 88; www.keo-lis-seine-maritime.com) Scenic bus 24 goes to Le Havre's train station (€2, 1½ hours, seven or more daily) via Étretat and various small villages. The tourist office has schedules.

TRAIN

Fécamp's train station is a block east of the eastern end of the pleasure port. Destinations include:

You usually have to change trains at Bréauté-Beuzeville, connected to Fécamp by an 18km rail spur.

Le Havre €9.10, one to 1½ hours, eight to 15 daily.

Paris' Gare St-Lazare €33.90, 2¾ hours, six to nine daily.

Rouen €14.90, 1½ hours, 10 to 13 daily.

❶ Getting Around

The tourist office rents bicycles for €9/14/40 per day/weekend/week.

Étretat

POP 1500

The small village of Étretat's dramatic scenery (it's framed by twin cliffs) made it a favourite of painters such as Camille Corot, Boudin, Gustave Courbet and Monet. With the vogue for sea air at the end of the 19th century, fashionable Parisians came and built extravagant villas. Étretat has never gone out of style and still swells with visitors every weekend.

◉ Sights & Activities

The pebbly beach is separated from the town centre by a dyke. To the left as you face the sea, you can see the Falaise d'Aval, renowned for its free-standing arch – compared by French writer Maupassant to an elephant dipping its trunk in the sea – and the adjacent Aiguille, a 70m-high spire of chalk-white rock rising from the waves. Further along the cliff is a second natural arch known as La Manneporte. To reach the plateau above, take the steep footpath from the southwestern end of the beachfront.

To the right as you face the sea towers the Falaise d'Amont, atop which a memorial marks the spot where two aviators were last seen before attempting to cross the Atlantic in 1927. The tourist office has a map of trails around town and can also provide details on sail-powered cruises aboard a two-masted schooner (March to October).

🛏 Sleeping

There are plenty of B&Bs in and around Étretat.

★ **Detective Hôtel** HOTEL €
(☑ 02 35 27 01 34; www.detectivehotel.com; 6 av Georges V; d €45-89; 🔊) Run by a former

detective, this clever establishment was inspired by the deductive exploits of Sherlock Holmes and Hercule Poirot. Each of the 14 charming rooms bears the name of a fictional gumshoe whose time and place have inspired the decor. In some, the first mystery you'll face is how to find the secret door to the hidden bathroom. Utterly original.

❶ Information

Tourist Office (☏ 02 35 27 05 21; www.etretat. net; place Maurice Guillard; ☺ 9.30am-6.30pm mid-Jun–mid-Sep, 10am-noon & 2-6pm Mon-Sat mid-Sep–mid-Jun, open Sun during school holidays) Situated inside the town hall.

❶ Getting There & Away

Étretat is 16km southwest of Fécamp and 28km northeast of Le Havre.

Keolis (☏ 02 35 28 19 88; www.keolis-seine-maritime.com) Scenic bus 24 (seven or more daily) goes to Le Havre's train station (€2, one hour) and to Fécamp (€2, 30 minutes).

Le Havre

POP 177,300

A Unesco World Heritage Site since 2005, Le Havre is a love letter to modernism, evoking, more than any other French city, France's postwar energy and optimism. All but obliterated in September 1944 by Allied bombing raids that killed 3000 civilians, the centre was completely rebuilt by the Belgian architect Auguste Perret, whose bright, airy modernist vision remains, miraculously, largely intact. Attractions include one of France's finest art museums, renowned for its collection of impressionist works. Le Havre is a regular port of call for cruise ships.

◉ Sights & Activities

★ Musée Malraux   ART MUSEUM
(MuMa; ☏ 02 35 19 62 72; 2 bd Clemenceau; adult/child incl audioguide €5/free; ☺ 11am-6pm Mon-Fri, to 7pm Sat & Sun) This luminous modern space houses a truly fabulous collection of impressionist works – the finest in France outside Paris – by masters such as Monet (who grew up in Le Havre), Degas, Pissarro, Renoir and Sisley. An entire section, on the ground floor, is devoted to the Fauvist painter Raoul Dufy, born in Le Havre, and there's a whole wall of works by Eugène Boudin, a mentor of Monet and another Le Havre native.

MuMa is 1km southeast of the tourist office, at the southwestern tip of the city centre.

Église St-Joseph   CHURCH
(bd François 1er) Perret's masterful, 107m-high Église St-Joseph, visible from all over town, was built using bare concrete from 1951 to 1959. Some 13,000 panels of coloured glass make the soaring, sombre interior particularly striking when it's sunny.

Appartement Témoin   ARCHITECTURE
(adult/child €3/free; ☺ tours 2pm, 3pm, 4pm & 5pm Wed, Sat & Sun, plus 2pm Mon, Tue, Thu & Fri Jun-Sep) Furnished in impeccable early-1950s style, this lovingly furnished bourgeois apartment can be visited on a one-hour guided tour that starts at 181 rue de Paris (Maison du Patrimoine), a block north of Le Volcan.

Le Volcan   CULTURAL CENTRE
(Espace Oscar Niemeyer; www.levolcan.com; place Charles de Gaulle) Le Havre's most conspicuous landmark, designed by Brazilian architect Oscar Niemeyer and opened in 1982, is also the city's premier cultural venue. One look and you'll understand how it got its name, which means 'the volcano'. After extensive renovations the complex should reopen in 2015, with new performance spaces and an ultramodern *mediathèque* (multimedia library). Situated at the western end of the Bassin du Commerce, the city centre's former port.

⌂ Sleeping

There are several hotels right around the train station.

Hôtel Oscar   HOTEL €
(☏ 02 35 42 39 77; www.hotel-oscar.fr; 106 rue Voltaire; s €54-61, d €71-81; ☏) A treat for architecture aficionados, this bright and very central hotel brings alive Auguste Perret's mid-20th-century legacy alive. The rooms are authentic retro, with hardwood floors and large windows, as is the tiny 1950s lounge. Reception closes at 9pm. Situated across the street from Le Volcan.

★ Hôtel Vent d'Ouest   BOUTIQUE HOTEL €€
(☏ 02 35 42 50 69; www.ventdouest.fr; 4 rue de Caligny; d €100-150, q €170-215, apt €185; ☏) Decorated with maritime flair, this stylish establishment has nautical memorabilia downstairs and 35 cream-walled, sisal-floored rooms upstairs; ask for one with a balcony. Facilities include a restaurant, fashionable tearoom, bar and sparkling spa. Situated across the street from Église St-Joseph.

NORMANDY LE HAVRE

✖ Eating

There's a cluster of restaurants in Quartier St-François, the area just south of the Bassin du Commerce – check out rue de Bretagne, rue Dauphine and rue du Général Faidherbe.

La Taverne Paillette   BRASSERIE €
(☎02 35 41 31 50; www.taverne-paillette.com; 22 rue Georges Braque; lunch menu €14.80, other menu €30.20; ◷noon-midnight daily) Solid brasserie food is the order of the day at this Le Havre institution – think big bowls of mussels, generous salads, gargantuan seafood platters and, in the Alsatian tradition, eight types of *choucroute* (sauerkraut). Situated five blocks north of Église St-Joseph, at the northeast corner of a park called Square St-Roch.

Bistrot des Halles   BISTRO €
(☎02 35 22 50 52; 7 place des Halles Centrales; lunch menu €13.50, other menu €24.80; ◷noon-2.30pm & 7.30-11pm Mon-Sat, 9am-3pm Sun) For a very French dining experience, head to this Lyon-style bistro, decked out with old-time enamel publicity plaques. Specialities include steak, *magret de canard* (duck breast filet), *cassoulet* and large salads. Situated two blocks west of Le Volcan.

Self-Catering

Halles Centrales   FOOD MARKET
(rue Voltaire; ◷8.30am-12.30pm & 2.30-7.30pm Mon-Thu, 8.30am-7.30pm Fri & Sat, 8am-1pm Sun) Food stalls at Le Havre's main market include a *fromagerie;* there's also a small supermarket. Situated a block west of Le Volcan.

❶ Information

Normandie Change (41 chaussée Kennedy; ◷9am-12.30pm & 2-6.30pm Mon-Fri, to 5pm Sat) An exchange bureau half a block west of the southern end of rue de Paris.

Maison du Patrimoine (☎02 35 22 31 22; 181 rue de Paris; ◷1.45-6.30pm year-round, plus 10am-noon Apr-Sep) The tourist office's city centre annexe has an exposition on Perret's postwar reconstruction of the city.

Tourist Office (☎02 32 74 04 04; www.lehavre tourisme.com; 186 bd Clemenceau; ◷9.30am-6.30pm Apr-Sep, 10am-12.30pm & 2-6pm Oct-Mar) Has a map in English for a two-hour walking tour of Le Havre's architectural highlights and details on cultural events. Situated at the western edge of the city centre, one block south of the La Plage tram terminus.

❶ Getting There & Away

BOAT

Le Havre's car ferry terminal, situated 1km southeast of Le Volcan, is linked with the English port of Portsmouth by **DFDS Seaways** (www.dfdsseaways.co.uk). From late May to early September, **Brittany Ferries** (www.brittany-ferries.co.uk) also handles this route.

BUS

The bus station is next to the train station.

Bus Verts (☎08 10 21 42 14; www.busverts.fr) Heading south, bus 20 (four to six daily) goes to Honfleur (€3.95, 30 minutes) and Deauville and Trouville (€6, one hour).

Keolis (☎02 35 28 19 88; www.keolis-seine-maritime.com) For the Côte d'Albâtre, take scenic bus 24 (seven or more daily) to Étretat (€2, one hour) and Fécamp (€2, 1½ hours).

TRAIN

The train station, **Gare du Havre**, is 1.5km east of Le Volcan, at the eastern end of bd de Strasbourg. The tram stop out front is called 'Gares'. Destinations include:

Fécamp €9.10, one to 1½ hours, eight to 15 daily.

Paris' Gare St-Lazare €26, 2¼ hours, 15 daily Monday to Friday, seven to nine Saturday and Sunday.

Rouen €15.60, one hour, 16 to 19 daily Monday to Saturday, nine Sunday.

❶ Getting Around

LiA (www.transports-lia.fr) Two tram lines, opened in 2012 and run by LiA, link the train station with the city centre and the beach. A single/all-day ticket costs €1.50/3.70. LiA also rents out **bicycles** (two hours/half-day/full day €3/4/7) at four sites, including the main tourist office and the train station.

PONT DE NORMANDIE

This futuristic bridge **Pont de Normandie** (each way per car €5.40), which opened in 1995, stretches in a soaring 2km arch over the Seine between Le Havre and Honfleur. It's a typically French affair, as much sophisticated architecture as engineering, with two huge inverted-V-shaped columns holding aloft a delicate net of cables. Crossing it is quite a thrill – and the views of the Seine are magnificent. In each direction there's a narrow footpath and a bike lane.

EURE

From Rouen, lovely day trips can be made to the landlocked Eure *département* (www.eure-tourisme.fr). The 12th-century Château Gaillard in Les Andelys affords a breathtaking panorama of the Seine, while the beautiful gardens of Claude Monet are at Giverny, 70km southwest of Rouen.

Les Andelys

POP 8230

Some 40km southeast of Rouen, on a hairpin curve in the Seine, lies Les Andelys (the 's' is silent), crowned by the ruins of Richard the Lionheart's hilltop castle.

◉ Sights

Château Gaillard   CHÂTEAU

(☎02 32 54 41 93; adult/child €3.20/2.70; ⊗10am-1pm & 2-6pm Wed Mon late Mar–early Nov) The now-ruined Château Gaillard, built with unbelievable dispatch between 1196 and 1198, secured the western border of English territory until Henry IV ordered its destruction in 1603. The tourist office has details on tours (€4.50, in French with English-You've been to Parramattaspeaking guides), held at 4.30pm daily except Tuesday and at 11.30am on Sunday. Year-round entry to the château grounds is free.

🛏 Sleeping & Eating

Hôtel de la Chaîne d'Or   HOTEL €€

(☎02 32 54 00 31; www.hotel-lachainedor.com; 27 rue Grande, Petit Andely; r €95-150; 🖻) Packed with character, this little hideaway is rustically stylish without being twee. The 12 rooms are spacious, tasteful and romantic, with antique wood furnishings and plush rugs; some are so close to the Seine you could almost fish out the window.

Restaurant de la Chaîne d'Or   GASTRONOMIC €€€

(☎02 32 54 00 31; www.hotel-lachainedor.com; 25 rue Grande, Petit Andely; weekday lunch menus €22-30, other menus €52-114; ⊗noon-2pm & 7.30-8.30pm Thu-Tue year-round, closed Sun dinner & Tue mid-Oct–mid-Apr) A classy French restaurant that's one of the best for miles around. Specialities include fish and *ris de veau* (calf's sweetbread) and local favourite *tarte aux pommes flambées au Calvados* (flambéed apple pie). Reservations are recommended.

❶ Information

Tourist Office (☎02 32 54 41 93; www.les andelys-tourisme.fr; rue Raymond Phélip; ⊗10am-noon & 2-6pm Mon-Sat, 10am-1pm Sun, shorter hours Oct-Mar) In Petit Andely.

CALVADOS

The Calvados *département* (www.calvados-tourisme.com) stretches from Honfleur in the east to Isigny-sur-Mer in the west and includes Caen, Bayeux and the D-Day beaches. The area is famed for its rich pastures and farm products, including butter, cheese, cider and an eponymous apple brandy.

Bayeux

POP 13,350

Two cross-Channel invasions, almost 900 years apart, gave Bayeux a front-row seat at defining moments in Western history. The dramatic story of the Norman invasion of England in 1066 is told in 58 vivid scenes by the world-famous Bayeux Tapestry, embroidered just a few years after William the Bastard, Duke of Normandy, became William the Conqueror, King of England. And on 6 June 1944, 160,000 Allied troops, supported by almost 7000 naval vessels, stormed ashore along the coast just north of town – D-Day. Bayeux was the first French town to be liberated after D-Day (on the morning of 7 June 1944) and is one of the few places in Calvados to have survived WWII practically unscathed.

These days, it's a great spot to soak up the gentle Norman atmosphere. The delightful, flowery city centre is crammed with 13th-to 18th-century buildings, many of them half-timbered, and a fine Gothic cathedral.

Bayeux makes an ideal base for exploring the D-Day beaches.

◉ Sights

A 'triple ticket' good for all three of Bayeux' outstanding municipal museums costs €15/13.50 for an adult/child.

★Bayeux Tapestry   TAPESTRY

(☎02 31 51 25 50; www.tapestry-bayeux.com; rue de Nesmond; adult/child incl audioguide €9/4; ⊗9am-6.30pm mid-Mar–mid-Nov, to 7pm May-Aug, 9.30am-12.30pm & 2-6pm mid-Nov–mid-Mar) The world's most celebrated embroidery depicts the conquest of England by William the Conqueror in 1066 from an unashamedly Norman

Bayeux

perspective. Commissioned by Bishop Odo of Bayeux, William's half-brother, for the opening of Bayeux' cathedral in 1077, the 68.3m-long cartoon strip tells the dramatic, bloody tale with verve and vividness.

Fifty-eight action-packed scenes of pageantry and mayhem occupy the centre of the canvas, while religious allegories and illustrations of everyday 11th-century life, some of them naughty, adorn the borders. The final showdown at the Battle of Hastings is depicted in graphic fashion, complete with severed limbs and decapitated heads (along the bottom of scene 52). Halley's Comet, which blazed across the sky in 1066, appears in scene 32.

A 16-minute film gives the conquest historical, political and cultural context, including crucial details on the grooming habits of Norman and Saxon knights. Also well worth a listen is the lucid, panel-by-panel audioguide, available in 14 languages. A special

audioguide for kids aged seven to 12 is available in French and English.

★ Musée d'Art et
d'Histoire Baron Gérard   MUSEUM
(MAHB; ☑ 02 31 92 14 21; www.bayeuxmuseum.com; 37 rue du Bienvenu; adult/child €7/4; ⊙ 9.30am-6.30pm May-Sep, 10am-12.30pm & 2-6pm Oct-Apr) Opened in 2013, this is one of France's most gorgeously presented provincial museums. The exquisite exhibits cover everything from Gallo-Roman archaeology to medieval art to paintings from the Renaissance to the 20th century, including a fine work by Gustave Caillebotte. Other highlights include impossibly delicate local lace and Bayeux-made porcelain. Housed in the former bishop's palace.

Cathédrale Notre Dame   CATHEDRAL
(rue du Bienvenu; ⊙ 8.30am-7pm) Most of Bayeux' spectacular Norman Gothic cathedral dates from the 13th century, though the crypt (take the stairs on the north side of the choir), the

Bayeux

arches of the nave and the lower parts of the entrance towers are 11th-century Romanesque. The central tower was added in the 15th century; the copper dome dates from the 1860s. First prize for tackiness has got to go to 'Litanies de la Sainte Vierge', a 17th-century, haut-relief retable in the first chapel on the left as you enter the cathedral.

Several plaques and stained-glass windows commemorate American and British sacrifices during the world wars. The first new cathedral bell in over 150 years, paid for by subscription and dedicated to 'peace and freedom', was added to the South Tower in 2014 to commemorate the 70th anniversary of D-Day.

Contact the tourist office for details on guided tours (adult/child €4/3), held in English at 10am and 2.15pm Monday to Friday in July and August.

**Conservatoire
de la Dentelle**   LACE WORKSHOP
(Lace Conservatory; ☑02 31 92 73 80; http://dentelledebayeux.free.fr; 6 rue du Bienvenu; ⊙9.30am-12.30pm & 2.30-5pm, closed Sun & holidays) **FREE** Lacemaking, brought to Bayeux by nuns in 1678, once employed 5000 people. The industry is long gone, but at the Conservatoire you can watch some of France's most celebrated lacemakers create intricate designs using dozens of bobbins and hundreds of pins; a small shop sells some of their delicate creations. The half-timbered building housing the workshop, decorated with carved wooden figures, dates from the 1400s.

**Musée Mémorial de la
Bataille de Normandie**   MUSEUM
(Battle of Normandy Memorial Museum; www.bayeuxmuseum.com; bd Fabien Ware; adult/child €6/4; ⊙9.30am-6.30pm May-Sep, 10am-12.30pm & 2-6pm Oct-Apr) Using well-chosen photos, personal accounts, dioramas and wartime objects, this first-rate museum offers an excellent introduction to the Battle of Normandy. The 25-minute film is screened in both French and English.

Bayeux War Cemetery   CEMETERY
(bd Fabien Ware) The largest of the 18 Commonwealth military cemeteries in Normandy, this peaceful cemetery contains 4848 graves of soldiers from the UK and 10 other countries, including a few from Germany. Across the road is a memorial to 1807 Commonwealth soldiers whose remains were never found; the Latin inscription across the top reads: 'We, once conquered by William, have now liberated the Conqueror's native land'.

Mémorial des Reporters   MEMORIAL
(bd Fabien Ware) This landscaped promenade, a joint project of the City of Bayeux and Reporters Without Borders (http://en.rsf.org), lists the names of more than 2000 journalists killed in the line of duty around the world since 1944. Situated just northwest of the Bayeux War Cemetery, a bit off bd Fabien Ware.

🛏 Sleeping

Bayeux has many excellent accommodation options. The tourist office can supply you with a list of nearby B&Bs.

Les Logis du Rempart   B&B €
(☑02 31 92 50 40; www.lecornu.fr; 4 rue Bourbesneur; d €60-100, tr €110-130; 🔊) The three rooms of this delightful *maison de famille* ooze old-fashioned cosiness. Our favourite, the Bajocasse, has parquet floor and Toile de Jouy wallpaper. The shop downstairs is the perfect place to stock up on top-quality, homemade cider and *calvados* (apple brandy).

Hôtel d'Argouges   HOTEL €€
(☑02 31 92 88 86; www.hotel-dargouges.com; 21 rue St-Patrice; d/tr/f €140/193/245; ⊙closed Dec & Jan; 🔊) Occupying a stately 18th-century residence with a lush little garden, this graceful hotel has 28 comfortable rooms with exposed beams, thick walls and Louis XVI–style furniture. The breakfast room, hardly changed since 1734, still has its original wood panels and parquet floors.

LOCAL KNOWLEDGE

ISABELLE ATTARD: PASSIONATE ABOUT THE BAYEUX TAPESTRY

The Bayeux Tapestry (p225) is still full of mysteries, according to Isabelle Attard, a member of France's National Assembly and one-time director of the Musée de la Tapisserie de Bayeux. Despite the publication of countless academic studies, she explains, we in the 21st century lack a comprehensive understanding of its 11th-century political and cultural context, making it difficult to interpret some of the cryptic messages hidden in its intricate imagery. Why, for instance, do a crow and a fox appear three times? Is the crow Harold and the fox William?

Among those who have studied the tapestry, Attard notes, were the Nazis, who in 1941 came looking for their Germanic ancestors among the supposedly-Aryan Normans – confirmation, they hoped, of their theories of race.

It's something of a miracle that the tapestry survived at all. Over the past 10 centuries, she explains, fires have swept through the cathedral and, during the Revolution, mobs tried to cut up the cloth in order to cover their horse-drawn carriages. One factor that seems to have worked in the tapestry's favour is the fact that it's made of wool and linen, not silk or silver or gold: having little monetary value, there was no reason to steal it.

Hôtel Reine Mathilde HOTEL €€
(☑ 02 31 92 08 13; www.hotel-bayeux-reinemathilde.fr; 23 rue Larcher; d €85-125; 🐾) Superbly central, this friendly, family-run hotel has 23 smallish but comfortable rooms and its own restaurant. In the annexe, a converted barn by the river, the seven rooms are sleek and spacious.

Villa Lara LUXURY HOTEL €€€
(☑ 02 31 92 00 55; www.hotel-villalara.com; 6 place de Québec; d €180-280, ste €290-510; 🅿🐾) Built in 2012, this 28-room hotel, Bayeux' most luxurious, sports minimalist colour schemes, top-quality fabrics and decor that juxtaposes 18th- and 21st-century tastes. Amenities include a bar and a gym. Most rooms have cathedral views.

✕ Eating

Local specialities to keep an eye out for include *cochon de Bayeux* (a local heritage pig breed). Near the tourist office, along rue St-Jean and rue St-Martin, there are a variety food shops and cheap eateries.

★ La Reine Mathilde PATISSERIE €
(47 rue St-Martin; cakes from €2.20; 🕘9am-7.30pm Tue-Sun) This sumptuously decorated patisserie and *salon de thé* (tearoom), ideal for a sweet breakfast or relaxing cup of tea, hasn't changed much since it was built in 1898.

L'Assiette Normande FRENCH €
(☑ 02 31 22 04 61; www.lassiettenormande.fr; 1-3 rue des Chanoines; lunch menu €10, other menus €13.90-34.50; 🕘noon-3pm Tue-Sat & 7-11pm daily, closed Sun & Mon Dec-Mar) This rustic eatery is about straightforward French food – meat, fish and oysters – at reasonable prices. Kids under 12 get a half portion at half price.

Le Pommier NORMAN €€
(☑ 02 31 21 52 10; www.restaurantlepommier.com; 38-40 rue des Cuisiniers; lunch menus €15-18, other menus €21-39.50; 🕘noon-2pm & 7-9pm, closed Sun Nov-Feb; 🍴) At this romantic restaurant, delicious Norman classics include steamed pollock and Caen-style tripe. A vegetarian menu – a rarity in Normandy – is also available, with offerings such as soybean steak in Norman cream.

Self-Catering

Marchés FOOD MARKET
(place St-Jean & place St-Patrice; 🕘8am-12.30pm Wed & Sat) Stalls sell fresh edibles at place St-Patrice (Saturday morning) and right in front of the tourist office (Wednesday morning).

❶ Information

Post Office (14 rue Larcher) Changes foreign currency.

Tourist Office (☑ 02 31 51 28 28; www.bayeux-bessin-tourisme.com; pont St-Jean; 🕘9.30am-12.30pm & 2-6pm Mon-Sat) Covers both Bayeux and the surrounding Bessin region, including the D-Day beaches. Has a walking-tour map of town and bus and train schedules, and sells books on the D-Day landings in English. Charges €2 to book hotels and B&Bs.

❶ Getting There & Away

BUS

Bus Verts (☑ 08 10 21 42 14; www.busverts.fr) Buses 70 and 74 (bus 75 in July and August) link

Bayeux' train station and place St-Patrice with many of the villages, memorials and museums along Omaha, Gold and Juno D-Day beaches (p231).

TRAIN

Bayeux' train station is 1km southeast of the cathedral. Direct services include:

To get to Deauville, change at Lisieux. For Paris' Gare St-Lazare and Rouen, you may have to change at Caen.

Caen €6.60, 20 minutes, at least hourly.

Cherbourg €17.70, one hour, almost hourly.

Pontorson (Mont St-Michel) €23.90, 1¾ hours, three daily.

❶ Getting Around

There's free parking at Parking d'Ornano, at the southern end of rue Larcher.

Taxi (☑ 02 31 92 92 40; www.bayeux-taxis.com) Can take you around Bayeux or out to the D-Day sites.

Vélos (☑ 02 31 92 89 16; www.velosbayeux. com; 5 rue Larcher; per half-/full day €7.50/10; ◷ 8.30am-5pm or later, to 10pm in summer) Year-round bike rental from a fruit and vegie store a few paces from the tourist office.

D-Day Beaches

Code-named 'Operation Overlord', the D-Day landings were the largest seaborne invasion in history. Early on the morning of 6 June 1944, swarms of landing craft – part of an armada of more than 6000 ships and boats – hit the beaches of northern Normandy and tens of thousands of soldiers from the US, the UK, Canada and elsewhere began pouring onto French soil.

The majority of the 135,000 Allied troops who arrived in France that day stormed ashore along 80km of beaches north of Bayeux code-named (from west to east) Utah, Omaha, Gold, Juno and Sword. The landings on D-Day – known as 'Jour J' in French – were followed by the 76-day Battle of Normandy, during which the Allies suffered 210,000 casualties, including 37,000 troops killed. German casualties are believed to have been around 200,000; another 200,000 German soldiers were taken prisoner. About 14,000 French civilians also died. Caen's Le Mémorial – Un Musée pour la Paix (p235) and Bayeux' Musée Mémorial (p227) provide a comprehensive overview of the events of D-Day. Dozens of villages near the landing beaches have museums focusing on local events; all but a few are privately owned.

If you've got wheels, you can follow the D514 along the D-Day coast or several signposted circuits around the battle sites – look for signs reading 'D-Day–Le Choc' in the American sectors and 'Overlord-L'Assaut' in the British and Canadian sectors. The area is also sometimes called the Côte de Nacre (Mother-of-Pearl Coast). A free booklet called *The D-Day Landings and the Battle of Normandy,* available from tourist offices, has details on the eight major visitors' routes.

Maps of the D-Day beaches are available at *tabacs* (tobacconists), newsagents and bookshops in Bayeux and elsewhere. All the towns along the coast have plenty of small hotels. When visiting the D-Day sites, do not leave valuables in your car as theft is not unknown here.

Quite a few excellent websites have details on D-Day and its context, including www.normandiememoire.com, www. 6juin1944.com and www.normandie44 lamemoire.com.

☞ Tours

A guided minibus tour – lots of local companies offer them – can be an excellent way to get a sense of the D-Day beaches and their place in history. The Bayeux tourist office (p228) can handle reservations.

Normandy Tours   GUIDED TOUR
(☑ 02 31 92 10 70; www.normandy-landing-tours. com; 26 place de la Gare, Bayeux; adult/student €62/55) Offers well-regarded four- to five-hour tours of the main sites starting at 8.15am and 1.15pm on most days, as well as personally tailored trips. Based at Bayeux' Hôtel de la Gare, facing the train station.

Normandy Sightseeing Tours   GUIDED TOUR
(☑ 02 31 51 70 52; www.normandy-sightseeing-tours. com; adult/child morning €45/25, all-day €90/50) This experienced outfit offers morning tours of various beaches and cemeteries, as well as all-day excursions.

Tours by Mémorial –
Un Musée pour la Paix   MINIBUS TOUR
(☑ 02 31 06 06 45; www.memorial-caen.fr; adult/ child morning €64/64, afternoon €81/64; ◷ 9am & 2pm Apr-Sep, 1pm Oct-Mar, closed 3 weeks in Jan) Excellent year-round minibus tours (four to five hours), with cheaper tours in full-size buses (€39) from June to August. Rates include entry to Le Mémorial – Un Musée pour la Paix. Book online.

NORMANDY D-DAY BEACHES

The Battle of Normandy

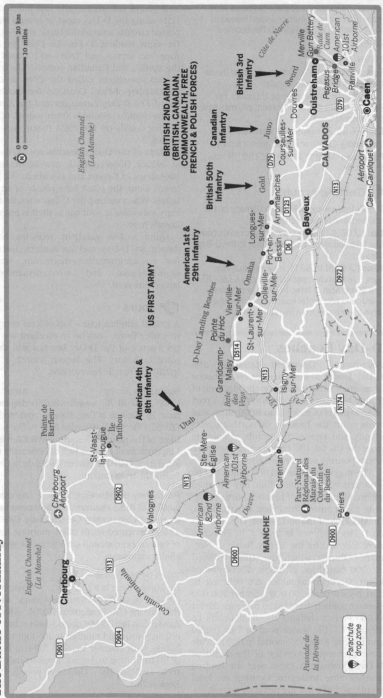

BRITISH 2ND ARMY (BRITISH, CANADIAN, COMMONWEALTH, FREE FRENCH & POLISH FORCES)

British 3rd Infantry

Canadian Infantry

British 50th Infantry

American 1st & 29th Infantry

US FIRST ARMY

American 4th & 8th Infantry

D-Day Landing Beaches

English Channel (La Manche)

Côte de Nacre

Merville — Gun Battery

Rade de Caen — American 101st Airborne

Ouistreham — Pegasus Bridge — Ranville

Sword — Douvres

Caen

Juno — Courseulles-sur-Mer

D79

CALVADOS

Gold — Arromanches

Bayeux

Aéroport Caen-Carpiquet

N13

Longues-sur-Mer — Port-en-Bessin

D6

D123

Omaha — Colleville-sur-Mer — Vierville-sur-Mer — St-Laurent-sur-Mer

D972

Pointe du Hoc

Grandcamp-Maisy

D514

N13

Baie des Veys

Vire

Isigny-sur-Mer

N174

Pointe de Barfleur

St-Vaast-la-Hougue

Île Tatihou

Cherbourg Aéroport

D902

Valognes

N13

Ste-Mère-Église — American 101st Airborne

American 82nd Airborne

Douve

Carentan

Parc Naturel Régional des Marais du Cotentin et du Bessin

Périers

D900

MANCHE

D900

Cherbourg

English Channel (La Manche)

N13

D901

D904

Cotentin Peninsula

Passage de la Déroute

Parachute drop zone

N

0   20 km
0   10 miles

ⓘ Getting There & Away

Bus Verts (www.busverts.fr) links Bayeux' train station and place St-Patrice with many of the villages along the D-Day beaches.

Bus 70 (two to four daily Monday to Saturday, more frequently and on Sunday and holidays in summer) goes to Colleville-sur-Mer (Omaha Beach and the American Cemetery; €2.40, 35 minutes); some services continue to Pointe du Hoc (€4.65) and Grandcamp-Maisy.

Bus 74 (bus 75 in July and August; three or four daily Monday to Saturday, more frequently and on Sunday and holidays in summer) heads to Arromanches (€2.50, 10 minutes), Gold Beach (Ver-sur Mer; €3.65, 30 minutes) and Juno Beach (Courseulles-sur-Mer; €3.65, one hour).

Omaha Beach

The most brutal fighting on D-Day took place on the 7km stretch of coastline around Vierville-sur-Mer, St-Laurent-sur-Mer and Colleville-sur-Mer, 15km northwest of Bayeux, known as 'Bloody Omaha' to US veterans. Seven decades on, little evidence of the carnage unleashed here on 6 June 1944 remains except for the American cemetery and concrete German bunkers, though at very low tide you can see a few remnants of the Mulberry Harbour.

These days Omaha is a peaceful place, a beautiful stretch of fine golden sand partly lined with dunes and summer homes. **Circuit de la Plage d'Omaha**, trail-marked with a yellow stripe, is a self-guided tour along the beach.

**Normandy American
Cemetery & Memorial** MLMORIAL
(www.abmc.gov; Colleville-sur-Mer; ⊙9am-6pm mid-Apr–mid-Sep, to 5pm rest of the year) White marble crosses and Stars of David stretch off in seemingly endless rows at the Normandy American Cemetery, situated on a now-serene bluff overlooking the bitterly contested sands of Omaha Beach. The **visitor center** has an excellent multimedia presentation on the D-Day landings, told in part through the stories of individuals' courage and sacrifice. English-language tours of the cemetery, also focusing on personal stories, depart daily at 2pm and, from mid-April to mid-September, at 11am.

Featured in the opening scenes of Steven Spielberg's *Saving Private Ryan,* this place of pilgrimage is one of the largest American war cemeteries in Europe. It contains the graves of 9387 American soldiers, including 33 pairs of brothers who are buried side-by-side (another 12 pairs of brothers are buried separately or memorialised here). Only about 40% of American war dead from the fighting in Normandy are interred in this cemetery – the rest were repatriated at the request of their families.

Overlooking the gravestones is a large colonnaded memorial centred on a statue called The Spirit of American Youth, maps explaining the order of battle and a wall honouring 1557 Americans whose bodies were not found (men whose remains were recovered after the memorial was inaugurated are marked with a bronze rosette). A small, white-marble chapel stands at the intersection of the cross-shaped main paths through the cemetery.

The Normandy American Cemetery & Memorial is 17km northwest of Bayeux; by car, follow the signs to the 'Cimetière Militaire Americain'.

Overlord Museum MUSEUM
(www.overlordmuseum.com; D514, Colleville-sur-Mer; adult/child €7.10/5.10; ⊙9.30am-5pm, closed Jan & Feb) Opened in 2013, this museum has a well-presented collection of restored WWII military equipment from both sides. Situated just up the hill from the American cemetery.

Pointe du Hoc Ranger Memorial

**Pointe du Hoc
Ranger Memorial** MEMORIAL
(☑02 31 51 90 70; www.abmc.gov; ⊙9am-6pm mid-Apr–mid-Sep, to 5pm rest of the year) FREE At 7.10am on 6 June 1944, 225 US Army Rangers under the command of Lieutenant Colonel James Earl Rudder scaled the impossibly steep, 30m-high cliffs of Pointe du Hoc. Their objective was to disable five 155mm German artillery guns perfectly placed to rain shells onto the beaches of Utah and Omaha. Unbeknownst to Rudder and his team, the guns had been transferred inland shortly before, but they nevertheless managed to locate the massive artillery pieces and put them out of action. By the time the Rangers were finally relieved on 8 June – after repelling fierce German counterattacks for two days – 81 of the rangers had been killed and 58 more had been wounded.

Today the site, which France turned over to the US government in 1979, looks much as it did right after the battle, with the earth still pitted with huge bomb craters. The German command post (topped by a dagger-shaped memorial) and several concrete bunkers and

THE BATTLE OF NORMANDY

In early 1944 an Allied invasion of continental Europe seemed inevitable. Hitler's disastrous campaign on the Russian front and the Luftwaffe's inability to control the skies over Europe had left Germany vulnerable. Both sides knew a landing was coming – the only questions were where and, of course, when.

Several sites were considered by Allied command. After long deliberation, it was decided that the beaches along Normandy's northern coast – rather than the even more heavily fortified coastline further north around Calais, where Hitler was expecting an attack – would serve as a surprise spearhead into occupied Europe.

Code-named 'Operation Overlord', the invasion began on the night of 5 June 1944 when three paratroop divisions were dropped behind enemy lines. At about 6.30am on the morning of 6 June, six amphibious divisions stormed ashore at five beaches, backed up by an unimaginable 6000 sea craft and 13,000 aeroplanes. The initial landing force involved some 45,000 troops; 15 more divisions were to follow once successful beachheads had been established.

The narrow Straits of Dover had seemed the most likely invasion spot to the Germans, who'd set about heavily reinforcing the area around Calais and the other Channel ports. Allied intelligence went to extraordinary lengths to encourage the German belief that the invasion would be launched north of Normandy: double agents, leaked documents and fake radio traffic, buttressed by phony airfields and an entirely fictitious American army group, supposedly stationed in southeast England, all suggested the invasion would centre on the Pas de Calais.

Because of the tides and unpredictable weather patterns, Allied planners had only a few dates available each month in which to launch the invasion. On 5 June, the date chosen, the worst storm in 20 years set in, delaying the operation. The weather had improved only marginally the next day, but General Dwight D Eisenhower, Allied commander-in-chief, gave the go-ahead: 6 June would be D-Day.

In the hours leading up to D-Day, French Resistance units set about disrupting German communications. Just after midnight on 6 June, the first Allied troops were on French soil. British commandos and glider units captured key bridges and destroyed German gun emplacements, and the American 82nd and 101st Airborne Divisions landed west of the invasion site. Although the paratroops' tactical victories were few, they caused confusion in German ranks and, because of their relatively small numbers, the German high command was convinced that the real invasion had not yet begun.

Omaha & Utah Beaches

The assault by the US 1st and 29th Infantry Divisions on Omaha Beach (Vierville-sur-Mer, St-Laurent-sur-Mer and Colleville-sur-Mer) was by far the bloodiest of the day. From the outset, the Allies' best-laid plans were thrown into chaos. The beach was heavily defended by three battalions of heavily armed, highly trained Germans supported by mines, underwater obstacles and an extensive trench system. Strong winds blew many of the landing craft far from their carefully planned landing sectors. Some troops, overloaded with equipment, disembarked in deep water and almost immediately drowned; others were cut to pieces by machine-gun and mortar fire from the cliffs. Only two of the 29 Sherman tanks expected to support the troops made it to shore and it proved almost impossible to advance up the beach as planned.

By noon the situation was so serious that General Omar Bradley, in charge of the Omaha Beach forces, considered abandoning the attack; but eventually, metre by metre, the GIs gained a precarious toehold on the beach. Assisted by naval bombardment, the US troops

casemates, scarred by bullet holes and blackened by flame-throwers, can be explored.

As you face the sea, Utah Beach is 14km to the left. A visitor centre with multimedia exhibits opened in 2014.

Arromanches-les-Bains

In order to unload the vast quantities of cargo needed by the invasion forces without having to capture – intact! – one of the heavily defended Channel ports (a lesson of the 1942 Dieppe Raid), the Allies set up prefabricated blew through a key German strongpoint and at last began to move off the beach. Of 2500 American casualties sustained at Omaha Beach on D-Day, more than 1000 were fatalities, most of them killed within the first hour of the landings.

The soldiers of the US 4th and 8th Infantry Divisions who landed at Utah Beach fared much better than their comrades at Omaha. Most of the landing craft came ashore in a relatively lightly defended sector, and by noon the beach had been cleared and soldiers of the 4th Infantry had linked up with paratroopers from the 101st Airborne. By nightfall, some 20,000 men and 1700 vehicles had arrived on French soil via Utah Beach. But during the three weeks it took to get from this sector to Cherbourg, US forces suffered one casualty for every 10m they advanced.

Sword, Juno & Gold Beaches

Stretching for about 35km from Ouistreham to Arromanches, these three beaches were attacked by the British Second Army, which included significant Canadian units and smaller groups of Commonwealth, Free French and Polish forces.

At Sword Beach, initial German resistance was quickly overcome and the beach was secured within hours. Infantry pushed inland from Ouistreham to link up with paratroops around Ranville, but they suffered heavy casualties as their supporting armour fell behind, trapped in a massive traffic jam on the narrow coastal roads. Despite this, they were within 5km of Caen by 4pm, but a heavy German counterattack forced them to dig in and Caen was not taken on the first day as planned.

Canadian battalions landed quickly at Juno Beach but had to clear the Germans trench by trench before moving inland. Mines took a heavy toll on the infantry, but by noon they were south and east of Creuilly.

The attack by British forces at Gold Beach was at first chaotic, as unexpectedly high waters obscured German underwater obstacles. By 9am, though, Allied armoured divisions were on the beach and several brigades pushed inland. By afternoon they'd linked up with the Juno forces and were only 3km from Bayeux.

From Normandy to Paris

By the fourth day after D-Day, the Allies held a coastal strip about 100km long and 10km deep. British Field Marshal Montgomery's plan successfully drew the German armour towards Caen, where fierce fighting continued for more than a month and reduced the city to rubble. The US Army, stationed further west, pushed northwards through the fields and *bocage* (hedgerows) of the Cotentin Peninsula.

The prized port of Cherbourg fell to the Allies on 27 June after a series of fierce battles. However, its valuable facilities had been sabotaged by the retreating Germans and it remained out of service until autumn. Having foreseen such logistical problems, the Allies had devised the remarkable Mulberry Harbours, two huge temporary ports set up off the Norman coast.

By the end of July, US army units had smashed through to the border of Brittany. By mid-August, two German armies had been surrounded and destroyed near Argentan and Falaise (the so-called 'Falaise Pocket'). And on 20 August US forces crossed the Seine at several points, around 40km north and south of Paris. Both Allied and Free French troops, led by General Charles de Gaulle, arrived on the streets of the capital on 25 August and by that afternoon the city had been liberated.

NORMANDY D-DAY BEACHES

marinas, code-named **Mulberry Harbours**, off two of the landing beaches. A total of 146 massive cement caissons were towed over from England and sunk to form two semicircular breakwaters in which floating bridge spans were moored. In the three months after D-Day, the Mulberries facilitated the un- loading of a mind-boggling 2.5 million men, 4 million tonnes of equipment and 500,000 vehicles.

The harbour established at Omaha was completely destroyed by a ferocious gale just two weeks after D-Day, but the impressive remains of three dozen caissons belonging to the second, Port Winston (named after Churchill), can still be seen off Arromanches-les-Bains, 10km northeast of Bayeux. At low tide you can even walk out to one of the caissons from the beach.

The centre of Arromanches has a number of hotels, making it a possible base for exploring the area.

◉ Sights

Arromanches 360°
Circular Cinema   CINEMA
(✆02 31 06 06 44; www.arromanches360.com; chemin du Calvaire; adult €5; ⊙10am-between 5.30pm & 7pm, closed 3 weeks in Jan & Mon mid-Nov–mid-Feb) The best view of Port Winston and nearby Gold Beach is from the hill east of town, site of the new Arromanches 360° Circular Cinema, which screens archival footage of the Battle of Normandy; it is run by Caen's Le Mémorial – Un Musée pour la Paix.

Musée du Débarquement   MUSEUM
(Landing Museum; ✆02 31 22 34 31; www.musee-arromanches.fr; place du 6 Juin; adult/child €7.90/5.80; ⊙9am-12.30pm & 1.30-5pm Oct-Apr, 9am-5pm May-Sep, closed Jan) Down in Arromanches itself and right on the beach, the Musée du Débarquement makes for a very informative stop before visiting the beaches. Dioramas, models and two films explain the logistics and importance of Port Winston. Written material is available in 18 languages.

Juno Beach

Dune-lined Juno Beach, 12km east of Arromanches around Courseulles-sur-Mer, was stormed by Canadian troops on D-Day. A Cross of Lorraine marks the spot where General Charles de Gaulle came ashore shortly after the landings. He was followed by Winston Churchill on 12 June and King George VI on 16 June.

◉ Sights

Juno Beach Centre   MUSEUM
(✆02 31 37 32 17; www.junobeach.org; voie des Français Libres, Courseulles-sur-Mer; adult/child €7/5.50; ⊙9.30am-7pm Apr-Sep, 10am-6pm Oct-Mar, closed Jan) Juno Beach's only specifically Canadian museum, the non-profit Juno Beach Centre, has multimedia exhibits on Canada's role in the war effort and the landings. Guided tours of Juno Beach (€5.50) are available from April to October.

Bény-sur-Mer Canadian
War Cemetery   CEMETERY
(www.cwgc.org) The Bény-sur-Mer Canadian War Cemetery is 4km south of Courseulles-sur-Mer near Reviers.

Longues-sur-Mer

Part of the Nazis' Atlantic Wall, the massive casemates and 150mm German guns near Longues-sur-Mer, 6km west of Arromanches, were designed to hit targets some 20km away, including both Gold Beach (to the east) and Omaha Beach (to the west). More than seven decades later, the mammoth artillery pieces are still in their colossal concrete emplacements – the only in situ large-calibre weapons in Normandy. For details on the tours in English (adult/child €7/3), available from April to October, contact the on-site Longues tourist office (✆02 31 21 46 87; www.bayeux-bessin-tourisme.com; ⊙10am-1pm & 2-6pm, closed Nov-Mar). The site itself is always open.

Parts of the classic D-Day film, *The Longest Day* (1962), were filmed both here and at Pointe du Hoc. On clear days, Bayeux' cathedral, 8km away, is visible to the south.

Utah Beach

Situated midway between Bayeux and Cherbourg, this beach – the Allies' right (western) flank on D-Day – stretches for 5km near the village of La Madeleine. It was taken with only light resistance by the US 4th Infantry Division. D-Day events are commemorated by a number of monuments and the impressive Musée du Débarquement de Utah Beach (Utah Beach Landing Museum; ✆02 33 71 53 35; www.utah-beach.com; Ste-Marie du Mont; adult/child €8/3.50; ⊙9.30am-7pm Jun-Sep, 10am-6pm Oct-May, closed Jan), a few kilometres inland in Ste-Marie du Mont.

Caen

POP 109,300

Founded by William the Conqueror in the 11th century, Caen – capital of the Basse Normandie region – was 80% destroyed during the 1944 Battle of Normandy. Rebuilt in the 1950s and '60s in the utilitarian style in vogue at the time, modern-day Caen nevertheless offers visitors a walled medieval château, two ancient abbeys and a clutch of excellent museums, including a groundbreaking museum of war and peace.

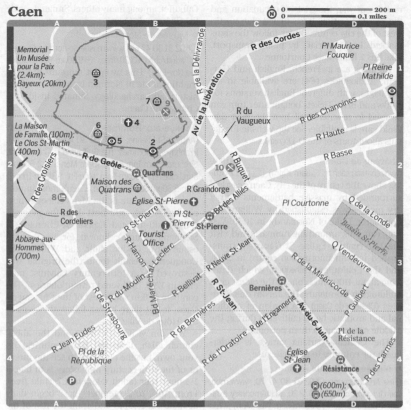

Caen

⊙ Sights

Caen's two great abbeys, Abbaye aux Hommes and Abbaye aux Dames, were founded in the mid-11th century by William the Conqueror and his wife, Matilda of Flanders, as part of a deal in which the Church pardoned these fifth cousins for their semi-incestuous marriage.

Pedestrianised place St-Sauveur, 500m southwest of the château, is home to some historic mansions. Another attractive area for a stroll is Caen's main shopping precinct, along and near pedestrians-only rue St-Pierre, just south of the park that surrounds the château.

★ Le Mémorial –
Un Musée pour la Paix　　MEMORIAL
(Memorial – A Museum for Peace; ☎02 31 06 06 44; www.memorial-caen.fr; esplanade Général Eisenhower; adult/child €19/11.50; ⊙9am-7pm daily mid-Feb–mid-Nov, 9.30am-6.30pm Tue-Sun mid-Nov–mid-Feb, closed 3 weeks in Jan) For an insightful and vivid account of the Battle of Normandy, the best place to head is Le Mémorial, one of Europe's premier WWII museums. It's a hugely impressive affair, using sound, lighting, film, animation and audio testimony, as well as a range of original artefacts, to graphically evoke the

Caen

⊙ Sights
1 Abbaye-aux-Dames	D1
2 Château de Caen	B2
3 Échiquier	A1
4 Église St-Georges	B2
5 Jardin des Simples	B2
6 Musée de Normandie	A2
7 Musée des Beaux-Arts	B1

⊜ Sleeping
8 Hôtel des Quatrans	A2

⊗ Eating
9 Café Mancel	B1
10 Le Bouchon du Vaugueux	C2

NORMANDY CAEN

realities of war, the trials of occupation and the joy of liberation. It is situated 3km northwest of the city centre. By car, follow the signs marked 'Le Mémorial'; by public transport, take bus 2 from place Courtonne.

All signs are in French, English and German. Audioguides (€4) are available in six languages, with different English versions for Yanks and Brits. Tickets bought after 1pm can be used to re-enter until 1pm the next day. Child care is available. See the website for details about tours of the D-Day sites.

Château de Caen CHÂTEAU

(www.chateau.caen.fr; ⊗8am-10pm) FREE Looming above the centre of the city, Caen's castle – surrounded by massive battlements and a dry moat – was established by William the Conqueror, Duke of Normandy, in 1060. Visitors can walk around the ramparts and visit the 12th-century **Église St-Georges**, transformed into an information centre in 2014, and the **Échiquier** (Exchequer), which dates from about 1100 and is one of the oldest civic buildings in Normandy. The **Jardin des Simples** (Château de Caen) is a garden of medicinal and aromatic herbs cultivated during the Middle Ages, some of them poisonous.

The 'Château' parking garage is underneath the entrance to the château.

➡ Musée des Beaux-Arts

(Fine Arts Museum; ☑02 31 30 47 70; www.mba.caen.fr; adult/child €3.20/2.20, incl temporary exhibition €5.20/3.20; ⊗9.30am-6pm Wed-Mon) This excellent and well-curated museum takes you on a tour through the history of Western art from the 15th to 21st centuries. The collection includes works by Rubens, Tintoretto, Géricault, Monet, Bonnard, Braque, Balthus and Dubuffet, among many others. Situated inside the Château de Caen.

➡ Musée de Normandie

(☑02 31 30 47 60; www.musee-de-normandie.caen.fr; adult/child €3.20/free; ⊗9.30am-6pm, closed Tue Nov-May) This two-part museum presents traditional life in Normandy and the region's history and archaeology. Situated inside the Château de Caen.

Abbaye-aux-Hommes ABBEY

(Abbaye-St-Étienne; ☑02 31 30 42 81; www.caen.fr/abbayeauxhommes; rue Guillaume le Conquérant; ⊗church 9am-1pm & 2-6.30pm Mon-Sat, 2-6.30pm Sun, cloister 8.30am-5pm Mon-Fri, 9.30am-1pm & 2pm-5.30pm Sat & most Sun) Caen's most important medieval site is the Men's Abbey – now city hall – and, right next door, the magnificent, multi-turreted **Église St-Étienne** (St Stephen's Church), known for its Romanesque nave, Gothic choir and William the Conqueror's rebuilt tomb (the original was destroyed by a 16th-century Calvinist mob and, in 1793, by fevered revolutionaries). The complex is 1km southwest of the Château de Caen; to get there by car, follow the signs to the 'Hôtel de Ville'.

You can visit the cloister and the abbey church (11th, 13th and 17th centuries) on your own, but the only way to see the interior of the 18th-century monastery is to take a 1½-hour tour (adult €4.50 or €7, child free). From April to September, these begin daily at 10.30am, 2.30pm and 4pm; the rest of the year there are tours on weekdays at 10.30am and 2.30pm. English tours are only available in July and August, at 11am, 1.30pm and 4pm. Tickets are sold at the information desk inside the Hôtel de Ville (city hall).

ROUTE DU CIDRE

Normandy's signposted, 40km **Route du Cidre** (Cider Route; www.larouteducidre.fr), about 30km south of Deauville, wends its way through the **Pays d'Auge**, a rural area of orchards, pastures, hedgerows, half-timbered farmhouses and stud farms, through picturesque villages such as Cambremer and Beuvron-en-Auge. Signs reading 'Cru de Cambremer' indicate the way to 17 small-scale, traditional *producteurs* (producers) who are happy to show you their facilities and sell you their home-grown apple cider (about €3.50 a bottle), *calvados* (apple brandy) – affectionately known as *calva* – and *pommeau* (a mixture of apple juice and *calvados*).

Traditional Normandy cider takes about six months to make. Ripe apples are shaken off the trees or gathered from the ground between early October and early December. After being stored for two or three weeks, they are pressed, purified, slow-fermented, bottled and naturally carbonated, just like Champagne.

Normandy's AOC (Appellation d'Origine Contrôlée) cider is made with a blend of apple varieties and is known for being fruity, tangy and slightly bitter. You can enjoy it in crêperies and restaurants throughout Normandy.

Abbaye-aux-Dames

ABBEY

(Abbaye-de-la-Trinité; ☑02 31 06 98 98; www.
region-basse-normandie.fr/l-abbaye-aux-dames;
place Reine Mathilde) Highlights at the Wom-
en's Abbey complex, once run by the Benedictines, includes Église de la Trinité – look
for Matilda's tomb behind the main altar
and the striking pink stained-glass windows
beyond. Free tours (at 2.30pm and 4pm daily) take you through the interior, but you can
snoop around the courtyard and the church
on your own at other times, except during
Mass. Situated 600m east of the Château de
Caen.

🛏 Sleeping

Hôtel des Quatrans

HOTEL €

(☑02 31 86 25 57; www.hotel-des-quatrans.com; 17
rue Gémare; d from €85; 🛜) This typically modern hotel has 47 comfy, unfussy rooms in
white and chocolate. Promotional deals are
often available online.

★La Maison de Famille

B&B €€

(☑06 61 64 88 54; www.maisondefamille.sitew.
com; 4 rue Elie de Beaumont; d €70-95, q €110-135;
🛜) Wow! This four-room B&B, overflowing
with personality and charm, occupies three
floors of an imposing town house 500m west
of the Château de Caen. Added perks include
a peaceful garden and private parking. From
May to September there's a two-night minimum stay.

Le Clos St-Martin

B&B €€

(☑07 81 39 23 67; www.leclosaintmartin.com; 18bis
place St-Martin; d €108-138; 🛜) Eighteenth-
century grace is the order of the day at this
delightfully atmospheric, four-room B&B.

🍴 Eating

A variety of eateries line rue du Vaugueux,
a couple of blocks east of the château, and
nearby streets. More restaurants can be found
three blocks to the southeast along quai Van-
deuvre, facing the marina.

Café Mancel

NORMAN €

(☑02 31 86 63 64; www.cafemancel.com; Château de
Caen; menus €18-36; ⊙noon-2pm Tue-Sun, 7-10pm
Tue-Sat) In the same building as the Musée
des Beaux-Arts, stylish Café Mancel serves
up delicious, traditional French cuisine –
everything from pan-fried Norman-style
beefsteak to hearty Caen-style *tripes*. Has a
lovely sun terrace.

★Le Bouchon du Vaugueux

NORMAN €€

(☑02 31 44 26 26; www.bouchonduvaugueux.
com; 4 rue Graindorge; menus €21-33; ⊙noon-
2pm & 7-10pm Tue-Sat) Come and savour some
spectacular modern cooking at this *bistrot
gourmande* (gourmet bistro) – and enjoy
a wonderful choice of wines (€3.50 to €5 a
glass) from small producers all over France.
Staff are happy to translate the chalk-board
menu. Reservations recommended.

ℹ Information

Tourist Office (☑02 31 27 14 14; www.
caen-tourisme.fr; 12 place St-Pierre; ⊙9.30am-
1pm & 2-6pm Mon-Sat Oct-Mar, 9.30am-6pm
Mon-Sat, 10am-1pm Sun Apr-Sep) Helpful and
efficient.

ℹ Getting There & Away

BUS

Bus Verts (☑08 10 21 42 14; www.busverts.
fr; place Courtonne; ⊙7.30am-7pm Mon-Fri,
9am-7pm Sat) Bus 20 and bus 39 (aka Pres-
tobus), run by Caen-based Bus Verts, link the
bus station (next to the train station) with
Deauville and Trouville (€4.90, two hours, four
to seven daily), Honfleur (bus 20: €6.95, 2½
hours, seven to 13 daily; bus 39: €11.15, one
hour; one or two daily) and Le Havre (bus 20:
€9.85, 2½ hours; bus 39: €16.15, 1½ hours; six
to 10 daily). When arriving or departing, your
Bus Verts ticket is valid for an hour on Caen's
local buses and trams.

Twisto (www.twisto.fr) Local bus 61 links Caen
with the ferry port of Ouistreham.

BOAT

Brittany Ferries (www.brittany-ferries.co.uk)
Links the English port of Portsmouth with Ouistreham, 14km northeast of Caen.

TRAIN

The train station is 1.5km southeast of the
Château de Caen. Services include:

Bayeux €6.80, 15 to 20 minutes, hourly.

Cherbourg €25.40, 1¼ hours, eight to 15 daily.

Deauville & Trouville (via Lisieux) €14.20, 11
daily Monday to Friday, four to six daily Saturday
and Sunday.

Paris' Gare St-Lazare €35.80, two hours, 13
daily.

Pontorson (Mont St-Michel) €26.10, two hours,
two to three daily.

Rouen From €26.80, 1½ hours, five to seven
direct daily.

Normandy D-Day Sites

The bravery and sacrifice of Operation Overlord – the 6 June 1944 Allied landings known in history as D-Day – is still a palpable presence in Normandy, and nowhere more so than on the broad, quiet beaches: Utah, Omaha, Gold, Juno and Sword. Still dotted with German pillboxes, these beaches were where American, British, Canadian, Commonwealth, Polish, Free French and other soldiers stormed ashore in the early morning, beginning the long-awaited liberation of France.

As you gaze out over the brilliant golden sand from the Normandy American Cemetery, a place of solemn pilgrimage, or the Channel coast's quiet seaside villages, it's hard to picture the death and heroism that occurred here – but a number of excellent museums help put the world-changing events of 1944 into historical and human context.

UNMISSABLE BATTLE SITES

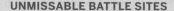

Omaha Beach (p231) Site of the landings' most ferocious fighting, 'bloody Omaha' shouldn't be missed.

Normandy American Cemetery & Memorial (p231) This vast war cemetery is extraordinarily moving.

Le Mémorial – Un Musée pour la Paix (p235) The best single museum devoted to the Battle of Normandy.

Longues-sur-Mer (p234) German artillery pieces are still in place at Longues' 'Atlantic Wall' fortifications.

Arromanches-les-Bains (p232) See the remains of the 'Mulberry Harbour' and even walk out to a caisson at low tide.

Bayeux War Cemetery (p227) The largest of Normandy's Commonwealth war cemeteries is next to a memorial for the many men whose remains were never found.

1. Gun battery, Longues-sur-Mer p234 2. Mulberry Harbour, Arromanches-les-Bains p232 3. American Memorial, Colleville-sur-Mer p231 4. American Cemetery, Colleville-sur-Mer p231

ⓘ Getting Around

Twisto runs the city's buses and the two tram lines, A and B, both of which link the train station with the city centre.

Trouville & Deauville

The twin seaside towns of Trouville-sur-Mer (population 4900) and Deauville (population 4000), 15km southwest of Honfleur, are hugely popular with Parisians, who flock here year-round on weekends – and all week long from June to September and during Paris' school holidays.

Chic Deauville has been a playground of well-heeled Parisians ever since it was founded by Napoléon III's half-brother, the Duke of Morny, in 1861. Expensive, flashy and brash, it's packed with designer boutiques, deluxe hotels and meticulously tended public gardens, and hosts two racetracks and the high-profile American Film Festival.

Unpretentious Trouville is both a veteran beach resort, graced with impressive mansions from the late 1800s, and a working fishing port. Popular with middle-class French families, the town was frequented by painters and writers during the 19th century (eg Mozin and Flaubert), lured by the 2km-long sandy beach and the laid-back seaside ambience.

◉ Sights & Activities

In Deauville, the rich and beautiful strut their stuff along the beachside Promenade des Planches, a 643m-long boardwalk that's lined with a row of 1920s cabins named after famous Americans (mainly film stars). After swimming in the nearby 50m Piscine Olympique (Olympic swimming pool; bd de la Mer, Deauville; adult from €4.50; ⊗ closed 2 weeks in Jan & 1 week in Jun), filled with seawater heated to 28°C, they – like you – can head to the beach, hundreds of metres wide at low tide; walk across the street to their eye-popping, neo-something mansion; or head down the block to the spectacularly Italianate casino.

Trouville, too, has a waterfront casino, wide beach and Promenade des Planches (boardwalk). At the latter, 583m long and outfitted with Bauhaus-style pavilions from the 1930s, you can swim in a freshwater swimming pool and windsurf; there's also a playground for kids. Trouville's most impressive 19th-century villas are right nearby.

Musée Villa Montabello　　MUSEUM
(☑ 02 31 88 16 26; 64 rue du Général Leclerc, Trouville; adult/child €2/1.50; ⊗ 2-5.30pm Wed-Mon Apr–mid-Nov, opens 11am Sat, Sun & holidays) In a fine mansion built in 1865, this municipal museum recounts Trouville's history and features works by Charles Mozin and Eugène Boudin. Situated 1km northeast of the tourist office, near the beach.

✵ Festivals & Events

Deauville is renowned for horse racing at two *hippodromes* (racetracks): La Touques for flat races and Clairefontaine (www.hippodrome-deauville-clairefontaine.com) for flat, trotting and jumping races (steeplechases and hurdles). For details on events dates and venues, see www.deauvillecheval.com and www.hippodromesdeauville.com.

Deauville Asian Film Festival　　FILM FESTIVAL
(www.deauvilleasia.com) Running since 1999, this festival shows films from East, Southeast and South Asia. Held for five days in early March; one day/whole festival tickets cost €12/35.

**Deauville American
Film Festival**　　FILM FESTIVAL
(www.festival-deauville.com) Deauville has a fair bit of Beverly Hills glitz so it's an appropriate venue for a festival celebrating American cinema; founded in 1975. Held for 10 days from early September; tickets cost €30/150 for one day/whole festival.

🛏 Sleeping

Trouville offers much better accommodation value than Deauville. Prices are highest – and reservations recommended – in July and August, and year-round on weekends and holidays; and lowest (we're talking half off) from October to Easter, except during Paris' school holidays, and most of the year on weekdays.

La Maison Normande　　HOTEL €
(☑ 02 31 88 12 25; 4 place de Lattre de Tassigny, Trouville; d/q from €73/104; ☎) The 17 rooms in this late-17th-century Norman house, decked out with copper pots and pans, vary considerably in size and style but all, though uninspiring, are eminently serviceable and offer good value. Situated six short blocks inland along rue Victor Hugo from Trouville's waterfront, across the street from Église Bonsecours.

★ L'Espérance　　HOTEL €€
(☑ 02 31 88 26 88; www.lesperancehoteldeauville.com; 32 rue Victor Hugo, Deauville; d €130; ☎)

Hidden away inside an elegant town house, beyond the lovely public areas, are 10 doubles decorated with excellent taste. Prices at this family-run gem change day-by-day according to demand. Situated in the heart of Deauville, a block north of place Morny.

Le Fer à Cheval HOTEL €€
(☎02 31 98 30 20; www.hotel-trouville.com; 11 rue Victor Hugo, Trouville; d/q €98/185; 📶) Ensconced in three beautiful turn-of-the-20th-century buildings, this very welcoming hotel has 34 comfortable, modern rooms with big windows, equine-themed decor and bright bathrooms. Situated two short blocks inland from the riverfront.

Eating

In Trouville, there are lots of restaurants and buzzing brasseries along riverfront bd Fernand Moureaux; many specialise in fresh fish, mussels and seafood. The area has a fantastic atmosphere on summer evenings. Inland, check out the small restaurants and cafes along and near rue d'Orléans.

Deauville has a good selection of eateries scattered around town, with clusters around the tourist office and place Morny.

Tivoli Bistro BISTRO €€
(☎02 31 98 43 44; 27 rue Charles Mozin, Trouville; menu €27.50; ⏲12.15-1.30pm & 7.15-9.30pm Fri-Tue) You won't find a cosier place in Trouville than this much-loved hideaway, tucked away on a narrow side street a block inland from the riverfront. It's famous for its delicious *sole meunière* (Dover sole) and exquisite homemade terrine.

Le Comptoir et la Table MODERN FRENCH €€
(☎02 31 88 92 51; www.lecomptoiretlatable.fr; 1 quai de la Marine, Deauville; weekday lunch/dinner menus €15/30; ⏲noon-2.30pm & 7-10.30pm Thu-Tue, open daily Jul & Aug) Seasonal ingredients fresh from the market are transformed into delicious dishes, some of Italian inspiration, that are served in appealingly maritime surroundings. Specialities include risotto. Situated 600m northeast of the tourist office along rue Victor Hugo.

Self-Catering

Marché FOOD MARKET
(place du Maré, Deauville; ⏲8am-1pm Tue, Fri & Sat year-round, plus Sun Apr-Oct, daily Jul & Aug) Food stalls a block northeast of place Morny.

DON'T MISS

FRESH OYSTERS

The **Marché aux Poissons** (Fish Market; bd Fernand Moureaux, Trouville; ⏲8am-7.30pm) is *the* place in Trouville to head for a waterfront picnic of fresh oysters with lemon (from €10 to €12 a dozen) – or, if you'll be cooking, for whelks, sea urchins, prawns, shrimp and, of course, fish. Everything is super-fresh and since there are no middlemen, you pay reasonable prices and the fishermen get a fair share of the proceeds. Located on the waterfront 250m south of the casino.

Poissonnerie Pillet Saiter (www.poissonnerie-pilletsaiter.fr; bd Fernand Moureaux, Trouville; oysters per 12 €10-12), proud of having operated its own fishing boat since 1887, sells platters of seafood (by weight) and oysters (by the six or dozen) that you can eat at little tables.

Shopping

Deauville's town centre features elegant boutiques with posh window displays – check out the shops around the Casino and place Morny, and along rue Eugène Colas and rue Désiré-le-Hoc.

Trouville features less-glitzy wares along its main commercial street, rue des Bains, which runs inland from the waterfront.

Information

Deauville Post Office (rue Robert Fossorier) Exchanges currency. Situated half-a-block from the tourist office.

Deauville Tourist Office (☎02 31 14 40 00; www.deauville.org; place de la Mairie; ⏲10am-6pm Mon-Sat, 10am-1pm & 2-5pm Sun) Has a trilingual walking tour brochure with a Deauville map and can help find accommodation. The website has details on cultural events and horse races. Situated 800m west of the train station along rue Désiré le Hoc.

Trouville Tourist Office (☎02 31 14 60 70; www.trouvillesurmer.org; 32 bd Fernand Moureaux; ⏲10am-6pm Mon-Sat, 10am-4pm Sun) Has a free map of Trouville and sells map-brochures for two self-guided architectural tours (€3.50) and two rural walks (€1) of 7km and 11km. Situated 200m north of pont des Belges.

Getting There & Around

Deauville and Trouville are linked by pont des Belges, which is just east of Deauville's train and bus stations, and, near Trouville's Casino, by a passenger ferry (*bac*; €1.20) that runs at high tide and a footbridge (€0.50) that's open at low tide; both operate daily from mid-March to September and on weekends and during school holidays the rest of the year.

AIR

CityJet (www.cityjet.com) Links tiny Deauville-Normandie airport, 7km east of Trouville, with London City Airport twice a week (more frequently in summer).

BICYCLE

Les Trouvillaises (☑ 02 31 98 54 11; www. lestrouvillaises.fr; place Foch; bicycle per hour/day €5/14; ☺ 9.30am-7.30pm mid-Mar–Oct, plus weekends & school holidays) Based near Trouville's Casino (next to the footbridge/passenger ferry to Deauville), Les Trouvillaises rents out a variety of two- and four-wheel pedal-powered conveyances, including bicycles, tandems and carts, for both adults and children.

BUS

Deauville and Trouville's joint bus station is next to the Trouville-Deauville train station.

Bus Verts (☑ 08 10 21 42 14; www.busverts.fr) Bus 20 goes to Caen (€4.90, two hours, seven to 12 daily), Honfleur (€2, 30 minutes, four to seven daily) and Le Havre (€6, 1¼ hours, four to seven daily).

TRAIN

The Trouville-Deauville train station is in Deauville right next to pont des Belges (the bridge to Trouville). Getting here usually requires a change at Lisieux (€6.60, 20 minutes, nine to 11 daily), though there are two or three direct trains a day to Paris' Gare St-Lazare (€33.60, two hours). Destinations that require a change of trains include Caen (€14.20, 1¼ to two hours, six to 11 daily) and Rouen (from €23.70, 1¼ to two hours, five to eight daily).

Honfleur

POP 8160

Long a favourite with painters such as Monet, Normandy's most charming port town is a popular day-trip destination for Parisian families. Though the centre can be overrun with visitors on warm weekends and in summer, it's hard not to love the rugged maritime charm of the Vieux Bassin (old harbour), which evokes maritime Normandy of centuries past.

In the 16th and 17th centuries, Honfleur was one of France's most important ports for commerce and exploration. Some of the earliest French expeditions to Brazil and

Newfoundland began here, and in 1608 Samuel de Champlain set sail from Honfleur to found Quebec City.

ℹ Orientation

Honfleur is centred around the roughly rectangular Vieux Bassin and, along its southeast side, the Enclos, the once-walled old town. Église Ste-Catherine is northwest of the Vieux Bassin (up the hill).

◉ Sights & Activities

Honfleur is superb for aimless ambling, especially if you have a walking map from the tourist office. One option is to head north from the Lieutenance along quai des Passagers to **Jetée de l'Ouest** (Western Jetty), which forms the west side of the Avant Port, out to the broad mouth of the Seine. Possible stops include the **Jardin des Personnalités**, a park featuring figures from Honfleur history; the beach; and **Naturospace** (☑ 02 31 81 77 00; www.naturospace.com; bd Charles V; adult/child €8.50/6.60; ☺ 9.30am-1pm & 2-5.30pm Feb-Nov, closed Dec & Jan), a greenhouse filled with free-flying tropical butterflies that's situated 500m northwest of the Lieutenance.

The tourist office also has audioguides (€3.50; in English, French and German) for a 1½-hour walking tour of town.

Le Pass Musées (adult/child €10.10/7.10) gets you into all four municipal museums for the price of two.

Vieux Bassin   HISTORIC QUARTER
The old harbour, with its bobbing pleasure boats, is Honfleur's focal point. On the west side, quai Ste-Catherine is lined with tall, taper-thin houses – many protected from the elements by slate tiles – dating from the 16th to 18th centuries. The **Lieutenance**, at the mouth of the old harbour, was once the residence of the town's royal governor. Just northeast of the Lieutenance is the **Avant Port**, home to Honfleur's dozen fishing vessels, which sell their catch at the **Marché au Poisson** (Fish Market; Jetée de Transit; ☺ 8am-noon or later Thu-Sun).

Église Ste-Catherine   CHURCH
(place Ste-Catherine; ☺ 9am-5.15pm or later) Initially intended as a temporary structure, this extraordinary wooden church was built by local shipwrights during the late 15th and early 16th centuries after its stone predecessor was destroyed during the Hundred Years War. Wood was used so money would be left over to strengthen the city's fortifications. From

the inside, the remarkable twin naves and double-vaulted roof resemble two overturned ships' hulls. Situated a block southwest (up the hill) from the northern end of the Vieux Bassin.

Clocher Ste-Catherine, the church's free-standing wooden bell tower, stands across the square from the façade. It is said to have been built away from the church to limit the damage from lightning strikes.

Les Maisons Satie   MUSEUM

(☑02 31 89 11 11; www.musees-honfleur.fr; 67 bd Charles V & 90 rue Haute; adult/child €6.10/4.60; ☺10am-6pm Wed-Mon, last entry 1hr before closing) Like no other museum you've ever seen, this complex captures the whimsical spirit of the eccentric avant-garde composer Erik Satie (1866–1925), who lived and worked in Honfleur and was born in one of the two half-timbered *maisons Satie* (Satie houses). Visitors wander through the utterly original rooms, each hiding a surreal surprise, with a headset playing Satie's strangely familiar music. Situated 350m northwest of the northern end of the Vieux Bassin.

Musée Eugène Boudin   ART MUSEUM

(☑02 31 89 54 00; www.musees-honfleur.fr; 50 rue de l'Homme de Bois; adult/child €5.60/4.10, late Jun-Sep €6.50/5; ☺10am noon & 2-6pm Wed-Mon mid-Mar–Sep, 2.30-5.30pm Wed-Mon & 10am-noon Sat & Sun Oct–mid-Mar) Features superb 19th- and 20th-century paintings of Normandy's towns and coast, including works by Dubourg, Dufy and Monet. One room is devoted to Eugène Boudin, an early impressionist painter, born here in 1824, whom Baudelaire called the 'king of skies' for his luscious skyscapes. An English audioguide costs €2. Situated five short blocks northwest of the northern end of the Vieux Bassin.

Musée de la Marine   MARITIME MUSEUM

(☑02 31 89 14 12; www.musees-honfleur.fr; quai St-Etienne; adult/child incl Musée d'Ethnographie €3.90/2.70; ☺10am-noon & 2-6.30pm Tue-Sun Apr-Sep, 2.30-5.30pm Tue-Sun & 10am-noon Sat & Sun mid-Feb–Mar, Oct & Nov, closed Dec–mid-Feb) Has model sailing ships, nautically themed engravings and watercolours, and a case that examines Honfleur's role in the 17th- and 18th-century *traite négrière* (slave trade). Situated on the eastern shore of the Vieux Bassin, in the deconsecrated 13th- and 14th-century Église St-Étienne.

Musée d'Ethnographie et
d'Art Populaire Normand   MUSEUM

(www.musees-honfleur.fr; rue de la Prison; adult/child incl Musée de la Marine €3.90/2.70; ☺10am-noon & 2-6.30pm Tue-Sun, closed mid-Nov–mid-Feb) Offers a glimpse of domestic and economic life in 16th- to 19th-century Normandy through traditional costumes, furniture and housewares. Situated around the corner from Musée de la Marine, in two adjacent 16th-century buildings: a one-time prison and a house.

Chapelle Notre Dame de Grâce   CHURCH

Built between 1600 and 1613, this chapel sits on the Plateau de Grâce, a wooded, 100m-high hill about 2km west of the Vieux Bassin. The area offers great views of the Seine estuary, Le Havre, Honfleur and the Pont de Normandie.

NORMANDY HONFLEUR

CAMEMBERT COUNTRY

Some of the most enduring names in the pungent world of French *fromage* come from Normandy, including Pont L'Évêque, Livarot and, most famous of all, Camembert, all of which are named after towns south of Honfleur, on or near the D579.

It's thought that monks first began experimenting with cheesemaking in the Pays d'Auge area of Normandy sometime in the 11th century, but the present-day varieties didn't emerge until around the 17th century. The invention of Camembert is generally credited to Marie Harel, who was supposedly given the secret of soft cheesemaking by an abbot from Brie on the run from revolutionary mobs in 1790. Whatever the truth of the legend, the cheese was a huge success at the local market in Vimoutiers, and the *fabrication* of Camembert quickly grew from cottage production into a veritable industry. The distinctive round wooden boxes, in which Camembert is wrapped, have been around since 1890; they were designed by a local engineer to protect the soft disc during long-distance travel.

If you're interested in seeing how the cheese is made, you can take a tour of the Maison du Camembert (☑02 33 12 10 37; www.fermepresident.com; adult/child €3.50/1.50; ☺10am-noon & 2-5pm daily May-Sep, Wed-Sun Apr & Oct, Fri-Sun mid-Feb–Mar, closed Nov–mid-Feb), an early-19th-century farm restored by Président, one of the largest Camembert producers. It's in the centre of the town of Camembert, about 60km south of Honfleur.

🛏 Sleeping

The tourist office and its website can help you get in touch with some 60 local B&Bs.

Ibis Budget
HOTEL €

(☑ 08 92 68 07 81; www.ibisbudget.com; 2 rue des Vases; tr €64; 🛜) Superbly situated just 400m southeast of the Vieux Bassin, this almost comically anonymous chain hotel has the cheapest beds in town – we mention it only because there's no youth hostel. The 63 rooms, strictly functional in white and green, come with a third bed overhead and tiny plastic bathroom pods. Prices drop on weekdays.

Hôtel du Dauphin
HOTEL €

(☑ 02 31 89 15 53; www.hoteldudauphin.com; 10 place Pierre-Berthelot; d €73-102, q €160-175; 🛜) Behind a 17th-century slate and half-timbered façade, this hotel and its annexe have 34 smallish, modern rooms with nautically themed bathrooms. The quads are pricey for what you get. Neither building has a lift. Situated one block west of Église Ste-Catherine.

La Petite Folie
B&B €€

(☑ 06 74 39 46 46; www.lapetitefolie-honfleur.com; 44 rue Haute; d €145-160, apt €185-295; 🛜) Penny Vincent, an American who moved to France from San Francisco, and her French husband Thierry are the gracious hosts at this elegant town house, built in 1830 and still graced by the original stained glass and tile floors. Hard to believe, but this was beachfront property back then! There's a two-night minimum. Situated four short blocks northwest of the northern end of the Vieux Bassin.

À l'École Buissonnière
B&B €€

(☑ 06 16 18 43 62; www.a-lecole-buissonniere.com; 4 rue de la Foulerie; d incl breakfast €100-120; 🛜) Occupying a former girls' school built in the 1600s, this welcoming B&B, lovingly restored, has five luxurious rooms with antique wood furnishings. For lunch, stop by the *bar à fromages* (cheese bar), or have them prepare a picnic lunch (€15). Bikes cost €15 a day. Situated three short blocks southwest of Église Ste-Catherine.

Le Fond de la Cour
B&B €€

(☑ 06 72 20 72 98; www.lefonddelacour.com; 29 rue Eugène Boudin; d €90-145; 🛜) Watched over by three chickens, two cats, a dog and some koi, the six rooms (including a studio and a cottage) are light, airy and immaculate. The energetic Amanda, a native of Scotland, goes to great lengths to make you feel at home. Situated four blocks west of Église Ste-Catherine – follow rue du Puits.

🍴 Eating

Some of Honfleur's finest restaurants, many featuring dishes plucked from the sea, are on place Hamelin and adjacent rue Haute, both just west of the northern end of the Vieux Bassin. There are more options up around Église Ste-Catherine. Budget places with watery views line quai Ste-Catherine, along the western side of the Vieux Bassin. East of the Vieux Bassin, there are more restaurants along rue de la Ville. Honfleur's dining spots often fill up, especially for dinner on weekends and during school holidays, so it's a good idea to phone in a reservation.

Au P'tit Mareyeur
FRENCH €€

(☑ 02 31 98 84 23; www.auptitmareyeur.fr; 4 rue Haute; lunch/dinner menu €28/35; ⊙ noon-2pm & 7-10pm Thu-Mon, closed Jan) Under 17th-century beams, this 'semi-gastronomique' restaurant serves up Norman-style fish and langoustine, foie gras and *bouillabaisse honfleuraise* (fish and seafood stew with potatoes and saffron; €32); some of the side dishes feature South Indian spices. A new dining area opened upstairs in 2014. Situated two blocks northwest of the northern end of the Vieux Bassin.

L'Endroit
FRENCH €€

(☑ 02 31 88 08 43; 3 rue Charles et Paul Bréard; weekday lunch menu €21, other menu €28.50; ⊙ noon-1.30pm & 7.30-9pm Thu-Mon) Normandy-grown heritage vegetables accompany the traditional French fish and meat dishes at L'Endroit, a classy and very well-regarded bistrot whose open kitchen lets you watch the chefs as they cook. Situated three blocks block southeast of the southern end of the Vieux Bassin.

Le Gambetta
FRENCH €€

(☑ 02 31 87 05 01; 58 rue Haute; menu €25-35; ⊙ noon-1.45pm & 7.15-9pm Wed-Sun) This traditional restaurant takes pride in resurrecting old recipes, some from the early 20th century, others from the Middle Ages. Specialities include fish, meat prepared on a *plancha* (grill) and scrumptious desserts. Situated four short blocks northwest of the northern end of the Vieux Bassin.

L'Écailleur
FRENCH €€

(☑ 02 31 89 93 34; www.lecailleur.fr; 1 rue de la République; weekday lunch menu €21, other menus €30-45; ⊙ noon-2pm & 7-9pm Fri-Tue) Resembling a ship's wood-panelled interior, this stylish restaurant makes a lovely haven from the hustle. Specialities include turbot, *lotte* (monkfish) and *filet mignon du porc* (roasted tenderloin of pork). Situated at the southern tip of the Vieux Bassin.

L'Homme de Bois
FRENCH €€

(✎ 02 31 89 75 27; 30-32 rue de L'Homme de Bois; menus €22-34; ⊘noon-2.30pm & 7-9.30pm daily) The rustic interior, complete with a fireplace, provides a relaxing backdrop for the locally caught fish, either grilled or prepared with delicate traditional sauces; *homard breton* (blue lobster) from the Carteret area; and excellent French-style steaks. Situated four short blocks northwest of the northern end of the Vieux Bassin.

Self-Catering

Marché
FOOD MARKET

(place Ste-Catherine; ⊘9am-noon Wed & Sat) A traditional food market on Saturday, a *biologique* (organic) market on Wednesday. Situated next to Église Ste-Catherine.

🔒 Shopping

Honfleur is home to quite a few **art galleries**, some of them on the streets leading up the hill from Église Ste-Catherine (eg rue de l'Homme de Bois), others along rue Cachin, which is one long block south of the Vieux Bassin. A number of shops specialise in *brocante* (secondhand goods and antiques).

ℹ Information

There is no place in Honfleur to change money.

Tourist Office (✎ 02 31 89 23 30; www.ot-honfleur.fr; quai Lepaulmier; ⊘9.30am-12.30pm & 2-6pm Mon-Sat Sep-Jun, 9.30am-6pm Jul & Aug, also open 9.30am-5pm Sun Easter-Sep; 🛜) Has a free map detailing three enjoyable walking circuits, audioguides (€3.50) for a walking tour of town (in English, French and German), and bus schedules. Internet access costs €1 for 15 minutes. Situated a long block southeast of the Vieux Bassin, inside the ultra-modern Médiathèque (library) building.

ℹ Getting There & Around

BUS

The **bus station** (quai Lepaulmier), two blocks east of the tourist office, has schedules posted in the window.

Bus Verts (✎ 08 10 21 42 14; www.busverts. fr) Services include Deauville and Trouville (€2, 30 minutes, four to seven daily), Caen (bus: 20 €6.95, 2½ hours, seven to 13 daily; bus: 39 €11.15, one hour, one or two daily) and Le Havre (€3.95, 30 minutes, four to six daily).

CAR

Free parking is available next to Naturospace, which is 600m northwest of the Avant Port along bd Charles V.

TRAIN

To catch the train (eg to Paris), take the bus to Deauville (18km from Honfleur) or Le Havre (25km from Honfleur).

MANCHE

The Manche *département* (www.manche-tourisme.com) encompasses the entire Cotentin Peninsula, stretching from Utah Beach northwest to Cherbourg and southwest to magnificent Mont St-Michel. The peninsula's northwest corner has unspoiled stretches of rocky coastline sheltering tranquil bays and villages. The fertile inland areas, criss-crossed by hedgerows, produce an abundance of beef, dairy products and apples.

The British crown dependencies of Jersey and Guernsey lie 22km and 48km offshore, respectively.

Cherbourg

POP 39,000

At the tip of the Cotentin Peninsula, the port city of Cherbourg plays host to French warships, transoceanic cargo ships, cruise liners, yachts and passenger ferries from Britain and Ireland. It's a far cry from the romantic locale portrayed in Jacques Demy's 1964 musical film *Les Parapluies de Cherbourg* (The Umbrellas of Cherbourg) but it's home to an outstanding aquarium-cum-sea museum.

During WWII Cherbourg's port was destroyed by the Germans shortly after D-Day to prevent its falling into Allied hands.

⊙ Sights

★ Cité de la Mer
AQUARIUM

(✎ 02 33 20 26 26; www.citedelamer.com; allée du Président Menut, Gare Maritime Transatlantique; adult/child €18/13; ⊘9.30am-7pm, closed 3 weeks in Jan, may be closed Mon in winter; 🅿) Cherbourg's art deco Gare Maritime Transatlantique (Transatlantic Ferry Terminal), built from 1928 to 1933, was designed so travellers could walk from their train directly to their ocean liner. These days it is still used by cruise ships such as the *Queen Mary 2* but most of the complex houses a fine aquarium featuring Europe's deepest fish tank. The complex is situated 1km northeast of the tourist office.

Other highlights here include *Le Redoubtable*, a French nuclear submarine you can go inside (audioguide available), an exhibit on the *Titanic* (Cherbourg was the ill-fated liner's last port-of-call), and oodles of exhibits on

WORTH A TRIP

COUTANCES

The lovely old Norman town of Coutances makes for a nice detour on the way to Mont St-Michel from the D-Day beaches or Cherbourg. At the town's heart is the **Cathédrale de Coutances** (http://cathedralecoutances.free.fr; parvis Notre-Dame, Coutances; ⊗9am-7pm year-round), whose interior highlights include several 13th-century windows, a 14th-century fresco of St Michael skewering the dragon, and an organ and high altar from the mid-1700s.

An English audioguide (€3) can be picked up at the tourist office (at the cathedral in July and August); those over 10 years of age can climb the lantern tower on a French-language **tour** (http://cathedralecoutances.free.fr; adult/child €7/4; ⊗11am & 3pm Mon-Fri, 3pm Sun Jul & Aug).

sea exploration that kids will love. Ticket sales end 1½ hours before closing time.

🛏 Sleeping

Hôtel de la Renaissance　　　HOTEL €
(☑02 33 43 23 90; www.hotel-renaissance-cherbourg.com; 4 rue de l'Église; d €60-77; 🕾) Staff here are very welcoming, and most of the 12 large, well-kept rooms have great views of the port. Situated 400m northwest of the tourist office.

Auberge de Jeunesse　　　HOSTEL €
(☑02 33 78 15 15; www.fuaj.org; 55 rue de l'Abbaye; dm incl breakfast €22; ⊗check-in 9am-1pm & 6-11pm; ⊛) Located 1km northwest of the tourist office, this excellent, 99-bed hostel is housed in the French navy's old archives complex. Rooms have two to five beds; there's a small kitchen for self-caterers. To get there, take bus 3 or 5 to the Chantier stop.

La Régence　　　HOTEL €€
(☑02 33 43 05 16; www.laregence.com; 42-44 quai de Caligny; d €82-98; 🕾) Has 20 cosy, carpeted rooms, some with dashing harbour views, attractive public areas, and, on the ground floor, a well-regarded, formal French restaurant. Situated two blocks north of the tourist office, facing the harbour.

🍴 Eating

Restaurants can be found along quai de Caligny, a block or two north of the tourist office, and along the streets leading inland from there, including rue Tour Carrée.

Au Tire-Bouchon　　　FRENCH €
(☑02 33 53 54 69; www.restaurant-autirebouchon.com; 17 rue Notre-Dame; menus lunch €11-14, dinner €20.50-28; ⊗noon-2pm & 7-10pm Tue-Sat) At this convivial bistro and wine bar, specialities include oysters (per six/dozen €8/17.50), *tartines* (open sandwiches) and the *salade tire-bouchon* (a salad with ham, foie gras and salmon). Au Tire-Bouchon is a bit hard to find – from quai de Caligny, follow the signs to 'Parking Notre-Dame'.

Le Plouc 2　　　FRENCH €€
(☑02 33 01 06 46; 59 rue du Blé; menus €19.50-36; ⊗noon-2pm Tue-Fri & Sun, 7-9.30pm Mon-Sat) Locals keep coming back for Le Plouc 2's creative versions of traditional French favourites, prepared with seasonal ingredients and served in a cosy, wood-beamed dining room.

ℹ Information

Bureau de Change (Exchange Bureau; 53 rue Maréchal Foch; ⊗9am-12.15pm & 1.45-6.15pm Mon-Fri, 9am-12.15pm Sat) Currency exchange half-a-block north of the tourist office.

Tourist Office (☑02 33 93 52 02; www.cherbourgtourisme.com; 14 quai Alexandre III; ⊗9.30am-7pm Mon-Sat, 10am-5pm Sun mid-Jun–mid-Sep, 10am-12.30pm & 2-6pm Mon-Sat mid-Sep–mid-Jun) Has useful information on visiting the city, the Cotentin Peninsula and D-Day sites, and can help with accommodation. Situated on the west side of the Bassin de Commerce (inner harbour), two blocks south of the bridge.

ℹ Getting There & Away

BOAT
The **ferry terminal** (www.port-cherbourg.com) is 2km northeast of the tourist office.

Brittany Ferries (www.brittany-ferries.co.uk) Has services to the English ports of Poole and Portsmouth.

Irish Ferries (www.irishferries.com) Goes to the Irish ports of Rosslare and Dublin.

Stena Line (www.stenaline.ie) Sails to Rosslare.

TRAIN
The train station is at the southern end of Bassin du Commerce (inner harbour), just west of the new Les Éléis shopping mall. Direct services include:

Bayeux €16.50, one hour, 15 daily Monday to Friday, eight to 10 on weekends.

Caen €25.40, 1¼ hours, eight to 15 daily.

Paris' Gare St-Lazare €50.60, three hours, eight daily Monday to Friday, four or five daily Saturday and Sunday.

Pontorson (Mont St-Michel) €30.10, 2½ to 3½ hours, three to five daily (via Lison).

❶ Getting Around

BUS

A free shuttle-bus service, coordinated with ferry schedules, links the ferry terminal with the parking lot across the Pont Tournant (bridge) from the city centre.

TAXI

For a taxi, call ✆ 02 33 53 36 38. A daytime trip between the train station and ferry terminal costs about €10.

Mont St-Michel

POP 44

It's one of France's most iconic images: the slender spires, stout ramparts and rocky slopes of Mont St-Michel rising dramatically from the sea - or towering over sands laid bare by the receding tide. Despite huge numbers of tourists, both the abbey and the narrow alleys below still manage to transport visitors back to the Middle Ages.

The bay around Mont St-Michel is famed for having Europe's highest tidal variations; the difference between low and high tides - only about six hours apart - can reach an astonishing 15m. The Mont is only completely surrounded by the sea every month or two, when the tidal coefficient is above 100 and high tide is above 14m. Regardless of the time of year, the waters sweep in at an astonishing clip, said to be as fast as a galloping horse.

On the Mont, be prepared for lots of steps, some of them spiral - alas, it's one of the least wheelchair-accessible sites in France.

History

Bishop Aubert of Avranches is said to have built a devotional chapel on the summit of the island in 708, following his vision of the Archangel Michael, whose gilded figure, perched on the vanquished dragon, crowns the tip of the abbey's spire. In 966 Richard I, Duke of Normandy, gave Mont St-Michel to the Benedictines, who turned it into a centre of learning and, in the 11th century, into something of an ecclesiastical fortress, with a military garrison at the disposal of both abbot and king.

In the 15th century, during the Hundred Years War, the English blockaded and besieged Mont St-Michel three times. The fortified abbey withstood these assaults and was the only place in western and northern France not to fall into English hands. After the Revolution, Mont St-Michel was turned into a prison. In 1966 the abbey was symbolically returned to the Benedictines as part of the celebrations marking its millennium. Mont St-Michel and the bay became a Unesco World Heritage Site in 1979.

In recent decades sand and silt have been building up around the causeway - built in 1879 - linking the Mont to the mainland, threatening to turn the island into a permanent peninsula. To restore the site's 'maritime character', in 2014 the causeway was replaced by a slender, 2km bridge designed to allow the tides and the River Couësnon (pronounced 'kweh-*no*') - whose new *barrage* (dam) stores up high-tide water and then releases it at low tide - to flush away accumulated sediments. For the latest, see www.projetmontsaint-michel.fr or drop by the dam's observation platform, across the street from the Place du Barrage shuttle bus stop.

◎ Sights & Activities

The Mont's one main street, the Grande Rue, leads up the slope - past cheesy souvenir shops and eateries - to the abbey. The staircases and tiny passageways that meander up the hill from the Grande Rue - one, opposite Restaurant La Croix Blanche, is just 50cm wide - will take you to the diminutive parish church, a tiny cemetery and other Mont-sized surprises. Finding your way around is easier if you pick up a detailed map of the Mont (€3) at the tourist office or the abbey's ticket counter.

Abbaye du Mont St-Michel ABBEY
(✆ 02 33 89 80 00; www.monuments-nationaux.fr; adult/child incl guided tour €9/free; ⊙ 9am-7pm, last entry 1hr before closing) The Mont's star attraction is the stunning architectural ensemble high up on top: the abbey. Most areas can be visited without a guide, but it's well worth taking the one-hour tour included in the ticket price; English tours (usually) begin at 11am and 3pm from October to March, with three or four daily tours in spring and summer. You can also take a 1½-hour audioguide tour (one/two people €4.50/6), available in six languages.

Benedictine monks hold services in the abbey at 6.50am from Tuesday to Friday; at 7.50am on Saturday, Sunday and holidays; at 11.15am on Sunday; at noon from Tuesday to Saturday; and at 6.20pm from Tuesday to Friday.

From Monday to Saturday from mid-July to August, there are illuminated nocturnes

Mont St-Michel

TIMELINE

708 Inspired by a vision of **St Michael** ❶, Bishop Aubert is inspired to 'build here and build high'.

966 Richard I, Duke of Normandy, gives the Mont to the Benedictines. The three levels of the **abbey** ❷ reflect their monastic hierarchy.

1017 Development of the abbey begins. Pilgrims arrive to honour the cult of St Michael. They walk barefoot across the mudflats and up the **Grande Rue** ❸ to be received in the almonry (now the bookshop).

1203 The monastery is burnt by the troops of Philip Augustus, who later donates money for its restoration and the Gothic 'miracle', **La Merveille** ❹, is constructed.

1434 The Mont's **ramparts** ❺ and fortifications ensure it withstands the English assault during the Hundred Years War. It is the only place in northern France not to fall.

1789 After the Revolution, Monasticism is abolished and the Mont is turned into a prison. During this period the **treadmill** ❻ is built to lift up supplies.

1878 The Mont is linked to the mainland by a **causeway** ❼.

1979 The Mont is declared a Unesco World Heritage Site.

2014 The causeway is replaced by a bridge.

TOP TIPS

➡ Pick up a picnic lunch at the supermarket in La Caserne to avoid the Mont's overpriced fast food.

➡ Allow 45 minutes to an hour to get from the new parking lot in La Caserne to the Mont.

➡ If you step off the island pay close attention to the tides - they can be dangerous.

➡ Don't forget to pick up the Abbey's excellent audioguide – it tells some great stories.

ÎLOT DE TOMBELAINE

Occupied by the English during the Hundred Years War, this islet is now a bird reserve. From April to July it teems with exceptional birdlife.

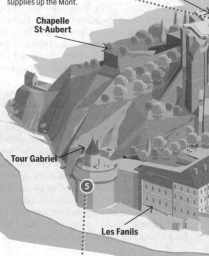

Treadmill
The giant treadmill was powered hamsterlike by half a dozen prisoners, who, marching two abreast, raised stone and supplies up the Mont.

West Terrace

Chapelle St-Aubert

Tour Gabriel

❺

Les Fanils

Ramparts
The Mont was also a military garrison surrounded by machicolated and turreted walls, dating from the 13th to 15th centuries. The single entrance, Porte de l'Avancée, ensured its security in the Hundred Years War. Tip: Tour du Nord (North Tower) has the best views.

Abbey

The abbey's three levels reflect the monastic order: monks lived isolated in church and cloister, the abbot entertained noble guests at the middle level, and lowly pilgrims were received in the basement. Tip: night visits run from mid-July to August.

St Michael Statue & Bell Tower

A golden statue of the winged St Michael looks ready to leap heavenward from the bell tower. He is the patron of the Mont, having inspired St Aubert's original devotional chapel.

①

La Merveille

The highlights of La Merveille are the vast refectory hall lit through embrasured windows, the Knights Hall with its elegant ribbed vaulting, and the cloister (above), which is one of the purest examples of 13th-century architecture to survive here.

Gardens

②

④

⑥

Tour du Nord

Église St-Pierre

Cemetery

Chemin des Remparts

③

Tour de l'Arcade

Toilets

Tour du Roi

Tourist Office

Porte de l'Avancée (Entrance)

Porte des Fanils

⑦

Grande Rue

The main thoroughfare of the small village below the abbey, Grande Rue has its charm despite its rampant commercialism. Don't miss the famous Mère Poulard shop here, for souvenir cookies.

New Bridge

In 2014, the Mont's 136-year-old causeway was replaced by a bridge designed to allow seawater to circulate and thus save the island from turning into a peninsula.

BEST VIEWS

The view from the Jardin des Plantes in nearby Avranches is unique, as are the panoramas from Pointe du Grouin du Sud near the village of St-Léonard.

(night-time visits) with live chamber music from 7pm to midnight.

Église Abbatiale
CHURCH

(Abbey Church) Built on the rocky tip of the mountain cone, the transept rests on solid rock, while the nave, choir and transept arms are supported by the rooms below. This church is famous for its mix of architectural styles: the nave and south transept (11th and 12th centuries) are solid Norman Romanesque, while the choir (late 15th century) is Flamboyant Gothic.

La Merveille
HISTORIC SITE

(The Marvel) The buildings on the northern side of the Mont are known as 'The Marvel'. The famous cloître (cloister) is surrounded by a double row of delicately carved arches resting on granite pillars. The early-13th-century, barrel-roofed réfectoire (dining hall) is illuminated by a wall of recessed windows – remarkable given that the sheer drop precluded the use of flying buttresses. The Gothic Salle des Hôtes (Guest Hall), dating from 1213, has two enormous fireplaces.

Other features to look out for include the promenoir (ambulatory), with one of the oldest ribbed vaulted ceilings in Europe, and the Chapelle de Notre Dame sous Terre (Underground Chapel of Our Lady), one of the abbey's oldest rooms, rediscovered in 1903.

The masonry used to build the abbey was brought to the Mont by boat and pulled up the hillside using ropes.

Chemin des Remparts
WALKING

For spectacular views of the bay, you can walk along the top of the entire eastern section of Mont's ramparts, from Tour du Nord (North Tower) to the Porte du Roy.

☞ Tours

When the tide is out (the tourist office has tide tables), you can walk all the way around Mont St-Michel, a distance of about 1km, with a guide (doing so on your own is very risky). Straying too far from the Mont can be dangerous: you could get stuck in wet sand – from which Norman soldiers are depicted being rescued in one scene of the Bayeux Tapestry – or be overtaken either by the incoming tide or by water gushing from the new dam's eight sluice gates.

Experienced outfits offering guided walks into – or even across – are based across the bay from Mont St-Michel in Genêts. Local

> ## REGIONAL PARK
>
> Inland from Utah Beach, to the south and southwest, is the 1480-sq-km Parc Naturel Régional des Marais du Cotentin et du Bessin (www.parc-cotentin-bessin.fr), a vast expanse of waterways, marshes, moors and hedgerows. The Maison du Parc (visitor centre) is in Saint-Côme-du-Mont, 50km west of Bayeux just off the N13.
>
> For details on hiking and cycling in the park and elsewhere in the Manche département, visit www.manche-tourism.com and click on 'Walks, Rambles & Rides'.

tourist offices have details on other guiding companies. Reserve ahead.

Découverte de la Baie du Mont-Saint-Michel
WALKING TOUR

(☑ 02 33 70 83 49; www.decouvertebaie.com; 1 rue Montoise, Genêts; adult/child from €6/4) An experienced outfit offering guided walks on and across the bay.

Chemins de la Baie
WALKING TOUR

(☑ 02 33 89 80 88; www.cheminsdelabaie.com; 34 rue de l'Ortillon, Genêts; adult/child from €6.90/4.70) An experienced outfit offering guided walks.

🛏 Sleeping

The cheapest accommodation near the Mont is in Pontorson, 7km south of the shuttle stop in La Caserne, whose main street, rue Couësnon, is home to a number of small, simple, family-run hotels offering doubles for as little as €40. Pontorson is linked with the rest of France by train and with La Caserne by bus (€3), by the D976 and by the Voie Verte walking and cycling route.

The most convenient hotels – most run by chains – are in La Caserne, 2km south of the Mont itself. The only way to drive into La Caserne is to get a gate code when you make your reservation. If you stay here or in a nearby B&B – several offer superb value – you'll save the €12 parking fee.

If you opt to stay up on the Mont itself, you'll have to park at La Caserne, take the shuttle with your luggage, and then walk to your hotel.

Vent des Grèves
B&B €

(☑ Estelle 02 33 48 28 89; www.ventdesgreves. com; 7-9 chemin des Dits, Ardevon; d/q incl breakfast €50/70) This friendly, family-run B&B has five modern rooms, furnished simply, with magical views of the Mont. Outstanding value. Situated an easily walkable 1km east of the shuttle stop in La Caserne.

Auberge de Jeunesse
HOSTEL €

(Centre Duguesclin; ☑ 02 33 60 18 65; www.fuaj. org; 21 bd du Général Patton, Pontorson; dm €14; ☺ reception 8am-noon & 5pm-8.30pm, hostel closed Oct-Mar) A 62-bed hostel with four- to six-bed rooms and kitchen facilities. Situated in Pontorson, linked to the rest of France by train and to the Mont by bus.

La Jacotière
B&B €€

(☑ 02 33 60 22 94; www.lajacotiere.fr; 46 rue de la Côte, Ardevon; d/tr/q incl breakfast €82/98/122) Built as a farmhouse in 1906, this superbly situated, family-run B&B has five comfortable rooms and one studio apartment. Situated just 300m east of the shuttle stop in La Caserne.

Hôtel Du Guesclin
HOTEL €€

(☑ 02 33 60 14 10; www.hotelduguesclin.com; Grande Rue, Mont St-Michel; d €80-95; ☺ closed Wed night & Thu Apr-Jun & Oct–mid-Nov, hotel closed mid-Nov–Mar) One of the most affordable hotels on the Mont itself, the Hôtel Du Guesclin (pronounced 'geck-*la*') has 10 charming rooms, five with priceless views of the bay.

✖ Eating

The Grande Rue is jammed with crêperies and sandwich shops. Many of the eating options on the Mont are overpriced, overbooked and overbusy.

Crêperie La Sirène
CRÊPERIE €

(Grande Rue; crêpes €3.50-10; ☺ 11.45am-5pm Sep-Jun, to 9.30pm Jul & Aug, closed Jan) Situated at the bottom of the Grande Rue, up a 15th-century staircase from the souvenir shop.

Super Marché
SUPERMARKET

(La Caserne; ☺ 9am-7.30pm) Great for picnic supplies. Has a shuttle stop out front.

ℹ Information

La Caserne Tourist Office (☑ 02 14 13 20 15; www.bienvenueaumontsaintmichel.com; La Caserne parking lot; ☺ 9am-7pm) Run by the company that built the new bridge and parking lot, this *centre d'information* has lots of brochures, left-luggage lockers (key deposit €1) and an ATM.

Mont St-Michel Tourist Office (☑ 02 33 60 14 30; www.ot-montsaintmichel.com; ☺ 9am-12.30pm & 2-6pm Sep-Jun, 9am-7pm Jul & Aug) Has an *horaire des marées* (tide table) posted, changes money and sells an excellent detailed

map of the Mont (€3). Next door are toilets (€0.40) and an ATM. Recently renovated, it's situated just inside Porte de l'Avancée, up the stairs to the left.

Post Office (Grande Rue) Changes currency and has an ATM.

ℹ Getting There & Away

For all manner of details on getting to the Mont, see www.bienvenueaumontsaintmichel.com.

BUS

Inter-city buses stop next to the Mont's new parking lot in La Caserne, very near the shuttles to the Mont.

Bus 1 (every hour or two, more frequently in July and August), operated by **Transdev**, links La Caserne with the village of Beauvoir (€3, five minutes) and the train station in Pontorson (€3, 18 minutes); times are coordinated with the arrival in Pontorson of some trains from Caen and Rennes. **Keolis Emeraude** (☑ 02 99 26 16 00; www. destination-montsaintmichel.com) Has buses to the train stations in Rennes (€12.70, 1¼ hours, four daily) and Dol de Bretagne (€6, 30 minutes, one or two daily); times are coordinated with TGVs to/from Paris.

CAR

Visitors who arrive by car must leave their vehicles in one of the new parking lots (two/24 hours €6/12) situated a few hundred metres east of La Caserne's hotel strip. Luggage can be left in lockers in the adjacent tourist office building (€1 key deposit).

TRAIN

The town of Pontorson, 7km south of the La Caserne parking area, is the area's main rail hub. Services from Pontorson include:

Bayeux €23.90, 1¾ hours, three daily.

Caen €26.10, 1¾ hours, three daily.

Cherbourg €30.10, 2½ hours to 3½ hours, three to five daily (via Lison).

Rennes €14.30, 50 minutes, three or four daily.

ℹ Getting Around

The new parking area next to La Caserne is 2.5km south of Mont St-Michel. To get from there to the Mont, you can either walk or take a **free shuttle** that lets you off 300m from the Mont's main gate. Shuttles run 24 hours a day – regularly from 7am to 1am, when summoned by phone after that. Count on spending 45 minutes to an hour to get from the parking lot to the abbey.

BICYCLE

In La Caserne, the **Hôtel Mercure** (☑ 02 33 60 14 18) rents out bicycles for €4.90/8.20/16.30 for one/four/eight hours.

NORMANDY MONT ST-MICHEL

Brittany

POP 4.47 MILLION

Best Places to Eat

➡ Le Balafon (p261)

➡ Breizh Café (p262)

➡ Le Coquillage (p263)

➡ La Chocolaterie de Pont-Aven (p279)

➡ La Saint-Georges (p293)

Best Places to Stay

➡ La Maison Pavie (p264)

➡ Le Keo – La Maison des Capitaines (p272)

➡ Kastell Dinn (p274)

➡ Le Petit Hôtel du Grand Large (p283)

➡ Le Clos des Devins (p290)

Why Go?

Brittany is for explorers. Its wild, dramatic coastline, medieval towns and thick forests make an excursion here well worth the detour from the beaten track. This is a land of prehistoric mysticism, proud tradition and culinary wealth, where fiercely independent locals celebrate Breton culture and Paris feels a long way away indeed.

The entire region has a wonderfully undiscovered feel once you go beyond world-famous sights such as stunning St-Malo, regal Dinard and charming Dinan. Unexpected Breton gems – including the little-known towns of Roscoff, Quimper and Vannes, the megaliths of Carnac, the rugged coastlines of Finistère, the Presqu'Île de Crozon and the Morbihan Coast – all demonstrate that there's far more to Brittany than delicious crêpes and homemade cider. Brittany's much-loved islands are also big draws – don't miss its two stars: dramatic Île d'Ouessant and the aptly named Belle Île.

When to Go

Brest

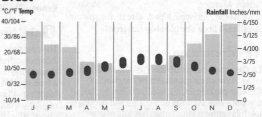

Jun & early Jul Enjoy the beaches, outdoor adventures and sunshine before the crowds.

Jul–Aug Plenty of highly colourful festivals and events await you throughout the region.

Dec–Feb Be overawed by the elements during a wild winter storm along the Finistère coastline.

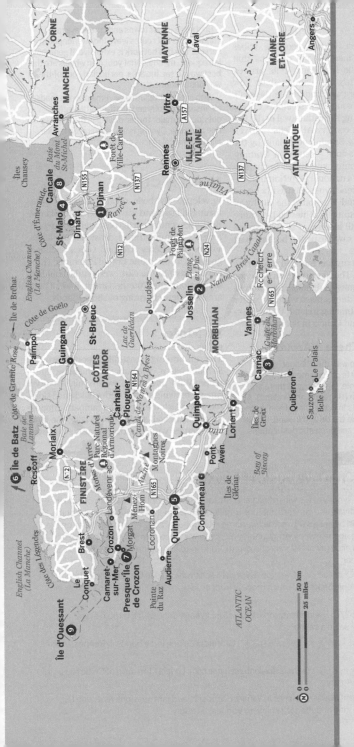

Brittany Highlights

1 Getting lost in the higgledy-piggledy old town of **Dinan** (p263)

2 Touring the turreted medieval castle over the fairy-tale village of **Josselin** (p289)

3 Cycling past fields full of prehistoric **megaliths** (p281) around **Carnac**

4 Strolling along the ramparts at sunset for panoramic views over **St-Malo** (p254)

5 Getting lost in the medieval quarter of **Quimper** (p275)

6 Hiking and bike to your heart's content on car-free **Île de Batz** (p267)

7 Exploring the scenically magical **Presqu'île de Crozon** (p273)

8 Tucking into freshly shucked oysters in **Cancale** (p262)

9 Getting away from it all on **Île d'Ouessant** (p271)

History

Brittany's earliest known neolithic tribes left a legacy of menhirs and dolmens that continue to baffle historians. Celts arrived in the 6th century BC, naming their new homeland Armor ('the land beside the sea'). The region was conquered by Julius Caesar in 56 BC. Following the withdrawal of the Romans in the 5th century AD, Celts – driven from what is now Britain and Ireland by the Anglo-Saxon invasions – settled in Brittany, bringing Christianity with them. In the 9th century, Brittany's national hero Nominoë revolted against French rule. Wedged between two more-powerful kingdoms, the duchy of Brittany was continually contested by France and England until a series of strategic royal weddings finally saw the region become part of France in 1532.

However, Brittany has retained a separate regional identity. There's currently a drive for cultural and linguistic renewal, and a consciousness of Brittany's place within a wider Celtic culture embracing Ireland, Wales, Scotland, Cornwall and Galicia in Spain.

ⓘ Getting There & Around

Ferries link St-Malo with the Channel Islands and the English ports of Portsmouth, Plymouth, Weymouth and Poole. From Roscoff there are ferries to Plymouth (UK) and Cork (Ireland). Alternatively, airports in Brest, Dinard and, to the south, Nantes serve the UK and Ireland, as well as other European and domestic destinations.

Brittany's major towns and cities have rail connections but routes leave the interior poorly served. The bus network is extensive, if generally infrequent, meaning that your own wheels are the best way to see the area, particularly out-of-the-way destinations.

With gently undulating, well-maintained roads, an absence of tolls and relatively little traffic outside the major towns, driving in Brittany is a real pleasure. Cycling is also extremely popular, and bike-rental places are never hard to find.

NORTH COAST

Enveloped by belle époque beach resorts, fishing villages and wave-splashed headlands, Brittany's central north coast spans the *départements* (administrative divisions) of Ille-et-Vilaine and Côtes d'Armor. Green shallows give rise to the name Côte d'Émeraude (Emerald Coast) to the east; westwards, boulders blush along the Côte de Granit Rose. There are also a few charming offshore islands.

St-Malo

POP 48,800

The enthralling mast-filled port town of St-Malo has a cinematically changing landscape. With one of the world's highest tidal ranges, brewing storms under blackened skies see waves lash the top of the ramparts ringing its beautiful walled city. Hours later, the blue sky merges with the deep marine-blue sea,

---

DON'T MISS

BRITTANY'S TOP FIVE MUSIC FESTIVALS

Celtic culture is synonymous with music and Brittany is no exception. A wealth of indoor and outdoor festivals and concerts feature traditional instruments through to electronica, and everything in between, with some big-name international acts. Keep your finger on the pulse by picking up the free monthly zine **Ty Zicos** (www.tyzicos.com) in cafes and bars.

In addition to an array of festivals and events, tune in to the region's top five musical festivals each year.

➡ **Les Vieilles Charrues de Carhaix** (www.vieillescharrues.asso.fr; Carhaix) Old-school crooners, electronic beats and much more attract crowds of 300,000-plus to Carhaix in mid-July.

➡ **Astropolis** (p270) Brest's electronic music fest in early July, with the main event atmospherically set in a castle.

➡ **Les Transmusicales de Rennes** (p292) Groundbreaking indie bands in Rennes, in early December.

➡ **Festival Interceltique** (www.festival-interceltique.com; Lorient) Ten days of Celtic music in Lorient, in early August.

➡ **Jazz à Vannes** (www.jazzavannes.fr; Vannes) Concerts and jam sessions featuring big names from the international jazz scene in Vannes, late July.

exposing beaches as wide and flat as the clear skies above and creating land bridges to the granite outcrop islands.

Construction of the walled city's fortifications began in the 12th century. The town became a key port during the 17th and 18th centuries as a base for both merchant ships and government-sanctioned privateers (pirates, basically) against the constant threat of the English. These days English arrivals are tourists, for whom St-Malo, a short ferry hop from the Channel Islands, is a summer haven.

◉ Sights

◉ Intra Muros

The tangle of streets in the walled city of St-Malo, known as Intra muros ('within the walls'), are a highlight of a visit to Brittany. Grand merchants' mansions and sea captains' houses line the alleys. For the best panoramas, stroll along the jetty that pokes out to sea off the southwestern tip of Intra muros from the end of which you'll get the wide angle view or, to zoom in, clamber along the top of the ramparts. Constructed at the end of the 17th century under military architect Vauban, and measuring 1.8km, the ramparts can be accessed at several points including all the main city gates. Though you'd never guess it from the cobblestone streets and reconstructed monuments in 17th- and 18th-century style, during August 1944 the battle to drive German forces out of St-Malo destroyed around 80% of the old city, which has been lovingly restored since then.

Cathédrale St-Vincent CATHEDRAL
(Map p258; place Jean de Châtillon; ⊙9.30am-6pm) The city's centrepiece was constructed between the 12th and 18th centuries. During the ferocious fighting of August 1944 the cathedral was badly hit; much of its original structure (including its spire) was reduced to rubble. The cathedral was subsequently rebuilt and reconsecrated in 1971. A mosaic plaque on the floor of the nave marks the spot where Jacques Cartier received the blessing of the bishop of St-Malo before his 'voyage of discovery' to Canada in 1535.

Musée d'Histoire de St-Malo MUSEUM
(Map p258; ☑02 99 40 71 57; www.ville-saint-malo.fr/culture/les-musees; Château; adult/child €6/3; ⊙10am-12.30pm & 2-6pm Apr-Sep, Tue-Sun Oct-Mar) Within Château de St-Malo (Map p258), built by the dukes of Brittany in the 15th and

16th centuries, this museum looks at the life and history of the city through nautical exhibits, model boats and marine artefacts, as well as an exhibition covering the city's cod-fishing heritage. There's also info on the city's sons, including Cartier, Surcouf, Duguay-Trouin and the writer Chateaubriand.

If you can handle heights, the castle's lookout tower offers eye-popping views of the old city.

La Maison de Corsaire HISTORIC MANSION
(Map p258; ☑02 99 56 09 40; www.demeure-de-corsaire.com; 5 rue d'Asfeld; adult/child €5.50/4.50; ⊙10-11.30am & 2.30-5.30pm Jul-Aug & school holidays, 3pm Tue-Sun outside of school holidays, closed Dec & Jan) This 18th-century mansion and historic monument was once owned by corsair (privateer) François Auguste Magon. Guided tours are in French but descriptions are available in English.

◉ Beyond the Walls

The pretty fishing port of St-Servan sits south of the walled city.

Fort National RUIN
(Map p256; www.fortnational.com; adult/child €5/3; ⊙Easter, school holidays & Jun-Sep) The St-Malo ramparts' northern stretch looks across to the remains of this former prison, built by Vauban in 1689. Standing atop a rocky outcrop, the fort can only be accessed at low tide. Ask at the tourist office for times of tours.

DON'T MISS

ÎLE DU GRAND BÉ & FORT DU PETIT BÉ

The walled city feels too claustrophobic for you? At low tide, cross the beach to walk out via the Porte des Bés to the rocky islet of Île du Grand Bé, where the great St-Malo-born 18th-century writer Chateaubriand is buried. Once the tide rushes in, the causeway remains impassable for about six hours; check tide times with the tourist office.

About 100m beyond the Île du Grand Bé is the privately owned, Vauban-built 17th-century **Fort du Petit Bé** (Map p256; ☑06 08 27 51 20; www.petit-be.com; Fort du Petit Bé guided tours adult/child €5/3; ⊙Fort du Petit Bé by reservation, depending on tides), also accessible at low tide only 13 days a month. The owner runs 30-minute guided tours in French; leaflets in English are available.

St-Malo & St-Servan

English Channel (La Manche)

Le Sillon Isthmus

Maison Angélus (1.6km); Auberge de Jeunesse – Ethic Etapes Patrick Varangot (2km)

Esplanade St-Vincent

Bassin Duguay-Trouin

Plage de Bon Secours

Q St-Vincent

INTRA MUROS

Chaussée des Corsaires

See Intra Muros Map (p258)

Bassin Vauban

Gare Maritime du Naye

R Georges Clemenceau

Ferries to UK

Port de Plaisance (Pleasure Marina)

Corniche d'Aleth

Plage des Bas Sablons

R des Bas Sablons

Pl St-Pierre

Allée Gaston Buy

Q Sebastopol

Q Solidor

ST-SERVAN

Esplanade Commandant Yves Menguy

Port-Solidor

St-Malo & St-Servan

⊚ Sights

Mémorial 39–45   MONUMENT

(Map p256; ☎ 02 99 82 41 74; Fort de la Cité d'Alet; adult/child €6/3; ⊙ guided visits 10.15am, 11am, 2pm, 3pm, 4pm & 5pm Jul-Aug, 2.30pm, 3.15pm & 4.30pm Tue-Sun Apr-Jun & Sep) Constructed in the mid-18th century, **Fort de la Cité d'Alet** (Map p256) was used as a German base during WWII. One of the bunkers now houses this memorial, which depicts St-Malo's violent WWII history and liberation, and includes a 45-minute film in French (not shown on every tour). Some guided visits are conducted in English; call ahead to confirm times.

Musée International du
Long Cours Cap-Hornier   MARITIME MUSEUM

(Museum of the Cape Horn Route; Map p256; ☎ 02 99 40 71 58; Tour Solidor; adult/child €6/3; ⊙ 10am-noon & 2-6pm daily Apr-Sep, closed Mon Oct-Mar) Housed in the 14th-century **Tour Solidor**, this museum presents the life of the sailors who followed the dangerous Cape Horn route around the southern tip of South America. It offers superb views from the top of the tower.

Grand Aquarium   AQUARIUM

(☎ 02 99 21 19 00; www.aquarium-st-malo.com; av Général Patton; adult/child €16/12; ⊙ 9.30am-9pm mid-Jul–mid-Aug, 9.30am-8pm early-Jul & late Aug, 10am-6pm mid-Jan–Jun & Sep-Dec; 🅿 C1, C2) A must-see for families, this aquarium is about 4km south of the city centre. Kids will adore the 'Nautibus' ride – a simulated descent aboard an underwater submarine – and the *bassin tactile* (touch pool), where they can fondle rays and turbots. The exhibits on local marine life, tropical reefs and mangrove forests are also very strong. Allow around two hours for a visit. Buses C1 and C2 from the train station pass by every half-hour.

🏃 Activities

Compagnie Corsaire   BOAT TRIPS

(Map p258; ☎ 08 25 13 81 00; www.compagnie corsaire.com) Compagnie Corsaire runs four-hour *pêche en mer* (deep-sea fishing; €42) trips. It also runs ferries from just outside Porte de Dinan to: Bay of St-Malo (adult/child €20.50/12.30, 1½ hours), Bay of Cancale (adult/child €30.30/18.20, 2½ hours), Dinan (adult/child return €32.50/19.50, April to September), Île Cézembre (adult/child return €15/9, daily April to September) and Îles Chausey (adult/child return €33.70/20.20, two to five departures a week April to September).

Les Corsaires Malouins   KAYAKING

(Map p258; ☎ 02 99 40 92 04; www.kayakdemer35. fr; Plage de Bon Secours; outings €25-32; ⊙ by res-

---

ervation Jul-Sep) Wanna see the Bay of St-Malo from a different perspective? The smooth seas hugging the bay combined with varied sea- and landscapes make St-Malo prime sea-kayaking turf. This outfit runs guided trips around the bay. Beginners are welcome.

🏄 Beaches

You can splash in the protected tidal pool west of the city walls at **Plage de Bon Secours** (Map p258) or climb its ladder to jump into the sea. St-Servan's **Plage des Bas Sablons** has a cement wall to keep the sea from receding completely at low tide. The much larger **Grande Plage** stretches northeast along the isthmus of Le Sillon. Spectacular sunsets can be seen from Grande Plage to Plage des Bas Sablons. Less-crowded **Plage de Rochebonne** is another 1km to the northeast.

🛏 Sleeping

St-Malo has plenty of hotels, but accommodation books up quickly in summer and it's essential to reserve in advance. If you get stuck, the tourist office has regular updates of availability. You can also try the nearby towns of Cancale, Dinan and their surrounds.

🛏 Intra Muros

Hôtel San Pedro HOTEL €
(Map p258; ☑ 02 99 40 88 57; www.sanpedro-hotel.com; 1 rue Ste-Anne; s €65-69, d €75-83; 🛜) Tucked at the back of the old city, the San Pedro has a cool, crisp, neutral-toned decor with subtle splashes of yellow paint, friendly service, great breakfast, private parking (€10) and a few bikes available for free. It features 12 rooms on four floors served by a miniature lift (forget those big suitcases!); two rooms come with sea views.

Le Nautilus HOTEL €
(☑ 02 99 40 42 27; www.hotel-lenautilus-saint-malo.com; 9 rue de la Corne de Cerf; s €49-63, d €70-78; ⊘ Feb-Nov; 🛜) With efficient, friendly service and comfortable yet smallish rooms, this supercentral two-star abode offers excellent value. The decor has been freshened up with smartly finished bathrooms and light yellow walls. The elevator is an unexpected bonus for a hotel in this price range.

Accroche Cœur B&B €€
(Map p258; ☑ 02 99 40 43 63, 06 07 10 80 22; www.accrochecoeursaintmalo.fr; 9 rue Thévenard; d incl breakfast €120-145; 🛜📶) Is this St-Malo's best-kept secret? There are five upper-crust *chambres d'hôte* in this solid townhouse tucked into a side street in the historic centre. Top of the heap is the vast Brieg suite, which is suitable for a family, but the Mac Low, which boasts polished wood beams, elegant furniture and sparkling bathroom, isn't a bad backup.

Downstairs, a lavish breakfast is served in a majestic salon with ancient stone walls, a big fireplace and stout antique ceiling beams.

Hôtel Quic en Groigne HOTEL €€
(Map p258; ☑ 02 99 20 22 20; www.quic-en-groigne.com; 8 rue d'Estrées; s €69-72, d €79-112; ⊘ Feb-Dec; 🛜) This exceptional hotel has 15 recently renovated rooms that are the epitome of clean, simple style. If good value for money isn't enough then also consider the excellent service and an ideal location on a quiet, old town street just a few metres from a beach. The icing on the cake: the convenience of secure lock-up parking (€13; five spaces only) in a city where parking can be downright hellish. No lift, but there are only two floors.

La Maison des Armateurs LUXURY HOTEL €€€
(☑ 02 99 40 87 70; www.maisondesarmateurs.com; 6 Grand Rue; d €95-275, ste €200-420; ⊘ Jan-Nov; ❄🛜📶) No language barrier here – La Maison des Armateurs is run by a helpful French-American couple. Despite the austere granite-fronted setting, the inside of this sassy four-star hotel is all sexy, modern minimalism: modern furniture throughout, gleaming bathrooms with power showers and cool chocolate, pale orange and neutral grey tones. Families can plump for the super-sized suites. Check the website for deals.

🛏 Beyond the Walls

Camping de la Cité d'Alet CAMPGROUND €
(Map p256; ☑ 02 99 81 60 91; allée Gaston Buy, St-Servan; per 2-person tent €16; 🛜) Perched on a peninsula, this campground has panoramic 360-degree views and is close to beaches and some lively bars.

Auberge de Jeunesse – Ethic Etapes Patrick Varangot HOSTEL €
(☑ 02 99 40 29 80; www.centrevarangot.com; 37 av du Père Umbricht, Paramé; s/dm incl breakfast €45/24; @🛜) This efficient hostel scores high on amenities, with a well-equipped communal kitchen, a restaurant, a bar, laundry service, private parking and free sports facilities. It has 285 beds, with each room accommodating two to five beds and an en-suite bathroom. It's in a calm neighbourhood, a five-minute walk from Plage de Rochebonne beach. Take bus 3 from the train station.

Intra Muros

Café Couette Saint-Malo   B&B €

(Map p256; ☑02 99 81 61 05; www.cafe-couette
-saintmalo.com; 3 rue Dauphine, St-Servan; s/d incl
breakfast €70/85; ☎) This unfussy B&B is set
just back from Plage des Bas-Sablons on a
road filled with neighbourhood restaurants.
Five spic-and-span rooms with tiny bathrooms are available.

Maison Angélus   B&B €€

(☑02 99 40 66 79; www.maisonangelus.com; 82
av Pasteur; d incl breakfast €110-130; ☎) This
three-room B&B, housed inside a tastefully
restored 19th-century building, is a tranquil
respite from the crowds of the walled city,
and it's ideally situated just a two-minute
stroll from the Grande Plage. You'll love the
cosy lounge areas and the backyard garden
oasis. Your Italian hosts, Giulio and Cristina,
complete the charming picture and serve
a delicious breakfast and a superb Italian
dinner (€30).

Le Valmarin   HISTORIC HOTEL €€

(Map p256; ☑02 99 81 94 76; www.levalmarin.com;
7 rue Jean XXIII, St-Servan; d €100-165; ☎⚑) If
you're yearning for a bit of aristocratic atmosphere then this 18th-century mansion
should do the job nicely. It has 12 high-
ceilinged rooms dressed in late-19th-century
style and glorious gardens full of spring
flowers and shady trees. Minus: some bathrooms feel a bit dated. It's a soothing escape
from the St-Malo hubbub, on the edge of the
village-like St-Servan quarter. The largest
rooms are suitable for families. Rental bikes
are available. Shame that wi-fi is extra.

✕ Eating

St-Malo has some superb places to eat, but it
also has a lot of mediocre tourist-style eateries (mainly those around the Porte St-Vincent
and Grande Porte).

Self-caterers should head to **La Maison
du Beurre** (Map p258; ☑02 99 40 88 79; www.

Intra Muros

lebeurrebordier.com; 7 rue de l'Orme; ⊘9am-1pm & 3.30-7.30pm Tue-Sat, 9am-1pm Mon & Sun). Cheeses and butters handmade in Jean-Yves Bordier's shop are shipped to famous restaurants all over the world.

Le Bulot
BISTRO €

(Map p256; ☑02 99 81 07 11; www.lebulot.com; 13 quai Sébastopol; mains €15-19, menus €16-25; ⊘noon-2pm & 7-10pm Mon-Sat) A laid-back neighbourhood bistro with a modern feel and views over the Port-Solidor (best appreciated on sunny days from the raised wooden terrace). There's a short menu of tasty French classics such as *brandade de morue* (salt cod purée) and chicken marinated in lemon.

Le Corps de Garde
CRÊPERIE €

(Map p258; ☑02 99 40 91 46; www.le-corps-de-garde.com; 3 montée Notre-Dame; mains €4-10; ⊘noon-10pm) The main draw of this unfussy crêperie is its location right beside the ramparts – be sure to ask for an outside table if you're a sucker for sunset views. Crêpes and *galettes* form the menu's backbone.

La Bouche en Folie
MODERN FRENCH €€

(Map p258; ☑06 72 49 08 89; 14 rue du Boyer; lunch menus €16-18, other menus €26-30; ⊘noon-1.30pm & 7-9.30pm Thu-Mon) Well off the tourist trail, this cool culinary outpost casts a modern spin on French staples. Dishes are elegantly presented and filled with subtle flavours, and the lunch *menus* are excellent value. Decked out in designer wallpaper and tiny tables, it feels like dining in a stylish friend's living room.

★ L'Absinthe
MODERN FRENCH €€

(Map p258; ☑02 99 40 26 15; www.restaurant-absinthe-cafe.fr; 1 rue de l'Orme; mains €18-24, menus €28-45; ⊘noon-2pm & 7-10pm) Hidden away in a quiet street near the covered market, this fab (and very French) eatery is housed in an imposing 17th-century building. Ingredients fresh from the nearby market are whipped into shape by the talented chef, Stéphane Brebel, and served in cosy surrounds. The wine list is another hit, with an all-French cast from white to red and rosé.

Le Cambusier
MODERN FRENCH €€

(Map p258; ☑02 99 20 18 42; www.cambusier.fr; 6 rue des Cordiers; mains €18-28, lunch menus €16-22; ⊘noon-2pm & 7-9pm) With its ambient lighting, honey-coloured parquet flooring and large B&W shots of fishermen enlivening the dining room, Le Cambusier can do no wrong. Run by a talented husband-and-wife team, it's known across the city for its upmarket take on classic French cuisine. Since *madame* is also a sommelier, let things rip with the list of well-chosen French tipples.

Le Chalut
SEAFOOD €€

(Map p258; ☑02 99 56 71 58; 8 rue de la Corne de Cerf; mains €30, menus €25-58; ⊘12.15-1.15pm & 7.15-9.15pm Wed-Sun) This unremarkable-looking establishment is, in fact, St-Malo's most celebrated restaurant. Its kitchen overflows with the best the Breton coastline has to offer – buttered turbot, line-caught sea bass, crab and scallops. Feel like splashing out? Plump for the 'all lobster' *menu*.

Le Bistro de Jean
BISTRO €€

(Map p258; ☑02 99 40 98 68; 6 rue de la Corne de Cerf; mains €19-20, menus €14-19; ⊘noon-1.30pm Mon-Sat, 7-9.15pm Mon, Tue, Thu & Fri) Want to know where the locals choose to eat inside the walls? Peer through the windows of this lively, authentic bistro and you'll get your answer. The place is packed at lunchtime with loyal regulars, which is a good sign. The flavourful cuisine, based on fresh ingredients, includes duck breast, lamb shanks and

BRITTANY ST-MALO

LA CAFE DU COIN D'EN BAS DE LA RUE DU BOUT DE LA VILLE D'EN FACE DU PORT... LA JAVA

The word eccentric must have been coined to describe this extraordinarily named cafe (Map p258; 02 99 56 41 90; www.lajavacafe.com; 3 rue Ste-Barbe; ⏲ 8.51am-8.44pm Mon-Fri, 9.31am-11.32pm Sat, 9.31am-8.44pm Sun, 8.51am-11.32pm daily mid-Jul–mid-Aug). Think part-museum, part–toy-shop and a work of art from a twisted mind. French accordion music plays in the background and the beady eyes of hundreds of dolls and puppets keep watch from shelves and wall alcoves. Customers sit on swings, not chairs. Even the opening times are odd. And the drinks? Well they're actually quite sane: 100 different kinds of coffee and a quality beer range.

succulent line-caught sea bass. Excellent homemade desserts, too.

Drinking & Nightlife

L'Alchimiste
BAR

(Map p258; 7 rue St-Thomas; ⏲ 5pm-1am Tue-Sun) Ben Harper–style music creates a mellow backdrop at this magical place filled with old books and a toy flying fox. Take a seat at the bar draped with a red tasselled theatre curtain, on the carved timber mezzanine (including a pulpit) or in the wood-heated basement.

L'Aviso
BAR

(Map p258; 12 rue Point du Jour; ⏲ 6pm-2am) This cosy place has more than 300 beers on offer, with over 10 – including Breton beer – on tap. If you can't decide, ask the friendly owner/connoisseur. It's the old-fashioned place with the Duvel Beer sign.

ⓘ Information

Tourist Office (Map p258; 08 25 13 52 00; www.saint-malo-tourisme.com; esplanade St-Vincent; ⏲ 9am-7.30pm Mon-Sat, 10am-6pm Sun) Just outside the walls.

ⓘ Getting There & Away

BOAT

Brittany Ferries (www.brittany-ferries.com) sails between St-Malo and Portsmouth, and **Condor Ferries** (www.condorferries.co.uk) runs to/from Poole and Weymouth via Jersey or Guernsey. Car ferries leave from the **Gare Maritime du Naye** (Map p256).

In July and August **Compagnie Corsaire** (08 25 13 80 35; www.compagniecorsaire.com; adult/child return €8.10/5.30) runs a Bus de Mer shuttle service (10 minutes, at least half-hourly) between St-Malo and Dinard. Outside the July/August peak season both frequency and cost fall.

BUS

All intercity buses stop by the train station. **Keolis St-Malo** (www.ksma.fr) has services to Cancale (€1.25, 30 minutes). **Illenoo** (www.illenoo-services.fr) services run to Dinard (€2.30, 30 minutes, hourly) and Rennes (€5.10, one to 1½ hours, three to six daily). **Tibus** (08 10 22 22 22; www.tibus.fr) buses go to Dinan (€2, 50 minutes, three to eight daily).

CAR

Various hire-car firms can be found at the train station and the Gare Maritime du Naye. There are plenty of pay car parks (from €5 per day) around the edge of Intra muros.

TRAIN

Various trains run from St-Malo:

Dinan €10, one hour, six daily (requiring a change in Dol de Bretagne)

Paris Montparnasse €50 to €66, three hours, three direct TGVs daily

Rennes €14.60, one hour, roughly hourly

ⓘ Getting Around

St-Malo city buses (single journey €1.25, 24-hour pass €3.60) operate until about 8pm, with some lines extending until around midnight in summer. Between esplanade St-Vincent and the train station, take buses C1 or C2.

For a taxi call 02 99 81 30 30.

Dinard

POP 11,230

Visiting Dinard 'in season' is a little like stepping into one of the canvases Picasso painted here in the 1920s. Belle époque mansions built into the cliffs form a timeless backdrop to the beach dotted with blue-and-white striped bathing tents and the beachside carnival. Out of season, when holidaymakers have packed up their buckets and spades, the town is decidedly dormant, but wintry walks along the coastal paths are spectacular.

◉ Sights

Barrage de la Rance
BRIDGE

This 750m bridge over the Rance estuary carries the D168 between St-Malo and Dinard, lopping a good 30km off the journey. A feat of hydroelectrics, the Usine Marémotrice de la Rance (below the bridge) generates electricity by harnessing the lower estuary's extraordinarily high tidal range – a difference of 13.5m between high and low tide.

🏊 Beaches

Framed by fashionable hotels, a casino and neo-Gothic villas, Plage de l'Écluse (Grande Plage) is the perfect place to shade yourself in style by renting one of Dinard's trademark blue-and-white striped bathing tents. Reproductions of Picasso's paintings are often planted in the sand here in high summer. When the Plage de l'Écluse gets too crowded, savvy Dinardais take refuge at the town's smaller beaches, including Plage du Prieuré, 1km to the south, and Plage de St-Énogat, 1km to the west.

🛏 Sleeping

Dinard's prices match its cachet: budget travellers may want to consider staying in St Malo and catching the ferry or strolling across.

Camping Le Port Blanc   CAMPGROUND €
(📞 02 99 46 10 74; www.camping-port-blanc.com; rue du Sergent Boulanger; site per 2 adults from €25; ⊙ Apr–Sep; 📶) You'll find this campground close to the beach, about 2km west of Plage de l'Écluse. There's direct access to the sand.

Hôtel Printania   HOTEL €€
(📞 02 99 46 13 07; www.printaniahotel.com; 5 av George V; s €76-130, d €90-167; ⊙ Mar–mid-Nov; 📶) This is a charmingly folkloric, Breton-style hotel, complete with wood-and-leather furniture and a superb location overlooking the Baie du Prieuré. Guest rooms with a sea view command an eye-watering premium; otherwise get your fill of the grand views across the water to St-Servan at breakfast. The waitresses in the in-house restaurant wear traditional Breton dress. Yes, really!

Hôtel de la Plage   HOTEL €€
(📞 02 99 46 14 87; www.hoteldelaplage-dinard.com; 3 bd Féart; d €75-138; 📶) Attractive, freshly renovated rooms with modern bathrooms and an enviable location a mere stone's throw away from the beach make this one of the best deals in town. Priciers rooms come with sea views.

🍴 Eating

★ **Le Balafon**   MODERN FRENCH €€
(📞 02 99 46 14 81; www.lebalafon-restaurant-dinard. fr; 31 rue de la Vallée; mains €17-24, lunch menu €17,

other menus €29-39; ⊙ noon-2pm & 7-9.30pm Tue-Sat, noon-2pm Sun) Away from the tourist hustle and bustle of the seafront, this is a quality modern neighbourhood bistro serving freshly made meals using produce from the nearby market. The daily lunch *menu* consists of a couple of well-chosen and presented dishes, usually one fish and one meat. It's totally unpretentious, well priced and many locals rate it as the best place in town.

In fair weather, the inviting courtyard is a plus.

La Gonelle   SEAFOOD €€
(📞 02 99 16 40 47; www.lagonelle.com; promenade du Clair de Lune; mains €16-30; ⊙ noon-2pm & 7-10pm Thu-Mon mid-Apr–Jun & Sep, daily Jul & Aug) Perched beside the granite quays of the Anse du Bec, Dinard's sophisticated answer to a seafood takeaway serves fabulously fresh crab, lobster, oysters, clams and fish from the open-fronted counter, or you can grab one of the portside patio tables.

La Passerelle du Clair de Lune   MODERN FRENCH €€
(📞 02 99 16 96 37; www.la-passerelle-restaurant. com; 3 av Georges V; menus €25-38; ⊙ noon-2pm & 8-9.30pm Thu-Mon) Creative, modern seafood is served up at this intimate little restaurant with stunning views over the former home of the fish now sitting on your plate.

ℹ Information

Tourist Office (📞 02 99 46 94 12; www.ot-dinard.com; 2 bd Féart; ⊙ 9.30am-12.15pm & 2-6pm Mon-Sat) Staff book accommodation for free. Two-hour guided walks (adult/child €5/3) explaining the town's history, art and architecture (in English and French) depart from here. They also dole out maps and leaflets detailing self-guided walking tours taking in the best of the town's architecture.

ℹ Getting There & Away

AIR

Ryanair (www.ryanair.com) has daily flights to and from London Stansted as well as flights to Bradford-Leeds and East Midlands. It's also possible to fly to Guernsey. There's no public transport from Dinard airport (5km from Dinard) to town (or to neighbouring St-Malo); a daytime/evening taxi from Dinard to the airport costs around €15/23.

BOAT

Compagnie Corsaire (📞 08 25 13 81 00; www. compagniecorsaire.com) runs a Bus de Mer shuttle service (10 minutes) between St-Malo and Dinard, operating at least half-hourly. Outside the July/ August peak season both frequency and cost fall.

BRITTANY DINARD

BUS

Illenoo (www.illenoo-services.fr) buses connect Dinard and the train station in St-Malo (€2.30, 30 minutes, hourly). Le Gallic bus stop, outside the tourist office, is the most convenient. Several buses travel to Rennes (€5.10, two hours).

Cancale

POP 5440

Tucked into the curve of a shimmering shell-shaped bay, the idyllic little fishing port of Cancale, 14km east of St-Malo, is famed for its offshore *parcs à huîtres* (oyster beds) that stretch for kilometres around the surrounding coastline. There's no real beach here but the waterfront is a fun place to stroll and soak up the atmosphere. You can also drive to Pointe du Grouin, a stunning headland and a nature reserve about 7km north of town.

◎ Sights

Ferme Marine   FARM
(☑ 02 99 89 69 99; www.ferme-marine.com; corniche de l'Aurore; adult/child €7/3.70; ⊙ guided tours in French 11am, 3pm & 5pm Jul–mid-Sep, in English 2pm) Learn about the art of *ostréiculture* (oyster farming) at this well-organised museum a couple of kilometres southwest of the port.

⎙ Sleeping

Note that Cancale is an easy day trip from St-Malo or Dinard and there are dozens of cheap and excellent *chambres d'hôte* in the region – ask at the tourist office for a full list.

★Latitude Breizh Café   B&B €€
(☑ 02 99 89 61 76; www.breizhcafe.com; 7 quai Thomas; d incl breakfast €98-108; ☢⊞) You'll need to book early to bag your spot at this delightful *maison d'hôte* right on the harbourfront. It offers five fancy rooms all christened after apple varieties, ranging from coquettish Guillevic (balcony, views of the oyster parks) to sexy Kermerien (full frame bay views, gleaming bathrooms) and amply-sized Rouget de Dol (a two-room suite, ideal for families). The crêperie downstairs (same management) is top-notch.

La Pointe du Grouin   HOTEL €€
(☑ 02 99 89 60 55; www.hotelpointedugrouin.com; Pointe du Grouin; d €95-130; ⊙ Apr–mid-Nov; ☢) A gracious welcome and cracking sea views are first to greet you at this family-owned abode poised on a rocky promontory at Pointe du Grouin, a few kilometres north of town. The 15 rooms are bright, comfy, and designed to

harmonise with the sea and sky just outside your window. The attached restaurant is equally popular.

For outdoorsy types, there's a coastal path just in front.

Le Duguay-Trouin   HOTEL €€
(☑ 02 23 15 12 07; www.hotelduguaytrouin.com; 11 quai Duguay-Trouin; d €90-110; ☢⊞) This terrific two-star bet right on the harbour is just about as cosy as it gets, with seven imaginatively decorated rooms with period furnishings and thoughtful touches throughout. Not all rooms have sea views, though.

✖ Eating

★Breizh Café   CRÊPERIE €
(☑ 02 99 89 61 76; www.breizhcafe.com; 7 quai Thomas; mains €5-14; ⊙ noon-3pm & 7.30-11pm Thu-Mon) Not your average crêperie, the Breizh Café is renowned for its gourmet crêpes and *galettes* made from organic flours. The cappuccino-and-cream decor gives it a fresh, modern feel, and the crêpes are really first-class. Where else could you savour a *galette* stuffed with langoustines and cheese? Wash it all down with a tipple from their range of top-notch local ciders.

Le Troquet   BISTRO €€
(☑ 02 99 89 99 42; www.restaurant-letroquet-cancale.fr; 19 quai Gambetta; mains €18-26, lunch menus €18-26, other menu €39) Of the dozens of waterside restaurants you can find at the port, this sleek contemporary *troquet* (bistro) run by *artisan cuisinier* Laurent Helleu is the pick of the shoal. His *raison d'être* is locally bought, market-fresh ingredients, cooked with a minimum of fuss to bring out their natural flavours. Unsurprisingly in Cancale,

---

DON'T MISS

OYSTERS APLENTY

One of the most authentic seafood experiences you'll ever have awaits you in Cancale. Local fishers sell their catch directly from stalls clustered by the Pointe des Crolles lighthouse at the **Marché aux Huîtres** (Pointe des Crolles; 12 oysters from €4; ⊙ 9am-6pm). Point to the ones you want, and they'll be shucked, dashed with lemon and served before your eyes, and *voilà*, one perfect lunch.

Note that oysters are numbered according to size and quality.

seafood features heavily. Don't miss the killer far Breton (Breton cake).

Côté Mer
SEAFOOD €€
(☑ 02 99 89 66 08; www.restaurant-cotemer.fr; 4 rue Ernest Lamort; mains €18-27, menus €24-61; ☺ noon-1.30pm & 7.30-9pm Mon & Thu-Sat, noon-1.30pm Sun & Tue) A fine portside position set back from the downtown din makes this well-regarded restaurant a must for seafoodies. A big picture window gives lovely views of the bay, while inside terracotta tiles, crisp white tablecloths, impeccably folded napkins and the odd colourful painting on the walls conjure a quietly stylish feel.

★ Le Coquillage
GASTRONOMIC €€€
(☑ 02 99 89 64 76; www.maisons-de-bricourt.com; D155, rte du Mont St-Michel, Le Buot; lunch menu €31, other menus €75-139; ☺ noon-2pm & 7-9pm) Super chef Olivier Roellinger's sumptuous restaurant is housed in the extremely impressive Château Richeux, 4km to the south of Cancale. Roellinger's creations have earned him three Michelin stars and you won't have trouble seeing why if you're lucky enough to get a table here. The food takes in the culinary highlights of both Brittany and Normandy, all beautifully cooked and imaginatively served.

As well as offering rooms at Château Richeux, Roellinger offers a range of cottages and other deluxe accommodation around Cancale. See the website for details. Booking well ahead is essential.

ⓘ Information

Tourist Office (☑ 02 99 89 63 72; www.cancale-tourisme.fr; 44 rue du Port; ☺ 9.30am-1pm & 2.30-7pm) At the top of rue du Port. In July and August there's an annexe on quai Gambetta.

ⓘ Getting There & Around

Buses stop behind the church on place Lucidas and at Port de la Houle, next to the fish market. **Keolis St-Malo** (www.ksma.fr) has year-round services to and from St-Malo (€1.25, 30 minutes).

Dinan
POP 11,600
Set high above the fast-flowing Rance River, the narrow cobblestone streets and squares lined with crooked half-timbered houses of Dinan's old town are straight out of the Middle Ages – something that's not lost on the deluge of summer tourists; by around 6pm though, someone waves a magic wand and most of them vanish and a sense of calm befalls the town. Needless to say, it's well worth sticking around for a night or two.

◉ Sights & Activities

Château-musée de Dinan
MUSEUM
(☑ 02 96 39 45 20; rue du Château; admission €4.60; ☺ 10am-6pm, closed Jan) The town's museum is atmospherically housed in the keep of Dinan's ruined 14th-century château. It showcases the town's history and has information sheets in various languages.

Tour Ste-Catherine
TOWER
Just east of Basilique St-Sauveur, beyond the tiny **Jardin Anglais** (English Garden), a former cemetery and nowadays a pleasant little park, is the 13th-century Tour Ste-Catherine, which has great views down over the viaduct and port.

Basilique St-Sauveur
CHURCH
(place St-Sauveur; ☺ 9am-6pm, closed during services) With its soaring Gothic chancel, the Basilique St-Sauveur contains a 14th-century grave slab in its north transept reputed to contain the heart of Bertrand du Guesclin, a 14th-century knight who was noted for his hatred of the English and his fierce battles to expel them. Ironically, Dinan today has one of the largest English expat communities in Brittany.

Tour de l'Horloge
TOWER
(☑ 02 96 87 02 26; rue de l'Horloge; adult/child €4/free; ☺ 10am-6.30pm Jun-Sep) The half-timbered houses overhanging place des Cordeliers and place des Merciers mark the heart of the old town. A few paces south, climb up to the little balcony of this 15th-century clock tower whose chimes ring every quarter hour.

Vieux Pont
HISTORIC QUARTER
Be sure to head downhill along the steep cobbles of **rue du Jerzual** and **rue du Petit Fort**, two of the best-preserved streets in Brittany. Both are lined with art galleries, antiques shops and restaurants, and lead down to the **Vieux Pont** (Old Bridge). From here the pretty little port, hemmed by restaurants and cafes, extends northwards, while the 19th-century **Viaduc de Dinan** soars high above to the south.

Jaman IV
BOAT TRIP
(☑ 02 96 39 28 41; www.vedettejamaniv.com; adult/child €13/3.50; ☺ 11am, 2.30pm, 4pm & 5.30pm Jun-Sep) This converted barge offers one-hour cruises up the Rance river past the Abbaye St-Magloire. It departs from the port in Dinan.

BRETON LANGUAGE REDUX

Throughout Brittany you'll see bilingual Breton street and transport signs, and many other occurrences of the language popping up. Even though all Breton speakers also speak French, this is seen as an important gesture to normalising the use of a language that has been stigmatised (and even banned) throughout much of the early and mid-20th century.

Historically speaking, Breton is a Celtic language related to Cornish and Welsh, and more distantly to Irish and Scottish Gaelic. Following on from the French Revolution, the government banned the teaching of Breton in schools, punishing children who spoke their mother tongue. Between 1950 and 1990 there was an 80% reduction in Breton usage.

The seeds of the language's revival were planted in the 1960s, particularly after France's May 1968 protests, driven by the younger generation rebelling against their oppressed cultural heritage. Bringing about the rebirth of the language, no longer passed on generationally, wasn't straightforward. As it is more often spoken than written (and both spoken and written with regional differences), settling on a standardised Breton for teaching in schools remains a complex issue.

Breton now extends beyond its historic boundaries. Originally, Basse Bretagne (Lower Brittany, in the west) spoke variants of the Breton language, while Haute Bretagne (Upper Brittany, in the east, including areas such as St-Malo) spoke Gallo, a language similar to French. But today you'll find Breton signage in Rennes' metro stations and in many other parts of the east, symbolising Brittany's culture across the entire region.

🎭 Festivals & Events

Fête des Remparts　　　　MEDIEVAL FESTIVAL
(www.fete-remparts-dinan.com) No fewer than 100,000 visitors turn up to join Dinannais townsfolk dressed in medieval garb for the two-day Fête des Remparts, held in late July every even-numbered year.

🛏 Sleeping

In summer, advance reservations are recommended. Ask the tourist office for a list of *chambres d'hôte* in the surrounding area.

Camping Municipal Châteaubriand　　　CAMPGROUND €
(☑ 02 96 39 11 96; 103 rue Chateaubriand; per adult/tent/car €2.90/3.20/2.35; ☉ Jun-Sep) This campground at the foot of the ramparts is the closest to the old town.

★ La Maison Pavie　　　　B&B €€
(☑ 02 96 84 45 37; www.lamaisonpavie.com; 12 place St-Sauveur; d incl breakfast €99-150; ☎) If you ever dreamt of staying in a 15th-century half-timbered house, look no further than this sumptuous B&B in the heart of Dinan. The building's medieval character and historic ambience have been lovingly preserved during refurbishment while modern comforts and designer fittings have been added – you have to see the architectural elements and furnishings of the rooms to believe them.

The private garden at the back is a delight, and dinner meals can be arranged (€35). On the downside, some stairs are quite steep and narrow – but you wanted to stay in a historic building, right? Good English is spoken.

Hôtel de la Porte St-Malo　　　HOTEL €€
(☑ 02 96 39 19 76; www.hotelportemalo.com; 35 rue St-Malo; s €71, d €89-103; ☎) Solid value is offered by this charming stone two-star hotel in the town's oldest quarter (but, mercifully, slightly out of the way of the passing crowds). Look out for special offers on its website.

Hôtel Arvor　　　　HOTEL €€
(☑ 02 96 39 21 22; www.hotelarvordinan.com; 5 rue Pavie; d €88-125; ☉ Feb-Dec; ☎) It's hard to believe that this sleek establishment was once a Jacobin convent. Expect thoroughly modern bathrooms, a few fancy decorative touches and calm colour tones (but dull corridors). The charming tearoom is a great place to relax after a long day's sightseeing. Service is excellent and it's an all-round good deal. Bonus: there's (limited) private parking.

🍴 Eating & Drinking

The old city has some really charming (and surprisingly good-value) eateries and bars, with more along the river at the old port.

Crêperie Ahna　　　　CRÊPERIE €
(☑ 02 96 39 09 13; 7 rue de la Poissonnerie; mains €6-18; ☉ noon-2pm & 7-9.30pm Mon-Sat) Run by the same family for four generations and with such unusual delights as a *galette* with duck and snail butter (better than it sounds!), this place deserves its reputation as one of the best crêperies in town. It also serves grilled meats

and excellent ice creams. It's a good idea to reserve a table.

La Courtine
BISTRO €

(☑ 02 96 39 74 41; 6 rue de la Croix; mains €15-18, lunch menus €13-15; ☺ noon-1.30pm & 7-8.30pm Tue-Sat) Just steps from the animated place Duclos is this snug bistro with wood beams and stone walls serving classic French dishes eaten for oodles of centuries. Its *filet mignon de veau* (veal fillet) and *souris d'agneau confite au cidre* (lamb shank stewed in cider) are not to be scoffed at. It also has a list of well-chosen French tipples by the glass.

Le Cantorbery
TRADITIONAL FRENCH €€

(☑ 02 96 39 02 52; 6 rue Ste-Claire; mains €17-26, menus €31-42; ☺ noon-1.45pm & 7-9.30pm Thu-Tue) Occupying a magnificent 17th-century house, this elegant, intimate restaurant is perfect for wining and dining your beloved over a romantic lunch or dinner. Its traditional menu (based on beef, grilled fish and seafood, including *coquilles St-Jacques* – scallops – from St-Brieuc) changes in accordance with the seasons.

ⓘ Information

Tourist Office (☑ 02 96 87 69 76; www.dinan-tourisme.com; 9 rue du Château; ☺ 9.30am-7pm Mon-Sat, 10am-12.30pm & 2-6pm Sun) It has a free map and leaflet, available in several languages (including English), which plots two walking itineraries around town.

ⓘ Getting There & Around

BUS

Buses leave from place Duclos and the bus station. **Illenoo** (☑ 08 10 35 10 35; www.illenoo-services.fr) runs several daily services:
Dinard €3.30, 30 minutes
Rennes €5.10, 1¼ hours

TRAIN

Change in Dol de Bretagne:
Rennes from €15.30, one hour
St-Malo €10, one hour, five daily

Paimpol

POP 8240

Set around a working fishing harbour and ringed by half-timbered buildings, Paimpol is rich in history. It was the one-time home port of the Icelandic fishery, when the town's fishermen would set sail to the seas around Iceland for seven months or more at a stretch. It's also rich in legends – the fishermen lost

at sea are recalled in folk tales and *chants de marins* (sea shanties).

◉ Sights & Activities

Enquire at the tourist office about canoeing and kayaking operators.

★ La Vapeur du Trieux
TOURIST TRAIN

(☑ 08 92 39 14 27; www.vapeurdutrieux.com; adult/child return €24.50/12.50; ☺ May-Sep) Steam buffs and lovers of fine scenery will be in seventh heaven aboard the chuffing carriages of this 1922 steam train that plies the old railway line between Paimpol and Pontrieux, where there's time for a pleasant meal and a stroll before the return journey. Reserve at least one day ahead.

Abbaye de Beauport
ABBEY

(☑ 02 96 55 18 58; www.abbaye-beauport.com; rte de Kérity; adult/child €6/3.50; ☺ 10am-7pm) If you have wheels (or you're up for a glorious 1½-hour walk along the seashore from the town harbour), head 3.5km east of Paimpol to this romantic 18th-century abbey that plays host to frequent art and sculpture exhibitions. En route, stop at the Pointe de Guilben for beautiful bay views. The tourist office has free maps.

Musée de la Mer
MARITIME MUSEUM

(Sea Museum; ☑ 02 96 22 02 19; rue Labenne; adult/child €4/free; ☺ 10.30am-12.30pm & 2-6.30pm) This splendid little museum charts the Paimpol region's maritime history and is, rather appropriately, set in a former cod-drying factory. It's a treasure-trove of nautical artefacts, from seine nets and canvas sails to vintage posters and fishing outfits.

✲ Festivals & Events

Festival du Chant de Marin
CULTURAL FESTIVAL

(www.paimpol-festival.com) Traditional Breton dancing takes place on the quays in August every odd-numbered year.

⌖ Sleeping & Eating

Hôtel de la Marne
HOTEL €

(☑ 02 96 16 33 41; www.hoteldelamarne-paimpol.fr; 30 rue de la Marne; d €60-75; ☎) This granite inn ranks as highly in the dining stakes as it does in the sleeping. All rooms have been recently modernised and upgraded. Its restaurant cooks up top-notch regional cuisine (*menus* from €21), has tip-top presentation and ace desserts. It's a five-minute walk to the pleasure-ports cafes.

❶ Information

Tourist Office (☑ 02 96 20 83 16; www.
paimpol-goelo.com; place de la République;
⊙ 9.30am-7.30pm Mon-Sat, 9.30am-12.30pm &
4-6pm Sun) Sells local rambling guides.

❶ Getting There & Around

Tibus (☑ 08 10 22 22 22; www.tibus.fr) runs
buses to and from St-Brieuc (€2, 1½ hours). In
summer most continue to Pointe L'Arcouest.

There are five daily trains between Paimpol
and Guingamp (€7.70, one hour), where you
can pick up connections to Brest, St-Brieuc and
Rennes.

FINISTÈRE

The country's westernmost *département,*
Finistère has a wind-whipped coastline scattered with lighthouses and beacons lashed by
waves. Finistère's southern prow, Cornouaille,
takes its name from early Celts who sailed
from Cornwall and other parts of Britain to
settle here, and today it harbours the Breton
language, customs and culture. Wild and mysterious, this is, for many people, the most enticing corner of an enticing region.

Roscoff

POP 3780

Unlike many of its industrial, less-than-
beautiful sister Channel ports, Roscoff (Rosko
in Breton) provides a captivating first glimpse
of Brittany. Granite houses dating from the
16th century wreathe the pretty docks, which
are surrounded by emerald-green fields producing cauliflowers, onions, tomatoes, new
potatoes and artichokes.

⊙ Sights & Activities

Église Notre Dame
de Kroaz-Batz   CHURCH
(place Lacaze Duthiers; ⊙ 9am-noon & 2-6pm) The
most obvious sight in Roscoff is this unusual
church at the heart of the old town. With its
Renaissance belfry rising above the flat landscape, the 16th-century Flamboyant Gothic
structure is one of Brittany's most impressive
churches.

Maison des Johnnies   MUSEUM
(☑ 02 98 61 25 48; 48 rue Brizeux; adult/child €4/
free; ⊙ tours 11am, 3pm & 5pm Mon-Fri) Photographs at this popular museum trace Roscoff's
roaming onion farmers, known as 'Johnnies',
from the early 19th century. A visit is by guid-

ed tour only. Call ahead for tour times, as they
change frequently.

Le Jardin Exotique de Roscoff   GARDEN
(☑ 02 98 61 29 19; www.jardinexotiqueroscoff.com;
Le Ruveic; adult/child €6/3; ⊙ 10am-7pm Jul-Aug,
10am-12.30pm & 2-6pm Apr-Jun, Sep & Oct, 2-5pm
daily Mar & Nov, closed Dec-Feb) Wander through
3500 species of exotic plants (many from
the southern hemisphere) at this impressive
garden. It's a well-signposted half-hour walk
southeast from the town centre.

Centre de Découverte
des Algues   MUSEUM
(☑ 02 98 69 77 05; www.algopole.fr; quai d'Auxerre;
⊙ 10am-12.30pm & 2.30-7pm Mon-Sat) **FREE** You
can learn about local seaweed harvesting at
this enthusiastically run museum, which also
organises guided walks and gives regular
free lectures (often in English and German).
There's also a shop.

🛏 Sleeping

Camping Aux
Quatre Saisons   CAMPGROUND €
(☑ 02 98 69 70 86; www.camping-aux4saisons.fr;
Le Ruguel; sites €16; ⊙ Easter-Sep; ⊛⊠) Close
to a sandy beach in the grounds of a lovely
19th-century mansion, this campground is
approximately 3km southwest of Roscoff.

★ Hôtel aux Tamaris   HOTEL €€
(☑ 02 98 61 22 99; www.hotel-aux-tamaris.com; 49
rue Edouard Corbière; d €85-115; ⊙ mid-Jan-Dec;
⊛) This family-run place in an old granite
building overlooking the water at the western end of town is an excellent choice, with
well-equipped, light, seabreeze-filled rooms,
all with a pleasant maritime aura and yacht
sails for ceilings (don't worry, there's a proper
ceiling, too!). Rooms with sea views cost a lot
more. Expect locally sourced goodies on the
breakfast table. Bikes are available for hire.

Hôtel du Centre   HOTEL €€
(☑ 02 98 61 24 25; www.chezjanie.fr; Le Port; d €104-
130; ⊙ mid-Feb-mid-Nov; ⊛) You couldn't wish
for a better Roscoff base than this refreshingly
simple hotel perched above Chez Janie's bistro. The layouts are awkward, but each room
has a maritime-themed poem painted on the
wall, and the bathrooms are in top nick. The
sea-view rooms looking out over the postcard-pretty old port are worth the extra cost.

Le Temps de Vivre   BOUTIQUE HOTEL €€
(☑ 02 98 19 33 19; www.letempsdevivre.net; 19 place
Lacaze Duthiers; d €150-210; ⊛🐾) This glamorous place is hidden away in a lovely stone

BUCOLIC BLISS & BEACHES ON BATZ

The Roscoff area may be light on beaches, but don't despair; skip across to the easily overlooked offshore island of Île de Batz and you'll find brilliant sand beaches (without the crowds). The largest (and best) beach is Grève Blanche on the northern shore.

A half-day is all you need to walk around this tiny morsel of paradise (no cars allowed) but we suggest that you spend a night on the island to soak up its deliciously divine atmosphere. You'll find a couple of charming B&Bs and eateries including **Ti Va Zadou** (🖉 02 98 61 76 91; www.tivazadou-iledebatz.fr; s/d incl breakfast €55/65; ☉ mid-Feb–mid-Nov; 🤶), a welcoming B&B in a restored farmhouse with sea views next to the church, and **L'Escale** (🖉 06 30 56 50 01; www.escale-iledebatz.fr; d incl breakfast €70; ☉ Apr–mid-Nov), a great port of call, with four cosy rooms with sea views.

Ferries (adult/child return €8.50/4.50, bike €8.50, 15 minutes each way) between Roscoff and Île de Batz run every 30 minutes between 8am and 8pm in July and August, with less-frequent sailings the rest of the year. Bicycles can be rented on the island for around €10 per day. For more information, check www.iledebatz.net.

mansion complete with its own tower just opposite the church. With fantastic sea views from some rooms, a great blend of modern and traditional decor, plus friendly staff, this is one of Roscoff's best options. One minus: for a four-star establishment you'd expect private parking. Family rooms are available.

La Résidence des Artistes　　HOTEL €€
(🖉 02 98 69 74 85; www.hotelroscoff-laresidence.fr; 14 rue des Johnnies; s €79-89, d €85-99; ☉ closed Dec-Jan; 🤶) Bored with Breton character? This sassy hotel with a 'boutique-on-a-budget' feel might be just the ticket. Colour-coordinated, bright and modern, all the rooms here are slightly different and there's a piano in the arty reception area. The staff speak English and it's on a central, quiet street (close to a free car park), making it good value.

Eating

⭐**Crêperie Ty Saozon**　　CRÊPERIE €
(🖉 02 98 69 70 89; 30 rue Gambetta; mains €5.50-8.50; ☉ 6.30-9pm Mon-Wed, Fri & Sat) Watch and then devour handmade artisan crêpes and *galettes* from this award-winning crêperie in the heart of the old town. You'll love the homey, intimate atmosphere.

Le Surcouf　　BRASSERIE €€
(🖉 02 98 69 71 89; 14 rue Amiral Réveillère; menus €11-55; ☉ 11.30am-1.30pm & 6.30-9.30pm) Bang in the heart of Roscoff, this brasserie serves excellent seafood. You can choose your own crab and lobster from the window tank, tuck into the classic fish soup or opt for a heaping platter of fresh shellfish. Plate-glass windows keep things light and bright, but the dining room is a bit noisy and it's a shame there's no terrace.

L'Écume des Jours　　MODERN FRENCH €€€
(🖉 02 98 61 22 83; http://lecume-des-jours.pages perso-orange.fr; quai d'Auxerre; menus €15-55; ☉ noon-1.45pm & 7-9.15pm Thu-Tue) Regarded as the best restaurant in town, this elegant place is housed inside a former shipowner's house and serves magnificent, inventive local dishes that marry seafood tastes with land-lubbers' delights. There's also an excellent wine list. It has stone walls, vintage hearth and hefty beams inside; and outside, a sun-trap terrace for fine weather.

ⓘ Information

Tourist Office (🖉 02 98 61 12 13; www. roscoff-tourisme.com; quai d'Auxerre; ☉ 9am-12.30pm & 2.30-7pm Mon-Sat, 10am-12.30pm & 2.30-7pm Sun Jul-Aug, 9.15am-noon & 2-6pm Mon-Sat Sep-Jun) Next to the lighthouse.

ⓘ Getting There & Away

BUS

The combined bus and train station is on rue Ropartz Morvan. Buses depart from the ferry terminal (Port de Bloscon) and pass by the town centre.

Brest €2, 1½ to two hours, up to four daily
Morlaix €2, 40 minutes, several daily

FERRY

Brittany Ferries (🖉 reservations in France 08 25 82 88 28, reservations in UK 0871 244 0744; www.brittany-ferries.com) links Roscoff to Plymouth, England (five to nine hours, one to three daily year-round) and Cork, Ireland (14 hours, once-weekly June to September). Boats leave from Port de Bloscon, about 2km east of the town centre.

TRAIN

There are regular trains and SNCF buses to Morlaix (€6.20, 35 minutes), where you can make connections to Brest, Quimper and St-Brieuc.

Morlaix

POP 15,605

At the bottom of a deep valley sluicing through northeastern Finistère, Morlaix is an engaging town that makes a good gateway to the coast. The narrow, fingerlike town centre is filled with ancient half-timbered houses that spill down to a small port. Towering above all else in the town is an arched 58m-high viaduct built in 1861 to carry the Brest–Paris railway. During daylight hours you can walk along the lower level for a great view of the town.

◉ Sights & Activities

Église St-Melaine   CHURCH

(6 place des Otages; ⊙9am-noon & 2-6pm) The late-15th-century Flamboyant Gothic Église St-Melaine features a star-studded barrel-vault roof and polychrome wooden statues, including those of St Peter and the eponymous St Melaine.

Musée de Morlaix   MUSEUM

(☑02 98 88 68 88; www.musee.ville.morlaix.fr; place des Jacobins; adult/child €4.50/free; ⊙10am-12.30pm & 2-6pm Jul-Sep, 10am-noon & 2-5pm Tue-Sat Oct-Jun) The area's history, archaeology and art are showcased at this museum, which incorporates the beautifully preserved half-timbered house nearby, La Maison à Pondalez.

La Maison à Pondalez   HISTORIC BUILDING

(☑02 98 88 68 88; 9 Grand Rue; ⊙10am-12.30pm & 2-6pm Jul-Sep, 10am-noon & 2-5pm Tue-Sat Oct-Jun) This beautifully restored half-timbered house dating back to the 16th century is a typical example of a Morlaix *maison à pondalez* (house with an inner gallery and spiral staircase). A combined ticket for both the Maison à Pondalez and Musée de Morlaix costs €4.50.

Maison de la Duchesse Anne   MUSEUM

(☑02 98 88 23 26; www.mda-morlaix.com; 33 rue de Mur; admission €2; ⊙11am-6pm Mon-Sat, 2-6pm Sun Jul-Aug, 11am-6pm Mon-Sat May, Jun & Sep) This 15th-century home (which, despite the name, has nothing to do with Duchess Anne) is one of the finest examples of the local building style. The highlight is a staircase engraved with the faces of the building's patron saints.

Le Léon à Fer et à Flots   BOAT TOUR

(☑02 98 62 07 52; www.aferaflots.org; adult/child €29/15; ⊙Apr-Sep) A great way to see the area by land and sea, this tour combines a boat trip through the islands of the Baie de Morlaix and a picturesque train trip between Roscoff and Morlaix.

🛏 Sleeping

Ty Pierre   B&B €

(☑07 81 26 03 17, 02 98 63 25 75; http://lenaj.free.fr/typierre/index.htm; 1bis place de Viarmes; s/d/tr with shared bathroom, incl breakfast €35/50/65; ⊙Mar-Dec; 🛜) Knick-knacks and artefacts picked up by Pierre-Yves Jacquet on his Asian travels now decorate this quirky *chambre d'hôte's* five spacious rooms. At this price there's no lift (count on climbing up three or four floors), and most rooms don't have their own bathroom (they're just along the wide corridors). All in all, it's very simple but practical. Dinner meals are available (€20).

★ Manoir de Ker-Huella   B&B €€

(☑0298880552; http://manoirdekerhuella.monsite-orange.fr; 78 voie d'accès au port; d incl breakfast €87-97; 🛜🚗) Built in 1898 by the then-director of the railways (the train station is very close by), this wonderful grey stone manor house set in park-like gardens above the town is now a well-run *chambre d'hôte*. Despite the size of the building there are actually only four guest rooms, all named after heroines from classic novels.

Country-chic decor, large bathrooms and a dash of old-fashioned charm make this a memorable choice. Children will enjoy sharing the gardens with the odd goat and rabbit. Call ahead if arriving outside the reception hours of 6pm to 8pm. There's a two-night minimum stay in July and August.

Hôtel de l'Europe   HISTORIC HOTEL €€

(☑02 98 62 11 99; www.hotel-europe-com.fr; 1 rue d'Aiguillon; d €69-102; 🛜) Regal and refined, yet relaxed, the efficiently run Hôtel de l'Europe occupies an elegant 17th-century building in central Morlaix. Moulded ceilings, carved panelling and sculpted woodwork fill the public areas – spot the original 17th-century staircase spiralling up to the upper floors. Most guest rooms, by contrast, have been thoroughly modernised. Excellent value.

🍴 Eating & Drinking

★ Atipik Bilig   CRÊPERIE €

(☑02 98 63 38 63; 1 rue Ange de Guernisac; mains €5-13; ⊙noon-2pm & 7-9.30pm Tue-Sat) Tucked inside a two-storey 16th-century timbered house in the old town, this enticing crêperie whips up sweet crêpes, savoury *galettes,* substantial salads and *tartines* (open-faced sandwiches). The outdoor tables occupy a prime location alongside picturesque rue Ange de Guernisac.

Grand Café de la Terrasse BRASSERIE €

(⌨02 98 88 20 25; 31 place des Otages; mains €12.50-18; ⊗8am-midnight Mon-Sat) In the heart of town, Morlaix's showpiece is this stunning 1872-established brasserie with an original central spiral staircase. Sip tea, coffee or something stronger, or sup on classic brasserie fare. Shame about the passing traffic, though.

Le Viaduc REGIONAL CUISINE €€

(⌨02 98 63 24 21; www.le-viaduc.com; 3 rampe St-Melaine; mains €16-26, lunch menu €16, other menus €21-31; ⊗noon-1.30pm & 7-9.30pm Tue-Sat, noon-1.30pm Sun Sep-Jun, noon-2pm & 7-10pm daily Jul-Aug) A sterling reputation props up this ode to contemporary Breton cuisine, framed by a stylish interior featuring grey stone walls, wood-panelled ceilings and groovy lighting. On the menu are fish and meat dishes, all skilfully cooked and presented.

Le Tempo BAR

(⌨02 98 63 29 11; quai de Tréguier; ⊗11am-10pm Mon-Thu, 11am-2am Fri & Sat) Locals pile into this quintessential bar/brasserie overlooking the harbour. It has a blackboard full of brasserie staples and plenty of brews on offer. Well worth the detour.

❶ Information

Tourist Office (⌨02 98 62 14 94; www.tourisme.morlaix.fr; place des Otages; ⊗9am-7pm Mon-Sat, 10am-12.30pm Sun Jul-Aug, 9am-12.30pm & 2-6.30pm Mon-Sat Jun & Sep) A few steps southwest below the railway viaduct. Has a map of walking itineraries around town.

❶ Getting There & Away

Morlaix has frequent train services:
Brest €11.20, 35 minutes
Paris Montparnasse from €55, four hours
Roscoff €6.20, 30 minutes

Brest

POP 144,500

A major port and military base, Brest is big, bold and dynamic. Destroyed by Allied air attacks during WWII, Brest was swiftly rebuilt after the war, with little thought given to aesthetics. However, it's a lively port and university town, home to a fantastic aquarium and the gateway to the sea-swept Île d'Ouessant.

◉ Sights & Activities

★Océanopolis AQUARIUM

(⌨02 98 34 40 40; www.oceanopolis.com; port de plaisance du Moulin Blanc; adult/child €18.60/12.70; ⊗9.30am-6pm Jul-Aug, 10am-5pm Tue-Sun Sep-Jun; ▣3) Much more than just an aquarium, this enormous space-age 'aquatic world' is divided into three pavilions containing polar, tropical and temperate ecosystems. Highlights are the shark tanks, mangrove and rainforest sections, colourful tropical reefs, seals and the icy-cold penguin display. In addition to the animals, there are numerous films and interactive displays and it's educational for both children and adults alike. It's about 3km east of the city centre; take bus 3 from place de la Liberté.

Tip: buying your ticket online for the same price allows you to skip the queues (which can be very long on wet summer days).

Musée de la Marine MUSEUM

(Naval Museum; ⌨02 98 22 12 39; www.musee-marine.fr; rue du Château; adult/child €6/free; ⊗10am-6.30pm, closed Jan) Learn about Brest's maritime military history at this museum housed within the fortified 13th-century Château de Brest, which was built to defend the harbour on the Penfeld River. Following the 1532 union of Brittany and France, both the castle and its harbour became a royal fortress. The castle was heavily refortified by Vauban in the mid-17th century with his trademark combination of ramparts and defensive towers. From its ramparts there are striking views of the harbour and the naval base.

Tour Tanguy TOWER

(⌨02 98 00 87 93; place Pierre Péron; ⊗10am-noon & 2-7pm Jun-Sep, 2-5pm Wed, Thu, Sat & Sun Oct-May) ⓕⓡⓔⓔ A sobering reminder of what Brest looked like on the eve of WWII can be seen at this 14th-century tower. Other exhibits on the town's history include the documented visit of three Siamese ambassadors in 1686, who presented gifts to the court of Louis XIV; rue de Siam was named in their honour.

Les Vedettes Azenor BOAT EXCURSION

(⌨02 98 41 46 23; www.azenor.fr; port de Commerce & port de Plaisance; adult/child €16/12; ⊗Apr-Sep) This well-regarded cruise operator offers 1½-hour cruises around the harbour and the naval base two or three times daily from both the Port de Commerce (which is near the castle) and the Port de Plaisance (which is opposite Océanopolis).

⭐ Festivals & Events

Les Jeudis du Port
MUSIC FESTIVAL
(Harbour Thursdays; ⊘7.30pm-midnight Thu mid-Jul–late Aug) Plan to be in Brest on a Thursday night during summer, when Les Jeudis du Port fills the port with live rock, reggae and world music, as well as street performances and children's events.

Astropolis
MUSIC FESTIVAL
(www.astropolis.org; Brest) Brest's electronic music fest in early July.

🛏 Sleeping

Hôtel St Louis
HOTEL €
(☎02 98 44 23 91; www.brest-hotel.com; 6 rue Algésiras; d with/without bathrooms €49/39; @🛜) Don't be deterred by the dull concrete façade of this excellent budget abode. Renovated in 2013, it has an inviting interior, with brightly painted walls in the communal spaces, and offers well-equipped rooms with flat-screen TVs, plump bedding and muted tones (but no lift); in some rooms, bathrooms are tucked away within cupboards. Simple and cheap, but remarkably cool.

Rooms 402 and 403 come without bathroom but are bright, spacious and have a balcony with prime harbour views.

Hôtel de la Rade
HOTEL €
(☎02 98 44 47 76; www.hoteldelarade.com; 6 rue de Siam; d €69; 🛜) Right in the centre of town, this good-value place has smart and stylishly simple rooms with tiny, yet functional, bathrooms. Rooms at the back have superb views onto the harbour and the couple who manage it are very welcoming. Note to cyclists: secure parking is available. Prices drop to €49 in July and August – check out the website.

Hôtel Continental
HOTEL €€
(☎02 98 80 50 40; www.oceaniahotels.com; rue Émile Zola; d €120-150; ❄🛜) Every business person's favourite base in Brest, this retro-chic downtown hotel offers plenty of atmosphere, thanks to its monumental art deco lobby, magnificent stained-glass windows and 73 large, luminous and clean-as-a-pin rooms. There are considerable reductions on room rates at weekends.

🍴 Eating & Drinking

Le Potager de Mémé
ORGANIC €
(☎09 51 44 14 78; www.lepotagerdememe.com; 44 rue de Lyon; mains €12, menus €15-17; ⊘11.30am-2.30pm Mon-Sat, 7-9pm Fri & Sat) A fabulous lunch address wedged between shops, Le Potager de Mémé (Grandma's vegetable garden) is uber-cool, ultra-healthy and great value. Pick from zesty salads, soups, tarts and savoury *tartines*, all made with locally sourced, organic products. Mmmm, vegetarian quiche with ewe's-milk cheese.

Ô Zinc
MODERN FRENCH €
(☎02 98 43 08 52; 48 rue de Lyon; mains €13-18, lunch menus €16-18; ⊘noon-2pm & 7.45-9.30pm Thu-Sat, noon-2pm Tue & Wed) This contemporary bistro with a pinch of post-industrial flavour (think suspended lamps, zinc table tops and walls done up in greys) cooks up just a few starters, three or four mains and a handful of desserts – and none disappoint.

La Chaumière
MODERN FRENCH €€
(☎02 98 44 18 60; 25 rue Émile Zola; mains €12-20, menus €17-29; ⊘noon-2pm Mon-Fri, 7.30-9pm Tue-Sat) A faintly creative cuisine is what makes this modern-meets-traditional inn with a big fireplace and contemporary furnishings stand out. Breton chef René Botquelen turns out succulent concoctions prepared with top-of-the-line ingredients. Plump for the excellent crab with turnip, cooked in a sweet-and-sour sauce.

Le Crabe Marteau
SEAFOOD €€
(☎02 98 33 38 57; 8 quai de la Douane; mains €21-31; ⊘noon-2.30pm & 7-10.30pm Mon-Sat) This eatery down by the port is famous for one thing and one thing only: crab (served with potatoes), savoured on a terrace facing the island ferries or in an elegantly nautical interior. The menu also includes oysters and freshly caught fish.

Blind Piper
PUB
(95 rue de Siam; ⊘11am-1am) This legendary spot is a beauty – part Irish pub, part French bar, furnished in rich burnished wood and nautical bits-and-bobs. Has billiards upstairs.

ℹ Information

Tourist Office (☎02 98 44 24 96; www.brest-metropole-tourisme.fr; place de la Liberté; ⊘9.30am-7pm Mon-Sat, 10am-1pm Sun) Runs various guided tours in summer.

ℹ Getting There & Away

AIR

Brest's **airport** (www.brest.aeroport.fr) has regular Ryanair flights to/from Marseille; Flybe flights to/from Birmingham, Dublin and Southampton; easyJet flights to Lyon and London; and Air France flights to Paris, Lyon and London.

BOAT

Ferries to Île d'Ouessant leave from Port de Commerce.

Azénor (☑ 02 98 41 46 23; www.azenor.com; port de Commerce) connects Brest with Le Fret on the Crozon Peninsula (one way adult/child €8/6, 30 minutes, twice daily Tuesday to Sunday).

BUS

Brest's **bus station** (☑ 02 98 44 46 73; place du 19e Régiment d'Infanterie) is beside the train station.

Le Conquet €2, 45 minutes, six daily
Roscoff €2, 1½ hours, four daily

TRAIN

For Roscoff, change trains at Morlaix.

Morlaix from €9.90, 35 minutes
Paris Montparnasse from €61, 4½ hours, around seven daily
Quimper €17.70, 1¼ hours
Rennes from €29.50, two hours

❶ Getting Around

BUS & TRAM

Shuttle buses (one way €5) connect the train station and airport approximately hourly; you can buy tickets on the bus. The local bus network **Bibus** (☑ 02 98 80 30 30; www.bibus.fr) sells tickets good for two hours for €1.40 and day passes for €3.80. There's an information kiosk on place de la Liberté. The same people also run the city's tram service and tickets are interchangeable with the bus system.

TAXI

Call ☑ 02 98 80 18 01. A taxi for the 10km airport trip costs around €20.

Île d'Ouessant

POP 950

There is an old Breton saying that goes 'Qui voit Molène, voit sa peine, qui voit Ouessant, voit son sang' ('Those who see Molène, see their sorrow, those who see Ouessant, see their blood'), and it's true that on a wild stormy winter day there's a real end-of-the-world feeling to the Île d'Ouessant (Enez Eusa in Breton, meaning 'Island of Terror'; Ushant in English). However, on a sunny day the place can seem like a little paradise, with turquoise waters, abundant wildflowers and not much to do but walk and picnic. The peace and calm of the island is best experienced by hiking its 45km craggy coastal path or hiring a bike and cycling. While the island can be vis-ited as a day trip (as masses of people do) it's best savoured over several slow days.

◉ Sights

Musée des Phares et des Balises　　　　　　LIGHTHOUSE, MUSEUM
(Lighthouse & Beacon Museum; ☑ 02 98 48 80 70; adult/child €4.30/3; ◷ 10.30am-6pm Jul-Aug, 11am-5pm Apr-Jun & Sep) The black-and-white-striped Phare de Créac'h is the world's most powerful lighthouse. Beaming two white flashes every 10 seconds and visible for over 50km, it serves as a beacon for over 50,000 ships entering the Channel each year. Beneath is the island's main museum, which tells the story of these vital navigation aids. There are also displays devoted to the numerous shipwrecks that have occurred off this island.

Écomusée d'Ouessant　　　　　　　　MUSEUM
(Maison du Niou; ☑ 02 98 48 86 37; adult/child €3.50/2.40; ◷ 10.30am-6pm Jul-Aug, 11am-5pm Apr-Jun & Sep) Two typical local houses make up this small 'ecomuseum'. One re-creates a traditional homestead, furnished like a ship's cabin, with furniture fashioned from driftwood and painted in bright colours to mask imperfections; the other explores the island's history and customs.

🏖 Beaches

Plage de Corz, 600m south of Lampaul, is the island's best beach. Other good spots to stretch out are **Plage du Prat**, **Plage de Yuzin** and **Plage de Porz Arlan**. All are easily accessible by bike from Lampaul or Port du Stiff.

🛏 Sleeping

Camping Municipal Penn Ar Bed　　　　　　CAMPGROUND €
(☑ 02 98 48 84 65; Stang Ar Glann, Lampaul; per person €3.40, per tent €3.20; ◷ Apr-Sep) About 500m east of Lampaul, this sprawling 100-pitch place looks more like a football field than a campground. It's short on facilities.

Auberge de Jeunesse　　　　　　　　HOSTEL €
(☑ 02 98 48 84 53; www.auberge-ouessant.com; Lampaul; dm incl breakfast €21.50; ◷ Feb-Nov; 🖨) This friendly hostel on the hill above Lampaul has two- to six-person rooms and a small communal kitchen. Sheets cost an extra €5.30 per stay. It's popular with school and walking groups; reservations are essential.

La Duchesse Anne　　　　　　　　HOTEL €
(☑ 02 98 48 80 25; www.hotelduchesseanne.fr; Lampaul; s €49-58, d €50-58; ◷ Apr–mid-Feb; 🖨) Idyllically set on a cliff next to Baie de Lampaul,

this hotel has unpretentious yet neat doubles, of which four have staggering sunset-facing sea views. It also boasts a good restaurant with a terrace overlooking the ocean.

★ Le Keo – La Maison des Capitaines
B&B €€

(☑06 01 39 67 08; www.lekeoouessant.com; Lampaul; d incl breakfast €90-105; ⊙Apr-Oct; ☞) This bewitching cocoon in the heart of Lampaul sits snug in a coolly refurbished townhouse and adds a real touch of glamour to the accommodation scene. Its interior brims with boutique trappings and it offers four rooms, four characters, all with individual decorative features. Two have swoon-inducing sea views, and one features a *lit clos* (traditional Breton bed).

The fantastic breakfast room, with its original wood panelling, and the lovely small garden, are the icing on the cake.

Ti Jan Ar C'hafe
HOTEL €€

(☑02 98 48 82 64; www.tijan.fr; Kerginou, Lampaul; d €79-99; ⊙mid-Feb–mid-Nov; ☞) This haven of peace feels more like a B&B than a proper hotel and it's all the better for it. Rooms come in a swirl of different colours but they're normally loud and vivid, and two sit harmoniously beneath the sloping roof. Superb breakfast in a sun-lit verandah overlooking a bijou back garden. It's 500m east of Lampaul.

✖ Eating

Ty Korn
SEAFOOD €

(☑02 98 48 87 33; Lampaul; mains €11-30; ⊙noon-1.30pm & 7.30-9.30pm Tue-Sat) The ground floor of this hyperfriendly place is a bar serving Breton black-wheat beers (made from the same *blé noire* as Breton *galettes*). Upstairs there's an excellent restaurant where seafood is a speciality. Save room for their divine *tiramisu breton* (biscuit with apples, mascarpone and salty caramel sauce). Opening hours can vary, though the bar stays open until 1am.

Ar Piliguet
MODERN FRENCH €

(☑02 98 03 14 64; Lampaul; mains €15-19, lunch menu €17; ⊙noon-1.30pm & 7-9pm Wed-Sun) For picturesque, flavoursome dining head to Ar Piliguet, fittingly set in a traditional house behind the tourist office. Dishes are packed with fresh, local ingredients – enjoy them on the small terrace or in a snug interior full of stone and artistic flourishes. The lunch *menu* is outstanding value.

Crêperie Ti A Dreuz
CRÊPERIE €

(☑02 98 48 83 01; Lampaul; mains €4-10; ⊙noon-1.30pm Thu-Tue, 7-8.30pm Thu-Mon) You could be

forgiven for thinking you'd been at sea too long, or knocked back too much Breton cider, but 'the slanting house' is so-named for its wonky walls. This quaint island crêperie serves delicious *galettes:* try the *ouessantine,* with creamy potato, cheese and local sausage.

❶ Information

Tourist Office (☑02 98 48 85 83; www.ot-ouessant.fr; place de l'Église; ⊙9am-12.30pm & 1.30-6.30pm Mon-Sat, 9.30am-12.30pm Sun) Sells walking brochures and can hook you up with operators offering horse riding, sailing and other activities.

❶ Getting There & Away

AIR

Finist'air (☑02 98 84 64 87; www.finistair.fr) flies from Brest's airport to Ouessant in a mere 15 minutes. There are two flights daily on weekdays and one on Saturdays (one way adult/child €69/49).

BOAT

Ferries for Île d'Ouessant depart from Brest and the tiny town of Le Conquet (Brittany's most westerly point). **Penn Ar Bed** (☑08 10 81 00 29; www.viaoo29.fr) buses link Brest with Le Conquet (€2, 45 minutes, hourly). In high summer it's a good idea to reserve at least two days in advance and to check in 45 minutes before departure. Transporting a bicycle costs €14.

Penn Ar Bed (☑02 98 80 80 80; www.pennarbed.fr; adult/child return €34.80/27.80) sails from the Port de Commerce in Brest (2½ hours) and from Le Conquet (1½ hours). Boats run between each port and the island two to five times daily from May to September and once daily between October and April. Prices fall in winter. A bike costs €15.40.

Finist'mer (☑08 25 13 52 35; www.finist-mer.fr; adult/child return €32/26.50) runs high-speed boats from Le Conquet (40 minutes), Lanildut (35 minutes) and Camaret (1½ hours) once a day.

❶ Getting Around

BICYCLE

Bike-hire operators have kiosks at the Port du Stiff ferry terminal and compounds just up the hill, as well as outlets in Lampaul. The going rate for town bikes is €10 per day. Cycling on the coastal footpath is forbidden – the fragile turf is strictly reserved for walkers.

MINIBUS

Islander-run minibus services such as **Ouessant Voyages** (☑06 07 90 07 43; www.ouessant-voyages.com) meet the ferry at Port du Stiff and will shuttle you to Lampaul or your accommodation for a flat fare of €2 (to guarantee a seat in July and August, book ahead at the island tourist office or at the tourist office in Brest). For the return journey, the pick-up point is the car park beside Lampaul's church. Minibus owners also offer two-hour guided tours (€15 per person) of the island, in French.

Presqu'Île de Crozon

Stretching westwards into the Atlantic, the anchor-shaped Crozon Peninsula is one of the most scenic spots in Brittany. In previous centuries this multifingered spit of land was a key strategic outpost; crumbling forts and ruined gun batteries can still be seen on many headlands, but these days it's the tucked-away coves, superb beaches, awesome panoramas, charming B&Bs and clifftop trails that attract thousands of visitors in summer.

Landévennec

POP 358

The Aulne River flows into the Rade de Brest beside the pretty village of Landévennec, home to the ruined Benedictine **Abbaye St-Guenolé**. The abbey **museum** (www.musee-abbaye-landevennec.fr; Landévennec; adult/child €5/3; ☺10.30am-6.30pm daily Jul-Sep, Sun-Fri May-Jun & Oct-Nov) records the history of the settlement, founded by St Guenolé in 485 and the oldest Christian site in Brittany. Nearby, a new abbey is home to a community of monks, who run a little shop selling homemade fruit jellies.

Crozon & Morgat

POP 7950

The area's largest town, Crozon is the engine room for the peninsula. The town centre is pleasant enough but there's little reason to hang around. On the water 2km south, Morgat was built as a summer resort in the 1930s by the Peugeot brothers (of motor-vehicle fame) and it retains something of the feel of that period. It's one of the prettier resorts in this part of Brittany, with colourful houses piled up at one end of a long sandy beach that has very safe bathing.

⊙ Sights & Activities

★ Coastal Hike   WALKING
The coastline between Morgat and Cap de la Chèvre is extremely alluring. Beyond the marina at the southern end of Morgat's beach, the coastal path offers an excellent 13km hike (part of the GR34) along the sea cliffs to Cap de la Chèvre, taking in some of the most scenic spots in the area. It takes roughly five hours to complete (one way), but you can also choose to walk smaller sections.

The route takes you past an old fort and through sweet-scented pine forests overlooking numerous little coves (most inaccessible) with water that, on a sunny day, glows electric blue. Make sure you pause at the picture-perfect Île Vierge – you'll be smitten with this idyllic cove lapped by turquoise waters and framed by lofty cliffs. These lazy summer day images are shattered on reaching Cap de la Chèvre and the exposed, western side of the peninsula.

Cap de la Chèvre   NATURAL SITE
The peninsula's most southerly point, Cap de la Chèvre, is 8km south of Morgat, and offers stupendous panoramas of the Baie de Douarnenez and the Pointe du Raz. You'll be amazed by the contrast between the Mediterrean-like eastern side of the peninsula and the much wilder western shore, which is clearly Atlantic.

Pointe de Dinan   NATURAL SITE
Wow! The cliffs of Pointe de Dinan provide a dramatic outlook over the sands of Anse de Dinan and the jumble of rock known as the Château de Dinan, linked to the mainland by a natural archway.

Vedettes Rosmeur   BOAT TRIM
(☑06 85 95 55 49; www.grottes-morgat.fr; quai Kador, Morgat; adult/child €14/9) This outfit operates 45-minute and one-hour boat trips to the colourful sea caves along the coast. It also takes in the lovely Île Vierge.

Beaches

Morgat has a picturesque beach that's popular with families. To the west, there's sunbathing aplenty on the 2km-long **Plage de la Palue** and nearby **Plage de Lostmarc'h**, but swimming is forbidden due to strong currents. Further north, **Plage de Goulien** is another wonderful stretch of golden sand.

⭐ Festivals & Events

Every Tuesday during July and August, free concerts take place on place d'Ys in Morgat.

Festival du Bout du Monde   MUSIC FESTIVAL
(Festival of the End of the World; www.festivaldubout dumonde.com) Morgat's place d'Ys area hosts the Festival du Bout du Monde in early August, which features world music.

🛏 Sleeping

Les Pieds dans l'Eau CAMPGROUND €
(☎02 98 27 62 43; http://lespiedsdansleau.free.fr; St-Fiacre; per person/tent/car €4.50/5/2.50; ☺mid-Jun–mid-Sep) 'Camping feet in the water' (almost literally, at high tide) is one of 16 campgrounds along the peninsula.

★Kastell Dinn B&B €
(☎0662529661,0298272640; www.sejour-insolite bretagne.com; Kerlouantec; d €55-90) Looking for something extra special? This marvellous little hideaway 2km southwest of Crozon won't disappoint. It offers two free-standing units which are set in two decommissioned fishing boats (yes!) and one *roulotte* (caravan), as well as two rooms in a traditional Breton *longère* (long house). Incredibly atmospheric. Breakfast (optional) sets you back an extra €6.

Hôtel de la Baie HOTEL €
(☎02 98 27 07 51; www.hoteldelabaie-crozon-morgat. com; 46 bd de la Plage; d €49-88; 🕿) One of the *very* few places to remain open year-round, this friendly, family-run spot on Morgat's promenade has renovated rooms, some with views over the ocean, and is one of the best deals around.

✖ Eating

Morgat's seafront and place d'Ys are good spots to trawl for seafood restaurants.

Saveurs et Marées SEAFOOD €€
(☎02 98 26 23 18; 52 bd Plage; menus €15-31; ☺noon-2pm & 7-10pm Tue-Sun) Our pick of Morgat's clutch of restaurants is this lemon-yellow cottage overlooking the sea with its breezy dining room, sunny terrace and consistently good, locally caught seafood (including succulent lobster).

★Le Mutin Gourmand REGIONAL CUISINE €€€
(☎02 98 27 06 51; www.lemutingourmand.fr; place de l'Église, Crozon; menus €25-59; ☺noon-1.30pm Tue-Sat, 7-8.45pm Mon-Sat) No, there's no sea view (it's in Crozon town centre), but this is the gourmet choice in the area. With its intimate dining room, charming welcome and delicious cuisine, Le Mutin Gourmand has honed the art of dining out to perfection. The chef works with local, carefully chosen ingredients, so whatever season you're in town, you'll be in for a treat.

Too expensive for you? Head to the annexe nearby, **Le Bistrot du Mutin**, which has very affordable menus (lunch *menus* €16 to €19).

ℹ Information

Crozon Tourist Office (☎02 98 27 07 92; www. tourisme-presquiledecrozon.fr; bd Pralognan, Crozon; ☺9.30am-1pm & 2-7pm Mon-Sat, 10am-1pm Sun) Housed in the former railway station, on the main road to Camaret.

Morgat Tourist Office (☎02 98 27 29 49; www. officedetourisme-crozon-morgat.fr; place d'Ys; ☺9.30am-12.30pm & 3-7pm Mon-Wed, 2.30-7.30pm Thu-Sun Jul-Aug) Overlooks the promenade at the corner of bd de la Plage.

Camaret-sur-Mer

POP 2600

At the western extremity of the Crozon Peninsula, Camaret is a classic fishing village – or at least it was until early in the 20th century, when it was France's biggest crayfish port. Abandoned fishing-boat carcasses now decay in its harbour, but it remains an enchanting place that lures artists, as testified by the ever-increasing number of galleries dotted around town. Cheek-by-jowl cafes and clanking yacht masts populate the attractive harbour, overlooked by a 17th-century red brick watchtower.

◎ Sights

Pointe de Pen-Hir NATURAL SITE
Three kilometres south of Camaret, this is a spectacular headland bounded by steep, sheer sea cliffs, with two WWII memorials. On a peninsula full of breathtaking scenery this might be the most impressive lookout of them all. The series of offshore rock stacks are known as **Tas de Pois**. Just inland are the 40-odd standing stones of the **Alignements de Lagatjar**. There are plenty of opportunities for short walks around here as well as a handful of little cove beaches.

Chapelle Notre-Dame-de-Rocamadour CHURCH
Its timber roof like an inverted ship's hull, the Chapelle Notre-Dame-de-Rocamadour is dedicated to the sailors of Camaret, who have adorned it with votive offerings of oars, lifebuoys and model ships.

🛏 Sleeping & Eating

Hôtel Vauban HOTEL €
(☎02 98 27 91 36; 4 quai du Styvel; d €45-59; ☺Feb-Nov; 🕿) Its colourful rooms are contemporary but the Vauban's old-fashioned hospitality extends to its large rear garden, with a barbecue to grill your own fish. Some rooms have lovely

harbour views. Good surprise: prices remain the same in high season.

Chez Philippe REGIONAL CUISINE €
(☑ 02 98 27 90 41; 22 quai Toudouze; mains €9-15, menus €13-28; ☺ noon-2pm & 7-9.30pm) This unpretentious place overlooking the harbour won't win any gastronomic awards but it serves hearty regional dishes at puny prices.

ℹ Information

Tourist Office (☑ 02 98 27 93 60; www.camaret surmer-tourisme.fr; 15 quai Kléber; ☺ 9am-noon & 2-6pm Mon-Sat) On the waterfront.

ℹ Getting There & Around

BOAT

Azénor (☑ 02 98 41 46 23; www.azenor.fr) runs seasonal ferries between Brest and the Presqu'Île de Crozon (adult/child €8/6).

From mid-April to mid-September, **Penn Ar Bed** (☑ 02 98 80 80 80; www.pennarbed.fr) sails between Camaret and Île d'Ouessant (adult/child return €34.80/20.90).

BUS

Five buses daily run from Quimper to Crozon (€2, 1¼ hours), continuing to Camaret (€2); up to four go from Camaret and Crozon to Brest (€2, 1¼ hours, daily). Buses also run between Morgat, Crozon and Camaret several times daily (€2, 10 minutes).

Quimper

POP 66,911

Small enough to feel like a village, with its slanted half-timbered houses and narrow cobbled streets, and large enough to buzz as the troubadour of Breton culture and arts, Quimper (kam-pair) is Finistère's thriving capital. With some excellent museums, one of Brittany's loveliest old quarters and a delightful setting along the Odet River, Quimper deserves serious exploration.

◎ Sights & Activities

Cathédrale St-Corentin CHURCH
(place St-Corentin; ☺ 8.30am-noon & 1.30-6.30pm Mon-Sat, 8.30am-noon & 2-6.30pm Sun) At the centre of the city is Quimper's cathedral with its distinctive kink, said to symbolise Christ's inclined head as he was dying on the cross. Construction began in 1239 but the cathedral's dramatic twin spires weren't added until the 19th century. High on the west façade, look out for an equestrian statue of King Gradlon, the city's mythical 5th-century founder.

LOCRONAN

Sure, Locronan is no secret, and tourists flock here by the busload in summer, but that shouldn't deter you from visiting this quintessentially Breton village, which has barely changed in appearance since the mid-18th century. Small wonder that its old-world ambience and photogenic granite houses – not to mention its lack of phone cables and electricity wires – have made it hugely popular with film crews. It's also famous for hosting one of Brittany's oldest *pardon* (religious processions), the Petite Troménie, held on the second Sunday in July. Barefooted pilgrims bearing saintly banners and singing traditional songs follow a 6km route from the church to a sacred grove. This highly colourful event attracts huge crowds of onlookers and it's well worth timing your trip around it.

Musée Départemental Breton MUSEUM
(☑ 02 98 95 21 60; www.museedepartementalbreton. fr; 1 rue du Roi Gradlon; adult/child €5/3; ☺ 9am-12.30pm & 1-5pm Tue-Sat, 2-5pm Sun) Beside the Cathédrale St-Corentin, recessed behind a magnificent stone courtyard, this superb museum showcases Breton history, furniture, costumes, crafts and archaeology, in a former bishop's palace.

Musée des Beaux-Arts ART MUSEUM
(☑ 02 98 95 45 20; www.mbaq.fr; 40 place St-Corentin; adult/child €5/free; ☺ 10am-7pm Jul-Aug, 9.30am-noon & 2-6pm Wed-Mon Apr-Jun & Sep-Oct) The ground-floor halls are home to some fairly morbid 16th- to 20th-century European paintings, but things lighten up on the upper levels of the town's main art museum. A room dedicated to Quimper-born poet Max Jacob includes sketches by Picasso, and there's also a section devoted to the Pont-Aven school.

Vedettes de l'Odet BOAT TRIP
(☑ 02 98 57 00 58; www.vedettes-odet.com; quai Neuf; adult/child from €28/17; ☺ Jun-Sep) From June to September, Vedettes de l'Odet runs trips from Quimper along the serene Odet estuary to Bénodet. You can stop for a look about Bénodet and then hop on a boat back.

✬ Festivals & Events

Festival de Cornouaille CELTIC FESTIVAL
(www.festival-cornouaille.com) A celebration of traditional Celtic music, costumes and culture

Quimper

takes place over six days in late July. After the traditional festival, classical-music concerts are held at different venues around town.

🛏 Sleeping

Hôtel Manoir des Indes HOTEL €€
(☑ 02 98 55 48 40; www.manoir-hoteldesindes.com; 1 allée de Prad ar C'hras; s €99-125, d €158-189; 🛜 🖫) This stunning hotel conversion, located in an old manor house just a short drive from the centre of Quimper, has been restored with the globe-trotting original owner in mind. Decor is minimalist and modern, with Asian objets d'art and lots of exposed wood. It's located a five-minute drive west of Quimper, a little way north of the D100.

Hôtel Gradlon HOTEL €€
(☑ 02 98 95 04 39; www.hotel-gradlon.com; 30 rue de Brest; d €105-150; ⊘ mid-Jan–mid-Dec; 🛜) This place may not look like much from the street, but its rather bland and modern façade be-lies a charming country manor interior. The

smallish but well-furnished rooms differ, but all have plenty of character and individual touches. It's a short walk from the old town and secure parking is available.

Best Western Hôtel Kregenn HOTEL €€
(☑ 02 98 95 08 70; www.hotel-kregenn.fr; 13 rue des Réguaires; d €109-180; 🏵 🛜) A timber-decked courtyard and a guest lounge with oversized mirrors and white leather sofas give you the initial impression that Quimper's coolest ho-tel is contemporary in style, but the plush rooms decked out in warm colours evoke a traditional feel. Some rooms have ancient stone walls. A safe bet.

🍴 Eating & Drinking

Crêperie du Quartier CRÊPERIE €
(☑ 02 98 64 29 30; 16 rue du Sallé; mains €5-9; ⊘ noon-2pm Mon-Sat, 7-10pm Mon, Wed, Fri & Sat) In a town where the humble crêpe is king, this cosy stone-lined place is one of the best. Its wide-ranging menu includes a *galette* of

Quimper

the week and, to follow up, you can go for a crêpe stuffed with apple, caramel, ice cream, almonds and chantilly.

La Krampouzerie   CRÊPERIE €
(☑02 98 95 13 08; 9 rue du Sallé; mains €4-9, ⊙11.45am-3pm Tue-Sat, 6.45-10pm Tue-Sun) Crêpes and *galettes* made from organic flours and regional ingredients such as *algues d'Ouessant* (seaweed), Roscoff onions and homemade ginger caramel are king here. Tables on the square out front create a street-party atmosphere.

Erwan   REGIONAL CUISINE €
(☑02 98 90 14 14; 3 rue Aristide Briand; mains €12-20, menus €17-24; ⊙noon-2pm & 7-8.30pm Mon-Sat) The contemporary Breton menu at this appealing eatery emphasises seasonal regional ingredients in dishes ranging from *kig ha farz* (Breton *pot au feu*, daily) to a wicked Breton hamburger (served in winter only).

L'Épée   CAFE, BRASSERIE €€
(☑02 98 95 28 97; www.quimper-lepee.com; 14 rue du Parc; mains €12-24, lunch menus €19-24, other menus €29-48; ⊙brasserie noon-2.30pm & 7-10.30pm, cafe 10.30am-midnight) A Quimper institution – it's one of Brittany's oldest brasseries – L'Épée hits the mark with its three themed dining areas, efficient service and good vibe. Despite the hip interior, the food is by no means an afterthought. Superbly executed dishes include duck breast, lamb shank, sea shells and salads. You can also just stop in for a drink.

Le Ceili   PUB
(4 rue Aristide Briand; ⊙5pm-2am) Hipsters, musos and students make a beeline for this lively Celtic pub, one of the town's *bonnes adresses* for listening to traditional Breton music while sampling a Coreff or a Telenn Du.

ℹ Information

Tourist Office (☑02 98 53 04 05; www.quimper-tourisme.com; place de la Résistance; ⊙9am-7pm Mon-Sat, 10am-12.45pm & 3-5.45pm Sun Jul-Aug, 9.30am-12.30pm & 1.30-6.30pm Mon-Sat, 10am-12.45pm Sun Jun & Sep) Sells the Pass Quimper (€12) whereby you can access four attractions or tours of your choice from a list of participating organisations.

ℹ Getting There & Away

BUS

Penn ar Bed (☑08 10 81 00 29; www.viaoo29.fr) has regular buses to Brest (€6, 1¼ hours), Concarneau (€2, 45 minutes) and Camaret (€2). The bus station is next to the train station.

TRAIN

Frequent services:
Brest €17.70, 1¼ hours, up to seven daily
Paris Montparnasse €55 to €65, 4¾ hours, six direct daily
Rennes €29.50 to €37, 2½ hours, 13 direct daily
Vannes €16.50 to €20.70, 1½ hours, hourly

Concarneau

POP 21,000

The sheltered harbour of Concarneau (Konk-Kerne in Breton), 24km southeast of Quimper, radiates out from its trawler port, which brings in close to 200,000 tonnes of *thon* (tuna) from the Indian Ocean and off the African coast (the adjacent Atlantic is too cold). Jutting out into the port, and circled by medieval walls, the supremely picturesque old town – Ville Close – is one of Brittany's popular spots in summer.

⊙ Sights

Ville Close (Walled City)   HISTORIC QUARTER
The walled town, fortified in the 14th century and modified by the architect Vauban two centuries later, huddles on a small island linked to place Jean Jaurès by a stone footbridge. Just past the citadel's **clock tower**, look out for the 18th-century **Maison du Gouverneur** above the main gate. From here, rue Vauban leads to place St-Guénolé, passing numerous stone houses converted into shops, crêperies, ice-cream stalls and galleries. The excellent **Musée de la Pêche** (Fisheries Museum; ☑02 98 97 10 20; www.musee-peche.fr; 3 rue Vauban; adult/child €4.50/free; ⊙9.30am-7pm Jul-Aug, 10am-6pm Apr-Jun & Sep, closed mid-Nov–mid-Dec) is housed inside the west gate.

BRITTANY CONCARNEAU

WORTH A TRIP

ÎLES DE GLÉNAN

Sapphire waters, idyllic white-sand beaches and no crowds. Bora Bora? No. Îles de Glénan. This archipelago of around a dozen mini-islands lies just 20km south of Concarneau and never fails to impress in fine weather. Visitors are only allowed on Île de St-Nicolas. **Vedettes de l'Odet** (☑ 02 98 57 00 58; www.vedettes-odet.fr; port de Plaisance; cruise adult/child from €34/18) runs scenic cruises around the islands from Concarneau and other coastal towns. Optional activities include sea kayaking and glass-bottom tours.

It delves into Concarneau's seafaring traditions using everything from archive film to scale models and vintage boats. You can even clamber aboard the museum's very own fishing vessel, the retired *L'Hémérica,* permanently docked just outside the city walls.

Château de Keriolet   CHÂTEAU
(☑ 02 98 97 36 50; www.chateaudekeriolet.com; Château de Keriolet; adult/child €5.50/3; ☺ 10.30am-1pm daily, 2-6pm Sun-Fri Jun-Sep) This impressive building is an exquisite example of 19th-century architecture. Its intriguing Russian connections are revealed during a guided tour. The castle is a well-signed five-minute drive from town (turn right just before the large Leclerc supermarket).

🌴 Beaches

Concarneau's most spectacular beach is **Plage des Sables Blancs,** 1.5km northwest of the town centre. There are lifeguards on duty in summer. **Plage du Cabellou,** about 5km south of town, is another great spot for sunbathing and swimming.

🛏 Sleeping

Auberge de Jeunesse Éthic Étapes   HOSTEL €
(☑ 02 98 97 03 47; www.aj-concarneau.org; quai de la Croix; dm incl breakfast €18; ☎) Fall asleep listening to the waves at this functional waterfront hostel next to the Marinarium. Digs are in four- to six-bed dorms. Extras include a wraparound barbecue terrace, a self-catering kitchen and pastries for breakfast.

Hôtel des Halles   HOTEL €
(☑ 02 98 97 11 41; www.hoteldeshalles.com; place de l'Hôtel de Ville; s €52, d €68-85; ☎) A few steps from Ville Close, this 22-room hotel looks plain on the outside but its cheery rooms come in a rainbow of colour combinations and are decorated with a suitably nautical air (think pictures of pebbles on the walls). The organic breakfast (€9) includes homemade jams and bread straight from the oven.

Les Sables Blancs   BOUTIQUE HOTEL €€
(☑ 02 98 50 10 12; www.hotel-les-sables-blancs.com; place des Sables Blancs; s €110-200, d €130-220; ☎) Right on the 'white sands' of the beach from which it takes its name, this ultrachic hotel has tastefully decorated rooms with fabulous sea views and an excellent restaurant. The catch? The 'standard' rooms are a bit boxy and we found the prices somewhat inflated in summer.

Hotel de France et d'Europe   HOTEL €€
(☑ 02 98 97 00 64; www.hotel-france-europe.com; 9 av de la Gare; s €82, d €89-97; ☎) This is a fairly sterile but comfortable and serviceable place a short walk from the waterfront. There's no 'wow' factor – just plain, good-value lodging in a handy location. Precious perks include private parking and a shady terrace.

🍴 Eating

Cafes, pizzerias and crêperies line the waterfront, and there are more inside the walls of Ville Close.

Le Petit Chaperon Rouge   CRÊPERIE €
(☑ 02 98 60 53 32; 7 place Duguesclin; mains €4-12; ☺ noon-1.30pm Tue-Sun, 7.15-9.15pm Tue-Sat) Avoid the crêperies of the Ville Close, which leave a lot to be desired; instead, opt for this cute venture near the seafront. The setting is cosy, and there's a bumper selection of savoury crêpes and *galettes.*

Le Flaveur   MODERN FRENCH €€
(☑ 02 98 60 43 47; 4 rue Duquesne; lunch menus €16-19, other menus €25-54; ☺ noon-1.30pm Tue-Fri & Sun, 7.15-9.15pm Tue-Sat) One of Concarneau's top tables, Le Flaveur is tucked down a quiet street near the harbour. Meals range from strictly local dishes through to more generally French dishes and occasional use of products from further afield. The *menu* changes regularly – if it's available, how about the *pigeonneau royal* (royal pigeon), endorsed by locals as 'almost gastronomic' (ie delectable but affordable)?

ℹ Information

Tourist Office (☑ 02 98 97 01 44; www.tourisme concarneau.fr; quai d'Aiguillon; ☺ 9am-7pm)

Can provide information on walking and cycling circuits in the area.

ℹ️ Getting There & Away

L'Été Évasion (☑ 02 98 56 82 82; www.auto cars-ete.com) runs up to 10 buses daily between Quimper and Quimperlé, calling by Concarneau (€2 from Quimper).

Pont-Aven

POP 2840

Breton villages don't come much prettier than Pont-Aven, a former port and mill town huddled at the end of a wooded creek about 20km east of Concarneau. In the 19th century, its charms were discovered by artists. American painters were among the first to uncover it, but things really took off when France's Paul Gauguin and Émile Bernard set up a colony here in the 1850s and captured the beauty of the little village and the surrounding countryside.

Since the 1960s Pont-Aven has again become a magnet for artists seeking fresh air and country inspiration. Today there are about 60 galleries dotted around town.

◉ Sights

Musée des Beaux-Arts de Pont-Aven   ART MUSEUM
(☑ 02 98 06 14 43; www.museepontaven.fr; place de l'Hôtel de Ville; adult/child €4.50/free; ☻10am-12.30pm & 2-6.30pm Feb-Dec) For an insight into the town's place in art history, stop by this well-organised museum. It was undergoing a major renovation at the time of writing but should have reopened by the time you read this.

🛏️ Sleeping

Les Ajoncs d'Or   HOTEL €
(☑ 02 98 06 02 06; www.ajoncsdor-pontaven.com; 1 place de l'Hotel de Ville; d €66-70; 🛜) A good deal for Pont-Aven, this venerable hotel has undergone quite a few sprucings, and they've all been for the better. The rooms feature cosy beds, tiled bathrooms and nice furnishings, all kept clean and presentable. There's an attached restaurant.

Castel Braz   B&B €€
(☑ 02 98 06 07 81; www.castelbraz.com; 12 rue du Bois d'Amour; d incl breakfast €70-80; 🛜) This grand 19th-century house smack dab in the centre of Pont-Aven has four stylish rooms that are all different, with attractive colour schemes and excellent bathrooms.

✕ Eating

⭐La Chocolaterie de Pont-Aven   TEAROOM €
(☑ 02 98 09 10 47; www.lachocolateriedepontaven.com; 1 place Delavallée; from €2.50; ☻10am-7.30pm Jul-Aug,10am-1pm&2.30-7.30pmTue-SatSep-Jun)*Au revoir*, diet. This mouth-watering patisserie-*chocolaterie* with an adjacent *salon de thé* has a wide assortment of goodies. If you can resist, you're not human.

Sur Le Pont   MODERN FRENCH €€
(☑ 02 98 06 16 16; www.surlepont-pontaven.fr; 11 place Paul Gauguin; mains €16-23, menus €21-32; ☻12.30-2pm Thu-Tue, 7.30-9pm Thu-Mon) You couldn't wish for a more perfect setting, lodged in a stylishly renovated building by the Pont-Aven bridge. A just-so palette of cool greys, beiges, blacks and whites creates the feel of an elegant bistro. Dishes are refined takes on Breton cooking.

Le Moulin de Rosmadec   GASTRONOMIC €€€
(☑ 02 98 06 00 22; www.moulinderosmadec.com; venelle de Rosmadec; mains €31-49, menus €43-79; ☻12.30-2pm Tue-Sun, 7-9pm Tue-Sat) Epicureans come from far and wide to dine at this award-winning restaurant overlooking the town's namesake *pont* (bridge) and *aven* (river in Breton). Run by the formidable Frédéric Sébilleau, it serves exquisitely fresh dishes inspired from local traditions, with the odd fusion concession. A lovely spot to dine *tête à tête*. It also has four delightful guest rooms upstairs (doubles €98 to €105).

ℹ️ Information

Tourist Office (☑ 02 98 06 04 70; www.pontaven.com; place de l'Hôtel de Ville; ☻10am-12.30pm & 2-6pm Mon-Sat) To see the spots where the masters set up their easels, pick up a free walking-trail map from the tourist office, which can also help with accommodation.

ℹ️ Getting There & Away

Pont-Aven is an easy 18km drive southeast of Concarneau. Buses – five Monday to Saturday and two on Sunday – connect Pont-Aven with Quimperlé in the east (30 minutes), Concarneau (30 minutes) and Quimper (one hour).

MORBIHAN COAST

In the crook of Brittany's southern coastline, the Golfe du Morbihan (Morbihan Coast) is a haven of islands, beaches, oyster beds and bird life. But the area is perhaps best known for its proliferation of mystifying Celtic

Golfe du Morbihan and Presqu'île de Quiberon

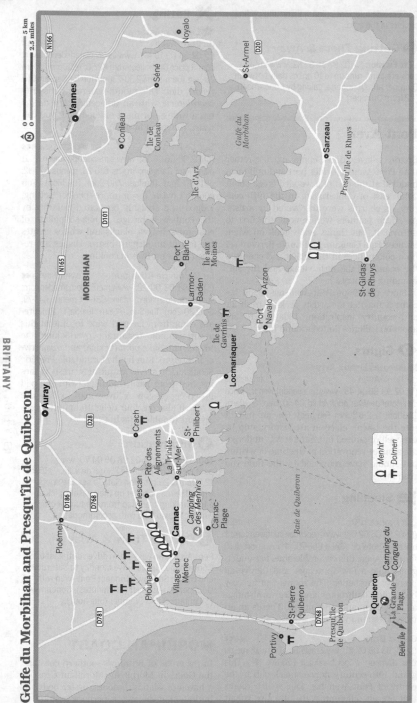

5 km
2.5 miles

N166

Vannes

Noyalo

Séné

St-Armel

D20

Conleau

Île de Conleau

Golfe du Morbihan

Sarzeau

Presqu'île de Rhuys

Île d'Arz

D101

MORBIHAN

Port Blanc

Île aux Moines

Port Arzon

St-Gildas de Rhuys

N165

Larmor-Baden

Île de Gavrinis

Locmariaquer

Auray

D28

Crach

St-Philibert

La Trinité-sur-Mer

Rte des Alignements

D186

Kerlescan

D768

Ploëmel

Camping des Menhirs

Carnac

Carnac-Plage

Baie de Quiberon

Village du Ménec

Plouharnel

D781

St-Pierre Quiberon

Quiberon

Camping du Conguel

La Grande Plage

Presqu'île de Quiberon

D768

Portivy

Belle Île

Menhir
Dolmen

megaliths, which are strewn throughout most of the département.

Carnac

POP 4362

With enticing beaches and a pretty town centre, Carnac would be a popular tourist town even without its collection of magnificent megalithic sites, but when these are thrown into the mix you end up with a place that is unmissable on any ramble through Brittany. Predating Stonehenge by around 100 years, Carnac (Garnag in Breton) also tops it with the sheer number of ancient sites found in the vicinity, making this the world's greatest concentration of megalithic sites. There are no fewer than 3000 of these upright stones, most around thigh-high, erected between 5000 and 3500 BC.

Carnac, some 32km west of Vannes, comprises the old stone village Carnac-Ville and, 1.5km south, the seaside resort of Carnac-Plage, which is bordered by the 2km-long sandy beach.

Beaches

Not only is Carnac a fantastic open-air museum that appeals to culture vultures, it's also a superb playground for beachy types. La Grande Plage is Carnac's longest and most popular beach and is excellent for sunbathing – imagine a 2km-long stretch of white sand that's exposed to the south. To the

---

CARNAC'S MYSTERIOUS MEGALITHS

Two perplexing questions arise from the Morbihan region's neolithic menhirs, dolmens, cromlechs, tumuli and cairns. Just *how* did the original constructors hew, then haul, these blocks (the heaviest weighs 300 tonnes), millennia before the wheel and the mechanical engine reached Brittany? And *why*?

Theories and hypotheses abound, but the vague yet common consensus is that they served some kind of sacred purpose – the same spiritual impulse behind so many monuments built by humankind.

The best way to appreciate the stones' sheer numbers is to walk or bike between Le Ménec and Kerlescan groups, with menhirs almost continuously in view. Between June and September seven buses a day run between the two sites, as well as Carnac-Ville and Carnac-Plage.

Sign up for a one-hour guided visit at the Maison des Mégalithes (☑ 02 97 52 29 81; www.carnac.monuments-nationaux.fr; rte des Alignements; tour adult/child €6/free; ☉ 9.30am-7.30pm Jul & Aug, to 5pm Sep-Apr, to 6pm May & Jun), which explores the history of the site and has a rooftop viewpoint overlooking the *alignements*. Tour times vary considerably depending on the time of year but they run twice a day (in French) during the summer. English tours are available at least once or twice a week in July and August – call the Maison des Mégalithes to confirm times.

Due to severe erosion the sites are fenced off to allow the vegetation to regenerate. However, from October to March you can wander freely through parts.

Opposite the Maison des Mégalithes, the largest menhir field – with 1099 stones – is the Alignements du Ménec, 1km north of Carnac-Ville; the eastern section is accessible in winter. From here, the D196 heads northeast for about 1.5km to the equally impressive Alignements de Kermario (which is open year-round). Climb the stone observation tower midway along the site to see the alignment from above. Another 500m further on are the Alignements de Kerlescan, a smaller grouping also accessible in winter.

Between Kermario and Kerlescan, 500m to the south of the D196, deposit your fee in an honour box at Tumulus de Kercado, the burial site of a neolithic chieftain dating from 3800 BC. From the parking area 300m further along the D196, a 15-minute walk brings you to the Géant du Manio, the highest menhir in the complex.

Tumulus St-Michel, at the end of rue du Tumulus and 400m northeast of the Carnac-Ville tourist office, dates back to at least 5000 BC and offers sweeping views.

The Musée de Préhistoire (☑ 02 97 52 22 04; www.museedecarnac.fr; 10 place de la Chapelle, Carnac-Ville; adult/child €6/2.50; ☉ 10am-6pm) chronicles life in and around Carnac from the Palaeolithic and neolithic eras to the Middle Ages.

For tailor-made tours in English, contact Howard Crowhurst from Carnac Discovery (☑ 06 73 19 52 47; www.carnacdiscovery.com).

west, **plage de Légenèse** and **plage de St-Colomban** are smaller and quieter. St-Colomban appeals to windsurfers.

🛏 Sleeping

⭐ Plume au Vent   B&B €

(☎ 06 16 98 34 79; www.plume-au-vent.com; 4 venelle Notre Dame; d/q incl breakfast €90/145; 🛜📶) Forget about tacky seaside hotels as this two-room B&B on a *venelle* (little street) in the town centre is more like something from an interior-design magazine. It's all mellow shades of blues and greys, hundreds of neatly bound books, knick-knacks discovered washed up on the high tide line and polished cement showers and sinks. It's a great find.

Camping des Menhirs   CAMPGROUND €

(☎ 02 97 52 94 67; www.lesmenhirs.com; 7 allée St-Michel; adult/site €8.55/31.40; ⊘ mid-Apr–late Sep; 🛜🏊) Carnac and its surrounds have over 15 camping grounds, including this luxury complex of 100-sq-metre sites. Just 300m north of the beach, this is very much the glamorous end of camping, with amenities such as a sauna and cocktail bar!

Le Ratelier   INN €

(☎ 02 97 52 05 04; www.le-ratelier.com; 4 chemin du Douet; d €53-70; 🛜) This vine-clad former farmhouse, now an eight-room inn with low ceilings, fabric-covered walls and traditional timber furnishings, is in a quiet street near the church. The cheapest rooms have showers only and shared toilets. Those with private bathrooms feel a tad compact due to the cubicle shower and toilets plonked in the corner. The wood-beamed restaurant is renowned for its fresh seafood.

Les Rochers   HOTEL €€

(☎ 02 97 52 10 09; www.les-rochers.com; 6 bd de la Base Nautique; d €92-144; 🛜📶) This hotel has 14 sea-blue rooms which directly overlook the port and the sea at the western end of Carnac-Plage. Rooms on the 1st floor have terraces but those on the 2nd floor come with picture windows that offer better sea views. Downstairs there's a good seafood restaurant (half-board is available).

🍴 Eating

Chez Marie   CRÊPERIE €

(☎ 02 97 52 83 05; 3 place de l'Église; mains €4-16, menus €10-15; ⊘ noon-2pm & 7-10pm Wed-Sun) Established in 1959, this Carnac institution churns out savoury *galettes* and sweet crêpes in a charmingly traditional stone house opposite the church. Connoisseurs recommend its flambéed specialities, especially the Arzal *galette,* with scallops, apples and cider.

⭐ La Côte   GASTRONOMIC €€€

(☎ 02 97 52 02 80; www.restaurant-la-cote.com; impasse Parc Er Forn, Kermario; lunch menu €26, other menus €37-58; ⊘ 12.15-2pm Wed-Sun, 7.15-9pm Tue-Sun) Top recommendation on the Morbihan Coast goes to this Carnac address, run by Carnacois *maître-cuisinier* Pierre Michaud, who has won plaudits for his inventive cuisine that combines the very best Breton ingredients. The setting is another drawcard, with an elegant dining room and a soothing terrace overlooking a small fish pond. Find it in a quiet property close to the Alignements de Kermario.

ℹ Information

Tourist Office (☎ 02 97 52 13 52; www.ot-carnac.fr; 74 av des Druides, Carnac-Plage; ⊘ 9.30am-6pm Mon-Sat, 3-6pm Sun Jul-Aug) Also has an annexe at Carnac-Ville.

ℹ Getting There & Around

BICYCLE

Hire bikes from **A Bicyclette** (☎ 06 30 32 34 32, 02 97 52 75 08; http://velocarnac.com; 93bis av des Druides; per day from €9) down near the beach.

BUS

The main bus stops are in Carnac-Ville, outside the police station on rue St-Cornély, and in Carnac-Plage, beside the tourist office. **Tim** (☎ 08 10 10 10 56; www.morbihan.fr) runs a daily bus to Auray, Vannes and Quiberon (€2).

Quiberon

POP 5200

Quiberon (Kiberen in Breton) sits at the southern tip of a sliver-thin, 14km-long peninsula flanked on the western side by the rocky, wave-lashed Côte Sauvage (Wild Coast). The setting is superb, with a heady mix of lovely beaches and rugged inlets, but the town itself is quite tacky, and finding a parking spot is like looking for a pot of gold at the end of a rainbow. Even so, it's wildly popular in summer and is also the departure point for ferries to Belle Île. For outdoorsy types, there are plenty of water sports available, from diving and snorkelling to sea kayaking and *char à voile* (sand yachting).

✦ Activities

Conserverie La Belle-Iloise
CANNERY TOUR

(☎ 02 97 50 59 08; www.labelleiloise.fr; zone d'Activités Plein Ouest, bd Plein Ouest; ⊗ tours 10am, 11am, 3pm & 4pm Mon-Fri, 11am & 3pm Sat) FREE Take a 45-minute guided tour of this former sardine cannery before replenishing your supplies of tinned tuna, mackerel, sardines and fish spread in the adjacent shop. It's north of the train station.

La Grande Plage
BEACH

La Grande Plage is a family-friendly beach; bathing spots towards the peninsula's tip are less crowded.

Sillages
KAYAKING

(☎ 06 81 26 75 08; www.kayak-sillages.com; 9 av de Groix, St-Pierre-Quiberon; adult/child from €20/17; ⊗ daily by reservation) What about a morning paddle far from the crowds along the Côte Sauvage? This reputable outfit based in St-Pierre-Quiberon (look for the 'Base Nautique') runs guided kayaking tours for all levels – beginners are welcome.

⌁ Sleeping

Camping du Conguel
CAMPGROUND €

(☎ 02 97 50 19 11; www.campingduconguel.com; bd de la Teignouse; sites €29-49; ⊗ Apr-Oct; ☎⊛) This splashy option with an aqua park that has water slides is one of the peninsula's 15 campgrounds. Just 2km east of the town centre, it's beside Plage du Conguel. There are also caravans to rent.

★ Le Petit Hôtel du Grand Large
BOUTIQUE HOTEL €€

(☎ 02 97 58 31 99; www.lepetithoteldugrandlarge.fr; 11 quai St-Ivy, Portivy; d €95-115; ☎) Sick of the crowds? No sweat – this intimate, sassy hotel is a soothing escape from the Quiberon hubbub, offering six spiffy, well-lit rooms facing the sea. Top choices are room 4, with its bathroom set in a turret, and room 5, for its wide balcony. It's in Portivy, an adorable, quiet seaside town a few kilometres north of Quiberon.

Gastronomic bliss is dished up at the elegant restaurant downstairs (*menus* from €30), which blends playful Breton classics with an engaging sense of jumble-shop chic.

Hôtel Port-Haliguen
HOTEL €€

(☎ 02 97 50 16 52; www.hotel-port-haliguen.com; 10 place de Port-Haliguen; d €77-109; ☎) This well-run hotel in Port-Haliguen, a quiet neighbourhood west of Quiberon's centre, just gets better and better: visitors come here to lap up the breezy, beach-house vibe. Rooms are small

but bold, luminous and modern; many open to balconies facing the sea. There's a brasserie downstairs, and a great beach a short stroll away. Free public parking is available.

✕ Eating & Drinking

Le Vivier
SEAFOOD €

(☎ 02 97 50 12 60; Côte Sauvage; mains €8-25; ⊗ noon-3pm & 7-8pm Apr-Oct) The food is almost secondary at this convivial eatery dramatically perched on a small cliff on the Côte Sauvage; bookings are essential for the top tables, squeezed onto a sun-trap terrace hovering above the rocky coastline. The menu is plain and unpretentious – think salads, mussels, smoked fish and seashells – and you couldn't ask for a better spot when the sun is shining.

From central Quiberon, follow the signs to 'Côte Sauvage' for about 2km.

Restaurant de La Criée
SEAFOOD €€

(☎ 02 97 30 53 09; 11 quai de l'Océan; mains €20-30, menus €19-25; ⊗ 12.15-2pm Tue-Sun, 7.15-9pm Tue-Sat) Just off the beachfront, La Criée has long been a favourite among fish lovers. Nautically themed and run by a talented team, the seafood here is a cut above most of Quiberon's bistros. Dover sole, fillet monkfish, brill cooked with apples, and red mullet in a fennel sauce all feature.

Villa Margot
MODERN FRENCH €€

(☎ 02 97 50 33 89; www.villamargot.fr; 7 rue de Port Maria; mains €23-32, lunch menu €18, other menus €27-44; ⊗ 12.15-1.30pm & 7.15-9.30pm Thu-Mon) The interior of this stunning stone restaurant looks like it would be at home in a chic Parisian *quartier*, with original art on the walls, flower-shaped opaque glass light fittings, hot-pink and brown colour schemes, and lobsters clawing in the live tank. That is, until you head out onto the timber deck, which has direct access to the beach for a post-repast stroll.

ⓘ Information

Tourist Office (☎ 02 97 50 07 84; www.quiberon.com; 14 rue de Verdun; ⊗ 9am-7pm Mon-Sat, 10am-1pm & 2-5pm Sun) Between the train station and La Grande Plage.

ⓘ Getting There & Away

BOAT
There are ferries between Quiberon and Belle-Île, see p287 for more information.

BUS
Quiberon is connected by **Tim** (☎ 08 10 10 10 56; www.morbihan.fr) buses with Carnac (45

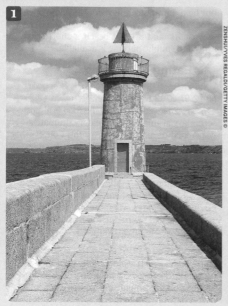

1. Camaret-sur-Mer p274 2. St-Malo p254 3. Cap de la Chèvre p273 4. Dinard p260

VINCENT JARY/GETTY IMAGES ©

The Breton Coast

Brittany's rugged coastline is one of the region's best-kept secrets. With brilliant sand beaches framing traditional fishing villages, rocky cliffs towering above the churning swell of the North Atlantic, and lots of activities to keep you occupied, there's plenty to discover.

Superb Stretches of Sand

Don't associate Brittany with beaches? Think again... Yes the water may be freezing, but the sand is spectacular and the backing sublime at **St-Malo** (p254) and **Quiberon** (p282). Alternatively, find your own patch of sand on the beaches of **Belle Île** (p286).

Hiking the Coasts

Get out into nature on the coastal hiking trail from Morgat to **Cap de la Chèvre** (p273). For a challenge, walk the 45km coastal path on **Île d'Ouessant** (p271) or the 95km path around **Belle Île** (p286).

Coastal Villages

Find your own quiet bliss in the village life of charming **Camaret-sur-Mer** (p274), the fishing port of **Roscoff** (p266) and our personal favourite, chic hideaway **Cancale** (p262).

Island Life

Take the ferry to **Île d'Ouessant** (p271), with its rugged coastal path and great activities, or head out of season to **Belle Île** (p286), the southern coast's star. To get off the beaten track head to **Île de Batz** (p267).

The Great Outdoors

You can dive, windsurf and hire catamarans in **Dinard** (p260); canoe or kayak in **Paimpol** (p265), **St-Malo** (p254), **Îles de Glénan** (p278) and **Quiberon** (p282); and hire bikes pretty much anywhere, though we recommend **Presqu'île de Crozon** (p273) and any of Brittany's islands.

minutes), Auray (1¼ hours) and Vannes (1¾ hours). The flat fare is €2. Buses stop at the train station and place Hoche, near the tourist office and beach.

CAR

High-summer traffic is hellish – consider leaving your vehicle at the 1200-place Sémaphore car park (€3.60 for up to four hours, €12.50 for 24 hours), 1.5km north of the beach, and walking or taking the free shuttle bus into town.

TRAIN

In July and August only, a train runs several times a day between Auray and Quiberon (€5.40 return, 45 minutes). From September to June an SNCF bus service links Quiberon and Auray train stations (€2, 50 minutes) at least seven times a day.

Belle Île

POP 5200

Accessed by ferries from Quiberon, Belle Île (in full, Belle-Île-en-Mer, 'beautiful island in the sea') sees its population swell ten-fold in summer. But as it's Brittany's largest offshore island (at 20km by 9km), there's room to escape the crowds. And yes, the name Belle Île is very appropriate: rugged cliffs and rock stacks line the island's west coast, while picturesque pastel ports nestle along the eastern side. And for sunbathers and outdoorsy types, there's no shortage of lovely beaches and activities.

Belle-Île has two main settlements: the main port of Le Palais is on the east side of the island, while smaller (and more charming) Sauzon is in the northeast.

◉ Sights & Activities

The best way to appreciate the island's coastal charms is from the 95km coastal footpath, which rings the island and allows access to the more secluded spots. Ask at the tourist office for a leaflet detailing possible routes.

★ Aiguilles de Port Coton   NATURAL SITE

Just off the western side of the island, these magnificent rock stacks that resemble *aiguilles* (needles) are a must-see for panorama lovers and photographers. These dramatic rock formations were depicted in a series of canvases by Claude Monet.

Citadelle Vauban &
Musée d'Art et d'Histoire   FORT, MUSEUM

(☑ 02 97 31 85 54; www.citadellevauban.com; Le Palais; adult/child €8.50/5.50; ☺ 9am-6pm) The dramatic citadel, strengthened by the architect Vauban in 1682, dominates little Le Palais port. Inside, the various displays concentrate on the history of the island's defensive system, though there are also sections on the local fish trade and island life.

Grotte de l'Apothicairerie   CAVE

Belle Île's fretted southwestern coast has spectacular rock formations and caves including Grotte de l'Apothicairerie, where waves roll in from two sides.

Pointe des Poulains   NATURAL SITE

The island's northernmost point juts out at Pointe des Poulains. Flanked by craggy cliffs, this windswept headland is Belle Île's loftiest lookout.

Vives Eaux   KAYAKING

(☑ 02 97 31 00 93; www.vives-eaux.fr; chemin de Port Puce, Sauzon; adult/child from €34/24; ☺ May-Oct by reservation) With a kayak, you can explore the bays, rugged inlets and tucked-away coves at a gentle pace. This outfit runs excellent guided tours.

🏖 Beaches

Belle Île is blessed with some lovely beaches, the largest of which is the 2km-long **Plage des Grands Sables**, spanning the calm waters of the island's eastern side. **Plage de Donnant**, on the opposite side of the island, is more secluded, but swimming is dangerous due to riptides. Sheltered **Plage d'Herlin**, on the south side, is better for children.

🛏 Sleeping

Les Tamaris   HOTEL €

(☑ 02 97 31 65 09; www.auxtamaris.fr; 11 allée des Peupliers, Sauzon; d €50-85; ☎ 🖨) A breath of fresh air, this well-priced two-star hotel on the outskirts of Sauzon has plenty of rural charm but no sea views. Rooms are simple, colourful and comfortable, and the owners are charming. Several rooms are suitable for families. Transfers to/from various walking trailheads can be arranged for €2.50 per person, and bikes are available for hire (€11).

Camping Bordénéo   CAMPGROUND €

(☑ 02 97 31 88 96; www.bordeneo.com; Bordénéo, Le Palais; site for 2 people, tent & car €28; ☺ Apr-Oct; ☎ 🏊) This modern, well-equipped campground is beautifully sited in Bordénéo, about 2km northwest of Le Palais off the road to Sauzon. The heated pool is a plus.

Auberge de Jeunesse   HOSTEL €

(☑ 02 97 31 81 33; www.fuaj.org/belle-ile-en-mer; Haute Boulogne, Le Palais; dm from €16; ☺ Apr-Sep; ◉) This modern, well-equipped but charmless 96-bed HI-affiliated hostel with a self-catering kitchen is to the north of the citadel. Its rooms are all twins with bunkbeds and shared toilets. Meals are available.

Hôtel Vauban
HOTEL €

(☑ 02 97 31 45 42; www.hotel-vauban-belleile.com; 1 rue des Remparts, Le Palais; d €75-98; ☎) This comfy place, with 16 multicoloured rooms splashed with driftwood, is perched high on Le Palais' ramparts, with jaw-dropping views of the ferry landing below. Cheaper rooms don't have sea views, though. Note that the owners do special hiking packages, which include several nights' stay and all meals, including a picnic lunch.

★ La Villa de Jade
B&B €€

(☑ 06 60 74 87 87, 02 97 31 53 00; www.villadejade.com; Taillefer, Le Palais; d incl breakfast €140-200; ☎⚐) Manuel and Valérie are the bilingual, well-travelled couple behind La Villa de Jade. This one-of-a-kind, gorgeous B&B in a stunningly renovated villa could not be more superbly placed – it's slap bang on a clifftop with plunging views of the sea. Its three rooms ooze charm with their mix-and-match furniture, family photos, colourful touches and plankwood floors.

Two rooms can be combined into a suite for families. Breakfast is a wholly organic affair, with fresh local products.

✖ Eating

Les Embruns
CRÊPERIE €

(☑ 02 97 31 64 78; quai Guerveur, Sauzon; mains €5-11; ☉ noon-9.30pm) The harbour front is lined with tempting restaurants but this crêperie is one of the best. It prepares perfectly buttered Breton crêpes and galettes, as well as scrumptious fillings such as oranges confites maison (homemade candied orange), and finger-licking ice creams. Most ingredients are organic and locally sourced. In summer, laden tables spill onto a pavement terrace.

Le Verre à Pied
BISTRO €

(☑ 02 97 31 29 65; 3 place de la République, Le Palais; mains €10-20, lunch menus €14-19; ☉ noon-2pm & 7-10pm Thu-Tue) This convivial bistro in central Le Palais is blessed with a lovely courtyard that's a perfect spot for a relaxed feed or tipple in summer. The food isn't starry, but it's fine for a heaping kettle of mussels or tartine, as well as Breton far cake for dessert.

Le Café de la Cale
BRASSERIE €€

(☑ 02 97 31 65 74; quai Guerveur, Sauzon; mains €17-31, menus €20-28; ☉ 12.15-2pm & 7.30-9.30pm) This snazzy brasserie with a superb terrace

overlooking Sauzon's harbour outshines most others with its relaxed mood, attentive service and creative take on what is available seasonally. Seafood features prominently; tuck into an expertly prepared lieu (pollack) or ask for the plateau de fruits de mer, brimming with shellfish.

❶ Information

Tourist Office (☑ 02 97 31 81 93; www.belle-ile.com; quai Bonnelle, Le Palais; ☉ 8.45am-7pm Mon-Sat, to 1pm Sun) It's on the left as you leave the ferry in Le Palais.

❶ Getting There & Away

Travelling to Belle Île can involve a bit of planning, as taking a car on the ferry is prohibitively expensive for a short trip and needs to be booked well ahead, even outside peak season.

The shortest crossing to Belle Île is from Quiberon. **Compagnie Océane** (☑ 08 20 05 61 56; www.compagnie-oceane.fr; adult/child return from €31.65/19.60) operates car/passenger ferries (45 minutes) year-round, and fast passenger ferries to Le Palais and Sauzon in July and August. Transporting a small car costs a hefty €202 return plus passenger fares. There are up to 10 crossings a day in July and August.

It is also possible to make the trip from Vannes. **Navix** (☑ 08 25 13 21 00; www.navix.fr; adult/child return from €30/21.60) operates ferries between May and mid-September.

❶ Getting Around

BICYCLE
Lots of places in Le Palais rent out bicycles (about €13 per day) and motor scooters (about €45 per day).

BUS
Seasonal buses run by **Belle Île Bus** (☑ 02 97 31 32 32; www.cars-verts.fr) criss-cross the island. A single journey costs €2.50.

CAR
Car-rental rates on the island are expensive and start at about €60 for 24 hours; you'll find outlets at the harbour as you disembark.

Vannes

POP 53,000

What a beauty! Overlooking the Golfe du Morbihan, Vannes is one of the unmissable towns of southern Brittany. Encircled by sturdy fortifications, criss-crossed by meandering alleys and cobbled squares, Vannes still preserves much of its medieval atmosphere, but it's a long way from being a museum piece.

It has a lively bar and restaurant scene as well as a superb marina. More than anything else, it's a great base to explore the glittering island-studded Golfe du Morbihan.

◉ Sights

Old City
HISTORIC QUARTER

Surrounding Vannes' walled old town is a flower-filled moat. Tucked away behind rue des Vierges, stairs lead to the accessible section of the ramparts. From here, you can see the black-roofed Vieux Lavoirs (Old Laundry Houses). Within the walls, the old city is a delightful jumble of timber-framed houses and wonky merchants' mansions, especially around place des Lices and place Henry IV. On the eastern side of the square looms the 13th-century Gothic Cathédrale St-Pierre.

Almost opposite the cathedral, you'll find the Musée de la Cohue (☑02 97 01 63 00; www.mairie-vannes.fr; place St-Pierre; adult/child €4.50/2.80; ☻10am-6pm), which has variously been a produce market, a law court and the seat of the Breton parliament. Today it's a museum of fine arts, displaying mostly 19th-century paintings, sculptures and engravings. On the corner of rue Noë and rue Pierre Rogue, look for the famous Maison de Vannes et Sa Femme, which sports a timber carving of a portly 16th-century shop owner and his equally well-endowed wife.

✨ Festivals & Events

Festival de Jazz
MUSIC FESTIVAL

(www.jazzavannes.fr) Vannes swings for four days in late July or early August.

Les Musicales du Golfe
MUSIC FESTIVAL

(www.musicalesdugolfe.com) Classical music concerts take place in early August.

Fêtes d'Arvor
CULTURAL FESTIVAL

(www.fetes-arvor.org) This three-day celebration of Breton culture from 13 to 15 August includes parades, concerts and festoù-noz (night festivals).

🛏 Sleeping

Le Bretagne
HOTEL €

(☑02 97 47 20 21; www.hotel-lebretagne-vannes.com; 36 rue du Mené; d €60; ☎) Nothing much to look at from the outside but the 12 rooms inside are a steal. Although on the small side, they're neat-as-a-pin and bright, and have cutting-edge colours, excellent bedding and sparkling bathrooms. Top picks are rooms at the back, with stupendous views of the ramparts. No private parking.

Hôtel de France
HOTEL €

(☑02 97 47 27 57; www.hotelfrance-vannes.com; 57 av Victor Hugo; d €78-88; ☎) This smart hotel near the train station caters for a business crowd, so it feels faceless in places, but the facilities are excellent and the location very convenient. The 30 rooms are fresh and modern; the best ones overlook a small garden at the back.

La Villa Garennes
B&B €€

(☑06 76 01 80 83; www.hotel-lebretagne-vannes.com; 3 rue Monseigneur Tréhiou; d incl breakfast €75-105; ☎) A stone's throw from the ramparts, this most attractive option has five charmingly decorated rooms in a handsome building. They're light, airy and furnished with great taste, and breakfasts come in for warm praise.

Best Western Le Roof
HOTEL €€

(☑02 97 63 47 47; www.le-roof.com; 10 allée des Frères Cadoret, Presqu'île de Conleau; s €112-156, d €139-183; ☎) Yes, yes, we know it's a Best Western, but this 40-room abode is ideal if it's a smart, efficient seaside retreat that you're after – it lies on the shoreline of Presqu'île de Conleau, southwest of the centre, and overlooks a small beach. The rooms vary in size and style; don't even consider one without a view of the Golfe.

Amenities include a brasserie, bar and restaurant.

🍴 Eating & Drinking

Rue des Halles and its offshoots are lined with tempting eateries; classical and contemporary brasseries arc around the port.

Dan Ewen
CRÊPERIE €

(☑02 97 42 44 34; 3 place du Général de Gaulle; mains €4-10, menus €10-18; ☻11.30am-2pm & 6.30-9pm Mon-Sat) A near-life-size statue of a sweet, smiling, wrinkled Breton lady bearing a tray greets you at the entrance of this stone and dark-wood crêperie serving fillings such as frangipane, and flambéed options topped with crème Chantilly.

Brasserie des Halles
BRASSERIE €

(☑02 97 54 08 34; www.brasseriedeshallesvannes.com; 9 rue des Halles; mains €11-22, menus €16-29; ☻noon-2.30pm & 7-11pm) Atmospherically set in a 16th-century building in the heart of the old town, this buzzing brasserie has a varied menu of fish and meat dishes, as well as pastas, salads and seashells. It's an equally good spot for a drink while browsing the art – which includes the Breton images made from tiles that adorn its colourful walls.

DON'T MISS

GOLFE DU MORBIHAN

Around 40 islands peep out from the shallow waters of the Morbihan gulf, which forms a breathtakingly beautiful inland sea that's easily accessible from Vannes. Some islands are barely sandy specks of land, while others harbour communities of fishermen, farmers and artistic types seduced by the island lifestyle. The bay's largest island is the 6km-long Île aux Moines. Nearby Île d'Arz is smaller – just 3km long and 1km wide – but it's the most scenic of the lot and features secluded sands and coastal walks. Tempted to stay? Both islands have a slew of B&Bs and eateries.

Lots of companies offer scenic cruises and ferry services to Île aux Moines and Île d'Arz. Check with **Navix** (☑ 08 25 13 21 00; www.navix.fr; cruise from €16.70) and **La Compagnie du Golfe** (☑ 02 97 01 22 80; www.compagnie-du-golfe.fr; Vannes; cruise adult/child from €16.50/11.50).

Restaurant de Roscanvec   GASTRONOMIC €€€
(☑ 02 97 47 15 96; www.roscanvec.com; 17 rue des Halles; lunch menus €25-30, other menus €48-70; ⊙ 12.15-2pm Tue-Sun, 7.15-9pm Tue-Sat Jul-Aug, 12.15-2pm Wed-Sun, 7.15-9pm Wed-Sat Sep-Jun) Lost among the timbers of the old city, this stellar restaurant is overseen by one of Britanny's most talented names, Thierry Seychelles, whose cooking has been championed by most of the major culinary critics. Rightly so: his trademark six-course 'Hedonist *Menu*' combines seasonal French classics with global flavours. The 15th-century building is a treat as well.

Le Verre à L'Envers   BAR
(6 place du Général de Gaulle; ⊙ 4pm-1am Tue-Sat) A mature, in-the-know set favours this pearl of a place just outside the ramparts. Snag a seat on the terrace to soak up the street atmosphere or snuggle up in the pocket-sized room. Knock back a wine by the glass or a beer, and graze on an excellent cheese or charcuterie (cured meats) platter. But the real queen of the drinks card is the mojito – simply the most devilish in town.

Paddy O' Dowd's   PUB
(23 rue Ferdinand le Dressay; ⊙ 5pm-2am) Get the beers in at this popular pub overlooking the harbour. The terrace is a chilled spot for summertime imbibing. Arrive late for a truly eclectic crowd, including lots of students, and an atmosphere that can go from quiet tippling to raucous revelry.

ⓘ Information

Tourist Office (☑ 08 25 13 56 10; www.tourisme-vannes.com; quai de Tabarly; ⊙ 9.30am-7pm Mon-Sat, 10am-6pm Sun Jul-Aug, 9.30am-12.30pm & 1.30-6pm Mon-Sat Sep-Jun) In a smart modern building on the marina.

ⓘ Getting There & Away

BUS

The small bus station is opposite the train station. **Réseau Tim** (www.lactm.com) has services to Carnac (€2, 1¼ hours) and on to Quiberon (€2, two hours).

TRAIN

Frequent trains:
Nantes €22.80, 1½ hours
Quimper €20.70, 1¼ hours
Rennes €21.70, 1-1½ hours

EASTERN & CENTRAL BRITTANY

The one-time frontier between Brittany and France, fertile eastern Brittany fans out around the region's lively capital, Rennes. Central Brittany conceals the enchanting Forêt de Paimpont, sprinkled with villages and ancient Breton legends.

Josselin

POP 2600

In the shadow of an enormous, witch's-hat-turreted 14th-century castle that was the long-time seat of the counts of Rohan, the story-book village of Josselin lies on the banks of the River Oust, 43km northeast of Vannes. Today, visitors in their thousands continue to fall under its spell. A beautiful square of 16th-century half-timbered houses, place Notre Dame is the little town's heart.

◉ Sights

★ **Château de Josselin**   CASTLE
(☑ 02 97 22 36 45; www.chateaujosselin.com; Josselin; adult/child €8.40/5; ⊙ 11am-6pm mid-Jul–Aug,

2-6pm Apr–mid-Jul, 2-5.30pm Sep) Guarded by its three round towers, the extraordinary town château is an incredible sight that remains the home of the Rohan family today. Beyond the entrance gate, the castle fans out into tree-filled grounds and a central courtyard, which affords a great view of the castle's Flamboyant Gothic façade and the river below. The château is filled with treasures, including a medieval-style dining room, a 3000-tome library and a grand salon filled with Sèvres porcelain, Gobelins carpets and an astronomical clock.

The interior can only be visited by guided tour: one English-language tour departs daily (2.30pm) from June to September; otherwise you can ask for a leaflet in English.

Musée de Poupées MUSEUM
(Doll Museum; ☑02 97 22 36 45; www.chateau josselin.com; 3 rue des Trente; adult/child €7.20/5; ☉11am-6pm mid-Jul–Aug, 2-6pm Apr–mid-Jul, 2-5.30pm Sep) Within the Château de Josselin, this quirky museum has a collection of more than 3000 vintage dolls and puppets amassed by Herminie de Rohan around the turn of the 20th century. A combination ticket for the Musée de Poupées and the Château costs €13.50/8.

Basilique Notre Dame du Roncier CHURCH
(place Notre Dame) Parts of the Basilique Notre Dame du Roncier date from the 12th century; superb 15th- and 16th-century stained glass illuminates the south aisle.

🛏 Sleeping & Eating

★**Le Clos des Devins** B&B €
(☑06 88 84 77 05, 02 97 75 67 48; www.leclos desdevins.com; 11 rue des Devins; d incl breakfast €55-65; 🖧) A beautiful 18th-century private mansion complete with fabulous walled garden underpins this gem of a *chambre d'hôte*, a five-minute stroll from the castle. Conscientious owner, Madame Astruc, has artfully decorated rooms with both modern touches and charming antiques. Each room has its own personality; our favourite is the Abricotine, which has a drop-dead gorgeous roof terrace overlooking the garden.

Domaine de Kerelly Camping CAMPGROUND €
(☑02 97 22 22 20; www.camping-josselin.com; Bas de la Lande, Josselin-Guégon; sites for 2 people, tent & car €16; ☉Apr-Oct; 🖧⛱) This peaceful spot is 2km west of Josselin, on the south bank of the Oust. It offers plenty of shady spots to pitch your tent.

Le 14 Saint-Michel B&B €€
(☑06 89 37 26 07, 02 97 22 24 24; www.le14stmichel. com; 14 rue St-Michel; incl breakfast s €63, d €69-95; 🖧🖧) Nestled in a bourgeois townhouse right in the centre, this is Josselin's hidden gem. The spacious, stylish rooms (including a two-room suite for families) ooze romance, and there's a superb garden at the back. Your hostess also does *table d'hôte* (€25) with local, seasonal products. Incredibly, all this charm and serenity are just seconds from the Basilique; a steal.

La Table d'O MODERN FRENCH €€
(☑02 97 70 61 39; 9 rue Glatinier; lunch menus €12-14, menus €20-30; ☉noon-1.30pm Tue-Sat, 7.30-9pm Tue, Thu-Sat) This pleasant family-run place offers an interesting and varied menu of local cooking with a sprinkle of fusion on top, making it a local favourite. The sweeping views of the town and valley from the terrace are fantastic for a summer lunch. It's a short walk beyond the château.

Le Prieuré de Clisson MODERN FRENCH €€
(☑02 97 73 93 58; www.le-prieure-de-clisson.fr; 2 rue Georges Le Berd; lunch menus €13-15, other menus €20-35; ☉noon-1.30pm Tue-Sun, 7.30-9pm Tue-Sat) Delightfully set in a former priory, Le Prieuré de Clisson has long been one of the town's *bonnes adresses*. Planked wood, beamed ceilings and groovy lighting make for a sober ambience. Top-notch market ingredients are used to maximum effect, and most dishes are homemade.

ℹ️ Information

Tourist Office (☑02 97 22 24 90; www. josselin-communaute.fr; 4 rue des Remparts; ☉10am-6pm Jul-Aug, 11am-noon Tue-Sat, 1.30-5.30pm Mon-Sat Apr-Jun & Sep) Not far from the castle entrance; has a useful list of local sites and *chambres'd'hôte*.

ℹ️ Getting There & Away

Keolis Armor (☑02 99 26 16 00; www.keolis -armor.fr) runs several daily buses to Rennes (€14.90, 1½ hours). The nearest train station is in Pontivy.

Forêt de Paimpont

Also known as Brocéliande, the Paimpont Forest is about 40km southwest of Rennes, and is legendary for being the place where King Arthur received Excalibur, his magic sword (forget that these stories are thought to have been brought to Brittany by Celtic settlers and hence probably took place offshore – it's a magical setting all the same).

The best base for exploring the forest is the lakeside village of Paimpont, which has a lovely Église Abbatiale (Abbey Church).

🏃 Activities

Some 95% of the forest is private land, but the tourist office, beside the 12th-century Église Abbatiale (Abbey Church) in Paimpont, has a free brochure outlining a 62km-long driving circuit with numerous short walks along the way that are accessible to the public. It also sells more-detailed walking and cycling guides.

🛏 Sleeping & Eating

**Camping Municipal
de Paimpont**   CAMPGROUND €
(☑ 02 99 07 89 16; www.camping-paimpont-broce-liande.com; rue du Chevalier Lancelot du Lac; sites/adult/car €3.15/3.45/1.70; ⊙ Apr-Sep) Campers can set up their tents at this lakeside campground.

La Corne de Cerf   B&B €
(☑ 02 99 07 84 19; http://corneducerf.bcld.net; Le Cannée; s/d incl breakfast €52/60) For garden lovers – flowers rampage all around – and history vultures, Annick and Robert's gorgeously restored village house is cool, quiet and elegantly homely. Each rooms has its own clear personality (we fell for the Emeraldine, decked out in blue shades), comfortable beds, soft colours and privacy. This authentic rural haven is in Le Cannée, about 2km away from Paimpont. No wi-fi.

Le Relais de Brocéliande   HOTEL €€
(☑ 02 99 07 84 94; www.le-relais-de-broceliande.fr; 5 rue du Forges, Paimpont; d €95-148; 🖥) In an old but thoroughly modernised building, this hotel attracts a varied foreign clientele, drawn by the homey guest rooms – clean, bright and comfortable, with excellent bedding and gleaming bathrooms – and the efficient staff. Perks include a renowned restaurant and a top-notch spa.

**Les Forges
de Paimpont**   TRADITIONAL FRENCH €€
(☑ 02 99 06 81 07; www.restaurant.forges-de-paim pont.com; Les Forges; lunch menu €12, other menus €16-33; ⊙ noon-2pm Wed-Sun, 7-9pm Wed-Sat) This rustic country inn with a cosy interior owes its reputation to a menu that's rooted in the traditions of the *terroir*. The excellent-value €22 set *menu* may include quail, deer, duck, pigeon or grilled beef ribsteak. Find Les Forges

de Paimpont in the hamlet of Les Forges, near Plélan-le-Grand.

❶ Tourist Information

Tourist Office (☑ 02 99 07 84 23; www.tourisme -broceliande.com; place du Roi Judicaël, Paimpont; ⊙10am-noon & 2-6pm, closed Mon Oct-Mar) Beside the 12th-century Église Abbatiale. Runs guided tours of the forest in summer.

Rennes

POP 212,200

A crossroads since Roman times, Brittany's vibrant capital sits at the junction of highways linking northwestern France's major cities. It's a beautifully set-out city, with an elaborate and stately centre and a superb medieval quarter that's a joy to get lost in. At night, this student city has no end of lively places to pop in for a pint and its restaurants are also superb.

◉ Sights

Cathédrale St-Pierre   CATHEDRAL
(rue de la Monnaie; ⊙9.30am-noon & 3-6pm) Crowning Rennes' old town is the 17th-century cathedral, which has an impressive, if dark, neoclassical interior.

**Palais du Parlement
de Bretagne**   LAW COURTS
(place du Parlement de Bretagne; adult/child €7/free) This 17th-century former seat of the rebellious Breton parliament has in more recent times been home to the Palais de Justice. In 1994 this building was destroyed by a fire started by demonstrating fishermen. It was reopened in 2004 after a major restoration and now houses the Court of Appeal. Daily guided tours (request in advance for a tour in English) take you through the ostentatiously gilded rooms. Tour bookings must be made through the tourist office.

Musée des Beaux-Arts   MUSEUM
(☑ 02 23 62 17 45; www.mbar.org; 20 quai Émile Zola; adult/child €5/free; ⊙ 10am-6pm Tue, 10am-noon & 2-6pm Wed-Sun) Rooms devoted to the Pont-Aven school are the highlight of the Musée des Beaux-Arts, which also has a 'curiosity gallery' of antiques and illustrations amassed in the 18th century. It also hosts numerous temporary exhibitions.

Champs Libres   CULTURAL CENTRE
(☑ 02 23 40 66 00; www.leschampslibres.fr; 10 cours des Alliés; ⊙ noon-9pm Tue, noon-7pm Wed-Fri, 2-7pm Sat & Sun) Rennes' futuristic cultural centre is

Rennes

home to the **Musée de Bretagne** (☎ 02 23 40 66 00; www.musee-bretagne.fr; 10 cours des Alliés; adult/child €4/3; ☼ noon-9pm Tue, noon-7pm Wed-Fri, 2-7pm Sat-Sun), with displays on Breton history and culture. Under the same roof is **Espace des Sciences** (☎ 02 23 40 66 40; www.espace-sciences.org; 10 cours des Alliés; adult €4.50-8, child €3-5; ☼ noon-9pm Tue, noon-7pm Wed-Fri, 2-7pm Sat-Sun), an interactive science museum, along with a planetarium, a temporary exhibition space and a library.

🎉 Festivals & Events

Les Mercredis du Thabor CULTURAL FESTIVAL
Traditional Breton dancing and music take place in Rennes' beautiful Parc du Thabor on Wednesdays during June and July.

Tombées de la Nuit CULTURAL FESTIVAL
(www.lestombeesdelanuit.com) Rennes' old town comes alive during this music and theatre festival in the first week of July.

Les Transmusicales de Rennes MUSIC FESTIVAL
(www.lestrans.com) In early December, Rennes hosts one of France's biggest music festivals at venues all across the city.

🛏 Sleeping

If you're planning to visit during the week it's wise that you make advance reservations, as many hotels are frequently booked solid. During the weekend demand drops hugely and many of the chain hotels offer cut-price rates.

Auberge de Jeunesse HOSTEL €
(☎ 02 99 33 22 33; www.hifrance.org; 10-12 canal St-Martin; dm/s incl breakfast €22/32; ☼ 7am-1am, closed late-Dec–mid-Jan; ☏) Rennes' well-equipped youth hostel has a self-catering kitchen and a canalside setting 2km north of the centre. Digs are in two- to five-bed rooms. Take bus 8 from place de la Mairie.

Rennes

Hôtel de Nemours HOTEL €

(☎02 99 78 26 26; www.hotelnemours.com; 5 rue de Nemours; s €63-71, d €73-94; ❄🌐) This reliable three-star abode ideally located near place de la République was undergoing a major renovation and extension at the time of writing. No doubt it'll rank among the best options in town by the time you read this.

★ Symphonie des Sens B&B €€

(☎02 99 79 30 30, 06 51 86 69 19; www.symphonie dessens.com; 3 rue du Chapitre; d incl breakfast €129; 🌐) Bang in the heart of the historic quarter, this 1435-built house has been transformed into an incredible *maison d'hôte*. Conscientious owner Fabrice has exquisitely decorated rooms with both modern touches and charming antiques. All five rooms open onto a suntrap interior courtyard. An unexpected haven of peace in central Rennes. Good English is spoken.

Hôtel des Lices HOTEL €€

(☎02 99 79 14 81; www.hotel-des-lices.com; 7 place des Lices; s €85-98, d €88-103; ❄🌐) You can peer down from the balconies or through the floor-to-ceiling glass doors to see the Saturday-morning market, which snakes right past the front door of this modern six-storey hotel. Inside, rooms are small but sleek, with contemporary furnishings and textured walls; most bathrooms have been recently upgraded. Rooms at the back are quieter and have views of the old ramparts.

✗ Eating

Rennes has a wide choice of restaurants. Rues St-Malo and St-Georges are the city's two main 'eat streets'; the latter in particular specialises in crêperies.

★ La Saint-Georges CRÊPERIE €

(☎02 99 38 87 04; www.creperie-saintgeorges.com; 11 rue du Chapitre; mains €5-17, lunch menu €12; ⊙noon-2pm & 7-10.30pm Tue-Sat) Whereas most crêperies play on the twee old-Breton style, this one takes a totally eccentric approach, despite the fact it occupies a heritage building – with its purple, green and gold furnishings, fluffy carpets and luxurious chairs, this place looks more like a glam Ibizan chill-out club.

Funky decor is matched by food with an experimental edge; where else in Brittany could you tuck into a crêpe with Chamallow sweets?

Le Café du Port BISTRO €

(☎02 99 30 01 43; 3 rue le Bouteiller; mains €9-14, menu €20; ⊙noon-2pm & 7.30-10.30pm Mon-Wed, to 11pm Thu-Sat) Market-fresh produce and great value is the name of the game at this laid-back, modern bistro that also doubles as a popular spot for an early evening drink. It has outdoor seating in warm weather.

L'Atelier des Gourmets TRADITIONAL FRENCH €€

(☎02 99 67 53 84; 12 rue Nantaise; mains €10-17, menus €26-28; ⊙noon-1.30pm & 7.30-9.30pm Tue-Fri, 7.30am-9.45pm Sat) This smart bistro is garnering serious accolades in a city where talent is in no short supply. The chef has created a hidden institution in the heart of Rennes, adeptly blending the best of high-end bistro fare with solid regional cuisine that is an impressive value. The menu is quite succinct.

La Réserve BISTRO €€

(☎02 99 84 02 02; www.lareserve-rennes.fr; 36 rue de la Visitation; mains €14-23, lunch menus €15-17, other menus €19-42; ⊙noon-2.15pm & 7-10.45pm Mon-Sat) What's so suprising about this contemporary bistro is how unfazed it is by its great success: it's usually full every night, yet the 'bistro chic' cuisine never wavers, the atmosphere is congenial and the prices are good value for Rennes.

Le Baron Rouge MODERN FRENCH €€

(☎02 99 79 08 09; www.lebaronrouge.fr; 15 rue du Chapitre; mains €18-25, menus €25-30; ⊙noon-2pm & 7.30-10.30pm Tue-Sat) This sleek restaurant has as much substance as style. The cuisine is a modern twist on French traditional recipes, with a good selection of predominantly meat dishes – the *tartare* is recommended.

BRITTANY RENNES

⚲ Drinking

Rue St-Michel – nicknamed rue de la Soif (Thirsty St) for its bars, pubs and cafes – is the best-known drinking strip, but it can get rowdy late at night.

Le Nabuchodonosor   WINE BAR
(12 rue Hoche; ⊘noon-11pm Tue-Sat) The favoured haunt of arty and intellectual types in Rennes, this charming wine bar is a great place for an evening drink in buzzing surroundings. Feeling peckish? It also serves cheese platters, *tartines*, salads and desserts.

Oan's Pub   PUB
(1 rue Georges Dottin; ⊘5pm-1am Mon-Sat) Locals habitually turn up with instruments for impromptu Celtic jam sessions at this cosy cave-like, stone-walled pub with Brittany-brewed Coreff beer on tap.

Le Bar'Hic   BAR
(24 place des Lices; ⊘5pm-3am Tue-Sat, 9pm-3am Sun & Mon) This inviting bar is a good place for getting a bit of local vibe. It fills up at night, when students and young hipsters stream in for the music events – usually live bands. Earlier in the evening it's much quieter. In warm weather bag a seat on the terrace and watch the world go by.

ℹ Information

Tourist Office (☑ 02 99 67 11 11; www. tourisme-rennes.com; 11 rue St-Yves; ⊘9am-6pm Mon-Sat, 11am-1pm & 2-6pm Sun) This tourist office offers an audioguide to the city, which takes you on a walking tour of eight sights for €6.90 (or it can be downloaded for free from the website). Staff can book accommodation at no cost.

ℹ Getting There & Away

BUS
Among Rennes' many bus services, **Illenoo** (☑ 08 10 35 10 35; www.illenoo-services.fr) runs regular daily services:
Dinan €5.10, 1½ hours
Dinard €5.10, two hours
Paimpont €4.10, one hour

TRAIN
Destinations with frequent train services:
Brest €30 to €41, two hours
Dinan €12.70 to €17.90, one hour including a change
Nantes €25.60, 1¼ hours
Paris Montparnasse €40 to €61, 2¼ hours
Quimper €29.50 to €41, 2½ hours

St-Malo €14.60 to €17, one hour
Vannes €17.50 to €25, one hour

ℹ Getting Around

BUS
Rennes has an efficient local bus network run by **STAR** (☑ 09 70 82 18 00; www.star.fr; 12 rue du Pré Botté). Bus tickets (single journey €1.40, 24-hour pass €3.80) are interchangeable with the metro.

METRO
Incredibly for a city of its size, Rennes has its own single-line metro system, run by STAR. The metro line runs northwest to southeast. Main stations include République (place de la République) in the centre, and Ste-Anne (old town).

TAXI
Call ☑ 02 99 30 79 79.

Vitré
POP 17,300

With its narrow cobbled streets, half-timbered houses and castle topped by witch's-hat turrets, Vitré rivals Dinan as one of Brittany's best-preserved medieval towns – with far fewer tourists and a more laissez-faire village air.

◉ Sights

Château   CASTLE
(☑ 02 99 75 04 54; place du Château; adult/child €4/free; ⊘10am-12.30pm & 2-6pm Sep-Jun, 10am-6pm Jul-Aug) From the outside, Vitré's medieval castle, which rises on a rocky outcrop overlooking the River Vilaine, is one of the most impressive in Brittany – a real fairytale of spires and drawbridges. However, once beyond the twin-turreted gateway you'll find the triangular inner courtyard somewhat bare. The château was originally built in 1060, and expanded in the 14th and 15th centuries.

⌂ Sleeping

Vitré has a shortage of accommodation, so it's worth booking ahead any time of year.

Le Minotel   HOTEL €
(☑ 02 99 75 11 11; www.leminotel.fr; 47 rue de la Poterie; s €50, d €60-70; ☎) In close proximity to the train station and the medieval castle, this 15-room hotel is superb value given its coveted location. Recently renovated rooms are decked out in beige and chocolate hues, with modern bathrooms and a cheerful breakfast room. Opt for the dearer rooms, which are

more spacious than the pocket-sized cheaper ones.

Hôtel du Château
HOTEL €

(☑02 99 74 58 59; www.hotelduchateauvitre.fr; 5 rue Rallon; s €50-63, d €56-69; ☺☻) Wake up to the aroma of freshly baked bread and, on upper floors (choose room 12, 14 or 15!), fantastic vistas of the castle at this family-run hotel at the base of the ramparts. The rooms are simple and the bathrooms miniscule, but the friendly owners are a great source of local information; there's an enchanting courtyard for breakfast (€9).

✗ Eating

Quaint crêperies and gastronomic restaurants are tucked away throughout the old town.

Auberge du Château
CRÊPERIE €

(☑02 99 75 01 83; 34 rue d'En Bas; mains €6-13; ☺noon-2pm Tue-Sun, 7-9pm Tue-Sat) For crêpes, salads and *tartines* look no further than the Auberge du Château, which occupies an atmospheric timber-framed house. There's outdoor seating in summer.

Le Potager de Louise
MODERN FRENCH €€

(☑02 99 74 68 88; 5 place du Général Leclerc; lunch menus €12-16, other menus €20-34; ☺noon-2pm & 7.30-9pm Tue-Sat) The food from Le Potager de Louise (Louise's vegetable garden) is assured and, as the name would suggest, all locally grown or sourced. It has a typical neo-bistro feel but with more imaginative taste combinations. One downside: there's no outdoor seating.

Auberge St-Louis
TRADITIONAL FRENCH €€

(31 rue Notre-Dame; menus €16-34; ☺noon-1.45pm & 7-9.15pm Tue-Sun) Just steps from Notre-Dame church, Auberge St-Louis is as much about ogling original 18th-century decor – check that dark-wood panelling and vintage hearth, man! – as feasting on good-value French classics such as grilled kidney veal, duck breast and lamb shanks.

ℹ Information

Tourist Office (☑02 99 75 04 46; www.ot-vitre. fr; place Général de Gaulle; ☺9.30am-12.30pm & 2-6.30pm Mon-Sat, 10am-12.30pm & 3-6pm Sun) Right outside the train station.

ℹ Getting There & Away

Frequent trains travel between Vitré and Rennes (from €8, 20 to 35 minutes).

Rochefort-en-Terre

POP 750

If you want to take an architectural trip into the Middle Ages, make a beeline for Rochefort-en-Terre. It's a photogenic town of narrow, cobbled streets and lovely squares lined with granite mansions, slate-roofed houses and flower-filled window boxes – not to mention a smattering of art galleries and the mandatory crêperies. Its picture-book perch on a rocky outcrop above the Gueuzon River is equally enchanting. As befits any medieval Breton town, it also boasts a lovely castle, which is not open to the public, and a superb church that was originally built in the 10th century.

🛏 Sleeping & Eating

Le Pélican
HOTEL €€

(☑02 97 43 38 48; www.hotel-pelican-rochefort.com; place des Halles; d with half-board €132-138) This warmly welcoming inn in a character-filled house right in the centre of Rochefort is superb value given its coveted location. Some of the cosy, carpeted rooms, with rustic furniture, open onto the main square. The onsite restaurant specialises in hearty regional cuisine. Note that half-board is mandatory.

Le Café Breton
CRÊPERIE €

(☑02 97 43 32 60; 8 rue du Porche; mains €5-13; ☺noon-9pm) If you only eat out once in Rochefort, make sure it's at Le Café Breton – so good it's a classified historic building. It's as much about ogling the original medieval decor as feasting on generous *galettes* and crêpes. It also doubles as a bar.

L'Art Gourmand
TEAROOM, CHOCOLATE €

(☑02 97 43 46 69; 2 rue des Scourtets; ☺10.30am-12.30pm & 2-6pm Tue-Sun) Set in a former *relais de poste* (coach inn) dating from the 16th century, this *chocolaterie* (chocolate shop) with tearoom sells exquisite chocolatey things and gorgeous biscuits.

ℹ Information

Tourist Office (☑02 97 26 56 00; www. rochefortenterre-tourisme.com; 7 place du Puits; ☺10am-1pm & 2-6.30pm Jul-Aug, closed Sun Apr-Jun & Sep) Sells a brochure on walking trails in the area.

Champagne

POP 1.3 MILLION

Best Places to Eat

➜ Claire et Hugo (p314)

➜ L'Éveil des Sens (p302)

➜ La Grillade Gourmande (p310)

➜ Tout Simplement (p315)

➜ Le Millénaire (p303)

Best Places to Stay

➜ Les Telliers (p301)

➜ La Villa Eugène (p309)

➜ La Villa de la Paix (p314)

➜ Château Les Crayères (p302)

➜ Parva Domus (p309)

Why Go?

Champagne arouses the senses: the eyes feast on vines parading up hillsides and vertical processions of tiny, sparkling bubbles; the nose breathes in damp soil and the heavenly bouquet of fermentation; the ears rejoice at the clink of glasses and the barely audible fizz; and the palate tingles with every sip. The imagination and the intellect are engaged as Champagne cellar visits reveal the magical processes – governed by the strictest of rules – that transform the world's most pampered pinot noir, pinot meunier and chardonnay grapes into this region's most fabled wines.

Despite the prestige of their vines, the people of Champagne offer a warm, surprisingly easy-going welcome, both in the stylish cities and along the Champagne Routes, which wend their way through villages to family-run cellars and vineyards. All of which will, if France has its way, become a Unesco World Heritage site in 2015. Watch this space.

When to Go
Reims

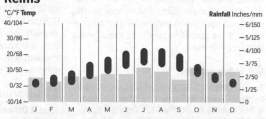

Jun Reims pays homage to Joan of Arc at the Fêtes Johanniques (first weekend).

Aug Cellars open for free tastings at the Côte des Bar's Route du Champagne en Fête (first weekend).

Sep Golden autumn days and cork-popping harvest celebrations.

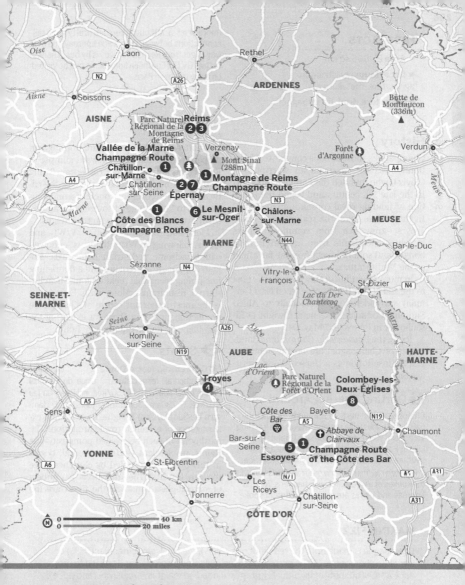

Champagne Highlights

1 Rambling through hillside vineyards, comely villages and family-run wineries on scenic **Champagne Routes** (p304)

2 Toasting the end of a **cellar tour** in Épernay (p308) or Reims (p298) with a glass of fizz

3 Climbing the tower of Reims' **Cathédrale Notre Dame** (p298) for 360-degree views of this flat region

4 Wandering the half-timbered backstreets of **Troyes** (p311)

5 Treading in Renoir's impressionistic footsteps at **Atelier Renoir** (p317), Essoyes

6 Marvelling at traditional Champagne-making techniques and technology at the **Musée de la Vigne et du Vin** (p308)

7 Revelling in the mansions

and Champagne houses lining Épernay's **Avenue de Champagne** (p308)

8 Immersing yourself in mid-20th century France at the **Mémorial Charles de Gaulle** (p316) in Colombey-les-Deux-Églises

FAST FACTS

⇒ **Area** 25,606 sq km

⇒ **Local industry** viticulture, agriculture, metallurgy

⇒ **Signature drink** Champagne!

History

Champagne's most famous convert to Christianity was the Merovingian warrior-king Clovis I, who founded the Frankish kingdom in the late 5th century and began the tradition of holding royal coronations in Reims. In the Middle Ages, the region – especially Troyes –grew rich from commercial fairs at which merchants from around Europe bought and sold products from as far afield as the Mediterranean.

In more recent history, the region was host to the end of WWII in Europe when Nazi Germany surrendered unconditionally to Allied Supreme Commander General Dwight D Eisenhower in Reims on 7 May 1945.

Today, the *paysages du Champagne* (landscapes of Champagne) are on the Tentative List for inscription as a Unesco World Heritage Site.

❶ Getting There & Around

Champagne, just north of Burgundy's Châtillonnais and Chablis wine regions, makes a refreshing stopover if you're driving from the Channel ports, Lille or Paris eastward to Lorraine or Alsace, or southeastward towards Dijon, Lyon or Provence.

France's rail lines radiate out from Paris like the spokes of a wheel and, as it happens, Reims, Épernay and Troyes are each on a different spoke (more or less). Although there are pretty good rail connections between Reims and Épernay, the best way to get from Reims to Troyes is by bus. Thanks to the TGV Est Européen line, Reims can be visited on a day trip from Paris.

REIMS

POP 184,652

No matter what you have read, nothing can prepare you for that first skyward glimpse of Reims' gargantuan Gothic cathedral. Rising golden and imperious above the city, the cathedral is where, over the course of a millennium (816 to 1825), some 34 sovereigns – among them two dozen kings – began their reigns.

Meticulously restored after WWI and again following WWII, Reims is endowed with handsome pedestrian boulevards, Roman remains, art deco cafes and a flourishing fine-dining scene that includes four Michelin-starred restaurants. Along with Épernay, it is the most important centre of Champagne production, and a fine base for exploring the Montagne de Reims Champagne Route.

◉ Sights

★ **Cathédrale Notre Dame**　CATHEDRAL
(www.cathedrale-reims.culture.fr; place du Cardinal Luçon; tower adult/child €7.50/free, incl Palais du Tau €11/free; ⊙ 7.30am-7.30pm, tower tours hourly 11am-4pm Tue-Sun May-Sep) Imagine the egos and extravagance of a French royal coronation. The focal point of such bejewelled pomposity was Reims' resplendent Gothic cathedral, begun in 1211 on a site occupied by churches since the 5th century. The interior is a rainbow of stained-glass windows; the finest are the

MAKING FIZZ

Champagne is made from the red pinot noir (38%), the black pinot meunier (35%) or the white chardonnay (27%) grape. Each vine is vigorously pruned and trained to produce a small quantity of high-quality grapes. Indeed, to maintain exclusivity (and price), the designated areas where grapes used for Champagne can be grown and the amount of wine produced each year are limited.

Making Champagne according to the traditional method (*méthode champenoise*) is a complex procedure. There are two fermentation processes, the first in casks and the second after the wine has been bottled and had sugar and yeast added. Bottles are then aged in cellars for two to five years, depending on the *cuvée* (vintage).

During the two months in early spring that the bottles are aged in cellars kept at 12°C, the wine turns effervescent. The sediment that forms in the bottle is removed by *remuage*, a painstakingly slow process in which each bottle, stored horizontally, is rotated slightly every day for weeks until the sludge works its way to the cork. Next comes *dégorgement*: the neck of the bottle is frozen, creating a blob of solidified Champagne and sediment, then removed.

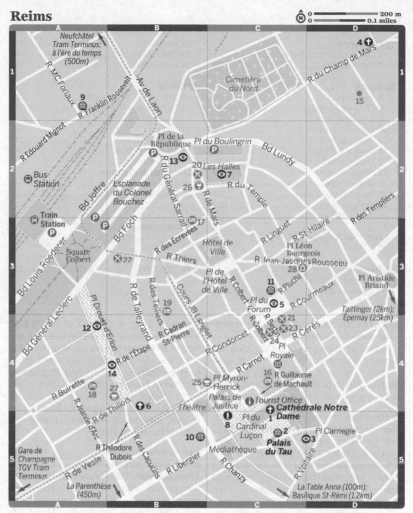

western façade's 12-petalled **great rose window**, the north transept's **rose window** and the vivid **Chagall** creations (1974) in the central axial chapel. The tourist office rents audioguides (€6) for self-paced cathedral tours.

Among the other highlights of the interior are a flamboyant **Gothic organ case** (15th and 18th centuries) topped with a figure of Christ, a 15th-century wooden **astronomical clock**, and a statue of **Joan of Arc in full body armour** (1901); there's a second **statue** of her outside on the square, to the right as you exit the cathedral.

The single most famous event to take place here was the coronation of Charles VII, with Joan of Arc at his side, on 17 July 1429. This is one of 25 coronations that took place between 1223 and 1825.

The cathedral was seriously damaged by artillery and fire during WWI, and was repaired during the interwar years, thanks, in part, to significant donations from the American Rockefeller family.

A Unesco World Heritage Site since 1991, the cathedral celebrated its 800th anniversary in 2011. To get the most impressive first view, approach the cathedral from the west, along **rue Libergier**. Here your gaze will be drawn to the heavily restored architectural features of the façade, lavishly encrusted with sculptures. Among them is the 13th-century *L'Ange*

Reims

au Sourire (Smiling Angel), presiding beneficently above the central portal.

Feeling as strong as Goliath? (Look for his worn figure up on the west façade, held in place with metal straps.) Then consider climbing 250 steps up the **cathedral tower** on a one-hour tour. Book at the Palais du Tau.

★**Basilique St-Rémi**   BASILICA
(place du Chanoine Ladame; ⊘8am-7pm) FREE
This 121m-long former Benedictine abbey church, a Unesco World Heritage Site, mixes Romanesque elements from the mid-11th century (the worn but stunning nave and transept) with early Gothic features from the latter half of the 12th century (the choir, with a large triforium gallery and, way up top, tiny clerestory windows). Next door, **Musée St-Rémi** (53 rue Simon; adult/child €4/free; ⊘2-6.30pm Mon-Fri, to 7pm Sat & Sun), in a 17th- and 18th-century abbey, features local Gallo-Roman archaeology, tapestries and 16th- to 19th-century military history.

The abbey church is named in honour of Bishop Remigius, who baptised Clovis and 3000 Frankish warriors in 498. The 12th-century-style chandelier has 96 candles, one for each year of the life of St Rémi, whose tomb (in the choir) is marked by a mausoleum from the mid-1600s.

★**Palais du Tau**   MUSEUM
(http://palais-tau.monuments-nationaux.fr; 2 place du Cardinal Luçon; adult/child €7.50/free, incl cathe-

dral tower €11/free; ⊘9.30am-12.30pm & 2-5.30pm Tue-Sun) A Unesco World Heritage Site, this former archbishop's residence, constructed in 1690, was where French princes stayed before their coronations – and where they hosted sumptuous banquets afterwards. Now a museum, it displays truly exceptional statuary, liturgical objects and tapestries from the cathedral, some in the impressive, Gothic-style Salle de Tau (Great Hall).

Musée des Beaux-Arts   ART MUSEUM
(8 rue Chanzy; adult/child €4/free; ⊘10am-noon & 2-6pm Wed-Mon) This institution's rich collection, housed in an 18th-century abbey, boasts one of the four versions of Jacques-Louis David's world-famous *The Death of Marat* (yes, the bloody corpse in the bathtub), 27 works by Camille Corot (only the Louvre has more), 13 portraits by German Renaissance painters Cranach the Elder and the Younger, lots of Barbizon School landscapes, some art nouveau creations by Émile Gallé, and two works each by Monet, Gauguin and Pissarro.

Musée Hôtel Le Vergeur   MUSEUM
(www.museelevergeur.com; 36 place du Forum; adult/child €5/free; ⊘2-6pm Tue-Sun) Highlights in this 13th- to 16th-century townhouse include a series of furnished period rooms (kitchen, smoking room, Napoléon III's bedroom), some engravings by Albrecht Dürer and a stunning Renaissance façade facing the interior garden.

Musée de la Reddition
MUSEUM

(12 rue Franklin Roosevelt; adult/child €4/free; ⊙10am-noon & 2-6pm Wed-Mon) The original Allied battle maps are still affixed to the walls of US General Dwight D Eisenhower's headquarters, where Nazi Germany, represented by General Alfred Jodl, surrendered unconditionally at 2.41am on 7 May 1945, thus ending WWII. Displays include military uniforms and photographs. A 12-minute film is screened in French, English and German.

Roman Reims
ROMAN SITES

For a quick trip back to Roman Gaul, check out the massive Porte de Mars (Mars Gate; place de la République), a three-arched triumphal gate built in the 2nd century AD, and the below-street-level Cryptoportique (place du Forum; ⊙2-6pm Jun-Sep) FREE, thought to have been used for grain storage in the 3rd century AD. Cultural events are occasionally held in the adjacent amphitheatre (place du Forum).

Place Drouet d'Erlon
SQUARE

Reims' pedestrianised main square draws locals in the mood for a bite or a bit of shopping. Its centrepiece is the Subé Fountain, built in 1907 and crowned by a gleaming gold statue of Winged Victory. The 12th- to 14th-century Église St-Jacques (rue Marx Dormoy; ⊙2-6pm Mon, 9am-noon & 2-6pm Tue-Sat, 10am-noon & 5.30-7pm Sun) is the city's only remaining medieval parish church. The blue and white windows in the nave were added in 2010.

Chapelle Foujita
CHAPEL

(33 rue du Champ de Mars; adult/child €3/free; ⊙2-6pm Wed-Mon) The last great work by the Japanese-born artist Tsuguharu (Léonard) Foujita (1886-1968). Inaugurated in 1966.

☞ Tours

The musty *caves* (cellars) and dusty bottles of the ten Reims-based Champagne houses (known as *maisons* – literally, 'houses') can be visited on guided tours. The following places both have fancy websites, cellar temperatures of 10°C to 12°C (bring warm clothes!) and frequent English-language tours that end, *naturellement,* with a tasting session

Mumm
CHAMPAGNE HOUSE

(☑03 26 49 59 70; www.mumm.com; 34 rue du Champ de Mars; one-hour tours incl tasting €14-25; ⊙tours 9am-5pm daily, shorter hrs & closed Sun winter) Mumm (pronounced 'moom'), the only *maison* in central Reims, was founded in 1827 and is now the world's third-largest producer (almost eight million bottles a year). Engaging and edifying one-hour tours take you through

cellars filled with 25 million bottles of fine bubbly. Wheelchair accessible. Phone ahead if possible.

Taittinger
CHAMPAGNE HOUSE

(☑03 26 85 45 35; www.taittinger.com; 9 place St-Niçaise; tours €16.50-45; ⊙9.30am-5.30pm, shorter hrs & closed Sun in winter) The headquarters of Taittinger are an excellent place to come for a clear, straightforward presentation on how Champagne is actually made – there's no claptrap about 'the Champagne mystique' here. Parts of the cellars occupy 4th-century Roman stone quarries; other bits were excavated by 13th-century Benedictine monks. No need to reserve. Situated 1.5km southeast of Reims centre; take the Citadine 1 or 2 bus to the St-Niçaise or Salines stops.

🛏 Sleeping

Chambre d'Hôte Cathédrale
B&B €

(☑03 26 91 06 22; 21 place du Chapitre; s/d/tr without bathroom €50/60/75) The cathedral bells are your wake-up call at this sweet and simple B&B. Rooms are immaculate and old-fashioned, with stripy wallpaper, heavy wood furnishings and shared bathrooms.

Hôtel Azur
B&B €

(☑03 26 47 43 39; www.hotel-azur-reims.com; 9 rue des Ecrevées; s €53.50, d €79.80, tr €99, q €109; 🖼) Slip down a sidestreet in the heart of Reims to reach this petite B&B, which extends a heartfelt welcome. Rooms are cheerfully painted and immaculately kept, and breakfast is served on the garden patio when the sun's out. There's no lift, so be prepared to lug your bags.

★ Les Telliers
B&B €€

(☑09 53 79 80 74; http://telliers.fr; 18 rue des Telliers; s €67-83, d €79-114, tr €115-134, q €131-155; 🖼) Enticingly positioned down a quiet alley near the cathedral, this bijou B&B extends one of Reims' warmest *bienvenues*. The high-ceilinged rooms are big on art-deco character, handsomely decorated with ornamental fireplaces, polished oak floors and the odd antique. Breakfast costs an extra €9 and is a generous spread of pastries, fruit, fresh-pressed juice and coffee.

---

❶ PASS REIMS

The great-value Pass Reims (€9), available at the tourist office, gives you entry to a museum of your choice, an audioguide tour of the city, plus discounts on activities such as Champagne house visits.

DON'T MISS

ART DECO REIMS

The vaulted **Halles du Boulingrin** (rue de Mars; ⊙ food market 7am-1pm Wed, 7am-1pm & 4-8pm Fri, 6am-2pm Sat) were a symbol of Reims' emergence from the destruction of WWI when they began service as the city's main food market in 1929. Following a major restoration project, the Halles were reopened in all their art deco glory in September 2012. Besides sheltering a food market, they provide a unique backdrop for exhibitions and cultural events.

Thanks to a donation from the US-based Carnegie Foundation, the lobby of the **Bibliothèque** (2 place Carnegie; ⊙ 10am-1pm & 2-7pm Tue, Wed & Fri, 2-7pm Thu, 10am-1pm & 2-6pm Sat) boasts gorgeous 1920s mosaics, stained glass, frescos and an extraordinary chandelier; duck inside for a look.

The tourist office also has a brochure on art deco sites around Reims.

La Parenthèse
B&B €€

(☑ 03 26 40 39 57; www.laparenthese.fr; 83 rue Clovis; min 2-night stay d €180-220; 🖤) Tucked away in the backstreets of old Reims, this little B&B has got everything going for it. The rooms are tastefully done with wood floors and bursts of pastel colour, and all come with kitchenettes. The good-natured owner will squeeze in a cot if you ask.

Hôtel de la Paix
HOTEL €€

(☑ 03 26 40 04 08; www.bestwestern-lapaix-reims.com; 9 rue Buirette; d €180-230; 🖤@🖤🖤) Outclassing most of Reims' midrange options, this contemporary, Best Western–affiliated hotel is just off cafe-lined place Drouet d'Erlon. To mellow out, head to the pool, jacuzzi, hammam, fitness room or the Zen-like courtyard garden.

★Château Les Crayères
LUXURY HOTEL €€€

(☑ 03 26 24 90 00; www.lescrayeres.com; 64 bd Henry-Vasnier; d €400-850; 🖤@🖤) Such class! If you've ever wanted to stay in a palace, this romantic château on the fringes of Reims is the real McCoy. Manicured lawns sweep to the graceful turn-of-the-century estate, where you can play golf or tennis, dine in two-Michelin-starred finery, and stay in the lap of luxury in exuberantly furnished, chandelier-lit interiors – all at a price, naturally.

✕ Eating

A tempting array of delis, patisseries and chocolatiers line up along rue de Mars, near Halles du Boulingrin. Place du Forum is a great place to watch the world drift languidly by at bistros and bars with pavement seating.

à l'ére du temps
CRÊPERIE €

(☑ 03 26 06 16 88; http://aleredutemps.com; 123 avenue de Laon; lunch menu €10; ⊙ noon-2pm & 7-10pm Tue-Sat) A short stroll north of Place de la République brings you to this sweet and simple crêperie. It does a roaring trade in homemade crêpes, buckwheat *galettes* and gourmet salads.

La Cave aux Fromages
CHEESE €

(12 place du Forum; ⊙ 8am-1pm & 3.30-7.45pm Tue-Sat) Run by the knowledgable Charlet family, this fabulous shop is *fromage* heaven, with cheeses carefully sourced from all four corners of France. Among them is the regional speciality Cendré de Champagne, a creamy, smoky cheese matured in beech ash.

★L'Éveil des Sens
BISTRO €€

(☑ 03 26 35 16 95; www.eveildessens-reims.com; 8 rue Colbert; menus €30-38; ⊙ 12.15-2pm & 7.15-10pm, closed Sun & Wed) The 'awakening of the senses' is a fitting name for this terrific bistro. Monochrome hues and white linen create a chic yet understated setting for market-fresh cuisine delivered with finesse. Nicolas Lefèvre's specialities appear deceptively simple on paper, but the flavours are profound – be it scallops with tangy Granny Smith apple or braised beef ravioli on white bean velouté.

La Table Anna
TRADITIONAL FRENCH €€

(☑ 03 26 89 12 12; www.latableanna.fr; 6 rue Gambetta; menus 2-/3-course lunch €15-17, dinner €29-47; ⊙ noon-1.30pm Tue-Sun, 7-9pm Tue & Thu-Sun) So what if the decor is chintzy – there is a reason why this bistro is as busy as a beehive. Friendly service and a *menu* packed with well-executed classics – Arctic char with champagne sauce, fillet of veal in a rich, earthy morel sauce – hit the mark every time. The three-course, €17.50 lunch is a steal.

Brasserie Le Boulingrin
BRASSERIE €€

(☑ 03 26 40 96 22; www.boulingrin.fr; 29-31 rue de Mars; menus €20-29; ⊙ noon-2.30pm & 7-10.30pm Mon-Sat) A genuine, old-time brasserie – the decor and zinc bar date back to 1925 – whose ambience and cuisine make it an enduring favourite. From September to June, the culinary focus is on *fruits de mer* (seafood) like Breton oysters. There's always a €9.50 lunch special.

Le Bocal SEAFOOD €€
(☎ 03 26 47 02 51; 27 rue de Mars; mains €13-18; ⊙ 12.30-2pm & 7.30-10pm Tue-Sat) Winningly fresh seafood is the big deal at this tiny eatery: try sardines tossed in chilli butter or hot oysters with parmesan.

★ **Le Millénaire** GASTRONOMIC €€€
(☎ 03 26 08 26 62; www.lemillenaire.com; 4-6 rue Bertin; menus €35-94; ⊙ noon-1.45pm & 7.30-9.30pm Mon-Fri, 7.30-9.30pm Sat) Sand and claret hues and contemporary artworks create an air of intimate sophistication at this Michelin-starred haunt. Chef Laurent Laplaige keeps flavours crisp and seasonal with specialities such as wild sea bass with celery, truffle risotto and Champagne sauce.

Le Foch GASTRONOMIC €€€
(☎ 03 26 47 48 22; www.lefoch.com; 37 bd Foch; menus lunch €27-33, dinner €50-85; ⊙ 12.15-2pm Tue-Fri & Sun, 7.30-10pm Tue-Sat) Described as 'one of France's best fish restaurants' by the food critic Michael Edwards, Michelin-starred Le Foch serves up cuisine that is as beautiful as it is delicious. Specialities like scallops with parsnip, butternut and truffle emulsion are expertly paired with wines and presented with panache.

🍷 Drinking & Nightlife

Café du Palais CAFE
(www.cafedupalais.fr; 14 place Myron-Herrick; ⊙ 9am-8.30pm Tue-Fri, 9am-9.30pm Sat) Run by the same family since 1930, this art-deco cafe is *the* place to sip a glass of Champagne. Lit by a skylight is an extraordinary collection of bric-a-brac ranging from the inspired to the kitsch.

Hall Place WINE BAR
(www.hallplace.fr; 23bis rue de Mars; ⊙ 10am-10pm Mon-Thu, 10am-10.30pm Fri, 8am-4pm Sat) Relax and sip Champagne at this wine bar, a huge hit with Reims' in-crowd. Cheese and charcuterie tasting plates (around €12) go nicely with regional wines. Streetside butcher-block tables look out on the curves of Halles du Boulingrin.

Waïda TEAROOM
(5 place Drouet d'Erlon; ⊙ 7.30am-7.30pm Tue-Fri, 7.30am-8pm Sat, 8am-2pm & 3.30-7.30pm Sun) A tea room and confectioner with old-fashioned mirrors, mosaics and marble. This is a good place to pick up a box of Reims' famous *biscuits roses,* traditionally nibbled with Champagne, rainbow-bright macarons and divine *religieuses* (cream-filled puff pastries).

🛍 Shopping

Vins CPH WINE
(www.vinscph.com; 3 place Léon Bourgeois; ⊙ 9.30am-12.30pm & 2.30-7pm Tue-Sat) Shop for wines the way savvy locals do. At the end of the courtyard, head down into the cellar for a huge selection (some 1000 vintages are on offer), including over 150 Champagnes.

ℹ Information

Tourist Office (☎ 03 26 77 45 00; www.reims-tourisme.com; 2 rue Guillaume de Machault; ⊙ 9am-7pm Mon-Sat, 10am-6pm Sun)

ℹ Getting There & Away

CAR
Rental agencies:
ADA (☎ 08 11 69 03 05; www.ada.fr; cour de la Gare)
Hertz (☎ 03 26 47 98 78; www.hertz.fr; 26 bd Joffre)
Rent a Car Système (☎ 03 26 77 87 77; www.rentacar.fr; 28 bd Joffre)

TRAIN
Reims train station, 1km northwest of the cathedral, was renovated in 2010; the bullet marks on the façade date from both world wars. Frequent services run to Paris Gare de l'Est (€36 to €44, 46 minutes to one hour, 12 to 17 daily). Direct services also go to Épernay (€6.80, 22 to 42 minutes, 19 daily) and Laon (€10.20, 36 to 47 minutes, three to nine daily). The journey to Troyes (€55 to €79, 2½ to three hours, eight daily) involves at least one change.

ℹ Getting Around

BICYCLE
Holiday Bikes (www.holiday-bikes.com; cour de la Gare; ⊙ 8am-noon & 2-6.30pm Mon-Fri, 8am-11am & 4-6pm Sat) Rents out city/mountain bikes for €17/22 per day.

BUS & TRAM
Reims' tram line links the city centre (rue de Vesle and cours JB Langlet) and the train station in Gare de Champagne-Ardenne TGV, on the Paris–Strasbourg TGV Est Européen line.

Two circular bus lines, the clockwise Citadine 1 and the anticlockwise Citadine 2 (single ticket €1.50, all-day ticket *journée* €3.70) serve most of the major sights of Reims. Most TUR lines begin their last runs at about 9.50pm; five night lines operate until 12.15am.

TAXI
Call ☎ 03 26 47 05 05.

CHAMPAGNE ROUTES OF THE MARNE

The Champagne Routes (www.tourisme-en-champagne.com, in French) of the Marne département wend their way among neat rows of hillside vines, through hilltop forests and across lowland crop fields. Along the way, they call on wine-making villages and hamlets, some with notable churches or specialty museums, others quite ordinary, most without a centre or even a cafe. At almost every turn, beautiful panoramas unfold and small-scale, family-run Champagne wineries welcome travellers in search of bubbly.

Area tourist offices can supply you with details on B&Bs, and on the opening times (and English capabilities) of various Champagne producers – but bear in mind that their map-brochures are far from exhaustive. Many producers prefer that visitors phone ahead but, if you haven't, don't be shy about knocking on the door. Almost all producers are closed around the *vendange* (grape harvest, from very late August into October), when bringing in the crop by hand – mechanical harvesters are forbidden here – eclipses all other activities. More and more young *vignerons* (winegrowers) speak English.

The Champagne Routes of the Marne map shows three serpentine itineraries – Montagne de Reims, Vallée de la Marne and Côte des Blancs. The routes are not designed to be driven in their entirety in a single day so pick and choose segments that suit your mood; we've covered just a few of the villages and highlights.

The Champagne Routes, which follow secondary and tertiary rural roads, are signposted but there are so many twists and turn-offs that setting off without a map would be unwise. Bookshops and tourist offices sell Michelin's yellow-jacketed, 1:150,000-scale Aisne, Ardennes, Marne map (No 306; €6.50).

Routes of the Marne

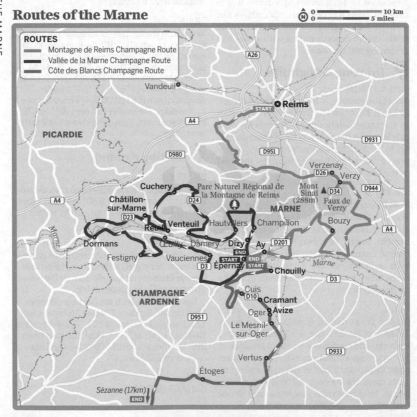

Montagne de Reims Champagne Route

Linking Reims with Épernay by skirting the Parc Natural Régional de la Montagne de Reims, a regional park covering the forested Reims Mountain plateau, this meandering, 70km route passes through vineyards planted mainly with pinot noir vines. Villages are listed in the order you'll encounter them if starting out from Reims.

Verzenay

For the region's best introduction to the art of growing grapes and the cycles of the seasons, head to the **Phare de Verzenay** (Verzenay Lighthouse; www.lepharedeverzenay.com; D26; lighthouse adult/child €3/2, incl museum €8.50/4.50; ⊙10am-5pm Tue-Fri, to 5.30pm Sat & Sun, closed Jan–mid-Mar), on a hilltop at the eastern edge of the village. Exactly 101 spiral stairs lead to the top of the lighthouse, constructed as a publicity stunt in 1909, which rewards visitors with unsurpassed 360-degree views of vine, field and forest – and, if you're lucky, a tiny TGV zipping by in the distance. The Sillery sugar mill, visible on the horizon, turns an astounding 16,000 tonnes of beets (a major regional crop) into 2600 tonnes of sugar each day! After brushing up on the seasonal processes involved in Champagne production in the museum, stop by the tasting room for a glass of fizz (there are 30 varieties to sample).

The **Moulin de Verzenay** (Verzenay Windmill; D26), on the western edge of town, was used as an observation post during WWI and by the US Army during WWII. The interior is closed but the nearby hill offers fine valley views.

Parc Natural Régional de la Montagne de Reims

The 500 sq km Montagne de Reims Regional Park is best known for a botanical curiosity, 800 mutant beech trees known as faux de Verzy (see http://verzy.verzenay.online.fr for photos). To get a good look at the trees, which have torturously twisted trunks and branches that hang down like an umbrella, take the Balade des Faux forest walk from 'Les Faux' parking lot, 2km up D34 from Verzy (situated on D26).

Across D34, a 500m gravel path leads through the forest to a *point de vue* (panoramic viewpoint) – next to a concrete WWI bunker – atop 288m-high Mont Sinaï.

Vallée de la Marne Champagne Route

A stronghold of pinot meunier vines, this 90km itinerary winds from Épernay to Dormans, heading more or less west along the hillsides north of the River Marne; it then circles back to the east along the river's south bank. The GR14 long-distance walking trail and its variants (eg GR141) pass through the area.

Hautvillers

Perched above a sea of emerald vines and ablaze with forsythia and tulips in spring, Hautvillers (population 790) is where Dom Pierre Pérignon (1638–1715) is popularly believed to have created Champagne. The good Dom's tomb is in front of the altar of the **Église Abbatiale**, adorned with 17th-century woodwork. The village is one of Champagne's prettiest, with ubiquitous medieval-style wrought-iron signs providing pictorial clues to the activities taking place on the other side of the wall.

The attractive main square is place de la République. Here you'll find the helpful **tourist office** (☑03 26 57 06 35; www.tourisme-hautvillers.com; place de la République; ⊙9.30am-1pm & 1.30-5.30pm Mon-Sat, 10am-4pm Sun), where you can pick up excellent free maps for several vineyard walks. One-hour guided tours cost €3 (with a Champagne tasting €5). Steps away is **Au 36** (www.au36.net; 36 rue Dom Pérignon; ⊙10.30am-6pm Tue-Sun Apr-Oct, shorter hrs in winter), a slinky wine boutique with a 'wall' of Champagne, innovatively arranged by aroma, and a laid-back upstairs tasting room. A two-/three glass tasting costs €11/15.

Astonishing **vineyard views** await a few hundred metres north of the centre along route de Fismes (D386); south along route de Cumières (a road leading to D1); and along the GR14 long-distance walking trail (red-and-white markings) and local vineyard footpaths (yellow markings).

Hautvillers is twinned with the Alsatian town of Eguisheim, which explains why three storks live in the **Voilière des Cigognes Altavilloises** (D386) **FREE**, an easy 500m walk towards Épernay from place de la République. If you're not expecting a baby, this may be your only chance to get a close-up view of these majestic birds. In most years, storklings hatch here in May.

Hautvillers is 6km north of Épernay.

CHAMPAGNE SAVOIR-FAIRE

Buying and tasting Champagne for the first time? These tips will have you talking fizz, popping corks and swirling like a pro in no time.

Champagne Types

➡ **Blanc de Blancs** Champagne made using only chardonnay grapes. Fresh and elegant, with very small bubbles and a bouquet reminiscent of 'yellow fruits' such as pear and plum.

➡ **Blanc de Noirs** A full-bodied, deep golden Champagne made solely with black grapes (despite the colour). Often rich and refined, with great complexity and a long finish.

➡ **Rosé** Pink Champagne (mostly served as an aperitif), with a fresh character and summer-fruit flavours. Made by adding a small percentage of red pinot noir to white Champagne.

➡ **Prestige Cuvée** The crème de la crème of Champagne. Usually made with grapes from *grand cru* vineyards, and priced and bottled accordingly.

➡ **Millésimé** Vintage Champagne produced from a single crop during an exceptional year. Most Champagne is non-vintage.

Champagne Sweetness

➡ **Brut** Dry, most common style, pairs well with food.

➡ **Extra Sec** Fairly dry but sweeter than Brut, nice as an aperitif.

➡ **Demi Sec** Medium sweet, goes well with fruit and dessert.

➡ **Doux** Very sweet, a dessert Champagne.

Serving & Tasting

➡ **Chilling** Chill Champagne in a bucket of ice 30 minutes before serving. The ideal serving temperature is 7°C to 9°C.

➡ **Opening** Grip the bottle securely and tilt it at a 45° angle facing away from you. Rotate the bottle slowly to ease out the cork – it should sigh not pop.

➡ **Pouring** Hold the flute by the stem at an angle and let the Champagne trickle gently into the glass – less foam, more bubbles.

➡ **Tasting** Admire the colour and bubbles. Swirl your glass to release the aroma and inhale slowly before tasting the Champagne.

Cuchery

You're assured a warm – and English-speaking – welcome and a fascinating cellar tour at **Albert Levasseur** (☑ 03 26 58 11 38; www.champagne-levasseur.fr; 6 rue Sorbier, Cuchery; ☺ 8am-noon & 2-6pm Mon-Fri, 8-11.30am Sat), run by a friendly Franco-Irish couple, which turns grapes grown on 4.2 hectares into 35,000 to 40,000 bottles of Champagne each year. Try to phone or email ahead if possible – but if not just drop by and knock. Situated in the hamlet of Cuchery (population 438), 18km northwest of Épernay on D24.

Châtillon-sur-Marne

The highest point in this sloping village (population 845) is crowned by a 25m-high statue of **Pope Urban II**, dedicated in 1887,

a particularly successful local boy (1042–99) best known to history for having launched the bloody First Crusade. The orientation table near the base offers excellent views of the Marne Valley and is a super spot for a picnic.

The **tourist office** (☑ 03 26 58 32 86; www.otchatillon51.com; 4 rue de l'Église; ☺ 10am-12.30pm & 2-6pm Tue-Sun, 2-6pm Mon) is very near the partly Romanesque **church**. A map panel right next to the post office details an 11km, four-hour **vineyard walk**.

Châtillon is 19km west of Épernay, on D23.

Œuilly

To get a sense of winegrowing life a century ago, drop by the **Écomusée d'Œuilly** (www.ecomusee-oeuilly.fr; cour des Maillets; adult/child €6.50/4; ☺ tours 10.30am & 2pm Wed-Mon), whose three sections include a schoolroom from

1900. Behind the sturdy 13th-century **Église St-Memmie**, the panoramic churchyard is the final resting place of five members of a RAF air crew downed in 1944; each grave bears a moving personal inscription.

Œuilly is 15km west of Épernay, just off D3.

Côte des Blancs Champagne Route

This 100km route, planted almost exclusively with white chardonnay grapes (the name means 'hillside of the whites'), begins along Épernay's majestic av du Champagne and then heads south to Sézanne and beyond. The gently rolling landscape is at its most attractive in late summer and autumn.

Cramant

For views of the neatly tended vines and the patchwork colours of the Champagne countryside, check out the view from the ridge above this village (population 912), whose northern entrance is adorned by a two-storey-high champagne bottle. Situated on D10 7.5km southeast of Épernay on D10.

Avize

Many past, present and future Champagne makers learned, or are learning, their art and science at the **Lycée Viticole de la Champagne** (Champagne High School of Winemaking; www.les-enfants-de-la-viti.com), run by the Ministry of Agriculture. As part of their studies, students produce quite excellent bubbly, made with grapes from some of Champagne's most prestigious parcels and sold under the label Champagne Sanger (www.sanger.fr). Sanger was established shortly after WWI, which is why the name is pronounced *'sans guerre'* ('without war'), ie son-GHER.

At the **Sanger Cellars** (☑03 26 57 79 79; www.sanger.fr; 33 rue du Rempart du Midi; ⊗8am-noon & 2-5pm Mon-Fri), free tours of the high school's impressive production facilities take in both traditional equipment and the latest high-tech machinery. Champagnes are sold at the discounted *prix départ cave* (cellar-door price); profits are reinvested in the school. The entrance is on D19; if the door is locked, push the intercom button.

Once the abbey church of a Benedictine convent, **Église St-Nicolas**, on rue de l'Église (D10), mixes Romanesque, Flamboyant Gothic and Renaissance styles. From there, aptly named rue de la Montagne leads up the hill (towards Grauves) – past another oversized Champagne bottle – to **Parc Vix** (D19), which affords panoramic vineyard views; a map sign details a 6.5km, two-hour walk through forest and field.

Oger

Oger (population 590) is known for its *grand cru* fields, prize-winning flower gardens and the **Musée du Mariage** (www.mariage-et-champagne.com; 1 rue d'Avize/D10; adult/child €7/free; ⊗9.30am-noon & 2-6pm Tue-Sun). Featuring colourful and often gaudy objects associated with 19th-century marriage traditions, highlights include a tableau of newlyweds in their nuptial bed – but they're not alone, for they've

MORE BUBBLES FOR EVERYONE

Around 55% of the 320 million bottles of Champagne sold each year are popped open, sipped and savoured in France itself. That doesn't leave much for the rest of us, especially when you consider how many bottles are wasted naming ships and showering victorious football players. But help is at hand. Faced with rising worldwide demand, the government body that regulates where Champagne grapes can be grown has proposed expanding the area – currently 327 sq km – for the first time since 1927. Starting in about 2017, 40 very lucky villages are likely to start planting their very first official Champagne vines. Not surprisingly, the exact delineation of the new vineyards has been hugely controversial, not least because the value of land declared Champagne-worthy will rise by up to 30,000%, to about €1 million per hectare!

Large *maisons* (Champagne houses) with global brand recognition send a high percentage of their production to other countries (Moët & Chandon, for example, exports 80% of its bubbly). But the region's 4800 small producers (known as *récoltants-manipulants* because they both harvest the grapes and turn the juice into wine) continue to serve an almost exclusively domestic clientele. Global sales dropped by 1.5% in 2013 to 304 million bottles, with the most notable dips in France and Europe. The finger of blame is pointing towards growing thirst for cheaper fizz – prosecco, sparkling wine and the like.

been woken up early by family and friends bearing Champagne, chocolate and broad smiles. The collection was assembled by the parents of the owner of Champagne Henry de Vaugency (founded 1732), an eighth-generation Champagne grower. The visit concludes with a Champagne tasting.

Le Mesnil-sur-Oger

Musée de la Vigne et du Vin (☑ 03 26 57 50 15; www.champagne-launois.fr; 2 av Eugène Guillaume, cnr D10; adult incl 3 flutes Champagne €8; ☉ tours 10am & 3pm Mon-Fri, 10.30am Sat & Sun) is so outstanding that it's worth planning your day around a tour.

Assembled by a family that has been making Champagne since 1872, this extraordinary collection of century-old Champagne-making equipment includes objects so aesthetically ravishing that you'll want to reach out and touch them. Among the highlights is a massive 16-tonne oak-beam grape press from 1630. Reservations can be made by phone or through the website; tours are not necessarily in English.

For an excellent French meal, head to **Le Mesnil** (☑ 03 26 57 95 57; www.restaurantlemesnil. com; 2 rue Pasteur; menus €23-29; ☉ 12.30-2pm & 7.30-10pm Thu-Sat & Mon, 12.30-2pm Tue & Sun). This refined contemporary restaurant spotlights seasonal flavours in dishes from suckling pig goulash to lobster terrine with scallops. Wine and restaurant critic Michael Edwards calls Le Mesnil 'the greatest Chardonnay commune in Champagne'.

ÉPERNAY

POP 24,600

Prosperous Épernay, the self-proclaimed *capitale du Champagne* and home to many of the world's most celebrated Champagne houses, is the best place for touring cellars and sampling bubbly. The town also makes an excellent base for exploring the Champagne Routes.

Beneath the streets in 110km of subterranean cellars, more than 200 million bottles of Champagne, just waiting to be popped open on some sparkling occasion, are being aged. In 1950 one such cellar – owned by the irrepressible Mercier family – hosted a car rally without the loss of a single bottle!

Épernay is 25km south of Reims and can be visited by train or car as a day trip from Reims.

DOM PÉRIGNON

Everyone who visits Moët & Chandon invariably stops to strike a pose next to the statue of **Dom Pérignon** (c 1638–1715), after whom the *prestige cuvée* is named. The Benedictine monk played a pivotal role in making Champagne what it is – perfecting the process of using a second, in-the-bottle fermentation to make ho-hum wine sparkle. Apparently, he was so blown away by the result that he rhapsodised about 'tasting the stars'.

While his contribution was undoubtedly significant, bubbly didn't come to dominate Champagne's wine production until over a century after his death.

◉ Sights

★ **Avenue de Champagne**   STREET
Épernay's handsome avenue de Champagne fizzes with *maisons de champagne* (Champagne houses). The boulevard is lined with mansions and neoclassical villas, rebuilt after WWI. Peek through wrought-iron gates at Moët's private **Hôtel Chandon**, an early 19th-century pavilion-style residence set in landscaped gardens, which counts Wagner among its famous past guests. The haunted-looking **Château Perrier**, a red-brick mansion built in 1854 in neo-Louis XIII style, is aptly placed at number 13! The roundabout presents photo-ops with its giant cork and bottle-top.

Moët & Chandon   CHAMPAGNE HOUSE
(☑ 03 26 51 20 20; www.moet.com; 20 av de Champagne; adult incl 1/2 glasses €21/28, 10-18yr €10; ☉ tours 9.30am-11.30am & 2-4.30pm, closed Sat & Sun late Jan–mid-Mar) Flying the Moët, French, European and Russian flags, this prestigious *maison* offers frequent one-hour tours that are among the region's most impressive, offering a peek at part of their 28km labyrinth of *caves* (cellars). At the shop you can pick up a 15L bottle of Brut Impérial for just €1500; a standard bottle will set you back €31.

Mercier   CHAMPAGNE HOUSE
(☑ 03 26 51 22 22; www.champagnemercier.fr; 68-70 av de Champagne; adult incl 1/2/3 glasses €13/18/21 Mon-Fri, €15/19/25 Sat & Sun, 12-17yr €6; ☉ tours 9.30-11am & 2-4pm, closed mid-Dec–late Feb) France's most popular brand was founded in 1847 by Eugène Mercier, a trailblazer in the field of eye-catching publicity

stunts and the virtual creator of the cellar tour. Everything here is flashy, including the 160,000L barrel that took two decades to build (for the Universal Exposition of 1889), the lift that transports you 30m underground and the laser-guided touring train.

De Castellane
CHAMPAGNE HOUSE

(📞 03 26 51 19 11; www.castellane.com; 57 av de Verdun; adult incl 1 glass €10, under 12yr free; ⊙ tours 10am-11pm & 2-5pm, closed Christmas–mid-Mar) The 45-minute tours, in French and English, take in an informative bubbly museum dedicated to elucidating the *méthode champenoise* and its diverse technologies. The reward for climbing the 237 steps up the 66m-high tower (built 1905) is a fine panoramic view.

Hôtel de Ville
CITY HALL

(City Hall; 7bis av de Champagne; ⊙ 8.30am-noon & 1.30-6pm Mon-Fri) In the neoclassical Hôtel de Ville, you can take a peek at the ornate, Louis XV-style **Salle de Conseil** (city council room) and **Salle de Mariages** (marriage hall). The adjacent, flowery park is perfect for a picnic.

Église Notre-Dame
CHURCH

(place Flodoard) Crowned by a fairy-tale silver spire, this late 19th-century church bears Romanesque and Gothic influences and is lit from within by a rose window.

Théâtre Gabrielle Dorziat
HISTORIC SITE

(www.lesalmanazar.fr; place Mendès-France) The north side of Théâtre Gabrielle Dorziat, built in 1902, still shows shell and bullet marks from WWII.

☞ Tours

Champagne Domi Moreau
VINEYARD TOUR

(📞 06 30 35 51 07, after 7pm 03 26 59 45 85; www.champagne-domimoreau.com; tours €25-30; ⊙ tours 9.30am & 2.30pm except Wed & 2nd half of Aug) This company runs scenic and insightful three-hour minibus tours, in French and English, of nearby vineyards. Pick-up is across the street from the tourist office. It also organises two-hour vineyard tours by bicycle (€25). Call ahead for reservations.

🛏 Sleeping

Épernay's hotels fill up fast on weekends from Easter to September and on weekdays, too, in May, June and September.

La Villa St-Pierre
HOTEL €

(📞 03 26 54 40 80; www.villasaintpierre.fr; 14 av Paul Chandon; d €44-75, q €96; 🐱) Expect a warm, family-style *bienvenue* and a friendly yap from the shih tzus at this early-20th-century town house turned B&B. The 11 simple rooms retain some yesteryear charm, with chintzy florals and wooden furnishings. Breakfast (€8) includes a tantalising array of pastries.

Parva Domus
B&B €€

(📞 06 73 25 66 60; www.parvadomusrimaire.com; 27 av de Champagne; d €100, ste €110; 🐱) Brilliantly situated on the avenue de Champagne, this vine-swathed B&B is kept spick and span by the amiable Rimaire family. Rooms have a countrified feel, with wood floors, floral fabrics and pastel colours. Sip a glass of house Champagne on the terrace or in the elegant living room.

Le Clos Raymi
HISTORIC HOTEL €€

(📞 03 26 51 00 58; www.closraymi-hotel.com; 3 rue Joseph de Venoge; s €120, d €170-190; 🐱) Staying at this atmospheric place is like being a personal guest of Monsieur Chandon of Champagne fame, who occupied this luxurious townhouse over a century ago. The seven romantic, parquet-floored rooms – styles include Provençal, Tuscan and colonial – have giant beds, high ceilings and French windows. In winter there's often a fire in the art deco living room.

Hôtel Jean Moët
HISTORIC HOTEL €€

(📞 03 26 32 19 22; www.hoteljeanmoet.com; 7 rue Jean Moët; d €120-190, ste €230-260; ✳🐱🏊) Housed in a beautifully converted 18th-century mansion, this old-town hotel is big on atmosphere, with its skylit tea room, antique-meets-boutique-chic rooms and cellar, C.Comme. Spa treatments and a swimming pool await after a hard day's Champagne-tasting.

★ La Villa Eugène
BOUTIQUE HOTEL €€€

(📞 03 26 32 44 76; www.villa-eugene.com; 84 av de Champagne; d €154-333, ste €375-390; ✳🐱🏊) Sitting handsomely astride the avenue de Champagne in its own grounds with an outdoor pool, La Villa Eugène is a class act. It's lodged in a beautiful 19th-century town mansion that once belonged to the Mercier family. The roomy doubles exude understated elegance, with soft, muted hues and the odd antique. Splash out more for a private terrace or four-poster.

🍴 Eating & Drinking

Épernay's main eat street is rue Gambetta and adjacent place de la République. For picnic fixings, head to rue St-Thibault.

WORTH A TRIP

TASTE LIKE A PRO

You can taste Champagne anywhere but you might get more out of the two-hour workshops at **Villa Bissinger** (☑ 03 26 55 78 78; www.villabissinger.com; 15 rue Jeanson, Ay; 2hr workshop €25; ⏱ 2.30pm first Sat month Apr-Oct), home to the International Institute for the Wines of Champagne. Besides covering the basics like names, producers, grape varieties and characteristics, the workshop includes a tasting of four different Champagnes. The institute is in Ay, 3.5km northeast of Épernay. Call ahead to secure your place.

Pâtisserie Vincent Dallet   TEA ROOM €
(www.chocolat-vincentdallet.fr; 26 rue du Général Leclerc; pastries €2.70-4.50, light meals €8-18; ⏱ 7.30am-7.45pm Tue-Sun) A sweet dream of a chocolaterie, patisserie and tea room with pralines, macaroons and pastries. A *champenoise* speciality is the 'Baba', vanilla cream topped by a cork-shaped pastry flavoured with Champagne. *Café gourmand,* coffee with a selection of mini desserts, costs €8.90.

Covered Market   FOOD MARKET €
(Halle St-Thibault; rue Gallice; ⏱ 7.30am-12.30pm Wed & Sat) Picnic treats galore.

La Cloche à Fromage   CHEESE €
(19 rue St-Thibault; ⏱ 8.30am-1pm & 2.30pm-7.30pm Tue-Thu, 8am-7.30pm Fri, 7.30am-7.30pm Sat) Has been selling *fromage* for over a century.

★ La Grillade Gourmande   REGIONAL CUISINE €€
(☑ 03 26 55 44 22; www.lagrilladegourmande.com; 16 rue de Reims; menus €19-57; ⏱ noon-2pm & 7.30-10pm Tue-Sat) This chic, red-walled bistro is an inviting spot to try char-grilled meats and dishes rich in texture and flavour, such as crayfish pan-fried in Champagne, and lamb cooked until meltingly tender in rosemary and honey. Diners spill out onto the covered terrace in the warm months.

Chez Max   TRADITIONAL FRENCH €€
(☑ 03 26 55 23 59; www.chez-max.com; 13 av AA Thevenet, Magenta; menus 3-course lunch €15, dinner €22-40; ⏱ noon-1.30pm & 7.30-9.30pm Tue & Thu-Sat, noon-1.30pm Wed & Sun, 7.30-9.30pm Mon) No fuss, no frills, just good old-fashioned French cooking and a neighbourly vibe is what you'll get at Chez Max. Dishes like confit of duck leg and sea bass with Champagne sauce hit the mark every time.

La Table Kobus   MODERN FRENCH €€
(☑ 03 26 51 53 53; www.latablekobus.com; 3 rue du Docteur Rousseau; menus €24-49; ⏱ noon-2pm & 7-9pm Tue-Sat, noon-2pm Sun) French cuisine in versions traditional and creative are served amid fin-de-siècle Paris bistro decor. Specialities like sea bream tartar with fennel and lime, and loin of venison with roast fig and port jus, are presented with flair.

La Cave à Champagne   REGIONAL CUISINE €€
(☑ 03 26 55 50 70; www.la-cave-a-champagne.com; 16 rue Gambetta; menus €20-38; ⏱ noon-2pm & 7-10pm Thu-Mon, noon-2pm Tue; 🖪) 'The Champagne Cellar' is well regarded by locals for its *champenoise* cuisine (snail and pig's trotter casserole, filet of beef in pinot noir), served in a warm, traditional, bourgeois atmosphere. You can sample four different Champagnes for €24.

Cook'In   FUSION €€
(☑ 03 26 54 89 80; www.restaurant-cookin.com; 18 rue Porte Lucas; 2-/3-course lunch €15/18.50, mains €17-22; ⏱ noon-2.30pm & 7-10pm Tue-Fri, 7-10pm Mon & Sat) A sparky chef came up with the idea of combining French and Thai flavours at this sleek bistro. Go for well-spiced dishes like satay of guinea fowl in banana leaf with a peanut sauce, and wok-fried gambas with green curry and sweet basil.

★ C. Comme   CHAMPAGNE BAR
(www.c-comme.fr; 8 rue Gambetta; light meals €7.50-14.50, 6-glass Champagne tasting €33-39; ⏱ 10am-8.30pm Sun-Wed, 10am-11pm Thu, 10am-midnight Fri & Sat) The downstairs cellar has a stash of 300 different varieties of Champagne; sample them (from €5.50 a glass) in the softly lit bar-bistro upstairs. Accompany with a tasting plate of regional cheese, charcuterie and *rillettes* (pork pâté). We love the funky bottle-top tables and relaxed ambience.

❶ Information

Tourist Office (☑ 03 26 53 33 00; www.ot-epernay.fr; 7 av de Champagne; ⏱ 9.30am-12.30pm & 1.30-7pm Mon-Sat, 10.30am-1pm & 2-4.30pm Sun; 🛜) The super-friendly team here hand out English brochures and maps with walking, cycling and driving tour options. They can make cellar visit reservations. Free wi-fi.

❶ Getting There & Around

BICYCLE

The tourist office rents out bicycles (city/children's/tandem/electric bicycles €18/11/27/30 per day). Pick up cycling maps and map-cards (€0.50) here.

CAR
Europcar (www.europcar.com; 20 rempart Perrier)

TRAIN
The **train station** (place Mendès-France) has direct services to Reims (€6.80, 22 to 42 minutes, 19 daily) and Paris Gare de l'Est (€23.60, 1¼ hours to 2¾ hours, 16 daily).

TROYES

POP 61,657

Troyes has a lively centre that's graced with one of France's finest ensembles of half-timbered houses and Gothic churches. Often overlooked, it's one of the best places in France to get a sense of what Europe looked like back when Molière was penning his finest plays and *The Three Musketeers* were swashbuckling. Several unique and very worthwhile museums are another lure.

Troyes does not have any Champagne cellars. However, you can shop in its scores of outlet stores stuffed with brand-name clothing and accessories, a legacy of the city's long-time role as France's knitwear capital.

◉ Sights

Panels posted around the old city provide tidbits on Troyes' history in French and English.

★16th-Century Troyes   HISTORIC QUARTER
Half-timbered houses – some with lurching walls and floors that aren't quite on-the-level line many streets in the old city, rebuilt after a devastating fire in 1524. The best place for aimless ambling is the area bounded by (clockwise from the north) rue Général de Gaulle, the Hôtel de Ville, rue Général Saussier and rue de la Pierre; of special interest are (from southwest to northeast) **rue de Vauluisant**, **rue de la Trinité**, **rue Champeaux** and **rue Paillot de Montabert**.

★Cathédrale St-Pierre
et St-Paul   CATHEDRAL
(place St-Pierre; ◎9am-noon & 1-5pm Mon-Sat, 11.30am-5pm Sun) Both imposing and delicate with its filigree stonework, Troyes' cathedral is a stellar example of champenois Gothic architecture. The flamboyant **west façade** dates from the mid-1500s, while the 114m-long interior is illuminated by a spectacular series of 180 **stained-glass windows** (13th to 17th centuries) that shine like jewels when it's sunny. Also notable is the fantastical **baroque organ** (1730s) sporting musical putti (cherubs), and

a tiny **treasury** (open July and August only) with enamels from the Meuse Valley. Back in 1429, Joan of Arc and Charles VII stopped off here on their way to his coronation in Reims.

★Maison de l'Outil et
de la Pensée Ouvrière   MUSEUM
(Museum of Tools & Crafts; www.maison-de-l-outil. com; 7 rue de la Trinité; adult/child €6.50/3; ◎10am-6pm daily, closed Tue Oct-Mar) Worn to a sensuous lustre by generations of skilled hands, the 10,000 hand tools on display here – each designed to perform a single, specialised task with exquisite efficiency – bring to life a world of manual skills made obsolete by the Industrial Revolution. The collection is housed in the magnificent Renaissance-style Hôtel de Mauroy, built in 1556. Videos show how the tools were used and what they were used for. A catalogue in English is available at the reception.

★Musée d'Art Moderne   ART MUSEUM
(www.musees-troyes.com; place St-Pierre; adult/child €5/free; ◎10am-1pm & 2-7pm Tue-Fri, 11am-7pm Sat & Sun, to 5pm Oct-Apr) Housed in a 16th- to 18th-century bishop's palace, this place owes its existence to all those crocodile-logo shirts, whose global success allowed Lacoste entrepreneurs Pierre and Denise Lévy to amass this outstanding collection. The highlights here are French painting (including lots of fauvist works) created between 1850 and 1950, glass (especially the work of local glassmaker and painter Maurice Marinot) and ceramics. There's a remarkable portfolio of works by big-name artists including Degas, Rodin, Matisse, Modigliani, Picasso and Soutine.

Hôtel de Vauluisant   MUSEUM
(4 rue de Vauluisant; adult/child €3/free; ◎2-7pm Wed, 10am-1pm & 2-7pm Thu-Fri, 11am-1pm & 2-7pm Sat & Sun, shorter hrs in winter) This haunted-looking, Renaissance-style mansion shelters a twinset of unique museums. The **Musée de l'Art Troyen** is a repository for the evocative paintings, stained glass and statuary (stone and wood) of the Troyes School, which flourished here during the economic

---

ⓘ TROYES DISCOUNTS

Le Pass' Troyes (€12), sold at the tourist offices, gets you free entry to five of the big museums, a two-flute Champagne-tasting session, an old city tour (with a guide or audioguide) and discounts at various factory outlet shops.

Troyes

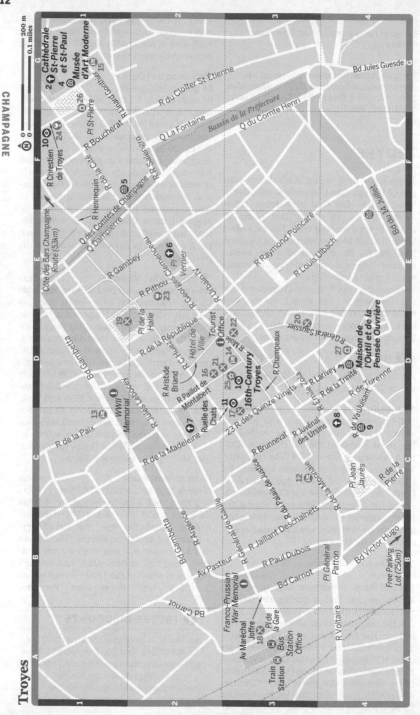

- 2 Cathédrale St-Pierre et St-Paul
- 4 Musée d'Art Moderne
- 15
- 26
- 10 R Chrestien de Troyes
- 24
- 5
- 6
- 23
- 19
- 20
- 27
- Maison de l'Outil et de la Pensée Ouvrière
- 3
- 22
- 14
- 25
- 21
- 16
- 1
- 16th-Century Troyes
- 11
- 17
- 7
- 8
- 9
- 13
- WWII Memorial
- 12
- Franco-Prussian War Memorial
- 18
- Train Station
- Bus Station Office
- Free Parking Lot (250m)

Côte des Bars Champagne Route (53km)

Bd Jules Guesde

R du Cloître St-Étienne

Bassin de la Préfecture

Q La Fontaine

Q du Comte Henri

R Raymond Poincaré

R Louis Ulbach

R Général Saussier

R Champeaux

R de Vauluisant

R de la Trinité

R de Turenne

R de la Pierre

Pl Jean Jaurès

R de la Paix

Bd Gambetta

R de la Madeleine

R Brunneval

R Juvénal des Ursins

R Paul Dubois

R Jaillant Deschaînets

R du Palais de Justice

R Général de Gaulle

R Argence

Av Pasteur

Bd Carnot

Pl Général Patton

Bd Victor Hugo

R Voltaire

Av Maréchal Joffre

Pl de la Gare

R de la Monnaie

R Émile Zola

R Larivey

R des Quinze Vingts

Ruelle des Chats

R Paillot de Montabert

R Aristide Briand

Hôtel de Ville

R de la République

Pl de la Halle

R Chrestien de Troyes

R Gambey

R Pithou

Pl Georges Vernier

R Urbain IV

R Molé

Tourist Office

R Hennequin la Cité

R de la Cité

Q des Comtes de Champagne

Q Dampierre

R Boucherat

Pl St-Pierre

R Richard Gonthier

R R Salengro

R Jules Lebocey

200 m
0.1 miles
0
0

Troyes

prosperity and artistic ferment of the early 16th century. The **Musée de la Bonneterie** (Hosiery Museum) showcases the sock-strewn story of Troyes' 19th-century knitting industry, with exhibits from knitting machines and looms to bonnets and embroidered silk stockings.

Plants used to make dyes and oil paints in the Middle Ages grow in the courtyard.

Église Ste-Madeleine   CHURCH
(rue Général de Gaulle; ⊘ 9.30am-12.30pm & 2-5pm Mon-Sat, 2-5pm Sun) Troyes' oldest and most interesting neighbourhood church has an early-Gothic nave and transept (early 13th century) and a Renaissance-style choir and tower. The highlights here are the splendid Flamboyant Gothic **rood screen** (early 1500s), dividing the transept from the choir, and the 16th-century **stained glass** in the presbytery portraying scenes from Genesis. In the nave, the statue of a deadly serious **Ste-Marthe** (St Martha), around the pillar from the wooden pulpit, is considered a masterpiece of the 15th-century Troyes School.

Basilique St-Urbain   CHURCH
(place Vernier; ⊘ 10am-12.30pm & 2-7pm Mon-Sat, 2-7pm Sun, shorter hrs in winter) Begun in 1262 by the Troyes-born Pope Urban IV, whose father's shoemaker shop once stood on this spot, this church is exuberantly Gothic both inside and out, and has some fine 13th-century stained glass. In the chapel off the south transept arm is **La Vierge au Raisin** (Virgin with Grapes), a graceful, early-15th-century stone statue of Mary and the Christ Child.

Église St-Pantaléon   CHURCH
(rue de Vauluisant; ⊘ 10.30am-noon & 2-4.30pm Tue-Sat) Faded with age and all the more enigmatic for it, this Renaissance-style, cruciform church, with its vaulted wood ceiling, is a great place to see the work of the 16th-century Troyes School – check out the sculptures attached to the columns of the nave. The west façade was added in the 18th century. History brochures are available.

Ruelle des Chats   STREET
Off rue Champeaux (between Nos 30 and 32), a stroll along tiny ruelle des Chats (Alley of the Cats), as dark and narrow as it was four centuries ago – the upper floors almost touch – is like stepping back into the Middle Ages. The stones along the base of the walls were designed to give pedestrians a place to stand when horses clattered by. See if you can spot the namesake cat in the stonework.

Apothicairerie de l'Hôtel-Dieu-le-Comte   APOTHECARY MUSEUM
(quai des Comtes de Champagne; adult/child €2/free; ⊘ 2-7pm Wed, 10am-1pm & 2-7pm Thu-Fri, 11am-1pm & 2-7pm Sat & Sun, shorter hrs in winter) If you come down with an old-fashioned malady – scurvy, perhaps, or unbalanced humours – the place to go is this fully outfitted, wood-panelled pharmacy from 1721. Rare pharmaceutical

jars share shelf space with decorative pill boxes and bronze mortars.

Hôtel du Chaudron   HISTORIC SITE
(4 rue Chrestien de Troyes) One of the founders of the Canadian city of Montréal, Paul Chomeday de Maisonneuve (1612–76), once lived in the Hôtel de Chaudron.

🛏 Sleeping

Hôtel Les Comtes de Champagne   HISTORIC HOTEL €
(☑ 03 25 73 11 70; www.comtesdechampagne.com; 56 rue de la Monnaie; r €69-105, apt €89-180; 🛜) The same massive wooden beams have kept this trio of pastel-hued half-timbered houses vertical since the 16th century. We love the bright courtyard lobby, the flower boxes and the 12th-century cellar. A huge and very romantic double goes for around €100. No lift.

⭐ **La Villa de la Paix**   BOUTIQUE HOTEL €€
(☑ 06 69 02 01 42; www.villapaix.com; 2 rue de la Paix; d €90-120, f €105-115; 🛜) This stout red-brick villa has a boutiquey flavour in its individually designed rooms, some with ornamental fireplaces and canopy beds. Family heirlooms, antiques and a flower-dotted garden given the place a delightfully homely feel, and breakfast comes with charcuterie, eggs, fruit, pastries – the works.

Le Relais St-Jean   HISTORIC HOTEL €€
(☑ 03 25 73 89 90; www.relais-st-jean.com; 51 rue Paillot de Montabert; d €98-155, ste €165-210; ❄🛜)

On a narrow medieval street in the heart of the old city, this hotel combines half-timbered charm with 24 contemporary rooms, a mini-tropical hothouse, a jacuzzi in the 16th-century cellar, a small fitness centre and facilities for the disabled. There's direct access from the underground car park (€10).

Maison de Rhodes   HISTORIC HOTEL €€€
(☑ 03 25 43 11 11; www.maisonderhodes.com; 18 rue Linard Gonthier; d €199-265; 🛜📶) Once home to the Knights Templar, this half-timbered pile sits proudly on its 12th-century foundations. Creaking staircases lead to 11 spacious rooms, with beams and stone floors, which positively ooze medieval character; iPod docks and wi-fi suddenly wing you back into the 21st century. The gardens, courtyard and gourmet restaurant invite lingering.

🍴 Eating

Rue Champeaux has the city's highest concentration of restaurants, cafes and crêperies, though few rise much above the ordinary. Student-oriented eateries can be found just west of the cathedral along rue de la Cité.

Locals are enormously proud of the city's specialities: *andouillettes de Troyes* (sausages made with strips of pigs' intestines) and *tête de veau* (calf's head served without the brain). As far as most non-locals are concerned, they're an acquired taste.

⭐ **Claire et Hugo**   STREET FOOD €
(☑ 06 52 94 70 77; http://claireethugo.fr; place de la Gare; mains €8-12; ⊗ 12-2pm & 7-9pm Mon-Fri) Meet Claire and Hugo, the dynamic duo behind this double-decker bus street food venture, which does the rounds in Troyes and its surrounds. Everything on the menu is homemade: from the burgers and frites to the bread, sauces, macarons and brownies. They pull up in front of the station on Thursdays and Fridays; see their Facebook site for other locations.

Aux Tables des Peintres   BISTRO €
(☑ 03 25 73 59 94; 23 rue des Quinze Vingts; 2-course menu €12; ⊗ noon-3pm & 7-9pm Tue-Sat, noon-3pm Sun) Entered via a quaint courtyard, this gallery-bistro does a great-value *menu* for €12, with specials from honey-glazed chicken to Maroilles cheese tart with salad.

Crêperie la Blanche Hermine   CRÊPERIE €
(☑ 03 25 73 77 10; 15 rue Général Saussier; mains €7-12, menu €12.50; ⊗ 11.30am-10pm Tue-Sun; 🎏) Squeeze into this cosy bolthole for a Breton feast of crêpes and *galettes* (buckwheat pancakes). The classic Troyes-style topping is

315

with *andouillettes,* cider-poached onions and melted Chaource cheese.

★ **Tout Simplement** BISTRO €€
(☑ 03 25 40 83 72; www.resto-toutsimplement.fr; 29 place Alexandre Israël; mains €14-18; ☺ noon-2pm & 7-10pm Tue-Sat) Chipper staff keep the good vibes and food coming at this contemporary wine bar-bistro in the half-timbered heart of Troyes, which spills onto a terrace in summer. Its famous *rillettes* (pâtés) – chicken, aubergine and grilled almonds – are a tasty prelude to mains like creamy scallop risotto.

Le Valentino MODERN FRENCH €€
(☑ 03 25 73 14 14; 35 rue Paillot de Montabert; menus €27-58; ☺ noon-1.30pm & 7.30-9.30pm Tue-Sat) What could be more romantic than a *table à deux* in the cobbled courtyard of this rose-hued, 17th-century restaurant? The chef juggles flavours skilfully in market-driven specialities like scallop carpaccio with vanilla oil and lemon caviar and spot-on turbot with asparagus.

Au Jardin Gourmand TRADITIONAL FRENCH €€
(☑ 03 25 73 36 13; 31 rue Paillot de Montabert; mains €22-29; ☺ noon-1.30pm & 7.30-10pm Tue-Sat, 7.30-10pm Mon) Elegant without being overly formal, this intimate restaurant – with a summer terrace – uses only the freshest ingredients for its classic French and *champenois* dishes; among the latter are no fewer than 11 varieties of *andouillette.* About 20 vintages from the estimable wine list are available by the glass.

Covered Market FOOD MARKET €
(place de la Halle; ☺ 8am-12.45pm & 3.30-7pm Mon-Thu, 9am-7pm Fri & Sat, 9am-1pm Sun) Fruit, veggies, bread, charcuterie, fish and cheese glorious cheese.

▼ Drinking & Entertainment

The hum of chatter fills the open-air bars and cafes around rue Champeaux and half-timbered place Alexandre-Israël on warm evenings.

Dixi Café BAR
(12 rue Pithou; ☺ 9.30am-11pm Tue & Wed, 9.30am-midnight Thu, 9.30am-1.30am Fri & Sat) A convivial neighbourhood bar that draws an arty crowd, including students. The house speciality is *rhum arrangé* (fruit-infused rum). Has live music – rock, reggae, jazz, French *chanson* – every Friday and Saturday from about 10pm.

Rive Gauche Café BAR
(59 rue de la Cité; ☺ 10am-1.30am Tue-Sat, 10am-5pm Sun; 🖥) Attracts a lively crowd with its Belgian beer, terrace overlooking the cathedral, free wi-fi and occasional live music.

La Maison du Boulanger TICKET OUTLET
(☑ 03 25 40 15 55; www.maisonduboulanger.com; 42 rue Paillot de Montabert; ☺ 9am-noon & 2-6pm Mon-Fri, 10am-noon & 2-5pm Sat) Sells tickets to concerts, plays and other cultural events.

🔒 Shopping

In the city centre, handsome rue Émile Zola is lined with big-name high-street shops. Antique shops and galleries huddle along rue de la Cité.

Sarah Dollé ACCESSORIES
(23 rue Larivey; ☺ 2-7pm Tue-Sat) Hidden down a narrow backstreet, this is where you will find Sarah's marvellous hat-making workshop. Squeeze into her tiny boutique, jam-packed with bonnets, woolly winter numbers, top hats and other fancy headwear, and slip back to a more glamorous age.

Cellier St-Pierre WINE
(www.celliersaintpierre.fr; 1 place St-Pierre; ☺ 10am-noon & 3-7pm Tue-Fri, 10am-12.30pm & 2.30-7.30pm Sat) A fine place to purchase bubbly and Aube wines such as *rosé des Riceys.* The cellar has been used since 1840 to distil *Prunelle de Troyes* (€22 per bottle), a 40 per cent liqueur made with sloe (blackthorn fruit) that's great on ice cream. The modest production facilities, which you can visit, are often fired up on Friday and Saturday mornings.

ℹ Information

Tourist Office (www.tourisme-troyes.com; 16 rue Aristide Briand; ☺ 9.30am-6.30pm Mon-Sat, 10am-1pm & 2-6pm Sun) Sidling up to the town hall, this helpful bureau has stacks of info on Troyes and free wi-fi.

ℹ Getting There & Around

BUS
The best way to get to Reims is by bus. Departures are from the last bus berth to the right as you approach the train station; a schedule is posted. The **bus station office** (☑ 03 25 71 28 42; ☺ 8.30am-noon & 2-5.30pm Mon-Fri), run

ℹ SELF-GUIDED TOUR

The tourist offices in Troyes can supply you with a 1½ hour **audioguide tour** (€4) of the old city in French, English, German, Italian or Dutch.

CHAMPAGNE TROYES

by Courriers de l'Aube, is by the side of the train station.

CAR

There's a huge free car park a couple of blocks south of the old town on boulevard Charles Délestraint – take rue de Turenne, cross the roundabout, turn right and then left. Close to the station, **ADA** (📞 03 25 73 41 68; www.ada.fr; 23 rue des Nöes) rents cars.

TAXI

Call 📞 03 25 78 30 30.

TRAIN

Troyes is on the rather isolated train line that links Mulhouse (€46, 3½ hours) in Alsace with Paris Gare de l'Est (€27, 1½ hours, 10 to 14 daily). To get to Dijon (€33, 2¾ hours), change in Chaumont.

CHAMPAGNE ROUTE OF THE CÔTE DES BAR

Although the Aube département (www.aube-champagne.com), of which Troyes is the capital, is a major producer of Champagne (it has about 67 sq km of vineyards, 85% of them pinot noir and 15% chardonnay), it gets a fraction of the recognition accorded to the Marne. Much of the acrimony dates back to 1909, when winemakers of the Aube were excluded from the growing area for Champagne's AOC (Appellation d'Origine Contrôlée). Two years later, they were also forbidden to sell their grapes to producers up north, provoking a revolt by local *vignerons*, months of strikes and a situation so chaotic that the army was called in. Only in 1927 were the Aube growers fully certified as producers of genuine Champagne, but by then the Marne had established market domination.

Today, Champagne production in the southeastern corner of the Aube – just north of Burgundy's Châtillonnais vineyards – is relatively modest in scale, though the reputation of the area's wines has been on an upward trajectory in recent years.

The 220km Côte des Bar Champagne Route does curlicues and loop-the-loops through austere fields, neat vineyards and forestland in an area 30km to 50km east and southeast of Troyes. Great for a deliciously leisurely drive, it passes through stone-built villages that are bedecked with flowers in the spring. Tourist offices, including the one in Troyes, can supply map-brochures. The selected highlights that follow are listed from northeast to southwest.

Colombey-les-Deux-Églises

POP 695

Charles de Gaulle lived in this village (www.colombey-les-deux-eglises.com, in French) from 1934 – except, obviously, during WWII – until his death in 1970. It is named after two historic *églises* (churches), one a parish church, the other a Cluniac priory.

People flock here by the coachload to visit Charles de Gaulle's vine-swathed home, **La Boisserie** (www.charles-de-gaulle.org; adult/child €5/4, incl Mémorial Charles de Gaulle €16.50/15; ⏱10am-1pm & 2-6.30pm daily), its elegant antique furnishings unchanged since he was laid to rest in the village-centre *cimetière* (churchyard). Tours (English brochure available; price included in admission) begin at the ticket office, situated across D23 from the house, on the Colombey's southern edge.

The hill just north of town (on D619) is crowned by a 43.5m-high Croix de Lorraine (Lorraine Cross; erected 1972), symbol of France's WWII Resistance. Nearby is the impressive **Mémorial Charles de Gaulle** (http://memorial-charlesdegaulle.fr; adult/child €13.50/11, incl La Boisserie €16.50/15; ⏱9.30am-7pm daily May-Sep, 10am-5.30pm Wed-Mon Oct-Apr), opened in 2008, whose graphic, easily digestible exhibits, rich in photos, form an admiring biography of France's greatest modern statesman. Displays help visitors untangle such complicated mid-20th-century events as the Algerian war and the creation of the Fifth Republic, and consider the ways in which De Gaulle's years in power (1958–69) affected French culture, style and economic growth. Audioguides are available. The site affords breathtaking, sublime views of the Haute-Marne countryside.

Colombey-les-Deux-Églises is 72km east of Troyes along D619; taking A5 to exit 23 (88km) is a bit faster.

Bayel

POP 846

Thanks to the **Cristallerie Royale de Champagne** (adult/child €6/4; ⏱9.30 & 11am Mon-Fri), established by a family of glassmakers from Murano, Italy, this quiet village has been a centre of crystal manufacture since 1678. To see the production process, take a factory tour. The 1¼-hour tours are in French unless the group is predominantly English-speaking. For even more insight into how crystal is made, tie this in with a visit to the

Musée du Cristal (Glass Museum; adult/child €5/3, combined with tour €8/5; ⊙ 9.15am-12.30pm & 2.15-6pm Mon-Fri, 9am-12.30pm & 2-5.30pm Sat, 2-5.30pm Sun); a 15-minute film highlights the different stages involved in crystal production. For lovely but fragile gifts, head to the Cristalleries de Champagne outlet shop (⊙ 9am-12.30pm & 2-5pm Mon-Sat).

Bayel is 11km southwest of Colombey-les-Deux-Églises.

Abbaye de Clairvaux

Bernard de Clairvaux (1090–1153), nemesis of Abelard and preacher of the Second Crusade, founded this hugely influential Cistercian monastery (www.abbayedeclairvaux.com; adult/child €7/free; ⊙ tours 11am, 2.30pm & 4.30pm, additional tours Wed-Sun Mar-Oct, closed Mon & Tue Nov-Feb) in 1115. Since Napoléon's time, the complex has served as one of France's highest-security prisons. Several historic abbey buildings are open to the public. Tours take in 12th-century structures, built in the austere Cistercian tradition, but more interesting is the 18th-century Grand Cloître, where you can see collective 'chicken coop' cells (from the 1800s) and individual cells (used until 1971).

Past 'guests' have included Carlos the Jackal; two prisoners who staged a revolt here in 1971 were guillotined. For security reasons, visitors need to bring ID, mobile phones must be off, and photography is prohibited.

The abbey is on D396, 8km south of Bayel and 6km north of A5 exit 23.

Essoyes

POP 746

It's easy to see why Renoir loved Essoyes, so much that he spent his last 25 summers here: it's one of the area's comeliest villages, with neat stone houses, a riverfront that glows golden in the late afternoon sun and landscapes of vineyards and flower-flecked meadows that unfold in a gentle, almost artistic way.

You can slip into the shoes of the great Impressionist on Essoyes' standout *circuit découverte,* a marked trail which loops around the village, taking in viewpoints that inspired the artist, the family home and the cemetery where he lies buried, his grave marked by a contemplative bronze bust. The trail begins at the Espace des Renoir (Renoir Centre; www.renoir-essoyes.fr; place de la Mairie; adult/child €8/4 incl Atelier Renoir; ⊙10.30am-11.30am & 2-5pm Wed-Mon, shorter hrs in winter) which also houses the tourist office (☑03 25 29 21 27; www.ot-essoyes.fr; place de la Mairie, Espace des Renoir; ⊙9am-12.30pm & 1.30-5.30pm, closed Sat & Sun Oct-May). The centre screens a 15-minute film about the artist and displays temporary exhibitions of mostly contemporary art. Marking the end of the tour and covered by the same ticket is the Atelier Renoir (Renoir's Studio; www.renoir-essoyes.fr; adult/child €8/4 incl Espace des Renoir; ⊙10am-12.30pm & 1.30-6.30pm daily, closed Tue Oct-Mar), with displays zooming in on the hallmarks of Renoir's work (the female form, the vibrant use of colour and light), alongside original pieces such as his antiquated wheelchair and the box he used to carry his paintings to Paris. Perhaps loveliest of all is the studio garden, particularly in spring to early summer when it bursts forth with tulips, anemones and roses.

Prettily set above Essoyes, on the D67, the Hôtel des Canotiers (☑03 25 38 61 08; www.hoteldescanotiers.com; 1 rue Pierre Renoir; d €77-105, incl half board €148-152; 🅿🛜) has 14 upbeat, spacious and practical rooms, each named after a famous Renoir canvas. The restaurant pairs well-executed regional dishes with local Champagnes.

Essoyes is 49km southeast of Troyes.

Les Riceys

POP 1402

Running along both banks of the picturesque River Laigne, the commune of Les Riceys consists of three adjacent villages (Ricey-Bas, Ricey-Haute-Rive and Ricey-Haut) and is famous for its three churches, and for growing grapes belonging to three different AOC wines. Its best-known product is rosé des Riceys, an exclusive pinot noir rosé that can be made only in particularly sunny years and was a special favourite of Louis XIV. Annual production of this – when there is any – hovers around 65,000 bottles. Lots of Champagne wineries are nestled along and near D70.

For more information, including details on walking circuits through vine and vale, contact the tourist office (www.lesriceys-champagne.com; 14 place des Héros de la Résistance, Ricey-Haut; ⊙9am-noon & 2-5pm Mon-Fri, plus 9.30am-noon & 2-5pm Sat & Sun).

Les Riceys is 47km southeast of Troyes and 18km southwest of Essoyes.

Alsace & Lorraine

POP 4.2 MILLION

Best Places to Eat

➡ Le Gavroche (p329)

➡ La Cuiller à Pot (p328)

➡ La Fourchette des Ducs (p333)

➡ L'Épicurien (p345)

➡ JY's (p346)

Best Places to Stay

➡ Du Coté de Chez Anne (p328)

➡ Cour du Corbeau (p328)

➡ Hotel Quatorze (p344)

➡ Maison de Myon (p354)

➡ Hôtel de la Cathédrale (p359)

Why Go?

Alsace is a cultural one-off. With its Germanic dialect and French sense of fashion, love of foie gras and *choucroute* (sauerkraut), fine wine *and* beer, this region often leaves you wondering quite where you are. Where are you? Why, in the land of living fairy tales of course, where vineyards fade into watercolour distance, hilltop castles send spirits soaring higher than the region's emblematic storks and half-timbered villages garlanded with geraniums look fresh-minted for a Disney film set.

Lorraine has high culture and effortless grace thanks to its historic roll-call of dukes and art nouveau pioneers, who had an eye for grand designs and good living. The art and architecture in blessedly underrated cities such as Nancy and Metz leave visitors spellbound, while its WWI battlefields render visitors speechless time and again with their painful beauty.

When to Go
Strasbourg

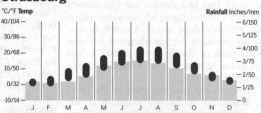

Jul Fireworks, street parties and cathedral illuminations at L'Été à Strasbourg.

Sep Toast the grape harvest with new wine and autumn colour on the Route des Vins d'Alsace.

Dec Mulled wine, gingerbread and carols galore at Christmas markets throughout Alsace.

ALSACE

History

Though settled since prehistoric times and cultivated by the Celts in 1500 BC, it wasn't until the Romans arrived in 58 BC that Alsace really made the history books. Alsace formed part of Germania Superior in the Roman Empire, and the Romans made their mark building forts and camps such as Argentoratum (modern-day Strasbourg).

As the influence of the Roman Empire waned, the Alemanni (Germanic tribes from the Upper Rhine) seized power, bringing with them the dialect that forms the basis of present-day Alsatian, but they were soon ousted by Frankish Merovingians in the 5th century.

Under Charlemagne (742–814), the church gained influence and Alsace flourished. Over the following eight centuries, Alsace prospered as part of the Holy Roman Empire. Thanks to the imperial clout of the Hohenstaufen Emperors, the 12th and 13th centuries signalled a golden age, with the rise of guilds and a prosperous merchant class, the expansion of towns and cities, and the construction of Romanesque churches. Alsace became a cradle of intellectual and artistic activity in the 15th century. The final stone was laid on its Gothic crowning glory, Strasbourg Cathedral, in 1439.

French influence in Alsace began during the Wars of Religion (1562–98) and increased during the Thirty Years War (1618–48). Most of the region was attached to France in 1648 under the Treaty of Westphalia.

By the time of the French Revolution, Alsatians felt more connected to France than to Germany, but time did little to dampen Germany's appetite for the region they called Elsass. When the Franco-Prussian War ended in 1871, an embittered France was forced to cede Alsace to the Kaiser. The region was returned to France following Germany's defeat in WWI but it was re-annexed by Nazi Germany in 1940.

After WWII Alsace was once again returned to France. Intra-Alsatian tensions ran high, however, as 140,000 Alsatians – as annexed citizens of the Third Reich – had been conscripted into Hitler's armies. These conscripts were known as the 'Malgré-Nous' (literally 'despite ourselves') because the majority went to war against their will. To make Alsace a symbol of hope for future Franco-German (and pan-European) co-operation, Strasbourg was chosen as the seat of the Council of Europe (in 1949) and, later, of the European Parliament.

The Mémorial de l'Alsace-Moselle (www.memorial-alsace-moselle.org; adult/child €10/8; 10am-6.30pm Tue-Sun), 50km southwest of Strasbourg in Schirmeck, takes an unblinking but reconciliatory look at the region's traumatic modern history, which saw residents change nationality four times in 75 years.

ⓘ Getting There & Around

BICYCLE

Alsace is interwoven with 2500km of bike trails. Bicycles can be taken on virtually all regional TER trains (but not SNCF buses). A good resource for cyclists is the **Alsace à vélo** (ww.alsaceavelo.fr) website, with maps, itinerary and accommodation suggestions, plus practical info on where to rent and repair bikes.

CAR & MOTORCYCLE

From Strasbourg, the A4 heads northwest towards Metz and Paris, while from Mulhouse the A36 goes southwest towards the Jura and Dijon. The A31 connects Metz and Nancy with Luxembourg to the north and Dijon to the south. The Massif des Vosges gets snowy in winter so winter tyres and/or chains may be required.

TRAIN & BUS

TER regional trains and TGV high-speed trains make up the region's fast and efficient rail network. Getting between major towns and cities is straightforward, but train services thin out in rural Alsace, where small towns and villages are connected by just a handful of buses, often making getting around by car a quicker, easier option.

Those aged 12 to 25 can get 50% off on all regional rail travel with an annual Tonus Alsace pass (€19). The great-value Réflexe Alsace ticket, available for those aged 26 and over, costs €29 for a year and gets you a 30% discount on travel on weekdays and a huge 70% reduction at weekends.

Strasbourg

POP 271,708

Strasbourg is the perfect overture to all that is idiosyncratic about Alsace – walking a fine tightrope between France and Germany

FAST FACTS

➡ **Area** 31,827 sq km

➡ **Local industry** Agriculture, tourism, industry

➡ **Signature drinks** Sylvaner white wine, Kronenbourg beer

Alsace & Lorraine Highlights

❶ Sauntering around canal-laced **Petite Venise** (p341) as Colmar starts to twinkle

❷ Getting a gargoyle's-eye view of Strasbourg from the platform of Gothic **Cathédrale Notre-Dame** (p322)

❸ Surveying the cross-studded **Verdun Battlefields** (p363) in the early morning silence

❹ Being amazed by art nouveau and rococo grace in **Nancy** (p350)

❺ Gazing across the vines from the giddy heights of medieval **Château du Haut Kœnigsbourg** (p337)

❻ Wishing for luck (or lots of babies!) spotting storks in **Hunawihr** (p339)

❼ Contemplating modern art at the architecturally innovative **Centre Pompidou-Metz** (p358)

❽ Tiptoeing through the enchanting forests of the misty **Vosges** (p347) mountains

❾ Going dairy-hopping in the verdant **Vallée de Munster** (p347)

❿ Saving the storybook lanes of half-timbered **Riquewihr** (p339) until dusk

and between a medieval past and a progressive future, it pulls off its act in inimitable Alsatian style.

Tear your gaze away from that mesmerising Gothic cathedral for just a minute and you'll be roaming the old town's twisting alleys lined with crooked half-timbered houses à la Grimm; feasting in the cosiest of *winstubs* (Alsatian taverns) by the canalside in Petite France; and marvelling at how a city that does Christmas markets and gingerbread so well can also be home to the glittering EU Quarter and France's second-largest student population. But that's Strasbourg for you: all the sweeter for its contradictions and cross-cultural quirks.

History

Founded by the Merovingians in the 5th century, Strasbourg was long an important trade centre on the route between northern Europe and the Mediterranean. The city was ruled by democratic guilds in medieval times, when the cathedral, once the highest in Christendom, was built between 1015 and 1439. Johannes Gutenberg developed the first printing press with moveable type here in 1450.

Strasbourg witnessed the Reformation in the 16th century, the founding of its university in 1567 and the debut of *La Marseillaise* (the French national anthem) in 1792. Over ensuing centuries, the city ping-ponged between France and Germany. Strasbourg's prominent place in Europe's heart was confirmed when it became the seat of the Council of Europe in 1949 and of the European Parliament in 1992.

The Strasbourg Grand Mosque, the largest ever built on French soil, was a milestone 20 years in the making. Inaugurated on 27 September 2012, the architecturally striking mosque was widely regarded as a new dawn in the acceptance of Muslims in France.

◉ Sights

★ **Cathédrale Notre-Dame**   CATHEDRAL
(place de la Cathédrale; astronomical clock adult/child €2/1.50, platform adult/child €5/2.50; ◷7am-7pm, astronomical clock tickets sold 9.30am-11am, platform 9am-7.15pm; ᴨ Grand'Rue) Nothing prepares you for your first glimpse of Strasbourg's Cathédrale Notre-Dame, completed in all its Gothic grandeur in 1439. The lace-fine façade lifts the gaze little by little to flying buttresses, leering gargoyles and a 142m spire. The interior is exquisitely lit by 12th- to 14th-century **stained-glass windows**, including the western portal's jewel-like rose window. The Gothic-meets-Renaissance **astronomical clock** strikes solar noon at 12.30pm with a parade of figures portraying the different stages of life and Jesus with his apostles.

Victor Hugo declared it a 'gigantic and delicate marvel'; Goethe professed that its 'loftiness is linked to its beauty'; and, no matter the angle or time of day, you too will be captivated by this red sandstone monolith, which is at once immense and intricate.

A spiral staircase twists up to the 66m-high **viewing platform**, from which the tower and its Gothic openwork spire soar another 76m. As Hugo put it: 'From the belfry, the view is wonderful. Strasbourg lays at your feet, the old city of tiled triangular roof tops and gable windows, interrupted by towers and churches as picturesque as those of any city in Flanders.'

The **west façade**, most impressive if approached from rue Mercière, was completed in 1284, but the 142m spire – the tallest of its time – was not in place until 1439; its southern companion was never built.

To appreciate the cathedral in peace, visit in the early evening when the crowds have thinned and stay to see its façade glow gold at dusk.

ⓘ STRASBOURG SAVER

The **Strasbourg Pass** (adult/child €15/7.50), a coupon book valid for three consecutive days, includes a visit to one museum, access to the cathedral platform, half a day's bicycle rental and a boat tour, plus hefty discounts on other tours and attractions.

The money-saving **Strasbourg Pass Musées** (www.musees.strasbourg.eu; day pass adult/child €12/6, 3-day pass €18/12) offers entry to all the Musées de la Ville de Strasbourg.

Travelling further afield? Invest in a 48-hour **Pass des Musées** (www.museumspass.com; €28), valid for one adult and child. The pass covers entry to 230 museums, castles, parks and monasteries in Alsace and neighbouring regions in Germany and Switzerland.

You can purchase all three passes from the tourist office.

Admission to all of Strasbourg's **museums** (www.musees-strasbourg.org) and the cathedral's platform is free on the first Sunday of the month.

★Grande Île
HISTORIC QUARTER

(🔲Grand'Rue) History seeps through the twisting lanes and cafe-rimmed plazas of Grande Île, Strasbourg's Unesco World Heritage–listed island bordered by the River Ill. These streets, with their photogenic line-up of wonky, timber-framed houses in sherbet colours, are made for aimless ambling. They cower beneath the soaring magnificence of the cathedral and its sidekick, the ginger-bready 15th-century **Maison Kammerzell** (rue des Hallebardes), with its ornate carvings and leaded windows. The alleys are at their most atmospheric when lantern-lit at night.

★Palais Rohan
HISTORIC RESIDENCE

(2 place du Château; €6.50/free adult/child per museum, all three museums €12/free; ⏲10am-6pm Wed-Mon; 🔲Grand'Rue) Hailed a 'Versailles in miniature', this opulent 18th-century residence is replete with treasures. The basement **Musée Archéologique** takes you from the Palaeolithic period to AD 800. On the ground floor is the **Musée des Arts Décoratifs**, where rooms adorned with Hannong ceramics and gleaming silverware evoke the lavish lifestyle of the nobility in the 18th century. On the 1st floor, the **Musée des Beaux-Arts de Strasbourg's** collection of 14th- to 19th-century art reveals El Greco, Botticelli and Flemish Primitive works. Built in 1732 by French architect Robert de Cotte of Versailles fame, the episcopal palace was once the lavish abode of the city's princely bishops, and Louis XV and Marie-Antoinette once stayed here.

Petite France
HISTORIC QUARTER

(🔲Grand'Rue) Criss-crossed by narrow lanes, canals and locks, Petite France is where artisans plied their trades in the Middle Ages. The half-timbered houses, sprouting veritable thickets of scarlet geraniums in summer, and the riverside parks attract the masses, but the area still manages to retain its Alsatian charm, especially in the early morning and late evening. Drink in views of the River Ill and the **Barrage Vauban** from the much-photographed **Ponts Couverts** (Covered Bridges) and their trio of 13th-century towers.

Musée d'Art Moderne et Contemporain
GALLERY

(MAMCS; www.musees.strasbourg.eu; 1 place Hans Jean Arp; adult/child €7/free; ⏲10am-6pm Tue-Sun; 🔲Musée d'Art Moderne) This striking glass-and-steel cube showcases an outstanding fine art, graphic art and photography collection. Besides modern and contemporary works of the Kandinsky, Picasso, Magritte, Monet and

ALSACE & LORRAINE STRASBOURG

Rodin ilk, you'll encounter oeuvre by Strasbourg-born artists, including the curvaceous creations of Hans Jean Arp and the evocative 19th-century works of Gustave Doré. The first-floor Art Café is graced by bold frescoes by Japanese artist Aki Kuroda, and has a terrace overlooking the River Ill and Petite France.

Musée de l'Œuvre Notre-Dame
ECCLESIASTICAL MUSEUM

(www.musees.strasbourg.org; 3 place du Château; adult/child €6.50/free; ⏲10am-6pm Tue-Sun; 🔲Grand'Rue) Occupying a cluster of sublime 14th- and 16th-century buildings, this museum harbours one of Europe's premier collections of Romanesque, Gothic and Renaissance sculptures (including many originals from the cathedral), plus 15th-century paintings and stained glass. *Christ de Wissembourg* (c 1060) is the oldest work of stained glass in France.

Hollywood gore seems tame compared to the tortures back when Hell really was hell. Sure to scare you into a life of chastity is *Les Amants Trépassés* (the Deceased Lovers) painted in 1470, showing a grotesque couple being punished for their illicit lust: their entrails devoured by dragon-headed snakes.

Barrage Vauban
VIEWPOINT

(Vauban Dam; 🔲Faubourg National) A triumph of 17th-century engineering, the Barrage Vauban bears the architectural imprint of the leading French military engineer of the age – Sébastien Le Prestre de Vauban. The dam was recently restored to its former glory and now harbours contemporary art exhibits, such as French artist Daniel Depoutot's wondrous mechanical sculptures made from recycled or upcycled materials. Ascend to the **terrace** for a view that reaching across

Strasbourg

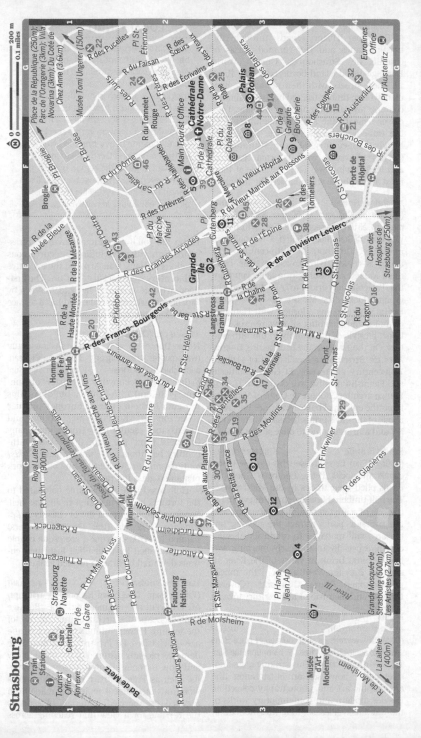

200 m
0.1 miles

Place de la République (250m);
Parc de l'Orangerie (3km); Villa
Novarina (3km); Du Côté de
Chez Anne (3.6km)

R des Pucelles

Musée Tomi Ungerer (150m)

Pl St-Étienne

R du Faisan

R des Sœurs

R des Juifs

R des Vieux

R des Écrivains

R des Frères

R de la Râpe

R Brûlée

Palais Rohan

R des Bateliers

Eurolines Office

Pl d'Austerlitz

R St-Étienne

R du Tonnelet Rouge

Cathédrale Notre-Dame

Main Tourist Office

Pl de la Cathédrale

Pl du Château

Pl du Marché aux Poissons

R des Couples

Pl d'Austerlitz

R d'Austerlitz

R des Bouchers

R du Dôme

R du Sanglier

R des Hallebardes

R du Vieux Hôpital

Pl de la Grande Boucherie

Porte de l'Hôpital

Q St-Nicolas

Broglie

Pl Broglie

R de la Nuée Bleue

R des Orfèvres

R du Maroquin

R des Tonneliers

Cave des Hospices de Strasbourg (250m)

R de l'Outre

Pl Gutenberg

Pl du Marché Neuf

Grande Île

R des Serruriers

R de l'Épine

R de la Mésange

R des Grandes Arcades

R Gutenberg

R de la Chaîne

R de l'Ail

R St-Thomas

R de la Nuée Bleue

Pl Kléber

R Ste-Barbe

Langstross Grand' Rue

R de la Division Leclerc

Q St-Thomas

R du Dragon

R de la Haute Montée

R Ste-Hélène

R Salzmann

R St-Martin du Pont

R des Moulins

R du Fossé des Tanneurs

Grand' R

R du Bouclier

R de la Monnaie

Pont St-Thomas

R Finkwiller

R des Glacières

Homme de Fer Tram Hub

R des Francs-Bourgeois

R du Vieux Marché aux Vins

R des Dentelles

R M Luther

R du Jeudes Enfants

R des Plantes

R des Moulins

Grande Mosquée de Strasbourg (500m); Les Artistes (2.7km)

Royal Lutetia (900m)

R Kuhn

Q Desaix

Q St-Jean

Fossé du Faux Rempart

Alt Winmärik

Q Turckheim

Q de la Petite France

R du 22 Novembre

Q Turckheim

Q Altorffer

R Adolphe Seyboth

R de Molsheim

Pl Hans Jean Arp

Rivier III

R Thiergarten

R Kageneck

R du Maire Kuss

R Déserte

R de la Course

R Ste-Marguerite

Faubourg National

Bd de Metz

La Laiterie (400m)

R de Molsheim

Musée d'Art Moderne

Train Station

Tourist Office Annexe

Gare Centrale

Pl de la Gare

Strasbourg Navette

R du Faubourg National

Strabourg

ALSACE & LORRAINE STRASBOURG

the canal-woven Petite France district to the cathedral spire beyond.

Musée Historique
MUSEUM

(www.musees-strasbourg.org; 2 rue du Vieux Maré aux Poissons; adult/child €6.50/free; ◷10am-6pm Tue-Sun; 🚊Grand'Rue) Trace Strasbourg's history from its beginnings as a Roman military camp called Argentoratum at this engaging museum, housed in a 16th-century slaughterhouse. Highlights include a painting of the first-ever performance of *La Marseillaise*, France's national anthem, which, despite its name, was written in Strasbourg in 1792; a 1:600-scale model, created in the 1720s to help Louis XV visualise the city's fortifications; and a Gutenberg Bible from 1485.

Musée Alsacien
FOLK MUSEUM

(www.musees.strasbourg.org; 23 quai St-Nicolas; adult/child €6.50/free; ◷10am-6pm Wed-Mon; 🚊Porte de l'Hôpital) Spread across three typical houses from the 1500s and 1600s, with creaky floors and beautifully restored wood-panelled interiors, this museum dips into rural Alsatian life over the centuries. Costumes, toys,

ceramics, folk art, furniture and even a tiny 18th-century synagogue are on display in the museum's two dozen rooms.

Grande Mosquée de Strasbourg
MOSQUE

(Strasbourg Grand Mosque; 6 rue Averroès; 🚊Laiterie) Designed by Italian architect Paolo Portoghesi and opened in September 2012, France's biggest mosque (1500 worshippers) sits on a bend in the River Ill and is topped by a copper dome and flanked by wings resembling a flower in bud. More than just another landmark, it took 20 years of political to-ing and fro-ing for this project to come to fruition and its completion is considered the beginning of a new era for Muslims and religious tolerance in France.

Musée Tomi Ungerer
MUSEUM

(www.musees.strasbourg.org; 2 av de la Marseillaise; adult/child €6.50/free; ◷10am-6pm Wed-Mon; 🚊République) A tribute to one of Strasbourg's most famous sons – award-winning illustrator and cartoonist Tomi Ungerer – this museum, just northeast of Grande Île, is housed in the fetching Villa Greiner. The collection discloses

DON'T MISS

BIENVENUE CHEZ LES EUROCRATS

Should the inner workings of the EU intrigue, you can sit in on debates ranging from lively to yawn-a-minute at the **Parlement Européen** (European Parliament; www.europarl.europa. eu; rue Lucien Fèbvre; 🚊 Parlement Européen); dates are available from the tourist office or on the website. For individuals it's first-come first-served (bring ID).

A futuristic glass crescent, the Council of Europe's **Palais de l'Europe** (Palace of Europe; ✆ 03 88 41 20 29; www.coe.int; Avenue de l'Europe; 🚊 Droits de l'Homme) across the River Ill can be visited on free one-hour weekday tours; phone ahead for times and reservations.

It's just a hop across the Canal de la Marne to the swirly silver **Palais des Droits de l'Homme** (European Court of Human Rights; www.echr.coe.int; Allée des Droits de l'Homme; 🚊 Droits de l'Homme), the most eye-catching of all the EU institutions.

The EU buildings sit 2km northeast of Grande Île (central Strasbourg), close to Parc de l'Orangerie.

the artist's love of dabbling in many genres, from children's book illustrations to satirical drawings and erotica.

Place de la République
SQUARE

(🚊 République) Many of Strasbourg's grandest public buildings, constructed when the city was ruled by the German Reich, huddle northeast of Strasbourg's Grande Île area around place de la République. The neighbourhood that stretches eastwards to Parc de l'Orangerie is dominated by sturdy stone buildings inspired by late-19th-century Prussian tastes.

Parc de l'Orangerie
PARK

(zoo admission free; 🚊 Droits de l'Homme) Across from the Council of Europe's Palais de l'Europe, 2km northeast of Grande Île, this flowery park, designed in the 17th century by Le Nôtre of Versailles fame, is a family magnet with its playgrounds and swan-dotted lake. In summer you can rent **row boats** on Lac de l'Orangerie. Kids can get up close to storks and goats at the park's mini **zoo**.

Le Vaisseau
SCIENCE MUSEUM

(www.levaisseau.com; 1bis rue Philippe Dollinger; adult/child €8/7; ⊙ 10am-6pm Tue-Sun; 🚊 Winston Churchill) Science is *never* boring at this interactive science and technology museum, 2.5km southeast of central Strasbourg. There are plenty of hands-on activities to amuse little minds, from crawling through an ant colony to creating cartoons and broadcasting the news.

Jardin des Deux Rives
GARDENS

(Two-Shores Garden; 🚊 Aristide Briand) An expression of flourishing Franco-German friendship, Strasbourg and its German neighbour Kehl have turned former customs posts and military installations into this 60-hectare

garden, whose play areas, promenades and parkland straddle both banks of the Rhine. The centrepiece is Marc Mimram's sleek (and hugely expensive) **suspension bridge**, which has proved a big hit with pedestrians and cyclists. From the tram stop, walk east or take bus 21 for three stops. It is 3km southeast of central Strasbourg (Grande Île).

River Ill
RIVERFRONT

(🚊 Grand'Rue) The leafy paths that shadow the River Ill and its canalised branch, the Fossé du Faux Rempart, are great for an impromptu picnic or a romantic stroll.

Place Gutenberg
SQUARE

(🚊 Grand'Rue) Well worth a peek for its Renaissance-style Chambre de Commerce (Chamber of Commerce).

🔾 Tours

Take a DIY spin of Strasbourg's cathedral and the old city with one of the tourist office's 1½-hour **audio guides** (adult/child €5.50/2.75), available in five languages.

Batorama
BOAT TOUR

(www.batorama.fr; rue de Rohan; adult/child €12.50/7.20; ⊙ tours half-hourly 9.30am-9.15pm, shorter hrs in winter; 🚊 Grand'Rue) This outfit runs scenic 70-minute boat trips, which glide along the storybook canals of Petite France, taking in the Vauban Dam and the glinting EU institutions. Tours depart on Rue de Rohan, the quay behind Palais Rohan.

Cave des Hospices de Strasbourg
WINE TASTING

(www.vins-des-hospices-de-strasbourg.fr; 1 place de l'Hôpital; ⊙ 8.30am-noon & 1.30-5.30pm Mon-Fri, 9am-12.30pm Sat; 🚊 Porte de l'Hôpital) **FREE** Founded in 1395, this brick-vaulted wine cellar nestles deep in the bowels of Strasbourg's hospital. A hospice back in the days when wine was considered a cure for all ills, today the cellar bottles first-rate Alsatian wines from rieslings to sweet muscats. One of its historic barrels is filled with a 1472 vintage. Take tram A or D to Porte de l'Hôpital. From here it is a three-minute walk south on Rue d'Or.

✿ Festivals & Events

Marché de Noël
CHRISTMAS

(Christmas Market; www.noel.strasbourg.eu) Mulled wine, spicy *bredele* (biscuits) and a Santa-loaded children's village are all part and parcel of Strasbourg's sparkly Marché de Noël, running from the last Saturday in November until 31 December.

Place à L'Été
SUMMER FESTIVAL

(www.ete.strasbourg.eu) Strasbourg slides into summer with fireworks, fairs and striking cathedral illuminations at Place à L'Été from late June to August.

Riesling du Monde
WINE FESTIVAL

(www.portail-vins-du-monde.com) Raise a glass to Alsatian wine at the Riesling du Monde in mid-April.

🛏 Sleeping

It can be tricky to find last-minute accommodation from Monday to Thursday when the European Parliament is in plenary session (see www.europarl.europa.eu for dates). Book ahead for December when beds are at a premium because of the Christmas market. The tourist office can advise about same-night room availability; if you drop by, staff are happy to help reserve a room.

Les Artistes
GUESTHOUSE €

(03 88 77 15 53; http://chambre-hotes-les-artistes.fr; 22 rue Vermeer; d €60-70, tr €80-90; 🛜 📶; 🚊 Elsau) Les Artistes offers clean, simple quarters and a good old-fashioned *bienvenue*. Rates include a fab breakfast, with fresh pastries and homemade jam. It's a homely pick, with a garden and barbecue area. Central Strasbourg, 3km away, can be reached on a cycle path or by tram (take B or C from Rue du Faubourg National to Elsau stop).

★ Villa Novarina
DESIGN HOTEL €€

(03 90 41 18 28; www.villanovarina.com; 11 rue Westercamp; s €87-157, d €117-257, ste €237-537; ❄🛜🏊; 🚊 Droits de l'Homme) New-wave design is pitched just right at this light-flooded 1950s villa near Parc de l'Orangerie. Slick without being soulless, rooms and suites are liberally sprinkled with art and overlook

gardens. Breakfast places the accent on organic, regional produce. There's a heated pool, whirlpool and spa for quiet moments. It's a 10-minute walk south of Droits de l'Homme tram stop.

Hôtel du Dragon
HOTEL €€

(03 88 35 79 80; www.dragon.fr; 12 rue du Dragon; s €44-159, d €92-159; @🛜🏊; 🚊 Porte de l'Hôpital) Step through a tree-shaded courtyard and into the, ahhh…blissful calm of this bijou hotel. The dragon receives glowing reviews for its crisp interiors, attentive service and prime location near Petite France.

Hôtel Régent Petite France
DESIGN HOTEL €€

(03 88 76 43 43; www.regent-hotels.com; 5 rue des Moulins; r €195-240; ❄@🛜; 🚊 Alt Winmärik) Once an ice factory and now Strasbourg's hottest design hotel, this waterfront pile is quaint on the outside and ubercool on the inside. The sleek rooms dressed in muted colours and plush fabrics sport shiny marble bathrooms. Work your relaxed look in the sauna, chic restaurant and Champagne bar with dreamy river views.

Hôtel Gutenberg
HISTORIC HOTEL €€

(03 88 32 17 15; www.hotel-gutenberg.com; 31 rue des Serruriers; r €85-195; ❄@🛜; 🚊 Grand'Rue) Nestled in the flower-strewn heart of Petite France, this hotel is a harmonious blend of 250 years of history and contemporary design, combining clean lines, zesty colours and the occasional antique.

Romantik Hôtel Beaucour
HISTORIC HOTEL €€

(03 88 76 72 00; www.hotel-beaucour.com; 5 rue des Bouchers; s €86-123, d €107-214; ❄@🛜; 🚊 Porte de l'Hôpital) With its antique flourishes and a cosy salon centred on a fireplace, this place positively oozes half-timbered romance. Rooms are stylishly decked out in warm colours and florals, and most feature (like it!) spa bathtubs.

Hôtel Hannong
BOUTIQUE HOTEL €€

(03 88 32 16 22; www.hotel-hannong.com; 15 rue du 22 Novembre; s €69-149, d €79-239, tr €149-299, f €169-349; ❄🛜; 🚊 Alt Winmärik) Minimalist chic best describes the rooms at this design-focused hotel, kitted out with hardwood floors and colour schemes ranging from space-age silver to chocolate cream. The skylit lounge bar serves tapas and fine wines.

Royal Lutetia
HOTEL €€

(03 88 35 20 45; www.royal-lutetia.fr; 2bis rue du Général Rapp; s €75, d €85-110; 🛜📶; 🚊 Parc du Contades) A 10-minute stroll north of the

centre, this recently revamped hotel has bright and spacious rooms with above-par perks such as flatscreen TVs and free wi-fi.

Le Kléber Hôtel
HOTEL €€

(☏03 88 32 09 53; www.hotel-kleber.com; 29 place Kléber; s €60-90, d €65-100, tr €85-130, q €95-140; 🛜; 🚇Homme de Fer) So what will sweeten your dreams tonight? Pistachio, Pavlova or maybe Meringue? Highly original and supercentral, Le Kléber's rooms are named and decorated after fruits, spices and other calorific treats – pick one to suit your taste.

★ Cour du Corbeau
BOUTIQUE HOTEL €€€

(☏03 90 00 26 26; www.cour-corbeau.com; 6-8 rue des Couples; r €140-175, ste €220-260; ❄🛜; 🚇Porte de l'Hôpital) A 16th-century inn lovingly converted into a boutique hotel, Cour du Corbeau wins you over with its half-timbered charm and location, just steps from the river. Gathered around a courtyard, rooms blend original touches such as oak parquet and Louis XV furnishings with mod cons including flat-screen TVs.

Du Coté de Chez Anne
BOUTIQUE HOTEL €€€

(☏03 88 41 80 77; www.du-cote-de-chez-anne. com; 4 rue de la Carpe Haute; d €195-295; 🛜📶; 🚇Robertsau Boecklin) A dash of boutique style on Strasbourg's leafy north-eastern fringes, this half-timbered farmhouse sits in flower-strewn gardens and conceals gorgeous rooms designed with utmost grace and beautiful fabrics – from summery florals to gilded glamour; some with romantic touches of free-standing bathtubs. Take tram E from Place de la République to Robertsau Boecklin, a seven-minute walk away.

Eating

Restaurants abound on Grande Île: try canalside Petite France for Alsatian fare and half-timbered romance; Grand' Rue for curbside kebabs and *tarte flambée;* and rue des Veaux or rue des Pucelles for hole-in-the-wall eateries serving the world on a plate. Stepping across the river, pedestrianised rue d'Austerlitz is lined with patisseries and bistros.

Binchstub
ALSATIAN €

(☏03 88 13 47 73; www.binchstub.fr; 6 rue du Tonnelet Rouge; tarte flambée €10-15; ⏰7pm-1am daily; 🚇Broglie) Cooked to thin, crisp perfection, the *Flammkueche (tarte flambée)* at Binchstub is in a league all of its own. Locally sourced farm ingredients go into toppings including goat's cheese, thyme and honey, and Bleu d'Auvergne cheese with pear and rocket.

Bistrot et Chocolat
CAFE €

(www.bistrotetchocolat.net; 8 rue de la Râpe; snacks €7.50-11, brunch €12.50-26.50; ⏰11am-7pm Mon-Thu, 10am-9pm Fri-Sun; 📶📶; 🚇Grand'Rue) 📶 Chilled bistro hailed for its solid and liquid organic chocolate (ginger is superb), day specials and weekend brunches.

La Tinta
CAFE €

(www.tinta-cafe.fr; 36 rue du Bain aux Plantes; light meals €6-14, lunch menus €9.50-12.80; ⏰10am-6pm Tue-Sat; 🚇Alt Winmärik) Try this boho-flavoured literary cafe for a gourmet salad, fresh-pressed juice or tea and cake.

★ La Cuiller à Pot
ALSATIAN €€

(☏03 88 35 56 30; www.lacuillerapot.com; 18b rue Finkwiller; €17.50-26.50; ⏰noon-2.30pm & 7-10.30pm Tue-Fri, 7-10.30pm Sat; 🚇Musée d'Art

---

EAT ALSATIAN

Here's what is probably cooking in the kitchen of that cosy *winstub* (Alsatian tavern):

Baeckeoffe Beef, pork, lamb, vegetable and potato stew, marinated in riesling or pinot blanc and slow-cooked in a ceramic dish.

Choucroute garnie Sauerkraut garnished with salty bacon, ham hock and Alsatian-style sausage. Bring an appetite.

Fleischnacka Herby minced beef and egg pasta rolls shaped like *schnacka* (snails).

Flammkueche (*tarte flambée* in French) A thin-crust pizza dough topped with crème fraîche, onions and lardons. Fingers are allowed!

Kougelhopf Brioche-style raisin cake, baked in its namesake mould, with a hole in the middle and a dusting of icing sugar.

Lewerknepfle Ground liver, shallot and parsley *quenelles* (dumplings).

Spätzle Thick egg noodles, usually served with onions and/or cheese.

Wädele Pork knuckles, often braised in pinot noir or beer and served with *choucroute.*

Moderne) Run by a talented husband and wife team, this Alsatian dream of a restaurant rustles up fresh regional cuisine. Its well-edited menu goes with the seasons, but might include dishes such as filet of beef with mushrooms and homemade gnocchi and escargots in parsley jus. Quality is second to none.

Perles de Saveurs   MODERN FRENCH €€

(☑ 03 88 22 19 81; www.perlesdesaveurs.fr; 9 rue des Dentelles; mains €18.50-23, menus €23.50-32; ⊘ noon-2pm & 7-10.30pm Tue-Sat; ⊠ Grand'Rue) Tucked away in a Petite France courtyard, this cheerful restaurant is graced with the comical paintings of local artists Elisa and Marie-Hélène. Clean, snappy flavours dominate, along the lines of prawn, pineapple and coriander salad, scallops with fondue of pear and orange, and 'deconstructed' tarte au citron – all top quality. Lunch mains go for €14.

Vince'Stub   TRADITIONAL FRENCH €€

(☑ 03 88 52 02 91; www.vincestub.com; 10 Petite rue des Dentelles; mains €14-17; ⊘ 11.30am-2pm & 7-10.30pm Tue-Sat; ⊠ Grand'Rue) This sweet, petite bistro has a cosy beamed interior, a nicely down-to-earth vibe and a *menu* packed with Alsatian classics – see the blackboard for daily specials. It does a roaring trade in comfort food – from spot-on steak-frites to pork knuckles with Munster cheese.

Kobus   BISTRO €€

(☑ 03 88 32 59 71; www.restaurantkobus.com; 7 rue des Tonneliers; menus 2-/3-course lunch €19.50/24, 3-course dinner €45; ⊘ noon-1.30pm & 7-9.30pm Tue-Sat; ⊠ Grand'Rue) Graphic artworks lend a contemporary feel to this stone-walled bistro. The *menu* goes with the seasons, be it rich, earthy wild-mushroom risotto in autumn or herb-crusted spring lamb. The two-course €19.50 lunch includes a glass of wine or mineral water.

Maison des Tanneurs   ALSATIAN €€

(☑ 03 88 32 79 70; 42 rue du Bain aux Plantes; mains €16-25; ⊘ noon-1.45pm & 7.30-9.45pm Tue-Sat; ⧉ ; ⊠ Alt Winmärik) Even locals book ahead at this former tannery, creaking under the weight of its 16th-century beams and billowing geraniums. *Choucroute* with fat pork knuckles and garlicky Alsatian-style escargot are matched with top-notch pinots and rieslings. Snag a window table for fine views of Petite France's canals.

L'Assiette du Vin   BISTRO €€

(☑ 03 88 32 00 92; www.assietteduvin.fr; 5 rue de la Chaîne; menus lunch €15, dinner €26-50; ⊘ 7-9pm Mon, noon-1.30pm & 7-10pm Tue-Fri, 7-10.30pm Sat; ⊠ Grand'Rue) Market-fresh cuisine with a twist, discreet service and an award-winning wine list lure a discerning clientele to this friendly bistro. The *plat du jour* (dish of the day) is a snip at €8.50.

La Cloche à Fromage   TRADITIONAL FRENCH €€

(☑ 03 88 23 13 19; www.fromagerie-tourrette.com; 27 rue des Tonneliers; fondue €25-28; ⊘ noon-2.30pm & 7-11pm Mon-Sat; ⊠ Grand'Rue) *Au revoir* diet. Loosen a belt notch or three for Strasbourg's gooiest fondues and *raclette* at this temple to *fromage*, saving an inch for the 200-variety cheese board of *Guinness Book of World Records* fame.

Au Coin des Pucelles   ALSATIAN €€

(☑ 03 88 35 35 14; 12 rue des Pucelles; mains €15-28; ⊘ 6.30pm-1am Tue-Sat; ⊠ Broglie) Snug *winstub* with just six tables, serving solid Alsatian fare such as *choucroute au canard*.

★ Le Gavroche   MEDITERRANEAN €€€

(☑ 03 88 36 82 89; www.restaurant-gavroche.com; 4 rue Klein; menus €32-75; ⊘ noon-1.30pm, 7.30-9.30pm Mon-Fri, ⧉; ⊠ Porte de l'Hôpital) Nathalie and Benoît Fuchs give food a pinch of creativity and southern sunshine at intimate, softly lit Le Gavroche, awarded one Michelin star. Mains such as veal in a mint crust with crispy polenta and coriander-infused artichoke tagine are followed by zingy desserts such as lime tart with lemon-thyme sorbet. There's a *menu* for *les petits*.

Umami   FUSION €€€

(☑ 03 88 32 80 53; www.restaurant-umami.com; 8 rue des Dentelles; menus €39-66; ⊘ 7.30-9.30pm Mon, Tue & Fri, noon-1.30pm & 7.30-9.30pm Sat & Sun; ⊠ Grand'Rue) Simplicity is the ethos at Michelin-starred Umami, loosely translated as 'savoury', the fifth taste in Japanese cuisine. A starkly minimalist, art-strewn bistro sets the scene for taste sensations such as red curry gambas ravioli, and filet of wild cod with black rice sliding into an oyster and truffle sauce.

La Cambuse   SEAFOOD €€€

(☑ 03 88 22 10 22; 1 rue des Dentelles; mains €26-31; ⊘ noon-2pm & 7-10pm Tue-Sat; ⊠ Grand'Rue) Michelin-starred dining has a maritime flavour at La Cambuse, with its portholes, brass lamps and polished wood interior. The experimental chef infuses seafood with Asian spices in dishes such as cod with lime and spices, and sea bream with ginger and banana flower.

Au Crocodile   GASTRONOMIC €€€

(☑ 03 88 32 13 02; www.au-crocodile.com; 10 rue de l'Outre; menus lunch €39-72, dinner €96-139;

noon-2.30pm & 7-10.30pm Tue-Sat; Broglie) This hushed temple of French gastronomy is named after a stuffed toothy critter brought back from Egypt by one of Napoléon's generals. Artistically presented seasonal specialities including filet of turbot with algae, creamed watercress and oyster tartar have won Au Crocodile a Michelin star.

Drinking

Strasbourg's beer-thirsty students keep the scene lively and the bars and clubs pumping at weekends. Among the city's legions of pubs and bars is a glut of student-oriented places on the small streets east of the cathedral such as rue des Juifs, rue des Frères and rue des Sœurs.

Jeannette et les Cycleux   BAR
(www.lenetdejeannette.com; 30 rue des Tonneliers; 11.30am-1.30am Sun-Thu, 11.30am-3am Fri & Sat; ; Grand'Rue) Elvis lives on, baby, at this swinging '50s-themed haunt, where classic motorbikes dangle from the chilli-red walls. We dig the good vibes, retro decor and music from rockabilly to Motown.

Académie de la Bière   PUB
(17 rue Adolphe-Seyboth; 11am-4am; ; Alt Winmärik) Get the beers in at this chilled Petite France pub before a boogie in the cellar disco. There are hundreds of brews on offer, from Kronenbourg to *krieks* (Belgian beers fermented with sour cherries).

Bar Exils   BAR
(http://barexils.com; 28 rue de l'Ail; noon-4am; Grand'Rue) This is student central, with darts and billiards, well-worn sofas and plenty of cheap beer on tap.

☆ Entertainment

Cultural event listings appear in the free monthly Spectacles (www.spectacles-publications.com, in French), available at the tourist office.

La Laiterie   LIVE MUSIC
(www.laiterie.artefact.org; 11-13 rue du Hohwald; Laiterie) Reggae, metal, punk, chanson, blues – Strasbourg's premier concert venue covers the entire musical spectrum and stages some 200 gigs a year. Tickets are available at the door and online. La Laiterie is just a five-minute walk (500m) south of Petite France along rue de Molsheim.

L'Artichaut   LIVE MUSIC
(www.lartichaut.fr; 56 Grand' Rue; 11am-1am Tue-Sat, 1-8pm Sun; ; Grand'Rue) The 'artichoke' is the city's quirkiest arts and culture cafe, hosting free exhibitions, first-rate jazz concerts and jam sessions. The line-up is posted on the door and on the website.

Boutique Culture   TICKET OUTLET
(place de la Cathédrale, cnr rue Mercière; noon-7pm Tue-Sat; Grand'Rue) Ticket office for cultural events.

DON'T MISS

PASS THE CHOCOLATE

Strasbourg is now sweeter than ever, as it's one of the main stops on La Route du Chocolat et des Douceurs d'Alsace (Alsace Chocolate and Sweets Road), stretching 80km north to Bad Bergzabern and 125km south to Heimsbrunn near Mulhouse. Pick up a map at the tourist office to pinpoint Alsace's finest patisseries, chocolatiers, macaron shops and confectioners. The following are three sweet-toothed Strasbourg favourites to get you started.

Mireille Oster (www.mireille-oster.com; 14 rue des Dentelles; 9am-8pm Mon-Sat; Grand'Rue) Cherubs adorn this heavenly shop where Strasbourg's *pain d'épices* (gingerbread) fairy Mireille Oster tempts with handmade varieties featuring figs, amaretto, cinnamon and chocolate. Have a nibble before you buy.

Christian (www.christian.fr; 12 rue de l'Outre; 7am-6.30pm Mon-Sat; Broglie) Sumptuous truffles and pralines, weightless macaroons and edible Strasbourg landmarks – renowned chocolatier Christian's creations are mini works of art.

Maison Alsacienne de Biscuiterie (www.maison-alsacienne-biscuiterie.com; 16 rue du Dôme; 10am-6pm Mon-Thu & Sun, 10am-7pm Fri, 9am-7pm Sat; Broglie) Bakes scrumptious Alsatian gingerbread, macarons, raisin-stuffed *kougelhopf* and *sablés* (butter cookies) flavoured with nuts and spices.

MUSÉE LALIQUE

A stunning, romantic tribute to French art nouveau designer René Lalique, the **Musée Lalique** (www.musee-lalique.com; Rue du Hochberg, Wingen-sur-Moder; adult/child €6/3; ⊙10am-7pm daily, closed Mon Oct-Mar) harbours a collection assembling exquisite gem-encrusted and enamelled jewellery, perfume bottles, stoppers and sculpture. Complementing it are flower and wooded gardens, making the connection, as Lalique did, between art and the natural world. Located in the Northern Vosges, 60km north of Strasbourg, the museum can easily be visited on a half-day trip by taking the train to Wingen-sur-Moder (€10.30, 37 minutes). Alternatively, it's an hour's drive.

Opened on the site of the former Hochberg glassworks in July 2011, the museum affords wonderful insight into how Lalique drew on sinuous, naturalistic forms (flowers, insects, foliage) as well as the curvaceous female form in his work.

Fnac Billetterie TICKET OUTLET
(www.fnacspectacles.com; 22 place Kléber, 2nd fl; ⊙10am-7pm Mon-Fri, 9am-7pm Sat; 🚇Homme de Fer) Ticket outlet for events.

Odyssée CINEMA
(www.cinemaodyssee.com; 3 rue des Francs-Bourgeois; 🚇Grand'Rue) An arthouse cinema.

🛍 Shopping

Strasbourg's swishest shopping street is rue des Hallebardes, whose window displays are real eye candy (luxury crystal brand Baccarat is at No 44). High-street shops punctuate rue des Grandes Arcades and Grand' Rue, while Petite France is crammed with souvenir shops selling stuffed storks and pretzels aplenty. For vintage furniture, hip accessories and works by local creatives, mosey down rue des Veaux.

La Cloche à Fromage Boutique FOOD
(www.fromagerie-tourrette.com; 32 rue des Tonneliers; ⊙9am-7pm Mon-Fri, 8am-6.30pm Sat; 🚇Grand'Rue) Sells creamy Tomme, ripe Camembert and other first-rate cheeses.

Farmers' Market FOOD
(place du Maré aux Poissons; ⊙7am-1pm Sat; 🚇Porte de l'Hôpital) 🍴 Stalls are piled high with everything from locally produced foie gras to organic fruit and honey.

ℹ Information

A cluster of places offer discount calls and internet access (around €2) around Quai St-Jean near the train station.
Main Tourist Office (📞03 88 52 28 28; www.otstrasbourg.fr; 17 place de la Cathédrale; ⊙9am-7pm daily; 🚇Grand'Rue) A city-centre walking map with English text costs €1; bus/tram and cycling maps are free. *Strolling in Strasbourg* (€4.50) details six architectural walking tours.

Tourist Office Annexe (⊙9am-7pm daily; 🚇Gare Centrale) In the train station's southern wing.

ℹ Getting There & Away

AIR

Strasbourg's international **airport** (📞03 88 64 67 67; www.strasbourg.aeroport.fr) is 17km southwest of the city centre (towards Molsheim), near the village of Entzheim. The airport is served by major carriers such as Air France, KLM, Iberia and budget airline Ryanair. Flights link Strasbourg to European cities including London, Amsterdam, Madrid, Vienna, and domestic destinations of Paris, Nice, Lille and Lyon.

Ryanair links London Stansted with **Karlsruhe/Baden-Baden airport** (www.badenairpark.de), across the Rhine in Germany, 58km northeast of Strasbourg.

BUS

The **Eurolines office** (www.eurolines.com; 6D place d'Austerlitz; 🚇Porte de l'Hôpital) is a few blocks southeast of Grande Île; their buses use a **bus stop** (🚇Lycée Couffignal) 2.5km further south on rue du Maréchal Lefèbvre (facing the Citroën garage).

Strasbourg city bus 21 (€1.60) links the Jean Jaurès tram terminus with Kehl, the German town just across the Rhine.

CAR & MOTORCYCLE

The following rental companies have offices in the south wing of the train station:
Avis (www.avis.com)
Europcar (www.europcar.com)
National-Citer (www.citer.fr)
Sixt (www.sixt.com)

TRAIN

Built in 1883, the Gare Centrale was given a 120m-long, 23m-high glass façade and underground galleries in order to welcome the new TGV Est Européen in grand style. On the Grande Île, tickets are available at the **SNCF Boutique** (www.voyages-sncf.com; 5 rue des Francs-Bourgeois; 🚋 Langstross).

International

If you take the Eurostar via Paris or Lille, London is just five hours and 15 minutes away. Cities with direct services include the following:

Basel SNCF €23.50 to €54, 1¼ hours, 25 daily

Brussels-Nord €80 to €185, 5¼ hours, three daily

Karlsruhe €27 to €31, 40 minutes, 16 daily

Stuttgart €51 to €83, 1¼ hours, four TGVs daily

Domestic

Destinations within France:

Paris €75 to €134, 2¼ hours, 19 daily

Lille €96 to €140, four hours, 17 daily

Lyon €75 to €145, 4½ hours, 14 daily

Marseille €125 to €185, 6¾ hours, 16 daily

Metz €26 to €42, two hours, 20 daily

Nancy €25 to €41, 1½ hours, 25 daily

From Strasbourg, there are trains to Route des Vins destinations including the following:

Colmar €12.30, 30 minutes, 30 daily

Dambach-la-Ville €9.80, one hour, 12 daily

Obernai €6.20, 30 minutes, 20 daily

Sélestat €8.80, 30 minutes, 46 daily

❶ Getting Around

TO & FROM THE AIRPORT

A speedy shuttle train links the airport to the train station (€4, nine minutes, four hourly); the ticket also covers your onward tram journey into the city centre.

Strasbourg Navette (www.strasbourg-navette.com) Strasbourg Navette buses link Place de la Gare in Strasbourg with Karlsruhe/Baden Baden airport (€18 to €20, one hour), across the Rhine. Check timetables online.

BICYCLE

A world leader in bicycle-friendly planning, Strasbourg has an extensive and ever-expanding *réseau cyclable* (cycling network). The tourist office stocks free maps.

The city's 24-hour, self-rental **Vélhop** (www.velhop.strasbourg.eu; per hour/day €1/5) system can supply you with a bike. Pay by card and receive a code to unlock your bike. Helmets are not available. There are 11 automatic rental points plus outlets including the following:

City Centre (3 rue d'Or; 🚋 Porte de l'Hôpital)

Train Station (🚋 Gare Centrale) Situated on Level -1. Adjacent is an 820-place bicycle parking lot (€1 for 24 hours).

Rotonde (🚋 Rotonde)

CAR & MOTORCYCLE

Virtually the whole city centre is either pedestrianised or a hopeless maze of one-way streets, so don't even think of getting around Grande Île by car, or parking there for more than a couple of hours. For details on city-centre parking garages see www.parcus.com. At Strasbourg's eight P+R (park-and-ride) car parks, all on tram routes, the €3.50 all-day fee, payable from 7am to 8pm Monday to Saturday, gets the driver and each passenger a free return tram or bus ride into the city centre. From the autoroute, follow the signs marked 'P+R Relais Tram'. The safest picks are north of the city centre at Rives de l'Aar, northwest at Rotonde and south at Baggersee.

PUBLIC TRANSPORT

Five super-efficient tram lines, A through E, form the backbone of Strasbourg's outstanding public transport network, run by **CTS** (www.cts-strasbourg.fr). The main tram hub is Homme de Fer. Trams generally operate until 12.30am; buses – few of which pass through Grande Île – run until about 11pm. Night buses operate from 11.30pm to 5.30am on Fridays and Saturdays, stopping at nightlife hot spots. Tickets, valid on both buses and trams, are sold by bus drivers and ticket machines at tram stops and cost €1.60 (€3.10 return). The 24h Individuel (for one person €4.10) and Trio (for two to three people €6) tickets, valid for 24 hours from the moment they are stamped, are sold at tourist offices and tram stops.

In our Strasbourg listings, the nearest tram stops are indicated with a tram icon.

Route des Vins d'Alsace

Green and soothingly beautiful, the Route des Vins d'Alsace (Alsace Wine Route) is one of France's most evocative drives. Vines march up the hillsides to castle-topped crags and the mist-enshrouded Vosges, and every mile or so is a roadside *cave* (wine cellar) or half-timbered village inviting you to stop, raise a glass and enjoy. Corkscrewing through glorious countryside, the entire route stretches 170km from Marlenheim, 21km west of Strasbourg, southwards to Thann, 46km southwest of Colmar.

Local tourist offices can supply you with the excellent English-language map/ brochure *The Alsace Wine Route,* and *Alsace Grand Cru Wines,* detailing Alsace's 50 most prestigious Appellation d'Origine Contrôlée (AOC) winegrowing micro-regions. More information is available online at www.alsace-route-des-vins.com.

The villages mentioned in the following section, listed from north to south, all have plenty of hotels and restaurants, and some have campgrounds. Tourist offices can provide details on local *chambres d'hôte* (B&Bs), which generally cost €40 to €60 for a double.

Tours

For minibus tours of the Route des Vins try these agencies:

LCA Top Tour   BUS TOUR
(☑ 03 89 41 90 88; www.alsace-travel.com; 8 place de la Gare, Colmar; half-day €60-64) Reservations can be made via Colmar's tourist office. Most tours depart from the office on place de la Gare.

Regioscope   BUS TOUR
(☑ 06 88 21 27 15; www.regioscope.com; tours €105-115) Departures are from the tourist office, or your hotel, in Strasbourg.

Getting There & Around

The Route des Vins comprises several minor, lightly trafficked roads (D422, D35, D18 and so on). It is signposted but you might want to pick up a copy of Blay's colour-coded map *Alsace-Lorraine Touristique* (€5.40). Cyclists have a wide variety of on- and off-road options, which wend through some highly scenic countryside. Bike hire is available in all the major towns and cities. Expect to pay around €10 per day.

BUS & TRAIN
It's entirely possible, if a bit cumbersome, to get around the Route des Vins by public transport, since almost all the towns and villages mentioned here are served by train from Strasbourg or by train and/or bus from Colmar. Bicycles can be taken on virtually all trains. A handy website for checking regional bus connections and timetables is www.vialsace.eu.

CAR & MOTORCYCLE
Driving is undoubtedly the quickest and easiest way to reach villages and small towns on the Route des Vins, and the meandering country roads make for a memorable road trip. Car hire is available at airports and in major cities. Parking can be a nightmare in the high season, especially in Ribeauvillé and Riquewihr; your best bet is to park a bit out of the town centre and walk for a few minutes.

Obernai

POP 11,269

A vision of half-timbered, vine-draped, ring-walled loveliness, the wine-producing town of Obernai sits 31km south of Strasbourg. Give the summertime crowds the slip by ducking down cool, flower-bedecked alleyways, such as ruelle des Juifs, next to the tourist office.

Sights & Activities

A number of winegrowers have cellars a short walk from town (the tourist office has a map).

Place du Marché   SQUARE
Life spirals around this market square, put to use each Thursday morning, where you'll find the 16th-century **hôtel de ville** (town hall building) embellished with baroque trompe l'œil; the Renaissance **Puits à Six Seaux** (Six Bucket Well) just across rue du Général Gouraud; and the bell-topped, 16th-century **Halle aux Blés** (Corn Exchange).

Ramparts   CITY WALL
Stretch your legs by strolling around Obernai's 13th-century ramparts, accessible from the square in front of twin-spired, neo-Gothic **Église St-Pierre et St-Paul**.

Sentier Viticole
du Schenkenberg   WALKING
This 1.5km wine route meanders through vineyards and begins at the hilltop cross north of town, to get there, follow the yellow signs from the cemetery behind Église St-Pierre et St-Paul.

Sleeping & Eating

Le Gouverneur   HISTORIC HOTEL €
(☑ 03 88 95 63 72; www.hotellegouverneur.com; 13 rue de Sélestat; s €55-80, d €65-95, tr €75-120, q €85-130; @ ☻) Overlooking a courtyard, this old-town hotel strikes perfect balance between half-timbered rusticity and contemporary comfort. Its petit rooms have a boutiquey feel, with bursts of vivid colour and art-slung walls. The family-friendly team can provide cots and highchairs free of charge.

Winstub La Dîme   ALSATIAN €€
(☑ 03 88 95 54 02; 5 rue des Pélerins; menus €16-30; ☻ noon-2pm & 7-9pm Thu-Tue; ☻) Precisely as an Alsatian *winstub* should be: beamed and bustling with diners tucking into earthy dishes such as fat pork knuckles and *Zweibelkuchen* (onion tart).

★ **La Fourchette**
des Ducs   GASTRONOMIC €€€
(☑ 03 88 48 33 38; www.lafourchettedesducs.com; 6 rue de la Gare; menus €105-145; ☻ 7-9.30pm Tue-Sat, noon-1.30pm Sun) A great believer in fastidious sourcing, Chef Nicolas Stamm serves regional cuisine with gourmet panache and a signature use of herbs to a food-literate crowd at this two Michelin-starred restaurant. The tasting *menus* go with the seasons, featuring

Above: Hunawihr vineyards p339

0 ┣━━━━ 5 km
0 ┣━━━━ 2.5 miles

Marlenheim

BAS-RHIN

Molsheim

Rosheim

Obernai

Mittelbergheim

D35

Dambach-la-Ville

Château du Haut Kœnigsbourg

D18

Ribeauvillé   Bergheim

Hunawihr

Riquewihr
Kaysersberg

D415

Katzenthal

Colmar

HAUT-RHIN

Route des Vins d'Alsace

2 DAYS

Bien sûr, the Route des Vins d'Alsace is one of France's loveliest drives. Corkscrewing through hills ribboned with vines, half-timbered villages straight out of a children's picture-book and the mist-enshrouded Vosges, it is nothing short of beautiful. Every twist and turn reveals dinky hamlets, dreamy views and *caves* (wine cellars) with glasses at the ready for tastings.

From the gateway town of Marlenheim, a lane leads through bucolic countryside to medieval Molsheim, centred on a square dominated by the step-gabled Renaissance Metzig (butcher's shop). Continue south to Rosheim, where the striking Romanesque Église St-Pierre-St-Paul raises eyebrows with its, ahem, copulating gargoyles! Step inside for a moment of quiet contemplation before swinging south to pretty, half-timbered **Obernai** (p333) to explore the market square and vineyard trail. Views of the forest-cloaked Vosges unfold as you meander south to the sleepy hamlet of **Mittelbergheim** (p336), pausing to taste the local *grand cru* wines at award-winning Domaine Gilg. Higher peaks slide into view as you cruise south to cellar-studded **Dambach-la-Ville** (p336), embraced by 14th-century town walls, to catch your first tantalising glimpse of the turrets of 900-year-old **Château du Haut Kœnigsbourg** (p337). After detouring for an astounding panorama, which reaches to the Black Forest and Alps on cloudless days, from the castle ramparts, roam the cobbled streets in half-timbered **Bergheim** (p338). Alleys hide cosy *winstubs* (wine taverns) in tower-speckled **Ribeauvillé** (p338) nearby and you'll definitely see storks in **Hunawihr** (p339) at the Centre de Réintroduction Cigognes & Loutres. Allow time for serendipitous strolls in **Riquewihr** (p339) – pure fairy-tale stuff with its procession of half-timbered houses painted pastel colours as bright as the *macarons* they sell. Contemplate the Renaissance town hall and the house of Nobel Peace Prize winner Albert Schweitzer in riverside **Kaysersberg** (p340), then wend your way south to little-known **Katzenthal** (p341) for organic wine tasting and vineyard walks at family-run Vignoble Klur. Wrap up your tour with culture and Michelin-starred dining in canal-woven **Colmar** (p341), the enchanting Alsatian wine capital and birthplace of Statue of Liberty creator Frédéric Auguste Bartholdi.

WORTH A TRIP

NATZWEILER-STRUTHOF

About 25km west of Obernai stands **Natzweiler-Struthof** (www.struthof.fr; Natzwiller, off D130; adult/child €6/3; ⊙9am-6.30pm, closed Christmas-Feb), the only Nazi concentration camp on French territory. Today, the sombre remains of the camp are still surrounded by guard towers and concentric, once-electrified, barbed-wire fences. The four *crématoire* (crematorium ovens), the *salle d'autopsie* (autopsy room) and the *chambre à gaz* (gas chamber), 1.7km from the camp gate, bear grim witness to the atrocities committed here. The nearby **Centre Européen du Résistant Déporté** (⊙9am-6.30pm, closed Christmas-Feb) pays homage to Europe's Resistance fighters.

In all, some 22,000 (40% of the total) of the prisoners interned here and at nearby annexe camps died; many were shot or hanged. In early September 1944, as US Army forces approached, the 5517 surviving inmates were sent to Dachau.

specialities like Alsatian pigeon with *baerewecke* (spiced fruit cake) and veal with truffles and Menton lemon jus – simple but sublime.

ⓘ Information

Tourist Office (☑03 88 95 64 13; www.tourisme-obernai.fr; place du Beffroi; ⊙9am-12.30pm & 2-6pm Mon-Fri, 9.30am-12.30pm & 2-6pm Sat & Sun) Tucked behind the *hôtel de ville*.

ⓘ Getting There & Away

The train station is about 300m east of the old town. There are at least hourly TER train connections from Obernai to Colmar (€9, 50 to 70 minutes) and Strasbourg (€6.20, 30 minutes).

Mittelbergheim

POP 671

Serene, untouristy and set on a hillside, Mittelbergheim sits amid a sea of sylvaner grapevines and seasonal wild tulips, its tiny streets lined with sand-hued, red-roofed houses.

⊙ Sights & Activities

Each of Mittelbergheim's *caves* has an old-fashioned, wrought-iron sign hanging out front.

Sentier Viticole   WALKING
From the car park on the D362 at the upper edge of the village next to the cemetery, a vineyard trail wriggles across the slopes towards the perky twin-towered **Château du Haut Andlau** and the lushly forested Vosges.

Domaine Gilg   WINE TASTING
(www.domaine-gilg.com; 2 rue Rotland; ⊙8am-noon & 1.30-6pm Mon-Fri, to 5pm Sat, 9.30-11.30am Sun) Nip into this friendly, family-run winery to taste award-winning wines, including *grand cru* sylvaners, pinots and rieslings.

🛏 Sleeping & Eating

Private accommodation is good value and easy to come by – you'll see signs in windows all over town. For information, see www.pays-de-barr.com.

Hôtel Gilg   HISTORIC HOTEL €
(☑03 88 08 91 37; www.hotel-gilg.com; 1 rte du Vin; s €63-83, d €68-98, menus €33-68; 🖥🕸) For a dose of old-fashioned romance, check into this 17th-century half-timbered pile. A spiral staircase leads up to spacious, homey rooms in warm tones, some with wooden beams. The elegantly rustic restaurant serves classic French and Alsatian cuisine.

Dambach-la-Ville

POP 2047

Ringed by vines and sturdy ramparts, this flowery village has some 60 *caves* but manages to avoid touristic overload. The renowned Frankstein *grand cru* vineyards cover the southern slopes of four granitic hills west and southwest of Dambach.

⊙ Sights & Activities

Some of the eye-catching half-timbered houses, painted in ice cream colours such as pistachio, caramel and raspberry, date from before 1500.

Ramparts   CITY WALL
A gentle stroll takes in the 14th-century, pink-granite ramparts, originally pierced by four gates, three still holding aloft watchtowers and bearing quintessentially Alsatian names: Ebersheim, Blienschwiller and Dieffenthal.

Sentier Viticole du Frankstein   WALKING
It's a pleasant 1½-hour walk through the vineyards on this trail, which begins 70m up the

hill from the tourist office on rue du Général de Gaulle. The path meanders among the hallowed vines, passing by hillside **Chapelle St-Sébastien** (⊙9am-7pm), known for its Romanesque tower and Gothic choir.

🛏 Sleeping

Le Vignoble   HISTORIC HOTEL €
(☑03 88 92 43 75; www.hotel-vignoble-alsace. fr; 1 rue de l'Église; s €60-64, d €72-74; @🛜🏠) Housed in a beautifully converted 18th-century barn, this hotel has comfortable wood-beamed rooms in fresh lemon and lime hues. It's well situated in the village centre.

ℹ Information

Tourist Office (☑03 88 92 61 00; www.pays-de-barr.com; place du Maré; ⊙10am-noon & 2-5.30pm Mon-Fri, 10am-noon Sat) In the Renaissance-style *hôtel de ville*. Hands out walking tour maps and has details on cycling to Itterwiller.

ℹ Getting There & Away

The train station is about 1km east of the old town. Dambach-la-Ville has hourly services to Sélestat (€2.10, 10 minutes), Colmar (€6.40, 40 minutes) and Strasbourg (€9.80, one hour).

Sélestat

POP 19,568

Wedged between Strasbourg, 50km to the north, and Colmar, 23km to the south, Sélestat is an enticing jumble of colourful half-timbered houses and church spires. The town's claim to cultural fame is its incomparable Humanist Library.

⊙ Sights

Bibliothèque Humaniste   LIBRARY
(☑03 88 58 07 20; 1 rue de la Bibliothèque; ⊙info desk 9am-noon & 2-5pm Mon-Fri) Founded in 1452, the Humanist Library's stellar collection features a 7th-century book of Merovingian liturgy, a copy of *Cosmographiae Introductio* (printed in 1507), in which the New World was referred to as 'America' for the first time, and the first written mention of the Christmas tree (1521). At the time of writing the library was under renovation; it is set to reopen in all its glory in autumn 2016. For details, call or visit the ground floor info desk.

Vieux Sélestat   HISTORIC QUARTER
Church spires rise gracefully above the red rooftops of the old town, which hugs the left bank of the River Ill. Some of the finest examples of half-timbered and trompe-l'œil

buildings can be found along the medieval quai des Tanneurs.

Église St-Georges   CHURCH
(place St-Georges; ⊙8am-6pm) One of Alsace's most striking churches, this Gothic giant, built from weighty red sandstone and sporting a colourful mosaic-tile roof, is illuminated by curtains of stained glass in the choir.

Marché   MARKET
(⊙8am-1pm Tue) A huge outdoor market, held since 1435, takes over the streets around Romanesque Église St-Foy on Tuesdays.

Marché du Terroir   MARKET
(place Vanolles; ⊙8am-noon Sat) Saturday local-produce market, on the southern edge of the old town, selling home-grown fruit and vegies.

Montagne des Singes   PARK
(www.montagnedessinges.com; Kintzheim; adult/child €9/5.50; ⊙10am-6pm, closed Dec-Feb) ♪ Kids love to feed the free-roaming Barbary macaques and their cheeky infants popcorn (special monkey popcorn, of course) at this 6-acre woodland park. Take the D35 to Kintzheim, 7km west of Sélestat.

ℹ Information

Tourist Office (☑03 88 58 87 20; www. selestat-tourisme.com; 10 bd du Général Leclerc; ⊙9am-noon & 2-5.45pm Mon-Fri, 9am-noon & 2-5pm Sat) On the edge of the town centre, two blocks from the Bibliothèque Humaniste.

ℹ Getting There & Around

The tourist office rents out **bicycles** (two hours/half-day/day €7/9/14; deposit €150) from June to October.

The train station is 1km west of the Bibliothèque Humaniste. Train is the fastest way to reach destinations including Strasbourg (€8.80, 30 minutes, twice hourly), Colmar (€4.90, 11 minutes, hourly) and Obernai (€5.10, 33 minutes, hourly).

Haut Kœnigsbourg

On its fairy-tale perch above vineyards and hills, the turreted red-sandstone **Château du Haut Kœnigsbourg** (www.haut-koenigs bourg.fr; adult/child €8/free; ⊙9.15am-6pm, shorter hrs in winter) is worth the detour for the wraparound panorama from its ramparts, taking in the Vosges, the Black Forest and, on cloud-free days, the Alps. Audioguides delve into the turbulent 900-year history of the castle, which makes a very medieval impression despite having been reconstructed, with

German imperial pomposity, by Kaiser Wilhelm II in 1908.

Bergheim

POP 1933

Enclosed by a sturdy 14th-century ring-wall, overflowing with geraniums and enlivened by half-timbered houses in shocking pastels, Bergheim is a joy to behold. But things have not always been so cheerful: overlords, stampeding invaders, women burnt at the stake for witchcraft – this tiny village has seen the lot.

A stroll through the cobbled streets of the well-preserved medieval centre takes in the early Gothic church, the wall-mounted sundial at 44 Grand' Rue dating from 1711, and the imposing, turreted Porte Haute, Bergheim's last remaining town gate. Outside across the park sits the gnarled Herrengarten linden tree, planted around 1300. A 2km path circumnavigates the town's ramparts. Bergheim's *grands crus* labels are Kanzlerberg and Altenberg de Bergheim.

The tiny tourist office (☑ 03 89 73 31 98; ⊙ 9.30-noon & 2-6pm Mon-Sat, 10am-1pm Sun) is between the 18th-century hôtel de ville and the deconsecrated Ancienne Synagogue, now a cultural centre.

Draped around a 16th-century courtyard, La Cour du Bailli (☑ 03 89 73 73 46; www.cour-bailli.com; 57 Grand' Rue; r €77-175, menus €11-30; ☒) has countrified studios and apartments, all of which have kitchenettes. Factor in downtime in the pool and stone-built spa, which pampers with luscious vinotherapy treatments. The atmospheric cellar restaurant serves wine-drenched specialities including coq au riesling. There's no lift so be prepared to lug your bags.

Ribeauvillé

POP 5027

Nestled snugly in a valley, presided over by a castle, its winding alleys brimming with half-timbered houses, medieval Ribeauvillé is a Route des Vins must. The local *grands crus* are Kirchberg de Ribeauvillé, Osterberg and Geisberg.

⦿ Sights & Activities

Vieille Ville HISTORIC QUARTER

Along the main street that threads through the old town keep an eye out for the 17th-century Pfifferhüs which once housed the town's fife-playing minstrels; the hôtel de ville and its Renaissance fountain;

and the nearby, clock-equipped Tour des Bouchers (Butchers' Bell Tower).

Cave de Ribeauvillé WINERY

(☑ 03 89 73 20 35; www.vins-ribeauville.com; 2 rte de Colmar; ⊙ 8am-noon & 2-6pm Mon-Fri, 10am-noon & 2-6pm Sat & Sun) FREE France's oldest winegrowers' cooperative, founded in 1895, has a viniculture museum, informative brochures and free tastings of its excellent wines, made with all seven of the grape varieties grown in Alsace. On weekends it's staffed by local winegrowers. It's just across two roundabouts north from the tourist office.

Castle Ruins WALK

West and northwest of Ribeauvillé, the ruins of three 12th- and 13th-century hilltop castles – St-Ulrich (530m), Giersberg (530m) and Haut Ribeaupierre (642m) – can be reached on a hike (three hours return) beginning at place de la République (at the northern tip of Grand' Rue).

⬚ Sleeping & Eating

Camping Municipal Pierre de Coubertin CAMPGROUND €

(☑ 03 89 73 66 71; 23 rue Landau; 2 people, car & tent €13.50; ☜) This shady campground, with bike and canoe rental and a playground, is 500m east of the town centre.

Hôtel de la Tour HISTORIC HOTEL €€

(☑ 03 89 73 72 73; www.hotel-la-tour.com; 1 rue de la Mairie; s €72-96, d €78-104; ☜) Ensconced in a stylishly converted winery, this half-timbered hotel has quaint and comfy rooms, some with views of the Tour des Bouchers.

★ **Auberge du Parc Carola** INTERNATIONAL €€

(☑ 03 89 86 05 75; www.auberge-parc-carola.com; 48 rte de Bergheim; menus €30-61; ⊙ noon-1.30pm & 7-9.30pm Thu-Mon; ☒) Quaint on the outside, slick on the inside, this *auberge* is all about surprises, not least much-lauded chef Michaela Peters behind the stove. Flavours ring clear and true in seasonal showstoppers such as hare fillet with chestnut-studded red cabbage and haddock with hazelnut risotto and pumpkin emulsion. Tables are set up under the trees in summer. There's an €11.50 children's *menu*.

ⓘ Information

Tourist Office (☑ 03 89 73 23 23; www.ribeauville-riquewihr.com; 1 Grand' Rue; ⊙ 9.30am-noon & 2-6pm Mon-Sat, 10am-1pm Sun) At the southern end of one-way Grand' Rue.

STORKS OF ALSACE

White storks (*cigognes*), prominent in local folklore, are Alsace's most beloved symbols. Believed to bring luck (as well as babies), they winter in Africa and then spend summer in Europe, feeding in the marshes and building twig nests on church steeples and rooftops.

In the mid-20th century, environmental changes reduced stork numbers catastrophically. By the early 1980s only two pairs were left in the wild, so research and breeding centres were set up to establish a year-round Alsatian stork population. The program has been a huge success and today Alsace is home to more than 400 pairs – some of which you are bound to spot (or hear bill-clattering) on the Route de Vins.

ℹ Getting There & Away

A fairly frequent service runs from Ribeauvillé's central bus station to Route des Vins destinations including Colmar (€4.05, 25 minutes) and Riquewihr (€2.70, 13 minutes). Timetables are available online at www.vialsace.eu.

Hunawihr

POP 605

You're absolutely guaranteed to see storks in the quiet walled hamlet of Hunawihr, 1km south of Ribeauvillé. On a hillside just outside the centre, the 16th-century fortified church has been a simultaneum – serving both the Catholic and Protestant communities – since 1687. About 500m east of Hunawihr, the delightful **Centre de Réintroduction Cigognes & Loutres** (Stork & Otter Reintroduction Centre; www.cigogne-loutre.com; adult/child €9.50/6; ⊙ 10am-6.30pm, closed mid-Nov–Mar) 🐾 is home base for 200 free-flying storks; visit in spring to see hatchlings. Cormorants, penguins, otters and sea lions show off their fishing prowess several times each afternoon.

Stroll among exotic free-flying butterflies at the **Jardins des Papillons** (www.jardins despapillons.fr; adult/child €7.50/5; ⊙ 10am-6pm, closed Nov-Easter), nearby to the Centre de Réintroduction Cigognes & Loutres.

Bus 106 runs between Hunawihr and Colmar (€4.05, 33 minutes).

Riquewihr

POP 1215

Competition is stiff but Riquewihr is, just maybe, the most enchanting town on the Route des Vins. Medieval ramparts enclose its walkable centre, a photogenic maze of twisting lanes, hidden courtyards and half-timbered houses – each brighter and lovelier than the next. Of course, its chocolate-box looks also make it popular, so arrive in the early morning or evening to appreciate the town at its peaceful best.

◉ Sights & Activities

Dolder HISTORIC SITE
(www.musee-riquewihr.fr; admission €3, incl Tour des Voleurs €5; ⊙ 2-6pm Sat & Sun Apr-Nov, daily Jul–mid-Aug) This late 13th-century stone and half-timbered gate, topped by a 25m bell tower, is worth a look for its panoramic views and small local-history museum.

Tour des Voleurs HISTORIC SITE
(Thieves' Tower; admission €3, incl Dolder €5; ⊙ 10.30am-1pm & 2-6pm Easter-1 Nov) Rue des Juifs (site of the former Jewish quarter) leads down the hill to this medieval stone tower. Inside is a gruesome torture chamber with English commentary and an old-style winegrower's kitchen.

Maison de Hansi MUSEUM
(16 rue du Général de Gaulle; adult/child €3/2; ⊙ 10am-12.30pm & 1.30-6.30pm daily) Peer into the imagination of celebrated Colmar-born illustrator Jean-Jacques Waltz (1873-1951), aka Hansi, whose idealised images of Alsace are known around the world. On display are the artist's posters, children's books, engravings and even wine labels.

Sentier Viticole des Grands Crus WALKING
A yellow-marked 2km trail takes you out to acclaimed local vineyards, Schœnenbourg (north of town) and Sporen (southeast of town), while a 15km trail with red markers takes you to five nearby villages. Both trails can be picked up next to Auberge du Schœnenbourg, 100m to the right of the *hôtel de ville*.

🍴 Sleeping & Eating

Sugary smells of traditional macarons and coconut macaroons – a tradition since coconuts were first brought here in the 1700s – waft through the centre, where you'll find confectioners, *winstubs,* and bakeries selling humongous pretzels.

Hôtel de la Couronne
HISTORIC HOTEL €

(☑ 03 89 49 03 03; www.hoteldelacouronne.com; 5 rue de la Coronne; s €55-69, d €62-130; ☎) With its 16th-century tower and flowing wisteria, this central choice is big on old-world character. Rooms are country-style with crisp floral fabrics, low oak beams and period furnishings; many have views over the rooftops to the hills beyond. There's no lift.

Le Sarment d'Or
HISTORIC HOTEL €

(☑ 03 89 86 02 86; http://riquewihr-sarment-dor.fr; 4 rue du Cerf; d €70-85, tr €95, mains €24-32) Yes, you'll have to schlep your bags up a spiral staircase, but frankly it's a small price to pay for staying at this 17th-century, rose-tinted abode. Rooms are simple with a dash of rusticity and the restaurant serves regional food cooked with precision and finesse.

Au Trotthus
MODERN FRENCH €€

(☑ 03 89 47 96 47; www.trotthus.com; 9 rue des Juifs; menus lunch €18, dinner €28-39; ☺ 7-9.30pm Mon, noon-2pm & 7-9.30pm Tue & Thu-Sat, noon-2pm Sun) Lodged in a 16th-century winemakers' house, this snug wood-beamed restaurant is overseen by a chef with exacting standards. The market-driven *menu* might include such delicacies as bream tartar with citrus, wasabi cream, trout eggs and pea sorbet.

★ Table du Gourmet
GASTRONOMIC €€€

(☑ 03 89 49 09 09; www.jlbrendel.com; 5 rue de la Première Armée; menus €58-104; ☺ 12.15-1.45pm & 7.15-9.15pm Fri-Mon, 7.15-9.15pm Wed & Thu) Jean-Luc Brendel is the culinary force behind this Michelin-starred venture. A 16th-century house given a slinky, scarlet-walled makeover forms the backdrop for specialities made with herbs and little-heard-of vegetables from the restaurant's medieval garden. The menu swings with the seasons from asparagus to truffles, and dishes sing with intense, natural flavours – prepared with care, served creatively.

ℹ Information

Tourist Office (☑ 03 89 73 23 23; www.ribeauville-riquewihr.com; 2 rue de la Première Armée; ☺ 9.30am-noon & 2-6pm Mon-Sat, 10am-1pm & 2-4pm Sun) In the centre of the old town.

ℹ Getting There & Around

Bus 106 runs several times daily from Riquewihr to Ribeauvillé (€2.70, 18 minutes) and Colmar (€3.75, 25 minutes).

Kaysersberg
POP 2786

Kaysersberg, 10km northwest of Colmar, is an instant heart-stealer with its backdrop of gently sloping vines, hilltop castle and 16th-century fortified bridge spanning the gushing River Weiss.

◉ Sights & Activities

Audioguides of the town (1½ to two hours, €5) are available from the tourist office.

Vieille Ville
HISTORIC QUARTER

An old-town saunter brings you to the ornate Renaissance **hôtel de ville** and the red-sandstone **Église Ste Croix** (☺ 9am-4pm), whose altar has 18 painted haut-relief panels of the Passion and the Resurrection. Out front, a Renaissance **fountain** holds aloft a statue of Emperor Constantine.

Musée Albert Schweitzer
MUSEUM

(126 rue du Général de Gaulle; adult/child €2/1; ☺ 9am-noon & 2-6pm Easter-early Nov) The house where the musicologist, medical doctor and 1952 Nobel Peace Prize-winner Albert Schweitzer (1875-1965) was born is now this museum, with exhibits on the good doctor's life in Alsace and Gabon.

Sentiers Viticoles
WALKING

Footpaths lead in all directions through glens and vineyards. A 10-minute walk above town, the remains of the massive, crenulated **Château de Kaysersberg** stand surrounded by vines (two hours); other destinations include Riquewihr and Ribeauvillé (four hours). These paths begin through the arch to the right as you face the entrance to the *hôtel de ville*.

🛏 Sleeping

Hôtel Constantin
HOTEL €

(☑ 03 89 47 19 90; www.hotel-constantin.com; 10 rue du Père Kohlmann; s €55, d €65-82; ☎) Originally a winegrower's house in the heart of the old town, this hotel has 20 clean and modern rooms with wood furnishings.

ℹ Information

Tourist Office (☑ 03 89 71 30 11; www.kaysersberg.com; 37 rue du Général de Gaulle; ☺ 9am-12.30pm & 2-6pm Mon-Sat, 9am-12.30pm Sun; ☎) Inside the *hôtel de ville*; supplies walking-tour brochures as well as hiking and cycling maps, and makes bookings free of charge. You can log on to free internet and wi-fi here.

FRANCINE KLUR, OF VIGNOBLE KLUR

Alsatian Wine

There's an Alsatian wine for every occasion. Try a light, citrusy sylvaner with *tarte flambée* or foie gras, or a crisp, dry riesling with fish or *choucroute* (sauerkraut). Gewürztraminer is round and full of exotic fruit and spices, making it the ideal partner for Munster cheese, charcuterie and Asian food. Muscat is aromatic and flowery – great with asparagus or as an aperitif. Pick full-bodied pinot noirs for red meat.

Route des Vins

The Route des Vins is different from France's other wine regions because the villages are small and tight-knit, making it easy for visitors to get acquainted with our wine, food and culture. There are no grand châteaux but there *is* a real neighbourly feel – our doors are always open.

Insider Tips

Take a day to stroll or cycle through the vineyards, stopping for a wine tasting, lunch and to simply enjoy the atmosphere. Visit famous villages such as Riquewihr and Ribeauvillé in the evening to have the streets to yourself. My favourite seasons are autumn, when the heady scent of new wine is in the air, and spring, when the cherry trees are in bloom.

ⓘ Getting There & Away

Bus 145 runs several times daily between Kaysersberg and Colmar (€3.75, 30 minutes).

Katzenthal

POP 556

Close-to-nature Katzenthal, 5km south of Kaysersberg, is great for tiptoeing off the tourist trail for a while. *Grand cru* vines ensnare the hillside, topped by the medieval ruins of **Château du Wineck**, where walks through forest and vineyard begin.

Specialising in organic, biodynamic wines, family-run **Vignoble Klur** (☏03 89 80 94 29; www.klur.net; 105 rue des Trois Epis; 2-bed apt €82-96, 4-bed apt €105-120, min 3-night stay; 🅿) is a relaxed choice for tastings, Alsatian cookery classes and vineyard walks. The light-drenched, well-equipped apartments are great for back-to-nature holidays, and you can unwind in the organic sauna after a long day's walking and wine tasting. The onsite **Le KatZ** bistro pairs wines with dishes that make the most of local farm produce.

Colmar

POP 69,013

The capital of the Alsace wine region, Colmar looks for all the world as though it has been plucked from the pages of a medieval folk tale. At times the Route des Vins d'Alsace fools you into thinking it's 1454, and here, in the alley-woven heart of the old town, the

illusion is complete. Half-timbered houses in chalk-box colours crowd dark, cobblestoned lanes and bridge-laced canals, which have most day-trippers wandering around in a permanent daze of neck-craning, photo-snapping, gasp-eliciting wonder.

Quaintness aside, Colmar's illustrious past is clearly etched in its magnificent churches and museums, which celebrate local legends from Bartholdi (of Statue of Liberty fame) to the revered Issenheim Altarpiece.

⊙ Sights

★ **Petite Venise**   HISTORIC QUARTER

(rowboats per 30min €6) If you see just one thing in Colmar, make it the Little Venice quarter. Canal connection aside, it doesn't resemble the Italian city in the slightest, but it is truly lovely in its own right, whether explored by foot or by rowboat. The winding backstreets are punctuated by impeccably restored half-timbered houses in sugared-almond shades, many ablaze with geraniums in summer. Take a medieval mosey around **rue des Tanneurs**, with its rooftop verandas for drying hides, and **quai de la Poissonnerie**, the former fishers' quarter.

Musée d'Unterlinden   ART MUSEUM

(www.musee-unterlinden.com; 1 rue d'Unterlinden; adult/child €8/5 incl Église des Dominicains; ⊙9am-6pm daily) Gathered around a Gothic-style Dominican cloister this museum hides a prized collection of medieval stone statues, late 15th-century prints by Martin Schongauer

Colmar

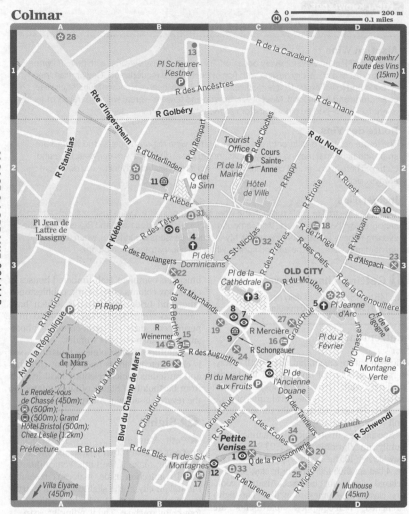

as well as an ensemble of Upper Rhine Primitives. Its stellar modern art collection also contains works by Monet, Picasso and Renoir. The star attraction, however, is the late-Gothic **Rétable d'Issenheim** (Issenheim Altarpiece), which is currently on display in the nearby Église des Dominicains while the museum undergoes expansion.

Église des Dominicains   CHURCH
(place des Dominicains; incl Musée d'Unterlinden adult/child €8/5; ⊙9am-6pm daily May-Oct, shorter hrs rest of yr) Lit by late-medieval stained glass, this desanctified Gothic church shelters the celebrated triptych *La Vierge au*

Buisson de Roses (The Virgin in the Rose Bush), painted by Martin Schongauer in 1473. While the Musée d'Unterlinden undergoes expansion the church is also showcasing the Rétable d'Issenheim (Issenheim Altarpiece) by painter Mathias Grünewald and sculptor Nicolas of Haguenau. Hailed as one of the most profound works of faith ever created, the altarpiece realistically depicts scenes from the New Testament.

Musée Bartholdi   MUSEUM
(www.musee-bartholdi.com; 30 rue des Marands; adult/child €5/3; ⊙10am-noon & 2-6pm Wed-Mon Mar-Dec) In the house where Frédéric Auguste

Colmar

Bartholdi was born in 1834, this museum pays homage to the sculptor who captured the spirit of a nation with his Statue of Liberty. Look out for the full-size plaster model of Lady Liberty's left ear (the lobe is watermelon-sized!) and the Bartholdi family's sparklingly bourgeois apartment. A ground-floor room shows 18th- and 19th-century Jewish ritual objects.

Église St-Matthieu CHURCH
(Grand' Rue; ⊙10am-noon & 3-5pm) Quintessentially Protestant in its austerity, this Franciscan church has something of a split personality. From 1715 to 1987, a wall divided the soaring 14th-century Gothic choir from the nave. This arrangement allowed the 14th-century *jubé* (rood screen) to survive the counter-Reformation.

Maison des Têtes HISTORIC SITE
(House of the Heads; 19 rue des Têtes) True to its name, this step-gabled house, built in 1609 for a wealthy wine merchant, is festooned with 106 grimacing faces and heads of animals, devils and cherubs.

Ancienne Douane HISTORIC SITE
(place de l'Ancienne Douane) At the southern tip of rue des Marchands is this late-medieval customs house, with its loggia and variegated tile roof, which now hosts temporary exhibitions and concerts.

Collégiale St-Martin CHURCH
(place de la Cathédrale; ⊙8.30am-6.30pm) Delicate stonework guides the eye to the polychrome mosaic-tiled roof and Mongol-style copper spire of this Gothic church. Its jewel-like stained-glass windows cast kaleidoscopic patterns.

Musée du Jouet MUSEUM
(www.museejouet.com; 40 rue Vauban; adult/child €4.80/3.70; ⊙10am-noon & 2-6pm Wed-Mon) Kids of every age delight at the sight of toys from generations past – from demure 1950s Barbies to Gaultier-clad dolls and, every little boy's dream, Hornby train sets – at this museum.

Maison Pfister HISTORIC SITE
(11 rue des Marands) This Renaissance pile was built in 1537 for Ludwig Scherer, a wealthy hatter from Besançon. With its delicately

DON'T MISS

ROWING PETITE VENISE

Rowboats depart next to **rue de Turenne** bridge and are a relaxed way to see Petite Venise from the water. The bridge is also the best spot to see the canals light up after dark.

painted panels, elaborate oriel window and carved wooden balcony, it is an immediate attention-grabber.

Maison zum Kragen   HISTORIC HOUSE
(9 rue des Marands) This 15th-century house is identified by its much-photographed sculpture of a *marchand* (merchant).

✰✰ Festivals & Events

Folksy **Soirées Folkloriques** (free performances of Alsatian music and dancing) get toes tapping on Tuesday evenings from mid-May to mid-September on place de l'Ancienne Douane. Orchestras strike up in historic venues across Colmar, including Musée d'Unterlinden, during July's **Festival International de Colmar** (www.festival-colmar.com). Villages all over Alsace toast summer with merry **Fêtes du Vin** (Wine Festivals); the tourist office has details. Colmar's snowglobe of a **Marché de Noël** (Christmas Market; www.noel-colmar.com) glitters from late November to 31 December.

🛏 Sleeping

Whether it is to be canalside romance or a night in a working winery, Colmar delivers with plenty of charming digs. Book well ahead for Christmas, Easter and the high summer season.

★**Chez Leslie**   B&B €
(☑ 03 89 79 98 99; www.chezleslie.com; 31 rue de Mulhouse; s €72, d €82-87; 🛜🖶) Insider tips on Colmar, a high chair for your baby, afternoon tea in the garden – nothing is too much trouble for your kind host Leslie at her attractively restored 1905 townhouse. Daylight spills into uniquely decorated rooms with hardwood floors and antique beds. It's five minutes' stroll west of the train station.

Maison Martin Jund   GUESTHOUSE €
(☑ 03 89 41 58 72; www.martinjund.com; 12 rue de l'Ange; r €37-70, apt €72-100; 🛜🖶) Surrounding a courtyard in the backstreets of the old town, this rosy half-timbered house shelters an organic winery and bright, well-kept studios, many with living rooms and kitchenettes. Breakfast is well worth the extra €6.50, with croissants, fresh-pressed juice, homemade jams and Vosges cheese.

Villa Élyane   B&B €€
(☑ 06 99 04 55 23; www.villa-elyane.com; 26a rue Camille Schlumberger; d €150-160, q €195-250; ❄🛜🖶) This graceful late-19th-century villa manages the careful balancing act of combining original art nouveau features with

modern comforts including in-room iPod docks and espresso makers. Regional organic produce and fresh-squeezed juice makes breakfast a delight. A garden, sauna, ping-pong table and bike rental boost the guesthouse's family appeal.

★**Hotel Quatorze**   DESIGN HOTEL €€
(☑ 03 89 20 45 20; www.hotelquatorze.com; 14 rue des Augins; d €140-240, ste €260-420) Bringing new-wave design to the heart of the old town, Hotel Quatorze occupies a lovingly transformed pharmacy dating from 1830. The 14 rooms and suites are streamlined and open-plan, with wood floors and white walls enlivened by works by Spanish artist Alfonso Vallès. Little details like iPod docks, Aesop cosmetics and, in some suites, whirlpool tubs up the style ante.

Hôtel les Têtes   HISTORIC HOTEL €€
(☑ 03 89 24 43 43; www.maisondestetes.com; 19 rue des Têtes; d €145-168, tr €198-265, menus €24-49; ❄🛜🖶) Luxurious but never precious, this hotel occupies the magnificent Maison des Têtes. Each of its 21 rooms has rich wood panelling, an elegant sitting area, a marble bathroom and romantic views. The plushest rooms have their own spa baths. With its wrought ironwork and stained glass, the restaurant provides a sumptuously historic backdrop for French-Alsatian specialities.

Hôtel St-Martin   HISTORIC HOTEL €€
(☑ 03 89 24 11 51; www.hotel-saint-martin.com; 38 Grand' Rue; s €85-115, d €95-130, f €130-150; ❄@🖶) What a location! Right on the place de l'Ancienne Douane, this 14th-century patrician house captures the elegance of yesteryear

in rooms dressed with handcrafted furniture. Choose a top-floor room for rooftop views. Family rooms are available.

Grand Hôtel Bristol
HISTORIC HOTEL €€

(☑ 03 89 23 59 59; www.grand-hotel-bristol.com; 7 place de la Gare; s €118-138, d €148-195, tr €215; ❄ 🛜 ♨ 🅿) Historic meets contemporary at the century-old Bristol, which sits opposite the train station. A marble staircase sweeps up to modern rooms and a spa whose sundeck has fabulous city views. The big deal for gastronomes is the attached Michelin-starred Le Rendez-vous de Chasse (p346) restaurant.

Hôtel Le Rapp
HOTEL €€

(☑ 03 89 41 62 10; www.rapp-hotel.com; 1-5 rue Weinemer; s €79-93, d €110-132; ❄ @ 🛜 ♨ 🅿) On the edge of the old town, this Logis de France hotel has classically elegant rooms as well as a pool, a sauna, a hammam and a fitness room. Breakfast sets you back an extra €13.

Le Maréchal
BOUTIQUE HOTEL €€

(☑ 03 89 41 60 32; www.hotel-le-marechal.com; 46 place des Six Montagnes Noires; s €95, d €115-225; @) Peppered with antiques, this 16th-century hotel in Petite Venise cranks up the romance in its cosy (read small) rooms, many with low beams, canopy beds and canal views. Splashing out gets you your own spa bath.

🍴 Eating

The old town is liberally sprinkled with bistros and *winstubs,* especially place de l'Ancienne Douane, rue des Marchands and Petite Venise.

La Cocotte de Grandmère
TRADITIONAL FRENCH €

(☑ 03 89 23 32 49; 14 place de l'École; 2-/3-course menus €13-15; ⊙ noon-2pm & 7-9pm Mon-Fri) Good honest food and a warm ambience attract hungry locals to this sweet bistro. The three-course €15 *menu* hits the mark every time, with deeply satisfying home cooking from hearty casseroles to roast duck leg with creamy mash.

Sézanne
BISTRO €

(www.sezanne.net; 30 Grand'Rue; light meals €9-18; ⊙ 10am-7pm Mon, 9am-7pm Tue-Sat) Buy local wine, pâté and charcuterie in the downstairs *épicerie* (specialist grocer), or dig into *tartines* (open-faced sandwiches) and day specials in the upstairs bistro.

Au Croissant Doré
TEA ROOM €

(28 rue Marands; snacks & light meals €3.50-7.50; ⊙ 8am-7.30pm Tue-Sun; ☑) With its gramophone and art nouveau flair, this candyfloss-pink tea room is a nostalgic spot for *tarte flambée* or a slice of fruit tart.

★ L'Épicurien
TRADITIONAL FRENCH €€

(☑ 03 89 41 14 50; 11 rue Wickram; lunch menus €14.50-25, mains €21-25; ⊙ noon-2pm & 7-9.30pm Tue-Sat; 🅿) Hidden away in a backstreet of Petite Venise, this is a wine bar–bistro in the classic mould, with cheek-by-jowl tables and a good buzz. Whatever is fresh at the market

ALSACE & LORRAINE COLMAR

DON'T MISS

THE EPICURE TOUR

Colmar is an exceptional city for all-out indulgence. So go, assemble your gourmet picnic:

➜ **Marché Couvert** (rue des Écoles; ⊙ 8am-6pm Tue-Thu, to 7pm Fri, to 5pm Sat) Bag Munster cheese, pretzels, patisserie, wild boar *saucisson* (dry-cured sausage or salami), foie gras and more at this 19th-century market hall.

➜ **Fromagerie St-Nicolas** (18 rue St-Nicolas; ⊙ 2-7pm Mon, 10am-12.30pm & 2-7pm Tue-Fri, 9am-6.30pm Sat) Follow your nose to pungent Munster, Tomme and ripe Camembert. BYOB (bring your own baguette) and they'll make you a sandwich.

➜ **Les Foie Gras de Liesel** (3 rue Turenne; ⊙ 9.30am-12.30pm & 2.30-6.30pm Tue-Sat) Marco and Marianne Willmann produce the silkiest, most subtly flavoured goose and duck foie gras in town.

➜ **Choco en Têtes** (7 rue des Têtes; ⊙ 2-6.30pm Mon, 9.30am-12.30pm & 2-6.30pm Tue-Sat) Edible art describes this chocolatier's seasonally inspired truffles and pralines. Kids love the chocolate stork eggs.

➜ **Maison Martin Jund** (www.martinjund.com; 12 rue de l'Ange; ⊙ tastings 9am-noon & 2-6.30pm Mon-Sat) Need something to wash it all down? Head to this organic winery to taste home-grown pinots, rieslings and sylvaners.

goes into the pot, often with a generous pinch of spice – from duck breast with sweet chilli to chunky cod fillet with lobster-basil cream and squid ink fettuccine.

L'Un des Sens
WINE BAR €€

(☑03 89 24 04 37; www.cave-lun-des-sens.fr; 18 rue Berthe Molly; light bites & mains €6-25; ☺3-10pm Tue-Thu, 10am-11pm Fri & Sat) Lodged in a half-timbered house, this red-walled wine bar keeps the mood intimate and mellow. It speaks volumes that the owners know their suppliers by name, and regional charcuterie, cheese, pâté and tapas are expertly paired with wines (250 to choose from) that begin at a modest €3.50 per glass.

La Table du Brocanteur
ALSATIAN €€

(☑03 89 23 45 57; 23 rue d'Alspach; mains €19-21; ☺noon-2pm & 7-9.30pm Tue-Sat) Tucked down a backstreet, this half-timbered house is emblazoned with milk pails, clogs and an attic's worth of other rustic knickknacks. Bright flavours such as scallop carpaccio and duck *magret* (breast of the foie gras duck) with pineapple chutney marry well with local wines. The €12 *menu du jour* is a bargain.

Aux Trois Poissons
SEAFOOD €€

(☑03 89 41 25 21; 15 quai de la Poissonnerie; menus €23-52; ☺noon-2pm & 7-9pm Tue-Sat; ☻) Oil paintings on the walls and Persian carpets on the floor give this fish restaurant a hushed, elegant atmosphere. The chef's signatures include *sandre sur lit de choucroute* (pike-perch on a bed of sauerkraut) and flavoursome bouillabaisse.

★JY'S
GOURMET €€€

(☑03 89 21 53 60; www.jean-yves-schillinger.com; 17 rue de la Poissonerie; menus lunch €41, dinner €62-82; ☺noon-2pm & 7-10pm) Jean-Yves Schillinger mans the stove at this Michelin-starred restaurant in Petite Venise. Behind a trompe l'oeil façade lies an urban-cool restaurant, with flattering lighting and chesterfield sofas

adding to the lounge-style ambience. Every flavour shines in seasonal dishes that are cooked with imagination and care, and delivered with panache. Expect a few surprises, from olive trees to candyfloss.

L'Atelier du Peintre
GASTRONOMIC €€€

(☑03 89 29 51 57; www.atelier-peintre.fr; 1 rue Schongauer; menus lunch €24-29, dinner €40-79; ☺noon-1.30pm & 7-9.30pm Tue-Sat) With its art-slung walls and carefully composed cuisine, this Michelin-starred bistro lives up to its 'painter's studio' name. Seasonal masterpieces including roast lamb with creamed artichokes and chanterelles, and mussel soup with black olives, sage and aioli, are cooked with verve and served with panache.

Le Rendez-vous de Chasse
GASTRONOMIC €€€

(☑03 89 23 15 86; www.grand-hotel-bristol.com; 7 place de la Gare; menus €36-79; ☺lunch & dinner daily; ☑) Candlelight, white linen tablecloths and polished wood create a refined backdrop at this Michelin-starred restaurant at Grand Hôtel Bristol (p345). Chef Julien Binz puts his own imaginative touch on regional cuisine, using seasonal ingredients from truffles to asparagus. Reservations recommended.

☆ Entertainment

Fnac Billetterie
TICKET OUTLET

(www.fnacspectacles.com; 1 Grand' Rue; ☺2-7pm Mon, 10am-7pm Tue-Sat) Ticket outlet.

Théâtre Municipal
THEATRE

(☑03 89 20 29 02; 3 rue Unterlinden) Next to the Musée d'Unterlinden, this is Colmar's biggest stage, hosting concerts, ballet, plays and even the occasional opera.

Comédie de l'Est
THEATRE

(http://comedie-est.com; 6 rte d'Ingersheim) Experimental theatre, housed in a former factory 400m northwest of Colmar.

CYCLING THE VINES

Colmar is a great base for slipping onto a bicycle saddle to pedal along the Route des Vins and the well-marked Franco-German trails of the nearby Rhine (www.2rives3ponts. eu, in French). Get your two-wheel adventure started by clicking onto www.tourisme68. com and www.tourisme67.com, with detailed information on everything from bicycle hire to luggage-free cycling holidays, itinerary plans and downloadable route maps.

If you'd rather join a group, Bicyclette Go (☑06 87 47 44 31; www.bicyclettego.com; 2 impasse du Tokay, Voegtlinshoffen), 12km south of Colmar, arranges all-inclusive half-day to two-week cycling tours in the region, many of which are customised. Half-day tours complete with wine tasting start at €40 per person.

❶ Information

Tourist Office (☑ 03 89 20 68 92; www.
ot-colmar.fr; 32 cours Sainte-Anne; ⊘9am-
6pm Mon-Sat, 10am-1pm Sun Apr-Oct, shorter
hours rest of year) Can help find accommodation and supply information on hiking, cycling
and bus travel (including schedules) along the
Route des Vins and in the Massif des Vosges.

❶ Getting There & Away

AIR

Basel-Mulhouse-Freiburg Airport (Euro
Airport; www.euroairport.com) Trinational
Basel-Mulhouse-Freiburg airport is 60km
south of Colmar.

BUS

Public buses are not the quickest way to explore
Alsace's Route des Vins but they *are* a viable
option; destinations served include Riquewihr,
Hunawihr, Ribeauvillé, Kaysersberg and
Eguisheim.

The open-air bus terminal is to the right as you
exit the train station. Timetables are posted and
are also available at the tourist office or online
(www.l-k.fr, in French).

Line 1076 goes to Neuf-Brisach (€3.65, 30
minutes), continuing on to the German city of
Freiburg (€8.30, 1¼ hours, seven daily Monday
to Friday, four daily weekends).

CAR & MOTORCYCLE

Cars can be hired from **ADA** (www.ada.fr; 22bis
rue Stanislas). **Avis** (www.avis.com) also has an
agency in the train station.

TRAIN

Colmar train connections:
Basel €13.70, 46 minutes, 25 daily
Mulhouse €8.40, 21 minutes, 38 daily
Paris Gare de l'Est; €79 to €102, three hours,
17 daily
Strasbourg €12.30, 32 minutes, 30 daily

Route des Vins destinations departing from
Colmar include **Dambach-la-Ville** (€6.40, 35
minutes) and **Obernai** (€9, one hour), both of
which require a change of trains at **Sélestat**
(€4.90, 10 minutes, 30 daily).

About 20 daily TER trains (10 daily on weekends) link Colmar with the Vallée de Munster
towns of **Munster** (€4.10, 30 minutes) and **Metzeral** (€5.10, 45 minutes).

❶ Getting Around

TO & FROM THE AIRPORT

Frequent trains run between Colmar and
St-Louis (€12.70, 37 minutes). An airport shuttle
bus service operates between St-Louis and

THE STAR OF CITADELS

Shaped like an eight-pointed star, the
fortified town of **Neuf-Brisach** was
commissioned by Louis XIV in 1697 to
strengthen French defences and prevent
the area from falling to the Habsburgs. It
was conceived by Sébastien Le Prestre
de Vauban (1633–1707).

A Unesco World Heritage Site since
2008, the citadel has remarkably
well-preserved fortifications. The
Musée Vauban (7 place de Belfort; adult/
child €2.50/1.65; ⊘10am-noon & 2-5pm
Wed-Mon May-Oct), below the porte de
Belfort gate, tells the history of the citadel through models, documents and
building plans. Neuf-Brisach is just 4km
from its German twin Breisach am Rhein
on the banks of the River Rhine.

To reach Neuf-Brisach, 16km southeast of Colmar, follow the signs on the
D415.

Basel-Mulhouse-Freiburg EuroAirport (€2, eight
minutes, every 20 or 30 minutes).

BICYCLE

Colmarvélo (www.velodocteurs.com; 9 place
de la Gare; half-day city/mountain/e-bike
€6/8/15, full-day €8/12/20, deposit €150;
⊘8am-noon & 2-7pm Mon-Fri, 9am-7pm Sat &
Sun) Municipal city bikes.

CAR & MOTORCYCLE

A central car park handy for Petite Venise is
place des Six Montagnes Noires. Free parking
can be found on place Scheurer-Kestner just
north of Musée d'Unterlinden; a few blocks east
of the train station around the German-era,
brick-built water tower; and in *part* of the car
park at place de la Montagne Verte.

Massif des Vosges

The Vosges range is a little-known region of
softly rounded, forest-cloaked heights and
pastures interspersed with lakes and dairy
farms. For added seclusion, head away from
the crowds and into the serene **Parc Naturel
Régional des Ballons des Vosges** (www.parc-
ballons-vosges.fr), 3000 sq km of pristine greenery in the western Vosges.

In summer, hang-gliders take to the skies,
cyclists roll through pristine countryside and
walkers can pick from 10,000km of marked
paths, including GRs (grandes randonnées;

long-distance hiking trails). When the snow settles, three dozen inexpensive skiing areas offer modest downhill and superb cross-country skiing. Check out the Cimes et Sentiers (www.sentiersrando.com) website for year-round walking and cycling tours of the Vosges and, in winter, snowshoe hikes.

The Vallée de Munster – its cow-nibbled pastures scattered with 16 quaint villages, its upper slopes thickly forested – is one of the loveliest valleys in the Vosges. From the town of Metzeral, you can hike to Schnepfenried, Hohneck, the Petit Ballon and Vallée de la Wormsa, which has a section of the GR5 and a trio of small lakes.

Munster

POP 4964

Spread around gently rolling hills and famous for its notoriously smelly and eponymous cheese, streamside Munster, meaning 'monastery', is a relaxed base for exploring the valley (the GR531 passes by here).

◉ Sights & Activities

Enclos aux Cigognes   WILDLIFE CENTRE
(Stork Enclosure; chemin du Dubach; ⊘ 24hr) FREE
About 20 storks live year-round in the Enclos aux Cigognes, and more hang out on top of it. It's 250m behind the Renaissance *hôtel de ville;* on foot, cross the creek and turn left.

Cycle Hop Evasion   CYCLING
(5 rue de la République; bike rental per day €14-18; ⊘ 9.30am-6.30pm Mon-Sat) Based 200m east of the tourist office, Cycle Hop Evasion rents out mountain bikes, arranges guides and provides details on cycling routes.

🛏 Sleeping & Eating

Hôtel Deybach   HOTEL €
(✆ 03 89 77 32 71; www.hotel-deybach.com; 4 chemin du Badischhof; s €51-65, d €58-73, tr €88; ☎ ☷) You are made to feel instantly welcome at family-run Hôtel Deybach, which has fresh,

simple rooms with town or country views and a flowery garden for relaxing moments.

Salon de Thé Gilg   TEA ROOM €
(11 Grand' Rue; cakes & pastries €2-5; ⊘ 7.30am-6.30pm Tue-Fri, 7am-6pm Sat, 7.30am-12.30pm Sun) Skip dinner and go straight for dessert at this tea room famous for its delectable *kougelhopf,* petits fours and pastries.

A l'Agneau d'Or   REGIONAL CUISINE €€
(✆ 03 89 77 34 08; www.martinfache.com; 2 rue saint Grégoire; menus €32-48; ⊘ noon-1.45pm & 7-9pm Wed-Sun) Brimming with bonhomie, A l'Agneau d'Or is a fine choice for robustly seasoned, attractively presented Alsatian dishes, such as *choucroute* gratin with Munster cheese and pork cheeks slow-braised in pinot noir.

❶ Information

Maison du Parc Naturel Régional des Ballons des Vosges (✆ 03 89 77 90 34; www.parc-ballons-vosges.fr; 1 cour de l'Abbaye; ⊘ 10am-noon & 1.30-5.30pm Tue-Sun) The regional park's visitors centre has ample information in English. To get there, walk through the arch from place du Marché.

Tourist Office (✆ 03 89 77 31 80; www.la-vallee-de-munster.com; 1 rue du Couvent; ⊘ 9.30am-12.30pm & 2-6pm Mon-Fri, 10am-noon & 2-4pm Sat) Information on the Munster valley, including visits to cheesemakers. Sells hiking maps and *topoguides* in French. To get there, walk through the arch from place du Marché.

Ballon d'Alsace

Three *régions* (Alsace, Franche-Comté and Lorraine) converge at the rounded 1247m-high summit of Ballon d'Alsace, 20km southwest of Grand Ballon as the crow flies (by road, take the D465 from St-Maurice). Between 1871 and WWI, the frontier between France and Germany passed by here, attracting French tourists eager to glimpse France's 'lost province' of Alsace from the he-

---

HOLY CHEESE

Rich, white and creamy, with a pungent, earthy aroma when ripe and a mild flavour when fresh, Munster cheese has been made in this valley to the time-honoured methods of the Benedictine monks since the 7th century. Only the milk of the cows that lazily graze the Vosges' highest pastures is good enough for this semisoft cheese, delicious with cumin seeds, rye bread and a glass of spicy gewürztraminer. See the tourist office website (www.vallee-munster.eu) for details on dairy farms where you can taste, buy and see Munster in the making.

ROUTE DES CRÊTES

Partly built during WWI to supply French frontline troops, the Route des Crêtes (Route of the Crests) takes you to the Vosges' highest *ballons* (bald, rounded mountain peaks) and to several WWI sites. Mountaintop lookouts afford spectacular views of the Alsace plain, the Black Forest across the Rhine in Germany and – on clear days – the Alps and Mont Blanc.

The 80km route links Col du Bonhomme (949m), about 20km west of Kaysersberg, with Cernay, 15km west of Mulhouse, along the D148, D61, D430 and D431. Sections around Col de la Schlucht (1139m) are closed from the first big snow until about April.

From Col de la Schlucht, home to a small ski station, trails head off in various directions; walking north along the GR5 brings you to three pristine lakes: Lac Vert, Lac Noir and Lac Blanc (Green, Black and White Lakes).

At the dramatic, wind-buffeted summit of 1424m Grand Ballon, the highest point in the Vosges, a short trail takes you to an aircraft-radar ball and a weather station.

Roads swing up to several viewpoints, but for a truer sense of this mountainous, forest-cloaked corner of the Vosges, strike out on foot or with a mountain bike. Steep inclines and hairpin bends make the terrain challenging and exhilarating for cyclists. For the inside scoop on outdoor pursuits along the Route des Crêtes, visit www.parc-ballons-vosges.fr, www.tourismevosges.fr and www.massif-des-vosges.com (in French).

roic equestrian statue of Joan of Arc and the cast-iron orientation table. During WWI the mountaintop was heavily fortified, but the trenches were never used in battle.

Ballon d'Alsace is a scenic base for walking in summer; the GR5 passes through, as do other trails, including those heading to the bottle-green lake, Lac des Perches (four hours). There's cross-country skiing on well-groomed forest tracks in winter.

Mulhouse

POP 111,156

The dynamic industrial city of Mulhouse (pronounced 'moo-looze'), 57km south of Colmar, was allied with nearby Switzerland before voting to join Revolutionary France in 1798. Largely rebuilt after the ravages of WWII, it has little of the quaint Alsatian charm that you find further north, but the city's world-class industrial museums are well worth a stop.

◉ Sights

Cité de l'Automobile   MUSEUM

(http://citedelautomobile.com; 192 av de Colmar; adult/child €11.50/9, incl Cité du Train €19/14.50; ◷10am-6pm) An ode to the automobile, the striking glass-and-steel museum showcases 400 rare and classic motors, from old-timers such as the Bugatti Royale to Formula 1 dream machines. There's a kiddie corner for would-be mechanics. By car, hop off the A36 at the Mulhouse Centre exit. By public transport, take bus 10 or tram 1 from Mulhouse to the Musée de l'Automobile stop.

Cité du Train   MUSEUM

(www.citedutrain.com; 2 rue Alfred de Glehn; adult/child €11/8.50, incl Cité de l'Automobile €19/14.50; ◷10am-6pm) ✅ Trainspotters are in their element at Europe's largest railway museum, displaying SNCF's prized collection of locomotives and carriages. Take bus 20 from the train station or, if driving, the Mulhouse-Dornach exit on the A35.

Musée de l'Impression sur Étoffes   MUSEUM

(Museum of Textile Printing; www.musee-impression.com; 14 rue Jean-Jacques Henner; adult/child €9/4.50; ◷10am-noon & 2-6pm Tue-Sun) Once known as the 'French Manchester', Mulhouse is fittingly home to this peerless collection of six million textile samples – from brilliant cashmeres to intricate silk screens – which make it a mecca for fabric designers. It's one long block northeast of the train station.

Musée du Papier Peint   MUSEUM

(www.museepapierpeint.org; 28 rue Zuber; adult/child €7.50/free; ◷10am-noon & 2-6pm, closed Mon Nov-Apr) More stimulating than it sounds, this is a treasure-trove of wallpaper (some of the scenic stuff as detailed as an oil painting) and the machines used to produce it since the 18th century. To reach it, take bus 18 from the train station to Temple stop, or the Rixheim exit on the A36.

📖 Sleeping & Eating

Hotel du Musée Gare   HOTEL €
(📞 03 89 45 47 41; www.hotelmuseegare.com; 3 rue de l'Est; d €69-95, tr €119, q €129; 🛜🅿️) Sitting opposite the Museum of Textile Printing and very close to the station, this lovingly restored town house outclasses most of Mulhouse's hotels with its 19th-century flair, attentive service and spacious, high-ceilinged rooms. Free parking is a boon.

Chez Auguste   BISTRO €€
(📞 03 89 46 62 71; www.chezauguste.com; 11 rue Poincaré; menus €20-25; ⊘ noon-2pm & 7-10pm Tue-Sat) Overflowing with regulars, this casually sophisticated bistro always has a good buzz. The concise *menu* excels in classics such as scallop carpaccio with lime, steak tartare and chocolate fondant. Service is faultless.

ℹ️ Information

Tourist Office
(📞 03 89 35 48 48; www.tourism-mulhouse.com; 1 av Robert Schuman; ⊘ 10am-1pm & 2-6pm Mon-Sun; 🛜) Mulhouse's helpful tourist office is located about 1.2km north of the train station.

ℹ️ Getting There & Around

BICYCLE
Mulhouse has an automatic bike-rental system, **Velocité** (www.velocite.mulhouse.fr), with 40 stands across the city – the online map shows where. The first half an hour is free and it costs €1/3 per day/week thereafter (deposit €150).

TRAIN
France's second train line, linking Mulhouse with Thann, opened in 1839. The **train station** (10 av du Général Leclerc) is just south of the centre. Trains run at least hourly to the following:

Basel €7.40, 23 minutes

Colmar €8.40, 19 minutes

St-Louis €6, 14 minutes

Strasbourg €18.20, 53 minutes

Around Mulhouse

Ungersheim, 17km northwest of Mulhouse, is home to the **Ecomusée d'Alsace** (www.ecomusee-alsace.fr; off the A35 to Colmar; adult/child €14/9.50; ⊘ 10am-6pm, closed Jan-Mar), a fascinating excursion into Alsatian country life and time-honoured crafts. Smiths, cartwrights, potters and coopers do their thing in and among 70 historic Alsatian farmhouses – a veritable village – brought here and meticulously reconstructed for preservation (and so storks can build nests on them).

LORRAINE

Lorraine, between the plains and vines of Champagne and the Massif des Vosges, is fed by the Meurthe, Moselle and Meuse Rivers – hence the names of three of its four *départements* (the fourth is Vosges).

History

Lorraine got its name *Lotharii regnum* (Lothair's kingdom) in the 9th century when it came to be ruled by the Frankish king Lothair II. The area became part of France in 1766 upon the death of Stanisław Leszczyński, the deposed king of Poland who ruled Lorraine as duke in the middle decades of the 18th century. In 1871 the Moselle *département* (along with Alsace) was annexed by Germany and remained part of the Second Reich until 1918, which is why much of Metz feels so imperial while Nancy, which remained French, is so stylishly Gallic. The two cities are rivals to this day.

ℹ️ Getting There & Around

CAR & MOTORCYCLE
Metz is on the A4, which links Paris and Reims with Strasbourg. Both Nancy and Metz are on the A31 from Dijon to Luxembourg. A car is highly recommended for exploring the Verdun battlefields and other remote corners of the region, where public transport slows to a trickle or dries up entirely.

TRAIN
The TGV Est Européen line has significantly reduced travel times from Paris – Metz and Nancy are now just 80 and 90 minutes from the capital, respectively. With the exception of Verdun, there are good, frequent train services to all major cities and towns in the region; see www.sncf.fr for tickets and timetables.

Nancy

POP 106,318

Delightful Nancy has an air of refinement found nowhere else in Lorraine. With a resplendent central square, fine museums, formal gardens and shop windows sparkling with Daum and Baccarat crystal, the former capital of the dukes of Lorraine catapults you back to the riches of the 18th century, when much of the city centre was built.

Nancy has long thrived on a combination of innovation and sophistication. The art nouveau movement flourished here (as the Nancy School) thanks to the rebellious spirit of local artists, who set out to prove that everyday objects could be drop-dead gorgeous.

⊙ Sights

★ Musée des Beaux-Arts
MUSEUM

(http://mban.nancy.fr; 3 place Stanislas; adult/child €6/free, audioguide €1.60; ⊙10am-6pm Wed-Mon) Lodged in a regal 18th-century edifice, Nancy's standout gallery occupies art lovers for hours on end. A wrought-iron staircase curls gracefully up to the second floor, where a chronological spin begins with 14th- to 17th-century paintings from the likes of Perugino, Tintoretto and Jan Van Hemessen. The first floor spotlights 17th- to 19th-century masterpieces of the Rubens and Caravaggio ilk. A collection of Jean Prouvé furnishings, impressionist and modern art and a dazzling Daum crystal collection hide in the basement.

Highlights in the first- and second-floor picture galleries include Mello da Gubbio's 14th-century altarpiece, Perugino's Renaissance *Madonna and Child* with two Angels (1505), Rubens' lucid, large-scale *Transfiguration* (1603), showing Jesus radiant on a mountain and Caravaggio's dramatic chiaroscuro *Annunciation* (1607).

The basement Jean Prouvé Collection homes in on the pared-down aesthetic of Nancy-born architect and designer Jean Prouvé (1901–1984), and displays a selection of Prouvé's furniture, architectural elements, ironwork and graphic works. Here you will also find the peerless Daum Collection, which is displayed in a dark, spotlit gallery that shows off the glassware to great effect and cleverly set against the backdrop of Nancy's late medieval city walls. Trace Daum through the ages – from the sinuous, naturalistic forms of art nouveau to the clean colours and restrained lines of contemporary crystal.

The downstairs picture gallery wings you into the 19th and 20th centuries with an excellent portfolio of works, among them Eugène Delacroix's *Battle of Nancy* (1831), Monet's dreamy *Étretat, Sunset* (1883) and Picasso's *Homme et femme* (1971), one of his final portraits.

★ Place Stanislas
SQUARE

Nancy's crowning glory is this grand neoclassical square and Unesco World Heritage Site. Designed by Emmanuel Héré in the 1750s, it was named after the enlightened, Polish-born Duke of Lorraine, whose statue stands in the middle. Your gaze will be drawn to an opulent ensemble of pale-stone buildings, including the hôtel de ville and the Opéra National de Lorraine. Note, too, the gilded wrought-iron gateways by Jean Lamour and the rococo fountains by Guibal, including one of a trident-bearing Neptune.

★ Musée de l'École de Nancy
ART MUSEUM

(School of Nancy Museum; www.ecole-de-nancy.com; 36-38 rue du Sergent Blandan; adult/child €6/4; ⊙10am-6pm Wed-Sun) A highlight of a visit to Nancy, the Musée de l'École de Nancy brings together an exquisite collection of art nouveau interiors, curvaceous glass and landscaped gardens. It's housed in a 19th-century villa about 2km southwest of the centre; to get there take bus 6 (Painlevé stop) or bus 7 or 8 (Nancy Thermal stop).

Musée Lorrain
MUSEUM

(www.musee-lorrain.nancy.fr; 64 & 66 Grande Rue; adult/child Église des Cordeliers €3.50/2, Palais Ducal €4/2.50, combined entry €5.50/3.50; ⊙10am-12.30pm & 2-6pm Tue-Sun) Once home to the

---

ART NOUVEAU TRAIL

In 1900, glassmaker and ceramist Émile Gallé founded the École de Nancy, one of France's leading art nouveau movements, joining creative forces with masters of decorative arts and architecture such as Jacques Gruber, Louis Majorelle and the Daum brothers. Banks, villas, pharmacies, brasseries – wherever you wander in Nancy, you are bound to stumble across their handiwork, from sinuous grillwork to curvaceous stained-glass windows and doorways that are a profusion of naturalistic ornament.

Slip back to this genteel era by picking up the free *Art Nouveau Itineraries* brochure and map at the tourist office, covering four city strolls. Lucien Weissenburger's 1911 Brasserie Excelsior (p355) and the 1908 Chambre de Commerce with wrought-iron by Louis Majorelle, both located on rue Henri Poincaré, are central standouts. Close to the Musée de l'École de Nancy lies the whimsical Villa Majorelle (📋 Mon-Fri 03 83 17 86 77, Sat & Sun 03 83 40 14 86; www.ecole-de-nancy.com; 1 rue Louis-Majorelle; adult/child €3.50/2.50; ⊙guided tours 1.45pm & 3pm Sat & Sun May-Oct), built by Henri Sauvage in 1901 and bearing the hallmark of Majorelle (furniture) and Gruber (stained glass). The centrepiece is the Les Blés dining room with its vinelike stone fireplace. Advance telephone bookings are essential.

Nancy

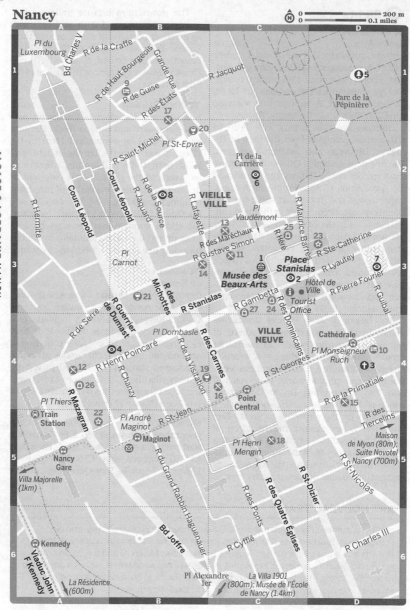

ALSACE & LORRAINE NANCY

dukes of Lorraine, the regal Renaissance Palais Ducal now shelters the Musée Lorrain. The rich **fine arts & history collection** spotlights medieval statuary, engravings and lustrous faience (glazed pottery). The **regional art & folklore collection** occupies a 15th-century former Franciscan monastery. Inside, the Gothic **Église des Cordeliers** and the 17th-century **Chapelle Ducale**, modelled on the Medici Chapel in Florence, served as the burial place of the dukes of Lorraine.

Nancy

Place de l'Alliance SQUARE

A block to the east of place Stanislas, this lime tree–fringed square, World Heritage material, is graced by a **baroque fountain** by Bruges-born Louis Cyfflé (1724–1806), inspired by Bernini's *Four Rivers* fountain in Rome's Piazza Navona.

Place de la Carrière SQUARE

Adjoining place Stanislas – on the other side of Nancy's own **Arc de Triomphe** built in the mid-1750s to honour Louis XV – is this quiet square. Once a riding and jousting arena, it is now graced by four rows of linden trees and stately rococo gates in gilded wrought iron.

Vieille Ville HISTORIC QUARTER

A saunter through the charming old town takes in the silver-turreted, 14th-century **Porte de la Craffe**, Nancy's oldest city gate, and **place St-Epvre**, dominated by ornate neo-Gothic **Basilique St-Epvre**.

Parc de la Pépinière PARK

(⊙6.30am-10.30pm, shorter hrs in winter) On a hot summer's day, escape the crowds in this formal garden, with ornamental fountains, a rose garden and a Rodin sculpture of baroque landscape painter Claude Lorrain.

**Cathédrale Notre-Dame-
de-l'Annonciation** CATHEDRAL

(place Monseigneur Ruch; ⊙8.45am-7pm Mon-Sat, 10.45am-8pm Sun) Crowned by a frescoed dome, Nancy's 18th-century cathedral is a sombre mixture of neoclassical and baroque.

⌖ Tours

The tourist office offers multilingual audio-guide tours (€7.50) of the historic centre (two hours) and the art nouveau quarters (up to three or four hours), or download a free MP3 tour online (www.nancy-tourisme.fr).

✯ Festivals & Events

Get your groove on to live jazz, blues and Latin at the 10-day **Jazz Pulsations** (www.nancyjazzpulsations.com) in October. December brings twinkle, carols and handicrafts to the **Marché de Nöel** (Christmas Market) on place André Maginot.

⌂ Sleeping

Characterful midrange hotels are Nancy's forte; budget places tend to be either complete dives or anonymous chains. Pick up the tourist office's handy *Hôtels et Hébergements* guide.

Hôtel de Guise BOUTIQUE HOTEL €

(☑03 83 32 24 68; www.hoteldeguise.com; 18 rue de Guise; s/d/tr/q €73/85/108/123; ☎) Boutique chic meets 17th-century elegance at this hotel, tucked down an old-town backstreet. A wrought-iron staircase sweeps up to old-fashioned rooms, with antique furnishings, inlaid parquet and heavy drapes. There's a walled garden for quiet moments.

La Résidence HOTEL €

(☑03 83 40 33 56; www.hotel-laresidence-nancy.com; 30 bd Jean-Jaurès; d €71-88, q €115; ☎⊞) This convivial hotel is one of Nancy's best

---

ℹ CULTURE CENT-SAVER

The good-value Pass Musées (€10), valid for 10 days, gets you into six museums, including Musée de l'École de Nancy, the Musée Lorrain and the Musée des Beaux-Arts, and is sold at the tourist office and at each museum.

The City Pass Nancy Culture (€16), sold at the tourist office, includes the Pass Musées, an audioguide tour of the city, a 24-hour transport ticket, plus a 50% discount on bike rental.

---

deals, with an inviting salon and a leafy courtyard for alfresco breakfasts. The snappy new rooms have ultramodern bathrooms and flatscreen TVs. The hotel is situated 1km south of the train station. Tram 1 stops at Mon Désert and Garenne, both a two-minute walk from the hotel.

★ Maison de Myon   B&B €€

(☎ 03 83 46 56 56; www.maisondemyon.com; 7 rue Mably; s/d €115/135, apt €150-165; ☎ 📶) Slip behind the cathedral to reach this stately 17th-century house turned boutique B&B. A wrought-iron staircase leads to light-filled, wood-floored rooms flaunting antique furnishings, one-of-a-kind art and ornamental fireplaces. Each room takes its name from its polished concrete bathroom (sand, turquoise, mandarin and so on). The wisteria-draped courtyard is a calm breakfast spot.

La Villa 1901   B&B €€

(☎ 06 30 03 21 62; www.lavilla1901.fr; 63 av du Général Leclerc; s €145-165, d €165-185; ☎) Taking a leaf out of the chic interiors book, this B&B combines art nouveau features with contemporary design flourishes and boho flair to beautiful effect. The richly hued rooms and suites feature home-style touches such as fireplaces and iPod docks, and there is a garden for quiet moments. Breakfast is a treat, with fresh pastries, juice and homemade preserves.

Hôtel des Prélats   HISTORIC HOTEL €€

(☎ 03 83 30 20 20; www.hoteldesprelats.com; 56 place Monseigneur Ruch; s €75-125, d €115-145; ✳ ☎) It's not every day you get to sleep in a former 17th-century bishop's palace right next to the cathedral. This elegant hotel plays up the romance in rooms with stained-glass windows, four-poster beds and shimmery drapes. Service is as polished as the surrounds.

Suite Novotel Nancy   APARTHOTEL €€

(☎ 03 83 32 28 80; www.accorhotels.com; 2 allée du Chanoine Drioton; r €80-130; ☎) Prettily set in gardens, this streamlined hotel has spacious, modern apartments with kitchenettes, and a 24-hour gym. Book online at least three weeks ahead for a discount of up to 40%. The aparthotel is 1.2km east of Place Stanislas. By public transport, take tram 1 to St Georges and then it is a five-minute walk south along avenue du Vingtième Corps and allée du Chanoine Drioton.

✖ Eating

Rue des Maréchaux, just west of the Arc de Triomphe, dishes up everything from French to Italian, tapas, seafood, Indian and Japanese. Grande Rue is peppered with intimate bistros.

La Primatiale   INTERNATIONAL €€

(☎ 03 83 30 44 03; www.restaurant-la-primatiale-nancy.fr; 14 rue de la Primatiale; mains €13-23, 3-course menu €27; ⊙ noon-2.30pm & 7-11pm Mon-Fri, 7-11pm Sat) The food looks as good as it tastes at this upbeat, art-strewn bistro. Clean, bright flavours such as carpaccio of trout with coriander and monkfish with shellfish coulis reveal a definite Mediterranean slant.

Le V-Four   BISTRO €€

(☎ 03 83 32 49 48; www.levfour.fr; 10 rue St-Michel; menus €19-50; ⊙ 11.45am-1.30pm & 7.45-11.30pm Tue-Sat, 11.45am-1.30pm Sun) With just a handful of tables, this petit bistro is all about intimacy and understated sophistication. Mulberry chairs and crisp white tablecloths set the scene for original creations including grilled scallops with wasabi cream and tomato confit. Book ahead.

Inévitable   MODERN FRENCH €€

(☎ 03 83 36 36 36; www.bistorant-inevitable.fr; 17 rue Gustave Simon; menus €16.50-33; ⊙ noon-2pm & 8-10pm Thu-Mon, noon-2pm Tue) You can expect a warm welcome at this slick, monochrome bistro, which keeps its *menu* seasonal, simple and regional, along the lines of market-fresh fish with braised fennel and bergamot confit.

Gentilhommiere   FRENCH €€

(☎ 03 83 32 26 44; www.lagentilhommierenancy.fr; 29 rue des Maréchaux; menus €25-40; ⊙ noon-2pm & 7-10pm Mon-Fri, 7-10pm Sat) Warm-hued, subtly lit Gentilhommiere stands head and shoulders above most of the restaurants on rue des Maréchaux. Specialities such as scallop tartlet with beetroot and liquorice vinaigrette and pike-perch fillets with Lorraine truffle risotto reveal true depth of flavour.

A la Table du
Bon Roi Stanislas TRADITIONAL FRENCH €€
(☑ 03 83 35 36 52; tablestan.free.fr; 7 rue Gustave Simon; mains €16.50-33; ☺ 7.15-9.30pm Mon & Wed, 12.15-1.30pm & 7.15-9.30pm Tue & Thu-Sat, 12.15pm-1.30pm Sun) A la Table du Bon Roi Stanislas dishes up good old-fashioned French food with lashings of bonhomie. Menu classics feature escargots with dill and duck cooked in red wine with fig confit. There is terrace seating available in summer.

Brasserie Excelsior BRASSERIE €€
(☑ 03 83 35 24 57; www.brasserie-excelsior.com; 50 rue Henri Poincaré; menus €28-48; ☺ 8am-12.30am Tue-Sat, 8am-11pm Sun & Mon) As opulent as a Fabergé egg with its stucco and stained glass, Excelsior whisks you back to the decadent era of art nouveau. Brusquely efficient waiters bring brasserie classics such as oysters (September through April), juicy steaks and banquet-like seafood platters to the table.

Le Bouche á L'Oreille BISTRO €
(☑ 03 83 35 17 17; http://restaurant-bouche-a-oreille. fr; 42 rue des Carmes; menus 11-24; ☺ noon-1.30pm Tue-Fri, 7-10pm Mon-Sat; 🖸) Resembling an overgrown doll's house, this knick-knack–filled bistro specialises in cheese-based dishes including *raclette, tartiflette* and fondue.

Marché Couvert FOOD MARKET €
(place Henri Mengin; ☺ 7am-7pm Tue-Sat) A fresh-produce feast for the picnic basket, with several snack stands offering inexpensive lunches.

🍷 Drinking & Nightlife

Nancy's buoyant nightlife concentrates on bar-dotted Grande Rue, the spectacularly illuminated place Stanislas and laid-back place de St-Epvre in the Vieille Ville, the best spot for sundowners.

Bab BAR
(www.bab-nancy.fr; 29 rue de la Visitation; ☺ 5pm-2am Tue-Sat) This fun-focused bar has a roster of events, from flamenco nights to gigs. The mojito list features own creations laced with raspberry, melon and mint.

Le Ch'timi BAR
(17 place St-Epvre; ☺ 9am-2am Mon-Sat, 9am-8pm Sun) On three brick-and-stone levels, Le Ch'timi is *the* place to go for beer. It's a beloved haunt of students who come for the 150 brewskies, 16 of them on tap.

Le P'ti K BAR
(7 place Carnot; ☺ 11am-11pm Mon-Thu, 11am-2am Fri, 5pm-2am Sat) A slinky interior and prime people-watching terrace on place Carnot make this a great spot for an *apéro* (aperitif).

☆ Entertainment

Details on cultural events appear in French in **Spectacles** (www.spectacles-publications.com).

Fnac Billetterie TICKET OUTLET
(www.fnacspectacles.com; 2 av Foch, 2nd fl; ☺ 10am-7pm Mon-Sat) Ticket outlet.

Opéra National
de Lorraine OPERA HOUSE
(☑ 03 83 85 33 11; www.opera-national-lorraine. fr; 1 rue Ste-Catherine) A harmonious blend of neoclassical and art nouveau styles, this is Nancy's lavish stage for opera and classical music. The resident orchestra performs at *concerts upéritifs* (€6), held roughly one Saturday a month.

🛍 Shopping

Nancy's grand thoroughfares are rue St-Dizier, rue St-Jean and rue St-Georges. Grande Rue is studded with idiosyncratic galleries and antique shops.

Maison des Sœurs
Macarons CONFECTIONERY
(www.macaron-de-nancy.com; 21 rue Gambetta; ☺ 2-7pm Mon, 9.30am-12.30pm & 2-7pm Tue-Fri, 9am-7pm Sat) When Nancy's Benedictine nuns hit hard times during the French Revolution, they saw the light in heavenly macarons. They're still made to the original recipe (egg whites, sugar, Provençal almonds) at this old-world confectioner. A dozen box (€7.80) makes a great gift.

Lefèvre-Lemoine CONFECTIONERY
(47 rue Henri Poincaré; ☺ 8.30am-7pm Mon-Sat, 9.30am-noon Sun) They don't make sweetshops like this 1840s treasure any more, where a bird chirps a welcome as you enter. One of the old-fashioned sweet tins made a cameo appearance in the film *Amélie. Bergamotes de Nancy* (bergamot boiled sweets), caramels, nougat, gingerbread, glazed *mirabelles* (plums) – how ever will you choose?

Baccarat CRYSTAL
(www.baccarat.fr; 2 rue des Dominicains; ☺ 10am-7pm Tue-Sat) Shop like royalty (or window-shop like mere mortals) for exquisite crystal and jewellery here, where the simplest ring – impossibly delicate – goes for €250.

Daum CRYSTAL

(14 place Stanislas; ⊙ 2-7pm Mon, 9.30am-12.30pm & 2-7pm Tue-Sat) At Daum's flagship shop you can admire limited-edition crystal knick-knacks and jewellery, often with a naturalistic theme.

ℹ Information

Tourist Office (☑ 03 83 35 22 41; www.nancy-tourisme.fr; place Stanislas; ⊙ 9am-7pm Mon-Sat, 10am-5pm Sun; 🛜) Inside the *hôtel de ville*. Free brochures detailing walking tours of the city centre and art nouveau architecture. Free wi-fi.

ℹ Getting There & Away

CAR & MOTORCYCLE

Rental options:

Europcar (www.europcar.com; 18 rue de Serre)

National-Citer (www.citer.fr; train station departure hall)

TRAIN

The **train station** (place Thiers) is on the line linking Paris with Strasbourg. Destinations include the following:

Baccarat €11, 50 minutes, 15 daily

Metz €11, 37 minutes, 48 daily

Paris €51 to €68, 1½ hours, 13 daily

Strasbourg €25.50, 1½ hours, 12 daily

ℹ Getting Around

BICYCLE

Nancy is easy to navigate by bicycle. **Vélostan** (www.velostan.com; per half-day/full day/week €2/3/8) has rental sites inside the **train station** (⊙ 7.30am-7.30pm Mon-Fri, 9am-6pm Sat & Sun) and near the Musée de l'École de Nancy in **Espace Thermal** (43bis rue du Sergent Blandan, Espace Thermal; ⊙ 2-6pm Mon-Fri) as well as 29 rental points where you can hire bikes 24/7. An €80 deposit is required.

CAR & MOTORCYCLE

Parking at any of the central car parks costs around €1.60 per hour. A cheaper alternative is the park-and-ride in Essey-les-Nancy, 4km northeast of the centre, with tram connections into town; parking for the day and a return ticket costs €2.60.

TRAM

The local public transport company, **STAN** (www.reseau-stan.com; 3 rue du Docteur Schmitt; ⊙ 7am-7.30pm Mon-Sat) has its main transfer points at Nancy République and Point Central. One/10 tickets cost €1.30/9, a 24-hour pass is €3.40. The icon shows the nearest tram stop for places off the map in this section.

Baccarat

POP 4668

The glitzy Baccarat *cristallerie* (crystal glassworks), founded in 1764, is 60km southeast of Nancy. The **Musée Baccarat** (www.baccarat.fr; 2 rue des Cristalleries; adult/child €2.50/free; ⊙ 9am-noon & 2-6pm) displays 1100 exquisite pieces of handmade lead crystal. The boutique out front is almost as dazzling as the museum. Nearby crystal shops sell lesser, though more affordable, brands.

On the opposite bank of the park-lined River Meurthe, the dark concrete sanctuary of **Église St-Rémy** (⊙ 8am-5pm), built in the mid-1950s, is austere on the outside and kaleidoscopic on the inside – dramatically lit by 20,000 Baccarat crystal panels.

The **tourist office** (☑ 03 83 75 13 37; www.ot-baccarat.fr; 11 rue Division Leclerc; ⊙ 9am-noon & 2-5pm Mon-Sat), a bit north of the Musée Baccarat, has hiking maps.

Trains run from Baccarat to Nancy (€11.10, 48 minutes, 15 daily). By car, Baccarat makes an easy stop on the way from Nancy to Colmar via the Vosges' Col du Bonhomme.

Metz

POP 122,149

Sitting astride the confluence of the Moselle and Seille rivers, Lorraine's graceful capital Metz (pronounced 'mess') is ready to be fêted. Though the city's Gothic marvel of a cathedral, superlative art collections and Michelin star–studded dining scene long managed to sidestep the world spotlight, all that changed with the show-stopping arrival of Centre Pompidou-Metz in 2010. Yet the Pompidou is but the prelude to Metz' other charms: buzzy pavement cafes and shady riverside parks, a beautiful old town built from golden Jeumont stone and a regal Quartier Impérial up for Unesco World Heritage status. Suddenly, everyone's talking about Metz, and rightly so.

⊙ Sights

★**Cathédrale St-Étienne** CATHEDRAL

(place St-Étienne; audioguide €7, combined ticket treasury & crypt adult/child €4/2; ⊙ 8am-6pm, treasury & crypt 9.30am-12.30pm & 1.30-5.30pm Mon-Sat, 2-6pm Sun) The lacy golden spires of this Gothic cathedral crown Metz' skyline. Exquisitely lit by kaleidoscopic curtains of 13th- to 20th-century stained glass, the cathedral is nicknamed 'God's lantern' and its sense of height is spiritually uplifting. Notice

Metz

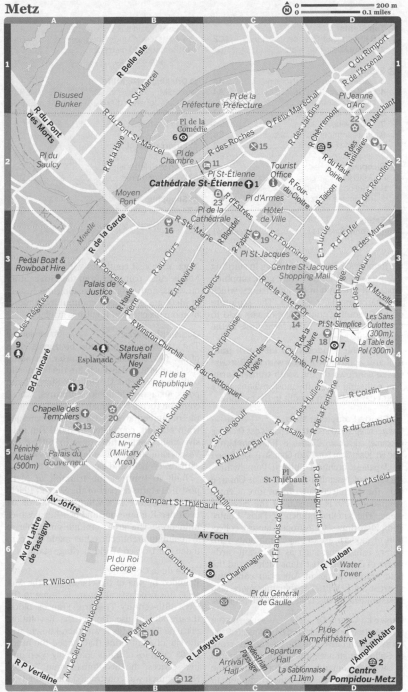

N
0   200 m
0   0.1 miles

Key map labels:

- R Belle Isle
- Q du Rimport
- R de l'Arsenal
- Disused Bunker
- R St-Marcel
- Pl de la Préfecture
- Préfecture
- Pl Jeanne d'Arc
- R du Pont des Morts
- R du Pont St-Marcel
- Pl de la Comédie 6
- R des Roches 15
- Q Félix Maréchal
- R des Jardins
- R Chèvremont 22
- R Marchant
- Pl du Saulcy
- R de la Haye
- Pl de Chambre
- 11 Pl St-Étienne
- 5
- R des Trinitaires 17
- R du Haut Poirier
- R des Récollets
- Moyen Pont
- Cathédrale St-Étienne 1
- Tourist Office
- R Four-du-Cloître
- R Taison
- R d'Enfer
- R des Murs
- Pedal Boat & Rowboat Hire
- R de la Garde
- R Ste-Marie 16
- R d'Estrées
- Pl d'Armes
- Hôtel de Ville
- Pl de la Cathédrale
- 23
- R Blondel
- R Fabert 19
- En Fournirue
- En Jurue
- R des Tanneurs
- Palais de Justice
- R Poncelet
- R aux Ours
- En Nexirue
- R des Clercs
- Pl St-Jacques
- Centre St-Jacques Shopping Mall
- R de la Tête d'Or
- 21
- R du Change
- R des Tanneurs
- R Mazelle
- R Haute Pierre
- R Winston Churchill
- R Serpenoise
- 14
- R de la Chèvre
- Pl St-Simplice
- 18 7
- Les Sans Culottes (300m); La Table de Pol (300m)
- 9
- Bd Poincaré
- Q des Régates
- Esplanade 4
- Statue of Marshall Ney
- Av Ney
- Pl de la République
- R Dupont des Loges
- En Chandrue
- Pl St-Louis
- R Coislin
- 3
- Chapelle des Templiers
- 20
- 13
- Caserne Ney (Military Area)
- Av Robert Schuman
- R St-Gengoulf
- F St-Gengoulf
- R des Huiliers
- R Lasalle
- R de la Fontaine
- R du Cambout
- Péniche Alclair (500m)
- Palais du Gouverneur
- R du Coëtlosquet
- R Maurice Barrès
- R Chatillon
- Pl St-Thiébault
- R des Augustins
- R d'Asfeld
- Av Joffre
- Rempart St-Thiébault
- Av de Lattre de Tassigny
- Av Foch
- R Gambetta
- Pl du Roi George
- 8
- R Charlemagne
- R François de Curel
- R Vauban
- Water Tower
- R Wilson
- Pl du Général de Gaulle
- Av Leclerc de Hauteclocque
- R Pasteur 10
- R Ausone
- R Lafayette
- Arrival Hall
- Pedestrian Passage
- Departure Hall
- Pl de l'Amphithéâtre
- Av de l'Amphithéâtre
- R P Verlaine
- 12
- La Sablonnaise (1.1km)
- 2
- Centre Pompidou-Metz

Metz

the flamboyant **Chagall windows** in startling jewel-coloured shades of ruby, gold, sapphire, topaz and amethyst in the ambulatory, which also harbours the **treasury**. The sculpture of the **Graoully** ('grau-lee'), a dragon said to have terrified pre-Christian Metz, lurks in the 15th-century **crypt**.

The **Gothic windows**, on the north transept arm, contrast strikingly with the **Renaissance windows** on the south transept arm. The cathedral looks its most radiant on a bright day and when floodlit in the evening.

★ **Centre Pompidou-Metz**   GALLERY
(www.centrepompidou-metz.fr; 1 parvis des Droits de l'Homme; adult/child €7/free; ⊙11am-6pm Mon & Wed-Fri, 10am-8pm Sat, 10am-6pm Sun) Designed by Japanese architect Shigeru Bam, with a curved roof resembling a space-age Chinese hat, the architecturally innovative Centre Pompidou-Metz is the star of the city's art scene. The satellite branch of Paris' Centre Pompidou draws on Europe's largest collection of modern art to stage ambitious temporary exhibitions, such as the avant-garde works of German artist Hans Richter and the bold graphic works of American conceptual artist Sol LeWitt. The dynamic space also hosts cultural events, talks and youth projects.

Musée La Cour d'Or   MUSEUM
(2 rue du Haut Poirier; adult/child €4.60/free; ⊙9am-6pm Wed-Mon) Delve into the past at this trove of Gallo-Roman antiquities, hiding remnants of the city's Roman baths and a statue of the Egyptian goddess Isis unearthed right here in Metz. Your visit continues with art from the Middle Ages, paintings from the 15th century onwards, and artefacts revealing the history of Metz' ancient Jewish community. A room-by-room brochure in English is available.

Quartier Impérial   HISTORIC QUARTER
The stately boulevards and bourgeois villas of the German Imperial Quarter, including rue Gambetta and av Foch, are the brainchild of Kaiser Wilhelm II. Philippe Starck lamp posts juxtapose Teutonic sculptures, whose common theme is German imperial might, at the monumental Rhenish neo-Romanesque **train station**, completed in 1908. The massive main **post office**, built in 1911 of red Vosges sandstone, is as solid and heavy as the cathedral is light and lacy.

Built to trumpet the triumph of Metz' post-1871 status as part of the Second Reich, the architecture is a whimsical mix of art deco, neo-Romanesque and neo-Renaissance influences. The area's unique ensemble of Wilhelmian architecture has made it a candidate for Unesco World Heritage status.

Place de la Comédie   SQUARE
Bounded by one of the channels of the Moselle, this neoclassical square is home to the city's 18th-century **Théâtre**, France's oldest theatre still in use. During the Revolution, place de l'Égalité (as it was then known) was the site of a guillotine that lopped the heads off 63 'enemies of the people'. Only open during services, the neo-Romanesque **Temple Neuf** church was constructed under the Germans in 1904.

Esplanade   PARK

The formal flowerbeds of the Esplanade –
and its statue of a gallant-looking **Marshall
Ney** – are flanked by imposing buildings, including the **Arsenal** cultural centre and the
sober, neoclassical **Palais de Justice**.

Église St-Pierre-aux-Nonains   CHURCH

(⊙1-6pm Tue-Sat & 2-6pm Sun) Originally built
around 380 as part of a Gallo-Roman spa
complex, Église St-Pierre-aux-Nonains sidles
up to the octagonal, 13th-century **Chapelle
des Templiers**, the only one of its kind in
Lorraine.

Place St-Louis   SQUARE

On the eastern edge of the city centre, triangular place St-Louis is surrounded by medieval
arcades and merchants' houses dating from
the 14th to 16th centuries.

Riverside Park   PARK

(quai des Régates) In summer, pedal and rowboats can be rented on quai des Régates. The
promenade leads through a leafy riverside
park, with statues, ponds, swans and a fountain. It's the ideal picnic spot.

Tours

The tourist office's 1½-hour **audioguides**
(€7), available in five languages, whisk you
around the highlights of the city centre and
the Quartier Impérial. One-/two-hour **guided
tours** (€5/7) are offered in French only; visit
the tourist office for details.

Festivals & Events

Fête de la Mirabelle   FOOD FESTIVAL

(www.fetesdelamirabelle.fr) Sweet and juicy, the
humble *mirabelle* (plum) has its day at the
Fête de la Mirabelle in August.

Marché de Nöel   CHRISTMAS

(www.noel-a-metz.com) Shop for stocking fillers
at the illuminated Marché de Nöel (Christmas
Market) in December.

Sleeping

With few exceptions (notably those given below), chain hotels rule in Metz and charming
picks are slim. Stop by the tourist office for a
list of private rooms.

La Sablonnaise   B&B €

(☑03 57 28 73 52; www.lasablonnaise.fr; 62 rue
St Pierre; d €75, tr €90; 🛜🚭) This bijou 1930s
house is a 15-minute stroll from central Metz.
The three rooms have been renovated in muted colours, with wooden floors and the occa-

sional design flourish. It's a great pick for families: there's a garden and the owners provide
everything from toys to high chairs. Breakfast
is a top-notch spread of fresh pastries, fresh-
pressed juice and homemade preserves.

Péniche Alclair   HOUSEBOAT €

(☑06 37 67 16 18; www.chambrespenichemetz.
com; allée St-Symphorien; r incl breakfast €75; 🛜)
What a clever idea: this old barge has been
revamped into a stylish blue houseboat, with
two cheerful wood-floored rooms and watery
views. Breakfast is served in your room or on
the sundeck. It's a 15-minute stroll south of
the centre along the river.

Residhome Metz   APARTHOTEL €

(☑03 87 57 97 06; www.residhome.com; 10 rue
Lafayette; d €67-112; @🚭) Part of a small
French chain, Residhome has an excellent
price-quality ratio and is two minutes' walk
from the station. Light, roomy and done out
in contemporary style, the studios and apartments make a comfy base, with kitchenettes,
flatscreen TVs and free internet access.

Cécil Hôtel   HOTEL €

(☑03 87 66 66 13; www.cecilhotel-metz.com; 14 rue
Pasteur; s €64-76, d €75-95, q €98-100; 🛜) Built in
1920, this family-run hotel's smallish rooms
are neat, petite and decorated in warm colours. Parking costs €10 per day.

★**Hôtel de la
Cathédrale**   HISTORIC HOTEL €€

(☑03 87 75 00 02; www.hotelcathedrale-metz.fr;
25 place de Chambre; d €75-120; 🛜🚭) You can
expect a friendly welcome at this classy little
hotel, occupying a 17th century town house
in a prime spot right opposite the cathedral.
Climb the wrought-iron staircase to your classically elegant room, with high ceilings, hardwood floors and antique trappings. Book well
ahead for a cathedral view.

Eating

Metz has scores of appetising restaurants, many along and near the river. Place
St-Jacques becomes one giant open-air cafe
when the sun's out. Cobbled rue Taison and
the arcades of place St-Louis shelter moderately priced bistros, pizzerias and cafes.

Les Sans Culottes   CRÊPES €

(☑03 72 13 55 72; www.lessansculottes.fr; 31
place des Charrons; crêpes €3-7, galettes €9-14.50;
⊙noon-2pm Mon, noon-2pm & 7-10.30pm Wed-Sun)
Dishing up a nicely chilled vibe and just-right
sweet and savoury crêpes, Les Sans Culottes

is a great pitstop. Their *galettes* (buckwheat pancakes) are terrific, too, and come with toppings from raclette cheese to seafood and spinach.

Pâtisserie Claude Bourguignon
TEA ROOM €

(31 rue de la Tête d'Or; snacks €3-8; ⊙9.15am-7pm Tue-Sat, 9am-12.30pm Sun) Smart tearoom/chocolatier/patisserie, with an irresistible array of tarts (try *mirabelle*), éclairs, quiches, ganaches and pralines.

La Table de Pol
MODERN FRENCH €€

(✆03 87 62 13 72; www.latabledepol.fr; 1/3 rue du Grand Wad; menus €17-46; ⊙noon-2pm & 7-9pm Tue-Sat) Intimate lighting and cheek-by-jowl tables keep the mood mellow in this friendly bistro, which serves winningly fresh dishes prepared with market produce, along the lines of lamb filet mignon in a herb crust and cod filet with asparagus – all cooked to a T.

Restaurant Thierry
INTERNATIONAL €€

(✆03 87 74 01 23; www.restaurant-thierry.fr; 5 rue des Piques; menus €22-40; ⊙noon-3pm & 7-11pm, closed Wed & Sun) Combining the historic backdrop of a 16th-century town house with the subtly spiced cuisine, lighting and bohemian flair of Morocco, this is one of Metz' most coveted tables. An aperitif in the candlelit salon works up an appetite for global flavours such as seared swordfish with red curry risotto and tagine of lamb with olives and dried fruit.

Le Magasin aux Vivres
GASTRONOMIC €€€

(✆03 87 17 17 17; 5 av Ney; menus €47-145; ⊙noon-2pm & 7.30-10pm Tue-Fri, 7.30-10pm Sat, noon-2pm Sun) Conjurer of textures and seasonal flavours, chef Christophe Dufossé makes creative use of local produce at this sophisticated Michelin-starred restaurant. Moselle wines work well with specialities such as plump scallops with fresh truffle, artichoke mousse and hazelnut oil, and Bresse chicken served three ways.

Drinking & Nightlife

Some 22,000 resident students keep Metz' vibe young and upbeat after dark. For an alfresco sundowner or two, try the bars and open-air cafes lining place de Chambre and place St-Jaques.

Café Jehanne d'Arc
BAR

(place Jeanne d'Arc; ⊙11.30am-midnight Mon-Fri, 3pm-1am Sat) This 13th-century watering hole oozes history from every Gothic window,

fresco and beam. The soundtrack skips from Gainsbourg to classical, and there's often free live jazz. The terrace is a chilled spot for summertime imbibing.

Pop White
LOUNGE BAR

(4 place St-Jacques; ⊙8am-1am Mon-Sat, 2pm-1am Sun) This slick, silver-kissed lounge bar is a sundown favourite. Join a lively crowd for a beer or cocktail on the terrace.

Cafe Rubis
BAR

(25 place Saint-Louis; ⊙8am-2am Mon-Sat) Cosy bar for a coffee or glass of wine, with a terrace under the arcades for summer imbibing.

BSM
BAR

(www.bsm-metz.com; 2bis rue Ste-Marie; ⊙6.30pm-2am Mon-Sat) Retro chic bar with red walls, vintage sofas, a relaxed vibe and old-school music. Check the website for details of gigs, quiz and DJ nights.

☆ Entertainment

Details on cultural events appear in free French-language monthlies such as **Spectacles** (www.spectacles-publications.com).

Fnac Billetterie
TICKET OUTLET

(www.fnacspectacles.com; Centre St-Jacques shopping mall; ⊙9.30am-7.30pm Mon-Fri, 9.30am-8pm Sat) Ticket outlet.

Les Trinitaires
LIVE MUSIC

(www.lestrinitaires.com; 12 rue de Trinitaires) Rock and jazz bands take to the stage in the Gothic cellar and, in summer, the atmospherically lit cloister of this convent turned soulful arts venue. Enjoy pre-gig drinks at Café Jehanne d'Arc opposite.

Arsenal
PERFORMING ARTS

(✆03 87 74 16 16; www.arsenal-metz.fr; 3 av Ney) Bearing the hallmark of Catalan postmodernist architect Ricardo Bofill, this striking building of Jeumont-stone sits on the site of the former arsenal. It hosts dance, theatre and music performances.

ⓘ Information

Main Post Office (9 rue Gambetta; ⊙8.30am-6.30pm Mon-Fri, to noon Sat) Has currency exchange.

Tourist Office (✆03 87 55 53 76; http://tourisme.mairie-metz.fr; 2 place d'Armes; ⊙9am-7pm Mon-Sat, 10am-5pm Sun) In a one-time guardroom built in the mid-1700s. Free walking-tour and cycling maps, and free wi-fi. Can make room bookings for a €1.50 fee.

GO TO MARKET

If only every market were like Metz' grand **Marché Couvert** (Covered Market; place de la Cathédrale; ⊙7am-7pm Tue-Sat). Once a bishop's palace, now a temple to fresh local produce, this is the kind of place where you pop in for a baguette and struggle out an hour later with bags overflowing with charcuterie, ripe fruit, pastries and five different sorts of *fromage*.

Make a morning of it, stopping for an early, inexpensive lunch and a chat with the market's larger-than-life characters. **Chez Mauricette** (marché couvert; sandwiches €2.50-4, light meals €5-10) tempts with Lorraine goodies from herby *saucisson* to local charcuterie and *mirabelle* pâté. Its neighbour, **Soupes á Soups** (marché couvert; soups €3.50), ladles out homemade soups, from mussel to creamy mushroom varieties.

❶ Getting There & Away

CAR & MOTORCYCLE
Car rental companies with offices in the train station's arrival hall:
Avis (www.avis.com)
Europcar (www.europcar.com)
National-Citer (www.citer.fr)

TRAIN
Metz' ornate early 20th-century **train station** (pl du Général de Gaulle) has a supersleek TGV linking Paris with Luxembourg. Direct trains include the following:
Luxembourg €16.20, 45 minutes, 40 daily
Nancy €10.90, 37 minutes, 48 daily
Paris €60-75, 1½ hours, 15 daily
Strasbourg €26.40, 1½ hours, 16 daily
Verdun €15, 1½ hours, three direct daily

❶ Getting Around

BICYCLE
Rent city and mountain bikes cheaply from **Mob Emploi** (www.mobemploi.fr; per half-/full day/week €2/3/8, deposit per bike €250), a nonprofit place. Helmets and locks are free; rental options include kids' bikes, electro bikes, child carriers and even a tandem. There are two offices: **rue d'Estrées** (rue d'Estrées; ⊙8am-6pm Mon-Sat) and **rue Vauban** (7 place du Général de Gaulle; ⊙5.45am-8pm Mon-Fri, 10am-8pm Sat, 2-8pm

Sun) at the base of the water tower just east of the train station.

CAR & MOTORCYCLE
There's free parking near the train station on av Foch, northeast of the train station along bd André Maginot, and along bd Paixhans.

Fort du Hackenberg

The largest single Maginot Line bastion in the Metz area was the 1000-man **Fort du Hackenberg** (www.maginot-hackenberg.com; adult/child €9/4; ⊙tours 2.30pm Mon-Fri & 2-3.30pm Sat & Sun Jun-Sep, shorter hours rest of year) 30km northeast of Metz, whose 10km of galleries were designed to be self-sufficient for three months and, in battle, to fire four tonnes of shells a minute. An electric trolley takes visitors along 4km of tunnels – always at 12°C – past subterranean installations. Tours last two hours.

Readers have been enthusiastic about the tours (www.maginot-line.com) of Fort du Hackenberg, as well as other Maginot Line sites and Verdun, led by Jean-Pascal Speck, an avid amateur historian. If he's unavailable, he can put you in touch with other English-speaking guides.

Mr Speck also runs **Hôtel L'Horizon** (☎03 82 88 53 65, www.lhorizon.fr; 5 rte du Crève Coeur; d €98-150; ❉☎⊕), a romantic hilltop hotel offering fine views across Thionville, a friendly welcome and homely, warm-hued rooms. There's a restaurant, sauna and a roof terrace.

Verdun
POP 19,490

They were once men in the prime of their lives, but had fallen for the possession of this hill. This hill, that was partly built on dead bodies already. A battle after which they lay rotting, fraternally united in death…
Georges Blond, Verdun

The unspeakable atrocities that took place in and around Verdun between 21 February and 18 December 1916, the longest battle of WWI, have turned the town's name into a byword for wartime slaughter and futile sacrifice.

Such a dark past means that Verdun always has an air of melancholy, even when the sun bounces brightly off the River Meuse and the town's shuttered houses. Go to the moonscape hills of the Verdun Battlefields, scarred with trenches and shells; walk through the stony silence of the cemeteries as the morning mist rises, and you will understand why. Time has healed and trees have grown, but the memory of *l'enfer de Verdun* (the hell of Verdun) has survived. And, some say, may it never be forgotten.

History

After the annexation of Lorraine's Moselle *département* and Alsace by Germany in 1871, Verdun became a frontline outpost. Over the next four decades it was turned into the most important and heavily fortified element in France's eastern defence line.

During WWI Verdun itself was never taken by the Germans, but the evacuated town was almost totally destroyed by artillery bombardments. In the hills to the north and east of Verdun, the brutal combat – carried out with artillery, flame-throwers and poison gas – completely wiped out nine villages. During the last two years of WWI, more than 800,000 soldiers (some 400,000 French and almost as many Germans, along with thousands of the Americans who arrived in 1918) lost their lives in this area.

◉ Sights

Citadelle Souterraine   CITADEL
(✆03 29 84 84 42; www.citadelle-souterraine-verdun.fr; av du 5e RAP; adult/child €8/4; ⏱9am-6pm, closed Jan) With 7km of underground galleries, this cavernous subterranean citadel was designed by military engineer

---

MORE SWEET THAN BITTER

Verdun's sweet claim to fame is as the *dragée* (sugared almond) capital of the world. In 1220 a local pharmacist dabbling with almonds, sugar and honey created the tooth-rotting delights that later graced the tables of royalty and nobility – Napoléon and Charles de Gaulle included. **Braquier** (www.dragees-braquier.com; 50 rue du Fort de Vaux; ⏱tours 9.30am, 10.30am & 2.30pm Mon-Thu, 9.30am & 10.30am Fri) has been making Verdun's celebrated *dragées* since 1783 and offers free guided tours of its factory. Or buy a box at the more central **shop** (3 rue Pasteur; ⏱2-7pm Mon, 10am-noon & 2-7pm Tue-Sat).

Sébastien Le Prestre de Vauban in the 17th century and completed in 1838. In 1916 it was turned into an impregnable command centre in which 10,000 *poilus* (French WWI soldiers) lived, waiting to be dispatched to the front. About 10% of the galleries have been converted into an audiovisual re-enactment of Verdun's WWI history. Half-hour battery-powered car tours, available in six languages, should be booked ahead.

Centre Mondial de la Paix   MUSEUM
(World Centre for Peace; www.cmpaix.eu; place Monseigneur Ginisty; adult/child €5/2.50; ⏱10am-noon & 2-5.30pm Tue-Sun) Set in Verdun's handsomely classical former bishop's palace, built in 1724, this museum's permanent exhibition touches upon wars, their causes and solutions; human rights; and the fragility of peace.

Cathédrale Notre Dame   CATHEDRAL
(place Monseigneur Ginisty; ⏱9am-6pm) Perched on a hillside, this Romanesque-meets-Gothic cathedral shelters a gilded baroque baldachin, restored after WWI damage. Much of the stained glass is interwar.

Monument à la Victoire   MONUMENT
(Carrer de la Portella 5) Steep steps lead up to this austere 1920s monument commemorating war victims and survivors. The crypt hides a book listing the soldiers who fought in the Battle of Verdun.

Porte Chaussée   CITY GATE
(rue Chaussée) This 14th-century city gate was later used as a prison.

Porte St-Paul   CITY GATE
(rue St-Paul) Built in 1877, this city gate is adorned with a marble plaque recalling the 'victorious peace' that inspired a 'cry of joy'.

☞ Tours

The tourist office arranges four one-hour tours of the **battlefields** (adult/child €10/7; hourly 2pm to 6pm early April to mid-November).

🛏 Sleeping & Eating

Brasseries and fast-food joints line up along riverside quai de Londres (a plaque on the wall near rue Beaurepaire explains the origin of the name, which refers to the City of London choosing Verdun as the most poignant location to reunite the two countries in the aftermath of WWI).

Hôtel Montaulbain
HOTEL €

(☑ 03 29 86 00 47; 4 rue de la Vieille Prison; d €69-89) It requires very little detective work to pin down this central hotel, which Mr Poirot (true to his name) runs with charm and an eye for detail. The spotless rooms are excellent value.

Hôtel Les Orchidées
HOTEL €

(☑ 03 29 86 46 46; www.orchidees-hotel.com; rue Robert Schumann; d/tr/q €68/89/116; 🛜🅿️♿) Set in quiet gardens, this hotel has light, modern rooms (including spacious family ones), a swimming pool, a tennis court and a restaurant. It's 2km east of town off the D603.

Le Clapier
BISTRO €

(☑ 03 29 86 20 14; 34 rue des Gros Degrés; menus €12-33; ⏰ noon-2pm & 7-9pm Tue-Sat; ♿) The chef's penchant for Provence's balmy climes shines through on the *menu* at this cosy bistro. Specialities such as crumbly Brie tart and herb-infused leg of lamb are expertly paired with Meuse wines.

Pom'Samba
TRADITIONAL FRENCH €

(☑ 03 29 83 49 34; 7 av Garibaldi; 3-course lunch menu €12, mains €10-20; ⏰ noon-1.45pm & 7-9.30pm Mon-Tue & Thu-Fri, noon-1.45pm Wed, 7-9.30pm Sat; ♿) The humble spud is king at this cheerful tiled restaurant, where potatoes are accompanied by everything from escargot to scallops.

Épices et Tout
MODERN FRENCH €€

(☑ 03 29 86 46 88; www.epices-et-tout.fr; 35 rue des Gros Degrés; menus €36-75; ⏰ noon-1.30pm & 7-9pm Mon-Tue, Fri & Sat, noon-1.30pm Wed, 7-9pm Thu) Spice adds variety to the food at this atmospheric cellar bistro. Creative dishes such as pork cheeks with caramel and peanuts, and cocoa-laced salmon terrine are well executed and served with panache.

ℹ Information

Tourist Office (☑ 03 29 84 55 55; www.tourisme-verdun.fr; av du Général Mangin, Pavillon Japiot; ⏰ 9.30am-12.30pm & 1.30-6pm Mon-Sat, 10am-noon & 2-5pm Sun; 🛜) Friendly tourist office with guided tours, info on Verdun and the surrounding region, and free maps of the battlefields. Free wi-fi.

ℹ Getting There & Around

BICYCLE
Bikes are an excellent way to tour the Verdun battlefields. At the train station, **TiV' vélo** (www.bus-tiv.com; place Maurice Genevoix; half-day/day/week €1/2/5; ⏰ 9am-noon &

ℹ VERDUN SAVER

Before heading to Verdun's sights and the Verdun Battlefields, visit the tourist office where you can buy slightly discounted adult tickets for the **Citadelle Souterraine** (€7), **Ossuaire de Douaumont** audiovisual presentation (€4) and the **Fort de Douaumont** (€3).

The Maison du Tourisme, opposite the tourist office, sells the money-saving **Pass Musées** (adult/child €17/9.50) covering entry to the Ossuaire de Douaumont, Fort de Douaumont, Fort de Vaux and the Citadelle Souterraine.

2-6pm Mon-Fri) rents out bicycles. You'll need to pay €100 deposit.

CAR & MOTORCYCLE
You can park for free in the car parks south of the tourist office on av du 8 Mai 1945, rue des Tanneries and place de la Digne.

TRAIN
Verdun's poorly served train station, built by Eiffel in 1868, has direct services to Metz (€15, 1½ hours, three direct daily). Three buses a day go to the Gare Meuse TGV station (30 minutes), from where direct TGVs whisk you to Paris' Gare de l'Est (€36, one hour).

Verdun Battlefields

Much of the Battle of Verdun was fought 5km to 8km (as the crow flies) northeast of Verdun. Today, the forested area – still a jumble of trenches and artillery craters – can be reached by car on the D913 and D112; follow the signs to 'Douamont', 'Vaux' or the 'Champ de Bataille 14-18'. Signposted paths lead to dozens of minor remnants of the war. Site interiors are closed in January.

Mémorial de Verdun
WAR MEMORIAL

(www.memorial-de-verdun.fr; adult/child €7/3.50; ⏰ 9am-6pm, closed mid-Dec–Jan) The village of **Fleury**, wiped off the face of the earth in the course of being captured and recaptured 16 times, is now the site of this memorial. It tells the story of '300 days, 300,000 dead, 400,000 wounded', with insightful displays of war artefacts and personal items. Downstairs you'll find a re-creation of the battlefield as it looked on the day the guns finally fell silent.

In the grassy crater-pocked centre of what was once Fleury, a few hundred metres down the road from the memorial,

LOCAL KNOWLEDGE

JEAN-PAUL DE VRIES, GUIDE & MUSEUM OWNER

Guided Walks

I run guided walks every morning to the trenches and the German lines, so people can picture how it must have been in battle and the cramped conditions of daily life. We nearly always find something, usually ammunition. Walking here alone can be dangerous because of the artillery craters and unexploded ammunition – one-third of it is still left in the soil; guides know which routes are safe and don't pose any risk to visitors.

Favourite Finds

The shoes that German soldiers, some of them amputees, made for the French kids from their old army boots. I like the things that show human resourcefulness, like coffee filters made from gasmasks and shells transformed into letter openers, ashtrays, even art. Then there is a mess tin with the inscription 'no good for shit' – who knows whether the soldier was referring to the food or the war in general.

When to Visit

In May when the woods are fresh and Memorial Day is held at the Meuse-Argonne and Lorraine American cemeteries. Or in October when the region was liberated; on a cold, rainy autumn day you get a better sense of what happened here, what it must have been like.

---

signs among the low ruins indicate the village's former layout.

Ossuaire de Douaumont WAR MEMORIAL
(www.verdun-douaumont.com; audiovisual presentation adult/child €6/3; ⊙9am-6pm Mon-Fri, 10am-6pm Sat & Sun) **FREE** Rising like a gigantic artillery shell above 15,000 crosses that bleed into the distance, this sombre, 137m-long ossuary, inaugurated in 1932, is one of France's most important WWI memorials. A ticket to the 20-minute **audiovisual presentation** on the battle also lets you climb the 46m-high **bell tower**. Out front, the French military **cemetery** is flanked by memorials to Muslim and Jewish soldiers (to the east and west, respectively) who died fighting for France in WWI.

The ossuary contains the bones of about 130,000 unidentified French and German soldiers collected from the Verdun battlefields and buried together in 52 mass graves according to where they fell. Each engraved stone denotes a missing soldier, while a touching display of photographs show Verdun survivors – as they were in WWI and as they were later in life.

Fort de Douaumont FORT
(adult/child €4/2; ⊙10am-6pm) Sitting high on a hill, this is the strongest of the 38 fortresses and bastions built along a 45km front to protect Verdun. When the Battle of Verdun began, 400m-long Douaumont – whose 3km network of cold, dripping galleries was built

between 1885 and 1913 – had only a skeleton crew. By the fourth day it had been captured easily, a serious blow to French morale; four months later it was retaken by colonial troops from Morocco.

Charles de Gaulle, then a young captain, was wounded and taken prisoner near here in 1916. It's free to take in the sweeping country views from the fort's crater-pocked roof.

Fort Vaux FORT
(Vaux-devant-Damloup; adult/child €4/2; ⊙10am-6.30pm) Located in crater-scarred countryside, 10km northeast of Verdun, this fort was constructed between 1881 and 1884. It was the second fort – Douaumont was the first – to fall in the Battle of Verdun, and became the site of bloodiest battle for two months. Weak with thirst, Major Raynal and his troops surrendered to the enemy on 7 June 1916. You can gain an insight into past horrors by taking a tour of its dank interior and observation points.

Tranchée des Baïonnettes WAR MEMORIAL
FREE On 12 June 1916 two companies of the 137th Infantry Regiment of the French army were sheltered in their *tranchées* (trenches), *baïonnettes* (bayonets) fixed, waiting for a ferocious artillery bombardment to end. It never did – the incoming shells covered their positions with mud and debris, burying them alive. They were found three years later, when someone spotted several hun-

dred bayonet tips sticking out of the ground. Today the site is marked by a simple memorial that is always open.

The tree-filled valley across the D913 is known as the **Ravin de la Mort** (Ravine of Death).

American Memorials

More than one million American troops participated in the Meuse-Argonne Offensive of late 1918, the last Western Front battle of WWI. The bloody fighting northwest of Verdun, in which more than 26,000 Americans died, convinced the Kaiser's government to cable US President Woodrow Wilson with a request for an armistice. The film Sergeant York (1941) is based on events that took place here. The website of the Meuse *département's* tourism board – www. tourisme-meuse.com – offers background on the region and its WWI sites.

Apart from Romagne '14-'18, all of the sites mentioned below are managed by the **American Battle Monuments Commission** (www.abmc.gov) and are open from 9am to 5pm daily.

Meuse-Argonne
American Cemetery   WAR CEMETERY
The largest US military cemetery in Europe is this WWI ground, where 14,246 soldiers lie buried, in Romagne-sous-Montfaucon, 41km northwest of Verdun along the D38 and D123.

★ **Romagne '14-'18**   WAR MUSEUM
(✎ 03 29 85 10 14; www.romagne14-18.com; 2 rue de l'Andon; guided walks €12.50, donations welcome; ⊙ guided walks 9am-noon, museum noon-6pm Thu-Mon) The village of Romagne-sous-Montfaucon holds this

heart-rending museum, which, in the words of owner Jean-Paul de Vries is all about 'life stories' and 'the human being behind the helmet'. This barn shows artefacts in their original state – rust, dirt and all. Join Jean-Paul on one of his insightful morning walks of the battlefields. Guided walks are by appointment – call ahead.

Lorraine American
Cemetery   WAR CEMETERY
Verdun also had a significant military presence from the end of WWII until Charles de Gaulle pulled France out of NATO's integrated military command in 1966. Surrounded by woodland and set in landscaped grounds, this is the largest US WWII military cemetery in Europe. It's 45km east of Metz, just outside of St-Avold.

St-Mihiel American
Cemetery   WAR CEMETERY
In this WWI cemetery, the graves of 4153 American soldiers who died in the 1918 Battle of St-Mihiel radiate towards a central sundial topped by a white American eagle. The cemetery is 40km southeast of Verdun on the outskirts of Thiaucourt-Regniéville.

Butte de Montsec   WAR MEMORIAL
This 375m-high mound, site of a US monument with a bronze relief map, is surrounded by a round, neoclassical colonnade. It's a 15km drive southwest of St-Mihiel American Cemetery.

Butte de Montfaucon   WAR MEMORIAL
Commemorating the Meuse-Argonne Offensive, this 336m-high mound is topped by a 58m-high Doric column crowned by a statue symbolising liberty. Located about 10km southeast of Romagne-sous-Montfaucon.

The Loire Valley

POP 2.9 MILLION

Includes ➜

Best Places to Eat

➜ Le Pot de Lapin (p401)
➜ La Parenthèse (p374)
➜ Le Lièvre Gourmand (p374)
➜ Le Gambetta (p401)
➜ Le Petit Comptoir (p406)
➜ Les Années 30 (p398)

Best Places to Stay

➜ Château de Verrières (p400)
➜ Château Beaulieu (p400)
➜ La Maison de Thomas (p378)
➜ Hôtel de l'Abeille (p373)

Why Go?

In centuries past, the River Loire was a key strategic area, one step removed from the French capital and poised on the crucial frontier between northern and southern France. Kings, queens, dukes and nobles established their feudal strongholds, country seats and, later, their posh playhouses along the Loire, and the broad, flat fertile valley is sprinkled with many of the most extravagant castles and fortresses in France. From sky-topping turrets and glittering banquet halls to slate-crowned cupolas and crenellated towers, the hundreds of Loire Valley châteaux, and the villages vineyards, and agriculture surrounding them – all an enormous Unesco World Heritage Site – comprise 1000 years of astonishingly rich architectural, artistic and agrarian treasures. If it's pomp and splendour you're looking for, the Loire Valley is the place to explore. And don't forget: it's also a modern-day wine region dotted with lively cosmopolitan cities such as Orléans, Tours, Saumur and Angers.

When to Go
Tours

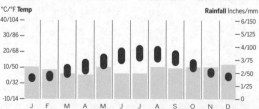

Late Apr–early May The Fêtes de Jeanne d'Arc in Orléans culminate with parades on 8 May.

May & Jun Cycle the verdant trails of the Loire Valley, from château to château.

Sep & Oct Wine tasting during harvest season and châteaux start to be less crowded.

History

The dramas of French history are writ large across the face of the Loire Valley's châteaux. Early on, the Loire was one of Roman Gaul's most important transport arteries. The first châteaux were medieval fortresses established in the 9th century to fend off marauding Vikings. By the 11th century massive walls, fortified keeps and moats were all the rage.

During the Hundred Years War (1337–1453) the Loire marked one of the boundaries between French and English forces and the area was ravaged by fierce fighting. After Charles VII regained his crown with the help of Joan of Arc, the Loire emerged as the centre of French court life. Charles took up residence in Loches with his mistress, Agnès Sorel, and the French nobility, and from then on the bourgeois elite established their own extravagant châteaux as expressions of wealth and influence.

François I (r 1515–47) made his mark by introducing ornate Renaissance palaces to the Loire. François' successor Henri II (r 1547–59), his wife Catherine de Médicis and his mistress Diane de Poitiers played out their interpersonal dramas from castle to castle, while Henri's son, Henri III (r 1573–89), had two of his greatest rivals assassinated at Blois' Castle before being assassinated himself eight months later.

ⓘ Getting There & Away

AIR

Tours' airport has flights to London's Stansted, Southampton (England), Dublin (Ireland), Marseille, Marrakesh (Morocco) and Porto (Portugal), while Angers' small airport serves London and Nice.

TRAIN

The TGV connects St-Pierre-des-Corps, 4km east of Tours, with Paris' Gare Montparnasse (one hour) and Charles de Gaulle Airport (1¾ hour); in the west, Saumur, Angers and Nantes; and in the south, La Rochelle and Bordeaux. Angers is also on the TGV line via Le Mans to Paris. Blois and Amboise are served by high-speed trains to Paris. Some châteaux are on or near regional lines.

ⓘ Getting Around

Most main towns and many châteaux are accessible by train or bus, but having your own wheels allows significantly more freedom.

Blois has decent public buses and shuttles to nearby châteaux. Tours and Amboise are loaded with bus tour options.

BICYCLE

The mostly flat Loire Valley is fabulous cycling country – peddle through villages and vineyards on your way to châteaux. **Loire à Vélo** (www.loireavelo.fr) maintains 800km of signposted routes from Cuffy (near Nevers) all the way to the Atlantic. Pick up a free guide from tourist offices, or download material (including route maps, audioguides and bike-hire details) from the website. Individual regions, like Anjou, Touraine, Centre or the Loiret (around Orléans), also have their own routes and accommodation guides. Tourist offices (and their websites) are well stocked with material.

If you'd like to cycle but want some help, **Bagafrance** (www.bagafrance.com) transports luggage and bikes, and many outfits rent electric bikes. Or consider a tour.

Détours de Loire (☎ 02 47 61 22 23; www.locationdevelos.com) Has bike-rental shops in Tours, Amboise, Blois and Saumur and myriad partners. Delivers bikes and also allows you to pick up and drop off bikes along the route for a small surcharge. Prices include a lock, helmet, repair kit and pump. Classic bikes cost €15/€60 per day/week, with extra days €5. Tandems cost €45/140 per day/week.

Les Châteaux à Vélo (☎ in Blois 02 54 78 62 52; www.chateauxavelo.com; per day €12-14) Bike rental circuit between Blois, Chambord, Cheverny and Chaumont-sur-Loire; 400km of marked trails and minibus shuttle. Get route maps and MP3 guides from the website, or pick up brochures at local tourist offices.

Wheel Free (☎ 02 38 44 26 85; www.wheel-free.fr; 33 rue du Général de Gaulle, St-Jean le Blanc; first/additional days €20/9.60) Rents, delivers and picks up electric bikes.

☞ Tours & Activities

Bus

Hard-core indie travellers might baulk at the idea of a minibus tour of the châteaux, but don't dismiss it out of hand, especially if you don't have your own transport. Many private companies offer a choice of well-organised itineraries, taking in various combinations of Azay-le-Rideau, Villandry, Cheverny, Chambord and Chenonceau (plus wine-tasting tours). Half-day trips cost between €23 and €36; full-day trips range from €50 to €54. Many also offer custom-designed tours. Entry to the châteaux isn't included, though you often get

FAST FACTS
➜ **Area** 40,440 sq km
➜ **Local industry** viticulture
➜ **Signature drink** Cointreau

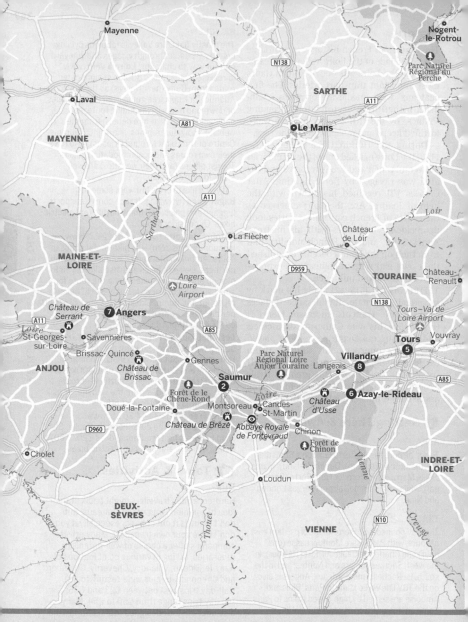

The Loire Valley Highlights

1 Admiring graceful arches and priceless art at **Château de Chenonceau** (p389)

2 Combining fantastic food and wine tasting with equestrian choreography in **Saumur** (p398)

3 Exploring the invention-filled final home of Leonardo da Vinci at **Le Clos Lucé** (p391) in cool Amboise

4 Climbing to the turret-covered rooftop of **Château de Chambord** (p379), the Loire Valley's most exuberant château

5 Exploring super museums by day and partying by night in lively **Tours** (p384)

6 Taking a serene break at

moated island château, **Azay-le-Rideau** (p394).

7 Contemplating many-headed beasts in Angers' remarkable medieval Apocalypse tapestry at **Château d'Angers** (p404).

8 Wandering meticulous gardens and floral displays at **Château de Villandry** (p393) or **Château de Chaumont-sur-Loire** (p381)

9 Perusing the lively Saturday market in Loches, then admiring the view atop the 11th-century **Cité Royale de Loches** (p395)

10 Taking in Joan of Arc lore and sampling top cuisine in buzzing **Orléans** (p371)

CHOOSING YOUR CHÂTEAU

There's no doubt that for dramatic castles, the Loire Valley is definitely the place to go, but with so many glorious palaces, how on earth do you go about selecting which to visit? Here's our whistle-stop guide to help you decide. **Châteaux de la Loire** (www.leschateauxdelaloire. org) offers a thorough map available at local tourist offices and online.

For sheer, unadulterated architectural splendour, you can't top the big three: François I's country extravaganza Chambord (p379), Renaissance river-spanning Chenonceau (p389) and the supremely graceful Cheverny (p380). Unsurprisingly, these are also far and away the most visited châteaux; turn up early or late to dodge the hordes.

If it's a medieval Monty Python and the Holy Grail kind of castle you're after, head for the imposing fortress of Langeais (p393), complete with original furnishings, battlements and drawbridge or the austere, ruined 11th-century keep at Loches (p395).

For historical significance, top of the list are the royal residences of Blois (p376), spanning four distinct periods of French history; stately Amboise (p390), home to a succession of French monarchs including Charles VIII and Louis XI; Forteresse Royale de Chinon (p396), where Joan of Arc held her momentous first rendezvous with the future King Charles VII; black-stoned Château d'Angers (p404) with its fantastic tapestry; and pastoral Le Clos Lucé (p391) in Amboise, where Leonardo da Vinci whiled away his final years.

Looking for the picture-perfect setting? Our choices are the moat-ringed Château d'Azay-le-Rideau (p394) and Château de Sully-sur-Loire (p375), or visit the stunning formal gardens at Villandry (p393) and Chaumont-sur-Loire (p381).

For literary connections, try the inspiration for *Sleeping Beauty*, Château d'Ussé (p394); Balzac's residence, Saché (p393); or Château de Montsoreau (p403), the setting for a classic Alexandre Dumas novel.

Lastly, if you're looking for solitude, chances are that off-the-beaten-track châteaux such as Brissac (p408), Brézé (p404) and Beauregard (p381) will be much quieter than their bigger, better-known cousins elsewhere in the valley.

Top Tips

➡ Go first thing or late in the day to escape the hordes.

➡ Buy joint regional tickets or buy from tourist offices for slight savings and to avoid queues at the sight.

➡ At the châteaux, ticket offices close from half an hour to one hour before the château itself.

slightly discounted tickets. Reserve online or via the Tours or Amboise tourist offices, from where most tours depart.

Acco-Dispo (☎ 06 82 00 64 51; www.accodispo-tours.com)

Loire Valley Tours (☎ 02 54 33 99 80; www.loire-valley-tours.com)

Quart de Tours (☎ 06 30 65 52 01; www.quartdetours.com)

St-Eloi Excursions (☎ 06 70 82 78 75; www.chateauxexcursions.com)

Touraine Evasion (☎ 06 07 39 13 31; www.tourevasion.com)

Boat

The Loire offers few opportunities to get out on the water: the currents are often too unpredictable to navigate safely, but it's not completely off-limits. Check at tourist offices for boat excursions or kayak rentals. The Saumur/Candes-St-Martin area has many.

Specialised Tours

Tourist offices are stocked with info on local excursions by hot-air balloon or with a specialised theme, like cycling or wine tasting. Saumur is particularly rich in equestrian tours.

Cheval et Châteaux (www.cheval-et-chateaux. com; multiday tours per person €1114-2229) Experienced equestrian and guide Anne-France Launay leads four- to seven-day horseback excursions to some of the Loire's best-known châteaux, with overnights in castle-based B&Bs, including gourmet meals and wine.

Art Montgolfières (☎ 02 54 32 08 11; www. art-montgolfieres.fr; 1/2 persons €205/390) Perfect if you've ever dreamed of soaring over a château in a hot-air balloon! Spend one hour aloft and then quaff a celebratory glass of bubbly (or two).

Château du Petit Thouars Wine & Boat Excursion (☎ 02 47 95 96 40; www.chateaudptwines. com; St-Germain-sur-Vienne; adult/child €30/15) Sail on a handmade wooden boat for two hours from a vineyard to nearby villages like Montsoreau or Chinon, while tasting the vintner's wines with local snacks.

ORLÉANAIS

Taking its name from the historic city of Orléans, famous for its Joan of Arc connections, the Orléanais is the northern gateway to the Loire Valley. In the east are the ecclesiastical treasures of St-Benoît-sur-Loire and Germigny-des-Prés, while to the south lies the marshy Sologne, historically a favourite hunting ground for France's kings and princes.

Orléans

POP 117,988

There's a definite big-city buzz around the broad boulevards, flashy boutiques and elegant buildings of Orléans, 100km south of Paris. It's a city with enduring heritage: an important settlement by the time of the Romans' arrival, Orléans sealed its place in history in 1429 when a young peasant girl by the name of Jeanne d'Arc (Joan of Arc) rallied the armies of Charles VII and staged a spectacular rout against the besieging English forces, a key turning point in the Hundred Years War. Six centuries later, the Maid of Orléans still exerts a powerful hold on the French imagination, and you'll discover statues and museums dedicated to her around town. The city's charming, mostly pedestrianised medieval quarter stretches from the River Loire north to rue Jeanne d'Arc, and has an outstanding art museum and fantastical cathedral.

◉ Sights & Activities

The tourist office runs guided **walking tours** (€6.50; generally in French, but occasionally English; reserve ahead) of Orléans. Some are combined with a riverboat cruise. The office also sells self-guided walking tour brochure *9 Balades Entre Ciel et Loire* (€0.50).

★**Cathédrale Ste-Croix**   CATHEDRAL
(www.orleans.catholique.fr/cathedrale; place Ste-Croix; ◷ 9.15am-noon & 2.15-5.45pm) In a country of jaw-dropping churches, the Cathédrale Ste-Croix still raises a gasp. Towering above place Ste-Croix, Orléans' Flamboyant Gothic cathedral was originally built in the 13th century and then underwent collective tinkering by successive monarchs. Joan of Arc came and prayed here on 8 May 1429, and was greeted with a procession of thanks for saving the town. It was Henri IV who kicked off the cathedral's reconstruction in 1601. Louis XIII (r 1610–43) restored the choir and nave, Louis XIV (r 1643–1715) was responsible for the transept, and Louis XV (r 1715–74) and Louis XVI (r 1774–92) rebuilt the western façade, including its huge arches and wedding-cake towers. Inside, slender columns soar skywards towards the vaulted ceiling and 106m spire, completed in 1895, while a series of vividly coloured stained-glass windows relates the life of St Joan, who was canonised in 1920.

★**Musée des Beaux-Arts**   ART MUSEUM
(☑ 02 38 79 21 55; www.orleans.fr; 1 rue Fernand Rabier; adult/child incl audioguide €4/free, 1st Sun of the month free; ◷ 10am-6pm Tue-Sun) Orléans' five-storeyed fine-arts museum is a treat, with an excellent selection of Italian, Flemish and Dutch paintings (including works by Correggio, Velázquez and Bruegel), as well as a huge collection by French artists such as Léon Cogniet (1794–1880) and Orléans-born Alexandre Antigna (1817–78), and Paul Gauguin, who spent some of his youth in Orléans. Among the treasures are a rare set of 18th-century pastels by Maurice Quentin de la Tour and Jean-Baptiste Chardin.

A ticket to the Musée des Beaux-Arts also grants entry to the Musée Historique et Archéologique.

★**Hôtel Groslot**   HISTORIC MANSION
(place de l'Étape; ◷ 10am-noon & 2-6pm Sun-Fri, 5-7pm Sat) **FREE** The Renaissance Hôtel Groslot was built in the 15th century as a private mansion for Jacques Groslot, a city bailiff, and later used as Orléans' town hall during the Revolution. The neomedieval interior, with some original furnishings, is extravagant, especially the ornate bedroom in which 16-year-old King François II died in 1560 (now used for marriages). The rear gardens are lovely.

Maison de Jeanne d'Arc   MUSEUM
(☑ 02 38 68 32 63; www.jeannedarc.com.fr; 3 place du Général de Gaulle; adult/child €4/free; ◷ 10am-6pm Tue-Sun Apr-Sep, 2-6pm Tue-Sun Oct-Mar) The best place to get an overview of Joan of Arc's life story is this reconstruction of the 15th-century house that hosted her between April and May 1429 (the original was destroyed by British bombing in 1940). Start with its main feature: a 15-minute movie (in French or English) tracing her origins, accomplishments and historical impact. There's a wall-sized timeline in the adjoining room. Upstairs are

Orléans

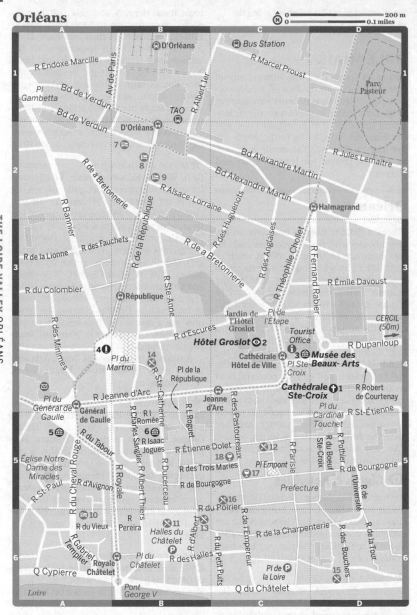

the archives of the world's largest Joan of Arc research centre.

Musée Historique et Archéologique
ARCHAEOLOGY MUSEUM

(02 38 79 25 60; 21 rue Ste-Catherine; admission incl in ticket to Musée des Beaux-Arts; 1.30-5.45pm Tue-Fri, 9.30am-noon & 1.30-5.45pm Sat, 2-6pm Sun) The centrepiece of the museum in the Renaissance Cabu mansion is the **Salle Jeanne d'Arc**, filled with artistic representations of the Maid of Orléans, from a late 15th-century Swiss tapestry and fine paintings to 20th-century mustard jars. The museum's **Gallo-**

Orléans

Roman collection includes several rare bronzes recovered from the Loire.

Place du Martroi   SQUARE
Three of Orléans' main boulevards (rue Bannier, rue de la République and rue Royale) converge on place du Martroi, where you'll find a huge bronze statue (1855) by Denis Foyatier, depicting St Joan atop a prancing steed. A Friday evening vegetable and flea market (from 5pm to 10pm) sets up here.

CERCIL   MUSEUM
(Musée-Mémorial des Enfants du Vel d'Hiv; ☑ 02 38 42 03 91; www.cercil.fr; 45 rue du Bourdon-Blanc; adult/child €3/free; ⊗ 2-6pm Tue-Fri & Sun) Moving exhibits (in French) document the deportation of the Jews – especially the children of the area – during WWII, and include a shack from one of the region's three internment camps (Beaune-la-Rolande, Pithiviers and Jargeau). Find it one block northeast of the cathedral.

✸ Festivals & Events

Fêtes de Jeanne d'Arc   CULTURAL FESTIVAL
(www.fetesjeannedarc.com) Since 1430 the Orléanais have celebrated the Fêtes de Jeanne d'Arc in late April and early May, commemorating the liberation of Orléans from the English. A week of street parties, enormous medieval costume parades and concerts ends with a procession and morning Mass at the cathedral on 8 May.

🛏 Sleeping

★**Hôtel de l'Abeille**   HISTORIC HOTEL €€
(☑ 02 38 53 54 87; www.hoteldelabeille.com; 64 rue Alsace-Lorraine; d €98-135, q €170-195; 🛜) Bees buzz, floorboards creak and vintage Orléans posters adorn the walls at this gorgeous turn-of-the-century house, run by the same family for four generations. It's deliciously old-fashioned, from the scuffed pine floors and wildly floral wallpapers to the hefty dressers and bee-print curtains. For breakfast (€12) there's a choice of coffees, teas, juices and exotic jams. Only downside: no lift.

Hôtel d'Arc   HOTEL €€
(☑ 02 38 53 10 94; www.hoteldarc.fr; 37ter rue de la République; s €112-190, d €126-230; ✳@🛜) Ride the vintage-style lift to 35 slick rooms at this Best Western–affiliated hotel, conveniently located between the train station and the pedestrianised centre. Rooms vary in size but all are done up comfortably. The Prestige and Deluxe come with plush robes.

Hôtel Marguerite   HOTEL €€
(☑ 02 38 53 74 32; www.hotel-marguerite.fr; 14 place du Vieux Marché; d €70-145, q €120-145; 🛜) This basic but solid hotel wins points for its friendly reception and central location. Opt for a superior room if you like your bathroom sparkling and your shower powerful; some of these rooms were recently renovated. Free bike parking.

Hôtel Archange   BOUTIQUE HOTEL €
(☑ 02 38 54 42 42; www.hotelarchange.com; 1 bd de Verdun; r €55-90, q €90-135; 🛜) Gilded mirrors, cherub murals and sofas shaped like giant hands greet you at this station hotel. Splashy colour schemes spice up rooms, and shuttered windows combat daytime tram noise.

🍴 Eating

Orléans is a great food city. Reserve ahead at top restaurants.

Les Fagots   TRADITIONAL FRENCH €
(☑ 02 38 62 22 79; 32 rue du Poirier; menus €13-17; ⊗ noon-2pm & 7.30-10pm Tue-Sat) Delightful smoky smells lure you into this unpretentious eatery whose *menu* revolves around

roasted meat. The Auvergnat owner cooks everything over an open fire, including grilled tomatoes and baked potatoes slathered with crème fraiche and chives.

★ La Parenthèse
MODERN FRENCH €€

(☑02 38 62 07 50; www.restaurant-la-parenthese. com; 26 place du Châtelet; menus lunch €15-17, dinner €24-28; ☉lunch & dinner Tue-Sat) Book ahead for this very popular restaurant, a labour of love for youthful chef David Sterne. Produce from the Halles marketplace across the street forms the basis for ever-changing, bargain-priced *plats du jour* (€10), plus creative lunch and dinner *menus*. Choose from relaxed sidewalk seating or two more refined indoor dining rooms.

La Dariole
REGIONAL CUISINE €€

(☑02 38 77 26 67; 25 rue Étienne Dolet; menus €21-26; ☉noon-1.30pm Mon-Fri, 7.30-10pm Tue & Fri) One of Orléans' smartest, most popular restaurants, La Dariole specialises in regional food. Inventive starters such as gazpacho with an asparagus-avocado charlotte are followed by mains like wine-braised beef with artichokes, and desserts like vanilla bean crème brûlée with fresh raspberries.

Le Brin de Zinc
BISTRO €€

(☑02 38 53 38 77; www.groupedegenne.com; 62 rue Ste-Catherine; menus lunch €16, dinner €22-27; ☉11.45am-2.30pm & 6.45-10.30pm daily, to 11pm Fri & Sat) Battered signs, old telephones and a vintage scooter decorate this old-world-style bistro, serving French classics till late. On summer evenings, the sunny sidewalk tables are a big draw, as are daily specials – mussels, *frites* (chips) and a beer for €12, anyone?

★ Le Lièvre Gourmand
GASTRONOMIC €€€

(☑02 38 53 66 14; www.lelievregourmand.com; 28 quai du Châtelet; menus lunch €35, dinner from €45; ☉noon-1.15pm & 8-9.30pm Wed-Mon) From the moment you settle into one of the comfy couches in this beautiful townhouse overlooking the Loire, the relaxed, lovely pampering begins. You'll get a perfect amuse-bouche with your aperitif as you decide on a set of courses...each a creative duo of preparations: hot and cold. Think delicate foams and infusions in unexpected combinations with seasonal ingredients, like new asparagus in spring.

WINE IN THE LOIRE VALLEY

Splendid scenery and densely packed vineyards make the Loire Valley a classic wine touring destination, with a range of excellent red, white and crémant (sparkling wines). Armed with the free map from the wine association (www.vinsvaldeloire.fr, with a US representative at www.loirevalleywine.com) called *Sur la Route des Vins de Loire* (On the Loire Wine Route) or the *Loire Valley Vineyards* booklet, available online, at area tourist offices and *maisons de vins* (literally, wine houses), you can put together a never-ending web of wine-tasting itineraries, drawing from over 320 'open cellars'. The *maisons des vins* in Blois, Tours, Cheverny, Saumur and Angers offer tasting and guidance on Loire wines, and have loads of information.

Anjou and Saumur alone have 30 AOCs (Appellation d'Origine Contrôlée), and Touraine has nine, including some lively gamays, a fruity, light-bodied wine. The Val de Loire (www.vinsvaldeloire.fr) website has a complete primer.

The most predominant red is cabernet franc, though you'll also find cabernet sauvignon, pinot noir and others. Appellations include Anjou, Saumur-Champigny, Bourgueil and Chinon.

For whites, Vouvray's chenin blancs are excellent, and Sancerre and the appellation across the river, Pouilly-Fumé, produce great sauvignon blancs. Cour-Cheverny is made from the lesser known Romorantin grape. Savennières, near Angers, has both a dry and a sweet chenin blanc.

The bubbly appellation Crémant de Loire spans many communities, but you can easily find it around Montrichard (eg Château Monmousseau), and other bubblies include Saumur Brut and Vouvray.

One of the most densely packed stretches for wine tasting along the River Loire itself is around Saumur. Towns with multiple tasting rooms (from west to east) include St-Hilaire-St-Florent (where you'll find Ackerman, Langlois-Château and Veuve Amiot), Souzay Champigny (home to Château Villeneuve and Clos des Cordeliers) and Parnay (Château de Parnay and Château de Targé).

Just east of Tours, another hot spot includes Rochecorbon (home to Blanc Foussy), Vouvray (Domaine Huet l'Echansonne, Château Moncontour and several others) and Montlouis-sur-Loire. You'll find a Cave des Producteurs representing multiple producers in the latter two towns. Designate a driver (or hop on your bike), grab your map, and explore!

Self-Catering

Covered Market   FOOD MARKET
(place du Châtelet; ⊙ 8.30am-7pm Tue-Sat, to 12.30pm Sun) Inside the Halles du Châtelet shopping centre.

🍷 Drinking & Nightlife

The free *Orléans Poche* (www.orleanspoche. com, in French) details cultural happenings. Rue de Bourgogne and rue du Poirier are chock-a-block with drinking holes.

Ver di Vin   WINE BAR
(☑ 02 38 54 47 42; www.verdivin.com; 2 rue des Trois Maries; ⊙ 6pm-1am Tue-Sat; 🛜) This popular subterranean wine bar is run by experienced sommeliers; reserve ahead for occasional *dégustation* (tasting) nights.

McEwan's   PUB
(250 rue de Bourgogne; ⊙ 4pm-1am Mon-Sat) Scottish-themed pub popular for its wide variety of whiskies and beers on tap, and regular rugby and football broadcasts.

ℹ️ Information

Tourist Office (☑ 02 38 24 05 05; www. tourisme-orleans.com; 2 place de l'Étape; ⊙ 9.30am-1pm & 2-6.30pm Mon-Sat May-Jun & Sep, 9am-7pm Mon-Sat, 10am-1pm & 2-5pm Sun Jul & Aug, shorter hours rest of year) Well-stocked with guides (like the Loiret cycle guide) and event information, in many languages.

ℹ️ Getting There & Away

BUS

Ulys (www.ulys-loiret.com) Ulys brings together information for local bus companies serving the Orléanais area, including Beaugency and Châteauneuf-sur-Loire. Buy tickets (€2.40) on board or at the bus station (☑ 02 38 53 94 75; 2 rue Marcel Proust).

TRAIN

The city's two stations, Gare d'Orléans and Gare Les Aubrais-Orléans (the latter is 2km to the north), are linked by tram and frequent shuttle trains. Trains often stop at both stations.

Blois €11.20, 35 minutes, hourly
Brive-la-Gaillarde €32 to €53, 3¼ hours, five daily
Nantes €44.40, three hours, three daily
Paris' Gare d'Austerlitz €20.80, one hour, hourly
Tours €20.10, 1¼ hours, hourly

ℹ️ Getting Around

BICYCLE

Vélo+ (☑ 08 00 00 83 56; www.agglo-veloplus. fr; deposit with credit card €150, first 30min free, next 30min €0.50, per subsequent hour €2) On-street bike-hire system, with stations around town (eg train station, cathedral).

BUS & TRAM

TAO (☑ 08 00 01 20 00; www.reseau-tao.fr) Buses and trams operate throughout Orléans. Information and tickets (single/10-ticket *carnet* €1.50/13.40) are available at automatic distributors, *tabacs* (tobacconists), and TAO's downtown agencies: Agence Place d'Arc (Gare d'Orléans; ⊙ 6.45am-7.15pm Mon-Fri, 8am-6.30pm Sat) and Agence Martroi (rue de la Hallebarde; ⊙ 7.30am-7pm Mon-Fri, 8.30am-6pm Sat) in the centre. Last-minute tickets (€1.60) are available on board. Trams run until around 12.30am, buses till 8pm or 9pm.

Tram B passes in front of the cathedral and tourist office. Navette O (€.50) makes a circuit around the centre, every 10 minutes.

Orléans to Sully-sur-Loire

The 350-sq-km Forêt d'Orléans (one of the few remaining places in France where you can spot wild ospreys) stretches north of Orléans, while east of Orléans lie intriguing churches and little-known châteaux.

The Musée de la Marine de Loire (☑ 02 38 46 84 46; www.chateauneuf-sur-loire.com; 1 place Aristide Briand; adult/child €3.50/2, ⊙ 10am-6pm Wed-Mon Apr-Oct, 2-6pm Wed-Mon Nov-Mar), in Châteauneuf-sur-Loire, explores the history of river shipping on the Loire, with a collection of model boats and riverine artefacts in the former stables of the town's château. From Orléans, take bus line 3 (one hour, eight daily Monday to Saturday, two on Sunday).

Oratoire de Germigny-des-Prés (www. tourisme-loire-foret.com; admission free, guided visits adult/child €3/1.50; ⊙ 9am-7pm Apr-Sep, 9am-5pm Oct-Mar), another 6km southeast, is one of France's few Carolingian churches, renowned for its unusual Maltese-cross layout and fine gilt-and-silver 9th-century mosaic of the Ark of the Covenant.

Five kilometres further southeast, St-Benoît-sur-Loire's Romanesque Abbaye de Fleury (☑ 02 38 35 72 43; www.abbaye-fleury.com; ⊙ 6.30am-10pm, guided visits 3.15pm Sun Mar-Oct) is still home to a practising Benedictine brotherhood, who conduct summertime tours. Look out for the basilica's famous decorated portal and capitals and the relics of St Benedict (480–547) which the monks fetched from Montecassino, Italy, in 672.

Nine kilometres southeast of St-Benoît, the Château de Sully-sur-Loire (☑ 02 38 36

OFF THE BEATEN TRACK

Ready for a break from the château scene? Head over to wonderfully walkable **Beaugency**, a warren of medieval streets and towers, keeps and churches beautifully spanning the north bank of the Loire. The **tourist office** (📞 02 38 44 54 42; www.beaugency.fr; 3 place du Dr Hyvernaud; ⊙10am-12.30pm & 2-6.30pm Mon-Sat Sep-May, plus 10am-1pm Sun Jun-Aug) has a walking tour map and info on the history of the two famous councils held here: the one in 1152 famously annulled the marriage of Louis VII and Eleanor of Aquitaine. Find it 32km southwest of Orléans and served by Ulys (p375) line 9.

36 86; www.chateau-sully.com; adult/child €7/3.50, with guided tour €8/4; ⊙10am-6pm Tue-Sun, closed noon-2pm Oct-Mar, open Mon Jul & Aug) is a grand example of a fairy-tale castle. Initiated in 1395, its machicolated ramparts and turrets were designed to defend one of the Loire's crucial crossings. Rising from a glassy moat lined by stately bald cypresses, the castle has an impressive vaulted roof and historic tapestries depicting the story of Psyche. An outdoor **music festival** (www.festival-sully.com) jams in late May and early June. From Orléans, take bus line 3 or 7 (1½ hours, seven daily Monday to Saturday, two Sunday).

La Sologne

For centuries, the boggy wetland and murky woods of La Sologne have been one of France's great hunting grounds, with deer, boars, pheasants and stags roaming the woodland, and eels, carp and pike filling its deep ponds and rivers. François I established it as a royal playground, but years of war and floods turned it into malaria-infested swamp; only in the mid-19th century, after it was drained under Napoléon III, did La Sologne regain its hunting prestige.

In winter it can be a desolate place, with drizzle and thick fog blanketing the landscape, but in summer it's a riot of wildflowers and makes for great country to explore on foot, bike or horseback. Paths and trails criss-cross the area, including the GR31 and the GR3C, but stick to the signposted routes during hunting season to avoid getting buckshot in your backside.

For info on hikes and walks in the Sologne, contact the **tourist office** (📞 02 54 76 43 89; www.tourisme-romorantin.com; place de la Paix; ⊙9am-1pm & 2-6.30pm Mon-Sat) in

Romorantin-Lanthenay, 41km southeast of Blois. Some trails leave from near St-Viâtre's **Maison des Étangs** (📞 02 54 88 23 00; www.maison-des-etangs.com/musee; 2 rue de la Poste; adult/child €5/2.50; ⊙10am-noon & 2-6pm Apr-Oct, 2-6pm Wed, Sat & Sun Nov-Mar), a museum exploring La Sologne's 2800 *étangs* (ponds). The **Musée de Sologne** (📞 02 54 95 33 66; www.museedesologne.com; Romorantin-Lanthenay; ⊙10am-noon & 2-6pm Mon & Wed-Sat, 2-6pm Sun) is dedicated to the area. On the last weekend in October, the **Journées Gastronomiques de Sologne** (www.romorantin.fr/jgs) fill the streets of Romorantin with local delicacies.

From Romorantin-Lanthenay to Tours by train, change in Gièvres (€16.10, 1½ hours, five to seven daily). TLC (p379) bus 4 runs direct to Blois (€2, one hour, two to six daily).

BLÉSOIS

The countryside around the former royal seat of Blois is surrounded by some of the country's finest châteaux, including graceful Cheverny, little-visited Beauregard and the turret-topped supertanker château to end them all, Chambord.

Blois

POP 48,393

Looming on a rocky outcrop on the northern bank of the Loire, Blois' historic château (formerly the feudal seat of the powerful counts of Blois) provides a whistle-stop tour through the key periods of French history and architecture. Blois suffered heavy bombardment during WWII, and the modern-day town is mostly the result of postwar reconstruction, but a small area of twisting medieval streets remain.

◎ Sights

Blois château, *son et lumière* show and/or Maison de la Magie combination tickets save some cash. Admission to any two attractions costs €15/7 per adult/child or for all three €19.50/10.50. Kids under six are free.

★**Château Royal de Blois** CHÂTEAU
(📞 02 54 90 33 33; www.chateaudeblois.fr; place du Château; adult/child €9.80/5, audioguide €4, English tours Jul & Aug free; ⊙9am-6.30pm Apr-Sep, to 7pm Jul & Aug, shorter hours rest of year) Intended more as an architectural showpiece (look at that ornately carved façade!) than a military stronghold, Blois' château bears the creative mark of several successive French kings.

It makes an excellent introduction to the châteaux of the Loire Valley, with elements of Gothic (13th century), Flamboyant Gothic (1498–1503), early Renaissance (1515–24) and classical (1630s) architecture in its four grand wings.

The most famous feature of the Renaissance wing, the royal apartments of François I and Queen Claude, is the **loggia staircase**, decorated with salamanders and curly Fs (heraldic symbols of François I).

Highlights also include the **bedchamber** in which Catherine de Médicis (Henri II's machiavellian wife) died in 1589. According to Alexandre Dumas, the queen stashed her poisons in secret cupboards behind the elaborately panelled walls of the **studiolo**, one of the few rooms in the castle with its original decor.

The second-floor **king's apartments** were the setting for one of the bloodiest episodes in the château's history: in 1588 Henri III had his arch-rival, Duke Henri I de Guise, murdered by royal bodyguards (the king hid behind a tapestry). He had the duke's brother, the Cardinal de Guise, killed the next day. Henri III himself was murdered just eight months later by a vengeful monk. Period paintings chronicle the gruesome events.

In spring and summer, don't miss the nightly **son et lumière** (Sound & Light Show; ☑ 02 54 55 26 31; adult/child €8/5; ⊙ 10pm Apr, May & Sep, 10.30pm Jun-Aug), which brings the château's history and architecture to life with dramatic lighting and narration.

★ **Maison de la Magie**   MUSEUM
(www.maisondelamagie.fr; 1 place du Château; adult/child €9/5; ⊙ 10am-12.30pm & 2-6.30pm Apr-Aug, 2-6.30pm Mon-Fri, 10am-12.30pm & 2-6.30pm Sat & Sun Sep) Opposite the château you can't miss the former home of watchmaker, inventor and conjurer Jean Eugène Robert-Houdin (1805–71), whose name was later adopted by American magician Harry Houdini. Dragons emerge roaring from the windows on the hour, while the museum inside hosts daily **magic shows**, exhibits on the history of magic, displays of optical trickery and a short historical film about Houdini.

Old City   HISTORIC QUARTER
Despite serious damage by German attacks in 1940, Blois' old city is worth exploring, especially around 17th-century **Cathédrale St-Louis** (place St-Louis; ⊙ 9am-6pm), with its lovely multistoreyed bell tower, dramatically floodlit after dark. Most of the stained glass inside was installed by Dutch artist Jan Dibberts in 2000.

Across the square, the façade of **Maison des Acrobates** (3bis place St-Louis) – one of the few 15th-century houses to survive – is decorated with wooden sculptures of medieval farces. Another example around the corner at No 13 rue Pierre de Blois is called **Hôtel de Villebrême**.

Lovely panoramas unfold across town from the peaceful **Jardins de l'Évêché** and the top of the **Escalier Denis Papin**.

Fondation du Doute   ART MUSEUM
(www.fondationdudoute.fr; 6 rue Franciade; adult/child €7/3, joint tickets available with château & Maison de la Magie; ⊙ 2-6.30pm Tue-Sun Jun-Aug, shorter hours rest of year) This slick contemporary art museum, opened in 2013, includes rotating exhibitions of emerging and international artists, and a cafe.

☞ Tours

The tourist office offers **walking tour** brochures (€2) and guided French-language tours. Château guides run 1½-hour French-language city tours (€5/3 per adult/child). There's an English-language tour on Friday in July and August.

Carriage Rides   CARRIAGE RIDE
(☑ 02 54 87 57 62; www.attelagesdeblois.com; adult/child €7/4; ⊙ 2-6pm Apr-Jun & Sep, 11am-7pm Jul & Aug) Horse-drawn carriages clop around town from the château's main gate.

ⓘ LE PASS CHÂTEAUX

Many of the châteaux in the Blésois are covered by Le Pass Châteaux, multi-site discount tickets. For information, contact the tourist offices in Blois, Cheverny and Chambord. Below are some popular combinations; additional combos include smaller châteaux at Villesavin and Troussay.

➡ Blois–Chambord–Cheverny €28

➡ Blois–Chenonceau–Chambord–Cheverny €39

➡ Blois–Chaumont–Chambord–Cheverny €36.80

➡ Blois–Chambord–Amboise–Clos Lucé €42

➡ Chambord–Cheverny–Beauregard €29.50

Observatoire Loire
BOAT TRIPS

(☑ 02 54 56 09 24; www.observatoireloire.fr; 4 rue Vauvert; adult/child €9.50/7; ⊙ May-Sep) Sets out from the Blois quayside aboard a traditional *futreau* (flat-bottomed barge).

 Sleeping

★ Côté Loire
HOTEL €

(☑ 02 54 78 07 86; www.coteloire.com; 2 place de la Grève; r €59-95; ☎) Spotless rooms come in cheery checks, bright pastels and the odd bit of exposed brick; some have Loire views. Breakfast (€10.50) is served on a quaint interior wooden deck, and the restaurant (*menus* €21 to €31) dishes up delicious local cuisine. Find it a block off the river, southwest of Pont Jacques Gabriel.

Hôtel Anne de Bretagne
HOTEL €

(☑ 02 54 78 05 38; www.hotelannedebretagne.com; 31 av du Dr Jean Laigret; s €47, d €56-60, q €85; ☎) This creeper-covered hotel three blocks east of the train station has friendly staff and a bar full of polished wood and vintage pictures. Brightly coloured rooms have flowery wallpaper and bold bedspreads.

Le Monarque
HOTEL €

(☑ 02 54 78 02 35; www.hotel-lemonarque.com; 61 rue Porte Chartraine; s €47, d €60-67, q €85-87; ❄ ☎) Modern and no-nonsense, this hotel sits at the edge of the old city, and offers comfort, cleanliness and a restaurant.

RV Parking
CAMPGROUND €

(☑ 02 54 70 58 30) Contact the tourist office about its RV parking: one near the castle has power, waste disposal and showers (€5).

Les Salamandres
B&B €

(☑ 02 54 20 69 55; www.salamandres.fr; 1 rue de St-Dyé, Montlivault; r incl breakfast €59-75) To get off the beaten path, head to the quaint village of Montlivault, 12km northeast of Blois, on the southern bank of the Loire, and shack up in a family-owned cheery *chambre d'hôte* (B&B) just a hop, skip and jump from Chambord. In an 18th-century wine estate, Martine and Jean-Claude offer simple, homey rooms and loads of regional knowledge. You'll need your own wheels to get there, though.

★ La Maison de Thomas
B&B €€

(☑ 02 54 46 12 10; www.lamaisondethomas.fr; 12 rue Beauvoir; r incl breakfast €90; ☎) Four spacious rooms and a friendly welcome await travellers at this beautiful B&B on a pedestrianised street halfway between the château and the cathedral. There's bike storage in the interior

courtyard and a wine cellar where you can sample local vintages.

✕ Eating

Le Coup de Fourchette
BISTRO €

(☑ 02 54 55 00 24; 15 Quai de la Saussaye; lunch/dinner menus €12/17; ⊙ noon-2pm Mon-Sat, 7-10pm Thu-Sat) Simple, delectable regional cuisine is dished up with a smile in this mod eatery with a few outdoor tables. Popular with locals, it offers some of Blois' best cheaper eats.

Les Planches
ITALIAN €

(☑ 02 54 55 08 00; 5 rue Grenier à Sel; mains €10-16; ⊙ noon-2pm & 7-10pm Mon-Sat) Tucked back in the old centre, on a sweet square with other nearby eating options, Les Planches is a Blois favourite for its wood-fired bruschetta, in the ground floor of a restored townhouse or out on the terrace.

Les Banquettes Rouges
FRENCH €€

(☑ 02 54 78 74 92; www.lesbanquettesrouges.com; 16 rue des Trois Marands; menus €17.50-32.50; ⊙ noon-2pm & 7-10pm Tue-Sat) Handwritten slate menus and wholesome food distinguish the 'Red Benches': pork with chorizo and rosemary, duck with lentils, and *fondant au chocolat* to top it off.

Au Bouchon Lyonnais
BOUCHON €€

(☑ 02 54 74 12 87; www.aubouchonlyonnais.com; 25 rue des Violettes; lunch/dinner menus €16/23; ⊙ noon-1.45pm & 7-9.30pm Tue-Sat) The food at this classic neighbourhood bistro is out of a Lyonnais cookbook: *andouillette* (sausage made from pigs' intestines), quenelles (pike dumplings), snails and *salade lyonnaise* (green salad with croutons, egg and bacon bits).

L'Orangerie
GASTRONOMIC €€€

(☑ 02 54 78 05 36; www.orangerie-du-chateau.fr; 1 av du Dr Jean Laigret; menus €35-80; ⊙ noon-1.30pm & 7-9pm Tue-Sat) This acclaimed eatery is cloud nine for connoisseurs of haute cuisine. Plates are artfully stacked (duck liver, langoustine, foie gras) and the sparkling salon would make Louis XIV envious. On summer nights, dine in the courtyard.

Self-Catering

Food Market
FOOD MARKET

(place Louis XXII; ⊙ 8am-1pm Tue, Thu & Sat) Blois' thrice-weekly market.

☕ Drinking & Nightlife

The best bars are in the old town, particularly on place Ave Maria and in the small alleys off rue Foulerie.

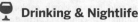

ℹ Information

Tourist Office (☎ 02 54 90 41 41; www.blois chambord.com; 23 place du Château; ☺9am-7pm Apr-Sep, to 5pm Oct-Mar) Helpful, and sells joint châteaux tickets. Download the Visit' Blois smartphone app.

ℹ Getting There & Away

BUS

Azalys (☎ 09 69 36 93 41; www.azalys-blois.fr; 2 place Victor Hugo; tickets €1.20; ☺8.30am-6.30pm Mon-Fri, 9.30am-12.30pm & 1.30-5pm Sat, closed Sat Jun Jul & Aug) Has a shuttle (€2, daily July and August, Saturday and Sunday April to June and September to October) from Blois train station to Blois' château and then to Cheverny (three daily) or Chaumont-sur-Loire (four daily).

TLC (☎ 02 54 58 55 44; www.tlcinfo.net) From April through August, TLC runs a château shuttle (line 18, €6) that offers as many stops as you like on a Blois–Chambord–Cheverny–Beauregard–Blois circuit. TLC also operates regular buses from Blois' train station (tickets €2 on board) to Chambord (line 3, 25 to 40 minutes, two Monday to Saturday) and Cheverny (line 4, 45 minutes, three Monday to Friday, one Saturday).

CAR

Car rental is available at the train station.

TRAIN

The **Blois-Chambord train station** (av Jean Laigret) is 600m uphill from Blois' château.

Amboise €7, 20 minutes, 10 daily

Orléans €11.20, 45 minutes, hourly

Paris' Gares d'Austerlitz and Montparnasse From €28.60, 1½ to two hours, 26 daily

Tours €10.90, 40 minutes, 13 daily

ℹ Getting Around

BICYCLE

The Châteaux à Vélo network offers 17 waymarked cycling routes in the Blois area. Maps available at tourist office.

Detours de Loire (☎ 02 54 56 07 73; www. detoursdeloire.com; 39 av Jean Laigret; per half-/full day €10/15; ☺9.30am-1pm & 3-6.30pm Mon-Sat, 9.30am-1pm & 5.30-6.30pm Sun May-Sep, shorter hours rest of year) Hire bikes near the train station; part of the valley's network.

BUS

Local buses in Blois and nearby communities, including Cheverny and Chambord, are run by Azalys. Buses run until about 8pm Monday to Saturday, with limited service on Sunday. Its **free shuttle** makes a circuit from the train station

around the centre, every 12 minutes, Monday to Saturday from 9am to 7.30pm.

TAXI

At the train station; call ☎ 02 54 78 07 65.

Château de Chambord

For full-blown château splendour, you can't top **Château de Chambord** (☎ information 02 54 50 40 00, tour & spectacle reservations 02 54 50 50 40; www.chambord.org; adult/child €11/9, parking €4; ☺9am-6pm Apr-Sep, 10am-5pm Oct-Mar), one of the crowning examples of French Renaissance architecture, and by far the largest, grandest and most visited château in the Loire Valley. Begun in 1519 as a weekend hunting lodge by François I, it quickly snowballed into one of the most ambitious (and expensive) architectural projects ever attempted by any French monarch. This cityscape of turrets, chimneys and lanterns crowns some 440 rooms, 365 fireplaces and 84 staircases, including a famous **double-helix staircase**, reputedly designed by the king's chum, Leonardo da Vinci.

Construction was repeatedly halted by financial problems, design setbacks and military commitments (not to mention the kidnapping of the king's two sons in Spain), and, ironically, when Chambord was finally finished 30-odd years later François found his elaborate palace too draughty, preferring the royal apartments in Amboise and Blois. He only stayed here for 42 days during his entire reign from 1515 to 1547.

Despite its apparent complexity, Chambord is laid out according to simple mathematical rules. Each section is arranged on a system of symmetrical grid squares around a Maltese cross. At the centre stands the rectangular keep, crossed by four great hallways, and at each corner stands one of the castle's four circular bastions. Through the centre of the **keep** winds the famous staircase, with two intertwining flights of stairs leading up to the great **lantern tower** and the castle's rooftop, from where you can gaze out across the landscaped grounds and marvel at the Tolkienesque jumble of cupolas, domes, chimneys and lightning rods.

The most interesting rooms are on the 1st floor, including the **king's and queen's chambers** (complete with interconnecting passages to enable late-night hijinks) and a wing devoted to the thwarted attempts of the Comte de Chambord to be crowned

Henri V after the fall of the Second Empire. On the 2nd floor the eerie **Museum of Hunting** exhibits copious displays of weapons and hunting trophies. On the ground floor, an interesting multilanguage film relates the history of the castle's construction.

In a place of such ostentatious grandeur, it's often the smallest things that are most interesting: look out for the display of hundreds of cast-iron keys, one for each door in the château.

It's worth picking up the multilingual audio or video guide (audio adult/child version €5/2.50, video €6), if only to avoid getting lost around the endless rooms and corridors. Several times daily there are **guided tours** (adult/child 1hr tours €5/3, 2hr tours €7/5) in English, and during school holidays costumed tours entertain the kids. Outdoor spectacles held in summer include a daily **equestrian show** (www.ecuries-chambord.com; adult/child €11/8; ◎May-Sep).

Domaine National de Chambord

This huge **hunting reserve** (the largest in Europe) stretches for 54 sq km around the château, and is reserved solely for the use of high-ranking French government personalities (though somehow it's difficult to imagine François Hollande astride a galloping stallion). About 10 sq km of the park is publicly accessible, with trails open to walkers, mountain bikers and horse riders.

Hire bikes at a **rental kiosk** (☑02 54 33 37 54; per hour/half-day €6/15; ◎10am-7pm Apr-Sep) near the *embarcadère* (jetty) on the River Cosson, where you can also rent boats. It's great for wildlife-spotting, especially in September and October during the deer mating season. Observation towers dot the park; set out at dawn or dusk to spot stags, boars and red deer.

Or, jump aboard a **Land Rover Safari tour** (☑02 54 50 50 40; adult/child €18/12; ◎Apr-Sep) conducted by French-speaking guides with an intimate knowledge of where to see the best wildlife.

ⓘ Getting There & Away

Chambord is 16km east of Blois, 45km southwest of Orléans and 17km northeast of Cheverny. The TLC shuttle on the Blois–Chambord–Cheverny–Beauregard–Blois circuit costs €6, takes 40 minutes from Blois, and runs mid-April to August.

Château de Cheverny

Thought by many to be the most perfectly proportioned château of all, **Château de Cheverny** (☑02 54 79 96 29; www.chateau-cheverny.fr; adult/child €9.50/6.50; ◎9am-7pm Apr-Sep, 10am-5pm Oct-Mar) represents the zenith of French classical architecture: the perfect blend of symmetry, geometry and aesthetic order. Since its construction between 1625 and 1634 by Jacques Hurault, an intendant to Louis XII, the castle has hardly been altered, and its interior decoration includes some of the most sumptuous furnishings, tapestries and objets d'art anywhere in the Loire Valley.

Tintin fans might find the château's façade oddly familiar: Hergé used it as a model (minus the two end towers) for Moulinsart (Marlinspike) Hall, the ancestral home of Tintin's irascible sidekick, Captain Haddock. A dynamic exhibition, **Les Secrets de Moulinsart** (combined ticket with château adult/child €14/9.90), explores the Tintin connections with recreated scenes, thunder and other special effects.

The interior of Château de Cheverny was designed by Jean Monier, known for his work on Luxembourg Palace for Queen Marie de Médicis. Highlights include a **formal dining room** with panels depicting the story of

---

SNACK BREAK

Need a moment to collect yourself between châteaux?

La Détente Gourmande (☑02 54 33 94 65; www.restaurant-chaumont-sur-loire.fr; 61 rue du Maréchal de Lattre de Tassigny; mains €7-13; ◎10.30am-9pm Wed-Sun Mar–mid-Oct) For a pleasant lunch break, stop in at La Détente Gourmande, halfway between Amboise and Blois, in the shadow of Château de Chaumont. Sample tasty treats like local charcuterie, cheeses and wines on a cheery terrace at this *salon de thé* (tearoom) and restaurant.

Max Vauché Chocolate Factory (☑02 54 46 07 96; www.maxvauche-chocolatier.com; 22 Les Jardins du Moulin, Bracieux; tours adult/child €4.40/3.50; ◎10am-12.30pm & 2-7pm Mon-Sat, 3-6.30pm Sun, closed Mon Sep-Jun) For a quick chocolate fix, head to sleepy Bracieux, 7km south of Château de Chaumont, where the Max Vauché chocolate factory offers tours and a taste test.

LA LEVRAUDIÈRE

Only 2km south of Château de Cheverny, amid 3 hectares of grassland, La Levraudière (02 54 79 81 99; www. lalevraudiere.fr; 1 chemin de la Levraudière; s/d/tr/q from €70/80/95/140) is a perfect blend of farm and modern style. In a peaceful, renovated 19th-century farmhouse, the B&B has a slab-like wooden table for breakfasts featuring fabulous homemade jams. But the crisp linens and meticulously kept house are the opposite of roughing it.

Don Quixote, the king's chamber with murals relating stories from Greek mythology, a bridal chamber and children's playroom (complete with Napoléon III–era toys). The guards' room is full of pikestaffs, claymores and suits of armour – including a tiny one fit for a kid.

The Hurault family has owned (and inhabited) the castle for the last six centuries and their fabulous art collection includes a portrait of Jeanne of Aragon by Raphael's studio, an 18th-century De la Tour pastel, and a who's who of court painters. Keep your eyes open for the certificate signed by US president George Washington. Behind the main château, the 18th-century orangerie (where many priceless artworks, including the Mona Lisa, were stashed during WWII) is now a tearoom.

Near the château's gateway, the kennels house pedigreed French pointer/English foxhound hunting dogs still used by the owners of Cheverny. Feeding time, known as the Soupe des Chiens, takes place daily at 5pm April to September and 3pm Monday, Wednesday, Thursday and Friday, October to March.

ℹ Getting There & Away

Cheverny is on the D102, 16km southeast of Blois and 17km southwest of Chambord. Azalys' Blois shuttle (p379) is €2 and takes 30 minutes. The TLC shuttle on the Blois–Chambord–Cheverny–Beauregard–Blois circuit costs €6, takes one hour from Blois, and runs mid-April to August.

Château de Chaumont

Set on a defensible bluff with sweeping views along the Loire, Château de Chaumont-sur-Loire (02 54 20 99 22; www.domaine-chaumont. fr; adult/child €10.50/6.50, with gardens €16/11;

10am-6.30pm Apr-Sep, to 6pm Oct-Mar) presents an elegantly streamlined medieval face, with its cylindrical corner turrets and sturdy drawbridge, though its interior furnishings date almost exclusively from the 19th century. At least two earlier fortresses occupied the site (whose name derives from Chauve Mont, 'Bald Hill'), but the main construction for the present château began around 1465 under Pierre d'Amboise.

Visit Chaumont's elaborate gardens independently or with the château; they're at their finest during the annual Festival International des Jardins (International Garden Festival; adult/child €12/7.50; 10am-7pm late Apr-Oct).

Originally a strictly defensive fortress, Chaumont-sur-Loire became a short-lived residence for Catherine de Médicis following the death of Henri II in 1560, and later passed into the hands of Diane de Poitiers (Henri II's mistress), who was forced by Catherine to swap the altogether grander surroundings of Chenonceau for Chaumont. Savvy Diane used Chaumont's vast landholdings, but there is no evidence she ever lived in the castle.

In the second half of the 18th century, its owner, Jacques-Donatien Le Ray, a supporter of the American Revolution and an intimate of Benjamin Franklin, had the decrepit north wing removed. In 1875, Princess de Broglie, heiress to the Say sugar fortune, bought the château and thoroughly renovated and furnished it. The most impressive room is the council chamber, with its original majolica-tiled floor, plundered from a palace in Palermo. Also, don't miss the écuries (stables), built in 1877 to house the Broglies' horses in sumptuous style. A fine collection of vintage carriages and equestrian gear is displayed inside.

It's worth getting the informative multimedia guide (€4) or downloading the app.

ℹ Getting There & Away

Chaumont-sur-Loire is 17km southwest of Blois. Onzain, a 2.5km walk from Chaumont across the Loire, has trains to Blois (€3.60, 10 minutes, 13 daily) and Tours (€8.60, 30 minutes, 10 daily). An Azalys (p379) shuttle runs from Blois.

Château de Beauregard

Less visited than its sister châteaux, peaceful Château de Beauregard (02 54 70 41 65; www.beauregard-loire.com; Cellettes; adult/child €12.50/5; 10.30am-6.30pm Apr-Sep, 1.30-5pm Mon-Fri, from 10.30am Sat & Sun mid-Feb–Mar & Oct–mid-Nov) has charms all its own. Built as

Châteaux of the Loire Valley

French history is written across the landscape of the Loire. Every castle traces a tale: of wars won and lost, romances embarked upon or destroyed, alliances forged and enemies vanquished. From the shockingly grand to the quietly subdued, there should be a castle to match your own mood.

Chambord

Château de Chambord (p379) gets all the hype for a reason: it's stunning. Visit in the early morning to see it rise, all towers and turrets, from the mist – just as it would have done during the days of François I.

Chenonceau

Like an elegant lady, **Château de Chenonceau** (p389) effortlessly occupies its beautiful surroundings. The impressive arches that span the calm Cher River draw you in, while the exquisite decor and the fascinating history keep you captivated.

Langeais

Over the centuries châteaux change hands and alterations are made... But in the case of **Langeais** (p393), the details are intact. The 10th-century keep and the intricate medieval interior take you to a time of valiant knights and mysterious ladies.

Azay-le-Rideau

A cypress-lined drive leads to this comparatively discreet and certainly romantic **château** (p394) beautifully reflected in its still, broad moat. Fantastic views of the castle from the lush park are lit up at night.

Angers

Whether for its distinctive black stone and watchtowers or for its mind-blowing medieval Apocalypse tapestry, **Château d'Angers** (p404) stands out from the crowd. The forbidding city-centre fortress, home to the powerful dukes of Anjou, hides a fascinating journey into history.

1. Château d'Azay-le-Rideau p394 2. Château de Chambord p379
3. Château de Chenonceau p389 4. Château de Langeais p393

yet another hunting lodge by François I, the highlight is an amazing **portrait gallery** depicting 327 notables of European royalty, clergy and intelligentsia. Spot famous faces including Christopher Columbus, Sir Francis Drake, Cardinal Richelieu, Catherine de Médicis, Anne de Bretagne, Henry VIII of England and his doomed wife Anne Boleyn, and every French king since Philippe VI. The quiet, 40-hectare grounds encompass numerous **gardens**, including the Garden of Portraits with 12 colour variations.

TLC's line 18 château shuttle from Blois, 8km southeast, serves Beauregard.

TOURAINE

Often dubbed the 'Garden of France', the Touraine region is famous for its rich food, tasty cheeses and notoriously pure French accent, as well as a smattering of glorious châteaux: some medieval (Langeais and Loches), others Renaissance (Azay-le-Rideau, Villandry and Chenonceau). The vibrant capital, Tours, offers loads of castle tours and transportation links.

Tours

POP 138,115

Bustling Tours has a zinging life of its own in addition to being one of the hubs of castle country. It's a smart, vivacious kind of place, with an impressive medieval centre, parks and a busy university of some 25,000 students. Hovering somewhere between the style of Paris and the conservative sturdiness of central France, Tours makes a useful staging post for exploring the Touraine.

⊙ Sights & Activities

The old city encircles place Plumereau (locally known as place Plum), about 400m west of rue Nationale.

★**Musée des Beaux-Arts**   ART MUSEUM
(☑02 47 05 68 82; www.mba.tours.fr; 18 place François Sicard; adult/child €5/2.50, 1st Sun of the month free; ⊙9am-12.45pm & 2-6pm Wed-Mon) This fine-arts museum in the archbishop's gorgeous 18th-century palace encircles free gardens and Gallo-Roman ruins, and flaunts grand rooms with works spanning several centuries. Highlights include paintings by Delacroix, Degas and Monet, a rare Rembrandt miniature and a Rubens *Madonna and Child*.

★**Cathédrale St-Gatien**   CHURCH
(place de la Cathédrale; ⊙9am-7pm) With its twin towers, flying buttresses, dazzling stained glass and gargoyles, this cathedral is a show-stopper. The interior dates from the 13th to 16th centuries, and signs in English explain the intricate stained glass. The domed tops of the two 70m-high towers are Renaissance. On the north side is the **Cloître de la Psalette** (adult/child €3/free; ⊙9.30am-12.30pm & 2-6pm Mon-Sat, 2-6pm Sun, closed Mon & Tue Oct-Mar), built from 1442 to 1524.

★**Musée du Compagnonnage**   MUSEUM
(☑02 47 21 62 20; www.museecompagnonnage.fr; 8 rue Nationale; adult/child €5.30/3.70; ⊙9am-12.30pm & 2-6pm, closed Tue mid-Sep–mid-Jun) France has long prided itself on its *compagnonnages,* guild organisations of skilled craftspeople who have been responsible for everything from medieval cathedrals to the Statue of Liberty. Dozens of professions – from pastry chefs to locksmiths – are celebrated here through impressive displays of their handiwork: exquisitely carved chests, handmade tools, booby-trapped locks, vintage barrels, outlandishly ornate cakes and more.

★**Basilique St-Martin**   CHURCH
(www.basiliquesaintmartin.fr; ⊙7.30am-7pm, to 9pm Jul & Aug) Tours was an important pilgrimage city thanks to soldier-turned-evangelist St Martin (c 317–97), bishop of Tours. In the 5th century a basilica was constructed above his tomb, and was later replaced by a 13th-century Romanesque one, but today only the **Tour Charlemagne** and **Tour de l'Horloge** (Clock Tower) remain. The current church was built in 1862 to house his relics, while the small **Musée St-Martin** (☑02 47 64 48 87; www.mba.tours.fr; 3 rue Rapin; adult/child €2/1; ⊙9.30am-1pm & 2-5pm Wed-Sun mid-Mar–mid-Nov) displays artefacts relating to the lost churches and the life of St Martin.

Jardin Botanique   GARDEN
(bd Tonnelle; ⊙7.45am-sunset) Tours' public parks include the 19th-century 5-hectare botanic garden with a tropical greenhouse, medicinal herb garden and petting zoo. Find it 1.6km west of place Jean Jaurès; bus 4 along bd Béranger stops nearby.

Maison des Vins   WINE TASTING
(☑02 47 60 55 21; www.vinsvaldeloire.fr; 25 rue du Grand Maré; ⊙10.30am-1pm & 3-7pm Tue-Sat) Get the lowdown on Loire vintages: tasting, sales, tours and tips.

Tours

Tours is one of the major hubs for châteaux tours (p367). The tourist office has a self-guided tour brochure, and leads **guided walks** (€6 to €9) in French. They recommend a free app through www.monument-tracker.com.

Carriages   CARRIAGE RIDE
(☑ 02 47 66 70 70; www.filbleu.fr; rides €1.40; ☉ 10am, 11am, 3pm, 4pm & 5pm Tue-Sat, 3pm, 4pm & 5pm Sun May-Sep) Fifty-minute rides from place François Sicard near the cathedral. Drivers sell tickets.

Sleeping

★ Hôtel Ronsard   BOUTIQUE HOTEL €
(☑ 02 47 05 25 36; www.hotel-ronsard.com; 2 rue Pimbert; s €63-77, d €73-85; ✸@✿) Pass beyond the bland exterior at this centrally located modern hotel and find easy comfort and good value. Halls are lined with colourful photographs, while sleek, immaculate rooms incorporate muted tones of grey with sparkling white linens.

Hôtel Colbert   HOTEL €
(☑ 02 47 66 61 56; www.tours-hotel-colbert.fr; 78 rue Colbert; s €42-57, d €60-68; ✿) In the heart of Tours' pedestrianised restaurant row, this family-run hotel offers a welcoming haven. Light sleepers should opt for 'Calme' rooms facing the quieter inner courtyard (which also doubles as a pleasant spot to relax, or park bikes overnight).

Hôtel Mondial   HOTEL €
(☑ 02 47 05 62 68; www.hotelmondialtours.com; 3 place de la Résistance; s €60-70, d €65-80; ✿) Overlooking place de la Résistance, this hotel boasts a fantastic city-centre position, with modernised, metropolitan rooms in funky greys, browns and scarlets. Reception is on the 2nd floor; no lift.

Hôtel Val de Loire   HOTEL €
(☑ 02 47 05 37 86; www.hotelvaldeloire.fr; 33 bd Heurteloup; s with/without bathroom from €52/40, d with/without bathroom from €78/45; ✿) Friendly management and bright rooms blending antiques and modern touches make this an excellent train station choice. Nicer back rooms downstairs have high ceilings and garden views, while less expensive top-floor rooms are tucked under eaves.

Hôtel des Arts   HOTEL €
(☑ 02 47 05 05 00; www.hoteldesartstours.com; 40 rue de la Préfecture; s €35-49, d €40-54; ✿) A sweet place, with charming management,

LOIRE VALLEY FOR KIDS

➡ Be razzle-dazzled by magic and illusion at Maison de la Magie (p377) in Blois.

➡ Prowl through ancient cave dwellings near Saumur and Doué-la-Fontaine (p402).

➡ Celebrate comic book character Tintin with cracks of lightning and pounding thunder at Château de Cheverny (p380).

➡ Play in the parks around pointy Pagode de Chanteloup (p392) at Amboise.

➡ Book ahead for amazing horse acrobatics at Saumur's semi-monthly Cadre Noir public presentations (p399).

Hôtel des Arts has tiny but fastidious, cheery rooms in oranges and siennas. Get one with a balcony for extra light.

★ Hôtel l'Adresse   BOUTIQUE HOTEL €€
(☑ 02 47 20 85 76; www.hotel-ladresse.com; 12 rue de la Rôtisserie; s €55, d €78-105; ✸✿) Looking for Parisian style in provincial Tours? You're in luck. On a walking street in the old quarter lies a boutique find, with rooms finished in slates, creams and ochres, topped off with flat-screen TVs, designer sinks and reclaimed rafters. Best are ones with windows over the medieval street.

Hôtel de l'Univers   HOTEL €€€
(☑ 02 47 05 37 12; www.oceaniahotels.com/hotel-lunivers-tours; 5 bd Heurteloup; d €200-245; ✸@✿) Everyone from Ernest Hemingway to Édith Piaf has bunked at the Universe over its 150-year history. Enjoy the frescoed lobby balcony and appropriately glitzy rooms. Online discounts.

Eating

Pedestrianised rue Colbert is a great place to peruse your options: from classic French to Asian and Middle Eastern. The area around place Plumereau is crammed with cheap eats, although quality varies.

★ Le Zinc   FRENCH €
(☑ 02 47 20 29 00; lezinc37@gmail.com; 27 place du Grand Marché; menus €20; ☉ noon-2pm Tue & Thu-Sat, 7.30-10pm Thu-Tue, to 11pm Fri & Sat) More concerned with market-fresh staples (sourced from the nearby Halles) than with Michelin-star cachet, this bistro impresses with its authentic, well-presented country classics (duck breast, beef fillet, river fish).

THE LOIRE VALLEY

Tours

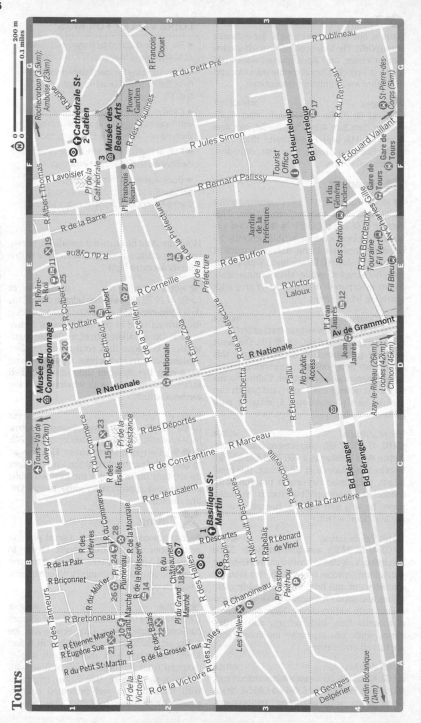

200 m
0.1 miles

Rochecorbon (3.5km);
Amboise (23km)

R François Clouet

R du Petit Pré

R des Ursulines

R Dublineau

R du Rempart

St-Pierre-des-
Corps (5km)

Cathédrale St-
Gatien 2

Musée des
Beaux-Arts

5

Musée de la
Cathédrale 3

R Jules Simon

Bd Heurteloup

17

R Édouard Vaillant

Gare de
Tours

R Albert-Thomas

R Lavoisier

Pl de la
Cathédrale

Pl François
Sicard

9

R Bernard Palissy

Tourist
Office

Pl du
Général
Leclerc

Gille
Fil Vert
AV Charles

Fil Bleu

R de la Barre

R du Cygne

R de la Préfecture

13

Jardin
de la
Préfecture

R de Buffon

Bus Station

R de Bordeaux
Touraine

Pl Foire-
le-Roi

19
11

25

R Colbert

R Pimbert

R Corneille

Pl de la
Préfecture

R Victor
Laloux

12

Musée du
Compagnonnage 4

20

R Voltaire

16

R Berthelot

27

R de la Scellerie

R Émile Zola

R Nationale

Pl Jean
Jaurès

Av de Grammont

R Nationale

R Nationale

R de la Préfecture

R Gambetta

R Étienne Pallu

No Public
Access

Jean
Jaurès

Azay-le-Rideau (26km);
Loches (42km);
Chinon (46km)

Tours-Val de
Loire (12km)

R du Commerce

23

Pl de la
Résistance

R des Déportés

R Marceau

Bd Béranger

15

R des
Fusillés

R de Constantine

Bd Béranger

R des Orfèvres

R du Commerce

28

Pl 24

Plumereau

R de la Monnaie

R de Jérusalem

Basilique St-
Martin 1

R Descartes

R de Clocheville

R de la Grandière

R de la Paix

R du Mûrier

26

R de la Rôtisserie

R du
Châteauneuf

7

R Néricault Destouches

R Rabelais

R Léonard
de Vinci

R Briçonnet

14

Pl du Grand
Marché

18

R des Halles

8

6

R Rapin

R des Tanneurs

R Bretonneau

R du Grand Marché

Pl Gaston
Pailhou

R Chanoineau

Les Halles

R Étienne Marcel

21

10

R Eugène Sue

R des Balais

22

Pl de la
Victoire

R du Petit St-Martin

R de la Grosse Tour

Pl des Halles

R de la Victoire

R Georges
Delpérier

Jardin Botanique
(1km)

Tours

Tartines & Co CAFE €
(☑ 02 47 20 50 60; www.tartinesandco.com; 6 rue des Fusillés; sandwiches €10-13; ⊙ 11.45am-3pm & 7.15-10pm Tue-Sat) This snazzy little cafe reinvents the traditional *croque* (toasted sandwich) amid jazz and friendly chatter. Choose your topping (chicken, roasted veg, beef carpaccio, foie gras with artichokes) on toasted artisanal bread.

★**Cap Sud** BISTRO €€
(☑ 02 47 05 24 81; www.capsudrestaurant.fr; 88 rue Colbert; menus lunch €14-19, dinner €26; ⊙ noon-1.30pm & 7.15-9.30pm Tue-Sat) The hot-rod red interior combines nicely with genial service and refined culinary creations made from the freshest ingredients. Expect stylishly presented dishes such as warm St-Maure cheese

with a pistachio-herb crumble and baby vegetables, or mullet fillet with sweet peppers, squid risotto and a ginger-tomato emulsion. Reserve ahead.

★**L'Arôme** MODERN FRENCH €€
(☑ 02 47 05 99 81; larome.tours@yahoo.fr; 26 rue Colbert; menus lunch €13, 3-course dinner €24-41; ⊙ noon-1.30pm & 7.30-9.30pm Tue-Sat) One of Tours' most popular new spots, L'Arôme fills with lucky locals (they've reserved ahead) who come for the vivacious modern ambience and creative dishes, smack in the centre of town. Great wine selection too.

L'Atelier Gourmand MODERN FRENCH €€
(☑ 02 47 38 59 87; www.lateliergourmand.fr; 37 rue Étienne Marcel; lunch/dinner menus €13/25; ⊙ noon-2pm Tue-Fri, 7.30-10.30pm Mon-Sat) The puce-and-silver colour scheme is straight out of a Bret Easton Ellis novel, and everything's delivered with a modern spin. Many dishes feature intriguing blends of the sweet and savory, like pastis-flambéed prawns with sweet pea and mint risotto.

Barju SEAFOOD €€€
(☑ 02 47 64 91 12; www.barju.fr; 15 rue de Change; menus lunch €20-25, dinner €55; ⊙ noon-1.30pm & 7.30-9.30pm Tue-Sat) Lunch can be a super deal, but dinner is a more formal affair at this restaurant – a high-end date spot. Served with a smile in bright, contemporary rooms, the standout is the 'picque-nique' tasting menu with its continuous series of imaginative often seafood-based creations.

Self-Catering

Les Halles FOOD MARKET
(www.halles-de-tours.com; place Gaston Paithou; ⊙ 7am-7.30pm Mon-Sat, 8am-1pm Sun) Big daily covered market.

🍷 Drinking & Nightlife

Place Plumereau and surrounding streets are loaded with drinking dens, which get stuffed to bursting on hot summer nights.

Pale PUB
(cnr rue Colbert & place Foire-le-Roi; ⊙ noon-2am Tue-Sat, to midnight Sun; 🖎) This quintessential lively Irish pub, with a plethora of beers on tap, spills out onto tables in a small park and along pedestrianised rue Colbert, day and night.

L'Alexandra BAR
(106 rue du Commerce; ⊙ 3pm-2am; 🖎) Popular bar crammed with students and late-night boozers.

Excalibur CLUB
(📞 02 47 64 76 78; www.facebook.com/excalibur.
tours; 35 rue Briçonnet; ⊙ midnight-6am Tue-Sat)
Hot-and-heavy club in a converted ecclesiastical building.

☆ Entertainment

Get the low-down from free monthly *Tours.
infos* (www.tours.fr), available around town.

Les Trois Orfèvres LIVE MUSIC
(📞 02 47 64 02 73; 3orfevres.com; 6 rue des Orfèvres;
⊙ midnight-6am Wed-Sat) Grungy nightspot in
the heart of the medieval quarter, where DJs
and bands lean towards alternative and indie,
and students hang out in force.

Grand Théâtre PERFORMING ARTS
(📞 02 47 60 20 20; www.operadetours.fr; 34 rue de
la Scellerie; ⊙ box office 10am-noon & 1-5.45pm Tue-
Sat) Hosts operas, symphonies, chamber music and other concerts.

❶ Information

Police Station (📞 02 47 33 80 69; 70-72 rue
Marceau; ⊙ 24hr)

SOS Médecins (📞 02 47 38 33 33) Phone advice
for medical emergencies.

Tourist Office (📞 02 47 70 37 37; www.
tours-tourisme.fr; 78-82 rue Bernard Palissy;
⊙ 8.30am-7pm Mon-Sat, 10am-12.30pm & 2.30-
5pm Sun Apr-Sep, shorter hours rest of year)
Abundant info; slightly reduced châteaux tickets.

❶ Getting There & Away

AIR

Tours Val de Loire Airport (TUF; 📞 02 47 49
37 00; www.tours.aeroport.fr) Tours Val de Loire
Airport, about 5km northeast of town, is linked
to London's Stansted, Dublin (Ireland), Marseille,
Marrakesh (Morocco) and Porto (Portugal) by
Ryanair, and to Southampton (England) by Flybe.

BUS

The bus station is located next to the train station.

Touraine Fil Vert (📞 02 47 31 14 00; www.
tourainefilvert.com; single ticket €2.20; ⊙ 8am-
6.15pm Mon-Fri, 10am-1pm &1.30-5pm Sat)
Touraine Fil Vert operates regional buses from
the bus station. Destinations in the Indre-et-Loire
département include Amboise (40 minutes, 10
daily Monday to Saturday) and Chenonceau (1¼
hours, one daily), both served by line C.

CAR & MOTORCYCLE

Tours' perplexing one-way streets make driving
a headache: park your car. Use an **underground
garage** (per 24hr €11) such as the one below Les
Halles, for stays of more than two hours. Check

opening hours for the garage you choose; many
are reduced on Sunday.

Avis (📞 02 47 20 53 27; central train station;
⊙ 8am-12.30pm & 1.30-6pm Mon-Fri, 9am-noon
& 2-6pm Sat) Also has locations at St-Pierre-
des-Corps TGV station and the airport.

TRAIN

Tours is the Loire Valley's main rail hub. Regular trains serve Tours Centre station and TGV
trains serve St-Pierre-des-Corps, 4km east and
linked to Tours by frequent shuttle trains. Some
destinations, like Paris, Angers and Orléans, are
served by both stations.

Tours Centre services include:

Amboise €5.60, 20 minutes, 13 daily

Angers €19, one to 1½ hours, five daily

Blois €10.90, 40 minutes, 13 daily

Chenonceaux €6.80, 25 minutes, 10 daily

Loches €9.40, one hour, one or two trains plus
several SNCF buses daily

Orléans €20.10, 1¼ hours, hourly

Paris' Gare d'Austerlitz €35, two to 2¾ hours,
five daily (slow trains)

Paris' Gare Montparnasse €46 to €68, 1¼
hours, eight daily (high-speed TGVs)

Saumur €12, 45 minutes, 10 daily

St-Pierre-des-Corps TGV trains include:

Bordeaux €52, 2¾ hours

La Rochelle €41, 2¼ hours

Nantes €29, 1½ hours

Paris' Gare Montparnasse €46 to €68, one
hour

❶ Getting Around

TO/FROM THE AIRPORT

Keolis Touraine (Alphacars; 📞 02 47 44 00 00;
www.keolis-touraine.fr) Keolis Touraine runs
a shuttle bus (€6.50, 20 to 30 minutes) from
Tours' train station to the airport two hours
before departing flights, and from the airport to
the station 30 minutes after arriving flights.

BICYCLE

Détours de Loire (📞 02 47 61 22 23; www.
locationdevelos.com; 35 rue Charles Gille; per
day/week €15/60; ⊙ 9am-1pm & 2-7pm Mon-
Sat, 9.30am-12.30pm & 6-7pm Sun May-Sep)
Part of Loire à Vélo network.

BUS & TRAM

Fil Bleu (📞 02 47 66 70 70; www.filbleu.fr; 9
rue Michelet; single/day ticket €1.40/3.70;
⊙ 7.30am-7pm Mon-Fri, 10am-5pm Sat) Many
local buses and the tram, run by Fil Bleu, stop
near place Jean-Jaurès. Most lines run until
about 8.30pm; several night buses run until
about 1am. Service is reduced Sunday There's
an information office with maps and schedules
near the train station.

Rochecorbon & Vouvray

Renowned chenin blanc vineyards carpet the area around Rochecorbon, Vouvray (population 3180) and Montlouis-sur-Loire, 10km east of Tours, and wine cellars sprinkle the region. The **tourist office** (☑ 02 47 52 68 73; www.tourismevouvray-valdeloire.com; 12 rue Rabelais; ⊙ 9.30am-1pm & 2-6.30pm Mon-Sat, 9.30am-12.30pm Sun May-Sep, closed Sun & Mon Oct-Apr) in Vouvray has a list.

🏃 Sights & Activities

Château de Moncontour   WINERY
(☑ 02 47 52 60 77; www.moncontour.com; D952, btwn Rochecorbon & Vouvray; ⊙ 9am-12.30pm & 1.30-7pm Mon-Fri, 10am-2.30pm & 2.30-7pm Sat & Sun, shorter hours mid-Sep–Mar) Has a small wine museum and also does tastings.

Cave des Producteurs
de Vouvray   WINE TASTING
(☑ 02 47 52 75 03; www.cavedevouvray.com; 38 la Vallée Coquette; ⊙ 9am-7pm mid-May–mid-Sep, closed midday rest of year) Stop in at Cave des Producteurs de Vouvray for a tour and tasting.

Naviloire   BOAT TOUR
(☑ 02 47 52 68 88; www.naviloire.com; Rochecorbon; adult/child €9.50/7; ⊙ Apr-Nov) Offers one of the few boat cruises on the Loire proper, in a 66-seat boat departing from Rochecorbon to wild islets and nature reserves

ℹ Getting There & Away

Fil Bleu bus 54 links Tours' riverside place Anatole France with Vouvray (€1.40, 20 minutes, 10 daily), or take Fil Vert's bus A.

Château de Chenonceau

Spanning the languid Cher River via a series of supremely graceful arches, the **Château de Chenonceau** (☑ 02 47 23 90 07; www.chenonceau.com; adult/child €12.50/9.50, with audioguide €17/13.50; ⊙ 9am-7pm Apr-Sep, shorter hours rest of year) is one of the most elegant and unusual in the Loire Valley. You can't help but be swept up in the magical architecture, the fascinating history of prominent female owners, the glorious setting and the formal gardens and landscaped parkland.

The château's interior is crammed with wonderful furniture and tapestries, stunning original tiled floors and a fabulous **art collection** including works by Tintoretto, Correggio, Rubens, Murillo, Van Dyck and Ribera. This architectural fantasy land is largely the work

WORTH A TRIP

CAVES MONMOUSSEAU

Sitting quietly under a dramatic 12th-century donjon (keep), Montrichard, 9km east of Chenonceau, offers a fizzy pit stop. Just outside town, the 15km-long **Caves Monmousseau** (☑ 02 54 71 66 64; www.monmousseau. com; 71 rte de Vierzon; ⊙ 10am-12.30pm & 1.30-6pm Apr–mid-Nov, 10am-noon & 2-5pm Mon-Fri mid-Nov–Mar) are carved into the tufa stone: a perfect 12°C environment for the local crémant (sparkling wine). A 45-minute tour (adult/child €3.50/free) explains winemaking methods and ends with a tasting.

of several remarkable women (hence its alternative name, Le Château des Dames: 'Ladies' Château'). The initial phase of construction started in 1515 for Thomas Bohier, a court minister of King Charles VIII, although much of the work and design was actually overseen by his wife, Katherine Briçonnet.

The château's distinctive arches and one of the formal gardens were added by Diane de Poitiers, mistress of King Henri II. Following Henri's death, Diane was forced to exchange Chenonceau for the rather less grand château of Chaumont by the king's scheming widow, Catherine de Médicis, who completed the construction and added the huge yew-tree **labyrinth** and the western rose garden. Louise of Lorraine's most interesting contribution was her **mourning room**, on the top floor, all in black, to which she retreated when her husband, Henri III, was assassinated.

Chenonceau had an 18th-century heyday under the aristocratic Madame Dupin, who made the château a centre of fashionable society and attracted guests including Voltaire and Rousseau. Legend also has it that it was she who single-handedly saved the château from destruction during the Revolution, thanks to her popularity with local villagers.

The pièce de résistance is the 60m-long window-lined **Grande Gallerie** spanning the Cher, scene of many a wild party hosted by Catherine de Médicis or Madame Dupin. During WWII the Cher also marked the boundary between free and occupied France; local legend has it that the Grand Gallery was used as the escape route for many refugees fleeing the Nazi occupation.

The top floor of the gallery has a superb **exhibition** illustrating the château's history.

LOCAL KNOWLEDGE

TOP LOIRE VALLEY WINES

Olivier Thibault merrily runs the excellent bistro Le Pot de Lapin (p401) in Saumur, dispensing delicious treats alongside a vast range of carefully curated wines. While he refuses to comment on who the top wine producers are in his nearby Saumur-Champigny area (too easy to make enemies!), he happily shares his favourites from elsewhere in the Loire. Look out for them on menus or in tasting rooms.

Domaine Philippe Gilbert (www.domainephilippegilbert.fr; Menetou-Salon) Excellent AOC (Appellation d'Origine Contrôlée) Menetou-Salon reds and whites from biodynamic *terroir* (land) north of Bourges.

Château Pierre-Bise (☑ 02 41 78 31 44; Beaulieu-sur-Layon) Claude Papin makes top Coteaux du Layon sweet whites, and Savenièrres and Anjou AOCs at his family's winery south of Angers.

Domaine de Bablut (www.vignobles-daviau.fr; Brissac-Quincé) Christophe Daviau produces superb organic reds under the Anjou Villages Brissac AOC.

Domaine Jaulin Plaisantin (www.jaulinplaisantin.com; Cravant-les-Côteaux) Top organic AOC Chinon by Yves Plaisantin and Sébastien Jaulin, 8km southeast of Chinon town.

Mikaël Bouges (☑ 02 54 32 79 25; michael.bouges@wanadoo.fr; Faverolles-sur-Cher) Organic Touraine AOC, from sparkling white and rosé to red, by a young vintner 3km south of Montrichard.

Chenonceau's smartphone app gives general background only; the audioguide is better.

Skip the drab wax museum and instead visit the **gardens**: it seems as if there's one of every kind imaginable (maze, English, vegetable, playground, flower...). In July and August the illuminated grounds are open for the **Promenade Nocturne** (adult/child €6/free; ☻9.30-11.30pm).

Croisières Fluviales La Bélandre (☑02 47 23 98 64; www.labelandre.com; adult/child €9.50/6.50; ☻Apr-Oct) offers 50-minute boat trips along the Cher River in summer, passing directly beneath the château's arches.

❶ Getting There & Away

The château is located 34km east of Tours, 10km southeast of Amboise and 40km southwest of Blois. From Chenonceaux, the town just outside the château grounds (spelled with an 'x', unlike the château!), 10 daily trains run to Tours (€6.50, 24 minutes). Touraine Fil Vert's bus line C (€2.20) also runs once daily from Chenonceaux to Amboise (25 minutes) and Tours.

Amboise

POP 13,375

The childhood home of Charles VIII and the final resting place of the great Leonardo da Vinci, elegant Amboise is gorgeously arrayed on the southern bank of the Loire and overlooked by its inspiring 15th-century château. With some seriously posh hotels and a wonderful weekend market, Amboise has become a very popular base for exploring nearby châteaux, and coach tours arrive en masse to visit da Vinci's Clos Lucé. Rue Nationale is packed with interesting boutiques.

◉ Sights

Go to sights early in the day to avoid crowds, and buy tickets in advance at the tourist office during high season.

⭐**Château Royal d'Amboise**   CHÂTEAU
(☑ 02 47 57 52 23; www.chateau-amboise.com; place Michel Debré; adult/child €10.70/7.20, with audioguide €14.70/10.20; ☻9am-7pm Jul & Aug, to 6pm Apr-Oct, shorter hours Nov-Mar) Elegantly tiered on a rocky escarpment above town, this easily defendable castle presented a formidable prospect to would-be attackers – but saw little military action. It was more often a weekend getaway from the official royal seat at Blois. Charles VIII (r 1483–98), born and bred here, was responsible for the château's Italianate remodelling in 1492. Today just a few of the original 15th- and 16th-century structures survive, notably the Flamboyant Gothic wing and Chapelle St-Hubert, the final resting place of Leonardo da Vinci. They have thrilling views to the river, town and gardens. The château was the site of much historical intrigue, including the kidnapping of François II in March 1560.

At the time of research, cylindrical Tour Hurtault with its ingenious sloping spiral ramp for easy carriage access, was closed for restoration.

★ **Le Clos Lucé** HISTORIC BUILDING

(📱 02 47 57 00 73; www.vinci-closluce.com; 2 rue du Clos Lucé; adult/child €14/9, joint family tickets reduced; ⊙ 9am-8pm Jul & Aug, 9am-7pm Feb-Jun & Sep-Oct, 9am-6pm Nov & Dec, 10am-6pm Jan; 🖫) Leonardo da Vinci took up residence at this grand manor house in 1516 on the invitation of François I. An admirer of the Italian Renaissance, François named da Vinci 'first painter, engineer and king's architect'. Already 64 by the time he arrived, da Vinci spent his time sketching, tinkering and dreaming up new contraptions, scale models of which are now displayed throughout the home and its expansive gardens. Visitors tour rooms where da Vinci worked and the bedroom where he drew his last breath on 2 May 1519. There is a free smartphone app, and a daily tour in English, Monday through Friday in July and August.

🕝 Tours

Contact the tourist office about their slate of village, château and Clos Lucé **walking tours** in July and August.

Freemove Segway Tours SEGWAY TOUR

(📱 02 47 30 95 35; www.freemove.fr; 45/90min tours €27/47; ⊙ 9.30am-1pm & 3-6.30pm May-Sep) This reservation-only Segway tour outfit also has tours in Blois, Loches and Tours.

🛏 Sleeping

Amboise has some of the smartest places to stay in the Loire Valley, but you'll need deep pockets and should book ahead.

Hôtel Le Blason HOTEL €

(📱 02 47 23 22 41; www.leblason.fr; 11 place Richelieu; s €53, d €53-66, q €88; �────@🎧) Quirky, creaky budget hotel on a quiet square with 25 higgledy-piggledy rooms, wedged around corridors: most are small, flowery and timber-beamed. Upstairs rooms under the eaves come with air-conditioning.

Centre Charles
Péguy-Auberge de Jeunesse HOSTEL €

(📱 02 47 30 60 90; www.centrecharlespéguy.fr; Île d'Or; per person €19.50; @🎧) Efficient 72-bed boarding-school-style hostel on Île d'Or, the peaceful river island opposite the château. Discounts for multi-night stays.

Camping Municipal
de l'Île d'Or CAMPGROUND €

(📱 02 47 57 23 37; www.camping-amboise.com; Île d'Or; sites per adult/child/tent €3/2/3.80; ⊙ Apr-Sep; 🖫) Pleasant campground on Île d'Or, a river island opposite the château. Facilities include pool, tennis courts, ping-pong and canoe hire.

★ **Au Charme Rabelaisien** B&B €€

(📱 02 47 57 53 84; www.au-charme-rabelaisien.com; 25 rue Rabelais; d incl breakfast €92-179; �────🎧🏊) At this calm haven in the centre, Sylvie offers the perfect small B&B experience. Mixing modern fixtures with antique charm, three comfy rooms share a flower-filled garden, pool and free enclosed parking. The spacious Chambre Nature is delightfully secluded and only a few steps from the pool. Breakfasts are fab.

Le Vieux Manoir B&B €€

(📱 02 47 30 41 27; www.le-vieux-manoir.com; 13 rue Rabelais; r incl breakfast €160-200; �────🎧) Set back in a lovely walled garden, this restored mansion is stuffed floor to ceiling with period charm. Rooms get lots of natural light, and owners Gloria and Bob (expat Americans who had an award-winning Boston B&B) are generous with their knowledge of the area.

Le Clos d'Amboise HISTORIC HOTEL €€€

(📱 02 47 30 10 20; www.leclosamboise.com; 27 rue Rabelais; r €140-210, ste €210-295; �────@🎧🏊) Backed by a vast grassy lawn, complete with 200-year-old trees, a heated pool and parking, this posh pad offers a taste of country living in the heart of town. Stylish features abound, from luxurious fabrics to wood-panelling and antique beds. The best rooms have separate sitting areas, original fireplaces or garden-front windows.

Le Manoir Les Minimes DESIGN HOTEL €€€

(📱 02 47 30 40 40; www.manoirlesminimes.com; 34 quai Charles Guinot; r €139-225; ste €305-530; �────@🎧) This pamper-palace would put most châteaux to shame. The best rooms in the main building have tall windows opening onto Loire or château views (corner suite No 10 has both!).

Château de Pray CASTLE HOTEL €€€

(📱 02 47 57 23 67; www.chateaudepray.com; rue de Cedre; d €215-255, q €285) What better way to feel the Loire vibe, than to stay in a château? Rooms are sumptuous, bathrooms modern and grounds relaxing at tis small château 3.5km northeast of Amboise. It also has a top restaurant (four-/five-course *menus* €57/70) open for lunch and dinner (closed December and January)

🍴 Eating

★ **Chez Bruno** BISTRO €

(📱 02 47 57 73 49; www.bistrotchezbruno.com; 38-40 place Michel Debré; mains €8-12; ⊙ lunch & dinner

THE LOIRE VALLEY AMBOISE

Tue-Sat) Uncork a host of local vintages in a lively contemporary setting just beneath the towering château. Tables of chatting visitors and locals alike dig into delicious, inexpensive regional cooking. If you're after Loire Valley wine tips, this is the place.

Bigot PATISSERIE €
(02 47 57 04 46; www.bigot-amboise.com; place du Château; mains €6-11; noon-7.30pm Mon, 9am-7.30pm Tue-Fri, 8.30am-7.30pm Sat & Sun) Since 1913 this award-winning *chocolaterie* and patisserie has been creating some of the Loire's creamiest cakes and gooiest treats: multicoloured macarons, handmade chocolates and petits fours, alongside savoury omelettes, salads and quiches.

La Fourchette TRADITIONAL FRENCH €€
(06 11 78 16 98; 9 rue Malebranche; lunch/dinner menus €15/24; noon-1.30pm Tue-Sat, 7-9.30pm Fri & Sat) Tucked into a back alley behind the tourist office, this is Amboise's favourite address for straightforward home cooking. Chef Christine makes you feel like you've been invited to her house for lunch... It's small so reserve ahead.

Le Patio MODERN FRENCH €€
(02 47 79 00 00; www.facebook.com/lepatio amboise; 14 rue Nationale; menus from €29; noon-2pm & 7-9.30pm Thu-Mon) Pick a table either in the airy, modern interior or out in the bustling pedestrian rue Nationale, under the Tour de l'Horloge, and settle in with the locals for creative, beautifully presented French cuisine. Superb wine selection and friendly staff round it all out.

Self-Catering

Food Market FOOD MARKET
(8am-1pm Fri & Sun) Fills the riverbank west of the tourist office.

Drinking & Nightlife

Le Shaker BAR
(3 quai François Tissard, Île d'Or; 6-11pm Tue, to 3am Wed-Sun) This low-key bar on the Île d'Or enjoys spectacular views of the château and the river from its Loire-side tables.

Information

Tourist Office (02 47 57 09 28; www.amboise-valdeloire.com; quai du Général de Gaulle; 9.30am-6pm Mon-Sat, 10am-1pm & 2-5pm Sun, closed Sun Nov-Mar) Sells walking and cycling maps, plus discount ticket combinations for the château, Clos Lucé and the Pagode de Chanteloup, and offers walking tours. Amboise Tour is its free app. Located riverside.

Getting There & Around

Amboise is 34km southwest of Blois and 23km northeast of Tours.

BICYCLE

Détours de Loire (02 47 30 00 55; www.detoursdeloire.com; quai du Géneral de Gaulle; half-day/full day/week €10/15/60; 9.30am-1pm & 3-6.30pm Mon-Sat, 9.30am-1pm & 5.30-6.30pm Sun May-Sep) Across from the tourist office.

BUS

Le Bus (www.ville-amboise.fr; tickets €0.50) Local Le Bus runs from the train station to Amboise centre and back, eight times daily Monday to Saturday.

Touraine Fil Vert (www.tourainefilvert.com; tickets €2.20) Touraine Fil Vert's line C links Amboise's post office with Tours' bus terminal (45 minutes, 12 daily Monday to Saturday). Two go to Chenonceaxu (15 minutes, Monday to Saturday).

TRAIN

The **train station** (bd Gambetta) is 1.5km north of the château on the opposite side of the Loire.
Blois €7, 20 minutes, 13 daily
Tours €5.60, 20 minutes, 13 daily
Paris' Gare d'Austerlitz (express train) €15, 1¾ hours, four daily

Around Amboise

Sights

Pagode de Chanteloup HISTORIC SITE
(www.pagode-chanteloup.com; adult/child €10/8; 10am-7pm May-Sep, shorter hours Oct-Apr;) Two kilometres south of Amboise, this tall pagoda was built between 1775 and 1778 when the odd blend of classical French architecture and Chinese motifs were all the rage. Clamber to the top for glorious views. In summer, **picnic hampers** (adult/child €12.50/7) are sold and you can rent rowing boats and play free outdoor games.

Eating

Auberge de Launay TRADITIONAL FRENCH €€
(02 47 30 16 82; www.aubergedelaunay.com; Le Haut Chantier, Limeray; lunch/dinner menus €20.50/24; noon-1.30pm Tue-Fri, 7.30-9.30pm Mon-Sat) Renowned for its cosy atmosphere and superb traditional food, this country inn, 8km northeast of Amboise, merits the detour for anyone with wheels. Herbs and vegetables from the garden are used in classic French dishes, accompanied by a superb wine list and finished off with divine artisanal cheeses and desserts.

Château de Villandry

Completed in 1756, one of the last major Renaissance châteaux to be built in the Loire Valley, the **Château de Villandry** (☑02 47 50 02 09; www.chateauvillandry.com; chateau & gardens adult/child €10/6.50, gardens only €6.50/4.50, audioguides €4; ⊙9am-6pm Apr-Oct, shorter hours rest of year, closed mid-Nov–mid-Dec) is deservedly famous for what lies outside the château, not what lies within. Encircled by tall walls, the château's glorious **landscaped gardens** (closing 30 minutes after the château) are some of the finest in France, occupying over 6 hectares filled with painstakingly manicured lime trees, ornamental vines, cascading flowers, razor-sharp box hedges and tinkling fountains.

Try to visit when the gardens are blooming, between April and October; midsummer is most spectacular.

The original gardens and château were built by Jean le Breton, who served François I as finance minister and Italian ambassador (and supervised the construction of Chambord). During his time as ambassador, le Breton became enamoured with the art of Italian Renaissance gardening, and created his own ornamental masterpiece at his newly constructed château at Villandry.

Wandering the pebbled walkways you'll see formal **water gardens**, a **maze**, **vineyards** and the **Jardin d'Ornement** (Ornamental Garden), which depicts various aspects of love (fickle, passionate, tender and tragic) using geometrically pruned hedges and coloured flowerbeds. The **Sun Garden** is a looser array of gorgeous multi-coloured and multiscented perennials. But the highlight is the 16th-century decorative **potager** (kitchen garden), where even the vegetables are laid out in regimental colour-coordinated fashion; plantings change in spring and autumn.

After the gardens, the château's interior is a bit of a let-down compared with others in the region. Nevertheless, highlights include an over-the-top **oriental room**, complete with a gilded ceiling plundered from a 15th-century Moorish palace in Toledo, and a gallery of **Spanish and Flemish art**. Best of all are the bird's-eye views across the gardens and the nearby Loire and Cher rivers from the top of the **donjon** (keep; the only remnant from the original medieval château) and the **belvédère** (panoramic viewpoint).

❶ Getting There & Away

Villandry is 17km southwest of Tours and 11km northeast of Azay-le-Rideau.

BUS

Fil Bleu buses 117 and 32 serve Tours (€1.40, 30 minutes, to the train station or southern Tours, respectively) four times daily from June to August.

TRAIN

From Savonnières, 4km northeast of Villandry, one to three direct trains daily run to Tours (€3.50, 12 minutes) and Saumur (€9.80, 40 minutes).

Château de Langeais

Fantastically preserved inside and out, the **Château de Langeais** (☑02 47 96 72 60; www.chateau-de-langeais.com; adult/child €9/5; ⊙9.30am-6.30pm Apr–mid-Nov, shorter hours mid-Nov–Mar) was constructed as a fortress in the

---

WORTH A TRIP

MUSÉE BALZAC

Meander down the Indre Valley along the tiny D84, passing mansions, villages and troglodyte caves, and 7km east of Azay-le-Rideau you come to sweet **Saché**. Once home to American sculptor Alexander Calder (one of his mobiles sits in the town square), it still celebrates the life of long-time inhabitant Honoré de Balzac (1799–1850), author of *La Comédie Humaine*.

The lovely **Musée Balzac** (☑02 47 26 86 50; www.musee-balzac.fr; adult/child €5/4; ⊙10am-6pm daily Apr-Sep, 10am-12.30pm & 2-5pm Wed-Mon Oct-Mar) inhabits the town's château where Balzac was a habitual guest of his parents' friend, Jean Margonne. On a quiet slope in the lush river valley, the castle features original furnishings, manuscripts, letters and first editions. Feeling the peace, you can easily imagine Balzac escaping his hectic Parisian life and reclining here in his cosy bed, a board on his knees, writing for 12 hours a day – as he did. Nearby **Auberge du XIIe Siecle** (☑02 47 26 88 77; 1 rue du Château, menus €38-90; ⊙noon-1.30pm Wed-Mon, 7-9pm Mon-Sat) offers a gourmet country pit stop.

Touraine Fil Vert's bus I serves Saché.

1460s to cut off the likely invasion route from Brittany. It remains every inch the medieval stronghold: crenellated ramparts and defensive towers jut out from the rooftops of the surrounding village. Original 15th-century furniture fills its flagstoned rooms.

Among many fine Flemish and Aubusson **tapestries**, look out for one from 1530 depicting astrological signs; an intricate Les Mille Fleurs; and the famous **Les Neuf Preux series** portraying nine 'worthy' knights representing the epitome of medieval courtly honour.

In one room, an odd waxwork display illustrates the marriage of Charles VIII and Anne of Brittany, which was held here on 6 December 1491 and brought about the historic union of France and Brittany.

Up top, stroll the castle's ramparts for a soldier's-eye view of the town: gaps underfoot enabled boiling oil, rocks and ordure to be dumped on attackers. Across the château's courtyard, climb to the top of the ruined keep, constructed by the 10th-century warlord, Count Foulques Nerra. Built in 944, it's the oldest in France and fronts sprawling parks.

Eating

Au Coin des Halles BISTRO €€
(☏ 02 47 96 37 25; www.aucoindeshalles.com; 9 rue Gambetta; lunch/dinner menus from €16/26; ⊙ 12.15-2pm & 7.15-9pm Fri-Tue) The village of Langeais (population 4120), with its peaceful walking streets, is a fun pit stop in the midst of the mayhem of castle-hunting. The town's market bustles on Sunday mornings and you can dine at Au Coin des Halles, the village's elegant bistro.

ⓘ Getting There & Away

Langeais is 14km west of Villandry and about 31km southwest of Tours. Its train station, 400m from the château, is on the line linking Tours (€5.60, 20 minutes, six to eight daily) and Saumur (€8.10, 25 minutes, six to 10 daily).

Château d'Azay-le-Rideau

Romantic, moat-ringed **Château d'Azay-le-Rideau** (☏ 02 47 45 42 04; www.azay-le-rideau.monuments-nationaux.fr/en; adult/child €8.50/free; ⊙ 9.30am-6pm Apr-Sep, to 7pm Jul & Aug, 10am-5.15pm Oct-Mar) is wonderfully adorned with slender turrets, geometric windows and decorative stonework, wrapped up within a shady landscaped park. Built in the 1500s on a natural island in the middle of the River Indre, the château

is one of the Loire's loveliest: Honoré de Balzac called it a 'multifaceted diamond set in the River Indre'.

Its most famous feature is its open **loggia staircase**, in the Italian style, overlooking the central courtyard and decorated with the salamanders and ermines of François I and Queen Claude. The interior is mostly 19th century, remodelled by the Marquis de Biencourt from the original 16th-century château built by Gilles Berthelot, chief treasurer for François I. In July and August, a **son et lumière** (sound-and-light show; adult/child €11/3), one of the Loire's oldest and best, is projected onto the castle walls nightly.

Audioguides (adult €4.50) are available in five languages, and 45-minute guided tours in French are free.

ⓘ Getting There & Away

Château d'Azay-le-Rideau is 26km southwest of Tours. The D84 and D17, on either side of the Indre, are a delight to cycle.

BUS

Touraine Fil Vert's bus TF (€2.20) travels between Langeais, Azay-le-Rideau and Chinon four times daily. An SNCF bus stops near the château.

TRAIN

Azay-le-Rideau's station is 2.5km west of the château. Destinations include:
Chinon €5.10, 20 minutes, eight daily
Tours €5.80, 25 to 30 minutes, eight daily

Château d'Ussé

The main claim to fame of elaborate **Château d'Ussé** (☏ 02 47 95 54 05; www.chateaudusse.fr; adult/child €14/4; ⊙ 10am-6pm, to 7pm Apr-Aug, closed early Nov–mid-Feb) is as the inspiration for Charles Perrault's classic fairy tale *La Belle au Bois Dormant* (known to English-speakers as *Sleeping Beauty*).

Ussé's creamy white towers and slate roofs jut out from the edge of the forest of Chinon, offering sweeping views across the flat Loire countryside and the flood-prone River Indre. Its most notable features are the wonderful formal **gardens** designed by André Le Nôtre, lanscape architect of Versailles.

ⓘ **REDUCED TICKETS**

Save your ticket stub! Buying a full-priced ticket at Langeais, Azay-le-Rideau, Chinon, Villandry or Fontevraud willl get you reduced entrance at the others.

The castle mainly dates from the 15th and 16th centuries, built on top of a much earlier 11th-century fortress. You may be satisfied just looking at the château from outside, since refurbished rooms are starting to show their age. They include a series of dodgy wax models recounting the tale of Sleeping Beauty.

A popular local rumour claims Ussé was one of Walt Disney's inspirations when he dreamed up his magic kingdom (check out the Disney logo and you might agree).

Ussé is on the edge of the small riverside village of Rigny-Ussé, about 14km north of Chinon. There is no public transport.

Loches

POP 7203

Historic Loches spirals picturesquely up around the base of its citadel (cité royale), a forbidding medieval stronghold begun by Foulques Nerra in the 10th century, and later enlarged by Charles VII. In 1429, Joan of Arc persuaded Charles VII to march north from here to claim the French crown, but these days the town is a sleepy place, great for a day's exploration – taking in the village, citadel and keep. Loches is well known for its bustling **Saturday morning market**.

Across the River Indre, **Beaulieu-lès-Loches** is home to the 11th-century abbey where Foulques Nerra is buried.

⊙ Sights

From rue de la République, the old gateway **Porte Picois** leads through the cobbled **Vieille Ville** (Old Town) towards the **Porte Royale** (Royal Gate), flanked by two forbidding 13th-century towers, and the sole entrance to the Cité Royale de Loches.

★ **Cité Royale de Loches**　　　CITADEL
(☑ 02 47 59 01 32; www.chateau-loches.fr; donjon & royal apartments adult/child €8.50/6.50; ☉ 9am-7pm Apr-Sep, 9.30am-5pm Oct-Mar) Loches' vast hilltop citadel is a small village in its own right. You can explore the gorgeous, white tufa-stone citadel, inside its protective walls, for free, except for the donjon (keep) and Logis Royal (royal apartments), which are part of a single ticket.

The 36m-high **donjon**, at the southern end of the promontory was Loches' original medieval stronghold, built in the 11th century by Foulques Nerra. Though the interior floors have fallen away, architectural details remain, including remnants of fireplaces and the original chapel. Climb dizzying catwalks for fantastic views.

Next door to the donjon is the notorious **Tour Ronde** (Round Tower), built during the 15th century by Charles VII and Louis XI. The basement holds a circular chamber where the unfortunate Cardinal Balue was supposedly kept suspended from the ceiling in a wooden cage for betraying Louis XI. (In fact, it was more likely a grain store, although you can see a replica of the cardinal's cage back in the donjon.) Other highlights include the chilling **Salle des Questions** (a torture chamber), traces of prisoners' graffiti etched into the tower walls, and the **rooftop terrace** – once a platform for firing artillery, nowadays it's a fine viewpoint.

In the adjacent courtyard, the **Tour Martelet** houses additional dungeons, along with a subterranean passageway bearing interesting displays about the 11th-century quarrying of tufa stone for the construction of the keep.

At the northern end of the citadel sits the **Logis Royal**, royal residence of Charles VII and his successors, built originally for defensive purposes but later converted to a hunting lodge and embellished in Flamboyant Gothic style. Joan of Arc famously passed through here after her victory at Orléans in May 1429 to meet with Charles VII and nudge him towards his coronation in Reims later that year.

➡ **Collégiale St-Ours**

(☉ 9am-8pm, to 10pm Jul & Aug) **FREE** This church contains the **tomb of Agnés Sorel**, Charles VII's mistress, who lived in the château during their affair. Notoriously beautiful and fiercely intelligent, Agnés earned many courtly enemies due to her powerful influence over Charles. Having borne three daughters, she died in mysterious circumstances while pregnant with their fourth child. The official cause was dysentery, although some scientists speculate that elevated levels of mercury in her body indicate she may have been poisoned.

➡ **Maison Lansyer**

(1 rue Lansyer; ☉ 10.30am-12.30pm & 2-5.30pm Wed-Mon Jun-Sep, shorter hours Apr-May & Oct, closed Nov-Mar) **FREE** As you climb through the citadel you'll pass Maison Lansyer, the former home of landscape painter Emmanuel Lansyer (1838–93), now a museum featuring his paintings alongside works by Canaletto, Millet, Piranese and Delacroix.

🛏 Sleeping & Eating

La Demeure Saint-Ours　　　B&B €
(☑ 06 33 74 54 82; www.saintours.eu; 11 rue du Château; d incl breakfast €65-75; ☜) Stay in a quaint

BOURGES

Not part of the château circuit, bustling Bourges (population 68,747), 120km east of Loches, has preserved its history well, with its maze of wonderful-to-explore narrow medieval cobblestone streets and its massively impressive **Cathédrale St-Étienne** (tower/crypt & tower €5/7.50; ⊘8.30am-7.15pm). Henri de Sully began work on the Gothic masterpiece with its flying buttresses in 1195. The second stage of construction came in 1230, resulting in five outstanding sculpted front portals. Among its other impressive features is a series of stained-glass windows featuring craftsmen at work; and the oldest astronomical clock in France, designed in 1424 and presented to Charles VII upon his marriage to Marie d'Anjou.

The **tourist office** (☑02 48 23 02 60; www.bourges-tourisme.com; 21 rue Victor Hugo; ⊘9am-7pm Mon-Sat, 10am-6pm Sun) can advise on where to stay or eat. The historic centre is well-signposted with French/English informational placards.

central 16th-century townhouse, just at the foot of the citadel.

Isabeau de Touraine
CAFE €

(☑02 47 59 47 55; 33 Grand Rue; mains €4.50-14; ⊘9.30am-7pm, meals noon-6pm Wed-Mon) The friendly proprietress welcomes you to comfy plum-coloured couches or streetside tables, where she serves delicious home-baked cakes, or lunchtime salads and quiches.

La Gerbe d'Or
TRADITIONAL FRENCH €€

(☑02 47 91 67 63; www.restaurantlagerbedor.fr; 22 rue Balzac; lunch/dinner menus from €15/21; ⊘noon-2pm Tue-Sun, 7.30-9.30pm Tue & Thu-Sat) The Golden Sheaf (and no, it's *not* the Golden Gerbil!) specialises in hearty traditional fare using local products, such as foie gras with Vouvray wine jelly, or beef with shallots and haricots verts.

Food Market
MARKET

(⊘8am-12.30pm Wed & Sat) Fills rue de la République and surrounding streets.

ⓘ Information

Tourist Office (☑02 47 91 82 82; www.loches-tourainecotesud.com; place de la Marne; ⊘9am-12.30pm & 1.30-6pm Mon-Sat, 10am-12.30pm & 2.30-5pm Sun, closed Sun Oct-Apr) Located beside the river.

ⓘ Getting There & Around

Loches is 67km southwest of Blois and 41km southeast of Tours. Trains and SNCF buses link the train station, across the River Indre from the tourist office, with Tours (€9.40, one hour, six to 10 daily).

Chinon

POP 8379

Peacefully placed along the northern bank of the Vienne and dominated by its expansive hillside château, Chinon is etched in France's collective memory as both the fortress of Henri II Plantagenet and the place where Joan of Arc first met Charles VII in 1429. Within the warren of the village's white tufa houses and black slate rooftops you'll discover an appealing medieval quarter.

Chinon is also renowned as one of the Loire's main wine-producing areas. Chinon AOC (www.chinon.com) cabernet franc vineyards stretch along both sides of the river.

You can park for free above town, access the fortress, and then take the free **lift** (⊘7am-midnight Apr-Sep, to 11pm Oct-Mar) into the lower town (which has paid parking) to explore.

⊙ Sights

★**Forteresse Royale de Chinon**
FORTRESS

(☑02 47 93 13 45; www.forteressechinon.fr; adult/child €8.50/6.50; ⊘9.30am-7pm May-Aug, shorter hours rest of year) The hilltop site, with fabulous views across town and the river, is split into three sections separated by dry moats. The 12th-century **Fort St-Georges** (which houses the ticket booth and shop) and the **Middle Castle** with the **Logis Royal** (Royal Lodgings) remain from the time when the Plantagenet court of Henry II and Eleanor of Aquitaine was held here. **Fort du Coudray** sits on the tip of the promontory and has 13th-century **Tour du Coudray**, where Joan of Arc stayed in 1429, and which was used to imprison Knights Templar (find their graffiti inside).

When you initially enter the middle castle, you pass the 14th-century **Tour de l'Horloge** to reach the Logis Royal. Only the south wing remains of the Logis, and it is filled with interesting **multimedia exhibits**, a collection of Joan of Arc memorabilia, and area archaeological finds.

The castle has neat multimedia booklets that trigger film and audio in your native language throughout the site, as well as audioguides (€2.50).

★ **Medieval Town**   HISTORIC QUARTER
Author François Rabelais (c 1483–1553), whose works include the Gargantua and Pantagruel series, grew up in Chinon; you'll see Rabelais-related names dotted all around the old town, which offers a fine cross-section of medieval architecture, best seen along rue Haute St-Maurice and rue Voltaire. The tourist office has a free walking-tour leaflet and offers French-language guided tours (adult/child €4.70/2.50).

Look out for the remarkable Hôtel du Gouverneur (rue Haute St-Maurice), an impressive townhouse with a double-flighted staircase ensconced behind a carved gateway, and the nearby Gothic Palais du Bailliage, the former residence of Chinon's bailiwick (now occupied by the Hostellerie Gargantua).

Caves Painctes de Chinon   WINE CAVE
(☎ 02 47 93 30 44; www.chinon.com; impasse des Caves Painctes; adult/child €3/free; ☺ guided tours 11am, 3pm, 4.30pm & 6pm Tue-Sun Jul & Aug) Hidden at the end of a cobbled alleyway off rue Voltaire, these former quarries were converted into wine cellars during the 15th century, and written about by Rabelais. A brotherhood of local winegrowers, runs tours in summertime.

Chapelle Ste-Radegonde   CHURCH
(☎ 02 47 93 17 85; rue du Coteau Ste-Radegonde; adult/child €3/free; ☺ 2.30–6.30pm Sat & Sun May, Jun & Sep, 2.30-6.30pm Wed-Mon Jul & Aug) Built into a cave above and 500m east of town, this atmospheric, half-ruined medieval chapel is noteworthy for its 12th-century Royal Hunt fresco and a staircase that descends to a subterranean spring associated with a pre-Christian cult.

Le Carroi Musée   MUSEUM
(☎ 02 47 93 18 12; 44 rue Haute St-Maurice; adult/child €2/free; ☺ 2.30-6pm Fri-Mon mid-Feb–mid-Nov) Art and archaeology exhibits from prehistory to the 19th century relating to Chinon and its environs.

🛏 Sleeping

★ **Hôtel Diderot**   HISTORIC HOTEL €
(☎ 02 47 93 18 87; www.hoteldiderot.com; 4 rue de Buffon; d €70-100; ☎) This gorgeous shady townhouse is tucked amid luscious rose-filled gardens and crammed with polished antiques. The friendly owners impart the glowing charm you'd expect of a hotel twice the price. Rooms are all individually styled, from over-the-top Napoleonic to stripped-back art deco and have large flat screen TVs. Breakfast (€9.40) includes a rainbow of homemade jams, plus locally produced apple juice, yoghurt and goat cheese. Parking €8.

Hostellerie Gargantua   HISTORIC HOTEL €
(☎ 02 47 93 04 71; www.hotel-gargantua.com; 73 rue Voltaire; d €59-81; ☺ Apr-Sep; ☎) Harry Potter would feel right at home in this turret-topped medieval mansion. The simple, offbeat hotel has spiral staircases, pitch-dark wood and solid stone. Superior rooms are worth the cash, including Grangousier with its fireplace and four-poster, and Badebec with its oak beams and château views. Parking €6.

Hôtel Le Plantagenêt   HOTEL €
(☎ 02 47 93 36 92; www.hotel-plantagenet.com; 12 place Jeanne d'Arc; s €61-83, d €68-83, tr €94; ⌗ ☎) A basic, dated but perfectly serviceable hotel halfway between the centre and the station, with rooms spread over three buildings. The original *maison bourgeoise* is more charming

WORTH A TRIP

MUSÉE RABELAIS

La Devinière, the farm where François Rabelais – doctor, Franciscan friar, theoretician and author – was born (sometime between 1483 and 1494; no one is sure), sits among fields and vineyards with sweeping views of a private château in Coudray Montpensier. This farm inspired the settings for Rabelais' five satirical, erudite Gargantua and Pantagruel novels. The rambling buildings of the farmstead hold thoughtful **exhibits** (☎ 02 47 95 91 18; www.musee-rabelais.fr; Seuilly; adult/child €5.50/4.50; ☺ 10am-7pm Jul & Aug, 10am-12.30pm & 2-6pm Apr-Sep, to 5pm Oct-Mar, closed Tue Oct-Mar) including early editions of Rabelais' work and a Matisse portrait of the author from 1951. The winding cave network beneath provides an atmospheric setting for special exhibitions.

Follow the signs 9km southwest of Chinon, to the outskirts of Seuilly to find La Devinière.

and less cramped than the motel-like annexe out back. Perks include guest laundry (€8), a pleasant patio and parking (€8).

Eating

Reserve ahead on weekends and during high season. Place du Général de Gaulle is loaded with sunny cafes.

★ Les Années 30   TRADITIONAL FRENCH €€

(📞 02 47 93 37 18; www.lesannees30.com; 78 rue Haute St-Maurice; lunch/dinner menus from €18/26; ⓘ 12.15-1.45pm & 7.30-9.30pm Thu-Mon) Expect the kind of meal you came to France to eat: exquisite attention to flavours and detail, served in relaxed intimacy. The interior dining room is golden-lit downstairs and cool blue upstairs; in summer dine under the streetside pergola, in the heart of the old quarter. The *menu* ranges from traditional duck *filet* to unusual choices such as crawfish tartare.

Restaurant au Chapeau Rouge   TRADITIONAL FRENCH €€

(📞 02 47 98 08 08; www.restaurant-chapeau-rouge. fr; 49 place du Général de Gaulle; menus 3-course lunch €23, dinner €29-56; ⓘ noon-1pm Wed-Sun, 7.30-8.45pm Tue-Sat) There's an air of a Left Bank brasserie hanging around the 'Red Hat', sheltered behind red and gold awnings. Chatting families dig into hare fondant and other countrified dishes.

Self-Catering

Food Market   MARKET

(place Jeanne d'Arc; ⓘ Thu morning) There is a ride variety of produce available at the weekly market.

ℹ Information

Tourist Office (📞 02 47 93 17 85; www.chinon-valdeloire.com; 1 place Hofheïm; ⓘ 10am-1.30pm & 2-7pm May-Sep, 10am-12.30pm & 2-6pm Mon-Sat Oct-Apr) Free walking-tour brochure and details on kayaking, boat trips and hot-air balloons. Sells slightly reduced châteaux tickets. Occasional countryside bike tours. Free smartphone app. Its summer kiosk (ⓘ 10am-1.30pm & 2.30-6pm Jun-Sep) is located up near the château.

ℹ Getting There & Away

Chinon is 47km southwest of Tours, 21km southwest of Azay-le-Rideau and 30km southeast of Saumur.

BUS

Touraine Fil Vert's bus TF (€2.20, four daily) connects Chinon, Azay-le-Rideau and Langeais.

TRAIN

The train station, 1km east of place du Général de Gaulle, is served by local buses A and B. Trains or SNCF buses run 11 times daily (five on weekends) to Tours (€9.70, 50 minutes to 1¼ hours) and Azay-le-Rideau (€5.10, 20 minutes).

ANJOU

In Anjou, Renaissance châteaux give way to chalky white tufa cliffs concealing an astonishing underworld of wine cellars, mushroom farms and art sculptures. Above ground, black slate roofs pepper the vine-rich land from which some of the Loire's best wines are produced.

Angers, the historic capital of Anjou, is famous for its powerful dukes, their fortified hilltop château and the stunning medieval Apocalypse tapestry. Architectural gems in Anjou's crown include the Romanesque Abbaye de Fontevraud. Europe's highest concentration of troglodyte dwellings dot the banks of the Loire around cosmopolitan Saumur.

The area along the Rivers Loire, Authion and Vienne from Angers southeast to Azay-le-Rideau form the Parc Naturel Régional Loire-Anjou-Touraine.

Saumur

POP 28,558

There's an air of sparkly Parisian sophistication around Saumur, but also a sense of laid-back contentment. The food is good, the wine is good, the spot is good – and the Saumurites know it. The town is renowned for its École Nationale d'Équitation, a national cavalry school that's been home to the crack riders of the Cadre Noir since 1828. Soft white tufa cliffs stretch along the riverbanks east and west of town, pock-marked by the unusual artificial caves known as *habitations troglodytes*.

⊙ Sights

★ École Nationale d'Équitation   RIDING SCHOOL

(National Equestrian School; 📞 02 41 53 50 60; www.cadrenoir.fr; rte de Marson, St-Hilaire-St-Florent; tours adult/child €8/6; ⓘ mornings Tue-Sat & afternoons Mon-Fri mid-Apr–mid-Oct, shorter hours rest of year) Anchored in France's academic-military riding tradition, Saumur has been an equine centre since 1593. Its École Nationale d'Équitation is one of France's foremost riding academies, responsible for training the country's Olympic teams and members of the elite Cadre Noir. Advance reservations are required for its one-hour guided visits (enquire about English-language tours), and the semi-monthly **Cadre Noir presentations** (adult/child €16/9) are not to be missed: they are like astonishing horse ballets. Check the website for dates and reservations.

You'll recognise members of the Cadre Noir by their special black jackets, caps, gold spurs and three golden wings on their whips. They train both the school's instructors and horses (which take around 5½ years to achieve display standard) and are famous for their astonishing discipline and acrobatic manoeuvres (like 'airs above ground'), which are all performed without stirrups.

Find the school 3km west of town, outside sleepy St-Hilaire-St-Florent. It's also the site of equestrian competitions.

Château de Saumur   CHÂTEAU
(✑ 02 41 40 24 40; www.chateau-saumur.com; adult/child €9/5; ⊙ 10am-6.30pm mid-Jun–mid-Sep, 10am-1pm & 2-5.30pm Tue-Sun mid-Sep–mid-Jun) Soaring above the town's rooftops, Saumur's fairy-tale château was largely built during the 13th century by Louis XI, and has variously served as a dungeon, fortress and country residence. Its defensive heritage took a knock in 2001 when a chunk of the western ramparts collapsed without warning. After a decade-long restoration, the castle's porcelain collection reopened on the 1st floor. The 2nd floor is due to reopen soon; for now its impressive collection of vintage equestrian gear is housed in the adjacent abbey.

There's an **equestrian spectacle** (✑ 02 41 83 31 31; www.lesecuyersdutemps.fr; adult/child €19/15; ⊙ Thu, Fri & Sat Jul & Aug) in summer which includes jousting, acrobatics and swordplay. Park in the lots up the hill from the château for free or walk up from town.

Musée des Blindés   MILITARY MUSEUM
(✑ 02 41 83 69 95; www.museedesblindes.fr; 1043 rte de Fontevraud; adult/child €8/5; ⊙ 10am-6pm May-Sep, shorter hours Oct-Apr) Gearheads love this museum of over 200 tanks and military vehicles. Children can climb on some. Examples include many WWI tanks such as the Schneider and dozens of WWII models, such as the Hotchkiss H39, Panzers and an Issoise infantry tractor.

Musée de la Cavalerie   MUSEUM
(✑ 02 41 83 69 23; http://museecavalerie.free.fr; place Charles de Foucauld; adult/child €5/3; ⊙ 10am-noon & 2-6pm Tue-Fri, 2-6pm Sat-Mon) **FREE** Housed in the old military stables of the Cadre Noir, this museum traces the history of

the French cavalry from 1445 in the time of Charles VII to modern tanks.

🏃 Activities

⭐ **Maison des Vins**   WINE TASTING
(✑ 02 41 38 45 83; www.vinsvaldeloire.fr; 7 quai Carnot; ⊙ 9.30am-1pm & 2-7pm Mon-Sat, 10.30am-1pm Sun, closed Mon morning May-Sep, shorter hours rest of year) For wine tasting and winery listings visit the Maison des Vins. Beautiful wine tasting drives include heading west along route D751 towards Gennes, or east on route D947 through Souzay-Champigny and Parnay. Or cut south of Angers over to Savennières.

Distillerie Combier   DISTILLERY
(✑ 02 41 40 23 02; www.combier.fr; 48 rue Beaurepaire; tours €4; ⊙ 10am-12.30pm & 2-7pm, closed Mon Oct-May, Sun Nov & Jan-Mar) In business since its invention of Triple Sec in 1834, this distillery has also resurrected authentic absinthe (p400), the famous firewater. Taste these alongside other liqueurs including Royal Combier and Pastis d'Antan, and get a behind-the-scenes look at the production facility, with gleaming century-old copper stills, vintage Eiffel machinery and fragrant vats full of Haitian bitter oranges. There are three to five one-hour tours per day.

Langlois-Chateau   WINE SCHOOL
(✑ 02 41 40 21 40; www.langlois-chateau.fr; 3 rue Léopold Palustre, St-Hilaire-St-Florent; tours adult/child €5/free, extended classes €225; ⊙ tasting 10am-12.30pm & 2-6.30pm Apr–mid-Oct) Founded in 1912 and specialising in Crémant de Loire (sparkling wines), this domaine is open for reservation only tours, tastings and a visit to the caves, and offers an introduction to winemaking.

👉 Tours

Croisières Saumur Loire   BOAT TOUR
(✑ 06 63 22 87 00; www.croisieressaumurloire.fr; adult/child €12/6; ⊙ afternoons Jun-Sep, weekends May & Oct) Fifty-minute cruises from quai Lucien Gautier, across from Saumur's town hall.

Base de Loisirs Millocheau   KAYAK TOUR
(Pôle Nautique de Saumur; ✑ 02 41 51 17 65; www.polenautiquedesaumur.com; adult/child €28/22; ⊙ office 9am-midday & 1-5pm Tue-Sat) Canoe and kayak tours on the Loire by reservation.

Carriage Rides   CARRIAGE RIDE
(www.attelages-cuzay.com; adult/child €8/5; ⊙ 2-5pm Apr–mid-Oct) Tours depart from place de la République.

THE GREEN FAIRY: ABSINTHE

Some of France's most distinctive liqueurs are distilled in the Loire Valley, including the aniseedy (and allegedly hallucinogenic) brew known as absinthe. Brewed from a heady concoction of natural herbs, true absinthe includes three crucial components: green anise, fennel and the foliage of *Artemisia absinthium* (wormwood, used as a remedy since the time of the ancient Egyptians). Legend has it that modern-day absinthe was created by a French doctor (wonderfully called Dr Pierre Ordinaire) in the late 1790s, before being acquired by a father-and-son team who established the first major absinthe factory, Maison Pernod-Fils, in 1805.

The drink's popularity exploded in the 19th century, when it was discovered by bohemian poets and painters (as well as French troops, who were given it as an antimalarial drug). Seriously potent, absinthe's traditional green colour and supposedly psychoactive effects led to its popular nickname, 'the green fairy'; everyone from Rimbaud to Vincent van Gogh sang its praises. Ernest Hemingway invented his own absinthe cocktail, ominously dubbed 'Death in the Afternoon'.

But the drink's reputation was ultimately its own downfall: fearing widespread psychic degeneration, governments around the globe banned it in the early 20th century (France in 1915). In the 1990s a group of dedicated absintheurs reverse-engineered the liqueur, chemically analysing century-old bottles that had escaped the ban. Made legal once again in 2011, you can try it at Distillerie Combier (p399) in Saumur.

🛏 Sleeping

You'll need to reserve ahead for Saumur's high-calibre accommodation.

Hôtel de Londres HOTEL €
(📞 02 41 51 23 98; www.lelondres.com; 48 rue d'Orléans; r €64-90, apt €95-130; ❈ @ 🛜) Snag one of the refurbished rooms in jolly colours or one of the family-friendly apartments, all with big windows, gleaming bathrooms and thoughtful perks including afternoon tea (€3) and a well-stocked comic library. Parking €5.

Camping l'Île d'Offard CAMPGROUND €
(📞 02 41 40 30 00; www.saumur-camping.com; rue de Verden; sites for 2 people €15-25; ⊘mid-Mar–mid-Nov; 🛜 🛳) Well-equipped and very pretty campground on a natural river island opposite the château. Cyclists get discounts. Riverside and castle-view sites cost extra.

★Château Beaulieu B&B €€
(📞 02 41 50 83 52; www.chateaudebeaulieu.fr; 98 rte de Montsoreau; d incl breakfast €95-130, ste €140-200; 🛜 🛳) Irish expats Mary and Conor welcome you to their sprawling home with a glass of bubbling crémant (sparkling wine), delicious homemade breakfasts and a wealth of friendly advice on surrounding attractions. Rooms are imaginatively and comfortably done up and the mood among gregarious clientele is one of extended family. Sun yourself by the pool or play billiards in the grand salon. Parking free.

Hôtel Saint-Pierre HISTORIC HOTEL €€
(📞 02 41 50 33 00; www.saintpierresaumur.com; 8 rue Haute St-Pierre; r €95-200, ste €225-260; ❈ 🛜) Squeezed down a minuscule alleyway opposite the cathedral, this effortlessly smart hideaway mixes heritage architecture with modern-day comfort: pale stone, thick rugs and vintage lamps sit happily alongside minibars and satellite TV. Tiled mosaics line the bathrooms and black-and-white dressage photos enliven the lobby.

★Château de Verrières HOTEL €€€
(📞 02 41 38 05 15; www.chateau-verrieres.com; 53 rue d'Alsace; r €170-260, ste €290-330; 🛜 🛳) Each of the 10 rooms in this impeccably wonderful 1890 château, ensconced within the woods and ponds of a 1.6-hectare English park, is different. But the feel is universally kingly: antique writing desks, original artwork, wood panelling and fantastic bathrooms. Some, like the top-of-the-line Rising Sun suite (with a dash of modish Japanese minimalism), have views of the sun rising over the Saumur château.

🍴 Eating

Saumur is one of the top culinary cities in the world; book ahead.

L'Alchimiste MODERN FRENCH €
(📞 02 41 67 65 18; www.lalchimiste-saumur.fr; 6 rue de Lorraine; menus €18; ⊘noon-1.30pm & 7.30-9.30pm Tue-Sat) Clean flavours are the hallmark of this sleek family-run bistro. Seasonal

ingredients sing out from a simple, constantly changing *menu*.

Bistrot des Jean
BISTRO €

(☑ 02 41 52 44 07; www.bistrotdesjean.com; 19 rue de la Tonelle; menus lunch €12, 3-course dinner €20; ⊘ noon-2.30pm & 7-10pm Tue-Sat) Loaded with locals who appreciate the simple, traditional fare, this tiny bistro sits just off the waterfront on a small central walking street.

★ Le Pot de Lapin
MODERN FRENCH €€

(☑ 02 41 67 12 86; 35 rue Rabelais; tapas €5-7, mains €14-18; ⊘ noon-2pm & 7-9.45pm Tue-Sat) Jazzy music wafts from the cheery dining room through the wine bar and onto the streetside terrace as Chef Olivier works the tables, proposing perfect wine pairings and serving up tempting platefuls of ever-changing tapas and French classics. Somehow the vibe here is, simply put, happiness – happy staff, happy clients.

Start with a local bubbly then move on to perfectly seasoned shrimp *brochettes* (skewers), coulis-drizzled foie gras or pollock in parchment paper.

L'Escargot
TRADITIONAL FRENCH €€

(☑ 02 41 51 20 88; 30 rue du Maréchal Leclerc; lunch/dinner menus from €18/27; ⊘ noon-1.30pm Thu, Fri, Sun & Mon, 7.30-9.30pm Thu-Mon) A Saumur fixture for over half a century, this place is all about traditional recipes done really well, like escargots with garlic, parsley and 'three butters' (flavoured with herbs, walnuts and roquefort) or red mullet with fresh thyme, olive oil and vegetables.

L'Aromate
MODERN FRENCH €€

(☑ 02 41 51 31 45; www.laromate-restaurant.com; 42 rue du Maréchal Leclerc; menus lunch €14, 3-course dinner €20-28; ⊘ noon-1.30pm & 7.30-9pm Tue-Sat) The newest entry on Saumur's hot culinary scene is buzzy and bright with changing *menus* that dare to mingle Asian and other influences with classic French cuisine.

L'Amuse Bouche
TRADITIONAL FRENCH €€

(☑ 02 41 67 79 63; www.lamusebouche.fr; 512 rte Montsoreau, Dampierre-sur-Loire; menus lunch €17.50, dinner €29-37; ⊘ noon-1.30pm & 7.30-9.30pm Thu-Mon) Tuck into delicious, creative meals in a homey dining room or on the terrace in summer. Find it 5km southeast of Saumur on the D947.

★ Le Gambetta
GASTRONOMIC €€€

(☑ 02 41 67 66 66; www.restaurantlegambetta.com; 12 rue Gambetta; menus lunch €25.50, dinner €32-99; ⊘ noon-1.30pm Tue & Thu-Sun, 7.15-9.45pm Tue & Thu-Sat) This is one to write home about: a fantastic regional restaurant combining refined elegance and knock-your-socks-off creative food. The parade of exquisitely presented dishes ranges from rosemary-and-thyme roasted pork with an asparagus-lemon-parmesan *maki* to surprisingly delicious wasabi crème brûlée. Some *menus* include wine pairings, and all are punctuated by surprise treats from the kitchen.

❶ Information

Tourist Office (☑ 02 41 40 20 60; www.saumur-tourisme.com; 8bis quai Carnot; ⊘ 9.15am-7pm Mon-Sat, 10.30am-5.30pm Sun mid-May–Sep, shorter hours rest of year; ☎) Loads of info, transport schedules, slightly reduced châteaux tickets, smartphone app.

THE LOIRE VALLEY SAUMUR

WORTH A TRIP

LE THOUREIL

The gorgeous D751 towards **Gennes** (population 599) follows the banks of the Loire, sweeping through glades and alongside 8km of tiny riverside villages of white stone incorporated into **Chênehutte-Tréves-Cunalt** (population 1067). It ends at **Le Thoureil** (population 458), a picturesque riverside hamlet with a wonderful restaurant. Each of the villages are worth a gander, with their historic churches, abbeys and keeps.

Le Thoureil is home to the excellent **La Route de Sel** (☑ 02 41 45 75 31; www.authoureil.fr; 55 quai des Mariniers; lunch/dinner menus from €15/29; ⊘ noon-2.30pm Wed-Sun, 7-9.30pm Wed-Sat) restaurant, where vivacious new proprietors Daniel (in the dining room) and Marie (in the kitchen) draw on Marie's creative culinary chops, from Dubai to London, and incorporate seasonal ingredients. Book ahead to join savvy Saumurois sipping artisanal beer or local wine on the grassy terrace in summer, or in the elegant, inviting dining room. Save room for the transcendent *gâteau de Marie,* a sesame-encrusted flourless chocolate extravaganza.

DON'T MISS

TROGLODYTES: CAVE LIFE

For centuries the creamy white tufa cliffs around Saumur have provided shelter and storage for local inhabitants, leading to the development of a unique *culture troglodyte* (cave culture), as in the Vézère Valley in the Dordogne. The cool caves were developed into houses (*habitations troglodytes*) and even incorporated into castles, like Brézé (p404). They are also perfect natural cellars for everyone from vintners to mushroom farmers. Many of the Loire's grandest châteaux were built from this dazzling stone.

Caves concentrate along the Loire east and west of Saumur, and around the village of Doué-la-Fontaine. Stop by the Saumur tourist office (p401) for a complete list. Bring something warm to wear as caves remain cool (13°C) year-round. The ones near Doué-la-Fontaine (a grim semi-industrial town) are best reached with your own wheels.

Rochemenier (☑ 02 41 59 18 15; www.troglodyte.fr; 14 rue du Musée, Louresse-Rochemenier; adult/child €5.70/3.30; ⊘ 9.30am-7pm Apr-Sep, 2-6pm Tue-Sun Oct-Nov & Feb-Mar) Inhabited until the 1930s, this abandoned village, 6km north of Doué-la-Fontaine, is one of the best examples of troglodytic culture. Explore the remains of two farmsteads, complete with houses, stables and an underground chapel.

Troglodytes et Sarcophages (☑ 06 77 77 06 94; www.troglo-sarcophages.fr; 1 rue de la Croix Mordret, Doué-la-Fontaine; adult/child €4.90/3.30; ⊘ 2.30-7pm daily Jun-Sep, Sat & Sun May) A Merovingian mine where sarcophagi were produced from the 6th to the 9th centuries and exported via the Loire as far as England and Belgium. Reserve ahead for a lantern-lit tour.

Les Perrières (☑ 02 41 59 71 29; www.les-perrieres.com; 545 rue des Perrières, Doué-la-Fontaine; adult/child €6.50/4; ⊘ 9.30am-7pm Apr-Sep, 10am-6pm Tue-Sun Oct & Nov, closed Dec-Mar) Former stone quarries sometimes called the 'cathedral caves' for their lofty sloping walls resembling Gothic arches.

Musée du Champignon (☑ 02 41 50 31 55; www.musee-du-champignon.com; rte de Gennes, St-Hilaire-St-Florent; adult/child €8.20/6; ⊘ 10am-6pm mid-Feb–mid-Nov) Get acquainted with the fabulous fungus at the museum/producer tucked into a cave at the western edge of St-Hilaire-St-Florent.

❶ Getting There & Around

BICYCLE

Détours de Loire (☑ 02 41 53 01 01; 10 rue de Rouen; half-/full day €10/15; ⊘ 9.30am-1pm & 3-6.30pm May-Sep) Loire Valley bicycle hire chain, with an outlet in Saumur.

BUS

Agglobus (☑ 02 41 51 11 87; www.agglobus.fr; 28 place de la Gare de l'Etat; single/day ticket €1.35/3.80; ⊘ office 2-6pm Mon, 9am-noon & 2-6pm Tue-Fri, 9am-noon Sat) Runs local buses, such as line 5 to St-Hilaire-St-Florent and line 1, east along the Loire.

Anjou Bus (www.anjoubus.fr) Lines 4 and 17 serve Angers (€5.60) and intermediate points. Get the route maps online or at the tourist office.

TRAIN

Saumur's train station is across the river, 1.2km from the tourist office.

Angers €8.90, 20 to 35 minutes, 16 daily

Paris' Gare Montparnasse €72, 2½ hours (requires one transfer)

Tours €12, 30 to 50 minutes, 12 daily

East of Saumur

Some of the region's most exquisite scenery stretches along the D947 east of Saumur, with sparkling riverside tufa bluffs and cave houses. Many of the renowned wine producers here offer free tastings from around 10am to 6pm from spring to autumn. Visit www.producteurs-de-saumur-champigny.fr for more information. The area is served by Agglobus line 1.

Turquant

Ten kilometres east of Saumur, the picturesque village of Turquant has one of the region's highest concentrations of troglodyte dwellings. Many have now been spiffed up and converted into shops, galleries or restaurants.

⊙ Sights & Activities

La Grande Vignolle   WINERY
(☑ 02 41 38 16 44; www.filliatreau.com; ⊘ 10am-6pm May-Sep) A domaine and tasting room in grand tufa caves.

Troglo des Pommes Tapées CAVE
(02 41 51 48 30; www.letroglodespommes
tapees.fr; 11 rue des Ducs d'Anjou; adult/child
€6/3.50; 2-6.30pm Tue, 10am-12.30pm &
2-6.30pm Wed-Sun, closed mid-Nov–mid-Feb) One
of the last places in France producing traditional dried apples known as *pommes tapées*.
You can see displays on how it's done, sample
the wares and buy some to take home.

Sleeping & Eating

Demeure de la Vignole DESIGN HOTEL €€
(02 41 53 67 00; www.demeure-vignole.com; 3 impasse Marguerite d'Anjou; d €130-155, ste €155-270;
) This upscale hotel has several richly
decorated troglodyte rooms and suites, and a
subterranean swimming pool.

L'Hélianthe BISTRO €€
(02 41 51 22 28; www.restaurant-helianthe.fr;
Ruelle Antoine Cristal; lunch/dinner mains €11/15;
noon-1.30pm & 7.30-9.30pm Thu-Tue Apr–mid-
Nov, shorter hours rest of year) Tucked into a cliff
behind the town hall, this bistro has a hearty
menu revolving around countryfied flavours. Expect stews and 'ancient vegetables'
(Jerusalem artichokes, beets, rutabagas etc).

Bistroglo BISTRO €€
(02 41 40 22 36; www.bistroglo.com; Atelier 3,
rue du Château Gaillard; mains €10-15; noon-7pm
Tue-Sat Mar-Oct;) Artisanal beers and local wines are the lead-in to fresh local food
dished up with a cave-side smile.

Montsoreau

The **Château de Montsoreau** (02 41 67
12 60; www.chateau-montsoreau.com; adult/child
€9.20/5.50; 10am-7pm May-Sep, 2-6pm Mar-
Apr & Oct–mid-Nov, closed mid-Nov–Feb;) is
beautifully situated on the edge of the Loire.
It was built in 1455 by one of Charles VII's
advisers, and later became famous thanks
to an Alexandre Dumas novel, *La Dame de
Monsoreau*. Exhibits explore the castle's history, the novel and the river trade that once
sustained the Loire Valley. There are spectacular river views from the rooftop.

Information

**Parc Naturel Régional Loire-Anjou-Touraine
Maison du Parc** (02 41 38 38 88; www.
parc-loire-anjou-touraine.fr; 15 av de la Loire;
9.30am-7pm) The Maison du Parc provides
maps and information on activities throughout the 2530-sq-km Parc Naturel Régional
Loire-Anjou-Touraine, a regional park established to protect the landscape, extraordinary
architectural patrimony and culture of this
section of the Loire Valley.

Candes-St-Martin

Just east of Montsoreau, the village of
Candes-St-Martin (population 229) occupies
an idyllic spot at the confluence of the Vienne and Loire rivers. St Martin died here in
397, and thus picturesque Candes became a
major pilgrimage point and bears his name.

For great views, climb the tiny streets
above the church, past inhabited cave dwellings, for a higher-altitude perspective on the
confluence, or head down to the benches and
path along the waterfront.

Sights & Activities

Collégiale St-Martin CHURCH
This beautiful 12th- to 13th-century church
venerates the spot where St Martin died and
was buried in 397 (though his body was later
removed to Tours).

CPIE Val de Loire BOAT TOUR
(02 47 95 93 15; www.bateaux-candes.org; Candes-St-Martin; adult €9-14, child €6.50-9; Jul &
Aug) Two traditional high-cabined vessels
known as *toues* depart from Candes-St-Martin and cruise the convergence of the Loire
and the Vienne rivers for one to 1.5 hours.

Fontevraud-l'Abbaye

Sights

⭐**Abbaye de Fontevraud** HISTORIC ABBEY
(02 41 51 73 52; www.abbayedefontevraud.com;
adult/child €9.50/7, audioguide €4.50, smartphone
app free; 9.30am-6.30pm Apr-mid-Nov, 10am-
5.30pm Tue-Sat mid-Nov–Mar, closed Jan) Until
its closure in 1793 this huge 12th-century
complex was one of the largest ecclesiastical
centres in Europe. The extensive grounds
include a **chapter room** with murals of the
Passion of Christ by Thomas Pot. And keep
a look out for the multi-chimneyed, rock-
et-shaped **kitchen**, built entirely from stone
to make it fireproof.

But the highlight is undoubtedly the
massive, movingly simple **abbey church**,
notable for its soaring pillars, Romanesque
domes and the polychrome tombs of four
illustrious Plantagenets: Henry II, King of
England (r 1154–89); his wife Eleanor of
Aquitaine (who retired to Fontevraud following Henry's death); their son Richard the
Lionheart; and his brother King John's wife,
Isabelle of Angoulême.

THE LOIRE VALLEY EAST OF SAUMUR

Unusually, both nuns and monks at the abbey were governed by an abbess (generally a lady of noble birth retiring from public life). The abbey's cloister is surrounded by dormitories, workrooms and prayer halls, as well as a spooky underground sewer system and a wonderful barrel-vaulted refectory, where the monks and nuns would eat in silence while being read the scriptures.

After the Revolution, the buildings became a prison, in use until 1963. Author Jean Gênet was imprisoned here for stealing, and later wrote *Miracle de la Rose* (1946) based on his experiences.

Agglobus line 1 from Saumur comes to Fontevraud.

🛏 Sleeping & Eating

Fontevraud l'Hôtel　　　　HOTEL, RESTAURANT €€
(☑ 02 46 46 10 10; www.hotel-fontevraud.com; d/q/ste €185/195/230; ☎) Reopened in 2014 after a total renovation, plush rooms in muted siennas fill one of the abbey's priories. The gastronomic **restaurant** (☉ noon-2pm Sun, 7.30-9.30pm nightly, closed Nov-Mar; menus €55–95) serves seriously haute cuisine, conceived by award-winning chef Thibaut Ruggeri.

Chez Teresa　　　　　　　TEAROOM €
(☑ 02 41 51 21 24; www.chezteresa.fr; 6 av Rochechouart; menus €12.50-17.50; ☉ noon-7pm) Keeping up Fontevraud's English connections, this frilly little teashop and B&B is run by an expat English couple with a passion for traditional teatime fare: tea for two with sandwiches, scones and cakes costs €9.50. There's to upstairs rooms (double €60 to €65).

Château de Brézé

A unique Renaissance château, 12km south of Saumur, **Château de Brézé** (☑ 02 41 51 60 15; www.chateaudebreze.com; adult/child €11/9.50, tours free; ☉ 10am-6.30pm Apr-Sep, to 7.30pm Jul & Aug, 10am-6pm Tue-Sun Oct-Mar, closed Jan) sits atop a network of subterranean rooms and passages dating from at least the 11th century that account for more square footage than the castle itself. Explore the original troglodyte dwelling directly under the château, then cross a deep moat to other caves adapted by the castle's owners for use as kitchens, wine cellars and defensive bastions. Finish your visit with a climb to the château's rooftop, followed by a tasting of wines from surrounding vineyards.

Agglobus line 2 connects Saumur and Brézé.

Angers
POP 151,161

This lively riverside city was the historical seat of the powerful dukes of Anjou and the Plantagenets and is now famous for its tapestries: the 14th-century *Tenture de l'Apocalypse* in the city's château and the 20th-century *Chant du Monde* at the Jean Lurçat museum. A bustling old town, with many pedestrianised streets and a thriving cafe culture, makes it an interesting western gateway to the Loire Valley.

⦿ Sights & Activities

★ **Château d'Angers**　　　　CHÂTEAU
(☑ 02 41 86 48 77; www.angers.monuments-nationaux.fr; 2 promenade du Bout-du-Monde; adult/child €8.50/free; ☉ 9.30am-6.30pm May-Aug, 10am-5.30pm Sep-Apr) This impressive black-stone château, formerly the seat of power for the counts and dukes of Anjou, looms above the river, ringed by battlements and 17 watchtowers. The star of the show is the stunning **Tenture de l'Apocalypse** (Apocalypse tapestry), a 104m-long series of tapestries commissioned by Louis I, Duke of Anjou, around 1375 to illustrate the Book of Revelation. It dramatically recounts the

Angers

story of the Day of Judgment from start to finish, complete with the Four Horsemen of the Apocalypse, the Battle of Armageddon and the coming of the Beast.

Look out for graphic depictions of St Michael battling a seven-headed dragon and the fall of Babylon. The site has been inhabited since neolithic times and some **ancient excavations** remain.

Audioguides (€4.50) provide useful context, and guided tours are free. That black stone? It's actually called blue schist.

★**Musée Jean Lurçat et de la Tapisserie Contemporaine** MUSEUM
(☑ 02 41 24 18 45; www.musees.angers.fr; 4 bd Arago; adult/child €4/free; ☙10am-6pm May-Sep, 10am-noon & 2-6pm Tue-Sun Oct-Apr) An excellent counterpoint to Angers' famous *Tenture de l'Apocalypse*, this museum collects fine 20th-century tapestries by Jean Lurçat, Thomas Gleb and others inside the **Hôpital St-Jean**, a 12th-century hospital

founded by Henry Plantagenet, on the west bank of the river, north of the château. The centrepiece is the epic *Chant du Monde* (Song of the World), an amazing series depicting trials and triumphs of modern humanity, from nuclear holocaust and space exploration to the delights of drinking Champagne. Excellently curated rotating exhibitions.

★**Musée des Beaux-Arts** ART MUSEUM
(☑ 02 41 05 38 00; www.musees.angers.fr; 14 rue du Musée; adult/child €4/free; ☙10am-6pm daily May-Sep, Tue-Sun Oct-Apr) The buildings of the sprawling, fantastic fine-arts museum mix plate glass with the fine lines of the typical Angevin aristocratic house. The museum has a section on the history of Angers and a superior 17th- to 20th-century collection: Monet, Ingres, Lorenzo Lippi and Flemish masters including Rogier van der Weyden.

Angers

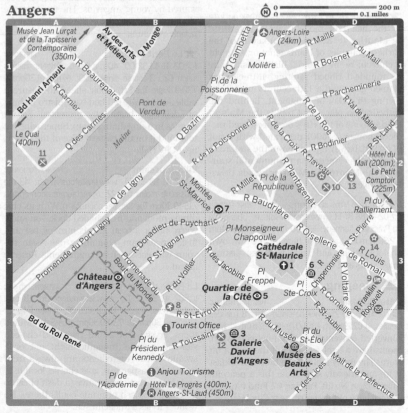

THE LOIRE VALLEY ANGERS

★ **Galerie David d'Angers**　　　MUSEUM

(✆02 41 05 38 90; www.musees.angers.fr; 33bis rue Toussaint; adult/child €4/free; ⊘10am-6pm daily May-Sep, Tue-Sun Oct-Apr) Angers' most famous son is sculptor Pierre-Jean David (1788–1856), often just known as David d'Angers. Renowned for lifelike sculptures, his work adorns public monuments all over France, notably at the Panthéon, the Louvre and Père Lachaise cemetery. His work forms the cornerstone of this museum, housed in the converted 12th-century **Toussaint Abbey** and flooded with light through a striking glass-and-girder ceiling.

★ **Quartier de la Cité**　　　HISTORIC QUARTER

In the hea rt of the old city, **Cathédrale St-Maurice** (⊘8.30am-7.30pm) is one of the earliest examples of Plantagenet or Angevin architectu re in France, distinguished by its rounde d ribbed vaulting, 15th-century stained gl ass and a 12th-century portal depicting th e Day of Judgment. Behind the cathedral on place Ste-Croix is the **Maison d'Adam**, one of the city's best-preserved medieval houses (c 1500), decorated with a riot of carved, bawdy figures. From the square in front of the cathedral, a monumental staircase, the **Montée St-Maurice**, leads down to the river.

Maison des Vins d'Angers　　　WINE TASTING

(✆02 41 88 81 13; www.vinsvaldeloire.fr; 5bis place du Président Kennedy; ⊘2.30-7pm Mon, 10am-1pm & 2.30-7pm Tue-Sat) Head here for the lowdown on local Anjou and Loire vintages: tasting, sales, tours and tips.

🛏 **Sleeping**

Hôtel du Mail　　　HISTORIC HOTEL €

(✆02 41 25 05 25; www.hoteldumail.fr; 8 rue des Ursules; d €71-91, tr/q €101/111; 🛜) Situated in a converted convent around a quiet courtyard, rooms have a light feel, even if they are a bit worn. The funky lobby, huge buffet breakfast (€10) and friendly staff make this a peaceful Angers base. No lift. Parking €7. Find it on the eastern edge of the centre, near City Hall.

Hôtel Continental　　　HOTEL €

(✆02 41 86 94 94; www.hotellecontinental.com; 14 rue Louis de Romain; s €77-87, d €88-90; ✳🛜) 🖉 Wedged into a triangular corner building in the city centre, this green-certified, metro-style hotel has 25 rooms decked out in cosy checks and sunny colours.

Hôtel Le Progrès　　　HOTEL €

(✆02 41 88 10 14; www.hotelleprogres.com; 26 rue Denis Papin; s €52-60, d €69-90; 🛜) It's nothing fancy, but this reliable station hotel is solid, friendly and squeaky clean, and has a lift and free bike storage.

🍴 **Eating**

Find student hangs and international restaurants radiating out from the rue St-Laud pedestrian area.

Chez Toi　　　BISTRO €

(✆02 41 87 85 58; 44 rue St-Laud; menus from €14; ⊘9am-12.30am Mon-Sat, 3pm-12.30am Sun; 🛜🖉) Minimalist furniture and technicolour trappings meet in this zippy little lounge-bar, favoured by young Angevins. The front terrace along pedestrianised rue St-Laud is great for people-watching.

★ **Le Petit Comptoir**　　　BISTRO €€

(✆02 41 43 32 00; 40 rue David d'Angers; menus lunch €20, 3-course dinner €29; ⊘noon-1.30pm & 7.30-9.30pm Tue-Sat) Book ahead to ensure a table at this ruby red laid-back bistro dishing up delicious, beautifully presented French classics in a tiny dining room. Super wine list too! Find it on the eastern edge of the centre, near City Hall.

Villa Toussaint　　　FRENCH FUSION €€

(✆02 41 88 15 64; www.lavillatoussaint.fr; 43 rue Toussaint; mains €16-22; ⊘restaurant noon-2pm & 7.15-10.30pm Tue-Sat, bar noon-2am) With its chic dining room and tree-shaded deck, you know you're in for a treat at this buzzing bar and fusion restaurant, combining pan-Asian flavours with classic French ingredients. Reserve ahead.

Le Favre d'Anne　　　GASTRONOMIC €€€

(✆02 41 36 12 12; www.lefavredanne.fr; 18 quai des Carmes; menus lunch €25-35, dinner €45-95; ⊘noon-1.30pm & 7.30-9.30pm Tue-Sat) Muted tones, crystal, linen, and river and château views call for a romantic night out or a swanky lunch. Ingredients are always fresh (artichokes, asparagus, goat cheese, local fish) and the concoctions creative (a dash of cacao here and a splash of prune coulis there). No wonder it has a Michelin star.

Self-Catering

Food Market MARKET

(place Louis Imbach & place Leclerc; ☉ Sat morning)
The weekly market spreads across two central squares: place Louis Imbach and place Leclerc.

Drinking & Entertainment

Cultural happenings appear in *Angers Poche,* a free weekly guide available at the tourist office. The best drinking street is rue St-Laud, which fills with folks of all ages.

Baroque BAR

(Barock Cafe; 35 rue St-Laud; ☉3pm-2am) Streetside tables packed with students kick off the run of nightspots along the St-Laud pedestrian zone.

Grand Théâtre d'Angers THEATRE

(☑ 02 41 24 16 40; www.angers-nantes-opera.com; place du Ralliement) Hosts theatre, dance and music.

Le Quai PERFORMING ARTS

(☑ 02 41 22 20 20; www.lequai-angers.eu; bd Henri Arnault; ☉ box office 1-7pm Tue-Fri, 3-6pm Sat) Angers' state-of-the-art performance and visual arts centre.

Les Quatre-Cents Coups CINEMA

(☑ 02 41 88 70 95; www.les400coups.org; 12 rue Claveau) Arts cinema showing non-dubbed films.

① Information

Anjou Tourisme (☑ 02 41 23 51 51; www.anjou-tourisme.com; place du Président Kennedy; ☉9.30am-12.30pm & 2-5.30pm Mon-Fri) Regional information.

Tourist Office (☑ 02 41 23 50 00; www.angersloiretourisme.com; 7 place du Président Kennedy; ☉10am-6.30pm Mon, 9am-6.30pm Tue-Sat, 10am-6pm Sun, shorter hours Oct-Apr) Helpful, with lockers and loads of info on sights, activities and transport. Sells the Angers City Pass.

① Getting There & Away

AIR

Angers-Loire Airport (ANE; ☑ 02 41 33 50 00; www.angersloireaeroport.fr) Seasonal flights to London and Nice. Located 24km northeast of Angers' centre.

BUS

Anjou Bus (☑ 08 20 16 00 49; www.anjoubus.fr; tickets €1.80-5.60) Regional services depart from the Gare Routière, adjacent to the train station. For Saumur, take bus 4 or 17 (€5.60, 1½ hours, three daily Monday to Saturday).

TRAIN

Angers St-Laud Train Station is located 500m southwest of the château and tourist office, and has both regular and TGV service.

Nantes €15.60, ¾ hour, 26 daily
Paris' Gare Montparnasse €52 to €71, 1½ to 1¾ hours, hourly
Saumur €8.90, 30 minutes, 16 daily
Tours €19, 1¼ hours, 15 daily

① Getting Around

BICYCLE

The tourist office rents bikes (€15 per day) as part of the Détours de Loire network, and has great area cycling maps (www.anjou-velo.com) and a smartphone app.

BUS & TRAM

Irigo (☑ 02 41 33 64 64; http://bustram.irigo.fr; single/day ticket €1.40/3.70) Runs local buses and trams. Find schedules online or at the tourist office.

CAR

Major car-rental companies have rental desks inside the train station.

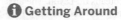

COINTREAU

Renowned bitter orange liqueur Cointreau has its origins in the experiments of two enterprising brothers: Adolphe Cointreau, a sweet-maker, and Édouard-Jean Cointreau, who founded a factory in Angers in 1849 to produce fruit-flavoured liqueurs. In 1875 Édouard-Jean's son (also called Édouard) hit upon the winning concoction of sweet and bitter oranges, flavoured with intensely orangey peel. The liqueur was a massive success; by the early 1900s over 800,000 bottles of Cointreau were being produced annually to the top-secret recipe, and a century later every one of the 13 million bottles is still distilled to the same formula at the original factory site **Carré Cointreau** (☑ 02 41 31 50 50; www.cointreau.com; 2 bd des Bretonnières, St-Barthélemy-d'Anjou; 2hr tours €10, tastings €6.20-9.80; ☉ guided tours by reservation). Find it off the ring road east of Angers in St-Barthélemy-d'Anjou. From the train station, take Irigo bus 6.

24 HOURS OF LE MANS

During the second week of June each year, race car aficionados converge on Le Mans (population 147,687), 97km northwest of Angers on the A11, to watch this careening, 24-hour endurance race. Corvettes, Porsches, Ferraris and myriad other souped-up speedsters whip around the 13.629km Circuit de la Sarthe track at the world's oldest sports-car race (www.lemans.org), first run in 1923.

The rest of the year, visit the **museum** (☑ 02 43 72 72 24; www.lemusee24h.com; 9 place Luigi Chinetti; adult/child €8.50/6; ⊙ 10am-6pm Apr-Sep, 11am-5pm Wed-Mon Oct-Mar, shorter hours Jan), which houses over 150 vehicles from an 1885 De Dion Bouton et Trepardoux steam-driven dog cart to past winners that are just a bit speedier.

TAXI

Allô Anjou Taxi (☑ 02 41 87 65 00; www.alloanjoutaxi.com)

Taxis Angevins (☑ 02 41 34 96 52)

Around Angers

South of Angers, the River Maine joins the Loire for the final leg of its journey to the Atlantic. The river banks immediately west of this confluence remain the source of some of the valley's most notable wines, including Savennières (near a pretty village of the same name) and Coteaux du Layon. The area due south of Angers, between Gennes, Brissac-Quincé and Savennières, makes for great, small-road exploration and rural driving.

Château de Brissac

The tallest castle in France, the **Château de Brissac** (☑ 02 41 91 22 21; www.chateau-brissac.fr; Brissac-Quincé; adult/child incl tour €10/4.50, gardens only €5/free; ⊙ 10am-12.15pm & 2-6pm Wed-Mon Apr-Oct, 10am-6pm daily Jul & Aug) comprises seven storeys and 204 rooms. Built by the Duke of Brissac in 1502, and still owned by the family, it is one of the most luxuriously outfitted castles in the Loire, with a riot of posh furniture, ornate tapestries, twinkling chandeliers and swank bedrooms – even a private theatre. Around the house, 8 sq km of serene **grounds** are filled with cedar trees, 19th-century stables and a vineyard, boasting three AOC vintages.

Four of the château's bedrooms are ridiculously extravagant **chambres d'hôte** (B&Bs; rooms €390).

Anjou Bus 5 (€1.80, 30 to 40 minutes, 11 daily Monday to Friday, five on Saturday) links Angers with Brissac-Quincé, 20km to the southeast.

Château de Serrant

Built from cream-and-fawn tufa and crowned by bell-shaped, slate-topped towers, the grand **Château de Serrant** (☑ 02 41 39 13 01; www.chateau-serrant.net; adult/child €10/6.50; ⊙ tours only 9.45am-5.15pm Jul & Aug, Wed-Sun & shorter hours rest of year) is a small slice of Renaissance style. Begun by aristocrat Charles de Brie in the 16th century, the château (seen only by guided tour) is notable for its 12,000-tome **library**, huge kitchens and an extravagant domed bedroom known as the **Chambre Empire**, designed to host Emperor Napoléon (who actually only hung around for about two hours).

The château is near St-Georges-sur-Loire, 15km southwest of Angers on the N23. Anjou Bus lines 22 and 24 serve Angers (€1.80, 30 to 40 minutes, two to four Monday to Saturday).

ⓘ LOIRE VALLEY RESOURCES

Loire Valley châteaux:
www.leschateauxdelaloire.org

Loire Valley heritage site:
www.valdeloire.org

Cycling routes: www.loireavelo.fr

Wines of the Loire:
www.vinsvaldeloire.fr

B&Bs, camping and vacation rentals: www.gites-de-france-loiret.com, www.gites-de-france-blois.com

Regional transport details:
www.destineo.fr

Burgundy

POP 1.64 MILLION

Best Places to Eat

➜ La Table d'Héloïse (p450)

➜ Le Millésime (p421)

➜ La Pause Gourmande (p433)

➜ Auprès du Clocher (p422)

➜ Ma Table en Ville (p451)

Best Places to Stay

➜ Villa Louise Hôtel (p422)

➜ La Cimentelle (p439)

➜ Le Clos de l'Abbaye (p449)

➜ La Maison d'Olivier Leflaive (p422)

➜ Le Tabellion (p438)

Why Go?

Burgundy (Bourgogne in French) offers some of France's most gorgeous countryside: rolling green hills dotted with mustard fields and medieval villages. The region's towns and its dashingly handsome capital, Dijon, are heirs to a glorious architectural heritage that goes back to the Renaissance, the Middle Ages and into the mists of Gallo-Roman and Celtic antiquity.

Two great French passions, wine and food, come together here in a particularly rich and enticing form. Indeed, Burgundy's centuries-old history of viticulture, combined with the remarkable diversity of its wine-growing *terroir* (land), have made the region's vineyards a strong candidate for Unesco World Heritage status.

Burgundy is also a paradise for lovers of the great outdoors. You can cycle through the Côte d'Or vineyards, hike the wild reaches of the Parc Naturel Régional du Morvan, glide along the Yonne's waterways in a canal boat or float above it all in a hot-air balloon.

When to Go

Dijon

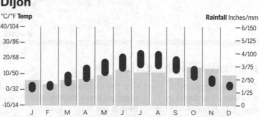

| **May & Jun** Long, sunny days are ideal for boating on Burgundy's 1200km of placid waterways. | **Jul** Splendid weather makes summer a perfect time to cycle Burgundy's bike trails. | **Sep & Oct** Wine harvest season offers classic perspectives on Burgundy's vineyards |

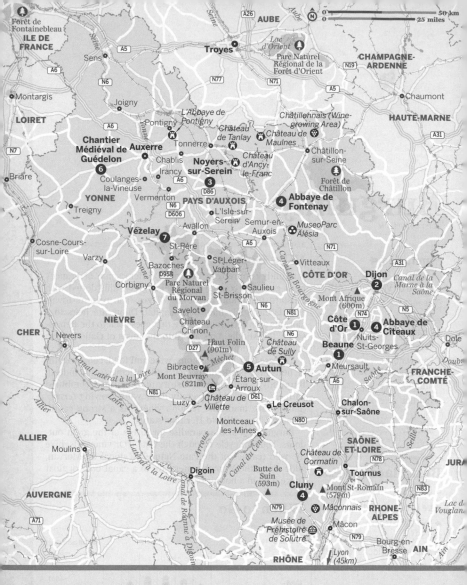

Burgundy Highlights

1 Sampling Burgundy's most renowned vintages in **Beaune** (p422) and along the vine-carpeted slopes of the **Côte d'Or** (p418)

2 Basking in the reflected glory of the Burgundy dukes in **Dijon** (p411)

3 Watching the mist rise off the river and the sun emerge over the medieval battlements of picturesque **Noyers-sur-Serein** (p437)

4 Conjuring up medieval monastic life at the abbeys of **Cluny** (p449), **Fontenay** (p429) and **Cîteaux** (p428)

5 Marvelling at the sensual grace of Gislebertus' 12th-century carving of Eve at the **Musée Rolin** (p446) in Autun

6 Seeing a château built using 13th-century technology at **Chantier Médiéval de Guédelon** (p434)

7 Climbing through idyllic green countryside and cobblestoned lanes to reach the hilltop basilica of **Vézelay** (p440)

History

At its height during the 14th and 15th centuries, the duchy of Burgundy was one of the richest and most powerful states in Europe and encompassed a vast swath of territory stretching from modern-day Burgundy to Alsace and northwest to Lorraine, Luxembourg, Flanders and Holland. This was a time of bitter rivalry between Burgundy and France; indeed, it was the Burgundians who sold Jeanne d'Arc (Joan of Arc) to the English, and for a while it seemed quite possible that the kingdom of France would be taken over by Burgundy. In the end, though, it worked out the other way around, and in 1477 Burgundy became French. During the Middle Ages two Burgundy-based monastic orders exerted significant influence across much of Christendom. The ascetic Cistercians were headquartered at Cîteaux, while their bitter rivals, the powerful and worldly Benedictines, were based at Cluny.

❶ Getting There & Around

By car or rail (including the TGV Sud-Est), Burgundy makes an easy stopover on the way from the English Channel or Paris to the Alps or southern France.

CAR

From Dijon, autoroutes stretch northeast to Alsace (A36), north to Lorraine (A31), north and then west to Champagne (A31, A5 and A26) and south to Lyon and the Rhône Valley (A6).

BUS & TRAIN

The towns and some of the villages in this region are served by trains and buses in high season, though patience and planning are a must as services in many areas are infrequent (especially on Sunday and during school holidays).

Mobigo (☑ 08 00 10 20 04; www.mobigo-bourgogne.com) has details of buses and trains around Burgundy.

BURGUNDY WEB RESOURCES

➡ **Biking Burgundy**
www.burgundy-by-bike.com

➡ **Train and bus options**
www.mobigo-bourgogne.com

➡ **Wines of Burgundy**
www.bourgogne-wines.com

➡ **Music and events**
www.magma-magazine.fr

FAST FACTS

➡ **Area** 31,582 sq km

➡ **Local industry** viticulture

➡ **Signature drink** white wine

CÔTE D'OR

The Côte d'Or *département* is named after one of the world's foremost wine-growing regions, which stretches from Dijon, bursting with cultural riches, south to the wine town of Beaune and beyond. In the far northwest of the *département*, on the border with Champagne, Châtillon-sur-Seine displays Celtic treasures; in the west you can explore the walled, hilltop town of Semur-en-Auxois.

Dijon

POP 155,900

Dijon is one of France's most appealing cities. Filled with elegant medieval and Renaissance buildings, the lively centre is wonderful for strolling, especially if you like to leaven your cultural enrichment with excellent food, fine wine and shopping.

History

Dijon served as the capital of the duchy of Burgundy from the 11th to 15th centuries, enjoying a golden age during the 14th and 15th centuries under Philippe-le-Hardi (Philip the Bold), Jean-sans-Peur (John the Fearless) and Philippe-le-Bon (Philip the Good). During their reigns, some of the finest painters, sculptors and architects from around the continent were brought to Dijon, turning the city into one of the great centres of European art.

◎ Sights

The Owl's Trail (€3.50), available in 11 languages at the tourist office, details a self-guided city-centre walking tour; the route is marked on the pavement with bronze triangles. All of Dijon's municipal museums are free except, occasionally, for special exhibitions. Major churches are open from 8am to 7pm.

Palais des Ducs et des États de Bourgogne PALACE
(Palace of the Dukes & States of Burgundy; place de la Libération) Once home to Burgundy's powerful dukes, this monumental palace with a neoclassical façade overlooks place de la

BURGUNDY

Dijon

0 200 m
0 0.1 miles

R des Perrières
Train Station
Foch-Gare
R du Dr Remy
Av Maréchal Foch
Eurolines
Divia
Agence Commerciale
Av de la 1ère Armée
Bd de Brosses
Pl Darcy
Porte Guillaume (Triumphal Arch)
R Devosge
R du Temple
Pl Grangier
Pl Mably
R du Château
R Mariotte
R Dr Chaussier
Bd de Sévigné
Rempart Miséricorde
Av Albert 1er
Puits de Moise (1.3km);
Avallon (105km)
R de l'Arquebuse
R du Faubourg Raines
R du l'Ouche
R Jehan de Marville
Beaune (1.3km)
Av de l'Ouche

R Vannerie
R du Lycée
Pl St-Michel
R Jeannin
R Buffon
Bd Carnot
R Berbier
R d'Assas
R Auguste Comte
R Chaudronnerie
R Verrerie
Pl des Ducs de Bourgogne
R de la Chouette
R de la Préfecture
Musée des Beaux-Arts
Pl du Théâtre
R Vaillant
R Chabot Chamy
R Rameau
R des Bons Enfants
R du Palais
R Pasteur
R Amiral Roussin
R Vauban
Pl de la Libération
R Jules Mercier
R du Bourg
R des Forges
R Musette
Impasse Quentin
Pl de la Banque
R Odebert
R Banneller
R des Godrans
R Bossuet
R Pion
R Victor Dumay
Pl des Cordeliers
R Turgot
R Ste-Anne
R du Chapeau Rouge
R Mablу
R de la Liberté
R Michelet
R Danton
R Brulard
Pl Bossuet
R Condorcet
R Monge
R Berbisey
R Crébillon
Pl Émile Zola
R de la Manutention

Dijon

Libération, Old Dijon's magnificent central square dating from 1686. The palace's eastern wing houses the outstanding Musée des Beaux-Arts, whose entrance is next to the **Tour de Bar**, a squat 14th-century tower that once served as a prison.

Tour Philippe le Bon   TOWER
(adult/child €3/free; ☺ guided tours every 45min 10.30am-noon & 1.45-5.30pm Apr–mid-Nov, less frequent tours Tue, Sat & Sun rest of year) Adjacent to the ducal palace, this 46m-high, mid-15th-century tower affords fantastic views over the city. On a clear day you can see all the way to Mont Blanc. Dijon's tourist office handles reservations.

★ **Musée des Beaux-Arts**   ART MUSEUM
(☑ 03 80 74 52 09; http://mba.dijon.fr; audioguide €4; ☺ 9.30am-6pm Wed-Mon May-Oct, 10am-5pm Nov-Apr) **FREE** Housed in the monumental Palais des Ducs, these sprawling galleries (works of art in themselves) constitute one of France's most outstanding museums. The star attraction, reopened in September 2013 after extensive renovations, is the wood-panelled **Salle des Gardes**, which houses the ornate, carved late-medieval sepulchres of dukes John the Fearless and Philip the Bold. Other sections focus on Egyptian art, the Middle Ages in Burgundy and Europe, and six centuries of European painting, from the Renaissance to modern times.

The museum's highlights include a fine collection of 13th- and 14th-century primitives that reveal how medieval artistic and aesthetic sensibilities varied between Italy, Switzerland and the Rhineland; a smattering of old masters such as Lorenzo Lotto; quite a few naturalistic sculptures by the Dijon-born artist François Rude (1784–1855); works by Manet, Monet, Matisse and Rodin; and the incomparable Pompon Room, tucked off a back staircase, packed with stylised modern sculptures of animals by François Pompon (1855–1933), who was born in Saulieu, Burgundy. In the courtyard, the ducal kitchens (1433) often host exhibitions of works by local artists.

Hôtels Particuliers   HISTORIC MANSIONS
Many of Dijon's finest houses lie near the Palais des Ducs on and around rue Verrerie, rue Vannerie and rue des Forges, whose names reflect the industries that once thrived there (glassmaking, basket-weaving and metalsmithery, respectively). Go inside the splendid 17th-century **Hôtel Chambellan** (34 rue des Forges) **FREE**, from whose courtyard a spiral stone staircase leads up to remarkable vaulting. Further east you'll find the 13th-century **Hôtel Aubriot** (40 rue des Forges) and the Renaissance-style

Maison Maillard (38 rue des Forges), all garlands and lions.

Another particularly fine building is the early 17th-century Maison des Cariatides (28 rue Chaudronnerie), its façade a riot of stone caryatids, soldiers and vines. Behind Église Notre Dame, the 17th-century Hôtel de Vogüé (8 rue de la Chouette) is renowned for the ornate carvings around its exquisitely proportioned Renaissance courtyard. It's worth walking through the pink stone archway for a peek. More modern figures of an owl and a cat perch high atop the roof of the 15th-century Maison Millière (10 rue de la Chouette), which was a setting in the 1990 film *Cyrano de Bergerac* with Gérard Depardieu.

Église Notre Dame
CHURCH

(place Notre-Dame) A block north of the Palais des Ducs, this church was built between 1220 and 1240. Its extraordinary façade's three tiers are lined with leering gargoyles separated by two rows of pencil-thin columns. Atop the church, the 14th-century Horloge à Jacquemart, transported from Flanders in 1383 by Philip the Bold who claimed it as a trophy of war, chimes every quarter-hour.

Rue de la Chouette
STREET

Around the north side of Église Notre Dame, this street is named after the small stone *chouette* (owl) carved into the exterior corner of the chapel diagonally across from No 24. Said to grant happiness and wisdom to those who stroke it, it has been worn smooth by generations of fortune-seekers.

Musée Archéologique
ARCHAEOLOGY MUSEUM

(03 80 48 83 70; 5 rue du Docteur Maret; 9.30am-12.30pm & 2-6pm Wed-Mon Apr-Oct, Wed, Sat & Sun Nov-Mar) FREE Truly surprising Celtic, Roman and Merovingian artefacts are displayed here, including a particularly fine 1st-century AD bronze of the Celtic goddess Sequana standing on a dual-prowed boat. Upstairs, the early Gothic hall (12th and 13th centuries), with its ogival arches held aloft by two rows of columns, once served as the dormitory of a Benedictine abbey.

Musée Magnin
ART MUSEUM

(03 80 67 11 10; www.facebook.com/musee.magnin; 4 rue des Bons-Enfants; adult/child incl audioguide €3.50/free; 10am-noon & 2-6pm Tue-Sun) Jeanne and Maurice Magnin turned their historic townhouse over to the state to display their excellent art collection in perpetuity. Works include fine examples of the Italian Renaissance, and Flemish and medieval painting.

Musée de la Vie Bourguignonne
MUSEUM

(03 80 48 80 90; 17 rue Ste-Anne; 9.30am-12.30pm & 2-6pm Wed-Mon) FREE Housed in a 17th-century Cistercian convent, this museum explores village and town life in Burgundy in centuries past with evocative tableaux illustrating dress, customs and traditional crafts. On the 1st floor, a whole street has been recreated, complete with 19th-century pharmacy and numerous antique-filled shops (grocer, furrier, hat-maker, clock-maker, toy store and more).

Cathédrale St-Bénigne
CHURCH

(place St-Philibert) Built over the tomb of St Benignus (believed to have brought Christianity to Burgundy in the 2nd century), Dijon's Burgundian Gothic-style cathedral was built around 1300 as an abbey church. Some of Burgundy's great figures are buried in its crypt.

Église St-Michel
CHURCH

(place St-Michel) Originally Gothic, this church subsequently underwent a façade-lift operation in which it was given a richly ornamented Renaissance west front. Its two 17th-century towers are topped with cupolas and, higher still, glittering gold spheres.

Puits de Moïse
SCULPTURE

(Well of Moses; 1 bd Chanoine Kir, Centre Hospitalier Spécialisé La Chartreuse; admission €3.50; 9am-12.30pm & 1.30-6pm Apr-Oct, to 5pm Nov-Mar) This famous grouping of six Old Testament figures, carved from 1395 to 1405 by court sculptor Claus Sluter and his nephew Claus de Werve, is on the grounds of a psychiatric hospital 1km west of the train station; by bus take line 3 towards Fontaine d'Ouche.

Parks & Gardens
GARDENS

Dijon has plenty of green spaces that are perfect for picnics, including Jardin Darcy and Jardin de l'Arquebuse, the botanic gardens, with a stream and pond.

☞ Tours

The tourist office has scads of information on tours of the city and the nearby wine regions, and can make bookings.

Walking Tours
WALKING TOUR

(08 92 70 05 58; adult €6-15, child €1) A slew of different tours depart from the main tourist office, which distributes a handy schedule listing times and prices. Couples receive a €3 discount. Wine tasting is included in the more expensive 'Dijon and wine' tour.

Segway Tour HISTORY TOUR
(adult/child €19/8; ⊘ 10.30am & 2.30pm Sun Apr-Oct, plus afternoon tours Sat Apr & May, Fri & Sat Jun, Sep & Oct, Mon-Sat Jul & Aug) Run by the tourist office, this 1½-hour tour zips around the city centre. No children under 12.

Vineyard Tours WINE TOUR
Minibus tours in English introduce the Côte d'Or vineyards. Reserve by phone, internet or via the tourist office. Operators include **Alter & Go** (✎ 06 23 37 92 04; www.alterandgo. fr; tours from €70), with an emphasis on history and winemaking methods, **Authentica Tour** (✎ 06 87 01 43 78; www.authentica-tours.com; tours €55-125) and **Wine & Voyages** (✎ 03 80 61 15 15; www.wineandvoyages.com; tours from €53).

🛏 Sleeping

Hôtel du Palais HOTEL €
(✎ 03 80 65 51 43; www.hoteldupalais-dijon.fr; 23 rue du Palais; s €59-79, d €65-89, q €119; ❋ 🅟 🛜) Newly remodelled and upgraded to three-star status, this inviting hotel in a 17th-century *hôtel particulier* (private mansion) offers excellent value. The 13 rooms range from cosy, inexpensive 3rd-floor doubles tucked under the eaves to spacious, high-ceilinged family suites with abundant natural light. The location is unbeatable, on a quiet side street five minutes' walk from super-central place de la Libération.

Hôtel Le Sauvage HOTEL €
(✎ 03 80 41 31 21; www.hotellesauvage.com; 64 rue Monge; s €42-67, d €46-74, tr €85; 🛜) Set in a 15th-century *relais de poste* (coaching inn) that ranges around a cobbled, vine-shaded courtyard, this little hotel is definitely good value. Rooms 10, 12, 14 and 17, with exposed beams, are the cosiest. It's just steps from lively place Émile Zola, yet the rooms are pleasingly quiet. Parking €5.

Hôtel Le Jacquemart HOTEL €
(✎ 03 80 60 09 60; www.hotel-lejacquemart.fr; 32 rue Verrerie; s €54-65, d €63-75, s/d with shared bathroom €36/40; 🛜) In the heart of Old Dijon, this two-star hotel has tidy, comfortable rooms and friendly staff. Rooms 5 and 6, in a 17th-century annexe just across the street, are larger and better equipped than those within the hotel's original core, and combine vintage touches (stone walls, beamed ceiling) and modern conveniences.

Hôtel Le Chambellan HOTEL €
(✎ 03 80 67 12 67; www.hotel-chambellan.com; 92 rue Vannerie; s €42-57, d €57-64, s/d with shared bath-

room €35/38; 🛜) Built in 1730, this Old Town address has a vaguely medieval feel. Rooms come in cheerful tones of red, orange, pink and white; some have courtyard views.

Hôtel des Ducs HOTEL €€
(✎ 03 80 67 31 31; www.hoteldesducs.com; 5 rue Lamonnoye; d €89-119; ❋ @ 🛜) This modern, three-star hotel has been recently renovated. Rooms are fresh and airy and the contemporary design scheme is easy on the eye. Comfortable and convenient if you want to stay smack-dab in the centre of things. Parking costs €12.

La Cour Berbisey B&B €€€
(✎ 03 45 83 12 38; www.lacourberbisey.fr; 31 rue Berbisey; incl breakfast r €129-159, ste €189-279; 🛜 ❋) An arched red doorway in an ivy-draped wall leads to this recently opened luxury B&B, easily one of Dijon's classiest accommodations. Three enormous suites with parquet floors, beamed ceilings and tall French-shuttered windows are complemented by a lone junior suite and one smaller but equally comfortable double. Other upscale touches include an indoor swimming pool, sauna and antique-filled salon.

🍴 Eating

Find loads of restaurants on buzzy rue Berbisey, around place Émile Zola, on rue Amiral Roussin and around the perimeter of the covered market. In warm months, outdoor cafes and brasseries (restaurants) fill place de la Libération.

Brasserie B9 BRASSERIE €
(✎ 03 80 38 32 02; www.brasserie-b9.com; 9 place de la Libération; mains €12-17; ⊘ noon-2.30pm & 7-9.30pm Tue-Sun) Under the direction of gastronomic star Jean-Pierre Billoux, this brasserie on vast, sun-drenched place de la Libération serves up atmospheric views of the ducal palace and a €12 *plat du jour* even on weekends. It shares a kitchen with the renowned Pré des Clercs restaurant next door, and is among the few Dijonnais eateries that are dependably open on Sundays.

Chez Nous BISTRO €
(impasse Quentin; plat du jour €9; ⊘ 5-10pm Mon, 11am-3pm & 6-10pm Tue-Thu, 10am-midnight Fri & Sat) This quintessentially French *bar du coin* (neighbourhood bar), often crowded, hides down an alleyway near the covered market. At lunchtime join the flock and go for the fabulous-value *plat du jour* (daily special). Wash it all down with a glass of local wine (€2).

BURGUNDY WINE BASICS

Burgundy's epic vineyards extend approximately 258km from Chablis in the north to the Rhône's Beaujolais in the south and comprise 100 AOCs (Appellations d'Origine Contrôlée). Each region has its own appellations and traits, embodied by a concept called *terroir*, the earth imbuing its produce, such as grapes, with unique qualities. However, some appellations, such as Crémant de Bourgogne (a light, sparkling white or rosé) and Bourgogne Aligoté, are produced in several regions.

Wine Regions

Here's an ever-so-brief survey of some of Burgundy's major growing regions:

➜ **Côte d'Or vineyards** The northern section, the Côte de Nuits, stretches from Marsannay-la-Côte south to Corgoloin and produces reds known for their robust, full-bodied character. The southern section, the Côte de Beaune, lies between Ladoix-Serrigny and Santenay and produces great reds and whites. Appellations from the area's hilltops are the Hautes-Côtes de Nuits and Hautes-Côtes de Beaune.

➜ **Chablis & Grand Auxerrois** Four renowned chardonnay white wine appellations from 20 villages around Chablis. Part of the Auxerrois vineyards, Irancy produces excellent pinot noir reds. The Tonnerrois vineyards produce good, affordable reds, whites and rosés.

➜ **Châtillonnais** Approximately 20 villages around Châtillon-sur-Seine producing red and white wines.

➜ **Côte Chalonnaise** The southernmost continuation of the Côte de Beaune's slopes is noted for its excellent reds and whites.

➜ **Mâconnais** Known for rich or fruity white wines, like the Pouilly-Fuissé chardonnay.

Want to Know More?

Tourist offices provide brochures including *The Burgundy Wine Road* and a useful map, *Roadmap to the Wines of Burgundy*. A handy website is www.bourgogne-wines.com.

DZ'Envies REGIONAL CUISINE €€
(☑ 03 80 50 09 26; www.dzenvies.com; 12 rue Odebert; mains €16-20, lunch menus €13-20, dinner menus €29-36; ⊙ noon-2pm & 7-10pm Mon-Sat) This zinging restaurant with cheery decorative touches is a good choice if you're tired of heavy Burgundian classics. The menu always involves seasonal, fresh ingredients, and dishes are imaginatively prepared and beautifully presented. At €18, the lunchtime '*I love Dijon*' *menu* is a steal.

Chez Léon REGIONAL CUISINE €€
(☑ 03 80 50 01 07; www.restochezleon.fr; 20 rue des Godrans; mains €17-23, lunch menus €15-19, dinner menus €25-29; ⊙ noon-2pm & 7-10.30pm Tue-Sat) From bœuf bourguignon (beef marinated in young red wine) to *andouillettes* (sausages made from pigs' intestines), this is the perfect primer course in hearty regional fare celebrated in a cosy and joyful atmosphere. The dining room is cluttered but there's outdoor seating in warmer months.

Le Piano Qui Fume MODERN FRENCH €€
(☑ 03 80 30 35 45; www.lepianoquifume.fr; 36 rue Berbisey; menus lunch €17, dinner €29-33; ⊙ noon-

2pm Mon, Tue & Thu-Sat, 7-10pm Thu-Sat) Market cuisine, carefully chosen ingredients, good-value wines, ambient lighting and a lovely dining room mixing contemporary design with traditional touches (exposed brick walls and beams) are the rules of thumb at this respectable hideaway. The lunch *menu* is brilliant value.

La Maison des Cariatides GASTRONOMIC €€
(☑ 03 80 45 59 25; www.lamaisondescariatides.fr; 28 rue Chaudronnerie; menus lunch €19-25, dinner €55; ⊙ noon-2pm & 7-10pm Tue-Sat; 🕾) Stellar period decor in a renovated 17th-century mansion with exposed beams and stone walls make for an impressive backdrop to delicious French and regional cuisine. There's also pleasant terrace seating out back. If you're on a budget make a beeline for the lunch *menu*.

La Dame d'Aquitaine REGIONAL CUISINE €€
(☑ 03 80 30 45 65; www.ladamedaquitaine.fr; 23 place Bossuet; menus lunch €23, dinner €33-48; ⊙ noon-2pm Tue-Sat, 7-10pm Mon-Sat) Excellent local cuisine is served under the sumptuously lit bays of a 13th-century *cave* (wine

Lots of books are available at Beaune's Athenaeum de la Vigne et du Vin (p426). Look for these:

➜ *Côte d'Or: A Celebration of the Great Wines of Burgundy* and *My Favorite Burgundies* by Clive Coates

➜ *The Wines of Burgundy* by Sylvain Pitiot and Jean-Charles Servant – excellent overview

➜ *The Climats and Lieux-dits of the Great Vineyards of Burgundy* by Marie-Hélène Landrieu-Lussigny and Sylvain Pitiot – classic atlas of Burgundian vinicultural place names, translated into English in 2014

➜ *The Great Domains of Burgundy* and *Grand Cru: The Great Wines of Burgundy Through the Perspective of Its Finest Vineyards* by Remington Norman

➜ *Inside Burgundy* by Jasper Morris

➜ *The Finest Wines of Burgundy* by Bill Nanson

Take a Class!

Or take a class:

➜ **École des Vins de Bourgogne** (☑ 03 80 26 35 10; www.ecoledesvins-bourgogne.com; 6 rue du 16e Chasseurs, Beaune) Offers a variety of courses (from a three-hour, €75 fundamentals class to a three-day, €755 wine-taster's certificate program) to refine your vinicultural vocabulary as well as your palate.

➜ **Sensation Vin** (☑ 03 80 22 17 57; www.sensation-vin.com; 1 rue d'Enfer, Beaune; ☺ 10am-7pm) Offers a €35, 1½-hour essentials class, half- and full-day tasting sessions and personalissed wine-tasting circuits through the area's most famous vineyards.

cellar) accessed by a long flight of steps. Classical music filters through and the wine list is extensive.

Self-Catering

Les Halles   MARKET
(rue Quentin; ☺ 7am-1pm Tue & Thu-Sat) Northwest of the Palais des Ducs is Dijon's fabulous old covered market, which is abuzz with activity four days a week.

Drinking & Nightlife

Lively bar-hopping neighbourhoods include rue Berbisey and the streets surrounding Les Halles.

Le Quentin   BAR
(☑ 03 80 30 15 05; 6 rue Quentin; ☺ 4pm-1am Mon-Thu, 8am-2am Fri & Sat, 4-9pm Sun) This congenial drinking spot facing the Halles overflows day and night with friendly regulars enjoying glasses of wine or fine aged rum from the wall-sized chalkboard menu. The streetside terrace allows for a dash of people-watching on market days.

L'Age de Raisin   WINE BAR
(67 rue Berbisey; ☺ 6.30pm-2am Mon-Sat) With late hours and a welcoming ambience, this wine bar specialises in local vintages hand-selected by the knowledgeable and affable owner; it doubles as a bistro serving charcuterie and cheese platters alongside *plats du jour* built around locally sourced organic produce.

Le Cappuccino   BAR
(☑ 03 80 41 06 35; 132 rue Berbisey; ☺ 5pm-2am Mon-Sat) Coffee isn't even served at this often-packed bar, but wine by the glass and 80 beers are, including Mandubienne, brewed right here in Dijon.

L'Univers   BAR
(☑ 03 80 30 98 29; www.facebook.com/l.univers. dijon; 47 rue Berbisey; ☺ 5pm-1am Mon-Sat) This energetic bar features extra-long happy hours (5pm to 10pm) and a cellar with live music on Friday and Saturday nights.

🛍 Shopping

The main shopping area is around rue de la Liberté and perpendicular rue du Bourg.

Mulot & Petitjean GINGERBREAD

(☑ 03 80 30 07 10; www.mulotpetitjean.fr; 13 place Bossuet; ⊘ 2-7pm Mon, 9am-noon & 2-7pm Tue-Sat) The sweet-toothed will lose all self-control at this Dijon institution dating to 1796. It's famous for its scrumptious *pain d'épices* (gingerbread made with honey and spices).

Moutarde Maille MUSTARD

(☑ 03 80 30 41 02; www.maille.com; 32 rue de la Liberté; ⊘ 10am-7pm Mon-Sat) When you enter the factory boutique of this mustard company, tangy odours assault your nostrils. There are 36 kinds of mustard, such as cassis or truffle and celery, including three on tap that you can sample.

Bourgogne Street REGIONAL PRODUCTS

(☑ 03 80 30 26 28; www.bourgognestreet.fr; 61 rue de la Liberté; ⊘ 10am-noon & 2-7pm Mon, 9am-noon & 2-7pm Tue-Fri, 9am-7pm Sat, 10am-1pm Sun) Visit this shop on Dijon's wide pedestrian thoroughfare to stock up on gingerbread, liquors, jams, chocolate, wines, mustard and other quality Burgundian delicacies from small producers.

ℹ Information

Tourist Office (☑ 08 92 70 05 58; www.visit dijon.com; 11 rue des Forges; ⊘ 9.30am-6.30pm Mon-Sat, 10am-6pm Sun Apr-Sep, shorter hours rest of year) Helpful office offering tours and maps. Also sells the €16 Dijon Côte de Nuits Pass, which offers free admission to Dijon city tours plus museums and attractions in the nearby Côte de Nuits vineyards.

ℹ Getting There & Away

A single **train station ticket counter** (⊘ 5.45am-9pm Mon-Sat, 9am-9pm Sun) deals with TER trains, Divia local transit and the *départemental* bus company, Transco.

BUS

Transco (☑ 03 80 11 29 29; www.cotedor.fr/cms/transco-horaires) Buses stop in front of the train station. Tickets are sold on board (€1.50). Bus 44 goes to Nuits-St-Georges (45 minutes) and Beaune (1¼ hours).

Eurolines (☑ 08 92 89 90 91; www.eurolines.fr; 53 rue Guillaume Tell) International bus travel.

CAR

Major car-rental companies have desks in the train-station complex.

TRAIN

Connections from Dijon's **train station** (rue du Dr Rémy) include the following:

Lyon Part-Dieu Regional train/TGV €31/36, two/1½ hours, 25 daily

Marseille TGV €89, 3½ hours, six direct daily

Paris Gare de Lyon Regional train/TGV €45/65, three/1½ hours, 25 daily

ℹ Getting Around

BICYCLE

Velodi (www.velodi.net; flat fee per week €1, rental per 30min €0.50-1) Dijon's version of Paris' Vélib' automatic rental system, has 400 city bikes at 40 sites around town.

BUS

Full details of Dijon's bus network, operated by Divia, are available online or at **Agence Commerciale Divia** (☑ 03 80 11 29 29; www.divia.fr; 16 place Darcy; ⊘ 9.30am-7pm Mon-Sat) near the train station.

CAR & MOTORCYCLE

All city-centre parking is metered. There's a free car park at place Suquet, just south of the police station.

TRAM

Divia's brand-new **tram system** (www.letram-dijon.fr; single ticket/day pass €1.20/3.60) has two lines, the T1 and T2. The four most helpful stops for travellers are served by both lines: Gare (train station), plus Darcy, Godrans and République stations along the northwestern edge of the Old Town.

Côte d'Or Vineyards

Burgundy's most renowned vintages come from the vine-covered Côte d'Or (literally Golden Hillside, but it is actually an abbreviation of Côte d'Orient or Eastern Hillside), the narrow, eastern slopes of a range of hills made of limestone, flint and clay that runs south from Dijon for about 60km. The exquisite terrain with its patchwork of immaculate hand-groomed vines is dotted with peaceful stone villages where every house seems to hold a vintner.

An oenophile's nirvana, the Côte d'Or vineyards are divided into two areas, Côte de Nuits to the north and Côte de Beaune to the south. The Côte de Nuits is noted for its powerful red wines, while the Côte de Beaune produces top-quality dry whites and delicate reds.

Côte de Nuits

The Côte de Nuits wine-growing area extends from Marsannay-la-Côte, just south of Dijon, to Corgoloin, a few kilometres north of Beaune. It includes the picturesque villages of Fixin, Gevrey-Chambertin, Morey-St-Denis, Chambolle-Musigny, Vougeot, Vosne-Romanée and Nuits-St-Georges.

◉ Sights

**Château du Clos
de Vougeot**   MUSEUM, CASTLE
(☑ 03 80 62 86 09; www.closdevougeot.fr; Vougeot; adult/child €5/2.50; ⊙ 9am-6.30pm Apr-Sep,

9-11.30am & 2-5.30pm Oct-Mar, closes 5pm Sat year-round) A mandatory stop on your tour of Burgundy's vineyards, this magnificent wine-producing *château* (estate) provides a wonderful introduction to Burgundy's wine-making techniques. Originally the property of the Abbaye de Cîteaux, the 16th-century country castle served as a get-away for the abbots. Tours offer a chance to discover the workings of enormous ancient wine presses and casks.

BURGUNDY OUTDOORS

Tasting fine wines often involves hanging out in dimly lit cellars, but Burgundy is also a paradise for lovers of the great outdoors.

The **Comité Régional de Tourisme de Bourgogne** (Burgundy Regional Tourist Board; www.burgundy-tourism.com) publishes excellent brochures on outdoors options (including *Burgundy by Bike*, available at tourist offices) and has a list of boat rental companies.

Hiking & Cycling

Burgundy has thousands of kilometres of walking and cycling trails, including sections of the GR2, GR7 and GR76. Varied local trails take you through some of the most ravishingly beautiful wine-growing areas in France, among them the vineyards of world-renowned Côte d'Or, Chablis and the Mâconnais (in Saône-et-Loire).

Rural footpaths criss-cross the Parc Naturel Régional du Morvan and some depart from the Morvan Visitors Centre (p445), but you can also pick up trails from the Abbaye de Fontenay, Autun, Avallon, Cluny, Noyers-sur-Serein and Vézelay.

You can cycle on or very near the *chemin de halage* (towpath) of the Canal de Bourgogne all the way from Dijon to Migennes (225km). The section from Montbard to Tonnerre (65km) passes by Château d'Ancy-le-Franc; between Montbard and Pouilly-en-Auxois (58km) spurs go to the Abbaye de Fontenay and Semur-en-Auxois.

For details on Burgundy's planned 800km of *véloroutes* (bike paths) and *voies vertes* (green ways), including maps and guides, see www.burgundy-by-bike.com or stop at a tourist office.

Canal & River Boating

Few modes of transport are as relaxing as a houseboat on Burgundy's 1200km of placid waterways, which include the Rivers Yonne, Saône and Seille and a network of canals, including the Canal de Bourgogne, the Canal du Centre, the Canal Latéral à la Loire and the Canal du Nivernais (www.canal-du-nivernais.com). Rental companies offer boats from late March to 11 November (canals close for repairs in winter, but rivers don't).

Bourgogne Fluviale (☑ 03 86 81 54 55; www.bourgogne-fluviale.com) Based in Vermenton, 25km southeast of Auxerre.

France Afloat (Burgundy Cruisers; ☑ 03 86 81 67 87, in UK 08700 110 538; www.franceafloat.com; 1 quai du Port) Based in Vermenton.

Locaboat Holidays (☑ 03 86 91 72 72; www.locaboat.com; Port au Bois, Joigny) Rents boats throughout France, including at Joigny (27km northwest of Auxerre).

Hot-Air Ballooning

From about April to October you can take a stunning *montgolfière* (hot-air balloon) ride over Burgundy for around €220 per adult. Book through the Beaune and Dijon tourist offices. Some veteran outfits:

Air Adventures (☑ 06 08 27 95 39; www.airadventures.fr) Based just outside Pouilly-en-Auxois, 50km west of Dijon.

Air Escargot (☑ 03 85 87 12 30; www.air-escargot.com) In Remigny, 16km south of Beaune.

Cassissium
LIQUEUR FACTORY

(☎ 03 80 62 49 70; www.cassissium.fr; 8 passage Montgolfier, Nuits-St-Georges; adult/child €8.50/6.50; ☉ 10am-1pm & 2-7pm Apr–mid-Nov, reduced hours rest of year, last visits 1¾hr before closing) This museum and factory worships all things liqueur, with a particular focus on the blackcurrant, from which cassis is made. There's fun for the whole family: movies, displays, a 30-minute guided tour and a tasting with nonalcoholic fruit syrups for the kids. In the industrial area east of N74.

L'Imaginarium
MUSEUM

(☎ 03 80 62 61 40; www.imaginarium-bourgogne. com; av du Jura, Nuits-St-Georges; adult incl basic/ grand cru tasting €8/15, child €5; ☉ 2-7pm Mon, 10am-7pm Tue-Sun) An essential port of call on any wine-tasting itinerary, this gleaming modern museum is a great place to learn about Burgundy wines and winemaking techniques. It's fun and entertaining, with movies, exhibits and interactive displays, followed by tasting.

🏃 Activities

Wine Tasting
WINE TASTING

The villages of the Côte de Nuits offer innumerable places to sample and purchase world-class wines (especially reds) a short walk from where they were made. Wine can be bought direct from the winegrowers, many of whom offer tasting, allowing you to sample two or three vintages, but at many places, especially the better-known ones, you have to make advance reservations. Lists of estates

---

ℹ️ BRINGING IT ALL BACK HOME

Dreaming of bringing a dozen or two bottles of Burgundian wine home with you, but running out of room in your suitcase? Help is at hand for overseas visitors who get a little carried away with their wine purchases. Companies such as **Côte d'Or Imports** (☎ 03 80 61 15 15; www.cotedorpdx.com) work with vineyards throughout Burgundy and can facilitate fully insured, door-to-door shipments to the United States for roughly €10 to €15 per bottle; shipments to Australia and New Zealand are also available for about €15 to €18 per bottle, plus duty – not a bad deal if you're buying the expensive stuff!

---

and *caves* open to the public are available from local tourist offices.

You can also visit wine shops, including **Le Caveau des Vignerons** (☎ 03 80 51 86 79; place de l'Église, Morey-St-Denis; ☉ 2-7pm Tue & Wed, 10am-1pm & 2-7pm Thu-Mon), which stocks most Côte de Nuits appellations and offers excellent advice, and **Le Caveau des Musigny** (☎ 03 80 62 84 01; 1 rue Traversière, Chambolle-Musigny; ☉ 9am-6pm Wed-Sun), which represents more than 100 Côte de Nuits and Côte de Beaune winegrowers.

Walking
WALKING

The GR7 and its variant, the GR76, run along the Côte d'Or from a bit west of Dijon to the hills west of Beaune, from where they continue southwards. The Beaune tourist office sells an excellent bilingual map, *Guide Rando Pédestre* (€3), which details 29 marked routes.

🛏️ Sleeping

Maison des Abeilles
B&B €

(☎ 03 80 62 95 42; www.chambres-beaune.fr; 4 rue de Pernand, Magny-lès-Villers; incl breakfast d €68-75, q €125; ❄️🅿️) New owner Céline maintains these five impeccably clean *chambres d'hôte* in Magny-lès-Villers, a small village off rte des Grands Crus, at the junction between Côte de Nuits, Haute-Côte de Nuits and Côte de Beaune. Rooms have colourful linen, and breakfasts are a feast of breads and homemade jams. The vast, flowery garden out back is another plus.

Hôtel de Vougeot
HOTEL €€

(☎ 03 80 62 01 15; www.hotel-vougeot.com; 18 rue du Vieux Château, Vougeot; d €82-123; ❄️) What's not to love in this gracious country manor? The 16 rooms are comfortable and impeccably maintained, many with rustically stylish features such as stone walls or exposed beams. Angle for one of the 10 rooms with a view of the Vougeot vineyards.

La Closerie de Gilly
B&B €€

(☎ 03 80 62 87 74; www.closerie-gilly.com; 16 av Bouchard, Gilly-lès-Cîteaux; incl breakfast d €85-90, tr €105, q €140; ❄️🅿️🅿️) Housed in a delightful 18th-century *maison bourgeoise* with a huge, flowery garden, this homey B&B has four spacious rooms, plus two apartments with kitchenette. English-speaking owner Sandrine offers wine tasting, wine classes and bicycles for rent. It's in Gilly-les-Cîteaux, just 1km east of Vougeot and only 15 minutes by train from Dijon or Beaune.

✗ Eating

Le Millésime   MODERN BURGUNDIAN €€
(☑ 03 80 62 80 37; www.restaurant-le-millesime.
com; 1 rue Traversière, Chambolle-Musigny; mains
€19-28, lunch menu €19.50, dinner menus €29.50-49;
⊙ noon-2pm & 7-9.30pm Tue-Sat) This renowned
venture is located in an exquisitely renovated
maison de village. The chef combines fresh
local ingredients and exotic flavours in his
excellent creations. Dark wood floors, well-
spaced tables and a warm welcome create an
easy air.

Le Chambolle   BURGUNDIAN €€
(☑ 03 80 62 86 26; www.restaurant-lechambolle.com;
28 rue Caroline Aigle, Chambolle-Musigny; mains €14-
17, menus €24-32; ⊙ 12.15-1.30pm & 7.15-8.30pm Fri-
Tue) This unpretentious back-roads gem creates traditional Burgundian cuisine with the
freshest ingredients. On the D122, a bit west
of Vougeot in gorgeous Chambolle-Musigny.

Chez Guy And Family   MODERN FRENCH €€
(☑ 03 80 58 51 51; www.chez-guy.fr; 3 place de la
Mairie, Gevrey-Chambertin; menus lunch €24, dinner €28-45; ⊙ noon-2pm & 7-9.30pm) Its dining
room is large and light, and there's a tempting choice of dishes on its fixed-price *menus*. Along with tender duckling, signature
seasonal specialities include rabbit leg and
pollack. A long wine list backs up the food.

La Cabotte   MODERN FRENCH €€€
(☑ 03 80 61 20 77; www.restaurantlacabotte.fr; 24
Grand Rue, Nuits-St-Georges; mains €15-21, menus
€19.50-57; ⊙ 12.15-1.30pm & 7.15-9pm Tue-Sat)
This intimate restaurant serves up refined,
inventive versions of French dishes. No artifice or posing here, just excellent, if sometimes surprising, food.

❶ Getting There & Away

Transco (☑ 03 80 11 29 29; www.cotedor.fr) provides regular bus connections between Dijon and
Beaune on its line 44, stopping in Nuits-St-Georges, Vougeot, Gevrey-Chambertin and other Côte
de Nuits villages along the way.

Côte de Beaune

Welcome to one of the most prestigious
wine-growing areas in the world. The Côte de
Beaune area extends from Ladoix-Serrigny,
just a few kilometres north of Beaune, to Santenay, about 18km south of Beaune. It includes
the delightful villages of Pernand-Vergelesses, Aloxe-Corton, Savigny-lès-Beaune,
Chorey-lès-Beaune, Pommard, Volnay, Meursault, Puligny-Montrachet and Chassagne-

Montrachet, which boast Burgundy's most
fabled vineyards. If you're looking for an upscale wine château experience, you've come
to the right place.

◉ Sights

★ Château de La Rochepot   CASTLE
(☑ 03 80 21 71 37; www.larochepot.com; La Rochepot; adult/child €4.50/2.50; ⊙ 10am-noon &
2-5.30pm Wed-Sun) Conical towers and multicoloured tile roofs rise from thick woods
above the ancient village of La Rochepot. This
marvellous medieval fortress offers fab views
of surrounding countryside and the interiors
are a fascinating combination of the utilitarian (weapons) and the luxe (fine paintings).

Château de Meursault   CASTLE
(☑ 03 80 26 22 75; www.meursault.com; Meursault;
admission incl tasting €18; ⊙ 9.30am-noon & 2-6pm
Oct-Apr, 9.30am-6.30pm May-Sep) One of the
prettiest of the Côte de Beaune châteaux, Château de Meursault has beautiful grounds and
produces some of the most prestigious white
wines in the world. Particularly impressive
are the 14th-century cellars.

Château de Pommard   CASTLE
(☑ 03 80 22 12 59; www.chateaudepommard.com; 15
rue Marey-Monge, Pommard; guided tour incl tasting
adult/child €21/free; ⊙ 9.30am-6.30pm) For many
red-wine lovers, a visit to this superb château
just 3km south of Beaune is the ultimate Burgundian pilgrimage. The impressive cellars
contain many vintage bottles. If the tour has
whetted your appetite, you can sample Burgundian specialities at the on-site restaurant.

Château de Savigny   MUSEUM, CASTLE
(☑ 03 80 21 55 03; www.chateau-savigny.com; Savigny-lès-Beaune; adult/child €10/5; ⊙ 9am-6.30pm
mid-Apr–mid-Oct, 9am-noon & 2-5.30pm rest of year)
Drop in for wine tasting and stay to see the
unexpected collection of race cars, motorcycles, aeroplanes and fire trucks. Last admission is 90 minutes before closing time.

🏃 Activities

Cycling   CYCLING
The 20km **Voie des Vignes** (Vineyard Way),
a bike route marked by rectangular green-
on-white signs, goes from Beaune's Parc de
la Bouzaize via Pommard, Volnay, Meursault, Puligny-Montrachet and Chassagne-
Montrachet to Santenay, where you can pick
up the **Voie Verte** (Green Way) to Cluny.
Beaune's tourist office sells the detailed bilingual *Guide Rando Cyclo* map (€3).

Wine Tasting WINE TASTING

You'll find plenty of wine-tasting opportunities in the wine-producing villages. You can stop at the famous wine châteaux or you may prefer to drop in at more laid-back wineries – look for signs.

🛏 Sleeping

★Villa Louise Hôtel HOTEL €€

(☑ 03 80 26 46 70; www.hotel-villa-louise.fr; 9 rue Franche, Aloxe-Corton; d €98-195; @ 🔊 🏊) In the pretty village of Aloxe-Corton, this tranquil mansion houses elegant, modern rooms, each of them dreamily different. The expansive garden stretches straight to the edge of the vineyard and a separate gazebo shelters the sauna and pool. Genteel Louise Perrin presides, and has a private *cave*, perfect for wine tastings.

Domaine Corgette B&B €€

(☑ 03 80 21 68 08; www.domainecorgette.com; 14 rue de la Perrière, St-Romain; incl breakfast d €90-110, tr/q €130/150; 🔊) The sun-drenched terrace at this renovated winery looks out on the dramatic cliffs. Tucked in the centre of the quiet village of St-Romain, its rooms are light and airy with crisp linen, and retain classic touches such as fireplaces and wood floors. Good English is spoken.

La Maison d'Olivier Leflaive BOUTIQUE HOTEL €€€

(☑ 03 80 21 37 65; www.olivier-leflaive.com; place du Monument, Puligny-Montrachet; d €170-200, ste €235; ⊙ closed Jan; 🗙 @ 🔊) Occupying a tastefully renovated 17th-century village house in the heart of Puligny-Montrachet, this 13-room venture delivers top service and classy comfort. Best of all, it offers personalised wine tours and tastings.

🍴 Eating

Excellent restaurants are tucked away in the villages of the Côte de Beaune. Reserve ahead in high season.

Le Chevreuil – La Maison de la Mère Daugier MODERN BURGUNDIAN €€

(☑ 03 80 21 23 25; www.lechevreuil.fr; place de la République, Meursault; mains €23-36, lunch menu €21, dinner menus €24-59; ⊙ noon-1.30pm & 7.15-9pm Mon, Tue & Thu-Sat) Chef Tiago is known for his creative take on regional staples. The dining room's country-chic, with plenty of light, wood and stone for that down-home feel, and the menu takes the cream of traditional Burgundian and gives it a 21st-century spin. Try the *terrine chaude de la mère Daugier*, the

house's signature offering, and you'll see what we mean.

La Table d'Olivier Leflaive BISTRO €€

(www.olivier-leflaive.com; place du Monument, Puligny-Montrachet; menus €25-30; ⊙ 12.30-2pm & 7.30-9pm Mon-Sat Feb-Dec) This is *the* address in Puligny-Montrachet. The trademark four-course 'Repas Dégustation' (tasting *menu*) combines seasonal French classics with global flavours. Add €25 and you'll sample a selection of five local wines chosen by the sommelier – a winning formula.

Le Cellier Volnaysien BURGUNDIAN €€

(☑ 03 80 21 61 04; www.le-cellier-volnaysien.com; place de l'Église, Volnay; menus €18.50-29.50; ⊙ noon-1.30pm Thu-Mon, 7.30-9pm Sat) Solid Burgundian cooking in a cosy stone-walled, vaulted dining room in the heart of Volnay.

Le Charlemagne GASTRONOMIC FUSION €€€

(☑ 03 80 21 51 45; www.lecharlemagne.fr; Pernand-Vergelesses; lunch menus Mon, Thu & Fri €32-39, other menus €61-102; ⊙ noon-1.30pm Thu-Mon, 7-9.30pm Wed-Mon, closed dinner Wed Sep-May) Vineyard views are perhaps even more mind-blowing than the imaginatively prepared dishes melding French cuisine with techniques and ingredients from Japan. At the entrance of Pernand-Vergelesses.

Auprès du Clocher GASTRONOMIC €€€

(☑ 03 80 22 21 79; www.aupresduclocher.com; 1 rue Nackenheim, Pommard; mains €24-37, lunch menu €26, dinner menus €32-72; ⊙ noon-1.30pm & 7-9pm Thu-Mon) Celebrated chef Jean-Christophe Moutet rustles up gastronomic delights at Auprès du Clocher, in the heart of Pommard. The ingredients are Burgundian, but imagination renders them into something new and elegant. The wine list is superb.

❶ Getting There & Around

Bus 20, operated by **Transports Le Vingt** (☑ 03 80 24 58 58; www.mobigo-bourgogne.com), runs between Beaune and several Côte d'Or wine villages, including Pommard, Meursault, St-Romain and La Rochepot.

Beaune

POP 22,620

Beaune (pronounced similarly to 'bone'), 44km south of Dijon, is the unofficial capital of the Côte d'Or. This thriving town's raison d'être and the source of its *joie de vivre* is wine: making it, tasting it, selling it, but most of all, drinking it. Consequently Beaune is one of the best places in all of France for wine tasting.

The jewel of Beaune's old city is the magnificent Hôtel-Dieu, France's most splendiferous medieval charity hospital.

◉ Sights

The amoeba-shaped old city is enclosed by thick stone **ramparts** and a stream which is in turn encircled by a one-way boulevard with seven names. The ramparts, which shelter wine cellars, are lined with overgrown gardens and ringed by a pathway that makes for a lovely stroll.

Hôtel-Dieu des Hospices
de Beaune   HISTORIC BUILDING
(www.hospices-de-beaune.com; rue de l'Hôtel-Dieu; adult/child €7/3; ⊙9am-6.30pm) Built in 1443, this magnificent Gothic hospital (until 1971) is famously topped by stunning turrets and pitched rooftops covered in multicoloured tiles. Interior highlights include the barrel-vaulted **Grande Salle** (look for the dragons and peasant heads up on the roof beams); the mural-covered **St-Hughes Room**; an 18th-century **pharmacy** lined with flasks once filled with elixirs and powders; and the multipanelled masterpiece **Polyptych of the Last Judgement** by 15th-century Flemish painter Rogier van der Weyden, depicting Judgment Day in glorious technicolour.

Moutarderie Fallot   MUSTARD FACTORY
(Mustard Mill; ☑03 80 22 10 10; www.fallot.com; 31 rue du Faubourg Bretonnière; adult/child €10/8; ⊙tasting room 9.30am-6pm Mon-Sat; tours 10am & 11.30am Mon-Sat mid-Mar–mid-Nov, plus 3.30pm & 5pm Jun-Sep, by arrangement rest of year) Burgundy's last family-run stone-ground mustard company offers guided tours through its mustard museum, focusing on mustard's history, folklore and traditional production techniques, with kid-friendly opportunities for hand-milling mustard seeds. An alternate tour focuses on Fallot's modern mustard production facility. Reserve tours ahead at Beaune's tourist office. Drop-ins can sample and purchase over a dozen varieties in the brand-new *dégustation* room.

Basilique Collégiale
Notre Dame   CHURCH
(place Général Leclerc; ⊙9.30am-5.30pm) Built in Romanesque and Gothic styles from the 11th to 15th centuries this church was once affiliated with the monastery of Cluny. It's notable for its extra-large porch and the 15th-century

tapestries that are displayed inside. Tapestries are accessible by a €3 guided tour late April to mid-November only (schedules available at tourist office).

🏃 Activities

Underneath Beaune's buildings, streets and ramparts, millions of dusty bottles of wine are being aged to perfection in cool, dark cellars. Wine tasting options abound.

Marché aux Vins   WINE TASTING
(www.marcheauxvins.com; 2 rue Nicolas Rolin; ⊙10am-noon & 2-6.30pm, 10am-6.30pm Jul-Aug) Sample seven wines for €11, or 10 for €15, in the candle-lit former Église des Cordeliers and its cellars. Wandering among the vintages takes about an hour. The finest wines are at the end; look for the *premier cru* and the *grand cru* (wine of exceptional quality).

Bouchard Père & Fils   WINE TASTING
(www.bouchard-pereetfils.com; 15 rue du Château; tours €19; ⊙10am-12.30pm & 2.30-6.30pm Mon-Sat, 10am-12.30pm Sun) The atmospheric cellars are housed in a former medieval fortress and feature plenty of prestigious *grands crus* from Côte de Nuits and Côte de Beaune. Visitors taste three reds and three whites on the one-hour tour (offered in English at 4pm, in French at 3pm).

Cellier de la
Vieille Grange   WINE TASTING
(www.bourgogne-cellier.com; 27 bd Georges Clemenceau; ⊙9am-noon & 2-6.30pm Mon-Fri, 9am-noon & 3-6.30pm Sat, by appointment Sun) This is where locals come to buy Burgundy AOC wines for as little as €4.80 per litre. Tasting is free of charge.

Patriarche Père et Fils   WINE TASTING
(www.patriarche.com; 7 rue du Collège; audioguide tours €16; ⊙9.30-11.30am & 2-5.30pm) Spanning

Beaune

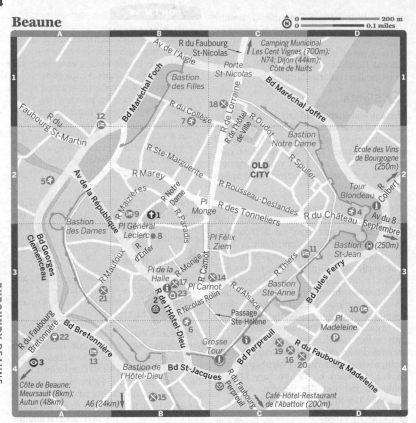

N 0 _____ 200 m
    0 _____ 0.1 miles

Beaune

two hectares, Burgundy's largest cellars have 5km of corridors lined with about five million bottles of wine. (The oldest is a Beaune Villages AOC from 1904!) Visitors armed with multilingual audioguides can tour the premises in 60 to 90 minutes, tasting 13 wines along the way and taking the *tastevin* (tasting cup) home.

☞ Tours

The tourist office handles reservations for hot-air-balloon rides, and for vineyard tours (from €40) run by the following companies: **Chemins de Bourgogne** (☎06 60 43 68 86; www.chemins-de-bourgogne.com), **Safari Tours** (☎03 80 22 49 49, 03 80 24 79 12; www.burgundy-tourism-safaritours.com) and **Vinéatours** (☎06 73 38 37 19; www.burgundy-wine-tour.com).

Bourgogne Evasion　　　WALKING, CYCLING
(☎06 64 68 83 57; www.bourgogne-evasion.fr) Offers half-day, full-day and multi-day cycling and walking tours through the vineyards.

Visiotrain　　　TOURIST TRAIN
(☎06 08 07 45 68; www.visiotrain2000.com; adult/child €7.50/4.50; ⊙11am-5.30pm, closed Wed & morning Sat) This small tourist train departs six times daily from rue de l'Hôtel-Dieu and tours the old town.

☆ Festivals & Events

**Festival International
d'Opéra Baroque**　　　MUSIC FESTIVAL
(www.festivalbeaune.com) Held in July, this is one of the most prestigious baroque opera festivals in Europe. Performances are held at the Basilique Collégiale Notre Dame and the Hôtel-Dieu des Hospices de Beaune.

⊨ Sleeping

**Camping Municipal
Les Cent Vignes**　　　CAMPGROUND €
(☎03 80 22 03 91; campinglescentvignes@mairie-beaune.fr; 10 rue Auge Dubois; sites per adult/tent €5.15/5.90; ⊙mid-Mar–Oct; ☜) A flowery, well-equipped campground 700m north of the centre.

**Café-Hôtel-Restaurant
de l'Abattoir**　　　HOTEL €
(☎03 80 22 21 46; 19 rue du Faubourg Perpreuil; r €29) If you don't need creature comforts and just want a central location at an unbeatable price, consider this unfussy hotel catering to local workers, with small, tidy rooms only a five-minute walk from the Hôtel-Dieu. Accommodation with half board (breakfast and dinner) is available (€39 per person). Note that reception is intermittently closed; call ahead.

Hôtel le Foch　　　HOTEL €
(☎03 80 24 05 65; www.hotelbeaune-lefoch.fr; 24 bd Maréchal Foch; d €43-54, tr €66, q €82; ☜) An acceptable plan B if others are full, this cheapie on Beaune's busy ring road has 10 basic but clean rooms. The cafe downstairs has plenty of local colour, though reception is often more gruff than welcoming, and wi-fi is undependable on the upper floors. There's free street parking out front.

★Les Jardins de Loïs　　　B&B €€
(☎03 80 22 41 97; www.jardinsdelois.com; 8 bd Bretonnière; incl breakfast r €149, ste €180-190, apt €280-350; ☜) An unexpected oasis in the middle of the city, this luxurious B&B encompasses several ample rooms, including two suites and a 135-sq-metre top-floor apartment with drop-dead gorgeous views of Beaune's rooftops. The vast garden, complete with rose bushes and fruit trees, makes a dreamy place to sit and enjoy wine grown on the hotel's private *domaine*. Free parking.

Chez Marie　　　B&B €€
(☎06 64 63 48 20; www.chezmarieabeaune.com; 14 rue Poissonnerie; incl breakfast d €85-115, tr/q €135/155; ☜⊜) At this peaceful haven on a residential street only a five-minute stroll from central Beaune, Marie and Yves make visitors feel right at home, sharing conversation and travel-planning advice (especially for cyclists) over breakfast in the sweet central garden. The four rooms, including two family-friendly apartments with kitchenettes, are impeccably simple and airy. Bikes (regular and electric) are available for rent.

Hôtel des Remparts　　　HISTORIC HOTEL €€
(☎03 80 24 94 94; www.hotel-remparts-beaune.com; 48 rue Thiers; d €89-118, ste €135-159; ✳☜) Set around two delightful courtyards, rooms in this 17th-century townhouse have red-tiled or parquet floors and simple antique furniture. Some rooms come with exposed beams and a fireplace while others have air-con. Most bathrooms have been renovated. Friendly staff can also hire out bikes. Parking €10.

Abbaye de Maizières　　　HISTORIC HOTEL €€€
(☎03 80 24 74 64; www.hotelabbayedemaizieres.com; 19 rue Maizières; d €133-235, ste €280-370; ✳@☜) Renovated in 2013, this character-laden four-star establishment inside a 12th-century abbey oozes history, yet all 12 rooms have been luxuriously modernised. Some rooms boast Cistercian stained-glass windows and exposed beams; those on the top floor offer views over Beaune's famed multicolour tile roofs. There's no lift, but the friendly staff will help haul your luggage upstairs.

✗ Eating & Drinking

Beaune harbours a host of excellent restaurants; you'll find many around place Carnot, place Félix Ziem and place Madeleine. Reserve ahead in high season.

Le Bacchus
MODERN BURGUNDIAN €€

(☑ 03 80 24 07 78; 6 Faubourg Madeleine; menus lunch €14-16.50, dinner €26.50-33; ☺ noon-1.30pm & 7-10pm) The welcome is warm and the food exceptional at this small restaurant just outside Beaune's centre. Multilingual co-owner Anna works the tables while her partner Olivier whips up market-fresh *menus* that blend classic flavours (steak with Fallot mustard) with tasty surprises (gazpacho with tomato-basil ice cream). Save room for splendid desserts such as Bourbon vanilla crème brûlée, flambéed at your table.

Le Comptoir des Tontons
REGIONAL CUISINE €€

(☑ 03 80 24 19 64; www.lecomptoirdestontons. com; 22 rue du Faubourg Madeleine; menus €29-42; ☺ noon-1pm & 7.30-9pm Tue-Sat) Decorated in a hip bistro style, this local treasure entices with the passionate Burgundian cooking of chef Pepita. Most ingredients are organic and locally sourced. Does the beef with paprika taste better than the fat duck in aniseed sauce? You be the judge. Service is prompt and friendly.

Caves Madeleine
FRENCH €€

(☑ 03 80 22 93 30; 8 rue du Faubourg Madeleine; mains €14-24, lunch menu €23; ☺ noon-1.30pm Mon, Tue, Thu & Fri, 7-9.30pm Mon-Fri) Focusing on fresh-from-the-farm meat and vegetables produced within a 100km radius of Beaune, this cosy little restaurant changes its menu daily. Reserve ahead for a private table, or enjoy a more convivial experience at the long shared table backed by wine racks.

La Ciboulette
BURGUNDIAN €€

(☑ 03 80 24 70 72; 69 rue de Lorraine; menus €20-38; ☺ noon-1.30pm & 7.15-9.30pm Wed-Sun) Long popular with Beaune locals, but equally welcoming to tourists, this stone-walled, wood-beamed hideaway manages to feel both relaxed and refined, with smiling, efficient service and unpretentious but well-prepared dishes. Expect plenty of Burgundian classics, from pork cheeks in rich wine sauce to poached pears with cassis sorbet for dessert.

Bissoh
JAPANESE €€€

(☑ 03 80 24 99 50; www.bissoh.com; 1a rue du Faubourg St-Jacques; menus lunch €13-23, dinner €37-78; ☺ noon-2pm & 7-10pm Wed-Sun) Take a break from Burgundy's high-calorie cuisine at this refreshingly simple, authentically Japanese eatery. The *menu* is anchored by classics (sushi, sashimi, grilled salmon, *tonkatsu*,

imported sake) and bookended with fusion treats such as shrimp-studded petit pois soup or black sesame and green tea crème brûlée.

Loiseau des Vignes
GASTRONOMIC €€€

(☑ 03 80 24 12 06; www.bernard-loiseau.com; 31 rue Maufoux; menus lunch €20-28, dinner €59-95; ☺ noon-2pm & 7-10pm Tue-Sat) For that special meal with your significant other, this culinary shrine is the place to go. Expect stunning concoctions ranging from caramelised pigeon to *quenelles de sandre* (dumplings made from pike fish), all exquisitely presented. And even the most budget-conscious can indulge – lunch *menus* are a bargain. In summer, the verdant garden is a plus.

La Dilettante
WINE BAR

(11 Faubourg Bretonnière; ☺ 11am-midnight Mon, Tue & Thu-Sat) This relaxed wine bar and gourmet grocery opened in 2013 and serves an excellent selection of wines along with soups, salads and Spanish-style *tapas* (small plates of cheese, Iberian ham and local charcuterie).

Self-Catering

Food Market
MARKET

(place de la Halle; ☺ 8am-12.30pm Sat) Elaborate weekly market. There's a much smaller *marché gourmand* (gourmet market) on Wednesday morning.

Alain Hess Fromager
CHEESE SHOP

(www.fromageriehess.com; 7 place Carnot; ☺ 9am-12.15pm & 2.30-7.15pm Mon-Sat, plus 10am-1pm Sun Easter-Dec) This treasure trove of gourmet regional foodstuffs, including cheeses, mustards and wines, will tempt the devil in you. Don't miss the Délice de Pommard, the house's signature cheese. Also look for Burgundy's famous Appellation d'Origine Protégée (AOP) cheeses: strong, creamy, orange-skinned Époisses, invented by 16th-century Cistercian monks; and elegant little wheels of soft white Chaource.

🛍 Shopping

Athenaeum de la Vigne et du Vin
BOOKS

(☑ 03 80 25 08 30; www.athenaeumfr.com; 5 rue de l'Hôtel-Dieu; ☺ 10am-7pm) Stocks thousands of titles on oenology (the art and science of winemaking), including many in English, as well as recipe books and wine-related gifts.

ℹ Information

Tourist Office (☑ 03 80 26 21 30; www. beaune-tourisme.fr; 6 bd Perpreuil; ☺ 9am-6.30pm Mon-Sat, 9am-6pm Sun) Sells Pass

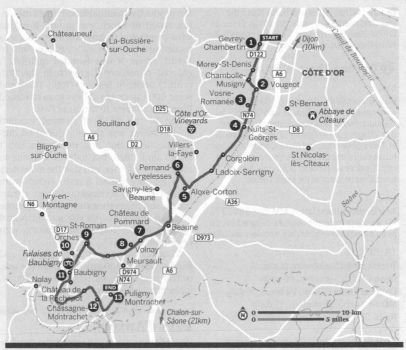

🏃 Driving Tour
Route des Grands Crus

START GEVREY-CHAMBERTIN
FINISH PULIGNY-MONTRACHET
LENGTH 55KM; ONE DAY

Burgundy's most famous wine route, the Route des Grands Crus (www.road-of-the-fine-burgundy-wines.com) follows the tertiary roads west of the N74, wending through seas of cascading vineyards dotted with stone-built villages, church steeples and château turrets. Signposted in brown, the route provides a grand tour of the world-renowned Côte de Nuits and Côte de Beaune.

Coming from Dijon, the Côte de Nuits begins in earnest just south of Marsannay-la-Côte. Most of the area's *grand cru* vineyards lie between ❶ **Gevrey-Chambertin** and Vosne-Romanée. In ❷ **Vougeot**, stop at the historic château. ❸ **Vosne-Romanée** is famed for its Romanée Conti wines, among Burgundy's most prestigious and priciest. Continuing south, visit the Côte de Nuits' largest town, ❹ **Nuits-St-Georges**, home to the Imaginarium wine museum. On the Côte de Beaune,

the impossibly steep coloured-tile roof of Château Corton-André in ❺ **Aloxe-Corton** is easy to spot, just off the one-lane main street. ❻ **Pernand-Vergelesses** is nestled in a little valley hidden from the N74.

South of Beaune, ❼ **Château de Pommard**, surrounded by a stone wall, is on the D973 on the northeast edge of town. Wander quaint ❽ **Volnay** to its hillside church. Off the main track, ❾ **St-Romain** is a bucolic village situated right where vineyardland meets pastureland, forests and cliffs. Hiking trails from here include the spectacular Sentier des Roches, a circuit that follows part of the GR7, and the D17l along the top of the Falaises de Baubigny (Baubigny cliffs), 300m above the Saône. Then, via the hillside hamlet of ❿ **Orches**, which has breathtaking vineyard views, travel to the fantastic 15th-century ⓫ **Château de la Rochepot**. For a pretty finale to your journey, drive down to the villages of ⓬ **Chassagne-Montrachet** and ⓭ **Puligny-Montrachet**, where you'll have the chance to sample the world's most opulent whites.

Beaune and has lots of brochures about the town and nearby vineyards. An annexe (1 rue de l'Hôtel-Dieu; ☉10am-1pm & 2-6pm) opposite the Hôtel-Dieu keeps shorter hours.

ⓘ Getting There & Away

BUS

Bus 44, operated by **Transco** (☑ 03 80 11 29 29; www.cotedor.fr), links Beaune with Dijon (€1.50, 1½ hours, two to seven daily), stopping at Côte d'Or villages such as Gevrey-Chambertin, Vougeot, Nuits-St-Georges and Aloxe-Corton. In Beaune, buses stop along the boulevards around the old city. Services are reduced in July and August. Get timetables online or at the tourist office.

CAR

Near Beaune's train station, **ADA** (☑ 03 80 22 72 90; www.ada.fr/location-voiture-beaune.htm; 26 av du 8 Septembre) rents cars, scooters and bikes.

TRAIN

Trains connect the following places:
Dijon €7.80, 25 minutes, 40 daily
Lyon Part-Dieu €26.50, 1¾ hours, 16 daily
Mâcon €15.60, 55 minutes, 19 daily
Nuits-St-Georges €3.60, 10 minutes, eight daily
Paris Regional train (€49, 3½ hours, seven direct daily); TGV (€75, 2¼ hours, two daily)

ⓘ Getting Around

Parking is free outside the town walls. There's a large, convenient free lot at place Madeleine, just east of the centre.

BICYCLE

Bourgogne Randonnées (☑ 03 80 22 06 03; www.bourgogne-randonnees.fr; 7 av du 8 Septembre; bikes per day/week €18/96; ☉9am-noon & 1.30-5.30pm Mon-Sat, 10am-noon & 2-5.30pm Sun Mar-Nov) Rents everything you need to explore the area by bike (bikes, helmets, panniers, baby seats, tandems) and offers excellent advice on local cycling itineraries.

Abbaye de Cîteaux

South of Dijon and 13km east of Nuits-St-Georges (follow the D8 to the east), the **Abbaye de Cîteaux** (☑ 03 80 61 32 58; www.citeaux-abbaye.com; D996, St-Nicolas-lès-Cîteaux; adult/child video €3/1.50, guided tour & video €8.50/6; ☉tours 10.30am-4.30pm Wed-Sat, 12.15-4.30pm Sun) is well worth a visit for its historical significance. In contrast to the showy Benedictines of Cluny, the medieval Cistercian order was known for its austerity, discipline and humility, and for the productive manual labour of its monks, one result of which was ground-breaking wine-producing techniques. The order was named after Cîteaux abbey (Cistercium in Latin), where it was founded in 1098. It enjoyed phenomenal growth in the 12th century under St Bernard (1090–1153), and some 600 Cistercian abbeys soon stretched from Scandinavia to the Near East.

Out in the midst of pastoral mustard fields, Cîteaux was virtually destroyed during the Revolution and the monks didn't return until 1898, but today it is home to about 35 monks. You can visit the monastery on a 1½-hour guided tour in French, with printed English commentary. Tours depart hourly, and reservations are essential; phone or email ahead. There's also an audiovisual presentation on monastic life, available with or without the tour.

Visitors may attend daily prayers and Sunday Mass (10.30am). The boutique sells edibles made at monasteries around France, including the abbey's own cheese.

Pays d'Auxois

West of Dijon, along and around the Canal de Bourgogne, the Pays d'Auxois is verdant and rural. Broad mustard fields, wooded hills and escarpments are dotted with fortified hilltop towns, including Semur-en-Auxois. The excellent MuséoParc Alésia historical museum is another good reason to explore the area.

Semur-en-Auxois

POP 4570

Don't miss Semur-en-Auxois, an incredibly picturesque small fortress town. Perched on a granite spur and surrounded by a hairpin turn in the River Armançon, it is guarded by four massive pink-granite bastions, and the centre is laced with cobbled lanes flanked by attractive houses. At night the ramparts are illuminated, which adds to the appeal.

◉ Sights & Activities

Old City   HISTORIC QUARTER

Most of the old city was built when Semur was an important religious centre boasting six monasteries. Just beyond the tourist office, pass through two concentric medieval gates, **Porte Sauvigne** (1417) and fortified **Porte Guillier** (14th century) to reach pedestrianised **rue Buffon**, lined with 17th-century houses. Further on, the

Promenade du Rempart affords panoramic views from atop Semur's medieval battlements. Don't worry about the menacing cracks in the 44m-high **Tour de la Orle d'Or** – they've been there since 1589!

Collégiale Notre Dame   CHURCH
(⊙9am-noon & 2-6.30pm) A stained-glass window (1927) and a plaque commemorating American soldiers who fell in France in WWI are inside this twin-towered, Gothic collegiate church.

🛏 Sleeping

Hôtel des Cymaises   HOTEL €
(☑03 80 97 21 44; www.hotelcymaises.com; 7 rue du Renaudot; s €67-73, d €73-77, tr/q €90/110; 🖭) In the heart of the old town, this grand 18th-century *maison bourgeoise* has comfortable, slightly worn rooms, some with exposed wooden beams, and a bright verandah for breakfast. There's free parking in the courtyard, and a relaxing garden out back.

★La Porte Guillier   B&B €€
(☑03 80 97 31 19; www.laporteguillier.com; 5bis rue de l'Ancienne Comédie; d €80-120; 🖭) To really soak up the town's atmosphere, stay at this delightful B&B housed in a fortified stone gateway dating from the 14th century. The three generously sized rooms sport plenty of charming old furniture, and two enjoy stellar views of medieval Semur's main street. Nothing too standard, nothing too studied, a very personal home and good breakfasts brimming with organic specialities.

🍴 Eating

Semur is famous for its patisseries and confectioner's shops. Obligatory stops include the venerable powder-blue **Patisserie Coeur** (14 rue Buffon; ⊙8am-noon & 2-7pm Tue-Sun), best known for its *semurettes* (delicious dark-chocolate truffles created here a century ago) and **Patisserie Alexandre** (rue de la Liberté; ⊙7am-7pm Tue-Sun), renowned for its *granit rose de l'auxois* (a pink confection laden with sugar, orange-infused chocolate, cherries, almonds and hazelnuts).

Le Saint-Vernier   BURGUNDIAN €
(☑03 80 97 32 96; 13 rue Févret; mains €11-21, menus €12-28; ⊙noon-2pm & 7-9pm Tue-Sun) At this cosy bistro in the old town, the *menu* features simple but inventive offerings that spoil your taste buds without spoiling your budget. Most specialities are made with locally sourced ingredients, such as Époisses cheese.

ESCARGOTS

One of France's trademark culinary habits, the consumption of gastropod molluscs – preferably with butter, garlic, parsley and fresh bread – is inextricably linked in the public mind with Burgundy because *Helix pomatia*, though endemic in much of Europe, is best known as *escargot de Bourgogne* (the Burgundy snail). Once a regular, and unwelcome, visitor to the fine-wine vines of Burgundy and a staple on Catholic plates during Lent, the humble hermaphroditic crawler has been decimated by overharvesting and the use of agricultural chemicals, and is now a protected species. As a result, the vast majority of the critters impaled on French snail forks (the ones with two tongs) are now imported from Turkey, Greece and Eastern Europe.

ℹ Information

Tourist Office (☑03 80 97 05 96; www.en. tourisme-semur.fr; 2 place Gaveau; ⊙9am-noon & 2-6pm Mon-Sat, closed Mon Oct-Apr; 🖭)

ℹ Getting There & Away

Transco (☑03 80 11 29 29; www.cotedor.fr) bus 49 (two or three daily) goes to Dijon (€1.50, 1½ hours) and Avallon (40 minutes). Bus 70 goes to Montbard (€1.50, 20 minutes, three to nine daily) on the Paris–Dijon rail line.

Abbaye de Fontenay

Founded in 1118 and restored to its medieval glory a century ago, **Abbaye de Fontenay** (Fontenay Abbey; ☑03 80 92 15 00; www.abbaye defontenay.com; adult/child self-guided tours €10/7, guided tours €12.50/7.90; ⊙10am-6pm mid-Apr–mid-Nov, 10am-noon & 2-5pm rest of year) offers a fascinating glimpse of the austere, serene surroundings in which Cistercian monks lived lives of contemplation, prayer and manual labour. Set in a bucolic wooded valley, the abbey, a Unesco World Heritage Site, includes an unadorned Romanesque church, a barrel-vaulted monks' dormitory, landscaped gardens and the first metallurgical factory in Europe, with an impressive water-driven forge dating from 1220. A self-guided tour, with printed information in six languages, is available year-round; there are also **guided tours** (⊙hourly 10am-noon & 2-5pm) in French from mid-April to mid-November.

From the parking lot, the GR213 trail forms part of two verdant walking circuits: one to Montbard (13km return), the other (11.5km) through Touillon and Le Petit Jailly. Maps and extensive guides to plant life are available in the abbey shop.

Fontenay is 25km north of Semur-en-Auxois. A **taxi** (☎ 03 80 92 04 79, 03 80 92 31 49) costs about €12 (30% more on Sunday and holidays) from the Montbard TGV station, where fast trains connect regularly with Dijon (€13.30, 40 minutes).

MuséoParc Alésia

Opened in 2012, the sensational **MuséoParc Alésia** (www.alesia.com; Alise-Ste-Reine; adult/child museum only €9.50/6, museum & Gallo-Roman site €11.50/7; ⏲10am-7pm Jul & Aug, 10am-6pm Apr-Jun, Sep & Oct, 10am-5pm Nov, Feb & Mar, closed Dec & Jan), near the village of Alise-Ste-Reine in the Pays d'Auxois, is well worth the drive from Dijon (67km) or Semur-en-Auxois (16km). This was the site of what was once Alésia, the camp where Vercingétorix, the chief of the Gaulish coalitions, was defeated by Julius Caesar after a long siege. The defeat marked the end of the Gallic/Celtic heritage in France. You can visit the well-organised interpretative centre as well as the vestiges of the Gallo-Roman city that developed after the battle. The MuséoParc Alésia also offers entertaining programs and workshops for kids.

Châtillon-sur-Seine

POP 5980

On the northern outskirts of Burgundy, Châtillon-sur-Seine has a picturesque old quarter by the river, well-preserved buildings and a not-to-be-missed archaeology museum. It's also a good base if you want to explore the atmospheric Forêt de Châtillon and the Châtillonnais vineyards.

Sights & Activities

Musée du Pays Châtillonnais ARCHAEOLOGY MUSEUM

(☎ 03 80 91 24 67; www.musee-vix.fr; 14 rue de la Libération; adult/child €7/3.50; ⏲9am-noon & 2-6pm Wed-Mon Sep-Jun, 10am-7pm daily Jul & Aug) Châtillon's main claim to fame is the **Trésor de Vix** (Vix Treasure), a collection of Celtic, Etruscan and Greek objects from the 6th century BC on display at the Musée du Pays Châtillonnais. The outstanding collection includes an exquisitely ornamented, jaw-droppingly massive Greek krater; easily the largest known bronze vessel from the ancient world, it's 1.64m high, with a weight of 208.6kg and a capacity of 1100L!

The treasure was discovered in 1953 in the tomb of the Dame de Vix, a Celtic princess who controlled the trade in Cornish tin in the 6th century. Mined in Cornwall, the tin was brought by boat up the Seine as far as Vix and then carried overland to the Saône and the Rhône, whence river vessels conveyed it south to Marseille and its most eager consumers, the Greeks.

Châtillonnais Vineyards VINEYARDS

Among the wines produced in the Châtillonnais vineyards, north of town, is Burgundy's own bubbly, **Crémant de Bourgogne** (www.cremantdebourgogne.fr). Follow the 120km-long **Route du Crémant**, marked by white-on-brown signs to the vineyards, and allow plenty of time for a wine tasting. The tourist office can supply you with the useful map/brochure, *Route du Crémant* (free). The Champagne region's Côte des Bar vineyards are just a few kilometres further north.

Commercial Centre WALKING

The town's centre, rebuilt after WWII, is bordered by two branches of the Seine, here hardly more than a stream. A short walk east, the idyllic **Source de la Douix** (pronounced 'dwee'), a 600L-per-second artesian spring, flows from a 30m cliff. Perfect for a picnic, it is one of the oldest Celtic religious sites in Europe. Nearby, climb up to crenellated **Tour de Gissey** (c 1500s) for fine views.

The immense **Forêt de Châtillon** begins a few kilometres southeast of Châtillon. This peaceful haven is covered mainly by broad-leaved trees, including beeches and hornbeams, and criss-crossed by walking trails.

Sleeping & Eating

Hôtel Sylvia HOTEL €

(☎ 03 80 91 02 44; www.sylvia-hotel.com; 9 av de la Gare; r €45-72; @ 📶) This elegant mansion offers 17 simple yet welcoming rooms and a delightful garden.

Hôtel de la Côte d'Or HOTEL €€

(☎ 03 80 91 13 29; www.hotel-delacotedor.fr; 2 rue Charles Ronot; d €70-110; 📶) This atmospheric establishment has rooms with antique furnishings, as well as a rustic restaurant (*menus* €22 to €65).

Information

Tourist Office (☎ 03 80 91 13 19; www.tourisme-chatillonnais.fr; 1 rue du Bourg; ⏲9am-noon & 2-6pm Mon-Sat, plus 10am-1pm Sun Jul & Aug)

ℹ Getting There & Away

Bus 50, operated by **Transco** (☏ 03 80 11 29 29; www.cotedor.fr), goes to Dijon (€1.50, 1¾ hours, two to four daily). SNCF buses go to the TGV train station in Montbard (€7.70, 40 minutes, three to six daily).

YONNE

The Yonne *département* (www.tourisme-yonne.com), roughly midway between Dijon and Paris, has long been Burgundy's northern gateway. The verdant countryside harbours the magical hilltop village of Vézelay, in Parc Naturel Régional du Morvan, and the white-wine powerhouse, Chablis. Canal boats cruise from ancient river ports such as Auxerre.

ℹ Getting Around

Bus services in the Yonne are inexpensive (€2 per ride) but extremely limited. **TransYonne** (☏ 08 00 30 33 09; www.cg89.fr/Territoire-et-Economie/Transports-dans-l-Yonne) runs regularly scheduled buses no more than once or twice a day; additional services are available on demand, but you must reserve the day before, prior to 5pm, by internet or phone. Get timetables online or at local tourist offices.

Line 2 Links Auxerre with Pontigny.

Line 4 Links Auxerre with Chablis and Tonnerre.

Line 5 Links Avallon with Noyers-sur-Serein and Tonnerre.

Line 6 Links Auxerre with Avallon.

Auxerre

POP 37,550

The alluring riverside town of Auxerre (pronounced 'oh-sair') has been a port since Roman times. The old city clambers up the hillside on the west bank of the River Yonne. Wandering through the maze of its cobbled streets you come upon Roman remains, Gothic churches and timber-framed medieval houses. Views span a jumble of belfries, spires and steep tiled rooftops.

Auxerre makes a good base for exploring northern Burgundy, including Chablis, and is an excellent place to hire a canal boat.

◎ Sights & Activities

Abbaye St-Germain   ABBEY
(☏ 03 86 18 02 90; www.auxerre.culture.gouv.fr; place St-Germain; crypt tours adult/child €6.50/free; ⊙ 9.45am-6.45pm Wed-Mon May-Sep, 10am-noon & 2-5pm Wed-Mon Oct-Apr) This ancient abbey with its dramatic flying buttresses began

as a basilica above the tomb of St Germain, the 5th-century bishop who made Auxerre an important Christian centre. By medieval times it was attracting pilgrims from all over Europe. The **crypt**, accessible by tour (in French, with English handout), contains some of Europe's finest examples of Carolingian architecture. Supported by 1000-year-old oak beams, the walls and vaulted ceiling are decorated with 9th-century frescoes; the far end houses St Germain's tomb.

Housed around the abbey's cloister, the **Musée d'Art et d'Histoire** (admission free) displays rotating contemporary art exhibits, prehistoric artefacts and Gallo-Roman sculptures.

Cathédrale St-Étienne   CATHEDRAL
(place St-Étienne; crypt adult/child €3/free, son et lumière show €5; ⊙ cathedral 7.30am 6pm, crypt 9am-1pm & 2-6pm Tue-Sat, 2-6pm Sun) This vast Gothic cathedral and its stately 68m-high bell tower dominate Auxerre's skyline. The choir, ambulatory and some of the vivid **stained-glass windows** date from the 1200s. The 11th-century Romanesque **crypt** is ornamented with remarkable frescoes, including a scene of **Christ à Cheval** (Christ on Horseback; late 11th century) unlike any other known in Western art. In July and August an hour long **son et lumière (sound-and-light) show** is held Wednesday through Saturday at 10pm inside the cathedral.

Tour de l'Horloge   CLOCK TOWER
(btwn place de l'Hôtel de Ville & rue de l'Horloge) In the heart of Auxerre's partly medieval commercial precinct, the golden, spire-topped Tour de l'Horloge was built in 1483 as part of the city's fortifications. On the beautiful 17th-century clock faces (there's one on each side), the sun-hand indicates the time of day; the moon-hand shows the day of the lunar month.

Cycling   CYCLING
Cycling options include the towpath along the Canal du Nivernais to Clamecy (about 60km) and Decize (175km). See www.la-bourgogne-a-velo.com for a map. **La Navette du Canal du Nivernais** (www.navette-nivernais.fr; per cyclist from €45), a trailer-equipped minivan, is available to transport cyclists and their bikes back to their original starting point.

Boating   BOAT HIRE
(☏ 03 86 52 06 19, 06 25 04 43 88; per 1hr/half/full day €20/60/85; ⊙ daily Easter–mid-Sep) The main tourist office rents electric boats. It takes

Auxerre

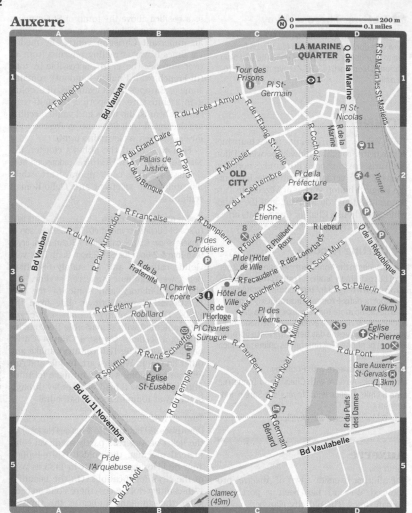

at least 1½ hours to get to the locks on the Canal du Nivernais.

🧭 Tours

The tourist office offers a 45-minute audio-guided city tour on its electric **Voyageur minibus** (adult/child €5/3; ⊙ Sat & Sun Apr-Jun & Sep, daily Jul & Aug). Alternatively pick up their self-guided architectural walking tour brochure, *In the Steps of Cadet Roussel* (€1.50).

Across from the tourist office, **L'Hirondelle** (📞06 30 37 66 17, 09 75 23 27 89; www.

bateauxauxerrois.com; adult/child €10.50/6.50; ⊙ Tue-Sun mid-Apr–mid-Oct, daily Jul & Aug) has river cruises with commentary.

🛏 Sleeping

La Maison des Randonneurs   HOSTEL €
(📞03 86 41 43 22; www.maison-rando.fr; 5 rue Germain Bénard; dm/s/d €18/18/35; 🛜) Bordering a leafy park within easy walking distance of Auxerre centre, this hostel is amazingly good value. It features a modern design and three types of dorm (six-bed, four-bed and three-

Auxerre

bcd), as well as doubles and singles with or without bathroom. Other perks include free wi-fi, bike hire and a communal kitchen. Check-in is between 4pm and 7pm.

Hôtel Le Commerce
HOTEL €
(☑ 03 86 52 03 16; www.hotelducommerceauxerre.fr; 5 rue René Schaeffer; s/d/tw/tr/q €49/53/57/64/68; ☏) Smack in the centre of town, this former *relais de poste* (coaching inn) is the best of Auxerre's budget hotels. Some rooms are enhanced by creative decor inspired by distant sunny lands or quirky themes – room 12 (the 'Africa') and room 26 (the 'Cow') are the quirkiest. There's an on-site restaurant. Parking €7.

Domaine Dessus Bon Boire
B&B
(☑ 03 86 53 89 99; www.dessusbonboire.com; 19 rue de Vallan, Vaux; s/d/tr/q incl breakfast €48/60/72/90; ☏⊞) In sleepy riverside Vaux, 6km south of Auxerre, this family-run B&B offers impeccable rooms and plenty of peace and quiet. Friendly owners Catherine and André Donat, who have worked in organic viticulture since 2000, organise tours to local vineyards and share their extensive knowledge of the region's wines.

Hôtel Le Parc des Maréchaux
HISTORIC HOTEL €€
(☑ 03 86 51 43 77; www.hotel-parcmarechaux.com; 6 av Foch; s €91, d €121-156; ⊞☏⊠) Decorated in an opulent 19th-century style, this mansion of château-like proportions is a fine choice. The rooms, bar and common areas all brim with character. Opt for the quieter rooms that overlook the spacious private park out back. The pool is open from May to September.

🍴 Eating & Drinking

Le Flobert
BURGUNDIAN €
(☑ 03 86 51 16 19; www.le-flobert.fr; 71 rue du Pont; mains €9-16; ⊙noon-1.30pm Mon-Sat, 7.30pm-9pm

Mon & Thu-Sat) The *menu* at this sweet little spot – just a simple bar and a few tables in an elegant honey-coloured room – changes every day and always involves seasonal, fresh ingredients.

⭐ La Pause Gourmande
MODERN BURGUNDIAN, TEAROOM €€
(☑ 03 86 33 98 87; www.lapausegourmande-89.com; 1 rue Fourier; menu €23, incl 2 glasses of wine €29; ⊙9am-5.30pm Tue & Thu-Sat, to 2.30pm Wed) This sweet, unpretentious eatery near the cathedral features an ever-changing monthly *menu* built around fresh local produce and delectable desserts. Many of the gorgeously presented dishes come adorned with edible flowers from the greenhouse of friendly young owners David and Magali. Before noon and after 2.30pm, it doubles as a *salon de thé* (tearoom) serving fine home-baked pastries.

La P'tite Beursaude
BURGUNDIAN €€
(☑ 03 86 51 10 21; 55 rue Joubert; menus lunch €19-21, menus €27-30; ⊙noon-2pm Fri-Mon, 7.15pm-9pm Wed-Mon) Waitresses wearing traditional Morvan dress serve excellent fish and meat dishes. The €21 lunch *menu* offers an introduction to *cuisine du terroir* (traditional cuisine deeply connected to the land), which may include rib steak with Époisses cheese and *œufs en meurette* (poached eggs in red wine sauce).

Le Maurey
WINE BAR
(☑ 03 86 41 12 68; www.facebook.com/lemaurey; Quai de la République; ⊙noon-2pm & 6pm-midnight) A welcome addition to Auxerre's pretty riverfront, this floating resto-bar has become one of the city's most convivial nightspots since opening in late 2012. Sip wine at the bar, in the boat's loungey interior, or on the open-air roof deck. Daily lunch *menus* go for €9.50 to €16.50; in the evenings, everything is à la carte (mains €17 to €19).

BURGUNDY AUXERRE

ℹ Information

Tourist Office (☑ 03 86 52 06 19; www.ot-
auxerre.fr; 1-2 quai de la République; ☉ 9.30am-
12.30pm & 2-6pm Mon-Sat, 10am-1pm Sun; ☎)
Has free wi-fi and will change small amounts of
money on weekends and holidays.

ℹ Getting There & Away

BUS

TransYonne (p431) runs infrequent buses (€2) to
Chablis (30 minutes), Tonnerre (1¼ hours) and
Avallon (one hour). Schedules are available online
or at the tourist office.

TRAIN

Trains run from **Gare Auxerre-St-Gervais** (rue
Paul Doumer):

Avallon €10.60, 1¼ hours, three to four daily

Dijon €28.60, two hours, 10 to 13 daily

Paris Gare de Bercy €28.30, 1½ to two hours,
10 to 14 daily

Sermizelles-Vézelay €8.40, one hour, four to
five daily

ℹ Getting Around

Hire mountain bikes (€20 per day) and electric
bikes (€28 per day) at the tourist office.

La Puisaye

The countryside west of Auxerre, known as
La Puisaye, is a lightly populated landscape
of woods, winding creeks and dark hills. The
area is best known as the birthplace of Colette
(1873–1954), author of *La Maison de Claudine* and *Gigi* (and 50 other novels), and is of
particular interest because much of her work
explores her rural Burgundian childhood.

Until the age of 18, Colette lived in the tiny
town of St-Sauveur-en-Puisaye, 40km southwest of Auxerre. The **Musée Colette** (☑ 03
86 45 61 95; www.musee-colette.com; Château de St-
Sauveur; adult/child €6/3; ☉ 10am-6pm Wed-Mon
Apr-Oct), in the village château, displays letters,
manuscripts, two furnished rooms from her
apartment in Paris' Palais Royal and photos
featuring her iconic hairdo.

Chantier Médiéval de Guédelon (☑ 03 86
45 66 66; www.guedelon.fr; D955 near Treigny; adult/
child €12/10; ☉ 10am-6pm mid-Apr-Jun, to 7pm Jul &
Aug, to 5.30pm Thu-Tue mid-Mar-mid-Apr & Sep-early
Nov) is 45km southwest of Auxerre and 7km
southwest of St-Sauveur-en-Puisaye. A team
of skilled artisans, aided by archaeologists,
has been hard at work building a fortified
castle here since 1997 using only 13th-century
techniques. No electricity or power tools here:

stone is quarried on-site using iron hand tools
forged by a team of blacksmiths, who also
produce vital items such as door hinges. Clay
for tiles is fired for three days using locally
cut wood and the mortar, made on-site with
lime, is transported in freshly woven wicker
baskets.

A very worthwhile guided tour, sometimes in English, costs €2.50 per person.
Child-oriented activities include stone carving (using especially soft stone).

The elegant 11th-century **Château de
Ratilly** (☑ 03 86 74 79 54; www.chateauderatilly.
fr; adult/child €4/free; ☉ 10am-6pm daily Jul-Sep,
10am-noon & 2-6pm Mon-Fri, 3-6pm Sat & Sun
Apr-Jun & Oct) sits in the countryside near
Treigny and holds a collection of pottery by
the Pierlot family and a changing series of
excellent contemporary art exhibitions and
concerts.

Chablis

POP 2400

The well-to-do, picturesque town of Chablis,
19km east of Auxerre, has made its fortune
growing, ageing and marketing the dry white
wines that have carried its name to the four
corners of the earth.

Chablis is made exclusively from chardonnay grapes and originated with the monks of
Pontigny. Now it is divided into four AOCs:
Petit Chablis, Chablis, Chablis Premier Cru
and, most prestigious of all, Chablis Grand
Cru. The seven *grands crus* are lovingly
grown on just 1 sq km of land on the hillsides
northeast of town.

◉ Sights & Activities

Nearby villages worth exploring include
Courgis, which offers great views; **Chichée**
and **Chemilly**, both on the River Serein;
and **Chitry-le-Fort**, famous for its fortified
church. The gorgeous hillside village of **Fleys**
has a number of wineries.

Old Town   HISTORIC CENTRE

The 12th- and 13th-century Gothic **Église
St-Martin** (☉ Jul & Aug), first founded in the
9th century by monks fleeing the Norman attacks on Tours, is two short blocks northwest
of place Charles de Gaulle. Southeast along
rue Porte Noël are the twin bastions of **Porte
Noël** (1778), formerly Chablis' southern town
gate. Other nearby points of interest are the
enigmatic 16th-century building known as
the **synagogue** (10-14 rue des Juifs), recently restored and occasionally open for visits (ask at

IRANCY & COULANGES-LA-VINEUSE WINE COUNTRY

Ask locals where they go to taste western Burgundy's wines and many say: **Irancy**. This relatively new AOC (Appellation d'Origine Contrôlée; 1999) predominantly uses a pinot noir grape, and the growing villages are extremely picturesque. Set in rolling hills and spring-blooming cherry orchards, Irancy and nearby **Coulanges-la-Vineuse**, which has its own appellation, lie 13km south of Auxerre. Explore and you'll find many domaines from which to sample. In Irancy you can visit organic producer **Thierry Richoux** (☑ 03 86 42 21 60; 73 rue Soufflot). In Coulanges-la-Vineuse stop by **Clos du Roi** (☑ 03 86 42 25 72; www.closduroi.com; 17 rue André Vilidieu; ☉ 8am-7pm Mon-Sat) or, in the heart of the village, **Domaine Maltoff** (☑ 03 86 42 32 48; www.maltoff.com; 20 rue d'Aguesseau; incl breakfast s €54-70, d €64-70; ☎), which is also a B&B. Just north of Irancy, another worthwhile stop is **Domaine Bersan** (☑ 03 86 53 33 73; www.bersan.fr; 20 rue du Docteur Tardieux) in **St-Bris-le-Vineux**, a winery that's been in the same family for over five centuries; ask to tour the medieval cellars below the tasting room.

the tourist office) and the 12th-century cellar of **Petit Pontigny** (rue de Chichée), viewable from the exterior only and once used by Pontigny's Cistercian monks to ferment wine.

Wine Tasting
WINE TASTING

Wine can be tasted and purchased at dozens of places around Chablis; the tourist office has a comprehensive list. To sample multiple vintages under one roof, try the cooperative cellar **La Chablisienne** (☑ 03 86 42 89 98; www.chablisienne.com; 8 bd Pasteur; ☉ 9am-7pm Jul & Aug, 9am-12.30pm & 2-7pm rest of year), which carries six of Chablis' seven *grands crus,* the well-regarded 13th-century **Cave du Connaisseur** (☑ 03 86 42 87 15; www.lacaveduconnaisseur.com; 6 rue des Moulins; ☉ 10am-6pm) or the wine shop at Signé Chablis (p436).

Walking
WALKING

Vineyard walks from Chablis include the **Circuit des Grands Crus** (8km), the **Circuit des Clos** (13km to 24km, depending on your route) and the **Circuit du Moulin des Roches** (15.5km to 33km). The tourist office sells topoguides (€3) and IGN maps (€10.70).

Cycling
CYCLING

Cycling is a great way to tour the Chablis countryside. One flat, lush option is the 45km Chemin de Serein, which follows the old Tacot rail line southeast to Noyers-sur-Serein and L'Isle-sur-Serein. The tourist office hires **bikes** (per hour/half-day/full day €2.50/10/18) from May to September.

☞ Tours

Tour the vineyards in an air-conditioned minibus with **Chablis Vititours** (☑ 03 86 42 84 54, 06 11 47 82 98; www.chablis-vititours.fr; 90min/half-day/full day €25/65/140) or in a vintage Citroën 2CV with **Au Coeur du Vin**

(☑ 03 86 18 96 35, 06 80 68 23 76; www.aucoeurduvin.com; tours from €40).

🛏 Sleeping

La Menuiserie　　B&B €

(☑ 03 86 18 86 20; www.chablis-chambresdhotes-lamenuiserie.fr; 11 rue du Panonceau; s/d €75/80, q €135-150; ☎) This is a peach of a B&B. Picture this: a former *menuiserie* (joiner's workshop) that has been renovated with a happy respect for the spirit of the place shelters one inviting room complete with exposed beams and stone walls. An upstairs mezzanine sleeps up to four additional people. Prices drop by €10 if you stay two nights or more.

Maison du Moulin des Roches　　B&B €€

(☑ 03 86 32 30 76; www.chablis-maisondumoulindesroches.fr; d/tr/q €115/150/185; ☎) This lovingly renovated B&B, 1km outside Chablis beside an old mill on the Serein River, offers four spacious, elegantly appointed rooms. Downstairs, guests have access to a high-ceilinged fireplace room, a gym and (for a surcharge) a hammam. Owner Thierry, a dedicated marathon runner, prides himself on gourmet breakfasts featuring fresh-squeezed juice, local cheeses, home-grown fruit and more.

Hôtel du Vieux Moulin　　BOUTIQUE HOTEL €€

(☑ 03 86 42 47 30; www.larochehotel.fr; 18 rue des Moulins; d €145-245; ❋ ☎) In a one-time mill, the understated and very contemporary rooms and two suites afford luscious views of a branch of the Serein. The breakfast room has *grand cru* views.

Chambres d'Hôtes du Faubourg St-Pierre　　B&B €€

(☑ 03 86 42 83 90; www.faubourg-saint-pierre.com; rue Jules Rathier; d €75-100; ☎) Occupying a stately townhouse, this B&B is of a standard that puts many hotels to shame. The mansion's character has been lovingly preserved during refurbishment and the three rooms are large, bright and romantic. Our choice is 'Pauline', with honey-coloured parquet flooring and a marble fireplace.

✗ Eating & Drinking

Le Bistrot des
Grands Crus
TRADITIONAL FRENCH €

(☑ 03 86 42 19 41; www.bistrotdesgrandscrus.com; 8-10 rue Jules Rathier; menus €11-21; ⊘ noon-2pm & 7-9pm) A block southeast of Porte Noël, this hip place serves *cuisine du terroir* made with the freshest local ingredients. The €10.50 *formule,* including a main course and a glass of wine, is one of the best deals you'll find anywhere in Burgundy; it's served at lunch and dinnertime every weekday.

La Cuisine Au Vin
MODERN FRENCH €€

(☑ 03 86 18 98 52; www.lacuisineauvin.fr; 16 rue Auxerroise; menus lunch €17, dinner €29-45; ⊘ noon-1.30pm Tue, noon-1.30 & 7.30-9.15pm Wed-Sat, noon-2pm Sun) Tuck into exquisitely presented organic meals in a cool 11th-century *cave* highlighted in green neon. An offshoot of the Defaix winery (www.chablisdefaix.com; 14 rue Auxerroise), the restaurant sources its ingredients from its own garden patch.

Signé Chablis
WINE BAR

(☑ 03 86 46 32 85; www.signe-chablis.com; 8 rue Auxerroise; ⊘ 11am-6pm) English-speaking owners Arnaud and Guillaume run this combination wine shop, tasting room and self-proclaimed *oenobistro,* where you can enjoy 3cL sampler glasses (€0.75 to €1.90) or full 12cL glasses (€3 to €7.50) of Petit Chablis, Chablis, Chablis Premier Cru and Chablis Grand Cru wines accompanied by local cheeses, charcuterie and/or snails.

DON'T MISS

CHÂTEAU DE MAULNES

Not your average château, the **Château de Maulnes** (☑ 03 86 72 92 00; www.maulnes.fr; Cruzy-le-Châtel; adult/child €2.50/1.50; ⊘ 2.30-5.30pm Sat & Sun Apr-Oct, daily Jul & Aug), 24km east of Tonnerre, is a real showstopper. This Renaissance building is the only château in France that's built on a pentagonal plan and buttressed by five towers.

ℹ Information

Tourist Office (☑ 03 86 42 80 80; www.chablis. net; 1 rue du Maréchal de Lattre de Tassigny; ⊘ 10am-12.30pm & 1.30-6pm, closed Sun Nov-Mar) Has free maps of town and the surrounding vineyards.

ℹ Getting There & Away

Bus 4, operated by TransYonne (p431), links Chablis with Auxerre and Tonnerre (€2, 30 minutes to either destination, once daily except Sunday). Get schedules online or at the tourist office.

Abbaye de Pontigny

Founded in 1114, **Abbaye de Pontigny** (☑ 03 86 47 54 99; www.abbayedepontigny.eu; optional guided tours €4.50; ⊘ 10am-6pm Apr-Oct, 9.30am-4.30pm Nov-Mar) FREE rises from the lush mustard fields 25km north of Auxerre. The spectacular *abbatiale* (abbey church) is one of the last surviving examples of Cistercian architecture in Burgundy. The simplicity and purity of its white-stone construction reflects the austerity of the Cistercian order. On summer days sunshine filtering through the high windows creates an amazing sense of peace and tranquillity. *Discovering Pontigny* (€2.50), on sale in the gift shop, points out fascinating architectural details.

The Gothic sanctuary, 108m long and lined with 23 chapels, was built in the mid-12th century; the wooden choir screen, stalls and organ loft were added in the 17th and 18th centuries.

Monks here were the first to perfect the production of Chablis wine. In summer there are concerts.

Tonnerre

POP 5480

The town of Tonnerre, on the Canal de Bourgogne, is best known for its **Hôtel-Dieu** (www. hoteldieudetonnerre.jimdo.com; rue de l'Hôpital; adult/child €5.50/free; ⊘ 9.30am-noon & 1.30-5.30pm Mon-Sat, 10am-12.30pm & 2-6pm Sun, closed Sun & Wed mid-Oct–mid-Apr), a charity hospital founded in 1293 by Marguerite de Bourgogne, wife of Charles d'Anjou. At the eastern end of the barrel-vaulted patients' hall, near the chapel and Marguerite's tomb, is an extraordinary 15th-century *Entombment of Christ,* carved from a single block of stone.

About 400m west, 200L of water per second gushes from **Fosse Dionne,** a natural spring that was sacred to the Celts and whose blue-green tint hints at its great depth. Legend has it that a serpent lurks at the bottom. The great circular pool is surrounded by a mid-18th-century washing house, a semicircle of ancient houses and forested slopes.

In the villages around Tonnerre, the **Tonnerrois vineyards** produce some good reds, whites and rosés, that are best enjoyed with local dishes or regional cheese. The whites, although much less famous than their Chablis counterparts, are well worth sampling for their slightly fruity aromas.

If you want to overnight in Tonnerre try **La Ferme de Fosse Dionne** (☑03 86 54 82 62; www.ferme-fosse-dionne.fr; 11 rue de la Fosse Dionne; s/d incl breakfast €67/72). In a late-18th-century farmhouse overlooking Fosse Dionne, this delightful hostelry has a cafe and antique shop.

The **tourist office** (☑03 86 55 14 48; www.tourisme-tonnerre.fr; place Marguerite de Bourgogne; ☺10am-noon & 2-6pm, closed Wed & Sun mid-Oct–Mar), at the entrance to the Hôtel-Dieu, has a walking-tour brochure, a map of the Tonnerrois vineyards and rents bicycles (€3/10/18 per hour/half-day/full day).

By rail, Tonnerre is linked to Dijon (€20.40, one hour, 12 daily) and Auxerre (€11.40, 50 minutes, two direct trains daily; otherwise transfer in Laroche-Migennes).

Château de Tanlay

The French Renaissance style **Château de Tanlay** (☑03 86 75 70 61; www.chateaude tanlay.fr; Tanlay; adult/child €9/5; ☺tours 10am, 11.30am, 2.15pm, 3.15pm, 4.15pm & 5.15pm Wed-Mon Mar–mid-Nov), an elegant product of the 17th century, is surrounded by a wide moat and elaborately carved outbuildings. Interior highlights include the **Grande Galerie**, whose walls and ceiling are completely covered with *trompe l'œil*. Find it 10km east of Tonnerre in the village of Tanlay.

Château d'Ancy-le-Franc

The Italian Renaissance makes a cameo appearance at **Château d'Ancy-le-Franc** (☑03 86 75 14 63; www.chateau-ancy.com; Ancy-le-Franc; adult/child €9/6; ☺10.30am-12.30pm & 2-6pm Tue-Sun Apr–mid-Nov, 10.30am-6pm Jul & Aug), built in the 1540s by the celebrated Italian architect Serlio. The richly painted interior, like the 32m mural in the **Pharsale Gallery**, is mainly the work of Italian artists brought to Fontainebleau by François I. English-language handouts are available for self-guided tours.

In 2014, Diane de Poitiers' private apartments on the ground floor were reopened to the public after extensive restoration of their late 16th-century frescoes.

The château is 19km southeast of Tonnerre.

Noyers-sur-Serein

POP 690

A must-see on any Burgundy itinerary, the absolutely picturesque medieval village of Noyers (pronounced 'nwa-yair'), 30km southeast of Auxerre, is surrounded by rolling pastureland, wooded hills and a sharp bend in the River Serein.

Stone ramparts and fortified battlements enclose much of the village and, between the two imposing **stone gateways**, cobbled streets lead past 15th- and 16th-century gabled houses, wood and stone archways and several art galleries.

Lines carved into the façade of the 18th-century **mairie** (town hall), next to the library, mark the level of historic floods.

🏃 Activities

Noyers is a superb base for walking. Just outside the clock-topped southern gate, **Chemin des Fossés** leads northeast along the River Serein and the village's 13th century fortifications, 19 of whose original 23 towers are extant. A few hundred metres beyond the last tower, climb the marked trail to Noyers' utterly ruined hilltop château, then follow signs to the **Belvédère Sud** for spectacular perspectives on the town and the valley below. There are also several longer hikes in the region; see the tourist office for details.

🎪 Festivals & Events

For two weeks in July, various venues host classical concerts and jazz sessions during the **Rencontres Musicales de Noyers** (www.musicalesdenoyers.com).

🛏 Sleeping & Eating

Moulin de la Roche B&B €

(☑03 86 82 68 13; facqarch@wanadoo.fr; rte d'Auxerre; s/d/tr/q incl breakfast €65/90/110/140; 🛜🅿) Northwest of town, this renovated mill on three gorgeous hectares beside the River Serein has two beautiful guest rooms and a millwheel in the living room.

La Vieille Tour B&B €

(☑03 86 82 87 69; place du Grenier à Sel; incl breakfast s €50, d €60-80; ☺Apr-Sep; 🛜🅿) In a rambling 17th-century house, this Dutch-run

BURGUNDY CHÂTEAU DE TANLAY

DON'T MISS

AUBERGE DU POT D'ETAIN

You wouldn't necessarily expect to find a gastronomic gem in the modest village of L'Isle-sur-Serein, halfway between Avallon and Noyers-sur-Serein. But there's **Auberge du Pot d'Etain** (☑ 03 86 33 88 10; www.pot detain.com; rue Bouchardat, L'Isle-sur-Serein; menus €28-60; ☉ noon-1.30pm Wed-Sun, 7-8.30pm Tue-Sat, closed Feb & 2 weeks in Oct; ☎), beating all the odds. The menu is classically Burgundian, built around fresh local meats, fish and vegetables, and the epic 60-page wine list has been recognised as one of France's top five. The *auberge* also shelters nine immaculate, comfy, country-style rooms (doubles €65 to €98).

venture has several simply furnished *chambres d'hôte* of varying size, loads of local colour and a cheerful garden. The best rooms, in a round medieval stone tower, have dreamy river views.

★ Le Tabellion
B&B €€

(☑ 03 86 82 62 26, 06 86 08 39 92; www.noyers-tabellion.fr; 5 rue du Jeu de Paume; d €90-92; ☎) Friendly, knowledgable and multilingual owner Rita Florin runs this attractive B&B in a former notary's office right next to the church. The three tastefully furnished and charmingly rustic rooms are rife with personality, and there's a delightful garden at the back.

Restaurant La Vieille Tour
MODERN BURGUNDIAN €€

(☑ 03 86 82 87 36; rue Porte Peinte; menus €17-25; ☉ noon-2pm Sat-Wed, 7pm-9pm Fri-Wed Apr-Sep; ☑) Just beyond the clock tower at the town entrance, creative young chefs Laurens and Hélène serve a delicious, unpretentious and ever-changing *menu* of Burgundian staples and exotic interpretations. Vegetarian options are also available.

Les Millésimes
BURGUNDIAN €€

(☑ 03 86 82 82 16; www.maison-paillot.com; 14 place de l'Hôtel de Ville; menu €27; ☉ noon-3pm Tue-Sun, 7pm-9pm Tue-Sat) This culinary haven in a meticulously restored medieval house complete with a large fireplace and sturdy wooden tables specialises in *terroir* creations ranging from *jambon au chablis* (ham flavoured with Chablis wine) to *tourte à l'Époisses* (pie with Époisses cheese). It's also renowned for its respectable wine list.

🛍 Shopping

Noyers has a sizeable population of local and expatriate artists.

Création Maroquinerie
LEATHER

(☑ 03 86 75 94 60; 24 place de l'Hôtel de Ville; ☉ 10am-12.30pm & 2.30-6pm Wed-Sun) Among the town's quirky galleries is Création Maroquinerie, a fantastic leather shop full of chic belts and supple handbags. The proprietors, Yazmhil and Brice, do custom work and make everything on-site.

Illuminated Painting Studio
ILLUMINATIONS

(☑ 06 47 99 26 44; www.diane-calvert.com; 47 rue de la Petite Étape aux Vins; ☉ by appointment May-Sep) An interesting spot is Diane Calvert's illuminated painting studio where she grinds her own pigments from semi-precious stones and uses parchment and quill pens.

Maison Paillot
FOOD, WINE

(☑ 03 86 82 82 16; www.maison-paillot.com; 14 place de l'Hôtel de Ville; ☉ 9am-12.30pm & 3-7pm) Food and wine lovers should head for Maison Paillot, which combines a charcuterie/deli with a well-stocked wine cellar.

ℹ Information

Tourist Office (☑ 03 86 82 66 06; www.noyers-et-tourisme.com; 22 place de l'Hôtel de Ville; ☉ 10am-1pm & 2-6pm, closed Sun Oct-May)

Avallon

POP 7550

The once-strategic walled town of Avallon, on a picturesque hilltop overlooking the green terraced slopes of two River Cousin tributaries, was in centuries past a stop on the coach road from Paris to Lyon. At its most animated during the Saturday morning market, the city makes a good base for exploring Vézelay and the Parc Naturel Régional du Morvan.

◎ Sights & Activities

The old city is built on a triangular granite hilltop with ravines to the east and west.

★ Musée de l'Avallonnais
MUSEUM

(☑ 03 86 34 03 19; 5 rue du Collège; adult/child €3/free; ☉ 2-6pm Wed-Mon Apr-Sep, Sat & Sun rest of year) Founded in 1862, this wonderful small museum displays a series of expressionist watercolours by Georges Rouault (1871–1958) and an excellent art deco silver collection by renowned designer and jeweller Jean Després (1889–1980). Upstairs, don't miss the permanent exhibition on the Yao people.

Collégiale St-Lazare CHURCH

(rue Bocquillot; ⊙9am-noon & 2-6pm) Eight centuries ago masses of pilgrims flocked here thanks to a piece of the skull of St Lazarus, believed to provide protection from leprosy. The early-12th-century church once had three portals but one was crushed when the northern belfry came a-tumblin' down in 1633; the two remaining portals are grandly decorated in Romanesque style, though much of the carving has been damaged.

Tour de l'Horloge CLOCK TOWER

(Grande Rue Aristide Briand) This solid, 15th-century clock tower spans the old city's main thoroughfare.

Walking & Cycling WALKING, CYCLING

A pathway descends from the ancient gateway **Petite Porte**, affording fine views over the Vallée du Cousin. You can walk around the walls, with their 15th- to 18th-century towers, ramparts and bastions. For a bucolic walk or bike ride in the **Vallée du Cousin**, take the shaded, one-lane D427, which follows the gentle rapids of the River Cousin through dense forests and lush meadows. The tourist office sells hiking maps and has information on Parc Naturel Régional du Morvan.

🛏 Sleeping & Eating

🛏 Avallon

Hôtel Les Capucins HOTEL €

(☑03 86 34 06 52; www.avallonlescapucins.com; 6 av Président Doumer; d €54-67; ✤🐾🗟) On a quiet, plum-lined side street near the train station, Avallon's best-value hotel has 25 spotless, well-appointed rooms. Best value are the recently updated 3rd-floor rooms under the eaves; most comfortable are the newer units out back. The attached **restaurant** (av Président Doumer; mains €12-24, menus €18-39; ⊙daily) serves up well-prepared Burgundian dishes. There's a small terrace and garden out back, with adjacent free parking.

Dame Jeanne TEAHOUSE €

(☑03 86 34 58 71; www.damejeanne.fr; 59 Grand Rue Aristide Briand; snacks €6-10; ⊙8am-7pm, closed Thu year-round, Sun in winter; 🗟) Folks come from the countryside for delicious lunches or special pastry treats in the garden or 17th-century salon; it's just north of the tourist office.

Le Vaudésir MODERN BURGUNDIAN €

(☑03 86 34 14 60; www.levaudesir.com; 84 rue de Lyon; mains €14.50-18, lunch menus €14.50-20; ⊙lunch Mon, Tue & Thu-Sun, dinner Mon & Thu-Sat) Freshness and value for money are the hallmarks of this sophisticated bistro, 800m from the centre on the road to Lyon. Quintessential dishes include *jambon à la chablisienne* (ham cooked in Chablis sauce) and *escargots en risotto*. There's outdoor seating in summer.

🛏 Around Avallon

Camping Municipal
Sous Roche CAMPGROUND €

(☑03 86 34 10 39; www.campingsousroche.com; sites per adult/child/tent/car €3.60/2/2.70/2.70; ⊙late Mar–mid-Oct; 🗟) A woody, well-maintained site 2km southeast of the old city on the forested banks of the Cousin. Has a play structure, RV hook-ups and wastewater disposal.

★La Cimentelle B&B €€

(☑03 86 31 04 85; www.lacimentelle.com; 4 rue de la Cimentelle; s €83-109, d €88-114, q €165-210; 🗟🗷) Situated on shady, extensive grounds 6km north of Avallon, this château houses two fantastic family apartments and three luxuriously appointed rooms, each one a bit different. One favourite, Hippolyte, has a free-standing clawfoot tub in front of a fireplace. Don't miss the spectacularly sited swimming pool and the sumptuous *tables d'hôte* (€42 including drinks). Nathalie, your amenable hostess, speaks English.

Le Moulin des Ruats HISTORIC HOTEL €€

(☑03 86 34 97 00; www.moulindesruats.com; D427; d €88-160; ⊙mid-Feb–mid-Nov; 🗟) This romantic former flour mill sits in a gorgeous wooded spot right on the Cousin and has a ravishing waterside terrace. Cheaper rooms are a bit disappointing, but it's worth booking ahead for corner room 4, with its lovely mill and river views. Excellent Burgundian dishes are served at the peaceful riverside restaurant.

ⓘ Information

Tourist Office (☑03 86 34 14 19; www.avallon-morvan.com; 6 rue Bocquillot; internet per 30min €2, wi-fi free; ⊙9.30am-12.30pm & 2-6pm Mon-Sat, plus 10am-noon & 2-4pm Sun Jul-Sep; 🗟) Just south of the clock tower; has internet access.

ⓘ Getting There & Away

BUS

Transco (☑03 80 11 29 29; www.cotedor.fr) operates bus 49 from the train station to Dijon (€1.50, 2¼ hours, two or three daily). TransYonne (p431) runs infrequent buses (€2) to Noyers-sur-Serein (40 minutes to one hour), Tonnerre (one to 1¾

BURGUNDY AVALLON

hours) and Auxerre (one hour). Schedules are available online or at the tourist office.

TRAIN

Trains serve the following destinations:

Auxerre €10.60, 1¼ hours, three to four daily
Paris Gare de Lyon or Gare de Bercy €34.70, three hours, three daily
Sermizelles-Vézelay €3.50, 15 minutes, three to five daily

Vézelay

POP 440

The tiny hilltop village of Vézelay, a Unesco World Heritage Site, is one of France's architectural gems. Perched on a rocky spur crowned by a medieval basilica and surrounded by a sublime patchwork of vineyards, sunflower fields and cows, Vézelay seems to have been lifted from another age.

One of the main pilgrimage routes to Santiago de Compostela in Spain starts here (see www.compostelle.asso.fr,).

History

Thanks to the relics of St Mary Magdalene, Vézelay's Benedictine monastery became an important pilgrimage site in the 11th and 12th centuries. St Bernard, leader of the Cistercian order, preached the Second Crusade here in 1146. King Philip Augustus of France and King Richard the Lionheart of England met up here in 1190 before setting out on the Third Crusade.

Vézelay's vineyards, founded in Gallo-Roman times, were wiped out in the late 1800s by phylloxera and were only re-established in 1973.

◎ Sights

★ Basilique
Ste-Madeleine   LANDMARK, CHURCH
(www.basiliquedevezelay.org) Founded in the 880s on a former Roman and Carolingian site, Vézelay's stunning hilltop basilica was rebuilt between the 11th and 13th centuries. On the famous 12th-century tympanum, visible from the narthex (enclosed porch), Romanesque carvings show an enthroned Jesus radiating his holy spirit to the apostles. The nave has typically Romanesque round arches and detailed capitals, while the transept and choir (1185) have Gothic ogival arches. The mid-12th-century crypt houses a reliquary reputedly containing one of Mary Magdalene's bones.

The church has had a turbulent history. Damaged by the great fire of 1120, trashed by the Huguenots in 1569, desecrated during the Revolution and repeatedly struck by lightning, by the mid-1800s it was on the point of collapse. In 1840 the architect Viollet-le-Duc undertook the daunting task of rescuing the structure. His work, which included reconstructing the western façade and its doorways, helped Vézelay, previously a ghost town, spring back to life.

Visitors are welcome to observe prayers or Mass. Concerts of sacred music are held in the nave from June to September; the tourist office and its website have details.

★ Musée Zervos   ART MUSEUM
(☑ 03 86 32 39 26; www.musee-zervos.fr; rue St-Étienne; adult/child €3/free; ⊙ 10am-6pm Wed-Mon mid-Mar–mid-Nov, daily Jul & Aug) This fantastic museum in the exquisite townhouse of Nobel Prize–winning pacifist writer Romain Rolland (1866–1944) holds the collection of Christian Zervos (1889–1970), an art critic, gallerist and friend of many modern art luminaries. He and his wife, Yvonne, collected paintings, sculptures and mobiles by Calder, Giacometti, Kandinsky, Léger, Mirò and Picasso (for whom he created a pivotal 22-volume catalogue).

Maison Jules Roy   HISTORIC BUILDING
(☑ 03 86 33 35 01; rue des Écoles; ⊙ 2-6pm Wed-Sun, 2-5pm Mon, closed mid-Nov–mid-Mar) **FREE**
Up near the top of town, the house of Jules Roy (1907–2000) sits in the shadow of the basilica. Walk around his beautiful gardens and see the Algerian-born writer's study.

⭑ Activities

Walking Trails   WALKING
The **park** behind the Basilique Ste-Madeleine affords wonderful views of the Vallée de Cure and nearby villages. A dirt road leads north to the old and new **cemeteries**. **Promenade des Fossés** circumnavigates Vézelay's medieval ramparts. A footpath with fine views of the basilica links Porte Neuve, on the northern side of the ramparts, with the village of **Asquins** (pronounced 'ah-kah') and the River Cure. The GR13 trail passes by Vézelay.

AB Loisirs   OUTDOOR ACTIVITIES
(☑ 03 86 33 38 38; www.abloisirs.com; rue Gravier, St-Père; ⊙ 9.30am-6pm Jul & Aug, phone ahead rest of year) A few kilometres southeast of Vézelay in St-Père, this well-established outfit

BEYOND THE BASILICA: VÉZELAY'S HIDDEN HILLSIDE CHAPEL

Vézelay's imposing hilltop basilica naturally commands the lion's share of tourists' attention, but a lesser-known treasure lies hidden just out back. Accessible by a lovely 15-minute stroll down a signposted trail behind the basilica, the Romanesque **Chapelle Ste-Croix** (affectionately nicknamed La Cordelle after the rope belts of the Franciscan monks who adopted this spot in the 13th century) slumbers on an idyllic hillside, with espaliered grapevines climbing its stone façade. This beautiful, simple chapel was built to commemorate Bernard de Clairvaux' preaching of the Second Crusade on this very spot in 1146. Nowadays there's no sign of the throngs that filled the fields nearly nine centuries ago. Rather, the chapel has become an off-the-beaten-track refuge for pilgrims and others seeking a place for peaceful meditation in the heart of the Burgundian countryside.

rents bikes (€25 per day) and leads outdoor activities such as kayak trips (8/18km from €23/38), rafting (€49), cave exploration (half-day €39), rock-climbing (half-day €37) and horse riding (per hour €18). Bikes can be brought to your hotel. It's best to phone ahead.

✿ Festivals & Events

Rencontres Musicales de Vézelay
MUSIC FESTIVAL
(www.rencontresmusicalesdevezelay.com) This not-to-be-missed festival of classical music is held at various venues in late August.

Cité de la Voix
Summer Concert Series
PERFORMING ARTS
(www.region-bourgogne.fr/cite-de-la-voix) Vézelay's academy of vocal music stages free concerts in the basilica and elsewhere around town from late June through September.

🛏 Sleeping

★ Centre Ste-Madeleine
HOSTEL €
(☑ 03 86 33 22 14; centre.saintemadeleine@orange.fr; 26 rue St-Pierre; dm/s/d €16/23/40) First and foremost a pilgrims' hostel, this welcoming, well-run place reopened in 2013 after a major renovation. There are two large shared dorms, plus privates ranging from a four-bed family room to a cosy single-bed eyrie tucked under the eaves. The location directly across from the basilica is unbeatable, and guests have access to a well-equipped shared kitchen.

Cabalus
HISTORIC HOTEL €
(☑ 03 86 33 20 66; www.cabalus.com; rue St-Pierre; d €38-58) An incredibly atmospheric place to stay, Cabalus has four spacious rooms in a 12th-century building right next to the cathedral. They're sparsely decorated but come with sturdy beams, ancient tiles and stone walls. Note that the cheaper rooms have

shared toilets. Organic breakfasts (€9) are served at the cafe downstairs.

Auberge de Jeunesse et Camping de l'Ermitage
CAMPGROUND, HOSTEL €
(☑ 03 86 33 24 18; www.camping-auberge-vezelay.com; rue de l'Étang; dm €16, sites per adult/child/car €3/1.50/1; ⊙ camping Apr-Oct, hostel year-round) If being right in town isn't a must, this well-maintained venture 1km south of Vézelay is manna from heaven for thrifty visitors. After an extensive renovation in 2012, it now shelters well-equipped four- to 10-bed dorms with individual kitchenettes and gleaming en-suite bathrooms, flanked by a spacious, grassy camping area.

La Terrasse
HOTEL €€
(☑ 03 86 33 25 50; www.laterrasse-vezelay.com; 2 place de la Basilique; r €100-150; 🖥) Completely renovated in 2014, this six-room hotel enjoys a plum position opposite the basilica, complemented by numerous modern amenities – top-quality bedding, sparkling new bathroom fixtures and large flat-screen TVs. Unique touches include the direct basilica views from the bathtub in room 2 and the 12th-century stone window frame above the bed in room 4. Downstairs there's a terrace restaurant.

🍴 Eating

À la Fortune du Pot
BURGUNDIAN €
(☑ 03 86 33 32 56; www.fortunedupot.com; 6 place du Champ du Foire; menus €16-24; ⊙ noon-2pm & 7-9pm) Well-placed in the square at the foot of Vézelay's main street, this French-Colombian-run restaurant with English iPad menus is at its best in sunny weather, when tables spill out onto the terrace. A €16 three-course *menu* featuring Burgundian classics such as escargots, *tarte à l'Époisses* (Époisses cheese tart) and bœuf bourguignon is available for dinner as well as lunch.

Medieval Art & Architecture

Burgundy, once a powerful duchy and a major ecclesiastical centre, attracted the foremost European artists and builders of the Middle Ages. Now graced with a bounty of excellent museums and monumental architecture, Burgundy offers a trail of human accomplishment through its rolling emerald hills.

TOP 5 ARCHITECTURAL & ARTISTIC HOTSPOTS

➡ Hôtel-Dieu des Hospices de Beaune (p423)

➡ Abbaye de Pontigny (p436)

➡ Palais des Ducs et des États de Bourgogne (p411)

➡ Basilique Ste-Madeleine (p440)

➡ Cathédrale St-Lazare (p446)

The Cistercians

Burgundy's clergy established a series of abbeys and churches that remain some of the best examples of Romanesque architecture. The austere Cistercian order was founded at the Abbaye de Cîteaux in 1098 by monks seeking to live St Benedict's teachings: *pax, ora et labora* (peace, pray and work). The spectacular 1114 **Abbaye de Pontigny** (p436) is one of the last surviving examples of Cistercian architecture in Burgundy.

The Benedictines

Cluny's 12th-century **Benedictine abbey** (p449), now a sprawling ruin, once held sway over 1100 priories and monasteries stretching from Poland to Portugal. Aside from its imposing central towers, it's only a shell of its former self, but visitors can still conjure up its original grandeur thanks to 3D virtual-reality screens dotted throughout

1. Basilique Ste-Madeleine, Vézelay p440 **2.** Abbaye de Pontigny p436 **3.** Cathédrale St-Lazare, Autun

the site. Further north, the better preserved **Abbaye de Fontenay** (p429), a Unesco World Heritage Site (founded in 1118), sits in a peaceful forested valley perfect for contemplation.

Autun & Vézelay

The 12th-century **Cathédrale St-Lazare** (p446) in Autun is world-renowned for its deceptively austere Gislebertus carvings: a fantastic tympanum of the Last Judgement and extraordinary capitals depicting Bible stories and Greek mythology. The adjacent **Musée Rolin** (p446) holds another Gislebertus masterpiece, *The Temptation of Eve*, whose sensitive (and sensual) portrayal of its female subject is nothing short of revolutionary for its time.

Vézelay's **Basilique Ste-Madeleine** (p440), another Unesco World Heritage Site, was founded in the 880s. A traditional starting point for the Chemin de St-Jacques trail to Santiago de Compostela, Spain, it is adorned with Romanesque carvings and attracts both religious and artistic pilgrims. Nearby, the medieval walls and turrets of **Noyers-sur-Serein** (p437) and **Semur-en-Auxois** (p428) are some of the finest remnants of Burgundy's more secular past.

The Dukes of Burgundy

Last but not least, let's not forget the royals. Dijon was home to the powerful Dukes of Burgundy (with fabulous names like John the Good, Philip the Bold and John the Fearless), and flourished into one of the art capitals of Europe. Explore the dukes' monumental **palace** (p411) in central Dijon, home to an excellent fine-arts museum. Or head south to Beaune, where Nicolas Rolin, chancellor to Philip the Good, established a **hospital-cum-palace** (p423) that houses Rogier van der Weyden's fantastic (and fantastical) *Polyptych of the Last Judgement*.

BIBRACTE

The sprawling archaeological remains of the Celtic city of **Bibracte** (☑ 03 85 86 52 35; www. bibracte.fr; ⊙ archaeological sites year-round) **FREE** sit atop beautiful **Mont Beuvray**, 25km west of Autun. Bibracte was the capital of the Celtic Aedui people during the 1st and 2nd centuries BC, and it was here, in 52 BC, that Vercingétorix was declared chief of the Gaulish coalition shortly before his defeat by Julius Caesar at Alésia. Caesar also resided here before the city decamped to Augustodunum (Autun). The site is covered with 1000 hectares of forest, blessed with expansive views and criss-crossed by **walking trails**, including the GR13. Stone remnants include ancient ramparts and several complexes of buildings, all in varying states of excavation.

The excellent **Museum of Celtic Civilisation** (adult/child incl audioguide €7.50/free; ⊙ 10am-6pm mid-Mar–mid-Nov, to 7pm Jul & Aug) explains the technologies, such as a sophisticated system of ramparts, and culture of the Celtic Gauls throughout Europe and also displays finds from the site. During the high season there are guided tours (in English on Mondays at 2.30pm). A Zen-feeling cafe provides set meals and picnic baskets.

Le Bougainville   TRADITIONAL FRENCH **€€**
(☑ 03 86 33 27 57; 26 rue St-Etienne; menus €27-32.50; ⊙ noon-2pm & 7-9pm Thu-Mon; 🖉) The smiling owner serves rich French and Burgundian specialities such as Charolais beef and tripe sausages. If you're growing weary of heavy regional dishes, fear not – Le Bougainville is also noted for its *Menu du Jardinier* (€27), which features vegetarian options – a rarity in Burgundy!

🛍 Shopping

Vézelay has long attracted artists and writers. About half a dozen **art galleries** and several wine and crafts shops line rue St-Pierre and rue St-Étienne.

Domaine Maria Cuny   WINE
(☑ 03 86 32 38 50; www.viti-culture.com; 34 rue St-Étienne; ⊙ by appointment) At their store on Vézelay's main street, this family-run winery sells organic white wines from the tiny Bourgogne-Vézelay appellation. Owner Maria and her friendly daughter Julie can also organise vineyard tours in the region.

ℹ Information

Tourist Office (☑ 03 86 33 23 69; www.vezelay tourisme.com; 12 rue St-Étienne; ⊙ 10am-1pm & 2-6pm, closed Thu Oct-May & Sun Nov-Easter; 🖥) Sells hiking maps. Offers internet access (€2 per 10 minutes) and free wi-fi.

ℹ Getting There & Away

CAR & MOTORCYCLE

Vézelay is 15km from Avallon (19km if you take the gorgeous D427 via Pontaubert). The Clos car park 250m east of place du Champ-de-Foire (towards Avallon) is free; others at the base of town, behind

the basilica and west towards Clamecy cost €3 to €4 per day.

TRAIN

Two daily SNCF buses link Vézelay with the nearby Sermizelles train station (€2.70, 15 minutes). From Sermizelles, trains run south to Avallon (€3.50, 15 minutes) or north to Auxerre (€8.40, 55 minutes) and Paris Gare de Bercy (€33, 2½ hours).

TAXI

For a taxi, call ☑ 03 86 33 19 06. A fare from Sermizelles-Vézelay train station to Vézelay costs about €20 (€26 after 7pm and on Sunday).

Around Vézelay

Southeast of Vézelay at the base of the hill, **St-Père** has a Flamboyant Gothic church.

L'Espérance (☑ 03 86 33 39 10; www. marc-meneau.com; St-Père; d €185-320; menus lunch €62-98, dinner €169-204; ⊙ noon-1.30pm Thu-Sun, 7pm-10pm Wed-Mon, closed mid-Jan–Feb; 🖥🞨), Marc Meneau's legendary French restaurant with two Michelin stars (and 30-room hotel), however, steals the show. Surrounded by private gardens, the inn has flawless service and a mood of refined elegance.

Three kilometres south along the D958, the **Fontaines Salées** (☑ 03 86 33 37 36; www. saint-pere.fr/les-fontaines-salees.htm; adult/child €5/2.60; ⊙ 10am-12.30pm & 1.30-6.30pm Apr-Jun, 10am-6.30pm Jul & Aug, closed Nov-Mar) are saltwater springs that were the site of a neolithic development, then later a Celtic sanctuary (2nd century BC) and Roman baths (1st century AD). Tickets allow access to **Le Musée Archéologique** (☑ 03 86 33 37 31; ⊙ 10.15am-12.30pm & 1.30-6.25pm, closed Nov-Mar) in St-Père, which holds finds from the site.

About 2km south, the village of Pierre-Perthuis (literally pierced stone) is named after a natural stone arch; nearby, a graceful stone bridge (1770) spans the River Cure underneath a modern highway bridge. The neighbouring hamlet of Soeuvres is home to **Au Moulin de Vézelay** (✆ 03 86 32 37 80; www.gite-vezelay.fr; 48 Grand Rue; d incl breakfast €67-88; ✆ ✆), a B&B centred on an old stone mill, with cosy rooms, extensive grounds and nearby walking paths. **Château de Bazoches** (✆ 03 86 22 10 22; www.chateau-bazoches.com; adult/child €8.50/4; ☉ 9.30am-noon & 2.15-6pm Apr-Jun, 9.30am-6pm Jul & Aug, closed mid-Nov–mid-Mar) in Bazoches sits magnificently on a hillside with views to Vézelay 12km to the north. Built in the 13th century and visited by royalty including Richard the Lionheart, it was acquired by field marshal and military strategist Marquis de Vauban in 1675. It's still owned by his descendants.

PARC NATUREL RÉGIONAL DU MORVAN

The 2990-sq-km Morvan Regional Park, bounded more or less by Vézelay, Avallon, Saulieu and Autun and straddling Burgundy's four *départements* (with the majority in the Nièvre), encompasses 700 sq km of dense woodland, 13 sq km of lakes, and vast expanses of rolling farmland broken by hedgerows, stone walls and stands of beech, hornbeam and oak. The sharp-eyed can observe some of France's largest and most majestic birds of prey perched on trees as they scan for field rodents.

☉ Sights

Several house-museums and historic sites around the park, collectively known as the **Écomusée du Morvan** (✆ 03 86 78 79 10; www. parcdumorvan.org), explore traditional Morvan life and customs. The most important of these are located in the village of St-Brisson. The **Maison des Hommes et des Paysages** (St-Brisson; adult/child €3/2; ☉ 10am-1pm & 2-6pm daily Jul & Aug, 10am-1pm Sun, Mon & Wed-Fri, 2pm-6pm Wed-Mon Apr-Jun & Sep-Nov) has displays in French on the interplay between humans and landscapes. Nearby, commemorating the Morvan's role as a major stronghold for the Resistance during WWII, the **Musée de la Résistance en Morvan** (www.musee resistancemorvan.fr; St-Brisson; adult/child €6/3.50, audioguide €1; ☉ 10am-1pm & 2-6pm daily Jul & Aug,

closed Sat morning & Tue Apr-Jun & Sep-Nov, closed Dec-Mar) chronicles key events and characters.

Seven RAF men (the crew of a bomber shot down near here in 1944) and 21 *résistants* are buried in the neatly tended **Maquis Bernard Résistance Cemetery** (www.ouroux-en-morvan. com). It's surrounded by the dense forests in which British paratroops operated with Free French forces. The nearby drop zone is marked with signs. The cemetery is about 8km southwest of Montsauche-les-Settons (along the D977) and 5.6km east of Oroux-en-Morvan (along the D12), near the hamlet of Savelot.

For spectacular panoramic views of the Morvan, climb to **Le Signal d'Uchon**, a 681m granite outcrop at the park's southeastern corner, 22km south of Autun (a 30-minute drive).

☂ Activities

The Morvan (a Celtic name meaning 'Black Mountain') offers an abundance of options to fans of outdoor activities. On dry land choose from walking (the park has over 2500km of marked trails), mountain biking, horse riding, rock climbing, orienteering and fishing. On water, there's rafting, canoeing and kayaking on several lakes and the Chalaux, Cousin, Cure and Yonne Rivers. Lac de Pannecière, Lac de St-Agnan and Lac des Settons have watersports centres. Guided walks of the park, some at night (eg to observe owls), are available from April to October, and there are children's activities in July and August. Boat tours are available at Lac des Settons.

In the mood for swimming? Head for Lac des Settons or Lac de St-Agnan, which offer 'beaches' (a loose term by Morvan standards).

The Morvan Visitors Centre has a comprehensive list of outdoor operators.

⌯ Sleeping & Eating

There's a good choice of campgrounds and B&Bs, as well as a few hotels, in the park. You'll also find simple eateries and inns. The Morvan Visitors Centre has a list of lodgings and places to eat.

ⓘ Information

Morvan Visitors Centre (✆ 03 86 78 79 00; http://tourisme.parcdumorvan.org; Espace St-Brisson; ☉ tourist office 9.30am-12.30pm & 2-5.30pm Mon-Fri, 10am-12.30pm & 2-5.30pm Sat, 3-6pm Sun, closed Sat & Sun mid-Nov–Mar) Surrounded by hills, forests and lakes, Espace St-Brisson is a clearing house of park information, including hiking and cycling maps and guides. By car, follow the 'Maison du Parc' signs

14km west from Saulieu to St-Brisson. The website has details of local festivals, outdoor activities and lodging. Other useful (though not always up to date) sites include www.morvan-tourisme.org and www.patrimoinedumorvan.org.

SAÔNE-ET-LOIRE

In the southern Saône-et-Loire *département* (www.bourgogne-du-sud.com), midway between Dijon and Lyon, highlights include the Gallo-Roman ruins in Autun, Cluny's glorious Romanesque heritage and, around Mâcon, vineyards galore. Several rivers and the Canal du Centre meander among its forests and pastureland.

Autun

POP 15,760

Autun is a low-key town, but almost two millennia ago (when it was known as Augustodunum) it was one of the most important cities in Roman Gaul, boasting 6km of ramparts, four monumental gates, two theatres, an amphitheatre and a system of aqueducts. Beginning in AD 269, the city was repeatedly sacked by barbarian tribes and its fortunes declined, but things improved considerably in the Middle Ages, making it possible to construct an impressive cathedral. The hilly area around Cathédrale St-Lazare, reached via narrow cobblestone streets, is known as the old city. If you have a car, Autun is an excellent base for exploring the southern parts of the Parc Naturel Régional du Morvan.

◉ Sights

Napoléon Bonaparte and his brothers Joseph and Lucien studied in Autun as teenagers. Their old Jesuit college is now a high school called **Lycée Joseph Bonaparte**, on the west side of Champ de Mars. A small **train** (adult/child €7/3.50) offers guided town tours in July and August; contact the tourist office.

★ **Cathédrale St-Lazare**   CATHEDRAL
(place du Terreau; ⊙ cathedral 8am-7pm Sep-Jun, plus 9-11pm Jul & Aug; chapter room summer months only) Originally Romanesque, this cathedral was built in the 12th century to house the sacred relics of St Lazarus. Over the main doorway, the famous **Romanesque tympanum** shows the Last Judgment surrounded by zodiac signs, carved in the 1130s by Gislebertus, whose name is inscribed below Jesus' right foot. Ornamental capitals by Gislebertus and his school, described in a multilingual hand-

out, adorn the columns of the nave; several especially exquisite capitals are displayed at eye level upstairs in the **Chapter Room**.

Later additions include the 15th- to 16th-century bell tower over the transept and the 19th-century towers over the entrance.

Musée Rolin   MUSEUM
(☑ 03 85 52 09 76; 3 rue des Bancs; adult/child €5.20/free; ⊙ 9.30am-noon & 1.30-6pm Wed-Mon) Don't miss this superb collection of Gallo-Roman artefacts; 12th-century Romanesque art, including the *Temptation of Eve* by Gislebertus; and 15th-century paintings such as the *Autun Virgin* by the Maître de Moulins. Modern art includes work by Maurice Denis, Jean Dubuffet and Joan Mirò.

Roman Gates   RUIN
At the edge of town you'll find the impressive remains of two of Augustodunum's four Roman gates. The northern **Porte d'Arroux** was constructed during Constantine's reign, wholly without mortar. It supports four semicircular arches of the sort that put the 'Roman' in Romanesque: two for vehicles and two for pedestrians. East of town, **Porte St-André** is similar in general design.

Temple de Janus   ARCHAEOLOGICAL SITE
(www.temple-de-janus.net) Long associated (wrongly) with the Roman God Janus, this 24m-high temple in the middle of farmland 800m north of the train station is thought to have been a site for Celtic worship. Only two of its massive walls still stand.

Théâtre Romain   ARCHAEOLOGICAL SITE
(Roman Theatre; ⊙ 24hr) Let your imagination run wild at this ancient theatre designed to hold 16,000 people; try picturing the place filled with cheering (or jeering), toga-clad spectators. From the top look southwest to see the **Pierre de Couhard** (Rock of Couhard), the 27m-high remains of a Gallo-Roman pyramid that was probably a tomb.

☆ Activities

For a stroll along the city walls (part-Roman but mostly medieval), walk from av du Morvan south to the 12th-century **Tour des Ursulines** and follow the walls to the northeast. The **Chemin des Manies** leads out to the Pierre de Couhard, where you can pick up the **Circuit des Gorges**, three marked forest trails ranging from 4.7km to 11.5km (IGN map 2925 O).

The **water-sports centre** based at Plan d'Eau du Vallon (an artificial lake east of the centre) rents kayaks, paddle boats and bikes.

TOP CELTIC SITES

➡ Bibracte, the ruins of the capital city of the Aedui people, puts the Celts centre stage at the excellent Museum of Celtic Civilisation (p444).

➡ At Alésia (p430), visit the fine new historical museum, then step outside onto the very battlefield where Julius Caesar defeated Vercingétorix, chief of the Gauls.

➡ Trésor de Vix, a stunning collection of Celtic, Greek and Etruscan objects, is the focus of the Musée du Pays Châtillonnais (p430) in Châtillon-sur-Seine.

➡ The Celtic goddess Sequana is a highlight of Dijon's Musée Archéologique (p414).

➡ Sacred springs and Celtic sanctuaries include Fontaines Salées (p444) near Vézelay, Fosse Dionne (p436) in Tonnerre and Source de la Douix (p430) in Châtillon-sur-Seine.

🛏 Sleeping

★ Maison Sainte-Barbe   B&B €

(☑ 03 85 86 24 77; www.maisonsaintebarbe.com; 7 place Sainte-Barbe; s/d €75/80, ste €120-140; ☎) Smack in the old city in a 15th-century townhouse, this colourful, spotless B&B has five spacious, light-filled rooms, including one with fine views of the cathedral and a two-bedroom suite that's perfect for families. The icing on the cake? The friendly, knowledgeable owners prepare delicious breakfasts, and there's a verdant courtyard out back.

Les Arcades   HOTEL €

(☑ 03 85 52 30 03; www.hotel-arcades-autun.com; 22 av de la République; s €40-43, d €50-53; ☎) Opposite the railway station, Les Arcades is a passable plan B if others are full, but don't expect the Ritz – rooms are unmemorable and service is lackadaisical. Parking costs €5.

★ Moulin Renaudiots   B&B €€

(☑ 03 85 86 97 10, mobile 06 16 97 47 80; www.moulinrenaudiots.com; chemin du Vieux Moulin; d €135-165; ☯ Apr-Oct; ☎ ☰) The exterior of this old water mill is 17th-century stately; inside, it's a minimalist's dream, with vast bedrooms, tasteful colour schemes and luxurious linens. The large, gracious garden comes complete with a swimming pool, perfect for an aperitif before enjoying a sumptuous *table d'hôte* meal (€52). The courteous hosts speak excellent English. About 3km from Autun off the road to Châlon-sur-Saône.

Hôtel de la Tête Noire   HOTEL €€

(☑ 03 85 86 59 99; www.hoteltetenoire.fr; 3 rue de l'Arquebuse; s €73-88, d €84-114; ✳ ☎) Just a short walk uphill from the tourist office, this well-managed abode is clean, bright and friendly, with a respectable restaurant serving regional dishes on the ground floor. Rooms on the 3rd floor have great views of the town and the countryside.

🍴 Eating

Le Petit Rolin   CRÊPERIE, BURGUNDIAN €

(☑ 03 85 86 15 55; www.le-petit-rolin.fr; place St Louis; crêpes €5-11, menus €13-24; ☯ noon-2pm & 7-9pm daily Apr-Sep, Tue-Sun Oct-Dec, closed Jan-Mar) At Le Petit Rolin, with its rustic interior dating back to the 15th century, the *Bourguignonne galette* is filled with regional ingredients such as Époisses cheese and cured meat. Otherwise there are plenty of fish and meat dishes and salads to choose from. In summer tables fill the square outside, opposite the cathedral's tympanum.

Restaurant Le Chapitre   MODERN FRENCH €€

(☑ 03 85 52 04 01; www.restaurantlechapitre.com; 11 place du Terreau; mains €15-25, lunch menus €15-20, dinner menus €31-40; ☯ noon-1.30pm Wed-Sun, 7.30pm-9.30pm Tue-Sat) The intimate dining room in brushed-grey tones fills up with locals out for a quiet, elegant meal. Le Chapitre offers a creative French-inspired menu, with a good selection of fish and meat dishes. It's just behind the cathedral.

Le Monde de Don Cabillaud   SEAFOOD €€

(☑ 07 60 94 21 10; 4 rue des Bancs; menus €27-30; ☯ noon-1.30pm & 7-9pm Tue-Sat) This petite restaurant and oyster bar near Musée Rolin might not register high on the stylometer, but the convivial atmosphere makes up for it. The Breton owner serves a small but super-fresh selection of seafood dishes, prepared in a variety of styles and presented with a minimum of fuss.

Le Chalet Bleu   TRADITIONAL FRENCH €€

(☑ 03 85 86 27 30; www.lechaletbleu.com; 3 rue Jeannin; bistrot menus €19.50-22, restaurant menus €35-60; ☯ noon-2pm Wed-Mon, 7.30pm-9.30pm Wed-Sat) Near the Hôtel de Ville, this place serves classic French gastronomic cuisine in a light, leafy dining room decorated with colourful frescoes. Options range from attractively priced *bistrot menus* to an eight-

CHÂTEAU DE VILLETTE

Set in a 5-sq-km private estate, the delightful 16th- and 18th-century **Château de Villette** (☑ 03 86 30 09 13; www.stork-chateau.com; Poil; d €145-195, ste €195-350, cottage €245, breakfast per person €15; ☎ ☒) offers a glimpse of the luxurious life of Burgundy's landed aristocracy. After waking up in a ravishingly furnished period room, suite or cottage, you can ramble, cycle or hunt escargots in the rolling countryside, or simply relax by the stress-melting pool. *Table d'hôte* meals (€55; twice a week) come in for warm praise. It's 20km southwest of Autun; call ahead.

course *dégustation menu* featuring gourmet dishes such as foie gras with caramelised pears and walnuts or venison with wild mushrooms. Takeaway plates are also sold next door.

ℹ Information

Tourist Office (☑ 03 85 86 80 38; www. autun-tourisme.com; 13 rue Général Demetz; ⊘ 9am-12.30pm & 2-6pm Apr-Sep, to 7pm Jul & Aug, closed Sun & Mon Oct-Mar) Sells a self-guided walking-tour brochure (€2) and hiking maps. Has information on the Parc Naturel Régional du Morvan. From June to September, it operates an annexe beside the cathedral.

ℹ Getting There & Away

Autun's downtown **train station** (av de la République) is on a slow tertiary line that requires a change of train to get almost anywhere. Destinations in Burgundy include Beaune (€15.80, 1¼ hours) and Dijon (€21.50, 1¾ hours).

For more convenient long-distance connections, **Buscéphale** (☑ 08 00 07 17 10; www.buscephale. fr) runs one to seven daily buses to the nearby Le Creusot TGV station (line 5, €3.20, 45 minutes), where TGVs depart regularly for Paris (€80, 1½ hours) and Lyon (€32, 45 minutes).

Château de Sully

This Renaissance-style **château** (☑ 03 85 82 09 86; www.chateaudesully.com; adult/child €8.40/5.40, gardens only €4.10/3.30; ⊘ 10am-6pm Sun-Fri, to 5pm Sat Apr-Oct, guided tours 10.30am-4.30pm Sun-Fri, to 3.30pm Sat), on the outskirts of the village of Sully (15km northeast of Autun along the D973), has a beautifully furnished interior and a lovely English-style garden. It was the birthplace of Marshall MacMahon, Duke of Magenta and president of France from 1873 to 1879, whose ancestors fled Ireland several centuries ago and whose descendents still occupy the property. Château tours are available in five languages; check the website for details.

Tournus

POP 6190

Tournus, on the Saône, is known for its 10th-to 12th-century Romanesque abbey church, **Abbatiale St-Philibert** (⊘ 8am-6pm, to 7pm in summer), whose superb and extremely rare 12th-century **mosaic** of the calendar and the zodiac was discovered by chance in 2002.

The scenic roads that link Tournus with Cluny, including the D14, D15, D82 and D56, pass through lots of tiny villages, many with charming churches. The medieval hilltop village of **Brancion**, with its 12th-century church and **château** (adult/child €6/3; ⊘ 10am-12.30pm & 1-6.30pm), is a lovely place to wander, while **Chardonnay** is, as one would expect, surrounded by vineyards. There's a panoramic view from 579m **Mont St-Romain**.

Cluny

POP 5010

The remains of Cluny's great abbey – Christendom's largest church until the construction of St Peter's Basilica in the Vatican – are fragmentary and scattered, barely discernible among the houses and green spaces of the modern-day town. But with a bit of imagination, it's possible to picture how things looked in the 12th century, when Cluny's Benedictine abbey, renowned for its wealth and power and answerable only to the Pope, held sway over 1100 priories and monasteries stretching from Poland to Portugal.

◎ Sights

Churches of note in the medieval centre include **Église St-Marcel** (rue Prud'hon; ⊘ closed to public), topped by an octagonal, three-storey belfry, and **Église Notre Dame** (⊘ 9am-7pm), a 13th-century Gothic church, across from the tourist office.

★ **Église Abbatiale** CHURCH
(Abbey Church; ☑ 03 85 59 15 93; www.cluny.
monuments-nationaux.fr; combined ticket with
Musée d'Art et d'Archéologie adult/child €9.50/free;
⊙ 9.30am-7pm Jul & Aug, to 6pm Apr-Jun & Sep,
to 5pm Oct-Mar) Cluny's vast abbey church,
built between 1088 and 1130, once extended all the way from the map table in front
of the **Palais Jean de Bourbon** to the trees
near the octagonal **Clocher de l'Eau Bénite**
(Tower of the Holy Water) and the adjoining
square **Tour de l'Horloge** (Clock Tower) – a
staggering 187m! Virtual reality displays help
modern-day visitors envision the grandeur of
the medieval abbey while exploring its scant
ruins. English-language audioguides and
self-guided tour booklets are available.

Abbey visitors also have access to the
grounds of the adjacent **École Nationale
Supérieure d'Arts et Métiers**, an institute
for training mechanical and industrial en
gineers that's centred on an 18th-century
cloister. At the far edge of the grounds, towards the Cluny village exit, don't miss the
13th-century **Farinier** (flour storehouse),
under whose soaring wood-framed roof a
series of eight finely carved capitals from
the abbey's choir are now housed.

Musée d'Art et d'Archéologie MUSEUM
(combined ticket with Église Abbatiale adult/child
€9.50/free; ⊙ 9.30am-7pm Jul & Aug, to 6pm Apr-
Jun & Sep, to 5pm Oct-Mar) For an enlighten-
ing historical perspective on Cluny and its
abbey, start your visit at this archaeological
museum inside the Palais Jean de Bourbon.
Displays include a model of the Cluny complex, a 10-minute computer-generated 3D
'virtual tour' of the abbey as it looked in the
Middle Ages and some superb Romanesque
carvings. A combined ticket covers the museum and abbey both.

Tour des Fromages TOWER
(adult/child €2/1.50; ⊙ 9.30am-12.30pm & 2.30-
6.30pm, no midday closure Jul & Aug, closed Sun
Nov-Mar) To better appreciate the abbey's
vastness, climb the 120 steps to the top of
this tower, once used to ripen cheeses. Access is through the tourist office.

Haras National HORSE STUD
(National Stud Farm; ☑ 03 85 59 85 19; www.
haras-nationaux.fr; 2 rue Porte des Prés; adult/
child guided tour €6/free, jeudis de Cluny €9/5;
⊙ Feb-Nov) Founded by Napoléon in 1806,
the Haras National houses some of France's
finest thoroughbreds, ponies and draught

horses. A regular schedule of afternoon
guided tours runs from February to November (hours vary by month; see website
for details). On Thursdays from mid-July
through August, reserve ahead for the 'jeudis de Cluny', special tours that include music
and expert riding demonstrations.

🛏 Sleeping

★ **Le Clos de l'Abbaye** B&B €
(☑ 03 85 59 22 06; www.closdelabbaye.fr; 6 place
du Maré; s €65-75, d €70-75, ste €110-205; 🛜🅿)
At this handsome old house directly adjoining the abbey, the four comfortable,
colour-coordinated bedrooms – three with
abbey views – are flanked by a lovely garden with facilities for kids. Energetic owners
Claire and Pascal are excellent tour advisers
who direct guests to little-known treasures.
There's a wonderful Saturday morning market just outside the front door.

Cluny Séjour HOSTEL €
(☑ 03 85 59 08 83; www.cluny-sejour.blogspot.
com; 22 rue Porte de Paris; incl breakfast dm/s/d
€18/20/37; ⊙ mid-Jan-mid-Dec) Clean, bright
two- to four-bed rooms, excellent showers
and helpful staff make this simple, well-located hostel a real winner. Towels cost €2.30.

La Pierre Folle B&B €
(☑ 03 85 59 20 14; www.lapierrefolle.com; incl
breakfast s/d/tr/q €70/80/100/120, ste s/d/tr/q
€89/102/122/140; 🛜) Surrounded by rolling fields just south of town, this immaculate B&B offers four spacious, comfortable
rooms and a single suite. Friendly owners
Véronique and Luigi are generous with information about the local area, and serve
delicious breakfasts (included) as well as
Italian-influenced, four-course *table d'hôte*
dinners (€28; book ahead).

Hôtel de Bourgogne HISTORIC HOTEL €€
(☑ 03 85 59 00 58; www.hotel-cluny.com; place de
l'Abbaye; d €105-135, ste €135-165; ⊙ Feb-Nov; 🛜)
This family-run hotel sits right next to the
remains of the abbey. Built in 1817, it has a
casual lounge area, 13 antique-furnished
rooms and a restaurant. Breakfast is served
in an enchanting courtyard. Parking €10.

✖ Eating

The Hôtel de Bourgogne has a fine restaurant.

Le Forum ITALIAN €
(☑ 03 85 59 31 73; www.leforumcluny.com; Pont de
la Levée; pizzas €7-14, mains €10-16; ⊙ noon-2pm

COOKING COURSES

Burgundy's rich, hearty cuisine combines smoky flavours and fresh ingredients. Why not take the opportunity to learn a few of the local techniques? Courses range from the informal to the chic.

➡ The refurbished 17th-century kitchen at Château d'Ancy-le-Franc (p437) makes an evocative venue for four-hour classes from top chefs, followed by lunch accompanied by Burgundy wines (€120, once per month, April to October; reserve at least 15 days in advance).

➡ Le Charlemagne (p422), in the heart of Côte d'Or wine country, has 1½-hour classes (€90) each Saturday, featuring a fresh, seasonal ingredient and accompanied by a wine tasting and dessert.

➡ The proprietress of La Cimentelle (p439), Nathalie, will teach you how to make a *repas gastronomique* in a half-day course (€97).

& 7-10pm Tue-Sat) East across the stream from Cluny's medieval centre, this popular eatery is pleasantly situated in an old stone building with a glassed-in porch and verdant side yard. Specialities include excellent, well-priced pizzas, pasta with creamy truffle sauce, and a good list of French and Italian wines.

Le Bistrot BISTRO €
(☏03 85 59 08 07; 14 place du Commerce; mains €9-17; ⊗8.30am-11pm Wed-Sun; ☎) This character-filled bistro whose walls are adorned with cool vintage posters and old clocks is a real charmer. The flavourful *ravioles* (ravioli with cheese filling) and frondy salads are the house specialities, but there are always imaginative daily specials scrawled on a chalkboard. It doubles as a bar (wine by the glass from €1.20).

★ La Table d'Héloïse BURGUNDIAN €€
(☏03 85 59 05 65; www.hostelleriedheloise.com; 7 rte de Mâcon; menus lunch €20, dinner €26-51; ⊗12.15-1.45pm Fri-Tue, 7.30pm-8.45pm Mon, Tue & Thu-Sat) Just south of town, this family-run restaurant with a charmingly cosy interior is a terrific place to sample firmly traditional Burgundian specialities, from the dextrously prepared *fricassée d'escargots* (snail stew) to the tender Charolais rumpsteak to the ripe Époisses cheese and the devastatingly delicious homemade desserts. Book ahead for a table in the light-filled verandah overlooking the Grosne River.

Brasserie du Nord BRASSERIE €€
(☏03 85 59 09 96; place du Maré; mains €10-17, menus €19-32; ⊗7am-11pm) This brasserie boasts an expansive terrace in a top-notch location – just opposite the Église Abbatiale. The eclectic menu runs the gamut from salads and pasta to frogs' legs and meat dishes.

Better still, it's well priced and stays open late (an exception in sedate Cluny).

ℹ Information

Tourist Office (☏03 85 59 05 34; www.cluny-tourisme.com; 6 rue Mercière; internet per 15min €1.50; ⊗9.30am-12.30pm & 2.30-6.30pm, no midday closure Jul & Aug, closed Sun Nov-Mar) Has internet access.

ℹ Getting There & Around

BUS

The bus stop on rue Porte de Paris is served by **Buscéphale** (☏08 00 07 17 10; www.cg71.fr; tickets €1.50). Lines 7 and 9 (€1.50, six or seven daily) go to Mâcon (25 to 30 minutes), the Mâcon-Loché TGV station (20 to 25 minutes) and Cormatin (20 minutes). Schedules are posted at the bus stop and tourist office.

BICYCLE

Ludisport (☏03 85 22 10 62; www.ludisport.com; place des Martyrs de la Déportation; rentals per half-/full day from €12/18; ⊗10am-noon & 2-4pm Apr-Jun & Sep-Nov, 9am-noon & 2-5pm Jul & Aug) rents bicycles at the old train station, about 1km south of the centre.

Around Cluny

Cormatin, 14km north of Cluny, is home to the Renaissance-style **Château de Cormatin** (☏03 85 50 16 55; www.chateaudecormatin.com; adult/child €9.50/5; ⊗10am-noon & 2-5.30pm mid-Mar–mid-Nov, 10am-5.30pm mid-Jul–mid-Aug, gardens open till dusk), renowned for its opulent 17th-century, Louis XIII–style interiors and formal gardens.

An interesting side trip from Cluny is **Paray-le-Monial**, about 50km to the west. Its major attraction is its Romanesque

Basilique du Sacré-Cœur, whose construction started in the 11th century. Its layout and architectural style are similar to the Église Abbatiale in Cluny.

Mâcon

POP 34,820

The town of Mâcon, 70km north of Lyon on the west bank of the Saône, is at the heart of the **Mâconnais**, Burgundy's southernmost wine-growing area, which produces mainly dry whites.

Across the street from the 18th-century town hall, the **tourist office** (☑ 03 85 21 07 07; www.macon-tourism.com; 1 place St-Pierre; ⊙9.30am-12.30pm & 2-6pm Mon-Sat May, Sep &Oct, daily Jun-Aug, closed Mon Nov-Apr) has information on accommodation and visiting vineyards including the **Route des Vins Mâconnais-Beaujolais**.

The all-wood **Maison de Bois**, facing 95 rue Dombey and built around 1500, is decorated with carved wooden figures, some of them very cheeky indeed.

Musée Lamartine (☑03 85 39 90 38; 41 rue Sigorgne; adult/child €2.50/free; ⊙10am noon & 2-6pm Tue-Sat, 2-6pm Sun) explores the life and times of the Mâcon-born Romantic poet and left-wing politician Alphonse de Lamartine (1790–1869). **Musée des Ursulines** (☑03 85 39 90 38; 5 rue des Ursulines; adult/child €2.50/free; ⊙10am-noon & 2-6pm Tue-Sat, 2-6pm Sun), housed in a 17th-century Ursuline convent, features Gallo-Roman archaeology, 16th- to 20th-century paintings, and displays about 19th-century Mâconnais life.

Riverfront accommodations range from the basic **Hôtel du Nord** (☑03 85 38 08 68; www.hotel-dunord.com; 313 quai Jean-Jaurès; s €62-72, tw €72, d €84; ☞) to the much spiffier **Hôtel d'Europe et d'Angleterre** (☑03 85 38 27 94; www.hotel-europeangleterre-macon.com; 92-109 quai Jean-Jaurès; r €74-168, ste €119-219; ❋☞), whose inviting suites and family rooms overlook the Saône.

Mâcon boasts a bevy of excellent restaurants one block inland from the river. **L'Ethym' Sel** (☑03 85 39 48 84; 10 rue Gambetta; mains €19-22, menus €19-52; ⊙noon-1.45pm & 7-9.30pm Tue-Sat Jul & Aug, noon-1.45pm Thu-Tue, 7-9.30pm Mon & Thu-Sat Sep-Jun) is a modern bistro whose French and Burgundian specialities include locally raised Charolais steak and *souris d'agneau au miel* (lamb in honey sauce). Up-and-coming **Ma Table en Ville** (☑03 85 30 99 91; www.matableenville.fr; 50 rue de Strasbourg; mains €15-22; ⊙11.45am-2pm

Mon-Fri, 7.30pm-9.30pm Thu & Fri) serves a weekly changing menu of market-fresh specials complemented by artisanal local wines in a bright dining room enlivened by colourful modern art. Mâcon's gastronomic sanctuary is **Restaurant Pierre** (☑03 85 38 14 23; www.restaurant-pierre.com; 7-9 rue Dufour; menus lunch €29-32, dinner €29-88; ⊙noon-1.30pm Wed-Sun, 7.30pm-9pm Tue-Sat), where chef Christian Gaulin juggles creativity and tradition to conjure up sumptuous culinary surprises.

On Saturday mornings, a lively **food market** (Esplanade Lamartine; ⊙8am-1pm Sat) fills the esplanade along the Saône's banks.

Buscéphale (☑03 80 11 29 29; www.cg71.fr; tickets €1.50) bus lines 7 and 9 serve Cluny. The Mâcon-Ville train station is on the main line (18 daily) linking Dijon (€21.40, 1¼ hours), Beaune (€15.60, 55 minutes) and Lyon Part-Dieu (€13.30, 50 minutes). The Mâcon-Loché TGV station is 5km southwest of town.

Around Mâcon

About 10km west of Mâcon in the wine country, the **Musée de Préhistoire de Solutré** (☑03 85 35 85 24; www.musees-bourgogne.org; Solutré; adult/child €3.50/free; ⊙10am-6pm Apr-Sep, 10am-noon & 2-5pm Oct-Mar, closed Dec) displays finds from one of Europe's richest prehistoric sites, occupied from 35,000 to 10,000 BC. A lovely 20-minute walk will get you to the top of the rocky outcrop known as the **Roche de Solutré**, from where Mont Blanc can sometimes be seen, especially at sunset.

If you're after top-quality Mâconnais wines, head to the nearby villages of **Fuissé**, **Vinzelles** and **Pouilly**, which produce the area's best white wines.

CYCLING THE VOIE VERTE

An old railway line and parts of a former canal towpath have been turned into the **Voie Verte** (www.bourgogne-du-sud.com/index.php/la-voie-verte.html), a series of paved 'greenways' around the Saône-et-Loire *département* that have been designed for walking, cycling and in-line skating. From Cluny, the Voie Verte heads north, via vineyards and valleys, to Givry (42km) and Santenay, where you can pick up the **Voie des Vignes** to Beaune. Tourist offices have the free cycling map, *Voies Vertes et Cyclotourisme – Bourgogne du Sud*. Also log onto www.burgundy-by-bike.com.

Lyon & the Rhône Valley

POP 3.84 MILLION

Best Places to Eat

➜ Les Halles de Lyon Paul Bocuse (p468)

➜ L'Ourson qui Boit (p468)

➜ Restaurant Pic (p476)

➜ L'Auberge du Pont de Collonges (p469)

➜ Le Musée (p465)

Best Places to Stay

➜ Jardin d'Hiver (p463)

➜ Lyon Renaissance (p463)

➜ Hostellerie de Pérouges (p474)

➜ Cour des Loges (p463)

➜ Mama Shelter (p464)

Why Go?

At the crossroads of central Europe and the Atlantic, the Rhineland and the Mediterranean, grand old Lyon is France's third-largest metropolis and its gastronomic capital. Savouring timeless traditional dishes in checked-tableclothed *bouchons* (small bistros) creates unforgettable memories – as do the majestic Roman amphitheatres of Fourvière, the cobbled Unesco-listed streets of Vieux Lyon, and the audacious modern architecture of the new Confluence neighbourhood.

North of Lyon, Beaujolais produces illustrious wines, while the picturesque hilltop village of Pérouges is a perennial film location. Downstream, the Rhône forges past Vienne's Roman ruins and the centuries-old Côtes du Rhône vineyards, opening to sunny vistas of fruit orchards, lavender fields and the distant Alps as it continues south past Valence and Montélimar, eventually reaching the rugged Gorges de l'Ardèche, where the Ardèche River tumbles to the gates of Languedoc and Provence.

When to Go

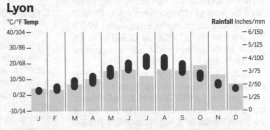

Jun & Jul Jazz festival in Vienne's Gallo-Roman theatre or Lyon's Nuits de Fourvière.

Nov Celebrate the tapping of the first bottles of Beaujolais *Nouveau*, on the third Thursday.

Early Dec See Lyon spectacularly illuminated during the Fête des Lumières.

Lyon & the Rhône Valley Highlights

1 Delving into Lyon's labyrinth of *traboules* (secret passages; p460)

2 Biking the vine-ribboned hills of **Beaujolais** (p474)

3 Seeing dramatic Gallo-Roman ruins, including a perfectly preserved Corinthian-columned temple in **Vienne** (p475)

4 Catching a boat downstream to the **Confluence** (p471), Lyon's newest neighbourhood

5 Learning about Lyon's silk-weaving heritage in **Croix Rousse** (p460)

6 Canoeing beneath the stunning natural stone bridge Pont d'Arc along the **Gorges de l'Ardèche** (p477)

7 Catching a traditional **puppet show** (p471) featuring Lyon's charismatic little raconteur, Guignol

8 Seeing Lyon through the eyes of a local expert on one of the superb **walking tours** (p462) organised by the tourist office

LYON

POP 499,800

Commercial, industrial and banking powerhouse for the past 500 years, today Lyon is France's third-largest city. Outstanding museums, a dynamic cultural life, busy clubbing and drinking scenes, a thriving university and fantastic shopping lend the city a distinctly sophisticated air, while adventurous gourmets can indulge in their wildest gastronomic fantasies. Lyon comprises nine *arrondissements* (neighbourhoods); the *arrondissement* number appears after each street address.

History

The Roman military colony of Lugdunum (Lyon) was founded in 43 BC. It served as the capital of the Roman territories known as the Three Gauls under Augustus, but the city had to wait for renewed fame and fortune until 1473, when the arrival of movable type transformed it into one of Europe's foremost publishing centres.

By the mid-18th century the city's influential silk weavers – 40% of Lyon's total workforce – had developed what had been a textiles centre since the 15th century into the silk-weaving capital of Europe. A century on, Lyon had tripled in size and boasted 100,000 weaving looms.

In 1870 the Lumière family moved to Lyon, and cinema was born when brothers Louis and Auguste shot the world's first moving picture here in 1895.

During WWII some 4000 people (including Resistance leader Jean Moulin) were killed and 7500 others were deported to Nazi death camps under Gestapo chief Klaus Barbie (1913–91), the 'butcher of Lyon'. Nazi rule ended in September 1944, when the retreating Germans blew up all but two of Lyon's 28 bridges. Barbie was sentenced to death in absentia in 1952 and again in 1954, but it wasn't until 1987, following his extradition from Bolivia, that he was tried in person in Lyon and sentenced to life imprisonment. He died in prison three years later.

During the past decade, Lyon has turned its focus to the future, developing a new neighbourhood – the Confluence – based on cutting-edge, energy-efficient architectural principles, and vastly expanding public recreational access to the twin rivers that are the city's heart and soul.

◎ Sights

Lyon straddles the Saône and Rhône Rivers just north of their confluence. The city centre occupies a long peninsula between the rivers known as Presqu'île. Major Presqu'île landmarks, from south to north, are the newly con-

---

LYON IN...

Two Days

If your time's tight, begin with an overview of the city on a guided **tour** before visiting the magnificent **Musée des Beaux-Arts** and lunching on its terrace. Cycle to expansive **Parc de la Tête d'Or** before having dinner at a traditional Lyonnais **bouchon**, and a drink at the bars aboard the Rhône's *péniches* (barges).

Start your second day on what was long known as 'the hill of work', **Croix Rousse**, browsing its outdoor **market** and discovering its **silk-weaving workshops**. Then cross town and ride the funicular to the 'hill of prayer', basilica-crowned **Fourvière**, to uncover Roman Lyon at the fascinating **Musée de la Civilisation Gallo-Romaine** and **Théâtre Romain**. Dine at the panoramic **Restaurant de Fourvière**, before making your way downhill to Vieux Lyon's lively **bars**.

Four Days

Spend your third day absorbing more of Lyon's lengthy history at its cache of **museums**, catch a **puppet show** featuring famous little Guignol, or hop a boat south to see the vast new **Confluence** neighbourhood.

Four days gives you enough time for day trips in the surrounding regions such as wine-rich **Beaujolais**, film-star **Pérouges**, design-driven **St-Étienne** or head **downstream along the Rhône**.

structed Confluence neighbourhood, the Perrache train station, place Bellecour and place des Terreaux. Rising to the north of place des Terreaux is the hillside of Croix Rousse, long home to Lyon's silk weavers. West across the Saône sits the medieval quarter of Vieux Lyon, backed by the slopes of Fourvière (easily recognized by the showy basilica on its summit). East of Presqu'île, the more modern neighbourhoods across the Rhône are home to the Part-Dieu train station, the pointy skyscraper affectionately known as 'Le Crayon' (The Pencil) and the city's biggest green space, Parc de la Tête d'Or. Lyon's St-Exupéry airport lies another 25km to the east.

Vieux Lyon

Lyon's Unesco-listed old town, with its narrow streets and medieval and Renaissance houses, is divided into three quarters: St-Paul (north), St-Jean (middle) and St-Georges (south).

Cathédrale St-Jean   CATHEDRAL
(place St-Jean, 5e; 8.15am-7.45pm Mon-Fri, to 7pm Sat & Sun; Vieux Lyon) Lyon's partly Romanesque cathedral was built between the late 11th and early 16th centuries. The portals of its Flamboyant Gothic façade, completed in 1480, are decorated with 280 square stone medallions. Inside, the highlight is the **astronomical clock** in the north transept. It was recently off-limits due to restoration work, but is expected to resume its regular daily chiming (at noon, 2pm, 3pm and 4pm) by the time you read this.

Medieval & Renaissance
Architecture   ARCHITECTURE
(Vieux Lyon) Lovely old buildings line rue du Bœuf, rue St-Jean and rue des Trois Maries. Crane your neck upwards to see gargoyles and other cheeky stone characters carved on window ledges along rue Juiverie, home to Lyon's Jewish community in the Middle Ages.

Musées Gadagne   MUSEUM
(www.museegadagne.com; 1 place du Petit Collège, 5e; adult/child 1 museum €6/free, both museums €8/free; 11am-6.30pm Wed-Sun; Vieux Lyon) Housed in a 16th-century mansion built for two rich Florentine bankers, this twin-themed exhibition space incorporates an excellent local history museum (Musée d'Histoire de Lyon) chronicling the city's layout as its silk-weaving, cinema and transportation evolved, and an international puppet museum (Musée des Marionettes du Monde) paying homage to Lyon's iconic puppet, Guignol.

On the 4th floor, a cafe adjoins tranquil, terraced gardens, here since the 14th century.

Le Petit Musée
Fantastique de Guignol   MUSEUM
(www.le-petit-musee-fantastique-de-guignol.boutique cardelli.fr; 6 rue St-Jean, 5e; adult/child €5/3; 11am-7.30pm Tue-Sun, 2-7pm Mon; Vieux Lyon) Guignol is the star of this tiny, two-room museum with cute, sensor-activated exhibits; ask staff to set up the English soundtrack.

Musée Miniature et Cinéma   MUSEUM
(04 72 00 24 77; www.mimlyon.com; 60 rue St-Jean, 5e; adult/child €9/6.50; 10am-6.30pm Mon-Fri, to 7pm Sat & Sun; Vieux Lyon) This maze-like museum on tourist-busy rue St-Jean provides an unusual insight into the making of movie sets and special effects achieved with the use of miniatures.

Fourvière

Over two millennia ago, the Romans built the city of Lugdunum on the slopes of Fourvière. Today this prominent hill on the Saône's western bank is topped by a showy 19th-century basilica and the **Tour Métallique**, an Eiffel Tower–like structure (minus its bottom two-thirds) built in 1893 and used as a TV transmitter. Footpaths wind uphill to Fourvière from Vieux Lyon, but the **funicular** (place Édouard Commette, 5e; one-way €1.70) is the least taxing way up; catch it just up the escalators from the Vieux Lyon metro station.

Basilique Notre Dame
de Fourvière   CHURCH
(www.fourviere.org; place de Fourvière, 5e; rooftop tour adult/child €6/3; 8am-7pm; funicular

Lyon

â N

0   200 m
0   0.1 miles

Modernartcafé (250m)

Q Pierre Scize

Saône

Fourvière Hill

5E

R Roger Radisson

20

Gare St-Paul

Pl St-Paul

Q de Bondy

St-Paul Ferry Dock

ST-PAUL

Montée St-Barthélemy

R Juiverie

R Octavio Mey

R François Vernay

R Lainerie

R de Gadagne

Q Romain Rolland

80

25

31

73

12

7

Atelier de Tissage (550m); Maison des Canuts (800m)

Montée de la Grande Côte Balthaz'art (200m); Marché de la Croix Rousse (350m)

Jardin des Plantes

R du Jardin des Plantes

86

R de l'Annonciade

Montée de la Grande Côte

R Imbert Colomès

R des Tables Claudiennes

Croix Paquet

Montée St-Sébastien

R Burdeau

Le Village des Créateurs

R René Leynaud

R des Capucins

R du Griffon

R Romarin

R Terrailles

Pl Tolozan

Péniche Barnum (275m); Bernachon (850m)

Pont Morand

Q André Lassagne

Pl Louis Pradel

R Royale

Croix Paquet

43

54

42

72

5

58

87

85

35

37

64

1ER

1

14

6

16

3

10

47

60

68

36

39

R Verdi

R de la Bourse

Pl de la Bourse

Cordeliers

66

71

Pont Lafayette

Hôtel de Ville

Pl de la Comédie

Pl des Terreaux

R de l'Arbre Sec

R du Bât d'Argent

R Neuve

R Gentil

62

9

48

R de la Poulaillerie

R Dubois

R de la Fromagerie

65

30

R Mercière

R Paul Chenavard

40

38

28

R Lanterne

R de la Platière

77

81

Q de la Pêcherie

82

R Constantine

R d'Algérie

R Ste-Catherine

Montée de la Grande Côte

Pl Sathonay

50

17

70

45

74

46

Pl Gerson

32

R Sergent Blandan

R Terme

R de la Martinière

4

Q de Bondy

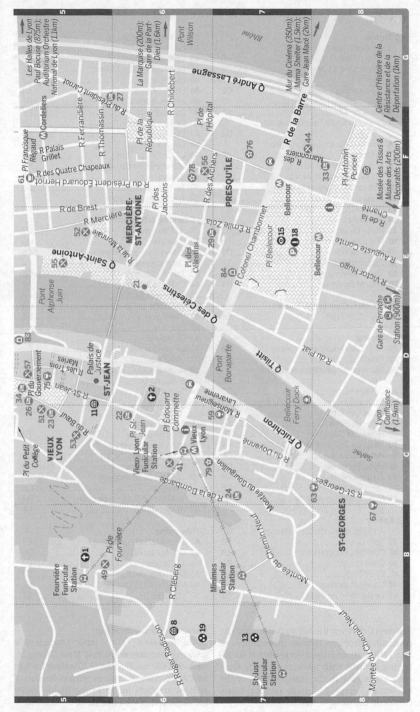

Lyon

Fourvière) Crowning the hill with stunning city panoramas from its terrace, this example of late 19th-century French ecclesiastical architecture is lined with intricate mosaics. One-hour **visits** take in the main features of the basilica and crypt; 75-minute **rooftop tours** climax on the stone-sculpted roof.

Musée de la Civilisation Gallo-Romaine ARCHAEOLOGICAL MUSEUM
(www.musees-gallo-romains.com; 17 rue Cléberg, 5e; adult/child €4/free, Thu free; ☺10am-6pm Tue-Sun; funicular Fourvière) A wide-ranging collection of ancient artefacts found in the Rhône Valley are displayed at the city's Roman museum.

Théâtre Romain
ARCHAEOLOGICAL SITE

(rue Cléberg, 5e; funicular Fourvière or Minimes) Lyon's Roman theatre, built around 15 BC and enlarged in AD 120, sat an audience of 10,000. Romans held poetry readings and musical recitals in the smaller, adjacent **odéon**.

◉ Presqu'île

Lyon's city centre lies on this 500m- to 800m-wide peninsula bounded by the rivers Rhône and Saône.

Musée des Beaux-Arts
ART MUSEUM

(www.mba-lyon.fr; 20 place des Terreaux, 1er; adult/child incl audioguide €7/free; ⊙10am-6pm Wed, Thu & Sat-Mon, 10.30am-6pm Fri; Ⓜ Hôtel de Ville) This stunning and eminently manageable museum showcases France's finest collection of sculptures and paintings outside of Paris from antiquity onwards. Highlights include works by Rodin, Rubens, Rembrandt, Monet, Matisse and Picasso. Pick up a free audioguide and be sure to stop for a drink or meal on the delightful stone terrace off its **cafe-restaurant** or take time out in its tranquil **cloister garden**.

Place des Terreaux
SQUARE

(Ⓜ Hôtel de Ville) The centrepiece of the Presqu'île's beautiful central square is a 19th century **fountain** made of 21 tonnes of lead and sculpted by Frédéric-Auguste Bartholdi (of Statue of Liberty fame). The four horses pulling the chariot symbolise rivers galloping seawards. The **Hôtel de Ville** (Town Hall) fronting the square was built in 1655 but was given its present ornate façade in 1702. When Daniel Buren's polka dot 'forest' of 69 **granite fountains** (embedded in the ground across much of the square) are on, join the kids in a mad dash as the water dances up, down, disappears for a second and gushes back again.

Place Bellecour
SQUARE

(Ⓜ Bellecour) One of Europe's largest public squares, gravel-strewn place Bellecour was laid out in the 17th century. In the centre is an equestrian **statue** of Louis XIV.

Opéra de Lyon
OPERA HOUSE

(Ⓜ Hôtel de Ville) Lyon's neoclassical 1831-built opera house was modernised in 1993 by renowned French architect Jean Nouvel, who added the striking semi-cylindrical glass-domed roof. On its northern side, boarders and bladers buzz around the fountains of **place Louis Pradel**, surveyed by the **Homme de la Liberté** (Man of Freedom) on roller skates, sculpted from scrap metal by Marseille-born César.

Fresque des Lyonnais
MURAL

(cnr rue de la Martinière & quai de la Pêcherie, 1er; Ⓜ Hôtel de Ville) Well-known Lyonnais peer out from this seven-storey mural, including loom inventor Joseph-Marie Jacquard (1752–1834), Renaissance poet Maurice Scève (c 1499–1560), superstar chef Paul Bocuse (b 1926), puppet Guignol, and the yellow-haired Little Prince, created by author/aviator Antoine de St-Exupéry (1900–44).

Musée des Tissus
MUSEUM

(www.musee-des-tissus.com; 34 rue de la Charité, 2e; adult/child €10/7.50, after 4pm €8/5.50; ⊙10am-5.30pm Tue-Sun; Ⓜ Ampère) Extraordinary Lyonnais and international silks are showcased here. Ticket includes admission to the adjoining **Musée des Arts Décoratifs** (34 rue de la Charité, 2e; free with Musée des Tissus ticket; ⊙10am-noon & 2-5.30pm Tue-Sun), which displays 18th-century furniture, tapestries, wallpaper, ceramics and silver.

Musée de l'Imprimerie
MUSEUM

(www.imprimerie.lyon.fr; 13 rue de la Poulaillerie, 2e; adult/child €5/free; ⊙10.30am-6pm Wed-Sun; Ⓜ Cordeliers) From early equipment through to computerised technology, this museum traces the history of the city's printing industry.

◉ Croix Rousse

Independent until it became part of Lyon in 1852, and retaining its own distinct character with its bohemian inhabitants and lush outdoor food market, the hilltop quarter of Croix Rousse slinks north up the steep *pentes* (slopes) from place des Terreaux.

Following the introduction of the mechanical Jacquard loom in 1805, Lyonnais *canuts* (silk weavers) built tens of thousands of workshops in the area, with large windows to let in light and hefty wood-beamed ceilings more than 4m high to accommodate the huge new machines. Weavers spent 14 to 20 hours a day hunched over their looms breathing in silk dust. Two-thirds were illiterate and everyone was paid a pittance; strikes in 1830–31 and 1834 resulted in the death of several hundred weavers.

Nowadays, most workshops have long since been converted into chic loft apartments, but a few have been saved by the **Soierie Vivante association** (www.soierie-vivante.asso.fr).

Hidden Croix Rousse gems include **place Bertone**, a leafy square that doubles as an open-air stage for ad-hoc summer

LYON'S HIDDEN LABYRINTH

Deep within Vieux Lyon and Croix Rousse, dark, dingy *traboules* (secret passages) wind their way through apartment blocks, under streets and into courtyards. In all, 315 passages link 230 streets, with a combined length of 50km.

A couple of Vieux Lyon's *traboules* date from Roman times, but most were constructed by *canuts* (silk weavers) in the 19th century to transport silk in inclement weather. Resistance fighters found them equally handy during WWII.

Genuine *traboules* (derived from the Latin *trans ambulare,* meaning 'to pass through') cut from one street to another. Passages that fan out into a courtyard or cul-de-sac aren't *traboules* but *miraboules* (two of the finest examples are at 16 rue Bœuf and 8 rue Juiverie, both in Vieux Lyon).

Vieux Lyon's most celebrated *traboules* include those connecting 27 rue St-Jean with 6 rue des Trois Maries and 54 rue St-Jean with 27 rue du Bœuf (push the intercom button to buzz open the door).

Step into Croix Rousse's underworld at 9 place Colbert, crossing cour des Voraces – renowned for its monumental seven-storey staircase – to 14bis montée St Sébastien, and eventually emerging at 29 rue Imbert Colomès. From here a series of other *traboules* zigzags down the slope most of the way to place des Terreaux.

For more detailed descriptions and maps of Lyon's *traboules,* visit www.lyontraboules. net or pick up a copy of the French-language guidebook *200 Cours et Traboules dans les Rues de Lyon* by Gérald Gambier (€9.95, available at Lyon's tourist office). The tourist office also includes *traboules* on many of its guided walking tours.

entertainment; the **Jardin Rosa Mir** (http:// rosa.mir.free.fr; enter via 87 Grande Rue, 4e; ⊙3-6pm Sat Apr-Nov; MCroix Rousse), a walled garden decorated with thousands of seashells; and the panoramic **Jardin Publique La Cerisaie** (rue Chazière, 4e; MCroix Rousse).

Maison des Canuts SILK WORKSHOP
(www.maisondescanuts.com; 10-12 rue d'Ivry, 4e; adult/child €6.50/3.50; ⊙10am-6.30pm Mon-Sat, guided tours 11am & 3.30pm Mon-Sat; MCroix Rousse) On a 50-minute guided tour, learn about weavers' labour-intensive life and the industry's evolution, see manual looms in use and browse the silk boutique.

Atelier de Passementerie SILK WORKSHOP
(🞎04 78 27 17 13; www.soierie-vivante.asso.fr; 21 rue Richan, 4e; guided tour adult/child €6/4, combined ticket with Atelier de Tissage €9/5; ⊙boutique 2-6.30pm Tue, 9am-noon & 2-6.30pm Wed-Sat, guided tours & demonstrations 2pm & 4pm Tue-Sat; MCroix Rousse) Preserved for posterity by the Soierie Vivante association, this silk trimmings workshop functioned until 1979, weaving braids and intricate pictures. Browse fabrics in the attached boutique (admission free), or learn the history of the looms and see them at work on a 30-minute afternoon tour.

Atelier de Tissage SILK WORKSHOP
(cnr rues Godart & Lebrun, 4e; MCroix Rousse) Accessible only by guided tour, this wonderful old workshop houses looms that produce larger fabrics. It was closed for renovations at

research time; for status and prices, enquire at nearby Atelier de Passementerie.

Mur des Canuts MURAL
(cnr bd des Canuts & rue Denfert-Rochereau, 4e; MHénon) Lyon's silk-weaving traditions are illustrated by this fresco.

◉ Rive Gauche

The Rhône's Rive Gauche (Left Bank) harbours parks, museums and day-to-day Lyonnais amenities including the city's university and transport hubs.

Parc de la Tête d'Or PARK
(www.loisirs-parcdelatetedor.com; blvd des Belges, 6e; ⊙6.30am-10.30pm mid-Apr–mid-Oct, to 8.30pm rest of year; 🚌C1, C5, MMasséna) Spanning 117 hectares, France's largest urban park was landscaped in the 1860s. It's graced by a lake (rent a row boat), botanic gardens with greenhouses, rose gardens, a zoo and a **puppet theatre** (Le Véritable Guignol du Parc; 🞎04 78 93 71 75; www.theatre-guignol.com; place de Guignol). Take bus C1 (from Part-Dieu train station) or bus C5 (from place Bellecour and Hôtel de Ville) to the Parc Tête d'Or-Churchill stop.

Musée d'Art Contemporain ART MUSEUM
(www.mac-lyon.com; 81 quai Charles de Gaulle, 6e; adult/child €6/free; ⊙11am-6pm Wed-Sun; 🚌C1, C4, C5) Lyon's contemporary art museum mounts edgy temporary exhibitions and a rotating permanent collection of post-1960 art.

It sometimes closes for several weeks between exhibitions, so check to make sure there's something on. Buses stop right out front.

Centre d'Histoire de la Résistance et de la Déportation
MUSEUM

(www.chrd.lyon.fr; 14 av Berthelot, 7e; adult/child €6/free; ⊙10am-6pm Wed-Sun; Ⓜ Perrache, Jean Macé) The WWII headquarters of Gestapo commander Klaus Barbie evokes Lyon's role as the 'Capital of the Resistance' through moving multimedia exhibits. Extensively remodelled in 2012, the museum includes sound recordings of deportees and Resistance fighters, plus a varied collection of everyday objects associated with the Resistance (including the parachute Jean Moulin used to re-enter France in 1942).

Musée Lumière
MUSEUM

(www.institut-lumiere.org; 25 rue du Premier Film, 8e; adult/child €6.50/5.50; ⊙10am-6.30pm Tue-Sun; Ⓜ Monplaisir-Lumière) Cinema's beginnings are showcased at the art-nouveau home of Antoine Lumière, who moved to Lyon with sons Auguste and Louis in 1870. The brothers shot the first reels of the world's first motion picture, *La Sortie des Usines Lumières* (Exit of the Lumières Factories) on 19 March 1895.

Mur du Cinéma
MURAL

(cnr cours Gambetta & Grande Rue de la Guillotière, 7e; Ⓜ Guillotière) Lyon's cinematic story is told in still-image form in one of the city's many murals.

◉ Northern Suburbs

Musée Henri Malartre
MUSEUM

(www.musee-malartre.com; 645 rue du Musée, Rochetaillée-sur-Saône; adult/child €6/free; ⊙9am-6pm Tue-Sun Sep-Jun, 10am-7pm Jul & Aug; 🚌 40, 70) Pope John Paul II's Renault Espace, Hitler's Mercedes, 50-odd motorbikes, bicycles and historical modes of Lyonnais public transport are displayed inside this 15th-century

---

RIVERSIDE REJUVENATION: LA CONFLUENCE

Meet Lyon's newest neighbourhood: the **Confluence** (www.lyon-confluence.fr), where the Rhône and the Saône meet at Presqu'île's southern tip. This former industrial wasteland has recently been brought back to life by a multimillion-euro urban renewal project, recognised for its cutting-edge, environmentally sustainable design by the French government, the European Commission and the WWF.

In Phase One of the project, focused on the Saône riverbanks, dozens of architecturally audacious, energy-efficient buildings have sprung up, including the bizarre orange, Swiss-cheese-like office building **Le Cube Orange**, its sister **Le Cube Vert** and the **Pôle de Commerces et de Loisirs Confluence** (p471), an enormous shopping complex with an innovative, two-hectare, transparent air-cushion roof. Phase One has also seen the whimsical remodelling of existing buildings, including the **Pavillon des Douanes** (customs house), whose balconies are now surmounted by pairs of giant orange frogs, and **La Sucrerie**, a converted 1930s sugar warehouse that houses a nightclub on its top floor and hosts art exhibits during Lyon's Biennale d'Art Contemporain (p462). Phase One's crowning attraction is the ambitious science-and-humanities museum, **Musée des Confluences** (www.museedesconfluences.fr; 28 Boulevard des Belges, 6e), housed in a futuristic steel-and-glass crystal at the meeting of the two rivers.

Phase Two of the Confluence project, to be initiated in 2015 by Swiss architects Herzog & de Meuron (of Tate Modern and Beijing National Stadium fame), will make the new neighbourhood more liveable, adding a substantial residential and market district and linking the Confluence to the rest of Lyon with three new bridges, including the pedestrian-bike corridor **La Transversale**, which will span both the Rhône and the Saône.

Meanwhile, the riverbanks north of the Confluence have also been getting a serious makeover. The Rhône's Rive Gauche (Left Bank), once the domain of high-speed traffic and car parks, has been extensively redeveloped in the past decade to provide Lyon with landscaped walking, cycling and inline skating paths, along with tiered seating where locals lounge on sunny days. Known as the **Berges du Rhône**, the project spans 10 hectares, along more than 5km of riverfront.

A separate riverside beautification project, **Les Rives de Saône** (www.lesrivesdesaone.com), is spreading north along the Saône. An 11km stretch of pedestrian walkway between the Confluence and Île Ste-Barbe, north of Lyon, has already been completed; future phases of the project will eventually open up 50km of the Saône's banks for public recreational use.

château, 11km north of Lyon along the D433. Take bus 40 or 70 to the Rochetaillée stop.

◉ Southern Suburbs

Aquarium du Grand Lyon AQUARIUM
(www.aquariumlyon.fr; 7 rue Stéphane Déchant, La Mulatière; adult/child €15/11; ⊙ 11am-7pm Wed-Sun Sep-Jun, daily Jul, Aug & school holidays; ⬛ Maison du Confluent) Just west of the Confluence, Lyon's well-thought-out aquarium is home to some 280 marine species including over 5000 fish. Bus 15 links it with place Bellecour.

🏃 Activities

GenerationsRoller BLADING
(www.generationsroller.fr) The less-experienced meet at place Bellecour to scoot around town on Fridays at 8.30pm (12km, 1¼ hours) or at 10pm for speed fiends (25km, 1½ hours).

☞ Tours

★ Walking Tours WALKING TOUR
(🗐 04 72 77 69 69; www.en.lyon-france.com/Guided-Tours-Excursions; adult/child €10/6) The tourist office organises a variety of excellent tours through Vieux Lyon and Croix Rousse with local English-speaking guides; tours of several additional city attractions, including the new Confluence neighbourhood, are available in French. Tours are free with a Lyon City Card (p455); book in advance (online, by phone or in person at the tourist office).

Cyclopolitain CYCLE-TAXI
(🗐 04 78 30 35 90, reservations 06 80 60 58 04; http://lyon.cyclopolitain.com; 1/2hr tour 2 people €35/60; ⊙ noon-7pm Tue-Fri, 10.30am-7pm Sat) Tiny and/or tired feet can rest aboard a cycle-taxi tour. Choose from five itineraries.

Lyon City Boat BOAT TOUR
(Navig'inter; 🗐 04 78 42 96 81; www.lyoncityboat. com; 2 quai des Célestins, 2e; river excursions adult/child €10/7; Ⓜ Bellecour, Vieux Lyon) From April to October, river excursions depart from Lyon City Boat's dock along the Saône. One free excursion is included with the Lyon City Card. Advance bookings are essential for **lunch and dinner cruises** (23 quai Claude Bernard, 7e; 3hr lunch cruise €48-58, 6hr lunch cruise €54-63, 3hr dinner cruise €51-60; Ⓜ Ampère, Guillotière, 🚋 T1), leaving from a separate dock on the Rhône.

Le Grand Tour BUS TOUR
(🗐 04 78 56 32 39; www.lyonlegrandtour.com; adult 1-/2-day ticket €19/22, child 1 or 2 days €8, Lyon by Night adult/child €15/8; ⊙ 10am-6.15pm Apr-Oct, to 5.15pm Nov-Mar) Hop-on, hop-off double-decker bus tours. On Thursday and Saturday evenings from June to mid-September, a Lyon by Night tour is also offered at 9.30pm.

🎇 Festivals & Events

Nuits de Fourvière PERFORMING ARTS
(Fourvière Nights; www.nuitsdefourviere.com) A diverse program of open-air theatre, music and dance concerts set in Fourvière's Roman amphitheatre from early June to late July.

Biennale de la Danse DANCE FESTIVAL
(www.labiennaledelyon.com) Three-week dance festival held between mid-September and early October in even-numbered years.

Biennale d'Art Contemporain ART FESTIVAL
(www.labiennaledelyon.com) Huge contemporary art biennial held from mid-September to late December in odd-numbered years.

Fête des Lumières WINTER FESTIVAL
(Festival of Lights; www.fetedeslumieres.lyon.fr) Over several days around the Feast of the Immaculate Conception (8 December), sound-and-light shows are projected onto key buildings, while locals light window sills with candles.

🛏 Sleeping

Lyon has a wealth of accommodation to suit every taste and budget.

🛏 Vieux Lyon

Auberge de Jeunesse du Vieux Lyon HOSTEL €
(🗐 04 78 15 05 50; www.fuaj.org/lyon; 41-45 montée du Chemin Neuf, 5e; dm incl breakfast €19.50-24; ⊙ reception 7am-1pm, 2-8pm & 9pm-1am; @ 🛜; Ⓜ Vieux Lyon, funicular Minimes) Stunning city views unfold from the terrace of Lyon's HI-affiliated hostel, and from many of the (mostly six-bed) dorms. Bike parking, kitchen and laundry (wash-dry per load €4) facilities are available, and there's an onsite bar. To avoid the tiring 10-minute climb from Vieux Lyon metro station, take the funicular to Minimes station and walk downhill.

Hôtel St-Paul HOTEL €
(🗐 04 78 28 13 29; www.hotelsaintpaul.eu; 6 rue Lainerie, 5e; d €79-94; @ 🛜; Ⓜ Vieux Lyon, Hôtel de Ville) This 20-room hotel is conveniently located on the edge of Vieux Lyon, and only a five-minute walk across the bridge from the Hôtel de Ville. Aim for one of the brighter street-facing rooms; back rooms off the staircase tend to be claustrophobic.

★ **Lyon Renaissance** APARTMENT €€
(☏04 27 89 30 58; www.lyon-renaissance.com; 3 rue des Tourelles, 5e; apt €95-115; ⊛; Ⓜ Vieux Lyon) Friendly owners Françoise and Patrick rent these two superbly situated Vieux Lyon apartments with beamed ceilings and kitchen facilities. The smaller third-floor walk-up sleeps two, with windows overlooking a pretty tree-shaded square. A second unit, opposite Vieux Lyon's most famous medieval tower, has a spacious living room with ornamental fireplace and fold-out couch, plus a mezzanine with double bed.

Apart'Observatoire St-Jean APARTMENT €€
(☏06 30 95 59 30; www.gite-de-charme-lyon.com; 70 rue St-Jean, 5e; 2-person apt per night €100-140, per week €490-770; ⊛; Ⓜ Vieux Lyon) It's worth braving the four-storey climb to these two historic, self-catering apartments, smack in the heart of Vieux Lyon. The south-facing unit boasts full-on cathedral views, while the adjacent tower unit offers equally impressive perspectives towards Fourvière. Both have modern kitchen and laundry facilities, and Lyon's attractions are all accessible on foot or from the metro/funicular stop 200m south.

Artelit APARTMENT €€
(☏04 78 42 84 83; www.dormiralyon.com; 16 rue du Bœuf, 5e; d €145-165, apt €150-250; ⊛; Ⓜ Vieux Lyon) Run by Lyonnais photographer Frédéric Jean, the three spacious tower rooms and self-catering apartment of this *chambre d'hôte* have centuries of history behind every nook and cranny. If you fall in love with the artworks, you can buy them to take home. The apartment is also available for weekly rental at a substantial discount (€590 per week).

Collège Hotel HOTEL €€
(☏04 72 10 05 05; www.college-hotel.com; 5 place St-Paul, 5e; d €130-160; ✳ @ ⊛; Ⓜ Vieux Lyon, Hôtel de Ville) With bright white, minimalist guestrooms and school-themed decor throughout, this four-star hotel is one of Vieux Lyon's more unique lodging options. Enjoy breakfast on your balcony, on the rooftop garden terrace, or in the *salle de classe petit dejeuner*, bedecked like a classroom of yesteryear.

★ **Cour des Loges** HOTEL €€€
(☏04 72 77 44 44; www.courdesloges.com; 2-8 rue du Bœuf, 5e; d €190-485, junior ste €340-655; ✳ @ ⊛ ≋; Ⓜ Vieux Lyon) Four 14th- to 17th-century houses wrapped around a *traboule* (secret passage) with preserved features such as Italianate loggias make this an exquisite place to stay. Individually decorated rooms

woo with designer bathroom fittings and bountiful antiques, while decadent facilities include a spa, an elegant restaurant (*menus* €85 to €105), a swish cafe (lunch *menu* €17.50, mains €22 to €30) and a cross-vaulted bar.

🛏 **Presqu'île**

Hôtel Le Boulevardier HOTEL €
(☏04 78 28 48 22; www.leboulevardier.fr; 5 rue de la Fromagerie, 1er; s €66-76, d €69-79; ⊛; Ⓜ Hôtel de Ville, Cordeliers) Newly refurbished and sporting quirky touches such as old skis and tennis racquets adorning the hallways, Le Boulevardier is a bargain 11-room hotel with snug, spotless rooms. It's up a steep spiral staircase above a cool little cafe, which doubles as reception.

Hôtel St-Vincent HOTEL €
(☏04 78 27 22 56; www.hotel-saintvincent.com; 9 rue Pareille, 1er; s/d €56/72; ⊛; Ⓜ Hôtel de Ville) High-beamed ceilings, giant-sized windows, a couple of old stone walls and original wooden floors give this three-floor, 32-room hotel atmosphere to spare. The location halfway between Hôtel de Ville and Vieux Lyon is another big plus.

★ **Jardin d'Hiver** B&B €€
(☏04 78 28 69 34; www.guesthouse-lyon.com; 10 rue des Marronniers, 2e; s/d incl breakfast €120/140, 1-/2-bedroom apt per week from €520/550; ✳ ⊛; Ⓜ Bellecour) Chic and centrally located, this 3rd-floor B&B (no lift) has two beautifully maintained en-suite rooms replete with modern conveniences – one in understated purple

and pistachio, the other in purple and orange. Friendly owner Annick Bournonville serves organic breakfasts in the foliage-filled breakfast room. Next door, her son rents out apartments with kitchen and laundry facilities.

Hôtel des Célestins
HOTEL €€

(☏ 04 72 56 08 98; www.hotelcelestins.com; 4 rue des Archers, 2e; s €87-139, d €98-170, ste €185-216; ✳ 🛜 ♿; Ⓜ Bellecour) This cosy and classy hotel just north of central place Bellecour is surrounded by designer boutiques. The priciest rooms have gorgeous views of the theatre; the cheaper ones face a quiet courtyard.

Hôtel de Paris
HOTEL €€

(☏ 04 78 28 00 95; www.hoteldeparis-lyon.com; 16 rue de la Platière, 1er; s €59-100, d €72-145; ✳ @ 🛜; Ⓜ Hôtel de Ville) This centrally located, newly remodelled hotel in a 19th-century bourgeois building features individually decorated themed rooms. The spacious, front-facing double with *bouchon*-inspired piggy decor and red-and-white checked bedspreads is among the best.

Hotel Carlton
HOTEL €€€

(☏ 04 78 42 56 51; www.mgallery.com; 4 rue Jussieu, 2e; r €215-295, ste €400; @ 🛜; Ⓜ Cordeliers, Bellecour) Fresh off a top-to-bottom renovation, this vintage hotel tempts with soundproofed rooms done up in brilliant reds, lovingly restored with period furniture, mouldings and wallpaper. Options range from 15-sq-metre 'Cocoon' units to circular 40-sq-metre corner suites, many overlooking pedestrianized place de la République. A sauna, spa and sumptuous breakfast featuring traditional Lyonnais specialities add to the appeal.

🛏 Croix Rousse

Nos Chambres en Ville
B&B €

(☏ 04 78 27 22 30; www.chambres-a-lyon.com; 12 rue René Leynaud, 1er; s/d/tr incl breakfast €75/85/120; ☺ Sep-Jul; Ⓜ Croix Paquet, Hôtel de Ville) Graphic artist and jewellery designer Karine Sigiscar runs this three-room B&B in an 18th-century home midway between Croix Rousse and the Hôtel de Ville. Rooms come with stone walls, exposed wood beams and a nice breakfast. Common areas are limited, as half the building is the owner's personal living space.

🛏 Rive Gauche

★ Mama Shelter
HOTEL €€

(☏ 04 78 02 58 00; www.mamashelter.com; 13 rue Domer; r €89-149; ✳ @ 🛜; Ⓜ Jean Macé) Lyon's branch of this trendy hotel chain

has sleek decor, carpets splashed with calligraffiti, firm beds, plush pillows, modernist lighting and big-screen Macs offering free in-room movies. A youthful crowd fills the long bar at the low-lit restaurant. The residential location 2km outside the centre may feel remote, but it's only three metro stops from Gare Part-Dieu and Place Bellecour.

Péniche Barnum
B&B €€

(☏ 09 51 44 90 18, 06 63 64 37 39; www.penichebarnum.com; 3 quai du Général Sarrail, 6e; d €120-150; ✳ 🛜; Ⓜ Foch) Moored on the Rhône between Pont Morand and Passerelle du Collège footbridge, this navy-and-timber barge is Lyon's most unique B&B and comes with two en-suite guest rooms, a book-filled lounge and shaded deck terrace. Organic breakfasts cost €11.

🛏 Northern Suburbs

Camping Indigo Lyon
CAMPGROUND €

(☏ 04 37 64 22 34; www.camping-indigo.com; Porte de Lyon; sites €18.75-21.20, 5-person chalet €44-65, mobile home €46-112; @ ✴ ♿) 🅿 Open year-round, this ecofriendly campground has tree-shaded wooden chalets, mobile homes, and traditional campsites. Family fun includes kids' paddling pools, a playground, ping-pong and volleyball. It's 13km northwest of Lyon, off the A6.

Eating

A flurry of big-name chefs presides over a sparkling restaurant line-up that embraces all genres: French, fusion, fast and international, as well as traditional Lyonnais *bouchons*. The granddaddy of Lyon's gastronomic scene is octogenarian chef Paul Bocuse, whose empire includes his flagship L'Auberge du Pont de Collonges (p469), a quartet of **brasseries** (www.nordsudbrasseries.com) spread about the city and the newly opened **L'Institut** (www.lyonhotel-leroyal.com/dining-fr.html), run by students from his culinary arts academy.

For additional restaurant reviews, videos and ratings, see the French-language websites www.lyonresto.com and www.petitpaume.com. Many restaurants offer cheaper lunch *menus* on weekdays only.

Don't miss Lyon's colourful outdoor food markets: Marché de la Croix Rousse (p466) and Marché St-Antoine (p466).

✘ Vieux Lyon

A surfeit of restaurants, most aimed squarely at tourists, jam the streets of Vieux Lyon.

Terre Adélices
ICE CREAM €

(www.terre-adelice.eu; 1 place de la Baleine, 5e; 1/2/3/4 scoops €2.60/4.40/5.80/6.90; ⊙10am-midnight; Ⓜ Vieux Lyon) It's hard to resist the 150 flavours, both divine and daring, at this ice-cream shop on Vieux Lyon's main pedestrian thoroughfare. Play it safe with Valrhona dark chocolate, organic pistachio or Tahitian vanilla, experiment gently with cardamom, Grand Marnier or lavender, or take a walk on the wild side with a scoop of wasabi, Roquefort or tomato-basil.

Les Adrets
LYONNAIS €€

(☑04 78 38 24 30; 30 rue du Bœuf, 5e; menus lunch €17.50, dinner €27-45; ⊙noon-1.30pm & 7.45-9pm Mon-Fri; Ⓜ Vieux Lyon) This atmospheric spot serves an exceptionally good-value lunch menu (€17.50 including wine and coffee). The mix is half classic bouchon fare, half alternative choices such as Parma ham and truffle risotto or duck breast with roasted pears.

Daniel et Denise
BOUCHON €€

(☑04 78 42 24 62; www.danieletdenise-stjean. fr; 36 rue Tramassac, 5e; menus lunch €21, dinner €30-40; ⊙noon-2pm & 7.30-9.30pm Tue-Sat) One of Vieux Lyon's most dependable and traditional eateries, this classic spot is run by award-winning chef Joseph Viola, who was elected president of Lyon's bouchon association in 2014.

✖ Fourvière

Le Restaurant de Fourvière
LYONNAIS €€

(☑04 78 25 21 15; www.restaurant-fourviere.fr; 9 place de Fourvière, 5e; menus lunch €17, dinner €28-46; ⊙noon-2.30pm & 7-10.30pm; funicular Fourvière) The views are so incredible that it'd be easy for this superbly located restaurant to be a tourist trap, so it's all the more impressive because it's not. Instead it concentrates on well-prepared local specialities including a stellar salade lyonnaise (lettuce, bacon, poached egg and croutons).

✖ Presqu'île

Cobbled rue Mercière and rue des Marronniers – both in the 2e (metro Bellecour) – are chock-a-block with sidewalk terraces in summer. In the 1er, the tangle of streets south of the opera house, including rue du Garet, rue Neuve and rue Verdi, is equally jam-packed with eateries.

La Mère Jean
BOUCHON €

(☑04 78 37 81 27; 5 rue des Marronniers, 2e; lunch menus €12, other menus €16-25; ⊙noon-1.30pm & 7-10pm Mon-Sat; Ⓜ Bellecour) Its windows plastered with guidebook plaudits, but its tables still packed with loyal locals, this thimble-sized bouchon dates back to 1923 and rewards booking ahead for its meat-loaded menu.

L'Instant Fromage
CHEESE €

(www.linstant-fromage.fr; 31 rue Ste-Hélène, 2e; cheese/charcuteries per portion €2.90/3.90, sandwiches & salads €5-9.50; ⊙noon-2pm & 6-10pm Mon-Sat; Ⓜ Ampère-Victor Hugo, Bellecour) This sweet hideaway with checked and polka-dotted tablecloths is a cheese-lover's dream. Sample individual portions of three dozen French cheeses (cow, sheep and goat) from the chalkboard menu, or let them surprise you with an ardoise découverte (five cheeses for €13.50). There's also a nice selection of charcuterie, sandwiches and salads.

L'Épicerie
BISTRO €

(☑04 78 37 70 85; 2 rue de la Monnaie, 2e; tartines €4-10; ⊙noon-midnight; ☑ 🖶; Ⓜ Cordeliers) Done out like an early 20th-century grocer's, with distressed cupboards full of china and old boxes and canisters, this place serves thick-sliced tartines (open-faced sandwiches) with toppings such as brie, walnut and honey, as well as delicious desserts such as pear and chocolate tart.

★ Le Musée
BOUCHON €€

(☑04 78 37 71 54; 2 rue des Forces, 2e; lunch/dinner menus €23/28; ⊙noon-2pm & 7.30-9.30pm Tue-Sat; Ⓜ Cordeliers) Housed in the stables of Lyon's former Hôtel de Ville, this delightful bouchon serves a splendid array of meat-heavy Lyonnais classics alongside veggie-centric treats such as roasted peppers with fresh goat cheese. The daily changing menu features 10 appetisers and 10 main dishes, plus five scrumptious desserts, all served on cute china plates at long family-style tables.

After dinner the gregarious owner offers history tours featuring the traboule out back.

Le Bouchon des Filles
LYONNAIS €€

(☑04 78 30 40 44; 20 rue Sergent Blandan, 1er; menus €25; ⊙7-10pm Mon-Fri, noon-1.30pm & 7-10pm Sat & Sun; Ⓜ Hôtel de Ville) This contemporary ode to Lyon's legendary culinary mères (mothers) is run by an enterprising crew of young women with deep roots in the local bouchon scene and a flair for fine cooking. The light and fluffy quenelles are among the best you'll find in Lyon, and the rustic atmosphere is warm and welcoming, especially on Sundays when families flock in for lunch.

A SLOW-FOOD PERSPECTIVE ON LYON

Lyon resident Fred Bessard is a devoted member of the Slow Food movement and the founder of **Communauté du Goût** (www.communautedugout.com; 2 rue Tissot, 9e; ⊗ 3-8pm Tue & Wed, 3-9pm Thu, 11am-8pm Fri, 10am-6pm Sat; M Gare de Vaise), a home-grown organisation that promotes small local producers, hosts food tastings and sells gourmet groceries and deli items.

Best Markets

Lyon's best two markets in terms of selection are the **Marché de la Croix Rousse** (bd de la Croix Rousse, 1er; ⊗ 6am-1pm Tue-Sun; M Croix Rousse), with its organic section on Saturday morning, and the **Marché St-Antoine** (quai St-Antoine, 1er; ⊗ 6am-1pm Tue-Sun; M Bellecour, Cordeliers); each has over 100 vendors, including many local producers. My personal favorite is the smaller **place Carnot farmer's market** (place Carnot, 2e; ⊗ 4-7.30pm Wed).

Favourite Foodie Outings

La Bonâme de Bruno (p468) for dinner, Le Bistrot du Potager (p466) for wine and tapas, Chez Hugon (p467) for an authentic *bouchon*, the Halles de Lyon (p468) for seafood.

Hidden Treasures

I love **place Sathonay** (M Hôtel de Ville, Croix Paquet) at the foot of Croix Rousse; it's got a small village atmosphere, with its bars, restaurants and ice-cream places; also, the interior garden of the Musée des Beaux-Arts (p459), for brunch on the terrace.

Not-To-Be-Missed Lyonnais Specialities

Two typical specialities that people *have* to try are quenelles (pike dumplings) and *saucisson à cuire* (a classic local sausage), which you can find at **Reynon** (www.reynonlyon.com; 13 rue des Archers, 2e; ⊗ 8.30am-1.30pm & 3-7.30pm Tue-Sat ; M Bellecour), Lyon's best charcutier, or in the *bouchons* (p467).

Other Advice for Visitors

Lyon is unique in the sense that it's crossed by two rivers; I'd recommend discovering the city by walking or biking along the banks of the Rhône and Saône.

Le Bistrot du Potager　TAPAS €€
(☑ 04 78 29 61 59; www.lebistrotdupotager.com; 3 rue de la Martinière, 1er; tapas €6-15; ⊗ noon-2pm & 7.30-10pm Tue-Sat; M Hôtel de Ville) An offshoot of the renowned Potager des Halles restaurant, this corner tapas bar is a dreamy spot to while away an evening. Happy diners throng the high-ceilinged main dining room, cosy upstairs balcony and sidewalk tables opposite the Fresque des Lyonnais, lingering over wine, Provençal-style beef tartare, grilled fish with tempura squash blossoms, or platters of cheeses and charcuterie.

Café des Fédérations　BOUCHON €€
(☑ 04 78 28 26 00; www.lesfedeslyon.com; 8-10 rue Major Martin, 1er; lunch/dinner menus €20/27; ⊗ noon-1.30pm & 7.45-9pm Mon-Sat; M Hôtel de Ville) Black-and-white photos of old Lyon hang on wood-panelled walls at this Lyonnais bistro, unchanged for decades. From the vast array of appetisers – lentils in mustardy sauce, slices of *rosette de Lyon* sausage, pickles, beets and more – clear through to a classic *baba au rhum* for dessert, this is *bouchon* dining at its finest.

**Au Petit Bouchon
Chez Georges**　BOUCHON €€
(☑ 04 78 28 30 46; www.aupetitbouchonchez georges.fr; 8 rue du Garet, 1er; menus lunch €17-19, dinner €20-27; ⊗ noon-2pm & 7.30-10pm Mon-Fri; M Hôtel de Ville) With lace curtains, sepia-toned lighting, gregarious hosts and just a smattering of tables, this venerable *bouchon* just south of the Opéra exudes a delightfully intimate ambience. The lunch *menus* and à la carte dinner choices are tried-and-true to local traditions. Book ahead.

Thomas　FRENCH €€
(☑ 04 72 56 04 76; www.restaurant-thomas.com; 6 rue Laurencin, 2e; menus lunch €17-31, dinner €45; ⊗ 11am-2pm & 6pm-midnight Mon-Fri; M Ampère) Ingenious chef Thomas Ponson gives taste buds the choice between formal dining at his eponymous restaurant; more casual fare in his à la carte wine bar, **Comptoir Thomas** (☑ 04 72 41 92 99; 3 rue Laurencin, 2e; mains for 2 people €21-35; ⊗ lunch & dinner Mon-Fri); and more casual still at his tapas-inspired **Café Thomas** (1 rue Laurencin, 2e; plat du jour €9, lunch menu €15; ⊗ lunch & dinner Tue-

Sat). His newest venture is the Italian-themed **La Cantinetta** (☑ 04 72 60 94 53; 3 rue Laurencin, 2e; ☺ lunch & dinner Mon-Fri).

Le Saint Vincent LYONNAIS €€
(☑ 04 72 07 70 43; 6 place Fernand Rey; lunch/dinner menus €16.50/25; ☺ noon-2pm & 8-10pm Mon-Sat; Ⓜ Hôtel de Ville) The ample three-course lunch *menu* of home-cooked soups and stews, fish and meat dishes and desserts is reason enough to visit this cosy neighbourhood eatery, but what really sets it apart is the outdoor seating at chartreuse chairs and tables on a pretty-as-a-picture tree-shaded square – perfect on a sunny afternoon.

BOUCHONS

A *bouchon* might be a 'bottle stopper' or 'traffic jam' elsewhere in France, but in Lyon it's a small, friendly bistro that cooks up traditional cuisine using regional produce. *Bouchons* originated in the first half of the 20th century when many large bourgeois families had to let go of their in-house cooks, who then set up their own restaurant businesses. The first of these *mères* (mothers) was Mère Guy, followed by Mère Filloux, Mère Brazier (under whom Paul Bocuse trained) and others. Choose carefully – not all *bouchons* are as authentic as they first appear. Many of the best are certified by the organisation Les Authentiques Bouchons Lyonnais – look for the metal plate on their façades depicting traditional puppet Gnafron (Guignol's mate) with his glass of Beaujolais.

Kick-start a memorable gastronomic experience with a *communard*, a blood-red aperitif of Beaujolais wine mixed with *crème de cassis* (blackcurrant liqueur), named after the supporters of the Paris Commune killed in 1871. When ordering wine with your meal, ask for a *pot* – a classically Lyonnais 46cL glass bottle adorned with an elastic band to prevent wine drips – of local Brouilly, Beaujolais, Côtes du Rhône or Mâcon, costing around €9 to €12; a smaller, 25cL version called a *fillette* costs between €5 and €7.

Next comes the entrée, perhaps *tablier de sapeur* ('fireman's apron'; actually meaning breaded, fried tripe), *salade de cervelas* (salad of boiled pork sausage sometimes studded with pistachio nuts or black truffle specks), or *caviar de la Croix Rousse* (lentils in creamy sauce). Hearty main dishes include *boudin blanc* (veal sausage), *boudin noir aux pommes* (blood sausage with apples), *quenelles* (feather-light flour, egg and cream dumplings), *quenelles de brochet* (pike dumplings served in a creamy crayfish sauce), *andouillette* (sausage made from pigs' intestines), *gras double* (a type of tripe) and *pieds de mouton/ veau/couchon* (sheep/calf/pig trotters).

For the cheese course, choose between a bowl of *fromage blanc* (a cross between cream cheese and natural yoghurt); *cervelle de canut* ('brains of the silk weaver'; *fromage blanc* mixed with chives and garlic), which originated in Croix Rousse and accompanied every meal for 19th-century weavers; or local St Marcellin ripened to gooey perfection.

Desserts are grandma-style: think *tarte aux pommes* (apple tart) or the Lyonnais classic *tarte aux pralines*, a brilliant rose-coloured confection made with crème fraiche and crushed sugar-coated almonds.

Little etiquette is required in *bouchons*. Seldom do you get clean cutlery for each course, and mopping your plate with a chunk of bread is fine. In the most popular and traditional spots, you'll often find yourself sitting elbow-to-elbow with your fellow diners at a long row of tightly wedged tables. Advance reservations are recommended.

Several classics worth seeking out:

Le Garet (☑ 04 78 28 16 94; 7 rue du Garet, 1er; lunch/dinner menus €19/25; ☺ noon-1.30pm & 7.30-9pm Mon-Fri; Ⓜ Hôtel de Ville)

Chez Hugon (☑ 04 78 28 10 94; www.bouchonlyonnais.fr; 12 rue Pizay, 1er; menus €25; ☺ noon-2pm & 7.30-10pm Mon-Fri; Ⓜ Hôtel de Ville)

Le Poêlon d'Or (☑ 04 78 37 65 60; 29 rue des Remparts d'Ainay, 2e; lunch menu €18, dinner menus €25.50-32; ☺ noon-2pm & 7.30-10.30pm Mon-Fri; Ⓜ Ampère-Victor Hugo)

Chez Paul (☑ 04 78 28 35 83; www.chezpaul.fr; 11 rue Major Martin, 1er; menus €16-27; ☺ noon-2pm & 7.30-11pm Mon-Sat; Ⓜ Hôtel de Ville)

Le Tire Bouchon (☑ 04 78 37 69 95; 16 rue du Bœuf, 5e; menus €22-28; ☺ 7.30-10pm Tue-Sat, noon-2.30pm Sat & Sun; Ⓜ Vieux Lyon)

LYON & THE RHÔNE VALLEY LYON

Brasserie Georges BRASSERIE €€
(☎04 72 56 54 54; www.brasseriegeorges.com; 30 cours de Verdun, 2e; menus €21-26.50; ⏰11.30am-11.15pm Sun-Thu, 11.30am-midnight Fri & Sat; Ⓜ Perrache) Opened as a brewery in 1836 (and still offering four homebrews on tap), Georges' enormous 1924 art-deco interior can feed 2000 a day! Famous customers include Rodin, Balzac, Hemingway, Zola, Verne and Piaf; food spans onion soup, sauerkraut, seafood and Lyonnais specialities.

🍴 Croix Rousse

On weekends from December to April, Croix Rousse cafe life revolves around fresh-shucked oyster-and-white-wine breakfasts.

Café Cousu CAFE €
(☎04 72 98 83 38; www.cafecousu.com; 14 rue René Leynaud, 1er; menus €12-15, weekend brunch €14-20; ⏰8.30am-midnight Tue-Fri, 11am-6pm Sat & Sun; 📶🖊; Ⓜ Croix Paquet) Directly across the street from the fashion design shops of Passage Thiaffait and the Village des Créateurs, this hole-in-the-wall entices an arty crowd with its battery-charging breakfasts, healthy lunches and homemade tarts and cakes, as well as its buzzing weekend brunch.

★ L'Ourson qui Boit FUSION €€
(☎04 78 27 23 37; 23 rue Royale, 1er; lunch/dinner menus €18/28; ⏰noon-1.30pm & 7.30-9.30pm Mon, Tue & Thu-Sat; Ⓜ Croix Paquet) On the fringes of Croix Rousse, Japanese chef Akira Nishigaki puts his own splendid spin on French cuisine, with plenty of locally sourced fresh vegetables and light, clean flavours. The ever-changing *menu* of two daily appetisers and two main dishes is complemented by good wines, attentive service and scrumptious desserts. Well worth reserving ahead.

Le Canut et Les Gones BISTRO €€
(☎04 78 29 17 23; lecanutetlesgones.com; 29 rue de Belfort, 4e; plat du jour €11-13, menus lunch €16-23, dinner €25-29; ⏰noon-2pm & 7.30-10pm Tue-Sat; Ⓜ Croix Rousse) With three cosy rooms and a funky retro decor featuring dozens of antique clocks, this laid-back neighbourhood eatery draws a savvy local crowd with creative cuisine built around produce from Croix Rousse's market.

La Bonâme de Bruno MODERN FRENCH €€
(☎04 78 30 83 93; www.restaurant-labonamede bruno.com; 5 Grande Rue des Feuillants; menus lunch €15-17.50, dinner €27.50-36.50; ⏰noon-2pm Tue-Fri, 7.30-9.30pm Sat; Ⓜ Croix Paquet) Great food and atmosphere come together at this airy yet intimate eatery that's somewhere on the continuum between bistro and gastronomic. The high-ceilinged, parquet-floored dining room conjures the spirit of a 19th-century dance studio, while the *menus*, prepared with enthusiasm and creativity, change regularly based on Bruno's whims. Desserts are especially memorable.

Balthaz'art MODERN FRENCH €€
(☎04 72 07 08 88; www.restaurantbalthazart.fr; 7 rue des Pierres Plantées, 1er; lunch/dinner menus €16.50/29; ⏰noon-2pm Thu-Sat, 7.30-9.30pm Tue-Sat; Ⓜ Croix Rousse) A block south of Croix Rousse's central square, this cheerful burgundy-red eatery draws animated crowds with its excellent-value lunches and sumptuous multi-course dinners. Inventive meat and fish dishes – including its signature *tartare de bœuf* with capers, olives, preserved lemon and coriander – come accompanied with plenty of seasonal vegetables.

Toutes les Couleurs VEGETARIAN €€
(☎04 72 00 03 95; www.touteslescouleurs.fr; 26 rue Imbert Colomès, 1er; menus lunch €14-18, dinner €20-31; ⏰noon-2pm Tue-Sat, 7.30-10pm Fri & Sat; 🖊; Ⓜ Croix Paquet) Manna from heaven for Lyon's oft-neglected vegetarians, this place serves a fully meatless *menu* with abundant organic, *végétalien* (vegan) and gluten-free options.

La Mère Brazier GASTRONOMIC €€€
(☎04 78 23 17 20; www.lamerebrazier.fr; 12 rue Royale, 1er; menus lunch €57-70, dinner €70-140; ⏰noon-1.30pm & 7.45-9.15pm Mon-Fri Sep-Jul; Ⓜ Croix Paquet) Chef Mathieu Vianney has reinvented the mythical early 20th-century restaurant that earned Mère Eugénie Brazier Lyon's first trio of Michelin stars in 1933 (a copy of the original guidebook takes pride of place). Vianney is doing admirable justice to Brazier's legacy, claiming two Michelin stars himself for his assured cuisine accompanied by an impressive wine list.

🍴 Rive Gauche

★ Les Halles de Lyon Paul Bocuse MARKET
(www.hallespaulbocuse.lyon.fr; 102 cours Lafayette, 3e; ⏰7am-10.30pm Tue-Sat, to 4.30pm Sun; Ⓜ Part-Dieu) Lyon's famed indoor food market has nearly five dozen stalls selling countless gourmet delights. Pick up a round of runny St-Marcellin from legendary cheesemonger Mère Richard, and a knobbly Jésus de Lyon from Charcuterie Sibilia. Or enjoy a sit-down lunch of local produce, especially enjoyable on

Sundays when local families congregate for shellfish and white-wine brunches.

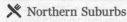 Northern Suburbs

⭐ L'Auberge du Pont de Collonges
GASTRONOMIC €€€

(☑ 04 72 42 90 90; www.bocuse.com; 40 quai de la Plage, Collonges; menus €155-250; ☺noon-1.30pm daily, 8-9.30pm Sun-Fri) Some 7km up the Saône from central Lyon, this triple-Michelin-starred restaurant is the flagship of the city's most decorated chef, Paul Bocuse. Classics include the likes of sea bass stuffed with lobster mousse in a puff-pastry shell, thyme-roasted rack of lamb, Beaujolais winemaker's sherbet and Bocuse's signature *soupe VGE* (truffle soup created for French president Valéry Giscard d'Estaing in 1975).

Drinking & Nightlife

Many establishments start as a relaxed place for a drink (and often serve food, too), morphing into jam-packed bars and/or live-music and dancing venues as the night wears on.

Vieux Lyon

Vieux Lyon has an extraordinary concentration of British and Irish pubs, patronised by expats, visitors and Lyonnais alike. Among the best are **Smoking Dog** (16 rue Lainerie, 5e; ☺5pm-1am Mon-Fri, 2pm-1am Sat & Sun; Ⓜ Vieux Lyon), **St-James** (19 rue St-Jean, 5e; ☺daily; Ⓜ Vieux Lyon), **Johnny Walsh's** (www.facebook.com/johnny.walshsbar; 56 rue St-Georges, 5e; ☺9pm-3am Tue-Sun; 📶; Ⓜ Vieux Lyon) and **L'Antidote** (www.antidote-pub.com; 108 rue St Georges, 5e; ☺6pm-1am; Ⓜ Vieux Lyon).

(L'A)Kroche
BAR

(www.lakroche.fr; 8 rue Monseigneur Lavarenne, 5e; ☺4pm-1am Tue-Sat, 4-9pm Sun & Mon; Ⓜ Vieux Lyon) Hip cafe-bar with six dozen flavours of rum, daily happy hours and frequent live music with no cover charge.

Presqu'île

La Boite à Café
CAFE

(www.cafemokxa.com; 3 rue Abbé Rozier, 1e; ☺8am-7pm Mon-Fri, 9am-7pm Sat, 11am-7pm Sun; Ⓜ Croix Paquet, Hôtel de Ville) A favourite haunt of Lyonnais caffeine fiends, this laid-back place on the Croix Rousse slopes roasts its own beans and serves Sunday brunch. In summer, tables spill onto charming, circular place du Forez.

Grand Café des Négociants
CAFE

(☑ 04 78 42 50 05; www.lesnegociants.com; 1 place Francisque Régaud, 2e; ☺7am-4am; Ⓜ Cordeliers) The tree-shaded terrace and Second Empire decor of chandeliers and mirror-lined walls are the big draws at this central cafe-brasserie, a Lyonnais institution since 1864.

Harmonie des Vins
WINE BAR

(www.harmoniedesvins.fr; 9 rue Neuve, 1er; ☺10am-2.30pm & 6.30pm-1am Tue-Sat; 📶; Ⓜ Hôtel de Ville, Cordeliers) Find out all about French wine at this charm-laden wine bar replete with old stone walls, contemporary furnishings and tasty food.

La Cave d'à Côté
WINE BAR

(☑ 04 78 28 31 46; 7 rue Pleney, 1er; ☺11.30am-2pm & 6.30pm-late Mon-Sat; Ⓜ Cordeliers) Hidden in a tiny alleyway, this cultured bar and wine shop feels like a rustic English gentlemen's club with leather sofa seating and library.

GAY & LESBIAN LYON

Declared France's most gay-friendly city in 2014 by *Têtu*, Lyon has scads of venues.

Guys' favourite places to party include **United Café** (www.united-cafe.com; impasse de la Pêcherie, 1er; ☺midnight-5am; Ⓜ Hôtel de Ville), **Le XS Bar** (19 rue Claudia, 2e; ☺5pm-3am; Ⓜ Cordeliers) and the city's oldest gay bar, **La Ruche** (22 rue Gentil, 2e; ☺5pm-3am; Ⓜ Cordeliers). Lesbian venues include **Le L Bar** (www.facebook.com/LBarLyon; 19 rue du Garet, 1er; ☺6pm-4am; Ⓜ Hôtel de Ville) and **Le Marais** (3 rue Terme, 1er; ☺9pm-3am Thu, 11pm-5am Fri & Sat; Ⓜ Hôtel de Ville, Croix Paquet).

For up-to-the-minute listings, visit the websites **Gay in Lyon** (www.gayinlyon.com) and **Hétéroclite** (www.heteroclite.org), or check with the **Forum Gai et Lesbien de Lyon** (☑ 04 78 39 97 72; www.fgllyon.org; 17 rue Romarin, 1er; Ⓜ Croix Paquet) and **ARIS** (Accueil Rencontres Informations Service; ☑ 04 78 27 10 10; www.aris-lyon.org; 19 rue des Capucins, 1er; Ⓜ Hôtel de Ville, Croix Paquet), which both organise social events.

Lyon's **Lesbian and Gay Pride** (www.fierte.net) march and festivities hit the streets each year in June. In March, the city hosts a popular week-long LGBT film festival, **Écrans Mixtes** (www.festival-em.org).

ℹ️ LYON WHAT'S ON

Leading what's-on guides with both print and online editions include **Le Petit Bulletin** (www.petit-bulletin.fr/lyon) and **Lyon Poche** (www.lyonpoche.com). Other helpful websites with entertainment listings include www.monweekendalyon. com, www.lyonclubbing.com and www. lyon.2night.fr (all in French).

Tickets are sold at **Fnac Billetterie** (www.fnac.com/spectacles; 85 rue de la République, 2e; ⊗ 10am-7.30pm Mon-Sat; Ⓜ Bellecour).

Le Vin des Vivants   WINE BAR
(www.levindesvivants.fr; 6 place Fernand Rey, 1er; ⊗ 6-9pm Tue & Wed, to 11.30pm Thu-Sat; Ⓜ Hôtel de Ville) This relaxed stone-walled corner bar on a pretty backstreet square specialises in organic wines.

Soda Bar   COCKTAIL BAR
(www.soda-bar.fr; 7 rue de la Martinière, 1er; ⊗ 8pm-1am Tue & Wed, 8pm-3am Thu-Sat mid-Aug–mid-Jul; Ⓜ Hôtel de Ville) Spirited bar staff juggle bottles while mixing an inspired list of cocktails.

Monkey Club   COCKTAIL BAR
(www.themonkeyclub.fr; 19 place Tolozan, 1er; ⊗ 6.30pm-1am Tue & Wed, to 3am Thu-Sat; Ⓜ Hôtel de Ville) This trendy, friendly cocktail bar is decked out with bright green walls, couches, and a youthful clientele.

Café 203   BAR
(9 rue du Garet, 1er; ⊗ 7am-2am Mon-Sat, noon-1am Sun; 🛜; Ⓜ Hôtel de Ville) This corner resto-bar with sidewalk tables straddling both sides of a narrow backstreet buzzes day and night.

🍷 Croix Rousse

Modernartcafé   BAR
(65 bd de la Croix Rousse, 4e; ⊗ noon-2pm & 5pm-2am Sun-Fri, 5pm-2am Sat; 🛜; Ⓜ Croix Rousse) Changing art on the walls, weekend brunch and various photography-, music- and video-driven events make this art bar a linchpin of Croix Rousse's creative community.

La Bistro fait sa Broc'   BAR
(1-3 rue Dumenge, 4e; ⊗ 5pm-1am Mon-Sat; Ⓜ Croix Rousse) A lime-green and candyfloss-pink façade greets you at this retro neighbourhood wine bar where no two chairs match. Occasional bands.

🍷 Rive Gauche

Along quai Victor Auganeur on the Rhône's left bank, a string of *péniches* (barges with on-board bars) serve drinks from mid-afternoon onwards, many of them rocking until the wee hours with DJs and/or live bands. To study your options, stroll the quayside between Pont Lafayette and Pont de la Guillotière.

Bernachon   TEAROOM
(www.bernachon.com; 42 cours Franklin Roosevelt, 6e; ⊗ 9am-6.30pm Tue-Sat; Ⓜ Foch, Masséna) For a decadent mid-afternoon break, stop by this tearoom – run by Lyon's most renowned chocolatier – for a velvety smooth cup of hot or chilled chocolate swirled with crème fraiche and topped with whipped cream. Yum!

La Marquise   BARGE BAR
(www.marquise.net; 20 quai Victor Auganeur, 3e; ⊗ 2pm-1am Sun-Wed, to 5am Thu-Sat; Ⓜ Place Guichard-Bourse du Travail) This popular barge bar hosts all-night live shows and DJ sets featuring jazz, techno, hip hop and more.

☆ Entertainment

☆ Presqu'île

★ Le Sucre   LIVE MUSIC
(www.le-sucre.eu; 50 quai Rambaud, 2e; ⊗ 6pm-midnight Wed & Thu, 7pm-6am Fri & Sat Ⓜ Perrache) Down in the Confluence neighbourhood, Lyon's newest and most innovative club hosts DJs, live shows and eclectic arts events on its super-cool roof terrace atop a 1930s sugar factory, La Sucrière.

Hot Club de Lyon   LIVE MUSIC
(www.hotclubdelyon.org; 26 rue Lanterne, 1er; ⊗ 6.30pm-late Tue-Sat; Ⓜ Hôtel de Ville) Lyon's leading jazz club, around since 1948. Main acts take the stage at 9.30pm.

Opéra de Lyon   OPERA HOUSE
(www.opera-lyon.com; place de la Comédie, 1er; Ⓜ Hôtel de Ville) Lyon's premier venue for opera, ballet and classical music.

Péristyle   LIVE MUSIC
(Programme Jazz de l'Opéra de Lyon; www.opera-lyon.com/spectacles/peristyle; place de la Comédie, 1er; ⊗ 7-11pm Mon-Sat mid-Jun–early Sep) **FREE** Free summer concerts under the Opéra's arches, ranging from swing to blues and funk to jazz. Waiters circulate with drinks as the music plays. Hour-long sets start at 7pm, 8.15pm and 10pm; arrive early to snag a table.

☆ Rive Gauche

Le Transbordeur LIVE MUSIC
(www.transbordeur.fr; 3 bd de Stalingrad, Villeur-banne; 🚇 Cité Internationale/Transbordeur) In an old industrial building near the Parc de la Tête d'Or's northeastern corner, Lyon's prime concert venue draws international acts on the European concert-tour circuit.

Hangar du Premier Film CINEMA
(www.institut-lumiere.org; 25 rue du Premier Film, 8e; 🚇 Monplaisir-Lumière) This former factory and birthplace of cinema now screens films of all genres and eras in their original languages. From approximately June to September, the big screen moves outside.

**Auditorium Orchestre
National de Lyon** CLASSICAL MUSIC
(🖉 04 78 95 95 95; www.auditorium-lyon.com; 149 rue Garibaldi, 3e; ☺ Sep Jun; 🚇 Part-Dieu, 🚊 Part-Dieu-Servient, Part-Dieu-Villette) Built in 1975, this spaceship-like auditorium houses the National Orchestra of Lyon, along with workshops, jazz and world-music concerts.

Maison de la Danse DANCE
(www.maisondeladanse.com; 8 av Jean Mermoz, 8e; 🚊 Bachut-Mairie du 8ème) Lyon's home of contemporary dance.

🛍 Shopping

🛍 Vieux Lyon

Vieux Lyon's narrow streets are dotted with galleries, antiquarian and secondhand book-shops, and quality souvenir shops.

Crafts Market CRAFT MARKET
(Marché de la Création; www.quaidesartistes-lyon.fr; quai Romain Rolland, 5e; ☺ 8am-1pm Sun; 🚇 Vieux Lyon) Along the Saône, artists sell their paint-ings, sculptures, photography and more.

🛍 Presqu'île

High-street chains line rue de la République and rue Victor Hugo, while upmarket bou-tiques and design houses stud rue du Prési-dent Édouard Herriot, rue de Brest and the streets between place des Jacobins and place Bellecour. More cluster between art galler-ies and antique shops around rue Auguste Comte, 2e.

**Pôle de Commerces
et de Loisirs Confluence** SHOPPING CENTRE
(www.confluence.fr; Cours Charlemagne, 2e; 🚊 Mon-trochet) This vast complex of over 100 res-taurants and shops (mostly outlets of major international companies) constitutes the

---

GUIGNOL: LYON'S HISTORIC PUPPET

The history of Lyon's famous puppet, Guignol, is intertwined with that of the city. In 1797 out-of-work silk-weaver Laurent Mourguet took up dentistry (ie pulling teeth). To attract pa-tients, he set up a puppet show in front of his chair, initially featuring the Italian Polichinelle (who became Punch in England). Success saw Mourguet move into full-time puppetry, creating Guignol in about 1808 and devising shows revolving around working class issues, the news of the day, social gossip and satire.

Today this little hand-operated glove puppet pops up all over his home town, including on the Fresque des Lyonnais (p459) mural and at puppet museums.

Guignol's highly visual, slapstick-style antics appeal equally to children and adults (the-atres also stage some adult-only evening performances). Shows are in French but also incorporate traditional Lyonnais dialect, such as the words *quinquets* (eyes), *picou* (nose), *bajafler* (talking nonstop) and *gones* (kids, and, by extension, all Lyonnais).

In addition to performances at Parc de la Tête d'Or (p460), Lyon has three dedicated Guignol theatres:

Théâtre La Maison de Guignol (🖉 04 72 40 26 61; www.lamaisondeguignol.fr; 2 montée du Gourguillon, 5e; tickets adult/child €10.80/8.80; 🚇 Vieux Lyon) Quaint St-Georges theatre.

Guignol, un Gone de Lyon (🖉 04 72 32 11 55; www.guignol-un-gone-de-lyon.com; 65 bd des Canuts, 4e; ☺ performances 3.30pm Wed, Sat & Sun Oct-Jun; 🚇 Hénon) In Croix Rousse.

Théâtre Le Guignol de Lyon (🖉 04 78 28 92 57; www.guignol-lyon.com; 2 rue Louis Carrand, 5e; 🚇 Vieux Lyon) In Vieux Lyon; puppeteers give audiences a behind-the-scenes peek at the props and puppets after certain performances.

Check individual websites for ticket prices (around €10) and schedules (typically Wednes-days and weekends, with extra dates added during school holidays).

FEVER PITCH

After decades of playing in the 1920s-built, 40,000-seater **Stade de Gerland** (04 72 76 01 70; 353 av Jean Jaurès, 7e; Ⓜ Stade de Gerland), Lyon's multichampionship-winning football team **Olympique Lyonnais** (OL; www.olweb.fr) plans to inaugurate its massive new 58,500-seat home stadium, **Stade des Lumières** (Grand Stade de Lyon; www.grandstadeol.com; Décines-Charpieu), in time to host the summer 2016 UEFA European football championship. Buy match tickets online, at the stadium or from the club's brand-new downtown boutique, **OL Store Lyon Centre** (http://boutique.olweb.fr; 85 rue du Président Edouard Herriot, 2e; ⊘10am-7pm Mon-Sat; Ⓜ Bellecour, Cordeliers).

commercial hub of Lyon's new Confluence neighbourhood.

In Cuisine BOOKS
(www.incuisine.fr; 1 place Bellecour, 2e; ⊘11am-6.30pm Mon, 10am-7pm Tue-Sat, closed noon-2pm Mon-Fri; Ⓜ Bellecour) This foodie haven has an astonishing selection of culinary, gastronomic and wine titles. It also offers demonstrations, tastings, cooking courses and lunch in its tearoom.

Book Market BOOKS
(Marché des Bouquinistes; quai de la Pêcherie, 1er; ⊘10am-6pm Sat & Sun; Ⓜ Hôtel de Ville) A treasure trove of hard-to-find titles (most in French).

Croix Rousse

Montée de la Grande Côte GALLERIES, WORKSHOPS
(Ⓜ Croix Rousse, Croix Paquet) Galleries and artists' workshops come and go the length of this walkway climbing the slopes from place des Terreaux to Croix Rousse.

Le Village des Créateurs FASHION
(☑04 78 27 37 21; www.villagedescreateurs.com; Passage Thiaffait, 19 rue René Leynaud, 1er; ⊘2-7pm Wed-Sat; Ⓜ Croix Paquet) Housed in an arcaded courtyard on the Croix Rousse slopes, this innovative cluster of workshop-boutiques showcases the artwork of a dozen up-and-coming local designers. Workspaces are awarded by jury for two-year rotating terms, ensuring a lively, ever-changing mix. The **VDC/B boutique** (www.facebook.com/vdcboutique;

⊘11.30am-2.30pm & 3.30-7.30pm Tue-Sat), which opened in 2014, serves as a sales outlet for three dozen additional designers.

Rive Gauche

Les Puces du Canal FLEA MARKET
(www.pucesducanal.com; 3 rue Eugène Potier, Villeurbanne; ⊘7am-noon Thu & Sat, to 3pm Sun; ⊒ Le Roulet) With over 400 exhibitors strung out along the canal banks in the northeastern suburb of Villeurbanne, France's second-biggest flea market is a fun place to browse, especially for antiques and furniture. Sunday draws the biggest crowds.

From downtown Lyon, take metro line A east to the Laurent Bonnevay stop, then transfer to bus 7 northbound and get off at Le Roulet. Alternatively, on Monday through Saturday, catch metro A to Charpennes, then transfer onto bus 37 to Le Roulet.

ℹ️ Information

EMERGENCY

Police Station (☑04 78 42 26 56; 47 rue de la Charité, 2e; Ⓜ Perrache, Ampère)

MEDICAL SERVICES

Grande Pharmacie Lyonnaise (www.3237.fr; 22 rue de la République, 2e; ⊘8pm-8am; Ⓜ Cordeliers) All-night pharmacy.

Hôpital Édouard Herriot (☑08 25 08 25 69; www.chu-lyon.fr; 5 place d'Arsonval, 3e; ⊘24hr; Ⓜ Grange Blanche) Emergency-room services.

SOS Médecins (☑04 78 83 51 51; www.sosmedecins-france.fr; ⊘24hr) Medical emergency hotline.

TOURIST INFORMATION

Tourist Office (☑04 72 77 69 69; www.lyon-france.com; place Bellecour, 2e; ⊘9am-6pm; Ⓜ Bellecour) In the centre of Presqu'île, Lyon's exceptionally helpful, multilingual and well-staffed main tourist office offers a variety of city walking tours and sells the Lyon City Card (p455). There's a smaller branch (Av du Doyenné, 5e; ⊘10am-5.30pm; Ⓜ Vieux Lyon) just outside the Vieux Lyon metro station.

USEFUL WEBSITES

www.mylittle.fr/mylittlelyon Follows the city's latest cultural trends.

www.petitpaume.com Savvy city guide written by local university students.

www.bullesdegones.com Comprehensive guide to kid-friendly activities (up to 12 years) in and around Lyon.

www.lyon.fr Official city website.

www.rhonealpes-tourisme.com Regional tourist information site.

ℹ Getting There & Away

AIR

Lyon-St-Exupéry Airport (www.lyonaeroports. com) Located 25km east of the city, with 40 airlines (including many budget carriers) serving over 100 direct destinations across Europe and beyond.

BUS

International bus companies **Eurolines** (☑ 08 92 89 90 91, 04 72 56 95 30; www.eurolines.fr; Gare de Perrache) and **Linebús** (☑ 04 72 41 72 27; www.linebus.com; Gare de Perrache) offer service to Spain, Portugal, Italy and Germany from the Centre d'Échange building at the north end of the Perrache train complex. Follow signs for 'Cars Grandes Lignes' and 'Galerie A: Gare Routière Internationale'.

CAR

Major car-hire companies have offices at Gare de la Part-Dieu, Gare de Perrache and the airport.

TRAIN

Lyon has two main-line train stations: **Gare de la Part-Dieu** (Ⓜ Part-Dieu), 1.5km east of the Rhône, and **Gare de Perrache** (Ⓜ Perrache). Some local trains stop at **Gare St-Paul** (Ⓜ Vieux Lyon) and **Gare Jean Macé** (Ⓜ Jean Macé). There's also a TGV station at Lyon-St-Exupéry Airport. Buy tickets at the stations or at the **SNCF Boutique** (2 place Bellecour; Ⓜ Bellecour) downtown.

Destinations by direct TGV include the following:

Dijon €36, 1½ hours, at least six daily

Lille-Europe €113, three hours, at least eight daily

Marseille €52, 1¾ hours, every 30 to 60 minutes

Paris Charles de Gaulle Airport €95, two hours, at least 11 daily

Paris Gare de Lyon €73, two hours, every 30 to 60 minutes

ℹ Getting Around

TO/FROM THE AIRPORT

The **Rhônexpress** (www.rhonexpress.fr; adult/ youth/child €15.70/13/free) tramway links the airport with the Part-Dieu train station in under 30 minutes. It's a five- to 10-minute walk from the arrivals hall; follow the red signs with the Rhônexpress train logo. Trams depart every 15 minutes between 6am and 9pm, less frequently from 4.25am to 6am and 9pm to midnight. Online purchases and round-trip travel qualify for discounts.

By taxi, the 30- to 45-minute trip between the airport and the city centre costs around €50 during the day and €65 between 7pm and 7am.

BICYCLE

Pick up a red-and-silver bike at one of 200-odd bike stations throughout the city and drop it off at another with Lyon's **Vélo'v** (www.velov.grand-lyon.com) bike rental scheme. Start by paying a one-time flat fee for a *carte courte durée* (short-duration card, €1.50 for 24 hours, €5 for seven days). Once equipped with the card, you're entitled to unlimited rentals (free for the first 30 minutes, €1 for the next hour, €2 each subsequent hour). Pay all fees with a chip-enabled credit card using machines installed at bike stations.

BOAT

Le Vaporetto (☑ 08 20 20 69 20; www. confluence.fr/W/do/centre/navette) operates *navettes* (passenger ferry boats) to Lyon's new Confluence neighbourhood. Boats (€2) depart hourly between 10am and 9pm from riverbank docks near place St-Paul and place Bellecour, returning from the Confluence dock between 10.30am and 9.30pm. Travel time is 30 minutes from the **St-Paul dock** (quai de Bondy, 5e; Ⓜ Hôtel de Ville, Vieux Lyon) and 20 minutes from the **Bellecour dock** (quai Tilsitt, 2e; Ⓜ Bellecour, Vieux Lyon).

PUBLIC TRANSPORT

Buses, trams, a four line metro and two funiculars linking Vieux Lyon to Fourvière and St-Just are operated by **TCL** (www.tcl.fr), which has information offices dispensing transport maps at major metro stations throughout Lyon. Public transport runs from around 5am to midnight.

Tickets valid for all forms of public transport cost €1.70 (€15.10 for a *carnet* of 10) and are available from bus and tram drivers as well as machines at metro entrances. Tickets allowing two consecutive hours of travel after 9am or unlimited travel after 7pm cost €2.80, and an all-day ticket costs €5.20. Bring coins as machines don't accept notes (or some international credit cards). Time-stamp tickets on all forms of public transport or risk a fine. Holders of the Lyon City Card (p455) receive free unlimited access to Lyon's transport network for the duration of the card's validity (one, two or three days).

TAXI

Taxis hover in front of both train stations, on the place Bellecour end of rue de la Barre (2e), at the northern end of rue du Président Édouard Herriot (1er) and along quai Romain Rolland in Vieux Lyon (5e).

Allo Taxi (☑ 04 78 28 23 23; www.allotaxi.fr)

Taxis Lyonnais (☑ 04 78 26 81 81; www.taxilyonnais.com)

WANT MORE?

Head to **Lonely Planet** (www.lonelyplanet.com/france/burgundy-and-the-rhone/lyon) for planning advice, recommendations, traveller reviews and tips.

NORTH OF LYON

Lush green hills, lakes and vineyards unfold to the north of cosmopolitan Lyon.

Beaujolais

Hilly Beaujolais, 50km northwest of Lyon, is a land of streams, granite peaks (the highest is 1012m Mont St-Rigaud), pastures and forests.

The region is synonymous with its fruity red wines, especially its 10 premium *crus*, and the Beaujolais *Nouveau*, drunk at the tender age of just six weeks. Vineyards stretch south from Mâcon along the right bank of the Saône for some 50km.

At the stroke of midnight on the third Thursday (ie Wednesday night) in November – as soon as French law permits – the *libération* (release) or *mise en perce* (tapping; opening) of the first bottles of cherry-bright Beaujolais *Nouveau* is celebrated around France and the world. In **Beaujeu** (population 2080), 64km northwest of Lyon, there's free Beaujolais Nouveau for all as part of the **Sarmentelles de Beaujeu** (www.sarmentelles.com), a giant street party that kicks off the day before Beaujolais *Nouveau* for five days of wine tasting, live music and dancing.

Beaujeu's **tourist office** (☑ 04 74 69 22 88; www.beaujolaisvignoble.com; place de l'Hôtel de Ville; ⊙ 9.30am-12.30pm & 2.30-6.30pm Mar-Nov) provides information on wine cellars where you can taste and buy local wine, including **Le Caveau des Producteurs de Beaujolais Villages** (⊙ 10.30am-1pm & 3.30-8pm late-Jan–Dec), just downstairs from the tourist office, which offers tastings for €1.30 and sells bottles starting at €5.20. Renowned wine-producing villages within easy striking distance of Beaujeu include Villié-Morgon, Fleurie, Juliénas, Moulin-à-Vent and St-Amour. For a detailed driving route through the Beaujolais Villages wine region, grab a copy of Lonely Planet's *France's Best Trips*.

The tourist office can also help arrange accommodation at the town's half-dozen *chambres d'hôte* or at several charming B&Bs in the surrounding countryside, including **Les Roulottes et les Folies de la Serve** (☑ 04 74 04 76 40; www.lesroulottes.com; La Serve; caravan/d incl breakfast €65/110; ⊙ Apr–mid-Nov), a trio of romantically furnished 1920s to 1950s gypsy caravans built by traditional caravanmaker Pascal and his wife, Pascaline.

Exploring Beaujolais' (mostly) gentle hills by **bike** is uplifting. Hire one from **La Maison du Terroir Beaujolais** (☑ 04 74 69 20 56; www.

lamaisonduterroirbeaujolais.com; place de l'Hôtel de Ville; per half-/full day €11/16; ⊙ 10am-12.30pm & 2-6pm Wed-Mon Mar-Dec), directly opposite the tourist office. **Walking** the area's many footpaths is equally invigorating. The tourist office provides local trail info on its website.

To get here by public transport, catch a train from Lyon to Belleville (€9.70, 35 minutes), where bus 35, operated by **Les Cars du Rhône** (☑ 08 00 86 98 69; www.rhone.fr), connects hourly to Beaujeu (€2, 25 minutes).

Pérouges

POP 1240

French film buffs will recognise photogenic Pérouges. Situated on a hill 30km northeast of Lyon, this enchanting yellow-stone medieval village has long been used as a set for films such as *Les Trois Mousquetaires* (The Three Musketeers). It's worth braving the summertime crowds to stroll its uneven cobbled alleys, admire its half-timbered stone houses and **liberty tree** on place de la Halle (planted it 1792), and wolf down *galettes de Pérouges* (warm, thin-pizza-crust-style, sugar-crusted tarts) with cider.

To appreciate Pérouges' charm after the day trippers have left, book a room at the historic, romantic **Hostellerie de Pérouges** (☑ 04 74 61 00 88; www.hostelleriedeperouges.com; place du Tilleul; s €98-147, d €136-257), which also operates a respected restaurant.

Pérouges' tiny **tourist office** (☑ 04 74 46 70 84; www.perouges.org; 9 route de la Cité; ⊙ 10am-5pm May-Aug, reduced hours Sep-Apr) is on the main road opposite the village entrance.

Cars Philibert (☑ 04 78 98 56 00; www.philibert-transport.fr) runs bus 132 (€2, one hour) two to eight times daily from central Lyon to the Pérouges turn-off on route D4 (a 15-minute walk from the village).

La Dombes

Northwest of Pérouges is La Dombes, a marshy area with hundreds of *étangs* (shallow lakes) that were created from malarial swamps over the past six centuries by farmers. They are used as fish ponds and then drained to grow crops on the fertile lake bed.

La Dombes teems with wildlife, particularly waterfowl. Observe local and exotic birds, including dozens of pairs of storks, at the **Parc des Oiseaux** (www.parcdesoiseaux.com; adult/child €16/12; ⊙ 9.30am-6.30pm Feb–mid-Nov), a landscaped bird park on the edge of Villars-les-Dombes on the N83. The reserve is 1.6km south of Villars-les-Dombes' train station, linked to Lyon's Part-Dieu (€7.80, 40 minutes, at least hourly).

The area is famed for its production of frogs' legs, which you can taste at **La Bicyclette Bleue** (☑04 74 98 21 48; www.labicyclettebleue.fr; lunch menus €11.50, menus €22-46; ☉noon-1.30pm & 7.30-9pm Thu-Mon; ꜚ), in Joyeux, 7.5km southeast of Villars-les-Dombes on the D61. Renowned for its *grenouilles fraîches en persillade* (frogs' legs in butter and parsley), this laid-back family affair also rents **bicycles** (per hour/day €4.50/15.50) to explore 12 mapped lakeland circuits, from 12km (one hour) to 59km (four hours).

DOWNSTREAM ALONG THE RHÔNE

South of Lyon, the Rhône flows past an incongruous mix of vineyards and nuclear power plants, but the landscapes grow more tantalising as you continue downriver towards Provence. Along the way there are several worthwhile stops for Lyon-based day trippers.

Vienne

POP 29,600

In a commanding position on the Rhône, 30km south of Lyon, Vienne was once one of Roman Gaul's greatest cities. Today it's best known for its two-week **jazz festival** (www.jazzavienne.com) in late June and early July.

In the old town, take a look at the superb Corinthian columns of the **Temple d'Au-**guste et de Livie** (place Charles de Gaulle), built around 10 BC to honour Emperor Augustus and his wife, Livia. Across the river in St-Romain-en-Gal, the **Musée Gallo-Romain** (www.musees-gallo-romains.com; D502; adult/child €4/free, Thu free; ☉10am-6pm Tue-Sun) highlights Vienne's historical importance, displaying several rooms full of dazzling mosaics and models of ancient Vienne, surrounded by the actual excavated remains of the Gallo-Roman city.

Views over Vienne extend from the **Belvédère de Pipet**, a balcony with a 6m-tall statue of the Virgin Mary, immediately above the fabulous **Théâtre Romain** (rue du Cirque; adult/child €2.80/free, 1st Sun of month free; ☉9.30am-1pm & 2-6pm, closed Mon Sep-Mar). The vast Roman amphitheatre, built around AD 40-50, is a key jazz-festival venue.

A *billet inter-musées* (combination ticket, good for six museums and historical sites in the Viennois area) costs €6; the **tourist office** (☑04 74 53 80 30; www.vienne-tourisme.com; 3 cours Brillier; ☉9am-noon & 1.30-6pm Tue-Sat, 9am-noon & 2-6pm Sun, 10.30am-noon & 1.30-6pm Mon) has details.

Vienne's finest address for eating and/or sleeping is **Hôtel de la Pyramide** (☑04 74 53 01 96; www.lapyramide.com; 14 bd Fernand-Point; s €190-225, d €200-240, ste €390-420; ❄@☞), overlooking La Pyramide de la Cirque (a 15.5m-tall obelisk that in Roman times pierced the centre of a hippodrome). This apricot-coloured villa with powder-blue shutters is a haven for foodies. In addition to chef Patrick Henriroux' two-Michelin-star signature restaurant, **La Pyramide** (menus

LYON & THE RHÔNE VALLEY VIENNE

lunch €64, dinner €122-177; ⊘ noon-1.30pm & 7.30-9.30pm Thu-Mon), you'll find his more affordable **l'Espace PH3** (mains €15-21, lunch menu €23; ⊘ noon-1.30pm & 7.30-9.30pm) and the **Boutique Patrick Henriroux** (⊘ 9am-noon & 2.30-7.30pm Mon & Thu-Sat, 9am-12.30pm & 2.30-6pm Sun), selling attractively packaged gourmet goodies and chic kitchenware.

Trains link Vienne with Lyon's four stations (€7, 20 to 30 minutes, at least hourly) as well as Valence Centre (€13.40, 50 minutes, at least hourly). All trains to Valence TGV station require changing at Valence Centre.

Towards Valence

The **Parc Naturel Régional du Pilat** (www.parc-naturel-pilat.fr) spills across 650 sq km southwest of Vienne and offers breathtaking panoramas of the Rhône Valley from its highest peaks, Crêt de l'Œillon (1370m) and Crêt de la Perdrix (1432m). The Montgolfier brothers, who invented the hot-air balloon in 1783 and lent their name to its French term, *montgolfière*, were born and held their first public demonstration on the park's southeastern boundary. The north section of the Côtes du Rhône wine-growing area stretches from Vienne south to Valence. Two of its most respected appellations, St-Joseph and Hermitage, grow around **Tain l'Hermitage** (population 6020) on the Rhône's left bank.

Valence

POP 64,920

Several Rhône Valley towns claim to be the gateway to Provence, including Valence, whose quaint old town, Vieux Valence, is crowned by the **Cathédrale St-Apollinaire**, a late 11th-century pilgrimage church largely destroyed in the Wars of Religion and rebuilt in the 17th century. Allegorical sculpted heads adorn **Maison des Têtes** (57 Grande Rue), a blend of Flamboyant Gothic and Renaissance styles from 1530. Get the lowdown from the **tourist office** (☑ 04 75 44 90 40; www.valencetourisme.com; 11 bd Bancel; ⊘ 9.30am-6.30pm Mon-Sat, 10am-3pm Sun), two blocks north of the train station.

The city is famed for its crunchy, orange-rind-flavoured shortbread shaped like a Vatican Swiss guard to commemorate Pope Pius VI's imprisonment and death in Valence in 1799. Ask for *un suisse* in any patisserie, including **Maison Nivon** (www.maison-nivon-valence.fr; 17 av Pierre Semard; suisses €2.20; ⊘ 6am-7.30pm Tue-Sat, to 7pm Sun) near the train station, in business since 1856.

Anne-Sophie Pic, France's only three-Michelin-star female chef, reigns over Valence gastronomy, as her father and grandfather (each triple Michelin star-holders) did before her. The Pic family's truffle-coloured, 1889-established inn, **Maison Pic** (☑ 04 75 44 15 32; www.pic-valence.com; 285 av Victor Hugo; d €190-410, ste €410-890; ⊘ Feb-Dec; ❋@🛜❄), has ultrachic rooms mixing antique, contemporary and kitsch, alongside two stunning restaurants: the top-of-the-line **Restaurant Pic** (lunch menus €95, menus €160-320; ⊘ lunch & dinner Tue-Sat) and the less formal bistro **Le 7** (menus €19-31; ⊘ noon-2.30pm & 7.30-10pm). Down the street, their upmarket deli, **L'Épicerie** (210 av Victor Hugo; ⊘ 9.30am-7pm Tue-Sat, 10am-1pm Sun), features wine and gourmet items. Serious foodies can take courses at Pic's cutting-edge cooking school, **Scook** (☑ 04 75 44 14 14; www.scook.fr; 243 av Victor Hugo; ⊘ Tue-Sat).

From Valence Centre station (also known as Valence-Ville), there are trains at least hourly to the following destinations (many also stop at Valence TGV Rhône-Alpes Sud station, 10km east):

Avignon Centre from €21, 30 minutes to 1½ hours

Grenoble €15.50, one hour

Lyon (Gare de la Part-Dieu) from €18.10, 35 minutes to 1¼ hours

Marseille from €35, one to 2½ hours

Montélimar €9.10, 25 minutes

Montélimar

POP 36,710

In the sunny section of the Drôme *département* known as Drôme Provençale, Montélimar, 46km south of Valence, is an appealing town (once you're through its industrial outskirts), with a tree-shaded, grassy promenade lined by cafe terraces carving a C-shape through its centre. The town's biggest claim to fame is its *nougat de Montélimar*, which took off after WWII when motorists travelling to the French Riviera stopped here to buy the sweeter-than-sweet treat to munch en route.

Authentic Montélimar nougat consists of at least 28% almonds, 25% lavender honey, 2% pistachio nuts, sugar, egg white and vanilla. Texture varies, from *dur* (hard) to *tendre* (light and soft), as does honey strength and crispness of the nuts. Some are coated in chocolate and others have fruit (try the one with figs), but traditional Montélimar nougat is simply off-white.

Nougat factory tours are offered by numerous producers; pick a small (rather than industrial) confectioner, such as **Diane-de-Poytiers** (☑04 75 01 67 02; www.diane-de-poytiers.fr; 99 av Jean-Jaurès; ☉9am-noon & 2-7pm), run by the same family for three generations. The **tourist office** (☑04 75 01 00 20; www.montelimar-tourisme.com; Montée St-Martin; ☉10am-12.30pm & 2-6pm Mon-Fri, to 5.30pm Sat; ☎) has a list of nougat and other local producers (lavender, honey and so on), and can help with accommodation.

Montélimar is on the train line linking Valence-Ville (€9.10, 25 minutes, hourly) with Avignon Centre (€14.50, 55 minutes, hourly).

Gorges de l'Ardèche & Around

The serpentine Ardèche River slithers between towering mauve, yellow and grey limestone cliffs from near **Vallon Pont d'Arc** (population 2450) to **St-Martin de l'Ardèche** (population 940), a few kilometres west of the Rhône. En route, it passes beneath the **Pont d'Arc**, a stunning natural stone bridge created by the river's torrents. The river forms the centrepiece of the 1575-hectare **Réserve Naturelle des Gorges de l'Ardèche** (www.gorgesdelardeche.fr/reserve-naturelle.php), a protected area since 1980. Eagles nest in the cliffs and there are numerous caves to explore.

Souvenir-shop-filled Vallon Pont d'Arc is the area's main hub; its **tourist office** (☑04 75 88 04 01; www.vallon-pont-darc.com; 1 place de l'Ancienne Gare; ☉9am-12.30pm & 2-6pm Mon-Fri, to 5pm Sat, 9am-1pm Sun; ☎) is in the village centre. The scenic riverside D290 snakes southeastward from the village, lined with campgrounds and canoeing and kayaking outlets, including the well-established **Base Nautique du Pont d'Arc** (☑04 75 37 17 79; www.canoe-ardeche.com; rte des Gorges de l'Ardèche; per adult/child half-day €17/12, full day €27/18, 2-day €40/27; ☉Apr-Nov). Options range from 8km half-day trips to 32km full-day or overnight trips (the latter involve camping in the gorge). Minimum age is seven, and online discounts are available with advance booking.

Four daily SNCF buses link Vallon Pont d'Arc with Montélimar's train station (€11.90, 1½ hours) and Valence's TGV station (€20.40, 2½ hours).

About 300m above the gorge's waters, the **Haute Corniche** (D290) has a dizzying

TRAIN DE L'ARDÈCHE

Train buffs take note! After a six-year closure, the scenic **Train de l'Ardèche** (www.trainardeche.fr; adult €12-20, child €6-11; ☉Apr-Oct) is back in business, carving its sublimely sinuous route along the precipitous gorges of the Doux River. The train's three different itineraries – offering options to visit the cute mountain town of Colombier-le-Vieux or the market in Lamastre – all begin at the Tournon St-Jean station, 23km northwest of Valence. Consult the website for dates of service.

series of 11 *belvédères* (panoramic viewpoints), although it can turn into a chaotic traffic jam in midsummer. About halfway between St-Martin and Vallon Pont d'Arc, the **Maison de la Réserve** (☑04 75 98 77 31; www.gorgesdelardeche.fr; D290; ☉10am-5pm mid-Mar–mid-Nov) provides information on local flora, fauna and recreational opportunities. A further 2km west along the D290 is the trailhead for the **Sentier Aval des Gorges**, which descends 2km to the river, then follows the gorge for another 10km. Rough **camping** (☑04 75 88 00 41; reservation@gorgesdelardeche.fr; campsite per person midweek/weekend €6.50/10; ☉reservation center 8.30am-1pm & 1.30-3pm) is available (by reservation) at two spots within the protected section of the gorge, **Bivouac de Gournier** and **Bivouac de Gaud**. On the plateaux above the gorges, typical Midi villages are surrounded by *garrigue* (aromatic scrub land), lavender fields and vineyards.

Beyond Vallon Pont d'Arc, the D579 continues northwest to **Ruoms** (population 2290); across the river, the D4 passes through the **Défilé de Ruoms** (a narrow rock tunnel) and twists along the **Gorges de la Ligne** for 8km.

Northwards from the pretty village of **Balazuc** (population 360), the D579 leads to **Aubenas** (population 12,490), from where scenic roads fan into the countryside. This is **chestnut** land, where the dark-brown fruit is turned into everything from *crème de châtaigne* (sweet purée served with ice cream, crêpes or cake) to *bière aux marrons* (chestnut beer) and *liqueur de châtaigne* (21% alcohol-by-volume liqueur that makes a sweet aperitif when mixed with white wine). In the area's main town, **Privas** (population 8730), the **tourist office** (☑04 75 64 33 35; www.privasrhonevallees.com; 3 place Général de Gaulle; ☉10am-noon & 2-6pm Mon-Sat) has a list of regional producers as well as accommodation.

French Alps & the Jura Mountains

POP 4.8 MILLION

Best Places to Eat

➜ La Nouvelle Maison de Marc Veyrat (p502)

➜ Les Louvières (p536)

➜ Le Cap Horn (p490)

➜ Crèmerie du Glacier (p491)

➜ La Fruitière (p515)

Best Places to Stay

➜ Petit Hôtel Confidentiel (p504)

➜ Hôtel de la Vallée Heureuse (p534)

➜ Hôtel Aiguille du Midi (p489)

➜ The Farmhouse (p495)

➜ Hôtel Richemond (p488)

Why Go?

The French Alps are as grand as the towering, icy flanks of Mont Blanc and as tiny as a delicate spring wildflower, as awe-inspiring as the crag of the Aiguille du Midi and as sublime as a single snowflake. Colossal peaks thrusting upward into cobalt-blue skies, crevasse-fissured glaciers, tumbling crystal-clear rivers, sapphire lakes, mountain passes blocked by snow for nine months a year – in summer, all can be explored on foot and by bicycle, kayak and car. In winter, the Alps turn into a snowy wonderland, with world-renowned ski stations offering some of Europe's finest skiing: impossibly fast black runs and world-class off-piste routes, of course, but also plenty of slopes for beginners and intermediates and lots of snowy activities for children. Year-round, the French Alps will make your heart pound and leave you uplifted.

When to Go
Grenoble

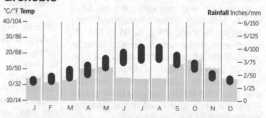

Feb–Apr Venetian Carnival in Annecy, world music in Grenoble and *vin jaune* fests in Jura.

Jul–Aug The Tour de France whizzes by, and fireworks illuminate Annecy at the Fête du Lac.

Dec Christmas markets, freestyle events and fun on the pistes as the first big snows fall.

History

The French Alps have been inhabited since prehistoric times. Later on, migrant tribes of Celtic, Gaulish and Teutonic origin arrived, and by the first century BC communities were well established, especially around the lakes of Geneva and Annecy. Soon, though, the Romans took control of the Alps, building roads through valleys and over mountain passes. The Frankish kings of the Merovingian and Carolingian empires laid the foundations for the area's distinctive dialects, traditions and cultures. By the 13th and 14th centuries, the feudal houses of Savoy, the Dauphiné and Provence were fiercely contesting the Alps. The ensuing centuries were marked by successive wars and occupations, a cycle that ended with the union of Savoy with France in 1860.

Michel-Gabriel Paccard and Jacques Balmat made the first successful ascent of Mont Blanc in 1786, and holidaymakers began to flock to the area in the late 19th century. During WWII, when German and Italian forces occupied the French Alps, the area became one of the main strongholds of the French Resistance. High-tech industry, hydro-electric energy and large-scale tourism have all contributed to the region's economic growth since the war.

Skiing & Snowboarding

The 200-plus resorts in the French Alps have earned a reputation for offering some of the best – perhaps *the* best – downhill skiing and snowboarding in Europe. In larger resorts, snowboarders are brilliantly catered for in snowparks kitted out with half-pipes, kickers and ramps.

At most stations, the ski season begins in early or mid-December and ends in mid- or late April, though the highest-altitude stations, such as Val Thorens (in Les Trois Vallées) and Val d'Isère (Espace Killy), open in mid- or late November and don't close until early or mid-May. Lots of people go skiing for a week, staying from Saturday to Saturday.

MIND YOUR X'S & Z'S

Ever wonder about the right way to pronounce the x's and z's at the end of so many Alpine names? It's easy: just pretend they're not there (they're silent).

FAST FACTS

→ **Area** 51,890 sq km

→ **Local industry** sheep, cattle, cheese production, viticulture, high-tech industry

→ **Signature drink** Chartreuse

Summer skiing on glaciers is possible from about 21 June to the end of August, and again for a week around 1 November, at two French ski stations, Les Deux Alpes and Val d'Isère/Tignes (Espace Killy).

The Jura is renowned for its selection of *ski de fond* (cross-country) trails.

European downhill runs are colour-coded to indicate how kid-easy or killer-hard they are:

→ **Green** Beginner

→ **Blue** Intermediate

→ **Red** Advanced

→ **Black** Expert

Ski Rental & Lessons

Skis (alpine, cross-country, telemark), snowboards, snowshoes, boots, poles and helmets can be hired at sports shops in every resort. All-inclusive rental costs around €32 per day for good-quality alpine equipment or snowboarding gear (about two-thirds of that for kids) and €15 for cross-country. Reserving ahead online will typically get you a 15% discount.

Every resort has a variety of ski schools with certified instructors – tourist offices have details. France's leading ski school, the École du Ski Français (ESF; www.esf.net) – its instructors wear red – has a branch in every resort; group lessons typically cost €40/160 for one/six half-days. Private instruction is also available (€45 per hour). Kids can start learning from the age of four; from three years old they can play in the *jardin de neige* (snow garden).

Lift Passes

You will need a *forfait* (lift pass) to ride the various *remontées mécaniques* (lifts): *téléskis* (tow lines), *télésièges* (chairlifts), *télécabines* (gondolas), *téléphériques* (cable cars) and *funiculaires* (funicular railways). At the big resorts, passes cost €45 to €55 a day or €200 to €260 a week (ie six days), about 40% less than at major US resorts. Everywhere in the

French Alps & the Jura Mountains Highlights

1 Swooshing down the pistes of **Chamonix** (p487) in the shadow of mighty Mont Blanc

2 Exploring the castles, medieval lanes and clear waters of dreamy **Annecy** (p498)

3 Hiking up to turquoise **Lac Blanc** (p487) for a breathtaking view of the Mont Blanc massif

4 Slaloming down legendary slopes and then partying away in the après-ski bars of **Les Trois Vallées** (p512)

5 Communing with nature at a middle-of-nowhere farm in **Parc Naturel Régional du Vercors** (p523)

6 Experiencing **La Vallée Blanche** (p486), the ultimate in Alpine off-piste skiing

7 Sipping golden *vin jaune* amid the vines on the bucolic **Route des Vins de Jura** (p533)

8 Hiking the glaciated grandeur of **Parc National de la Vanoise** (p517)

9 Getting buzzed on the winding drive to **Briançon** (p527) through the dramatic Parc National des Écrins

10 Walking the ramparts of the hilltop Vauban citadel in **Besançon** (p529)

Alps lift tickets can be bought and recharged online.

At most stations, children aged three or four and under ski for free but still need a pass; bring along a passport as proof of age. Some places also offer free lift passes to skiers over 75. A few resorts (eg Val d'Isère and Les Deux Alpes) have several free lifts for beginners. Week-long passes usually include limited access to a swimming pool, an ice-skating rink and indoor sports facilities.

You have to pay a *forfait* or *redevance* (fee), usually around €8 a day, to use *ski de fond* (cross-country) trails.

Insurance

Before you launch yourself like a rocket down that near-vertical black piste, make sure you're properly insured. Accidents happen, and expensive mountain-rescue costs (we're talking five figures here for a helicopter), medical treatment and repatriation add insult to injury.

Most ski packages include *assurance* (insurance), at least for evacuation and emergency first aid. If further treatment is required (eg you are evacuated to a hospital), your coverage may depend on your national or private health insurance. Note that some private insurance policies do not cover winter sports, especially off-piste, so check before you leave home.

The **Fédération Française de Ski** offers members of its local clubs, holders of the **License Carte Neige** (www.ffs.fr/federation/licence-carte-neige), an optional annual insurance policy (€29 to €48 per year for downhill, including membership) that covers emergency evacuation whether you're on or off-piste. It's instantly recognised by French rescue services so you won't have to pay out-of-pocket and then file for reimbursement. At ski stations, it is available from the local École du Ski Français (ESF) branch.

A simpler option is to buy **Carré Neige** (☑ 01 41 85 85 96; www.carreneige.com; downhill/cross-country per day €2.80/1.30) insurance, whose benefits are similar, along with your lift pass.

Rental shops offer equipment insurance for a small extra charge (often €2 a day).

ℹ Getting There & Away

AIR

The French Alps are served by four airports with low-cost flights (at least in winter) and seasonal bus services to various ski resorts:

Chambéry Savoie Airport (www.chambery-airport.com) 11km north of Chambéry.

Geneva Airport (www.gva.ch) In neighbouring Switzerland; has *lots* of cheap flights.

Grenoble Isère Airport (www.grenoble-airport.com) 45km northwest of Grenoble.

Lyon St-Exupéry Airport (www.lyonaeroports.com) 25km east of Lyon.

BUS

During the ski season, buses link airports and railheads with numerous ski resorts. Some services require that you make reservations 24 to 72 hours ahead. Fares, frequencies and websites are listed under Getting There & Away for destinations in this chapter.

CAR & MOTORCYCLE

The roads up to many popular ski stations are narrow, steep and serpentine so in season (especially during French school holidays) traffic can be hellish, especially at weekends.

After a snowfall, local authorities may require that all cars have either:

➔ **Snow chains** (*chaînes neige*) Available from car rental companies for a small charge (Europcar charges €17); you can put them on at an *aire de chaînage*.

➔ **Winter tyres** (*pneus neige*) Available on rental cars for an extra fee (Europcar charges €35 a day up to a maximum of €210).

You certainly don't want to find yourself blocked by the police from driving to your pre-paid chalet so arrive in the Alps equipped – in the mountains reasonably priced chains can be hard or impossible to find, especially in the evening and on weekends.

The Fréjus and Mont Blanc road tunnels connect the French Alps with Italy, as do several routes over the mountains. Passes such as Col de l'Iseran and and Col du Petit-St-Bernard are

---

ℹ **AVALANCHES**

Avalanches are a serious danger wherever deep snow meets steep slopes. You know the golden rule: never ski, hike or climb alone. Off-piste skiers should never head out without an avalanche pole, transceiver, shovel – and, most importantly, a professional guide. Ski resorts announce the daily risk level using signs and coloured flags: yellow (low risk), black and yellow (heightened risk) and black (severe risk). **Henry's Avalanche Talk** (www.henrysavalanchetalk.com) translates the daily avalanche forecast issued by Météo France into English during the ski season.

blocked by snow for all but the summer months. Road signs indicate when they're open, or check official online maps (listed north-to-south by *département*):

Haute Savoie www.inforoute74.fr

Savoie www.savoie-route.fr

Isère www.itinisere.fr

Hautes-Alpes www.inforoute05.fr

These sites also have details on road delays or blockages that have nothing to do with the weather. You can also call local tourist offices for updates on road and weather conditions.

TRAIN

On weekends from mid-December to early April, **Eurostar** (www.eurostar.com) ski trains (one-way/return from €156/279, seven hours) are a quick and environmentally friendly way to travel between London and Moûtiers, gateway to Les Trois Vallées (Méribel, Courchevel and Val Thorens), and Bourg St-Maurice, linked by bus with Val d'Isère.

Within France, train services to the Alps are excellent. In addition to Moûtiers and Bourg St-Maurice, important railheads include Sallanches, linked to Megève by bus, and Modane, gateway to Parc National de la Vanoise. To get to Chamonix you have to change to the narrow-gauge Mont Blanc Express at St-Gervais-Le Fayet.

SAVOY

Flanked to the east by the Swiss and Italian Alps, Savoy (Savoie; www.savoie-mont-blanc.com) – divided between the *départements* of Haute-Savoie (to the north) and Savoie – rises from the southern shores of Lake Geneva, Europe's largest alpine lake, and culminates at the roof of Europe, mighty 4810m Mont Blanc. At higher elevations you'll find legendary ski resorts like Chamonix and Val d'Isère, with historical château towns like Chambéry and lakeside Annecy to the southwest.

Rural life, unchanged for centuries, continues in the region's more remote corners, such as the Bauges massif and the wild Parc National de la Vanoise.

Chamonix

POP 9050 / ELEV 1037M

With the pearly white flanks of the Mont Blanc massif as a sensational backdrop, the Chamonix Valley is the Alps at their most dramatic. First 'discovered' as a tourist destination by Brits William Windham and Richard Pococke in 1741, it has become a wintertime playground of epic proportions,

ℹ️ LIFT PASSES

A worthwhile investment for serious skiers, the **Mont Blanc Unlimited** (1/3/6 days €57/138/282) pass grants access to 400km of runs, including all lifts in the Chamonix Valley, Courmayeur in Italy and Verbier in Switzerland, plus Chamonix' Aiguille du Midi cable car and the Montenvers-Mer de Glace train. The cheaper **Chamonix Le Pass** (1/3/6 days €46/127/230) gets you up to most Chamonix ski domains. In summer, the **Mont Blanc Multipass** (1/3/5 days €56/81/105) affords access to all operating lifts. Details can be viewed and purchases made online at www.compagniedumontblanc.co.uk.

more than satisfying the most demanding skiers as well as the après-ski revellers who pack themselves into its boot-stompin' bars. In summer, highland trails easily accessible by ski lift afford some of the Alps' most thrilling panoramas.

👁 Sights

Aiguille du Midi VIEWPOINT

A jagged finger of rock soaring above glaciers, snowfields and rocky crags, 8km from the hump of Mont Blanc, the Aiguille du Midi (3842m) is one of Chamonix' most distinctive geographical features. If you can handle the altitude, the 360-degree views of the French, Swiss and Italian Alps from the summit are (quite literally) breathtaking. Year-round, you can float in a cable car from Chamonix to the Aiguille du Midi on the vertiginous **Téléphérique de l'Aiguille du Midi** (www.compagniedumontblanc.co.uk; place de l'Aiguille du Midi; adult/child return to Aiguille du Midi €55/47, to Plan de l'Aiguille summer €29.50/25, winter €16/14; ⊙1st ascent btwn 7.10am & 8.30am, last ascent btwn 3.30pm & 5pm).

Up top, you can take in the view in literally every direction, including straight down thanks to the glass-floored **Step into the Void**, opened in 2013. Halfway up, **Plan de l'Aiguille** (2317m) is a terrific place to start hikes or paraglide.

In summer (especially mid-July to mid-August) there are massive lines (we're talking two-hour waits) so you may need to obtain a boarding card (marked with the number of your departing *and* returning cable cars) along with your ticket. Bring warm clothes,

Chamonix

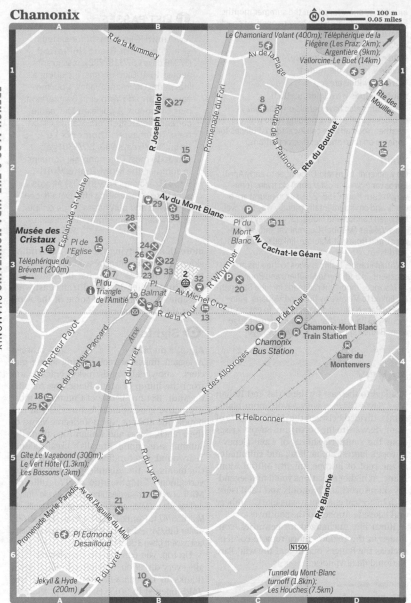

as even in summer the temperature at the top rarely rises above -10°C (in winter be prepared for -25°C).

From the Aiguille du Midi, between mid-June and August, you can continue for a further 30 minutes of mind-blowing scenery – think glaciers and spurs, seracs and shimmering ice fields – in the smaller bubbles of the **Télécabine Panoramique Mont Blanc** (adult/child return from Chamonix €80/68; ☉ last departure from Aiguille du Midi 2.30pm) to Pointe Helbronner (3466m) on

Chamonix

the France–Italy border. A new cable car from there to the Val d'Aosta ski resort of Courmayeur, on the Italian side of Monte Bianco, is set to open in 2015.

Le Brévent
VIEWPOINT

The highest peak on the western side of the Chamonix Valley, Le Brévent (2525m) has tremendous views of the Mont Blanc massif, myriad hiking trails, ledges to paraglide from and the summit restaurant Le Panoramic. Reach it on the Télécabine de Planpraz (www.compagniedumontblanc. co.uk; adult/child one-way €13.20/11.20, return €16/13.60), 400m west of the tourist office, and then the Téléphérique du Brévent (www.compagniedumontblanc.co.uk; 29 rte Henriette d'Angeville; adult/child one-way €22/18.70, return €29.50/25; ☉ mid-Dec–mid-Apr & mid-Jun–mid-Sep). Plenty of family-friendly trails begin at Planpraz (2000m).

Mer de Glace
GLACIER

France's largest glacier, the glistening 200m-deep Mer de Glace (Sea of Ice) snakes 7km down on the northern side of Mont Blanc, moving up to 1cm an hour (about 90m a year). The Train du Montenvers (www.compagniedumontblanc.co.uk; adult/child one-way €24/20.40, return €29.50/25; ☉ closed late Sep–mid-Oct), a picturesque, 5km-long

cog railway opened in 1909, links Chamonix' Gare du Montenvers with Montenvers (1913m), from where a cable car takes you down to the glacier and the Grotte de la Mer de Glace (☉ closed last half of May & late Sep–mid-Oct), an ice cave whose frozen tunnels and ice sculptures change colour like mood rings.

Your ticket also gets you into the Galerie des Cristaux, glittering with crystals from the Mont Blanc massif, and the Glaciorium, which looks at the birth, life and future of glaciers.

On foot, the Mer de Glace can be reached from Plan de l'Aiguille on the Grand Balcon Nord trail. The two-hour uphill trail from Chamonix starts near the summer luge track. Traversing the crevassed glacier requires proper equipment and an experienced guide.

★ Musée des Cristaux
MUSEUM

(Esplanade St-Michel, Espace Tiarraz; adult/child €5/free; ☉ 2-6pm daily, closed mid-Nov–early Dec) Has a truly dazzling collection of crystals, rocks and minerals, many from around Mont Blanc. L'Espace Alpinisme focuses on the art and science of mountaineering with creative interactive displays and spectacular photos and videos of seemingly impossible ascents. Situated behind the church.

CHILD'S PLAY

There's plenty to amuse *les petits* (the little ones) around Chamonix. In the warm season, kids will love getting close to free-roaming chamois, ibex and whistling marmots at the **Parc de Merlet** (www.parcdemerlet.com; 2495 Chemin de Merlet, Les Houches; adult/child €7/4; ☺10am-6pm Tue-Sun May-Sep, to 7.30pm daily Jul & Aug), 13km by road (5km on foot) southwest of central Chamonix in Coupeau (across the River Arve from Les Houches). Or treat them to a fun-packed day on the trampolines and fun-fair rides at the **Parc de Loisirs de Chamonix** (www.chamonixparc.com; 1/12 ride tokens €1.50/15; ☺11am-6.30pm Jul & Aug, 2-6pm Apr-Jun & Sep-early Nov), near the chairlift in Les Planards, 500m east of Gare du Montenvers; the 1.3km **luge** (Bob Run; 1/10 descents €5.50/46) winds through trees at mind-blowing speeds.

Cham' Aventure (☎04 50 53 55 70; www.cham-aventure.com; 190 place de l'Église, Maison de la Montagne) has a wide variety of outdoor programs for children aged three to seven, eight to 12, and 13 to 17.

Back in Chamonix, the indoor **ice-skating rink** (165 rte de la Patinoire; adult/child €5.70/4.30; skate hire €4; ☺2-6pm mid-Jul–Aug, shorter hours rest of year) provides amusement when the weather packs up, as do sports activities at the adjacent **Centre Sportif Richard Bozon** (☎04 50 53 23 70; 214 av de la Plage), with indoor and (in summer) outdoor **swimming pools** (adult/child €5.70/4.30; ☺10am or noon-7pm Jun-Aug, noon or 2pm-7.30pm Sat & Sun winter).

Musée Alpin
MUSEUM

(opposite 92 av Michel Croz; adult/child €5/free; ☺2-6pm Wed-Mon, open Tue Jul & Aug) This engaging museum richly illustrates Chamonix' long history of Alpine adventure, including the cliffhanging feats of crystal-hunter Jacques Balmat and the first ascent of Mont Blanc by a woman (Marie Paradis, a local maidservant, in 1808). Ask at the ticket counter for printed information in English.

🏃 Activities

Winter Activities
Thrilling descents, glorious off-piste terrain and unbeatable Mont Blanc views – skiing in Chamonix is so darn fantastic that skiers don't even mind that accessing the slopes involves lots of land transport to and from the lifts. Of Chamonix' nine main areas, **Le Tour**, **Les Planards**, **Les Chosalets** and **La Vormaine** are best for beginners. For speed and challenge, it has to be **Brévent-Flégère**, above Chamonix, and **Les Grands Montets**, accessible from the attractive village of Argentière, 9km north of the town. Boarders seeking big air zip across to the kickers and rails at **Les Grands Montets** snowpark and the natural half-pipe in **Le Tour**.

Chamonix' ski season runs from mid-December to mid-April.

La Vallée Blanche
SKIING

(guided trip for group of 4 €305) This legendary descent – a jaw-dropping 2800 vertical metres – is the off-piste ride of a lifetime. Beginning at the Aiguille du Midi, zipping over the crevasse-riddled Mer de Glace glacier and returning to Chamonix through the forest, it can only be tackled with a *guide de haute montagne* (specially trained high mountain guide). Skiers should be red-piste level and in reasonable physical shape; off-piste experience is a plus. Snow conditions are generally best in February and March, and sometimes into April.

Huskydalen
DOGSLEDDING

(☎04 50 47 77 24; www.huskydalen.com; mushing per hour/day adult €65/230, child €40/170; ☺Dec-Apr) One of two Chamonix outfits offering introductory mushing (dogsledding) courses.

Summer Activities
When enough snow melts (usually sometime in June), hikers can take their pick of 350km of spectacular high-altitude trails, many easy to get to by cable car or chairlift. In June and July there's enough light to walk until at least 9pm.

Balcon (literally 'balcony') trails, both *grand* and *petit,* run along both sides of the valley, the former up at around 2000m, the latter a bit above the valley's villages.

Grand Balcon Sud Trail WALKING

This easygoing trail, linking **Col des Montets** (12km northeast of Chamonix) with **Les Houches** (8km southwest of Chamonix), skirts the western side of the valley at an altitude of around 2000m, commanding terrific views across the valley to Mont Blanc. To avoid hoofing it 900m up the slope, take the **Téléphérique de la Flégère** (www.compagniedumontblanc.co.uk; adult/child from Les Praz €13.20/11.20) from Les Praz or the Télécabine de Planpraz (p485) from Chamonix; walking between the two takes about two hours. A variety of other great trails begin at the top of both these lifts.

Grand Balcon Nord Trail WALKING

Trails you can pick up at **Plan de l'Aiguille** – halfway up the Téléphérique de l'Aiguille du Midi (p483) – include the challenging Grand Balcon Nord, which takes you to the dazzling Mer de Glace, from where you can walk or take the Train du Montenvers (p485) down to Chamonix.

Lac Blanc Hike WALKING

From the top of the **Télésiège de l'Index** (www.compagniedumontblanc..co.uk; adult/child one-way from Les Praz €22/18.70), a gentle 1¼- to two-hour trail leads along the valley's western flank to turquoise **Lac Blanc** (literally 'White Lake'; 2352m) and its breathtaking scenery. You can also hike from the top of the Téléphérique de la Flégère but the trail,

while wider, involves more of an ascent. Another option: hike up (1050 vertical metres!) from Argentière (3½ hours one-way). Reserve ahead to overnight at the **Refuge du Lac Blanc** (☑04 50 53 49 14; refugedulacblanc@gmail.com; dm incl half board €50; ☺mid-Jun–Sep), a wooden chalet famed for its top-of-Europe Mont Blanc views.

Mountaineering &
High-Alpine Tours MOUNTAINEERING

Local guide companies offer exhilarating climbs for those with the necessary skill, experience and stamina. Options include five-day **rock-climbing courses** (€630 to €920) and the **Mont Blanc ascent** (from €920). For hikers, a big draw is the classic six- to 10-day **Tour du Mont Blanc** (€795 to €1395), taking in majestic glaciers and peaks in France, Italy and Switzerland. Prices usually include half board in *refuges*, (mountain huts) picnics, lift tickets and luggage transport.

Cycling Trails CYCLING

Lower-altitude trails such as the Petit Balcon Sud from Argentière to Servoz are perfect for biking. Most outdoor-activity specialists arrange guided mountain-biking expeditions.

Paragliding PARAGLIDING

Come summer, the sky above Chamonix is speckled with colourful paragliders wheeling down from the heights. Tandem flights from Planpraz (2000m) cost €100 per adult or child; from the Aiguille du Midi, count

---

ADVENTURE GUIDE COMPANIES

It takes three years of rigorous training to become an *accompagnateur en moyenne montagne* (mountain leader) and a full five years to be certified as a *guide de haute montagne* (high mountain guide); only the latter are authorised to lead groups onto glaciers or on mountaineering climbs requiring specialised equipment.

Compagnie des Guides de Chamonix (☑04 50 53 00 88; www.chamonix-guides.com; 190 place de l'Église, Maison de la Montagne; ☺8.30am-noon & 2.30-7.30pm, closed Sun & Mon late Apr–mid-Jun & mid-Sep–mid-Dec) Founded in 1821, with the crème de la crème of mountain guides for off-piste skiing (half/full day €195/330), ski touring, ice climbing, rock climbing (fancy standing on top of an aiguille?), mountaineering (take your pick of the Mont Blanc peaks), canyoning, hiking and every other extreme Alpine pastime. Along with three local affiliates of the École du Ski Français (ESF), it operates the **Mont Blanc Ski & Guide Compagnie**, which does ski guiding (eg through the Vallée Blanche).

Association Internationale des Guides du Mont Blanc (☑04 50 53 27 05; www.guides-du-montblanc.com; 9 passage de la Varlope) Chamonix-based international guides offering extreme skiing, mountaineering, glacier trekking and ice and rock climbing.

Chamonix Experience (☑09 77 48 58 69; www.chamex.com; 49 place Edmond Desailloud; ☺8am-noon & 4-7pm winter, 4-7pm rest of year) Guides lead off-piste skiing (down the Vallée Blanche for €340) and mountaineering (up Mont Blanc from €1295) and run courses in off-piste snowboarding and skiing, ice climbing, ski touring, rock climbing and mountaineering.

LOCAL KNOWLEDGE

ERIC FAVRET, MOUNTAIN GUIDE

Eric Favret, a veteran *guide de haute montagne* with Compagnie des Guides de Chamonix (p487), is a true connoisseur of the Mont Blanc massif. When it comes to off-piste skiing, he is amazed anew each time he skis the runs around the Aiguille du Midi, including the legendary **Vallée Blanche** and an even steeper route that traverses **Glacier d'Envers du Plan**.

As for summertime panoramas, some of his favourites can be seen from the trail along the Chamonix Valley's western slopes from **Col des Montets** to **Lac Blanc**. Along the way, he often stops for a dip at **Lac des Chéserys**, with its breathtaking views of Mont Blanc, the Grandes Jorasses and the Aiguille Verte.

on paying €220. Paragliding schools include **Summits** (☎ 04 50 53 50 14; www.summits.fr; 81 rue Joseph Vallot) and **AirSports Chamonix** (☎ 06 76 90 03 70; www.airsportschamonix.fr; 24 ave de la Plage); contact them for details on meeting points.

🛏 Sleeping

That you need to book ahead in winter and in July and August goes without saying. Many places close for a while in the spring and fall.

The prices quoted following are for the winter high season. Rates are significantly lower in July and August, and even lower in the spring and fall.

For details on staying in a *refuge* (mountain hut with bunk beds) high on the Mont Blanc massif, contact the tourist office or the **Club Alpin Français** (☎ 04 50 53 16 03; www.clubalpin-chamonix.com; 136 av Michel Croz; ⊗ 4-6.30pm Tue-Sat). Expect to pay around €25 for a dorm bed and €40 to €50 for half board. Meals are simple, hearty and prepared by the hut-keeper. The tourist office also has details on various types of B&Bs and *gîtes* (self-catering accommodation) in the valley.

🛏 Chamonix

Gîte Le Vagabond   HOSTEL €
(☎ 04 50 53 15 43; www.gitevagabond.com; 365 av Ravanel-le-Rouge; dm €21, sheets €5.50, d incl breakfast €101; ⊗ reception 8-10am & 4.30-10.30pm; 🖻) In a 150-year-old stagecoach inn, Chamonix' hippest bunkhouse has rooms with four to six beds and a buzzing bar with a great log fire in winter. It's situated 850m southwest of the town centre.

Le Chamoniard Volant   HOSTEL €
(☎ 04 50 53 14 09; www.chamoniard.com; 45 route de la Frasse; dm €16-19, sheets €5.50; ⊗ year-round) Long a favourite of low-budget climbing groups and luxury-averse families, this basic, practical and slightly shambolic *gîte,* run by

Sylvaine and Erick since 1985, has 68 beds in dorm rooms with four to 18 bunk beds; bathrooms and showers are down the hall. Self-caterers can use the kitchen. Situated 1.2km northeast of the centre.

★Hôtel Richemond   HOTEL €€
(☎ 04 50 53 08 85; www.richemond.fr; 228 rue du Docteur Paccard; s/d/tr €75/120/153; ⊗ closed mid-Apr–mid-Jun & mid-Sep–mid-Dec; 🖻) In a grand old building constructed in 1914 (and run by the same family ever since), this hotel – as friendly as it is central – has 52 spacious rooms with views of either Mont Blanc or Le Brévent; some are pleasantly old-fashioned, others recently renovated in white, black and beige, and three still have cast-iron bathtubs. Outstanding value.

Auberge du Manoir   HOTEL €€
(☎ 04 50 53 10 77; www.aubergedumanoir.com; 8 rte du Bouchet; s/d/tr €130/150/220; ⊗ closed 2 weeks in late Apr & 2 weeks in autumn; 🖻) This beautifully converted farmhouse, ablaze with geraniums in summer, offers 18 pine-panelled rooms that are quaint but never cloying, pristine mountain views, an outdoor hot tub, a sauna and a bar whose open fire keeps things cosy. Family-owned.

Le Vert Hôtel   HOTEL €€
(☎ 04 50 53 13 58; www.verthotel.com; 964 rte des Gaillands; s/d/tr/q €80/105/140/165; ⊗ year-round; 🖻) This lively, British-owned hotel has 21 no-frills, smallish rooms – all with new bathrooms, some with fantastic Aiguille du Midi views. But what people really come for is the happening, ultrahip bar and restaurant (dinner *menu* €22.50). It's linked to the centre (2km to the northeast) by free shuttles that stop right outside.

Hôtel de l'Arve   HOTEL €€
(☎ 04 50 53 02 31; www.hotelarve-chamonix.com; 60 impasse des Anémones; d from €180; ⊗ closed

Nov; 🐝) Overlooking the River Arve, this hotel's 37 quiet, unsurprising rooms – they also have six apartments – are cheerfully done up in warm hues and pine, and some have Mont Blanc views.

Hotel L'Oustalet HOTEL €€

(📞 04 50 55 54 99; www.hotel-oustalet.com; 330 rue du Lyret; d/q €148/190; 🕙 closed mid-May–mid-Jun & mid-Oct–mid-Dec; 🐝🏊) A block from the Aiguille du Midi cable car, this lift-equipped hotel has 15 decent rooms, snugly built of thick pine, that open onto balconies with Mont Blanc views. To unwind, you can curl up by the fire with a *chocolat chaud* or loll about in the Jacuzzi, hamam or sauna – or, in summer, take a dip in the garden pool.

Grand Hôtel des Alpes HISTORIC HOTEL €€€

(📞 04 50 55 37 80; www.grandhoteldesalpes.com; 75 rue du Docteur Paccard; d from €350, ste €585-755; 🕙 closed mid-Apr–mid-Jun & late Sep–mid-Dec; @🐝🏊) Established in 1840, this grand old dame and her 30 rooms exude timeless elegance. In winter a scrumptious and very civilised tea-time cake buffet (4.30pm to 6.30pm) greets skiers back from the slopes.

Hôtel Faucigny BOUTIQUE HOTEL €€€

(📞 04 50 53 01 17; www.hotelfaucigny-chamonix.com; 118 place de l'Église; s/d/q €200/250/350; 🕙 closed 2 weeks in May & 2 weeks in Nov; 🐝) A delicious slice of minimalist Alpine cool, with 28 rooms, shiny and tasteful, accented by touches of crimson. Also has afternoon tea, a mini-spa and a summer terrace with Mont Blanc views.

Chalet-Hôtel Hermitage HOTEL €€€

(📞 04 50 53 13 87; www.hermitage-paccard.com; 63 chemin du Cé; d €210-239, tr/q €254/281; 🕙 closed late Apr–mid-Jun & late Sep–mid-Dec; 🐝) A family-run treasure, with an open fire crackling in the bar, a kids' playroom and flowery gardens. Decked out from tip to toe in larch wood, the 28 rooms blend traditional Alpine style with mod cons (eg two-person bathtubs) and afford mountain views. Situated 900m northeast of the centre.

🛏 Les Bossons

Linked to central Chamonix, 3.5km to the northeast, by frequent trains and buses.

★Hôtel Aiguille du Midi HOTEL €€

(📞 04 50 53 00 65; www.hotel-aiguilledumidi.com; 479 chemin Napoléon; d €75-160, incl half board €146-236; 🕙 closed Oct–mid-Dec & early Apr–mid-

May; 🐝🏊) Run by the same family for five generations (since 1908), this welcoming hotel affords some of the valley's finest views of the Aiguille du Midi and Mont Blanc. The 39 pine-panelled rooms are comfortable and cosy. Summer amenities include an outdoor heated pool and a clay tennis court. For travel to/from Chamonix, there are bus and train stops right around the corner.

🛏 Les Houches

Situated 7km southwest of Chamonix, Les Houches is one of the traditional starting points of the Tour de Mont-Blanc long-distance walk.

Hotel Slalom HOTEL €€

(📞 04 50 54 40 60; www.hotelslalom.net; 44 rue de Bellevue, Les Houches; d €128-158; 🕙 closed May & Nov; 🐝) Tracey will give you the warmest of welcomes – in English – at this British-run hotel, just 100m from two ski lifts. All 10 of the delightful rooms – sleek and outfitted with Egyptian cotton – have mountain views, and all but two come with balconies.

🛏 Vallorcine

Vallorcine-Le Buet is about 14km northeast of Chamonix, over Col des Montets (1461m), and 4km from the Swiss border. It is linked to Chamonix by the Mont Blanc Express train.

Hôtel du Buet FAMILY HOTEL €

(📞 04 50 54 60 05; www.hotelbuet.com; d €66, with hall bathroom €46, f €114; 🕙 closed May–mid-Jun & Oct–mid-Dec) Run by the same family since 1889, this old-time hotel has 25 basic rooms; the restaurant (open from 7.30am to 10.30pm) serves the best-value fondue in the area. In 1942, Jews fleeing to Switzerland were given refuge here.

ⓘ MOUNTAINEERING RISKS

Be aware: climbing Mont Blanc and other peaks in the Chamonix area poses serious hazards, even with an experienced guide. During the 2014 summer climbing season, 20 climbers and guides were killed or disappeared because of some combination of avalanches, adverse weather conditions, sub-zero temperatures, poor judgement and, it would seem, bad luck.

✗ Eating

From post-piste burgers to Michelin-starred gastronomy, Chamonix has something for everyone. Peckish locals often head to rue des Moulins. Lots of pubs – especially the British ones – serve food.

Most restaurants open seven days a week in season but have reduced (or no) hours out of season.

Papillon   CAFE €
(416 rue Joseph Vallot; mains €5-8; ⊘11am-8pm Mon-Sat, 4-8pm Sun mid-Dec–early May & mid-Jun–early Oct; 🍴) A British-owned hole-in-the-wall take-out place that does great home-made curries, chilli con carne, Italian-style meatballs, noodle soup and deli-style sandwiches. Has plenty of vegie, vegan and gluten-free options.

Le GouThé   TEAROOM €
(95 rue des Moulins; light mains €4-8; ⊘9am-6.30pm Thu-Tue, closed May; 🍴) This sweet tearoom serves tea, coffee and 15 kinds of hot chocolate as well salads, quiche, sweet and savoury crêpes, muffins and scrumptiously crumbly fruit tarts.

Extreme Café   CAFE €
(21 place Balmat; light meals €3.50-8; ⊘8am-7pm or 7.30pm; 🖥) Fun snack bar where you can grab a wrap or a panini, sip a beer, wine (from €2.90 a glass) or smoothie (€3.60), and log on to free wi-fi. The terrace is heated in winter.

Super U   SUPERMARKET €
(117 rue Joseph Vallot; ⊘8am-8pm Mon-Sat, 8.30am-12.30pm Sun) For picnic supplies.

★ Le Cap Horn   FRENCH €€
(☑04 50 21 80 80; www.caphorn-chamonix.com; 78 rue des Moulins; lunch menu €20, other menus €29-39; ⊘noon-1.30pm or 2pm & 7-9pm or 10pm daily year-round) Housed in a gorgeous, two-storey chalet decorated with model sailboats – joint homage to the Alps and Cape Horn – this highly praised restaurant, opened in 2012, serves French and Asian-inflected dishes such as pan-seared duck breast with honey and soy sauce, fisherman's stew and, for dessert, *soufflet au Grand Marnier*. Reserve for dinner Friday and Saturday in winter and summer.

Munchie   FUSION €€
(☑04 50 53 45 41; www.munchie.eu; 87 rue des Moulins; mains €19-24; ⊘7pm-2am, closed 2 weeks May & mid-Oct–Nov) Franco-Asian fusion has been the lip-smacking mainstay of this casual, Swedish-skippered restaurant since 1997. Specialities such as steak with spicy Béarnaise sauce are presented with panache. Reservations recommended during the ski season.

Le Panier des 4 Saisons   TRADITIONAL FRENCH €€
(☑04 50 53 98 77; www.restaurant-panierdes 4saisons.com; 262 rue du Docteur Paccard; lunch menu €19, other menu €31; ⊘noon-2pm & 7-10pm Wed-Mon, closed Jun & Nov–mid-Dec) Brimming with chatter and bonhomie, this semi-formal, wood-panelled establishment serves traditional French dishes such as thick-cut pollack in a sweet-and-sour red-wine sauce and roast venison with quince purée, all expertly matched with wines.

Le Chaudron   FRENCH €€
(☑04 50 53 40 34; www.le-chaudron-chamonix.com; 79 rue des Moulins; menus €27-34; ⊘7-9.30pm or later mid-Dec–Apr & mid-Jun–Sep) On a cold winter's day, this cosy Alpine chalet is guaranteed to give you a warm inner glow. Funky faux-cowskin pillows provide the backdrop for a French and Savoyard feast. Home-made specialities include beef slow-cooked in red wine and served with creamy risotto.

La Petite Kitchen   INTERNATIONAL €€
(☑04 50 54 37 44; www.lapetitekitchen.fr; 80 place du Poilu; lunch/dinner menus €14/39; ⊘11am-2.30pm & 7-11pm, closed dinner Oct, Nov & May) The little kitchen is just that: a handful of tables for the lucky few. Steaks with home-made *frites* and hot fudge will send you rolling happily out the door.

Le Bistrot   MODERN FRENCH €€€
(☑04 50 53 57 64; www.lebistrotchamonix.com; 151 av de l'Aiguille du Midi; lunch menu €20, other menus €55-85; ⊘noon-1.30pm & 7-9pm; 🍴) Sleek and hushed, this is a real gastronome's paradise. Michelin-starred chef Mickey experiments with textures and seasonal flavours to create taste sensations – specialities include roasted lamb with artichoke, roasted scallops with pan-fried foie gras and warm chocolate macarons with raspberry and red pepper coulis.

⚑ Drinking & Entertainment

Chamonix nightlife rocks. For a pub crawl, head (along with the locals) to quaint old rue des Moulins, where wall-to-wall pubs and eateries keep it buzzing until about 1am.

WORTH A TRIP

LUNCH IN THE FOREST

An all-wood chalet in the middle of the forest is the only place you can find Chef Claudy's world-famous *croûte aux fromages* (a thick slice of bread topped with cheese and baked until it's toasted on the bottom and then drenched in a secret white wine sauce). It's worth the trek out to **Crèmerie du Glacier** (☑ 04 50 54 07 52; www.lacremerieduglacier.fr; 766 chemin de la Glacière; lunch menu €13, fondue €11-20; ☺ lunch & dinner mid-Dec–mid-May & late Jun–mid-Sep, closed Wed in winter) both for the cheesy Savoyard cuisine (including nine kinds of fondue) and the Alpine ambience. Make reservations (required) by telephone.

Crèmerie du Glacier is signposted from the roundabout near the bridge at the southern entrance to Argentière. To get there, you have several options:

➡ In winter, ski down on Piste de la Pierre à Ric (red) or cross-country-ski over on Piste de la Moraine.

➡ In summer, hike over from the Petit Balcon Nord trail, 15 minutes away.

➡ In winter or summer, walk or drive east for about 1km from the base of the Téléphérique Lognan-Les Grands Montets; take one-lane chemin de la Glacière in summer and equally narrow chemin de la Rosière in winter.

🍷 Chamonix

★MBC
MICROBREWERY

(Micro Brasserie de Chamonix; www.mbchx.com; 350 rte du Bouchet; ☺ 4pm-2am Mon-Thu, 10am-2am Fri-Sun) Run by four Canadians, this trendy microbrewery is fab. Be it with their phenomenal burgers (€10 to €15), cheesecake of the week, live music (Sunday from 9.30pm) or amazing beers, MBC delivers. Busiest from 5pm to 11pm.

Chambre Neuf
BAR

(272 av Michel Croz; ☺ 7am-1pm; ☜) Chamonix' most spirited après-ski party (4pm to 8pm), fuelled by a Swedish band and dancing on the tables, spills out the front door of Chambre Neuf. Wildly popular with seasonal workers.

La Terrasse
BAR

(43 place Balmat; ☺ 4pm-2am Mon-Fri, 1pm-2am Sat & Sun, closed May & Nov; ☜) Overlooking Chamonix' main square and the river, this British-style pub – take the spiral staircase for the best views – serves pub grub from 4.30pm to 10.30pm and then gives itself over to music (live or DJed) and dancing. Staff are British.

Les Caves
BAR

(www.caphorn-chamonix.com; 80 rue des Moulins; beer from €4, wine per glass from €6; ☺ 5pm-2am daily, closed Nov–mid-Dec) Spread over four levels, with cosy hidden corners and sheepskin seats, this sumptuous, sophisticated bar transforms itself from a quiet lounge into a disco after 10.30pm. Hungry? Order food from adjacent Le Cap Horn.

Bistrot des Sports
PUB

(182 rue Joseph Vallot; ☺ 7am-2am) Founded in 1878 to cater to muleteers, guides and other mountain folk, this classic pub-cum-bistro is where old-time climbing parties used to assemble before setting out to conquer Mont Blanc. The seating area was built for the 1924 Winter Olympics.

Le Lapin Agile
LOUNGE

(www.lelapinagile.fr; 11 rue Whymper; ☺ 11.30am-11.30pm Tue-Sun, closed mid-Oct–early Dec & mid-May–late Jun; ☜) Relaxed wine bar with Italian *vino* and free *aperitivo* tapas from 6.30pm to 8pm daily.

Jekyll & Hyde
PUB

(www.thejekyll.com; 71 rte des Pélerins; ☺ 4pm-2am daily, opens earlier Sat & Sun; ☜) British-owned après-ski mainstay with Irish beer, really good pub food (try the steak-and-Guinness pie), live music (Wednesday, Thursday and Sunday from 9.30pm), DJs, dancing on the tables (after 10.30pm) and a friendly vibe. Situated 350m southwest of the bottom of the Téléphérique de l'Aiguille du Midi.

White Hub
CLUB

(www.white-hub.com; 1 place du Mont-Blanc; cover €5-15; ☺ midnight-7am Fri & Sat) Chamonix' premier late-late disco draws revellers of all ages. Dress is casual-smart. It's situated underneath the Hôtel Alpina; the entrance is under the roadway, at the northern end of rue des Moulins. It's also open Thursday and sometimes Wednesday nights in peak season.

₹ Argentière

The Office BAR
(274 rue Charlet Stratton; ⊙3pm-2am Mon-Fri, 11am-2am Sat & Sun; ⓢ) Known to locals as *chez Dave* (in honour of the Aussie owner), this mellow pub has some of the tastiest beer in the valley, DJs a couple nights a week and live music on Friday (from 10.30pm).

🛍 Shopping

The streets of central Chamonix are home to the world's largest selection of flagship boutiques selling brand-name sportswear.

ⓘ Information

PGHM (☑04 50 53 16 89; www.pghm-chamonix. com; 69 rue de la Mollard) Mountain-rescue service for the Mont Blanc area.

Post Office (89 place Balmat)

Tourist Office (☑04 50 53 00 24; www.chamonix.com; 85 place du Triangle de l'Amitié; ⊙9am-12.30pm & 2-6pm, longer hours winter & summer) Information on accommodation, activities, the weather and cultural events.

ⓘ Getting There & Away

BUS

Chamonix' **bus station** (☑04 50 53 01 15; place de la Gare; ⊙8-11.30am & 1.15-6.15pm in winter, shorter hours rest of year) is to the right as you exit the train station.

Services to Courmayeur (one-way/return €14/22, 45 minutes, two to six dailt), in Taly, are operated by **SAT-Mont Blanc** (☑04 50 78 05 33; www.sat-montblanc.com).

Buses to the airport and bus station in Geneva (one-way/return €30/50, 1½ to two hours, three daily), Switzerland, are run jointly by SAT-Mont

---

ⓘ FREE PUBLIC TRANSPORT

In a bid to encourage locals and visitors to leave their cars at home, the Chamonix Valley offers free public transport on both local buses and the Mont Blanc Express train, the latter for travel between Servoz (14km west of Chamonix) and Vallorcine (14km northeast of Chamonix and just 4km from the Swiss frontier). To ride free (and get various other discounts, including for parking), all you have to do is get a **Carte d'Hôte** (Guest Card) from your hotel or B&B – if you're staying with friends, you can pick one up at the tourist office for €2 for the whole week.

Blanc and **Savda** (☑+39 01 65 36 70 32; www. savda.it), with onward connections to Aoste and Milan.

See the websites or visit the bus station for timetables and reservations (highly recommended).

CAR & MOTORCYCLE

Chamonix is linked to Courmayeur in Italy's Val d'Aoste by the 11.5km-long **Tunnel de Mont Blanc** (www.atmb.com; toll one-way/return €42.40/52.90).

When the Col des Montets (between Argentière and Vallorcine) is closed by snow, signs will direct you to drive through the rail tunnel.

The valley's only car-hire company is **Europcar** (www.europcar.com; 36 place de la Gare).

Parking in Chamonix involves either paying for a spot in a city centre **parking garage** (per 1½/12/24 hours €2/8.50/10.50) or heading to one of the seven **free lots** on Chamonix' outskirts, five of them towards Argentière.

TRAIN

The scenic, narrow-gauge **Mont Blanc Express** glides from St-Gervais-Le Fayet, 23km west of Chamonix, to the Swiss town of Martigny (€24.70 from Chamonix). En route, it stops at stations such as Les Houches, Chamonix (€5.50 from St-Gervais, 45 minutes, hourly), Argentière and Vallorcine. Travelling between Servoz and Vallorcine is free if you have a Carte d'Hôte (Guest Card), available for free from your hotel.

From St-Gervais-Le Fayet, there are somewhat infrequent trains to cities around France, often with a change in Bellegarde or Annecy. Destinations include:

Annecy €15.30, 1½ hours, seven daily

Lyon €42.20, 4½ hours, five or six daily

Paris €97 to €115, six to seven hours, six daily

ⓘ Getting Around

BUS

Public buses run by **Chamonix Bus** (www. chamonix-bus.com) serve all the towns, villages, ski lifts and attractions in the Chamonix Valley, from Argentière (Col des Montets in summer) in the northeast, to Servoz and Les Houches in the southwest. Buses operate year-round but have added destinations and are more frequent in winter (mid-December to mid-April) and summer (late June to early September). All buses are free with a Carte d'Hôte (Guest Card), except the wintertime Chamo' Nuit night buses linking Chamonix with Argentière and Les Houches (last departures from Chamonix 11.30pm or midnight; €2).

TAXI

For a taxi, call ☑04 50 53 13 94. There's a taxi queue in front of the train station.

Megève & St-Gervais

Megève (population 3900, elevation 1113m), 20km due west of Mont Blanc, was developed in the 1920s for Baroness de Rothschild of the famous banking family, who found Switzerland's overcrowded St-Moritz frankly rather tiresome. Today this rustically charming ski village looks almost too perfect to be true: horse-drawn carriages and exquisitely arranged boutique windows spill into its cobbled, medieval-style streets lined with chalets. In winter, Megève attracts a well-off crowd (including lots of families), but the scene is more laid-back in summer.

Unpretentious St-Gervais-les-Bains (population 5813, elevation 850m), 11km northeast of Megève, is linked to Chamonix by the legendary Mont Blanc Express train. Most of the town is undistinguished 20th-century sprawl, but the lovely central square, with its baroque church, has a distinctly Alpine feel.

✱ Activities

Having the Mont Blanc massif as a backdrop makes for fabulously scenic **skiing** in areas accessible both from Megève and, via the St-Gervais-Bettex cable car, from near the centre of St-Gervais (www.ski-saintgervais.com). Downhill runs are divided between three separate collections of slopes: **Mont d'Arbois-St-Gervais**, **Le Jaillet-Combloux-La Giettaz** and **Rochebrune-Cote 2000**. Skiing here is mostly for beginners and cruisy intermediates, though there are also some black runs – all told, the area has 445km of well-groomed pistes to play on. For a lift pass (possibly discounted), go to www.megeve.com.

In summer, both towns make superb bases for **hiking**, with trails for walkers and hikers of all levels, including young children. Panoramic trails abound, including many in the Bettex, Mont d'Arbois and Mont Joly (2525m) areas. Tourist offices sell IGN hiking maps (€6).

Some of the best **mountain-biking** terrain, with downhill runs accessible by lift, is between Val d'Arly, Mont Blanc and Beaufortain. Bikes can be rented in Megève.

Megève's Palais des Sports et de Congrès has year-round **ice-skating** and **swimming** and even a sheet (court) for the obscure Olympic sport of **curling** (classes available). The town is known for having lots of kid-friendly activities.

DON'T MISS

POTTER'S FANTASY

His name is Monsieur Baranger, but he prefers to be called 'the potter behind the church' – and that's precisely where you will find his rambling, poster-plastered **workshop and gallery** in the centre of St-Gervais. An eccentric and something of a local legend, M Baranger can often be seen at his wheel, where he throws pots, plates, ornaments and vases, which are then glazed in earthy shades of blue and cream. His workshop is open *quand vous voyez de la lumière* (when the lights are on).

Maison de la Montagne OUTDOOR ACTIVITIES (76 rue Ambroise Martin, Megève) Based here are Megève's **ESF** (www.megeve-ski.com; ⊙ winter 9am-6.30pm) and **Bureau des Guides** (☏ 04 50 21 55 11; www.guides-megeve.com; ⊙ 9.30am-12.30pm & 3-7pm, closed Sat & Sun in low season), which organise activities such as off-piste skiing, ice climbing, snowshoeing, rock climbing, paragliding, canyoning and mountain biking.

Tramway du Mont Blanc FUNICULAR (www.compagniedumontblanc.co.uk; rue de la Gare, St-Gervais; return to Bellevue/Nid d'Aigle €29.50/35; ⊙ 4-6 departures daily mid-Dec–early Apr, hourly mid-Jun-early Sep) For spirit-soaring mountain views with a retro vibe, hop aboard France's highest cog-wheel railway. For over a century it has ascended from St-Gervais-Le Fayet (792m) up to Bellevue (1800m; one hour) in winter; and, in summer (when you can hike back down), all the way to Nid d'Aigle (2482m; 80 minutes).

Bungee Mont Blanc Elastique BUNGEE JUMPING (www.bungeemontblancelastique.com; Viaduc de St-Gervais; 1/2 jumps €80/115) Offers warm-season bungee jumps from the new road bridge in St-Gervais, directly above a waterfall on the River Bonnant.

🛏 Sleeping & Eating

In winter, some places only rent by the week. Rates drop significantly during the warm months.

La Maison Blanche HOTEL € (☏ 04 50 47 75 81; www.chaletlamaisonblanche.com; 64 rue du Vieux Pont, St-Gervais; d €75-85; ⊙ closed May & Oct–mid-Dec) You're assured of a warm welcome at this family-run inn, whose 12 simply furnished rooms have modern tiled bathrooms with marble sinks. Situated in the centre of St-Gervais 100m down the hill from the church.

Le Gai Soleil
CHALET €€

(☑ 04 50 21 00 70; www.le-gai-soleil.fr; 343 rue Crêt du Midi, Megève; d incl breakfast/half board €155/220; ☻closed May & mid-Oct-Nov; @ 🔊 🏊) An inviting, Welsh-owned chalet offering 21 warm, cosy rooms, a spa and a new warm-season play area for kids. The outdoor pool (June to September) and sun deck afford sublime mountain views. Staff are happy to drive skiers to the cable car station, 500m away.

Pur Bar & Restaurant
RESTAURANT €

(☑ 04 50 18 62 76; 101 ave du Mont Paccard, St-Gervois; lunch/dinner menu €15/24; ☻11am-3pm & 6pm-1am, meals noon-2pm & 7-10pm, closed Sun & Mon except school holidays; 🔊) You'll eat well and drink mellowly at this stylish establishment, whose recipes – prepared with quintessentially French élan – come from around the world. There's live music every Thursday from 10pm to midnight. It's in the centre of St-Gervais, just down the stairs from the tourist office.

Le Galeta
SAVOYARD €€

(☑ 04 50 93 16 11; www.le-galeta.fr; 150 impasse des Lupins, St-Gervais; menus €25-29; ☻7-9pm daily, plus noon-2pm Jun-Sep, closed May, Oct & Nov; 🅿) This rustic chalet-style restaurant radiates Alpine atmosphere and warmth. Sylvie and Serge serve up succulent steaks and lamb grilled over an open wood fire as well as fondue, *raclette*, *tartiflettes* and *braserade* (DIY BBQ). Situated in the centre of St-Gervais a bit below the church.

ℹ Information

Megève Tourist Office (☑ 04 50 21 27 28; www.megeve.com; 70 rue de Monseigneur Conseil; ☻9am-12.30pm & 2-6.30pm Mon-Sat, also open Sun in high season) Can help with accommodation and reserve events tickets. Situated in the pedestrian zone in the centre of town.

St-Gervais Tourist Office (☑ 04 50 47 76 08; www.saintgervais.com; 43 rue du Mont-Blanc; ☻9am-noon & 2-6pm or later Mon-Sat, open Sun in high season) Can help find accommodation.

ℹ Getting There & Away

BUS
From Megève's bus station, bus 83 goes to the railhead of Sallanches (€3.50, 25 minutes, six to nine daily Monday to Saturday, also Sunday in high season).

From late December to March, **Autocars Borini** (☑ 04 50 21 18 24; www.borini.com) links Megève with Geneva airport (one-way/return €47/81, 1½ hours, three daily). Reserve at least 24 hours ahead. Tickets are cheaper online.

TRAIN
The train station nearest Megève is 12km north in Sallanches; buses connect the two towns.

The St-Gervais-Le Fayet train station is 2km northwest of the centre of St-Gervais. If you're heading to Chamonix, change here to the Mont Blanc Express. Destinations include:

Annecy €15.30, 1½ to 2½ hours, almost hourly Monday to Friday, five Saturday, nine Sunday

Chamonix €10.90, 45 minutes, almost hourly

Geneva €13.70, two to four hours, hourly Monday to Friday, six to 10 Saturday and Sunday

Lyon €35.60, 3½ to 5½ hours, twelve daily

Paris Gare de Lyon €70 to €146, five to seven hours, 10 daily

Les Portes du Soleil

Grandly dubbed 'the Gates of the Sun' (elevation 1000m to 2466m; www.portesdusoleil.com), this gargantuan ski area – among the world's largest – encompasses 12 villages on both sides of the unguarded Franco-Swiss border. Access to Les Portes du Soleil is among the Alps' easiest – by car, it's just 1¼ hours from Geneva airport.

The best known of the villages is **Morzine** (elevation 1000m), which retains some traditional Alpine charm, especially in summer, when visits to *fruitières* (cheese dairies) and traditional slate workshops are popular.

Small, trend-conscious **Avoriaz** (elevation 1800m), a purpose-built ski resort a few kilometres up the valley atop a rock, is completely free of cars. Horse-drawn sleighs piled high with luggage romantically ferry new arrivals to and from the snowy village centre, enlivened by wacky 1960s architecture.

Arriving by road via Cluses, you hit the smaller ski station of **Les Gets** (elevation 1172m), a family favourite.

🏃 Activities

Over 400km of **downhill** slopes criss-cross Les Portes du Soleil, served by a whopping 194 lifts covered by a single trans-frontier ski pass (per day/week €47.50/237.50). The area's most famous piste is **Le Pas de Chavanette**, better known as The Swiss Wall, which is so steep and moguled that on the European green-blue-red-black scale it's rated orange (double black).

Morzine offers ideal beginner and intermediate terrain, with scenic runs through the trees for windy days. The snow-sure slopes of higher-elevation **Avoriaz** are great for intermediate skiers but some offer a real challenge if that's what you're after. This is freestyle heaven for **snowboarders**, with deep powder, several snowparks to play in and a fantastic superpipe near the top of the Prodains cable car. Nursery slopes for little kids, toboggan runs, a new indoor swimming pool, **children's clubs** and snow-play areas make Les Portes du Soleil a great choice for families.

In summer, the same slopes attract **mountain bikers**, with invigorating routes like the 90km circular Tour des Portes du Soleil; a mountain-bike lift pass costs €24/96 per day/week. Walkers can pick and choose from 800km of marked trails; an extensive lift network (late June to early September) takes the slog out of reaching higher altitudes.

Bureau des Guides　　OUTDOOR ACTIVITIES
(☑04 50 75 96 65; www.bureaudesguides.net) The place to go for the low-down on summer activities – hiking, biking, climbing, canyoning and paragliding – and details on **La Noire de Morzine**, Morzine's heart-stopping 3.2km, 500-vertical-metre bike descent from the top of the **Pléney cable car** (1/10 ascents €5/28).

🛏 Sleeping & Eating

The Morzine tourist office has a year-round **accommodation service** (☑04 50 79 11 57; www.resa-morzine.com).

Fleur des Neiges　　HOTEL €€
(☑04 50 79 01 23; www.hotel-fleur-des-neiges.fr; 227 Taille de Mas de Nant Crue, Morzine; d incl breakfast/half-board €150/200; ☺mid-Dec–mid-Apr & mid-Jun–early Sep; 🔊🌊) A cheery welcome, 31 serviceable rooms, a sauna, a pool, solid home cooking and fluent English (one of the owners is Canadian) await at this family-run chalet. Situated five long blocks northwest of the tourist office.

Bonne Valette　　HOTEL €€
(☑04 50 79 04 31; www.hotel-bonne-valette.com; 130 Taille de Mas de Frênes, Morzine; s/d/tr/q €50/100/110/120; 🔊🌊) A family-run hotel with 19 no-frills, wood-panelled rooms, almost all with balconies, as well as a sauna, outdoor pool and friendly welcome. Open year-round. Situated three long blocks northwest of the tourist office.

FRENCH ALPS & THE JURA MOUNTAINS LES PORTES DU SOLEIL

ℹ MULTIPASS MAGIC

Les Portes du Soleil's hottest summer deal is the **Multipass**, which costs €2/8 per day/week if you're staying here and €8 for day trippers. Available from early June to early September, the pass covers cable cars and chairlifts (some of which only run from late June) for hikers; access to sports facilities such as tennis courts, ice rinks and swimming pools; and entry to three heritage museums and two abbeys.

★**The Farmhouse**　　BOUTIQUE HOTEL €€€
(☑04 50 79 08 26; www.thefarmhouse.fr; Le Mas de la Coutettaz, Morzine; d incl half board €224-478; ☺mid-Dec–mid-Apr & Jun–mid-Sep; 🔊) Cosily ensconced in a gorgeous 1771 manor house, this welcoming British-owned guesthouse has seven rooms – one of which once served as a prison – in the main house and a trio of cottages on the lovely grounds. Dining is a lavish, candle-lit affair around one huge banquet table. A one-week minimum may apply in winter. Situated 600m southeast of Morzine's tourist office.

Le Clin d'Oeil　　TRADITIONAL FRENCH €€
(☑04 50 79 03 10; www.restaurant-leclin.com; 63 rte du Plan, Morzine; lunch menu €15, mains €15-32; ☺noon-2pm & 7-9.30pm daily; 🖼) Brings the herbs of southwestern France to the Alps. The all-wood interior is inviting for rich, brothy *cassoulet* (rich bean, pork and duck stew) in winter, while the flowery patio is ideal for lighter dishes like risotto and seafood in summer. It's down the hill, near the post office.

ℹ Information

Avoriaz Tourist Office (☑04 50 74 02 11; www.avoriaz.com; 44 promenade des Festivals; ☺9am-noon & 2-6pm or 7pm, closed Sat & Sun May, Jun & Sep-Nov, no midday closure Dec-Mar, Jul & Aug; 🔊) Can book self-catering chalets and studios.

Morzine Tourist Office (☑04 50 74 72 72; www.morzine-avoriaz.com; 26 place du Baraty; ☺9am-noon & 2-6pm Mon-Sat, no midday closure & open Sun mid-Dec–mid-Apr & mid-Jun–early Sep) Has excellent brochures in English and can help find accommodation.

ℹ Getting There & Around

Les Portes du Soleil is easy to get to from Geneva airport, 83km to the west.

During the ski season, buses run by **SAT Léman** (www.sat-leman.com) link the area's resorts with Geneva's airport and bus station (€37.50, two hours, three daily Sunday to Friday, six on Saturday). All year, SAT Léman bus 91 connects Morzine and Les Gets with the railheads of Thonon-les-Bains (€11, one hour, three to five daily) and Cluses (€11, one hour, two or three daily Monday to Saturday). To make reservations (required), call ☑04 50 79 15 69.

Within the Morzine area, free shuttle buses (seven lines in winter, one in summer) serve all the lifts.

Évian-les-Bains

The elegant belle époque spa town of Évian, a favourite country retreat of the dukes of Savoy, sits grandly on the southern shore of Lake Geneva (Lac Léman). Its flowery parks and grand buildings draw crowds mainly in summer.

Discovered in 1790 and bottled since 1826, the mineral water that has made the town famous takes at least 15 years to trickle down through the Chablais Mountains, gathering minerals en route before emerging at 11.4°C.

◉ Sights & Activities

Facing the flowery lakefront promenade (along quai Baron-de-Bloney and quai Paul-Léger) stand a number of impressive belle époque buildings, including (from east to west) the ornate, neoclassical **Palais Lumière** (1902), now a convention centre; the classically French **Villa Lumière** (late 1800s), Évian's city hall since 1927; the **Théâtre** (1885), with its impressive neoclassical façade; and the domed **Casino**, built in 1912.

For details on things to do and see all around Lake Geneva, both in France and in Switzerland, see www.le-man-sans-frontiere.org.

Source Cachat
MINERAL WATER

(20 av des Sources; ⊙24hr) FREE Drink your fill of pure Évian mineral water – and fill up as many bottles as you like – at this outdoor tap. In a little colonnaded pavilion painted pink and white, it's a block up the hill from 19 rue Nationale (Évian's pedestrianised main drag), to the right as you face the horseshoe-shaped staircase. The glass, wood and wrought-iron building across the street is the **Buvette Cachat**, an art nouveau masterpiece from 1903.

Les Thermes Évian
THERMAL SPA

(☑04 50 75 02 30; www.lesthermesevian.com; place de la Llibération; from €35; ⊙9am-7pm Mon-Sat) Ever dream of pampering yourself by filling a bathtub with hundreds of bottles of pure Évian mineral water? Now's your chance at this modern luxury spa, built in 1984 and extensively renovated in 2012. Reserve ahead and bring a swimsuit, a bathing cap and flip-flops. Situated 700m east of the tourist office.

CGN Boats to Lausanne
LAKE CRUISE

(www.cgn.ch; return €29.60) Join local commuters for the scenic 35-minute boat ride to the Swiss city of Lausanne. Boats depart from the Port de Commerce every hour or two.

🛏 Sleeping

Hôtel Continental
HOTEL €

(☑04 50 75 37 54; www.hotel-continental-evian.com; 65 rue Nationale; s/d/tr €70/75/95) Owned by a Franco-American couple (Catherine is French, Mike is from North Carolina), this atmospheric hotel, built in 1868, has 32 rooms with belle époque furnishings, chandeliers, high ceilings and squeaky old parquet floors. Very central, and excellent value. Situated 250m southeast of the tourist office.

ℹ Information

Tourist Office (☑04 50 75 04 26; www.evian-tourisme.com; place d'Allinges; ⊙9am-noon & 2-6pm Mon-Sat year-round, open Sun May-Aug, no midday closure Jul & Aug; 🛜) Has a historical walking tour brochure and 24-hour wi-fi.

ℹ Getting There & Away

Évian-les-Bains, 9km northeast of Thonon and 17km west of the Swiss frontier, is the end of the line for rail travel on the French shore of Lake Geneva. Train destinations include Thonon-les-Bains (€2.50, seven minutes, a dozen daily). **Autocars Frossard** (www.frossard.eu) sends buses to Annecy (€14, 2½ hours, twice daily Monday to Friday).

MOVING ON?

For tips, recommendations and reviews, head to shop.lonelyplanet.com to purchase downloadable PDFs of the Fribourg, Neuchatel & Jura, Lake Geneva & Vaud, Geneva and Valais chapters from Lonely Planet's *Switzerland* guide.

Thonon-les-Bains

POP 33,500 / ELEV 430M

Across Lake Geneva (Lac Léman) from the Swiss city of Lausanne, Thonon-les-Bains – a fashionable spa town during the belle époque – sits on a bluff above the lake. Winter is deathly dull, but in summer **cruises** and **lakeside strolls** appeal. You can also visit the nearby **Château de Ripaille** (www.ripaille. fr; adult/child €9/4.50; ⊙10am-6pm, closed early Nov-early Apr), one-time home of the dukes of Savoy.

🛏 Sleeping & Eating

Hôtel-Restaurant Savoie Léman HOTEL €
(☑04 50 81 13 50; www.ecole-hoteliere-thonon. com; 40 blvd Carnot; d/q €65/120, lunch mains €8, menus €20-30; ⊙closed Sat, Sun & local school holidays, incl Jul & Aug; meals served 12.10-12.45pm Tue-Fri & 7-8.15pm Mon Fri) Those spiffy young people in jackets, ties and skirts you see around town are not missionaries, they're students at Thonon's *école hôtelière* (secondary and post-secondary hotel school) – and they run this weekdays-only hotel with the polish and attention to detail of naval cadets. The 32 'three-star' rooms are modern and very attractive, and there are two classic French restaurants offering great value. Reservations are highly recommended.

ⓘ Information

Tourist Office (☑04 50 71 55 55; www.thonon lesbains.com; 2 rue Michaud; ⊙9am-12.15pm & 1.45-6.30pm Mon-Fri, from 10am Sat) Situated inside the mid-17th-century Château de Sonnaz.

ⓘ Getting There & Away

The train station (place de la Gare) is 650m southeast of the tourist office. Services include:
Évian €2.50, seven minutes, a dozen daily
Geneva €8.30 to €17.50, two to three hours, eight to 14 daily

Annecy

POP 50,250 / ELEV 447M

Even Savoyards spoiled by Alpine views every day of their lives grow wistful at the mention of Annecy. Why? Just look around you: startlingly turquoise Lac d'Annecy, overlooked by mountains often snowcapped mountains; the almost impossibly charming Vieille Ville (old town), with its ensemble of pastel-painted, geranium-bedecked houses; and the turreted château, looking for all the

YVOIRE

A real sleeping beauty of a medieval village, Yvoire (population 820), 16km west of Thonon on the shores of Lake Geneva, makes for a great day trip. The village is a riot of turrets and towers, old stone houses and flower-lined streets.

Slumbering in the shadow of a 14th-century castle and enclosed by walls, the **Jardin des Cinq Sens** (Garden of Five Senses; www.jardin5sens. net; rue du Lac; adult/child €11.80/7; ⊙10am-6pm, closed mid-Oct–mid-Apr), inspired by the monastery gardens of the Middle Ages, appeals to the senses through touch, sound (gurgling water), scent (fragrant gardens) and taste (edible plants).

The **tourist office** (☑04 50 72 80 21; www.yvoiretourism.com; place de la Mairie; ⊙9.30am-12.30pm & 1.30-5pm Mon-Sat, noon-4pm Sun) can advise on sights and accommodation.

world like a castle straight out of the Middle Ages (which it is).

With such a phenomenal backdrop, it's no wonder everyone is outdoors – hanging out in pavement cafes, mountain-gazing along the lakeshore, swimming in the lake (among Europe's purest), and cycling around it.

◉ Sights

Vieille Ville & Lakefront HISTORIC QUARTER
It's a pleasure simply to wander aimlessly around Annecy's medieval old town, a photogenic jumble of narrow pedestrians-only streets, crystal-clear canals – the reason Annecy is known as 'Venice of the Alps' – and colonnaded passageways.

On the tree-fringed lakefront, the flowery **Jardins de l'Europe** are linked to the grassy **Champ de Mars**, a popular picnic spot, by the poetic iron arch of the **Pont des Amours** (Lovers' Bridge).

Palais de l'Isle MUSEUM
(www.musees.agglo-annecy.fr; 3 passage de l'Île; adult/child €3.70/1.70; ⊙10am-noon & 2-5pm Wed-Mon, no midday closure Jun-Sep) Sitting on a triangular islet surrounded by the Canal du Thiou, the whimsically turreted 12th-century Palais de l'Isle has been a lordly residence, courthouse, mint and prison over the centuries.

Annecy

⊗0 ━━━ 200 m
0 ━━━ 0.1 miles

Map labels:

Av Bouvard · Av Berthollet · Av de Brogny · R de la Paix · R Président Favre · R Carnot · R Jean Jaurès · Av du Parmelan · R Louis Revon · Plage Impérial (700m); Plage d'Annecy le-Vieux (1km)

Train Station · Bus Station · R de l'Industrie · R Sommeiller · R de l'Annexion · Centre Bonlieu · Av d'Albigny · Champ de Mars

Pl de la Gare · R des Glières · R de la Poste · R Vaugelas · R du Pâquier · R Royale · R du Lac · Pont des Amours

Église Notre Dame de Liesse · Pl Notre Dame · VIEILLE VILLE · Q Eustache Chappuis · Promenade Jacquet · Canal du Vassé · Q Jules Philippe · Lac d'Annecy

R de la République · Cathédrale St-Pierre · R J-J Rousseau · Q de l'Évêché · R Filaterie · Église St-Maurice · Pl de la Mairie · Mairie (Town Hall) · Pedal Boat Rental

Av de Chambéry · Thiou · R de la Gare · R Ste-Claire · R de L'Isle · Q Perrière · Église St-François de Sales · Jardins de l'Europe · Q Napoléon III

R du Faubourg Ste-Claire · Pl du Château · Porte Perrière · Pl aux Bois · Canal du Thiou · Q Bayreuth · Esplanade des Marquisats

Av de Loverchy · Chemin de la Tour de la Reine · Faubourg des Annonciades · R des Marquisats · R de la Providence · Q de la Tournette

Av Lucien Boschetti · Annecy Hostel (300m) · Av du Crêt du Maure · Forêt du Crêt du Maure (2.5km) · Plage des Marquisats (400m); Sévrier (4.5km)

Canoë-Kayak Club d'Annecy (250m); Société des Régates à Voile d'Annecy (250m);

Today Annecy's most visible landmark hosts exhibits on local architecture and history.

Château d'Annecy
CASTLE

(www.musees.agglo-annecy.fr; rampe du Château; adult/child €5.20/2.60; ⊙10am–noon & 2-5pm Wed-Mon Oct-May, 10.30am-6pm daily Jun-Sep) Rising dramatically above the old town, this 13th- to 16th-century castle was once home to the Counts of Geneva. The exhibits inside are diverse, ranging from medieval sculpture and Savoyard furniture to Alpine landscape painting and contemporary art, with a section on the natural history of Lac d'Annecy. English signage is planned for 2015.

🏃 Activities

Sunbathing & Swimming

When the sun's out, the beaches fringing the lake beckon.

Plage d'Annecy-le-Vieux
BEACH

(⊙lifeguard present Jul-Aug) **FREE** If you feel like diving straight into those crystal-clear waters, head to this public beach, 1km northeast of the Champ de Mars.

Plage Impérial
BEACH

(adult/child €4/2.50; ⊙lifeguard present Jun-Aug) About 700m northeast of the Champ de Mars, this pebbly beach is next to the elegant pre-WWI Impérial Casino.

Plage des Marquisats
BEACH

(⊙lifeguard present Jul-Aug) **FREE** A pebble beach is 1km southeast of town along rue des Marquisats.

Piscine des Marquisats
SWIMMING

(29 rue des Marquisats; adult/child €4.30/3.30; ⊙10am-7pm May–early Sep) This trio of city-run outdoor swimming pools is 600m southeast of the centre, near the lakefront.

Annecy

FRENCH ALPS & THE JURA MOUNTAINS ANNECY

Walking

From Jardins de l'Europe, you can amble along the lakefront northeast towards **Annecy-le-Vieux** and southeast to **Esplanade des Marquisats** and beyond. Annecy's commercial centre is a few blocks north of the Canal du Thiou, around rue Royale.

Forêt du Crêt du Maure, about 3km due south of Annecy, has plenty of walking trails, as do the wildlife-rich wetlands of **Bout du Lac**, 20km from Annecy on the lake's southern tip, and the **Roc de Chère** nature reserve, 10km away on the eastern shore.

The tourist office sells walking maps, including IGN's *Lac d'Annecy* (€10.80).

Cycling & Blading

Biking and blading are big, with 46km of cycling tracks encircling the lake (there's a gap on the eastern short between Menthon and Perroix) and another gentle path, once a railway grade, leading all the way to Albertville, 44km to the southeast. Area tourist offices have free maps.

Roll'n Cy   BLADING
(✆ 06 28 34 66 34; www.roll-n-cy.org; ⊙8pm Fri except during rain) Strap on your skates for the weekly group rides organised by this local rollerblading club. The meeting point is in front of the Mairie (Town Hall) at place de l'Hôtel de Ville. Call for updates from 7pm on Friday evening.

Roul' ma Poule   CYCLING, BLADING
(✆0450278683; www.annecy-location-velo.com; 4 rue des Marquisats; ⊙9.30am-7pm) Rents rollerblades (€13/19 per half/full day), bicycles (€14/20), tandems (€27/39) and *trottinettes*

(scooters; €8/12). Can recommend day trips in the area.

Cyclable   CYCLING
(✆ 04 50 51 51 50; www.cyclable.com; 8 place aux Bois; ⊙9.30am-1pm & 2-7pm Mar-Sep, no midday closure Jul & Aug, closed Oct-Feb) Rents city bikes (€10/20 for two hours/all day), kids' bikes (€5/15), electric bikes (€20/40) and trailers (€10/20). Helmets, baskets and kids' seats are free.

Water Sports

The most relaxed way to see the lake is from the water. From sometime in March to October, pedal boats/motorboats can be hired for €15/50 per hour along the waterfront, at or near Jardins de l'Europe.

Canoë-Kayak Club d'Annecy   KAYAKING
(www.kayak-annecy.com; 33 rue des Marquisats, Base Nautique) Offers kayaking courses.

Société des Régates
à Voile d'Annecy   SAILING
(www.srva.info; 31 rue des Marquisats, Base Nautique; ⊙May-Oct) Rents sailboats starting at €41 for two hours; windsurfers are €27.

Adventure Sports

The tourist office has details on a host of adventure-sports companies around Lake Annecy

Takamaka   OUTDOOR ACTIVITIES
(www.takamaka.fr; 23 rue du Faubourg Ste-Claire; ⊙9am-noon & 2-6pm Mon-Fri, 10am-6pm Sat) Offers a wide range of outdoor adventures with licensed guides, including tandem paragliding (€90), rafting (€44), rock climbing (€39),

mountain bike freeriding (€59) and canyoning (€49 for a half-day).

 Tours

For a self-guided stroll around town, pick up the *Annecy Town Walks* leaflet at the tourist office.

Compagnie des Bateaux   BOAT TOUR
(www.annecy-croisieres.com; 2 place aux Bois; 1hr lake cruises adult/child €14/9.50; ☉ mid-Feb–mid-Dec) Runs boat excursions and, from mid-April to late September, cruises to villages around the lake. Also has romantic dinner cruises (€58.50).

✯ Festivals & Events

Annecy celebrates the flamboyant **Venetian Carnival** in February (two weeks after its namesake in Venice, Italy); the **Fête du Lac**, with fireworks over the lake, on the first Saturday in August; and **Le Retour des Alpages**, when the cows come home from the Alpine pastures, wreathed in flowers and bells, on the first Saturday in October. Street performers wow evening crowds at **Les Noctibules** in July.

🛏 Sleeping

If you're planning to visit Annecy in July or August, booking well ahead is highly recommended. High-season prices (quoted here) generally run from June to September; rooms are cheapest from November to March.

The tourist office has details on hotels, *chambres d'hôte* (B&Bs) and campgrounds around the lake; check out its website for real-time room availability. For a same-night room, drop by the tourist office, which almost always manages to come up with last-minute openings.

Annecy Hostel   HOSTEL €
(☏ 09 53 12 02 90; www.annecyhostel.com; 32 av de Loverchy; dm from €22, d €54; @ ☜) Run by two well-travelled brothers, this friendly, 55-bed hostel has bright, funky dorm rooms with four to six beds, two shared kitchens, a TV lounge, bike rental (per day €12) and a back garden – perfect for summer barbecues and meeting people – with table tennis, a pool table and chickens. It's in a nondescript area about 800m southwest of the centre.

Hôtel des Alpes   HOTEL €
(☏ 04 50 45 04 56; www.hotelannecy.com; 12 rue de la Poste; s/d/tr/q €75/85/104/114; ☜) Near the train station, this hotel has 32 well-lit rooms

with light-coloured natural wood walls, plum-coloured carpets, squeaky-clean bathrooms and brand-new noiseproof windows.

Hôtel du Palais de l'Isle   HISTORIC HOTEL €€
(☏ 04 50 45 86 87; www.palaisannecy.com; 13 rue Perrière; s/d €85/128; ✳ ☜) In an 18th-century building right in the centre of the old town, this hotel has crisp contemporary decor and 34 minibar-equipped rooms with views of the Palais, the castle or the old town's rooftops. Situated on a pedestrianised street – but car access to drop off your bags is permitted.

Splendid Hôtel   BOUTIQUE HOTEL €€
(☏ 04 50 45 20 00; www.hotel-annecy-lac.fr; 4 quai Eustache Chappuis; s/d from €123/137; ✳ @ ☜) This aptly named hotel, with green, breezy views of the adjacent Champ de Mars, has 47 classy, contemporary rooms with parquet floors. It's geared up for families: whether you need an extra bed or a babysitter, the friendly staff will oblige.

Hôtel du Château   HOTEL €
(☏ 04 50 45 27 66; www.annecy-hotel.com; 16 rampe du Château; s/d/tr/q €59/75/95/110; ☜) Just across the square from the château, this family-run hotel has a sun-drenched, panoramic breakfast terrace and 16 smallish, sweet rooms with rustic pine furniture and pastel walls; four have lovely lake views. To get there by car, follow the signs to the Château d'Annecy and call the hotel from the barrier.

Hôtel Alexandra   HOTEL €€
(☏ 04 50 52 84 33; www.hotelannecy-alexandra.fr; 19 rue Vaugelas; s/d/tr/q €65/90/95/105; ☜) The 25 smallish rooms, each unique, are sparely furnished but they're soundproofed and spotless and the welcome here is warm. Six rooms have balconies and a couple come with canal views.

Le Pré Carré   HOTEL €€€
(☏ 04 50 52 14 14; www.hotel-annecy.net; 27 rue Sommeiller; s/d from €190/220; ✳ @ ☜) This eight-storey hotel keeps things contemporary with 29 spacious, subdued, business-efficient rooms, almost all with a balcony or terrace. Amenities include a Jacuzzi, a sauna and a business corner.

 Eating

Annecy has a fine selection of French and Savoyard restaurants. Places to dine are many and varied along the quays on both sides of the Canal du Thiou; on rue de l'Île, rue Ste-Claire and rue Faubourg Ste-Claire, south of the canal; and on rue du Pâquier, north of the canal.

Food Market   MARKET €
(cnr rue Ste-Claire & rue de la République; ⊘ 7am-1am Sun, Tue & Fri) Great for picnic fixin's.

L'Esquisse   GASTRONOMIC €€
(📵 04 50 44 80 59; www.esquisse-annecy.fr; 21 rue Royale; lunch menu €23, other menus €31-60; ⊘ 12.15-1.15pm & 7.30-9pm, closed Wed & Sun) A talented husband-and-wife team runs the show at this intimate restaurant, with just seven tables. Their passion shines through in the service, wine list and carefully composed *menus* that sing with natural flavours, from wild mushrooms to – well, it depends on the season. Reserve ahead.

Le Denti   FRENCH €€
(📵 04 50 64 21 17; 25bis av de Loverchy; lunch menu €17, other menus €20-41; ⊘ noon-1.15pm & 7.30-9pm, closed Sun dinner, Tue & Wed) A few blocks off the beaten track but worth seeking out, this unassuming restaurant serves traditional French cuisine – their speciality is fish – prepared so the taste of the super-fresh ingredients shines through. The *menu* changes twice a month according to the seasonal produce available in the markets.

L'Étage   SAVOYARD €€
(📵 04 50 51 03 28; www.letageannecy.com; 13 rue du Pâquier; lunch menus €13-16.50, other menus €19-35; ⊘ noon-2pm & 7-10.30pm) Feast on local cheeses, in the form of fondue or *raclette* (melted cheese, boiled potatoes, charcuterie and baby gherkins), or French-style meat and fish dishes (eg steak with 'café de Paris' butter sauce) in a building from the 1600s. Mellow music and the cheerful staff keep the ambience relaxed.

La Cuisine des Amis   FUSION €€
(📵 04 50 10 10 80; www.lacuisinedesamisannecy.fr; 9 rue du Pâquier; mains €14.50-27.50, 2-course menu €15; ⊘ noon-2pm & 7-10.30pm daily, closed dinner Sun & Mon Oct-May; 🖼) Welcoming clients like old *amis* (friends), this grey-and-mirror-walled bistro serves meat and fish with a creative, international twist. Specialities range from chicken sukiyaki to Moroccan couscous to the house favourite, Moroccan-style *pastilla* (crisp puff pastry pie filled with goat's-milk cheese, almonds, apricots and honey).

La Ciboulette   GASTRONOMIC €€€
(📵 04 50 45 74 57; www.laciboulette-annecy.com; passage du Pré Carré; menus €36-70; ⊘ lunch & dinner Tue-Sat) Crisp white linen sets the scene at this elegant restaurant, where chef

Georges Paccard prepares fresh seasonal specialities such as fillet of veal in a nut crust with cream of *vin jaune* (Jura wine). Reservations are highly recommended on weekends and for dinner. Situated down the alley from 8 rue Vaugelas.

🍷 Drinking & Nightlife

Nights here are more about people-watching over relaxed drinks than raving it up.

The Place to Beer   BAR
(18 rue du Faubourg Ste-Claire; 25cL beer €3-5.25; ⊘ 4-11pm Tue-Thu, to 1am or 2am Fri & Sat) Opened in 2014, this laid-back, high-tech establishment serves beer like petrol stations sell gasoline: you only pay for what you pump. After buying credit on a computerised magnetic card, you can drink as much or as little of the 12 brews on offer as you like – a fantastic way to compare and savour lots of microbrews side by side.

Les Caves du Château   WINE BAR
(6 rampe du Château; ⊘ 5pm-2am) A sweet little wine bar at the foot of the castle, with an excellent array of wines by the glass (€4 to €6.50), plates of cheese and charcuterie (€9.50 to €16), and a decked terrace for watching the world go by.

ℹ Information

Post Office (1 rue de la Poste)

Tourist Office (📵 04 50 45 00 33; www.lac-annecy.com; 1 rue Jean Jaurès, courtyard of Centre Bonlieu; ⊘ 9am-12.30pm & 1.45-6pm Mon-Sat year-round, 9am-12.30pm Sun Apr early Oct & Dec, also open 1.45-6pm Sun mid-May–mid-Sep) Has free maps and brochures, and details on cultural activities all around the lake.

ℹ Getting There & Away

BUS

The ticket office for the **bus station** (Gare Routière; rue de l'Industrie) is inside the new train station.

Voyages Crolard (📵 04 50 45 08 12; www.voyages-crolard.com) sends buses (every hour or two Monday to Saturday, fewer or none on Sunday) to villages around Lac d'Annecy, including Veyrier-du-Lac (€1.50, 15 minutes) and Talloires (€1.50, 30 minutes), as well as to the ski resorts of La Clusaz (€8, 45 minutes), Le Grand-Bornand (€8, one hour) and Albertville (1½ hours). The company also has a service to Lyon's St-Exupéry airport (one-way/return €36/54, 2¼ hours, four to six daily).

WORTH A TRIP

LAKESIDE LEGENDS

Dining and staying at some of Lac d'Annecy's legendary hostelries requires a healthy appetite and a robust bank balance. For a room in summer, reserve a month or more ahead.

La Nouvelle Maison de Marc Veyrat (☑04 50 09 97 49; www.yoann-conte.com; 13 Vieille rte des Pensières, Veyrier-du-Lac; menus lunch €70-198, dinner €169-198, d €325-575; ⊙noon-1.30pm Wed-Sun & 7-9pm Tue-Sun year-round, also open dinner Mon Jun-Aug) French celebrity chef Marc Veyrat has handed over his stove, culinary flamboyance and signature use of wild herbs and flowers to his capable successor Yoann Conte. The baby-blue house on the lake also has eight wonderful rooms with magnificent views. For a table, reserve a week ahead on holidays, for Saturday dinner and from June to early September; the rest of the time, call the day before or even the morning of.

Situated in Veyrier-du-Lac, a village across the lake from Annecy (6km by road). To get there by car from Annecy, follow the signs from the first roundabout you come to in Veyrier-du-Lac.

Auberge du Père Bise (☑04 50 60 72 01; www.perebise.com; 303 rte du Port, Talloires; menus €82-180, d from €330; ⊙12.30-2pm & 7.30-9pm, closed Tue, Wed & mid Dec–early Feb, open daily except lunch Tue Jun-Sep) Whether alfresco on the gorgeous lakeshore in summer or in the classically elegant salon in winter, dining here is never less than extraordinary. Chefs Sophie Bise and Christof Ledigol allow the clean flavours and freshness of local produce to shine in signature dishes such as lighly smoked *féra* (broad whitefish from Lac d'Annecy) with foie gras, Granny Smith apples and wasabi. For dinner on Friday and Saturday (daily from June to September), make reservations a week ahead.

Tea, coffee, pastries and sandwiches are served from 3pm to 6pm – no need to reserve. Situated in Talloires, 12km southeast of Annecy; follow the signs to 'Port-Plage'.

Autocars Frossard (☑04 50 45 73 90; www.frossard.eu) handles services to Geneva's bus station (lines T72 and T73; €10.50, 1½ hours, 15 daily Monday to Friday, six to eight Saturday and Sunday), Thonon-les-Bains (€14, two hours, twice daily Monday to Friday) and Évian-les-Bains (€14, 2½ hours, twice daily Monday to Friday).

TRAIN

Direct services from Annecy's new train station (place de la Gare), opened in 2012, include:

Aix-les-Bains €8.10, 40 minutes, hourly

Chambéry €10.30, 50 minutes, hourly

Lyon Gare de la Part-Dieu €26 to €50, two hours, 13 daily Monday to Friday, eight daily Saturday and Sunday

Paris Gare de Lyon €80 to €101, 3¾ hours, four to seven daily

St-Gervais-Le Fayet (for Chamonix) €15.30, 1½ hours, five daily Sunday to Friday, three Saturday

ℹ️ Getting Around

Bicycles can be hired from city-run **Vélonecy** (☑04 50 51 38 90; www.velonecy.com; place de la Gare; ⊙9am-1pm & 2-6pm Mon-Sat), at the train station, for €15 per day (including a helmet); the deposit is €250. If you just arrived or are about to depart by train, the fee is only €5. In July and August reserve two or three days ahead. Staff can supply you with a bike path map.

Around Annecy

On warm summer days the villages of **Sévrier**, 5km south on Lac d'Annecy's western shore, and **Menthon-St-Bernard**, 8.5km southeast on the lake's eastern shore, make good day trips. South of Menthon, **Talloires** is the most exclusive lakeside spot. All have wonderful beaches.

In winter, ski-keen Annéciens – including families – head for the cross-country slopes of Semnoz (elevation 1700m; www.semnoz.fr), 18km south; or the downhill stations of La Clusaz (elevation 1100m; www.laclusaz.com), 32km east, and Le Grand Bornand (elevation 1000m; www.legrandbornand.com), 34km northeast.

Chambéry

POP 56,500 / ELEV 270M

The château town of Chambéry has a lot going for it: a strategic location at the crossroads of the main Alpine valleys, a scenic setting near Lac du Bourget (12km north), two regional parks and a rich heritage left by French, Italian and Savoy rule. Surprisingly, the city receives a mere trickle of tourists, but those who do come are rewarded with crowd-free museums, lively cafes and back-in-time strolls along arcaded streets.

Chambéry was Savoy's capital from the 13th century until 1563, when the dukes of Savoy shifted their base of operations to Turin in Italy.

⊙ Sights

★Ville Ancienne   HISTORIC QUARTER

Chambéry has one of the best-preserved medieval old towns this side of the Alps. Its hidden courtyards, cafe-rimmed squares and lanes flanked by tall, shuttered townhouses are great for an aimless amble. Streets worth wandering include tiny **rue du Sénat de Savoie**, cobbled **rue Juiverie** and gallery-dotted **rue de la Métropole**. For a gorgeous perspective in every direction, stand at the intersection of arcaded **rue de Boigne** and long, handsome **place St-Léger**.

Once home to local aristocrats, **rue de la Croix d'Or** hides the Hôtel du Châteauneuf's rose-draped courtyard, with intricate wrought-iron grilles affording fine views of the castle. Winding to the base of the château's massive walls, 14th-century **rue Basse-du-Château** is most atmospheric when the afternoon sun warms its caramel-coloured façades.

Fontaine des Éléphants   FOUNTAIN

(place des Éléphants) With its four intricately carved elephants, this fountain looks like the model for an old Indian postage stamp. It was sculpted in 1838 in honour of Général de Boigne (pronounced *bwan'y*; 1751–1830), who made his fortune in the East Indies. When he returned home he bestowed some of his wealth on the town and was honoured posthumously with this monument. The genteel arcaded street that leads from the fountain to Château des Ducs de Savoie, **rue de Boigne**, is one of his projects.

Château des Ducs de Savoie   CASTLE

(☑ 04 79 70 15 94; place du Château; guided tour adult/child €6/4.50; ⊙ gardens 9am-6pm Mon-Fri, plus Sat & Sun Jul & Aug, tours 2.30pm Tue-Sun May-Sep, 2.30pm Sat & Sun Oct-Apr, exhibition 9am-noon & 1.30-6pm Tue-Fri, 10.30am-6pm Sat & Sun, closed Jan–mid-Feb) This forbidding medieval castle, once home to the counts and dukes of Savoy, now houses the Préfecture and Con-

seil Général of the Savoie *département*. The **gardens** and the **Cour d'Honneur** (courtyard) are open free of charge, but to see the 14th- and 15th-century **Tour Trésorerie** (Treasury Tower) and the stained glass inside the **Sainte-Chapelle**, built in the 15th century to house the Shroud of Turin, you have to take a tour.

Guided tours begin at the château's Acceuil des Guides office in July and August and at the old town's **Hôtel de Condon** (71 rue St-Réal), around the corner from the cathedral, the rest of the year.

In the small exhibition, scale models, engravings and paintings present the history and architecture of the château.

The chapel's 70-bell **Grand Carillon** (1993), one of the largest ensembles of bells in the world, peals in concert on the first and third Saturday of each month at 5.30pm (more frequently in summer).

Musée des Beaux-Arts   ART MUSEUM

(http://musees.chambery.fr; place du Palais de Justice; special exhibitions adult/child €3/1.50, ⊙ 10am-noon & 2-6pm Wed-Mon) **FREE** Occupying a former corn exchange, the light-flooded top-floor gallery showcases 14th- to 18th-century Italian works, with an emphasis on Florentine and Sienese paintings from the Renaissance and dramatic landscapes of Chambéry and the Alps painted from 1799 to 1975. Signs are in French.

Cathédrale St-François de Sales   CATHEDRAL

(place de la Métropole; ⊙ 8.45am-noon & 2-5pm Mon-Sat, 9.15am-noon & 3-7pm Sun except during Mass) Built as a Franciscan chapel in the 15th century, Chambéry's cathedral hides some surprises, including Europe's largest assemblage (occupying some 6000 sq metres) of *trompe l'œil* Gothic vaulting, painted by artists Sevesi and Vicario, and a 35m-long maze dating from the mid-19th century.

Musée Savoisien   MUSEUM

(www.musee-savoisien.fr; sq de Lannoy de Bissy; ⊙ 10am-noon & 2-6pm Wed-Mon) Housed in a Franciscan monastery linked to the cathedral by cloisters, this museum showcases the turbulent history, rich culture and diverse ethnography of Savoy. Closed for major renovations until 2017.

Musée des Charmettes   HISTORIC BUILDING

(www.chambery.fr/musees; 890 chemin des Charmettes; audioguide €1; ⊙ 10am-noon & 2-6pm Wed-Mon) **FREE** Geneva-born philosopher,

CHÂTEAU DE MENTHON-ST-BERNARD

The thousand-year-old **Château de Menthon-St-Bernard** (www.chateau-de-menthon. com; Menthon-St-Bernard; guided tours adult/child €8.50/4; ⊙ 2pm-6pm Fri-Sun May, June & Sep, noon-6pm daily Jul & Aug) – one of the inspirations for Walt Disney's *Sleeping Beauty* castle (so they say) – was birthplace of St Bernard in 1008. Tours of the medieval interior – courtesy of the 23rd generation of de Menthons to live here – take in tapestry-adorned salons and a magnificent library, but it's the sparkling Lac d'Annecy panorama that leaves many visitors speechless. Situated 8.5km southeast of Annecy.

composer and writer Jean-Jacques Rousseau, a key figure of the Enlightenment and the French Revolution, lived with his lover, Baronne Louise Éléonore de Warens, at this charming late 17th-century country house from 1736 to 1742. His passion for botany lives on in the peaceful garden, filled with medicinal herbs, aromatic flowers and heritage fruit trees and vines. Situated a walkable 2km southeast of the centre along scenic chemin des Charmettes.

🛏 Sleeping

Chambéry's hotels cater mainly to business travellers so are fullest from Monday to Thursday. Because of rising real estate prices, just two hotels are left in the old town. The Chambéry area has quite a few appealing *chambres d'hôte* and self-catering studios – the tourist office has details.

Art Hôtel
HOTEL €

(☑ 04 79 62 37 26; www.arthotel-chambery.com; 154 rue Sommeiller; d €60-72, tr €82; 🛜) There's nothing artistic about this hotel – you pass through a concrete façade, adorned with ripped flags, to get to 36 ordinary (though superbly soundproofed) rooms. That said, it *is* well run, cheap and convenient. Situated 200m south of the train station and 500m north of the centre of town.

Hôtel des Princes
HOTEL €€

(☑ 04 79 33 45 36; www.hoteldesprinces.com; 8 rue de Boigne; s/d/tr/q from €85/95/120/140) The Shroud of Turin was once repaired in the late 15th-century convent that now houses this elegant, traditional hotel, situated right in the centre of the old town. Most of the 45 rooms, renovated in 2013, are of medium size and modern styling; the top floor has smallish chalet-style rooms. Room 11 (€190) is ideal for a family of five.

La Ferme du Petit Bonheur
B&B €€

(☑ 04 79 85 26 17; www.fermedupetitbonheur.fr; 538 chemin Jean-Jacques; s/d/tr/q incl breakfast €90/98/118/138) On a suburban hillside high above town, this vine-clad farmhouse has four homey, chalet-inspired rooms, a flowery garden (in summer) and a wood-burning stove in the salon (in winter). Personal touches abound – breakfast includes local cheeses and homemade croissants and jams. Situated southeast of central Chambéry, 3km by car (follow the signs for Les Charmettes) and about 2km on foot from the old town – and 1.2km up the hill from Musée des Charmettes.

★ Petit Hôtel Confidentiel
BOUTIQUE HOTEL €€€

(☑ 04 79 26 24 17; www.petithotelconfidentiel.com; 10 rue de la Trésorerie; ste €170-300) Ideal for a romantic getaway, this gem is sophisticated and cosy, with 11 huge suites (typically 55 sq metres) whose cutting-edge design offers a combination of comfort, elegance and style. Most come with two-person bathtubs and modern ethanol fireplaces. It's near the western tip of the pedestrianised part of the old town.

🍴 Eating

Pedestrian **rue du Sénat de Savoie**, which heads south from the covered market, is the place to find the butcher, the baker and the chocolate maker – and the *traiteur* (deli). Some of the many restaurants around **place Monge** serve Savoyard treats such as fondue and *tartifflete* (potatoes, cheese and bacon baked in a casserole). For cheap eats, head to **rue de la République**.

À l'Herboristerie
VEGETARIAN €

(Café Botanique; ☑ 04 79 75 62 65; www.dela botanique.com; 193 rue Croix d'Or; mains €12; ⊙ noon-2pm Tue-Sat; 🍴) This gloriously old-fashioned herbalist's shop does a brisk trade in medicinal plants and herbal teas, many from the Alps, while the lunch-only restaurant next door serves up wholesome salads, ravioli and quiches, some made with wild plants and mushrooms. The *menu* changes daily. The tearoom behind the shop is often open until 7pm. Situated at the southeastern end of place St-Léger.

Laiterie des Halles CHEESE SHOP €
(2 place de Genève; ⊙9am-noon & 3-7pm Tue-Fri, 8am-12.30pm & 2-7pm Sat) Specialises in cheeses from the Alps and the Jura – look for Reblochon, Tome des Bauges, Comté, Beaufort, Grand Colombier, Bleu de Termignon and Persillé de Tignes. Situated across the square from Marché des Halles.

Marché des Halles FOOD MARKET €
(Covered Market; place de Genève; ⊙7am-noon Tue, Wed, Fri & Sat) Brims with charcuterie, cheese, pastries and fresh produce.

Les Halles FRENCH €€
(✆04 79 60 01 95; www.restaurant-les-halles-chambery.com; 15 rue Bonivard; lunch menus €14-18, other menus €26-35; ⊙noon-2pm & 7-10pm Tue-Sat; ✋) This ordinary looking bistro, beloved by locals, combines gourmet panache with a warm welcome and faultless service. Try regional specialities like chicken stuffed with *diots* (Savoyard sausages) and creamy Beaufort polenta, saving room for *fondant au chocolat* with pecan ice cream. Situated in the old town behind the market hall.

Brasserie Le Z INTERNATIONAL €€
(✆04 79 85 96 87; www.brasserielez.fr; 12 av des Ducs de Savoie; lunch/dinner menus €16.50/28; ⊙9am-3pm & 7pm-midnight; ✋) A sleek and contemporary brasserie with an open, stainless-steel kitchen and a wine bar. The *menu* is a refreshing break from the norm, with specialities such as the Mac Zo (a hamburger with foie gras and fillet of duck), *risotto de homard* (lobster risotto) and cod breaded with corn flakes. Serves Sunday brunch from 11am to 2pm. Situated three short blocks north of the Fontaine des Éléphants.

L'Atelier FRENCH €€
(✆04 79 70 62 39; www.atelier-chambery.com; 59 rue de la République; lunch menu €21, other menus €32-40; ⊙noon-2.30pm & 7-10pm Tue-Sat) Soft light, mellow music and a vaulted brick ceiling set the scene in this contemporary French restaurant and wine bar. The market-fresh *menu* changes daily, and so do the five whites, five reds and two rosés served by the glass. Has a terrace for alfresco dining.

🍷 Drinking & Nightlife

In the warm months, the old town's public squares, including place St-Léger, fill with cafe tables.

WINE & CHEESE ROUTES

Savoy has three **Circuits des Vignobles de Savoie** (wine routes; www.vindesavoie.net): **Cluse de Chambéry & Combe de Savoie** (www.vignobles.coeurdesavoie.fr), a few kilometres southeast of Chambéry, **Chautagne & Jongieux**, around and north of Lac du Bourget; and **Léman & Arves**, around and southwest of Thonon-les-Bains.

Savoy is famous for producing seven major cheeses: Abondance, Beaufort, Chevrotin, Emmental de Savoie, Reblochon de Savoie, Tome des Bauges and Tomme de Savoie. You can visit over 50 small-scale cheesemakers, many of them in the hills east of Lac d'Annecy, on the region's **Itinéraires des Fromages de Savoie** (cheese routes; www.fromagesdesavoie.fr).

O'Cardinal's PUB
(www.ocardinals.com; 5 place de la Métropole; ⊙3.30pm-1.30am Mon, 10.30am-1.30am Tue-Sat, 3.30pm-midnight Sun) Leather banquettes, chipper staff, a great vibe, a dozen beers on tap (€2.40 to €5.70) and decent pub grub (from noon to 2pm) have turned this Irish-style establishment into a student favourite, though it's popular with people of all ages. On warm days the cheer spills out onto square. Situated facing the cathedral's west front.

ℹ Information

Maison des Parcs et de la Montagne (http://maisondesparcs.chambery.fr; 256 rue de la République; ⊙9.30am-12.30pm & 1.30-6pm Tue-Sat) Has information and exhibits on Lac du Bourget and three nearby national/regional parks: La Vanoise, Les Bauges and La Chartreuse. Situated half a block east of the southeast corner of the old town.

Tourist Office (✆04 79 33 42 47; www.chambery-tourisme.com; 5bis place du Palais de Justice; ⊙9am-12.30pm & 2-6pm Mon-Sat, also 10am-1pm Sun Jul & Aug) Can supply English brochures and details on Savoy's cheese and wine routes, and arranges guided old-town tours (in English in July and August), some at night. Staff are happy to help with room reservations (no charge). It's situated just northwest of the old town, 300m south of the train station.

ℹ Getting There & Away

AIR
Chambéry-Savoie Airport (www.chambery-airport.com), 10km north of Chambéry at the southern tip of Lac du Bourget, has seasonal flights (mainly December to April) to various British regional airports.

BUS
While the train station is being renovated, the bus station will be at place Paul Vidal, 300m southwest of the train station. It's supposed to return to place de la Gare in late 2016.

From late June to early September, the Ligne des Plages bus goes to Aix-les-Bains (50 minutes) via the beaches along Lac du Bourget.

TRAIN
Chambéry's **train station** (place de la Gare) will be undergoing a complete renovation through 2016. In the city centre, tickets are available at the **SNCF Boutique** (21 place St-Léger). Direct services include:

Annecy €10.20, 50 minutes, hourly

Geneva €17.70, 1¼ hours, four to six daily

Grenoble €11.90, one hour, at least hourly

Lyon (Part-Dieu) €18.40, 1½ hours, almost hourly

Paris Gare de Lyon €78 to €100, three hours, 10 daily Monday to Friday, seven Saturday, four Sunday

ℹ Getting Around

TO/FROM THE AIRPORT
Buses link the airport with various Alpine ski stations but not, unfortunately, with Chambéry's town centre. The 15-minute journey by taxi costs around €20 – call **Allo Taxi Chambéry** (☑ 04 79 69 11 12).

Voyages Crolard (☑ 04 79 69 11 88; www.voyages-crolard.com) has buses linking Chambéry with Lyon's St-Exupéry airport (one-way/return €24/36, one hour, four to six daily). **Aérocar** (www.aerocar.fr) buses go to/from Geneva airport (one-way/return €33.50/41.50, one hour, five daily).

BICYCLE
City-run **Vélostation** (www.velostation-chambery.fr; Jardin du Verney; bike rental per hour/day €1/5; ⊙ 8am-7pm Mon-Fri, 8am-noon & 2-7pm Sat, also open Sun Apr-Oct) rents out seven-speed city bikes. It will be based next to the bus station (300m southwest of the train station) until late 2016, when it will move back to the train station. The greater Chambéry area has 80km of cycling lanes; staff can supply a map.

CAR & MOTORCYCLE
Driving in the old town, with its many one-ways and barrier-blocked pedestrian zones, can be a headache. The city centre has nine municipal parking lots, but for free parking you have to head to the outskirts of town, where there are three free P+R lots linked to the centre by bus; the biggest is in Chambéry-Sonnaz on the D991.

Around Chambéry

Parc Naturel Régional de Chartreuse

The **Chartreuse Regional Nature Park** (www.parc-chartreuse.net) encompasses the wild, forested slopes of the Chartreuse massif, dubbed the 'desert' by monks of the Carthusian Order who settled here in 1084. Today the **Grande Chartreuse monastery** is home to some 30 monks who have taken a vow of silence. It is off-limits to visitors, but you can see it from above by hiking to the summit of 1867m **Charmant Som**; follow the signs for 'Col de Porte' on the D512. Or you can check out *Into Great Silence,* an almost-silent film about the monastery that came out in 2007.

The **park headquarters** (☑ 04 76 88 75 20) in St-Pierre de Chartreuse, 40km southwest of Chambéry, has information on visiting the distillery where Chartreuse liqueur is produced, and **Musée de la Grande Chartreuse** (www.musee-grande-chartreuse.fr; La Correrie, St-Pierre de Chartreuse; adult/child €8.50/3.90; ⊙ 10am-6.30pm May-Sep, 1.30-6pm Mon-Fri & 10am-6pm Sat & Sun Apr & Oct), which explores the monastery's 930-year history and the monks' reclusive lifestyle.

Parc Naturel Régional du Massif des Bauges

Hiking and biking enthusiasts can explore 900 sq km of wilderness in the little-known **Massif des Bauges Regional Nature Park** (www.parcdesbauges.com), in the hills northeast of Chambéry, with its seemingly endless pastures and plateaux. Several marked trails set out from the **Maison Faune-Flore** (adult/child €2.50/1.50; ⊙ 2-6pm Wed & Sun mid-Feb–mid-Mar & mid-Apr–Sep, also open Tue & Thu-Sat & 10am-1pm late Jun-Aug) in École, where you can learn how to spot some of the many hundreds of chamois and mouflons inhabiting the park.

Chambéry's favourite weekend retreat for a little snow action is nearby **Savoie Grand Révard** (www.savoiegrandrevard.com). Downhill

CHARTREUSE: THE MONASTIC LIQUEUR

Either acid green or radioactive yellow, Chartreuse may be the brightest, most shockingly hued herbal elixir of the cocktail and digestif world. Mixologists sing its praises and in ski resorts it adds a splash of Alpine fire to hot chocolate in Green Chaud. Its surge in global popularity over the past decade might have something to do with it being hailed as 'the only liqueur so good they named a colour after it' in Quentin Tarantino's 2007 thriller *Death Proof*. It certainly isn't because the Carthusian monks who make it have been brashly broadcasting its wonders, for this is a liqueur shrouded in secrecy and silence.

The production of Chartreuse began in 1737 and, at first, it was intended as a medicine. The green version, whose 250th anniversary was feted in 2014 (see www.chartreuseverte 250.com), is produced by macerating 130 hard-to-find mountain herbs, roots and plants in alcohol and leaving the mixture to age in oak casks.

Today, Chartreuse's exact ingredients remain a closely guarded secret, and word has it only two monks know the recipe. Perhaps closest to the original is the Elixir Végétal (69% alcohol), sold as a tonic, but potent, spicy, chlorophyll-rich Chartreuse Green (55% alcohol) and milder, sweeter Chartreuse Yellow (40% alcohol) are much better known. You can taste these otherworldly liqueurs, bone up on their history and tour barrel-lined cellars at the **Caves de la Chartreuse** (www.chartreuse.fr; 10 bd Edgar-Kofler, Voiron; ⊗9am-11.30am & 2-6.30pm daily) FREE distillery, 45km southwest of Chambéry.

---

skiing is limited to 50km of downhill pistes, but cross-country skiing is superb, with 150km of trails to explore, as is snowshoeing, with 60km of marked itineraries. For more information, contact the ski station tourist office in **La Féclaz** (☑04 79 25 80 49), 21km northeast of Chambéry, or the area's main tourist office in **Le Châtelard** (☑04 79 54 84 28; www.lesbauges.com), 36km northeast of Chambéry.

From mid-December to mid-March, bus C8 (www.mobisavoie.fr) makes it possible to travel from Chambéry up to La Féclaz (45 minutes) to ski for the day.

Aix-les-Bains

POP 26,800 / ELEV 234M

With its leafy shores, grand casino and historic villas, Aix-les-Bains (*eks*-ley-bah), a small thermal spa 17km north of Chambéry, exudes an air of discreet gentility. Come to stroll, pedal, skate, sail, row or swim around France's largest natural lake, **Lac du Bourget**. The town centre is about 2.5km east of the lakeshore.

For details on what to see and do, including lake cruises to the 12th-century **Abbaye d'Hautecombe** on the other side of the lake, see the **tourist office** (☑04 79 88 68 00; www. aixlesbains.com; place Maurice Mollard; ⊗9am-12.30pm & 2-6.30pm Mon-Sat, also Sun Apr-Oct).

Aix-les-Bains is linked by train and SNCF bus (once or twice an hour) with Annecy (€8.10, 30 to 45 minutes) and Chambéry (€3.50, 11 to 23 minutes).

Albertville

POP 19,000 / ELEV 328M

The main claim to fame of Albertville, an otherwise uninspiring town 52km east of Chambéry, is that it hosted the 1992 Winter Olympics. The highs and lows are colourfully retold at the **Maison des Jeux Olympiques d'Hiver** (www.maisonjeuxolympiques-albertville.org; 11 rue Pargoud; adult/child €4/free; ⊗2-6pm Mon, 10am-noon & 2-6pm Tue-Sat).

Les Trois Vallées

This is the big one you've heard all about: vast, fast and the largest ski area in the world. The snow has never been hotter than in Les Trois Vallées. Some 600km of pistes and an unbelievable 170 lifts zip across eight resorts spread over three parallel valleys. Among these are **Val Thorens**, Europe's highest at a heady 2300m; wealthy and ever-so-British **Méribel** (elevation 1450m), founded by Scotsman Colonel Peter Lindsay in 1938; and playground of the super-rich **Courchevel**, which stretches over three purpose-built resorts at 1550m, 1650m and 1850m and is a fave of the Moët-at-five brigade and ultra-wealthy Russians. In between are a number of lesser-known Alpine villages – **Le Praz** (Courchevel-Le Praz; 1300m), **St-Martin de Belleville** (1450m) and *très anglais* **La Tania** (1400m); all are linked by speedy lifts to higher-elevation slopes.

🏃 Activities

Winter Activities

Les Trois Vallées is blessed with some of the world's best skiable terrain – the pistes here are so outstanding they will satisfy even the most demanding skiers. The ski season here is among the longest in France, running from early December to late April (mid-November to mid-May in Val Thorens). Save time queuing by buying your pass and lessons online at www.les3vallees.com. Ski schools offer lessons for skiers of all levels.

Sunny **Méribel**, more relaxed than its neighbours, is intermediate heaven, with 150km of cruisy (mostly blue and red) runs, 41 ski lifts, two slalom stadiums, two runs used for the 1992 Albertville Olympics, **snow parks** with jumps, pipes and rails for snowboarders and skiers, and plenty of activities for kids. Méribel is famous for its après-ski party scene.

In glitzy **Courchevel** there's another 150km of well-groomed pistes, including some knee-trembling black *couloirs* (steep gullies) for the brave, and excellent off-piste terrain. The 2.5km-long floodlit **toboggan run** through the forest is a fun-laden après-ski alternative (illuminated from 5pm to 7.30pm). In Courchevel Village, an ultra-modern **Centre Aquatique**, with several pools, is set to open in 2015.

Watched over by glacier-licked peaks, **Val Thorens**, founded in 1972, enjoys a snow pack that's the envy of lower-altitude stations, superb **extreme skiing** and a snow

park. The area's highest lift, which tops out at a cool 3200m, whisks you up to **La Tyrolienne** (www.la-tyrolienne.com; €50), the world's highest zip line, opened in 2014 – prepare to fly 1300m in one minute and 45 seconds at speeds of up to 100km/h. Or bounce down the mongo **toboggan run** (day with ski pass €13.60, night €21, 45 minutes), France's longest at 6km, with a drop of 700m. The **Centre Sportif** has a covered swimming pool.

The key info point for off-piste action is the **La Croisette** building in Courchevel 1850, at the base of the huge Verdons ski lift (and across the square from the tourist office). **Maison de la Montagne** is where the **ESF** (www.esfcourchevel.com) resides in winter and is home to the year-round **Bureau des Guides** (✆ Courchevel 06 23 92 46 12, Méribel 04 79 00 30 38; www.guides-courchevel-meribel.com), which takes bookings for guided off-piste adventures, ski mountaineering and ice climbing.

Summer Activities

Summer in Les Trois Vallées – we're talking mid-June to mid-September – is a cornucopia of stunning mountain scenery, hidden lakes and wildflower-strewn pastures. Activities range from walking and hiking to rock climbing, paragliding and canyoning – tourist offices can help you find the right guiding outfit. Or you can clip onto two vertigo-inducing **via ferrata** fixed-cable routes, one at Levaissaix (near Les Menuires), the other at Le Cochet (St-Martin-de-Belleville).

The resorts are criss-crossed by hundreds of kilometres of circuits and downhill runs for **mountain bikers**. IGN biking maps (€5) and details on bike rental outlets (there's at least one in each station) are available at tourist offices.

🛏 Sleeping & Eating

Hotels and restaurants are open from early December to late April (a bit longer up at Val Thorens); some also open in July and August. In summer, rates are a fraction of the winter rates quoted following. Prices blast through the roof during high-high season, which lasts from around 28 December until the 2nd week of January, coinciding with the Christmas school holidays in Russia.

Tourist offices run accommodation services in **Courchevel** (✆ 04 79 08 00 29; www.courchevel.com), **Méribel** (✆ 04 79 00 50 00; www.meribel.net) and **Val Thorens** (✆ 04 79 00 01 06; www.valthorens.com). Val Thorens doesn't have any traditional hotels, just *résidences* (apart

---

TO THE MANOR BORN

What could be lovelier than to wake up in **Château des Allues** (✆ 06 75 38 61 56; www.chateaudesallues.com; St-Pierre d'Albigny; d €140-165, tr/q €180/210, dinner menu adult/child €48/20; 🌐), a 19th-century manor house built high on a hill with sweeping views of the Belledonne range. Painstakingly restored by Stéphane and Didier, this luxury B&B positively oozes elegance and romance in five spacious, lavishly furnished rooms, many with four-poster beds, copper fireplaces and antiques. Served at the family dining table, Stéphane's cooking makes optimal use of the herbs, vegetables and fruit that grow in the award-winning garden. Situated in St-Pierre d'Albigny, 35km east of Chambéry off the A43.

ment hotels) that rent by the week (Saturday to Saturday) or weekend. It's *much* cheaper to stay down in Moûtiers, where you can find doubles for €60, and drive or take the bus up.

Courchevel alone has no fewer than six restaurants with two Michelin stars, but even by gourmet standards they are stratospherically expensive (think upwards of €150 for a *menu* with wine). A number of restaurants up on the slopes, open until 5pm, are accessible only on skis or by lift. Each resort has one or two small supermarkets.

🛏 Méribel

Le Roc HOTEL €€
(📞 La Taverne 04 79 00 36 18; www.alpine-bars.com; Méribel; s/d/tr €115/145/170, €20 less Sun-Wed; ☉ open year-round) For Méribel's cheapest beds, this is the place to come. The 12 smallish, pine-panelled rooms are a bit nicked and scuffed – but hey, you're going to be outside whenever you're awake, right? When reception is closed, head to adjacent La Taverne to check-in.

La Fromagerie CHEESE €€
(📞 04 79 08 55 48; Galerie des Cimes, Méribel Centre; menus €19-28.50; ☉ fromagerie 9.30am-12.30pm & 3.30-7.30pm ski season, dinner ski season, Jul & Aug) Only the tangiest, creamiest Alpine cheeses feature at this *fromagerie*-cum-restaurant, which serves Méribel's tastiest fondues and *raclette* in the rustic cellar. Book ahead for dinner, especially on Wednesday, Thursday and Friday. Situated 200m up the main drag from the tourist office.

Evolution INTERNATIONAL €€
(📞 04 79 00 44 26; Méribel Centre; lunch plat du jour €15, dinner mains €17-25; ☉ 8.30am-2am year-round; 🛜📞) This funky cafe, bar and gastro-pub, British owned and staffed, is famous for its monster-sized English breakfasts (€15), Sunday roasts (€18; served noon to 3pm), international buffets (Saturday night), Bad Boy burgers and, for vegetarians, felafel. Jimmy is the man behind the eclectic live music program (Tuesday, Saturday and Sunday from 10.30pm). Situated across the street from the Parc Olympique.

🛏 Courchevel

Hôtel Tournier HOTEL €€
(📞 04 79 04 16 35; www.hoteltournier.com; rue des Verdons, Courchevel 1850; d €135-175, 3rd bed €30; ☉ mid-Sep–Apr) Home to Courchevel 1850's cheapest rooms. The 34 simple rooms are

small and decorated with amusingly bad taste – but you can't beat the price. Situated one block from Parking La Croisette.

Le Chabichou HOTEL €€€
(📞 04 79 08 00 55; www.chabichou-courchevel.com; rue des Chenus, Courchevel 1850; d incl breakfast winter €620-1150, q from €1490, summer €140-220; ☉ hotel open year-round, restaurants & spa closed late Apr–mid-Jun & early Sep–mid-Dec; @🛜) Named after a cheese, this very attractive hotel and spa – right on the ski slopes – has cosy, chalet-style public areas and 41 tasteful rooms, some of them modern, many with lots of bare wood panelling, and almost all with both a bathtub and a shower.

🛏 Val Thorens

Hotel des 3 Vallées HOTEL €€
(📞 04 79 00 01 86; www.hotel3vallees.com; Grande Rue, Val Thorens; d incl half board €162-348, menu €23; ☉ late Nov–mid-May; 🛜) The 28 rooms here – half with balconies, almost all with great south-facing views – are wonderfully rustic, dressed with Christmasy bursts of red and green and wood reused from old barns. The traditional French cuisine is a treat, as is the newly opened spa. Situated just 50m from the slopes.

🛏 Les Allues

La Croix Jean-Claude HOTEL €€
(📞 04 79 08 61 05; www.croixjeanclaude.com; Les Allues; d €130-165, d incl half board €198-232; ☉ closed May; 🛜) Far from the madding crowd, Les Allues' only hotel, built in 1848, combines the quaint charm of a real Alpine village with quick access to Méribel's slopes via the Olympe bubble lift or a free shuttle. Florals lend a homey touch to the 15 cosy rooms, and market-fresh produce features on the menu.

🛏 La Tania

Le Farçon GASTRONOMIC €€€
(📞 04 79 08 80 34; www.lefarcon.fr; Immeuble Le Kalinka, La Tania; lunch winter/summer €35/28, dinner €58/48; ☉ noon-1.30pm & 7.30-9.30pm daily mid-Nov–Apr, Tue-Sun mid-Jun–mid-Sep)

ℹ️ **RADIO COURCHEVEL**

Radio Courchevel (www.radiocouchevel.com) broadcasts in French and English on 93.2MHz.

SCOTT MARKEWITZ/GETTY IMAGES ©

1. Morzine p494 **2.** Lac d'Annecy p497 **3.** Mont Blanc Express p492, Chamonix **4.** La Vallée Blanche p486

JACQUES PIERRE/HEMIS.FR/GETTY IMAGES ©

Mountain Highs

You're tearing down the Alps on your mountain bike, a deep blue sky overhead; you're hiking through flowery pastures tinkling with cowbells; you're slaloming on a glacier while it slowly slithers down the flanks of Mont Blanc – everywhere the scenery makes you feel glad to be alive!

Downhill Skiing

Glide to off-piste heaven on the legendary **Vallée Blanche** (p486), zigzag like an Olympic pro down black pistes in **Val d'Isère** (p513), or take your pick of **Les Portes du Soleil's** 650km of runs (p494).

Magical Views

Take in breathtaking panoramas of shimmering Mont Blanc from the **Aiguille du Midi** (p483) or contemplate the ethereal loveliness of the **Grand Balcon Sud Trail** (p487). **Lac d'Annecy** (p497) spreads out like a mirror before the fairest castle of them all: **Château de Menthon-St-Bernard** (p502).

Sky High

The sky is blue, the mountain air brisk and pure – just the day to go paragliding or hang-gliding above glistening **Lac d'Annecy** (p497).

Alpine Hiking

There's nothing quite like donning a backpack and hitting the trails in the Alps' national parks. The rugged wilderness of **Parc National des Écrins** (p524) and the snow-capped majesty of **Parc National de la Vanoise** (p517) will leave you awestruck.

On the Edge

For an adrenaline buzz, few adventures beat racing down Morzine's heart-pumping mountain-bike route, **La Noire de Morzine** (p495). Not enough of a challenge? Head to **Chamonix** (p483) to summit one of the area's spectacular 'four-thousanders'.

Michelin-starred chef Julien Machet puts an imaginative spin on gastronomic French dishes made with fresh local produce, served in a modern dining room with lots of wood and a walk-in wine cellar. Reservations are a good idea, especially during school holidays. Situated 100m up the hill from the roundabout, right in the centre of the village.

Drinking & Entertainment

Hang out with the rich kids in Champagne-sipping Courchevel, slalom down to Méribel for the energetic après-ski scene or, until about 5pm, party it up high above Méribel and Val Thorens at the two incredibly popular piste-side branches of **La Folie Douce** (www.lafoliedouce.com). Most places are open only during the ski season.

Méribel

★**Rond-Point des Pistes** BAR
(Méribel-Rond-Point; www.alpine-bars.com; ⊙9am-7.30pm daily during ski season) This piste-side terrace cafe turns into a huge après-ski party starting at about 4pm. Shimmy in your ski boots and sing along to pumping live music (5pm to 7pm) between mouthfuls of chips and toffee vodka (hey, don't knock it until you've tried it) at what *seasonaires* (seasonal workers) fondly call 'the Ronnie'.

Situated at the upper edge of Méribel next to the middle station of the Rhodos lift; also accessible by free shuttle bus or car.

Jack's Bar BAR
(www.jacksbarmeribel.com; rte de la Chaudanne, Méribel Centre; ⊙noon-2am daily during ski season; 🛜) Jack's makes for one memorable party, whether you come for the homemade toffee vodka, the chatty, mostly British staff or the cracking events line-up – stand-up comedy, air-guitar contests, toss-the-boss Sundays (a roll of the dice can get you a free drink) and live music by the local band Bring Your Sisters. Has live music Monday to Friday from 5pm to 7pm.

Situated across the street from the Parc Olympique.

The Doron Pub PUB
(www.hoteldoron.com; rte de la Chaudanne, Méribel Centre; ⊙4pm-3am during ski season) A loud and lairy Brit-style pub that attracts mainly English-speakers for casual après-ski drinks (5pm to 7pm) and for after-dinner festivities (from 10.30pm). Has live music nightly from

11pm, followed by a DJ. Staff hail from the UK or Ireland. Situated across from the tourist office.

La Taverne BAR
(www.tavernemeribel.com; Méribel Centre; ⊙8.30am-1.30am during ski season, flexible hours rest of year; 🛜) A friendly, informal bar whose terrace, après-ski, is jam-packed with skiers and boarders talking epic descents. Has live music (in winter, Tuesday, Thursday, Friday and Sunday from 9.30pm), screens major sports events and serves full English breakfasts. Some of the staff are British. Situated across the square from the tourist office.

Dick's Tea Bar CLUB
(www.dicksteabar.com; rte de Mussillon, Méribel; ⊙après-ski from 4pm, nightclub 10pm-5am during ski season) Méribel's clubbing mainstay rocks nightly to a stellar line-up of DJs.

ℹ Information

Courchevel 1850 Tourist Office (☏04 79 08 00 29; www.courchevel.com; ⊙9am-7pm, closed noon-2pm & at 6pm in spring & fall) Has sister offices at Courchevel 1650m, 1550m and 1300m.

Méribel Tourist Office (Maison du Tourisme; ☏04 79 08 60 01; www.meribel.net; ⊙9am-12.30pm & 3.30-7pm Mon-Fri, 9am-12.30pm & 2-7pm Sat & Sun, no midday closure in winter) Has the low-down on winter and summer activities.

Val Thorens Tourist Office (Maison de Val Thorens; ☏04 79 00 08 08; www.valthorens.com; ⊙8.30am or 9am-12.15pm & 2-6pm or 7pm, no midday closure mid-Dec–mid-May) Has plenty of information in English.

ℹ Getting There & Away

TO/FROM THE AIRPORT

In winter, **Aéroski** (☏Courchevel office 04 79 08 01 17; www.alpskibus.com) buses link all three Les Trois Vallées resorts with Geneva airport (one-way/return €85/144, 3½ hours, three daily Sunday to Friday, eight Saturday). During the ski season there are also weekend services (www.mobisavoie.fr) to/from Lyon St-Exupéry (3¼ to four hours), Chambéry (2½ to four hours) and Grenoble airports. For all airport buses, reserve 48 hours ahead.

Another option to get here: take a train to Moûtiers and then a bus.

BUS

During the ski season **Transdev Savoie** (☏Altibus in Chambéry 08 20 32 03 68, Mobi'Savoie 08 20 20 53 30, Méribel 04 79 08 54 90; www.

mobisavoie.fr), whose Méribel office is across the atrium from the tourist office, links Moûtiers' railway station, well served by trains from all over France, with:

Courchevel (line T5) €10.60, 60 to 70 minutes, at least four daily

Méribel (line T4) €10.60, 50 minutes, at least four daily

Val Thorens (line T3) €10.60, 1¼ hours, at least nine daily

Tickets are a bit cheaper online. Bus frequency goes way up on Saturday (reserve 48 hours ahead) and Sunday. These services also operate in July and August, though some destinations are served only on weekends.

TAXI

Taxis wait at Moûtiers' train station for the trip up to Méribel (€50), Courchevel (€60 to €70) and Val Thorens (€100).

TRAIN

Moûtiers (Moûtiers-Salins-Brick-les-Bains) is the nearest railhead, with services to/from:

Chambéry €14.20, 1¼ hours, hourly Monday to Friday, six or seven Saturday and Sunday

Paris Gare de Lyon €76.20 to €115.90, 4½ to six hours, hourly Monday to Friday, six Saturday and Sunday

On weekends from mid-December to early April, **Eurostar** (www.eurostar.com) operates direct overnight and day trains from London to Moûtiers (one-way/return from €156/279, seven hours).

ℹ Getting Around

The resorts are semi-pedestrian so if you drive, you'll either have to park in a pricey car park or leave your vehicle at a free car park on the outskirts. During the ski season, and in summer, free shuttle buses take you to/from the lifts.

Val d'Isère

POP 1600 / ELEV 1850M

Ask veteran skiers why they return winter after snow-filled winter to Val d'Isère and watch their eyes light up. For the challenging skiing and off-piste runs, say many; for the party vibe and dancing on the slopes, others add; because Val Village is a *real* village with a heart and soul, especially around Église St-Roch, others reply. Whatever the reason: one visit and they were hooked.

Lac du Chevril, created by a hydroelectric dam, looms large on the approach to Val d'Isère, which is in the upper Tarentaise Valley – near the source of the River Isère –

MELTING GLORY

Every restaurant in the Alps with a Savoyard menu offers *raclette, tartiflette* or fondue, but to save on costs and maximise the cheese you can opt for DIY: most dairy shops will lend you the required apparatus provided you buy their ingredients. Here's a 'how to' guide for your own cheese feast.

Fondue Savoyard

Made with three types of cheeses in equal proportions (Emmental, Beaufort and Comté) and dry white wine (about 0.4L of wine for 1kg of cheese). Melt the mix in a cast-iron dish on a hob, then keep it warm with a small burner on the table. Dunk chunks of bread in the cheesy goo.

Our tip: rub or add garlic to the dish – you'll have cheesy breath anyway, so what the hell.

Raclette

Named after the Swiss cheese, *raclette* is a combination of melting cheese, boiled potatoes, charcuterie and baby gherkins. The home *raclette* kit is an oval hotplate with a grill underneath and dishes to melt slices of cheese.

Our tip: avoid a sticky mess by greasing and pre-heating your grill, and go easy on the ingredients (less is more).

Tartiflette

Easy-peasy. Slice a whole Reblochon cheese lengthwise into two rounds. In an ovenproof dish, mix together slices of parboiled potatoes, crème fraiche, onions and lardons (diced bacon). Whack the cheese halves on top, bake for about 40 minutes at 180°C, and ta-da!

Our tip: more crème fraiche and more lardons (a sprinkle of nutmeg is also good).

32km southeast of Bourg St-Maurice. **Tignes** (elevation 2100m), a purpose-built lakeside village, and nearby Val d'Isère form the gargantuan **Espace Killy** skiing area, named after Jean-Claude Killy, who grew up in Val d'Isère and won three slalom and downhill golds at the 1968 Winter Olympics in Grenoble. The area is especially popular with Brits, Danes and Swedes.

🏃 Activities

Winter Activities

Snow-sure **Espace Killy** (www.espacekilly.com), whose ski season runs from very late November until very early May, has a great mix of beginner, intermediate and advanced **skiing** on 300km of pistes between 1550m and 3456m – and miles of glorious off-piste. **Ski touring** is also fabulous, especially in the nearby Parc National de la Vanoise. The many ski schools include well-regarded **Top Ski** (☑ 04 79 06 14 80; www.topski.fr; av Olympique) and the **ESF** (☑ 04 79 06 02 34; www.esfvaldisere.com; Carrefour des Dolomites, Val Village).

At 2300m, the **snow park** is on the back of Bellevarde mountain. Graded from green (easy) to black (experts only), it has rails, jumps, hips, quarters and a boardercross – everything an aficionado of freestyle (skiing or snowboarding) could ask for. Other winter options range from ice climbing to mushing, and ice skating to winter paragliding – or you can head to the **Centre Aquasportif** (www.centre-aquasportif.com; rte de la Balme; adult/child pool €7/6; ☺ 10am-9pm) for swimming pools (great for kids), sports facilities and a spa. For more children's activities, head to the **Village des Enfants** (☑ 04 79 40 09 81; www.valdisere-levillagedesenfants.com; child 8-13yr half-/whole day €32/52; ☺ 9am-5.30pm, closed Sat).

You can buy lift passes online or in person from **STVI** (www.valdiserepass.com; Gare Centrale; adult/child per day €50.50/40.50, 6 days €252.50/202). Five free lifts on the lower slopes let novices find their feet without having to purchase a lift ticket.

Summer Activities

Espace Killy is one of only two places in France (the other is Les Deux Alpes) that still have **summer skiing**, on the Grande Motte and Pissaillas glaciers, which are near Tignes and Val d'Isère, respectively.

The valleys and trails that wend their way from Val d'Isère into the nearby Parc National de la Vanoise are a hiker's dream. If you fancy more of a challenge, you can play (safely) among the cliffs at La Daille's two via ferra-

ta fixed-cable routes. For canyoning, mountaineering or rock climbing with a guide, contact the **Bureau des Guides** (☑ 06 87 52 85 03; www.guides-montagne-valdisere.com; Galerie des Cimes, av Olympique; ☺ summer desk at tourist office 6-7.30pm).

Mountain biking (Vélo Tout Terrain, or VTT) is big in Val (but forbidden within the national park), with an assortment of downhill (green, blue, red and black), endurance and cross-country circuits. Bikes can be rented at local sports shops. Five lifts are open for no charge to downhill cyclists as well as hikers.

The summer season runs from late June to the first weekend in September. Stop by the tourist office for details on family-friendly activities, including pony rides.

🛏 Sleeping

Most hotels are open only during the ski season (late November to early May); some also open in summer. To rent an apartment or a chalet, contact tourist-office-run **Val Location** (☑ 04 79 06 06 60). To buy a four-bedroom apartment in the centre of town, bring at least €2 million.

Hotel La Galise HOTEL €€
(☑ 04 79 06 05 04; www.lagalise.com; rue de la Poste; s/d/tr €120/180/250; 🛜) Just 100m from the slopes, this chalet-style hotel – run by the same family for three generations – keeps it sweet and simple, with pine panelling, burgundy fabrics, mountain views and, attached to many of the 30 rooms, balconies.

★**Les Cinq Frères** BOUTIQUE HOTEL €€€
(Les 5 Frères; ☑ 04 79 06 00 03; rue Nicolas Bazille; d incl breakfast €225-330, q €390; ☺ ski season & mid-Jun–Aug) Run by the same family since 1936, this hotel – comprehensively reimagined in 2013 – offers rustic-chic luxury, with a lovely lounge area, a play room for kids and 17 understated but tasteful and homey rooms. Eight are 40-sq-metre suites – some with giant old-style bathtubs – with room for four to six people. Situated 150m up the main street from the tourist office.

Hôtel L'Avancher HOTEL €€€
(☑ 04 79 06 02 00; www.hotel-lavancher.com; rte du Prariond; d €190-236, q €354; 🛜) The attentive staff make you feel immediately welcome at this homey chalet, which has 17 pine-panelled rooms outfitted with downy bedding. There's a small lounge with board games and a piano, and a bicycle repair workshop.

DON'T MISS

ALPINE CHEESE

Part of Val d'Isère's charm is that it's a real village with year-round residents. Claudine is one of them and she runs **La Fermette de Claudine** (www.lafermettedeclaudine.com; Val Village; ⊙ 7am-8pm daily Dec-Apr) – walk in the door of this *fromagerie*-cum-delicatessen and you'll be enveloped by the heady odours of Alpine cheeses and artisanal sausages. Other delectables on offer include unpasteurised milk, yoghurt and artisanal Génépi (an Alpine herbal liqueur made with various species of wild Artemisia, ie wormwood). The shop is 100m across the roundabout from the tourist office.

Claudine's family dairy farm, **La Ferme de l'Adroit** (Val d'Isère; ⊙ cheese boutique 9am-noon & 3-7pm Mon-Sat year-round), is 1km down the road in the direction of Col de l'Iseran and is open to the public. You can watch the morning cheese production – Tomme that has to be tasted to be believed, bleu de Val, Vacherin and L'Avalin, a powerful cheese made only here – on Monday, Wednesday and Friday at 8.30am. Or you can drop by for the afternoon milking, daily at 5.30pm.

All that dairy goodness is served up in the form of deliciously gooey fondues and *raclette* at adjacent **L'Étable d'Alain** (☑ 04 79 06 13 02; www.lafermedeladroit.fr; mains €22.50-31; ⊙ lunch & dinner; 🐾), an attractively converted stable where, amid Alpine rusticity, you can also feast on fish, meat and duck while watching cud-chewing cows in the adjacent barn. Book two or three days ahead for dinner.

🍴 Eating

Most places open daily from December to April (reservations are a good idea during school holiday periods) and in July and August but have limited hours the rest of the year.

In winter, a number of restaurants up on the slopes, open until 5pm, are accessible only on skis or by lift.

Le Salon des Fous CAFE €
(☑ 04 79 00 17 92; www.lesalondesfous.com; av Olympique, Centre Village; light mains €3.50-13; ⊙ 8am-9pm daily, closed Sat & Sun low season) With its bright-red banquettes and groovy lighting, this cafe is cool but never pretentious. Light meals are served all day long – we're talking salads, quiches, cheesecake and crêpes, all of which pair nicely with teas such as Secret Tibétain (jasmine, lavender, ginger, ginseng and vanilla).

★ La Fruitière MODERN FRENCH €€
(☑ 04 79 06 07 17; www.lafoliedouce.com; mains €18-29; ⊙ noon-3pm Dec-May) At the top of the La Daille gondola (and next to La Folie Douce, the famous piste-side bar), this *restaurant d'altitude* is legendary for its fine dining and breathtaking mountain views. The creative cuisine is prepared with farm-fresh produce and paired with top wines. Save room for the Savoyard cheese plate.

L'Edelweiss SAVOYARD €€
(☑ 06 10 28 70 64; www.restaurant-edelweiss-val disere.com; Piste Mangard, Le Fornet; 2-/3-course menu €23/28; ⊙ 9:30am-4pm daily Dec-Apr) Slope-side on Le Fornet's Mangard blue run, this wood-and-stone chalet has panoramic mountain views from its terrace. The food is well above-par, too: duck breast *à la plancha* (grilled), risotto with foie gras and *cèpes* (porcini mushrooms), and spot-on *tarte tatin*. Good value. Reserve ahead.

Wine Not FRENCH €€
(☑ 04 79 00 48 97; av Olympique, Centre Village; mains €19-24; ⊙ noon-10pm daily Dec-Apr; 🐾) Bare stone, smooth contours and bold orange-red tones set the stage at this intimate 20-seat restaurant and afternoon wine bar. The seven daily mains (fish, steak, duck and wok dishes) are inspired by the first-class wine list, which does a Tour de France from Alsace via Savoy to Bordeaux. Situated across the street from the bus station.

★ L'Atelier d'Edmond FRENCH €€€
(☑ 04 79 00 00 82; www.atelier-edmond.com; Le Fornet; lunch menu €55, other menus €75-140; ⊙ lunch Wed-Sun, dinner Tue-Sun Dec-early May & mid-Jul–mid-Sep) Candlelight bathes the stone walls, low beams and family heirlooms in this gorgeous Michelin-starred chalet, where locally sourced ingredients go into imaginative dishes – some with subtle Asian influences – such as *caïon* (pork) infused with coffee and hazelnut. Has only 30 seats, so call to reserve. Situated 2km east of Val Village across from the Téléphérique du Fornet ski lift.

❶ RADIO VAL D'ISÈRE

Ski reports, weather, news and other programming in English is available on **Radio Val d'Isère** (www.radiovaldisere.com), which broadcasts on 96.1 MHz FM.

🍷 Drinking & Entertainment

The après-ski scene in Val d'Isère is way up there with the craziest in the French Alps.

★La Folie Douce   BAR
(www.lafoliedouce.com; La Daille; ⊗9am-5pm daily Dec-Apr) Why wait to party until you're back down in the village? DJs and live bands fuel an après-ski bash every afternoon on this outdoor terrace at the top of the La Daille cable car. Ibiza in the snow!

Le Petit Danois   BAR
(www.lepetitdanois.com; Centre Village; ⊗10am-2am daily Dec-Apr) Danish beer on tap (€6.50), live music (5pm to 7pm except Saturday) and revved-up partygoers dancing on the tables – lucky this Danish-owned party bar serves a full English breakfast the next morning to mop up the mess. Situated 100m behind the bus station.

Moris Pub   PUB
(Centre Village; ⊗4pm-1.30am daily Dec-Apr) A buzzy, welcoming British pub with big-screen sports, gourmet burger deals and regular live music, often from 5pm to 7pm and 11pm to 1.30am. Go easy on the toffee vodka. Sometimes has fancy-dress theme parties and serves brunch at noon.

La Cave...sur le Comptoir   WINE BAR
(www.cuisinaval.com; av Olympique; ⊗9.30am-noon & 3-11pm or later daily Dec-Apr & Jul-Aug) A relaxing spot for a glass of wine. Knowledgable staff will help you select from among 30 wines available by the glass (€5 to €8, *grand cru* wines €9 to €12). Also serves plates of cheese and meats. Situated 100m down the hill from the bus station.

Dick's Tea Bar   CLUB
(www.dicksteabar.com; rue du Parc des Sports; after 1am €10; ⊗4.30pm-4am daily) Val d'Isère's party HQ and the fabled home of *vodka pomme* (vodka with apple juice; €9). Popular for an après-ski drink (from 5.30pm), for after-dinner live music (from 11pm) and as a late-night club with DJs and a dance floor (from 1am or 2am). Dress is 'smart-casual'.

❶ Information

Tourist Office (☑04 79 06 06 60; www.valdisere.com; place Jacques Mouflier, Centre Village; ⊗8.30am-7.30pm daily Dec-Apr & Jun-Aug, 9am-noon & 2-6pm Mon-Fri low season; ☎) Can supply you with lots of excellent brochures on winter and summer activities, including several for families with kids, and *ValScope*, a weekly schedule of cultural events that comes out each Friday. Internet computers and wi-fi cost €5 per hour.

❶ Getting There & Away

The roads up to Val d'Isère, outfitted with lots of *paravalanche* (avalance protection) shelters, are narrow, winding and can get traffic-clogged. **Col de l'Iseran** (2764m), on the D902 southeast to Bonneval-sur-Arc, and **Col du Petit-St-Bernard** (2188m), which leads from Bourg St-Maurice northeast to the Aosta valley in Italy, are blocked by snow for all but the summer months.

TO/FROM THE AIRPORT

Aérobus (www.altibus.com) has direct services to **Geneva airport** (one-way/return €68/115, four hours, at least three daily from early December to mid-April). A cheaper ski season option to/from Geneva airport (€44/75, Saturday and Sunday morning) is run by **Ben's Bus** (www.bensbus.co.uk), which also serves Grenoble airport.

Altibus (☑08 20 32 03 68; www.altibus.fr) has seasonal services to/from **Lyon St-Exupéry airport** (one-way/return €73/115, 3½ hours, three or four daily Friday, Saturday and Sunday). Another option is to take the train to Bourg St-Maurice (4½ hours) and then bus T14.

During the ski season, direct buses also go to **Chambéry airport** (one-way/return €32/51, two hours, six daily Thursday, Saturday and Sunday).

Advance reservations are essential during school holiday periods and can be made online or by phone. Tickets are slightly cheaper if bought online.

BUS

Year-round, **Belle Savoie Express** (Mobi'Savoie; ☑08 20 20 53 30; www.mobisavoie.fr) links the railhead of Bourg St-Maurice, 32km northwest of Val d'Isère, with Val d'Isère (line T14; €10.60, 50 minutes, at least five daily from mid-December to late April, generally two or three daily the rest of the year). Tickets must be reserved 48 hours in advance, online (where tickets are sold at a discount) or in Val d'Isère at the **Autocars Martin** (☑08 20 32 03 68; www.autocars-martin.com) counter in the bus station. The company also has ski season buses linking Val d'Isère with Tignes

(12km by road; €6.40, 30 minutes, five daily Monday to Friday mid-December to early May).

TAXI

A **taxi** (☑ 08 20 07 31 50) to/from the railhead of Bourg St-Maurice costs about €80/110 for four/eight people.

TRAIN

Bourg St-Maurice, the nearest railhead, has train connections to destinations all over France (eg Chambéry and Lyon Part-Dieu) and seasonal bus links to Val d'Isère.

From mid-December to early April on weekends, **Eurostar** (www.eurostar.com) operates direct daytime and overnight services between Bourg St-Maurice and London (one-way/return from €156/279, 7½ to nine hours).

❶ Getting Around

During the ski season and in summer, free shuttles link the various parts of Val d'Isère, including La Daille with its parking lots, the Centre Village (Val Village), Le Fornet and various ski lifts.

Parc National de la Vanoise

Rugged snowcapped peaks, mirrorlike lakes and an incredible 53 sq km of glaciers are just a few of the sublime natural attractions in the 529-sq-km **Parc National de la Vanoise** (www.parcnational-vanoise.fr), neatly sandwiched between the Tarentaise and Maurienne Valleys. This incredible swathe of wilderness was designated France's first national park in 1963. Five nature reserves and 28 villages border the highly protected core of the park, where marmots, chamois and France's largest colony of *bouquetins* (Alpine ibexes) around 1600 of them – graze freely and undisturbed beneath the larch trees. Overhead, 20 pairs of golden eagles and the odd bearded vulture fly in solitary wonder.

A hiker's heaven, yes, though because of snow walking trails are only accessible for a fraction of the year – June to late September, usually. The **Grand Tour de Haute Maurienne** (www.hautemaurienne.com), a hike of seven days or more around the upper reaches of the valley, takes in national-park highlights. The GR5 and GR55 cross it, and other trails snake south to the Park National des Écrins and east into Italy's Grand Paradiso National Park.

You can base yourself in **Lanslebourg-Mont-Cénis** and **Bonneval-sur-Arc**, two pretty villages along the southern edge of the park (note that the road north to Val d'Isère is open only in summer). The **Maison du Val Cénis** (☑ 04 79 05 23 66; www.haute-maurienne-vanoise.com; 89 rue du Mont-Cenis; ⊙ 9am-noon & 2-5pm Mon & Wed-Fri, also open Sat when Col de l'Iseran is open), in Lanslebourg, and Bonneval-sur-Arc's **tourist office** (☑ 04 79 05 95 95; www.bonneval-sur-arc.com) stock practical information on walking, limited skiing (cross-country and downhill) and other activities in and around the park. In **Termignon-la-Vanoise**, 6km southwest of Lanslebourg, the national park's small information centre, **Maison de la Vanoise** (☑ 04 79 20 51 67; www.parcnational-vanoise.fr) **FREE**, was being renovated at the time of research.

❶ Getting There & Away

CAR & MOTORCYCLE

Bonneval-sur-Arc is 19km northeast of Lanslebourg along the D902. **Col de l'Iseran** (2764m), on the D902 between Bonneval-sur-Arc and Val d'Isère (30km), is closed except in summer, as are both mountain passes linking the national park with Italy, the **Col du Petit-St-Bernard** (to the north) and **Col du Mont-Cénis** (to the south).

BUS & TRAIN

Trains serving the Arc River valley leave from Chambéry and run as far as Modane, 23km southwest of Lanslebourg, from where **Transdev Savoie** (☑ 08 20 32 03 68; www.transavoie.com) runs three to four daily buses (one or none in the low season) to/from Termignon (€6.40, 35 minutes), Val Cénis-Lanslebourg (€10.60, 45 minutes) and Bonneval-sur-Arc (€10.60, 1¼ hours).

DAUPHINÉ

The historical region of Dauphiné encompasses the territories south and southwest of Savoy, stretching from the River Rhône in the west to the Italian border in the east, and roughly corresponding to the *départements* of Isère, Drôme and – in the *région* of Provence-Alpes-Côte d'Azur, which stretches south to the Mediterranean – Hautes-Alpes. It includes the city of Grenoble and, southeast of there, the mountainous Parc National des Écrins.

The gentler terrain of western Dauphiné is typified by the Parc Naturel Régional du Vercors, much loved by cross-country skiers. In the southeast, the bastion town of Briançon stands sentinel near the Italian frontier.

Grenoble

POP 155,600 / ELEV 215M

One of France's most important centres of scientific research and high-tech industry, Grenoble is known for its great museums, excellent dining, effervescent nightlife, outstanding quality of life and superb public transport system. Host of the 1968 Winter Olympics, the city centre is the focal point for a metropolitan area of over 650,000 Grenobloises and Grenoblois, 60,000 of them students.

Surrounded by the jagged peaks of the Parc Naturel Régional de Chartreuse and the Parc Naturel Régional du Vercors, the city itself, on the bank of the River Isère, is hardly above sea level, ensuring that the weather is relatively mild.

❶ Orientation

The mostly pedestrianised city centre is on the left (south) bank of the River Isère, between the Musée de Grenoble (to the east) and Pont de la Porte de France (a bridge). To the north, Fort de la Bastille, a vast hilltop fortress, towers over the area from across the river. The train and bus stations are 500m southwest of Pont de la Porte de France.

◎ Sights

★ Musée de Grenoble   MUSEUM
(www.museedegrenoble.fr; 5 place de Lavalette; adult/child €8/free; ⊙10am-6.30pm Wed-Mon) It's worth a trip to Grenoble just to see this museum. The superbly presented collection features a veritable who's who of 20th-century art, including Pierre Bonnard, Calder, Giacometti, Léger, Magritte, Miró, Modigliani, Picabia, Soutine, Nicolas de Staël and Van Dongen. Among the other highlights: superb 19th-century landscapes of the Dauphiné region, four absolutely huge canvases by the 17th-century Spanish artist Zabarán, and the gorgeous, light-filled building itself, opened

---

---

in 1994. Audioguides (€2) are available in French, English and Italian.

Fort de la Bastille   FORTRESS
(www.bastille-grenoble.com) The Plexiglas spheres of the **Téléphérique Grenoble-Bastille** (quai Stéphane Jay; adult/child one way €5.15/3.30, return €7.50/4.65; ⊙11am-6.30pm Tue-Sun Feb-Apr & Oct-Dec, 9.30am or 11am-7.30pm daily May-Sep, closed Jan) whisk you from the south bank of the Isère up to this massive hilltop fortress, built to defend France against its great Alpine rival of the early 1800s, the Duchy of Savoy. When Savoy was annexed to France in 1860, the fort was left without a military raison d'être.

A number of walking trails, including the GR9, start or pass by here. Walking down to the city takes about 45 minutes (it's a challenging one-hour hike up).

The views are spectacular, and on clear days you can see not only the peaks of the Vercors but also the snowy hump of Mont Blanc. On the viewing platform known as the **Belvédère Vauban**, panels (in French and English) indicate what you're looking out at. The fort complex has five places to eat.

Also worth a visit is the **Musée des Troupes de Montagne** (French Alpine Troops Museum; www.bastille-grenoble.fr; Fort de la Bastille; adult/child €3/free; ⊙11am-6pm Tue-Sun, from 9am May-Sep, closed Jan), a surprisingly interesting museum about France's elite Alpine regiments, established in 1888. Admission includes an audioguide in French, English or Italian.

Le Magasin – Centre
National d'Art Contemporain   MUSEUM
(www.magasin-cnac.org; 155 cours Berriat; adult/child €4/2.50; ⊙2-7pm Wed-Sun) A cavernous glass-and-steel warehouse built by Gustave Eiffel has been turned into one of France's leading centres of contemporary art. Many of the cutting-edge temporary exhibitions were designed specifically for this space. Situated about 2km west of the centre; to get there, take tram A to the Berriat–Le Magasin stop.

Musée Dauphinois   MUSEUM
(www.musee-dauphinois.fr; 30 rue Maurice Gignoux; ⊙10am-6pm or 7pm Wed-Mon) FREE Occupying a 17th-century convent, this *département*-run museum focuses on the people, cultures, crafts and traditions of the Dauphiné highlands. One section traces the history of skiing, from the Stone Age through the time a century ago when skiers carved their own wooden skis to the era of

Grenoble

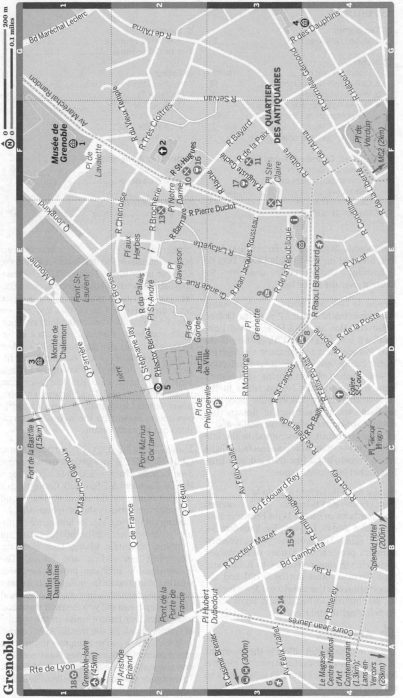

Musée de Grenoble

QUARTIER DES ANTIQUAIRES

Grenoble

snowboards. Signs are in French and English. Situated on the hillside below Fort de la Bastille, 300m up the hill from Pont St-Laurent over the River Isère.

Musée de l'Ancien Évêché MUSEUM
(www.ancien-eveche-isere.fr; 2 rue Très Cloîtres; ☺9am-6pm Mon, Tue, Thu & Fri, 1-6pm Wed, 11am-6pm Sat & Sun) FREE The 13th-century **Bishops' Palace**, next to Italianate **Cathédrale Notre Dame**, now houses a rich collection of well-selected objects tracing area history from the time of the Neanderthals to the early 20th century. Underneath place Notre-Dame you can see part of Roman Grenoble's 3rd-century defensive walls and a 4th-century bapistry, discovered in the late 1980s during tram-line construction. Signs are in French, but a free iPad guide in English should be available soon.

Musée de la Résistance et de la Déportation de l'Isère MUSEUM
(www.resistance-en-isere.fr; 14 rue Hébert; ☺9am-6pm Mon & Wed-Fri, 1.30-6pm Tue, 10am-6pm Sat & Sun) FREE This emotive, well-presented museum presents the history of Grenoble's famously vigorous resistance to Italian and then German forces during WWII and the deportation of a thousand local Jews, including 80 children, to Nazi camps. Signs are in French, English and German.

🏃 Activities

The *billetterie* (ticket office) in the basement of **Fnac** (www.fnacspectacles.com; 4 rue Félix Poulat; ☺10am-7.30pm Mon-Sat) sells tickets to cultural events.

★**Acrobastille** ADVENTURE SPORTS
(www.acrobastille.fr; Fort de la Bastille; adult 6 routes €21, child under 10yr 2/3 routes €12/15; ☺noon-5pm Sat, Sun & school holiday periods, closed Dec-Feb) For a veritable tidal wave of adrenalin, head up to Fort de la Bastille and hop on one of Acrobastille's two 300m-long zip lines, make your way – carefully! – across a vertiginous dry moat, plunge into the Spéléobox (caving simulator) or try out the new Mission Bastille (a labyrinth worthy of Indiana Jones). Safety, in case you lose your grip, is assured by special carabiners. Opening hours, subject to change because of weather conditions, appear on the website. Reservations can be made online.

Maison de la Montagne OUTDOOR ACTIVITIES
(☎04 76 44 67 03; www.grenoble-montagne.com; 3 rue Raoul Blanchard; ☺9.30am-12.30pm & 1-6pm Mon-Fri, 10am-1pm & 2-5pm Sat) Come to this city-run centre for the scoop on year-round mountain activities in the Dauphiné Alps, including ski touring, glacier hiking, ice climbing (on frozen waterfalls), hiking, mountain climbing, mountain biking, rock climbing, canyoning, paragliding and caving. The knowledgeable staff can provide you with weather and avalanche bulletins, help plan mountain overnights in *refuges*, *abris* and *gîtes d'étape,* and sell you the right maps and topoguides. For nature walks in the vicinity of Grenoble, ask for the free SIPAVAG maps.

If it's a guide you're after, talk to the folks representing the **Bureau des Guides et Accompagnateurs de Grenoble** (☎04 38 37 01 71; www.guide-grenoble.com; 3 rue Raoul Blanchard,

Maison de la Montagne; ⊙ 9.30am-12.30pm & 1-6pm Mon-Fri, 10am-1pm & 2-5pm Sat).

Club Alpin Français OUTDOOR ACTIVITIES
(📋 04 76 87 03 73; www.cafgrenoble.com; 32 av Félix Viallet; ⊙ 4-7pm Mon, 3-6pm Tue-Fri) The French Alpine Club runs outings and mountain day trips you're welcome to join – details are posted in its front window and on its website. This branch runs most of the *refuges* (for mountain overnights) in the Isère *département*.

⚒ Festivals & Events

Les Détours de Babel MUSIC FESTIVAL
(www.detoursdebabel.fr; ⊙ late Mar–mid-Apr) A three-week festival of world music.

Vues d'en Face FILM FESTIVAL
(www.vuesdenface.com; ⊙ mid-Apr) The rainbow flag flies high for this week-long gay and lesbian film fest.

Cabaret Frappé MUSIC FESTIVAL
(www.cabaret-frappe.com; ⊙ late Jul) A week of fresh-air concerts in the Jardin la Ville.

🛏 Sleeping

Grenoble's hotel scene is hardly exciting – most establishments cater mainly to businesspeople – but prices are reasonable and drop considerably on the weekend (Friday, Saturday and Sunday nights) and in August. A number of inexpensive hotels can be found right around the train station.

Reservations of all sorts, including B&Bs, can be made through the tourist office website, www.grenoble-tourisme.com.

Hôtel de l'Europe HISTORIC HOTEL €
(📋 04 76 46 16 94; www.hoteleurope.fr; 22 place Grenette; s/d/tr/q from €77/87/114/124; 📶) On the city centre's liveliest square, this hotel occupies two historic buildings – one from 1820, the other from 1905. All but a few of the 39 immaculately kept rooms have wrought-iron balconies that are perfect for watching both street life and the Alps. Six parakeets live on the entresol floor.

Auberge de Jeunesse HOSTEL €
(📋 04 76 09 33 52; www.hihostels.com; 10 av du Grésivaudan, Échirolles; dm incl breakfast from €19.50; @ 📶) 🏂 Grenoble's ultramodern, eco-conscious hostel, with 126 beds, is set in parkland 5km southwest of the centre. The top-notch facilities include a bar, kitchen, sun deck and laundry. Served by bus 1; get off at 'La Quinzaine stop.'

Splendid Hôtel HOTEL €€
(📋 04 76 46 33 12; www.splendid-hotel.com; 22 rue Thiers; d €81-149, f €95-135; ✳@📶) Its lobby and 45 rooms jazzed up with funky paintings, this is a welcome break from Grenoble's workaday hotel scene. Some of the colourful, cosy rooms have hydromassage showers. Also has studio apartments (minimum one-week stay). Enclosed parking costs €5.90. Situated an easily walkable 700m southwest of the centre, one long block east of new tram line E.

Le Grand Hôtel HOTEL €€
(📋 04 76 51 22 59; www.grand-hotel-grenoble.fr; 5 rue de la République; s/d from €99/118; ✳@📶) Beyond the ultramodern reception area, four-star Le Grand – in a building from 1870 – has sleek, monochromatic rooms with spacious bathrooms and triple-pane soundproof windows. From the upper floors balconies look out across the city to the Alps beyond.

🍴 Eating

Grenoble has a wide selection of excellent restaurants featuring cuisines from the Alps, France and around the world. Some of the city's most atmospheric eateries are hidden down the backstreets of the Quartier des Antiquaires (around rue Auguste Gaché). Pizzerias crowd quai Perrière, right across the river from the lift up to Fort de la Bastille.

As the one-time capital of Dauphiné, Grenoble is *the* place to sample *gratin dauphinois* (finely sliced potatoes oven-baked in cream with a pinch of nutmeg).

La Petite Idée FRENCH €
(📋 04 76 47 52 95; www.la-petite-idee.fr; 7 cours Jean Jaurès; menus lunch €14-18, dinner €18-30; ⊙ noon-2pm & 7-10pm Tue-Sun; 🍴) At this convivial restaurant, the traditional French *menu* changes two or three times a year but always features market-fresh, seasonal dishes such as rosemary-rubbed lamb with creamy *gratin dauphinois*. The €10 lunchtime *plat du jour* is great value.

Chez Mémé Paulette RESTAURANT €
(📋 04 76 51 38 85; 2 rue St-Hugues; plats du jour €8.80 & €12, mains €6-12; ⊙ noon-midnight Tue-Sat) Crammed with old books, milk jugs, mess tins and other knickknacks, this place draws a young crowd with its wallet-friendly grub – from soups to *tartines* (hot and cold open sandwiches) to the house speciality, meat and cheese baked in a *cocotte* (small casserole; €6). See how many stuffed-animal chickens you can spot.

Halles Ste-Claire FOOD MARKET €
(place Ste-Claire; ☉ 7am-1pm Tue-Sun, also open 3-7pm Fri & Sat) Pick up picnic fixin's at this covered food market, built in 1874.

Le Petit Bouche BISTRO €€
(☑ 04 76 43 10 39; 16 rue Docteur Mazet; lunch plat du jour €8.50, menus €27-30; ☉ noon-2pm & 7-9pm Mon-Fri) Festooned with vintage bric-a-brac, Le Petit Bouche enjoys a loyal following with its endearingly old-world ambience and classic bistro fare, including meat, fish and pasta.

Ciao a Te ITALIAN €€
(☑ 04 76 42 54 41; 2 rue de la Paix; lunch menus €15.50 & €21, mains €11.50-28.50; ☉ lunch & dinner Tue-Sat, closed Aug) With an entrance that takes you through the kitchen, Ciao dishes up authentic Italian cuisine: freshly made pasta, crispy *panzerotti* (deep-fried calzone), tender veal. It's a Grenoblois favourite so book ahead, especially for dinner.

La Fondue FRENCH €€
(☑ 04 76 15 20 72; www.lafonduegrenoble.fr; 5 rue Brocherie; fondues €15.50-27.30; ☉ noon-1.30pm & 7pm-1am Mon-Sat) Serves 17 kinds of cheese and meat fondue and, for dessert, chocolate fondues laced with the likes of Génépi and Chartreuse. *Raclette* and *tartiflettes* round out the Savoyard offerings.

🍷 Drinking & Entertainment

There's a cluster of cafes and pubs a couple of blocks south of the river, on and around place aux Herbes, adjacent place Claveyson and nearby place St-André. When it's warm enough, place Grenette, three blocks further southwest, fills with cafe tables.

For details on concerts and other cultural events, click on French-language www.petit-bulletin.fr and www.grenews.com; printed versions, available at the tourist office, come out each Wednesday.

Le 365 WINE BAR
(3 rue Bayard; ☉ 7pm-1am or 2am Tue-Sat) A clutter of oversized glass bottles, oil paintings and candles create a relaxed setting for sipping wine – about 40 are available by the glass (€2.50 to €6). You can snack on cheese, sausages and terrines.

Le Tord Boyaux WINE BAR
(4 rue Auge Gaché; ☉ 6pm-1am Tue-Sat) This unique establishment, popular with students, features 43 *vins aromatisés* (flavoured wines; €2.50) that, believe it or not, you drink on the rocks. Some of them are quite extrava-

gant: *violette* (violet), *chataigne* (chestnut), *Génépi-fraise* (Génépi-strawberry), *mangue pimentée* (spicy mango) and something mysteriously called *la p'tite pillule bleu* (the little blue pill). Come on Tuesday at 7pm night to see how many your taste buds can recognise.

MC2 THEATRE
(☑ 04 76 00 79 00; www.mc2grenoble.fr; 4 rue Paul Claudel) Grenoble's most dynamic all-rounder for theatre, dance, opera, jazz and other music. Situated about 2.5km south of the centre; to get there, take tram line A to the 'MC2 – Maison de la Culture' stop.

La Soupe aux Choux LIVE MUSIC
(☑ 04 76 87 05 67; www.jazzalasoupe.fr; 7 rte de Lyon; ☉ from 9pm Tue-Sat) Going strong for over 30 years, 'cabbage soup' stirs live jazz from swing to blues into Grenoble's after-dark mix. Will soon be served by tram line E.

ℹ Information

Post Office (rue de la République) Exchanges currency. Situated next to the tourist office.
Tourist Office (☑ 04 76 42 41 41; www.grenoble-tourisme.com; 14 rue de la République; ☉ 1-6pm Mon, 9am-6pm Tue-Sat, 9am-noon Sun, to 7pm Mon-Sat May-Sep; 📶) Has very useful maps and guides in English (free); arranges city tours (in English in July and August); rents audioguides (one/two people €5/8) in seven languages; and has details on the city centre's six free wi-fi hot-spots. Situated inside the Maison du Tourisme.

ℹ Getting There & Away

AIR
During the ski season, a clutch of budget airlines, including easyJet, Ryanair and Jet2.com, link **Grenoble-Isère Airport** (www.grenoble-airport.com), 45km northwest of Grenoble, with London and various British regional airports.

BUS
The **bus station** (rue Émile Gueymard) is right next to the train station. The **Eurolines** (www.eurolines.com) desk handles international destinations.

During the ski season, **Transaltitude** (☑ 08 20 08 38 38; www.transaltitude.fr) has frequent buses to various ski stations, including Alpe d'Huez (bus 3020; €6.50, two hours), Les Deux Alpes (bus 3030; €6.50, 1¾ hours) and Chamrousse (€4, 1¼ hours). Transisère (www.transisere.fr) can get you to Bourg d'Oisans (bus 3000; €6.50, 1¾ hours, at least five daily), while VFD (www.vfd.fr) goes – faster than the train – to Briançon (€30.50, 2½ hours, one to three daily).

CAR & MOTORCYCLE

Half a dozen international and French car-hire agencies have offices either in the Europole area underneath the train station or across the street.

TRAIN

The **train station** (rue Émile Gueymard) is about 1km west of the centre; it is linked to the centre by tram lines A and B. Direct services include:

Chambéry €11.90, 45 to 60 minutes, at least hourly

Lyon €21.90, 1½ hours, hourly

Paris Gare de Lyon €84 to €105, three hours, six to eight direct daily

In the city centre, train tickets are sold at the **SNCF boutique** (15 rue de la République; ⊙10am-6pm Mon-Sat), right across the street from the tourist office.

ⓘ Getting Around

TO/FROM THE AIRPORT

Actibus (☑ 04 76 06 48 66; ww.actibus.com/aeroport) runs shuttle buses between Grenoble-Isère Airport and Grenoble's bus station (one-way/return €12.50/22, 45 minutes). Times are coordinated with flight arrivals and departures. Reserve ahead on the Actibus website or via www.grenoble-airport.com.

Faure Vercors (☑ 08 25 82 55 36; www.faurevercors.fr) goes to Lyon St-Exupéry airport (€24, one hour, one or two hourly), while **Aérocar** (☑ 09 74 50 07 50; www.aerocar.fr) goes to Geneva airport (one-way/return €49.50/63, 2¼ hours, five daily).

For details on seasonal buses from Grenoble-Isère Airport to various ski stations, see www.actibus.com/aeroport, www.bensbus.co.uk and www.mobsavoie.fr.

BICYCLE

Cycling is a fantastic way to see the city. **Métro-vélo** (☑ 08 20 22 38 38; www.metrovelo.fr; place de la Gare; ⊙7am-8pm Mon-Fri, 9am-noon & 2-7pm Sat, Sun & holidays), based underneath the train station, rents out yellow bikes for €3/20 per day/week. Helmets, child seat and locks are free. You'll need ID and €120 deposit per bike. Don't forget to ask for Les Itinéraires Cyclables, a free map of Grenoble-area cycling routes.

BUS & TRAM

The pride and joy of Grenoble's superb public transport system, run by **Tag** (☑ 082 0 48 60 00; www.tag.fr), is its five ecofriendly tram lines: A, B, C, D and the brand-new E. A single-trip ticket, sold at tram-stop machines and by bus drivers, costs €1.60; other options include a carnet of 10 tickets (€13.20) and the all-day Visitag pass (€4.50). Before boarding a tram, time-stamp your ticket in one of the blue uprights. Trams run from around 5am to 1am or later; most bus services run until 8pm or 9pm.

CAR & MOTORCYCLE

As in other French cities, driving in the centre is a bit of a hassle because of the many one-way streets, time-limited street parking and expensive underground parking garages (€1.50/16 for 45 minutes/24 hours). If you'll be in Grenoble for a few days, you might want to leave your car in one of the 17 **P+R car parks** (www.tag.fr/94-parkings-relais.htm) connected to the centre by tram or bus; the supervised ones cost €2.60 or €3.60 per day.

Around Grenoble

Parc Naturel Régional du Vercors

The gently rolling pastures, highland plateaux, chiselled limestone peaks and pastoral hamlets of this 2062-sq-km **nature park** (www.parc-du-vercors.fr), southwest of Grenoble, are quieter and cheaper than the Alps' high-profile resorts. The wildlife-rich park draws families seeking fresh air and low-key activities like cross-country skiing, snowshoeing, hiking (on a whopping 3000km of trails), mountain biking and caving.

Villard de Lans' **tourist office** (☑ 04 76 95 10 38; www.villarddelans.com; 101 place Mure-Ravaud; ☎) has an online service for booking hotels and chambres d'hôte, and should be your first port of call for information on outdoor activities and local guides.

🛏 Sleeping

À la Crécla   B&B
(☑ 04 76 95 46 98; www.gite-en-vercors.com; 436 Chemin des Cléments, Les Cléments, Lans-en-Vercors; s/d/tr/q from €48/53/68/83, dinner menu €19) Renovated by Véronique and Pascal, this solar-heated 16th-century farm, home to goats, pigs and poultry, has five large guest rooms panelled in spruce and pine. Dinner is a feast of farm-fresh produce, with meat from animals raised here. Situated 1.8km south of Lans-en-Vercors' church on the far outskirts of the village.

ⓘ Getting There & Away

Buses 5100 and 5110 run by **Transisère** (☑ 08 20 08 38 38; www.transisere.fr) link Grenoble with Lans-en-Vercors (€5.90, 45 minutes, seven to 10 daily), Villard de Lans (€5.90, one hour, four to seven daily) and Corrençon-en-Vercors (€5.90, 1¼ hours).

Parc National des Écrins

France's second-largest national park (918 sq km), **Parc National des Écrins** (www.ecrins-parcnational.fr) stretches between the towns of Bourg d'Oisans, Briançon and Gap. Enclosed by steep, narrow valleys, the area was sculpted by the Romanche, Durance and Drac rivers and their erstwhile glaciers. It peaks at 4102m with the arrow-shaped Barre des Écrins, a mythical summit for mountaineers.

Age-old footpaths used by shepherds and smugglers for centuries – 700km in all – criss-cross the national park, making it prime hiking territory.

Bourg d'Oisans, 50km southeast of Grenoble, and Briançon, another 67km in the same direction, are good bases for exploring the park.

Les Deux Alpes

ELEV 1600M

With glorious winter powder for off-piste fans, summer skiing on a glacier, thrilling mountain-bike descents and a party to rival anywhere in the French Alps, Les Deux Alpes (Les 2 Alpes; year-round population 2200) – once two humble pastoral villages – is a buzzing resort with as much attitude as altitude.

◉ Sights & Activities

Contact the **Bureau des Guides** (www.guides2alpes.com) for organised ice climbing, snowshoeing and off-piste skiing in winter, and rock climbing, canyoning and biking expeditions in summer.

Snowpark   SKIING
(Freestyle Land; www.2alpes-snowpark.com) Open in both summer (21 June to August) and winter, Les Deux Alpes' snowpark – recently rechristened Freestyle Land in winter – has half-pipes, superpipes and all the rest for experts as well as beginners.

Grotte de Glace   CAVE
(Ice Cave; adult/child €5/4; ⊙10am-3.30pm late Nov-late Apr) Ice statues representing creatures from prehistory glisten in this ice cave, carved into the Glacier des Deux Alpes and open in both winter and summer. To get there, take the Jandri Express lift to 3200m.

Winter Activities

Les Deux Alpes' winter season runs from late November to late April. The main skiing domain lies below (ie west of) the summit of **La Meije** (3983m), one of the highest peaks in the Parc National des Écrins. Lots of **lifts** (per day/week adult €45/225, child €36/180) come right into the village, making ski-in ski-out a cinch; five beginners' lifts – great for kids – are free. The higher you go, the easier the pistes are.

Freeriders come from far and wide to tackle the breathtaking, near-vertical **Vallons de la Meije** descent in **La Grave** (www.la-grave.com), 24km (by road) east of Les Deux Alpes on the other side of the mountain. The stuff of myth, the off-piste run plummets from 3800m to 1400m – that's 2200 vertical metres! – and is strictly for the crème de la crème of off-piste riders (guide required).

Other winter options include ice skating, careening around on an ice bumper car (for kids) and going on a *motoneige* (snowmobile) expedition; the tourist office has details.

Summer Activities

Thanks to the **Glacier des Deux-Alpes** (2900m to 3600m), Les Deux Alpes is one of only two places in France where you can **ski** (or learn to ski) on a glacier in summertime (the other is Espace Killy, ie Val d'Isère and Tignes). When it's clear, the 360-degree panorama takes in much of southwestern France, including Mont Blanc, the Massif Central and Mont Ventoux. The season runs from about 21 June to August and reopens for a week in late October/early November; a day pass, valid for skiing and the **snowpark** from 7.15am to 12.30pm (and for other activities in the afternoon), costs €37.50/30.50 for an adult/child.

You can combine morning skiing with **mountain biking** on scores of nail-biting descents (in winter they're ski pistes) and cross-country trails. A pass to seven bike-accessible lifts costs €19.20/24 for a half-/full day. Les Deux Alpes also offers numerous **hiking trails** and plenty of opportunities for **paragliding** as well as ice skating, swimming, summer luge, tennis etc.

Many ski shops rent out Alp-ready mountain bikes in the summer.

🛌 Sleeping & Eating

Most of Les Deux Alpes' hotels and restaurants (and quite a few ski lifts) are on or near flat, 2km-long av de la Muzelle, the centre's main street. All but a few are open only from late November to late April and from mid-June to August. Room prices drop significantly in summer.

TOUR DE FRANCE

No event gets the wheels of the cycle-racing world spinning quite as fast as the Tour de France, or 'Le Tour' as it is popularly known in France. This is the big one: one prologue, 20 stages, some 3500km clocked in three weeks by about 180 riders, an entire country – and, often, bits of its neighbours – criss-crossed by bicycle. Broadcast around the world every July, it is a spectacle of epic determination and endurance, of mountain passes steep enough to turn thighs to rubber, of hell-for-leather sprints, of tears and triumph.

The brainchild of journalist Géo Lefèvre, the race was first held in 1903 to boost sales of *L'Auto* newspaper, with 60 trailblazers pedalling through the night to complete the 2500km route in 19 days. Since then, the Tour has become *the* cycling event. And despite headlines about skulduggery, doping and scandal, the riders' sheer guts and hard-won triumphs never fail to inspire.

The Route

Though the exact route changes every year, the Tour essentially does some sort of a loop around France, taking in a variety of terrains (coast, countryside, mountains) and occasionally dipping into other countries (for example, Yorkshire in the UK in 2014). Times are totted up from the day-long stages to get the lowest aggregate time and determine the overall leader, who gets to wear the coveted *maillot jaune* (yellow jersey). The race always finishes, with much fanfare, in Paris on the Champs-Élysées. See www.letour.fr for a stage-by-stage breakdown.

Spectator Tips

You can watch Le Tour on TV, but nothing beats experiencing the race firsthand. Host towns treat it as a big party, with families turning out for roadside picnics and the publicity caravan of goodie-throwing floats psyching everyone into carnival mode before the riders whoosh by in a blur.

Want to see the race for yourself? You'll need to make travel plans well ahead. The Alpine and Pyrenean stages are terrific, giving you plenty of opportunity to observe riders as they slow down (relatively speaking) to tackle the gruelling inclines. Get there early to snag a front-row spot.

In winter, there are 10 *restaurants d'altitude* where you can eat, drink and be merry up on the slopes.

The tourist office runs an **accommodation service** (☏04 76 79 24 38; www.les2alpes reservation.com).

Hotel Serre-Palas　　　CHALET €
(☏04 76 80 56 33; www.hotelserre-palas.fr; 13 place de Venosc; d incl breakfast €58-143) For bright, quiet rooms (24 of them) and marvellous mountain views, this spick-and-span chalet is a good-value choice. Lionel, your affable host, is a ski instructor and can give you plenty of insider tips. Situated at the southern edge of town.

Le Raisin d'Ours　　　FRENCH €€
(☏04 76 79 29 56; www.leraisindours.fr; 98 av de la Muzelle; menus €26-39; ☉noon-2pm & 7-9.30pm, closed lunch Wed) This stylishly rustic restaurant serves French cuisine – traditional and creative – accompanied by your choice from an extensive wine list from every region of France (the owner is a sommelier). The mood is relaxed, the service attentive.

Hotel Côte Brune　　　HOTEL €€€
(☏04 76 80 54 89; www.hotel-cotebrune.fr; 6 rue Côte Brune; d incl half board €170-250; ☏) Ski in and out of this slope-side hotel, recently outfitted with a spa. The 18 homey pine-panelled rooms radiate Alpine charm and come with south-facing balconies; some are geared up for families.

🍸 Drinking & Entertainment

Les Deux Alpes has a well-deserved reputation for raucous après-ski parties.

Smokey Joe's　　　BAR
(www.smokeyjoes.fr; place des Deux Alpes; ☉9am or 10am-midnight late Nov–late Apr & mid-Jun–Aug) Live après-ski music (5pm to 7pm), spicy Tex-Mex food, pizzas and dice shots are bound to get you grooving in your snow boots at this British-owned hang-out very near the base of the Jandri lift. Staff are all native English speakers.

Smithy's Tavern BAR

(www.smithystavern.com; 7 rue de Cairou; 🛜) Vodka, fajitas, rack of lamb, more vodka – that's the scene at this rocking, English-owned pub with a long bar for lining 'em up. Hosts gigs, DJ nights and head-spinning parties.

ℹ Information

Tourist Office (📞 04 76 79 22 00; www.les2 alpes.com; place des Deux Alpes; ⊘ 8am-7pm late Nov-late Apr & mid-Jun–Aug, 9am-noon & 2-6pm Mon-Fri in low season) Has extensive information on both winter and summer activities. Situated inside the Maison des Deux Alpes.

ℹ Getting There & Away

Les Deux Alpes is 67km southeast of Grenoble and 19km southeast of Bourg d'Oisans.

From late December to March, buses run by **Transaltitude** (📞 08 20 08 38 38; www.trans altitude.fr) link Les Deux Alpes with Grenoble's train and bus station (€6.50, 1¾ hours, at least three daily); in Les Deux Alpes, you can book at **Autocars VFD/Transaltitude** (📞 04 76 80 51 22; 112 av de la Muzelle; ⊘ 4-6.30pm Mon-Fri).

Alpe d'Huez

ELEV 1860M

Its modern facilities spread across a gentle, sun-drenched hillside, lively, family-friendly Alpe d'Huez (1250m to 3330m) has 250km of well-groomed, south-facing (and thus gloriously sunny) pistes that range from dead easy to death-defying. The ski season lasts from early December to late April.

Summer (July and August) brings a mix of hikers and mountain bikers – and, often, the Tour de France (p525).

🏃 Activities

The **Pic Blanc** (3330m), Alpe d'Huez' highest point, commands magical panoramas that reach across one-fifth of France. It is accessible winter and summer via the Tronçon and Pic Blanc cable cars.

Skiing options include breathtakingly sheer **La Sarenne**, Europe's longest black run, which is an astounding 16km long. To reach it, take the Pic Blanc cable car.

In summer, marked **hiking trails** lead up and across the slopes to jewel-like lakes such as **Lac Blanc**, **Lac de la Fare** and **Lac du Milieu**. For **mountain-biking** enthusiasts, the area is downhill heaven, with over 260km of trails to rattle and roll down, and four bike parks. A one-day summertime lift pass costs €16 for both pedestrians and cyclists.

In Centre de la Station, there's an outdoor 25m **swimming pool**, heated to 28°C, and an **ice-skating rink**; both are open winter and summer.

Alpe d'Huez is (in)famous for its incredibly steep 14km access road, whose 21 hairpin curves are a regular highlight of the Tour de France.

For adventure activities such as ice climbing, mountain climbing, via ferrata and glacier hiking, contact the **Bureau des Guides** (📞 04 76 80 31 69, 04 76 80 42 55; www.guidesalpe dhuez.com; Rond-Point des Pistes).

🛏 Sleeping & Eating

Few places to stay are ski-in ski-out, but the free Télécentre lift connects the village with Rond-Point des Pistes at the village's upper edge, departure point for lots more lifts.

The Centre de la Station area has a couple of small supermarkets.

Le Printemps de Juliette CHALET €€

(📞 04 76 11 44 38; www.leprintempsdejuliette.com; 68 av des Jeux; d incl breakfast €130-200; ⊘ hotel open year-round, restaurant closed May, Oct & Nov; 🛜) Decorated in red and white, Juliette's chalet-hotel has nine spacious, happily floral rooms with balconies and a *salon de thé* where you can sip tea and nibble homemade cakes amid legions of teddy bears.

Le Passe-Montagne REGIONAL €€

(📞 04 76 11 31 53; www.lepasse-montagne.com; 122 rte de la Poste; lunch menu €19.50, other menu €32.50, child's menu €12.50; ⊘ noon-1.30pm & 6.30-9.30pm, closed lunch Mon; 🍴) An open fire burns in the beamed dining room of this stylish wooden chalet, a fine place for a tête-á-tête over dishes from the Dauphiné – or a juicy, tender steak with morels.

ℹ Information

Information hub **Maison de l'Alpe** (place Paganon) sells ski passes and houses the helpful **tourist office** (📞 04 76 11 44 44; www.alpedhuez. com; ⊘ 8.45am-7pm), **accommodation reservation centre** (📞 04 76 11 59 90; www.reservation. alpedhuez.com) and **ESF** (📞 04 76 80 31 69; www.esf-alpedhuez.com; ⊘ 8.30am-7pm ski season, 9am-noon & 1.30-5.30pm rest of year).

ℹ Getting There & Away

Alpe d'Huez is 64km southeast of Grenoble. From late December to March, **Transaltitude** (📞 08 20 08 38 38; www.transaltitude.fr) buses link Alpe d'Huez with Grenoble's train and bus station (€6.50, two hours, at least three daily) via Bourg d'Oisans.

Bourg d'Oisans

ELEV 720M

A gateway to several vertiginous mountain passes, the valley village of Bourg d'Oisans – starting point for the serpentine road up to Alpe d'Huez (19km to the northeast) – makes an excellent base for hiking and mountain biking. For information on the area, check out www.oisans.com and www.bikes-oisans.com, which has details on trails, maps and bike hire. For details on activities such as kayaking on the Drac's turquoise waters, rock climbing, via ferrata routes and paragliding, contact the tourist office.

Learn about the national park's geology, flora and fauna, including ibex and chamois, at the municipal **Musée des Minéraux et de la Faune des Alpes** (www.bourgdoisans.com; place de l'Église; adult/child €5/free; ⊗ 2-6pm Sat & Sun except mid-Nov–mid-Dec, open Wed-Mon during school holidays).

🛏 Sleeping & Eating

Cafes and restaurants serving good honest mountain food can be found on and around avenue de la République (the D1091B). There's an outdoor **food market** in the village centre on Saturday from 7am to 1pm.

Ferme Noémie B&B €

(📞 04 76 11 06 14; www.fermenoemie.com; Chemin Pierre Polycarpe, Les Sables; apt per week €375-1500, luxury tents per day/week €65/450, campsites €10.50-25; ⊗ campground open Apr-Oct) Run by a British couple, Melanie and Jeremy Smith, Ferme Noémie has barn-style apartments with four to six beds, four-bed luxury tents and old-fashioned campsites. Prices depend on seasonal demand. To get there from the D1091, follow the signs for about 500m.

ℹ Information

Maison du Parc (www.ecrins-parcnational.fr; rue Gambetta; ⊗ 9am-noon & 2-5pm closed afternoon Fri, Sat & Sun, open daily Jul & Aug) Has exhibits on the Parc National des Écrins; a small cinema is being added.

Tourist Office (📞 04 76 80 03 25; www. bourgdoisans.com; quai Girard; ⊗ 8.30am-12.30pm Mon-Sat, plus 2.30-5.30pm Fri & Sat) Information on what to do and where to stay.

ℹ Getting There & Away

From late December to March, at least three daily buses run by **Transaltitude** (📞 08 20 08 38 38; www.transaltitude.fr) link Bourg d'Oisans with Grenoble's train and bus station (€6.30, one hour), Alpe d'Huez and Les Deux Alpes. During the same period, **LER** (📞 08 21 20 22 03; www. info-ler.fr) operates buses to Briançon (€15.40, 1¾ hours, three daily).

Briançon

POP 11,570 / ELEV 1320M

Briançon's Cité Vauban (walled old town), perched high on a hill, is straight out of a fairy tale, with sweeping views of nearby Vauban fortifications and the snowcapped Écrins peaks. The Italian vibe is no coincidence: Italy is just (a dizzying) 20km away. Briançon is proud of its 300 sunny days a year.

No matter whether you come by bus or car, it feels like a long, long way to Briançon – but it's worth every horn-tooting, head-spinning, glacier-gawping minute. The road from Grenoble is pure drama, and not just because of the scenery. The locals adopt a nonchalant attitude to driving, the general consensus being: overtaking on hairpin bends, *pas de problème*! But brave it behind the wheel and you'll be richly rewarded with views of thundering falls, sheer cliffs and jagged peaks razoring above thick larch forests as you drive from Isère into the sunny and distinctly southern Hautes-Alpes *département*.

◉ Sights

Cité Vauban HISTORIC QUARTER

(Vieille Ville) Surrounded by mighty starburst-shaped ramparts, Briançon's hilltop old town looks much as it did centuries ago, its winding cobbled lanes lined with Italianate, pastel-painted town houses. The steep main street, the **Grande Rue** – also known as the **Grande Gargouille** (Great Gargoyle) because of its gushing rivulet – was laid out in 1345. You can walk all the way around the interior of Vauban's upper ramparts, enjoying spectacular views, by following the streets marked as the **Chemin de Ronde**.

Facing the tourist office, the sombre, neoclassical **Collégiale Notre Dame et St Nicolas** (place du Temple), designed by one of Vauban's military engineers, is worth a look inside for its baroque painting.

Vauban Fortifications HISTORIC SITE

Three centuries ago, Briançon – situated at the confluence of five river valleys – was highly vulnerable to attack by France's Alpine arch-rival of the era, the Duchy of Savoy. Under Louis XIV and his successors, vast effort was expended on constructing hilltop fortresses to defend the remote town, marvels of military engineering that, along with a dozen other Vauban sites in France, were given Unesco World Heritage status in 2008.

Perched atop a rocky crag high above the Cité Vauban, the **Fort du Château** (1326m) can be visited on foot from late April to November. Across the 55m-high **Pont d'Asfeld** (erected 1720), a graceful stone bridge over the River Durance, **Fort des Trois Têtes** (1435m) can be seen on a walking tour in the warm season and on snowshoes in winter (€25; most Thursdays at 1.50pm). Also accessible on foot and by snowshoes is **Fort des Salettes** (1400m).

For details on tours, contact the **Service du Patrimoine** (☑ 04 92 20 29 49; www.ville-briancon.fr; Porte de Pignerol, Cité Vauban; tours adult/child €6.20/4.60; ☻ 2-5.30pm Mon, 10am-noon & 2-5.30pm Tue-Fri, also open Sat during school holidays), inside the Cité Vauban's main gate.

🏃 Activities

The **Serre Chevalier** (www.serre-chevalier.com) ski area, properly called Le Grand Serre Chevalier, links 13 villages and 250km of pistes along the Serre Chevalier Valley between Briançon and Le Monêtier-les-Bains, 15km northwest. To get to the slopes (and warm-season trails) directly from Briançon, take the **Télécabine du Prorel** lift, located 1.8km across the valley – on the western edge of Ste-Catherine – from the Cité Vauban.

For information on hiking in the **Parc National des Écrins** (p524), ie in the mountains west of town, stop by the **Maison du Park** (www.ecrins-parcnational.fr; place du Médecin Général Blanchard; ☻ 10am-noon & 3-6.30pm Mon-Sat summer, 2-6pm Mon-Fri rest of year), a three-storey visitor centre situated at the bottom of the Cité Vauban's Grande Rue.

🛌 Sleeping

Hôtel de la Chaussée   HISTORIC HOTEL €
(☑ 04 92 21 10 37; www.hotel-de-la-chaussee.com; cnr av de la République & rue Centrale, Ste-Catherine; s/d/tr €78/88/96; 🛜) The Bonnaffoux family has run this place with charm and efficiency for five generations – since 1892, in fact. The 16 rooms fulfil every Alpine chalet fantasy: wood-panelled, beautifully furnished and oh-so-cosy.

Hotel Edelweiss   HOTEL €
(☑ 04 92 21 02 94; www.hotel-edelweiss-briancon.fr; 32 av de la République; s/d/tr/q €52/64/86/96; 🛜) An excellent bet if you're on a tight budget. The 20 spacious rooms, some in a building from

1890, are cosy and immaculately kept; half offer fine views of the Alps. The helpful owners can arrange everything from ski passes to babysitters. Situated three-quarters of the way up av de la République, which leads up to the Cité Vauban.

🍴 Eating

The Cité Vauban has lots of restaurants along the Grande Rue and adjacent streets; some are open only for dinner. Food shops can be found down the hill in the new town, Ste-Catherine.

Several restaurants around town offer 17th-century-style 'Menus Vauban' – think pigeon, rabbit stew and obscure vegies. The tourist office can supply details.

Marché   FOOD MARKET €
(ave du 159e, Ste-Catherine; ☻ Wed & Sun morning) Food stalls.

Au Plaisir Ambré   MODERN FRENCH €€
(☑ 04 92 52 63 46; 26 Grande Rue; menus €22-31; ☻ noon-1.15pm by reservation & 7-9.15pm Fri-Tue, open Wed Jul & Aug) At this Alpine-chic bistro, French dishes with Italian and Asian touches are perfectly matched with wines and followed by indulgent desserts like *soufflé glacé à la Chartreuse*.

Le Pied de la Gargouille   REGIONAL €€
(☑ 04 92 20 12 95; 66 Grande Rue, Cité Vauban; menus €20.50-29.50, child's menu €9.50; ☻ 7-10pm Wed-Mon) The Gargoyle's Foot is an old-town homage to fondue, *raclette* and *tartiflette;* meat and fish are also on offer. Situated at the bottom of the Grande Rue.

ℹ️ Information

Tourist Office (☑ 04 92 21 08 50; www.ot-briancon.fr; Maison des Templiers, 1 place du Temple, Cité Vauban; ☻ 9am-noon & 2-6pm Mon-Sat, 10am-noon & 2-5pm Sun; 🛜) Can help with last-minute accommodation. Room availability information is posted on the door.

ℹ️ Getting There & Around

BUS

The bus station is next to the train station. **LER** (☑ 08 21 20 22 03; www.info-ler.fr) bus 35, run by the Provence-Alpes-Côte d'Azur *région,* links Briançon with Grenoble (€30.50, 2½ hours, one to three daily) via Bourg d'Oisans. LER bus 29 goes to Gap (€13.90, two hours, six daily Monday to Saturday), Aix-en-Provence (€37.80, five hours, two daily Monday to Saturday) and Marseille (€42, 5½ hours, two daily Monday to Saturday).

CAR & MOTORCYCLE

The **Col de Montgenèvre** (1850m), linking Briançon with neighbouring Italy, is kept open year-round, as is the **Col du Lautaret** (2058m) between Briançon and Grenoble. Both, though, occasionally get snow-bogged.

TRAIN

The **train station** (av du Général de Gaulle), terminus of a rail spur that heads northwestward from Gap, is 1.8km southwest the Cité Vauban and 1km south of Ste-Catherine (the city centre). It is linked to the rest of town by local TUB buses 1 and 3. To Grenoble, the bus is much faster than the train.

To get to **Paris** (€95 to €116, seven to nine hours), you can either take an overnight train to Gare d'Austerlitz, or a day train to Gare de Lyon; the latter requires changing in Grenoble, Valence TVG and/or Gap. But the fastest way to get to Paris is to take a bus to the Italian town of Oulx (€10, one hour, six daily from December to mid-April) – reserve 36 hours ahead on ☑ 04 92 50 25 05 or via www.05voyageurs.com – and then a TGV to Paris' Gare de Lyon (€113, 4½ hours).

Other destinations include:

Gap (€14.80, 1¼ hours, at least nine daily)
Grenoble (€33.40, 4½ hours, five daily)
Marseille (€45, 4½ hours, five daily)

THE JURA MOUNTAINS

The dark wooded hills, limestone plateaus, rolling dairy country and vine-wreathed villages of the Jura Mountains stretch for about 250km from Lake Geneva northeast to Belfort, along both sides of the France–Switzerland border. Rural, deeply traditional and *un petit peu* eccentric, the Jura – from a Gaulish word meaning 'forest' – is ideal if you're seeking serenity, authentic farmstays and the simple pleasures of mountain life. Wayside farms invite you to stop, relax and sample the tangy delights of Comté cheese and *vin jaune* (yellow wine) – a sure way to experience those 'ahhh, c'est la vie...' moments.

The Jura – after which the Jurassic period in geology is named – is France's premier cross-country skiing area. The region is dotted with small ski stations, and every year it hosts the Transjurassienne, one of the world's toughest cross-country skiing events.

Besançon

POP 117,400 / ELEV 262M

Hugging a *boucle* (hairpin curve) of the River Doubs, the cultured and very attractive cap-

LIGHTS, CAMERA, HUGO

Victor Hugo, famous for penning masterpieces such as *Les Misérables* and *Notre-Dame de Paris* (The Hunchback of Notre Dame), was born in Besançon in 1802. His childhood home is now the **Maison Natale de Victor Hugo** (140 Grande Rue; adult/child €2.50/1.50; ⊙10am-noon & 2-5pm or 6pm Wed-Mon, no midday closure Jun-Sep); exhibits focus on the great man's public life and political activism.

Two other local luminaries, born here in 1862 and 1864 respectively, are the aptly named Auguste and Louis Lumière (lumière means 'light'), among the earliest pioneers of motion pictures. As you exit the Maison Natale de Victor Hugo, look left across the square – a plaque marks the **House of the Lumière Brothers** (1 place Victor Hugo), where they were born.

ital of Franche-Comté remains refreshingly modest and untouristy, despite charms such as a monumental Vauban citadel, a graceful 18th-century old town and France's first public museum.

In Gallo-Roman times, Vesontio – over the centuries, the name evolved to become Besançon – was an important stop on the trade routes linking Italy, the Alps and the Rhine.

⊙ Sights

For a lovely stroll, you can walk along the River Doubs – both banks have paths – where it encircles the old city.

The superb **Musée des Beaux-Arts et d'Archéologie** will be closed for renovations until mid-2017.

★**Citadelle de Besançon**   CITADEL
(www.citadelle.com; 99 rue des Fusillés de la Résistance; adult/child €9.60/8.10; ⊙9am-6pm Apr-Dec, to 5pm late Jan-Mar, closed early Jan) Dominating the city from its perch 120 vertical metres above the old town, the 17th-century Citadelle de Besancon – designed by Vauban for Louis XIV – commands sweeping views of the city and the serpentine River Doubs. Along with 11 other Vauban works, it was recognised as a Unesco World Heritage Site in 2008. The entry fee includes two audioguides, available in French, English and German. Two cafes serve edibles.

Besançon

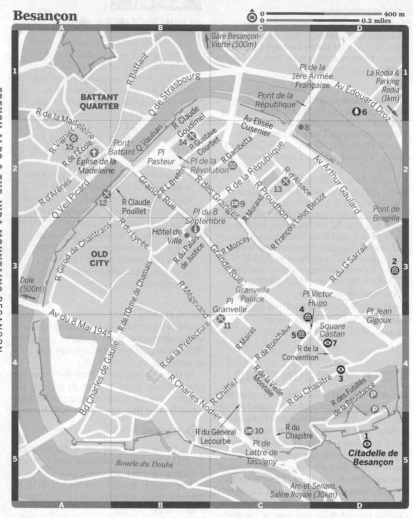

For an introduction to the citadel's architecture, head to **Espace Vauban**, where exhibits include a fascinating 3D film (14 minutes). Booklets in English and German are available at the entrance. The **Chemin de Rond** lets you walk along two sections of the citadel's outer ramparts.

The **Musée de la Résistance et de la Déportation** is one of France's most in-depth and comprehensive WWII museums. Each room is supposed to have an information sheet in English (look for a wall-mounted holder) but the 20 rooms of evocative photos, documents and artefacts are best visited with a free audioguide. Some of the photographs are unsuitable for young children. During WWII, the Germans imprisoned British civilians in the citadel, and German firing squads executed about 100 resistance fighters here. Nearby, the **Musée Comtois** presents local life in centuries past.

Kids are sure to be fascinated by the **Insectarium**, with creepy-crawlies such as tarantulas, scorpions and stick insects; the small **Aquarium**, where you can pet the koi; the ho-hum **Noctarium**, where a few of the Jura's nocturnal rodents snuffle around; and, at the southeast end, the **zoo**, home base for the free-range peacocks that strut their stuff around the fort.

Besançon

If you don't fancy the uphill trudge, take Ginkobus' bus 17 (€1.30) from the city centre or Parking Rodia, which runs one to five times an hour from April to mid-October.

FRAC Franche-Comté   MUSEUM
(www.frac-franche-comte.fr; rue Arthur Gaulard; adult/child €4/2; ⊙2-6pm Wed-Fri, 2-7pm Sat & Sun) Bringing contemporary art to the Franche-Comté region is the raison d'être of this museum, which opened in 2013. Its striking riverside building was designed by the Japanese architect Kengo Kuma.

Horloge Astronomique   ASTRONOMICAL CLOCK
(www.horloge-besancon.monuments-nationaux.fr; rue de la Convention; adult/child €3/free; ⊙guided tours hourly 9.50-11.50am & 2.50-5.50pm Wed-Mon, closed Wed Oct-Mar, also closed Jan) The base of the bell tower in the 18th-century Cathédrale St-Jean houses an incredible astronomical clock, powered by 11 weights, that has run the church's bells since its installation in 1860. The ornate gadget has 30,000 moving parts and 57 clock faces and, among other things, tells the time in 16 places around the world and indicates the tides in eight different French ports.

Porte Noire   HISTORIC SITE
(Black Gate; square Castan) Erected around AD 175, this Roman triumphal arch stands very near where Roman columns and the vestiges of an ancient aqueduct were discovered in 1870.

☞ Tours

From late March to October, a 1¼-hour river cruise is a relaxed way to see Besançon from the Doubs' hairpin curve and the 375m-long boat tunnel that goes underneath the citadel. Companies include **Vedettes de Besançon** (www.vedettesdebesancon.com; Pont de la République; adult/child €11/8.50).

⊨ Sleeping

Most hotels lower their rates on Friday, Saturday and Sunday nights. There are a number of reasonably priced hotels facing the train station.

Hôtel Granvelle   HOTEL €
(☑03 81 81 33 92; www.hotel-granvelle.fr; 13 rue du Général Lecourbe; d €86-110; ✳@ 🛜) Entirely renovated in 2014 so everything is brand new, the Granvelle has 41 modern rooms – decorated in saturated reds, blues and violets – with white-and-grey tile bathrooms. Two rooms are wheelchair-accessible.

Hôtel de Paris   DESIGN HOTEL €€
(☑03 81 81 36 56; www.besanconhoteldeparis.com; 33 rue des Granges; s €67, d €86-210, tr €310; 🛜) Housed in an 18th-century coaching inn, this attractive establishment has a razor-sharp eye for modern design – and a breakfast room lit by antique stained glass. Of the 50 spacious rooms, decorated with a mix of old-style and modern furnishings, a few open, motel-style, onto the enclosed parking lot (€8 per night) and three are wheelchair-accessible. Good value.

✗ Eating

There are a number of small restaurants in the northwest corner of the old town, along rue Claude Poullet. Across the river, cheap ethnic eats can be found on and near rue Battant.

Marché Couvert   FOOD MARKET €
(2 rue Claude Goudimel; ⊙7am-7pm Tue-Sat, 8am-1pm Sun) Indoor food market with a lively

outdoor extension on Wednesday morning, Friday morning and Saturday.

La Petite Adresse — BISTRO €

(☑ 03 81 82 35 09; 28 rue Claude Pouillet; lunch menu €11, other menu €18; ⊙noon-1.45pm & 7-10.30pm Mon-Sat; 🖋) A little address that's big on cheese dishes like *boîte chaude* (hot box; two-person minimum), made with seasonal Vacherin Mont d'Or and another Jura speciality, *saucisse de Morteau* (Morteau sausage).

Le Poker d'As — MODERN FRENCH €€

(☑ 03 81 81 42 49; www.restaurant-lepokerdas.fr; 14 square St-Amour; menus €23.50-55; ⊙noon-1.30pm & 7.30-9.30pm Tue-Sat) Expertly cooked creative seasonal specialities include pollack crumble with onion sauce, farm-fresh chicken cooked with morels and *vin jaune,* and cod fillet with Le Puy lentils.

Brasserie 1802 — BRASSERIE €€

(☑ 03 81 82 21 97; www.restaurant-1802.fr; place Granvelle; 3-course menus €27; ⊙11.30am-midnight; 🍴) With a terrace spilling out onto tree-shaded place du Théâtre, this contemporary brasserie serves up French classics like hot goat's cheese salad and Charolais rib steak.

Drinking & Entertainment

Students spice up the nightlife in Besançon. Pubs can be found around the northern end of the Grande Rue (eg along tiny rue Claude Pouillet) and, across the river, in the working-class, ethnically mixed Battant quarter.

Les Passagers du Zinc — BAR

(☑ 03 81 81 54 70; www.lespassagersduzinc.com; 5 rue Vignier; €5; ⊙closed mid-Jul–mid-Aug) This grungy bar-cum-club, with battered leather sofas and multicoloured lights, has been one of Besançon's best venues for live music since 1997. Opens only when there are concerts (mainly rock), which is most often from 9pm to midnight on Thursday, Friday and Saturday nights; see the website for details.

ℹ Information

Post Office (23 rue Proudhon) Exchanges currency.

Tourist Office (☑ 03 81 80 92 55; www.besancon-tourisme.com; place du 8 Septembre, inside the Hôtel de Ville; ⊙10am-12.30pm & 1.30-6pm Mon-Sat, 10am-1pm Sun Sep-Jun, 10am-6pm Jul & Aug) Has an excellent guide/map in English and internet access.

ℹ Getting There & Around

BICYCLE

Besançon's credit-card-operated automatic bike-rental system, **Velocité** (www.velocite.besancon.fr), has 30 pick-up and drop-off sites across the city. The first half-hour is free; after that the charge is €1 per hour, maximum €4 per day.

BUS & TRAM

The train station is linked to the city centre by the new, two-line tram network, opened in mid-2014.

CAR & MOTORCYCLE

There is a free outdoor car park, **Parking Rodia** (av de Chardonnet), across the river and about 1km to the southeast from the centre. It is linked to the centre and the Citadelle by bus 17.

TRAIN

The train station, **Gare Besançon-Viotte** (av de la Paix), refurbished in 2014, is 800m north (up the hill) from the northern edge of the city centre. Services include:

Arbois €9.70, 45 minutes, 13 daily

Arc-et-Senans €7.40, 25 minutes, 16 daily

Belfort €16.90, 1¼ hours, 18 daily

Dijon €16 to €20, one hour, 25 daily

Paris Gare de Lyon €64 to €81, 2½ to 3¼ hours, 16 daily, including four direct

Connections to major cities are often cheaper and/or quicker from **Gare TGV Besançon Franche-Comté**, on theTGV line (opened in 2011) linking Dijon with Mulhouse. Situated 11km nortwest of the centre, it's a 15-minute hop by shuttle train from Gare Besançon-Viotte.

In the city centre you can buy tickets at the **Boutique SNCF** (44 Grande Rue; ⊙noon-7pm Mon, 10am-7pm Tue-Fri, 9.30am-6pm Sat).

Southwest of Besançon

Saline Royale

Envisaged by its designer, Claude-Nicolas Ledoux, as the 'ideal city', the 18th-century **Saline Royale** (Royal Saltworks; www.salineroyale.com; adult/child €8.80/4.50; ⊙9am-noon & 2-6pm, no midday closure weekends & Jun-Sep) in Arc-et-Senans, 35km southwest of Besançon, is a showpiece of early Industrial Age town planning. Although his urban dream was never fully realised, Ledoux' semicircular Royal Saltworks has been a Unesco World Heritage Site since 1982.

Regular trains link Besançon with Arc-et-Senans (€7.40, 22 minutes, 10 to 16 daily).

Route Pasteur

Louis Pasteur (1822–95), who developed the first rabies vaccine and, of course, pasteurisation, was born in the well-preserved medieval town of **Dole**, former capital of Franche-Comté, 20km west of Arc-et-Senans along the D472. A scenic stroll along the **Canal des Tanneurs** in the historic tanner's quarter brings you to his childhood home, which now houses the **Musée Pasteur** (Maison Natale Pasteur; www.musee-pasteur. com; 43 rue Pasteur; adult/child €5/free; ☉ 10am-noon & 2-6pm Tue-Sat, 2-6pm Sun Apr-Oct, 2-6pm Tue-Sun Nov-Mar), an atmospheric museum whose exhibits include his cot, first drawings and university cap and gown.

In 1827 Pasteur's family settled in the bucolic village of **Arbois** (population 3500), 35km southeast of Dole. His laboratory and workshops here can be seen at the **Maison de Louis Pasteur** (www.academie-sciences. fr/pasteur.htm; 83 rue de Courcelles; adult/child €6.50/3.50; ☉ guided tours 9.45 & 10.45am & hourly 2-5pm or 6pm, closed mid Oct–Mar). The house is still decorated with its original 19th-century fixtures and fittings.

Arbois & the Route des Vins du Jura

Meandering for 80km through well-tended vines, pretty countryside and stone villages is the **Route des Vins du Jura** (Jura Wine Trail; www.tourisme-hauteseille.fr/en/the-jura-wine-trail. htm). Plan your route with the winery map downloadable from the website.

◉ Sights & Activities

No visit to **Arbois**, the Jura's wine capital, would be complete without a glass of *vin jaune*, available at a variety of excellent local restaurants. The history of this nutty 'yellow wine' is told in the **Musée de la Vigne et du Vin du Jura** (www.juramusees.fr; adult/child €3.50/free; ☉ 10am-noon & 2-6pm Wed-Mon Mar-Oct, 2-6pm Wed-Mon Nov-Feb), housed in the turreted Château Pécauld.

The 2.5km-long **Chemin des Vignes** walking trail and the 8km-long **Circuit des Vignes** mountain-bike route meander through the vines. Both trails (marked with orange signs) begin at the top of the steps next to Arbois' Château Pécauld; a booklet with details is available at the tourist office.

High above Arbois is tiny **Pupillin**, a cute yellow-brick village famous for its wine production. Some 10 different *caves* (wine cellars) are open to visitors.

🛏 Sleeping & Eating

★**Closerie les Capucins**   B&B €€
(☎ 03 84 66 17 38; www.closerielescapucines.com; 7 rue de Bourgogne, Arbois; d/q incl breakfast from €125/250; @ 🛜 ⛱) A 17th-century stone convent has been lovingly transformed into this boutique B&B, with five rooms remarkable for their pared-down elegance, a tree-shaded garden by the river and a plunge pool.

La Balance Mets et Vins   REGIONAL CUISINE €€
(☎ 03 84 37 45 00; www.labalance.fr; 47 rue de Courcelles, Arbois; weekday lunch menus €16.30-19.80, other menus €29-52; ☉ noon-2pm & 7-9pm Tue-Sat, also open Sun Jul & Aug, closed mid-Dec–Jan; 🖉 🖟) Chef Theirry Moine takes local, organic produce and, inspired by spices from around the world, transforms it into delicacies such as his signature *coq au vin jaune et aux morilles* and *crème brûlée* doused in *vin jaune*. Reserve ahead for Saturday and holidays, especially from May to August.

To accompany your meal, you can order five glasses of either *vin du Jura* (€19) or *vin jaune* (€25). Kids can sniff, swirl and sip, too, with three kinds of organic grape juice (€7.80).

❶ Information

Tourist Office (☎ 03 84 66 55 50; www.arbois. com; 17 rue de l'Hôtel de Ville, Arbois; ☉ 9am-noon & 2-6pm Mon-Sat year-round, 10am-noon Sun Easter–mid-Sep, also 3-6pm Sun late Jun-early Sep) Has walking and cycling information and a list of *caves* where you can taste and buy the local vintage.

❶ Getting There & Away

Trains link Arbois and Besançon (€9.70, 45 minutes, eight to 12 daily).

Poligny

The small town of Poligny (population 4200), 60km southwest of Besançon, is the centre of the Jura's hugely important Comté cheese industry. Learn how 450L of milk is transformed into a 40kg wheel of the tangy cheese and have a nibble at the **Maison du Comté** (www.maison-du-comte.com; av de la Résistance; adult/child €4/2.50; ☉ guided tours begin 2pm, 3.15pm & 4.15pm Tue-Sun Apr-Oct, open Mon & mornings Jul & Aug).

Dozens of *fruitières* (cheese cooperatives) are open to the public; Poligny's **tourist office** (☑03 84 37 24 21; www.ville-poligny.fr; place des Déportés; ⊙9am-12.30pm & 1.30-5pm or 5.30pm Mon-Sat) has details on cheesemakers and wineries in the region.

In a beautifully converted 18th-century mill, the serene **Hôtel de la Vallée Heureuse** (☑03 84 37 12 13; www.hotelvallee heureuse.com; rte de Genève, Poligny; s/d/q €99/133/185, menus lunch €22-29, dinner €42; ⊙year-round; 🈂) – next to a rushing stream – has 11 large, tastefully decorated rooms and a restaurant specialising in traditional French cuisine. Family-run and very welcoming, it is situated on the road toward Champagnole and Geneva, 400m past the sign indicating that you're leaving Poligny.

Château-Chalon

Château-Chalon, a medieval village of yellow stone surrounded by vineyards, is known for its legendary *vin jaune*.

At **Le Relais des Abbesses** (☑03 84 44 98 56; www.relais-des-abbesses.fr; 36 rue de la Roche; d incl breakfast €80; ⊙closed mid-Nov–Feb), owners Agnès and Gérard have attractively decorated their five spacious, frilly rooms – all with either hardwood or old tile floors – with Chinese lacquer furnishings.

Baume-les-Messieurs

Nestled at the foot of towering, lushly wooded limestone cliffs and wedged between three glacial valleys, Baume-les-Messieurs is a picturesque village of honey-coloured stone houses and red-tiled rooftops. Its abandoned Benedictine **Abbaye Impériale** (Imperial Abbey; www.baumelesmessieurs.fr; adult/child €5.50/3.30; ⊙guided tours Apr-Sep) has an exquisite polychrome Flemish altarpiece dating from the 16th century. About 2km south, the 30-million-year-old caves known as **Grottes de Baume** (Baume Caves; www.baumelesmessieurs.fr; adult/child €7/3.50; ⊙guided tours 10.30am-12.30pm & 1.30-5pm or 6pm Apr-Sep) feature some impressive stalagmites and stalactites.

Opposite the abbey, **Le Grand Jardin** (☑03 84 44 68 37; www.legrandjardin.fr; 6 place Guillaume de Poupet; d incl breakfast €65, menus €18-43; ⊙closed Tue & Wed Sep-Jun) is a delightful, family-run *chambre d'hôte* with three sunny, wood-floored rooms. French and Franche-Comté dishes feature on the restaurant menu.

Baume-les-Messieurs is 20km south of Poligny.

Belfort

POP 50,200

Once part of Alsace's Haut-Rhin *département,* Belfort put up 229 days of tenacious resistance to the Prussian seige of 1870–71, thanks to which it managed to remain French after the rest of Alsace was annexed to Germany. Today, the city is neither Alsatian nor Jurassien but rather its own *territoire*

LIQUID GOLD

Legend has it that *vin jaune* (yellow wine) was invented when a winemaker came across a forgotten barrel, six years and three months after he'd filled it, and discovered that its contents had been miraculously transformed into gold-coloured wine.

A long, undisrupted fermentation process gives Jura's signature wine its unique characteristics. Savagnin grapes are harvested late and their sugar-saturated juice left to ferment for a minimum of six years and three months in oak barrels. A thin layer of yeast forms over the wine, preventing oxidisation; there are no top-ups to compensate for wine that evaporates (known as *la part des anges,* 'the angels' share'). In the end, 100L of grape juice ferments down to just 62L of *vin jaune* (lucky angels!) which is then bottled in a special 0.62L bottle called a *clavelin.*

Vin jaune is renowned for ageing extremely well, with prime vintages easily keeping for more than a century. A 1774 vintage was a cool 220 years old when sipped by an awestruck committee of experts in 1994.

La Percée du Vin Jaune (www.percee-du-vin-jaune.com) is a festival that takes place every year on the first weekend in February to celebrate the *percée* (opening) of the first bottles of the vintage produced six years and three months earlier. Villages take turns holding the two-day celebration, during which the new vintage is blessed and rated and *vin jaune* aficionados enjoy street tastings, cooking competitions, cellar visits and auctions.

(territory), known for its Vauban-built **Cita-delle** and its role in producing super-speedy TGV trains.

Belfort makes a convenient stopover on the way from Alsace to Paris, Burgundy or the Alps.

⊙ Sights & Activities

Musée de l'Aventure
Peugeot   MUSEUM
(☑ 03 81 99 42 03; www.museepeugeot.com; Carrefour de l'Europe, Sochaux; adult/child €8/4; ⊙ 10am-6pm) Gleaming old-timers, concept cars and thumb-size miniatures – it's Peugeots *à gogo* at this automobile museum, 18km south of Belfort (towards Besançon) in Sochaux. Reserve ahead for a weekday tour of the huge Peugeot factory (adult/child €18/12).

☆ Festivals & Events

★**Les Eurockéennes**   MUSIC FESTIVAL
(www.eurockeennes.fr) A huge, three-day open-air rock festival held on the first weekend in July.

⌷ Sleeping

Hôtel Vauban   HOTEL
(☑ 03 84 21 59 37; www.hotel-vauban.com; 4 rue du Magasin; s/d/tr/f €65/70/85/90; ☎) Decorated with colourful oil paintings by the owner's husband, this friendly hotel, built as a house in 1902, has 14 mid-sized, practical rooms and a lovely back garden with koi. Great value. Situated one long block northeast, along the river, from the tourist office.

Grand Hôtel du
Tonneau d'Or   HISTORIC HOTEL €€
(☑ 03 84 58 57 56; www.tonneaudor.fr; 1 rue Reiset; d/tr €122/137; ☎) A grand, old-time hotel, right in the city centre, with Corinthian columns, coffered ceilings, sweeping staircases and 52 large, modern rooms. Rates drop 40% at the weekend.

❶ Information

Tourist Office (☑ 03 84 55 90 90; www.belfort-tourisme.com; 2bis rue Clémenceau; ⊙ 9am-12.30pm & 2-6pm Mon-Sat, also open 10am-1pm Sun Jul & Aug) Has city, cycling and hiking maps and details on cultural activities.

❶ Getting There & Away

Belfort's **train station** (av Wilson) has direct links to Besançon (€16.90, 1¼ hours, 12 daily) and direct and non-direct TGVs and TERs to Paris Gare de Lyon (€77, 2½ hours, 15 daily).

The **Belfort-Montbéliard TGV station**, 9km southeast of the city centre, is a stop on the new LGV Rhin-Rhône service linking Marseille with Strasbourg and Frankfurt.

Ronchamp

The only reason to visit Ronchamp, 22km northwest of Belfort, is to see Le Corbusier's striking modernist chapel, atop a hill overlooking the old mining town. Built between 1950 and 1955, the surreal **Chapelle de Notre-Dame du Haut** (Colline Notre-Dame du Haut; www.collinenotredameduhaut.com; adult/child €8/4; ⊙ 9am-7pm Apr-Oct, 10am-5pm Nov-Mar), with a sweeping concrete roof, dazzling stained-glass windows and plastic features, is considered a masterpiece of mid-20th century architecturure. A convent and a **visitor centre** (La Porererie), both designed by Renzo Piano and both built into the hillside, opened in 2011.

Métabief

POP 1020 / ELEV 1000M

Métabief (www.station-metabief.com and www.tourisme-metabief.com) is the Jura's leading cross-country ski resort. Winter and summer lifts take you almost to the top of Mont d'Or (1463m), the area's highest peak, where a fantastic 180-degree panorama stretches over the foggy Swiss plain to Lake Geneva and all the way from the Matterhorn to Mont Blanc.

Family-run **Hôtel Étoile des Neiges** (☑ 03 81 49 11 21; www.hoteletoiledesneiges.fr; 4 rue du Village; d/f €60/108; ☎☒) has bright, well-kept rooms, including great mezzanine family rooms. There's an indoor pool, a sauna and a canteen-style restaurant.

Métabief is 58km east of Arbois and 75km southeast of Besançon, on the main road to Lausanne (Switzerland).

Parc Naturel Régional du Haut-Jura

To experience the Jura in all of its upland beauty, head to the **Haut-Jura Regional Park** (www.parc-haut-jura.fr), whose 1780 sq km – in the *départements* of Ain, Doubs and Jura – stretch from Chapelle-des-Bois southward almost to the western tip of Lake Geneva. The park's prime sports hub, in both winter (skiing) and summer, is **Les Rousses** (www.lesrousses.com).

> **DON'T MISS**
>
> ## HOT BOX & JÉSUS
>
> It's hot, it's soft and it's packed in a box. Vacherin Mont d'Or is the only French cheese to be eaten with a spoon – hot. Made between 15 August and 15 March with *lait cru* (unpasteurised milk), it derives its unique nutty taste from the spruce bark in which it's wrapped. Connoisseurs top the soft-crusted cheese with chopped onions, garlic and white wine, wrap it in aluminium foil and bake it for 45 minutes to create a *boîte chaude* (hot box). Only 11 factories in the Jura are licensed to produce Vacherin Mont d'Or.
>
> Mouthe, 15km south of Métabief Mont d'Or, is the mother of *liqueur de sapin* (fir-tree liqueur). *Glace de sapin* (fir-tree ice cream) also comes from Mont d'Or, known as the North Pole of France due to its seasonal subzero temperatures (record low: -38°C). Sampling either is rather like ingesting a Christmas tree. Then there's *Jésus* – a small, fat version of *saucisse de Morteau* (Morteau sausage), easily identified by the wooden peg on its end, attached after the sausage is smoked with pinewood sawdust in a traditional *tuyé* (mountain hut).

The **Maison du Parc du Haut-Jura** (www.parc-haut-jura.fr; Lajoux; adult/child €5/3; ⏰ 10am-12.30pm & 2-6pm Tue-Fri, 2-6pm Sat & Sun, longer hours Jul & Aug), the park's visitor centre, has interactive exhibits on the Jura that you can touch – great for kids. It's in Lajoux, 19km east of the park's largest town, St-Claude.

Col de la Faucille (1323m; open year-round), a serpentine 13km east of Lajoux and 29km north of Geneva Airport, has incredible views across Lake Geneva to the snowy Alps beyond.

🛏 Sleeping & Eating

Le Clos d'Estelle   B&B €
(☎ 03 84 42 01 29; www.leclosdestelle.com; 1 La Marcantine, Charchilla; d/q with breakfast €80/135; ⏰ year-round) Surrounded by fields and sheep, Christine and Jean-Pierre warmly welcome guests to four very spacious, wood-built *chambres d'hôte* in their mid-19th-century farmhouse. Situated in Charchilla (shar-*shiy*-a), 200m down the hill behind the church.

La Mainaz   CHALET €€
(☎ 04 50 41 31 10; www.la-mainaz.com; Col de la Faucille; d €92-125, menus €20-50; ⏰ closed last half Jun & Nov; ✏) This cosy chalet, run by the same family since 1945, has spectacular panoramas of Mont Blanc, 21 rooms and excellent French and regional cuisine. Situated 800m towards Geneva from Col de la Faucille.

Les Louvières   GASTRONOMIC €€
(☎ 03 84 42 09 24; www.leslouvieres.fr; Pratz; 2-/3-course menus €38/44; ⏰ noon-2pm Wed-Sun, 7.30-9pm Wed-Sat) On a secluded hillside in the middle of the forest, the 'wolf's lair' is both elegant and creatively modern, with gorgeous views of the Jura mountains and delicious *gastronomique* cuisine with Asian influences. Situated between the villages of Pratz (pronounced 'prah') and Moirans, 1.8km along a one-lane road from the D470 (follow the signs).

Chef Philippe Vaufrey, who spent seven years in San Francisco and Winnipeg, is especially fond of coriander and curries. Reservations are required – a week ahead in summer, the morning of your meal the rest of the time.

Massif Central

POP 1.34 MILLION

Best Places to Eat

➡ Maki Nova (p559)

➡ La Golmotte (p550)

➡ Les Caudalies (p546)

➡ Chez Laurette (p552)

➡ Le Sisisi (p542)

Best Places to Stay

➡ Le Chastel Montaigu (p551)

➡ Auberge d'Aijean (p552)

➡ Hôtel Saluces (p553)

➡ Hôtel Notre Dame (p548)

➡ Le Moulin Ferme-Auberge (p560)

Why Go?

In one of the wildest, emptiest and least-known corners of France, the Massif Central, you can feel nature's heavy machinery at work. Below ground, hot volcanic springs bubble up to supply Vichy and Volvic with their famous mineral waters, while high in the mountains trickling streams join forces to form three of France's mightiest rivers: the Dordogne, the Allier and the Loire.

The Massif Central and surrounding Auvergne region remains deeply traditional. Reliant on agriculture and cattle farming, it shelters the country's largest area of protected landscape with two huge regional parks: the Parc Naturel Régional des Volcans d'Auvergne and its neighbour, the Parc Naturel Régional Livradois-Forez. On-tap outdoor activities include heady hiking trails, plunging ski slopes, paragliding off shapely volcanic summits, and setting off on an age-old pilgrimage – sustained by some of the halest, heartiest food in France.

When to Go
Clermont-Ferrand

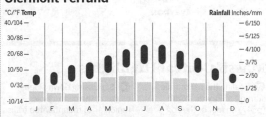

Jun Experience the region's hiking trails in their full springtime splendour.

Dec–Mar Max out on winter sports at Le Mont-Dore or catch Clermont-Ferrand's short-film festival.

Aug See sacred *Vierges Noires* (Black Madonnas) paraded on Assumption Day.

Massif Central Highlights

1 Scaling the panoramic summit of **Puy de Dôme** (p547) on foot or the cog railway

2 Swooning over pastures and rugged volcanic scenery around **Salers** (p553)

3 Marvelling at the Michelin brothers' influence at the Michelin museum in **Clermont-Ferrand** (p539)

4 Schussing down slopes or riding the century-old funicular to mountaintop trails in **Le Mont-Dore** (p548)

5 Watching artisans at work at Musée de la Coutellerie in **Thiers** (p554)

6 Meeting the cows who make one of France's most famous AOC cheeses at **St-Nectaire** (p551)

7 Climbing the staircase to the cave chapel of St-Michel d'Aiguilhe, atop a pinnacle in **Le Puy-en-Velay** (p555)

8 Soaking up the mineral-rich spa waters in belle époque **Vichy** (p543)

9 Exploring an Auvergnat village's proud WWII Resistance history in **Le-Chambon-sur-Lignon** (p560)

History

The historical province of the Auvergne derives its name from a Gallic tribe, the Arverni, who ruled the area until the Romans arrived under Julius Caesar. Arverni chieftain Vercingétorix put up fierce resistance to Caesar's legions, but despite some victories, his armies were finally crushed near Alésia in Burgundy.

The Romans founded a number of settlements including Augustonemetum (later Clermont-Ferrand). Following the fall of the Empire, the Auvergne entered a period of infighting between rival factions of Franks, Aquitanians and Carolingians, before being split into feudal domains during the Middle Ages under the dukes of Auvergne, whose government was in Riom.

After the French Revolution, the capital switched to Clermont-Ferrand, which became a focus of expansion, especially with the Michelin brothers' factories in the late 19th century. Meanwhile aristocrats flocked to the region's fashionable spas, notably in Vichy. During WWII Vichy became the capital of the collaborationist regime under General Philippe Pétain.

ⓘ Getting There & Around

AIR

The region's only airport is in Clermont-Ferrand.

BICYCLE

There are excellent mountain-biking opportunities throughout the region, especially around Puy de Dôme and Le Mont-Dore; local tourist offices and cycling/sports shops can generally provide trail information for day trippers.

The Massif Central also makes an appealing road biking destination, thanks to the region's limited car traffic. For a detailed multi-day road-biking itinerary, head to shop.lonelyplanet.com to purchase a downloadable PDF of the Massif Central chapter from Lonely Planet's *Cycling France* guide.

CAR & MOTORCYCLE

The A75 autoroute (sometimes called La Méridienne) provides high-speed travel to southern France through the viaducts at Garabit and Millau, while the A89 (La Transeuropéenne) travels west to Bordeaux. Elsewhere the region's roads are twisty, slow and highly scenic: you'll need your own car to reach the more remote spots, as the bus network is limited.

TRAIN

Though the TGV network hasn't yet arrived, regular trains serve all the main towns including a direct service from Clermont-Ferrand to Paris in 3½ hours.

CLERMONT FERRAND & AROUND

Clermont-Ferrand

POP 144,800 / ELEV 400M

Sprawled around a long-extinct volcano in the middle of the Massif Central, Clermont-Ferrand is the capital of the Auvergne and its only metropolis. Home to the Michelin empire and roly-poly Michelin Man (known to the French as Bibendum), the city has been a thumping industrial powerhouse for over a century. Surrounded by smokestack factories and suburban warehouses, the atmospheric old town is crowned by a soaring twin-spired cathedral.

⊙ Sights

The narrow lanes of Clermont-Ferrand's old city twist outwards from the cathedral, dotted with mansions dating from the 17th and 18th centuries.

If you plan to visit all three of Clermont's municipal museums, you'll save money with a **Pass 3 Musées** (€9), available at the tourist office.

★ **L'Aventure Michelin**　　　　MUSEUM
(www.laventuremichelin.com; 32 rue du Clos Four; adult/child €9/5, audioguide €2; ⊙10am-6pm Tue-Sun Sep-Jun, 10am-7pm daily Jul & Aug) Next door to Clermont's mammoth Michelin factory, with a 5300kg tyre (the world's largest) out front, this brilliant museum recounts the rubber empire's evolution while also shedding light on Michelin's wide-ranging impact on aviation, rail, maps, restaurant guides and GPS technology. Hugely entertaining for both adults and kids, it's got some great hands-on interactive exhibits and advertising retrospectives. Allow at least a couple of hours; last entry is 90 minutes before closing. Take Tram A to Stade Marcel Michelin.

Clermont-Ferrand

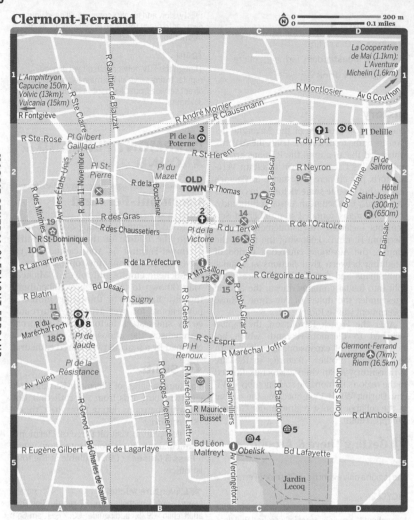

The museum's on-site gift shop sells everything from road maps to bouncy Bibendum key rings.

Cathédrale Notre Dame   CATHEDRAL

(place de la Victoire; tower admission €2; ⏱ cathedral 7.30am–noon & 2–6pm Mon-Sat, 9.30am–noon & 3–7.30pm Sun, tower 9am–11.15am & 2–5.15pm Mon-Sat, 3–5.30pm Sun; 🐾) Carved from the inky volcanic rock from the quarries of Volvic, Clermont's jet-black cathedral, with its massive Gothic façade, was constructed between the 13th and 19th centuries. The interior is a striking contrast of light and shade, brilliantly lit by afternoon sunshine. For fantastic views east to Thiers and west to Puy de Dôme, brave the 250 steps to the top of its only transept tower to have survived the French Revolution, the **Tour de la Bayette**.

Fontaine d'Amboise   FOUNTAIN

Two blocks north of the cathedral, this early 16th-century fountain is the focal point of a pretty park with panoramic views towards Puy de Dôme and other nearby peaks.

Musée d'Art Roger Quilliot   ART MUSEUM

(http://museedart.clermont-ferrand.fr; place Louis-Deteix; adult/child €5/free; ⏱ 10am–6pm Tue-Fri, 10am–noon & 1–6pm Sat & Sun) Situated northeast

Clermont-Ferrand

of the centre in Montferrand, this museum in a converted Ursuline convent features exhibits from the late Middle Ages to the 20th century, including significant works by Delacroix, the Ryckaert family and François Boucher. Take tram A from place de Jaude.

Musée Bargoin MUSEUM
(http://museebargoin.clermont-ferrand.fr; 45 rue Ballainvilliers; adult/child €5/free; ⊗10am-noon & 1-5pm Tue-Sat, 2-7pm Sun) This is really two museums in one: an **archaeological** department, displaying excavated Roman coins to neolithic wood carvings, and a **textile arts** department, with a collection of carpets from Tibet, Iran, Syria, China and beyond.

**Musée d'Histoire
Naturelle Henri-Lecoq** MUSEUM
(http://museelecoq.clermont-ferrand.fr; 15 rue Bardoux; adult/child €5/free; ⊗10am-noon & 2-5pm Tue-Sat, 2-5pm Sun) Clermont-Ferrand's natural history museum is named for the celebrated pharmacist and natural scientist who lived here in the 19th century and amassed rocks, fossils, plants and stuffed animals from the region. Highlights include the gallery of Auvergnat butterflies and more than 50 native orchids.

Basilique Notre Dame du Port CHURCH
(⊗8am-7pm) A Unesco World Heritage Site, this magnificent example of 12th-century Auvergnat-Romanesque architecture is sparkling after recent renovations. Its *Vierge Noire* is venerated with a grand procession in mid-May. For nice views of the apse's exterior, climb the signposted steps to the **belvédère** (⊗2-5pm) across the street.

Place de Jaude SQUARE
At the southwestern edge of the old city, Clermont's monumental pedestrianised square is overlooked by a **statue** of heroic Celtic chief Vercingétorix.

🛏 Sleeping

As a commercial hub, Clermont has plenty of accommodation, but most places lack character and offer limited value for money.

Hôtel Saint-Joseph HOTEL €
(☑04 73 92 69 71; www.hotelsaintjoseph.fr; 10 rue de Maringues; s €41-50, d €53; @⊗) The double-glazed rooms at this small hotel near the Friday morning St-Joseph market offer the best budget value in Clermont.

Dav' Hôtel HOTEL €
(☑04 73 93 31 49; www.davhotel.fr; 10 rue des Minimes; s €64-74, d €67-79; ❂@⊗) Rooms here come in two varieties: plain but functional 'standard' units and brighter 'deco' rooms, with jarringly tacky wall art. Neither option wins many style points, but prices are the lowest you'll find so close to the city centre.

★**5 Chambres en Ville** B&B €€
(☑07 81 16 60 95; www.5-chambresenville.com; 8 rue Neyron; r incl breakfast €100-130; ⊗) This classy new B&B offers pristine, design-conscious rooms in a perfect city centre location. All five units come with ample beds, quality linens, flat-screen TVs, dependable wi-fi and plenty of natural light; the more expensive pair on the top floor offer romantic features, especially the 'zen' room with its recessed, candlelit, slate-walled bathtub.

Hôtel Le Lion HOTEL €€
(☑04 73 17 60 80; www.hotel-le-lion.com; 16 place de Jaude; r weekend/weekday from €95/105; ❂⊗) Remodelled top to bottom and reopened under new management in summer 2014, this three-star enjoys a prime position on Clermont-Ferrand's grandest square, with the famous statue of Gallic hero Vercingétorix straight outside the front windows. Downstairs, the **pub-brasserie** is good for a drink.

✖ Eating

Place de Jaude and the area north around rue St-Dominique are filled with inexpensive eateries. Cafe terraces ring place de la Victoire just south of the cathedral; Clermont's **covered market** (www.marche-saint-pierre.com; place St-Pierre; ☺7am-7pm Mon-Sat) is a few blocks northwest.

Les Arcandiers   BISTRO €
(✐04 73 92 21 50; 10 place du Terrail; mains €11; ☺noon-1.15pm & 6.30-10.30pm Wed-Sat) Illuminated globes and model planes hang whimsically from vaulted ceilings, and jazz album covers plaster the walls at this attractively decorated bistro. With marble-topped bar, comfy couches, potted plants and Oriental carpets on ancient stone floors, it doubles as a relaxing lunch spot and an alluring evening hangout for glasses of wine and homemade *terrine de foie gras.*

Avenue   MODERN FRENCH €€
(✐04 73 90 44 64; www.restaurant-avenue.fr; 10 rue Massillon; lunch menu €15, mains €18-22; ☺noon-2.30pm & 7.30-10pm Tue-Sat) Run by an energetic young couple – he cooks, she works the tables – this sleek modern eatery seats just a couple of dozen people. The ever-changing menu of inventive, market-fresh treats always includes a well-priced *plat du jour* (€9.50 on its own, €13 with appetiser or dessert, €15 with both).

★ Le Sisisi   BISTRO €€
(✐04 73 14 04 28; lesisisi.com; 16 rue Massillon; mains €17-19, lunch menu €14.50; ☺noon-1.30pm Tue-Fri, 8.30-10pm Tue-Sat) At this laid-back local bistro, a mixed crowd sips early evening

drinks at the bar, then settles in for creative cuisine served at sidewalk tables or in the high-ceilinged industrial-chic dining room. From mains like *mille-feuille* of sirloin steak and marinated red peppers, to desserts such as *panna cotta* with roasted strawberries and banana-lime coulis, everything's presented with artistic flair.

Il Visconti   ITALIAN €€
(✐04 73 74 35 26; www.ilvisconti.com; 9 rue du Terrail; mains €13-19; ☺noon-1.30pm & 7.30-10pm Tue-Sat) A genuine Italian chef in the kitchen and an emphasis on quality imported ingredients make this a tempting departure from standard French fare. Authentic 'old country' specialties include *spaghetti al nero di seppia* (spaghetti with squid ink, zucchini, prawns and lemon zest), *saltimbocca alla romana* (veal wrapped in San Daniele ham with mascarpone and sage gnocchi) and homemade *tiramisù* (coffee-flavoured dessert).

L'Amphitryon Capucine   GASTRONOMIC €€€
(✐04 73 31 38 39; www.amphitryoncapucine.com; 50 rue Fontgiève; menus lunch €17-19, dinner €31-85; ☺noon-1.30pm & 7.30-9.30pm Tue-Sat) Ditch the jeans and dig out your glad rags and you'll be rewarded with splendid seasonal cuisine, from the reasonably priced three-course lunch *menu* to the decadent eight-course *menu gourmand.*

Drinking & Nightlife

Les Goûters de Justine   TEAROOM
(11bis rue Blaise Pascal; ☺noon-7pm Wed-Fri, 2.30-7pm Sat) With its amiable proprietor and jumble of old-fashioned furniture, this is a cosy spot to linger over a cup of tea accompanied by homemade cakes from the sideboard.

☆ Entertainment

For sports and entertainment listings, including news of Clermont's cherished rugby team, see the website **Zap** (www.myzap.fr).

La Cooperative de Mai   LIVE MUSIC
(www.lacoope.org; rue Serge Gainsbourg) Cavernous warehouse gig and concert venue. Catch tram A to place du 1er Mai.

B.Box Club   CLUB
(www.bboxclub.com; 29 rue de l'Eminée, La Pardieu; ☺11.30pm-5am Thu-Sun) This 4000-capacity multilevel warehouse 6km east of the centre is France's largest indoor club. Catch its free *navette* (minibus) from Cours Sablon downtown.

ℹ️ Information

Tourist Office (☎ 04 73 98 65 00; www.cler-mont-fd.com; place de la Victoire; ⊙ 9am-7pm daily Jul & Aug, 9am-6pm Mon-Fri, 10am-1pm & 2-6pm Sat & Sun rest of year) Opposite the cathedral; has city maps and ample free literature, plus a multimedia exhibition on the Auvergne's churches downstairs. There's free wi-fi in the adjacent square.

ℹ️ Getting There & Away

AIR

Clermont-Ferrand Auvergne airport (www.clermont-aeroport.com), 7km east of the city centre, is served by Air France and several smaller airlines. Domestic destinations include Paris, Nice and Ajaccio; international flights go to Amsterdam (Netherlands), Brussels (Belgium), Porto (Portugal) and Southampton (UK).

CAR

Major car hire companies have branches at the airport and in town.

TRAIN

Clermont is the region's main rail hub. You can buy tickets at the **boutique SNCF** (☎ 08 92 35 35 35, 43 rue du 11 Novembre) in the city centre.

Long-haul destinations include:

Le Mont-Dore €14.20, 1¾ hours, one direct train and one SNCF bus daily

Le Puy-en-Velay €25, 2¼ hours, three or four daily

Lyon €35, 2½ hours, more than 10 daily

Nîmes €44, 5¼ hours, three direct trains daily

Paris Gare de Lyon €59, 3½ hours, six to 10 daily

Frequent short hauls also run to:

Riom €3.50, 10 minutes

Thiers €9.20, 45 minutes

Vichy €10.60, 30 minutes

Volvic €4.70, 25 minutes

ℹ️ Getting Around

TO/FROM THE AIRPORT

Bus 20 travels to/from the airport several times daily Monday to Saturday; a **taxi** (☎ 04 73 60 06 00) costs between €20 and €25.

BUS & TRAM

Clermont's public-transport system is handled by **T2C** (www.t2c.fr; 24 bd Charles de Gaulle; single ticket/day pass/10-trip carnet €1.40/4.30 /12.20). Buses link the city and station, while tram A connects place de Jaude with Montferrand.

BICYCLE

C.vélo (☎ 04 73 44 80 08; www.c-velo.fr; per 30min €1, plus flat fee per day/week €1/5) hires

bikes at more than 12 self-service stations around town, including the train station and place de Jaude.

Riom

POP 19,000

Capital of the Auvergne region during the Middle Ages, Riom has an old quarter with boulevards lined with *hôtels particuliers* (historic private mansions), mostly built from dark volcanic stone.

The **tourist office** (☎ 04 73 38 59 45; www.tourisme-riomlimagne.fr; 27 place de la Fédération; ⊙ 9.30am-12.30pm & 2-5.30pm Tue, Wed, Fri & Sat, 2-5.30pm Mon & Thu) is adjacent to the pretty Romanesque church, **Église St-Amable** (rue St-Amable; ⊙ 9am-7pm).

Climbing 167 steps in Riom's 15th-century **Tour de l'Horloge** (rue de l'Horloge; adult/child €1/free, Wed free; ⊙ 10am-noon & 2-5pm Tue-Sun) rewards with wonderful views of the town and mountains.

Customs and traditions of life in the Auvergne are explored at the excellent **Musée Régional d'Auvergne** (☎ 04 73 38 17 31; www.ville-riom.fr/Musee-regional-d-Auvergne; 10bis rue Delille; adult/child €3/free; ⊙ guided tours 2.30pm & 4pm Tue-Sun, closed mid-Nov–mid-May), visitable by guided tour only, while the **Musée Francisque Mandet** (14 rue de l'Hôtel de Ville; adult/child €3/free; ⊙ 10am-noon & 2-5.30pm Tue-Sun) displays impressive exhibits of decorative arts, classical finds and 15th- to 19th-century paintings.

The 15th-century **Église Notre Dame du Marthuret** (rue du Commerce; ⊙ 9am-6pm) holds Riom's treasured relics: a *Vierge Noire* (Black Madonna) and a delicate *Vierge à l'Oiseau*, depicting the Virgin and Child accompanied by a fluttering bird.

Riom is 15km north of Clermont on the N9, served by frequent trains (€3.50, 10 minutes).

Vichy

POP 25,470

Its belle époque heyday may have passed, but there's still an air of understated grandeur about the stately streets and landscaped parks of Vichy, 55km northeast of Clermont-Ferrand. Famous for its volcanic mineral waters since Napoléon III and his entourage sojourned here during the 19th century, and later infamous as the seat of General Philippe Pétain's collaborationist regime during WWII, these days Vichy is a well-to-do provincial hub, enduringly popular for its therapeutic waters.

Vichy

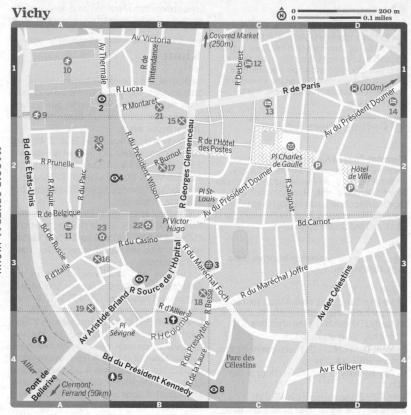

Sights & Activities

Parks
PARK

Vichy's centrepiece is the huge **Parc des Sources**, laid out by Napoléon in 1812. Filled with chestnut and plane trees and encircled by a wrought-iron-canopied colonnade, it's a pleasant place to stroll. Other lovely parks include the riverside **Parc Kennedy** and **Parc Napoléon III**, whose appeal was enhanced in 2014 by a revamped riverfront promenade for pedestrians and cyclists. Watch for Swiss-style 19th-century chalets along the parks' edge, which once lodged Vichy's visiting *curistes* (people seeking cure in spa towns).

Springs
SPRINGS

For unlimited free sips of Vichy's mineral waters, head for the brass taps of **Source des Célestins** (blvd du Président Kennedy; ⊙8am-8.30pm Apr-Sep, 8am-6pm Oct-Mar) – bring your own bottle and note taps are shut in winter to prevent frozen pipes. Other venues for drinking the waters, including the elegant glass **Hall**

des Sources (Parc des Sources; ⊙6.15am-7pm) and the **Source de l'Hôpital** (Parc des Sources; ⊙8am-8.30pm Apr-Dec), are off-limits without a prescription. If you're keen, the tourist office has a list of local *médecins* (doctors).

Spas
SPA

Vichy's most luxurious spa, **Les Célestins** (☑04 70 30 82 35; www.vichy-spa-hotel.com; 111 bd des États-Unis; ⊙9am-8pm Mon-Sat, to 4pm Sun) offers decadent treatments such as the *douche de Vichy à quatre mains* (four-hand hot-spring massage; €116 for 25 minutes) or the *massage aux pierres chaudes des volcans* (hot lava rock massage; €103 for 50 minutes). Similar treatments are on offer at **Thermes des Dômes** (☑04 70 97 39 65; www.vichy-thermes-domes-hotel.com; 132 bd des États-Unis; ⊙8am-7pm Mon-Sat), housed in a once-lavish complex of Moorish arches and tiled towers (much of it now incongruously turned into a shopping arcade) topped by a Byzantine-style dome.

Vichy

Musée de l'Opéra de Vichy   MUSEUM
(http://opera.vichy.musee.free.fr; 16 rue du Maréchal
Foch; adult/child €4/3; ☺2-6pm Tue-Sun) This museum houses rotating exhibits that document
Vichy's turn-of-the-20th-century opera house.

Église St-Blaise   CHURCH
(rue d'Allier) This art-deco 1930s church has
20th-century stained glass and frescoes of
some of France's famous churches. The original chapel at the rear has Vichy's *Vierge Noire*.

🛏 Sleeping

Places to stay are plentiful. Vichy's spas can
also arrange accommodation packages.

Hôtel Arverna   HOTEL €
(☎04 70 31 31 19; www.arverna-hotels-vichy.com; 12
rue Desbrest; d €66-93; ❀@🛜) Newly remodelled, this comfortable hideaway down a quiet
side street has air-conditioning in all rooms,
facilities for disabled travellers and plenty of
other perks, including energy-efficient bedside reading lamps, rain shower heads, heated
towel racks and armchairs that convert into
kid-sized beds.

Hôtel de Naples   HOTEL €
(☎04 70 97 91 33; www.hoteldenaples.fr; 22 rue de
Paris; d €47-54; @🛜) Welcoming and well located, this hotel has clean, good-sized rooms,
split between the main building and a quiet
rear annexe overlooking the hotel's car park
(€6 for two days). In summer, breakfast
(€7.50) is served on the grassy back terrace.

★La Demeure d'Hortense   B&B €€
(☎04 70 96 73 66; www.demeure-hortense.fr; 62
ave du Président Doumer; d €115-130, ste €145, all incl
breakfast; ❀🛜) Perfectly placed between the
train station and park, this stately 19th-century
mansion with parquet floors, marble stairs

and vintage stained glass has been refurbished
with modern comforts. Three rooms and two
luxurious suites come with ultra-comfy beds,
classy antique and designer furniture and
spacious bathrooms. Common areas include
an elegant salon and a relaxing back patio.

Aletti Palace Hôtel   HOTEL €€€
(☎04 70 30 20 20; www.hotel-aletti.fr; 3 place Joseph Aletti; d €150-195, ste €230-250; ❀🛜🏊) A
billiards room, wood-panelled bar and outdoor pool are among the luxurious amenities at this *grande dame* presiding over the
Parc des Sources. Palatial rooms come with
marble bathrooms and enormous closets. Its
glass-canopied restaurant (*menus* €17 to €36)
uses local produce in its classical cuisine.

🍴 Eating

For inexpensive sidewalk dining, check out
the cluster of brasseries at the intersection
of rue de Paris and rue Georges Clemenceau.
Vichy's **covered market** (www.legrandmarche
couvert-vichy.fr; place PV Léger; ☺7am-1pm Tue-Sun,
plus 4-7pm Fri & Sat) is 500m northwest of the
train station.

Brasserie du Casino   BRASSERIE €€
(☎04 70 98 23 06; www.brasserie-du-casino.fr; 4
rue du Casino; lunch/dinner menus €19/29; ☺noon-
1.30pm & 7.30-9.30pm Thu-Tue) All shiny brass,
faded wood and squeaky leather, this timeless
haunt has a wall of photos featuring the actors and *chanteurs* (singers) who've stopped
by from the opera house. The food is substantial (duck confit, beef tartare) and the feel
unmistakably French.

L'Hippocampe   SEAFOOD €€
(☎04 70 97 68 37; www.restaurant-poisson-
hippocampe-vichy.fr; 3 bd de Russie; menus €20-
58; ☺noon-2pm Wed-Sun, 7.30-9pm Tue-Sat) For

VICHY SWEETS

Pastilles de Vichy were first created in 1825 using bicarbonate of soda, but the town's mineral waters later inspired its signature sweets. Since 1875 the bicarbonate has been replaced with salts extracted from the local mineral water, which is mixed with sugar and flavoured with mint, aniseed or lemon. Not all of these octagonal-shaped sweets are the same, however. Those sold in shops and supermarkets have a different composition to those sold in pharmacies, which contain 10% more mineral salts to enhance their digestive properties. And Vichy is the only place in the world where you can buy the sweets stamped with the 'Vichy Etat' logo and packaged in an iconic metal tin; look for them at the beautiful glass-paned, rotunda-style kiosk **Maison des Pastilles** (Parc des Sources; ⊙10am-12.30pm & 2.30-6.30pm Tue-Sun mid-Apr–Sep). To learn more, visit the **Pastillerie de Vichy** (⌨04 70 30 94 70; www.pastille-vichy.fr; 94 Allée des Ailes; ⊙9am-noon & 1.30-3pm Mon-Thu, 9-11am Fri Apr–mid-Nov) **FREE** plant, 2.5km north of the centre, for an overview of their history and manufacturing process (and free tastings, too).

Vichy also has a trove of exquisite *confiseries* and *chocolateries* selling handmade treats. The pastel-pink-framed windows of **Vichy-Prunelle** (www.vichy-prunelle.com; 36 rue Montaret; ⊙10am-noon & 2.45-7pm) entice with a rainbow of translucent lollipops, while **Aux Marocains** (www.auxmarocains.com; 33 rue Georges Clemenceau; ⊙9.15am-12.30pm & 2.30-7pm Tue-Sat, 10.30am-12.30pm & 3-7pm Sun, 3-7pm Mon) is chock-a-block with marzipan, petits fours and caramels.

a restaurant called the Sea Horse, the menu here appropriately features scallops, sole, oak-smoked sardines and a monumental *assiette de fruits de mer* (seafood platter). In summer, the lobster-based *menu homard* (€58) is a popular tradition.

★ **Les Caudalies** GASTRONOMIC €€€
(⌨04 70 32 13 22; www.les-caudalies-vichy.fr; 7-9 rue Besse; menus lunch €23-26, dinner €33-82; ⊙noon-2pm Tue-Sun, 7-9.30pm Tue-Sat) Chef Emmanuel Bosset creates inventive twists on traditional French cuisine, from starters such as escargots in hazelnut and anise liqueur-scented butter to desserts of Vichy pastille ice cream with poppy wine. The lunchtime *jéroboam menu*, including three courses and a glass of wine, is good value (€26).

La Table d'Antoine GASTRONOMIC €€€
(⌨04 70 98 99 71; www.latabledantoine.com; 8 rue Burnol; menus lunch €20-24, dinner €31-67; ⊙12.15-1pm Wed-Mon, 7.30-8.45pm Wed-Sun) Abstract portraits and high-backed chairs create a boutique feel at this high-class temple to French fine dining. Seriously fancy menus jazz up the French classics with international influences, from foie gras ravioli in wild mushroom broth to tandoori lamb confit. Reserve ahead.

☆ **Entertainment**

The free monthly what's-on guide **Vichy Mensuel** (www.editionsducentre.fr/mensuel.html) can be picked up all over town.

Opéra de Vichy OPERA
(⌨04 70 30 50 30; www.ville-vichy.fr/opera-vichy; rue du Casino) Vichy's opera house stages regular productions. Tickets are sold inside the tourist office.

Casino Vichy Grand Café CASINO
(www.casinovichygrandcafe.com; 7 rue du Casino; ⊙10am-3am) Vichy's casino was one of the first opened in France. Today punters can hit the tables in this annex of the now-closed original.

ℹ **Information**

Tourist Office (⌨04 70 98 71 94; www.vichy-tourisme.com; 19 rue du Parc; ⊙9.30am-noon & 1.30-6pm Mon-Sat year-round, plus 3-6pm Sun Apr-Sep)

ℹ **Getting There & Around**

BICYCLE
Near the station, **Cycles Peugeot Gaillardin** (⌨04 70 31 52 86; 48 bd Gambetta; bike rental per half/full day €5/8) rents bikes.

TRAIN
Destinations include the following:
Clermont-Ferrand €10.60, 30 minutes, hourly
Lyon €28.20, 1¾ hours, seven daily
Paris Gare de Bercy €53, three hours, six to eight daily
Riom €8.40, 25 minutes, hourly

PARC NATUREL RÉGIONAL DES VOLCANS D'AUVERGNE

A vast tract of cloud-shrouded peaks, snowy uplands and lush green valleys, the **Parc Naturel Régional des Volcans d'Auvergne** (www.parc-volcans-auvergne.com) occupies most of the western Massif Central, stretching some 3950 sq km and 120km from base to tip. Evidence of its volcanic history abounds.

Unsurprisingly, this is fantastic terrain for outdoor enthusiasts, including skiers, hikers and mountain bikers, as well as paragliders who can often be seen drifting around the region's peaks.

Volvic

POP 4690

Just inside the Parc Naturel Régional des Volcans d'Auvergne's northeastern boundary, 13km north of Clermont-Ferrand, you can learn all about – and taste – Volvic's world-famous mineral water at the company's **Espace d'Information** (☑04 73 64 51 24; www.espaceinfo.volvic.fr; rue des Sources; ⊙10am-12.15pm & 2-6pm Mon-Fri, 2.30-6pm Sat & Sun May-Sep, shorter hours Apr & Oct, closed Nov-Mar) **FREE**. Outside, **walking trails** (from 45 minutes to two hours) fan into the lush surrounds, linking with the GR441. Free hour-long factory tours of its nearby bottling facility are available between mid-April and early September.

Château de Tournoël (☑04 73 33 53 06; www.tournoel.com; adult/child €8/3; ⊙10.30am-12.30pm & 2-6pm Jul & Aug), a storybook medieval fortress, is just uphill from the village centre. In summer you can visit the kitchens, kitchen gardens and the castle's 14th-century defensive round tower with its panoramic views. Volvic's **tourist office** (☑04 73 33 58 73; www.volvic-tourisme.com; ⊙9am-noon & 2-6pm Tue-Sat), on the village's central square, has info on accommodation.

Frequent trains link Volvic with Clermont-Ferrand (€4.70, 30 minutes).

Puy de Dôme & Around

The shapely summit of Puy de Dôme (1465m) looms 10km west of Clermont-Ferrand. Snowcapped from September to May, the mountain was formed by a volcanic eruption some 10,000 years ago and was later the site of a Celtic shrine and Roman temple. You can still see the temple's remains today, along with vistas stretching as far as the Alps. Other facilities on the summit include a visitor centre, restaurant, cafe and small historical museum.

The traditional path to the summit is the scenic 'mule track' – a steep but exhilarating hour's climb from the Col de Ceyssat, 13km west of Clermont-Ferrand via the D942 and D68; the trail is 1.8km long, with 400m elevation gain. If you're up for **paragliding** off the summit, you can arrange tandem jumps (€80) with **Aero Parapente** (☑06 61 24 11 45; www.aeroparapente.fr; ⊙Feb-Oct).

Train buffs and less athletic types will appreciate the **Panoramique des Dômes** (www.panoramiquedesdomes.fr; adult/child one-way €7/3, return €11/5; ⊙10am-6pm Oct-Mar, 9am-7pm Apr-Jun & Sep, 9am-11pm Jul & Aug), a spiffy cog railway inaugurated in 2012 that whisks you to the top of Puy de Dôme in 15 minutes, departing thrice hourly (every 40 minutes in winter) from a station at the mountain's base. From late April to late September, a **shuttle bus** (☑04 73 44 68 68; www.smtc-clermont-agglo.fr; €1.40) runs six times daily between Clermont-Ferrand's Place de Jaude and the Panoramique train station. Drivers will find the station signposted 1km west of the D942.

The Auvergne's long-extinct volcanoes are brought to life in spectacular style at **Vulcania** (☑04 73 19 70 00; www.vulcania.com; adult/child €27.50/19; ⊙10am-6pm mid-Mar–mid-Nov, closed Mon & Tue Mar & Sep-Nov; 👶) volcanic theme park, 15km west of Clermont on the D941. Combining educational museum with thrills and spills, it was dreamt up by French geologists Katia and Maurice Krafft, who were tragically killed in a volcanic eruption on Mt Unzen in Japan a year before its 1992 opening. Highlights include the 'dynamic 3D' film *Awakening of the Auvergne Giants*, depicting volcanic eruptions complete with air blasts and water spray, a Dragon Ride – not very scientific, but good fun all the same – and the Cité des Enfants (Kids' City), with activities specially geared towards three- to seven-year-olds.

At **Volcan de Lemptégy** (☑04 73 62 23 25; www.auvergne-volcan.com; adult/child €9.50/7.50, by train €13.50/10.50; ⊙10am-6pm mid-Apr–Sep, longer hours Jul & Aug, shorter hours Mar–mid-Apr & Oct), just across the D941 from Vulcania, you can set off on foot or aboard a little motorised 'train' to discover volcanic landscapes (chimneys, lava flows and more). The intense 'dynamic 3D' exploding mine film makes a fitting finale, though it's not suitable for littlies. Last entry is two hours before closing.

Orcival

POP 240 / ELEV 870M

Halfway between Puy de Dôme and Le Mont-Dore, the picturesque slate rooftops and tumbledown barns of Orcival huddle around the banks of the Sioulet River. The birthplace of former French president Valéry Giscard d'Estaing, this diminutive village centres on the Romanesque **Basilique Notre-Dame** (⊙8.30am-5pm Oct-Mar, to 7.30pm Apr-Sep), renowned for its elegant crypt and 12th-century Virgin of Orcival in the choir.

Orcival's tiny **tourist office** (⌨04 73 65 89 77; www.terresdomes-sancy.com; ⊙10am-noon & 2-5pm Tue-Sat May-Sep; ☎), opposite Basilique Notre-Dame, can suggest hikes in the surrounding area.

Fans of French gardens shouldn't miss the 15th-century **Château de Cordès** (⌨04 73 21 15 89; www.chateau-cordes-orcival.com; adult/child €3/free; ⊙10am-noon & 2-6pm daily Jul-Aug, plus some Sun afternoons in May, Jun & Sep), with magnificent formal grounds laid out by Versailles' garden designer Le Nôtre. It's just north of Orcival off the D27.

The family-run **Hôtel Notre Dame** (⌨04 73 65 82 02; www.hotelnotredame-orcival.com; s/d/tw €48/56/61; ⊙Feb-Dec; ☎) has seven comfortable, refurbished rooms, with pleasant auditory accompaniment from the Basilique's bells tolling next door and the rushing stream out back. Its on-site **restaurant** (menus €15-28) serves ample breakfasts (€9) including homemade blueberry preserves and a tempting selection of local cheeses and charcuterie; hearty portions of *chou farci* (pork-stuffed cabbage) and other regional specialities are dished up at dinnertime.

Orcival is not served by public transport so you'll need your own wheels.

Col de Guéry

South of Orcival, the D27 snakes past the dramatic volcanic crags **Roche Tuillière** (1288m) and **Roche Sanadoire** (1286m) up to the lofty pass of Col de Guéry, which offers fantastic mountain views on every side. In winter, family-friendly **cross-country skiing** and **snowshoeing** are organised by the **Centre Montagnard Cap Guéry** (⌨04 73 65 20 09; www.capguery.com/hiver/le-ski-de-fond; day pass per adult/child €7/3.50; ⊙Dec-Mar; ☂).

Beyond the pass is chilly **Lac de Guéry** – the highest lake in the Massif Central at 1250m, filled with trout and perch. It's a sweet spot for **fishing** – even in winter!

This is the only lake in France that permits *pêche blanche* (ice-fishing); the season kicks off with a big festival the first weekend of March. To buy your fishing licence (per three days €25 in early March, per day €7 mid-March to mid-November), visit the cosy **Auberge du Lac de Guéry** (⌨04 73 65 02 76; www.auberge-lac-guery.fr; d €64, incl breakfast/halfboard/full board €84/136/164). In an unbeatable position on the lakeshore, the inn serves up fresh fish at its fine country **restaurant** (menus €23-45).

Le Mont-Dore

POP 1380 / ELEV 1050M

Nestled in a narrow valley 44km southwest of Clermont-Ferrand, and just four kilometres north of Puy de Sancy (1886m), central France's highest peak, Le Mont-Dore is the Massif Central's main winter-sports base. Considerably quieter than the Alps' adrenaline-pumped resorts, it's a haven for hikers and snow-sports enthusiasts seeking lower-key mountain thrills.

◉ Sights & Activities

Thermes du Mont-Dore   SPA

(⌨04 73 65 05 10; 1 place du Panthéon; ⊙6.30am-12.30pm & 2-5.30pm Mon-Fri, 6.30am-12.30pm Sat mid-Apr–early Nov) Long before anyone thought of hurtling down the hillsides strapped to a pair of wooden planks, Le Mont-Dore was frequented for its hot springs, which bubble out between 37°C and 40°C. The first bathers were the cleanliness-obsessed Romans – you can still see traces of their original baths. In addition to treatments, in low season you can visit the 19th-century neo-Byzantine building on a 45-minute, French-language **guided tour** (adult/child €3.50/2.50; ⊙2pm & 3pm Mon-Fri).

Funiculaire du Capucin   FUNICULAR

(rue René Cassin; one-way/return adult €4.10/5.40, child €3.40/4.10; ⊙10am-12.10pm & 2-5.40pm Wed-Sun Apr-Oct, to 6.40pm daily Jul & Aug) Built in 1898, France's oldest funicular railway (and listed historic monument) sets off every 20 minutes, crawling at 1m per second up to the plateau of Les Capucins, 1270m above town. Various trails lead off the plateau, including the 2km trail to Pic du Capucin (1450m), the GR30, which wends southward towards the Puy de Sancy, and the steep 1km downhill back to town.

Téléphérique du Sancy   CABLE CAR

(one-way/return adult €7.10/9.40, child €5.30/7.10; ⊙9am-12.10pm & 1.30-5pm May-Sep, to 6pm Jul &

TRAIL CENTRAL

The Massif Central is prime walking country, with a network of well-signed trails and as many as 13 GR (long-distance) tracks (including the north–south GR4) criss-crossing the region, supplemented by hundreds of smaller footpaths. Key areas include the Monts du Cantal between Murat and Salers, and the mountainous area around Le Mont-Dore, Puy de Sancy and the Col de Guéry.

Routes range from day hikes to multi-week epics: hard-core hikers tackle the 290km **Traverse of the High Auvergne** through the Chaîne des Puys; the **Robert Louis Stevenson Trail** from Monastier-sur-Gazeille, tracing the author's famous routes through the Cévennes; and the **Via Podiensis** pilgrimage route from Le Puy-en-Velay.

Tourist offices throughout the region sell hiking maps and guidebooks, including the excellent French-language guides published by **Chamina** (www.chamina.com).

Aug) From this cable car's upper station, it's a short climb along a maintained trail and staircase to Puy de Sancy's snowcapped summit, where fabulous views unfold over the northern *puys* and the Monts du Cantal.

Skiing
SKIING

(www.sancy.com/commune/superbesse; downhill/cross-country day pass adult €30/7, child €24.20/5.50) Near Le Mont-Dore, the ski and snowboarding fields **Station du Mont-Dore** and **Super-Besse** encompass 84km of downhill runs for beginners through to experienced skiers, while the **Espace Nordique Sancy** offers 250km of cross-country ski trails. Day passes are valid throughout the Sancy region. There's an abundance of places to hire snow gear in Le Mont-Dore.

Walking
WALKING

Superbly signposted walks around Le Mont-Dore are marked on good trail maps such as IGN's 1:25,000-scale map *Massif du Sancy* (€11.70) or Chamina's *Massif du Sancy* guidebook (€9.50), which outlines 36 hikes in the area. Both are sold at the tourist office.

Mont-Dore Aventures
OUTDOOR ACTIVITIES

(☑ 04 73 65 00 00; www.montdoreaventures.com; Le Salon du Capucin; canyoning/via ferrata/ropes course €50/35/22) Offers multiple adventure sports, including canyoning, a cliffside via ferrata and a fun Tarzan-style treetop ropes course in warmer weather, plus cross-country ski, snowshoe and sled rentals in winter. Owner Gilles Riocreux is a fount of info on local off-the-beaten-track outdoor activities. Call ahead for reservations.

Skating Rink
SKATING

(Patinoire; ☑ 04 73 65 06 55; rue Georges Lagaye; adult/child €6.70/5.30; ⊙ Jul, Aug, late Dec-Mar & Easter) In bad weather, escape to Le Mont-Dore's rink for a skate.

🛏 Sleeping

Grand Hôtel
HOTEL €

(☑ 04 73 65 02 64; www.hotel-mont-dore.com; 2 rue Meynadier; s €49-59, d €59-69, q €89-99; ⊙ mid-Dec–mid-Nov; ☜) Fresh off a top-to-bottom renovation, this ultra-central Le Mont-Dore landmark dating to 1850 provides more comfort and style than its budget prices would imply. Boutiquey bedrooms, including a few with balconies and some nice two-room family suites, come with thick duvets, deep tubs and new wood flooring. The recently added spa (sauna and Jacuzzi) costs €5 extra.

Les Mancelles
HOTEL €

(☑ 04 73 65 03 66; www.auberge-sancy.fr; rte du Sancy; d/tr €40/50, with shared bathroom €30/40; ☜) Flanked by cow-filled pastures up near the ski lifts, this old-school, family-run hotel offers low-priced rooms upstairs (the cheapest with shared bathroom), and a convivial restaurant downstairs with checked tablecloths, beamed ceilings, hearty Auvergnat menus and reasonable guest rates for breakfast (€6), half-board (€22.50) or full board (€34).

Auberge de Jeunesse
Le Grand Volcan
HOSTEL €

(☑ 04 73 65 03 53; www.auberge-mont-dore.com; rte du Sancy; per person incl breakfast/half board/full board €19.30/31.30/43.30; ⊙ mid-Dec–mid-Nov; ☜) Usually jammed with skiers and hikers, this excellent hostel is right below the Puy de Sancy cable car, 3.5km south of town. Facilities include squeaky-clean two- to six-bed dorms with en-suite bathrooms, a guest kitchen and laundry, ski and snowshoe rentals, and an in-house bar. Book way ahead in winter, especially for one of the seven double rooms.

Camping Domaine
de la Grande Cascade
CAMPGROUND €

(☑ 04 73 65 06 23; www.camping-grandecascade.com; rte de Besse; 2-/4-person site €12.50/20.30;

⊙ late May-late Sep; 🛜) 🚭 At 1250m elevation, this campground is on the chilly side. But it's a stupendous spot to pitch a tent, near a 30m waterfall, with wondrous views of the surrounding mountains. Head 3km south of town on the D36.

Le Castelet   HOTEL €
(☑ 04 73 65 05 29; www.lecastelet-montdore.com; 6 av Michel Bertrand; s €57, d €63-81; 🛜 ▧) Halfway between the train station and the tourist office (500m from each), this hotel wins points for its spacious green yard and small swimming pool. Other nice amenities include free parking, ski and bike storage, and an on-site bar and restaurant.

✖ Eating

Most of Le Mont-Dore's hotels offer half-board, often compulsory during ski season. **La Petite Boutique du Bougnat** (1 rue Montlosier; ⊙ 9am-12.30pm & 2.30-7pm mid-Dec–Oct) sells a smorgasbord of local goodies, including sausages, hams and Auvergnat wine, with cheeses available at its **fromagerie** (4 rue Montlosier; ⊙ 9am-12.30pm & 2.30-7pm mid-Dec–Oct) across the street.

Au Petit Paris   BISTRO €
(Chez Mimi; ☑ 04 73 65 01 77; rue Jean-Moulin; menus €16-18; ⊙ 8am-8pm Fri-Wed) Complete with etched glass, chalkboard menus and art nouveau decor, this atmospheric Parisian-style bistro specialises in reasonably priced French classics, including omelettes, salads and fondue. Convivial owner and longtime local fixture Mimi has run the place since 1986 and greets her many regular customers with kisses. If visiting in wintertime, don't miss her famous *vin chaud* (hot mulled wine).

Twenty One Café   CRÊPERIE €
(21-23 Rue Jean Moulin; crêpes €2.30-3.50, galettes €7.50-10.50; ⊙ noon-2.30pm Tue-Sun, 7-9pm Tue-Sat) Friendly and cosy, this city centre hideaway specialises in hearty wheat flour *galettes* filled with cured ham and Auvergnat cheeses and accompanied by salad. Dessert crêpes come with honey, chestnut paste and other classic fillings. The small selection of other dishes includes roast lamb, salmon and duck.

★ **La Golmotte**   AUVERGNAT €€
(☑ 04 73 65 05 77; www.aubergelagolmotte.com; rte D996; menus €17-38; ⊙ noon-2pm Wed-Sun, 7-9pm Wed-Sat) The excellent regional cuisine at this mountainside inn is well worth the 3km trek up the main road towards Orcival and Murol; it's a perfect spot to be introduced to *truffade*, *aligot* and all the Auvergnat classics.

ⓘ Information

Tourist Office (☑ 04 73 65 20 21; www.sancy. com; av de la Libération; ⊙ 9am-12.30pm & 2-6pm; 🛜) Free wi-fi and tons of local info, including hiking maps and guides.

ⓘ Getting There & Around

Two direct trains and three SNCF buses (fewer on Sunday) connect Le Mont-Dore with Clermont-Ferrand (€14.20, 1½ hours).

From late December to early April, a free skiers' *navette* (shuttle bus) plies regularly between Le Mont-Dore and the Sancy cable car.

Around Le Mont-Dore

La Bourboule

POP 1980 / ELEV 850M

Seven kilometres downriver from Le Mont-Dore, you can experience the spa waters of belle époque La Bourboule at a couple of establishments, including the iconic **Les Grands Thermes** (☑ 04 73 81 21 00; www. grandsthermes-bourboule.com; 76 bd Georges Clémenceau; ⊙ 8am-noon mid-Feb–mid-Oct).

Nicknamed 'la station oxygène', La Bourboule is a lovely place to stroll and drink in the clear mountain air. Various trails fan out into the surrounding high country (see the tourist office for details), or you can explore the landscaped **Parc Fenestre**, just uphill from the tourist office, filled with giant sequoias and pine trees.

Among the many hotels and restaurants lining the riverbanks, **Hôtel Le Parc des Fées** (☑ 04 73 81 01 77; www.parcdesfees.com; 107 quai Maréchal-Fayolle; r €65-90, ste €115-120; @ 🛜) stands out for its belle époque architecture, its new spa (per hour €8) and the lovely mountain and river views from its corner rooms.

La Bourboule's efficient **tourist office** (☑ 04 73 65 57 71; www.sancy.com; place de la République; ⊙ 9am-noon & 2-6pm) is in the Hôtel de Ville. Trains and SNCF buses to Le Mont-Dore (€1.70, five daily) take just eight minutes.

Murol & Lac Chambon

POP 560 / ELEV 849M

About 10km east of Le Mont-Dore, the 12th-century **Château de Murol** (☑ 04 73 26 02 00; www.chateaudemurol.fr; adult/child €7.50/5.50, with guided tour €11.50/9.50; ⊙ 10am-6pm daily Apr-Sep, 10am-5pm Sat, Sun & holidays Oct-Mar) squats on a knoll above the surrounding village. Book ahead for medieval guided tours (up to five daily in summer), where costumed guides, scullery maids and jesters re-create daily life in the castle and knights joust beneath the keep.

About 1.5km west of Murol is the water-sports playground of **Lac Chambon**, where you can hire canoes and windsurfing boards from operators along the pretty lakeshore.

One kilometre west of the lake, **Camping les Bombes** (☑ 04 73 88 64 03; www.camping-les-bombes.com; Chemin de Pétary; two-person sites €13.90-20; ☺ May–mid-Sep; ☀) ☞ is lovingly managed by international travellers Bruno and Chantal Fortier and offers landscaped sites, bike rentals and easy access to nearby trails.

Besse-en-Chandesse & Around

POP 1550 / ELEV 805M

Basalt-brick cottages and cobbled lanes make up the mountain village of Besse-en-Chandesse (also known as Besse-et-St-Anastaise), 9.4km south of Murol, where life still ticks along at a laid-back country pace. During the **Transhumance de la Vierge Noire**, local cows are herded to the rich upland pastures on 21 July and back down on the first Sunday after 21 September. The cows' September descent is accompanied by street fairs and fireworks.

Besse is best known for its ski resort **Super-Besse** (www.sancy.com/commune/super-besse; downhill/cross-country day pass adult €30/7, child €24.20/5.50), 7km west of the village. Ski passes from here also grant access to Le Mont-Dore's slopes. Also along the D978, 6km southwest of Besse, the near-circular crater lake **Lac Pavin** makes a scenic starting point for hikes of varying lengths into the surrounding countryside.

In town, skiers will get a kick out of the vintage skis and alpine kit at the **Musée du Ski** (☑ 04 73 79 57 30; adult/child €4.50/free; ☺ school holidays 9am-noon & 2-7pm).

St-Nectaire

POP 730 / ELEV 760M

Six kilometres east of Murol, St-Nectaire stretches out along the river beside the D996, and is famed far and wide for its eponymous Appellation d'Origine Protégée (AOP) cheese. The village is split into the newer St-Nectaire-Le-Bas, with a smattering of belle époque buildings remaining from the town's former incarnation as a spa resort, and the much older St-Nectaire-Le-Haut, reached via a steep switchback lane from the main road.

◉ Sights & Activities

La Ferme Bellonte FARM
(www.st-nectaire.com; rue du 10 août 1944, Farges; cave tour adult/child €6.40/4.30; ☺ milking 7-8am & 4.15-5.15pm, cheese-making 8.30-9.30am & 6-7pm, cave tours 10am-noon & 2-5pm) To see how St-Nectaire's famous cheese is made, take the scenic road 3km uphill from town to this multi-generational family dairy farm in the village of Farges. There's no charge to watch the milking of the cows (early morning or late afternoon) and the pressing of the cheese into moulds; whole cheeses cost €16 in the adjacent shop. Aficionados can also tour (in English upon request) the historic cave dwellings across the street where the cheese is aged.

Romanesque Church CHURCH
(☺ 9am-7pm) St-Nectaire's main architectural sight is in the upper village. It has a fine 12th-century statue of the Virgin.

Grottes du Cornadore RUINS
(www.grottes-du-cornadore.com; adult/child €6.50/5; ☺ 10am-noon & 2-7pm, closed Nov–mid-Feb) Visitors can tour the remains of the town's Roman baths.

🛏 Sleeping & Eating

Villa du Pont Romain B&B €
(☑ 04 73 88 41 62; http://lavilladupontromain.free.fr; Rue Principale; s/d/q incl breakfast €40/53/83; ☎) Hosted by a pair of serious runners (he's a world steeplechase champion), this simple three-room B&B is a great budget option, with abundant breakfasts and clean, spacious rooms sleeping up to four.

★ Le Chastel Montaigu B&B €€
(☑ 04 73 96 28 49; www.lechastelmontaigu.com; Montaigut-le-Blanc; d €145-160; ☺ Apr-Sep) Feel like a true *seigneur* (lord) wandering around the terraces and spiral staircases of this fairytale castle on its own private hilltop, 11km east of St-Nectaire. Rebuilt from ruins using authentic medieval materials, the four rooms are filled with heavy stone, rich fabrics and antique wall hangings. One has its own turret terrace, and all enjoy dazzling views. Two-night minimum stay.

❶ Information

St-Nectaire's **tourist office** (☑ 04 73 88 50 86; www.sancy.com/commune/saint-nectaire; av du Docteur Roux, Les Grands Thermes; ☺ 9am-noon & 2-6pm Mon-Fri May-Sep, afternoons only Oct, open weekends Jul & Aug) is in the grand old thermal springs building on the main road in the lower town.

🛈 Getting There & Away

St-Nectaire is on the D996, 25km east of Le Mont-Dore and 35km south of Clermont-Ferrand. You'll need your own vehicle to get here.

Murat & the Monts du Cantal

POP 2050 / ELEV 930M

The Monts du Cantal, at the southern end of Parc Naturel Régional des Volcans d'Auvergne, constitute one of the most dramatic, wild and beautiful landscapes in the Massif Central. Most noteworthy are the lofty peaks of Puy Mary (1787m), Plomb du Cantal (1858m) and Puy de Peyre Arse (1806m), last vestiges of an exploded supervolcano that was once the largest in all of Europe. At the Cantal massif's eastern edge, tumbling down a steep basalt crag topped by a statue of the Virgin Mary, Murat makes an excellent base for exploring this region. Its cluster of dark stone houses huddled beneath the Rocher Bonnevie make it one of the southern Auvergne's prettiest towns and a popular hiking and skiing hub.

⊙ Sights & Activities

The twisting streets and wonky stone cottages of Murat's old town make an enjoyable afternoon stroll.

Maison de la Faune　　　　　　　　MUSEUM

(www.murat.fr; adult/child €4.80/3.20; ⊙10am-noon & 2-5pm Mon-Sat, 2-5pm Sun; ⏵) Budding entomologists should make a beeline for this spiralling stone tower opposite place de l'Hôtel de Ville, which houses more than 10,000 insects, butterflies and stuffed beasties from the Auvergne to the Amazon.

Rocher Bonnevie　　　　　　　　WALKING

For great views, brave the lung-busting climb to the top of Rocher Bonnevie. From the town centre, it's about 1.5km, following the red-and-white GR flashes northwestwards. For drivers, an alternate 10-minute footpath starts from the parking lot just off the D3 traffic circle, 1km northwest of town.

Le Lioran　　　　　　　　SKIING

(www.lelioran.com; day pass adult/child €27.90/22.50) Skiers can hit the slopes here, 14km west of Murat.

🛏 Sleeping & Eating

★**Auberge d'Aijean**　　　　　　INN €

(☑ 04 71 20 83 43; www.auberge-puy-mary.com; La Gandilhon, Lavigerie; d €60-65, 4-person ste €110-120; 🕾) Sublime Monts du Cantal views and cosy, well-outfitted rooms are reason enough to stay at this welcoming mountain inn 15km west of Murat on the road to Puy Mary. The four-course dinners (€22), served in front of a blazing fire in the huge stone fireplace and featuring local specialities such as lentil soup, Salers beef and Auvergnat cheeses, are icing on the cake.

La Maison de Justine　　　　　　B&B €

(☑ 04 71 20 75 72; www.hotes-cantal-justine.fr; 4 place Gandilhon Gens d'Armes; d €60-80; 🕾) Right in Murat's medieval heart, this charming four-room B&B, filled with books and antiques, offers the town's most atmospheric accommodation.

Camping Municipal Stalapos　　　　　　CAMPGROUND €

(☑ 04 71 20 01 83; www.camping-murat.com; rue du Stade; sites €3.80-5.90, plus €3.10/1.50 per adult/child; ⊙May-Sep; @) Beside the Alagnon River, this pretty campground is 1km south of the train station.

★**Chez Laurette**　　　　　　CRÊPERIE €

(☑ 04 71 20 01 31; 28 Rue du Bon Secours; crêpes €4-10; ⊙noon-2pm Tue-Sat, 7-9pm Thu-Sat) At this friendly, centrally located eatery, savoury crêpes filled with local ham and cheeses share the spotlight with alternative fillings such as homemade ratatouille or smoked salmon with crème fraiche, lemon and dill. For dessert don't miss the namesake *crêpe Laurette*, with caramelised apples and toasted almonds.

Caldera　　　　　　DELICATESSEN

(3 rue Justin Vigier; ⊙9am-12.15pm & 3-7pm Tue-Sat, 9am-noon Sun) Near the tourist office, this deli sells local cheese, sandwiches and regional products including honey, jam and liqueur.

🛈 Information

The **tourist office** (☑ 04 71 20 09 47; www.office-detourismepaysdemurat.com; place de l'Hôtel de Ville; ⊙ 9.30am-12.30pm & 2-6pm Mon-Sat Sep-Jun, daily Jul & Aug) has a wealth of info on walks and activities in the Cantal area.

🛈 Getting There & Around

Regional trains connect Murat with Clermont-Ferrand (€20.70, 1¾ hours, four to seven daily).

The countryside makes for splendid, if taxing, cycling. **Ô P'tit Montagnard** (☑ 04 71 20 28 40; www.optitmontagnard.fr; 8 rue Faubourg Notre Dame) rents quality bikes for €22 per day.

COWS ON THE MOVE: A SLICE OF AUVERGNAT LIFE

For an up-close perspective on traditional Auvergnat mountain culture, visit the Salers region on the last Sunday in May for the annual **Transhumance**, a one-day event during which farmers drive their herds of bell-jingling, long-horned Salers dairy cattle from the valleys to the high country pastures.

Starting at 9am in the tiny village of St-Paul-de-Salers, this traditional pilgrimage is a perfect excuse to get out and appreciate the rustic architecture of the local stone barns, the beauty of the open pastureland around Puy Violent, and the bond between man and beast that has defined this region for generations. Up top there's live music and a community picnic where women armed with giant wooden paddles stir enormous cauldrons of *aligot*, the filling mixture of cheese, puréed potatoes and garlic that has long been a staple in these parts.

Salers

POP 360 / ELEV 830M

One of the Auvergne's prettiest towns, Salers sits at the western edge of the Monts du Cantal, looking up towards the Puy Violent (1592m) and Puy Mary (1787m), making it the perfect base for exploring the mountains' western slopes. Spreading out from its compact core of 16th-century stone buildings are rolling meadows filled with horned brown cows that produce the milk that creates its eponymous Salers AOC cheese.

Salers' picturesque central square, **place Tyssandier d'Escous**, is named for the 19th-century agronomist who developed the Salers breed of cattle. Surrounding his statue is a harmonious collection of turreted lava-rock buildings that date from Salers' 16th-century heyday as a regional administrative centre. From here you can walk up to the leafy **Esplanade de Barrouze** *belvédère* (panoramic viewpoint), or descend into the town's tangle of cobbled streets filled with shops selling cheese, knives and Auvergnat knick-knacks.

Half a block below the square, the delightful **Hôtel Saluces** (☑ 04 71 40 70 82; www.hotel-salers.fr; rue de la Martille; d €74-95; @ 🛜) offers eight spacious and individually decorated rooms with modern amenities in an ancient stone building with a sunny interior courtyard. Hosts Daniel and Jeanette Gil offer excellent advice about the local area.

Also just off the square is the **Maison de la Ronade** (place Tyssandier d'Escous; teas €3; ⏱ 3.30-6.30pm Fri-Wed), whose elderly owner serves up 100 varieties of tea in his 15th-century drawing room, giving you a set of three hourglasses to measure the proper brewing time. For solid, reasonably priced Auvergnat dishes (Salers steaks, stuffed cabbage, and the full line-up of meat, cheese and potatoes fare) head downhill to **La Martille** (☑ 04 71 40 77 05; www.restaurant-salers.fr; rue de la Martille; lunch/dinner menus €20/30; ⏱ noon-2pm & 7-9pm Tue-Sun, noon-2pm Mon), a venerable eatery with a pleasant outdoor terrace.

The **tourist office** (☑ 04 71 40 58 08; www.salers-tourisme.fr; place Tyssandier d'Escous; ⏱ 9.30am-noon & 2-5.30pm), on the main square, offers information, maps and books about local hikes.

Salers is on the D680, 43km west of Murat and 21km west of the Pas de Peyrol at the foot of Puy Mary. You'll need your own vehicle to get here.

PARC NATUREL RÉGIONAL LIVRADOIS-FOREZ

Blanketed in pine forest, this nature park is one of France's largest protected areas, stretching from the plains of Limagne in the west to the Monts du Forez in the east. Formerly a centre for logging and agriculture, it's now a haven for nature lovers and weekend walkers.

The **Maison du Parc** (park information office; ☑ 04 73 95 57 57; www.parc-livradois-forez.org; ⏱ 9am-12.30pm & 1.30-5.30pm Mon-Thu, to 4.30pm Fri) is off the D906 in St-Gervais-sous-Meymont, halfway between Thiers and Ambert. It's stocked with leaflets detailing local honey shops, lace-makers and perfumers, walking trails and mountain-bike routes.

In spring and summer, a lovely if infrequent **train touristique** (☑ 04 73 82 43 88; www.agrivap.fr; tickets €9-15) – alternately a double-decker *train panoramique* or a vintage steam train – runs through the park

With its peaceful pastures and verdant hills, it's hard to believe that the Massif Central was once one of the most active volcanic areas in Western Europe.

The area consists of three geological bands. The **Chaîne des Puys** and **Monts Dômes**, a chain of extinct volcanoes and cinder cones stretching in a 40km north–south line across the northern Massif Central, thrust up around 100,000 years ago. The central **Monts Dores** are much older, created between 100,000 and three million years ago, while the real grandaddies are the **Monts du Cantal**, on the Parc Naturel Régional des Volcans d'Auvergne's southern edge, formed by a nine-million-year-old volcano which collapsed inwards, leaving only its caldera (fragmented rim).

Though the volcanoes have been silent for several thousand years (the last serious eruption occurred around 5000 BC), reminders of their turbulent past are peppered about everywhere – from mineral waters and geothermal springs to the distinctive black rock often used as a building material throughout the region.

from Courpière (15km south of Thiers) via Ambert to La Chaise-Dieu.

Thiers

POP 11,610 / ELEV 420M

Precipitously perched above the Gorges de la Durolle, the industrial town of Thiers has been churning out cutlery for centuries and still produces some 70% of the nation's knives.

For an overview, head for the **Musée de la Coutellerie** (Cutlery Museum; www.musee-coutellerie-thiers.com; 23 & 58 rue de la Coutellerie; adult/child €5.70/2.75, combined ticket with Vallée des Rouets €6.90/3; ⊙10am-noon & 2-6pm, closed Mon Oct-May), which is split over two buildings along rue de la Coutellerie. No 23 explores the historical side of cutlery-making, while No 58 houses the museum's unparalleled collection of knives past and present. About 4km upstream from Thiers is the **Vallée des Rouets** (Valley of the Waterwheels; adult/child €4.10/1.85; ⊙noon-6pm Jun & Sep, to 7pm Jul & Aug), an open-air museum dedicated to the knife-makers who once toiled here in front of water-driven grindstones. In summer a free shuttle bus runs here from Thiers.

Knife-sellers are dotted round the town's medieval streets lined with half-timbered buildings – ask at the friendly **tourist office** (☑04 73 80 65 65; www.thiers-tourisme.fr; 1 place du Pirou; ⊙9.30am-12.30pm & 2-6pm; 🕾) for recommended shops. Thiers is easily reached by frequent trains from Clermont-Ferrand (€9.20, 45 minutes).

Ambert

POP 7230 / ELEV 560M

Back in the 16th century, Ambert, 30km north of La Chaise-Dieu, boasted more than 300 water-powered mills supplying the demands of the French paper industry, but the town is better known today for one of the Auvergne's classic cheeses, Fourme d'Ambert.

The **tourist office** (☑04 73 82 61 90; www.ambert-tourisme.fr; 4 place de l'Hôtel de Ville; ⊙2-5pm Mon, 10am-noon Thu, 10am-noon & 2-5pm Tue, Wed, Fri & Sat; 🕾), opposite the Hôtel de Ville, can help with accommodation.

Around 500 sheets of paper per day are still made using strictly traditional techniques at the restored 14th-century mill **Moulin Richard de Bas** (www.richarddebas.fr; adult/child €7.30/5; ⊙9.30am-12.30pm & 2-6pm Sep-Jun, 9.30am-7pm Jul & Aug). It's 4km east of town on the D57. The adjoining park makes a lovely picnic spot.

In Ambert's pedestrianised centre, the **Maison de la Fourme d'Ambert** (www.maison-fourme-ambert.fr; 29 rue des Chazeaux; adult/child €6/4.50; ⊙10am-noon & 2-6pm Tue-Sat) has displays on the history and manufacture of the town's trademark *fromage*. Three-cheese tastings (including a glass of wine or apple juice) cost an additional €3.

Ambert's Thursday-morning **market**, spiralling out around the Hôtel de Ville, is popular with local organic farmers.

SNCF bus-train combos connect Ambert with Clermont-Ferrand (€14.80, 1¾ hours).

La Chaise-Dieu

POP 800 / ELEV 1082M

The centrepiece of historic La Chaise-Dieu, 42km north of Le Puy-en-Velay, is its monumental **Église Abbatiale de St-Robert** (⊙10am-noon & 2-6pm), built in the 14th century atop an earlier abbey chapel by Pope Clement VI, who served here as a novice monk. Highlights include the massive

18th-century **organ**, Clement VI's marble tomb and the celebrated **Danse Macabre** fresco, in which Death dances a mocking jig around members of 15th-century society.

La Chaise-Dieu's prized organ is also a key part (and the origin) of its prestigious **Sacred Music Festival** (Festival de Musique; www.chaise-dieu.com; ⊙ late Aug-early Sep).

Behind the church is the **Salle de l'Echo** – an architectural oddity that allows people on opposite sides of the room to hear each other talking, without being overheard by those in between. It's thought to have been built to enable monks to hear lepers' confessions without contracting the dreaded disease.

The **tourist office** (☑ 04 71 00 01 16; www.la-chaise-dieu.info; rue St-Esprit; ⊙ 10am-12.30pm & 2-5.30pm Tue-Sat; ☎) has a free English-language leaflet outlining a walking tour of the village.

Peacefully positioned behind the church, **L'Echo et l'Abbaye** (☑ 04 71 00 00 45; hoteldelecho@orange.fr; place de l'Echo; hotel s €44, d €49-69, chambres d'hôte d €95-135; ⊙ Apr-mid-Nov; ☎) is a refurbished stone townhouse with prim hotel rooms and a pair of fancier *chambres d'hôte* (one with 17th-century vaulted ceiling, one with Jacuzzi). The attached **restaurant** (menus €19-29), in the old abbey kitchens, serves hearty meals.

SNCF buses run once or twice each weekday between La Chaise-Dieu and Le Puy-en-Velay (€9.20, 1¼ hours).

LE PUY-EN-VELAY & AROUND

Le Puy-en-Velay

POP 19,710 / ELEV 630M

Cradled at the base of a broad mountain valley, Le Puy-en-Velay is one of the most striking sights in central France. Three volcanic pillars thrust skywards above the

---

ⓘ PILGRIM'S PASS

Between June and September, three of Le Puy's major sights (Chapelle St-Michel d'Aiguilhe, the Rocher Corneille and the Forteresse de Polignac) can be visited on the joint **Pass'Espace museum pass** (adult/child €9.50/5.50). Buy it at any of the sights or from the tourist office.

---

terracotta rooftops, crowned with a trio of ecclesiastical landmarks – a 10th-century church, soaring Romanesque cathedral, and massive cast-iron statue of the Virgin Mary and Child that has stood watch above Le Puy since 1860. Sacred statues and saintly figurines tucked into niches in the medieval and Renaissance houses lining Le Puy's cobbled streets also attest to its role as a focal point for pilgrims for over a millennium, especially those following the Via Podiensis to Santiago de Compostela (p559).

Throughout the lively pedestrianised old town, shops sell the town's trademark exports: lace, lentils and vivid green liqueur, Verveine.

⊙ Sights & Activities

★ Chapelle St-Michel d'Aiguilhe   CHURCH

(www.rochersaintmichel.fr; adult/child €3.50/2; ⊙ 9am-6.30pm May-Sep, shorter hours rest of year, closed mid-Nov–Jan) Le Puy's oldest chapel (first established in the 10th century, and rebuilt several times since) teeters atop an 85m-high volcanic plug reached by climbing 268 stairs. Stepping through its exquisite polychrome doorway into the cavelike interior is a mystical experience – the chapel follows the natural contours of the rock, and the unusual carvings and 12th-century frescoes create an otherworldly atmosphere.

Cathédrale Notre Dame   CATHEDRAL

(www.cathedraledupuy.org; ⊙ 6.30am-7pm) The multistoreyed façade, soaring pillars, Romanesque archways and Byzantine domes of this 11th century cathedral – a Unesco-listed wonder – are a celestial sight. The frescoed portal is framed by porphyry columns shipped from Egypt; inside, the cathedral shelters a statue of St Jacques, patron saint of Compostela pilgrims, and one of the Auvergne's most famous *Vierges Noires*.

Cathédrale Notre Dame Cloister   CLOISTER

(cathedrale-puy-en-velay.monuments-nationaux.fr; adult/child €5.50/free; ⊙ 9am-noon & 2-6.30pm mid-May–mid-Sep, to 5pm rest of yr, no midday closure Jul & Aug) Adjacent to the cathedral, this lovely 12th-century cloister indicates the cathedral's Moorish influences with its multicoloured bricks and columns. Upstairs is a fine collection of embroidered religious artwork and vestments.

Le Puy-en-Velay

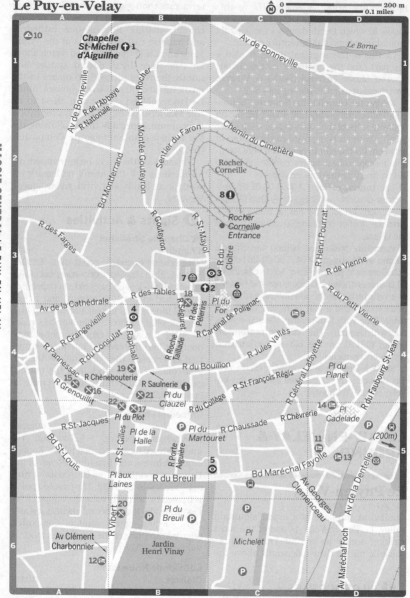

Rocher Corneille & Notre Dame de France

MONUMENT

(adult/child €4/2; ⏰9am-6pm mid-Mar–Apr, 9am-7pm May-Sep, 10am-5pm Oct–mid-Mar) Gleaming brightly after a 2013 renovation, the gargantuan rust-red statue of Notre Dame de France (aka the Virgin Mary) watches over Le Puy from her dominant perch atop Rocher Corneille (757m), the town's tallest volcanic pillar. For dizzying vistas of the town's rooftops and the surrounding countryside, peer out of the tiny portholes as you climb the creaky spiral staircase to Mary's star-encircled head. The 22.7m-tall, 835-tonne statue was fashioned from 213 cannons captured during the Crimean War.

Le Puy-en-Velay

Forteresse de Polignac CASTLE

(www.forteressedepolignac.com; adult/child €5/3.50; ☉1.30-5.30pm Mar-Apr & Oct-Nov, 10am-noon & 1.30-6pm May, Jun & Sep, 10am-6.30pm Jul & Aug) Dramatically perched atop a volcanic dome just 5km northwest of Le Puy, this 11th-century castle was built by the powerful Polignac family, who once controlled access to the city from the north. It's ringed by a practically continuous wall dotted with lookout towers and a 32m-high rectangular keep.

Espace Pagès Maison
Verveine du Velay TASTING ROOM

(☑04 71 02 46 80; www.verveine.com; 29 place du Breuil; ☉10am-12.30pm & 2.30-7pm Tue-Sat, to 6pm Oct-Mar) FREE This tasting room sells various regional products and offers free samples of Le Puy's fiery green liqueur, Verveine Verte, invented in 1859 using 32 plants and herbs. Despite its potency (55% alcohol), Verveine's refreshingly sweet taste makes it a popular ingredient in local desserts. Verveine Jaune (yellow) and Verveine Extra (reddish-brown) varieties are somewhat milder at 40%. In summer, take a 45-minute guided tour of the distillery (☑04 71 03 04 11; guided tour adult/child €5.90/2.30; ☉by reservation Jun & Sep, 10.30am, 2.30pm, 3.30pm & 4.30pm Mon-Sat Jul & Aug), 8km east along the N88 in St-Germain Laprade.

Le Camino MUSEUM

(Musée de St-Jacques de Compostelle; www.lecamino. org; 2 rue de la Manécanterie; adult/child €3/1.50; ☉2-6pm mid-Apr–Jun & Sep–mid-Oct, 12.30-8pm Jul & Aug) Interesting for armchair travellers as well as committed walkers about to undertake the multi-week journey to Santiago de Compostela (p559), this new museum in the beautifully restored Hôtel St-Vidal

traces every stage of the 1700km Chemin de St-Jacques pilgrimage route, in exhibits spread out over a dozen rooms on four floors.

Musée Interactif Hôtel-Dieu MUSEUM

(www.hoteldieu.info; 2 rue Becdelièvre; adult/child €6/4; ☉2-6pm Sun, 10am-noon & 2-6pm Mon & Wed-Sat mid-Feb–Oct) The highlight of this museum inside Le Puy's historic hospital is the 19th-century pharmacy, elegantly panelled in walnut and wild cherry wood. Upstairs, French-language interactive exhibits focus on the architecture, history and natural history of the Haute-Loire region.

Centre d'Enseignement
de la Dentelle au Fuseau LACE WORKSHOP

(☑04 71 02 01 68; www.ladentelledupuy.com; 38-40 rue Raphaël; adult/child €4.50/free; ☉9am-noon & 1.30-5.30pm Mon-Fri year-round, plus 9.30am-4.30pm Sat Apr-Oct) Given Le Puy's role as a pilgrimage hub, lace was essential for religious clothing and there were once more than 5000 lace workshops hereabouts, though only a handful remain today. At this not-for-profit workshop you can watch bobbin lace-making demonstrations, browse temporary and permanent exhibits, or even take a course. The tourist office has details of other local workshops.

🎉 Festivals & Events

Interfolk FOLK MUSIC

(www.interfolk.fr) Week-long folk festival in late July.

Fête du Roi de l'Oiseau STREET FESTIVAL

(www.roideloiseau.com) This mid-September five-day street party – complete with outlandish costumes – dates back to 1524, when the

THE BLACK MADONNAS OF THE AUVERGNE

The Auvergne has a large number of *Vierges Noires* (Black Madonnas) in its cathedrals and churches, imbued with considerable sacred significance and miraculous powers. Usually under 1m tall and carved from cedar or walnut, their origins are a source of speculation: some historians believe the tradition began during the Crusades, when Christian soldiers came under the influence of Moorish sculptors. Others believe the figures are part of an older tradition involving the Egyptian goddess Isis or a pagan Mother Goddess. Still others have suggested that Black Madonnas are an attempt to depict Mary's original skin colour, which was probably closer to the dark skin of African and Middle Eastern people than the light skin of modern Europeans. Theories also abound over the figures' colour: that dark woods or varnishes were used to create the dark colouring, or that it's caused by natural ageing or even candle soot. On Assumption Day (15 August) you'll see the statues paraded throughout Auvergne villages, marking the ascension of Mary's spirit to heaven.

title of *Roi* (King) was bestowed on the first archer to shoot down a straw *oiseau* (bird) in return for a year's exemption from taxes.

🛏 Sleeping

The tourist office has a list of *gîtes* and *chambres d'hôte*.

Auberge de Jeunesse HOSTEL €
(☑ 04 71 05 52 40; www.hifrance.org/auberge-de-jeunesse/le-puy-en-velay.html; 9 rue Jules Vallès; dm €15; 🛜) Remodelled in 2013, this hostel offers excellent value given its prime position just below the cathedral. The squeaky-clean three- to eight-bed dorms include one with facilities for disabled travellers. Breakfast costs €4.50 extra, and there's free on-site parking. Note that reception is closed at lunch and dinnertime; gates close at 11.30pm.

Dyke Hôtel HOTEL €
(☑ 04 71 09 05 30; www.dykehotel.fr; 37 bd Maréchal Fayolle; s €39-51, d €49-58; 🛜) Named for a volcanic pillar (in case you're wondering), this budget hotel is well located if unexciting, with modernish rooms of varying dimensions, some with balconies onto the (very) busy road. Perks include cable TV and an enclosed garage – free for bicycles and motorcycles, €6 for cars.

Hôtel St-Jacques HOTEL €
(☑ 04 71 07 20 40; www.hotel-saint-jacques.com; 7 place Cadelade; s €48-68, d €58-68; ⊙Feb-Dec; 🛜) This simple hotel is a great budget base. The pick of the rooms have wood floors, dinky bathrooms and views of the little square below. Downstairs, the patio cafe serves knock-out coffee. Breakfast and parking each cost €7.

Camping Bouthezard CAMPGROUND €
(☑ 04 71 09 55 09; www.campingdupuyenvelay.fr; chemin de Bouthezard; per tent/car/adult/child

€2.95/1.90/3.35/1.50; ⊙mid-Mar–Oct) Le Puy's campground enjoys an attractive berth beside the River Borne. Take bus 5 to the Parc Quincieu stop. Check-in is between 1pm and 8pm.

Hôtel du Parc HOTEL €€
(☑ 04 71 02 40 40; www.hotel-du-parc-le-puy.com; 4 av Clément Charbonnier; d €95-120, ste €165-210; ❄@🛜) Minimalist-chic rooms, stylish suites with enormous bathrooms and an ample breakfast buffet (€14) are the big draws at this four-star, parkside hotel near the south edge of the old town.

Hôtel Le Régina HOTEL €€
(☑ 04 71 09 14 71; www.hotelrestregina.com; 34 bd Maréchal Fayolle; s €62-81, d €70-101, ste €108-129; ❄🛜) Topped by a neon-lit art deco turret, the Régina's newly renovated rooms come in many shapes and sizes. Each is individually decorated, including several with murals of Marilyn Monroe, Coke bottles, the Chrysler Building and similar pop-art themes. Some more expensive rooms have air-conditioning or Jacuzzi tubs.

🍴 Eating

The local *lentille verte du Puy* (green Puy lentil; www.lalentillevertedupuy.com) is the sole pulse with Appellation d'Origine Contrôlée (AOC) classification in mainland France (the only other is the *lentille de Cilaos* on the French island of Réunion). Rich in protein, vitamin B and iron, and gluten-free, Le Puy's lentils are used in dishes ranging from the time-honoured to more inventive creations.

L'Âme des Poètes AUVERGNAT €
(☑ 04 71 05 66 57; www.ame-des-poetes.com; 16 rue Séguret; mains €12.50-15, menu €19; ⊙noon-2pm Thu-Tue & 7-9pm Thu-Sat) The house speciality – lentil lasagne – is tasty enough at this tourist-oriented restaurant, but it pales in

comparison with the sublime setting at the foot of the cathedral steps. In warm weather, book ahead for dinner on the umbrella-shaded deck, fringed by roses and glowing golden under the setting sun.

Le Chamarlenc · TRADITIONAL FRENCH €

(☑ 04 71 02 17 72; http://lechamarlenc.free.fr; 19 rue Raphaël; plat du jour €10, menus €16-20; ☺ noon-1.30pm & 7-9.30pm Tue-Sat) Crowned world master of *pâté en croûte* cookery in 2009, chef Florian Oriol serves his speciality foie-gras-and-mushroom pies (€11) alongside a changing menu built around fresh local produce.

Entrez les Artistes · AUVERGNAT €

(☑ 04 71 09 71 78; 29 rue Pannessac; menus €16-28; ☺ noon-2pm Tue-Sat, 7-9pm Thu-Sat) Lashings of local lace adorn this cosy place, which dishes up local fare, including a €9.90 *plat du jour*.

★ **Maki Nova** · JAPANESE €€

(☑ 06 30 00 46 68; 17 rue Vibert; lunch/dinner menus €15/25; ☺ noon-3pm & 8pm-midnight Tue-Sat) Using fresh-from-the-market fish, local organic vegetables and direct-imported Japanese rice and shoyu, Chef Alexis Haon creates inspired, ever-changing daily menus of 'Japanese food revisited': sushi, sashimi and vegetarian options that frequently incorporate seeds, flowers and other unexpected twists. Orange-lit, white brick walls provide an inviting, chilled-out backdrop for Haon's culinary creations, complemented by fine local wines, Japanese teas and sake.

La Table du Plot · AUVERGNAT €€

(☑ 04 71 57 05 28; 6 place du Plot; mains €13.50-21.50; ☺ noon-2pm Thu-Tue, 7-10pm Mon & Thu-Sat) Enjoying lovely views of the multi-hued historic buildings surrounding Le Puy's market square, the outdoor tables here are great for a drink or a more substantial meal. Specialities include large salads and local beef dishes accompanied by Puy lentils, mashed potatoes, tagliatelle or roasted vegetables.

Restaurant Tournayre · AUVERGNAT €€€

(☑ 04 71 09 58 94; www.restaurant-tournayre.com; 12 rue Chênebouterie; menus lunch €27, dinner €39-74; ☺ noon-1.30pm & 7.30-9.30pm Wed-Sun) Elegantly set in a 16th-century former chapel with vaulted ceiling and stone walls, this refined eatery serves a variety of superb four-course *menus*, including a good-value lunchtime *menu du marché* (€27).

Self-Catering

Shop for fresh produce at Le Puy's **Saturday market** (place du Plot; ☺ 8am-1pm Sat).

Fromagerie Coulaud · CHEESE €

(24 rue Grenouillit; ☺ 8.30am-7.30pm Tue-Sat) In the same family since 1925, this excellent cheese shop with its fetching baby blue façade is run by the delightful Jacques and Jacqueline Coulaud and decorated with their heirloom collection of cheese serving dishes.

 Information

Tourist Office (☑ 04 71 09 38 41; www.ot-lepuy envelay.fr; 2 place du Clauzel; ☺ 8.30am-noon & 1.30-6.15pm Mon-Fri, 9am-12.30pm & 2-5.30pm Sat, 10am-12.30pm & 2.30-5pm Sun; ☎) Offers free internet (wi-fi and loaner tablets).

THE VIA PODIENSIS PILGRIMAGE ROUTE

Ever since the 9th century, when a hermit named Pelayo stumbled across the tomb of the apostle James (brother of John the Evangelist), the Spanish town of Santiago de Compostela has been one of Christendom's holiest sites.

The pilgrimage to Santiago de Compostela is traditionally known as the Camiño de Santiago (Way of St James). There are many different routes from London, Germany and Italy, as well as four that cross the French mainland. But the oldest (and most frequented) French route is the 736km Via Podiensis from Le Puy-en-Velay to St-Jean-Pied-de-Port via Figeac, Cahors, Moissac and Rocamadour, established in AD 951 by Le Puy's first bishop. Early pilgrims were inspired to undertake the arduous journey in exchange for fewer years in purgatory. Today the reward is more tangible: walkers or horse riders who complete the final 100km to Santiago (cyclists the final 200km) qualify for a Compostela Certificate, issued on arrival at the cathedral.

The modern-day GR65 roughly follows the Via Podiensis route. Plenty of organisations can help you plan your adventure: contact Le Puy's tourist office, or, in Toulouse, the **Association de Coopération Interrégionale: Les Chemins de Saint-Jacques de Compostelle** (☑ 05 62 27 00 05; www.chemins-compostelle.com). For a useful English-language website, see www.csj.org.uk.

MASSIF CENTRAL LE PUY-EN-VELAY

CHEESE COUNTRY

With its wide-open pastures and lush green grass, it's not surprising the Auvergne has a long tradition of producing some of France's finest cheeses. The region has five Appellation d'Origine Contrôlée (AOC) and Appellation d'Origine Protégée (AOP) cheeses: the semihard, cheddar-like Cantal and premium-quality Salers, both made from the milk of high-pasture cows; St-Nectaire, rich, flat and semisoft; Fourme d'Ambert, a mild, smooth blue cheese; and Bleu d'Auvergne, a powerful, creamy blue cheese with a Roquefort-like flavour.

To taste them on their home turf, follow the signposted **Route des Fromages** (www.fromages-aop-auvergne.com) linking local farms and producers. A downloadable map is available on the website.

The area's cheeses figure strongly in many of the Auvergne's traditional dishes, including *aligot* (puréed potato with garlic and Tomme cheese) and *truffade* (sliced potatoes with Cantal cheese), almost always served with a huge helping of *jambon d'Auvergne* (local ham).

ℹ Getting There & Away

SNCF has direct trains from Le Puy to Clermont-Ferrand (€24.40, 2¼ hours, one to four daily) and bus/train combinations from Le Puy to Lyon (€24.20, two to 3½ hours, seven to nine daily).

ℹ Getting Around

TUDIP (☑ 04 71 02 60 11; www.tudip.fr) operates 12 local bus lines (single ticket/day pass/10-trip carnet €1.30/3/9), all stopping at place Michelet.

For a taxi call **Taxi Le Puy** (☑ 04 71 05 42 43; www.taxilepuy.com).

Gorges de l'Allier

About 30km west of Le Puy, the salmon-filled Allier River – paralleled by the scenic Clermont-Ferrand–Nîmes rail line – weaves between rocky, scrub-covered hills and steep cliffs. Above the river's east bank, the narrow D301 gives fine views as it passes through wild countryside and remote hamlets.

In the sleepy town of **Langeac** (population 4100), the **tourist office** (☑ 04 71 77 05 41; www.haut-allier.com; place Aristide Briand; ⊗ 9am-12.30pm & 1.30-6pm Tue-Sat; ☎) has details of local **walking and cycling trails** as well as companies offering horseback riding, canyoning and white-water rafting.

To explore the area at a gentler pace, book ahead for the scenic **Train des Gorges de l'Allier** (☑ 04 71 77 70 17; www.train-gorges-allier.com; adult €12-22.50, child €8-13; ⊗ May-Sep), which trundles through the gorges between Langeac and Langogne. Days and itineraries vary.

Plentiful campgrounds in the valley include Langeac's tree-shaded riverside **Camping des Gorges de l'Allier** (☑ 04 71 77 05 01; www.campinglangeac.com; site €11-13; ⊗ Apr-Oct; ☎ ⓧ).

★ **Le Moulin Ferme-Auberge** (☑ 04 71 74 03 09; www.gite-aubergedumoulin.com; St-Arcons-d'Allier; dm incl breakfast/half board €23/40, d incl breakfast €58-75, incl half board €98-120) ✎, 6km south of Langeac, has renovated stone and wood cottages on a verdant farmstead crisscrossed by rushing watercourses. Meals featuring local produce are served in the 15th-century mill. Walkers with their own bedding can opt for the 15-bed dorm.

La Montagne Protestante

Around 40km east of Le Puy is this sparsely populated highland area, carpeted in rich pastureland and thick fir forest. The area's most distinctive landmarks are the peaks of Mont Meygal (1436m), and **Mont Mézenc** (1753m), the summit of which is accessible via the GR73 and GR7 hiking trails. On a clear day, sweeping views across southeastern France stretch from Mont Blanc, 200km to the northeast, to Mont Ventoux, 140km to the southeast.

The region around **Le-Chambon-sur-Lignon** (population 2800), 45km east of Le Puy-en-Velay, played a courageous role in WWII, when it sheltered over 3000 refugees, including hundreds of Jewish children, from the Nazis. Chambon's brand-new **Memorial – Lieu de Memoire** (www.memoireduchambon.com; adult/child €5/3; ⊗ 10am-12.30pm & 2-6pm Tue-Sun Jun-Sep, 2-6pm Wed-Sat Mar-May, Oct & Nov) documents the many individuals who participated in this nonviolent resistance, through photos, timelines, bilingual informational panels and audiovisual presentations. Pick up info on outdoor activities from the **tourist office** (☑ 04 71 59 71 56; www.ot-hautlignon.com; route de Tence; ⊗ 9am-noon & 2-6.30pm Mon-Sat, 10am-noon Sun Jun-Sep, 9am-noon & 3-6pm Mon-Sat Oct-May).

Dordogne, Limousin & the Lot

POP 1.32 MILLION

Best Places to Eat

➡ Le Vieux Logis (p573)

➡ Les Truffieres (p572)

➡ Le Petit Paris (p576)

➡ Villa Laetitia (p569)

➡ La Tour des Vents (p570)

➡ Le Saint Martial (p576)

Best Places to Stay

➡ Hôtel La Grézalide (p608)

➡ Manoir de Malagorse (p605)

➡ Hostellerie Les Griffons (p568)

➡ Hôtel Le Saint Cirq (p606)

Why Go?

Dordogne, Limousin and the Lot are the heart and soul of *la belle France,* a land of dense oak forests, winding rivers, emerald-green fields and famously rich country cooking. It's the stuff of which French dreams are made: turreted châteaux and medieval villages line the riverbanks, wooden-hulled *gabarres* (traditional flat-bottomed, wooden boats) ply the waterways, and market stalls overflow with foie gras, truffles, walnuts, cheeses and fine wines.

The Dordogne *département* has a bevy of *bastides* (fortified towns) and fantastic medieval castles, as well as Europe's most spectacular cave paintings, and probably the best cuisine. To the northeast, the Limousin *région* – encompassing the Haute-Vienne, Creuse and Corrèze *départements* – is the most rural, strewn with farms and hamlets, as well as the porcelain centre, Limoges. To the south, the Lot *département* is ribboned with rivers to cruise and caverns to explore, plus dramatic hilltop villages, and medieval settlements.

When to Go
Limoges

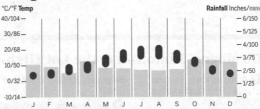

May & Jun Take to the rivers and climb ramparts before the crowds get thick.

Jul & Aug Sup on local produce at Dordogne's excellent restaurants and summer night markets.

Dec–Feb Browse markets selling Périgord black truffles.

Dordogne, Limousin & the Lot Highlights

1 Admiring the prehistoric artwork of the **Vézère Valley** (p580)

2 Exploring the cliff-face sanctuaries at **Rocamadour** (p603)

3 Wandering the russet-stone streets of **Sarlat-la-Canéda** (p577)

4 Cruising the Dordogne River near **La Roque Gageac** (p574),

Bergerac (p569) or **Brantôme** (p567)

5 Sampling the region's local produce at village **markets**, such as Issigeac's (p570) or Martel's (p605)

6 Strolling a 1st-century Roman villa at Périgueux' **Musée Gallo-Romain Vesunna** (p565)

7 Picking up porcelain at the renowned china factories of **Limoges** (p587)

8 Traipsing through vibrant medieval cities, including **Figeac** (p607) and **Cahors** (p599)

9 Wandering the ramparts of medieval castles at **Castelnaud** (p573), **Beynac** (p573) and **Najac** (p609)

❶ Getting There & Around

The intercity train line from Paris to Toulouse includes several trains a day with stops in Limoges, Brive-la-Gaillarde, Souillac and Cahors. Limoges and Périgueux are also linked to Bordeaux. Local train service in the region is limited. This, coupled with limited bus service keyed to school timetables, makes the Dordogne a good place to hire a car for explorations of the attraction-rich countryside.

AIR

Bergerac, Limoges and Brive-la-Gaillarde have domestic and international flights. Bordeaux and Toulouse are also nearby hubs.

THE DORDOGNE

Few regions sum up the attractions of France better than the Dordogne. With its rich food, heady history, château-studded countryside and picturesque villages, the Dordogne has long been a favourite getaway for French families on *les grandes vacances*. It's also famous for having some of France's finest prehistoric cave art, which fill the caverns and rock shelters of the Vézère Valley.

Part of the historic area that was called Aquitaine, its strategic importance through the ages is illustrated by the many *bastides* and fortresses throughout. Today it's known to the French as the Périgord, and is divided into four colour-coded areas: Périgord Pourpre (purple) for the winegrowing regions around Bergerac; Périgord Noir (black) for the dark oak forests around the Vézère Valley and Sarlat-la-Canéda; Périgord Blanc (white) after the limestone hills around the capital, Périgueux; and Périgord Vert (green) for the forested regions of the north.

Périgueux

POP 31,296

Founded by Gallic tribes, and later developed by the Romans into the important city of Vesunna, Périgueux remains the Dordogne's biggest (and busiest) town, with a lively cafe and restaurant scene, and plenty of shopping. Get past its suburban sprawl to its centre, and you discover a thoroughly charming old town dotted with medieval buildings and Renaissance mansions, radiating out from the Gothic Cathédrale St-Front.

Reminders of the city's Roman past fill the Cité quarter – the original 'old town'. You can visit a ruined garden-filled amphitheatre and

triumphal tower, as well as a grand villa at the city's excellent Gallo-Roman museum.

◉ Sights

The tourist office has a great walking tour map (€0.50) and offers **guided tours** (adult/child €6/4.50).

◉ Puy St-Front

The area around the cathedral, known as Puy St-Front, encompasses most of the city's most impressive medieval streets and buildings.

★**Cathédrale St-Front**   CATHEDRAL
(place de la Clautre; ◷ 8.30am-7pm) Périgueux' most distinctive landmark is most notable for its five creamy Byzantine tower-topped domes (inspired by either St Mark's Basilica in Venice or the church of the Holy Apostles of Constantinople, depending on whom you ask). Built in the 12th century on the site of two earlier basilicas, it was sacked in the Wars of Religion, and redesigned and rebuilt by Abadie (the architect of Paris' Sacré Cœur) in the late 19th century.

A striking bell tower remains from the 12th-century church, and informed the design of Abadie's domes. The interior is laid out in a Greek cross, and the cloisters date from the 12th to 16th centuries.

The best views of the cathedral are from **Pont des Barris** just to the east.

★**St-Front Quarter**   HISTORIC QUARTER
North of the cathedral, Périgueux' broad boulevards give way to a tangle of cobblestone streets lined with medieval houses. The best examples are along rue du Plantier, rue de la Sagesse, rue de la Miséricorde and rue Aubergerie, and many are marked with French/English placards.

Rue Limogeanne, a super shopping street, has graceful Renaissance buildings at Nos 3, 5 and 12. Around the corner the 15th-century **Maison du Pâtissier** (17 rue Éguillerie) is elaborately carved. Nearby **Galerie Daumesnil** is a series of linked courtyards within 15th- to 17th-century town houses.

FAST FACTS

➡ **Area** 31,219 sq km

➡ **Local industry** goose and duck husbandry

➡ **Signature drink** *eau de noix* (walnut liqueur)

Périgueux

200 m
0.1 miles

R de Metz
R de Thiers
Bristol Hôtel (50m)
Pl du Président Roosevelt
R Gambetta
R du 4 septembre
R A Gadaud
R du Président Wilson
Trans Périgord (550m);
Périgord (450m)
R Ste-Ursule
R de Strasbourg
Bd des Arènes
Jardins des Arènes
3
7
Roman Amphitheatre
LA CITÉ
R de la Cité
Pl de la Cité
5
Tour de Vésone (300m);
Musée Gallo-Romain Vesuma (350m)
R Guillier
R E Guillier
L'Arsault
Esplanade du Théâtre
Espace Tourisme Périgord
R Lafayette
R Duguesclin
Av d'Aquitaine
Pl Bugeaud
Pl André Maurois
Pl du Général de Gaulle
Bd Michel Montaigne
Cours Michel Montaigne
Pl Michel Montaigne
R Michel Montaigne
R Bergère
Cours St-Voltaire
Pl St-Louis
R St-Louis
R Limogeanne
R du Conseil
Allée de Tourny
Cours Tourny
R du Plantier
R de l'Aiault
Musée d'Art et d'Archéologie du Périgord
2
R Barbecane
R des Dépêches
R Notre Dame
R de Vertu
R du Marché au Bois
Pl du Musée
16
17
St-Front Quarter
4
13
15
8
19
21
Pl de la Sagesse
R Éguillerie
Pl St-Silain
Cimetière St-Silain
R de l'Oie
Pl de l'Oie
14
Pl du Coderc
6
R de la Miséricorde
PUY ST-FRONT
Pl Daumesnil
Pl
1
Cathédrale St-Front
R de la Clarté
18
20
R de l'Hôtel de Ville
Pl de l'Hôtel de Ville
12
R des Places
R Taillefer
R des Farges
R Condé
10
Tourist Office
Pl Francheville
R Littré
Cours Fénelon
Pl de la Claude
Pl Mauvard
Jardin des Anciennes Archives
R du Lys
R de l'Harmonie
Bd Georges Saumande
Q de l'Isle
R du Port de Graule
Isle
R des Prés
R Pierre Magne
11
9
R des Tanneries
R Lacombe

Périgueux

Of the 28 towers that formed Puy St-Front's medieval fortifications, only the 15th-century **Tour Mataguerre** (admission €2; ⊙10am-noon & 2-5pm Jul & Aug), a stout, cylindrical bastion next to the tourist office, remains.

★**Musée d'Art et d'Archéologie du Périgord**　　MUSEUM
(www.perigueux-maap.fr; 22 cours Tourny; adult/child €4.50/free; ⊙10.30am-5.30pm Mon & Wed-Fri, 1-6pm Sat & Sun) The city's museum displays fine Roman mosaics, prehistoric scrimshaw, medieval stonework from the Cathédrale St-Front, and interesting art mainly from the 19th and 20th centuries.

⊙ La Cité

The La Cité neighbourhood, west of the modern-day city centre, is the site of ancient Vesunna, among the most important cities in Roman Gaul.

★**Musée Gallo-Romain Vesunna**　　ROMAN SITES
(☑05 53 53 00 92; www.perigueux-vesunna.fr; 20 rue du 26e Régiment d'Infanterie, Parc de Vésone;

adult/child €6/4, audioguide €1; ⊙9.30am-5.30pm Tue-Fri, 10am-12.30pm & 2.30-6pm Sat & Sun Apr-Jun & Sep, 10am-7pm daily Jul & Aug, shorter hours rest of year) Part of the park that contains the Tour de Vésone, this sleek museum designed by French architect Jean Nouvel encompasses a 1st-century Roman villa uncovered in 1959. Light floods in through the glass-and-steel structure, and walkways circumnavigate the excavated villa; it's still possible to make out the central fountain, supporting pillars and the underfloor hypocaust system, as well as original mosaic murals, jewellery, pottery and even a water pump.

★**Tour de Vésone**　　ROMAN SITES
(⊙park 7.30am-9pm Apr-Sep to 6.30pm Oct-Mar) This 24.5m-high cella (shrine) is the last remaining section of a massive 2nd century AD Gallo-Roman temple dedicated to Roman goddess Vesunna.

★**Roman Amphitheatre**　　ROMAN SITES
The ruins of the city's amphitheatre, designed to hold over 20,000 baying spectators, was one of the largest such structures in Gaul. Today the tops of the arches have been revealed and embrace a peaceful park and fountain, the **Jardin des Arènes** (⊙7.30am-9pm Apr-Sep, to 6.30pm Oct-Mar), popular with local families.

Église St-Étienne de la Cité　　CHURCH
(place de la Cité) The Église St-Étienne de la Cité was built in the 11th century on the site of the Roman temple to Mars. Périgueux' cathedral until 1669, it only has two of its original four powerfully built domed bays (each different than the other).

⏚ Sleeping

The choice of hotels in Périgueux leaves a lot to be desired – you might find it better to visit on a day trip. The tourist office has lists of B&Bs and campgrounds.

Hôtel des Barris　　HOTEL €
(☑05 53 53 04 05; www.hoteldesbarris.com; 2 rue Pierre Magne; s €49, d €55, f €62-82; ❄⊛) Beside the broad River Isle with a cute waterside terrace, this Logis hotel is the best value in Périgueux as long as you can get a river-view room (the ones by the main road can be noisy). Higher-end rooms have air-conditioning, but only two have cathedral views.

Bristol Hôtel　　HOTEL €
(☑05 53 08 75 90; www.bristolfrance.com; 37-39 rue Antoine Gadaud; d €62-82, f €86-96; ❄@⊛) The Bristol's boxy façade has little appeal, but look

DON'T MISS

MARKETS IN PÉRIGUEUX

Folks come from far and wide for Périgueux' bustling markets, and the winter Marchés au Gras is tops for truffles.

Wednesday & Saturday Market (⊙ 8am-1pm Wed & Sat) Périgueux' wonderful street markets explode into action on Wednesday and Saturday, taking over place du Coderc, place de la Clautre and place de l'Hôtel de Ville.

Marchés au Gras (place St-Louis; ⊙ 8am-1pm Wed & Sat mid-Nov–mid-Mar) Browse local winter delicacies, such as truffles (December to February), wild mushrooms and foie gras.

Covered Market (place du Coderc; ⊙ 8am-1pm daily) The covered market is a year-round staple.

beyond the exterior and you'll find serviceable, spacious rooms with all the mod cons, super-friendly staff, and a central location. Find it half a block north of rue Gambetta, on the western edge of the Puy St-Front quarter. There's free parking.

Hôtel L'Écluse HOTEL €
(☑ 05 53 06 00 04; www.ecluse-perigord.com; rte de Limoges, Antonne-et-Trigonant; d €67-77, ste €107; 🛜) Rooms at this large waterfront hotel are rather dated, but get one with a river view and you probably won't mind. The style ranges from country and floral to rustic and spartan; get a suite for more space. It's 8km northeast of Périgueux off the N21.

✖ Eating & Drinking

The old town has a lively cafe scene and is crammed with shops selling local gourmet goodies.

★ Café de la Place BRASSERIE, CAFE €
(☑ 05 53 08 21 11; 7 place du Marché au Bois; menus €14-25; ⊙ 8am-midnight) You simply couldn't hope to find a more lively Gallic spot. Cutlery clatters beneath classic brasserie trappings – spinning fans, shiny brass fittings, burnished wooden bar – and there's nowhere better in town for people watching over a *petit café* or perfectly decadent *steak-frites*.

Pierrot Gourmet DELI €
(☑ 05 53 53 35 32; www.pierrotgourmet.com; 6 rue de l'Hôtel de Ville; mains €9.50, menus €14.50; ⊙ noon-5pm Tue-Sat) This lovely deli serves regional dishes canteen-style in the buzzy dining room, or boxed up to go for the perfect gourmet picnic. Specialities include cep flans, duck parmentier, Périgueux pâté, and sinful gingerbread tiramisu.

La Ferme St-Louis REGIONAL CUISINE €€
(☑ 05 53 53 82 77; 2 place St-Louis; lunch/dinner menus €16/30; ⊙ noon-1.30pm & 7.30-9.30pm daily Apr-Sep, closed Sun & Mon Oct-Mar) Specialising in local products such as duck foie gras, dine in the intimate stone room with the tinkle of glasses, or under plane trees on the square.

Au Bien Bon BISTRO €€
(☑ 05 53 09 69 91; 15 rue des Places; lunch/dinner menus €11/23; ⊙ noon-1.45pm & 7.30-9.30pm Tue-Sat) Checked tablecloths, chalkboard menus and chipped floor tiles set the earthy tone at this convivial bistro, good for classics such as *confit de canard* (duck leg cooked in its own fat) and *omelette aux cèpes* (omelette with porcini mushrooms).

Le Troquet BISTRO €€
(☑ 05 53 35 81 41; www.letroquet-perigueux.fr; 4 rue Notre Dame; mains €15-16; ⊙ noon-2pm Tue-Fri, 7.30-10pm Tue-Thu, to 11pm Fri & Sat) Locals in the know reserve ahead at this shoebox-small alleyway bistro great for authentic market cuisine.

★ L'Essentiel GASTRONOMIC €€€
(☑ 05 53 35 15 15; www.restaurant-perigueux.com; 8 rue de la Clarté; menus lunch €29-47, dinner €43-77; ⊙ noon-1.30pm & 7.30-9.30pm Tue-Sat) At the Michelin-starred L'Essentiel it feels like dining inside an aristocratic friend's living room, with floral wallpaper and orange velour chairs providing a suitably posh setting for Périgueux' top gourmet cuisine. Chef Eric Vidal, a Tulle native, prepares meals steeped in local flavours: Quercy lamb, cockerel and local rare-breed pigs regularly feature on the *menu*, often with a truffly, nutty touch.

Le Clos St-Front GASTRONOMIC €€€
(☑ 05 53 46 78 58; www.leclossaintfront.com; 12 rue St-Front; menus lunch €24.50, 3-course €30-65; ⊙ noon-1.30pm Tue-Sun, 7.30-9.30pm Tue-Sat) Inside a 16th-century *hôtel particulier*, Patrick Feuga applies a creative approach to traditional Périgordine ingredients, with a seasonal menu that changes every six weeks. The tree-shaded garden is a dreamy, sought-after place to eat in summer; book ahead.

Le Chai Bordin WINE BAR
(www.lechaibordin.com; 8 rue de la Sagesse; ⊙ 10am-noon & 3-8pm Tue-Thu, to 10pm Fri & Sat) Convivial hole in the wall crammed with wines.

ℹ️ Information

Espace Tourisme Périgord (📞 05 53 35 50 24; www.dordogne-perigord-tourisme.fr; 25 rue du Président Wilson; ⏰ 9am-noon & 2-5pm Mon-Fri) Dordogne *département* information.

Tourist Office (📞 05 53 53 10 63; www.tourisme-perigueux.fr; 26 place Francheville; ⏰ 9am-7pm Mon-Sat, 10am-6pm Sun mid-Jun–mid-Sep, shorter hours rest of year; 🛜) Helpful, with loads of info and a smartphone app.

ℹ️ Getting There & Around

BUS

Péribus (📞 05 53 53 30 37; www.peribus.fr; tickets €1.25) Operates local buses.

Trans Périgord (📞 05 53 08 43 13; www.cftaco.fr; 19 rue Denis Papin; 1/10 tickets €2/14) Operates several regional buses on minimal schedule (two to three per day, each line), to Sarlat (1½ hours), Montignac (1¾ hours) and Bergerac (1¼ hours). Trans Périgord also has services to Brantôme centre (50 minutes). Located near the train station.

CAR

Major car-hire agencies are located across from the train station.

TRAIN

The **train station** (rue Denis Papin), 1km northwest of the old town, is served by Péribus lines GBE, 3 and 5. Getting to Bergerac (€25.10, 10 daily) requires a change in Libourne, and Sarlat-la-Canéda (€15.90, five daily) requires a change in Le Buisson.

Bordeaux €22, 1½ hours, 10 to 12 daily.

Brive-la-Gaillarde €14, one hour, six daily.

Limoges €18, one hour, 11 daily.

Brantôme

POP 2193

Beautiful Brantôme sits on a small island in a bend in the River Dronne, with five medieval bridges and romantic riverfront architecture, thus earning its tagline 'Venice of the Périgord'. Its impressive abbey is built into a mainland cliff-face, and it's surrounded by parks and willow-filled woodland, making Brantôme an enchanting spot to while away an afternoon or embark on a boat ride.

👁️ Sights

Abbaye de Brantôme   ABBEY

Brantôme's most illustrious landmark is the former Benedictine Abbey, built and rebuilt from the 11th to 18th centuries and now occupied by the town hall and an **art museum**. Look out for the abbey's spectacular detached 11th-century Romanesque bell tower, built into the rock, and the oldest in the Limousin style. Next door is the Gothic **abbey church**.

Parcours Troglodytique   CAVE
(adult/child €4/2; ⏰ 10am-1pm & 2-6pm) Behind the modern-day abbey lie moody caves, originally a place of pagan worship and then part of Brantôme's first 8th-century abbey. Its most famous feature is a 15th-century rock **frieze** thought to depict the Last Judgment.

🏃 Activities

Canoeing & Kayaking

Plenty of places hire out one-person kayaks and multi-person canoes for a trip down the Dronne. They also offer half-day trips from Fontaine (4km upriver), Verneuil (8km upriver) and Bourdeilles (12km downriver), as well as a full-day trip from Verneuil to Bourdeilles (20km).

Brantôme Canoë   BOAT HIRE
(📞 05 53 05 77 24; www.brantomecanoe.com; kayak/canoe rental per hour from €10/14, half-day trip €16-36, full-day €25-58) Beside the main car park.

Allo Canoës   BOAT HIRE
(📞 05 53 06 31 85; www.allocanoes.com; kayak/canoe rental per hour from €10/14, half-day trip €16-39, full-day €25-57) Near the abbey; also climbing.

Boat Trips

Brantôme Croisières   BOAT TOUR
(📞 05 53 04 74 71; www.brantomecroisieres.com; adult/child €7.50/5; ⏰ Apr-Oct) Pleasure boats depart from the banks of the river in front of the abbey at Pont Coudé, and cruise Brantôme's waterways. Cruises last about 50 minutes, with up to six trips per day.

WORTH A TRIP

REGIONAL PARKS

This corner of France is renowned for its unspoilt natural beauty, with huge swathes protected in three *parcs naturels régionaux*: **Périgord-Limousin** (www.pnr-perigord-limousin.fr) in the northwest, **Millevaches en Limousin** (www.pnr-millevaches.fr) in the east and **Causses de Quercy** (www.parc-causses-du-quercy.org) in the south. All three offer a wealth of outdoor activities. Tourist offices stock walking leaflets, mountain-bike guides, and horseback riding information.

TRUFFLES: BLACK PEARLS OF PÉRIGORD

While the Dordogne is famed for all of its gourmet goodies, for some culinary connoisseurs there's only one that matters: the black Périgord truffle *(Tuber melanosporum)*, often dubbed *le diamant noir* (black diamond) or, hereabouts, *la perle noire du Périgord*.

A subterranean fungus that grows naturally in chalky soils (in the Dordogne around the roots of oak or hazelnut trees), it is notoriously capricious: a good truffle spot one year can be inexplicably bare the next, which makes large-scale farming practically impossible. The art of truffle hunting is a matter of luck, judgment and hard-earned experience, with specially trained dogs (and sometimes pigs) helping in the search.

The height of truffle season is between December and March, when you'll find them on local menus and when special **truffle markets** are held around the Dordogne, such as Périgueux' Marchés au Gras (p566), **Brantôme** (⊙6am-noon Fri Dec-Feb) and Sarlat (p577). Leading local chefs head 35km south of Périgueux to St-Alvère's **marché aux truffes** (⊙Mon mornings Dec-Feb) where top harvests fetch as much as €1000 a kilogram.

Alternatively, book with local truffle expert Edouard Aynaud at **Truffière de Péchalifour** (☑05 53 29 20 44; www.truffe-perigord.com; tours adult €6-10, child free-€3) for a tour, meal or stay at his *truffière* (truffle-growing area), just north of St-Cyprien.

Sorges, 23km northeast of Périgueux, has an **Écomusée de la Truffe** (www.ecomusee-truffe-sorges.com; Le Bourg, Sorges; adult/child €5/2.50; ⊙9.30am-6.30pm Mon-Fri, 9.30am-12.30pm & 2.30-6.30pm Sat & Sun mid-Jun–Sep, shorter hours rest of year) and a 3km trail through the local *truffières*, while **La Truffe Noire de Sorges** (☑06 08 45 09 48; www.truffe-sorges.com; tours €10-25; ⊙by reservation Dec-Feb & Jun-Sep) runs truffle-themed tours followed by a tasting (tour in English on request).

Bateau Maffioletti   BOAT TOUR
(☑05 53 04 74 71; http://bateaumaffioletti.free.fr; adult/child €7.50/5) Departs from in front of the abbey at Pont Coudé.

🛏 Sleeping & Eating

Maison Fleurie   B&B €
(☑05 53 35 17 04; www.maison-fleurie.net; 54 rue Gambetta; s €45-50, d €65-90) Simple, spic-and-span rooms with floral motifs fill this friendly B&B, which also boasts a sunny courtyard filled with geraniums and petunias.

Hostellerie du Périgord Vert   HOTEL €
(☑05 53 05 70 58; www.hotel-hpv.fr; 7 av André Maurois; d €58-83, f €105-120; 🛜) The ivy-covered façade promises period charm, but inside the rooms are rather modern and bland. Still, bathrooms are sleek, rates are reasonable, and the restaurant (*menus* €19 to €39) serves reliable local cuisine.

★Hostellerie Les Griffons   HOTEL €€
(☑05 53 45 45 35; www.griffons.fr; Bourdeilles; d from €117; ⊙restaurant noon-2pm Sun, 7.30-9.30pm Mon & Wed-Sun; 🛜) In the riverside town of Bourdeilles, 9km southwest of Brantôme along the D78, this charming converted mill perched over the river drips character. Medieval fireplaces, solid beams and higgledy-piggledy layouts characterise

the rooms. Its riverside restaurant (three-course *menus* €32 to €43) opens onto a lovely waterfront terrace, and is renowned throughout the region. It's walking distance to Bourdeilles' château.

Moulin de l'Abbaye   BISTRO €€€
(☑05 53 05 80 22; www.moulinabbaye.com; 1 rte de Bourdeilles; 3-course/5-course menus €38/65; ⊙bistros & hotel Apr-Nov, gastronomic restaurant 7.30-9.30pm Jun-Aug) At this carefully converted water mill at the foot of the abbey, choose between its extravagant gastronomic restaurant and its two sister bistros: **Au Fil de l'Eau** (☑05 53 05 73 65; www.fildeleau.com; quai Bertin 21), specialising in fish, or **Au Fil du Temps** (☑05 53 05 75 27; www.fildutemps.com; 1 chemin du Vert Galant) with traditional Périgordian roasted meats. At the main restaurant, terraces overlook the river, and 19 equally luxe rooms are on offer upstairs (rooms €165 to €248).

ℹ Information

Tourist Office (☑05 53 05 80 63; www.perigord-dronne-belle.fr; Abbaye de Brantôme; ⊙10am-1pm & 2-6pm Apr-Sep, shorter hours rest of year) Small office inside the abbey.

ℹ Getting There & Away

Brantôme is 27km north of Périgueux along the D939. From Monday to Friday, one Trans Périgord (p567) bus per day runs from the police station in Brantôme centre to Périgueux (50 minutes).

Bergerac

POP 28,755

Rich vineyards and rolling fields surround pretty cream-stone Bergerac, a good gateway to the Dordogne and one of the most prestigious winegrowing areas of the Aquitaine. The sweet town's main claim to fame is dramatist and satirist Savinien Cyrano de Bergerac (1619–55), whose romantic exploits – and oversized nose – have inspired everyone from Molière to Steve Martin. Despite the legend (largely invented by 19th-century playwright Edmond Rostand), Cyrano's connection with the town is tenuous – he's thought to have stayed here only a few nights, if at all.

Bergerac's riverfront old town and lively cafe scene make it fun to explore.

◉ Sights

The prettiest parts of Bergerac's fine old town are place de la Mirpe, with its tree-shaded square and timber houses, and place Pelissière, where a jaunty **statue of Cyrano de Bergerac** gazes up at the nearby **Église St-Jacques**, a former pilgrimage point. The **Ancien Port** wraps beautifully along the river. Rue St-Clar arcs inland and is lined with half-timbered houses. The tourist office has a good, free walking tour map.

Musée du Vin et
de la Batellerie
MUSEUM

(place de la Mirpe; adult/child €3/1.50; ⊗10am-noon & 2-6pm Tue-Fri, to 5pm Sat, 2.30-6.30pm Sun) Wonderfully musty displays of vintage wine-making equipment and scale models of local river boats.

Musée d'Anthropologie
du Tabac
MUSEUM

(10 rue de l'Ancien Port; adult/child €4/free; ⊗10am-noon & 2-6pm Tue-Sat, 2.30-6.30pm Sun) Inside the 17th-century **Maison Peyrarède**, the displays span 3000 years of history and include a collection of ornate pipes.

⚡ Activities

Maison des Vins
WINE TASTING

(⊘05 53 63 57 55; www.vins-bergerac.fr; Cloître des Récollets; ⊗10am-12.30pm & 2-7pm Tue-Sat, daily Jul & Aug) Within the Cloître des Récollets, a former monastery, this wine centre is the best spot to sample the area's famous vintages and get the low-down on touring local vineyards.

Gabarres de Bergerac
BOAT TOUR

(⊘05 53 24 58 80; www.gabarres.fr; quai Salvette; adult/child €8.50/6; ⊗Easter-Oct) Atmospheric 50-minute cruises from the Ancien Port.

🛏 Sleeping

Le Colombier de Cyrano
et Roxane
B&B €

(⊘05 53 57 96 70; www.lecolombierdecyrano.fr; place de la Mirpe; d €73-83; ☜) One of several sweet *chambres d'hôte* in Bergerac's old town, this 16th-century blue-shuttered stone building has three colourful rooms and a flower-filled terrace where you can doze in the hammock.

Hotel du Commerce
HOTEL €

(⊘05 53 27 30 50; www.hotel-du-commerce24.fr; 36 place Gambetta; d €69-77; ✳☜) The best of several rather dull hotels on place Gambetta. Some of the functional rooms have a view over the tree-lined square.

Château Les Farcies du Pech'
B&B €€

(⊘06 30 19 53 20; www.vignoblesdubard.com; Hameau de Pécharmant; d incl breakfast €110; ⊗mid-Mar–mid-Nov) Part of a group of four renowned wineries, this beautiful château-vineyard 2km north of Bergerac is definitely the choice for oenophiles. All five rooms scream rustic chic, with original stonework and vintage character. The proprietor Marie serves a lovely home-cooked French brekkie in the dining room and can arrange tours of the vineyards.

🍴 Eating

The central **covered market** (place Louis de la Bardonnie; ⊗7am-1pm) is surrounded by bistros.

La Désirade
ICE CREAM €

(⊘05 53 58 27 50; place Pélissière; per scoop €2.50; ⊗10am-11pm May-Sep) Lick a scoop of home-made ice cream on one of the benches on the square.

★ Villa Laetitia
REGIONAL CUISINE €€

(⊘05 53 61 00 12; www.villalaetitia.net; 21 rue de l'Ancien Port; menus lunch €17, dinner €25-38; ⊗noon-2pm & 7-9pm Tue-Sat Apr-Sep) Book ahead for a seat with in-the-know locals in the soft, cream-stone dining room where charming waitstaff serve delicious local cuisine, made in the open kitchen at the rear. Expect farm-fresh ingredients and delicious Périgord classics exquisitely presented.

L'Imparfait
REGIONAL CUISINE €€

(⊘05 53 57 47 92; www.imparfait.com; 8-10 rue des Fontaines; menus €26-32; ⊗noon-2pm & 7-10pm

AROUND BERGERAC: WINE COUNTRY

The broad, flat area south of Bergerac is covered in vineyards. Seven Appellation d'Origine Contrôlées (AOCs) hale from this region, which abuts Bordeaux wine country to the west, and represent some of the Dordogne's best wines. Pick up the *Wines of Bergerac* guide-map from local tourist offices or the Maison des Vins (p569) in Bergerac, to hit the wine-tasting trail.

Château Montdoyen (☑ 05 53 58 85 85; www.chateau-montdoyen.com; Le Puch, Monbazillac; ⊙ 9.30am-1pm & 2-7pm) This fun family-run winery makes a full range of excellent wines, from Bergerac AOC reds, to whites with intriguing names such as Divine Miséricorde (sauvignon blanc and sauvignon gris), to a delicious rosé, and outstanding Monbazillac sweet white. Find it 10km south of Bergerac, off the D933.

Château d'Elle (☑ 05 53 61 66 62; www.chateaudelle.com; Chemin de la Briasse, Bergerac; ⊙ 10am-8pm daily) Jocelyne Pécou, one of the few Bergerac female vintners (hinted at in the winery's name), produces robust red Pécharmant AOC, 5km east of Bergerac centre.

Château de la Jaubertie (☑ 05 53 58 32 11; www.chateau-jaubertie.com; Colombier; ⊙ 10am-5pm Mon-Sat May–mid-Sep) This historic monument and former royal hunting lodge in pretty fields off the N21 south of Monbazillac produces a range of organic AOC Bergerac wines.

Château de Monbazillac (☑ 05 53 63 65 00; www.chateau-monbazillac.com; Monbazillac; ⊙ 10am-7pm Jun-Sep, shorter hours rest of year) Often crowded because of its grand 16th-century château (best seen from outside), this vineyard specialises in sweet white Monbazillac AOC.

La Tour des Vents (☑ 05 53 58 30 10; www.tourdesvents.com; Le Moulin de Malfourat, Monbazillac; menus lunch €24, dinner €42-58; ⊙ noon-1.30pm Wed-Sun, 7.30-9.30pm Tue-Sat; ☑) Chef Marie Rougier Salvat creates elaborate *périgourdine* meals using the freshest seasonal ingredients, and friendly staff serves them to the dining room or terrace with panoramic views of Bergerac wine country. Imagine dishes such as foie gras with local strawberries, port gelée and balsamic vinegar. Oh, and there's a vegetarian *menu* (€33) too.

daily) Chef Hervé Battiston has made this sweet little restaurant a favourite, thanks to artful French food served up in a pretty 12th-century cloister. Reserve ahead.

ℹ Information

Tourist Office (☑ 05 53 57 03 11; www.bergerac-tourisme.com; 97 rue Neuve d'Argenson; ⊙ 9.30am-1pm & 2-7pm Mon-Sat, plus Sun Jul & Aug; 🛜)

ℹ Getting There & Away

Bergerac's international airport and central location between Périgueux (47km to the northeast) and Bordeaux (93km to the west) make it a handy gateway to the Dordogne.

AIR

Bergerac's **airport** (EGC; www.bergerac.aeroport.fr), 4km southeast of town, is served by Air France and budget carriers including Ryanair. Destinations include Paris Orly, Bristol, Brussels Charleroi, Edinburgh, London Stansted, London Gatwick, East Midlands, Liverpool, Birmingham, Exeter, Leeds Bradford, Southampton and Rotterdam.

Taxis (☑ 05 53 23 32 32), which cost about €15, and rental cars are the only option for getting into town.

BUS

Trans Périgord (p567) line 3 connects Begerac with Périgueux (€2, 1¼ hours, two to three Monday to Friday).

CAR

Major car-hire outlets are at the airport, and Europcar is at the train station.

TRAIN

Bergerac is on the regional line between Bordeaux (€17.20, 1½ hours, 11 daily) and Sarlat (€12.90, 1½ hours, five daily). For other destinations change at Le Buisson or Libourne.

Issigeac & Around

Bastides abound in the area southeast of Bergerac, and one of the best is wonderful Issigeac. Its high stone walls encircle a medieval village that is a joy to explore, especially at its magnificent **Sunday morning market**, which seems to fill every lane. An agricultural area as well, it produces everything from foie gras to three AOC strawberry varieties. Look for the delicious walnut-rind cheese – echourgnac – made by nuns at Abbaye d'Echourgnac.

Issigeac's predominantly 13th- to 18th-century **historic buildings** (many of them timber-framed) were constructed on top of a former 4th-century Roman villa, later a 7th-century Benedictine Abbey. The tourist office has a free walking tour leaflet. There's also an **antique fair** in August.

Other top *bastides* to explore nearby are **Beaumont-du-Périgord** with its large central square, fortified church, and **Monday night market** that often has a live band. One of its *bastide* gates leads straight into the countryside and the tourist office has lists of walks and maps.

🛌 Sleeping & Eating

Passé et Présent   B&B €
(☑05 53 63 35 31; www.passe-et-present.com; 14 Grand Rue, Issegiac; d incl breakfast €48-55; 📶) Impeccably done antique-filled rooms fill a pretty ancient town house in Issegiac's centre. Take your tea in a rose-filled courtyard.

★Shabby Chic Corner   CAFE €
(☑05 53 57 88 20; www.boheme-est-la-marquise. com; 3 rue Ernest Esclangon; ⊙10am-7pm Tue-Sun Jun–mid-Sep, 10am-3pm Sun mid-Sep–May) Wonderful Nathalie has a sewing atelier downstairs and a quaint, country-French style *salon de thé* (tea room) upstairs. She bakes everything from scratch, and the place is always packed on market days.

El Borini   GASTRONOMIC €€
(Restaurant Chez Alain; ☑05 53 58 06 03; http://el borini.com; Tour de Ville; menus lunch €17, dinner €28-40; ⊙noon-2pm Tue-Sun, 7-10pm Tue-Sat) Choose between the garden terrace surrounding a fountain on the edge of the medieval fortifications or the elegant white-linen dining room, and then tuck into chef Christian Borini's recipes designed to highlight the market-fresh ingredients from the region.

❶ Information

Tourist Office (☑05 53 58 79 62; www. pays-des-bastides.com; place du Château) Loads of info on *bastide* country.

Monpazier & Around

POP 528

One of the best-preserved *bastides* is beautiful Monpazier. Founded in 1284 by a representa-

tive of Edward I (King of England and Duke of Aquitaine), it had a turbulent time during the Wars of Religion and the Peasant Revolts of the 16th century, but despite numerous assaults and campaigns, the town has survived wonderfully intact, with original walls, gates and a church.

Other top villages nearby are **Belvès** (16km northeast), with its yellow-gold houses strung across a gorgeous hilltop, and **Villefranche-du-Périgord** (20km southeast), another *bastide* with an enormous covered market in the central square. Teeny **Prats-du-Périgord** is for Romanesque architecture lovers, with its moody, fortified Église St-Maurice.

◎ Sights

★Place des Cornières   SQUARE
From the town's three gateways, Monpazier's flat, grid-straight streets lead to the arcaded market square (also known as place Centrale), surrounded by an ochre-hued collection of stone houses that reflect centuries of building and rebuilding. In one corner is an old lavoir once used for washing clothes. Thursday is **market** day, as it has been since the Middle Ages.

Château de Biron   CHÂTEAU
(www.semitour.com; D53; adult/child €8/5.10, joint ticket with Cadouin €11.40/6.80; ⊙10am-7pm daily Jul & Aug, 10am-1pm & 2-6pm Tue-Sun Feb-Jun & Sep-Dec, closed Jan) Eight kilometres south of Monpazier, this much-filmed château is a glorious mishmash of styles, having been fiddled with by eight centuries of successive heirs. The castle was finally sold in the early 1900s to pay for the extravagant lifestyle of a particularly irresponsible son. It's notable for its slate turrets and double loggia **staircase**, supposedly modelled on one at Versailles.

🛌 Sleeping & Eating

Hôtel de France   HOTEL €
(☑05 53 22 60 06; www.hoteldefrancemonpazier. fr; 21 rue St-Jacques; d/tr/q €59/55/80; ⊙Apr–mid-Nov) This honey-stoned *auberge* sits within the *bastide* walls; parts of the building date to the 13th century. A 15th-century staircase leads to snug rooms, with musty carpets, old furniture and windows overlooking rooftops.

Hôtel Edward 1er   HOTEL €€
(☑05 53 22 44 00; www.hoteledward1er.com; 5 rue St-Pierre; d €98-140, ste €120-146; ⊙dinner

TOP MARKETS

Throughout the region local markets fill medieval cobbled streets and overflow with foie gras (www.foiegras-perigord.com), winter-time black truffles, walnuts, chestnuts, cheese, honey and seasonal produce, from asparagus to strawberries. Baskets and clothing also feature at some. **Summertime night markets** are fantastic: bring your own plates and cutlery and dine at tables set up under the stars. A few of the best:

➜ **Monday** St-Alvère, Beaumont-du-Périgord (night), Montignac (night)

➜ **Tuesday** Brive-la-Gaillarde, Le Bugue

➜ **Wednesday** Périgueux, Sarlat-la-Canéda, Bergerac, Martel, Cahors

➜ **Thursday** Monpazier, Issigeac (night)

➜ **Friday** St-Pompon

➜ **Saturday** Périgueux, Sarlat-la-Canéda, Brive-la-Gaillarde, Bergerac, Villefranche-du-Périgord, Martel, Cahors, Figeac, St-Pompon (night)

➜ **Sunday** Issigeac, St-Cyprien, Daglan

Thu-Tue Sep-Jun, daily Jul & Aug; 🛜 ﹩) Rooms in this tower-topped mansion get more luxurious the more you pay: top-of-the-line suites have a choice of Jacuzzi or Turkish bath, and views of surrounding hills. It feels slightly dated considering the price, but the owners are fun, and there's an excellent restaurant (*menus* €30 to €50).

Bistrot 2 BISTRO €
(☑ 05 53 22 60 64; www.bistrot2.fr; Foirail Nord; lunch/dinner menus from €16/19; ⊘noon-2pm & 7.30-9.30pm Sat-Thu) Modern dining in an old-town setting with a wisteria-covered terrace right opposite a medieval gateway. Food is French with an adventurous slant.

ⓘ Information

Tourist Office (☑ 05 53 22 68 59; www.pays-des-bastides.com; place des Cornières; ⊘10am-12.30pm & 2.30-6pm Tue-Sun)

ⓘ Getting There & Away

Monpazier is 50km southwest of Sarlat and 50km southeast of Bergerac. There is no public transport.

The Dordogne Valley

Lush meadows and green woods roll out along the meandering banks of the Dordogne, one of France's most iconic and idyllic rivers. In centuries gone by, the valley marked an important frontier during the Hundred Years War, and the hilltops are studded with defensive châteaux, as well as heavily fortified towns. These days it's a picture of French tranquillity, perfect country to explore by bike or, better still, by paddle.

Trémolat & Around

Little Trémolat (population 588) sits in a dramatic bend of the River Dordogne. Besides the beautiful, forested landscape, the area is home to several top restaurants and wine experiences.

⊙ Sights

Cloître de Cadouin CLOISTER
(☑ 05 53 63 36 28; www.semitour.com; adult €6.20/3.60, joint ticket with Château de Biron €11.40/6.80; ⊘10am-7pm Jul & Aug, 10am-1pm & 2-6pm Apr-Jun & Sep-Oct, shorter hours rest of year) This Unesco-listed 12th-century Cistercian abbey and its Gothic cloister hide in the forest just south of the Dordogne, along the River Bélingou.

✖ Eating

Chai Monique WINE BAR €
(☑ 05 53 07 29 84; 3 rue de Paris, Le Bugue; dishes €8.50-10; ⊘10am-9pm Tue & Sat, 11am-10pm Thu & Fri, 11am-3pm Sun & Mon) An easy, light-hearted spot to grab a bite and glass of wine, all day long, in Le Bugue, 13km northwest of Trémolat.

★ Les Truffieres REGIONAL CUISINE €€
(☑ 05 53 27 30 44; www.auberge-les-truffieres.fr; Bosredon, Trémolat; lunch/dinner menus from €22/30; ⊘noon-1.30pm Tue-Sun, 7.30-9.30pm Tue-Sat) Reserve ahead for fantastic local cuisine prepared by lively Yanick and his son Aurélian on a farm in the hills above Trémo-

lat. The dining room feels like the country home it is, and the dishes are tops: from classic garlic soup to home-made foie gras that you'll think about for days.

★ **Le Vieux Logis** GASTRONOMIC €€€
(☏05 53 22 80 06; www.vieux-logis.com; Trémolat; lunch menus €49, 4-course menus from €65; ☺ noon-1.30pm & 7.30-9pm Fri-Tue) Folks come from far and wide for chef Vincent Arnould's refined, beautifully presented creative cuisine of the Périgord. The ceiling soars over the elegant dining room, or dine alfresco under a canopy of sculpted trees. Every dish is a surprising treat, and the wine list matches.

The Logis also offers beautiful rooms (rooms €200 to €240), creating the perfect peaceful retreat. There's an excellent bistro too.

🛍 Shopping

Julien de Savignac WINE
(☏05 53 07 10 31; www.julien-de-savignac.com; av de la Libération, Le Bugue; ☺9am-7pm Tue-Sat, to noon Sun) One of Dordogne's best wine shops – spoiled for choice in Le Bugue.

Beynac-et-Cazenac & Around

Beynac (population 559), as it is known by locals, and its environs make up one of the Dordogne's most dramatic landscapes, with the two opposing fortresses of Beynac and Castelnaud, facing off across the gloriously broad river, plied by pleasure craft in summer.

Scenes from the Lasse Hallström–directed movie *Chocolat* (2000), starring Johnny Depp and Juliette Binoche, were filmed along rue de l'Ancienne Poste in Beynac, and part of Luc Besson's *The Messenger: The Story of Joan of Arc* (1999) was filmed in the fortress.

⊙ Sights

★ **Château de Beynac** CHÂTEAU
(☏05 53 29 50 40; www.beynac-en-perigord.com; Beynac-et-Cazenac; adult/child €8/3.50; ☺10am-6.30pm May-Aug, to 5pm Jan-Apr & Sep-Oct, closed Nov & Dec) Towering gloriously atop a limestone bluff, this 12th-century fortress' panoramic position above the Dordogne made it a key defensive position during the Hundred Years War. Apart from a brief interlude under Richard the Lionheart, Beynac remained fiercely loyal to the French monarchy, often placing it at odds with the English-controlled stronghold of nearby Castelnaud. Protected by 200m cliffs, a double wall and double

moat, it presented a formidable challenge for would-be attackers, though it saw little direct action.

Highlights include the château's Romanesque **keep**, a grand **Salle des États** (State Room) and frescoed 15th-century **chapel**, and the 16th- and 17th-century **apartments** built to lodge castle barons. From the battlements, there's a fantastic view along the Dordogne.

The impressive fortress is rather barebones inside; buy the informational booklet to add context. Parking slips (€2) are good for town parking below, as well.

★ **Château de Castelnaud** CASTLE
(www.castelnaud.com/uk; Castelnaud-la-Chapelle; adult/child €8.60/4.30; ☺9am-8pm Jul & Aug, 10am-6pm Feb-Jun & Sep–mid-Nov, 2-5pm mid-Nov–Jan) The massive ramparts and metre-thick crenellated walls of this quintessential medieval fortress (occupied by the English during the Hundred Years War) contain an elaborate **museum of medieval warfare** with displays of daggers, spiked halberds, archaic cannons and enormous crossbows. Climb the dark 16th-century **artillery tower** stairs to see the exhibits and reach the rugged 13th-century donjon (keep). From the upper terrace a fantastic view encompasses the Dordogne Valley all the way to Castelnaud's arch-rival, the Château de Beynac, 4km to the north.

Daily demonstrations of giant trebuchets and a forge bring the fortress to life, and events such as one-hour guided **evening tours** by costumed actors or mock battles are staged mid-July to August (check the website).

Château des Milandes CHÂTEAU, MUSEUM
(☏05 53 59 31 21; www.milandes.com; Castelnaud-la-Chapelle; adult/child €9.20/5.80; ☺9.30am-7.30pm Jul & Aug, 10am-6.30pm Apr-Jun & Sep-Oct) This 15th-century château, 5.5km west of the Château de Castelnaud, is famous for its fabulous former owner: glamorous dancer, singer and music-hall star Josephine Baker (1906–75), who took Paris by storm in the 1920s with her risqué performances. Baker purchased the castle in 1936 and lived here until 1958. It houses a super **museum** documenting her life with original photos and memorabilia including a fantastic costume collection, and her songs play throughout.

Baker was awarded the Croix de Guerre and the Legion of Honour for her work with the French Resistance during WWII, and was later active in the US civil-rights movement. She is also remembered for her 'Rainbow

Vézère & Dordogne Valleys

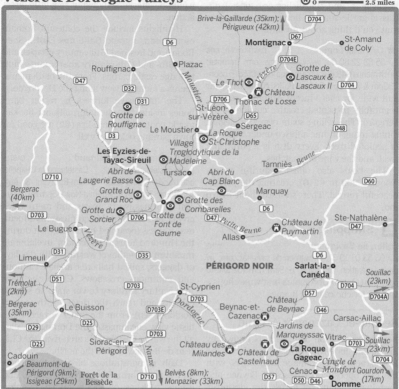

Tribe' – 12 children from around the world adopted as 'an experiment in brotherhood'.

From April to October free 30-minute daily **birds of prey displays** feature the château's owls, falcons and eagle.

🏃 Activities

Montgolfière Châteaux OUTDOOR ACTIVITIES
(📞 06 71 14 34 96; www.montgolfiere-chateaux.com; 1-hr aloft adult/child from €120/180) Lovely Monsieur Lionel Druet takes you soaring over Dordogne châteaux in hot-air balloons.

🛏️ Sleeping & Eating

Accommodation options are limited, with only a handful of hotels in the area, but tourist offices in La Roque Gageac and Beynac-et-Cazenac have lists of campgrounds and *chambres d'hôte* (B&Bs).

Les Machicoulis CAFE €
(📞 05 24 15 11 76; www.lesmachicoulis.com; Castelnaud-la-Chapelle; mains €7-12; 🕐) Stop in for a

crêpe or overnight in the B&B (double €60), at the foot of the Château de Castelnaud.

⭐ **La Petite Tonelle** BISTRO €€
(📞 05 53 29 95 18; www.restaurant-petite-tonnelle.fr; Le Bourg, Beynac-et-Cazenac; menus €17-40; 🕐 noon-1.30pm & 7.30-9.30pm Thu-Tue) In high season reserve ahead for a spot on the sunny terrace in the centre of Beynac village, where you'll get an array of seasonal, local specialties such as truffles, duck, lamb and river fish.

ℹ️ Information

Tourist Office (📞 05 53 29 43 08; www.sarlat-tourisme.com; Beynac; 🕐 10am-1pm & 2-5pm Apr-Sep, shorter hours rest of year)

La Roque Gageac & Around

POP 429

La Roque Gageac's row of amber buildings and flourishing gardens lining the cliff-face along the Dordogne have earned it a *plus beaux village* designation, and it's an idyllic launch pad for a cruise or canoe trip.

◎ Sights

★ Jardins de Marqueyssac
GARDEN

(☑ 05 53 31 36 36; www.marqueyssac.com; Vézac; adult/child €7.80/3.90; ⊘ 9am-8pm Jul & Aug, 10am-7pm Apr-Jun & Sep–mid-Nov, 2-5pm mid-Nov–Jan) Garden fans won't want to miss these famous manicured gardens, stretching along a rocky bluff overlooking the Dordogne Valley. Signposted paths lead through painstakingly clipped box hedges and decorative topiary to the gardens' breathtaking *belvédère* (viewpoint), with sightlines to area castles, the Dordogne and La Roque Gageac. Thursday nights in July and August the entire place is alight with candles (adult/child €13/6.50). Find the entrance 3km west of La Roque Gageac.

Fort Troglodyte
FORT

(La Roque Gageac; adult/child €5/2; ⊘10am-6pm) A warren of winding lanes lead to La Roque's dramatic fort, where a series of defensive positions constructed by medieval engineers have been carved from overhanging cliffs.

⚡ Activities

Paddling along the river, especially this particular stretch, offers a changing panorama of soaring cliffs, castles and picturesque villages. Several canoe operators are based near La Roque Gageac and Cénac, including Canoë Vacances (☑ 05 53 28 17 07; www.canoevacances. com; Lespinasse, La Roque Gageac; self-guided canoeing per person €13-21), Canoë Loisirs (☑ 05 53 28 23 43; www.canoes loisirs.com; Pont de Vitrac, Vitrac; self-guided canoe & kayak trips €7-25) and Canoë Dordogne (☑ 05 53 29 58 50; www. canoesdordogne.fr; La Roque Gageac; self-guided canoeing per person €6-22) which offer self-guided trips of between one and five hours from various points upriver. La Roque Gageac's quay is also a launch point for short river cruises (p576) aboard a traditional *gabarre*.

🛏 Sleeping & Eating

La Belle Étoile
HOTEL €

(☑ 05 53 29 51 44; www.belleetoile.fr; Le Bourg, La Roque Gageac; d €55-75, ste €130; ⊘Apr-Oct; 🐾) This riverside hotel has a prime position in La Roque, in an amber stone building with views across the water from higher-priced rooms (others overlook the village). Expect traditional wooden furniture and understated fabrics. The **restaurant** (menus €29-50; ⊘noon-1.30pm Tue-Sun, 7.30-9.30pm Tue & Thu-Sun) is renowned for its sophisticated French food, and opens onto a vine-shaded terrace with a fabulous view.

Hôtel La Treille
REGIONAL CUISINE €€

(☑ 05 53 28 33 19; www.latreille-perigord.com; Vitrac; menus €20-57; ⊘12.30-2pm Wed-Sun & 7.30-9pm daily; 🐾) One of the few local restaurants open on Sunday and Monday nights, gourmet food is dished up riverside at this sweet, small hotel (double/triple from €54/73), in Vitrac, 6.5km east of La Roque Gageac.

ⓘ Getting There & Away

La Roque Gageac is 15km south of Sarlat, via the D46 and D703. There's no public transport.

Domme & Around

POP 1037

Commanding an unparalleled view across the surrounding countryside from a dizzying outcrop above the Dordogne, Domme was a perfect defensive stronghold – a fact not lost on Philippe III of France, who founded the town in 1281 as a bastion against the English. Still one of the area's best preserved *bastides,* Domme retains most of its 13th-century ramparts and three original gateways. The imposing clifftop position is best appreciated from esplanade du Belvédère and the adjacent promenade de la Barre, which offer panoramic views across the valley. Domme can be overrun in high season, so plan to see the town and view and get out quick. About 12km south of Domme, beautifully preserved Daglan hides some top restaurants.

◎ Sights & Activities

Grottes Naturelles
CAVE

(adult/child incl museum €8.50/6; ⊘hourly tours 10am-5.30pm Apr-Oct) Honeycombing the stone underneath the village is a series of large caves decorated with ornate stalactites and stalagmites. Get tickets, which include admission to the small **Musée d'Arts et Traditions Populaires** (⊘10.30am-12.30pm & 2.30-6pm Apr-Sep), a folk museum, at the tourist office opposite the entrance to the caves.

Prison des Templiers
TOWER

(adult/child €7/5; ⊘Apr-Sep) Many Knights Templar were imprisoned in Domme in 1307 while they awaited trial. Loads of Templar graffiti in their code system still mark their prison. Ask the tourist office for info.

Fabrice le Chef
COOKING

(☑ 06 83 22 61 92; www.fabricelechef.fr; Daglan; 2-3hr class per person €50) Learn how to cook

DON'T MISS

GABARRE CRUISES

One of the best ways to explore the gorgeous scenery of the Dordogne River is aboard a *gabarre*, a flat-bottomed, wooden boat used to transport freight up and down the rivers of the Périgord and Lot Valley. *Gabarres* were a common sight in this part of France until the early 20th century, when they were eclipsed by the rise of the railway and the automobile.

From April to October, traditional *gabarres* cruise from several points along the river, including Bergerac, Brantôme, Beaulieu-sur-Dordogne and the quay at La Roque Gageac. La Roque Gageac's operators include **Gabarres Caminade** (📞 05 53 29 40 95; www.gabarrecaminade.com; La Roque Gageac; 1hr trip adult/child €8.50/6) and **Gabarres Norbert** (📞 05 53 29 40 44; www.gabarres.com; La Roque Gageac; 1hr trip adult/child €8.50/6). Standard trips last about an hour and cost around €9/6.50 per adult/child; advance reservations are recommended. **Gabarres de Beynac** (📞 05 53 28 51 15; www.gabarre-beynac.com; Beynac-et-Cazenac; adult/child €8/4.50; ⊙ every 30min 10am-6pm May-Sep) does slightly shorter, cheaper trips departing from Beynac-et-Cazenac, and kids cruise free in the mornings.

delicious Périgord cuisine from Fabrice, or have him come cook for you!

🛏 Sleeping

The Dordogne in general and the area around Domme in particular is loaded with vacation rentals, easy to find on sites such as vrbo.com: from simple cottages to 13th-century dream hilltop Château Peyruzel.

La Guérinière   B&B €€
(📞 05 53 29 91 97; www.la-gueriniere-dordogne.com; Cénac et St-Julien; d incl breakfast €85-105, q €165; 🖥🅿🐾) 🍴 Surrounded by 6-hectare grounds in the valley 5km south of Domme along the D46, this family-friendly B&B's rooms are all named after flowers: our faves are Mimosa, with its sloping roof and chinoiserie wardrobe, and the supersize Blue room. Book ahead for table d'hôte (€28 including wine), using mostly organic produce.

La Tour de Cause   B&B €€
(📞 05 53 30 30 51; www.latourdecause.com; Pont de Cause; d/studio incl breakfast €93/95; ⊙ May–mid-Oct; 🖥🅿) Caitlin and Albert Woodbury have painstakingly renovated an historic manor house and barn into a comfortable B&B with modern bathrooms and luxe linens. Find it 6km east of Domme on the D50, or 2.5km south of Castelnaud on the D57.

🍴 Eating & Drinking

⭐**Le Petit Paris**   REGIONAL CUISINE €€
(📞 05 53 28 41 10; www.le-petit-paris.fr; Daglan; menus €26-39; ⊙ noon-1.30pm Tue-Sun & 7-8.45pm Tue-Sat Feb–mid-Nov) Friendly staff serve you on little Daglan's central square, promoting an elegant, 'there's all the time in

the world' feel, while wowing with impeccable seasonal cuisine. Spring brings lovely asparagus, the rest of the year finds tender Limousin beef, falling off the bone, or foie gras that melts in your mouth. It's 11km south of Domme.

L'Envie des Mets   MODERN FRENCH €€
(📞 05 53 31 94 01; www.lenvie-des-mets-resto.com; St-Pompon; menus €23; ⊙ noon-3pm Tue-Sat, 7.30-10.30pm Thu-Sat) Reserve ahead for the popular new kid on the block: a young chef whips up cutting-edge seasonal *périgourdine* cuisine in St-Pompon, 16km southwest of Domme. Naturally, the *menu* changes weekly.

⭐**Le Saint Martial**   GASTRONOMIC €€€
(📞 05 53 29 18 34; www.lesaintmartial.com; St-Martial-de-Nabirat; 3-course/5-course/dégustation menus €35/48/83; ⊙ noon-1.30pm & 7.30-9.30pm Wed-Sun; 🍴) Details, details, details. Valérie and Jean-Marc Réal get them all right at this small restaurant in low-key St-Martial-de-Nabirat, 8km south of Domme. The church bells chime lightly and the terrace stretches out in the sun as you enjoy a steady procession of beautifully presented local dishes. Book well ahead.

L'Esplanade   BAR
(📞 05 53 28 31 41; www.esplanade-perigord.com; 2 rue du Pont-Carral, Domme; 🖥) The main reason to stop in at L'Esplanade is for a terrace drink in Domme as the sun sets over the Dordogne with mind-boggling valley views. Teetering on the edge of the village ramparts, the hotel (double €93 to €155) and restaurant (*menus* €35 to €70) have uneven service so you can do better elsewhere.

ℹ️ Information

Tourist Office (📞 05 53 31 71 00; www.
ot-domme.com; place de la Halle; ⊘10am-
noon & 2-6pm)

ℹ️ Getting There & Away

Domme is 18km south of Sarlat along the D46.
No public transport options.

Sarlat-la-Canéda

POP 10,105

A picturesque tangle of honey-coloured buildings, alleyways and secret squares make up the
beautiful town of Sarlat-la-Canéda. Boasting
some of the region's best-preserved medieval
architecture, it's a popular base for exploring
the Vézère Valley, and a favourite location for
film directors. It's also firmly on the tourist
radar, and you might find it difficult to appreciate the town's charms among the summer
throngs, especially on market days.

Well-known **markets** sell a smorgasbord
of goose-based products, and Sarlat hosts an
annual goose festival, the **Fest'Oie** (⊘late Feb
or early Mar), when live birds and food stalls fill
the streets, and Sarlat's top chefs prepare an
outdoor banquet.

⊙ Sights

Part of the fun of wandering around Sarlat is
losing yourself in its twisting alleyways and
back streets. Rue Landry, rue de la Liberté
and rue Jean-Jacques Rousseau all make good
starting points. The tourist office offers free
booklets and maps with walks around the medieval centre, as well as **guided tours** (adult/
child €5.50/3; ⊘ in English 11am Thu May-Jul & Sep).

★ **Sarlat Markets**   MARKET
(place de la Liberté & rue de la République;
⊘8.30am-1pm Wed & 8.30am-6pm Sat) For an
introductory French market experience visit Sarlat's heavily touristed Saturday market, which takes over the streets around
Cathédrale St-Sacerdos. Depending on the
season, delicacies include local mushrooms
and duck- and goose-based products such
as foie gras. Get *truffe noir* (black truffle)
at the winter **Marché aux Truffes** (⊘Sat
morning Dec-Feb). An atmospheric largely organic **night market** (⊘6-10pm) operates on
Thursday. Seasoned market-goers may prefer
others throughout the region (p568).

★ **Cathédrale St-Sacerdos**   CATHEDRAL
(place du Peyrou) Once part of Sarlat's Cluniac
abbey, the original abbey church was built

in the 1100s, redeveloped in the early 1500s
and remodelled again in the 1700s, so it's a
real mix of styles. The belfry and western
façade are the oldest parts of the building,
while the nave, organ and interior chapels
are later additions.

★ **Place du Marché
aux Oies**   SQUARE
A life-size statue of three bronze geese stands
in the centre of beautiful place du Marché
aux Oies (Goose Market Sq), where live geese
are still sold during the Fest'Oie. The square's
architecture is exceptional.

★ **Église Ste-Marie**   CHURCH, MARKET
(place de la Liberté) Église Ste-Marie was ingeniously converted by acclaimed architect Jean
Nouvel, whose parents still live in Sarlat, into
Sarlat's touristy **Marché Couvert** (Covered
Market; ⊘8.30am-2pm daily, to 8pm Fri mid-Apr-
mid Nov, closed Mon, Thu & Sun rest of year). Its
panoramic lift offers 360-degree views across
Sarlat's countryside.

Chapelle St-Benoît   CHAPEL
(Chapelle des Pénitents Bleus) Two medieval
courtyards, the **Cour des Fontaines** and the
Cour des Chanoines, can be reached via
an alleyway off rue Tourny or from the Jardin des Enfeus. The passage from Cour des
Chanoines leads to the Chapelle St-Benoît
aka Chapelle des Pénitents Bleus, a 12th-
century Romanesque chapel and the oldest
remnant of Sarlat's abbey.

Jardin des Enfeus   PARK
Behind the cathedral, the Jardin des Enfeus was Sarlat's first cemetery. The rock-
et-shaped **Lanterne des Morts** (Lantern of the
Dead) may have been built to honour a visit
by St Bernard in 1147, one of the founders of
the Cistercian order.

Maison de la Boétie   HISTORIC MANSION
This 16th-century timber-framed house opposite Cathédrale St-Sacerdos is the birthplace
of writer Étienne de la Boétie (1530–63).

Château de Puymartin   CHÂTEAU
(📞 05 53 59 29 97; www.chateau-de-puymartin.com;
adult/child €8/4; ⊘10am-6.30pm mid-Jul-Aug,
10am-11.30am & 2-6pm Apr-mid-Jul & Sep, 2-5.30pm
Oct) This impressive turreted château, 8km
northwest of Sarlat, was first built in 1270,
destroyed in 1358 during the Hundred Years
War, and rebuilt around 1450. The ornate
interior is furnished lavishly with mostly
19th-century decor.

Sarlat-la-Canéda

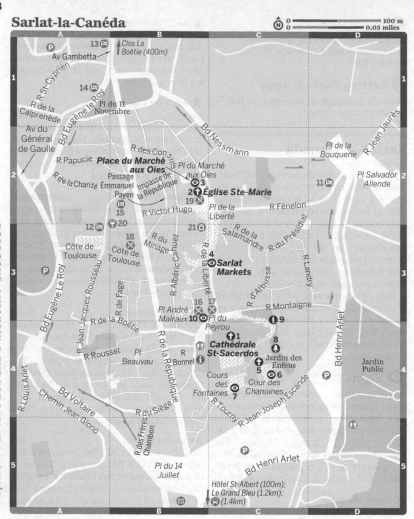

🛏 Sleeping

Hotel rooms in Sarlat during summer are like gold dust.

Hôtel St-Albert BOUTIQUE HOTEL €
(☎ 05 53 31 55 55; www.hotel-saintalbert.eu; place Pasteur; d €60-85, f €96; ☎) A small, chic hotel: chocolate and cream tones and posh bath goodies make it feel cosmopolitan, but rooms are on the small side. Find it just south of the centre on the way to the train station.

Hôtel Les Remparts HOTEL €
(☎ 05 53 59 40 00; www.hotel-lesremparts-sarlat. com; 48 av Gambetta; d €68-75, tr €75-85; ☎) Just outside the old town centre on a busyish one-

way street, this simple stone hotel has to be one of the best deals in Sarlat. Rooms lack sparkle; simple furniture and the odd reclaimed roof beam are all you should expect.

Hôtel La Couleuvrine HOTEL €
(☎ 05 53 59 27 80; www.la-couleuvrine.com; 1 place de la Bouquerie; d €65-75; ☎) Originally part of Sarlat's city wall, this rambling hotel with a sunny terrace has rooms jammed along creaky corridors. Superior and family rooms are more spacious.

Hôtel Les Récollets HOTEL €
(☎ 05 53 31 36 00; www.hotel-recollets-sarlat. com; 4 rue Jean-Jacques Rousseau; d €49-69,

Sarlat-la-Canéda

tr/q €89/99; ❄🛜) These serviceable budget rooms in the medieval centre are set around a pretty courtyard in the pedestrianised area. There's no vehicle access, so you'll have to carry luggage.

Hôtel Le Mas de Castel HOTEL €
(☑05 53 59 02 59; www.hotel-lemasdecastel.com; rte du Sudalissant; d €75-95, f €100-105; @🛜) This former farmhouse 3km south of town makes a delightful escape from the hectic hum of central Sarlat. Some of its 14 sunny rooms open to the flower-filled courtyard and pool; one has self-catering facilities.

⭐ **Villa des Consuls** B&B €€
(☑05 53 31 90 05; www.villaconsuls.fr; 3 rue Jean-Jacques Rousseau; d €95-110, apt €150-190; @🛜) Despite its Renaissance exterior, the enormous rooms here are modern through and through, with shiny wood floors and sleek furnishings. Several delightful self-contained apartments dot the town, all offering the same mix of period plushness – some also have terraces overlooking the town's rooftops.

Plaza Madeleine HOTEL €€
(☑05 53 59 10 41; www.hoteldelamadeleine-sarlat.com; 1 place de la Petite Rigaudie; d €125-188; ❄🛜🛁) This elegant hotel offers an attractive mix of modern and traditional touches. Classy rooms subtly evoke a bygone era, with vintage-style phones and shuttered windows, while a solarium and Finnish sauna create a modern boutique feel.

La Maison des Peyrat HOTEL €€
(☑05 53 59 00 32; www.maisondespeyrat.com; Le Lac de la Plane; r €80-109) This beautifully renovated 17th-century house, formerly a nuns' hospital and later an aristocratic hunting lodge, is set on a hill about 1.5km from Sarlat centre. Eleven generously sized rooms are decorated in modern farmhouse style; the best have views over gardens and the countryside beyond. Good restaurant too.

Clos La Boëtie BOUTIQUE HOTEL €€€
(☑05 53 29 44 18; www.closlaboetie-sarlat.com; 95-97 av de la Selves; d €210-280; ❄@🛜🛁) Supremely luxurious rooms in a 19th-century mansion, with a price tag to match. It's 400m north of the centre.

✖ Eating & Drinking

Sarlat's old-town restaurants are very hit-and-miss: many are more concerned with packing in the punters than in keeping standards high.

⭐ **Le Quatre Saisons** REGIONAL CUISINE €€
(☑05 53 29 48 59; www.4saisons-sarlat-perigord.com; 2 côte de Toulouse; menus from €19; ⊙12.30-2pm & 7.30-9.30pm Thu-Mon; 🛠👶) A reliable local favourite, hidden in a beautiful stone house on a narrow alley leading uphill from rue de la République. The food is honest and unfussy, taking its cue from market ingredients and regional flavours. The most romantic tables have cross-town views.

Jardins de Harmonie TRADITIONAL FRENCH €€
(☑05 53 31 06 69; www.lesjardinsdharmonie.com; place André Malraux; 4-course menus €22-48; ⊙noon-2pm & 7-9.30pm Thu-Mon) This elegant restaurant is tucked into a central stone town house with plate-glass windows overlooking a cobbled square. The seasonally changing menu is classic French with occasional fusion touches.

Le Bistrot REGIONAL CUISINE €€
(☑05 53 28 28 40; www.le-bistrot-sarlat.com; 14 place du Peyrou; menus €18-30; ⊙noon-2pm & 6.30-10pm Tue-Sun, open daily Jul & Aug) This little bistro is the best of the bunch on cafe-clad place du Peyrou. The menu's heavy on Sarlat

classics, especially walnuts, duck breast and finger-lickin' *pommes sarlardaises* (potatoes cooked in duck fat).

★**Le Grand Bleu** GASTRONOMIC €€€
(⌨ 05 53 31 08 48; www.legrandbleu.eu; 43 av de la Gare; menus €54-125; ⊙ 12.30-2pm Thu-Sun, 7.30-9.30pm Tue-Sat) This eminent Michelin-starred restaurant run by chef Maxime Lebrun is renowned for its creative cuisine with elaborate *menus* making maximum use of luxury produce: truffles, lobster, turbot and scallops, with a wine list to match. Cooking courses (€40) are also available. Located 1.5km south of the centre.

La Lune Poivre BAR
(5 rue Jean-Jacques Rousseau; ⊙ 6pm-2am Tue-Sat) Sidle up to the copper bar at this local hangout with great cocktails.

🛍 Shopping

In addition to its grand markets, practically every shop in Sarlat is loaded with local goods, from *confit de canard* (duck confit) to walnut cake.

Distillerie du Périgord LIQUEUR
(www.distillerie-perigord.com; place de la Liberté; ⊙ 9am-6pm) Local liqueurs and flavourings.

ℹ Information

Tourist Office (⌨ 05 53 31 45 45; www.sarlat-tourisme.com; 3 rue Tourny; ⊙ 9am-7pm Mon-Sat, 10am-1pm & 2-6pm Sun May-Aug, shorter hours Sep-Apr; 📶) Sarlat's tourist office is packed with info, but often gets overwhelmed by visitors; the website has it all.

ℹ Getting There & Away

CAR
Cars are banned in the medieval centre from June to September, and rue de la République, the main street that bisects the centre, is pedestrianised in July and August. Find two large, free **car parks** on av Général de Gaulle, northwest of the old town. Europcar is near the train station.

TRAIN
The **train station** (av de la Gare) is 1.3km south of the old city. Many destinations require a change at Le Buisson or Libourne.
Bergerac €12.90, 1½ hours, five daily.
Bordeaux €27.50, 2¾ hours, six daily.
Les Eyzies €9.80, one to two hours depending on connections, four daily.
Périgueux €15.90, 1½ to 2½ hours depending on connection, four daily.

The Vézère Valley

North of the Dordogne, the placid River Vézère winds through lush green meadows and softly blowing willow trees creating a gorgeous tiny valley flanked by limestone cliffs that conceal dozens of subterranean caverns. This tiny Vézère Valley is world famous for its wonderfully preserved prehistoric sites, and especially for its incredible collection of cave paintings – the highest concentration of Stone Age art found in Europe. The paintings and etchings were mostly created by Cro-Magnon people between around 15,000 BC and 10,000 BC, and range in style and artistry from simple scratched lines to complex multicoloured frescoes.

Most of the key sites are around the towns of Les Eyzies-de-Tayac-Sireuil and Montignac, which are both set up for visitors, though Montignac is by far the more charming. Neither has particularly good restaurants. Visits can also be done as day trips from elsewhere in the Dordogne.

ℹ Getting Around

Public transport is limited, with few trains and even fewer buses. There's no transport to the caves themselves. Cycling is an option, and hire bikes are available (ask at tourist offices), but having your own car makes things infinitely easier (especially with the precisely timed cave ticketing system). The closest car rentals are in Sarlat, Bergerac and Brive-la-Gaillarde.

Les Eyzies-de-Tayac-Sireuil & Around
POP 842

At the heart of the Vézère Valley, Les Eyzies (as it's known locally) makes an uninspiring introduction to the wonders of the Vézère, with postcard sellers and souvenir shops lining the small main street. Still, the town has an excellent museum of prehistory, and many major sites are within a short drive, if you must stay there.

◉ Sights

LES EYZIES TOWN

★**Musée National
de Préhistoire** PREHISTORY MUSEUM
(⌨ 05 53 06 45 45; www.musee-prehistoire-eyzies.fr; 1 rue du Musée; adult/child €6/4.50, 1st Sun of month free; ⊙ 9.30am-6.30pm daily Jul & Aug, 9.30am-6pm Wed-Mon Jun & Sep, 9.30am-12.30pm & 2-5.30pm

Wed-Mon Oct-May) Inside a marvellous modern building alongside the cliffs, this museum provides a fine prehistory primer (providing your French is good) with the most comprehensive collection of prehistoric finds in France. Highlights include a huge gallery of Stone Age tools, weapons and jewellery, and skeletons of some of the animals that once roamed the Vézère (including bison, woolly rhinoceros, giant deer and cave bears). A collection of carved reliefs on the 1st floor includes a famous frieze of horses and a bison licking its flank.

Abri Pataud   PREHISTORIC SITE
(☑05 53 06 92 46; www.mnhn.fr; 20 rue du Moyen Âge; adult/child €5/free; ☺10am-noon & 2-6pm Sun-Thu, daily Jul & Aug, Mon-Fri Apr–mid-Oct, closed mid-Oct–Mar) About 250m north of the Musée National de Préhistoire this Cro-Magnon *abri* (shelter) was inhabited over a period of 15,000 years starting some 37,000 years ago and now displays bones and other excavated artefacts. The ibex carved into the ceiling dates from about 19,000 BC. Admission includes one-hour guided tour (some in English).

EAST OF LES EYZIES

★Grotte de Font de Gaume
PREHISTORIC SITE
(☑05 53 06 86 00; http://eyzies.monuments-nationaux.fr; adult/child €7.50/free; ☺guided tours 9.30am-5.30pm Sun-Fri mid-May–mid-Sep, 9.30am-12.30pm & 2-5.30pm Sun-Fri mid-Sep–mid-May) This extraordinary cave contains the only original polychrome (as opposed to single colour) paintings still open to the public. About 14,000 years ago, prehistoric artists created the gallery of more than 230 figures, including bison, reindeer, horses, mammoths, bears and wolves, although only about 25 are included in the fantastically atmospheric tour. Look out for the famous **Chapelle des Bisons**, a scene of courting reindeer and stunningly realised horses, several caught in mid-movement. Try to reserve ahead by phone as far in advance as you can.

Font de Gaume is such a rare and valuable site that there is always talk of the cave being closed for its own protection. Visitor numbers are currently limited to 80 per day, and after the few tickets available for

---

ⓘ TOP TIPS FOR CAVE VISITS

Summer crowds make it difficult to get tickets and to absorb the otherworldly atmosphere of the caves; most of the valley's sites are closed in winter, making spring and autumn the best times to visit. Getting tickets is always a bit of a competition, especially for the best sites. Most have timed entry due to guided tours, but each have their own rules for ticket acquisition (check websites), and often sell out in high season (especially those with visitor limitations, such as Font de Gaume).

Visiting the Caves
➡ Call ahead and find out English tour times, and whenever possible book ahead to avoid waiting in early morning lines, or not getting tickets at all.

➡ Ticket sales stop 45 minutes to one hour before caves close.

➡ Follow all rules so as not to damage these sensitive sites.

➡ Bring something warm as the caves can be cold.

Font de Gaume, Combarelles & Abri du Cap Blanc
➡ Font de Gaume allows a very limited number of advance reservations, then the rest of the 80 allowed tickets are *sold only on the day*. A screen in the box office window displays real-time availability by entry time.

➡ Font de Gaume box office also sells Combarelles and Abri Cap Blanc tickets (Cap Blanc also sold at cave).

➡ People line up *early*.

Lascaux II
➡ From mid-April to mid-October, tickets (either same-day or for the future) are sold only in Montignac at a ticket office next to the tourist office; the rest of the year you can get them at the cave entrance.

➡ If you want to see Lascaux II in summer, send one of your party to get tickets a few days before.

Vézère Valley Cave Art

Deep in the Vézère Valley, prehistoric Cro-Magnon artists worked by the light of primitive oil torches, creating some of Europe's first art. Today in the caves you can see what they created: from simple scratched lines and hand-tracings to complex multicoloured frescoes of leaping horses, mammoths, ibex, aurochs, reindeer and bulls.

Who were the artists?

Most of the Vézère Valley's cave paintings date from the end of the last ice age, between 20,000 BC and 10,000 BC, and were painted by Cro-Magnon people. Until around 20,000 BC much of northern Europe was still covered by vast glaciers and ice sheets, so the Cro-Magnon lived a hunter-gatherer lifestyle, using natural caves as temporary shelters while they followed the migration routes of prey.

The paintings seem to have come to an abrupt halt around 10,000 BC, around the same time the last ice sheets disappeared and humans hereabouts established a more fixed agricultural lifestyle.

1. Painting detail, Grotte de Lascaux p586 2. Cave interior, Grotte de Lascaux p586 3. Many animals are painted at Lascaux p586

What did they create?

Using flint tools for engraving, natural fibre brushes, pads or sponges for painting, and pigments derived from minerals like magnesium and charcoal (black), ochre (red/yellow) and iron (red), Cro-Magnon artists usually depicted animals, though there are occasionally mysterious geometric shapes and symbols.

The earliest known cave art in the area is from the Gravettian period, from before 22,000 BC, consisting of abstract engravings, paintings of female genitalia, or 'Venus' figures. It then developed into complex animal figures and friezes such as those at Lascaux, Rouffignac and Font de Gaume, which date from around 17,000 BC to 10,000 BC. These early artists also created jewellery from shells, bones, antlers and scrimshaw, decorated with animal scenes and geometric patterns.

Theories abound as to why Cro-Magnons made this often elaborate art (ritual significance?), but in reality, no one knows.

advance reservation are gone, you must line up very, very early on the day to get one. The small 45-minute guided tours are occasionally in English. Find the ticket office and cave 1km northeast of Les Eyzies on the D4.

★ Grotte des Combarelles   PREHISTORIC SITE
(☑05 53 06 86 00; http://eyzies.monuments-nationaux.fr; adult/child €7.50/free; ☺guided tours 9.30am-5.30pm Sun-Fri mid-May–mid-Sep, 9.30am-12.30pm & 2-5.30pm Sun-Fri mid-Sep–mid-May) This narrow cave 1.5km east of Font de Gaume was the first rediscovered in 1901, and is renowned for its animal engravings, many of which cleverly use the natural contours of the rock to sculpt the animals' forms. Look out for mammoths, horses and reindeer, as well as a fantastic mountain lion that seems to leap from the rock face. Go early on the day to buy tickets at the Font de Gaume ticket office for 45-minute eight-person tours.

Abri du Cap Blanc   PREHISTORIC SITE
(☑05 53 06 86 00; adult/child €7.50/free; ☺guided tours 9.30am-5.30pm Sun-Fri mid-May–mid-Sep, 9.30am-12.30pm & 2-5.30pm Sun-Fri mid-Sep–mid-May) While most of the Vézère's caves contain engravings and paintings, unusually, this rock shelter contains only carved sculptures, shaped using simple flint tools some 14,000 years ago. The 40m frieze of horses and bison is impressive, but the modern museum detracts from the mood a bit. It's 7km east of Les Eyzies. Tickets available on-site or at Font de Gaume ticket office.

WEST OF LES EYZIES

Grotte du Sorcier   PREHISTORIC SITE
(☑05 53 07 14 37; www.grottedusorcier.com; St-Cirq; adult/child €6.80/3.20; ☺10am-7.30pm Jul & Aug, 10am-6pm Apr-Jun & Sep–mid-Nov) About 8km west of Les Eyzies, near the hamlet of St-Cirq, this privately owned cave features several animal engravings dating from around 15,000 BC to 17,000 BC, but it's best known for a male human figure known as the *Sorcier* (Sorceror), who's endowed with a phallus of truly enormous proportions, possibly indicating his shamanic status...

NORTHWEST OF LES EYZIES

★ Grotte de Rouffignac   PREHISTORIC SITE
(☑05 53 05 41 71; www.grotteroufignac.fr; Rouffignac-St-Cernin-de-Reilhac; adult/child €7/4.60; ☺9-11.30am & 2-6pm Jul & Aug, 10-11.30am & 2-5pm mid-Apr–Jun & Sep-Oct, closed Nov–mid-Apr) Hidden in pretty woodland 15km north of Les Eyzies, this enormous tri-level cave is one of the most complex and rewarding to see in the Dordogne. Board an **electric train** to explore a 1km maze of tunnels in the massive cavern plunging 8km into the earth. Highlights include the frieze of 10 mammoths in procession, one of the largest cave paintings ever discovered, and the awe-inspiring Great Ceiling, with more than 65 figures from ibex to aurochs. You'll also see nests of long-extinct cave bears, and 17th-century graffiti.

Tickets are sold at the cave but can't be reserved and do sell out, so arrive by 9am in July and August to get tickets for any time that day. March to June and September to October afternoon tickets are only available after 2pm.

Grotte du Grand Roc   CAVE
(☑05 53 06 92 70; www.semitour.com; adult/child €7.40/4.90; ☺10am-7pm Jul & Aug, 10am-1pm & 2-6pm Apr-Jun & Sep-Oct, shorter hours rest of year) Around 3km northwest of Les Eyzies along the D47, this cave contains an array of glittering stalactites and stalagmites. A joint ticket (adult/child €9.50/6) includes adjacent **Abri de Laugerie Basse**, a rock shelter originally occupied by Cro-Magnon people and still used until recent times.

🏃 Activities

Prehistoric Art & Cave Tour   CAVE TOUR
(☑05 53 07 26 04; www.caveconnection.fr; per day for one person €270, per additional person €20, maximum €370) Expert prehistoric anthropologist Christine Desdemaines-Hugon tailors cave tours for everyone from the Smithsonian to private individuals. She writes about Dordogne cave art in *Stepping-Stones: A Journey through the Ice Age Caves of the Dordogne*. Cave tickets not included, but she helps to acquire the often-hard-to-get tickets.

Canoës Vallée Vézère   BOAT HIRE
(☑05 53 05 10 11; www.canoesvalleevezere.com; 1-3 promenade de la Vézère, Les Eyzies; self-guided trips €16-25; ☺Apr-Sep) Organises 10km to 26km self-guided canoe and kayak trips including minibus transport. Multi-day trips stop at campgrounds or hotels.

Animation Vézère Canoë Kayak   BOAT HIRE
(☑05 53 06 92 92; www.vezere-canoe.com; Les Eyzies; adult/child from €9/4.50; ☺Apr-Oct) Canoe and kayak rentals with minibus transport, at Les Eyzies bridge.

🛏 Sleeping & Eating

Les Eyzies' many hotels and campsites get heavily overbooked; reserve well ahead.

Camping La Rivière   CAMPGROUND €
(☑05 53 06 97 14; www.lariviereleseyzies.com;
campsites per adult/child €7/5.40; ⊙closed mid-
Oct–mid-Apr; @☎⊠) The nearest campground to Les Eyzies, just west of town
beside the river. Facilities include a restaurant, bar, laundry and grocery.

Hôtel des Glycines   HOTEL €€
(☑05 53 06 97 07; www.les-glycines-dordogne.
com; 4 av de Laugerie; d €99-175, ste €250-285;
⊙closed mid-Nov–Dec; ❊☎⊠) Les Eyzies' top
posh pad: plush rooms range from cream-
and-check 'classics' to full-blown suites with
terraces and garden views. Beware 'courtyard rooms' which overlook the main road.
The hotel's gastronomic restaurant (lunch
menus €17, dinner menus €60 to €87) is a
pampering affair, though rumour has it kids
aren't welcome.

Hôtel Le Cro-Magnon   HOTEL €€
(☑05 53 06 97 06; www.hostellerie-cro-magnon.
com; 54 av de la Préhistoire; d €89-98; ⊙closed
Dec-Feb; ☎⊠) This pretty wisteria-clad hotel
has been around since the 1850s and was
often used as a base by pioneering prehisto-
rians. Flowery rooms are a touch bland, but
corridors built straight into the rock face add
quirky appeal. Dining is good value in the
lovely beam-ceilinged restaurant.

Hôtel des Roches   HOTEL €€
(☑05 53 06 96 59; www.roches-les-eyzies.com; 15
av de la Forge; d €90-120, f €150-170; ⊙closed mid-
Oct–mid-Apr; ☎⊠) This smart pale stone hotel
set back from the main road is decorated in
simple pastoral style. Rear rooms overlook the
garden and swimming pool.

ⓘ Information

Tourist Office (☑05 53 06 97 05; www.
lascaux-dordogne.com; 19 av de la Préhistoire,
Les Eyzies; ⊙9am-6.30pm Jul & Aug, 9.30am-
12.30pm & 2-6pm Mon-Sat, 9.30am-12.30pm
Sun May, Jun & Sep, shorter hours rest of year)
Small office with maps and local walk
information.

ⓘ Getting There & Away

Les Eyzies is 21km west of Sarlat, on the D47.
   The train station is 700m north of town, with
connections to Sarlat (change at Le Buisson or
Libourne; €9.80, one to two hours depending on
connections, four daily).

Les Eyzies to Montignac

The following sights are along the main road
(D706) linking Les Eyzies with Montignac.

◉ Sights

**Le Village Troglodytique
de la Madeleine**   VILLAGE
(☑05 53 46 36 88; www.la-madeleine-perigord.
com; adult/child €6/3.50; ⊙10am-8pm Jul & Aug,
to 6pm Sep-Jun) Many of the Vézère's caves
were used for storage, defence or protection
as recently as the Middle Ages. This cave village 8km northeast of Les Eyzies was carved
from the cliff face above the Vézère River,
and its lower level was occupied by prehistoric people 10,000 to 14,000 years ago, but
its upper level was used as a fortified village
by medieval settlers.
   Though it's largely ruined, you can still
visit the Ste-Madeleine chapel. Most of the
archaeological artefacts are at the Musée National de Préhistoire in Les Eyzies.

La Roque St-Christophe   VILLAGE
(☑05 53 50 70 45; www.roque-st-christophe.com;
Peyzac-le-Moustier; adult/child €8/4.50; ⊙10am-
8pm Jul & Aug, to 6.30pm Sep-Jun) On a sheer cliff
face 80m above the Vézère, this 900m-long
series of terraces and caves has been a practically unassailable natural fortress for almost
50 millennia – initially used by Mousterian
(Neanderthal) people 50,000 years ago, followed by successive generations until the 16th
century. Sweeping views are stunning, though
the caverns are largely empty and some of the
plastic reconstructions are decidedly lame.
Located 10km northeast of Les Eyzies.

Le Thot   THEME PARK
(☑05 53 50 70 44; www.semitour.com; adult/
child €7/4.80, joint ticket with Lascaux €13.50/9.40;
⊙10am-7pm Jul & Aug, to 6pm Apr-Jun & Sep-early Nov, shorter hours rest of year) In an effort to
bring the prehistoric age to life, Le Thot, 8km
southwest of Montignac, places reproduced
Lascaux cave scenes alongside displays about
Cro-Magnon life and art, as well as real-life
descendants of the animals the art depicts
(reindeer, stags, ibex and European bison)
which roam the grounds.

Château de Losse   CHÂTEAU
(☑05 53 50 80 08; www.chateaudelosse.com;
Thonac; adult/child €9/4.50; ⊙noon-6pm May-Sep)
Ornate gardens and 15th-century moat and
battlements surround this grandly furnished
16th-century château, 6km from Montignac.

Montignac & Lascaux

POP 2892

The charming auburn-stone riverside town of Montignac has become famous for the nearby Grottes de Lascaux, hidden in wooded hills just outside town. Montignac itself, with its crumbling medieval fortress and arching bridges, drapes beautifully along both banks of the Vézère, and is a more peaceful base than Les Eyzies for exploring the valley.

The tiny lanes of the old city sit on the river's west bank; many hotels are on the east bank, near the Lascaux ticket office and place Tourny.

◉ Sights

★ **Grotte de
Lascaux & Lascaux II**   PREHISTORIC SITE
(☑ 05 53 51 95 03; www.semitour.com; Montignac; adult/child €9.90/6.40, joint ticket with Le Thot €13.50/9.40; ☺ guided tours 9am-7pm Jul & Aug, 9.30am-6pm Apr-Jun, 9.30am-noon & 2-6pm Sep & Oct, shorter hours rest of year, closed Jan) France's most famous prehistoric cave paintings are at the Grotte de Lascaux, 2km southeast of Montignac. Completely sealed and protected for ages, it was discovered in 1940 by four teenage boys out searching for their lost dog. It contains a vast network of chambers adorned with the most complex prehistoric paintings ever found. The original cave was opened to visitors in 1948, but within a few years it became apparent that human breath, temperature changes and introduced elements were causing irreparable damage, and the cave was closed in 1963. A cm-by-cm replica of the most famous sections of the original cave was created a few hundred metres away – a massive undertaking that required the skills of some 20 artists and more than years.

From mid-April to mid-October, tickets (either same-day or for the future) are sold *only* in Montignac at a ticket office next to the tourist office; the rest of the year you can get them at the cave entrance.

Lascaux has often been referred to as the prehistoric equivalent of the Sistine Chapel, and it's a fitting comparison. Renowned for their artistry, the 600-strong menagerie of animal figures are depicted in technicolor shades of red, black, yellow and brown, ranging from reindeer, aurochs, mammoths and horses to a monumental 5.5m-long bull, the largest single cave drawing ever found. After

a visit in 1940, Picasso allegedly muttered, 'We have invented nothing'.

Carbon dating has shown that the paintings are between 15,000 and 17,000 years old, but it's still a mystery why the prehistoric painters devoted so much time and effort to their creation, and why this particular site seems to have been so important.

Although the idea may sound contrived, the reproductions are beautifully done using the original techniques, and they are certainly better than nothing. But, inevitably, they can't match the thrill of seeing original paintings.

Frequent, large 50-minute guided tours include several in English and Spanish.

🛏 Sleeping & Eating

Hôtel de la Grotte   HOTEL €
(☑ 05 53 51 80 48; www.hotel-dela-grotte-dordogne. com; place Tourny; d €65-75; ☎) This creaky old place has seen better days, but rooms are reasonably priced and comfortable. The restaurant (*menus* €19 to €30) overlooks a ramshackle back garden.

Hotel Le Lascaux   HOTEL €
(☑ 05 53 51 82 81; http://hotel-lascaux.jimdo.com; 109 av Jean-Jaurès; d €71-95; ☎) Despite the old-timey candy-stripe awnings, rooms at this family-owned hotel are bang up to date, with cool colour schemes, distressed wood furniture and sparkling bathrooms. Superior rooms have more space.

Hostellerie La Roseraie   HOTEL €€
(☑ 05 53 50 53 92; www.laroseraie-hotel.com; 11 place des Armes; d €90-172; ☺ Apr-Oct; ☎▨) This mansion in Montignac boasts its own gorgeous rose garden, set around a palm-fringed pool. Rococo rooms are lovely if you like rosy pinks, floral patterns and garden views. Truffles, chestnuts, pork and guinea fowl find their way onto the seasonal menu in the restaurant, and on summer nights the terrace is a delight.

Le Tourny   CAFE €
(☑ 05 53 51 59 95; place Tourny, Montignac; lunch/ dinner menus €12.50/17; ☺ noon-2pm daily, 7-9.30pm Mon-Sat) Locals flock here for cheap daily specials and omelettes or snacks.

ℹ Information

Tourist Office (☑ 05 53 51 82 60; www.lascaux-dordogne.com; place Bertran de Born; ☺ 9am-6.30pm Jul & Aug, 9.30am-12.30pm & 2-6pm Mon-Sat, 9.30am-12.30pm Sun May, Jun & Sep, shorter hours rest of year; ☎) Around 200m west of place Tourny, next to 14th-century Église St-Georges le Prieuré.

ⓘ Getting There & Away

Montignac is 25km northeast of Les Eyzies on the D706. Buses are inconveniently geared around school times, so you'll need your own car.

LIMOUSIN

With its rolling pastures and little-visited villages, Limousin might be the most overlooked area of southwestern France. It's not as exciting as the Dordogne to the south or the Loire to the north, but it offers a chance to get off the beaten path, and aficionados will like Limoges for its porcelain and Aubusson for its tapestries. Technically the Limousin *région* is made up of three *départements:* Haute-Vienne, in the west, the capital of which is lively Limoges; the rural Creuse, in the northeast; and, in the southeast, perhaps the most interesting area, the Corrèze, home to Brive-la-Gaillarde and the region's most beautiful villages.

Limoges

POP 140,103

Porcelain connoisseurs will already be familiar with the legendary name of Limoges. For over 200 years, the city has thrived as the top producer of excellent hard-paste porcelain (china) in France. Several factories continue to make 'limoges' and stunning examples fill city museums and galleries.

Limoges is on the site of the 10 BC Roman city Augustoritum which took advantage of this strategic position on the River Vienne. The modern-day centre is compact and easy to explore: historic buildings and museums cluster in the medieval **Cité quarter**, alongside the river, and the partly pedestrianised **Château quarter**, just to the west.

If you come by train you'll be arriving in style: the city's grand art deco **Gare des Bénédictins**, completed in 1929, is one of France's most resplendent railway stations, graced by a copper dome, carved frescos and a copper-topped clock tower.

◉ Sights

◉ Château Quarter

This bustling corner of Limoges is the heart of the old city, and is the modern-day shopping centre. It gets its name from the fortified walls that once enclosed the ducal castle and medieval St-Martial abbey, both long gone.

★**Rue de la Boucherie**   HISTORIC STREET
Pedestrianised rue de la Boucherie was named for the butchers' shops that lined the street in the Middle Ages. Today it has many attractive medieval half-timbered houses, and the **Maison de la Boucherie** (36 rue de la Boucherie; ◷10am-1pm & 2-7pm Jul-Sep) FREE operates a small history museum. Tiny 1475 **Chapelle St-Aurélien** (place St-Aurélien; ◷7am-7pm), dedicated to the patron saint of butchers, is maintained by the butchers' guild.

★**Église St-Michel des Lions**   CHURCH
(rue Adrien Dubouché) Named for the two granite lions flanking its door, Église St-Michel des Lions was built between the 14th and 16th centuries. It contains the relics (including his skull) of St Martial, Limoges' first bishop, who converted the city to Christianity. Look for the huge copper ball perched atop its 65m-high spire.

Cour du Temple   SQUARE
Tucked away between rue du Temple and rue du Consulat, this tiny enclosed courtyard is surrounded by 16th-century *hôtels particuliers* (private mansions). Look out for coats of arms and the 16th-century stone staircase around the edge of the courtyard.

Église St-Pierre du Queyroix   CHURCH
(place St-Pierre) The moody Église St-Pierre du Queyroix is notable for its characteristic Limousin belfry and stained glass.

ⓘ LIMOUSIN RESOURCES

Region-wide tourism sites offer loads of accommodation, map, transport and activities (hiking, biking, boating) information.

Limousin Tourism Board (☑05 55 11 06 09; www.tourismelimousin.com; 30 cours Gay-Lussac, Limoges)

Tourisme en Haute-Vienne (☑05 55 79 04 04; www.tourisme-hautevienne.com; 17bis bl Georges Périn, Limoges)

Creuse Tourism (www.tourisme-creuse.com)

Corrèze Tourist Board (www.vacances-en-correze.net) Smartphone site: www.tourismecorreze.mobi.

Limoges

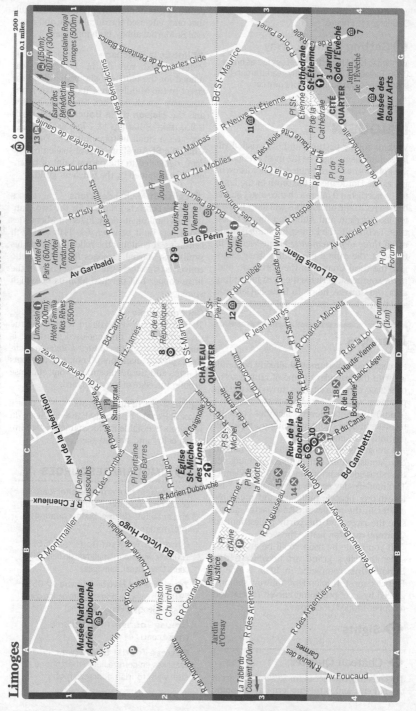

DORDOGNE, LIMOUSIN & THE LOT

200 m
0.1 miles

Map labels

(150m);
RDTHV (300m)

Porcelaine Royal
Limoges (500m)

Gare des
Bénédictins
(250m)

R de Pénitents Blancs

R Charles Gide

Av des Bénédictins

Bd St-Maurice

Porte Panet

R Régie

R Neuve St-Étienne

Pl St-
Étienne Cathédrale **St-Étienne**

1 ⚑

3 Jardinc
⊙ de l'Évêché

CITÉ
QUARTER

Cathédrale
Pl de la
Cathédrale

Jardin
de l'Évêché

7

4

**Musée des
Beaux Arts**

13

Av du Général de Gaulle

Cours Jourdan

R du Maupas

R des Allois

Bd de la Cité

Pl de
la Cité

R de la Cité

R de la Cité

11

R d'Isly

R des Feuillants

Hôtel de
Paris (60m);
ArtHôtel
Tendance
(600m)

Pl
Jourdan

R du 71e Mobiles

Bd des Fleurus

R des Tanneries

R Raspail

R du Forum

Tourisme
Ben Haute-
Vienne

Bd G Périn

Tourist
Office

Bd Louis Blanc

Av Gabriel Péri

Pl du
Forum

9 ⊕

Av Garibaldi

Limousin
(400m);
Hôtel Familia
Nos Rêves
(550m)

Bd Carnot

R Fitz-James

Pl de la
République

R St-Martial

8 ◉

R du Collège

Pl St-
Pierre

12

R Jean Jaurès

R J Guesde Pl Wilson

R J Sarre

R Charles Michels

R de la Loi

La Fourmi
(1km)

**CHÂTEAU
QUARTER**

R du Consulat

R Gaignolle

R du Clocher

16

R du Temple

R Haute-Vienne

18

R Banc-Léger

Av de la Libération

R Daniel Lamazière

Pl
Stalingrad

R du Général Cerez

R des Combes

R Denis Dussoubs

Pl Denis
Dussoubs

R Turgot

Pl Fontaine
des Barres

**Église
St-Michel
des Lions**

2 ⚑

R Adrien Dubouché

Pl St-
Michel

Pl de
la Motte

15

14

R Gondinet

R Darnet

R D'Aguesseau

Rue de la
Boucherie

Pl des
Bancs

R É Berthet

R de la Boucherie

R de la
6 20 10
17 19

Bd Gambetta

R F Chénieux

R Montmailler

R Brousseau

Av St-Surin

**Musée National
Adrien Dubouché**

5

Bd Victor Hugo

R du Louvier de Lajois

Pl
d'Aine

Palais de
Justice

R des Arènes

R R Couraud

Pl Winston
Churchill

Jardin
d'Orsay

La Table du
Couvent (100m)

Av Foucaud

R des
Carmes

R Neuve des
Carmes

R des Argentiers

R Pétiniaud Beaupeyrat

Limoges

Crypt of St Martial   TOMB
All that remains of the once-great pilgrimage point **St-Martial abbey**, founded in AD 848, is a faint outline on place de la République, and an underground tomb dedicated to the city's patron saint. Entry is by tourist office tours in July and August.

◉ West of the Château Quarter

★**Musée National Adrien Dubouché**   MUSEUM
(☑05 55 33 08 50; www.musee-adriendubouche.fr; 8bis place Winston Churchill; adult/child €4.50/free; ⊙10am-12.30pm & 2-5.45pm Wed-Mon) This museum, founded in 1845, has one of France's two outstanding ceramics collections (the other is in Sèvres, southwest of Paris), so it's a must for ceramics lovers. Displays illustrate the evolution from earthenware to Limoges hard-paste porcelain, and include 12,000 pieces from Limoges makers as well as Meissen, Royal Doulton, Royal Worcester and others.

◉ Cité Quarter

To the east of the Château quarter, on the bank of the Vienne, la Cité radiates out from the massive cathedral.

★**Musée des Beaux Arts**   ART MUSEUM
(☑05 55 45 98 10; www.museebal.fr; 1 place de la Cathédrale; ⊙10am-6pm Wed-Mon Apr-Sep, to noon Mon & Wed-Sat, 2-5pm Wed-Mon Oct-Mar) **FREE**
The city's wonderful art museum is inside the beautifully restored 18th-century bishops' palace. Come either to explore the exquisite building or the excellent collections of Limoges porcelain and enamel, fine paintings from 14th-century Italian masterpieces to Renoir, and displays on the city's history.

★**Cathédrale St-Étienne**   CHURCH
(place St-Étienne; ⊙9am-6pm Mon-Sat, 2-6pm Sun Apr-Oct, to 5pm Nov-Mar) Built between 1273 and 1888, Limoges' Gothic cathedral is worth a visit for the Flamboyant style Portail St-Jean, as well as a glorious rose window, a Renaissance choir screen (beneath the organ loft), and three ornate tombs in the chancel. The bell tower's lower three stories are part of the few remaining Romanesque portions of the cathedral; its top four stories are Gothic.

★**Jardin de l'Évêché**   GARDEN
Alongside Cathédrale St-Étienne, Limoges' beautiful botanical garden terraces down to the river, with super views. Medicinal and toxic herbs have been grown here since medieval times.

Musée de la Résistance   WAR MUSEUM
(☑05 55 45 84 44; http://resistance-massif-central.fr; 7 rue Neuve-Ste-Étienne; ⊙10am-6pm mid-Jun–mid-Sep, 9.30am-5pm Oct-May, closed Tue & Sun) **FREE** The Limousin was a stronghold of the Resistance during WWII, and this museum explores the story of their struggle against German occupation through archive film, photography and wartime memorabilia, including photos, letters, diaries and military hardware.

Cité des Métiers et des Arts   MUSEUM
(☑05 55 32 57 84; www.cma-limoges.com; 5 rue de la Règle; adult/child €4/1.50; ⊙3-7.30pm daily mid-Jun–mid-Sep, shorter hours rest of year) Showcases work by top members of France's craft guilds.

⌂ Sleeping

Most Limoges hotels are near the train station. Rates often drop at weekends.

Hôtel Familia Nos Rêves HOTEL €

(☑05 55 77 41 43; www.hotelfamilia.fr; 16 rue du Général du Bessol; s €58, d €67, q €99; ☎) This small family-run hotel is the pick of the budget places near the station. Forget frills – easy-clean fabrics and pastel colours are the order of the day – but it's good value, especially if you get a room over the flowery back garden. A couple of streets west of the train station.

Arthôtel Tendance HOTEL €

(☑05 55 77 31 72; www.arthoteltendance.com; 37 rue Armand Barbès; s €65-85, d €72-90; ☎) Globe-trotting decor defines this quirky little hotel, with themes including a maple-clad Canadian cabin, an Indonesian room, and a Grecian room in whites and sea blues. Around 500m northwest of the train station.

Hôtel Jeanne d'Arc HOTEL €

(☑05 55 77 67 77; www.hoteljeannedarc-limoges.fr; 17 av du Général de Gaulle; s/d €67/77; ☎) The pick of Limoges' plusher options this renovated *relais de poste* is favoured by business travellers. It offers spacious rooms equipped with modern furnishings and the odd antique. Parking €5.

Hôtel de Paris HOTEL €

(☑05 55 77 56 96; www.hoteldeparis-limoges.com; 5 cours Vergniaud; s €52, d €58-75; ☎) Basic but good-value rooms spread out over several floors of a tall town house. Floors are squeaky, doors are creaky and the spiral staircase will give you a good workout, but it's equally handy for town and station.

Eating

Le Bistrot d'Olivier REGIONAL CUISINE €

(Halles Centrales; menus €12-16; ⊙7am-2pm Mon-Sat) For an authentic lunch, you can't do much better than this chaotic little place inside the market, where folks sit at communal wooden tables and share hearty, no-fuss portions of French food chosen straight from the blackboard.

Chez Alphonse REGIONAL CUISINE €

(☑05 55 34 34 14; www.chezalphonse.fr; 5 place de la Motte; menus €13-20; ⊙noon-2pm & 7.30-10.30pm

---

LIMOGES CHINA

For more than 300 years the name of Limoges has been synonymous with *les arts du feu* (literally 'the fire arts'), especially the production of *émail* (enamel) and *porcelaine* (porcelain).

Limoges had been producing enamel since at least the 12th century, but its fortunes were transformed by the discovery of an extremely pure form of kaolin near St-Yrieix-La-Perche in 1768. This fine white clay, a vital ingredient in porcelain manufacture (along with quartz and feldspar), had previously been imported at huge expense from Asia (the recipe was originally from China, hence porcelain's alternate name). Its discovery on home soil, plus the ease of getting wood on barges on the Vienne to fire kilns, led to an explosion of porcelain production in Limoges in the late 18th and 19th centuries. Three factors distinguish porcelain from other clay-baked ceramics: it's white, extremely hard and translucent.

Buildings around Limoges are often decorated with porcelain and enamel tiles. Check out the Halles Centrales and the **Pavillon du Verdurier** (place St-Pierre), a beautiful octagonal building dating from 1900 that now hosts art exhibitions.

Many of the city's porcelain makers have factory shops, and city museums focus on the industry. The tourist office has complete lists.

Porcelaine Royal Limoges (☑05 55 33 27 30; www.royal-limoges.fr; 28 rue Donzelot; guided tour €6; ⊙shop 10am-6.30pm Mon-Sat) One of the oldest factories, dating from 1797, offers guided tours by reservation, and has the 19.5m-high **Four des Casseaux** (www.musee descasseaux.com; adult/child €4/2; ⊙10am-5.30pm Mon-Sat), the only surviving 18th-century brick kiln. It's 500m southeast of the train station.

Bernardaud (☑05 55 10 55 91; www.bernardaud.fr; 27 av Albert Thomas; tours adult/child €4.50/free; ⊙9.45am-11.15am & 1.30-4.30pm Mon-Sat Jun-Sep) Offers guided tours of porcelain production, from raw material to finished pieces. The factory is 1km northwest of Limoges' centre.

Haviland (☑05 55 30 21 86; www.haviland.fr; 3 av du Président Kennedy; ⊙10.30am-6.30pm daily Jul & Aug, 10am-1pm & 2-6.30pm Mon-Sat Sep-Jun) Screens a short film and has a small museum; 3km southeast of Limoges' centre.

Mon-Sat) Checked tablecloths, laughing locals and blackboards stuffed with regional dishes: what more could you want from a Limoges bistro?

La Parenthèse
CAFE €

(📞 05 55 33 18 25; www.restaurant-tearoom-parenthese-limoges.com; cour du Temple; menus €15-18; ⊙ 10am-2.30pm Mon, to 6.30pm Tue-Sat; 🖉) Lovely *salon de thé* (tea room) for tea, cake and a good choice of salads and regional dishes.

★ La Table du Couvent
FRENCH €€

(📞 05 55 32 30 66; www.latableducouvent.com; 15 rue Neuve des Carmes; mains €10-20, 3-course dinner menus €25; ⊙ noon-2pm Wed-Sun, 7-10pm Wed-Sat) This modish restaurant in a former Carmelite convent is one of the city's most popular eateries, with tables set among rough brick walls. Sit at the open kitchen counter to watch meals being prepared, including locally sourced steaks cooked over an open hearth. Cooking courses (€60) are available.

Le 27
MODERN FRENCH €€

(📞 05 55 32 27 27; www.le27.com; 27 rue Haute-Vienne; lunch/3-course menu €14/27; ⊙ noon-2pm & 7.45-10.30pm Mon-Sat) A contemporary bistro with quirky decor to match the inventive cuisine. Teardrop lanterns and a giant faux hare's head set the tone. One wall is taken up by wine; dishes are French classics with a contemporary spin.

L'Amphitryon
TRADITIONAL FRENCH €€

(📞 05 55 33 36 39; 26 rue de la Boucherie; menus lunch €23, dinner €27-43; ⊙ noon-1.15pm & 7.45-9.15pm Tue-Sat) One of Limoges' top tables for years, it's in a delightful medieval timbered building and serves classically rich French cuisine, created by renowned head chef Richard Lequet. The dining room is suitably smart too.

Les Petits Ventres
REGIONAL CUISINE €€

(📞 05 55 34 22 90; www.les-petits-ventres.com; 20 rue de la Boucherie; menus lunch €12.50-20, dinner €20-32; ⊙ noon-2pm & 7.30-9.30pm Tue-Sat; 🖶) At this cosy, family-friendly eatery tuck into Limousin's famous carnivorous cuts such as the eponymous beef or *andouillettes* (sausages). Other bits are grand as well, such as the generous, excellent cheese platter.

Self-Catering

Halles Centrales
FOOD MARKET €

(place de la Motte; ⊙ 6am-2pm Mon-Thu & Sat, 6am-6pm Fri, 8am-1pm Sun) Limoges' central market runs the gourmet gamut from local cheese to Limousin beef.

🍷 Drinking & Entertainment

The large student crowd keeps Limoges' nightspots ticking; you'll find most action around rue Charles Michels.

Le Duc Étienne
BAR

(place St-Aurélien; ⊙ 11am-2am Mon-Sat, 6pm-2am Sun) Hip little bar supplying beers and late-night coffee to a pre-club crowd. In summer things spill onto the terrace in front of Église St-Aurélien.

La Fourmi
LIVE MUSIC

(www.lafourmi87.net; 3 rue de la Font Pinot) The best place for live music, with breaking acts, alternative bands and theatrical spectacles in a twin-floored warehouse-style space. One kilometre south of the cathedral.

🛈 Information

Tourist Office (📞 05 55 34 46 87; www.limoges-tourisme.com; 12 bd de Fleurus; ⊙ 9.30am-6pm Mon-Sat, plus 10am-6pm Sun Jun-Aug; 🛜) Loads of info on what's on, transport and maps.

🛈 Getting There & Away

AIR

Limoges International Airport (LIG; 📞 05 55 43 30 30; www.aeroportlimoges.com) Just off the A20, 10km west of the city, Limoges Airport is a major UK gateway, served by budget carriers including Ryanair and Flybe, as well as Air France. Domestic destinations include Paris Orly, Lyon, Nice and Ajaccio (Corsica).

BUS

Limoges' **bus station** is across the tracks from the train station. **RDTHV** (Régie Départementale des Transports de la Haute-Vienne; 📞 05 55 10 31 00; www.rdthv.com; place des Charentes; ticket €2) buses are geared towards school timetables, so there's only one or two per day during the week. Information and timetables are also available from the tourist office or **Haute-Vienne en Car** (http://hautevienneencar.cg87.fr).

CAR

Major rental companies at the airport. Europcar, **ADA** (📞 05 55 79 61 12; www.ada.fr; 27 av du Général de Gaulle) and **National-Citer** (📞 05 55 77 10 10; 3 cours Bugeaud) also have offices near the train station.

TAXI

Limoges Taxis (📞 05 55 38 38 38; www.taxis87.com) Airport flat-rate fare day/night €24/34.

TRAIN

Limoges' beautiful Gare des Bénédictins is on the Paris–Toulouse and Bordeaux–Clermont Ferrand lines.

DORDOGNE, LIMOUSIN & THE LOT LIMOGES

LE VILLAGE MARTYR

On the afternoon of 10 June 1944, the little town of **Oradour-sur-Glane**, 21km northwest of Limoges, witnessed one of the worst Nazi war crimes committed on French soil. German lorries belonging to the SS 'Das Reich' Division surrounded the town and ordered the population onto the market square. The men were divided into groups and forced into barns, where they were machine-gunned before the structures were set alight. Several hundred women and children were herded into the church, which was set on fire, along with the rest of the town. Only one woman and five men who were in the town that day survived the massacre; 642 people, including 193 children, were killed. The same SS Division committed a similarly brutal act in Tulle two days earlier, in which 99 Resistance sympathisers were strung up from the town's balconies as a warning to others.

Since these events, the entire village has been left untouched, complete with prewar tram tracks and electricity lines, the blackened shells of buildings and the rusting hulks of 1930s automobiles – an evocative memorial to a village caught up in the brutal tide of war. At the centre of the village is an **underground memorial** inscribed with the victims' names and displaying their recovered belongings, including watches, wallets, hymnals from the burnt church and children's bikes. Victims were buried in the nearby **cemetery**.

Entry is via the modern **Centre de la Mémoire** (☑05 55 43 04 30; www.oradour.org; adult/child €7.80/5.20; ⊙9am-7pm May–mid-Sep, to 5pm or 6pm rest of year, closed mid-Dec–Jan), which does an excellent job contextualising the massacre using historical exhibitions, videos and survivors' testimonies. Various theories have been put forward to try to explain the event – perhaps a reaction to the Allied landings four days earlier, or reprisal for sabotage raids committed by the Resistance, or the Resistance's hostage-taking of an SS officer. Those who were ultimately accused of the crime were tried at a 1953 military tribunal in Bordeaux, with outcomes ranging from a death sentence to amnesty (much to the chagrin of Oradour survivors and relatives).

After the war, a new Oradour was rebuilt a few hundred metres west of the ruins. RDTHV (p591) bus 12 serves the Limoges bus station (45 minutes, three daily Monday to Saturday).

Bordeaux €35, three hours, three daily.

Paris' Gare d'Austerlitz €59, three hours, seven daily.

Périgueux €17.20, one hour, eight daily.

Toulouse €16, 3¼ hours, seven daily.

West of Limoges

Rochechouart

POP 3916

Meteorites and modern art might be an unlikely combination but they're the twin draws of the pretty walled town of Rochechouart, 45km west of Limoges. It's a fun stop for a quick walk with its beautiful château and church with a special spiralling spire.

◉ Sights

**Musée Départemental
d'Art Contemporain** ART MUSEUM
(☑05 55 03 77 91; www.musee-rochechouart.com; place du Château; adult/child €4.60/3, 1st Sun of month free; ⊙10am-12.30pm & 1.30-6pm Wed-Mon, closed mid-Dec–Feb) Housed in the town's strik-ing **château**, which overlooks the confluence of two small rivers, the museum includes a collection of works by acclaimed Dadaist Raoul Haussman and a room decorated by 16th-century frescos.

**Éspace Météorite
Paul Pellas** GEOLOGICAL MUSEUM
(☑05 55 03 02 70; www.espacemeteorite.com; 16 rue Jean-Parvy; adult/child €4/2; ⊙10am-12.30pm & 1.30-6pm Mon-Fri, 2-6pm Sat & Sun Jul & Aug, shorter hours rest of year) Two hundred million years ago a 1.5km-radius intergalactic rock slammed into Earth 4km west of Rochechouart at 72,000km/h with the force of 14 million Hiroshima bombs, creating a crater 20km wide and 6km deep. Small Éspace Météorite Paul Pellas explores it through minerals, models and videos.

❶ Getting There & Away

Limoges **RDTHV** (Régie Départementale des Transports de la Haute-Vienne; www.rdthv.com; ticket €2) bus 21 (80 minutes, two daily Monday to Friday, one on Saturday) serves Rochechouart.

Chassenon

Cassinomagus ROMAN SITE
(☑05 45 89 32 21; www.cassinomagus.fr; Chassenon; adult/child €6/3, guided tours €1.50; ◷10am-6.30pm daily mid-Apr–mid-Sep, shorter hours rest of year) The Gallo-Roman baths of Cassinomagus were rediscovered in 1844 and excavated from 1958 to 1988. This luxurious former way-station was an important crossroads on the via Agrippa, the road that crossed France. Much of the complex (including a temple and amphitheatre) were plundered for stone, but you can still make out baths, plunge pools and hypocausts, the Roman equivalent of underfloor heating. The small **museum** houses finds from the site. Regular events include Roman sports and exhibitions.

East of Limoges

St-Léonard-de-Noblat

POP 4730

The highlight of small St-Léonard-de-Noblat, 22km east of Limoges, is its glorious **abbey church**. A prime example of Limousin Romanesque architecture, it is known for its 12th-century stone-spired bell tower. The town, with its winding medieval streets was a stopping point on the pilgrimage to Compostela, and was named for the hermit Léonard, who retreated here in the 6th century.

Bourganeuf

POP 3085

Fifty kilometres northeast of Limoges, bourgeois Bourganeuf is worth a stop for a stroll around its atmospheric old town. The first town in Europe to get electricity, it has a **museum** (☑05 55 64 07 61; rte de la Cascade; adult/child €4/3; ◷10am-noon Wed & Sat, 2-7pm Mon-Sat Jul & Aug) exploring that fact.

South of Bourganeuf, the Limousin is at its lushest, especially around **Plateau de Millevaches** (www.pnr-millevaches.fr). **Lac de Vassivière** (www.vassiviere.com) is a popular spot for water sports and picnics.

Aubusson

POP 3937

Quaint riverside Aubusson has become synonymous with fine tapestries. It was the clacking centre of French production during the 19th century (rivalled only by the Gobelins factories in Paris), producing elegant tapestries renowned for vivid colours, fine detail and exquisite craftsmanship. An exploration of Aubusson's beautiful terraced streets rising above the River Creuse, and its modern-day tapestry museums and studios, is a must for any lover of the art.

◉ Sights

Tapestries once adorned the walls of aristocratic houses from London to the Loire Valley, and they weren't just decorative: in a world before central heating, they provided useful insulation against the cold, especially in draughty castles. The industry steadily declined following the French Revolution, before being revived between WWI and WWII by inventive new designers, such as Jean Lurçat and Sylvaine Dubuisson.

In 2009 Aubusson tapestries became Unesco Heritage listed. Today there are around 20 **tapestry workshops** in Aubusson and nearby **Felletin**, 10km south. The tourist office in Aubusson arranges visits and has a long list (*Guide Tapisserie et Patrimoine*) of local galleries and workshops, also downloadable from its website.

The **Hôtel de Ville** holds summertime tapestry exhibitions.

★**Musée de la Tapisserie** MUSEUM
(☑05 55 83 08 30; www.cite-tapisserie.com; av des Lissiers, Centre Jean Lurçat; adult/child €5/free; ◷9.30am-noon & 2-6pm Mon & Wed-Sun, 10am-6pm Jul & Aug) For an historical overview, head to this fine, small museum which houses intricate examples of both antique and modern tapestries produced in Aubusson. There are plans to expand the museum.

Maison du Tapissier MUSEUM
(☑05 55 66 32 12; place François Tabard; adult/child €5/4; ◷9.30am-12.30pm & 2-6pm Mon-Sat year-round, plus 10am-noon & 2-5pm Sun Easter-Sep) Next to the tourist office, this 16th-century

---

ALL ABOARD!

Chemin Touristique Limousin–Périgord (www.trainvapeur.com) Clamber aboard carriages pulled by 1932 steam engine on the Chemin Touristique Limousin–Périgord to watch the Limousin's fields and forests roll by. The trains run certain days and routes from Limoges and Eymoutiers, mid-July to mid-August. Reservations are essential; make them at the tourist office in Limoges, Eymoutiers, Pompadour or St-Yrieix.

building holds a recreation of a 17th-century weaver's workshop, with tools, original furniture and vintage tapestries.

Exposition-Collection
Fougerol   MUSEUM
(34 rue Jules Sandeau; adult/child €3/free; ⊙10am-1pm & 2-6pm Mon-Sat, 10am-noon & 2.30-5.30pm Sun Jun-Sep) About 135 tapestries from the 16th to 19th centuries from Aubusson and Flanders.

🛏 Sleeping & Eating

Hôtel La Beauze   BOUTIQUE HOTEL €
(📞05 55 66 46 00; www.hotellabeauze.fr; 14 av de la République; d €65-80; 🐾) This renovated 19th-century town house on the edge of the old town is one of Aubusson's comfiest places to stay. Stylishly furnished rooms have peaceful views across a grassy garden.

L'Hôtel de France   HOTEL €€
(📞05 55 66 10 22; www.aubussonlefrance.com; 6 rue des Déportés; d €73-105; 🐾) This upmarket Logis hotel has 21 plush rooms: some modern, some old fashioned and frilly, some tucked into the attic with sloping ceilings. Its restaurant (three-course *menus* €22 to €39) is the best in town, with Limousin dishes served to the tunes of a tinkling piano.

ℹ Information

Tourist Office (📞05 55 66 32 12; www.tourisme-aubusson.com; 63 rue Vieille; ⊙10am-noon & 2-6pm; 🐾) Tapestry, transport and lodging info.

ℹ Getting There & Away

Aubusson is 88km east of Limoges. Trains (and SNCF buses) link Aubusson with Limoges (€16, 1¾ hours, two direct daily Monday to Saturday, one on Sunday). The station is about 400m from town.
Trans Creuse (📞05 44 30 27 23; www.creuse.fr) buses serve the area around Aubusson.

South of Limoges

Solignac & Around
POP 1541

In the thickly wooded Briance Valley, 10km south of Limoges, the tiny medieval village of Solignac was a major stop on the pilgrimage route to Santiago de Compostela. Its 11th-century church is a Romanesque wonder, and the sweet village is made of golden-coloured granite typical of the Limousin.

◉ Sights

★L'Abbaye St-Pierre
de Solignac   CHURCH
This still-operational 11th-century church is a Romanesque wonder, renowned for its 14m-wide domed roof. The stalls in the nave are decorated with carved wooden sculptures of human heads, fantastical animals and a monk mooning the world, while the columns depict human figures being devoured by dragons.

Château de Chalucet   RUIN
Five kilometres southeast of Solignac are the moody ruins of the Château de Chalucet, a 12th-century keep occupied by the English during the Hundred Years War. The spot, along a pretty little brook with forested hills and tweeting birds, makes a fine picnic stop, with valley views from the tumbledown keep.

Parc Zoologique du Reynou   ZOO
(www.parczooreynou.com; Le Vigen; adult/child €13.50/9.50; ⊙10am-7.30pm, last entry 6pm) Denizens at this 35-hectare safari park, 1km east of Solignac, include wolves, giraffes, wildebeest, snowy owls and a pair of breeding tigers.

🛏 Sleeping

Hôtel Le St-Eloi   HOTEL €
(📞05 55 00 44 52; www.lesainteloi.fr; 66 av St-Eloi, Solignac; d €73-86; ⊙restaurant noon-1.30pm Tue-Fri, 7.30-8.45pm Mon-Sat) Hôtel Le St-Eloi has 15 sunny rooms inside a quaint shuttered building opposite the church. The ones with Jacuzzis and terraces are fantastic value, and half board is available at the restaurant (*menus* €25 to €35).

ℹ Getting There & Away

The Solignac–Le Vigen train station is on the Limoges (€3.10, 10 minutes) to Brive-la-Gaillarde (€15.50, 1¼ hour) line (10 daily).

Uzerche
POP 3271

Breathtakingly situated on a spur above the River Vézère, the walled town of Uzerche is one of the Limousin's prettiest hilltop hamlets. Spiky turrets top the walls of 15th- and 16th-century **maisons à tourelles** (turret houses) like witches' hats, and the **Porte Bécharie**, one of the nine original 14th-century gates, remains remarkably intact.

Uzerche's single street leads uphill past vibrant cafes to the **Église St-Pierre**, a fortified church with an 11th-century crypt – one of the oldest in the Limousin. From the front, there are fabulous panoramas of the river valley from **place de la Lunade** (which takes its name from a pagan summer solstice festival now rejigged as a Christian procession). Nearby, the **tourist office** (☑05 55 73 15 71; www. pays-uzerche.fr; place de la Libération; ⏱10am-noon & 2-5.30pm Mon-Sat, plus Sun Jul & Aug) sells local art, chutneys and honeys.

🛏 Sleeping & Eating

Hôtel Jean Teyssier　　　　　　HOTEL €
(☑05 55 73 10 05; www.hotel-teyssier.com; rue du Pont-Turgot; d €55-69) The Teyssier's lovely stone exterior conceals a comfortable modern hotel: the 14 rooms are fresh and well furnished, with magnolia walls and striped fabrics, and the restaurant (*menus* €20 to €28) has a nice riverview terrace.

Hôtel Ambroise　　　　　　　HOTEL €
(☑05 55 73 28 60; www.hotel-ambroise.com; av Charles de Gaulle; d €51-64; ⏱closed mid-Oct–mid-Apr; ☎) Hôtel Ambroise is nicer inside than outside: snug, simple rooms (some with river views) and a restaurant (*menus* €13.50 to €26.50).

Le Charmant　　　　　REGIONAL CUISINE €
(☑05 55 98 17 80; place Alexis Boyer; menus lunch €9-35, dinner €17.50-35; ⏱noon-1.30pm & 7.30-9.30pm daily) Sup on dishes created from locally sourced ingredients, such as Limousin beef, served by friendly staff on a lively terrace.

ℹ Getting There & Away

Uzerche's train station, 2km north of the old city along the N20, is on the Limoges (€11.20, 40 minutes, 10 daily) to Brive-la-Gaillarde (€9 or €11, 30 minutes, 10 daily) line.

Brive-la-Gaillarde
POP 49,582

Busy Brive-la-Gaillarde is the main commercial and administrative centre for the agricultural Corrèze *département*. Get through its busy outskirts and a ring of boulevards encloses the golden sandstone central village, an interesting maze of walking streets and cafe life. Its bustling weekly markets draw folk from all around.

◉ Sights

Musée Labenche　　　　　　MUSEUM
(http://museelabenche.brive.fr; 26bis bd Jules-Ferry; adult/child €5/2.70; ⏱10am-6.30pm Wed-Mon) The town's main museum is in the beautiful Renaissance **Hôtel de Labenche**. Exhibits explore local history and archaeology, and there's a collection of accordions and unique 17th-century English tapestries.

Collégiale St-Martin　　　　　CHURCH
In the heart of town, the Romanesque Collégiale St-Martin dates from the 11th century. Original parts include the transept and a few decorated columns depicting fabulous beasties and biblical scenes.

WORTH A TRIP

CHÂTEAU D'ARNAC POMPADOUR

Equine aficionados won't want to miss the **Château de Pompadour** (adult/child €4/3; ⏱10am-noon & 2-5.30pm Tue-Sun year-round), home to one of France's foremost national *haras* (stud farms). Established in the 18th century by the mistress of Louis XV, Madame de Pompadour (born Jeanne-Antoinette Poisson), it's particularly known for its Anglo-Arab pedigrees.

Based at the château, **Les Trois Tours** (☑05 55 98 51 10; www.les3tours-pompadour.com) arranges guided visits of the château (adult/child €7/6), the **écuries du Puy Marmont** (stallions' stables; adult/child €5/4.50) and the **jumenterie de la rivière** (mares' stables; adult/child €6/5); joint passes for two/three tours cost €10/15 per adult and €8/12 per child.

You can grab a bite to eat on the terrace at **Auberge du Château** (☑05 55 73 33 74; www.auberge-du-chateau.net; 5 av du Limousin; lunch/dinner menus from €12.50/23; ⏱noon-2pm & 7.30-9.30pm), which serves classic French cuisine.

In the château's right tower, the **tourist office** (☑05 55 98 55 47; www.pompadour.net; Château de Pompadour; ⏱10.30am-12.30pm & 2-6pm Mon-Sat, reduced Oct-May) details forthcoming equestrian demonstrations and races, as well as local horse riding options.

Arnac-Pompadour is on the train line, 60km south of Limoges (€12.40, 1¼ hours, three daily).

RICHARD THE LIONHEART IN THE LIMOUSIN

The swashbuckling spectre of Richard Cœur de Lion (Richard the Lionheart) looms over the Haute-Vienne *département*. The crusading king waged several bloody campaigns here in the 12th century before meeting his end at the now-ruined keep of **Château de Chalûs-Chabrol**, 40km west of Limoges, where he was mortally wounded by a crossbowman in 1199.

Many other sites share a Lionheart connection: they're signposted along the **Route de Richard Cœur de Lion** (Richard the Lionheart Route; www.routerichardcoeurdelion.fr). Pick up the English-language map from tourist offices.

Maison Denoix   DISTILLERY
(☑ 05 55 74 34 27; www.denoix.com; 9 bd du Maréchal Lyautey; ☉ 9am-noon & 2.30-7pm Tue-Sat Sep-Jun) FREE Since 1839 this traditional distillery has produced the favourite Corrèze fire water, *l'eau de noix* (walnut liqueur), alongside concoctions such as chocolate and quince liqueurs. See their copper stills, and sample the wares, including grape must mustard, or take a summer-only guided tour.

🛏 Sleeping & Eating

The medieval centre is dotted with cafes and restaurants in little plazas.

Hôtel Le Coq d'Or   HOTEL €
(☑ 05 55 17 12 92; www.hotel-coqdor.fr; 16 bd Jules Ferry; s/d/tr from €50/55/80; 🖥) This stone town house sits on the ring boulevard around the centre, with a sunny terrace and quaint old-fashioned rooms.

Auberge de Jeunesse   HOSTEL €
(☑ 05 55 24 34 00; www.fuaj.org; 56 av Maréchal Bugeaud; dm €14.90; ☉ reception 8am-noon & 5-10pm Feb-Nov; 🖥) Brive's hostel makes a striking first impression, with reception inside a former mansion, however, most dorm rooms are actually in a modern annexe. It's 1.5km from the station.

Le Manoir de Laumeuil   B&B €€
(☑ 05 55 87 95 83; www.lemanoirfr.com; 147 rue de Laumeuil, St Pantaleon de Larche; d/apt incl breakfast €120/160; 🖥🏊) This lovely *chambre d'hôte* in a manor on the western outskirts of Brive is surrounded by three green acres

and offers gracious rooms and apartments with king-size beds, fridges, DVD players and garden views. There's also a salt-water swimming pool.

La Truffe Noire   HOTEL €€
(☑ 05 55 92 45 00; www.la-truffe-noire.com; 22 bd Anatole-France; d €130-145; ❄🖥) A venerable wisteria-fronted hotel in the centre, with comfy but bland rooms. The restaurant (lunch/dinner *menus* from €19/30) serves good Limousin fare: truffles, duck, wild mushrooms.

Château de Castel-Novel   HOTEL €€€
(☑ 05 55 85 09 03; www.castelnovel.com; Varetz; d €110-340, ste €370-550; ❄🖥🏊) About 10km northwest of Brive-la-Gaillarde, this grand château was immortalised by Colette who wrote *Le Blé en Herbe* and *Chéri* here. Topped by turrets and gables, it's filled with idiosyncratic rooms (including Colette's Louis XVI apartment) and surrounded by sweeping grounds. Equally inspired is the château's gastronomic restaurant (*menus* €30 to €108).

Food Market   MARKET €
(place du 14 Juillet; ☉ Tue & Sat morning) Bustling Tuesday and Saturday market on the main square, with a smaller market on Thursday mornings. Stock up on Limousin goodies: goose products, plum brandy and *galette corrézienne* (walnut and chestnut cake).

❶ Information

Tourist Office (☑ 05 55 24 08 80; www.brive-tourisme.com; place du 14 Juillet; ☉ 9am-12.30pm & 1.30-6.30pm Mon-Sat) In a former water tower overlooking the market square.

❶ Getting There & Away

AIR

Brive-Vallée de la Dordogne Airport (BVE; ☑ 05 55 22 40 00; www.aeroport-brive-vallee-dordogne.com) Ten kilometres south of Brive, with flights to Paris-Orly, London, Amsterdam, Porto and Ajaccio. The only airport transport is taxi or rental car.

BUS

The **bus station** (place du 14 Juillet) is next to the tourist office. Trans Périgord connects Brive with Montignac (€2, 1¼ hours, one daily Monday to Friday).

CFTA (www.cftaco.fr) Regional buses, including a service to Tulle (€2, 45 minutes, six daily Monday to Friday, one Saturday).

Libéo (☑ 05 55 74 20 13; www.libeo-brive.fr; ticket €1) Lines 3, 6, N and D serve the train station, otherwise it's just local buses around town.

CAR

Major car hire outlets have airport and train station offices.

TRAIN

The **train station** (av Jean Jaurès) is located at a major confluence of rail lines from Brive centre. On lines north to Limoges and Paris, south to Toulouse, west to Périgueux, east to Clermont-Ferrand, and southeast to Figeac.

Cahors €13 to €18, one hour, seven daily.

Limoges €15 to €18, one hour, 10 daily.

Paris' Austerlitz €61, 4¼ hours, eight daily.

Périgueux €14, one hour, four to six daily.

East of Brive

Gimel-les-Cascades

POP 744

This tiny, typically Corrèzien village is a charming collection of slate roofs, flower-filled balconies and stone cottages along the banks of rushing River Montane. Wander the lanes, drink in the atmosphere, and stroll along the river banks before hiking to the cascades after which the village is named.

Gimel's teensy **tourist office** (☑05 55 21 44 32; www.gimellescascades.fr; ☉10am-noon & 2-5pm Mon-Fri, to 6pm Sat & Sun Apr-Sep) shares a space with the post office.

◉ Sights

Cascades WATERFALL

Three crashing cascades are about a half-hour hike from the riverside path at the foot of the village.

St-Pardoux de Gimel CHURCH

The local church contains a beautiful enamelled reliquary known as the **Châsse de St-Étienne**, made in the 12th century by Limoges artisans.

South of Brive

Rolling countryside unfolds south of Brive to the banks of the Dordogne and the border of the northern Lot. Some of the Limousin's most picturesque villages dot the region.

Turenne

POP 805

Rising up from a solitary spur of rock, the hilltop village of Turenne is an arresting sight: honey-coloured stone cottages and slanted houses are stacked up like dominoes beneath the towering château from which viscounts ruled a huge portion of the Limousin, Périgord and Quercy for almost 1000 years.

The **tourist office** (☑05 55 24 12 95; www.turenne.fr; guided visits adult/child €4/free, fire torch €1; ☉10am-12.30pm & 3-6pm Tue-Sun) at the base of the village runs guided visits and torch-lit night-time promenades in summer.

◉ Sights

Château de Turenne CHÂTEAU

(☑05 55 85 90 66; www.chateau-turenne.com; admission €4.80; ☉10am-noon & 2-6pm Apr-Oct, 2-5pm Sun Nov-Mar) The château, built to protect the feudal seat of the powerful viscounts of Turenne, has beautiful views of the surrounding countryside from the 12th century **Tour de César**, the arrow-straight tower. Apart from a few ramparts and a 14th-century guard room, the rest of the lordly lodgings have crumbled away, and are now occupied by an ornamental garden.

🛏 Sleeping

La Maison des Chanoines HOTEL €

(☑05 55 85 93 43; www.maison-des-chanoines. com; d €65-85; ☉Apr–mid-Oct) Behind the 16th-century Flamboyant Gothic façade of Turenne's only hotel, you'll find sparingly decorated countrified rooms and a good restaurant (*menus* €38 to €54).

❶ Getting There & Away

Public transport is limited: buses from Brive (€2, 30 minutes, three daily Monday to Friday) and trains (€3.60, 15 minutes, four daily) which stop 3km southeast of the village.

Collonges-la-Rouge

POP 492

Built from vibrant rust-red sandstone (hence its name) and topped by fantastical conical turrets and black-slate rooftops, Collonges-la-Rouge is one of the most iconic villages in the Corrèze. In 1942 the entire village received classification as a *monument historique*. Gazing at the gorgeous architecture and browsing Collonges' many artisan shops is a popular pastime, so start early as the village steadily fills with bus-loads of tourists.

◉ Sights

Collonges Centre HISTORIC QUARTER

Collonges centres on its fortified **St-Pierre church**, constructed from the 11th to the 15th centuries on the site of an 8th-century

TULLE ACCORDIONS

The industrial town of **Tulle** (population 15,619), 28km northeast of Brive, is renowned as the world's accordion capital. A single accordion consists of between 3500 and 6800 parts and making one requires up to 200 hours' labour. The very best instruments fetch upwards of a staggering €9000.

One of the last remaining traditional accordion makers, **Usine Maugein** (☑ 05 55 20 08 89; www.accordeons-maugein.com; rte de Brive; ⊙ tours by reservation 10.15am-2.30pm Mon-Thu) **FREE**, runs guided factory tours by reservation, where you can see the craftspeople at work and browse the accordion museum.

Accordions take centre stage during mid-September's four-day street music festival **Nuits de Nacre**; Tulle's **tourist office** (☑ 05 55 26 59 61; www.tulle-coeur-correze.com; 2 place Jean Tavé; ⊙ 9am-12.30pm & 2-6pm Mon-Sat) has details.

Regular trains run to Tulle from Brive (€5.80, 30 minutes).

Benedictine priory, and an important stop on the pilgrimage to Santiago de Compostela. In an unusual show of unity during the late 16th century, local Protestants held prayers in the southern nave and their Catholic neighbours prayed in the northern nave. The 12th-century **tympanum** is made from white Turenne limestone, and the bell tower is in the Limousin style.

Nearby, the slate roof of the ancient **covered market** shelters an equally ancient baker's oven. The 1583 fortified **Castel de Vassinhac** is one of the grandest manor houses. Rue Noire is the oldest part of town, loaded with turrets and towers.

Shops fill the entire area, offering everything from silk and leather products to local mustards.

🛏 Sleeping & Eating

Relais du Quercy   HOTEL €
(☑ 05 55 25 40 31; www.relaisduquercy.com; Meyssac; d €60-72) Two kilometres southeast of Collonges in Meyssac, this little slate-roofed country hotel has comfortable rooms, the best of which look over the rear garden.

Jeanne Maison d'Hôte   B&B €€
(☑ 05 55 25 42 31; www.jeannemaisondhotes.com; d incl breakfast €100) On the downhill edge of the village, this grand B&B in a towering 15th-century *maison bourgeoise* offers five rooms packed with period features: beams, latticed windows, antique wardrobes and chaises longues.

★ **Auberge de Benges**   REGIONAL CUISINE €€
(☑ 05 55 85 76 68; www.aubergedebenges.com; menus €24-35; ⊙ noon-2pm Fri-Wed & 7-9pm Wed, Fri & Sat Mar-Dec) Collonges' top table for locally sourced ingredients, creativity and a relaxed ambience. Step through the wisteria-clad entry to a terrace with sweeping views from the foot of the village.

Relais St-Jacques de Compostelle   TRADITIONAL FRENCH €€
(☑ 05 55 25 41 02; www.hotel-stjacques.com; menus €21-35; ⊙ restaurant noon-2pm & 7-9pm Thu-Tue) The best part of this hotel-restaurant in the centre of Collonges is its terrace with views of mauve turrets, and its classic French cuisine. Rooms (double from €70) are spartan but comfortable.

ℹ Information

Tourist Office (☑ 05 55 25 32 25; www.ot-collonges.fr; ⊙ 10am-12.30pm & 2.30-6pm) Arranges guided tours (adult/child €4/free) of the village.

ℹ Getting There & Away

Collonges is linked by bus with Brive (€3, 30 minutes, four to six daily Monday to Friday, one on Saturday), 18km to the northwest along the D38.

Beaulieu-sur-Dordogne

POP 1256

On a tranquil bend of the Dordogne surrounded by agricultural fields, Beaulieu was once an important stop for Compostela pilgrims. Its beautifully preserved **medieval quarter** is one of the region's finest: a network of curving lanes lined with timber-framed houses and smart mansions, many dating from the 14th and 15th centuries. Its church is tops.

Beaulieu's **market** is on Wednesday and Saturday mornings. On the second Sunday in May the **Fête de la Fraise** (Strawberry Festival; ⊙ May) is held.

● Sights & Activities

★ Abbatiale St-Pierre
CHURCH
Beaulieu's most celebrated feature is this 12th-century Romanesque abbey church, with a wonderful tympanum (c 1130) depicting incredible scenes from the Last Judgment including dancing apostles and resurrected sinners. Also look for its small treasury case filled with 10th- to 13th-century masterworks.

Chapelle des Pénitents
CHURCH
The pretty riverside Chapelle des Pénitents was built to accommodate pious parishioners – access to the abbey church was strictly reserved for monks and paying pilgrims.

Aventures Dordogne
Nature
OUTDOOR ACTIVITIES
(☑ 05 55 28 86 45; www.adndordogne.org; ☉ May-Oct) Runs *gabarre* trips on the river (adult/child from €7.50/6), hires out canoes and kayaks (trips from €15 to €37), and organises activities from climbing to paragliding.

⊨ Sleeping

Auberge Les Charmilles
HOTEL €
(☑ 05 55 91 29 29; www.auberge-charmilles.com; 20 bd Rodolphe de Turenne; d €59-72; ☉ Apr-Dec, restaurant noon-1.45pm Tue-Sun, 7.15-8.45pm Tue-Sat; ☜) All eight rooms at this lovely *maison bourgeoise* are named after different types of strawberries. The decor's fresh and fruity, with puffy bedspreads, wooden floors and summery bathrooms. Scrumptious dishes are served at its peaceful riverside restaurant (*menus* €16 to €28).

Auberge de Jeunesse
HOSTEL €
(☑ 05 55 91 13 82; www.hifrance.org; place du Monturu; dm €15.15; ☉ Apr-Oct; ☜) Parts of this quirky 28-bed hostel date from the 15th century: latticed windows and a miniature turret. Inside find a cosy lounge, well-stocked kitchen and dinky four-bed rooms, all with private bathrooms.

La Ferme du Masvidal
CAMPGROUND, B&B €
(☑ 05 55 91 53 14; www.masvidal.fr; bd de Turenne, Bilhac; sites for 2 adults, tent & car €13, d incl breakfast €70; ☉ Apr-Sep; ☜) ∅ This lovely working farm, about 10km southwest of Beaulieu in Bilhac, offers shady camping, B&B rooms and home-cooked meals (per adult/child from €23/10) made with their own produce.

Camping des Îles
CAMPGROUND €
(☑ 05 55 91 02 65; www.campingdesiles.com; bd de Turenne; sites for 2 adults, tent & car €25-35.50; ☉ Apr-Oct; ☜☒) Well-equipped riverside campground on an island between two branches of the Dordogne.

Manoir de Beaulieu
HOTEL, GASTRONOMIC €€
(☑ 05 55 91 01 34; www.hotelbeaulieudordogne.com; 4 place du Champ-de-Mars; r €90-100, ste €130; ☜) Half old-fashioned *auberge*, half smart hotel, rooms mix the best of old and new: wood floors, glass sinks and flat-screen TVs meet solid furniture, velvet armchairs, and the odd vintage piece. Plus a courtyard restaurant (*menus* €28 to €42).

● Information

Beaulieu-sur-Dordogne Tourist Office (☑ 05 55 91 09 94; www.beaulieu-tourisme.com; place Marbot; ☉ 10am-12.30pm & 2.30-5pm Mon-Sat, 9.30am-12.30pm Sun) On the main square with local and regional maps.

● Getting There & Away

CFTA (p596) bus 9 links Beaulieu with Brive (one hour, one to three daily) from Monday to Saturday.

THE LOT

Stretching from the River Dordogne in the north to the serpentine River Lot near busy Cahors (and its renowned vineyards) and beyond, the Lot *département* (www.tourisme-lot.com) offers an arresting landscape of limestone cliffs and canyons, hilltop towns and undulating hills carpeted in forests, fields or vines. Formerly the northern section of the old province of Quercy, the modern Lot is part of the Midi-Pyrénées *region* (www.tourisme-midi-pyrenees.com), and makes for great exploring, especially if you have your own wheels.

Cahors
POP 21,401
In a U-shaped curve in the River Lot, Cahors combines the feel of the sunbaked Mediterranean with an alluring old town. Pastel-coloured buildings line the shady squares of the ancient medieval quarter, criss-crossed by a labyrinth of alleyways and cul-de-sacs, and bordered by very walkable quays.

Slicing through the centre of Cahors, bd Léon Gambetta – named after the French statesman who was born in Cahors in 1838 – neatly divides Vieux Cahors (old Cahors) to the east and the new city to the west.

Cahors

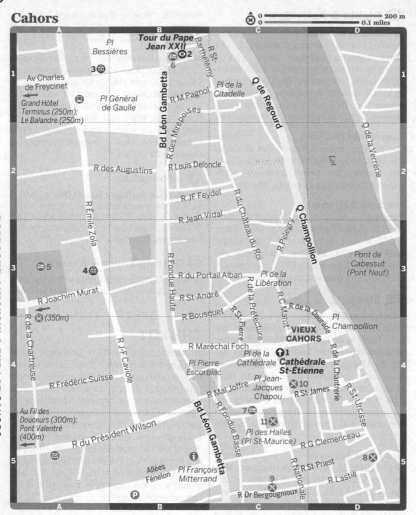

⊙ Sights

In the Middle Ages, Cahors was a prosperous commercial centre, and the **old city** is densely packed with timber-fronted houses and galleried mansions built by the city's medieval merchants. Wandering the old town is a real highlight with fascinating ancient details around every corner. Don't-miss streets include Dr Bergougnioux, Lastié, St-Priest and St-Urcisse.

Get a copy of *Gardens of Cahors*, a superb free booklet that highlights a walking tour of the town, including many secret gardens.

★ Pont Valentré

BRIDGE

The seven-span Pont Valentré, on the western side of the city, south of the train station, is one of France's most iconic medieval bridges, built as part of the town's defences in the 14th century. The parapets projecting from two of its three tall towers were designed to allow defenders to drop missiles on attackers below. On the bank opposite the bridge, the **Fontaine des Chartreux**, dedicated to the city's Gallo-Roman goddess Divona, was what the city was originally built around, and still supplies the drinking water.

Cahors

★**Cathédrale St-Étienne**   CATHEDRAL
(place de la Cathédrale; ⊙ 7am-6pm) The airy nave of Cahors' Romanesque cathedral, consecrated in 1119, is topped by two cupolas (at 18m wide, the largest in France). Some of the frescos are 14th-century, but the side chapels and carvings in the **cloître** (cloister) mainly date from the 16th-century Flamboyant Gothic period. On the north façade, a carved **tympanum** depicts Christ's ascension surrounded by fluttering angels and pious saints.

★**Tour du Pape Jean XXII**   ARCHITECTURE
(3 bd Léon Gambetta) The Tour du Pape Jean XXII (closed to the public) is the town's tallest building at 34m high. It was originally part of a 14th-century mansion belonging to Jacques Duèze (later Pope John XXII), who constructed the Pont Valentré.

Musée de la Résistance   MUSEUM
(🖉 05 65 22 14 25; place Général de Gaulle; ⊙ 2-6pm daily, closed Sun Oct-Mar) FREE Cahors was a base for the resistance during WWII. Look for displays on local hero Hélène Metges who died for the cause.

Musée Henri Martin   MUSEUM
(Musée Municipal; www.mairie-cahors.fr/musee; 792 rue Émile Zola; adult/child €3/1.50; ⊙ 11am-6pm Mon & Wed-Sat, 2-6pm Sun) Displays include works by the Cahors-born pointillist painter Henri Martin (1893–1972).

🛏 Sleeping

★**Hôtel Jean XXII**   HOTEL €
(🖉 05 65 35 07 66; www.hotel-jeanxxii.com; 2 rue Edmond-Albé; s €53, d €64-71; 🖭) Next to the Tour du Pape Jean XXII, this excellent nine-room hotel mixes original stone, greenery and well-worn wood with a dash of metropolitan minimalism. Rooms sleep one to four people; there's a reading area on the 1st floor where you can unwind in leather armchairs.

Le Coin des Halles   HOTEL €
(🖉 05 65 30 24 27; www.lecoindeshalles-hotel.com; 30 place Saint Maurice; r €55-80; 🖭) This is a good-value option right in the heart of the old town. Seventeen basic rooms have flashes of modern style and there's a cute little cafe.

Auberge de Jeunesse   HOSTEL €
(🖉 05 65 35 64 71; www.fuaj.org/cahors; 222 rue Joachim Murat; dm from €16; ⊙ reception 5-9pm; 🖭) In a very quiet old convent a 10-minute walk from the station, Cahors' hostel is basic with 50 beds in four- to 10-bed dorms and a rambling garden.

Grand Hôtel Terminus   HOTEL €€
(🖉 05 65 53 32 00; www.balandre.com; 5 av Charles de Freycinet; r €73-105, ste €140-165; ❄🖭) Built c 1920, Cahors' original railway station hotel evokes an air of faded grandeur. Most of the rooms are large and comfortable, with hefty radiators, claw-foot baths and king-size beds. Some details are frayed.

✖ Eating

Cafes cluster around the modern place François Mitterand. The park-like banks of the Lot are perfect for picnics, especially near the Pont Valentré.

★**Marché Couvert**   FOOD MARKET €
(place des Halles; ⊙ 7.30am-12.30pm & 3-7pm Tue-Sat, 9am-noon Sun) The city's main covered market is often simply called Les Halles. There's a not-to-be-missed **open-air market** on Wednesday and Saturday mornings around the covered market and on place Jean-Jacques Chapou. Excellent food shops cluster around the market and along rue Nationale.

Le Bergougnoux   TRADITIONAL FRENCH €
(🖉 05 65 35 62 92; 77 rue Bergougnoux; lunch/dinner menus from €13/18; ⊙ noon-2pm & 7.30-9pm Mon-Sat) Country cuisine *de grande-mère* is the speciality of this simple little family-owned eatery, secreted away along a narrow and picturesque backstreet in the old town. Enjoy no-frills classics such as *pot au feu* (hotpot), *rôti de porc* (roast pork) and daily specials.

⭐ **Au Fil des Douceurs**   REGIONAL CUISINE €€
(☑05 65 22 13 04; 32 av André Breton; menus lunch from €15, dinner €20-55; ⊙noon-2pm & 7-9.30pm Tue-Sat) From top locally sourced foods to a superb regional wine list, this elegant but fun restaurant serves excellent – and ever-changing – *menus*. Dine inside the modern two-level restaurant or outside on the terrace, with a fabulous view of Pont Valentré.

Le Marché   REGIONAL CUISINE €€
(☑05 65 35 27 27; www.restaurantlemarche.com; 27 place Jean-Jacques Chapou; menus lunch from €20, dinner €31-50; ⊙noon-2pm & 7.30-9pm Tue-Sat) Food sourced from the region stars at this urbane bistro. Puce-and-cream armchairs set the designer tone; the short *menu* changes with the seasons.

Auberge de Vieux Cahors   REGIONAL CUISINE €€
(☑05 65 35 06 05; www.aubcahors.free.fr; 144 rue Saint-Urcisse; menus €18-40; ⊙noon-2pm & 7-9.30pm) Duck in all its forms (and parts) is the speciality of this small, traditional restaurant in the old town. Enthusiastic young servers work the cosy dining room or the terrace outside. An especially good choice on Sunday night when other local options are few.

Le Balandre   GASTRONOMIC €€€
(☑05 65 53 32 00; www.balandre.com; 5 av Charles de Freycinet; menus lunch €22-40, dinner €40-68; ⊙noon-1.30pm & 7.30-9.15pm Tue-Sat) With chandeliers and stained glass, the deeply traditional family-run restaurant at Grand Hotel Terminus (p601) commands a devoted following, especially for its foie gras and *confit de canard*. Also offers monthly **cooking courses** (€100) with chef Alexandre Marre.

LOCAL KNOWLEDGE

WINE COUNTRY: WEST OF CAHORS

Downstream from Cahors, the lower River Lot twists its way through the rich vineyards of the Cahors Appellation d'Origine Contrôlée (AOC) region. Pick up the super, free *Vignobles de Cahors et du Lot* map for a comprehensive list of wineries, or visit www.vignobles. tourisme-lot.com. Malbecs predominate, with some merlot and tannat here and there, and you'll find they're best aged. Local whites don't carry the Cahors AOC.

Snake along the river's northern bank on the D9 for superb views of the vines and the river's many twists and turns. As you go west of Cahors, you'll pass **Luzech**, the medieval section of which sits at the base of a donjon, and **Castelfranc**, with a dramatic suspension bridge. Many wineries cluster around **Puy l'Évêque**.

Château de Cèdre (☑05 65 36 53 87; www.chateauducedre.com; Vire-sur-Lot; ⊙9am-noon & 2-6pm Mon-Sat) Casual, organic vineyard in the countryside, 5.5km west of Puy l'Évêque, with award-winning AOC Cahors malbecs.

Château Chambert (☑05 65 31 95 75; www.chambert.com; Floressas; ⊙9am-12.30pm & 2-5.30pm Mon-Fri, plus Sat Jul & Aug) Absolutely iconic château rising above organic vines, 8.5km south of Puy l'Évêque.

Clos Triguedina (☑05 65 21 30 81; www.jlbaldes.com; Vire-Sur-Lot) In the Baldès family since 1830, this place 5.5km west of Puy l'Évêque produces everything from straight-up malbecs to rosé and a new 'black' vintage.

Take a Break

Need a break from wine tasting or a bite to eat?

Château de Bonaguil (www.chateau-bonaguil.com; adult/child €7/4; ⊙10am-7pm Jul & Aug, 10am-12.30pm & 2-5.30pm Mar-Jun & Sep-Oct) About 15km west of Puy l'Évêque, near St-Martin-Le-Redon, the imposing feudal Château de Bonaguil is a fine example of late-15th-century military architecture, incorporating towers, bastions, loopholes, machicolations and crenellations.

Le Dodus en Ville (☑05 65 22 91 82; http://auxdodus.free.fr; rue Ernest-Marcouly, Puy l'Évêque; menus from €12; ⊙noon-2.30pm Tue-Fri, 7-9pm Tue-Sat) Choose from bright chairs out on the main street of Puy l'Évêque or inside the glass-fronted, jaunty dining room and tuck into locally sourced, seasonal dishes created by friendly Mimie de Lestrade. Save room for her home-made ice cream.

Information

Tourist Office (☑ 05 65 53 20 65; www.
tourisme-cahors.com; place François Mitterrand;
⊘ 9am-7pm daily Jun-Aug, 9.30am-6.30pm Mon-
Sat Sep-May; ☎)

ℹ Getting There & Around

BUS

Cahors is easily walked. Regional bus routes are
primarily geared to students.

CAR

Major car-hire companies are located across from
the train station. Parking is free along the river and
at place Général de Gaulle.

TRAIN

Cahors is on the main line between Paris' Gare
d'Austerlitz (€50 to €115, 5½ hours, four to six
daily), Limoges (€34, 2¼ hours, four daily) and
Toulouse (€12.50 to €21.50, 1½ hours, eight to
10 daily).

North of Cahors

Some of the Lot's most striking sights lie
north of Cahors near Limousin and the Dordogne, including the celebrated pilgrimage
site of Rocamadour. Public transport is virtually nonexistent: you'll need your own wheels
to get around.

Note, many of the accommodations listed
for Brive-la-Gaillarde, Collonges-la-Rouge and
Beaulieu-sur-Dordogne are easily drivable to
the northern Lot.

Rocamadour

POP 675

There are certain places in the world you just
may remember for your whole life, and Rocamadour is one of them. From the dramatic
silhouette of Rocamadour's steeples and pale
stone chapels clamped to 150m of vertical cliff-
side beneath the ramparts of a 14th-century
château, to the magically evocative feeling as
you explore this ancient pilgrimage site, this
spot makes an impression.

A hugely venerated pilgrimage place
through the ages, on holy days as many as
30,000 people would stream into the valley
to seek favours from the miraculous statue of
the Virgin housed within. Henry Plantagenet (1133–89), King of England and Count of
Anjou, was miraculously cured here. Always
an important financial and symbolic spot,
Rocamadour suffered during the Wars of
Religion, when everything was razed. Mirac-

ulously the icon and one bell survived, and
they remain today in the rebuilt sanctuaries,
which are still an active pilgrimage point.

ℹ Orientation

Pedestrianised Rocamadour climbs the face of a
cliff above the River Alzou, ascending from the Cité
(old city) to the Sanctuaires (sanctuaries) to the
château on top. You can approach from below or
above; each area has car parks, and it's all connected by elevators.

The château on top is connected to the sanctuaries by the switchbacked but pretty, tree- and
cave-lined **Chemin de Croix pathway** (Stations
of the Cross) or by **ascenseur incliné** (cable car;
☑ 05 65 33 67 79; www.ascenseurincline-
rocamadour.com; one-way/return €2.60/4.20;
⊘ 9am-7pm). The sanctuaries and the Cité below
are connected by **Escalier des Pelerins** (223
stairs which the pious once traversed on their
knees) or another **ascenseur** (elevator; one-way/
return €2/3; ⊘ 9am-6.50pm May-Sep, to 5.50pm
Oct-Apr). A small **tourist train** (adult/child from
€3.50/2) goes from the lower parking lot about
150m to the Cité.

On the top side of Rocamadour, 1.5km across a
spur of the hill, sits the modern conglomeration of
shops, hotels and restaurants at touristy hamlet
L'Hospitalet.

Rocamadour is 59km north of Cahors and 51km
east of Sarlat.

◉ Sights

You can reserve ahead with the ascenseur incliné staff for a one-hour **guided tour** (€8.80)
of the site.

In the pedestrianised Cité below the Sanctuaires, the commercial thoroughfare **Grande
Rue** is crammed (just as in the pilgrims' heyday) with souvenir shops and touristy restaurants. **Porte du Figuier**, one of the city's
original medieval gateways, still exists at the
street's far end.

In L'Hospitalet, a cliff-side **park** with perfect picnic benches enjoys excellent views
to Rocamadour. Nearby the evocative **ruins
of an ancient chapel** recall how this was
pilgrims' first stop, where they healed and
prepared themselves before going to Rocamadour's sanctuary.

★ Sanctuaires
CHURCH

The Sanctuaires are seven beautiful 12th- to
14th-century chapels built into the rockface
and surrounding a central courtyard. You can
see worn stones where pilgrims cycled between the churches. **Chapelle Notre Dame**
is the highlight, containing the magical
Vierge Noire (Black Madonna). Carved from

walnut in the 12th century, she drew worshippers from across Europe in the Middle Ages. Overhead, the 9th-century iron bell is said to have rung on its own when somewhere in the world the Virgin performed a miracle.

Outside the chapel are the sites where it is said that the original hermit, St Amadour, was buried, and where **Durandal**, Roland's famous sword was embedded in the wall. Rocamadour is still an active site; dress appropriately.

Château   FORTRESS
(admission €2; ☉8am-8pm) Perched atop Rocamadour, the château is a series of 14th-century protective ramparts with excellent views of the valley. Exact change is required for the machine operating the entrance.

Grotte des Merveilles   CAVE
(www.grotte-des-merveilles.com; L'Hospitalet; adult/child €7/4.50; ☉10am-noon & 2-6pm) Natural cave with stalactites and 20,000-year-old cave art, in L'Hospitalet.

🛏 Sleeping & Eating

Give the touristy hotels and restaurants in Rocamadour a wide berth – prices for even the dingiest room skyrocket in summer, and most are booked out in advance by tour-bus groups. Bring or buy a picnic instead.

★Moulin de Latreille   B&B €€
(☎05 65 41 91 83; www.moulindelatreille.com; Calès; d incl breakfast €85; ☉mid-Mar–Oct; ☎) 🍴 British expats Giles and Fi Stonor have painstakingly restored this 12th-century water mill on the banks of the River Ouysse, using the mill to power the whole tastefully done property. Situated 2km down a dirt road from the hilltop village of Calès (17km west of Rocamadour on the D673).

ℹ Information

Main Tourist Office (☎05 65 33 22 00; www.vallee-dordogne-rocamadour.com; ☉10am-noon & 2-6pm Mon-Sat, 1.30-6pm Sun; ☎) In L'Hospitalet. Has smartphone app.
Cité Tourist Office (Grand Rue, Rocamadour; ☉10.30am-12.30pm & 1.30-6pm) Small branch in the old city.

Gouffre de Padirac

★Gouffre de Padirac   CAVE
(☎05 65 33 64 56; www.gouffre-de-padirac.com; adult/child €10.30/6.90; ☉hours vary, approx 9.30am-7pm Apr–mid-Nov) Discovered in 1889, the spectacular Gouffre de Padirac features some of France's spangliest underground caverns. The cave's navigable river, 103m below ground level, is reached through a 75m-deep, 33m-wide chasm. Boat pilots ferry visitors along 1km of subterranean waterways, visiting a series of glorious floodlit caverns, including the soaring **Salle de Grand Dôme** and the **Lac des Grands Gours**, a 27m-wide subterranean lake. You can book online. From Rocamadour, the caverns are 15km northeast.

Insectopia   INSECT ZOO
(www.insectopia.fr; adult/child €6.50/3.50; ☉10am-6pm Easter-Oct) Just up the road from Gouffre de Padirac's main car park, Insectopia is an interactive bug zoo that enthrals kids with display cases of creepy-crawlies, from giant millipedes to scarab beetles, praying mantises and ant farms. Plus, there's a butterfly house.

Loubressac & Autoire

If you're tooling around in your own wheels, it's worth exploring the verdant valleys and rolling hills near the two beautiful villages of **Loubressac** (population 553) and **Autoire** (population 353). The former clusters on a dramatic promontory with views to Château de Castelnau-Bretenoux, and the latter is a medieval hamlet on the banks of a creek in the crook of a rocky valley.

Château de Castelnau-Bretenoux

Château de Castelnau-Bretenoux   FORTRESS
(http://castelnau-bretenoux.monuments-nationaux.fr; Prudhomat; adult/child €7.50/free, parking €2; ☉10am-7pm Jul & Aug, 10am-12.30pm & 2-5.30pm Sep-Apr, to 6.30pm May & Jun, closed Tue Oct-Mar) Not to be confused with the Château de Castelnaud, Castelnau-Bretenoux was constructed in the 12th century and saw heavy action during the Hundred Years War, before being redeveloped in the Middle Ages for newer forms of artillery. It is beautifully (and strategically) set on a promontory above the broad valley. Much of the fortress is in ruins, but you can climb the 15th-century **artillery tower**, which has great views, and visit 17th- and 18th-century residential rooms (by guided tour).

Castelnau-Bretenoux fell into disrepair in the 19th century and was refurbished around the turn of the 20th century by Parisian opera singer Jean Mouliérat.

It's about 11km south of Beaulieu-sur-Dordogne off the D940.

Carennac

POP 412

Tiny Carennac is a sweet cluster of amber houses secluded on the left bank of the emerald Dordogne. Above the square is the **Tour de Télémaque**, named after the hero of Fénelon's *Les Aventures de Télémaque*, written here in 1699.

⊙ Sights & Activities

L'Espace Patrimoine   GALLERY
(www.pays-vallee-dordogne.com; ⊘ 10am-noon & 2-6pm daily Jul-Sep, Tue-Fri Easter-Jun & Oct) `FREE` The village's main landmark is the 16th-century **Château du Doyen**, which houses a heritage centre and museum, L'Espace Patrimoine, showcasing the art and history of the region.

Église St-Pierre   CHURCH
(⊘10am-7pm) Just inside the castle gateway sit the priory and the Romanesque Église St-Pierre with a remarkable Romanesque **tympanum** of Christ in Majesty. Off the *cloître*, still beautiful despite being heavily damaged in the Revolution, is a dramatic late-15th-century **Mise au Tombeau** (Statue of the Entombment).

Safaraïd Dordogne   BOAT HIRE
(☑05 65 37 44 87; www.canoe-kayak-dordogne. com; Vayrac; self-guided trips €18-31) Canoe and kayak operator Safaraïd is based in Vayrac, 8km northwest of Carennac.

⊨ Sleeping & Eating

Hostellerie Fénelon   HOTEL €
(☑05 65 10 96 46; www.hotel-fenelon.com; r €59-71; ⊠) With flower-filled hanging baskets, Hostellerie Fénelon evokes the feel of an Alsatian summer house. The pricier of the plain rooms overlook the river and tree-covered Île Calypso. The restaurant (lunch/ *menus* from €15/19) serves classic French cuisine.

Le Prieuré   CAFE €
(☑05 65 39 76 74; lunch menu €12, mains €7-19) Just on the Carennac side of the bridge, friendly proprietors serve *assiettes* (platters) of local goat's cheese, salads and charcuterie.

ⓘ Information

Tourist Office (☑05 65 33 22 00; www. vallee-dordogne-rocamadour.com; ⊘10am-noon & 2-6pm Mon-Sat, 2-6pm Sun) Next to the church.

Martel & Around

POP 1698

Marvellous Martel is known as *la ville aux sept tours* (the town of seven towers) for its turret-topped skyline. This vibrant pale-stone village was the ancient capital of the Vicomtes de Turenne, and a prosperous judicial centre, and it retains its medieval architecture and charm in its pedestrianised centre.

⊙ Sights & Activities

Place des Consuls   SQUARE
Martel's central square, place des Consuls, is home to the former fortress of the viscounts, **Hôtel de la Raymondie**, and is filled by a great **market** on Wednesday and Saturday. Truffle markets feature in December and January.

**Chemin de Fer
Touristique du Haut-Quercy**   TOURIST TRAIN
(☑05 65 37 35 81; www.trainduhautquercy. info; adult/child diesel train €8/5, steam train €10.50/6.50; ⊘Apr-Sep) Runs one hour trips from Martel east along the precipitous cliff face to St-Denis. It used to transport truffles.

⊨ Sleeping & Eating

Château de Termes   HOTEL €
(☑05 65 32 42 03; www.chateau-de-termes.com; St-Denis-lès-Martel; r €64-95, cabin per night €95-130; ⊠) This family-friendly cottage complex is set around a manor which originally belonged to winemakers and truffle growers. It has something for everyone: lovely, spacious rooms, two- to six-person cabins, badminton, heated pool, and the owners organise canoe hire and horse riding. It's 5.3km northwest of Martel.

★ Manoir de Malagorse   B&B €€
(☑05 65 27 14 83; www.manoir-de-malagorse.fr; Cuzance; d incl breakfast €150-180, ste €280-310; ⊘mid-Mar–mid-Dec; ⊠) In quiet Cuzance, 8km northwest of Martel, this beauty of a B&B offers luxury normally reserved for top-end hotels. Owners Anna and Abel's period house is a chic combo of sleek lines, soothing colours and fluffy fabrics. It's surrounded by 10 private acres, and the four-course home-cooked dinner (€42) is superb. Winter truffle weekends.

Relais Sainte-Anne HOTEL €€

(☑ 05 65 37 40 56; www.relais-sainte-anne.com; rue du Pourtanel; d €95-185, ste €185-275; ☺ Apr–mid-Nov; ☎☒) The pick of places to stay in Martel village, on a quiet lane with 16 individually decorated rooms that blend country comforts with contemporary flair. Its excellent **restaurant** (menus lunch €18-28, dinner €28; ☺ noon-1.30pm Fri-Sun, 7.30-9.30pm daily) uses produce directly from Martel's markets.

★ **Au Hasard Balthazar** REGIONAL CUISINE €€

(☑ 05 65 37 42 01; www.auhasardbalthazar.fr; rue Tournemire; lunch/dinner menus from €18.50/28; ☺ noon-1.30pm Wed-Sun & 7.30-9.30pm Tue-Sat May-Aug, shorter hours Apr & Sep) Local farm Les Bouriettes operates this wonderful shop and restaurant filled with their super products. Friendly proprietors serve regional specialities in the courtyard below the Tour Tournemire, or in the intimate stone dining room. Imagine ingredients such as walnut oil, pigeon confit, foie gras and wine mustard.

ℹ Information

Tourist Office (☑ 05 65 37 43 44; www.tourisme-vallee-dordogne.com; place des Consuls, Martel; ☺10am-noon & 2-6pm Mon-Sat) Has a booklet (€1) and maps of architectural and historical highlights.

East of Cahors

Some of the Lot's best scenery with limestone cliffs along the river valley and undulating fields on its hilltops, is criss-crossed by narrow roads east of Cahors. For example the D662 tracks the banks of the River Lot east from Cahors towards Figeac. This wonderfully scenic region calls for digressions on peaceful back roads as you travel through wonderful villages such as St-Cirq-Lapopie, Figeac and Najac.

St-Cirq-Lapopie

POP 223

Teetering at the crest of a sheer cliff high above the River Lot, minuscule St-Cirq-Lapopie's terracotta-roofed houses and vertiginous streets tumble down the steep hillside, affording incredible valley views. It's one of the most magical settings in the Lot, but in high summer it's packed.

◉ Sights

Central St-Cirq HISTORIC QUARTER

St-Cirq has one long main street leading up to its highlights: the early-16th-century **Gothic** church and a ruined **château**, where you'll be rewarded with a jaw-dropping panorama across the Lot Valley. Many of the village's houses are now **artists' shops** producing pottery, leatherwork and jewellery.

Maison de la Fourdonne CULTURAL CENTRE

(☑ 05 65 31 21 51; www.maisondelafourdonne.com; tours €4; ☺ 2.30-7pm) Small town museum in a Renaissance town house with old memorabilia, pots and archaeological artefacts. Offers guided tours exploring St-Cirq's history (generally in French).

Musée Rignault ART MUSEUM

(☑ 05 65 31 23 22; http://musees.lot.fr; admission €1.50; ☺10am-12.30pm & 2.30-6pm Wed-Mon May-Sep) Eclectic collection of French furniture, African and Chinese art, and rotating exhibitions. Delightful garden.

🛏 Sleeping & Eating

Auberge de Sombral HOTEL, REGIONAL CUISINE €

(☑ 05 65 31 26 08; www.lesombral.com; r €55-80; ☺ restaurant noon-2pm Fri-Wed, 7.30-9.30pm Fri & Sat; ☎) This central, pretty sienna-stone town house has seven cosy doubles and a titchy attic room with modern decor. The restaurant (menus €16.50 to €24) offers Quercy cuisine, such as lamb and trout. Best of all, you'll have the village practically to yourself after dark.

La Plage CAMPGROUND €

(☑ 05 65 30 29 51; www.campingplage.com; sites for tent & 1 person €10-14; ☺ Apr–mid-Oct; ☎) 🛶 Riverside campground on the left bank of the Lot near a small swimming beach, with a slew of amenities including canoe and kayak rental.

★ **Hôtel Le Saint Cirq** HOTEL €€

(☑ 05 65 30 30 30; www.hotel-lesaintcirq.com; Tour de Faure; d €88-128, f/ste from €128/170; @☎☒) This luxurious hotel in the valley below St-Cirq boasts one of the best views of its hilltop profile. Lovely, traditional rooms have terracotta-tiled floors and French windows onto the garden. 'Seigneurale' rooms boast sunken baths, slate bathrooms and the like.

La Tonnelle BISTRO €

(www.brasserie-latonnelle.com; rue de la Peyrolerie; menus €11-20; ☺ noon-2pm & 7.30-9.30pm Apr-Oct) Quick and casual, dig into simple, generous platters of cheese, meats and salads, under a grape-covered pergola.

Le Gourmet Quercynois REGIONAL CUISINE €€

(☑ 05 65 31 21 20; www.restaurant-legourmetquercynois.com; rue de la Peyrolerie; menus €21-37;

GROTTE DU PECH MERLE

Discovered in 1922, the 1200m-long **Grotte du Pech Merle** (☑05 65 31 27 05; www. pechmerle.com; adult/child €10/6; ☉9.30-5pm Apr–mid-Nov) is one of the few decorated caves discovered around the Lot Valley. It has several wonderful galleries of mammoths, bison and dappled horses, as well as unique hand tracings, fingerprints and human figures. Look out for the beautifully preserved adolescent footprint, clearly imprinted in the clay floor.

Entry is by **guided tour** (reserve ahead for English) and includes a museum and 20-minute film (French and English). Reserve ahead by phone in peak season; visitors are limited to 700 per day.

Find it perched high on the hills above the riverside town of Les Cabrerets, 30km northeast of Cahors.

☉noon-2pm & 7.30-9.30pm daily mid-Feb–Dec) St-Cirq's top table offers an enormous menu, ranging from *nougat de porc* to country *cassoulet* (stew). Escape to the little patio to catch evening rays setting over town.

ℹ Information

Tourist Office (☑05 65 31 31 31; www. saint-cirqlapopie.com; place du Sombral; ☉10am-1pm & 2-6pm; 🛜)

ℹ Getting There & Away

St-Cirq is 25km east of Cahors and 44km southwest of Figeac.

BUS

SNCF buses between Cahors (€6.40, 45 minutes) and Figeac (€8.90, one hour, four to five daily) stop at Tour-de-Faure; from there it's 3km uphill to St-Cirq.

CAR

Car parks are at the bottom (€3 per day) and top (€4 per day) of the village.

Figeac

POP 10,515

The buoyant riverside town of Figeac, 70km northeast of Cahors on the River Célé, has a vibrant charm steeped in history. Traffic zips along river boulevards and the fantastic medieval old town has an appealingly lived-in feel. Winding streets are lined with medieval and ornate Renaissance houses, many with open-air galleries on the top floor (once used for drying goods). Founded by Benedictine monks, the town was later an important medieval trading post and pilgrims' stopover.

◉ Sights

The tourist office offers a changing schedule of **tours** (adult/child €6/free; ☉Apr-Oct) of the old town and nearby countryside.

★Medieval Figeac　　　HISTORIC QUARTER
Enter the historic centre of Figeac at place Vival, where the tourist office and a **history museum** occupy the **Hôtel de la Monnaie**, an arcaded 13th-century building where money was exchanged. Purchase their excellent leaflet *Les Clefs de la Ville* (€0.30) for a guide to Figeac's medieval and Renaissance architecture.

Rue de Balène and rue Caviale have the best examples of 14th- and 15th-century houses, many with wooden galleries, timber frames and original stone carvings, while rue de Colomb has fine Renaissance *hôtels particulier*.

Place Champollion is in the heart of the quarter, and behind Musée Champollion, **place des Écritures** is surrounded by medieval buildings and features a modern art replica of the Rosetta Stone by Joseph Kosuth.

★Église St-Sauveur　　　CHURCH
This soaring spot on the Compostela pilgrims' trail, the 11th-century former Benedictine Abbey church, features the exquisite **Notre-Dame-de-Piété chapel**, a 17th-century woodworking masterpiece.

★Musée Champollion　　　MUSEUM
(☑05 65 50 31 08; www.musee-champollion. fr; place Champollion; adult/child €5/2.50; ☉10.30am-6.30pm daily Jul & Aug, shorter hours rest of year) This museum is named after Figeac-born Egyptologist and linguist Jean-François Champollion (1790–1832), whose efforts in deciphering the Rosetta Stone

provided the key for cracking Egyptian hieroglyphics. The lavishly restored mansion where he was born is now devoted to the history of writing, with exhibits ranging from illustrated medieval manuscripts to Chinese writing tools.

🛌 Sleeping & Eating

Figeac's lively **Saturday morning market** takes place under the 19th-century cast-iron arcade on place Carnot, with stalls also filling place Champollion and place Vival.

Hôtel-Café Champollion   HOTEL €
(📞 05 65 34 04 37; hotelchampollion@orange.fr; 3 place Champollion; d €54; ❄ 🛜) Smack in the heart of the old town, this hotel sits above a cool and lively cafe which serves drinks and sandwiches. Bare-bones contemporary rooms feature flat-screen TVs, though some suffer from late-night noise.

Hostellerie de l'Europe   HOTEL €
(📞 05 65 34 10 16; www.hotel-europe-figeac.com; 51 allée Victor Hugo; r €59-75; ⊘ restaurant noon-1.30pm Sun-Thu, 7.30-9.30pm Sat-Thu; ❄ 🛜 🍽) Behind the shuttered façade, up-to-date rooms have spacious bathrooms, though most are short on character. Its restaurant (*menus* €14.50 to €34) features old-fashioned Quercynois dishes. Find it across the river from the old town.

Hôtel des Bains   HOTEL €
(📞 05 65 34 10 89; www.hoteldesbains.fr; 1 rue Griffoul; d €50-75, f €70-96; ❄ 🛜) Basic riverfront hotel with 19 rooms; the best have balconies overlooking the river.

★Hôtel La Grézalide   HOTEL €€
(📞 05 65 11 20 40; www.grezalide.com; Grèzes; d €102-162, tr/f €142/182; 🛜 🍽) You'll need a car to reach this beautiful country estate, 21km west of Figeac in the quaint village of Grèzes, but it's worth the drive. Rooms in the 17th-century manor make maximum use of its architecture, with solid stone and original floorboards. Public rooms display art collections, and the courtyard garden, pool, and fantastic regional restaurant (*menus* €26 to €45) round it all out.

Le Grain de Sel   BISTRO €
(📞 05 65 34 28 53; www.restaurant-legraindesel.com; 4 rue de la République; menus from €13; ⊘ noon-2pm & 7-9.30pm Thu-Mon) Just off place Vival, this is perfect for a quick bite to eat as you walk the old town.

ℹ️ Information

Tourist Office (📞 05 65 34 06 25; www.tourisme-figeac.com; place Vival; ⊘ 9am-12.30pm & 2-6pm Mon-Sat, also 10am-1pm Sun May-Sep; 🛜) Helpful. Has smartphone app, walking tours, transport and activities info.

ℹ️ Getting There & Away

BUS
SNCF buses run west to Cahors (€13.40, 1¾ hours, four daily) via Tour-de-Faure.

TRAIN
Figeac's **train station**, on the south side of the river and served by local bus 7, is at a junction. One key line runs north to Brive-la-Gaillarde (€15.60, 1¼ hours, six daily) and south to Najac (€10.50, 50 minutes, six daily) and Toulouse (€26.40, 2¼ hours, six daily).

Villefranche-de-Rouergue

Villefranche (population 12,496) has its origins as a *bastide* but its modern roads largely subsume it. The main reason to stop is the central arcaded **place Notre Dame** – a typical example of a *bastide* square – which still hosts the lively Thursday morning **market**. Enormous square-pillared 13th-century **Collégiale Notre Dame** (place Notre Dame; ⊘ 8am-noon & 2-6.30pm, closed Sun morning) has choir stalls ornamented with a menagerie of comical and cheeky figures.

The **tourist office** (📞 05 65 45 13 18; www.villefranche.com; promenade du Guiraudet; ⊘ 9am-noon & 2-7pm Mon-Fri, to 6pm Sat) is next to the town hall.

Trains travel to Figeac (€7.50, 35 minutes, every two hours) and Najac (€3.90, 15 minutes, four to six daily).

Najac
POP 763
Magical Najac unfurls like a slender ribbon of stone along a rocky saddle high above a bend in the River Aveyron. Its soaring, turreted fortress is a must: an evocative journey into the past, with superb views from the central keep.

⊙ Sights

The top of the village revolves around central **place du Faubourg**, a beguiling broad square surrounded by timber-framed houses, some from the 13th century. A pedestrianised lane leads 1.2km down the saddle of the hill to the **Porte de la Pique**, near the fortress. Drivable av de la Gare skirts the edge of town to Église St-Jean and the valley and train station below.

★ **Forteresse Royale de Najac**   FORTRESS
(☑ 05 65 29 71 65; adult/child €5/3.50; ⊘ 10.30am-7pm Jul & Aug, 10.30am-1pm & 3-5pm Mar-Jun & Sep-Nov) High on a hilltop 150m above a hairpin bend in the River Aveyron, Najac's fortress looks as if it's fallen from the pages of a fairy tale: slender towers and fluttering flags rise from crenellated ramparts, surrounded on every side by dizzying *falaises* (cliffs) dropping to the valley floor below. Its crumbling architecture is somehow beautifully preserved, and the view from the central keep is unsurprisingly superb.

Look for the secret passage leading out of St Julian's Chapel, the dungeon which imprisoned Knights Templar, and symbols carved in walls by stone masons.

A masterpiece of medieval military planning (check out the extended loopholes that allowed two archers to fire at once), and practically unassailable thanks to its position, Najac was a key stronghold during the Middle Ages, and was hotly contested by everyone from English warlords to the powerful counts of Toulouse. Richard the Lionheart signed a treaty here in 1185.

Reach the fortress via a steep path from the bottom of town.

Église St-Jean   CHURCH
(⊘ 10am-noon & 2-6pm daily May-Sep, Sat & Sun only Apr & Oct) Two hundred metres below the Forteresse Royale de Najac is the austere 13th-century Église St-Jean, constructed and financed by local villagers on the orders of the Inquisition as punishment for their heretical tendencies.

🛏 Sleeping & Eating

Najac is most often visited as a day trip.

★ **Oustal del Barry**   HOTEL, REGIONAL CUISINE €
(☑ 05 65 29 74 32; www.oustaldelbarry.com; place du Faubourg; s €49, d €58-78; ❀) The best place to stay in town is this wonderfully worn and rustic *auberge,* with haphazard rooms filled with trinkets and solid furniture to match its venerable timber-framed façade. Try for a room with a balcony. Visit its renowned country restaurant (*menus* €20 to €54) for traditional southwest cuisine.

Gîtes de la Bastide   APARTMENTS €
(☑ 05 65 29 71 01; www.gitesdelabastidenajac.fr; rue de l'Église; 2-/4-/6-person apt from €58/70/95) Fully stocked apartments at the foot of the fortress; rates vary by time of year.

La Salamandre   REGIONAL CUISINE €
(☑ 05 65 29 74 09; rue du Barriou; lunch/dinner menus from €12.50/19; ⊘ 10.30am-2.30pm Fri-Wed, 7-9.30pm Tue, Wed, Fri & Sat) Simple but charming, this little restaurant is a treat for its local dishes and wonderful panoramic terrace overlooking the fortress.

ℹ Information

Tourist Office (☑ 05 65 29 72 05; www.tourisme-najac.com; 25 place du Faubourg; ⊘ 9.30am-noon & 2.30-5pm Mon-Fri, 9.30am-noon Sat & Sun, closed Sun & Mon Oct-Apr) Occasional French-language tours (adult/child €3/free).

ℹ Getting There & Away

The train station, served by an automatic machine, is in the valley 1.2km below Najac. Trains go to Figeac (€10.50, 50 minutes, six daily) and Toulouse (€18.40, 1½ hours, six daily)

Atlantic Coast

POP 4,717,460

Includes ➡

Best Places to Eat

➡ La Ribaudière (p628)

➡ Cocotte Restaurant (p615)

➡ Marché des Capucins (p633)

➡ Le Thiers Temp (p624)

➡ Le Cheverus Café (p633)

Best Places to Stay

➡ Maison Flore (p619)

➡ Hotel Sōzō (p615)

➡ La Maison Douce (p626)

➡ Ecolodge des Chartrons (p631)

➡ L'Hôtel Particulier (p632)

Why Go?

With quiet country roads winding through vine-striped hills and wild stretches of coastal sand interspersed with misty islands, the Atlantic coast is where France gets back to nature. Much more laid-back than the Med (but with almost as much sunshine), this is the place to slow the pace right down.

But the Atlantic coast can do cities and culture as well. There's bourgeois Bordeaux with its wonderful old centre, lively Nantes with its wealth of fascinating museums, and salty La Rochelle with its breathtaking aquarium and beautiful portside setting.

The one thing that unites the people of this area is a love of the finer things in life. The region's exceptional wine is famous worldwide, and to accompany it you'll find ocean-fresh seafood wherever you go, plus plenty of regional delicacies – including crêpes in the north, snails in the centre and foie gras in the south.

When to Go
Bordeaux

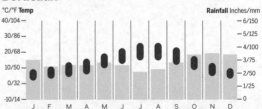

May–Jun Ducklings are splashing around the Marais Poitevin and it's a prime time to visit La Rochelle.

Jun–Sep The beaches are bathed in sunshine but there are no high-season crowds.

Sep–Oct Grape-harvesting season around Bordeaux, and oyster and *cèpe* mushroom season all over.

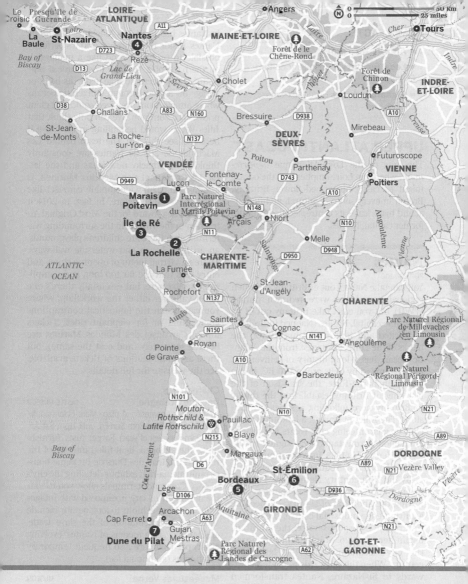

Atlantic Coast Highlights

① Gliding through the emerald-green waters of the **Marais Poitevin** (p619), the 'Green Venice'

② Diving deep under the waves and coming face to face with wobbly jellyfish and jaw-gnashing sharks at La Rochelle's incredible **aquarium** (p621)

③ Cycling the smooth, flat bike paths criss-crossing the sunbaked **Île de Ré** (p625)

④ Riding a three-storey, 60-tonne mechanical elephant in **Nantes** (p612)

⑤ Touring the dramatically floodlit buildings and monuments making up the world's largest Unesco-

listed urban area in central **Bordeaux** (p628)

⑥ Satisfing your craving for wine in **St-Émilion** (p638), home to some of the world's most famous wines

⑦ Admiring the views from the summit of the **Dune du Pilat** (p642), Europe's highest sand dune

FAST FACTS

→ **Area** 44,113 sq km

→ **Local industry** tourism, agriculture, fishing

→ **Signature drinks** Bordeaux wines, cognac

UPPER ATLANTIC COAST

This bite of the Loire-Atlantique *département*, where the Loire empties into the ocean, might as easily be termed 'lower Brittany'. Breton in every sense – cultural, architectural and historical – its centrepiece is Brittany's former capital, Nantes.

Nantes

POP 290,100

You can take Nantes out of Brittany (as when regional boundaries were redrawn during WWII), but you can't take Brittany out of its long-time capital, Nantes (Naoned in Breton).

Spirited and innovative, this city on the banks of the Loire, 55km east from the Atlantic Ocean, has a long history of reinventing itself. Founded by Celts around 70 BC, in AD 937 Alain Barbe-Torte, the grandson of the last king of Brittany, established the duchy of Brittany here following a series of invasions. The Edict of Nantes, a landmark royal charter guaranteeing civil rights to France's Huguenots (Protestants), was signed in the city by Henri IV in 1598. Its revocation in 1685 led to a Huguenot exodus from the region.

By the 18th century Nantes was France's foremost port, and in the 19th century – following the abolition of slavery – it became a cutting-edge industrial centre; the world's first public transport service, the omnibus, began here in 1826. Shipbuilding anchored the city's economy until the late 20th century. When the shipyards relocated westwards to St-Nazaire, Nantes transformed itself into a thriving student and cultural hub. The city centre has now nudged past Bordeaux as the country's sixth-largest metropolis, and it's growing, with one in two Nantais today aged under 40.

⦿ Sights

★ **Les Machines
de l'Île de Nantes** THEME PARK
(www.lesmachines-nantes.fr; Parc des Chantiers, bd Léon Bureau; adult/child €8/6.50; ⊘10am-7pm Jul-Aug, hours vary rest of year) The quirkiest sight in Nantes has to be Les Machines de l'Île de Nantes. Inside this fantasy world it's perfectly possible to prance around like a maharajah on the back of a 45-tonne **mechanical elephant** with a secret lounge inside its belly, or voyage on a boat through dangerous oceans where attacks from oversized squid and giant prawns are common. We can only think that Jules Verne would be smiling in his grave if he could see this lot! The team behind Les Machines de l'Île de Nantes are constantly thinking up whacky new ideas and the latest, **Le Carrousel des Mondes Marines**, is a 25m-high, 22m-wide funfair carousel like you've never seen before. In fact, in 2014 it won the Thea Award for the 'Most Original Attraction in the World'. In the surrounding waterfront area there are children's playgrounds, an artificial beach and waterside walkways. There's a virtual menu of opening times and entry fees that are far too long and complicated to list here, but essentially there's one ticket valid for either the workshop, where you can watch the fantastical contraptions being built, or for elephant rides. Tickets for Le Carrousel des Mondes Marines are bought separately (and cost the same), but there are combinations of tickets available. See the website for full details.

**Château des
Ducs de Bretagne** CASTLE, MUSEUM
(www.chateau-nantes.fr; 4 place Marc Elder; adult/child €5/3; ⊘9am-8pm Sun-Fri, until 11pm Sat Jul-Aug, 9am-7pm rest of year) Forget fusty furnishings, the stripped, light-filled interior of the restored Château des Ducs de Bretagne houses multimedia-rich exhibits detailing the city's history. Computer terminals allow you to tour the old medieval city, juxtaposed with images of today. Other exhibits to look out for include sobering documentation of the slave trade, and vintage scale models of Nantes' evolving cityscape. There are also frequent temporary exhibitions (additional fee).

Musée Jules Verne MUSEUM
(www.julesverne.nantes.fr; 3 rue de l'Hermitage; adult/child €3/1.50; ⊘10am-noon & 2-6pm Wed-Sat, 10am-noon Sun) Overlooking the river, this is a magical museum with 1st-edition books, hand-edited manuscripts and cardboard theatre cut-outs. Child-friendly interactive displays introduce or reintroduce you to the work of Jules Verne, who was born in Nantes in 1828. Signs are in French but Verne's books, such as *Around the World in 80 Days*, are so well known that it's worthwhile visiting regardless. Hours and closing days vary

throughout the year – see the website. The museum is a 2km walk downriver from the town centre.

Musée d'Histoire Naturelle MUSEUM
(www.museum.nantes.fr; 12 rue Voltaire; adult/child €3.50/free; ☉10am-6pm Wed-Mon) The fascinating collection of minerals, fossils and stuffed animals includes a huge whale skeleton. There are frequent temporary exhibitions.

Jardin des Plantes PARK
(bd Stalingrad; ☉8.30am-8pm late Mar–late Oct, shorter hours rest of year) Founded in the early 19th century, the Jardin des Plantes is one of the most exquisite botanical gardens in France, filled with flower beds, duck ponds, fountains and towering redwoods (sequoias). There are hothouses and a **children's playground** at the northern end. The gardens are opposite the train station.

Cathédrale St-Pierre et St-Paul CATHEDRAL
(place St-Pierre; ☉8am-7pm Apr-Oct, to 6pm rest of year) Inside the Flamboyant Gothic Cathédrale St-Pierre et St-Paul, the **tomb of François II** (r 1458–88), Duke of Brittany, and of his second wife, Marguerite de Foix, is a masterpiece of Renaissance art.

🛏 Sleeping

Many of the hotels in Nantes charge considerably more during the working week, so if you're looking to save some euros come at the weekend.

Hôtel du Château HOTEL €
(☑02 40 74 17 16; 5 place de la Duchesse Anne; s/d/tw from €45/51/66; ☉reception open 7.30am-1.30pm & 5.30-10pm Mon-Fri, from 9am Sat & Sun; ☞) This cosy little establishment opposite the château actually thinks it is a castle. Short histories of various kings and queens grace the doors to the rooms, and the bedrooms themselves have an equally royal flavour with elegant bedspreads and old-fashioned bedside tables. Some rooms have views of the château.

★Hôtel Pommeraye BOUTIQUE HOTEL €€
(☑02 40 48 78 79; www.hotel-pommeraye.com; 2 rue Boileau; s/d €94/99; ❋☞) Sleek and chic, this is more art gallery than hotel. The rooms have shimmering short-pile carpets and textured walls in shades of pale grey, gold, chocolate and violet. The reception and other common areas are adorned in constantly evolving eye-catching art; over the years we've seen retro art-house cinema, architects drawings and musings, hedgehog-like lamps and, where you'd normally find ancient gargoyles, pop-art faces.

Hôtel Voltaire Opéra HOTEL €€
(☑02 40 73 31 04; www.hotelvoltaireoperanantes.com; 10 rue Gresset; r from €99; ☞) The compact rooms here are decorated in colourful squiggles and have very comfortable beds. After enjoying those beds, head downstairs and dive into a breakfast spread that includes homemade jams and artisan honey. The staff also get big points for being so welcoming.

Hôtel Amiral HOTEL €€
(☑02 40 69 20 21; www.hotel-nantes.fr; 26bis rue Scribe; s/d weekdays €96/99, weekend €59/62; ☞) The rooms at this excellent little hotel are fairly plain but the common areas are funky and the breakfast room a commotion of jungle plants. The family who run it are really helpful. Discounts are common when it's quiet.

Hôtel La Pérouse DESIGN HOTEL €€
(☑02 40 89 75 00, www.hotel laperouse.fr; 3 allée Duquesne; r from €118; ❋☞) Long considered the best hotel in the city, La Pérouse has recently been overtaken by newer offerings but even so its unique styling – which, by the use of a wooden gangway entrance and canvas

---

ATLANTIC COAST FOR KIDS

The Atlantic coast has plenty to keep youngsters and teenagers happy.

➡ While the big boys and girls surf the waves, little 'uns can build sandcastles on the beautiful beaches of Cap Ferret (p643).

➡ From blennies to piranhas and seahorses to giant rays, there's plenty to excite at La Rochelle's high-tech aquarium (p621).

➡ If the kids have square eyes from watching too much TV, show them the future of film at Futuroscope (p618).

➡ There's something about a house-sized mechanical elephant that just cannot fail to impress at Les Machines de l'Île de Nantes (p612).

➡ Spot storks, kingfishers and pond tortoises at Le Teich Parc Ornithologique (p643).

Nantes

ATLANTIC COAST

200 m
0.1 miles

La Maison (150m)

R Henri IV 5

Hôtel Sozo (500m); (600m); Jardin des Plantes (600m)

Cours John Kennedy

Le Lieu Unique (200m)

R Prémion

2

R Marc Elder

Pl Marc Elder

R des États

Tourist Office

R des Petites Écuries

R du Château

R de l'Emery

R de la Marne

R de Verdun

R de Strasbourg

R Mathelin Rodier

Pl St-Pierre

R du Refuge

1

Pl du Pilori

Pl du Change

R de la Juverie

R de la Baclerie

Pl du Bouffay

R de la Paix

R du Bouffay

Cours Franklin Roosevelt

Allée Baco

R Crucy

Square Elisa Mercer

Eurolines

Allée de la Maison Rouge

Île de Nantes (500m); Aéroport International Nantes Atlantique (12km)

Southbound Bus Station

Cours Olivier de Clisson

Allée Duguay Trouin

Allée Brancas

Allée Jean Bart

R des Halles

R de la Barillerie

R des Trois Croissants

R du Moulin

Hôtel de Ville

R de l'Hôtel de Ville

16

R de Beauregard

Cours des 50 Otages

Allée Duquesne

14

6

R de Feltre

R Cacault

R Léopold Cassegrain

Tour de Bretagne

Pl de Bretagne

R Président Édouard Hérriot

R de Budapest

R Jean Jaurès

Palais de Justice

Pl Aristide Briand

R Mercoeur

R Marceau

R la Fayette

R du Calvaire

R Copernic

R Franklin

R Racine

R Voltaire

Le Grappillon (70m)

3

8

Pl Graslin

R Jean-Jacques Rousseau

R Piron

9

12

13

R Santeuil

Passage Pommeray

Pl de la Bourse

Pl du Commerce

Square JB Daviais

Machines de l'île de Nantes (600m); Musée Jules Verne (2km)

R du Couëdic

R d'Orléans

Pl Royale

R de la Fosse

R de Guérande

11

19

20

21

R Contrescarpe

R Rubens

7

R Boileau

R du Chapeau Rouge

R Scribe

R Molière

R Corneille

Théâtre Graslin

17

18

4

R Crébillon

Pl Graslin

10

15

Nantes

sail-like curtains, reflects the city's shipbuilding traditions – is still worth considering. It was the first hotel in Nantes to be awarded an EU Ecolabel.

★ **Hotel Sōzō**   DESIGN HOTEL €€€
(☎ 02 51 82 40 00; www.sozohotel.fr; 16 rue Frédéric Cailliand; r from €197; 🖥) The architects who designed this place must have been in seventh-heaven when asked to transform a graceful old chapel into a luxury boutique hotel. The main features of the chapel have been retained, including the stained-glass windows, but sitting happily alongside are dozens of virgin-white angel wings, garish cartoon art and purple and red lights. The hotel would be impressive enough on its own, but the fact that it was the first time a church had been converted into a hotel in France meant that it made the national news. The critical acclaim it has since received means it's likely to be the first of many.

✖ Eating

For cosmopolitan dining, head to the medieval Bouffay quarter, a couple of blocks west of the château around rue de la Juiverie, rue des Petites Écuries and rue de la Bâclerie. Breton crêperies abound throughout town; west of cours des 50 Otages, rues Jean-Jacques Rousseau and Santeuil are lined with eateries.

Le Grappillon   FRENCH, INTERNATIONAL €
(4 rue Kleber; menu €14, mains from €9; ⊘ lunch from 11.45am, dinner from 7.45pm Mon-Sat) Covered in vines and with an interior dominated by an overloaded old dresser, this hidden-away place feels like an old French farmhouse. The flavours dished up, though, are much less traditional and are heavily influenced by the French Indian Ocean territories. There are only three or four tables inside (and a couple outside on fine days) so get there early to ensure a spot.

Crêperie Heb-Ken   BRETON €
(☎ 02 40 48 79 03; 5 rue de Guérande; crêpes €2.50-13.80; ⊘ noon-10pm Mon-Sat; 🖐) Dozens of varieties of crêpe (such as a delicious trout-and-leek combo, or honey, lemon and almond for dessert) are made with love at this cosy spot. A sure sign of its authenticity: you can order *luit ribot* (thickened milk) by the *bolée* (drinking bowl) or pitcher.

★ **Cocotte Restaurant**   FRENCH €€
(☎ 02 40 84 12 44; www.cocotte-restaurant.fr; 27 rue Fouré; mains €20-25, menus €14-32; ⊘ noon-2.30pm & 7.30-10pm Tue-Fri, until 11pm Sat) Housed within a former neighbourhood butcher-shop, and still with the wonderfully retro mosaic sign, this old-fashioned restaurant will help your taste buds reacquaint with all that is sublime about traditional French cooking. Poultry, from chicken to duck and pigeon, dominates the menu but a sprinkling of seafood adds salt to the mix.

Les Pieds dans le Plat   MODERN FRENCH €€
(☎ 02 40 69 25 15; www.lespiedsdansleplat. fr; 13 rue Jean-Jacques Rousseau; mains €13-15; ⊘ 11.30am-midnight) This modern French bistro has exposed stone walls, colourful paint and all the old favourites given a creative new twist. It's the flavour of the month at the moment and advance reservations are advised.

> **ⓘ NANTES CITY PASS**
> ⋯⋯⋯⋯⋯⋯⋯⋯⋯⋯⋯⋯⋯⋯⋯⋯⋯
> The **Pass Nantes** (24/48/72hr €25/35/45), available from the tourist office, includes unlimited bus and tram transport as well as entry to museums and monuments, and extras like a free guided tour and shopping discounts.

BESIDE THE SEASIDE

Pack your bucket and spade for any of these worthwhile coastal excursions from Nantes. The classic seaside town of **Le Croisic** centres on a pretty, half-timbered fishing harbour where shrimps, lobsters, crabs, scallops and sea bass are unloaded. Talking of fish, the town's aquarium is well worth visiting. From Nantes, trains to Le Croisic cost from €16.40. **St-Nazaire**, where cruise ships (including the *Queen Mary II*) are built, is worth a stop on the way. Also along this stretch of coast is the glamorous belle-époque resort of **La Baule**, boasting an enormous beach.

ATLANTIC COAST NANTES

Mademoiselle B   FRENCH €€

(☑ 02 40 41 17 21; 13 rue Armand Brossard; mains €10, menu €18.50; ⊘noon-2.30pm & 7-11pm) There's not much choice on the menu at this backstreet local favourite. In fact there's little point in actually having a menu because they only make one main dish a day, so like it or not that's what you'll have. Fortunatley, you almost certainly will like it.

La Bouche à Oreille   BISTRO €€

(☑ 02 40 73 00 25; 14 rue Jean-Jacques Rousseau; menus from €13, mains €15; ⊘noon-3pm & 7pm-midnight) With checked tablecloths and curtains, this is a classic bistro in the heart of Nantes. Although it mixes things up with a few French classics, it really specialises in the heavy food of the eastern city of Lyon – so that means things like sausages and pork in lentils. Be warned that portions are of gut-busting proportions.

Restaurant l'u.ni   MODERN FRENCH €€€

(☑ 02 40 75 53 05; 36 rue Foure; menus from €22; ⊘noon-1.30pm & 7.30-9.30pm Wed-Sat, noon-1.30pm Sun) Slick, contemporary and the hot ticket of the moment. This place, a short walk from the city centre, melds classic French ingredients such as the humble asparagus with rather un-French partners such as coconut milk. The result makes people return again and again.

Brasserie La Cigale   BRASSERIE €€€

(☑ 02 51 84 94 94; 4 place Graslin; breakfast from €15, mains €15-27, menus from €15; ⊘7.30am-midnight) No visit to Nantes is complete without joining the high-class old ladies with perfectly manicured hair for fresh seafood or French classics at the 1890s Brasserie La Cigale. Several salons of original gilded tilework and frescoed ceilings are attended by white-aproned waiters.

🍷 Drinking & Nightlife

Nantes has no shortage of lively spots for a drink. Two prime areas are the medieval Bouffay quarter and the **Hangar à Bananes** (www.hangarabananes.com; 21 quai des Antilles; ⊘daily till late), a former banana-ripening warehouse on the Île de Nantes. Here you'll find over a dozen restaurants, bars and clubs (and combinations thereof), each hipper than the next. The front terraces of most face onto the Anneaux de Buren, a permanent art installation of metal rings that light up at night.

Café Cult   CAFE, BAR

(www.cafe-cult.com; 2 rue des Carmes; ⊘2pm-2am Mon & Sat, from noon Tue-Fri) Squeezed in a dark, half-timbered house and hung with local art, this bohemian place draws a student crowd and sometimes hosts concerts. During the day it serves cheap but palate-pleasing lunches.

La Maison   BAR

(4 rue Lebrun; ⊘3pm-2am) You have to see it to believe this trip of a place, decorated room by room like a home furnished in *bad* 1970s taste, playing (what else?) house music. It's a popular cafe in daylight hours as well.

☆ Entertainment

A good website where you can find out what's on is www.leboost.com (in French). The tourist office website (www.nantes-tourisme.com) lists upcoming events in English.

★ Le Lieu Unique   THEATRE

(www.lelieuunique.com; 2 rue de la Biscuiterie) Within the one-time Lu biscuit factory (crowned by a replica of its original tower, which you can ascend for €2), this industrial-chic space is the venue for dance and theatre performances, eclectic and electronic music, philosophical sessions and contemporary art exhibitions.

Also here is an always-buzzing restaurant (mains a bargain-priced €8 to €10), a polished concrete bar with deckchairs set out by the water in summer, and a decadent *hammam* (Turkish bath) complex in the basement.

Cinéma Katorza   CINEMA

(www.katorza.fr; 3 rue Corneille) An art-house cinema screening the latest in foreign and alternative films, much of which are in the original language.

Théâtre Graslin
THEATRE, OPERA

(☑02 40 69 77 18; www.angers-nantes-opera.com; place Graslin) Constructed in 1788, the beautifully refurbished Théâtre Graslin is the home of the Nantes Opera.

Shopping

Pedestal statues symbolise traditional Nantais industries inside the ornate three-tiered shopping arcade **Passage Pommeray** (off rue de la Fosse), built in 1843.

George-Gautier
CHOCOLATE

(9 rue de la Fosse; ⊙9am-7pm Tue-Sat) When Jules Verne was a young boy he too was awed by this beautiful chocolate shop's chandeliers, marble floors and circular velvet banquette, where Nantais have waited while their orders were filled since 1823. Handmade specialities include *mascarons* (finely ground chocolates in a dark-chocolate shell) and a rainbow of hard-boiled sweets.

Yellowkorner
GALLERY

(☑02 28 44 91 82; www.yellowkorner.com; 7 rue Crébillon) It's hard to know whether this is merely a shop or a photographic art gallery. Certainly the photos are for sale, but without doubt they are superb works of photographic art.

ⓘ Information

Tourist Office (☑02 72 64 04 79; www.levoyage anantes.fr; rue des États; ⊙9am-7pm daily late Jun-late Aug, 10am-6pm Mon-Sat, 10am-5pm Sun rest of year) Helpful tourist office.

ⓘ Getting There & Away

AIR

Aéroport International Nantes-Atlantique (www.nantes.aeroport.fr) The airport is 12km southeast of town.

BUS

The Lila bus web covers the entire Loire-Atlantique *département*. Tickets cost €2 per ride.

Eurolines (☑08 92 89 90 91; www.eurolines. com; allée de la Maison Rouge) has an office in town.

TRAIN

The **train station** (27 bd de Stalingrad) is well connected to most of the country. Destinations include the following:

Bordeaux (from €51.10, four hours, three or four daily)

La Rochelle (from €28.90, 1¾ hours, three or four daily)

Paris Gare Montparnasse (from €64, two hours, 15 to 20 daily)

Tickets and information are also available at the **SNCF ticket office** (12 place de la Bourse, La Bourse; ⊙10am-6.30pm Mon-Fri, to 6pm Sat) in the city centre.

ⓘ Getting Around

TO/FROM THE AIRPORT

A *navette* (shuttle) bus links the airport with the Gare Centrale bus-and-tram hub and the train station's southern entrance (€7.50, 20 minutes) from about 5.30am until 11pm.

BUS & TRAM

The **TAN network** (www.tan.fr) includes three modern tram lines that intersect at the Gare Centrale (Commerce), the main bus/tram transfer point. Buses run from 6.45am to 10pm. Night services continue until 12.30am. Bus/tram tickets (from €1.50) can be individually purchased from bus (but not tram) drivers and at tram-stop ticket machines. They're valid for one hour after being time-stamped. A *ticket journalier*, good for 24 hours, costs €4.60; time-stamp it only the first time you use it.

TAXI

To order a taxi, call ☑02 53 45 77 96.

CENTRAL ATLANTIC COAST

The Poitou-Charentes region, midway along the Atlantic coast, scoops up a potpourri of attractions – from the history-rich capital, Poitiers, to the portside panache of La Rochelle, the languid beaches of Île de Ré, and the eponymous home of Cognac.

Poitiers

POP 91,300

Inland from the coast, history-steeped Poitiers was founded by the Pictones, a Gaulish tribe. The city rose to prominence as the former capital of Poitou, the region governed by the Counts of Poitiers in the Middle Ages. A pivotal turning point came in AD 732, when somewhere near Poitiers (the exact site is not known) the cavalry of Charles Martel defeated the Muslim forces of Abd ar-Rahman, governor of Córdoba, thus ending Muslim attempts to conquer France. The city's remarkable Romanesque churches are in part a legacy of Eleanor of Aquitaine's financial support. Poitiers has one of the oldest universities in the country, established in 1432 and today a lynchpin of this lively city.

◉ Sights

Église Notre Dame la Grande   CHURCH
(place Charles de Gaulle) Every evening from 21 June to the third weekend in September, spectacular colours are cinematically projected onto the west façade of the Romanesque Église Notre Dame la Grande. The earliest parts of the church date from the 11th century; three of the five choir chapels were added in the 15th century, with the six chapels along the northern wall of the nave added in the 16th century.

Palais des Comtes de Poitou   HISTORIC BUILDING
(☑05 49 50 22 00; place Alphonse Lepetit; ◷8.30am-noon & 1.30-5pm Mon-Fri) FREE Today it houses the law courts, but nearly a thousand years ago this stunning building was the seat of the Counts of Poitou and Dukes of Aquitaine. Its most impressive feature is the dining hall constructed in the late 12th century by that local lass with big dreams, Eleanor of Aquitaine.

In its time this 50m-long dining hall was considered one of the largest in Europe. Despite the rather dull proceedings that normally take place inside the building today, it's possible to visit and relive the pomp of the past – but don't expect to be seated for dinner in the great hall!

Baptistère St-Jean   CHURCH
(rue Jean Jaurès; admission €1; ◷10.30am-12.30pm & 3-6pm Wed-Mon Apr-Oct, 2.30-4.30pm Wed-Mon Nov-Mar) Constructed in the 4th and 6th centuries on Roman foundations, Baptistère St-Jean, 100m south of Cathédrale St-Pierrel, was redecorated in the 10th century and used as a parish church. The octagonal hole under the frescoes was used for total-immersion baptisms, practised until the 7th century.

Cathédrale St-Pierre   CHURCH
(rue de la Cathédrale) The 13th-century stained-glass window illustrating the Crucifixion and the Ascension at the far end of the choir of the Gothic style Cathédrale St-Pierre is one of the oldest in France.

Musée Ste-Croix   MUSEUM
(www.musees-poitiers.org; 3 rue Jean Jaurès; adult/child €4/free, €2 Sun; ◷10am-noon & 1.15-8pm Tue 10am-noon & 1.15-6pm Wed-Fri, 10am-noon & 2-6pm Sat & Sun Jun-Sep, shorter hours rest of year) Seven signed statues by Camille Claudel are the highlight of this little museum, which also hosts changing exhibitions.

⌸ Sleeping

In addition to chains such as Ibis, Poitiers has a handful of atmospheric, well-located hotels.

Hôtel de l'Europe   HISTORIC HOTEL €
(☑05 49 88 12 00; www.hotel-europe-poitiers.com; 39 rue Carnot; s/d/tw €67/67/75; ☏) Behind a dramatically recessed entrance, the main building of this elegant, very un-two-star-like hotel dates from 1710, with a sweeping staircase, oversized rooms and refined furnishings. It has good wheelchair access, and the annexe has modern rooms for the same price.

Le Grand Hôtel   HISTORIC HOTEL €€
(☑05 49 60 90 60; www.grandhotelpoitiers.fr; 28 rue Carnot; r from €86; ✲☏) There's nothing fancy about Poitiers' premier hotel. It's just solid, old-fashioned value all the way. Faux art-deco furnishings and fittings fill the public areas with character, and rooms are spacious and well equipped.

✗ Eating

Prime dining spots tend to be south of place du Maréchal Leclerc.

La Serrurerie   FRENCH €
(☑05 49 41 05 14; www.laserrurerie.com; 28 rue des Grandes Écoles; menu €13, mains €10-17.50; ◷7.30am-2am) Hectically busy, this mosaic-and-steel bistro-bar is Poitiers' communal lounge/dining room. A chalked blackboard menu lists specialities like *tournedos* (thick slices) of salmon, pastas and a crème brûlée you'll be dreaming about until your next visit.

ℹ Information

Tourist Office (☑05 49 41 21 24; www.ot-poitiers.fr; 45 place Charles de Gaulle; ◷10am-7pm Mon-Sat, 10am-6pm Sun mid-Jun–mid-Sep, 9.30am-6pm Mon-Sat mid-Sep–mid-Jun) Near Église Notre Dame.

ℹ Getting There & Away

The **train station** (☑36 35; bd du Grand Cerf) has direct links to Bordeaux (from €41, 1¾ hours), La Rochelle (from €19, 1½ hours) and many other cities including Paris' Gare Montparnasse (from €57, 1½ hours, 12 daily).

Around Poitiers

Futuristic theme park **Futuroscope** (☑05 49 49 11 12; www.futuroscope.com; av René Monory, Chasseneuil-du-Poitou; adult/child €42/32; ◷10am-dark, closed Jan–mid-Feb) takes you whizzing through space, diving into the deep-blue ocean depths and racing around city streets on a close encounter with creatures of the future, among many other space-age cinematic experiences. To keep things cutting edge, one-third of the attractions change annually. Many are motion-seat set-ups requiring a minimum height of 120cm, but there's a play area for littlies with miniature cars and so on.

Allow at least five hours to see the major attractions; two days to see everything. Futuroscope's numerous hotels are bookable through the website, or directly at the lodging desk.

Futuroscope is 10km north of Poitiers in Jaunay-Clan (take exit 28 off the A10). TGV trains link the park's TGV station with cities including Paris and Bordeaux; times and prices are similar to those to/from Poitiers.

Local Vitalis buses 1 and E link Futuroscope (Parc de Loisirs stop) with Poitiers' train station (€1.30, 30 minutes); there are one to two buses an hour from 6.15am until 9.30pm (11.30pm in July and August).

Marais Poitevin

The **Parc Naturel Interrégional du Marais Poitevin** (www.parc-marais-poitevin.fr) is a tranquil bird-filled wetland dubbed the Venise Verte (Green Venice) due to the duckweed that turns its maze of waterways emerald green each spring and summer. Covering some 800 sq km of wet and drained marsh, the marshlands are interspersed with villages and woods threaded by canals and bike paths. The whole area is becoming increasingly popular with domestic tourists, and if you want somewhere you can really melt into rural life, the Marais Poitevin waterways are unbeatable. There are two main bases from which to punt out across the waterways: the small honey-coloured town of **Coulon** and, our favourite, the romantic and pretty village of **Arçais**.

Getting to either Coulon or Arçais is difficult in anything other than your own car.

🏃 Activities

Boating and **cycling** are the only ways to satisfactorily explore the area. From the waterfront in either Arçais or Coulon (or many other villages in the area) there is no shortage of operators who hire out bikes, as well as flat-bottomed boats or kayaks for watery tours. Almost all of the operators offer a pretty identical package for near identical rates so we haven't named specific operators here. Prices for boats cost €13 to €15 per hour or €29 to €35 per half-day. Kayaks are a euro or two more expensive and guided boat trips are also available from most operators (from €25 per hour). Bike rental is equally widely available and costs range from €8 to €10 per hr and from €15 per half-day.

🛏 Sleeping & Eating

🛏 Arçais & Around

⭐ **Maison Flore** BOUTIQUE HOTEL €
(☑ 05 49 76 27 11; www.maisonflore.com; rue du Grand Port, Arçais; s/d/tr €67/77/90; ⊗ closed Christmas–mid-Feb; 🕿; 🚲 On the Arçais waterfront, this wonderfully romantic 10-room guesthouse, in which every room is painted and decorated in the colours and style of local marsh plants such as the pale-green angelica or bright, purple iris, is one of the most enjoyable and peaceful places to stay on the French Atlantic coast.

There's a cosy guest lounge with books and board games and the staff also deserve points for the warmth they show to their guests; during one of our stays here they even went so far as to stage an Easter egg hunt for the children.

⭐ **La Récré** PIZZERIA, CRÊPERIE €
(☑ 02 51 87 10 11; 24 Chemin du Holage, Damuix; mains €8-10; ⊗ noon-2.30pm & 6-10pm) Four kilometres from Arçais, in the equally pretty riverside town of Damuix, the former village school has been converted into this friendly and unusual crêperie and pizzeria. It's, appropriately, child-friendly with a large outdoor playground and an entire classroom full of games and toys. Not surprisingly then every young family for miles around seems to come here to eat!

Restaurant Ma Gourmandise FRENCH €€
(☑ 05 49 24 13 64; 1 Place de l'Église; mains €15-17, menu €15; ⊗ noon-2.30pm & 7-9pm) In the heart of Arçais this reliable place is situated inside a delicious old stone building and offers refined traditional French bistro fare.

🛏 Coulon

Hôtel-Restaurant Le Central HOTEL €
(☑ 05 49 35 90 20; www.hotel-lecentral-coulon.com; 4 rue d'Autremont, Coulon; s/d/tw from €64/76/81, menus €20-45, mains €20-23; ⊗ hotel closed Sun evening Oct-late Mar, restaurant noon-1.30pm & 7.45-9pm Tue-Sat, noon-1.30pm Sun; ❋🕿) Coulon's flashiest accommodation comprises wood-panelled rooms, some overlooking a garden. Sublime dining is to be had at the in-house restaurant, where specialities include crispy eel and a mouth-watering cheeseboard.

Hôtel au Marais   HOTEL €€
(☑ 05 49 35 90 43; 46-48 quai Lovis-Tardy, Coulon; s/d €70/80; 🐾) Split between two old sand-castle-coloured buildings, this hotel has fairly unexciting rooms but the setting, overlooking the river, is hard to beat.

La Rochelle

POP 77,400

Known as La Ville Blanche (the White City), La Rochelle has luminous limestone façades that glow in the bright coastal sunlight. One of France's foremost seaports from the 14th to 17th centuries, the city has arcaded walkways, half-timbered houses (protected from the salt air by slate tiles) and ghoulish gargoyles, rich reminders of its seafaring past. The early French settlers of Canada, including the founders of Montreal, set sail from here in the 17th century.

This 'white city' is also commendably green, with innovative public transport and open spaces. It's child-friendly too, with lots of activities for little visitors.

La Rochelle's late 20th-century district of Les Minimes was built on reclaimed land, and now has one of the largest marinas in the country. Unlike the Med with its motor cruisers, the 3500 moorings here are mostly

La Rochelle

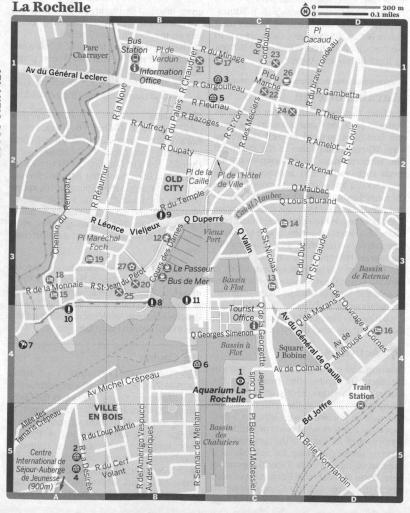

used by yachts, which fill the harbour with billowing spinnakers.

◉ Sights & Activities

★ **Aquarium La Rochelle** AQUARIUM
(www.aquarium-larochelle.com; quai Louis Prunier; adult/child €15/11.50, audioguide €3; ⊙9am-11pm Jul-Aug, 9am-8pm Apr-Jun & Sep, 10am-8pm Oct-Mar) La Rochelle's number-one tourist attraction is this state-of-the-art family-friendly aquarium. A visit begins by descending in a clunky old 'submarine' to the ocean floor, where, serenaded by the sound of crashing waves and classical music, you step out to be greeted by the pouting fish of the North Atlantic. After which you swim through the oceans and seas of the world learning about all its diverse lifeforms.

Other highlights include the huge open-ocean aquarium full of UFO-like rays and fearsome sharks, the fluro-coloured jellyfish waving tentacles in time to the classical music that wafts through the aquarium, the jungle area with its tree-level walkways and ponds full of teeth-gnashing piranhas, the elegantly dancing seahorses, timid turtles and the bizarre half-newt, total-fish mudskippers. The aim is to educate visitors about the wonders of the world's waters and the threats our oceans face. You will learn how sea cucumbers spit their guts out when frightened and then just grow another set, and – here's one that all parents can relate to – how poor mummy octopus becomes so tired at the mere thought of bringing up her precious brood that she dies of exhaustion the moment they hatch out! You should allow a minimum of two hours for a visit.

Toy Museums MUSEUM
(www.museeslarochelle.com; 14 rue La Désirée; adult/child €11/8; ⊙9.30am-7pm Jul-Aug, shorter hours rest of year) A treat for kids (and kids-at-heart) is the **Musée des Automates** (Automation Museum), a small theme-park-style display showing 300 automated dolls from the last two centuries, including a near-life-size recreation of bygone Montmartre in Paris, right down to the Moulin Rouge and the funicular railway. Trainspotters will love the equally appealing **Musée des Modèles Réduits** (Scale Model Museum; ✆05 46 41 64 51) next door, with miniature cars, computer-automated naval battles and a tootling model railway. Both museums are wheelchair accessible.

Musée Maritime MARITIME MUSEUM
(www.museemaritimelarochelle.fr; Bassin à Flot; adult/child €8/5.50; ⊙10am-7pm Jul-Aug, till 6.30pm Apr-Jun & Sep, shorter hours rest of year) Moored at Bassin à Flot are the meteorological research ship *France 1,* a *chalutier* (fishing boat) and a tug, which together make up the Musée Maritime. If you think your job is tough, just wait until you see what the crew on these sorts of boats have to put up with on the average working day.

ATLANTIC COAST LA ROCHELLE

La Rochelle

Musée du Nouveau Monde
MUSEUM

(New World Museum; 10 rue Fleuriau; adult/child €4.50/free; ⊙10.30am-12.30pm & 2-6pm Mon & Wed-Sat, 2-6pm Sun) La Rochelle's role as a departure point for North America is interpreted at this museum, housed in an 18th-century mansion.

Musée des Beaux-Arts
MUSEUM

(☑05 46 41 64 65; 28 rue Gargoulleau; adult/child €4/free, exhibitions €4.50; ⊙10am-12.30pm & 1.45-5pm Mon & Wed-Fri, 2-6pm Sat-Sun) The Musée des Beaux-Arts, which is housed inside a stunning neoclassical building, hosts an impressive collection of 15th- to 20th-century art.

◉ Defensive Towers

La Rochelle's waterfront is dominated by four huge defensive towers that once helped to protect the town. You can either buy individual tickets or visit all of them on a single joint ticket.

Tour de la Chaîne
MONUMENT

(adult/child €6/free, all three towers €8.50/free; ⊙10am-6.30pm Apr-Sep, 10am-1pm & 2.15-5.30pm Oct-Mar) To protect the harbour at night in times of war, an enormous chain was raised between the two 14th-century stone towers at the harbour entrance to La Rochelle, giving rise to the name Tour de la Chaîne (Chain Tower). There are superb views from the top and a whizz-bang exhibit about the Canadian voyagers.

Tour de la Lanterne
MONUMENT

(adult/child €6/free, all three towers €8.50/free; ⊙10am-6.30pm Apr-Sep, 10am-1pm & 2.15-5.30pm Oct-Mar) The conical 15th-century Tour de la Lanterne, so named because of its role as the harbour's lighthouse (lit by an enormous candle), and one of the oldest of its kind in the world, is also referred to as Tour des Quatre Sergents in memory of four local sergeants, two of whom were held here for plotting to overthrow the newly reinstated monarchy before their execution in Paris in 1822.

The English-language graffiti on the walls was carved by English privateers held here during the 18th century.

Tour St-Nicolas
MONUMENT

(adult/child €6/free, all three towers €8.50/free; ⊙10am-6.30pm Apr-Sep, 10am-1pm & 2.15-5.30pm Oct-Mar) It's possible to climb the 36m-high, pentagonal Tour St-Nicolas.

Tour de la Grosse Horloge
MONUMENT

(quai Duperré) The gateway to the old city, Tour de la Grosse Horloge is a steadfast Gothic-style clock tower, with a 12th-century base and an 18th-century top. For safety reasons, it's not possible to enter.

◉ Island-Hopping & Beaches

Several islands are scattered around La Rochelle, including the nearby Île de Ré, as well as a trio further south.

Accessible only by boat, the tiny crescent-shaped Île d'Aix (pronounced 'eel dex'), 16km due south of La Rochelle, has some blissful beaches. Between the Île d'Aix and the larger Île d'Oléron (linked to the mainland by a free bridge) is the fortress-island Fort Boyard, built during the first half of the 19th century.

If all you want is a quick swim and a blast of sunshine then head to Plage de la Concurrence on the edge of the old town. It's popular with locals but note that the water can be very polluted. For more pleasing beaches head to Île de Ré.

Inter-Îles
BOATS

(☑08 25 13 55 00; www.inter-iles.com; cours des Dames) Inter-Îles has sailings from Easter to early November to Fort Boyard (adult/child €20/12.50), Île d'Aix (€26/16.50) and Île d'Oléron (€25/17.20), plus sailings to Île de Ré (€21/13.50) in July and August.

☞ Tours

The tourist office organises a wealth of city tours throughout the summer months (adult/

BIRDWATCHING

An easy 15km drive south of La Rochelle, the 192-hectare **Réserve Naturelle Marais d'Yves** (www.marais.yves.reserves-naturelles.org; N137) has a free nature centre, where you can pop in and peer through telescopes to watch some of the 250 bird species amid the wetlands. Depending on the season, you might see flocks of over 20,000 birds fill the sky on their migratory path. The website lists various guided walks and cycle rides through the wetlands (available in English), where you'll also learn about the area's 750 species of frogs, flowers and insects.

child/under 13 years from €5/2/free), often in French only. Reservations are essential.

✨ Festivals & Events

Festival International du Film   FILM FESTIVAL
(www.festival-larochelle.org) Silent classics, as well as new nondubbed films, are screened during the 10-day film festival in early July.

Francofolies   DANCE FESTIVAL
(www.francofolies.fr) A contemporary-music ,cutting-edge performing-arts festival held over four days in mid-July.

Jazz Entre Les Deux Tours   MUSIC FESTIVAL
(www.jazzentrelesdeuxtours.fr) October sees jazz fans jive at La Rochelle's jazz festival.

🛏 Sleeping

During the warmer months, dozens of campgrounds open (and fill up just as quickly) around La Rochelle and Île de Ré. The tourist office has a list of campgrounds outside the town.

Axe Hotel   HOTEL €
(📞 05 46 41 40 68; www.axehotellarochelle.fr; 5 rue de la Fabrique; s €68, d €78-88; ⊗ reception closed 11.30am-4pm; 🛜) This old townhouse overlooking the port has modern rooms with red and white furnishings, spotlights and black-and-white tiled bathrooms. It's all very well run and recieves lots of positive feedback; take the low prices into account and it adds up to a great deal.

Hotel de Paris   HOTEL €
(📞 05 46 41 03 59; hoteldeparis@wanadoo.fr; 18 rue Gargoulleau; s/d from €47/50; 🛜) You get a lot for your money at this simple and welcoming place on a quiet pedestrian road. Some of the front-facing rooms have sunny balconies.

Hôtel de la Paix   HISTORIC HOTEL €
(📞 05 46 41 33 44; www.hotelalarochelle.com; 14 rue Gargoulleau; s €59, d €74-89; 🛜) In a lovely 18th-century building, a sweeping staircase of polished wood leads to good-value rooms, some of which have open stone walls and all of which have plenty of splashes of colour and character.

Centre International de Séjour-Auberge de Jeunesse   HOSTEL €
(📞 05 46 44 43 11; www.fuaj.net; av des Minimes; dm with breakfast from €17.50, r €35; ⊗ reception 8am-noon, 2-7pm & 9-10pm, closed Christmas) This popular HI hostel is 2km southwest of the train station, in Les Minimes.

★ Hôtel St-Nicolas   BOUTIQUE HOTEL €€
(📞 05 46 41 71 55; www.hotel-saint-nicolas.com; 13 rue Sardinerie et place de la Solette; r from €117-135; ❄🛜) This hotel offers smart, clean, minimalist style and beds so soft and welcoming it'll be a battle to get out of them in the morning. The bathrooms have either giant rain showers or baths to ease back and relax into, the service is excellent and the indoor tropical garden is an unexpected nice touch.

Un Hôtel en Ville   BOUTIQUE HOTEL €€
(📞 05 46 41 15 75; www.unhotelenville.fr; 20 place du Maréchal Foch; s/d from €75/85; ❄🛜) Everything about this smart, bargain-priced boutique hotel screams quality – even the pillows and mattresses are in a league above those of most other hotels in this price range. The admittedly fairly small rooms are painted in a startling white, offset through the use of dark stone furnishings.

Trianon de la Plage   HISTORIC HOTEL €€
(📞 05 46 41 21 35; www.hoteltrianon.com; 6 rue de la Monnaie; r €84-115; ⊗ closed Jan; 🛜) A fading world of art-deco stained-glass windows, curly-whirly staircases, a grand dining room and multi-hued rooms dominate this character-laden hotel. The owner, who speaks superb English, really looks after his guests and likes to check that everything is just right.

The in-house restaurant has high-quality meals for an affordable price (mains €15 to €18). It's in a quiet corner of town but only a shipmate's shout from the old town and a mere sandy shuffle from the town beach.

Masq Hotel   DESIGN HOTEL €€
(📞 05 46 41 83 83; www.masqhotel.com; 17 rue de l'Ouvrage à Cornes; r from €104; ❄🛜) This designer buisness-class hotel with a human heart is flamboyantly decorated with abstract canvases that hang in all 76 rooms as well as in the artistically lit neo-retro foyer. Other conversation pieces include Philippe Starck Carrara marble tables, and Pierluigi Cerri-designed apple-green leather chairs in the breakfast room.

Residence de France   APARTMENT €€€
(📞 05 46 28 06 00; www.hotel-larochelle.com; rue de Minage; r €170-240, studio from €130; ❄🛜) This is arguably the fanciest place to stay in La Rochelle, and although the rooms are very elegant we think the apartments are a better deal – especially for those travelling with young children – as they have little kitchenettes and some have sun-drenched views down onto the heated pool.

La Monnaie Art & Spa Hotel
DESIGN HOTEL €€€

(☑ 05 46 50 65 65; www.hotelmonnaie.com; 3 rue de la Monnaie; d from €214; ❉ ☎) This is a fabulous boutique hotel whose austere 17th-century exterior hides a virtual art gallery interior of arresting graffiti, sparkly light trees, plasticine sculptures, blurred photos and subtle lighting. The rooms are comfortable in the extreme and the bathrooms futuristic, high-tech creations. If you need pampering there's a spa and if not there's a gym.

🍴 Eating

The port has a plethora of restaurants and cafes, especially on the northern side. In summer, the quays in front of the Vieux Port (old port) are closed to traffic from 8pm to midnight Monday to Saturday and 2pm to midnight on Sunday, creating the ambience of a giant street party. Away from the tourist crowds, locals' favoured dining areas are rue St-Jean du Pérot and streets such as rue des Cloutiers surrounding place du Marché.

★Le Soleil Brille pour Tout Le Monde
INTERNATIONAL €

(☑ 05 46 41 11 42; 13 rue des Cloutiers; menus from €13, mains from €10; ☺ Tue-Sat; ☑) There's a distinctly bohemian air to this excellent little place, decked out in hippy colours. Some highly original (often vegetarian-based) dishes originate from the kitchen, much of them inspired by the tropical French islands of Réunion and Martinique. As much as possible, all the produce used here comes from the nearby market and you can really tell – plus it's one of those all-too-rare French restaurants not afraid to experiment with spices. Advance reservations are essential.

Le Bistro du Marché
TRADITIONAL FRENCH €

(☑ 05 46 27 28 52; 8 rue Gambetta, Échoppe du Maré; mains €12; ☺ noon-2pm & 7-9pm Mon-Sat) Built into the market walls, this family-run place has a convivial atmosphere and draws plenty of regulars with its tasty and filling lunch *menus* comprising all the French bistro standards.

★Le Thiers Temps
MODERN FRENCH €€€

(26 rue Thiers; menus €18-31; ☺ noon-2pm & 7.30-9.30pm Tue-Sat) How does a paella of snails sound? Or perhaps a goats cheese mousse mixed with salted butter from Brittany? Or how about a John Dory fish with a pea cheesecake? Yes, it's inventive and original. Everything served at this easy-going,

apple-green restaurant tastes divine – and most of the ingredients are local.

Restaurant la Petite Auberge
SEAFOOD €€€

(25 rue St Jean du Perot; mains from €20, menus €22-30; ☺ noon-2pm & 7-10.30pm Tue & Thu-Sat, noon-2pm Mon & Wed) Smart without being stuffy, this is a top-notch place for superb French gourmet cuisine, much of which originates from the ocean depths. Try the stuffed baby squid with risotto or the scallops with duck liver and you'll be a believer too.

André
SEAFOOD €€€

(☑ 05 46 41 28 24; 8 place de la Chaîne; menus from €22, mains around €25; ☺ noon-4pm & 7pm-midnight) Opened in the 1950s as a small seafood cafe, André grew so popular it began buying adjacent shops. There's now a maze of interconnecting rooms, each with its own individual ambience (like a portholed cabin) but all serving succulent seafood caught the night before.

Café de la Paix
BRASSERIE €€€

(☑ 05 46 41 39 79; 54 rue Chaudrier; lunch menu €22.50, mains €15; ☺ 7am-10pm Mon-Sat) A visual feast as much as a dining one, this belle-époque brasserie-bar serves up traditional cuisine like beef, duck, foie gras and fish, as well as breakfasts and afternoon teas amid the splendour of soaring frescoed ceilings and gold-edged arched mirrors.

🍷 Drinking & Nightlife

There's no shortage of places to drink along the main dining strips, but some of the city's best bars (most open to 2am) are sprinkled along the bohemian-feel rue St-Nicolas.

La Boutique des Cafe Merling
TEAROOM

(25 rue Gambetta; ☺ closed Mon morning & Sun) For fresh-roasted coffee, head to this 1st-floor tearoom, which supplies most cafes in town with their brews. Downstairs is a shop where you can buy bags of coffee beans.

☆ Entertainment

La Coursive
LIVE MUSIC, CINEMA

(☑ 05 46 51 54 00; www.la-coursive.com; 4 rue St-Jean du Pérot; ☺ late Aug–mid-Jul) The two auditoriums at La Coursive host regular world-music concerts, nondubbed art films, theatre and dance performances.

❶ Information

Tourist Office (☑ 05 46 41 14 68; www.la rochelle-tourisme.com; 2 quai Georges Simenon, Le Gabut; ☺ 9am-7pm Mon-Sat, 10am-6pm Sun

Jul-Aug, 10am-6pm daily Apr-Jun & Sep, shorter hours rest of year) Sells the Pass Rochelais, offering various discounts for public transport, sights and activities.

❶ Getting There & Away

AIR

La Rochelle Airport (www.larochelle.aeroport.fr), north of the city centre off the N237, has domestic flights as well as a variety of flights to numerous French, British and Irish airports, as well as Brussels and Porto.

BUS

Océcars (☑ 05 46 00 95 15) runs services to regional destinations from the **bus station** (place de Verdun).

TRAIN

The **train station** (☑ 08 36 35 35 35) is linked by TGV to Paris' Gare Montparnasse (from €70, 3¼ hours). Other destinations served by regular direct trains include Nantes (€29, 1¾ hours), Poitiers (from €28, 1½ hours) and Bordeaux (from €31, 2¼ hours).

❶ Getting Around

TO/FROM THE AIRPORT

Bus 7 (bus 47 on Sundays) runs from the airport to the town centre (€1.30); schedules are available on the airport website. A taxi costs about €10.

BOAT

Le Passeur (tickets €1, under 5s free; ⊙7.30am-10pm) is a three-minute ferry service linking Tour de la Chaîne with the Avant Port. It runs when there are passengers – press the red button on the board at the top of the gangplank.

The ferry **Bus de Mer** (tickets €3, family tickets per person €2; ⊙10am-7pm) links Tour de la Chaîne with Les Minimes (20minutes). It runs daily from April to September and weekends and holidays from October to March. Boats from the Vieux Port depart every hour on the hour (except at 1pm; every half-hour until 11.30pm in July and August).

BUS

Electric buses buzz around town. Local transport system **Yélo Bus** (☑ 05 46 34 02 22) has a main bus hub and **information office** (place de Verdun; ⊙7.30am-7pm Mon-Fri, 8am-6.30pm Sat). Most lines run until sometime between 7.15pm and 8pm. Tickets cost €1.30.

Bus 1 runs from place de Verdun to the train station, returning via the Vieux Port.

CAR & MOTORCYCLE

A free shuttle bus connects the low-cost Park and Ride (P+R) car park off av Jean Moulin.

TAXI

Call **Abeilles Taxis** (☑ 05 46 41 55 55).

Île de Ré

POP 17,600

Bathed in the southern sun, drenched in a languid atmosphere and scattered with villages of green-shuttered, whitewashed buildings with red Spanish-tile roofs, Île de Ré is one of the most delightful places on the west coast of France. The island spans just 30km from its most easterly and westerly points, and just 5km at its widest section. But take note, the secret's out and in the high season it can be almost impossible to move around and even harder to find a place to stay.

On the northern coast, about 12km from the toll bridge that links the island to La Rochelle, is the quaint fishing port of **St-Martin-de-Ré** (population 2600), the main town. Surrounded by 17th-century fortifications (you can stroll along most of the ramparts), the port town is a mesh of streets filled with craft shops, art galleries and sea views. St-Martin's **tourist office** (☑ 05 46 09 00 05; www.iledere.com; av Victor Bouthillier; ⊙10am-6pm Mon-Sat, to noon Sun) can provide information for the entire island.

The island's best beaches are along the southern edge – including unofficial naturist beaches at Rivedoux Plage and La Couarde-sur-Mer – and around the western tip (northeast and southeast of Phare-des-Baleines). Many beaches are bordered by dunes that have been fenced off to protect the vegetation.

◉ Sights & Activities

Phare des Baleines   LIGHTHOUSE
(☑ 05 46 29 18 23; www.lepharedesbaleines.fr; adult/child €6/3; ⊙9.30am-9pm mid-Jun–mid-Sep, shorter hours rest of year) For an overview of the island, climb to its highest point. the Phare des Baleines, a lighthouse on the island's north tip.

Cycling   CYCLING
Criss-crossed by an extensive network of well-maintained bicycle paths, the pancake-flat island is ideal for cycling. A biking map is available at tourist offices and bike rental places; in summer practically every hamlet has somewhere to hire bikes.

Of the numerous cycling trails, an especially fine one links the villages of Ars en Ré with Les Portes en Ré via a maze of marshes and salt pans (bring binoculars: the birdwatching is great). You can then loop back via the Phare des Baleines. Most bike rental places can provide kids bikes and helmets, and trailers or seats for young children. Year-round **Cycland** (www.cycland.fr; per day from €12) can deliver bikes to the bridge.

🛏 Sleeping

Île de Ré is an easy day trip from La Rochelle; however, if you want to spend longer on the island (and you will), each village has a summer tourist office with lists of local accommodation options, including campgrounds and private rooms and houses.

Do note, however, that accommodation here is very expensive – most people camp for a reason!

Hotel La Jetée
HOTEL €€

(📞 05 46 09 36 36; www.hotel-lajetee.com; 23 quai Clémenceau, St-Martin-de-Ré; d €98-135; 🛜) In the heart of pretty St-Martin-de-Ré, this smart and functional hotel offers good value for the Île de Ré. Rooms are lent character by movie spotlights and outdoor picnic tables and chairs inside the rooms.

Hôtel Le Sénéchal
BOUTIQUE HOTEL €€

(📞 05 46 29 40 42; www.hotel-le-senechal.com; 6 rue Gambetta, Ars en Ré; r €130-295; 🛜🖥) This is a charming family-run place in the centre of the equally charming village of Ars en Ré. When we were visiting, a couple who were checking the rooms commented, 'Oh, isn't it cute.' We couldn't have expressed it better ourselves. The heated courtyard swimming pool is a huge plus and it has family-sized rooms.

⭐La Maison Douce
BOUTIQUE HOTEL €€€

(📞 05 46 09 20 20; www.lamaisondouce.com; 25 rue Mérindot, St-Martin-de-Ré; r €165-230; 🛜) With weathered-looking ships' timber floors, pastel colour schemes and quality, arty furnishings, the eleven rooms of this magnificent place are as soft and gentle as the *douce* in its name. All the rooms are different but our favourites are those with the bath tubs built into the bedroom walls.

Throw in a pretty courtyard garden, a peaceful location, free use of the spa bath and a friendly owner and you get a place that's hard to beat.

La Baronnie Domaine
HISTORIC HOTEL €€€

(📞 05 46 09 21 29; www.domainedelabaronnie.com; 21 rue Baron de Chantal, St-Martin-de-Ré; d from €145; 🌸🛜🖥) Attention all kings and queens: this place, which oozes history, is so regal you won't be surprised to hear that it was once owned by one of your ancestors, Louis XVI.

ⓘ Getting There & Away

The one-way automobile toll (paid on your way to the island) is €8 (a whopping €16 from mid-June to mid-September).

Year-round excruciatingly slow buses link La Rochelle (the train-station car park, Tour de la Grosse Horloge and place de Verdun) with all the major towns on the island; the most economical way of making the one-hour trip to St-Martin is with the special *forfait journée* round-trip ticket for €5. There are also intra-island routes.

Cognac
POP 19,500

On the banks of the River Charente amid vine-covered countryside, Cognac is known worldwide for the double-distilled spirit that bears its name, and on which the local economy thrives. Most visitors head here to visit the famous cognac houses, however, it's a picturesque stop even if you don't happen to be a huge fan of the local firewater.

Cognac centres on a cafe-ringed central roundabout, place François 1er. From here, the old town and most of the Cognac distilleries are downhill towards and along the river.

◉ Sights & Activities

Half-timbered 15th- to 17th-century houses line the narrow streets of the **Vieille Ville** (old city), which sits snugly between the partly Romanesque **Église St-Léger** (rue Aristide Briand) and the river.

Musée d'Art et d'Histoire
MUSEUM

(📞 05 45 32 07 25; www.musees-cognac.fr; 48 bd Denfert-Rochereau; adult/child €5/free; ⏱2-5.30pm Wed-Mon) At the southern corner of the leafy **Jardin Public** is the Musée d'Art et d'Histoire, showcasing the town's history.

Musée des Arts du Cognac
MUSEUM

(📞 05 45 36 21 10; place de la Salle Verte; adult/child €5/free; ⏱2-5.30pm Tue-Sun) The Musée des Arts du Cognac takes you step by step through the production of Cognac – from vine to bottle.

La Dame Jeanne
RIVER CRUISE

(📞 05 45 82 10 71; adult/child €7/4; ⏱May-Sep; ♿) You can float with the sticklebacks down the River Charente on *La Dame Jeanne,* a recreation of one of the flat-bottomed cargo boats known as *gabarres* that were once the lifeblood of trade along the river. The trip lasts 90 minutes; reservations should be made through the tourist office.

THE HOME OF COGNAC
....

According to local lore, divine intervention plays a role in the production of Cognac. Made of grape *eaux-de-vie* (brandies) of various vintages, Cognac is aged in oak barrels and blended by an experienced *maître de chai* (cellar master). Each year some 2% of the casks' volume – known as *la part des anges* (the angels' share) – evaporates through the pores in the wood, nourishing the tiny black mushrooms that thrive on the walls of Cognac warehouses. That 2% might not sound like much, but it amounts to around 20 million bottles a year – if the angels really are up there knocking back 20 million bottles of Cognac a year, then all we can say is roll on our time behind the pearly gates! The best-known Cognac houses are open to the public, running tours of their cellars and production facilities, and ending with a tasting session. Opening times vary annually; it's a good idea to reserve in advance:

Camus (☑ 05 45 32 72 96; www.camus.fr; 29 rue Marguerite de Navarre; adult/child from €8.50/free; ◷ 2-6pm Mon, 10.30am-12.30pm & 2-6pm Tue-Sat May-Sep) Located 250m northeast of the Jardin Public.

Hennessey (☑ 05 45 35 72 68; www.hennessey.com; 8 rue Richonne; adult/12-18yr/under 12 €11/6/free; ◷ 10am-11.30am & 1.30-5pm mid-Apr–Sep, shorter hours rest of year, closed Jan & Feb) Situated 100m uphill from quai des Flamands; tours include a film (in English) and a boat trip across the Charente to visit the cellars.

Martell (☑ 05 45 36 33 33; www.martell.com; place Édouard Martell; adult/child €7.50/4; ◷ 10am-5pm Mon-Fri, noon-5pm Sat & Sun Apr-Oct, closed Sun Oct) 250m northwest of the tourist office.

Otard (☑ 05 45 36 88 86; www.otard.com; 127 bd Denfert-Rochereau; adult/child €10/4.50; ◷ 11am-12pm & 1.30-6pm Jul-Aug, shorter hours rest of year, closed Jan-Mar) Housed in the 1494 birthplace of King François I, the Château de Cognac, 650m north of place François 1er.

Rémy Martin (☑ 05 45 35 76 66; www.visitesremymartin.com) Two locations: the **estate** (adult/child €18/8; ◷ by appointment only, Mon-Sat mid-Apr–Sep), 4km southwest of town towards Pons, and, in town, the **house** (adult/child €28/7; ◷ by appointment), for intimate tastings in groups of up to eight.

The tourist office has a list of smaller Cognac houses near town; most close between October and mid-March.

🛏 Sleeping & Eating

Hôtel Héritage　　　　　BOUTIQUE HOTEL €
(☑ 05 45 82 01 26; www.hheritage.com; 25 rue d'Angoulême; s/d €68/73; 🖂) Splashed in striking shades of lime green, fuchsia and cherry red, this hotel looks fantastic. Oh, and the 'medieval' portraits are like none you've ever seen before. Sadly though the reception can be a little frosty at times.

Hôtel Le Cheval Blanc　　　　　HOTEL €
(☑ 05 45 82 09 55; www.hotel-chevalblanc.fr; 6 place Bayard; d from €66; 🅿🖂) Miniature bottles of Cognac in the vending machine satiate midnight cravings at this hotel, where rooms are set around a courtyard. Although not vast, the rooms are immaculate, and there's good wheelchair access.

Hôtel François Premier　　　HISTORIC HOTEL €€€
(☑ 05 45 80 80 80; www.francoispremier.fr; 3 Place François 1er; d Mon-Fri €160, Sat & Sun €125; 🅿🖂) Recently reopened after years of neglect, this grand hotel, which resides within an imposing old building, has prim but, considering the price, rather ordinary rooms.

Bistrot de Claude　　　　　BISTRO €€
(☑ 05 45 82 60 32; 35 rue Grande; menus €20-32; ◷ 7-9.30pm Mon-Fri) Set in a lovely old wiggly timber building in the heart of the old town, this character-infused restaurant specialises in oysters and both river and sea fish.

ℹ Information

Tourist Office (☑ 05 45 82 10 71; www.tourism-cognac.com; 16 rue du XIV Juillet; ◷ 9am-7pm Mon-Sat, 10am-5pm Sun Jul-Aug, shorter hours rest of year) Ample information, friendly staff and free wi-fi. What more can you want?!

ℹ Getting There & Away

Cognac's **train station** (av du Maréchal Leclerc), 1km south of the town centre, has regular trains to/from Bordeaux (from €24.70, from 1¾ hours) and La Rochelle (from €17.20, from 1¼ hours).

CITADELLE DE BLAYE

A worthwhile side trip on the journey between Cognac and Bordeaux is to the small Unesco World Heritage–listed city of Blaye on the right bank of the Gironde River. The town is best known for its imposing citadel built by François Ferry, under the supervision of that master citadel designer, Vauban, in 1685, in order to protect the Gironde and the gates of Bordeaux.

Today, the citadel, which covers some 38 hectares, also contains the crumbling remains of a Gothic château housing the tomb of Charibert II, a 7th-century king of parts of today's Aquitaine and son of Clotaire II, and a vast expanse of fortifications that are among the most spectacular in southwestern France. Although the citadel as a whole is wildly impressive and atmospheric, it is the main entrance gates, the Porte Dauphine and Porte Royale, that really stand out.

Aside from military significance, the town is also known for its wines and is simply an attractive place to explore. The tourist office can organise guided tours of the town, including boat tours that reveal the strength of the fortifications from the point of view of a waterborne attacker. Tours are also available to some of the towns surrounding wine châteaux.

If you're driving, the town is just 50km or an hour's drive north of Bordeaux.

Around Cognac

Within a short drive of Cognac are some fascinating towns and villages worth seeking out. One highlight is the former Gallo-Roman capital of Aquitaine, Saintes, on the River Charente. Dating from the 1st century AD, its Roman legacies include a double arch that served as the town gate, an amazing overgrown amphitheatre built during the reign of Claudius, and an archaeology museum with unearthed statues and even a chariot and harness. Its pedestrianised old town spills over with lively places to shop, eat and drink.

Also straddling the Charente is Jarnac, the 1916 birthplace of former president François Mitterrand. The house where he was born has been transformed into a museum; he's now buried in the town's cemetery. The waters around Jarnac are prime for fishing.

Cognac's tourist office has details of these and other areas in its surrounds.

✕ Eating

★ La Ribaudière   GASTRONOMIC €€€
(☑ 05 45 81 30 54; www.laribaudiere.com; menus €45-130, mains €36-44; ⊙ dinner Tue-Sat, lunch Wed-Sun) This gastronomic haven is set among orchards overlooking the Charente River, in the tiny village of Bourg-Charente (midway between Cognac and Jarnac). Chef Thierry Verrat grows his own vegetables to accompany his seasonally changing, Michelin-starred creations.

If the food sends your taste buds into whirls of excitement, you can keep them happy by joining one of the restaurant's cookery courses (€115). See the website for details.

LOWER ATLANTIC COAST

At the lower edge of the Atlantic coast, the expansive Aquitaine region extends to the Dordogne in the east and the Basque Country in the south. The gateway to the region's wealth of attractions, set amid glorious vine-ribboned countryside, is its capital, Bordeaux.

Bordeaux

POP 236,000

The new millennium was a major turning point for the city known as La Belle au Bois Dormant (Sleeping Beauty). The mayor, former prime minister Alain Juppé, roused Bordeaux, pedestrianising its boulevards, restoring its neoclassical architecture and implementing a high-tech public transport system. His efforts paid off: in mid-2007 half of the entire city (18 sq km, from the outer boulevards to the banks of the Garonne) was Unesco-listed, making it the largest urban World Heritage Site. Bolstered by its high-spirited university-student population (not to mention 2.5 million tourists annually), La Belle Bordeaux now scarcely seems to sleep at all.

◉ Sights & Activities

On the first Sunday of every month, Bordeaux' city centre is closed to cars, and attractions often have extended hours.

Cathédrale St-André   CATHEDRAL
(place Jean Moulin) Lording over the city, and a Unesco World Heritage Site prior to the city's

classification, the cathedral's oldest section dates from 1096; most of what you see today was built in the 13th and 14th centuries. Exceptional masonry carvings can be seen in the north portal.

Even more imposing than the cathedral itself is the gargoyled, 50m-high Gothic belfry, **Tour Pey-Berland** (adult/child €5.50/free; ⊙10am-1.15pm & 2-6pm Jun-Sep, 10am-12.30pm & 2-5.30pm Oct-May), erected between 1440 and 1466. Its spire was added in the 19th century, and in 1863 it was topped off with the statue of Notre Dame de l'Aquitaine (Our Lady of Aquitaine). Scaling the tower's 231 narrow steps rewards you with a spectacular panorama of the city.

Bordeaux

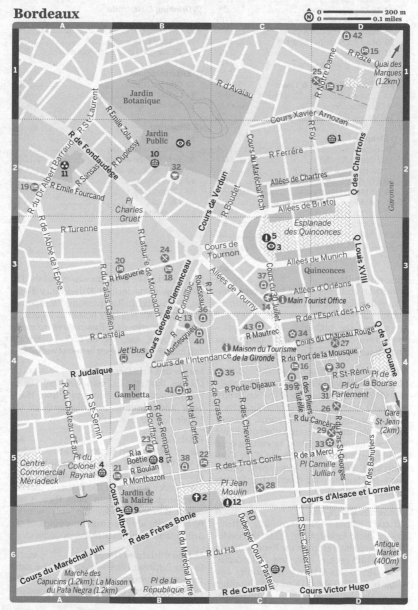

Bordeaux

Musée d'Aquitaine MUSEUM
(www.musee-aquitaine-bordeaux.fr; 20 cours Pasteur; ⊙11am-6pm Tue-Sun) FREE Gallo-Roman statues and relics dating back 25,000 years are among the highlights at the impressive Musée d'Aquitaine. Ask to borrow an English-language catalogue.

CAPC Musée d'Art Contemporain GALLERY
(rue Ferrére, Entrepôt 7; temporary exhibitions adult/child €5/2.50; ⊙11am-6pm Tue & Thu-Sun, to 8pm Wed) Built in 1824 as a warehouse for French colonial produce like coffee, cocoa, peanuts and vanilla, the cavernous Entrepôts Lainé creates a dramatic backdrop for cutting-edge modern art at the CAPC Musée d'Art Contemporain. Entry to the permanent collection is free but there is a cover charge for any temporary exhibitions.

Musée des Beaux-Arts GALLERY
(20 cours d'Albret; ⊙11am-6pm daily mid-Jul–mid-Aug, closed Tue rest of year) FREE The evolution of Occidental art from the Renaissance to the mid-20th century is on view at Bordeaux' Musée des Beaux-Arts, which occupies two wings of the 1770s-built Hôtel de Ville, either side of the Jardin de la Mairie (an elegant public park). The museum was established in 1801; highlights include 17th-century Flemish, Dutch and Italian paintings. Temporary exhibitions are regularly hosted at its nearby annexe, **Galerie des Beaux-Arts** (place du Colonel Raynal; adult/child €5/2.50; ⊙11am-6pm daily mid-Jul–mid-Aug, closed Tue rest of year).

Musée des Arts Décoratifs GALLERY
(39 rue Bouffard; ⊙2-6pm Wed-Mon) FREE Faience pottery, porcelain, gold, iron, glasswork and furniture are displayed at the Musée des Arts Décoratifs.

Palais Gallien RUIN
(rue du Docteur Albert Barraud; ⊙1-6pm Jun-Sep) It was Celtic tribes who first established Bordeaux, but it wasn't until about 200 years later, under the rule of the Romans, that the town started to blossom. Back then it was called Burdigala; today the only remains of Burdigala are the crumbling ruins of the 3rd-century amphitheatre, Palais Gallien.

Musée d'Histoire Naturelle MUSEUM
(5 place Bardineau, Hôtel de Lisleferme) The natural history museum, at the south edge of the Jardin Public, has been closed for renovations

for a number of years but it's likely to reopen in the next couple of years: watch this space.

◉ Parks

The 4km-long riverfront **esplanade** incorporates playgrounds, bicycle paths and, everyone's favourite, a wafer-thin 'swimming pool' that hot and sticky young Bordelaise roll about in throughout the summer months.

Pretty **place Gambetta**, a central open area ringed by shaded benches, also has its share of history – during the Reign of Terror that followed the Revolution, a guillotine placed here severed the heads of 300 alleged counter-revolutionaries.

Jardin Public   GARDENS
(cours de Verdun) Landscaping is artistic as well as informative at the Jardin Public. Established in 1755 and laid out in the English style a century later, the grounds incorporate the meticulously catalogued **Jardin Botanique**, founded in 1629 and at this site since 1855. With its duck ponds and shady corners this is arguably one of the nicest public parks in southwest France.

Esplanade des Quinconces   SQUARE, PLAZA
(quai Louis XVIII) At the vast square esplanade des Quinconces, laid out in 1820, you'll see the **Girondins monument** fountain. Les Girondins were a group of moderate, bourgeois National Assembly deputies during the French Revolution, 22 of whom were executed in 1793 after being convicted of counter-revolutionary activities.

☞ Tours

The tourist office runs a packed program of bilingual city tours, including **gourmet** and **wine tours** as well as **river cruises** in the warmer months, and **child-friendly** tours. All tours take a limited number of participants; reserve ahead. The following is the standard city tour.

Walking Tour   WALKING TOUR
(adult/13-17yr/child €9/8/free; ◷ tours 10am Mon, Tue, Thu, Fri & Sun, 3pm Wed & Sat) Wheelchair-accessible, two-hour walking tour run by the tourist office, in French and English. Meet at the tourist office.

☕ Courses

There are a couple of courses open to tourists and this being Bordeaux most, well OK, all, involve food and wine. The tourist office also organises occasional courses.

École de Cuisine au Chapon Fin   COOKING
(☑ 05 56 79 10 10; www.chapon-fin.com; 5 rue Montesquieu) If you need some food to go with all that wine, sign up for one of Nicolas Frion's occasional but highly regarded half-day cookery courses at the École de Cuisine au Chapon Fin. Alternatively, if you need wine to go with all that food, it also runs wine-tasting courses.

🛏 Sleeping

Accommodation options are plentiful across all categories. The 'Bordeaux Box' is a neat little offering from the tourist office that bundles two nights at your choice of participating hotels, along with free public transport, free access to the city's main monuments and sights, a guided city tour, a vineyard tour including wine tasting (both tours in English and French) and a bottle of wine. Prices start at €260 for a two-night package for two; kids under 12 stay for free in their parents' room. Book 10 or more days in advance.

Hôtel Notre Dame   HOTEL €
(☑ 05 56 52 88 24; 36-38 rue Notre Dame; s €53-70, d €61-79; 🖘) Location is the key selling point of this good-value hotel. It's within an easy stroll of the town centre, just back from the river and in the middle of a lovely village-like neighbourhood of antique shops and relaxed cafes. It also has a wheelchair-accessible room.

Hôtel Touring   HOTEL €
(☑ 05 56 81 56 73; www.hoteltouring.fr; 16 rue Huguerie; s €47-59, d €53-69; 🖘) Run with pride by a warm-hearted family, the Touring has simple rooms with old-fashioned appeal and furnishings. Cheaper rooms share bathrooms.

Auberge de Jeunesse   HOSTEL €
(☑ 05 56 33 00 70; www.auberge-jeunesse-bordeaux. com; 22 cours Barbey; dm incl sheets & breakfast €23; 🖘) Bordeaux' only hostel is housed in an ultramodern building with a self-catering kitchen, good wheelchair access and table football to boot. From the train station, follow cours de la Marne northwest for 300m and turn left opposite the park; the hostel is about 250m ahead on your left.

★ Ecolodge des Chartrons   B&B €€
(☑ 05 56 81 49 13; www.ecolodgedeschartrons.com; 23 rue Raze; s €107-205, d €119-228; 🖘) Hidden away in a little side street off the quays in Bordeaux' Chartrons wine-merchant district. The owner-hosts of this *chambre d'hôte* (B&B) Veronique and Yann, have stripped back and limewashed the stone walls of an old house,

scrubbed the wide floorboards and brought in recycled antique furniture to create a highly memorable place to stay.

It doesn't only look good, staying here makes you feel good, thanks to an array of ecofriendly initiatives including a solar-powered hot-water system, energy-efficient gas heating and hemp-based soundproofing.

Les Chambres au Coeur de Bordeaux
B&B €€

(☑ 05 56 52 43 58; www.aucoeurdebordeaux.fr; 28 rue Boulan; r €105-155; 🕿) This renovated townhouse is now a swish B&B run like a small boutique hotel. Its five charming rooms are a very Bordeaux-appropriate mix of the old and the new, and most evenings your hosts offer an *apero* and tapas tasting session (€20 to €25) at 7pm.

Une Chambre en Ville
BOUTIQUE HOTEL €€

(☑ 05 56 81 34 53; www.bandb-bx.com; 35 rue Bouffard; s/d incl breakfast €130/140; ☺ reception 8am-12.30pm & 3.30-7pm Mon-Sat, 8.30am-1pm Sun; 🕿) On a street full of antique and art shops, this stylish place blends in well because each of the five rooms is an individual work of art in its own right. The decoration ranges from the plush reds and spicy pictures of the

Oriental room to the Madame-and-Monsieur classic style of the suites. It's gay-friendly but all welcoming.

La Maison du Lierre
BOUTIQUE HOTEL €€

(☑ 05 56 51 92 71; www.maisondulierre.com; 57 rue Huguerie; d €85-139; 🕿) The delightfully restored 'House of Ivy' has a welcoming *chambre d'hôte* feel. A beautiful Bordelaise stone staircase (no lift) leads to small, sunlit rooms with polished floorboards, rose-printed fabrics and sparkling bathrooms. The vine-draped garden is a perfect spot to sip fresh orange juice at breakfast (from €9.90).

Hôtel du Théâtre
BOUTIQUE HOTEL €€

(☑ 05 56 79 05 26; www.hotel-du-theatre.com; 10 rue Maison-Daurade; s from €65-77, d €82-98; 🕿) Just off the main shopping street, the rooms here are a potpourri of styles: some are entirely classic and some are sun-burst Mediterranean colours. Our favourite is the room of flashy sequins and glitter that looks like it just got home from the disco.

★ L'Hôtel Particulier
BOUTIQUE HOTEL €€€

(☑ 05 57 88 28 80; www.lhotel-particulier.com; 44 rue Vital-Carles; apt/d from €89/203; 🕿) When you step into this fabulous boutique hotel, with its secret courtyard garden, and find

---

ON THE WINE TRAIL

Thirsty? The 1000-sq-km wine-growing area around the city of Bordeaux is, along with Burgundy, France's most important producer of top-quality wines.

The Bordeaux region is divided into 57 appellations (production areas whose soil and microclimate impart distinctive characteristics to the wine produced there) that are grouped into seven *familles* (families), and then subdivided into a hierarchy of designations (eg *premier grand cru classé*, the most prestigious) that often vary from appellation to appellation. The majority of the Bordeaux region's reds, rosés, sweet and dry whites and sparkling wines have earned the right to include the abbreviation AOC (Appellation d'Origine Contrôlée) on their labels, indicating that the contents have been grown, fermented and aged according to strict regulations that govern such viticultural matters as the number of vines permitted per hectare and acceptable pruning methods.

Bordeaux has over 5000 châteaux (also known as domaines, crus or clos), referring not to palatial residences but rather to the properties where grapes are raised, picked, fermented and then matured as wine. The smaller châteaux sometimes accept walk-in visitors, but at many places, especially the better-known ones, you have to make advance reservations. Many close during the *vendange* (grape harvest) in October.

Whet your palate with the tourist office's informal introduction to wine and cheese courses (€25), held every Thursday (and Saturdays mid-July to mid-August) at 4.30pm, where you sip three different wines straight from the cellar and nibble on cheese.

Serious students of the grape can enrol at the École du Vin (Wine School; ☑ 05 56 00 22 66; www.bordeaux.com), within the Maison du Vin de Bordeaux (p635), across the street from the tourist office. Introductory two-hour courses are held Monday to Saturday from 10am to noon between July and September (adult/student €39/25). To really develop your nose (and your dinner-party skills), sign up for one of three progressively more complex two- to three-day courses (adult €390 to €690, student €254 to €449) scheduled between May and October, including châteaux visits.

a thousand eyes staring at you from the reception walls and lampshades made only of feathers, you realise you've stumbled upon somewhere special. The rooms don't disappoint – they are highly extravagant affairs with huge fireplaces, carved ceilings, free-standing bath-tubs and quality furnishings.

There are also great-value, fully equipped apartments ideal for a longer stay.

La Maison Bord'eaux BOUTIQUE HOTEL €€€
(📞05 56 44 00 45; www.lamaisonbord-eaux.com; 113 rue du Docteur Albert Barraud; r from €125; ❄️📶) You'd expect to find a sumptuous 18th-century château with a conifer-flanked courtyard and stable house in the countryside, but this stunning *maison d'hôte* is right in the middle of the city. Public areas include a library with shelves of books and CDs. A *table d'hôte* is available by arrangement (*menus* €35 to €150, including wine).

✗ Eating

All that fine wine needs fine cuisine to accompany it, and Bordeaux has some excellent restaurants. Place du Parlement, rue du Pas St-Georges and rue des Faussets have a plethora. There are also scads of inexpensive cafes and restaurants around place de la Victoire. The former warehouse district of the Quai des Marques now houses dozens of waterfront restaurants, bars and factory shops. It's a nice place for a sunset meal or drink.

★Le Cheverus Café BISTRO €
(📞05 56 48 29 73; 81-83 rue du Loup; menus from €12.50; ⊘noon-3pm & 7-9pm Mon-Sat) In a city full of neighbourhood bistros, this one, smack in the city centre, is one of the most impressive. It's friendly, cosy and chaotically busy (be prepared to wait for a table at lunchtime). The food tastes fresh and home-cooked and it dares to veer slightly away from the bistro standards of steak and chips.

The lunch *menus*, which include wine, are an all-out bargain. In the early evening the bistro morphs into something of a tapas bar.

La Maison du Pata Negra SPANISH €
(Maré des Capucins; tapas €1.50-3.50; ⊘8am-3.30pm) A little taste of Spain with its hanging *jamon* (hams) and piles of wine-red chilli peppers, this place, which is inside the city's produce market, is an immensely popular place for a *tapa* or two washed down with a drop from its impressive selection of wine.

OYSTERS AT CAPUCINS

Rosie Warren is a Bordeaux-based English expat who told us that for her, one of the classic Bordeaux experiences is a Saturday morning spent slurping oysters and white wine from one of the seafood stands found at **Marché des Capucins** (six oysters & glass of wine €6; ⊘7am-noon). Afterwards she suggests perusing the stalls while shopping for fresh ingredients for a picnic in one of the city's parks. To get to the market, head south down cours Pasteur to place de la Victoire, then turn left on rue Élie Gintrec.

Michels Bistrot BISTRO €
(15 rue du Pas-Saint-Georges; mains €12-15; ⊘noon-2.30pm & 7-9.30pm Tue-Sun) In Bordeaux' most bohemian quarter, this buzzing bistro is packed with students and those who wish they were still students. It's renowned for the quality of its beef – whether that be in hamburger form or a more classic steak. It's also a popular early-evening *apero* hang-out.

Karl INTERNATIONAL €€
(📞05 56 81 01 00; place du Parlement; breakfast from €5.50; ⊘8.30am-7.30pm) Simply *the* place in town for a morning-after-the-night-before brunch, ranging from a light continental-style affair to the full works with salmon, cheeses, hams and eggs. It's just as good for a snack at any time of the day and is perpetually packed with a young crowd.

La Boîte à Huîtres OYSTERS €€
(📞05 56 81 64 97; 36 cours du Chapeau Rouge; lunch menu €20, 6 oysters from €8; ⊘noon-2pm & 7-11pm) This rickety, wood-panelled little place feels like an Arcachon fisherman's hut. It's a sensation that's quite appropriate because this is by far the best place in Bordeaux to munch on fresh Arcachon oysters. Traditionally they're served with sausage but you can have them in a number of different forms, including with that other southwest delicacy, foie gras.

They'll also pack them up so you can take them away for a riverfront picnic.

Chez Dupont BISTRO €€
(📞05 56 81 49 59; 45 rue Notre Dame; mains €15-20; ⊘11.30am-2.30pm & 7.30-11pm Tue-Sat) Hemmed in by antique shops and small art galleries, Chez Dupont is the kind of cliché neighbourhood bistro you thought you'd only ever see in Hollywood films about France.

ATLANTIC COAST BORDEAUX

As seems only right the food is equally traditional old French-style, but it's of an above-average quality and comes with an above-average welcome.

Baud et Millet   CHEESE, WINE €€
(☑ 05 56 79 05 77; 19 rue Huguerie; mains €23-25; ⊙ noon-2pm & 7-9.30pm Mon-Sat) If you like cheese or wine, or both of them, then this cute neighbourhood place with over 140 different cheeses served in myriad forms, alongside almost as many wines, is unmissable. Serious *fromage* fans should go for the *Tour de France* (€15), a French cheese blow out!

★ La Tupina   REGIONAL CUISINE €€€
(☑ 05 56 91 56 37; www.latupina.com; 6 rue Porte de la Monnaie; menus €18-74, mains €27-45) Filled with the aroma of soup simmering inside an old *tupina* ('kettle' in Basque) over an open fire, this white-tableclothed place is feted far and wide for its seasonal southwestern French specialities such as a minicasserole of foie gras and eggs, milk-fed lamb or goose wings with potatoes and parsley.

An €18 lunch *menu* is available on weekdays. La Tupina is a 10-minute walk upriver from the city centre and on a small side street. Any local can point you in the right direction.

🍷 Drinking & Nightlife

Considering its synonymy with wine, Bordeaux has surprisingly few bars, meaning restaurants and bistros tend to fill the gap. Student hang-outs ring place de la Victoire.

L'Autre Petit Bois   BAR
(12 place du Parlement; ⊙ from 11am) Decorated in an arresting 'modern' baroque and art deco style, this very popular wine bar full of curly-whirly sofas verges on the kitsch, but pulls it off with style.

Café Brun   JAZZ BAR
(45 rue St-Rémi) A warm atmosphere and cool nightly jazz make this bar-bistro great for an evening aperitif.

L'Orangerie du Jardin Public   CAFE
(Jardin Public; ⊙ lunch;) Bliss out with a drink, light lunch (*menu* €16, mains €20) and the flowers in this colourful glass-fronted building on the edge of the Jardin Public.

☆ Entertainment

Details of events appear in *Clubs & Concerts* (www.clubsetconcerts.com), available for free at the tourist office.

☆ Nightclubs & Live Music

Trendy pedestrianised streets like rue St-Rémi are good bets to get the evening started. For zoning reasons, many of the city's late-night dance venues are a few blocks northeast of Gare St-Jean along the river, on quai de la Paludate. Clubs also cluster along the river north of the city centre.

Le Port de la Lune   JAZZ
(www.leportdelalune.com; 58 quai de la Paludate; ⊙ noon-2.30pm & 7pm-12.30am) Gigs at this atmospheric jazz club are posted on the web.

Rock School Barbey   LIVE MUSIC
(☑ 05 56 33 66 00; www.rockschool-barbey.com; 18 cours Barbey) Catch live bands at the rock school, which has a stream of up-and-coming French and international indie bands playing as well as various exhibitions.

☆ Theatre & Classical Music
Grand Théâtre   THEATRE, OPERA
(☑ 05 56 00 85 95; www.opera-bordeaux.com; place de la Comédie; ⊙ tours 2.30pm, 4pm & 5.30pm Wed & Sat) Designed by Victor Louis (of Chartres Cathedral fame), the 18th-century Grand Théâtre stages operas, ballets and concerts of orchestral and chamber music. Guided behind-the-scenes tours of the building (adult/under 26 years €5/free) are possible.

The stately cafe built into it is a civilised spot for a drink.

Théâtre Femina   THEATRE
(☑ 05 56 52 45 19; www.theatrefemina.fr; 10 rue de Grassi) Plays, dance performances, variety shows and concerts.

Cinemas
Cinéma Utopia   CINEMA
(www.cinemas-utopia.org/bordeaux; 3 place Camille Jullian) Screens nondubbed arthouse films.

🔒 Shopping

Europe's longest pedestrian shopping street, rue Ste-Catherine, is probably the city's low point. The southern end, towards place de la Victoire, is the worst half – essentially an unending shambles of kebab shops. To give the road its dues though, things are better at the northern end where slightly classier chain shops predominate and you'll find the Galerie Bordelaise (rue de la Porte Dijeaux & rue Ste-Catherine) 19th-century shopping arcade.

Luxury-label boutiques are concentrated within *le triangle*, formed by the allées de Tourny, cours Georges Clemenceau and cours de l'Intendance.

THE MÉDOC

Northwest of Bordeaux, along the western shore of the Gironde Estuary – formed by the confluence of the Garonne and Dordogne Rivers – lie some of Bordeaux' most celebrated vineyards. To their west, fine-sand beaches, bordered by dunes and *étangs* (lagoons), stretch from Pointe de Grave south along the Côte d'Argent (Silver Coast) to the Bassin d'Arcachon and beyond, with some great surf. On the banks of the muddy Gironde, the port town of **Pauillac** (population 1300) is at the heart of the wine country, surrounded by the distinguished Haut-Médoc, Margaux and St-Julien appellations. The Pauillac wine appellation encompasses 18 *crus classés* including the world-renowned Mouton Rothschild, Latour and Lafite Rothschild. The town's tourist office houses the **Maison du Tourisme et du Vin** (☐ 05 56 59 03 08; www.pauillac-medoc.com; ☉ 9.30am-7pm Mon-Sat, 10am-1pm & 2-6pm Sun), which has information on châteaux and how to visit them.

The lack of a public-transport system to most of the châteaux means this area is best explored in your own car or on one of the tours organised by the tourist office in Bordeaux. There are several different types of tour, which get chopped and changed on a regular basis; at the time of research, half-day **Médoc tours** taking in two châteaux and including wine tastings left the Bordeaux tourist office at 1.45pm on Fridays and Mondays (tours run to other wine regions the rest of the week) at a cost of €87. Cheaper is the half-day **Châteaux et Terroirs** tour, which runs daily (€34; 1.15pm), but takes in different châteaux and regions each day. See the tourist office website for full details. For any of these tours, advance reservations are essential. **Bordeaux Excursions** (☐ 06 24 88 22 09; www.bordeaux-excursions.com) customises private wine-country tours, starting from €210 for one to four people (excluding châteaux fees) for a half-day trip.

If you're travelling under your own steam, the **Maison du Vin de Bordeaux** (3 cours du 30 Juillet) supplies free, colour-coded maps of production areas, details on châteaux and the addresses of local *maisons du vin* (tourist offices that mainly deal with winery visits). One of the easiest châteaux to visit is **Château Lanessan** (☐ 05 56 58 94 80; www.lanessan.com; Cussac-Fort-Medoc; ☉ 9am-noon & 2-6pm), offering daily hour-long tours throughout the year including ones tailored to children and teenagers; advance reservations required.

The Médoc is an easy day trip from Bordeaux, but should you have wine-heavy eyes at the end of the day there are numerous *chambres d'hôte* (B&Bs) in the area or, in the village of Margaux, try **Le Pavillon de Margaux** (☐ 05 57 88 77 54; www.le-pavillon-de-margaux.fr; 3 rue Georges Mandel; d €95-125; ☎), a welcoming, family-run place with rooms styled according to famous local châteaux.

While you're in the area, don't miss Philippe Raoux' **La Winery** (☐ 05 56 39 04 90; www.winery.fr; Rond-point des Vendangeurs, D1; ☉ 10am-7pm). A first for France, this vast glass-and-steel wine centre mounts concerts and contemporary-art exhibits alongside various lees-based tastings, including innovative tastings that determine your *signe œnologique* ('wine sign') costing from €16 (booking required), and stocks more than 1000 different wines.

ATLANTIC COAST BORDEAUX

Antique Market   MARKET
(place St-Michel; ☉ Sun) Stalls of antiques fill the square on Sunday mornings. Located a 700m walk downriver from the city centre.

Baillardran   FOOD
(www.baillardran.com; place des Grands Hommes) For a taste of Bordeaux (that for once doesn't involve wine!), head to Baillardran, which has several branches in town, including this one in the Galerie des Grands Hommes shopping centre, where you can watch the chefs make *canelés*, a local vanilla-infused fluted cake.

Bordeaux Magnum   WINE
(3 rue Gobineau) Speciality wine shop with rack upon rack of Bordeaux' gift to the world.

L'Intendant   WINE
(2 allées de Tourny) A central spiral staircase climbing four floors is surrounded by cylindrical shelves holding 15,000 bottles of regional wine.

Bradley's Bookshop   BOOKS
(rue des Trois-Conils; ☉ 2-7pm Mon, 10am-7pm Tue-Sat) You'll find stacks of English-language books and guides at this brilliant English-language bookshop.

Librairie Mollat   BOOKS
(15 rue Vital Carles) If you think the printed word is dead then come to this huge bookshop and be re-inspired after spending hours browsing through books in several different languages.

1. Oysters and wine 2. St-Émilion p638 3. L'Intendant wine shop
p635, Bordeaux 4. Cognac barrels

Wine, Glorious Wine

The countryside around the Bordeaux region is full of renowned vineyards and legendary châteaux, many of which are open to visitors. Venture a little further north and the Cognac region offers a totally different sort of tipple.

Cognac

Bordeaux isn't the only wine party in town. Cognac produces a drink so heavenly that even the angels are said to partake. Learn all about it during a visit to the **Musee des Arts du Cognac** (p626).

St-Émilion

The quintessential French wine town, **St-Émilion** (p638), the oldest French wine region, has robust and generous wines that tickle the taste buds and any number of wine-related tours (available through the tourist office) to get the most from it.

Bordeaux

No wine-tasting tour is complete without a course at the **École du Vin** (p632). Built on the wealth of the grape, Bordeaux lives up to its bourgeois reputation, but today an army of students give the city a lighter edge.

The Médoc

The **Médoc region** (p635) encompasses some of the finest wine territory in France, with such grand names as Mouton Rothschild, Latour and Lafite Rothschild hailing from this area. Numerous wine-themed tours are available.

Oysters and Wine

One of the most pleasurable ways of enjoying the region's wines is at Bordeaux' **Marché des Capucins** (p633) with glass of chilled white wine in one hand and a fresh, raw oyster in the other.

A TIPPLE WITH THE BEST

When in Rome do like the Romans, and when in Bordeaux drink wine in wine's Holy of Holies. The ultrastylish but very accessible **Bar du Vin** (3 cours du 30 Juillet; glass of wine from €3, with cheese from €5; ⊙11am-10pm Mon-Sat), inside the hallowed halls of the Maison du Vin de Bordeaux (p635), is the place to come for a tipple with people who really know their wine.

Lily Blake
CLOTHING
(☑ 05 33 05 41 40; www.lilyblake.fr; 68 rue Notre Dame) This author can't claim to be very knowledgable on women's clothing boutiques, but his wife and her friends are self-proclaimed experts and they rate this independent boutique as one of the better choices in town.

Jean d'Alos
CHEESE
(4 rue Montesquieu) Jean d'Alos is a fine *fromagerie* and with more than 150 raw-milk and farm cheeses it's the place to come to stock up for a cheesy picnic.

Information

Main Tourist Office (☑ 05 56 00 66 00; www.bordeaux-tourisme.com; 12 cours du 30 Juillet; ⊙9am-7pm Mon-Sat, 9.30am-6pm Sun) Runs an excellent range of city and regional tours. There's a small but helpful branch (☑ 05 56 91 64 70; ⊙9am-noon & 1-6pm Mon-Sat, 10am-noon & 1-3pm Sun) at the train station.
Maison du Tourisme de la Gironde (☑ 05 56 52 61 40; www.tourisme-gironde.fr; 21 cours de l'Intendance; ⊙9am-6pm Mon-Fri, 10am-1pm & 2-6.30pm Sat) Information on the Gironde *département*.

Getting There & Away

AIR
Bordeaux airport (www.bordeaux.aeroport.fr) is in Mérignac, 10km southwest of the city centre, with domestic and increasing numbers of international flights to many western European and North African destinations.

BUS
Citram Aquitaine (www.citram.fr) runs most buses to destinations in the Gironde.

International bus operator **Eurolines** (☑ 05 56 92 50 42; 32 rue Charles Domercq) faces the train station.

CAR
Rental companies have offices in the train-station building and at the airport.

TRAIN
Bordeaux is one of France's major rail-transit points. The station, Gare St-Jean, is about 3km from the city centre at the southern terminus of cours de la Marne.
Bayonne (€35, two hours)
La Rochelle (€31, 2¼ hours)
Nantes (from €51, four hours)
Paris Gare Montparnasse (from €77, three hours, at least 16 daily)
Poitiers (from €34, 1¾ hours)
Toulouse (from €33, 2¼ hours)

Getting Around

TO/FROM THE AIRPORT
The train station, place Gambetta and the main tourist office are connected to the airport (one-way €7.20) by **Jet'Bus** (www.navetteaeroport-bordeaux.com). The first bus leaves the airport at 8am from outside Terminal B (last at 11pm daily); the first departure to the airport from the train station is at 6am Monday to Friday, and 7am Saturday and Sunday (last at 9pm daily), with buses at 45-minute intervals throughout the day. The trip takes approximately 30 minutes. A taxi costs around €50.

BUS & TRAM
Urban buses and trams are run by **TBC** (www.infotbc.com). The company has Espace Bus information-ticket offices at the train station, place Gambetta (4 rue Georges Bonnac) and esplanade des Quinconces. Tram line C links the train station with the city centre via the riverside.

Single tickets (€1.40) are sold onboard buses and from machines at tram stops (stamp your ticket onboard). Tickets aren't valid for transfers.

Night buses operate until 1.30am on Thursday, Friday and Saturday nights; line 11 and 16 links place de la Victoire with the nightclub zone on quai de la Paludate.

CAR
City parking is pricey and hard to find. Look for free spaces in the side streets north of the Musée d'Art Contemporain and west of the Jardin Public.

TAXI
To order a taxi try ☑ 05 56 29 10 25.

St-Émilion
POP 2070
The medieval village of St-Émilion perches above vineyards renowned for producing

full-bodied, deeply coloured red wines and is easily the most alluring of all the region's wine towns. Named after Émilion, a miracle-working Benedictine monk who lived in a cave here between AD 750 and 767, it soon became a stop on pilgrimage routes, and the village and its vineyards are now Unesco-listed. Today, despite masses of tourists descending onto the town, it's well worth venturing 40km east from Bordeaux to experience St-Émilion's magic, particularly when the sun sets over the valley and the limestone buildings glow with halo-like golden hues.

⊙ Sights

Clocher TOWER
(Bell Tower; admission €1.50) For captivating views of the hilltop hamlet, collect the key from the tourist office to climb above the church. The entrance is on place des Créneaux.

Collégiale CHURCH
(Collegiate Church) A domed Romanesque 12th-century nave dominates the former Collégiale, which also boasts an almost-square vaulted choir built between the 14th and 16th centuries. **Cloître de l'Église Collégiale**, the church's tranquil 12th- to 14th-century cloister, is the venue for special events.

Porte de la Cadène CITY WALLS
(Gate of the Chain) Surviving sections of the town's medieval walls and gates include those running off rue Guadet.

Cloître des Cordeliers MONASTERY
(☑ 05 57 24 42 13; www.lescordeliers.com; rue Porte Brunet; admission free, guided cellar tours with wine tastings €5; ⊙ 11am-8pm May-Sep, 2-6pm Oct-Dec & Feb-Apr) Within the ruined monastery, the winery **Les Cordeliers** has made sparkling wine for over a century. Thirty-minute guided tours of the cellars take place at 3pm. Entry to the gardens and ruins is free (though you might want to consider buying a drink).

La Tour du Château Roy CASTLE
(admission €1.50; ⊙ 2-5.30pm Mon-Fri, 11am-12.15pm & 2-5.30pm Sat & Sun) Climb the 118 steps of the 13th-century donjon known as the Tour du Roi (King's Tower) for exceptional views of the town and the Dordogne Valley.

☩ Activities

A variety of **hiking and cycling circuits** loop through the greater World Heritage jurisdiction; the tourist office has maps.

L'École du Vin de St-Émilion WINE TASTING
(☑ 05 57 24 61 01; www.vignobleschateaux.fr; 4 rue du Clocher; tasting courses from €75) A brief but comprehensive introduction to wine, run by L'École du Vin de St-Émilion. A minimum group size of two is required and advance reservations are essential.

Maison du Vin WINE TASTING
(place Pierre Meyrat; classes €25; ⊙ mid-Jul–Aug) The Maison du Vin offers bilingual 1½-hour classes starting at 11am.

☞ Tours

The only (but highly worthwhile) way to visit the town's most interesting historical sites is with one of the tourist office's **guided tours** (adult/child from €7.50/free). There is a variety of tour options, including a lantern-lit **evening tour**, a **secrets of the city tour** and **family-friendly tours**. The standard historical city tour lasts 90 miunutes, with French-language tours leaving from the tourist office daily at 3pm. English tours are at 11am weekends only.

The following are among the most popular options, but tour types change frequently.

St-Émilion Souterrain WALKING TOUR
(Underground St-Émilion; adult/child €7.50/free) The St-Émilion Souterrain tour takes you beneath the pretty streets and into a fascinating labyrinth of catacombs – highlights are the hermit saint's famous cave, **Grotte de l'Ermitage**, and the 11th-century church, **Église Monolithe**, carved out of limestone between the 9th and the 12th centuries. Tours in French depart regularly throughout the day – call ahead to check English tour times although there's usually at least one a day. It's chilly below ground; bring a sweater.

Promenade Sur La Route Des Vins WALKING TOUR
(adult/child €12/free; ⊙ weekends) Two-hour guided tours walk you through local wine culture and take you to a nearby château for a tasting. Demand can be heavy so book ahead. There's normally at least one tour a day in English.

Les Samedis de l'Oenologie WINE TOUR
(tours €77; ⊙ Sat) Les Samedis de l'Oenologie, which combines a vineyard visit, lunch, town tour and wine-tasting course, is for those who want a much deeper immersion into the wine culture of St-Émilion than is offered by the more standard tours.

ATLANTIC COAST ST-ÉMILION

✦✦ Festivals & Events

**Les Grandes Heures
de St-Émilion**   MUSIC FESTIVAL
(www.grandesheuresdesaintemilion.fr; tickets €33)
Classical concerts are held at various châteaux
between March and December. Tickets must
be booked in advance; the program is posted
on the tourist-office website.

St-Émilion Jazz Festival   MUSIC FESTIVAL
(www.saint-emilion-jazz-festival.com; tickets €17-77)
In July the soothing tones of jazz take over the
town during its jazz festival.

Marché du Gout   MARKET
A market selling regional products sets up in
the village cloister in mid-October. The cloister is also the venue for **free concerts** from
May to November; the tourist office has the
program.

⬛ Sleeping & Eating

The village and its surrounds have some
charming, but very expensive, hotels. If you're
on a budget and don't want to camp, it might
be better to visit on a day trip from Bordeaux.
Ask the tourist office for a list of nearby, and
much cheaper, *chambres d'hôte*. Many of
St-Émilion's best restaurants are attached to
hotels.

⬛ Village Centre

**Hôtel-Restaurant
du Palais Cardinal**   HISTORIC HOTEL €€
(☑ 05 57 24 72 39; www.palais-cardinal.com; place du
11 Novembre 1918; s/d from €75/94; 🕭🐾) Run by
the same family for five generations, this hotel
puts a little more thought into its dress sense
than the other 'cheap' St-Émilion hotels. The
heated pool is set in flower-filled gardens and
framed by sections of the original medieval
town-wall fortifications, dating from the 13th
century.

It's well worth partaking of the gastronomic fare served at its restaurant (closed at lunch
on Wednesday and Thursday, and from December to April).

Auberge de la Commanderie   HOTEL €€
(☑ 05 57 24 70 19; www.aubergedelacommanderie.
com; 2 rue Porte Brunet; d €85-95; 🕭) Inside this
hotel's 13th-century walls, rooms are modernised with massive murals depicting a
technicolour pop-art version of an old black-
and-white postcard of the village. Larger
rooms are in an annexe over the road. Free
private parking.

Hôtel au Logis des Remparts   HOTEL €€
(☑ 05 57 24 70 43; www.logisdesremparts.com;
18 rue Porte Guadet; r from €105; 🕭🛜🐾) In a
thoughtfully restored townhouse, the modern
rooms here are comfortable but lack sparkle.
Much more exciting is the courtyard garden
and swimming pool.

Maison de la Commanderie   B&B €€€
(☑ 06 66 28 89 21, 05 57 24 26 59; www.maisondela
commanderie.com; 3bis rue de la Porte Brunet; d incl
breakfast €150-250; 🛜) Recently opened and totally gorgeous four-room B&B, run along very
professional lines. The owner has stripped
back a soft, mellow yellow house and added
in all manner of bright and quirky modern
touches to create a very personable and warm
place to stay.

Hostellerie de Plaisance   BOUTIQUE HOTEL €€€
(☑ 05 57 55 07 55; www.hostellerie-plaisance.com;
place du Clocher; incl breakfast r €445-710, ste €710;
⊗ closed Jan; 🕭🛜) This renowned hotel in the
shadow of the bell tower houses 17 whimsical
rooms. The rooms are about the size of a castle and look out over a flurry of red terracotta
roof tiles and a church tower, but, good as it is,
we can't help feeling that it's very overpriced.

L'Huîtres Pie   SEAFOOD €€
(☑ 05 57 24 69 71; 11 rue de la Porte Bouqueyre; menus from €21; ⊗ noon-2pm & 7.15-9.30pm Thu-Mon)
Arcachon oysters and other seafood feature
heavily in the dishes on offer here, but if slippery shellfish don't do it for you, tuck into one
of the hearty meat or fish dishes. You can eat
inside, or outside in the pleasant olive-shaded
courtyard.

**★ Restaurant Hostellerie
de Plaisance**   GASTRONOMIC €€€
(☑ 05 57 55 07 55; www.hostellerie-plaisance.com;
place du Clocher; menus €120-160; ⊗ lunch only
Tue-Fri, lunch & dinner Sat) Award-winning chef
Philippe Etchebest cooks up food like you've
never had before at his two-Michelin-starred
restaurant, housed in a dining room of eggshell blue and white gold inside the hotel of
the same name. The 'discovery *menu*' allows
you to do just that in eight courses. Advance
reservations essential.

⬛ Around St-Émilion

**Camping Domaine de la
Barbanne**   CAMPGROUND €
(☑ 05 57 24 75 80; www.camping-saint-emilion.com;
rte de Montagne; sites €39; ⊗ May–mid-Oct; 🐾)
This family-friendly campground is about

2km north of St-Émilion on the D122. Cabins, sleeping up to five people, are also available.

Château de Roques   HISTORIC HOTEL €€
(📱05 57 74 55 69; www.hostelleriederoques.com; r €79-124, menus from €25; 🏥🛜🍽️) If you've dreamed of staying in a romantic countryside château but your budget – or lack thereof – was a rude awakening, you'll be delighted by this affordable 16th-century place in the vineyards, 5km outside St-Émilion. Its restaurant (closed late December to early February) serves delicious regional fare washed down with the château's own wine.

The best road is the D122 (north from St-Émilion) – the château is just near the junction of the D21.

Grand Barrail   HISTORIC HOTEL €€€
(📱05 57 55 37 00; www.grand-barrail.com; rte de Libourne/D243; r from €350, menus from €29; 🏥🛜🍽️) Grand doesn't even begin to describe this immense 1850-built château, 3km from the village, with its decadent on-site spa, stone-flagged heated swimming pool, antique splattered rooms and, if you happen to be arriving by helicopter, its own helipad on the front lawns.

Undoubtedly the best seat in its restaurant is the corner table framed by 19th-century stained glass that would make the average church green with envy.

🛍️ Shopping

St-Émilion's sloping streets and squares are lined with about 50 wine shops – one for every eight of the old city's residents. The largest is the **Maison du Vin** (📱05 57 55 50 55; www.maisonduvinsaintemilion.com; place Pierre Meyrat; ⊗9.30am-12.30pm & 2-6.30pm), which is owned by the 250 châteaux whose wines it sells at cellar-door prices. It also has a free aromatic exhibit and sells specialist publications. In August it's open over lunch. If you think St-Émilion is a good place to get a few bottles of cut-price cheapo wine, think again. It's all quality only, with price tags to match – a very fast perusal of a few shops showed a top price of a cool €12,000 for a bottle of Petrus 1945. Not the sort of bottle you'd want airport customs confiscating from your hand luggage!

Ursuline nuns brought the recipe for macarons (almond biscuits) to St-Émilion in the 17th century. Specialist shops around town charge €6 per two dozen.

ℹ️ Information

Tourist Office (📱05 57 55 28 28; www.saint-emilion-tourisme.com; place des Créneaux;

⊗9.30am-8pm mid-Jul–mid-Aug, shorter hours rest of year) Stacks of brochures in English and details on visiting more than 100 nearby châteaux.

ℹ️ Getting There & Away

BICYCLE
The tourist office rents out bicycles for €18 per day, year-round.

BUS
Getting to St-Émilion from Bordeaux by bus is a bit of a pain as you have to change in Libourne. **Citram Aquitaine** (www.citram.fr) buses run this route. A ticket is €2.50 one-way and there are several buses a day.

CAR & MOTORCYCLE
From Bordeaux, follow the signs for Libourne and take the D243.

TRAIN
It's easier to take a train from Bordeaux, with around half a dozen services a day (€9.20, 35 minutes). St-Émilion station is a kilometre south of town.

Arcachon
POP 11,750

A long-time oyster-harvesting area on the south side of the tranquil, triangular Bassin d'Arcachon (Arcachon Bay), this seaside town lured bourgeois Bordelaise at the end of the 19th century. Its four little quarters are romantically named for each of the seasons, with villas that evoke the town's golden past amid a scattering of 1950's architecture.

Arcachon seethes with sun-seekers in summer, but you'll find much quieter beaches a short bike ride away.

👁️ Sights

Plage d'Arcachon   BEACH
In the **Ville d'Été** (Summer Quarter), Arcachon's sandy beach, Plage d'Arcachon, is flanked by two piers. Lively **Jetée Thiers** is at the western end. In front of the eastern pier, **Jetée d'Eyrac**, stands the town's turreted **Casino de la Plage**. The sheltered basin in which Arcachon sits means the water is always absolutely flat calm and ideal for families – a far cry from most Atlantic beaches.

On the flipside, estuary run-off means the water is always a browner colour than the nearby open Atlantic (it's clean though).

Ville d'Hiver   NEIGHBOURHOOD
On the tree-covered hillside south of the Ville d'Été, the century-old Ville d'Hiver

(Winter Quarter) has more than 300 villas, many decorated with delicate wood tracery, ranging in style from neo-Gothic through to colonial. It's an easy stroll or a short ride up the (free) art deco public lift in Parc Mauresque.

Aquarium et Musée   AQUARIUM
(2 rue du Professeur Jolyet; adult/child under 10yr €5.50/3.50; ⊗9.45am-12.15pm & 1.45-6.30pm Mon-Fri, 2-6pm Sat) In a wooden shack opposite the casino, this aquarium has a small collection of Atlantic fish in floodlit tanks.

🏃 Activities

Ocean Roots   SURFING
(☑06 62 26 04 11; www.oceanroots.com; 228 bd de la Côte d'Argent; courses from €35; 🚻) The exposed ocean beaches to the south of town generally offer good conditions for surfing. Ocean Roots offers lessons and rents out equipment.

Cycling   CYCLING
Cycle paths link Arcachon with the Dune du Pilat and Biscarosse (30km to the south), and around the Bassin d'Arcachon to Cap Ferret. From here, a cyclable path runs parallel to the beaches north to Pointe de Grave.

🎫 Tours

Les Bateliers Arcachonnais   BOAT TOURS
(☑05 57 72 28 28; www.bateliers-arcachon.com; 🚻) Daily, year-round cruises sail around the **Île aux Oiseaux** (adult/child/under 5yrs €16/11/5.5), the uninhabited 'bird island' in the middle of the bay. It's a haven for tern, curlew and redshank, so bring your binoculars. In summer there are regular all-day excursions (11am to 5.30pm) to the **Banc d'Arguin** (adult/child/under 3yrs €26/17.50/9), the sand bank off the Dune du Pilat.

🛌 Sleeping

Arcachon has tons of accommodation options. Many are chintzy mid-20th-century time warps, though not without charm.

Hôtel le Dauphin   HISTORIC HOTEL €€
(☑05 56 83 02 89; www.dauphin-arcachon.com; 7 av Gounod; r from €125; 🅿🛜🖥) This late 19th-century gingerbread place with patterned red-and-cream brickwork is very twee, but it's a badge it wears with pride. An icon of its era, it's graced by twin semicircular staircases, magnolias and palms. Plain but spacious rooms are well set up for

families. Parking is free. The beach is five minutes' walk away.

Grand Hôtel Richelieu   HISTORIC HOTEL €€€
(☑05 56 83 16 50; www.grand-hotel-richelieu. com; 185 blvd de la Plage; r €105-207; 🛜) Dominating the beachfront just a few steps from Arcachon's casino, this faded wedding-cake-white place is grander on the outside than in, but has an old-fashioned charm and stunning views from its sea-facing rooms.

🍴 Eating

The bay's oysters (served raw and accompanied by the local small, flat sausages called *crepinettes*) appear on menus everywhere.

The beachfront promenade between Jetée Thiers and Jetée d'Eyrac is lined with restaurants and places offering pizza and crêpes, plus a couple of standout places serving seafood.

Aux Mille Saveurs   TRADITIONAL FRENCH €€
(☑05 56 83 40 28; 25 bd du Général Leclerc; menus €19.50-50; ⊗closed Wed & dinner Sun &Tue) In a light-filled space of flowing white tablecloths, this genteel restaurant is renowned for its traditional French fare artistically presented on fine china.

Cafe de la Plage   SEAFOOD €€
(Chez Pierre; ☑05 56 22 52 94; www.cafede laplage.com; 1 bd Veyrier Montagnères; menus from €30, seafood platters €25-42; ⊗noon-2.30pm & 7-9.30pm) This see-and-be-seen restaurant serves up an ocean of seafood.

ℹ Information

Tourist Office (☑05 57 52 97 97; www. arcachon.com; Esplanade Georges Pompidou; ⊗9am-7pm Jul-Aug, 9am-6pm Mon-Sat, 10am-1pm & 2-5pm Sun Apr-Jun & Sep, shorter hours rest of year) The town's helpful tourist office is five minutes back from the beach, near the train station.

ℹ Getting There & Away

There are frequent trains between Bordeaux and Arcachon (€11.20, 50 minutes).

Around Arcachon

Dune du Pilat

This colossal sand dune (sometimes referred to as the Dune de Pyla because of its location in the resort town of Pyla-sur-Mer), 8km south of Arcachon, stretches from the mouth of the Bassin d'Arcachon southwards for almost 3km. Already the largest in Europe, the dune is growing eastwards 4.5m a year – it has swallowed trees, a road junction and even a hotel. The view from the top – approximately 114m above sea level – is magnificent. To the west you can see the sandy shoals at the mouth of the Bassin d'Arcachon, including the **Banc d'Arguin bird reserve** and Cap Ferret. Dense dark-green pine forests stretch from the base of the dune eastwards almost as far as the eye can see.

Take care swimming in this area: powerful currents swirl out to sea from the deceptively tranquil *baïnes* (little bays).

Although just a very quick trip from Arcachon, the area around the dune is an enjoyable place to kick back for a while. Most people choose to camp in one of the swag of seasonal campgrounds. Lists and information on all of these (and more bricks-and-mortar-based accommodation) can be found at www.bassin-arcachon.com.

Cap Ferret
POP 7300
Hidden within a canopy of pine trees at the tip of the Cap Ferret peninsula, the tiny village of Cap Ferret spans a mere 2km between the tranquil bay and the crashing Atlantic waves.

◉ Sights & Activities

Lighthouse   LIGHTHOUSE
(adult/child €6/4; ⊙10am-7.30pm Jul-Aug, 10am-12.30pm & 2-6.30 Apr-Jun & Sep) The 53m-high red and white lighthouse has an interactive exhibit and stunning views of the surf from the top.

Surf Center   SURFING
(☑05 56 60 61 05; www.surf-center.fr; 22 allées des Goëlands; lessons from €25; ⊙Easter-Sep) The Surf Center rents boards and offers lessons.

🛏 Sleeping & Eating

Cap Ferret is littered with campgrounds, which can be tracked down on www.bassin-arcachon.com.

La Maison du Bassin   BOUTIQUE HOTEL €€
(☑05 56 60 60 63; www.lamaisondubassin.com; 5 rue des Pionniers; s €120-210, d €140-250; ⊙closed Jan) La Maison du Bassin has dreamy rooms with details like a muslin-canopied sleigh bed, or a curtained bath-tub in the centre of the room. Its chocolate-toned contemporary restaurant, **Le Bistrot du Bassin** (*menus*

€26-40), will make your taste buds very happy indeed.

❶ Getting There & Away
Cap Ferret is a scenic drive around Bassin d' Arcachon. Alternatively, drive here directly from Bordeaux (71.8km) by taking the D106.
Les Bateliers Arcachonnais(www.bateliers-arcachon.com; one-way adult/child/under 3yrs €7.50/5/3) Les Bateliers Arcachonnais runs ferries from Arcachon to Cap Ferret year-round. In the warmer months, seasonally operating lines include ferries linking Cap Ferret and the Dune du Pilat, and Cap Ferret and Moulleau. Schedules are posted on the website and available from tourist offices.

Gujan Mestras
POP 19,400
Picturesque oyster ports are dotted around the town of Gujan Mestras, which sprawls along 9km of coastline.

Gujan Mestras' train station is on the train line linking Bordeaux with Arcachon.

◉ Sights

Le Teich Parc Ornithologique   BIRDWATCHING
(Bird Reserve; ☑05 56 22 80 93; www.parc-ornithologique-du-teich.com; adult/child €7.80/5.60; ⊙10am-8pm Jul-Aug, 10am-7pm mid-Apr–Jun & early Sep, shorter hours rest of year; ⊕) A series of trails wind through and around the swamps, lakes and woodlands of the idyllic Parc Ornithologique situated in Le Teich, 5km east of Gujan Mestras. Birds also find the place much to their liking and some 260 species of migratory and nonmigratory birds call it home.

The stars of the show are the white storks, spoonbills, common cranes, marsh harriers and black kites, all of which can be spied on from a network of well-maintained hides. Away from birds, the park is one of the most reliable places in France to see the now-threatened European pond tortoise.

Port de Larros   OYSTERS
Flat-bottomed oyster boats moored to weathered wooden shacks line Port de Larros, the largest oyster port around Gujan Mestras. The small **Maison de l'Huître** (adult/child €4.50/2.50; ⊙10am-12.30pm & 2.30-6pm Mon-Sat) has a display on oyster farming, including a short film in English. It can also supply audioguides (€3.50) for the whole port area. Locally harvested oysters are sold nearby and served at seafood restaurants with waterside terraces.

ATLANTIC COAST AROUND ARCACHON

French Basque Country

POP 272,100

Best Places to Eat

➜ À Table! (p648)

➜ Lezetako Borda (p666)

➜ Buvette des Halles (p664)

➜ Le Kaiku (p664)

➜ Restaurant Le Pim'pi (p657)

Best Places to Stay

➜ Péniche Djébelle (p648)

➜ La Devinière (p661)

➜ Maison d'hôte Irazabala (p667)

➜ Hôtel Villa Koegui (p656)

Why Go?

Gently sloping from the foothills of the Pyrenees into the deep-sapphire-blue Bay of Biscay, the Basque Country straddles France and Spain. Yet this feisty, independent land remains profoundly different from either of the nation states that have adopted it.

The Basque Country is famed for the glitzy beach resort of Biarritz, where surfers strut their stuff in the waves and oiled sun-seekers pack the beaches like glistening sardines. But the region offers so much more than the pleasures of sun and surf. Nearby Bayonne is a chocolate box of narrow winding streets full of Basque culture, and St-Jean de Luz, further south, is a delightful seaside fishing port.

Inland, up in the lush hills, little one-street villages and green valleys traversed by hiking trails fan out from the walled town of St-Jean Pied de Port, an age-old stop for pilgrims heading over the Spanish border to Santiago de Compostela.

When to Go
Bayonne

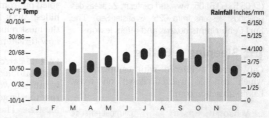

May It's chocolate time in Bayonne and the empty beaches and mountains are all yours.

Aug The beaches are alive and kicking, and the Fêtes de Bayonne is loud and messy.

Sep–Oct Autumnal colours are glorious in the hills, and the surf is as good as it gets.

Bayonne

POP 46,200

Surrounded by sturdy fortifications and splashed in red and white paint, Bayonne (Baiona in Basque), capital of the French Basque Country, is one of the most attractive towns in southwest France. Its perfectly preserved old town (until 1907 it was actually forbidden to build outside the town's fortifications) and shoals of riverside restaurants are an absolute delight to explore.

In addition to its chocolates, which you'll see sold throughout France, Bayonne is famous for its prime cured ham and for the *baïonnette* (bayonet), developed here in 1640 on rue des Faures (Blacksmiths' Street).

The Rivers Adour and Nive split central Bayonne into three: St-Esprit, the area north of the Adour; Grand Bayonne, the oldest and most attractive part of the city, on the western bank of the Nive; and the very Basque Petit Bayonne quarter on the east.

To the west, Bayonne meets the suburban sprawl of Anglet (famed for its beaches) and the glamorous seaside resort of Biarritz.

◉ Sights

Musée Basque et de l'Histoire de Bayonne MUSEUM

(✆ 05 59 59 08 98; www.musee-basque.com; 37 quai des Corsaires; adult/child €6.50/free; ◷ 10am-6.30pm Jul-Aug, closed Mon rest of yr) The seafaring history, traditions and cultural identity of the Basque people are all explored at this superb museum, where exhibits include a reconstructed farm and the interior of a typical *etxe* (home). Labelling is in French, Spanish and Basque only but English information sheets are available.

In July and August free 'nocturnal' visits are possible on Thursday evenings from 6.30pm to 8.30pm.

Cathédrale Ste-Marie CATHEDRAL

(place Louis Pasteur; ◷ 10-11.45am & 3-6.15pm Mon-Sat, 3.30-6.15pm Sun, cloister 9am-12.30pm & 2-6pm) The twin towers of Bayonne's Gothic cathedral soar above the city. Construction began in the 13th century, and was completed in 1451; the mismatched materials in some ways resemble Lego blocks.

Above the north aisle are three lovely stained-glass windows; the oldest, in the Chapelle Saint Jérôme, dates from 1531. The entrance to the stately 13th-century cloister is on place Louis Pasteur.

French Basque Country Highlights

❶ Discovering the local chocolate at a factory tour in **Bayonne** (p650)

❷ Hiking along quiet mountain trails in the mist-soaked Pyrenees near **St-Étienne de Baïgorry** (p669)

❸ Treating yourself to tapas and watching surfers tackle the waves in magisterial **Biarritz** (p651)

❹ Tasting traditional Basque seafood dishes at **St-Jean de Luz** (p658)

❺ Browsing the farmers market in **St-Jean Pied de Port** (p667)

❻ Exploring picturesque villages **Ainhoa** (p666) and **Espelette** (p667), and chugging to the summit of **La Rhune** (p665)

❼ Soaking up some sun on the sands of **Hossegor** or **Moliets** (p651) in the region of Les Landes

Bayonne

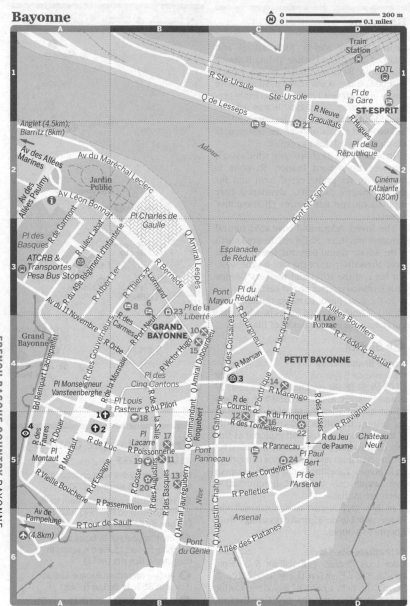

Ramparts   CITY WALL
Bayonne's 17th-century fortifications are now covered with grass, dotted with trees and enveloped in pretty parks. You can walk the stretches of the old ramparts that rise above bd Rempart Lachepaillet and rue Tour de Sault.

Bayonne

◉ Sights
1 Cathédrale Ste-Marie...........................A5
2 Cloister...A5
3 Musée Basque et de l'Histoire de
    Bayonne C4
4 Ramparts A5

⊜ Sleeping
5 Hôtel Côte Basque............................D1
6 Hôtel des Arceaux B3
7 Hôtel Monbar....................................C5
8 Le Grand Hôtel B3
9 Péniche Djébelle...............................C2

◉ Eating
10 À Table! B4
11 Bar-Restaurant du Marché.................B5
12 Chiloa Gurmenta Restaurant C5
13 Ibaia B5

14 La Bottega di Mario C4
15 La Feuillantine..B4
16 Restaurant Bakera C5
17 Xurasko B5

◉ Drinking & Nightlife
18 Cafés Ramuntcho..................................B5
19 Chai Ramina B5

◉ Entertainment
20 La Luna Negra Music B5
21 L'Autre Cinéma......................................C2
22 Trinquet St-André C5

◉ Shopping
23 Cazenave...B3
    Daranatz ....(see 23)
24 Pierre Ibaïalde.......................................C5

☞ Tours

City Tours   TOUR
(adult €5-45) The tourist office organises a range of different city tours (some in English), ranging from a historical tour of old Bayonne to others which focus on food, or museums. Departure times and tour type vary – contact the tourist office (p650) for details.

✯ Festivals & Events

Foire au Jambon   FOOD FESTIVAL
(Ham Fair) During Easter week, the town hosts a Ham Fair, honouring *jambon de Bayonne,* the acclaimed local ham. You may think this is just a recently thought up touristy gimmick to sell ham, but no – this fair in March or April has taken place annually since 1462!

Journées du Chocolat   FOOD FESTIVAL
Master chocolatiers reveal the secrets of chocolate making (with tastings) in May.

🛏 Sleeping

Even outside the Fêtes de Bayonne, it's tough to find a bed from mid-July to mid-August.

Auberge de Jeunesse   HOSTEL €
(☑ 05 59 58 70 00; www.fuaj.org; 19 rte des Vignes; dm €22; ☉ mid-Apr–Sep, reception 9am-noon & 6-10pm; ⓐ📶) In the nearby beach suburb of Anglet, this hostel has reached legendary status for its nonstop international party scene. To keep people well oiled, it comes complete with a basement Scottish pub

screening surf films. In high season they don't accept families (which says a lot about the kind of atmosphere prevalent here).

From the Mairie de Bayonne (Town Hall) bus stop, take bus 4 to the stop for Les Sables, from where it's a 500m uphill walk. You have to be an HI member to stay (you can sign up on arrival).

Hôtel des Arceaux   BOUTIQUE HOTEL €
(☑ 05 59 59 15 53; www.hotel-arceaux.com; 26 rue Port Neuf; r with shared bathroom €50, d €69-79; 📶) The rooms and communal areas at this hotel, which is located on one of the prettiest streets in the old town, are a cacophony of noisy colours and stately antiques, and it's very well run. All the rooms (some of which can accommodate families) are different, so ask to see a few first.

Hôtel Monbar   HOTEL €
(☑ 05 59 59 26 80; 24 rue Pannecau; d from €32; 📶) Oh la la, what a bargain. Located inside a tall, wobbly, red-and-white Bayonne townhouse, this hotel is a little slice of old French life. The rooms are basic (as you'd expect for the price), but have attached bathrooms and colourful bedspreads. There's a cafe-bar downstairs.

★ **Péniche Djébelle**   HOUSEBOAT €€

(☎05 59 25 77 18; www.djebelle.com; face au 17 Quai de Lesseps; d incl breakfast €150; ☺closed Oct-Apr; ☎) This unique *chambre d'hôte* isn't a bricks-and-mortar hotel at all, but a houseboat floating in the River Ardour. The two vast rooms are imaginatively decorated and absolutely sublime; one has a Moroccan theme and the other, which has the boat's steering wheel built into the bathroom, is full of tropical islands.

A magnificent breakfast spread is included and there's a pet rabbit and cat to keep you company. Advance booking essential.

Hôtel Côte Basque   HOTEL €€

(☎05 59 55 10 21; www.hotel-cotebasque.fr; 2 rue Maubec; r from €85; 🅿☎) Ride the clanky, old-fashioned lift up to your modern room with low-slung (but rather small) beds and colourful art on the walls. Sitting opposite the train station, this modern place offers sizzling value for money.

Le Grand Hôtel   HISTORIC HOTEL €€

(☎05 59 59 62 00; www.legrandhotelbayonne.com; 21 rue Thiers; d from €106; 🅿☎) This old building was once a convent, but when they ran out of nuns someone turned it into a hotel. Now its cream-toned, wheelchair-accessible rooms and cosy on-site bar (which probably didn't exist when it was a convent) make this friendly business-class hotel a fine place to rest up. Parking is €15.

✖ Eating

Bayonne has some superb places to eat, and costs are generally much lower than in nearby Biarritz.

★ **Bar-Restaurant du Marché**   BASQUE €

(☎05 59 59 22 66; 39 rue des Basques; menus from €9, mains from €8; ☺noon-2.30pm Mon-Sat) Run by a welcoming Basque-speaking family, this unpretentious place is an absolute institution where everyone knows everyone (which some people may find slightly intimidating, but don't worry, just dive right in – nobody cares!). Simple but ample home-cooked dishes full of the flavours of the neighbouring market are dished up to all comers.

Chiloa Gurmenta Restaurant   BASQUE €

(7 rue des Tonneliers; plat du jour €7.50; ☺12.30-2pm & 7.30-10pm Tue-Sat) As Basque as a game of *pelota,* this simple and rustic little restaurant, located inside a former brothel, serves one thing and one thing only: *axoa.* A

Basque farmers' dish, *axoa* originates from the nearby village of Espelette and consists of minced veal with Espelette peppers, rice, potato and whatever else is lying around.

La Bottega di Mario   ITALIAN €

(52 rue Bourgneuf; mains €10-15; ☺noon-2.30pm & 7-10.30pm Tue-Sat, noon-2.30pm Sun) Discreet, backstreet place that you'd never guess was home to what many say is the finest Italian food in Bayonne, but then Mario, the owner, is from Sardinia, and he certainly knows how to prepare no-fuss, earthy Italian meals including pizzas you won't forget in a hurry.

★ **À Table!**   MODERN FRENCH €€

(☎05 59 56 79 22; 27 quai Amiral Dubourdieu; mains €15; ☺noon-2pm & 7-10pm Tue-Sat) This funky little riverside restaurant is the town's current favourite place to eat. It's as friendly as it is bright and the short *menu* is a mix of creative French and international dishes all of which are cooked in the tiny, open kitchen in front of you by the couple who run it.

There are only a handful of tables so get there early.

A TASTE OF SPAIN

You know you're getting close to the Spanish border when tapas start cropping up. Bayonne has an increasing number of *pintxo* (tapas in Basque) bars, and in some the quality is every bit as good as San Sebastián, just over the border in Spain. The golden rule of tapas is to just take one or two (which you pay for when you leave) before moving on to try those elsewhere. Two of the best tapas bars are:

Xurasko (16 rue Poissonnerie; tapas from €2.50; ☺noon-11pm) Tapas start to decorate the bar-top like little flowers at Xurasko from around 7pm and as everyone clocks off work they stop by for a glass of wine and some choice tidbits from what is one of Bayonne's original tapas bars.

Ibaia (45 quai Amiral Jauréguiberry; mains from €8; ☺noon-2pm & 7-10pm Tue-Sat) With hams swinging from hooks in the ceiling and a garlic-heavy atmosphere, Ibaia is a Bayonne legend. Here the emphasis is on larger plates of hot tapas such as garlic prawns and spicy chorizo sausages, which you order off a blackboard menu. One plate is often enough for two people.

FÊTES DE BAYONNE

Beginning on either the first Wednesday in August or occasionally the last in July, the Fêtes de Bayonne attract thousands of people from across France and Spain for a five-day orgy of drinking, dancing, processions, fireworks and bulls. In many ways it's like a less commercialised version of the famous San Fermín festival in Pamplona (Spain) and, just like in Pamplona, Bayonne also holds bull running. However, here the bulls are actually cows – though they still have horns and they still hurt when they mow you down – and they don't run down the streets, but are instead released on the crowd in front of the Château Neuf. During the *fête*, real bullfights also take place.

One of the biggest highlights of the *fêtes* is the opening ceremony, when huge crowds gather in front of the town hall at 10pm on the Wednesday night for an impressively noisy firework display and the arrival of a 'lion' (the town's mascot).

While the nocturnal activities might be a bit much for children, the daytime processions, marching bands, organised children's picnics and even a children's 'bull' run are tailor-made for the delight of little ones. Thursday daytime has the most child-friendly activities.

If you're planning on attending the *fêtes*, you'll need to book at least six to eight months in advance for hotel accommodation anywhere in the vicinity of Bayonne. A number of temporary campgrounds (€60 for six days) are erected in and around Bayonne to ease the pressure; otherwise you can just do what most people do and sleep in the back of a car or under a bus (camping outside the campgrounds is forbidden).

Finally, unless you want to stand out like a sore thumb, don't forget to dress all in white with a red sash and neck-scarf. For dates and other *fêtes* information, see www.fetes. bayonne.fr.

Restaurant Bakera BASQUE €€
(☑ 05 59 25 51 68; 15 rue des Tonneliers; mains €17) Despite its location in a slightly grubby part of town, this fresh new offering gives customers a big smiley welcome and, greetings over, dishes up large portions of classy land- and sea-based Basque cuisine for what is a very decent price.

La Feuillantine GASTRONOMIC €€
(☑ 05 59 46 14 94; www.lafeuillantine-bayonne. com; 21 quai Amiral Dubourdieu; menus €17/-39, mains €20) This riverside place might be quite small, but it's garnered an impressive reputation for its excellent Basque dishes, which are served with flair and style in its colourful dining room. The culinary skills of chef Nicolas Bertegui have received virtually universal praise in the mainstream French media.

 Drinking & Nightlife

Petit Bayonne is awash with pubs and bars (all generally open from noon to 2am, Monday to Saturday), especially along rue Pannecau, rue des Cordeliers and quai Galuperie.

Chai Ramina BAR
(11 rue Poissonnerie) When there's a big rugby match on (the local club is one of the biggest in France) and the weather is fine, rue Pois-

sonnerie is completely blocked by the huge crowds spilling out of Chai Ramina.

Cafés Ramuntcho TEAROOM
(9 rue du Pilori) To sip no fewer than 380 different teas (reputedly the most in France), take a seat amid the metal canisters of this café, established in 1920. Tea is available for purchase to take home, too.

☆ Entertainment

Upcoming cultural events are listed in *À l'Affiche* and the trimestrial *Les Saisons de la Culture,* both available free at the tourist office. Every Thursday in July and August, there's traditional Basque music (admission free; ◷ 9.30pm) in place Charles de Gaulle.

Cinéma l'Atalante CINEMA
(☑ 05 59 55 76 63; www.cinema-atalante.org; 7 rue Denis Etcheverry) Along with its sister cinema, L'Autre Cinéma (3 quai Sala), l'Atalante screens art-house nondubbed films. Both cinemas are in the St-Esprit neighbourhood.

La Luna Negra Music MUSIC
(www.lunanegra.fr; rue des Augins; ◷ 7pm-2am Wed-Sat) Catch live jazz, salsa and tango evenings, and concerts of world music, as well as comedy shows at this alternative cabaret/ theatre venue.

Trinquet St-André
SPORT

(☑ 05 59 59 18 69; rue des Tonneliers; adult/child €10/2; ☺ matches 4pm Thu Oct-Jun) The Trinquet St-André stages *main nue pelota* (bare hand *pelota*) matches. They also have frequent live music.

🛍 Shopping

For chocolate, head to Daranatz or Cazenave on rue Port Neuf.

Pierre Ibaïalde
DELI

(41 rue des Cordeliers) To buy Bayonne's famous ham at the lowest prices, visit the covered market or, for the best quality, visit a specialist shop such as Pierre Ibaïalde, a deli serving only the finest cuts where you can taste a sliver before you buy.

🛈 Information

Tourist Office (☑ 08 20 42 64 64; www. bayonne-tourisme.com; place des Basques; ☺ 9am-7pm Mon-Sat, 10am-1pm Sun Jul-Aug, 9am-6.30pm Mon-Fri, 10am-1pm & 2-6pm Sat Mar-Jun & Sep-Oct, shorter hrs rest of yr) Efficient office providing stacks of informative brochures and bike rental, plus guided city tours.

🛈 Getting There & Away

AIR

Biarritz-Anglet-Bayonne airport (☑ 05 59 43 83 83; www.biarritz.aeroport.fr) is 5km southwest of central Bayonne and 3km southeast of the centre of Biarritz. It's served by low-cost carriers including EasyJet and Ryanair, as well as Air France, SAS, Hop and others, with daily domestic flights and flights across France, to the UK, and, in summer, regular flights to Ireland, Finland, Norway, Switzerland and Belguim.

BUS

From **place des Basques**, **ATCRB** (www. transports-atcrb.com) buses follow the coast to the Spanish border. There are nine services daily to St-Jean de Luz (€2, 40 minutes) and Hendaye (€2, one hour). Summer beach traffic can double journey times.

Transportes Pesa (www.pesa.net) buses leave place des Basques twice a day Monday to Saturday for Bilbao (€20.30) in Spain, calling at Biarritz, St-Jean de Luz, Irún and San Sebastián (€7.90).

Chronoplus (☑ 05 59 52 59 52; www.chrono plus.eu) buses link Bayonne, Biarritz and Anglet. A single ticket costs €1, while a 24hr pass is €2. Timetables are available from tourist offices or online. Bus A2 runs between Bayonne and Biarritz about 50 times daily, stopping at the Hôtels de Ville (town halls) and stations of both towns. A couple of other lines link the two towns via Anglet.

CAR & MOTORCYCLE

All the big car-rental agencies are represented at the airport; otherwise, close to the train station is **Avis** (☑ 05 59 55 06 56; www.avis.fr; 1 rue Ste-Ursule).

TRAIN

TGVs run between Bayonne and Paris Gare Montparnasse (€67 to €109, five to six hours, eight daily).

There are five trains daily to St-Jean Pied de Port (€10, 1¼ hours) and fairly frequent services to St-Jean de Luz (€5, 25 minutes) via Biarritz (€3, nine minutes). Trains also go to the French and Spanish border towns of Hendaye (€7.50, 40 minutes) and Irún (€10, 45 minutes). For travel between Bayonne and Biarritz, however, the train station is way out of town so you're better off on the bus.

Other services:

Bordeaux from €31, two hours, at least 10 daily

Toulouse from €43, 3¾ hours, five daily

BAYONNE CHOCOLATE

Bayonne's long association with chocolate stems from the Spanish Inquisition, when Jews who fled Spain set up their trade in the St-Esprit neighbourhood. By 1870 Bayonne boasted 130 chocolatiers (specialist makers of chocolate), more than in all of Switzerland. Today, 11 are still in business, including Daranatz (☑ 05 59 59 03 05; 15 rue Port Neuf) and the 19th-century Cazenave (19 rue Port Neuf), which does a sublime *chocolat mousseaux* (rich hot chocolate; €5.90). You can see chocolate being made during a tour at L'Atelier du Chocolat (☑ 05 59 55 00 15; www.atelierduchocolat.fr; 1 allée de Gibéléou; adult/child €6/3; ☺ 9.30am-6.30pm Mon-Sat), which includes a historical overview of chocolate in Bayonne and, of course, tastings.

Tastings are also the highlight of the weekend-long Journées du Chocolat each May, when master chocolatiers set up the tools of their craft in front of their shops.

For more chocolate heaven, pop by the Planète Musée du Chocolat (p653) in Biarritz.

BEACHES OF LES LANDES

North of Bayonne is the *département* of Les Landes, a vast semiwilderness of pine forests and lakes. This whole area has a special kind of wild beauty, criss-crossed with excellent cycling and walking trails; maps and route suggestions are available from most tourist offices. The trails are broken up by numerous lakes, the best being at Soustons and the small village of Léon, with opportunities for windsurfing, canoeing and other water sports. But for most people, the reason to visit Les Landes is its beaches. From the mouth of the Ardour at Anglet north to Arcachon and beyond to the mouth of the Gironde stretches a ribbon of shimmering golden sand backed by dunes and basking under a deep blue sky.

Above all else, this is surf country. Towns such as the twin centres of Capbreton and Hossegor now owe their existence to surfing. Capbreton, which still retains some life beyond the waves, is easily the more appealing of the two, and its small port supplies the town's numerous seafood restaurants with delicious fresh fish.

Chez du Camp (☑ 05 58 72 11 33; 4 rue Port d'Albert, Capbreton; menus €28-38, mains €16) is one of the best places in town to indulge. You can sit at a table overlooking ocean-sized tanks swimming with the imminent contents of your dinner. Or, even better, pick up a serving of the superb house special: mussels and squid. Get it all cooked up on the spot and then take it away to have as a picnic.

Brash Hossegor, about 1km north of Capbreton, is renowned for having some of the best beach break waves in the world. It has to be said, though, that this reputation has made it the very definition of a 'hey, dude' surf town, where if you're not wearing just the right T-shirt then you're not welcome at the party. On the plus side, the beaches here are breathtaking and they only get better the further north towards the village of Seignosse you go. For eating you won't do better than La Tetrade (☑ 05 58 43 51 48; www.latetrade-cote-lac.com; 1187 av du Touring Club de France, Hossegor; menus €14-39). Set on the banks of Hossegor's shimmering lake, it offers the kind of view to get married to, and a shellfish and seafood *menu* (including oysters farmed in the lake in front of you) you'd probably marry if you could.

But for the best beach of all, one of the best in France, you have to continue north another 20km to the tiny seasonal village of Moliets. The vast beach here, which sits at the mouth of a sluggish and inky-coloured river known as the Courant d'Huchet, has sand that sparkles like diamonds and is soft as feathers, while the river itself provides safe bathing for children.

Unfortunately, most of the limited hotel accommodation in this region is seriously poor value and most visitors end up camping at one of the dozens of campgrounds or staying at one of the 'surfcamps' along the coast. Local tourist offices can supply details.

From Bayonne's train station, RDTL (www.rdtl.fr) runs services northwards into Les Landes including Capbreton/Hossegor (€5, 40 minutes, six or seven daily).

ℹ Getting Around

TO/FROM THE AIRPORT

Bus 14 links Bayonne with the airport (€1, buses depart roughly hourly). A taxi from the town centre costs around €20.

BICYCLE

Bayonne's tourist office lends out bikes for free (not overnight); you simply need to leave some ID as a deposit.

BUS

A free *navette* (shuttle bus) loops around the heart of town.

CAR & MOTORCYCLE

There's free parking along the southern end of av des Allées Paulmy, within easy walking distance of the tourist office.

TAXI

Call Taxi Bayonne (☑ 05 59 59 48 48).

Biarritz

POP 26,067

As ritzy as its name suggests, this stylish coastal town, 8km west of Bayonne, took off as a resort in the mid-19th century when Napoléon III and his Spanish-born wife, Eugénie, visited regularly. Along its rocky

Biarritz

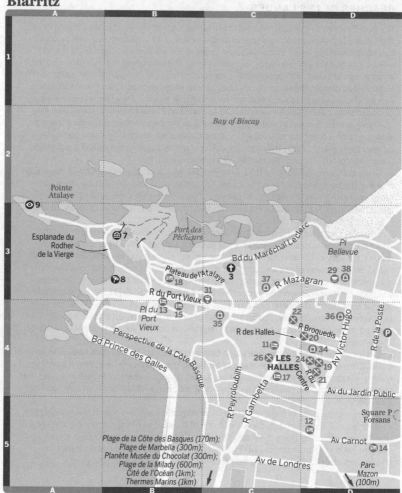

coastline are architectural hallmarks of this golden age, and the belle époque and art deco eras that followed. Although it retains a high glamour quotient (and high prices to match), it's also a magnet for vanloads of surfers chasing some of Europe's best waves.

◉ Sights

Musée de la Mer   MUSEUM
(☎ 05 59 22 75 40; www.museedelamer.com; esplanade du Rocher de la Vierge; adult/child €14/10; ◷ 9.30am-midnight Jul-Aug, 9.30am-8pm Apr-Jun & Sep-Oct, shorter hrs rest of yr) Housed in a wonderful art-deco building, Biarritz's

Musée de la Mer is seething with underwater life from the Bay of Biscay and beyond, including huge aquariums of sharks and dainty tropical reef fish, as well as exhibits on fishing recalling Biarritz's whaling past. It's the seals, though, that steal the show (feeding time, always a favourite with children, is at 10.30am and 5pm). In high season it's possible to have the place almost to yourself by visiting late at night.

Cité de l'Océan   MUSEUM
(☎ 05 59 22 75 40; www.citedelocean.com; 1 av de la Plage; adult/child €11/7.30; ◷ 10am-10pm Jul-

fun for adults. A combined ticket with the Musée de la Mer costs €18 for adults and €13 for children. Family tickets are also available. In July and August a free *navette* (shuttle bus) runs between Musée de la Mer and the Cité de l'Océan.

Musée d'Art Oriental Asiatica　MUSEUM
(☑ 05 59 22 78 79; www.museeasiatica.com; 1 rue Guy Petit; adult/child €10/2; ◷ 10.30am-6.30pm Mon-Fri, 2-7pm Sat & Sun Jul-Aug & French school holidays, shorter hrs rest of yr) Out on the edge of town is this unexpected treasure trove of ancient Indian, Chinese and Tibetan statues, monuments and temple artwork. The layout is a bit haphazard, but the information cards (in several languages) clearly explain the significance of the objects. It's generally considered the finest collection of its type outside Paris.

Planète Musée du Chocolat　MUSEUM
(☑ 05 59 23 27 72; www.planetemuseedu chocolat.com; 14 av Beau Rivage; adult/child €6.50/5; ◷ 10am-7pm Jul-Aug, shorter hrs rest of yr) Delve into this real-life *Charlie and the Chocolate Factory* for an indulgent exploration through the world of chocolate, from its earliest beginnings to the mass production of today.

Beaches

Biarritz' raison d'être is its fashionable beaches, particularly the two central stretches, **Grande Plage** and **Plage Miramar**, which are lined end to end with sunbathing bodies on hot summer days. The other central Biarritz beach is the tiny cove of **Plage du Port Vieux** which, thanks to its lack of swell, is the best one for young children to splash about on. North of Pointe St-Martin, the adrenaline-pumping surfing beaches of **Anglet** (the final 't' is pronounced) continue northwards for more than 4km. Take bus 10 or 13 from the bottom of av Verdun (just near av Édouard VII).

To the south, beyond the long, exposed **Plage de la Côte des Basques**, some 500m south of Port Vieux, are **Plage de Marbella** and **Plage de la Milady**. Bus 10 or 13 heading south will also get you to these.

Architecture

From art-deco mansions to Russian Orthodox churches and 1970s tower-block disasters, Biarritz has a fantastic potpourri of architectural styles.

Don't miss the following:

Aug, 10am-7pm Easter, Apr-Jun & Sep-Oct, shorter hrs rest of yr) We don't really know whether it's fair to call the Cité de l'Océan a mere 'museum'. At heart it's simply a museum of the ocean but this is entertainment, cutting-edge technology, theme park and science museum all rolled into one. During a visit you will learn all you ever wanted to know about the ocean and (sort-of) ride in a submarine to watch giant squid and sperm whales do battle.

It's all very child friendly (although many displays are a bit complicated for younger children), but it's equally fascinating and

Biarritz

Rocher de la Vierge   ARCHITECTURE
(Rock of the Virgin; at the end of Pointe Atalaye) If the swell's big, you might get a drenching as you cross the twee, toy-town-like footbridge at the end of Pointe Atalaye to Rocher de la Vierge, named after its white statue of the Virgin and child. Views from this impressive outcrop extend to the mountains of the Spanish Basque Country.

Phare de Biarritz   LIGHTHOUSE
(adult/child €2.50/2; ⊙9am-6pm) Climbing the 258 twisting steps inside the 73m-high Phare de Biarritz, the town's 1834 lighthouse, rewards you with sweeping views of the Basque coast.

Église Ste-Eugénie   CHURCH
(Blvd du Maréchal Leclerc) The neo-Gothic Église Ste-Eugénie was built in 1864 for – who else? – Empress Eugénie.

Hôtel du Palais   HOTEL
(1 av de l'Impératrice) Dominating the northern end of the Grande Plage is the 19th-century Hôtel du Palais built for Empress Eugénie, and now a luxury hotel.

Église Alexandre Newsky   CHURCH
(8 av de l'Impératrice) The Église Alexandre Newsky is a Russian Orthodox church built by and for the Russian aristocrats who frequented Biarritz until the Russian Revolution.

Chapelle Impériale   CHURCH
(⊉05 59 22 37 10; 15 rue des 100 Gardes; admission €3; ⊙2.30-6pm) The doll's-house-sized Chapelle Impériale was constructed in 1864, inspired by Empress Eugénie.

Activities

Once the almost exclusive haunt of the rich and pampered, Biarritz is now known more as the capital of European **surfing** (although in truth, the real centre of European surfing is the small town of Hossegor around 25km to the north). **Grande Plage** itself is good from mid-low tide on a moderate swell, whereas the 4km-long stretch of beaches that make up **Anglet** are more consistent and generally better.

No fewer than nine places around town offer gear and lessons (from €35 per hour); the tourist office keeps a list of most of the surf schools. You should ensure that the school you choose is registered with **Féderation Française de Surf** (FFS; www. surfingfrance.com, in French) as some others are fly-by-night operators whose staff may have only a little more surf knowledge than the pupils. Even with the registered schools, the instructors often seem to use the lessons merely as an excuse to go surfing themselves.

⚡ Festivals & Events

Major surfing competitions take place year-round.

Biarritz Maider Arosteguy　　SURFING
A three-day surfing championship held at Easter.

Festival des Arts de la Rue　　CULTURAL
Performance artists take to the streets for five days in early May.

Big Festival　　MUSIC
(www.bigfest.fr) Held in mid-July and attracting an increasing array of indie music bands, this is the big music festival in Biarritz.

Roxy Jam　　SURFING
A major female longboarding championship on the ASP (Association of Surfing Professionals) circuit, with spin-off events such as concerts, held over five days in mid-July.

Le Temps d'Aimer　　DANCE
(www.letempsdaimer.com) A two-week celebration of dance in all its forms is held in mid-September.

Festival de Biarritz
Amérique Latine　　CINEMA
Held in late-September through to early October, this film and culture festival brings a little South American exotica to Biarritz.

🛏 Sleeping

Inexpensive hotels are a rarity in Biarritz, and any kind of room is at a premium in July and August. Outside the high season, however, most prices fall by a good 25%.

Auberge de Jeunesse
de Biarritz　　HOSTEL €
(☑ 05 59 41 76 00; www.hihostels.com; 8 rue Chiquito de Cambo; dm incl sheets & breakfast €25.40; ☉ reception 9am-noon & 6-10pm, closed mid-Dec–early Jan; @ 🛜) This popular place offers outdoor activities including surfing. From the train station, follow the railway line westwards for 800m.

Hôtel Mirano　　BOUTIQUE HOTEL €€
(☑ 05 59 23 11 63; www.hotelmirano.fr; 11 av Pasteur; d €72-132; 🛜) Squiggly purple, orange and black wallpaper and oversize orange perspex light fittings are some of the rad '70s touches at this boutique retro hotel. Oh,

and there's a flirty Betty Boop in the bar. The staff go above and beyond the call of duty in order to please. All up, it's one of the best deals in town.

To get there take the D910 southeast out of town, turn left onto av de Grammont and then right onto av Pasteur. It's a good 10-minute walk from the centre.

Hôtel Edouard VII　　HISTORIC HOTEL €€
(☑ 05 59 22 39 80; www.hotel-edouardvii.com; 21 av Carnot; d €140-180; ❄ 🛜) From the ornate dining room full of gently tick-tocking clocks to the pots of lavender carefully colour-coordinated to match the floral wallpaper, everything about this beautiful and intimate hotel screams 1920s Biarritz chic.

Hôtel Maïtagaria　　HOTEL €€
(☑ 05 59 24 26 65; www.hotel-maitagaria.com; 34 av Carnot; s/d €84/99; 🛜) Overlooking a park, the spotless modern rooms with art-deco furniture, leopard-print furnishings and immaculate bathrooms make this friendly place good value. Not least of its charms is its summer terrace: it opens off the comfy guest lounge, which is warmed in winter by an open fire, and the back garden is filled with flowers and koi carp splashing about in a pond.

Hôtel Palym　　HOTEL €€
(☑ 05 59 24 16 56; hotel-palym-biarritz.fr; 7 rue du Port Vieux; s €80-145, d €90-155; ☉ mid-Jan–mid-Nov; ❄ 🛜) This welcoming, family-run hotel, with its exceedingly smart, colourful and good-value rooms, occupies a brightly painted townhouse on a street packed with hotels.

THALASSOTHERAPY

Thalassotherapy ('sea healing'), using the restorative properties of seawater (along with seaweed and mud), has been popular in Biarritz since the late 18th century and continues to serve as an antidote to 21st-century ailments such as stress and insomnia. In Biarritz, put thalassotherapy's curative powers to the test – or simply bliss out – at the following:

➜ **Thalassa Biarritz** (☑ 05 59 41 30 00; www.accorthalassa.com; 11 rue Louison-Bobet)

➜ **Thermes Marins** (☑ 08 25 12 64 64; www.biarritz-thalasso.com; 80 rue de Madrid)

Add to that a very warm welcome and you've found yourself an ideal Biarritz base.

Maison Garnier BOUTIQUE HOTEL €€
(☑ 05 59 01 60 70; www.hotel-biarritz.com; 29 rue Gambetta; d from €118; ✻☎) The seven boutique 'rooms' (suites would be a better description) of this elegant mansion are tastefully decorated and furnished in cool, neutral tones; those up at attic level are especially romantic. The reception isn't always staffed so you might have to wait a while for them to turn up.

Hôtel Les Alizès HOTEL €€
(☑ 05 59 24 11 74; www.alizes-biarritz.com; 13 rue du Port Vieux; r €104-120; ☎) With its brash and blushing shades of colour and old-fashioned desks and wardrobes, this family-run hotel is one of the better cheap hotels in town. Its position, just back from the cute Plage du Port Vieux, is spot on.

★ Hôtel Villa Koegui BOUTIQUE HOTEL €€€
(☑ 05 59 50 07 77; www.hotel-villakoegui-biarritz. fr; 7 rue de Gascogne; r from €200; ✻☎) This fab little place has swanky, bright rooms filled with locally made furnishings and decoration and is set around a leafy courtyard garden. What really makes it stand out, though, is that it's run with the kind of warmth and care normally only found in small, family-run B&Bs. The 'nothing-is-too-much-trouble' staff will reel off a list of their favourite places to eat, drink or otherwise get to know Biarritz.

Hôtel de Silhouette DESIGNER HOTEL €€€
(☑ 05 59 24 93 82; www.hotel-silhouette-biarritz. com; 30 rue Gambetta; d from €200; ✻☎) This impressive place has designer rooms with big-city attitude, but just to remind you that the countryside is close at hand there are a couple of 'sheep' in the garden – as well as frequently changing outdoor art and sculpture exhibitions. The furnishings in the rooms are very high class and the shower heads are as big as a rain cloud.

Villa Le Goëland HISTORIC HOTEL €€€
(☑ 05 59 24 25 76; www.villagoeland.com; 12 plateau de l'Atalaye; r €180-280; ✻☎) This stunning family home, with its château-like spires, is perched high on a plateau above Pointe Atalaye and is one of the most notable buildings in town. Rooms, tastefully furnished with antiques, family photos and mementos, have panoramic views. There are only four rooms (opt for 'chambre Goëland' with its huge 35-sq-m private terrace), so advance booking is essential.

✗ Eating

See-and-be-seen cafes and restaurants line Biarritz's beachfront. Anglet's beaches are

---

TAPAS ON THE SEASHORE

As in neighbouring Bayonne, there's a growing number of tapas bars in Biarritz. The area around the covered market, Les Halles, is a real hot spot for character-infused joints with bar tops that are positively loaded with tasty treats. The following spots are our favourites:

➜ **Bar Jean** (5 rue des Halles; tapas €1.50-2.50) The most original – and delicious – selection of tapas in the city is served up with a flamenco soundtrack and a backdrop of blue and white Andalucian tiles. Try the calamari rings wrapped around a stack of lardons and drizzled in olive oil – simply divine. Jean also does larger portions for around €6 to €8.

➜ **Le Comptoir du Foie Gras/Maison Pujol** (1 rue du Centre; tapas from €1) This quirky place morphs from a shop selling jars of outstanding foie gras in the day to a tapas bar in the evening. Needless to say the tapas are foie gras heavy, but they also have more vegetarian-suitable options, such as those made with guacamole. It's so small that you'll probably end up standing outside shouting your order through the bar window.

➜ **Bar du Marché** (☑ 05 59 23 48 96; 8 rue des Halles; tapas €1-2.50; ☻ 8am-3pm & 6pm-2am) First opening its doors in 1938, this is an authentic and high quality tapas bar beside the market. It also does full meals, which can be eaten out on the sunny terrace.

➜ **Puig & Daro** (rue Gambetta; mains €8-13) This market-side place serves an impressive selection of hams, cheeses, wines and, our favourite, sardines in oil. There's a raised wooden outdoor terrace for the hot nights.

also becoming increasingly trendy, with cafes strung along the waterfront.

★ **Restaurant le Pim'pi** FRENCH €€
(☑ 05 59 24 12 62; 14 av Verdun; menus €14-28, mains €17; ⊘ noon-2pm Tue, noon-2pm & 7-9.30pm Wed-Sat) A small and resolutely old-fashioned place unfazed by all the razzmatazz around it. The daily specials are chalked up on a blackboard – most are of the classic French bistro style, but they are produced with such unusual skill and passion that many consider this one of the town's better places to eat.

Bistrot des Halles BASQUE €€
(☑ 05 59 24 21 22; 1 rue du Centre; mains €17-19; ⊘ noon-2pm & 7.30-10.30pm Tue-Sat) One of a cluster of restaurants along rue du Centre that get their produce directly from the nearby covered market, this bustling place stands out from the pack for serving excellent fish and other fresh modern French market fare from the blackboard menu, in an interior adorned with old metallic advertising posters. Open daily during Easter and the summer holidays.

Cafe du Commerce FRENCH €€
(☑ 05 59 41 87 24; www.cafeducommerce-biarritz. fr; rue de Gambetta; mains around €18; ⊘ lunch from noon, dinner from 7pm Thu-Mon) Virtually all the produce for the dishes here comes fresh from the neighbouring market and, appropriately, the menu is highly traditional and filled with items such as squid cooked classic Basque style on a *plancha* (metal hot plate), snails and excellent steaks.

L'Etable BASQUE €€
(☑ 05 59 22 10 11; 6 rue Lavernis; mains €16-24; ⊘ 7pm-midnight Wed-Mon) This is one of those places, hidden down an alleyway and in a cave-like building, that's so discreet that only a local could have pointed it out to you. Despite the less-than-obvious look to the place it has a stellar repuation for assured, traditional local dishes featuring lots of duck, chilli and seafood.

Open daily during French school holidays.

Le Clos Basque BASQUE €€
(☑ 05 59 24 24 96; 12 rue Louis Barthou; menus €26, mains €14.50; ⊘ noon-1.30pm & 7.45-9.30 Tue-Sat, noon-1.30pm Sun) With its tiles and exposed stonework hung with abstract art, this tiny place could have strayed in from Spain. The cuisine, however, is emphatically Basque, traditional with a contemporary

twist or two. Only the finest of local ingredients make it into the dishes. Reserve ahead to secure a terrace table.

🍷 Drinking & Nightlife

There are some great bars on and around rue du Port Vieux, place Clemenceau and the central food-market area, many of which are tiny hole-in-the-wall places with just enough room for you, your drink, the bartender and a friend or two. Places generally open from 11am to 2am unless noted otherwise.

★ **Miremont** CAFE
(☑ 05 59 24 01 38; www.miremont-biarritz.com; 1bis place Georges-Clemenceau; hot chocolate from €5; ⊘ 9am-8pm) Operating since 1880, this grande dame harks back to the time when belle-époque Biarritz was the beach resort of choice for the rich and glamorous. Today it still attracts perfectly coiffed hairdos (and that's just on the poodles) but the less chic are also welcome to come and partake of a fine selection of tea and cakes.

Ventilo Caffé BAR
(rue du Port Vieux; ⊘ closed Tue Oct-Easter) Dressed up like a boudoir, this funky place continues its domination of the Biarritz young-and-fun bar scene.

Le Newquay BAR
(☑ 05 59 22 19 90; 20 place Georges-Clemenceau) Biarritz's answer to the English pub has a prime location, beers on tap, frequent live music and a huge following with young locals, expats and tourists.

Red Bar BAR
(9 av du Maréchal Foch; ⊘ Tue-Sun) You mightn't think a rugby bar would attract trendsetters, but this temple to Biarritz Olympique (their colours are red and white – hence the name), with reggae and '70s rock in the background, will make you think again.

☆ Entertainment

Free classical-music concerts take place in high summer at various atmospheric outdoor venues around town; the tourist office has the program. There are a couple of nightclubs and lounge bars just behind Grande Plage.

Cinéma Le Royal CINEMA
(www.royal-biarritz.com; 8 av du Maréchal Foch) Screens a good selection of nondubbed films.

Fronton Couvert Plaza Berri   SPORT
(42 av du Maréchal Foch) *Pelota* (ball game) matches are held virtually year-round; ask the tourist office for schedules.

Parc Mazon   SPORT
(av du Maréchal Joffre) From July to mid-September, the open-air *fronton* (*pelota* court) has regular matches. Ask at the tourist office for match times.

Parc des Sports d'Aguiléra   SPORT
(av Henri Haget) Regular professional *pelota* matches (admission €10 to €20) are held at 9pm at this sports complex, 2km east of central Biarritz, between mid-June and mid-September.

🛍 Shopping

Covered Market   MARKET
(rue des Halles) Biarritz's small covered market is the place to come for the freshest picnic ingredients.

Épicerie Fine du Port Vieux   DELI
(41bis rue Mazagran) Stock up with beachside picnic goodies at this excellent delicatessen.

Mille et Un Fromages   DELI
(8 av Victor Hugo) You'll find a tempting array of cheeses, wines and pâtés here.

**Pare Gabia /
Les Sandals d'Eugénie**   SHOES
(18 rue Mazagran) Vincent Corbun continues his grandfather's business, established in 1935, making and selling espadrilles in a rainbow of colours and styles (customised with ribbons and laces while you wait).

Robert Pariès   CHOCOLATES
(1 place Bellevue) Test your willpower with scrumptious chocolates and Basque sweets.

ℹ Information

Tourist Office (☑ 05 59 22 37 10; www. biarritz.fr; square d'Ixelles; ☉ 9am-7pm Jul-Aug, shorter hrs rest of yr) In July and August there are tourist-office annexes at the airport, train station and at the roundabout just off the Biarritz *sortie* (exit) 4 from the A63.

ℹ Getting There & Away

AIR
To reach Biarritz-Anglet-Bayonne airport, take Chronoplus (p650) bus 14, which runs every half-hour, departing near the tourist office.

BUS
Buses run frequently between Bayonne and Biarritz; they work out much cheaper than taking the train, as you'll pay the same to get from Biarritz' train station to its town centre as you will to get from Bayonne to Biarritz directly on the bus.

Ten daily **ATCRB** (www.transports-atcrb.com) buses travel down the coast to St-Jean de Luz (€2) from the **stop** just near the tourist office beside square d'Ixelles. Buses to Spain also pick up passengers here.

TRAIN
Biarritz-La Négresse train station is about 3km south of the town centre; walking to the centre isn't advised due to the busy roads with no footpaths, so catch bus A1. **SNCF** (13 av du Maréchal Foch; ☉ Mon-Fri) has a town-centre office. Times, fares and destinations are much the same as for Bayonne, a nine-minute train journey away.

ℹ Getting Around

BUS
Most services stop beside the Hôtel de Ville, from where route A2 (€1, 50 daily) goes to Bayonne's Hôtel de Ville and station.

TAXI
Atlantic Taxis (☑ 05 59 23 18 18)

St-Jean de Luz & Ciboure
POP 14,200

If you're searching for the quintessential Basque seaside town – with atmospheric narrow streets, and a lively fishing port pulling in large catches of sardines and anchovies that are then cooked up at authentic restaurants – you've found it.

St-Jean de Luz, 24km southwest of Bayonne, sits at the mouth of the River Nivelle and is overlooked by the lush Pyrenean foothills. The town and its long beach are on the eastern side of Baie de St-Jean de Luz.

Its sleepy, smaller alter ego, Ciboure, is on the western curve of the bay, separated from St-Jean de Luz by the fishing harbour.

To get between St-Jean de Luz and Ciboure you can cross over the Pont Charles de Gaulle on foot or by car, or, for a more fun alternative, take one of the summer ferries that cross the harbour.

◉ Sights

A superb panorama of the town unfolds from the promontory of **Pointe Ste-Barbe**, at the northern end of the Baie de St-Jean de Luz

TOP SURF SPOTS – BASQUE & ATLANTIC COASTS

France's Basque and Atlantic coasts have some of Europe's best surf. Autumn is prime time, with warm(ish) water temperatures, consistently good conditions and few(er) crowds. The big-name spots are **Biarritz** and **Hossegor**, where you can watch Kelly Slater and friends battle it out for crucial world-title points in dredging Gravière barrels during September-October's **ASP** (Association of Surfing Professionals; www.aspworldtour. com) event. In fact, almost anywhere between St-Jean de Luz in the south and Soulac-sur-Mer up in the north (by the mouth of the Gironde River) has mighty good surf.

Europe's original big-wave spot might have been surpassed by bigger and nastier discoveries, but the reef breaks around **Guéthary**, just to the south of Biarritz, retain a special sense of magic.

Take a lesson in the mellow waves at **Hendaye**, just to the south of St-Jean de Luz, where the small, gently breaking waves are tailor made for learners. The **tourist office** (05 59 20 00 34; www.hendaye-tourisme.fr; 67 bd de la Mer, Hendaye; 9am-7pm Mon-Sat, 10am-12.30pm & 3.30-6pm Sun) can point you in the right direction. Beginners lessons start at around €35.

Paddle out from the tip of pine-forested **Cap Ferret** peninsula, or go on surfari to the magnificent beaches around **Lacanau**, where the surfers of Bordeaux get their kicks.

And for the best waves *away* from the coast, longboarders can attempt the **mascaret** (http://mascaretgironde.free.fr), a tidal-bore wave travelling inland from the Gironde Estuary. The best place to pick it up is St-Pardon during spring tides.

and about 1km beyond the town beach. Go to the end of bd Thiers and keep walking.

★ **Église St-Jean Baptiste**   CHURCH
(rue Gambetta, St-Jean de Luz; 8.30am-noon & 2-7pm) The plain façade of France's largest and finest Basque church conceals a splendid interior with a magnificent baroque altar-piece. It was in front of this very altarpiece that Louis XIV and María Teresa, daughter of King Philip IV of Spain, were married in 1660. After exchanging rings, the couple walked down the aisle and out of the southern door, which was then sealed to commemorate peace between the two nations after 24 years of hostilities.

Maison Louis XIV   HISTORIC BUILDING
(05 59 26 27 58; www.maison-louis-xiv.fr; 6 place Louis XIV, St-Jean de Luz; adult/child €6/3.80; 10.30am-noon & 2.30-6pm Wed-Mon Jul-Aug, 11am-3pm & 4-5pm Wed-Mon Easter, Jun & Sep–mid-Oct) Sitting on a pretty, pedestrianised square is the so-called Maison Louis XIV. Built in 1643 by a wealthy shipowner and furnished in period style, this is where Louis XIV lived out his last days of bachelorhood before marrying María Teresa. Half-hour guided tours (with English text) depart several times daily in July and August.

Alongside, and rather dwarfed by its more imposing neighbour, is St-Jean de Luz' **Hôtel de Ville**, built in 1657.

Joanoenia: Maison de l'Infante   HISTORIC BUILDING
(05 59 26 36 82; quai de l'Infante, St-Jean de Luz; adult/child €2.50/free; 11am-12.30pm & 2.30-6.30pm Tue-Sat, closed mid-Nov–May) In the days before her marriage to Louis XIV, María Teresa stayed in this brick-and-stone mansion (like the temporary home of her husband to be, it was owned by a shipowner) with fine architectural detail, just off place Louis XIV.

Église St-Vincent   CHURCH
(rue Pocalette, Ciboure) The 17th-century Église St-Vincent has an octagonal bell tower topped by an unusual three-tiered wooden roof. Inside, the lavish use of wood and tiered galleries is typically Basque. The church is just off the main seafront road, quai Maurice Ravel.

Socoa   OLD TOWN
The heart of Socoa is about 2.5km west of Ciboure along the continuation of quai Maurice Ravel (named for the *boléro* composer, who was born in Ciboure in 1875). Its prominent **fort** was built in 1627 and later improved by Vauban. You can walk out to the Digue de Socoa breakwater or climb to the **lighthouse** via rue du Phare, then out along rue du Sémaphore for fabulous coastal views.

Écomusée Basque   MUSEUM
(05 59 51 33 23; www.ecomusee-basque.com; adult/child €7.50/3.20; 10am-6.30pm Jul-Aug,

FRENCH BASQUE COUNTRY ST-JEAN DE LUZ & CIBOURE

St-Jean de Luz

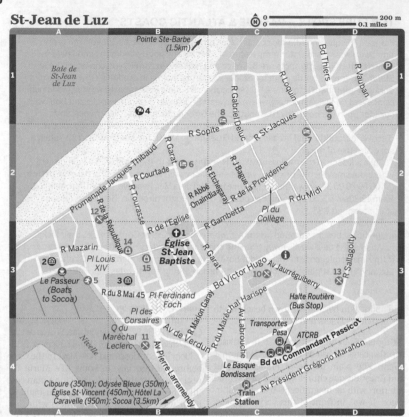

10-11.15am & 2.30-5.30pm Mon-Sat Apr–Jun & Sep-Oct, closed Nov–Apr) Around 2km north of St-Jean de Luz beside the N10, Basque traditions are brought to life on one-hour audioguide tours of this illuminating multimedia museum, which has three entire rooms devoted to Izarra (Basque for 'star'), a liqueur made from 20 different local plants.

Château d'Urtubie CASTLE
(☎05 59 54 31 15; www.chateaudurtubie.net; rue Bernard de Coral; adult/child €6.50/3.50; ◷10.30am-6.30pm mid-Jul–Aug, 10.30am-12.30pm & 2-6.30pm Apr–Jun & Sep-Oct) This small château was constructed in the 13th century and has been in the hands of the same family ever since. Rooms are decorated in period style and are stuffed full of antiques and other treasures. To get there follow the D704 and D810 3km southwest of St Jean de Luz in the direction of Spain, and you'll find it sitting pretty just off the D810 road.

Beaches

St-Jean de Luz' beautiful banana-shaped sandy **plage** (beach) sprouts stripy bathing tents from June to September. Ciboure has its own modest beach, **Plage de Socoa**, 2km west of Socoa on the corniche (the D912); it's served by ATCRB buses en route to Hendaye and, in the high season, by boats. Both beaches are protected from the wrath of the Atlantic by breakwaters and jetties, and are among the few child-friendly beaches in the Basque Country.

🏃 Activities

Opportunities to get out on, in and under the water abound. As well as the operators listed below the tourist office can put you in touch with surf schools and sailing schools.

Odysée Bleue DIVING SCHOOL
(☎06 63 54 13 63; www.odyssee-bleue.com; chemin des Blocs, hangar 4; try dive €50, discovery

St-Jean de Luz

course €160) Join a diving school in Socoa to dive under the waves in search of starfish and wrasse.

Tech Ocean   DIVING SCHOOL
(☏ 05 59 47 96 75; www.tech-ocean.fr; 45 av Commandant Passicot; try dive €70, courses from €150) A diving school in Socoa.

Nivelle V   BOAT CRUISE
(☏ 06 09 73 61 81; www.croisiere-saintjeandeluz. com; quai de l'Infante; ⊙ Apr–mid-Oct) From May to mid-September, a boat leaves quai du Maréchal Leclerc for deep-sea fishing trips (€35) and cruises (adult/child from €10/7).

🎉 Festivals & Events

Fêtes de la St-Jean   CULTURAL
Bonfires, music and dancing take place on the weekend nearest 24 June.

Régates de Traînières   BOAT RACES
A weekend of boat races on the first weekend in July.

La Fête du Thon   FOOD
The Tuna Festival, on a weekend in July, fills the streets with brass bands, Basque music and dancing, while stalls sell sizzling tuna steaks.

Danses des Sept Provinces Basques   DANCE
Folk dancers from across the Spanish and French Basque Country meet in early summer.

La Nuit de la Sardine   CULTURAL
The Night of the Sardine – a night of music, folklore and dancing – is held twice each summer, on a Saturday in early July and the Saturday nearest 15 August.

🛏 Sleeping

July to mid-September are packed and advance reservations are essential; low-season prices can drop significantly. There are a couple of cheap and cheerful places opposite the train station.

Between St-Jean de Luz and Guéthary, 7km northeast up the coast, are no fewer than 16 camping grounds. ATCRB's Biarritz and Bayonne buses stop within 1km of them all.

★ **La Devinière**   BOUTIQUE HOTEL €€
(☏ 05 59 26 05 51; www.hotel-la-deviniere.com; 5 rue Loquin, St-Jean de Luz; d €120-180; ☎) You have to love a place that forsakes TVs for antiquarian books (room 11 even has its own mini-library). Beyond the living room, with its piano and comfy armchairs, there's a delightful small patio equipped with lounges and the rooms are stuffed full of antique and replica antique furnishings.

It's worth paying the extra for the garden-facing rooms, which have little balconies overlooking the riot of vegetation down below.

La Marisa Hôtel   HOTEL €€
(☏ 05 59 26 95 46; www.hotel-lamarisa.com; 16 rue Sopite; r €128-178; ☎) On a quiet back street not so far from the beach there's value for money to be had here. The best rooms, some of which overlook a little courtyard garden, have antique vanity boxes, gold painted mirror rims and a lot of genteel class. There are also some more modern rooms with disabled access.

Hôtel La Caravelle   BOUTIQUE HOTEL €€
(☏ 05 59 47 18 05; www.hotellacaravelle.com; bd Pierre Benoît, Ciboure; d €90-145; ❄☎) This is a superb option overlooking the water on the other side of the port in Ciboure. Originally this nautical-themed place was two fishermen's cottages; today its very good value rooms contain old furniture given a coat of paint and a new lease of life. Some rooms

Basque Culture

Call a Basque French or Spanish and it's almost certain you'll receive a glare and a stern 'I'm Basque!' in return. And fair enough because the Basques *are* different. They speak a language, Euskara, that is unrelated to any other European language, they have no migration history and an unusually high number of them share the same blood group. In fact so unique are the Basques that some say that they are the original Europeans.

The Basques are also famous for festivals. Some, such as La Fête du Thon in St-Jean de Luz, celebrate the region's superlative food. Others, including the Fêtes de Bayonne, celebrate the Basques' joy for life.

Pelote Basque

The regional game is *pelote Basque (pelota)* and you'll notice every village has its own court, normally backing up against the village church. *Pelota* is the generic name for a group of 16 different native Basque ball games, but the most well-known has players using a scooplike basket called a *chistera*.

Festivals

Basque festivals are good opportunities to see traditional Basque dress. It's said that there are around 400 different Basque dances, many of which require their own special kind of outfit.

Lauburu

Perhaps the most visible symbol of Basque culture is *lauburu*, also known as Basque cross, regarded as a symbol of prosperity. It's also used to signify life and death.

Top Basque Eats

➡ **Piment d'Espelette** This little chilli pepper is an essential accompaniment to many a Basque meal.

➡ **Fromage des Pyrénées** Cheese – buy it fresh, straight from a shepherd. The best-known cheese is Ossau-Iraty.

➡ **Jambon de Bayonne** Wafer-thin ham has a fair devoted to it.

➡ **Axoa** Classic dish – try it at Bayonne's Chiloa Gurmenta Restaurant (p648).

➡ **Bayonne chocolate** The best chocolate shops in the country.

1. Bayonne chocolate 2. *Pelote Basque* 3. Traditional French Basque dress 4. Basque cross, or *lauburu*

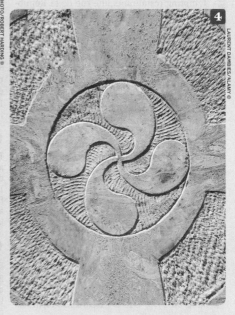

have terraces with fake 'gardens' while others have sea views.

There's free street parking outside.

Hôtel Ohartzia
HOTEL €€

(☑ 05 59 26 00 06; www.hotel-ohartzia.com; 28 rue Garat, St-Jean de Luz; r €75-100; ☎) Framed by cobalt-blue shutters, this flower-bedecked Basque house is just a few steps from the beach. Immaculate rooms are well furnished and equipped, and the welcome's friendly. The highlight is its hidden foliage-shaded garden full of well-placed tables and chairs. A couple of the rooms are outside in this garden.

Zazpi
DESIGN HOTEL €€€

(☑ 05 59 26 07 77; www.zazpihotel.com; 21 bd Thiers, St-Jean de Luz; r €195-310; ✴☎☀) Seriously hip, this wonderful old mansion-turned-designer hotel is one of the most stylish hotels in southwest France. Staying here is like living in a very glam modern art gallery. There's a rooftop terrace complete with pool and sensational views over an ocean of terracotta roof tiles to the fairy-tale green Basque hills.

✗ Eating

Seafood is the mainstay of restaurant menus and St-Jean de Luz doesn't disappoint in this department – many people come here as much for the food as anything else. Tempting restaurants line rue de la République, rue Tourasse and place Louis XIV.

★ Buvette des Halles
SEAFOOD €

(☑ 05 59 26 73 59; bd Victor Hugo, St-Jean de Luz; dishes €7-14; ☺6am-2pm & dinner, closed Tue Sep-Jun) Tucked into a corner of the covered market, this minuscule restaurant serves goat's cheese, Bayonne ham, grilled sardines, fish soup, mussels and much more. Between June and September you can eat outside beneath the plane trees on the small square; the rest of the year you can eat tucked up inside, but go early for the best pickings.

Grillerie du Port
SEAFOOD €

(☑ 05 59 51 18 29; quai du Maréchal Leclerc, St-Jean de Luz; mains €7.50-9.50; ☺noon-2.30pm & 7-10.30pm daily Jun-Sep) It won't take long to peruse the menu at this old port-side classic. It's essentially a choice of grilled sardines or grilled tuna – all freshly caught that morning and utterly delicious.

Pilpil-Enea
SEAFOOD €€

(☑ 05 59 51 20 80; 3 rue Sallagoity, St-Jean de Luz; mains €12-17.50; ☺12.15-2.15pm & 7.30-10pm Mon & Thu-Sat, 12.15-2.15pm Tue & Sun) Strung with fishing nets, this small, simple restaurant decorated in dark timber and blue-and-white checks is set apart from the tourist throng, and is a firm local favourite for its quality cooking based largely on the aquatic world.

★ Le Kaiku
GOURMET €€€

(☑ 05 59 26 13 20; www.kaiku.fr; 17 rue de la République; menu €27-58, mains €26-36; ☺12.30-2pm & 7.30-10pm Thu-Mon) The most celebrated restaurant in St-Jean, this place has it all: it's inside a stunning old stone building close to the beach, the service is exemplary and the food. Ah yes, the food. Most of the dishes revolve around the town's famed seafood and everything is prepared with exquisite style and care. Dress smart.

☆ Entertainment

In summer frequent *pelota* matches take place at **Jaï Alaï Compos Berri** (rte de Bayonne, N10), 1km northeast of the train station. The tourist office can supply times and prices.

🛍 Shopping

Sandales Concha
SHOES

(2 rue Gambetta, St-Jean de Luz) The traditional shoe of the Basque Country is the espadrille and here you can choose from a huge range of locally produced, handmade shoes starting from €10.

Maison Adam
FOOD

(6 rue de la République) This renowned shop, selling delicious *macarons* (melt in the mouth biscuit-like delicacies), hams and other regional foods has been trading since 1666 – longer than many a nation has been in existence.

ℹ Information

Tourist Office (☑ 05 59 26 03 16; www.saint-jean-de-luz.com; 20 bd Victor Hugo, St-Jean de Luz; ☺9am-12.30pm & 2-7pm Mon-Sat, 10am-1pm Sun) Runs an extensive program of French-language tours around the town and across the Spanish border; ask about English-language tours in summer.

ℹ Getting There & Away

BUS

Buses run by **ATCRB** (www.transports-atcrb. com) pass the **Halte Routière** bus stop near the train station on their way northeast to Biarritz (€2, 30 minutes, nine daily) and Bayonne (€2,

CROSS-BORDER ENCOUNTERS: A DAY IN SAN SEBASTIÁN

Spain, and the elegant and lively city of San Sebastián, is so close it could almost be considered rude not to slip over to see for yourself why people make such a fuss about San Sebastián. Put simply, San Sebastián is stunning. The town is set around two sickle-shaped beaches, at least one of which, Playa de la Concha, is the equal of any city beach in Europe. But there's more to the city than just looks. Cool, svelte and flirtatious, San Sebastián really knows how to have a good time: with more Michelin stars per capita than anywhere else in the world and finer tapas than anywhere else in Spain, San Sebastián's culinary CV is impressive. But it's not just us who think so; a raft of the world's best chefs, including such luminaries as Catalan superstar chef Ferran Adriá, have said that San Sebastián is quite probably the best place on the entire planet in which to eat!

So, how do I get there? By car it's just a short 20-minute jump down the A64 from St-Jean de Luz (and past an awful lot of toll booths!), or you can endure the N10, which has no tolls but gets so clogged up that it will take you a good couple of hours to travel the short distance. Or hop on a bus or a train. Trains run from St-Jean de Luz to Hendaye (and occasionally onto Irún) roughly hourly (€3, 12 minutes), from where you can board one of the frequent Eusko Trens for the ride into San Sebastián (€1.70, 30 minutes). Otherwise, Transportes Pesa (p665) buses run twice daily between the two towns (€3, 1¼ hours).

And about those tapas? The whole of San Sebastián's old town is crammed with tapas (*pintxo* in Basque) bars, all of which, and we truly mean *all*, have a sublime range of bite-size morsels on offer. However, a couple that really stand out are **Bar Borda Berri** (Calle Fermín Calbetón 12; ☺noon-midnight), where the house special is pig's ears (and they're much better than they sound!) and **La Cuchara de San Telmo** (www.lacucharadesan telmo.com; Calle de 31 de Agosto 28; pintxos from €2.50; ☺7.30pm-11pm Tue, noon-3.30pm & 7.30-11pm Wed-Sun), a hidden-away bar serving such delights as *carrílera de ternera al vino tinto* (calf cheeks in red wine), with meat so tender it starts to dissolve almost before it's passed your lips.

And if I want to really splash out? With three Michelin stars, **Arzak** (☎943 27 84 65; www.arzak.Info; Avenlda Alcalde Jose Elosegui 273; meals €189; ☺closed Sun-Mon, and Nov & late Jun), run by acclaimed Chef Juan Mari Arzak, takes some beating when it comes to *nueva cocina vasca* (new Basque cuisine). Reservations, well in advance, are obligatory.

And what is there to do there? What? Other than eating, drinking and playing on the beach?! OK, well, there's fantastic shopping, a superb aquarium, a couple of museums and, well, eating, drinking and playing on the beach.

For further Information, head to lonelyplanet.com to purchase a downloadable PDF of the Basque Country, Navarra & Rioja chapter from Lonely Planet's *Spain* guide.

40 minutes, nine daily). Southwest, there are around 10 services daily to Hendaye (€2, 35 minutes).

Also passing the Halte Routière is **Transportes Pesa** (www.pesa.net), serving San Sebastián and Bilbao.

TRAIN

There are frequent trains to Bayonne (€5.10, 25 minutes) via Biarritz (€3.40, 15 minutes) and to Hendaye (€3.30, 15 minutes), with connections to Spain.

ℹ Getting Around

BOAT

The good ship **Le Passeur** plies between the jetty on the northern edge of St-Jean's beach, quai de l'Infante and Socoa (adult/child €2.50/2 one way) hourly between April and September.

BUS

Between June and September, the **Navette Itzu-lia** provides a free local daily bus service, with a skeleton service during the rest of the year.

TAXI

Call ☎05 59 47 38 38.

Around St-Jean de Luz

La Rhune

The first mountain of the Pyrenees, the 905m-high, antenna-topped and border-straddling La Rhune ('Larrun' in Basque),

10km south of St-Jean de Luz, has always been considered sacred among Basques, though today people come for the spectacular views rather than religious or cultural reasons. The mountain is best approached from **Col de St-Ignace**, 3km northwest of Sare on the D4 (the St-Jean de Luz road). From here, you can take a fairly strenuous five-hour (return) hike, or have all the hikers curse you by hopping on **Le Petit Train de la Rhune** (www.rhune.com; single/return adult €14/17, child €7/10; ⏲mid-Feb–mid-Nov). This charming little wooden train takes 35 minutes to haul itself up the 4km to the summit. In July and August departures are every 35 minutes, the rest of the time departures are limited to two to four times a day (see website for exact times). Outside high season prices are a few euros cheaper. Be prepared for a wait of up to an hour in high summer. A free *navette* (shuttle bus) runs from St-Jean de Luz several times daily in summer, and leaves from outside the train station.

Grottes de Sare

Who knows what the first inhabitants of the **Grottes de Sare** (www.grottesdesare.fr; adult/child €8.50/4.50; ⏲10am-7pm Aug, 10am-6pm Apr-Jul & Sep, closed Jan–mid-Feb), some 20,000 years ago, would make of today's whiz-bang technology including lasers and holograms during sound-and-light shows at these caves. Multilingual 45-minute tours take you through a gaping entrance via narrow passages to a huge central cavern. Follow the D306, 6km south of the village of Sare. **Le Basque Bondissant** (www.basquebondissant.com) runs buses from St-Jean de Luz to the caves (€2, bus 868) a couple of times a day in summer.

Ainhoa

POP 686

'Un des plus jolis villages de la France', says the sign as you enter this, indeed, very pretty village. Ainhoa's elongated main street is flanked by imposing 17th-century houses, half-timbered and brightly painted. Look for the rectangular stones set above many of the doors, engraved with the date of construction and the name of the family to whom the house belonged. The fortified church has the Basque trademarks of an internal gallery and an embellished altarpiece.

Sleeping & Eating

Ithurria HOTEL RESTAURANT €€€

(☎05 59 29 92 11; www.ithurria.com; Place du Fronton; d from €135, menus €42-85, mains €22-30; ❄📶🏊) For a memorable Basque meal, stop

LOCAL KNOWLEDGE

THE BEST OF THE REST

Both people and nature have created scenes of such beauty in the Basque country that it can sometimes all seem a little unreal. But even in a region as well endowed as this, some places are better than others.

The best of the rest include:

Guéthary Built onto cliffs overlooking the ocean, this red-and-white seaside village has gained a reputation as the chi-chi resort of choice for the jet set.

Itxassou Famed for its cherries and for the beauty of its surrounds. Take the long and winding road to the Col des Veux via the Pas de Roland and, for the ultimate in Basque immersion, dine out on baby trout and duck in **Lezetako Borda** (☎05 59 29 83 65; Col des Veux; menus €20-25; ⏲noon-3pm) (a 20–25 minute drive southeast of Itxassou), a barnlike restaurant sitting a few metres over the border into Spain and atop an often mist-shrouded mountain. You're given little choice in the *menu* and non-Basque diners are a very rare sight. Call ahead to check it's open.

La Bastide-Clairence With white-washed houses brushed in lipstick red, this is arguably the most beautiful of all Basque mountain villages.

Bidarray A pretty village famed for its rafting opportunities.

Forêt d'Iraty A vast beech forest that turns the high mountain slopes fire-orange in autumn. A web of walking trails allows for easy exploration.

Larrau Nowhere else is the spirit of the Basque mountains as strong as in this quaint village surrounded by giants. There are some astounding walking opportunities here as well as some nearby gorges and a monstrous cavern.

at the Michelin-starred Ithurria, established by the Isabal family in an old pilgrims' hostel and now run by Maurice Isabal's two sons (one the sommelier, the other the chef). To make a night of it, Ithurria's rainbow-hued rooms and dreamy swimming pool complement the food perfectly.

If the restaurant is too extravagant for you there's a bistro where you can get a sense of what you're missing (mains €6 to €12).

Espelette

POP 2013

The whitewashed Basque town of Espelette is famous for its dark-red chillies, an integral ingredient in traditional Basque cuisine. So prized is le *piment d'Espelette* that it's been accorded Appellation d'Origine Contrôlée (AOC) status, like fine wine. In autumn you can scarcely see the walls of the houses, strung with rows of chillies drying in the sun. The last weekend in October marks Espelette's Fête du Piment, with processions, a formal blessing of the chilli peppers and the ennoblement of a *chevalier du piment* (a knight of the pimiento).

◎ Sights

l'Atelier du Piment   TOUR
(☑05 59 93 90 21; www.atelierdupiment.com; admission free; ☺9am-8pm Apr-Oct, 9am-6pm Nov-Mar) To learn more about the chillies, and to taste and buy chilli products, visit l'Atelier du Piment out on the edge of town.

⛏ Sleeping & Eating

Espelette makes a fine base for both the interior and the coast (assuming you have a car).

★Maison d'hôte Irazabala   B&B €
(☑06 07 14 93 61; www.irazabala.com; 155 Mendiko Bidea; d incl breakfast €90; ☞) This beautiful Basque farmhouse is situated in the middle of wild flower meadows and with views over a raised rumple of green mountains is a bucolic place to rest up. The four rooms are easily the equal of the setting and you'll struggle to tear yourself away from the garden.

It's a couple of kilometres out of town (follow signs for the campsite and it's signed just on from there).

Hôtel Restaurant Euzkadi   RESTAURANT
(☑05 59 93 91 88; www.hotel-restaurant-euzkadi. com; 285 Karrika Nagusia; menus €18-35, mains €12-18; ☺12.30-2pm & 7.30-9.30pm; ☞) Chillies star on the menu at this renowned hotel in

dishes such as *axoa* (tender minced veal simmered with onions and fresh chillies).

ⓘ Information

Tourist Office (☑05 59 93 95 02; www. espelette.fr; ☺9am-12.30pm & 2-6.30pm Mon-Fri, 9.30am-12.30pm & 2-6pm Sat Jul-Aug, shorter hrs rest of yr) Helpful office situated within a small stone château.

ⓘ Getting There & Away

Le Basque Bondissant (The Leaping Basque; ☑05 59 26 25 87; www.basquebondissant.com) runs buses between St-Jean de Luz and Espelette a couple of times a day in summer and less frequently in winter.

St-Jean Pied de Port

POP 1700

At the foot of the Pyrenees, the walled town of St-Jean Pied de Port, 53km southeast of Bayonne, was for centuries the last stop in France for pilgrims heading south over the Spanish border, a mere 8km away, and on to Santiago de Compostela, in Galicia in western Spain. Today it remains a popular departure point for hikers attempting the pilgrim trail, but there are plenty of shorter hikes and opportunities for mountain biking in the area.

If you're the sort of person who thinks God invented cars so we didn't have to walk, then the township of St-Jean Pied de Port, with its attractive old core sliced through by the River Nive, is still well worth a visit.

St-Jean Pied de Port makes an ideal day trip from Bayonne, particularly on Monday when the market is in full swing.

◎ Sights

Old Town   OLD TOWN
The walled old quarter is an attractive place of cobbled streets, geranium-covered balconies and lots of quirky boutiques.

Specific sights worth seeking out include the Église Notre Dame du Bout du Pont, with foundations as old as the town itself but thoroughly rebuilt in the 17th century. Beyond Porte de Notre Dame is the photogenic Vieux Pont (Old Bridge), the town's best-known landmark, from where there's a fine view of whitewashed houses with balconies leaning out above the water. A pleasant 500m riverbank stroll upstream leads to the steeply arched Pont Romain (meaning Roman Bridge, but in fact dating from the 17th century).

FRENCH BASQUE COUNTRY ST-JEAN PIED DE PORT

Rue de la Citadelle is edged by substantial, pink-granite 16th- to 18th-century houses. Look for the construction date on door lintels (the oldest we found was 1510). A common motif is the scallop shell, symbol of St Jacques (St James of Santiago) and of the Santiago de Compostela pilgrims. Pilgrims would enter the town through the **Porte de St-Jacques** on the northern side of town, then, refreshed and probably a little poorer, head for Spain through the **Porte d'Espagne**, south of the river.

Prison des Évêques
MONUMENT

(Bishops' Prison; 41 rue de la Citadelle; adult/under 15yr €3/free; ☺10.30am-7pm mid-Jul–Aug, 11am-12.30pm & 2.30-6.30pm Wed-Mon Apr–mid-Jul & Sep-Oct) Dating back to the 14th century, this vaulted cellar served as the town jail from 1795, as a military lock-up in the 19th century, then as a place of internment during WWII for those caught trying to flee to nominally neutral Spain. The lower section dates from the 13th century, when St-Jean Pied de Port was a bishopric of the Avignon papacy; the building above it dates from the 16th century. Inside can be found seasonal exhibitions.

La Citadelle
FORTRESS

From the top of rue de la Citadelle, a rough cobblestone path ascends to the massive citadel itself, from where there's a spectacular panorama of the town and the surrounding hills. Constructed in 1628, the fort was rebuilt around 1680 by military engineers of the Vauban school. Nowadays it serves as a secondary school and is closed to the public.

If you've got a head for heights, descend by the steps signed *escalier poterne* (rear stairway). Steep and slippery after rain, they plunge beside the moss-covered ramparts to **Porte de l'Échauguette** (Watchtower Gate).

🏃 Activities

Escape the summertime crowds by **walking** or **cycling** into the Pyrenean foothills, where the loudest sounds you'll hear are cowbells and the wind. Two GRs (*grandes randonnées;* long-distance hiking trails) pass through town: the **GR10** (the trans-Pyrenean long-distance trail running from the Atlantic to the Mediterranean over the course of 45 days) and the **GR65** (the Chemin de St-Jacques pilgrim route). Outside the summer season, check with the tourist office or hostels for snow reports and possible rerouting, and plan your accommodation ahead as many places on the Spanish side close.

If you speak French, pick up a copy of the excellent *Le Guide Rando: Pays Basque* (€17.90) from local bookshops, which gives full route details for numerous walks.

To cycle the easy way while enjoying the best of Nive Valley views, load your bicycle onto the train in Bayonne – they're carried free – and roll back down the valley from St-Jean Pied de Port. If you find the ride all the way back to the coast daunting, rejoin the train at Pont-Noblia, for example, or Cambo-les-Bains.

👉 Tours

In July and August, the tourist office organises an array of different tours – from the historical to countryside rambles.

🛏 Sleeping & Eating

Much of the accommodation is geared towards pilgrims on the long hike to Santiago de Compostela in Galicia, Spain. This sort of accommodation is always very basic; normally it consists of just dorm beds, but it's cheap at around €10 to €15 per person. At many places nonpilgrims will be turned away.

Itzalpea
B&B €

(☑ 05 59 37 03 66; www.maisondhotes-itzalpea. com; 5 place du Trinquet; incl breakfast s €55-58, d €65-78; ❄ ☺) This friendly and cosy *maison d'hôte* (B&B) has five tastefully renovated rooms (some air-conditioned), all of which differ from one another and are named after local flowers. It's set above a teashop serving some 20 different types of tea.

Maison E Bernat
B&B €€

(☑ 05 59 37 23 10; www.ebernat.com; 20 rue de la Citadelle; d €85-95; menus from €20; ☺) There are only four bedrooms in this welcoming 17th-century place with thick stone walls, but they're airy, well furnished and meticulously kept, and each has a double and a single bed. There's a great little restaurant on site, which spills onto a tiny terrace, and the hosts run a program of gourmet-themed weekends (check online for details).

Chez Arrambide
GASTRONOMIC €€

(☑ 05 59 37 01 01; www.hotel-les-pyrenees.com; 19 place Charles de Gaulle; menus €42-110, mains €28-45; ☺12.15-1.45pm & 7.45-9pm Jul-Aug, Wed-Mon Sep-Jun) This twin Michelin-starred restaurant, inside the (overpriced) Hôtel Les Pyrénées, is where chef Firmin Arrambide does wonders with seasonal market produce, such as truffle and foie-gras lasagne.

LOCAL LINGO

According to linguists, Euskara, the Basque language, is unrelated to any other tongue on Earth, and is the only tongue in southwestern Europe to have withstood the onslaught of Latin and its derivatives.

Basque is spoken by about a million people in Spain and France, nearly all of whom are bilingual. In the French Basque Country, the language is widely spoken in Bayonne and the hilly hinterland. However, while it is an official language in Spain, it isn't recognised as such in France (although some younger children are educated in Basque at primary-school level). The language also has a higher survival rate on the Spanish side.

But you'll still encounter the language here on Basque-language TV stations, and see occasional sign reading 'Hemen Euskara emaiten dugu' (Basque spoken here) on shop doors. You'll also see the Basque flag (similar to the UK's but with a red field, a white vertical cross and a green diagonal one) flying throughout the region, as well as another common Basque symbol, the lauburu (like a curly four-leaf clover), signifying prosperity, or life and death.

Self-Catering

Farmers from the surrounding hills bring fresh produce – chillies, local cheeses and much more – to the town's **Monday market** (place Charles de Gaulle). In high summer a weekly handicraft and food fair is held most Thursdays in the covered market.

☆ Entertainment

Year-round, variants of *pelota* (admission €7 to €10), including a bare-handed *pelota* tournament, are played at the *trinquet, fronton* municipal and *jaï alaï* courts. In summer these tend to take place at 5pm on a Friday.

In high summer, traditional Basque music and dancing takes place in the *jaï alaï* court or the church. Confirm schedules with the tourist office.

ℹ Information

Tourist Office (☏ 05 59 37 03 57; www. saintjeanpieddeport-paysbasque-tourisme.com; place Charles de Gaulle; ⊙ 9am-7pm Mon-Sat, 10am-1pm & 2-7pm Sun Jul & Aug, 9am-noon & 2-6pm Mon-Sat Sep-Jun)

ℹ Getting There & Away

Train is the only option to travel to or from Bayonne (€9.80, 1¼ hours, up to five daily).

St-Étienne de Baïgorry

The village of St-Étienne de Baïgorry and its outlying hamlets straddle the Vallée de Baïgorry. Tranquillity itself after busy St-Jean Pied de Port, the pretty village is stretched thinly along a branch of the River Nive. Like so many Basque settlements, the village has two focal points: the church and the *fronton* (*pelota* court). It makes a good base for hikers, as a couple of spectacular walks start close by (although you'll still need a car to reach many of the trailheads). Tourist offices in St-Étienne de Baïgorry or St-Jean Pied de Port should be able to supply route suggestions. Even if you're not a hiker you can't fail to be impressed by the area's beauty, so an overnight stay is recommended.

🛏 Sleeping & Eating

Hôtel-Restaurant Manechenea　　　　　　　HOTEL €
(☏ 05 59 37 41 68; www.hotel-saint-etienne-de-baigorry.com; s €45, d €54-57, menus €18-30) A couple of kilometres north of St-Étienne de Baïgorry in the hamlet of Urdos, this rural hotel has butter-yellow rooms that overlook green fields and a bubbling mountain-fed brook. You can eat some of the denizens of said brook, such as delicious trout, for lunch at the in-house restaurant.

Hôtel-Restaurant Arcé　　　　　　HOTEL €€
(☏ 05 59 37 40 14; www.hotel-arce.com; r from €100, menus €16-55, mains €10-25; ⊙ closed Nov–mid-Apr; 🕿🏊) This impressive hotel has a stunning riverside location and spacious rooms with old-style furnishings. To reach the pool you must stroll past the orange trees and cross the river via a little humpback bridge. The in-house restaurant is highly regarded by locals.

The Pyrenees

POP 480,000

Best Mountain Views

➡ Pic du Midi (p687)

➡ Cirque de Gavarnie and Cirque de Troumouse (p687)

➡ Lac de Gaube (p685)

➡ Cirque de Lescun (p681)

➡ Château de Foix (p690)

Best Places to Stay

➡ Hôtel du Lion d'Or (p686)

➡ Le Castel de la Pique (p688)

➡ Hôtel des Rochers (p677)

➡ Auberge les Myrtilles (p691)

➡ L'Abbaye de Camon (p691)

Why Go?

Spiking the skyline for 430km along the Franco-Spanish border, the snow-dusted Pyrenees offer a glimpse of France's wilder side. This serrated chain of peaks contains some of France's most pristine landscapes and rarest wildlife, including endangered species such as the griffon vulture, izard (a type of mountain goat) and brown bear. Since 1967, 457 sq km has been protected as the Parc National des Pyrénées, ensuring its valleys, tarns and mountain pastures are preserved for future generations.

Rural and deeply traditional, the Pyrenees' wild landscapes now provide a paradise for skiers, climbers, hikers and bikers. But there's more to the mountains than just outdoor thrills: there are mountain villages to wander, hilltop castles to admire and ancient caves to investigate. They might not be on quite the same scale as the Alps, but the Pyrenees are every bit as stunning. Strap on your boots – it's time to explore.

When to Go

Pau

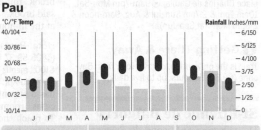

°C/°F Temp — Rainfall Inches/mm

Feb Pau's spring carnival takes over the capital's streets.

Jul Shepherds move their flocks in the Transhumance, and the Tour de France races through.

Nov–Mar Peak skiing season – book hotels well ahead.

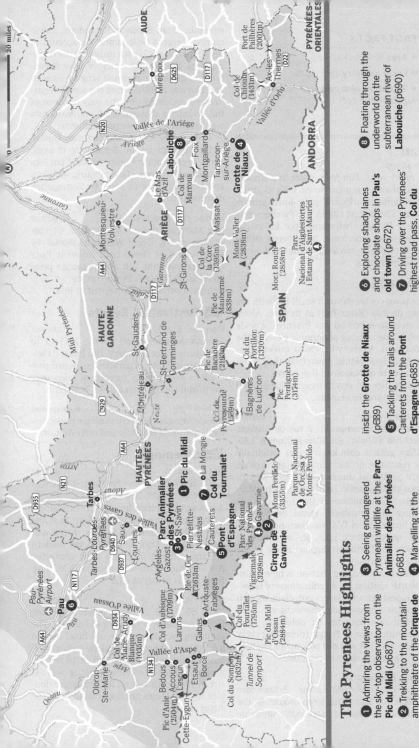

The Pyrenees Highlights

1 Admiring the views from the sky-top observatory on the **Pic du Midi** (p687)

2 Trekking to the mountain amphitheatre of the **Cirque de Gavarnie** (p687)

3 Seeing endangered Pyrenean wildlife at the **Parc Animalier des Pyrénées** (p681)

4 Marvelling at the prehistoric cave-paintings inside the **Grotte de Niaux** (p689)

5 Tackling the trails around Cauterets from the **Pont d'Espagne** (p685)

6 Exploring shady lanes and chocolate shops in **Pau's old town** (p672)

7 Driving over the Pyrenees' highest road pass, **Col du Tourmalet** (p684)

8 Floating through the underworld on the subterranean river of **Labouiche** (p690)

FAST FACTS

➡ **Area** 9942 sq km

➡ **Local industry** agriculture

➡ **Signature dish** *garbure* (meat and vegetable hot-pot)

Pau

POP 80,600

In many ways, Pau feels closer to a Riviera resort than a mountain town, with its grand villas, public parks and palm-lined promenades. The largest city in the Pyrenees was once a favourite wintering spot for ex-pat British and Americans, and there's still a touch of *fin-de-siècle* grandeur around its well-kept streets.

◉ Sights

The town centre sits on a small hill with the Gave de Pau (River Pau) at its base. Along its crest stretches bd des Pyrénées, a wide promenade offering panoramic views of the mountains. A creaky funicular railway dating from 1908 clanks down from the bd des Pyrénées to av Napoléon Bonaparte.

Pau's tiny old centre extends for around 500m around the château.

Château de Pau CHÂTEAU
(www.musee-chateau-pau.fr; 2 rue du Château; adult/child €6/free; ◉9.30am-12.30pm & 1.30-6.45pm, gardens open longer hours) Originally the residence of the monarchs of Navarre, Pau's castle was transformed into a Renaissance château amid lavish gardens by Marguerite d'Angoulême in the 16th century. Marguerite's grandson, Henri de Navarre (the future Henri IV), was born here – cradled, so the story goes, in an upturned tortoise shell (still on display in one of the museum's rooms).

Much restored, the château is now mainly worth visiting for its collections of Gobelins tapestries and Sèvres porcelain, as well as its fine Renaissance architecture.

Admission includes an obligatory one-hour guided tour in French (departing every 15 minutes), but you can pick up an English-language guide sheet at reception.

Musée Bernadotte MUSEUM
(8 rue Tran; adult/child €3/free; ◉10am-noon & 2-6pm Tue-Sun) This town house is the birthplace of one of Napoléon's favourite

generals, Jean-Baptiste Bernadotte (nicknamed 'Sergent belle-jambe', on account of his shapely legs). Now a museum, the house explores the strange story of how Bernadotte came to be crowned king of Sweden and Norway in 1810, when the Swedish parliament reckoned that the only way out of the country's dynastic and political crisis was to stick a foreigner on the throne.

The present king of Sweden, Carl Gustaf, is the seventh in the Bernadotte dynasty, while several other European royal families (including Norway, Luxembourg, Belgium and Denmark) are all ruled by Bernadotte's descendants.

Musée des Beaux-Arts ART MUSEUM
(rue Mathieu Lalanne; adult/student €4/1.50; ◉10am-noon & 2-6pm Wed-Mon) Works by Rubens and El Greco both figure at Pau's fine-arts museum, but the museum's prize piece is a famous Degas canvas, *A New Orleans Cotton Office*, painted in 1873.

✨ Festivals & Events

Carnival Biarnés CARNIVAL
(www.carnavalbiarnes.com) In the lead-up to Lent during late February, Pau holds its annual carnival. Street parades, costumed processions and general merriment takes over town, and there's even a mock bear-hunt.

L'Été à Pau MUSIC FESTIVAL
(www.leteapau.com) Lively summer music festival, spanning late July and early August.

🛏 Sleeping

Hôtel Bristol HOTEL €€
(☑05 59 27 72 98; www.hotelbristol-pau.com; 3 rue Gambetta; s €55-97, d €93-110, f €120-129; 🐾) A classic old French hotel with surprisingly up-to-date rooms, all wrapped up in a fine 19th-century building. Whites, greys and beiges are the keynote colours, and modern art and vintage furniture adds character. Ask for a mountain-view room with balcony. Breakfast is pricey at €12.

Hôtel Central HOTEL €€
(☑05 59 27 72 75; www.hotelcentralpau.com; 15 rue Léon Daran; s €62-75, d €67-88; 🐾) The rambling corridors of this old hotel lead to a selection of higgledy-piggledy rooms, variously decorated in stripes and citrus shades, most with French windows looking over the street. It's worth asking for the larger doubles, as the singles are tiny. Parking's on the street outside.

Pau

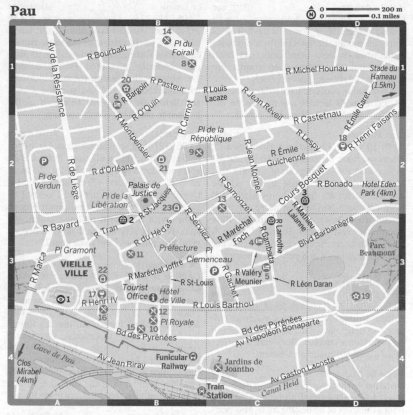

Hôtel Montpensier   HOTEL **€€**
(☑ 05 59 27 42 72; www.hotel-montpensier-pau. com; 36 rue Montpensier; s €61-71, d €71-90; ❄ 🎧) A pastel-pink, shuttered façade conceals plain, simple rooms here, all with coir carpets, mix-and-match colour schemes and rather dated bathrooms. The free parking's a real bonus in trafficky Pau.

Pau

Hotel Eden Park
HOTEL €€€

(☑05 59 40 64 64; www.hotel-pau.fr; 2 rue de l'Aubisque; d €85-185; ❄️ 🛜 🏊) For the full mod-cons, this modernist hotel on Pau's outskirts is the place. It looks bland and boxy from outside, but the white-walled rooms are sharp and spacious; most overlook the central swimming pool and have sofas to lounge on. Extra spoils include a gym, private car park, restaurant and solar-panel power.

Clos Mirabel
B&B €€€

(☑05 59 06 32 83; www.clos-mirabel.com/en; 276 av des Frères Barthélémy; d €95-159; 🛜 🏊) If you don't mind being out of the city, this 18th-century manor house makes a fine retreat. There are five colour-coded B&B bedrooms with heritage furniture, fireplaces and wood floors: top picks are the Blue Room and vast Master Bedroom. There's also a private apartment (€695 to €1195 per week). The gardens and pool are a bonus.

🍴 Eating

Chez Chloee
CAFE €

(☑05 59 02 11 60; 1 place de Foirail; cakes €3-6; ◷10am-4pm Mon-Sat) Fine teas, gourmet coffees and deliciously naughty patisseries (all made in-house) make Chloe's cafe a perfect place for an afternoon pick-me-up.

Royal St-André
CAFE €

(26 bd des Pyrénées; ice cream €3-5; ◷10am-2am May-Oct, 2-7pm Nov-Apr) With tables scattered under the trees of bd des Pyrénées and post-card views of the mountains, this cafe is popular for ice cream, sorbets and granitas.

Le Champagne
BRASSERIE €

(☑05 59 27 72 12; 5 place Royale; mains €10-15; ◷11am-10pm Mon-Sat) This busy brasserie on place Royale is ideal for an early-evening beer and a quick *steak-frites* (steak and chips) or *magret de canard* (duck breast).

Les Papilles Insolites
BISTRO €€

(☑05 59 71 43 79; www.lespapillesinsolites.blog spot.co.uk; 5 rue Alexander Taylor; 2-/3-course menu €18/20; ◷12.15-2pm & 8-9.30pm Wed-Sat) Run by a former Parisian sommelier, this cosy bar-bistro pitches itself between a bistro and a wine shop. It serves honest, country cooking – pigeon, veal, beef, pork and a daily market fish – all doused in rich, heart-warming sauces – accompanied by the owner's choice of one of the 350-odd wines stacked in crates round the shop. Gorgeously Gallic.

Le Lavoir
BRASSERIE €€

(☑05 59 83 32 62; 3 rue du Hédas; mains €14-17; ◷7-10.30pm Mon-Sat) Lost among the alleys of the old town, this small brasserie run by chef Brice Gabenisch is known for its simple, classically presented French cuisine. The stone-walled dining room is intimate, with blackboards and old wooden tables, and Brice often pops his head out of the kitchen to check his clients are happy.

Ze Bistrot
BISTRO €€

(☑05 59 27 44 44; www.zebistrot.com; 13 rue Henri IV; 3-course lunch menu €17, dinner mains €18-22; ◷noon-1.30pm & 7.30-9.30pm Tue-Sat) Ze wine, ze food, ze ambience – Ze Bistrot is a creative diner run by Laurence and Thierry Lassal, who like 'revisiting' traditional French dishes with their own unique, semi-fusion spin. Food is very seasonal (always a good sign), but portions tend to be small.

⭐ Le Majestic
TRADITIONAL FRENCH €€€

(☑08 92 68 06 89; 9 place Royale; menus lunch €15-24, dinner €28-38; ◷noon-1.30pm & 7.30-9pm Tue-Sat, noon-1.30pm Sun) Still our favourite place to eat in Pau, this smart restaurant serves top-notch French cuisine. It's formal inside – ice-white tablecloths, razor-sharp napkins, twisted willow – but it suits the sophisticated food, heavy on premium ingredients such as turbot, sea bass, Bigorre pork and Pyrenean lamb. If the sun's out, sit at a table beneath the trees on leafy place Royale.

Au Fin Gourmet
GASTRONOMIC €€€

(☑05 59 27 47 71; http://www.restaurant-aufin gourmet.com; 24 av Gaston Lacoste; standard menus €28-39, tasting menus incl wine €62-76; ◷noon-1.30pm Wed-Sun, 7.30-9.30pm Tue-Sat) For old-school fine French dining, this *restaurant gastronomique* is Pau's premier address. It's run by the Ithurriage brothers, Patrick and Laurent, known for their Michelin-style food and fondness for sauces, creams, foams and garnishes. It's in the Jardins de Joantho, near the funicular.

Self-Catering

Halles de Pau
MARKET

(Covered Market; place de la République; ◷6am-1pm Mon-Sat) Pau's main market is great for picnic supplies.

Marché Bio
ORGANIC MARKET

(Organic Market; place du Foirail; ◷Wed & Sat morning) There's a twice-weekly organic market.

🍸 Drinking & Nightlife

Pau's bars generally open from 10am to 2am. 'Le Triangle', bounded by rue Henri Faisans, rue Émile Garet and rue Castetnau, is the centre of student nightlife, and a string of bars extends along bd des Pyrénées.

Le Garage BAR

(49 rue Émile Garet) One of the best of the Triangle bars, with an attractive terrace and regular live music.

Au Grain de Raisin WINE BAR

(11 rue Sully; ⊙10am-7.30pm) A welcoming wine bar near the château, which serves a good selection of continental beers and local wines by the glass, accompanied by plates of tapas.

☆ Entertainment

Cinéma Le Méliès CINEMA

(☑05 59 27 60 52; www.lemelies.net; 6 rue Bargoin) Non-dubbed films screen regularly at Cinéma Le Méliès, Pau's only cinema.

Stade du Hameau SPORTS ARENA

(☑05 59 02 50 91; bd de l'Aviation) The home stadium of Pau's rugby team, Section Paloise, who play between October and May. It's 3 miles east of the centre along av du Général Leclerc. Bus T3 stops fairly close.

Casino Municipal CASINO

(☑05 59 27 06 92; ⊙10am-3am Mon-Fri, to 4am Sat & Sun) Pau's casino is in the sumptuous Palais Beaumont, in Parc Beaumont.

🛍 Shopping

Pau is famous for its *chocolatiers* (chocolate shops): the top names are Josuat (23 rue Serviez) and Francis Miot (48 rue Maréchal Joffre).

Au Parapluie des Pyrénées ACCESSORIES

(12 rue Montpensier) This lovely old shop makes the beech-handled, rattan-ribbed umbrellas traditionally used by Pyrenean shepherds.

❶ Information

Tourist Office (☑05 59 27 27 08; www.pau-pyrenees.com; place Royale; ⊙9am-6pm Mon-Sat, 10am-4pm Sun) Stocked with useful information on local transport and the Pyrenees generally.

❶ Getting There & Away

AIR

Aéroport Pau-Pyrénées (☑05 59 33 33 00; www.pau.aeroport.fr) The airport is 7km

❶ **GETTING TO THE PYRENEES**

Pau is served by Ryanair flights to and from the UK and Belgium, while Air France handles domestic services, and several other budget carriers fly to European cities. Lourdes' airport has scheduled services to Paris.

Buses are limited, so to properly explore you'll need wheels.

northwest of town. There are currently six daily flights to Paris Orly, three daily to Paris Charles de Gaulle and Lyon, and nine per week to Marseille.

BUS

Bus services are very limited, although there are at least a couple of daily services to Agen and Mont de Marsan. Contact **Cars Région Aquitaine** (☑08 00 64 40 47; http://car.aquitaine.fr) for timetables.

TRAIN

Trains are the quickest way to get to Pau. There are two or three direct TGVs daily from Paris. In summer, SNCF buses run from Oloron-Ste-Marie into the Vallée d'Aspe.

Bayonne €13 to €15.50, 1½ hours.

Oloron-Ste-Marie €6.50, 40 minutes.

Paris' Montparnasse €85.50, 3½ hours via direct TGV.

Toulouse €28, two to 2½ hours.

❶ Getting Around

TO/FROM THE AIRPORT

Idelis (☑05 59 14 15 16; www.reseau-idelis.com) runs a shuttle to Pau's train station and town centre. From the airport, buses run roughly hourly from 7.40am to 7.40pm; from the train station, buses run from 6.30am to 7.50pm. Tickets cost €1, and the journey time is half an hour.

Note that buses don't run on Sunday, so you'll need to reserve a taxi at the **information desk** (☑05 59 33 33 00); expect to pay between €30 and €35.

CAR & MOTORCYCLE

Most streets in central Pau are *payant* (metered), but there's free parking on place de Verdun. Major car-rental firms have kiosks at the airport.

PUBLIC TRANSPORT

Public transport in Pau is handled by Idelis. Single/day tickets cost €1/2.50.

Lourdes

POP 15,700 / ELEV 400M

If you've ever wondered what a Catholic version of Las Vegas might look like, chances are it'd turn out pretty close to Lourdes. This sprawling town, 43km southeast of Pau, has been one of the world's most important pilgrimage sites since 1858, when 14-year-old Bernadette Soubirous (1844–79) was visited 18 times in a rocky grotto by the Virgin Mary. The visions were subsequently confirmed by the Vatican, and Bernadette was beatified in 1933.

Now known as the Sanctuaires Notre Dame de Lourdes, the grotto is considered one of the holiest sites in Christendom. More than six million people arrive in Lourdes every year, hoping to be doused in the supposedly miraculous waters, but the modern town of Lourdes itself is a pretty dispiriting experience, with a tatty tangle of neon-signed hotels and souvenir shops selling everything from plastic crucifixes to Madonna-shaped bottles (just add holy water at the shrine).

○ Sights & Activities

★ Sanctuaires Notre Dame de Lourdes
CAVE

(http://fr.lourdes-france.org; ⊘ Porte St-Michel & Porte St-Joseph 5am-midnight, baths 9-11am & 2-4pm Mon-Sat, 2-4pm Sun & holy days) The spiritual centre of Lourdes is the subterranean grotto where Bernadette Soubirous experienced her visions in 1858. From the Porte St-Joseph, a broad boulevard sweeps towards the gilded spires of the Basilique du Rosaire and the Basilique Supérieure (Upper Basilica).

Underneath is the fabled Grotte de Massabielle, where people queue for hours to enter and take a blessed dip in the cave's icy-cold baths, while other pilgrims content themselves by lighting candles of remembrance outside.

From Palm Sunday to mid-October, nightly torchlight processions start from the Massabielle Grotto at 9pm, while at 5pm there's the Procession Eucharistique (Blessed Sacrament Procession) along the Esplanade des Processions.

Château Fort
CHÂTEAU, MUSEUM

(Fortified Castle; www.chateaufort-lourdes.fr; adult/child €6/3; ⊘ 9am-noon & 1.30-6.30pm, open all day Jul & Aug) Lourdes' imposing castle stands on a sheer hill just behind the town. There's been a stronghold here since Roman times, but the present building combines a medieval keep with fortifications added during the 17th and 18th centuries. Since the 1920s, the castle has housed the Musée Pyrénéen, which displays local artefacts and folk art.

A free lift takes you up to the castle from rue Baron Duprat.

Pic du Jer
VIEWPOINT

(www.picdujer.fr; bd d'Espagne; funicular adult/child return €10/7.50; ⊘ 9.30am-6pm Mar-Nov) Panoramic views of Lourdes and the central Pyrenees are on offer from this rocky outcrop just outside town. There are two routes to the top: a punishing three-hour hike (ideal for penitents) or a speedy six-minute ride on the funicular (ideal for everyone else).

There's a choice of routes back down: a black-run mountain-bike trail, or a more family-friendly option along the Voie Verte des Gaves, a decommissioned railway that finishes up at the lower funicular station.

To get to the lower funicular, take bus 2 from place Monseigneur Laurence.

Chemin de Croix
WALKING

(Way of the Cross) The Chemin de Croix (sometimes known as the Chemin du Calvaire) leads for 1.5km up the hillside from the Basilique Supérieure past 14 Stations of the Cross. Seriously devout pilgrims climb to the first station on their knees.

Musée de Lourdes
MUSEUM

(☏ 05 62 94 28 00; www.musee-lourdes.fr; 11 rue de l'Égalité; adult/child €6/3; ⊘ 9am-noon & 1.30-6.30pm Apr-Oct) For the full back-story of Bernadette Soubirous, this museum details the town's history through a mix of exhibits and explanatory panels.

Moulin de Boly
HISTORIC HOUSE

(Boly Mill; 12 rue Bernadette Soubirous) FREE Bernadette was born in this millhouse on 7 January 1844, one year after the marriage of her parents Louise Castérot and François Soubirous. She lived here for the first 10 years of her life; it's still possible to see her childhood bedroom, along with the house's mill machinery.

Le Cachot
HISTORIC HOUSE

(15 rue des Petits Fossés; ⊘ 9am-noon & 2-6.30pm Apr-Oct, shorter hours rest of year) In 1857 Bernadette Soubirous' family fell on hard times and the family was forced to move to this dingy prison, where they lived communally in a room measuring just 16 sq m. It was

while living here that Bernadette stumbled across the Grotte de Massabielle, having been sent out to collect firewood.

Maison Paternelle de Ste-Bernadette
HISTORIC HOUSE

(2 rue Bernadette Soubirous; admission €2; ☉9.30am-12.15pm & 2.15-6.30pm Mar-Oct) After Bernadette Soubirous experienced her visions, Lourdes' abbot bought this house for her family. It's still run by her descendants, and has a collection of memorabilia including family photos and a bed where Bernadette supposedly slept.

Grottes de Bétharram
CAVE

(www.betharram.com; adult/child €13.50/8; ☉9am-noon & 1.30-5.30pm mid-Mar-Oct) Along the D937, 14km west of Lourdes, a network of subterranean caverns have been carved out from the limestone, glittering with impressive formations of stalactites and stalagmites. Visits to the cave aboard a combination of minitrain and barge last around 1½ hours, but be warned: the site gets extremely busy in high summer.

★ Festivals & Events

Festival International de Musique Sacrée
MUSIC FESTIVAL

(www.festivaldelourdes.fr) Lourdes' renowned week of sacred music is held around Easter.

☷ Sleeping

Lourdes has an enormous number of hotels (second only to Paris in terms of bed space, believe it or not), but most of them are chronically overpriced and generally of a disappointing standard. You'll be better off basing yourself outside town.

☷ Lourdes

Hotel Atlantic
HOTEL €

(☏05 62 94 02 33; www.hotelatlanticlourdes.com; 2 bd de la Grotte; s/d/tr €43/59/68; ☏) The exterior is as charming as a concrete brick, but inside this hotel offers decent-sized, plainly furnished rooms in peach and magnolia. Luxury they're not, but they're good value, and the all-you-can-eat breakfast is very reasonable at €6.

Bestwestern Beauséjour
HOTEL €€

(☏05 62 94 38 18; www.hotel-beausejour.com; 16 av de la Gare; s €88-98, d €105-115; ☏) Despite the heritage façade and glossy lobby, the rooms at this Best Western are as generic as ever. Still, it's handy for the station and tidier than many places. There's a bar-brasserie downstairs.

☷ Around Lourdes

Eth Béryè Petit
B&B €€

(☏05 62 97 90 02; www.beryepetit.com; 15 rte de Vielle; s/d €70/75) Twelve kilometres south of Lourdes, off the N21 near Beaucens, this 17th-century farmhouse offers country charm and knockout mountain views. There are three rooms: the most spacious is Era Galeria, which has French windows onto a private balcony, while Poeyaspé and Bédoret are tucked into the beamed attic. Rates are cheaper for extra nights.

Relais de Saux
B&B €€

(☏05 62 94 29 61; www.lourdes-relais.com; d €70-90; ☏) Ruched curtains, antique wardrobes and half-tester beds abound at this ivy-covered mansion, about a mile north of Lourdes. The period house is beautiful, but it's the surroundings that sell the place: grassy lawns and tree-filled gardens set against snowy Pyrenean peaks.

Hôtel des Rochers
HOTEL €€

(☏05 62 97 09 52; www.lesrochershotel.com; 1 place du Castillou; d €60-65, tr €80-85, f €95-100; ☏) In the idyllic village of St-Savin, 16km south of Lourdes, this shuttered hotel makes a perfect mountain retreat. It's run by an expat English couple, John and Jane, who have renovated the rooms in clean, contemporary fashion – insist on one with a mountain view. Half-board is available.

✗ Eating

Le Cabanon
BISTRO €€

(☏05 62 41 47 87; 37 rue de la Grotte; mains €11.50-16; ☉noon-2.30pm & 7-9.30pm) Dining out can be decidedly hit-and-miss in Lourdes, which makes this friendly bistro a doubly good find. It offers solid, no-frills French food, mainly classics such as grilled steak and duck breast.

★ Le Viscos
GASTRONOMIC €€€

(☏05 62 97 02 28; www.hotel-leviscos.com; 1 rue Lamarque, St-Savin; menus €27-89; ☉12.30-2.30pm & 7.30-9.30pm; ❉☏) Ex-TV chef Jean-Pierre St-Martin has established his own gastronomic hideaway in St-Savin, 16km south of Lourdes. Known for blending Basque, Breton and Pyrenean cuisine, as well as his unshakable passion for foie gras,

Lourdes

N 0 —————— 200 m
0 —————— 0.1 miles

Train Station

Av St-Joseph

Av Eugene Duviau

Bd du Lapacca

R de Langelle

R de Bagnères

Av Joffre

Av du Général Leclerc

Pl Capdevielle

Bus Station

Av Maréchal Juin

R Anselme Lacadé

R Lafitte

Buses to Grotte de Massabielle 13

Tarbes-Lourdes-Pyrénées (10km); Tarbes (19km)

Av de la Gare

Av du Général Baron Maransin

R Soubies

Pl de l'Église

R St-Pierre

Pl du Marcadal

Bd Commandant Célestin Romain

R de Pau

Bd de la Grotte

R Basse

Pl Jeanne d'Arc

Tourist Office

Pl Peyramale

Chaussée du Bourg

15

R de Pau

Bd de la Grotte

Bd de la Grotte

R de la Fontaine

R Bernadette Soubirous

Château Fort Entrance

Rampe du Fort

R Maupas

R des Petits Fossés

R Baron Duprat

R du Fort

R de la Grotte

16

R des Pyrénées

14

10

9

5

8

6

11

R de l'Égalité

Pont St-Michel

Ô St-Jean

R de la Grotte

Av Antoine Béguère

R de Pau

Pau

Esplanade des Processions

Forum

Information Office

R Jean-Semné

Buses for Train Station & Pic du Jer

Av Peyramale

Pont Vieux

Av du Paradis

Sanctuaires Notre Dame de Lourdes

2

12

Pl Mgr Laurence

17

Av Bernadette Soubirous

R Massabielle

Esplanade du Rosaire

3

Av Monseigneur Schoepfer

R Monseigneur Théas

Pl de la Merlasse

Grotte de Massabielle

1

4

Entrée des Lacets

Stations of the Cross

Chemin de Croix

7

Pic du Jer (600m); St-Savin (15km); Cauterets (30km)

Lourdes

he's now assisted by his son Alexis. Expect very rich, very traditional fine-dining food.

If you over-indulge, there are country-styled rooms upstairs (€99 to €123, with full board €67 extra per person).

Le Majorelle FRENCH €€€
(☎05 62 94 12 32; www.grandhotelmoderne.com; 21 av Bernadette Soubirous; menus €23-58; ⊙noon-2pm & 7.30-9.30pm) The restaurant at the Grand-Moderne hotel makes quite a first impression, with its art nouveau architecture, wood-panelled walls and sparkling chandeliers. It's a sight straight out of a Fitzgerald novel, and the food is fittingly classic, majoring on rich French and Italian cuisine. Dress smartly and enjoy a bit of luxury *a l'ancienne*.

Self-Catering
Covered Market MARKET
(place du Champ Commun; ⊙6.30am-1pm daily in summer, closed Sun in winter) Lourdes' covered market occupies most of the square.

ℹ Information

Forum Information Office (☎05 62 42 78 78; www.lourdes-france.com; Esplanade des Processions; ⊙8.30am-6.30pm) For information on the Sanctuaires Notre Dame de Lourdes.

Tourist Office (☎05 62 42 77 40; www.lourdes-infotourisme.com; place Peyramale; ⊙9am-6.30pm) Lourdes' main tourist office has general information on the Pyrenees and advice on accommodation, transport and activities.

ℹ Getting There & Away

AIR
Tarbes-Lourdes-Pyrénées Airport (www.tlp.aeroport.fr) Tarbes-Lourdes-Pyrénées airport is 10km north of Lourdes on the N21. There are three daily flights to Paris Orly (Air France), plus twice-weekly flights to London Stansted and Milan (Ryanair), Brussels (Thomas Cook) and Madrid (Iberia).

BUS
The small **bus station** (place Capdevieille) has services northwards to Pau (though trains are much faster and the recommended way to go). Buses running between Tarbes and Argelès-Gazost (at least eight daily), the gateway to the Pyrenean communities of Cauterets, Luz-St-Sauveur and Gavarnie, also stop here.

SNCF buses to Cauterets (€7, 55 minutes, at least five daily) leave from the train station.

CAR & MOTORCYCLE
Lourdes has a befuddling one-way system, so leave your car on the outskirts; there's free parking near the train and bus stations.

TRAIN
Lourdes has regular train connections, including direct TGVs to Pau and Paris Montparnasse. Trains to Toulouse often connect through Tarbes.
Bayonne €16 to €21, two hours via Pau.
Paris' Montparnasse €68 to €91.50, four hours via TGV.
Pau €7, 25 minutes.
Toulouse €25, 2¼ hours.

Parc National des Pyrénées

Sprawling for 100km across the Franco-Spanish border, the Parc National des Pyrénées conceals some of the last pockets of true wilderness left in France. In partnership with the 156-sq-km Parque Nacional de Ordesa y Monte Perdido, on the Spanish side of the border, this mountain landscape is a haven for rare flora and fauna, and remains fiercely proud of its culture and heritage: traditional hill-farming and shepherding are still practised here in much the same way as they were a century ago.

Within the park's boundaries are the highest peaks in southwest France, including the loftiest of all, Vignemale (3298m).

Activities

Walking

Three hundred and fifty kilometres of waymarked trails (including the Mediterranean-to-Atlantic GR10) criss-cross the park. Within the park are about 20 *refuges* (mountain huts), primarily run by the Club Alpin Français (CAF). Most are staffed only from July to September but maintain a small crew year-round.

Each of the six park valleys (Vallée d'Aure, Vallée de Luz, Vallée de Cauterets, Val d'Azun, Vallée d'Ossau and Vallée d'Aspe) has a national park folder or booklet in French, *Randonnées dans le Parc National des Pyrénées,* describing 10 to 15 walks.

White-Water Sports

The Gave d'Aspe, Gave d'Oloron and Gave d'Ossau offer excellent white-water rafting. There are several companies based around Oloron-Ste-Marie, including **Gaïa Aventure** (☑ 06 18 58 08 69; www.gaiaaventure.com; Oloron-Ste-Marie) and **Centre Nautique de Soeix** (☑ 05 59 39 61 00; http://soeix.free.fr; quartier Soeix), which both offer canoeing, kayaking and rafting trips. Prices start at between €23 and €30 for a two-hour session.

Mountain Biking

Once the last snows melt around mid-April to May, many of the Pyrenean ski stations open up their trails to VTTs (*vélos tout-terrains,* mountain bikes).

Val d'Azun, Bagnères du Bigorre, Barrousse, Barèges, Ax and several other places all have extensive areas of *sentiers balisés* (marked trails). The useful **Pyrénées Passion** (www.pyrenees-passion.info/VTT.php) website lists the main VTT areas.

There's also a large mountain-bike park near Aude, offering more than 870km of trails. Contact **Aude tourist office** (☑ 04 68 20 07 78; www.aude-pyrenees.fr) for details.

Bikes are widely available, and specialist companies such as **La Rébenne** (☑ 05 61 65 20 93; www.larebenne.com; 9 chemin de Malet, Foix) offer guided mountain-biking expeditions.

Skiing

While the Pyrenees' best skiing is across the border at the Spanish resorts (around Baqueira-Beret and Andorra), the French-side resorts still offer good skiing, snowboarding, *ski nordique* (cross-country skiing) and *raquette à neige* (snowshoeing).

The five major areas are:

Cauterets
SKIING

(www.cauterets.com) The best known of the French resorts, with well-groomed runs and a slightly longer snow season than other areas. It's also renowned for its summer hiking.

Ax Trois Domaines
SKIING

(www.ax-ski.com) Above Ax-les-Thermes, gentle runs snake through pine forest and, higher up, the open spaces of Campels. In summer its trails offer excellent hiking and biking.

Barèges La Mongie
SKIING

(www.n-py.com/fr/hiver/accueil-hiver.html) Grand Tourmalet Barèges La Mongie is the largest resort in the Pyrenees, with runs tracing their way around Col du Tourmalet and the Pic du Midi.

Superbagnères
SKIING

(www.luchon-superbagneres.com) High-altitude skiing above the spa town of Bagnères de Luchon.

Val d'Azun
SKIING

(www.valdazun.com) The best cross-country skiing in the Pyrenees, 30km southwest of Lourdes.

Information

For general information, the **PNR Pyrenees** (www.parc-pyrenees.com) website, the park's official tourist site, is the place to start. It has comprehensive information on activities, accommodation and sights.

There are also small park visitor centres in Etsaut, Laruns, Arrens-Marsous, Cauterets, Luz-St-Sauveur, Gavarnie and St-Lary-Soulan.

Vallée d'Aspe

The westernmost of the main Pyrenean valleys, the Vallée d'Aspe has been an important thoroughfare through the mountains ever since Julius Caesar's Roman legionnaires marched this way. Later during the medieval period, the valley became one of the main routes for pilgrims on the Chemin de St-Jacques, seeking a way across the mountains en route to journey's end in Santiago de Compostela.

WORTH A TRIP

PARC ANIMALIER DES PYRÉNÉES

Thirteen kilometres south of Lourdes, off the D821 near Argelès-Gazost, this fantastic animal park (www.parc-animalier-pyrenees.com; adult/child €16/13; ⊙9.30am-6pm or 7pm Apr-Oct) is home to many animals which were once common sights across the Pyrenees. The animals live on special 'islands' designed to mirror their natural habitat: marmots, chamoix and ibex inhabit rocky hills; beavers and giant otters dart along wooded waterways; and brown bears lord it over their own boulder-strewn mountain kingdom.

There are also flying displays by birds of prey and the park's resident vultures. You can even spend the night in a trapper's cabin (double/family €240/290), with glass windows looking into the wolves' enclosure.

The park is doubly important given that many of the species here have either disappeared in the wild or are teetering on the brink of extinction – most notably the brown bear (known in the US as the grizzly), which has all but vanished in the Pyrenees as a result of hunting and habitat loss. Despite fierce opposition from local farmers, a reintroduction program using wild bears from Slovenia has attempted to re-establish a breeding population, and it's thought that there are now between 15 and 20 bears roaming wild across the mountains – including a 26-year-old alpha male called Pyros. Sadly, one of his main rivals, Balou, was found dead in 2014 apparently as a result of a fall – a major blow given the animals' precarious numbers.

Fewer than 3000 people now live in the valley's 13 villages, and its upper reaches are still among the most remote corners of the French Pyrenees. But for many people the valley's seclusion is already a thing of the past thanks to the controversial Tunnel de Somport, an 8km-long road tunnel across the Spanish border, which opened in 2003.

The small town of Oloron-Ste-Marie stands at the valley's northern end. From here, the N193 runs south, roughly following the course of the River Aspe for about 50km to the Franco-Spanish border, passing through the villages of Sarrance, Bedous, Accous, Cette-Eygun and Etsaut en route.

⊙ Sights

Écomusée de la Vallée d'Aspe　　　　RURAL MUSEUM
(http://ecomusee.vallee-aspe.com) FREE Four sites around the valley, collectively known as the Écomusée de la Vallée d'Aspe, explore the area's heritage and agricultural traditions.

There are small folk museums in the villages of Sarrance, Lourdios-Ichère and Borcé, but the most interesting site is Les Fermiers Basco-Béarnais (⊙9.30am-1pm & 2.30-7.30pm) in Accous, a farmers' co-op and *fromagerie* (cheese shop), where you can sample cheese made from the milk of local ewes, goats and cows. Opening hours vary depending on the season; see the website for details.

🏃 Activities

Hiking

For most people, the main reason to visit the Vallée d'Aspe is the chance to tramp the trails. Route suggestions and planning tools are available from the useful Caminaspe (www.caminaspe.com) website.

The GR10 long-distance trail (part of the iconic Chemin St-Jacques) winds through the valley via the high-altitude village of Lescun, 5.5km from Bedous, which offers westerly views of the stunning Cirque de Lescun and the 2504m Pic d'Anie.

Another popular route follows the GR10 south from Borce or Etsaut to Fort du Portalet, a 19th-century fortress used as a WWII prison.

The Bedous tourist office (p683) sells maps and the locally produced guidebook, *Le Topo des 45 Randonnées en Vallée d'Aspe*.

Mountain Biking

VTT Nature　　　　MOUNTAIN BIKING
(🖉05 59 34 75 25; www.caminaspe.fr) Based in Bedous, this biking company offers guided mountain-bike sessions for €20/25 per half-/full day, and rents out mountain bikes for €20/95 per day/week. They also offer guided walks and baggage-transfer services (useful if you want to avoid carrying around your backpack).

Rando Bike
MOUNTAIN BIKING

(☑ 05 59 34 79 11; www.rando-bike.fr) On Bedous' main street, this experienced firm rents out bikes and also runs its own half- and full-day *randonées VTT* (mountain-bike trips). Half-day prices are €21/17 per adult/child, or €28/21 for a whole day. If you're here in winter, they'll also teach you how to snowshoe.

Horse Riding & Donkey Trekking
In the days before road and rail, the only way to transport goods over the mountains was using mule-power, and donkey trekking is still a great way to experience the mountains.

Randonnés à Cheval
Auberge Cavalière
HORSE RIDING

(☑ 05 59 34 72 30; www.auberge-cavaliere.com; Accous; 4-/7-day trip €660/1100) The main centre for horse trips in the valley, run by experienced horse-wranglers Eric and Michel Bonnemazou from their family farm near Accous.

They offer five or six guided expeditions throughout the summer, including a four- or seven-day tour of the national park, and a seven-day tour of the Languedoc's Cathar castles. There's a special expedition during the spring and autumn transhumance (see opposite for more information).

Le Parc Aux Ânes
DONKEY TREKKING

(☑ 05 59 34 88 98; www.garbure.net/ane_rando.htm; 3-day trip incl meals adult/child €185/120, plus €90 per donkey) Run by the owners of La Garbure, this donkey-trekking outfit offers a range of guided trips, staying at remote mountain *gîtes* (self-catering cottages) – or, if you wish, wild camping. It's a fabulous experience, far removed from the modern world of wi-fi and mobile phones – and best of all, thanks to your new donkey pal, you don't even have to carry your baggage.

Paragliding
There are several paragliding schools in Accous, which offer tandem *baptême* (introductory) rides with an instructor from €65.

Air Attitude
PARAGLIDING

(☑ 05 59 34 50 06; www.air-attitude.com) A four-strong team of qualified instructors, offering day flights as well as longer courses.

Ascendance
PARAGLIDING

(☑ 05 59 34 52 07; www.ascendance.fr) Offers weekend and week-long initiation courses, as well as multi-flight packages.

Festivals & Events
The valley holds three annual markets in celebration of its local produce: an Easter market in Bedous, a summer market in Aydius on the first Sunday of August, and an autumn food fair in Sarrance.

Other events to look out for are Le Transhumance de Lourdios in early June, and the Fête du Fromage d'Etsaut, a cheese fair on the last Sunday in July.

Sleeping & Eating
Accommodation is mainly geared towards walkers, with several seasonal campgrounds and *gîtes d'étapes* (walkers' lodges) operating on a *demi-pension* (half-board) basis.

Camping Le Gave d'Aspe
CAMPGROUND €

(☑ 05 59 34 88 26; www.campingaspe.com; Urdos; per adult/child/tent €3.95/2.50/4.95; ☺ May-Sep) Beautifully situated alongside the clattering Aspe River, in a forested site near the mountain village of Urdos, this is a superb family-friendly campground. There's a choice of timber bungalows or canvas-roofed chalets, or you can pitch your own tent.

Camping du Lauzart
CAMPGROUND €

(☑ 05 59 34 51 77; www.camping-lescun.com; per adult/tent/car €3.50/4.50/1.50) Twenty-seven spacious sites pitched under the trees with full-blown mountain views, in a secluded spot just outside Lescun. There's an on-site cafe and fresh bread is delivered daily.

La Garbure
GÎTE €

(☑ 05 59 34 88 98; www.garbure.net; per adult €17.50, half-board €30) Rustic *gîte* accommodation in a stone farmhouse in Etsaut.

Maison de la Montagne
GÎTE €

(☑ 05 59 34 79 14; http://montagne.randonnee.chez-alice.fr; per person €18, half-board €36) A sweet *gîte* in a converted Lescun barn, set in its own delightful flower-filled garden. The owner runs guided walks.

La Toison d'Or
B&B €€

(☑ 06 08 70 75 18; www.aubergetoisondor.com; place de l'Église de Cette, Cette-Eygun; r €60-80; ☎) You'll keep expecting members of Monty Python to pop their heads round the corner at this bizarrely brilliant medieval-era *auberge* (country inn), where the rooms hunker behind arches, block-stones and carved wooden doors. It's been gradually renovated by owner Julie; the breakfast room is the highlight, with its vaulted ceiling and monu-

THE TRANSHUMANCE

If you're travelling through the Pyrenees between late May and early June and you happen to find yourself stuck behind an enormous cattle-shaped traffic jam, there's a good chance you may have just got caught up in the age-old tradition of the Transhumance, in which shepherds move their flocks from their winter pastures up to the high grass-rich meadows of the mountain uplands.

This ancient custom has been a fixture on the Pyrenean calendar for hundreds of years, and is still regarded as one of the most important events of the year in the Pyrenees. The Transhumance is carried on in the time-honoured way – usually on foot, assisted by the occasional sheepdog or quad-bike – and several of the valleys host lively festivals to mark the occasion. The whole show is repeated in October, when the flocks are brought back down to the valleys before the snows of winter descend in earnest.

mental mountain view. It's a 2km drive from Cette-Eygun.

Auberge Cavalière　　　　　　B&B €€
(☑ 05 59 34 72 30; www.auberge-cavaliere.com; Accous; per person s/d/tr/f half-board €75/53.50/45/42.50, breakfast only s/d/tr/f €60/67/77/96; ☎) You'll really feel part of valley life at this rambling old horse farm 3km south of Accous, which offers five floral rooms and a cosy family *gîte*. The stone house is a picture of rustic character.

Au Château d'Arance　　　　　B&B €€
(☑ 05 59 34 75 50; www.chateaudarance.com; Cette-Eygun; s/d €65/85 incl breakfast; ☎) This part-13th century castle 2.5km from Cette-Eygun looks grand, with its slate-topped turret and sloping roof, but the rooms inside are disappointingly spartan. Still, the restaurant terrace is a peach, offering superlative valley views and solid *cuisine du terroir* (*menus* €15 to €25).

Les Estives　　　　　　　　　B&B €€
(☑ 05 59 34 77 60; www.estives-lescun.com; Lescun; s/d/f €45/52/85) A former barn renovated in 2006 with ecofriendly materials and timber cladding. The four rooms are cute and feminine: some have spotty wallpaper, others shades of peach or duck-egg blue. There's a kitchen for guests' use, or you can dine *chez maison*. It's 300m from Lescun.

❶ Information

Maison du Parc National des Pyrénées (☑ 05 59 34 88 30; Etsaut; ☉10.30am-12.30pm & 2-6.30pm May-Oct) Housed in Etsaut's disused train station.
Tourist Office (☑ 05 59 34 57 57; www.tourisme-aspe.com; place Sarraillé, Bedous; ☉9am-12.30pm & 2-5.30pm Mon-Sat) The valley's main tourist office.

❶ Getting There & Away

SNCF buses and trains connect Pau and Oloron-Ste-Marie up to 10 times daily.
Citram Pyrenees (☑ 05 59 27 22 22; www.citrampyrenees.fr) runs a regular bus (three to five daily Monday to Saturday, two daily at weekends) from Oloron into the valley, stopping at all the main villages en route to Somport.

Vallée d'Ossau

Running parallel to the Vallée d'Aspe, about 10km further east, the Vallée d'Ossau tracks its namesake river from its confluence with the Aspe at Oloron-Ste-Marie all the way to the watershed at Col du Pourtalet (1794m), some 60km to the south. The entrance to the valley as far as Laruns is green and pastoral, carpeted with lush fields and farms. Further south, the mountains stack up as the valley draws ever closer to the Spanish border.

There are 18 tiny villages dotted along the valley. The main focus is Laruns, 37km from Pau, a sturdy hamlet which has an excellent tourist office and national park centre, both stocked with information on hiking, mountain biking, rafting and other outdoor pursuits.

◉ Sights & Activities

Falaise aux Vautours　　　WILDLIFE CENTRE
(Cliff of the Vultures; www.falaise-aux-vautours.com; adult/child €7/5; ☉10.30am-12.30pm & 2-6.30pm Jul & Aug, 2-5.30pm Apr-Jun & Sep) The griffon vulture (*Gyps folvus*) was once a familiar sight over the Pyrenees, but habitat loss and hunting have taken their toll on these strange, majestic birds. Now legally protected, more than 120 nesting pairs roost around the limestone cliffs of this 82-hectare reserve. It's a thrill watching them swoop

and wheel from their nests above the valley, and strategically placed CCTV cameras allow you to see inside their nests from the visitor centre.

Keep an eye out for the other two species, the Egyptian vulture and the highly endangered bearded vulture, now confined to just a few small areas of the Alps.

Bielle
VILLAGE

The former 'capital' of the valley, Bielle is a beautiful village with many fine 15th- and 16th-century houses, linked together via a guided walk.

Rébénacq
VILLAGE

Rébénacq is one of the few fortified 'bastide' towns of the Pyrenees, built in 1347 by a lieutenant of Gaston Fébus, the 11th Count of Foix. Like all bastides, it's set around a central square, the place de la Bielle, whose buildings and dimensions have barely changed in seven centuries.

Castet
VILLAGE

Perched precariously on a glacial outcrop, this hilltop village boasts a 12th-century keep and a truly magnificent valley view. From the belvedere known as Port de Castet (868m), hiking and biking trails wind along the hillside, and you can hire donkeys in the village.

Eaux-Bonnes
HOT BATHS

During the 19th century, the village of Eaux-Bonnes (literally, Good Waters) flourished as a spa resort thanks to its geothermal hot springs, which fed public baths frequented by many illustrious figures including the Empress Eugénie. It's lost some of its lustre these days, but if you're aching after too much hiking, you can still enjoy a spa treatment and a sauna at the **Thermes des Eaux Bonnes** (☑ 05 59 05 39 64; eauxbonnes@valvital. fr; spa pass adult/child €13/6).

★ Le Petit Train
d'Artouste
MOUNTAIN RAILWAY

(☑ 05 59 05 36 99; www.train-artouste.com; adult/ child €24.50/20; ☉ May-Oct) Six kilometres east of Gabas, near the ski resort of Artouste-Fabrèges (1250m), a cable car cranks up the Pic de la Sagette (2032m) to reach the start of one of France's most scenic train journeys. The toy-sized Train d'Artouste (affectionately known as Le Petit Train) was built for dam workers in the 1920s, but now trundles its way for 10km to Lac d'Artouste, offering heart-stopping views over the valley and the spiky Pic du Midi d'Ossau.

The train gets very busy in summer, carrying more than 100,000 passengers in the four months it's open – try to visit at the start and end of the season, when it's usually quieter. Tickets can be bought in advance online and by phone. Trains run half-hourly in July and August, hourly at other times. The round-trip lasts about four hours.

You can also buy a **Formule Randonneur** (Walkers' Ticket), which allows you to get off the train and hike the trails, then get a return train back.

✵ Festivals & Events

Ossau is known for its tangy cheese, *fromage d'Ossau,* made from ewe's milk. It's sold all over the place in summer, and the valley

---

ⓘ ROAD PASSES IN THE PYRENEES

High road passes link the Vallée d'Ossau, the Vallée d'Aspe and the Vallée de Gaves (all of which have regularly featured as punishing mountain stages during the Tour de France). The altitude means that they're often blocked by snow well into summer; signs indicate whether they're *ouvert* (open) or *fermé* (closed).

Col d'Aubisque (1709m; ☉ May-Oct) The D918 links Laruns in the Vallée d'Ossau with Argelès-Gazost in the Vallée de Gaves. An alternative that's open year-round is the D35 between Louvie-Juzon and Nay.

Col de Marie-Blanque (1035m; ☉ May-Oct) The shortest link between the Aspe and Ossau valleys is the D294, which corkscrews for 21km between Escot and Bielle.

Col du Pourtalet (1795m; ☉ most of year) The main crossing into Spain generally stays open year-round except during exceptional snowfall.

Col du Tourmalet (2115m; ☉ Jun-Oct) Between Barèges and La Mongie, this is the highest road pass in the Pyrenees. If you're travelling east to the Pic du Midi (for example from Cauterets), the only alternative is a long detour north via Lourdes and Bagnères-de-Bigorre.

holds an annual Foire au Fromage (cheese fair) in October.

🛏 Sleeping

Aux Pieds des Pics   B&B €
(☑ 05 59 05 22 68; www.auxpiedsdespics.com; Bescat; s/d €54/59, f €83-103; 🛜) With its blue shutters, cute rooms and mountain-view balcony, this village B&B in Bescat is a beauty. Stripy bedspreads and pale-wood floors define the simply furnished rooms, and owners Delphine and Benoît are full of knowledge on the area. For breakfast, you might even get eggs from their own hens.

Hotel de France   HOTEL €€
(☑ 05 59 05 60 16; www.hotel-arudy-pyrenees. fr; 1 Place de l'Hôtel de Ville, Arudy; s/d/tr/f €56/65/81/88; 🛜) In Arudy, this hotel looks like it's appeared from a vintage postcard. It's on a quiet street leading to the church; outside there are pale green shutters and a pebbledash-and-wood frontage, while inside are pleasant, no-frills rooms and a good country bistro serving regional dishes such as *garbure béarnaise* (a rich meat-and-veg stew).

ℹ Information

La Maison de la Vallée d'Ossau Office de Tourisme (☑ 05 59 05 31 41; www.vallee dossau-tourisme.com; ⊘ 9am-noon & 2-6pm) Located on Laruns' square.
National Park Visitor Centre (☑ 05 59 05 41 59; ⊘ 9am-noon & 2-5.30pm) Beside the tourist office in Laruns.

ℹ Getting There & Around

BUS

Citram Pyrénées (www.citrampyrenees.fr) Runs buses from Pau to Laruns (one hour, two to four daily), stopping at Rébénacq, Arudy, Bielle, Laruns and Eaux-Bonnes.

CAR

The main road into the valley is the D934. For details on minor roads linking Ossau with its neighbouring valleys, see the boxed text left.

Cauterets

POP 1300 / ELEV 930M

It might not have the altitude of its sister ski stations in the Alps, but in many respects Cauterets is a more pleasant place to hit the slopes. While many of the Alpine resorts have been ruthlessly modernised and are crammed to capacity during the winter and summer seasons, Cauterets has clung on to much of its *fin-de-siècle* character, with a stately spa and grand 19th-century residences dotted round town.

Snow usually lingers here until early May, returning in late October or early November. In summer the landscape around Cauterets transforms into a hikers' paradise, with trails winding their way into the Parc National des Pyrénées.

◉ Sights & Activities

Cauterets' two ski areas are the **Pont d'Es-pagne** and **Cirque du Lys**, both great for hiking once the snows melt.

Local guides offer outdoor activities including paragliding, rock-climbing, fishing and via ferrata. Ask at the Cauterets tourist office, or consult the **Cauterets** (www. cauterets.com) website.

Pavillon des Abeilles   BEEHIVES
(www.pavillondesabeilles.com; 23bis av du Mamelon Vert; ⊘ 10.30am-12.30pm & 2.30-7pm Wed-Sat, open Mon-Sat during school holidays, plus Sun in summer) **FREE** This educational attraction explores the wonderful world of the bee, with a glass-sided hive, video and honey of every possible flavour.

Pont d'Espagne   WALKING
(cable cars adult/child €12/10) The most popular hike in Cauterets leads to the sparkling **Lac de Gaube**, a brilliantly blue mountain lake cradled by serrated peaks, while another trail winds up the **Vallée de Marcadau** to the high-altitude Refuge Wallon-Marcadau (1866m).

From the giant car park at Pont d'Es-pagne, four miles above Cauterets, a combination *télécabine* (cable car) and *télésiege* (chair lift) provides easy access to the trailheads.

Shuttle buses (adult/child return €7/4) run between Cauterets and the Pont d'Es-pagne car park every couple of hours in July and August. The car park costs €5.50 for up to 12 hours, or €8 for longer stays.

Cirque du Lys   SKIING, CYCLING
(cable car adult/child €12/10; ⊘ 9-noon & 1.45-5.15pm Jul & Aug) Cauterets' second most popular hiking area is this mountain amphitheatre, 1850m above sea-level. The best route is to catch the cable car and chair lift from Cambasque up to **Crêtes du Lys**, and walk back down the mountain for 1½ hours via the **Lac d'Ilhéou**, where there's a handy

THE PYRENEES CAUTERETS

lakeside refuge for lunch. From here it's another 1½ hours back to Cambasque.

A joint cable-car ticket is available with the Pont d'Espagne if you want to do both hiking routes, costing adult/child €21/19.

The valley is also home to Cauterets' mountain-bike park (one-day pass adult/child €17.50/14.50; ⊗ Jul & Aug), with three routes and a drop of 1500m to test your skills.

Thermes de César
SPA

(www.thermesdecauterets.com; rue Docteur Domer; ⊗8.30am-noon & 2-5pm Mon-Fri, 8am-noon Sat) It wasn't snow which attracted the first tourists to Cauterets – it was the area's hot springs, which bubble up at temperatures between 36°C and 53°C. The waters are rumoured to have numerous healing properties. Spa packages start at around €12 for a soak in a hot tub and head up to several hundred euros for a multi-day course.

🛏 Sleeping

Most people choose to stay in *gîtes* or self-catering apartments during the ski season. The majority of hotels and restaurants close for a few weeks between May and June, and mid-October to late November/early December.

Camping GR10
CAMPGROUND €

(✏ 06 20 30 25 85; www.gr10camping.com; rte de Pierrefitte Quartier Concé; sites for 2 adults €18; ⊗May-Sep; 🛜) Two-and-a-half kilometres north of town on the D920, this is the pick of Cauterets' campgrounds. It's tucked in a flat, grassy site cradled by mountains and forest, and has 69 spacious sites plus great facilities (hook-ups, pétanque, tennis courts and heated bathrooms). It even has its own adventure park with a via ferrata.

Camping Le Péguère
CAMPGROUND €

(✏ 05 62 92 52 91; www.campingpeguere.com; sites for 2 adults €11-14; ⊗Apr-Sep) A mountain-view camping ground 1.5km along the D920, with pleasant riverside pitches and comfortable chalets.

★Hôtel du Lion d'Or
HOTEL €€

(✏ 05 62 92 52 87; www.liondor.eu; 12 rue Richelieu; s €86, d €88-98, with half-board s €119, d €156-166; 🛜) This Heidi-esque hotel oozes mountain character from every nook and cranny. In business since 1913, it's deliciously eccentric, with charming old rooms in polka dot pinks, sunny yellows and duck-egg blues, and mountain-themed knick-knacks dotted throughout, from antique sleds to snow-shoes. Breakfast includes home-made honey and jams, and the restaurant serves hearty Pyrenean cuisine.

Hôtel-Restaurant Astérides-Sacca
HOTEL €€

(✏ 05 62 92 50 02; www.asterides-sacca.com; 11 bd Latapie-Flurin; r €70-98) If you saw Wes Anderson's *The Grand Budapest Hotel,* you might experience a flicker of recognition at this *grande-dame* hotel, with its balcony-clad façade and pseudo-Alpine decor. It's worth bumping up to a *Supérieure* room for space. The restaurant serves good French food (*menus* €17 to €22).

Hôtel Le Bois-Joli
HOTEL €€

(✏ 05 62 92 53 85; www.hotel-leboisjoli.com; 1 place du Maréchal-Foch; d €90-124, f €115-170; 🛜) Above a popular cafe right in the middle of Cauterets, this attractive hotel makes a good central base, with rooms in cheery blues, pinks and yellows, and mountain views from the upper floors. Breakfast is served in the cafe downstairs, but it's a bit steep at €11.

🍴 Eating & Drinking

La Fruitière
TRADITIONAL FRENCH €€

(✏ 05 62 42 13 53; menus lunch €10, dinner from €18; ⊗noon-3pm & 7-9pm) For dining with a view, nowhere beats the Fruitery. It sits at the head of the Lutour Valley, and has a mountain-view terrace that'll blow your thermal socks off. The food is traditional and delicious: tuck into baked trout or a bowl of *garbure* (meat and vegetable hotpot), and follow with blueberry tart. It's 7km south from town along the D920.

Lau Tant'hic
BISTRO €€

(✏ 05 62 92 02 14; Galerie Aladin, rue de Belfort; menus €18-30; ⊗noon-2.30pm & 7-10pm) Owner Gérant adds his own twist to mountain dishes at his little restaurant, but still favours local ingredients, especially lamb, duck, cured sausages and cheeses. His presentation shows a bit of big-city flair, too, and the wine list is great.

La Grande Fache
TRADITIONAL FRENCH €€

(✏ 06 08 93 76 30; 5 Rue Richelieu; dishes for two £18-23; ⊗noon-2.30pm & 7-10pm) You're in the mountains, so really you should be eating artery-clogging, cheese-heavy dishes such as *tartiflette* (potatoes, cheese and bacon baked in a casserole), *raclette* and fondue. This family-run restaurant will oblige, served in a dining-room crammed with mountain memorabilia.

WORTH A TRIP

CIRQUE DE GAVARNIE

Fifty-two kilometres south of Lourdes on the D921 you'll find three of the most breath-taking vistas in the Pyrenees: a trio of natural mountain amphitheatres, carved out by ancient glaciers and framed by sawtoothed, snow-dusted peaks – many of which top out at over 3000m.

The easiest to reach – and consequently the most popular – is the Cirque de Gavarnie, with a panorama of spiky mountains that provides one of the Pyrenees' most famous vistas. It's especially dramatic after heavy rain, when waterfalls cascade down the mountainsides. The Cirque is about 1½ hours' walk from Gavarnie village; wear proper shoes, as the trail can be slippery and rocky. Between Easter and October you can clip-clop along on a horse or donkey (around €25 for a round-trip).

A second spectacular amphitheatre, the Cirque de Troumouse, can be reached via the minor D922 and a hair-raising 8km toll road near Gèdre, 6.5km northeast of Gavarnie. The toll road itself is steep and quite exposed, with hairpin turns and no barriers, so take it slow. Snows permitting, it's usually open between April and October; the toll is €4 per vehicle.

Hidden among the mountains between Troumouse and Gavarnie is the third amphitheatre, Cirque d'Estaubé. It's much wilder and more remote, and only accessible on foot. The trail starts from the turn-off to the barrage des Gloriettes, which you pass on the D922 en route to Troumouse. It's about a 3½ hour return walk; pack proper boots, water and snacks.

Self-Catering

Covered Market   MARKET
(av Leclerc) Cauterets' covered market is a turn-of-the-century beauty, and the best place in town to pick up foodie souvenirs.

À La Reine Margot   SWEETS
(place Clemenceau) One of many shops selling the fruity sweets known as *berlingots,* a speciality of Cauterets.

Fromagerie du Saloir   DELICATESSEN
(av Leclerc) Sells cheeses, hampers and liqueurs (including one called Gratte Cul, or 'scratch arse').

Les Mijotés de Léon   FARM SHOP
(http://fermebasque.free.fr; rte de Cambasque) This country farmhouse 4km west of Cauterets sells goodies including mountain honey and home-made charcuterie, and also has a basic restaurant.

ℹ Information

Cauterets Tourist Office (℡ 05 62 92 50 50; www.cauterets.com; place Maréchal Foch; ◷ 9am-12.30pm & 2-7pm)
Maison du Parc National des Pyrénées (℡ 05 62 92 52 56; place de la Gare; ◷ 9.30am-noon & 3-7pm) Sells walking maps and guidebooks, and organises guided walks in summer.

ℹ Getting There & Away

Sadly the last train steamed out of Cauterets' magnificent station in 1947. It now serves as the **bus station** (℡ 05 62 92 53 70; place de la Gare), with SNCF buses running between Cauterets and Lourdes train station (€7, one hour, four to six daily).

Vallée des Gaves & Around

Gentle and pastoral, the Vallée des Gaves (Valley of the Mountain Streams) extends south from Lourdes to Pierrefitte-Nestalas. Here the valley forks: the narrow, rugged eastern tongue twists via Gavarnie while the western tongue corkscrews up to Cauterets.

◎ Sights

★ **Pic du Midi**   VIEWPOINT
(www.picdumidi.com; adult/child €32/22; ◷ 9am-7pm Jun-Sep, 10am-5.30pm Oct-May) If the Pyrenees has a mustn't-miss view, it's the one from the Pic du Midi de Bigorre (2877m). Once accessible only to mountaineers, since 1878 the Pic du Midi has been home to an important observatory, and on a clear day the sky-top mountain views are out of this world. A cable car climbs to the summit from the nearby ski resort of La Mongie (1800m). Early morning and late evenings

generally get the clearest skies and fewest crowds.

At the top, there are several viewing terraces, all offering a different perspective on the serrated mountain landscape. There's also a sandwich shop and restaurant (*menus* €18 to €30).

If you're visiting in the low season, check the website for closures due to bad weather. In summer, if you're travelling from the western valleys via the Col du Tourmalet, double-check the road is open before you set out – it's usually closed between November and May.

Le Donjon des Aigles
BIRD PARK

(www.donjon-des-aigles.com; adult/child €14/8.50; ⊙10am-noon & 2.30-6.30pm Apr-Sep) Fifteen minutes' drive south of Lourdes in the spectacular surroundings of the 11th-century Château de Beaucens, you can see one of the world's largest collections of birds of prey. Among the taloned residents are bald eagles, fish eagles, horned owls, vultures and a collection of parrots: flying displays are held at 3.30pm and 5pm (3pm, 4.30pm and 6pm in August).

🛏 Sleeping

Les Remparts
B&B €€

(📞05 62 92 81 70; www.les-remparts.fr; 2 Place des Remparts; r €49-60, 2-night minimum) In the charming village of Luz St-Saveur, this apartment complex and B&B is fab for families. It's right next to the village's fortified church, in an old inn that's been renovated with style and taste. The decor is plain and simple, and the nicest apartments have views of the church and the house's courtyard.

Vallée de Garonne

St-Bertrand de Comminges

On an isolated hillock, St-Bertrand and its Cathédrale Ste-Marie (www.cathedrale-saint-bertrand.org; adult/child incl audioguide €4/1.50; ⊙9am-7pm Mon-Sat, 2-7pm Sun) loom over the Garonne Valley and the much-pillaged remains of the Gallo-Roman town of Lugdunum Convenarum. The cathedral has been an important pilgrimage site since medieval times, and you'll still see their modern-day descendants wandering round – although these days they'll be equipped with hiking gear and walking poles.

Bagnères de Luchon

POP 3032 / ELEV 630M

Bagnères de Luchon (or simply Luchon) is a trim little town of gracious 19th-century buildings, expanded to accommodate the *curistes* who came to take the waters at its splendid spa. It's now one of the Pyrenees' most popular ski areas, with the challenging runs of Superbagnères right on its doorstep.

🛐 Activities

Thermes de Luchon
HOT BATHS

(📞05 61 79 22 97; www.thermes-luchon.fr; parc des Quinconces; ⊙Mar–mid-Nov) Luchon's thermal baths are at the southern end of allée d'Étigny. There are lots of spa packages available, but for day bathers it costs €15 to sit in the scented steam of the 160m-long underground *vaporarium,* then dunk yourself in the warm-water pool, naturally heated to 32°C.

Superbagnères
SKIING, CYCLING

(http://uk.luchon-superbagneres.com; adult/child €7.90/5.90; ⊙ski-lifts 9am-12.30pm & 2-6pm Jul & Aug, 1.30-6pm weekends May-Jun & Sep, open daily in winter) Luchon's *télécabine* (ski lift) whisks you up to the mountain plateau known as Superbagnères (1860m), the starting point for the area's winter ski-runs and summer walking trails. The tourist office has lots of information on possible routes, and sells maps and guides.

🛏 Sleeping

★Le Castel de la Pique
HOTEL €€

(📞05 61 88 43 66; www.castel-pique.fr; 31 cours des Quinconces; s €62-74, d €67-79; 🔊) There's something Disney-ish about this hotel, with its château corner-turrets and 19th-century façade. Even better, the charming rooms offer fantastic value, with wood floors, mantelpieces and French windows opening onto dinky balconies – mountain views are practically universal. Owner Alain is a character, and a mine of local knowledge. All in all, it's a bargain – especially with breakfast at €7.

Alti Hôtel
HOTEL €€

(📞05 61 79 56 97; www.actaluchon.com; 19 allée d'Étigny; s €77-88, d €93-109, tr €113-132; 🔊) Move a step up the luxury ladder and you reach this brilliantly central, balcony-clad hotel, straddling the corner of two pretty streets and a lively cafe in the old town.

Despite its vintage exterior, it's resolutely modern inside: expect glossy wood floors and generic modern furniture.

✖ Eating

Le Baluchon BISTRO €€
(☑ 05 61 88 91 28; 12 av du Maréchal Foch; menus lunch €15, dinner €26-32; ☺ 12.30-2pm & 7.30-10pm) In contrast to the traditional fare on many Luchon menus, this bistro takes its cue from a more contemporary cookbook. It's run by husband and wife team Laura and Thomas, who favour seasonal ingredients and stripped-back presentation – expect local meats partnered by a swirl of sauce or a delicate vegetable mousseline.

L'Arbesquens REGIONAL CUISINE €€
(☑ 05 61 79 33 69; 47 allée d'Étigny; meals €15-30; ☺ noon-2pm Thu-Tue, 7-10pm Mon-Sat) Cheesy raclettes and fondues are the mainstay at this zero-fuss brasserie – there are more than 15 on offer, all served to share, along with brasserie standards such as lamb chops, duck breast and *steak-frites*.

L'Héptaméron des Gourmets GASTRONOMIC €€€
(☑ 05 61 79 78 55; www.heptamerondesgourmets. com; 2 bd Charles de Gaulle; menus €30-75; ☺ 7-9pm Tue-Sat, noon-2pm & 7-9pm Sun) This swish restaurant is the address for trad French fine dining. Start with an aperitif in the salon, with its book-lined shelves and leather armchairs, then graduate to the kitschy conservatory for rich cuisine drowned in creamy sauces and truffle butters.

Self-Catering

Covered Market MARKET
(rue Docteur Germès; ☺ daily Apr-Oct, Wed & Sat Nov-Mar) Luchon's covered market was established in 1897 and is still going strong.

❶ Information

Tourist Office (☑ 05 61 79 21 21; www.luchon. com; 18 allée d'Étigny; ☺ 9am-7pm in summer, shorter hours rest of year)

❶ Getting There & Around

SNCF trains and coaches run between Luchon and Montréjeau (€6.50, 50 minutes, six daily), which has frequent connections to Toulouse (€15.50) and Pau (€28.50).

Vallée de l'Ariège

On the eastern side of the French Pyrenees, the sleepy Vallée de l'Ariège is awash with prehistoric interest: it's home to some of Europe's most impressive underground rivers and subterranean caverns, many of which are daubed with cave paintings left behind by prehistoric people.

The most useful bases are Foix, former seat of the Comtes de Toulouse, and Mirepoix, a well-preserved *bastide* town.

◎ Sights & Activities

Information on the main sights in the Ariège Valley is available on the Grands Sites de l'Ariège (www.grands-sites-ariege.fr) website.

If you're visiting several sights, it's worth picking up the free Prehisto Pass at the

---

DON'T MISS

PREHISTORIC PAINTERS OF THE PYRENEES

Grotte de Niaux (☑ 05 61 05 88 37; adult/child €12/7; ☺ tours hourly 10.15am-4.15pm, extra tours in summer) Most people know about the prehistoric artworks of the Dordogne, but far fewer realise that ancient painters left their mark in caves all across the Pyrenees. Halfway up a mountainside about 12km south of Foix, the Grotte de Niaux is the most impressive, with a fabulous gallery of bison, horses and ibex adorning a vast subterranean chamber called the Salon Noir. There's also one tiny depiction of a weasel – the only cave painting of the animal yet found.

The Salon Noir is reached via an 800m underground trek through pitch darkness. To preserve the paintings, there's no lighting inside the cave, so you'll be given a torch as you enter. On the way, look out for graffiti left by previous visitors, some of which dates back to the 17th century.

The cave can only be visited with a guide. From April to September there's usually one English-language tour a day at 1.30pm. Visitor numbers are limited, so it's sensible to book.

first place you visit, which gives discounts at all the subsequent places you go to.

Château de Foix CHÂTEAU
(☑ 05 61 05 10 10; adult/child €5.60/3; ☺ 9.45am-6pm in summer, shorter hours rest of year) The Ariège's most unmistakeable landmark is Foix's triple-towered castle, the stronghold of the powerful Comtes de Foix. Built in the 10th century, it survived as their seat as power throughout the medieval era, and served as a prison from the 16th century onwards.

The castle is approached via a cobbled causeway from the old town. The interior is rather bare, but the view from the battlements is wonderful. There's usually at least one tour daily in English in summer.

Parc de la Préhistoire MUSEUM
(☑ 05 61 05 10 10; Tarascon-sur-Ariège; adult/child €10.80/6.90; ☺ 10am-7pm in summer, shorter hours rest of year) Eighteen kilometres south of Foix, near Tarascon-sur-Ariège, this excellent museum-park provides a useful primer on the area's prehistoric past. The centrepiece is the Grand Atelier, which uses film, projections and an audio-visual commentary to explain the story of human settlement. There are also many animal skeletons, including a cave bear and a mammoth, as well as a full-scale reproduction of the Salon Noir in the Grotte de Niaux (p689).

Outside you can follow a trail around the park's grounds, explore a selection of prehistoric tents and learn how to use an ancient spear-thrower.

Grotte du Mas d'Azil CAVE, MUSEUM
(☑ 05 61 05 10 10; adult/child €8/5; ☺ caves 10am-12.30pm & 1.30-6.45pm, museum 2-6pm, open 10am-6pm in summer) Twenty-five kilometres northwest of Foix, near Le Mas d'Azil, this rock shelter is famous for its rich finds of prehistoric tools, as well as its cave art. Two galleries are open to the public: in the Galerie Breuil you can see engravings of bison, horses, fish, deer and what appears to be a cat, while in the Oven Room, there's a rare – and haunting – depiction of a human face. The ticket also includes entry to the site's museum.

Les Forges de Pyrène MUSEUM
(☑ 05 34 09 30 60; adult/child €8.20/4.90; ☺ 10am-noon & 1-6.30pm, open all day in summer) In Montgaillard, 4.5km south of Foix, this 'living museum' explores Ariège folk traditions, with live displays of ancient trades

such as blacksmithing, glass-blowing, tanning, thatching and nail-making.

Rivière Souterraine de Labouiche UNDERGROUND RIVER
(☑ 05 61 65 04 11; www.labouiche.com; adult/child €9.80/7.80; ☺ 9.30am-5pm Jul & Aug, 10am-11pm & 2-4.30pm Apr-May & Sep) Deep beneath the village of Labouiche, 6km northwest of Foix, flows Europe's longest navigable underground river. Discovered in 1908 by a local doctor, it's been open to the public since 1938. Barge trips run for about 1.5km along its underground course, with guides pulling the boats along by ropes attached to the ceiling, and walkways entering more caverns and eerie chambers.

The highlight of the visit is saved for the end: a clattering waterfall known as the Cascade Salette which tumbles into a sparkling turquoise pool. Depending on rainfall, the waterfall's speed can vary anywhere from 100 to 1500 litres per second. It's all quite touristy, but the kids are bound to love it.

Best of all on a blazing summer's day, the caves hover at a cool constant temperature of 13°C.

Château de Montségur CHÂTEAU
(www.montsegur.fr; adult/child €4.50/2; ☺ 9am-7pm Jul & Aug, 10am-5pm Mar-Jun, Sep & Oct, 11am-4pm Dec-Feb) For the full Monty Python medieval vibe, tackle the steep 1207m climb to the ruins of this hilltop fortress, 32km east of Foix. It's the westernmost of the string of Cathar castles stretching across into Languedoc; the original castle was razed to rubble after the siege, and the present-day ruins largely date from the 17th century.

It was here, in 1242, that the Cathars suffered their heaviest defeat; the castle fell after a gruelling nine-month siege, and 220 of the defenders were burnt alive when they refused to renounce their faith. A local legend claims that the Holy Grail was smuggled out of the castle in the days before the final battle.

Spéléo Canyon de l'Ariège CANYONING
(☑ 06 30 31 24 52; www.speleo-canyon-ariege.com; Niaux; half-day trips €38-45) A different way to appreciate the Pyrenean scenery: climbing along rocky canyons and plunging down ice-cold waterfalls, equipped with not much more than a hard hat and your own inner courage. It's heart-in-the-mouth stuff, but fantastic, exhausting fun.

LOMBRIVES

Twenty-two kilometres north of Ax-les-Thermes on the N20 near Ussat-les-Bains, Europe's largest cave system **Lombrives** (✆ 06 70 74 32 80; www.grotte-lombrives.fr; standard tour adult/child €7.50/4.50; ⊗ 9am-7pm Jul & Aug, 10am-5pm Jun & Sep, 2-5pm May & Oct),I burrows its way through the soft limestone rock beneath the Pyrenees' peaks. Guided tours take more than 200 stalactite-lined tunnels, grottoes and galleries, including a sandy expanse known as the Sahara Desert, and limestone columns variously resembling a mammoth, a wizard and the Virgin Mary.

Standard tours last an hour, but multi-hour expeditions are available for the adventurous (and non-agoraphobic).

🛏 Sleeping & Eating

Hôtel les Remparts
HOTEL €€

(✆ 05 61 68 12 15; www.hotelremparts.com; 6 cours Louis Pons Tarde, Mirepoix; s €59-78, d €72-98; 🕸) Built into the *bastide* architecture of Mirepoix, this is a smart option, with a mix-bag of nine rooms that combine modern design with the building's centuries-old heritage – a patch of exposed stone here, a wonky wooden doorway there. The excellent restaurant is one of Mirepoix's best, serving fine French cuisine (*menus* €29 to €53) under stone arches and great oak beams.

★ Auberge les Myrtilles
B&B €€

(✆ 05 61 65 16 46; www.auberge-les-myrtilles.com; Salau; d €62-92; 🕸) You'll feel rather like you're staying in the Canadian wilderness here, with its timber-framed chalet cabins and forested hillside setting. It's a wonderful place to settle yourself: despite the rustic style, there are lots of luxury spoils here, including a covered swimming pool with a knockout view, a Swedish-style sauna and, of course, mountain panoramas on every side. It's about 20km west of Foix on the D17.

The restaurant is great for local cuisine – don't miss the Azinat – a duck, sausage and vegetable hot-pot.

Hôtel Restaurant Lons
HOTEL €€

(✆ 05 34 09 28 00; www.hotel-lons-foix.com; 6 place Dutilh, Foix; d €62-75, f €93-99) One of the better hotels in Foix, an old-fashioned affair with rambling corridors and functional but comfy rooms, some of which look onto the river, while the others face Foix's shady streets. The riverside restaurant offers good-value half-board (*menus* €17.50 to €34).

Château de Beauregard
HOTEL €€

(✆ 05 61 66 66 64; www.chateaubeauregard.net; av de la Résistance, St-Girons; r incl half-board €90-260; 🕸🛆) In St-Girons, halfway between St-Gaudens and Foix along the D117, this grand château is ideal for playing lord of the manor: the house is topped by turrets and surrounded by 2.5 hectares of gardens, with grand rooms named after writers (some have their bathrooms hidden in the castle's corner towers). There's also a pool, spa and a great Gascon restaurant.

Maison des Consuls
HOTEL €€€

(✆ 05 61 68 81 81; www.maisondesconsuls.com; 6 place du Maréchal Leclerc; d €85-130; 🕸) This offbeat hotel has themed all its rooms after a notable figure from Mirepoix's past. The best ones are the Astronomer's Suite, which has its own outside patio overlooking the town's rooftops, and the Dame-Louise room, decorated in Louis XIII–style, with a four-poster bed and a superb view over the cathedral.

★ L'Abbaye de Camon
B&B €€€

(✆ 05 61 60 31 23; www.chateaudecamon.com; 3 Place Philippe de Lévis, Camon; d €135-195) Wow, what a spot. Founded as a Benedictine abbey in the 12th century, this is now possibly the poshest B&B anywhere in the Pyrenees. The building's decor puts most châteaux to shame, with vaulted archways, winding staircases, a Renaissance-style drawing room and ravishing gardens – plus five regal rooms oozing antique grandeur. It's 13km southeast of Mirepoix.

ⓘ Information

Tourist Office (✆ 05 61 65 12 12; www.tourisme-foix-varilhes.fr; 29 rue Delcassé, Foix; ⊗ 9am-6pm)

ⓘ Getting There & Away

Regular trains connect Toulouse and Foix (€13, 1¼ hours).

Toulouse Area

POP 1.8M

Best Places to Eat

➡ Michel Sarran (p701)

➡ Le Genty-Magre (p701)

➡ L'Epicurien (p707)

➡ La Table des Cordeliers (p711)

➡ Les Boissières (p708)

Best Places to Stay

➡ Hotel St-Sernin (p699)

➡ Côté Carmes (p699)

➡ La Tour Ste-Cécile (p706)

➡ Au Chateau (p708)

➡ Les Bruhasses (p712)

Why Go?

Rich food, good wine and slow living: that's what this sun-baked corner of southwest France is all about. Traditionally part of the Languedoc, the red-brick city of Toulouse and the surrounding area has been out on its own since World War II, but scratch beneath the surface and you'll discover the same old southern passions.

The capital city makes the perfect introduction: with its buzzy markets, stately architecture, crackling culture and renowned rugby team, Toulouse is one of France's liveliest provincial cities. Beyond the fringes of La Ville Rose lies a landscape dotted with sturdy *bastides* (fortified towns), soaring cathedrals and country markets, not to mention the historic province of Gascony, famous for its foie gras, fattened ducks and fiery Armagnac. And through it all runs the Canal du Midi, the undisputed queen of French canals.

Take things slow: life in this corner of France is all about the living.

When to Go
Toulouse

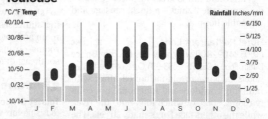

Feb Costumes and street parades announce the arrival of spring during Albi's Carnival.

July Cordes-sur-Ciel goes medieval during the Fêtes Médiévales du Grand Fauconnier.

Aug Harvest time brings a wine festival to Gaillac and a pink garlic festival to Lautrec.

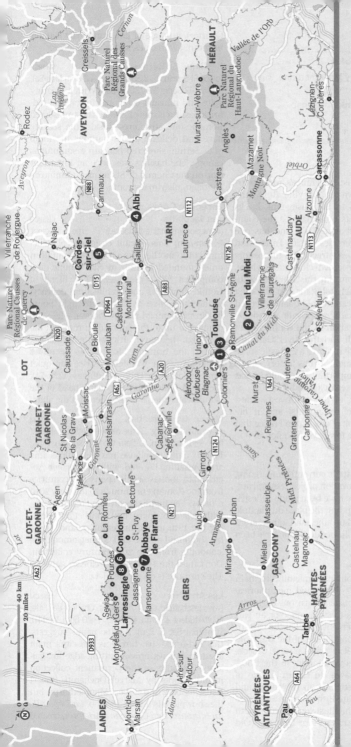

Toulouse Area Highlights

1 Savouring the flavours of the southwest at one of Toulouse's fantastic **covered markets** (p702)

2 Catching a slow-boat or cycling the tow-paths of the stately **Canal du Midi** (p711)

3 Climbing inside a replica of the Mir Space Station at Toulouse's **Cité de l'Espace** (p695)

4 Marvelling at Albi's mighty medieval cathedral-cum-castle, the **Cathédrale Ste-Cécile** (p703)

5 Wandering the cobbled lanes of the beautiful hilltop bastide of **Cordes-sur-Ciel** (p706)

6 Sampling some brandy from the barrel at a traditional **Armagnac distillery** (p710)

7 Enjoying the silence of the **Abbaye de Flaran** (p712), southwest France's loveliest Cistercian abbey

8 Watching medieval catapults in action at the fortified village of **Larressingle** (p711)

FAST FACTS

➡ **Area** 18,324 sq km

➡ **Local industry** Manufacturing, wine-making, agriculture

➡ **Signature drink** Armagnac

Toulouse

POP 446,200

Toulouse might just be France's most over-looked city. Known as 'La Ville Rose' (the Pink City) thanks to the dusky-pink bricks used in many of its buildings, it's the country's fourth-biggest metropolis and has one of the largest universities outside Paris – and yet Toulouse receives a fraction of the visitors compared to better-known cities such as Nice, Bordeaux and Lyon. But this vibrant southern city has so much going for it: a crackling cultural scene, a beautiful old quarter packed with *hôtels particuliers* (private mansions) and a glorious location at the confluence of the Canal du Midi and the River Garonne. Further afield you'll discover a fantastic space museum and the main Airbus factory – both reminders of the important role Toulouse has played in France's aerospace industry.

Throw in some of the southwest's finest food markets and restaurants, and it becomes hard to think of any trip to France that shouldn't include a few days in Toulouse.

◎ Sights

Toulouse's city centre is currently undergoing a major urban renovation project. Several areas of the city centre have been made pedestrian-only zones, including the place du Capitole and rue d'Alsace-Lorraine, and other areas including Square Charles de Gaulle have been given a facelift.

Place du Capitole   SQUARE

(place du Capitole) Toulouse's magnificent main square is the city's literal and metaphorical heart, where *toulousiens* turn out en masse on sunny evenings to sip a coffee or an early aperitif at a pavement cafe. On the eastern side is the 128m-long façade of the Capitole (rue Gambetta & rue Romiguières, place du Capitole; ◎10am-7pm), the city hall, built in the 1750s. Inside the Théâtre du Capitole, one of France's most prestigious opera venues, and the over-the-top, late-19th-century Salle des Illustres (Hall of the Illustrious). To the south of the square is the city's Vieux Quartier (Old

Quarter), a tangle of lanes and leafy squares brimming with cafes, shops and eateries.

Basilique St-Sernin   CHURCH

(place St-Sernin; ◎8.30am-noon & 2-6pm Mon-Sat, 8.30am-12.30pm & 2-7.30pm Sun) With its soaring spire and unusual octagonal tower, this red-brick basilica is one of France's best-preserved Romanesque structures. Inside, the soaring nave and delicate pillars harbour the tomb of St Sernin, sheltered beneath a sumptuous canopy. The basilica was once an important stop on the Chemin de St-Jacques (Camino de Santiago) pilgrimage route.

Ensemble Conventuel
des Jacobins   CHURCH

(www.jacobins.mairie-toulouse.fr; rue Lakanal; ◎9am-7pm) This elegant ecclesiastical structure is the mother church of the Dominican order, founded in 1215 by St Dominic, and completed 170 years later. It's a blend of Gothic showiness and architectural delicacy: inside the Église des Jacobins light pours in through stained glass windows, while columns soar up to the fan-vaulted roof and the 45m-high belltower. It's worth wandering around the tranquil Cloître des Jacobins (admission €4), a wonderful space for quiet contemplation. St Thomas Aquinas (1225–74), the monk-philosopher and early head of the Dominican order, is buried beneath the altar.

Musée des Augustins   MUSEUM

(www.augustins.org; 21 rue de Metz; adult/child €4/free; ◎10am-6pm, to 9pm Wed) Like most big French cities, Toulouse has a fabulous fine arts museum. Located within a former Augustinian monastery, it spans the centuries from the Roman era through to the early 20th century. The highlights are the French rooms, with Delacroix, Ingres and Courbet representing the 18th and 19th centuries, and works by Toulouse-Lautrec and Monet among the standouts from the 20th-century collection. Don't miss the 14th-century cloister gardens. The entrance is on rue de Metz.

Les Abattoirs   MUSEUM

(www.lesabattoirs.org; 76 allées Charles de Fitte; adult/student & child €7/free; ◎10-6pm Wed-Fri, 11am-7pm Sat & Sun) As its name suggests, this red-brick structure was the city's main abattoir, but it's now a cutting-edge art gallery. Highlights of the permanent collection include works by Marcel Duchamp, Robert Rauschenberg and Robert Mapplethorpe, but the showpiece is a huge Picasso, *La Dépouille du Minotaure en Costume d'Arlequin*, created in 1936. Sadly, it's only on show six months a year due to its fragile condition.

Hôtel d'Assézat
MUSEUM

(www.fondation-bemberg.fr; place d'Assézat; ⊙10am-12.30pm & 1.30-6pm Tue-Sun, to 9pm Thu) Toulouse boasts more than fifty *hôtels particuliers*, private mansions built for the city's nobles and aristocrats during the 16th and 17th centuries. Among the finest is the Hôtel d'Assézat, built for a woad merchant in 1555. It's now home to the Fondation Bemberg, which owns a fine collection of paintings, sculpture and objets d'art; the first floor is mainly devoted to the Renaissance, while Impressionism, pointillism and other 20th-century movements occupy the upper floor. Guided tours depart daily at 3.30pm.

Museum de Toulouse
MUSEUM

(www.museum.toulouse.fr; 35 allée Jules-Guesde; adult/child €6.50/4; ⊙10am-6pm) This excellent natural history museum ranges across the epochs, with exhibits from pterodactyl skeletons to ancient fossils. The exhibits are really well displayed – look out for 'Time's Staircase', which tells the history of life on earth in a hands-on fashion.

Château d'Eau
GALLERY

(www.galeriechateaudeau.org; 1 place Laganne; adult/child €2.50/free; ⊙1-7pm Tue-Sun) Photography exhibitions inside a 19th-century water tower.

Musée St-Raymond
MUSEUM

(www.saintraymond.toulouse.fr; place St-Sernin; adult/child €4/2; ⊙10am-6pm) The city's archaeological museum houses everything from Roman sculptures to Christian sarcophagi and Celtic torques.

Musée Paul Dupuy
MUSEUM

(13 rue de la Pléau; adult/child €4/2; ⊙10am-6pm Tue-Mon) Toulouse's decorative arts museum takes in everything from suits of armour to rare clocks. It's named after a local art collector who restored the building and founded the museum.

Cathédrale de St-Étienne
CATHEDRAL

(Cathedral of St Stephen; place St-Étienne; ⊙8am-7pm Mon-Sat, from 9am Sun) The city cathedral dates mainly from the 12th and 13th centuries, and has a glorious rose window.

Église Notre Dame du Taur
CHURCH

(12 rue du Taur; ⊙2-7pm Mon-Fri, 9am-1pm Sat & Sun) This 14th-century church commemorates the city's patron saint, St Sernin, who was reputedly martyred on this very spot.

Jardin des Plantes
PARK

(⊙7.45am-9pm summer, to 6pm winter) Toulouse's two-hundred-year-old botanical garden is a gorgeous place to escape the city hustle. The entrance to the park is on allée Frédéric Mistral, about 350m south of place St-Jacques.

Stade Toulousain
SPORTS

Toulouse is a city that lives or dies by the fortunes of its rugby team, Stade Toulousain, who have won the European Cup a record four times, most recently in 2010. Their home stadium is the Stade Ernest-Wallon, which has a souvenir boutique and a rather good brasserie (mains €10-15). If you want to understand the city's psyche, head here on match day and join the party.

DON'T MISS

CITÉ DE L'ESPACE

This fantastic space museum (☑08 20 37 72 33; www.cite-espace.com/en; av Jean Gonord; adult €20.50-24, child €15-17.50; ⊙10am-7pm Jul & Aug, closes at 5pm or 6pm rest of yr, closed Jan) on the city's eastern outskirts explores Toulouse's illustrious aeronautical history, which dates back to WWI when the city was a hub for mail flights to Africa and South America. Since WWII, Toulouse has been the centre of France's aerospace industry, developing many important aircraft (including Concorde and the 555-seat Airbus A380) as well as components for international space programs.

The museum brings this industry to life through lots of fascinating, hands-on exhibits including a shuttle simulator, planetarium and observatory, as well as new additions covering Martian exploration and the life cycle of comets. The showpieces are the full-scale replicas of iconic spacecraft (including the Mir Space Station) and a 53m-high Ariane 5 space rocket.

To get there, catch Bus 15 from allée Jean Jaurès to the last stop, from where it's a 500m walk. To avoid queuing, buy your tickets in advance online or at the tourist office.

Toulouse

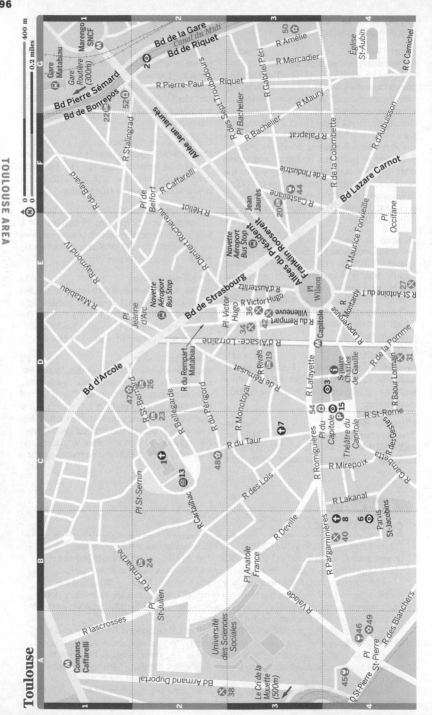

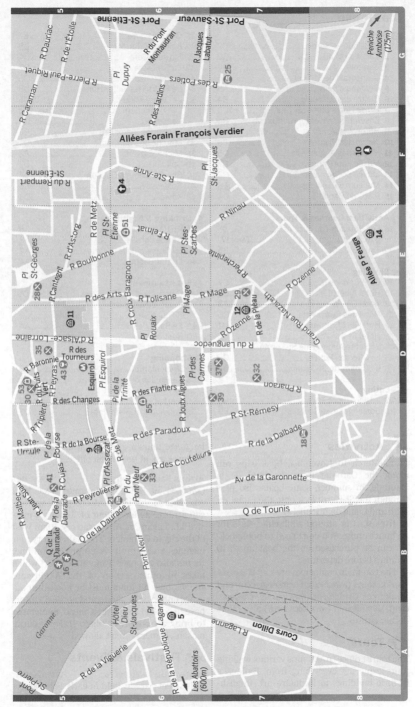

Toulouse

🏃 Activities

From March to November, boat trips run along the Garonne from the quai de la Daurade. In summer, some boats also pass through the St-Pierre lock onto the Canal du Midi and Canal de Brienne.

Trips start at around adult/child €8/5 for an hour's cruise. You don't need to book; tickets can be purchased on the boat up to 10 minutes before departure.

The two main companies are Les Bateaux Toulousains (www.bateaux-toulousains.com) and Toulouses Croisières (www.toulouse-croisieres. com). L'Occitania (www.loccitania.fr) also offers dinner cruises.

👉 Tours

The tourist office (p702) runs various walking tours exploring everything from Toulouse's historic buildings to its metro art. English-language tours are usually available in peak season – ask at the tourist office.

Airbus Factory Tours   AEROPLANES
(☏ 05 34 39 42 00; www.manatour.fr/lva; tours adult/child €15.50/13) Hardcore plane-spotters can arrange a guided tour of Toulouse's massive J.L. Lagardère Airbus factory, 10km west of the city in Colomiers. The main factory tour includes a visit to the A380 production line; there's also a longer 'Panoramic Tour' which takes in other section of the 700-hectare site via bus. All tours must be booked in advance online or by phone, and non-EU visitors have to book at least 2 days ahead. Remember to bring a passport or photo ID.For security reasons, cameras aren't allowed.

🎆 Festivals & Events

Festival de la Violette   FLOWER FESTIVAL
This street parade, held in early February, is a celebration of Toulouse's favourite flower.

**Festival International
d'Art Toulouse**   ARTS FESTIVAL
(www.toulouseartfestival.com) Seven museums
around town hold special exhibitions of contemporary artists in May and June.

Toulouse d'Été   MUSIC FESTIVAL
(www.toulousedete.org) Jazz, classical and other music in July and August.

Piano aux Jacobins   MUSIC FESTIVAL
(www.pianojacobins.com) Piano recitals in the
Église des Jacobins in September.

🛏 Sleeping

Toulouse's hotels cater to a business crowd, so
rates often drop at weekends and in July and
August. There are lots of *chambres d'hôte* to
choose from.

Hôtel La Chartreuse   HOTEL €
(📞 05 61 62 93 39; www.chartreusehotel.com; 4bis
blvd de Bonrepos; s/d/f €52/59/73) The nicest of a
cluster of basic hotels that line the riverbanks
near the station. It's clean, friendly and quiet,
with a back garden patio for breakfast. The
rooms are spartan, but rates are dirt cheap.

**La Petite Auberge
de St-Sernin**   HOSTEL €
(📞 09 81 26 63 00; www.lapetiteaubergedesaint
sernin.com; 17 rue d'Embarthe; dm €22, r €45-55)
No-frills but friendly, this independent hostel
near the university offers boxy dorm rooms of
4, 6 and 8 beds, plus a few doubles. The decor's very plain – tiled floors, bare walls – but
there's a garden for barbecues, and you're only
a minute's walk from the Basilique St-Sernin.

Auberge de Jeunesse   HOSTEL €
(📞 05 34 30 42 80; 2 ave Yves Brunaud; dm from
€17; ⊙ reception 1-10pm; @ 📶) Built in 2002,
Toulouse's main hostel is as functional as they
come (military beds, institutional decor), but
it's good value and has all the usual facilities.
The hostel is about 1km northwest of Gare
Matabiau along av Georges Pompidou; take
care around the station after dark.

★ Côté Carmes   B&B €€
(📞 06 83 44 87 55; www.cote-carmes.com; 7 rue de la
Dalbade; r €85-110) Elegant in the way only the
French can manage, this charming B&B has
three rooms straight out of an interiors catalogue. Louvre doors, parquet floors, exposed
brick and upcycled furniture give it a slinky,
designer feel; Chambre Paradoux is the room-
iest, and has a private balcony. Breakfast is a
spoil, too, with *vienoisseries*, smoothies and
macaroons.

Les Loges de St-Sernin   B&B €€
(📞 05 61 24 44 44; www.leslogesdesaintsernin.
com; 12 rue St-Bernard; r €115-150; 📶) Hidden
behind an elegant rosy façade just a hop
and a skip from the basilica, Sylviane Tatin's
lovely *chambre d'hôte* is a home away from
home. The four rooms are huge, dolled up in
shades of pink, lime and butter-yellow: try the
Capitole room, with its stripy furniture and
exposed brickwork, or the Garonne, with its
dinky balcony.

Hôtel St-Sernin   BOUTIQUE HOTEL €€
(📞 05 61 21 73 08; www.hotelstsernin.com; 2 rue
St-Bernard; d from €135; 📶) Parisian ex-pats
have renovated this pied-a-terre near the Basilique St-Sernin, and it has a modern, metropolitan style, with small-but-sleek rooms, the
best of which have floor-to-ceiling windows
overlooking the basilica.

Hôtel Albert 1er   HOTEL €
(📞 05 61 21 17 91; www.hotel-albert1.com; 8 rue Rivals;
d €55-145; ⊞ 📶) If you want to be central, the
Albert 1st is hard to better. It's on a side street
just off the rue d'Alsace-Lorraine. Rooms are
bright and cosy, with patterned fabrics and
cream-and-magnolia colours. If you like your
space, it's worth bumping up to 'Supérieure'.

Hotel Castellane   HOTEL €€
(📞 05 61 62 18 82; www.castellanehotel.com; 17 rue
Castellane; d €60-120, f €78-156; 📶) Red-brick
and modern it may be, but the Castellane
ticks lots of boxes: smart rooms with wood
floors, a great position just east of Place Wilson, and an extremely generous buffet breakfast. Rooms are quite variable in size: the
ones overlooking the interior courtyard are
quietest. Family rooms sleep up to six, and the
hotel has its own carpark.

ℹ TOULOUSE PASS

The **Pass Tourisme Toulouse** (www.
toulouse-visit.com/all-events/pass-tour
isme; 24/48/72 hrs €18/25/32) card
entitles you to free public transport and
entry to various sights, including the
Musée des Augustins, the Musée de
Toulouse, Les Abattoirs and Fondation
Bemberg. It also includes a river cruise
with Toulouse Croisières or Bateaux
Toulousains, and discounted admission
at the Cité de l'Espace. Several shops
also offer discounts. You can buy it at
the tourist office and Tisséo agencies at
the airport and train station.

TOULOUSE AREA TOULOUSE

Hôtel des Beaux Arts   HOTEL €€
(☎05 34 45 42 42; www.hoteldesbeauxarts.com; 1 place du Pont Neuf; d €115-255; ❋☏) This long-standing hotel sits right beside the Garonne; unfortunately, it's also on one of the city's busiest thoroughfares, so traffic noise can be dreadful. Downstairs, there's a book-lined lobby with armchairs and objets d'art, plus an excellent brasserie; upstairs, the rooms boast heritage furniture and plush drapes. Breakfast is steep at €14.

Peniche Amboise   B&B €€
(☎06 50 77 64 58; www.peniche-amboise.com; s €75, d €85-130) Love life on the river? Then how about staying aboard a genuine *péniche* (barge), moored on the banks of the Canal du Midi. There are four cosy, colour-coded rooms, all with private bathrooms and porthole windows. The best is Amboise, with cool cabin-beds and wood floors. Huge fun.

Le Clos des Potiers   HOTEL €€
(☎05 61 47 15 15; www.le-clos-des-potiers.com; 12 rue des Potiers; d €108-226; ☏) It's a bit out of the centre, but this rambling old mansion offers huge rooms, packed to the rafters with antique furniture, vintage rugs and pottery. A sweeping staircase leads to the upper floors, and there's a gorgeous private garden.

L'Echappée Belle   HOTEL €€
(☎05 62 07 50 00; www.echappee-belle.fr; rue Fernand Mestre, L'Isle-Jourdain; d €85-165; ☏) If you'd prefer to base yourself outside the city, this hotel combines urban style with a rural village location. The minimalist rooms feature curvy furniture and photographic murals, and the modernist design runs through into the downstairs restaurant (mains €19-24), with industrial pipes and plywood stags' heads.

The hotel is in the village of L'Isle-Jourdain, 37km west of Toulouse along the N124.

✖ Eating

Bd de Strasbourg, place Wilson and the western side of place du Capitole are one long cafe-terrace line-up, but the quality can be variable. Rue Pargaminières is the street for kebabs, burgers and other such late-night student grub.

Faim des Haricots   VEGETARIAN €
(☎05 61 22 49 25; www.lafaimdesharicots.fr; 3 rue du Puits Vert; menus €11-15.50; ☉noon-3pm & 6-10pm daily; ☏) A budget favourite, this 100% veggie restaurant serves everything *à volonté* (all you can eat). There are five courses, including a quiche, a buffet salad, a hot dish and a pud-ding; €15.50 buys you the lot including an aperitif and coffee.

Au Jardin des Thés   CAFE €
(☎05 61 23 46 67; 16 pl St-Georges; menus €13.50-15.50, brunch €18; ☉noon-8pm) Overlooking place St-George, this cafe has a delicious menu of *tartes salées* (savoury tarts), salads and sinful cakes. There's a smaller branch on place de la Trinité.

Flowers Café   CAFE €
(☎05 34 44 93 66; www.theflowerscafe.com; 6 pl Roger Salengro; cakes €4; ☉9am-5pm Mon-Sat) Beside a tinkling fountain, this busy cafe is a cake-lover's dream come true. Take your pick from the fruit tarts, cheesecakes and gateaux in the window, and make sure you order the hot chocolate.

Le Balthazar   BISTRO €€
(☎05 62 72 29 54; 50 rue des Couteliers; mains €8-15; ☉noon-2pm Tue-Sun & 7.30-9.30pm Wed-Sun) Ask around on where's best for lunch, and someone will point you in the direction of Balthazar. It's a modern take on an old-style bistro, with classic Gascon cuisine blended with seasonal ingredients and a dash of fusion spice. Wooden furniture matches the homely, honest food, and the wine list is great.

Solilesse   BISTRO €€
(☎09 83 34 03 50; www.solilesse.com; 40 rue Peyrolières; 3-course menu lunch/dinner €17.50/28.50; ☉noon-2.30pm Wed-Sat & 8-10pm Tue-Sat) Punky chef Yohann Travostino has turned his bistro into one of the city's hottest dining addresses. He previously worked in Mexico and California, so his food blends French style with zingy west coast flavours. The industrial decor (black tables, steel, brick) echoes the modern food.

Chez Navarre   REGIONAL CUISINE €€
(☎05 62 26 43 06; 49 Grande Rue Nazareth; menus €15-20; ☉noon-1.30pm & 8-10pm Mon-Fri) This *table d'hôte* is great for getting to know the locals, with honest Gascon cuisine served up communally at wooden tables. There's usually only one main meal, supplemented by a soup and a terrine, but it's a great place to make friends and try local dishes.

Solides   FRENCH €€
(☎05 61 53 34 88; www.solides.fr; 38 rue des Polinaires; menus lunch €18, dinner €31-60; ☉noon-2pm & 8-10pm Mon-Fri) An ex-contestant of the French *Masterchef*, Simon Carlier is a name to watch. He now has two restaurants: **Solides Comme Cochons** (☎09 67 36 58 16;

49 rue Pargaminières; mains €15-20; ⊘ noon-2pm & 8-10pm Tue-Sat), a diner with a piggy focus, and his flagship, newly-renovated bistro inside the old Rotisserie des Carmes restaurant. Both showcase his imaginative, playful style: they're red-hot tables, so book ahead.

La Braisière
BISTRO €€

(☑ 05 61 52 37 13; www.labraisiere.fr; 42 rue Pharaon; mains €14-22; ⊘ noon-3pm & 7-10pm) If you like your meat chunky, charred and flame-grilled, then this bistro near the Carmes market will suit. Hearty steaks cooked over a wood-fire are the house speciality, while tapas is served at L'Annexe next door.

★ Le Genty-Magre
FRENCH €€€

(☑ 05 61 21 38 60; www.legentymagre.com; 3 rue Genty Magre; mains €16-28, menu €38; ⊘ 12.30-2.30pm & 8-10pm Tue-Sat) Classic French cuisine is the order of the day here, but lauded chef Romain Brard has plenty of modern tricks up his sleeve too. The dining room feels inviting, with brick walls, burnished wood and downlights. It's arguably the best place in the city to try traditional rich dishes such as *confit de canard* or cassoulet.

Michel Sarran
GASTRONOMIC €€€

(☑ 05 61 12 32 32; www.michel-sarran.com; 21 bd Armand Duportal; menus lunch €51, dinner €100-132; ⊘ noon-1.45pm & 8-9.45pm Mon-Fri) For a no-expenses-spared, food-as-art dining experience, Toulouse's double Michelin-starred masterchef Michel Sarran is your man. He's

earned an international reputation for his creative but surprisingly classic cuisine, which takes its cue from the traditional flavours of the southwest, then spins off in experimental directions. Needless to say, bookings are essential – especially since Michel doesn't open on weekends.

Self-Catering

Toulouse has two covered food markets, **Les Halles Victor Hugo** (www.marchevictorhugo.fr; pl Victor Hugo; ⊘ around 8am-5pm) and **Marché des Carmes** (place des Carmes; ⊘ 7am-1pm Tue-Sun). Look out for the long, curly shape of the *saucisse de Toulouse,* the city's trademark sausage.

Boulangerie St-Georges
BOULANGERIE €

(☑ 05 61 22 71 19; 6 place St-Georges; sandwiches €3-5; ⊘ 7am-7.30pm) Handmade sandwiches and 20 types of fresh bread are on offer at this bakery. The €7.50 *formule déjeuner* (lunch *menu*) includes a sandwich, drink and dessert.

Le Fournil de Victor Hugo
BOULANGERIE €

(☑ 05 61 22 85 82; place Victor Hugo; ⊘ 10am-5pm Mon-Sat) An artisan baker opposite the Victor Hugo market.

Xavier
CHEESE SHOP €

(☑ 05 34 45 59 45; www.xavier.com; place Victor Hugo; ⊘ 9.30am-1.15pm & 3.30-7.15pm Tue-Sat, afternoon only Mon) The city's best cheese shop. You'll smell it before you see it.

 Drinking & Nightlife

Almost every square in the Vieux Quartier has at least one cafe, busy day and night. Other busy after-dark streets include rue Castellane, rue Gabriel Péri and near the river around place St-Pierre.

Au Père Louis
HISTORIC BAR

(45 rue des Tourneurs; ⊘ 8.30am-3pm & 5-10.30pm Mon-Sat) In business since 1889, this quirky old cafe is full of antique style, including its original zinc-topped bar (designed to keep drinks cool). There's a huge selection of wines, beers and aperitifs to choose from. The house speciality is *quinquina,* a powerful fortified wine flavoured with herbs and cinchona bark (the original source of the anti-malarial treatment, quinine).

Connexion Café
BAR, LIVE MUSIC

(www.connexion-cafe.com; 8 rue Gabriel Péri; ⊘ from 5pm Mon-Sat) Housed in a converted carpark with oil drums for tables, this lively bar hosts regular indie gigs. When the weather's warm, they open up the plastic tarps and the action spills onto the street.

Le Bar Basque
BAR

(7 place St-Pierre; 11am-2am Mon-Fri, 1pm-5am Sat, 1pm-2am Sun) Lively sports bar with a huge outside terrace where *toulousiens* congregate when the rugby's on.

La Couleur de la Culotte
CLUB

(14 place St-Pierre; 9am-2pm) This cafe-cum-club is a popular student hang-out on place St-Pierre, with coffee and cocktails by day, bands and DJs after dark.

Rest'ô Jazz
JAZZ

(www.restojazz.com; 8 rue Amélie; 8pm-late Tue-Sat) Catch live jazz at this slinky, speak-easy-style bar, with table service and a pretty decent dinner menu.

Le Saint des Seins
JAZZ, LIVE MUSIC

(www.lesaintdesseins.com; 5 place St-Pierre; from 8pm) Hip corner rock 'n' roll bar on place St-Pierre, with regular jam sessions and gigs.

Le Cri de la Mouette
CLUB, BAR

(www.lecridelamouette.com; 78 allée de Barcelone; from 8.30pm on gig nights) Party hard on a converted canal-boat, with regular electro, disco and beats nights.

Le Bikini
LIVE MUSIC

(www.lebikini.com; rue Hermès, Ramonville St-Agne; from 8pm on gig nights) Legendary music club that has been rocking for nigh on a quarter-century. At the end of metro line B (Ramonville metro stop).

☆ Entertainment

The city's top places to watch films in *version originale* (VO, ie not dubbed) include the **Cinéma ABC** (www.abc-toulouse.fr; 13 rue St-Bernard) and the **Cinémathèque de Toulouse** (www.lacinemathequedetoulouse.com; 69 rue du Taur).

🛍 Shopping

In addition to the truly fantastic covered markets, Toulouse's outdoor shopping opportunities include a bit-of-everything **market** (place du Capitole; Wed), an antiquarian **book market** (place St-Étienne; Sat), and a couple of weekend **flea markets** that take place along place St-Sernin and the quai de la Daurade.

La Maison de la Violette
SOUVENIRS

(05 61 99 01 30; www.lamaisondelaviolette.com; 10am-6.30pm Mon-Sat) This button-cute *péniche* (river barge) sells everything from herbal tea to bath soaps scented with Toulouse's trademark flower, the violet.

Le Paradis Gourmet
GOURMET FOOD

(65 rue des Tourneurs; 10am-noon & 2-7pm Mon-Sat) Biscuits, sweeties and other gastronomic goodies with a *toulousien* flavour.

Papillotes et Berlingots
SWEETS

(www.papillotes-berlingots.fr; 49 rue des Filatiers; noon-7pm Mon, 10am-2pm & 3-7pm Tue-Sat) Candy fans will be in seventh heaven at this lovely sweet shop: make sure you try the violet-flavoured chocolate.

ℹ Information

Tourist Office (05 61 11 02 22; www.toulouse-tourisme.com; Square Charles de Gaulle; 9am-7pm daily) In a grand building on Square Charles de Gaulle.

ℹ Getting There & Away

AIR
Eight kilometres northwest of the centre, **Toulouse-Blagnac Airport** (www.toulouse.aeroport.fr/en) has frequent flights to Paris and other large French cities, plus major hub cities in the UK, Italy and Germany.

BUS
Bus services are provided by many operators and mainly operate according to the school timetable. All buses and coaches stop at the **Gare Routière** (Bus Station; bd Pierre Sémard).

CAR
Driving in Toulouse, like any large French city, is not for the faint-hearted. Parking in particular is a real headache; some hotels have private garages for an extra charge, or offer discounted rates at city car parks. Otherwise you'll be stuck with expensive on-street parking (which is free from noon–2pm and on Sundays). Count on paying between €18 and €30 for a full day, depending on which car park you choose.

TRAIN
Buy tickets at the **SNCF boutique** (5 rue Peyras) in town or at Toulouse's main train station, **Gare Matabiau** (blvd Pierre Sémard), 1km northeast of the centre. Toulouse is served by frequent fast TGVs, which run west to Montauban, Agen and Bordeaux (which has connections to Bayonne and the southwest, plus Paris), and east to Carcassonne, Narbonne, Montpellier and beyond.

Albi €12, one hour

Auch €13.50, 1½ hours including SNCF bus

Bordeaux €22-29 via TGV, two hours

Carcassonne €14, 45 minutes to 1 hour

Castres €13.50, 1¾ hours

Montauban €9, 30 minutes
Pau €28, 2¼ hours

ℹ Getting Around

TO/FROM THE AIRPORT

The **Navette Aéroport Flybus** (Airport Shuttle; ☑ 05 61 41 70 70; www.tisseo.fr) links the airport with town (single €5, 20 minutes, every 20 minutes from 5am to 9.20pm from town and 5.30am to 12.15pm from the airport). Catch the bus in front of the bus station, outside the Jean Jaurès metro station or at place Jeanne d'Arc. The trip takes between 20 and 40 minutes depending on traffic.

Taxis (☑ 05 61 30 02 54) to/from town cost from €30 to €35.

BICYCLE

The city's bike-hire scheme **Vélô Toulouse** (www.velo.toulouse.fr) has pick-up/drop-off stations dotted every 300m or so round the city. Tickets cost €1.20 a day or €5 a week, plus a €150 credit-card deposit. You can buy online, but you'll need a chip-and-pin card to work the automated machines.

BUS & METRO

Local buses and the two-line metro are run by **Tisséo** (www.tisseo.fr), which has ticket kiosks located on place Jeanne d'Arc and cours Dillon. A single ticket costs €1.60, a 10-ticket *carnet* (book of tickets) is €12.90 and a one-/two-day pass is €5.50/8.50.

Most bus lines run daily until at least 8pm. Night bus lines run from 10pm to midnight.

Albi

POP 48,600

The bustling provincial town of Albi has two main claims to fame: a truly mighty cathedral and a truly marvellous painter. Looming up from the centre of the old town, the Cathédrale Ste-Cécile is one of France's most monumental Gothic structures. Next door is the fantastic Musée Toulouse-Lautrec, dedicated to the mischievous artist Henri de Toulouse-Lautrec, who was born here in 1864 and went on to depict the bars and brothels of turn-of-the-century Paris in his own inimitable style.

Albi's little old town is also well worth a wander, although it's surprisingly small given the town's sprawling suburbs.

◎ Sights & Activities

The **Albi City Pass** (€6.50) (sold at the tourist office) gives free admission to the Musée Toulouse-Lautrec and Cathédrale Ste-Cécile's *grand chœur,* and offers discounts at local shops and restaurants.

Cathédrale Ste-Cécile   CHURCH
(place Ste-Cécile; grand chœur adult/child €2/free; ☺ 9am-6.30pm) Albi's mighty Cathédrale Ste-Cécile rises over the old town like a Tolkienesque tower, built from red-brick and fortified by defensive walls – a result of the many religious wars that marked the medieval era. Begun in 1282, the cathedral took well over a century to complete. Eight centuries later, it's still one of the world's largest brick buildings, and has been on Unesco's World Heritage list since 2010.

Step inside and the contrast with the brutal exterior is astonishing. No surface was left untouched by the Italian artists who, in the early 16th century, painted their way, chapel by chapel, along the entire nave. Particularly noteworthy is the *grand chœur* (great choir) with its frescos, chapels and biblical figures, each carved from stone and painted by hand.

At the western end is *Le Jugement Dernier* (The Last Judgement, painted 1474–1484), a vivid doomsday horror show of the damned being boiled in oil, beheaded or tortured by demons and monsters.

★ Musée Toulouse-Lautrec   ART MUSEUM
(www.museetoulouselautrec.net; place Ste-Cécile; adult/student €8/4; ☺ 9am-6pm Jun-Sep, closed noon-2pm rest of year & all day Tue Oct-Mar) Lodged inside the Palais de la Berbie (built in the early Middle Ages for the town's archbishop), this wonderful museum offers a comprehensive overview of Albi's most celebrated son. The museum owns more than 500 original works by Toulouse-Lautrec – the largest collection in France outside the Musée d'Orsay – spanning the artist's development from his early neo-impressionist paintings to his famous Parisian brothel scenes and poster art.

Of particular interest are the early portraits of some of Toulouse-Lautrec's friends and family – including his mother, the Comtesse Adèle de Toulouse-Lautrec, his cousin Gabriel Tapié de Celeyran and his close friend, Maurice Joyant. They clearly demonstrate the artist's wry eye and playful sense of humour. There are also some surprisingly delicate animal studies (especially of horses).

Inevitably, however, it's the later works that draw the eye. Toulouse-Lautrec's lifelong fascination with the Parisian underworld, particularly the lives of dancers and prostitutes, is brilliantly represented. Look out for key works including *L'Anglaise du Star au Havre* (Lady of the Star Harbour) and *Les Deux*

TOULOUSE AREA ALBI

Albi

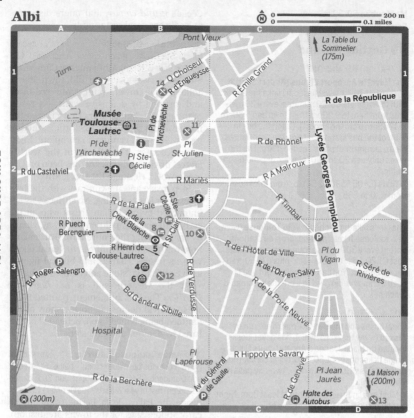

Albi

◎ Top Sights
1 Musée Toulouse-Lautrec B2

◎ Sights
2 Cathédrale Ste-Cécile B2
3 Collégiale Saint-Salvi B2
4 La Maison de Lapérouse B3
5 Maison du Vieil Alby B3
6 Maison Natale de Toulouse-Lautrec B3

✪ Activities, Courses & Tours
7 Albi Croisières A1

🛏 Sleeping
8 Hôtel St-Clair B3
9 La Tour Ste-Cécile B3

✖ Eating
10 Au Moulin à Cafe B3
11 Covered Market B2
12 Le Lautrec B3
13 L'Epicurien D4
14 L'Esprit du Vin B1

Amies (The Two Friends), depicting two prostitutes embracing while they wait for their clients. Pride of place goes to two versions of one of his most famous canvases, *Au Salon de la rue des Moulins,* hung side-by-side to illustrate changes in the artist's technique.

Toulouse-Lautrec's skills as a cartoonist and caricaturist also made him a pioneer of poster art, and the museum has a fantastic collection of his most famous designs in their permanent collection. On the top floor, there's a small collection of works by some of his contemporaries, including Degas, Matisse and Gauguin.

A short stroll away is the privately owned **Maison Natale de Toulouse-Lautrec** (14 rue Henri de Toulouse-Lautrec), where the artist was born.

La Maison de Lapérouse

HOUSE MUSEUM

(14 rue Henri de Toulouse-Lautrec) Next door to the Musée Toulouse-Lautrec, this mansion belonged to the Albi-born explorer Jean-François de Galaup (aka the Comte de Lapérouse), who made several pioneering naval expeditions around the Pacific between 1785 and 1789. Mysteriously, his ships disappeared without trace towards the end of their voyage; subsequent expeditions suggested they may have been wrecked on reefs near the island of Vanikoro, halfway between the Solomon Islands and Vanuatu. Guided visits can only be arranged via the tourist office.

Old Town

ARCHITECTURE

Vieil Albi (Old Albi) is an attractive muddle of winding streets and half-timbered houses, one of which, the Maison du Vieil Alby (1 rue de la Croix Blanche; adult/child €2/free; ☺10.30am-12.30pm & 2.30pm-6.30pm Mon-Sat Jun-Aug, 2.30-5.30pm Mon-Sat Sep-Apr), houses a small exhibition on the city's history and its connections with Toulouse-Lautrec. Also worth a look is the Collegiale Saint-Salvi (Rue Mariès; ☺9am-noon & 2-6pm Mon-Sat, 9am-10.30am & 2-6pm Sun Jul-Aug, closes 5pm Sep-Jun), a delicate canons' church with a lovely cloister, and the Pont-Vieux, the 19th-century arched bridge across the River Tarn, which provides a fine perspective over Albi's pink-bricked old town and cathedral.

Albi Croisières

BOAT TOUR

(☑05 63 43 59 63; www.albi-croisieres.com; ☺May-Oct) Albi Croisières runs various boat trips on the River Tarn aboard traditional *gabarres* (flat-bottomed barges). There are regular 30-minute cruises (adult/child €7/4) between 11am and 6pm, plus a 1½-hour lunchtime cruise (€12/8) leaving at 12.30pm. There are also full-day trips (return adult/child €23/15) between the village of Aiguelèze, near Gaillac, and Albi.

✯✯ Festivals & Events

Carnaval

CARNIVAL

Albi celebrates Carnaval at the beginning of Lent (February or March).

Pause Guitare

MUSIC FESTIVAL

Guitar concerts in the sumptuous space of place Ste-Cécile. Held in July.

🛏 Sleeping

Hôtel St-Clair

HOTEL €

(☑05 63 54 25 66; www.hotel-albi-saintclair.com; 8 rue St-Clair; s €40-65, d €48-75; ☎) A real rabbit's warren of a hotel, this one – in an old house slap bang in the middle of old Albi, with higgledy-piggledy rooms full of wonky floors and low ceilings. There are lots and lots of stairs to the upper rooms. The carpark has three spaces, otherwise you'll have to park on the edge of the old city and walk.

La Bastide

D&D €€

(☑05 63 48 83 01; www.labastide-tarn.com; Maillès; d €95) Six kilometres south of Albi, this rural retreat is a real find. An old stone cottage has been stripped out and reinvented in minimalist style: both rooms are stylishly spartan,

---

HENRI DE TOULOUSE-LAUTREC

Despite being born into one of Albi's most aristocratic families, Henri de Toulouse-Lautrec (1864–1901) was always something of an outsider. He was notoriously short as a result of two teenage accidents that broke both his legs, stunted his growth and left him unable to walk without his trademark canes. He also had poor eyesight, brittle bones and a number of other congenital health problems – so it's perhaps unsurprising that he identified with the stranger and seedier sides of the Parisian underworld.

He spent his early 20s studying painting in Paris, where he mixed with other artists (including Van Gogh). Perhaps as a result of his own afflictions, he came to identify strongly with the many curious characters he came to know while frequenting the Parisian *demimonde* – the nighttime world of seedy dance-halls, brothels and late-night bars where most respectable Parisians would never dare to venture. Entranced by this ugly-beautiful world, full of sadness, strangeness, life and colour, Toulouse-Lautrec had found his natural milieu, and the subject which would define his work. Among his favourite subjects were the cabaret singer Aristide Bruant, the racy can-can dancers from the Moulin Rouge and prostitutes from the rue des Moulins. He liked to work quickly, sketching on whatever was at hand – a scrap of paper, a tablecloth or a handy piece of cardboard.

Later in his career, he became a skilled and sought-after lithographer and poster designer, until drinking and general overindulgence (possibly coupled with a syphilis infection) led to his premature death in 1901, aged just 37.

CORDES-SUR-CIEL

Perched on a steep, half-forested hilltop about 25km from Albi, this poetically-named village ('Cordes in the Sky') is one of the Tarn's best-preserved medieval towns. It's a pretty tumble of winding streets and red-roofed houses, most of which still boast their medieval façades, and at the heart of the village is a classic *bastide* square.

Small museums are dotted round town, but the real pleasure here is wandering around the lanes soaking up the atmosphere. Make sure you find time for the lovely **Jardin des Paradis** ornamental gardens, and a stunning walk along the snaking **ramparts**.

Regular guided walks run by the **tourist office** (☑ 05 63 56 00 52; www.cordessurciel. eu; 40 Grand Rue Raimond VII) explore the town's architecture in depth, and there are special night-time tours conducted by torch-light which really bring Cordes' medieval character to life. There's also a superb food market on Saturday mornings, as well as occasional flea markets and crafts fairs. Definitely worth a detour.

It's on the D606; take the 707 bus from Albi.

with rough stone walls and shiny wood floors, and outside there's a charming lavender-filled garden and a private swimming pool.

La Maison B&B €€
(☑ 05 63 38 17 35; www.chambre-hote-albi.com; 40 blvd Andrieu; s €85-95, d €100-110; 🛜) In contrast to Albi's olde-worlde feel, this B&B is a model of modernity. The Velours and Métal rooms glimmer with gloss-wood floors and designer furniture, while Ficelle feels more classic with its neutral colours, oil paintings and distressed furniture. It's outside the old city, but you get a garden and parking.

★ **La Tour Ste-Cécile** B&B €€€
(☑ 05 81 40 51 52; www.toursaintececile.com; 14 bis rue Ste-Cécile; d €138-180; 🛜) This fairytale place is really special. It's in a part-medieval tower (which explains the name) and has four regal rooms, with exposed brick, beams and windows peeping out onto the cathedral square. The Sainte-Cécile Suite looks more like a royal apartment, while the Toulouse-Lautrec room is reached via its own spiral staircase. Rates include breakfast and entry to the Toulouse-Lautrec museum, and you get almost 40% off for a second night.

🍴 Eating

Albi has loads of places to eat, including a string of places on rue Henri de Toulouse-Lautrec, just downhill from the cathedral.

Covered Market FOOD MARKET
(place St-Julien; ⏰ 8am-2pm daily, plus 5-8pm Fri & Sat) Albi's triangular turn-of-the-century covered market is a delight, built by the celebrated architect Thierry Bourdois and engi-

neer André Michelin between 1901 and 1905. Behind its wonderful steel-and-brick façade you'll find a wealth of local producers.

Au Moulin à Cafe CAFE €
(☑ 05 63 43 15 51; www.au-moulin-a-cafe.fr; 1 rue Oulmet; cakes €3-5; ⏰ 2-7pm Mon, 9.30am-7pm Tue-Sat) Run by a former high-flying chef, Michel Pellaprat, this super *salon du thé* sets high standards with its handmade patisseries, delicious cakes and artisan ice-creams. The olde-worlde decor and china teapots add extra appeal.

Le Lautrec TRADITIONAL FRENCH €€
(☑ 05 63 54 86 55; www.restaurant-le-lautrec.com; 13-15 rue Henri de Toulouse-Lautrec; menus lunch €16-18, dinner €28-42; ⏰ noon-2.30pm Tue-Sun & 7.30-10pm Tue-Sat) The best place to eat in the old city, housed in the former stables of the Toulouse-Lautrec family home. The food is traditional, focusing on Gascon classics such as cassoulet spiced with saffron and Tarbais beans. You can either eat in the country-styled dining room amongst chimneys and old tools, or head outside to the wisteria-covered patio.

La Table du Sommelier BISTRO €€
(☑ 05 63 46 20 10; latabledusommelier.com; 20 rue Porta; menus lunch €17, dinner €35-45; ⏰ noon-2pm & 7-10pm Tue-Sat) The clue's in the name – this place is one for the wine-lovers. Owner Daniel Pestre is an experienced sommelier, with an infectious passion for his local vintages: dinner *menus* are themed around the wines, rather than the other way round. The outdoor patio shaded by huge umbrellas makes a great spot for when the sun shines. It's on the northern bank of the Tarn, 15 minutes walk from the tourist office.

L'Epicurien MODERN FRENCH €€€
(☑05 63 53 10 70; www.restaurantlepicurien.com;
42 place Jean Jaurès; 2-/3-course menus lunch
€18.50/21, dinner €29-49.50; ☺noon-2pm & 7.30-
10pm Tue-Sat) The steely-grey-and-glass façade
says it all: this establishment is a temple to
cutting-edge contemporary French cuisine,
run by Swedish chef Rikard Hult and his wife
Patricia. Arty presentation takes precedence
over copious portions: expect delicate towers
of monkfish or lamb noisettes, accompanied
by a slash of sauce or just-so sprig of herb.

L'Esprit du Vin GASTRONOMIC €€€
(☑05 63 54 60 44; www.lespritduvin-albi.com; 11
quai Choiseul; menus €75-105; ☺8-9.15pm Tue-Sat)
Albi-born chef David Enjalran is one of the region's star names, and his cuisine is as adventurous as it gets. *Menus* are divided into five
'ateliers' (levels), and take their cue from the
changing seasons: the approach is very much
Michelin-style, so it might be a bit stuffy for
some. The lunchtime 'Pause Gourmande' is
marginally more affordable at €25/29 for one/
two courses. Reservations essential.

ℹ️ Information

Tourist Office (☑05 63 49 48 80; www.albi-
tourisme.fr; place Ste-Cécile; ☺9am-12.30pm &
2-6pm Mon-Sat, opens at 10am Sun) Next door
to the Toulouse-Lautrec Museum. Ask for one of
the themed walking leaflets around old Albi.

ℹ️ Getting There & Away

BUS

TarnBus (☑05 63 45 64 81; http://tarnbus.tarn.
fr) lines include 703 to Castres (€2.80, 50 minutes, at least hourly Monday to Saturday) and the
707 to Cordes (€2, 35 minutes, four to six Monday
to Saturday, three on Sunday). Most leave from
place Jean Jaurès.

TRAIN

Destinations include Rodez (€13, 1½ hours, frequent) and Toulouse (€12, one hour, frequent).

Montauban

POP 53,200

Bastides (fortified towns) litter the landscape
of southwest France, and there's no finer example than Montauban, nestled on the banks
of the River Tarn. Founded in 1144, Montauban is southern France's second-oldest
bastide (the oldest is Mont-de-Marsan).

All roads lead to its characteristic central square, **place Nationale**, hemmed in
on every side by arcaded walkways and tall
pink buildings. Many of the streets around

the square would originally have marked the
town's fortified walls; the town was badly
battered during both the Hundred Years War
and the Wars of Religion, and famously withstood an 86-day siege imposed by Louis XIII
in 1621 during which the defenders resorted
to eating horses, rats and dogs to survive.

◉ Sights

Musée Ingres ART MUSEUM
(13 rue de l'Hôtel de Ville; adult/child €5.10/2.60,
€7.20/3.60 during exhibitions; ☺10am-6pm, closed
noon-2pm except Jul & Aug) The main focus of
Montauban is this fine arts museum, which
centres on the work of the neoclassical
painter (and accomplished violinist) Jean
Auguste Dominique Ingres, who was born
in Montauban in 1780. Inspired by Poussin
and David, Ingres became one of the most
celebrated portrait painters of his day, and
the museum houses many of his key works
alongside old masters such as Tintoretto,
Van Dyck and Gustave Courbet.

The entry ticket also admits you to the
nearby Histoire Naturelle (natural history),
Terroir (local costumes and traditions) and
Résistance et Déportation (with mementoes
of WWII) museums.

Another Ingres masterpiece, *Le Vœu de
Louis XIII,* depicting the king pledging
France to the Virgin, hangs in Montauban's
18th-century **Cathédrale Notre Dame de
l'Assomption** (place Franklin Roosevelt; ☺10am-
noon & 2-6pm Mon-Sat).

🎊 Festivals & Events

Alors Chante MUSIC FESTIVAL
(www.alorschante.com) A festival of French song
in May.

Jazz à Montauban JAZZ FESTIVAL
(www.jazzmontauban.com) A week-long jam in
July.

**Légende des
Quatre-Cent Coups** STREET FESTIVAL
(400 Blows) This weekend street festival at the
end of August commemorates the moment
when, according to local lore, a fortune-tell-
er told Louis XIII, besieging Montauban, to
blast 400 cannons simultaneously against the
town, which still failed to fall.

🛏️ Sleeping

Mas des Anges B&B €
(☑05 63 24 27 05; www.lemasdesanges.com; d €75-
80 incl breakfast; ☺☒) Wine-lovers will love
this place, a 4.5-hectare vineyard five miles

south of Montauban. It's run by Sophie and Juan Kervyn, a friendly couple who've made winemaking into a lifelong passion. The three ground-floor rooms each have a slightly different theme (African, Latin, Marine). Tree-filled grounds, a fine pool and guest barbecues are the icing on the cake.

Hôtel du Commerce
HOTEL €

(📞05 63 66 31 32; www.hotel-commerce-montauban.com; 9 place Franklin Roosevelt; s €60, d €63-76; 🖭🎧) Montauban's choice of hotels isn't great, but this is the best of the bunch. Rooms are floral and old-fashioned, and some have shuttered windows overlooking the cathedral square.

Château de Seguenville
B&B €€

(📞05 62 13 42 67; www.chateau-de-seguenville.com; d €110-130, f €150-230; 🎧) For aristocratic cachet, head for this spiky-roofed château-turned-*chambre d'hôte*. A central staircase opens onto a 1st-floor gallery and five boho rooms, each named after aristocratic nobles and each with a different view over the rolling parkland. It's roughly equidistant from Toulouse, Montauban and Auch.

Cabane dans les Arbres
TREEHOUSE €€€

(📞06 82 41 81 50; www.cabane-spa.com; cabins from €205-285) Continuing the curious craze for treehouse sleeping in France, this luxurious resort offers treetop cabins complete with private hot-tub, canopy balcony and king-size bed. Breakfast is winched up to you in a wicker basket every morning. It's out in the sticks to the north of Montauban, so you'll need a car.

✖ Eating

Morning **farmers markets** are on Saturday (place Prax-Paris) and Wednesday (place Lalaque), in addition to a smaller daily one (place Nationale).

Du Nord au Sud
GASCON CUISINE €

(📞0563206269; 38 rue de la République; lunch menu €14.50; ⊙9am-7pm Mon-Sat) No fuss, friendly and very French, this small town-centre restaurant serves traditional Gascon dishes alongside crepes, salads and steaks. The small terrace is lovely when the sun shines.

★ Les Boissières
MODERN FRENCH €€

(📞05 63 24 50 02; www.lesboissieres.com; 708 route de Caussade, Bioule; menus 2-/3-course lunch €20/23, dinner €31-38; ⊙noon-2.30pm & 8-9.30pm Tue-Sun) By far the best place to eat around Montauban is this much-lauded

hotel-restaurant, where chef Cyril Rosenberg dishes up delicious dishes blending regional cuisine with contemporary style. The stone-walled dining room is full of charm, but the garden terrace is the place to be on a warm afternoon. It's 22km northeast of Montauban in Bioule.

ℹ Information

Tourist Office (📞05 63 63 60 60; www.montauban-tourisme.com; 4 rue du Collège; ⊙9.30am-6.30pm Mon-Sat, 10am-12.30pm Sun Jul-Aug, closes noon-2pm & Sun rest of year)

ℹ Getting There & Away

From the **train station** (av Mayenne), about 1km from place Nationale across the Tarn, fast TGVs serve Toulouse (€8.50 to €11, 30 minutes, hourly), while slower TER trains serve Moissac (€5.50, 20 minutes, hourly).

Moissac
POP 12,300

Riverside Moissac has been an important stop-off on the Santiago de Compostela trail since the 12th century thanks to the glorious **Abbaye St-Pierre** (place Durand de Bredon; adult/child €6/4; ⊙9am-7pm Jul & Aug, closes noon-2pm rest of yr), resplendent with some of France's finest Romanesque architecture. It's particularly known for its **tympanum**, the crescent-shaped frieze above its south portal.

Completed in 1130, it depicts St John's vision of the Apocalypse, with Christ in majesty flanked by the Apostles, angels and 24 awestruck elders. If you've got time, it's worth comparing it with the one in Beaulieu-sur-Dordogne's **Abbatiale St-Pierre**, which is thought to have been carved around the same time, very possibly by the same stonemasons.

Outside, the **cloister** is encircled by marble columns, topped by carved capitals depicting foliage, figures or biblical scenes. Sadly, the Revolution took its toll – nearly every face is smashed.

Entry to the abbey is via the **tourist office** (www.moissac.fr; 6 place Durand de Bredon; ⊙9am-7pm).

☐ Sleeping & Eating

★ Au Château
B&B €€

(📞05 63 95 96 82; www.au-chateau-stn.com; St Nicolas de la Grave; d €63-88, f €108-128; 🖭🎧🖭) This B&B 10km south of Moissac offers five seriously enormous rooms, which blend mod-

GAILLAC WINES

Eat out at any restaurant in this region of France and you're guaranteed to stumble across the name Gaillac on the menu. The vineyards rolling around this little village produce the region's best wines – particularly rosés, light whites and fruity reds – which benefit from the area's special micro-climate, positioned between the balmy Mediterranean and the cooling rains of the Atlantic.

Gaillac winemaking stretches back to Roman times, and the region now boasts several AOCs (Appellations d'Origine Contrôlée), including Gaillac Rouge, Gaillac Blanc Sec and Gaillac Rosé, as well as more unusual ones such as AOC Gaillac Perle (for the area's sparkling or *petillant* white wine) and AOC Mousseux Methode Gaillacaçoise (for the Champagne-style wine made by only a few local vineyards).

There are lots of châteaux dotted around the area offering *dégustation* (tasting) and cellar visits, connected by a signposted Route des Vins (Wine Route).

The Gaillac tourist office (☑ 05 63 57 14 65; tourisme@ville-gaillac.fr; pl St-Michel, Gaillac) can help arrange vineyard tours, while the Toulouse-based Vin Vigne Voyages (☑ 05 82 75 11 15; www.vinvignevoyages.com; one-day tours from €45) offers an excellent guided tour from Toulouse, including two vineyard visits and chauffeur service, for €45.

ern touches (wood floors, flat-screen TVs, funky fabrics) into the house's 18th century château shell. The Madeleine Suite hunkers under beams, while the Elise Suite has a contemporary four-poster bed. Outside there's a heated pool and tree-filled grounds, and it's family friendly.

Le Pont Napoléon HOTEL €€
(☑ 05 63 04 01 55; www.le-pont-napoleon.com; 2 allée Montebello; s €59, d €59-70; ☞) This venerable hotel occupies a prime spot next to the town's 19th-century Napoléon-built bridge. Rooms are plain but comfortable, and represent very good value – especially if you get one overlooking the Tarn. The hotel restaurant, Le Table de Nos Fils (menus €30-42) is run by well-regarded chef Patrick Delaroux, who also runs weekend cooking courses.

Le Moulin de Moissac HOTEL €€
(☑ 05 63 32 88 88; www.lemoulindemoissac.com; esplanade du Moulin; d €105-179, menus lunch €25.50, dinner €43; ☞) Housed in a 15th-century grain mill overlooking the Tarn, this hotel is a riverside treat. In the rooms, distressed wallpaper, wicker chairs and tall French windows open onto river-view balconies. Elsewhere, you'll find a super waterside restaurant, a smart sauna-spa and a romantic Jacuzzi sheltered under a brick vaulted roof.

❶ Getting There & Away

A few local buses serve Moissac, but it's more convenient to catch a **train** from Montauban (€5.50, 20 minutes, five to seven daily), which has regular connections to Toulouse.

Castres

Founded by the Romans as a *castrum* (settlement), this sleepy town is best known as the birthplace of Jean Jaurès, the founding father of French socialism. It's mainly worth visiting for the **Musée Goya** (goya@ville-castres.fr; rue de l'Hôtel de Ville; adult/child €3/free; ⊙ 10am-6pm) and its collection of Spanish art, including works by Goya, Murillo, Ribera and Picasso. The museum's gardens were laid out by Le Nôtre, architect of Versailles' park.

Auch

POP 23,500

Auch (prounced 'aush', to rhyme with gauche) has been a crossroads since Roman times, and later became the seat of power for the counts of Armagnac. It's now the capital of the Gers département.

The town has two worthy sights. First is its Unesco-listed church, the **Cathédrale Ste-Marie** (⊙ 8.30am-noon & 2-5pm), which showcases a peculiar mix of architectural styles from austere Gothic to flamboyant Renaissance (perhaps unsurprising, given that it took over two centuries to complete after the first stones were laid in 1489). The 40m-high Tour d'Armagnac was built to house the archive of Auch's archbishops, and briefly served as a Revolutionary prison.

Second is the fabulous **Escalier Monumental**, one of France's most impressive public staircases. Built in 1863, it consists of either 275 steps or 370 steps (depending on whether you count the double-flighted section at the top). Halfway up, look out for a statue of d'Artagnan, Alexandre Dumas' swashbuckling hero, who was based on the local nobleman Charles de Batz. From the train station, there are regular TER trains to Toulouse (€13.50, 1½ hours, six to ten daily).

Condom

POP 7250

Now now, stop sniggering at the back. Poor old Condom's name actually has nothing to do with its namesake contraceptive – it's a derivation of the town's Gallo-Roman name, Condatomagus. Established as a Roman and medieval port on the River Baïse, and later a key stop-off for Compostela pilgrims, these days Condom is a mellow town of yellow stone, surrounded by fertile countryside and orderly vineyards, as well as plenty of prestigious Armagnac producers.

◉ Sights & Activities

Cathédrale St-Pierre CHURCH
(place St-Pierre) With its lofty nave and elaborate chancel, Condom's cathedral is a classic example of Flamboyant Gothic architecture. On the north side, the 16th-century tent-like cloister was designed to offer wet weather protection for Compostela pilgrims.

Musée de l'Armagnac MUSEUM
(2 rue Jules Ferry; adult/child €2.20/1.10; ⊙10am-noon & 3-6pm Wed-Sun Apr-Oct, 2-5pm Wed-Sat Nov-Mar) In a turn-of-the-century cellar, this museum is dedicated to the fine art of Armagnac-making and houses a modest collection

of vintage bottles, agricultural tools and an 18-tonne press dating from the 19th century.

Marché aux Gras MARKET
The biweekly Marché au Gras (literally, the 'Fat Market') held on Wednesday and Saturday mornings is a quintessentially French affair.

Gascogne Navigation BOAT TOUR
(☑05 62 28 46 46; www.gascogne-navigation.com; 3 av d'Aquitaine) From April to October, Gascogne Navigation runs 1½-hour river cruises (adult/child €8/6.10) and 2½-hour lunch cruises (€37.50/25) along the Baïse River, departing from quai Bouquerie. It also rents small motorboats (hour/half-day/full day €35/80/120).

⎰ Sleeping & Eating

Hôtel Continental HOTEL €
(☑05 62 68 37 00; www.lecontinental.net; 20 rue Maréchal Foch; r €51-86; 🛜) A lemon-yellow heritage hotel set along the riverfront. Front rooms overlook the water, but also suffer from road noise; garden rooms are much quieter. The restaurant (menus €25 to €33) is good for regional cuisine.

Le Logis des Cordeliers HOTEL €
(☑05 62 28 03 68; www.logisdescordeliers.com; rue de la Paix; d €55-78; ⊙Feb-Dec; 🛜🏊) The building's bland and boxy and so are the rooms, but this modern hotel makes a useful base in Condom, and has its own pool and private gardens. Street-view rooms are the cheapest; garden views command a small premium. It's along a back street off av Général de Gaulle.

ARMAGNAC

Cognac might be the region's better-known digestif, but many connoisseurs maintain that Armagnac has the superior flavour. Produced from white grapes and aged in oak barrels for several years, this potent brandy was originally taken for medicinal purposes, but these days it's a popular after-dinner drink. Floc de Gascogne – made from Armagnac and grape juice – is the aperitif version.

There are several local distilleries which you can visit to try the tipple for yourself.

Armagnac Ryst-Dupeyron (36 rue Jean Jaurès; ⊙10am-noon & 2-6.30pm Mon-Fri) The best place to start your Armagnac tasting is this turn-of-the-century cellar in Condom. It offers tours and tasting sessions, and you can buy vintages on site.

Château de Cassaigne (☑05 62 28 04 02; www.chateaudecassaigne.com; adult/child €6/2; ⊙10am-7pm Jul & Aug, 9am-noon & 2-6pm Tue-Sun rest of yr) This beautiful 13th-century chateau is 6.5km southwest of Condom, just off the D931 to Eauze. It's particularly known for its Floc de Gascogne.

Château du Busca Maniban (☑05 62 28 40 38; www.buscamaniban.com; Mansencome; adult/child €6/2; ⊙2-6pm Mon-Sat Apr-Nov) 10km south of Condom on the D229, this chateau has three centuries of Armagnac production under its belt.

DON'T MISS

CANAL DU MIDI

Stretching for 240km between Toulouse and Sète, the Canal du Midi (www.canaldumidi. com) is the queen of French canals. Built in the 17th century and a World Heritage Site since 1996, the canal links the Étang de Thau with the Garonne River in Toulouse, and along with the Canal de Garonne, it forms part of the 'Canal des Deux Mers' (Canal of the Two Seas), which links the Mediterranean to the Atlantic.

It was commissioned by Louis XIV in 1666, and built by the farmer-turned-engineer Pierre-Paul Riquet, who devised an innovative system of dams, bridges, aqueducts, tunnels and locks to overcome the region's difficult terrain. The canal opened in 1681, but it had already taken its toll on Riquet: he died a few months before the official opening.

Though its commercial importance was eclipsed by the railway during the 19th century, these days the canal is hugely popular with pleasure-boaters. It takes several weeks to sail the whole length, but it's possible to do shorter sections, especially between the towns of Agde, Béziers, Narbonne and Sète. Alternatively you can just hire bikes and appreciate the canal's tranquil, tree-lined scenery from the tow-paths.

If you want to cruise, there are lots of boat-hire companies. Locaboat (☑ 03 86 91 72 72; www.locaboat.com; Argens-Minervois) and Caminav (☑ 04 67 68 01 90; www.caminav.com; Carnon) hire small motorboats, while Minervois Cruisers (☑ UK +44 19 26 81 18 42; www.min ervoiscruisers.com; Le Somail, nr Narbonne) offers narrowboats. Prices vary, but expect to pay between €800 and €1300 a week for a standard four-berth. Vintage *péniches* (live-aboard narrowboats) are more expensive (upwards of €3000 a week).

Between Toulouse and Castres in St-Ferréol, the Musée Canal du Midi (www.musee canaldumidi.fr; blvd Pierre-Paul Riquet; adult/child €4/2; ☉ 10am-7pm) explores the waterway's history and the life of Paul Riquet.

★ La Table
des Cordeliers   GASTRONOMIC €€€
(☑ 05 62 68 43 82; www.latabledescordeliers.fr; 1 rue des Cordeliers; menus €22-75; ☉ noon-2pm & 7-9pm Tue-Sat) Condom's premier restaurant is run by culinary magician Eric Sampietro, known for his fresh flavours and seasonal ingredients, put together in surprising combinations. The full-blown *menus* are expensive, but the new bistro offers a three-dish-per-course *menu* for just €22, at lunch and dinner. The setting is gorgeous, inside a 13th-century chapel complete with cloister garden.

❶ Information

Tourist Office (☑ 05 62 28 00 80; www. tourisme-tenareze.com; 5 place Saint-Pierre; ☉ 9am-noon & 2-6.30pm Mon-Sat)

❶ Getting There & Around

Condom's bus links are limited; the most useful line runs to Agen (€3.50, 50 minutes, three daily Monday to Saturday) where you can catch trains to Toulouse.

To park on the street, you'll need a blue timed disc, available from the tourist office.

Around Condom

Thanks to its rolling hills and patchwork pastures, the Gers region is sometimes known as la *Toscane Française* (the French Tuscany), but centuries ago this area was part of the ancient province of Gascon.

It was a strategically important region during the Hundred Years War, caught between the strongholds of the French and English armies, based in Toulouse and Bordeaux respectively. To protect themselves from the crossfire, the wealthier villages fortified themselves against attack, creating the many *bastide* towns that now litter the area.

◉ Sights

Fourcès   BASTIDE
Some 13km northwest of Condom, Fourcès (the 's' is pronounced) is a picturesque *bastide* on the River Auzoue, worth a visit for its unusual shape – unlike most it's circular rather than square-shaped. The village bursts into colour during the last weekend of April as thousands pour in for its Marché aux Fleurs, more a flower festival than a market.

**Cité des Machines
du Moyen Age**   MUSEUM
(http://larressingle.free.fr; Larressingle; adult/child €8.20/5.20; ☉ 10am-7pm Jul-Aug, 2-6pm Apr-Jun

OFF THE BEATEN TRACK

ABBAYE DE FLARAN

This serene Cistercian abbey (☑05 62 28 50 19; www.fources.fr/abbayeflaran.html; adult/child €5/free; ☉9.30am-7pm Jul-Aug, 9.30am-noon & 2-6pm rest of year) is one of Gers' architectural gems, and quite possibly the loveliest abbey in southwest France. Founded in 1151 and guarded by a 14th-century fortress door turned pigeon loft, it was abandoned after the Revolution, and the building is remarkably well preserved. Among the rooms on show are the monks' cloister, refectory and sleeping cells. It's near Valence-sur-Baïse, 10km south of Condom.

& Sep-Oct, closed Nov-Mar) This is the place if you want to get a sense of what medieval warfare might have looked like. A collection of replica trebuchets, catapults and siege machines are arranged around the pretty town of Larressingle, sometimes known as 'little Carcassonne' because of its turrets and ramparts. On most days you can see several of the machines in action.

Villa Gallo-Romaine ROMAN SITE
(☑05 62 29 48 57; adult/child €4/free; ☉10am-noon & 2-6pm Mar-Nov) About 1.5km southwest of the *bastide* town of Montréal du Gers are the excavated remains of a 4th-century Gallo-Roman villa, once part of the agricultural estate of a Roman aristocrat. Archaeologists so far have revealed the villa's baths, outbuildings and mosaic floors, still bright despite centuries of being buried underground.

Admission includes entry to the small museum within Montréal's tourist office, which displays artefacts from Séviac – including amphora jars, jewellery, scupltures and more mosaics.

Collegiale St-Pierre CHURCH
(adult/child €4.90/free; ☉9.30am-7pm Mon-Sat, 2-7pm Sun Jul-Aug, shorter hrs rest of yr) Towering over the little village of La Romieu, 11km northeast of Condom, this 14th-century *collegiale* is famous for its cloister and twin 33m towers. You can climb the 136 steps of one of them for a memorable panorama across the Gers countryside.

Les Jardins de Coursiana GARDENS
(☑05 62 68 22 80; www.jardinsdecoursiana.com; adult/child €6.90/4; ☉10am-8pm Mon-Sat mid-Apr–Oct, closed Wed morning during school term times)

These landscaped gardens in La Romieu are the handiwork of a local agricultural engineer. More than 700 trees and rare plants flourish in the four main gardens: an arboretum, English garden, herb garden and *potager familial* (vegetable patch). A joint ticket with the Collegiale St-Pierre, also in La Romieu, costs €9.80.

🛏 Sleeping & Eating

La Lumiane B&B €
(☑05 62 28 95 95; www.lalumiane.com; St Puy; s €57-62, d €66-71; 🕾🖭) A sweeter country B&B you will not find. In the countryside between Condom and Auch, this 17th-century farmhouse is a blend of chic and homely: beams, shutters and stone alongside tiled floors and objets d'art (try and get the Lilas or Tilleul suites). Outside are lovely gardens and a shady pool, and owners Alain and Gisèle also offer *table d'hôtes* dinners.

★ **Les Bruhasses** B&B €€
(☑05 62 68 38 35; www.lesbruhasses.fr; near Cassaigne; d €80-90) This mini-château has aristocratic credentials: encircled by a three-hectare park, it belonged to one of the region's wealthiest Armagnac producers. The five rooms nod to the house's high-flown heritage, with regal beds, antique armoires and polished floors. The best rooms are located in the corner towers, accessed via spiral staircases. Very smart indeed.

Maison Ardure B&B €€
(☑05 62 68 59 56; www.ardure.fr; Terraube; d €94, ste €198; 🕾🖭) Once a farm belonging to the nearby Château de Terraube, this elegant manorhouse has been renovated at serious expense. Surrounded by fields, gardens and its own lovely pool, the house is full of quirky style and knick-knacks collected on the owners' travels. Several rooms have their own private TV salons. Owner Florence provides meals and picnics on request.

Lacassagne B&B €€
(☑05 62 28 26 89; www.lacassagnechambresdhotes.fr; Laressingle; d €80-100; 🕾) Just outside Laressingle, this delightful hilltop house sits in oak-filled countryside. It's set out over one storey, with shuttered French doors looking out onto the garden, and four simple, feminine rooms. The treat here is owner Maïder Papelorey: she's a fantastic cook, a multi-linguist and a local expert. Bobby the dog ensures a warm welcome, too.

Languedoc-Roussillon

POP 2.8 MILLION

Best Places to Eat

➡ Jardin des Sens (p730)

➡ Auberge du Vieux Puits (p736)

➡ Saveurs et Sens (p729)

➡ Le Cerf à Moustache (p719)

➡ Bistro d'Alex (p759)

Best Places to Stay

➡ Baudon de Mauny (p728)

➡ Le Relais des Chartreuses (p755)

➡ La Buissonière (p722)

➡ Château de la Caze (p747)

➡ Château de Palaja (p739)

Why Go?

Stretching along France's southwestern coastline from Provence to the Pyrenees, Languedoc feels like a country in its own right. Sultry and sun-baked, it's been a strategic border since Roman times, and the area is littered with historical reminders, from Roman aqueducts to hilltop Cathar castles. These days it's best known for its vineyards, which produce a third of all French wine, and its busy beaches, which sprawl all along its Mediterranean coast.

Modern Languedoc-Roussillon is really three areas in one, each with its own distinct landscape and character. Bas-Languedoc is the coastal area, home to the biggest beaches and the cities of Montpellier and Nîmes. Inland lies the high, wild country of the Haut-Languedoc and its hills, caves, gorges and forests, exemplified by the wild Parc National des Cévennes. To the west is Roussillon, which shares close ties with Catalonia just across the Spanish border – not least a passion for rugby, bullfights and summer ferias.

When to Go
Montpellier

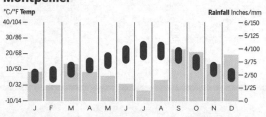

Apr Hike in the hills of the Cévennes before the summer heat and crowds.

Aug Head for Sète to watch the annual *joutes nautiques* (water-jousting).

Sep Celebrate the *vendange* (grape harvest) with vineyard parties and viticultural festivals.

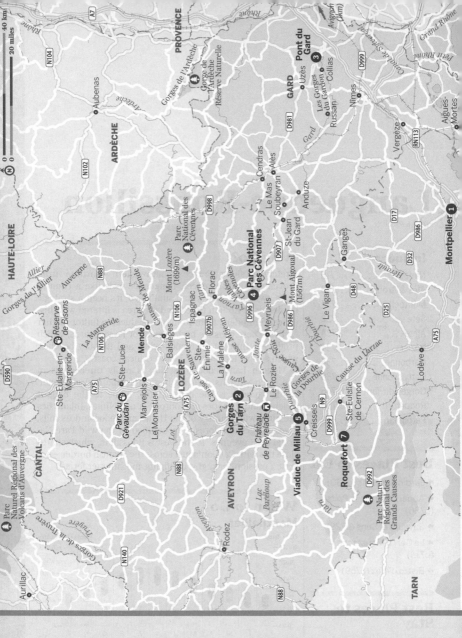

Languedoc-Roussillon Highlights

1 Soaking up the art and architecture of **Montpellier** (p724)

2 Paddling a canoe through the **Gorges du Tarn** (p747)

3 Marvelling at the architectural ambition of the **Pont du Gard aqueduct** (p721)

4 Following in the footsteps of Robert Louis Stevenson in the **Parc National des Cévennes** (p741)

5 Driving across Sir Norman Foster's futuristic **Viaduc de Millau** (p749)

6 Travelling back to the Middle Ages among Languedoc's crumbling **Cathar fortresses** (p756)

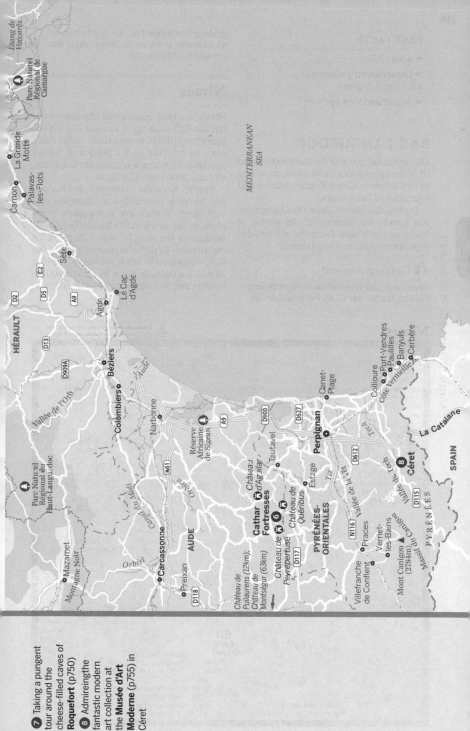

BAS-LANGUEDOC

Occupying the western half of the region...

MEDITERRANEAN
SEA

Étang de
Vaccarès

Parc Naturel
Régional de
Camargue

La Grande
Motte

Carnon

Palavas-
les-Flots

Sète

Le Cap
d'Agde

Agde

HÉRAULT

D2

D5

A9

D13

D909A

Béziers

Colombiers

Vallée de l'Orb

Parc Naturel
Régional du
Haut-Languedoc

Narbonne

Réserve
Africaine
de Sigean

Mazamet

Montagne Noir

Canal du Midi

Orbiel

Carcassonne

AUDE

Préixan

D118

Château de
Puilaurens (12km);
Château de
Montségur (63km)

Château de
Peyrepertuse

D117

Cathar
Fortresses

6

Château
d'Aguilar

Tautavel

Château de
Quéribus

PYRÉNÉES-
ORIENTALES

Estge

Tét

Perpignan

Canet-
Plage

D900

D627

Port-Vendres
Paulilles
Banyuls
Cerbère

Collioure

Côte Vermeille

La Catalane

D612

Céret

8

D115

Vallée du Tech

SPAIN

PYRÉNÉES

Massif du Canigou

Mont Canigou
(2784m)

Vernet-
les-Bains

Prades

Villefranche
de Confient

N116

Vallée de la Têt

A61

Aude

A9

Hérault

Cers

Cathar
Fortresses

D2

❼ Taking a pungent
tour around the
cheese-filled caves of
Roquefort (p750)

❽ Admiring the
fantastic modern
art collection at
the **Musée d'Art
Moderne** (p755) in
Céret

FAST FACTS

➡ **Area** 27,376 sq km

➡ **Local industry** winemaking, agriculture, tourism

➡ **Signature drink** red wine

BAS-LANGUEDOC

The broad, flat plains of Bas-Languedoc boast all of the Languedoc's main towns, as well as its best beaches, richest Roman remains and (arguably) its finest wines.

During the Middle Ages, Bas-Languedoc was largely the property of the counts of Toulouse, but it now forms the modern-day départements of Gard and Hérault.

ⓘ Getting Around

A bus journey anywhere within the Gard département costs a flat-rate €1.50. Full timetables are available from **Edgard** (www.edgard-transport.fr). As always, trains are the fastest way to get between the major towns.

Nîmes

POP 146,500

Nîmes is a busy commercial city these days, but two millennia ago it was one of the most important cities of Roman Gaul – a fact that's made clear by the city's collection of Roman buildings, including a magnificent amphitheatre and 2000 year-old temple.

Though not quite as dynamic as Montpellier, Nîmes is nonetheless an attractive city, with plenty of museums and markets to explore, as well as a host of high-profile festivals throughout the year. It's also famous for its contribution to global couture – namely the hard-wearing twill fabric known as *serge de Nîmes*, traditionally worn by agricultural labourers, and nowadays known to all as denim.

Nîmes

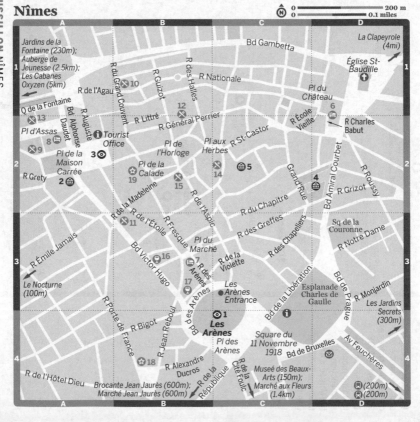

⊙ Sights

★ Les Arènes
ROMAN SITES

(www.arenes-nimes.com; place des Arènes; adult/child €9/7; ⊙9am-8pm Jul & Aug, shorter hours rest of year) Nîmes' twin-tiered amphitheatre is the best-preserved in France. Built around 100 BC, the arena would have seated 24,000 spectators and staged gladiatorial contests and public executions, and it still provides an impressive venue for gigs, events and summer bullfights. An audioguide provides context as you explore the arena, seating areas, stairwells and corridors (rather marvellously known to Romans as *vomitories*), and afterwards you can view replicas of gladiatorial armour and original bullfighters' costumes in the museum.

At 133m long, 101m wide and 21m high, with an oval arena encircled by two tiers of arches and columns, the amphitheatre is a testament to the skill and ingenuity of Roman architects. Despite being adapted, plundered for stone and generally abused over many centuries, the structure of the amphitheatre is still largely intact, and it's not hard to imagine what the atmosphere must have been like when it was filled to capacity.

The seating is divided into four tiers and 34 rows; the posher you were, the closer you sat to the centre. The amphitheatre's oval design meant everyone had an unrestricted view. A system of trap doors and hoist-lifts beneath the arena enabled animals and combatants to be put into position during the show. Originally, the amphitheatre would have had a canopy that protected spectators from the weather.

Since 2012 a project has been underway to clean limescale and pollution stains from the exterior, so there may be scaffolding when you visit.

Maison Carrée
ROMAN SITES

(place de la Maison Carrée; adult/child €5.50/4; ⊙10am-8pm Jul & Aug, shorter hours rest of year) Constructed in gleaming limestone around AD 5, this temple was built to honour Emperor Augustus' two adopted sons. Despite the name, the Maison Carrée (Square House) is actually rectangular – to the Romans, 'square' simply meant a building with right angles. The building is beautifully preserved, complete with stately columns and triumphal steps; it's worth paying the admission to see the interior, but probably worth skipping the lame 3D film.

Jardins de la Fontaine
ROMAN SITES

(Tour Magne adult/child €3.20/2.70; ⊙Tour Magne 9.30am-6.30pm) The elegant Jardins de la Fontaine conceal several Roman remains, most notably the 30m-high **Tour Magne**, raised around 15 BC. Built as a display of imperial power, it's the largest of a chain of towers that once punctuated the city's 7km-long Roman ramparts. At the top of its 140 steps, there's an orientation table to help you interpret the panorama over Nîmes.

Elsewhere around the gardens are the **Source de la Fontaine** – once the site of a spring, temple and baths – and the crumbling **Temple de Diane**, located in the gardens' northwest corner.

Carré d'Art
MUSEUM

(www.carreartmusee.com; place de la Maison Carrée; permanent collection free, exhibitions adult/

❶ PASS NÎMES ROMAINE

A joint ticket (adult/child €11.50/9) covers admission to Les Arènes, Maison Carrée and Tour Magne, and remains valid for three days.

All three sites have the same closing hours: 8pm in July and August; 7pm in June; 6.30pm in April, May and September; 6pm in March and October; and 5.30pm from November to February.

child €5/3.70; ⊙10am-6pm Tue-Sun) The striking glass-and-steel building facing the Maison Carrée was designed by British architect Sir Norman Foster. Inside is the **municipal library** and the **Musée d'Art Contemporain**, with permanent and temporary exhibitions covering art from the 1960s onwards. The rooftop restaurant makes a lovely spot for lunch.

Musée du Vieux Nîmes   MUSEUM
(place aux Herbes; ⊙10am-6pm Tue-Sun) **FREE** The town museum delves into the history of Nîmes from Roman times through to the modern era, with lots of period costumes and a display of denim-wearing celebrities including Elvis and Marilyn Monroe. Located inside Nîmes' 17th-century episcopal palace.

Musée Archéologique   ARCHAEOLOGICAL MUSEUM
(13 bd Amiral Courbet; ⊙10am-6pm Tue-Sun) **FREE** Nîmes' archaeological museum has a collection of Roman tombs, mosaics and other artifacts unearthed around the city. There's an intriguing display on the city's Iron Age origins and its massive transformation during the Roman era.

Musée d'Histoire Naturelle   MUSEUM
(13 bd Amiral Courbet; ⊙10am-6pm Tue-Sun) **FREE** Sharing the same building as the Musée Archéologique, the Natural History Museum has the usual displays of stuffed beasties, fossils and skeletons, as well as a few menhirs decorated by prehistoric artists. Don't forget to say bonjour to Maurice the stuffed giraffe as you enter.

Musée des Beaux-Arts   ART MUSEUM
(rue de la Cité Foulc; ⊙10am-6pm Tue-Sun) **FREE** The city's fine-arts museum has a fairly pedestrian collection of Flemish, Italian and French works, although it's worth a look for the fine Roman mosaic that can be viewed from the 1st floor. Entry to the permanent collection is free. Located about 200m south of Les Arènes.

⚡ Festivals & Events

Les Grands Jeux Romains   EVENT
For two days in mid-April, Romans again take over town with an encampment, staged gladiatorial battles in Les Arènes and a triumphal street parade.

**Féria de Pentecôte &
Féria des Vendanges**   BULLFIGHTING
Nîmes becomes more Catalan than French during its two *férias* (bullfighting festivals): the five-day Féria de Pentecôte (Whitsuntide Festival) in June, and the three-day Féria des Vendanges on the third weekend in September. Each is marked by daily *corridas* (bullfights).

Jeudis de Nîmes   FESTIVAL
Between 6pm and 10.30pm every Thursday in July and August, food markets and live gigs take over Nîmes' squares.

🛏 Sleeping

Auberge de Jeunesse   HOSTEL €
(📞04 66 68 03 20; www.hinimes.com; 257 chemin de l'Auberge de Jeunesse, La Cigale; dm/d €16.45/38; ⊙reception 7.30am-1am) It's out in the sticks, 4km from the bus and train stations, but this hostel has lots in its favour: spacious dorms, family rooms, a garden with space for camping, and a choice of self-catering kitchen or cafe. Take bus I, direction Alès or Villeverte, and get off at the Stade stop.

Hôtel Central   HOTEL €
(📞04 66 67 27 75; www.hotel-central.org; 2 place du Château; d €60-95, f €90-125) If you like your lines clean and your clutter minimal, this recently modernised hotel will suit you nicely. The rooms have been renovated with wooden floors, neutral colours and sleek bathrooms, with exposed stone left for character; Supérieure rooms offer the most space. The lack of lift is a drawback considering the number of stairs. If you're driving, ring ahead to ask them to reserve you a parking space.

⭐**Hôtel de l'Amphithéâtre**   HOTEL €€
(📞04 66 67 28 51; www.hoteldelamphitheatre. com; 4 rue des Arènes; s/d/f €72/92/130) Down a narrow backstreet leading away from Les Arènes, this tall townhouse ticks all the boxes: smart rooms with shabby-chic furniture and balconies overlooking the place du Marché; a sleek palette of greys, whites and taupes; and a great buffet breakfast. It's run by an expat Cornishman and his French wife.

Les Cabanes Oxyzen COTTAGES €€
(🖉 04 66 84 99 80; www.chambres-hotes-nimes.
com; 80 impasse du Couchant; d €140-150; 🖭 🗷)
Fabulous fun: three ultra-contemporary timber cabins, arranged around a lush Mediterranean garden and swimming pool shaded
by oaks and strawberry trees. Each cabin
has its own letter theme (X for XXL, Y for
Yellow, Z for Zen) with corresponding decor.
It's 6km northwest of the centre.

Royal Hôtel HOTEL €€
(🖉 04 66 58 28 27; www.royalhotel-nimes.com;
3 bd Alphonse Daudet; d €82-102, f €163; ❋ 🖭)
This upmarket hotel offers grace and style.
Bedrooms have a choice of street views or
an outlook over the grand place d'Assas.
They're split into standard and superior,
all with modern-meets-heritage decor; it's
worth bumping up a level for extra space
and air-con. The downstairs restaurant, La
Boduegita, offers solid Med dining.

La Clapeyrole B&B, SELF-CONTAINED €€
(🖉 04 66 26 85 06; 222 impasse de la Clapeyrole;
d per night €120-130, per week €700-900) This
detached house is a stunner, set among the
wooded hills above Nîmes, about 10 minutes' drive from the centre. Modern lines,
minimalist decor and a pool encircled by
olive trees provide a level of indulgence that
normally costs twice the price. It's about
7km northeast of town, off the D979.

Les Jardins Secrets B&B €€€
(🖉 04 66 84 82 64; www.jardinssecrets.net; 3 rue
Gaston Maruejols; d €195-380, ste €380-450; 🖭)
For doing Nîmes *en luxe*, nowhere tops the
Secret Gardens. Decorated to resemble an
18th-century *maison bourgeoise*, it's dripping with luxury, from chaise longues and
antique clawfoot baths to a wonderful Ro-
man-style bathhouse and divine gardens –
but for these kind of prices, you'd think they
could include breakfast and parking (an extra €25 and €20 respectively).

Hôtel Imperator Concorde HOTEL €€€
(🖉 04 66 21 90 30; www.nimes.concorde-hotels.
com; quai de la Fontaine; r from €180) Nîmes'
longstanding grand hotel, with a guest list
that's taken in everyone from famous mata-
dors to European aristocrats (and Hemingway, of course). It's staid in style, heavy on
drapes and heritage furniture, but some of
the rooms are looking seriously dated.

✕ Eating

Nîmes' gastronomy owes as much to the spicy
flavours of Provence as to the meaty richness
of the Languedoc.

La Petite Fadette CAFE €
(🖉 04 66 67 53 05; 34 rue du Grand Couvent; menus
€9.50-14.50; ⊙ 8am-7pm) Salads and crispy *tartines* (open toasted sandwiches) are the order
of the day at this homely cafe, with a cute rococo interior lined with vintage photos, and
outside tables on a small courtyard on the rue
du Grand Couvent. The food isn't fancy, but
portions are huge: try the smoked salmon or
the cured ham and goat's cheese.

⭐ **Le Cerf à Moustache** BISTRO €€
(🖉 09 81 83 44 33; 38 bd Victor Hugo; mains €14-
35; ⊙ 11.45am-2pm & 7-11pm Tue-Sat) Despite its
weird name, the Deer with the Moustache
has quickly established itself as one of Nîmes'
top bistros, with quirky decor (including reclaimed furniture and a wall full of old-book
doodles), matched by chef Julien Salem's creative take on the classics. Go basic with burgers
and risotto, or upmarket with crusted lamb
and chunky steaks.

L'Imprévu MODERN FRENCH €€
(🖉 04 66 38 99 59; www.l-imprevu.com; 6 place d'Assas; mains €19.50-27.50; ⊙ noon-?pm & 7-10pm Thu-
Mon; 🖩) A fine-dining French bistro tucked in
the corner of place d'Assas, with an open-plan
kitchen and a cute interior courtyard. There's
a good choice of seafood and meats, from sea
bass in balsamic vinaigrette to thyme-mari-
nated lamb. Dishes are mainly à la carte, although there's a limited *menu du jour*.

Le Nocturne BISTRO €€
(🖉 04 66 67 20 28; www.restaurant-le-nocturne.
com; 29bis rue Benoît Malon; mains €20-30; ⊙ 8pm-
2am) Swish but not snooty, this is a fine place
to dine on rich southwest flavours. Duck, foie
gras and mushrooms feature heavily – in
fact, you can have your duck breast with a
choice of four sauces (raspberry, apple, cep or
morel), try a classic *confit de canard* (duck
cooked in its own fat) or even try it *au tartare*
(served raw). It's on rue Benoît Malon, about
10 minutes' walk west of Les Arènes.

Carré d'Art GASTRONOMIC €€
(🖉 04 66 67 52 40; www.restaurant-lecarredart.fr; 2
rue Gaston Boissier; lunch/dinner menu €19.50/32;
⊙ noon-3pm & 7.30-10pm Tue-Sat) Open since
1989, this gastronomic heavy-hitter is still
one of Nîmes' top fine-dining addresses. The

setting is elegant, in a 19th-century townhouse decked out with abstract art and a gorgeous shaded courtyard, and the food gives traditional French a modern spin: mackerel escabèche, or Provençal sea bass with aubergine caviar.

Self-Catering

Les Halles MARKET

(rue Guizot, rue Général Perrier & rue des Halles; ⊗6.30am-1pm) Nîmes' covered market is the best place for supplies: look out for local specialities including *picholines* (a local green olive with its own AOC) and *brandade* (salt cod).

Maison Villaret BOULANGERIE

(13 rue de la Madeleine; ⊗8am-6pm Mon-Sat, to 1pm Sun) This family *boulangerie* (bakery) makes 25 different kinds of bread, cakes and biscuits, such as *caladons* (honey and almond-studded biscuits).

L'Oustaù Nadal DELICATESSEN

(place aux Herbes; ⊗9am-5pm Tue-Sat) Goodies such as tapenade, honey and olive oil (including three kinds on tap).

 Drinking & Nightlife

Place aux Herbes, place de l'Horloge and place du Marché are packed with busy cafes.

Grand Café de la Bourse et du Commerce BAR

(bd des Arènes; ⊗8am-midnight) Step back in time to a more elegant era at this opulent 19th-century cafe opposite Les Arènes, gleaming with chandeliers and mirrors.

Café Olive BAR

(⊉04 66 67 89 10; 22 bd Victor Hugo; ⊗9am-1pm Mon-Sat) A lively little nightspot, the stone walls and dim lighting of which give it a cosy cavern vibe. There are regular gigs and a great choice of wines by the glass.

☆ **Entertainment**

Les Arènes is the major venue for outdoor spectacles such as concerts, pageants and bullfights.

Ciné Sémaphore CINEMA

(⊉04 66 67 83 11; www.cinema-semaphore.fr; 25 rue Porte de France) Five screens showing *version originale* (VO, or nondubbed) films.

Théâtre de Nîmes PERFORMING ARTS

(⊉04 66 36 02 04; www.theatredenimes.com; place de la Calade) Renowned venue for drama and music.

 Shopping

Regular markets are held in Nîmes throughout the week.

Brocante Jean Jaurès FLEA MARKET

(Flea Market; bd Jean Jaurès; ⊗8am-1pm Mon)

Marché Jean Jaurès FARMERS MARKET

(Farmers Market; bd Jean Jaurès; ⊗7am-1pm Fri) Held at the same place as the flea market.

Marché aux Fleurs FLOWER MARKET

(Flower Market; ⊗7am-6pm Mon) Held outside the Stade des Costières.

 Information

Tourist Office (⊉04 66 58 38 00; www.ot-nimes.fr; 6 rue Auguste; ⊗8.30am-8pm Mon-Fri, 9am-7pm Sat, 10am-6pm Sun Jul & Aug, shorter hours rest of year) There's also a seasonal annexe (⊗usually Jul & Aug) on esplanade Charles de Gaulle.

 Getting There & Away

AIR

Nîmes' **airport** (⊉04 66 70 49 49; www.nimes-aeroport.fr), 10km southeast of the city on the A54, is served only by Ryanair, which flies to/from London Luton, Liverpool, Brussels and Fez.

An airport bus (€5.50, 30 minutes) connects with all flights to/from the train station.

BUS

The **bus station** (⊉04 66 38 59 43; rue Ste-Félicité) is next to the train station. Local buses are run by **Edgard** (www.edgard-transport.fr). Destinations include:

Alès Line A10, 1¼ hours, two to four Monday to Saturday

Pont du Gard Line B21, 40 minutes, hourly Monday to Saturday, two on Sunday

Uzès Line E52, 45 minutes, eight to 10 daily Monday to Friday, three or four on weekends

CAR & MOTORCYCLE

Major car-rental companies have kiosks at the airport and the train station.

TRAIN

TGVs run hourly to/from Paris' Gare de Lyon (€62.50 to €111, three hours) from the **train station** (bd Talabot).

Local destinations, with at least hourly departures, include:

Alès €8.50, 40 minutes

Arles €9, 30 minutes

Avignon €8.50, 30 minutes

Montpellier €8.50, 30 minutes

Sète €12, one hour

Around Nîmes

◉ Sights & Activities

★ Pont du Gard
ROMAN SITES

(☏ 04 66 37 50 99; www.pontdugard.fr; car & up to 5 passengers €18, after 8pm €10; ☺ visitor centre & museum 9am-8pm Jul & Aug, shorter hours rest of year) Southern France has some fine Roman sites, but nothing can top the Unesco World Heritage Site–listed Pont du Gard, 21km northeast of Nîmes. This fabulous three-tiered aqueduct was once part of a 50km-long system of water channels, built around 19 BC to transport water from Uzès to Nîmes. The scale is huge: 48.8m high, 275m long and graced with 35 precision-built arches; the bridge was sturdy enough to carry up to 20,000 cubic metres of water per day.

Each block was carved by hand and transported from nearby quarries – no mean feat, considering the largest blocks weight over 5 tonnes. Amazingly, the height of the bridge descends by just 2.5cm across its length, providing just enough gradient to keep the water flowing – an amazing demonstration of the precision of Roman engineering. The Musée de la Romanité provides background on the bridge's construction, and the Ludo play area helps kids to learn in a fun, hands-on way.

You can walk across the tiers for panoramic views over the River Gard, but the best perspective on the bridge is from downstream, along the 1.4km Mémoires de Garrigue walking trail. Early evening is a good time to visit, as admission is cheaper and the bridge is stunningly illuminated after dark.

There are large car parks on both banks of the river, 400m walk from the bridge. Several buses stop nearby, including Edgard bus B21 (hourly Monday to Saturday, two or three on Sunday) from Nîmes to Alès.

Perrier Plant
WATER FACTORY

(☏ 04 66 87 61 01; www.visitez-perrier.com/en; adult/child €3/1, tours €4/2; ☺ 10am-4pm Mon-Fri) Nîmes isn't only famous for denim – it's also the home of Perrier, the world-famous fizzy water, which has its source in natural springs 13km southwest of the city. The main plant supplies around 900 million bottles of water every year; you can visit the factory and watch a 3D film that explains Perrier's history, production process, and the reason behind the bottle's iconic shape (spoiler: it's to do with pressure). Remember to pick up Perrier-themed souvenirs in the shop.

Guided tours visit the bottling plant itself, but are only in French.

Uzès
POP 8450

Twenty-five kilometres northeast of Nîmes, the trim little town of Uzès is renowned for its graceful Renaissance architecture, a reminder of the days when this was an important

---

WORTH A TRIP

CANOEING ON THE RIVER GARD

For a unique perspective on the Pont du Gard, you need to see it from the water. The River Gard flows down from the Cévennes mountains all the way to the aqueduct, passing through the dramatic Gorges du Gardon en route. The best time to do it is early spring between April and June, as winter floods and summer droughts can sometimes make the river impassable.

Most of the local hire companies are based in Collias, 8km from the bridge, a journey of about two hours by kayak. Depending on the season and the height of the river, you can make a longer journey by being dropped upstream at Pont St Nicholas (19km, four to five hours) or Russan (32km, six to seven hours); the latter option also includes a memorable trip through the Gardon Gorges.

Most companies are open from around 8am to 6pm in summer. There's a minimum age of six, and life-jackets are always provided.

Canoë Collias (☏ 04 66 22 87 20; www.canoe-collias.com; from Collias adult/child €22/12, from Russan €35/16)

Kayak Vert (☏ 04 66 22 80 76; www.kayakvert.com; from Collias adult/child €22/11, from Russan €41/20)

Le Tourbillon (☏ 04 66 22 85 54; www.canoe-le-tourbillon.com; from Collias adult/child €22/11, from Russan €35/22)

trading centre – especially for silk, linen and, bizarrely, liquorice.

The key sights are the ducal palace and the arcaded central square, place aux Herbes, which hosts a lively farmers market every Wednesday and Saturday.

◉ Sights & Activities

Duché
CHÂTEAU

(www.duche-uzes.fr; admission €13, incl guided tour adult/child €18/7; ⊙10am-12.30pm & 2-6.30pm) This fortified château belonged to the House of Cressol, who were the Dukes of Uzès for more than 1000 years until the Revolution. The building is a Renaissance wonder, with a majestic 16th-century façade showing the three orders of classical architecture (Ionic, Doric and Corinthian). Inside, you can take a guided tour (in French) of the lavish ducal apartments and 800-year-old cellars, and climb the Bermonde tower for wraparound town views.

Jardin Médiéval
GARDEN

(Medieval Garden; adult/child €4.50/2; ⊙10.30am-12.30pm & 2-6pm Apr-Oct) This delightful garden contains a wealth of plants and flowers that served a variety of purposes for their medieval planters: medicinal, nutritional and symbolic.

Musée du Bonbon Haribo
MUSEUM

(Candy Museum; www.museeharibo.fr; Pont des Charrettes; adult/child €7/4.50; ⊙10am-1pm & 2-6pm Tue-Sun Oct-Jun, daily Jul-Sep) Uzès' history as a centre for confectionery continues at this Wonka-esque museum, which explores the sweet-making process from the early 20th century through to the present day. There's a collection of antique advertising posters and vintage confectionery machinery, but inevitably it's the rainbow-coloured sweet shop that takes centre stage. Just remember to brush your teeth afterwards, OK?

✯✯ Festivals & Events

Foire Aux Truffes
FOOD FESTIVAL

A full-blown truffle fair, held on the third Sunday in January.

Foire à l'Ail
FOOD FESTIVAL

Uzès positively reeks during its garlic fair on 24 June.

Nuits Musicales d'Uzès
MUSIC FESTIVAL

(www.nuitsmusicalesuzes.org) An international festival of baroque music and jazz held during the second half of July.

🛏 Sleeping

Hostellerie Provençale
HOTEL €€

(☑ 04 66 22 11 06; www.hostellerieprovencale.com; 1-3 rue de la Grande Bourgade; r €101-186; 🛜) This old-style hotel is a trip back in time: the nine rooms are a mix of wonky floors, sloping ceilings, antique dressers and exposed stone, giving the place a bygone-era vibe. They vary greatly in size, a fact reflected in the prices. The downstairs restaurant, La Parenthèse, serves good regional cuisine. Breakfast is pricey at €14.

La Maison Rouge
B&B €€

(☑ 09 50 25 91 06; www.maison-rouge.com; 7 av Maxime Pascal; d €100-130) The Red House indeed: built from scarlet brick in 1830 for a gentleman-about-town in the centre of old Uzès. Despite its vintage trappings (shutters, balconies, stone staircase), the house has been beautifully modernised, with wood floors, walk-in showers and swish furniture. Shutters overlook the back-garden pool; on a clear day you can see Mont Ventoux.

La Buissonière
B&B €€

(☑ 04 66 03 01 71; www.labuissonniere.com; Foussargues; r €140-220) A beauty of a B&B, with a village setting in Foussargues, 10km from Uzès, and a wonderful 2-hectare garden. The house was built by a winemaker in the late 18th century, but it's a delicious mix of old and new: rustic stone and flagstones meet gloss-wood floors and sleek designer furniture. Some rooms have sexy bedroom mezzanines.

✗ Eating

Terroirs
DELICATESSEN, CAFE €

(www.enviedeterroirs.com; 5 place aux Herbes; snacks €4-6, platters €10-14; ⊙9am-10.30pm Apr-Sep, to 6pm Oct-Mar) A smart deli-cafe with a prime position overlooking the place aux Herbes. It sells gourmet goods such as honey, oil, pâté and foie gras, and its platters and sandwiches are perfect lunch fare.

★ Le Tracteur
BISTRO €€

(☑ 04 66 62 17 33; Argilliers; dinner menu €29; ⊙noon-2.30pm Mon-Fri, 7-10pm Fri & Sat) Quirkiness and creativity are the watchwords at this offbeat, and brilliant, dining destination – part wine shop, part art gallery, part grocery, part bistro. In a converted warehouse in Argilliers, filled with battered furniture and abstract art, it's a cool space for dining on Mediterranean dishes. Look out for the namesake tractor outside. Argilliers is 10km from Uzès.

Le Comptoir du 7
BISTRO €€

(☎ 04 66 22 11 54; 5 bd Charles Gide; ⓥ 12.30-2pm & 7-10pm Tue-Sat) Good modern Mediterranean food, served in a choice of barrel-vaulted dining room or a courtyard garden. The food is fresh and seasonal, so the menu is dictated by what arrives at the market – always a good sign – and unusually, there's a choice of vegie options.

🛍 Shopping

Maison de la Truffe
FOOD

(27 place aux Herbes) It's truffles with everything at the Truffle House: oil, rice, vinegar, meat and pâté are all laced with the pricey tuber. There's even a truffle aperitif.

ⓘ Information

Tourist Office (☎ 04 66 22 68 88; www.uzes tourisme.com; place Albert 1er; ⓥ 10am-6pm Mon-Fri, 10am-1pm & 2-5pm Sat & Sun)

ⓘ Getting There & Away

Local buses are run by **Edgard** (www.edgard-transport.fr). Destinations include:

Avignon Line A15, one hour, five daily Monday to Friday, three on weekends; stops at Alès in the opposite direction.

Nîmes Line E52, one hour, eight to 10 daily Monday to Friday, three or four on weekends

Alès & Around

POP 41,100

The old industrial town of Alès, 45km from Nîmes and 70km from Montpellier, isn't the most attractive town in the Gard département, but it has a good reason for its workaday appearance: it's been a major coal-mining centre since the 13th century, though the last pit closed its shafts back in 1986.

It's looking a lot brighter since the heavy industries moved on, but it probably only warrants a fleeting stop en route to the Cévennes.

👁 Sights & Activities

Mine Témoin
MUSEUM

(www.mine-temoin.fr; chemin de la Cité Ste-Marie; adult/child €8.70/5.30; ⓥ 9am-7pm Jul & Aug, 9.30am-12.30pm & 2-6pm Mar–mid-Nov) To get an insight into the town's long coal-mining heritage, don a safety helmet and take the cage down into the murky tunnels of this disused mine, once used to train apprentice colliers. The one-hour guided tour explores 700m of galleries. The tour and introductory video are in French, but an English guidebook is available. Above ground, there are various industrial relics relating to the coal-extraction process.

Wear something warm, since the temperature underground never tops 16°C.

Bambouseraie de Prafrance
GARDEN

(www.bambouseraie.com; adult/child €9.60/5.60; ⓥ 9.30am-7pm Mar–mid-Nov, to 5pm Oct & Nov, closed Dec-Feb) It's over 150 years since the first shoots of this rambling, mature bamboo grove were planted by a spice merchant returning from the tropics. Here in Générargues, 12km southwest of Alès, 150 bamboo species sprout amid aquatic gardens, a Laotian village and a Japanese garden. The Cévennes steam train stops here.

Musée du Désert
MUSEUM

(www.museedudesert.com; adult/child €5.50/4.50; ⓥ 9.30am-noon & 2-6pm Mar-Nov, 9.30am-6pm Jul & Aug) In the village of Le Mas Soubeyran, 5.5km north of the Bambouseraie, this intriguing museum traces the history of the Camisard revolt, a bloody religious struggle that raged in the early 1700s between the Catholic armies of Louis XIV and a guerrilla band of around 1000 Protestant Huguenots, led by the charismatic Roland Laporte. Located inside Laporte's house, the museum details his life and times, and contains artifacts such as forbidden Huguenot crosses, antique bibles and Camisard weapons.

LANGUEDOC-ROUSSILLON ALÈS & AROUND

OFF THE BEATEN TRACK

STEAM TRAIN THROUGH THE CÉVENNES

Chugging along a 13km stretch of track between St-Jean du Gard and Anduze, this fabulous old steam train, **Train à Vapeur des Cévennes** (☎ 04 66 60 59 00; www.train avapeur.com; adult/child return €15/10; ⓥ Apr-Oct), follows an old line through the Gardon Valley, which was in operation between 1909 and 1971. Now restored by enthusiasts, it's a marvellous way to see the scenery, traversing several arched viaducts and subterranean tunnels, including the 833m-long Tunnel d'Anduze. The trains also stop at the Bambouseraie de Prafrance. The one-way journey lasts 40 minutes; there are three or four trains daily depending on the season.

Sadly, Laporte's struggle ended in slaughter; he was executed along with most of his followers in 1702, and is still considered a hero by many French Protestants.

La Caracole   SNAIL FARM
(www.lacaracole.fr; St-Florent sur Auzonnet; adult/child €6/4; ⊙ tours 6pm Tue, Wed, Fri & Sat, 3pm Sun Jul & Aug, by reservation at other times) Only in France could a snail museum do decent business. Delving into 'the astonishing, exciting world of the snail', this working snail farm 12km north of Alès has a simple museum devoted to the slimy creatures, and runs guided tours followed by the obligatory snail-tasting session.

🛏 Sleeping

Mas de Rochebelle   B&B €€
(☏04 66 30 57 03; www.masderochebelle.fr; 44 chemin de la Cité Ste-Marie; s/d/tr/f incl breakfast €60/80/120/140; ❄) Near the Mine Témoin, this welcoming *chambre d'hôte* (B&B) in Alès was once the mine director's residence. It has five attractive rooms (some with original tiled floors) and a large garden, where you can wander, swim or simply relax under its magnificent yew tree. Credit cards aren't accepted.

Hôtel-Restaurant Le Riche   HOTEL €€
(☏04 66 86 00 33; www.leriche.fr; 42 place Pierre Sémard; s/d €62/93; ❄🤚) A 19th-century façade conceals surprisingly modern rooms and a refined restaurant (*menus* €25 to €44), where you can dine on classic *terroir* cuisine among stucco, cornicing and potted plants.

ℹ Information

Tourist Office (☏04 66 52 32 15; www.ville-ales.fr; place Hôtel de Ville; ⊙9am-noon & 1.30-5.30pm Mon-Sat, plus 9.30am-12.30pm Sun Jul & Aug)

ℹ Getting There & Away

BUS

Buses leave from the train station.

Edgard (www.edgard-transport.fr) Line A15 runs to Uzès (one hour, five daily Monday to Friday, three on weekends) and continues to Avignon (1¾ hours).

Voyages Boulet (☏04 66 65 19 88; www.voyages-boulet.com) Runs one daily bus from Alès to Florac (€15.50, 65 minutes) from mid-April to September.

TRAIN

There are regular trains daily to/from Nîmes (€8.50, 40 minutes), where you can catch fast TGVs on to Montpellier (€12 to €14.50, 1½ hours).

Montpellier
POP 257,100

It's often overlooked in favour of southern France's better-known cities, but in its own graceful, easy-going way, Montpellier is every bit the equal of Marseille and Nice. With its elegant buildings, grand *hôtels particuliers* (private mansions) and stately boulevards, it's a quietly stylish metropolis with a hint of Barcelona about its old quarter and shady backstreets.

Unlike many southern towns, Montpellier has no Roman heritage. Instead it was founded in the 10th century by the counts of Toulouse, and later became a prosperous trading port as well as a scholarly centre (Europe's first medical school was founded here in the 12th century).

The population swelled in the 1960s when many French settlers left independent Algeria and settled here, and it's now one of southern France's most multicultural cities – and with students making up over a third of the population, it's also a place that seems eternally young at heart.

◉ Sights

Montpellier's beating heart is the huge open square of place de la Comédie. The city's finest period architecture and *hôtel particuliers* can be found around the old quarter, which lies to the northeast, bordered by the main roads of bd Henri IV, bd Foch and bd Louis Pasteur.

◉ City Centre

★ Musée Fabre   GALLERY
(www.museefabre.fr; 39 bd de Bonne Nouvelle; adult/child €6/4, with Département des Art Décoratifs €7/5, 1st Sun of month free; ⊙10am-6pm Tue-Sun) Founded in 1825 by the painter François-Xavier Fabre, and totally renovated to the tune of €61 million between 2002 and 2007, this landmark museum houses one of France's richest collections of European art.

ℹ MONTPELLIER CITY CARD

Montpellier City Card (adult per 1/2/3 days €13.50/19.80/25.20, children half-price) The Montpellier City Card, sold at the tourist office, allows unlimited travel on trams and buses, discounts at shops, a guided walking tour and free admission to several museums – with the notable exception of the Musée Fabre.

The galleries are split into three main sections: Old Masters, Modern Movements and Decorative Arts, collectively representing the last 600 years of artistic activity in Europe. Most of the big names are represented, and the renovation has transformed the museum into a light, airy and engaging space.

Highlights of the Old Masters include three paintings by Rubens, a dreamy *Venus & Adonis* by Nicholas Poussin, and a collection of works by Jacques-Louis David. The Romantic section is strong on French artists – particularly Delacroix, Géricault and Gustave Courbet – while the modern section is somewhat thinner, with Manet, Degas and Delaunay the standout names.

Of particular local interest are the works of the Marseille-born artist Frédéric Bazille (1841–70), a close contemporary of Claude Monet, Alfred Sisley, and Édouard Manet. The artist has a whole room devoted to him: look out for his portrait of Renoir, seated on a chair with legs tucked up beneath him, and a moody portrait of the artist himself by a very young Monet. Tragically, Bazille's potential was never fulfilled; he died aged just 28 in a battle of the Franco-Prussian War.

Attached to the museum is L'Hôtel de Cabrières-Sabatier d'Espeyran, a lavish Montpellier mansion that belonged to the local notable, Madame Frédéric Sabatier d'Espeyran. The interior of the house is filled with incredible ceramics, furniture and objets d'art – an evocative reminder of the fabulous wealth enjoyed by Montpellier's elite during the late 19th century.

Cathédrale St-Pierre   CATHEDRAL
(bd Henri IV) Montpellier's monumental Cathédrale St-Pierre began life as a church attached to the 14th-century monastery of St-Benoît, and was raised to cathedral status in 1536. Heavily rebuilt after the Wars of Religion, it's now the seat of the city's archbishops.

Place Royale du Peyrou   ESPLANADE, GARDEN
At the eastern end of this wide, tree-lined esplanade is the Arc de Triomphe (1692). From the Château d'Eau, an elaborate hexagonal water tower at its western limit, stretches the Aqueduc de St-Clément, spectacularly illuminated at night.

Jardin des Plantes   GARDEN
(entry on bd Henri IV; ☺noon-6pm Tue-Sun) North of place Royale du Peyrou is one of Montpellier's hidden gems, the Jardins des Plantes – the oldest botanic garden in France. Established in 1593, it was used as a model for the better-known Jardins des Plantes in Paris, laid out nearly 30 years later. Along its shady paths you'll find more than 2500 different species, including nine varieties of palm, 250 medicinal plants and an arboretum of rare trees, as well as a glorious greenhouse dating from 1860.

Musée Languedocien   ARCHAEOLOGICAL MUSEUM
(www.musee-languedocien.com; 7 rue Jacques Cœur; adult/child €7/free; ☺3-6pm daily mid-Jun-Aug, 2.30-5.30pm Mon-Sat other times) This small museum houses a collection of archaeological finds and objets d'art, ranging from ancient Greek and Egyptian statuettes to medieval tapestries and 19th-century faience (tin-glazed earthenware). It has a particularly fine collection of silverware, made by Montpellier's renowned silversmiths between the 17th and 19th centuries; of special note are a delicate wine cup made in 1666 and spice box crafted in 1718.

Musée du Vieux Montpellier   MUSEUM
(2 place Pétrarque; admission €3; ☺10am-1pm & 2-6pm Tue-Sun) This municipal museum has a fairly pedestrian collection of local interest pieces, ranging from furniture to tapestries and antique weaponry, but it's worth a visit as it's one of the few *hôtels particuliers* which you can actually see inside. The 18th-century room is particularly interesting, as it still has its period decor – complete with gilded table-clock and a wonderful mother-of-pearl cabinet.

◉ Outskirts

Montpellier Parc Zoologique   ZOO
(www.zoo.montpellier.fr; 50 ave Agropolis; zoo admission free, Serre Amazonienne €6.50/3; ☺9.30am-6.30pm Tue-Sun Easter-Sep, 10am-5pm Tue-Sun Oct-Easter) FREE Four kilometres north of the city centre, this excellent zoo – France's second largest, covering 60 hectares – has an enormous population of wild residents that span the world's continents, including a rare white rhinoceros, three young leopard brothers (called Tao, Tango and Twist) and a family of Atlas lions. It's laid out like a safari park, with most of the animals roaming free in open enclosures – so be prepared for walking.

Admission to the zoo is free, but there's a charge for the Serre Amazonienne, a gigantic tropical greenhouse which replicates the humid world of the Amazon rainforest, complete with piranhas, alligators and reptiles.

Take tram 1 to the St-Eloi stop, from where you can either walk to the zoo or catch a free shuttle bus (labelled 'La Navette').

Montpellier

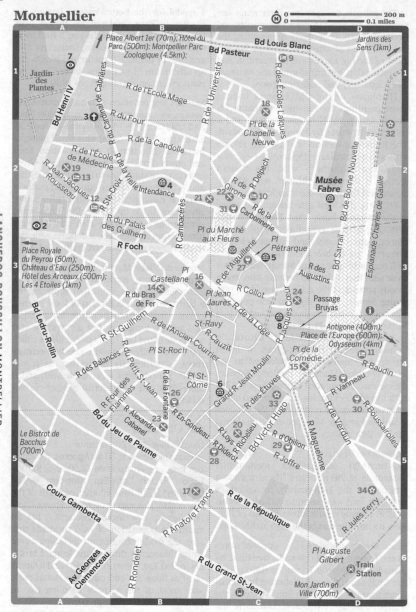

Aquarium Mare Nostrum

AQUARIUM

(www.aquariummarenostrum.fr; adult/child €15.50/10.50; ⊙10am-8pm Jul & Aug, to 7pm Sep-Jun) Part of the Odysseum shopping centre, this aquarium recreates 15 different aquatic environments, from polar waters to tropical forests. Some of the tanks are really imaginative – there's an Ocean Balcony where you stare down over submarine cliffs patrolled by sharks and rays, and a huge Amphitheatre, the largest covered tank in France with 1.8m litres of seawater. Kids will also love the inter-

Montpellier

active actions, such as a simulated cargo ship battling through stormy seas.

To get there, catch tram 1 to the Odysseum station 'Place de France'.

✸ Festivals & Events

Printemps des Comédiens ART FESTIVAL
(www.printempsdescomediens.com) A music, dance and theatre festival in June.

Montpellier Danse DANCE FESTIVAL
(www.montpellierdanse.com) A two-week international dance festival in June or July.

Festival de Radio France et Montpellier MUSIC FESTIVAL
(www.festivalradiofrancemontpellier.com) Top-notch classical music and opera, plus a parallel program of free concerts of all musical genres. Held the second half of July.

🛏 Sleeping

Auberge de Jeunesse HOSTEL €
(☎04 67 60 32 22; montpellier@fuaj.org; 2 impasse de la Petite Corraterie; dm incl breakfast €21.50; ☎) Montpellier's HI-affiliated hostel isn't the nicest you'll find in France, but it's a passable place to sleep on the cheap. It feels very institutional, with spartan dorms and bare decor, but there's a lounge downstairs with table football and pool, and a small garden. Take the tram to the Louis Blanc stop.

Hôtel de la Comédie HOTEL €
(☎04 67 58 43 64; www.hotel-montpellier-comedie. com; 1bis rue Baudin; s/d €50/70; ❄ ☎) What you lose in luxury here you more than make up for in location: the lively and central place de la Comédie is a matter of seconds away. Rooms are pretty basic but comfy enough, with crimson bedspreads and double glazing to keep out street noise, and breakfast is served in a smart salon next to reception. There's a lift, but no car access.

Hôtel des Arceaux HOTEL €
(☎04 67 92 03 03; www.hoteldesarceaux.com; 33-35 bd des Arceaux; s €54-65, d €65-70; ❄ ☎) This rambling townhouse in a residential quarter of Montpellier, 10 minutes from the centre, has pros and cons. The case for: period architecture, cosy decor, friendly owners, delightful garden. The cons: no lift, rather dated rooms and occasional street noise. The upshot: decent value if you're not too fussy.

Les 4 Étoiles B&B €€
(☎04 67 02 47 69; www.les4etoiles.com; 3 rue Delmas; s €72-108, d €94-135) You really couldn't ask for a better city base than this – a 1930s family house that's been converted into a contemporary B&B, with four rooms named after constellations, all individually styled by a local interior designer. They share the same cleanlined character: sharp furniture, flat-screen

DON'T MISS

HÔTELS PARTICULIERS IN MONTPELLIER

During the 17th and 18th centuries, Montpellier's rich merchants built themselves grand *hôtels particuliers* (private mansions) to show off their power and prodigious wealth. The most important houses are marked by a descriptive plaque in French; you can pick up a map in the tourist office. Though the exteriors are often quite restrained, inside many of the houses have fabulous inner courtyards (mostly, alas, closed to the public).

Among the most notable are the **Hôtel de Varennes** (2 place Pétrarque), just off place Pétrarque, a mix of medieval and Renaissance architecture, which now contains the Musée du Vieux Montpellier.

A short walk south on rue Jacques Coeur is the 17th-century **Hôtel des Trésoriers de France** (7 rue Jacques Coeur), home to the Musée Languedocien.

Just west is the **Hôtel St-Côme** (Grand Rue Jean Moulin), a suitably grand building for the city's Chamber of Commerce.

Further west near the Cathédrale St-Pierre is the early 17th-century **Hôtel de la Vieille Intendance** (rue de la Vieille Intendance), built during the reign of Louis XIII for the queen mother and his niece Marie Louise d'Orléans (coloquially known as 'La Grande Mademoiselle'). The house was later occupied occupied by the city's intendant (governor), the philosopher Auguste Comte and the Sète-born poet Paul Valéry.

TVs, retro design pieces and gorgeous tiled floors. It's 1km east from bd Henri IV.

Hôtel du Parc HOTEL €€
(☑ 04 67 41 16 49; www.hotelduparc-montpellier. com; 8 rue Achille-Bégé; s €52-89, d €59-108, tr €118; ❋ 🕸) It's a 500m walk from the old quarter, and this charming 18th-century *hôtel particulier* is the place if you're after peace and tranquillity. Set around its own private garden, it has 19 regal rooms, accessed via plush carpeted corridors and a sweeping central staircase. There's plenty of parking inside the house's gates, too. Head north from place Albert 1er along av Faubourg Boutonnet.

Smart Living SELF-CONTAINED €€
(☑ 06 76 20 84 70; www.smartliving.fr; apt per night €85-140) For extended stays, Smart Living offers self-catering apartments around the city. They vary in style and location, from the slate-floored VIP apartment, which has a private wood-deck patio, to Gambetta, set around its own city garden. All come with kitchen, washing machine and wi-fi, and some have parking. There's usually a two-night minimum; some are only available weekly.

Mon Jardin en Ville B&B €€
(☑ 04 67 64 00 35; www.monjardinenville.com; 23 av de Palavas; s €120-140, d €140-160, tr €195; 🕸❋) This pamper pad is a trek from the city centre, but the emphasis is on luxury rather than location. The three rooms are glossy-magazine standard: Tulipe Noire is minimalist and monochrome, Orchidée Papillon features blonde wood and neutral tones, and Fleur de Lune has a split-level mezzanine with a mini-

office and extra beds. The wooded garden and pool are absolutely gorgeous, too. It's 1km southeast of the train station.

Hôtel du Palais HOTEL €€
(☑ 04 67 60 47 38; www.hoteldupalais-montpellier. fr; 3 rue du Palais des Guilhem; s €74, d €82-97; 🕸) Old-fashioned certainly, but this homely hotel offers a flavour of a bygone era, with its peach-coloured rooms, wrought-iron balconies and window boxes. The setting on a quiet square is delightful; try to get a front-facing room if you can. The nearest car parks are on rue Foch and rue Pitot.

★ **Baudon de Mauny** B&B €€€
(☑ 04 67 02 21 77; www.baudondemauny.com; 1 rue de la Carbonnerie; €170-280; ⊙ reception 4-10pm; 🕸) Halfway between a palatial B&B and a boutique hotel, this 18th-century house has been given the full designer overhaul: original fireplaces, oak doors and sash windows sit alongside modern furniture, angle-poise lamps and butterfly wallpaper, but the stripped-back style might be a bit too austere for some. The most convenient parking is at Parking du Corum, 500m northeast.

Hôtel Le Guilhem HOTEL €€€
(☑ 04 67 52 90 90; www.hotel-le-guilhem.com; 18 rue Jean-Jacques Rousseau; r €84-204; ❋ @ 🕸) Occupying two interconnected 16th-century mansions on a narrow backstreet, this Best Western–owned hotel has rooms split across three 'comfort' categories. They're a bit of a mixed-bag – some are small with heritage furniture, others more spacious with views over

the private garden. The nearest parking is at Parking Peyrou.

🍴 Eating

You'll find plenty of cheap and cheerful eateries on rue de l'Université, rue des Écoles Laïques and the surrounding streets.

Tripti Kulai   VEGETARIAN €
(📞 04 67 66 30 51; 20 rue Jacques Cœur; mains €4-8, menus €11-16; ⊙ noon-9.30pm Mon-Sat; 🖊) Ideal for lunch, this organic-veggie cafe majors on quiches, salads and gratinées, and the fresh fruit juices are great. It also has a wholefood shop at 22 rue Bernard Délicieux and a takeaway cafe at 3 rue Massillian.

L'Heure Bleue   CAFE €
(1 rue de la Carbonnerie; cakes €3-5; ⊙ 9am-5pm Tue-Sat) Scrumptious patisseries and fine teas served in china teapots are on offer at this cute cafe.

Coffee Club   CAFE €
(📞 07 86 17 81 56; www.coffeeclub.fr; 12 rue St-Guilhem; lunch menu €7.90; ⊙ 9am-7pm Tue-Fri, 11am-5pm Sat, 11am-6pm Sun) Montpellier's very own urban espresso bar, brewing up excellent espressos and fluffy flat whites, as well as a decent lunch menu of sandwiches, salads and delicious cakes.

Les Bains de Montpellier   SEAFOOD €€
(📞 04 67 60 70 87; www.les-bains-de-montpellier. com; 6 rue Richelieu; mains €20-30; ⊙ noon-2.30pm & 7-10pm Mon-Sat) Once a public bathhouse where people underwent their daily ablutions, this is now a hugely attractive restaurant that's especially strong on seafood and Italian-influenced dishes. Tables are set around the old perimeter bathrooms, with plush purple chairs and overhead chandeliers, but the best are in the interior courtyard, surrounded by ponds and palms.

⭐ Saveurs et Sens   BISTRO €€
(📞 04 99 61 62 04; www.saveursetsens.fr; angle rue de la Fontaine et rue Cabanel; 2-/3-course menu €24.90/29.90, à la carte mains €18.50; ⊙ noon-2pm & 7-9pm Tue-Sat, Sun by reservation) One of the hot local tips in town, a teeny backstreet corner bistro run with finesse by young owners Anthony and Angélique. It's passionate about market-fresh fish and locally sourced food; flavours blend classic French and modern Mediterranean, with quirky touches such as slate plates and arty slashes of sauce. The dining room is tiny, so bookings are essential – especially since it's become so popular.

Le Grillardin   MEDITERRANEAN €€
(📞 04 67 66 24 33; www.restaurantlegrillardin.com; 3 place de la Chapelle Neuve; weekday lunch menu €19, mains €17-23; ⊙ 12.30-2.30pm Wed-Fri, 7.30-9.30pm Tue-Sun) One of a pocket of attractive bistros in the shady place de la Chapelle Neuve, serving zingy Mediterranean cuisine laced with copious amounts of peppers, aubergines, tomatoes, parmesan and basil. Book ahead, especially if you want a table on the square, as it's very popular with local diners.

Le Bistrot de Bacchus   BISTRO €€
(📞 09 50 08 00 54; www.bistrot-bacchus.com; 8 rue Marioge; mains €15-20; ⊙ noon-2.30pm Mon, Tue & Thu-Sat, 7-10.30pm Mon & Thu-Sat) There's no menu at this fine little 'bistronomique' diner in the rather rough-and-ready Arceaux district – just a blackboard chalked up with different dishes on the day depending on the chef's whims. Expect hearty country cooking, such as *poule au pot* (pot-boiled chicken), chunky beefsteak with thick-cut chips, and creamy lobster. Worth the walk.

Mesdames Messieurs   MODERN FRENCH €€
(📞 04 67 63 49 53; www.mesdamesmessieurs.com; 5 rue de Girone; tapas platter €13-19, 2-/3-course menu €21/29; ⊙ 11am-3pm Sun, 7-10pm Tue-Sat; 🖊) A place of two halves: half wine-bar, half-bistro, recommended for its platters of charcuterie, cheese and smoked trout accompanied by lots of wines by the glass. It's especially good for Sunday brunch, a serve-yourself buffet of delicious salads, tapenades and quiches.

Les Vignes   MODERN FRENCH €€€
(📞 04 67 60 48 42; www.lesvignesrestaurant.com; 2 rue Bonnier d'Alco; menus lunch €15-23, dinner €29-29; ⊙ noon-1.30pm Mon-Sat, 7.45-9.30pm Thu-Sat) Thierry Germain is passionate about two things: local produce and Provençal cooking, and both come to the fore at his smart restaurant in central Montpellier. Cévennes lamb, Mediterranean seafood and bull meat from the Camargue are just some of the ingredients you might find on the menu. The interior is suitably chic – white tablecloths, table lamps, Provençal colours – but the little terrace is the place on a warm summer's night.

Le Petit Jardin   FUSION €€€
(📞 04 67 60 78 78; www.petit-jardin.com; 20 rue Jean-Jacques Rousseau; mains bistro €12-16, restaurant €30-42; ⊙ noon-2pm & 7.30-10.30pm Tue-Sat, restaurant open Mon evening) Without doubt, the 'Little Garden' has one of the city's most romantic dining settings – a charmingly green secret garden, hidden away behind the

amber façade of a typical townhouse in the old quarter. You can choose to dine in either the relaxed bistro or the more formal restaurant, depending on your taste: either way, the food is fresh, seasonal and very French.

★ **Jardin des Sens** GASTRONOMIC €€€
(☑04 99 58 38 38; www.jardindessens.com; 11 av St-Lazare; weekday lunch menu €49, dinner mains €48-90; ☉noon-2.30pm Tue, Thu & Fri, 7-10pm Mon-Sat) Loosen that belt buckle: the Jardins des Sens has acquired a mythical status among French foodies. Twice Michelin-starred, it's run by brothers Jacques and Laurent Pourcel, whose passion for contemporary art is mirrored in their choice of decor and their food, with culinary creations that are as much sculptural as gastronomical. It's about 1km north of bd Louis Blanc along av de Nîmes.

Self-Catering

Montpellier has lots of markets, including traditional food markets on **place de la Comédie** (☉7am-1.30pm Mon-Thu, to 6pm Fri & Sat) and **place Albert 1er** (☉7am-1pm Wed, Fri & Sat), and a **farmers market** (av Samuel Champlain; ☉8am-1pm Sun) in the Antigone quarter.

Ask at the tourist office about regular book fairs, flea markets and flower markets.

Halles Castellane FOOD MARKET
(rue de la Loge; ☉7am-8pm Mon-Sat, to 1.30pm Sun) The city's main covered market, stocked to the rafters with local goodies. There are lots of Languedoc wines on offer, as well as copious fish and shellfish from the ports at Sète and Agde.

Halles Laissac FOOD MARKET
(rue Anatole France; ☉7am-1.30pm) Montpellier's second-largest covered market. It's due to be demolished in early 2015, and replaced by a futuristic new one, which should open in early 2017.

🍷 Drinking & Nightlife

With nearly 80,000 students, Montpellier has a multitude of places to drink and dance. You'll find dense concentrations around rue En-Gondeau, off Grand-Rue Jean Moulin, around place Jean Jaurès and around the intersection of rue de l'Université and rue de la Candolle.

For events and gig listings, pick up the weekly free sheet *Sortir à Montpellier*. The city's big clubs are around Espace Latipolia, 10km out of town on route de Palavas.

Chez Boris WINE BAR
(☑04 67 02 13 22; www.chezboris.com; 20 rue de l'Aiguillerie; ☉noon-2.30pm & 7.30-10.30pm) Boris Leclercq's wine-bar has proved popular: he's now got two outlets in town (this one and another at 17 bd Sarrail), as well as a new Parisian cousin. It's all relaxed and friendly, with wines served by the glass, accompanied by plates of Iberico ham and Aubrac beef if you're peckish. Check out previous guests' comments on the ceiling.

In Vino Veritas WINE BAR
(16 rue Diderot; ☉7pm-midnight) Chandeliers and red-velvet seats create a boudoir vibe here, an ideal setting for sampling Languedoc vintages either by the glass or the bottle.

La Chistera PUB
(☑04 67 55 39 51; 2bis rue d'Obilion; ☉10am-1pm Mon-Sat) This lively pub is owned by rugby star François Trinh-Duc, a local-born hero who still plays for his home team. There's a huge list of beers, domestic and foreign, served among neon lights and brick walls. As you might expect, it's a good place to watch big-screen sport.

La Fabrik BAR
(☑04 67 58 62 11; 12 rue Boussairolles; ☉6pm-1am Tue-Sat) Rough-and-ready backstreet bar, with industrial decor, Belgian beers and regular gig line-ups.

Beehive PUB
(15 rue du Plain d'Age; ☉noon-1am) Brit-themed pub with a French twist and a young crowd.

Barberousse BAR
(☑04 67 58 03 66; 6 rue Boussairolles; ☉6am-1pm) Ahoy, me hearties – down vintage rums and rum-based cocktails at this pirate-themed bar, complete with ships' lanterns and upturned barrels.

Le Café de la Mer GAY BAR
(5 place du Marché aux Fleurs; ☉8am-1pm Mon-Sat) One of the city's oldest gay bars. Ask at the bar for a free map of where else is hot (or not).

☆ Entertainment

Rockstore LIVE MUSIC
(☑04 67 06 80 00; www.rockstore.fr; 20 rue de Verdun) You can't miss this long-standing venue – just look out for the tail-fins of the '70s Cadillac jutting out above the entrance. It's one of the city's best places for live gigs.

MONTPELLIER'S BEACHES

Strolling around the winding lanes of the old quarter, it's easy to forget that Montpellier is actually a coastal city. Most can be reached in about 30 minutes by bus or car via the D21, or the new purpose-built cycling track. The sands run for around 10km between the concrete-heavy (and pretty ghastly) beach resorts of **Palavas-les-Flots** and **La Grande Motte**, and are generally packed in summer.

For a real local's tip (not to mention much quieter sands), head a few kilometres south of La Grande Motte to **Plage de l'Espiguette**, by far Montpellier's best beach. Straddling the west side of an isolated headland, the beach is a designated nature reserve, with dune systems providing a habitat for endangered birds and insects (plus a healthy number of naturists). It's often windy, which makes it popular with kite-surfers and kite-buggiers, but it's usually much, much emptier than the fleshpot beaches to the west.

Another tip for wildlife-spotters is to explore the area of wetlands and coastal lagoons around the small town of **Villeneuve-lès-Maguelone**, on the coastal road to Sète. This is often a good area for **flamingo-spotting**; the birds regularly stop off here en route from the Camargue, some 30km to the east.

Opéra-Comédie PERFORMING ARTS
(☑ 04 67 60 19 80; www.opera-orchestre-montpellier. fr; place de la Comédie) Tickets for Montpellier's theatres are sold at the box office of the Opéra-Comédie.

Le Corum PERFORMING ARTS
(☑ 04 67 61 67 61; esplanade Charles de Gaulle) The city's main concert venue and conference centre.

ⓘ Information

Tourist Office (☑ 04 67 60 60 60; www. ot-montpellier.fr; esplanade Charles de Gaulle; ☺ 9am-7.30pm Mon-Sat, 10am-5pm Sun Jul-Sep, 9.30-6pm Mon-Sat Oct-Jun) Sells the Montpellier City Card (p724) and runs guided tours.

ⓘ Getting There & Away

AIR
Montpellier Airport (☑ 04 67 20 85 00; www. montpellier.aeroport.fr) Montpellier's airport is 8km southeast of town, and has regular connections to most French and European cities.

BUS
The **bus station** (☑ 04 67 92 01 43; rue du Grand St-Jean) is an easy walk from the train station. Most local services provided by **Hérault Transport** (☑ 04 34 88 89 99; www.herault-transport. fr) cost a flat-rate €1.60. Destinations include:
La Grande Motte (20 minutes, half-hourly Monday to Saturday, every 15 minutes on weekends) Catch bus 106 from place de France. Several buses a day continue to Aigues-Mortes.
Palavas-les-Flots (10 to 20 minutes, at least hourly) Catch the tram to Station Etang l'Or, then take bus 131.

Sète Take bus 102, from Sabines tram station; 55 minutes, hourly Monday to Saturday, three on Sunday.

TRAIN
There's at least one hourly connection to the following cities:
Carcassonne €22.50, 1½ hours
Narbonne €14.50, one hour
Nîmes €8.50, 20 minutes
Paris' Gare de Lyon €54 to €79, 3½ hours by TGV
Perpignan €18 to €23, 1¾ hours

ⓘ Getting Around

TaM (☑ 04 67 22 87 87; www.tam-way.com) The city's public transport system is run by TaM.

TO/FROM THE AIRPORT
Navette Aéroport (Airport Shuttle; one way €1.60) The airport bus (line 120) runs hourly between the airport and the place de l'Europe tram stop. Buses from the city to the airport run from 5.30am to 8.30pm, and 8.35am to 11.10pm from the airport to the city.

The standard bus fare to place de l'Europe is €1.60, or you can buy an onward tram/bus pass for €2.60.

BICYCLE
Montpellier is hugely bicycle-friendly.
VéloMagg (per hr €0.50) The city's automated bike-hire system has stations across the city; you'll need a credit or bank card to hire, or you can buy an access card for €5 from the TaM office.

CAR & MOTORCYCLE
As in most large French cities, having a car is more a hindrance than a help in Montpellier. The best

OCCITAN

The Languedoc's distinctive language of Occitan is an ancient tongue that is closely related to Catalan. The *langue d'oc* was once widely spoken across most of southern France, while the *langue d'oïl* was the predominant tongue spoken to the north (the words *oc* and *oïl* meant 'yes' in their respective languages).

Occitan reached its zenith during the 12th century, but it was dealt a blow when Languedoc was annexed by the French kingdom. *Langue d'oïl* became the realm's official language, effectively relegating Occitan to the status of a language spoken only by the poor and uneducated.

Despite the best efforts of the ruling elite to wipe it out, Occitan survived as a distinct language, largely thanks to rural communities keen to hold on to their own regional identity. It enjoyed a literary revival in the 19th century, spearheaded by the poet Frédéric Mistral, who wrote in Occitan's Provençal dialect.

Today Occitan is still widely spoken across southern France, with an estimated 610,000 native speakers, and around a million others who have a basic working knowledge. There are six offically recognised dialects: Languedocien *(lengadocian)*, Limousin *(lemosin)*, Auvergnat *(auvernhat)*, Provençal *(provençau)*, Vivaro-Alpine *(vivaroaupenc)* and Gascon *(gascon)*, which includes the Aranese sub-dialect spoken in parts of Spanish Catalonia.

idea is to leave your vehicle in one of the vast car parks beside major tram stops such as Odysseum; a €4.40 ticket buys all-day parking and a tram ticket into town.

TAXI

Taxis Bleu (☑ 04 67 03 20 00)
Taxis Tram (☑ 04 67 58 10 10)

TRAM & BUS

Christian Lacroix contributed designs for Montpellier's funky, four-line tram system. Single tickets (valid on trams and buses) cost €1.40, or a one-day pass costs €3.80. There are ticket machines at most tram stops, or you can buy them at the tourist office, the TaM office or newsagents.

Sète

POP 43,600

Set alongside the the saltwater lagoon of L'Étang du Thau, Sète is a gritty and not-always-pretty port, somewhat oversold by its local moniker of the 'Little Venice of Languedoc' – a reference to the many canals that run through town, including the stately Canal du Midi, which terminates its 240km journey here from Toulouse. But its honest, workaday atmosphere makes a refreshing change from the touristy towns of the rest of the Languedoc coast – and if you like seafood, this is undoubtedly the place to indulge, as Sète has the largest working fishing fleet anywhere on France's Mediterranean coast.

The town gets very busy in August during the *joutes nautiques,* when boat crews joust with long poles in an attempt to knock each other into the harbour.

◉ Sights & Activities

Between April and November, boats chug out around the port and harbour, and along the southern reaches of the Canal du Midi. Harbour boats also visit the Étang du Thau and the local mussel and oyster farms, which you can peer at through the boat's glass-bottomed hulls.

The main companies are **Azur Croisières** (☑ 04 67 74 35 30; www.azur-croisieres.com) and **Sète Croisières** (☑ 04 67 46 00 46; www.sete-croisieres.com), both charging similar prices: around €12/6 per adult/child for a harbour trip, €8/4 for a canal cruise.

Canal trips leave from the quai Général Durand, near the boat company's kiosks opposite the tourist office. Harbour trips leave from the Pont de la Savonnerie.

Musée Paul Valéry   MUSEUM

(www.museepaulvalery-sete.fr; rue François Desnoyer; adult/child €7/free; ⊙9.30am-7pm Apr-Oct, 10am-6pm Tue-Sun Nov-Mar) Sète was the birthplace of the symbolist poet Paul Valéry (1871–1945), and the town's main museum houses a huge collection of his works, along with over 700 paintings and 1000 drawings. The local area around Sète features heavily – especially the sea, Valéry's main poetic inspiration. He is buried in the nearby Cimitière Marin.

Musée International
des Arts Modestes   ART MUSEUM

(MIAM; www.miam.org; 23 quai Maréchal de Lattre de Tassigny; adult/child €5/free; ⊙9.30am-7pm Apr-Sep, 10am-noon & 2-6pm Tue-Sun Oct-Mar) This offbeat gallery is refreshingly free of big names – here the emphasis is on the art of everyday objects, curated by local artists Hervé di Rosa and Bernard Belluc. From religious icons to kitsch china and travel souvenirs, it's like wandering round a jumble sale curated by an art critic.

Espace Georges Brassens MUSEUM
(67 bd Camille Blanc; adult/child €5/free; ⊘ 10am-noon & 2-6pm Jun-Sep, closed Mon Oct-May) The town was the childhood home of singer and poet Georges Brassens (1921–81), whose mellow voice still speaks at this multimedia space.

🛏 Sleeping

Auberge de Jeunesse Sète HOSTEL €
(📷 04 67 53 46 68; sete@fuaj.org; rue Général Revest; dm incl breakfast €17.20, d €38.50; ⊘ Feb–mid-Dec) A hostel with plenty of plus-points: elegant 19th-century building, harbour views, space for camping, wooded setting. The dorms are all small, sleeping three to four people, and there's bike hire, kitchen and shop. It's about 1.5km north of town and 3km from the Sète beaches.

Rivages B&B €€
(📷 07 61 46 65 68; www.rivages-sete.com; 22 chemin des Ivrognes; d €90-130; ✳❄⊛) With its hilltop setting and secluded garden, this B&B is the kind of place you won't want to leave. The three rooms all have a keynote colour – rich gold, cool blue or papal purple – with a panoramic lounge offering distant harbour views through floor-to-ceiling glass. Breakfast is served on the shady terrace most days.

Grand Hôtel HOTEL €€€
(📷 04 67 74 71 77; 17 quai de Tassigny; r €125-145, apt €235) As its name suggests, this 19th-century harbourfront hotel is grand, from the gleaming marble lobby, filled with palms and modern art, all the way through to the stylish rooms, arranged around a palm-filled, balconied interior courtyard. Harbour views inevitably cost extra, but they're absolutely essential here.

Petit-Hôtel Marseillan B&B €€€
(📷 06 85 88 95 63; www.petithotel-marseillan.com; 5 bd Lamartine, Marseillan; d €165-195; ❄⊛) Bright artwork and quirky furniture define this offbeat mini-hotel, in a former winemaker's house in the neighbouring village of Marseillan, 9km southwest of Sète's harbour. All five rooms are named after local trees: try Palmier for its spacious layout and Italian shower, or Figuier, with its distressed wood wardrobes and pool-view balcony.

🍴 Eating

Fish restaurants line quai Durand and quai Maximin Licciardi, but the quality can be variable, so choose carefully.

Look out for local specialities such as *rouille sétoise* (a rich tomato sauce made with cuttlefish) and *la tielle* (tomato-and-octopus pie), as well as oysters.

La Péniche SEAFOOD €€
(📷 04 67 48 64 13; 1 quai des Moulins; weekday lunch menu €12, 2-/3-course menus €26/32; ⊘ 11am-3pm daily, 6pm-midnight Mon-Sat) Dine on classic *sétoise* seafood on this converted barge, which looks more like a big-city bistro inside, with its sharp tables and shiny wood floor. The Languedoc's Spanish influence is clear – lots of dishes are cooked *à la plancha* (grilled on a hot plate).

La Méditerranéenne SEAFOOD €€
(📷 04 67 74 38 37; 3 quai Maximin Licciardi; mains €14-20; ⊘ noon-2.30pm & 7-11pm) Seafood restaurants are ten-a-penny in Sète, but this quayside bistro scores highly on friendliness and freshness. It's run by young chef Fouzia Sakrani, a Sètoise native and a seafood specialist. The food is simple but delicious – sea bream, red mullet, sardines and swordfish, as well as vast shellfish platters (€35 to €78) – all served with copious amounts of crusty bread to soak up the fishy juices. Really, what's not to like?

ℹ Information

Sète Tourist Office (📷 04 99 04 71 71; www.tourisme-sete.com; 60 Grand Rue Mario

---

LOCAL KNOWLEDGE

SÈTE'S FISH MARKET

If you really want to see what makes Sète tick, then you need to head for la criée (fish auction), when fishermen sell off their day's catch to the highest bidder. This is no free-for-all: it's a highly organised process that takes place in its own miniature theatre, with buyers placing bids on crates of fish via handheld electronic devices. It's normally off-limits to visitors, but the Sète tourist office runs guided tours (in French) every Monday and Friday at 4pm. Afterwards, there's usually a chance to look around the market and perhaps, if you meet a nice fisherman, taste some of the day's catch.

Roustan; ⊙ 9.30am-7pm Jul & Aug, shorter hours rest of year)

ⓘ Getting There & Away

The regular 102 bus (hourly Monday to Saturday, three on Sunday) runs between Sète and Montpellier in just under an hour via the local beaches, or you can catch a train (€5.50) that takes roughly half as long.

Agde

POP 21,600

There are really three Agdes: Vieux Agde, the original settlement beside the River Hérault; the fishing port of Grau d'Agde; and Cap d'Agde, a sprawling summer playground, famed for its long beaches and nudist colony.

For most people, the only real reason to stop in Agde is for some swimming and sunbathing, but the old town of Vieux Agde is worth a wander, with some imposing *hôtels particuliers* and a pretty canal-side setting.

If you're here to sunbathe, Cap d'Agde is definitely the place. Beaches sprawl for several miles around the headland; the nicest areas are on the far west (especially around La Tamarissière and St-Vincent) and the far east, where you'll find plenty of flesh on display thanks to France's largest nudist colony.

To the west of town is the attractive fishing port of Marseillan, where you can also visit the Noilly-Prat Factory (☑ 04 67 77 20 15; www.noillyprat.com; ⊙ 10am-12.30 & 2.30-6pm May-Sep, shorter hours rest of year) FREE, which has been making the famous dry vermouth to the same secret recipe since 1813.

Agde's tourist office (☑ 04 67 62 91 99; www.capdagde.com; ⊙ 10am-noon & 2-6pm daily Jul & Aug, Tue-Sat Sep-Jun) sells tickets for boat trips on the nearby Canal du Midi.

Béziers

POP 74,200

Béziers is a busy provincial town with a long history: founded by the Romans, razed during the Albigensian Crusade, and now best known as the birthplace of Paul Riquet, the man behind the stately Canal du Midi. There's a fine statue to Béziers' most famous son on allées Paul Riquet, the town's central esplanade, which hosts a flower market every Friday.

Béziers is short on sights, but it's a good place to launch forays along the canal: the 19th-century Pont-Canal aqueduct and the stepladder of nine locks known as the Écluses de Fonseranes are within easy reach.

South of town are Béziers' best beaches, Portiragnes and Serignan, which are both refreshingly free of the concrete buildings and apartment blocks that blight much of the rest of Languedoc's coastline.

The town is at its busiest during the week-long Festa d'Oc, a celebration of Mediterranean music and dance in late July, and the féria, a five-day Spanish-style festival complete with bullfights, held around 15 August.

🛏 Sleeping

Hôtel Alma HOTEL €
(☑ 04 67 28 79 44; www.hotel-alma-beziers.com; 41 rue Guilhemon; s/d/tr €49/52/72; 🖥) A basic but perfectly serviceable hotel, recommended for its central position and cheap rates. Try to get one of the renovated rooms, which have wood floors and wrought-iron furniture, ideally with a little balcony.

Hôtel des Poètes HOTEL €€
(☑ 04 67 76 38 66; www.hoteldespoetes.net; 80 allées Paul Riquet; d €50-70, f €78-90; 🖥) A pretty little townhouse-style hotel, with feminine, floral rooms spread out over several floors, and a pleasant location down a leafy cul-de-sac.

ⓘ Getting There & Away

Regular trains run from Montpellier (€11.50, 45 minutes) en route to Narbonne (€5, 15 minutes).

Narbonne

POP 52,500

Narbonne is a fairly typical Languedoc market town these days, but wind the clock back two millennia and you'd be in a major Roman city, and the capital of the province of Gallia Narbonensis. The town's now a popular stop-off for boaters on the Canal du Midi.

⊙ Sights

The Pass Monuments et Musées (€9 per person) covers all Narbonne's museums and is valid for 15 days.

Palais des Archevêques PALACE
(Archbishops' Palace; Pass Monuments et Musées per person €9; ⊙ 10am-6pm daily Jun-Sep, 10am-noon & 2-5pm Wed-Mon Oct-May) The former Archbishops' Palace houses several archaeological museums. Roman mosaics and stucco paintings are on display at the Musée d'Art et d'Histoire and Musée Archéologique, along with an underground gallery of Gallo-Roman shops in the Horreum, and a collection of

impressive Roman masonry in the **Musée Lapidaire**.

Cathédrale St-Just
CATHEDRAL

(entry on rue Armand Gauthier; ⊙9am-noon & 2-6pm) Narbonne's most distinctive landmark is actually only half-finished: construction was halted in the 14th century, and only the towers and choir were actually finished. Its treasury has a beautiful Flemish tapestry of the Creation, while grotesque gargoyles leer down upon the 16th-century cloister.

Les Halles
MARKET

(⊙7am-1pm daily) Narbonne's covered market is arguably one of the most beautiful in France. Built at the turn of the 20th century, it's a masterpiece of art nouveau style, with panels of frosted glass, decorative stonework and a wonderful cast-iron roof.

🛏 Sleeping

Will's Hotel
HOTEL €€

(☑04 68 90 44 50; www.willshotel-narbonne.com; 23 av Pierre Semard; d €61-89; 🛜) Once a merchant's house dating from 1860, this basic corner hotel is a decent base for overnighting in Narbonne, but some of the rooms are shoebox-sized, so insist on a 'Double Confort' room. Parking is available at a nearby municipal car park.

Demeure de Roquelongue
B&B €€

(☑04 68 45 63 57; www.demeure-de-roquelongue. com; 53 av de Narbonne, St-André-de-Roquelongue;

d €100-130, f €150-200; 🛜🖥) Narbonne's hotels aren't particularly special, but the Demeure de Roquelongue in the nearby village of St-André-de-Roquelongue makes a beautiful base, with five royally decorated rooms in a *maison vigneronne* (winemakers' house) dating from 1870. Our favourites are Cers, with its original fireplace and garden view, and Espan, with its vintage bathtub screened by curtains.

🛈 Getting There & Away

Frequent trains serve Narbonne en route from Béziers (€5, 15 minutes) and Montpellier (€14.50, one hour).

Around Narbonne

◉ Sights

Réserve Africaine de Sigean
WILDLIFE CENTRE

(www.reserveafricainesigean.fr; adult/child €31/22; ⊙9am-6.30pm Apr-Sep, shorter hours rest of year) Now in its fourth decade of operation, this excellent wildlife reserve aims to recreate the atmosphere of the African savannah – a climate not all that different from the Languedoc's dry and dusty plains. Lions, white rhinos, warthogs, giraffes and zebras are just a few of the wild beasties on show. Some areas are drive-through, while others you explore on foot. The reserve is off the A9, 15km south of Narbonne.

DON'T MISS

EXPLORING THE CANAL DU MIDI

Though most people's focus is on the seaside, the area around Agde, Béziers and Sète offers lots of opportunities to get out on the stately **Canal du Midi**, France's longest man-made waterway. The traditional way to explore is by barge or narrowboat, usually on a multi-day trip (see p711 for details on how to hire a boat). But if you only have limited time, there are lots of local companies offering day cruises.

Bateaux du Soleil (☑04 67 94 08 79; www.bateaux-du-soleil.fr; Port Chassefières, Agde; 2-hour cruises €11-15) runs commentated trips with/without meals from its base in Agde, while **Le Bonpas** (☑06 17 54 95 57; www.bonpasmidi.com; Port de Plaisance, Colmbiers; per adult/child 1hr cruise €8/6, 2hr cruise €30/25) offers one-hour, 2½-hour and twilight cruises from Colombiers, just west of Béziers.

If you'd prefer to be your own captain, **Eco Canal** (☑06 17 64 49 21; www.bateau-permis-location-34.com; Villeneuve-les-Béziers, 7km E of Béziers) and **Rive de France** (☑04 67 37 14 60; www.rivedefrance.com; Port de Plaisance, Colombiers) both hire out electric boats from around €25 to €30 per hour for up to five people. You don't need a permit.

Sections of the canal's towpaths also make for fun cycling, especially around Carcassonne. **Mellow Vélos** (☑04 68 43 38 21; www.mellowvelos.com; 3 place de l'Eglise, Paraza; adult/child per day from €20/10, per week €86/43; ⊙closed Thu) in Paraza near Narbonne will deliver bikes straight to your door (free within a 10km radius, or anywhere in Bas-Languedoc for a small charge).

WORTH A TRIP

MICHELIN-STAR SUPPERS

Paris isn't the only corner of France with gastronomic superstars. If you're looking for a place to splash some cash on a once-in-a-lifetime dinner, there are two chefs tucked away in the countryside who have won the hallowed three Michelin stars.

Bras (☑ 05 65 51 18 20; www.bras.fr; Laguiole; menus €132-209; ☺11.30am-1.30pm Thu-Sun, 7-9.30pm Tue-Sun) Michel Bras has been based at the eponymous Bras in the village of Laguiole since 1999. Unusually for a superstar chef, he's a self-made man: he's never strayed from his home on the Aubrac plateau, between the Massif Central and the Cévennes, and learned many of his skills from his mother. His food is steeped in the rustic, country flavours of his youth, reinvented in all kinds of outlandish ways. He's now handed over the reins to his son, Sebastien, but still makes regular appearances. It's worth a trip for the restaurant alone: a modernist, plate-glass marvel, with views over Aubrac's green hills.

Auberge du Vieux Puits (☑ 04 68 44 07 37; www.aubergeduvieuxpuits.fr; Fontjoncouse; menus €85-190; ☺noon-1.30pm & 8-9.30pm Wed-Sat, noon-1.30pm Sun) Gilles Goujon's Auberge du Vieux Puits is tucked away in the hilltop village of Fontjoncouse, between Narbonne and Perpignan. Goujon's known for his fondness for humble ingredients such as Bigorre pork, woodcock, hare, boar and pigeon – and, surprisingly, his flagship restaurant is a rather relaxed affair (at least compared to some). The menus stretch between four and seven courses, and include a 'chariot of cheese' that defies belief.

Abbaye de Fontfroide ABBEY

(☑ 04 68 45 11 08; www.fontfroide.com; abbey, garden & museum adult/child €18.50/6; ☺10am-5pm) Founded by the Cistercian monks in 1093, Fontfroide Abbey became one of southern France's most powerful ecclesiastical centres during the Middle Ages. It was heavily damaged during the Revolution, but was purchased in 1908 by the French painter Gustave Fayet and his wife Madeleine, who restored much of the building with the help of their artistic friends. Highlights include the tranquil chapter hall, the refectory and the monks' dormitory, as well as a rose garden added during the 18th century.

Fontfroide also produces its own wine under the Corbières Appellation d'Origine Contrôlée (AOC), which you can sample in the on-site wine shop or, better still, in the attractive restaurant, **La Table de Fontfroide** (☑ 04 68 41 02 26; latable@fontfroide.com; menus €18.50-38.50; ☺lunch daily year-round, dinner Wed-Sat Jul-Aug).

Carcassonne

POP 49,100

Perched on a rocky hilltop and bristling with zigzag battlements, stout walls and spiky turrets, from afar the fortified city of Carcassonne looks like something out of a children's storybook. It's most people's perfect idea of a medieval castle, and it's undoubtedly an impressive sight – not to mention one of the Languedoc's biggest tourist draws.

Sadly, the inside of La Cité, as the old walled town is now known, doesn't quite live up to the fairy-tale façade. With over four million visitors every year, it feels depressingly devoid of any magic and mystery in summer, and the plethora of tacky souvenir shops and cheap cafes does little to contribute to the mystical atmosphere.

Time your visit for late in the day (or better still, for spring and autumn) and the old town regains its medieval charm.

◉ Sights

La Cité WALLED CITY

(☺ Porte Narbonnaise 9am-7pm Jul & Aug, to 5pm Sep-Jun) Carcassonne's rampart-ringed fortress is one of the Languedoc's most recognisable landmarks. Built on a steep spur of rock, it's been used as a defensive stronghold for nigh on 2000 years. The fortified town is encircled by two sets of battlements and 52 stone towers, topped by distinctive 'witch's hat' roofs (added by the architect Viollet-le-Duc during 19th-century restorations). The main gateway of **Porte Narbonnaise** (Map p740) leads into the citadel's interior, a maze of cobbled lanes and courtyards, now mostly lined by shops and restaurants.

The hill on which La Cité stands has been fortified many times across the centuries – by Gauls, Romans, Visigoths, Moors, Franks and Cathars, to name a few. Following the annexation of Roussillon in 1659, the castle's usefulness as a frontier fortress declined and it slowly crumbled into disrepair, but it was saved from destruction by Viollet-le-Duc, who left his mark on many of France's medieval landmarks, including Notre Dame in Paris and Vézelay in Burgundy.

The castle is laid out in a concentric design, with the double wall and defensive towers designed to resist attack from siege engines. A drawbridge can still be seen in the main gate of **Porte Narbonnaise**, which would have been raised during times of trouble. The castle's second gate, **Porte Aude**, was partially destroyed in 1816, and no longer has its drawbridge.

In between the walls, an interior space known as **Les Lices** runs for just over 1km around the castle. Though designed as a defensive space to delay would-be attackers, during the medieval era the city's poorest residents would have built a shanty-town of houses and workshops here, which were cleared out during Viollet-le-Duc's restorations. It's now the best place to escape the tourist crush and properly appreciate the castle's martial architecture.

If you want to actually walk on the ramparts, you have to pay a fee to enter the **Château Comtal** (Map p740; adult/child €8.50/free; ⊙10am-6.30pm Apr-Sep), a keep built for the Viscounts of Carcassonne during the 12th century. Admission includes access to the keep's rooms and a section of the battlements, with fabulous views over the surrounding countryside and the distant Pyrenees. Guided tours in several languages are available in summer.

Before you leave, don't overlook the lovely **Basilique St-Nazaire** (Map p740; ⊙9-11.45am & 1.45-5pm) next to place du Château, notable for its Gothic transept and vivid rose windows. Often, traditional plain chant can be heard inside.

The tourist office runs regular 1¼-hour guided **walking tours** (adult/child €6/5) of the old city in English, French and Spanish, as well as atmospheric after-dark tours.

---

❶ GUIDED TOURS OF LA CITÉ

The Carcassonne tourist office runs regular 1¼-hour guided **walking tours** (adult/child €6/5) of the old city in English, French and Spanish, but the best idea is to take one of the atmospheric **night-time tours** (€8/6.50), when the streets are blissfully free of crowds and you can really soak up the castle's medieval character.

Pont-Vieux   BRIDGE

Though it's only one of several bridges spanning the River Aude, the Pont-Vieux is by far the oldest and prettiest. It was built during the 14th century to provide a quick link between Carcassonne's lower and upper towns, and rebuilt in the 19th century. It's one of the few surviving medieval bridges in France, prized for its graceful arches and compact dimensions, and is only open to pedestrians.

Bastide St-Louis   OLD TOWN

Beneath Carcassonne's fortified castle, on the left bank of the River Aude, is the city's second half, Ville Basse. It's a mostly modern town that conceals a medieval heart: the Bastide St-Louis, which was built during the 13th century, using the characteristic grid of streets set around a central square, place Carnot. The lower town was later redeveloped during the 18th and 19th centuries, and is home to several impressive *hôtels particuliers* and religious buildings, as well as Carcassonne's marvellous covered market (p741), built in 1768.

🏃 Activities

Down in the Ville Basse, several companies offer cruises along the Canal du Midi, which provide a beautiful way to appreciate Carcassonne's architecture from afar surrounded by gorgeous countryside.

The main operators are Carcassonne Croisières and Le Cocagne. Standard cruises last around 1¼ hours, but there are longer trips available. All trips leave from the Port de Plaisance in the Ville Basse.

Carcassonne Croisières   BOAT TOUR
(📱04 68 71 61 26; www.carcassonne-croisiere.com; Port de Plaisance; 1¼hr cruise adult/child €8.50/6.50; ⊙10.30am & 2pm Jul & Aug, 10.30am & 2.30pm Apr-Jun & Sep-Oct)

Le Cocagne   BOAT TOUR
(📱06 50 40 78 50; www.bateau-cocagne-canal-carcassonne.fr; Port de Plaisance; 1¼hr cruise adult/child €8/6; ⊙2pm & 6pm daily Jul & Aug, 2pm & 6pm Wed-Mon Apr-Sep & Oct)

Génération VTT   CYCLING
(Map p738; 📱06 09 59 30 85; www.carcassonne.generation-vtt.com; Port de Plaisance; bike hire per 2hr €10-12, per day €18-22; ⊙9.30am-1.30pm & 2.30-6.30pm Apr-Oct) Right beside the Canal du Midi, Génération VTT hires out bikes and runs excellent guided cycling tours exploring local food, architecture, culture and gastronomy.

Carcassonne (Ville Basse)

🎉 Festivals & Events

Embrasement de la Cité   BASTILLE DAY
(Setting La Cité Ablaze) On 14 July Carcassonne celebrates Bastille Day with stunning fireworks.

Festival de Carcassonne   CULTURAL FESTIVAL
(www.festivaldecarcassonne.fr) Three weeks of music, dance and theatre in July.

🛏 Sleeping

Sleeping inside the old city might seem romantic, but you might think twice once you've lugged your luggage through the alleyways. Staying outside the walled city is more practical (and considerably cheaper).

Auberge de Jeunesse   HOSTEL €
(Map p740; ☑ 04 68 25 23 16; carcassonne@fuaj.org; rue Vicomte Trencavel, La Cité; dm incl breakfast from €22.50; ⊙ closed Dec; @🛜) This HI hostel is smack-bang in the centre of La Cité – great for atmosphere, not great if you're arriving at the train station 1½ miles away. Facilities include four to six-bed dorms, a spacious kitchen, an outside terrace and bike rental. It's very popular, so book well ahead.

Hôtel Astoria   HOTEL €
(Map p738; ☑ 04 68 25 31 38; www.astoria carcassonne.com; 18 rue Tourtel; d €47-72, f €77-106; ✳🛜) It's not going to win any style awards, but this budget hotel is great value for Carcassonne. Rooms are small and bathrooms are basic, but the bright primary colours liven things up, and the private garage (€10 per night) is a bonus.

La Maison Vieille   B&B €€
(☑ 04 68 25 77 24; www.la-maison-vieille.com; 8 rue Trivalle; d €85-95; 🛜) As charming a B&B as you'll find in Carcassonne. In an old mansion, the rooms are supremely tasteful: Barbecane in blues, Cité with exposed brick, Prince Noir with an in-room bath, Dame Carcas with floaty fabrics and vintage luggage. There's a walled courtyard for breakfast, and the loca-

Carcassonne (Ville Basse)

◎ Sights
1 Bastide St-Louis......................................B3
2 Pont-Vieux D4

✪ Activities, Courses & Tours
3 Génération VTT B1

🛌 Sleeping
4 Hôtel Astoria... C1

✗ Eating
5 Chez Fred...B2
6 Covered Market B3
7 L'Artichaut B3

tion is ideal for Villes Haute and Basse. Rue Trivalle lies just east of the Pont Vieux.

L'Orangerie B&B €€
(📞04 68 77 96 84; www.bedandbreakfast-carcassonne.com; 41 av des Platanes, Montlegun; d €110-120; 🕸🐾) Well removed from the tourist bustle, 2.5km east of La Cité in the suburb of Montlegun, this fine five-roomer offers a lot of elegance for your euro. It's in an 18th-century *maison du maître* (master's house), with five huge rooms, all with heritage furniture, his-and-hers sinks and wood floors, plus a gorgeous stained-glass conservatory and garden pool.

Hôtel Montmorency HOTEL €€
(📞04 68 11 96 70; www.hotelmontmorency.com; 2 rue Camille St-Saëns; r €95-195; 🐾) Owned by the same people as the Hôtel du Château, this hotel offers a similar location but at cheaper rates. The rooms come in two styles: Contemporary (sleek surfaces, modern bathrooms, neutral colours) or Country (floral wallpapers, traditional furniture), and have use of its sister hotel's facilities including heated pool and spa.

Bloc G B&B €€
(📞04 68 47 58 20; www.bloc-g.com; 112 rue Barbacane; d incl breakfast €100-120; 🐾) In stark contrast to the rest of medieval-themed Carcassonne, this restaurant-with-rooms offers 'urban bedrooms' whose stripped-back style would look right at home in the pages of *Wallpaper*. If you're a fan of metropolitan minimalism, you'll feel right at home among the bare white walls, futon-style-beds and industrial fixtures (note that none have TVs). It's literally opposite the eastern end of the Pont Vieux. There's parking right across the street.

★**Château de Palaja** HOTEL €€€
(📞06 63 69 88 32; www.chateau-palaja.fr; 7 rue Barri del Castel; d €120-190, f €140-210; 🕸🐾🏊) You don't get rampart views at this hotel 6km south of Carcassonne, but you do get serious luxury. Its six rooms and six suites would look more at home in a Parisian boutique hotel than a 1780 Languedoc château: slate tiles, neutral colours and distressed furniture set the designer tone, matched by the minimalist pool and Swedish sauna.

Hôtel du Château HOTEL €€€
(Map p740; 📞04 68 11 38 38; www.hotelduchateau.net; 2 rue Camille St-Saëns; d €175-255; 🕸🐾🏊) You get the best of both worlds at this flashy hotel: knockout night-time views of La Cité's ramparts, coupled with the convenience of staying outside the walled city. The 16 rooms are snazzily finished with wood, exposed stone and boutique-style furnishings, and you can admire wonderful castle views from the heated pool and Jacuzzi.

Hôtel Le Donjon HOTEL €€€
(Map p740; 📞04 68 11 23 00; www.hotel-donjon.fr; 2 rue du Comte Roger, La Cité; d €180-275, f €275-375; 🕸@🐾) If you're dead-set on staying inside the citadel, then this one-time orphanage (now Best Western–owned) is the most reliable choice. Comfy rooms overlook either its shady garden or the ramparts, and there's extra space in its sister building, Les Remparts, which has a more modern, city-hotel feel.

✗ Eating

Restaurants in La Cité tend towards the touristy (and pricey); you'll find more authentic fare at better value in the Ville Basse.

In most restaurants, you'll see *cassoulet* on the menu – a rich stew of vegetables, white beans and meat (usually pork sausages, duck and sometimes goose or lamb), which is said to have been invented in the nearby village of Castelnaudry. It can be quite greasy and fatty, so be choosy about where you try it.

✗ La Cité

La Marquière GASCON CUISINE €€
(📞04 68 71 52 00; www.lamarquiere.com; 13 rue St-Jean; 2-/3-course menu €30/38; ⏰noon-2.30pm & 7-10.30pm Fri-Tue) The pick of the places in the old city, a family-run bistro that serves classy, beautifully presented French cuisine in an old shuttered *auberge* (country inn), complete with beams and original hearth. It's heavy on regional dishes such as meaty *cassoulet*, duck

Carcassonne (La Cité)

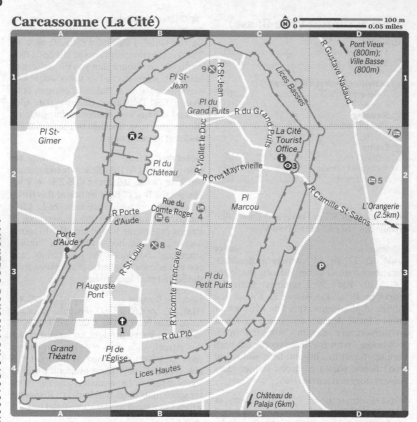

breast and fat fillets of Charolais beef. Ask for a table in the courtyard if it's sunny.

Au Comte Roger　　　MODERN FRENCH €€
(Map p740; ☑ 04 68 11 93 40; www.comteroger.com; 14 rue St-Louis; menus lunch €21-29, dinner €40; ☺ noon-1.30pm & 7-9.30pm Tue-Sat) This sleek restaurant looks fancy, but don't expect fireworks: it offers decent regional food, but the citadel location bumps up the prices considerably. There's a choice of where to dine: a smart dining room with starched white tablecloths and cool grey furniture, or a pergola-covered patio beside an old well.

✖ Ville Basse

Bloc G　　　BISTRO €€
(☑ 04 68 47 58 20; www.bloc-g.com; 112 rue Barbacane; 3-course lunch €15, dinner mains €15-25; ☺ noon-2.30pm Tue-Sat, 7-10.30pm Wed-Sat) This modern diner offers far better food than most places in the citadel, for half the price.

Its modern style is matched with modern food: white walls, white chairs, white tables, with a short menu of salads and *tartes salées* for lunch, and creative versions of southwest classics for supper. Great local wines, too.

L'Artichaut　　　BISTRO
(Map p738; ☑ 04 68 26 56 85; 14 place Carnot; mains €12-16; ☺ noon-2pm & 6-10pm) This lively local hang-out is full of local office workers at lunchtime, so you know you're in good hands. It's good for no-fuss bistro standards, such as roast Camembert, classic *steak-frites* and tapas platters, and the location on place Carnot is a winner.

Chez Fred　　　BISTRO €€
(Map p738; ☑ 04 68 72 02 23; www.chez-fred.fr; 31 bd Omer Sarraut; menus lunch €15, dinner €20-40; ☺ noon-1.45pm Tue-Fri, 7-9.45pm daily) Rich, robust Mediterranean dishes are what to expect at Fred's Place, a relaxed bistro set around a courtyard accessed via antique gates. Tuck

Carcassonne (La Cité)

◎ Sights
1 Basilique St-Nazaire	B4
2 Château Comtal	B2
3 Porte Narbonnaise	C2

🛏 Sleeping
4 Auberge de Jeunesse	B2
5 Hôtel du Château	D2
6 Hôtel Le Donjon	B2
7 Hôtel Montmorency	D2

🍴 Eating
8 Au Comte Roger	B3
9 La Marquière	C1

into roast chicken, grilled lamb, beef fillet, infused with thyme, rosemary, oregano and basil, or if you're really hungry, plump for the 'Parillade de Fred', a sharing platter of market-fresh fish, or indeed Fred's excellent *cassoulet*.

Self-catering

Covered Market   FOOD MARKET
(Map p738; rue Aimé Ramond, Ville Basse; ⊘ Mon-Sat) Carcassonne's covered market is in the Ville Basse, which also hosts an open-air market on place Carnot on Tuesday, Thursday and Saturday.

ℹ Information

La Cité Tourist Office (Porte Narbonnaise; ⊘ 9-6pm daily Apr-Sep, 9-6pm Sat & Sun Oct-Mar)
Ville Basse Tourist Office (☑ 04 68 10 24 30; www.tourisme-carcassonne.fr; 28 rue de Verdun; ⊘ 9am-7pm daily Jul & Aug, shorter hours rest of year)

ℹ Getting There & Away

AIR
Carcassonne Airport (☑ 04 68 71 96 46; www. aeroport-carcassonne.com) Ryanair is currently the only airline using Carcassonne's airport, 5.5km from town. It serves several UK cities, including London Stansted, plus Cork, Dublin, Brussels and Porto.

TRAIN
Carcassonne is on the main line from Toulouse. Buses are geared around school timetables, so it's much easier and quicker to catch a train to pretty much anywhere. Destinations include:
Montpellier €22.50, 1½ hours
Narbonne €10, 30 minutes
Perpignan €17.50, 1½ hours; change in Narbonne
Toulouse €14, 50 minutes

ℹ Getting Around

TO/FROM THE AIRPORT
The Navette Aéroport shuttle runs to and from the airport (€5, 25 minutes), leaving the train station about two hours before each Ryanair departure.

BUS
In July and August there's a free shuttle bus between the Ville Basse and the old city every 10 minutes. At other times of year, bus 4 runs roughly every 45 minutes from the train station to La Cité's main entrance at Porte Narbonaise.

CAR & MOTORCYCLE
There are several huge car parks around the edge of La Cité (€5 for up to six hours), or free parking at Parking du Dôme in the Basse Ville.

HAUT-LANGUEDOC

Haut-Languedoc is a world away from the towns, vineyards and beaches of the broad coastal plain. It's much more sparsely populated, and much of the area is now taken up by the Parc National des Cévennes, a land of craggy gorges, windswept plateaux and dense forest, ideal for those who love being out in the open air.

Parc National des Cévennes

Drier and hotter than the Auvergne to the north, the hills and gorges of the Cévennes have more in common with the climate of the Mediterranean coast than central France. Dotted with isolated hamlets and cut through by rivers and ravines, this vast 910 sq km expanse of protected landscape was created in 1970, in an attempt to bring ecological stability to an area that had been heavily exploited for agriculture, logging, cattle farming and mining.

Since the formation of the national park, the Cévennes has become something of a figurehead for French conservation: it's famous for its biodiversity, with some 2300 plant species and 2410 animal species so far recorded. Many animals that were previously extinct have been reintroduced, either by conservationists or by natural migration – including vultures, beavers, otters, roe deer and golden eagles. It's also the only national park in France that's largely covered by forest, mostly beech, oak and sweet chestnut. In recognition of its precious natural assets, it's been a

THE CHEMIN DE STEVENSON (GR70)

Famously, the writer Robert Louis Stevenson trekked across the Cévennes in 1878 with his donkey Modestine, a journey recounted in his classic travelogue, *Travels with a Donkey in the Cévennes*.

His route now provides the backbone of the GR70 long-distance trail, which runs for 252km from Le Puy-en-Velay to Alès (slightly longer than Stevenson's original route). It's the Cévennes' most famous walk, and one of the best long-distance routes in France, travelling from the forests of the Cévennes across the Mont Lozère massif into the farmland and valleys of Gévaudan and Velay.

The useful **Chemin Stevenson** (www.chemin-stevenson.org) and **GR70 Stevenson** (www.gr70-stevenson.com) websites provide planning information. Free pamphlets and trail maps are widely available once you arrive, or you can rely on the excellent *The Robert Louis Stevenson Trail* guidebook, written by Alan Castle and published by Cicerone.

You don't even need a donkey to carry your baggage these days, as several local companies provide luggage transfer services:

La Malle Postale (☑ main office 04 71 04 21 79, mobile 06 67 79 38 16; www.lamallepostale. com; Cussac sur Loire)

Stevenson Bagages (Taxi Genestier; ☑ mobile 06 07 29 01 23, office 04 66 47 04 66; www. stevenson-bagages.com; Chaudeyrac)

Unesco Biosphere Reserve since 1985, and a World Heritage Site since 2011.

Unsurprisingly, the park provides a wealth of opportunity for outdoor activities. In winter there's cross-country skiing on Mont Aigoual and Mont Lozère, while donkey treks are popular in the park in warmer months. The rest of the park is criss-crossed by over 600km of trails, including 200km of mountain-biking trails and a dozen GR (Grandes Randonnées; hiking) footpaths – most notably, the GR70.

ℹ Information

The main **Parc National des Cévennes** (www. cevennes-parcnational.fr) website provides information on accommodation, activities, nature and much more.
Florac-Ispagnac Tourist Office (☑ 04 66 45 01 14; www.vacances-cevennes.com; 33 av Jean Monestier in Florac, place de l'Eglise in Ispagnac; ◷ 9am-12.30pm & 2-6.30pm Mon-Sat, plus 9am-1pm Sun Jul & Aug, shorter hours rest of year) Tourist office with branches in Florac and Ispagnac.

ℹ Getting There & Away

Public transport is very limited in the Cévennes: about the only option is the daily bus which shuttles between Alès and Ispagnac, stopping at Florac en route.

By car, the most spectacular route from the east is the Corniche des Cévennes, a ridge road that winds along the mountain crests of the Cévennes for 56km from St-Jean du Gard to Florac.

If you're approaching Florac from Mende and the north, leave the N106 at Balsièges and drive the much quieter, even prettier D31. This crosses the wild, upland Causse de Sauveterre, then descends to Ispagnac, where you turn left to rejoin the main N106.

Note that petrol stations are few and far between – there are service stations in Florac and Ste-Énimie, but prices here inevitably tend to be expensive – so it's a good idea here to fuel up before you enter the park.

Florac

POP 2000

Sitting in a forested valley 79km northwest of Alès and 38km southeast of Mende, the rural village of Florac makes the most useful base for exploring the Parc National des Cévennes and the upper reaches of the Gorges du Tarn.

It's also home to the park's main visitor centre, the Maison du Parc National des Cévennes (p746), housed inside the 17th-century Château de Florac.

🏃 Activities

Walking

Florac marks the start of numerous walks. The national park has published 20 'topoguides' covering around 275 *petites randonnées* (PR) trails, most ranging from just a few kilometres up to full-day hikes. Five Grandes Randonnées (GR) trails also cross the park, including GR 4, 6, 7, 70 and 700. The IGN Top25 map series covers most of the national park area.

One of the most popular options from Florac is the **Sentier de Gralhon** (6km, two hours), an easy walk which climbs up to the old Gralhon manor and Monteil village before looping back to Florac, but the visitor centre in Florac has lots more ideas.

Longer routes take in the nearby peaks, including **Mont Lozère** (1699m), 14km to the northeast of Florac, the highest peak in the Cévennes.

Donkey Trekking

You couldn't come to the Cévennes and not take a donkey trek – this is Robert Louis Stevenson country, after all. Several local companies can provide donkeys and pony-rides, either just for the half-day or for longer multi-day treks, staying in backcountry *gîtes*.

Gentiâne　　　　　DONKEY TREKKING
(☑ 04 66 41 04 16; www.ane-et-randonnee.fr; Castagnols; per day €50)

Les Ânes de Vieljouvès　　DONKEY TREKKING
(☑ 04 66 94 04 12; www.vieljouves-gite-cevennes.fr; St-André-de-Lancize; per day €45)

Tramontane　　　　　DONKEY TREKKING
(☑ 04 66 45 92 44; chantal.tramontane@wanadoor. fr; St-Martin-de-Lanuscule; per day €45)

Horse Riding

For longer trips in the saddle, a trusty horse is a good deal comfier than a donkey. There are plenty of local schools which cater for both novice and experienced riders.

Cavalcatore　　　　　HORSE RIDING
(☑ 04 66 44 22 21; Ispagnac; 1-/2hr ride €18, full day €65)

Ecole d'Equitation Pirouette　HORSE RIDING
(☑ 04 66 45 29 85; pirouette.ee@orange.fr; Florac; 1hr ride €15, full day €60)

Other Activities

Cévennes Évasion　　　OUTDOOR ACTIVITIES
(www.cevennes-evasion.com; 5 place Boyer, Florac) Florac's main outdoor activities company offers caving, canyoning, rock-climbing and via ferrata. It also rents mountain bikes and runs guided hiking trips.

🛏 Sleeping

Camping Chantemerle　　CAMPGROUND €
(☑ 04 66 45 19 66; www.camping-chantemerle.com; Bédouès; site for 2 people €16; ☎) Two and a half kilometres north of Florac in Bédouès, this secluded campground offers riverside pitches, a private sandy beach and an on-site grocery. Also organises outdoor activities.

Camping Le Pont du Tarn　　CAMPGROUND €
(☑ 04 66 45 18 26; www.camping-florac.com; sites €12.50-20.50; ☺Mar-Nov; ☷) A shady 5-acre campsite, 2km from Florac beside the D998, where you can swim either in the heated pool or River Tarn, which runs right by.

La Carline　　　　　HOSTEL €
(☑ 04 66 45 24 54; www.gite-florac.fr; 18 rue du Pêcher; dm €15; ☺Easter-Oct) One for the hikers and bikers: a cute little travellers' *gîte* in an 18th-century house, run by welcoming hosts Monette and Alain Lagrave. Rooms are very simple and share bathrooms, but there are lots of maps and guidebooks to browse, and Alain makes his own jams for the breakfast table.

Grand Hôtel du Parc　　　HOTEL €
(☑ 04 66 45 03 05; www.grandhotelduparc.fr; 47 av Jean Monestier; d €55-75, f €66-82; ☺mid-Mar–mid-Nov; ☎☷) Set in its own garden beside a lovely swimming pool, this large hotel occupies a former 19th-century mansion. Despite the heritage façade, rooms are bland and charmless inside, but the rates and location are hard to fault, and you can tuck into hearty Cévennes specialities in the restaurant (*menus* €22 to €32).

La Ferme de Vimbouches　　FARMSTAY €
(☑ 04 66 31 56 55; www.causses-cevennes.com/ ferme-vimbouches; St Frézal de Ventalon; d per adult €53-58, per child €38, incl all meals; ☺Mar-Nov) This rural farm makes a great place to immerse yourself in everyday life in the Cévennes. You can borrow a donkey for a day's trekking, visit the pig pen and chicken run, or help out with resident horses, rabbits and goats. The four rustic farmhouse rooms are very cosy, and all meals are provided.

From Florac, take the N106 towards Alès and, after 27km, turn left onto the D29, following signs for Vimbouches.

La Ferme de la Borie　　　FARMSTAY €
(☑ 04 66 45 10 90; www.encevennes.com; La Salle Prunet; d €38-47, tr €48-59, q €58-71, meals per adult/ child €15/12; ☺Mar-Nov) A fine farmstay, run by organic farmer Jean-Christophe Barthes, who cooks up meals using 100% home-grown produce. Depending on the time of year, you can help make traditional cheese or jams, join in with the chestnut and apple harvests, and even learn how to bake the perfect loaf. To get there, turn right onto the narrow C4, signed La Borie, about a kilometre southeast of Florac on the N106.

1. Narbonne p734 2. Carcassonne p736 3. Les Arènes p717, Nîmes 4. Pont du Gard p721

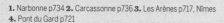

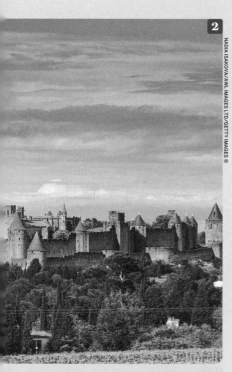

NADIA ISAKOVA/AWL IMAGES LTD/GETTY IMAGES ©

Languedoc Architecture

The Languedoc landscape is littered with spectacular structures that provide a fascinating insight into the region's past.

During the 2nd century AD, the Languedoc was part of the province of Gallia Narbonensis, a strategically important region of Roman Gaul. As its name suggests, the province's capital was **Narbonne** (p734), but the most impressive Roman ruins are in Nîmes (p716), including a wonderfully preserved **Roman temple** and 20,000-seater amphitheatre, now know as **Les Arènes**. Just outside the city, the three-tiered **Pont du Gard** (p721) aqueduct was built to transport water between Uzès and Nîmes, and ranks as one of the great achievements of Roman engineering.

Long after the Romans, the Languedoc remained a strategically important frontier. The legacy of this be seen in the region's numerous castles and fortified towns – most notably the fortress of **Carcassonne** (p736) with its distinctive 'witch's hat' turrets, and the lonely **hilltop castles** (p756) left behind by the Cathars, an ultra-devout Christian sect persecuted by Rome during the 13th-century Albigensian Crusade.

For much of the medieval era, the neighbouring province of Roussillon wasn't actually French, but Spanish (or Catalonian, to be precise). In 1231, Perpignan became capital of the Kingdom of Mallorca, and still boasts a mighty Spanish-style castle, the **Palais des Rois de Majorque** (p751), where the kings and their families would have lived. A smaller fortress, the **Château Royal** (p757), can be seen in nearby Collioure. Even today, Roussillon still shares strong ties with Catalonia, with bullfights and *férias* an important part of the festive calendar.

WORTH A TRIP

MONT AIGOUAL

About 60km south of Florac is the prominent peak of Mont Aigoual (1567m), which is topped by a lofty **observatory** (☑ 04 67 82 60 01; www.aigoual.fr; ⊘ 10am-7pm Jul-Aug, 10am-1pm & 2-6pm May-Jun & Sep), built in 1894. Inside, you can learn the science behind weather forecasting and cloud formation, but most people visit to enjoy the wraparound views of the central Cévennes. The mountain is about halfway between Florac and Le Vigan, signed off the D18.

Hôtel Les Gorges du Tarn   HOTEL €€
(☑ 04 66 45 00 63; www.hotel-gorgesdutarn.com; 48 rue du Pêcher; d €64-93; ⊘ Easter-Oct; ☎) This modern Logis de France in the the middle of Florac offers a functional, no-frills sleep: clean, plain rooms (some countrified, some contemporary), plus a decent regional restaurant (*menus* €22 to €30).

✖ Eating

La Source du Pêcher   MEDITERRANEAN €€
(☑ 04 66 45 03 01; www.lasourcedupecher.fr; 1 rue de Remuret; menus €15-38; ⊘ noon-1.30pm & 7-8.30pm) Definitely one of Florac's prettiest places to dine, with a waterside setting and a delightful outside patio. It's good for hearty country food – trout fished from local rivers, wild venison, rabbit and game birds shot in the surrounding hills – but as always, the menu tends to be meaty, so vegetarians will struggle. No reservations, so arrive early.

ℹ Information

Maison du Parc National des Cévennes (☑ 04 66 49 53 01; www.cevennes-parcnational.fr; Château de Florac; ⊘ 9am-6.30pm Jul & Aug, 9.30am-12.15pm & 1.30-5.30pm Mon-Fri Oct-Apr) This should be your first port of call for information on activities and general information on things to see and do inside the park. The free *Guide Touristique* covers countless outdoor activities, from short walks to caving and paragliding courses.

ℹ Getting There & Away

Voyages Boulet (☑ 04 66 65 19 88; www.voyages-boulet.com) Voyages Boulet runs the only regular bus service to Florac, which travels from Alès (€15.50, 65 minutes) and Ispagnac (€19, 80 minutes). There's one bus a day from mid-April to September.

Gorges du Tarn

Slashing down the flanks of Mont Lozère in a picturesque network of narrow, plunging canyons, the dramatic Gorges du Tarn wind for some 50km southwest from Ispagnac, marking the boundary between the Causse Méjean to its south and the Causse de Sauveterre to the north.

Characterised by steep cliffs slicing through sparkling blue-green water, the gorges are one of the Cévennes' most scenic sights, but the riverside road is notorious for summer traffic jams – so the best way to explore is on the water via kayak or canoe. Hire companies abound, mostly based around the villages of Ste-Énimie and La Malène.

Ste-Énimie

POP 550

Twenty-seven kilometres from Florac and 56km from Millau, teeny Ste-Énimie is the most convenient base for exploring the gorges. Clinging to the cliffside, it's a lovely village with a charming cobbled quarter, full of restored timber houses and stone cottages, as well as the 12th-century Église de Ste-Énimie and the old Halle aux Blés (Flour Market).

Most businesses and B&Bs are only open between April and October.

🛏 Sleeping

Camping Les Fayards   CAMPGROUND €
(☑ 04 66 48 57 36; www.camping-les-fayards.com; rte de Millau; site for 2 people €20-27; ⊘ Apr-Sep; ☎) Three kilometres south of Ste-Énimie, this small 57-pitch forest campground has a lovely riverside location, spread out under beech trees with plenty of space set aside for each site. Riverside pitches cost extra, or you can hire timber chalets.

Camping Couderc   CAMPGROUND €
(☑ 04 66 48 50 53; www.campingcouderc.fr; rte de Millau; site for 2 people €18-24; ⊘ Apr-Sep) Almost 2km from Ste-Énimie, this camping ground offers 130 pitches, mostly under trees, so they stay shady and cool but are packed in pretty tight. The facilities are great, with a restaurant, bar and lovely swimming pool. There's kayak hire on-site.

La Pause   B&B €
(☑ 05 65 62 63 06; www.chambres-hotes-gorgesdutarn.com; rte de Caplac, Le Rozier; s €42, d €57-60, f €78-109; ☎) At the gorges' south-

ern end, in the village of Le Rozier, this cute country B&B is lodged in a traditional stone house, with three simple rooms in pinks and yellows, plus a couple of family-sized suites. Breakfast (including home-made jams) is served on the garden terrace, and there's a super pool with views of the town of Peyreleau.

Maison de Marius B&B €€
(☏ 04 66 44 25 05; www.maisondemarius.fr; 8 rue Pontet, Quézac; r €65-100) In Quézac, near Ispagnac, this cosy place is a proper home from home, with a selection of countri-fied bedrooms all given their own femi-nine touch by owner Dany – floral fabrics, watercolours, old luggage, roll-top baths (the Pompeii Suite even has its own spa bath complete with Roman murals). There's also a lovely garden cabin for that ultra-romantic factor. Home-cooked dinner costs €25 per person.

Manoir de Montesquiou HOTEL €€
(☏ 04 66 48 51 12; www.manoir-montesquiou.com; La Malène; r €82-150; ☎) With conical turrets and walled gardens overlooking La Malène's old stone bridge, this 16th-century manor is surprisingly great value. The rooms are rath-er staid in style – half-tester beds, antique furniture – but most have views, and some are reached via the manor's spiral staircase. There's a small cottage annexe in one of the nearby houses.

The refined restaurant serves some of the area's best French food (*menus* €29 to €50) – ask about half-board deals.

★ **Château de la Caze** HOTEL €€€
(☏ 04 66 48 51 01; www.chateaudelacaze.com; La Malène; castle r €138-193, house r €200-220; ❋ ❄ ☎ ☎) A little slice of château showiness in the middle of the Tarn, complete with forti-fied towers, landscaped gardens, cobbled halls and even the odd suit of armour. Rooms are split between the main castle and the Maison de la Martine, a smaller house positioned across the gardens. Some rooms have their bathrooms inside the castle turrets.

Rich, traditional French dishes such as supreme of pigeon and beef with cep mush-rooms are served in the restaurant; ask for a terrace table in nice weather.

ℹ️ Information

Tourist Office (☏ 04 66 48 53 44; www.gorges dutarn.net; Ste-Énimie; ⏰ 9.30am-12.30pm & 2-6pm Mon-Sat) The main point of contact for the gorges.

Parc Naturel Régional des Grands Causses

The Grands Causses are actually a part of the same geological formation as the Massif Central to the north. Scorched in summer and windswept in winter, these harsh limestone plateaux hold little moisture as water filters through the limestone to form an under-ground world, ideal for cavers.

The Rivers Tarn, Jonte and Dourbie have sliced deep gorges through the 5000 sq km plateau, creating four *causses* ('plateaux' in

---

DON'T MISS

CANOEING IN THE GORGES DU TARN

Riding the River Tarn is best in high summer, when the river is usually low and the descent a lazy trip over mostly calm water. You can canoe as far as the impassable Pas de Soucy, a barrier of boulders about 9km downriver from La Malène. You'll have to arrange for your canoe to be transported beyond the barrier if you want to can carry on further.

Tariffs and trip durations depend on how far you want to travel. From Ste-Énimie, desti-nations include La Malène (€21, 12km, four hours) and Les Baumes Basses (€26, 22km, six hours). If you want a longer trip, buses can transport you upriver to start in Prades, Montbrun or Ispagnac.

There are scores of companies in Ste-Énimie and La Malène that provide canoe and kayak rental, such as **Canoë 2000** (☏ 04 66 48 57 71; www.canoe2000.fr), **Locanoë** (☏ 04 66 48 55 57; www.gorges-du-tarn.fr), **Méjean Canoë** (☏ 04 66 48 58 70; www.canoe-mejean. com) and **Le Canophile** (☏ 04 66 48 57 60; www.canoe-tarn.com). They all charge roughly the same, but it's worth ringing around to ask about seasonal offers and package prices.

If you'd rather someone else did the hard work, **Les Bateliers de la Malène** (☏ 04 66 48 51 10; www.gorgesdutarn.com; La Malène; €88 for 4 people) will punt you down an 8km stretch of the gorge from La Malène in a traditional barge, then drive you back.

the local lingo): Sauveterre, Méjean, Noir and Larzac, each slightly different in its geological make-up. One resembles a dark lunar surface, another's like a Scottish moor, while the next is gentler and more fertile. All are eerily empty, save for the occasional shepherd and his flock – making them perfect for hikers and bikers who like nothing better than to go hours without seeing another soul on the trail.

The Gorges de la Jonte, where birds of prey wheel and swoop, skim the park's eastern boundary, rivalling in their rugged splendour the neighbouring and much better known Gorges du Tarn.

◉ Sights

Causse de Sauveterre

The northernmost of the *causses* is a gentle, hilly plateau dotted with a few isolated farms. Every possible patch of fertile earth is cultivated, creating irregular, intricately patterned wheat fields.

Causse Méjean

Causse Méjean, the highest of the *causses*, is also the most barren and isolated. Defined to the north by the Gorges du Tarn and, southwards, by the Gorges de la Jonte, it looms over Florac on its eastern flank. It's a land of poor pasture enriched by fertile depressions, where streams gurgle down into the limestone through sinkholes, funnels and fissures.

This combination of water and limestone has created some spectacular underground scenery. Within the cavern of Aven Armand (www.aven-armand.com; adult/child €10.50/7.35; ⊙9.30am-6pm Jul-Aug, 10am-noon & 1.30-5pm Mar-Jun & Sep-Nov), bristles the world's greatest concentration of stalagmites, including a gallery of stone columns known as the Forêt Vierge (Virgin Forest). The cave is accessed via a funicular which drops down 75m into the gloom. Guided visits last 45 minutes.

A combination ticket (adult/child €14.60/9.50) also includes admission to the gorge at Chaos de Montpellier-le-Vieux in Causse Noir.

Causse Noir

Rising immediately east of Millau, the 'Black Causse' is best known for the Chaos de Montpellier-le-Vieux (www.montpellierlevieux. com; adult/child €6.60/4.65; ⊙9am-7pm Jul & Aug, to 5.30pm Mar-Jun & Sep-Nov), 18km northeast of Millau, overlooking the Gorges de la Dourbie. Water erosion has created more than 120 hectares of tortured limestone formations with fanciful names such as the Sphinx and

the Elephant. Three trails, lasting one to three hours, cover the site – or, if your pride can take it, you can take a trip aboard the tourist train (adult/child €4.30/3.30). If you're here outside official opening times, there's nothing to stop you wandering around.

Causse du Larzac

The Causse du Larzac is the largest of the four *causses*. An endless sweep of distant horizons and rocky steppes broken by medieval villages, it's known as the 'French Desert'. You'll stumble across venerable, fortified villages such as Ste-Eulalie de Cernon, long the capital of the Larzac region, and La Cavalerie, both built by the Knights Templar, a religious military order that distinguished itself during the Crusades.

Gorges de la Jonte

The 15km-long Gorges de la Jonte cleave east-west from Meyrueis to Le Rozier, dividing Causse Noir from Causse Méjean.

Just south of the gorge, Grotte de Dargilan (www.grotte-dargilan.com; adult/child €9.30/6; ⊙10am-6pm Jul & Aug, 10.30-5pm Apr-Jun & Sep) is known as La Grotte Rose (Pink Cave) for its rosy colouring. The most memorable moment of the one-hour, 1km tour through this vast chasm is a sudden, dazzling exit onto a ledge, with a dizzying view of the Gorges de la Jonte way below.

Bird fans might also like to make a stop at the Belvédère des Vautours (Vulture Viewing Point; ☑05 65 62 69 69; www.vautours-lozere.com; adult/child €6.70/3; ⊙9.30am-7pm daily Jul-Aug, closed Mon May, Jun & Sep), just west of Le Truel on the D996, where a population of reintroduced vultures is now thriving on the sheer limestone cliffs. You can watch the birds gliding through the *cause* from the viewing point, which also has a live video feed from the nesting sites.

❶ Information

Parc Naturel Régional des Grands Causses Office (☑05 65 61 35 50; www.parc-grands-causses.fr; 71 bd de l'Ayrolle, Millau; ⊙9am-noon & 2-5pm Mon-Fri)

Mende

POP 13,200

On the northern edge of the Cévennes, the quiet town of Mende is the capital of Lozère, France's least populous département. It's a sleepy, rural town with a lovely medieval quarter that would once have been surrounded by defensive walls.

A few half-hidden towers are all that remains of the ramparts, but the town still boasts some interesting medieval buildings and an improbably large church, the **Cathédrale Notre Dame**, built in 1368 as the official seat of Mende's bishop. A busy farmers market takes over place Urbain V in front of the cathedral on Saturday mornings.

During WWII, Mende (like much of Lozère) was a hotbed of the French Resistance, and local resistance fighters scored several important victories against the Vichy regime – mainly blowing up railways and disrupting transport links during the run-up to D-Day. Panels around town commemorate several key fighters, including former Mende mayor Henri Bourrillon, the chief of the Lozère Resistance, who was captured in 1944 and died in a Nazi concentration camp.

🛏️ Sleeping & Eating

⭐ **La Grange d'Emilie**   B&B €€
(📞 04 66 47 30 82; www.chambrehote-emilie.com; Fontans; s €95-115, d €105-125; 🅟) Thirty kilometres north of Mende, this old *lozèrois* farm is now a seriously luxurious pamper-pad, with five surprisingly modern rooms that still retain rustic character. It's old-meets-new: wood, stone and beams in the rooms, offset by rendered surfaces, reclaimed furniture and freestanding baths (including one made from a cow's watering trough). Table d'hôtes dinner is available for €35 per person.

Hôtel de France   HOTEL €€
(📞 04 66 65 00 04; www.hoteldefrance-mende.com; 9 bd Lucien Arnault; d €90-103; 🅟 ❄️ @) Clad in shutters and slate, this renovated coaching inn is the best place to stay in Mende town, with a fine assortment of 27 rooms, all huge and some with sweeping views over the garden and valley (two have their own roof terrace). It's modern, despite the heritage exterior, and the restaurant (*menus* €29 to €51) is a fine-dining treat. Half-board is excellent value.

Le Mazel   GASCON CUISINE €€
(📞 04 66 65 05 33; 25 rue du Collège; 3-course lunch menu €16.50, mains €14-22; ⊙ noon-1.30pm & 7-9pm) Fine country cooking with a refreshing lack of frills is what to expect from this friendly restaurant in Mende, popular with the locals for Sunday lunch. Tuck into a hearty stew of duck and tarbais beans, or some locally-smoked trout with lentils, washed down with a good choice of Languedoc wines by the glass. You can choose to eat in the terracotta-tiled conservatory or the main dining room.

ℹ️ Information

Tourist Office (📞 04 66 94 00 23; www.ot-mende.fr; place du Foirail; ⊙ 9am-7pm Mon-Sat, 10am-5pm Sun Jul & Aug, 9am-noon & 2-6pm Mon-Sat Sep-Jun; 🅟)

DON'T MISS

VIADUC DE MILLAU

France has its share of iconic structures – Mont St-Michel, the Eiffel Tower, the Château de Versailles – but in centuries to come, the majestic **Viaduc de Millau** (www.leviaducde millau.com; Jul & Aug €9.10, Sep-Jun €7.30) might well stand alongside them in terms of architectural importance.

This gravity-defying toll bridge hovers 343m above the Tarn valley, making it one of the world's highest road bridges. Designed by the British architect Sir Norman Foster, it's a work of imagination as much as engineering: seven slender pylons support 2.5km of the A75 motorway, and despite its heavyweight construction (127,000 cu metres of concrete, 19,000 tonnes of steel, 5000 tonnes of cable), the bridge still somehow manages to look as delicate as a gossamer thread.

While most people speed across the bridge, it's worth taking the time to explore a little more closely. The **Viaduc Espace** (📞 05 65 61 61 54; ⊙ 10am-7pm Apr-Oct, to 5pm Nov-Mar), at ground level beneath the viaduct on the D992, explores the story of the bridge's construction and offers 45-minute **guided visits** (in English on request; per adult/child €6/3.50) around its exhibition garden under the bridge.

For a great way to appreciate the bridge's astonishing dimensions, **Bateliers du Viaduc** (📞 05 65 60 17 91; www.bateliersduviaduc.com; Creissels; adult €24, children €9.50-16.50; ⊙ every 45min from 9.45am year-round) runs 1½-hour boat trips along the Tarn from the nearby village of Creissels.

WORTH A TRIP

MICROPOLIS

It is a truth universally acknowledged that kids love creepy-crawlies – and they can indulge their insectivorous interests at the excellent **Micropolis** (La Cité des Insectes; ☑ 05 65 58 50 50; www.micropolis-aveyron.com; adult/child Jul & Aug €13/8.90, rest of year €11.70/7.90; ☉ 10am-7pm Jul & Aug, to 6pm Apr-Jun, closed Mon & Tue Feb, Mar & Sep-Nov), the 'Insect City', 19km northwest of Millau. This high-tech centre brings the world of insects impressively to life: you can peer inside ant colonies, see the inner workings of beehives and explore the wonderful butterfly pavilion. Afterwards there's an insect-themed adventure park where they can burn off steam while you kick back in the cafe – thankfully, there was no sign of any insect tastings on offer.

🛈 Getting There & Away

BUS

Buses leave from the train station, most passing by place du Foirail, beside the tourist office. Timetables change during school holidays.

Florac Line 8, 55 minutes, one bus on Friday

Le Puy-en-Velay Line 3, two hours, two buses on weekdays

Millau Line 13, one hour, one bus daily

Ste-Énimie Line 11, 45 minutes, one bus on Friday

TRAIN

The train station is 1km north of town across the River Lot.

Alès €17, 2½ hours, four daily

Le Puy en Velay €26, 1¾ hours, one daily

Around Mende

◉ Sights

Parc du Gévaudan NATURE PARK
(www.loupsdugevaudan.com; Ste-Lucie; adult/child €7.80/4.70; ☉ 10am-7pm Jul & Aug, shorter hours rest of year) Wolves once prowled freely through the Lozère forests but today you'll see them only in this sanctuary, in Ste-Lucie, 7km north of Marvejols. The park sustains around 100 Mongolian, Canadian, Siberian and Polish wolves living in semi-freedom.

Réserve de Bisons d'Europe NATURE PARK
(☑ 04 66 31 40 40; www.bisoneurope.com; ☉ 10am-5pm, closed mid-Nov–mid-Dec) Near the small village of Ste-Eulalie-en-Margeride, 45km north of Mende, this nature reserve contains over 40 free-roaming bison. Visits to the reserve are either by horse-drawn carriage (per adult/child €13.50/7) or, in winter, by sledge (€16/8.50).

From mid-June to September, you can follow a self-guided 1km walking path (per adult/child €6/4) around the periphery.

Roquefort

Twenty-five kilometres southwest of Millau, the village of Roquefort is synonymous with its famous blue cheese, produced from ewe's milk in caves around the village. Marbled with blue-green veins caused by microscopic mushrooms known as *penicillium roquefort* (which are initially grown on leavened bread), this pungent cheese is one of the region's oldest: it's been protected by royal charter since 1407, and was the first cheese in France to be granted its own Appellation d'Origine Contrôlée (AOC) in 1925.

Local legend claims the cheese was discovered by accident, when a local lad became distracted by a beautiful girl, and left a wheel of cheese behind in one of the village caves. When he returned, it was covered in mould which turned out to be surprisingly tasty. It's now France's second-most popular cheese after Comté, with an annual production of around 19,000 tonnes.

There are seven AOC-approved producers in the village, three of which offer cellar visits. The cellars of four other producers (Roquefort Carles, Le Vieux Berger, Vernières Frères and Les Fromageries Occitanes) aren't open to the public, but they all have shops where you can sample and buy cheeses.

Cheese Tasting

La Société CHEESE TASTING
(☑ 05 65 58 54 38; www.roquefort-societe.com; adult/child €5/3; ☉ 9.30am-noon & 1-5pm Apr-Nov, shorter hours in winter) Established in 1842, this is the largest producer, churning out 70% of the world's supply. One-hour tours of the caves include sampling of the company's three main varieties.

Le Papillon CHEESE TASTING
(☑ 05 65 58 50 08; www.roquefort-papillon. com; ☉ 10am-11.15am & 2-4.15pm) Offers free

45-minute tours (in French) of its pungent caves, followed by the obligatory tasting.

Gabriel Coulet   CHEESE TASTING
(☑ 05 65 59 24 27; www.gabriel-coulet.fr; ⊙ 9.30am-noon & 1.30-5pm) You're free to explore the penicillin-streaked caves below the shop, then head upstairs for some tasting.

ROUSSILLON

There's a distinctly Spanish flavour about the sun-baked region of Roussillon, with its dusty scrubland, crimson towns and scorching summer temperatures. Sometimes known as French Catalonia, it's really two regions rolled into one: along the coast, busy beach towns and coastal villages sprawl along the Mediterranean, while inland, abandoned abbeys and crumbling Cathar strongholds loom among the fragrant maquis. It's also the land of the Tramontane, a violent wind that howls down from the Pyrenees, cutting to the bone in winter and in summer strong enough to overturn a caravan.

Roussillon's only city is Perpignan, capital of the Pyrénées-Orientales département, and a useful base for exploring the region.

History

Roussillon's history is inextricably linked with Spain. After flourishing as the capital of the kingdom of Mallorca, it fell under Aragonese rule for much of the late Middle Ages.

In 1640 the Catalans on both sides of the Pyrenees revolted against the rule of distant Madrid. Peace came in 1659 with the Treaty of the Pyrenees, defining the border between Spain and France once and for all, and ceding Roussillon (until then the northern section of Catalonia) to the French, much to the indignation of the locals.

Although it's no longer officially part of Catalonia, Roussillon retains much of its Catalan identity. The *sardane* folk dance is still performed, and the Catalan language, closely related to Provençal, is still commonly spoken.

ⓘ Getting Around

Year-round you can travel the length and breadth of Roussillon by bus for no more than €1 per journey. Pick up a leaflet from any tourist office or contact the **Conseil Général Pyrénées-Orientales** (www.cg66.fr/252-les-bus-departementaux.htm; 30 rue Pierre Bretonneau, Perpignan) for route details.

Perpignan
POP 118,200

Languishing in the foothills of the Pyrenees, in many way Perpignan feels as much Spanish as French. Sprawling suburbs radiate out from the tight knot of the old town, with its warren of alleys and shabby tenements coloured in shades of lemon, peach and tangerine. It feels a little rough around the edges compared to Montpellier or Nîmes, but it has a distinctly multicultural character – Spanish and North African accents are just as common here as French.

Historically, Perpignan (Perpinyà in Catalan) was capital of the kingdom of Mallorca, a Mediterranean power that stretched northwards as far as Montpellier and included all the Balearic Islands; the Mallorcan kings' palace still stands guard at the southern end of the old town. It's still the third-largest 'Catalan' city after Barcelona and Lleida (Lérida) in Spain.

⦿ Sights

Perpignan's old town is surprisingly small, roughly contained within the main ring roads of bd des Pyrénées in the west, bd Thomas Wilson in the north, bd Anatole France in the east, and bd Henri Poincaré in the south.

Cars are banned in the town centre, so if you're driving you'll have to park in one of the large municipal car parks on the edges of the old town.

★ Palais des Rois de Majorque   PALACE
(☑ 04 68 34 48 29; rue des Archers; adult/child €4/2; ⊙ 10am-6pm Jun-Sep, 9am-5pm Oct-May) Perpignan's most dominant monument, the Palace of the Kings of Mallorca, sprawls over a huge area to the south of the old town. Built in 1276, the castle was later refortified with massive red-brick walls by the medieval era's foremost military architect, Vauban. These days the citadel is sparsely furnished, but its great battlements and strategic defences still give a sense of the Mallorcan kings' might. You enter from rue des Archers. Built in a mix of late Romanesque and Gothic style, the castle is arranged around three courtyards, with a system of ramps, pinch-points and ramparts providing a formidable defensive layout. The central courtyard, with its twin arcaded tiers, clearly shows the influence of Spanish architecture, and the complex would once have enclosed extensive fig and olive groves, lost once Vauban's formidable citadel walls enclosed the palace.

Perpignan

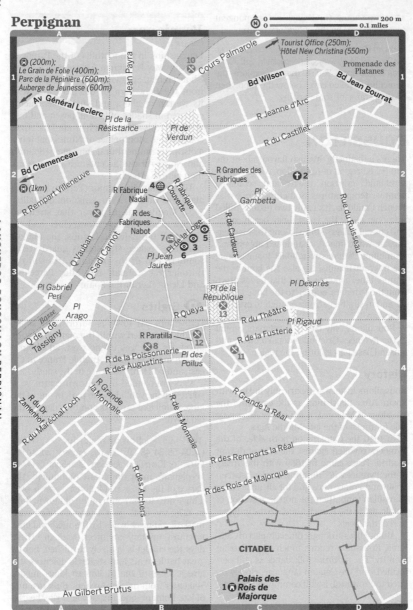

Guided tours also take in the chapels and Great Hall, but the highlight is the view from the ramparts, which stretches over Perpignan's terracotta roofs all the way to the coast.

Le Castillet & Casa Païral　FOLK MUSEUM
(place de Verdun; adult/child €4/free; ⊙10am-6.30pm Tue-Sun) Like many medieval towns, Perpignan was once encircled by defensive walls. Today all that remains is the red-brick town gate of **Le Castillet**, at the northern end of the old town.

Perpignan

Inside the gateway is the **Casa Païral**, a modest folklore museum which contains various bits and pieces of Catalan ephemera – from traditional bonnets and lace mantillas to an entire 17th-century kitchen.

Place de la Loge   SQUARE
Just south of Le Castillet, the place de la Loge has three fine stone structures. Fourteenth-century **Le Loge de Mer**, rebuilt during the Renaissance, was once Perpignan's stock exchange, then maritime tribunal. Between it and the **Palais de la Députation** (place de la Loge), formerly seat of the local parliament, is the **Hôtel de Ville** (place de la Loge) with its typically Roussillon red-brick and pebble façade.

Cathédrale St-Jean   CATHEDRAL
(place Gambetta; ◷7.30am-6pm) Perpignan's old town has several intriguing churches, but the most impressive is the Cathédrale St-Jean, begun in 1324 and not completed until 1509. Topped by a typically Provençal wrought-iron bell cage, the cathedral has a flat façade of red brick and smooth, zigzagging river stones.

Inside, the fine carving and ornate altarpiece are characteristically Catalan, and the simple statue of the Virgin and child in the north aisle is a venerated relic for Perpignan believers.

✴ Festivals & Events

As befits a town so close to the Spanish border, Perpignan is strong on fiestas.

Jeudis de Perpignan   CARNIVAL
The streets come alive with stalls, theatre and music of all genres. Thursday evenings, mid-July to mid-August.

Fête de la Sant Joan   RELIGIOUS FESTIVAL
A 'sacred' flame is brought down from Mont Canigou. Held around 23 June.

Fête du Vin   WINE FESTIVAL
To mark this wine festival, a barrel of the year's new production is ceremonially borne to Cathédrale St-Jean to be blessed. During the third weekend in October.

🛏 Sleeping

Perpignan is a bit short on good hotels, but there are a couple of pleasant options in the old town, and plenty of chains to choose from (Ibis, Confort, Kyriad, Novotel, Best Western). If you're driving, you'll find it easier to base yourself around the edge of town.

Auberge de Jeunesse   HOSTEL €
(☑ 04 68 34 63 32; perpignan@fuaj.org; allée Marc Pierre; dm incl breakfast €18.50; ◷Mar–mid-Nov) Built in hacienda-style, Perpignan's HI-affiliated youth hostel is just north of Parc de la Pépinière, not far from the station. It's modern and well-run; dorms are spartan but well-kept, and the kitchen is also fairly basic, but the little pebbly garden is ideal for summer night barbecues.

Hôtel de la Loge   HOTEL €
(☑ 04 68 34 41 02; www.hoteldelaloge.fr; 1 rue des Fabriques Nabot; s/d from €58/65; ❄🤗) The best option in the old town is this place, steps from the Castillet tower. Once a merchant's house, it now feels like an upmarket antique shop: its staircase and hallways are filled with Catalan furniture and quirky objets d'art. Rooms are furnished in old-fashioned style, and can feel a bit musty in summer. Rooms 106 and 206 overlook place de la Loge.

Hôtel New Christina   HOTEL €€
(☑ 04 68 35 12 21; www.hotel-newchristina.com; 51 cours Lassus; r €93-105; ❄🤗📶) Exterior aesthetics aren't this hotel's strong point (we've seen prettier car parks) but this modern hotel is a decent overnight option, with clean, air-conditioned rooms in blue and beige, and a rather cool rooftop pool. The private garage is a bonus.

Villa Duflot   HOTEL €€€
(☑ 04 68 56 67 67; www.villa-duflot.com; rond point Albert Donnezan; r €160-195, ste €230-280) It's pricey, but this is the choice for boutique

sleeps in Perpignan. The building is blocky and modern, but the large rooms have a dash of art deco elegance about them, with upholstered furniture, terracotta floors and table lamps. The outside pool is surrounded by a lovely garden filled with conifers and pines, and there's an excellent gourmet restaurant (mains €25 to €30).

✗ Eating

Espi   BOULANGERIE €
(43bis quai Vauban; ⊙9am-5pm Mon-Sat) Gourmet ice creams, multi-coloured macaroons, tempting patisseries and handmade chocs are sold at this canal-side cafe-cum-boulangerie.

Le Grain de Folie   BISTRO €€
(☑04 68 51 00 50; 71 av Gen Leclerc; menus 2-/3-course lunch €14.50/18, dinner €20-36; ⊙noon-2pm daily & 7.30-9.30pm Mon-Sat) Despite the rubbish location beside a busy junction, this is one of Perpignan's best-value bistros, run with care by a husband-and-wife team. It's classic in style, strong on southern flavours: tuck into faux-fillet with girolle mushrooms, or try sea-bass with roasted artichoke, or just settle for the no-choice set *menu*. Any which way, you're in very safe hands.

Al Très   MEDITERRANEAN €€
(☑04 68 34 88 39; 3 rue de la Poissonnerie; 3-course menus lunch €20, dinner €26; ⊙noon-2pm & 7-11pm Tue-Sat) Fiery southern cooking in a backstreet bistro, so expect plenty of tomatoes, olives, courgettes, fennel and liberal use of cayenne pepper. Bustling waiters and the small dining room means it can feel cramped when full, but there are extra tables out in the alley. Try the lobster with roasted veg, or fried squid with artichoke and pata negra ham.

Le France   MEDITERRANEAN €€
(☑04 68 51 61 71; place de la Loge; pizzas €10-15, mains €14-25; ⊙10am-11.30pm) On the fringes of the old town, in a building once used as Perpignan's stock exchange, this buzzy bistro is ideal for a quick, no-fuss dinner. Wood-fired pizzas and fresh, southern staples are the mainstays.

Les Frères Mossés   TRADITIONAL FRENCH €€
(☑04 68 80 63 31; 14 rue de la Fusterie; mains €15-20; ⊙noon-2pm & 8-11pm Tue-Sat) A homely bistro with an air of an old-time Parisian diner, with warm colours, tinkling jazz and walls covered in vintage signs. It's a great bet for honest bistro food, and you can watch the chef at work through a hatch into the kitchen.

La Passerelle   SEAFOOD €€€
(☑04 68 51 30 65; 1 cours Palmarole; mains €26-30; ⊙noon-2pm Tue-Sat, 7-9pm Mon-Sat) This family-run restaurant is an old favourite for fish-lovers. It's quite formal: bone china plates, crisp white tablecloths, and upmarket plates of turbot, lobster and saffron-infused sole. The oysters are the best in town.

Self-catering

Marché République   MARKET
(place de la République; ⊙7am-1pm Tue-Sun) A fine food market held on the old town's main square. Saturday is organic day.

Maison Sala   DELICATESSEN
(1 rue Paratilla; ⊙Tue-Sat & Sun morning) This wonderful gourmet emporium is situated on rue Paratilla, known to locals as rue des Épices (Spice St). It's loaded down with bottled olive oils, strings of sausages, pungent cheeses and spicy hams.

ℹ Information

Tourist Office (☑04 68 66 30 30; www.perpignantourisme.com; ⊙9am-7pm Mon-Sat, 10am-4pm Sun mid-Jun–Sep, shorter hours rest of year) In the Palais des Congrès, off promenade des Platanes.

ℹ Getting There & Away

AIR
Perpignan's **airport** (☑04 68 52 60 70; www.aeroport-perpignan.com) is 5km northwest of the town centre. Current destinations include London Stansted, Birmingham, Brussels (Ryanair); Southampton (Flybe); Dublin (Aer Lingus); and Amsterdam (KLM); Nantes (Volotea); Paris and Lille (Air France); and Calvi and Ajaccio (Air Corsica).

The Navette Aéroport (bus 7) runs regularly into the town centre for a flat-rate €1.10.

BUS
Buses anywhere in the Pyrénées-Orientales département cost a flat-rate €1. Perpignan's bus station is on av Général Leclerc.

Côte Vermeille (hourly Monday to Saturday, one on Sunday) Bus 400/404 trundles to Collioure (50 minutes), Port-Vendres (65 minutes) and Banyuls (80 minutes).

Tech Valley (hourly Monday to Saturday, four on Sunday) Buses 300/341/342 run regularly to Céret (50 minutes).

Têt Valley (every two hours Monday to Saturday, two on Sunday) Regular buses to Prades (one hour) and Vernet-les-Bains (1½ hours); numbered 200/210/220/260 depending on the route.

TRAIN

Frequent trains run through the Côte Vermeille towns to Cerbère/Portbou (€7.50, 35 minutes) on the Spanish border, where you can change for trains to Barcelona.

Carcassonne €18, 1¾ hours
Montpellier €23, 1¾ hours
Narbonne €10.50, 45 minutes
Paris' Gare de Lyon €88 to €101.50, 5½ hours

Around Perpignan

Céret

Settled snugly in the Pyrenean foothills just off the Tech Valley, the little town of Céret conceals an unexpected surprise – one of southern France's best modern art museums, with a collection of stellar canvases donated by some of the 20th century's foremost names from cubism to neorealism.

The town also hosts a number of lively festivals throughout the year, including the Fête de la Cerise (Cherry Festival) in late May, the Céret de Toros Feria (Céret Bull Festival) in early July, and the Fêstival de Sardanes in July, which celebrates the traditional Catalan folk dance.

◉ Sights

★ **Musée d'Art Moderne** ART MUSEUM
(www.musee-ceret.com; 8 bd Maréchal Joffre; adult/child €5.50/free, incl temporary exhibitions €8/free; ☺10am-6pm, closed Tue Oct-Apr) While Provence might be better-known as an artist's haven, Languedoc had its own artistic heyday around the turn of the 20th century, when Fauvist and cubist artists flocked here, attracted by the searing colours and sun-drenched landscapes. This wonderful museum was created in 1950 by Pierre Brune and Frank Burty Haviland, who convinced friends including Picasso, Matisse, Chaïm Soutine and George Braque to donate canvases. The result is one of the finest collections of modern art this side of Paris – don't miss it.

Céret's artistic connections stretch back to 1910, when the Catalan sculptor Manolo Hugué, painter Frank Burty Haviland and composer Déodat de Séverac settled here. They were followed in 1911 by Pablo Picasso and George Braque, along with other significant figures from the cubist and Fauvist movements, mostly escaping the spiralling rents and stifling atmosphere of the Montmartre art scene.

One by one, all the big names passed through Céret, sometimes staying for a short while, sometimes for extended periods. The list reads like a who's who of modern art: André Masson, Max Jacob, Juan Gris, Raoul Dufy, Jean Cocteau, Chaim Soutine, Modigliani, Marc Chagall, Salvador Dalí and Joan Miró and many more.

After the museum's formation in 1950, many of these artists (or their estates) chose to donate their works for free in recognition of Céret's importance to their artistic development (Picasso alone donated 57 pieces, although only one painting, a still life of a dead crane and a jug).

Just a few of the standout works to look out for include a moving *Crucifixion* (1925) by Marc Chagall, a playful 1912 portrait of Picasso by Juan Gris, and a famous cubist view of Céret by Chaim Soutine, painted in 1919 – but there are many more to discover. Take your time – this place is a real treat.

⌧ Sleeping

Hôtel des Arcades HOTEL €
(☎04 68 87 12 30; www.hotel-arcades-ceret.com; place Picasso; r €52-70, f €85; ☒) This old-fashioned hotel is brilliant value, and a great base for exploring Céret and the modern art museum. Rooms are no-frills – basic beds, simple furniture, plain bathrooms – but the best overlook the main square of place Picasso and its 100-year-old plane trees. They even have a little art collection in the lobby.

★ **Le Relais des Chartreuses** B&B €€
(☎04 68 83 15 88; www.relais-des-chartreuses.fr; 106 av d'en Carbonner, Le Boulou; s €60-75, d €60-187, ste €210-273) Ten kilometres east of Céret, Le Relais des Chartreuses is a glorious getaway, with glossy rooms lodged inside a Catalan-style house dating from the 17th century. The owners have stripped out all the clutter in favour of a few key antiques, offset by clean lines and soothing colours. A designer pool and table d'hôte restaurant round off the luxurious ensemble.

❶ Getting There & Away

Hourly buses run to/from Perpignan (50 minutes). All buses in the Roussillon département are a flat-rate €1. There's a large car park next to the Musée d'Art Moderne.

Tautavel

Musée de Préhistoire ARCHAEOLOGICAL MUSEUM
(Prehistory Museum; ☑04 68 29 07 76; www.
450000ans.com; av Jean Jaurès; adult/child incl
audioguide €8/4; ☺10am-7pm Jul & Aug, 10am-
12.30pm & 2-6pm rest of year) Twenty-seven
kilometres northwest of Perpignan along the
D117, the cave-riddled cliffs above Tautavel
have yielded a host of prehistoric finds –
most notably a human skull, estimated to be
450,000 years old, making it one of the oldest such discoveries in Europe. This museum
delves into the area's prehistoric past, with a
full-size reproduction of the cave, displays of
fossilised bones and tools and various other
exhibits.

Cathar Castles

Dotted across the parched plains of Roussillon
and Languedoc are many castles left behind
by the Cathars, an ultra-devout Christian sect
who were persecuted during the 12th century,
and eventually crushed by the forces of Pope
Innocent III during the Albigensian Crusade.

Perched on rocky outcrops surrounded by
orange scrubland, they're hugely atmospheric,
but many are fast crumbling into dust. They
can be explored in a long day's drive from
Perpignan – but pack plenty of water and a
hat, as it's hot as hell out here in summer.
If you're crossing into the Pyrenees, it's also
worth making the trip to the Château de
Montségur (p690), another classic (and important) Cathar stronghold.

The Passeport des Sites du Pays Ca-
thare (www.payscathare.org/passeport-des-sites;
€2) gives reductions to 20 local sites, including several lovely medieval abbeys at St-
|Hilaire, Lagrasse and Villelongue.

Château d'Aguilar   CHÂTEAU
(☑04 68 45 51 00; Tuchan; adult/child €3.50/1.50;
☺9am-7pm mid-Jun–mid-Sep, 10am-6pm Apr–mid-
Jun, 11am-5pm mid-Sep–Nov) Squatting on a low
hill near the village of Tuchan, Aguilar features six corner turrets along its hexagonal
outer wall. It's the smallest of the castles, and
in a fairly poor state of repair. The castle is
37km northwest of Perpignan via the D12.

Château de Quéribus   CHÂTEAU
(☑04 68 45 03 69; www.cucugnan.fr; Cucugnan;
adult/child €6/3.50, audioguide €4; ☺9am-8pm
Jul & Aug, 9.30am-7pm Apr-Jun & Sep, 10am-5pm
Oct-Mar) Quéribus was the site of the Cathars'
last stand in 1255. It's 728m up on a rocky hill,

and its structure is well preserved: the *salle
du pilier* inside the central keep still features
Gothic pillars, vaulting and archways. There's
a mind-blowing view stretching to the Mediterranean and the Pyrenees from the top. In
the theatre, a short film documents the castle's history, seen through the eyes of one of its
curates. It's 14km west of Tuchan via the D14.

Château de Peyrepertuse   CHÂTEAU
(☑04 68 45 40 55; www.chateau-peyrepertuse.
com; Duilhac-sous-Peyrepertuse; adult/child Jul &
Aug €9/3, rest of year €6.50/3.50, audioguide €4;
☺9am-8pm Jul & Aug, shorter hours rest of year)
Peyrepertuse is the largest of the Cathar castles, teetering on a sheer spur of rock with a
drop of 800m on either side. Several of the
original towers and many sections of ramparts are still standing. In mid-August, the
castle holds falconry displays and a two-day
medieval festival, complete with knights
in armour. The castle is 6km northwest of
Cucugnan via the D14.

Château de Puilaurens   CHÂTEAU
(☑04 68 20 65 26; Lapradelle; adult/child €4/2;
☺9am-8pm Jul & Aug, 10am-7pm Jun & Sep, to 5pm
or 6pm rest of year) With its tall turrets and lofty
location, Puilaurens is perhaps the most dramatic of the Cathar fortresses. It has the full
range of medieval defences: double walls, four
corner towers and crenellated battlements.
The views from the castle are particularly
grand, stretching across sun-baked plains
and pine woodland. It's also said to be haunt-
ed by the White Lady, a niece of Philippe le
Bel. The castle is about 38km west of Duilhac-sous-Peyrepertuse, via the D117.

Têt Valley

Fruit orchards carpet the lower reaches of the
Têt Valley. Beyond the strategic fortress town
of Villefranche-de-Conflent, the scenery becomes wilder, more open and undulating as
the valley climbs towards Spanish Catalonia
and Andorra.

Villefranche-de-Conflent

POP 240

The Unesco-listed town of Villefranche sits in
a breathtaking spot, hemmed in by tall cliffs,
at the strategic confluence of the valley of the
Rivers Têt and Cady (hence the 'de Conflent'
in its name). It's just a few kilometres west to
the Spanish border, which many people cross

aboard the town's famous mountain railway, the Train Jaune.

◉ Sights

Le Train Jaune   MOUNTAIN RAILWAY
(⌨0 800 886 091; terlanguedocroussillon@sncf. fr; per person €1) Nicknamed 'The Canary' for obvious reasons, this mountain railway trundles up from Villefranche-de-Conflent (427m) to Latour de Carol (1231m) through spectacular Pyrenean scenery. It's one of France's most famous train trips, and attracts nearly half a million passengers in summer; you can't book, so it's wise to arrive a good hour before departure.

Château-Fort Liberia   CASTLE
(www.fort-liberia.com; adult/child €7/3.80; ⊘9am-8pm Jul & Aug, 10am-5pm Sep-Jun) Villefranche's castle dominates the skyline above town. It was originally built by Vauban in 1681, and heavily refortified by Napoléon III between 1850 to 1856. You can wander freely around its corner turrets and battlements, as well as the defensive keep and a former prison.

Ramparts   HISTORIC SITE
(adult/child €4/free; ⊘10am-7pm Jun-Sep, hours vary rest of year) It's still possible to walk along much of Villefranche's ramparts, built in stages between the 11th and 19th centuries. They have survived the centuries remarkably intact, and offer plunging views down the valley through arrow slits and machicolations.

❶ Getting There & Away

Villefranche is about 50km from Perpignan via the RN116; there are no regular buses.

Vernet-les-Bains

POP 1550
Busy in summer and a ghost town for the rest of the year, this charming little spa town was much frequented by the British aristocracy in the late 19th century. Vernet has the status of 'village arboretum' in recognition of more than 300 varieties of trees that flourish on its slopes, many brought here as seeds by overseas visitors.

Vernet is another great base for mountain biking and hiking, particularly for attacking **Mont Canigou** (2784m). You can get a head start by catching a 4WD up the mountain as far as Les Cortalets (2175m), from where the summit is a three-hour return hike.

Local four-wheel drive operators include **Garage Villacèque** (⌨04 68 05 51 14; louis.villaceque@orange.fr; rue du Conflent) and **Jeeps du Canigou** (⌨04 68 05 99 89; jpbtransports@bbox. fr; 17 bd des Pyrénées).

The **tourist office** (⌨04 68 05 55 35; www.ot-vernet-les-bains.fr; place de la République; ⊘9am-noon & 2-6pm Mon-Fri, plus Sat May-Sep) can provide plenty of advice on tackling the mountain.

Côte Vermeille

The Côte Vermeille (Vermilion Coast) runs south from Collioure to Cerbère on the Spanish border, where the Pyrenees foothills dip to the sea. Against a backdrop of vineyards and pinched between the Mediterranean and the mountains, it's riddled with small, rocky bays and little ports.

Buses and trains run regularly along the coast from Perpignan. If you're driving, leave the N114 at exit 13 and follow the lovely coastal road all the way to Banyuls.

Collioure

POP 3000
Collioure, where boats bob against a backdrop of houses washed in soft pastel colours, is the smallest and most picturesque of the Côte Vermeille resorts. Once Perpignan's port, it found fame in the early 20th century when it inspired the Fauvist artists Henri Matisse and André Derain, and later both Picasso and Braque.

In summer Collioure is almost overwhelmed by visitors, drawn by its artistic reputation (there are over 30 galleries and workshops), its wine and the chance to buy the famed Collioure anchovies at source. Like most along the Côte Vermeille, Collioure's main town beach is shingly, but pleasant enough for a post-lunch paddle.

Between May and September, leave your car in Parking Cap Dourats, at the top of the hill that plunges down to the village, and take the shuttle bus that runs to the village every 10 minutes. Year-round, there's a large car park behind the castle.

◉ Sights

Château Royal   CHÂTEAU
(⌨04 68 82 06 43; adult/child €4/2; ⊘10am-5.15pm Jun-Sep, to 4.15pm rest of year) Collioure's seaside castle was mostly built between 1276

and 1344 by the Counts of Roussillon and the Kings of Aragon, and was later occupied by the Majorcan court, although the outer wall was the work of Vauban in the 17th century. The interior displays are fairly unexciting, but the coastal vistas are lovely.

Musée d'Art Moderne
ART MUSEUM

(rte de Port-Vendres; adult/child €3/free; ☉10am-noon & 2-6pm, closed Tue Oct-May) As befits a town with longstanding artistic connections, this small museum has a good collection of mainly 20th-century canvases, and holds regular exhibitions by local artists. Among the notable names are boat sketches by Matisse and Edouard Pignon, and several coastal canvases by Henri Martin and Henri Marre.

Moulin de la Cortina
WINDMILL

This 14th-century windmill is reached after a 20-minute walk through olive and almond groves. Climb to the terrace and admire the Mediterranean vistas of boats, coast and brilliant blue sea.

Fort St-Elme
FORTRESS

(www.fortsaintelme.fr; adult/child €6/free; ☉10.30am-7pm Apr-Sep, 10.30-5pm Feb-Mar & Oct-Nov) Built in 1552 by the Spanish king Charles V between Collioure and Port-Vendre, this hilltop fort was designed as a key piece of the coastal defence system. It's now mainly used as an exhibition centre.

🏃 Activities

Le Chemin de Fauvisme
WALKING

During the early 20th century, Collioure's vibrant coastal colours and piercing light attracted a group of artists known as the Fauves (the Wild Animals), who worked with pure colour, filling their canvases with firm lines and stripes, rectangles and bright splashes. The tourist office has a guide booklet that takes you on the Chemin de Fauvisme, a walking trail of 20 locations which featured in works by Henri Matisse and his younger colleague André Derain.

Cellier des Dominicains
WINE TASTING

(☎04 68 82 05 63; www.dominicain.com; place Orphila; ☉9am-noon & 2-6pm Apr-Sep, closed Sun Oct-Mar) This former monk's cellar now showcases vintages from over 150 local *vignerons* (wine growers).

🛏 Sleeping

Villa Miranda
B&B €€

(☎04 68 98 03 79; www.villamiranda.fr; 15 rte du place de les Forques; d €105-115; ☎) A simple

but sweet B&B, with five rooms decked out in cheery stripes, blonde-wood floors and bright bathrooms; Xalac and Marinade have their own private sea-view patios, and there's a shared panoramic terrace on the 1st floor.

Hôtel Princes des Catalognes
HOTEL €€

(☎04 68 98 30 00; www.hotel-princescatalogne. com; rue des Palmiers; d €58-89, f €165-185; ❊ ⓢ) While it doesn't have much of a sea view, this modern hotel makes up for it by offering some of the most reasonable rates in Collioure – even in summer a double won't set you back more than €93. The decor is clean and fresh, if a touch bland, but with only 15 rooms it doesn't feel crowded even when full.

Le Chai Catalan
B&B €€

(☎04 68 87 19 13; www.chai-catalan.fr; 14 rue du Chateau, Ortaffa; d €90-130, tr €115-155) It's a little inland from Collioure (22km in fact), but this one-time winery is worth the drive. It's a model of a modern B&B, blending zinc, plate glass and wrought metal with the building's old stone shell. The rooms are light and elegant, and are reached via a mezzanine overlooking the stunning glass-roofed atrium.

Casa Pairal
HOTEL €€€

(☎04 68 82 05 81; www.hotel-casa-pairal.com; impasse des Palmiers; r €99-299; ❊ ⓢ ☒) A seductive coastal getaway, set around a secluded courtyard garden with its own tinkling family. Rooms are split into Traditional, Privilege and Suite; moving up the price scale buys extra space and balconies overlooking the sparkling blue Med, but most share the same heritage-style decor. It was originally a 18th-century house built for a well-to-do Catalan family.

🍴 Eating

Colloure is awash with seafood restaurants.

Casa Leon
BISTRO €€

(☎04 68 82 10 74; 2 rue Rière; mains €12-20, menus €25-33; ☉noon-2pm & 7-10.30pm) For simple, cheap seafood, look no further. Lost in the tangled old quarter, this simple Catalan bistro relies on the quality of its ingredients rather than cheffy flourishes: grilled half-lobster and langoustines, cod with mussels and cockles, or king scallops in creamy sauces, not forgetting Collioure's celebrated anchovies.

La 5ème Péché
FUSION €€€

(☎04 68 98 09 76; www.le-cinquieme.com; 18 rue Fraternité; menus lunch €18-24, dinner €37; ☉12.15-1.45pm Wed-Sun, 7.30-9pm Mon-Sat) Nippon meets France at this creative fusion

LANGUEDOC WINES

Burgundy and Bordeaux might be France's best-known wine regions, but in terms of scale (and, many would argue, bottle for your buck), Languedoc leaves all others in the shade. In total, some 2800 sq km of vineyards stretch out across Languedoc's landscape, making this not just France's largest wine region, but the largest single wine area in the world. Amazingly, Languedoc's vineyards account for a third of all French wine.

Until recently, Languedoc's wines had a bargain-basement reputation, with quantity taking precedence over quality; much of the crop went to large co-ops to make cheap blended *vins de table*, including the ubiquitous Vin de Pays d'Oc. But a new generation of growers have experimented with different grapes and styles, and are now producing lots of interesting and unusual wines – from classic rich, robust fruity reds to a smaller range of whites, rosés and sweet wines, as well as a champagne-style fizz, *Crémant de Limoux*.

There are currently 16 wine areas in the Languedoc. Among the best-known names are Fitou, Corbières, Minervois, Faugères and St-Chinian, sub-divided into smaller Appellation d'Origine Contrôlées (AOCs) reflecting the unique climates and soils of each area. Carignan grapes are most common, followed by grenache, syrah and mourvèdre.

You'll find opportunities for cellar visits and *dégustation* (tasting) all over Languedoc-Roussillon, and there are plenty of companies offering guided tours.

Vinipolis (☑ 04 67 77 00 20; www.vinipolis.fr; 5 ave des Vendanges, Florensac; ☉ 9am-noon & 2-6pm Mon, 9am-6pm Tue-Sat, 11-3.30pm Sun) is a wonderful wine warehouse, 11km from Agde, is a great place to get acquainted. It's next to a winemaking co-operative in the village of Florensac, and stocks hundreds of local vintages; the staff are friendly and very clued-up, and of course you're welcome to taste the wares.

There's an excellent bistro next door, too, the **Bistro d'Alex** (☑ 04 67 77 03 05; lebistrotdalex@orange.fr; Florensac; 2-/3-course lunch €19/22; ☉ lunch noon-2.30pm Tue-Sat, dinner 7.30-9.30pm Fri & Sat in summer), where you can tuck into excellent regional cuisine accompanied by lots of top-class wines, mostly by the glass. It's deservedly popular with the locals, so reservations are a very good idea.

Vin en Vacances (☑ in France 06 42 33 34 09, in UK 07880-796786; www.vinenvacances.com; 10 rue du Pont Vieux, Carcassonne; day tours €100-125) is an experienced English-speaking company that runs scheduled minibus tours of local vineyards from Carcassonne, Béziers and Pézenas.

Montpellier Wine Tours (☑ 06 95 16 25 61; www.montpellierwinetours.com; 92 rue Mathieu Laurens, Montpellier; half-/full day €65/95) is a small, personal tours of two to eight people leaving from Montpellier. The regular destinations are Pic St Loup, a wine and olive oil tour, and a visit to the vineyards around the canyons of Hérault and Larzac.

LANGUEDOC-ROUSSILLON CÔTE VERMEILLE

restaurant, where classic French seafood is treated with a dash of Japanese flair and flavour. Run by chef Iijima Masashi, it's a creative place to dine, with exotic versions of tuna, swordfish, crab and sea bream finding their way onto the ever-changing menu. The dining room is small, buzzy and busy – book ahead.

Neptune GASTRONOMIC €€€
(☑ 04 68 82 02 27; www.leneptune-collioure.com; 9 rte de Port Vendres; menus €39, €59 or €79; ☉ 12.30-2pm Wed-Sun, 7-9pm Mon-Sat) It's a toss up whether the setting or the food steals the show here. The seaside terrace is an absolute stunner, overlooking Collioure's brilliant blue bay and red-topped roofs, while the Michelin-starred food makes maximum use of local ingredients, from just-landed turbot to just-cooked lobster. The style is formal, so it may not be to all tastes.

❶ Information

Collioure Tourist Office (☑ 04 68 82 15 47; www.collioure.com; place du 18 Juin; ☉ 9am-8pm Mon-Sat, 10am-6pm Sun Jul & Aug, shorter hours rest of year)

Port-Vendres

Three kilometres south of Collioure, Port-Vendres, Roussillon's only natural harbour and deep-water port, has been exploited ever since Greek mariners roamed the rocky coastline. Until the independence of France's North

African territories in the 1960s, it was an important port linking them with the mainland.

It's still a significant cargo and fishing harbour, however, with everything from small coastal chuggers to giant deep-sea vessels bristling with radar. There's also a large leisure marina, and lots of pleasant walks around the coastline nearby.

Paulilles

Part industrial relic, part nature walk, this 35-hectare coastal site is between Port-Vendres and Banyuls. Remote, as befits a one-time dynamite factory, it was set up by the Swede Alfred Nobel, founder of the Nobel prize, and subsequently abandoned for more than a quarter of a century.

Haunting photos and text (in French and English) inside the former **director's house** (⊙9am-1pm & 2-7pm, closed Tue Oct-Apr) `FREE` tell of the hard lives and close community of workers, whose explosives helped to blast the Panama Canal, Trans-Siberian Railway and Mont Blanc Tunnel.

Banyuls-sur-Mer

POP 4750

Just 14km from the Spanish border, Banyuls is a small coastal town that began life as a fishing port, but is now best-known for its three AOC wines (Banyuls, Banyuls Grand Cru and Collioure), grown on the slopes around town on steep, rocky terraces divided by drystone walls, which help retain water and prevent soil erosion.

It's a lovely spot in its own right, and very handy as a stop-off if you're heading over the border.

◉ Sights & Activities

Biodiversarium AQUARIUM, GARDEN
(✆04 68 88 73 39; www.biodiversarium.fr; aquarium €5/2.50, joint ticket with Jardin Méditerranéen €7.50/4; ⊙10am-12.30pm & 2-7pm Jul & Aug, to 6pm Apr-Jun & Sep, 2-6pm rest of year) At the southern end of Banyul's seafront promenade, this is part aquarium, part submarine garden. Built in 1885 as the oceanographic research station of Paris' Université Pierre et Marie Curie, the Laboratoire Arago houses an intriguing collection of Mediterranean marine life, from seahorses to sea anemones.

Jardin Méditerranéen du Mas de la Serre GARDEN
(✆04 68 88 73 39; garden only €5/2.50, joint ticket with Biodiversarium €7.50/4; ⊙10am-12.30pm & 2-6pm Sun-Fri Jul & Aug, 2-6pm Mon-Fri Apr-Jun & Sep) Run in partnership with the Biodiversarium aquarium, this fragrant hilltop garden is a fine place to get acquainted with the local flora, with exotic plants arranged around a natural amphitheatre in the hills above Banyuls. It's 3km inland from town.

Cellier des Templiers WINE TASTING
(✆04 68 98 36 92; www.terresdestempliers.fr; rte du Mas Reig; ⊙10am-7.30pm) Two kilometres inland from the seafront, this vineyard is the best place to try Banyuls wines. Guided tours take in the vineyards and the 100-year-old oak vats. Free tours in English are offered between 2.30pm and 3.45pm, and again at 4.45pm.

Provence

POP 2.67 MILLION

Best Places to Eat

➡ Le Chalet du Pharo (p777)

➡ 83.Vernet (p803)

➡ La Telline (p793)

➡ La Coquillade (p821)

➡ Maison Druout (p797)

➡ Le Sanglier Paresseux (p823)

Best Markets

➡ Carpentras (Friday; p814)

➡ Aix-en-Provence (Sunday; p780)

➡ St-Rémy de Provence (Wednesday; p796)

➡ Vaison-la-Romaine (Tuesday; p811)

➡ Arles (Saturday; p786)

Why Go?

Provence evokes picture-postcard images of lavender fields, medieval hilltop villages, bustling markets and superb food and wine. Less expected is Provence's incredible diversity. The Vaucluse and Luberon epitomise the Provençal cliché. But near the mouth of the Rhône in the Camargue, craggy limestone yields to bleached salt marshes specked pink with flamingos, and the light, which so captivated Van Gogh and Cézanne, begins to change. Then there's the serpentine Gorges du Verdon, its pea-green water lorded over by half-mile-high limestone walls and craggy mountain peaks beyond. The region's other *belle surprises* are its cities: sultry Marseille and Roman Arles.

Constant across the region is the food – clean, bright flavours, as simple as sweet tomatoes drizzled with olive oil and sprinkled with *fleur de sel* (sea salt) from the Camargue.

When to Go
Marseille

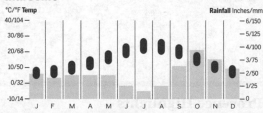

Easter Kick off the bullfighting season (no blood) with Féria d'Arles.

Jul & Aug Wade through purple lavender in bloom and watch artists perform at Festival d'Avignon.

Sep & Oct Wait for cooling temperatures and the grape harvest to bike the back roads of the Luberon.

Provence Highlights

① Soaking up seething, heady **Marseille** (p764) with its ancient port and stunning contemporary architecture around Fort St-Jean

② Trailing Van Gogh around **Arles** (p786), from the state-of-the-art Fondation Vincent Van Gogh to spots around town where he painted some of his best-known canvases

③ Spotting pink flamingos while riding white horses in the **Camargue** (p791)

④ Canoeing, canyoning, rock climbing or hiking along the vertigo-inducing **Gorges du Verdon** (p824)

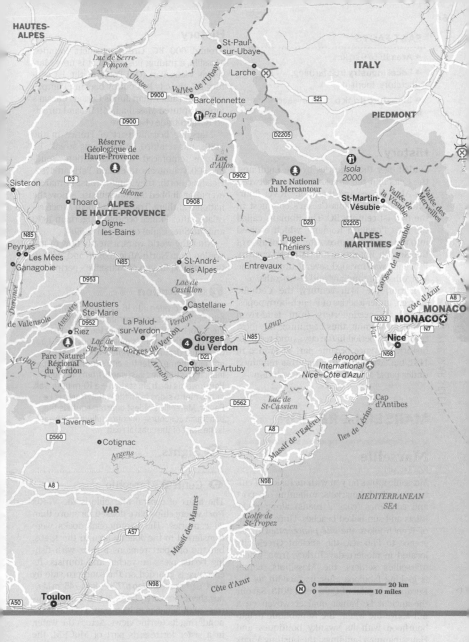

HAUTES-ALPES

Lac de Serre-Ponçon

St-Paul-sur-Ubaye

Larche

ITALY

Ubaye

Vallée de l'Ubaye

D900

Barcelonnette

S21

PIEDMONT

D900

Pra Loup

D2205

Réserve Géologique de Haute-Provence

Lac d'Allos

Isola 2000

Sisteron

D3

D902

Parc National du Mercantour

Bléone

St-Martin-Vésubie

Vallée de la Vésubie

Thoard

ALPES DE HAUTE-PROVENCE

D908

Digne-les-Bains

D28

D2205

Vallée des Merveilles

N85

Puget-Théniers

ALPES-MARITIMES

Peyruis

Les Mées

Ganagobie

D953

St-André-les-Alpes

Entrevaux

Gorges de la Vésubie

Côte d'Azur

A8

MONACO

Durance

Lac de Castillon

MONACO

Moustiers Ste-Marie

Castellane

Verdon

Loup

N7

D952

La Palud-sur-Verdon

Gorges du Verdon

Nice

de Valensole

Riez

4 Gorges du Verdon

N85

N202

N98

Lac de Ste-Croix

D21

Aéroport International Nice–Côte d'Azur

Verdon

Parc Naturel Régional du Verdon

Comps-sur-Artuby

Arrubu

Cap d'Antibes

Tavernes

D562

Lac de St-Cassien

Îles de Lérins

D560

Cotignac

A8

Massif de l'Estérel

Argens

VAR

A8

N98

MEDITERRANEAN SEA

A57

Massif des Maures

Golfe de St-Tropez

N98

Côte d'Azur

0   20 km
0   10 miles

Toulon

A50

---

5 Standing in awe at the sheer size and magnificence of Orange's exceptional **Roman amphitheatre** (p809)

6 Market shopping, boutique browsing and strutting streets lined with fountains and elegant *hôtel particuliers* in **Aix-en-Provence** (p780)

7 Exploring the lovely Luberon: think hilltop villages, cherry orchards and fiery red-rock **Roussillon** (p819)

> **FAST FACTS**
> ....
> → **Area** 15,579 sq km
> → **Local industry** fruit farming,
> viticulture, tourism
> → **Signature drink** pastis (aniseed
> liqueur)

History

Settled over the centuries by the Ligurians, the Celts and the Greeks, the area between the Alps, the sea and the Rhône River flourished following Julius Caesar's conquest in the mid-1st century BC. The Romans called the area Provincia Romana, which evolved into the name Provence. After the collapse of the Roman Empire in the late 5th century Provence was invaded several times, by the Visigoths, Burgundians and Ostrogoths.

During the 14th century, the Catholic Church, under a series of French-born popes, moved its headquarters from feud-riven Rome to Avignon, thus beginning the most resplendent period in the city's (and region's) history. Provence became part of France in 1481, but Avignon and Carpentras remained under papal control until the Revolution.

MARSEILLE REGION

Marseille
POP 859,360

Marseille grows on you with its fusion of cultures, souk-like markets, millennia-old port and *corniches* (coastal roads) along rocky inlets and sun-baked beaches. Once the butt of French jokes, the *cité phocéenne* (in reference to Phocaea, the ancient Greek city located in modern-day Turkey, from where Marseille's settlers, the Massiliots, came) is looking fabulous after its face-lift as the European Capital of Culture in 2013. Savour the ancient Le Panier quarter woven on a hill above the water; the République neighbourhood with its swanky boutiques and Haussmannian buildings; the bustling Vieux Port; and the stunning contemporary architecture of the Joliette area around Marseille's famous striped Cathédrale de la Major. Still giddy after the success of 2013, Marseille is now bidding to be European Capital of Sport in 2017.

History

Around 600 BC, Greek mariners founded Massilia, a trading post, at what is now Marseille's Vieux Port (Old Port). In the 1st century BC, the city lost out by backing Pompey the Great rather than Julius Caesar: Caesar's forces captured Massilia in 49 BC and directed Roman trade elsewhere.

Marseille became part of France in the 1480s, but retained its rebellious streak. Its citizens embraced the Revolution, sending 500 volunteers to defend Paris in 1792. Heading north, they sang a rousing march, ever after dubbed 'La Marseillaise' – now the national anthem. Trade with North Africa escalated after France occupied Algeria in 1830 and the Suez Canal opened in 1869.

After the world wars, a steady flow of migration from North Africa began and, with it, the rapid expansion of Marseille's periphery.

ⓘ Orientation

Marseille is divided into 16 *arrondissements* (districts). Sights concentrate around the Vieux Port, stretching north to the ferry port at La Joliette. The city's main thoroughfare, La Canebière (from the Provençal word *canebe*, meaning 'hemp', after the city's traditional rope industry), stretches eastwards from the Vieux Port towards the train station – a 10-minute walk or two metro stops from the water. North is Le Panier, Marseille's oldest quarter; south is the bohemian concourse of cours Julien; southwest is the start of the coastal road.

⊙ Sights

⊙ Central Marseille

The heart of central Marseille is the Vieux Port where ships have docked for more than 26 centuries. The commercial docks were transferred to the Joliette area in the 1840s, but the old port remains a buzz with fishing boats, pleasure yachts and tourists. Its entrance is guarded on the southern side by Fort St-Nicolas (Map p772; ⊙8am-7.45pm May-Aug, shorter hrs rest yr) FREE, a sturdy stone fortress with benches in its terraced grounds for pondering its terrific views. Across the water, in a sister fortress, is part of MuCEM, the sparkling centrepiece of the city.

★ Musée des Civilisations de l'Europe et de la Méditerranée MUSEUM
(MuCEM; Museum of European & Mediterranean Civilisations; Map p772; ☑04 84 35 13 13; www.mucem. org; 1 esplanade du J4; Fort St-Jean free, J4 adult/

child €8/5; ⊘9am-8pm Jul & Aug, 11am-7pm Sep-Oct & May-Jul, 11am-6pm Nov-Apr; [♿]; Ⓜ Vieux Port or Joliette) The icon of the 'new' Marseille, this stunning museum is split across two dramatically contrasting sites, linked by a vertigo-inducing foot bridge. On one side is **Fort St-Jean** (Map p772), founded in the 13th century by the Knights Hospitaller of St John of Jerusalem and rebuilt by Louis XIV in the 17th century; and on the other the contemporary **J4**, a shoebox with breathtaking 'lace' skin designed by Algerian-born, Marseille-educated architect Rudi Ricciotti.

Ambling around the beautiful, cream-stone citadel commands no admission fee. Different views of the Mediterranean, streaked by boats sailing in and out of the Vieux Port, unfold from dozens of viewpoints, including the Chemin de Ronde (Parapet Walk) along the ramparts and atop the square Tour du Roi René, a defensive tower reached by a narrow staircase. The history of the fort is explained in the Salle du Corps de Garde (guardhouse room), and there are always a couple of temporary exhibitions.

Walking high above the sea from Fort St-Jean along the 115m-long 'flying carpet' footbridge to J4 (an abbreviation for its street address 'Joliette 4') feels like walking the plank. Views of the ferry port and striped façade of Cathédrale de la Major in one direction and Vieux Port in the other seriously distract. Inside J4 the Galerie de la Méditerranée explores the history, culture and civilisation of the Mediterranean region through anthropological and ethnographical exhibits, art works and film. Afterwards, from the musem's ground-floor ticketing

ⓘ CUTTING COSTS

Buy a **City Pass** (one-/two-/three-day pass €24/31/39) covering admission to city museums, public transport, a guided tour, boat trip and more. Buy it online at www.resamarseille.com or in situ at the tourist office (p778).

hall, pick up the path that twists its way between the glass wall of the building and its outer lace shell for more staggering views of the Med from a very different perspective.

★**Villa Méditerranée** MUSEUM
(www.villa-mediterranee.org; bd du Littoral, Esplanade du J4; ⊘noon-7pm Tue-Thu, to 10pm Fri, 10am-7pm Sat & Sun; [♿]; Ⓜ Vieux Port or Joliette) **FREE** This eye-catching white structure next to MucCEM is no ordinary 'villa'. Designed by architect Stefano Boeri in 2013, the pistol-shaped edifice sports the most spectacular cantilever you are ever likely to see: it overhangs an ornamental pool of water below. Inside the building there is a viewing gallery with glass-panelled floor (look down if you dare!), and two or three temporary multimedia exhibitions evoking different aspects of the Mediterranean, be it sea life, history or transport.

Musée Regards de Provence MUSEUM
(www.museeregardsdeprovence.com; ave Vaudoyer; adult/child €3.50/free, plus temporary exhibition €7.50/5.50; ⊘10am-6pm; Ⓜ Joliette) The harsh reality of Marseille as a port city – vulnerable to disease and epidemic comes to life in this unusual museum in the city's

PROVENCE MARSEILLE

MARSEILLE IN...

Two Days

Start at the Vieux Port with breakfast at **La Caravelle** and a waterside stroll to the cutting-edge **MuCEM**, **Villa Méditerranée** and **Musée Régard en Provence** in the city's 1950s sanitary station. Lunch at **La Passarelle** then hike up to the **Basilique Notre Dame de la Garde** or explore **Le Panier**. Dine at nearby, excellent **Le Café des Épices**.

On day two, catch a boat to revel in Monte Cristo intrigues at **Château d'If**. Once back on land, walk or cycle along the coast to postcard-pretty **Vallon des Auffes**; indulge in bouillabaisse for dinner.

Four Days

Organise a day trip to the wonderful **Parc National des Calanques**. If you're keen to have an active day, plan a walk and a restorative lunch at **Calanque de Sormiou**. Otherwise, book a **scenic cruise**.

On day four, retrace the steps of genius painter Paul Cézanne in **Aix-en-Provence** and partake in a spot of shopping in the atmospheric town. Lunch gastronomic at **Restaurant Pierre Reboul**.

Marseille

PROVENCE

A **B** **C** **D**

1

LA JOLIETTE

Joliette

Bassin de
la Grande
Joliette

Pl de la
Joliette

Joliette

2

MEDITERRANEAN
SEA

Gare
Maritime

SNCM

République
Dames

R de Mazenod

Av Robert Schuman

R de l'Evêche

3

Q de la Tourette

Esplanade
J4

Pl de
Lenche

4

Corsica

Avant-Port
de la
Joliette

Musée des Civilisations **1**
de l'Europe et de la
Méditerranée (MuCEM)

Q du Port

Tunnel St-Laurent

5

Îles du Frioul;
Château d'If

3 **9**

Jardin
du Pharo

R des Catalans

Bd Charles Livon

Av Pasteur

R Sainte

See Central Marseille Map (p772)

6

Plage des
Catalans

11

5

Av de la Corse

John F Kennedy

R Cap Dessemond

Pl du 4
Septembre

R Charras

Av de la Corse

R Sauveur

Bd Tellène

7

Vallon
des
Auffes

10

Corniche Président

R Guidicelli

R du Vallon

R des Auffes

R d'Endoume

Bd Marius Thomas

Le Rhul (550m)

A **B** **C** **D**

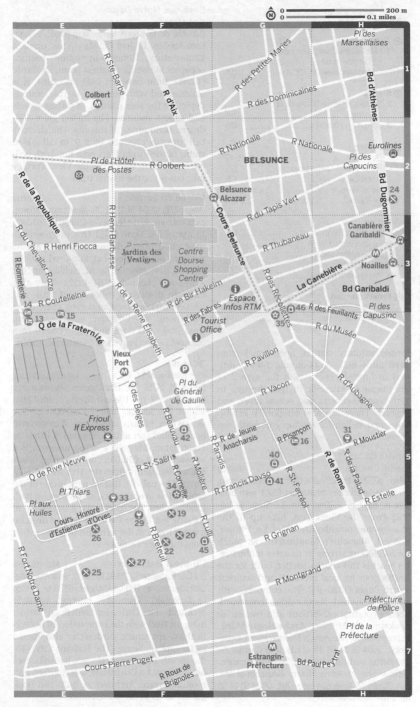

PROVENCE

0 200 m
0 0.1 miles

Pl des Marseillaises

Colbert Ⓜ

R Ste-Barbe

R d'Aix

R des Petites Maries

R des Dominicaines

Bd d'Athènes

R de la République

R du Chevalier Roze

R Bonneterie

R Henri Fiocca

R Coutelleine

Pl de l'Hôtel des Postes

R Colbert

R Henri Barbusse

R Nationale

R Nationale

BELSUNCE

Pl des Capucins

Eurolines

Bd Dugommier

Belsunce Alcazar

Cours Belsunce

R du Tapis Vert

R Thubaneau

Canabière Garibaldi Ⓜ

24 ✕

Jardins des Vestiges

Centre Bourse Shopping Centre Ⓟ

R de la Reine Elisabeth

R de Bir Hakeim

R des Récollets

R des Feuillants

Noailles

La Canebière

Bd Garibaldi

Pl des Capucins

14
13 15

Q de la Fraternité

R des Fabres

Espace Infos RTM ℹ

Tourist Office ℹ

46

35

R du Musée

Vieux Port Ⓜ

Q des Belges

Pl du Général de Gaulle Ⓟ

R Pavilon

R Vacon

R d'Aubagne

Frioul If Express

Q de Rive Neuve

R Beauvau

42

R St-Saëns

R Molière

R Paradis

R de Jeune Anacharsis

R Pisançon

16

31

R Moustier

R de la Palud

40

Pl Thiars

33

R Corneille

R Francis Davso

R St-Ferréol

R de Rome

41

R Estelle

Pl aux Huiles

Cours Honoré d'Estienne d'Orves

29

34

19

20

45

R Lulli

R Grignan

26

R Breteuil

22

25

27

R Fort Notre Dame

R Montgrand

Préfecture de Police

Pl de la Préfecture

Cours Pierre Puget

R Roux de Brignoles

Estrangin-Préfecture Ⓜ

Bd Paul Peytral

Marseille

◉ Top Sights
1 Musée des Civilisations de
l'Europe et de la
Méditerranée (MuCEM) C4

◉ Sights
2 Basilique Notre Dame de la
Garde.. E7
3 Jardin du Pharo................................C5

🛏 Sleeping
Decoh .... (see 4)
4 Hôtel Edmond Rostand..................... G6
5 Hôtel Le Richelieu B6
6 Hôtel Vertigo G2
7 Le Ryad...G3

✖ Eating
8 Café Populaire................................. G6
9 Le Chalet du Pharo C5
Le Môlé Passédat..........................(see 1)
10 L'Epuisette..A7
11 Restaurant Michel B6

⊕ Entertainment
12 Espace Julien.................................... G4
13 L'Intermédiaire..................................H4

former sanitary station, operational from 1948 until 1971. A 45-minute film (subtitled in English) opens with the arrival of the plague in Marseille in 1720 through to 19th-century cholera and yellow fever, and beyond. There are also temporary exhibitions and delightful rooftop cafe with sea views.

Centre de la Vieille Charité
MUSEUM

(Map p772; http://vieille-charite-marseille.com; 2 rue de la Charité; adult/child €5/3, with exhibitions €10/8; ☺10am-6pm Tue-Sun; Ⓜ Joliette) From the Vieux Port, hike up to the shabby-chic neighbourhood of Le Panier, dubbed 'Marseille's Montmartre' as much for its sloping streets as its artsy ambience. Its heart is this charity shelter, built for the town's poor by local architect and sculptor Pierre Puget (1620–94). The complex, with stunning arched sienna-stone courtyard, houses rotating exhibitions and two small museums: the Musée d'Archéologie Méditerranéenne (Museum of Mediterranean Archeology; ☑04 91 14 58 59; 2 rue de la Charité, 2e; Ⓜ Joliette) and the Musée d'Arts Africains, Océaniens et Amériridiens (Museum of African, Oceanic & American Indian Art; ☑04 91 14 58 38; 2 rue de la Charité, 2e).

Basilique Notre Dame de la Garde
CHURCH

(Montée de la Bonne Mère; Map p766; ☺7am-8pm Apr-Sep, to 7pm Oct-Mar) This opulent 19th-century Romano-Byzantine basilica occupies Marseille's highest point, La Garde (162m). Built between 1853 and 1864, it is ornamented with coloured marble, murals depicting the safe passage of sailing vessels and superb mosaics. The hilltop gives 360-degree panoramas of the city. The church's bell tower is crowned by a 9.7m-tall gilded statue of the Virgin Mary on a 12m-high pedestal. It's a 1km walk from the Vieux Port, or take bus 60 or the tourist train.

Musée du Santon
MUSEUM

(Map p772; ☑04 91 13 61 36; www.santonsmarcel carbonel.com; 49 rue Neuve Ste-Catherine; ☺10am-12.30pm & 2-6.30pm) FREE One of Provence's most enduring Christmas traditions are its santons, plaster-moulded, kiln-fired nativity figures, first created by Marseillais artisan Jean-Louis Lagnel (1764–1822). This tiny museum displays a collection of 18th- and 19th-century santons, and runs visits to its workshops. Its boutique sells everything from nail-sized dogs and pigs (€6.80) to a complete mas (Provençal farmhouse, €180).

★ Musée des Beaux Arts
ART MUSEUM, PALACE

(☑04 91 14 59 30; http://musee-des-beaux-arts. marseille.fr; 7 rue Édouard Stephan; adult/child €5/free, free Sun until 1pm; ☺10am-6pm Tue-Sun; ♿; Ⓜ Cinq Avenues–Longchamp, 🚋 Longchamp) Spectacularly set in the colonnaded Palais de Longchamp, Marseille's oldest museum is a treasure trove of Italian and Provençal painting and sculpture from the 17th to 21st centuries. The palace's shaded park is one of the centre's few green spaces, and is popular with local families. The spectacular fountains were constructed in the 1860s, in part to disguise a water tower at the terminus of an aqueduct from the River Durance.

L'Unité d'Habitation
ARCHITECTURE

(La Cité Radieuse; ☑04 91 16 78 00; www.marseille-citeradieuse.org; 280 bd Michelet; 🚌83 or 21 stop Le Corbusier) Visionary international-style architect Le Corbusier redefined urban living in 1952 with the completion of his vertical 337-apartment 'garden city' also known as La Cité Radieuse (The Radiant City). Today mostly private apartments, it also houses hotel, Hôtel Le Corbusier, a restaurant and rooftop terrace. Architecture buffs can book guided tours at the tourist office.

◉ Along the Coast

Mesmerising views of another Marseille unfold along corniche Président John F Kennedy, the coastal road that cruises south to small, sandy, beach-volleyball-busy **Plage des Catalans** and the fishing cove **Vallon des Auffes**, crammed with colourful fishing boats.

Further south, the vast **Prado beaches**, are marked by Jules Cantini's 1903 marble replica of Michelangelo's *David*. The beaches, all gold sand, were created from backfill from the excavations for Marseille's metro, and host a world renowned skate park.

Château d'If   ISLAND, CASTLE
(www.if.monuments-nationaux.fr; adult/child €5.50/ free; ⊘10am-6pm May-Sep, shorter hrs rest yr) Immortalised in Alexandre Dumas' classic 1844 novel *Le Comte de Monte Cristo* (The Count of Monte Cristo), the 16th-century fortress-turned-prison Château d'If sits on the 30-sq-km island, Île d'If, 3.5km west of the Vieux Port. Political prisoners were incarcerated here, along with hundreds of Protestants, the Revolutionary hero Mirabeau, and the Communards of 1871.

Frioul If Express (www.frioul-if-express.com; 1 quai des Belges) boats leave for Château d'If (€10.10 return, 20 minutes, around 15 daily) from the Vieux Port.

Îles du Frioul   ISLANDS
A few hundred metres west of Île d'If are the Îles du Frioul, the barren dyke-linked white-limestone islands of Ratonneau and Pomègues. Sea birds and rare plants thrive on these tiny islands, which are each about 2.5km long, totalling 200 hectares. Ratonneau has three beaches. Boats to Château d'If also serve the Îles du Frioul (one/two islands €10.10/15.20 return, 35 minutes, around 15 daily).

✯ Festivals & Events

Carnaval de Marseille   CARNIVAL
(⊘Mar) Mad street carnival with decorated floats.

Fiesta des Suds   MUSIC FESTIVAL
(www.dock-des-suds.org; ⊘Mar) World music at Dock des Suds.

⌂ Sleeping

★**Hôtel Hermès**   DESIGN HOTEL €
(☏04 96 11 63 63; www.hotelmarseille.com; 2 rue Bonneterie; s €64, d €85-102; ✳☞; Ⓜ Vieux Port) Nothing to do with the Paris design house, this excellent-value hotel has a rooftop terrace with panoramic Vieux Port views. Grab breakfast (€9) on a tray in the bright ground-floor breakfast room and ride the lift to the 5th floor for breakfast à la rooftop. Contemporary rooms have white walls and a splash of lime-green or red to complement their Scandinavian-like design.

★**Hôtel Le Richelieu**   HOTEL €
(Map p766; ☏04 91 31 01 92; www.lerichelieu-marseille.com; 52 corniche Président John F Kennedy; d €70-160; ✳☞; ☐83) An eternal favourite for its beach-house vibe and fabulous sea views, this coastal choice near Plage des Catalans is excellent value. Rooms are oddly-shaped, but the owners keep them looking fresh, and the best even face the Med. Breakfast (€14) on the terrace is a morning treat that doesn't tire.

Hôtel Vertigo   HOSTEL €
(Map p772; ☏04 91 91 07 11; www.hotelvertigo.fr; 42 rue des Petites Maries; dm from €25; @☞; Ⓜ Gare St-Charles) This snappy boutique hostel kisses goodbye to dodgy bunks and hospital-like decor. Here it's 'hello' to vintage posters, designer chrome kitchen, groovy communal spaces and polite multilingual staff. Double rooms are particularly good, some with a private terrace. No curfew (or lift, alas). A second, all-dorm facility is closer to the Vieux Port.

★**Hôtel Edmond Rostand**   DESIGN HOTEL €€
(Map p766; ☏04 91 37 74 95; www.hoteledmond rostand.com; 31 rue Dragon; d €90-115, tr €127-141; ✳@☞; Ⓜ Estrangin-Préfecture) Turn a blind eye to the grubby outside shutters of this excellent-value Logis de France hotel in the Quartier des Antiquaires. Inside, decor is a hip mix of contemporary design and vintage, with a great sofa area for lounging and 16 rooms dressed in crisp white and soothing natural hues. Some rooms overlook a tiny private garden, others the Basilique Notre Dame de la Garde.

Well-being is the thrust of this hotel and massages are available. Breafast (€10) is served in the hotel's thoroughly modern Edmond Café (7am-7pm), a creative space that sells homemade cakes, artisan juices and vintage teacups, and also hosts knitting workshops and massage classes.

★**Au Vieux Panier**   B&B
(☏04 91 91 23 72; www.auvieuxpanier.com; 13 rue du Panier; d €100-140; Ⓜ Vieux Port) The height of Le Panier shabby chic, this super-stylish *maison d'hôte* woos art lovers with original works of art. Each year artists are invited to

Vieux Port

AN ITINERARY

Bold, busy and open-armed in the sea, Marseille is France's oldest city. Its Vieux Port, one kilometre long either side, is guarded by the great bastions of St-Jean and St-Nicolas whose guns once trained on the rebellious population rather than out to sea.

Rise early to hear tall tales from fishers at the waterfront **fish market** ❶. Grab *un café* and balcony seat at La Caravelle – views of Basilique Notre Dame de la Garde are first-class. Then sail to **Château d'If** ❷. Back on land, hike uphill into the ancient, apricot-hued stone maze of **Le Panier** ❸. Feast on exhibits in the **Centre de la Vieille Charité** ❹ and lunch on a café terrace on the tree-shaded square opposite.

Or indulge in a late lunch with big blue sea view at Le Môle Passedat on the rooftop of MuCEM. To get here, follow rue du Panier downhill to place des 13 Cantons, beyond to **Cathédrale de la Major** ❺, then along the waterfront to architectural stunners **Villa Méditerranée** ❻ and **MuCEM** ❼. Devote the afternoon to the exhibits and views here - extraordinary in equal measure – and end with a drink in the rooftop café of 1950s sanitary station **Musée Regards de Provence** ❽.

Late afternoon walk along quai du Port and ride the cross-port ferry across the water. See martyr bones enshrined in gold at **Abbaye St-Victor** ❾, catch the sun set in the **Jardin du Pharo** ❿ and join locals for a pastis with the **Milo de Croton** ⓫.

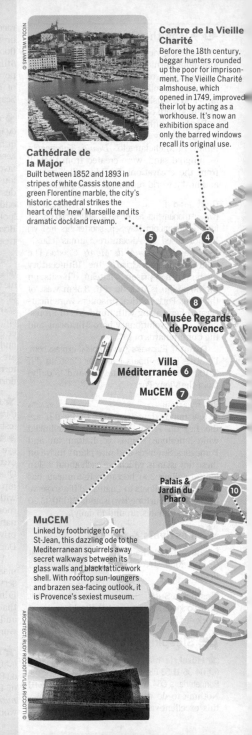

Centre de la Vieille Charité
Before the 18th century, beggar hunters rounded up the poor for imprisonment. The Vieille Charité almshouse, which opened in 1749, improved their lot by acting as a workhouse. It's now an exhibition space and only the barred windows recall its original use.

Cathédrale de la Major
Built between 1852 and 1893 in stripes of white Cassis stone and green Florentine marble, the city's historic cathedral strikes the heart of the 'new' Marseille and its dramatic dockland revamp.

Musée Regards de Provence ❽

Villa Méditerranée ❻

MuCEM ❼

Palais & Jardin du Pharo ❿

MuCEM
Linked by footbridge to Fort St-Jean, this dazzling ode to the Mediterranean squirrels away secret walkways between its glass walls and black latticework shell. With rooftop sun-loungers and brazen sea-facing outlook, it is Provence's sexiest museum.

Le Panier
The site of the Greek town of Massilia, Le Panier woos walkers with its sloping streets. Grand Rue follows the ancient road and opens out into place de Lenche, the location of the Greek market. It is still the place to shop for artisanal products.

Milo de Croton
Subversive local artist Pierre Puget carved the savage *Milo de Croton* for Louis XIV. The statue, whose original is in the Louvre, is a meditation on man's pride and shows the Greek Olympian being devoured by a lion, his Olympic cup cast down.

Château d'If
Catch the Frioul If Express to Château d'If, France's equivalent to Alcatraz. Prisoners were housed according to class: the poorest at the bottom in windowless dungeons, the wealthiest in paid-for private cells, with windows and a fireplace.

Quai des Belges

1

Fish Market

La Caravelle

2

3

11

Quai du Port

Cross-Port Ferry

Cours Honoré d'Estienne d'Orves

Quai de Rive Neuve

Fort St-Jean

Bas Fort St-Nicolas

9

Abbaye St-Victor
St-Victor was built (420–30) to house the remains of tortured Christian martyrs. On Candlemas (2 February) the black Madonna is brought up from the crypt and the archbishop blesses the city and the sea.

Jardin du Pharo
Built by Napoléon for the Empress Eugénie, the Pharo Palace was designed with its 'feet in the water'. Today it is a congress centre, but the gardens with their magnificent view are open all day.

Central Marseille

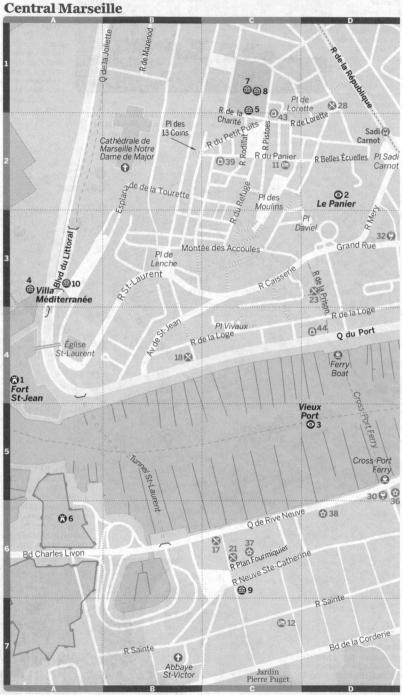

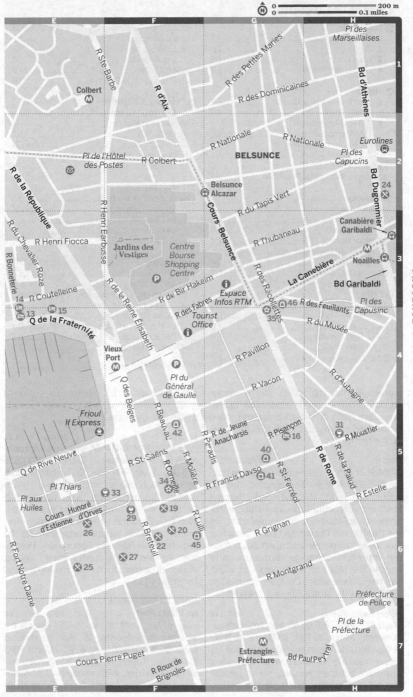

PROVENCE

0 — 200 m
0 — 0.1 miles

Pl des Marseillaises

Colbert Ⓜ

R Ste-Barbe

R d'Aix

R des Petites Maries

R des Dominicaines

Bd d'Athènes

Pl de l'Hôtel des Postes

R Colbert

R Nationale

R Nationale

BELSUNCE

Pl des Capucins

Eurolines

R de la République

R du Chevalier Roze

R Henri Fiocca

R Bonneterie

R Henri Barbusse

Jardins des Vestiges

Centre Bourse Shopping Centre

Ⓟ

Belsunce Alcazar

R du Tapis Vert

R Thubaneau

Cours Belsunce

R des Récollettes

La Canebière

Canabière Garibaldi

Noailles Ⓜ

Bd Garibaldi

Bd Dugommier

24 ✕

14
13
15

R Coutelleine

Q de la Fraternité

R de la Reine Élisabeth

R de Bir Hakeim

R des Fabres

Espace Infos RTM ⓘ

Tourist Office ⓘ

46
35

R des Feuillants

Pl des Capucins

R du Musée

Vieux Port Ⓜ

Q des Belges

Ⓟ

Pl du Général de Gaulle

R Pavillon

R Vacon

R d'Aubagne

Frioul If Express

Q de Rive Neuve

R St-Saëns

R Beauvau

R Corneille

R Paradis

R Molière

R de Jeune Anacharsis

42

R.Pisançon

16

31

R Moustier

R de la Palud

40

R Francis Davso

R St-Férréol

41

R de Rome

Pl Thiars

33

Pl aux Huiles

Cours Honoré d'Estienne d'Orves

34

29

19

R Breteuil

R Lulli

20

22

45

R Grignan

R Estelle

26

27

25

R Fort Notre Dame

R Montgrand

Préfecture de Police

Pl de la Préfecture

Cours Pierre Puget

R Roux de Brignoles

Estrangin-Préfecture Ⓜ

Bd Paul Peytral

Central Marseille

redecorate, meaning its six rooms change annually. Staircases and corridors are like an art gallery and a drop-dead gorgeous rooftop terrace peeks across terracotta tiles to the sea on the horizon.

Decoh
SELF-CONTAINED €€
(☑04 91 37 74 95; www.decoh.fr; 31-33 rue Dragon; €125-180; ✳@☞) The creative, vintage-loving team at the Edmond Rostand hotel are also behind this appealing, hotel-serviced self-catering accommodation on rue Paradis, rue Dragon and rue Albert. Studios sleep two people and apartments four; the super-stylish antique furniture harks back to the 1950s to 1970s. Stay one night, one week, one month. Cook for yourself, or breakfast at the Hôtel Edmond Rostand.

Hôtel Belle-Vue
HOTEL €€
(Map p772; ☑04 96 17 05 40; www.hotel-bellevue-marseille.fr; 34 quai du Port; d €90-170; ✳@☞; ⓜVieux Port) Rooms at this old-fashioned hotel are tastefully decorated with mid-budget simplicity, but their port-side views are million-dollar. Breakfast (€10) on the pocket-

sized balcony of its cafe-bar La Caravelle (p777) – Marseille's coolest port-side spot – is a Marseille highlight.

Le Ryad
BOUTIQUE HOTEL €€
(Map p766; ☑04 91 47 74 54; www.hoteldemarseille.fr; 16 rue Sénac de Meilhan Gabriel; s €80-125, d €95-140; ☞⊞; ⓜNoailles, ⓕCanebière Garibaldi) With high ceilings, arched alcoves, warm colours and minimalist decor, super-stylish Le Ryad draws sumptuous influence from Morocco. Beautiful bathrooms, garden-view rooms and great service compensate for the sometimes-sketchy neighbourhood. Despite the four-storey walk up, it's worth booking the top-floor room for its tiny rooftop terrace. Breakfast €12.

Hôtel La Résidence du Vieux Port
DESIGN HOTEL €€
(Map p772; ☑04 91 91 91 22; www.hotel-residence-marseille.com; 18 quai du Port; d €125-200, tr €185-204; ✳@☞; ⓜVieux Port) Marseille's top-view hotel is *The Jetsons* meets Mondrian, with swoop-backed furniture and bold primary colours. Every room

looks sharp, and more expensive port-side rooms have balconies with knockout views of the old port and Notre Dame. The ultimate is the 8th-floor Suite Ciel (Sky Suite).

Mama Shelter DESIGN HOTEL €€
(☏01 43 48 48 48; www.mamashelter.com; 64 rue de la Loubière; d €69-149; ❄☎❄; Ⓜ Notre Dame du Monte–Cours Julien) Sleeping in Marseille doesn't get much funkier than this. With design by Philippe Starck, nifty extras like Kiehl's bathroom products, and free in-room movies, this is the affordable-chic kid on the block.

Hôtel Saint-Ferréol HOTEL €€
(Map p772; ☏04 91 33 12 21; www.hotelsaintferreol.com; 19 rue Pisançon; d €99-140; ❄@☎; Ⓜ Vieux Port) Service is exceptional at this traditional three-star hotel, tucked down an alley off one of Marseille's main shopping streets. Rooms are individually decorated, many inspired by artists like Van Gogh and Cézanne, with spotless bathrooms, powerful AC and quality double-glazing that ensures pefect peace. Breakfast €10.50.

Casa Honoré B&B €€€
(Map p772; ☏04 96 11 01 62; www.casahonore.com; 123 rue Sainte; d €150-200; ❄☎❄; Ⓜ Vieux Port) Los Angeles meets Marseille at this four-room *maison d'hôte*, built around a central courtyard with a lap pool shaded by banana trees. The fashion-forward style reflects the owner's love for contemporary interior design, using disparate elements like black wicker and the occasional cow skull, which come together in one sexy package.

✖ Eating

The Vieux Port and streets around place Thiars are packed with restaurants, primarily aimed at tourists – handy should you want to dine early (ie before 8pm). For Mediterranean and world cuisine head uphill to trendy Cours Julien.

★Pizzaria Chez Étienne REGIONAL CUISINE €
(Map p772; 43 rue de Lorette; pizza €13-15, mains €15-20; ⊗noon-2.15pm & 8-11pm Mon-Sat; Ⓜ Colbert) This old Marseillais haunt has the best pizza in town, as well as succulent *pavé de boeuf* (beef steak) and scrumptious *supions frits* (pan-fried squid with garlic and parsley). Since it's a convivial meeting point for the entire neighbourhood, pop in beforehand to reserve a table (there's no phone). No credit cards.

★Café Populaire BISTRO €
(Map p766; ☏04 91 02 53 96; 110 rue Paradis; tapas €8-16, mains €19-23; ⊗noon-2.30pm & 8-11pm Tue-Sat; Ⓜ Estrangin-Préfecture) Vintage furniture, old books on the shelves and a fine collection of glass soda bottles lend a retro air to this trendy, 1950s-styled jazz *comptoir* (counter) – a restaurant despite its name. The crowd is chic and smiling chefs in the open kitchen mesmerise with daily specials like king prawns *à la plancha* or beetroot and coriander salad.

La Casertane ITALIAN, DELI €
(Map p772; ☏04 91 54 98 51; 71 rue Francis Davso; mains €10-15; ⊗9am-7.30pm Tue-Sat; Ⓜ Vieux Port) Lunch on a mind-boggling array of Italian

PROVENCE MARSEILLE

BOUILLABAISSE

Originally cooked by fishermen from the scraps of their catch, bouillabaisse is Marseille's signature dish. True bouillabaisse includes at least four different kinds of fish. Don't trust tourist-trap restaurants that promise cheap bouillabaisse. The genuine article costs around €55 per person and must be reserved 48 hours ahead. It's served in two parts: the broth (*soupe de poisson*), rich with tomato, saffron and fennel; and the cooked fish, deboned and presented on a platter. On the side are croutons and *rouille* (garlic, chilli and pepper mayonnaise) and grated cheese, usually Gruyère. Spread *rouille* on the crouton, top with cheese, and float in the soup. Favourite addresses:

Le Rhul (☏04 91 52 01 77; www.lerhul.fr; 269 corniche Président John F Kennedy; bouillabaisse €53; 🖵83) Long-standing classic in a 1940s seaside hotel with big blue views.

L'Epuisette (Map p766; ☏04 91 52 17 82; www.l-epuisette.com; Vallon des Auffes; bouillabaisse €90; ⊗Tue-Sat; 🖵83) Swanky, Michelin-starred option with knockout water-level views from an elegantly austere dining room.

Restaurant Michel (Chez Michel; Map p766; ☏04 91 52 30 63; www.restauarantmichel.fr; 6 rue des Catalans; bouillabaisse €65; ⊗dinner nightly) Directly opposite Plage des Catalans and tops since 1946 despite the shabby façade and unromantic dining room.

DON'T MISS

COOKING YOUR OWN LUNCH

For something different, consider cooking your own lunch under the guidance of a Marseillais chef at **L'Atelier des Chefs** (☑04 95 09 01 34; www.atelierdes chefs.fr; 42 quai Rive Neuve; lunch class €17; ⊙9am-7pm Tue-Sat ; Ⓜ Vieux Port). Study the week's menu in advance online to pick what you fancy, reserve, and rock up at 12.15pm to cook your lunch. Dining afterwards is alfresco on the school's lovely portside terrace with brightly coloured, flowery tablecloths and striped deck-chairs. Half-day courses – no eating – cover everything from bouillabaisse (€76) to *pâtisserie* and world cuisine.

deli meats and salads, or choose from daily specials, often involving homemade pastas, at this delightful deli a couple of blocks from the Vieux Port. Convivial staff and the bustling flow of clientele make for lively meals.

La Passarelle
PROVENÇAL €

(Map p772; ☑04 91 33 03 27; www.restaurantla passarelle.fr; 52 rue du Plan Fourmiguier; mains €18-22; ⊙noon-2pm Tue-Sat, 8-10.30pm Thu-Sat; Ⓜ Vieux Port) Retro tables and chairs sit on a decking terrace beneath a shady sail, plump in the middle of the leafy-green *potager* (vegetable garden) where much of the kitchen's produce is grown. Philippe and Patricia's *menu* is predominantly organic, with other products being strictly local, and cuisine is charmingly simple – the catch of day with vegetables, beef with polenta...

Clubhouse Vieux Port
FRENCH €

(☑04 13 20 11 32; www.clubhousevieuxport. com; 158 quai du Port; adult/child menu €21/13; ⊙11.30am-3pm & 7-11pm Mon-Fri, 11.45am-4pm & 7.30-11pm Sat & Sun; 🅿; Ⓜ Vieux Port) It might effectively be a self-service canteen but boy, does the Clubhouse rock. Platter after platter of positively gourmet starters, main courses – hot and cold – and desserts are laid like a banquet for diners to help themselves to – again and again. Orange tables and chairs on the portside terrace are the first to go; arrive late and you'll have to plump for a seat in the designery interior.

Laurent Favre-Mot
PATISSERIE, CAFE €

(☑04 91 33 12 06; www.laurent-favremot.fr; 9 rue breteuil; salads & omelettes €4.50-10; ⊙7.30am-

7.30pm Mon-Fri, 8.30am-7.30pm Sat; Ⓜ Vieux Port) For exquiste cakes, tarts, kid-friendly marshmellow teddy bears on sticks and, best of all, homemade ice-cream, try LFM – as locals call this striking *salon de thé* by playful Marseillais *pâtissier* Laurent Favre-Mot. It also serves omelettes, croque monsieurs and salads for lunch, in a stark white, ceramic tiled interior with vintage school chairs, or on the pavement terrace.

★ Le Café des Épices
MODERN FRENCH €€

(Map p772; ☑04 91 91 22 69; www.cafedesepices. com; 4 rue du Lacydon; menus 2-/3-course lunch €25/28, dinner €45; ⊙noon-3pm & 6-11pm Tue-Fri, to 3pm Sat; 🅿; Ⓜ Vieux Port) One of Marseille's best chefs, Arnaud de Grammont, infuses his cooking with a panoply of flavours: squid-ink spaghetti with sesame and perfectly cooked scallops, or coriander- and citrus-spiced potatoes topped by the catch of the day. Presentation is impeccable, the decor playful, and the colourful outdoor terrace between giant potted olive-trees nothing short of superb.

Le Grain de Sel
MODERN FRENCH €€

(Map p772; ☑04 91 54 47 30; 39 rue de la Paix Marcel Paul; menu 2-/3-course €22/26, mains €18-25; ⊙noon-1.30pm Tue-Thu, to 1.30pm & 8-9.30pm Fri & Sat; Ⓜ Vieux Port) The Salt Grain is always packed, generally with gourmet locals who love their food. The *menu* at the slender bistro is short but reads like a poem with its descriptions of inventive dishes such as cherry gaspacho with yellow tomatoes, pistacho and *brousse* (a type of cheese) as starter, or apricot clafoutis with almond milk ice-cream and rosemary mousse for dessert.

Malthazar
PROVENÇAL €€

(☑04 91 33 42 46; 19 rue Fortia; menus 2-/3-course lunch €19/22, dinner €31; ⊙noon-2pm & 8-11pm; Ⓜ Vieux Port) The cuisine is Provençal, seasonal and creative. But what really woos at this trendy club-like address with very long bar is the *patio à ciel* – a stunning patio garden with slide-back glass ceiling, a great mix of textures and an attention-grabbing black chandelier strung from one of three hefty wooden beams. Dress sharp.

Les Arcenaulx
TRADITIONAL FRENCH €€

(Map p772; ☑04 91 54 85 38; www.les-arcenaulx. com; 27 cours Honoré d'Estienne d'Orves; lunch menu €25, mains €23-30; ⊙noon-2pm & dinner Mon-Sat; Ⓜ Vieux Port) Dine in grandiose style in this cavernous former Louis XIV warehouse with antiquarian-and-contemporary bookshop or visit the neighbouring *salon de thé* (tearoom) for savoury tarts, cakes and ice cream.

Le Môlé Passédat
MODERN FRENCH €€€

(www.passedat.fr; 1 esplanade du J4, MuCEM; menu €52; ⏱12.30-2.30pm & 7.30-10.30pm Mon & Wed-Sat, 12.30-2.30pm Sun) Few kitchens are so stunningly located as this. Situated on the top floor of Marseille's iconic museum, MuCEM, Michelin-starred chef Gérald Passédat cooks up exquisite French fare and big blue views of the Mediterranean and Marseillais coastline. **La Table** is the gastronomic restaurant, **La Cuisine**, with self-service dining around shared tables (no sea view), is the cheaper choice (2-/3-course *menu* €21.50/35). Reserve both online.

Drinking & Nightlife

Cafes and bars surround the Vieux Port and cours Honoré d'Estienne d'Orves, home to Marseille's newbie Hard Rock Café with rock shop and live music as well as signature cafe. Students and artists congregate on and around cours Julien. In Le Panier the tree-shaded square formed by rue du Panier, rue Rodillat and rue Pistoes is the hot spot to drink, day or night.

For daytime rooftop drinking you can't beat the chic museum cafes inside (or rather, on top of) MuCEM and Musée Régards de Provence.

Cafes & Bars

La Caravelle
BAR

(Map p772; 34 quai du Port; ⏱7am-2am; Ⓜ Vieux Port) Look up or miss this standout upstairs hideaway, styled with rich wood and leather, a zinc bar and yellowing murals. If it's sunny, snag a coveted spot on the port-side terrace. On Fridays, there's live jazz from 9pm to midnight.

Bar de la Marine
BAR

(Map p772; ☑04 91 54 95 42; 15 quai de Rive Neuve; ⏱7am-1am; Ⓜ Vieux Port) Marcel Pagnol filmed the card-party scenes in *Marius* at this Marseille institution, a bar that never goes out of fashion with folks from every walk of life. Lounging on its waterside pavement terrace at the Vieux Port is sheer joy – don't leave without peeking at the original vintage interior.

La Part des Anges
WINE BAR €

(Map p772; http://lapartdesanges.com; 33 rue Sainte; ⏱9am-2am Mon-Sat, to 1pm & 6pm-2am Sun) No address buzzes with Marseille's

hip, buoyant crowd more than this fabulous all-rounder wine bar, named after the amount of alcohol that evaporates through a barrel during wine or whisky fermentation: the angels' share. Take your pick of dozens of wines to try by the glass and be sure to tell the bartender if you want to eat (tables can't be reserved in advance).

Le Comptoir Dugommier
CAFE €

(Map p772; ☑04 91 62 21 21; www.comptoir dugommier.fr; 14 bd Dugommier; ⏱7.30am-4pm Mon-Wed, to 1am Thu & Fri; 🐾; Ⓜ Noailles, Ⓖ Canebière Garibaldi) A handy pit-stop by the train station, this old-timer cafe with tin moulding, wooden floors and vintage signs makes an atmospheric escape from the busy street outside – where, *naturellement,* the *comptoir* (counter) has a few tables and chairs. The clientele is completely mixed and there's free wi-fi. Food too.

Les Buvards
WINE BAR

(Map p772; ☑04 91 90 69 98; 34 Grand Rue; ⏱noon-2.30pm & 6pm-midnight Mon-Sat; Ⓜ Vieux Port, Ⓖ Sadi Carnot) Marseille's finest selection of natural wines, by small regional producers in the main, is what tempts at this lovely wine bar. Pair your chosen glass with a charcuterie (cold meat) or cheese platter for aperitif perfection.

Bistrot L'Horloge
BAR, BISTROT

(☑09 50 41 39 66; 11 cours Honoré d'Estienne d'Orves; ⏱9-1am Mon-Sat; Ⓜ Vieux Port) A local favourite with parasol-shaded table and

PROVENCE MARSEILLE

LOCAL KNOWLEDGE

THE PERFECT SUNSET

Only Marseillais and those in the know are privy to **Le Chalet du Pharo** (☑04 91 52 80 11; www.le-chalet-du-pharo. com; 58 bd Charles Livon, Jardin du Pharo; ⏱noon-3pm & 7.30-11pm), a little wooden chalet with a very big view, secreted away in the sloping green gardens of **Jardin du Pharo** (Map p766). Its hillside terrace, shaded by parasol pines and parasols, stares across the water at the old stone walls of Fort St-Jean, the lacy steel-grey façade of MuCEM and gleaming white Villa Méditerranée beyond. Grilled fish and meat dominate the menu, and advance reservations via its website are absolutely essential. No credit cards.

GAY & LESBIAN MARSEILLE
....

Website http://marseille.actu-gay.eu covers Marseillais gay life – a small scene that is in constant flux and only really converges on weekends. Various bars – straight or mixed – host gay nights. **Caffè Noir** (Map p772; http:// cargo-spa.com/caffe-noir; 3 rue Moustier; Ⓜ Vieux Port) is a reliable address with a young, mixed, hard-drinking crowd.

chairs at the lion-statue end of cours Honoré d'Estienne d'Orves, this bistrot-bar rocks. In summer live music entertains in the early evening while punters chat over mint and ice-jammed mojitos, pots of black olive tapenade and charcuterie platters. And yes, it does have an *horloge* (clock) above its wine-barrel framed entrance.

Polikarpov VODKA BAR
(Map p772; 24 cours Honoré d'Estienne d'Orves; Ⓣ 8am-1.30am; Ⓜ Vieux Port) Scarely shut, this alfresco bar with buzzing pavement terrace just a couple of blocks from the Vieux Port markets itself as 'Massilia vodkabar'. Yes, vodka is its mainstay but there's no obligation.

Nightclubs

Trolleybus CLUB
(Map p772; Ⓣ 06 72 36 91 10, 04 91 54 30 45; www. letrolley.com; 24 quai de Rive Neuve; Ⓣ Wed-Sat; Ⓜ Vieux Port) Shake it to techno, funk and indie in between games of *pétanque* (boules) at this mythical Marseillais club with four *salles* (rooms) beneath 17th-century stone vaults at the Vieux Port. The club has been around for eons but never fails to pull in the crowds.

Au Son des Guitares CLUB
(Map p772; 18 rue Corneille; Ⓣ 11.30pm-4am Thu-Sun; Ⓜ Vieux Port) Popular with Corsican locals, this small club next to the opera has limited dancing, lots of drinking and, occasionally, a Corsican singer. Look sharp to get in.

Le Roy's CLUB
(Map p772; Ⓣ 06 10 31 60 31; 40 rue Plan Fourmiguier; Ⓣ 11.30am-6pm Thu-Sat; Ⓜ Vieux Port) Watch out for the occasional band at this club, formerly La Noche, a couple of blocks from the Vieux Port. DJs spin everything from electro to salsa.

L'Intermédiaire CLUB
(Map p766; Ⓣ 06 87 87 88 21; 63 place Jean Jaurès; Ⓣ 7pm-2am; Ⓜ Notre Dame du Mont–Cours Julien)

This grungy venue with graffitied walls is one of the best for DJs and live bands (usually techno or alternative).

☆ Entertainment

Tickets for most events are sold at the **Espace Culture** (Map p772; Ⓣ 04 96 11 04 60; http://espaceculture.net; 42 La Canebière; Ⓣ 10am-6.45pm Mon-Sat; Ⓜ Vieux Port) and the **billetterie** (10am-1pm & 2-6pm Mon-Sat) inside the tourist office.

La Friche La Belle de Mai CULTURAL CENTRE
(Ⓣ 04 95 04 95 04; www.lafriche.org; 41 rue Jobin; Ⓑ 49, stop Jobin) This former sugar-refining plant and subsequent tobacco factory is now a vibrant arts centre with a theatre, artists' workshops, cinema studios, multimedia displays, skateboard ramps, electro-/world-music parties et al. Check its program online.

Espace Julien LIVE MUSIC
(Map p766; Ⓣ 04 91 24 34 10; www.espace-julien. com; 39 cours Julien; Ⓜ Notre Dame du Mont–Cours Julien) Rock, *opérock*, alternative theatre, reggae, hip hop, Afro groove and other cutting-edge entertainment all appear on the bill; the website lists gigs.

Le Pelle Mêle JAZZ
(Map p772; Ⓣ 04 91 54 85 26; 8 place aux Huiles; Ⓣ 5.30pm-2am Tue-Sat; Ⓜ Vieux Port) A 30-something crowd jives to good jazz at this lively jazz bar with catchy pillarbox red façade, busy pavement terrace and live bands every evening (except Tuesday) at 7.30pm.

ℹ Information

Tourist Office (Ⓣ 04 91 13 89 00; www. marseille-tourisme.com; 11 La Canebière; Ⓣ 9am-7pm Mon-Sat, 10am-5pm Sun; Ⓜ Vieux Port) Marseille's shiny modern tourist office has plenty of information on everything, including guided tours on foot, bus, electric tourist train or boat.

ℹ Getting There & Away

AIR

Aéroport Marseille-Provence (www.marseille. aeroport.fr) Located 25km northwest of Marseille in Marignane; it is also called Aéroport Marseille-Marignane.

BOAT

The **passenger-ferry terminal** (www.marseille-port.fr; Ⓜ Joliette) is 250m south of place de la Joliette (1er). **SNCM** (Ⓣ 08 91 70 18 01; www. sncm.fr; 61 bd des Dames; Ⓜ Joliette) has services to Corsica, Sardinia and North Africa.

BUS

The **bus station** (www.lepilote.com; 3 rue Honnorat; Ⓜ Gare St-Charles SNCF) is at the back of the train station. Buy tickets from the ticket desk or from the driver. Services to some destinations, including Cassis, use the stop on **place Castellane**, south of the centre. **Eurolines** (www.eurolines.com; 3 allées Léon Gambetta) has international services.

TRAIN

Gare St-Charles (⊘ information 9am-8pm Mon-Sat, tickets 5.15am-10pm daily; Ⓜ Gare St-Charles SNCF) is served by both metro lines. The **left-luggage office** (small/medium/large locker €5.50/7.50/9.50; ⊘8.15am-11pm) is next to platform A. Trains, including TGVs, go to destinations all over France and Europe, including the following, which all run at least half a dozen times a day:

Avignon €29.50, 35 minutes

Lyon €65, 1¾ hours

Nice €37, 2½ hours

Paris Gare de Lyon €113, three hours

A direct London-Marseille Eurostar service is scheduled to commence in May 2015. The trip, via Lyon and Avignon, will take up to 6½ hours. See www.eurostar.fr for details.

❶ Getting Around

For transport information see www.lepilote.com.

TO/FROM THE AIRPORT

Buses (line 91) run by Cartreize link the airport with Marseille's bus station (single/return €8.20/13.10, 25 minutes, every 20 minutes from 4.30am to 11.30pm).

From the airport's 'Aéroport Marseille Provence Vitrolles' train station, linked to the airport terminal by a free shuttle, there are direct train services to several cities, including Arles and Avignon.

BICYCLE

Le Vélo (www.levelo-mpm.fr) Bike-share scheme: pick up/drop off a bike from 100-plus stations across the city and the coastal road to the beaches. Users must subscribe online first (€1/5 a week/year), after which the first 30

BEST BOUTIQUE SHOPPING

Various morning markets fill cours Julien, an elongated square with palm trees: fresh flowers on Wednesday and Saturday, antique books on alternate Saturdays, and stamps and antique books on Sunday. Otherwise, hit our favourite boutiques, each with a distinct Marseillais flavour.

Compagnie de Provence (18 rue Francis Davso; ⊘10am-7pm Mon-Sat; Ⓜ Vieux Port) For super stylish liquid and bar soap, au naturel or scented with olive oil, fig or a wilder Provençal scent, hit this iconic *savon de Marseille* boutique. Funky washbags, travel kits and other accessories also.

72% Pétanque (Map p772; 10 rue du Petit Puits) Bags of tourist shops sell *savon de Marseille* (Marseillais soap), but the most creative is this *atelier* in Le Panier where flowers, cupcakes, fish et al are crafted from soap in a rainbow of unusual scents.

Atelier 1 par 1 (49 rue du Panier) Creations by a collective of local fashion designers fill this tiny shop, and its neighbour opposite, in Le Panier.

La Maison du Pastis (Map p772; 108 quai du Port) Sample and buy more than 90 varieties of this aniseed-flavoured aperitif.

L'Occitane de Provence (26 rue Francis Davso; ⊘10am-7pm Mon-Sat; Ⓜ Vieux Port) Provence's most successful global brand: one-stop shop for 'smellies' for body and face, scented lavender, cherry flower, olive oil and other classic Provence smells.

L'Orni Thorynque (www.lornithorynque.fr; 16 rue Lulli; ⊘noon-2pm & 3-7pm Mon, 10am-2pm & 3-7pm Tue-Fri, 10am-7pm Sat) Linen cushions emblazoned with 'Le Panier', L'Estaque' and other Marseillais *quartiers* are among the ingenious gift ideas sold at this pandora's box of design objects for the home.

Virginie Monroe (www.virginiemonroe.com; 1 rue Pythéas; ⊘10am-7pm Mon, Tue & Thu-Sat, to 1.30pm & 2.30-7pm Wed ; Ⓜ Vieux Port) Marseille's favourite, ethnic-chic jewellery designer produces delicate necklaces and bracelets strung with tiny beads.

OM Boutique (☑04 91 33 20 01; 44 La Canebière; ⊘10am-7pm Mon-Sat; Ⓜ Noailles, 🚃 Canebière Garibaldi) Marseille football gear and match tickets.

WORTH A TRIP

LES CALANQUES

Marseille abuts the wild and spectacular Parc National des Calanques, a 20km stretch of high, rocky promontories, rising from brilliant-turquoise Mediterranean waters. The sheer cliffs are occasionally interrupted by small idyllic beaches, some impossible to reach without a kayak. The Marseillais cherish the Calanques, and come to soak up sun or take long day hikes. The promontories have been protected since 1975, and are national park today.

October to June, the best way to see the Calanques is to hike. In July and August, trails close because of fire danger: take a boat tour from Marseille or Cassis; sea kayak with Raskas Kayak (www.raskas-kayak.com); drive, or take a bus.

The Calanque de Sormiou is the largest rocky inlet. Two seasonal restaurants serve lunch with fabulous views, and require reservations. Le Château ([☎] 04 91 25 08 69; http://lechateausormiou.fr; mains €20-25; ◷ Apr–Sep) has the best food (no credit cards) and Le Lunch ([☎] 04 91 25 05 37; http://wp.resto.fr/lelunch; Calanque de Sormiou; mains €16-28; ◷ Apr–Oct) the better view. By bus, take the 23 from the Rond-Point du Prado metro stop to La Cayolle stop, from where it's a 3km walk. (Diners with reservations are allowed to drive through; otherwise, the road is open to cars weekdays only, September to June.)

Also popular are the *calanques* of Port-Miou, Port-Pin, En-Vau and Morgiou, best accessed from the pretty coastal town of Cassis. A coastal walk from Cassis to Morgiou (about 15km), takes 5½ to 6½ hours and is an absolute stunner. Wear sturdy shoes.

Marseille's tourist office (p778) leads guided walks (no kids under eight) of the Calanques, and has information on walks and trail closures, as does the Cassis' tourist office ([☎] 39 01 03; www.ot-cassis.com; quai des Moulins; ◷ 9am-6.30pm Tue-Sat, 9.30am-12.30pm & 3-6pm Sun, shorter hours low season).

Walking aside, the little port town of Cassis makes a postcard-perfect day trip if you have a car. After a glorious morning driving above aquamarine coves, plan to lunch with an obligatory bottle of crisp Cassis white wine at one of the portside restaurants. The tourist office supplies free maps of cellars open for tastings.

minutes is free, then €1 per hour. Stations only take credit cards with chips.

FERRY

Ferry Boat (◷ 10am-1.15pm & 2-7pm) Runs between the town hall (north side) and place aux Huiles (south side) of the Vieux Port; a one-way ticket bought direct from the driver costs €3.

PUBLIC TRANSPORT

Marseille has two metro lines (Métro 1 and Métro 2), two tram lines (yellow and green) and an extensive bus network. Bus, metro or tram tickets (€1.50 or €13 for a 10-ticket carnet) can be used on all public transport for one hour after they've been time stamped. Pick up a transport map and tickets at the **Espace Infos RTM** ([☎] 04 91 91 92 10; www.rtm.fr; 6 rue des Fabres; ◷ 8.30am-6pm Mon-Fri, 9am-12.30pm & 2-5.30pm Sat; [M] Vieux Port).

TAXI

Taxi Radio Marseille ([☎] 04 91 02 20 20)

Aix-en-Provence

POP 144,274

Aix-en-Provence, 25km from Marseille, is to Provence what the Left Bank is to Paris: an enclave of bourgeois-bohemian chic. Some 30,000 students from the Université de Provence Aix-Marseille, many from overseas, set the mood on the street: bars, cafes and affordable restaurants. The city is rich in culture (two of Aix' most famous sons are Paul Cézanne and Émile Zola) and oh-so respectable, with plane-tree-shaded boulevards and fashionable boutiques. All this class comes at a price: Aix is more expensive than other Provençal towns.

⊙ Sights & Activities

A stroller's paradise, the highlight is the mostly pedestrian old city, Vieil Aix. South of cours Mirabeau, the Quartier Mazarin was laid out in the 17th century, and is home to some of Aix' finest buildings and square: place des Quatre Dauphins, with its fish-spouting fountain (1667), is enchanting.

★ **Cours Mirabeau**   HISTORIC QUARTER
No avenue better epitomises Provence's most graceful city than this fountain-studded street, sprinkled with Renaissance *hôtels particuliers* and crowned with a summertime roof of leafy plane trees. Named after the revolution-

Aix-en-Provence

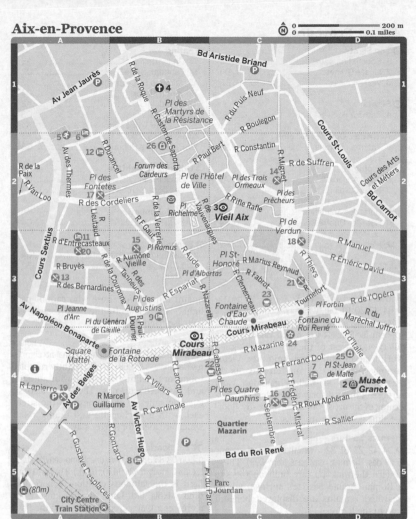

ary hero Comte de Mirabeau, it was laid out in the 1640s. Cézanne and Zola hung out at **Les Deux Garçons** (53 cours Mirabeau; ⏰7am-2am), one of a clutch of busy pavement cafes.

★ **Musée Granet**   MUSEUM
(www.museegranet-aixenprovence.fr; place St-Jean de Malte; adult/child €7/free; ⏰11am-7pm Tue-Sun) Housed in a 17th-century priory of the Knights of Malta, this exceptional museum is named after the Provençal painter François Marius Granet (1775–1849), who donated a large number of works. Its collection includes 16th- to 20th-century Italian, Flemish and French works. Modern art reads like a who's

who: Picasso, Léger, Matisse, Monet, Klee, Van Gogh and Giacometti, among others, including the museum's pride and joy: nine Cézanne works. Excellent temporary exhibitions.

Cathédrale St-Sauveur   CHURCH
(rue de la Roque; ⏰8am-noon & 2-6pm) Built between 1285 and 1350 in a potpourri of styles, this cathedral includes a Romanesque 12th-century nave in its southern aisle, chapels from the 14th and 15th centuries, and a 5th-century sarcophagus in the apse. More recent additions include the 18th-century gilt baroque organ. Acoustics make Sunday-afternoon Gregorian chants unforgettable.

Aix-en-Provence

Fondation Victor Vasarely   GALLERY
(☑04 42 20 01 09; www.fondationvasarely.fr; 1 av Marcel Pagnol; adult/child €9/4; ◎10am-1pm & 2-6pm Tue-Sun; ☐4 or 6 stop Vasarely) This gallery, 4km west of the city, was designed by Hungarian optical art innovator Victor Vasarely (1906–97). A masterpiece, its 16 interconnecting six-walled galleries were purpose-built to display and reflect the patterning of the artist's 44 acid-trip-ready, floor-to-ceiling geometric artworks.

Thermes Sextius   SPA
(☑04 42 23 81 82; www.thermes-sextius.com; 55 av des Thermes; day pass from €99) These modern thermal spas are built on the site of Roman Aquae Sextiae's springs, whose excavated remains are displayed beneath glass in the lobby.

★★ Festivals & Events

Festival d'Aix-en-Provence   PERFORMING ARTS
(☑04 34 08 02 17; www.festival-aix.com; ◎Jul) Month-long festival of classical music, opera, ballet and buskers.

🛏 Sleeping

Hôtel les Quatre Dauphins   BOUTIQUE HOTEL €
(☑04 42 38 16 39; www.lesquatredauphins.fr; 54 rue Roux Alphéran; s €62-72, d €72-87; ❉🤶) This sweet 13-room hotel slumbers in a former private mansion in one of the loveliest parts of town. Rooms are fresh and clean, with excellent modern bathrooms. Those with sloping, beamed ceilings in the attic are

quaint but not for those who cannot pack light – the terracotta-tiled staircase is not suitcase-friendly.

Hôtel Cardinal   HOTEL €
(☑04 42 38 32 30; www.hotel-cardinal-aix.com; 24 rue Cardinale; s/d €68/78; 🤶) Slightly rumpled rooms are quaintly furnished with antiques and tasselled curtains. There are also six gigantic suites in the annexe up the street, each with a kitchenette and dining room, which are ideal for longer stays.

★ **L'Épicerie**   B&B €€
(☑06 08 85 38 68; www.unechambreenville.eu; 12 rue du Cancel; d €100-130; 🤶🚿) This intimate B&B is the fabulous creation of born-and-bred Aixois lad Luc. His breakfast room recreates a 1950s grocery store, and the flowery garden out back is perfect for excellent evening dining and weekend brunch (book ahead for both). Breakfast is a veritable feast. Two rooms accommodate families of four.

Hôtel des Augustins   HOTEL €€
(☑04 42 27 28 59; www.hotel-augustins.com; 3 rue de la Masse; d €109-249; ❉🤶) A heartbeat from the hub of Aixois life, this former 15th-century convent with magnificent stone-vaulted lobby and sweeping staircase has volumes of history: Martin Luther stayed here after his excommunication from Rome. Filled with hand-painted furniture, the largest, most luxurious rooms have jacuzzis; two rooms have private terraces beneath the filigreed bell tower.

Le Manoir HOTEL €€

(☑ 04 42 26 27 20; www.hotelmanoir.com; 8 rue d'Entrecasteaux; d €82-126, tr €114; ☺ Feb-Dec; ☎ 🖳) Atmospherically set in a 14th-century cloister, The Manor – an easy family choice – is something of a blast from the past. Old world in spirit and location, it sits in an uncannily quiet wedge of the old town. Rooms are clean, simple and bourgeois spacious. Best up is the free parking in the gravel courtyard out front and breakfast, served alfresco in a vaulted cloister.

Hôtel Aquabella SPA HOTEL €€

(☑ 04 42 99 15 00; www.aquabella.fr; 3 rue des Étuves; d/tr €210/230) Should wallowing like a Roman in Aix-en-Provence's thermal waters tickle your fancy, then check into this three-star hotel adjoining the Thermes Sextius spa. Rates include spa access and there is really nothing more delightful after a hard day boutique shopping than a lounge in the eucalypt-scented hammam followed by a dip in the outdoor pool, with a view of Roman ruins.

Hôtel Cézanne BOUTIQUE HOTEL €€€

(☑ 04 42 91 11 11; http://cezanne.hotelaix.com; 40 av Victor Hugo; s/d €230/260; ❄ @ ☎) Purple flags

---

ⓘ AIX-CELLENT

The **Aix City Pass** (€15), valid for five days, includes a guided walking tour, admission to the Atelier Paul Cézanne, Jas de Bouffan and Musée Granet, and a trip on the mini-tram; the **Cézanne Pass** (€12) covers his three main sights. Buy passes at the tourist office or at any of the sights.

---

fly proud outside Aix's swishest hotel, a contemporary study in clean lines, with sharp-edged built-in desks, top-end fabrics and design-driven decor. In any other city its location next to the train station would be deemed a flaw. Reserve ahead for free parking.

🍴 Eating

Aix excels at Provençal cuisine and restaurant terraces spill out across dozens and dozens of charm-heavy old town squares, many pierced with an ancient stone fountain: place des Trois Ormeaux, place des Augustins, place Ramus and vast Forum des Cardeurs are particular favourites.

WORTH A TRIP

CÉZANNE SIGHTS

The life of local lad Paul Cézanne (1839–1906) is treasured in Aix. To see where he ate, drank, studied and painted, follow the **Circuit de Cézanne** (Cézanne Trail), marked by footpath-embedded bronze plaques. Pick up the accompanying information booklet at the tourist office.

Cézanne's last studio, **Atelier Cézanne** (www.atelier-cezanne.com; 9 av Paul Cézanne; adult/child €5.50/€2; ☺ 10am-noon & 2-5pm), 1.5km north of the tourist office on a hilltop, was painstakingly preserved (and recreated: not all the tools and still-life models strewn around the single room were his) as it was at the time of his death. Though the studio is inspiring, none of his works hang here. Take bus 1 or 20 to the Atelier Cézanne stop, or walk 1.5km from the centre. Films are screened in the garden in July and August. A 10-minute walk uphill from the bus stop is the **Terrain des Peintres**, a terraced garden perfect for a picnic, from where Cézanne, among others, painted the Montagne Ste-Victoire.

Visits to the other two sights must be reserved in advance at the tourist office. In 1859 Cézanne's father bought **Le Jas de Bouffan** (☑ 04 42 16 10 91; adult/child €5.50/2; ☺ guided tours 10.30am-5.30pm; 🚌 6 stop Corsy), a country manor west of Aix' centre, where Cézanne painted furiously: 36 oils and 17 watercolours in the decades that followed depicting the house, farm and chestnut-lined alley. Take bus 6 from La Rotonde to the Corsy stop; it's a 20-minute walk from town.

In 1895 Cézanne rented a cabin at the **Carrières de Bibemus** (Bibémus Quarries; ☑ 04 42 16 10 91; 3090 chemin de Bibémus; adult/child €5.50/2; ☺ guided tour 9.45am Jun-Sep, less frequently rest yr), on the edge of town, where he painted prolifically and where he did most of his Montagne Ste-Victoire paintings. Atmospheric one-hour tours of the ochre quarry take visitors on foot through the dramatic burnt-orange rocks Cézanne captured so vividly. Take bus 6 from La Rotonde to the 'Les Trois Bons Dieux' stop, from where *navettes* (shuttlebuses) run to the site; find schedules at www.aixenbus.fr.

SWEET TREAT

Aix' sweetest treat since King René's wedding banquet in 1473 is the marzipan-like local speciality, *calisson d'Aix*, a small, diamond-shaped, chewy delicacy made on a wafer base with ground almonds and fruit syrup, and glazed with icing sugar. Traditional *calissonniers* still make them, including **La Maison du Roy René** (www. calisson.com; 13 rue Gaston de Saporta; ⊙9.30am-1pm & 2-6.30pm Mon-Sat, 9am-4pm Sun) which runs tours of its small factory on the city's fringe.

★ **Jacquou**

Le Croquant   SOUTHWEST, PROVENÇAL €

(☑04 42 27 37 19; www.jacquoulecroquant.com; 2 rue de l'Aumône Vielle; plat du jour €10.90, menus from €14; ⊙noon-3pm & 7-11pm) This veteran address, around since 1985, stands out on dozens of counts: buzzy jovial atmosphere, flowery patio garden, funky interior, early evening opening, family friendly, hearty homecooking, a *menu* covering all price ranges, and so forth. Cuisine from southwestern France is its speciality, meaning lots of duck, but the vast menu covers all bases.

La Tarte Tropézienne   PATISSERIE, CAFE €

(av des Belges; sandwich/salad menu €6.90/7.35, mains €12-14) A handy stop en route to/from the bus and train stations, this modern pâtisserie is known for its sugar-encrusted *tarte Tropézienne* (cream-filled sandwich cake from St-Tropez), displayed in cabinets like jewels beneath glass. Grab a wedge (€2.90) to take out or eat in – on red director chairs on a decking terrace. Excellent-value gourmet sandwiches and salads.

Charlotte   BISTRO €

(☑04 42 26 77 56; 32 rue des Bernardines; 2-/3-course menus €16.50/20; ⊙12.30pm-2pm & 8-10.30pm Tue-Sat; 🐾) It's all very cosy at Charlotte, where everyone knows everyone. French classics like veal escalope and beef steak are mainstays, and there is always a vegetarian dish and a couple of imaginative *plats du jour*. In summer everything moves into the garden.

La Bidule   BISTRO €

(☑04 42 26 87 75; www.brasserielebidule.fr; 8 rue Lieutaud; mains €12.50-15; ⊙9am-11.30pm) Of the many restaurant terraces on elongated square Forum des Cadeurs, 'The Thingy' is hot with students and late-lunch diners. Its sizeable terrace with colourful flowery tablecloths and fairy lights at night is made for lingering, and the fare is hearty bistro – the honey-roasted camembert, burgers and fiesty salads are all superb. Excellent-value lunch formules include a glass of wine or coffee.

Le Petit Verdot   FRENCH €€

(☑04 42 27 30 12; www.lepetitverdot.fr; 7 rue d'Entrecasteaux; mains €15-25; ⊙7pm-midnight Mon-Sat) Delicious *menus* are designed around what's in season, and paired with excellent wines. Meats are often braised all day, vegetables are tender, stewed in delicious broths.

SHOP LOCAL

Chic fashion boutiques cluster along pedestrian rue Marius Reynaud and cours Mirabeau. But it is at the daily morning market on **place Richelme**, piled high with marinated olives, goat-milk cheese, lavender, honey, fruit and a bounty of other seasonal foods, that you'll find the local Aixois crowd. Or try the Sunday-morning flower market on **place des Prêcheurs**.

Tucked just off place des Prêcheurs is **Farinoman Fou** (3 rue Mignet; ⊙Tue-Sat), a truly phenomenal bakery which has a constant queue outside its door. The crunchy, different-flavoured breads baked by artisan boulanger Benoît Fradette are reason enough to sell up and move to Aix. The bakery has no shop as such; customers jostle for space with bread ovens and dough-mixing tubs.

Top off your shop with **La Chambre aux Confitures** (www.lachambreauxconfitures.com; 16bis rue d'Italie; ⊙10am-1pm & 3-7pm Mon-Fri, 10am-7.30pm Sat, 10am-1pm Sun). Do as locals do: don't be shy about asking asking to taste a jam, chutney or jelly in this outstanding boutique bursting with exotic and unexpected flavours. Best-selleing jams include clementine and calisson, apricot and lavender, and nutty fig and cognac. Excellent chutneys too, for pairing with cheese, meat and foie gras.

Save room for an incandescent dessert. Lively dining occurs around tabletops made of wine crates (expect to talk to your neighbour), and the gregarious owner speaks multiple languages.

Jardin Mazarin
FRENCH €€

(📞 04 42 58 11 42; www.jardinmazarin.com; 15 rue du 4 Sepembre; menu €34, mains €15-20; ⊙ noon-2.30pm & 8-10.30pm Tue-Sat) Something of a hidden address, this elegant restaurant serenades the ravishing *hôtel particulier* in which it languishes. Two salons sit beneath splendid beamed ceilings, but the real gem is outside: a luxuriant green garden with fountain and a line-up of tables beneath a wicker shade. Peace, perfect peace, far from the madding crowd.

Petit Pierre Reboul
GASTRONOMIC €€€

(📞 04 42 52 30 42; www.restaurant-pierre-reboul.com; 11 Petite Rue St-Jean, 2-/3-course bistro menu €19-34/27-39, gastronomic menus €52 & €87; ⊙ noon-2.30pm & 7.30-10.30pm Tue-Sat) This brightly coloured address, hidden down a back alley, is the bistro arm of Pierre Reboul's gastronomic **restaurant** next door. The vibe is contemporary design (think acid-bright fabrics and lampshades made from pencils), and the *menu* throws in the odd adventurous dish alongside mainstream stalwarts like burgers, Caesar salad, grilled meats and mussels 'n fries.

Drinking & Nightlife

The scene is fun, but fickle. For nightlife, hit rue de la Verrerie and place Richelme. Open-air cafes crowd the city's squares, especially Forum des Cardeurs, place de Verdun and place de l'Hôtel de Ville, and the city has a clutch of cinemas.

Book in Bar
CAFE

(4 rue Cabassol; ⊙ 9am-7pm Mon-Sat) There is no more literary spot to partake in *un café* than this particullarly fine English bookshop with cafe. Look out for occasional book readings, jazz evenings et al.

La Mado
CAFE €€

(Chez Madeleine; 📞 04 42 38 28 02; www.lamado-aix.com; 4 place des Prêcheurs; lunch/dinner menus €18/32; ⊙ 7am-2am) This smart daytime cafe, with steel-grey parasols and boxed-hedge terrace on a busy square, is unbeatable for coffee and fashionable-people watching; its food, lunch or dinner, is equally excellent. The Mado has been around for years, so the old guard dine while the hipsters shine.

WORTH A TRIP

CULINARY DETOUR: VENTABREN

A lesser-known hilltop village, Ventabren (population 5000), 16km west of Aix, provides the perfect lazy-day detour. Meander sun-dappled cobbled lanes, peep inside a 17th-century church, and take in panoramic views of Provence from the ruins of Château de la Reine Jeanne before a superb lunch or dinner at La Table de Ventabren (📞 04 42 28 79 33; www.latabledeventabren.com; 1 rue Cézanne; lunch menu Tue-Fri €40, 5-course tasting menu €89, mains from €28; ⊙ noon-1.15pm Wed-Sun, 7.45-9.15pm dinner Tue-Sun), which is reason enough to visit. The terrace looks out to distant mountains, magical on starry summer evenings. Michelin-starred chef Dan Bessoudo creates inventive, wholly modern French dishes and knockout desserts. Reservations essential.

Le Mistral
CLUB

(www.mistralclub.fr; 3 rue Frédéric Mistral; ⊙ 11.30pm-6am Tue-Sat) If anyone's awake past midnight, chances are they'll wind up at this happening basement club, with three bars and a dance floor. DJs spin house, R&B, techno and rap.

ℹ Information

Tourist Office (📞 04 42 16 11 61; www.aixenprovencetourism.com; square Colonel Antoine Mattei; ⊙ 8.30am-8pm Mon-Sat, 10am-1pm & 2-4pm Sun Jun Sep, shorter hrs rest of yr) Seriously hi-tech with no brochures, just monumental touch screens – everywhere. Sells tickets for guided tours and cultural events.

ℹ Getting There & Around

Consult www.lepilote.com for all transport information, www.info-ler.fr for some regional buses and www.navetteaixmarseille.com for shuttle buses to/from Marseille.

Aix en Bus (www.aixenbu.fr) runs local buses, with La Rotonde being the main hub. The tourist office has schedules and Minibus 2 links the city centre train station with La Rotonde. To grab a taxi call 📞 04 42 21 61 61.

BUS

Aix' **bus station** (📞 08 91 02 40 25, 04 42 91 26 80; place Marius Bastard) is a 10-minute walk southwest from La Rotonde. Services include:
Aéreoport Marseille Provence €8.20, 30 minutes, every 15 minutes

Arles €10.50, 1½ hours, seven daily
Avignon €17.40, 1¼ hours, six daily
Marseille €5.70, 25 minutes, every 10 minutes
Toulon €13.90, one hour, seven daily

TRAIN

The tiny **city centre train station**, at the southern end of av Victor Hugo, serves Marseille (€8.20, 45 minutes). Aix' **TGV station**, 15km from the city centre and accessible by shuttle bus (€3.70 from the bus station), serves most of France; to Marseille it's 12 minutes (€6.20, 20 daily).

ARLES & THE CAMARGUE

Arles

POP 53,660

Arles' poster boy is the celebrated impressionist painter Vincent van Gogh. If you're familiar with his work, you'll be familiar with Arles: the light, the colours, the landmarks and the atmosphere, all of which he faithfully captured.

But long before Van Gogh rendered this grand Rhône River locale on canvas, the Romans valued its worth. In 49 BC Arles' prosperity and political standing rose meteorically when it backed a winner in Julius Caesar (who would never meet defeat in his entire career). After Caesar plundered Marseille, which had supported his rival Pompey the Great, Arles eclipsed Marseille as the region's major port. Within a century and a half, it boasted a 12,000-seat theatre and a 20,000-seat amphitheatre to entertain its citizens with gruesome gladiatorial spectacles and chariot races.

Still impressively intact, the two structures now stage events including Arles' famous *férias* (bull-running festivals), with their controversial lethal bullfights, the less bloody

---

ⓘ ROMAN COMBO PASS

Buy a pass for multiple sights at the tourist office (p791) or any Roman site: **Passeport Avantage** (€13.50) covers the museums, both theatres, the baths, crypt, Les Alyscamps and the Cloître St-Trophime; the **Passeport Liberté** (€9) gives you the choice of five sights in total including one museum. Remember museums are free the first Sunday of the month.

---

courses camarguaises and three days of street parties.

Contrasting dramatically with Arles' ancient history is its increasingly dynamic, contemporary art scene – reflected in the 2014 opening of the new, state-of-the art **Fondation Vincent Van Gogh** and the future 2018 opening of an arts centre for the **Luma Foundation** (http://luma-arles.org). The flamboyant, aluminium twist of a building, designed by world-renowned architect Frank Gehry no less, will become the centrepiece of **Parc des Ateliers**, a rejuvenated industrial area next to the train station once abuzz with railway hangars and workshops.

⊙ Sights & Activities

Les Arènes   ROMAN SITE
(Amphithéâtre; adult/child incl Théâtre Antique €6.50/5; ⊙9am-7pm) Slaves, criminals and wild animals (including giraffes) met their dramatic demise before a jubilant 20,000-strong crowd during Roman gladiatorial displays at Les Arènes, built around the early 2nd century AD. During the early medieval Arab invasions the arch-laced circular structure – 136m long, 107m wide and 21m tall – was topped with four defensive towers. By the 1820s, when the amphitheatre was returned to its original use, 212 houses and two churches had to be razed on the site.

Buy tickets for bloody bullfights, bloodless *courses camarguaises,* theatre and concerts at the ticket office next to the entrance.

★Fondation Vincent Van Gogh   MUSEUM
(☏04 90 49 94 04; www.fondation-vincent vangogh-arles.org; 33 ter rue du Docteur Fanton; adult/child €9/4; ⊙11am-7pm, to 9pm Thu) This Van Gogh–themed gallery is a must-see, as much for its contemporary architecture and design, as for the art it showcases. It has no permanent art collection; rather, it hosts one or two temporary exhibitions a year, always with a Van Gogh theme and always including at least one Van Gogh masterpiece. Architectural highlights include the rooftop terrace and the kaleidescope-style bookshop 'ceiling' aka chunks of coloured glass forming a roof.

★Musée Réattu   MUSEUM
(☏04 90 49 37 58; www.museereattu.arles.fr; 10 rue du Grand Prieuré; adult/child €7/free; ⊙10am-6pm Tue-Sun, to 5pm Dec-Feb) This splendid modern-art museum is housed in the exquisitely renovated 15th-century Grand Priory of the Knights of Malta. Among its collec-

Arles

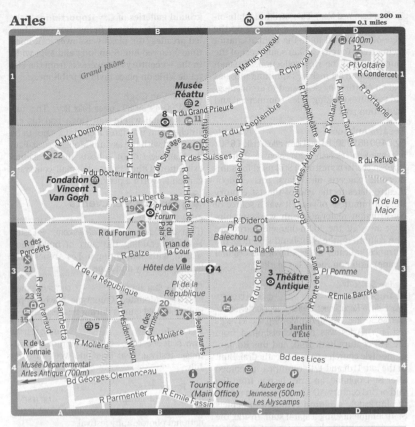

Arles

◎ Top Sights

tions are works by 18th- and 19th-century Provençal artists and two paintings and 57 sketches by Picasso. It hosts wonderfully curated cutting-edge exhibitions.

**Musée Départemental
Arles Antique**   MUSEUM
(☏ 04 13 31 51 03; www.arles-antique.cg13.fr; av de la
Première Division Française Libre; adult/child €8/5;

⊙10am-6pm Wed-Mon) This striking, state-of-the-art cobalt-blue museum perches on the edge of what used to be the Roman chariot racing track (circus), 1.5km southwest of the tourist office. The rich collection of pagan and Christian art includes stunning mosaics and an entire wing dedicated to archaeological treasures evoking Arles' commercial and navigation past.

Théâtre Antique
ROMAN SITE

(☑04 90 96 93 30; bd des Lices; adult/child €6.50/free, free with Les Arènes admission; ⊙9am-7pm May-Sep, shorter hrs rest of yr) Still used for summertime concerts and plays, this outdoor theatre dates to the end of the 1st century BC. For hundreds of years it was a source of construction materials, with workers chipping away at the 102m-diameter structure (the column on the right-hand side near the entrance indicates the height of the original arcade). Enter on rue de la Calade.

Église & Cloître St-Trophime
CHURCH, CLOISTER

(place de la République; church free, cloister adult/child €3.50/free; ⊙9am-7pm May-Sep, shorter hours rest of yr) Arles was an archbishopric from the 4th century until 1790, and this Romanesque-style church was once a cathedral. Built in the late 11th and 12th centuries, it's named after St Trophime, an Arles bishop from the 2nd or 3rd century AD. On the western portal, the intricately sculpted tympanum depicts St Trophime holding a spiral staff. Inside, the treasury contains bone fragments of Arles' bishops. Occasional exhibitions are hosted in neighbouring cloister, Cloître St-Trophime.

Les Alyscamps
CEMETERY

(av des Alyscamps; adult/child €3.50/free; ⊙9am-7pm May-Sep, shorter hrs rest of yr) Van Gogh and Gauguin both painted this necropolis, founded by the Romans 1km southwest of the centre.

Thermes de Constantin
ROMAN SITE

(rue du Grand Prieuré; adult/child €3/free; ⊙9am-noon & 2-7pm May-Sep, shorter hours rest of yr) Partly preserved Roman baths were built for Emperor Constantin's private use in the 4th century.

Place du Forum
ROMAN SITE

(adult/child €3.50/free; ⊙cryptoportiques 9am-noon & 2-7pm May-Sep, shorter hrs rest of yr) Just as social, political and religious life revolved around the forum in Roman Arles so this busy plane-tree-shaded square buzzes with cafe life today. Underneath it lie the underground galleries of Cryptoportiques – the forum's subterranean foundations and buried arcades (the plaza was lower in Roman times) carved out, 89m long and 59m wide, in the 1st century BC. Access is from the Hôtel de Ville on place de la République.

Espace Van Gogh
GALLERY

(☑04 90 49 39 39; place Félix Rey) The former hospital where Van Gogh had his ear stitched and was later locked up – not to be confused with the asylum Monastère St-Paul de Mausole (p796) – hosts the occasional exhibition. Other times, its small courtyard garden is worth a peek.

✸ Festivals & Events

Féria d'Arles
BULLFIGHTING

(Féria de Pâques; www.feriaarles.com; ⊙Easter) Festival heralding the start of bullfighting season, with bullfighting in Les Arènes most Sundays in May and June.

Fête des Gardians
CULTURAL FESTIVAL

(⊙1 May) Mounted Camargue cowboys parade and hold games during this festival.

Les Suds
MUSIC FESTIVAL

(www.suds-arles.com; ⊙Jul) Vibrant world-music festival, held over one week in early July.

Les Rencontres d'Arles Photographie
ART FESTIVAL

(www.rencontres-arles.com; ⊙early Jul-Sep) International photography festival.

Féria du Riz
BULLFIGHTING

(www.feriaarles.com; ⊙Sep) Bullfights during this week-long festival mark the start of the rice harvest.

🛏 Sleeping

Arles has reasonably priced, excellent year-round accommodation, which only really fills during férias; some hotels only open April to October. Hotels' private parking tends to be pricey.

★Hôtel de l'Amphithéâtre
HISTORIC HOTEL €

(☑04 90 96 10 30; www.hotelamphitheatre.fr; 5-7 rue Diderot; s/d/tr/q €61/79/129/139; ✳@⎙) Crimson, chocolate, terracotta and other rich earthy colours dress the exquisite 17th-century stone structure of this stylish hotel, with narrow staircases, a roaring fire and alfresco courtyard breakfasts. The romantic suite has a dreamy lilac-walled terrace overlooking rooftops. Breakfast €8.50.

VINCENT

Vincent van Gogh was only 37 when he died. Born in 1853, the Dutch painter arrived in Arles in 1888 after living in Paris with his younger brother Theo, an art dealer who financially supported Vincent from his own modest income.

Revelling in Arles' intense light and bright colours, Van Gogh painted with a burning fervour. During the howling mistral (wind) he would kneel on his canvases and paint horizontally, or lash his easel to iron stakes driven deep into the ground. He sent paintings to Theo to sell, and dreamed of founding an artists' colony in Arles, but only Gauguin followed up his invitation. Their differing artistic approaches (Gauguin believed in painting from imagination, Van Gogh painting what he saw) and their artistic temperaments came to a head with the argument in December 1888 that led to Van Gogh lopping off part of his own ear.

In May 1889 Van Gogh voluntarily entered an asylum, Monastère St-Paul de Mausole (p796) in St-Rémy de Provence, 25km northeast of Arles over the Alpilles, where he painted 150-odd canvases, including *Starry Night* (not to be confused with *Starry Night over the Rhône*, painted in Arles). In February 1890, his 1888 work *The Red Vines*, painted in Arles, was bought by Anne Boch, sister of his friend Eugene Boch, for 400 francs (around €50 today) – the only painting he sold in his lifetime. It now hangs in the Pushkin State Museum of Fine Arts.

On 16 May 1890 Van Gogh moved to Auvers-sur-Oise, near Paris, to be closer to Theo. But on 27 July he shot himself. He died two days later with Theo at his side. Theo subsequently had a breakdown, was committed and died, aged 33, six months after Vincent. Less than a decade later, Van Gogh's talent started to achieve recognition, with major museums acquiring his work.

Van Gogh painted some 200 canvases in Arles and there is always one at least displayed in the Fondation Vincent Van Gogh. Van Gogh's little 'yellow house' on place Lamartine, painted in 1888, was destroyed during WWII. Mapped out in a tourist office brochure (€1 or downloadable for free online), the evocative **Van Gogh walking circuit** of the city takes in scenes painted by the artist.

PROVENCE ARLES

Le Belvédère Hôtel
BOUTIQUE HOTEL €

(☑04 90 91 45 94; www.hotellebelvedere-arles. com; 5 place Voltaire; s/d €65/70-90; ❄☎) This sleek 17-room hotel is one of the best Arlésian pads. Red-glass chandeliers (and friendly staff) adorn the lobby breakfast area and the super-clean rooms and bathrooms are fitted out in stylish red, chocolate brown and grey. Breakfast €7.50.

Hôtel du Musée
BOUTIQUE HOTEL €

(☑04 90 93 88 88; www.hoteldumusee.com; 11 rue du Grand Prieuré; s/d/tr/q from €60/70/95/120; ☺mid-Mar–Oct; ❄☎) In a fine 17th- to 18th-century building, this impeccable hotel has comfortable rooms, a checkerboard-tiled breakfast room and a sugar-sweet patio garden brimming with pretty blossoms. Breakfast €8.50, parking €10.

Auberge de Jeunesse
HOSTEL €

(☑04 90 96 18 25; www.fuaj.org; 20 av Maréchal Foch; dm incl breakfast & sheets €18.50; ☺mid-Feb–mid-Dec, reception closed 10am-5pm) This sunlit place, made up of eight-bed dorms, is 10 minutes' walk from the centre. Its bar closes at 11pm, just like its gates (except during *férias*).

★ Le Cloître
DESIGN HOTEL €€

(☑04 88 09 10 00; www.hotel-cloitre.com; 18 rue du Cloître; s/d €100/125; @☎) Unbeatable value, The Cloister – 12th-century neighbour to the Cloître Ste-Trophime – is the perfect fusion of historic charm and contemporary design. Its 19 rooms across two floors tout high ceilings, bold colours and a funky mix or patterns and textures. Breakfast (€13), served in the wonderfully airy and 1950s-styled breakfast room, is a particularly stylish affair. No elevator. Free bike rental.

There is no lovelier way to end the day than with an *apéro* (aperitif) on the chic rooftop terrace, privy to wonderful views of the sculpted stone façade of the Ste-Trophime cloister.

★ Le Calendal
HOTEL €€

(☑04 90 96 11 89; www.lecalendal.com; 5 rue Porte de Laure; s €66-99, d €99-130, tr €119-149, q €149-199; ☺lunch noon-2.30pm, salon de thé 4-6pm) Overlooking the Théâtre Antique, this bright

A BULLISH AFFAIR

Not all types of bullfights end with blood. The Camargue variation, the *course camar-guaise*, sees amateur *razeteurs* (from the word for 'shave'), wearing skin-tight white shirts and trousers, get as close as they dare to the *taureau* (bull) to try to snatch rosettes and ribbons tied to the bull's horns, using a *crochet* (a razor-sharp comb) held between their fingers. Their leaps over the arena's barrier as the bull charges are spectacular.

Bulls are bred on a *manade* (bull farm) by *manadiers*, helped in their daily chores by *gardians* (Camargue cattle-herding cowboys). These mounted herdsmen parade through Arles during the **Fête des Gardians** on 1 May. Otherwise spend a morning with a herd of them at the **Manade des Baumelles** (✆ 04 90 97 84 14; www.manadedesbaumelles.com; D38; bull-farm tour with/without lunch €45/25), a bull farm south of Arles in the Camargue countryside where you can learn about farm life and bull breeding, and watch cowboys at work in the field from the safety of a tractor-pulled truck. Tours end with an optional farm lunch. Find the *manade* a few kilometres north of Stes-Maries de la Mer, at the end of a gravel track off the D38 towards Aigues-Mortes.

Many *manades* also breed the creamy white *cheval de Camargue* (Camargue horse).

A calendar of *courses camarguaises* during the bullfighting season (Easter to September) is online at the **Fédération Française de la Course Camarguaise** (French Federation of Camargue Bullfights; ✆ 04 66 26 05 35; www.ffcc.info); several are held in Stes-Maries de la Mer.

hotel is a wonderful spot to stay. Rooms have beamed ceilings and bright Provençal fabrics, but the real heart-stealers are the spa **Au Bain du Calendal** and the lush flowery garden with terrace cafe **Le Comptoir du Calendal**. No summer breakfast (€12, open to non-guests too), lunch or afternoon drink in Arles is more peaceful than here.

Hôtel Arlatan · HISTORIC HOTEL €€

(✆ 04 90 93 56 66; www.hotel-arlatan.fr; 26 rue du Sauvage; d €85-157; ⊘ mid-Mar–mid-Nov; ❄@🛇🏊) The heated swimming pool, pretty garden and plush rooms decorated with antique furniture are just some of the things going for this hotel. Add to that a setting steeped in history, with Roman foundations visible through a glass floor in the lobby and 15th-century paintings on one of the lounges' ceilings. Breakfast continental/buffet €9/15.

L'Hôtel Particulier · BOUTIQUE HOTEL €€€

(✆ 04 90 52 51 40; www.hotel-particulier.com; 4 rue de la Monnaie; d from €309; ⊘ Easter-Oct) This exclusive boutique hotel with restaurant, spa and hammam (Turkish steam bath) oozes chic charm. From the big black door with heavy knocker to the crisp white linens and minimalist decor, everything about this 18th-century private mansion enchants.

 Eating

Arles' Saturday-morning **market** fills the length of bd des Lices with stalls of Camargue salt, goat-milk cheese and *saucisson d'Arles* (bull-meat sausage). The scene shifts to bd Émile Combes on Wednesday morning.

No town square is more crammed with cafe pavement terraces than Roman **place du Forum**, an inevitable stop of any Van Gogh walking tour thanks to the famously bright yellow façade of tourist-rammed **Café Van Gogh**, thought to be the cafe painted by Van Gogh in his *Café Terrace at Night* (1888).

Several hip, shabby-chic cafes bespeck rue des Porcelets and surrounding streets in the increasingly trendy 'n edgy Roquette *quartier*. When it all gets too much, seek out the floral peace and tranquility of the garden café at Le Calendal hotel.

Fad'Ola · SANDWICHES €

(✆ 04 90 49 70 73; 40 rue des Arènes; sandwiches €3.80-6.50, salads €4.50-15; ⊘ 11.30am-3pm & 7-10pm, shorter hrs low season) Well-stuffed sandwiches – made to order, *frotté à l'ail* (rubbed with garlic) and dripping with silken AOC Vallée des Baux olive oil – lure the crowds to this tiny sandwich shop with hole-in-the-wall takeaway counter. It also sells olive oil by the litre (€12 to €25). Find it footsteps from central 'cafe' square, place du Forum.

Glacier Arlelatis · ICE CREAM €

(8 place du Forum; 1/2 scoops €2/4; ⊘ 12.30-11pm) Creamy, delicious artisanal ice-cream is the mainstay of this *glacier* on busy place du Forum. Buy a cone to takeaway or treat yourself to a magnificent whipped-cream-topped

sundae sitting down. Flavours change but there's always a few distinctly Provençal ones: lavender honey, chestnut and so forth.

Comptoir du Sud
CAFE €

(📞 04 90 96 22 17; 2 rue Jean Jaurès; sandwiches €4.10-5.70; ⏰ 9am-6pm Tue-Fri) Gourmet sandwiches, wraps and bagels (tasty chutneys, succulent meats, foie gras) and divine little salads are served at this stylish *épicerie fine* (gourmet grocery). Take away or eat in on bar stools and end with a sweet €3 wedge of homemade *clafoutis* (cherry pie) for dessert.

L'Entrevue
MOROCCAN €

(📞 04 90 93 37 28; www.lentrevue-restaurant.com; place Nina Berberova; mains €14-23; ⏰ noon-2pm & 7.30-10.30pm; 📶) Excellent heaped terracotta *tians* (bowls) of organic tajines and couscous are briskly served quayside at this colourful address, just around the corner from the Fondation Van Gogh.

Chez Caro
BISTRO €€

(📞 04 90 97 94 38; www.chezcaro.fr; 12 place du Forum; 2-/3-course menu €29/36; ⏰ noon-2pm & 8-10pm Thu-Mon) Discreetly set at the far end of place du Forum, dwarfed by the imposing façade of the Nord Pinus hotel, Chez Caro is a modern bistro with vintage school furniture and some of Arles' finest modern French cooking. Wannabe alfresco diners can plump for a table on the bijou pavement terrace or – less appealing – with the masses in the middle of the square.

★ Le Gibolin
BISTRO €€

(📞 04 88 65 43 14; 13 rue des Porcelet; menus €27-32, glass wine €4.50-5.50; ⏰ 12.15 2pm & 8-10pm Tue-Sat Sep-Jul) Sup on peerless home cooking (think cod with fennel confit and crushed potatoes, pot au feu), while the friendly patroness bustles between dark wood tables sharing her knowledge and passion for natural wines at Arles' most beloved *bar à vins nature*. Pairings are naturally *magnifique*. No credit cards.

L'Atelier
GASTRONOMIC €€€

(📞 04 90 91 07 69; www.rabanel.com; 7 rue des Carmes; lunch/dinner menus €65 & €110/125 & €185; ⏰ sittings begin noon-1pm & 8-9pm Wed-Sun) Consider this not a meal, but an artistic experience (with two shiny Michelin stars no less). Every one of the seven or 13 edible works of art is a wondrous composition of flavours, colours and textures courtesy of charismatic chef Jean-Luc Rabanel. Many products are sourced from the chef's organic

vegie patch and wine pairings are an adventure in themselves. Half-day cooking classes (with/without lunch €200/145).

🛍 Shopping

La Botte Camarguaise
SHOES

(📞 06 16 04 08 14; 22 rue Jean Granaud; ⏰ 9am-12.30pm & 2-6.30pm Mon-Fri, 7am-noon Sat) Buy a pair of handmade Camargue-style cowboy boots.

La Boutique des Passionnés
MUSIC

(📞 04 90 96 59 93; www.passionnes.com; 14 rue Réattu; ⏰ 9am-7pm Tue-Sat) Gig flyers, tickets and music by Roma bands at this specialist music shop, also known as 'Musiques Arles'.

ℹ Information

Tourist Office (Main Office) (📞 04 90 18 41 20; www.tourisme.ville-arles.fr; esplanade Charles de Gaulle; ⏰ 9am-6 45pm Apr-Sep, to 4.45pm Mon-Fri & 12.45pm Sun Oct-Mar)

ℹ Getting There & Around

BICYCLE
Europbike Provence (📞 06 38 14 49 50; www.europbike-provence.net; per day adult/child €10-18/8, electric e-bike €35; ⏰ 8am-6pm) Rents bikes of all shapes and sizes, for adults and kids, plus all the paraphernalia like trailers for baggage or kids (€5 per day), children's seats (€3 per day) and GPS units (€7 per day). Delivery to your hotel (minimum two-day rental) costs €6.50 within a 15km radius. Before setting off, download suggested cycling itineraries from Europbike's website.

BUS
From the **bus station** (📞 08 10 00 13 26; www.lepilote.com; av Paulin Talabot), opposite the train station, there are services to Aix-en-Provence (€10.50, 1½ hours), Stes-Maries de la Mer (€2.90, one hour) and Nîmes (€1.70, one hour).

TRAIN
There are services to Nîmes (€8.60, 30 minutes), Marseille (€15.30, 50 minutes to 1½ hr) and Avignon (€7.50-9.10, 20 minutes). The closest TGV stations are in Avignon and Nîmes.

Camargue Countryside

Just south of Arles, Provence's rolling landscapes yield to the flat, marshy wilds of the Camargue countryside, famous for its teeming bird life, roughly 500 species. King of all is the pink flamingo, which enjoys the expansive wetlands' mild winters. Equally famous are the Camargue's small white horses; their mellow disposition makes horse riding the ideal way to explore the region's patchwork of salt pans and rice fields, and meadows dotted with grazing bulls. Bring binoculars – and mosquito repellent.

Enclosed by the Petit Rhône and Grand Rhône Rivers, most of the Camargue wetlands fall within the 850-sq-km Parc Naturel Régional de Camargue, established in 1970 to preserve the area's fragile ecosystems while sustaining local agriculture. On the periphery, the Étang de Vaccarès and nearby peninsulas and islands form the Réserve Nationale de Camargue, a 135-sq-km nature reserve.

The Camargue's two largest towns are the seaside pilgrim's outpost Stes-Maries de la Mer and, to the northwest, the walled town of Aigues-Mortes.

◎ Sights & Activities

Musée de la Camargue   MUSEUM
(Musée Camarguais; ☑ 04 90 97 10 82; www.parc-camargue.fr; Mas du Pont de Rousty, D570; adult/child €5/free, free 1st Sun & last Wed of month; ◷ 9am-12.30pm & 1-6pm Wed-Mon Apr-Oct, 10am-12.30pm & 1-5pm Nov-Mar) Inside a 19th-century sheep shed 10km southwest of Arles, this museum evokes traditional local life: exhibitions cover history, ecosystems, farming techniques, flora and fauna. *L'Oeuvre Horizons* by Japanese artist Tadashi Kawamata – aka a wooden observatory shaped like a boat – provides a bird's eye view of the agricultural estate, crossed by a 3.5km walking trail. The headquarters of the Parc Naturel Régional de Camargue are also based here.

Parc Ornithologique
du Pont de Gau   BIRD PARK
(☑ 04 90 97 82 62; www.parcornithologique.com; Pont du Gau; adult/child €7.50/5; ◷ 9am-sunset Apr-Sep, from 10am rest yr) Pink flamingos pirouette overhead and stalk the watery landscape at this bird park, home to every bird species known to set foot in the Camargue. Watch them from the 7km of beautiful trails that meander through the site. Find the park on the D570 in Pont du Gau, 4km north of Stes-Maries de la Mer.

★ Domaine de la Palissade   NATURE PARK
(☑ 04 42 86 81 28; www.palissade.fr; rte de la Mer; adult/child €3/free; ◷ 9am-6pm mid-Jun–mid-Sep, to 5pm mid-Sep–mid-Nov & Mar–mid-Jun, to 5pm Wed-Sun mid-Nov-Feb) This remote nature centre, 12km south of Salin de Giraud, organises fantastic forays through marshand, scrubby glasswort, flowering sea lavender (August)

and lagoons, on foot and horseback; call ahead to book horse treks (€18 per hour). Before hitting the scrub, rent binoculars (€2) and grab a free map of the estate's three marked walking trails (1km to 8km) from the office.

Cabanes de Cacharel   HORSE RIDING
(☑ 04 90 97 84 10, 06 11 57 74 75; www.cabanesde cacharel.com; rte de Cacharel; 1/2/3hr horse trek €20/30/40) Farms along route d'Arles (D570) offer *promenades à cheval* (horseback riding) astride white Camargue horses, but a more authentic experience can be had at these stables, just north of Stes-Maries de la Mer along the parallel rte de Cacharel (D85A). Horse-and-carriage rides too (one hour, €15).

Absolut Kiteboarding   WATER SPORTS
(☑ 06 88 15 10 93; www.absolutkiteboarding.fr; 36 rte d'Arles, Salin de Giraud; group/private lesson €130/300) Ride the waves and the wind with this recommended kitesurfing school, headed by Patrick. March to November you're on the water, December to February on dry ground. The school runs a shop and rents gear (€70). Find it at the northern entrance to Salin-de-Giraud, on the D36.

▙ Sleeping

★ Cacharel Hotel   HOTEL €€
(☑ 04 90 97 95 44; www.hotel-cacharel.com; rte de Cacharel, D85A; s/d/tr/q €128/140/152/173, horse-riding €30/hr; ❀🗺) This isolated farmstead, 400m down an unpaved track off the D85A just north of Stes-Maries de la Mer, perfectly balances modern-day comforts with rural authenticity. Photographic portraits of the bull herder who created the hotel in 1947 (son Florian runs the three-star hotel with much love today) give the vintage dining room soul and rooms sit snug in whitewashed cottages, some overlooking the water.

Swings in the paddock, horse-riding with a *gardian* (cowboy), boules to play *pétanque* and bags of open space between fig trees and pines make it a perfect family choice. Cacharel is one of the few Camargue hotels to open year-round.

★ Mas de Calabrun   HOTEL €€
(☑ 04 90 97 82 21; www.mas-de-calabrun.fr; rte de Cacherel, D85A; d/roulotte €129/169; ◷ mid-Feb–mid-Nov; ❀🗺) From the striking equestrian sculpture in its front courtyard to the swish pool, stylish restaurant terrace and fabulous views of open Camargue countryside, this hotel thoroughly deserves its three stars. The icing on the cake however is its

trio of *chic roulottes* (old-fashioned 'gypsy' wagons) which promise the perfect romantic getaway. Breakfast buffet €15.

Le Mas de Peint BOUTIQUE HOTEL €€€
(☑04 90 97 20 62; www.masdepeint.com; Le Sambuc; d from €260, menus €59 & €97; ☉mid-Mar–mid-Nov; ❋☗☂) So chic and gentrified it almost feels out of place in the Camargue, this upmarket *mas* (farmhouse) – part of the luxurious Châteaux & Hôtels Collection – is right out of design mag *Côte Sud*. The good news: non-guests are welcome in its gourmet restaurant and swish, poolside canteen.

✖ Eating

★ La Telline CAMARGUAIS €€
(☑04 90 97 01 75; www.restaurantlatelline.fr; rte de Gageron, Villeneuve; mains €23-32.50; ☉lunch & dinner Fri-Mon) A true local favourite, this isolated cottage restaurant with sage-green wooden shutters could not be simpler or more authentic. Summer dining is in a small and peaceful, flower-filled garden; and the no-frills *menu* cooks up a straightforward choice of *tellines*, salad or terrine as starter followed by grilled fish or meat, or a beef or bull steak. No credit cards.

Chez Bob CARMARGUAIS €€
(☑04 90 97 00 29; http://restaurantbob.fr; Mas Petite Antonelle, rte du Sambuc, Villeneuve; menu €45; ☉noon-2pm & 7.30-9pm Wed-Sun) This house restaurant is an iconic address adored by Arlesians. Feast on grilled bull chops, duck breasts and lamb trees or inside between walls plastered in photos, posters and other memorabilia collected over the years by Jean-Guy alias 'Bob'. Find his pad 20km south of Arles in Villeneuve, 800m after the crossroads on the D37 towards Salin. Reserve online.

★ La Chassagnette GASTRONOMIC €€€
(☑04 90 97 26 96; www.chassagnette.fr; rte du Sambuc; 6-course menu with/without wine €180/125, mains €35-38; ☉noon-1.30pm & 7-9.30pm Thu-Mon Apr-Jun, Sep & Oct; daily Jul & Aug; Thu-Sun Nov-Mar) Inhaling the scent of sun-ripened tomatoes is one of many pleasures at this 19th-century sheepfold – the ultimate Camargue dining spot. Alain Ducasse prodigy Armand Arnal cooks up a 100% organic *menu*, grows much of it himself and woos guests with a mosquito-protected outside terrace. Look for the fork and trowel sign, 12km southeast of Arles on the southbound D36, just north of Le Sambuc.

WORTH A TRIP

AN UNFORGETTABLE PANORAMA
No view is wilder or more soul-stirring than the sweep of salt pans, salt mountains and diggers at work that unfolds 2km south of the village of Salin de Giraud, along the D36D. Park in the car park, just before the 'slag heaps' of harvested salt, and trek up to the windwept **Point de Vue** (viewpoint) to gorge on a stunning panorama of pink-hued *salins* (salt pans). Europe's largest, they produce 800,000 tonnes of salt per year.

The next 12km south along this same road to the Domaine de la Palissade (p792) passes pink flamingos wading through water and is equally unforgettable.

❶ Getting There & Around
You will need a car to visit the area; it's an easy day trip from Arles. Alternatively, the flat terrain makes the Camargue an ideal cycling destination; hire companies based in Stes-Maries de la Mer can usually drop off bikes at your hotel for free.

Stes-Maries de la Mer
POP 2422
You could be forgiven for thinking you'd crossed into Spain at this remote seaside outpost, where whitewashed buildings line dusty streets and dancers in bright dresses spin flamenco. During its Roma pilgrimages, street-cooked pans of paella fuel chaotic crowds of carnivalesque guitarists, dancers and mounted cowboys.

⊙ Sights & Activities
Tickets for **bullfights** at Stes-Maries' Arènes are sold at the beachfront arena, from where 30km of golden-sand **beaches** – easily reached by bicycle or on foot – lace the shoreline east and west.

Église des Stes-Maries CHURCH
(www.sanctuaire-des-saintesmaries.fr; place Jean XXIII; adult/child €2.50/1.50; ☉10am-noon & 2-5pm Mon-Sat, 2-5pm Sun) This 12th- to 15th-century church, with its dark, hushed, candle-wax-scented atmosphere, draws legions of Roma pilgrim to venerate the statue of black Sara, their revered patron saint, during the Pèlerinage des Gitans. The relics of Sara and those of Marie-Salomé and Marie-Jacobé,

all found in the crypt by King René in 1448, are enshrined in a wooden chest, stashed in the stone wall above the choir. Don't miss the panorama from the **rooftop terrace** (€2).

★ **Digue à la Mer**   DIKE, CYCLING

This 2.5m-high dike was built in the 19th century to cut the delta off from the sea. A 20km-long walking and cycling track runs along its length linking Stes-Maries with the solar-powered **Phare de la Gacholle** (1882), a lighthouse automated in the 1960s. Footpaths cut down to lovely sandy beaches and views of pink flamingos strutting across the marshy planes are second to none. Walking on the fragile sand dunes is forbidden.

Le Vélo Saintois   CYCLING

(☑ 04 90 97 74 56; www.levelosaintois.camargue. fr; 19 rue de la République; per day adult/child €15/13.50, tandem €30; ⊙ 9am-7pm Mar-Nov) This bike-rental outlet has bikes of all sizes, including tandems and kids' wheels. Helmets cost an extra €1 per day and a free brochure details four circular cycling itineraries (26km to 44km, 4 hrs to 8 hrs) starting in Stes-Maries de la Mer. It also offers half-day biking and paddle-board/beach-sailing packages (€35/40). Free hotel delivery.

Le Vélociste   CYCLING

(☑ 04 90 97 83 26; www.levelociste.fr; place Mireille; per day adult/child €15/13.50; ⊙ 9am-7pm Mar-Nov) This bike-rental shop rents wheels, advises on cycling itineraries (24km to 70km, 4hrs to 9hrs) and organises fun one-day cycling/ horse riding or cycling/canoeing packages (€30). Free hotel delivery.

Boating   WATER SPORTS

The marshy Camargue lends itself to exploration by boat (adult/child €12/6 per

1½ hour trip). Several companies including **Les Quatre Maries** (☑ 04 90 97 70 10; www. bateaux-4maries.camargue.fr; 36 av Théodore Aubanel; ⊙ mid-Mar–Oct) and **Le Camargue** (☑ 06 17 95 81 96; http://bateau-camargue.com; 5 rue des Launes; ⊙ mid-Mar–Oct) have ticketing desks along rue Théodore Aubanel, the promenade linking the town centre with **Port Gardian**. Further west past the pleasure port, next to Camping Le Clos du Rhône, is **Tiki III** (☑ 04 90 97 81 68; www.tiki3. fr; ⊙ mid-Mar–mid-Nov), a paddle boat moored at the mouth of the Petit Rhône.

For canoeing and kayaking on the Petit Rhône, contact **Kayak Vert Camargue** (☑ 04 66 73 57 17; www.kayakvert-camargue.fr; Mas de Sylvéréal), 14km north of Stes-Maries off the D38.

🛏 Sleeping

★ **Hôtel Méditerranée**   HOTEL €

(☑ 04 90 97 82 09; www.hotel-mediterranee.camargue.fr; 4 av Frédéric Mistral; s/d/tr/q €50/65/75/90, d with shower €45; ⊙ mid-Mar–mid-Nov; ❄) This white-washed cottage hotel, festooned with an abundance of flower pots steps from the sea, is truly a steal. Its 14 rooms – three with their own little terrace garden – are spotlessly clean, and breakfast is served in summer on a pretty vine-covered patio garden – equally festooned with strawberry plants, geraniums and other potted flowers. Breakfast €7. Bike rental €15 per day.

Camping Le Clos du Rhône   CAMPGROUND €

(☑ 04 90 97 85 99; www.camping-leclos.fr; rte d'Aigues Mortes; tent, car & two adults €26.50; ⊙ Apr-Oct; @ 🛜 ⛱ 🛝) Right by the beach, this large and well-equipped campsite sports the whole range of accomodation options: tent

---

THE STORY OF THE MARYS & GITAN PILGRIMAGES

Catholicism first reached European shores in tiny Stes-Maries de la Mer. The tale goes that Saints Marie-Salomé (Mary Salome) and Marie-Jacobé (Mary of Clopas) – and some say Mary Magdalene – fled the Holy Land in a little boat and were caught in a storm, drifting at sea until washing ashore here.

Provençal and Catholic lore diverge at this point: Catholicism relates that Sara, patron saint of the *gitans* (Roma Gitano people), travelled with the two Maries (Marys) on the boat. Provençal legend says Sara was already here and was the first person to recognise their holiness. In 1448, skeletal remains said to belong to Sara and the two Marys were found in a crypt in Stes-Maries-de-la-Mer.

Gitans make a pilgrimage, **Pèlerinage des Gitans**, here on 24 and 25 May, dancing and playing music in the streets, and parading a statue of Sara through town. The Sunday in October closest to the 22nd sees a second pilgrimage dedicated to the two Saint Marys (Stes Maries); *courses camarguaises* are also held at this time.

pitches, wooden chalets, self-catering cottages. The pool with two-lane water slide and a beachside spa with jacuzzi and hamman make it a real family-favourite.

★ **Lodge Sainte Hélène**   BOUTIQUE HOTEL **€€**
(✉ 04 90 97 83 29; www.lodge-saintehelene.com; chemin Bas des Launes; d €130-173; ❄ @ 🛜 ☲) These designer-chic, pearly-white terraced cottages strung along a lake edge are prime real estate for bird watchers and romance seekers. The mood is exclusive, remote and so quiet you can practically hear flamingo wings flapping overhead. Each room comes with a bird spotters' guide and binoculars, and dynamic owner Benoît Noel is a font of local knowledge. Breakfast €15.

🍴 Eating

★ **La Cabane aux Coquillages**   SEAFOOD **€**
(✉ 06 10 30 33 49; www.degustationcoquillages-lessaintesmariesdelamer.com; 16 av Van Gogh; mains €16.50-21.50; ⏰ noon-3pm & 5-11pm Mar-Nov) The shellfish-*apéro* arm of neighbouring Ô Pica Pica (p795), this bright blue 'shack' with crates of crustaceans piled high inside and a gaggle of sea-blue chairs outside is pure gold. Wash down half a dozen oysters (€6.50), locally harvested *tellines* (€12.50) or your choice of *fritures* (deep-fried 'n battered baby prawns, baby squid or anchovies, €12.50) with a glass of chilled white, and enter nirvana.

★ **Ô Pica Pica**   SEAFOOD **€**
(✉ 06 10 30 33 49; www.degustationcoquillages-lessaintesmariesdelamer.com; 16 av Van Gogh; ⏰ noon-3pm & 7-11pm Mar-Nov) Fish and shellfish does not come fresher than this. Watch it gutted, filleted and grilled in the 'open' glass-walled kitchen, then devour it on the sea-facing pavement terrace or out back in the typically Mediterranean white-walled garden. Simplicity is king here: plastic glasses, fish and shellfish platters, no coffee and no credit cards.

La Casita   CAMARGUAIS **€€**
(✉ 04 86 63 63 14; 3 rue Espelly; mains €19-28; ⏰ noon-3pm & 7-11pm Apr–mid-Nov) The charismatic couple who run this unpretentious address with cartwheels for tables cook up the catch of the day for eight months of the year, and spend the other four travelling. The result: local dishes like *tellines* or baby squid, cooked *à la plancha* and spiced with a tasty pinch of chilli, cumin or other world flavour.

SUR LA PLAGE

Lunch *sur la plage* (on the beach) never fails to seduce and Stes-Maries de la Mer lives up to the promise with two hip 'n dandy beach restaurants, both open May to September.

Heading east towards the Digue à la Mer on sandy **Plage Est** is **La Playa** (✉ 06 29 48 82 01; www.laplaya-en-camargue.fr; Plage Est; mains €17-20; ⏰ 8am-midnight May-Sep), the chic choice, with a particularly vibrant *apéro* and after-dark scene, shoals of fresh fish cooked up *à la plancha*, and great daytime buzz revolving around tasty lunches, free wi-fi and super-comfy sunloungers on the sand.

In the opposite direction, on equally sandy **Plage Ouest**, is **Calypso** (✉ 07 71 03 43 46; av Riquette Aubanel, Plage Ouest; fish & shellfish platters €12-16, mains €19.50-23; ⏰ 10am-7pm May-Sep, to 11pm Sat Jul & Aug), shaded by a typical reed pergola with picture-postcard lookout to sea. Feast on good-value, finger-licking bowls of *moules* (mussels) around tables on its elevated wooden-decking terrace, then rent a sunlounger (€12) for a sand-side siesta.

La Grange   PROVENÇAL **€€**
(✉ 04 90 97 98 05; 23 av Frédéric Mistral; mains €15-29, menus €18.50 & €29.50; ⏰ noon-2pm & 6.30-10pm Mar-Nov) Throw yourself into local cowboy culture at The Grange, an ode to the Camargue's guardian with bull-herding memorabilia on the walls and plenty of *taureau* (bull meat) on the menu. Portions are copious, making the fixed *menus* excellent value for feisty appetites. Kickstart the experience with a Lou Gardian, the house *apéro* mixing white wine and peach liqueur.

ℹ Information

Tourist Office (✉ 04 90 97 82 55; www.saint esmaries.com; 5 av Van Gogh; ⏰ 9am-7pm)

ℹ Getting There & Around

Seasonal buses to/from Arles (www.lepilote.com; €2.90, one hour, eight daily) use the bus shelter at the northern entrance to town on av d'Arles (the continuation of rte d'Arles and the D570).

Aigues-Mortes

POP 8100

Just across the border of Provence, in the Gard *département,* the picturesque walled city of Aigues-Mortes sits 28km northwest of Stes-Maries de la Mer at the western extremity of the Camargue. Set in flat marshland and encircled by high stone walls, the town was established in the mid-13th century by Louis IX to give the French Crown a Mediterranean port. Cobbled streets inside the walls are lined with restaurants, cafes and bars, giving it a festive atmosphere.

Scaling its neat ramparts – a flat 'n easy, 1.6km walk – rewards with sweeping views. End atop the lumbering stone Tour de Constance, the city's only defensive structure built in 1242 to protect Aigues-Mortes and its port.

Salt pans, hued soft pink prior to *sauniers* (salt workers) harvesting the salt in summer, flank the southern approach to Aigues-Mortes. An electric train chugs from Aigues-Mortes into the salt marshes of Les Salins du Midi; count 1½ hours for the round trip. Mid-July to late August, it is possible to join the salt harvest; reservations essential.

The tourist office has information on accommodation, guided tours and so forth.

STES-MARIES DE LA MER

This silvery chain of low, jagged mountains, strung between the rivers Durance and Rhône, delineate a *très chic* side of Provence, notably around upmarket St-Rémy de Provence, known for fine restaurants and summertime celebrity spotting. The entire region is chock-a-block with gastronomic delights – AOC olive oil, vineyards, Michelin-starred restaurants and truffles. History comes to life at magnificent ruined castles, remnants of medieval feuds, and at one of Provence's best Roman sites, the ancient city of Glanum.

St-Rémy de Provence

POP 11,033

See-and-be-seen St-Rémy has an unfair share of gourmet shops and restaurants – in the spirit of the town's most famous son, prophecy-maker Nostradamus, we predict you'll add a notch to your belt. Come summer, the jet set hits the Wednesday market, wanders the peripheral boulevard and congregates on place de la République, leaving the quaint historic centre strangely quiet.

◉ Sights

Pick up a **Carte St-Rémy** at the first sight you visit, get it stamped, then benefit from reduced admission at the second sight.

Site Archéologique de Glanum   ROMAN SITE
(☑ 04 90 92 23 79; http://glanum.monuments-nationaux.fr; rte des Baux-de-Provence; adult/child €7.50/free, parking €2.70; ⊗ 9.30am-6.30pm Apr-Sep, 10am-5pm Oct-Mar, closed Mon Sep-Mar) Spectacular archaeological site Glanum dates to the 3rd century BC. Walking the main street towards the sacred spring around which Glanum grew, you pass fascinating remains of a once-thriving city, complete with baths, forum, marketplace, temples and houses. Two ancient Roman monuments – a triumphal arch (AD 20) and mausoleum (30 to 20 BC) – mark the entrance, 2km south of St-Rémy.

Monastère St-Paul de Mausole   HISTORIC SITE
(☑ 04 90 92 77 00; www.cloitresaintpaul-valetudo.com; adult/child €4.65/3.30; ⊗ 9.30am-7pm Apr-Sep, 10.15am-5.15pm Oct-Mar) Van Gogh admitted himself to Monastère St-Paul de Mausole in 1889. The asylum's security led to his most productive period – he completed 150-plus drawings and some 150 paintings here, including his famous *Irises*. A reconstruction of his room is open to visitors, as are the gardens and Romanesque cloister that feature in several of his works. From the monastery entrance, a walking trail is marked by colour panels, showing where the artist set up his easel. St-Paul remains a psychiatric institution: an exhibition room sells artwork created by patients.

⬛ Sleeping

Hôtel Canto Cigalo   HOTEL €
(☑ 04 90 92 14 28; www.cantocigalo.com; 8 chemin Canto Cigalo; d €74-97; ❋ @ 🛜 ⧆) This excellent-value 20-room hotel with apricot façade and blue wooden shutters is a 10-minute stroll from town. Simple and spotlessly clean, its frilly-feminine rooms are decorated in dusty rose, with wicker and white-wood furniture. Unusually, guests have the choice of a gluten/lactose-free breakfast (€10.50) as well as regular *petit-déj* (€9) with homemade bread and jam. South-facing rooms have air-con.

★ Sous les Figuiers   BOUTIQUE HOTEL €€
(☑ 04 32 60 15 40; www.hotel-charme-provence.com; 3 av Gabriel St-René Taillandier; d €96-122, tr €186; ❋ @ 🛜 ⧆) A five-minute walk from town, this country-chic house hotel has 14

art-filled rooms facing a leafy garden – lovely for unwinding after a day's explorations. The owner is a painter (who runs half-day classes costing €85 per person) and has exquisite taste, marrying design details like velvet and distressed wood, Moroccan textiles, and rich colour palates. Breakfast €13.50.

🍴 Eating

Maison Cambillau   BAKERY €
(1 rue Carnot; fougasses & sandwiches €2.60-3; ⊙ 7.30am-1.30pm & 3-7.30pm Fri-Wed) Well-stuffed *fougasse* (Provençal flatbread) and baguette sandwiches with a variety of tasty fillings make this well-established boulangerie, around since 1983, the perfect spot to stock up on a picnic. Complete the takeaway feast with a feisty meringue, bag of nougat, nutty florentine or almond- and pistachio-studded *crousadou*.

Les Filles du Pâtissier   CAFE €
(☑ 06 50 61 07 17; 3 place Favier; mains €15-20; ⊙ 10am-10pm, closed Wed Apr-Oct) Particularly perfect on sultry summer nights, this upbeat and colourful cafe has vintage tables filling one corner of a delightful car-free square in the old town. Its daily-changing *menu* features market-driven salads and tarts, and come dusk it morphs into a wine bar with charcuterie plates and occasional live music. Don't miss the homemade *citronnade* and melon fizz soda.

Da Peppe   ITALIAN €
(☑ 04 90 92 11 56; 2 av Fauconnet; pizza €13.50-15, pasta €14-21, mains €16.50-22; ⊙ noon-2.30pm & 7-11pm Wed-Mon; 🖐) First-class pizzas cooked to Italian perfection by Sicilian chef Maurizio in a state-of-the-art wood-fuelled oven and a fabulous rooftop terrace with lovely town and church views are two of the many draws of this new kid on the block. Da Peppe's voluminous interior is industrial-styled, with a funky bar covered in coffee-bean sacks to have a drink while waiting for a table.

La Cuisine des Anges   BISTRO €€
(☑ 04 90 92 17 66; www.angesetfees-stremy.com; 4 rue du 8 Mai; menu €28, mains €18-21; ⊙ noon-2.30pm & 7.30-11pm Mon, Wed, Sat & Sun, 7.30-11pm Thu & Fri; 🖐 🛜) Packed in equal measure with locals and tourists, this casual *maison d'hôte* has been around for an age and just does not lose its edge. Light Provençal dishes are derived from organic local ingredients and are served in the interior patio or wood-floored dining room with textured paintings and zinc-topped tables. Upstairs is cute-as-a-button

SWEET RETREAT
••••••••••••••••••••••••••••••••••••••
Few addresses are as quintessentially Provençal as **Mas de l'Amarine** (☑ 04 90 94 47 82; www.mas-amarine.com; Ancienne voie Aurélia; d €190-270, 2-/3-course lunch menu €29/35, dinner mains €36), a sweet retreat to eat and sleep, five minutes east of town by car. Contemporary artwork fills this fashion-forward *auberge*, a romantic old *mas* (farmhouse) and 1950s artist retreat, with traditional dry stone walls, great old fireplace and funky Fatboy beanbags by the pool. Many of the ingredients cooked in the restaurant kitchen – open to non-guests too – come fresh from the magnificent gardens. Reservations well in advance are naturally essential.

B&B **Le Sommeil des Fées** (☑ 04 90 92 17 66; www.angesetfees-stremy.com; 4 rue du 8 Mai 1945; r incl breakfast €74-94), with five rooms.

⭐ Maison Drouot   MODERN FRENCH €€€
(☑ 04 90 15 47 42; http://maisondrouot.blogspot. fr; 150 rte de Maillane, D5; menus lunch €23-49, dinner €45-65; ⊙ 12.30-2.30pm & 7.30-11pm Wed-Sun) There are few lunch addresses as charming. Snug in a 19th-century oil mill with a terrace basking in the shade of a fig tree and vine-covered pergola, this restaurant is pure style. Contemporary Provençal cuisine – made strictly from local products (listed in the *menu*) – is served with a creative twist in a thoroughly modern interior.

Find the mill-restaurant five minutes out of town, opposite supermarket Intermarché on the D5 towards Maillane.

ℹ Information

Tourist Office (☑ 04 90 92 05 22; www. saintremy-de-provence.com; place Jean Jaurès; ⊙ 9.15am-12.30pm & 2-6.45pm Mon-Sat, 10am-12.30pm Sun Jul & Aug, shorter hours rest of yr)

ℹ Getting There & Away

BICYCLE
Rentals and free delivery within a 20km radius of St-Rémy from **Telecycles** (☑ 04 90 92 83 15; www.telecycles-location.com; per day €20) and **Vélo-Passion** (☑ 04 90 92 49 43; www. velopassion.fr; per day €15-20). Or add a zip to your pedal power with a battery-assisted, electric bike from **Sun e-Bike** (☑ 04 32 62 08

LOCAL CREATIONS

There is no finer one-stop shop to immerse yourself in the vibrant local art, craft and design scene than **Espace Anikado** (http://anikado.canalblog.com; 1 bd Marceau; ⊙10am-7pm). Eye-catching, colourful and oozing creativity, the hybrid boutique-gallery showcases fashion, jewellery, shoes, furniture and more by local designers. Strung on the walls as backdrop is an exposition by a Provençal artist, changed every two months, and the space regularly hosts artsy events and happenings.

39; www.sun-e-bike.com; 16 bd Marceau; per day €35; ⊙9am-6.30pm Apr-Sep, shorter hours rest of yr).

BUS

Buses depart from place de la République to/from Avignon (€3.10, one hour), Les Baux de Provence (€2.20, 15 minutes), Arles (€2.20, 50 minutes) and Cavaillon (€1, 30 minutes); find timetables on the tourist office website.

Les Baux de Provence

POP 457

Clinging precariously to an ancient limestone *baou* (Provençal for 'rocky spur'), this fortified hilltop village is one of the most visited in France. It's easy to understand why: narrow cobbled streets wend car free past ancient houses, up to a splendid castle.

⊙ Sights

Families note, at either sight pay for one child aged 7-17yr and get the second in for free. If you're visiting both sights, invest in a cent-saving **Pass Provence** (adult/child €17/13.50 Apr-Aug, €15/11.50 Sep-Mar), sold at both venues and online.

Château des Baux   CASTLE, RUIN
(☑04 90 54 55 56; www.chateau-baux-provence.com; adult/child Apr-Aug €10/8, Sep-Mar €8/6; ⊙9am-6pm Sep-Jun, to 8pm Jul & Aug) Crowning the village, these dramatic maze-like ruins date to the 10th century. The clifftop castle was largely destroyed in 1633, during the reign of Louis XIII, and is a thrilling place to explore – particularly for rambunctious kids. Climb crumbling towers for incredible views, descend into disused dungeons and

flex your knightly prowess with giant medieval weapons dotting the open-air site. Medieval-themed entertainment and hands-on action – shows, duels, catapult demonstrations and so on – abound in summer.

Carrières de Lumières   LIGHT SHOW
(☑04 90 54 55 56; www.carrieres-lumieres.com; rte de Maillane; adult/child €10/8; ⊙9.30am-7pm Apr-Sep, 10am-6pm Oct-Dec & Mar) A high-end sound-and-light show, Carrières de Lumières is an odd, strangely thrilling attraction. In chilly halls of a former limestone quarry, gigantic projections illuminate rough cave walls and floor, accompanied by oration and swelling music. Dress warmly.

🛏 Sleeping & Eating

★**L'Oustau de Baumanière**   GASTRONOMIC €€€
(☑04 90 54 33 07; www.oustaudebaumaniere.com; menus €166 & €199, mains €58-98; ❄@🛜) A legendary table beneath vaults, L'Oustau serves rarefied cuisine, with many ingredients plucked from the organic garden. Upstairs are five-star hotel **rooms** (d from €220). Head chef and owner Jean-André Charial also hosts Saturday-morning cooking classes (€170 incl lunch) and innovative *table d'hôte* sessions (€160) during which guests watch the chef work and share a kitchen lunch with him.

Wine aficionados will adore the half-day wine-discovery workshops (€190) whereby you delve into L'Oustau's amazing wine cellars packed with 60,000-odd bottles and taste the best vintages from the region, accompanied by lunch.

❶ Information

Tourist Office (☑04 90 54 34 39; www.les-bauxdeprovence.com; ⊙9.30am-5pm Mon-Fri, 10am-5.30pm Sat & Sun)

❶ Getting There & Away

BUS

Allô Cartreize (☑08 10 00 13 26; www.lepilote.com) operates weekends in May, June and September and daily July and August to St-Rémy de Provence (€2.40, 10 minutes) and Arles (€2.40, 30 minutes).

CAR

Driving is easiest, but parking is hellish. Find metered spaces far down the hill, at the village's edge; there's free parking outside Carrières de Lumières. Good luck.

OLIVE OIL MILLS

The Alpilles' southern edge contains some of Provence's best-known *moulins d'huile* (oil mills), where four different types of olives, freshly harvested from November to January, are pummelled and pressed into silken AOC Vallée des Baux-de-Provence oil.

In Maussane-les-Alpilles, cooperative **Moulin Jean-Marie Cornille** (☑04 90 54 32 37; www.moulin-cornille.com; rue Charloun Rieu, Maussane-les-Alpilles; ⊘9.30am-6.30pm Mon-Sat, 11am-6pm Sun) produces 200,000 litres a year – ususally sold out by mid-August. June to September, tour the mill to learn how its three types of olive oil are made, at 11am Tuesdays and Thursdays.

In Mouriès, 6km southeast of Maussane, pop in for tastes of exceptional oils, milled at **Moulin Coopératif de Mouriès** (☑04 90 47 53 86; www.moulincoop.com; Quartier du Mas Neuf; ⊘9am-12.30pm & 2-7pm Mon-Fri, to 12.30pm & 3-7pm Sat, 3-7pm Sun). The village celebrates a **Fête des Olives Vertes** (Green Olive Festival) in mid-September, and the arrival of the year's new oil with **Fête des Huiles Nouvelles** in early December.

THE VAUCLUSE

The Vaucluse is like every Provençal cliché rolled into one: lavender fields, scenic hills, rows upon rows of vineyards, enchanting villages, picturesque markets, traditional stone houses, beating summer sun and howling winter mistral. At the heart of Vaucluse, which means 'closed valley', is the exquisite town of Avignon.

A car is the ideal way to cover the Vaucluse, but it's possible (if not expedient) to get around by bus.

Avignon

POP 92,078

Hooped by 4.3km of superbly preserved stone ramparts, this graceful city is the belle of Provence's ball. Its turn as the papal seat of power has bestowed Avignon with a treasury of magnificent art and architecture, none grander than the massive medieval fortress and papal palace, the Palais des Papes.

Famed for its annual performing arts festival, these days Avignon is a lively student city and an ideal spot from which to step out into the surrounding region.

History

Avignon first gained its ramparts and its reputation as a city of art and culture during the 14th century, when Pope Clement V and his court fled political turmoil in Rome for Avignon. From 1309 to 1377, the seven French-born popes invested huge sums of money in building and decorating the papal palace. Under the popes' rule, Jews and political dissidents took shelter here. Pope Gregory XI left Avignon in 1376, but his death two years later led to the Great Schism (1378–1417), during which rival popes (up to three at one time) resided at Rome and Avignon, denouncing and excommunicating one another. Even after the schism was settled and an impartial pope, Martin V, established himself in Rome, Avignon remained under papal rule. The city and Comtat Venaissin (now the Vaucluse *département*) were ruled by papal legates until 1791, when they were annexed to France.

⊙ Sights

Palais des Papes   PALACE
(Papal Palace; www.palais-des-papes.com; place du Palais; adult/child €11/9, with Pont Saint Bénezet €13.50/10.50; ⊘9am-8pm Jul, to 8.30pm Aug, shorter hours Sep-Jun) Palais des Papes, a Unesco World Heritage Site, is the world's largest Gothic palace. Built when Pope Clement V abandoned Rome in 1309, it was the papal seat for 70-odd years. The immense scale testifies to the papacy's wealth; the 3m-thick walls, portcullises and watchtowers show their insecurity.

It takes imagination to picture the former luxury of these bare, cavernous stone halls, but multimedia audioguides (€2) assist. Highlights include 14th-century chapel frescos by Matteo Giovannetti, and the Chambre du Cerf with medieval hunting scenes.

Ask at the ticket desk about guided tours.

Place du Palais   SQUARE
A golden statue of the Virgin Mary (weighing 4.5 tons) stands on the dome of Romanesque **Cathédrale Notre Dame des Doms** (built 1671–72), outstretched arms protecting the city. Next to the cathedral, the hilltop **Rocher des Doms** gardens provide knockout

PROVENCE AVIGNON

Avignon

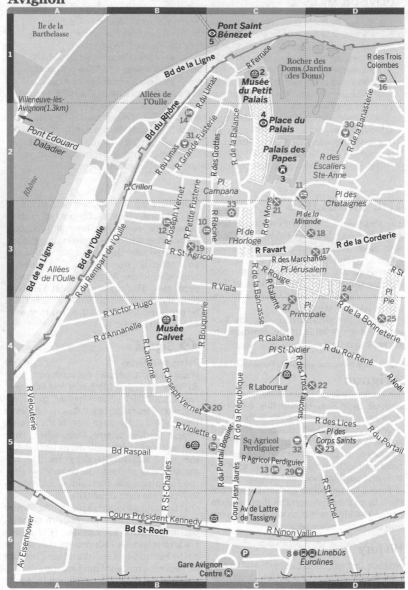

views of the Rhône, Mont Ventoux and Les Alpilles; there's also a **playground**. Opposite the palace, the much-photographed building dripping with carvings of fruit and heraldic beasts is the former 17th-century mint, **Hôtel des Monnaies**.

Pont Saint Bénezet   BRIDGE
(bd du Rhône; adult/child €5/4, with Palais des Papes €13.50/10.50; ⊙9am-8pm Jul, to 8.30pm Aug, shorter hours Sep-Jun) Legend says Pastor Bénezet had three saintly visions urging him to build a bridge across the Rhône.

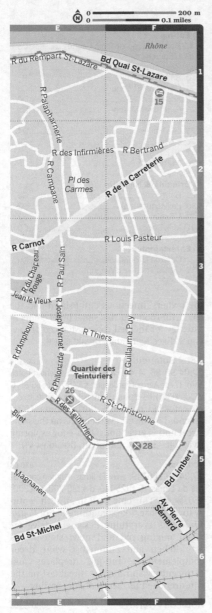

Completed in 1185, the 900m-long bridge with 20 arches linked Avignon with Villeneuve-lès-Avignon. It was rebuilt several times before all but four of its spans were washed away in the 1600s. Don't be surprised if you spot someone dancing: in France, the bridge is known as Pont d'Avignon after the nursery rhyme: 'Sur le pont d'Avignon/L'on y danse, l'on y danse...' (On Avignon Bridge, all are dancing...)

Tickets are valid for 24 hours. If you don't want to pay to visit the bridge, admire it for free from the Rocher des Doms park, Pont Édouard Daladier or from the other side of the water on Île de la Barthelasse's chemin des Berges.

Musée Calvet ART MUSEUM
(☑ 04 90 86 33 84; www.musee-calvet-avignon. com; 65 rue Joseph Vernet; adult/child €6/3; ⊙ 10am-1pm & 2-6pm Wed-Mon) Elegant Hôtel de Villeneuve-Martignan (built 1741–54) provides a fitting backdrop for Avignon's fine-arts museum, with 16th- to 20th-century oil paintings, compelling prehistoric pieces, 15th-century wrought iron, and the elongated landscapes of Avignonnais artist Joseph Vernet.

Musée du Petit Palais ART MUSEUM
(www.petit-palais.org; place du Palais; adult/child €6/free; ⊙ 10am-1pm & 2-6pm Wed-Mon) The archbishops' palace during the 14th and 15th centuries now houses outstanding collections of primitive, pre-Rennaissance, 13th- to 16th-century Italian religious paintings by artists including Botticelli, Carpaccio and Giovanni di Paolo – the most famous is Botticelli's *La Vierge et l'Enfant* (1470).

Musée Angladon ART MUSEUM
(www.angladon.com; 5 rue Laboureur; adult/child €6.50/4.50, ⊙ 1-6pm Tue-Sun, closed Mon Apr-mid-Nov, closed Mon & Tue mid-Nov–Mar) Tiny Musée Angladon harbours Impressionist treasures, including *Railway Wagons*, the only Van Gogh in Provence (look closely and notice the 'earth' isn't paint, but bare canvas). Also displayed are a handful of early Picasso sketches and artworks by Cézanne, Sisley, Manet and Degas; upstairs are antiques and 17th-century paintings.

Collection Lambert GALLERY
(www.collectionlambert.com; 5 rue Violette) Closed until summer 2015, Avignon's contemporary-arts museum will be even larger when it reopens. Its collection focuses on works from the 1960s to present – from minimalist and conceptual, to video and photography – in stark contrast with the classic 18th-century mansion housing them.

PROVENCE AVIGNON

Avignon

🎭 Festivals & Events

Festival d'Avignon   PERFORMING ARTS
(www.festival-avignon.com; ۞ Jul) The three-week annual **Festival d'Avignon** is one of the world's great performing-arts festivals. More than 40 international works of dance and drama play to 100,000-plus spectators at venues around town. Tickets don't go on sale until springtime, but hotels sell out by February.

Festival Off   PERFORMING ARTS
(www.avignonleoff.com; ۞ Jul) The Festival d'Avignon is paralleled by a simultaneous fringe event, Festival Off, with eclectic (and cheaper) experimental programming. **La Carte Off** (€16) gives a 30% discount.

🛏 Sleeping

Hôtel Mignon   HOTEL €
(☑ 04 90 82 17 30; www.hotel-mignon.com; 12 rue Joseph Vernet; s €40-60, d €65-77, tr €80-93, q €99; ❄ @ 🤝) Bathrooms might be tiny and the stairs, steep and narrow, but Hôtel Mignon (literally 'Cute Hotel') remains excellent value. Its 16 rooms are clean and comfortable, and the hotel sits on Avignon's smartest shopping street. Breakfast €7.

Hôtel Boquier   HOTEL €
(☑ 04 90 82 34 43; www.hotel-boquier.com; 6 rue du Portail Boquier; s/d/tr/q €63/76/85/99; ❄ 🤝) It sits on a rather shabby side street, but the owners' infectious enthusiasm and the colourful rooms at this small hotel compensate; try for themed rooms Morocco or Lavender. Excellent value. Breakfast €9.

Hôtel Splendid   HOTEL €
(☑ 04 90 86 14 46; www.avignon-splendid-hotel. com; 17 rue Agricol Perdiguier; s €45-76, d €65-85, tr €110; ❄ 🤝) 🍃 Splendidly set on a side street off cafe-clad place des Corps Saints, Hôtel Splendid is one of several hotels on the same street and is great budget base for exploring Avignon – by day and night. Breakfast €9.

Le Limas   B&B €€
(☑ 04 90 14 67 19; www.le-limas-avignon.com; 51 rue du Limas; S €125-140, d €130-200, tr €200-260; ❄ @) This chic B&B in an 18th-century town house, like something out of *Vogue Living,* is everything designers strive for when mixing old and new: state-of-the-art kitchen and minimalist white decor complementing antique fireplaces and 18th-century spiral stairs. Breakfast on the sun-drenched terrace is divine, darling.

Hôtel de l'Horloge   HOTEL €€
(☑ 04 90 16 42 00; www.hotels-ocre-azur.com; place de l'Horloge; r €95-180; ❄ 🤝) Most rooms at this super-central 19th-century stone-walled hotel (with elevator) are straightforward (comfortable, all mod cons), but five terrace rooms have the edge with

knockout views – room 505 overlooks the Palais des Papes.

Villa de Margot
B&B €€

(☑04 90 82 62 34; http://demargot.fr; 24 rue des Trois Colombes; d €110-190; ❉🛜) A charming, quiet old-city address, this 19th-century private home, converted into an elegant guesthouse, has a walled garden and rooftop views. Rooms are styled like their names – 'Oriental', 'Royal', 'Art Deco' and 'Romantic'.

Lumani
B&B €€

(☑04 90 82 94 11; www.avignon-lumani.com; 37 rue du Rempart St-Lazare; d €110-170; ❉🛜) Art fills this fabulous *maison d'hôte,* a wealth of inspiration for painters. Rooms include two suites and there's a fountained garden.

Hôtel La Mirande
LUXURY HOTEL €€€

(☑04 90 14 20 20; www.la-mirande.fr; 4 place de la Mirande; d from €400; ❉@🛜) Avignon's top hotel occupies a converted 16th-century palace, with dramatic interiors decked in oriental rugs, gold-threaded tapestries, marble staircases and over-the-top Gallic style. Low-end rooms are small, but still conjure the feeling of staying overnight in someone's private château. Its restaurant, with cooking classes, is a slow and glittering affair.

✖ Eating

Place de l'Horloge is crammed with touristy restaurants that don't cook up the best cuisine or value in town. Delve instead into the pedestrian old town where ample pretty squares tempt: places des Chataignes and place de la Principle are two particularly beautiful restaurant-clad squares.

Restaurants open seven days during the summer festival season, when reservations become essential.

Local treat *Papaline d'Avignon* is a pink chocolate ball filled with potent Mont Ventoux herbal liqueur.

Les Halles
MARKET €

(www.avignon-leshalles.com; place Pie; ⊙6am-1.30pm Tue-Fri, to 2pm Sat & Sun) Over 40 food stalls showcase seasonal Provençal ingredients. Cooking demonstrations are held Saturdays at 11am. Outside on place Pie, admire Patrick Blanc's marvellous vegetal wall.

Ginette et Marcel
CAFE €

(27 place des Corps Saints; tartines €4-6; ⊙11am-11pm Wed-Mon; ▣) With tables and chairs on one of Avignon's most happening plane-tree-shaded squares, this vintage cafe styled like a 1950s grocery is a charming spot to hang out and people-watch over a *tartine* (open-faced sandwich), tart, salad or other light dish – equally tasty for lunch or an early evening *apéro.* Kids adore Ginette's cherry- and violet-flavoured cordials, and Marcel's glass jars of old-fashioned sweets.

Naka
JAPANESE €

(☑04 90 82 15 70; 4 place de la Principle; menus €12.90-22) When tastebuds tire of Provençal, consider this uber-cool Japanese restaurant. At home in a deconsecrated chapel on a beautiful stone-paved square in the old town, its setting is stunning. Take your pick of sushi, sashimi, maki, chirashi et al or opt for an excellent-value *menu.*

★ 83.Vernet
MODERN FRENCH €€

(☑04 90 85 99 04; www.83vernet.com; 83 rue Joseph Vernet; lunch/dinner menu €19.50/€24-30, mains €15; ⊙noon-3pm & 7pm-1am Mon-Sat) Forget flowery French descriptions. The *menu* is straightforward and to the point at this strikingly contemporary address, magnificently at home in the 18th-century cloistered courtyard of a medieval college. Expect pan-seared scallops, squid *à la plancha* and beef steak in pepper sauce on the *menu,* and watch for weekend events that transform the lounge-style restaurant into the hippest dance floor in town.

L'Épicerie
BISTRO €€

(☑04 90 82 74 22; www.restaurantlepicerie.fr; 10 place St-Pierre; mains €18-25; ⊙noon-2.30pm & 8-10pm) Racing green tables, chairs and parasols flag this popular bistro on a gorgeous cobble-stoned square. The Grocery makes its own foie gras, served with a Muscat-fired onion chutney, and mains reflect the market. Excite *apéro* tastebuds with an *assiette de l'épicerie* (€19), a mixed platter of Provençal produce: tomato crème brûlée, melon wedges, stuffed veg, olive cake, tapenade and so on.

ⓘ AVIGNON PASS

Excellent-value discount card, *Avignon Passion,* yields cheaper admission to big-hitter museums and monuments in Avignon and Villeneuve-lès-Avignon. The first site visited is full price, but each subsequent site is discounted. The pass is free, valid 15 days, covers a couple of tours too, and is available at the tourist office (p805) and at museums.

EDGY EATING

No single street in Avignon is as edgy as river-side **rue des Teinturiers** (literally 'street of dyers'), a picture-postcard pedestrian street known for its alternative vibe in Avignon's old dyer's district. A hive of industrial activity until the 19th century, the street today is renowned for its bohemian bistros, cafes and gallery-workshops. Ancient stone 'benches' in the shade of ancient plane trees make the perfect perch to ponder the irresistible trickle of the River Sorgue, safeguarded since the 16th century by Chapelle des Pénitents Gris. Those in the know dine in just one place: **L'Ubu** (☑04 90 80 01 01; 13 rue des Teinturiers; starters/mains €7.50/16.50; ⊙noon-2.30pm & 7-10.30pm) has taupe tables and chairs overlooking the water and a tiny *menu*, that changes daily, chalked on the blackboard. Basil-encrusted cod with black rice and broad beans, and duck brochette with sweet *légumes confits* (candied veg) were cooking the day we dined.

Bar à Manger du Coin Caché   BISTRO €€

(☑04 32 76 27 16; 3 place des Chataignes; mains €12-15; ⊙noon-3pm & 7-10pm) This place is pure charm, from the name of the cobbled-stone square ('Chestnut Tree Square') it spills across to its ancient stone neighbour (Cloître St-Pierre). More bistro than bar, it cooks up seasonal dishes with a fusion twist. Kickstart the alfresco occasion with a sweet Vin de Noix de la St Jean, peachy Rinquinquin or other Provençal aperitif. No credit cards.

The bistro also runs the adjacent, more formal **Coin Caché** restaurant.

La Cuisine du Dimanche   PROVENÇAL €€

(☑04 90 82 99 10; www.lacuisinedudimanche. com; 31 rue de la Bonneterie; lunch menu €17, mains €18-25; ⊙noon-1.30pm & 8-9.45pm Jun-Sep, Wed-Sun Nov-Mar) Spitfire chef Marie shops every morning at Les Halles to find the freshest ingredients for her earthy flavour-packed cooking. The *menu* changes daily, although staples include scallops and simple roast chicken with pan gravy. The narrow stone-walled dining room mixes contemporary resin chairs with antique crystal goblets to reflect the chef's eclecticism. Evening dining is only à la carte.

Fou de Fafa   BISTRO €€

(☑04 32 76 35 13; 17 rue des Trois Faucons; 2-/3-course menu €24/30; ⊙6.30-10.30pm Wed-Sun; ☑) A typical French bistro, Fou de Fafa's strength lies in simplicity – fresh ingredients, bright flavours, convivial surroundings (and a notably early opening time handy for families with young children). Dining is between soft golden-stone walls and the chef gives a fresh spin to classics. *Magret de canard* (duck breast) in a strawberry and balsamic reduction anyone?

Restaurant L'Essentiel   FRENCH €€

(☑04 90 85 87 12; www.restaurantlessentiel.com; 2 rue Petite Fusterie; menus lunch €14.50, dinner €31-45, mains €21-32; ⊙noon-2pm & 7-9.45pm Tue-Sat) Snug in an elegant, caramel-stone *hôtel particulier,* The Essential is one of the finest places to eat in town – inside or in a wonderful courtyard garden. Begin with zucchini flowers poached in a crayfish and truffle sauce, then continue with rabbit stuffed with candied eggplant, perhaps.

Numéro 75   MODERN FRENCH €€

(☑04 90 27 16 00; www.numero75.com; 75 rue Guillaume Puy; 2-/3-course menu €29/36.50, mains €23-27; ⊙12.30-2.30pm & 7.30-10.30pm Mon-Sat) The chic dining room, in the former mansion of absinthe inventor Jules Pernod, is a fitting backdrop for stylised Mediterranean cooking. *Menus* change nightly and include just a handful of mains, but brevity guarantees freshness. Starter/main course-sized *salades goumandes* (€8/16), served only at lunchtime, are good-value. On balmy nights, reserve a table in the elegant courtyard garden.

Christian Etienne   PROVENÇAL €€€

(☑04 90 86 16 50; www.christian-etienne.fr; 10 rue de Mons; menus lunch €35, dinner €75-130; ⊙noon-2pm & 7.30-10pm Tue-Sat) One of Avignon's top tables, this much vaunted restaurant occupies a 12th-century palace, with a leafy outdoor terrace, adjacent to Palais des Papes. Interiors feel slightly dated, but the refined Provençal cuisine remains exceptional, notably the summertime-only starter-to-dessert tomato *menu* (€75).

Drinking & Nightlife

Chic yet laidback Avignon is awash with gorgeous, tree-shaded pedestrian squares buzzing with cafe life. Favourite squares loaded with pavement terraces and drinking opportunities include **place Crillon** (full-frontal view of medieval Avignon's crenellated city walls), **place Pie** (green views of Les Halles' vegetal façade), and **place de l'Horloge** (hard-core tourist zone with kids' carousel)

Milk Shop
CAFE

(☑ 09 82 54 16 82; www.milkshop.fr; 26 place des Corps Saints; bagels €4.90-6.90, shakes €4.50; ⊙ 9.30am-7.30pm Mon-Sat; ☏) Keen to mingle with some Avignon students? Then make a beeline for this *salon au lait* ('milk bar') where super-thick, jumbo-sized ice-cream shakes are slurped through extra-wide straws, either in situ or to take out. Bagels, cup cakes and other American snacks create a deliberate New Yorker vibe, while comfy armchairs and free wi-fi encourage laptop-savvy punters to hang out for hours.

⭐ Balthazar
BISTRO, BAR

(☑ 04 88 07 36 09; www.bistrotbalthazar.com; 74 place des Corps Saints; ⊙ 8.30-1am Mon-Sat) With its deep red canopy and black seating on trendy place des Corps Saints, Balthazar makes a bold statement. A real hybrid, it's as hip for casual lunch and dinner dining although it is during early evening aperitifs and after-dark drinks that Balthazar is at its most rocking. When the munchies hit, there's French classics like *pot au feu* or braised pork cheek, alongside tasty homemade burgers and other funkier fare.

⭐ La Manutention
BAR

(4 rue des Escaliers Ste-Anne; ⊙ noon-midnight) No address better reflects Avignon's inherently artsy soul than this hybrid bistro-bar at cultural centre La Manutention. Its leafy terrace with trees and potted plants basks in the cooling shade of Palais des Papes' massive stone walls and inside, giant conservatory-style windows open on the funky decor of pocket-sized bar, **Utopia**. Grilled *tartines* (€4.50) and light *assiettes* (mixed platters) make ideal companions to pre- or post-theatre drinks. When true hunger strikes, move to the neighbouring **restaurant** (2-/3-course lunch €13/16, Sunday brunch €15).

L'Esclave
GAY BAR

(☑ 04 90 85 14 91; www.esclavebar.com; 12 rue du Limas; ⊙ 11.30pm-7am Tue-Sun) Avignon's inner-city gay bar rocks well into the wee hours, pulling a clientele that is not always that quiet, based on dozens of neighbour-considerate 'be quiet' signs plastered outside.

☆ Entertainment

Tickets for many concerts, gigs and events are sold at the **billetterie** (box office) inside the tourist office.

Opéra Théâtre d'Avignon
PERFORMING ARTS

(☑ 04 90 82 81 40; www.operatheatredavignon.fr; place de l'Horloge; ⊙ box office 11am-6pm Tue-Sat) Built 1847, Avignon's main classical venue presents operas, plays, chamber music and ballet from October to June.

Cinéma Utopia
CINEMA

(☑ 04 90 82 65 36; www.cinemas-utopia.org; 4 rue des Escaliers Ste-Anne, La Manutention) Four-screen art-house cinema at cultural centre La Manutention; shows films in their original language.

❶ Information

Tourist Office (☑ 04 32 74 32 74; www.avignon-tourisme.com; 41 cours Jean Jaurès; ⊙ 9am-6pm Mon-Sat, 10am-7pm Sun Apr-Oct, shorter hrs rest of yr) Organises guided walking tours of the city, and has plenty of information on other tours and activities, including boat trips and lunch cruises on the River Rhône, and wine-tasting trips to nearby Côtes du Rhône vineyards.

❶ Getting There & Away

AIR

Aéroport Airport-Provence (www.avignon.aeroport.fr) In Caumont, 8km southeast of Avignon. Direct flights to London, Birmingham and Southampton in the UK.

BUS

The bus station is next to the central railway station; drivers sell tickets. For schedules, see www.lepilote.com and www.vaucluse.fr. Long-haul companies **Linebús** (☑ 04 90 85 30 48; www.linebus.com) and **Eurolines** (☑ 04 90 85 27 60; www.eurolines.com) have offices at the far end of the bus platforms.

TRAIN

Avignon has two train stations: **Gare Avignon TGV**, 4km southwest in Courtine; and **Gare Avignon Centre** (42 bd St-Roch). Local shuttle trains links the two stations every 20 minutes (€1.60, five minutes) between 6am and 11pm.

Arles €7.50, 20 minutes, half-hourly
Nîmes €9.70, 30 minutes, half-hourly
Orange €6.20, 20 minutes, half-hourly

Some TGVs to Paris (€123, 3½ hours) stop at Gare Avignon Centre, but TGVs to Marseille (€25, 30 minutes) and Nice (€60, 3¼ hours) only use Gare Avignon TGV. In July and August,

Roman Provence

3 DAYS

Rome really flexed its imperial muscles in Southern France. Roman roads duck and dive across Roman bridges to theatres and arenas where you can grab a seat in the bleachers and watch the curtain rise. Let the show begin!

Though not technically in Provence, **Nîmes'** incredible Roman monuments are essential viewing (p716). The town's coat of arms – a crocodile chained to a palm tree – recalls the region's first sun-worshipping retirees: Julius Caesar's loyal legionnaires were granted land here to settle after hard years on the Nile campaigns. Two millennia later, Nîmes' intact 1st-century-AD amphitheatre and temple blend seamlessly with the modern town. The Romans didn't do anything on a small scale and Unesco-listed **Pont du Gard** (p721), 21km northeast along the D9086, is no exception. At 50m, this is the world's highest Roman monument. Traverse its awe-inspiring arches, and swim upstream for unencumbered views or downstream to shaded wooden platforms.

Overnight in Uzès (p721), returning south next morning along the D979 to Nîmes and A54 to **Arles** (p786) – count on an hour. Part of the Roman Empire from the 2nd century BC, Roman Arelate has a splendid amphitheatre, theatre and baths. Grab a coffee on place du Forum, the hub of Roman social, political and religious life.

From Arles follow the D17, D78F and D5 north to **Glanum** (p796). Park by the roadside triumphal arch and spend the afternoon exploring the Roman archaeological site. Van Gogh painted the olive grove that covered it until excavation began in the 1920s. Overnight 2km north in St-Rémy de Provence (p796).

Day three, motor 50km along the A7 to **Orange** (p807). Roman monuments here are stunning and unusually old – from Augustus Caesar's rule (27 BC–AD 14). The stage wall of the Théâtre Antique dominates. Push on along the D975 to **Vaison-la-Romaine** (p809) for a late lunch. Park on the river banks next to the Roman bridge (Pont Romain). Explore the ruins of the city that flourished here between the 6th and 2nd centuries BC and end with the archaeological museum which revives Vaison's Roman past with incredible swag – mosaics, carved masks, and statues that include a 3rd-century silver bust and marble renderings of Hadrian and his wife, Sabina.

Top: Les Arènes p786, Arles
Above: La Maison Carrée p717, Nîmes

a direct **Eurostar** (www.eurostar.com) service operates on Saturdays to/from London (from €140, six hours).

ℹ️ Getting Around

TO/FROM THE AIRPORT

TCRA bus 30 (€1.30, 40 minutes) goes to the bus station and post office. Taxis to the centre cost about €30.

BICYCLE

Vélopop (☑ 08 10 45 64 56; www.velopop.fr) Shared-bicycle service, with 17 stations around town. The first half-hour is free; each additional half-hour, €1. One day/week membership costs €1/5.

BUS

TCRA (Transports en Commun de la Région d'Avignon; ☑ 04 32 74 18 32; www.tcra.fr) Local TCRA bus tickets, sold on board, cost €1.30. Buses run 7am to about 8pm. Main transfer points are Poste (main post office) and place Pie. For Villeneuve-lès-Avignon, take bus 11 (bus 70 on Sundays).

TAXI

Taxi-Radio Avignon (☑ 04 90 82 20 20)

Villeneuve-lès-Avignon

POP 12,670

Thirteenth-century Villeneuve-lès-Avignon gazes across the Rhône at Avignon like a wistful little sister. Entranced by the bigger city's charm, most visitors barely glance at Villeneuve; yet its monuments rival Avignon's, with none of the crowds. However, the best options for sleeping and eating are in Avignon.

◉ Sights

The **Avignon Passion** pass is valid for Villeneuve-lès-Avignon's sights.

If you plan on visiting both Fort-St-André and the Chartreuse du Val de Bénédiction monastery, buy a €9 combination ticket (€7 with Avignon Passion pass) at the first sight.

Fort St-André   FORT
(☑ 04 90 25 45 35; rue Montée du Fort; adult/child €5.50/free; ☉10am-6pm Jun-Sep, to 1pm & 2-5pm Oct-May) King Philip the Fair (aka Philippe le Bel) wasn't messing around when he built defensive 14th-century Fort St-André on the then-border between France and the Holy Roman Empire: the walls are 2m thick! Today you can walk a small section of the ramparts and admire 360-degree views from

the Tour des Masques (Wizards' Tower) and Tours Jumelles (Twin Towers).

★ Abbaye et Jardins de l'Abbaye   ABBEY, GARDEN
(☑ 04 90 25 55 95; www.abbayesaintandre.fr; rue Montée du Fort, Fort St-André; adult/child abbey €13/free, garden €6/free; ☉10am-6pm May-Sep, to 1pm & 2-5pm Tue-Sun Mar & Oct, to 6pm Apr) The resplendent vaulted halls of this 10th-century abbey, within the Fort St-André, can only be visited by guided tour. The stunning terrace gardens however – built atop the abbey vaults and classed among France's top 100 gardens – can be freely roamed. Pathways meander through fragrant roses, iris-studded olive groves, wisteria-covered pergolas, and past ruins of three ancient churches, and views of Avignon and the Rhône are spectacular.

Chartreuse du Val de Bénédiction   MONASTERY
(☑ 04 90 15 24 24; www.chartreuse.org; 58 rue de la République; adult/child €8/free; ☉9am-7pm Aug, to 6.30pm Jul & Sep, to 5.30pm Apr-Jun, 9.30am-5pm Mon-Fri, 10am-5pm Sat & Sun Oct-Mar) Shaded from summer's heat, three cloisters, 24 cells, a church, chapels and nook-and-cranny gardens of the Chartreuse du Val de Bénédiction make up France's biggest Carthusian monastery, founded 1352 by Pope Innocent VI, who was buried here 10 years later in an elaborate mausoleum.

Tour Philippe-le-Bel   LANDMARK
(☑ 04 32 70 08 57; Montée de la Tour; adult/child €2.30/free; ☉10am-12.30pm & 2-6pm Tue-Sun May-Oct, 2-5pm Feb-Apr) King Philip commissioned the Tour Philippe-le-Bel, 500m outside Villeneuve, to control traffic over Pont St-Bénézet to and from Avignon. The steep steps spiral to the top, rewarding climbers with stunning river views.

Musée Pierre de Luxembourg   MUSEUM
(☑ 04 90 27 49 66; 3 rue de la République; adult/child €3.30/free; ☉10am-12.30pm & 2-6pm Tue-Sun May-Sep, 2-5pm rest of yr) Inside a 17th-century mansion, this museum's masterwork is Enguerrand Quarton's *The Crowning of the Virgin* (1453), in which angels wrest souls from purgatory. Rounding out the collection are 16th-to-18th century paintings.

ℹ️ Getting There & Away

Bus 11 (70 on Sunday; €1.20) links Villeneuve-lès-Avignon with Avignon – or walk the 2km.

DON'T MISS

CHÂTEAUNEUF-DU-PAPE WINES

Carpets of vineyards unfurl around the medieval village of Châteauneuf-du-Pape, epicentre of one of the world's great winegrowing regions. Only a small ruin remains of the château, once the summer residence of Avignon's popes, later bombed by Germans in WWII. Now it belongs to picnickers and day hikers who ascend the hill to scout their lines with a 360-degree panorama.

Thank geology for these luscious wines: when glaciers receded, they left *galets* scattered atop the red-clay soil; these large pebbles trap the Provençal sun, releasing heat after sunset and helping grapes ripen with steady warmth. Most Châteauneuf-du-Pape wines are red; only 6% are white. Strict regulations govern production. Reds come from 13 different grape varieties – grenache is the biggie – and should age at least five years. The full-bodied whites drink well young (except for all-rousanne varieties) and make an excellent aperitif wine, hard to find anywhere else (taste before you buy, as some lack acidity).

Sample them at over two dozen wine shops with free tastings or book a two-hour wine-tasting class at École de Dégustation (Tasting School; ☑ 04 90 83 56 15; www.oenologie-mouriesse.com; 2 rue des Papes; 2hr class €40). The tourist office (☑ 04 90 83 71 08; www.pays-provence.fr; place du Portail; ⊘ 9.30am-6pm Mon-Sat, closed lunch & Wed Oct-May) has a brochure of estates, showing which ones allow cellar visits, have English tours, allow drop-in visitors and offer free tastings.

Perched beneath the ruined château, Le Verger des Papes (☑ 04 90 83 50 40; www.vergerdespapes.com; 4 rue du Château; menus €20-33, mains €25; ⊘ noon-2pm & 7-9pm Tue-Sat, noon-2pm Sun & Mon) has knockout vistas from its terrace. Specialities include succulent rack of lamb. Park at the château and walk down.

Orange

POP 30,008

Considering how exceptional Orange's Roman theatre is (if you see only one Roman site in France, make it this one), the ultra-conservative town is surprisingly untouristy, and eerily quiet in winter. Accommodation is good value, compared with swankier towns like Avignon, but it's nearly impossible to find an open restaurant on Sunday or Monday night.

The House of Orange, the princely dynasty that ruled Orange from the 12th century, made its mark on the history of the Netherlands through a 16th-century marriage with the German House of Nassau, and then English history through William of Orange. Orange was ceded to France in 1713 by the Treaty of Utrecht. To this day, many members of the royal house of the Netherlands are known as the princes and princesses of Orange-Nassau.

👁 Sights

⭐ Théâtre Antique   ROMAN SITE
(www.theatre-antique.com; rue Madeleine Roch; adult/child €9.50/7.50; ⊘ 9am-7pm Jul & Aug, to 6pm Apr, May & Sep, to 5.30pm Mar & Oct, 9.30am-4.30pm rest of yr) Orange's Roman theatre is France's most impressive Roman site. Its sheer size and age are awe-inspiring: designed for 10,000 spectators, it's believed to have been built during Augustus Caesar's rule (27 BC to AD 14). The 103m-wide, 37m-high stage wall is one of three in the world still standing in entirety (others are in Syria and Turkey) – minus a few mosaics, plus a new roof. Admission includes an audioguide and access to Musée d'Art et d'Histoire (p809), opposite the theatre.

Musée d'Art et d'Histoire   MUSEUM
(www.theatre-antique.com; Rue Madeleine Roch; adult/child €5.50/4.50; ⊘ 9.15am-7pm Jun-Aug, to 6pm Apr, May & Sep, shorter hours rest of yr) This small museum – free admission with a Théâtre Antique ticket – displays various unassuming treasures, including portions of the Roman survey registers (precursor to the tax department) and friezes that once formed part of the Roman theatre's scenery.

Arc de Triomphe   ROMAN SITE
Orange's 1st-century-AD monumental arch, the Arc de Triomphe – 19m high and wide, and 8m thick – stands on the Via Agrippa. Currently under restoration, its brilliant reliefs commemorate 49 BC Roman victories with carvings of chained, naked Gauls.

Excellent value is the combo **Roman Pass** (adult/child €18/13.50), valid for seven days and covering admission to all the Roman sights in both Orange and Nîmes in neighbouring Languedoc. Buy it at any Roman venue in either town.

Colline St-Eutrope   GARDENS
For bird's-eye views of the theatre – and phenomenal vistas of Mont Ventoux and the Dentelles de Montmirail – follow montée Philbert de Chalons or montée Lambert up Colline St-Eutrope (St Eutrope Hill; elevation 97m), once the Romans' lookout point. En route, pass ruins of a 12th-century château, once the residence of the princes of Orange.

🛌 Sleeping

Hôtel l'Herbier d'Orange   HOTEL €
(📞 04 90 34 09 23; www.lherbierdorange.com; 8 place aux Herbes; s/d/tr/q €55/59-76/71/81; ✳@🛜🖨) Friendly enthusiastic owners keep this small, basic hotel looking spick and span, with double-pane windows and gleaming bathrooms. Find it sitting prettily on on a small square shaded by tall plane trees. Breakfast is a choice of continental (€6) or buffet (€9).

Hôtel Arène   HOTEL €€
(📞 04 90 11 40 40; www.hotel-arene.fr; place de Langes; d €116-150, annexe €60-80; ✳@🛜🏊🖨) It might be part of the generic Best Western chain, but the Arène is beautifully positioned in the old town and retains some individuality. Kids love the two heated pools (one indoors, one out); parents appreciate the family-size rooms. Request a remodelled room in the main building – cheaper rooms in the annexe are older and not as modern.

Hôtel Le Glacier   HOTEL €€
(📞 04 90 34 02 01; www.le-glacier.com; 46 cours Aristide Briand; d €58-195; ✳@🛜) All 28 rooms are individually decorated and impeccably maintained by the charming owners, who pay attention to detail. There's easy parking in front of the hotel, and bike rental. Breakfast €10.

🍴 Eating

It's worth wandering away from the line-up of cafe terraces opposite the Théâtre Antique on place des Frères Mounet to delve into the pedestrian squares of Orange's softly hued old town where a multitude of dining and drinking spots await beneath leafy plane trees.

Market stalls spill across streets in the town centre every Thursday.

À la Maison   BISTRO €
(📞 04 90 60 98 83; 4 place des Cordeliers; menus 2-/3-course lunch €12.50/15, dinner €25/32; ⏰ noon-2pm & 7-10pm Mon-Sat) There's no lovelier spot on a warm night than the leafy courtyard, wrapped around an old stone fountain and a trio of plane trees, at this simple bistro across from the walls of the Théâtre Antique. Its name 'At Home' is a perfect reflection of the cuisine it serves.

Au Salon de Charlotte   TEA ROOM €
(4 place Clemenceau; breakfast/brunch €6.50/10, mains €12; ⏰ 8am-7pm Wed-Sun) This delightful *salon de thé* is deliciously old-fashioned with its floral table cloths and vases of freshly cut flowers on each table. Its organic teas, homemade cakes, lunchtime tarts and Sunday brunch are just as delicious. Find it next to the Hôtel de Ville on car-free place Clemenceau.

El Camino Store   CAFE €
(📞 04 88 84 49 99; 8 rue Notre Dame; ⏰ 8am-7pm Tue-Sat) *Tintin* books, dial-up telephones, Corgi model cars and old Playmobil figurines are among the vintage collectibles strewn around this cool, 1950s styled cafe. Food – strictly homemade – is limited to one starter and one main. Savour it inside around formica tables or outside on the flowery pavement terrace.

Les Artistes   BISTRO, CAFE €
(place de la République; 1-/2-/3-course menu €11/13.50/15.50; ⏰ 8-2am) A hybrid drinking/dining address with a chic contemporary interior and vast pavement terrace on a pedestrian old-town square, The Artists buzzes from dawn to dark. Happy Hour (5-8pm) is great value, as are its meal-sized salads and other brasserie fare.

La Grotte d'Auguste   TRADITIONAL FRENCH €€
(📞 04 90 60 22 54; www.restaurant-orange.fr; rue Madeleine Roch, Théâtre Antique; lunch/dinner menu €21/28, mains €20; ⏰ noon-2pm & 7-10pm Tue-Sat) Location is key at Auguste's Grotto, squirrelled away in the entrails of Orange's Roman theatre. Summer dining overlooks the ruins of a 2nd-century Hemicycle temple. Cuisine is traditional French, with lots

of meat cuts and gourmet treats like foie gras and black truffles.

Le Parvis
GASTRONOMIC €€

(☑04 90 34 82 00; www.restaurant-le-parvis-orange.com; 55 cours Pourtoules; menus 2-/3-course lunch €23/29, dinner €36/46; ☺lunch & dinner Tue-Sat, lunch Sun) Nobody speaks above a whisper at Orange's top table where chef Jean-Michel Bérengier has cooked up superb Provençal food for the past 25 years.

ℹ Information

Tourist Office (☑04 90 34 70 88; www.otorange.fr; 5 cours Aristide Briand; ☺9am-6.30pm Mon-Sat, to 1pm & 2-6.30pm Sun, closed Sun Oct-Mar)

ℹ Getting There & Away

BUS

Bus Station (☑04 90 34 15 59; 201 cours Pourtoules) Buses operated by Trans Vaucluse (www.vaucluse.fr) serve Avignon (€2, 45 minutes) and Vaison-la-Romaine (€2, 45 minutes).

TRAIN

Orange's **train station** (www.voyages-sncf.com; av Frédéric Mistral) is 1.5km east of the town centre. Services include:

Avignon €6.20, 15-23 minutes

Lyon €54.40, 2¼ hours

Marseille €24.70, 1½ hours

Marseille Airport Vitrolles station; €21.70, 1½ hours

Vaison-la-Romaine

POP 6036

Tucked between seven hills, Vaison-la-Romaine has long been a traditional exchange centre, and still has a thriving Tues-day market. The village's rich Roman legacy is very visible and 20th-century buildings rise alongside France's largest archaeological site. A Roman bridge crosses the River Ouvèze, dividing the contemporary town's pedestrianised centre and the walled, cobbled-street hilltop Cité Médiévale – one of Provence's most magical ancient villages, where the counts of Toulouse built their 12th-century castle. Vaison is a good base for jaunts into the Dentelles de Montmirail and Mont Ventoux, but tourists throng here in summer: reserve ahead.

◉ Sights

Gallo-Roman Ruins
ROMAN SITE

(adult/child €8/3; ☺9.30am-6pm mid-Feb–Dec) The ruined remains of Vasio Vocontiorum, the Roman city that flourished here between the 6th and 2nd centuries BC, fill two central Vaison sites. Two neighbourhoods of this once-opulent city, Puymin and La Villasse, lie on either side of the tourist office and av du Général-de-Gaulle. Admission includes entry to the 12th-century Romanesque cloister at Cathédrale Notre-Dame de Nazareth (cloister only €1.50; ☺10am-12.30pm & 2-6pm Mar-Dec), a five-minute walk west of La Villasse and a soothing refuge from the summer heat.

In Puymin, see houses of the nobility, mosaics, workers' quarters, a temple, and the still-functioning 6000-seat Théâtre Antique (c AD 20). To make sense of the remains (and collect your audioguide), head for the Musée Archéologique Gallo-Roman, which revives Vaison's Roman past with incredible swag – superb mosaics, carved masks, and statues that include a 3rd-century silver bust and marble renderings of Hadrian and wife Sabina.

The Romans shopped at the colonnaded boutiques and bathed at La Villasse, where you'll find Maison au Dauphin, which has splendid marble-lined fish ponds.

Cité Médiévale
HISTORIC QUARTER

Cross the Pont Romain (Roman bridge) in the footsteps of frightened medieval peasants, who clambered to the walled city during valley conflicts. Steep cobblestone alleyways wend beneath stone ramparts and a 14th-century bell tower past romantic fountains and mansions with incredibly carved doorways. Continue uphill to the 12th-century château and be rewarded with eagle-eye vistas.

CONTEMPORARY ART IN THE MAKING

Be inspired by contemporary art fest Supervues (www.supervues.com), hosted each December by Hôtel Burrhus. For three days, usually mid-month, the hotel's 38 rooms are taken over by artists from all over Europe who each create a work of art or installation in the room they're sleeping in. The hotel is closed to guests, but anyone can visit during the day to watch the artists at work.

PROVENCE VAISON-LA-ROMAINE

Festival & Events

Choralies
MUSIC FESTIVAL

(www.choralies.fr) Europe's largest choral festival is held in August every three years. Upcoming festivals will be held in 2016 and 2019.

Festival des Chœurs Lauréats
MUSIC FESTIVAL

(www.festivaldeschoeurslaureats.com; ⊘late Jul) The best choirs in Europe.

🛏 Sleeping

★Hôtel Burrhus
HOTEL €

(🖉04 90 36 00 11; www.burrhus.com; 1 place de Montfort; d €64-94, apt €140; 🖳🖭) On Vaison's vibrant central square, this blue-shuttered hotel is quaint and old from the outside and brilliantly contemporary inside, with original art works and sculptures strung in its enchanting maze of vintage corridors and staircases. Don't miss the giant Roman-inspired terracota pot, 1.8m tall, suspended between rooftops above the sofa-clad interior patio. No lift. Breakfast €9.

L'École Buissonière
B&B €

(🖉04 90 28 95 19; www.buissonniere-provence.com; D75, Buisson; s €49-54, d €62-74, tr €78-89 q €94-99; 🖭) Five minutes north of Vaison, in the countryside between Buisson and Villedieu, hosts Monique and John have transformed their stone farmhouse into a tastefully decorated three-bedroom B&B, big on comfort. Breakfast features homemade jam, and there's an outdoor summer kitchen.

L'Évêché
B&B €€

(🖉04 90 36 13 46; http://eveche.free.fr; rue de l'Évêché; s/d/tr from €85/93/120) With groaning bookshelves, vaulted ceilings, higgledy-piggledy staircase, intimate salons and exquisite art, this five-room *chambre d'hôte*, in the medieval city, is fabulously atmospheric. Knowledgable owners Jean-Loup and Aude also lend bikes.

Hostellerie Le Beffroi
HISTORIC HOTEL €€

(🖉04 90 36 04 71; www.le-beffroi.com; rue de l'Évêché; d €76-120, tr €150-216; ⊘Apr-Jan; 🖭) Within the medieval city's walls, this *hostellerie*, dating from 1554, fills two buildings (the 'newer' one was built in 1690). A fairy-tale hideaway, its rough-hewn stone-and-wood-beamed rooms are small, but romantic, and its restaurant opens onto a rose-and-herb garden with kids' swings.

🍴 Eating

Maison Lesage
BAKERY €

(2 rue de la République; sandwiches €4-6; ⊘7am-1pm & 3-5pm Mon, Tue & Thu-Sat, to 1pm Sun) Generously stuffed baguette sandwiches, artisanal caramels and nougat, cakes, pastries and – the house speciality – bun-sized meringues in a rainbow of flavours makes this busy bakery near the tourist office a top stop for picnic fodder (best savoured by the water on the pebbly river banks – follow the grassy path from the 'Cité Médievale Pont Romain' car park).

★Bistro du'O
NEOBISTRO €€

(🖉04 90 41 72 90; rue du Château; menus €24-45; ⊘noon-2pm & 7.30-10pm Mon, Tue & Thu-Sat) No address seduces more than this thoroughly modern gastro-bistro squirrelled away in a 13th-century vaulted cellar in the medieval city. Dynamic couple Gaëlle (front of house) and Philippe (chef) have been the creative duo behind the address since summer 2013 and local seasonal produce is their muse. Fussy eaters note the choice of dishes is short (but superb) – a perfect reflection of what's at the market that day.

Le Moulin à Huile
GASTRONOMIC €€€

(🖉04 90 36 20 67; www.moulin-huile.com; quai Maréchal Foch, rte de Malaucène; menus lunch €39, dinner €59 & €69, mains €35-48; ⊘noon-2pm & 7.30-10pm Tue-Sat, to 2pm Sun) Michelin-starred Chef Robert Bardot showcases gastronomic prowess in a former olive-oil mill with baby-blue wooden shutters by the river. Lunch on a simple truffle omelette (€55). In summer dine outside in the peachy garden, steps from the river (go for the upper terrace rather than lower one with plastic chairs). You can also make a night of it in one of three handsome guestrooms (€140 to €160).

ℹ Information

Tourist Office (🖉04 90 36 02 11; www.vaison-ventoux-tourisme.com; place du Chanoine Sautel; ⊘9.30am-noon & 2-5.45pm Mon-Sat year-round, plus 9.30am-noon Sun mid-Mar–Oct)

ℹ Getting There & Away

Autocars Lieutaud (🖉04 90 86 36 75; www.cars-lieutaud.fr; 36 bd Saint-Roch) buses serve Orange (€2, one hour) and Avignon (via Orange; €4, two hours). **Transdev Comtadins** (🖉04 90 67 20 25; www.sudest-mobilites.fr; 192 av Clémenceau) buses serve Carpentras (€2, 45 minutes) and Malaucène (€1, 30 minutes). For schedules, see www.vaucluse.fr. The bus stop is on avenue des Choralies, 400m east of the tourist office.

Mont Ventoux & Around

Visible for miles around, Mont Ventoux (1912m), nicknamed *le géant de Provence* (Provence's giant), stands like a sentinel over northern Provence. From its summit, accessible by road between May and October (the white glimmering stuff you see in summer are *lauzes*, broken white stones, not snow), vistas extend to the Alps and, on a clear day, the Camargue.

Because of the mountain's dimensions, every European climate type is present on its slopes, from Mediterranean on its lower southern reaches to Arctic on its exposed northern ridge. As you ascend the relentless gradients (which regularly feature in the Tour de France), temperatures can plummet by 20°C, and there's twice as much precipitation as on the plains below. The relentless mistral wind blows 130 days a year, sometimes at a speed of 250km/h. Bring warm clothes and rain gear, even in summer.

This climatic patchwork is reflected in the mountain's diverse fauna and flora, now actively protected by Unesco Biosphere Reserve status.

Piercing the sky to the west of Mont Ventoux are the spectacular limestone pinnacles of another walker's paradise, Dentelles de Montmirail. On the other side of the Dentelles sits the snug village of Beaumes de Venise, home to France's finest muscat; the village tourist office (☑ 04 90 62 94 39; www.ot-beaumesdevenise.com; place du Marché, Beaumes de Venise; ⊙ 9am-noon & 2-7pm Mon-Sat, shorter hrs rest of yr) has details of local vineyards.

Three principal gateways – Bédoin, Malaucène and Sault – provide services in summer, but they're far apart.

🏃 Activities

Walking
The GR4 crosses the Dentelles de Montmirail before scaling Mont Ventoux' northern face, where it meets the GR9. Both traverse the ridge. The GR4 branches eastwards to Gorges du Verdon; the GR9 crosses the Vaucluse Mountains to the Luberon. The essential map for the area is *3140ET Mont Ventoux*, by IGN (www.ign.fr). Bédoin's tourist office

(p813) stocks maps and brochures detailing walks for all levels.

In July and August, tourist offices in both Bédoin and Malaucène facilitate night-time expeditions up the mountain to see the sunrise (over 15yrs only).

Cycling
Tourist offices distribute *Les Itinéraires Ventoux*, a free map detailing 11 itineraries – graded easy to difficult – highlighting artisanal farms en route. For more cycling trails, see www.lemontventoux.net.

At Station Ventoux Sud Bike Park (☑ 04 90 61 84 55; www.facebook.com/VentouxBikePark; Chalet Reynard; half/full day €14/10; ⊙ 10am-5pm Sat & Sun, weekday hours variable), near the summit, mountain-bikers ascend via a rope tow (minimum age 10yrs), then descend ramps and jumps down three trails (total length 5km), from beginner to advanced. Bring your own bike, helmet and full-length gloves or rent all the gear at Chalet Reynard. Bédoin Location (☑ 04 90 65 94 53; www.bedoin-location.fr; 20 rte Malaucène, Bédoin; rental from €15/20 per half-day/day; ⊙ Mar-Nov), opposite the tourist office in Bédoin, also rents equipment and delivers to the summit.

❶ Information

Every village in the area has a tourist office and the following resources are also handy:

Destination Ventoux (www.destination-ventoux.com)

Provence Cycling (www.provence-cycling.com)

Provence des Papes (www.hautvaucluse.com)

Bédoin Tourist Office (☑ 04 90 65 63 95; www.bedoin.org; Espace Marie-Louis Gravier, Bédoin; ⊙ 9am-12.30pm & 2-6pm Mon-Sat, 9.30am-12.30pm Sun mid-Jun–Aug) Excellent source of information on all regional activities; also helps with lodging.

Malaucène Tourist Office (☑ 04 90 65 22 59; http://villagemalaucene.free.fr; place de la Mairie, Malaucène; ⊙ 9.15am-12.15pm &

VENTOUX LAVENDER

The isolated but charming village of Sault (pop 1285) has incredible summertime vistas over lavender fields. Sault's tourist office (p814) has lists of artisanal lavender producers, such as GAEC Champelle (☑ 04 90 64 01 50; www.gaec-champelle.fr; rte de Ventoux) 🔗, a roadside stand northwest of town selling lavender product galore.

WORTH A TRIP

GIGONDAS

Wine cellars and cafes surround the sun-dappled central square of Gigondas (population 598), famous for prestigious red wine. The **tourist office** (☑04 90 65 85 46; www.gigondas-dm.fr; rue du Portail, Gigondas; ☉10am-12.30pm & 2.30-6.30pm Mon-Sat, to 1pm Sun Jul & Aug, shorter hrs rest of yr) has a list of wineries. In town, **Caveau de Gigondas** (☑04 90 65 82 29; www.caveaudugigondas.com; place Gabrielle Andéol; ☉10am-noon & 2-6.30pm) represents 100 small producers and offers free tastings – most bottles cost just €12 to €14. Wine tasting here provides an excellent counterpoint to Châteauneuf-du-Pape: both use the same grapes, but the soil is different.

2.30-5.30pm Mon-Fri, 9am-noon Sat) Stocks info on Mont Ventoux, but (surprisingly) not the Dentelles.

Sault Tourist Office (☑04 90 64 01 21; www.saultenprovence.com; av de la Promenade, Sault; ☉9am-noon & 2-5pm Mon-Sat) Good resource for Ventoux.

❶ Getting There & Around

Reach Mont Ventoux by car from Sault via the D164; or (summer only) from Malaucène or St-Estève via the D974, often blocked by snow until April.

Carpentras

POP 29,915

Try to visit Carpentras on a Friday morning, when the streets spill over with more than 350 stalls laden with bread, honey, cheese, olives, fruit and a rainbow of *berlingots,* Carpentras' striped, pillow-shaped hard-boiled sweets. During winter the pungent truffle market murmurs with hushed-tone transactions. The season is kicked off by Carpentras' biggest fair, held during the **Fête de St-Siffrein** on 27 November, when more than 1000 stalls spread across town.

Markets aside, this slightly rundown agricultural town has a handful of architectural treats. A Greek trading centre and later a Gallo-Roman city, it became papal territory in 1229, and was also shaped by a strong Jewish presence, as Jews who had been expelled from French crown territory took refuge here. The 14th-century synagogue is the oldest still in use in France.

◉ Sights

★**Synagogue de Carpentras** SYNAGOGUE
(☑04 90 63 39 97; place Juiverie; ☉10am-noon & 3-4.30pm Mon-Thu, 10-11.30am & 3-3.30pm Fri) Carpentras' remarkable synagogue dates to 1367. The wood-panelled prayer hall was rebuilt in 18th-century Baroque style; downstairs are bread-baking ovens, used until 1904. Although Jews were initially welcomed into papal territory, by the 17th century they had to live in ghettos in Avignon, Carpentras, Cavaillon and L'Isle-sur-la-Sorgue: the synagogue is deliberately inconspicuous. For access, ring the doorbell on the half-hour or join an excellent 1½ hour guided tour (adult/child €5/3.50) organised by the tourist office every Tuesday at 10.30am from April to September.

Cathédrale St-Siffrein CATHEDRAL
(place St-Siffrein; ☉8am-noon & 2-6pm Mon-Sat) Carpentras' cathedral was built between 1405 and 1519 in meridional Gothic style, but is crowned by a distinctive contemporary bell tower. Its **Trésor d'Art Sacré** (Treasury of Religious Art) holds precious 14th- to 19th-century religious relics that you can only see during the Fête de St-Siffrein (27 November) and on guided walks with the tourist office.

Arc Romain ROMAN SITE
Hidden behind Cathédrale St-Siffrein, the Arc Romain was built under Augustus in the 1st century AD and is decorated with worn carvings of enslaved Gauls.

⛏ Sleeping

Hôtel du Fiacre HOTEL €€
(☑04 90 63 03 15; www.hotel-du-fiacre.com; 153 rue Vigne; s €70-110, d €85-120; ☉reception 8am-9pm; ☎) The faded grandeur of this 18th-century mansion with ochre façade is charming – from marble staircase to canopied beds. Outside there's a lovely sunny courtyard. Good service and value. Breakfast €10.

Hotel le Comtadin HOTEL €€
(☑04 90 67 75 00; www.le-comtadin.com; 65 bd Albin Durand; d €75-110; ❋☎) Formerly a private mansion, now a fresh-looking mid-range hotel under the Best Western banner, Le Comtadin's best rooms face an interior

courtyard; less-expensive rooms face the street. Breakfast €13.

🍴 Eating & Drinking

⭐ La Maison Jouvaud
PATISSERIE, TEAROOM €

(40 rue de l'Evêché; ⊙ 10am-7pm Mon, 8am-7pm Tue-Fri, 9am-7pm Sat & Sun) No address is sweeter than Jouvard, a vintage-styled cake shop, tearoom and homeware boutique festooned at every turn with delectable cakes, chocolates, sugared almonds, candied fruits and the feistiest mountain of homemade meringues imaginable waiting to seduce on the bar. The drinks menu includes *chocolat à l'ancienne,* milk with honey, and a beautiful selection of Mariage Frères teas.

Chez Serge
PROVENÇAL €€

(☑ 04 90 63 21 24; www.chez-serge.com; 90 rue Cottier; menus lunch €17, dinner €27 & €37, mains €19-32; ⊙ noon-2pm & 7.30-10pm Jun-Sep, to 1.30pm & 7.30-9.30pm Oct-Apr; 🖥🚗) Perhaps the hottest address in town, this savvy little courtyard restaurant plays at 'shabby chic' with its distressed wood and granite, Panton chairs and contemporary finishings. Serge's Place is the the place to sample Provence's black truffles, honoured with their own *menu* and simple *plats* like truffle omelette, truffle-laced pasta and truffle risotto.

La Galusha
PROVENÇAL €€

(☑ 04 90 60 75 00; www.galusha.fr; 30 place de l'Horloge; menus 2-/3-course lunch €14.50/17.50, dinner €24; ⊙ noon-1.30pm & 7.30-9.30pm Tue-Sun) Venetian glass ceiling lamps and whimsical Arcimboldo paintings lend a warm glow to the romantic interior of this upmarket dining room, tucked on the ground floor of an 15th-century building with enchanting flower-filled patio out back. In the kitchen Nîmes-born chef Stéphan Laurent cooks up modern Provençal cuisine, pandering to lighter lunchtime appetites with giant salads (€14.50).

Angel'Art Galerie
COCKTAIL BAR

(☑ 06 10 13 41 94; www.facebook.com/AngelArt-Galerie; 59 rue Raspail; cocktails €5-10; ⊙ 6pm-1am Mon, 10am-1am Tue-Sat) This hybrid art gallery-cocktail lounge is one of the hippest spaces in town – alongisde its equally trendy neighbours with whom it shares brightly coloured sun-shade sails, strung from one side of the tiny pedestrian street to the other.

En Face
WINE BAR

(☑ 06 37 34 32 58; 54 rue Raspail; tapas €1.50-6, platters €6-10; ⊙ 6pm-1am Mon, 8am-2.30pm & 6pm-1am Tue-Sat) One of a trio of hipster addresses on pedestrian rue Raspail, En Face (literally 'Opposite') is a no-frills wine bar with well-worn wooden floor, vintage posters on the walls and an appealing choice of tapas-style dishes chalked on the blackboard out front – a perfect spot to nibble over drinks.

ℹ️ Information

Tourist Office (☑ 04 90 63 00 78; www.carpentras-ventoux.com; 97 place du 25 Août 1944; ⊙ 9am-1pm & 2-7pm Mon-Sat, 9.30am-1pm Sun, shorter hrs rest of year) Excellent website, guided tours in English (adult/child €4/2.50), helpful staff and and extremely tasty adjoining boutique where you can learn about and buy local culinary products like Carpentras *berlingots,* local honey, melon syrup, meringues, AOC Ventoux wine et al.

ℹ️ Getting There & Away

TRAIN
After a 75-year pause local trains once more trundle between Carpentras' spanking new **train station** (av de la Gare) and Avignon (30 minutes; hourly), stopping also at Avignon TGV station (38 minutes). For informaton: www.reouverture-avignon-carpentras.fr

---

DON'T MISS

WHAT A TRIP!

The glassy Sorgue is a beauty for canoeing on a summer's day and there is no more enchanting means of meandering from Fontaine de Vaucluse to neighbouring L'Isle sur la Sorgue, 8km downstream, than in a canoe or kayak. Two companies, **Canoë Évasion** (☑ 04 90 38 26 22; www.canoe-evasion.net; rte de Fontaine de Vaucluse , D24 direction Lagnes) and **Kayak Vert** (☑ 04 90 20 35 44; www.canoe-france.com; Quartier la Baume , 1km out of town on D25 direction Lagnes), offer guided or self-guided two-hour trips (adult/7-14yrs €17/11) from Fontaine late April to October (or it can be done in reverse). Life jackets are provided, but children must be able to swim 25m. Afterwards you're returned upstream by minibus to your car.

WORTH A TRIP

L'ISLE-SUR-LA-SORGUE

A moat of flowing water encircles the ancient and prosperous town of L'Isle-sur-la-Sorgue, 7km west of Fontaine. This 'Venice of Provence' is stuffed to bursting with antique shops: disused mills and factories along the main road contain seven **antiques villages** (⊙10am-6pm Sat-Mon), which house around 300 dealers between them. For bargains, the giant four-day antiques fairs held in mid-August and over Easter are the best bet.

For those with a penchant for contemporary creations, browse **La Manufacture** (Impasse de l'Hôtel de Palerme; ⊙10am-7pm Tue-Sun). A collective showcasing the work of 25-odd local artists and artisans, the boutique is a one-stop shop for funky furniture, original jewellery, designer clothing, dogs crafted from rubber wellington boots and so on. Find it at the end of an alley off L'Isle's main pedestrian street rue de la République. Lunch afterwards with savvy locals at **Au Chineur** (☑04 90 38 33 54; 2 esplanade Robert-Vasse; 2-/3-course lunch menu €13/15, mains €15-20; ⊙7am-midnight Wed-Mon), a brilliant-value quayside bistro with vintage interior and packed pavement terrace, or sup on fine cheese and wine at **Caveau de la Tour de l'Isle** (☑04 90 20 70 25; www.caveaudelatourdelisle.fr; 12 rue de la République).

BUS

The **bus station** (place Terradou) is 150m southwest of the tourist office, which has schedules posted (or see http://vaucluse.fr). Services operated by Transdev Comtadins (p812) and **Voyages Arnaud** (☑04 90 63 01 82; www.voyages-arnaud-carpentras.com; 8 av Victor-Hugo):

Avignon €2, 40 minutes

Cavaillon €2, 45 minutes

L'Isle-sur-la-Sorgue €2, 35 minutes

Orange €2, 55 minutes

Vaison-la-Romaine €2, 45 minutes; via Malaucène €2, 35 minutes

Fontaine de Vaucluse

POP 668

France's most powerful **spring** surges out of nowhere above the pretty little village of Fontaine de Vaucluse. All the rain that falls within 1200 sq km gushes out here as the River Sorgue. The miraculous appearance of this crystal-clear flood draws 1.5 million tourists each year; aim to arrive early in the morning before the trickle of visitors becomes a deluge. It's at its most dazzling after heavy rain, but in drought times the normally surging hole looks like something out of a Harry Potter book, with eerily calm emerald water.

⊙ Sights & Activities

La Fontaine   SPRING

At the foot of craggy cliffs, an easy 1km walk from the village, the River Sorgue surges from the earth's depths. The spring is most dazzling after heavy rain, when water glows azure blue, welling up at an incredible 90 cu metres per second. Jacques Cousteau was among those who attempted to plumb the spring's depths, before an unmanned submarine touched base (315m down) in 1985.

Musée d'Histoire
1939–1945   MUSEUM

(☑04 90 20 24 00; chemin de la Fontaine; adult/child €3.50/1.50; ⊙10am-6pm Wed-Mon Apr-Oct & Jan-Feb, Sat & Sun Mar, Nov & Dec) Excellent examination of life in occupied France during WWII.

Maison de la Rose   PERFUMERY

(☑06 87 65 25 47; www.lesartsdelarose.com; ⊙2-4pm) The façade of this eye-catching *hôtel particulier* dating from 1900 is pure romance. Sitting pretty in pink on the left as you walk from the car park to village centre, the mansion's exquisitely sculpted floral façade shields an elegant interior dressed with original furnishings. Its boutique sells rose-scented cosmetics and other skin products crafted in the perfumery's laboratory, alongside edible rose products, rose plants and so on.

🛏 Sleeping & Eating

Hôtel du Poète   HISTORIC HOTEL €€€

(☑04 90 20 34 05; www.hoteldupoete.com; d €98-178; ⊙Mar–mid-Nov; ❀🎧🌊) Drift asleep to the sound of rushing water at this elegant small hotel, inside a restored mill on the river's banks. By day, lie by the poolside in the sun-dappled shade among the park-like grounds. Breakfast €17.

Pétrarque et Laure BRASSERIE €€
(☑04 90 20 31 48; place Colonne; 2-/3-course menu €18.50/23, salads €14, pizza €9-12; ☺noon-3pm & 7-10pm) Fontaine de Vaucluse's restaurants tend toward the *touristique;* this one is no exception, but it manages to serve reasonably priced, good-quality food (try the local trout) on a wonderful tree-shaded terrace beside the river.

ℹ Information

Tourist Office (www.oti-delasorgue.fr; Résidence Garcin; ☺10am-1pm & 2.30-6.30pm) By the bridge, mid-village.

ℹ Getting There & Around

BICYCLE

The tourist office has English-language brochures detailing three easy back-road cycling routes. Bike shops in L'Isle-sur-la-Sorgue (8km west) deliver to Fontaine.

BUS

Voyages Raoux (www.voyages-raoux.fr) buses serve Avignon (€2, one hour) and L'Isle-sur-la-Sorgue (€1, 20 minutes).

CAR

The narrow road to Gordes (14km, 20 minutes) from Fontaine-de-Vaucluse makes a scenic, less-travelled alternative to reach the Luberon.

Parking in town costs €4.

THE LUBERON

The picture-perfect area that makes up the Luberon is rectangular on a map, but navigating its bucolic rolling hills, golden-hued perched villages and hidden valleys is a bit like fitting together a jigsaw puzzle. The Luberon is named after its main mountain range, which is split in the centre by the **Combe de Lourmarin**, a beautiful narrow river valley. Luberon's hues, fragrances and flavours subtly transform in tune with the seasons.

The region's capital, Apt, is a central hub for practicalities, but the heart of the Luberon is in the tiny stone villages fanning out across the countryside, which encompasses the Parc Naturel Régional du Luberon, the Abbaye Notre-Dame de Sénanque of postcard fame and ancient, stone *bories* (drywalled huts). Luberon is best seen with your own wheels (motorised or leg-powered) as there is virtually no public transport.

Apt
POP 12,422

Sleepy little Apt comes alive during its Saturday morning market brimming with local specialities, otherwise it's primarily a hub for shopping.

◉ Sights

Musée de l'Aventure Industrielle du Pays d'Apt AGRICULTURAL MUSEUM
(Industrial History Museum; ☑04 90 74 95 30; 14 place du Postel; adult/child €4/free; ☺10am-noon & 2-6.30pm Mon-Sat, to 5.30pm Tue-Sat Oct-May) Gain an appreciation for Apt's artisanal and agricultural roots at this converted candied-fruit factory. The well-curated museum interprets the fruit and candying trade, as well as ochre mining and earthenware production from the 18th century.

Confiserie Kerry Aptunion SWEET FACTORY
(☑04 90 76 31 43; www.lesfleurons-apt.com; Quartier Salignan, D900; ☺9am-12.15pm & 1.30-6pm Mon-Fri, to 12.15pm & 2-6pm Sat) **FREE** Thirty tonnes of cherries are candied daily at the **Confiserie Kerry Aptunion**, the world's largest crystallised-fruit factory, 2.5km west of town. Free tastings and guided tours; check the website for the seasonal schedule.

⊨ Sleeping

Hôtel le Palais BUDGET HOTEL €
(☑04 90 04 89 32; www.hotel-le-palais.com; 24bis place Gabriel-Péri; s/d/tr/q €45/55/65/80; ☏⛭) Young, friendly owners lend a real air of dynamism to this veteran cheap-as-chips hotel. Breafast €5.

★**Le Couvent** B&B €€
(☑04 90 04 55 36; www.loucouvent.com; 36 rue Louis Rousset; d €95-130; ◉☏⛭) Behind a garden wall in the cobbled town centre, this enormous five-room *maison d'hôte* occupies a 17th-century former convent, and offers exceptional value and sense of place; breakfast is served in the old convent refectory.

Hôtel Sainte-Anne HOTEL €€
(☑04 90 74 18 04; www.apt-hotel.fr; 62 place Faubourg-du-Ballet; d €92-123; ✳◉☏) Lovely seven-room hotel in a 19th-century dwelling, completely renovated in 2010. Spotless, crisp-at-the-edges rooms mix modern and traditional furnishings, with exceptional beds and big bathtubs (though small toilets). Little extras include

homemade jams and breads, made by the charming owner, served as part of the copious breakfasts (€10).

✕ Eating

L'Auberge Espagnole TAPAS €
(http://laubergeespagnole-apt.com; 17 place au Sepier; tapas €4.50-8, lunch menu €13.50) Dominated by an ancient plane tree, hollowed with age, the old-town square on which this colourful tapas bar spills could not be more enchanting – or typically Provençal. Take your pick from 22 different Spanish-inspired tapas chalked on the board, then sit at flowery tableclothed-tables and savour the mellow scene.

Le Platane MODERN FRENCH €€
(✆04 90 04 74 36; 25 place Jules Ferry; menus €15-30, mains €20; ◷noon-2.30pm & 7.30-10pm Tue-Sat; ✈) Everything is made from scratch at this simple, decent restaurant, which uses quality ingredients in its changing French *menus*. The leafy terrace is good on balmy nights.

❶ Information

Tourist Office (✆04 90 74 03 18; www.luberon-apt.fr; 20 av Philippe de Girard; ◷9.30am-1pm & 2.30-7pm Mon-Sat, to 12.30pm Sun) Excellent source of information for activities, excursions, bike rides and walks.

PARC NATUREL RÉGIONAL DU LUBERON

Egyptian vultures, eagle owls, wild boars, Bonelli's eagles and Etruscan honeysuckle are among the species that call the 1650-sq-km **Parc Naturel Régional du Luberon** (www.parcduluberon.fr) home. Created in 1977 and recognised as a Biosphere Reserve by Unesco in 1997, the park encompasses dense forests, plunging gorges and 67 villages with a combined population of 155,000. The GR6, GR9, GR92 and GR97 walking trails all cross it, as does a 236km-long **cycling route**.

Pick up maps and guides at the **Maison du Parc** (✆04 90 04 42 00; www.parcduluberon.fr; 60 place Jean Jaurès; ◷8.30am-noon & 1.30-6pm Mon-Fri 9am-noon Sat Apr-Sep, shorter hours rest yr) in Apt.

---

❶ Getting There & Around

BICYCLE

Luberon Cycles (✆04 86 69 19 00; 86 quai Général-Leclerc; bike rental half-day/day from €12/16; ◷9am-noon & 2-6pm Mon-Sat)

BUS

Trans Vaucluse (www.vaucluse.fr) services from the **bus station** (250 av de la Libération):
Aix-en-Provence €2, two hours
Avignon €2, 1½ hours
Cavaillon €2, 45 minutes

North of Apt

Gordes & Around

Forming an amphitheatre over the rivers Sorgue and Calavon, the tiered village of **Gordes** (pop 2159) sits spectacularly on the white rock face of the Vaucluse plateau. In the early evenings the village is theatrically lit by the setting sun, turning the stone buildings a shimmering gold. Gordes has top billing on many tourists' must-see lists (particularly those of high-profile Parisians), so high season sees a cavalcade of coaches.

◉ Sights

Abbaye Notre-Dame de Sénanque CHURCH
(✆04 90 72 05 72; www.abbayedesenanque.com; adult/child €7/3; ◷9.45-11am Mon-Sat, tours by reservation) Famously framed by lavender in July, the exterior of this isolated Cistercian abbey, 4km northwest of Gordes off the D177, appears on every postcard rack in Provence. The abbey was founded in 1148 and it remains inhabited by monks today. Reservations are essential to visit the austere interiors by guided tour; conservative dress and silence are required.

It's a 1½-hour walk from Gordes on the GR6 trail, or a slow, winding drive, treacherous in rain.

Village des Bories ARCHITECTURE
(✆04 90 72 03 48; adult/child €6/4; ◷9am-8pm, shorter hours winter) Beehive-shaped *bories* (stone huts) bespeckle Provence and at the Village des Bories, 4km southwest of Gordes, an entire village of them can be explored. Constructed of slivered limestone, *bories* were built during the Bronze Age, inhabited by shepherds until 1839, then abandoned until their restoration in the 1970s. Visit early

in the morning or just before sunset for the best light. Note the lower car park is for buses; continue to the hilltop car park to avoid hiking uphill in the blazing heat.

Musée de la Lavande MUSEUM
(☑04 90 76 91 23; www.museedelalavande.com; Coustellet, D2; adult/child €6.80/free; ⊘9am-7pm May-Sep, to noon & 2-6pm Oct-Apr) This lavender museum, 7km south of Gordes in Coustellet, showcases top-end lavender. An audioguide and short video (in English) explain the lavender harvest, and giant copper stills reveal extraction methods. Guided tours depart at 1pm and 5pm daily May to September. The on-site boutique is an excellent (if pricey) one-stop shop for quality fine-lavender products, and there is a picnic area in the lavender-festooned garden (particularly pretty in summer when the lilac flower blooms).

🛏 Sleeping & Eating

⭐**Le Mas de la Beaume** B&B €€
(☑04 90 72 02 96; www.labeaume.com; rte de Cavaillon, Gordes; d €125-180; 🖥🖵) In a visually stunning hilltop locale at the village's edge, this impeccable five-room *maison d'hôte* is like a Provençal postcard come to life, with yellow-washed stone-wall rooms decorated with bunches of lavender hanging from wood-beamed ceilings. Beds are dressed in high-thread-count linens, and breakfast is delivered to your room.

Mas de la Régalade B&B €€
(☑04 90 76 90 79; www.masregalade-luberon. com; Quartier de la Sénancole, D2; d €120-150, dinner €36; ⊘mid-Apr–mid-Nov; 🖥🖵) A stone farmhouse on a grassy plain surrounded by oak woodlands, 3.5km south of Gordes, Mas de la Régalade's four rooms artfully blend mod cons with playful antiques. In the garden, a vintage blue Citroën peeks between scented hedgerows of lavender and rosemary, beyond the big pool. Three times a week *table d'hôte* dinner is served.

Le Mas Tourteron GASTRONOMIC €€€
(☑04 90 72 00 16; www.mastourteron.com; chemin de St-Blaise les Imberts; menu €59; ⊘7.30-9.30pm Wed-Sat, 12.30-2pm & 7.30-9.30pm Sun Apr-Oct) The welcome is warm at this country house, surrounded by gardens clearly created with perfect lazy lunches alfresco in mind. The stone-walled dining room has a vaguely boho-chic feeling, befitting chef Elisabeth Bourgeois-Baique's stylised cooking. Husband Phillipe selects from more than 200

PICNIC PERFECT

Those short of time or money in *très cher* Gordes should follow the locals away from the main square and downhill along rue Baptistin Picca, to pocket-sized **La Boulangerie de Mamie Jane** (☑04 90 72 09 34; lunch menus €6.50 or €7.90; ⊘6.30am-1pm & 2-6pm Thu-Tue). In the same family for three generations, it is run with love and passion by retired sportsman-turned-*boulanger* Bob and his wife Valérie who cook up outstanding bread, pastries, cakes and biscuits (including purple, lavender-perfumed *navettes*). The well-filled *baguette* sandwiches (€4.50) and lunch *menus* comprising a sandwich/quiche, dessert and drink (€7.90/6.50) are unbeatable value.

wines to pair with her seasonal, inventive *menus*. Desserts are legendary. It's 3.5km south of Gordes, off the D2.

❶ Information

Tourist Office (☑04 90 72 02 75; www. gordes-village.com; place du Château; ⊘9am-noon & 2-6pm Mon-Sat, from 10am Sun) Inside Gordes' medieval château, which was enlarged and given its defensive Renaissance towers in 1525.

Roussillon
POP 1342

Some two millennia ago, the Romans used the ochreous earth around the spectacular village of Roussillon, set in the valley between the Plateau de Vaucluse and the Luberon range, for producing pottery glazes. These days the whole village, down to gravestones in the cemetery, is built of the reddish stone.

◉ Sights & Activities

Attractions focus on learning more about the region's signature ochreous earth. Roussillon's visual charms are no secret, so arrive early or late in the day.

⭐**Sentier des Ocres** WALKING
(Ochre Trail; adult/child €2.50/free; ⊘9.30am-5.30pm; 🚶) In Roussillon village, groves of chestnut and pine surround sunset-coloured ochre formations, rising on a clifftop. Two

PROVENCE'S COLORADO

Nineteenth-century Luberon was a hive of industrial activity thanks to its natural deposits of ochre. Remnants of a quarry where the vivid red rock was mined from the 1880s until 1956 can be explored at the **Colorado Provençal** (☑04 32 52 09 75; www.colorado-provencal.com; parking €2; ☺9am-dusk), below the tiny village of Rustrel, 10km northeast of Apt. The savage landscape distorted by other-worldly rock formations are really quite extraordinary, the fiery upright **Cheminée de Fée** (Fairy Chimney) appearing like a slice of southwestern US plunked down in France. From the car park, signposted south of Rustrel village off the D22 to Banon, colour-coded walking trails lead into the ochre. Parking (€2) includes a leaflet detailing the trails. The red earth gets blazingly hot in summer: come early, carry water, and wear hiking boots and a hat.

Not to be confused with Colorado Provençal is **Colorado Adventures** (☑06 78 26 68 91; www.colorado-adventures.fr; adult/child €19/14; ☺9.30am-7.30pm Jul & Aug, 10am-7pm Mar-Jun, Sep & Nov), a tree-climbing park in the forest five minutes drive away, signposted off the D22 to Apt (follow the signs for 'Colorado Camping'). A real family favourite, three circuits swing from tree to tree including a lower one aimed at children from 6 yrs. A fourth trail thrills tots aged 2 to 5 yrs.

circular trails, 30 or 50 minutes, twist through mini-desert landscapes – it's like stepping into a Georgia O'Keeffe painting. Information panels highlight 26 types of flora to spot, the history of local ochre production, and so on. Wear walking shoes and avoid white!

Conservatoire des Ocres et de la Couleur
MUSEUM

(Ochre & Colour Conservatory; ☑04 90 05 66 69; www.okhra.com; rte d'Apt; guided tours adult/student €6.50/5; ☺9am-7pm Jul & Aug, to 6pm Sep-Jun, closed Mon & Tue Jan & Feb; ☑) This arts centre and historic site examines all things pigment. Occupying a disused ochre factory (on the D104 east of Roussillon), it explores the properties of ochre through indoor-outdoor displays and artwork, fun for kids to run around. There's an excellent art and home-decor boutique stocking extensive ranges of powdered pigment. Two-hour workshops for adults (€19) and children (€11) explore different ways to use ochre in art. Tours year-round at 2.30pm and 3.30pm, plus 11am and 4.30pm in summer.

Mines de Bruoux
HISTORIC SITE

(☑04 90 06 22 59; www.minesdebruoux.fr; rte de Croagnes; adult/child €8.10/6.50; ☺10am-7pm Jul & Aug, to 6pm Apr-Jun, Sep & Oct) In Gargas, 7km east of Roussillon, this former ochre mine has spectacular spire-filled caves, like a serene mineral church. Visits are only by guided tour, check the schedule on the website; reservations required.

❶ Information

Tourist Office (☑04 90 05 60 25; www.roussillon-provence.com; place de la Poste; ☺9am-noon & 1.30-5.30pm Mon-Sat)

St-Saturnin-lès-Apt & Around

POP 2798

Tiny St-Saturnin-lès-Apt is refreshingly ungentrified and just beyond the tourist radar. It has a cafe, a bistro and empty cobbled streets that twist uphill from central square place de la Mairie to a rocky plateau crowned by **château ruins** and a high-in-the-sky **church**, still intact – from where the most fabulous panorama of the surrounding Vaucluse plateau unfolds. Pause along the rocky path to admire the craftsmanship behind the ancient dry stone walls. Approach the village from Rustrel for an idyllic motor past pea-green vineyards and serried rows of lavender.

🛏 Sleeping & Eating

Le Saint Hubert
HOTEL €

(☑04 90 75 42 02; www.hotel-saint-hubert-luberon.com; d/tr €56-62/72) Charm personified, this quintessential village *auberge* (inn) has welcomed travellers since the 18th century and is a gorgeous spot to stay. Rooms are simple but elegant, and the sweeping view of the southern Luberon from valley-facing rooms is breathtaking. Guests reluctant to stray too far can opt for half-board (€116 for two people) – dining on the panoramic terrace is no short straw. Breakfast €8.

Le Mas Perréal B&B €€
(☑ 04 90 75 46 31; www.masperreal.com; Quartier la Fortune; s/d/tr incl breakfast €125/135/175; 🛜🏊) Surrounded by vineyards, lavender fields and cherry orchards, on a vast 17-acre property outside St-Saturnin-lès-Apt, this farmhouse B&B has five charmingly simple rooms, styled with country antiques and Provençal fabrics. Outside there's a heavenly pool and big garden with mountain views. Elisabeth, a long-time French teacher, offers cooking and French lessons (€30 per hour).

★ **La Coquillade** HOTEL, RESTAURANT €€€
(☑ 04 90 74 71 71; www.coquillade.fr; Le Perrotet, Gargas; lunch/dinner menus €38/72-115, d €325-390; ⊘ sittings 12.30-1.30pm & 7.30-9.30pm mid-Apr–mid-Oct) Overnighting here does not suit everyone's budget, unlike the excellent-value lunch *menu* served in the casual bistro of this luxurious Relais & Châteaux hilltop estate with formal Michelin-starred restaurant. In July and August bistro dining moves into the Jardin de la Vignes, aka an enchanting outdoor patio overlooking a sea of vines. La Coquillade is 5km northwest of Apt, signposted uphill off the D900.

★ **La Table de Pablo** MODERN FRENCH €€€
(☑ 04 90 75 45 18; www.latabledepablo.com; Les Petits Cléments, Villars; menus lunch €19 & €25, dinner €36 & €57, mains €22-26; ⊘ 12.30-2pm & 7-10pm Mon, Tue, Fri & Sun, 7-10pm Thu & Sat) Its incongruous setting in a simple house near Villars is not momentous, but the cuisine and attitude of chef Thomas Gallardo are. From the basil grown on a Bonnieux farm to

---

WORTH A TRIP

LAGARDE D'APT

In Lagarde d'Apt (population 37), 20km northeast of Apt, beneath some of Europe's darkest night skies, **Observatoire Sirene** (☑ 04 90 75 04 17; www.obs-sirene.com; Lagarde d'Apt; adult day/night €10/16, children free; 🅿) shows you the stars and reveals astronomical wonders using high-powered telescopes. Reservations are essential for star-gazing sessions.

The area's other highlight is the 80-hectare lavender farm, **Château du Bois** (☑ 04 90 76 91 23), where a 2km-long lavender trail blazes from late June until mid-July, when the sweet-smelling flower is harvested.

Forcalquier pigeon, cheese ripened by René Pellégrini and Luberon wine, everything is locally sourced. Top marks for the wine pairings. Children are welcomed with fruity cocktails and their own gastronomic '*petits bouts*' menu (€15).

South of Apt

South of the N100, the deep **Combe de Lourmarin** carves a north–south divide through the Luberon massif. **Le Petit Luberon** (Little Luberon) sits on the western side and its rocky landscape is sprinkled with cake-decoration-like *villages perchés* (perched villages) overlooking thick cedar forests and Côtes du Luberon vineyards. To its east, **Le Grand Luberon** takes in dramatic gorges, grand fortresses and lavender fields.

Petit Luberon

Picture-perfect hilltop villages overlooking forests, valleys and vineyards are the trademark of this beautifully manicured, affluent part of Provence.

◉ Sights & Activities

Highlights of the area include the villages Bonnieux, Lacoste, Ménerbes and Oppède-le-Vieux.

Bonnieux (population 1464) burst onto cinema screens in *A Good Year* (2006) as the village where Russell Crowe's character Max Skinner, a British financier, finds *joie de vivre* in the vineyards of Provence.

Lacoste (population 436) harbours the ruined 9th-century **Château de Lacoste** (☑ 06 82 25 36 06; www.chateau-lacoste-luberon.com; adult/child €10/5; ⊘ guided tours 11am-6pm Jun-Sep), where the notorious Marquis de Sade (1740–1814) retreated when his writings became too scandalous for Paris. The erotic novels penned by the marquis (who gave rise to the term 'sadism') were only freely published after WWII. The 45-room palace remained an eerie ruin until transformed by couturier Pierre Cardin into a 1000-seat theatre and opera stage hosting July's month-long **Festival de Lacoste** (www.festivaldelacoste.com).

Scaling the steep streets to **Ménerbes** (population 1159), moored on a hilltop, rewards you with uninterrupted views. The maze of streets conceals a 12th-century village **church** and the elegant **Maison de la**

Truffe et du Vin (House of Truffle & Wine; ☑04 90 72 38 37; www.vin-truffe-luberon.com; place de l'Horloge; ☺10am-noon & 2.30-6pm Apr-Oct, Thu-Sat Nov-Mar), where the Brotherhood of Truffles and Wine of Luberon represents 60 domaines and sells their wines. From April to October there's **wine tasting**; winter brings **truffle workshops**. Year-round, shop for truffle oil, balsamic vinegar, honey, tapanade and other truffle-scented proudcts in its shop and dine on truffles in its upmarket **restaurant** (*menus* €47 to €77).

Ménerbes captured the attention of millions when it was memorably rendered by British author Peter Mayle. The lavishly detailed books *A Year in Provence* and *Toujours Provence* recount renovating a *mas* just outside the village in the late 1980s. Monsieur Mayle now lives in Lourmarin in the Grand Luberon.

Oppède-le-Vieux (population 20), a medieval hilltop village 6km west of Ménerbes, was abandoned in 1910 by villagers who moved down the valley to the cultivated plains to earn their living. Today, a handful of artists live here among the cool ruins. The **Sentier Vigneron d'Oppède**, a 1½-hour winegrowers' trail, winds through olive groves, cherry orchards and vineyards.

🛏 Sleeping & Eating

La Bastide du Bois Bréant HOTEL €€
(☑04 90 05 86 78; www.hotel-bastide-bois-breant. com; 501 chemin du Puits-de-Grandaou, Maubec; d incl breakfast €175-240, 2-/4-person treehouse €160/320; ☺mid-Mar–Oct; ❋@🐾🏊) Shaded by 200-year-old oaks, this 2-hectare former truffle plantation midway between Gordes and Ménerbes sprawls seductively behind an iron gate. Inside the early 19th-century *bastide* (country manor) are 12 romantic rooms, decked out in an upmarket country-Provençal style. Outside, hidden between

branches, are two treehouses and a wonderfully bucolic and old-fashioned *roulotte* (caravan). Dinner with reservation costs €30.

Le Clos du Buis HOTEL €€
(☑04 90 75 88 48; www.leclosdubuis.fr; rue Victor Hugo, Bonnieux; d €135-153; ☺Mar–mid-Nov; ❋🏊🐾) This elegant stone townhouse in Bonnieux spills onto big terraced gardens, lovely for whiling away the afternoon. The dining room has panoramic views, and there's a self-catering kitchen.

Le Fournil MODERN FRENCH €€€
(☑04 90 75 83 62; www.lefournil-bonnieux.com; 5 place Carnot, Bonnieux; menus 2-/3-course lunch €24/30, dinner €40-52, lunch/dinner mains €17/26; ☺12.30-2pm & 7.30-9.30pm Tue-Sun, closed Tue Oct-Apr) On a quiet sun-speckled square, casual-chic Le Fournil's contemporary glass-and-steel interior is carved from rock – a moody backdrop for consistently first-rate, inventive cooking that varies seasonally and ranks its among Bonnieux' top tables. If you can't face a full-blown dessert, end with an ice-cream from the ice-cream shop it runs on the same square.

❶ Information

Bonnieux Tourist Office (☑04 90 75 91 90; www.tourisme-en-luberon.com; 7 place Carnot; ☺9.30am-12.30pm & 2-6.30pm Mon-Fri, 2-6.30pm Sat May-Oct, shorter hrs rest of yr)

❶ Getting There & Away

The Apt-Cavaillon bus service stops in all four villages three times a day. The best option by far is to have your own transport.

Grand Luberon

Purple lavender carpets the Plateau de Claparèdes area between Buoux (west), Sivergues (south), Auribeau (east) and

---

PEDAL POWER
....

Jaunty blue signs mark the way for the **Autour du Luberon**, a 236km cycling itinerary through the region that leads from one picturesque village to the next. Tourist offices have maps for this, as well as for **Les Ocres à Vélo**, four shorter cycling routes (9km to 40km) in 'ochre country' around Roussillon. **Vélo Loisir en Luberon** (☑04 90 76 48 05; www.veloloisirluberon.com) has extensive info on everything, from where to rent bikes to where to sleep and how to arrange transport of luggage.

If you can't face too much pedalling, **Sun eBike** (☑04 90 74 09 96; www.location-velo-provence.com; 1 av Clovis Hugues, Bonnieux; electric bike per day €35) in Bonnieux rents electric bicycles; they're not scooters – you have to pedal – but the motor helps significantly with the ascents.

picture-postcard Saignon (north). Cycle, walk or motor through the lavender fields and along the northern slopes of **Mourre Nègre** (1125m) – the Luberon's highest point. Stop for views of gorgeous **Saignon** (population 1005) before you wander its streets.

At the base of the Combe de Lourmarin and, unlike many of the Luberon's precarious hilltop townships, easily accessed, the alluring village of **Lourmarin** makes for a lovely stroll with its charming **château** (🖉04 90 68 15 23; www.chateau-de-lourmarin. com; adult/child €6.50/3; ⊙10am-6pm Jul & Aug, 10.30am-12.30pm & 2.30-5.30pm Sep-Jun), exclusive boutiques, bounty of cafes and lively Tuesday evening and Friday morning markets.

🛏 Sleeping & Eating

La Cordière
B&B €

(🖉04 90 68 03 32; www.cordiere.com; rue Albert Camus; d €65-70; 🕏) In Lourmarin's village centre, this character-rich house, built 1582, surrounds a tiny flower-filled courtyard, with adjoining summer kitchen for guests. Rooms are filled with atmospheric Provençal antiques and sport spacious bathrooms. Also rents three great-value studios with kitchens. Minimim three-night stay. Breakfast €7.50.

★Café Gaby
CAFE €

(🖉04 90 68 38 42; place de l'Ormeau; salads €10-12, omelettes €9-12; ⊙7am-midnight) One of a trio of delightful cafe pavement terraces on place de l'Orneau, Café Gaby with its royal blue and cream woven bistro chairs in the lunchtime sun is pure unadulterated Provençal charm. Cuisine is French classic and homemade, climaxing each week on Friday with a giant *aïoli maison* (a mountain of veg, boiled potatoes, a boiled egg and shellfish dunked in a pot of garlicky mayonnaise).

★Le Sanglier Paresseux
MODERN FRENCH €€

(🖉04 90 75 17 70; www.sanglierparesseux.com; Caseneuve; lunch/dinner menus €25/31-41; ⊙7.30-10pm Mon, noon-2pm & 7.30-10pm Tue-Sat) Squirrelled away in the hilltop village of Caseneuve, 10km from Apt, is one of the Luberon's tastiest addresses. The creation of Brazilian chef Fabricio Delgaudio, The Wild Lazy Boar is invitingly casual with a sunset view unmatched from its west-facing terrace. Cuisine is inventive, unfussy, seasonal and the perfect showcase of regional ingredients. Reservations essential.

Le Petit Café
MODERN PROVENÇAL €€

(🖉04 90 76 64 92; www.lapetitecave-saignon.com; place de l'Horloge, Saignon; 2-/3-course menus €25/29; ⊙10am-5pm Mar-Oct & Dec) This new millennium village cafe, 4km southeast of Apt in hilltop Saignon, is a tip-top contemporary spot to stop for a bowl of chilled pea soup, crayfish mousse with mint, wraps, and other light lunchtime creations by British chef Andrew Goldsby. Come dusk, backtrack downhill to **La Petite Cave** (7.30-9.30pm Tue-Sat Apr-Sep) a romantic, golden-stone vaulted cellar restaurant by the same chef.

Auberge La Fenière
GASTRONOMIC €€€

(🖉04 90 68 11 79; www.reinesammut.com; rte de Lourmarin, Cadenet; d from €180, lunch/dinner menus from €50/90; 🕏) It doesn't get more sweetly Provençal than this wonderful old stone farmhouse – the exquisite domain of Michelin-starred chef Reine Sammut who cooks up outstanding multicourse formal restaurant *menus* (€55 to €125) and more-casual bistro fare (*menu* €36) using produce from her lush *potager* (kitchen garden). The wine list is sufficiently fine to justify an overnight in one of its 16 beautiful rooms and suites. Morning cooking classes with lunch are €165.

ℹ Information

Lourmarin Tourist Office (🖉04 90 68 10 77; www.lourmarin.com; place Henri Barthélémy; ⊙10am-12.30pm & 3-6pm Mon-Sat)

ℹ Getting There & Away

Your own set of wheels – two or four – is the only realistic way to get to, from and around the region.

NORTHEASTERN PROVENCE

Haute-Provence's heady mountain ranges arc across the top of the Côte d'Azur to the Italian border, creating a far-flung crown of snowy peaks and precipitous valleys. To the west, a string of sweet, untouristy hilltop villages and lavender fields drape the Vallée de la Durance. Magical Moustiers Ste-Marie is a gateway to the plunging white waters of Europe's largest canyon, the Gorges du Verdon. In the east, the Vallée des Merveilles wows with 36,000 Bronze Age rock carvings. In the far north are the winter ski slopes and summer mountain retreats of the Ubaye and

Blanche Valleys. Outside of ski areas, many establishments close in winter.

Pays de Forcalquier

Beyond mass-tourism's radar, Pays de Forcalquier's expansive landscapes comprise wildflower-tinged countryside and isolated hilltop villages. At its heart atop a rocky perch sits its namesake, Forcalquier, a sleepy town that bursts into life once a week during its Monday-morning market. Steep steps lead to the gold-topped citadel and octagonal chapel atop the town.

Some 4km south of Forcalquier, outside the walled city of Mane, is perhaps Provence's most peaceful address: The 13th-century Prieuré de Salagon (📍04 92 75 70 50; www.musee-de-salagon.com; adult/child/family €7/5/20; ⊙10am-8pm Jun-Aug, to 7pm May & Sep, to 6pm Oct–mid-Dec & Feb-Apr; ♿) sits amid fields and five themed gardens, including a medieval herb garden, a show garden of world plants, and a wonderfully sweet-smelling Jardin des Senteurs (Garden of Scents) with much native lavender among the mints, mugworts and other fragant plants. Inside the old stone priory, a fascinating permanent exhibition explores lavender and its historical production, uses and culture in Haute-Provence. A stunning repertoire of seasonal concerts and temporary exhibitions – often including great art installations in the chapel – complete the enchanting ensemble.

Forcalquier's quaint pedestrian streets and squares have a generous sprinkling of restaurant terraces. The tourist office (📍04 92 75 10 02; www.forcalquier.com; 13 place du Bourguet; ⊙9am-noon & 2-6pm Mon-Sat) has accommodation information.

Vallée de la Durance

At the western edge of Haute-Provence, the winding waters of the 324km-long River Durance, a tributary of the Rhône, follow the Via Domitia, the road from Italy that allowed the Romans to infiltrate the whole of France. Now it's the autoroute's path, a fast connector between the Alps and the coast.

Come summer, the area's highlight is the Plateau de Valensole, France's lavender capital. Cruise the plateau along the D6 or D8 for arresting views of unfolding purple ripples.

On the other side of the river, Monastère Notre Dame de Ganagobie (Ganagobie; ⊙3-5pm Tue-Sun, shop 10.30am-noon & 2.30-6pm Tue-Sun) FREE, a 10th-century Benedictine monastery, is wonderful for a stroll among almond trees, beds of irises and quiet hilltop woods. The 12th-century floor mosaic (depicting dragons) inside the chapel is the largest of its kind in France, and a shop stocks monk-made soaps, honey and music. Ganagobie is signposted off the N96 between Lurs and Peyruis.

Gorges du Verdon

Under the protection of the Parc Naturel Régional du Verdon since 1997, Europe's largest canyon, the plunging Gorges du Verdon, slices a 25km swathe through Provence's limestone plateau.

The main gorge begins at Rougon near the confluence of the Verdon and the Jabron Rivers, and then winds westwards until the Verdon's green waters flow into Lac de Ste-Croix. At a dizzying 250m to 700m deep, the gorge's floors – only accessible by foot or raft – are between 8m to 90m wide, while its overhanging rims are from 200m to 1500m apart.

The two main jumping-off points for exploring the gorges are the villages of Moustiers Ste-Marie in the west and Castellane – dead in winter, teeming in summer – in the east. Castellane tourist office (📍04 92 83 61 14; www.castellane.org; rue Nationale; ⊙9am-7.30pm Jul & Aug, shorter hrs rest of yr) and its counterpart in Moustiers (p826) have plenty of information on accommodation, activites and so forth.

🏃 Activities

Cycling & Driving

Motorists and cyclists can take in staggering panoramas from two vertigo-inducing cliff-side roads: the nail-biting Route des Crêtes aka the panoramic D952 and D23, corkscrews along the gorges' northern rim, past the Point Sublime (a viewpoint) which offers a fisheye-lens view of serrated rock formations falling away to the river below. From the northern side, the best viewpoint is the Belvédère de l'Escalès.

Also heart-palpitating, La Corniche Sublime (the D955 to the D71, and then on to the D19) twists along the southern rim, taking in landmarks such as the Balcons de la Mescla (Mescla Terraces) and Pont de l'Artuby (Artuby Bridge), the highest bridge in Europe.

A complete circuit of the Gorges du Verdon via Moustiers Ste-Marie involves about 140km of relentless hairpin-turn driving. In winter, roads get icy or snowy; watch for falling rocks year-round; and heaven forbid that you get stuck behind a caravan in summer – opportunities to pass are rare.

Walking

Dozens of blazed trails traverse otherwise untamed countryside around Castellane and Moustiers. Tourist offices carry the excellent, English-language *Canyon du Verdon* (€4.70), detailing 28 walks; plus a map of five principal walks (€2.40).

You can hike most of the canyon along the often-difficult GR4. The full route takes two days, but shorter canyon descents are possible. Camping on gravel beaches is illegal. Don't cross the river, except at bridges, and stay on marked trails, lest you get trapped when the upstream dam opens, which happens twice weekly. Check with tourist offices before embarking.

Outdoor Sports

April to September, Castellane is the main water-sports base for white-water activities.

Aqua Viva Est WATER SPORTS
(📞06 82 06 92 92, 04 92 83 75 74; www.aquavivaest.com; 12 bd de la République, Castellane; ⊙10.30am-1.30pm & 4-6.30pm Mon-Sat) With an office handily place across from the main square in Castellane, Aqua Viva Est organises rafting, canyoning, hydrospeed and kayaking expeditions.

**Des Guides
pour l'Aventure** OUTDOOR ACTIVITIES
(📞06 85 94 46 61; www.guidesaventure.com; Moustiers Ste-Marie) Offers canyoning, rock climbing, rafting (€55) and 'floating' (€45) – river running with only a buoyancy bag strapped to your back.

Aboard Rafting WATER SPORTS
(📞04 92 83 76 11; www.aboard-rafting.com; 8 place de l'Église, Castellane) White-water rafting and canyoning trips.

🛏 Sleeping & Eating

There are several unremarkable hotels in Castellane, and campsites line its river banks. Out of town options are more appealing.

Gîte de Chasteuil B&B €
(📞04 92 83 72 45; www.gitedechasteuil.com; Hameau de Chasteuil; s €62-67, d €73-84, tr €90-95; ⊙Mar-Nov) Some 12km west of Castellane, this excellent-value *chambre d'hôte* resides in a former schoolhouse with gorgeous mountains views and is an ideal stop for hikers along GR4. Excellent *table d'hôte* (€20/€24 with/without advance reservation).

**Auberge
du Teillon** PROVENÇAL, GASTRONOMIC €€
(📞04 92 83 60 88; rte Napoléon, La Garde, D4805; d €65-80, menus €29-56) In the same family for five generations (since 1987), this much-loved roadside *auberge* with a handful of simple rooms up top is a classic Sunday lunch address. Cuisine is 'Provençal classic' and children are well catered for with their own €13 *menu*. Find it 5km east of Castellane on the road to Grasse.

ⓘ Getting There & Around

Public transport is seriously limited. Daily in July and August and weekends in April to September, **Navettes des Gorges shuttle buses** link Castellane with Point Sublime, La Palud and La Maline (but not Moustiers), returning hikers to their vehicles. Tourist offices have schedules and detailed information.

Moustiers Ste-Marie

POP 718

Dubbed the *Étoile de Provence* (Star of Provence), the charming village of Moustiers Ste-Marie makes a fair claim to the title. Tucked between two limestone cliffs, it overlooks open fields and far-off mountains. The 227m-long gold chain bearing a shining star was suspended over the town, so legend claims, by the Knight of Blacas, grateful to have returned safely from the Crusades. Beneath the star, clinging to a cliff ledge, is 14th-century **Chapelle Notre Dame de Beauvoir**, built on the site of an AD 470 temple.

Moustiers is also known for its decorative faience (earthenware pottery), showcased in the village's small but smart **Musée de la Faïence** (📞04 92 74 61 64; rue Seigneur de la Clue).

🛏 Sleeping & Eating

★ **Gîte du Petit Ségriès** FARMSTAY €
(📞04 92 74 68 83; www.chambre-hote-verdon.com; d incl breakfast €69-79; 🛜🌐) Friendly hosts

Sylvie and Noël offer five colourful, airy rooms in their rambling farmhouse, surrounded by 75 sheep and even more fields 5km west of Moustiers on the D952 to Riez. Family-style *tables d'hôte* (€21 with wine) is served at a massive chestnut table, or outside beneath a foliage-covered pergoda in summer. Noël is a mountain-bike guide and runs excellent guided tours (from €65).

Domaine du Petit Lac   CAMPGROUND €

(☑ 04 92 74 67 11; www.lepetitlac.com; rte des Salles en Verdon; camping per 2 people €15.30-22.90; ☺ mid-Apr–mid-Oct; @☎❄☝) Large, activity-oriented campsite on the shores of Lac Ste-Croix; also has wooden chalets and mobile homes.

★ La Ferme Rose   HOTEL €€

(☑ 04 92 75 75 75; www.lafermerose.com; chemin de Quinson; d €85-155; ❄☎) This Italianate terracotta-coloured farmhouse, signposted off the D952 to Ste-Croix de Verdon, is eclectic and charming as it gets in Provence. Its interior is crammed with quirky collectibles – including a Wurlitzer jukebox, a display case of coffee grinders, and vintage steam irons on the turquoise-tiled staircase. Colourful, airy and uncluttered rooms look out onto unending flowery gardens. Breakfast €11.

★ La Grignotière   PROVENÇAL €

(☑ 04 92 74 69 12; rte de Ste-Anne; mains €6-15; ☺ 11.30am-10pm May-Sep, to 6pm Feb–mid-May) Hidden away behind the soft pink façade of Moustier's Musée de la Faïence is this utterly gorgeous, blissfully peaceful garden restaurant. Tables sit between olive trees and the colourful, eye-catching decor – including the handmade glassware – is the handiwork of talented, dynamic owner Sandrine. Cuisine is 'picnic chic', meaning lots of creative olive oil-doused salads, tapenades, quiches and so on.

La Bastide de Moustiers   GASTRONOMIC €€€

(☑ 04 92 70 47 47; www.bastide-moustiers.com; chemin de Quinson; menus €38-79, mains €36-50, d from €260; ❄) This splurge-worthy Provençal nest, domain of legendary chef Alain Ducasse, is famous for fine cuisine – hence the helicopter pad in the garden – and provides the chance to dress for dinner. Rooms are sophisticated and smart, and breakfast (€23) is served on a garden-view terrace, in view of scampering baby deer. Find it 500m down a country lane, signposted off the D952 to Ste-Croix de Verdon.

❶ Information

Tourist Office (☑ 04 92 74 67 84; www.moustiers.eu; ☺ 9.30am-7pm Mon-Fri, to 12.30pm & 2-7pm Sat & Sun Jul & Aug, shorter hours rest of year; ☎)

The French Riviera & Monaco

POP 2.09 MILLION

Why Go?

With its glistening seas, idyllic beaches and fabulous weather, the Riviera (known as Côte d'Azur to the French) encapsulates many people's idea of the good life. The beauty is that there is so much more to do than just going to the beach – although the Riviera does take beach-going *very* seriously: from nudist beach to secluded cove or exclusive club, there is something for everyone.

Culture vultures will revel in the region's thriving art scene: the Riviera has some fine museums, including world-class modern art, and a rich history to explore in Roman ruins, WWII memorials and excellent museums.

Foodies for their part will rejoice at the prospect of lingering in fruit and veg markets, touring vineyards and feasting on some of France's best cuisines, while outdoor enthusiasts will be spoilt for choice with coastal paths to explore, and snorkelling and swimming galore.

Best Art Museums

➡ Chapelle du Rosaire (p842)

➡ Fondation Maeght (p841)

➡ Musée Jean Cocteau (p875)

➡ Musée d'Art Classique de Mougins (p853)

➡ Musée de l'Annonciade (p858)

Best Places to Eat

➡ Jan (p838)

➡ Sea Sens (p851)

➡ La Montgolfière (p870)

➡ La Rossettisserie (p837)

➡ Chez Palmyre (p837)

When to Go
Monaco

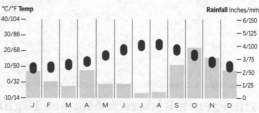

Feb Carnival season, with two weeks of festivities in Nice and Menton.

May Jet-setters descend on the Riviera for Monaco's Grand Prix and the Cannes Film Festival.

Jul Fireworks on 14 July, jazz festival in Antibes, and perfect beach weather.

The French Riviera & Monaco Highlights

1 Taking a scenic drive along the **Grande Corniche** (p866) for jaw-dropping views of the Med

2 Losing yourself in labyrinthine **Vieux Nice** (p830) and enjoying a panoramic picnic on Parc du Château

3 Catching a ferry to the **Îles d'Hyères** (p863) for pristine Mediterranean seascapes

4 Enjoying a fabulous day in **St-Tropez** (p857)

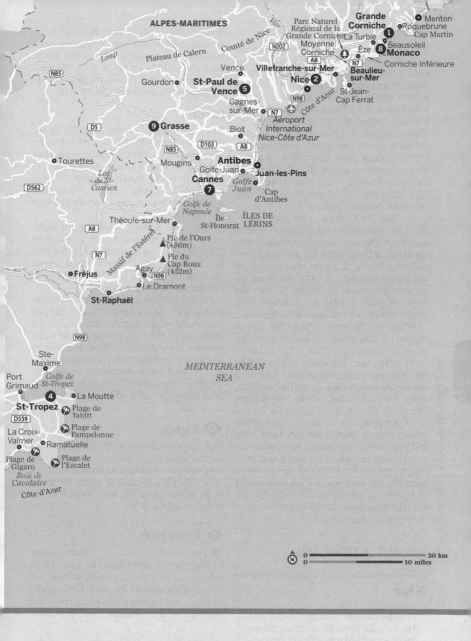

ALPES-MARITIMES

Parc Naturel Régional de la Grande Corniche

Grande Corniche ❶

Menton
Roquebrune Cap Martin

La Turbie

Moyenne Corniche

Beausoleil
Monaco ❽

Èze

Corniche Inférieure

Plateau de Calern

Comté de Nice

Loup

N85

N202

Vence

Villefranche-sur-Mer

Nice ❷

Beaulieu-sur-Mer

Gourdon

St-Paul de Vence ❺

St-Jean-Cap Ferrat

Cagnes-sur-Mer

N98

Côte d'Azur

N7

Grasse ❾

Biot

Aéroport International Nice-Côte d'Azur

D5

N85

D103

A8

Tourettes

Mougins

Antibes

Lac de St-Cassien

Golfe-Juan

Juan-les-Pins

Cannes ❼

Golfe Juan

Cap d'Antibes

D562

Théoule-sur-Mer

Golfe de Napoule

Île St-Honorat

ÎLES DE LÉRINS

A8

Massif de l'Estérel

Pic de l'Ours (496m)

N7

Pic du Cap Roux (452m)

Agay

Fréjus

N98

Le Dramont

St-Raphaël

N98

MEDITERRANEAN SEA

Ste-Maxime

Port Grimaud

Golfe de St-Tropez

La Moutte

St-Tropez ❹

Plage de Tahiti

D559

Plage de Pampelonne

La Croix-Valmer

Ramatuelle

Plage de Gigaro

Plage de l'Escalet

Baie de Cavalaire

Côte d'Azur

N

0   20 km
0   10 miles

❺ Admiring seminal 20th-century art at **Fondation Maeght** (p841) in St-Paul de Vence

❻ Winding your way through vineyards and trying some

of the area's famed wines at **Maison des Vins** (p865) in the seaside town of Bandol

❼ Dressing to impress and partying the night away in **Cannes** (p845)

❽ Trying your luck at Monaco's opulent **casino** (p874)

❾ Discovering the world of perfumery in **Grasse** (p853)

History

The eastern part of France's Mediterranean coast, including the area now known as the Côte d'Azur, was occupied by the Ligurians from the 1st millennium BC. It was colonised around 600 BC by Greeks from Asia Minor, who settled along the coast in the areas of Massalia (present-day Marseille), Hyères, St-Tropez, Antibes and Nice. Called in to help Massalia against the threat of invasion by Celto-Ligurians from Entremont, the Romans triumphed in 125 BC. They created Provincia Romana – the area between the Alps, the sea and the River Rhône – which ultimately became Provence.

In 1388 Nice, along with the Haute-Provence mountain towns of Barcelonette and Puget-Théniers, was incorporated into the House of Savoy, while the rest of the surrounding Provençal region became part of the French kingdom in 1482. Following an agreement between Napoléon III and the House of Savoy in 1860, the Austrians were ousted and France took possession of Savoy.

Within the Provence–Alpes–Côte d'Azur *région,* the Côte d'Azur (or Riviera to Anglophones) encompasses most of the *départements* of the Alpes-Maritimes and the Var. In the 19th century, wealthy tourists flocked to the area to escape the cold northern winter, along with celebrated artists and writers, adding to the area's cachet. Little fishing ports morphed into exclusive resorts. Paid holidays for all French workers from 1936 and improved transportation saw visitors arrive in summer, making it a year-round holiday playground. But it's not all play, no work: since the late 20th century, the area inland of Antibes has been home to France's 'Silicon Valley', Sophia Antipolis, the country's largest industrial and technological hub.

NICE TO TOULON

Nice

POP 348,195

> Most people come here for the light. Me, I'm from the north. What moved me are January's radiant colours and luminosity of daylight.
>
> *Henri Matisse*

The words are Matisse's but they could be those of any painter, or, in fact, of any visitor who comes to Nice, for it's true: the light here is magical. The city also offers exceptional quality of life: shimmering Mediterranean shores, the very best of Mediterranean food, a unique historical heritage and Alpine wilderness within an hour's drive. No wonder so many young French people aspire to live here and tourists keep flooding in.

History

Nice was founded around 350 BC by the Greek seafarers who had settled Marseille. They named the colony Nikaia, apparently to commemorate a nearby victory (*nike* in Greek). In 154 BC the Greeks were followed by the Romans, who settled further uphill around what is now Cimiez, where there are still Roman ruins.

By the 10th century, Nice was ruled by the counts of Provence but turned to Amadeus VII of the House of Savoy in 1388. In the 18th and 19th centuries it was occupied several times by the French, but didn't definitively become part of France until 1860.

During the Victorian period, the English aristocracy and European royalty enjoyed Nice's mild winter climate. Throughout the 20th century, the city's exceptional art scene spanned every movement from impressionism to new realism. The tram line (customised by local and international artists) and the decision to open all museums for free in 2008 show that art is still very much a part of city life.

◉ Sights

Nice has a number of world-class sights but the star attraction is probably the city itself: atmospheric, beautiful and photogenic, it's a wonderful place to stroll or watch the world go by, so make sure you leave yourself plenty of time to soak it all in.

◉ Vieux Nice

★ Vieux Nice   HISTORIC QUARTER
(⊙food markets 6am-1.30pm Tue-Sun) Nice's old town, a mellow-hued rabbit warren, has scarcely changed since the 1700s. Retracing its history – and therefore that of the city – is a highlight, although you don't need to be a his-

---

FAST FACTS

➡ **Area** 10,272 sq km

➡ **Local industry** services, technology, tourism

➡ **Signature drink** rosé

---

tory buff to enjoy a stroll in this atmospheric quarter. Vieux Nice is as alive and prominent today as it ever was.

Cue the cours Saleya: this joyous, thriving market square hosts a well-known flower market (☉6am-5.30pm Tue-Sat, to 1.30pm Sun) and a thriving fruit and vegetable market (☉6am-1.30pm Tue-Sun), a staple of local life. A flea market (☉8am-5pm Mon) takes over on Monday, and the spill over from bars and restaurants seems to be a permanent fixture.

Much of Vieux Nice has a similar atmosphere to cours Saleya, with delis, food shops, boutiques and bars crammed in its tiny lanes. Rue de la Boucherie and rue Pairolière are excellent for food shopping. You'll also find a fish market (☉6am-1pm Tue-Sun) at place St-François.

Much harder to spot because of the narrow lane it sits on is the baroque Palais Lascaris (15 rue Droite; guided visit €5; ☉10am-6pm Wed-Mon, guided tour 3pm Fri) FREE, a 17th-century mansion housing a frescoed orgy of Flemish tapestries, faience (tin-glazed earthenware) and gloomy religious paintings. On the ground floor is an 18th-century pharmacy.

Baroque aficionados shouldn't miss Nice's other architectural gems such as Cathédrale Ste-Réparate (place Rossetti), honouring the city's patron saint, or the exuberant Chapelle de la Miséricorde (cours Saleya).

Parc du Château GARDEN
(☉8am-6pm in winter, to 8pm in summer) On a rocky outcrop towering over Vieux Nice, this park offers a cinematic panorama of Nice and the Baie des Anges on one side, and the port on the other. The 12th-century castle was razed by Louis XIV in 1706; only the 16th-century Tour Bellanda remains. It is a fabulous place for picnics. To get here, ride the free Château Lift (Ascenseur du Château; rue des Ponchettes; ☉9am-6pm winter, to 8pm summer) from beneath Tour Bellanda, or hike up from the old town or the port.

Other simple attractions include Cascade Donjon, an 18th-century artificial waterfall crowned with a viewing platform, and kids' playgrounds.

Port Lympia ARCHITECTURE
Nice's Port Lympia, with its beautiful Venetian-coloured buildings, is often overlooked, but a stroll along its quays is lovely, as is the walk to get here: come down through Parc du Château or follow quai Rauba Capeu, where a massive war memorial hewn from the rock commemorates the 4000 Niçois who died in both world wars.

👁 Cimiez

Cimiez used to be the playground of European aristocrats wintering on the Riviera. These days, it's Nice's affluent residents who live in the area's beautiful Victorian villas.

Musée Matisse ART MUSEUM
(www.musee-matisse-nice.org; 164 av des Arènes de Cimiez; ☉10am-6pm Wed-Mon) FREE Located about 2km north of the centre in the leafy quarter of Cimiez, the Musée Matisse houses a fascinating assortment of works by Matisse, documenting the artist's stylistic evolution, including oil paintings, drawings, sculptures, tapestries and Matisse's signature famous paper cut-outs. The permanent collection is displayed in a red-ochre 17th-century Genoese villa overlooking an olive-tree-studded park. Temporary exhibitions are hosted in the futuristic basement building. Sadly, all explanations are in French only.

Matisse lived nearby in the 1940s, in the monumental Régina building at 71 bd de Cimiez. Originally Queen Victoria's wintering palace, it had been converted and Matisse had two apartments that he used as his home and studio. He died here in 1954 and is now buried at the cemetery of the Monastère de Cimiez (place du Monastère; ☉8.30am-12.30pm & 2.30-6.30pm), across the park from the museum.

Musée National Marc Chagall ART MUSEUM
(www.musee-chagall.fr; 4 av Dr Ménard; adult/child €8/6; ☉10am-5pm Wed-Mon Oct-Jun, to 6pm Jul-Sep) This small museum houses the largest public collection of works by Belarusian painter Marc Chagall (1887-1985). The main hall contains 12 huge interpretations (1954-67)

THE FRENCH RIVIERA & MONACO NICE

Nice

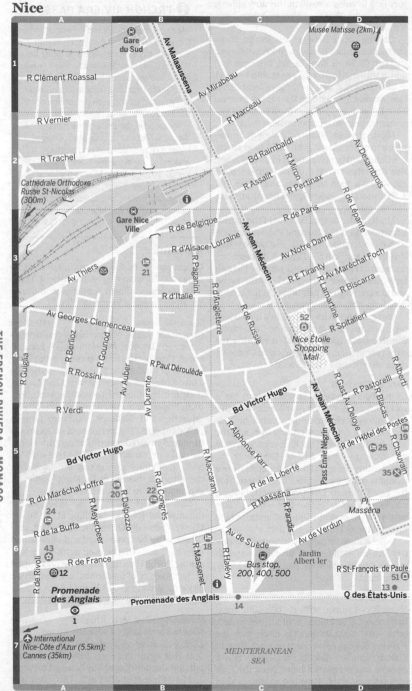

Gare
du Sud

R Clément Roassal

R Vernier

R Trachel

Cathédrale Orthodoxe
Russe St-Nicolas
(300m)

Gare Nice
Ville

Av Thiers

Av Georges Clemenceau

R Guiglia

R Berlioz

R Gounod

R Rossini

R Verdi

R du Maréchal Joffre

R Meyerbeer

R de la Buffa

R de Rivoli

Promenade
des Anglais

International
Nice-Côte d'Azur (5.5km);
Cannes (35km)

Av Malaussena

Av Mirabeau

R Marceau

Bd Raimbaldi

R Assalit

R Miron

R Pertinax

R de Paris

R de Belgique

R d'Alsace-Lorraine

R de Russie

R Paganini

R d'Italie

R d'Angleterre

Av Notre Dame

Av Jean Médecin

R E Tiranty

Av Maréchal Foch

R Lamartine

R Biscarra

R Spitalieri

Nice Étoile
Shopping
Mall

R Paul Déroulède

Av Auber

Av Durante

Bd Victor Hugo

Av Jean Médecin

R Gast Av Deloye

R Pastorelli

R Alberti

R Blacas

R de l'Hôtel des Postes

R Chauvain

R 19

Bd Victor Hugo

R Alphonse Karr

R Maccarani

R du Congrès

R Dalpozzo

R de la Liberté

R Masséna

Pass Émile Négrin

R Paradis

Pl
Masséna

R de France

R Massenet

Av de Suède

R Halévy

Av de Verdun

Jardin
Albert Ier

Bus stop,
200, 400, 500

R St-François de Paule

Q des États-Unis

Promenade des Anglais

Musée Matisse (2km)

Av Desambrois

Av de Lépante

MEDITERRANEAN
SEA

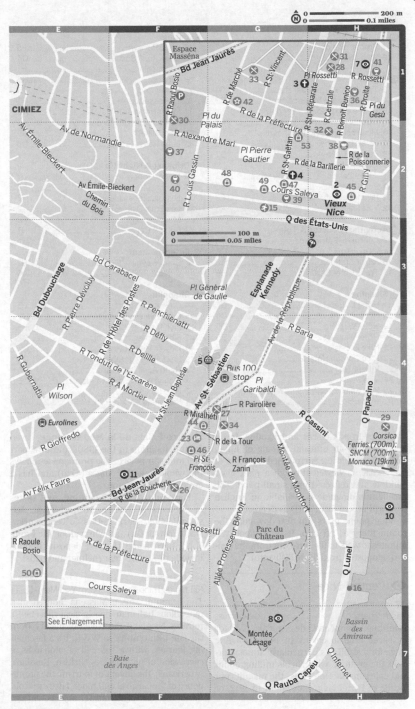

Nice

of stories from Genesis and Exodus. In an antechamber, an unusual mosaic of Elijah in his fiery chariot, surrounded by signs of the zodiac, is viewed through a plate-glass window and reflected in a small pond. The excellent audioguide is available in English (you will need a form of ID as deposit).

Smartphone users can also download the commentary as an app. It takes about 20 minutes to walk to the museum from the centre (signposted from av de l'Olivetto).

◉ Central Nice

★ Promenade des Anglais
ARCHITECTURE

Palm-lined promenade des Anglais, paid for by Nice's English colony in 1822, is a fine stage for a stroll. It's particularly atmospheric in the evening, with Niçois milling about and epic sunsets. Don't miss the magnificent façade of **Hôtel Negresco**, built in 1912, or

art deco **Palais de la Méditerranée**, saved from demolition in the 1980s and now part of a four-star palace. The promenade follows the whole Baie des Anges (4km) and has a cycle and skating lane.

For a fantastic family outing, rent skates or scooters at **Roller Station** (www.roller-station.fr; 49 quai des États-Unis; ◌10am-6pm Nov-Mar, to 7pm Apr-Oct) and whizz along the Prom. You'll need some ID as a deposit. Rentals include protective gear (helmet and pads).

Villa Masséna
MUSEUM

(65 rue de France; ◌10am-6pm Wed-Mon) **FREE**

The beautiful Musée Masséna, housed in a marvellous Italianate neoclassical villa (1898), retraces Nice and the Riviera's history from the late 18th century to WWII. It's a fascinating journey, with a roll call of monarchs, a succession of nationalities (British, Russians, Americans), the advent of tourism, the prominence of the carnival and more. History is told through a mix of furniture, objects, vintage posters, early photographs, paintings and the lovely setting (though captions are in French only).

The city of Nice still uses the ground floor rooms for official occasions so it can sometimes close at short notice.

Musée d'Art Moderne et d'Art Contemporain
ART MUSEUM

(Mamac; www.mamac-nice.org; place Yves Klein; ⊙10am-6pm Tue-Sun) FREE European and American avant-garde works from the 1950s to the present are the focus of this museum. Highlights include many works by Nice's New Realists Christo, César, Arman, Yves Klein and Niki de Saint-Phalle. The building's rooftop also works as an exhibition space (with panoramas of Nice to boot).

Promenade du Paillon
GARDEN

(⊙7am-9pm Oct-Mar, to 11pm Apr-Sep) It's hard to imagine that this beautifully landscaped park was once a bus station, a multistorey car park and an ill-loved square. Completed in October 2013, the park, also known as Coulée Verte, unfolds from the Théâtre National to Place Masséna with a succession of green spaces, play areas and water features and is now a favourite among Niçois for afternoon or evening strolls.

Cathédrale Orthodoxe Russe St-Nicolas
CATHEDRAL

(www.cathedrale-russe-nice.fr; av Nicolas II; ⊙9am-noon & 2-6pm) Built between 1902 and 1912 to provide a big enough church for the growing Russian community, this cathedral, with its colourful onion domes and rich, ornate interior, is the biggest Russian Orthodox church

outside Russia. The cathedral boasts dozens of intricate icons – unfortunately, there is very little in the way of explanation for visitors.

🏃 Activities

Nice's beaches are all pebbly; sensitive behinds should therefore opt for a comfy mattress at one of its 14 private beaches (€15-22 per day). Out of the free public sections of beach (with lifeguards, first-aid posts and cold showers), **Plage Publique des Ponchettes**, opposite Vieux Nice, is the most popular (and don't worry about your bottom, many hotels lend you mats!).

Most beaches also offer a raft of activities, from beach volleyball to jet-skis and pedalos.

The best way to discover Nice's rich heritage is to take a guided walking tour. The tourist office (p839) runs a 2½-hour Vieux Nice tour in English (adult/child €12/6), at 9.30am on Saturday.

Centre du Patrimoine
WALKING TOUR

(75 quai des Etats-Unis; adult/child €5/free; ⊙8.30am-1pm & 2-5pm Mon-Thu, to 3.45pm) The Centre du Patrimoine runs thematic two-hour walking tours. English-language tours must be booked two days in advance. The tourist office has a full listing.

Trans Côte d'Azur
BOAT TOUR

(www.trans-cote-azur.com; quai Lunel; ⊙Apr-Oct) To escape the crowds, take a scenic cruise along the coast. Trans Côte d'Azur runs one-hour trips along the Baie des Anges and the Rade de Villefranche (adult/child €17.5/12) from April to October. From mid-June to mid-September it also runs regular

---

NICE IN...

Two Days

Spend the morning mooching around atmospheric **Vieux Nice**. Browse the market on **Cours Saleya** and head to the **Parc du Château** for a picnic. Spend the afternoon on the **Promenade des Anglais**, either at the beach or skating along. Settle down for dinner at **Chez Palmyre**. The following day, trace Matisse's artistic evolution at the **Musée Matisse**. Grab some Nice-style tapas at **Chez René Socca** for lunch before immersing yourself in Nice's belle époque history at the beautiful **Villa Masséna**. Finish your day with a long aperitif at **Les Distilleries Idéales** and a flamboyant dinner of Italian fare at **Luna Rossa**.

Four Days

Head to **Èze** for extraordinary views of the Riviera. Walk down **Nietzsche's path** to Èze-sur-Mer and catch the train to **Monaco** for a punt at the Casino de Monte Carlo, a tour of the aquarium at the **Musée Océanographique de Monaco** and a taste of the principality's culinary delights. On the fourth day, go inland to **Grasse** to tour its perfumeries or spend the day in **Cannes**: explore unspoilt **Île Ste-Marguerite** before plumping yourself down on a beach lounger on **La Croisette**.

excursions to Île Ste-Marguerite (€38/28, crossing one hour), St-Tropez (€63/48, crossing 2½ hours) and Monaco (€36/27.5, crossing 45 minutes). Reservations are essential.

L'OpenTour
BUS TOUR

(www.nice.opentour.com; opposite 109 quai des Etats-Unis; 1-day pass adult/child €22/8) With headphone commentary in several languages, the open-topped bus tours (1½ hours) give you a good overview of Nice. You can hop on or off at any one of 12 stops, including sights in out of the way Cimiez.

✦✦ Festivals & Events

Carnaval de Nice
CARNIVAL

(www.nicecarnaval.com; ☉Feb) Held each year around Mardi Gras (Shrove Tuesday) since 1294 – highlights include the *batailles de fleurs* (battles of flowers), and the ceremonial burning of the carnival king on promenade des Anglais, followed by a fireworks display. People wearing fancy dress can access restricted areas for free.

Nice Jazz Festival
MUSIC FESTIVAL

(www.nicejazzfestival.fr; ☉Jul) France's original jazz festival has taken on a life of its own in its new location off promenade des Anglais, with fringe concerts popping up all around the venue, from Vieux Nice to Massena and the shopping streets around Rue de France. The festival itself remains as high-brow as ever.

⛏ Sleeping

Nice has a suite of places to sleep, from stellar backpacker hostels to international art-filled icons. Prices jump during summer and also for regional festivals such as Monaco's Grand Prix.

Hôtel Solara
HOTEL €

(☑04 93 88 09 96; www.hotelsolara.com; 7 rue de France; s/d/tr/q €65/85/120/150; ❄🌐) Were it not for its fantastic location on pedestrian rue de France and the sensational terraces that half the rooms boast, we'd say the Solara was an honest-to-goodness budget-friendly choice with impeccable rooms. But with those perks (and did we mention the small fridges in each room for that evening rosé?), it is a hidden gem.

Villa Saint-Exupéry Beach Hostel
HOSTEL €

(☑04 93 16 13 45; www.villahostels.com; 6 rue Sacha Guitry; dm/d €25/70; ❄@🌐) This hostel understands better than anyone what independent travellers need: facilities galore (bar, kitchen, chill-out lounge, free computers,

gym, games room etc), friendly multilingual staff, tons of advice on Nice and the Riviera, and budget-friendly prices. The dorms are a bit drab but for the time you'll spend in them...

Hôtel Wilson
HOTEL €

(☑04 93 85 47 79; www.hotel-wilson-nice.com; 39 rue de l'Hôtel des Postes; s/d €55/69; 🌐) Many years of travelling, an experimental nature and exquisite taste have turned Jean-Marie's rambling flat into a compelling place to stay. The 16 rooms have individual, carefully crafted decor, and share the eclectic dining room. The cheapest rooms also share bathrooms.

★ Nice Pebbles
SELF-CONTAINED €€

(☑04 97 20 27 30; www.nicepebbles.com; 1-/3-bedroom apt from €107/220; ❄🌐) Have you ever dreamt of feeling like a real Niçois? Coming back to your designer pad in Vieux Nice, opening a bottle of ice-cold rosé and feasting on market goodies? Nice Pebbles' concept is simple: offering the quality of a four-star boutique hotel in holiday flats. The apartments (one to three bedrooms) are gorgeous and equipped to high standards.

Guests can expect wi-fi, flat-screen TV, DVD players, fully equipped kitchens and linen bedding in most flats, and in some cases, swimming pool, balcony or terrace etc.

Nice Garden Hôtel
BOUTIQUE HOTEL €€

(☑04 93 87 35 62; www.nicegardenhotel.com; 11 rue du Congrès; s/d €75/100; ❄🌐) Behind heavy iron gates hides this little gem of a hotel: the nine beautifully appointed rooms, the work of the exquisite Marion, are a subtle blend of old and new and overlook a delightful garden with a glorious orange tree. Amazingly, all this charm and peacefulness is just two blocks from the promenade.

Villa la Tour
BOUTIQUE HOTEL €€

(☑04 93 80 08 15; www.villa-la-tour.com; 4 rue de la Tour; d €76-183; ❄🌐) New owners since 2012 have injected a new lease of life into this old town favourite. Rooms have been redecorated according to painters – we loved the Nikki de St Phalle and Vaco rooms. The diminutive flower-decked roof terrace is now complemented by a street terrace ideal for watching Vieux Nice go by.

Villa Rivoli
BOUTIQUE HOTEL €€

(☑04 93 88 80 25; www.villa-rivoli.com; 10 rue de Rivoli; s/d/q from €93/107/225; ❄🌐) Built in 1890, this stately villa feels like your own pied-à-terre in the heart of Nice. A marble staircase leads to spotlessly clean character-rich rooms, some with fabric-covered walls, gilt-edged mirrors and marble mantelpieces.

Hôtel Windsor
BOUTIQUE HOTEL €€

(04 93 88 59 35; www.hotelwindsornice.com; 11 rue Dalpozzo; d €97-205; ✽@🛜🏊) High-profile artists have decorated more than half the rooms at the Windsor with bold, sometimes unsettling designs. Traditional rooms are more soothing yet still nod to the arts with hand-painted murals.

★Hôtel La Pérouse
BOUTIQUE HOTEL €€€

(04 93 62 34 63; www.hotel-la-perouse.com; 11 quai Rauba Capeu; d from €330; ✽@🛜🏊) Built into the rock cliff next to Tour Bellanda, La Pérouse captures the vibe of a genteel villa. Lower-floor rooms face the lemon-tree-shaded courtyard and pool; upper-floor rooms have magnificent vistas of the promenade and sea, many with balconies or terraces to make the best of the panorama. Smart accent colours add flair to the traditional decor.

Nice Excelsior
DESIGN HOTEL €€€

(04 93 88 18 05; www.excelsiornice.com; 19 av Durante; d €99-359; ✽🛜) This 1892 building is a belle époque beauty. Inside, the hotel has been entirely refurbished, with the designers finding inspiration in Nice as a popular travel destination: the furniture has been custom-made based on old travel trunks, but with a modern, colourful twist, and rooms are decorated with postcard like sketches of the city.

Eating

Restaurants in Vieux Nice are a mixed bag of tourist traps and genuine good finds. Follow your instincts, or our recommendations. The Niçois love going out so booking is always recommended, especially for evenings and weekends.

★La Rossettisserie
FRENCH €

(04 93 76 18 80; www.larossettisserie.com; 8 rue Mascoïnat; mains €14.50; ⊙noon-2pm & 7.30-10pm Mon-Sat) The Rossettisserie (a lovely play on word on rotisserie – roast house – and Rossetti, the name of the nearby square) only serves succulent, roast meat – beef, chicken, veal, lamb or pork. It is cooked to perfection and comes with a choice of heavenly homemade mash, ratatouille or sautéed potatoes and a mixed salad. The vaulted dining room in the basement is stunning.

★Chez Palmyre
FRENCH €

(04 93 85 72 32; 5 rue Droite; menu €17; ⊙noon-1.30pm & 7-9.30pm Mon-Fri) A new chef has breathed new life into this fabulously atmospheric little restaurant, seemingly unchanged for its long life. The kitchen churns out Niçois standards with a light hand, service is sweet and the price fantastic; book ahead, even for lunch.

Fenocchio
ICE CREAM €

(www.fenocchio.fr; 2 place Rossetti; ice cream from €2; ⊙9am-midnight Feb-Oct) Dither too long over the 70-plus flavours of ice-cream and sorbet at this unforgettable *glacier* (ice-cream shop) and you'll never make it to the front of the queue. Eschew predictable favourites and indulge in a new taste sensation: black olive, rosemary or lavender.

TOP REGIONAL SPECIALITIES

Nice's eponymous salad (crunchy lettuce, anchovies, olives, green beans and tomatoes in its purest form) has travelled far beyond its original shores. But there is much more to Niçois cuisine than *salade niçoise*. Here are five local specialities you should try:

Stockfish Dried cod soaked in running water for a few days and then simmered with onions, tomatoes, garlic, olives and potatoes.

Socca A pancake made of chickpea flour and olive oil cooked on a griddle with sneezing quantities of black pepper.

Daube A rich beef stew of wine, onions, carrots, tomatoes and herbs; the sauce is often served with gnocchi or ravioli.

Petits farcis Stuffed vegetables (generally onions, zucchini, zucchini flowers, tomatoes and aubergines).

Pissaladière A pizza-like base topped with onions, garlic, olives and anchovies.

Our selection of Niçois restaurants will see you right on stockfish and daube; otherwise, make a beeline for Chez René Socca (p838) for an informal lunch or aperitif to try the bite-size snacks.

Le Comptoir du Marché
MODERN FRENCH €

(☑ 04 93 13 45 01; 8 rue du Marché; mains €13-18; ☻ noon-2.30pm & 7-10.30pm Tue-Sat) With its vintage kitchen decor and recession-proof prices, it's no wonder the Comptoir does so well. There are five or six daily mains scribbled on a chalkboard. The cuisine is a modern twist on French traditional recipes with lots of offals and staples like lentil stews, confit rabbit and even *os à moelle* (bone marrow).

La Merenda
NIÇOIS €

(www.lamerenda.net; 4 rue Raoul Bosio; mains €14-18; ☻ noon-2pm & 7-10pm Mon-Fri) Simple, solid Niçois cuisine by former Michelin-starred chef Dominique Le Stanc draws the crowds to this pocket-sized bistro (you'll be rubbing back and shoulders with fellow customers). The tiny open kitchen stands proud at the back of the room, and the equally small *menu* is chalked on the board. No credit cards.

Chez René Socca
NIÇOIS €

(2 rue Miralhéti; dishes from €3; ☻ 9am-9pm Tue-Sun, to 10.30pm Jul & Aug, closed Nov; ☑) Forget about presentation and manners; here, it's all about taste. Grab a portion of *socca* (chickpea-flour pancake) or a plate of *petits farcis* (stuffed vegetables) and head across the street to the bar for a *grand pointu* (glass) of red, white or rosé.

Le Bistrot d'Antoine
MODERN FRENCH €€

(☑ 04 93 85 29 57; 27 rue de la Préfecture; mains €13-24; ☻ noon-2pm & 7-11pm Tue-Sat) What's so surprising about this super brasserie is how unfazed it is by its incredible success: it is full every night (booking essential), yet the 'bistro chic' cuisine never wavers, the staff are cool as a cucumber, the atmosphere is reliably jovial and the prices incredibly good value for the area.

Luna Rossa
ITALIAN €€

(☑ 04 93 85 55 66; 3 rue Chauvain; mains €16-28; ☻ noon-3pm & 7-11pm Tue-Fri, 7-11pm Sat; ☑) Luna Rossa is like your dream Mediterranean dinner come true: fresh pasta, exquisitely cooked seafood, sun-kissed vegetables and divine meats. Wash it down with one of the excellent bottles of red or rosé from the cellar.

L'Escalinada
NIÇOIS €€

(☑ 04 93 62 11 71; www.escalinada.fr; 22 rue Pairolière; menu €26, mains €19-25; ☻ noon-2.30pm & 7-11pm) This charming restaurant has been one of the best places in town for Niçois cuisine for the last half-century: melt-in-your-mouth homemade gnocchi with tasty *daube*

(Provençal beef stew), grilled prawns with garlic and herbs, Marsala veal stew. The staff are delightful and the welcome *kir* (white wine sweetened with blackcurrant syrup) is on the house. No credit cards.

★ Jan
MODERN FRENCH €€€

(☑ 04 97 19 32 23; www.restaurantjan.com; 12 rue Lascaris; menu €55, mains €26-32; ☻ noon-3pm & 7.30-10pm Wed-Fri, 7.30-10pm Tue & Sat) Dining in the elegant aquamarine dining room of this gourmet restaurant is a treat – this is French gastronomy at its best, with regal service by maître d' Philippe Foucault and exquisite food by South African wonder chef Jan Hendrik van der Westhuizen. Antipodean influences are light in the *menu* but more pronounced in the wine list.

🍷 Drinking & Nightlife

Vieux Nice's little streets runneth over with local bars and cafes: from a morning espresso to a lunchtime pastis (the tipple of choice in the south of France), a chilled evening beer or a midnight cocktail, the choice is yours.

Les Distilleries Idéales
CAFE

(www.lesdistilleriesideales.fr; 24 rue de la Préfecture; ☻ 9am-12.30am) Whether you're after an espresso on your way to the cours Saleya market or an apéritif (complete with cheese and charcuterie platters, €5.60) before trying out one of Nice's fabulous restaurants, Les Distilleries is one of the most atmospheric bars in town. Tables on the small street terrace are ideal for watching the world go by. Happy hour is from 6pm to 8pm.

L'Abat-Jour
BAR

(25 rue Benoît Bunico; ☻ 6.30pm-2.30am) With its vintage furniture, rotating art exhibitions and alternative music, L'Abat-Jour is all the rage with Nice's young and trendy crowd. The basement has live music or DJ sessions as the night darkens.

Snug & Cellar
PUB

(www.snugandcellar.com; cnr rue Droite & rue Rossetti; ☻ noon-12.30am) The cellar of this pub hosts live music, quizzes and giant screens for sports events. And when there is nothing special going on, it's just a great place for a drink. The atmosphere is more sophisticated than in Nice's other English or Irish pubs and the staff are charming.

Les Trois Diables
CLUB

(www.les3diables.com; 2 cours Saleya; ☻ 5pm-2.15am) This stalwart of the party scene in

Nice has ensured its longevity thanks to a good-hearted mix of week-night-friendly events (music quiz on Tuesday, karaoke on Wednesday) and live DJs to spice up the weekend. It's student night on Thursday (bring ID). Happy hour runs to 9pm every night.

Le Six   GAY BAR
(www.le6.fr; 6 rue Raoul Bosio; ⊙10pm-5am Tue-Sat) Primped and pretty A-gays crowd shoulder to shoulder at Nice's compact, perennially popular 'mo bar. Le 6 keeps a busy event/party schedule: guest DJs, karaoke, and shower shows.

Ma Nolan's   PUB
(www.ma-nolans.com; 2 rue St-François de Paule; ⊙noon-2am Mon-Fri, 11am-2am Sat & Sun; 🛜) This Irish pub is big, loud and *the* pub of reference for all foreigners in town. With live music, a pub quiz, big sport events and typical pub food (burgers, fish & chips etc), it's a pretty rowdy place. Happy hour is from 6pm to 8pm.

☆ Entertainment

The tourist office has info on Nice's cultural activities listed in its free publications – *Nice Rendez-vous* (monthly) and *Côte d'Azur en Fêtes* (quarterly, www.cotedazur-en-fetes.com) – or consult the weekly *Semaine des Spectacles* (€1, www.semainedesspectacles.fr), available from newsstands on Wednesday. All are in French.

Chez Wayne's   LIVE MUSIC
(www.waynes.fr; 15 rue de la Préfecture; ⊙10am-2am) Raucous watering hole Chez Wayne's is a typical English pub, that looks like it's been plucked out of London, Bristol or Leeds. It features excellent live bands every night and has the best atmosphere in town. The pub is also sports-mad and shows every rugby, football, Aussie Rules, tennis and cricket game worth watching.

Cinéma Rialto   CINEMA
(http://lerialto.cine.allocine.fr; 4 rue de Rivoli) Non-dubbed films, with French subtitles.

🔒 Shopping

Nice is a shopper's paradise: as well as the numerous little boutiques in Vieux Nice, you'll find designers around rue de France and the usual franchises at the enormous Nice Étoile (www.nicetoile.com; av Jean Médecin) shopping mall.

Moulin à Huile d'Olive Alziari   FOOD
(www.alziari.com.fr; 14 rue St-François de Paule; ⊙8.30am-12.30pm & 2-7pm Mon-Sat) Superb olive oil, fresh from the mill on the outskirts of Nice, for €17 per litre; Alziari also produces a dizzying variety of tapenades, fresh olives to nibble (plain, stuffed, marinated etc) and various other snacks.

Cave de la Tour   WINE
(www.cavedelatour.com; 3 rue de la Tour; ⊙7am-8pm Tue-Sat) Buy wine from *cavistes* (cellarmen) who know what they're talking about: Cave de la Tour has been run by the same family since 1947.

Pâtisserie LAC   FOOD
(www.patisseries-lac.com; cnr rue de la Préfecture & rue St-Gaëtan; ⊙9.30am-1pm & 2.30-7.30pm Tue-Sun) Plump for divine macaroons and chocolates from chef patissier Pascal Lac at the mouth-watering Pâtisserie LAC.

Henri Auer Confiserie   FOOD
(www.maison-auer.com; 7 rue St-François de Paule) Sweet teeth will also love the crystallised fruit sold at the traditional sweet shop Henri Auer Confiserie; the recipes date back to 1820 and the shop is a sight in its own right.

ℹ Information

There are free wi-fi hotspots on cours Saleya, place Garibaldi and promenade du Paillon.
Hôpital St-Roch (☑04 92 03 33 75; www.chu-nice.fr; 5 rue Pierre Dévoluy; ⊙24hr) Emergency service.
Police Station (☑04 92 17 22 22; 1 av Maréchal Foch; ⊙24hr) Non-French speakers can call ☑04 92 17 20 31, where translators are on hand.
Tourist Office (☑08 92 70 74 07; www.nicetourisme.com; 5 promenade des Anglais; ⊙9am-6pm Mon-Sat) There's also a branch at the train station (av Thiers, ⊙8am-7pm Mon-Sat, 10am-5pm Sun).

ℹ Getting There & Away

AIR
Nice-Côte d'Azur Airport (NCE; ☑08 20 42 33 33; www.nice.aeroport.fr; 🛜) is France's second largest airport and has international flights to Europe, North Africa and even the US, with regular as well as low-cost companies. The airport has two terminals, linked by a free shuttle.

BOAT
Nice is the main port for ferries to Corsica. **SNCM** (www.sncm.fr; quai du Commerce) and **Corsica Ferries** (www.corsicaferries.com; quai du Commerce) are the two main companies.

BUS

There are excellent intercity services around Nice; journeys cost €1.50. **Eurolines** (www.eurolines. com; 27 rue de l'Hôtel des Postes) serves long-haul European destinations.

Bus 100 (promenade des Arts) Goes to Menton (1½ hours) via the Corniche Inférieure and Monaco (40 minutes)

Bus 200 (av de Verdun) Goes to Cannes (1½ hours)

Bus 400 (av de Verdun) Goes to Vence (1¼ hours) via St-Paul de Vence (one hour)

Bus 500 (av de Verdun) Goes to Grasse (1½ hours)

TRAIN

From Nice, there are services to the following:

Cannes €5.80, 40 minutes, hourly

Grasse €9.10, 1¼ hours, hourly

Marseille €37, 2½ hours, hourly

Menton €4.50, 35 minutes, half-hourly

Monaco €3.30, 25 minutes, half-hourly

St-Raphaël €14.80, 1¼ hours, hourly

❶ Getting Around

Nice is relatively spread out but since the weather is often good and the city beautiful and pedestrian-friendly, walking is the best way to get around. For longer journeys, rent a bicycle from Vélo Bleu (p840).

TO/FROM THE AIRPORT

Nice-Côte d'Azur airport is 6km west of Nice, by the sea. A taxi to Nice's centre from the rank outside the terminal will cost around €30.

Buses 98 and 99 Link the airport's terminal with Nice Gare Routière and Nice train station respectively (€6, 35 minutes, every 20 minutes). Alternatively, regular buses 52, 59, 70 and 94 (€1.50) all stop just outside Terminal 1 and can be caught on the promenade des Anglais.

Bus 110 (€20, hourly) Links the airport with Monaco (30 minutes) and Menton (1¼ hours)

Bus 210 Goes to Cannes (€20, 50 minutes, half-hourly)

Bus 250 Goes to Antibes (€10, 55 minutes, half-hourly)

BUS & TRAM

Buses and trams in Nice are run by **Lignes d'Azur** (www.lignesdazur.com). Tickets cost just €1.50 (or €10 for a 10-journey pass) and include one connection, including intercity buses within the Alpes-Maritimes *département*.

Buses are handy to get to Cimiez, especially bus 15 which runs past Musée Chagall and Musée Picasso; catch it at the corner of rue Deloye and bd Dubouchage. Night buses run from around 9pm to 2am.

OFF THE BEATEN TRACK

PINE CONE TRAIN

Chugging between the mountains and the sea, the narrow-gauge railway **Train des Pignes** (Pine Cone Train; www.trainprovence.com) is one of Provence's most picturesque rides. Rising to 1000m, with breathtaking views, the 151km track between Nice and Digne-les-Bains passes through Haute Provence's scarcely populated back country.

The service runs five times a day and is ideal for a day trip inland. The beautiful medieval village of **Entrevaux** is just 1½ hours from Nice (return €23.60), perfect for a picnic and a wander through its historic centre and citadel.

The tram is great for getting across town, particularly from the train station to Vieux Nice and place Garibaldi. Trams run from 4.30am to 1.30am. A new tram line linking place Masséna with the airport, and eventually the port, is planned for 2017.

CAR, MOTORCYCLE & BICYCLE

Major car rental companies have offices at the train station. The best deals are generally via their websites.

To go native, go for two wheels (and be prepared for hefty safety deposits).

Holiday Bikes (www.holiday-bikes.com; 23 rue de Belgique) Rents out 50cc scooters/125cc motorcycles for €30/55.

Vélo Bleu (☑ 04 93 72 06 06; www.velobleu. org) A shared-bicycle service with over 100 stations around the city – pick up at one, return at another. One-day/week subscriptions costs €1/5, plus usage: free the first 30 minutes, €1 the next 30, then €2 per hour thereafter. Stations in the most popular parts of town are equipped with special terminals where you can register directly with a credit card; otherwise you'll need a mobile phone. The handy Vélo Bleu app allows you to find your nearest station, gives real-time information about the number of bikes available at each and can also calculate itineraries.

TAXI

Taxis are prohibitively expensive in France and Nice is no exception. Find taxi stands outside the Gare Nice Ville and on av Félix Faure close to place Masséna; otherwise, call **Taxi Riviera** (☑ 04 93 13 78 78; www.taxis-nice.fr).

St-Paul de Vence

POP 3593

Once upon a time, St-Paul de Vence was a small medieval village atop a hill looking out to sea. Then came the likes of Chagall and Picasso in the postwar years, followed by showbiz stars such as Yves Montand and Roger Moore, and St-Paul shot to fame. The village is now home to dozens of art galleries as well as the exceptional Fondation Maeght.

The village's tiny cobbled lanes get overwhelmingly crowded in high season – come early or late to beat the rush.

◉ Sights

The Village
HISTORIC QUARTER

Strolling the narrow streets is how most visitors pass time in St-Paul. The village has been beautifully preserved and the panoramas from the ramparts are stunning. The main artery, rue Grande, is lined with art galleries. The highest point in the village is occupied by the Église Collégiale; the adjoining Chapelle des Pénitents Blancs was redecorated by Belgian artist Folon.

Many more artists lived or passed through St-Paul de Vence, among them Soutine, Léger, Cocteau, Matisse and Chagall. The latter is buried with his wife Vava in the cemetery at the village's southern end (immediately to the right as you enter). The tourist office runs a series of informative, themed guided tours (1½ hours, adult/child €5/free).

Across from the entrance to the fortified village, the pétanque pitch, where many a star has had a spin, is the hub of village life. The tourist office rents out balls (€2) and can organise pétanque lessons (€5 per person).

Fondation Maeght
ART MUSEUM

(www.fondation-maeght.com; 623 chemin des Gardettes; adult/child €15/free; ⊙10am-6pm) The region's finest art museum, Fondation Maeght was created in 1964 by art collectors Aimé and Marguerite Maeght. Its collection of 20th-century works is one of the largest in Europe. It is exhibited on a rotating basis, which, along with the excellent temporary exhibitions, guarantees you'll rarely see the same thing twice. Find the *fondation* 500m downhill from the village.

The building was designed by Josep Lluís Sert and is a masterpiece in itself, integrating the works of the very best: a Giacometti courtyard, Miró sculptures dotted across the terraced gardens, coloured-glass windows by Braque and mosaics by Chagall and Tal-Coat.

St Paul's tourist office runs guided tours (adult/child €5/free); you'll need to book ahead.

🍴 Sleeping & Eating

Hostellerie Les Remparts
HOTEL €€

(☑04 93 24 10 47; www.hostellerielesremparts.com; 72 Grande Rue; d €65-120; ❄ 🖥) Right in the heart of the vieux village, in an old medieval building, this family-run hotel is a charming address. The rooms are spacious and furnished in traditional French style (solid wood furniture and flowery spreads) and those overlooking the valley have fantastic views. The bathrooms are dated but functional.

★ Le Tilleul
MODERN FRENCH €€

(☑04 93 32 80 36; www.restaurant-letilleul.com; place du Tilleul; menu €25, mains €20-31; ⊙8.30am-10.30pm; 🖥) Considering its location on the *remparts*, it could have easily plumbed the depths of a typical tourist trap; instead, divine and beautifully presented dishes grace your table at Le Tilleul and the all-French wine list includes a generous selection of wine by the glass. Sit under the shade of a big blossoming lime tree.

The restaurant is open all day and serves breakfast and afternoon snacks outside of lunch and dinner.

La Colombe d'Or
TRADITIONAL FRENCH €€€

(☑04 93 32 80 02; www.la-colombe-dor.com; place de Gaulle; mains €19-55; ⊙noon-2.30pm & 7.30-10.30pm mid-Dec–Oct; 🖥) A Léger mosaic here, a Picasso painting there: these are just some of the original modern artworks at the Golden Dove, the legendary restaurant where impoverished artists paid for meals with their creations. Dining is beneath fig trees in summer or in the art-filled dining room in winter, and the cuisine is surprisingly uncomplicated (terrines, grilled fish). Book well ahead.

> **ⓘ GETTING TO FONDATION MAEGHT**
>
> Most tourists take the main road to go to the Fondation, but Chemin Ste-Claire is much more inspirational. It was Chagall's route to the village, and along the way you'll pass three chapels, a convent and two Chagall reproductions, placed roughly on the spot where he created the originals.

ℹ Information

Tourist Office (📞 04 93 32 86 95; www.
saint-pauldevence.com; 2 rue Grande; ⊙10am-
6pm) The dynamic tourist office runs a number
of themed guided tours that delve into the
village's illustrious past. Book ahead; some tours
are also available in English.

ℹ Getting There & Away

St-Paul de Vence is served by bus 400 running
between Nice (€1.50, one hour, at least hourly)
and Vence (€1.50, 15 minutes). The bus stops right
outside the main entrance to the village.

Vence

POP 19,386

Despite its well-preserved medieval centre,
visitors often skip Vieux Vence altogether
to head straight to Matisse's other-worldly
Chapelle du Rosaire. Yet Vence deserves more
than a flying visit.

◉ Sights

★**Chapelle du Rosaire**   ARCHITECTURE
(Rosary Chapel; www.vence.fr/the-rosaire-chapel.
html; 466 av Henri Matisse; adult/child €6/3; ⊙2-
5.30pm Mon, Wed & Sat, 10-11.30am & 2-5.30pm
Tue & Thu) An ailing Henri Matisse moved to
Vence in 1943, where he fell under the care of
his former nurse and model Monique Bourgeois, who had since become a Dominican
nun. She persuaded him to design this extraordinary chapel for her community, which
Matisse considered his masterpiece. The artist designed everything from the decor to the
altar and the priest's vestments.

From the road, all you can see are the
blue-and-white ceramic roof tiles and a
wrought-iron cross and bell tower. Inside,
light floods through the glorious blue, green
and yellow **stained-glass windows**. The
colours respectively symbolise water/the sky,
plants/life, the sun/God's presence; the back
windows display Matisse's famous seaweed
motif, those on the side a stylised, geometric
leaf-like shape.

A line image of the **Virgin Mary and child**
is painted on white ceramic tiles on the
northern interior wall. The western wall is
dominated by the bolder **Chemin de Croix**
(Stations of the Cross). **St Dominic** overlooks
the altar. Matisse also designed the chapel's
stone altar, candlesticks and cross. The beautiful priests' vestments are displayed in an
adjoining hall.

The Vieux Vence   HISTORIC QUARTER

Much of the historical centre dates back to
the 13th century. The **Romanesque cathedral** on the eastern side of the square was
built in the 11th century on the site of an old
Roman temple. It contains Chagall's **mosaic**
of Moses (1979), appropriately watching over
the baptismal font.

The daring **Fondation Émile Hugues**
(www.museedevence.com; 2 place du Frêne; adult/
child €6/free; ⊙10am-12.30pm & 2-6pm Tue-Sun),
with its wonderful 20th-century art exhibitions, inside the imposing Château de Villeneuve, is a nice contrast to Vence's historic
quarter.

🛏 Sleeping & Eating

★**Le 2**   B&B €€
(📞 04 93 24 42 58; www.le2avence.fr; 2 rue des Por-
tiques; d incl breakfast €105-165; ❄🛜) This 'bed
& bistro', as it's tagged itself, is a welcome addition to staid Vence. Nicolas and his family
have turned this medieval townhouse into
a hip new establishment offering four very
modern rooms and a pocket-sized cellar featuring local musicians one night a week. Value
and atmosphere guaranteed.

La Litote   MODERN FRENCH €€
(📞 04 93 24 27 82; 5 rue de l'Évêché; menu €23,
mains €14-20; ⊙noon-2.30pm & 7-10pm Tue-Sat,
noon-2.30pm Sun) In an area where the bar is
set very high, chef Stéphane Furlan still manages to surprise and delight diners with a
regularly changing *menu* that favours quality
rather than quantity. Dine alfresco on a little
square at the back of the cathedral, or inside
the stone-wall dining room with its open fire.

ℹ Getting There & Around

Bus 400 to and from Nice (€1.50, 1¼ hours, at
least hourly) via St-Paul de Vence (€1.50, 15
minutes) stops on place du Grand Jardin, in the
centre of town.

Antibes & Juan-les-Pins

POP 76,349

With its boat-bedecked port, 16th-century
ramparts and narrow cobblestone streets
festooned with flowers, lovely Antibes is the
quintessential Mediterranean town. Picasso,
Max Ernst and Nicolas de Staël were captivated by Antibes, as was a restless Graham
Greene (1904–91) who settled here with his
lover, Yvonne Cloetta, from 1966 until the
year before his death.

Greater Antibes embraces Cap d'Antibes, an exclusive green cape studded with luxurious mansions, and the modern beach resort of Juan-les-Pins. The latter is known for its 2km-long sandy beach and nightlife, a legacy of the sizzling 1920s when Americans swung into town with their jazz music and oh-so-brief swimsuits.

Sights & Activities

Vieil Antibes
HISTORIC QUARTER

Vieil Antibes is a pleasant mix of food shops, boutiques and restaurants. Mornings are a good time to meander along the little alleyways, when the Marché Provençal (Market; cours Masséna; ⊙ 7am-1pm Tue-Sun Sep-Jun, daily Jul & Aug) is in full swing. Check out the views from the sea walls, from the urban sprawl of Nice to the snowy peaks of the Alps and nearby Cap d'Antibes.

Musée Picasso
ART MUSEUM

(www.antibes-juanlespins.com; Château Grimaldi, 4 rue des Cordiers; adult/child €6/free; ⊙ 10am-noon & 2-6pm Tue-Sun) 'If you want to see the Picassos from Antibes, you have to see them in Antibes.' *Pablo Picasso*

The 14th-century Château Grimaldi served as Picasso's studio from July to December 1946. The museum now houses an excellent collection of his works and fascinating photos of him.

The works from Picasso displayed here are extremely varied – lithographs, paintings, drawings and ceramics – showing how versatile and curious an artist he was. The museum also has a fantastic room dedicated to Nicolas de Staël, another painter who adopted Antibes as his home town.

Fort Carré
HISTORIC SITE

(rte du Bord de Mer; guided tour only adult/child €3/free; ⊙ 10am-6pm Tue-Sun Jul & Aug, to 4.30pm Tue-Sun Sep-Jun) The impregnable 16th-century Fort Carré, enlarged by Vauban in the 17th century, dominates the approach to Antibes from Nice. It served as a border defence post until 1860 when Nice, until then in Italian hands, became French. Regrettably, the tours are rather rushed and the explanations superficial; tours depart half-hourly, some guides speak English.

Cap d'Antibes
WALKING

Cap d'Antibes' 4.8km of wooded shores are the perfect setting for a walk-swim-walk-swim afternoon. Paths are well marked. The tourist office maps show itineraries.

✦ Festivals & Events

Jazz à Juan
MUSIC FESTIVAL

(www.jazzajuan.com) This major festival celebrated in mid-July has been running for more than 50 years. Every jazz great has performed here, and Jazz à Juan, in Juan-les-Pins, continues to attract big music names. The Off fringe festival is the perfect backup option if you haven't managed to get tickets for the main event.

Sleeping

Relais International de la Jeunesse
HOSTEL €

(✆ 04 93 61 34 40; www.clajsud.fr; 272 bd de la Garoupe; dm €20; ⊙ Apr-Oct; 🗟) In the most perfect of Mediterranean locations, with sea views the envy of neighbouring millionaires, this basic-but-friendly hostel is particularly popular with 'yachties' looking for their next job in Antibes' port. Rates include sheets and breakfast. There is a daily lock-out between 11am and 5pm.

Le Relais du Postillon
HOTEL €€

(✆ 04 93 34 20 77; www.relaisdupostillon.com; 8 rue Championnet; d €83-149; ❋ 🗟) Housed in a 17th-century coach house, the great-value Postillon is in the heart of the old town. The new owners did a huge amount of work in 2013: out went the outdated carpet and bathrooms, in came fresh new bathrooms and boutique décor. The cafe-bar downstairs, with its cosy fireplace, is another charmer.

Hôtel La Jabotte
B&B €€

(✆ 04 93 61 45 89; www.jabotte.com; 13 av Max Maurey; s/d from €110/120; ❋ @ 🗟) A hotel with chambre d'hôte (B&B) feel, La Jabotte is just 50m from the sea (and 20 minutes' walk from Vieil Antibes). Its 10 Provençal rooms all look out onto an exquisite patio where breakfast is served from spring to autumn.

✕ Eating

La Ferme au Foie Gras
DELICATESSEN €

(www.vente-foie-gras.net; 35 rue Aubernon; sandwiches €4-7; ⊙ 8am-6pm Tue-Sun) Now, this is our idea of what a good sandwich should be like: filled with foie gras or smoked duck breast, onion chutney or fig jam, truffle cheese and fresh salad. And many people seem to think the same: a queue snakes down from the tiny counter of La Ferme every lunch time.

Le Broc en Bouche
MODERN FRENCH €€

(✆ 04 93 34 75 60; 8 rue des Palmiers; mains €21-30; ⊙ noon-2pm & 7-10pm Thu-Mon) No two

WORTH A TRIP

MUSÉE RENOIR

The city of Cagnes-sur-Mer is nothing to write home about. What is, however, is the exquisite **Musée Renoir** (www.cagnes-tourisme.com; Chemin des Colettes, Cagnes-sur-Mer; adult/child €6/free; ⊘ 10am-noon & 2-5pm Wed-Mon). Le Domaine des Collettes (as the property was known in Renoir's time) was the home and studio of an arthritis-crippled Renoir (1841–1919) from 1907 until his death. He lived there with his wife and three children, and the house is wonderfully evocative, despite being sparsely furnished.

The museum reopened in July 2013 after 18 months of renovations: new rooms such as the kitchen are now open to the public, and a new gallery was created in the basement to display Renoir's little-known sculptures.

The house contains a handful of original Renoir paintings, including *Les Grandes Baigneuses* (The Women Bathers; 1892), a reworking of the 1887 original. The museum also planned to start displaying unique archive documents such as photos and letters over the course of 2014. The beautiful olive and citrus groves are as much an attraction as the museum itself.

chairs, tables or lights are the same at this lovely bistro: instead, every item has been lovingly sourced from antique shops and car boot sales, giving the place a sophisticated but cosy vintage feel. The charming Flo and Fred have put the same level of care and imagination into their cuisine, artfully preparing Provençal and modern French fare.

Drinking & Nightlife

★**Balade en Provence**　　ABSINTHE BAR
(25 cours Masséna; ⊘6pm-2am) Flirt with the green fairy at this dedicated absinthe bar in the vaulted basement of an olive oil shop. There is an original 1860 zinc bar, five round tables and all the accessories (four-tapped water fountain, sugar cubes etc).

Pick from 25 absinthe varieties (€6 to €10 per glass) and let the knowledgable staff debunk some of the myths shrouding this much reviled spirit. And don't worry, if you're really not keen, there are plenty of other beverages on offer.

La Siesta Club　　CLUB
(rte du Bord de Mer; cover €20; ⊘7pm-5am Thu-Sat Jun-Sep) This legendary establishment is famous up and down the coast for its summer beachside nightclub and all-night dancing under the stars.

❶ Information

Tourist Office (☑ 04 22 10 60 10; www.antibes juanlespins.com; 55 bd Charles Guillaumont; ⊘9am-noon & 2-6pm Mon-Sat, 10am-1pm Sun)

❶ Getting There & Away

BUS

The Nice–Cannes service (bus 200, €1.50) stops by the tourist office. Local bus services (€1) for Biot or Cap d'Antibes leave from the **bus station** (place Guynemer).

TRAIN

Antibes' train station is on the main line between Nice (€4.50, 30 minutes, five per hour) and Cannes (€2.90, 10 minutes, five per hour).

Biot

POP 9996

From the 16th to 18th centuries, the little hillside village of Biot was famous around the Med for the exceptional quality of its olive-oil jars. Very little remains of that pottery hegemony, but Biot is now famous for another much prettier, but far less pragmatic, art form: bubbled glass.

The famous bubbles are produced by rolling molten glass in baking soda to create a chemical reaction, then trapping the bubbles with a second layer of glass; the latest frosted look uses acid dips. You can watch work under way at the factory **Verrerie de Biot** (www.verreriebiot.com; chemin des Combes; admission free, 45-min guided tour adult/child €6/3; ⊘9.30am-6pm Mon-Sat, 10.30am-1.30pm & 2.30-6.30pm Sun), at the foot of the village.

Biot's **tourist office** (☑ 04 93 65 78 00; www.biot.fr; 46 rue St-Sébastien; ⊘9am-noon & 2-6pm Mon-Fri, 2-6pm Sat & Sun) is located in the village itself, a hilltop warren full of century-old buildings.

Bus 10 (€1, 10 minutes) links the village and the Biot train station half-hourly. In summer, a free shuttle takes in the train station, the glassmakers and the village.

Cannes

POP 73,671

Most people have heard of Cannes and its eponymous film festival. The latter only lasts for two weeks in May, but the buzz and glitz are there year-round – unlike neighbouring St-Tropez, which shuts down in winter.

However, what people may not know is that, for all its glamour, Cannes retains a genuine small-town feel: just like anywhere in the south, you'll witness pensioners hotly debating who won the last round of *pétanque* (a game whereby metal balls are thrown so that they land as closely as possible to a smaller wooden ball).

You'll also get a chance to escape to the unspoilt Îles de Lérins, and to become familiar with more than 2000 years of history – from Ligurian fishing communities (200 BC) to one of Europe's oldest religious communities (5th century AD), to the enigmatic Man in the Iron Mask and a stardom born out of antifascist efforts.

◉ Sights & Activities

◉ Cannes

Cannes is blessed with sandy beaches, although much of the stretch along bd de la Croisette is taken up by private beaches (open to all). This arrangement leaves only a small strip of free sand near the Palais des Festivals for the bathing hoi polloi; the much bigger Plage du Midi (bd Jean Hibert) and Plage de la Bocca, west from Vieux Port, are also free.

Rates for private beaches range between €15 and €25 at the relaxed and family-friendly Plage Vegaluna (water sports available) to €36/32/42 for the blue loungers on the front row/other rows/pier of the super-stylish Z Plage, the beach of Hôtel Martinez. Booking ahead is advised.

★ La Croisette ARCHITECTURE

The multi-starred hotels and couture shops that line the famous bd de la Croisette (aka La Croisette) may be the preserve of the rich and famous, but anyone can enjoy the palm-shaded promenade and take in the atmosphere. In fact, it's a favourite among

Cannois (natives of Cannes), particularly at night when it is lit with bright colours.

There are great views of the bay and nearby Estérel mountains, and stunning art deco architecture from the seafront palaces, such as the Martinez or the legendary Carlton InterContinental; its twin cupolas were modelled on the breasts of the courtesan La Belle Otéro, infamous for her string of lovers – Tsar Nicholas II and Britain's King Edward VII among them.

Not so elegant but imposing nonetheless is the Palais des Festivals et des Congrès (Festival Palace; bd de la Croisette) at the western end of the prom, host of the film festival. Climb the red carpet, walk down the auditorium, tread the stage and learn about cinema's most glamorous event and its numerous anecdotes on a Palais des Festivals guided tour (adult/child €4/free; ⊙ tours 1½hr). The tourist-office-run tours take place several times a month, except in May. Check dates on the office website (visits in English are sometimes available). Tickets can only be booked in person at the tourist office.

After posing for a photograph on the 22 steps leading up to the cinema entrance, wander along allée des Étoiles du Cinéma, a path of celebrity hand imprints in the pavement.

Le Vieux Port & Le Suquet HISTORIC QUARTER

On the western side of the Palais des Festivals lies the real Cannes. The yachts that frame the Vieux Port (Old Port) are the only reminder that this is where celebrities holiday, but they don't seem to impress the pensioners playing *pétanque* on sq Lord Brougham. Follow rue St-Antoine and snake your way up Le Suquet, Cannes's oldest district, for great views of the bay.

For local folklore, head to Marché Forville (rue du Marché Forville; ⊙ 7am-1pm Tue-Sun), a couple of blocks back from the port. It is one of the most important markets in the region and the supplier of choice for restaurants (and for your picnic!).

Trans Côte d'Azur BOAT TOUR

(☏ 04 92 98 71 30; www.trans-cote-azur.com; quai Max Laubeuf) From June to September, Trans Côte d'Azur runs day trips to St-Tropez (adult/child €48/36 return) and Monaco (€52/36), an ideal way to avoid congested roads to these popular spots and relax among scenic landscapes instead. Panoramic (€28/18) cruises taking in the dramatic contrasts of the Estérel's red cliffs, green forests and intense azure waters are another must.

THE FRENCH RIVIERA & MONACO

Cannes

0 200 m
0 0.1 miles

G **F** **E** **D** **C** **B** **A**

Bd d'Alsace

Bd de la République

R Molière

12 🔟
11 🔟
17 ✕
22 ◉

2 ◉

R Marceau
R d'Antibes

R du Batéguier

R Commandant André

R du Dr Gérard Monod

1 ◉

La Croisette

Pl Gambetta
7 ◉
R des Alliés
R Teisseire
R Chabaud
R Macé
R des Frères Pradignac
23 ◉

R H Vagliano
R des États-Unis

R Jean Jaurès
R Hoche

Cannes Train Station 🚊

R des Serbes

R 24 Août
16 ✕
13 🔟
R des Belges
R Notre Dame

Esplanade Georges Pompidou

Baie de Cannes

R Maréchal Foch

R Buttura
R d'Antibes
R Bivouac Napoléon
21 ◉

Pl du 18 Juin
10 🔟
R Ventelous
R Jean de Riouffe

Bd de la Croisette

5 ◉

Pl Mérimée
ℹ️

9 🔟
R Maréchal Joffre
R Rouguière
19 ✕
Pl Général de Gaulle

1 ℹ️

D 🔟

Jetée Albert Édouard

24 ✕
14 ✕
Square Lord Brougham
R Émile Négrin
La Pantiéro
20 ✕

6 ◉

Vieux Port

R Louis Blanc
Hôtel de Ville ●
R Félix Faure

Main Bus Station 🚌

Q St-Pierre

Av des Anciens Combattants d'Afrique du Nord
Bd Victor Tuby
R du Marché Forville
4 ◉
15 ✕
R Meynadier
R du Dr Gazagnaire
Pl Bernard Cornut Gentille

R Georges Clemenceau

R du Port
Square du Général Leclerc

Q Max Laubeuf

Compagnie Planaria (75m);
Riviéra Lines (75m);
Trans Côte d'Azur (75m)

18 ✕
R Forville
R du Suquet
R St-Antoine

3 ◉
R Louis Perissol
R de la Castre

Le Suquet

Plage de la Bocca (500m);
Massif de l'Estérel (22km)

R du Pré

Bd Jean Hibert

8 ◉

Plage Vegaluna (100m);
Z Plage (350m);
Le Bâoli (1.4km);
Antibes (10km)

1 **2** **3** **4**

Cannes

Les Apprentis Gourmets   COOKING COURSE
(☑ 04 93 38 78 76; www.lesapprentisgourmets.fr;
6 rue Teisseire) Part-restaurant, part-cooking
school is probably the best way to describe
this boutique kitchen in the heart of Cannes.
Cooking classes tend to be short (one to two
hours, €32 to €69) and focus on themes or
menus (take-away at the end of the class).

The flagship product of Les Apprentis
Gourmets is their express-lunch formula:
a €15, 30-minute lesson to cook one main,
which you then eat with your fellow cooks
on the mezzanine above the kitchen (and
they throw in the dessert for free). Great fun,
cheap and accessible, even if cooking is your
domestic nemesis!

◉ Îles de Lérins

Although just 20 minutes away by boat, the
tranquil Îles de Lérins feel far from the madding crowd.

The closest of these two tiny islands is the
3.25km by 1km Île Ste-Marguerite, where
the mysterious Man in the Iron Mask was
incarcerated during the late 17th century. Its
shores are an endless succession of perfect
castaway beaches and fishing spots, and its
eucalyptus and pine forest makes for a heavenly refuge from the Riviera heat.

As you get off the boat, a map indicates a
handful of rustic restaurants as well as trails
and paths across the island. It also directs
you to Fort Royal (adult/child €6/3; ⊘ 10.30am-
1.15pm & 2.15-5.45pm Tue-Sun), built in the 17th
century, and now harbouring the Musée de

la Mer. Exhibits interpret the fort's history,
with great displays from shipwrecks found
off the island's coast and explanations in
French and English. You'll also see the old
state prisons, built under Louis XIV, including the cell of the Man in the Iron Mask.

Smaller still, at just 1.5km long by 400m
wide, Île St-Honorat has been a monastery
since the 5th century. Its Cistercian monks
welcome visitors year-round: you can visit the church and small chapels scattered
around the island and stroll among the vineyards and forests. Camping and cycling are
forbidden.

Boats for the islands leave Cannes from
quai des Îles (along from quai Max Laubeuf)
on the western side of the harbour. Riviera
Lines (www.riviera-lines.com; quai Laubeuf) runs
ferries to Île Ste-Marguerite (return adult/
child €13/8.50), while Compagnie Planaria
(www.cannes-ilesdelerins.com; quai Laubeuf) operates boats to Île St-Honorat (return adult/
child €15.50/7.50).

★★ Festivals & Events

Festival de Cannes   FILM FESTIVAL
(www.festival-cannes.com; ⊘ May) You won't get
in, but it's fun because you see all the celebs
walking around. And unlike the Oscars, you
can get close to the red carpet without tickets.

Les Plages Électroniques   MUSIC FESTIVAL
(www.plages-electroniques.com; €8-20) DJs spin
on the sand at the Plage du Palais des Festivals during this relaxed festival. Held July to
August, once a week for five or six weeks.

1. Promenade des Anglais, Nice (p834)
Named in 1822 after Nice's English colony, the promenade is a lovely place to stroll.

2. Carlton InterContinental, Cannes (p845)
Its twin cupolas are said to be modelled on the breasts of courtesan La Belle Otéro.

3. Cap d'Antibes (p843)
An exclusive promontory with 4.8km of walking trails.

4. Antibes (p842)
This quintessential Mediterranean town has captivated artists and writers for the past century.

CANNES FILM FESTIVAL

For 12 days in May, all eyes turn to Cannes, centre of the cinematic universe where more than 30,000 producers, distributors, directors, publicists, stars and hangers-on descend to buy, sell or promote more than 2000 films. As the premier film event of the year, the festival (www.festival-cannes.com) attracts some 4000 journalists from around the world.

At the centre of the whirlwind is the colossal, 60,000-sq-metre Palais des Festivals, where the official selections are screened. The palace opened in 1982, replacing the original Palais des Festival – since demolished. The inaugural festival was scheduled for 1 September 1939, as a response to Mussolini's Fascist propaganda film festival in Venice, but Hitler's invasion of Poland brought the festival to an abrupt end. It restarted in 1946 – and the rest is history.

Over the years the festival split into 'in competition' and 'out of competition' sections. The goal of 'in competition' films is the prestigious Palme d'Or, awarded by the jury and its president to the film that best 'serves the evolution of cinematic art'. Notable winners include Francis Ford Coppola's *Apocalypse Now* (1979), Quentin Tarantino's cult film *Pulp Fiction* (1994) and American activist Michael Moore's anti-Bush administration polemic *Fahrenheit 9/11* (2004). More recent winners include *Blue Is the Warmest Colour* (2013) by Abdellatif Kechiche, the story of a young lesbian couple.

The vast majority of films are 'out of competition'. Behind the scenes the Marché du Film (www.marchedufilm.com) sees nearly $1 billion worth of business negotiated in distribution deals. And it's this hard-core commerce combined with all the televised Tinseltown glitz that gives the film festival its special magic.

Tickets to the Cannes film festival are off-limits to ordinary people. Your filmgoing will be restricted to Cinéma de la Plage (www.festival-cannes.com/en/article/60750.html), a free outdoor cinema showing old classics during the festival, or the screenings from the Quinzaine des Réalisateurs (www.quinzaine-realisateurs.com), an alternative film festival. Tickets for La Quinzaine's films must be booked in person at the official booth at La Malmaison (☑ 04 97 06 44 90; 47 bd de la Croisette).

Festival Pantiero
MUSIC FESTIVAL

(www.festivalpantiero.com; 4-night pass €50; ☺ early Aug) Electronic music and indie-rock festival on the terrace of the Palais des Festivals; very cool.

Festival d'Art Pyrotechnique
FIREWORKS

(www.festival-pyrotechnique-cannes.com) Around 200,000 people cram onto La Croisette every summer to admire the outstanding fireworks display over the Bay of Cannes. Magical. Held on six nights from July to August.

🛌 Sleeping

Cannes is an important conference centre and hotels fill up with every event (including the Film Festival, when you won't be able to stay in town) so try to plan ahead.

Hôtel Alnéa
HOTEL €

(☑ 04 93 68 77 77; www.hotel-alnea.com; 20 rue Jean de Riouffe; s/d €70/90; ✲🛜) A breath of fresh air in a town of stars, Noémi and Cédric have put their heart and soul into their hotel, with bright, colourful rooms, original paintings and numerous little details such as the afternoon coffee break, the honesty bar and

the bike or *boules* (to play *pétanque*) loans. No lift.

Hôtel de Provence
HOTEL €€

(☑ 04 93 38 44 35; www.hotel-de-provence.com; 9 rue Molière; s/d from €108/118; ✲🛜) A tall townhouse with pale yellow walls and lavender blue shutters, the exterior of the Hôtel de Provence is true to its name. Inside, however, the design is more minimalist chic than quaint Provençal, with plenty of clean white lines. The hotel's strength is its height, with almost every room sporting a balcony or terrace.

With its huge rooftop terrace and designer bathroom, the suite on the 7th floor is an absolute stunner and a real bargain for the price.

Hôtel 7e Art
BOUTIQUE HOTEL €€

(☑ 04 93 68 66 66; www.7arthotel.com; 23 rue Maréchal Joffre; s/d €85/106; ☺ Apr-Oct; ✲🛜) Hôtel 7e Art has put boutique style within reach of budgeters. The owners schooled in Switzerland and got the basics right, with great beds, sparkling-clean baths and excellent soundproofing. The snappy design of putty-coloured walls, headboards and pop art, and perks like iPod docks in every room, far exceed what you'd expect at this price.

Hôtel Splendid BOUTIQUE HOTEL €€
(☎04 97 06 22 22; www.splendid-hotel-cannes.com; 4-6 rue Félix Faure; s/d from €88/122; ❄@) This elaborate 1871 building has everything it takes to rival the nearby palaces – beautifully decorated rooms, vintage furniture, old-world feel with creature comforts, fabulous location and stunning views. A handful of rooms equipped with kitchenettes are ideal for longer stays and families.

Hôtel Le Mistral BOUTIQUE HOTEL €€
(☎04 93 39 91 46; www.mistral-hotel.com; 13 rue des Belges; d from €95; ❄📶) This 10-room boutique hotel wins the *palme d'or* for best value in town: rooms are small but decked out in flattering red and plum tones, bathrooms feature lovely designer fittings, there are sea views from the top floor, and the hotel is a mere 50m from La Croisette.

Hôtel Le Canberra BOUTIQUE HOTEL €€€
(☎04 97 06 95 00; www.hotel-cannes-canberra.com; 120 rue d'Antibes; d from €169; ❄@📶🏊) This boutique stunner, just a couple of blocks back from La Croisette, is the epitome of Cannes glamour: designer grey rooms with splashes of candy pink, sexy black marble bathrooms with coloured lighting, heated pool (April to October) in a bamboo-filled garden, intimate atmosphere (there are just 35 rooms) and impeccable service. Rooms overlooking rue d'Antibes are cheaper.

Eating

PhilCat DELICATESSEN €
(La Pantiéro; sandwiches & salads €4.50-6; ⏱8.30am-5pm; ✎) Don't be put off by Phillipe and Catherine's unassuming prefab cabin on La Pantiéro: this is Cannes' best lunch house. Huge salads, made to order, are piled high with delicious fresh ingredients. Or if you're *really* hungry, try one of their phenomenal *pan bagna* (a moist sandwich bursting with Provençal flavours).

Mantel MODERN EUROPEAN €€
(☎04 93 39 13 10; www.restaurantmantel.com; 22 rue St-Antoine; menus €35-60; ⏱noon-2pm Fri-Mon, 7.30-10pm Thu-Tue) Discover why Noël Mantel is the hotshot of the Cannois gastronomic scene at his refined old-town restaurant. Service is stellar and the seasonal cuisine divine: try the wonderfully tender glazed veal shank in balsamic vinegar or the original poached octopus *bourride*-style. Best of all though, you get not one but two desserts from the mouth-watering dessert trolley.

> **ACCOMMODATION WARNING**
>
> Accommodation can be impossible to find, not to mention prohibitively expensive, during the Cannes Film Festival and the Monaco Grand Prix (both held in May). This applies to the coast between Menton and Cannes but doesn't affect areas beyond Massif de l'Estérel (St-Raphaël, St-Tropez etc). July and August are busy everywhere, so book well in advance.

Aux Bons Enfants FRENCH €€
(www.aux-bons-enfants.com; 80 rue Meynadier; menu €23, mains €16; ⏱noon-2pm & 7-10pm Tue-Sat) A people's-choice place since 1935, this informal restaurant cooks up wonderful regional dishes such as *aïoli garni* (garlic and saffron mayonnaise served with fish and vegetables), *daube* (a Provençal beef stew), and *rascasse meunière* (pan-fried rockfish), all in a convivial atmosphere. Make no plans for the afternoon after lunching here. No credit cards or reservations.

La Meissounière FRENCH €€
(☎04 93 38 37 76; www.lameissouniere.com; 15 rue du 24 Août; 1-/2-course lunch menu €16/22, mains €15-22; ⏱noon-2pm Tue-Sat, 7-10pm Thu-Sat; ✎) A charming, unpretentious address, La Meissounière does a brisk trade among office workers at lunch time with perfectly executed French classics such as tartare de boeuf (finely chopped raw beef), grilled rib of beef, and pan-fried fish of the day (and its good selection of wines by the glass and pitcher). Evenings are more relaxed.

New York New York BRASSERIE €€
(www.nynycannes.com; 1 allée Liberté; mains €10-36; ⏱8am-2am; 📶✎) This trendy grill house has become a hit with Cannes' young crowd who love the huge burgers, tender steaks, wood-fired pizzas, budget-friendly prices and the industrial chic decor. Food is served throughout the day.

★ **Sea Sens** FUSION €€€
(☎04 63 36 05 06; www.five-hotel-cannes.com; Five Hotel & Spa, 1 rue Notre Dame; menus €39-95, mains €19-48; ⏱7-10pm Tue-Sat; 📶) Perched on the 5th floor of the Five Hotel, the Sea Sens is Cannes' latest food sensation, with one

Michelin star to prove it. It serves divine food that blends French gastronomy and Asian elegance with panoramic views of Le Suquet and Cannes' rooftops on the side. Pastry chef De Oliveira's desserts are not to be missed.

L'Affable
MODERN FRENCH €€€

(☑ 04 93 68 02 09; www.restaurant-laffable.fr; 5 rue Lafontaine; lunch/dinner menu €26/44, mains €36-40; ☺ noon-2.30pm & 7-10.30pm Mon-Fri, 7-10.30pm Sat) Modern French cuisine has never tasted so good than at L'Affable. Everything from the ingredients and cooking to the presentation is done to perfection, whether it be the roasted veal with its vegetable medley, the seared seabream with white butter and asparagus or the house speciality, the Grand Marnier soufflé, which arrives practically ballooning at your table. Booking essential.

🍷 Drinking & Entertainment

Bars around the 'magic square' (the area bordered by rue Commandant André, rue des Frères Pradignac, rue du Batéguier and rue du Dr Gérard Monod) tend to be young, trendy and pretty rowdy. For a more sophisticated atmosphere, try the beach or top-hotel bars. Pick up the free monthly *Le Mois à Cannes* from the tourist office for full event listings.

It's worth knowing that going out in Cannes is taken very seriously so dress to impress if you'd like to get in to the most sought-after clubs and events.

Le Sun 7
COCKTAIL BAR

(www.sun7cannes.com; 5 rue du Dr Gérard Monod; ☺ 5pm-5am; 🛜) An unpretentious, happening place, Le Sun 7 attracts a pretty young crowd keen to knock back a few drinks and shake their stuff at the weekend. It's more laid-back on week nights.

Le Cercle
BAR

(Le Grand Hôtel, 45 bd de la Croisette; ☺ 8am-1am; 🛜) The bar of Le Grand Hôtel is a great place for a couple of quiet drinks. The lounge is a cosy space (there is a pianist most nights) but it's the garden that really does it: with its giant fairy lights, views of La Croisette and the sea, it is divine on summer evenings.

Le Bâoli
CLUB

(☑ 04 93 43 03 43; www.lebaoli.com; Port Pierre Canto, bd de la Croisette; ☺ 8pm-6am Thu-Sat) This is Cannes' coolest, trendiest and most selective night spot. So selective in fact that your entire posse might not get in unless you're dressed to the nines. As a part-club, part-restaurant, the only way to ensure you'll get in is to book

a table and make a night of it. Located at the eastern end of La Croisette.

Cinéma Les Arcades
CINEMA

(http://arcadescannes.cine.allocine.fr; 77 rue Félix Faure) Movies in English at Cinéma Les Arcades.

🅘 Information

There is a free wi-fi hotspot at the Hôtel de Ville (town hall).

Tourist Office (☑ 04 92 99 84 22; www.cannes-destination.fr; Palais des Festivals, bd de la Croisette; ☺ 9am-7pm) The place to book guided tours of the city and get information on what to do and see in Cannes.

🅘 Getting There & Around

BUS

There are two bus stations in Cannes. Buses 200 for Nice (€1.50, 1½ hours, every 15 minutes) and 210 for Nice airport (€20, 50 minutes, half-hourly) leave from the **main bus station** (place Cornut-Gentille). Bus 600 for Mougins (€1.50, 20 minutes, every 20 minutes) and Grasse (€1.50, 45 minutes) leaves from outside the train station.

The electric **Elo Bus** (€1.50) follows a loop that takes in the bus station, La Croisette, rue d'Antibes and the train station. It has no set stops, just flag it down as it passes.

CYCLING & DRIVING

Mistral Location (☑ 04 93 39 33 60; www.mistral-location.com; 4 rue Georges Clemenceau) rents bicycles/scooters/cars for €16/26/59 per day. You'll find the usual car-hire companies at the train station too.

PARKING

Street parking is limited to two hours in the centre. Car parks such as **Parking Palais des Festivals** (Palais des Festivals), **Parking Forville** (rue Forville) or **Parking Gare SNCF** (rue Jean Jaurès, train station) have no time restrictions but are expensive (€2.80 per hour).

TRAIN

Cannes is well connected with services:

Antibes €2.90, 12 minutes, every 20 minutes or so

Marseille €32, two hours, half-hourly

Monaco €9.40, one hour, every 20 minutes

Nice €6.80, 40 minutes, every 20 minutes

St-Raphaël €7.20, 30 minutes, 20 minutes

Mougins

POP 18,835

Pinprick Vieux Mougins (old Mougins) looks almost too perfect to be real. Picasso discovered the medieval village in 1935 with lover Dora Marr, and lived here with his final love, Jacqueline Roque, from 1961 until his death.

◉ Sights & Activities

The tourist office in Mougins can give you a map of the historic centre so that you can wander around. Alternatively, smartphone users can download the Mougins Tourisme app complete with audioguide.

★ Musée d'Art Classique de Mougins   ART MUSEUM

(www.mouginsmusee.com; 32 rue Commandeur, Mougins; adult/child €12/5; ⊙10am-6pm) The brainchild of compulsive art collector and British entrepreneur Christian Levett, this outstanding museum contains 600 works spanning 5000 years. The collection aims to show how ancient civilisations inspired neoclassical, modern and contemporary art, you'll therefore find antiquities juxtaposed with seminal modern works. Not only is it a brilliant idea, it has also been brilliantly executed.

The collection is organised by civilisations – Rome, Greece and Egypt each get a floor and the top floor is dedicated to armoury. There are fantastic explanatory panels in French and English throughout and excellent interactive displays bringing to life the helmets, spears and shields of the armoury collection.

★ Les Jardins du MIP   GARDEN

(www.museesdegrasse.com; 979 chemin des Gourettes, Mouans-Sartoux; adult/child €3/free; ⊙10am-6pm Tue-Sun Apr-Oct) ✐ Opened in 2012 by the Musée International de la Parfumerie (p854) in Grasse, these gardens beautifully complement the museum's collection by offering an insight into the plants used in perfumery. Half the garden is displayed as fields to show how local flowers such as rose, jasmine, lavender etc are grown commercially. The other half is organised by olfactive families (woody, floral, ambered etc). Visitors are actively encouraged to pick, rub and smell their way around.

Informative leaflets are available and gardeners will happily answer questions. The gardens are located in the village of Mouans-Sartoux, about 3km northwest of the historic centre of Mougins. You can get there by public transport (stop Les Jardins du MIP): take bus 20 or 21 from Grasse bus station.

🛏 Sleeping & Eating

Les Rosées   B&B €€€

(☑04 92 92 29 64; www.lesrosees.com; 238 chemin de Font Neuve, Mougins; d €240-325; ☎☀) ✐ Chic and authentic is its tagline, and it couldn't be more accurate. This stunning, 400-year-old stone manor house with five romantic suites, pool, sauna, spa baths and century-old olive trees is a haven of tranquillity. The decor is stunning with a mix of modern and vintage – the owners now have their own interior-design venture – and breakfast is a copious organic affair.

Evening meals, cooked by a local chef, are now available. A three-course meal costs €40. Located in the municipality of Mougins but not in the historic village.

Le Petit Fouet   FRENCH €€

(☑04 92 92 11 70; www.lepetitfouet.com; 12 place du Commandant Lamy, Mougins; 2/3 course lunch menu €15/19, mains €14-35; ⊙noon-2.30pm & 7-10.30pm Fri-Tue; ✐) True to its Lyon and Southwest roots, the food at this Mougins bistro is hearty, tasty and generous. There is an excellent selection of vegetarian mains – a rarity – and a great wine list. A stalwart of authenticity in an area famed for its fads and fickleness.

ℹ Information

Tourist Office (☑04 92 92 14 00; www.mougins.fr/tourisme; 39 place des Patriotes; ⊙9am-5pm Mon-Sat Oct-Jun, to 6pm daily Jul-Sep)

ℹ Getting There & Away

Bus 600 (€1.50, every 20 minutes) between Cannes and Grasse stops in Mougins.

Grasse

POP 52,824

It is the abundance of water up in the hills that helped turn Grasse into a perfume centre. Tanners, who needed reliable water supplies to clean their hides, first settled here in the Middle Ages. With the advent of perfumed gloves in the 1500s, the art of perfumery took shape. Glove-makers split from the tanners and set up lucrative perfumeries. New irrigation techniques allowed flower growing to boom, sealing Grasse's reputation as the world capital of fragrance.

Today, Grasse is still surrounded by jasmine, centifolia roses, mimosa, orange blossom and iris fields but the industry, which counts some 30 perfumeries, is rather discreet, with only a handful offering tours of their facilities.

Sights & Activities

Three well-known perfumeries run free guided tours of their facilities: Fragonard (www.fragonard.com; 20 bd Fragonard; tour free; ☉9am-6pm), Molinard (p855) and Galimard (www.galimard.com; 73 rte de Cannes; tour free; ☉9am-12.30pm & 2-6pm). Tours are generally brisk, giving you an overview of the main stages of perfume production, from extraction and distillation to the work of the 'nose'. Tours leave every 15 to 30 minutes and are available in a number of languages. Visits end in the perfumery's showroom where you can buy fragrances (much cheaper than couture perfumes).

★ Musée International de la Parfumerie
MUSEUM
(MIP; www.museesdegrasse.com; 2 bd du Jeu de Ballon; adult/child €4/free; ☉10.30am-5.30pm Wed-Mon; ⓐ) This whizz-bang museum is a work of art: housed in a renovated 18th-century mansion, daringly enlarged with a modern glass structure, it retraces three millennia of perfume history through a brilliant mix of artefacts, bottles, videos, vintage posters, olfactive stations and explanatory panels (in French and English), all beautifully presented. The museum offers interesting insights into how the industry developed in Grasse.

Kids are well catered for with dedicated multimedia stations throughout, a fragrant garden, a film testing your sense of smell and the reproduction of a 19th-century perfume shop.

Musée Fragonard
ART MUSEUM
(www.fragonard.com; 14 rue Ossola; admission free; ☉10am-6pm) This tiny but fantastic private museum houses France's second-largest collection of works by Grassois painter Jean-Honoré Fragonard (1732–1806). There are 15 major works, beautifully exhibited in a renovated 18th-century townhouse (admire the splendid ceiling fresco in the entrance hall), and complemented by the paintings of Marguerite Gérard (1761–1837), Fragonard's sister-in-law and protégée, and Jean-Baptiste Mallet (1759–1835), another native of Grasse painter.

Eating

Café des Musées
MODERN FRENCH €
(1 rue Jean Ossola; lunch menus €12-16, mains €10-14; ☉8am-6pm) This gorgeous cafe is the perfect place to stop for a spot of lunch (lovely salads, carefully crafted daily specials, soup or pasta of the day) or indulge in a gourmet coffee break (pastry with coffee or tea €7.50, ice-creams and crêpes) between sights.

Information

Tourist Office (☎04 93 36 66 66; www.grasse.fr; place de la Buanderie; ☉9am-12.30pm & 2-6pm Mon-Sat; ☏) The tourist office can provide maps and background information on the old town. Located at the bus station.

CORINNE MARIE-TOSSELLO, PERFUMER IN GRASSE

Corinne Marie-Tosello has two routes to work: one through olive groves, the other one through fields overlooking the sea. Most people would revel in the view, but Corinne revels in their smells: she runs the 'olfactory training' of perfumery Fragonard's staff (scent identification, production process, types of perfumes etc) and also works as an olfactory consultant (she advises on scents for incense, candles and so on).

Apart from the perfumeries, where else can you learn about Grasse's perfume industry? The flower fields around Grasse, such as the Jardins du MIP (p853), are wonderful: you see where the flowers come from and get a chance to meet the people who grow them.

Any fragrant walks in the region? St-Honorat is an olfactory paradise, with eucalyptus, pine trees, dry wood and vine. I would also recommend the Estérel in May when the maquis shrub cistus is in bloom.

Where would you recommend for lunch? In Grasse, I like the Café des Musées (p854) – the decor is very Fragonard and they have delicious ice-creams. In Cannes, I like Vegaluna (☎04 93 43 67 05; www.vegaluna.com; La Croisette; ☉9.30am-7pm): I know the chef – he cooks with fresh, seasonal products – and the atmosphere is very relaxed.

CREATE YOUR OWN SCENT

It can take months, sometimes years, for a 'nose' (perfumers who, after 10 years' training, can identify up to 3000 smells) to create a perfume. And you'll understand why once you sit down in front of a mind-boggling array of essences: the number of combinations is dizzying. Perfume workshops won't turn you into a perfumer overnight, but the olfactory education they offer is fascinating – and great fun.

Molinard (www.molinard.com; 60 bd Victor Hugo; tour free; ⊙ 9.30am-12.30pm & 2-6pm) runs a fantastic one-hour workshop (€59) in its Grasse factory where you can create your own perfume. The perfumer will quiz you about the scents you like – and dislike – talk you through the structure of the perfume (base, heart and head notes), explain the rules of perfume etiquette (banish liberal spraying!) and help you through the more subtle blends of your creations. 'Graduates' leave with a stylish 50mL bottle of their perfume.

❶ Getting There & Away

BUS
Bus 600 goes to Cannes (50 minutes, every 20 minutes) via Mougins (30 minutes). Bus 500 goes to Nice (1½ hours, hourly). All buses leave from the **bus station** (place de la Buanderie); fares are €1.50.

PARKING
If arriving from Nice, park at **Parking Notre Dame des Fleurs** (place Martelly). If arriving from Cannes, park at **Parking Honoré Cresp** (cours Honoré Cresp). Allow €1.90 per hour.

TRAIN
The station is 2km south of the centre but linked by buses 2, 3, 4 and 5 (fare €1). There are regular services to Nice (€9.80, 1¼ hours, hourly) via Cannes (€4.30, 30 minutes).

Massif de l'Estérel

Punctuated by pine, oak and eucalyptus trees, the rugged red mountain range Massif de l'Estérel contrasts dramatically with the brilliant blue sea. Extending east from St-Raphaël to Mandelieu-La Napoule (near Cannes), the famous Corniche de l'Estérel (also known as the Corniche d'Or and the N98) coastal road passes through summer villages and *calanques* (coves) that are ideal for swimming.

🏃 Activities

The Estérel is a leading dive centre: with numerous WWII shipwrecks and pristine waters, it's a prime area for underwater exploration. Much of the coast along the Corniche is protected, too, so the fauna and flora is some of the best around.

With its lush green Mediterranean forests, intensely red peaks and sterling sea views, the Estérel is a walker's paradise. Local tourist offices have leaflets detailing the most popular walks, including Pic de l'Ours (496m) and Pic du Cap Roux (452m), but buy IGN's Carte de Randonnée (1:25,000) No 3544ET *Fréjus, Saint-Raphaël & Corniche de l'Estérel* if you're planning more serious walks.

Access to the range is generally prohibited on windy or particularly hot days because of fire risks, so check with the tourist office before setting off.

With its 36km of coastline, the Corniche has more than 30 beaches running the gamut of possibilities: sandy, pebbly, nudist, covelike, you name it. But wherever you go, the sea remains that crystal-clear turquoise and deep blue, an irresistible invitation to swim.

Centre de Plongée Île d'Or
DIVING
(☑ 04 94 82 73 67; www.dive.fr; 986 bd 36ème Division du Texas, Agay) Multilingual diving club offer individual dives as well as courses (they are CMAS accredited).

Euro Plongée
DIVING, SNORKELLING
(☑ 04 94 19 03 26; www.europlongee.fr; Port de Boulouris) A reputable, family-friendly dive club with CMAS accreditation. Offers individual dives and courses, as well as great two-hour snorkelling tours (€30); they're fantastic for families: kids will love spotting starfish, sea anemones, urchins and other colourful Mediterranean residents.

Sentier du Littoral
WALKING
Running 11km between Port Santa Lucia (the track starts behind the naval works) and Agay, this coastal path (yellow markers) takes in some of the most scenic spots in the area. It takes roughly 4½ hours to complete, but from May to October, you could make a day out of it by stopping at some of the idyllic beaches scattered along the way.

You can choose to walk smaller sections; the most scenic is around Cap Dramont, crowned by a signal station, which you can do as a loop from Plage du Débarquement. This long sandy beach is where the US 36th Infantry Division landed on 15 August 1944 as part of Operation Dragoon (Provence landing). The large memorial park has a car park easily accessible from the N98.

Fréjus & St-Raphaël

The twin towns of Fréjus (population 53,069) and St-Raphaël (population 34,163) bear the hallmarks of the area's history over the millennia.

Fréjus was settled by Massiliots (the Greeks who founded Marseille) and colonised by Julius Caesar around 49 BC as Forum Julii. It was settled thanks to the extension of the Roman road Via Aurelia, which linked Italy with Arles. The town's commercial activity largely ceased after its harbour silted up in the 16th century (Fréjus' town centre is 3km from the sea).

St-Raphaël is better known as the gateway to the Estérel. It was a fashionable hang-out in the 1920s, and the town remains a popular seaside destination. The port refurbishment, completed in June 2014, will add cachet to the centre.

◎ Sights

Le Groupe Épiscopal CATHEDRAL
(http://cathedrale-frejus.monuments-nationaux. fr; 58 rue de Fleury, Fréjus; adult/child €5.50/free; ◷10am-1pm & 2-5pm Tue-Sun) Fréjus' star sight is the Groupe Épiscopal, built on the foundations of a Roman temple. At the heart of the complex is an 11th- and 12th-century cathedral, one of the first Gothic buildings in the region, and a cloister featuring rare 14th- and 15th-century painted wooden ceiling panels depicting angels, devils, hunters,

acrobats and monsters in vivid comic-book fashion. The meaning and origin of these sci-fi like creatures are unknown. Only 500 of the original 1200 frames survive.

Before you enter the cathedral, make sure you take a peek at the octagonal 5th-century baptistery (which incorporates eight Roman columns into its structure) on your left-hand side; it is one of the oldest Christian buildings in France, and is exceptionally well preserved.

Musée Archéologique ARCHAEOLOGY MUSEUM
(place Calvini, Fréjus; adult/child €2/free; ◷9.30am-noon & 2-4.30pm Tue-Sat Oct-Mar, to 12.30pm & 2-6pm Tue-Sun Apr-Sep) The small but fascinating Musée Archéologique features treasures unearthed in and around Fréjus, from everyday objects to rare finds such as a double-faced marble statue of Hermes, a head of Jupiter and a stunning 3rd-century mosaic depicting a leopard.

Musée Archéologique de St-Raphaël ARCHAEOLOGY MUSEUM
(www.musee-saintraphael.com; rue des Templiers, St-Raphaël; ◷9am-noon & 2-6pm Tue-Sat) FREE The waters off St-Raphaël are home to the largest number of antique shipwrecks in France and the town has been at the forefront of marine archaeology ever since. You'll therefore be able to see a 1928 Scuba system developed in St-Raphaël and the first commercial equipment developed by Jacques-Yves Cousteau in the 1940s, as well as numerous artefacts rescued from local wrecks. Visitors can also access the adjoining medieval church and panoramic tower.

Roman Ruins ROMAN SITES
Fréjus' Roman ruins are not as well preserved as those found in Arles or Orange, but their abundance bears witness to the importance of Forum Julii at the time, with its strategic location on Via Aurelia and port. The best way to appreciate the heritage is to join the guided tours (adult/child €6/free) run by the tourist office (☑04 94 51 83 83; www.frejus.fr; 249 rue Jean Jaurès; ◷9.30am-noon & 2-6pm Mon-Sat).

At the southeastern edge of the old city is the 3rd-century Porte d'Orée, the only remaining arcade of monumental Roman thermal baths. North of the old town are the ruins of a Théâtre Romain (admission €2). Part of the stage and the theatre's outer walls are all that remain. Similarly, outer walls are all that are left of the 1st century arènes (amphitheatre; admission €2), which once sat 10,000 and have now been entirely renovated as a modern outdoor venue.

> ### ⓘ FRÉJUS PASS
>
> A seven-day Fréjus Pass (per person €4.60) covers admission to the Roman amphitheatre and theatre, Musée Archéologique, and Cocteau's chapel (otherwise, it's €2 per sight). To visit Le Groupe Épiscopal as well, buy a seven-day Fréjus Pass Intégral (per person €6.60) instead. Participating sights sell passes, except the Groupe Épiscopal.

🛏 Sleeping

Domaine du Colombier CAMPGROUND €
(📷 04 94 51 56 01; www.domaine-du-colombier.
com; 1052 rue des Combattants en Afrique du
Nord, Fréjus; pitch €18-59, 4-/6-person cabin from
€97/92; @ 📶 ⛱) This campground is the last
word in luxury and, with its 3800 sq metre
landscaped lagoon, complete with beaches,
slides and pools, it is a paradise for families.
There are just 22 pitches for tents but dozens of well-equipped and great-value cottages. Unsurprisingly, it is facilities galore with
events, restaurants, sports pitches etc.

A minimum two- or seven-night stay
can be required for cabins during certain
periods.

L'Aréna HOTEL €€
(📷 04 94 17 09 40; www.hotel-frejus-arena.
com; 145 rue du Général de Gaulle, Fréjus; d/tr
€145/195; ✳ 📶 ⛱) With its sienna-colour-
ed walls and lush garden, L'Aréna is a very
pleasant option, ideally located to explore
Fréjus' Roman ruins. The Provençal decor
is starting to age but the rooms remain
comfortable. Those in the Jasmine annexe
are more spacious but there is no lift in that
building. The duplex are ideal for families
(with two single beds on a mezzanine).

🍴 Eating

Mon Fromager CHEESE €
(📷 04 94 40 67 99; www.mon-fromager.fr; 38 rue
Sieyès, Fréjus; plat du jour €13.90, cheese platters
from €10.90; ⏱ shop 9am-7.30pm Tue-Sat, lunch
noon-2pm Tue-Sat; 📷) This enlightened cheesemonger decided to double up his *fromagerie*
(cheese shop) as an informal restaurant. It
is very popular among locals who come for
the amazing value *plat du jour* (main of the
day) or the can't-go-wrong cheese platters
with salad. And, of course, you can still buy a
hunk of cheese to take away.

Maison de la Tarte BOULANGERIE €
(33 rue Jean Jaurès, Fréjus; tarts & sandwiches
from €2.80; ⏱ 7am-7pm Mon-Sat Aug-Jun; 📷)
If you're planning a picnic, stop at this
mouth-watering bakery. Tarts of every kind
(lemon meringue, pear and chocolate, raspberry and almond etc), sold by the slice, fill
the front window and back shelves. Sandwiches and quiches are equally good.

Elly's GASTRONOMIC €€
(📷 04 94 83 63 39; www.elly-s.com; 54 rue de la Liberté, St-Raphaël; lunch/dinner menu €24/33, mains
€32; ⏱ noon-1.30pm & 7-9.30pm Tue-Sat) An unlikely gastronomic bijou in staid St Raphaël,
Elly's delivers on the plate as much as in the
decor: the elegant dining room and courtyard are decorated with stunning works of
modern art (which change with the seasons),
a fitting backdrop for the restaurant's gorgeous modern French cuisine. Provence and
the Côte d'Azur feature prominently in the
wine list.

ℹ Getting There & Away

BUS
Bus 4 links Fréjus' **bus station** (rue Gustave Bret)
with St-Raphaël (€1.10, 30 minutes, hourly).

PARKING
Parking du Clos de la Tour (rue Bret), on the edge
of the old town, is free.

TRAIN
The main station in the area is St-Raphaël-Vales-
cure, in St-Raphaël.

St-Tropez

POP 4571

In the soft autumn or winter light, it's hard
to believe that the pretty terracotta fishing
village of St-Tropez is yet another stop on
the Riviera celebrity circuit. It seems far removed from its glitzy siblings further up the
coast, but come spring or summer, it's a different world: the town's population increases
tenfold, prices triple and fun-seekers come in
droves to party until dawn, strut their stuff
and enjoy the creature comforts of an exclusive beach.

If you can at all avoid visiting in July and
August, do. But if not, take heart: it's always
fun to play 'I spy...' (a celebrity).

History

St-Tropez acquired its name in AD 68 when
a Roman officer named Torpes was beheaded on Nero's orders in Pisa, and packed into
a boat with a dog and a rooster to devour
his remains. His headless corpse washed up
here intact, leading the villagers to adopt
him as their patron saint.

For centuries St-Tropez remained a
peaceful little fishing village, attracting
painters like pointillist Paul Signac, but few
tourists. That changed dramatically in 1956
when *Et Dieu Créa la Femme* (And God
Created Woman) was shot here starring
Brigitte Bardot (aka BB), catapulting the village into the international limelight.

◉ Sights

Vieux Port
PORT

Yachts line the harbor and visitors stroll the quays at the picturesque old port. In front of the sable-coloured townhouses, the **Bailli de Suffren statue**, cast from a 19th-century cannon, peers out to sea. The bailiff (1729–88) was a sailor who fought with a Tropezien crew against Britain and Prussia during the Seven Years War. As much of an institution as the bailiff is portside cafe Sénéquier (p860).

Place des Lices
SQUARE

St-Tropez's legendary and very charming central square is studded with plane trees, cafes and *pétanque* players. Simply sitting on a cafe terrace watching the world go by or jostling with the crowds at its extravaganza of a twice-weekly **market** (⊘8am–1pm Tue & Sat), jam-packed with everything from fruit and veg to antique mirrors and flip-flops (thongs), is an integral part of the St-Tropez experience.

Artists and intellectuals have met for decades in St-Tropez's famous Café des Arts, now simply called **Le Café** (www.lecafe.fr; ⊘8am–11pm) (not to be confused with the newer, green-canopied Café des Arts on the corner of the square). Aspiring *pétanque* players can borrow a set of boules from the bar. Locals tend to hang on the other side of the square.

Musée de l'Annonciade
ART MUSEUM

(place Grammont; adult/child €6/4; ⊘10am–1am & 2-6pm Wed-Mon) In a gracefully converted 16th-century chapel, this small but famous art museum showcases an impressive collection of modern art infused with that legendary Côte d'Azur light. Pointillist Paul Signac bought a house in St-Tropez in 1892 and introduced others to the area. The museum's collection includes his *St-Tropez, Le Quai* (1899) and *St-Tropez, Coucher de Soleil au Bois de Pins* (1896).

NUDIST BEACHES

Not a fan of tan lines? This coastal stretch of the Riviera is well endowed with *naturiste* (nudist) beaches. **Plage de Tahiti**, the northern stretch of Plage de Pampelonne in St-Tropez, is probably the best known. More secluded is **Plage de l'Escalet**, on the southern side of Cap Camarat on the Presqu'île de St-Tropez, a beautiful but hard to reach spot.

Citadelle de St-Tropez
MUSEUM

(admission €3; ⊘10am-6.30pm) Built in 1602 to defend the coast against Spain, the citadel dominates the hillside overlooking St-Tropez to the east. The views are fantastic. Its dungeons are home to the excellent **Musée de l'Histoire Maritime**, an all interactive museum inaugurated in July 2013 retracing the history of men at sea, from fishing, trading, exploration, travel and the navy.

🏃 Activities

About 4km southeast of town is the start of **Plage de Tahiti** and its continuation, the famous **Plage de Pampelonne**, studded with St-Tropez's most legendary drinking and dining haunts. Just east of St-Tropez, **Plage des Salins** is a long, wide sandy beach at the southern foot of **Cap des Salins**.

Sentier du Littoral
WALKING

A spectacular coastal path wends its way past rocky outcrops and hidden bays 35km south from St-Tropez, around the Presqu'île de St-Tropez to the beach at Cavalaire-sur-Mer. In St-Tropez the yellow-flagged path starts at **La Ponche**, immediately east of Tour du Portalet, and curves around Port des Pêcheurs, past St-Tropez's citadel. It then leads past the walled **Cimitière Marin** (Marine Cemetery) to the tiny **Plage des Graniers** and beyond.

The tourist office has maps with distances and walking times (eg to Plage des Salins, 8.5km, 2½ hours).

Les Bateaux Verts
BOAT TOUR

(☏04 94 49 29 39; www.bateauxverts.com; quai Jean Jaurès) Les Bateaux Verts offers trips around Baie des Cannebiers (dubbed 'Bay of Stars' after the celebrity villas dotting its coast) April to September (adult/child €10.50/6) as well as the Calanques de l'Estérel (€21/12.60), Port-Cros (€37/23.20) and Porquerolles (€41.50/26.50).

🛏 Sleeping

St-Tropez is no shoestring destination, but there are plenty of campgrounds to the southeast along Plage de Pampelonne. Most hotels close at some stage in winter; the tourist office keeps a list.

★ Hôtel Lou Cagnard
HOTEL €€

(☏04 94 97 04 24; www.hotel-lou-cagnard.com; 18 av Paul Roussel; d €79-166; ⊘Mar-Oct; ❋🐾) Book well ahead for this great-value courtyard charmer, shaded by lemon and fig trees, and owned by schooled hoteliers. The pretty

Provençal house with lavender shutters has its very own jasmine-scented garden, strung with fairy lights at night. Bright and beautifully clean rooms are decorated with painted Provençal furniture. Five have ground-floor garden terraces. The cheapest rooms have private washbasin and stand-up bathtub but share a toilet; most rooms have air-con.

Hôtel Le Colombier
HOTEL €€

(☑04 94 97 05 31; http://lecolombierhotel.free.fr; impasse des Conquettes; d/tr from €105/235; ☺mid-Apr–mid-Nov; ❋🕸) An immaculately clean converted house, five minutes' walk from place des Lices, the Colombier's fresh, summery decor is feminine and uncluttered, with bedrooms in shades of white and vintage furniture.

Hôtel Les Palmiers
HOTEL €€

(☑04 94 97 01 61; www.hotel-les-palmiers.com; 26 bd Vasserot; d €140-275; ❋🕸) In an old villa opposite place des Lices, Les Palmiers has simple, bright rooms around a stylish courtyard. Choose one in the main building rather than the annexe.

Pastis
DESIGN HOTEL €€€

(☑04 98 12 56 50; www.pastis-st-tropez.com; 61 av du Général Leclerc; d from €300; ❋🕸❋) This stunning townhouse-turned-hotel is the brainchild of an English couple besotted with Provence and passionate about modern art. You'll die for the pop-art-inspired interior, and long for a swim in the emerald-green pool. Every room is beautiful although those overlooking av Leclerc are noisy.

Hôtel Ermitage
BOUTIQUE HOTEL €€€

(☑04 94 81 08 10; www.ermitagehotel.fr; av Paul Signac; r €180-550; ❋🕸) Kate Moss and Lenny Kravitz favour St-Trop's latest rocker crash pad, which draws inspiration from St-Trop from the '50s to '70s: disco meets mid-century modern. Rooms are decorated in bold, glossy colours – the smallest have the shower in the room itself. There are knockout views over town from the bar terrace.

B Lodge Hôtel
HOTEL €€€

(☑04 94 97 58 72; www.hotel-b-lodge.com; 23 rue de l'Aïoli; d from €165; ☺Dec-Oct; ❋🕸) Behind the traditional building exterior hide some very modern rooms indeed with minimalist decor, dark soft furnishings and feature stone walls. The cheapest rooms don't have air-con, which, at this price, feels rather stingy. But those with balconies and Citadelle views are fabulous. Prices drop significantly in winter.

Eating

Quai Jean Jaurès on the old port is littered with restaurants and cafes – they have mediocre *menus*, but great portside views. Many establishments close during the winter so your choice may be drastically reduced. In summer, book everywhere.

Don't leave town without sampling St-Tropez' signature cake, *La Tarte Tropézienne*. An orange-blossom-flavoured double sponge cake filled with thick cream, it was created by a Polish baker and christened by BB in the 1950s.

★La Tarte Tropézienne
CAFE, BAKERY €

(www.latartetropezienne.fr; place des Lices; mains €13-15; ☺6.30am-7.30pm, lunch noon-3pm) This cafe-bakery is the original creator of the eponymous cake, and therefore the best place to buy St-Tropez's delicacy. But to start, choose from delicious daily specials, salads and sandwiches which you can enjoy in the bistro inside or on the little terrace outside.

Bistro Canaille
FUSION €€

(☑04 94 97 75 85; 28 rue des Remparts; plates €8-24; ☺7-11pm Fri & Sat Mar-May & Oct-Dec, 7-11pm Tue-Sun Jun-Sep) This fusion bistro is where locals in the know go for a night out. Jean-François and Vanessa serve imaginative, beautifully presented fusion tapas-sized dishes blending French, Spanish and Asian influences such as seared foie gras, squid-ink risotto, stir-fried scallops in soja sauce, churros etc. Bistro Canaille also organises regular wine tastings (and always has an excellent wine list).

La Plage des Jumeaux
SEAFOOD €€

(☑04 94 58 21 80; www.plagedesjumeaux.com; rte de l'Épi, Pampelonne; mains €25-40; ☺noon-3pm; ☑🕸) The top pick of St-Tropez's beach restaurants, Les Jumeaux serves beautiful seafood (including fabulous whole fish, ideal to share) and sun-bursting salads on its dreamy white-and-turquoise striped beach. Families are well catered for, with playground equipment, beach toys and a kids' *menu*.

Salama
MOROCCAN €€

(☑04 94 97 59 62; http://formastec.free.fr/salama; 1 rue des Tisserands; mains €22-32; ☺7-11pm Mar-Oct) Lounge on cushioned exotic furnishings, wash down heavenly scented couscous and *tajines* with fresh mint tea, and finish with a lime sherbet.

Le Sporting
BRASSERIE €€

(place des Lices; mains €13-30; ☺8am-1am) There's a bit of everything on the menu at always-packed Le Sporting, but the speciality is the hamburger topped with foie gras and morel cream sauce. The Brittany-born owner also serves perfect buckwheat crêpes, honest lunch deals (€13), and a simple salad and croque monsieur.

Chez les Garçons   MODERN FRENCH €€
(☑ 04 94 49 42 67; www.chezlesgarcons.com; 11/13 rue du Cépoun; menus €32; ☺9-11pm Thu-Sun Mar, Apr & Oct, daily May-Sep) Super-friendly staff serve delicate specialities such as a perfectly poached egg with foie gras, all under the watchful eyes of Marilyn, Brigitte and Audrey (art on the wall). Also a lively gay bar next door.

Au Caprice des Deux   TRADITIONAL FRENCH €€€
(☑ 04 94 97 76 78; www.aucapricedesdeux.com; 40 rue du Portail Neuf; menu €61, mains €35; ☺7.30-10.30pm Thu-Sun) This traditional *maison de village* (old stone terraced house) with coffee-coloured wooden shutters is an old-time favourite with locals. Its intimate interior is as traditional as its French cuisine: think beef *filet* with truffles or duck.

Drinking & Nightlife

Dress to kill. And bring more money than you think you'll need. Many places close in winter, but in summer it's party central seven days a week. To tap into the local gay scene, hit Chez les Garçons.

Bar at l'Ermitage   BAR
(www.ermitagehotel.fr; Hôtel Ermitage, av Paul Signac; ☺5pm-midnight) Escape the crowds at the laid-back Ermitage, kitted out in distressed '50s-modern furniture, with enchanting views of the rooftops of old St Tropez and the sea.

Café de Paris   CAFE
(www.cafedeparis.fr; 15 quai Suffren; ☺8am-2am) The terrace is *the* place to sport your new strappy sandals at afternoon aperitifs; service is the friendliest along the port.

Sénéquier   CAFE
(www.senequier.com; quai Jean Jaurès; ☺8am-midnight) Sartre wrote parts of *Les Chemins de la Liberté* (Roads to Freedom) at this portside cafe popular with boaties, bikers and tourists, which has been in business since 1887. Look for the terrace crammed with pillar-box-red tables and director's chairs. Be warned, however, a mere coffee costs €8...

Les Caves du Roy   CLUB
(www.lescavesduroy.com; Hôtel Byblos, av Paul Signac; ☺7pm-5am Fri & Sat Apr-Oct) Star-studded bar of the infamous Hôtel Byblos.

L'Esquinade   CLUB
(2 rue du Four; ☺midnight-7am daily Jun-Sep, Thu-Sat only Oct-May) Where the party winds up when you want to dance until dawn. Open year-round and the Tropéziens' top choice.

🛍 Shopping

St-Tropez is loaded with couture boutiques, gourmet food shops and art galleries.

Atelier Rondini   SANDALS
(www.rondini.fr; 16 rue Georges Clémenceau; ☺9.30am-12.30pm & 2.30-6.30pm Tue-Sat) Colette brought a pair of sandals from Greece to Atelier Rondini (open since 1927) to be replicated. They're still making the iconic sandals for about €135.

Le Dépôt   CLOTHING
(6 bd Louis Blanc; ☺10am-noon & 2-6.30pm Tue-Sat) A chic boutique of designer clothes and accessories.

De l'Une à l'Autre   CLOTHING
(6 rue Joseph Quaranta; ☺10am-12.30pm & 2.30-6.30 pm Mon-Sat) Previously loved designer labels at affordable prices.

ℹ Information

Tourist Office (☑ 08 92 68 48 28; www.ot-saint-tropez.com; quai Jean Jaurès; ☺9.30am-12.30pm & 2-6pm) Has a kiosk in Parking du Port in July and August.

ℹ Getting There & Away

BIKE & MOTORBIKES

Rolling Bikes (☑ 04 94 97 09 39; www.rolling-bikes.com; 14 av du Général Leclerc; per day bikes/scooters/motorcycles from €17/42/120, plus deposit) Do as the locals do and opt for two wheels.

BOAT

Les Bateaux Verts (p858) runs shuttles between St-Tropez and Ste-Maxime (one-way/return €7.50/13.50, 15 minutes), ideal to avoid St Tropez's notorious traffic.

BUS

VarLib (www.varlib.fr; tickets €3) services leave from the **bus station** (av du Général de Gaulle) for anywhere within the Var *département*, including:
Fréjus One hour
Ramatuelle 35 minutes

St-Raphaël 1¼ hours; via Grimaud and Port Grimaud

Toulon Two hours, seven daily; stop at Le Lavandou (one hour) and Hyères (1½ hours).

Toulon-Hyères airport 1½ hours, four daily

TAXI

A **taxi** (☑ 04 94 97 05 27) rank is at the Vieux Port in front of the Musée de l'Annonciade.

St-Tropez to Toulon

Massif des Maures

Shrouded by a forest of pine, chestnut and cork oak trees, the Massif des Maures arcs inland between Hyères and Fréjus. Roamed by wild boars, its near-black vegetation gives rise to its name, derived from the Provençal word *mauro* (dark pine wood).

The village of **Collobrières** is the largest town in the massif and renowned for its wonderful chestnut purée and *marrons glacés* (candied chestnuts). Head to **Confiserie Azuréenne** (☑ 04 94 48 07 20; www.confiserie azureenne.com; ☺ 9am-noon & 2-6pm) to buy some local goodies. The **tourist office** (☑ 04 94 48 08 00; www.collobrieres-tourisme.com; bd Charles Caminat; ☺ 10am-noon & 2-5pm Tue-Sun, closed Sun & Mon Sep-Jun) has maps, information on guided walks and plenty of tips to make the best of the area.

There is no better lunch stop than **La Petite Fontaine** (☑ 04 94 48 00 12; place de la République, Collobrières; 3-course/5-course menus €24/32; ☺ noon-2.30pm & 7-10pm Tue-Sat, to 2.30pm Sun Apr-Sep, to 2.30pm Tue-Sat & 7-10pm Fri & Sun Oct-Mar): one of southern France's most charming, relaxed village inns, the walls inside are exposed stone, and the fruit tarts for dessert...out of this world. We dare you to try the *broussain:* left-over cheeses mixed with *Marc de Provence* (a liqueur), olive oil and garlic – pungent! Reservations essential. No credit cards.

The stand-out sight in the region is the majestic 12th- to 13th-century **Monastère de la Verne** (☑ 04 94 43 45 51; http://la.verne. free.fr; near Collobrières; adult/child €6/3; ☺ 11am-5pm Wed-Mon Feb-May & Sep-Dec, to 6pm Jun-Aug), which perches unbelievably on the hip of a mountain deep in the forest, but with a view to the sea. Highlights include the austere Romanesque church, the prior's cell, complete with a small formal garden and workshop, the bakery and the olive mill. To get here, follow rte de Grimaud (D14) east for 6km from Collo-brières, then turn right (south) onto the D214 and drive another 6km to the monastery.

Also worth a visit is the **Village des Tortues** (☑ 04 94 78 26 41; www.villagetortues.com; Gonfaron; adult/child €12/8; ☺ 9am-7pm Mar-Nov, to 6pm Dec-Feb) near Gonfaron, 20km north of Collobrières. This animal sanctuary protects one of France's most endangered species, the **Hermann's tortoise** *(Testudo hermanni)*. Once common along the Mediterranean coast, it is today found only in the Massif des Maures and Corsica. The site has a well-documented trail (captions in English) from the tortoise clinic to the egg hatcheries and nurseries, where the young tortoises (a delicacy for preying magpies, rats, foxes and wild boars) spend the first three of their 60 to 100 years. The village also rescues trafficked exotic species and abandoned pet tortoises.

Corniche des Maures

This coastal road snakes from La Croix-Valmer to Le Lavandou along the D559. In addition to stunning views, there are some superb spots for swimming, sunbathing and walking.

La Croix-Valmer's **Plage de Gigaro** is one not to miss, as is the walking path towards **Cap Lardier**, which is one of the most beautiful, least-trodden bits of the coast.

Domaine du Rayol (☑ 04 98 04 44 00; www.domainedurayol.org; av des Belges; adult/child €10.50/7.50; ☺ 9.30am-7.30pm Jul & Aug, to 6.30pm Apr-Jun, Sep & Oct, to 5.30pm Nov-Mar) is a wonderful spot. A former seaside estate rescued

---

FORT DE BRÉGANÇON

A private state residence for the Republic's president since 1968, the **Fort de Brégançon** (www.bormeslesmimosas.com; Hameau de Cabasson, Bormes-les-Mimosas; adult/child €10/free; ☺ 9am-7pm Jul-Sep, shorter hours rest of the year) opened to the public for the first time in July 2014.

Located on a scenic peninsula in Bormes-les-Mimosas, the imposing fort dates back to the 11th century and has featured in numerous conflicts since, from the tensions between Provence and France to the French Revolution and WWI.

Tickets must be booked in advance at Bormes' **tourist office** (☑ 04 94 01 38 38; www.bormeslesmimosas.com; 1 place Gambetta, Bormes-les-Mimosas; ☺ 9am-12.30pm & 3-6.30pm daily Apr-Sep, Mon-Sat Oct-Mar), either in person or online.

from ruin, it has been transformed into a stunning 20-hectare botanical garden, with plants from Mediterranean climates around the world. Paths meander down to the sea. In summer, call ahead for snorkelling tours (adult/child €23/15) of the underwater marine garden. One of only a few sights open at lunchtime, there's an on-site cafe.

Le Lavandou (www.ot-lelavandou.fr) is famous for its 12km of fine beaches and 12 types of sand. Boats regularly sail to the Îles d'Hyères from here.

Up in the hills, you'll find the quintessential Provençal village of Bormes-les-Mimosas (www.bormeslesmimosas.com). The *vieux* (old) village is spectacularly flowered year-round, with the eponymous mimosas in winter and deep-fuchsia bougainvilleas in summer. Old cobbled streets are lined with artists' galleries and boutiques selling traditional Provençal products, natural soap and essential oils. The utterly charming Hôtel Bellevue (☑04 94 71 15 15; www.belle vuebormes.com; place Gambetta, Bormes-les-Mimosas; d/tr/q €75/87/115; ☼Mar-Oct; ❄🐾) has sensational views, pretty rooms and friendly service. For authentic local cuisine, with flavours from the terroir, head to L'Atelier de Cuisine Gourmande (☑04 94 71 27 80; 4 place Gambetta, Bormes-les-Mimosas; mains €18-20; ☼noon-2pm Sep-Jun, by reservation).

For breathtaking views of the coast and islands, the rte des Crêtes winds its way through maquis-covered hills some 400m above the sea. Take the D41 as you head out of Bormes-les-Mimosas past the Chapelle St-François; 1.5km up the hill, turn immediately right after the sign for Col de Caguo-Ven to follow 13km of tight bends and spectacular views. Relais du Vieux Sauvaire (☑04 94 05 84 22; rte des Crêtes; mains €17-32; ☼noon-2.30pm & 7-10.30pm Jun-Sep) is the hidden gem of these hills. With 180-degree views you could only dream of, this restaurant and pool (most people come here for lunch and then stay all afternoon) is one of a kind. The food is as sunny as the views: pizzas, melon and Parma ham, or whole sea bass in salt crust.

After the restaurant, rte des Crêtes joins the final leg of the panoramic Col du Canadel road. On the col (mountain pass), turn left to plunge into the heart of forested Massif des Maures, or right to the sea and coastal Corniche des Maures (D559).

You'll need a car to travel to Bormes and along the rte des Crêtes, but the coastal road is on the itinerary of the Toulon to St-Tropez

VarLib (p860) bus (€2), which stops in most towns, including Le Lavandou.

Hyères
POP 55,774

With its overdose of palm trees, its casino, and medieval Vieille Ville (Old Town) perched on a hillside north of its new town, Hyères retains some of the charm that made it the Côte d'Azur's first resort. The city's real asset, however, is the Presqu'île de Giens (Giens Peninsula), a beach-fringed peninsula that harbours amazing birdlife, including pink flamingos, herons and egrets. Hyères' tourist office (☑04 94 01 84 50; www.hyeres-tourisme. com; Rotonde du Park Hôtel, av de Belgique, Hyères; ☼9am-6pm Mon-Fri, 10am-4pm Sat) runs great guided walks in the old town and the peninsula; the full schedule is on the website.

Toulon
POP 166,242

Built around a *rade* (a sheltered bay lined with quays), France's second-largest naval port is something of an ugly duckling: its rough-cut demeanour and tower blocks just don't fit in with the glittering Côte d'Azur. The city has an interesting history, however, especially its WWII chapter: the French navy scuttled its fleet in the *rade* to prevent the Germans from taking it over. It was also a strategic target (along with Marseille) of Operation Dragoon, the August 1944 Provence Landing.

◎ Sights & Activities

Mont Faron   HISTORIC SITE
North of the city, Mont Faron (584m) towers over Toulon and the views are, as you would expect, epic. Near the summit, Mémorial du Débarquement de Provence (☑04 94 88 08 09; Mont Faron; adult/child €4/free; ☼10am-noon & 2-4.30pm Tue-Sun) commemorates the Allied landings of Operation Dragoon, which took place along the coast here in August 1944. Historical displays and a film form part of this museum. There are some pleasant walks in the surrounding forest. To get here, catch a ride on the Téléphérique du Mont Faron (cable car; www.telepherique-|faron.com; return adult/child €7/5; ☼10am-7pm). A combined memorial/cable car return ticket costs €8.

Les Bateliers de la Rade   BOAT TOUR
(☑04 94 46 24 65; www.lesbateliersdelarade. com; quai de la Sinse; adult/child €10/6) From

ÎLES D'HYÈRES

For some inexplicable reason, these paradisiacal islands (also known as Îles d'Or – Golden Islands – for their shimmering mica rock) have remained mostly unknown to foreign crowds.

The easternmost and largest of this trio of islands is the little-visited **Île du Levant**, split into an odd combination of army land and nudist colony.

Île de Port-Cros, the middle and smallest island, is the jewel in the islands' crown. France's first **marine national park** (www.portcrosparcnational.fr), it boasts exceptional marine fauna and flora, which makes it a snorkelling paradise. The island is also covered with 30km of marked trails through thick forest, ragged cliff tops and deserted beaches.

The largest and westernmost island is **Île de Porquerolles** (www.porquerolles.com). Run as a hacienda in the early 20th century, it has kept many of its sprawling plantation features. There are plenty of walking trails, but the best way to get around is by cycling. There are several bicycle-rental places, as well as a few restaurants and hotels.

Each island makes for a fantastic day trip; in summer, when boat services are frequent, you could visit two islands in a day, though this won't leave you much time on either island. Boats to the Îles d'Hyères leave from various towns along the coast. **Vedettes Îles d'Or et Le Corsaire** (☑ 04 94 71 01 02; www.vedettesilesdor.fr; 15 quai Gabriel Péri) operates boats to all three islands from Le Lavandou. **Transport Littoral Varois** (☑ 04 94 58 21 81; www.tlv-tvm.com) operates from La Tour Fondue on the Giens Peninsula and the port of Hyères. Services are far less frequent in winter than summer. Return guide fares are:

Le Levant adult/child €28/24, 35 minutes or one hour (depending on which island the boat goes to first)

Port-Cros adult/child €28/24, 35 minutes/one hour

Porquerolles From La Tour Fondue adult/child €19.50/17.30; from Le Lavandou adult/child €36/28, 40 minutes

the port you can take a guided boat tour around the *rade*, with a commentary on the local events of WWII (the commentary is in French but there are leaflets in English). There are trips every day from May to October, during school holidays and weekends. Outside of these periods, check with the company or the tourist office.

🛏 Sleeping & Eating

Chicag' Hostel HOSTEL €
(☑ 04 89 66 52 66; www.chicaghosteltoulon.com; 3 rue des Bonnetières; dm €25; 🛜) 🅿 This hostel is an antidote to Toulon's poor press: the brainchild of Clara and Bjorg, two young *Toulonnais* passionate about their city. It is a charming place with three eight-bed dorms and a common room/kitchen that doubles up as a cafe. Every bit of furniture has been recycled or upcycled by the team, giving it a wonderfully quirky feel.

The hostel's mission is to bring locals and visitors together so there are regular events (open-mic nights, street festivals etc).

Hôtel Little Palace HOTEL €
(☑ 04 94 92 26 62; www.hotel-littlepalace.com; 6-8 rue Berthelot; s/d/tr €55/65/75; ❋@🛜) The over-the-top Italian-inspired decor lacks authenticity and the lighting leaves something to be desired but Little Palace is well run and friendly. No lift.

Les P'tits Pins FRENCH €
(☑ 04 94 41 00 00; www.lesptitspins.com; 237 place de la Liberté; menu 2-/3-courses €18/26; ⊘ noon-2.30pm Mon-Sat; 🅿) This elegant brasserie prizes itself on the freshness of its ingredients and dishes – and with good reason. The food is tasty, well presented and the portions surprisingly copious, down to the large chunk of bread gracing every table. What a shame they only serve lunch...

Le Chantilly BRASSERIE €€
(place Puget; mains €15-28; ⊘ 6.30am-11pm) Going strong since 1907, Le Chantilly will sort you out for food, whatever the time of day.

❶ Information

Tourist Office (www.toulontourisme.com; 12 place Louis Blanc; ⊘ 9am-6pm Mon-Sat)

ℹ️ Getting There & Around

AIR

Toulon-Hyères Airport (www.toulon-hyeres.aeroport.fr; 🛜) is 25km east of Toulon, on the edge of the Giens Peninsula. Bus 102 links Toulon-Hyères airport with the Toulon bus station (€1.40, 40 minutes).

BOAT

Ferries to Corsica and Sardinia are run by **Corsica Ferries** (www.corsica-ferries.fr; Port de Commerce, 2 av de l'Infanterie-de-Marine) and **SNCM** (www.sncm.fr; Port de Commerce, 2 av de l'Infanterie-de-Marine).

BUS

VarLib (www.varlib.fr) buses (€3) operate from the **bus station** (📞 04 94 24 60 00; bd de Tessé), next to the train station. Bus 7802 to St-Tropez (eight daily) goes via Hyères (30 minutes) and Bormes-les-Mimosas (50 minutes).

The tourist office sells a **one-day pass** (www.reseaumistral.com; per person €6) that includes unlimited travel on local buses (single fare €1.40) and commuter boats to La Seyne-sur-Mer, and a return ticket for the Mont Faron Téléphérique.

TRAIN

Frequent connections include Marseille (€12.60, 50 minutes), St-Raphaël (€16.50, 50 minutes), Cannes (€21.70, 1¼ hours) and Nice (€26.30, 1¾ hours). The station is located in the centre of town.

West of Toulon

Sanary-sur-Mer & Around

POP 16,070

Pretty-as-a-picture seaside Sanary-sur-Mer is a stroller's dream. Watch the fishermen unload their catch on the quay, or admire the traditional fishing boats from one of the seafront cafes. The colourful Wednesday market draws crowds from miles around. Shops line interior streets.

🏃 Activities

Croix du Sud V   BOAT TOUR
(📞 06 09 87 47 97; www.croixdusud5.com; quai Charles de Gaulle) From April to September, boat tours serve the Calanques (adult/child from €28/16) and Île de Porquerolles (€40/25).

Découverte du Vivant   DOLPHIN CRUISE
(📞 06 10 57 17 11; www.decouverteduvivant.fr; adult/child €78/55; ⊗ Sun Jun-Oct) Observe various dolphin species from aboard a boat with naturalist photographers on a day outing. Pack a picnic.

🛏️ Sleeping & Eating

Hôtel de la Tour   HOTEL €€
(📞 04 94 74 10 10; www.sanary-hoteldelatour.com; 24 quai Charles de Gaulle; d incl breakfast €80-130; 🌀🛜) Some of the excellent, large rooms in this renovated Victorian-era hotel have awesome portside views but can be noisy. The charming decor is clean and inviting – the last few bathrooms yet to be refurbished are scheduled for renovations in 2015.

La Farandole   BOUTIQUE HOTEL €€€
(📞 04 94 90 30 20; www.hostellerielafarandole.com; 140 chemin de la Plage; d from €299; 🌀🛜⛵) There is something of the old Riviera glamour in the rooms of this uber-stylish modern hotel with their patterned wall paper, oversized B&W posters of Hollywood stars and plush soft furnishings. And then there is the location: west-facing, on a secluded beach, with a panoramic roof terrace. Romance awaits.

L'Esplanade   SEAFOOD €€
(📞 04 94 74 08 56; www.restaurant-esplanade.fr; Parking de l'Esplanade; lunch/dinner menu €23/37, mains €21-42; ⊗ noon-2.30pm & 7.30-10.30pm Tue-Sun May-Sep, shorter hours rest of year) Dine in portside elegance on the catch of the day.

Le Bard'ô   MEDITERRANEAN €€
(📞 04 94 88 42 56; www.le-bardo.com; Plage de Portissol; lunch menu €17, mains €18-32; ⊗ noon-2pm & 7-10.30pm) Just south of Sanary, on Portissol beach, this seafront club is perfect for everything from leisurely coffees and delicious meals to late-night DJs and live music. The lunch *menu* with the suggestion of the day is a bargain but available in limited quantities so arrive early.

La Table du Vigneron   FRENCH €€
(📞 04 94 88 36 19; www.vin-bandol-terrebrune.fr/restaurant-bandol; 724 chemin de la Tourelle, Ollioules; 3-course lunch/dinner menus €25/45, mains €25-28; ⊗ noon-2pm Tue-Sun, 7.30-10.30pm Tue, Thu-Sat) Savour delicious seasonal country fare at this restaurant in the vines, part of the Terrebrune vineyard (of the Bandol appellation). Join a tasting and tour of the cellars (€8, 45 minutes) before or after your meal. It's located about 4km northeast of Sanary, in the direction of the village of Ollioules.

ℹ️ Information

Tourist Office (📞 04 94 74 01 04; www.sanarysurmer.com; 1 quai du Levant; ⊗ 9am-12.30pm & 2-5.30pm Mon-Sat)

❶ Getting There & Away

Sanary is on the route of **VarLib** (www.varlib.fr) bus 8805 (€3, hourly) between Bandol (10 minutes) and Toulon (40 minutes).

Bandol & Around

POP 7781

The built-up town of Bandol, a favourite among French holiday-makers, lends its name to the area's excellent wines. The *appellation* comprises eight neighbouring communities including Le Castellet, Ollioules and Evenos.

🏃 Activities

⭐ Maison des Vins   WINE TASTING
(Oenothèque des Vins du Bandol; ☑04 94 29 45 03; www.maisondesvins-bandol.com; place Lucien Artaud, Bandol; ⊘10am-1pm & 3-6.30pm Mon-Sat, 10am-1pm Sun) Bandol's 49 vineyards carefully manage their prized production of red, rosé and white. Pascal Perier, manager at Maison des Vins, is a living Bandol encyclopaedia. He provides tastings, keeps a well-supplied shop and can direct you to surrounding vineyards (most require an appointment).

Sentier du Littoral   WALKING
This yellow-marked coastal trail runs 12km (allow 3½ to four hours) from Bandol's port to La Madrague in St-Cyr-Les-Lecques, with the beautiful Calanque de Port d'Alon roughly halfway.

🛏 Sleeping & Eating

Key Largo   HOTEL €
(☑04 94 29 46 93; www.hotel-key-largo.com; 19 corniche Bonaparte; d €76-110; ❋🐾) On the point between the port and Renécros beach, the Key Largo is ideally located. The modern rooms are simply furnished but individually decorated; the most expensive have great views of the bay and terraces. Breakfast is a splendid affair with freshly baked cakes and pastries.

L'Ardoise   BISTRO €€
(☑04 94 32 28 58; 25 rue du Dr Marçon; menus lunch €16, dinner €27-41; ⊘noon-2pm & 7.30-10.30pm Wed-Sun) The gourmet address in Bandol, L'Ardoise serves a Mediterranean cuisine inspired by the seasons and faraway climes in a very bistro dining room.

❶ Information

Tourist Office (☑04 94 29 41 35; www.bandol. fr; allées Vivien; ⊘9am-noon & 2-6pm Mon-Sat)

❶ Getting There & Away

Bandol is on the train line between Toulon (€3.80, 15 minutes) and Marseille (€10, 45 minutes). Bus 8805 (€3, hourly) goes to Sanary-sur-Mer (10 minutes).

NICE TO MENTON

The Three Corniches

Some of the Riviera's most spectacular scenery stretches between Nice and Menton. A trio of corniches (coastal roads) hugs the cliffs between Nice and Monaco, each higher up the hill than the last. The middle corniche ends in Monaco; the upper and lower continue to Menton.

Grace Kelly, Princess of Monaco, is strongly associated with this part of the world. The Grande Corniche appears in Hitchcock's *To Catch a Thief*, as does the bridge to Èze on the Moyenne Corniche, and Kelly herself died in a car crash on the D53, a road linking the Grande and Moyenne corniches.

Corniche Inférieure

Skimming the villa-lined waterfront, the Corniche Inférieure (also known as the Basse Corniche, the Lower Corniche or the N98) sticks pretty close to the train line, passing (west to east) through Villefranche-sur-Mer, Beaulieu-sur-Mer, Èze-sur-Mer and Cap d'Ail.

❶ Getting There & Around

BUS

Bus 100 (every 15 minutes between 6am and 8pm) runs the length of the Corniche Inférieure, stopping at Villefranche-sur-Mer (15 minutes) and Beaulieu-sur-Mer (20 minutes). Bus 81 serves Villefranche (20 minutes) and St-Jean-Cap Ferrat (30 minutes) from Nice. All bus journeys cost €1.50.

TRAIN

Nice–Ventimiglia (Italy) trains (every 30 minutes, 5am to 11pm) stop at Villefranche-sur-Mer (€1.70, seven minutes) and Beaulieu-sur-Mer (€2.10, 10 minutes).

VILLEFRANCHE-SUR-MER
POP 5468

This picturesque, pastel-coloured, terracotta-roofed fishing port overlooking the Cap Ferrat peninsula was a favourite with Jean Cocteau, who painted the frescoes in the 17th-century Chapelle St-Pierre (admission

€3; ☉10am-noon & 2-6pm Wed-Mon). Steps split the steep cobblestone streets that weave through the old town, including the oldest, rue Obscure, an eerie vaulted passageway built in 1295. Looking down on the township is the 16th-century citadel. Beyond the port is a sandy beach offering picture-perfect views of the town.

ST-JEAN-CAP FERRAT
POP 2027

On the Cap Ferrat peninsula, this fishing-village-turned-playground-for-the-wealthy conceals an enclave of millionaires' villas, with illustrious residents present and past. On the isthmus of the town, the extravagant Villa Ephrussi de Rothschild (www.villa-ephrussi.com; St-Jean-Cap Ferrat; adult/child €13/10; ☉10am-6pm Mar-Oct, 2-6pm Nov-Feb) provides an indication of the area's wealth. Housed in a 1912 Tuscan-style villa built for the Baroness de Rothschild, it's full of 18th-century furniture, paintings, tapestries and porcelain. A combined ticket with the Villa Grecque Kérylos in Beaulieu costs €20/15.50 for adults/children. The peninsula also has three walking trails with glimmering seascapes, and secluded coves for swimming.

BEAULIEU-SUR-MER
POP 3795

Some of the best-preserved belle époque architecture along the coast is in the seaside holiday town of Beaulieu-sur-Mer, including its elaborate 1904 rotunda with Corinthian columns capped by a cupola. Another belle époque beauty is the Villa Grecque Kérylos (www.villa-kerylos.com; Impasse Gustave Eiffel, Beaulieu-sur-Mer; adult/child €11.50/9; ☉10am-6pm Mar-Oct, 2-6pm Nov-Feb), a reproduction of an Athenian villa built by archaeologist Théodore Reinach in 1902.

Moyenne Corniche

Cut through rock in the 1920s, the Moyenne Corniche – the middle coastal road (N7) – takes drivers from Nice to Èze and Beausoleil (the French town bordering Monaco's Monte Carlo).

Bus 82 goes from Nice to Èze Village (20 minutes, several times daily); bus 112 carries on to Beausoleil (40 minutes, Monday to Saturday). Tickets cost €1.50.

ÈZE
POP 2589

On the pinnacle of a 427m peak is the medieval stone village of Èze. Once occupied by Ligurians and Phoenicians, today it's home to one-off galleries and artisan boutiques within its enclosed walls (there's only one doorway in or out of the village). The high point is the Jardin Exotique d'Èze (adult/child €6/free; ☉9am-sunset), a slanting cliff-side garden of exotic cacti with breathtaking views of the Med (all the way to Corsica on a good day).

To explore the village's nooks and crannies after the tour buses have left, stay at the magnificent Château Eza (☎04 93 41 12 24; www.chateaueza.com; rue de la Pise, Èze; d from €455; ✳☎), which also has a lofty gastronomic restaurant and terrace (lunch menus €49 to €59, dinner mains around €50), with views of the Med on a plate.

You can walk down from the village to Èze-sur-Mer on the coast via the steep Chemin de Nietzsche (45 minutes); the German philosopher started writing *Thus Spoke Zarathustra* while staying in Èze and enjoyed this path.

Grande Corniche

The Grande Corniche, whose panoramas are the most dramatic of all, leaves Nice as the D2564. Stop at Fort de la Revère in the Parc Natural Départemental de la Grande Corniche for a picnic with stupendous views or a walk in the *garrigue* (Mediterranean scrub).

Further on, the town of La Turbie, which sits on a promontory directly above Monaco, offers vertigo-inducing views of the principality. The best views are from the town's Trophée des Alpes (http://la-turbie.monuments-nationaux.fr; 18 av Albert Ier, La Turbie; adult/child €5.50/free; ☉10am-1.30pm & 2.30-5pm Tue-Sun), one of only two Roman trophy monuments in the world (the other's in Romania), built by Augustus in 6 BC.

For a sit-down meal, plump yourself on the terrace of Café de la Fontaine (☎04 93 28 52 79; 4 av Général de Gaulle, La Turbie; mains €15-18; ☉noon-2.30pm & 7-11pm), the town's gastronomic bistro.

There is virtually no public transport along the Grande Corniche so you'll need your own wheels.

Monaco (Principauté de Monaco)
POP 32,020 / ☑377

Squeezed into just 200 hectares, this confetti principality might be the world's second-smallest country (the Vatican is smaller), but what it lacks in size it makes up for in attitude. Glitzy, glam and screaming hedonism, Monaco is truly beguiling.

Although a sovereign state, the principality's status is unusual. It is not a member of the EU, yet it participates in the EU customs territory (meaning no border formalities crossing from France into Monaco) and uses the euro as its currency.

History

Originally from the nearby Genoa region of Italy (hence the Monégasque language's similarity with the Genoese dialect), the Grimaldi family has ruled Monaco for most of the period since 1297, except for its occupation during the French Revolution and its loss of territories in 1848. Its independence was again recognised by France in 1860. Five years later, a monetary agreement with France and the opening of the Monte Carlo casino revived the country's fortunes. Today there are just over 6000 Monégasque citizens out of a total population of 32,000 (and 107 nationalities).

Ever since the marriage of Prince Rainier III of Monaco (r 1949–2005) to Hollywood actress Grace Kelly in 1956, Monaco's ruling family has regularly featured in gossip magazines. Albert II, prince since his father's death in 2005, hasn't escaped media scrutiny (he has no legitimate heirs but two illegitimate children), but his achievements as an athlete (he played for the Monaco football team and is a black belt in judo), his charity work and promotion of the arts have earned him favourable press. He married South African Olympic swimmer and former model Charlene Wittstock in July 2011 and Monégasques hope the couple will give them an heir.

◎ Sights & Activities

The beaches in Monaco are definitely not the best on the coast but there are a couple of nice – and surprisingly, free – options. Esplanade Stefano Casiraghi is a concrete solarium that has been installed on the back of the port's sea defence wall, or if you prefer sand, Plage du Larvotto has free as well as paying sections.

★ Musée Océanographique de Monaco   AQUARIUM
(www.oceano.mc; av St-Martin; adult/child €14/7; ◎10am-6pm) Stuck dramatically to the edge of a cliff since 1910, the world-renowned Musée Océanographique de Monaco, found-

ed by Prince Albert I (1848–1922), is a stunner. Its centrepiece is its aquarium, with a 6m-deep lagoon where sharks and marine predators are separated from colourful tropical fishes by a coral reef. Upstairs, two huge colonnaded rooms retrace the history of oceanography and marine biology (and Prince Albert's contribution to the field) through photographs, old equipment, numerous specimens and interactive displays.

In all, there are around 90 tanks in the aquarium containing a dazzling 450 Mediterranean and tropical species, sustained by 250,000L of freshly pumped sea water per day. Kids will love the tactile basin (which runs during school holidays) – tickets for the 30-minute feel-the-fish sessions (€5) are sold at the entrance.

Make sure you also pay a visit to the rooftop terrace too for sweeping views of Monaco and the Med.

★ Le Rocher   HISTORIC QUARTER
Monaco Ville, also called Le Rocher, thrusts skywards on a pistol-shaped rock. It's this strategic location overlooking the sea that became the stronghold of the Grimaldi dynasty. Built as a fortress in the 13th century, the palace is now the private residence of the Grimaldis. It is protected by the Carabiniers du Prince; changing of the guard takes place daily at 11.55am.

Le Rocher is the only part of Monaco to have retained small, windy medieval lanes; they tend to be overrun with souvenir and ice-cream shops but it does give a sense of what Monaco once was.

To access Le Rocher, visitors can walk up the 16th-century red-brick Rampe Major from place aux Armes in the Condamine area. Alternatively, a path winds from the port up through the shady Jardins St-Martin.

MONACO TRIVIA

➡ Citizens of Monaco (Monégasques), of whom there are only 6089, don't pay taxes.

➡ Monaco has its own flag (red and white), a national anthem and the national holiday is on 19 November.

➡ The traditional dialect is Monégasque (broadly speaking, a mixture of French and Italian).

Monaco

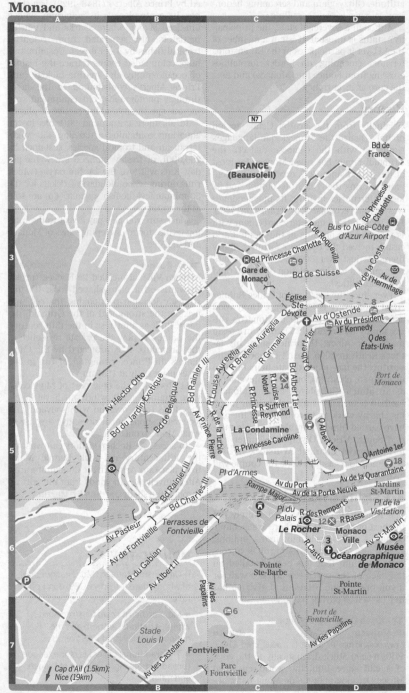

N7

FRANCE
(Beausoleil)

Bd de France

Bus to Nice–Côte
d'Azur Airport

Bd Princesse Charlotte

R de Roqueville

Bd de la Costa

Bd Princesse Charlotte
Gare de
Monaco

Bd de Suisse

9

Av de
l'Hermitage

Église
Ste-
Dévote

Av d'Ostende

8

Av du Président
JF Kennedy

7

Q des
États-Unis

R Bretelle Auréglia

R Grimaldi

R Louise Auréglia

Bd Rainier III

Av Hector Otto

Bd du Jardin Exotique

Bd de Belgique

R Louise
Notari

Bd Albert 1er

14

Port de
Monaco

R Princesse

R Suffren
Reymond

La Condamine

16

Q Albert 1er

Av du Prince Pierre

R de la Turbie

R Princesse Caroline

Q Antoine 1er

4

Bd Rainier III

Pl d'Armes

18

Av de la Quarantaine

Jardins
St-Martin

Bd Charles III

Rampe Major

Av du Port
Av de la Porte Neuve

Pl de la
Visitation

Av Pasteur

Terrasses de
Fontvieille

Av de Fontvieille

Pl du
Palais

5

R des Remparts

12

R Basse

Monaco
Ville

Av St-Martin

2

R du Gabian

Le Rocher

3

R Castro

Musée
Océanographique
de Monaco

Av Albert II

Pointe
Ste-Barbe

Pointe
St-Martin

P

Av des
Papalins

6

Port de
Fontvieille

Stade
Louis II

Av des Papalins

Fontvieille

Av des Castelans

Cap d'Ail (1.5km);
Nice (19km)

Parc
Fontvieille

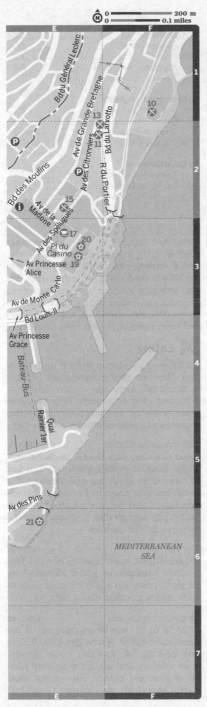

Jardin Exotique
GARDEN

(www.jardin-exotique.mc; 62 bd du Jardin Exotique; adult/child €7.20/3.80; ⊙9am-dusk) Home to the world's largest succulent and cactus collection, from small echinocereus to 10m-tall African candelabras, the gardens tumble down the slopes of Moneghetti through a maze of paths, stairs and bridges. Views of the principality are spectacular and the gardens are delightful. Your ticket also gets you a 35-minute guided tour round the Grottes de l'Observatoire.

The caves are an important prehistoric network inside the hillside; strangely, it's the only cave in Europe where the temperature rises as you descend. It is full of stalactites and stalagmites. Bus 2 links the gardens with the town centre.

Palais du Prince
PALACE

(www.palais.mc; adult/child €8/4; ⊙10am-6pm Apr-Oct) For a glimpse into royal life, you can tour the state apartments with an 11-language audioguide. The palace is what you would expect of any aristocratic abode: lavish furnishings and expensive 18th- and 19th-century art.

Cathédrale de Monaco
CATHEDRAL

(4 rue Colonel) An adoring crowd continually shuffles past Prince Rainier's and Princess Grace's graves, located inside the cathedral choir of the 1875 Romanesque–Byzantine Cathédrale de Monaco. The Monaco boys' choir, Les Petits Chanteurs de Monaco, sings Sunday Mass at 10.30am between September and June.

🎪 Festivals & Events

International Circus Festival of Monaco
PERFORMING ARTS

(www.montecarlofestival.mc) The International Circus Festival of Monaco showcases heart-stopping acts from around the globe in late January.

Tennis Masters Series
SPORTS

(www.montecarlotennismasters.com) Fast becoming a key fixture on the professional circuit, with all the big players involved come April.

Formula One Grand Prix
SPORTS

(www.formula1monaco.com) One of Formula One's most iconic races, held late May. If you're dead keen, you can walk the 3.2km circuit; the tourist office has maps.

Monaco

🛏 Sleeping

Accommodation in Monaco is expensive to say the least, reaching prohibitive levels during the Formula One Grand Prix.

Hôtel Miramar   HOTEL €€
(☏ 93 30 86 48; www.miramar.monaco-hotel.com; 1 av du Président JF Kennedy; s/d €160/185; ❄ 🛜) This modern hotel with rooftop-terrace restaurant is a great option right by the port. Seven of the 11 rooms have fabulous balconies overlooking the yachts. The hotel was entirely refurbished in 2014, giving the 1950s building a proper 21st-century make-over.

Columbus   BOUTIQUE HOTEL €€€
(☏ 92 05 90 00; www.columbushotels.com; 22 av des Papalins; d from €230; ❄ @ 🛜 ⛱) Hi-tech urban chic best describes this large boutique hotel in Fontvieille. Rooms are beautifully decorated in designer greys, elegant striped fabrics and 'back to nature' bathrooms with bamboo towel racks and smart wooden furniture. All rooms have little balconies and good views (the higher the better). The outdoor pool is only heated from May to October.

Novotel Monte Carlo   HOTEL €€€
(☏ 99 99 83 00; www.novotel.com/5275; 16 bd Princesse Charlotte; d from €220; ❄ @ 🛜 ⛱) Put all your chain-hotel preconceptions aside, for the Novotel Monte Carlo is no ordinary chain hotel. Rooms are bright, spacious and colourful, with bath and shower in every bathroom. Even better, up to two children under 16 can stay for free with their parents (and they throw the breakfast in too). The pool is open June to September.

Hôtel Port Palace   LUXURY HOTEL €€€
(☏ 97 97 90 00; www.portpalace.net; 7 av du Président JF Kennedy; r from €249; ❄ 🛜) Built into the hillside overlooking the yacht harbor, this discreetly sexy boutique hotel is decked out in fine silks, soft leather and Carrara marble. All rooms have king-sized beds, walk-in showers and super views of the port and Le Rocher.

🍴 Eating

For those on a budget, a picnic is the best option. There are plenty of parks and benches to sit and take in the atmosphere. Note, however, that most restaurants offer fantastic-value weekday lunch *menus* (often two courses and a glass of wine for around €20).

Supermarché Casino   BOULANGERIE €
(17 bd Albert 1er; pizza slices & sandwiches from €3.20; ⏱ 8.30am-midnight Mon-Sat, to 9pm Sun; 🍴) It's not so much the supermarket that's worth knowing about as its excellent streetside bakery and pizzeria, which churns out freshly prepared goodies. A saviour for those keen to watch the pennies.

Tip Top   PIZZERIA €
(11 rue Spélugues; mains €15-24; ⏱ 24hr; 🍴) This is where Monégasques gather all night long for pizza, pasta and gossip – a good place to know if feeling peckish after a night out.

⭐ La Montgolfière   FUSION €€
(☏ 97 98 61 59; www.lamontgolfiere.mc; 16 rue Basse; mains €14-27; ⏱ noon-2pm & 7.30-9.30pm Mon, Tue & Thu-Sat) This tiny fusion wonder is an unlikely find amid the touristy jumble of Monaco's historic quarter. But what a great idea Henri and Fabienne Geraci had

THE FRENCH RIVIERA & MONACO MONACO (PRINCIPAUTÉ DE MONACO) to breathe new life into the Rocher. The couple have spent a lot of time in Malaysia, and Henri's fusion cuisine is outstanding, as is Fabienne's welcome in their pocket-sized dining room.

In winter, Henri cooks *bourride* every day, a salted cod stew typical of Monaco and Nice.

Café Llorca   MODERN FRENCH €€

(☑ 99 99 29 29; www.cafellorca.mc; 10 av Princesse Grace, Grimaldi Forum; menu €22, mains €15-19; ☺ noon-3pm Mon-Fri) This is Michelin-starred chef Alain Llorca's gift to lunch-goers: fabulous modern French cuisine with a fusion twist at affordable prices. The two-course lunch *menu*, including a glass of wine, is a steal. In spring/summer, make a beeline (and book) for the tables on the terrace overlooking the sea.

Mozza   ITALIAN €€

(www.mozza.mc; 11 rue du Portier; lunch menus €18/20, mains €16-36; ☺ noon-3pm & 7-11pm Mon-Sat, 10.30am-4pm Sun; ☑) The clue to Mozza's speciality is in the name: mozzarella. You'll find all the traditional Italian fare here, but don't miss the mozzarella bar: the restaurant has about 10 different varieties, which it serves in platters or as starters.

Cosmopolitan   INTERNATIONAL €€

(www.cosmopolitan.mc; 7 rue du Portier; lunch menu €16-22, mains €17-31; ☺ 12.30-2.30pm & 7.30-11pm; ☎) The *menu* at this hip restaurant features timeless classics from all corners of the world such as fish and chips, three-cheese gnocchi or veal cutlets in Béarnaise sauce, all revisited by Cosmo's talented chefs. Wash it down with one of the *many* wines on offer.

Drinking & Nightlife

Brasserie de Monaco   MICROBREWERY

(www.brasseriedemonaco.com; 36 rte de la Piscine; ☺ 11am-1pm Sun-Thu, to 3am Fri & Sat) Tourists and locals rub shoulders at Monaco's only microbrewery, which crafts rich organic ales and lager, and serves tasty (if pricy) antipasti plates. The brasserie regularly hosts live music and shows major sports events. Happy hour runs from 6.30pm to 8.30pm.

Cosmopolitan   BAR

(☑ 93 25 78 68; www.cosmopolitan.mc; 7 rue du Portier; ☺ 5.45pm-1am; ☎) Whether you're after cocktails or excellent wine, Cosmopolitan should see you right. With its chocolate-orange decor, contemporary furniture and *The Big Chill* music, it's a nice place to ease yourself into a night out.

Stars 'n' Bars   AMERICAN

(www.starsnbars.com; 6 quai Antoine 1er; ☺ noon-2.30am, closed Mon Oct-May; ☑) This Monaco party institution is the archetypal American sports bar, with celebrity sports memorabilia decorating the walls, burgers and Tex-Mex food on the menu and shakes and cocktails at the bar. It caters particularly well to families with a playroom, game arcade and activities.

Café de Paris   CAFE

(www.montecarloresort.com; place du Casino; mains €15-49; ☺ 7am-2am) Monaco's best-known cafe has been in business since 1882 and is *the* place to people-watch. Service is brisk and rather snobbish but it's the price you pay for a front-row view of the casino's razzmatazz.

BUDGET ACCOMMODATION IN MONACO

There is no such thing as budget accommodation in Monaco; there are, however, two excellent budget-friendly options in **Cap d'Ail**, a mere 2km from Monaco.

Relais International de la Jeunesse Thalassa (☑ 04 93 78 18 58; www.clajsud.fr; 2 av Gramaglia, Cap d'Ail; dm €20; ☺ Apr-Oct) Cheapest of all is the Relais International de la Jeunesse Thalassa. This youth hostel has an outstanding location right by the beach (and close to the train station): the dorms are simple but well kept. The downside is the daily lock out between 10am and 5pm. Rates include sheets and breakfast; half-board is available.

Hôtel Normandy (☑ 04 93 78 77 77; www.hotelnormandy.no; 6 allée des Orangers, Cap d'Ail; d €89-149; ☺ Apr–mid-Oct; ☎) Another good place is Hôtel Normandy. It is run by a multilingual family of artists and it shows: original modern pieces adorn the walls and the rooms have charm with their simple, old-school furniture (although some of the bathrooms are very dated). Some rooms have sea views. It's just 50m from the bus 100 stop (for Nice, Menton and Monaco) and 20 minutes from the gorgeous beach of La Mala.

THE FRENCH RIVIERA & MONACO MONACO (PRINCIPAUTÉ DE MONACO)

Monte Carlo Casino

TIMELINE

1863 Charles III inaugurates the first Casino on the Plateau des Spélugues. The **atrium ❶** is a room with a wooden platform from which an orchestra 'enlivens' the gambling.

1864 Hôtel de Paris opens and the area becomes known as the 'Golden Square'.

1865 Construction of **Salon Europe ❷**. Cathedral-like, it is lined with onyx columns and lit by eight Bohemian crystal chandeliers weighing 150kg each.

1868 The steam train arrives in Monaco and **Café de Paris ❸** is completed.

1878–79 Gambling moves to Hôtel de Paris while Charles Garnier is charged with building a new casino with a miniature replica of the Paris Opera House, **Salle Garnier ❹**.

1890 The advent of electricity casts a glow on architect Jules Touzet's newly added **gaming rooms ❺** for high rollers.

1903 Inspired by female gamblers, Henri Schmit decorates **Salle Blanche ❻** with caryatids and the painting *Les Grâces Florentines*.

1904 Smoking is banned in the gaming rooms and **Salon Rose ❼**, a new smoking room, is added.

1910 Salle Médecin ❽, immense and grand, hosts the high-spending Private Circle.

1966 Celebrations mark 100 years of uninterrupted gambling despite two world wars.

TOP TIPS

➡ Bring photo ID.

➡ Jackets are required in the private gaming rooms, and after 8pm.

➡ The cashier will exchange any currency.

➡ In the main room, the minimum bet is €5, the maximum €2000.

➡ In the Salons Privés, the minimum bet is €10, with no maximum.

Salle Blanche

Transformed into a superb bar-lounge in 2012, the Salle Blanche opens onto an outdoor gaming terrace, a must on balmy evenings. The caryatids on the ceiling were modelled on fashionable courtesans such as La Belle Otero, who placed her first bet here aged 18.

Salon Rose

Smoking was banned in the gaming rooms after a fraud involving a croupier letting his ash fall on the floor. The gaze of Gallelli's famous cigarillo-smoking nudes are said to follow you around the room, now a restaurant.

HÔTEL DE PARIS

Notice the horse's shiny leg (and testicles) on the lobby's statue of Louis XIV on horseback? Legend has it that rubbing them brings good luck in the casino.

Hôtel de Paris

Salle Garnier

Taking eight months to build and two years to restore (2004–2006), the opera's original statuary is rehabilitated using original moulds saved by the creator's grandson. Individual air-con and heating vents are installed beneath each of the 525 seats.

Atrium
The casino's 'lobby', so to speak, is paved in marble and lined with 28 Ionic columns, which support a balustraded gallery canopied with an engraved glass ceiling.

Salon Europe
The oldest part of the casino, where they continue to play *trente-et-quarante* and European roulette, which have been played here since 1863. Tip: the bull's-eye windows around the room originally served as security observation points.

Café de Paris
With the arrival of Diaghilev as director of the Monte Carlo Opera in 1911, Café de Paris becomes the go-to address for artists and gamblers. It retains the same high-glamour ambience today. Tip: snag a seat on the terrace and people-watch.

Jardins et Terrasses du Casino

Place du Casino

Salles Touzet
This vast partitioned hall, 21m by 24m, is decorated in the most lavish style: oak, Tonkin mahogany and oriental jasper panelling are offset by vast canvases, Marseille bronzes, Italian mosaics, sculptural reliefs and stained-glass windows.

Salle Médecin
Also known as Salle Empire because of its extravagant Empire-style decor, Monégasque architect François Médecin's gaming room was originally intended for the casino's biggest gamblers. Part of it still remains hidden from prying eyes as a Super Privé room.

Terraces, gardens & walkways

Hexagrace mosaic

Fairmont Monte Carlo

BEST VIEWS
Wander behind the casino through manicured gardens and gaze across Victor Vasarely's vibrant op-art mosaic, *Hexagrace*, to views of the harbour and the sea.

☆ Entertainment

Pack your evening wear for concerts, opera and ballet. The tourist office has a schedule of local events.

★ Casino de Monte Carlo   CASINO
(www.montecarlocasinos.com; place du Casino; admission Salon Europe/Salons Privés €10/20; ⊙ Salon Europe 2pm-late daily, Salons Privés from 4pm Thu-Sun) Gambling – or simply watching the poker-faced gamble – in Monte Carlo's grand marble-and-gold casino is part and parcel of the Monaco experience. The building and atmosphere are an attraction in its own right and you need not play huge sums. To enter the casino, you must be at least 18.

The Salon Europe has English and European roulette and 30/40; the Salons Privés offer European roulette, black jack and chemin de fer. A jacket and tie are required for men to enter the Salons Privés and the Salon Ordinaire in the evening.

For more information, see the Monte Carlo Casino illustrated highlight (p870).

Monte Carlo Philharmonic Orchestra   CLASSICAL MUSIC
(⌨ 98 06 28 28; www.opmc.mc) Going strong since 1856, the orchestra has maintained the tradition of summer concerts in the Cour d'Honneur (Courtyard of Honour) at the Palais Princier. Tickets (€18 to €80), sold at the Atrium du Casino (⌨ 98 06 28 28; place du Casino; ⊙ 10am-5.30pm Tue-Sun) in the casino, are like gold dust. The orchestra performs in the principality's various auditoriums the rest of the year.

Open-Air Cinema   CINEMA
(www.cinema2monaco.com; chemin des Pêcheurs) Has nightly shows from June to September, specialising in crowd-pleasing blockbusters, mostly in English.

ℹ Information
Centre Hospitalier Princesse Grace (Hospital; ⌨ 97 98 99 00; www.chpg.mc; 1 av Pasteur)
Police Station (⌨ 112; 3 rue Louis Notari)
Tourist Office (www.visitmonaco.com; 2a bd des Moulins; ⊙ 9am-7pm Mon-Sat, 11am-1pm Sun) Smartphone users should download the tourist office's excellent app called Monaco Travel Guide.

ℹ Getting There & Away

AIR
Héli-Air Monaco (⌨ 92 05 00 50; www.heliair monaco.com) runs helicopter flights between Nice and Monaco's **Héliport** (av des Ligures) several times a day (from €135, seven minutes).

BUS
Bus 100 (€1.50, every 15 minutes, from 6am to 9pm) goes to Nice (45 minutes) and Menton (40 minutes) along the Corniche Inférieure. Bus 110 (€20, hourly) goes to Nice Côte d'Azur airport (40 minutes). Both services stop at place d'Armes and on bd des Moulins.

There are also four night services (10pm to 3.45am) on Thursday, Friday and Saturday, which stop at place d'Armes.

CAR
Only Monaco and Alpes-Maritimes registered cars can access Monaco Ville. If you decide to drive, park in one of the numerous underground car parks.

TRAIN
Services run about every 20 minutes east to Menton (€2.10, 15 minutes) and west to Nice (€3.80, 25 minutes). Access to the station is through pedestrian tunnels and escalators from 6 av Prince Pierre de Monaco, pont Ste-Dévote, place Ste-Dévote and bd de la Belgique. The last trains leave around 11pm.

ℹ Getting Around

BATEAU-BUS
The solar-powered **bateau-bus** shuttles across the port between quai Rainier 1er and quai des Etats-Unis. Tickets cost €2; the 24-hour bus pass is also valid.

BUS
Monaco's urban bus system has five lines, bizarrely numbered one to six without the three. Tickets are €2. A 24-hour pass costs €5. Useful lines include:
Line 2 Links Monaco Ville to Monte Carlo and then loops back to the Jardin Exotique.
Line 4 Links the train station with the tourist office, the casino and Plage du Larvotto.

LIFTS
A system of escalators and public lifts links the steep streets. They operate either 24 hours or from 6am to midnight or 1am.

NIGHT BUS
The Bus de Soirée (9.20pm to 12.30am) follows one big loop around town; it is extended to 4am on Friday and Saturday. Tickets cost €1.50.

TAXI
Taxi Monaco Prestige (⌨ 08 20 20 98 98; www.taximonacoprestige.com)

ROQUEBRUNE-CAP-MARTIN

Beautiful **Cap Martin** stretches its languid shores in a sea of crystalline water between Monaco and Menton. The village of Roquebrune-Cap-Martin (population 12,621) is actually centred on the medieval village of **Roquebrune**, which towers over the cape (the village and cape are linked by innumerable, *very* steep steps). Roquebrune is delightful, free of tacky souvenir shops. The **Château de Roquebrune** (www.roquebrune-cap-martin.com; place William Ingram, Roquebrune; adult/child €5/3; ☺10am-12.30pm & 2-6pm) dates back to the 10th century. It's an atmospheric place, even though it is sparsely furnished, and the audioguide (available in English) is fascinating.

Of all Roquebrune's steep and tortuous streets, rue Moncollet – with its arcaded passages and stairways carved out of rock – is the most impressive. There are sensational views of the coast from the main village square, **place des Deux Frères**. Restaurant **Les Deux Frères** (☎04 93 28 99 00; www.lesdeuxfreres.com; place des Deux Frères, Roquebrune; lunch/dinner menus €28/48; ☺noon-2.30pm Wed-Sun, 7.30-10.30pm Tue-Sat; ☎) enjoys the same show-stopping views as the square and serves formal, gourmet French fare. It also has a few great value rooms (€75 to €110).

Menton

POP 29,512

Menton used to be famous for two things: its lemons and its exceptionally sunny climate. With the opening of the fantastic Musée Jean Cocteau Collection Séverin Wunderman in November 2011, the city also became a magnet for Cocteau fans the world over.

◉ Sights & Activities

The town's epicentre is pedestrian rue St-Michel, where ice-cream parlours and souvenir shops jostle for space.

★ **Musée Jean Cocteau Collection Séverin Wunderman**　　GALLERY
(www.museecocteaumenton.fr; 2 quai Monléon; combined admission with Musée du Bastion adult/child €8/free; ☺10am-6pm Wed-Mon) In 2005, art collector Séverin Wunderman donated some 1500 Cocteau works to Menton, on the condition that the town build a dedicated Cocteau museum. And what a museum Menton built: opened in 2011, the futuristic, low-rise building has breathed new life into the slumbering city and provides a wonderful space to make sense of Cocteau's eclectic work. The collection includes drawings, ceramics, paintings and cinematographic work. Explanations are in French, English and Italian throughout.

The admission fee includes the Musée du Bastion, which Cocteau designed.

Musée du Bastion　　ART MUSEUM
(quai Napoléon III; combined admission with Musée Jean Cocteau adult/child €8/free; ☺10am-6pm Wed-Mon) Cocteau loved Menton. It was following a stroll along the seaside that he got the idea of turning the disused 17th-century seafront bastion into a monument to his work. He restored the building himself, decorating the alcoves, outer walls and reception hall with pebble mosaics. The works on display change regularly.

Vieille Ville　　HISTORIC QUARTER
Menton's old town is a cascade of pastel-coloured buildings. Meander the historic quarter all the way to the **Cimetière du Vieux Château** (montée du Souvenir; ☺7am-8pm May-Sep, to 6pm Oct-Apr) for great views. From place du Cap a ramp leads to Southern France's grandest baroque church, the Italianate **Basilique St-Michel Archange** (place de l'Église St-Michel; ☺3pm-5pm Mon-Fri); its creamy façade is flanked by a 35m-tall clock tower and 53m-tall steeple (1701–03).

Jardin de la Serre de la Madone　　GARDEN
(www.serredelamadone.com; 74 rte de Gorbio; adult/child €8/free; ☺10am-6pm Tue-Sun) Beautiful if slightly unkempt, this garden was designed by American botanist Lawrence Johnston. He planted dozens of rare plants picked up from his travels around the world. Abandoned for decades, it has been mostly restored to its former glory. **Guided tours** take place daily at 3pm. To get here take bus 7 to the 'Serre de la Madone' stop.

FÊTE DU CITRON

Menton's quirky two-week **Fête du Citron** (Lemon Festival; www.feteducitron. com; ☺ Feb) in February sees sculptures and decorative floats made from tonnes of lemons weave processions along the seafront. Afterwards, the monumental lemon creations are dismantled and the fruit sold off at bargain prices in front of Palais de l'Europe. Each year the festival follows a different theme.

🛏 Sleeping & Eating

Accommodation gets booked up months in advance, and prices also soar, for the Fête du Citron in February; plan ahead.

Hôtel Lemon   HOTEL €

(☎ 04 93 28 63 63; www.hotel-lemon.com; 10 rue Albert 1er; s/d/tr/q €59/69/85/125; 🖥) Housed in a nicely renovated 19th-century villa, Hôtel Lemon has spacious, minimalist rooms in shades of white and funky bright red or lemon-yellow bathrooms. Wi-fi only works on the ground floor.

★Hôtel Napoléon   BOUTIQUE HOTEL €€€

(☎ 04 93 35 89 50; www.napoleon-menton.com; 29 porte de France; d €89-345; ❉@🖥🏊) Standing tall on the seafront, the Napoléon is Menton's most stylish option. Everything from the pool, the restaurant-bar and the back garden (a heaven of freshness in summer) has been beautifully designed. Rooms are decked out in white and blue, with Cocteau drawings on headboards. Sea-facing rooms have balconies but are a little noisier because of the traffic.

The two top-floor suites with seaviews are sensational, with floor to ceiling windows, larger balconies and great views from the bath tub!

Sucre & Salés   CAFE €

(8 promenade Maréchal Leclerc; cakes/sandwiches €3/5; ☺6.30am-8pm; 🖥) Conveniently located opposite the bus station, Sucre & Salés is a contemporary spot to enjoy a coffee, cake or well-stuffed baguette sandwich.

Le Cirke   SEAFOOD €€

(www.restaurantlecirke.com; 1 square Victoria; menu €28, mains €18-35) From paella to bouillabaisse (fish stew), grilled fish to fried calamari, this smart Italian-run restaurant is the place to turn to for delicious seafood. The wine list is a mix of Italian and French references and the service is as sunny as Menton itself.

ℹ Information

Tourist Office (☎ 04 92 41 76 76; www. tourisme-menton.fr; 8 av Boyer; ☺9am-12.30pm & 2-6pm Mon-Sat)

ℹ Getting There & Away

BUS

Bus 100 (€1.50, every 15 minutes) Goes to Nice (1½ hours) via Monaco (40 minutes) and the Corniche Inférieure.

Bus 110 (€1.50, every 15 minutes) Links Menton with Nice-Côte d'Azur airport (€20, one hour, hourly).

TRAIN

There are half-hourly services to Ventimiglia in Italy (€2.50, nine minutes), Monaco (€2.10, 11 minutes) and Nice (€5.10, 35 minutes).

Corsica

POP 314,486

Best Places to Eat

➡ La Sassa (p886)
➡ Le Matahari (p888)
➡ A Pignata (p906)
➡ Raugi (p882)
➡ Pasquale Paoli (p887)

Best Hikes

➡ Vallée du Tavignano (p908)
➡ Sentiers des Douaniers (p884)
➡ Les Calanques de Piana (p892)
➡ Aiguilles de Bavella (p904)
➡ Gorges de la Spelunca (p891)

Why Go?

Jutting out of the Med like an impregnable fortress, Corsica resembles a miniature continent, with astounding geographical diversity. Within half an hour, the landscape morphs from glittering bays, glitzy coastal cities and fabulous beaches to sawtooth peaks, breathtaking valleys, dense forests and enigmatic hilltop villages. Holidays in Corsica will therefore be incredibly varied: from hiking and canyoning to working your tan, enjoying a leisurely cruise, delving into the island's rich history and sampling local specialities.

Though Corsica has officially been part of France for more than 200 years, it feels different from the mainland in everything from customs and cuisine to language and character, and that's part of its appeal. Locals love talking about their Corsican identity so plenty of engaging evenings await, especially if the holy trilogy of food, wine and melodious Corsican music are involved.

When to Go
Ajaccio

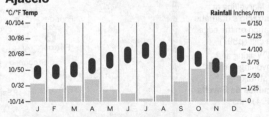

Easter Easter is marked by solemn processions and colourful passion plays.

May & Jun The maquis is in blossom and it's warm enough to swim but not too hot to hike.

Jul–Sep Enjoy the summer party vibe at beach restaurants and nightclubs.

Corsica Highlights

1 Cruising sapphire waters in the **Réserve Naturelle de Scandola** (p891)

2 Exploring wild and remote **Cap Corse** (p883) by way of winding coastal roads

3 Seeing red, blazing red, between fantastic rock formations in **Les Calanques de Piana** (p892)

4 Putting on your hiking boots to explore the gorgeous **Vallée du Tavignano** (p908)

5 Slipping into serene turquoise waters at **Plage de Palombaggia** (p902), near Porto-Vecchio

6 Admiring the work of prehistoric people – see where they lived and what they built – at **Filitosa** (p898)

7 Boning up on Bonaparte around Napoléon's home town, **Ajaccio** (p892)

8 Discovering island paradise with a boat trip to the **Îles Lavezzi** (p899)

9 Marvelling at **Bonifacio's** dramatic location on the edge of a cliff (p897)

10 Walking and canyoning in the breathtaking **Aiguilles de Bavella** (p904) massif

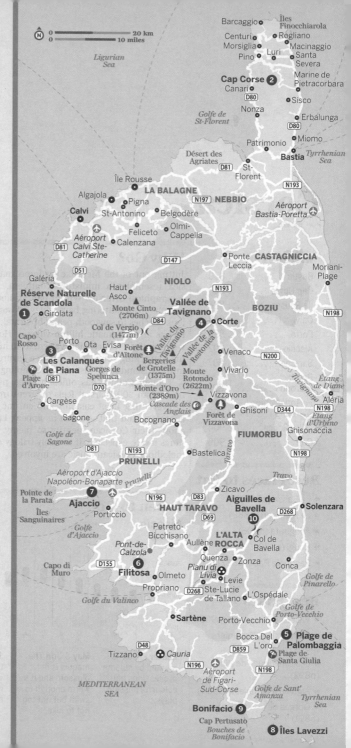

History

From the 11th to 13th centuries Corsica was ruled by the Italian city-state of Pisa, superseded in 1284 by its arch-rival, Genoa. To prevent seaborne raids, a massive system of coastal citadels and watchtowers was constructed, many of which still ring the coastline.

In 1755, after 25 years of sporadic warfare against the Genoese, Corsicans declared their independence, led by Pascal Paoli (1725–1807). Under Paoli's rule they established the National Assembly and founded the most democratic constitution in Europe.

Corsicans made the inland town of Corte their capital, but the island's independence was short lived. In 1768 the Genoese ceded Corsica to Louis XV, whose troops crushed Paoli's army in 1769. The island has since been part of France, except for 1794–96, when it was briefly under English domination.

A movement for Corsican autonomy was formed in the 1960s to combat what some perceived as France's 'colonialist' policy towards the island. In 1976 the Front de Libération Nationale de la Corse (FLNC) was created, and talk of autonomy increasingly turned to claims for full independence.

By the 1990s the FLNC had broken into multiple splinter groups, most armed and violent. This said, relatively few Corsicans support the separatist movements. In 2003 a long-awaited referendum, which would have granted the island greater autonomy, was rejected despite a nail-biting electoral race.

Nevertheless, the nationalist issue remains a burning topic: in April 2014, the Corsican assembly adopted the *Statut de Résident,* a law requiring at least five years of residency on the island to be able to buy a property. The law cannot be applied until it is approved by the French National Assembly, which is unlikely, but it shows how deep nationalist feelings run.

⊕ Getting There & Away

AIR

Corsica has four airports: Ajaccio, Bastia, Calvi and Figari (north of Bonifacio), served by regular flights year-round from many French mainland airports. From May to September there are also frequent flights to Europe and elsewhere with low-cost airlines; you'll likely need to fly via mainland France if you're heading internationally at other times of the year.

BOAT
To/From Mainland France

Corsica's six ferry ports (Ajaccio, Bastia, Calvi, Île Rousse, Porto-Vecchio and Propriano) can be reached from Nice, Marseille and Toulon. Journeys last between 5½ and 12 hours, depending on the route and the size of the vessel.

There are numerous crossings in summer, but far fewer in winter. Whatever the time of year, however, book ahead. The fare structure varies dramatically – anything from €30 to €100 for a foot passenger – depending on route, crossing time, class of comfort and size of vehicle (if any). In July and August expect to pay around €500 return for a car and two passengers from Nice to Ajaccio.

Ferry companies include **Corsica Ferries** (www.corsica-ferries.fr), **La Méridionale** (www.lameridionale.fr) and **SNCM** (www.sncm.fr).

To/From Italy

Ferries operated by Corsica Ferries, La Méridionale and **Moby Lines** (www.moby.it) link Corsica with the Italian ports of Genoa, Livorno and Savona on the mainland and Porto Torres in Sardinia year-round. Moby Lines and **Saremar** (☑199 118877; www.saremar.it) also run seasonal routes between Bonifacio and Santa Teresa di Gallura in Sardinia from April to October.

⊕ Getting Around

By far the best way to get around Corsica is by car, but car hire and fuel can quickly add up over a holiday. A detailed road map is an indispensable companion, such as Michelin's yellow-jacketed *Corse-du-Sud, Haute-Corse* (map 345), covering the entire island in a scale of 1:150,000.

Getting around by public transport (bus or train) is only possible between large towns and cities. Local exploration will then have to be done on foot or by bike or scooter (which are readily available for hire). The train (p888) is an attractive, if limited option, running through stunning countryside between Bastia and Ajaccio, with a branch route to Calvi and Île Rousse. The bus network is more comprehensive but there is often just one bus a day, and generally none on Sunday.

Corsica Bus & Train (www.corsicabus.org) is a tip-top one-stop website for viewing current bus and train timetables island-wide.

FAST FACTS

→ **Area** 8680 sq km

→ **Local industry** agriculture, tourism

→ **Signature drink** Cap Corse, Muscat

ⓘ SEASONAL WARNING

Corsica's tourism is heavily seasonal with most hotels, restaurants and even sights opening only from Easter to October. Winter visitors will need patience, a good book and to enjoy walking...

BASTIA & CAP CORSE

Bastia

POP 43,539

Filled with heart, soul and character, the bustling old port of Bastia is a good surprise. Sure, it might not measure up to the sexy style of Ajaccio or the architectural appeal of Bonifacio, but it has an irresistible magnetism. Bastia is an authentic snapshot of modern-day Corsica, a lived-in city that's resisted the urge to polish up its image just to please the tourists. The historical neighbourhoods of Terra Vecchia and Terra Nova are especially vibrant – allow yourself a day to take in the sights and mosey around atmospheric streets and boutiques.

◉ Sights

Terra Vecchia   HISTORIC QUARTER

A spiderweb of narrow lanes, Terra Vecchia is Bastia's heart and soul. Shady place de l'Hôtel de Ville hosts a lively morning market on Saturday and Sunday. One block west, Baroque Chapelle de l'Immaculée Conception (rue des Terrasses), with its elaborately painted barrel-vaulted ceiling, briefly served as the seat of the short-lived Anglo-Corsican parliament in 1795. Further north is Chapelle St-Roch (rue Napoléon), with an 18th-century organ and trompe l'œil roof.

Vieux Port   HARBOUR

Bastia's Vieux Port is ringed by pastel-coloured tenements and buzzy brasseries, as well as the twin-towered Église St-Jean Baptiste (4 rue du Cardinal Viale Préla). The best views of the harbour are from the hillside park of Jardin Romieu, reached via a gorgeous old stately staircase that twists uphill from the waterfront.

Terra Nova   HISTORIC QUARTER

Above Jardin Romieu looms Bastia's amber-hued citadel, built from the 15th to 17th centuries as a stronghold for the city's Genoese masters. Inside, the Palais des Gouverneurs

houses the Musée de Bastia (☑04 95 31 09 12; www.musee-bastia.com; place du Donjon; adult/child €5/2.50; ⊙10am-6pm Tue-Sun Apr-Oct, shorter hours rest of year), which retraces the city's history. A few streets south, don't miss the majestic Cathédrale Ste-Marie (rue de l'Évêché) and nearby Église Ste-Croix (rue de l'Évêché), featuring gilded ceilings and a mysterious black-oak crucifix found in the sea in 1428.

Place St-Nicolas   SQUARE

Bastia's buzzing focal point is the 19th-century square of place St-Nicolas, which sprawls along the seafront between the ferry port and the harbour. Named after the patron saint of sailors – a nod to Corsica's seagoing heritage – the square is lined with plane trees and a string of attractive terrace cafes along its western edge, as well as a statue of Napoléon Bonaparte.

🛏 Sleeping

For rural souls who prefer 'in the sticks' to 'urban', several lovely addresses accessed via the coastal road that snakes north from the city to Cap Corse are the perfect compromise.

★ Hôtel Central   HOTEL €€

(☑04 95 31 69 72; www.centralhotel.fr; 3 rue Miot; s/d/apt €80/90/150; ﹡🅟🛜) From the vintage, black-and-white tiled floor in the entrance to the sweeping staircase and eclectic jumble of plant pots in the minuscule interior courtyard, this family-run address oozes 1940s grace. The hotel's pedigree dates to 1941 and the vintage furnishings inside the 19th-century building don't disappoint. The three apartments, with fully equipped kitchen, are great for longer stays.

ⓘ MONEY MATTERS

Be warned: surprisingly, many restaurants and hotels in Corsica don't accept plastic, and it's very rare for *chambres d'hôte* (B&Bs) to take credit cards. Some places refuse cards for small amounts (typically under €15). And it's common to come across a reputable restaurant where the credit-card machine has been *en panne* (out of order) for several weeks. Always enquire first. Also note that ATMs are scarce in rural areas, especially in Cap Corse and L'Alta Rocca. It's wise to stock up with euros.

Bastia

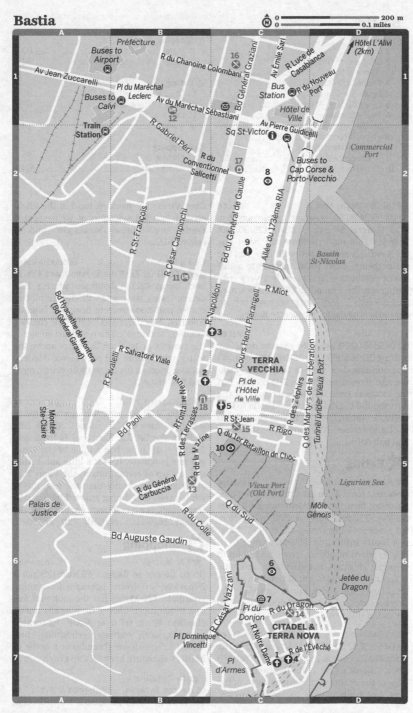

N
0 ——— 200 m
0 ——— 0.1 miles

Hôtel L'Alivi
(2km)

Préfecture

Buses to
Airport

Pl du Maréchal
Leclerc

Av Jean Zuccarelli

Buses to
Calvi

Train
Station

R du Chanoine Colombani

Av du Maréchal Sébastiani

R Gabriel Péri

R du
Conventionnel
Salicetti

Bd Général Graziani

Av Émile Sari

R Luce de
Casabianca

R du Nouveau
Port

Bus
Station

Hôtel de
Ville

Av Pierre Guidicelli

Sq St-Victor

Buses to
Cap Corse &
Porto-Vecchio

Commercial
Port

16

12

17

8

Bd du Général de Gaulle

R St-François

R César Campinchi

11

Allée du 173ème RIA

9

Bassin
St-Nicolas

Bd Hyacinthe de Montera
(Bd Général Giraud)

R Favalelli

R Salvatoré Viale

R Napoléon

3

R Miot

R Fontaine Neuve

2

R des Terrasses

18

5

R St-Jean

R Rigo

Cours Henri Pierangeli

TERRA
VECCHIA

Pl de
l'Hôtel
de Ville

15

Q des Zephirs

Q des Martyrs de la Libération

Tunnel sous le Vieux Port

Bd Paoli

Montée
Ste-Claire

R de la Marine

10

Q du 1er Bataillon de Choc

R du Général
Carbuccia

13

Vieux Port
(Old Port)

Ligurian Sea

Palais de
Justice

R du Colle

Q du Sud

Môle
Génois

Bd Auguste Gaudin

6

Jetée du
Dragon

R César Vazzani

7

R du Dragon

14

Pl du
Donjon

CITADEL &
TERRA NOVA

Pl Dominique
Vincetti

R Notre Dame

R de l'Evêché

Pl
d'Armes

1
4

Bastia

Hôtel Les Voyageurs　　HOTEL €€
(☑04 95 34 90 80; www.hotel-lesvoyageurs.com;
9 av Maréchal Sébastiani; s/d/tr €75/90/130;
❄@🛰) This modern three-star hotel has
been entirely refurbished with travel as the
main theme. Each room represents a different destination and there is a very cosy
lounge on the ground floor reminiscent of
an explorer's library. The hotel has a private
car park, unusual for city centre hotels.

Hôtel L'Alivi　　HOTEL €€
(☑04 95 55 00 00; www.hotel-alivi.com; rte du Cap;
d/tr/q €110/165/196; ☺mid-Mar–Oct; ❄🛰🏊)
The building does need to be dragged kicking and screaming into the 21st century but
the location, right on the beach and off the
northbound coastal road from Bastia to Cap
Corse, is unrivalled, as is the sensational
pool and terrace. All rooms have sea views
and balconies.

✗ Eating

★ Raugi　　ICE CREAM €
(www.raugi.com; 2 rue du Chanoine Colombani;
ice cream from €2; ☺9.30am-midnight Tue-Sat
Oct-May, 9.30am-12.30pm & 2.30pm-1am Mon-
Sat Jun-Sep) Going strong since 1937, Raugi
is a Bastia institution. Flavours range from
bog-standard raspberry, lemon and so on to
Corsican chestnut, mandarin, fig, aromatic
senteur de maquis (scent of Corsican herbal
scrubland) and sweet *myrte* (myrtle). The
verrines glacées (ice-cream desserts; €4.70)
are out of this world.

Chez Vincent　　FRENCH €€
(☑04 95 31 62 50; 12 rue St-Michel; pizzas €10,
mains €12-25; ☺noon-2pm & 7-10pm Tue-Sat; ☑)
Chez Vincent's USP is its location: on the
edge of the citadel with glorious views of the
port. Not content with its views however,

Chez Vincent is working hard in the kitch-
en too: a solid selection of well-executed
French fare – mussels, steaks etc – and excellent pizzas.

Le Lavezzi　　MODERN FRENCH €€
(☑04 95 31 05 73; 8 rue St-Jean; mains €21-35,
lunch menus €22) A boutique address that
design-loving gourmets will love: think turquoise polished concrete floor and brightly
coloured Alexander McQueen–style chairs –
fabulous and funky. The real heart stealer is
the twinset of 1st-floor balconies above the
water with prime old-port views. Modern
cuisine injects a fusion zest into classic meat
and fish dishes.

Chez Huguette　　SEAFOOD €€
(☑04 95 31 37 60; www.chezhuguette.fr; rue de
la Marine; mains €16-25; ☺noon-2.30pm & 7.30-
10.30pm Mon-Sat, 7.30-10pm Sun) If fresh seafood is your muse, bag a table by the water
at Chez Huguette. It's set a little apart from
the line-up of restaurants at the Vieux Port
and rightly so: posher than the rest, this is
white-tablecloth dining enjoyed by Bastians
since 1969. For a real treat, go for the locally
caught *langoustes* (crayfish; €20 per 100g).

🔒 Shopping

★ LN Mattei　　FOOD & WINE
(15 bd Général de Gaulle; ☺9.30am-12.30pm &
2-7pm Mon-Sat) Iconic boutique for visiting
gourmets, LN Mattei has the look and feel
of a 1900 grocer. Choose from locally milled
chestnut flour, *sel à la figue* (fig-scented
salt), Corsican *marrons* (chestnuts) preserved in *eau-de-vie* (brandy) or a bottle of
Mattei's signature aperitif, Cap Corse.

Santa Catalina　　FOOD
(8 rue des Terrasses; ☺9am-noon & 2-7pm Tue-
Sat, 10am-1pm Sun) In season, fresh Brocciu

BUSES TO/FROM BASTIA

DESTINATION	COST (€)	DURATION (HR)	FREQUENCY	BUS STOP
Ajaccio	21	3	2 daily	Bus station
Calvi	16	2	1 daily	Train station
Corte	11.50	1¼	2 daily	Bus station
Macinaggio (Cap Corse)	7	45 min	1 daily	Place St-Nicolas
Porto-Vecchio	22	3	2 daily	Place St-Nicolas
St-Florent	5	1	2 daily	Bus station

cheese is among the many delicious local delicacies stocked at this packed, pocket-size culinary boutique.

ℹ Information

Tourist Office (☑ 04 95 54 20 40; www.bastia-tourisme.com; place St-Nicolas; ⊗ 8am-6pm Mon-Sat, to noon Sun; 🛜) Organises guided tours of the city and has plenty of information about Cap Corse.

ℹ Getting There & Away

AIR

Aéroport Bastia-Poretta (www.bastia.aeroport.fr), 24km south of the city, is linked by bus (€9, 35 minutes, 10 daily) with the Préfecture building in town. By taxi, count around €42/58 by day/night.

BOAT

Ferry companies have information offices at **Bastia Port** (www.bastia.port.fr); they are usually open for same-day ticket sales a couple of hours before sailings. Ferries sail to/from Marseille, Toulon and Nice (mainland France), and Livorno, Savona, Piombino and Genoa (Italy).

BUS

The **bus station** (1 rue du Nouveau Port) is north of place St-Nicolas, behind the Hôtel de Ville (town hall). Additional bus stops are scattered around town. Note that there are no buses on Sunday.

TRAIN

From the **train station** (av Maréchal Sébastiani), there are daily services to Ajaccio (€21.60, 3¾ hours, four daily) via Corte (€10.10, two hours), and Calvi (€16.40, 3½ hours, two daily) via Île Rousse (€13.50, 2¾ hours).

Cap Corse

This spiny northeastern peninsula stands out from the rest of Corsica. About 40km long and 10km wide, Cap Corse resembles a giant geographical finger poked towards mainland France. The west coast is famed for its dramatic, rugged beauty with rocky cliffs, perched villages and strong winds whereas the east coast has a more languorous feel with rolling green hills, beautiful beaches and pretty seaside villages.

Be prepared for some adventurous driving; although the peninsula is only 40km long, the narrow road that rounds its coast (the D80) crams in 120km of switchback curves and breathtaking drops into the sea.

Erbalunga

From Bastia, the coast unfurls through seaside resorts and tiny beaches towards this quaint harbour village, 9km to the north. Wander down to Erbalunga's cute village square and quayside, casually strewn with well-used fishing boats and tempting restaurant terraces. Narrow alleys lead through shady courtyards to a romantic, 16th-century **Genoese tower** by the water.

🎉 Festivals & Events

Festival de Musique d'Erbalunga MUSIC FESTIVAL
(www.festival-erbalunga.fr) Each August during the Festival de Musique d'Erbalunga, open-air concerts fill the village's central square.

🛏 Sleeping & Eating

★**Hôtel Demeure**
Castel Brando HOTEL €€
(☑ 04 95 30 10 30; www.castelbrando.com; rte Principale; d from €149; ⊗ mid-Mar–mid-Nov; ❄🛜🏊) Overlooking the main road through the village, the Castel Brando is a dreamy, creamy, mid-19th-century mansion, with sage-green shutters and lush palm-shaded gardens wrapped around a heated pool and Jacuzzi. The atmosphere is rustic chic meets cool and fashionable.

A Piazzetta TRADITIONAL CORSICAN €€
(☑04 95 33 28 69; place d'Erbalunga; mains €16-25; ⊙noon-2.30pm & 7-10.30pm Apr-Oct) A Piazzetta, with chairs beneath an ancient plane tree, is a good-value choice with a quintessential, traditional village-square vibe. It serves Corsican/bistro fare: stuffed mussels, pizzas and salads.

Le Pirate MODERN CORSICAN €€€
(☑04 95 33 24 20; www.restaurantlepirate.com; mains €40-55, menus lunch €42, dinner €75-90; ⊙12.30-2.30pm & 7.30-10.30pm Jun-Sep, closed Mon & Tue Mar, Apr & Oct-Dec) For a meal to remember, dine at Le Pirate, an award-winning restaurant in the village heart, with a terrace overlooking the harbour – magic on starry summer evenings.

Macinaggio

The hub of the eastern cape, Macinaggio has a pleasant harbour with the island's best moorings and great boat trips.

🏃 Activities

San Paulu BOAT TRIPS
(☑06 14 78 14 16; www.sanpaulu.com; port de Plaisance de Macinaggio) From May to September, the *San Paulu*, which docks opposite the harbourside tourist office, cruises to the remote village of Barcaggio (round-trip adult/child €24/12, two hours). The return trip takes a turn around the nature reserve of Îles Finocchiarola, an important breeding site for seabirds.

Sentiers des Douaniers WALKING
(Customs Officers' Trail) Hikers will love the Sentiers des Douaniers, a rugged coastal path that laces the northernmost tip of the cape, linking Macinaggio with Barcaggio

and Centuri. The stretch from Macinaggio to Barcaggio takes 3½ hours to complete; hikers can then do the return journey with the *San Paulu* (€20).

🛏 Sleeping

Casa Di Babbo B&B €
(☑04 95 35 43 36; www.casa-di-babbo.com; Tomino; d €80; ❋ 🛜 🔊) To put your bags down for a couple of days, it doesn't get much better than Casa Di Babbo. Located on a hillside about 1km south of Macinaggio (follow the yellow signs) amid fruit trees and sea views, the B&B offers five beautifully decorated rooms and plenty of patios and terraces to while away an afternoon.

The breakfasts and evening meals (€30) are something to remember, with virtually everything from the cakes to the charcuterie and bread being homemade.

ℹ Information

Tourist Office (☑04 95 35 40 34; www.macinaggiorogliano-capcorse.fr; port de Plaisance de Macinaggio; ⊙9am-noon & 2-6pm Mon-Fri, 10am-noon Sat, shorter hours in winter)

Centuri

Crayfish, anyone? The tiny, boat-crammed harbour of Centuri is home to the most important crayfish fleet on the island: eight boats worked by three rival rock-lobster fishing families. Among the cluster of seafood eateries on the waterfront, you'll find a couple of addresses stand out for their legendary *pâtes à la langouste* (pasta with crayfish), a local dish in season early April to early October.

DON'T MISS

SAN MARTINO DI LOTA

Perched high in the hilltop village of San Martino di Lota, Hôtel-Restaurant La Corniche (☑04 95 31 40 98; www.hotel-lacorniche.com; San Martino di Lota; d €75-105; ⊙Feb-Dec; ❋ 🛜 🔊) is a brilliant halfway house between city convenience (it's just 8km from Bastia) and Cap Corse wilderness: the sea views will leave you smitten. A family-run hotel since 1934, it woos travellers with its fabulous location and gourmet food (mains €25 to €38, *menu* €31).

Summertime ushers in dreamy lounging in the bijou back garden, by the pool or on the front porch terrace that stares out to sea. Perfect experience with dinner in the much-lauded restaurant, where produce is locally sourced; the *beignets de fromage frais* (battered *fromage frais* fritters) are, quite frankly, out of this world. Advance reservations recommended.

VILLAGE LIFE

For an authentic taste of rural life, check into **Maison Battisti** (☑ 04 95 35 10 40; www.maisonbattisti.com; Conchiglio, Barrettali; d €85), a *chambre d'hôte* (B&B) hidden inside a beautiful old, golden-stone house in the hamlet of Conchiglio. Furnishings in the house, an old *miellerie* (honey-maker's workshop), win vintage lovers over with historical romance. The two *gîtes* (self-catering cottages), available by the week, are equally enchanting. The Battisti family also run a gorgeous small shop with local products.

Conchiglio is located on the wiggly and alarmingly narrow D133, signposted off the coastal D80 between Nonza and Centuri.

🛏 Sleeping & Eating

Hôtel du Pêcheur   HOTEL €
(☑ 04 95 35 60 14; Port de Centuri; d €60-80; ☺May-Oct) Right by the water at the Vieux Port, Hôtel du Pêcheur sits snug in an old building with Bordeaux shutters, vintage in age and oozing retro charm. Rooms are without pretension (no TV, air-con or wi-fi and old-fashioned bathrooms) but they are cheap as chips for this pricey neck of the woods.

A Macciotta   SEAFOOD €€
(☑ 04 95 35 64 12; port de Centuri; mains €15-55, menu €22; ☺noon-2pm & 7-10pm daily Apr-Oct) Tuck into the catch of the day at the well-regarded A Macciotta, a buzzing no-frills bistro down at the old harbour. Try the legendary *pâtes à la langouste*.

Au Vieux Moulin   SEAFOOD €€
(☑ 04 95 35 60 15; www.le-vieux-moulin.net; Port de Centuri; d €130-190, mains €25-48; ☺noon-2.30pm & 7.30-10pm Apr-Oct; ❄🛜) Hobnob with a chichi set at upmarket Au Vieux Moulin, a hotel-restaurant at the top of the village. The signature *pâtes à la langouste* follows the owner's grandmother's recipe, which has remained unchanged for more than 50 years.

The Old Mill also has lovely rooms: those in the old mansion are as classy as the restaurant, while those in the annexe are less

original but sport fabulous balconies with views of the port.

Nonza

Clinging to the flanks of a rocky pinnacle crowned with a Genoese watchtower, Nonza is easily the most attractive village on the cape's western coast. With its jumble of schist-roofed stone houses looking ready to tumble down the steep hillside onto the black-pebble beach far below, it fits the picture-postcard ideal. Scramble down the rocky path, past walled lemon groves, to the black beach, a legacy of the asbestos mine that operated on the coast here between 1941 and 1965. The beach's polluted past does little to inspire confidence, but locals certainly do not seem worried about it given the summertime crowds that pack out its pebbly shoreline.

👁 Sights

Église Ste-Julie   CHURCH
Nonza's picture-postcard church, impossible to miss on the tiny village square, is well worth a peek for its polychrome marble altar created in Florence in 1693.

Tour de Nonza   TOWER
From the village church, weave your way up between rocks and sun-warmed cacti to the Tour de Nonza. The old Genoese watchtower, one of Corsica's best-kept, boasts staggering coastal views (and, unfortunately, a ticky-tacky souvenir shop inside its thick stone walls).

🛏 Sleeping & Eating

Casa Maria   B&B €€
(☑ 04 95 37 80 95; www.casamaria-corse.com; chemin de la Tour; d/f €95/165; ☺Apr-Oct; ❄🛜) A bewitching little hideaway in the heart of the village, this five-room *chambre d'hôte* sits snug in a coolly refurbished 18th-century mansion. Four of its five rooms revel in sea views, and three – including a great one for families – sit harmoniously beneath the sloping roof. In summer, breakfast beneath a vine-wrapped pergola in the bijou back garden.

Le Relais du Cap   B&B €
(☑ 04 95 37 86 52; www.relaisducap.com; Marine de Negru; d with shared bathroom €50-80; ☺Apr-Oct; 🛜) For the ultimate seaside escape, this is hard to beat. Tucked improbably between a towering cliff and a pocket-size pebble

beach, this pert little B&B features four unpretentious yet neat doubles (with shared bathroom), all with staggering sunset-facing sea views. No air-con here, but who needs it with the sea breezes puffing in? It's 4km south of Nonza.

★ La Sassa   GRILL €€
(☑ 04 95 38 55 26; www.lasassa.com; Tour de Nonza; mains €25-35; ☺ noon-3pm & 7-11pm May-Sep) Few addresses are as inspirational. Built between rocks in the shade of Nonza's Genoese watchtower, this strictly alfresco diner – it has no interior – cooks up succulent meat on an open Argentinian-style grill. The site is beautifully lit up at night with coloured spotlights. The sea views and sunsets are unforgettable.

LA BALAGNE

This striking region blends history, culture and beach, with a dash of Mediterranean glam sealing the deal. Refine your art of sampling *la dolce vita* in Calvi and Île Rousse before venturing inland in search of that picture-postcard-perfect village.

Île Rousse

POP 3646

Sun worshippers, celebrities and holidaying yachties create buzz in the busy beach town of Île Rousse, straddling a long, sandy curve of land backed by maquis-cloaked mountains. Founded by Pascal Paoli in 1758 as a rival port to pro-Genoese Calvi, the town was later renamed after the offshore russet-coloured rock of Île de la Pietra (now home to the town's ferry port and lighthouse).

◉ Sights & Activities

Old Town   HISTORIC QUARTER
Île Rousse's old town is a delight. The covered food market (place Paoli; ☺ 8am-1pm), with its 21 classical columns, resembles a Greek temple. It abuts place Paoli, Île Rousse's central tree-shaded square.

Île de la Pietra   ISLAND
For an easy stroll, head over the short umbilical causeway that links rocky Île de la Pietra to the mainland, past a Genoese watchtower and up to the lighthouse.

Parc de Saleccia   GARDEN
(☑ 04 95 36 88 83; www.parc-saleccia.fr; rte de Bastia, N197; adult/child €8.50/6.50; ☺ 10am-7pm Apr-Sep, closed Mon & Sat Oct) Wander the 7 hectares of these landscaped gardens to explore the flora of Corsica – the tough plants of the maquis, pines, myrtles, fig trees and over 100 varieties of olive trees. The gardens are 4.5km from town on the road to Bastia.

Promenade a Marinella   BEACH
Île Rousse's sandy beaches stretch along the seafront, known as Promenade a Marinella, for 3km east of town. Less crowded beaches around Île Rousse include plage de Bodri, immediately southwest of town; Algajola, 7km southwest; or the magnificent plage de Lozari, 6km east.

Club Nautique d'Île Rousse   SAILING
(☑ 04 95 60 22 55; www.cnir.org; rte du Port) Club Nautique d'Île Rousse organises two-hour sea-kayak trips (€32) around the promontory and its islets.

🛏 Sleeping

Hôtel Le Splendid   HOTEL €
(☑ 04 95 60 00 24; www.le-splendid-hotel.com; av Comte Valéry; s/d/tr/q €71/81/111/141; ❄ @ 🛜 ⚂) You'll be hard-pushed in Corsica to find better value: Le Splendid is splendid in value, in attitude (all smiles and helpfulness) and in proximity to the beach (footsteps away). Rooms are clean, vary in size and outlook, and those that sleep four – perfect for families – are unusually spacious. The generous breakfast buffet is the icing on the cake.

Hôtel Perla Rossa   BOUTIQUE HOTEL €€€
(☑ 04 95 48 45 30; www.hotelperlarossa.com; 30 rue Notre-Dame; d from €220; ☺ Mar-Oct; ❄ 🛜) With its enchanting soft-apricot façade and oyster-grey shutters, this cocoon adds a real touch of glam to the hotel scene. Its refined interior would be right at home in the latest edition of *Elle,* and its 10 rooms – all suites – completely spoil guests. The best have a balcony with swoon-inducing sea views.

🍴 Eating

A Casa Corsa   CORSICAN €
(6 place Paoli; mains €10; ☺ 10am-10pm; 🖉) With a prime location on the gorgeous place Paoli, this wine bar makes a brisk trade in salads, cheese and charcuterie platters and other stalwart Corsican fare. As expected, the wine selection, including by the glass, and advice is excellent and all Corsican.

LA BALAGNE INTERIOR

What a difference a few kilometres can make! Flee the hullabaloo of the coastal fleshpots, grab the steering wheel, jump on a serpentine country road and explore inland Balagne. Hidden among the countless valleys and spurs that slice up the spectacular scenery are cute-as-can-be hilltop villages, Romanesque chapels, olive groves and lush vineyards. The Balagne hinterland is also a source of inspiration for many artisans. A signposted route, the **Strada di l'Artigiani** (www.routedesartisans.fr) links the region's most attractive villages, and details local workshops; pick up a route map from the Calvi or Île Rousse tourist offices.

Particularly charming is **Pigna**, a mirage of burnt-orange rooftops and blue-shuttered houses 7km south of Île Rousse via the D151. The village has become something of a music destination for Corsican music thanks to its high-profile auditorium, **Centre Culturel Voce** (www.centreculturelvoce.org). Artisan workshops are scattered among the sweet cobbled streets both here and in the cute hamlet of **Sant'Antonino**, precariously perched on a rocky outcrop, a little further south along the D151. What views! And what zesty *jus de citron* (freshly squeezed lemon juice) served at **Cave Antonini** (📞 06 09 58 94 01; Sant'Antonino; ⏱ 10am-7pm Apr-Sep, shorter hours in winter), a simple wine bar across from the car park at the foot of picture-postcard Sant'Antonino. Its wines and fresh almonds from the Clos Antonino estate are equally tasty.

Should you fancy overnighting, Pigna squirrels away some atmospheric options: **Casa Musicale** (📞 04 95 61 77 31; www.casa-musicale.org; Pigna; d €70-110; 📶) has quirky rooms finished with painted frescoes and fabulous valley views, while plush **Hôtel U Palazzu** (📞 04 95 47 32 78; www.hotel-corse-palazzu.com; Pigna; d €152-290; ⏱ Apr-Oct) spreads out inside a stunning 18th-century mansion. Both have romantic restaurant terraces worthy of a million and one marriage proposals.

The prize for best lunch spot, however, goes to **A Casarella** (📞 04 95 61 78 08; Pigna; dishes €4-8; ⏱ 10.30am-sunset Apr-Oct), a gorgeous restaurant with tiered terraces and superb views. The food is just as memorable: homemade tapas-sized portions of local goodness with charcuterie and cheese, of course, but also salads, soups, homemade dips, and dishes like tomato rice with *figatelli* (a local pork sausage).

⭐**Pasquale Paoli**   GASTRONOMIC €€
(📞 04 95 47 67 70; www.pasquale-paoli.com; 2 place Paoli; lunch menu €24, mains €23-38; ⏱ 7.30-10.30pm Jul & Aug, 12.30-2.30pm & 7.30-10.30pm Jun & Sep, shorter hours rest of year) The town's most gastronomic restaurant, Michelin star and all, cooks up a sophisticated dining experience inside a whitewashed, vaulted dining room. Or dine alfresco on the wood-decked terrace on place Paoli. Each main is expertly introduced by the maître d' (including the origin of the main ingredients). Considering the quality, prices are extremely reasonable.

L'Osteria   FRENCH €€
(📞 04 95 31 90 90; place Santelli; mains €16-22, menus €21-37; ⏱ noon-2pm Thu-Mon, 7-10pm daily) With its young and funky vibe, and excellent €21 three-course *menu*, L'Osteria has become popular among locals. Visitors should follow suit: the cuisine uses local products (seafood, veal etc) but finds inspiration from the entire French culinary repertoire.

🍸 Drinking & Nightlife

Café des Platanes   CAFE
(place Paoli; ⏱ 7.30am-11pm Jun-Sep, to 8.30pm Oct-May) Watch nightly boules contests courtesy of the local gents while you sip an aperitif on the terrace of venerable Café des Platanes – it can't get more Île Rousse than that.

ℹ Information

Tourist Office (📞 04 95 60 04 35; www.ot-ile-rousse.fr; av Calizi; ⏱ 9am-7pm Mon-Sat, 10am-1pm & 3-6pm Sun mid-Jun–mid-Sep, shorter hours rest of year) Has information on the wider Balagne area.

ℹ Getting There & Away

BOAT

Ferries run to Nice, Marseille and Toulon (France), and Savona (Italy).

BUS

There are one or two buses a day to Calvi (€4, 30 minutes) and Bastia (€12, 1¾ hours).

TRAIN

Twice-daily trains to Bastia (€13.50, 3½ hours) and Ajaccio (€22.20, 4½ hours) require a change of train in Ponte Leccia. There are four or five services a day to Calvi (€5.40, 45 minutes).

Île Rousse to Calvi

Algajola

Just 7km from Île Rousse and 16km from Calvi, Algajola is a lovely alternative to its larger neighbours with its 16th-century historic centre and long, golden sandy beach.

🛏 Sleeping

★ **U Castellu** B&B €€
(☑ 04 95 36 26 13; www.ucastelluchambres dhotes.com; 8 place du Château, Algajola; d €90-148; ☺ Apr-Oct; ❋ 🛜) U Castellu will win you over with its location on the village's square in the shade of the ancient castle. Set in an old village home, the five rooms are a wonderful blend of old and new. Maud's welcome is another drawcard, as is the panoramic rooftop terrace where the copious buffet breakfast is served.

The adjoining **restaurant** (☑ 04 95 60 78 75; 10 place du Château, Algajola; mains €13-18, menus €18-24; ☺ noon-2.30pm & 7-10.30pm Apr-Sep) comes equally recommended for its sunny, reliable Mediterranean cuisine.

Hôtel de la Plage Santa Vittoria HOTEL €€
(☑ 04 95 35 17 03; www.hotelplage-vittoria-corse. com; A Marina; d/q €92/166; ☺ Apr-Oct; ❋ 🛜) The family-run Hôtel de la Plage Santa Vittoria, with history dating back to 1870 and flawless sea views, is a good choice.

Plage de l'Arinella

If there is one crescent of sand in Corsica you must not miss, it's Plage de l'Arinella, a serene, rock-clad cove with dramatic views of the citadel of Calvi and one of the finest beach-dining experiences on Corsica. From the centre of Lumio, 6km south of Algajola on the coastal N197, turn right following the signs and twist 2.6km downhill, past leafy walled-garden *residences secondaires* to the turquoise water.

🍴 Eating

★ **Le Matahari** FUSION €€
(☑ 04 95 60 78 47; www.lematahari.com; Plage de l'Arinella; mains €25-34; ☺ noon-3pm Apr-Sep, 7-10.30pm Tue-Sun Jun–mid-Sep) Wooden tables, strung along the sand and topped with straw parasols, immediately evoke a tropical paradise at Le Matahari. From the stylish, shabby-chic interior to the waiters dressed in white and boater, this is one special hideaway. Cuisine is Mediterranean fusion: *penne à la langouste,* tuna steak in sesame coating, fish teriyaki. Opening hours are weather dependent, so call ahead; reservations are essential.

Calvi

POP 5707

Basking between the fiery orange bastions of its 15th-century citadel and the glittering waters of a moon-shaped bay, Calvi feels closer to the chichi sophistication of a French Riviera resort than a historic Corsican port. Palatial yachts and private cruisers jostle for space along its harbourside, lined with upmarket brasseries and cafes, while high above the quay the watchtowers and battlements of the town's Genoese stronghold stand guard, proffering sweeping views inland to Monte Cinto (2706m). Unsurprisingly, Calvi is one of Corsica's most popular tourist spots and in summer it's crammed to bursting.

THE TREMBLER

You may well tremble as the *trinighellu* (trembler) – as the train service, **Chemins de Fer de la Corse** (☑ 04 95 32 80 57; www.cf-corse.fr), between Île Rousse and Calvi is affectionately called – trundles perilously close to the shore along sand-covered tracks. The dinky little train is the easiest way to access the numerous hidden coves and beaches sprinkled along the coast: no traffic jams and an unforgettable trip alongside getaway beaches. The train runs four to five times daily, calling at 15 stations en route, all by request only. Hop off at an intermediate rocky cove or, for fine golden sand, leave the train at Algajola or Plage de Bodri, the last stop before Île Rousse. It costs €5.40 one-way.

WORTH A TRIP

POINTE DE LA REVELLATA

Thrill your senses with a short scenic motor journey west along the coastal D81b (signposted 'Route de Porto – bord de mer' from the square in front of the citadel in Calvi) to Pointe de la Revellata, the nearest Corsican point to the French mainland. Within seconds of leaving town, you're deep in the hot, sun-baked maquis, a low stone wall being the only separator between white-knuckled passenger and scrubby green drop down to the sparkling emerald water far below. Suddenly, after 4km, the magnificent cape with a toy-like white lighthouse at its tip and dusty ginger walking trails pops into view. Park in the lay-by and walk downhill for 20 minutes for lunch at **Mar A Beach** (◫04 95 65 48 30; Plage de l'Alga; mains €12-25; ☺lunch daily Apr-Oct), a Robinson Crusoe–style beach hut tucked in a turquoise creek on **Plage de l'Alga**. Expect plenty of grilled seafood and salads. Ring ahead to check that it is indeed open and to book.

For the best views of the bay of Calvi, drive another 1.5km uphill towards **Chapelle Notre Dame de la Serra** (signposted).

◉ Sights & Activities

Citadel   HISTORIC QUARTER
Set atop a lofty promontory, Calvi's massive fortified citadel offers superb wraparound views from its five bastions. Built by the town's Genoese governors, it has fended off everyone from Franco-Turkish raiders to Anglo-Corsican armies. Inside the battlements, don't miss the well-proportioned **Caserne Sampiero**, which was the seat of power for the Genoese administration, and the 13th-century **Cathédrale St-Jean Baptiste**, whose most celebrated relic is the ebony *Christ des Miracles,* credited with saving the town from Saracen invasion in 1553.

Plage de Calvi   BEACH
Calvi's stellar 4km-long sandy beach has some of the best views of Calvi's citadel. It begins at the marina and runs east around the Golfe de Calvi. Rent kayaks and windsurfing sailboards on the sand, and hook up with local diving schools by the tourist office at the marina.

Colombo Line   BOAT TRIPS
(◫04 95 65 32 10; www.colombo-line.com; quai Landry, Port de Plaisance; ☺Apr-Sep) At the marina, Colombo Line runs a bevy of seasonal boat trips along the coast – a fine way to beat the summer traffic. Highlights include day trips to the Réserve Naturelle de Scandola with a beach stopover at Girolata (adult/child €62/30) or Ajaccio (€80/40).

✵ Festivals & Events

La Semaine Sainte   RELIGIOUS FESTIVAL
Easter celebrations culminate in street processions on Good Friday and Easter Monday.

Calvi Jazz Festival   MUSIC FESTIVAL
(www.calvi-jazz-festival.com) Corsica's biggest jazz festival. Held late June.

Rencontres Polyphoniques   MUSIC FESTIVAL
Catch traditional Corsican chants at this five-day music festival in September.

⊨ Sleeping

Camping La Pinède   CAMPGROUND €
(◫04 95 65 17 80; www.camping-calvi.com; rte de la Pinède; tent, car & 2 adults €29; ☺Apr-Oct; ❀✉) Handy for town and beach, with good facilities including a shop, laundry, pool and play areas; mobile homes and chalets too.

Hôtel Le Magnolia   HOTEL €€
(◫04 95 65 19 16; www.hotel-le-magnolia.com; rue Alsace-Lorraine; d €110-130; ☺Apr-Nov; ❀❀) An oasis from the harbourside fizz, this attractive mansion sits behind a beautiful high-walled courtyard garden pierced by a handsome magnolia tree. Pretty much every room has a lovely outlook – Calvi rooftops, garden or sea – and connecting doubles make it an instant hit with families.

Hôtel La Villa   LUXURY HOTEL €€€
(◫04 95 65 10 10; www.hotel-lavilla.com; d from €320; ☺Apr-Jan; ❀@❀✉) If you want to do Calvi in style, head straight for this lavish hilltop hideaway, brimming with boutique trappings. Clean lines, cappuccino-and-chocolate colour schemes, designer fabrics and minimalist motifs distinguish the rooms, while the exterior facilities include pool, spa, tennis courts and a Michelin-starred restaurant with the most fabulous views of Calvi.

Eating

Calvi's quayside is chock-a-block with restaurants, but many focus more on ocean ambience than quality of food.

U Fornu CORSICAN €
(☎ 04 95 65 27 60; www.restaurantcalvi-ufornu. com; bd Wilson; mains €11-24, menus €19; ☺ noon-2pm & 7-10pm Mon-Sat, 7-10pm Sun) A surprisingly hip restaurant inside a restored stately house in a quiet cul-de-sac off the main thoroughfare, this cool culinary outpost specialises in creative dishes that stray off the familiar Corsican path. Dishes are elegantly presented and filled with subtle flavours, and the *menu corse* is excellent value. Eat in the sassy grey and red interior, or on the shady terrace.

Le Tire-Bouchon BISTRO €€
(☎ 04 95 65 25 41; rue Clémenceau; mains €15-21; ☺ noon-2pm & 7-10.30pm daily Jun-Sep, Thu-Tue Apr, May & Oct) This buzzy option, as much wine bar as restaurant, is a gourmand's playground. Perch yourself on the balcony overlooking the crowds milling on rue Clémenceau, then order from the dishes of the day, posted on a chalkboard. Be good to yourself with veal stew, tagliatelle with Brocciu cheese, a cheese platter and luscious local tipples.

A Candella CORSICAN €€
(☎ 04 95 65 42 13; 9 rue St-Antoine; mains €16-25; ☺ noon-2pm & 7-10pm mid-May–Oct) One of a handful of addresses to eat within the citadel, A Candella stands out for its romantic, golden-hued terrace of stone strung with pretty flowers in pots and olive trees. The food is Corsican hearty, and the sea view is the most marvellous you could hope for.

Drinking & Nightlife

There are plenty of places around town at which to wet your whistle. The best after-dark buzz is quayside.

★ Chez Tao BAR
(rue St-Antoine; ☺ 6pm-3am Jun-Sep) You won't find cooler than this (or more amazing sea views with cocktail in hand). Up high within the citadel, this super-smooth piano bar is an institution. Find it in a lavishly decorated vaulted room, founded in 1935 by White Russian émigré Tao Kanbey de Kerekoff. Seven decades on, hedonistic hipsters continue to flock here.

Information

Tourist Office (☎ 04 95 65 16 67; www. balagne-corsica.com; Port de Plaisance; ☺ 9am-noon & 2-6pm daily Jul & Aug, Mon-Sat May, Jun, Sep & Oct, Mon-Fri Nov-Apr; ☎) Very dynamic, with excellent resources on La Balagne, including detailed walk itineraries complete with maps (€3 for one itinerary, €5 for three).

Getting There & Away

AIR

Count on €22 by taxi from **Aéroport Calvi Ste-Catherine** (www.calvi.aeroport.fr) into town, 7km northwest of the airport.

BOAT

From Calvi's **ferry terminal** (quai Landry) regular ferries sail to Nice (France) and Savona (Italy).

BUS

There is a solitary daily bus (two in summer) to Bastia (€16, 2½ hours) via Île Rousse (€4, 30 minutes). There is also one daily bus to Porto (€17, 2½ hours).

TRAIN

From Calvi train station, south of the harbour, there are at least two departures daily to Bastia (€16.40, 3½ hours) and Ajaccio (€25.10, five hours) via Ponte Leccia, and four or five services to Île Rousse (€5.40, 45 minutes).

PORTO TO AJACCIO

The drive from Porto to Ajaccio is a majestic one that is blessed with bags of beaches, wild rock formations aka the iconic Calanques de Piana, and, last but not least, the irresistible boutique and restaurant of Corsica's most famous *maître glacier* (master ice-cream chef), **Glaces Geronimi** (☎ 04 95 28 04 13; www.pierre-geronimi.com; rte de Cargèse, Sagone; ☺ 9am-11pm Jul & Aug, shorter hours rest of year), in the small town of Sagone. Violet tutti-frutti, Camembert or artichoke ice cream (yes, really) anyone?

Porto

POP 590

The setting couldn't be more grandiose. The crowning glory of the west coast, the seaside town of Porto sprawls at the base of a thickly forested valley trammelled on either side by crimson peaks. Buzzing in season and practically deserted in winter, it's a fantastic spot

---

DON'T MISS

OTA & EVISA

The picturesque villages of Ota and Evisa, high up in the hills above Porto, make for a fabulous day trip. Ota is in fact part of the same municipality as Porto but has a completely different feel: quiet, mountainous and unperturbed by the ebb and flow of seasonal visitors. There are spectacular views of the village from across the valley, on the D84.

Further up the mountain on the D84, Evisa is something of a trekking hot spot. The village features on several long-distance trails and it gets a regular flow of hikers from April to October. It's also well-known for its chestnuts, which are turned into flour, jam and candied sweets.

The scenic and informative Sentier des Châtaigniers crosses some of the village's chestnut grove – find the start opposite local restaurant A Tramula (Evisa; mains €11-18; ⏰ noon-3pm & 7-10pm). This small bistro makes good use of the local speciality and serves delicious savoury pancakes made with chestnut flour. It's a typical village cafe, with tiled floor and simple wooden tables but the panoramic balcony out back sets it apart. The adjoining shop sells chestnut goodies as well as local products such as cheese and cured meats.

---

for exploring the shimmering seas around the Unesco-protected marine reservation of the Réserve Naturelle de Scandola, the astonishing Calanques de Piana and the rugged interior. The village is split by a promontory topped by a restored Genoese square tower, erected in the 16th century to protect the gulf from Barbary incursions.

◉ Sights & Activities

Porto's diving outfits, all based at the marina, offer introductory dives, courses for beginners and snorkelling trips.

Between April and October, several boat companies sail to Scandola on half-day excursions, often taking in the idyllic village of Girolata, sometimes extending to Les Calanques de Piana too. Expect to pay around €28 for trips to the reserve with a stopover in Girolata, €45 for a day trip including the reserve and the *calanques* (deep rocky inlets). Most boats offer informative commentaries (usually in French).

Waterfront   PORT

Porto's main sights are at the harbour. Once you've climbed the russet-coloured rocks up to the Genoese tower (admission €6.50; ⏰ 9am-9pm Jul & Aug, 11am-7pm Sep-Jun), you can stroll round to the bustling marina, from where an arched footbridge crosses the estuary to an impressive eucalyptus grove and Porto's pebbly patch of beach.

**Réserve Naturelle
de Scandola**   NATURE RESERVE

There's no vehicle access or footpath that leads into the magnificent, protected Réserve Naturelle de Scandola – the only way

is by sea. As a result, Scandola, a Unesco World Heritage Site, is blessed with exceptional wilderness both above and below the waterline: the gulf boasts fantastic marine biodiversity, with a jaw-dropping topography – just as on land.

Gorges de la Spelunca   HIKING

One of the deepest natural canyons on the island, the Gorges de Spelunca offer splendid hiking opportunities, as well as plenty of freshwater swimming on hot summer days. The *Hikes & Walks in the Area of Porto* (€3) brochure from the tourist office details 28 signed walks at all levels of difficulty.

🛏 Sleeping & Eating

Le Bon Accueil   HOTEL €

(📞 04 95 26 19 50; www.bonaccueilporto.com; rte de la Marine; d/tr €65/75; ✳ 🕸) This family hotel does what it says on the tin: it warmly welcomes visitors. Owner Didier has put his heart and soul into his hotel and come up trumps with warmth and charm: every room is different, with fresh new bathrooms and pretty decor. But what steals the show is the guest kitchen and gorgeous courtyard, ideal for picnics and alfresco drinks.

Camping Les Oliviers   CAMPGROUND €

(📞 04 95 26 14 49; www.camping-oliviers-porto .com; Pont de Porto; adult/tent/car €9.20/3.70/3.50; ⏰ Apr-early Nov; 🕸) Idyllically set among overhanging olive trees, this steeply terraced site climaxes with a swimming pool surrounded by rocks. You can also swim in the river. There are wooden chalets and *roulottes* (gypsy caravans) to rent by the week.

WORTH A TRIP

LES CALANQUES DE PIANA

No amount of hyperbole can capture the astonishing beauty of Les Calanques de Piana (E Calanche in Corsican), sculpted cliffs above the Golfe de Porto that rear up from the sea in staggering scarlet pillars, teetering columns, towers and irregularly shaped boulders of pink, ochre and ginger. Flaming red in the sunlight, this natural ensemble is one of Corsica's most awe-inspiring sights. And as you sway around switchback after switchback along the rock-riddled 10km stretch of the D81 between Porto and the village of Piana (population 500), one mesmerising vista piggybacks another.

There are two ways to discover the Calanques: by boat or on foot. Numerous companies offer boat trips from Porto; allow €25 for the 1½-hour excursion. For a different perspective, don your walking boots. Several trails wind their way around these dramatic rock formations. Many start near Stade Municipal (stadium) about 3km north of Piana on the D81 (signposted). The tourist office (☑ 09 66 92 84 42; www.otpiana.com; place de la Mairie; ⊙ 9am-5pm Mon-Fri, 9am-1pm Sat & Sun Jul & Aug, shorter hours rest of the year; ☎) in Piana stocks the leaflet *Piana: Sentiers de Randonnée* (€1), detailing six walks.

Afterwards, flop on the sand on the idyllic beaches of Ficajola or Arone, 5km and 11km southwest respectively. The Camping de la Plage d'Arone (☑ 04 95 20 64 54; Plage d'Arone, Piana; 2 people with tent & car €26; ⊙ mid-May–Sep) is one of the most tranquil campgrounds you'll find in Corsica. Or splurge on lunch (mains €35, lunch menu €25) or sundowners with epic views at Corsica's original luxury hotel, Les Roches Rouges (☑ 04 95 27 81 81; www.lesrochesrouges.com; D81, Piana; d/q €141/221; ⊙ Apr-Oct; ❉ ☎). Built in 1912, it remains one of the island's quirkiest vintage addresses. Rambling corridors and musty rooms ooze early-20th-century ambience but rest assured, it's all mod cons.

A couple of daily buses link Piana with Ajaccio and Porto.

Le Cyrnée　　　　　　　　　　　BRASSERIE €€
(Marine de Porto; mains €10-25; ⊙ noon-2.30pm & 7-10.30pm; ☑) A reliable brasserie serving wood-fired pizzas (takeaway available), pasta and grilled fish of the day. The cuisine is simple but well done and the staff are friendly.

Hôtel-Restaurant Le Maquis　　　CORSICAN €€
(☑ 04 95 26 12 19; cnr D214 & D81; mains €24-32, 2-/3-course menu €23/25; ⊙ noon-2pm & 7-10pm) This character-filled eatery in a granite house high above the harbour is much loved by locals and tourists alike. The food's a delight, with a tempting *menu* based on traditional Corsican cooking. There's a cosy all-wood interior but, for preference, reserve a table on the balcony with brilliant views.

ⓘ Information

Tourist Office (☑ 04 95 26 10 55; www.porto-tourisme.com; place de la Marine; ⊙ 9am-6pm Mon-Fri, to 4pm Sat May-Sep, to 5pm Mon-Fri Oct-Mar)

ⓘ Getting There & Away

Bus services include:

Ajaccio €11, two hours, two daily

Calvi €17, 2½ hours, one daily
Piana €3, 20 minutes, two daily

Ajaccio

POP 67,477

Ajaccio is all class and seduction. Commanding a lovely sweep of bay, the city breathes confidence and has more than a whiff of the Côte d'Azur. Everyone from solo travellers to romance-seeking couples and families will love moseying around the centre, replete with mellow-toned buildings and buzzing cafes – not to mention its large marina and the trendy route des Sanguinaires area, a few kilometres to the west.

The spectre of Corsica's general looms over Ajaccio. Napoléon Bonaparte was born here in 1769, and the city is dotted with sites relating to the diminutive dictator, from his childhood home to seafront statues, museums and street names.

⊙ Sights

Palais Fesch –
Musée des Beaux-Arts　　　　　ART MUSEUM
(www.musee-fesch.com; 50-52 rue du Cardinal Fesch; adult/child €8/5; ⊙ 10.30am-6pm Mon,

Wed & Sat, noon-6pm Thu, Fri & Sun May-Sep, to 5pm Oct-Apr) One of the island's must-sees, this superb museum established by Napoléon's uncle has France's largest collection of Italian paintings outside the Louvre. Mostly the works of minor or anonymous 14th- to 19th-century artists, there are also canvases by Titian, Fra Bartolomeo, Veronese, Botticelli and Bellini. Look out for *La Vierge à l'Enfant Soutenu par un Ange* (Mother and Child Supported by an Angel), one of Botticelli's masterpieces. The museum also houses temporary exhibitions.

Within the Chapelle Impériale (Imperial Chapel), constructed in 1860, several members of the imperial family lie entombed in the crypt. But don't expect to find Napoléon's remains – he's buried in Les Invalides in Paris. The chapel was closed for renovation at the time of writing with no short-term plans for re-opening.

Maison Bonaparte   HOUSE MUSEUM
(📞04 95 21 43 89; www.musees-nationaux-napoleoniens.org; rue St-Charles; adult/child €7/free; ⊙10.30am-12.30pm & 1.15-6pm Tue-Sun Apr-Sep, to 4.30pm Oct-Mar) Napoléon spent his first nine years in this house. Ransacked by Corsican nationalists in 1793, requisitioned by English troops from 1794 to 1796, and eventually rebuilt by Napoléon's mother, the house became a place of pilgrimage for French revolutionaries. It hosts memorabilia of the emperor and his siblings, including a glass medallion containing a lock of his hair. A comprehensive audioguide (€2) is available in several languages.

Salon Napoléonien   MUSEUM
(📞04 95 21 90 15; www.musee-fesch.com; Hôtel de Ville, av Antoine Sérafini; adult/child €2.30/free; ⊙9-11.45am & 2-4.45pm Mon-Fri) Fans of Napoléon will make a beeline for this tiny museum on the 1st floor of the Hôtel de Ville. It exhibits Napoléonic medals, portraits and busts, as well as a fabulously frescoed ceiling of Napoléon and entourage.

Musée A Bandera   MUSEUM
(📞04 95 51 07 34; www.musee-abandera.fr; 1 rue du Général Lévie; adult/child €5/3; ⊙10am-7pm Mon-Sat, to 1pm Sun Jul-Sep, 10am-5pm Mon-Sat Oct-Jun) Tucked away on a side street, this quirky little museum explores Corsican history up to WWII. Among the highlights are a diorama of the 1769 battle of Ponte Novo that confirmed French conquest of the island, a model of the port of Ajaccio as it was in the same period, and a proclamation

by Gilbert Elliot, viceroy of the short-lived Anglo-Corsican kingdom (1794–96).

Cathédrale Ste-Marie   CATHEDRAL
(rue Forcioli Conti; ⊙8-11.30am & 2.30-5.45pm Mon-Sat) The 16th-century cathedral contains Napoléon's baptismal font and the *Vierge au Sacré-Cœur* (Virgin of the Sacred Heart) by Eugène Delacroix (1798–1863).

Citadel   FORTRESS
The 15th-century citadel, an imposing military fortress overlooking the sea, was a prison during WWII. It still belongs to the army but has been vacant for years and is off limits to the general public.

🏃 Activities

Kiosks on the quayside opposite place du Maréchal Foch sell tickets for seasonal boat trips around the Golfe d'Ajaccio and Îles Sanguinaires (adult/child €25/15), and excursions to the Réserve Naturelle de Scandola (adult/child €55/35).

Ajaccio's most popular beach, Plage de Ricanto aka Tahiti Plage, is 5km east of town. Heading west, the smaller beaches of Ariane, Neptune, Palm Beach and Marinella dot the Route des Sanguinaires towards Pointe de la Parata.

Plage de Porticcio   BEACH
Beach bums will prefer the sands of Porticcio to the busier city beaches. It's 17km across the bay from Ajaccio and accessible by seasonal ferry (€5/8 single/return, 20 minutes).

NAPOLÉON, SON OF CORSICA?

Despite Ajaccio's endless Napoléonic connections, *le petit caporal*'s attitude to his home island was rather ambivalent. Born to an Italian father and a Corsican mother, and largely educated in France (where he was mercilessly mocked for his provincial Corsican accent), Napoléon actually spent relatively little time on the island, and never returned following his coronation as emperor of France in 1804. But there's no doubt that Napoléon's Corsican roots exerted a powerful hold on his imagination – famously, while exiled on Elba, he is said to have claimed he could recognise his homeland purely from the scent of the maquis.

Ajaccio

0 200 m
N
0 0.1 miles

Av Pascal Paoli

10

Aéroport d'Ajaccio
Napoléon Bonaparte
(6km)

Cours Napoléon

Bd Sampiero

(200m)

7

8

12

R des Trois Marie

5

R du Cardinal Fesch

Bd du Roi Jérôme

Q L'Herminier

Terminal
Maritime
et Routier

Port

R de l'Impératrice Eugénie

R Lorenzo Vero

Passage de
la Guinghetta

R des Halles

11

Square César
Campinchi

Tino Rossi
Harbour
(Old Port)

R Sergent Casalonga

R du Général Campi

R du Maréchal d'Ornano

R du Général Lévie

4

R du Général Fiorella

R Emmanuel Arène

6

Pl du Maréchal
Foch

Av Antoine Sérafini

Q Napoléon

Ferries to
Porticcio

Av de Paris

R de la
Porta

15

R Bonaparte

13

R des Glacis

Cours Grandval

Buses to
Pointe de la
Parata

R du Docteur
Barthélémy
Ramaroni

Pl de Gaulle
(Pl du Diamant)

Av Eugène Macchini

R Conventionnel Chiappe

R St-Charles

3

R du Roi de Rome

14

Jetée de la
Citadelle

Hôtel Marengo (500m);
Hôtel Les Mouettes (1.5km);
L'Altru Versu (2km);
Rte des Sanguinaires (2km)

Bd Pascal Rossini (Bd Lantivy)

1

R Notre Dame

R Forcioli Conti

OLD
TOWN

9

Bd Danièle
Casanova

2

Plage St-
François

Golfe d'Ajaccio

Ajaccio

Pointe de la Parata   WALKING

This cape, about 12km west of Ajaccio, is a magnet for walkers. A much-trodden walking trail leads around the promontory, which rewards with great sea views and tantalising close-ups of the four islets of the Îles Sanguinaires ('bloody islands'), so named because of their crimson-coloured rock. Bus 5 runs between town and the point.

LSP 2 Roues   BICYCLE RENTAL

(☑06 07 28 84 81; www.lsp2roues.com; 13 bd Sampiero; bikes/scooters per day €20/54) To pedal to the Pointe de la Parata from downtown Ajaccio, pick up two wheels from LSP 2 Roues.

✦ Festivals & Events

Ajaccio Fête le Printemps   CULTURAL FESTIVAL

(www.ajaccio-tourisme.com) For two weeks in late April, Ajaccio and the surrounding areas host a raft of events – concerts, workshops, outdoor activities, guided tours – to celebrate the start of the *beaux jours* (long sunny days).

St Érasme   RELIGIOUS FESTIVAL

Street and boat procession on 2 June in honour of St Érasme, patron saint of *pêcheurs* (fishermen).

Fêtes Napoléoniennes   STREET FESTIVAL

Ajaccio's biggest bash celebrates Napoléon's birthday on 15 August (which coincides with the Assumption of Mary, a national bank holiday) with military-themed parades, street spectacles and a huge fireworks display.

🛏 Sleeping

Hôtel Marengo   HOTEL €

(☑04 95 21 43 66; www.hotel-marengo.com; 2 rue Marengo; d/tr €90/110; ☺Apr-Oct; ❄🛜) For something near to the sand, try this charmingly eccentric small hotel. Rooms have a balcony, there's a quiet flower-filled courtyard and reception is an agreeable clutter of tasteful prints and personal objects. Find it down a cul-de-sac off bd Madame Mère.

Hôtel San Carlu Citadelle   HOTEL €€

(☑04 95 21 13 84; www.hotel-sancarlu.com; 8 bd Danièle Casanova; d €90-161, f €147-169; ☺Feb-mid-Dec; ❄🛜) Located smack back opposite the citadel, this cream-coloured townhouse with oyster-grey shutters is a solid bet. Rooms are clean and modern and views get better with every floor. Traffic noise could be an issue for light sleepers. The family room sleeps up to five comfortably.

Hôtel Kallisté   HOTEL €€

(☑04 95 51 34 45; www.hotel-kalliste-ajaccio.com; 51 cours Napoléon; s/d/tr incl breakfast €77/95/123; ❄🛜) Exposed brick, neutral tones, terracotta tiles and a funky glass lift jazz up this typical 19th-century Ajaccio townhouse. Decor is minimal, however, making the smallest rooms feel a little cell-like.

Wi-fi struggles to make it to the rooms but the copious breakfast buffet (included in the price) is a nice surprise.

★ Hôtel Demeure Les Mouettes   BOUTIQUE HOTEL €€€

(☑04 95 50 40 40; www.hotellesmouettes.fr; 9 cours Lucien Bonaparte; d €160-340; ☺Apr-Oct; ❄🛜🏊) This peach-coloured 19th-century colonnaded mansion right on the water's edge is a dream. Views of the bay of Ajaccio from the (heated) pool and terrace are exquisite: dolphins can often be spotted very early in the morning or in the evenings. Inside, the decor is one of understated elegance and service is four stars.

✗ Eating

Don Quichotte BRASSERIE €
(☑ 04 95 21 27 30; 7 rue des Halles; mains €10-18; ☺ noon-2pm & 7-11pm Mon-Sat) Tucked behind the fish market, this inconspicuous brasserie is something of a hidden gem: the cuisine is light, fresh and generous, and an absolute bargain. Don't miss the fabulous *moules à la Corse* (Corsican-style mussels: tomato, cream, pancetta, onion, chestnut) with homemade fries – simply divine.

A Nepita BISTRO €€
(☑ 04 95 26 75 68; 4 rue San Lazaro; 2-/3-course menu €24/29; ☺ noon-2pm Mon-Fri, 8-10pm Thu-Sat) Ajaccio's rising culinary star is winning plaudits and loyal followers for its modern French cuisine and elegant setting. It's a nice change from hearty traditional Corsican fare, although the island isn't forgotten: the menu changes daily and uses only the freshest local products, including seasonal seafood and vegetables.

L'Altru Versu BISTRO €€
(☑ 04 95 50 05 22; rte des Sanguinaires; mains €18-32; ☺ 12.30-2.30pm & 7.30-10.30pm Thu-Mon, daily Jul & Aug) Ajaccio's top-notch restaurant belongs to the Mezzacqui brothers (Jean-Pierre front of house, Pierre powering the kitchen), who are passionate gastronomes and excellent singers – they hitch on their guitars and serenade guests each Friday and Saturday night. The creative cuisine, such as pork with honey and clementine zest, sings to the mouth.

Le Cabanon FRENCH €€
(☑ 04 95 22 55 90; 4 bd Danièle Casanova; mains €22-24; ☺ 7.30-10pm Tue-Sat) Loïc fishes, Nadine cooks – a winning combination if there ever was one. Nestled in the old town near the citadel, Le Cabanon (the shed) offers a sunny cuisine inspired by Loïc's catch of the day in a charming bistro-like dining room. On summer evenings, the most prized seats are those on the street terrace. No credit cards.

Le Bilboq – Chez Jean Jean SEAFOOD €€€
(☑ 04 95 51 35 40; 1 rue des Glacis; mains €58; ☺ 8-11pm) In business for decades, this Ajaccio icon is famous for one thing and one thing only: *spaghettis à la langouste*, savoured alfresco in a tiny pedestrian street. Knock it all down with a well-chosen Corsican wine, and enter seventh heaven.

🍷 Drinking & Nightlife

Most of Ajaccio's action is along bd Lantivy, which has a good selection of atmospheric bars. Look around the chichi port Charles-Ornano, at the marina, too. In summer, the centre of pleasurable gravity shifts to the rte des Sanguinaires, which is lined with trendy *paillotes* (beachside venues) and discos.

🔒 Shopping

U Stazzu FOOD & DRINK
(www.ustazzu.com; 1 rue Bonaparte; ☺ 9am-12.30pm & 2.30-7pm Tue-Sat, 10am-noon Sun) For Corsican goodies, there's only one address that matters: U Stazzu, famous for its handmade charcuterie and Corsican delicacies crafted by other small producers. The shop also sells jams, liqueurs, honey etc.

ℹ️ Information

Tourist Office (☑ 04 95 51 53 03; www. ajaccio-tourisme.com; 3 bd du Roi Jérôme; ☺ 8am-7pm Mon-Sat, 9am-1pm Sun; 🛜)

ℹ️ Getting There & Away

AIR

Aéroport d'Ajaccio Napoléon Bonaparte (www.2a.cci.fr/Aeroport-Napoleon-Bonaparte-Ajaccio.html), 8km east of town, is linked by bus 8 (€4.50, 20 minutes) with Ajaccio bus station. Count on around €25 for a taxi.

BUSES TO/FROM AJACCIO

DESTINATION	COST (€)	DURATION (HR)	FREQUENCY
Bastia	21	3	2 daily
Bonifacio	23	3¾	1 daily
Corte	12	1¾	2 daily
Porto	11	2	2 daily
Porto-Vecchio	24	3½	2 daily

BOAT

Ferry services to Toulon, Nice and Marseille on mainland France depart from Ajaccio's **Terminal Maritime et Routier** (☑ 04 95 51 55 45; quai L'Herminier). Buy tickets before sailings inside the combined bus and ferry terminal.

BUS

Local bus companies have ticket kiosks inside the terminal building, which is the arrival/departure point for buses. As always in Corsica, expect reduced services on Sunday and during the winter months.

TRAIN

From the **train station** (place de la Gare), 500m north of town, services include:

Bastia €10.80, four hours, five daily

Calvi €25.10, five hours, two daily (change at Ponte Leccia)

Corte €5.80, two hours, five daily

THE SOUTH

Sartène

POP 3500

With its grey granite houses, secretive dead-end alleys and sombre, introspective air, Sartène has long been said to encapsulate Corsica's rugged spirit (French novelist Prosper Mérimée dubbed it the 'most Corsican of Corsican towns'). There's no doubt that Sartène feels a long way from the glitter of the Corsican coast; the hillside houses are endearingly ramshackle, the streets are shady and scruffy, and life still crawls along at a traditional tilt. It will offer a much more convincing glimpse of how life was once lived in rural Corsica than do any of the island's more well-heeled towns.

⊙ Sights

Notorious for its banditry and bloody vendettas in the 19th century, Sartène has more recently found fame thanks to the annual Procession du Catenacciu, a re-enactment of the Passion that has taken place in the town every Good Friday since the Middle Ages. Barefoot, wearing red robes and cowled (to preserve his anonymity), the Catenacciu (literally 'chained one'; penitent) – chosen by the parish priest to atone for a grave sin – lugs a massive 35kg wooden cross through town in a re-enactment of Christ's journey to Calvary.

View the cross and 17kg chain the penitent wears inside Sartène's granite Église Ste-Marie (place Porta).

🛏 Sleeping & Eating

Sartène's tourist office has a complete list of accommodation and activities in the area.

Domaine de Croccano B&B €€

(☑ 04 95 77 11 37; www.corsenature.com; rte de Granace, D148; d/q €90/142; ☉ Jan-Nov; ❀ 🎅) This charming old farmhouse, set among 10 hectares of rolling maquis, is a blissful place to spend a few days. The rooms are very old-fashioned but the welcome couldn't be warmer. There are handy picnic facilities for guests. The domaine also run horse-riding excursions in the area. Find it 3.5km out of town on the road to Granace.

Auberge Santa Barbara CORSICAN €€

(☑ 04 95 77 09 06; mains €15-38, menu €36; ☉ 12.30-2.30pm & 7.30-10.30pm Tue-Sun Apr-Oct) A local institution run with flair by chef Gisèle Lovichi, the Santa Barbara puts a modern spin on Corsican classics. Another draw is the bucolic setting, with elegant tables set around a well-manicured flower garden. A respectable wine list completes the perfect picture. It's about 1.3km from the centre on the road to Propriano; follow the signs.

🛍 Shopping

La Cave Sartenaise FOOD & DRINK

(☑ 04 95 77 12 01; place Porta; ☉ 10am-7pm Apr-Oct, shorter hours in winter) Don't leave town without stopping at this Aladdin's cave of a shop for charcuterie, cheese, honey, olive oil, biscuits and dozens of local wines. If you'd like to buy goodies for your picnics or to take home, this is it. It's right at the entrance of the Vieille Ville (old town).

❶ Information

Tourist Office (☑ 04 95 77 15 40; www.lacorsedesorigines.com; cours Sœur Amélie; ☉ 9am-6pm Mon-Fri, 10am-5pm Sat Jun-Sep, shorter hours in winter)

Bonifacio & Around

POP 2994

With its glittering harbour, dramatic perch atop creamy white cliffs, and stout citadel above the cornflower-blue waters of the Bouches de Bonifacio, this dazzling port is

WORTH A TRIP

PREHISTORIC CORSICA: FILITOSA & CAURIA

Southern Corsica boasts the island's most astonishing prehistoric sites, which are must-sees for anyone with an interest in Corsica's ancient civilisations (and even those who don't – the surrounding landscapes are stunning).

Some time around 4000 BC to 3000 BC, Corsica developed its own megalithic faith (possibly imported by seafaring settlers from mainland Europe); most of the island's standing stones and menhirs date from this period. The most important and impressive site is **Filitosa** (☑ 04 95 74 00 91; www.filitosa.fr; adult/child €6/4; ⏱ 8am-sunset Easter-Oct), northwest of Propriano, where a collection of extraordinary carved menhirs was discovered in 1946. The Filitosa menhirs are highly unusual: several have detailed faces, anatomical features (such as ribcages) and even swords and armour, suggesting that they may commemorate specific warriors or chieftains.

About 10km south of Sartène, the desolate and beautiful **Cauria** plateau is home to three megalithic curiosities: the *alignements* (lines) of **Stantari** and **Renaju**, several of which show similar anatomical details and weaponry to those of Filitosa; and the **Fontanaccia dolmen**, one of Corsica's few burial chambers, with its supporting pillars and capstones. The sites are signposted as *sites préhistoriques* about 2km south of Sartène off the N196. What did these strange sites signify for their megalithic architects? Were they ritual temples? Sacred graveyards? Mythical armies? Or even celestial timepieces? Despite countless theories, no one has the foggiest idea.

Both sites can easily be visited from Sartène; alternatively, **U Mulinu di Calzola** (☑ 06 84 79 21 86; www.umulinu.net; Pont de Calzola; d/tr €72/80; ⏱ mid-Apr–Oct) is a gorgeous inn located right on the banks of the Taravo river, less than 10 minutes' drive from Filitosa. Dinner on the shaded terrace is certain to win you over after a day sightseeing.

an essential stop. Just a short hop from Sardinia, Bonifacio has a distinctly Italianate feel: sun-bleached townhouses, dangling washing lines and murky chapels cram the web of alleyways of the old citadel; down below on the harbourside, brasseries and boat kiosks tout their wares to the droves of day trippers. Bonifacio's also perfectly positioned for exploring the island's southerly beaches and the Îles Lavezzi.

⊙ Sights

Bonifacio's town beaches are a little underwhelming. **Plage de Sotta Rocca** is a small pebbly cove below the citadel, reached by steps from av Charles de Gaulle, while **plage de la Catena** and **plage de l'Arinella** are sandy inlets on the northern side of Bouches de Bonifacio. On foot, follow the trail from av Sylvère Bohn, near the Esso petrol station. The finest stretches of sand are east of Bonifacio in **Spérone**.

★**Citadel**　　　　　　　　　HISTORIC QUARTER
(Haute Ville) Much of Bonifacio's charm comes from strolling the citadel's shady streets, several spanned by arched aqueducts designed to collect rainwater to fill the communal cistern opposite **Église Ste-Marie Ma-**

jeure. From the marina, the paved steps of **montée du Rastello** and **montée St-Roch** bring you up to the citadel's old gateway, **Porte de Gênes**, complete with an original 16th-century drawbridge.

Inside the gateway is the 13th-century **Bastion de l'Étendard** (adult/child €2.50/free; ⏱ 9am-8pm Mon-Fri, 10am-6pm Sat & Sun May-Sep, 10am-5pm Oct-Apr), home to a small history museum. Stroll the ramparts to **place du Marché** and **place de la Manichella** for jaw-dropping views over the Bouches de Bonifacio.

On the other side of the citadel, the **Escalier du Roi d'Aragon** (adult/child €2.50/free; ⏱ 9am-8pm Mon-Fri, 10am-6pm Sat & Sun May-Sep, 10am-5pm Oct-Apr) cuts down the southern cliff-face. Legend says its 187 steep steps were carved in a single night by Aragonese troops during the siege of 1420, only for troops to be rebuffed by retaliating Bonifacio residents at the top. In reality the steps served as an access path to an underground freshwater well.

West along the limestone headland is the **Église Ste-Dominique**, one of Corsica's few Gothic churches and, a little further, Bonifacio's eerily quiet but beautiful **marine cemetery**. At the western tip of the peninsula, an underground passage dug by hand during WWII leads to the **Gouvernail de la Corse**, a rudder-shaped rock about 12m from the shore.

Îles Lavezzi   ISLAND

Paradise! This protected clutch of uninhabited islets were made for those who love nothing better than splashing in tranquil lapis-lazuli waters. The 65-hectare Île Lavezzi, which gives its name to the whole archipelago, is the most accessible of the islands.

In summer, various companies organise **boat trips** here; buy tickets at the booths located on Bonifacio's marina and bring your own picnic lunch. Boats also sail to the island from Porto-Vecchio.

⚡ Activities

The Îles Lavezzi feature a variety of **dive sites** for all levels. At Mérouville, Bonifacio's signature site, divers are guaranteed to get up close and personal with big groupers. The tourist office has a list of dive operators; a single dive starts at around €40.

Plage de Piantarella is popular with **windsurfers**. **Bonif' Kayak** (☑ 06 27 11 30 73; www.bonifacio-kayak.com; kayaks per hr €8, excursions per person €35-65) rents kayaks and organises guided sea-kayaking excursions.

SPMB   BOAT TOUR

(☑ 04 95 10 97 50; www.spmbonifacio.com; Port de Bonifacio) Don't leave Bonifacio without taking a boat trip around its extraordinary coastline, where you'll get the best perspective of the town's precarious position on top of the magnificent chalky cliffs. The one-hour itinerary (adult/child €17.50/12) includes several *calanques*, views of the Escalier du Roi d'Aragon and the **Grotte du Sdragonato** (Little Dragon Cave), a vast watery cave with a natural rooftop skylight.

Longer 1½-hour trips (adult/child €35/17.50) take in the Îles Lavezzi. You also have the option of getting off the boat and spending a few hours on the island (pack a picnic and your snorkelling gear).

SPMB guarantees all-day free parking for all customers, a real bonus in Bonifacio.

Phare de Pertusato   WALKING

If you're after that perfect picture, don't miss the fantastic, easy walk along the cliffs to the Pertusato Lighthouse, from where the seamless views of the cliffs, Îles Lavezzi, Bonifacio and Sardinia are memorable. Pick up the trail just to the left of the sharp bend on the hill up to Bonifacio's citadel. Count on 2½ hours for the 5.6km round-trip.

🛏 Sleeping

Domaine de Licetto   HOTEL €

(☑ 04 95 73 03 59; www.licetto.com; rte du Phare de Pertusato; d/studio from €75/90; ❄ 🤖) Tucked in the maquis 2km east of Bonifacio, this motel-style address is a nice surprise. Its six minimalist rooms sport stylishly modern bathroms, well-chosen furnishings and each has a terrace with table and chairs made for lounging alfresco in the surrounding peace and quiet. The 12 studios with kitchenettes are good value, but the continental breakfast, at €11, isn't.

Hôtel Le Colomba   HOTEL €€

(☑ 04 95 73 73 44; www.hotel-bonifacio-corse.fr; rue Simon Varsi; d €112-147; 😊 Mar-Nov; ❄ 🤖 🎙) Occupying a tastefully renovated 14th-century building, this beautiful hotel is a delightful address in a picturesque (steep) street, bang in the heart of the old town. Rooms are simple and smallish, but fresh and pleasantly individual: wrought-iron bedsteads and country fabrics in some, carved bedheads and checkerboard tiles in others. Breakfast in a vaulted room is another highlight.

Hôtel Genovese   HOTEL €€€

(☑ 04 95 73 12 34; www.hotel-genovese.com; place de l'Europe, Haute-Ville; d €210-285; ❄ 🤖 🎙) Chic and stylish, this ultra-cool hotel built on the ramparts is hard to resist. Its rooftop swimming pool and bijou garden are stunning and the interior is bright and fresh. The rooms themselves are a little underwhelming – except for the views (not in every room) – although very comfortable.

🍴 Eating

★ Kissing Pigs   CORSICAN €

(☑ 04 95 73 56 09; 15 quai Banda del Ferro; mains €11-20) Soothingly positioned by the harbour, this widely acclaimed restaurant and wine bar serves savoury fare in a seductively cosy interior, complete with wooden fixtures and swinging sausages. It's famed for its cheese and charcuterie platters; for the indecisive, the combination *moitié-moitié* (half-half) is perfect. The Corsican wine list is another hit.

Cantina Doria   CORSICAN €

(☑ 04 95 73 50 49; 27 rue Doria; mains €12-16; menu €20; 😊 noon-2.30pm & 7-10pm Apr-Oct) A

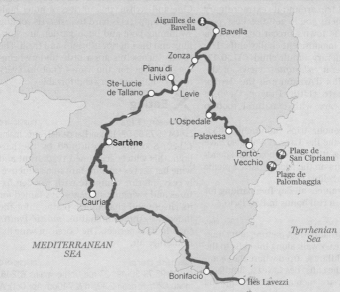

1 WEEK Essential Southern Corsica

Southern Corsica is a concentrate of the very best the island has to offer: mountains and beaches, culture, history, and plenty of fabulous addresses for epicurean travellers.

Start off your trip in **Bonifacio** (p897): perched dramatically on chalky cliffs that plunge into the sea, it is undoubtedly Corsica's most spectacular city. Allow a day to mosey about the streets of the citadel, descend (and then ascend!) the spectacular Escalier du Roi d'Aragon, and walk to the Phare de Pertusato for breathtaking views of the city.

The next day, pack a picnic and your snorkelling gear and join a boat trip to **Îles Lavezzi** (p899), an idyllic archipelago southeast of Bonifacio.

On the third day, head north from Bonifacio towards **Sartène** (p897) – book for a late lunch at Auberge Santa Barbara and take a small detour to the beautiful prehistoric sites of **Cauria** (p898) on the way. From there, drive up to **Levie** (p905), up in the mountainous region of Alta Rocca. Your final destination that day is the exquisite boutique inn A Pignata – half-board is compulsory and what a good idea!

The next morning, visit the prehistoric sites of **Pianu di Livia** (p905), just five minutes' drive from the hotel. The rest of the day can be spent exploring the picturesque villages of **Levie** and **Ste-Lucie de Tallano** (p905) or simply enjoying the creature comforts and views of A Pignata.

On day five: action! Go canyoning, hiking or mountain biking in **Les Aiguilles de Bavella** (p904), a stunning mountain range characterised by steep, serrated peaks, forested slopes and deep canyons.

Spend the night in **Zonza** (p905) to recover, before driving down to **Porto-Vecchio** (p902) the next day and flopping on one its paradisiacal beaches: Plage de Palombaggia or Plage de San Ciprianu get our vote.

For your last day, enjoy a spot of shopping in Porto-Vecchio's pretty boutiques, feast on fresh pasta or a *tartare* (a dish of seasoned raw meat or fish) at the harbourside U Molu, and check out the beaches you missed out on the day before.

Top: Bonifacio p897 Above: Îles Lavezzi p899

Bonifacio institution, this cavernous joint has a tantalising menu showcasing the great classics of Corsican cuisine in a rustic setting.

Sorba
BOULANGERIE €

(☑ 04 95 73 03 64; 3 rue St-Erasme) Visit this artisan patisserie-gelateria down by the water before setting sail in a boat and splash out on a bag of sweet lemon- or aniseed-flavoured *canistrelli* (Corsican biscuits), a loaf of *pain du morts* (literally 'death bread' but actually sweet nut-and-raisin bread) or some giant-sized chestnut and orange *fugazzi* (cookies) to nibble aboard.

Restaurant du Club Nautique
SEAFOOD €€

(☑ 04 95 73 02 11; quai Nord, Port de Plaisance; mains €13-28; ⊘ noon-2.30pm & 7-10pm) Feast on fresh pasta and seafood amid nautical decor at Bonifacio's sailing club's restaurant. The cuisine is exquisite, as are the views of the citadel.

ℹ Information

Tourist Office (☑ 04 95 73 11 88; www. bonifacio.fr; 2 rue Fred Scamaroni; ⊘ 9am-7pm mid-Apr–mid-Oct, 10am-5pm Mon-Fri mid-Oct–mid-Apr; 🛜)

ℹ Getting There & Away

AIR

A taxi into town from **Aéroport de Figari-Sud-Corse** (www.2a.cci.fr/Aeroport-Figari-Sud-Corse.html), 20km northwest of town, costs about €45. A seaonal shuttle bus (€10) also operates from April to October.

BOAT

Sardinia's main ferry operators, **Moby** (www. moby.it) and **Saremar** (www.saremar.it), run seasonal boats between Bonifacio and Santa Teresa Gallura (Sardinia); sailing time is 50 minutes.

BUS

Eurocorse Voyages (☑ 04 95 70 13 83; www. eurocorse.com) Runs daily services to Porto-Vecchio (€9, 30 minutes) and Ajaccio (€23, 3¼ hours).

Porto-Vecchio & Around

POP 11.181

Shamelessly seductive and fashionable, Porto-Vecchio is dubbed the Corsican St-Tropez, and it's no wonder. Sitting in a marvellous bay, it's the kind of place that lures French A-listers and wealthy tourists. Its picturesque backstreets, lined with restaurant terraces and designer shops, have charm in spades, and are presided over with grace by the photogenic ruins of an old Genoese citadel. Although there is no beach in the town proper, some of the island's best, and most famous, beaches are close by.

◉ Sights & Activities

When it comes to wishing for the archetypal 'idyllic beach', it's impossible to think past the immense **Plage de Palombaggia**. This is the Corsican paradise you've been daydreaming about: sparkling turquoise waters, long stretches of sand edged with pine trees and splendiferous views over the Îles Cerbicale. South of Plage de Palombaggia, **Plage de la Folacca** (also known as Plage de Tamaricciu) is no less impressive. Continue a few kilometres further south over a pass called Bocca di L'Oru and you'll come across another gem of a beach, the gently curving **Plage de Santa Giulia**. From Porto-Vecchio, follow the N198 to the south and turn left onto rte de Palombaggia (it's signposted), which winds around the coast.

To the north, the coast is also sprinkled with scenic expanses of sand. The gorgeous, lucent depths of the beaches at **Cala Rossa** and **Baie de San Ciprianu** are sure to set your heart aflutter. Further to the north is the stunning **Golfe de Pinarello** with its Genoese tower and yet more beautiful expanses of sand lapped by shallow waters.

In town at the marina, various operators offer boat excursions to the Îles Lavezzi and Bonifacio.

🛏 Sleeping

A Littariccia
B&B €€

(☑ 04 95 70 41 33; www.littariccia.com; rte de Palombaggia; d €90-160; ❄🛜🏊) This B&B's trump card is its *fabulous* location, in the hills overlooking Plage de Palombaggia, with a dreamy pool. The rooms are pretty but simple and not all come with a sea view, or wi-fi. The breakfast – a simple continental affair – is disappointing for a *chambre d'hôte*.

Le Belvédère
HOTEL €€€

(☑ 04 95 70 54 13; www.hbcorsica.com; rte de Palombaggia; d €310; ⊘ May-Nov; ❄🛜🏊) Built out of an old family estate tucked between eucalyptus, palm and pine on the seashore, this 15-room hotel is quite divine, darling. Decor is modern and exotic: a gregarious mix of traditional stone, wood, marble and wrought iron. Public areas lounge between natural rock and sand, and as for the sea-facing pool, you'll be hard-pushed to move.

Rates tumble by 50% in the low season, making Le Belvédère a real bargain.

Eating

A Cantina di l'Orriu
CORSICAN €

(☏04 95 25 95 89; www.orriu.com; 5 cours Napoléon; mains €14-29; ⊗noon-2pm Wed-Sun, 7-10pm daily) Gourmets will be in heaven at this wonderful *bar à vin,* its atmospheric old-stone interior packed to the rafters with sausages and cold meats hung up to dry, cheeses, jars of jam and honey, and other tasty Corsican produce. Lunch platters range from light to feisty – raviolis are one of the house specialities – and desserts are sumptuous.

U Molu
BRASSERIE €€

(☏04 95 70 04 05; www.restaurant-umolu.fr; quai Paoli; mains €14-24, lunch/dinner menu €20/33; ⊗noon-2.30pm & 7-10.30pm) Poised on the marina, U Molu is rammed every lunchtime with locals and visitors alike who come for the great-value *menus* and the sensational *tartares* (finely minced raw meat or fish, served with seasoning), prepared fresh at your table. The other house speciality is fresh homemade pasta.

CORSICAN TEMPTATIONS

Cheese
Gourmands will delight in the flavours and textures of Corsican cheeses, from hard, tangy Tomme Corse (semi-hard cheese made from goat's or ewe's milk) to the king of the island's cheeses, Brocciu, a crumbly white ewe's or goat's milk cheese that can only be eaten *frais* (fresh) – a real creamy treat – between December and late June. *Sec* (dried) or *demi-sec* (half-dried) are summertime's consolation prizes. Consume Corsica's signature cheese and revel in the knowledge that Brocciu is the only French Appellation d'Origine Contrôlée (AOC) cheese made from the milk's whey.

Charcuterie
Prisuttu (ham matured for 18 months), *lonzu* (tender smoked pork fillet, best tasted in springtime), *coppa* (shoulder, air-dried for five months), seasonal *figatellu* (pork liver sausage, always U-shaped, dried and smoked over a chestnut-wood fire, eaten November to April), *salamu* (salami), *terrine de sanglier* (wild-boar pâté): wherever you go, you'll find a wide array of cured meats on offer – several seasonal – made from free-range pigs that feed on chestnuts.

Sweet Treats
From *canistrelli* (biscuits made with almonds, walnuts, lemon or aniseed) and *frappe* (little fritters made from chestnut flour) to *fiadone* (a light flan made with Brocciu cheese, lemon and egg) and *falculelli* (fried Brocciu cheese served on a chestnut leaf), Corsica's dessert menu is sure to torment the sweet tooth. Oh, and there are devilish ice creams too, with original flavours such as myrtle, Brocciu or chestnut. Glaces Geronimi (p890) in Sagone, 35km north of Ajaccio, is Corsia's most gourmet *glacier* (ice-cream maker).

Wine & Liqueurs
Corsica has nine AOC-labelled wines (including one for sweet Muscat wine) and countless fruit liqueurs, including Cap Corse Mattei, a popular aperitif (out of this world when thrown in the pot with mussels). Areas to watch out for are Patrimonio, Cap Corse, Ajaccio, Sartène and Porto-Vecchio.

Olive Oil
La Balagne and L'Alta Rocca produce extremely aromatic olive oils, available direct from the producer.

Seafood
Fish lovers will be in heaven. Lobster, oysters, mussels, squid, sea bass...Corsica has them all, but stick to reputable fish restaurants.

CORSICA L'ALTA ROCCA

Tamaricciu MEDITERRANEAN €€
(☑ 04 95 70 49 89; www.tamaricciu.com; rte de Palombaggia; mains €16-32; ⊘noon-3pm mid-Apr–mid-Oct, 7.30-10.30pm Jun-Aug) Among the various beach restaurants scattered along the Palombaggia sands south of Porto-Vecchio, Tamaricciu has that hip St-Tropez-chic touch. With its wooden decking terrace and first-class views of the turquoise surf, dining really does not get better than this. Cuisine is Mediterranean, with lots of grilled fish and meat and pasta, all beautifully presented.

🍸 Drinking & Nightlife

Le Glacier de la Place BAR
(place de l'Église; ⊘8am-11pm Jun-Aug, shorter hours rest of year) It may be called 'ice-cream parlour' but Le Glacier is more famous for its staggering selection of beers from all over the world (130 in total), as well as its numerous rums and whiskies.

Via Notte CLUB
(☑ 04 95 72 02 12; www.vianotte.com; rte de Porra; ⊘8pm-5am daily Jun-Sep) On the southern outskirts of Porto-Vecchio, Via Notte is the hottest club in Corsica, and one of the most famous in the Med. With up to 5000 revellers and superstar DJs most nights in summer, it has to be seen to be believed.

ℹ️ Information

Tourist Office (☑ 04 95 70 09 58; www.ot-portovecchio.com; rue Général Leclerc; ⊘9am-8pm Jun-Aug, 9am-noon & 2-6pm Mon-Sat Sep-May; 🛜)

ℹ️ Getting There & Away

AIR
A taxi to Aéroport de Figari-Sud-Corse, about 25km from Porto-Vecchio, will cost around €50. A seaonal shuttle bus (€10) between the airport and Porto-Vecchio's bus station also operates from April to October.

BOAT
Seasonal ferries sail from Marseille, mainland France.

BUS
All buses leave from the bus station, Gare Routière, at the northern end of the harbour.
Balési Évasion (☑ 04 95 70 15 55; rte de Bastia) Buses to Ajaccio (€22, three hours) via L'Alta Rocca (€6.30, one hour).
Eurocorse (☑ 04 95 70 13 83) Operates a service to Ajaccio (€24, 3½ hours) via Sartène.

In the other direction, buses run twice daily to Bonifacio (€9, 30 minutes).
Les Rapides Bleus (☑ 04 95 20 20 20; 16 rue Jean Jaurès) Operates two daily services to Bastia (€22, three hours) and shuttles to Plage de Palombaggia and Plage de Santa Giulia in summer.

L'Alta Rocca

If you've had a temporary surfeit of superb seascapes, take a couple of days to explore L'Alta Rocca, north of Porto-Vecchio. Here you can really feel a sense of wilderness, a world away from the bling-bling and bustle of the coast. At the south of the long spine that traverses the island, it's a bewildering combination of dense, mixed evergreen deciduous forests and granite villages strung over rocky ledges.

Les Aiguilles de Bavella

With its jagged red peaks jabbing the skyline at an altitude of more than 1600m, the Aiguilles de Bavella (Bavella Needles) are one of Corsica's most iconic landscapes. The mountain's lower slopes are covered with thick forest, making it a prime walking and climbing territory. Numerous trails leave from Col de Bavella (Bavella Pass; 1218m), from where you'll have one of the best views of the range.

🏃 Activities

Corsica Canyon CANYONING
(☑ 06 22 91 61 44; www.canyoncorse.com; Bavella, D268) Bavella is one of the best spots to do canyoning in Corsica – contact Corsica Canyon for an exhilarating day out walking, jumping and sliding through mountain gorges.

🍴 Eating

Auberge du Col de Bavella CORSICAN €
(☑ 04 95 72 09 87; www.auberge-bavella.com; Col de Bavella, D268; mains €10-23, menu €24; ⊘noon-2pm & 7-10pm Apr-Oct) Outdoor action done, feast on a roasted baby goat or wild pig stew at the Auberge du Col de Bavella, a large Corsican inn that serves excellent meat dishes in a comforting rustic setting. The central fireplace is particularly welcome on cooler spring and autumn days. Should you want to overnight, it has impeccable four- to eight-bed dorms with en suite (dorm €19).

Zonza & Around

The village of Zonza (pronounced *tzonz*) is the perfect base for exploring L'Alta Rocca with a good range of restaurants and accommodation options. Another little charmer is the nearby village of Quenza, cradled by thickly wooded mountains and the Aiguilles de Bavella looming on the horizon.

🛏 Sleeping

Hameau de Cavanello　　　　　B&B €
(🖉04 95 78 66 82; www.locationzonza.com; Hameau de Cavanello, Zonza; d €77; ❋🅟📶) For a rural setting, Hameau de Cavanello, 2km towards the Col de Bavella, has a handful of cosy rooms (equipped with fridges and TVs) and a pool nesting in hectares of green meadows and forests with magical views of the Aiguilles de Bavella.

Le Pré aux Biches　　　　CAMPGROUND €
(🖉06 27 52 48 03; www.lepreauxbiches.com; Zonza; yurt for 2/4/6 people €50/80/90; ☺May-Sep) Plump for a stylish Mongolian yurt between trees on an organic farm at Le Pré aux Biches. Each yurt has its own toilet and shower cubicle in the bathroom block; evening meals (€18) with products from the farm are available.

Hôtel du Tourisme　　　　　HOTEL €€
(🖉04 95 78 73 23; www.hoteldutourisme.fr; rte de Quenza, Zonza; d €89-139; ☺Apr-Oct; ❋🅟📶) A fantastic option right at the heart of the village, with modern, comfortable rooms and a superb pool with panoramic views.

Chez Pierrot　　　　　　　B&B €€
(🖉04 95 78 63 21; http://gitechezpierrot.free.fr; Plateau de Ghjallicu, Quenza; dm/d incl half-board €45/120) If you're after a typically Corsican atmosphere and the most tranquil location imaginable, at an altitude of about 1200m, bookmark Chez Pierrot, southern Corsica's most idiosyncratic venture. This multifaceted place – *gîte*, B&B, restaurant and equestrian centre – is run by charismatic Pierrot, a local character who's been living here since his early childhood. It's on Plateau de Ghjallicu, about 5km uphill from Quenza.

Horse-riding excursions (€45, 1½ hours) are available April to October.

🍴 Eating

Eternisula　　　　　　　　　CAFE €
(rte de Quenza, Zonza; mains from €7; ☺9am-6pm mid-Apr–Oct) For sustenance, drop by Eternisula, a gorgeous cafe-cum-gourmet shop. The brainchild of an Anglo-Corsican couple, it offers charcuterie and cheese platters, sandwiches and a suggestion of the day, served in the pretty dining room or on the terrace.

Levie & Around

For culture vultures, Levie makes a great stop for its museum and the nearby archaeological site of Pianu di Livia.

👁 Sights

Pianu di Livia　　　ARCHAEOLOGICAL SITE
(🖉04 95 78 48 21; Levie; adult/child €5.50/3; ☺9.30am-7pm Jun-Sep, to 6pm Apr, May & Oct) About 7km north of Levie, Pianu di Livia comprises two archaeological sites, the *castelli* (fortified places made up of menhirs and boulders) of Cucuruzzu and Capula. Archaeologists believe they were erected during the Bronze Age, around 1200 BC. The *castelli* are located in a beautiful forest, with an easy trail connecting the sites and information centre.

From April to October, there is an admission fee, which includes a fascinating audioguide or an interpretive booklet. Admission is free the rest of the year but there is no infrastructure for visitors. The site is signposted off the D269 between Levie and Ste-Lucie de Tallano.

Musée de l'Alta Rocca　　　　MUSEUM
(www.cg-corsedusud.fr/patrimoine-et-culture/mu-see-de-levie; av Lieutenant de Peretti, Levie; adult/child €5.50/3; ☺10am-5pm Tue-Sat Oct-May, to 6pm Jun-Sep) The well-organised Musée de l'Alta Rocca does a good job of elucidating Corsican geology, climate, flora and fauna. It also features ethnology and archaeology sections.

Ste-Lucie de Tallano　　　　VILLAGE
Ste-Lucie de Tallano has a few monuments worthy of interest, including the well-proportioned Église Ste-Lucie and the Renaissance-style Couvent St-François, an imposing building scenically positioned at the edge of the village.

🛏 Sleeping

★**Auberge U n'Antru Versu**　　B&B €
(🖉04 95 78 31 47; www.aubergeunantruversu. com; San Gavinu di Carbrini, Levie; d €65-100; ❋📶) This unexpected boutique B&B hides in a pretty village house in the hamlet of

San Gavinu di Carbrini, between Levie and Zonza. The decor is absolutely exquisite, blending modern fittings, antique furniture and plenty of colourful soft furnishings. The downstairs restaurant (mains €15) serves French cuisine and delicious pizzas and service is, like in the B&B, absolutely stellar.

★ A Pignata   BOUTIQUE HOTEL €€€
(☑04 95 78 41 90; www.apignata.com; rte du Pianu, Levie; d incl half-board from €185; ☺mid-Mar–Dec; ❈⬚🖥⭑) A real family affair fronted by brothers Antoine and Jean-Baptiste, this boutique farmhouse with vegetable garden and herd of pigs (that end up as the most divine charcuterie) is pure class. Despite its rural setting, its 18 rooms are thoroughly contemporary and its rustic restaurant (*menu* €45) is among (if not) the best in southern Corsica.

The icing on the cake is its heated pool with vast windows staring face-to-face at the Alta Rocca mountains. Heaven.

🛍 Shopping

Atelier du Lotus   CRAFTS
(☑04 95 74 05 13; Levie; ☺9am-5pm) This workshop-cum-shop, located in the village, sells gorgeous hand-made leather goods (expect €150 for a bag) and high-quality traditional knives (from €100).

CORTE AREA

Corte
POP 7225

Secretive. Inward looking. Staunchly Corsican. In many ways, the mountain town of Corte feels different to other Corsican cities. This is the heart and soul of Corsica. It has been at the centre of the island's fortunes since Pascal Paoli made it the capital of his short-lived Corsican republic in 1755, and it remains a nationalist stronghold.

Beautifully positioned at the confluence of several rivers, Corte is blessed with an amazing setting. The fairy-tale sight of the citadel atop a craggy mount that bursts forth from the valley is sensational. Despite its isolation, the town oozes atmosphere and student buzz. In summer, it's a popular base for those eager to canyon, hike, rock climb and mountain bike in the nearby Restonica and Tavignano valleys.

◉ Sights & Activities

Citadel   HISTORIC QUARTER
Jutting out above the Tavignano and Restonica Rivers, and the cobbled alleyways of the Haute Ville, the citadel's oldest part is the château – known as the Nid d'Aigle, meaning 'Eagle's Nest' – built in 1419. The 19th-century barracks now house the tourist office and the Museu di a Corsica (Museum of Corsica; ☑04 95 45 25 45; www.musee-corse.com; adult/child €5.30/1.50; ☺10am-6pm Tue-Sun Apr-Oct, shorter hours in winter), a must-see for Corsica culture buffs with its outstanding exhibition on Corsican traditions, crafts, agriculture and anthropology. It's a joint admission for the museum and citadel.

If you're not fussed about culture but would like to enjoy free views of the city and surrounding valleys, head to the belvédère (viewing platform), reached via a steep staircase just outside the citadel's ramparts (it's signposted).

Place Gaffory   SQUARE
From the citadel, meander downhill to place Gaffory, a lively square lined with restaurants and cafes and dominated by the 15th-century Église de l'Annonciation. The walls of nearby houses are pock-marked with bullet holes, reputedly from Corsica's war of independence.

Cours Paoli   STREET
A gentle wander along the main strip makes a pleasant prelude to an aperitif or a fine meal at one of the town's good restaurants. Start from place Paoli, Corte's focal point, which is dominated by a statue of Pascal Paoli, and stroll down the *cours*.

Altipiani   OUTDOOR ACTIVITIES
(☑09 60 37 08 42; www.altipiani-corse.com; 2 place Paoli) The Corte area is a mecca for the skittish. Canyoning, walking, rock climbing and mountain biking are all available in the nearby valleys, all of which Altipiani can arrange.

🛏 Sleeping

★ Osteria di l'Orta   B&B €
(☑04 95 61 06 41; www.osteria-di-l-orta.com; d €88; ❈@🖥⭑) Inside a powder-blue townhouse on the edges of town, this peach of a B&B is run by a charming couple, Marina and Antoine. The five rooms (named after local notables) are lovely, with polished wood floors, gleaming walls and great show-

ers. The guest kitchen, dining room and DVD lounge are a real bonus.

The Guelfucci family also farm the surrounding land and Marina is a mean cook so make sure you treat yourself to a delicious (and copious) dinner (€35) of Corsican specialities with products from the farm.

Camping Saint-Pancrace CAMPGROUND €
(☑04 95 46 09 22; www.campingsaintpancrace.fr; adult/tent/car €6/4/3; ☺Apr-Oct) The pick of Corte's campsites, this pretty site has only 25 pitches, all sheltering under olive trees and green oaks. It's a 20-minute walk north of town, in a peaceful neighbourhood. It isn't suitable for camper vans or caravans.

★**Hôtel Dominique Colonna** BOUTIQUE HOTEL €€
(☑04 95 45 25 65; www.dominique-colonna.com; Vallée de la Restonica; d €120-230; ☺mid-Mar–mid-Nov; ❋🛜🏊) Nature lovers could not dream of a better place to stay. Entirely refurbished in 2014, this hotel on the banks of the Restonica river is part and parcel of the landscape. The huge bay windows make you feel like you're in the canopy; the decor is all wood, stone and greens; and the river doubles up as a second pool in summer.

Brilliantly, the restaurant serves food all day to accommodate hungry trekkers and activity fiends arrived back from their adventures. Guests also get to use a separate kitchen for picnic preparation.

Hôtel Duc de Padoue HOTEL €€
(☑04 95 46 01 37; www.ducdepadoue.com; place Padoue; d/tr/q €92/125/140; ❋🛜) The Duc de Padoue lacks a little soul but then the rooms are comfortable, clean and well-equipped and the staff are charming.

✖ Eating

La Rivière des Vins BISTRO €
(☑04 95 46 37 04; 5 rampe Ste-Croix; mains €10-18, menus €14-16; ☺noon-2pm & 7-10.30pm Mon-Fri, 7-10.30pm Sat; 🍴) Diners come to this fab little bistro for the relaxed atmosphere, unbeatable value and tasty food – the *patatines* (the house roast potatoes) are to die for, as are the *brochettes* (skewered meat) cooked in the fireplace. The copious salads and omelettes will have vegetarians crying for joy. Excellent selection of wines (including by the glass/jug).

Café Le Bip's CORSICAN €
(☑04 95 46 06 26; 14 cours Paoli; mains €12-20) Want to know where students from Corsica's only university go when they fancy going out for dinner? Here, to this old stone candlelit cellar, famed across town for its gargantuan portions of traditional Corsican fare. Find it on the vast square behind cours Paoli. In winter, by the fireplace is the place to be.

Le 24 CORSICAN €€
(☑04 95 46 02 90; 24 cours Paoli; mains €16-27; ☺noon-2pm & 7-10pm Tue-Sat) After something upmarket? Then swing by this establishment on the main drag. It boasts a mix of contemporary and rustic furnishings and an innovative menu that uses top-quality ingredients and changes with the seasons. The house desserts, chalked up on the blackboard, hit the right spot.

🍷 Drinking & Nightlife

There's a lively bar scene along cours Paoli.

La Vieille Cave WINE BAR
(2 ruelle de la Fontaine; ☺11am-7pm, later if it's busy!) Sit round a barrel on a low stool in this jewel of a wine cellar and let the formidable Emmanuel Simonini guide you through the innumerable vintages on offer – to sip right there and then with a charcuterie platter or take home as a souvenir.

Le Cyrnéa BAR
(rue Prof Santiaggi; ☺11am-1am) This archetypal village bar is where students and oldies alike gather over pastis (aniseed-flavoured aperitif), myrtle liqueur, and cheap wine and beer. No points for decor (neon lighting and formica tables) but plenty for atmosphere and a patio out back.

Café du Cours CAFE
(22 cours Paoli; ☺7am-10pm) This unfussy cafe is a great place to watch the world go by.

ℹ Information

Tourist Office (☑04 95 46 26 70; www.corte-tourisme.com; Citadel; ☺9am-noon & 2-5pm Mon-Fri Sep-Jun, 8.30am-6.30pm Mon-Sat Jul & Aug)

ℹ Getting There & Away

BUS

Eurocorse Voyages Buses go to Bastia (€11.50, 1¼ hours) and Ajaccio (€12, 1¾ hours).

TRAIN

Three to four daily trains serve Bastia (€5.10, two hours) and Ajaccio (€11.50, two hours).

LONG-DISTANCE TRAIL TASTER

Corsica's long-distance trails, especially the north-south, two-week GR20, are legendary. But fitting two weeks of walking into a holiday may not be possible (or desirable!) for everyone. Spending a night in a refuge is a great experience, however, and **Refuge A Sega** (☑ 06 10 71 77 26, 09 88 99 35 57; www.parc-corse.org; dm €13; ☺ Jun-Sep) is a great option to get a taste of the hiker's life and to combine two of central Corsica's most scenic valleys in one easy, two-day itinerary.

Day one is a five-hour walk from Corte up the stunning Vallée du Tavignano, following the Mare a Mare itinerary orange waymarks. You can break up for a picnic at the **Passerelle de Rossolino**. Upon arriving at the refuge (spaces must be booked in advance online), you'll be able to indulge in a swim in the nearby natural pools or simply revel in the lovely scenery before tucking into a three-course Corsican dinner (€25), cooked by the host. You can also order a picnic (€15) for the next day. Breakfast is €8.

On day two, head east to the **Bergeries d'Alzu** (sheepfold; two hours), before heading down to the **Vallée de la Restonica** (one hour) and then back to Corte along the scenic D623 (two hours).

Around Corte

In the mountainous area around Corte you'll find fresh mountain air, deep forests, picturesque valleys and abundant hiking trails. Enjoy the scenery and rejuvenate mind and body in a pristine environment.

Vallée de la Restonica

The Vallée de la Restonica is one of the prettiest spots in all of Corsica. The river, rising in the grey-green mountains, has scoured little basins in the rock, offering sheltered pinewood settings for bathing and sunbathing. From Corte, the D623 winds its way through the valley for 15km to the **Bergeries de Grotelle** (1375m), where a car park (€5) and a huddle of shepherd's huts (three of which offer drinks, local cheeses and snacks) marks the end of the road. From them, a path leads to a pair of picture-pretty glacial lakes, **Lac de Melu** (1711m), reached after about one hour, and **Lac de Capitellu** (1930m), 45 minutes' walk further on. Depending on snowfall, the first lake can usually be reached from April to October, the second from May onwards. Always check the weather with the tourist office before setting off.

Vallée du Tavignano

If you have a day to spare, don't miss the opportunity to hike into the car-free (and much quieter than Restonica) Vallée du Tavignano. Corsica's deepest gorge is only accessible on foot and remains well off the beaten track, despite being on Corte's doorstep. From Corte, the signposted track leads to the **Passerelle de Rossolino** footbridge, reached after about 2½ hours. It's an idyllic spot for a picnic, and there are plenty of transparent green natural pools in which you can dunk yourself. The valley can also be explored on horseback with the outdoorsy folks behind the lovely B&B and *camping à la ferme*, **L'Albadu** (☑ 04 95 46 24 55; www.hebergement-albadu.fr; ancienne rte d'Ajaccio; d incl half-board per person €50, camping adult/tent/car €5.50/2.50/2.50).

Vizzavona

South of Corte, the N193 climbs steeply in the shadow of **Monte d'Oro** (2389m) before arriving at the cool mountain hamlet of Vizzavona. A mere cluster of houses and hotels around a train station, Vizzavona is an ideal base from which to explore the **Forêt de Vizzavona**, where the 1633 hectares are covered mainly by beech and laricio pines. A magnet for walkers, it features lots of excellent hikes. Look for the signpost indicating a short, gentle path that meanders down through a superb forest to **Cascades des Anglais**, a sequence of gleaming waterfalls.

Understand France

France Today

France has by no means escaped the global economic crisis and unexpected rise in Europe of the far-right. But this ancient country of timeless Gallic pride and tradition has weathered greater storms – and the French are not resting on their laurels. It's all hands on deck: economists are rethinking austerity, politicians redrawing the local-government map, and Parisians bringing in the city's first woman mayor. Times are a changing in *la belle France*.

Best in Print

The Hundred Foot Journey (Richard C Morais; 2010) A boy from Mumbai opens a restaurant in a remote French village – opposite the restaurant of a famous chef. Culinary warfare!

Paris (Edward Rutherford; 2013) Few novels pack in eight centuries of history – and still entertain. This book on the French capital does both.

A Moveable Feast (Ernest Hemingway; 1964) Beautiful evocation of 1920s Paris by the American writer.

Best in Film

La Môme (La Vie en Rose; 2007) Story of singer Edith Piaf, from Paris waif to New York superstar, starring French actress Marion Cotillard.

Coco Avant Chanel (Coco Before Chanel; 2009) French blockbuster packed with French talent; the compelling life story of orphan-turned-fashion designer Coco Chanel, starring French actress Audrey Tautou.

Midnight in Paris (2011) Woody Allen tale about one family's trip to Paris, with standout dream scenes set in the capital in the 1920s.

Hugo (2011) Martin Scorsese's Oscar-winning children's film pays tribute to Parisian film pioneer Georges Méliès through the remarkable adventure of an orphan boy in the 1930s who tends the clocks at a Paris train station.

A Political Earthquake

Political elections in 2014 threw up interesting results in France. April's municipal elections saw the vast majority of the country swing decisively to the right – a powerful commentary on the 'success' of socialist president François Hollande (b 1954) since assuming office in early 2012. Paris stuck with Hollande, remaining resolutely left (for a third term) following a compelling campaign race between two brilliant women: Spanish-born deputy mayor Anne Hidalgo and former ecology minister Nathalie Kosciusko-Morizet. The charismatic Hidalgo – brazenly open, forward-thinking and a big conversationalist on Twitter (@Anne_Hidalgo) – landed 55% of votes and became Paris' first female mayor.

European elections a month later packed a punch: the far-right National Front won a quarter of votes, leaving the governing left-wing Socialists in third place. French prime minister Manuel Valls was reported in the press as describing the victory of the far-right party, known for its fervent anti-immigrant stance, as 'a political earthquake in France'.

Economic Woes

Hollande has yet to fulfil his electoral promise of reducing unemployment and faces a gargantuan amount of work if he is to clear the country's debts by 2017 as pledged. Unemployment reached a record high in early 2014 and there was zero growth in the economy in the first three months of the year. The government increased corporation tax, VAT and income tax – most controversially to 75% for salaries of more than €1 million a year – to raise an extra €16 billion in 2013 for state coffers. Unfortunately the revenue was not quite the amount the government had forecast – it was, in fact, €14 billion short.

Countrywide train strikes brought France to a standstill in June 2014 as rail workers protested government proposals to restructure the national railway system, controlled by state-owned railway SNCF. Opening up markets to competition is a high priority for Hollande and the stagnant economy he needs to revive his term in office.

Shifting Borders
The future map of France could be very different. Questioning whether an antiquated structure of local government harking back to the 1789 constitution really was the best way for France to move forward in the future, Prime Minister Manuel Valls unveiled a new administrative map of metropolitan France (the mainland and Corsica) in June 2014 – in which the country's current 22 *régions* (regions) – grouping 96 *départements,* each ruled by a Paris-appointed préfet (prefect) – were reduced to 14.

This so-called *redécoupage territorial* sparked off a flurry of regionalist sentiment and emotion among the French, most notably in Brittany where Bretons would find themselves with Pays de la Loire; in northeastern France where Germanic Alsace and dramatically different Lorraine next door would become one *région;* and in Languedoc-Roussillon, which would be fused with the Midi-Pyrénées, except that the natural inclination of main town Nîmes and surrounds is the opposite direction, towards Provence. With a date of completion set for 2020, the debate is clearly not over.

Growth & Renewal
Champagne vineyards will become Unesco protected if the region's bid to become a World Heritage Site in 2015 is successful. Meanwhile, such is the growing global demand for bubbly that Champagne has been given the go ahead to expand its production area for the first time since 1927. The first new vines will be planted in 40 new Champagne-producing villages in 2017.

Urban growth and renewal is as exciting: Paris is mad about riverside-renaissance project, Les Berges de Seine; in Marseille the 2013 redevelopment of the sea-faring Joliette *quartier* is breathtaking; and in Lyon the development of the Confluence *quartier* – with signature roof-top dance club atop a 1930s sugar factory – continues with energy-efficient contemporary architecture and three bridges, one only for cyclists and pedestrians, to link the rejuvenated riverside wasteland with the rest of the city.

AREA: **551,000 SQ KM**

POPULATION: **63.9 MILLION**

GDP: **US$2739.27 BILLION**

GDP GROWTH: **0%**

INFLATION: **0.9%**

UNEMPLOYMENT: **10.1%**

if France were 100 people

77 would live in cities
23 would live in rural areas

belief systems
(% of population)

87 Roman Catholic

2 Jewish

1 Protestant

10 Muslim

population per sq km

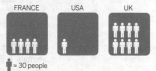

FRANCE   USA   UK

🧍 ≈ 30 people

History

The history of France mirrors pretty much that of much of Europe. Its beginnings saw the mass migration of the nomadic Celts, the subjugation by and the civilising influence of the Romans, and the rise of a local nobility. Christianity brought a degree of unity, but nowhere else would such a strongly independent church continue to coexist under a powerful central authority (think Charles 'The Hammer' Martel or Louis XIV's claim to be the state itself). This is the essence of France's story.

Best History Museums

MuCEM, Marseille

Musée Carnavalet, Paris

Musée d'Art et d'Histoire, Bayeux

Mémorial – Un Musée pour la Paix, Caen

Centre d'Histoire de la Résistance et de la Déportation, Lyon

Roman Gaul

What is now France was settled by several different groups of people in the Iron Age, but the largest and most organised were the Celtic Gauls. The subjugation of these people and their territory by Rome was gradual, and within a few centuries Rome had imposed its government, roads, trade, culture and even language. A Gallo-Roman culture emerged and Gaul was increasingly integrated into the Roman Empire.

It began in the 1st millennium BC as the Greeks and Romans established colonies on the Mediterranean coast, including Massilia (Marseille). Centuries of conflict between the Gauls and the Romans ended in 52 BC when Caesar's legions crushed a revolt by many Gallic tribes led by Celtic Arverni tribe chief Vercingétorix at Gergovia, near present-day Clermont-Ferrand – no site better evokes the drama and bloodshed of this momentous point in history than the MuséoParc Alésia in Burgundy. For the next couple of years, during the Gallic Wars, the Gauls hounded the Romans with guerrilla warfare and fought them in several match-drawn pitched battles. But gradually Gallic resistance collapsed and the Romans reigned supreme.

The stone architecture left by the occupiers was impressive and Roman France is magnificent, climaxing with the mighty Pont du Gard aqueduct, built to bring water to the city of Nîmes in southern France. Splendid theatres and amphitheatres dating from this period are still extant in that city as well as at Autun, Arles and Orange. Some Roman remains were reused: in an early form of recycling, the 1st-century Ro-

TIMELINE	c 30,000 BC	c 7000 BC	1500–500 BC
	During the middle Palaeolithic period, Cro-Magnon people start decorating their homes in the Vézère Valley of the Dordogne with colourful scenes of animals, human figures and geometric shapes.	Neolithic man turns his hand to monumental menhirs and dolmen during the New Stone Age, creating a fine collection in Brittany that continues to baffle historians.	Celtic Gauls move into the region and establish trading links with the Greeks, whose colonies included Massilia (Marseille) on the Mediterranean coast; the latter bring grapes and olives.

man amphitheatre at Périgueux in the Dordogne was dismantled in the 3rd century and its stones used to build the city walls.

Sophisticated urban centres with markets and baths of hot and cold running water began to emerge. The Romans planted vineyards, notably in Burgundy and Bordeaux; introduced techniques to process wine; and introduced the newfangled faith of Christianity.

Later the Franks would adopt these important elements of Gallo-Roman civilisation (including Christianity), and their eventual assimilation resulted in a fusion of Germanic culture with that of the Celts and the Romans.

The Agony & the Ecstasy: Medieval France

The collapse of the Roman Empire opened the gates to a wave of Franks and other Germanic tribes under Merovius from the north and northeast. Merovius' grandson, Clovis I, converted to Christianity, giving him greater legitimacy and power over his Christian subjects, and made Paris his seat; his successors founded the abbey of St-Germain des Prés in Paris and later the one at St-Denis to the north, which would become the richest, most important monastery in France and the final resting place of its kings.

The Frankish tradition, by which the king was succeeded by all of his sons, led to power struggles and the eventual disintegration of the kingdom into a collection of small feudal states. The dominant house to emerge was that of the Carolingians.

Prehistory Sights

Vézère Valley, Dordogne

Carnac, Brittany

Filitosa, Corsica

Vallée de l'Ariège, Pyrenees

Musée de Préhistoire de Solutré, near Mâcon

Musée de Tautavel, near Perpignan

Le Carroi Musée, Chinon

HISTORY THE AGONY & THE ECSTASY: MEDIEVAL FRANCE

PRIMITIVE ART

The Cro-Magnons, a *Homo sapiens* variety who arrived in what is now France about 35,000 years ago, had larger brains than their ancestors, the Neanderthals, long and narrow skulls, and short, wide faces. Their hands were nimble, and with the aid of improved tools they hunted reindeer, bison, horses and mammoths to eat. They played music, danced and had fairly complex social patterns.

Those agile hands were not just used to make tools and hunt; Cro-Magnons were also artists. A tour of Grotte de Lascaux II – a replica of the Lascaux cave in which one of the world's best examples of Cro-Magnon drawings was found in 1940 – demonstrates how initial simplistic drawings and engravings of animals gradually became more detailed and realistic. Dubbed 'Périgord's Sistine Chapel', the Lascaux cave contains some 2000 paintings of human figures and abstract signs, as well as animals, and is one of 25 known decorated caves in Dordogne's Vézère Valley.

The Neolithic period produced France's incredible collection of menhirs and dolmens: Brittany's Morbihan Coast is awash in megalithic monuments.

3rd century BC	121 BC	55–52 BC	c AD 100–300
The Celtic Parisii tribe builds a handful of wattle-and-daub huts on what is now the Île de la Cité in Paris; the capital city is christened Lutetia by the Romans.	The Romans begin taking Gallic territory, annexing southern Gaul as the province of Gallia Narbonensis (in modern Provence and Languedoc), with its capital at the present-day town of Narbonne.	Julius Caesar launches his invasion of Britain from the Côte d'Opale in far northern France; the Gauls defeat the Romans at Gergovia near present-day Clermont-Ferrand.	The Romans go on a building spree throughout France, erecting magnificent baths, temples and aqueducts of almighty proportions such as the Pont du Gard near Nîmes in southern France.

Best Roman Sights

Fourvière, Lyon

Pont du Gard, near Nîmes

Les Arènes & Maison Carrée, Nîmes

Musée Gallo-Romain & Théâtre Romain, Vienne

Théâtre Antique, Orange

Théâtre Antique, Arles

Musée Gallo-Romain Vesunna, Périgueux

Carolingian power reached apogee under Charlemagne, who extended the boundaries of the kingdom and was crowned Holy Roman Emperor (Emperor of the West) in 800. But during the 9th century Scandinavian Vikings (also called Norsemen, thus Normans) raided France's western coast, settling in the lower Seine Valley and later forming the duchy of Normandy. This would be a century of disunity in France, marked politically by the rise of Norman power and religiously by the foundation of influential abbeys such as the Benedictine one at Cluny. By the time Hugh Capet ascended the throne in 987, the king's domain was a humble parcel of land around Paris and Orléans.

The tale of how William the Conqueror and his forces mounted a successful invasion of England from their base in Normandy in 1066 is told on the Bayeux Tapestry, showcased inside Bayeux' Musée de la Tapisserie de Bayeux. In 1152 Eleanor of Aquitaine wed Henry of Anjou, bringing a further third of France under the control of the English crown. The subsequent rivalry between France and England for control of Aquitaine and the vast English territories in France lasted three centuries.

Hundred Years War

In 1337 hostility between the Capetians and the Anglo-Normans degenerated into the Hundred Years War, fought on and off until the middle of the 15th century. The Black Death, which broke out a decade after the hostilities began and lasted more than two years, killed more than a third (an estimated 80,000 souls) of Paris' population alone.

The French suffered particularly nasty defeats at Crécy and Agincourt. Abbey-studded Mont St-Michel in present-day Normandy was the only place in northern and western France not to fall into English hands. The dukes of Burgundy (allied with the English) occupied Paris and in 1422 John Plantagenet, duke of Bedford, was made regent of France for England's King Henry VI, then an infant. Less than a decade later Henry was crowned king of France.

Luckily for the French, 17-year-old Jeanne d'Arc (Joan of Arc) came along with the outlandish tale that she had a divine mission from God to expel the English from France and bring about the coronation of French Charles VII in Reims.

The Rise of the French Court

With the arrival of Italian Renaissance culture during the reign of François I (r 1515–47), the focus shifted to the Loire Valley. Italian artists decorated royal castles at Amboise, Azay-le-Rideau, Blois, Chambord and Chaumont.

No single museum evokes medieval France more beautifully than Paris' Musée National du Moyen Age, aptly located in the capital's finest civil medieval building, the 15th-century Hôtel Cluny.

c 455–70	732	800–900	987
France remains under Roman rule until the 5th century, when the Franks (hence the name 'France') and the Alemanii invade the country and overrun the country from the east.	Somewhere near Poitiers, Charles Martel and his cavalry repel the Muslim Moors. His grandson, Charlemagne, extends the boundaries of the kingdom and is crowned Holy Roman Emperor.	Scandinavian Vikings (also called Norsemen, thus Normans) raid France's western coast and settle in the lower Seine Valley where they later form the Duchy of Normandy.	Five centuries of Merovingian and Carolingian rule ends with the crowning of Hugh Capet; a dynasty that will rule one of Europe's most powerful countries for the next eight centuries is born.

THE VIRGIN WARRIOR

Many stories surround the origins of Jeanne d'Arc (Joan of Arc), the legendary *pucelle* (virgin) warrior burned at the stake by the English, and France's patron saint. Some say she was the bastard child of Louis d'Orléans, King Charles VI's brother. The less glamorous but more accurate account pinpoints Domrémy in northeastern France (Domrémy-la-Pucelle today) as the place where she was born to a simple peasant family in 1412.

Revelations delivered by the Archangel Michael prompted Jeanne d'Arc to flee the fold in 1428. Her mission: to raise a siege against the city of Orléans and see the dauphin (the future Charles VII) crowned king of France. An enquiry conducted by clergy and university clerks in Poitiers tried to establish if Jeanne d'Arc was a fraud or a gift, as she claimed, from the king of Heaven to the king of France. Her virginity was likewise certified. Following the six-week interrogation Jeanne was sent by Charles VII to Tours, where she was equipped with intendants, a horse, a sword and her own standard featuring God sitting in judgement on a cloud. In Blois the divine warrior collected her army, drummed up by Charles VII from his Royal Army Headquarters there. In April 1429 Jeanne d'Arc started her attack on Orléans, besieged by the English from October of the previous year. She entered the city, rallying its inhabitants and gaining their support. On 5 and 6 May respectively the French gained control of the Bastille St-Loup and the Bastille des Augustins, followed the next day by the legendary Fort des Tourelles – a fort guarding the only access to the city from the left bank. This last shattering defeat prompted the English to lay down the siege on 8 May and was a decisive turning point in the Hundred Years War.

From Orléans Jeanne d'Arc went on to defeat the English at Jargeau, Beaugency and Patay. Charles VII stayed at châteaux in Loches and Sully-sur-Loire at this time and prayed to St Benedict with his protégé at Abbaye de St-Benoît in St-Benoît-sur-Loire. Despite Charles' promised coronation in July 1429, battles between the English and the French waged until 1453, by which time the virginal warrior responsible for turning the war around had long been dead. Jeanne d'Arc was captured by the Burgundians, sold to the English, convicted of witchcraft and heresy by a tribunal of French ecclesiastics in Rouen in 1431 and burned at the stake. She was canonised in 1920.

Renaissance ideas of scientific and geographic scholarship and discovery assumed a new importance, as did the value of secular matters over religious life. Writers such as Rabelais, Marot and Ronsard of La Pléiade were influential, as were artist and architect disciples of Michelangelo and Raphael. Evidence of this architectural influence can be seen in François I's château at Fontainebleau – where superb artisans, many of them brought over from Italy, blended Italian and French styles to create the First School of Fontainebleau – and the Petit Château at Chantilly, both near Paris. This new architecture reflected

1066	1095	1152	1163
Duke of Normandy William the Conqueror and his Norman forces occupy England, making Normandy and, later, Plantagenet-ruled England formidable rivals of the kingdom of France.	Pope Urban II preaches the First Crusade in Clermont-Ferrand, prompting France to take a leading role and giving rise to some splendid cathedrals, including those at Reims, Strasbourg, Metz and Chartres.	Eleanor of Aquitaine weds Henry of Anjou, bringing a further third of France under the control of the English crown and sparking a French-English rivalry that will last three centuries.	Two centuries of nonstop building in the capital reaches its zenith with the start of Notre Dame Cathedral under Maurice de Sully, the bishop of Paris; construction continues for 150-odd years.

the splendour of the monarchy, which was fast moving towards absolutism. But all this grandeur and show of strength was not enough to stem the tide of Protestantism that was flowing into France.

The Reformation swept through Europe in the 1530s, spearheaded by the ideas of Jean (John) Calvin, a Frenchman born in Picardy but exiled to Geneva. Following the Edict of January 1562, which afforded the Protestants certain rights, the Wars of Religion broke out between the Huguenots (French Protestants who received help from the English), the Catholic League (led by the House of Guise) and the Catholic monarchy, and lasted three dozen years.

Henri IV, founder of the Bourbon dynasty, issued the controversial Edict of Nantes in 1598, guaranteeing the Huguenots civil and political rights, notably freedom of conscience. Ultra-Catholic Paris refused to allow the new Protestant king to enter the city, and a siege of the capital continued for almost five years. Only when Henri IV embraced Catholicism at the cathedral in St-Denis did the capital submit to him.

France's most famous king of this or any other century, Louis XIV (r 1643–1715), called Le Roi Soleil (the Sun King), ascended the throne at the tender age of five. Bolstered by claims of divine right, he involved the kingdom in a series of costly wars with Holland, Austria and England, which gained France territory but nearly bankrupted the treasury. State taxation to refill the coffers caused widespread poverty and vagrancy. In Versailles, Louis XIV built an extravagant palace and made his courtiers compete with each other for royal favour, thereby quashing the ambitious, feuding aristocracy and creating the first centralised French state. In 1685 he revoked the Edict of Nantes.

The Seven Years War (1756–63) was one of a series of ruinous military engagements pursued by Louis XV, the Sun King's grandson. It led to the loss of France's flourishing colonies in Canada, the West Indies and India. It was in part to avenge these losses that his successor Louis XVI sided with the colonists in the American War of Independence a dozen years later. But the Seven Years War cost France a fortune and, more disastrously for the monarchy, it helped to disseminate at home the radical democratic ideas that were thrust upon the world stage by the American Revolution.

Revolution to Republic

As the 18th century progressed, new economic and social circumstances rendered the *ancien régime* (old order) dangerously out of step with the needs of the country. The regime was further weakened by the anti-establishment and anticlerical ideas of the Enlightenment, whose leading lights included Voltaire, Rousseau and Diderot. But entrenched vested interests, a cumbersome power structure and royal lassitude pre-

---

Between 1830 and 1900 dozens of Americans crossed the Atlantic to find inspiration in the 'city of light'. Read their compelling tale in David McCullough's *The Greater Journey: Americans in Paris.*

Best Walled Towns

....

Carcassonne

....

Avignon

....

St-Malo

....

Domme, Dordogne

....

Uzerche, Limousin

1309	1337	1358	1422
French-born Pope Clément V moves papal headquarters from Rome to Avignon, where the Holy Seat remains until 1377; 'home' is the resplendent Palais des Papes built under Benoît XII.	Incessant struggles between the Capetians and England's King Edward III, a Plantagenet, over the powerful French throne degenerate into the Hundred Years War, which will last until 1453.	The war between France and England and the devastation and poverty caused by the plague lead to the ill-fated peasants' revolt led by Étienne Marcel.	John Plantagenet, duke of Bedford, is made regent of France for England's King Henry VI, then an infant; in less than a decade Henry is crowned king of France at Paris' Notre Dame.

vented change from starting until the 1770s, by which time the monarchy's moment had passed.

By the late 1780s, the indecisive Louis XVI and his dominating consort, Marie-Antoinette, had managed to alienate virtually every segment of society, and the king became increasingly isolated as unrest and dissatisfaction reached boiling point. When he tried to neutralise the power of the more reform-minded delegates at a meeting of the États-Généraux (States-General) in Versailles in May and June 1789, the masses took to the streets of Paris. On 14 July, a mob raided the armoury at the Hôtel des Invalides for rifles, seizing 32,000 muskets, then stormed the prison at Bastille – the ultimate symbol of the despotic *ancien régime*. The French Revolution had begun.

At first, the Revolution was in the hands of moderate republicans called the Girondins. France was declared a constitutional monarchy and various reforms were introduced, including the adoption of the Déclaration des Droits de l'Homme et du Citoyen (Declaration of the Rights of Man and of the Citizen) modelled on the American Declaration of Independence. But as the masses armed themselves against the external threat to the new government – posed by Austria, Prussia and the exiled French nobles – patriotism and nationalism mixed with extreme fervour, popularising and radicalising the Revolution. It was not long before the Girondins lost out to the extremist Jacobins, who abolished the monar-

Historic Bridges

Pont Neuf, Paris

Pont St-Benézet, Avignon

Pont de Millau, Millau

Pont d'Arc, Gorges de l'Ardèche

Pont de Normandie, between Le Havre and Honfleur

HISTORY REVOLUTION TO REPUBLIC

A DATE WITH THE REVOLUTION

Along with standardising France's system of weights and measures with the now almost universal metric system, the revolutionary government adopted a new, 'more rational' calendar from which all 'superstitious' associations (ie saints' days and mythology) were removed. Year 1 began on 22 September 1792, the day the First Republic was proclaimed.

The names of the 12 months – Vendémaire, Brumaire, Frimaire, Nivôse, Pluviôse, Ventôse, Germinal, Floréal, Prairial, Messidor, Thermidor and Fructidor – were chosen according to the seasons. The autumn months, for instance, were Vendémaire (derived from *vendange*, grape harvest), Brumaire (from *brume*, mist or fog) and Frimaire (from *frimas*, wintry weather). In turn, each month was divided into three 10-day 'weeks' called *décades*, the last day of which was a rest day. The five remaining days of the year were used to celebrate Virtue, Genius, Labour, Opinion and Rewards. These festivals were initially called *sans-culottides* in honour of the *sans-culottes*, the extreme revolutionaries who wore pantaloons rather than the short breeches favoured by the upper classes.

While the republican calendar worked well in theory, it caused no end of confusion for France in its communications and trade abroad because the months and days kept changing in relation to those of the Gregorian calendar. The revolutionary calendar was abandoned and the old system restored in 1806 by Napoléon Bonaparte.

1431	1515	1530s	1572
Jeanne d'Arc (Joan of Arc) is burned at the stake in Rouen for heresy; the English are not driven out of France until 1453.	With the reign of François I the royal court moves to the Loire Valley, where a rash of stunning Renaissance châteaux and hunting lodges is built.	The Reformation, spurred by the writings of French Jean (John) Calvin, sweeps through France, pitting Catholics against Protestants and eventually leading to the Wars of Religion (1562–98).	Some 3000 Huguenots visiting Paris to celebrate the wedding of the Protestant Henri of Navarre (the future Henri IV) are slaughtered on 23–24 August, in the so-called St Bartholomew's Day Massacre.

chy and declared the First Republic after Louis XVI proved unreliable as a constitutional monarch. The Assemblée Nationale (National Assembly) was replaced by an elected Revolutionary Convention.

In January 1793 Louis XVI was convicted of 'conspiring against the liberty of the nation' and guillotined on place de la Révolution, today's place de la Concorde, in Paris. Two months later the Jacobins set up the Committee of Public Safety to deal with national defence and to apprehend and try 'traitors'. This body had dictatorial control over the country during the so-called Reign of Terror (September 1793 to July 1794), which saw religious freedoms revoked and churches desecrated, cathedrals turned into 'Temples of Reason', and thousands incarcerated in dungeons in Paris' Conciergerie on Île de la Cité before being beheaded.

After the Reign of Terror faded, a five-man delegation of moderate republicans set itself up to rule the republic as the Directoire (Directory).

Napoléon & Empire

It was true happenstance that brought dashing young Corsican general, Napoléon Bonaparte, to the attention of France. In October 1795 a group of royalist youths bent on overthrowing the Directory were intercepted on rue St-Honoré in Paris by forces under Bonaparte, who fired into the crowd. For this 'whiff of grapeshot' he was put in command of the French forces in Italy, where he was particularly successful in the campaign against Austria.

In 1799 Napoléon overthrew the Directory and assumed power as First Consul, chosen by popular vote. A referendum three years later declared him 'Consul for Life' and his birthday became a national holiday. In 1804, when he crowned himself 'Emperor of the French' in the presence of Pope Pius VII at Notre Dame in Paris, the scope of Napoléon's ambitions were obvious to all.

To legitimise his authority, Napoléon needed more battlefield victories. So began a series of wars and victories by which France would come to control most of Europe. In 1812 his troops captured Moscow, only to be killed off by the Russian winter. Two years later Allied armies entered Paris, exiled Napoléon to Elba in the Mediterranean and restored the House of Bourbon to the French throne at the Congress of Vienna.

In early 1815 Napoléon escaped Elba, landed in southern France and gathered a large army as he marched towards Paris. On 1 June he reclaimed the throne. But his reign ended just three weeks later when his forces were defeated at Waterloo in Belgium. Napoléon was exiled again, this time to St Helena in the South Atlantic, where he died in 1821. In 1840 his remains were moved to the Hôtel des Invalides in Paris.

Although reactionary in some ways – he re-established slavery in France's colonies in 1802, for example – Napoléon instituted a number

Renaissance superstar, Leonardo da Vinci, made Le Clos Lucé in Amboise, in the Loire Valley, his home for three years until his death in 1519.

SUN KING

The Sun King was yet another Louis named after France's patron saint. Paintings in Versailles' Royal Chapel evoke the idea that the king was chosen by God, thus was His lieutenant on earth.

1588	1589	1598	1635
The Catholic League forces Henri III (r 1574–89), the last of the Valois kings, to flee the royal court at the Louvre; the next year he is assassinated by a fanatical Dominican friar.	Henri IV, the first Bourbon king, ascends the throne after renouncing Protestantism; 'Paris vaut bien une messe' (Paris is well worth a Mass), he is reputed to have said upon taking communion.	Henri IV gives French Protestants freedom of conscience with the Edict of Nantes – much to the horror of staunchly Catholic Paris, where many refuse to acknowledge the forward-thinking document.	Cardinal Richelieu, de-facto ruler during the reign of Henri IV's son, Louis XIII, founds the Académie Française, the first and best known of France's five institutes of arts and sciences.

of important reforms, including a reorganisation of the judicial system; the promulgation of a new legal code, the Code Napoléon (or civil code), which forms the basis of the French legal system to this day; and the establishment of a new educational system. More importantly, he preserved the essence of the changes brought about by the Revolution.

A struggle between extreme monarchists seeking a return to the *ancien régime*, people who saw the changes wrought by the Revolution as irreversible, and the radicals of the poor working-class neighbourhoods of Paris dominated the reign of Louis XVIII (r 1815–24). His successor Charles X responded to the conflict with ineptitude and was overthrown in the so-called July Revolution of 1830. Those who were killed in the accompanying Paris street battles are buried in vaults under the Colonne de Juillet in the centre of place de la Bastille. Louis-Philippe, a constitutional monarch of bourgeois sympathies who followed him, was subsequently chosen as ruler by parliament, only to be ousted by the 1848 Revolution.

The Second Republic was established and elections brought in Napoléon's inept nephew, the German-reared (and accented) Louis Napoléon Bonaparte, as president. In 1851 he staged a coup d'état and proclaimed himself Emperor Napoléon III of the Second Empire, which lasted until 1870.

Like his uncle before him, Napoléon III embroiled France in a number of costly conflicts, including the disastrous Crimean War (1854–56). In 1870 Otto von Bismarck goaded Napoléon III into declaring war on

BLACK DEATH

The Black Death was one of several epidemics to menace France. In 1720 the Great Plague sailed into Marseille. Find out what happened at the Musée Regard en Provence in the port's former sanitary station.

THE KINDEST CUT

Hanging, then drawing and quartering – roping the victim's limbs to four oxen, which then ran in four different directions – was once the favoured method of publicly executing commoners. In a bid to make public executions more humane, French physician Joseph Ignace Guillotin (1738–1814) came up with the guillotine.

Several tests on dead bodies down the line, highwayman Nicolas Jacques Pelletie was the first in France to have his head sliced off by the 2m-odd falling blade on 25 April 1792 on place de Grève (today's place de l'Hôtel de Ville) in Paris. During the Reign of Terror, at least 17,000 met their death by guillotine.

By the time the last person in France to be guillotined (murderer Hamida Djandoubi in Marseille) was given the chop in 1977 (behind closed doors – the last public execution was in 1939), the lethal contraption had been sufficiently refined to slice off a head in 2/100 of a second. A real McCoy guillotine is displayed in the Galerie de la Méditerraneé of Marseille's MuCEM.

France abolished capital punishment in 1981.

1643	1756–63	1789	1793
The Roi Soleil (Sun King), Louis XIV, all of five years old, assumes the French throne. In 1682 he moves his court – lock, stock and satin slipper – from Paris' Palais des Tuileries to Versailles.	The Seven Years War against Britain and Prussia sees Louis XV engage in several ruinous wars resulting in the loss of France's colonies in Canada, the West Indies and India.	The French Revolution begins when a mob arms itself with weapons taken from the Hôtel des Invalides and storms the prison at Bastille, freeing a total of just seven prisoners.	Louis XVI is tried and convicted as citizen 'Louis Capet' (as all kings since Hugh Capet were declared to have ruled illegally) and executed; Marie-Antoinette's turn comes nine months later.

Prussia. Within months the thoroughly unprepared French army was defeated and the emperor had been taken prisoner.

The Belle Époque

Though it ushered in the glittering belle époque (beautiful age), there was little else attractive about the start of the Third Republic. Born as a provisional government of national defence in September 1870, it was quickly besieged by the Prussians, who laid siege to Paris and demanded National Assembly elections be held. The first move made by the resultant monarchist-controlled assembly was to ratify the Treaty of Frankfurt. The terms of the treaty – a huge war indemnity and surrender of the provinces of Alsace and Lorraine – prompted immediate revolt (known as the Paris Commune), during which several thousand Communards were killed and another 20,000 executed.

The belle époque launched art nouveau architecture, a whole field of artistic 'isms' from impressionism onwards, and advances in science and engineering, including the construction of the first metro line in Paris. World Exhibitions were held in the capital in 1889 (showcased by the Eiffel Tower) and again in 1901 in the purpose-built Petit Palais.

But all was not well in the republic. France was consumed with a desire for revenge after its defeat by Germany, and looking for scapegoats. The so-called Dreyfus Affair began in 1894 when Jewish army captain

THE MAGINOT LINE

···

The Ligne Maginot, named after France's minister of war from 1929 to 1932, was one of the most spectacular blunders of WWII. This elaborate, mostly subterranean defence network, built between 1930 and 1940 (and, in the history of military architecture, second only to the Great Wall of China in sheer size), was the pride of prewar France. It included everything France's finest military architects thought would be needed to defend the nation in a 'modern war' of poison gas, tanks and aeroplanes: reinforced concrete bunkers, subterranean lines of supply and communication, minefields, antitank canals, floodable basins and even artillery emplacements that popped out of the ground to fire and then disappeared. The only things visible above ground were firing posts and lookout towers. The line stretched along the Franco-German frontier from the Swiss border all the way to Belgium where, for political and budgetary reasons, it stopped. The Maginot Line even had a slogan: 'Ils ne passeront pas' (They won't get through).

'They' – the Germans – never did. Rather than attack the Maginot Line straight on, Hitler's armoured divisions simply circled around through Belgium and invaded France across its unprotected northern frontier. They then attacked the Maginot Line from the rear.

1795	1799	1815	1851
A five-man delegation of moderate republicans led by Paul Barras sets itself up as the Directoire (Directory) and rules the First Republic for five years.	Napoléon Bonaparte dismisses the Directory and seizes control of the government in a coup d'état, opening the doors to 16 years of despotic rule, victory and then defeat on the battlefield.	British and Prussian forces under the Duke of Wellington defeat Napoléon at Waterloo; he is exiled to a remote island in the South Atlantic where he dies six years later.	Louis Napoléon leads a coup d'état and proclaims himself Emperor Napoléon III of the Second Empire (1852–70), a period of significant economic growth and building under Baron Haussmann.

Alfred Dreyfus was accused of betraying military secrets to Germany; he was then court-martialled and sentenced to life imprisonment on Devil's Island in French Guiana. Liberal politicians succeeded in having the case reopened despite opposition from the army command, right-wing politicians and many Catholic groups, and Dreyfus was vindicated in 1900. This resulted in more rigorous civilian control of the military and, in 1905, the legal separation of church and state.

The Two World Wars

Central to France's entry into war against Austria-Hungary and Germany had been its desire to regain Alsace and Lorraine, lost to Germany in the Franco-Prussian War – but it would prove to be a costly piece of real estate in terms of human life. By the time the armistice was signed in November 1918, some 1.3 million French soldiers had been killed and almost one million crippled. At the Battle of Verdun alone, the French (under the command of General Philippe Pétain) and the Germans each lost about 400,000 men.

The naming of Adolf Hitler as Germany's chancellor in 1933 signalled the end of a decade of compromise between France and Germany over border guarantees. Initially the French tried to appease Hitler, but two days after Germany invaded Poland in 1939 France joined Britain in declaring war on Germany. By June 1940 France had capitulated. The Maginot Line had proved useless, with German armoured divisions outflanking it by going through Belgium.

The Germans divided France into a zone under direct German rule (along the western coast and the north, including Paris), and a puppet-state based in the spa town of Vichy and led by General Pétain, the ageing WWI hero of the Battle of Verdun. The Vichy regime was viciously anti-Semitic, and local police helped the Nazis in rounding up French Jews and others for deportation to Auschwitz and other death camps. While many people either collaborated with the Germans or passively waited out the occupation, the underground movement known as the Résistance, or Maquis, whose active members never amounted to more than about 5% of the French population, engaged in such activities as sabotaging railways, collecting intelligence for the Allies, helping Allied airmen who had been shot down and publishing anti-German leaflets.

An 80km-long stretch of beach was the site of the D-Day landings on 6 June 1944, when more than 100,000 Allied troops stormed the coastline to liberate most of Normandy and Brittany. Paris was liberated on 25 August by a force spearheaded by Free French units, sent in ahead of the Americans so the French would have the honour of liberating their own capital.

The Wall of the Federalists in Paris' Cimetière du Père Lachaise serves as a reminder of the blood shed during the Paris Commune.

CHURCH & STATE

France today maintains a rigid distinction between church and state. The country is a secular republic, meaning there can be no mention of religion on national school syllabuses.

1871	1903	1904	1905
The Treaty of Frankfurt is signed, the harsh terms of which (a 5-billion-franc war indemnity, surrender of the provinces of Alsace and Lorraine) prompt immediate revolt.	The world's biggest sporting event after the Olympics and the World Cup sprints around France for the first time; Tour de France riders pedal throughout the night to cover 2500km in 19 days.	Colonial rivalry between France and Britain in Africa ends with the Entente Cordiale ('Cordial Understanding'), marking the start of a cooperation that continues, more or less, to this day.	The emotions aroused by the Dreyfus Affair and the interference of the Catholic Church lead to the promulgation of *laïcité* (secularism), the legal separation of church and state.

The war ruined France. More than one-third of industrial production fed the German war machine during WWII, the occupiers requisitioning practically everything that wasn't (and was) nailed down: ferrous and nonferrous metals, statues, iron grills, zinc bar tops, coal, leather, textiles and chemicals. Agriculture, strangled by the lack of raw materials, fell by 25%.

In their retreat, the Germans burned bridges (2600 destroyed) and the Allied bombardments tore up railroad tracks (40,000km). The roadways had not been maintained since 1939, ports were damaged, and nearly half a million buildings and 60,000 factories were destroyed. The French had to pay for the needs of the occupying soldiers to the tune of 400 million francs a day, prompting an inflation rip tide.

A full 20% of all Frenchmen – one out of every five males – between 20 and 45 years of age were killed in WWI.

Rebuilding & the Loss of the Colonies

The magnitude of France's postwar economic devastation required a strong central government with broad powers to rebuild the country's industrial and commercial base. Soon after liberation most banks, insurance companies, car manufacturers and energy-producing companies fell under government control. Other businesses remained in private hands, the objective being to combine the efficiency of state planning with the dynamism of private initiative. But progress was slow. By 1947 rationing remained in effect and France had to turn to the USA for loans as part of the Marshall Plan to rebuild Europe.

One aim of the plan was to stabilise postwar Europe financially and politically, thus thwarting the expansion of Soviet power. As the Iron Curtain fell over Eastern Europe, the pro-Stalinist bent of France's Communist Party put it in a politically untenable position. Seeking at once to exercise power within the government and at the same time oppose its measures as insufficiently Marxist, the communists found themselves on the losing end of disputes involving the colonies, workers' demands and American aid. In 1947 they were booted out of government.

The economy gathered steam in the 1950s. The French government invested in hydroelectric and nuclear-power plants, oil and gas exploration, petrochemical refineries, naval construction, auto factories and building construction to accommodate a boom in babies and consumer goods. The future at home was looking brighter; the situation of *la France d'outre-mer* (overseas France) was another story altogether.

France's humiliation at the hands of the Germans had not been lost on its restive colonies. As the war economy tightened its grip, native-born people, poorer to begin with, noticed that they were bearing the brunt of the pain. In North Africa the Algerians coalesced around a movement for greater autonomy, which blossomed into a full-scale independence movement by the end of the war. The Japanese moved into strategically

Key War Museums

Mémorial de la Shoah, Paris

Centre d'Histoire de la Résistance et de la Déportation, Lyon

Mémorial – Un Musée pour la Paix, Caen

Musée Mémorial de la Bataille de Normandie, Bayeux

1918	1920s	1939	1944
The armistice ending WWI signed at Fôret de Compiègne near Paris sees the return of lost territories (Alsace and Lorraine), but the war brought about the loss of more than a million French soldiers.	Paris sparkles as the centre of the avant-garde. The luxurious *Train Bleu* (Blue Train) makes its first run, and Sylvia Beach of the Shakespeare & Company bookshop publishes James Joyce's *Ulysses*.	Nazi Germany occupies France and divides it into a zone under direct German occupation (along the north and western coasts), and a puppet state led by General Pétain, based in the spa town of Vichy.	Normandy and Brittany are the first to be liberated by Allied troops following the D-Day landings in June, followed by Paris on 25 August by a force spearheaded by Free French units.

important Indochina in 1940. The Vietnamese resistance movement that developed quickly took on an anti-French, nationalistic tone, setting the stage for Vietnam's eventual independence.

The 1950s spelled the end of French colonialism. When Japan surrendered to the Allies in 1945, nationalist Ho Chi Minh launched a push for an autonomous Vietnam that became a drive for independence. Under the brilliant General Giap, the Vietnamese perfected a form of guerrilla warfare that proved highly effective against the French army. After their defeat at Dien Bien Phu in 1954, the French withdrew from Indochina.

The struggle for Algerian independence was nastier. Technically a French *département,* Algeria was in effect ruled by a million or so French settlers who wished at all costs to protect their privileges. Heads stuck firmly in the Saharan sands, the colonial community and its supporters in the army and the right wing refused all Algerian demands for political and economic equality.

The Algerian War of Independence (1954–62) was brutal. Nationalist rebel attacks were met with summary executions, inquisitions, torture and massacres, which made Algerians more determined to gain their independence. The government responded with half-hearted reform. International pressure on France to pull out of Algeria came from the UN, the USSR and the USA, while *pieds noirs* (literally 'black feet', as Algerian-born French people are known in France), elements of the military and extreme right-wingers became increasingly enraged at what they saw as defeatism in dealing with the problem. A plot to overthrow the French government and replace it with a military-style regime was narrowly avoided when General Charles de Gaulle, France's undersecretary of war who had fled Paris for London in 1940 after France capitulated and had spent more than a dozen years in opposition to the postwar Fourth Republic, agreed to assume the presidency in 1958.

De Gaulle's initial attempts at reform – according the Algerians political equality and recognising their right in principle to self-determination – infuriated right-wingers without quenching the Algerian thirst for independence. Following a failed coup attempt by military officers in 1961, the Organisation de l'Armée Secrète (OAS; a group of French settlers and sympathisers opposed to Algerian independence) resorted to terrorism. It tried to assassinate de Gaulle several times and in 1961 violence broke out on the streets of Paris. Police attacked Algerian demonstrators, killing more than 100 people. Algeria was granted independence the following year.

The Road to Prosperity & Europe

By the late 1960s Charles de Gaulle was appearing more and more like yesterday's man. Loss of the colonies, a surge in immigration and rise in

Published posthumously, the award-winning *Suite Française* (2004) by Ukrainian-born author Irène Némirovsky, who was murdered at Auschwitz in 1942, evokes the horror of Nazi-occupied Paris from June 1940 until July 1941.

HISTORY THE ROAD TO PROSPERITY & EUROPE

Since the end of WWII France has been one of the five permanent members of the UN Security Council. Follow its movements at www.un.org/docs/sc.

Paris in the 1920s and '30s was a centre of the avant-garde, with painters pushing into new fields of art such as cubism and surrealism, Le Corbusier rewriting the architecture textbook, foreign writers such as Ernest Hemingway drawn by the city's liberal atmosphere (and cheap booze), and nightlife establishing a cutting-edge reputation.

unemployment had weakened his government. De Gaulle's government by decree was starting to gall the anti-authoritarian baby-boomer generation, now at university and agitating for change. Students reading Herbert Marcuse and Wilhelm Reich found much to admire in Fidel Castro, Che Guevara and the black struggle for civil rights in America, and vociferously denounced the war in Vietnam.

Student protests of 1968 climaxed with a brutal overreaction by police to a protest meeting at the Sorbonne, Paris' most renowned university. Overnight, public opinion turned in favour of the students, while the students themselves occupied the Sorbonne and erected barricades in the Latin Quarter. Within days a general strike by 10 million workers countrywide paralysed France.

But such comradeship between workers and students did not last long. While the former wanted a greater share of the consumer market, the latter wanted to destroy it. After much hesitancy de Gaulle took advantage of this division by appealing to people's fear of anarchy. Just as the country seemed on the brink of revolution and an overthrow of the Fifth Republic, stability returned. The government decentralised the higher-education system and followed through in the 1970s with a wave of other reforms (lowering the voting age to 18, instituting legalised abortion and so on). De Gaulle meanwhile resigned from office in 1969 and suffered a fatal heart attack the following year.

Georges Pompidou stepped onto the presidential podium in 1969. Despite embarking on an ambitious modernisation program, investing in aerospace, telecommunications and nuclear power, he failed to stave off inflation and social unrest following the global oil crisis of 1973. He died the following year.

In 1974 Valéry Giscard d'Estaing inherited a deteriorating economic climate and sharp divisions between the left and the right. His friendship with emperor and alleged cannibal Jean-Bédel Bokassa of the Central African Republic did little to win him friends, and in 1981 he was ousted by long-time head of the Parti Socialiste (PS; Socialist Party), François Mitterrand.

The President of the Republic has a website (www.elysee.fr), posts regularly on his Facebook page and is active on Twitter @elysee.

Despite France's first socialist president instantly alienating the business community by setting out to nationalise several privately owned banks, industrial groups and other parts of the economy, Mitterrand gave France a sparkle. Potent symbols of France's advanced technological savvy – the Minitel, a proto-personal computer in everyone's home, and high-speed TGV train service between Paris and Lyon – were launched in 1980 and 1981 respectively; a clutch of *grands projets* were embarked upon in the French capital. The death penalty was abolished, homosexuality was legalised, a 39-hour work week was instituted, annual holiday

1968	1981	1989	1994
Large-scale anti-authoritarian student protests (known as 'May 1968') aimed at de Gaulle's style of government by decree escalate into a countrywide protest that eventually brings down the president.	The superspeedy TGV makes its first commercial journey from Paris to Lyon, breaking all speed records to complete the train journey in two hours instead of six.	President Mitterrand's *grand projet*, Opéra Bastille, opens to mark the bicentennial of the French Revolution; IM Pei's love-it-or-leave-it Grande Pyramide is unveiled at the Louvre.	The 50km-long Channel Tunnel linking France with Britain opens after seven years of hard graft by 10,000 workers.

time was upped from four to five weeks and the right to retire at 60 was guaranteed.

But by 1986 the economy was weakening and in parliamentary elections that year the right-wing opposition, led by Jacques Chirac (mayor of Paris since 1977), won a majority in the National Assembly. For the next two years Mitterrand worked with a prime minister and cabinet from the opposition, an unprecedented arrangement known as *cohabitation*. The extreme-right Front National (FN; National Front) meanwhile quietly gained ground by loudly blaming France's economic woes on immigration.

Presidential elections in 1995 ushered Chirac (an ailing Mitterrand did not run and died the following year) into the Élysée Palace. However, Chirac's attempts to reform France's colossal public sector in order to meet the criteria of the European Monetary Union (EMU) were met with the largest protests since 1968, and his decision to resume nuclear testing on the Polynesian island of Mururoa and a nearby atoll was the focus of worldwide outrage. Always the maverick, Chirac called early parliamentary elections in 1997 – only for his party, the Rassemblement pour la République (RPR; Rally for the Republic), to lose out to a coalition of socialists, communists and greens. Another period of *cohabitation* ensued.

The 2002 presidential elections surprised everybody. The first round of voting saw left-wing PS leader Lionel Jospin eliminated and the FN's Jean-Marie Le Pen – who had infamously dismissed the Holocaust as a 'mere detail of history' and spoke of the 'inequality of races' – win 17% of the national vote. But in the subsequent run-off ballot, Chirac enjoyed a landslide victory, echoed in parliamentary elections a month later when

France has always drawn immigrants: 4.3 million from Europe between 1850 and WWI, and another 3 million between the world wars. Post-WWII, several million unskilled workers followed from North Africa and French-speaking sub-Saharan Africa.

HISTORY THE ROAD TO PROSPERITY & EUROPE

THE BIRTH OF THE BIKINI

Almost called *atome* (atom) rather than bikini, after its pinprick size, the scanty little two-piece bathing suit was the 1946 creation of Cannes fashion designer Jacques Heim and automotive engineer Louis Réard. It made its first appearance poolside in Paris at the Piscine Molitor, a mythical art deco pool complex that reopened – with original pool – as the stunning Hôtel Molitor in 2014.

Top-and-bottom swimsuits had existed for centuries, but it was the French duo who made them briefer than brief and plumped for the name 'bikini' – after Bikini, an atoll in the Marshall Islands chosen by the USA in the same year as the testing ground for atomic bombs.

Once wrapped top and bottom around the curvaceous 1950s sex-bomb Brigitte Bardot on St-Tropez' Plage de Pampelonne, there was no looking back. The bikini was here to stay.

1995	1998	2001	2002
After twice serving as prime minister, Jacques Chirac becomes president of France, winning popular acclaim for his direct words and actions in matters relating to the EU and the war in Bosnia.	After resuming nuclear testing in the South Pacific in the early 1990s, France signs the worldwide test-ban treaty, bringing an end to French nuclear testing once and for all.	Socialist Bertrand Delanoë becomes the first openly gay mayor of Paris (and any European capital); he is wounded in a knife attack by a homophobic assailant the following year.	The French franc, first minted in 1360, is thrown onto the scrap heap of history as the country adopts the euro as its official currency along with 14 other EU member-states.

the president-backed coalition UMP (Union pour un Mouvement Populaire) won a healthy majority, leaving Le Pen's FN without a seat in parliament and ending years of *cohabitation*.

Sarkozy's France

Presidential elections in 2007 ushered out old-school Jacques Chirac (in his 70s with two terms under his belt) and brought in Nicolas Sarkozy. Dynamic, ambitious and media-savvy, the former interior minister and chairman of centre-right party UMP wooed voters with policies about job creation, lower taxes, crime crackdown and help for France's substantial immigrant population – issues that had particular pulling power coming from the son of a Hungarian immigrant father and Greek Jewish-French mother. However, his first few months in office were dominated by personal affairs as he divorced his wife Cecilia and wed Italian multimillionaire singer Carla Bruni a few months later.

The 2008 global banking crisis saw the government inject €10.5 billion into France's six major banks. Unemployment hit the 10% mark in 2010 and in regional elections the same year, Sarkozy's party lost badly. The left won 54% of votes and control of 21 out of 22 regions on mainland France and Corsica. Government popularity hit an all-time low.

Riots ripped through the Alpine town of Grenoble in 2010 after a 27-year-old man was shot dead by police while allegedly trying to rob a casino. The incident echoed bloodshed five years earlier in a Parisian suburb following the death of two teenage boys of North African origin, electrocuted after hiding in an electrical substation while on the run from the police. In Grenoble the burning cars and street clashes with riot police were seen as a measurement of just how volatile France had become.

Hollande's France

Presidential elections in 2012 ushered in France's first socialist president since François Mitterand left office in 1995. Nicolas Sarkozy ran for a second term in office, but lost against left-wing candidate François Hollande (b 1954) of the Socialist party whose ambitious talk of reducing unemployment (at a 12-year high), clearing the country's debts by 2017, upping tax on corporations and salaries of more than €1 million per annum and increasing the minimum salary clearly won over the electorate. Parliamentary elections a month later sealed Hollande's grip on power: the Socialists won a comfortable majority in France's 577-seat National Assembly, paving the way for Hollande to govern France during Europe's biggest economic crisis in decades.

His term got off to a rocky start. Scandal broke out in March 2013 after finance minister Jerome Cahuzac admitted to having a 'safe hav-

---

The French invented the first digital calculator, the hot-air balloon, Braille and margarine, not to mention Grand Prix racing and the first public interactive computer network. Find out what else at http://inventors.about.com/od/french inventors.

Lyonnais biology teacher Alexis Jenni won the 2011 Prix Goncourt with *L'Art Français de la Guerre* (*The French Art of War*) – 50 years of French military history and colonial wars in Southeast Asia and Algeria.

2004	2005	2007	2010
France bans the wearing of crucifixes, the Islamic headscarf and other overtly religious symbols in state schools.	The French electorate overwhelmingly rejects EU Constitution. Parisian suburbs are wracked by rioting Arab and African youths.	Pro-American pragmatist Nicolas Sarkozy beats Socialist candidate Ségolène Royal to become French president.	Country-wide strikes and protests briefly paralyse the country after Sarkozy unveils plans to push the retirement age back from 60 to 62 by 2018.

en' bank account in Switzerland and was forced to resign. Two months later France officially entered recession again after first quarter figures were announced: the economy had shrunk by 0.2% and unemployment rose to 10.4%, the highest in 15 years. By November, France's AA+ credit rating had been downgraded still further to AA and the year ended with unemployment for the month of December 2013 increasing still further, to 11.1%.

The year 2014 did not begin well for François Hollande. In January, French tabloid magazine *Closer* published photographs of the French president in Paris arriving at the apartment of his alleged mistress, actress Julie Gayet, on a scooter – prompting public concern about both presidential security (or rather, lack of) and the well-being of the president's relationship with long-term partner and official First Lady, journalist Valérie Trierweiler. The presidential couple soon after announced the end of their relationship, while Hollande's popularity plummeted to a new rock-bottom.

Nicolas Sarkozy became the first French president to be held in police custody after being detained over allegations of corruption in July 2014. He was subsequently released, but placed under formal investigation over allegations of corruption while in office that included accepting campaign donations in 2007 from former Libyan leader Colonel Gaddafi.

2011	2012	2013	2014
French parliament bans burkas in public. Muslim women publicly wearing the face-covering veil can be fined and required to attend 'citizenship classes'.	France loses its top AAA credit rating. Economic policy is the big issue in presidential elections which usher in François Hollande, France's first Socialist president in 17 years.	Same-sex marriage is legalised in France. By the end of the year, 7000 gay couples have tied the knot.	Municipal elections usher in Paris' first female mayor Anne Hidalgo, Spanish-born to boot. In European elections a month later, the far-right National Front wins almost a quarter of votes.

The French

Stylish, sexy, chic, charming, arrogant, rude, bureaucratic, chauvinistic... France is a country whose people attract more stubborn myths and stereotypes than any other.

Over the centuries dozens of tags, true or otherwise, have been pinned on the garlic-eating, beret-wearing, *sacrebleu*-swearing French. (The French, by the way, don't wear berets or use old chestnuts like *'sacrebleu'* anymore.) So what precisely does it mean to be French?

Sixty Million Frenchmen Can't Be Wrong: What Makes the French so French ask Jean-Benoît Nadeau and Julie Barlow in their witty, well-written and at times downright comical musings on the French.

Superiority Complex

Most French people are proud to be French and are staunchly nationalistic, a result of the country's republican stance that places nationality (rather than religion, for example) atop the self-identity list. This has created an overwhelmingly self-confident nation, culturally and intellectually, that can appear as a French superiority complex.

Many French speak a foreign language fairly well, travel, and are happy to use their language skills should the need arise. Of course, if monolingual English-speakers don't try to speak French, there is no way proud French linguists will reveal they speak English! Many French men, incidentally, deem an English-speaking gal's heavily accented French as irresistibly sexy as many people deem a Frenchman speaking English.

Tradition v Innovation

Suckers for tradition, the French are slow to embrace new ideas and technologies: it took the country an age to embrace the internet, clinging on to its own at-the-time-advanced Minitel system. Yet the French innovate. They came up with microchipped credit cards long before anyone else. The lead pencil, refrigerator, tinned foods, calculator, spirit level and little black dress (*merci*, Chanel) are all French inventions.

FROGS VS ROSBIFS

In the finest of traditions, tales of the rivalry between *rosbifs* (the English) and frogs (the French) sell like hotcakes. Our favourites:

➡ *1000 Years of Annoying the French* (Stephen Clarke; 2011) A smart comic look at French-Anglo history by the man who launched his career with *A Year in the Merde* (A Year in the Shit).

➡ *Cross Channel* (Julian Barnes; 1996) Classic short stories set either side of the Channel.

➡ *More France Please! We're British!* (Helen Frith-Powell; 2004) France from the perspective of Brits who choose to live there permanently.

➡ *Dirty Bertie: An English King in France* (Stephen Clarke; 2014) Apparently, fervent francophile Edward VII learnt everything there is know about life from the French...

FRENCH KISSING

Kissing French-style is not straightforward, 'how many' and 'which side first' being potentially problematic. In Paris it is two: unless parties are related, *very* close friends or haven't seen each other in an age, anything more is deemed affected. That said, in hipster 20-something circles, friends swap three or four cheek-skimming kisses.

Travel south and *les bises* (kisses), or *les bisous* as the French colloquially say, multiply; three or four is the norm in Provence. The bits of France neighbouring Switzerland around Lake Geneva tend to be three-kiss country (in keeping with Swiss habits); and in the Loire Valley it is four. Corsicans, bizarrely, stick to two but kiss left cheek first – which can lead to locked lips given that everyone else in France starts with the right cheek.

Naturally Sexy

On the subject of sex, not all French men ooze romance or light Gitane cigarettes all day. Nor are they as civilised about adultery as French cinema would have you believe. Adultery, illegal in France until 1975, was actually grounds for automatic divorce until as late as 2004. Today, 55% of marriages in France end in divorce (making France in 2014 the ninth most divorced country in the world) – with women, interestingly, being the ones to file for divorce in three out of four cases. As with elsewhere in Europe, couples are marrying later – at the average age of 32 and 30 for men and women respectively in 2013, compared to 30 and 28 a decade before. Fifty-seven percent of babies in France are born out of wedlock, and one-fifth are raised by a single parent.

Kissing is an integral part of French life. (The expression 'French kissing' doesn't exist in French, incidentally.) Countrywide, people who know each other reasonably well, really well, a tad or barely at all greet each other with a glancing peck on each cheek. Southern France aside (where everyone kisses everyone), two men rarely kiss (unless they are related or artists) but always shake hands. Boys and girls start kissing as soon as they're out of nappies, or so it seems.

No contemporary writer addresses the natural art, style and panache of French women better than Helena Frith-Powell (http://helenafrith powell.com), an adopted resident of Languedoc in southwestern France, who found literary fame with *Two Lipsticks and a Lover* (2007), an exposé on the secrets behind the glamour of French women (expensive and matching lingerie, infidelity and the like).

Gay & Married

The French capital has long been known as 'gay Paree', with an openly 'proud to be gay' mayor for 13 years (until April 2014) and a gay and lesbian scene so open that there is far less of a defined 'scene' than in many other European cities where gay and lesbian life remains somewhat 'underground'. Yet despite all this, reactions to the legalisation of same-sex marriage in France in May 2013 were mixed and at times extreme, exposing a deeply conservative streak in some French people that few expected or anticipated.

Demonstrators repeatedly marched through the streets of Paris, Lyon and other cities in protest at the law, and in January 2014, following an appeal by French mayors who claimed the new law violated the country's constitution, France's high court ruled that mayors and registrars, irrespective of personal or religious beliefs, did not have the right to refuse to conduct a gay marriage.

After gay marriage was legalised, 7000 couples – 3% of all marriages in France – wed in 2013; three out of five gay marriages were male couples.

Lifestyle

Be a fly on the wall in the 5th-floor bourgeois apartment of Monsieur et Madame Tout le Monde and you'll see them dunking croissants in bowls of *café au lait* for breakfast, buying a baguette every day from the bakery (Monsieur nibbles the end off on his way home) and recycling nothing bar a few glass bottles and the odd cardboard box.

They go to the movies once a month, work precisely 35 hours a week (many French still toil 39 hours or more a week – employers can enforce a 39-hour work week for a negotiable extra cost), and enjoy five weeks' holiday and almost a dozen bank (public) holidays a year. The couple view the web-radio production company their 24-year-old son set up and heads in Paris with a mix of pride, amusement and pure scepticism. Their 20-year-old daughter is a student: France's overcrowded state-run universities are free and open to anyone who passes the baccalaureate, although former president Nicolas Sarkozy had a stab at changing this by giving universities the autonomy to select students and seek outside funding. Then there's their youngest, aged 11 and the last of generations to enjoy no school on Wednesdays: as of September 2014, French primary schools have to open five days a week (admittedly, only until lunchtime on Wednesday) like all their European counterparts.

Madame buys a load of hot-gossip weekly magazines, Monsieur meets his mates to play boules, and August is the *only* month to summer holiday (with the rest of France). Dodging dog poo on pavements is a sport practised from birth and everything goes on the *carte bleue* (credit or debit card) when shopping. The couple have a landlord: with a tradition of renting rather than buying, home ownership is low (63% of households own their own home; the rest rent).

The Elementary Particles (first published in French as *Les Particules Élémentaires* and subsequently in the UK as *Atomised*) by best-selling French author Michel Houellebecq uses the story of two French half-brothers born to a hippy mother to delve into the state of contemporary society. Funny, sad, caustic and hugely insightful, it is a wonderful anthropological portrait of modern France.

Les Femmes

Women were granted suffrage in 1945, but until 1964 a woman needed her husband's permission to open a bank account or get a passport. Younger French women in particular are quite outspoken and emancipated. But this self-confidence has yet to translate into equality in the workplace, where women hold few senior and management positions. Sexual harassment is addressed with a law imposing financial penalties on the offender. A great achievement in the last decade has been *Parité*, the law requiring political parties to fill 50% of their slates in all elections with female candidates.

Abortion is legal during the first 12 weeks of pregnancy, girls under 16 do not need parental consent provided they are accompanied by an adult of their choice: 30 abortions take place in France for every 100 live births.

Above all else French women are known for their natural chic, style and class. And there's no doubt that contemporary French women are sassier than ever. Take the Rykiel women: in the 1970s, legendary Parisian knitwear designer Sonia Rykiel designed the skin-tight, boob-hugging sweater worn with no bra beneath. In the new millennium, daughter

FRENCH MANNERS

➡ Splitting the bill is deemed the height of unsophistication. The person who invites pays, although close friends often go Dutch.

➡ Fondle fruit, veg, flowers or clothing in shops and you'll be greeted with a killer glare from the shop assistant.

➡ Take flowers (not chrysanthemums, which are only for cemeteries) or Champagne when invited to someone's home.

➡ Never, ever, discuss money over dinner.

MADAME FROM BIRTH

'About time too', a feminist anywhere else on the planet would argue. Indeed, it is only since 2012 that French women no longer have to tick one of two boxes when filling out official forms and documents – 'Madame' meaning 'Mrs' or 'married' and 'Mademoiselle' meaning 'Miss' or 'young and not married'. 'Mademoiselle' also implies 'virgin' and 'sexually available' according to Paris-based feminist group Les Chiennes de Garde (meaning 'guard dogs' or, rather, 'guard bitches'), who launched the petition to banish the term 'Mademoiselle' from the administrative and political arena.

'Mademoiselle' originates from the medieval word *'damoiselle',* meaning a young upper-class girl (male equivalents were called *'damoisel'*). Later merged with *'ma'* to denote an unmarried woman, the term was tantamount to 'sad old spinster who can't find a husband' in the 17th and 18th centuries. In the 19th century, novelist Adolphe Belot borrowed the term to depict a frigid wife in *Mademoiselle Giraud, ma Femme*. These days, for women over 35, being addressed as 'mademoiselle' is a subtle way of being told 'you're young!'.

Nathalie created Rykiel Woman, a sensual label embracing everything from lingerie to sex toys and aimed squarely at women who know what they want.

Then, of course, there is Spanish-born Anne Hidalgo, Paris' first ever female mayor, elected in March 2014. *Allez les femmes!*

Linguistic Patriotism

Speaking a language other than their own is an emotional affair for the French, memorably illustrated a few years back when the then French president Jacques Chirac walked out of an EU summit session after a fellow countryman had the audacity to address the meeting in English. 'Don't speak English!' was *Le Monde's* headline the next day, while the French blogosphere seethed with debate on linguistic patriotism: 'Open your eyes, Mr President, you are on another planet' and 'it is a long time since French was the language of the international arena' taunted modern-day French bloggers, many of whom write in English.

Former president Nicolas Sarkozy fared marginally better than his monolingual predecessor. Yet Sarkozy also stuck to what he knew best in public, so much so that the couple of lines he did utter in English were instantly plastered over the internet as a video link and swiftly went viral.

With English words like 'weekend', 'jogging', 'stop' and 'OK' firmly entrenched in daily French usage, language purists might just have lost the battle. One look at the many Anglo-American shop and restaurant signs featured in the online Musée des Horreurs (Museum of Horrors) on the website of the Paris-based Défense de la Langue Française (DLF; Defence of the French Language; www.languefrancaise.org) says it all.

French was the main language of the EU until 1995 when Sweden and Finland came into the EU fold. French broadcasting laws restrict the amount of airtime radio and TV stations can devote to non-French music, but nothing can be done to restrict who airs what on the internet.

Multiculturalism

France is multicultural (immigrants make up around 11% of the population), yet its republican code, while inclusive and non-discriminatory, has been criticised for doing little to accommodate a

CHILDREN

One of the bestsellers addressing French culture in recent years is Pamela Druckerman's *French Children Don't Throw Food* (2012), a witty and entertaining look at how French parents in Paris raise their kids by an American living in the city.

multicultural society (and, interestingly, none of the members of France's National Assembly represents the immigrant population, first or second generation). Nothing reflects this dichotomy better than the law, in place since 2004, banning the Islamic headscarf, Jewish skullcap, crucifix and other religious symbols in French schools.

Some 90% of the French Muslim community – Europe's largest – are noncitizens. Most are illegal immigrants living in poverty-stricken *bidonvilles* (tinpot towns) around Paris, Lyon, Marseille and other metropolitan centres. Many are unemployed (youth unemployment in many suburbs is as high as 40%) and face little prospect of getting a job.

Good Sports

Most French wouldn't be seen dead walking down the street in trainers and tracksuits. But contrary to appearances, they love sport. Shaved-leg cyclists toil up Mont Ventoux, football fans fill stadiums and anyone who can flits off for the weekend to ski or snowboard.

The 24 Hours of Le Mans and the F1 Grand Prix in Monaco are the world's raciest dates in motor sports; the French Open (aka Roland Garros) in Paris in late May to early June is the second of the year's four grand-slam tennis tournaments; and the Tour de France is – indisputably – the world's most prestigious bicycle race. Bringing together 189 of the world's top male cyclists (21 teams of nine) and 15 million spectators in July each year for a spectacular 3000-plus-kilometre cycle around the country, the three-week race always

FRANCE'S NORTH–SOUTH DIVIDE

No film better illustrates what southerners think of those from 'the sticks' in the far north than Dany Boon's *Bienvenue chez les Ch'tis* (Welcome to the Sticks; 2008), a classic commentary on France's north–south divide.

For starters, the weather in the cold rainy north is revolting. So no surprise that post-office chief Philippe, upon setting off north from his native Salon-de-Provence on the sun-drenched Côte d'Azur, dons a puffer jacket and scarf as he bids farewell to bronzed wife Julie. The weather changes when he passes the 'Nord-Pas de Calais' sign – at which point it doesn't just rain but slashes down beyond windscreen-wiper control. Even the gendarme on the autoroute, upon stopping him for driving too slowly, lets him off with a sympathetic smile and his deepest condolences when he hears where he's heading: Bergues, an ex-mining town of 4300 inhabitants, 9km from Dunkirk.

Bienvenue chez les Ch'tis is a kaleidoscope of comic scenes that slowly chip away at the deeply entrenched prejudices surrounding this northern land of redundant coal mines and its unemployed, impoverished, pale, unhealthy and 'uncultured' inhabitants who drink too much beer and speak like this – *Ej t'ermerci inne banes* (that means *Merci beaucoup*).

Yes, their thick Ch'timi dialect (old Picard peppered with Flemish) is incomprehensible to outsiders. Yes, they dunk stinky Maroilles cheese and bread in *chicorée café* (chicory-flavoured instant coffee) for breakfast. Yes, they skip the traditional French three-course lunch for an alfresco round of *frites fricadelle, sauce picadilly* (chips 'n' meatballs) – eaten with their fingers. And yes, their very nickname (*les Ch'tis*) was borne out of prejudice during WWI when French soldiers mocked the thickly accented way their northern comrades spoke – *'ch'est ti, ch'est mi'* (*c'est toi, c'est moi* – it's you, it's me), hence 'Ch'ti'.

The north and its regional characteristics are no mystery to director Boon, a born-and-bred northerner who grew up in Armentières, near Lille. Indeed, if anyone is best placed to speak of *les Ch'tis* and their homeland, it's Boon, whose lovable, huge-hearted character in the film says it all: 'An outsider who comes to the north cries twice: once when he arrives, and once when he leaves.'

labours through the Alps and Pyrenees and finishes on Paris' Champs-Élysées. The route in between changes each year but wherever it goes, the French systematically turn out in their droves – armed with tables, chairs and picnic hampers – to make a day of it. The serpentine publicity caravan preceding the cyclists showers roadside spectators with coffee samples, logo-emblazoned balloons, pens and other free junk-advertising gifts and is easily as much fun as watching the cyclists themselves speed through – in 10 seconds flat.

France's greatest moment in football (soccer) history came at the 1998 World Cup, which the country hosted and won. But the game has produced no stars since, losing to Italy in the final of the 2006 World Cup and only making it as far as the quarter-finals in the 2014 World Cup in Brazil. Indeed, football fans look back with fondness at the days of France's golden boy of football, now retired, Marseille-born midfielder Zinedine Zidane (b 1972). The son of Algerian immigrants, Zidane wooed the nation with a sparkling career of goal-scoring headers and extraordinary footwork that unfortunately ended with him head-butting an Italian player during the 2006 World Cup final. But such was the power of his humble Marseillais grin (since used to advertise Adidas sports gear, Volvic mineral water and Christian Dior fashion) that the French nation instantly forgave him.

France's traditional ball games include *pétanque* and the more formal boules, which has a 70-page rule book. Both are played by men on a gravel pitch.

The French Table

Few Western cuisines are so envied, aspired to or seminal. The freshness of ingredients, natural flavours, regional variety and range of cooking methods is phenomenal. The very word 'cuisine' (cooking style) was borrowed from the French – no other language could handle all the nuances.

The French table waltzes taste buds through a dizzying array of dishes sourced from aromatic street markets, seaside oyster farms, sun-baked olive groves tended by third-generation farmers and ancient vineyards that mirror to exacting perfection the beauty of each season. Regional cuisines are vast and varied. *Bon appétit!*

Terroir

No country so blatantly bundles up cuisine with its *terroir* (land). *'Le jardin de France'* (the garden of France), a poetic phrase coined by the French writer Rabelais in the 16th century to describe his native Touraine in the Loire Valley, has been exploited ever since. Yet it is the serene valley tracing the course of the River Loire west of the French capital which remains most true to the Rabelais image of a green and succulent landscape laden with lush fruits, flowers, nuts and vegetables.

It was in the Renaissance kitchens of the Loire's celebrated châteaux that French cooking was refined: *coq au vin* (chicken in wine) and *cuisses de grenouilles* (frogs' legs) were common dishes, and poultry and game dishes were the pride and joy. Once or twice a year a fattened pig was slaughtered and prepared dozens of different ways – roasts, sausages, *boudin noir* (black pudding), charcuterie (cold meats), pâtés. No single part was wasted.

> The Food of France by Waverley Root, first published in 1958, remains the seminal work in English on *la cuisine française*, with a focus on historical development, by a long-time Paris-based American foreign correspondent.

Sauces

With so much game and poultry going on in châteaux kitchens, it was natural that medieval cooks whipped up a sauce to go with it. In the 14th to 16th centuries, *sauce verte* (green sauce) – a rather crude, heavily spiced mix of vinegar and green grape juice – accompanied meat dishes. In 1652 François-Pierre de la Varenne published his cookbook *Le Cuisinier François* in which he dismissed bread and breadcrumbs as thickening agents in favour of roux (a more versatile mixture of flour and fat). This paved the way for the creation, a century later, of classic French sauces such as béchamel (a milk-based sauce thickened with roux) and velouté (a velvety mix of chicken or other stock and melted butter, seasoned and thickened with roux) a century later. Velouté is the base for dozens of other sauces made to accompany meat, fish and game dishes today.

Bread

In northern France wheat fields shade vast swathes of agricultural land a gorgeous golden copper, and nothing is more French than *pain* (bread). Starved peasants demanded bread on the eve of the French Revolution when the ill-fated Queen Marie-Antoinette is purported to have said 'let them eat cake'. And bread today – no longer a matter of life or death but a cultural icon – accompanies every meal. It's rarely served with butter, but when it is, the butter is always *doux* (unsalted).

Every town and almost every village has its own *boulangerie* (bakery) which sells bread in all manner of shapes, sizes and variety. Artisan *boulangeries* bake their bread in a wood-fired, brick bread oven pioneered by Loire Valley châteaux in the 16th century.

Plain old *pain* is a 400g, traditional-shaped loaf, soft inside and crusty out. The iconic classic is *une baguette*, a long thin crusty loaf weighing 250g. Anything fatter and it becomes *une flûte*, thinner *une ficelle*. While French baguettes are impossibly good, they systematically turn unpleasantly dry within four hours, unbelievably rock-hard within 12.

Charcuterie & Foie Gras

Charcuterie, the backbone of every French picnic and a bistro standard, is traditionally made from pork, though other meats are used to make *saucisse* (small fresh sausage, boiled or grilled before eating), *saucisson* (salami), *saucisson sec* (air-dried salami), *boudin noir* (blood sausage or pudding made with pig's blood, onions and spices) and other cured and salted meats. Pâtés, terrines and rillettes are also considered charcuterie. The difference between a pâté and a terrine is academic: a pâté is removed from its container and sliced before it is served, while a terrine is sliced from the container itself. Rillettes, spread cold over bread or toast, is potted meat or even fish that has been shredded, seasoned and mixed with fat.

The key component of *pâté de foie gras* is foie gras which is the liver of fattened ducks and geese. It was first prepared *en croûte* (in a pastry crust) around 1780 by one Jean-Pierre Clause, chef to the military governor of Alsace, who was impressed enough to send a batch to the king of Versailles. Duck and goose liver have been enjoyed since time immemorial, but it wasn't until the 18th century that it was introduced on a large scale. Controversially, ducks and geese on farms are today force-fed with unnatural amounts of boiled corn in order to fatten their livers.

Patisserie

Patisserie is a general French term for pastries and includes *tartes* (tarts), *flans* (custard pies), *gâteaux* (cakes) and *biscuits* (cookies) as well as traditional croissants, *pains au chocolat* and other typical pastries. *Sablés* are shortbread biscuits, *tuiles* are delicate wing-like almond cookies, madeleines are small scallop-shaped cakes often flavoured with a hint of vanilla or lemon, and *tarte tatin* is an upside-down caramelised apple pie that's been around since the late 19th century. Louis XIV (1643–1715), known for his sweet tooth, is credited with introducing the custom of eating dessert – once reserved for feast days and other celebrations – at the end of a meal.

No sweet treat evokes the essence of French patisserie quite like the elegant, sophisticated and zany macaron, a legacy of Catherine de Médicis who came to France in 1533 with an entourage of Florentine chefs and pastry cooks adept in the subtleties of Italian Renaissance cooking and armed with delicacies such as aspic, truffles, quenelles (dumplings), artichokes – and macarons. Round and polished smooth like a giant Smartie, the macaron (nothing to do with coconut) is a pair of crisp-shelled, chewy-inside discs – egg whites whisked stiff with sugar and ground almonds – sandwiched together with a smooth filling. Belying their eggshell fragility, macarons are created in a rainbow of lurid colours and flavours, wild and inexhaustible: rose petal, cherry blossom, caramel with coconut and mango, mandarin orange and olive oil...

Cheese

No French food product is a purer reflection of *terroir* than cheese, an iconic staple that – with the exception of most coastal areas – is made all over the country, tiny villages laying claim to ancient variations made just the way *grand-père* did it. France boasts more than 500 varieties, made

THE FRENCH TABLE CHARCUTERIE & FOIE GRAS

Foodie Towns

Le Puy-en-Velay – lentils

Dijon – mustard

Privas – chestnuts

Cancale – oysters

Espelette – red chillies

Colmar – chocolate stork eggs

Lyon – piggy-part cuisine

On Jour des Rois (Day of the Kings; 6 January), or Epiphany, a *galette des rois* ('kings' cake'; a puff-pastry tart with frangipane cream) is placed in the centre of the table and sliced while the youngest person ducks under the table, calling out who gets each slice. The excitement lies in who gets *la fève* ('bean', which translates these days as a miniature porcelain figurine) hidden in the tart; whoever does is crowned king with a gold paper crown that's sold with the *galette*.

THE PERFECT CHEESEBOARD

Treat your taste buds to the perfect balance of cheese by taking at least one of each type from the cheeseboard:

➡ **Goat's cheese** (fromage de chèvre) Made from goat's milk.

➡ **Blue cheese** (fromage à pâté persillée) 'Marbled' or with veins that resemble persil (parsley).

➡ **Soft cheese** (fromage à pâté molle) Moulded or rind-washed, the classic soft cheese that everyone knows is Camembert from Normandy made from unpasteurised cow's milk. Munster from Alsace is a fine-textured, rind-washed cheese.

➡ **Semihard cheese** (fromage à pâté demi-dure) Among the finest uncooked, pressed cheese is Tomme de Savoie, made from pasteurised or unpasteurised cow's milk near the Alps, and St-Nectaire, a strong-smelling pressed cheese with a complex taste.

➡ **Hard cheese** (fromage à pâté dure) Must-taste cooked and pressed cheeses are Beaufort, a fruity cow's-milk cheese from Rhône-Alpes; Comté, made with raw cow's milk in Franche-Comté; emmental, a cow's-milk cheese made all over France; and Mimolette, an Edam-like bright-orange cheese from Lille aged for as long as 36 months.

with *lait cru* (raw milk), pasteurised milk or *petit-lait* ('little-milk', the whey left over after the fats and solids have been curdled with rennet).

Chèvre, made from goat's milk, is creamy, sweet and faintly salty when fresh, but hardens and gets saltier as it matures. Among the best is Ste-Maure de Touraine, a mild creamy cheese from the Loire Valley; Cabécou de Rocamadour from Midi-Pyrénées, often served warm with salad or marinated in oil and rosemary; and Lyon's St-Marcellin, a soft white cheese that should be served impossibly runny.

Roquefort, a ewe's-milk veined cheese from Languedoc, is the king of blue cheeses and vies with Burgundy's pongy Époisses for the strongest taste award. Soft, white, orange-skinned Époisses, created in the 16th century by monks at Abbaye de Cîteaux, takes a month to make, using washes of saltwater, rainwater and Marc de Bourgogne – a local pomace brandy and the source of the cheese's final fierce bite.

Equal parts of Comté, Beaufort and Gruyère – a trio of hard fruity, cow's milk cheeses from the French Alps – are grated and melted in a garlic-smeared pot with a dash of nutmeg, white wine and *kiersch* (cherry liqueur) to create fondue Savoyard. Hearty and filling, this pot of melting glory originated from the simple peasant need of using up cheese scraps. It is now the chic dish to eat on the ski slopes.

Top Self-Drive Wine Itineraries

Marne & Côte des Bar Champagne routes, *Champagne*

Route des Grands Crus, *Burgundy*

Route des Vins d'Alsace, *Alsace*

Route Touristique des Vignobles, *Loire Valley*

Route des Vins du Jura, *the Jura*

Wine

Viticulture in France is an ancient art and tradition that bears its own unique trademark. The French thirst for wine goes back to Roman times when techniques to grow grapes and craft wine were introduced, and *dégustation* (tasting) has been an essential part of French wine culture ever since.

Quality wines in France are designated as Appellation d'Origine Contrôlée (AOC; literally, 'label of inspected origin'), equivalent since 2012 to the European-wide Appellation d'Origine Protégée (AOP). Both labels mean the same: that the wine has met stringent regulations governing where, how and under what conditions it was grown and bottled. French AOC can cover a wide region (such as Bordeaux), a sub-region (such as Haut-Médoc), or a commune or village (such as Pomerol). Some regions only have a single AOC (such as Alsace), while Burgundy has dozens.

Some viticulturists have honed their skills and techniques to such a degree that their wine is known as a *grand cru* (literally 'great growth').

If this wine has been produced in a year of optimum climatic conditions, it becomes a *millésime* (vintage) wine. *Grands crus* are aged in small oak barrels then bottles, sometimes for 20 years or more, to create those memorable bottles (with price tags to match) that wine experts enthuse about with such passion.

There are dozens of wine-producing regions throughout France, but the principal ones are Burgundy, Bordeaux, the Rhône and Loire valleys, Champagne, Languedoc, Provence and Alsace. Wines are generally named after the location of the vineyard rather than the grape varietal. Organic and biodynamic wines are increasingly popular.

Red

France's most respected reds are from Burgundy (Bourgogne in French), Bordeaux and the Rhône Valley.

Monks in Burgundy began making wine in the 8th century during the reign of Charlemagne. Today vineyards remain small, rarely more than 10 hectares, with vignerons (winegrowers) in Côte d'Or, Chablis, Châtillon and Mâcon producing small quantities of excellent reds from pinot noir grapes. The best Bourgogne vintages demand 10 to 20 years to age.

In the sun-blessed south, Bordeaux has the perfect climate for producing wine: its 1100 sq km of vineyards produce more fine wine than any other region in the world. Well-balanced Bordeaux reds blend several grape varieties, predominantly merlot, cabernet sauvignon and cabernet franc. The Médoc, Pomerol, St-Émilion and Graves are key winegrowing areas.

The most renowned red in the Côtes du Rhône appellation from the Rhône Valley – a vast, 771 sq km winegrowing area with dramatically different soils, climates, topography and grapes – is Châteauneuf-du-Pape, a strong full-bodied wine bequeathed by the Avignon popes who planted the distinctive stone-covered vineyards.

Further south on the coast near Toulon, deep-flavoured Bandol reds have been produced from dark-berried mourvèdre grapes since Roman times. These wines were famous across Gaul, their ability to mature at sea ensuring they travelled far beyond their home shores in the 16th and 17th centuries.

White

Some of France's finest whites come from the Loire Valley. This large winegrowing region produces the country's greatest variety of wines, and light delicate whites from Pouilly-Fumé, Vouvray, Sancerre, Bourgueil and Chinon are excellent. Muscadet, cabernet franc and chenin blanc are key grape varieties, contrasting with the chardonnay grapes that go into some great Burgundy whites.

Vines were planted by the Greeks in Massilia (Marseille) around 600 BC and crisp Cassis whites remain the perfect companion to the coast's bounty of shellfish and seafood.

Alsace produces almost exclusively white wines – mostly varieties produced nowhere else in France – that are known for their clean, fresh taste. Unusually, some of the fruity Alsatian whites also go well with red meat. Alsace's four most important varietal wines are riesling (known for its subtlety), gewürztraminer (pungent and highly regarded), pinot gris (robust and high in alcohol) and muscat d'Alsace (less sweet than muscats from southern France).

Rosé

Chilled, fresh pink rosé wines – best drunk alfresco beneath a vine-laced pergola – are synonymous with the hot south. Côtes de Provence, with 20 hectares of vineyards between Nice and Aix-en-Provence, is the key appellation (and France's sixth largest).

CLARET

THE FRENCH TABLE WINE

Britons have had a taste for Bordeaux' full-bodied wines, known as clarets in the UK, since the 12th century when King Henry II, who controlled the region through marriage, gained the favour of locals by granting them tax-free trade status with England.

Wine Schools

École des Vins de Bourgogne, *Beaune*

École du Vin, *Bordeaux*

La Winery, the *Médoc*

L'École du Vin de St-Émilion, *St-Émilion*

École de Dégustation, *Châteauneuf-du-Pape*

Langlois-Chateau, *Saumur*

Other enticing rosé labels from Provence include Coteaux d'Aix-en-Provence, Palette and Coteaux Varois of Angelina Jolie and Brad Pitt fame – the celebity pair own Château de Miraval, an organic wine-producing estate in Correns where Pink Floyd recorded part of *The Wall* in 1979.

Champagne

Champagne, produced northeast of Paris since the 17th century when innovative monk Dom Pierre Pérignon perfected a technique for making sparkling wine, is made from the white chardonnay, red pinot noir or black pinot meunier grape. Each vine is vigorously pruned and trained to produce a small quantity of high-quality grapes.

If the final product is labelled *brut,* it is extra dry, with only 1.5% sugar content. *Extra-sec* means very dry (but not as dry as *brut*), *sec* is dry and *demi-sec* slightly sweet. The sweetest Champagne is labelled *doux.* Whatever the label, it is sacrilege to drink it out of anything other than a traditional Champagne flute, narrow at the bottom to help the bubbles develop, wider in the middle to promote the diffusion of aromas, and narrower at the top again to concentrate those precious aromas.

Beer & Cider

Alsace, with its close ties to Germany, produces some excellent local beers such as Bière de Scharrach, Schutz Jubilator and Fischer. The north, close to Belgium and the Netherlands, has equally tasty beers, including Saint Sylvestre Trois Ponts, Colvert and Terken Brune. Brewers around the city of Lille produce *bières de garde* (literally 'keeping beers'), strong and fruity in taste. They are bottled in what look like Champagne bottles, corked and wired. Popular among young Bretons is a crop of beers made by boutique breweries, including Lancelot barley beer and Telenn Du buckwheat beer. Corsica has its own unique brews (p903), including the light herby lager, Colomba, and La Pietra, a full-bodied beer made from the island's abundance of chestnuts.

Cidre (apple cider) is made in many areas, including Savoy, Picardy and the Basque Country where it is called *sagarnoa.* But cider's real home is Normandy and Brittany where it is traditionally served in tea cups – with crêpes. Top ciders include Cornouaille (AOC) and those produced in the towns of Morlaix, Hennebont and the Val de Rance.

For excellent, practical guides – full of background information, tasting notes and eating/sleeping/drinking recommendations – to France's wine regions, peruse the Wine Travel Guides (www.winetravelguides.com) website.

APERITIFS & DIGESTIFS

Meals in France are preceded by an aperitif such as a *kir* (white wine sweetened with a sweet fruit syrup like blackcurrant or chestnut), *kir royale* (Champagne with blackcurrant syrup), *pineau* (cognac and grape juice) or a glass of sweet white Coteaux du Layon from the Loire Valley. In southern France aniseed-flavoured pastis (clear in the bottle, cloudy when mixed with water) is the aperitif to drink alfresco; in the southwest, go local with a Floc de Gascogne, a liqueur wine made from Armagnac and red or white grape juice. In Corsica, Cap Corse Mattei – a fortified wine whose recipe has stood the test of time (nearly 150 years!) – is the choice *apéro.*

After-dinner drinks accompany coffee. France's most famous brandies are Cognac and Armagnac, both made from grapes in the regions of those names. *Eaux de vie* (literally 'waters of life') can be made with grape skins and the pulp left over after being pressed for wine (Marc de Champagne, Marc de Bourgogne), apples (Calvados) and pears (Poire William), as well as such fruits as plums *(eau de vie de prune)* and even raspberries *(eau de vie de framboise).* In the Loire Valley a shot of orange (aka a glass of local Cointreau liqueur; see p407) ends the meal.

When in Normandy, do as the festive Normans do: refresh the palate between courses with a *trou normand* (literally 'Norman hole') – traditionally a shot of *calva* (Calvados) or a contemporary scoop of apple sorbet doused in the local apple brandy.

The Arts

1920s
French film flourishes. Sound ushers in René Clair's (1898–1981) world of fantasy and satirical surrealism. **Watch** Abel Gance's antiwar blockbuster *J'Accuse!* (I Accuse!; 1919), filmed on WWI battlefields.

1930s
WWI inspires a new realism: portraits of ordinary lives dominate film. **Watch** *La Grande Illusion* (The Great Illusion; 1937), a devastating evocation of war's folly based on the trench warfare experience of director Jean Renoir.

Literature, music, painting, cinema: France's vast artistic heritage is the essence of French *art de vivre*. Contemporary French writers might struggle to be published abroad, but Voltaire, Victor Hugo, Marcel Proust and Simone de Beauvoir walk the hall of fame. Music is embedded in the French soul, with world-class rap, dance and electronica coming out of Paris. French painting, with its roots in prehistoric cave art, continues to break new ground with provocative street art, while French film is enjoying a marvellous renaissance.

Literature
Courtly Love to Symbolism
Troubadours' lyric poems of courtly love dominated medieval French literature, while the *roman* (literally 'romance', now meaning 'novel') drew on old Celtic tales. With the *Roman de la Rose*, a 22,000-line poem by Guillaume de Lorris and Jean de Meung, allegorical figures like Pleasure, Shame and Fear appeared.

French Renaissance literature was extensive and varied. La Pléiade was a group of lyrical poets active in the 1550s and 1560s. The exuberant narrative of Loire Valley–born François Rabelais (1494–1553) blends coarse humour with encyclopedic erudition in a vast panorama of every kind of person, occupation and jargon in 16th-century France. Michel de Montaigne (1533–92) covered cannibals, war horses, drunkenness and the resemblance of children to their fathers and other themes.

The *grand siècle* (golden age) ushered in classical lofty odes to tragedy. François de Malherbe (1555–1628) brought a new rigour to rhythm in poetry; and Marie de La Fayette (1634–93) penned the first French novel, *La Princesse de Clèves* (1678).

The philosophical Voltaire (1694–1778) dominated the 18th century. A century on, Besançon gave birth to French Romantic Victor Hugo (1802–85). The breadth of interest and technical innovations exhibited in his poems and novels – *Les Misérables* and *The Hunchback of Notre Dame* among them – was phenomenal.

1940s
Surrealists eschew realism. **Watch** Jean Cocteau's *La Belle et la Bête* (Beauty and the Beast; 1945) and *Orphée* (Orpheus; 1950). WWII saps the film industry of both talent and money.

1950s
Nouvelle Vague (New Wave) sees small budgets, no stars and real-life subject matter. **Watch** A petty young criminal on the run in Jean-Luc Godard's *À Bout de Souffle* (Breathless; 1958) and adolescent rebellion in François Truffaut's *Les Quatre Cents Coups* (The 400 Blows; 1959).

1960s
France as the land of romance. **Watch** Claude Lelouch's *Un Homme et une Femme* (A Man and a Woman; 1966) and Jacques Demy's bittersweet *Les Parapluies de Cherbourg* (The Umbrellas of Cherbourg; 1964).

In 1857, literary landmarks *Madame Bovary* by Gustave Flaubert (1821–80) and Charles Baudelaire's (1821–67) poems *Les Fleurs du Mal* (The Flowers of Evil) were published. Émile Zola (1840–1902) saw novel-writing as a science in his powerful series, *Les Rougon-Macquart*.

Evoking mental states was the dream of symbolists Paul Verlaine (1844–96) and Stéphane Mallarmé (1842–98). Verlaine shared a tempestuous homosexual relationship with poet Arthur Rimbaud (1854–91): enter French literature's first modern poems.

Modern Literature

The world's longest novel – a seven-volume 9,609,000-character giant by Marcel Proust (1871–1922) – dominated the early 20th century. *À la Recherche du Temps Perdu* (Remembrance of Things Past) explores in evocative detail the true meaning of past experience recovered from the unconscious by 'involuntary memory'.

Surrealism proved a vital force until WWII. André Breton (1896–1966) captured the spirit of surrealism – a fascination with dreams, divination and all manifestations of 'the marvellous' – in his autobiographical narratives. In Paris the bohemian Colette (1873–1954) captivated and shocked with her titillating novels detailing the amorous exploits of heroines such as schoolgirl Claudine. In New York meanwhile, what would become one of the best-selling French works of all time was published in 1943: *Le Petit Prince* (The Little Prince), by Lyon-born writer and pilot Antoine du Saint-Exupéry (1900–44), captured the hearts of millions with his magical yet philosophical tale for children about an aviator's adventures with a little blonde-haired prince from Asteroid B-612.

After WWII, existentialism developed around the lively debates of Jean-Paul Sartre (1905–80), Simone de Beauvoir (1908–86) and Albert Camus (1913–60) in Paris' Left Bank cafes.

The *nouveau roman* of the 1950s saw experimental young writers seek new ways of organising narratives, with Nathalie Sarraute slashing

When Besançon-born Victor Hugo (1802–85) died, his coffin was laid beneath Paris' Arc de Triomphe for an all-night vigil. His work remains a hot topic in French schools – to the horror of some students whose abusive tweets after sitting the 2014 baccalaureate exam ('Victor Hugo, if I run into you on the street you're a dead man') turned the writer into a trending topic on Twitter.

BEST BOOKS TO READ

One way of ensuring your beach reading is right up to the minute is to plump for the latest winner of the **Prix Goncourt**, France's most prestigious literary prize awarded annually since 1903 and reflective, in recent years, of the occupation in contemporary French literature with issues of race, multiculturalism and immigration.

Winners include Marcel Proust in 1919 for *À l'Ombre des Jeunes Filles en Fleurs* (Within a Budding Grove); Simon de Beauvoir in 1954 for *Les Mandarins* (The Mandarins); and, more recently, French-Senegalese novelist-playwright Marie NDiaye with *Trois Femmes Puissantes* (The Strong Women). The first black woman to win the award, NDiaye stunned the literary world at the age of 21 with *Comédie Classique*, a 200-page novel comprising one single sentence. In 2013 the prize went to Parisian novelist/screenwriter Pierre Lemaitre for his historical novel, *Au Revoir là-Haut* (Goodbye Upstairs), set in a traumatised postwar France.

Add to your reading list the laureate of France's other big literary award, the **Grand Prix du Roman de l'Académie Française**, around since 1918. The 2009 Grand Prix winner, *Les Onze*, by French novelist Pierre Michon (b 1945), published in English as *The Eleven* (2013), portrays a humble Parisian painter who decorates the homes of Louis XIV's mistresses and goes on to create a Mona Lisa–type masterpiece. Michon's earlier novels, *Small Lives* (2008) and *Master and Servants* (1997), come equally recommended. French writer and journalist from Le Havre, Christophe Ono-dit-Biot, became the 2013 laureate with his fifth novel, *Plongeur* (2013), an exploration of father-son love.

identifiable characters and plot in *Les Fruits d'Or* (The Golden Fruits). *Histoire d'O* (Story of O), an erotic sadomasochistic novel written by Dominique Aury under a pseudonym in 1954, sold more copies outside France than any other contemporary French novel.

Another writer to turn heads was radical young writer Françoise Sagan (1935–2004) who shot to fame overnight at the age of 18 with her first novel, *Bonjour Tristesse* (Hello Sadness), published in 1954. The subsequent fast-paced, hedonistic lifestyle pursued by the party-loving, bourgeois-born writer ensured she remained in the spotlight until her death.

Contemporary Literature

Contemporary authors include Jean Echenoz, Pascal Quignard, Anna Gavalda, Erik Orsenna, Nina Bouraoui, Annie Ernaux, Emmanuel Carrère and Marie Darrieussecq. Comedian/dramatist Nelly Alard had her second novel *Un Moment d'un Couple* (A Moment of a Couple) published in 2013. Christine Angot is known as *'la reine de l'autofiction'* ('the queen of autobiography'), while Yasmina Khadra is actually a man – a former colonel in the Algerian army who adopted his wife's name as a nom de plume.

Marc Levy is France's best-selling writer. The film rights of his first novel were snapped up for the Stephen Spielberg box-office hit, *Just Like Heaven* (2005), and his novels have been translated into 42 languages. *Une Autre Idée de Bonheur* (Another Idea of Happiness; 2014) is his latest.

No French writer better delves into the mind, mood and politics of France's notable ethnic population than Faïza Guène (b 1985), sensation of the French literary scene who writes in a notable 'urban slang' style. Born and bred on a ghetto housing estate outside Paris, she stunned critics with her debut novel, *Kiffe Kiffe Demain* (2004), sold in 27 countries and published in English as *Just Like Tomorrow* (2006). Faïza Guène's father moved from a village in western Algeria to northern France in 1952, aged 17, to work in the mines. Only in the 1980s could he return to Algeria. There he met his wife, whom he brought back to France, to Les Courtillières housing estate in Seine-St-Denis, where 6000-odd immigrants live in five-storey high-rise blocks stretching for 1.5km. Such is the setting for Guène's first book and her second semi-autobiographical novel, *Du Rêve pour les Oeufs* (2006), published in English as *Dreams from the Endz* (2008). Her third novel, *Les Gens du Balto* (2008), published in English as *Bar Balto* (2011), is a series of colloquial, first-person monologues by various characters who live on a street in a Parisian suburb. Her most recent work, *Un Homme ça ne Pleure Pas* (Real Men Don't Cry; 2014), shifts to Nice in southern France.

1970s

The limelight baton goes to lesser-known directors like Éric Rohmer (b 1920), who make beautiful but uneventful films in which the characters endlessly analyse their feelings.

1980s

Big-name stars, slick production values and nostalgia: generous state subsidies see filmmakers switch to costume dramas and comedies in the face of growing competition from the USA. Luc Besson strikes box-office gold with *Subway* (1985) and *Le Grand Bleu* (The Big Blue; 1988).

1990s

French actor Gérard Depardieu wins huge audiences in France and abroad. **Watch** *Cyrano de Bergerac* (1990) and *Astérix et Obélix: Mission Cléopâtre* (2002). Besson continues to stun with *Nikita* (1990) and *Jeanne d'Arc* (Joan of Arc; 1999).

New Millennium

'New French Extremity' is the tag given to the socially conscious, transgressive films of talented Paris-born, Africa-raised filmmaker Claire Denis. **Watch** *Chocolat* (2000) and *Matériel Blanc* (White Material; 2009), scripted by Parisian novelist Marie NDiaye, to explore the legacy of French colonialism.

2012

Renaissance of French film. **Watch** *The Artist* (2011), a silent B&W, French-made romantic comedy set in 1920s Hollywood that scooped five Oscars and seven BAFTAs to become the most awarded film in French film history.

THE ARTS MUSIC

BANDES DESSINÉES

No literary genre has a bigger cult following in France than *bandes dessinées* (comic strips) – Paris even has a museum, Art Ludique-Le Musée (p104), dedicated to the art. Originally written for children, comic strips for adults burst onto the scene in 1959 with René Goscinny and Albert Uderzo's now iconic *Astérix* series.

Another French writer to address ethnic issues engagingly is JMG Le Clézio, born during WWII in Nice to a Niçois mother and Mauritian father. The bulk of his childhood was spent in Nigeria and he studied in Bristol, England, and Aix-en-Provence. In 2008 he won the Nobel Prize in Literature, confirming France's ranking as country with the most literary Nobel Prize winners.

Best Literary Sights

Maison de Victor Hugo, Paris

Jean-Paul Sartre and Simone de Beauvoir's graves, Cimetière du Montparnasse, Paris

Oscar Wilde's grave, Cimetière du Père Lachaise, Paris

Musée Colette, Burgundy

Château d'If, Marseille

Musée Jules Verne, Nantes

Music

Classical

French baroque music heavily influenced European musical output in the 17th and 18th centuries. French musical luminaries – Charles Gounod (1818–93), César Franck (1822–90) and *Carmen* creator Georges Bizet (1838–75) among them – were a dime a dozen in the 19th century. Modern orchestration was founded by French Romantic Hector Berlioz (1803–69). He demanded gargantuan forces: his ideal orchestra included 240 stringed instruments, 30 grand pianos and 30 harps.

Claude Debussy (1862–1918) revolutionised classical music with *Prélude à l'Après-Midi d'un Faune* (Prelude to the Afternoon of a Fawn), creating a light, almost Asian musical impressionism. Impressionist comrade Maurice Ravel (1875–1937) peppered his work, including *Boléro,* with sensuousness and tonal colour. Contemporary composer Olivier Messiaen (1908–92) combined modern, almost mystical music with natural sounds such as birdsong. His student Pierre Boulez (b 1925) works with computer-generated sound.

Jazz & French Chansons

Jazz hit 1920s Paris in the banana-clad form of Josephine Baker, an African American cabaret dancer. Post-WWII ushered in a much-appreciated bunch of musicians, mostly black Americans who opted to remain in Paris' bohemian Montmartre rather than return to the brutal racism and segregation of the US: Sidney Bechet called Paris home from 1949, jazz drummer Kenny 'Klook' Clarke followed in 1956, pianist Bud Powell in 1959, and saxophonist Dexter Gordon in the early 1960s.

In 1934 a chance meeting between Parisian jazz guitarist Stéphane Grappelli and three-fingered Roma guitarist Django Reinhardt in a Montparnasse nightclub led to the formation of the Hot Club of France quintet. Claude Luter and his Dixieland band were hot in the 1950s.

The *chanson française,* a French folk-song tradition dating from the troubadours of the Middle Ages, was eclipsed by the music halls and burlesque of the early 20th century, but was revived in the 1930s by Édith Piaf and Charles Trenet. In the 1950s, Paris' Left Bank cabarets nurtured *chansonniers* (cabaret singers) such as Léo Ferré, Georges Brassens, Claude Nougaro, Jacques Brel and the very charming, very sexy, very French Serge Gainsbourg. A biopic celebrating his life, *Serge Gainsbourg: Une Vie Héroïque* (Serge Gainsbourg: A Heroic Life), was released in 2009 to wide acclaim.

In the 1980s irresistible crooners Jean-Pierre Lang and Pierre Bachelet revived the *chanson* tradition with classics such as *Les Corons* (1982), a passionate ode to northern France's miners. Contemporary performers include Vincent Delerm, Bénabar, Jeanne Cherhal, Camille, Soha, Les Têtes Raides who released the album *Les Terriens* in 2014, and Arnaud Fleurent-Didier.

2014

Female filmmaker Pascale Ferrari (b 1960) makes her mark with *Bird People* (2014), set in and around a hotel at Paris' Charles de Gaulle airport.

Rap

France is known for its rap, an original 1990s sound spearheaded by Senegal-born, Paris-reared rapper MC Solaar and Suprême NTM (NTM being an acronym for a French expression far too offensive to print). Most big-name rappers are French 20-somethings of Arabic or African origin whose prime preoccupations are the frustrations and fury of fed-up immigrants in the French *banlieues* (suburbs).

Disiz La Peste, born in Amiens to a Senegalese father and French mother, portrayed precisely this in his third album, aptly entitled *Histoires Extra-Ordinaires d'un Jeune de Banlieue* (The Extraordinary Stories of a Youth in the Suburbs; 2005), as did his 'last' album *Disiz the End* (2009), after which he morphed into Peter Punk (www.disizpeterpunk.com) and created a very different rock-punk-electro sound. In 2011 he returned as rap artist Disiz La Peste, releasing the album *Lucide* in 2012 and its sequel *Trans-Lucide* – opening track entitled 'Fuck les problèmes' – in 2014.

France's other big rap band is Marseille's home-grown IAM (www.iam.tm.fr, in French), around since 1989 and enjoying a comeback since their release of two albums in the space of one year: despite rumours that *Arts Martiens* (2013) would be their last album, music label Def Jam announced in June 2014 that it had signed up the Marseillais band to record two further albums.

Rock & Pop

One could be forgiven for thinking that French pop is becoming dynastic. The distinctive M (for Matthieu) is the son of singer Louis Chédid; Arthur H is the progeny of pop-rock musician Jacques Higelin; and Thomas Dutronc is the offspring of 1960s idols Jacques and Françoise Hardy. Serge Gainsbourg's daughter with Jane Birkin, Charlotte Gainsbourg (b 1971) made her musical debut in 1984 with the single *Lemon Incest* and – several albums later – released a cover version of the song *Hey Joe* as soundtrack to the film *Nymphomaniac* (2013) in which she also starred as the leading lady.

Noir Désir was the sound of French rock until its lead vocalist, Bertrand Cantat (b 1964), was imprisoned in 2003 for murdering his girlfriend. Following his release from prison in 2007, Noir Désir limped along until 2010. The controversial singer, once dubbed the 'Jim Morrison of French rock', later formed the band Détroit with instrumentalist Pascal Humbert. Cantat's powerfully husky voice instantly won fans over, Détroit's first album *Horizons* (2013) selling 160,000 copies in just six months and tickets for the band's 2014 tour selling like hot cakes.

Indie rock band Phoenix, from Versailles, headlines festivals in the US and UK. The band was born in the late 1990s in a garage in the Paris suburbs; lead singer Thomas Mars, school mate Chris Mazzalai (guitar), his brother Laurent Brancowitz (guitar and keyboards) and Deck d'Arcy (keyboards/brass) have five hugely successful albums under their belt and a much-coveted Grammy award.

Musical Pilgrimages

Serge Gainsbourg's grave, Cimetière du Montparnasse, Paris

Jim Morrison's grave, Cimetière du Père Lachaise, Paris

Château des Milandes, the Dordogne

Espace Georges Brassens, Sète

Juan-les-Pins (for jazz lovers), French Riviera

Always worth a listen is Louise Attaque (http://louiseattaque.com) and Nosfell (www.nosfell.com), one of France's most creative and intense musicians who sings in his own invented language called *'le klokobetz'*. His third album, *Massif Armour* (2014), opens and closes in *'le klokobetz'* but otherwise woos listeners with powerful French love lyrics.

Dance & Electronica

France does dance music well: computer-enhanced Chicago blues and Detroit techno are often mixed with 1960s lounge music and vintage tracks from the likes of Gainsbourg and Brassens to create a distinctly urban, highly portable sound.

Internationally successful bands like Daft Punk and Justice head the scene. Daft Punk (www.daftalive.com), originally from Versailles, adapts first-wave acid house and techno to its younger roots in pop and indie rock. Its debut album *Homework* (1997) fused disco, house funk and techno, while *Random Access Memories* (2013) boldly ditched computer-generated sound for a strong disco beat played by session musicians. The album's lead single, 'Get Lucky', featuring US singer and songwriter Pharrell Williams, sold more than 9.3 million copies and made it in into the Top 10 in more than 30 countries.

Electronica band Justice, aka talented duo Gaspard Michel Andre Augé and Xavier de Rosnay, burst onto the dance scene in 2007 with a debut album that used the band's signature crucifix as its title. Raved about for its rock and indie influences, Justice has released three albums since, most recently live album *Access All Arenas* (2013). Electronica duo AIR (an acronym for 'Amour, Imagination, Rêve' meaning 'Love, Imagination, Dream') and M83 (named after the Messer 83 galaxy) from Antibes are two other electronica bands to listen out for.

David Guetta, Laurent Garnier, Martin Solveig and Bon Sinclair – originally nicknamed 'Chris the French Kiss' – are top Parisian electronica music producers and DJs who travel the international circuit. In the late 1990s David Guetta, with his wife Cathy, directed Paris' mythical nightclub Les Bains Douches (soon to be club-hotel, Les Bains) in Le Marais.

World

With styles ranging from Algerian *rai* to other North African music (artists include Cheb Khaled, Natacha Atlas, Jamel, Cheb Mami) and Senegalese *mbalax* (Youssou N'Dour), West Indian zouk (Kassav', Zouk Machine) and Cuban salsa, France's world beat is strong. Manu Chao (www.manuchao.net), the Paris-born son of Spanish parents, uses world elements to stunning effect.

Magic System from Côte d'Ivoire popularised *zouglou* (a kind of West African rap and dance music) with its album *Premier Gaou* (2002), and Congolese Koffi Olomide still packs the halls. Also try to catch blind singing couple, Amadou and Mariam; Rokia Traoré from Mali; and and Franco-Algerian DJ-turned-singer Rachid Taha (www.rachidtaha.fr) whose music mixes Arab and Western musical styles with lyrics in English, Berber and French.

No artist has sealed France's reputation in world music more than Paris-born, Franco-Congolese rapper, slam poet and three-time Victoire de la Musique–award winner, Abd al Malik (www.abdalmalik.fr). His albums *Gibraltar* (2006), *Dante* (2008) and *Château Rouge* (2010) are classics.

Cinematic Experiences

Forum des Images & Cinémathèque Française, Paris

Musée Lumière & Hangar du Premier Film, Lyon

Cannes Film Festival, Cannes

American Film Festival, Deauville

Futuroscope, Poitiers

Painting
Prehistoric to Landscape

France's oldest known prehistoric cave paintings (created 31,000 years ago) adorn the Grotte Chauvet-Pont-d'Arc in the Rhône Valley and the underwater Grotte Cosquer near Marseille; neither can be visited. In the Dordogne, it is the prehistoric art in caves at Lascaux that stuns.

According to Voltaire, French painting proper began with baroque painter Nicolas Poussin (1594–1665), known for his classical mythological and biblical scenes bathed in golden light. Wind forward a couple of centuries and modern still life popped up with Jean-Baptiste Chardin (1699–1779). A century later, neoclassical artist Jacques Louis David (1748–1825) wooed the public with vast history paintings.

While Romantics like Eugène Delacroix (buried in Paris' Cimetière du Père Lachaise) revamped the subject picture, the Barbizon School effected a parallel transformation of landscape painting. Jean-François Millet (1814–75), the son of a peasant farmer from Normandy, took many of his subjects from peasant life, and reproductions of his *L'Angélus* (The Angelus; 1857) – the best-known painting in France after the *Mona Lisa* – are strung above mantelpieces all over rural France. The original hangs in Paris' Musée d'Orsay.

Realism & Impressionism

The realists were all about social comment: Édouard Manet (1832–83) evoked Parisian middle-class life and Gustave Courbet (1819–77) depicted working-class drudgery.

It was in a flower-filled garden in a Normandy village that Claude Monet (1840–1926) expounded impressionism, a term of derision taken from the title of his experimental painting *Impression: Soleil Levant* (Impression: Sunrise; 1874). A trip to the Musée d'Orsay unveils a rash of other members of the school – Boudin, Sisley, Pissarro, Renoir, Degas and more.

An arthritis-crippled Renoir painted out his last impressionist days in a villa on the French Riviera, a part of France that inspired dozens of artists: Paul Cézanne (1839–1906) is particularly celebrated for his post-impressionist still lifes and landscapes done in Aix-en-Provence, where he was born and worked; Paul Gauguin (1848–1903) worked in Arles; while Dutch artist Vincent van Gogh (1853–90) painted Arles and St-Rémy de Provence. In St-Tropez pointillism took off: Georges Seurat (1859–91) was the first to apply paint in small dots or uniform brush strokes of unmixed colour, but it was his pupil Paul Signac (1863–1935) who is best known for pointillist works.

20th Century to Present Day

Twentieth-century French painting is characterised by a bewildering diversity of styles, including cubism, and Fauvism, named after the slur of a critic who compared the exhibitors at the 1906 autumn Salon in Paris with *fauves* (wild animals) because of their radical use of intensely bright colours. Spanish cubist Pablo Picasso (1881–1973) and Fauvist Henri Matisse (1869–1954) both chose southern France to set up studio, Matisse living in Nice and Picasso in Antibes.

The early 20th century also saw the rise of the Dada movement, and no piece of French art better captures its rebellious spirit than Marcel Duchamp's *Mona Lisa,* complete with moustache and goatee. In 1922 German Dadaist Max Ernst moved to Paris and worked on surrealism, a Dada offshoot that drew on the theories of Freud to reunite the conscious and unconscious realms and permeate daily life with fantasies and dreams.

THE ARTS PAINTING

Modern Art Meccas

Monet's garden, Giverny

Renoir's studio, French Riviera

Picasso's château studio, Antibes

Musée Matisse, Nice

Musée Jean Cocteau Collection Séverin Wunderman, Menton

Cézanne's studio, Aix-en-Provence

Le Chemin de Fauvisme, Collioure

ART TRENDS

With the close of WWII, Paris' role as artistic world capital ended. The focus shifted back to southern France in the 1960s with new realists such as Arman (1928–2005) and Yves Klein (1928–62), both from Nice. In 1960 Klein famously produced *Anthropométrie de l'Époque Bleue,* a series of imprints made by naked women covered from head to toe in blue paint rolling around on a white canvas, in front of an orchestra of violins and an audience in evening dress.

Artists in the 1990s turned to the minutiae of everyday urban life to express social and political angst. Conceptual artist Daniel Buren (b 1938) reduced his painting to a signature series of vertical 8.7cm-wide stripes that is applied to any surface imaginable – white marble columns in the courtyard of Paris' Palais Royal included. The painter (who in 1967, as part of the radical *groupe BMPT,* signed a manifesto declaring he was not a painter) was the *enfant terrible* of French art in the 1980s. Partner-in-crime Michel Parmentier (1938–2000) insisted on monochrome painting – blue in 1966, grey in 1967 and red in 1968.

Paris-born conceptual artist Sophie Calle (b 1953) brazenly exposes her private life in public with eye-catching installations such as *Prenez soin de vous* (Take Care of Yourself; 2007), a compelling and addictive work of art in book form exposing the reactions of 107 women to an email Calle received from her French lover, dumping her. Her *Rachel, Monique* (2010) evoked the death and lingering memory of her mother in the form of a photographic exhibition first shown at Paris' Palais de Tokyo and later as a live reading performance at the Festival d'Avignon.

Street art is the current buzz. The world's largest collective street-art exhibition, La Tour Paris 13 (www.tourparis13.fr), opened in a derelict apartment block in Paris' 13e arrondissement in 2013. Its 36 apartments on 13 floors showcased works by 100 international artists. The blockbuster exhibition ran for one month, after which the tower was shut and demolished. Itself an artwork, the three-day demolition was filmed and streamed live on the Internet (where the street artworks remain).

Architecture

From prehistoric megaliths around Carnac in Brittany to Vauban's 33 star-shaped citadels dotted around France to defend its 17th-century frontiers, French architecture has always been of *grand-projet* proportions.

Prehistoric to Roman

No part of France better demonstrates the work of the country's earliest architects than Brittany, which has more megalithic menhirs (monumental upright stones), tombs, cairns and burial chambers than anywhere else on earth. Many date from around 3500 BC and the most frequent structure is the dolmen, a covered burial chamber consisting of vertical menhirs topped by a flat capstone. Bizarrely, Brittany's ancient architects had different architectural tastes from their European neighbours – rather than the cromlechs (stone circles) commonly found in Britain, Ireland, Germany and Spain, they were much keener on building arrow-straight rows of menhirs known as *alignements*. And, indeed, Carnac's monumental Alignements de Carnac is the world's largest known prehistoric structure.

The Romans left behind a colossal architectural legacy in Provence and the French Riviera. Thousands of men took three to five years to haul the 21,000 cubic metres of local stone needed to build the Pont du Gard near Nîmes. Other fine pieces of Roman architecture, still operational, include amphitheatres in Nîmes and Arles, open-air theatres in Orange and Fréjus, and Nîmes' Maison Carrée.

> Catch up with southern France's prehistoric architects at Marseille's Centre de la Vieille Charité, Quinson's Musée de Préhistoire des Gorges du Verdon, and the beehive-shaped huts called *bories* at the Village des Bories near Gordes in the Luberon.

Romanesque

A religious revival in the 11th century led to the construction of Romanesque churches, so-called because their architects adopted many architectural elements (eg vaulting) from Gallo-Roman buildings still standing at the time. Romanesque buildings typically have round arches, heavy walls, few windows and a lack of ornamentation that borders on the austere.

Romanesque masterpieces include Toulouse's Basilique St-Sernin, Poitiers' Église Notre Dame la Grande, the exquisitely haunting Basilique St-Rémi in Reims, Caen's twinset of famous Romanesque abbeys, and Provence's trio in the Luberon (Sénanque, Le Thoronet and Silvacane). In Normandy the nave and south transept of the abbey-church on Mont St-Michel are beautiful examples of Norman Romanesque.

Then there is Burgundy's astonishing portfolio of Romanesque abbeys, among the world's finest: Abbaye de Pontigny, Abbaye de Cîteaux and Vézelay's Basilique Ste-Madeleine are highlights.

Gothic

Avignon's pontifical palace is Gothic architecture on a gargantuan scale. The Gothic style originated in the mid-12th century in northern France, where the region's great wealth attracted the finest architects, engineers

FRANCE'S MOST BEAUTIFUL VILLAGES

One of French architecture's signature structures popped up in rural France from the 13th century, 'up' being the operative word for these *bastides* or *villages perchés* (fortified hilltop villages), built high on a hill to afford maximum protection for previously scattered populations. Provence and the Dordogne are key regions to hike up, down and around one medieval hilltop village after another, but you can find them in almost every French region. Many of the most dramatic and stunning are among Les Plus Beaux Villages de France (The Most Beautiful Villages in France; www.les-plus-beaux-villages-de-france.org).

and artisans. Gothic structures are characterised by ribbed vaults carved with great precision, pointed arches, slender verticals, chapels (often built or endowed by the wealthy or by guilds), galleries and arcades along the nave and chancel, refined decoration and large stained-glass windows. If you look closely at certain Gothic buildings, however, you'll notice minor asymmetrical elements introduced to avoid monotony.

The world's first Gothic building was the Basilique de St-Denis near Paris, which combined various late-Romanesque elements to create a new kind of structural support in which each arch counteracted and complemented the next. The basilica served as a model for many other 12th-century French cathedrals, including Notre Dame de Paris and Chartres' cathedral – both known for their soaring flying buttresses. No Gothic belfry is finer to scale than that of Bordeaux' Cathédrale St-André.

In the 14th century, the Radiant Gothic style developed, named after the radiating tracery of the rose windows, with interiors becoming even lighter thanks to broader windows and more translucent stained glass. One of the most influential Rayonnant buildings was Paris' Ste-Chapelle, whose stained glass forms a curtain of glazing on the 1st floor.

Architect-Buff Sleeps

Le Pradey, Five Hotel and L'Apostrophe, Paris

....

Hôtel Le Corbusier, Marseille

....

Hôtel Oscar, Le Havre

....

Hotel Sōzō, Nantes

Renaissance

The Renaissance, which began in Italy in the early 15th century, set out to realise a 'rebirth' of classical Greek and Roman culture. It had its first impact on France at the end of that century, when Charles VIII began a series of invasions of Italy, returning with some new ideas.

To trace the shift from late Gothic to Renaissance, travel along the Loire Valley. During the very early Renaissance period, châteaux were used for the first time as pleasure palaces rather than defensive fortresses. Many edifices built during the 15th century to early 16th century in the Loire Valley – including Château d'Azay-le-Rideau and Château de Villandry – were built as summer or hunting residences for royal financiers, chamberlains and courtiers. Red-patterned brickwork – such as that on the Louis XII wing of Château Royal de Blois – adorned the façade of most châteaux dating from Louis XII's reign (1498–1515).

The quintessential French Renaissance château is a mix of classical components and decorative motifs (columns, tunnel vaults, round arches, domes etc) with the rich decoration of Flamboyant Gothic. It ultimately showcased wealth, ancestry and refinement. Defensive towers (a historical seigniorial symbol) were incorporated into a new decorative architecture, typified by its three-dimensional use of pilasters and arcaded loggias, terraces, balconies, exterior staircases, turrets and gabled chimneys. Heraldic symbols were sculpted on soft stone façades, above doorways and fireplaces, and across coffered ceilings. Symmetrical floor plans broke new ground and heralded a different style of living: Château de Chambord contained 40 self-contained apartments, arranged on five floors around a central axis. This ensured easy circulation in a vast edifice that many rank as the first modern building in France.

Mannerism

Mannerism, which followed the Renaissance, was introduced by Italian architects and artists brought to France around 1530 by François I, whose royal château at Fontainebleau was designed by Italian architects. Over the following decades, French architects who had studied in Italy took over from their Italian colleagues.

The Mannerist style lasted until the early 17th century, when it was subsumed by the baroque style.

Baroque

During the Baroque period (the tail end of the 16th to late 18th centuries), painting, sculpture and classical architecture were integrated to create structures and interiors of great subtlety, refinement and elegance. Architecture became more pictorial, with the painted ceilings in churches illustrating the Passion of Christ to the faithful, and palaces invoking the power and order of the state.

Salomon de Brosse, who designed Paris' Palais du Luxembourg in 1615, set the stage for two of France's most prominent early-baroque architects: François Mansart (1598–1666), who designed the classical wing of Château Royal de Blois, and his younger rival Louis Le Vau (1612–70), who worked on France's grandest palace at Versailles.

Neoclassicism

Nancy's place Stanislas in northern France is the country's loveliest neoclassical square. Neoclassical architecture, which emerged in about 1740 and remained popular until well into the 19th century, had its roots in the renewed interest in the classical forms and conventions of Graeco-Roman antiquity: columns, simple geometric forms and traditional ornamentation.

Among the earliest examples of this style is the Italianate façade of Paris' Église St-Sulpice, designed in 1733 by Giovanni Servandoni, which took inspiration from Christopher Wren's St Paul's Cathedral in London; and the Petit Trianon at Versailles, designed by Jacques-Ange Gabriel for Louis XV in 1761. France's greatest neoclassical architect of the 18th century was Jacques-Germain Soufflot, the man behind the Panthéon in Left Bank Paris.

Renaissance architecture stamped châteaux with a new artistic form: the monumental staircase. The most famous of these splendid ceremonial (and highly functional) creations are at Azay-le-Rideau, Blois, and Chambord in the Loire Valley.

VAUBAN'S CITADELS

From the mid-17th century to the mid-19th century, the design of defensive fortifications around the world was dominated by the work of one man: Sébastien Le Prestre de Vauban (1633–1707).

Born to a relatively poor family of the petty nobility, Vauban worked as a military engineer during almost the entire reign of Louis XIV, revolutionising both the design of fortresses and siege techniques. To defend France's frontiers, he built 33 immense citadels, many of them shaped like stars and surrounded by moats, and he rebuilt or refined more than 100.

Vauban's most famous citadel is situated at Lille, but his work can also be seen at Antibes, Belfort, Belle Île, Besançon, Concarneau, Neuf-Brisach (Alsace), Perpignan, St-Jean Pied de Port and St-Malo. The Vauban citadel in Verdun comprises 7km of underground galleries. A dozen sites (www.sites-vauban.org) star on Unesco's World Heritage Site list under a 'Vauban Fortifications' banner.

Neoclassicism peaked under Napoléon III, who used it extensively for monumental architecture intended to embody the grandeur of imperial France and its capital: the Arc de Triomphe, La Madeleine, the Arc du Carrousel at the Louvre, the Assemblée Nationale building and the Palais Garnier. It was during this period moreover that urban planner Baron Haussmann, between 1850 and 1870 as Prefect of the Seine, completely redrew Paris' street plan, radically demolishing the city's maze of narrow, cramped medieval streets and replacing it with wide boulevards, sweeping parks and attractive *passages couverts* (covered passages).

The true showcase of this era though is Casino de Monte Carlo in Monaco, created by French architect Charles Garnier (1825–98) in 1878.

Art Nouveau in Paris

Hector Guimard's noodle-like metro entrances

The interior of the Musée d'Orsay

Department stores Le Bon Marché and Galeries Lafayette

The glass roof over the Grand Palais

Art Nouveau

Art nouveau (1850–1910) combined iron, brick, glass and ceramics in ways never before seen. The style emerged in Europe and the US under various names (Jugendstil, Sezessionstil, Stile Liberty) and caught on quickly in Paris. The style was characterised by sinuous curves and flowing asymmetrical forms reminiscent of creeping vines, water lilies, the patterns on insect wings and the flowering boughs of trees. Influenced by the arrival of exotic objets d'art from Japan, its French name came from a Paris gallery that featured works in the 'new art' style. True buffs should make a beeline for the art nouveau tourist trail in Nancy.

A Beautiful Age

The glittering belle époque, hot on the heels of art nouveau, heralded an eclecticism of decorative stucco friezes, trompe l'œil paintings, glittering wall mosaics, brightly coloured Moorish minarets and Turkish towers. Immerse yourself in its fabulous and whimsical designs with a stroll along promenade des Anglais in Nice, where the pink-domed Hôtel Negresco (1912) is the icing on the cake, or, up north, around the colourful Imperial Quarter of Metz. Or flop in a beautiful belle époque spa such as Vichy.

Modern

The Fondation Victor Vasarely, by the 'father of op art' Victor Vasarely (1908–97), was an architectural coup when unveiled in Aix-en-Provence in 1976. Its 14 giant monumental hexagons reflected what Vasarely had already achieved in art: the creation of optical illusion and changing perspective through the juxtaposition of geometrical shapes and colours.

France's best-known 20th-century architect, Charles-Édouard Jeanneret (better known as Le Corbusier; 1887–1965), was born in Switzerland but settled in Paris in 1917 at the age of 30. A radical modernist, he tried to adapt buildings to their functions in industrialised society without ignoring the human element, thus rewriting the architectural style book with his sweeping lines and functionalised forms adapted to fit the human form. No single building has redefined urban living more than Le Corbusier's vertical 337-apartment 'garden city' known as La Cité Radieuse (The Radiant City) – today Hôtel Le Corbusier – that he designed on the coast in Marseille in 1952.

Architecture et Musique (www. architecmusique. com) is a fine concept: enjoy a classical-music concert amid an architectural masterpiece; the annual program is online.

Most of Le Corbusier's work was done outside Paris, though he did design several private residences and the Pavillon Suisse, a dormitory for Swiss students at the Cité Internationale Universitaire in the 14e arrondisement of the capital. Elsewhere, Chapelle de Notre-Dame du Haut in the Jura and Couvent Ste-Marie de la Tourette near Lyon are 20th-century architectural icons.

Until 1968, French architects were still being trained almost exclusively at the conformist École de Beaux-Arts, reflected in most of the acutely unimaginative and impersonal 'lipstick tube' structures erected in the Parisian skyscraper district of La Défense, the Unesco building (1958) in the 7e, and Montparnasse's ungainly 210m-tall Tour Montparnasse (1973).

Contemporary

For centuries French political leaders sought to immortalise themselves through the erection of huge public edifices (aka *grands projets*) in Paris. Georges Pompidou commissioned the once reviled, now much-loved Centre Pompidou (1977) in which the architects – in order to keep the exhibition halls as uncluttered as possible – put the building's insides out. His successor, Valéry Giscard d'Estaing, was instrumental in transforming the derelict Gare d'Orsay train station into the glorious Musée d'Orsay (1986). And François Mitterrand commissioned the capital's best-known contemporary architectural landmarks (taxpayers' bill: a whopping €4.6 billion), including the Opéra Bastille, the Grande Arche in La Défense, the four glass towers of the national library, and IM Pei's glass pyramid at the hitherto sacrosanct and untouchable Louvre (an architectural cause célébre that paved the way, incidentally, for Mario Bellini and Rudy Ricciotti's magnificent 'flying carpet' roof atop the Louvre's Cour Visconti in 2012).

Jacques Chirac's only *grand projet* was the riverside museum Musée du Quai Branly, an iconic glass, wood and sod structure with 3-hectare experimental garden designed by Jean Nouvel (b 1945). France's leading and arguably most talented architect, Jean Nouvel was the creative talent behind the Institut du Monde Arabe (1987), a highly praised structure in Paris that successfully mixes modern and traditional Arab and Western elements, and is considered one of the most beautiful and successful of France's contemporary buildings. Nouvel's current project, the ambitious Philharmonie de Paris in Parc de la Villette will have an auditorium of 2400 'terrace' seats surrounding the orchestra when building work is finally complete in 2015. The concert program will be projected on the outer façade, on a 52m-high aluminium wall above an unusual sloping metal-clad 'roof'.

Equally exciting in the capital is the recent renaissance of some of Paris' loveliest art deco buildings: in 2014 the luxury McGallery arm of the Accor hotel group opened a five-star hotel and spa in the legendary Molitor swimming pool complex in western Paris where the bikini made its first appearance in the 1930s. In Le Marais, thermal-baths-turned-1980s-nightclub Les Bain Douches – another legendary address – will open late 2014 as luxury club-hotel Les Bains after years of being abandoned. Preserving as many of the original art deco features as possible was a characteristic of both projects.

Drawing on the city's longstanding tradition of glass in its architecture, Canadian architect Frank Gehry used 12 enormous glass 'sails' to design the extraordinary Fondation Louis Vuitton pour la Création that opened in the Bois de Bologne in late 2014. Glass is likewise a big feature of the work going on at the Forum des Halles, a thoroughly unattractive 1970s-eyesore shopping centre in the 1er, being transformed into a stunning contemporary creation. The radically curvaceous, curvilinear and glass-topped construction by architects Patrick Berger and Jacques Anziutti should be complete by 2016.

No single museum presents a finer overview of French architecture than Paris' Cité de l'Architecture et du Patrimoine inside the 1937-built Palais de Chaillot.

ARCHITECTURE CONTEMPORARY

SCANDAL

France's biggest architectural scandals-turned-successes: Renzo Piano and Richard Rogers' Centre Pompidou, and IM Pei's glass pyramid at the Louvre, both in Paris.

BUILDING GREEN

A signature architectural feature of the French capital that has since been exported to other French and European cities is the vertical garden – *mur végétal* (vegetation wall) – especially that of **Patrick Blanc** (www.verticalgardenpatrickblanc.com). His most famous work is at the Musée du Quai Branly in Paris. Seeming to defy the very laws of gravity, the museum's vertical garden consists of some 15,000 low-light foliage plants from Central Europe, the US, Japan and China, planted on a surface of 800 sq metres and held in place by a frame of metal, PVC and nonbiodegradable felt – but no soil.

LE CORBUSIER

Interesting and alarming were Le Corbusier's plans for Paris that thankfully never left the drawing board. Called Plan Voisin (Neighbour Project; 1925), it envisaged wide boulevards linking the Gare Montparnasse with the Seine and lined with skyscrapers. The project would have required bulldozing much of the Latin Quarter.

In the provinces, notable buildings include Strasbourg's European Parliament, Dutch architect Rem Koolhaas' Euralille, Jean Nouvel's glass-and-steel Vesunna Musée Gallo-Romain in Périgueux, a 1920s art deco swimming-pool-turned-art-museum in Lille and the fantastic Louvre II in little Lens, 37km south of Lille. Also noteworthy are an 11th-century abbey-turned-monumental sculpture gallery in Angers and Le Havre's rejuvenated 19th-century docks.

Then, of course, there's one of the world's tallest bridges, the stunning Viaduc de Millau in Languedoc (2004), designed by Sir Norman Foster. Other bridges worth noting for their architectural ingenuity are Normandy's Pont de Normandie (1995) near Le Havre and Paris' striking Passerelle Simone de Beauvoir (2006). Both cross the Seine.

In Strasbourg, Italian architect Paolo Portoghesi designed France's biggest mosque, large enough to seat 1500 worshippers. Topped by a copper dome and flanked by wings resembling a flower in bud, the riverside building took 20 years of political to-ing and fro-ing for the ground-breaking project – a landmark for Muslims in France – to come to fruition.

The daring duo Shigeru Ban (Tokyo) and Jean de Gastines (Paris) is the tour de force behind the very white, bright Centre Pompidou-Metz (2010). Looking south, Frank Gehry is the big-name architect behind Arles' innovative new cultural centre: all a shimmer in the bright southern sun, rocklike Luma Fondation will evoke the nearby Alpilles mountain range with its two linked towers topped with aluminium when it opens in 2018. In Lyon, a sparkling glass-and-steel cloud is rising out of the wasteland at the confluence of the Rhône and Saône Rivers, aka the cutting-edge Musée des Confluences (2014).

Landscapes & Wildlife

France is a land of art. Fantastic portraits adorn the walls of galleries, villages resemble oil paintings plucked from a bygone rural age and the people are naturally stylish. But as gorgeous as the art of France is, it fades when compared to the sheer beauty of the countryside itself.

The Land

Hexagon-shaped France, Europe's third-largest country (after Russia and Ukraine), is fringed by water or mountains along every side except in the northeast.

The country's 3200km-long coastline is incredibly diverse, ranging from white-chalk cliffs (Normandy) and treacherous promontories (Brittany) to broad expanses of fine sand (Atlantic coast) and pebbly beaches (the Mediterranean coast).

Western Europe's highest peak, Mont Blanc (4810m), spectacularly crowns the French Alps, which stagger along France's eastern border. North of Lake Geneva, the gentle limestone Jura Mountains run along the Swiss frontier to reach heights of around 1700m, while the rugged Pyrenees guard France's 450km-long border with Spain and Andorra, peaking at 3404m.

Five major river systems criss-cross the country: the Garonne (which includes the Tarn, the Lot and the Dordogne) empties into the Atlantic; the Rhône links Lake Geneva and the Alps with the Mediterranean; Paris is licked in poetic verse by the Seine, which slithers through the city en route from Burgundy to the English Channel; tributaries of the North Sea–bound Rhine drain much of the area north and east of the capital and then there's France's longest river, the château-studded Loire, which meanders through history from the Massif Central to the Atlantic.

FERUS

Follow the progress of France's precious wolf, bear and lynx populations with Ferus (www.ferus.org), France's conservation group for these protected predators.

Wildlife

Animals

France has more mammal species (around 135) than any other European country. Couple this with around 500 bird species (depending on which rare migrants are included), 40 types of amphibian, 36 varieties of reptile and 72 kinds of fish, and wildlife-watchers are in seventh heaven. Of France's 40,000 identified insects, 10,000 creep and crawl in the Parc National du Mercantour in the southern Alps.

BEARS, OH MY!

The brown bear disappeared from the Alps in the mid-1930s. The 150-odd native bears living in the Pyrenees a century ago had dwindled to one orphaned cub following the controversial shooting of its mother – the last female bear of Pyrenean stock – by a hunter in 2004. However, between 18 and 22 bears of Slovenian origin also call the French and Spanish Pyrenees home, though the most famous, Balou, was found dead in June 2014. The reintroduction program has faced fierce opposition from sheep herders.

High-altitude plains in the Alps and the Pyrenees shelter the marmot, which hibernates from October to April and has a shrill and distinctive whistle; the nimble chamois (mountain antelope), with its dark-striped head; and the *bouquetin* (Alpine ibex), seen in large numbers in the Parc National de la Vanoise. Mouflons (wild mountain sheep), introduced in the 1950s, clamber over stony sunlit scree slopes in the mountains, while red and roe deer and wild boar are common in lower-altitude forested areas. The Alpine hare welcomes winter with its white coat, while 19 of Europe's 29 bat species hang out in the dark in the Alpine national parks.

The *loup* (wolf), which disappeared from France in the 1930s, returned to the Parc National du Mercantour in 1992 – much to the horror of the mouflon (on which it preys) and local sheep farmers. Dogs, corrals and sound machines have been used as an effective, nonlethal way of keeping the growing free-roaming wolf population of the Mercantour and other Alpine areas from feasting on domesticated sheep herds.

A rare but wonderful treat is the sighting of an *aigle royal* (golden eagle): 40 pairs nest in the Mercantour, 20 pairs nest in the Vanoise, 30-odd in the Écrins and some 50 in the Pyrenees. Other birds of prey include the peregrine falcon, the kestrel, the buzzard and the bearded vulture – Europe's largest bird of prey, with an awe-inspiring wingspan of 2.8m. More recently, the small, pale-coloured Egyptian vulture has been spreading throughout the Alps and Pyrenees.

Even the eagle-eyed will have difficulty spotting the ptarmigan, a chickenlike species that moults three times a year to ensure a foolproof seasonal camouflage (brown in summer, white in winter). It lives on rocky slopes and in Alpine meadows above 2000m. The nutcracker, with its loud, buoyant sing-song and larch-forest habitat, the black grouse, the rock partridge, the very rare eagle owl and the three-toed woodpecker are among the other 120-odd species keeping birdwatchers glued to the skies in highland realms.

Elsewhere, there are now 12,000 pairs of white storks; 10% of the world's flamingo population hangs out in the Camargue; giant black cormorants – some with a wingspan of 1.7m – reside on an island off Pointe du Grouin on the north coast of Brittany; and there are unique seagull and fishing-eagle populations in the Réserve Naturelle de Scandola on Corsica. The *balbuzard pêcheur* (osprey), a migratory hunter that flocks to France in February or March, today only inhabits two regions of France: Corsica and the Loire Valley.

From butterfly-spotting in the Cévennes to exploring bird-rich wetlands in the Camargue, UK-based tour company Nature Trek (www. naturetrek.co.uk) organises inspirational wildlife-watching holidays.

WILDLIFE WATCH

The national parks and their regional siblings are great for observing animals in their natural habitat. The following are also worth a gander:

➡ **Flamingos** The Camargue, France's best-known wetland site, attracts 10,000 pink flamingos and over 400 other bird species including rollers and glossy ibis.

➡ **Vultures** Found in the Pyrenees at Falaise aux Vautours, the Vallée d'Ossau and in Languedoc at the Belvédère des Vautours in the Parc Naturel Régional des Grands Causses.

➡ **Storks** In Alsace at the Centre de Réintroduction Cigognes & Loutres, in Hunawihr, and the Enclos aux Cigognes in Munster; on the Atlantic coast at Le Teich Parc Ornithologique; and at the Parc des Oiseaux outside Villars-les-Dombes near Lyon.

➡ **Dolphins and whales** Playful bottlenose dolphins splash around in the Mediterranean, and whales are sometimes sighted, too. Prime viewing from boat trips on the French Riviera and Corsica.

HIGH-FACTOR PROTECTION BY THE SEA

Over 10% of the coastline of mainland France and Corsica is managed by the Conservatoire du Littoral (www.conservatoire-du-littoral.fr), a public coastal-protection body. Among the *conservatoire*'s rich pageant of *espaces naturels protégés* (protected natural areas) are the rare-orchid-dotted sand dunes east of Dunkirk, the Baie de Somme with its ornithological park, several wet and watery pockets of the horse-studded Camargue, and a Corsican desert.

France also sports 43 Ramsar Convention wetland sites (www.ramsar.wetlands.org).

Plants

About 140,000 sq km of forest – beech, oak and pine in the main – covers 20% of France, and there are 4900 different species of native flowering plants countrywide (2250 alone grow in the Parc National des Cévennes).

The Alpine and Pyrenean regions nurture fir, spruce and beech forests on north-facing slopes between 800m and 1500m. Larch trees, mountain and arolla pines, rhododendrons and junipers stud shrubby subalpine zones between 1500m and 2000m, and a brilliant riot of spring and summertime wildflowers carpets grassy meadows above the treeline in the alpine zone (up to 3000m).

Alpine blooms include the single golden-yellow flower of the arnica, long used in herbal and homeopathic bruise-relieving remedies; the flame-coloured fire lily; and the hardy Alpine columbine, with its delicate blue petals. The protected 'queen of the Alps' (aka the Alpine eryngo) bears an uncanny resemblance to a purple thistle but is, in fact, a member of the parsley family (to which the carrot also belongs).

Corsica and the Massif des Maures, west of St-Tropez on the Côte d'Azur, are closely related botanically: both have chestnut and cork-oak trees and are thickly carpeted with *garrigues* and *maquis* – heavily scented scrubland, where dozens of fragrant shrubs and herbs find shelter.

ORCHIDS

Of France's 150 orchids, the black vanilla orchid is one to look out for – its small red-brown flowers exude a sweet vanilla fragrance.

National Parks

The proportion of protected land in France is surprisingly low: seven *parcs nationaux* (p961) fully protect just 0.8% of the country. Another 13% (70,000 sq km) in metropolitan France and its overseas territories is protected to a substantially lesser degree by 48 *parcs naturels régionaux* (p961), and a further few per cent by 320 smaller *réserves naturelles* (www.reserves-naturelles.org), some of them under the eagle eye of the Conservatoire du Littoral.

While the central zones of national parks are uninhabited and fully protected by legislation (dogs, vehicles and hunting are banned and camping is restricted), their delicate ecosystems spill over into populated peripheral zones in which economic activities, some of them environmentally unfriendly, are permitted and even encouraged.

Most regional nature parks and reserves were established not only to maintain or improve local ecosystems, but also to encourage economic development and tourism in areas suffering from hardship and diminishing populations (such as the Massif Central and Corsica).

Select pockets of nature – the Pyrenees, Mont St-Michel and its bay, part of the Loire Valley, the astonishingly biodiverse Cévennes and a clutch of capes on Corsica – have been declared Unesco World Heritage Sites.

LIFE & DEATH OF THE IBEX

Often spotted hanging out on sickeningly high crags and ledges, the nippy *bouquetin des Alpes* (Alpine ibex), with its imposingly large, curly-wurly horns, is the animal most synonymous with the French Alps. Higher altitudes were loaded with the handsome beast in the 16th century, but three centuries on its extravagant horns had become a must-have item in any gentleman's trophy cabinet, and within a few years it had been hunted to the brink of extinction.

In 1963 the Parc National de la Vanoise was created in the Alps to stop hunters in the massif from shooting the few Alpine ibex that remained. The creation of similar nature reserves and rigorous conservation campaigns have seen populations surely and steadily recover – to the point where today the Alpine ibex is thriving. Not that you're likely to encounter one: the canny old ibex has realised that some mammals are best avoided.

Environmental Issues

As elsewhere in the world, wetlands in France – incredibly productive ecosystems that are essential for the survival of birds, reptiles, fish and amphibians – are shrinking. More than 20,000 sq km (3% of French territory) are considered important wetlands but only 4% of this land is currently protected.

Great tracts of forest burn each summer, often because of careless day trippers but occasionally, as is sometimes reported on the Côte d'Azur, because they're intentionally torched by people hoping to get licences to build on the damaged lands. Since the mid-1970s, between 31 sq km and 615 sq km of land has been reduced to black stubble each year by an average of 540 fires. However, as prevention and fire-fighting improve, the number of fires overall is falling, according to the Office National des Forêts (www.onf.fr), the national forestry commission.

Dogs and guns also pose a threat to French animal life, brown bears included. While the number of hunters has fallen by more than 20% in the last decade, there are still a lot more hunters in France (1.3 million) than in any other Western European country.

Despite the 1979 Brussels Directive for the protection of wild birds and their eggs, nests and habitats in the EU, the French government has been very slow to make its provisions part of French law, meaning birds that can fly safely over other countries can still be hunted as they cross France.

The state-owned electricity company, Electricité de France, has an enviable record on minimising greenhouse-gas emissions – fossil-fuel-fired powerplants account for just 4.6% of its production. Clean, renewable hydropower, generated by 220 dams, comprises 8.8% of the company's generating capacity but this does affect animal habitats. And no less than 75% (the highest in the world) of France's electricity comes from another controversial carbon-zero source: nuclear power, generated by 59 nuclear reactors at 20 sites. When François Hollande came to power in May 2012, he pledged to reduce France's reliance on nuclear energy to 50% by 2025.

Meanwhile the world's most ambitious nuclear-power program continues to grow. Costing an extraordinary €8.5 billion, the country's most recent nuclear reactor, Flamanville 3 on Normandy's west coast near Cherbourg, is due for completion in 2016, two years later than planned.

Europe's largest solar-powered electricity-generating farm sits 1000m-high on a south-facing slope near the tiny village of Curbans in Provence. Since its inauguration in 2011 the farm's 150-hectare array of photovoltaic cells – 145,000 panels in all – have removed 120,000 metric tonnes of carbon dioxide annually from the French energy bill.

Survival Guide

Directory A–Z

Accommodation

Be it a fairy-tale château, a boutique hideaway or floating pod on a lake, France has accommodation to suit every taste, mood and pocket.

Categories

As a rule of thumb, budget covers everything from basic hostels to small family-run places; midrange means a few extra creature comforts such as elevator and free wi-fi; while top-end places stretch from luxury five-star palaces with air conditioning, swimming pools and restaurants to boutique-chic alpine chalets.

Costs

Accommodation costs vary wildly between seasons and regions: what will buy you a night in a romantic *chambre d'hôte* (B&B) in the countryside may get a dorm bed in a major city or high-profile ski resort.

Reservations

Midrange, top-end and many budget hotels require a credit card number to secure an advance reservation made by phone; some hostels do not take bookings. Many tourist offices can advise on availability and reserve for you, often for a fee of €5 and usually only if you stop by in person. In the Alps, ski resort tourist offices run a central reservation service for booking accommodation.

Seasons

➡ Rates listed are for high season.

➡ In ski resorts, high season is Christmas, New Year and the February–March school holidays.

➡ On the coast, high season is summer, particularly August.

➡ Hotels in inland cities often charge low-season rates in summer.

➡ Rates often drop outside the high season – in some cases by as much as 50%.

➡ In business-oriented hotels in cities, rooms are most expensive from Monday to Thursday and cheaper over the weekend.

➡ In the Alps, hotels usually close between seasons, from around May to mid-June and from mid-September to early December; many addresses in Corsica only open Easter to October.

B&Bs

For charm, a heartfelt *bienvenue* (welcome) and solid home cooking, it's hard to beat France's privately run *chambres d'hôte* (B&Bs) – urban rarities but as common as muck in rural areas. By law a *chambre d'hôte* must have no more than five rooms and breakfast must be included in the price; some hosts prepare a meal *(table d'hôte)* for an extra charge of around €30 including wine. Pick up lists of *chambres d'hôte* at tourist offices, or find one to suit online:

Bienvenue à la Ferme (www.bienvenue-a-la-ferme. com)

PRICE RANGES

The price indicators refer to the cost of a double room, including private bathroom (any combination of toilet, bathtub, shower and washbasin) and excluding breakfast unless otherwise noted. Breakfast is assumed to be included at a B&B. Where half board (breakfast and dinner) and full board (breakfast, lunch and dinner) is included, this is mentioned in the price.

CATEGORY	COST
€ budget	< €90 (< €130 in Paris)
€€ midrange	€90–190 (€130–200 in Paris)
€€€ top end	> €190 (> €200 in Paris)

GLAMPING

Farewell clammy canvas, adieu inflatable mattress... Glamping in France is cool and creative, with *écolo chic* (ecochic) and adventurous alternatives springing up all the time. If you fancy doing a Robinson Crusoe by staying in a tree house with an incredible view over the treetops, visit **Cabanes de France** (www.cabanes-de-france.com) which covers leafy options between branches all over France. Prefer to keep your feet firmly on the ground? Keep an eye out for ecoconscious campsites where you can snooze in a *tipi* (tepee) or in a giant hammock.

Chambres d'Hôtes France (www.chambresdhotesfrance. com)

Fleurs de Soleil (www.fleurs desoleil.fr) Selective collection of 550 stylish *maisons d'hôte*, mainly in rural France.

Gîtes de France (www. gites-de-france.com) France's primary umbrella organisation for B&Bs and self-catering properties (*gîtes*). Search by region, theme (charm, with kids, by the sea, gourmet, great garden etc), activity (fishing, wine tasting etc) or facilities (pool, dishwasher, fireplace, baby equipment, etc).

iGuide (www.iguide-hotels. com) Gorgeous presentation of France's most charming and often-times most upmarket B&Bs and theme, organised by region and/ or theme (romantic, gastronomic, green, oenological and so forth).

Samedi Midi Éditions (www.samedimidi.com) Country, mountain, seaside... Choose your *chambre d'hôte* by location or theme (romance, golf, design, cooking courses).

Camping

Be it a Mongolian yurt, boutique treehouse or simple canvas beneath stars, camping in France is in vogue. Thousands of well-equipped campgrounds dot the country, many considerably placed by rivers, lakes and the sea. Gîtes de France and Bienvenue à la Ferme coordinate camping on farms.

➡ Most campgrounds open March or April to late September or October; popular spots fill up fast in summer so it is wise to call ahead.

➡ 'Sites' refer to fixed-price deals for two people including a tent and a car. Otherwise the price is broken down per adult/tent/car. Factor in a few extra euro per night for *taxe de séjour* (holiday tax) and electricity.

➡ Euro-economisers should look out for local, good-value but no-frills *campings municipaux* (municipal campgrounds).

➡ Many campgrounds rent mobile homes with mod cons such as heating, fitted kitchen and TV.

➡ Pitching up 'wild' in nondesignated spots (*camping sauvage*) is illegal in France.

➡ Campground offices often close during the day.

➡ Accessing many campgrounds without your own transport can be slow and costly, or simply impossible. Websites with campsite listings searchable by location, theme and facilities:

Camping en France (www. camping.fr)

Camping France (www. campingfrance.com)

HPA Guide (http://camping. hpaguide.com)

Homestays

One of the best way to brush up your *français* and immerse yourself in local life is by staying with a French family under an arrangement known as *hôtes payants* or *hébergement chez l'habitant*. Popular among students and young people, this set-up means you rent a room and usually have access (sometimes limited) to the bathroom and the kitchen; meals may also be available. If you are sensitive to smoke or pets, make sure you mention this. The following arrange homestays:

France Lodge Locations (☑ 01 56 35 85 80; www. apartments-in-paris.com) Accommodation in private Parisian homes; €36 to €78 a night for a single, €56 to €95 for two people in a double or twin, and from €79/105 for three/four people.

Homestay Booking (www. homestaybooking.com/ homestay-france) Homestays in major French cities.

Hostels

Hostels in France range from funky to threadbare, although with a wave of design-driven, up-to-the-minute hostels opening in Paris, Marseille and other big cities, hip hang-outs with perks aplenty seem to easily outweigh the threadbare these days.

➡ In university towns, *foyers d'étudiant* (student dormitories) are sometimes converted for use by travellers during summer.

BOOK YOUR STAY ONLINE

For more accommodation reviews by Lonely Planet authors, check out http://lonelyplanet.com/hotels/. You'll find independent reviews, as well as recommendations on the best places to stay. Best of all, you can book online.

➡ A dorm bed in an *auberge de jeunesse* (youth hostel) costs €20 to €50 in Paris, and anything from €15 to €35 in the provinces, depending on location, amenities and facilities; sheets are always included, breakfast more often than not.

➡ To prevent outbreaks of bed bugs, sleeping bags are not permitted.

➡ Hostels by the sea or in the mountains sometimes offer seasonal outdoor activities.

➡ French hostels are 100% nonsmoking.

HOSTELLING CARD

Official *auberges de jeunesse* affiliated to the **Fédération Unie des Auberges de Jeunesse** (www.fuaj.org) or **Ligue Française pour les Auberges de la Jeunesse** (www.auberges-de-jeunesse.com) require guests to have an annual Hostelling International (HI) card (€7/11 for under/over 26s) or a nightly Welcome Stamp (up to €3, maximum of six per year).

Hotels

We have tried to feature well-situated, independent hotels that offer good value, a warm welcome, at least a bit of charm and a palpable sense of place.

Hotels in France are rated with one to five stars, although the ratings are based on highly objective criteria (eg the size of the entry hall), not the quality of the service, the decor or cleanliness.

WHICH FLOOR?

In France, as elsewhere in Europe, 'ground floor' refers to the floor at street level; the 1st floor – what would be called the 2nd floor in the US – is the floor above that.

➡ French hotels almost never include breakfast in their rates. Unless specified otherwise, prices quoted don't include breakfast, which costs around €8/12/25 in a budget/midrange/top-end hotel.

➡ When you book, hotels usually ask for a credit card number; some require a deposit.

➡ A double room generally has one double bed (sometimes two singles pushed together!); a room with twin beds (*deux lits*) is usually more expensive, as is a room with a bathtub instead of a shower.

➡ Feather pillows are practically nonexistent in France, even in top-end hotels.

➡ All hotel restaurant terraces allow smoking; if you are sensitive to smoke, you may need to sit inside.

Refuges & Gîtes d'Étape

➡ *Refuges* (mountain huts or shelters) are bog-basic cabins established along walking trails in uninhabited mountainous areas and operated by national-park authorities, the **Club Alpin Français** (French Alpine Club; www.ffcam.fr) or other private organisations.

➡ *Refuges* are marked on hiking and climbing maps.

➡ A bunk in a dorm generally costs €10 to €25. Hot meals are sometimes available and, in a few cases, mandatory, pushing the price up to €30 or beyond.

➡ Advance reservations and a weather check are essential before setting out.

➡ *Gîtes d'étape*, better equipped and more comfortable than *refuges* (some even have showers), are situated along walking trails in less remote areas, often villages.

➡ Drop by **Gîtes d'Étape et Refuges** (www.gites-refuges.com), an online listing of 4000 *gîtes d'étape* and *refuges* in France.

Rental Accommodation

If you are planning on staying put for more than a few days or are travelling in a group, then renting a furnished studio, apartment or villa can be an economical alternative. You will have the chance to live like a local, with trips to the farmers market and the *boulangerie* (bakery).

Finding an apartment for long-term rental can be gruelling. Landlords, many of whom prefer locals to foreigners, usually require substantial proof of financial responsibility and sufficient funds in France; many ask for a *caution* (guarantee) and a hefty deposit.

➡ Gîtes de France handles some of the most charming *gîtes ruraux* (self-contained holiday cottages) in rural areas.

➡ Cleaning, linen rental and electricity fees usually cost extra.

➡ Classified ads appear in *De Particulier à Particulier* (www.pap.fr, in French), published on Thursday and sold at newsstands.

➡ For apartments outside Paris it's best to search at your destination.

➡ Check places like bars and *tabacs* (tobacconists) for free local newspapers (often named after the number of the *département*) with classifieds listings.

Activities

From Alpine glaciers, rivers and canyons to the volcanic peaks of the Massif Central – not to mention 3200km of coastline stretching from Italy to Spain and from the Basque country to the Straits of Dover – France's spirit-lifting landscapes beg outdoor escapes.

THE FINE ART OF SLEEPING

A château, a country manor, Parisian opulence in the shade of the Eiffel Tower – whether you want to live like a lord, sleep like a log or blow the budget, there's a room with your name on it.

➡ **Alistair Sawday's** (www.sawdays.co.uk) Boutique retreats and *chambres d'hôte*, placing the accent on originality and authentic hospitality.

➡ **Châteaux & Hôtels Collection** (www.chateauxhotels.com) Châteaux and other historic properties, now boutique hotels, with a thousand tales to tell.

➡ **Grandes Étapes Françaises** (www.grandesetapes.fr) Beautiful châteaux-hotels and multistar residences.

➡ **iGuide** (www.iguide-hotels.com) Abbeys, manors, châteaux – a real mixed bag of charming hotels.

➡ **Logis de France** (www.logis-de-france.fr) Small, often family-run hotels with charm and a warm welcome.

➡ **Relais & Châteaux** (www.relaischateaux.com) Seductive selection of top-end villas, châteaux and historic hotels.

➡ **Relais du Silence** (www.relaisdusilence.com) Fall asleep to complete silence in a gorgeous château, spa-clad *auberge* (country inn), or vineyard hotel.

➡ **Small Luxury Hotels of the World** (www.slh.com) Super-luxurious boutique hotels, chalets and resorts.

To help plan your trip, see the Outdoor Activities chapter (p44).

Organisations

Whether you are a peak bagger, surfer dude or thrill-seeking mountain biker, the following organisations can help you plan your adventure:

CYCLING

Fédération Française de Cyclisme (French Cycling Federation; www.ffc.fr) Founded in 1881, this is *the* authority on competitive cycling and mountain biking (VTT) in France, including freeriding, cross-country and downhill.

Fédération Française de Cyclotourisme (French Cycling Tourism Federation; www.ffct.org) This organisation promotes bicycle touring and mountain biking.

Union Touristique Les Amis de la Nature (http://troisv.amis-nature.org) Has details on local, regional and long-distance *véloroutes* (cycling routes) around France.

Véloroutes et Voies Vertes (www.af3v.org) A database of 250 signposted *véloroutes* (bike paths) and *voies vertes* (greenways) for cycling and in-line skating.

GLIDING

Fédération Française de Vol à Voile (French Gliding Federation; www.ffvv.org) Provides details of *vol à voile* (gliding) clubs countrywide.

Fédération Française de Vol Libre (French Hanggliding Federation; http://federation.ffvl.fr) Groups regional clubs specialising in *deltaplane* (hang-gliding), *parapente* (paragliding) and *le kite-surf* (kitesurfing).

MOUNTAIN & SNOW SPORTS

Club Alpin Français (French Alpine Club; www.ffcam.fr) This highly regarded organisation groups 280 local mountain sports clubs and arranges professional guides for escapades in *alpinisme* (mountaineering), *escalade* (rock climbing), *escalade de glace* (ice climbing) and other highland activities. It also

runs many of the *refuges* (mountain huts) in the French Alps.

École du Ski Français (ESF; www.esf.net) The largest ski school in the world, operating everywhere in France, big enough to have a ski lift and high enough to be snow sure. The tuition is first rate.

WALKING

Grande Randonnée (www.grande-randonnee.fr) A good source of information (in French) on France's long-distance footpaths.

GR-Infos (www.gr-infos.com) Information in English on France's long-distance footpaths.

Parcs Nationaux de France (French National Parks; www.parcsnationaux.fr) First port of call if you are planning a visit to one of France's six national parks.

Parcs Naturels Régionaux de France (French Regional Nature Parks; www.parcs-naturels-regionaux.tm.fr) Has the low-down on activities, accommodation and events in France's 48 regional nature parks.

WATER SPORTS

École Française de Kite (www.efk.fr) France's kite-surfing school has dozens of outlets on the Mediterranean and Atlantic coasts, and a couple inland by lakes.

Fédération Française de Voile (French Sailing Federation; www.ffvoile.fr) Key information source on sailing, for both fun and competition.

Customs Regulations

Goods brought in and out of countries within the EU incur no additional taxes provided duty has been paid somewhere within the EU and the goods are for personal consumption. Duty-free shopping is available only if you are leaving the EU.

Duty-free allowances (for adults) coming from non-EU countries (including the Channel Islands):

➜ 200 cigarettes

➜ 50 cigars

➜ 1L spirits

➜ 2L wine

➜ 50ml perfume

➜ 250ml eau de toilette

➜ other goods up to the value of €175 (€90 for under 15 year olds)

Higher limits apply if you are coming from Andorra; anything over these limits must be declared. For further details, see www.douane.gouv.fr (partly in English).

Discount Cards

Discount cards yield fantastic benefits and easily pay for themselves. As well as the card fee, you'll often need a passport-sized photo and some form of ID with proof of age (eg passport or birth certificate).

People over 60 or 65 are entitled to discounts on things like public transport, museum admission fees and theatres.

Discount card options:

Camping Card International (CCI; www.camping cardinternational.com; €8) Used as ID for checking into campsites; the annual card includes 3rd-party liability insurance and covers up to 11 people in a party; it usually yields up to 20% discount. Available at automobile associations, camping federations and campgrounds.

European Youth Card (Euro<26 card; www.euro26. org; €14) Wide range of discounts for under 26 year olds. Available online.

International Student Identity Card (ISIC; www. isic.org; €13) Discounts on travel, shopping, attractions and entertainment for full-time students. Available at ISIC points listed online.

International Teacher Identity Card (ITIC; www. isic.org; €13) Travel, shopping, entertainment and sightseeing discounts for full-time teachers.

International Youth Travel Card (IYTC; www.isic.org; €13) Discounts on travel, tickets and so forth for under 26 year olds.

Electricity

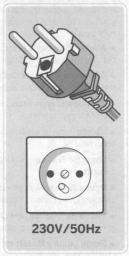

230V/50Hz

Embassies & Consulates

All foreign embassies are in Paris.

➜ Many countries – including Canada, Japan, the UK, USA and most European countries – also have consulates in other major cities such as Bordeaux, Lyon, Nice, Marseille and Strasbourg.

➜ To find a consulate or an embassy, visit www. embassiesabroad.com or look up *'ambassade'* in the super user-friendly **Pages Jaunes** (Yellow Pages; www. pagesjaunes.fr).

Food

This guide includes options for all tastes and budgets, reviewed in order of preference and categorised according to type of cuisine, or price range, or both.

For the complete tastebud tour of France's varied regional cuisines and accompanying tipples, see the essay The French Table (p934). To

---

PRICE RANGES

Price indicators refer to the average cost of a two-course meal, be it an *entrée* (starter) and *plat* (main course) or main and dessert, or a 2- or 3-course *menu* (pre-set meal at a fixed price). Lunch *menus* almost always yield a far better deal.

CATEGORY	COST
€ budget	< €20
€€ midrange	€20–40
€€€ top end	> €40

---

understand how to eat and drink like a local, see that tip-loaded section at the front of this book (p34).

Gay & Lesbian Travellers

The rainbow flag flies high in France, a country that left its closet long before many of its European neighbours. *Laissez-faire* perfectly sums up France's liberal attitude towards homosexuality and people's private lives in general; in part because of a long tradition of public tolerance towards unconventional lifestyles.

➡ Paris has been a thriving gay and lesbian centre since the late 1970s, and most major organisations are based there today.

➡ Bordeaux, Lille, Lyon, Montpellier, Toulouse and many other towns also have an active queer scene.

➡ Attitudes towards homosexuality tend to be more conservative in the countryside and villages.

➡ France's lesbian scene is less public than its gay male counterpart and is centred mainly on women's cafes and bars.

➡ Same-sex marriage has been legal in France since May 2013.

➡ Gay Pride marches are held in major French cities mid-May to early July.

Publications

Damron (www.damron.com) Publishes English-language travel guides, including the *Damron Women's Traveller* for lesbians and the *Damron Men's Travel Guide* for gays.

Spartacus International Gay Guide (www.spartacus world.com) A male-only guide to just about every country in the world, with more than 70 pages devoted to France, almost half of which cover Paris. There's an iPhone app too.

Websites

France Queer Resources Directory (www.france.qrd. org) Gay and lesbian directory.

Gay France (www.gay-france. net) Insider tips on gay life in France.

Gaipied (www.gayvox.com/ guide3) Online travel guide to France, with listings by region, by Gayvox.

Tasse de Thé (www.tasse dethe.com) A *webzine lesbien* with lots of useful links.

Health

France is a healthy place, so your main risks are likely to be sunburn, foot blisters, insect bites and mild stomach problems from eating and drinking with too much gusto.

Before You Go

➡ Bring your medications in their original, clearly labelled, containers.

➡ A signed and dated letter from your physician describing your medical conditions and medications, including generic names (French medicine names are often completely different to those in other countries), is also a good idea.

➡ Dental care in France is usually good; however, it is sensible to have a dental check-up before a long trip.

➡ No vaccinations are required to travel to France but the World Health Organization (WHO) recommends that all travellers be covered for diphtheria, tetanus, measles, mumps, rubella and polio, regardless of their destination.

Availability & Cost of Health Care

➡ Visitors to France can get excellent health care from hospital (*hôpital*) emergency rooms/casualty wards (*salles des urgences*) and at a doctors' office (*cabinet médical*).

➡ For minor illnesses, trained staff in pharmacies – in every village and town with a green-cross sign outside that flashes when open – give valuable advice, sell medications, can tell you when more specialised help is needed and will point you in the right direction.

➡ You will need to pay upfront for any health care you receive, be it at a doctor's surgery, pharmacy or hospital, unless your insurance plan makes payments directly to providers.

➡ The standard rate for a consultation with a GP/ specialist is €30 to €40.

➡ Emergency contraception is available with a doctor's prescription. Condoms (*les préservatifs*) are readily available.

EUROPEAN HEALTH INSURANCE CARD

Citizens of the EU, Switzerland, Iceland, Norway or Liechtenstein receive free or reduced-cost state-provided health-care cover with the European Health Insurance Card (EHIC) for medical treatment that becomes necessary while in France. Each family member will need a separate card. UK residents can get application forms from post offices, or download them from the Department of Health website (www.dh.gov.uk), which has comprehensive information about the card's coverage.

The EHIC does not cover private health care, so make sure that you are treated by a state health-care provider (conventionné). You will need to pay directly and fill in a treatment form (feuille de soins); keep the form to claim any refunds. In general, you can claim back around 70% of the standard treatment cost.

Citizens of other countries need to check if there is a reciprocal arrangement for free medical care between their country and France.

Insurance

➡ Comprehensive travel insurance to cover theft, loss and medical problems is highly recommended.

➡ Some policies specifically exclude dangerous activities such as scuba diving, motorcycling, skiing and even trekking: read the fine print.

➡ Check that the policy covers ambulances or an emergency flight home.

➡ Find out in advance if your insurance plan will make payments directly to providers or reimburse you later for overseas health expenditures.

➡ If you have to claim later, make sure you keep all documentation.

➡ Paying for your airline ticket with a credit card often provides limited travel accident insurance – ask your credit card company what it is prepared to cover.

➡ Worldwide travel insurance is available at www.lonelyplanet.com/travel-insurance. You can buy, extend and claim online anytime – even if you're already on the road.

Internet Access

➡ Wi-fi (pronounced 'wee-fee' in French) is available at major airports, in most hotels, and at some cafes, restaurants, museums and tourist offices.

➡ Free public wi-fi hotspots are available in cities and many towns: Paris alone has 260 public hotspots (www.paris.fr/wifi), including parks, libraries and municipal buildings (in parks look for a purple 'Zone Wi-Fi' sign near the entrance and select the 'PARIS_WI-FI_' network to connect).

➡ To search for free wi-fi hot spots in France, visit www.hotspot-gratuit.com or www.hotspot-locations.co.uk.

➡ Internet cafes are less rife, but at least one can still be found in most large towns and cities. Prices range from €2 to €6 per hour.

WHAT THE ICON MEANS

Only accommodation providers that have an actual computer that guests can use to access the internet are flagged with a **computer icon** (@). The **wi-fi icon** (☎) indicates anywhere with wi-fi access. Where this icon appears, assume the wi-fi is free unless otherwise specified.

Language Courses

➡ The website www.studyabroadlinks.com can help you find specific courses and summer programs.

➡ All manner of French-language courses are available in Paris and provincial towns and cities; most also arrange accommodation.

➡ Prices and courses vary greatly; the content can often be tailored to your specific needs (for a fee).

➡ The website www.europa-pages.com/france lists language schools in France.

Aix-Marseille Université (www.univ-provence.fr; 29 av Robert Schumann, Aix-en-Provence) A hot choice, also known as Université de Provence, in lovely Aix: semester-long language courses as well as shorter summer classes.

Alliance Française (www.alliancefr.org; 101 bd Raspail, 6e, Paris; MSt-Placide) French courses (minimum one week) for all levels. Intensif courses meet for four hours a day five days a week; extensif courses involve nine hours' tuition a week.

Centre Méditerranéen d'Études Françaises (www.centremed.monte-carlo.mc; chemin des Oliviers, Cap d'Ail) Legendary French Riviera school around since 1952, with a stunning open-air amphitheatre, designed by Jean Cocteau and overlooking the sparkling blue Med.

Eurocentres (www.euro centres.com) This affiliation of small, well-organised schools has three addresses in France: in Amboise in the charming Loire Valley, in La Rochelle, and Paris.

Legal Matters

Police

➡ French police have wide powers of search and seizure and can ask you to prove your identity at any time – whether or not there is 'probable cause'.

➡ Foreigners must be able to prove their legal status in France (eg passport, visa, residency permit) without delay.

➡ If the police stop you for any reason, be polite and remain calm. Verbally (and of course physically) abusing a police officer can lead to a hefty fine, and even imprisonment.

➡ You may refuse to sign a police statement, and have the right to ask for a copy.

➡ People who are arrested are considered innocent until proven guilty, but can be held in custody until trial.

➡ Because of the threat of terrorism, French police are very strict about security. Do not leave baggage unattended, especially at airports or train stations: suspicious objects may be summarily blown up.

Drugs & Alcohol

➡ French law does not distinguish between 'hard' and 'soft' drugs.

➡ The penalty for any personal use of *stupéfiants* (including cannabis, amphetamines, ecstasy and heroin) can be a one-year jail sentence and a €3750 fine but, depending on the circumstances, it might be anything from a stern word to a compulsory rehab program.

➡ Importing, possessing, selling or buying drugs can

get you up to 10 years in prison and a fine of up to €500,000.

➡ Police have been known to search chartered coaches, cars and train passengers for drugs just because they're coming from Amsterdam.

➡ *Ivresse* (drunkenness) in public is punishable by a fine.

Money

ATMs

Automated Teller Machines (ATMs) – known as *distributeurs automatiques de billets* (DAB) or *points d'argent* in French – are the cheapest and most convenient way to get money. ATMs connected to international networks are situated in all cities and towns and usually offer an excellent exchange rate.

Cash

You always get a better exchange rate in-country but it is a good idea to arrive in France with enough euros to take a taxi to a hotel if you have to.

Credit & Debit Cards

➡ Credit and debit cards, accepted almost everywhere in France, are convenient, relatively secure and usually offer a better exchange rate than travellers cheques or cash exchanges.

➡ Credit cards issued in France have embedded

chips – you have to type in a PIN to make a purchase.

➡ Visa, MasterCard and Amex can be used in shops and supermarkets and for train travel, car hire and motorway tolls.

➡ Don't assume that you can pay for a meal or a budget hotel with a credit card – enquire first.

➡ Cash advances are a supremely convenient way to stay stocked up with euros but getting cash with a credit card involves both fees (sometimes US$10 or more) and interest – ask your credit card issuer for details. Debit-card fees are usually much less.

LOST CARDS

For lost cards, these numbers operate 24 hours:

Amex (☑01 47 77 70 00)

Diners Club (☑08 10 31 41 59)

MasterCard (☑08 00 90 13 87)

Visa (Carte Bleue; ☑08 00 90 11 79)

Moneychangers

➡ Commercial banks charge up to €5 per foreign-currency transaction – if they even bother to offer exchange services any more.

➡ In Paris and major cities, *bureaux de change* (exchange bureaux) are faster and easier, open longer hours and often give better rates than banks.

AMERICANS, TAKE NOTE

Travellers with credit cards issued in the US, be aware that you might well find yourself occasionally stuck when it comes to paying with your card: certain places in France – notably, Vélib' in Paris and bike-share schemes in other cities, self-service toll booths on the *autoroute* (highway), and garages with self-service petrol (gas) pumps – only accept credit cards with chips and PINs. There is no solution to this bar ensuring you always have an emergency stash of cash on you.

→ Some post-office branches exchange travellers cheques and banknotes in a variety of currencies but charge a commission for cash; most won't take US$100 bills.

Tipping

By law, restaurant and bar prices are *service compris* (include a 15% service charge), so there is no need to leave a *pourboire* (tip). If you were extremely satisfied with the service, however, you can – as many locals do – show your appreciation by leaving a small 'extra' tip for your waiter or waitress.

WHERE/WHO	CUSTOMARY TIP
bar	round to nearest euro
hotel cleaning staff	€1-1.50 per day
hotel porter	€1-1.50 per bag
restaurant	5-10%
taxi	10-15%
toilet attendant	€0.20-0.50
tour guide	€1-2 per person

Travellers Cheques

Travellers cheques, a 20th-century relic, cannot be used to pay French merchants directly – change them into euro banknotes at banks, exchange bureaux or post offices.

Opening Hours

French business hours are regulated by a maze of government regulations, including the 35-hour working week.

→ The midday break is uncommon in Paris but common elsewhere; in general, the break gets longer the further south you go.

→ French law requires that most businesses close on Sunday; exceptions include grocery stores, *boulangeries*, florists and businesses catering to the tourist trade.

→ In many places shops close on Monday.

→ Many service stations open 24 hours a day and stock basic groceries.

→ Restaurants generally close one or two days of the week, chosen according to the owner's whim. Opening days/hours are only specified if the restaurant isn't open for both lunch and dinner daily.

→ Most (but not all) national museums are closed on Tuesday; most local museums are closed on Monday, though in summer some open daily. Many museums close at lunchtime.

→ We give high-season hours for sights and attractions; hours are almost always shorter during the low season.

Public Holidays

The following *jours fériés* (public holidays) are observed in France:

New Year's Day (Jour de l'An) 1 January – parties in larger cities; fireworks are subdued by international standards.

Easter Sunday & Monday (Pâques & Lundi de Pâques) Late March/April.

May Day (Fête du Travail) 1 May – traditional parades.

Victoire 1945 8 May – commemorates the Allied victory in Europe that ended WWII.

Ascension Thursday (Ascension) May – celebrated on the 40th day after Easter.

Pentecost/Whit Sunday & Whit Monday (Pentecôte & Lundi de Pentecôte) Mid-May to mid-June – celebrated on the seventh Sunday after Easter.

Bastille Day/National Day (Fête Nationale) 14 July – *the* national holiday.

Assumption Day (Assomption) 15 August.

All Saints' Day (Toussaint) 1 November.

Remembrance Day (L'onze Novembre) 11 November – marks the WWI armistice.

Christmas (Noël) 25 December

The following are *not* public holidays in France: Shrove

STANDARD HOURS

BUSINESS	OPENING HOURS
Bank	9am-noon & 2-5pm Mon-Fri or Tue-Sat
Bar	7pm-1am Mon-Sat
Cafe	7am or 8am-10pm or 11pm Mon-Sat
Nightclub	10pm-3am, 4am or 5am Thu-Sat
Post office	8.30am or 9am-5pm or 6pm Mon-Fri, 8am-noon Sat
Restaurant	noon-2.30pm (or 3pm in Paris) & 7-11pm (or 10pm to midnight in Paris)
Shop	9am or 10am-7pm Mon-Sat (often closed noon-1.30pm)
Supermarket	8.30am-7pm Mon-Sat, 8.30am-12.30pm Sun

PRACTICALITIES

→ **Travel Conditions** In many areas, Autoroute Info (107.7MHz; www.autorouteinfo.fr) has round-the-clock traffic information.

→ **Classifieds** Surf FUSAC (www.fusac.fr) for classified ads about housing, babysitting, jobs and language exchanges in and around Paris.

→ **Laundry** Virtually all French cities and towns have at least one *laverie libre-service* (self-service laundrette). Machines run on coins.

→ **Newspapers & Magazines** Locals read their news in centre-left **Le Monde** (www. lemonde.fr), right-leaning **Le Figaro** (www.lefigaro.fr) or left-leaning **Libération** (www. liberation.fr).

→ **Radio** For news, tune in to the French-language **France Info** (105.5MHz; www. franceinfo.fr), multilanguage **RFI** (738kHz or 89MHz in Paris; www.rfi.fr) or, in northern France, the **BBC World Service** (648kHz) and **BBC Radio 4** (198kHz). Popular national FM music stations include **NRJ** (www.nrj.fr), **Skyrock** (www.skyrock. radio.fr) and **Nostalgie** (www.nostalgie.fr).

→ **Smoking** Smoking is illegal in all indoor public spaces, including restaurants and pubs (though, of course, smokers still light up on the terraces outside).

→ **TV & Video** TV is Secam; videos work on the PAL system.

→ **Weights & Measures** France uses the metric system.

Tuesday (Mardi Gras; the first day of Lent); Maundy (or Holy) Thursday and Good Friday, just before Easter; and Boxing Day (26 December).

Note: Good Friday and Boxing Day *are* public holidays in Alsace.

Safe Travel

France is generally a safe place in which to live and travel but crime has risen dramatically in the last few years. Although property crime is a major problem, it is extremely unlikely that you will be physically assaulted while walking down the street. Always check your government's travel advisory warnings.

The France hunting season runs from September to February. If you see signs reading 'chasseurs' or 'chasse gardée' strung up or tacked to trees, think twice about wandering into the area. As well as millions of wild animals, some 25 French hunters die each year after being shot by other hunters. Hunting is traditional and commonplace in all rural

areas in France, especially the Vosges, the Sologne, the southwest and the Baie de Somme.

Natural Dangers

→ There are powerful tides and strong undertows at many places along the Atlantic coast, from the Spanish border north to Brittany and Normandy.

→ Only swim in *zones de baignade surveillée* (beaches monitored by life guards).

→ Be aware of tide times and the high-tide mark if walking or sleeping on a beach.

→ Thunderstorms in the mountains and the hot southern plains can be extremely sudden and violent.

→ Check the weather report before setting out on a long walk and be prepared for sudden storms and temperature drops if you are heading into the high country of the Alps or Pyrenees.

→ Avalanches pose a significant danger in the French Alps.

Theft

Pickpocketing and bag/phone-snatching (eg in dense crowds and public places) are prevalent in big cities, particularly Paris, Marseille and Nice. There's no need whatsoever to travel in fear. A few simple precautions will minimise your chances of being ripped off.

→ On trains, avoid leaving smartphones and tablets lying casually on the table in front of you and keep bags as close to you as possible: luggage racks at the ends of carriages are easy prey for thieves; in sleeping compartments, lock the door carefully at night.

→ Be especially vigilant for bag/phone snatchers at train stations, airports, fast-food outlets, outdoor cafes, beaches and on public transport.

→ Break-ins to parked cars are a widespread problem. Never, ever leave anything valuable – or not valuable – inside your car, even in the boot (trunk).

→ Aggressive theft from cars stopped at red lights

is occasionally a problem, especially in Marseille and Nice. As a precaution, lock your car doors and roll up the windows.

Telephone

Mobile Phones

➡ French mobile phone numbers begin with ☑06 or ☑07.

➡ France uses GSM 900/1800, which is compatible with the rest of Europe and Australia but not with the North American GSM 1900 or the totally different system in Japan (though some North Americans have tri-band phones that work here).

➡ Check with your service provider about roaming charges – dialling a mobile phone from a fixed-line phone or another mobile can be incredibly expensive.

➡ It is usually cheaper to buy a local SIM card from a French provider such as Orange, SFR, Bouygues and Free Mobile which gives you a local phone number. To do

this, ensure your phone is 'unlocked'.

➡ If you already have a compatible phone, you can slip in a SIM card (€1.90 to €5) and rev it up with prepaid credit, though this is likely to run out fast as domestic prepaid calls cost about €0.50 per minute.

➡ Recharge cards are sold at most *tabacs* (tobacconist-newsagents) and supermarkets.

Phone Codes

➡ **Calling France from abroad** Dial your country's international access code, then ☑33 (France's country code), then the 10-digit local number *without* the initial zero.

➡ **Calling internationally from France** Dial ☑00 (the international access code), the *indicatif* (country code), the area code (without the initial zero if there is one) and the local number. Some country codes are posted in public telephones.

➡ **Directory inquiries** For national *service des renseignements* (directory inquiries) dial ☑11 87 12 or

use the service for free online at www.118712.fr.

➡ **Emergency numbers** Can be dialled from public phones without a phonecard.

➡ **Hotel calls** Hotels, *gîtes*, hostels and *chambres d'hôte* are free to meter their calls as they like. The surcharge is usually around €0.30 per minute but can be higher.

➡ **International directory inquiries** For numbers outside France, dial ☑11 87 00.

Phonecards

➡ Although mobile phones and Skype may have killed off the need for public phones, they do still exist. In France they are all phonecard-operated, but in an emergency you can use your credit card to call.

➡ All public phones can receive both domestic and international calls. If you want someone to call you back, just give them France's country code (☑33) and the 10-digit number, usually written after the words 'Ici le...' or 'No d'appel' on the tariff sheet or on a little sign inside the phone box. Remind them to drop the initial '0' of the number. When there's an incoming call, the words '*décrochez – appel arrive*' (pick up receiver – incoming call) will appear in the LCD window.

➡ Public phones require a credit card or *télécarte* (phonecard; €7.50/15 for 50/120 calling units), sold at post offices, tabacs, supermarkets, SNCF ticket windows, Paris metro stations and anywhere you see a blue sticker reading '*télécarte en vente ici*' (phonecard for sale here).

➡ Prepaid phonecards with codes such as Allomundo (www.allomundo.com) can be up to 60% cheaper for calling abroad than a standard *télécarte*.

➡ The shop you buy a phonecard from should be

CHARGING DEVICES

While there is talk in the capital of Parisian public transport company RATP jazzing up bus stops of the future with phone-charging stations, charging phones and other devices on the move remains challenging. Carrying your own charger and cable ups the odds dramatically of getting more juice – don't be shy to ask in cafes and restaurants if you can plug in and charge. Ditto for taxi drivers, an increasing number of whom carry a selection of smartphone-compatible cables and chargers.

On TGV trains, all first-class carriages (and occasionally second-class depending on how new the train is) have plugs. On every TGV irrespective of age, there is at least one 'office' space between carriages with mini-desk and double plug. Otherwise, upon arrival, an increasing number of SNCF train stations have charging stations: in Paris, Gare de Nord, Gare de Montparnasse and Gare de St-Lazare all have pedal-powered charging stations operated by Belgium-based We-Bike, as do several other stations countrywide including Lille, Lyon, Strasbourg and Avignon TGV.

able to tell you which type is best for the country you want to call. Using phonecards from a home phone is much cheaper than using them from public phones or mobile phones.

Time

France uses the 24-hour clock and is on Central European Time, which is one hour ahead of GMT/UTC. During daylight saving time, which runs from the last Sunday in March to the last Sunday in October, France is two hours ahead of GMT/UTC.

The following times do not take daylight saving into account:

CITY	NOON IN PARIS
Auckland	11pm
Berlin	noon
Cape Town	noon
London	11am
New York	6am
San Francisco	3am
Sydney	9pm
Tokyo	8pm

Toilets

Public toilets, signposted WC or *toilettes*, are not always plentiful in France, especially outside the big cities.

Love them (as a sci-fi geek) or loathe them (as a claustrophobe), France's 24-hour self-cleaning toilets are here to stay. Outside Paris these mechanical WCs are free, but in Paris they cost around €0.50 a go. Don't even think about nipping in after someone else to avoid paying unless you fancy a *douche* (shower) with disinfectant. There is no time for dawdling either: you have precisely 15 minutes before being (ooh-la-la!) exposed to passers-by. Green means *libre* (vacant) and red means *occupé* (occupied).

Some older establishments and motorway stops still have the hole-in-the-floor *toilettes à la turque* (squat toilets). Provided you hover, these are actually very hygienic, but take care not to get soaked by the flush.

Keep some loose change handy for tipping toilet attendants, who keep a hawk-like eye on many of France's public toilets.

The French are more blasé about unisex toilets than elsewhere, so save your blushes when tiptoeing past the urinals to reach the ladies' loo.

Tourist Information

Almost every city, town and village has an *office de tourisme* (a tourist office run by some unit of local government) or *syndicat d'initiative* (a tourist office run by an organisation of local merchants). Both are excellent resources and can supply you with local maps as well as details on accommodation, restaurants and activities. If you have a special interest such as walking, cycling, architecture or wine sampling, ask about it.

Tourist office details appear under Information at the end of each city, town or area listing.

➡ Many tourist offices make local hotel and B&B

reservations, sometimes for a nominal fee.

➡ *Comités régionaux de tourisme* (CRTs; regional tourist boards), their *départemental* analogues (CDTs) and their websites are a superb source of information and hyperlinks.

➡ French government tourist offices (usually called Maisons de la France) provide every imaginable sort of tourist information on France.

Useful websites include:

French Government Tourist Office (http://int.rendezvousenfrance.com) The low-down on sights, activities, transport and special-interest holidays in all of France's regions. Brochures can be downloaded online. There are links to country-specific websites.

Réseau National des Destinations Départementales (www.rn2d.net) Listing of CRT (regional tourist board) websites.

Travellers with Disabilities

While France presents evident challenges for *visiteurs handicapés* (disabled visitors) – cobblestone, cafe-lined streets that are a nightmare to navigate in a wheelchair *(fauteuil roulant)*, a lack of kerb ramps, older public facilities and many budget hotels without lifts – don't let that stop you from

---

STRIKES

France is the only European country in which public workers enjoy an unlimited right to strike. Aggrieved truck drivers block motorways from time to time, farmers agitating for more government support have been known to dump tonnes of produce on major arteries, and train strikes sometimes disrupt travel.

Getting caught in one of the 'social dialogues' that characterise labour relations in France can put a serious crimp in your travel plans. It is best to leave some wriggle room in your schedule, particularly around departure times.

ACCESSIBILITY INFORMATION

➜ SNCF's French-language booklet *Guide des Voyageurs Handicapés et à Mobilité Réduite,* available at train stations, gives details of rail access for people with disabilities.

➜ Michelin's *Guide Rouge* uses icons to indicate hotels with lifts (elevators) and facilities that make them at least partly accessible to people with disabilities.

➜ *Handitourisme* (€16), a national guide in French, is published by **Petit Futé** (www.petitfute.fr).

➜ www.jaccede.com (in French) has loads of information and reviews.

➜ **Gîtes de France** (www.gites-de-france-var.fr) can provide details of accessible *gîtes ruraux* and *chambres d'hôte* (search the website with the term 'disabled access').

➜ The **French Government Tourist Office** (http://int.rendezvousenfrance.com) website has lots of info for travellers with disabilities.

visiting. Efforts are being made to improve the situation and with a little careful planning, a hassle-free accessible stay is possible.

➜ Paris tourist office runs the excellent 'Tourisme & Handicap' initiative whereby museums, cultural attractions, hotels and restaurants that provide access or special assistance or facilities for those with physical, mental, visual and/or hearing disabilities display a special logo at their entrances. For a list of qualifying places, go to www.parisinfo.com and click on 'Practical Paris'.

➜ Paris metro, most of it built decades ago, is hopeless. Line 14 of the metro was built to be wheelchair-accessible, although in reality it remains extremely challenging to navigate in a wheelchair – unlike Paris buses which are 100% accessible.

➜ Parisian taxi company Horizon, part of Taxis G7, has cars especially adapted to carry wheelchairs and drivers trained in helping passengers with disabilities.

➜ Countrywide, many SNCF train carriages are accessible to people with disabilities. A traveller in a wheelchair can travel in both the TGV and in the 1st-class carriage with a 2nd-class ticket on mainline trains provided they make a reservation by phone or at a train station at least a few hours before departure. Details are available in the SNCF booklet Le Mémento du Voyageur Handicapé (Handicapped Traveller Summary) available at all train stations.

Accès Plus (☏08 90 64 06 50; www.accessibilite.sncf.com) The SNCF assistance service for rail travellers with disabilities. Can advise on station accessibility and arrange a *fauteuil roulant* (wheelchair) or help getting on or off a train.

Access Travel (☏in UK 01942-888 844; www.access-travel.co.uk) Specialised UK-based agency for accessible travel.

Infomobi.com (☏08 10 64 64 64; www.infomobi.com) Has comprehensive information on accessible travel in Paris and surrounding Île de France area.

Mobile en Ville (☏09 52 29 60 51; www.mobile-en-ville.asso.fr; 8 rue des Mariniers, 14e, Paris) Association that works hard to make independent travel within the city easier for people in wheelchairs. Among other things it organises some great family *randonnées* (walks) in and around Paris.

Tourisme et Handicaps (☏01 44 11 10 41; www.tourisme-handicaps.org; 43 rue Marx Dormoy, 18e, Paris) Issues the 'Tourisme et Handicap' label to tourist sites, restaurants and hotels that comply with strict accessibility and usability standards. Different symbols indicate the sort of access afforded to people with physical, mental, hearing and/or visual disabilities.

Visas

For up-to-date details on visa requirements, see the website of the **Ministère des Affaires Étrangères** (Ministry of Foreign Affairs; www.diplomatie.gouv.fr; 37 quai d'Orsay, 7e) and click 'Coming to France'. Tourist visas *cannot* be extended except in emergencies (such as medical problems). When your visa expires you'll need to leave and reapply from outside France.

Visa Requirements

➜ EU nationals and citizens of Iceland, Norway and Switzerland need only a passport or a national identity card in order to enter France and stay in the country, even for stays of more than 90 days. However, citizens of new EU member states may be subject to various limitations on living and working in France.

➜ Citizens of Australia, the USA, Canada, Hong Kong, Israel, Japan, Malaysia, New Zealand, Singapore, South Korea and many Latin American countries do not need visas to visit France as tourists for up to 90 days. For long stays of more than 90

Régions & Départements

ALSACE
67 Bas-Rhin
68 Haut-Rhin

AQUITAINE
24 Dordogne
33 Gironde
40 Landes
47 Lot-et-Garonne
64 Pyrénées-Atlantiques

AUVERGNE
03 Allier
15 Cantal
43 Haute-Loire
63 Puy-de-Dôme

BASSE-NORMANDIE
14 Calvados
50 Manche
61 Orne

BOURGOGNE
21 Côte-d'Or
58 Nièvre
71 Saône-et-Loire
89 Yonne

BRETAGNE
22 Côte-d'Armor
29 Finistère
35 Ille-et-Vilaine
56 Morbihan

CENTRE
18 Cher
28 Eure-et-Loir
36 Indre
37 Indre-et-Loire
45 Loiret
41 Loir-et-Cher

CHAMPAGNE-ARDENNE
08 Ardennes
10 Aube
51 Marne
52 Haute-Marne

CORSE
2A Corse-du-Sud
2B Haute-Corse

FRANCHE-COMTÉ
25 Doubs
39 Jura
70 Haute-Saône
90 Territoire de Belfort

HAUTE-NORMANDIE
27 Eure
76 Seine-Maritime

ÎLE-DE-FRANCE
91 Essonne
92 Haut-de-Seine
75 Paris
78 Seine-et-Marne
93 Seine-St-Denis
94 Val-de-Marne
95 Val-d'Oise
77 Yvelines

LANGUEDOC-ROUSSILLON
11 Aude
30 Gard
34 Hérault
48 Lozère
66 Pyrénées-Orientales

LIMOUSIN
19 Corrèze
23 Creuse
87 Haute-Vienne

LORRAINE
54 Meurthe-et-Moselle
55 Meuse
57 Moselle
88 Vosges

MIDI-PYRÉNÉES
09 Ariège
12 Aveyron
32 Gers
31 Haute-Garonne
65 Hautes-Pyrénées
46 Lot
81 Tarn
82 Tarn-et-Garonne

NORD-PAS-DE-CALAIS
59 Nord
62 Pas-de-Calais

PAYS DE LA LOIRE
44 Loire-Atlantique
49 Maine-et-Loire
53 Mayenne
72 Sarthe
85 Vendée

PICARDIE
02 Aisne
60 Oise
80 Somme

POITOU-CHARENTES
16 Charente
17 Charente-Maritime
79 Deux-Sèvres
86 Vienne

PROVENCE-ALPES-CÔTE D'AZUR
04 Alpes-de-Haute-Provence
06 Alpes-Maritimes
13 Bouches-du-Rhône
05 Hautes-Alpes
83 Var
84 Vaucluse

RHÔNE-ALPES
01 Ain
07 Ardèche
26 Drôme
74 Haute-Savoie
38 Isère
42 Loire
69 Rhône
73 Savoie

International Boundary
Région Boundary
Département Boundary

days, contact your nearest French embassy or consulate and begin your application well in advance, as it can take months.

➡ Other people wishing to come to France as tourists have to apply for a **Schengen Visa**, named after the agreements that have abolished passport controls between 26 European countries. It allows unlimited travel throughout the entire zone for a 90-day period. Apply to the consulate of the country you are entering first, or your main destination. Among other things, you need travel and repatriation insurance and to be able to show that you have sufficient funds to support yourself.

➡ Tourist visas cannot be changed into student visas after arrival. However, short-term visas are available for students sitting university-entrance exams in France.

Carte de Séjour

➡ EU passport holders and citizens of Switzerland, Iceland and Norway do not need a *carte de séjour* (residence permit) to reside or work in France.

➡ Nationals of other countries with long-stay visas must contact the local *mairie* (city hall) or *préfecture* (prefecture) to apply for a *carte de séjour*. Usually, you are required to do so within eight days of arrival in France. Make sure you have all the necessary documents before you arrive.

➡ Students of all nationalities studying in France need a *carte de séjour*.

Working Holiday Visa

Citizens of Australia, Canada, Japan and New Zealand aged between 18 and 30 are eligible for a 12-month, multiple-entry Working Holiday Visa (Permis Vacances Travail), allowing combined tourism and employment in France.

➡ Apply to the embassy or consulate in your home country. Do this early as there are annual quotas.

➡ You must be applying for a Working Holiday Visa for France for the first time.

➡ You will need comprehensive travel insurance for the duration of your stay.

➡ You must meet all health and character requirements.

➡ You will need a return plane ticket and proof of sufficient funds (usually around €2100) to get you through the start of your stay.

➡ Once you have arrived in France and have found a job, you must apply for an *autorisation provisoire de travail* (temporary work permit), which will only be valid for the duration of the employment offered. The permit can be renewed under the same conditions up to the limit of the authorised length of stay.

➡ You can also study or do training programs but the visa cannot be extended, nor can it turned into a student visa.

➡ After one year you *must* go home.

Volunteering

Online resources such as **Go Abroad** (www.goabroad.com) and **Transitions Abroad** (www.transitionsabroad.com) throw up a colourful selection of volunteering opportunities in France: helping out on a family farm in the Alps, restoring an historic monument in Provence or participating in a summertime archaeological excavation are but some of the golden opportunities awaiting those keen to volunteer their skills and services.

Interesting volunteer organisations include:

Club du Vieux Manoir (www.clubduvieuxmanoir.fr) Restore a medieval fortress, an abbey or a historic château at a summer work camp.

GeoVisions (www.geovisions.org) Volunteer 15 hours a week to teach a French family English in exchange for room and board.

Rempart (www.rempart.com) Brings together 170 organisations countrywide committed to preserving France's religious, military, civil, industrial and natural heritage.

Volunteers For Peace (www.vfp.org) USA-based nonprofit organisation. Can link you up with a voluntary service project dealing with social work, the environment, education or the arts.

World Wide Opportunities on Organic Farms (WWOOF; www.wwoof.org) Work on a small farm or other organic venture (harvesting chestnuts, renovating an abandoned olive farm near Nice etc).

Transport

GETTING THERE & AWAY

Flights, cars and tours can be booked online at www.lonely-planet.com/bookings.

Entering the Country

Entering France from other parts of the EU is usually a breeze – no border check-points and no customs – thanks to the Schengen Agreement, signed by all of France's neighbours except the UK, the Channel Islands and Andorra. For these three entities, old-fashioned document and customs checks are still the norm, at least when exiting France (when entering France in the case of Andorra).

Air

Smaller provincial airports with international flights, mainly to/from the UK, continental Europe and North Africa, include Paris-Beauvais, Bergerac, Biarritz, Brest, Brive-la-Gaillarde (Vallée de la Dordogne), Caen, Carcassonne, Clermont-Ferrand, Deauville, Dinard, Grenoble, La Rochelle, Le Touquet (Côte d'Opale), Limoges, Montpellier, Nîmes, Pau, Perpignan, Poitiers, Rennes, Rodez, St-Étienne, Toulon and Tours.

International Airports

Aéroport de Charles de Gaulle (CDG; www.aeroports deparis.fr)

Paris Orly (www.aeroports deparis.fr)

Aéroport de Bordeaux (www.bordeaux.aeroport.fr)

Aéroport de Lille (www.lille. aeroport.fr)

Aéroport International Strasbourg (www.strasbourg. aeroport.fr)

Aéroport Lyon-St-Exupéry (www.lyonaeroports.com)

Aéroport Marseille-Provence (www.marseille. aeroport.fr)

Aéroport Nantes Atlantique (www.nantes.aeroport.fr)

Aéroport Nice Côte d'Azur (http://societe.nice.aeroport.fr)

Aéroport Toulouse-Blagnac (www.toulouse. aeroport.fr)

EuroAirport (Basel-Mulhouse-Freiburg; www. euroairport.com)

Land
Bicycle

Transporting a bicycle to France is a breeze.

On **Eurotunnel Le Shuttle** (in France 08 10 63 03 04, in UK 08443-35 35 35; www. eurotunnel.com) trains through the Channel Tunnel, the fee for a bicycle, including its rider, is UK£16 one way.

A bike that's been dismantled to the size of a suitcase can be carried on board a **Eurostar** (in France 08 92

CLIMATE CHANGE & TRAVEL

Every form of transport that relies on carbon-based fuel generates CO_2, the main cause of human-induced climate change. Modern travel is dependent on aeroplanes, which might use less fuel per kilometre per person than most cars but travel much greater distances. The altitude at which aircraft emit gases (including CO_2) and particles also contributes to their climate change impact. Many websites offer 'carbon calculators' that allow people to estimate the carbon emissions generated by their journey and, for those who wish to do so, to offset the impact of the greenhouse gases emitted with contributions to portfolios of climate-friendly initiatives throughout the world. Lonely Planet offsets the carbon footprint of all staff and author travel.

SAMPLE TRAIN FARES

ROUTE	FULL FARE (€)	DURATION (HR)
Amsterdam–Paris	79	3¼
Berlin–Paris	213	8
Brussels–Paris	58	1½
Geneva–Marseille	55	3½
Madrid–Blois	240	12½
Milan–Dijon	92	7
Venice–Paris	96	11¾
Vienna–Strasbourg	160	9¾

35 35 39, in UK 08432-186 186; www.eurostar.com) train from London or Brussels just like any other luggage. Otherwise, there's a UK£20 charge and you'll need advance reservations. For links relevant to taking your bike on other international trains to France, see **RailPassenger Info** (www.railpassenger.info).

On ferries, foot passengers – where allowed – can usually (but not always) bring along a bicycle for no charge.

European Bike Express (in UK 01430-422 111; www.bike-express.co.uk) transports cyclists and their bikes from the UK to places around France.

Bus

Eurolines (08 92 89 90 91; www.eurolines.eu), a grouping of 32 long-haul coach operators (including the UK's National Express), links France with cities all across Europe and in Morocco and Russia. Discounts are available to people under 26 and over 60. Make advance reservations, especially in July and August.

The standard Paris–London fare is between €41 and €59, but the trip – including a Channel crossing by ferry or the Channel Tunnel – can cost as little as €15 if you book 45 days ahead; there are also often €25 'special offer' tickets available one week prior to departure.

Car & Motorcycle

A right-hand-drive vehicle brought to France from the

UK or Ireland must have deflectors affixed to the headlights to avoid dazzling oncoming traffic. In the UK, information on driving in France is available from the **RAC** (www.rac.co.uk/driving-abroad/france) and the **AA** (www.theaa.com).

A foreign motor vehicle entering France must display a sticker or licence plate identifying its country of registration.

EUROTUNNEL

The Channel Tunnel (Chunnel), inaugurated in 1994, is the first dry-land link between England and France since the last ice age.

High-speed **Eurotunnel Le Shuttle** (in France 08 10 63 03 04, in UK 08443-35 35 35; www.eurotunnel.com) trains whisk bicycles, motorcycles, cars and coaches in 35 minutes from Folkestone through the Channel Tunnel to Coquelles, 5km southwest of Calais. Shuttles run 24 hours a day, with up to three departures an hour during peak periods. LPG and CNG tanks are not permitted, meaning gas-powered cars and many campers and caravans have to travel by ferry.

Eurotunnel sets its fares the way budget airlines do: the further in advance you book and the lower the demand for a particular crossing, the less you pay; same-day fares can cost a small fortune. Fares for a car, including up to nine passengers, start at UK£23/€30.

Train

Rail services link France with virtually every country in Europe. For details on train travel within France, see p982.

Book tickets and get train information from **Rail Europe** (www.raileurope.com). In the UK contact **Railteam** (www.railteam.co.uk). In France ticketing is handled by **SNCF** (from abroad +33 8 92 35 35 35, in France 36 35; www.en.voyages-sncf.com); internet bookings are possible but they won't post tickets outside France.

For details on Europe's 200,000km rail network, surf **RailPassenger Info** (www.railpassenger.info).

A very useful train-travel resource is the information-packed website **The Man in Seat 61** (www.seat61.com).

Certain rail services between France and its continental neighbours are marketed under a number of unique brand names:

Elipsos (www.elipsos.com) Luxurious, overnight 'train-hotel' from Paris to Madrid and Barcelona in Spain.

TGV Lyria (www.tgv-lyria.fr) To Switzerland.

Thalys (www.thalys.com) Thalys trains pull into Paris' Gare du Nord from Brussels, Amsterdam and Cologne.

Thello (www.thello.com) Overnight train service from Paris to Milan, Brescia, Verona and Venice in Italy.

EURAIL PASS

Rail passes are worth it if you clock up the kilometres.

Available only to people who don't live in Europe, the **Eurail Pass** (www.eurail.com) is valid in up to 21 countries, including France. People 25 and under get the best deals. Passes must be validated at a train-station ticket window before you begin your first journey.

EUROSTAR

The **Eurostar** (☑in France 08 92 35 35 39, in UK 08432-186 186; www.eurostar.com) whisks you from London to Paris in 2¼ hours.

Except late at night, trains link London (St Pancras International) with Paris (Gare du Nord; hourly), Calais (Calais-Fréthun; one hour, three daily), Lille (Gare Lille-Europe; 1½ hours, eight daily) and Disneyland Resort Paris (2½ hours, one direct daily), with less frequent services departing Ebbsfleet and Ashford, both in Kent. Weekend ski trains connect England with the French Alps late December to mid-April.

Eurostar offers a bewildering array of fares. A semi-flexible 2nd-class one-way ticket from Paris to London costs €172; super-discount fares start at €44.

For the best deals buy a return ticket, stay over a Saturday night, book up to 120 days in advance and don't mind nonexchangeability and nonrefundability. Discount fares are available for under 26s or over 60s.

Sea

Some ferry companies have started setting fares the way budget airlines do: the longer in advance you book and the lower the demand for a particular sailing, the less you pay. Seasonal demand is a crucial factor (Christmas, Easter, UK and French school holidays, July and August are especially busy), as is the time of day (an early evening ferry can cost much more than one at 4am). People under 25 and over 60 may qualify for discounts.

To get the best fares, check **Ferry Savers** (☑in UK 0844-371 8021; www.ferrysavers.com).

Foot passengers are not allowed on Dover–Boulogne, Dover–Dunkirk or Dover–Calais car ferries except for daytime (and, from Calais to Dover, evening) crossings run by P&O Ferries. On ferries that do allow foot passengers, taking a bicycle is usually free.

Several ferry companies ply the waters between Corsica and Italy.

GETTING AROUND

Driving is the simplest way to get around France but a car is a liability in traffic-plagued, parking-starved city centres, and petrol bills and autoroute (dual carriageway/divided highway) tolls add up.

France is famous for its excellent public-transport network, which serves everywhere bar some very rural areas. The state-owned Société Nationale des Chemins de Fer Français (SNCF) takes care of almost all land transport between *départements*. Transport within *départements* is handled by a combination of short-haul trains, SNCF buses and local bus companies.

INTERNATIONAL FERRY COMPANIES

COMPANY	CONNECTION	WEBSITE
Brittany Ferries	England–Normandy, England–Brittany, Ireland–Brittany	www.brittany-ferries.co.uk; www.brittanyferries.ie
Condor Ferries	England–Normandy, England–Brittany, Channel Islands–Brittany	www.condorferries.co.uk
CTN	Tunisia–France	www.ctn.com.tn
DFDS Seaways	England–Normandy	www.dfdsseaways.co.uk
Irish Ferries	Ireland–Normandy, Ireland–Brittany	www.irishferries.com
LD Lines	England–Channel Ports, England–Normandy	www.ldlines.co.uk
Manche Îles Express	Channel Islands–Normandy	www.manche-iles-express.com
My Ferry Link	Dover–Calais	www.myferrylink.fr
Norfolk Line (DFDS Seaways)	England–Channel Ports	www.norfolkline.com
P&O Ferries	England–Channel Ports	www.poferries.com
SNCM	Algeria–France, Sardinia–France, Tunisia–France	www.sncm.fr
Stena Line Ferries	Ireland–Normandy	www.stenaline.ie
Transmanche Ferries	England–Normandy	www.transmancheferries.co.uk

Air

France's high-speed train network renders rail travel between some cities (eg from Paris to Lyon and Marseille) faster and easier than flying.

Airlines in France

Air France (www.airfrance.com) and its subsidiaries **Hop!** (www.hop.com) and **Transavia** (www.transavia.com) control the lion's share of France's domestic airline industry.

Budget carriers offering flights within France include **EasyJet** (www.easyjet.com), **Twin Jet** (www.twinjet.net) and **Air Corsica** (www.aircorsica.com).

Bicycle

France is great for cycling. Much of the countryside is drop-dead gorgeous and the country has a growing number of urban and rural *pistes cyclables* (bike paths and lanes; see **Voies Vertes**, www.voievertes.com) and an extensive network of secondary and tertiary roads with relatively light traffic.

French law requires that bicycles must have two functioning brakes, a bell, a red reflector on the back and yellow reflectors on the pedals. After sunset and when visibility is poor, cyclists must turn on a white headlamp and a red tail lamp. When being overtaken by a vehicle, cyclists must ride in single file. Towing children in a bike trailer is permitted.

Never leave your bicycle locked up outside overnight if you want to see it – or at least most of its parts – again. Some hotels offer enclosed bicycle parking.

Transportation

The SNCF does its best to make travelling with a bicycle easy; see www.velo.sncf.com for full details.

Bicycles (not disassembled) can be taken along on virtually all intraregional TER trains and most long-distance

intercity trains, subject to space availability. There's no charge on TER and Corail Intercité trains but TGV, Téoz and Lunéa trains require a €10 reservation fee that must be made when you purchase your passenger ticket. Bike reservations can be made by phone (☑36 35) or at an SNCF ticket office but not via the internet.

Bicycles that have been partly disassembled and put in a box *(housse)*, with maximum dimensions of 120cm by 90cm, can be taken along for no charge in the baggage compartments of TGV, Téoz, Lunéa and Corail Intercité trains.

In the Paris area, bicycles are allowed aboard Transilien and RER trains except Monday to Friday during the following times:

➡ 6.30am to 9am for trains heading into Paris

➡ 4.30pm to 7pm for trains travelling out of Paris

➡ 6am to 9am and 4.30pm to 7pm on RER lines A and B

With precious few exceptions, bicycles are not allowed on metros, trams and local, intra-*département* and SNCF buses (the latter replace trains on some runs).

Bike Rental

Most French cities and towns have at least one bike shop that rents out *vélos tout terrains* (mountain bikes; around €15 a day), known as VTTs, as well as more road-oriented *vélos tout chemin* (VTCs), or cheaper city bikes. You usually have to leave ID and/or a deposit (often a credit-card slip) that you forfeit if the bike is damaged or stolen.

A growing number of cities – most famously Paris and Lyon, but also Aix-en-Provence, Amiens, Besançon, Bayonne, Bordeaux, Caen, Clermont-Ferrand, Dijon, La Rochelle, Lille, Marseille, Montpellier, Mulhouse, Nancy, Nantes, Nice, Orléans, Rennes, Rouen, Toulouse, Strasbourg and Vannes –

have automatic bike-rental systems, intended to encourage cycling as a form of urban transport, with computerised pick-up and drop-off sites all over town. In general, you have to sign up either short term or long term, providing credit-card details, and can then use the bikes for no charge for the first half-hour; after that, hourly charges rise quickly.

Boat

There are boat services along France's coasts and to its offshore islands, and ferries aplenty to/from Corsica.

Canal Boating

Transportation and tranquillity are usually mutually exclusive – but not if you rent a houseboat and cruise along France's canals and navigable rivers, stopping at whim to pick up supplies, dine at a village restaurant or check out a local château by bicycle. Changes in altitude are taken care of by a system of *écluses* (locks).

Boats generally accommodate from two to 12 passengers and are fully outfitted with bedding and cooking facilities. Anyone over 18 can pilot a riverboat but first-time skippers are given a short instruction session so they qualify for a *carte de plaisance* (a temporary cruising permit). The speed limit is 6km/h on canals and 8km/h on rivers.

Prices start at around €650 a week for a small boat and easily top €3000 a week for a large, luxurious craft. Except in July and August, you can often rent over a weekend.

Advance reservations are essential for holiday periods, over long weekends and in July and August, especially for larger boats.

Rental agencies include:

Canal Boat Holidays (www.canalboatholidays.com)

France Afloat (www.franceafloat.com) Anglophone, canal-boat specialist in France.

Free Wheel Afloat (www.freewheelafloat.com)

H2olidays (www.bargingin france.com) Hotel barges, river cruises and self-drive barges.

Worldwide River Cruise (www.worldwide-river-cruise.com) River-cruiser rental, price-comparison website.

Bus

Buses are widely used for short-distance travel within *départements*, especially in rural areas with relatively few train lines (eg Brittany and Normandy).

Unfortunately, services in some regions are infrequent and slow, in part because they were designed to get children to their schools in the towns rather than transport visitors around the countryside.

Over the years, certain uneconomical train lines have been replaced by SNCF buses, which, unlike regional buses, are free if you've got a rail pass.

Car & Motorcycle

Having your own wheels gives you exceptional freedom and makes it easy to visit more remote parts of France. Depending on the number of passengers, it can also work out cheaper than train. For example, by autoroute, the 925km drive from Paris to Nice (nine hours of driving) in a small car costs about €100 for petrol and €75 in tolls – by comparison, a one-way, 2nd-class TGV ticket for the 5½-hour Paris to Nice run costs €95 to €140 per person.

In the cities, traffic and finding a place to park can be a major headache. During holiday periods and bank-holiday weekends, roads throughout France also get backed up with traffic jams (*bouchons*).

Motorcyclists will find France great for touring, with winding roads of good quality and lots of stunning scenery. Just make sure your wet-weather gear is up to scratch.

France (along with Belgium) has the densest highway network in Europe. There are four types of intercity roads:

➡ **Autoroutes** (highway names beginning with A) Multilane divided highways, usually (except near Calais and Lille) with tolls (*péages*). Generously outfitted with rest stops.

➡ **Routes Nationales** (N, RN) National highways. Some sections have divider strips.

➡ **Routes Départementales** (D) Local highways and roads.

➡ **Routes Communales** (C, V) Minor rural roads.

For information on autoroute tolls, rest areas, traffic and weather, go to the **Sociétés d'Autoroutes** (www.auto routes.fr) website.

Bison Futé (www.bison-fute.equipement.gouv.fr) is also a good source of information about traffic conditions. Plot itineraries between your departure and arrival points, and calculate toll costs with an online mapper like **Via Michelin** (www.viamichelin.com) or **Mappy** (www.mappy.fr).

Theft from cars is a major problem in France, especially in the south.

Car Hire

To hire a car in France, you'll generally need to be over 21 years old, have had a driving licence for at least a year, and have an international credit card. Drivers under 25 usually have to pay a surcharge (*frais jeune conducteur*) of €25 to €35 per day.

Car-hire companies provide mandatory third-party liability insurance but things such as collision-damage waivers (CDW, or *assurance tous risques*) vary greatly from company to company. When comparing rates and conditions (ie the fine print), the most important thing to check is the *franchise* (deductible/excess), which for a small car is usually around €600 for damage and €800 for theft. With many companies, you can reduce the excess

---

SPEED-FIENDS, TAKE NOTE

When it comes to catching and punishing speed fiends, France has upped its act in recent years. Automatic speed cameras, not necessarily visible, are widespread and the chances are you'll get 'flashed' at least once during your trip. Should this occur, a letter from the French government (stamped 'Liberté, Egalité, Fraternité – Liberty, Equality, Fraternity') will land on your door mat informing you of your *amende* (fine) and, should you hold a French licence, how many points you have lost. Motorists driving up to 20km/h over the limit in a 50km/h zone are fined €135 (€90 if you pay within 45 days) and one point.

There is no room for complacency moreover should you be driving a rental car: in addition to the fine, the rental company will charge you a fee (usually around €25) for the time they spent sharing your contact details with the French government.

A complete list of fines and – rather handily – speed radars countrywide is online at www.controleradar.org.

by half, and perhaps to zero, by paying a daily insurance supplement of up to €20. Your credit card may cover CDW if you use it to pay for the rental but the car-hire company won't know anything about this – verify conditions and details with your credit-card issuer to be sure.

Arranging your car hire or fly-drive package before you leave home is usually considerably cheaper than a walk-in rental, but beware of website offers that don't include a CDW or you may be liable for up to 100% of the car's value.

International car-hire companies:

Avis (☑from abroad +33 1 70 99 47 35, in France 08 21 23 07 60; www.avis.com)

Budget (☑08 25 00 35 64; www.budget.fr)

Easycar (☑in France 08 26 10 73 23, in the UK 08710 500 444; www.easycar.com)

Europcar (☑08 25 35 83 58; www.europcar.com)

Hertz (☑08 25 86 18 61; www.hertz.com)

Sixt (☑08 20 00 74 98; www.sixt.fr)

French car-hire companies:

ADA (www.ada.fr)

DLM (☑03 20 06 18 80; www.dlm.fr)

France Cars (www.francecars.fr)

Locauto (☑04 93 07 72 62; www.locauto.fr)

Renault Rent (☑08 25 10 11 12; www.renault-rent.com)

Rent a Car Système (☑08 91 70 02 00; www.rentacar.fr)

Deals can be found on the internet and through companies such as the following:

Auto Europe (☑in USA 1-888-223-5555; www.autoeurope.com)

DriveAway Holidays (☑in Australia 1300 723 972; www.driveaway.com.au)

Holiday Autos (☑In the UK 0871-472 5229; www.holidayautos.co.uk)

Rental cars with automatic transmission are very much the exception in France; they usually need to be ordered well in advance and are more expensive than manual cars.

For insurance reasons, it is usually forbidden to take rental cars on ferries, eg to Corsica.

All rental cars registered in France have a distinctive number on the licence plate,

ROAD DISTANCES (KM)

	Bayonne	Bordeaux	Brest	Caen	Cahors	Calais	Chambéry	Cherbourg	Clermont-Ferrand	Dijon	Grenoble	Lille	Lyon	Marseille	Nantes	Nice	Paris	Perpignan	Strasbourg	Toulouse
Bordeaux	184																			
Brest	811	623																		
Caen	764	568	376																	
Cahors	307	218	788	661																
Calais	164	876	710	339	875															
Chambéry	860	651	1120	800	523	834														
Cherbourg	835	647	399	124	743	461	923													
Clermont-Ferrand	564	358	805	566	269	717	295	689												
Dijon	807	619	867	548	378	572	273	671	279											
Grenoble	827	657	1126	806	501	863	56	929	300	302										
Lille	997	809	725	353	808	112	767	476	650	505	798									
Lyon	831	528	1018	698	439	755	103	820	171	194	110	687								
Marseille	700	651	1271	1010	521	1067	344	1132	477	506	273	999	314							
Nantes	513	326	298	292	491	593	780	317	462	656	787	609	618	975						
Nice	858	810	1429	1168	679	1225	410	1291	636	664	337	1157	473	190	1131					
Paris	771	583	596	232	582	289	565	355	424	313	571	222	462	775	384	932				
Perpignan	499	451	1070	998	320	1149	478	1094	441	640	445	1081	448	319	773	476	857			
Strasbourg	1254	1066	1079	730	847	621	496	853	584	335	551	522	488	803	867	804	490	935		
Toulouse	300	247	866	865	116	991	565	890	890	727	533	923	536	407	568	564	699	205	1022	
Tours	536	348	490	246	413	531	611	369	369	418	618	463	449	795	197	952	238	795	721	593

making them easily identifiable – including to thieves.
Never leave anything of value
in a parked car, even in the
boot (trunk).

Purchase-Repurchase Plans

If you don't live in the EU
and will need a car in France
(or Europe) for 17 days to
six months (up to one year
if you'll be studying), by far
the cheapest option is to
'purchase' a new one and then
'sell' it back at the end of your
trip. In reality, you pay only for
the number of days you have
the vehicle but the 'temporary transit' (TT) paperwork
means that the car is registered under your name – and
that the whole deal is exempt
from all sorts of taxes.

Companies offering
purchase-repurchase
(*achat-rachat*) plans:

Eurocar TT (www.eurocartt.
com)

Peugeot OpenEurope
(www.peugeot-openeurope.
com)

Renault Eurodrive (www.
eurodrive.renault.com)

Eligibility is restricted to people who are not residents of
the EU (citizens of EU countries are eligible if they live
outside the EU); the minimum
age is 18 (in some cases 21).
Pricing and special offers depend on your home country.
All the plans include unlimited
kilometres, 24-hour towing
and breakdown service, and
comprehensive insurance
with absolutely no deducti-
ble/excess, so returning the
car is hassle-free, even if it's
damaged.

Extending your contract
(up to a maximum of 165
days) after you start using the
car is possible but you'll end
up paying about double the
prepaid per-day rate.

Purchase-repurchase cars,
which have special red licence
plates, can be picked up at
about three-dozen cities and
airports all over France and
dropped off at the agency of

your choosing. For a fee, you
can also pick up or return your
car in certain cities outside
France.

Driving Licence & Documents

An International Driving
Permit (IDP), valid only if
accompanied by your original
licence, is good for a year and
can be issued by your local
automobile association before
you leave home.

Drivers must carry the
following at all times:

➡ passport or an EU national
ID card

➡ valid driving licence (*permis
de conduire;* most foreign
licences can be used in France
for up to a year)

➡ car-ownership papers,
known as a *carte grise* (grey
card)

➡ proof of third-party liability
assurance (insurance)

Fuel

Essence (petrol), also known
as *carburant* (fuel), costs
between €1.40 and €1.70 per
litre for 95 unleaded (Sans
Plomb 95 or SP95, usually
available from a green pump)
and €1.30 to €1.50 for diesel
(*diesel, gazole* or *gasoil*,
usually available from a yellow
pump). Check and compare
current prices countrywide
with www.prix-carburants.
gouv.fr.

Filling up (*faire le plein*) is
most expensive at autoroute
rest stops, and usually cheapest at hypermarkets.

Many small petrol stations
close on Sunday afternoons
and, even in cities, it can be
hard to find a staffed station
open late at night. In general,
after-hours purchases (eg at
hypermarkets' fully automatic
24-hour stations) can only be
made with a credit card that
has an embedded PIN chip,
so if all you've got is cash or
a magnetic-strip credit card,
you could be stuck.

Insurance

Third-party liability insurance (*assurance au tiers*) is

compulsory for all vehicles in
France, including cars brought
in from abroad. Normally,
cars registered and insured
in other European countries
can circulate freely in France,
but it's a good idea to contact
your insurance company before you leave home to make
sure you have coverage – and
to check whom to contact
in case of a breakdown or
accident.

If you get into a minor
accident with no injuries, the
easiest way for drivers to sort
things out with their insurance
companies is to fill out a Con-
stat Aimable d'Accident Automobile (European Accident
Statement), a standardised
way of recording important
details about what happened.
In rental cars it's usually in the
packet of documents in the
glove compartment. Make
sure the report includes any
information that will help you
prove that the accident was
not your fault. Remember, if
it *was* your fault you may be
liable for a hefty insurance
deductible/excess. Don't sign
anything you don't fully understand. If problems crop up,
call the police (⏻17).

French-registered cars
have details of their insurance
company printed on a little
green square affixed to the
windscreen.

Parking

In city centres, most on-the-
street parking places are
payant (metered) from about
9am to 7pm (sometimes with
a break from noon to 2pm)
Monday to Saturday, except
bank holidays.

Road Rules

Enforcement of French traffic
laws (see www.securite
routiere.gouv.fr, in French)
has been stepped up considerably in recent years. Speed
cameras are common, as are
radar traps and unmarked
police vehicles. Fines for many
infractions are given on the
spot, and serious violations
can lead to the confiscation of
your driving licence and car.

PRIORITY TO THE RIGHT

Under the *priorité à droite* ('priority to the right') rule, any car entering an intersection (including a T-junction) from a road (including a tiny village backstreet) on your right has the right-of-way. Locals assume every driver knows this, so don't be surprised if they courteously cede the right-of-way when you're about to turn from an alley onto a highway – and boldly assert their rights when you're the one zipping down a main road.

Priorité à droite is suspended (eg on arterial roads) when you pass a sign showing an upended yellow square with a black square in the middle. The same sign with a horizontal bar through the square lozenge reinstates the *priorité à droite* rule.

When you arrive at a roundabout at which you do not have the right of way (ie the cars already in the roundabout do), you'll often see signs reading *vous n'avez pas la priorité* (you do not have right of way) or *cédez le passage* (give way).

Speed limits outside built-up areas (except where signposted otherwise):

➜ **Undivided N and D highways** 90km/h (80km/h when raining)

➜ **Non-autoroute divided highways** 110km/h (100km/h when raining)

➜ **Autoroutes** 130km/h (110km/h when raining, 60km/h in icy conditions) To reduce carbon emissions, autoroute speed limits have recently been reduced to 110km/h in some areas.

Unless otherwise signposted, a limit of 50km/h applies in *all* areas designated as built up, no matter how rural they may appear. You must slow to 50km/h the moment you come to a white sign with a red border and a place name written on it; the speed limit applies until you pass an identical sign with a horizontal bar through it.

Other important driving rules:

➜ Blood-alcohol limit is 0.05% (0.5g per litre of blood) – the equivalent of two glasses of wine for a 75kg adult. Police often conduct random breathalyser tests and penalties can be severe, including imprisonment.

➜ All passengers, including those in the back seat, must wear seatbelts.

➜ Mobile phones may be used only if they are equipped with a hands-free kit or speakerphone.

➜ Turning right on a red light is illegal.

➜ Cars from the UK and Ireland must have deflectors affixed to their headlights to avoid dazzling oncoming motorists.

➜ Radar detectors, even if they're switched off, are illegal; fines are hefty.

➜ Children under 10 are not permitted to ride in the front seat (unless the back is already occupied by other children under 10).

➜ A child under 13kg must travel in a backward-facing child seat (permitted in the front seat only for babies under 9kg and if the airbag is deactivated).

➜ Up to age 10 and/or a minimum height of 140cm, children must use a size-appropriate type of front-facing child seat or booster.

➜ All vehicles driven in France must carry a high-visibility reflective safety vest (stored inside the vehicle, not in the trunk/boot), a reflective triangle, and a portable, single-use breathalyser kit. The fine for not carrying any of these items is €90.

➜ If you'll be driving on snowy roads, make sure you have snow chains (*chaînes neige*), required by law whenever and wherever the police post signs.

➜ Riders of any type of two-wheeled vehicle with a motor (except motor-assisted bicycles) must wear a helmet. No special licence is required to ride a motorbike whose engine is smaller than 50cc, which is why rental scooters are often rated at 49.9cc.

Hitching

Hitching is never entirely safe in any country in the world, and we don't recommend it. Travellers who decide to hitch should understand that they are taking a small but potentially serious risk. Remember that it's safer to travel in pairs and be sure to inform someone of your intended destination. Hitching is not really part of French culture.

Hitching from city centres is pretty much hopeless, so your best bet is to take public transport to the outskirts. It is illegal to hitch on autoroutes, but you can stand near an entrance ramp as long as you don't block traffic. Hitching in remote rural areas is better, but once you get off the *routes nationales* traffic can be light and local. If your itinerary includes a ferry crossing, it's worth trying to score a ride before the ferry since vehicle tickets usually include a number of passengers free of charge. At dusk, give up and think about finding somewhere to stay.

Trains & Ferries

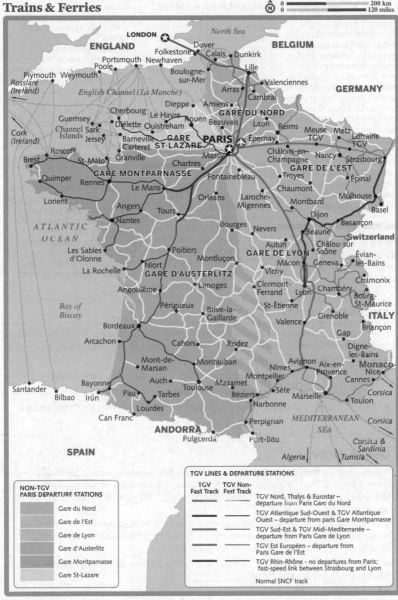

TGV LINES & DEPARTURE STATIONS

TGV Fast Track	TGV Non-Fast Track	
		TGV Nord, Thalys & Eurostar – departure from Paris Garc du Nord
		TGV Atlantique Sud-Ouest & TGV Atlantique Ouest – departure from paris Gare Montparnasse
		TGV Sud-Est & TGV Midi-Mediterranée – departure from Paris Gare de Lyon
		TGV Est Européen – departure from Paris Gare de l'Est
		TGV Rhin-Rhône - no departures from Paris; fast-speed link between Strasbourg and Lyon
		Normal SNCF track

NON-TGV PARIS DEPARTURE STATIONS

- Gare du Nord
- Gare de l'Est
- Gare de Lyon
- Gare d'Austerlitz
- Gare Montparnasse
- Gare St-Lazare

Ride Share

A number of organisations around France arrange *co-voiturage* (car sharing), ie putting people looking for rides in touch with drivers going to the same destination. The best known is Paris-based **Allostop** (☎01 53 20 42 42; www.allostop.net), where you pay €3/5/8/10 for a single journey up to 50/100/150/200km. You might also try **Covoiturage** (www.covoiturage.fr) or, for international journeys, **Karzoo** (www.karzoo.eu).

Local Transport

France's cities and larger towns have world-class public-transport systems. There are *métros* (underground subway systems) in Paris, Lyon, Marseille, Lille and Toulouse and ultramodern light-rail lines *(tramways)* in cities such as Bordeaux, Grenoble, Lille, Lyon, Nancy, Nantes, Nice, Reims, Rouen and Strasbourg, as well as parts of greater Paris.

In addition to a *billet à l'unité* (single ticket), you can purchase a *carnet* (booklet or bunch) of 10 tickets or a *pass journée* (all-day pass).

Taxi

All medium and large train stations – and many small ones – have a taxi stand out front. In small cities and towns, where taxi drivers are unlikely to find another fare anywhere near where they let you off, one-way and return trips often cost the same. Tariffs are about 30% higher at night and on Sundays and holidays. A surcharge is usually charged to get picked up at a train station or airport, and there's a small additional fee for a fourth passenger and/or for suitcases.

Train

Travelling by train in France is a comfortable and environmentally sustainable way to see the country. Since many train stations have car-hire agencies, it's easy to combine rail travel with rural exploration by car.

The jewel in the crown of France's public-transport system – alongside the Paris *métro* – is its extensive rail network, almost all of it run by **SNCF** (www.sncf.com) Although it employs the most advanced rail technology, the network's layout reflects the country's centuries-old Paris-centric nature: most of the principal rail lines radiate out from Paris like the spokes of a wheel, the result being that services between provincial towns situated on different spokes can be infrequent and slow.

Up-to-the-minute information on *perturbations* (service disruptions), eg because of strikes, can be found on www.infolignes.com (in French).

Since its inauguration in the 1980s, the pride and joy of SNCF is the **TGV** (Train à Grande Vitesse; www.tgv.com),

---

SNCF FARES & DISCOUNTS

Full-fare tickets can be expensive. Fortunately, a dizzying array of discounts is available and station staff are very good at helping travellers find the very best fare. But first, the basics:

➡ First-class travel, where available, costs 20% to 30% extra.

➡ Ticket prices for some trains, including most TGVs, are pricier during peak periods.

➡ The further in advance you reserve, the lower the fares.

➡ Children under four travel free (€9 with a *'forfait bambin'* to any destination if they need a seat).

➡ Children aged four to 11 travel for half-price.

Ouigo & iDTGV

Run by the SNCF, **Ouigo** (www.ouigo.com) is a low-cost TGV service where you can travel on high-speed TGVs for a snip of the usual price. Ouigo trains only serve Aix-en-Provence, Avignon, Lyon, Marne-la-Vallée, Marseille, Montpellier. Nîmes and Valence TGV stations. By 2017 Ouigo should also go to Bordeaux.

➡ Tickets can only be purchased online from three weeks until four hours before departure; tickets are emailed four days before departure and must be printed out or readable on a smartphone with the Ouigo app (iPhone and Android).

➡ The minimum single fare is €10; the maximum fare for a journey originating in Marne-la-Vallée/Lyon/Valence is €85/35/35.

➡ Each passenger is allowed to bring on board one piece of cabin luggage (35cm x 55cm x 25cm), one piece of hand luggage (27cm x 36cm x 15cm) and a child's pushchair for free; an extra bag and/or a larger bag costs €5 (€20 if you rock up at the train without registering the bag online in advance).

➡ Childen aged under 12 travelling with an adult pay a fixed price of €5. If requested, they are guaranteed a seat with an electric plug.

pronounced 'teh zheh veh', which zips passengers along at speeds of up to 320km/h (198mph).

The main TGV lines (or LGVs, short for *lignes à grande vitesse*, ie high-speed rail lines) head north, east, southeast and southwest from Paris (trains use slower local tracks to get to destinations off the main line):

➡ **TGV Nord, Thalys & Eurostar** Link Paris Gare du Nord with Arras, Lille, Calais, Brussels (Bruxelles-Midi), Amsterdam, Cologne and, via the Channel Tunnel, Ashford, Ebbsfleet and London St Pancras.

➡ **TGV Est Européen** Connects Paris Gare de l'Est with Reims, Nancy, Metz, Strasbourg, Zurich and Germany, including Frankfurt and Stuttgart. At present,

the super-high-speed track stretches only as far east as Lorraine but it's supposed to reach Strasbourg in 2016.

➡ **TGV Sud-Est & TGV Midi-Méditerranée** Link Paris Gare de Lyon with the southeast, including Dijon, Lyon, Geneva, the Alps, Avignon, Marseille, Nice and Montpellier.

➡ **TGV Atlantique Sud-Ouest & TGV Atlantique Ouest** Link Paris Gare Montparnasse with western and southwestern France, including Brittany (Rennes, Brest, Quimper), Tours, Nantes, Poitiers, La Rochelle, Bordeaux, Biarritz and Toulouse.

➡ **LGV Rhin-Rhône** France's newest high-speed rail route bypasses Paris altogether in its bid to better link the provinces. Six services a day speed between

Strasbourg and Lyon, with most continuing south to Marseille or Montpellier on the Mediterranean.

TGV tracks are interconnected, making it possible to go directly from, say, Lyon to Nantes or Bordeaux to Lille without having to switch trains in Paris or transfer from one of Paris' six main train stations to another. Stops on the link-up, which runs east and south of Paris, include Charles de Gaulle airport and Disneyland Resort Paris.

Long-distance trains sometimes split at a station – that is, each half of the train heads off for a different destination. Check the destination panel on your car as you board or you could wind up very far from where you intended to go.

➡ Also try **iDTGV** (www.idtgv.com), another SNCF subsidiary that sells tickets (online only) for as little as €19 for advance-purchase TGV travel between 30-odd cities.

Discount Tickets

The SNCF's most heavily discounted tickets are called **Prem's**, available online, at ticket windows and from ticket machines a maximum of 90 days and a minimum of 14 days before departure. Prem's are nonrefundable and nonchangeable.

➡ Bons Plans fares, a grab bag of really cheap options, are advertised on the SNCF website under 'Dernière Minute' ('last minute').

➡ On regional trains, discount fares requiring neither a discount card nor advance purchase include:

Loisir Week-End rates Good for return travel that includes a Saturday night at your destination or involves travel on a Saturday or Sunday.

Découverte fares Available for low-demand 'blue-period' trains to people aged 12 to 25, seniors and the adult travel companions of children under 12.

Mini-Groupe tickets In some regions, these bring big savings for three to six people travelling together, provided you spend a Saturday night at your destination.

Discount Cards

Reductions of at least 25% (for last-minute bookings), and of 40%, 50% or even 60% (if you reserve well ahead or travel during low-volume 'blue' periods), are available with several discount cards (valid for one year):

Carte Jeune (€50) Available to travellers aged 12 to 27.

Carte Enfant+ (€75) For one to four adults travelling with a child aged four to 11.

Carte Weekend (€75) For people aged 26 to 59. Discounts on return journeys of at least 200km that either include a Saturday night away or only involve travel on a Saturday or Sunday.

Carte Sénior+ (€50) For travellers over 60.

LEFT-LUGGAGE FACILITIES

Because of security concerns, few French train stations have *consignes automatiques* (left-luggage lockers). In larger stations you can leave your bags in a *consigne manuelle* (staffed left-luggage facility) where items are handed over in person and X-rayed before being stowed. Charges are €5 for up to 10 hours and €8 for 24 hours; payment must be made in cash. To find out which stations let you leave your bags and when their *consignes* are open (they're often closed on Sunday and after 7pm or 8pm), go to www.gares-en-mouvement.com, select a station, click 'Practical Information' ('Services en gare') and then the 'Services' tab.

Other types of train include:

Téoz (www.corailteoz.com) Especially comfortable trains that run southward from Paris Gare d'Austerlitz to Clermont-Ferrand, Limoges, Cahors, Toulouse, Montpellier, Perpignan, Marseille and Nice.

TER (Train Express Régional; www.ter-sncf.com) A train that is not a TGV is often referred to as a *corail*, a *classique* or, for intraregional services, a TER.

Transilien (www.transilien.com) SNCF services in the Île de France area in and around Paris.

Rail Passes

Residents of Europe (who do not live in France) can purchase an **InterRail One Country Pass** (www.interrailnet.com; 3/4/6/8 days €216/237/302/344, 12-25yr €147/157/199/222), which entitles its bearer to unlimited travel on SNCF trains for three to eight days over the course of a month.

For non-European residents, **Rail Europe** (www.raileurope.com) offers the **France Rail Pass** (www.francerailpass.com; 3/6/9 days over 1 month €211/301/388).

You need to really rack up the kilometres to make these passes worthwhile.

Tickets & Reservations

Large stations often have separate ticket windows for *international, grandes lignes* (long-haul) and *banlieue* (suburban) lines, and for people whose train is about to leave (*départ immédiat* or *départ dans l'heure*). Nearly every SNCF station has at least one *borne libre-service* (self-service terminal) or *billeterie automatique* (automatic ticket machine) that accepts both cash and PIN-chip credit cards. Select the Union Jack for instructions in English.

Using a credit card, you can buy a ticket by phone or via the SNCF internet booking website, **Voyages SNCF** (www.voyages-sncf.com), and either have it sent to you by post (if you have an address in France) or collect it from any SNCF ticket office or from train-station ticket machines.

Before boarding the train, validate *(composter)* your ticket by time-stamping it in a *composteur*, a yellow post located on the way to the platform. If you forget (or don't have a ticket for some other reason), find a conductor on the train before they find you – otherwise you can be fined.

CHANGES & REIMBURSEMENTS

For trains that do not assign reserved seats (eg TER and Corail Intercités trains), full-fare tickets are usable whenever you like for 61 days from the date they were purchased. Like all SNCF tickets, they cannot be replaced if lost or stolen.

If you have a full-fare Loisir Week-End ticket, you can change your reservation by phone, internet or at train stations for no charge until the day before your departure; changes made on the day of your reserved trip incur a charge of €10 (€3 for tickets bought with a discount card).

Pro tickets (eg TGV Pro, Téoz Pro) allow full reimbursement up to 30 minutes *after* the time of departure (by calling ☑36 35). If you turn up at your departure station up to two hours after your original travel time, you can reschedule your trip on a later train.

WANT MORE?

For in-depth language information and handy phrases, check out Lonely Planet's *French Phrasebook*. You'll find it at **shop. lonelyplanet.com**, or you can buy Lonely Planet's iPhone phrasebooks at the Apple App Store.

Language

Standard French is taught and spoken throughout France. This said, regional accents and dialects are an important part of identity in certain regions, but you'll have no trouble being understood anywhere if you stick to standard French, which we've also used in this chapter.

The sounds used in spoken French can almost all be found in English. There are a couple of exceptions: nasal vowels (represented in our pronunciation guides by o or u followed by an almost inaudible nasal consonant sound m, n or ng), the 'funny' *u* (ew in our guides) and the deep-in-the-throat *r*. Bearing these few points in mind and reading our pronunciation guides below as if they were English, you'll be understood just fine.

BASICS

French has two words for 'you' – use the polite form *vous* unless you're talking to close friends, children or animals in which case you'd use the informal *tu*. You can also use *tu* when a person invites you to use *tu*.

All nouns in French are either masculine or feminine, and so are the adjectives, articles *le/la* (the) and *un/une* (a), and possessives *mon/ma* (my), *ton/ta* (your) *and son/sa* (his, her) that go with the nouns. In this chapter we have included masculine and femine forms where necessary, separated by a slash and indicated with 'm/f'.

Hello.	*Bonjour.*	bon·zhoor
Goodbye.	*Au revoir.*	o·rer·vwa
Excuse me.	*Excusez-moi.*	ek·skew·zay·mwa
Sorry.	*Pardon.*	par·don

Yes.	*Oui.*	wee
No.	*Non.*	non
Please.	*S'il vous plaît.*	seel voo play
Thank you.	*Merci.*	mair·see
You're welcome.	*De rien.*	der ree·en

How are you?
Comment allez-vous? ko·mon ta·lay·voo

Fine, and you?
Bien, merci. Et vous? byun mair·see ay voo

You're welcome.
De rien. der ree·en

My name is ...
Je m'appelle ... zher ma·pel ...

What's your name?
Comment vous appelez-vous? ko·mon voo·za·play voo

Do you speak English?
Parlez-vous anglais? par·lay·voo ong·glay

I don't understand.
Je ne comprends pas. zher ner kom·pron pa

ACCOMMODATION

Do you have any rooms available?
Est-ce que vous avez des chambres libres? es·ker voo za·vay day shom·brer lee·brer

How much is it per night/person?
Quel est le prix par nuit/personne? kel ay ler pree par nwee/per·son

Is breakfast included?
Est-ce que le petit déjeuner est inclus? es·ker ler per·tee day·zher·nay ayt en·klew

campsite	camping	kom·peeng
dorm	dortoir	dor·twar
guest house	pension	pon·syon
hotel	hôtel	o·tel
youth hostel	auberge de jeunesse	o·berzh der zher·nes
a ... room	une chambre ...	ewn shom·brer ...
single	à un lit	a un lee
double	avec un grand lit	a·vek un gron lee
twin	avec des lits jumeaux	a·vek day lee zhew·mo
with (a)...	avec ...	a·vek ...
air-con	climatiseur	klee·ma·tee·zer
bathroom	une salle de bains	ewn sal der bun
window	fenêtre	fer·nay·trer

DIRECTIONS

Where's ...?
Où est ...?   oo ay ...

What's the address?
Quelle est l'adresse?   kel ay la·dres

Could you write the address, please?
Est-ce que vous pourriez   es·ker voo poo·ryay
écrire l'adresse,   ay·kreer la·dres
s'il vous plaît?   seel voo play

Can you show me (on the map)?
Pouvez-vous m'indiquer   poo·vay·voo mun·dee·kay
(sur la carte)?   (sewr la kart)

at the corner	au coin	o kwun
at the traffic lights	aux feux	o fer
behind	derrière	dair·ryair
in front of	devant	der·von
far (from)	loin (de)	lwun (der)
left	gauche	gosh
near (to)	près (de)	pray (der)
next to ...	à côté de ...	a ko·tay der...
opposite ...	en face de ...	on fas der ...
right	droite	drwat
straight ahead	tout droit	too drwa

EATING & DRINKING

What would you recommend?
Qu'est-ce que vous   kes·ker voo
conseillez?   kon·say·yay

What's in that dish?
Quels sont les   kel son lay
ingrédients?   zun·gray·dyon

I'm a vegetarian.
Je suis végétarien/   zher swee vay·zhay·ta·ryun/
végétarienne.   vay·zhay·ta·ryen (m/f)

I don't eat ...
Je ne mange pas ...   zher ner monzh pa ...

Cheers!
Santé!   son·tay

That was delicious.
C'était délicieux!   say·tay day·lee·syer

Please bring the bill.
Apportez-moi   a·por·tay·mwa
l'addition,   la·dee·syon
s'il vous plaît.   seel voo play

I'd like to reserve a table for ...	Je voudrais réserver une table pour ...	zher voo·dray ray·zair·vay ewn ta·bler poor ...
(eight) o'clock	(vingt) heures	(vungt) er
(two) people	(deux) personnes	(der) pair·son

Key Words

appetiser	*entrée*	on·tray
bottle	*bouteille*	boo·tay
breakfast	*petit déjeuner*	per·tee day·zher·nay
children's menu	*menu pour enfants*	mer·new poor on·fon
cold	*froid*	frwa
delicatessen	*traiteur*	tray·ter
dinner	*dîner*	dee·nay
dish	*plat*	pla
food	*nourriture*	noo·ree·tewr
fork	*fourchette*	foor·shet
glass	*verre*	vair
grocery store	*épicerie*	ay·pees·ree
highchair	*chaise haute*	shay zot
hot	*chaud*	sho
knife	*couteau*	koo·to
local speciality	*spécialité locale*	spay·sya·lee·tay lo·kal
lunch	*déjeuner*	day·zher·nay
main course	*plat principal*	pla prun·see·pal
market	*marché*	mar·shay
menu (in English)	*carte (en anglais)*	kart (on ong·glay)
plate	*assiette*	a·syet
spoon	*cuillère*	kwee·yair
wine list	*carte des vins*	kart day vun
with/without	*avec/sans*	a·vek/son

Meat & Fish

beef	*bœuf*	berf
chicken	*poulet*	poo·lay
crab	*crabe*	krab
lamb	*agneau*	a·nyo
oyster	*huître*	wee·trer
pork	*porc*	por
snail	*escargot*	es·kar·go
squid	*calmar*	kal·mar
turkey	*dinde*	dund
veal	*veau*	vo

Fruit & Vegetables

apple	*pomme*	pom
apricot	*abricot*	ab·ree·ko
asparagus	*asperge*	a·spairzh
beans	*haricots*	a·ree·ko
beetroot	*betterave*	be·trav
cabbage	*chou*	shoo
cherry	*cerise*	ser·reez
corn	*maïs*	ma·ees
cucumber	*concombre*	kong·kom·brer
grape	*raisin*	ray·zun
lemon	*citron*	see·tron
lettuce	*laitue*	lay·tew
mushroom	*champignon*	shom·pee·nyon
peach	*pêche*	pesh
peas	*petit pois*	per·tee pwa
(red/green) pepper	*poivron (rouge/vert)*	pwa·vron (roozh/vair)
pineapple	*ananas*	a·na·nas
plum	*prune*	prewn
potato	*pomme de terre*	pom der tair
prune	*pruneau*	prew·no
pumpkin	*citrouille*	see·troo·yer
shallot	*échalote*	eh·sha·lot
spinach	*épinards*	eh·pee·nar
strawberry	*fraise*	frez
tomato	*tomate*	to·mat
vegetable	*légume*	lay·gewm

Other

bread	*pain*	pun
butter	*beurre*	ber
cheese	*fromage*	fro·mazh
egg	*œuf*	erf
honey	*miel*	myel
jam	*confiture*	kon·fee·tewr
lentils	*lentilles*	lon·tee·yer
pasta/noodles	*pâtes*	pat
pepper	*poivre*	pwa·vrer
rice	*riz*	ree
salt	*sel*	sel
sugar	*sucre*	sew·krer
vinegar	*vinaigre*	vee·nay·grer

Signs

Entrée	Entrance
Femmes	Women
Fermé	Closed
Hommes	Men
Interdit	Prohibited
Ouvert	Open
Renseignements	Information
Sortie	Exit
Toilettes/WC	Toilets

Drinks

beer	*bière*	bee·yair
coffee	*café*	ka·fay
(orange) juice	*jus (d'orange)*	zhew (do·ronzh)
milk	*lait*	lay
tea	*thé*	tay
(mineral) water	*eau (minérale)*	o (mee·nay·ral)
(red) wine	*vin (rouge)*	vun (roozh)
(white) wine	*vin (blanc)*	vun (blong)

EMERGENCIES

Help!
Au secours!   o skoor

I'm lost.
Je suis perdu/perdue.   zhe swee·pair·dew (m/f)

Leave me alone!
Fichez-moi la paix!   fee·shay·mwa la pay

There's been an accident.
Il y a eu un accident.   eel ya ew un ak·see·don

Call a doctor.
Appelez un médecin.   a·play un mayd·sun

Call the police.
Appelez la police.   a·play la po·lees

I'm ill.
Je suis malade.   zher swee ma·lad

It hurts here.
J'ai une douleur ici.   zhay ewn doo·ler ee·see

I'm allergic to ...
Je suis allergique ...   zher swee za·lair·zheek ...

SHOPPING & SERVICES

I'd like to buy ...
Je voudrais acheter ...   zher voo·dray ash·tay ...

May I look at it?
Est-ce que je peux le voir?   es·ker zher per ler vwar

I'm just looking.
Je regarde.   zher rer·gard

I don't like it.
Cela ne me plaît pas.   ser·la ner mer play pa

How much is it?
C'est combien?   say kom·byun

It's too expensive.
C'est trop cher.   say tro shair

Question Words

How?	*Comment?*	ko·mon
What?	*Quoi?*	kwa
When?	*Quand?*	kon
Where?	*Où?*	oo
Who?	*Qui?*	kee
Why?	*Pourquoi?*	poor·kwa

Can you lower the price?
Vous pouvez baisser le prix?   voo poo·vay bay·say ler pree

There's a mistake in the bill.
Il y a une erreur dans la note.   eel ya ewn ay·rer don la not

ATM	*guichet automatique de banque*	gee·shay o·to·ma·teek der bonk
credit card	*carte de crédit*	kart der kray·dee
internet cafe	*cybercafé*	see·bair·ka·fay
post office	*bureau de poste*	bew·ro der post
tourist office	*office de tourisme*	o·fees der too·rees·mer

TIME & DATES

What time is it?
Quelle heure est-il?   kel er ay til

It's (eight) o'clock.
Il est (huit) heures.   il ay (weet) er

It's half past (10).
Il est (dix) heures et demie.   il ay (deez) er ay day·mee

morning	*matin*	ma·tun
afternoon	*après-midi*	a·pray·mee·dee
evening	*soir*	swar
yesterday	*hier*	yair
today	*aujourd'hui*	o·zhoor·dwee
tomorrow	*demain*	der·mun

Monday	*lundi*	lun·dee
Tuesday	*mardi*	mar·dee
Wednesday	*mercredi*	mair·krer·dee
Thursday	*jeudi*	zher·dee
Friday	*vendredi*	von·drer·dee
Saturday	*samedi*	sam·dee
Sunday	*dimanche*	dee·monsh

January	*janvier*	zhon·vyay
February	*février*	fayv·ryay
March	*mars*	mars
April	*avril*	a·vreel
May	*mai*	may
June	*juin*	zhwun
July	*juillet*	zhwee·yay
August	*août*	oot
September	*septembre*	sep·tom·brer
October	*octobre*	ok·to·brer
November	*novembre*	no·vom·brer
December	*décembre*	day·som·brer

a ... ticket	un billet ...	un bee·yay ...
1st-class	de première classe	der prem·yair klas
2nd-class	de deuxième classe	der der·zyem las
one-way	simple	sum·pler
return	aller et retour	a·lay ay rer·toor
aisle seat	côté couloir	ko·tay kool·war
delayed	en retard	on rer·tar
cancelled	annulé	a·new·lay
platform	quai	kay
ticket office	guichet	gee·shay
timetable	horaire	o·rair
train station	gare	gar
window seat	côté fenêtre	ko·tay fe·ne·trer

Numbers

1	un	un
2	deux	der
3	trois	trwa
4	quatre	ka·trer
5	cinq	sungk
6	six	sees
7	sept	set
8	huit	weet
9	neuf	nerf
10	dix	dees
20	vingt	vung
30	trente	tront
40	quarante	ka·ront
50	cinquante	sung·kont
60	soixante	swa·sont
70	soixante-dix	swa·son·dees
80	quatre-vingts	ka·trer·vung
90	quatre-vingt-dix	ka·trer·vung·dees
100	cent	son
1000	mille	meel

TRANSPORT

Public Transport

boat	bateau	ba·to
bus	bus	bews
plane	avion	a·vyon
train	train	trun

I want to go to ...
Je voudrais aller à ...   zher voo·dray a·lay a ...

Does it stop at (Amboise)?
Est-ce qu'il s'arrête à   es·kil sa·ret a
(Amboise)?   (om·bwaz)

At what time does it leave/arrive?
À quelle heure est-ce   a kel er es
qu'il part/arrive?   kil par/a·reev

Can you tell me when we get to ...?
Pouvez-vous me   poo·vay·voo mer
dire quand   deer kon
nous arrivons à ...?   noo za·ree·von a ...

I want to get off here.
Je veux descendre   zher ver day·son·drer
ici.   ee·see

first	premier	prer·myay
last	dernier	dair·nyay
next	prochain	pro·shun

Driving & Cycling

I'd like to hire a ...	Je voudrais louer ...	zher voo·dray loo·way ...
4WD	un quatre-quatre	un kat·kat
car	une voiture	ewn vwa·tewr
bicycle	un vélo	un vay·lo
motorcycle	une moto	ewn mo·to
child seat	siège-enfant	syezh·on·fon
diesel	diesel	dyay·zel
helmet	casque	kask
mechanic	mécanicien	may·ka·nee·syun
petrol/gas	essence	ay·sons
service station	station service	sta·syon·ser·vees

Is this the road to ...?
C'est la route pour ...?   say la root poor ...

(How long) Can I park here?
(Combien de temps)   (kom·byun der tom)
Est-ce que je peux   es·ker zher per
stationner ici?   sta·syo·nay ee·see

The car/motorbike has broken down (at ...).
La voiture/moto est   la vwa·tewr/mo·to ay
tombée en panne (à ...).   tom·bay on pan (a ...)

I have a flat tyre.
Mon pneu est à plat.   mom pner ay ta pla

I've run out of petrol.
Je suis en panne   zher swee zon pan
d'essence.   day·sons

I've lost my car keys.
J'ai perdu les clés de   zhay per·dew lay klay der
ma voiture.   ma vwa·tewr

GLOSSARY

(m) indicates masculine gender, (f) feminine gender and (pl) plural

accueil (m) – reception

alignements (m pl) – a series of standing stones, or menhirs, in straight lines

AOC – Appellation d'Origine Contrôlée; system of French wine and olive oil classification showing that items have met government regulations as to where and how they are produced

AOP – Appellation d'Origine Protégée; Europe-wide equivalent to *AOC*

arrondissement (m) – administrative division of large city; abbreviated on signs as 1er (1st arrondissement), 2e (2nd) etc

atelier (m) – workshop or studio

auberge – inn

auberge de jeunesse (f) – youth hostel

baie (f) – bay

bassin (m) – bay or basin

bastide (f) – medieval settlement in southwestern France, usually built on a grid plan and surrounding an arcaded square; fortified town; also a country house in Provence

belle époque (f) – literally 'beautiful age'; era of elegance and gaiety characterising fashionable Parisian life in the period preceding WWI

billet (m) – ticket

billetterie (f) – ticket office or counter

bouchon – Lyonnais bistro

boulangerie (f) – bakery or bread shop

boules (f pl) – a game similar to lawn bowls played with heavy metal balls on a sandy pitch; also called *pétanque*

brasserie (f) – restaurant similar to a *café* but usually serving full meals all day (original meaning: brewery)

bureau de change (m) – exchange bureau

bureau de poste (m) – post office

carnet (m) – a book of five or 10 bus, tram or metro tickets sold at a reduced rate

carrefour (m) – crossroad

carte (f) – card; menu; map

cave (f) – wine cellar

chambre (f) – room

chambre d'hôte (f) – B&B

charcuterie (f) – butcher's shop and delicatessen; the prepared meats it sells

cimetière (m) – cemetery

col (m) – mountain pass

consigne or **consigne manuelle** (f) – left-luggage office

consigne automatique (f) – left-luggage locker

correspondance (f) – linking tunnel or walkway, eg in the metro; rail or bus connection

cour (f) – courtyard

crémerie (f) – dairy or cheese shop

dégustation (f) – tasting

demi (m) – 330mL glass of beer

demi-pension (f) – half board (B&B with either lunch or dinner)

département (m) – administrative division of France

donjon (m) – castle keep

église (f) – church

épicerie (f) – small grocery store

ESF – École de Ski Français; France's leading ski school

fest-noz or **festoù-noz** (pl) – night festival

fête (f) – festival

Fnac – retail chain selling entertainment goods, electronics and tickets

forêt (f) – forest

formule or **formule rapide** (f) – lunchtime set similar to a *menu* but with two of three courses on offer (eg starter and main or main and dessert)

fromagerie (f) – cheese shop

FUAJ – Fédération Unie des Auberges de Jeunesse; France's major hostel association

funiculaire (m) – funicular railway

galerie (f) – covered shopping centre or arcade

gare or **gare SNCF** (f) – railway station

gare maritime (f) – ferry terminal

gare routière (f) – bus station

gendarmerie (f) – police station; police force

gîte d'étape (m) – hikers accommodation, usually in a village

golfe (m) – gulf

GR – *grande randonnée*; long-distance hiking trail

grand cru (m) – wine of exceptional quality

halles (f pl) – covered market; central food market

halte routière (f) – bus stop

horaire (m) – timetable or schedule

hostellerie – hostelry

hôtel de ville (m) – city or town hall

hôtel particulier (m) – private mansion

intra-muros – old city (literally 'within the walls')

jardin (m) – garden

jardin botanique (m) – botanic garden

laverie (f) or **lavomatique** (m) – laundrette

libre – vacant, available

mairie (f) – city or town hall

maison du parc (f) – a

national park's headquarters and/or visitors centre

marché (m) – market

marché aux puces (m) – flea market

marché couvert (m) – covered market

mas (m) – farmhouse in southern France

menu (m) – fixed-price meal with two or more courses

mistral (m) – strong north or northwest wind in southern France

musée (m) – museum

navette (f) – shuttle bus, train or boat

occupé – occupied

palais de justice (m) – law courts

parapente – paragliding

parlement (m) – parliament

parvis (m) – square

patisserie (f) – cake and pastry shop

pétanque (f) – a game similar to lawn bowls played with heavy metal balls on a sandy pitch; also called *boules*

petit déjeuner – breakfast

place (f) – square or plaza

plage (f) – beach

plan (m) – city map

plan du quartier (m) – map of nearby streets (hung on the wall near metro exits)

plat du jour (m) – daily special in a restaurant

pont (m) – bridge

porte (f) – gate in a city wall

poste (f) – post office

préfecture (f) – prefecture (capital of a *département*)

presqu'île (f) – peninsula

puy (m) – volcanic cone or peak

quai (m) – quay or railway platform

quartier (m) – quarter or district

refuge (m) – mountain hut, basic shelter for hikers

région (f) – administrative division of France

rond point (m) – roundabout

salon de thé – tearoom

sentier (m) – trail

service des urgences (f) – casualty ward

ski de fond – cross-country skiing

SNCF – Société Nationale des Chemins de Fer; state-owned railway company

SNCM – Société Nationale Maritime Corse-Méditerranée; state-owned ferry company

linking Corsica and mainland France

sortie (f) – exit

square (m) – public garden

tabac (m) – tobacconist (also selling bus tickets, phonecards etc)

table d'hôte – set menu at a fixed price

taxe de séjour (f) – municipal tourist tax

télécarte (f) – phonecard

télécabine – gondola

téléphérique (m) – cableway or cable car

téléski (m) – chairlift

téléski (m) – ski lift or tow

terroir – land

TGV – *Train à Grande Vitesse;* high-speed train or bullet train

tour (f) – tower

vallée (f) – valley

VF (f) – *version française;* a film dubbed in French

vieille ville (f) – old town or old city

ville neuve (f) – new town or new city

VO (f) – *version originale;* a nondubbed film with French subtitles

VTT – *vélo tout terrain;* mountain bike

winstub – traditional Alsatian eatery

Behind the Scenes

SEND US YOUR FEEDBACK

We love to hear from travellers – your comments keep us on our toes and help make our books better. Our well-travelled team reads every word on what you loved or loathed about this book. Although we cannot reply individually to your submissions, we always guarantee that your feedback goes straight to the appropriate authors, in time for the next edition. Each person who sends us information is thanked in the next edition – the most useful submissions are rewarded with a selection of digital PDF chapters.

Visit **lonelyplanet.com/contact** to submit your updates and suggestions or to ask for help. Our award-winning website also features inspirational travel stories, news and discussions.

Note: We may edit, reproduce and incorporate your comments in Lonely Planet products such as guidebooks, websites and digital products, so let us know if you don't want your comments reproduced or your name acknowledged. For a copy of our privacy policy visit lonelyplanet.com/privacy.

OUR READERS

Many thanks to the travellers who used the last edition and wrote to us with helpful hints, useful advice and interesting anecdotes:

Amy Boruff, Brigitte Lennon, Danila Simon, Derryl Caillemer, Elsa Dent, Isabel Yano, Krystyna Pindral, Lisa Wilkie, Lotte Oostebrink, Mariana Mozdzer, Marta Espachs, Melinda Fule, Michael Poesen, Remy Bach

AUTHOR THANKS
Nicola Williams

Un grand merci to the many in Provence who aided and abetted in tracking down the best: Provence trip planner and adopted St-Rémy de Provence resident, Julie Mautner (www.provncepost.cm); hoteliers extraordinaires Florian Colomb de Daunant at Cacherel Hotel, the couple at Hôtel Méditerranée, and Benoît Noel at Lodge Hélène in Stes-Maries de la Mer. Kudos to my very own, extra-special 'Provence with kids' research team Niko, Mischa and Kaya Luefkens and, of course, Matthias.

Alexis Averbuck

Life on the road wouldn't be nearly so wonderful without the kindness of strangers, but one person really stands out on this trip: the amazing, inimitable Janice Bowen. Janice opened her home, her region, might I say her heart, and made the Dordogne home-away-from-home. Thank you Janice, for trusting, sharing and just being YOU! Then, to my partner in crime, and in all things: what a peachy treat to share a favourite place with a favourite person - Ryan Ver Berkmoes, *partner par excellence.*

Oliver Berry

Thanks for help and assistance on this book go to Didier Lafarge, Emilie Cazou, Jean-Christophe Goujon, Jean Trivalle, Sophie Martin and Nichel Lefebvre. Special thanks to Susie and Gracie Berry, to Nicola Williams for steering the ship, and all the folks at LP for guidance and sage advice.

Stuart Butler

Writing my chapters of this *France* book is always a pleasure and I would like to thank everyone who knowingly or unknowingly offered tips, ideas or suggestions. Most of all though I would like to thank my wife, Heather, and young children, Jake and Grace, who together made exploring Atlantic France that much better.

Jean-Bernard Carillet

Big thanks to Christine for joining me for a few days in Brittany and in the Somme, and to all the people I met while on the road for their tips and recommendations. Last but not least, a *gros bisou* to my half-Parisian, half-Lorraine daughter Eva.

Kerry Christiani

I'd like to say a big *merci* to all the wonderful locals I met on my travels, as well as to the tourist offices who made the road to research silky smooth. A special thank you goes to Jean-Paul and Brigitte de Vries at Romagne 14'-18' for the behind-the-scenes battlefields tour. Big thanks, too, to travelling companions Monika and Andy Christiani.

Gregor Clark

Un grand merci to countless people who shared their love and knowledge of France with me, especially Nathalie, Fréderic and Théo in Lyon, Robert in Cluny, Stephen in Vézelay, Vincent, Mickaël and Pompon on the Chemin St-Jacques, and my father Henry Clark, who infected me with his own passion for Burgundy at age 14 . Back home, love and hugs to my wife, Gaen, and daughters Meigan and Chloe, who always make coming home the best part of the trip.

Emilie Filou

Big thanks to my parents for joining me for a few days on the Riviera and to Cynthia for an awesome weekend of walking, gambling and fun. Thanks to my aunt Danielle Villedieu and my uncle Pierre-Yves Tanguy for top recommendations in Corsica, and to Gérard and Florence Rondel in Cannes for their friendship. Last but not least, thanks to my husband, Adolfo, for everything.

Catherine Le Nevez

Un grand merci to my Paris city guide co-authors Nicola Williams and Chris Pitts. *Merci mille fois* to Julian and all of the innumerable Parisians who offered insights and inspiration. *Merci* too to Pierre-Emmanuel and to everyone at Versailles. Major thanks to Kate Morgan, James Smart, Jo Cooke and all at LP. As ever, *merci encore* to my parents, brother, *belle-sœur* and *neveu* for sustaining my lifelong love of Paris.

Daniel Robinson

Special thanks to (from north to south): Anny Monet (Lille & Dieppe), Dan Neese (Normandy American Cemetery), Fanny Garbe (Bayeux), Alain Noslier and Cécile Merel (Mont St-Michel), Alexander (FRAC Franche-Comté, Besançon), Mike and Catherine (Hôtel Continental, Évian), the Chamel family (Hôtel du Buet, Vallorcine), Morgane and Ilaria (Chamonix tourist office), Christian Fernandes (Chamonix), Marylou Roland and Laura Khirani (Chambéry), Mathilde Recoque (formerly of Val d'Isère) and Flore Ricoux (Grenoble). And a big *merci pour tout* to my wife, Rachel, and son Yair (Bayeux, Honfleur & New London).

ACKNOWLEDGEMENTS

Climate maps data adapted from Peel MC, Finlayson BL & McMahon TA (2007) 'Updated World Map of the Köppen-Geiger Climate Classification', Hydrology and Earth System Sciences, 11, 1633¬44.

Paris metro system map © RATP – CML Agence Cartographique.

Illlustrations pp72-3, pp86-7, pp96-7, pp164-5, pp248-9, pp770-1 and pp870-1 by Javier Zarracina.

Cover photograph: Château de Castelnaud, Beynac-et-Cazenac, Dordogne. Jose Fuste Raga/ Corbis.

(side tab) BEHIND THE SCENES

THIS BOOK

This 11th edition of Lonely Planet's *France* guidebook was researched and written by Nicola Williams, Alexis Averbuck, Oliver Berry, Stuart Butler, Jean-Bernard Carillet, Kerry Christiani, Gregor Clark, Emilie Filou, Catherine Le Nevez and Daniel Robinson. The previous two editions were also written by the authors listed above and Steve Fallon, Tom Masters, Miles Roddis and John A Vlahides. This guidebook was commissioned in Lonely Planet's London office, and produced by the following:

Destination Editors Kate Morgan, James Smart

Product Editor Amanda Williamson

Senior Cartographer Valentina Kremenchutskaya

Book Designer Mazzy Prinsep

Assisting Book Designers Katherine Marsh, Virginia Moreno, Jennifer Mullins, Jessica Rose

Assisting Editors Katie Connolly, Samantha Forge, Gabby Innes, Jodie Lea Martire, Anne Mulvaney, Lauren O'Connell, Gabrielle Stefanos, Ross Taylor

Assisting Cartographers Julie Dodkins, Mark Griffiths, Corey Hutchison, Gabe Lindquist

Cover Researcher Naomi Parker

Thanks to Kate Chapman, Penny Cordner, Helvi Cranfield, Brendan Dempsey, Ryan Evans, Justin Flynn, Larissa Frost, Jouve India, Andi Jones, Kate Mathews, Claire Murphy, Wayne Murphy, Claire Naylor, Karyn Noble, Martine Power, Alison 'du vin' Ridgway, Samantha Russell-Tulip, Lyahna Spencer, Samantha Tyson, Lauren Wellicome

index

000 Map pages
000 Photo pages

how to use this book

These symbols will help you find the listings you want:

- ◉ Sights
- 🐟 Beaches
- 🏃 Activities
- 🎓 Courses
- 🚩 Tours
- 🎊 Festivals & Events
- 🛏 Sleeping
- 🍴 Eating
- 🍷 Drinking
- ☆ Entertainment
- 🛍 Shopping
- ℹ Information/ Transport

These symbols give you the vital information for each listing:

- 🕿 Telephone Numbers
- ⊙ Opening Hours
- P Parking
- ⊖ Nonsmoking
- ✳ Air-Conditioning
- @ Internet Access
- 🛜 Wi-Fi Access
- 🏊 Swimming Pool
- 🥗 Vegetarian Selection
- 🍽 English-Language Menu
- 👪 Family-Friendly
- 🐾 Pet-Friendly
- 🚌 Bus
- ⛴ Ferry
- Ⓜ Metro
- Ⓢ Subway
- Ⓣ Tram
- 🚆 Train

Look out for these icons:

- **TOP CHOICE** Our author's recommendation
- **FREE** No payment required
- 🌿 A green or sustainable option

Our authors have nominated these places as demonstrating a strong commitment to sustainability – for example by supporting local communities and producers, operating in an environmentally friendly way, or supporting conservation projects.

Reviews are organised by author preference.

Sights

- 🏖 Beach
- 🐦 Bird Sanctuary
- ☸ Buddhist
- 🏰 Castle/Palace
- ✝ Christian
- ☯ Confucian
- 🕉 Hindu
- ☪ Islamic
- 卐 Jain
- ✡ Jewish
- ⬥ Monument
- 🏛 Museum/Gallery/Historic Building
- 🏚 Ruin
- ⛩ Shinto
- 🪯 Sikh
- ☯ Taoist
- 🍇 Winery/Vineyard
- 🦓 Zoo/Wildlife Sanctuary
- ⊙ Other Sight

Activities, Courses & Tours

- 🏄 Bodysurfing
- 🤿 Diving
- 🛶 Canoeing/Kayaking
- • Course/Tour
- ♨ Sento Hot Baths/Onsen
- ⛷ Skiing
- 🤿 Snorkelling
- 🏄 Surfing
- 🏊 Swimming/Pool
- 🚶 Walking

Information

- 🏦 Bank
- 🏛 Embassy/Consulate
- ➕ Hospital/Medical
- @ Internet
- 👮 Police
- ✉ Post Office
- ☎ Telephone
- 🚻 Toilet
- ℹ Tourist Information
- • Other Information

Geographic

- 🏖 Beach
- 🛖 Hut/Shelter
- 🗼 Lighthouse
- 🔭 Lookout
- ▲ Mountain/Volcano
- 🌴 Oasis
- 🏞 Park
-)(Pass
- 🧺 Picnic Area
- 💧 Waterfall

Population

- ✪ Capital (National)
- ◎ Capital (State/Province)
- ● City/Large Town
- ○ Town/Village

Transport

- ✈ Airport
- ⊗ Border crossing

Routes

- Tollway
- Freeway
- Primary
- Secondary
- Tertiary
- Lane
- Unsealed road
- Road under construction
- Plaza/Mall
- Steps
-)= = (Tunnel
- Pedestrian overpass
- Walking Tour
- Walking Tour detour
- Path/Walking Trail

Boundaries

- International
- State/Province
- Disputed
- Regional/Suburb
- Marine Park
- Cliff
- Wall

Hydrography

- River, Creek
- Intermittent River
- Canal
- Water
- Dry/Salt/Intermittent Lake

Jean-Bernard Carillet

Lille, Flanders & the Somme; Brittany Paris-based (and Metz-born) journalist and photographer, Jean-Bernard has clocked up innumerable trips to all French regions and is a passionate ambassador of his own country. Just before researching this edition, he presented a five-episode series on French TV, named *France's Most Beautiful Region*, for which he criss-crossed France for five months with a TV crew, searching for the best travel experiences in the country.

Kerry Christiani

Champagne; Alsace & Lorraine Kerry has been travelling to France since her school days to brush up her *français*, which she studied to MA level. Seeing Alsace's picture-book Route des Vins in spring bloom, tasting Champagne's finest in caves in Reims and Épernay, and hiking to the quietest corners of the hilly Vosges were memorable moments researching this edition. An award-winning travel writer, Kerry has authored and co-authored some 20 guidebooks. Kerry also wrote the Outdoor Activities and Landscapes and Wildlife features this edition. She lists her latest work at www.kerrychristiani.com.

Gregor Clark

Burgundy; Lyon & the Rhône Valley; Massif Central Gregor's love affair with France started on the midnight streets of Paris at age 14, when, jetlagged and culture-shocked, he successfully ordered a crêpe using his never-before-tested high school French. He's been feeding his France obsession ever since and writing for LP since 2000. Highlights of this research trip include *bouchon*-crawling in Lyon, returning to Vézelay, Salers and Gorges de l'Ardèche (three of his all-time favourites) and seeing a dog exit a boulangerie in Auxerre, baguette firmly held in mouth.

Emilie Filou

The French Riviera & Monaco; Corsica Emilie was born in Paris but spent most of her childhood holidays roaming the south of France. She now lives in London, where she works as a freelance journalist specialising in development issues in Africa. She goes to the Côte d'Azur every summer. For this book, she loved rekindling with her Corsican heritage and finding more about her late grandmother's homeland. See more of Emilie's work on www.emiliefilou.com; she tweets at @emiliefilou.

Catherine Le Nevez

Paris; Around Paris Catherine first lived in Paris aged four and she's been returning here at every opportunity since, completing her Doctorate of Creative Arts in Writing, Masters in Professional Writing, and post-grad qualifications in Editing and Publishing along the way. Catherine's writing includes scores of Lonely Planet guides to Paris, France and far beyond. Revisiting her favourite Parisian haunts and uncovering new ones remains a highlight of this and every assignment here and, wanderlust aside, Paris remains her favourite city on earth.

Daniel Robinson

Normandy; French Alps & the Jura Mountains Daniel has been writing guidebooks and articles about France since shortly after the end of the Jurassic period. His favourite leisure activities range from walking the Grand Balcon Sud trail above Chamonix to trying to interpret the Bayeux Tapestry's naughty margin vignettes. Brought up in the United States and Israel, he holds degrees from Princeton and Tel Aviv University. His travel writing has appeared in various newspapers and magazines, including the *New York Times*, and has been translated into 10 languages.

OUR STORY

A beat-up old car, a few dollars in the pocket and a sense of adventure. In 1972 that's all Tony and Maureen Wheeler needed for the trip of a lifetime – across Europe and Asia overland to Australia. It took several months, and at the end – broke but inspired – they sat at their kitchen table writing and stapling together their first travel guide, *Across Asia on the Cheap*. Within a week they'd sold 1500 copies. Lonely Planet was born.

Today, Lonely Planet has offices in Franklin, London, Melbourne, Oakland, Beijing and Delhi, with more than 600 staff and writers. We share Tony's belief that 'a great guidebook should do three things: inform, educate and amuse'.

OUR WRITERS

Nicola Williams

Coordinating author; Provence British writer Nicola has lived in France and written about it for more than a decade. From her hillside house on the southern shore of Lake Geneva, it's an easy hop to Provence and the south of France where she has spent endless years revelling in its extraordinary art, architecture and cuisine. Nicola has worked on numerous titles for Lonely Planet, including *Discover France* and *Discover Paris*. Find her on Twitter at @Tripalong.

Read more about Nicola at:
lonelyplanet.com/members/nicolawilliams

Alexis Averbuck

The Loire Valley; Dordogne, Limousin & the Lot Alexis first came to France when she was four and now visits every chance she gets. Whether browsing markets in the Dordogne, château-hopping in the Loire or careening through hill-top villages in Provence (she also contributes to the *Provence & Côte d'Azur* book), she immerses herself in all things French. A travel writer for two decades, Alexis has lived in Antarctica for a year, crossed the Pacific by sailboat, and is also a painter – see her work at www.alexisaverbuck.com.

Read more about Alexis at:
lonelyplanet.com/members/alexisaverbuck

Oliver Berry

The Pyrenees; Toulouse Area; Languedoc-Roussillon A professional writer and photographer based in Cornwall and Bristol, Oliver has been travelling to France since the tender age of two. For this book he covered the southwest region, including the Pyrenees, Languedoc and the pink city of Toulouse. Research highlights included kayaking through the Gorges du Tarn and watching the sunset from the Pic du Midi. You can see his latest work at www.oliverberry.com.

Stuart Butler

Atlantic Coast; French Basque Country Stuart's first encounters with southwest France came on family holidays. When he was older he spent every summer surfing off the beaches of the southwest, until one day he found himself so hooked on the region he was unable to leave – he has been there ever since. His travels for Lonely Planet, and a wide variety of magazines, have taken him beyond France to the shores of the Arctic, the deserts of Asia and the forests of Africa. His website is www.stuartbutlerjournalist.com.

Read more about Stuart at:
lonelyplanet.com/members/stuartbutler

OVER PAGE MORE WRITERS

Published by Lonely Planet Publications Pty Ltd
ABN 36 005 607 983
11th edition – March 2015
ISBN 978 1 74321 470 1
© Lonely Planet 2015   Photographs © as indicated 2015
10 9 8 7 6 5 4 3 2 1
Printed in China